Fundamentals of Mathematics

Functions and Graphs

Second Edition

Sanjay Mishra

B.Tech.
Indian Institute of Technology, Varanasi

G K Publications (P) Ltd

Title : Fundamentals of Mathematics Functions and Graphs

Language : English

Author : Sanjay Mishra

Typeset & Published by :

Career Launcher Infrastructure (P) Ltd.

A-45, Mohan Cooperative Industrial Area, Near Mohan Estate Metro Station, New Delhi - 110044

Marketed by :

G.K. Publications (P) Ltd.

Plot No. 63, Sector-27A, Near Sector - 28 Metro Station, Faridabad, Haryana-121003

ISBN : **978-81-93975-92-3**

Printer's Details : Printed in India, New Delhi.

For product information :
Visit ***www.gkpublications.com*** or email to ***gkp@gkpublications.com***

Preface

Calculus is a branch of mathematics which is considered as gateway course for almost all career streams closely associated with mathematics like Engineering, Applied physics, Astrophysics, Computer Science, Electronics etc. It is the most basic mathematical tool dealing with rate of changes (variations). Indeed this beautiful branch was not born in a moment of divine inspiration ,rather it gradually came in to existence as a variety of apparently different ideas and procedures merged together to form a systematic coherent pattern.

Over the years, scientists, economists, and other researchers have studied the relationships existing between various quantities. For example, an engineer may need to know how the illumination from a light source on an object is related to the distance between the object and the source; a biologist may wish to investigate how the population of a bacterial colony varies with time in the presence of a toxin; an economist may wish to determine the relationship between consumer demand for a certain commodity and its market price. The mathematical study of such relationship involves the concept of a ***function***. The concept of function is an essential pre-requisite for understanding the most basic idea of calculus. The purpose of this book is to lay foundation for the same to understand Calculus.

Functions are "the central objects of investigation" in most fields of modern mathematics. , It can be understood as a "machine" which for each input x returns exactly one corresponding output. $f(x)$. There are many ways to represent a function. Some functions may be defined by formula or algorithm that tells how to compute the output for a given input.

Since the input and output of a function can be expressed as an ordered pair, ordered such that the first element is the input (or tuple of inputs, if the function takes more than one input), and the second is the output. For instance, given a function $f(x) = x^2$, we have the ordered pair (1, 1), (−2, 4) etc satisfying it. If both input and output are real numbers, this ordered pair can be viewed as the Cartesian coordinates of a point on the graph of the function. Therefore, functions can also be represented by a picture, called its graph. Graph of Function is set of all those points (input x, output y) that satisfy the relation $y = f(x)$. Graphs last longer in our mind(s) as they provide a visual impact to our memory. They also reveal information about functions which may not be readily evident from verbal or an algebraic description.

Calculus constitutes a major share in the syllabus of IIT JEE MAINS/ADVANCED & other competitive engineering examinations therefore its in-depth analysis is essential. This book has been written to serve as a basic text book as well as an exercise book for Calculus; having a special focus on problem solving. I feel this will not only fulfill the needs of a beginner pre-college students (i.e., students of Class XIth & XIIth) but will also meet the advanced requirements of students who are preparing for various engineering entrance examinations like IIT-JEE MAINS /ADVANCED, BIT-SAT, and other state engineering entrance examinations.

Fundamentals of Mathematics (Vol-V) "Functions and Graphs" develop a deep insight of topics, such as Relations, Functions; their classifications and their exhaustive properties. Topic on Graph Theory provides details about various functions, their graphical nature and the variation observed in their graphs as they pass through different mathematical transformations. Method of sketching an unknown curve(s) using calculus shall be an essential skill to be learned which is sufficiently discussed in detail. I have personally experienced in my teaching career that if the core concepts of functions and their graphs is well laid upon in the mind of students from beginning then then mastering the Giant like calculus becomes very convenient. From a JEE aspirant's point of view, this topic is highly scoring in Mathematics as far as competitive exams are concerned. It's commonly observed among many students that they tend to develop a "phobia" against calculus. This is due to the non familiarity with the detail concepts of functions and their properties. Further, there exists a lack of good books that lay down these core concepts in a lucid and student friendly manner.

This book has a well arranged content list which will help students and teachers both to conveniently access the chapters & sub topics of their interest. Each chapter is divided in to several topics. Each topic contains its theory with sufficient number of worked out illustrative problems. This will enable the students to develop an applicative understanding of the concepts. This is then followed by a textual exercise of both objective and subjective problems, testing the student's understanding of concepts taught. At the end of the theory of each chapter, a large set of solved examples of both objective & subjective type is given. This will involve application of all the concepts learnt in the chapter so that students can develop expertise over the chapter.

The tutorial exercise given at the end contains a large number of multiple choice problems of single & multiple correct options, comprehension passage, column matching problems, numerical integer type questions to facilitate the students to do the thorough revision of entire chapter for raising their level of understanding of these topics. For teachers, this text book will be quite helpful as it will provide a set of well graded problems, arranged topic and sub-topic wise, that can then be used as a home assignment given to their students.

I must add that although this book contains not much work that might strictly be called original yet it will be found to be quite different from many existing books on this subject, through various innovative ways.

Any suggestions for improving the content of this book are most welcome and will be gratefully acknowledged.

—Sanjay Mishra

Acknowledgements

I am really grateful to the GK Publications, for showing their faith in me and for providing me an opportunity to transform my yearning, my vast experience of years of teaching and my knowledge in to the present comprehensive text book, "Fundamentals of Mathematics". I would like to thank all my friends and teachers, for their valuable criticism, support and advice that was really helpful to carve out this work. I have pleasure to award special acknowledgement to all my pupils. During my interactions with my students, I have got much of the inspiration for writing this text book. I feel that by interacting with them, I have learnt much more than I could have ever taught them. I wish to thank my parents and all my family members, for their patience & support in bringing out this book and donating their valuable share of time for such cause. I extend my special thanks to my team, including my assisting teachers, managers and computer operators, for their hard work and dedication in completing this task.

—Sanjay Mishra

Contents

Chapter 3 Graph Theory 3.1—3.191

CHAPTER 1

Relations

■ INTRODUCTION

To study relation between two sets we must do nothing but to look around different relations in our day to day business, e.g., friendship relation, relation between two countries, relationship between two families etc. For the existence of all the above relations there must be some method or rule (correspondence) of association by which the relation is actually established. So relation between two sets can be defined as a rule by which elements of first set actually correspond with the elements of the second set. In my view without the study of relations the actual understanding of functions and further study of calculus is not possible.

So this chapter which includes study of sets and relations between sets prepares a strong foundation for further study of calculus.

Cartesian Product of Two Sets

Cartesian product of two sets A and B is a set containing the ordered pairs (a, b) such that $a \in A$ and $b \in B$. It is denoted by $A \times B$. That is, $A \times B = \{ (a, b): a \in A \text{ and } b \in B\}$. If set $A = \{ a_1, a_2, a_3\}$ and $B = \{b_1, b_2\}$, then

$A \times B = \{(a_1, b_1),(a_1, b_2),(a_2, b_1), (a_2, b_2), (a_3, b_1), (a_3, b_2)\}$, and

$B \times A = \{(b_1, a_1), (b_1, a_2), (b_1, a_3), (b_2, a_1), (b_2, a_2), (b_2, a_3)\}$.

Clearly $A \times B \neq B \times A$ until A and B are equal.

REMARKS:

1. *Since $A \times B$ has elements as ordered pairs therefore it can be geometrically located on X-Y plane by considering set A on X-axis and set B on Y-axis.*
2. *Cartesian product of n sets $A_1, A_2, A_3,....,A_n$ is denoted by $A_1 \times A_2 \times A_3 \times .... \times A_n$ and is the set of n ordered tuples i.e., $A_1 \times A_2 \times A_3 \times .... \times A_n = \{(a_1, a_2, a_3, ..., a_n) : a_i \in A_i, i = 1, 2, 3, .., n\}$. Cartesian product of n sets represents n dimensional space.*
3. *$A \times B \times C$ and $(A \times B) \times C$ are not same.*
   $A \times B \times C = \{(a, b, c) : a \in A, b \in B, c \in C\}$, whereas $(A \times B) \times C = \{((a, b), c) : a \in A, b \in B, c \in C\}$

Number of Elements in Cartesian product $A \times B$

If number of elements in A denoted by $n(A) = m$ and number of elements in B denoted by $n(B) = n$, then number of elements in $(A \times B) = m \times n$. i.e., $n(A \times B) = n(A) \times n(B)$.

Since $A \times B$ contains all such ordered pairs of the type (a, b) such that $a \in A$ and $b \in B$, that means it includes all possibilities in which the elements of set A can be related with the elements of set B. Therefore, $A \times B$ contains $n(A) \times n(B)$ number of elements.

Properties and laws of Cartesian Product

Distributive Laws

(a) Cartesian product distributes over union and intersection of sets.

i.e., $A \times (B \cup C) = (A \times B) \cup (A \times C)$ and $A \times (B \cap C) = (A \times B) \cap (A \times C)$ for every group of sets A, B and C.

Proof: Let $(x, y) \in A \times (B \cup C)$

$\Rightarrow x \in A$ and $y \in (B \cup C)$

$\Rightarrow x \in A$ and $y \in B$ or $y \in C$

$\Rightarrow x \in A$ and $y \in B$ or $x \in A$ and $y \in C$

$\Rightarrow (x, y) \in (A \times B) \cup (A \times C)$

$A \times (B \cup C)$ is a subset of $(A \times B) \cup (A \times C)$

Similarly, we can prove that $(A \times B) \cup (A \times C)$ is subset of $A \times (B \cup C)$.

therefore, $A \times (B \cup C) = (A \times B) \cup (A \times C)$

Similarly, we can prove $A \times (B \cap C) = (A \times B) \cap (A \times C)$ for every group of sets A, B and C.

(b) Cartesian product distributes over subtraction of sets i.e., $A \times (B - C) = (A \times B) - (A \times C)$

Proof: Let $(x, y) \in A \times (B - C)$

$\Rightarrow x \in A$ and $y \in B - C$

$\Rightarrow x \in A$ and $y \in B$ but $y \notin C$

$\Rightarrow x \in A, y \in B$ and $x \in A, y \notin C$

$\Rightarrow (x, y) \in (A \times B)$ but $(x, y) \notin (A \times C)$

$\Rightarrow (x, y) \in (A \times B) - (A \times C)$

$\Rightarrow A \times (B - C) \subseteq (A \times B) - (A \times C)$

Similarly $(A \times B) - (A \times C) \subseteq A \times (B - C)$

$\Rightarrow A \times (B - C) = (A \times B) - (A \times C)$.

2. **Cartesian Product is not Associative:** Cartesian product of sets is not associative in nature, i.e., $A \times (B \times C) \neq (A \times B) \times C$

As the elements of $A \times (B \times C)$ are of the type $(a, (b, c))$, whereas the elements of $(A \times B) \times C$ are of the type $((a, b), c)$; $a \in A$, $b \in B$, $c \in C$.

3. **Cartesian Product is not Commutative:** Cartesian product of sets is not commutative in nature.

i.e., $A \times B \neq B \times A$ until $A = B$.

4. **Cardinality of Cartesian Product:**

(a) If A and B are two sets, then $n(A \times B) = n(A) \times n(B)$.

(b) If A and B are sets having k number of common elements, i.e., $n(A \cap B) = k$, then the number of elements common to $A \times B$ and $B \times A = k^2$.

Proof: Let $C \subset B$ and $C \subset A$ and C is largest such set and let $n(C) = k$

Now, $C \times C \subset A \times B$ and $C \times C \subset B \times A$

$\Rightarrow n[(A \times B) \cap (B \times A)] = n(C) \cdot n(C) = k \cdot k = k^2$.

5. Intersection of cross product is equal to cross product of intersection:

That is, for sets A, B, S and T : $(A \times B) \cap (S \times T) = (A \cap S) \times (B \cap T)$

6. **For subset A of B and C of D:** We have

(a) $(A \times C) \subseteq (B \times C)$ for every set C.

(b) $(A \times C) \subseteq (B \times D)$

(c) $(A \times A) \subseteq (A \times B) \cap (B \times A)$

7. For complementary sets B' and C' of sets B and C

(a) $A \times (B' \cup C')' = (A \times B) \cap (A \times C)$

(b) $A \times (B' \cap C')' = (A \times B) \cup (A \times C)$

Proof: (a) $A \times (B' \cup C')'$

$= A \times (B \cap C)$ [By Demorgan's Law]

$= (A \times B) \cap (A \times C)$

(b) $A \times (B' \cap C')'$

$= A \times (B \cup C)$ [By Demorgan's Law]

$= (A \times B) \cup (A \times C)$

8. $A \times (B \Delta C) = (A \times B) \Delta (A \times C)$

Proof: $A \times (B \Delta C) = A \times [(B - C) \cup (C - B)]$

$= [A \times (B - C)] \cup [A \times (C - B)]$

$(\because A \times (B \cup C) = (A \times B) \cup (A \times C))$

$= [(A \times B) - (A \times C)] \cup [(A \times C) - (A \times B)]$

$(\because A \times (B - C) = (A \times B) - (A \times C))$

$= (A \times B) \Delta (A \times C)$

ILLUSTRATION 1: If the number of elements in A is 2 and number of elements in B is 3, then find

(i) the number of elements in the power set of $A \times B$.

(ii) the number of elements in the power set of $(A \times B) \times (A \times B)$

SOLUTION: (i) Since $n(A) = 2$; $n(B) = 3$, then $n(A \times B) = 6$

So number of subsets of $A \times B = 2^6$ $\Rightarrow n(P(A \times B)) = 2^6 = 64$

(ii) Number of subsets of $[(A \times B) \times (A \times B)] = 2^{[n(A \times B)]^2} = 2^{36}$.

$\therefore n(P[(A \times B) \times (A \times B)]) = 2^{36}$.

ILLUSTRATION 2: Let A and B be two non-empty sets having n elements in common, then prove that $A \times B$ and $B \times A$ have n^2 elements in common.

SOLUTION: We have $(A \times B) \cap (C \times D) = (A \cap C) \times (B \cap D)$

On replacing C by B and D by A, we get $(A \times B) \cap (B \times A) = (A \cap B) \times (B \cap A)$

It is given that A and B have n elements in common, so $[(A \cap B) \times (B \cap A)]$ has n^2 elements

But $(A \times B) \cap (B \times A) = (A \cap B) \times (B \cap A)$

$\therefore$ $[(A \times B) \cap (B \times A)]$ has n^2 elements. Hence $A \times B$ and $B \times A$ have n^2 elements in common.

ILLUSTRATION 3: Given two sets A and B defined as $A = \{a : a \in \mathbb{Z} \text{ and } |a - 2| \leq 3\}$ and $B = \{b : b \in \mathbb{Z} \text{ and } |b - 4| \leq 2\}$.

Find $A \times B$ and $B \times A$. Represent them geometrically and also find number of elements common in $A \times B$ and $B \times A$.

SOLUTION: $A = \{a : a \in \mathbb{Z} \text{ and } |a - 2| \leq 3\}$; $B = \{b : b \in \mathbb{Z} \text{ and } |b - 4| \leq 2\}$.

To find: $A \times B$ and $B \times A$

Here $-3 \leq a - 2 \leq 3 \Rightarrow -1 \leq a \leq 5$ and $-2 \leq b - 4 \leq 2 \Rightarrow 2 \leq b \leq 6$

$\therefore$ $A = \{-1, 0, 1, 2, 3, 4, 5\}$; $B = \{2, 3, 4, 5, 6\}$

$(A \times B)$ can be represented geometrically by taking the set A along x-axis and set B along y-axis as shown below in Figure 1.1.

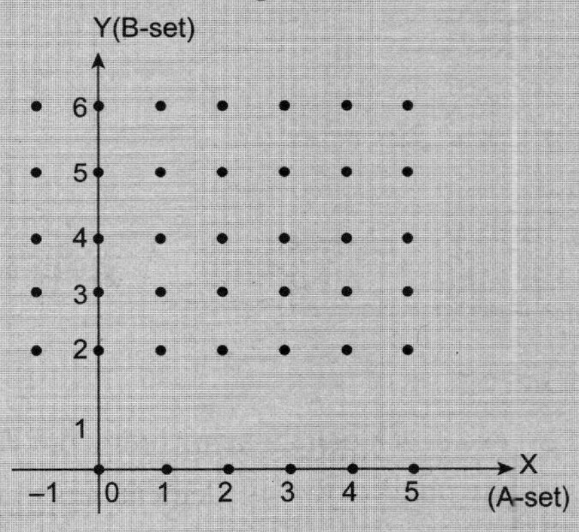

FIGURE 1.1

Now, $(B \times A)$ can be represented geometrically by taking set B along x-axis and set A along y-axis as shown below in Figure 1.2.

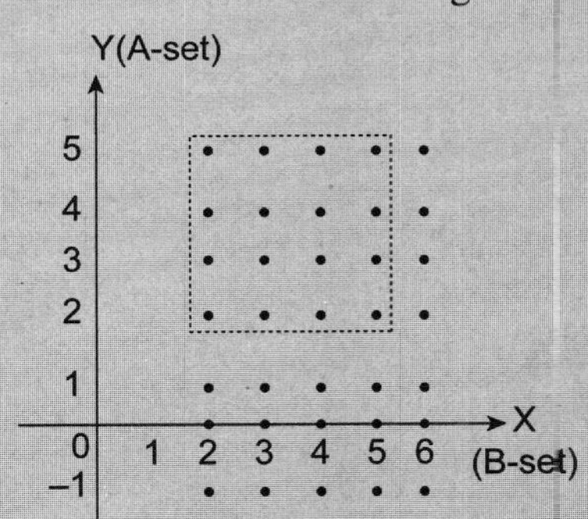

FIGURE 1.2

Clearly, $A \times B$ and $B \times A$ have 16 elements in common as represented enclosed by rectangular region in above graph. Note that A and B have 4 elements in common.

$\therefore$ $(A \times B)$ and $(B \times A)$ have $(4)^2$ elements in common

ILLUSTRATION 4: Given two sets A and B defined as $A = \{a : a \in \mathbb{R} \text{ and } |a - 2| \le 3\}$ and $B = \{b : b \in \mathbb{Z} \text{ and } |b - 2| \le 4\}$. Find $A \times B$ and $B \times A$. Represent them geometrically and also find number of elements common in $A \times B$ and $B \times A$. Fiind the answer if $b \in \mathbb{R}$.

SOLUTION: $A = \{a : a \in \mathbb{R} \text{ and } |a - 2| \le 3\}$; $B = \{b : b \in \mathbb{Z} \text{ and } |b - 2| \le 4\}$.

Here $|a - 2| \le 3 \Rightarrow -3 \le a - 2 \le 3 \Rightarrow -1 \le a \le 5 \Rightarrow A = [-1, 5]$

And $|b - 2| \le 4 \Rightarrow -4 \le b - 2 \le 4 \Rightarrow -2 \le b \le 6; b \in \mathbb{Z} \Rightarrow B = \{-2, -1, 0, 1, 2, 3, 4, 5, 6\}$

$\therefore$ $(A \times B)$ can be represented geometrically by taking set A along x-axis and set B along y-axis as shown below in Figure 1.3.

Further, $(B \times A)$ can be represented geometrically by taking set B along x-axis and set A along y-axis as shown in Figure 1.4.

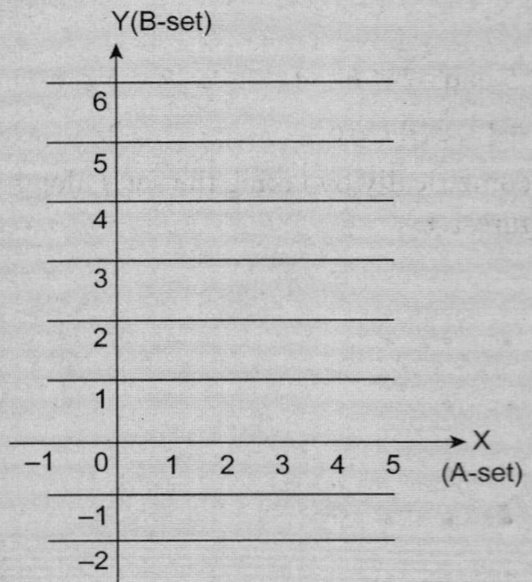

FIGURE 1.3

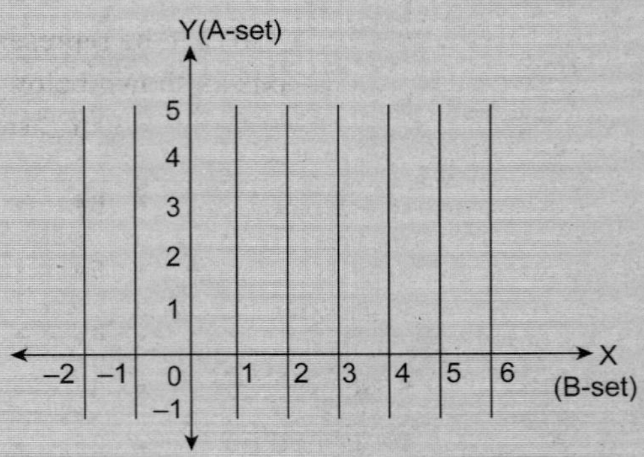

FIGURE 1.4

Since A and B have seven elements in common, i.e., –1, 0, 1, 2, 3, 4, 5.

$\therefore$ $(A \times B)$ and $(B \times A)$ have $(7)^2 = 49$ elements in common.

Further, if $b \in \mathbb{R}$, then $B = [-2, 6]$.

Then $(A \times B)$ and $(B \times A)$ can be represented geometrically as shown in Figure 1.5 and 1.6 respectively.

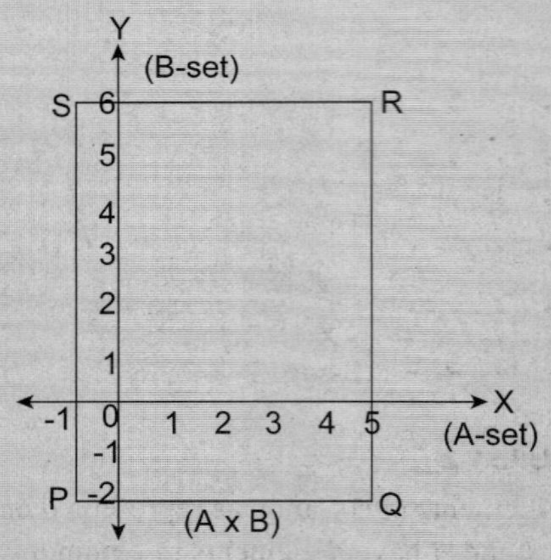

FIGURE 1.5

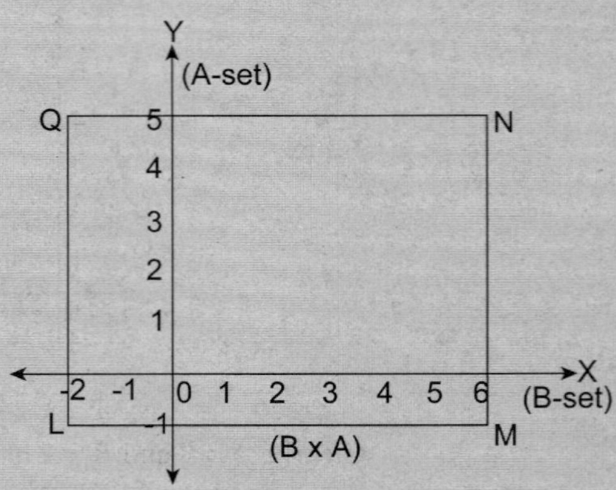

FIGURE 1.6

In above case when $A = [-1, 5]$ and $B = [-2, 6]$; $A \times B$ and $B \times A$ have infinitely many uncountable number of common elements each occurring in square bounded by straight lines $x = -1$, $x = 5$, $y = -1$ and $y = 5$. That is, $A \times B$ and $B \times A$ have 36 square units area in common.

ILLUSTRATION 5: Given two sets A and B defined as $B = \{y : y \in \mathbb{R} \text{ and } |y| \le 4\}$ and $A = \{x : x \in \mathbb{R} \text{ and } |x| \le 3$ and $x^2 + 3x \ge 0\}$. Find the region common to $R : A \to B$ and $A \times B$; where $R = \left\{(x, y) : \frac{x^2}{9} + \frac{y^2}{4} \le 1 \text{ and } (x, y) \in (A \times B)\right\}$.

SOLUTION: $A = \{x : x \in \mathbb{R} \text{ and } |x| \le 3; x^2 + 3x \ge 0\}$; $B = \{y : y \in \mathbb{R} \text{ and } |y| \le 4\}$.

Now for $x \in A$; $x \in [-3, 3]$ and $(x)(x + 3) \ge 0$

$\Rightarrow x \in [-3, 3]$ and $x \in (-\infty, -3] \cup [0, \infty)$

$\Rightarrow x \in [0, 3]$

$\therefore A = [0, 3]$ and for $y \in \mathbb{R}$; $|y| \le 4$

$\Rightarrow y \in [-4, 4] \Rightarrow B = [-4, 4]$

$\therefore A \times B = [0, 3] \times [-4, 4]$ is the rectangular region bounded by straight lines $x = 0$; $x = 3$; $y = -4$ and $y = 4$ as shown in Figure 1.7.

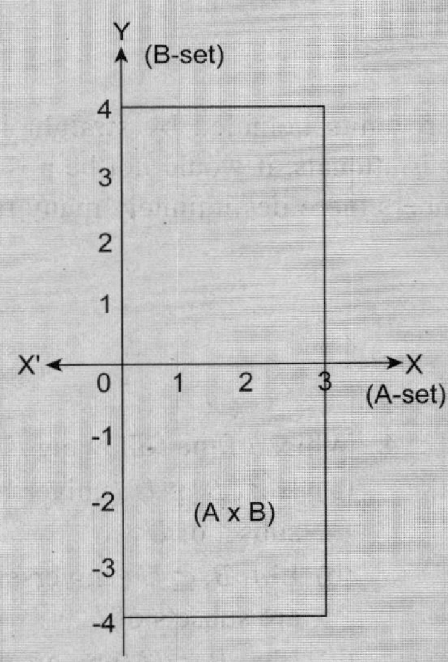

FIGURE 1.7

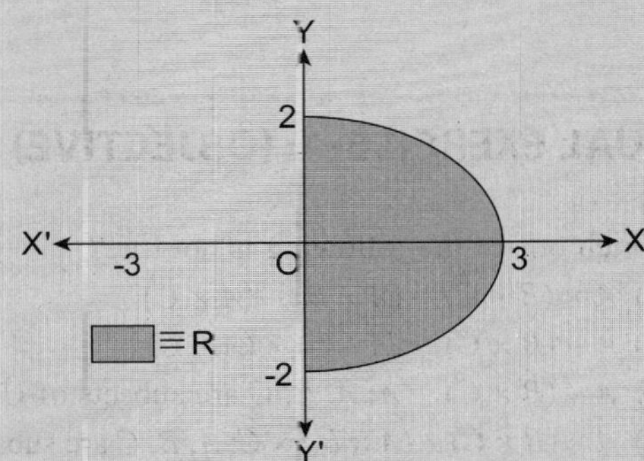

FIGURE 1.8

Further $R : A \longrightarrow B$ is defined by $R = \left\{(x, y) : \frac{x^2}{9} + \frac{y^2}{4} \le 1\right\}$, represents the right half of the interior region of standard ellipse with length of semi major axis 3 and semi minor axis 2 as shown in Figure 1.8.

$\because$ R lies wholly inside the region $(A \times B)$.

Thus, $R \cap (A \times B) = R$

$= 1/2 \times \pi \times (3) \times (2) = 3\pi$ square units ($\because$ Area of ellipse $= \pi AB$).

TEXTUAL EXERCISE–1: (SUBJECTIVE)

1. If $A = \{x : x \in \mathbb{N}, x \leq 4\}$; $B = \{y : y \in W, y \leq 2\}$; W = set of whole numbers.
   (a) Find $A \times B$ (b) Find $n(A \times B)$
2. Plot $A \times B$ and $B \times A$ on x-y plane, if
   (a) $A = \{x : x \in \mathbb{R}, 1 \leq x \leq 4\}$; $B = \{y : y \in W, y \leq 2\}$
   (b) $A = \{y : y \in \mathbb{R}, 0 \leq y \leq 2\}$; $B = \{x : x \in \mathbb{N}, x \leq 4\}$
3. Find the area of common region represented by following two relations.
   (a) $A \times B$; where $A = \{x : x \in \mathbb{R}, -1 \leq x \leq 1\}$; $B = \{y : y \in \mathbb{R}, -1 \leq y \leq 1\}$ and $|x| + |y| \leq 1$
4. Find out $n[(A \times B) \cap (B \times A)]$ iff $A = \{x : x \in$ non-negative integers and $x^2 - 2x - 8 \leq 0\}$ and $B = \{x : x \in \mathbb{N}$ and $x^2 - 5x + 4 \leq 0\}$
5. What will be the number of elements in $[(A \times B) \cap (B \times A)]$ if
   (i) Elements of set A are natural numbers and that of B in above problem are real numbers
   (ii) Elements of set A and B are real numbers.
   And how $A \times B$ and $B \times A$ can be geometrically represented and is it possible to represent the same in case elements are rationals or irrational numbers?

Answer Keys

1. (a) $A \times B = \{(1,0),(1,1), (1,2), (2,0),(2,1),(2,2), (3,0),(3,1),(3,2),(4,0),(4,1),(4,2)\}$ (b) 12
3. 2 Square units
4. 16
5. (i) 16
   (ii) Infinitely many found in square of area 9 square units bounded by straight lines $x = 1$, $x = 4$, $y = 1$ and $y = 4$. If elements of A and B are rationals or irrationals, it would not be possible to represent $A \times B$ and $B \times A$ geometrically as between any two real numbers there lies infinitely many rationals and irrationals.

TEXTUAL EXERCISE–1: (OBJECTIVE)

1. Which one of the following is not true?
   (a) $A \times (B - C) = (A \times B) - (A \times C)$
   (b) $A - (B \times C) = (A - B) \times (A - C)$
   (c) $A - (B \times C) = A$; A, B, C are subsets of U
   (d) $A \times (B \times C) \neq (A \times B) \times C$; A, B, C are subsets of U
2. Which of the following is/are not true?
   (a) $(A \cap B) \cap C = A \cap (B \cap C)$
   (b) $(A \cup B) \cup C = A \cup (B \cup C)$
   (c) $(A \times B) \times C = A \times B \times C = A \times (B \times C)$
   (d) $(A - B) - C = A - (B - C)$
3. Which of the following is/are not true?
   (a) $A \cap (B \cup C) = (A \cap B) \cup (A \cap C)$
   (b) $A \cup (B \cap C) = (A \cup B) \cap (A \cup C)$
   (c) $A \cup (B \cup C) = (A \cup B) \cup (A \cup C)$ and $A \cap (B \cap C) = (A \cap B) \cap (A \cap C)$
   (d) $A \times (B \times C) = (A \times B) \times (A \times C)$
4. Which of the following is/are not true?
   (a) If $A, B \subseteq U$ (universal set), then $A \times B$ is also a subset of U
   (b) If $A, B, \subseteq U$ (universal set), then $A \cup B$ and $A \cap B$ are subsets of U
   (c) If $A, B \subseteq U$ (universal set), then $A - B$ and $A \Delta B$ are subsets of U
   (d) If $A, B \subseteq U$, then $A \times B$ is a subset of $U \times U$
5. Which of the following is/are true?
   (a) If $A \subseteq B \subseteq C$, then $(A \times B) \subseteq (A \times C)$
   (b) If $A \subseteq B \subseteq C$, then $(A \times B) \subseteq (B \times C)$
   (c) If $A \subseteq B \subseteq C$, then $(A \times B) \cup (B \times C) = (B \times C)$
   (d) If $A \subseteq B \subseteq C$, then $(A \times B) \cap (A \times C) = (A \times B)$
6. Which of the following is/are true?
   (a) $A \times C \subseteq B \times C \Rightarrow A \subseteq B$
   (b) $A \times C \subseteq B \times C \Rightarrow A \subseteq B \subseteq C$

(c) $A \times B \subseteq B \times C \quad \Rightarrow A \subseteq B \subseteq C$
(d) $A \times B = B \times C \quad \Rightarrow A = B = C$

7. If $A = \{2, 3, 4, 5\}$; $B = \{x : x$ is a letter of English alphabet$\}$, then $n(A \times B)$ is
(a) 26 (b) 52
(c) 104 (d) $(4)^{26}$

8. If $A = \{2, 3, 4, 5\}$; $B = \{a, e, i, o, u\}$, then number of subsets of $A \times B$ is
(a) $(2)^{20}$ (b) $(4)^{10}$
(c) $(16)^5$ (d) None of these

9. If $A = \{\phi\}$; $B = \{\{\{\}\}\}$, then $n(A \times B)$ is
(a) 0 (b) 3
(c) 1 (d) Can't be defined

10. If $(A \times B)$ is an infinite set, then what can be said about A and B ?
(a) A and B both must be infinite sets
(b) A is finite and B is infinite
(c) A is infinite and B is finite
(d) At least one of A and B is an infinite set

11. Let $A = \{(x, y): x, y \in \mathbb{R}$ and $x^2 = 4y\}$ and $B = \{(x, 4); x \in \mathbb{R}\}$, then the set $(A \cap B) \cup \{(0,0)\}$ forms
(a) vertices of an equilateral triangle
(b) vertices of an isosceles triangle
(c) vertices of an square
(d) vertices of an scalene triangle

12. Let $A = \{(x, y); x, y \in \mathbb{R}$ and $x^2 = 4y\}$ and $B = \{(x, y), x\, y \in \mathbb{R}$ and $y = |x|\}$, then the area of triangle joining the points represented by $A \cap B$ is
(a) 16 (b) 4
(c) $4\sqrt{2}$ (d) None of these

13. If $A = \{\phi, \{\{\{\}\}\}\}$, then $n[P(P(A \times A))]$ is
(a) 2^{16} (b) $(16)^4$
(c) $(256)^2$ (d) None of these

14. If $n(A) = 50$; $n(B) = 60$; $n(A \cup B) = 100$, then $n[(A \times B) \cap (B \times A)]$ is
(a) 10 (b) 100
(c) $(50 \times 60)^2$ (d) None of these

15. If $n(A \cap B) = 2$; $n(B \cap C) = 3$; $n(C \cap A) = 5$; $n(A \cap B \cap C) = 1$, then $n[(A \times B \times C) \cap (B \times C \times A)]$ is
(a) 6 (b) 8
(c) 30 (d) None of these

Answer Keys

1. (b)	**2.** (c,d)	**3.** (d)	**4.** (a)	**5.** (a,b,c,d)	**6.** (a,c,d)	**7.** (c)	**8.** (a,b,c)	**9.** (c)	**10.** (d)
11. (b)	**12.** (a)	**13.** (a,b,c)	**14.** (b)	**15.** (c)					

■ BASIC DEFINITIONS

1. **Quantity:** Any thing on which mathematical operation such as addition, subtraction, multiplication, division can be performed is called a Quantity.
2. **Constant:** A constant is a quantity whose value does not change under different mathematical circumstances.

   Such a quantity retains the same value through out a mathematical operation.
3. **Absolute Constant:** When a quantity represents the same elements in all circumstances, then it is known as absolute constant. Such a constant retains the same value in every mathematical operation.

   Thus, 1, 2, 3, ..., $\sqrt{2}$, $\sqrt{3}$, π, e, etc, are the absolute constant.
4. **Arbitrary Constant:** A constant which retains the same value throughout in one problem but may have different values for different problems is called arbitrary constant. It is usually denoted by a, b, c, ..., l, m, n etc.

   For example in the equation of a straight line $y = mx + c$; m and c are arbitrary constant as they have same values for one line and other values for the other lines.
5. **Variable:** A quantity which varies, i.e., a quantity x, which assumes different values from a given set X, is called as a variable over the set X. For example in the equation: $y = mx + c$; $ax + by + c = 0$; $x^2 + y^2 = a$, x and y are variables. There are two types of variables as given below:

   (i) **Independent Variable:** A quantity (say x) which represents any arbitrary member belonging to a set, is called an independent variable this nomenclature is based upon the fact that the values of x can be arbitrarily chosen.

(ii) **Dependent Variable:** A quantity (say y) whose value depends upon some chosen values of an independent variable (x), is named as dependent variable.

For example, volume of sphere $V = (4/3)\ \pi r^3$ and surface area $S = 4\pi r^2$, here V and S are dependent variables and r is an independent variable.

6. **Domain of a Variable:** The set of all possible values of variable x is called the domain of the variable x.

7. **Continuous Variable:** Continuous variable is a variable that can take all the numerical values from one real number to another real number or between two given real numbers. For a continuous variable domain is an interval (open, closed or semi-open, semi-closed).

8. **Discrete Variable:** Quantities which are incapable of taking all possible values between two given numbers are called discrete or discontinuous variables.

■ RELATIONS

A relation R from set X to $Y(R : X \to Y)$ is a correspondence between set X to set Y by which none, one or more elements of X are associated with none, one or more elements of Y. Therefore a relation (or binary relation) R, from a non-empty set X to another non-empty set Y, is a subset of $X \times Y$. i.e., $R : X \to Y$ is nothing but subset of $A \times B$. For example, consider a set X and Y as set of all males and females members respectively of a royal family of the kingdom Ayodhya.

Thus X = {Dashrath, Ram, Bharat, Laxman, Shatrughan} and Y = {Koshaliya, Kaikai, Sumitra, Sita, Mandavi, Urmila, Shrutkirti} and a relation R is defined as x was husband of y from set X to set Y.

Then R = {(Dashrath, Koshaliya), (Ram, Sita); (Bharat, Mandavi); (Laxman, Urmila); (Shatrughan, Shrutkirti); (Dashrath, Kaikai); (Dashrath, Sumitra)}

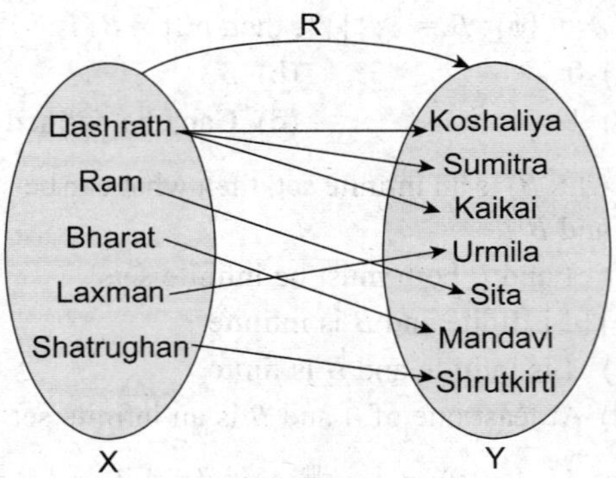

FIGURE 1.9

ILLUSTRATION 6: Are the following set of ordered pairs (correspondences) are relations from set A to set B?

(i) $R = \{(2, 4), (3, 6), (2, 6), (4, 8)\}$; $A = \{2, 3, 4\}$; $B = \{4, 6, 8\}$

(ii) If $A = \{a, b, c, d)\}$ and $B = \{p, q, r, s\}$

(a) $R_1 = \{(a, p), (b, r),(c, s)\}$ (b) $R_2 = \{(q, b), (c, s), (d, r)\}$

(c) $R_3 = \{(a, p), (a, q), (d, p), (c, r), (b, r)\}$

SOLUTION: (i) R is a relation from A to B as every ordered pair of R is an element of $A \times B$.

(ii) (a) Clearly $R_1 \subseteq A \times B$. So, R_1 is a relation from A to B.

(b) Since $(q, b) \in R_2$ but $(q, b) \notin A \times B$. So $R_2 \nsubseteq A \times B$. Thus, R_2 is not a relation from A to B.

(c) Clearly $R_3 \subseteq A \times B$. So, R_3 is a relation from A to B.

Note: (i) If a is related to b, then symbolically it is written as $(a\ R\ b)$ or $(a, b) \in \mathbb{R}$; where a is pre-image and b is image.

(ii) If a is not related to b, then symbolically it is written as a R b or $(a, b) \notin \mathbb{R}$.

ILLUSTRATION 7: A relation '~' from $\mathbb{C}$ to $\mathbb{R}$ is defined as $z \sim x$ iff $|z| = x$; $z \in \mathbb{C}, x \in \mathbb{R}$. Which of the following are correct?

(a) $(3 + 4i) \sim 5$ (b) $2 \sim -2$

(c) $1 + i \sim 2$ (d) $i \sim 1$

SOLUTION: As $|3 + 4i| = \sqrt{3^2 + 4^2} = 5$, therefore, $(3 + 4i) \sim 5$ ⇒ (a) holds

Also, $|2| = 2 \neq -2$, therefore, $2 \sim -2$ is not true. ⇒ (b) is incorrect.

and $|1+i| = \sqrt{1^2+1^2} = \sqrt{2} \neq 2$, therefore, $1+i \sim 2$ is not true. $\Rightarrow$ (c) is incorrect

Next $i \sim 1$ as $\sqrt{0^2+1^2} = 1$. $\Rightarrow$ (d) holds.

DOMAIN, CO-DOMAIN AND RANGE OF RELATION

Domain: Domain of a relation R from set A to set B is the collection of elements of set A which are participating in the correspondence. That is, it is set of all pre-images under the relation R. For example, Domain of $R = \{(1, 5), (2, 10), (3, 6)\}$ is

$D_R = \{1,2,3\}$ where R is a relation from set $A = \{1,2,3,4\}$ to set $B = \{5,6,7,8,9,10\}$.

Co-Domain: Co-domain of a relation R from set A to set B is set B itself irrespective of the fact whether an element of set B is related with any element of A or not. For example, $B = \{5, 6, 7, 8, 9, 10\}$ is co-domain of above relation R.

Range: Range of a relation R from set A to set B is the set of those elements of set B which are participating in the correspondence, i.e., set of all images under the relation R. For the above relation range is given by the set $R_R = \{5,6,10\}$

ILLUSTRATION 8: Let R be the relation from the set of whole numbers W to $\mathbb{N}$ the set of natural numbers defined by

$R = \{(x, y)\} : x + 3y = 12, x \in W, y \in \mathbb{N}\}$

Find (i) R (ii) Domain of R

(iii) co-domain of R (iv) Range of R

SOLUTION: (i) We have, $x + 3y = 12$

$\Rightarrow x = 12 - 3y$

Putting $y = 1, 2, 3, 4$, we get $x = 9, 6, 3, 0$ respectively.

Also for $y > 4$, $x \notin W$

$\therefore R = \{ (9, 1), (6, 2), (3, 3), (0,4)\}$

(ii) Domain of $R = D_R = \{ 0, 3, 6, 9\}$

(iii) Co-domain of $R = \mathbb{N}$ (set of natural numbers)

(iv) Range of $R = R_R = \{1,2,3,4\}$.

ILLUSTRATION 9: If $A = \{2, 3, 4, 5\}$; $B = \{2, 3, 4, 6, 7\}$, then find the domain, co-domain and range of the relations from A to B defined below.

(a) $R_1 = \{(x, y) : y = x + 1\}$ (b) $R_2 = \{(x, y) : x + y > 6\}$

(c) $R_3 = \{(x, y) : y < x\}$ (d) $R_4 = \{(x, y) : x + y = 7\}$

SOLUTION: (a) $R_1 = \{(x, y) : y = x + 1\} = \{(2, 3), (3, 4), (5, 6)\}$

$\Rightarrow$ Domain of $R_1 = D_{R_1} = \{2,3,5\}$; Co-domain $= B$;

Range of $R_1 = R_{R_1} = \{3,4,6\}$

(b) $R_2 = \{(x, y) : x + y > 6\}$

$= \{(2, 6), (2, 7), (3, 4), (3, 6), (3, 7), (4, 3), (4, 4), (4, 6), (4, 7), (5, 2), (5, 3), (5, 4), (5, 6), (5, 7)\}$

$\Rightarrow$ Domain of $R_2 = D_{R_2} = \{2,3,4,5\} = A$; Co-domain $= B$;

Range of $R_2 = R_{R_2} = \{2,3,4,6,7\} = B$

(c) $R_3 = \{(x, y) : y < x\} = \{(3, 2), (4, 2), (4, 3), (5, 2), (5, 3), (5, 4)\}$

$\Rightarrow$ Domain of $R_3 = D_{R_3} = \{3,4,5\}$; Co-domain $= B$; Range of $R_3 = R_{R_3} = \{2,3,4\}$

(d) $R_4 = \{(x, y) : x + y = 7\} = \{(3, 4), (4, 3), (5, 2)\}$

$\Rightarrow$ Domain of $R_4 = D_{R_4} = \{3,4,5\}$; Co-domain $= B$; Range of $R_4 = R_{R_4} = \{2,3,4\}$

■ UNIVERSAL RELATION FROM SET *A* TO SET *B*

Since $A \times B$ contains all possible ordered pairs which relate each element of A to every element of B, therefore $(A \times B)$ is largest possible relation defined from set A to set B, and hence also known as Universal relation from A to B.

■ NUMBER OF RELATIONS FROM SET *A* TO SET *B*

Since each relation from A to B is a subset of Cartesian product $A \times B$, therefore number of relations that can be defined from set A to set B is equal to the number of subsets of $A \times B$. Thus number of relations from A to $B = 2^{n(A \times B)} = 2^{n(A) \times n(B)}$.

■ RELATION ON *A* SET

A relation R from a set A to itself is called relation on set A.

For example, let $A = \{1,2,3,4,9,16\}$. Define a relation from set A to itself as 'a R b, if b is square of a but $a \neq b$', then

$R = \{(2, 4), (3, 9),(4, 16)\}$. Here domain $= \{2, 3, 4\}$; co-domain $= A$; range $= \{4, 9, 16\}$.

ILLUSTRATION 10: Let R be the relation of $\mathbb{N}$ defined as $x\ R\ y$ iff $x + 2y = 8$. Find the domain and range of R.

SOLUTION: Domain of $R = \{ x \in \mathbb{N} : x \text{ R } y \text{ for some } y \in \mathbb{N}\}$.

$$\text{Hence, } x = 8 - 2y,\ y \in \mathbb{N} = \begin{Bmatrix} 6 \text{ when } y=1 \\ 4 \text{ when } y=2 \\ 2 \text{ when } y=3 \end{Bmatrix}$$

Thus, $R = \{(2, 3), (4, 2), (6, 1)\}$.

$\Rightarrow D_R = \{2, 4, 6\}$; $R_R = \{1, 2, 3\}$

■ REPRESENTATION OF RELATION IN DIFFERENT FORMS

(i) **By representing the relation as a set of ordered pairs (Roster form):**
In this method we represent the relation by a set containing ordered pairs (a, b), where $a \in A$ and $b \in B$ such that ***aRb*** as shown below for the relation R from $A = \{1, 2, 3, 4\}$ to set $B = \{2, 3, 4, 5, 6, 7\}$ when $b \in B$ is to be related to $a \in A$ such that $b = 2a + 1$.
$R = \{(1,3), (2, 5), (3, 7)\}$.

(ii) **Analytical method or set builder from:** In this method we represent the relation as
$R = \{(a, b) : a \in A, b \in B; a....b\}$; where the dots are replaced by an equation connecting image b with its pre-image a. For example, let R be a relation from set $A = \{1, 2, 3, 4\}$ to set $B = \{2, 3, 4, 5, 6, 7\}$ given by $R = \{(1,3),(2,5),(3,7)\}$, then it can be represented by $R = \{(x, y) : x \in A, y \in B; x\ R\ y \text{ iff } y = 2x + 1\}$.

(iii) **Graphical representation or representation by lattice:** In this method we take set X along x-axis and set B along y-axis, then plot the points $(a, b) \in$

$\mathbb{R}$ in x-y plane. For example, in above illustration the relation can be represented as shown in the diagram given below.

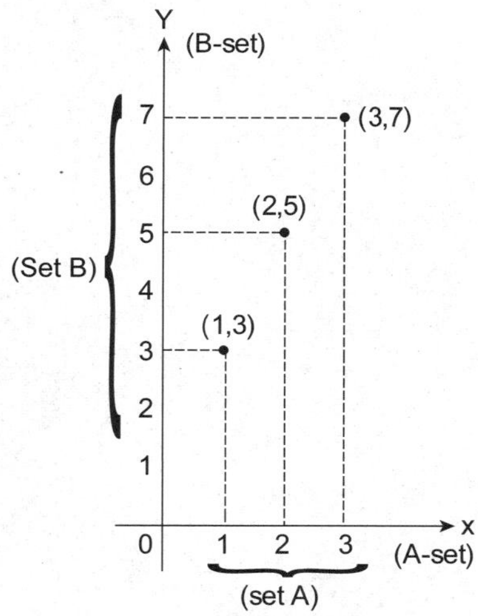

FIGURE 1.10

(iv) **By arrow Diagram:** In this method, we represent the set A and set B by two circles or by two ellipses and join the images and their pre-images by using arrows as shown below for above illustration.

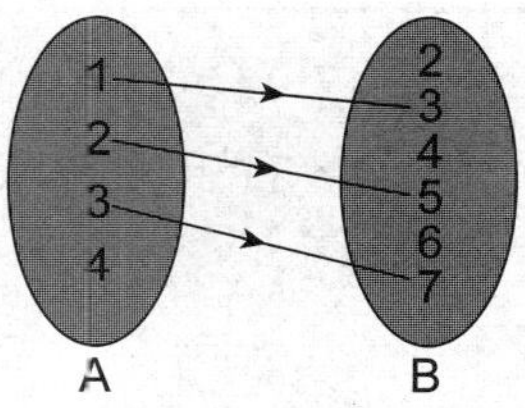

FIGURE 1.11

(v) **Tabular form:** In this form of representation of a relation R from set A to set B, elements of A and B are written in the first column and first row respectively. If $(a, b) \in \mathbb{R}$, then we write '1' in the row containing a and the column containing b and if $(a, b) \notin \mathbb{R}$, then we write '0' in the row containing a and the column containing b.

For example, for the relation $R = \{(1, 3), (2, 5), (3, 7)\}$ from set $A = \{1, 2, 3, 4\}$ to set $B = \{2, 3, 4, 5, 6, 7\}$ we have following tabular representation.

R	2	3	4	5	6	7
1	0	1	0	0	0	0
2	0	0	0	1	0	0
3	0	0	0	0	0	1
4	0	0	0	0	0	0

ILLUSTRATION 11: Given $A = \{1, 2, 3, 4\}$ and $B = \{x : x \in \mathbb{Z}$ and $0 < |x| \leq 4\}$, then represent the relations R_1, R_2, R_3 defined from A to B by using ordered pairs and by arrow diagrams.

(a) $y\, R_1\, x$ iff $y = x + 1$

(b) $y\, R_2\, x$ iff $y = 2x$

(c) $y\, R_3\, x$ iff $y^2 = x$

SOLUTION: $A = \{1, 2, 3, 4\}$ and $B = \{x : x \in \mathbb{Z}$ and $0 < |x| \leq 4\}$

$= \{x : x \in \mathbb{Z}; -4 \leq x \leq 4; x \neq 0\}$

$= \{-4, -3, -2, -1, 1, 2, 3, 4\}$

(a) Ordered pair representation of $R_1 = \{(1, 2), (2, 3), (3, 4)\}$

Arrow diagram representation of R_1

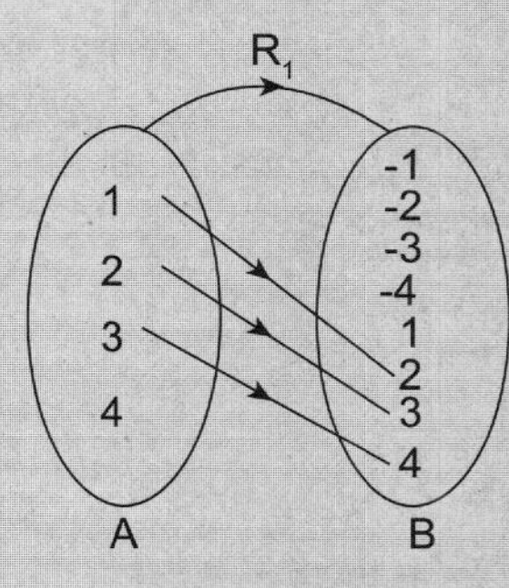

FIGURE 1.12

(b) Ordered pair representation of $R_2 = \{(1, 2), (2, 4)\}$

Arrow diagram representation of R_2

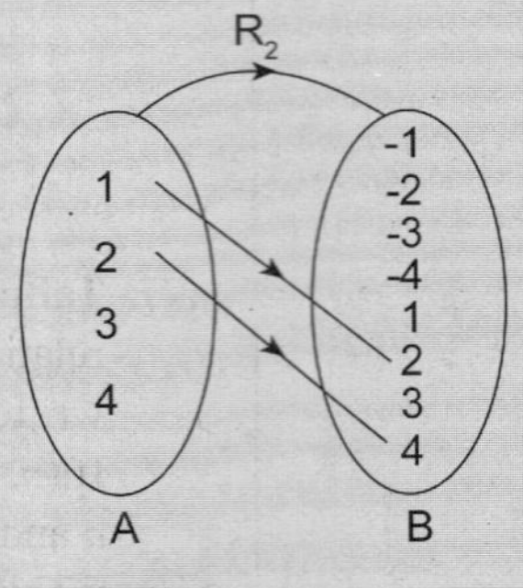

FIGURE 1.13

(c) Ordered pair representation of $R_3 = \{(1, 1), (1, -1), (4, 2), (4, -2)\}$

Arrow diagram representation of R_3

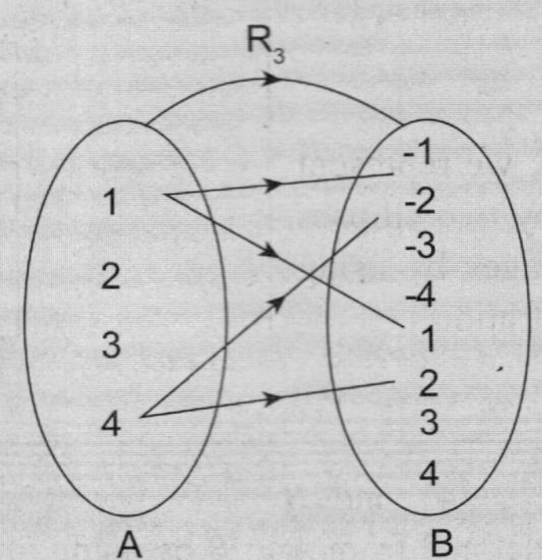

FIGURE 1.14

ILLUSTRATION 12: The relations R_1 and R_2 are defined from $\mathbb{R}$ to $\mathbb{R}$ as given below:

$R_1 = \{(x, y) : |x - 3| \leq 1, |y - 3| \leq 1\}$ and

$R_2 = \{(x, y) : 4x^2 + 9y^2 - 32x - 54y + 109 \leq 0\}$. Show that $R_1 \subset R_2$.

SOLUTION: $|x - 3| \leq 1$

$\Rightarrow -1 \leq x - 3 \leq 1$

$\Rightarrow 2 \leq x \leq 4$ and $|y - 3| \leq 1$

$\Rightarrow 2 \leq y \leq 4$

Therefore, the relation R_1 consists of the points, on and inside the square bounded by the lines

$x = 2, x = 4, y = 2$ and $y = 4$.

Now for relation R_2.

Also $4x^2 + 9y^2 - 32x - 54y + 109 \leq 0$

$\Rightarrow 4(x^2 - 8x + 16) + 9(y^2 - 6y + 9) \leq 36$

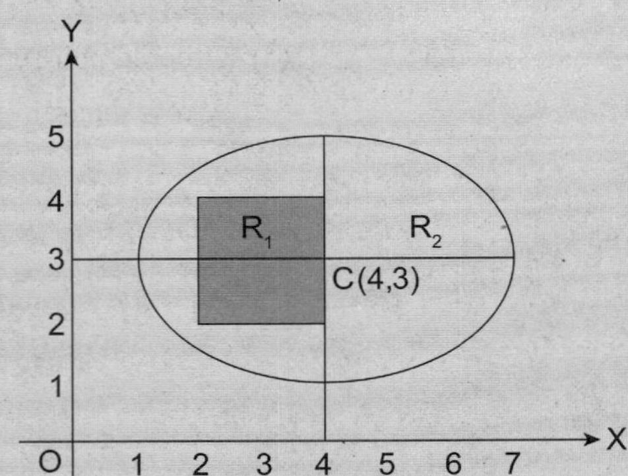

FIGURE 1.15

$$\Rightarrow \frac{(x-4)^2}{9} + \frac{(y-3)^2}{4} \le 1$$

$\Rightarrow$ The set R_2 consists of all the points inside or on the ellipse with centre (4, 3) and semi-major and semi-miner axes of lengths three and two units respectively as shown in the above Figure 1.15. From above Figure 1.15 it is clear that $R_1 \subseteq R_2$

■ CLASSIFICATION OF RELATIONS

One–One or Injective Relation

If different elements of set X are related with different elements of set Y. That is,, no two different elements of domain are related to same element of set Y, then R is said to be one-one relation or injective relation from set X to set Y.

For example, R_1: $\{(x_1, y_1), (x_2, y_2)\}$.

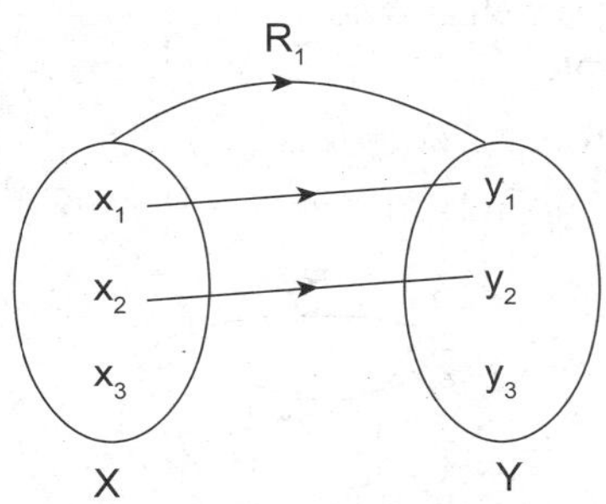

FIGURE 1.16

Many–One Relation

When there exists at least one group having more than one element of set X which are related with same element of set Y, then R is said to be many–one relation from set X to set Y.

For example, R_2 : $\{(x_1, y_1), (x_2, y_1), (x_3, y_3)\}$.

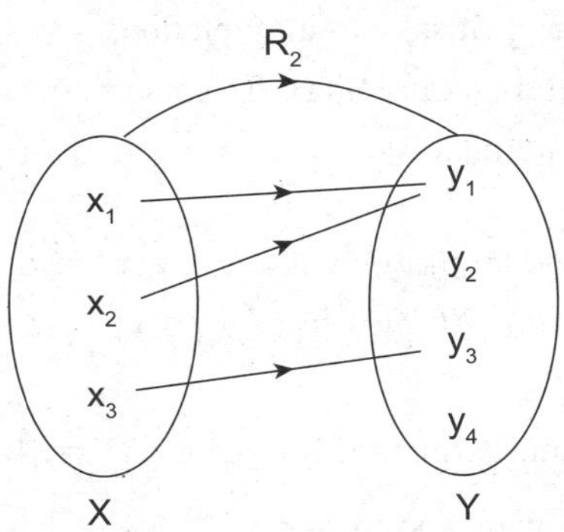

FIGURE 1.17

One–Many Relation

Relation R from set X to set Y is said to be one–many if there exists an element in set X which is related with more than one element of set Y.

For example, R_3 : $\{(x_1, y_1), (x_1, y_2), (x_2, y_3)\}$

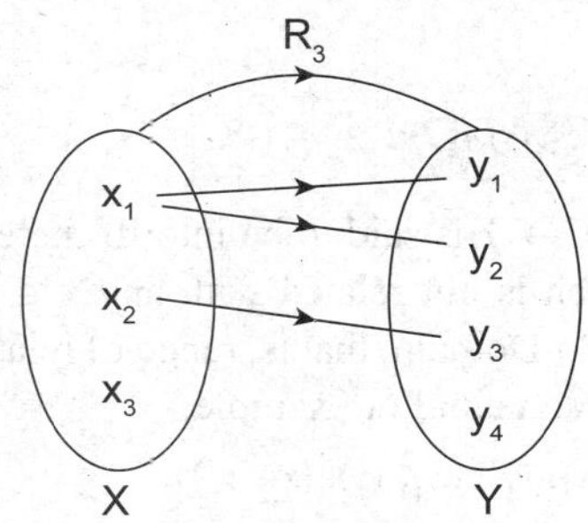

FIGURE 1.18

Many–Many Relation

Relation R from set X to set Y is said to be many–many if it is many–one as well as one–many.

For example, R_4: $\{(x_1, y_1), (x_1, y_2), (x_2, y_3), (x_3, y_3)$.

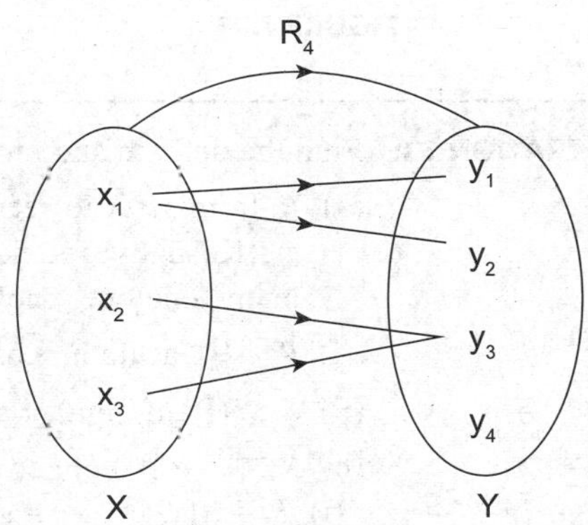

FIGURE 1.19

Onto Relation (Surjective Relation)

A relation $R : X \rightarrow Y$ is said to be onto or surjective relation if there is no such element $y \in Y$ which is not related with any $x \in X$, that is, for each $y \in Y$ there exist at least one element x in X which is related with y. In such a relation,

Range (R_R) = Co-Domain, That is, range of onto relation is nothing but the co-domain of the relation.

For example, R_5: $\{(x_1, y_1), (x_1, y_2), (x_2, y_3), (x_2, y_4)\}$

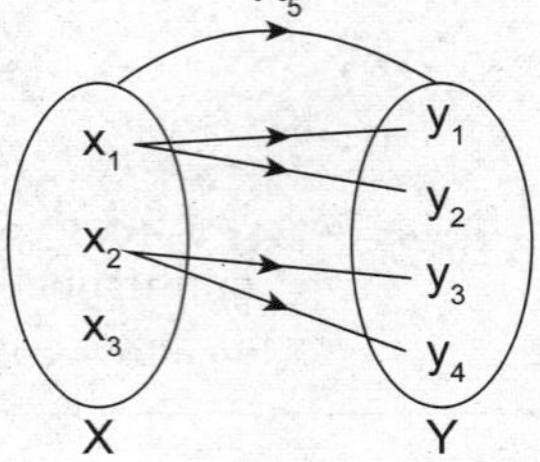

FIGURE 1.20

REMARK:

In onto relation all elements of set X may or may not participate in relation but all elements of co-domain set Y participate in relation.

INTO RELATION

A relation $R : X \rightarrow Y$ is said to be into iff there exist at least one $y \in Y$ which is not related with any $x \in X$. That is, if Range $(R_R) \subset$ Co-Domain, that is, range of relation is a proper subset of co-domain. For example,

$$R_6: \{(x_1, y_1), (x_1, y_2), (x_2, y_3)\}$$

Clearly under relation R_6, y_4 has no pre-image in X.

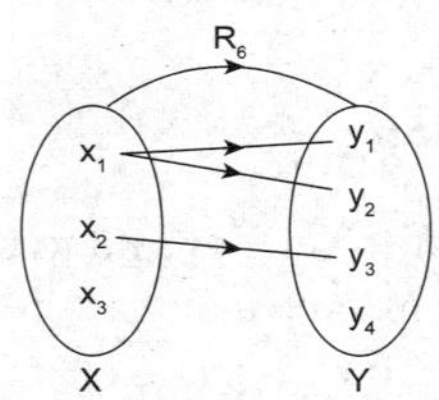

FIGURE 1.21

One–One–Onto Relation (Bijective Relation)

A relation $R : X \rightarrow Y$ is said to be bijective relation iff it is both one–one as well as onto.

For example,

$$R_7: \{(x_1, y_2), (x_2, y_1), (x_3, y_3),$$

where $X = \{x_1, x_2, x_3, x_4\}$ and $Y = \{y_1, y_2, y_3\}$

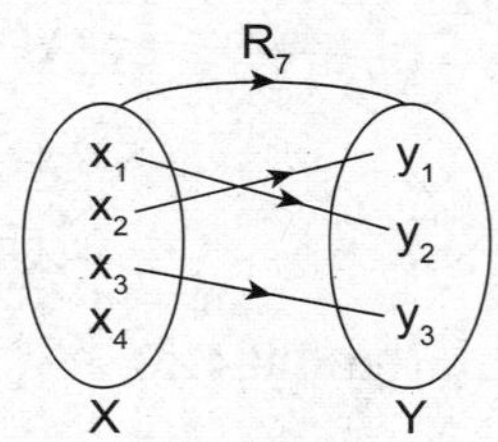

FIGURE 1.22

ILLUSTRATION 13: Find the domain and range of following relations

(a) R_i from set X to set Y; where X = {Dashrath, Ram, Bharat, Laxman, Shatrughan} and Y = {Koshaliya, Kaikai, Sumitra, Sita, Mandavi, Urmila, Shrutkirti} and classify them as many–one/one–one/one–many/many–many as well as onto/into relations.

(i) R_1 : {(Dashrath, Koshaliya), (Dashrath, Sumitra), (Ram, Sita), (Laxman, Urmila)}

(ii) R_2: {(Ram, Sita),(Laxman, Urmila), (Bharat, Mandavi)}

(b) $R : \mathbb{R} \rightarrow \mathbb{R}$ defined as

(i) $R_1 = \{(x, y) : x^2 = y^2\}$

(ii) $R_2 = \{(x, y): y \geq 0, y \leq x, x + y \leq 1\}$

(iii) $R_3 = \{(x, y) : x^2 + y^2 \leq 1 \,;\, x \geq 0\}$

(iv) $R_4 = \{(x, y) : |y| \leq |x| \leq 1\}$

(v) $R_5 = \{(x, y) : |y| = \sin x\}$

SOLUTION: (a) (i) For R_1: Domain $= D_{R_1}$ = {Dashrath, Ram, Laxman}; Range $= R_{R_1}$ = {Koshaliya, Sumitra, Sita, Urmila}. Clearly R_1 is one–many and into.

(ii) For R_2: Domain $= D_{R_2} = \{\text{Ram, Laxman, Bharat}\}$; Range $= R_{R_2}$ $= \{\text{Sita, Urmila, Mandavi}\}$. Clearly R_2 is one-one and into.

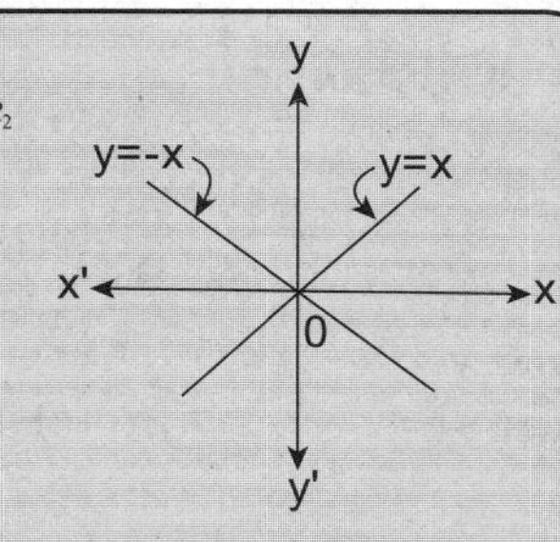

FIGURE 1.23

(b) (i) $R_1 = \{(x, y) : x^2 = y^2\}$

Now, $y^2 = x^2$

$\Rightarrow$ $y = \pm x$

$\Rightarrow$ the given relation contains a pair of straight lines given by $y = x$ and $y = -x$.

That is, $R = \{(x, y) : y = x \text{ or } y = -x\}$

Therefore, domain and range of relation R are $\mathbb{R}$ (set of real numbers) and the relation is many–many and onto.

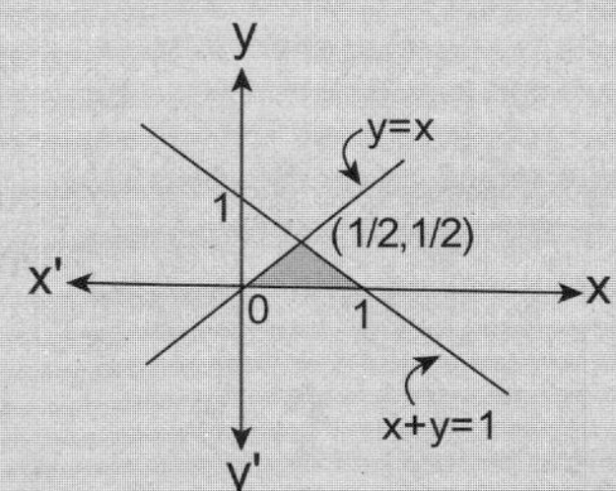

FIGURE 1.24

(ii) $R_2 = \{(x, y) : y \geq 0, y \leq x, x + y \leq 1\}$;

R_2 represents the shaded region bounded by x-axis, the straight line $y = x$ and the straight line $x + y = 1$ as shown in Figure 1.24 given.

Therefore, Domain of $R_2 = [0, 1]$; Range $= [0, 1/2]$.

Clearly R_2 is many–many and into.

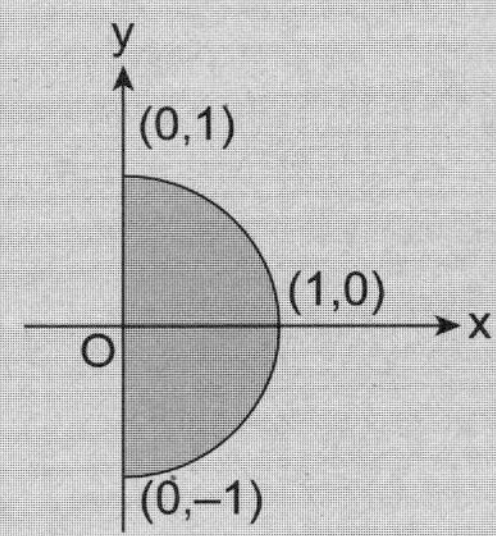

FIGURE 1.25

(iii) $R_3 = \{(x, y) : x^2 + y^2 \leq 1; x \geq 0\}$; R_3 represents the region of semi circle (interior and semi circular arc) of circle $x^2 + y^2 = 1$ on right side of y-axis as shown below.

Therefore, Domain of $R_3 = [0, 1]$; Range $= [-1, 1]$; many–many and into

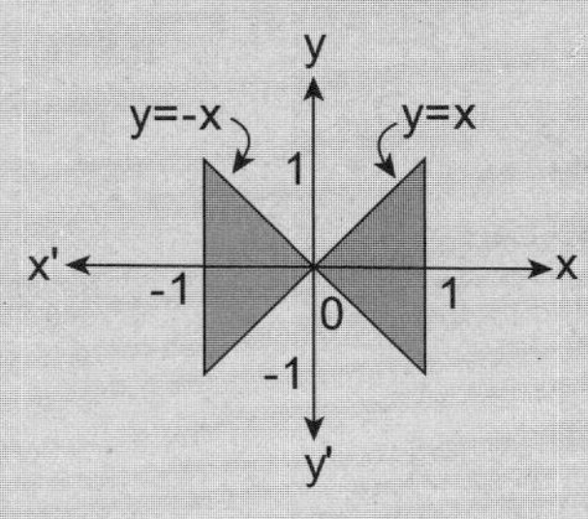

FIGURE 1.26

(iv) $R_4 = \{(x, y) : |y| \leq |x| \leq 1\}$; R_4 represents the area bounded by straight lines $y = \pm x$ and $x = \pm 1$ as shown below

Therefore, Domain $R_4 = [-1, 1]$; Range $= [-1, 1]$; many–many and into

(v) $R_5 = \{(x, y) : |y| = \sin x\}$; R_5 represents the positive portion of sine curve along with its reflection on x-axis as shown below.

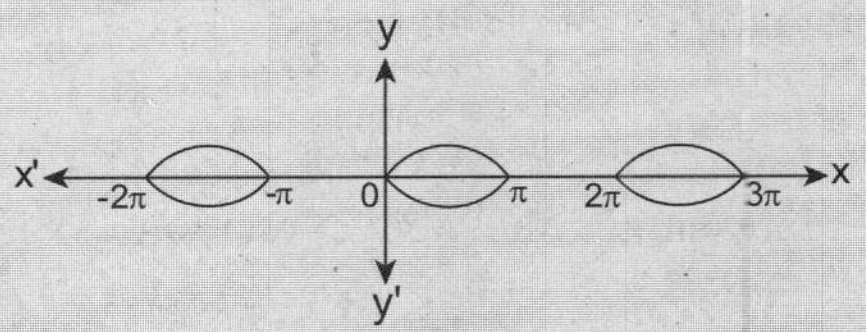

FIGURE 1.27

Therefore, Domain of $R_5 = \bigcup_{n \in \mathbb{Z}} [2n\pi, (2n+1)\pi]$; Range of $R_5 = [-1, 1]$;

The relation R_5 is many–many and into.

ILLUSTRATION 14: Test for injectivity and surjectivity the following relations

(a) $y^2 = 2x - 4$ (b) $x^2 = 2y + 1$

(c) $y = |x| + 2$ (d) $y = \sqrt{(x-2)(x-4)}$

(e) $y^2 = x^2 - 4$ (f) $xy = 4$

(g) $y = x + \frac{1}{x}$ (h) $|y| = |\tan x|$

SOLUTION: (a) $y^2 = 2x - 4 = 2(x - 2)$. The above equation represents a right handed parabola with its vertex at (2, 0) as jhshown below.

Clearly we have infinitely many pairs of points on the curves having same abscissa in $(2, \infty)$, one such pair P and Q having co-ordinates (x_1, y_1) and (x_1, y_2) is shown in above diagram.

Thus the given equation represents one–many relation, that is, not an injective relation (one–one). Domain of above relation is $[2, \infty)$ and range is $(-\infty, \infty)$. Thus the relation is surjective (onto) from $\mathbb{R} \to \mathbb{R}$.

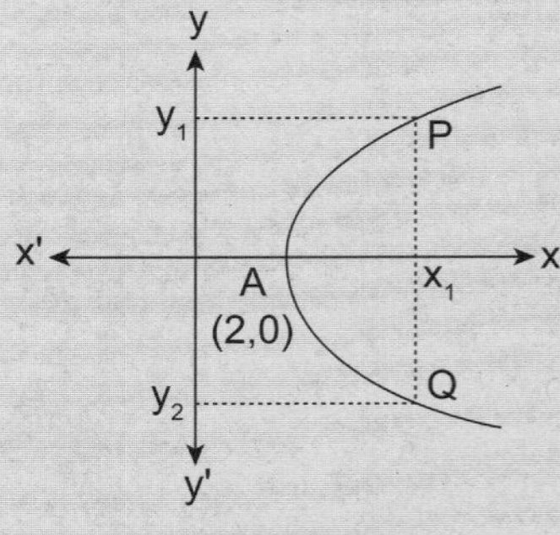

FIGURE 1.28

(b) $x^2 = 2y + 1 = 2\left(y + \frac{1}{2}\right)$.

The above equation represents an upwards parabola with its vertex at $\left(0, -\frac{1}{2}\right)$ as shown below.

Clearly for every input x, output $y = \frac{1}{2}(x^2 - 1)$ is unique however we get infinitely many pairs of points on the curve having same ordinate but different abscissae one such pair of points P and Q is shown on the graph having their co-ordinates (x_1, y_1) and (x_2, y_1) respectively.

Thus the given equation represents many–one relation and hence not an injective relation. Clearly domain of relation is $\mathbb{R}$ and range of relation is $\left[-\frac{1}{2}, \infty\right)$. Thus the relation from $\mathbb{R} \to \mathbb{R}$ is not surjective (onto).

However the relation from $\mathbb{R}$ to $\left[-\frac{1}{2}, \infty\right)$ is surjective.

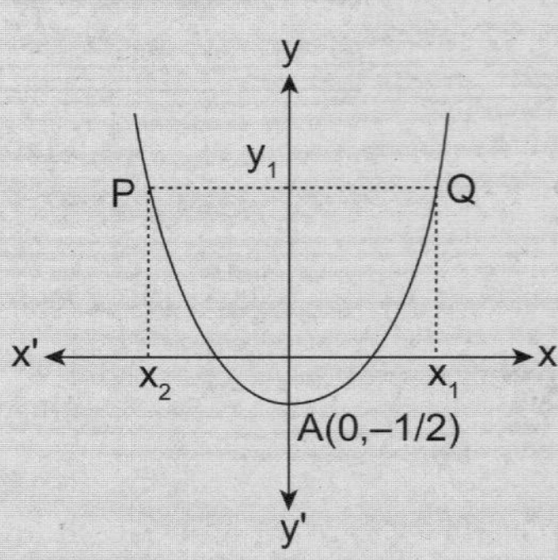

FIGURE 1.29

(c) $y = |x| + 2$

The graph representing the above relation is as shown below

Clearly the relation is many–one and hence not injective. Also domain of relation is $(-\infty, \infty)$ and range $(2, \infty)$. Thus, the given relation is not surjective from $\mathbb{R}$ to $\mathbb{R}$. But it is surjective from $\mathbb{R}$ to $[2, \infty)$.

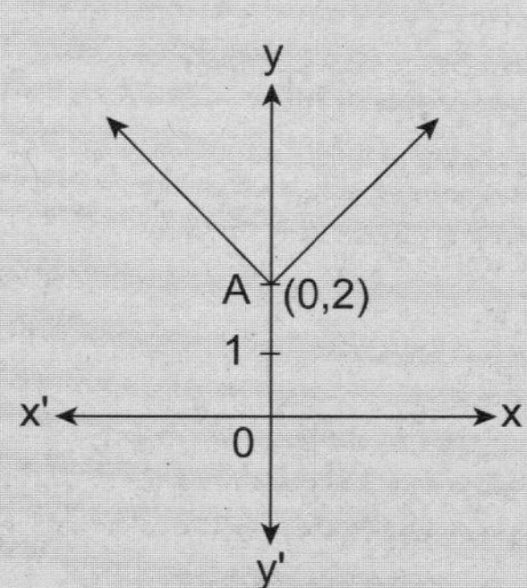

FIGURE 1.30

(d) $y=\sqrt{(x-2)(x-4)}$; Domain of relation = $(-\infty, 2] \cup [4, \infty)$ and range = $[0, \infty)$

Thus, the relation is not surjective from $\mathbb{R}$ to $\mathbb{R}$. But it is so from $\mathbb{R}$ to $[0, \infty)$.

Also $y = 0$ at $x = 2$ and at $x = 4$

$\Rightarrow$ the relation is many–one and hence not injective.

(e) $y^2 = x^2 - 4$

$\Rightarrow x^2 - y^2 = 4$

$\Rightarrow \frac{x^2}{4} - \frac{y^2}{4} = 1$

which represents a rectangular hyperbola as shown below.

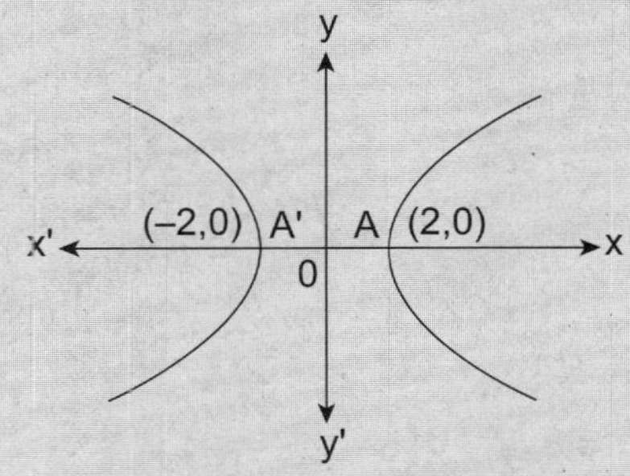

FIGURE 1.31

Clearly the relation is one–many as well as many–one with domain $(-\infty, -2] \cup [2, \infty)$ and range = $(-\infty, \infty)$.

Thus, the relation is not injective but it is surjective from $\mathbb{R} \to \mathbb{R}$.

(f) $xy = 4$

$\Rightarrow y = 4/x$

The graph of above relation is as shown below:

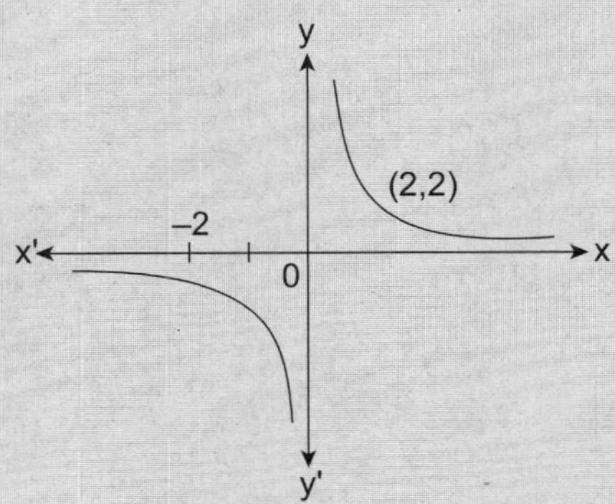

FIGURE 1.32

Clearly the given equation represents one-one relation, i.e., injective with domain $\mathbb{R} \sim \{0\}$ and range $\mathbb{R} \sim \{0\}$.

Thus the given relation is not surjective from $\mathbb{R}$ to $\mathbb{R}$, but it is so from $\mathbb{R} \sim \{0\}$ to $\mathbb{R} \sim \{0\}$.

(g) $y = x + \frac{1}{x}$.

The above equation represents the graph as shown below

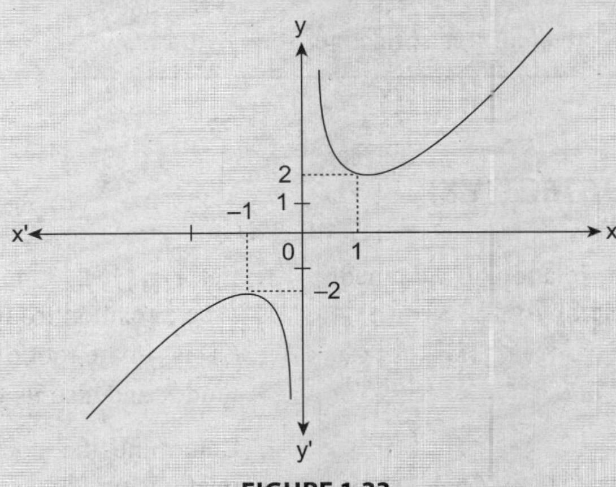

FIGURE 1.33

Clearly the given relation is many–one and hence not an injective relation with domain = $\mathbb{R} \sim \{0\}$ and range = $\mathbb{R} \sim (-2, 2)$.

Thus, the relation from $\mathbb{R}$ to $\mathbb{R}$ is not surjective.

(h) $|y| = |\tan x|$

Let $|\tan x| = g(x)$

$\Rightarrow$ $|y| = g(x)$

The graph of $g(x)$ is as shown below

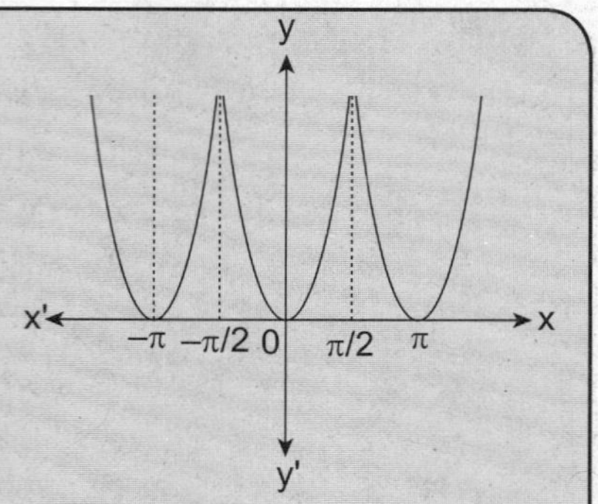

FIGURE 1.34

Now $|y| = g(x)$

$\Rightarrow$ $y = \pm g(x)$

Thus, graph of $|y| = g(x)$ can be obtained by reflecting the graph of $g(x)$ on x-axis and also considering the graph of $g(x)$ along with as shown below.

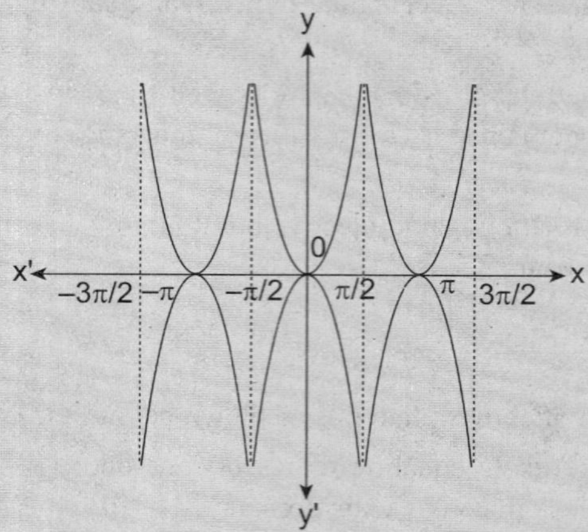

FIGURE 1.35

Graph of $|y| = |\tan x|$

Clearly the given relation represents one–many as well as many–one relation. Domain of relation is $\mathbb{R} \sim \left\{(2n+1)\frac{\pi}{2}; n \in \mathbb{Z}\right\}$ and range of relation is $(-\infty, \infty)$. Thus the relation is not injective but it is surjective from $\mathbb{R}$ to $\mathbb{R}$.

TEXTUAL EXERCISE–2: (SUBJECTIVE)

1. Let $A = \{1, 2, 3, 4, 6\}$. Let R is the relation on A defined by $\{(a, b): a, b \in A, b$ is divisible by $a\}$
   (i) Write R in roster form
   (ii) Find the domain of R
   (iii) Find the range of R.

2. Let $R = \{(x, y) : x, y \in \mathbb{Z}; (x + y)(y + 2004) + 1 = 0\}$.
   (i) Write R in roster form
   (ii) Find the domain of R
   (iii) Find the range of R.

3. Let $A = \{1, 2, 3, 4, 5\}$ and $B = \{1, 2, 3, ..., 66, 67\}$. If R be a relation from the set A to the set B defined by
   (i) is square root of (ii) is cube root of
   Find R and also its domain and range.

4. Determine the domain and range of the following relations on $\mathbb{N}$.
   (i) $R = \{(x, x^3) : x$ is a prime number less than $10\}$
   (ii) $R = \{(4x + 3, 1 - x) : x \leq 4; x \in \mathbb{N}\}$
   (iii) $R = \left\{\left(x, \frac{1}{x}\right) : 0 < x < 4 \text{ and } x \text{ is natural number}\right\}$

5. Let $R = \{(x, y) : x, y \in W; y = 2x - 4\}$. If $(a, -2) \in R$ and $(4, b^2) \in R$, then find the relation $R_1 = \{(a, b)\}$.

6. Find a linear relation between the components of the ordered pairs of relation R given by
$R = \{(0, 2), (-1, 5), (2, -4), ...\}$

7. Let $A = \{1, 2, 3, 4\}$, $B = \{1, 2, 3, 4, 5\}$ and R be a relation from A to B defined by $a\ R\ b$ iff $a|b$
   (i) represent R by lattice
   (ii) represent R in tabular form

8. Let $A = \{1, 2, 3\}$, $B = \{4, 5\}$ and R be a relation from A into B given by $R = \{(2, 4), (2, 5), (3, 5)\}$. Represent R:
   (i) in tabular form (ii) by arrow diagram

9. Figure 1.36 shows a relation R from set A to set B. Write this relation in
   (i) set builder form (ii) roster form

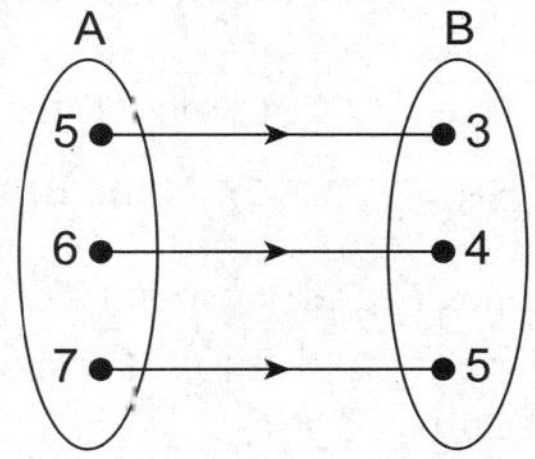

FIGURE 1.36

10. Test the given relations for injectivity and surjectivity.
   (a) $y^2 = 2x - 3$ (b) $y = x^2 + 4$
   (c) $y = ax^2 + bx + c$ (d) $y^3 = 5x + 4$
   (e) $y = \sqrt{3x-4}$

Answer Keys

1. $R = \{(1, 1), (1, 2), (1, 3), (1, 4), (1, 5), (1, 6), (2, 2), (2, 4), (2, 6), (3, 3), (3, 6), (4, 4), (6, 6)\}$; $D_R = R_R = A$
2. $R = \{(2002, -2003), (2006, -2005)\}$, $D_R = \{2002, 2006\}$, $R_R = \{-2003, -2005\}$.
3. (i) $R = \{(1, 1), (2, 4), (3, 9), (4, 16), (5, 25)\}$; $D_R = A$; $R_R = \{1, 4, 9, 16, 25\}$
   (ii) $R = \{(1, 1), (2, 8), (3, 27), (4, 64)\}$; $D_R = \{1, 2, 3, 4\}$; $R_R = \{1, 8, 27, 64\}$
4. (i) $D_R = \{2, 3, 5, 7\}$; $R_R = \{8, 27, 125, 343\}$ (ii) $D_R = \{ \}$; $R_R = \{ \}$
   (iii) $D_R = \{\}$; $R_R = \{\}$
5. $R_1 = \{(1, 2), (1, -2)\}$ 6. $3x + y = 2$
9. (i) $R = \{(x, y) : y = x - 2 \text{ and } x \in \{5, 6, 7\}\}$ (ii) $R = \{(5, 3), (6, 4), (7, 5)\}$
10. (a) injective, surjective (b) neither injective nor surjective, many–one
   (c) neither injective nor surjective, many–one (d) injective, surjective
   (e) injective but not surjective.

TEXTUAL EXERCISE–2: (OBJECTIVE)

1. Let $A = \{2, 3, 4, 5\}$, then how many relations can be defined on set A?
   (a) $(16)^2$ (b) $(2)^{16}$
   (c) $(16)^4$ (d) $(4)^{16}$

2. Let $A = \{a, e, i, o, u\}$, then how many relations can be defined on power set of A?
   (a) $(2)^{10}$ (b) $(2^{10})^2$
   (c) $(2)^{2^{10}}$ (d) None of these

3. Let $A = \{1, 2, 3\}$ and $B = \{a, b, c, d\}$; then the number of relations that can defined from set A to set B is
   (a) $(2)^{12}$ (b) $(12)^2$
   (c) $(2)^7$ (d) None of these

4. If $n(A) = m$ and $n(B) = n$ and $m > n$. Let k = number of relations defined from set A to set B and p = number of relations defined from set B to set A, then
   (a) $k > p$ (b) $k < p$
   (c) $k = p$ (d) Can't be predicted surely

5. Define a relation R on set $A = \{2, 3, 5, 6, 10\}$ as 'xRy if $x < y$ and x divides y', then the domain of relation is
   (a) $\{2, 3, 5, 6, 10\}$ (b) $\{2, 3, 5\}$
   (c) $\{2, 3, 5, 6\}$ (d) None of these

6. Define a relation R on set of natural numbers defined as xRy if '$3x + 5y = 53$', then the range set of relation is
   (a) {1, 4} (b) {1, 4, 8}
   (c) {1, 4, 7, 10} (d) None of these

7. Define relations R_1 and R_2 on set $A = \{2, 3, 5, 7, 10\}$ as xR_1y if $x|(y - 1)$ and xR_2y if $x + y = 10$, then the relation R given by $R = R_1 \cap R_2$ is
   (a) { } (b) {(3, 7)}
   (c) {(3, 7), (5, 5)} (d) None of these

8. Define a relation R on set of natural numbers as $x\ Ry$ if '$x + y$ divides 10', then the relation is
   (a) One–one (b) Many–one
   (c) One–many (d) None of these

9. Define a relation R on set $A = \{2, 7, 9, 11\}$ defined as $x\ R\ y$ if 'x divides y' then the relation R is
   (a) Many–one
   (b) One–many
   (c) One–one
   (d) A function from set A to set A

10. For a relation to be a function from set A to set B, it should be
   (a) One–one
   (b) One–many
   (c) Many–one
   (d) Domain of relation should be A

11. If $A = \{x : x^2 - 3x + 2 = 0; x \in \mathbb{R}\}$, and R is a universal relation on A, then R is;
   (a) {(1,1),(2,2)} (b) {(1,1)}
   (c) { } (d) {(1,1),(1,2),(2,1),(2,2)}

12. If $A = \{1,2,3\}$ and $R_1 = \{(1,2),(3,2),(1,3)\}$; $R_2 = \{(1,3), (3,6), (2,1), (1,2)\}$, then
   (a) R_1 is a relation and R_2 is not on A
   (b) R_1 and R_2 both are relations on A
   (c) R_1 and R_2 both are not relations on A
   (d) None of these

13. Let $A = \{a, b, c, d\}$, $B = \{b, c, d, e\}$. Then $n[(A \times B) \cap (B \times A)]$ is equal to
   (a) 3 (b) 6
   (c) 9 (d) None of these

Answer Keys

1. (b,c) **2.** (c) **3.** (a) **4.** (c) **5.** (b) **6.** (c) **7.** (b) **8.** (b,c) **9.** (c,d)
10. (a,c,d) **11.** (d) **12.** (a) **13.** (c)

TYPES OF RELATIONS

Reflexive Relation

$R : X \to Y$ is said to be reflexive iff $x\ R\ x\ \forall\ x \in X$. That is, every element of X, must be related to itself.

Therefore if for each $x \in X$; $(x, x) \in R$, then relation R is called reflexive relation. For a relation to be reflexive from set X to set Y, X must be a subset of Y.

REMARK:

If $R : X \to Y$ is a reflexive relation, then its domain is X. For example, if R is a relation on set of integers ($\mathbb{Z}$) defined by 'xRy iff x divides y', then it is reflexive and hence its domain set is $\mathbb{Z}$.

ILLUSTRATION 15: If $X = \{x_1, x_2, x_3\}$ and $Y = \{x_1, x_2, x_3, x_4, x_5\}$, then find which of the following is/are reflexive relation.

(a) R_1: $\{(x_1, x_1), (x_2, x_2)\}$ (b) R_2: $\{(x_1, x_1), (x_2, x_2), (x_3, x_3)\}$
(c) R_3: $\{(x_1, x_1), (x_2, x_2), (x_3, x_3), (x_1, x_3), (x_2, x_4)\}$ (d) R_4: $\{(x_1, x_1), (x_2, x_2), (x_3, x_4)\}$

SOLUTION: (a) Not reflexive as (x3, x3) $\notin$ R1 (b) Reflexive
(c) Reflexive (d) Non-reflexive because $(x_3, x_3) \notin R_4$.

Identity Relation

A relation $R : X \to Y$ is said to be an identity relation if each element of X is related to it self only. For example, if $X = \{x_1, x_2, x_3\}$ and $Y = \{x_1, x_2, x_3, x_4\}$, then the relation $R = \{(x_1, x_1), (x_2, x_2), (x_3, x_3)\}$ is an identity relation from set X to set Y.

REMARKS

1. *Every identity relation from set X to set Y is reflexive relation from set X to set Y, but converse is not true. that is, every reflexive relation need not be identity. For example, $R : X \to Y$; where $X = \{x_1, x_2, x_3\}$ and $Y = \{x_1, x_2, x_3, x_4\}$, then the relation $R = \{(x_1, x_1), (x_2, x_2), (x_3, x_3), (x_1, x_2)\}$ is reflexive but not identity relation from set X to set Y because $x_1 R x_1$ as well as $x_1 R x_2$.*
2. *If R is a relation from set X to itself, then the relation is called relation on set X.*
   (a) R is said to be reflexive on set X if $xRx \ \forall\ x \in X$
   (b) R is said to be identity relation on set X if $xRx \ \forall\ x \in X$ and x is not related to any other element and it is denoted by I_x.
3. ***Symmetric Relation:*** *$R : X \to Y$ is said to be symmetric iff $(x, y) \in R \Rightarrow (y, x) \in R$*
   That is, $x R y \Rightarrow y R x$. For example, perpendicularity of lines in a plane is symmetric relation.

ILLUSTRATION 16: If $X = \{a, b, c\}$ and $Y = \{a, b, c, d, e, f\}$; then find which of the following relations is/are symmetric relation (s).

(i) $R_1 = \{\ \}$ that is, void relation (ii) $R_2 = \{(a, b)\}$

(iii) $R_3 = \{(a, b), (b, a), (a, c), (c, a), (a, a)\}$

SOLUTION: (i) R_1 is symmetric relation by default i.e., we have no counter example such that $(a, b) \in R_1$ but $(b, a) \notin R_1$.

(ii) R_2 is not symmetric because $(a, b) \in R_2$ but $(b, a) \notin R_2$ and

(iii) R_3 is symmetric as $(a, b), (a, c), (a, a) \in R$ and $(b, a), (c, a), (a, a) \in R$

Transitive Relation

$R : X \to Y$ is said to be transitive iff $(x, y) \in R$ and $(y, z) \in R \Rightarrow (x, z) \in R$

i.e., $x R y$ and $yR z$

$\Rightarrow x R z$

For example, the relation 'being sister of' among the members of a family is always transitive.

ILLUSTRATION 17: If $X = \{a, b, c\}$ and $Y = \{a, b, c, d, e\}$; then which of the following is/are transitive relation(s).

(a) $R_1 = \{\ \}$ (b) $R_2 = \{(a, a)\}$

(c) $R_3 = \{(a, a), (c, d)\}$ (d) $R_4 = \{(a, b), (b, a), (a, c), (a, a), (c, a)\}$

SOLUTION: (a) R_1 is transitive relation because it is null relation, i.e., we have no counter example to disprove its non-transitivity.

(b) R_2 is transitive relation because all singleton relations are transitive.

(c) R_3 is transitive relation as we have no counter example to prove its non-transitivity, that is, R_3 does not contain ordered pairs of the type (x, y) and (y, z) for which (x, z) is not contained in R_3.

(d) R_4 is not transitive relation as (b, a); $(a, c) \in R_4$ but $(b, c) \notin R_4$.

NOTE:

(i) Every null relation is a transitive relation.
(ii) Every singleton relation is a transitive relation.
(iii) Universal and identity relations are reflexive as well as transitive.

Anti-symmetric Relation

A relation R from set X to set Y is said to be an anti-symmetric relation iff $(a, b) \in R$ and $(b, a) \in R \Rightarrow a = b$ i.e., for two different elements $x \in X$ and $y \in Y$, the relation R does not contain the ordered pairs (x, y) and (y, x) simultaneously.

e.g., Relations 'being subset of'; 'is greater than or equal to' and 'identity relation' are anti-symmetric relations.

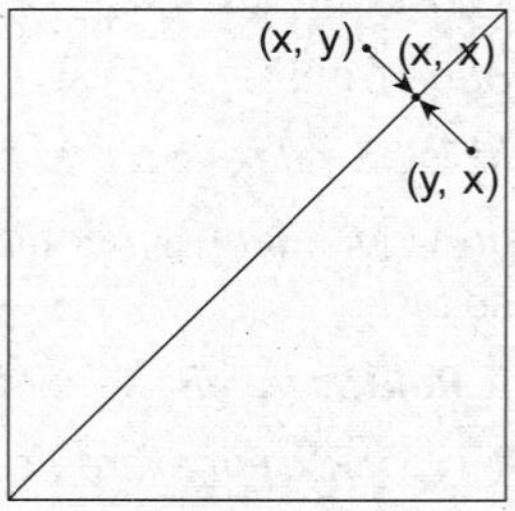

FIGURE 1.37

REMARK:

A relation R from set X to set Y may be both symmetric as well anti-symmetric, any one or not both e.g. let X = {1, 2, 3, 4} and Y = {1, 2, 3, 4, 5, 6}

R:AA, where n(A) = m

Number of reflexive relation $= 2^{m^2-m}$

Number of symmetric relation $= 2^{\frac{m}{2}+m} = 2^{\frac{m^2+m}{2}}$

From m × m matrix choose all diagonal element and rest element have two choices each. Each elements on diagonal and above have two choices, then their symmetric pair is always to be taken.

Consider the relations:

(i) $R_1 = \{(1,1), (2,2)\}$
(ii) $R_2 = \{(1, 2), (2, 1), (2, 3), (3, 2)\}$
(iii) $R_3 = \{(1, 1), (2, 2), (3, 4)\}$
(iv) $R_4 = \{(1, 2), (2, 1), (3, 4)\}$

(i) R_1 is symmetric as whenever ordered pair $(x, y) \in R_1 \Rightarrow (y, x) \in R_1$.
Also R_1 is anti-symmetric as for no two different elements x, y the ordered pairs (x, y) and (y, x) occur in R_1.

(ii) R_2 is symmetric but not anti-symmetric as $(1, 2), (2, 3) \in R_2$
$\Rightarrow$ $(2, 1), (3, 2) \in R_2$ but $1 \neq 2$ and $2 \neq 3$.

(iii) R_3 is anti-symmetric but not symmetric as $(3, 4) \in R_3$ but $(4, 3) \notin R_3$.

(iv) R_4 is neither symmetric nor anti-symmetric as $(3, 4) \in R_4$ but $(4, 3) \notin R_4$ and $(1, 2), (2, 1)$ both are in R_4 but $1 \neq 2$.

ILLUSTRATION 18: Let R be a relation on the set $\mathbb{N}$ of natural numbers defined by $xRy \Leftrightarrow$ 'x divides y' for all $x, y \in \mathbb{N}$.

SOLUTION: This relation is an anti-symmetric relation on set $\mathbb{N}$.

Since for any two numbers $a, b \in \mathbb{N}$, $.a \mid b$ and $b \mid a \Rightarrow a = b$

i.e., $a\ R\ b$ and $b\ R\ a$

$\Rightarrow\ a = b.$

It should be noted that this relation is not anti-symmetric on the set $\mathbb{Z}$ of integers, because we find that for any non-zero integer a, $aR\,(-a)$ and $(-a)\ R\ a$. but $a \neq -a$.

ILLUSTRATION 19: Let a relation R_1 on the set $\mathbb{R}$ of real numbers be defined as $(a, b) \in R_1 \Leftrightarrow 1 + ab > 0$ $\forall\ a, b \in \mathbb{R}$.

Show that R_1 is reflexive and symmetric but not transitive.

SOLUTION: We observe the following properties:

Reflexivity: Let a be an arbitrary element of $\mathbb{R}$. Now $1 + a\,.\,a = 1 + a^2 > 0$

$\Rightarrow\ (a, a) \in R_1$ Thus $(a, a) \in R_1$ for all $a \in \mathbb{R}$. So R_1 is reflexive on $\mathbb{R}$

Symmetry: Let $(a, b) \in R_1$ $\qquad \Rightarrow\ 1 + ab > 0$

$\Rightarrow\ 1 + ba > 0$ $\qquad \Rightarrow\ (b, a) \in R_1$.

$\therefore\ R_1$ is symmetric relation on $\mathbb{R}$

Transitivity: Let $a = 4$, $b = -1/5$, $c = -1$, then $1 + ab = 1 + 4(-1/5) = 1/5$

$\Rightarrow\ 1 + ab > 0$ $\qquad \Rightarrow\ (a, b) \in R_1$.

Also $1 + bc = 1 + (-1/5)(-1) = 6/5$

$\Rightarrow\ 1 + bc > 0$ $\qquad \Rightarrow\ (b, c) \in R_1$

Now $1 + ac = 1 + 4(-1) = -3 < 0$

$\Rightarrow\ (a, c) \notin R_1$.

$\therefore\ R_1$ is not transitive.

Equivalence Relation

A relation R from a set X to set Y (R: $X \to Y$) is said to be an equivalence relation iff it is reflexive, symmetric as well as transitive. The equivalence relation is denoted by ~. *e.g* Relation 'is equal to' (Equality). Similarity and congruency of triangles, parallelism of lines are equivalence relations.

ILLUSTRATION 20: Let $A = \{1, 2, 3\}$. Which of the following is not an equivalence relation on A?

(a) $\{(1, 1), (2, 2), (3, 3)\}$
(b) $\{(1, 1), (2, 2), (3, 3), (1, 2), (2, 1)\}$
(c) $\{(1, 1), (2, 2), (3, 3), (2, 3), (3, 2)\}$
(d) None of these

SOLUTION: All the subsets of $A \times A$, given in (a), (b) and (c) are equivalence relation on A, as they are reflexive, symmetric and transitive.

ILLUSTRATION 21: Prove that the relation R on the set $\mathbb{Z}$ of all integer numbers defined by $(x, y) \in R$ $\Leftrightarrow x - y$ is divisible by n is an equivalence relation on $\mathbb{Z}$, where n is a fixed integer.

SOLUTION: We observe the following properties

Reflexivity: For any $a \in \mathbb{Z}$, we have $a - a = 0 \times n \Rightarrow a - a$ is divisible by $n \Rightarrow (a, a) \in R$

Thus, $(a, a) \in R$ for all $a \in \mathbb{Z}$. So, R is reflexive on $\mathbb{Z}$.

Symmetricity: Let $(a, b) \in R. \Rightarrow (a - b)$ is divisible by n

$\Rightarrow (a - b) = np$ for some $p \in \mathbb{Z} \Rightarrow b - a = n(-p)$

$\Rightarrow b - a$ is divisible by n $\Rightarrow (b, a) \in R$

Thus $(a, b) \in R$ $\Rightarrow (b, a) \in R$ for all $a, b \in R$. So R is symmetric on $\mathbb{Z}$.

Transitivity: Let $a, b, c \in \mathbb{Z}$, such that $(a, b) \in R$ and $(b, c) \in R$. Then $(a, b) \in R$

$\Rightarrow (a - b)$ is divisible by n $\Rightarrow a - b = np$ for some $p \in \mathbb{Z}$, $(b, c) \in R$

$\Rightarrow (b - c)$ is divisible by n $\Rightarrow b - c = nq$ for some $q \in \mathbb{Z}$

$\therefore$ $(a, b) \in R$ and $(b, c) \in R$ $\Rightarrow a - b = np$ and $b - c = nq$

$\Rightarrow (a - b) + (b - c) = np + nq$ $\Rightarrow a - c = n(p + q)$

$\Rightarrow a - c$ is divisible by n $\Rightarrow (a, c) \in R$

Thus, $(a, b) \in R$ and $(b, c) \in R$ $\Rightarrow (a, c) \in R$ for all $a, b, c \in \mathbb{Z}$

So, R is transitive relation on $\mathbb{Z}$.

Thus, R being reflexive, symmetric and transitive is an equivalence relation on $\mathbb{Z}$

ILLUSTRATION 22: Given the relation $R = \{(1, 2), (2, 4)\}$ on set of natural numbers $\mathbb{N}$, add a minimum number of ordered pairs so that the enlarged relation is symmetric, transitive and reflexive, i.e., equivalence.

SOLUTION: The enlarged relation $= \{(1, 2), (2, 1), (2, 4), (4, 2), (1, 4), (4, 1), (1, 1), (2, 2), (4, 4)\}$ is reflexive, symmetric and transitive i.e., equivalence.

ILLUSTRATION 23: A relation R on the set of complex numbers $\mathbb{C}$ is defined by $z_1 R z_2$ iff $\frac{z_1 - z_2}{z_1 + z_2}$ is real. Show that R is an equivalence relation.

SOLUTION: Given $z_1\ R\ z_2$ iff $\frac{z_1 - z_2}{z_1 + z_2}$ is real.

Reflexivity: Now $z_1 R z_1$ if $\frac{z_1 - z_1}{z_1 + z_1}$ is real. i.e., iff 0 is real, which is true.

$\Rightarrow$ The relation R is reflexive

For Symmetry: Also $z_1\ R\ z_2$ $\Rightarrow \frac{z_1 - z_2}{z_1 + z_2}$ is real

$\Rightarrow \frac{z_2 - z_1}{z_1 + z_2}$ is real $\Rightarrow z_2\ R\ z_1$.

$\Rightarrow$ the relation R is symmetric.

For Transivity: Let $z_1 = a + ib$, $z_2 = c + id$, $z_3 = e + if$ be any three complex numbers, where a, b, c, d, e, f are reals.

Then $z_1\ R\ z_2$ iff $\frac{z_1 - z_2}{z_1 + z_2}$ is real, i.e., iff $\frac{(a-c)+i(b-d)}{(a+c)+i(b+d)}$ is real.

That is, iff $\frac{(a-c)+i(b-d)}{(a+c)+i(b+d)} \times \frac{(a+c)-i(b+d)}{(a+c)-i(b+d)}$ is real

That is, iff $\frac{(a^2-c^2+b^2-d^2)+i[(a+c)(b-d)-(a-c)(b+d)]}{(a+c)^2+(b+d)^2}$ is real.

i.e., iff $(a + c)(b - d) - (a - c)(b + d) = 0$

i.e., iff $(ab - ad + bc - cd - ab - ad + bc + cd) = 0$

i.e., iff $2bc - 2ad = 0$ i.e., $ad = bc$.

Now $z_1 R z_2$ and $z_2 R z_3$ $\Rightarrow ad = bc$ and $cf = ed$

$\Rightarrow adcf = bced$ $\Rightarrow af = be$ when $cd \neq 0$

$\Rightarrow z_1 R z_3$ and when $cd = 0$, then transitivity is obvious

$\Rightarrow$ the relation R is transitive.

Hence, the given relation R is an equivalence relation.

ILLUSTRATION 24: If R_1 and R_2 are two equivalence relations on a non-empty set A, then show that $R_1 \cup R_2$ need not be an equivalence relation.

SOLUTION: When R_1 and R_2 are equivalence relations, then both R_1 and R_2 are reflexive as well as symmetric.

Also $R_1 \cup R_2$ will be reflexive and symmetric, but $R_1 \cup R_2$ need not be transitive.

For example, on set $A = \{1, 2, 3\}$

Both $R_1 = \{(1, 1), (2, 2), (3, 3), (1, 2), (2, 1)\}$ and $R_2 = \{(1, 1), (2, 2), (3, 3), (2, 3), (3, 2)\}$ are equivalence relations but $R_1 \cup R_2$ is not an equivalence relation as $(1, 2) \in R_1 \cup R_2$ and $(2, 3) \in R_1 \cup R_2$ but $(1, 3) \notin R_1 \cup R_2$ thus showing that $R_1 \cup R_2$ is not transitive.

ILLUSTRATION 25: Which of the following is not an equivalence relation on $\mathbb{Z}$, the set of integers?

(a) $xRy \Leftrightarrow x + y$ is an even integer.
(b) $xRy \Leftrightarrow x < y$.
(c) $xRy \Leftrightarrow x - y$ is an even integer.
(d) $xRy \Leftrightarrow x = y$

SOLUTION: (a) **Reflexivity:** Let xRx iff $x + x$ is an even integer iff $2x$ is an even integer, which is true.

Symmetry: Let $xRy \Rightarrow x + y$ is even integer $\Rightarrow y + x$ is even integer

$\Rightarrow yRx$

Transitivity: Let xRy and $yRz \Rightarrow x + y$ is even integer and $y + z$ is even integer.

$\Rightarrow (x + y) + (y + z)$ is even integer

$\Rightarrow x + 2y + z$ is even integer

$\Rightarrow x + z$ is even integer as the sum of two even integers is an even integer.

$\Rightarrow xRz$.

Thus, the given relation is an equivalence relation

(b) **Reflexivity:** Let xRx iff $x < x$ which is false. Thus R is non-reflexive.

Symmetry: Let $xRy \Rightarrow x < y \not\Rightarrow y < x$ i.e., $y \not R x$. Thus R is non-symmetric.

Transitivity: Let xRy and $yRz \Rightarrow x < y$ and $y < z \Rightarrow x < z$. Thus R is transitive.

Thus, the given relation is not an equivalence relation.

(c) Reflexivity: Let xRx iff $x - x$ is an even integer.

Iff zero is an even integer, which is true.

Symmetry: Let $xRy \Rightarrow x - y$ is even integer $\Rightarrow y - x$ is even integer.

$\Rightarrow yRx$

Transitivity: Let xRy and $yRz \Rightarrow x - y$ is even integer and $y - z$ is even integer.

$\Rightarrow (x - y) + (y - z)$ is even integer

$\Rightarrow$ $x - z$ is even integer

$\Rightarrow$ xRz $\Rightarrow$ R is transitive

Thus the given relation is an equivalence relation

(d) **Reflexivity:** Let xRx iff $x = x$ which is true. Thus, R is reflexive.

Symmetry: Let $xRy \Rightarrow x = y \Rightarrow y = x$. Thus, R is symmetric.

Transitivity: Let xRy and $yRz \Rightarrow x = y$ and $y = z$

$\Rightarrow$ $x = z$. Thus, R is transitive.

Thus, the given relation is an equivalence relation.

ILLUSTRATION 26: Let $A = \{a, b, c\}$ and $R = \{(a, a), (b, b), (c, c), (b, c)\}$ be a relation on A. Show that R is

(a) reflexive (b) non-symmetric

(c) Anti-symmetric (d) transitive

SOLUTION: (a) **Reflexivity:** Since $x\ R\ x$ for all $x \in A$, therefore, R is reflexive.

(b) **Non-symmetry:** As bRc but $c \not R b$ i.e., $(b, c) \in \mathbb{R}$ but $(c, b) \notin \mathbb{R}$, therefore, R is not symmetric.

(c) **Anti-symmetry:** As for any two distinct $x, y \in \mathbb{R}$, both (x, y) and (y, x) do not belong to R.

Therefore, R is anti-symmetric.

(d) **Transitivity:** Further R is transitive as whenever xRy and yRz, then xRz.

(Here, bRb and $bRc \Rightarrow bRc$).

Equivalence class of an element: If R is an equivalence relation on a set A i.e., $R : A \rightarrow A$ is an equivalence relation, then for an element $x \in A$, equivalence class of element x is denoted by $[x]$ and is defined as $[x] = \{a \in A : (a, x) \in R\}$.

Further various equivalence classes of elements of A are either identical or disjoint and their union covers the set A.

If $A_1, A_2, A_3, \ldots, A_n$ are equivalence classes on set A, then either $A_i = A_j$ or $A_i \cap A_j = \phi\ \forall$ i, j and $\bigcup_{i=1}^{n} A_i = A$.

The sequence $A_1, A_2, A_3, \ldots, A_n$ called a partition of A if each A_i represents a different equivalence class,

i.e., $Ai \cap Aj = \phi$ and $\bigcup_{i=1}^{n} Ai = A$.

ILLUSTRATION 27: In the set W of whole numbers an equivalence relation R is defined as follows. '$a\ R\ b$ iff both a and b leave same remainder when divided by 5'.

SOLUTION: Equivalence class of $1 = [1] = \{a \in W; a\ R\ 1\} = \{a \in W; a = 5p + r; 1 = 5q + r$, for some $p, q \in W)\}$

$= \{a \in W; a = 5p + 1\}$ as $1 = 5q + r$

$\Rightarrow$ $q = 0, r = 1$

$\therefore$ $[1] = \{1, 6, 11, 16, 21 \ldots\}$

■ COMPOSITION OF RELATIONS

Let R and S be two relations from set A to B and B to C respectively. Then we can define a relation SoR from A to C such that $(a, c) \in So\ R \Leftrightarrow \exists\ b \in B$ such that $(a, b) \in R$ and $(b, c) \in S$.

This relation is called the composition of R and S. Diagrammatically it is as shown bellow.

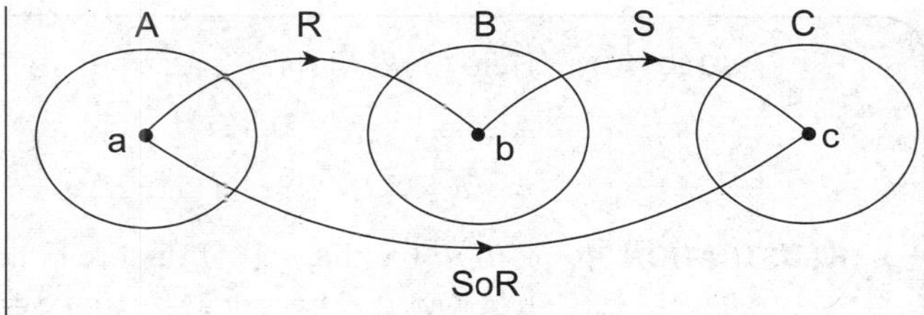

FIGURE 1.38

ILLUSTRATION 28: If $A = \{1, 2, 3\}$, $B = \{a, b, c, d\}$, $C = \{p, q, r, s\}$ be three sets such that $R = \{(1, a), (2, c), (1, c), (2, d)\}$ is a relation from A to B and $S = \{(a, s), (b, q), (c, r)\}$ is relation from B to C. Then find SoR and RoS.

SOLUTION: $SoR = \{(1, s), (2, r), (1, r)\}$. In this case RoS does not exist as S is a relation from B to C and R is a relation from A to B. RoS exists if S is a relation from B to C, than R should be from C to other set A. In general $RoS \neq SoR$.

■ INVERSE OF A RELATION

Let A, B be two sets and let R be a relation from a set A to B. Then the inverse of R, denoted by R^{-1}, is a relation from B to A and is defined by $R^{-1} = \{(b, a): (a, b) \in R\}$. Clearly, $(a, b) \in R \Leftrightarrow (b, a) \in R^{-1}$.

Also, Dom (R) = Range (R^{-1}) and range (R) = Dom (R^{-1}).

e.g. Let $A = \{1, 2, 3, 4\}$ and $B = \{2, 3, 4, 5\}$.

Define a relation R from A to B as xRy iff $y = x + 1$, then $R = \{(1, 2), (2, 3), (3, 4), (4, 5)\}$.

$\Rightarrow\ R^{-1} = \{(2, 1), (3, 2), (4, 3), (5, 4)\}$

Thus, we can define R^{-1} a relation (say R_1) from B to A as xR_1y iff $y = x - 1$. The arrow diagram given below represents the relations R and R^{-1}.

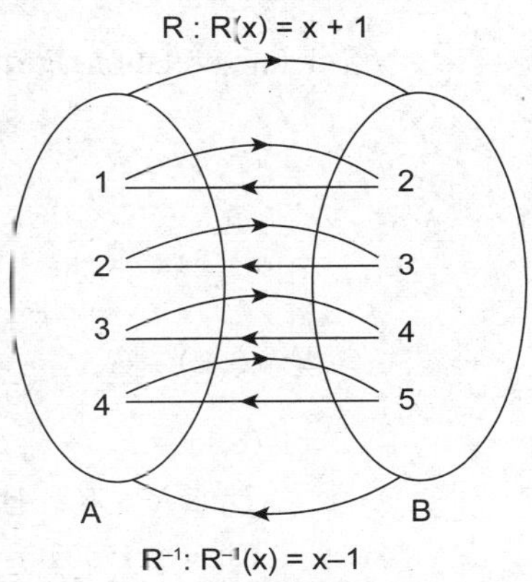

FIGURE 1.39

REMARK:

$(SoR)^{-1} = R^{-1}oS^{-1}$; where R is a relation from A to B and S is a relation from B to C.

Proof: Let $(x, y) \in (SoR)^{-1}$

$\Leftrightarrow (y, x) \in (SoR) \Leftrightarrow (SoR)(y) = x$

$\Leftrightarrow S[R(y)] = x \Leftrightarrow (R(y), x) \in S \Leftrightarrow (x, R(y)) \in S^{-1}$

$\Leftrightarrow S^{-1}(x) = R(y) \Leftrightarrow R(y) = S^{-1}(x) \Leftrightarrow R^{-1}(S^{-1}(x)) = y$

$\Leftrightarrow R^{-1}oS^{-1}(x) = y \Leftrightarrow (x, y) \in R^{-1}oS^{-1}$

$\Leftrightarrow SoR^{-1} = R^{-1}oS^{-1}$.

ILLUSTRATION 29: Let $A = \{1, 2, 3, 4\}$; $B = \{5, 6, 7, 8\}$; $C = \{9, 10, 11, 12\}$ and let $R = \{(1, 5), (2, 6), (3, 7)\}$ and $S = \{(5, 9), (6, 11), (8, 12)\}$, be the relations from A to B and B to C respectively. Then prove that $(SoR)^{-1} = R^{-1}oS^{-1}$.

SOLUTION: Here $(SoR) = \{(1, 9), (2, 11)\}$ $\Rightarrow (SoR)^{-1} = \{(9, 1), (11, 2)\}$

Also $S^{-1} = \{(9, 5), (11, 6), (12, 8)\}$ and $R^{-1} = \{(5, 1), (6, 2), (7, 3)\}$

$\Rightarrow R^{-1}oS^{-1} = \{(9, 1), (11, 2)\}$ $\therefore (SoR)^{-1} = R^{-1}oS^{-1}$.

ILLUSTRATION 30: Let A be the set of first ten natural numbers and let R be a relation on A defined by $(x, y) \in R \Leftrightarrow x + 2y = 10$. i.e., $R = \{(x, y): x \in A, y \in A \text{ and } x + 2y = 10\}$.

Express R and R^{-1} as sets of ordered pairs. Determine also

(i) Domains of R and R^{-1} (ii) Range of R and R^{-1}.

SOLUTION: We have $(x, y) \in R \Leftrightarrow x + 2y = 10 \Leftrightarrow y = \dfrac{10-x}{2}, x, y \in A$;

where $A = \{1, 2, 3, 4, 5, 6, 7, 8, 9, 10\}$

Now, for $x = 1, y = \dfrac{10-1}{2} = \dfrac{9}{2} \notin A$

This shows that 1 is not related to any element in A.

Similarly, we can observe that 3, 5, 7, 9 and 10 are not related to any element of A under the defined relation. Further, we find that for $x = 2, y = \dfrac{10-2}{2} = 4 \in A$

$\therefore (2, 4) \in R.$ $\Rightarrow$ For $x = 4, y = \dfrac{10-4}{2} = 3 \in A$

$\Rightarrow (4, 3) \in R$ $\Rightarrow$ For $x = 6, y = \dfrac{10-6}{2} = 2 \in A$

$\Rightarrow (6, 2) \in R$ $\Rightarrow$ For $x = 8, y = \dfrac{10-8}{2} = 1 \in A$

$\Rightarrow (8,1) \in R$

Thus $R = \{(2, 4), (4, 3), (6, 2), (8, 1)\}$ $\Rightarrow R^{-1} = \{(4, 2), (3, 4), (2, 6), (1, 8)\}$

Clearly, Domain $(R) = \{2, 4, 6, 8\}$ = Range (R^{-1}) and range $(R) = \{4, 3, 2, 1\}$ = Domain (R^{-1}).

■ IMPORTANT REMARKS AT A GLANCE

- ❑ If number of elements in A: $n(A) = m$ and $n(B) = n$, then number of elements in $(A \times B) = m \times n$.
- ❑ Since $A \times B$ contains all such ordered pairs of the type (a, b) such that $a \in A$ and $b \in B$, that means it includes all possibilities in which the elements of set A can be related with the elements of set B. Therefore, $A \times B$ is termed as largest possible relation defined from set A to set B, also known as universal relation from A to B.
- ❑ If $A \subseteq B$, then $(A \times B) \cap (B \times A) = A^2 = A \times A$
- ❑ If A has m elements and B has n elements, then number of relations that can be defined from A to $B = 2^{m \times n}$.
- ❑ If A is a set containing n elements, then the number of relations that can be defined on set $A = (2)^{n^2}$.
- ❑ If A and B are two non-empty sets having n elements in common, then $A \times B$ and $B \times A$ have n^2 elements in common.
- ❑ If A is related to B, then symbolically it is written as (aRb), where a is pre-image and b is image.
- ❑ If A is not related to B, then symbolically it is written as $a \not{R}\, b$.
- ❑ Every relation from $A \to B$ is a subset of $A \times B$.
- ❑ Every function is a relation but every relation cannot be a function.
- ❑ Relations can be represented in following 5 ways
  1. **As a set of ordered pair:** (Roster form)
  2. Graphically (by lattice) $\to$ Plotting the points on $x - y$ plane
  3. Diagrammatically (by using arrow diagrams)

4. Analytically (set builder form) → Representing relation as an equation in x and y. e.g., $y = \sqrt{x}$
5. **Tabular form:** Arranging the elements of set A along first column and the elements of set B along first row and putting '1' in the row containing a and column containing b if $(a, b) \in R$ and 0 if $(a, b) \notin R$

- ❑ All identity relations are reflexive but all reflexive relations are not identity.
- ❑ If a relation comes out to be neither One–many nor Many–one, then it is classified as One–one relation.
- ❑ ϕ or { } is called null or void relation. i.e., relation having no element. e.g. If $A = \{2, 3, 5\}$, $B = \{7, 11\}$, then the relation R from A to B defined by $(a, b) \in R$, if 'a divides b' is a null or void relation, because there is no element in A which divides any element of B. i.e., $R = \{\ \}$ or ϕ.
- ❑ Every null relation is a transitive relation.
- ❑ Every singleton relation is a transitive relation.
- ❑ Universal and identity relations are reflexive, as well as transitive.
- ❑ Identity relation is symmetric as well as anti-symmetric both.
- ❑ Union of two reflexive (or symmetric) relations on a set A also reflexive (or symmetric) on set A.
- ❑ Union of two transitive relations need not be transitive on set A.
- ❑ Union of two equivalence relations need not be equivalence.

TEXTUAL EXERCISE–3: (SUBJECTIVE)

1. Let R be a relation from $\mathbb{N}$ to $\mathbb{N}$ defined by $R = \{(a, b): a^2 + b^2 = ab\}$. Are the following true?
   (i) $(a, a) \in R \ \forall\ a \in \mathbb{N}$
   (ii) $(a, b) \in R \Rightarrow (b, a) \in R$
   (iii) $(a, b) \in R$; $(b, c) \in R \Rightarrow (a, c) \in R$
2. Let R be a relation from $\mathbb{Q}$ to $\mathbb{Q}$ defined by $R = \{(a, b): a, b \in \mathbb{Q}$ and $a - b \in \mathbb{Z}\}$. Show that
   (i) $(a, a) \in R$ for all $a \in \mathbb{Q}$
   (ii) $(a, b) \in R \Rightarrow (b, a) \in R$
3. Let $A = \{2, 3, 6\}$. Which of the following relations on A are reflexive?
   (i) $R_1 = \{(2, 2), (3, 3), (6, 6)\}$
   (ii) $R_2 = \{(2, 2), (3, 3), (3, 6), (6, 3)\}$
   (iii) $R_3 = \{(2, 2), (3, 6), (2, 6)\}$
   (iv) $R_4 = \{(2, 2), (3, 3), (3, 6), (6, 6)\ (6, 3)\}$
4. Let $A = \{1, 2, 3, 5\}$. Which of the following relations on A are symmetric?
   (i) $R_1 = \{(1, 2), (2, 3)\}$
   (ii) $R_2 = \{(1, 2), (2, 3), (3, 5), (3, 2), (5, 3), (2, 1)\}$
   (iii) $R_3 = \{(1, 1), (2, 2), (3, 3), (5, 5), (3, 5)\}$
   (iv) $R_4 = A \times A$
5. Let $A = \{2, 3, 4, 5, 6\}$. Which of the following relations on A are transitive?
   (i) $R_1 = \{(2, 3), (3, 6)\}$
   (ii) $R_2 = \{(2, 2), (3, 4), (4, 4), (4, 5)\}$
   (iii) $R_3 = \{(2, 4), (4, 5), (2, 5)\}$
   (iv) $R_4 = \{(2, 3), (3, 2), (4, 5), (5, 4)\}$
6. Let $A=\{1, 2, 3, 4\}$.Which of the following relations on A are reflexive, symmetric and transitive
   (i) $R_1 = \{(1, 1), (2, 2), (3, 3), (4, 4), (1, 3), (3, 4)\}$
   (ii) $R_2 = \{(2, 4), (4, 2)\}$
   (iii) $R_3 = \{(4, 3), (2, 4)\}$
   (iv) $R_4 = A \times A$
7. Let R be the relation on the set R of real numbers defined by $(a, b) \in R$ if $1 - ab > 0$. Show that the relation R is symmetric, but not reflexive and transitive.
8. Test whether the following relations are reflexive, symmetric and transitive.
   (i) R_1 on $\mathbb{Z}$ defined by $(a, b) \in R_1$ iff $|a - b| \le 7$
   (ii) R_2 on $\mathbb{Q}$ defined by $(a, b) \in R_2$ iff $ab = 4$.
   (iii) R_3 on $\mathbb{R}$ defined by $(a, b) \in R_3$ iff $a^2 - 4ab + 3b^2 = 0$.
9. Classify the following relations in terms of Reflexive (A) Symmetric (B) and Transitive (C) relations also state which of them are equivalence relation.
   R_1: $\mathbb{Z} \to \mathbb{Z}$, $\{a\ R_1\ b$ iff a is divisible by b;$\}$ where $\mathbb{Z}$ is set of all integers.
   R_2: $\Delta \to \Delta$ where Δ is set of all triangles defined as $\{\Delta_1\ R_2\ \Delta_2$ iff Δ_1 and Δ_2 are similar$\}$ similarity of triangles.
   R_3: $L \to L$, where L is set of all lines on a given plane defined as $\{L_1\ R_3\ L_2$ iff L_1 is $\parallel L_2\}$ parallelism of lines
   R_4: $L \to L$, where L is set of all lines on a given plane defined as $\{L_1\ R_4\ L_2$ if $L_1 \perp L_2\}$ perpendicularity of lines

R_5: $H \to H$, where H is set of all members of a family and relation is being sister of. i.e., $\{a\ R_5\ b$ iff a is sister of $b\}$

R_6: $\mathbb{N} \to \mathbb{N}$, where $\mathbb{N}$ is a natural numbers defined as $\{a\ R_6\ b$ iff $a - b \in \mathbb{N}\}$

R_7: $\mathbb{R} \to \mathbb{R}$; where $\mathbb{R}$ is set of real numbers defined as $\{a\ R_7\ b$ iff $a \geq b\}$

10. Let $\mathbb{N}$ denote the set of all natural numbers and R a relation on $\mathbb{N} \times \mathbb{N}$. Which of the following is an equivalence relation?

(a) $(a, b)\ R\ (c, d)$ iff $ad\ (b + c) = bc\ (a + d)$
(b) $(a, b)\ R\ (c, d)$ iff $a + d = b + c$
(c) $(a, b)\ R\ (c, d)$ iff $ad = bc$
(d) None of these

11. For real numbers x and y, we write $x\ R\ y \Leftrightarrow x^2 - y^2 + \sqrt{3}$ is an irrational number. Then the relation R is

(a) reflexive (b) symmetric
(c) transitive (d) None of these

Answer Keys

1. (i) False (ii) True (iii) True
3. (i) and (iv) **4.** (ii) and (iv) **5.** (iii)
6. (i) only reflexive (ii) only symmetric (iii) Nothing
(iv) Reflexive, symmetric as well as transitive i.e., equivalence.
7. (i) Reflexive and symmetric but not transitive. (ii) only symmetric. (iii) only transitive.
9. $R_1 \to C$; $R_2 \to A, B, C$; $R_3 \to A, B, C$; $R_4 \to B$; $R_5 \to C$; $R_6 \to C$; $R_7 \to A, C$
10. a, b, c **11.** a

TEXTUAL EXERCISE-3: (OBJECTIVE)

1. Define a relation R on set $A = \{2, 3, 4, 9, 16\}$ as xRy if '$x^2 = y$', then ROR^{-1} is

(a) Identity relation on set A
(b) Identity relation on Domain set of R^{-1}
(c) Reflexive relation on A
(d) Reflexive and symmetric relation on Domain of R^{-1}

2. Define two relations R_1 and R_2 on set $\{10, 20, 30, 40, 50\}$ as xR_1y if '$y - x = 10$' and xR_2y if x divides $(x + y)$; then the relation $(R_1\ o\ R_2)^{-1}$ is

(a) $\{(20, 10), (30, 10), (30, 20), (40, 10), (40, 30), (50, 10), (50, 20), (50, 40)\}$
(b) $\{(20, 10), (30, 20), (40, 30), (50, 20)\}$
(c) $\{(20, 10), (30, 30), (40, 40), (50, 20)\}$
(d) None of these

3. The relation on set of natural numbers defined as xRy if '$x + y + 4xy$' is an even number, then R is

(a) reflexive (b) symmetric
(c) transitive (d) equivalence

4. Let $A = \{2, 3, 4, 5\}$ and let $R = \{(2, 2), (3, 3), (4, 4)$ $(5, 5), (2, 3), (3, 2), (3, 5), (5, 3)\}$ be a relation in A. Then R is

(a) reflexive and transitive
(b) reflexive and symmetric
(c) reflexive and anti-symmetric
(d) None of the above

5. If R is a relation on A such that $R = R^{-1}$, then R is

(a) reflexive (b) symmetric
(c) transitive (d) None of these

6. Let R and S be two relations on a set A. Then:

(a) R and S are transitive, then $R \cup S$ is also transitive
(b) R and S are reflexive, then $R \cup S$ is equivalence
(c) R and S are symmetric, then $R \cup S$ is equivalence
(d) R and S are reflexive, then $R \cup S$ is reflexive

7. A set of points in a plane is denoted by P. Let $P_1, P_2 \in P$, then $P_1\ R\ P_2 \Leftrightarrow P_1$ and P_2 are equidistant from origin; then which statement(s) is/are correct?

(a) R is reflexive but not symmetric.
(b) R is reflexive, symmetric but not transitive
(c) R is reflexive, symmetric and transitive
(d) R is not an equivalence relation.

8. $\mathbb{N}$ is the set of natural numbers. The relation R is defined on $\mathbb{N}$ as follows $(a, b)\ R(c, d) \Leftrightarrow a + d = b + c$ is

(a) reflexive (b) symmetric
(c) transitive (d) All of these

9. The relation R defined on the set $\mathbb{N}$ of natural numbers by $xRy \Leftrightarrow 2x^2 - 3xy + y^2 = 0$ is
(a) symmetric but not reflexive
(b) only symmetric
(c) not symmetric but reflexive
(d) None of these

10. The minimum number of elements that must be included to the relation $R = \{(1,2), (2,3)\}$ on the set $\{1,2,3\}$ so that it is equivalence is
(a) 4 (b) 7
(c) 6 (d) 5

11. If R is a relation from a set A to a set B and S is a relation from set B to a set C, then the relation SoR:
(a) is from A to C (b) is from C to A
(c) Does not exist (d) None of these

12. If $R \subseteq A \times B$ and $S \subseteq B \times C$ be two relations, then $(SoR)^{-1}$ is equal to
(a) $S^{-1}oR^{-1}$ (b) $R^{-1}oS^{-1}$
(c) SoR (d) RoS

13. Consider the following statements:
(1) Identify relation on a finite set A is the greatest relation on A
(2) The universal relation on a set containing at least two elements is not anti-symmetric.
(3) The union and intersection of two symmetric relations are also symmetric relations.
(a) only 1 (b) only 2 and 3
(c) only 3 and 1 (d) All of these

14. If R and R' are symmetric relations (not disjoint) on a set A, then the relation $R \cap R'$ is
(a) reflexive (b) symmetric
(c) transitive (d) None of these

15. Let m = number of elements in a reflexive relation defined on set A and n = number of elements in an identity relation defined on set A, then
(a) $m \geq n$ (b) $m \leq n$
(c) $m = n$ (d) None of these

16. The set $S = \{1, 2, 3, \ldots, 12\}$ is to be partitioned into three sets A, B, C of equal size. Thus, $A \cup B \cup C = S$, $A \cap B = B \cap C = A \cap C = \phi$. The number of ways to partition S is
(a) $\dfrac{12!}{3!(3!)^4}$ (b) $\dfrac{12!}{(4!)^3}$
(c) $\dfrac{12!}{(3!)^4}$ (d) $\dfrac{12!}{3!(4!)^3}$

Answer Keys

1. (b,d)	**2.** (a)	**3.** (a,b,c,d)	**4.** (b)	**5.** (b)	**6.** (d)	**7.** (c)	**8.** (d)	**9.** (c)	**10.** (b)
11. (a)	**12.** (b)	**13.** (b)	**14.** (b)	**15.** (a)	**16.** (b)				

MULTIPLE-CHOICE QUESTIONS

SECTION–I

OBJECTIVE-TYPE SOLVED EXAMPLE

1. If $A = \{1, 2, 5, 6\}$ and $B = \{1, 2, 3\}$, then $(A \times B) \cap (B \times A)$ equals.

(a) $\{(1, 1), (2, 1), (6, 1), (3, 2)\}$
(b) $\{(1, 1), (1, 2), (2, 1), (2, 2)\}$
(c) $\{(1, 1), (2, 2)\}$
(d) $(1, 1), (1, 2), (2, 5), (2, 6)\}$

Solution: (b) $A = \{1, 2, 5, 6\}$ and $B = \{1, 2, 3\}$
Now $(A \times B) \cap (B \times A) = (A \cap B) \times (B \cap A)$
$[\because (A \times B) \cap (C \times D) = (A \cap C) \times (B \cap D)]$
$= (A \cap B) \times (A \cap B) = \{1, 2\} \times \{1, 2\}$
$= \{(1, 1), (1, 2), (2, 1), (2, 2)\}$.

2. If A, B, C are non-empty sets such $A \cap C = \phi$, then what is $(A \times B) \cap (C \times B)$?

(a) $A \times C$ (b) $A \times B$
(c) $B \times C$ (d) ϕ

Solution: **(d)** $(A \times B) \cap (C \times B)$
$= (A \cap C) \times (B \cap B)$
$= \phi \times B = \phi$

3. If $A = \{a, b\}$, $B = \{c, d\}$, $C = \{d, e\}$, then $\{(a, c), (a, d), (a, e), (b, c), (b, d), (b, e)\}$ is equal to

(a) $A \cap (B \cup C)$ (b) $A \cup (B \cap C)$
(c) $A \times (B \cup C)$ (d) $A \times (B \cap C)$

Solution: (c) Clearly $A \cap (B \cup C)$ and $A \cup (B \cap C)$ do not contain ordered pairs.
So the answer can't be (*a*) and (*b*)
Now $(B \cap C) = \{d\}$ and $A \times (B \cap C)$
$= \{a, b\} \times \{d\} = \{(a, d), (b, d)\}$
So (d) is incorrect.
Next $(B \cup C) = \{c, d, e\}$
$\Rightarrow A \times (B \cup C) = \{a, b\} \times \{c, d, e\} = \{(a, c), (a, d), (a, e), (b, c), (b, d), (b, e)\}$
$\therefore$ (c) is correct.

4. If $S_1 = \{1, 2, 3, ..., 20\}$, $S_2 = \{a, b, c, d\}$, $S_3 = \{b, d, e, f\}$. The number of elements of $(S_1 \times S_2) \cup (S_1 \times S_3)$ is

(a) 100 (b) 120
(c) 140 (d) 40

Solution: (b) $S_1 \times S_2$ has $20 \times 4 = 80$ elements
$S_1 \times S_3$ has $20 \times 4 = 80$ elements
Number of common elements $= 20 \times 2 = 40$
$[\because b$ and d are common elements in S_2 and $S_3]$
$\therefore$ Number of elements of $(S_1 \times S_2) \cup (S_1 \times S_3)$
$= 80 + 80 - 40 = 160 - 40 = 120$.

5. Let $A = \{(x, y) : y = e^x, x \in \mathbb{R}\}$, $B = \{(x, y) : y = e^{-x}, x \in \mathbb{R}\}$. Then:

(a) $A \cap B = \phi$ (b) $A \cap B \neq \phi$
(c) $A \cup B = \mathbb{R}$ (d) None of these

Solution: (b) $y = e^x$ and $y = e^{-x}$
$\Rightarrow e^x = e^{-x}$ $\Rightarrow e^{2x} = 1$
$\Rightarrow e^{2x} = e^0$ $\Rightarrow 2x = 0$
$\Rightarrow x = 0$
$\therefore y = e^0 = 1$
$\therefore$ A and B meet at (0, 1)
Hence, $A \cap B \neq \phi$

6. Let $A = \{(x, y) : y = e^x, x \in \mathbb{R}\}$, $B = \{(x, y) : y = x, x \in \mathbb{R}\}$. Then:

(a) $B \subseteq A$ (b) $A \subseteq B$
(c) $A \cap B = \phi$ (d) $A \cup B = A$

Solution: (c) $y = e^x$ and $y = x$
$\Rightarrow e^x = x$
$\Rightarrow$ No $x \in \mathbb{R}$ as e^x and $y = x$ do not intersect each other.
Hence $A \cap B = \phi$.

7. Consider the following with regard to a relation R on a set of real numbers defined by xRy if and only if $3x + 4y = 5$. Consider the following three statements:

1. $0R1$ **2.** $1R\frac{1}{2}$

3. $\frac{2}{3}R\frac{3}{4}$

Which of the above are correct?

(a) 1 and 2 only (b) 1 and 3 only
(c) 2 and 3 only (d) 1, 2 and 3

Solution: (c) $3x + 4y = 5$
$\Rightarrow y = \frac{5-3x}{4}$

we are to find y for $x = 0, 1, \frac{2}{3}$ (By given options)

$\Rightarrow y = \frac{5}{4}$ for $x = 0$; $y = \frac{1}{2}$ for $x = 1$ and

$y = \frac{3}{4}$ for $x = \frac{2}{3}$

$\Rightarrow 1R\frac{1}{2}$ and $\frac{2}{3}R\frac{3}{4}$

$\Rightarrow$ (2) and (3) are true

$\Rightarrow$ (c) is correct option.

8. If the set A and B are defined as: $A = \left\{(x, y) : y = \frac{1}{x}, 0 \neq x \in \mathbb{R}\right\}$, $B = \{(x, y) : y = -x, x \in \mathbb{R}\}$, then

(a) $A \cap B = A$ (b) $A \cap B = B$

(c) $A \cap B = \phi$ (d) None of these

Solution: (c) $y = \frac{1}{x}$ and $y = -x$

$\Rightarrow \frac{1}{x} = -x$

$\Rightarrow x^2 = -1$

$\Rightarrow x \notin \mathbb{R}$.

$\therefore A \cap B = \phi$.

9. What is the set of points (x, y) satisfying the equation $x^2 + y^2 = 4$ and $x + y = 2$?

(a) {(2, 0), (–2, 0), (0, 2)}

(b) {(0, 2), (0, –2)}

(c) {(0, 2), (2, 0)}

(d) {(2, 0), (–2, 0), (0, 2), (0, –2)}

Solution: (c) $x^2 + y^2 = 4$; $x + y = 2$

$\Rightarrow x^2 + (2 - x)^2 = 4$

$\Rightarrow 2x^2 - 4x = 0$

$\Rightarrow x = 0$ or $x = 2$

$\therefore$ for $x = 0, y = 2$ and for $x = 2, y = 0$

$\therefore \{(x, y) : x^2 + y^2 = 4; x + y = 2\} = \{(0, 2), (2, 0)\}$

10. Let $R = \{(1, 3), (4, 2), (2, 4), (2, 3), (3, 1)\}$ be a relation on the set $A = \{1, 2, 3, 4\}$. The relation R is

(a) a function (b) reflexive

(c) not symmetric (d) transitive

Solution: (c) R is not a function as element 2 has two images 4 and 3.

Also R is not reflexive as no element of A is related with itself.

Further $(2, 3) \in R$ but $(3, 2) \notin R$

Hence, R is not symmetric.

Also R is not transitive as $(2, 4), (4, 2) \in R$ but $(2, 2) \notin R$.

11. Let $R = \{(3, 3), (6, 6), (9, 9), (12, 12), (6, 12), (3, 9), (3, 12), (3, 6)\}$ be a relation on the set $A = \{3, 6, 9, 12\}$.

The relation is

(a) reflexive and transitive only

(b) reflexive only

(c) an equivalence relation

(d) reflexive and symmetric only

Solution: (a) R is reflexive and transitive only.

Since $(3, 3), (6, 6), (9, 9), (12, 12) \in R$

$\Rightarrow R$ is Reflexive

and $(3, 6), (6, 12), (3, 12) \in R$

$\Rightarrow R$ is transitive. Further R is not symmetric as $(3, 9), (6, 12), (3, 6), (3, 12) \in R$ but their inverses $(9, 3), (12, 6), (6, 3), (12, 3) \notin R$.

12. Let W denotes the set of words in the English dictionary. Define the relation R by: $R = \{(x, y) \in W \times W \mid$ the words x and y have at least one letter in common$\}$. Then R is

(a) not reflexive, symmetric and transitive

(b) reflexive, symmetric and not transitive

(c) reflexive, symmetric and transitive

(d) reflexive, not symmetric and transitive

Solution: (b) **Reflexivity:** Clearly $(x, x) \in R\ \forall x \in W$ as every word has all letters common to itself. So, R is reflexive.

Symmetricity: Let $(x, y) \in R$, then $(y, x) \in R$ as x and y have at least one letter in common.

So, R is symmetric.

Transitivity: But R is not transitive for example let x = DELHI, y = CHANDIGARH and z = AMBALA, then $(x, y) \in R$ and $(y, z) \in R$ but $(x, z) \notin R$.

13. Let X be the set of all graduates in India. Elements x and y in X are said to be related if they are graduates of the same university. Which one of the following statements is correct?

(a) Relation is symmetric and transitive only

(b) Relation is reflexive and transitive only

(c) Relation is reflexive and symmetric only

(d) Relation is reflexive, symmetric and transitive.

Solution: (d) **Reflexivity:** xRx iff x and x are graduates of same university, which is true.

Symmetricity: $xRy \Rightarrow x$ and y are graduates from same university

$\Rightarrow$ y and x are graduates from same university

$\Rightarrow yRx$

Transitivity: xRy and yRz

$\Rightarrow$ x and y are graduates from same university as well as y and z are graduates from same university.

$\Rightarrow$ x, y and z are graduates from same university

$\Rightarrow$ x and z are graduates from same university

$\Rightarrow xRz$.

14. Let M be set of men and R is a relation 'is son of' defined on M. Then R is

(a) an equivalence relation
(b) a symmetric relation only
(c) a transitive relation only
(d) None of the above

Solution: (d) **Reflexivity:** As nobody can be son of himself so the relation R can't be reflexive

Symmetric: xRy

$\Rightarrow$ x is son of y

$\Rightarrow$ y is father of x

$\Rightarrow$ y can't be son of x

$\Rightarrow y \not R x$.

Transitivity: Let xRy and yRz

$\Rightarrow$ x is a son of y and y is a son of z

$\Rightarrow$ x is a grand son of z

$\Rightarrow x \not R z$.

$\therefore$ The given relation is neither reflexive nor symmetric, transitive

15. Let $\mathbb{R}$ be the real line. Consider the following subsets of the plane $\mathbb{R} \times \mathbb{R}$.

$S = \{(x, y) : y = x + 1 \text{ and } 0 < x < 2\}$, $T = \{(x, y) : x - y \text{ is an integer}\}$. Which one of the following is true?

(a) neither S nor T is an equivalence relation on $\mathbb{R}$
(b) both S and T are equivalence relations on $\mathbb{R}$
(c) S is an equivalence relation on $\mathbb{R}$ but T is not
(d) T is an equivalence relation on $\mathbb{R}$ but S is not

Solution: (d) **Reflexivity:** $T = \{(x, y): x - y \in \mathbb{Z}\}$

xTx iff $x - x = 0 \in \mathbb{Z}$; which is true

$\Rightarrow$ T is a reflexive relation

Symmetricity: Let xTy

$\Rightarrow x - y \in \mathbb{Z}$ $\quad\Rightarrow y - x \in \mathbb{Z}$

$\Rightarrow yTx$ $\quad\therefore$ T is symmetrical also

Transitivity: Let xTy, yTz

$\Rightarrow x - y \in \mathbb{Z}$ and $y - z \in \mathbb{Z}$

$\Rightarrow (x - y) + (y - z) \in \mathbb{Z}$

$\Rightarrow x - z \in \mathbb{Z}$ $\quad\Rightarrow xTz$

$\Rightarrow$ T is also transitive.

Hence, T is an equivalence relation.

Clearly, $x \neq x + 1 \Rightarrow (x, x) \notin S$

$\therefore$ S is not reflexive

$\Rightarrow$ S can't be an equivalence relation.

16. Consider the following relations. $R = \{(x, y) \mid x, y$ are real numbers and $x = wy$ for some rational number $w\}$

$S = \{\left(\frac{m}{n}, \frac{p}{q}\right) \mid m, n, p$ and q are integers such that, $q \neq 0, n \neq 0$ and $qm = pn\}$. Then

(a) Neither R nor S is an equivalence relation
(b) S is an equivalence relation but R is not an equivalence relation
(c) R and S both are equivalence relations
(d) R is an equivalence relation but S is not an equivalence relation.

Solution: (b) **Reflexivity:** xRx as $x = 1.x$ and 1 is a rational number.

$\frac{m}{n} S \frac{m}{n}$ iff $m.n = m.n$, which is true.

Thus, R and S are reflexive relations.

Symmetricity: Let xRy

$\Rightarrow x = wy$ for some rational number w

$\Rightarrow y = \frac{1}{w} x$

$\Rightarrow yRx$ provided $w \neq 0$, but if $x = 0$ and y is any non-zero integer, then $x = 0y$ and there exist no rational number w for which $y = wx$.

$\Rightarrow y \not R x$ thus R is not symmetric.

Next let $\frac{m}{n} S \frac{p}{q}$

$\Rightarrow mq = pn$ $\quad\Rightarrow pn = mq$

$\Rightarrow \frac{p}{q} S \frac{m}{n}$

$\Rightarrow$ S is a symmetric relation.

Transitivity: Let xRy and yRz

$\Rightarrow x = w_1 y$ and $y = w_2 z$ for some $w_1, w_2 \in \mathbb{Q}$

$\Rightarrow x = w_1(w_2 z) = (w_1.w_2)z$

$\Rightarrow xRz$ as $w_1.w_2 \in \mathbb{Q}$

Now let $\frac{m}{n} S \frac{p}{q}$ and $\frac{p}{q} S \frac{r}{t}$; where $n, q, t \neq 0$

$\Rightarrow mq = np$ and $pt = qr$

$\Rightarrow mqpt = npqr$

$\Rightarrow mt = nr$, as $q \neq 0, p \neq 0$ (as if $p = 0$, then $mq = 0$

$\Rightarrow m = 0 \Rightarrow \frac{m}{n} = \frac{p}{q} = \frac{r}{t} = 0$)

$\Rightarrow \frac{m}{n} S \frac{r}{t}$

$\Rightarrow S$ is transitive.

$\Rightarrow S$ is an equivalence relation but R is not an equivalence relation

17. Consider the following relation R on the set of real square matrices of order 3.

$\{(A, B) | A = P^{-1} BP$ for some invertible matrix $P\}$

A: R is an equivalence relation.

R: For any two invertible 3×3 matrices M and N, $(MN)^{-1} = N^{-1}M^{-1}$. Now answer

(a) If both assertion and reason are correct, and reason is the correct explanation of the assertion.

(b) If both assertion and reason are correct, but reason is not correct explanation of the assertion.

(c) If assertion is correct, but reason is incorrect

(d) If assertion is incorrect, but reason is correct

Solution: (a) **Reflexivity:** As $A = P^{-1}AP$ when $P = I_3$, the identity matrix of order 3,

we get $(A, A) \in R\ \forall$ real square matrix A of order 3.

$\therefore$ R is reflexive.

Symmetricity: Let us assume $(A, B) \in R$

$\Rightarrow$ There exists a non-singular matrix P such that $A = P^{-1} BP$

$\Rightarrow B = PAP^{-1} = (P^{-1})^{-1} AP^{-1}$

$\left(\because |P^{-1}| = \frac{1}{|P|} \neq 0 \Rightarrow P^{-1} \text{ is invertible}\right)$

Thus, $(B, A) \in R$

$\therefore$ R is symmetric

Next, assume that $(A, B) \in R$ and $(B, C) \in R$.

$\Rightarrow A = P^{-1} BP$ and $B = Q^{-1} CQ$ for some invertible matrices P and Q

$\therefore A = P^{-1} (Q^{-1} C Q)P = (P^{-1} Q^{-1}) C (QP)$

$= (QP)^{-1} C (QP)$ [using Reason]

$\Rightarrow (A, C) \in R$. [$\because |QP| = |Q|.|P| \neq 0$ as $|P| \neq 0, |Q| \neq 0$

$\therefore$ Assertion is true and Reason is true and is correct explanation for Assertion.

SECTION–II

SUBJECTIVE-TYPE SOLVED EXAMPLE

1. Let $A = \{1, 2\}$ and $B = \{3, 4\}$. Write all subsets of $A \times B$.

Solution: Given, $A = \{1, 2\}$ and $B = \{3, 4\}$

$\therefore A \times B = \{(1, 3), (1, 4), (2, 3), (2, 4)\}$

Subsets of $A \times B$ are ϕ, $\{(1, 3)\}$, $\{(1, 4)\}$, $\{(2, 3)\}$, $\{(2, 4)\}$, $\{(1, 3), (1, 4)\}$, $\{(1, 3), (2, 3)\}$, $\{(1, 3), (2, 4)\}$, $\{(1, 4), (2, 3)\}$, $\{(1, 4), (2, 4)\}$, $\{(2, 3), (2, 4)\}$, $\{(1, 3), (1, 4), (2, 3)\}$, $\{(1, 3), (1, 4), (2, 4)\}$, $\{(1, 4), (2, 3), (2, 4)\}$, $\{(1, 3), (2, 3), (2, 4)\}$, $A \times B$

2. If $A = \{2, 3\}$, $B = \{4, 5\}$ and $C = \{5, 6\}$, then find

(i) $A \times (B \cup C)$ (ii) $A \times (B \cap C)$

(iii) $(A \times B) \cup (B \times C)$

Solution: (i) $B \cup C = \{4, 5, 6\}$

$A \times (B \cap C) = \{2, 3\} \times \{4, 5, 6\} = \{(2, 4), (2, 5), (2, 6), (3, 4), (3, 5), (3, 6)\}$

(ii) $B \cap C = \{5\}$

$A \times (B \cap C) = \{2, 3\} \times \{5\} = \{(2, 5), (3, 5)\}$

(iii) $A \times B = \{2, 3\} \times \{4, 5\} = \{(2, 4), (2, 5), (3, 4), (3, 5)\}$

$B \times C = \{4, 5)\} \times \{5, 6\} = \{(4, 5), (4, 6), (5, 5), (5, 6)\}$

$\therefore$ $(A \times B) \cup (B \times C) = \{(2, 4), (2, 5), (3, 4), (3, 5), (4, 5), (4, 6), (5, 5), (5, 6)\}$

3. Let $A = \{1, 2, 3, 4\}$ and $S = \{(a, b) : a \in A, b \in A, a$ divides $b\}$. Write S explicitly

Solution: Since 1 divides 2, 3, 4 and 2 divides 4

3 does not divide any of 1, 2 and 4

4 does not divide any of 1, 2 and 3

Also 1 divides 1, 2 divides 2, 3 divides 3 and 4 divides 4.

Hence, $S = \{(a, b) : a \in A, b \in A, a$ divides $b\}$

$= \{(1, 1), (1, 2), (1, 3), (1, 4), (2, 2), (2, 4), (3, 3), (4, 4)\}$

4. If $\mathbb{R}$ is the set of all real numbers, what do the Cartesian products $\mathbb{R} \times \mathbb{R}$ and $\mathbb{R} \times \mathbb{R} \times \mathbb{R}$ represent?

Solution: $\mathbb{R} \times \mathbb{R} = \{(x, y) : x \in \mathbb{R}, y \in \mathbb{R}\}$
Hence $\mathbb{R} \times \mathbb{R}$ represents the coordinates of all the points in x-y plane
Again $\mathbb{R} \times \mathbb{R} \times \mathbb{R} = \{(x, y, z)\} : x, y, z \in \mathbb{R}\}$
Hence $\mathbb{R} \times \mathbb{R} \times \mathbb{R}$ represents the coordinates of all the points in three dimensional space.

5. If $A \times B = \{(a, x), (a, y), (b, x), (b, y)\}$. Find A and B

Solution: Given $A \times B = \{(a, x), (a, y), (b, x), (b, y)\}$
$\therefore$ A = set of first components of all ordered pairs in $A \times B = \{a, b\}$ and B = set of second components of all ordered pairs in $A \times B = \{x, y\}$

6. If A and B are two sets such that $A \times B$ consists of 6 elements and if three elements of $A \times B$ are (3, 3), (1, 3) and (2,5), then what are its remaining elements?

Solution: Since $(1, 3), (2, 5), (3, 3) \in A \times B$. So clearly $1, 2, 3 \in A$ and $3, 5 \in B$
Given $n(A \times B) = 6 \quad \Rightarrow n(A).\ n(B) = 6$
But $1, 2, 3 \in A$ and $3, 5 \in B$
Hence, $A = \{1, 2, 3\}$ and $B = \{3, 5\}$
$\therefore$ $A \times B = \{(1, 3), (1, 5), (2, 3), (2, 5), (3, 3), (3, 5)\}$
$\therefore$ Remaining elements of $A \times B$ are (3, 5), (1, 5) and (2, 3).

7. Let A and B be two sets such that $n(A) = 5$ and $n(B) = 2$. If a, b, c, d, e are distinct elements and $(a, 2), (b, 3), (c, 2), (d, 3), (e, 2)$ are in $A \times B$, then find the sets A and B.

Solution: Since a, b, c, d, e are distinct and $(a, 2), (b, 3), (c, 2), (d, 3), (e, 2)$ are elements of $A \times B$.
Therefore, a, b, c, d, e are in A.
But $n(A) = 5$
$\therefore$ $A = \{a, b, c, d, e\}$
Again $n(B) = 2$ and $(a, 2), (b, 3) \in A \times B$
$\therefore$ $B = \{2, 3\}$.

8. The Cartesian product $A \times A$ has 9 elements among which two are $(-1, 0)$ and $(0, 1)$. Find the set A and the remaining elements of $A \times A$.

Solution: Let $n(A) = m$
Given, $n(A \times A) = 9 \quad \Rightarrow n(A).\ n(A) = 9$
$\Rightarrow m \cdot m = 9 \quad \Rightarrow m = 3$
$\therefore$ $n(A) = 3$.
Now $(-1, 0) \in A \times A$
$\Rightarrow -1 \in A$ and $0 \in A$
Again $(0, 1) \in A \times A$
$\Rightarrow 0 \in A$ and $1 \in A$
Thus, $-1 \in A$, $0 \in A$ and $1 \in A$
But A has exactly three elements, therefore $A = \{-1, 0, 1\}$
Remaining elements of $A \times A$ are $(-1, -1), (-1, 1), (0, -1), (0, 0), (1, -1), (1, 0), (1, 1)$.

9. Prove that $A \times \phi = \phi$ for any set A.

Solution: $(x, y) \in A \times \phi \Rightarrow y \in \phi$ (contradiction)
Thus there is no element (x, y) in $A \times \phi$
$\therefore$ $A \times \phi = \phi$

10. Prove that $A \times B = \phi \Leftrightarrow A = \phi$ or $B = \phi$

Solution: Let $A \times B = \phi$. Then it is to prove that either $A = \phi$ or $B = \phi$
Suppose, if possible, neither $A = \phi$ nor $B = \phi$.
Then there are elements $x \in A$ and $y \in B$ so that $(x, y) \in A \times B = \phi$ i.e., $(x, y) \in \phi$
This is a contradiction
Hence, our supposition is wrong. So either $A = \phi$ or $B = \phi$
Thus, $A \times B = \phi \Rightarrow A = \phi$ or $B = \phi$ ...(1)
Conversely, let either $A = \phi$ or $B = \phi$, then it is to prove that $A \times B = \phi$.
Suppose, if possible $A \times B \neq \phi$, then there is an element $(x, y) \in A \times B$ so that $x \in A$ and $y \in B$, i.e., $A \neq \phi$ and $B \neq \phi$
This is contradictory to our supposition
$\therefore$ $A \times B \neq \phi$ is impossible
$\therefore$ $A \times B = \phi$
Thus $A = \phi$ or $B = \phi$
$\Rightarrow A \times B = \phi$ ....(2)
From (1) and (2), we have $A \times B = \phi \Leftrightarrow A = \phi$ or $B = \phi$.

11. If A and B are two sets, then prove $A \times B$ and $B \times A$ have an element in common iff A and B have an element in common.

Solution: $(A \times B) \cap (C \times D) = (A \cap C) \times (B \cap D)$
$\therefore$ $(A \times B) \cap (B \times A) = (A \cap B) \times (B \cap A)$
$= (A \cap B) \times (A \cap B) = C \times C$, where $C = A \cap B$
$\therefore$ $(A \times B) \cap (B \times A) \neq \phi \Leftrightarrow C \times C \neq \phi \Leftrightarrow C \neq \phi$
$\Leftrightarrow A \cap B \neq \phi$

12. If A and B are any two non-empty sets, then prove that $A \times B = B \times A \Leftrightarrow A = B$.

Solution: If part: Let $A = B$ ...(1)
To prove $\quad A \times B = B \times A$
Now, $\quad A \times B = A \times A \quad [\because B = A]$

$= B \times A$ $[\because A = B]$

Only if part: Let $A \times B = B \times A$ .....(2)

To prove $A = B$. Let $a \in A$ and $b \in B$

$\Rightarrow (a, b) \in A \times B$

$\Rightarrow (a, b) \in B \times A$ [From (2)]

$\Rightarrow a \in B$ and $b \in A$

Thus $a \in A \Rightarrow a \in B$

$\Rightarrow A \subseteq B$ and $b \in B \Rightarrow b \in A \Rightarrow B \subseteq A$ .....(3)

Thus $A \subseteq B$ and $B \subseteq A \Rightarrow A = B$

13. Let A and B be non-empty sets such that $A \times B = A \times C$. Show that $B = C$

Solution: Given, $A \times B = A \times C$ ....(1)

A and B are non-empty sets. We are to prove $B = C$.

Let b be an arbitrary element of B. A is non-empty

$\Rightarrow$ there exists $a \in A$

Now, $a \in A$ and $b \in B$

$\Rightarrow (a, b) \in A \times B$

$\Rightarrow (a, b) \in A \times C$ $[\because A \times B = A \times C]$

$\Rightarrow b \in C$

Thus, $b \in B \Rightarrow b \in C$

$\Rightarrow B \subseteq C$ .... (2)

Again, let c be an arbitrary element of C.

A is non-empty

$\Rightarrow$ there exist $a \in A$.

Now, $a \in A$ and $c \in C$

$\Rightarrow (a, c) \in A \times C$

$\Rightarrow (a, c) \in A \times B$ [From (1)]

$\Rightarrow c \in B$

Thus $c \in C \Rightarrow c \in B$

$\Rightarrow C \subseteq B$ ... (3)

From (2) and (3), $B = C$.

16. Find the linear relation between the components of the ordered pairs of the relation R, where $R = \{(2, 1), (4, 7), (1, -2),\ldots\}$

Solution: Given $R = \{(2, 1), (4, 7), (1, -2)\ldots\}$

Let $y = ax + b$ be the linear relation between the components of R.

Since $(2, 1) \in R$

$\Rightarrow y = ax + b \Rightarrow 1 = 2a + b$ ...(1)

Also $(4, 7) \in R$

$\Rightarrow y = ax + b \Rightarrow 7 = 4a + b$ ....(2)

Subtracting (1) from (2), we get $2a = 6 \Rightarrow a = 3$

Substituting $a = 3$ in (1), we get $b = -5$

Substituting these values of a and b in $y = ax + b$, we get $y = 3x - 5$, which is the required linear relation between the components of the given relation.

17. Let $A = \{1, 2, 3, 4\}$ and $B = \{x, y, z\}$. Let R be a relation from A into B defined by

$R = \{(1, x), (1, z), (3, x), (4, y)\}$

(i) Draw arrow diagram of relation R.

(ii) Represent R in the tabular form

Solution: (i) Given $R = \{(1, x), (1, z), (3, x), (4, y)\}$

As $1Rx$, $1Rz$, $3Rx$ and $4Ry$

Therefore, the given figure below is the arrow diagram of relation R.

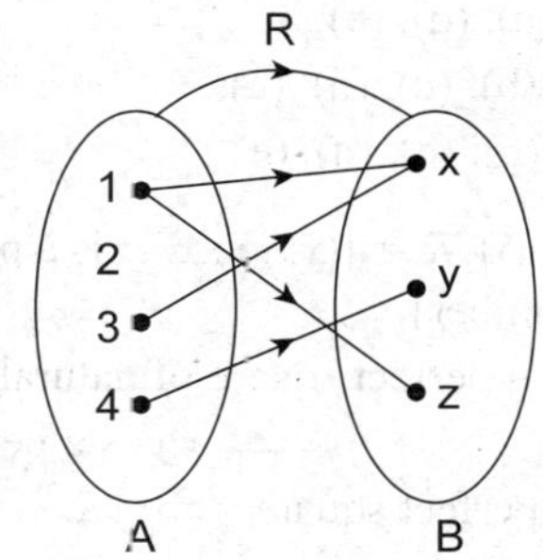

(ii) Given $A = \{1, 2, 3, 4\}$ and $B = \{x, y, z\}$, $R = \{(1, x), (1, z), (3, x), (4, y)\}$

Here $1Rx$, $1Rz$, $3Rx$ and $4Ry$

While representing a relation R from A to B in tabular form, we write elements of A in first column and elements of B in first row, keeping the position corresponding to first row and first column to represent relation R.

If $(a, b) \in R$, we write 1 in the row containing a and column containing b and if $(a, b) \notin R$, then we write 0 in the row containing a and the column containing b. The tabular form of relation R has been shown in the table given below.

R	x	y	z
1	1	0	1
2	0	0	0
3	1	0	0
4	0	1	0

Solved Column Matching

1. **Column I**

(i) $R = \{(x, y) : (x. y)$ is a perfect square of a natural number and $x, y \in \mathbb{N}\}$ is

(ii) $R = \{(x, y) : y = (x)^{1/n}$ for some $n \in \mathbb{N}$; $x, y \in \mathbb{N}\}$ is

(iii) $R = \{(x, y) : (x, y)$ is a point on circle of radius $2\sqrt{2}$ units having centre at origin and $x^2 - y^2 = 0\}$ is

(iv) $R = \{(x, y) : |x - y| \leq 4; x, y \in \mathbb{R}\}$ is

Column II

(a) Reflexive
(b) Symmetric
(c) Transitive
(d) One–many
(e) Many–one

Ans. (i) → (a), (b), (c), (d), (e);
(ii) → (a), (c), (d), (e);
(iii) → (a), (b), (c), (d), (e);
(iv) → (a), (b), (c), (d), (e)

Solution: (i) $R = \{(x. y) : x . y$ is a perfect square of a natural number$\}$

xRx as x^2 is a perfect square of natural number x

Now xRy ⇒ $x.y$ is a perfect square

⇒ $y.x$ is a perfect square ⇒ yRx

Also xRy, yRz

⇒ $x \cdot y = k_1^2$, $y \cdot z = k_2^2$ for some $k_1, k_2 \in \mathbb{N}$

Now $(x \cdot y)(y \cdot z) = k_1^2 . k_2^2$

⇒ $x.z = \dfrac{k_1^2 k_2^2}{y^2} = \left(\dfrac{k_1 k_2}{y}\right)^2$,

which must be square of a natural number as left hand side is also a natural number.

⇒ xRz ⇒ R is transitive.

Since $2.2 = 4 = (2)^2$ ⇒ $2R2$

Also $2.8 = 16 = (4)^2$ ⇒ $2R(16)$

Thus the relation is one–many. Also the relation is symmetric

⇒ The relation is many–one

∴ (i) → (a), (b), (c), (d), (e)

(ii) $R = \{(x, y) : y = (x)^{1/n}$ for some $n \in \mathbb{N}; x, y \in \mathbb{N}\}$

Since $x = (x)^{1/1}\ \forall\ x \in \mathbb{N}$

⇒ xRx

⇒ R is reflexive.

Now if we consider $3 = (27)^{1/3}$

⇒ $27 = (3)^3$

⇒ $27 \not R 3$ as the power of 3 is not of the form $\dfrac{1}{n}$; $n \in \mathbb{N}$.

⇒ R is not symmetric.

Now xRy, yRz

⇒ $x = (y)^{1/n}$ for some $n \in \mathbb{N}$,

and $y = (z)^{1/m}$ for some $m \in \mathbb{N}$,

⇒ $x = (z)^{1/nm}$ ⇒ R is transitive.

Also $2 = (8)^{1/3}$ and $2 = (64)^{1/6}$

⇒ $2R8$ and $2R(64)$

⇒ R is one–many

Also, $8 = (64)^{1/2}$ and $4 = (64)^{1/3}$

⇒ $8R(64)$ and $4R(64)$

⇒ R is many–one.

⇒ (ii) → (a), (c), (d), (e)

(iii) $R = \{(x, y) : (x, y)$ is a point on circle of radius $2\sqrt{2}$ units having centre at origin and $x^2 - y^2 = 0\}$

$= \{(x, y) : x^2 + y^2 = 8, x^2 - y^2 = 0\}$

$= \{(x, y) : x^2 + y^2 = 8, y = \pm x\} = \{(x, \pm x) : x^2 = 4\}$

$= \{(x, \pm x) : x = \pm 2\} = \{(2, -2), (2, 2), (-2, 2), (-2, -2)\}$

∵ $(2, 2), (-2, -2) \in \mathbb{R}$

⇒ R is reflexive.

Also aRb

⇒ $bRa\ \forall\ a, b \in \{2, -2\}$

⇒ R is symmetric

Also aRb and bRc

⇒ $aRc\ \forall\ a, b, c \in \{2, -2\}$

⇒ R is transitive

Also $2R(-2)$ and $2R2$

⇒ R is One–many

∴ R is symmetric

⇒ R is Many–one

⇒ (iii) → (a), (b), (c), (d), (e)

(iv) $R = \{(x, y) : |x - y| \leq 4; x, y \in \mathbb{R}\}$

Since $|x - x| = 0 \leq 4$

⇒ $xRx\ \forall\ x \in \mathbb{R}$ ⇒ R is reflexive.

Further xRy ⇒ $|x - y| \leq 4$

⇒ $|y - x| \leq 4$ ⇒ R is symmetric.

Now let xRy and yRz

⇒ $|x - y| \leq 4$ and $|y - z| \leq 4$

Now $|x - z| = |(x - y) + (y - z)| \leq |x - y| + |y - z| \leq 4 + 4 = 8$ (∵ $|a + b| \leq |a| + |b|$)

∴ xRz

⇒ R is transitive

Now $2R2$ and $2R4$ as $|2 - 2| \leq 4$ and $|2 - 4| \leq 4$

⇒ R is one–many

∵ R is symmetric

⇒ R is many–one

⇒ (iv) → (a), (b), (c), (d), (e)

TUTORIAL EXERCISE

SECTION–III

OBJECTIVE-TYPE QUESTIONS (ONLY ONE CORRECT ANSWER)

1. If a set A has n distinct elements, the number of all relations on A is
(a) 2^{n^2} (b) n^2
(c) 2^n (d) None of these

2. Let $A = \{2, 3, 4, 5\}$ and let $R = \{(2, 2), (3, 3), (4, 4)$ $(5, 5), (2, 3), (3, 2), (3, 5), (5, 3)\}$ be a relation on A. Then R is
(a) reflexive and transitive
(b) reflexive and symmetric but not transitive
(c) reflexive and anti-symmetric
(d) none of the above

3. If R is a relation on A such that $R = R^{-1}$, then R is
(a) reflexive (b) symmetric
(c) transitive (d) None of these

4. If $A = \{x : x^2 - 3x + 2 = 0\}$, and R is a universal relation on A, then R is
(a) $\{(1, 1), (2, 2)$ (b) $\{1, 1)\}$
(c) $\{\phi\}$ (d) $\{(1,1), (1,2), (2,1), (2,2)\}$

5. An integer m is said to be related to another integer n if m is a multiple of n. Then the relation $\mathbb{R} : \mathbb{Z} \sim \{0\} \to \mathbb{Z}$ is
(a) reflexive and symmetric
(b) reflexive and transitive
(c) symmetric and transitive
(d) equivalence relation

6. If $A = \{5, 6, 7\}$ and $B = \{1, 2, 3, 4\}$, then number of elements in set $(A \times B) \times B$ is equal to
(a) 36 (b) 48
(c) 16 (d) None of these

7. If R be a relation from $A = \{2, 3, 4\}$ to $B = \{3, 5\}$ such that $a < b$ $((a, b) \in R)$, then RoR^{-1} does not contain
(a) (3, 3) and (5, 5) (b) (3, 3)
(c) (5, 5) (d) None of these

8. If R and R' are symmetric relations (not disjoint) on a set A, then the relation $R \cap R'$ is
(a) reflexive (b) symmetric
(c) transitive (d) None of these

9. A and B are two sets having 3 and 4 elements respectively and having 2 elements in common. The number of non-empty relations which can be defined from A to B is equal to
(a) 2^5 (b) $2^{10} - 1$
(c) $2^{12} - 1$ (d) None of these

10. If the relation $R : A \to B$, where $A = \{1, 2, 3, 4\}$ and $B = \{1, 3, 5\}$ is defined by $R = \{(x, y); x < y, x \in A,$ $y \in B\}$, then $R^{-1} o R$ is equal to
(a) $\{(1, 3), (1, 5), (2, 3), (2, 5), (3, 5), (4, 5)\}$
(b) $\{(3, 1), (5, 1), (5, 2), (5, 3), (5, 4)\}$
(c) $\{(3, 3), (3, 5), (5, 3), (5, 5)\}$
(d) None of these

11. The relation 'less than' in the set of natural numbers is
(a) only symmetric
(b) only transitive
(c) only reflexive
(d) equivalence relation

12. Let $P = \{(x, y)| x^2 + y^2 = 1, x, y \in \mathbb{R}\}$. Then P is
(a) reflexive (b) symmetric
(c) transitive (d) anti-symmetric

13. Let R be an equivalence relation on a finite set A having n elements. Then the number of ordered pairs in R is
(a) less than n
(b) greater than or equal to n
(c) less than or equal to n
(d) None of these

14. For real numbers x and y, we write $xRy \Leftrightarrow x - y + \sqrt{5}$ is an irrational number. Then the relation R is
(a) reflexive (b) symmetric
(c) transitive (d) None of these

15. Let X be a family of sets and R be a relation on X defined by 'A is disjoint from B'. Then R is
(a) reflexive (b) symmetric
(c) anti-symmetric (d) transitive

16. The relation R defined on the set $A = \{1, 2, 3, 4, 5\}$ by $R = \{(x, y) : |x^2 - y^2| < 16\}$ is given by
(a) $\{(1, 1), (2, 1), (3, 1), (4, 1), (2, 3)\}$
(b) $\{(2, 2), (3, 2), (4, 2), (2, 4)\}$
(c) $\{(3, 3), (3, 4), (5, 4), (4, 3), (3, 1)\}$
(d) None of these

17. A relation R is defined from $\{2, 3, 4, 5\}$ to $\{3, 6, 7, 10\}$ by $xRy \Leftrightarrow$ x is relatively prime to y. Then domain of R is
(a) $\{2, 3, 5\}$ (b) $\{3, 5\}$
(c) $\{2, 3, 4\}$ (d) $\{2, 3, 4, 5\}$

18. If $R = \{(x, y) \mid x, y \in \mathbb{Z}, x^2 + y^2 \leq 4\}$ is a relation on $\mathbb{Z}$, then domain of R is
(a) $\{0, 1, 2\}$ (b) $\{0, -1, -2\}$
(c) $\{-2, -1, 0, 1, 2\}$ (d) None of these

19. Let R be a reflexive relation on a set A and I be the identity relation on A. Then
(a) $R \subset I$ (b) $I \subset R$
(c) $R = I$ (d) None of these

20. The relation 'is subset of' on the power set $P(A)$ of a set A is
(a) symmetric
(b) anti-symmetric
(c) equivalence relation
(d) None of these

21. The relation R defined on a set A is anti-symmetric if $(a, b) \in R \Rightarrow (b, a) \in R$ for
(a) every $(a, b) \in R$
(b) no $(a, b) \in R$
(c) no $(a, b) \in R, a \neq b$
(d) None of these

22. The void relation on a set A is
(a) reflexive
(b) symmetric and transitive
(c) reflexive and symmetric
(d) reflexive and transitive

23. Which one of the following relations on $\mathbb{R}$ is an equivalence?
(a) $aR_1b \Leftrightarrow |a| = |b|$
(b) $aR_2b \Leftrightarrow a \geq b$
(c) $aR_3b \Leftrightarrow a$ divides b
(d) $aR_4b \Leftrightarrow a < b$

24. If R an equivalence relation on a set A, then R^{-1} is
(a) reflexive only
(b) symmetric but not transitive
(c) equivalence
(d) None of these

25. The relation 'congruence modulo m' is
(a) reflexive only
(b) transitive only
(c) symmetric only
(d) an equivalence relation

26. Let R and S be two equivalence relations on a set A. Then
(a) $R \cup S$ is an equivalence relation on A
(b) $R \cap S$ is an equivalence relation on A
(c) $R - S$ is an equivalence relation on A
(d) None of these

27. Let $R = \{(1, 3), (2, 2), (3, 2)\}$ and $S = \{(2, 1), (3, 2), (2, 3)\}$ be two relations on set $A = \{1, 2, 3\}$. Then $RoS =$
(a) $\{(1, 3), (2, 2), (3, 2), (2, 1), (2, 3)\}$
(b) $\{(3, 2), (1, 3)\}$
(c) $\{(2, 3), (3, 2), (2, 2)\}$
(d) $\{(2, 3), (3, 2)\}$

28. $x^2 = xy$ is a relation which is
(a) symmetric (b) reflexive
(c) transitive (d) None of these

29. The number of reflexive relations of a set with four elements is equal to
(a) 2^{16} (b) 2^{12}
(c) 2^8 (d) 2^4

30. If A is the set of even natural numbers less than 8 and B is the set of prime numbers less than 7, then the number of relations from A to B is
(a) 2^9 (b) 9^2
(c) 3^2 (d) $2^9 - 1$

31. If $A = \{(x, y) : x^2 + y^2 = 25\}$ and $B = \{(x, y) : x^2 + 9y^2 = 144\}$, then $A \cap B$ contains
(a) one point (b) three points
(c) two points (d) four points

32. Let R be the relation on the set R of all real numbers defined by aRb iff $|a - b| \leq 1$. Then R is
(a) reflexive and symmetric
(b) symmetric only
(c) transitive only
(d) anti-symmetric only

SECTION–IV

OBJECTIVE-TYPE QUESTIONS (MORE THAN ONE CORRECT ANSWER)

1. Let $X = \{1, 2, 3, 4, 5\}$ and $Y = \{1, 3, 5, 7, 9\}$. Which of the following is/are relations from X to Y?
   (a) $R_1 = \{(x, y) | y = 2 + x, x \in X, y \in Y\}$
   (b) $R_2 = \{(1, 1), (2, 1), (3, 3), (4, 3), (5, 5)\}$
   (c) $R_3 = \{(1, 1), (1, 3), (3, 5), (3, 7), (5, 7)\}$
   (d) $R_4 = \{(1, 3), (2, 5), (2, 4), (7, 9)\}$

2. $\mathbb{N}$ is the set of natural numbers. The relation R is defined on $\mathbb{N}$ as follows $(a, b)\ R(c, d) \Leftrightarrow a + d = b + c$ is
   (a) reflexive
   (b) symmetric
   (c) transitive
   (d) anti-symmetric

3. If $A = \{(x, y): y = e^{2x}, x \in \mathbb{R}\}$ and $B = \{(x, y): y = e^{-2x}, x \in \mathbb{R}\}$, then:
   (a) $(A \cap B) = \phi$
   (b) $(A \cap B) \neq \phi$
   (c) $A \cap B$ is a singleton set
   (d) None of these

4. If $A = \{(x, y): x^2 + y^2 \leq 1; x, y \in \mathbb{R}\}$ and $B = \{(x, y): x^2 + y^2 \geq 4; x, y \in \mathbb{R}\}$, then:
   (a) $A - B \neq \phi$ (b) $B - A = \phi$
   (c) $(A \cap B) \neq \phi$ (d) $(A \cap B) = \phi$

5. A relation $R : \mathbb{R} \to \mathbb{R}$ such that aRb iff $a \leq b^2$ is.
   (a) reflexive (b) not symmetric
   (c) non-transitive (d) not equivalence

6. A relation R on set $A = \{1, 2, 3, 4, 5, 6\}$ given by $R = \{(x, y) : y = x + 1\}$ is.
   (a) not reflexive
   (b) symmetric
   (c) non-transitive
   (d) not an equivalence relations.

7. Let R and be two relations on a set A. Then
   (a) R and S are transitive, then $R \cup S$ is also transitive
   (b) R and S are transitive, then $R \cap S$ is also transitive
   (c) R and S are reflexive, then $R \cap S$ is also reflexive
   (d) R and S are symmetric, then $R \cup S$ is also symmetric

8. Let n be a fixed positive integer. Define a relation R on the set $\mathbb{Z}$ of integers by $aRb \Leftrightarrow n\,|(a - b)$. Then R is
   (a) reflexive
   (b) symmetric
   (c) transitive
   (d) an equivalence relation

9. Let A be the non-void set of the children in a family. The relation 'x is a brother of y' on A is
   (a) reflexive (b) symmetric
   (c) transitive (d) None of these

SECTION–V

ASSERTION AND REASON-TYPE QUESTION

1. **A:** A relation $R : \mathbb{Z} \to \mathbb{Z}$ defined such that aRb iff $a|b$ (a divides b), then R is reflexive relation.
   R: A relation $R : A \to B$ is called reflexive iff $aRa\ \forall\ a \in A$.

2. **A:** If $n(A) = m$ and $n(B) = k$, then total number of relations that can be defined from set A to set $B = 2^{km}$.
   R: Every relation $R : A \to B$ is a subset of $A \times B$.

3. **A:** A relation $R : \mathbb{C} \to \mathbb{C}$ such that $(a, b) \in R$ iff $|a - b| \leq 1$, then R is an equivalence relation.
   R: A relation is called equivalence iff it is reflexive, symmetric as well as transitive.

4. **A:** A relation $A \times B$ is universal relation (largest relation) defined from set A to set B.
   R: Any relation $R : A \to B$ is always a subset of $A \times B$.

5. **A:** A relation $R : \mathbb{R} \to \mathbb{R}$ such that aRb iff $2|(a - b)$ is not an equivalence relation.
   R: For a relation to be an equivalence it has to be reflexive, symmetric as well as transitive.

SECTION–VI

LINKED COMPREHENSION-TYPE QUESTIONS

A: A relation R on a set 'B' is a subset of $B \times B$, i.e., $R = \{(x, y) : x, y \in B\} \subseteq B \times B$. If $(x, y) \in R$, then we write this fact as xRy (read as 'x is related to y'). Now R is called Reflexive, if $x R x \ \forall \ x \in B$, symmetric if xRy

$\Rightarrow$ yRx and transitive if

xRy and $yRz \Rightarrow xRz$. If R is reflexive, symmetric and transitive, then it is called an equivalence relation. Let R_1 and R_2 be two relations on the set ($\mathbb{N} \times \mathbb{N}$ where $\mathbb{N}$ is set) of natural numbers defined as $R_1 = \{((a, b) (c, d)) : ad = bc\}$ and $R_2 = \{((a, b), (c, d)) : a + d = b + c \}$. Now, choose the most appropriate alternative in the following

1. (a) R_1 is relfexive but R_2 is not reflexive
(b) R_1 is not reflexive but R_2 is reflexive
(c) R_1 and R_2 both are reflexive
(d) R_1 and R_2 both are not reflexive

2. Which of the following is true?
(a) R_1 is symmetric but R_2 is not symmetric
(b) R_1 and R_2 both are symmetric
(c) R_2 is symmetric but R_1 is not symmetric
(d) R_1 and R_2 both are not symmetric

3. Which of the following is correct?
(a) R_1 is transive but R_2 is not transitive
(b) R_1 and R_2 both transitive
(c) R_1 is not transitive but R_2 is transitive
(d) R_1 and R_2 both are not transitive

4. Which of the following is true?
(a) R_1 and R_2 both are equivalence relations
(b) R_1 is equivalence but R_2 is not
(c) R_1 is not equivalence but R_2 is equivalence
(d) R_1 and R_2 both are not equivalence.

SECTION–VII

COLUMN MATCHING-TYPE QUESTION

1. **Column A**
(i) R : $A \to A$ where $A = \{1, 2, ..., 14\}$ defined by $R = \{(x, y) : 3x - y > 0\}$ is
(ii) R : $\mathbb{N} \to \mathbb{N}$ defined by $R = \{(x, y) : y = x + 4 \text{ and } x < 4\}$ is
(iii) R : $\mathbb{Z} \to \mathbb{Z}$ defined by $R = \{(x, y): x - y \in \mathbb{Z}\}$ is
(iv) R : $A \to A$, where A is set of humans in a town defined by $R = \{(a, b)$:a and b work in same place$\}$ is

Column B
(a) Reflexive relation
(b) Symmetric relation
(c) Transitive relation
(d) Equivalence relation
(e) Anti-symmetric relation

2. **Column A**
(i) R: $\mathbb{R} \to \mathbb{R}$: defined as aRb iff $a \le b$
(ii) $R : \mathbb{R} \to \mathbb{R}$: defined as aRb iff $a \le b^3$ is
(iii) $R : A \to A$ defined as $R = \{(a, b):|a - b| \text{ is even}\}$; $A = \{1, 2, 3, 4, 5\}$ is
(iv) R : $H \to H$ where H is set of Human beings defined as $R = \{(x, y) : x \text{ and } y \text{ have same age}\}$ is

Column B
(a) Reflexive
(b) Symmetric
(c) Transitive
(d) Equivalence
(e) Anti-symmetric
(f) None of these

3. **Column A**
(i) $R = \{(X, Y) : X, Y \in P(A); X \cap Y \ne \phi\}$, where $P(A)$ denotes the power set of A, is
(ii) R : $\{(x, y) : x, y \in \mathbb{N}$ and L.C.M. $(x, y) = 12\}$ is
(iii) $R = \{(x, y) : x, y \in \mathbb{C}$ and y is complex conjugate of $x\}$; $\mathbb{C}$ is the set of complex numbers.
(iv) $R = \{(x, y) : 2x^2 + 3y^2 - 5xy = 0; x, y \in \mathbb{R}\}$ is

Column B
(a) Reflexive
(b) Symmetric
(c) Transitive
(d) Surjective
(e) Injective.

Answer Keys

SECTION–III

1. (a)	**2.** (b)	**3.** (b)	**4.** (d)	**5.** (b)	**6.** (b)	**7.** (d)	**8.** (b)	**9.** (c)	**10.** (d)
11. (b)	**12.** (b)	**13.** (b)	**14.** (a)	**15.** (b)	**16.** (d)	**17.** (d)	**18.** (c)	**19.** (b)	**20.** (b)
21. (c)	**22.** (b)	**23.** (a)	**24.** (c)	**25.** (d)	**26.** (b)	**27.** (c)	**28.** (b)	**29.** (b)	**30.** (a)
31. (d)	**32.** (a)								

SECTION–IV

1. (a,b,c) **2.** (a,b,c) **3.** (b,c) **4.** (a,d) **5.** (b,c,d) **6.** (a,c,d) **7.** (b,c,d) **8.** (a,b,c,d) **9.** (c)

SECTION–V

1. (d) **2.** (a) **3.** (d) **4.** (a) **5.** (d)

SECTION–VI

1. (c) **2.** (b) **3.** (b) **4.** (a)

SECTION–VII

1. (i) → (a) (ii) → (c),(e) (iii) → (a,b,c,d) (iv) → (a,b,c,d)
2. (i) → (a,c,e) (ii) → (f) (iii) → (a,b,c,d) (iv) → (a,b,c,d)
3. (i) → (b) (ii) → (b) (iii) → (b,d,e) (iv) → (a,d)

HINTS AND SOLUTIONS

TEXTUAL EXERCISE-1: (SUBJECTIVE)

1. $A = \{x: x \in \mathbb{N}, x \leq 4\} = \{1, 2, 3, 4\}$; $B = \{y: y \in W, y \leq 2\} = \{0, 1, 2\}$.

   (a) $A \times B = \{(1, 0), (1, 1), (1, 2), (2, 0), (2, 1), (2, 2), (3, 0), (3, 1), (3, 2), (4, 0), (4, 1), (4, 2)\}$

   (b) $n(A \times B) = n(A) \times n(B) = 4 \times 3 = 12$

2. **(a)** $A = \{x : x \in \mathbb{R};\ 1 \leq x \leq 4\}$; $B = \{y : y \in W, y \leq 2\}$

   $\Rightarrow$ $A = [1, 4]$ and $B = \{0, 1, 2\}$

   $\therefore$ $(A \times B)$ will be plotted in shown below.

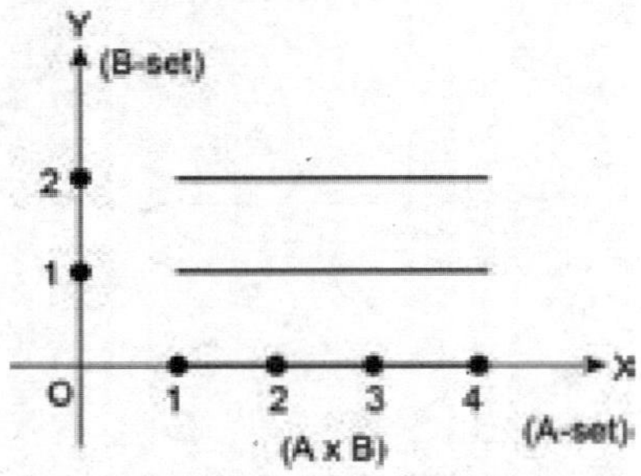

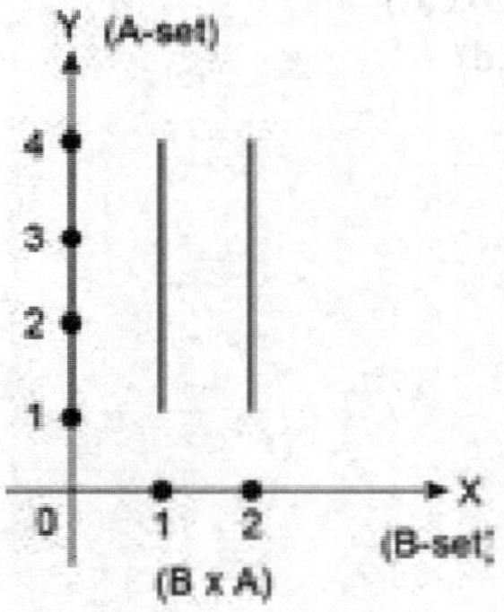

   (b) $A = \{y: y \in \mathbb{R};\ 0 \leq y \leq 2\}$; $B = \{x: x \in \mathbb{N}, x \leq 4\}$

   $\Rightarrow$ $A = [0, 2]$ and $B = \{0, 1, 2, 3, 4\}$

   $\therefore$ $(A \times B)$ and $(B \times A)$ will be plotted in shown below.

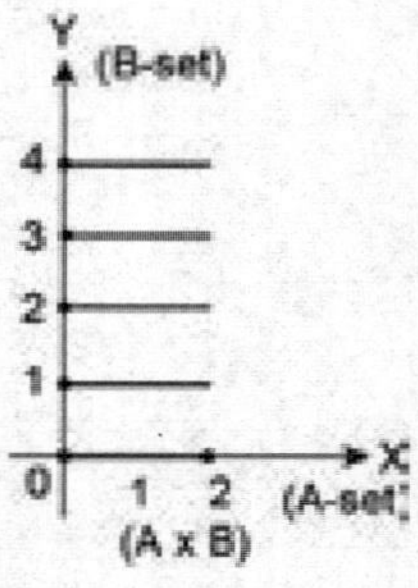

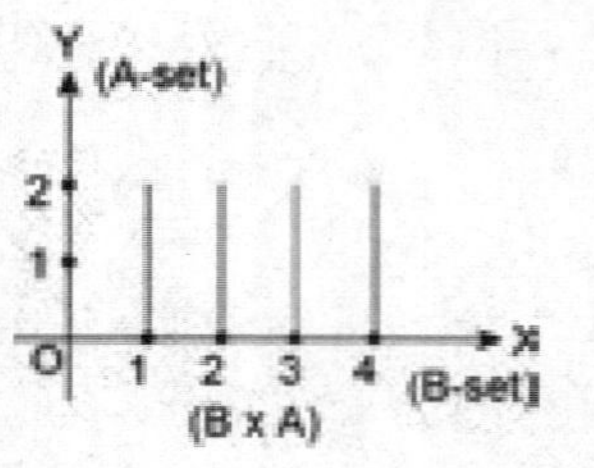

3. $A = \{x: x \in \mathbb{R}, -1 \leq x \leq 1\}$; $B = \{y: y \in \mathbb{R}, -1 \leq y \leq 1\}$

   $\Rightarrow$ $x \in A = [-1, 1]$ and $y \in B = [-1, 1]$ and $|x| + |y| \leq 1$.

   The common region is shown by shaded portion and equals $4\left(\frac{1}{2}(1)(2)\right) = 2$ sq. units.

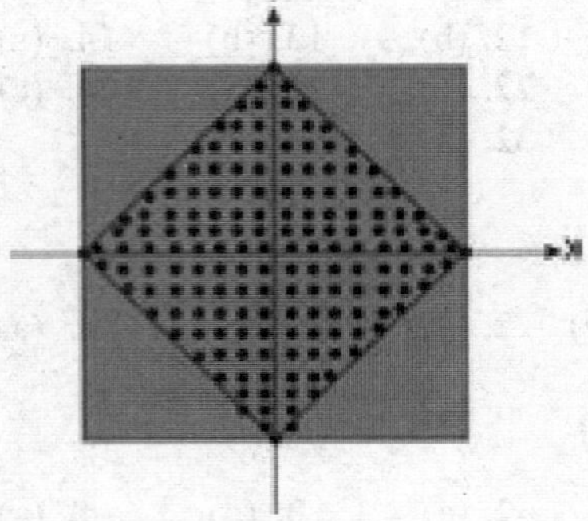

   Here ■ $= (A \times B)$; ▦ $= \{(x, y): |x| + |y| \leq 1\}$ = common Area.

4. $A = \{x: x \in$ non-negative integers and $x^2 - 2x - 8 \leq 0\}$ and $B = \{x: x \in \mathbb{N}$ and $x^2 - 5x + 4 \leq 0\}$

   $\Rightarrow$ $A = \{x: x \geq 0, x \in \mathbb{Z}$ and $(x - 4)(x + 2) \leq 0\} = \{0, 1, 2, 3, 4\}$ and $B = \{x: x\ \mathbb{N}$ and $(x - 1)(x - 4) \leq 0\} = \{1, 2, 3, 4\}$

   $\Rightarrow$ $A \cap B = \{1, 2, 3, 4\}$

   $\Rightarrow$ We know that $[(A \times B) \cap (B \times A)] = [(A \cap B) \times (B \cap A)]$

   $\Rightarrow$ $n[(A \times B) \cap (B \times A)] = n[(A \cap B) \times (B \cap A)] = [n(A \cap B)]^2 = (4)^2 = 16$

5. **(i)** If elements of set A are natural, and that of B are real in above problem, then

   $A = \{1, 2, 3, 4\}$ and $B = [1, 4]$; then $(A \cap B) = \{1, 2, 3, 4\}$

   $\Rightarrow$ $n[(A \times B) \cap (B \times A)] = n[(A \cap B) \times (B \cap A)] = [n(A \cap B)]^2 = (4)^2 = 16$

   (ii) If elements of the set A and B are real numbers, then $A = [-2, 4]$; $B[1, 4]$

   $\Rightarrow$ $(A \cap B) = [1, 4]$ having infinitely many uncountable numbers of elements

   $\Rightarrow$ $n[(A \times B) \cap (B \times A)] = [n(A \cap B)]^2$ = infinitely many found in area of 9 square units bounded by straight lies $x = 1$,

   $x = 4$, $y = 1$, $y = 4$.

   $\therefore$ $(A \times B)$ and $(B \times A)$ will be plotted as shown below.

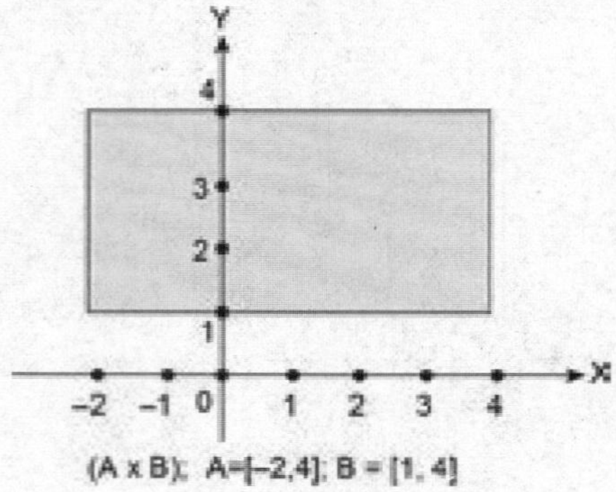

(A x B); A=[-2,4]; B = [1, 4]

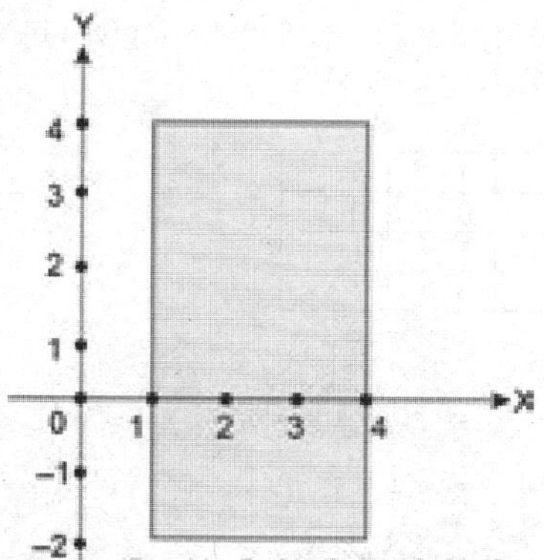

(B x A); B=[1,4]; A = [–2, 4]

If elements of A and B are rational or irrational, then it is impossible to represent $A \times B$ and $B \times A$. Geometrical as between any two real numbers, there lie infinitely many rationals and irrationals .

TEXTUAL EXERCISE–1: (OBJECTIVE)

1. (b) $\because A-(B \times C)$ is a subset of A; where as $(A-B) \times (A-C)$ is a subset $A \times A$

Thus the equality is invalid.

2. (c, d) $\because (A \times B) \times C = \{((x, y), z): x \in A, y \in B, z \in C\}$, similarly $A \times (B \times C)$

Where as $A \times B \times C = \{(x, y, z): x \in A, y \in B, z \in C\}$,

$\therefore$ $(A \times B) \times C \neq A \times B \times C \neq A \times (B \times C)$

$\Rightarrow$ (c) is not true.

Also (d) is not true.

See the Venn–Diagrams

Clearly, $(A-B)-C \neq A-(B-C)$

3. (d) $\therefore A\times (B \times C) = \{(x, (y, z)): x \in A, y \in B, z \in C\}$, where as $(A \times B) \times (A \times C) = \{((x, y), (z, w)); x, z \in A, y \in B, w \in C\}$

Clearly, then elements of two sets are of different forms, thus equality for two sets is invalid.

4. (a) $\therefore A \times B$ is a subset of $U \times U$

$\Rightarrow$ (a) is not true.

5. (a, b, c, d) Each of the options can be verified by using the results

That (i) If $A \subseteq B$ and $C \subseteq D$, then $(A \times C) \subseteq (B \times D)$

(ii) If $A \subseteq B$, then $A \cap B =$ A and $A \cup B = B$.

6. (a), (c), (d) It is standard result that if $(A \times B) \subseteq (C \times D)$, then A $\subseteq C$ and $B \subseteq D$,

$\Rightarrow$ (a), and (c) are true, but (b) is not true.

Also, $A \times B = C \times D \Leftrightarrow A = C$ and $B = D$

$\Rightarrow$ (d) is also true.

7. (c) $n(A \times B) = n(A) \times n(B) = 4 \times 26 = 104$

8. (a), (b), (c) $n(P(A \times B) = (2)^{n(A \times B)} = (2)^{n(A) \times n(B)} = (2)^{4 \times 5} = (2)^{20} = (4)^{10} = (16)^5$

9. (c) A $= \{\phi\}$, $B = \{\{\{\}\}\}$, $n(A \times B) = n(A) \times n(B) = 1 \times 1 = 1$

10. (d) If none of A and B is infinite, $A \times B$ can't have infinitely many elements. Thus at least one of A and B must be infinite set for $A \times B$ to be infinite.

11. (b) A $= \{(x, y) : x, y \in \mathbb{R}$ and $x^2 = 4y\}$ and $B = \{(x, 4); x \in \mathbb{R}\}$

A represents an upwards parabola and B represents a straight line $y = 4$.

$\therefore$ $A \cap B$ represents two points of intersection of parabola and straight line which are (–4, 4) and (4, 4).

$\therefore$ $(A \cap B) \cup \{(0, 0)\} = \{(-4, 4), (4, 4), (0, 0)\}$ forms an isosceles triangle which is not equilateral.

12. (a) $A = \{(x, y) : x, y \in \mathbb{R}$ and $x^2 = 4y\}$

$B = \{(x, y): x, y \in \mathbb{R}$ and $y = |x|\}$

A represents upwards parabola $x^2 = 4y$, where as B represents curve $y = |x|$

$\Rightarrow$ $A \cap B$ is the set of their points of intersection.

$\Rightarrow$ $\frac{x^2}{4} = \pm x$ $\qquad$ $\Rightarrow$ $x(x \pm 4) = 0$

$\Rightarrow$ $x = 0$ or $x = \pm 4$

$\Rightarrow$ $\{(0, 0), (4, 4)$ and $(-4, 4)\}$ is the set $(A \cap B)$.

$\Rightarrow$ Area of Δ formed by these points of intersection $= \frac{1}{2}$ (8) (4) = 16 square units.

13. (a), (b), (c) A $= \{\phi, \{\{\{\}\}\}\}$

$n(A \times A) = n(A) \times n(A) = 4$

$\Rightarrow$ $n\{P(P(A \times A))\} = (2)^4 = 16$

$\Rightarrow$ $n\{P(P(A \times A))\} = (2)^{16} = (16)^4 = (256)^2$

14. (b) $n(A) = 50$, $n(B) = 60$, $n(A \cup B) = 100$

$\Rightarrow$ $n(A \cap B) = n(A) + n(B) - n(A \cup B) = 50 + 60 - 100 = 10$

$\Rightarrow$ $n[(A \times B) \cap (B \times A)] = [n(A \cap B)]^2 = (10)^2 = 100$

15. (c) $n[(A \times B \times C) \cap (B \times C \times A)] = n(A \cap B) \times n(B \cap C) \times n(C \cap A) = 2 \times 3 \times 5 = 30$

TEXTUAL EXERCISE–2: (SUBJECTIVE)

1. $A = \{1, 2, 3, 4, 6\}$ and $R = \{(a, b): a, b \in A, b$ is divisible by $a\}$

(i) $R = \{(1, 1), (1, 2), (1, 3), (1, 4), (1, 6), (2, 2), (2, 4) (2, 6), (3, 3), (3, 6), (4, 4), (6, 6)\}$

(ii) Domain of $R = D_R = \{1, 2, 3, 4, 6\} = A$

(iii) Range of $R = P_R = \{1, 2, 3, 4, 5, 6\} = A$

2. $R = \{(x, y): x, y \in \mathbb{Z}; (x + y) (y + 2004) + 1 = 0\}$

$\therefore$ $(x + y) (y + 2004) = -1$ and $x, y \in \mathbb{Z}$

$\Rightarrow$ $x + y = -1, y + 2004 = 1$ or $x + y = 1, y + 2004 = -1$

$\Rightarrow$ $x = 2002, y = -2003$ or $x = 2006, y = -2005$

(i) $R = \{(2002, -2003), (2006, -2005)\}$

(ii) Domain $R = D_R = \{2002, 2006\}$

(iii) Range of $R = R_R = \{-2003, -2005\}$

3. $A = \{1, 2, 3, 4, 5\}$ and $B = \{1, 2, 3\dots 66, 67\}$.

(i) $a R b \Leftrightarrow$ a is square root of b and $R \subseteq (A \times B)$

$\Rightarrow$ $R = \{(1, 1), (2, 4), (3, 9), (4, 16), (5, 25)\}$

$\Rightarrow$ $D_R = \{1, 2, 3, 4, 5\} = A$ and $R_R = \{1, 4, 9, 16, 25\}$

(ii) a R b ⇔ a is cube root of b and $R \subseteq (A \times B)$

⇒ $R = \{(1, 1), (2, 8), (3, 27), (4, 64)\}$

⇒ $D_R = \{1, 2, 3, 4\}$ and $R_R = \{1, 8, 27, 64\}$

4. (i) $R = \{(x, x^3) : x$ is a prime number less than $10\}$

$= \{(2, 8), (3, 27), (7, 343)\}$

⇒ $D_R = \{2, 3, 5, 7\}$: $R_R = \{8, 2, 7, 125, 343\}$

(ii) $R = \{(4x + 3, 1 - x); x \le 4; x \in \mathbb{N}\} \subseteq \mathbb{N} \times \mathbb{N}$ (given)

$= \{\ \}$ as $1 - x \in \mathbb{N}$ ⇒ $1 - x \ge 1$

⇒ $x \le 0$

Which is impossible as $x \in \mathbb{N}$.

⇒ $D_R = \{\}$, $R_R = \{\}$

(iii) $R = \{(x, \frac{1}{x}); 0 < x < 4$ and $x \in \mathbb{N}\} \subseteq \mathbb{N} \times \mathbb{N}$ (given)

⇒ $x, \frac{1}{x} \in \mathbb{N}$, which is impossible.

⇒ $R = \{\ \}$ ⇒ $D_R = \{\}$ and $R_R = \{\}$.

5. $R = \{(x, y); x, y \in W; y = 2x - 4\}$; $(a, -2) \in \mathbb{R}$ and $(4, b^2) \in \mathbb{R}$

⇒ $-2 = 2a - 4$ and $b^2 = 8 - 4$

⇒ $2a = 2$ and $b^2 = 4$ ⇒ $a = 1$ and $b = \pm 2$

∴ $R_1 = \{(a, b)\} = \{(1, 2), (1, -2)\}$

6. Let $R = \{(x, y)\} = \{(0, 2), (-1, 5), (2, -4)\}$ and for linear relation between x and y.

Let $y = ax + b$ ⇒ $2 = b$ and $5 = -a + b$

⇒ $a = b - 5 = 2 - 5 = -3$

⇒ $y = -3x + 2$ ⇒ $3x + y = 2$

7. $A = \{1, 2, 3, 4\}$; $B = \{1, 2, 3, 4, 5\}$ and $R \subseteq A \times B$; where $a\ R\ b \Leftrightarrow a / b$

⇒ $R = \{(1, 1), (1, 2), (1, 3), (1, 4), (1, 5), (2, 2), (2, 4), (3, 3), (4, 4)\}$

(i) (Representation of R by Lattice diagram)

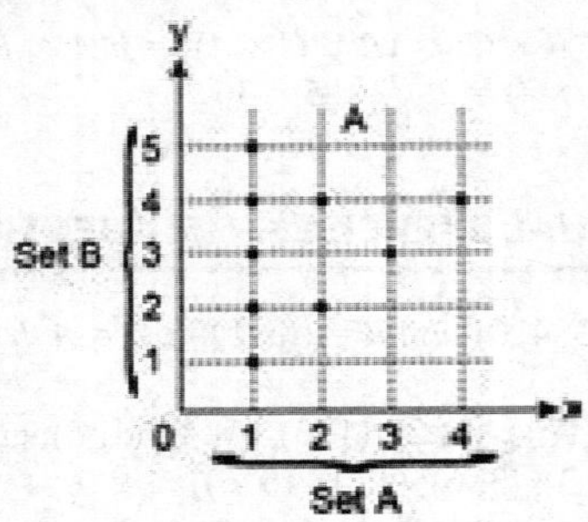

(ii) (Representation of R by tabular form)

$B \rightarrow$

R	1	2	3	4	5
1	1	1	1	1	1
2	0	1	0	1	0
3	0	0	1	0	0
4	0	0	0	1	0

$A \uparrow$

8. $A = \{1, 2, 3\}$; $B = \{4, 5\}$; $R \subseteq A \times B$ given by $R = \{(2, 4), (2, 5), (3, 5)\}$

(i)

R	4	5
1	0	0
2	1	1
3	0	1

(ii)

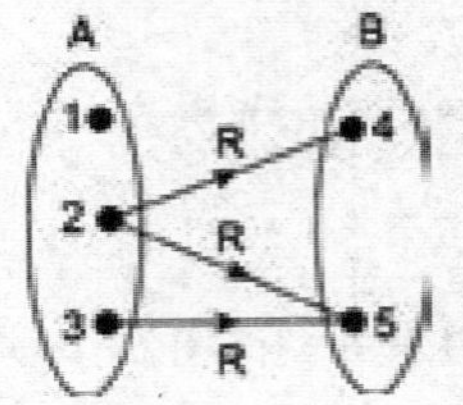

9. (i) $R = \{(x, y) : y = x - 2$ and $x \in \{5, 6, 7\}\}$

(ii) $R = \{(5, 3), (6, 4), (7, 5)\}$

10. (a) $y^2 = 2x - 3$

∵ $(2, -1)$ and $(2, 1) \in \mathbb{R}$

⇒ R is one–many.

From graph of $y^2 = 2x - 3$

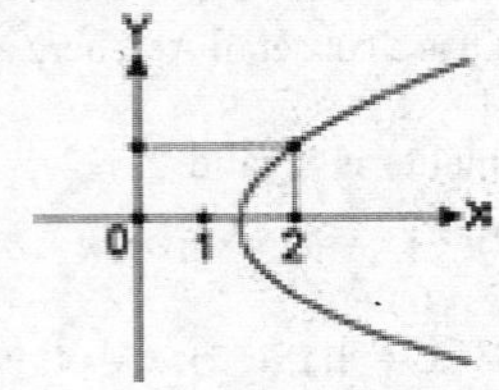

Clearly by horizontal line test, the relation is injective but range of $R = (-\infty, \infty)$ ⇒ R is subjective with co-domain $\mathbb{R}$.

(b) $y = x^2 + 4$

∵ $(-1, 5)$ and $(1, 5) \in \mathbb{R}$

⇒ R is many–one ⇒ R is not injective

Also $y \ge 4$

⇒ R is not surjective with co-domain $\mathbb{R}$.

(c) $y = ax^2 + bx + c$

∵ $\left(\frac{-b}{2a} - k, y\right)$ and $\left(\frac{-b}{2a} + k, y\right) \in \mathbb{R}\ \forall \in \mathbb{R}$ as graph is symmetric about the line $x = \frac{-b}{2a}$.

⇒ Relation R is many–one, i.e., not injective.

Also $y \ge -\frac{(b^2 - 4ac)}{4a}$ for $a >$ o and $y \le -\frac{(b^2 - 4ac)}{4a}$ for $a < 0$

⇒ Range ≠ $\mathbb{R}$ R is not subjective with co-domain $\mathbb{R}$.

(d) $y^3 = 5x + 4$

⇒ $y = 3\sqrt{5x + 4} \in \mathbb{R}$ and range of relation = $\mathbb{R}$.

⇒ R is subjective.

Now, $x_2 > x_1$ ⇒ $5x_2 > 5x_1$

⇒ $5x_2 + 4 > 5x_1 + 4$

⇒ $3\sqrt{5x_2 + 4} > 3\sqrt{5x_1 + 4}$

⇒ $y_2 > y_1$ where (x_1, y_1) and $(x_2, y_2) \in \mathbb{R}$

$\Rightarrow$ For $x_1 \neq x_2$ and $y_1 \neq y_2$

$\Rightarrow$ Relation is injective.

(e) $y = \sqrt{3x-4}$

Clearly range of relation = $[0, \infty) \neq \mathbb{R}$

$\Rightarrow$ Relation is not subjective,

Also for $x_2 > x_1$, $\sqrt{3x_2 - 4} > \sqrt{3x_1 - 4}$

$\Rightarrow$ $y_2 > y_1$ for $(x_1, y_1), (x_2, y_2) \in \mathbb{R}$

$\Rightarrow$ For $x_1 \neq x_2, y_1 \neq y_2$

$\Rightarrow$ Relation R is injective.

TEXTUAL EXERCISE-2: (OBJECTIVE)

1. (b), (c) No. of relations from A to A; where $A = \{2, 3, 4, 5\}$
= number of subset $A \times A$

$= (2)^{n(A \times A)} = (2)^{(4)^2} = (2)^{16} = (16)^4$

2. (c) $A = \{a, e, i, o, u\}$,

Number of relations on power set of $A = (2)^{n(P(A) \times P(A))}$

$= (2)^{[n(P(A))]^2}$

$= (2)^{\left[2^{n(A)}\right]^2} = (2)^{\left[2^5\right]^2} = (2)^{2^{10}}$

3. (a) $A = \{1, 2, 3\}$ and $B = \{a, b, c, d\}$;

Number of relations from set of set A to set B

$= 2^{n(A \times B)} = 2^{3 \times 4} = (2)^{12}$

4. (c) $n(A) = m$, $n(B) = n$ and $m > n$.

$k = n[P(A \times B)] = (2)^{n(A \times B)} = (2)^{mn}$ and $P = n[P(B \times A)]$
$= (2)^{n(B \times A)} = (2)^{nm}$

$\Rightarrow$ $k = p$

5. (c) $A = \{2, 3, 5, 6, 10\}$ and '$x\ R\ y$ if $x < y$ and x divides y';
$R \subseteq (A \times A)$

$\Rightarrow$ $R = \{(2, 3), (2, 5), (2, 6), (2, 10), (3, 5), (3, 6), (3, 10), (5, 6), (5, 10), (6, 10)\}$

$\Rightarrow$ Domain of $R = \{2, 3, 5, 6\}$

6. (c) $R \subseteq \mathbb{N} \times \mathbb{N}$; $x\ R\ y$ if '$3x + 5y = 53$'

For $x = 1, y = 10$; For $x = 6, y = 7$; For $x = 11, y = 4$; For $x = 16, y = 1$

$\Rightarrow$ Range of relation = $\{1, 4, 7, 10\}$

7. (b) $A = \{2, 3, 5, 7, 10\}$

$R_1 = \{(x, y): x/(y-1)\}$; $R_1 \subseteq A \times A$ and $R_2 = \{(x, y): x + y = 10\}$; $R_2 \subseteq A \times A$

$\Rightarrow$ $R_1 = \{(2, 3), (2, 5), (2, 7), (3, 7), (3, 10)\}$ and $R_2 = \{(3, 7), (5, 5), (7, 3)\}$

$\Rightarrow$ $R = R_1 \cap R_2 = \{(3, 7)\}$

8. (b), (c) $R \subseteq \mathbb{N} \times \mathbb{N}$ and $x\ R\ y$ if '$x + y$ divides 10'

$\Rightarrow$ $R = \{(1, 1), (1, 4), (2, 3), (3, 2), (4, 1), (1, 9), (2, 8), (3, 7), (4, 6), (5, 5), (6, 4), (7, 3), (8, 2), (9, 1)$

Clearly the relation is one–many as well as many–one.

9. (c), (d) $R \subseteq A \times A$; where $A = \{2, 7, 9, 11\}$ and $x\ R\ y$ if 'x divides y'

$\Rightarrow$ $R = \{(2, 2), (7, 7), (9, 9), (11, 11)\}$

Clearly R is one–one.

Also each element of set A has a unique image in A.

Thus R is also a function from set A to itself.

10. (a), (c), (d) For a relation to be a function from set A to set B, it must be one–one or many–one and must have its domain A.

11. (d) $A = \{x : x^2 - 3x + 2 = 0; x \in \mathbb{R}\}$

$\Rightarrow$ $A = \{1, 2\}$ and $R = A \times A$

$\Rightarrow$ $R = \{(1, 1), (1, 2), (2, 1), (2, 2)\}$

12. (a) $A = \{1, 2, 3\}$

$R_1 = \{(1, 2), (3, 2), (1, 3)\}$

$R_2 = \{(1, 3), (3, 6), (2, 1), (1, 2)\}$

Clearly R_1 is one–many relation as well as many–one but R_2 is one–many as $(1, 3), (1, 2) \in R_2$

But $6 \notin$ A, implies R_2 is not a relation on A.

13. (c) $A = \{a, b, c, d\}$; $B = \{b, c, d, e\}$

$n[(A \times B) \cap (B \times A)] = n\,[(A \cap B) \times (B \cap A)]$

$= [n(A \cap B)]^2 = (3)^2 = 9$

TEXTUAL EXERCISE-3: (SUBJECTIVE)

1. $R \subseteq \mathbb{N} \times \mathbb{N}$ such that $R = \{(a, b); a^2 + b^2 = ab\}$

(i) $(a, a) \in \mathbb{R}\ \forall\ a \in \mathbb{N}$

$\Rightarrow$ $a^2 + a^2 = a^2$ $\quad\Rightarrow$ $a^2 = 0$, which is impossible

$\Rightarrow$ False

(ii) $(a, b) \in \mathbb{R}$ $\quad\Rightarrow$ $a^2 + b^2 = ab$

$\Rightarrow$ $b^2 + a^2 = ba$ $\quad\Rightarrow$ $(b, a) \in \mathbb{R}$

$\Rightarrow$ True

(iii) $(a, b) \in \mathbb{R}$ $\quad\Rightarrow$ $a^2 + b^2 = ab$

$\Rightarrow$ $a^2 - ab + b^2 = 0$

It is a quadratic in 'a' (or b) with discriminate $= b^2 - 4b^2 = -3b^2 < 0$

$\Rightarrow$ No real values of a and b satisfy $a^2 + b^2 = ab$

$\Rightarrow$ $R = \{\ \}$

Thus, by default R is transitive \

$\Rightarrow$ True

2. (i) For every $a \in \theta$, $a - a = 0 \in \mathbb{Z}$

$\Rightarrow$ $(a, a) \in \mathbb{R}\ \forall\ a \in \theta$

(ii) For $a, b \in \theta$, $a - b \in \mathbb{Z}$

$\Rightarrow$ $(b - a) \in \mathbb{Z}$

$\therefore$ $(a, b) \in \mathbb{R}$ $\quad\Rightarrow$ $(b, a) \in \mathbb{R}\ \forall\ a, b \in \theta$

3. $\therefore$ $(2, 2), (3, 3), (6, 6) \in R_1, R_4$ and $A = \{2, 3, 6\}$

$\Rightarrow$ R_1 and R_4 represented in (i) and (iv) respectively reflexive.

4. $A = \{1, 2, 3, 5\}$

Clearly, whenever $(a, b) \in R_2$

$\Rightarrow$ $(b, a) \in R_2$

$\Rightarrow$ R_2 is symmetric

Also $R_4 = A \times A$ being universal relation on A is symmetric.

5. $\therefore$ $(2, 6) \notin R_1 \Rightarrow R_1$ is not transitive. Similarly $(3, 5) \notin R_2$

$\Rightarrow$ R_2 is not transitive.

Also $(2, 2), (3, 3), (5, 5) \notin R_4$

$\Rightarrow$ R_4 is not transitive.

$\therefore$ R_3 is the only transitive relation.

6. (i) Only reflexive

(ii) Only symmetric

(iii) Only transitive
As there are no ordered pairs (a, b) and $(b, c) \in \mathbb{R}$.
(iv) $R_4 = A \times A$, being universal relation is reflexive, Symmetric as well as transitive, i.e., equivalence.

7. (i) Let a = 2
$\Rightarrow 1 - a^2 = 1 - 4 = -3 \not> 0$
$\Rightarrow (a, a), (2, 2) \notin \mathbb{R}$
$\Rightarrow$ R is not reflexive on $\mathbb{R}$.
(ii) Clearly $(a, b) \in \mathbb{R}$
$\Rightarrow 1 - ab > 0$
$\Rightarrow 1 - ba > 0 \quad \Rightarrow (b, a) \in \mathbb{R}$
$\Rightarrow R$ is symmetric
(iii) Let $a = \frac{1}{2}, b = \frac{1}{5}, c = 4$
$\Rightarrow 1 - ab = 1 - \frac{1}{10} = \frac{9}{10} > 0$
$\Rightarrow (a, b) \in \mathbb{R}$
Also $1 - bc = 1 - \frac{4}{5} = \frac{1}{5} > 0$
$\Rightarrow (b, c) \in \mathbb{R}$
Now, $1 - ac = 1 - 2 = -1 < 0$
$\Rightarrow (a, c) \notin \mathbb{R}$
$\Rightarrow R$ is not transitive.

8. R_1 and $\mathbb{Z}$ and $(a, b) \in R_1 \Leftrightarrow |a - b| \le 7$
$(a, a) \in R_1 \Leftrightarrow |a - b| \le 7 \Leftrightarrow 0 \le 7$, which is true.
$\Rightarrow R_1$ is reflexive.
Now, $(a, b) \in R_1 \Leftrightarrow |a - b| \le R_1$
$\Leftrightarrow |b - a| \le 7 \Leftrightarrow (b, a) \in R_1$
$\Rightarrow R_1$ is symmetric.
Further, let $a = 2$, $b = 8$, $c = 12$, then $|a - b| = 6 \le 7$
$\Rightarrow (a, b) \in R_1$
And $|b - c| = 4 \le 7$
$\Rightarrow (b, c) R_1$
But $|a - c| = 10 \not< 7 \Rightarrow (a, c) R_1$
$\Rightarrow R_1$ is not transitive.

10. R_1: $a/a \ \forall \ a \in \mathbb{Z}$ and $a \neq 0$, but 0 does not divide 0
$\Rightarrow R_1$ is not reflexive
But $a/b \not\Rightarrow b/a$
$\Rightarrow (b, a) \in R_1 \not\Rightarrow (a, b) \in R_1$
$\Rightarrow R_1$ is not symmetric.
Clearly, a/b and b/c
$\Rightarrow a/c$
$\Rightarrow$ transitivity of R_1
$\Rightarrow R_1 \to$ (c)
R_2: Since each triangle is similar to itself
$\Rightarrow$ Reflexivity holds
Also $\Delta_1 \sim \Delta_2$
$\Rightarrow \Delta_2 \sim \Delta_1 \quad \Rightarrow$ Symmetricity
Also $\Delta_1 \sim \Delta_2$ and $\Delta_2 \sim \Delta_3$
$\Rightarrow \Delta_1 \sim \Delta_3 \quad \Rightarrow$ Transitivity
$\Rightarrow R_2$ is equivalence relation
$\Rightarrow R_2 \to A, B, C$

R_3: $L_1 \parallel L_1$, $L_1 \parallel L_2 \quad \Rightarrow L_2 \parallel L_1$
And $L_1 \parallel L_2 \parallel L_3 \quad \Rightarrow L_1 \parallel L_3$
$\Rightarrow R_3$ is equivalence relation
$\Rightarrow R_3 \to A, B, C$
R_4: No line is $\perp$r to itself
$\Rightarrow R_4$ is not reflexive. Also $L_1 \perp r\, L_2$
$\Rightarrow L_2 \perp r\, L_1$
$\Rightarrow L_1 \parallel L_3 \quad \Rightarrow R_4$ is not transitive.
$\therefore R_4 \to (B)$
R_5: No girl can be sister of herself
R_5 is not reflexive
Also if 'a is sister of b', then it is not necessary that 'b is sister of a' as, 'b may be brother of a'.
Thus, $a\, R_5\, b$
$\Rightarrow b\, R_5\, a$
$\Rightarrow R_5$ is not symmetric.
Further $(a, b), (b, c) \in R_5$
$\Rightarrow$ 'a is sister b' and 'b is sister of c'
$\Rightarrow$ 'a is also sister of c'. Thus, R_5 is transitive.
$\therefore R_5 \to$ (c)
$\Rightarrow R_6$: $a - a = 0 \ \forall \ a \in \mathbb{N}$
$\Rightarrow (a, a) \notin R_6$ for any $a \in \mathbb{N}$
$\Rightarrow R_6$: is not reflexive
Now $(a - b) \in \mathbb{N} \quad \Rightarrow -(a - b) \notin \mathbb{N}$
$\Rightarrow (b - a) \notin \mathbb{N} \quad \Rightarrow R_6$ is not symmetric.
Also $a - b \in \mathbb{N} \quad \Rightarrow a \ge b + 1$ and $b - c \in \mathbb{N}$
$\Rightarrow b \ge c + 1 \quad \Rightarrow a \ge (c + 1) + 1$
$\Rightarrow (a - c) \ge 2$ and $a, c \in \mathbb{N}$
$\Rightarrow (a, c) \in \mathbb{N} \quad \Rightarrow R_6$ is transitive
Thus $R_6 \to$(c)
R_7: $\because a = a \ \forall \ a \in \mathbb{R}$
$\Rightarrow R_7$ is reflexive.
Also $a \ge b \not\Rightarrow b\, a$ e.g., $7 > 2 \not\Rightarrow 2 > 7$
$\Rightarrow R_7$ is not symmetric.
Now $a \ge b$ and $b \ge c$
$\Rightarrow a \ge c \quad \Rightarrow R_7$ is transitive.
$\therefore R_7 \to (A), (C)$

11. (a) $(a, b)\, R\, (c, d) \Leftrightarrow ad\,(b + c) = bc\,(a + d)$
Reflexivity: $(a, b)\, R\, (a, b)$
$\Leftrightarrow ab\,(b + a) = ba\,(a + b)$, which is true
$\Rightarrow R$ is reflexive.
Symmstricity: $(a, b)\, R\, (c, d)$
$\Leftrightarrow ad\,(b + c) = bc\,(a + d)$
$\Leftrightarrow bc\,(a + d) = ad\,(b + c)$
$\Leftrightarrow cb\,(d + a) = da\,(c + b)$
$\Leftrightarrow (c, d)\, R\, (a, b)$
$\Rightarrow R$ is symmetric
Transitivity: Let $(a, b)\, R\, (c, d)$ and $(c, d)\, R\, (e, f)$
$\Rightarrow ad\,(b + c) = bc\,(a + d)$
$\Rightarrow \left(\frac{1}{c} + \frac{1}{b}\right) = \left(\frac{1}{d} + \frac{1}{a}\right)$ (dividing by $abcd$)
And $cf\,(d + f) = de\,(c + f)$
$\Rightarrow \left(\frac{1}{e} + \frac{1}{d}\right) = \left(\frac{1}{f} + \frac{1}{c}\right)$ (dividing by $cdef$)

$\Rightarrow \frac{1}{c}-\frac{1}{d}=\frac{1}{a}-\frac{1}{b}=\frac{1}{e}-\frac{1}{f} \Rightarrow \frac{1}{a}-\frac{1}{b}=\frac{1}{e}-\frac{1}{f}$

$\Rightarrow \frac{1}{a}+\frac{1}{f}=\frac{1}{b}+\frac{1}{e}$ $\Rightarrow$ be $(a+f)=af(b+e)$

$\Rightarrow (a, b) R (e, f)$ $\Rightarrow$ R is transitive.

(b) $(a, b) R (c, d)$ iff $a+d=b+c$

Reflexivity: $(a, b) R (a, b) \Leftrightarrow a+b=b+a$, which is true

Symmetricity: $(a, b) R (c, d) \Leftrightarrow a+d=b+c$

$\Leftrightarrow b+c=a+d$

$\Leftrightarrow (c+b)=(d+a)$ $\Leftrightarrow (c, d) R (a, b)$

$\Leftrightarrow$ R is symmetric.

Transitivity: $(a, b) R (c, d)$ and $(c, d) R (e, f)$

$\Leftrightarrow a+d=b+c$ and $c+f=d+e$

$\Leftrightarrow a-b=c-d=e-f$

$\Leftrightarrow a-b=e-f$ $\Leftrightarrow a+f=b+e$

$\Leftrightarrow (a, b) R (e, f)$

$\Leftrightarrow$ R is transitive

Thus (a), (b), (c), all represent equivalence relations.

12. $x R y \Leftrightarrow x^2-y^2+\sqrt{3}$ is an irrational number

Reflexivity: $x R x$

$\Leftrightarrow x^2-x^2+\sqrt{3}$ i.e., $\sqrt{3}$ is irrational, which is true.

Symmetricity: $x R y$

$\Leftrightarrow x^2-y^2+\sqrt{3}$ is irrational, but $\not\Rightarrow y^2-x^2+\sqrt{3}$ is also irrational.

e.g., let $x=\sqrt{2.4\sqrt{3}}; y=4\sqrt{3}$

$\Rightarrow x^2-y^2+\sqrt{3}=2\sqrt{3}-\sqrt{3}+\sqrt{3}=2\sqrt{3}$ which is irrational .

$\Rightarrow x R y$, but $y^2-x^2+\sqrt{3}=\sqrt{3}-2\sqrt{3}+\sqrt{3}=0$ which is rational.

$\Rightarrow (y, x) \notin R$ $\Rightarrow R$ is not symmetric.

Transitivity: Let $x R y$ and $y R Z$. We claim that $x R z$ is nodal ways true.

Consider, $x=\sqrt[4]{3}, y=1, z=\sqrt{2}\sqrt[4]{3}$,

then $x^2-y^2+\sqrt{3}=\sqrt{3}-1+\sqrt{3}=2\sqrt{3}-1\in\overline{\mathbb{Q}} \Rightarrow xRy$

Now, $y^2-z^2+\sqrt{3}=1-2\sqrt{3}+\sqrt{3}=1-\sqrt{3}\in\overline{\mathbb{Q}}$

$\Rightarrow y R z$

Further, $x^2-z^2+\sqrt{3}=\sqrt{3}-2\sqrt{3}+\sqrt{3}=0\in\mathbb{Q}$

$\not\Rightarrow x R z$

$\Rightarrow$ R is not transitive.

TEXTUAL EXERCISE-3: (OBJECTIVE)

1. (b, d) $R=\{(2, 4), (3, 9), (4, 16)\}$

$\Rightarrow R^{-1}=\{(4, 2), (9, 3), (16, 4)\}$

$\Rightarrow R_0 R^{-1}=\{(4, 4), (9, 9), (16, 16)\}$

Which is identify relation on domain set of R^{-1}.

Also it is reflexive and symmetric on domain of R^{-1}

2. (a) $R_1=\{(10, 20), (20, 30), (30, 40), (40, 50)\}$

$R_2=\{(10, 10), (10, 20), (10, 30), (10, 40), (10, 50), (20, 20), (20, 40), (30, 30), (40, 40), (50, 50)\}$

$\Rightarrow (R_1\ 0\ R_2)^{-1}=R_2^{-1}\ 0\ R_1^{-1}=\{(20, 10), (30, 10), (30, 20), (40, 10), (40, 30), (50, 10), (50, 20), (50, 40)\}$

3. (a), (b), (c), (d)

$x R y \Leftrightarrow x+y+4xy$ is even number

Reflexivity: $x R x \Leftrightarrow x+x+4x^2=2x+4x^2$ is even, which is true.

Symmetricity: $x R y$

$\Leftrightarrow x+y+4xy=2k$; for some $k\in\mathbb{N}$.

$\Leftrightarrow y+x+4xy=2k$

$\Leftrightarrow y R x$

Transitivity: $x R y$

$\Leftrightarrow x+y+4xy$ is even and $y R z$

$\Leftrightarrow y+z+4xy$ is even

$\Leftrightarrow x+y=2k_1$ and $y+z=2k_2$ for some $k_1, k_2\in\mathbb{N}$

Case (i): If y is odd, then x, z are odd

$\Rightarrow (x+z)$ is even

$\Rightarrow x+z+4xz$ is even

$\Rightarrow x R z$

Case (ii): If y is even, then x, z are even

$\Rightarrow (x+z)$ is even

$\Rightarrow x+z+4xz$ is even

$\Rightarrow x R z$

4. (b) $A=\{2, 3, 4, 5\}$

$R=\{(2, 2), (3, 3), (4, 4), (5, 5), (2, 3), (3, 2), (3, 5), (5, 3)\}$

Clearly R is reflexive and symmetric, but $(2, 3), (3, 5)\in\mathbb{R}$ and $(2, 5)\notin\mathbb{R}$

$\Rightarrow R$ is not transitive.

Also $(3, 2), (2, 3)\ \mathbb{R}$ and $2\neq 3$

$\Rightarrow R$ is not anti-symmetric

5. (b) $R=R^{-1}$

$\Rightarrow (x, y)\in R$

$\Leftrightarrow (x, y)\in R^{-1}$

$\Rightarrow (x, y)\in R$ and $(y, x)\in R$

$\Rightarrow R$ is symmetric.

6. (d) (b) and (c) are wrong as if

$A=\{2, 3, 5\}$ and R, S are relation on set A defined by $R=\{(2, 2), (3, 3), (5, 5)\}$ and $S=\{(2, 2), (3, 3), (5, 5), (2, 5)\}$, then $(R\cup S)$ is not equivalence, also union of two transitive.

$\Rightarrow$ (a) is false .

7. (c) Clearly $OP_i=OP_i$ for each $P_i\in P$

$\Rightarrow P_i R P_i\ \forall P_i\in P$

$\Rightarrow R$ is reflexive.

Also $OP_1=OP_2$ $OP_2=OP_1$

$\therefore P_1 R P_2$ $P_2 R P_1$

$\Rightarrow R$ is symmetric.

Also $OP_1=OP_2$ and $OP_2=OP_3$

$\Rightarrow OP_1=OP_3$ $\Rightarrow R$ is transitive.

8. (d) $(a, b) R (c, d)$ $\Leftrightarrow a+d=b+c$

$(a, b) R (a, b)$ $\Leftrightarrow a+b=b+a$

Which is true $\Rightarrow$ R is reflexive.

$(a, b) R (c, d)$ $\Leftrightarrow a+d=b+c$

$\Leftrightarrow b+c=a+d$ $\Leftrightarrow c+b=d+a$

$\Leftrightarrow (c, a) R (a, d)$ $\Rightarrow R$ is symmetric

Also, $(a, b) R (c, d)$ and $(c, d) R (e, f)$

$\Leftrightarrow$ $a + d = b + c$ and $c + f = d + e$
$\Leftrightarrow$ $a - b = c - d$ and $c - d = e - f$
$\Leftrightarrow$ $a - b = e - f$ $\quad\Leftrightarrow$ $a + f = b + e$
$\Leftrightarrow$ $(a, b)\ R\ (e, f)$ $\quad\Rightarrow$ R is transitive.

9. (c) $2x^2 - 3xy + y^2 = 0$
$\Leftrightarrow$ $2x^2 - 2xy - xy + y^2 = 0$
$\Leftrightarrow$ $2x(x - y) - y(x - y) = 0$
$\Leftrightarrow$ $(2x - y)(x - y) = 0$
$\Leftrightarrow$ $2x = y$ or $x = y$
R is reflexive as $x = x\ \forall\ x \in \mathbb{N}$
$\therefore$ $(2, 4) \in \mathbb{R}$ as $2x = y$ holds, but $(4, 2) \notin \mathbb{R}$
$\Rightarrow$ R is not symmetric.
Also (2, 4) and (4, 8) $\in \mathbb{R}$ as $2x = y$ in each pair, but (2, 8) $\notin \mathbb{R}$
$\Rightarrow$ R is not transitive.

10. (b) $R = \{(1, 2), (2, 3)\}$; $A = \{1, 2, 3\}$ and $R \subseteq A \times A$.
<u>To make *R* reflexive:</u> (1, 1), (2, 2), (3, 3) must be included.
<u>To make *R* symmetric:</u> (2, 1), (3, 2) must be included.
<u>To make *R* transitive:</u> (1, 3), (3, 1) must be included.
Thus total 7 elements are required to be included in *R*.

11. (a) $R : A \to B$ and $S : BC$;
$(S\ O\ R)(x) = S(R(x))$
$\Rightarrow$ $x \in A$
Also $R(x) \in B$ $\quad\Rightarrow$ $S(R(x) \in C$
$\therefore$ $S\ O\ R: A \to C$

12. (b) $R \subseteq A \times B$ and $S \subseteq B \times C$
$(SOR)^{-1} = R^{-1}\ O\ S^{-1}$ (standard result of composition of two relations)

13. (b) Universal relation on set *A*, i.e., $A \times A$ is the greatest on set *A*
$\Rightarrow$ 1 is incorrect
Let $A = \{a_1, a_2, \ldots, a_n\}$; $n \geq 2$
$\Rightarrow$ $A \times A = \{(a_1, a_1), (a_1, a_2), (a_1, a_3), \ldots, (a_1, a_n), (a_2, a_1), (a_2, a_2), (a_2, a_3), \ldots, (a_2, a_n), \ldots, (a_n, a_1), (a_n, a_2), \ldots, (a_n, a_n)\}$
$\therefore$ $(a_1, a_2), (a_2, a_1) \in R$, but $a_1 \neq a_2$
$\Rightarrow$ R is not anti-symmetric
$\Rightarrow$ (2) is correct
We know that union and intersection of two is also symmetric
$\Rightarrow$ (3) is correct
$\therefore$ If $(a, b) \in R \cup S$
$\Rightarrow$ $(a, b) \in R$ or S
$\Rightarrow$ $(b, a) \in R$ or S ($\because$ R, *S* are symmetric)
$\Rightarrow$ $(b, a) \in R \cup S$ $\quad\Rightarrow$ $R \cup S$ is symmetric
Parallely if $(a, b) \in R \cap S$
$\Rightarrow$ $(a, b) \in R$ and S
$\Rightarrow$ $(b, a) \in R$ and S
$\Rightarrow$ $(b, a) \in R \cap S$
$\Rightarrow$ $R \cap S$ is symmetric

14. (b) Intersection of two symmetric relations is symmetric.

15. (a) In an identity relation a *R* a and $a\ R\ b$ for $a \neq b$, however in a reflexive relation a *R* a and *a* may be related to any other element different from *a*
$\Rightarrow$ n (reflexive relation) $\geq n$ (identify relation)
$\Rightarrow$ $m \geq n$

16. (b) $S = \{1, 2, 3, \ldots, 12\}$
Let a_1 = number of elements in set *A*
a_2 = number of elements in set *B*
a_3 = number of elements in set *C*
$\therefore$ *A*, *B*, *C* are of equal size
$\Rightarrow$ $a_1 = a_2 = a_3 = 4$
Thus, we are to divide 12 elements equally among 3 naming groups.
By the knowledge of permutations, number of ways = $\dfrac{12!}{4!4!4!} = \dfrac{12!}{(4!)^3}$

SECTION-3: (ONLY ONE CORRECT ANSWER)

1. (a) Relation from A to A is a subset of $A \times A$
Number of relation on A = Number of subsets of $A \times A$
$= (12)^{n(A) \times n(A)} = (2)^{n^2}$

2. (b) $A = \{2, 3, 4, 5\}$
$\because$ (2, 2), (3, 3), (4, 4), (5, 5), $\in R$
$\Rightarrow$ R is reflexive.
$\because$ (2, 3), (3, 2), (3, 5) and (5, 3) $\in R$
$\Rightarrow$ R is symmetric.
$\because$ (2, 3), (3, 5) $\in$ R, but (2, 5) $\notin R$
$\Rightarrow$ R is not transitive.

3. (b) $R \subseteq A \times A$ and $R = R^{-1}$
$\Rightarrow$ $(a, b) \in R, R^{-1}$ $\quad\Rightarrow$ $(b, a) \in R, R^{-1}$
$\Rightarrow$ R must be symmetric

4. (d) $A = \{x : x^2 - 3x + 2 = 0\}$ $\quad\Rightarrow A = \{1, 2\}$
$\Rightarrow$ $R = A \times A = \{(1, 1), (1, 2), (2, 1), (2, 2)\}$

5. (b) $R = \{(m, n) : m = k_n; k \in \mathbb{Z}; k \neq 0\}$
<u>Reflexivity:</u>
$\because$ $m = 1.m\ \forall\ m \in \mathbb{Z} - \{0\}$
$\Rightarrow$ $(m, m) \in \forall\ m \in \mathbb{Z} - \{0\}$
$\Rightarrow$ R is reflexive
<u>Symmetric:</u>
$\because$ $(4, 2) \in R$ as $4 = 2(2)$, but $2 \neq k(4)$ for any $k \in \mathbb{Z}$
$\Rightarrow$ $(2, 4) \notin R$ $\quad\Rightarrow$ R is not symmetric
<u>Transitive:</u>
Let $(m, n) \in R$ and $(n, k) \in R$
$\Rightarrow$ $m = k_1 n$ and $n = k_2 k$; $k_1, k_2 \in \mathbb{Z}$
$\Rightarrow$ $(m, k) \in$
$\Rightarrow$ R is transitive.

6. (b) $A = \{5, 6, 7\}$ and $B = \{1, 2, 3, 4\}$;
$n[(A \times B) \times B] = n(A \times B) \times n(B)$
$= n(A) \times n(B) \times n(B)$
$= 3 \times 4 \times 4 = 48$

7. **(d)** $A = \{2, 3, 4\}$ and $B = \{3, 5\}$
$R = \{(a, b): (a < b)\} \subseteq A \times B$
$\Rightarrow R = \{(2, 3), (2, 5), (3, 5), (4, 5)\}$
$\Rightarrow R^{-1} = \{(3, 2), (5, 2), (5, 3), (5, 4)\}$
$\Rightarrow R \text{ o } R^{-1} = \{(3, 3), (3, 5), (5, 3), (5, 5)\}$

8. **(b)** R and R' are symmetric
Let $(R \cap R')$ contains (a, b)
$\Rightarrow (a, b) \in R$ and R′
$\Rightarrow (b, a) \in R$ and R′
$\Rightarrow (b, a) \in R \cap R'$
$\Rightarrow (R \cap R')$ is symmetric.

9. **(c)** n (Relations form A to B) $= 2^{n(A\times B)} = (2)^{3\times 4} = (2)^{12}$
$\Rightarrow$ Number of non-empty relations $2^{12} - 1$

10. **(d)** $R = \{(x, y); x < y\}\ A \times B$
$\Rightarrow R = \{(1, 3), (1, 5), (2, 3), (2, 5), (3, 5), (4, 5)\}$
$\Rightarrow R^{-1} = \{(3, 1), (5, 1), (3, 2), (5, 2), (5, 3), (5, 4)\}$
$\Rightarrow R^{-1}OR = \{(1, 1), (1, 2), (1, 3), (1, 4), (2, 1), (2, 2), (2, 3), (2, 4), (3, 1), (3, 2), (3, 3), (3, 4), (4, 1), (4, 2), (4, 3), (4,4)\}$
$\Rightarrow$ None of these

11. **(b)** $\because a \nless a, a < b \nRightarrow b < a$ and $a < b; b < c \Rightarrow a < c$
$\Rightarrow R$ is only transitive.

12. **(b)** $P = \{(x, y) : x^2 + y^2 = 1, x, y \in \mathbb{R}\}$, then clearly $x\,R\,x$ only for $x = \pm\frac{1}{\sqrt{2}}$
$\Rightarrow R$ is not reflexive.
$\therefore x^2 + y^2 = 1 \quad \Rightarrow y^2 + x^2 = 1$
$\Rightarrow R$ is symmetric
If $x = 1, y = 0$
$\Rightarrow x\,R\,y$ and $y = 0, z = 1$
$\Rightarrow y\,R\,z$
But $1 \not R\, 1$, i.e., $x \not R\, z \Rightarrow$ R is not transitive.

13. **(b)** R is any Equivalence relation on A and $n(A) = n$
$\Rightarrow a\,R\,a\ \forall\ a \in A \quad \Rightarrow n(R) \geq n$

14. **(a)** $x\,R\,y \Leftrightarrow x - y + \sqrt{5}$ is irrational .
Reflexivity: $x\,R\,x$
$\Leftrightarrow x - x + \sqrt{5}$ is irrational, i.e., $\sqrt{5}$ is irrational, which is true,
Symmetricity: Let $x = 2\sqrt{5}, y = \sqrt{5}$, then $x - y + \sqrt{5} = 2\sqrt{5} - \sqrt{5} + \sqrt{5} = 2\sqrt{5}$ which is irrational
$\Rightarrow x\,R\,y.$
But $y - x + \sqrt{5} = \sqrt{5} - 2\sqrt{5} + \sqrt{5} = 0$ which is rational
$\Rightarrow (y, x) \notin R$
$\Rightarrow$ R is not symmetric.
Let $x = 2\sqrt{5}, y = \sqrt{5}, z = 3\sqrt{5}$, then $x - y + \sqrt{5} = 2\sqrt{5}$
$\Rightarrow (x, y) \in \mathbb{R}$
Now, $x - z + \sqrt{5} = 0$
$\Rightarrow (x, z) \notin \mathbb{R} \quad \Rightarrow$ R is not transitive.

15. **(b)** $A, B\ X$ and $A\,R\,B \Leftrightarrow A \cap B = \phi$
Reflexivity: $A \cap A = A \neq \phi\ \forall\ A\ X$
$\Rightarrow A$ is not reflexive.
Symmtricity: $A \cap B = \phi$
$\Rightarrow B \cap A = \phi \quad \Rightarrow R$ is symmetric.
Transitivity: Let $A = \{1, 2, 3\}, B = \{4, 5, 6\}, C = \{2, 7, 8\}$
Clearly $A \cap B = \phi; B \cap C = \phi; A \cap C \neq \phi$
$\Rightarrow R$ is not transitive.

16. **(d)** $A = \{1, 2, 3, 4, 5\}$
$R = \{(x, y): |x^2 - y^2| < 16\}$
$R = (x, y): -16 < x^2 - y^2 < 16\}$
$R = \{(x, y): x^2 - y^2 < 16$ and $x^2 - y^2 > -16$
$R = \{(1, 1), (1, 2), (1, 3), (1, 4), (1, 5), (2, 1), (2, 2), (2, 3), (2, 4), (3, 1), (3, 2), (3, 3), (3, 4), (4, 1), (4, 2), (4, 3), (4, 4), (4, 5), (5, 4), (5, 5)\}$

17. **(d)** $R = \{(x, y) : x$ is relatively prime to $y\}$
$= \{(2, 3), (2, 7), (3, 7), (3, 10), (4, 3), (4, 7), (5, 3), (5, 7)\}$
$\Rightarrow$ Domain of $R = \{2, 3, 4, 5\}$

18. **(c)** $x^2 + y^2 \leq 4 \quad \Rightarrow x \in [-2, 2]$
But $x \in \mathbb{Z} \quad \Rightarrow x \in \{-2, -1, 0, 1, 2\}$

19. **(b)** Identify relation is always not true
$\Rightarrow I \subset R$

20. **(b)** $A\ A, A\ B \nRightarrow B\ A$
And $A\ B, B\ C \quad \Rightarrow A\ C$
$\Rightarrow R$ is reflexive and transitive.
Also $A\ B$ and $B\ A$
$\Rightarrow A = B$
$\Rightarrow R$ is anti-symmetric.

21. **(c)** $\because R$ is anti-symmetric iff (a, b) and $(b, a) \in \mathbb{R}$
$\Rightarrow a = b$

22. **(b)** $\because$ o contains no elements
$\Rightarrow (a, a) \notin R$ for any $a \in A$
Also by default three is no pair $(a, b) \in R$ for which $(b, a) \notin R$
$\Rightarrow R$ is symmetric. Similarly by default R is transitive.

23. **(a)** Clearly R_1 is equivalence as $|a| = |a|, |a| = |b|$
$\Rightarrow |b| = |a|$
And $|a| = |b|, |b| = |c|$
$\Rightarrow |a| = |c|$
R_2 is not equivalence as $a \leq b$
$\nRightarrow b \leq a$
R_3 is not equivalence as a/b
$\nRightarrow b/a$
R_4 is not equivalence as $a < b$
$\nRightarrow b < a$

24. **(c)** Since R^{-1} of equivalence relation R is also equivalence.

25. **(d)** $\because a \equiv a \pmod m$ as $m/(a - a)$
Also $a \equiv b \pmod m$ as $m/(a - b)$
$\Rightarrow m/(b - a) \quad \Rightarrow b \equiv a \pmod m$
Further $m/(a - b)$ and $m/(b - c)$
$\Rightarrow m/(a - b) + (b - c) \quad \Rightarrow m/(a - c)$
$\Rightarrow a \equiv c \pmod m$

26. **(b)** $\because$ Union of two equivalence relations need not be equivalence, but intersection of two equivalence relation is equivalence

27. (c) $R = \{(1, 3), (2, 2), (3, 2)\}$ and $S = \{(2, 1), (3, 2), (2, 3)\}$
$\Rightarrow$ Ros $= \{(2, 3), (2, 2), (3, 2)\}$

28. (b) $\because x^2 = xy \quad \Rightarrow x(x - y) = 0$
$\Rightarrow x = 0$ or $x = y$
$\because \quad x = x \; \forall \; x \in A \quad \Rightarrow R$ is reflexive.
Also $x \; R \; y \quad \Rightarrow x = 0$ or $x = y$
When $x = 0$, then $x^2 = xy$; $y \neq 0$, then $y^2 \neq yx$ as L.H.S. $\neq 0$, R.H.S $= 0$
$\Rightarrow R$ is not symmetric.
Let $x \; R \; y$ and $y \; R \; z$
$\Rightarrow$ Either $x = 0$ or $x = y$ and $y = 0$ or $y = z$
Case (i): $x = 0$, $y = 0$ and $z \neq 0$, then $x^2 = xz$
Case (ii): $x = 0$, $y = z \neq = 0$, then $x^2 = xz$
$\Rightarrow x \; R \; z$
Case (iii): $x = y \neq 0$; $y = z$
$\Rightarrow x = z \quad \Rightarrow \quad x \; R \; z$
$\Rightarrow R$ is transitive.

29. (b) Let $A = \{a_1, a_2, a_3, a_4\}$, then reflexive relation.
R must contain atleast (a_1, a_1), (a_2, a_2), (a_3, a_3) and (a_4, a_4)
$A \times A$ has 16 elements, out of these 16 elements, 4 elements of type (a_i, a_i) are include in reflexive relation.
Now out of remaining 12 elements 0, 1, 2, 3, …., 12 elements can be include in reflexive relation.
Thus number of ways $= {}^{12}C_0 + {}^{12}C_1 + {}^{12}C_2 + {}^{12}C_3 + \ldots + {}^{12}C_{12} = (2)^{12}$

30. (a) $A = \{2, 4, 6\}$ and $B = \{2, 3, 5\}$
$\Rightarrow$ Number of relation from A to $B = n[P(A \times B)] = 2^{n(A \times B)} = 2^{(3) \times (3)} = (2)^9$.

31. (d) $A = \{(x, y) : x^2 + y^2 = 25\}$ and $B = \{(x, y) : x^2 + 9y^2 = 144\}$
A represents of circle of radius 5 and with centre at origin. B represents an ellipse with centre at origin with major axis length 12 and minor axis length 4.

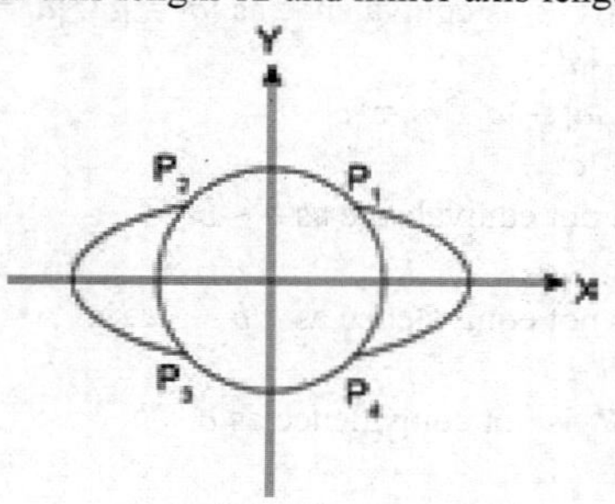

$\Rightarrow A$ and B have exactly 4 points common.

32. (a) $a \; R \; b \quad \Leftrightarrow \quad |a - b| \leq 1$
$\therefore \quad a \; R \; b$ as $|a - a| = 0 \leq 1$
$\Rightarrow$ R is reflexive.
Let $a = 2$, $b = 2.5$, $c = 3.4$, then $|a - b| = 0.5 < 1$ and $|b - c| = 0.9 < 1$
But $|a - c| = |2 - 3.4| = 1.4 \nleq 1$
$\Rightarrow (a, c) \notin R$
$\Rightarrow$ R is not transitive.
Clearly $|a - b| \leq 1$
$\Rightarrow |b - a| \leq 1$
$\Rightarrow$ R is symmetric.

SECTION–IV: (MORE THAN ONE ARE CORRECT)

1. (a), (b), (c) $X = \{1, 2, 3, 4, 5,\}$; $Y = \{1, 3, 5, 7, 9\}$
(a) $R_1 = \{(1, 3), (3, 5), (5, 7)\}$ is a relation for X to Y.
(b) $R_2 \; X \times Y \Rightarrow R_2$ is a relation from X to Y.
(c) $R_3 \; X \times Y \Rightarrow R_3$ is also a relation from X to Y.
(d) $R_4 \nsubseteq X \times Y$ as $7 \notin X$ and $4 \notin Y$.
$\Rightarrow R_4$ is not a relation from X to Y.

2. (a), (b), (c)
$\because \quad (a, b) \; R \; (a, b) \quad \Leftrightarrow \; a + b = b + a$
$\Rightarrow R$ is reflexive.
Also $(a, b) \; R \; (c, d)$
$\Rightarrow (a + d) = (b + c)$
$\Rightarrow (b + c) = (a + d) \quad \Rightarrow \quad (c + b) = (d + a)$
$\Rightarrow (c, d) \; R \; (a, b) \quad \Rightarrow \quad$ R is symmetric
$(a, b) \; R \; (c, d)$ and $(c, d) \; R \; (e, f)$
$\Rightarrow a + d = b + c$ and $c + f = d + e$
$\Rightarrow a - b = c - d$ and $c - d = e - f$
$\Rightarrow a - b = e - f \quad \Rightarrow \quad a + f = b + e$
$\Rightarrow (a, b) \; R \; (e, f) \quad \Rightarrow \quad R$ is transitive.

3. (b), (c) $A = \{(x, y) : y = e^{2x}, x \in \mathbb{R}\}$ and $B = \{(x, y) : y = e^{-2x}, x \in \mathbb{R}\}$
Clearly $(0, 1) \in A \cap B \quad \Rightarrow \quad A \cap B \neq \phi$
Also $e^{2x} = e^{-2x} \quad \Leftrightarrow \quad e^{4x} = 1$
$\Leftrightarrow x = 0$
$\Rightarrow (A \cap B)$ is singleton set.

4. (a), (d) $A = \{(x, y) : x^2 + y^2 \leq 1, x, y \in \mathbb{R}\}$ and $B = \{(x, y) : x^2 + y^2 \geq 4, x, y \in \mathbb{R}\}$
$\Rightarrow A$ is interior of circle $x^2 + y^2 = 1$ and B is exterior of circle $x^2 + y^2 = 4$
$\Rightarrow A \cap B = \phi$
$\Rightarrow A - B = A$ and $B - A = B$
$\Rightarrow B - A \neq \phi$ and $A - B \neq \phi$

5. (b), (c), (d)
$a \; R \; a \quad \Leftrightarrow a^2 \leq a^2$
$\Leftrightarrow a = 0$ or $a = 1$
$\Rightarrow R$ is not reflexive.
$a \; R \; b \quad \Leftrightarrow \quad a \leq b^2$
$\nRightarrow \; b \leq a^2 \quad \Leftrightarrow \quad (b, a) \notin R$
$\Rightarrow R$ is not symmetric
$\therefore \quad a \leq b^2$ and $b \leq c^2 \quad \nRightarrow \quad a \leq c^2$
Let $a = 2$, $b = -3$, $c = 1$, then $a = 2$, $b^2 = 9$, $c^2 = 1$, $b = -3$
$\Rightarrow a < b^2$ and $b < c^2$ but $a > c^2$
$\Rightarrow$ Thus, $(a, b) \in R$ and (b) $\in R$
$\nRightarrow \; (a, c) \in R$
$\Rightarrow R$ is not transitive and equivalence

6. (a), (c),(d) $R = \{(1, 2), (2, 3), (3, 4), (4, 5), (5, 6)\}$
$\Rightarrow R$ is not reflexive, not symmetric and not transitive.

7. (b), (c), (d) If R, S are reflexive, then $R \cup S$ and $R \cap S$ are also reflexive.

Same is true when R and S are symmetric. If R and S are both transitive, then $R \cap S$ is also transitive but not $R \cup S$.

8. (a), (b), (c), (d)

$a\,R\,b \Leftrightarrow n \mid (a-b)$

$\because n/(a-a)$ i.e., $n|0 \Rightarrow R$ is reflexive.

$\Rightarrow a\,R\,b \Leftrightarrow n \mid (a-b)$

$\Rightarrow n \mid (b-a) \Rightarrow b\,R\,a$

$\Rightarrow R$ is symmetric.

$a\,R\,b$ and $b\,R\,c$

$\Rightarrow n \mid (a-b) \Rightarrow n \mid (a-c)$

$\Rightarrow a\,R\,c \Rightarrow R$ is transitive.

$\Rightarrow R$ is equivalence.

9. (c) $A \neq$

$\Rightarrow (x, x) \notin R; (x, y)\,R$

$\Rightarrow (y, x)\,R$ as x is brother of y may imply that y is sister of x

$\Rightarrow (x, y)\,R, (y, z)\,R$

$\Rightarrow (x, z)\,R$ as x is brother and y is brother of Z

$\Rightarrow x$ is brother of z

$\Rightarrow R$ is transitive.

SECTION–V: (ASSERTION AND REASON TYPE)

1. (d) Clearly R is correct.

Further $a \mid a\ \forall\ a\ \mathbb{Z} - \{0\}$, but 0 does not divide itself.

So R is not reflexive

$\Rightarrow$ Assertion is incorrect.

2. (a) Reason is true

$\Rightarrow$ Number of relation A to B

$= n[P(A \times B)] = (2)^{n(A\times B)} = 2^{n(A)\times n(B)} = (2)^{\text{km}}$

$\Rightarrow$ Assertion is true.

3. (d) Clearly reason is true

$|a-a| \leq 1 \Rightarrow R$ is reflexive.

$|a-b| \leq 1 \Rightarrow |b-a| \leq 1$

$\Rightarrow R$ is symmetric.

If $a = 1, b = 1.5, c = 2.4$

$\Rightarrow |a-b| < 1, |b-c| < 1$, but $|a-c| \nless 1$

$\Rightarrow R$ is not transitive and hence not equivalence.

Assertion is incorrect.

4. (a) $\because A \times B = \{(a, b) : a\ A$ and $b\ B\}$ and $R : A \to B$ is a relation having some ordered pairs (x, y), such that $x\ A$ and $y\ B$ satisfying some given condition.

$\Rightarrow$ Every relation is a subset of $A \times B$

$\Rightarrow A \times B$ is the largest relation from A to B, i.e., universal relation.

$\Rightarrow$ Both assertion and reason are correct and reason correctly explains assertion.

5. (d) Clearly the reason is correct

$\because 2/(a-a)$ and $2/(a-b)$

$\Rightarrow 2/-(a-b) \Rightarrow 2/(b-a)$

$\Rightarrow R$ is reflexive and symmetric, also $2/(a-b)$ and $2/(b-c)$

$\Rightarrow a\,R\,c$

$\Rightarrow$ R is transitive and hence equivalence. Thus assertion is incorrect.

SECTION–VI: (COMPREHENSION)

A:

1. (c)

2. (b)

3. (b)

4. (a)

Reflexivity: $(a, b)\,R_1\,(a, b)$

$\Leftrightarrow ab = ba$, which is true

$\Rightarrow R_1$ is reflexive.

Again $(a, b)\,R_2\,(a, b)$

$\Rightarrow a - b = b + a$, which is true

$\Rightarrow R_2$ is reflexive.

Symmetric: $(a, b)\,R_1\,(c, d)$

$\Rightarrow ad = bc \Rightarrow bc = ad$

$\Rightarrow cb = da \Rightarrow (c, d)\,R_1\,(a, b)$

$\Rightarrow R_1$ is symmetric

Again $(a, b)\,R_2\,(c, d)$

$\Rightarrow a - d = b + c \Rightarrow b + c = a + d$

$\Rightarrow c + d = d + a \Rightarrow (c, d)\,R_2\,(a, b)$

$\Rightarrow R_2$ is symmetric.

Transitivity: Let $(a, b)\,R_1\,(c, d)$ and $(c, d)\,R_1\,(e, f)$

$\Rightarrow ad = bc$ and $cf = de \Rightarrow \frac{a}{b} = \frac{c}{d}$ and $\frac{c}{d} = \frac{e}{f}$

$\Rightarrow \frac{a}{b} = \frac{e}{f} \Rightarrow af = be$

$\Rightarrow (a, b)\,R_1\,(e, f) \Rightarrow R$ is transitive.

Again $(a, b)\,R_2\,(c, d)$ and $(c, d)\,R_2\,(e, f)$

$\Rightarrow a + d = b + c$ and $c + f = d + e$

$\Rightarrow a - b = c - d$ and $c - d = e - f$

$\Rightarrow (a - b) = (e - f)$

$\Rightarrow a + f = b + e$

$\Rightarrow (a, b)\,R_2\,(e, f)$ R_2 is also transitive.

$\Rightarrow R_1$ and R_2 both are equivalence relation.

SECTION–VII: (COLUMN–MATCHING TYPE I)

1. (i) → (a); (ii) → (c), (e); (iii) → (a), (b) , (c), (d); (iv) → (a), (b), (c), (d)

(i) $R: A \to A; A = \{1, 2, 3, \ldots, -14\}$

$R = \{(x, y): 3x - y > 0\}$

Reflexivity: $3x - x > 0 \Leftrightarrow 2x > 0$

$\Leftrightarrow x > 0$, which is true for x A

$\Rightarrow$ R is reflexive.

Symmeticity: Let $y = 1 \Rightarrow 3y = 3$ and $x = 4$

$\Rightarrow 3x = 12$, then $3x - y = 12 - 1 = 11 > 0$

$\Rightarrow x\,R\,y$

And $3y - x = 3 - 4 = -1 < 0$

$\Rightarrow (y, x) \notin R$

Transitivity: Let $x = 1$

$\Rightarrow 3x = 3$ and $y = 2$

$\Rightarrow 3y = 6$ and let $z = 5$, then $x\,R\,y$ as $3x - y = 3 - 2 = 1 > 0$, $y\,R\,z$ as $3y - z = 6 - 5 = 1 > 0$, but $(x, z) \notin R$ as $3x - z = 3 - 5 = -2 < 0$

$\Rightarrow$ R is not transitive.
$\Rightarrow$ R is not Equivalence, also (1, 2) R as $3(1) - 2 > 0$ and (2, 1) R as $3(2) - 1 > 0$
However $1 \neq 2$ $\Rightarrow$ R is not anti-symmetric

(ii) $R: \mathbb{N} \rightarrow \mathbb{N}$; $R = \{(x, y): y = x + 4 \text{ and } x < 4\}$
$\Rightarrow$ $R = \{(1, 5), (2, 6), (3, 7)\}$
$\Rightarrow$ R is not reflexive, not symmetric, but transitive and anti-symmetric by default.

(iii) $R: \mathbb{Z} \rightarrow \mathbb{Z}$; $R = \{(x, y); x - z \in \mathbb{Z}\}$
$\because$ $x - x = 0 \in \mathbb{Z}$ $\Rightarrow$ R is reflexive and $x - y \in \mathbb{Z}$
$\Rightarrow$ $y - x \in \mathbb{Z}$ $\Rightarrow$ R is symmetric
Also $x - y, y - z \in \mathbb{Z}$ $\Rightarrow$ $(x - y) + (y - z) \in \mathbb{Z}$
$\Rightarrow$ $(x - z) \in \mathbb{Z}$ $\Rightarrow$ R is transitive.
$\because$ $(2, 4), (4, 2) \in \mathbb{Z}$, but $2 \neq 4$
$\Rightarrow$ R is not anti-symmetric.

(iv) ($a R a$) as same person work with himself at same place.
Also $a R b$ $\Rightarrow$ $b R$ a and a $R b$ is $b R c$
$\Rightarrow$ $a R c$
$\Rightarrow$ (R) is reflexive, symmetric, transitive and equivalence.
However $(a, b), (b, a) \in R$, but $a \neq b$ is possible for two different person a and b.
$\Rightarrow$ R is not anti-symmetric.

2. (i) $\rightarrow$ (a), (c), (e); (ii) $\rightarrow$(f); (iii) $\rightarrow$(a), (b), (c), (d); (iv) $\rightarrow$ (a), (b), (c), (d)

(i) $R = \{(a, b); a \leq b;\ a, b \in \mathbb{R}\}$
$\because$ $a R a$ as $a = a$ $\Rightarrow$ R is reflexive
However, $a \leq b$ $\not\Rightarrow$ $b \leq a$, e.g., $2 < 3$
$\not\Rightarrow$ $3 < 2$
$\Rightarrow$ R is not symmetric, also $a \leq b$ and $b \leq c$
$\Rightarrow$ $a \leq c$
$\Rightarrow$ R is transitive, also $2 < 3$ and $3 < 2$ can't hold simultaneously.
$\Rightarrow$ R is anti-symmetric by default.

(ii) $R = \{(a, b): a \leq b^3\}$
$\because$ $a \leq a^3$ $\Rightarrow$ $a^3 - a\ 0$
$\Rightarrow$ $a(a^2 - 1)\ 0$ $\Rightarrow$ $a(a + 1)(a - 1)\ 0$
$\Rightarrow$ $a \in [-1, 0] \cup [1, \infty)$
$\Rightarrow$ R is not reflexive.
Also for $a = 4$, $b = 65$
$a < b^3$ as $4 < (65)^3$, but $b \not< a^3$ as $65 \not< 64$
$\Rightarrow$ R is not symmetric.
Further for $b = 4$, $b^3 = 64$, $c = 2$
$\Rightarrow$ $c^3 = 8$ and a = 10, we have $a < b^3$ as $10 < 64$
$\Rightarrow$ $(a, b)\ R$
$\Rightarrow$ $b < c^3$ as $4 < 8$ $\Rightarrow$ $(b, c) \in R$ but $a \not< c^3$ as $10 \not< 8$
$\Rightarrow$ $(a, c) \notin R$
R is not transitive.
Also (2, 3) and (3, 2) $\in R$ as $2 < (3)^3$ and $3 < (2)^3$
$\Rightarrow$ R is not anti-symmetric.

(iii) R: A $\rightarrow$ A; A = {1, 2, 3, 4, 5}
$R = \{(a, b): |a - b| \text{ is even}\}$
$\Rightarrow$ $R = \{(1, 3), (3, 1), (1, 5), (5, 1), (2, 4), (4, 2), (3, 5)\ (5, 3), (1, 1), (2, 2), (3, 3), (4, 4)\}$
$\Rightarrow$ R is reflexive, symmetric,
Also $|a - b|$ = even
$\Rightarrow$ $a - b = 2k_1$ and $|b - c|$ = even
$\Rightarrow$ $b - c = 2k_2$
$\Rightarrow$ $a - c = 2(k_1 + k_2)$ $\Rightarrow$ $|a - c|$ = even
$\Rightarrow$ $a R c$ $\Rightarrow$ R is transitive.
Also (2, 4), (4, 2) R, but $4 \neq 2$
$\Rightarrow$ R is not anti-symmetric.

(iv) $R = \{(x, y): x$ and have same age$\}$
Clearly, R will be reflexive, symmetric and transitive but $a R b$ and $b R$ a and $a \neq b$ is possible
$\Rightarrow$ R is not anti-symmetric.

3. (i) $\rightarrow$ (b); (ii)$\rightarrow$ (b), (iii)$\rightarrow$ (b), (d), (e); (iv) $\rightarrow$(a), (d)

(i) $R = \{(X, Y): X, Y \in P(A); X \cap Y \neq \phi\}$
Reflexivity: $\because$ For $X \neq \phi$, $X \cap X = X = \phi$, but $\phi \cap \phi = \phi$
$\Rightarrow$ $\phi R \phi$
Subjectivity: $\Rightarrow$ R is not reflexive, also $X \cap \phi = \phi\ \forall\ X \in P(A)$
$\Rightarrow$ $\phi \notin$ range of Relation.
$\Rightarrow$ R is not subjective.
Symmetricity: $X R Y$
$\Rightarrow$ $X \cap Y \neq \phi$
$\Rightarrow$ $Y \cap X = \phi$ $\Rightarrow$ $Y R X$
$\Rightarrow$ R is symmetric.
Transitivity: $X RY$ and $Y R Z$
$\Rightarrow$ $X \cap Y \neq \phi$ and $Y \cap Z \neq \phi$, but $(X \cap Z)$ may be empty.
e.g., if $X = \{1, 2, 3\}$; $Y = \{2, 5, 6\}$; $Z = \{5, 8\}$, then $X \cap Y = \{2\}$; $Y \cap Z = \{5\}$, but $X \cap Z = \{\} = \phi$
$\Rightarrow$ R is not transitive
Injectivity: If X, Y, Z such that $X \cap Z \neq \phi$, $X \cap Z \neq \phi$
$\Rightarrow$ $(X, Z)\ (Y, Z)$

(ii) $R = \{(x, y): x, y \in \mathbb{N}$ and R is not injective. L.C.M $(x, y) = 12\}$
Reflexivity: $\because$ L.C.M $(x, x) = 12$
$\Leftrightarrow$ x = 12 $\Rightarrow$ R is not reflexive
Symmetric: If L.C.M $(x, y) = 12$, then L.C.M $(y, x) = 12$
$\Rightarrow$ R is symmetric
Transitive: If L.C.M $(x, y) = 12$, then $(x, y) \in R$
$\Rightarrow$ R = {(1, 12), (3, 4), (4, 3), (4, 6), (6, 4), (2, 12), (12, 2), (12, 1)}
$\therefore$ $(3, 4), (4, 6) \in R$ but $(3, 6) \notin R$
$\Rightarrow$ R is not transitive.
Also $(3, 4), (4, 3) \in R$ but $3 \neq 4$
$\Rightarrow$ R is not anti-symmetric.
$\because$ Range $\neq \mathbb{N}$
$\Rightarrow$ R is not surjective, also $(3, 4), (6, 4) \in R$
$\Rightarrow$ R is not injective

(iii) $R = \{(x, y): x, y \in \mathbb{C}$ and $y = \overline{x}\}$; $\mathbb{C}$ is the set of complex numbers.
Reflexivity: $x R x$ $\Rightarrow$ $x = \overline{x}$
$\Rightarrow$ $x \in \mathbb{R}$ i.e., $(x, x) \in R$ holds only when x is purely real
$\Rightarrow$ R is not reflexive.
Symmetricity: If $x R$ y, then $y = \overline{x}$
$\Rightarrow$ $\overline{y} = x$ $\Rightarrow$ $(y, x) \in R$
$\Rightarrow$ R is symmetric.
Transitive: $x R y$ $\Rightarrow$ $y = \overline{x}$ and $y R z$
$\Rightarrow$ $z = \overline{y}$

$\Rightarrow$ $x = z$ $\nRightarrow$ $z = \overline{x}$

$\Rightarrow$ R is not transitive.

Anti-symmetric: $x\ R\ y$ and $y\ R\ x$ for $x\ y$ e.g., $(2 + 3i)\ R\ (2 - 3i)$, but $2 + 3i \neq 2 - 3i$

$\Rightarrow$ R is not anti-symmetric.

Surjectivity: Let $a + ib \in \mathbb{C}$ then, $(a - ib) \in \mathbb{C}$ such that $(a - ib)\ R\ (a + ib)$

$\Rightarrow$ R is subjective.

Injectivity: Let $(z_1, z_2) \in R$ and $(z_3, z_2) \in R$ i.e., $z_2 = \overline{z_1}$ and $z_2 = \overline{z_3}$

$\Rightarrow$ $\overline{z_1} = \overline{z_3}$ $\Rightarrow$ $z_1 = z_3$

$\Rightarrow$ R is injective.

(iv) $R = \{(x, y): 2x^2 + 3y^2 - 5xy = 0; x, y \in \mathbb{R}\}$

Reflexivity: $x\ R\ x$ $\Leftrightarrow$ $2x^2 + 3x^2 - 5x^2 = 0$, which is true

$\Rightarrow$ R is reflexive.

Symmetricity: $2x^2 - 5xy + 3y^2 = 0$

$\Rightarrow$ $2x^2 - 2xy - 3xy + 3y^2 = 0$

$\Rightarrow$ $2x(x - y) - 3y(x - y) = 0$

$\Rightarrow$ $(2x - 3y)(x - y) = 0$

$\Rightarrow$ $2x = 3y$ or $x = y$

Let $x = 3$, $y = 2$, then $2(x) = 6$ and $3(y) = 6$

$\therefore$ $2x = 3y$

$\Rightarrow$ $x\ R\ y$, but $y \not R\ x$ as $2y = 4$ and $3x = 9$

$\therefore$ R is not symmetric.

Transitivity: Let $x = 3$, $y = 2$, $z = \frac{4}{3}$, then $2x = 3y$

$\Rightarrow$ $x\ R\ y$

And $2y = 3z$ $\Rightarrow$ $y\ R\ z$; but $x\ z$ and $2x\ 3z$

$\Rightarrow$ $(x, z) \notin R$

$\Rightarrow$ R is not transitive.

Surjective: Let $y \in \mathbb{R}$; then $x = \frac{3}{2}y \in \mathbb{R}$ and $2x = 3y$

$\Rightarrow$ $(x, y) \in \mathbb{R}$ $\Rightarrow$ R is surjective

Injective: $\because$ $(x, y) \in \mathbb{R}$ and $\left(\frac{3}{2}y, y\right) \in \mathbb{R}$

$\Rightarrow$ R is not injective.

CHAPTER 2

Functions

INTRODUCTION

The term function was first used by Leibnitz to denote the dependence of one quantity on other quantities.

Examples

1. The area of a circle depends on its radius r through the equation $A = \pi r^2$. Thus, we say that A is a function of r and to denote this we write $A = f(r)$.
2. If you are traveling on a motor bike, the distance covered by you will depend upon how long you have been driving. So, we say that distance covered is a function of time. Further, the distance covered will also depend upon the speed with which you are driving. Here, we are expressing the distance covered to be a function of speed and time, because if the speed or the time increases the distance covered will increase and vice versa. The symbol f does not have a special meaning, it simply indicates dependence of one physical quantity over the other.

So, the concept of function is useful in defining the dependence of one thing (called dependent variable) on other things (called independent variables). In certain cases the dependent variables may not always increase with the increase in the independent variables. Also, the independent variable for one function may be a dependent variable for other function, which is studied under monotonicity of functions and composition of functions.

We need to understand that any relationship between two phenomenons is not necessarily a function. Actually the functions are specific type of relations. In this chapter we will also learn how to graphically represent the function and its applications to find out the solution of various problems.

DEFINITION OF FUNCTION

Let X and Y be two non-empty sets. Then a function f from set X to set Y is denoted as $f : X \to Y$ or $y = f(x)$; $x \in X$ and $y \in Y$. A function $f(x)$ from X (domain) to Y (co-domain) is defined as a relation f from set X to set Y such that each and every element of X is related with exactly one element of set Y.

Therefore, mathematically the function $f: X \to Y$ is infact a specific relation satisfying the following three conditions.

(i) $f \subset X \times Y$
(ii) for each $x \in X \Rightarrow (x, f(x)) \in f$
(iii) $(x, y_1) \in f$ and $(x, y_2) \in f \Rightarrow y_1 = y_2$

Pictorially

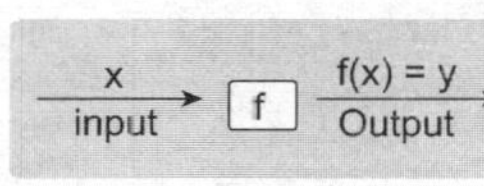

FIGURE 2.1

e.g.: Let $X = \{0, 1, 2, 3\}$ and $Y = \{1, 3, 5, 7, 9, 11\}$; define a function $f : X \to Y$ by $f(x) = 2x + 3$; then

$f = \{(0, 3), (1, 5), (2, 7), (3, 9)\}$. Clearly f is a function. But above is not a function when:

Set $Y = \{y: y$ is prime and $y \leq 15\}$, because 9 does not belong to Y in that case.

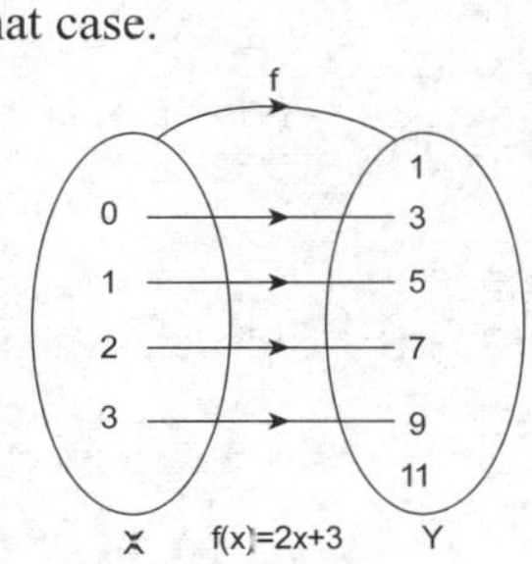

FIGURE 2.2

Machine Model of Function: $(x \in X) \to f \to (y \in Y)$ is called as function of x and abbreviated as 'y' is f of 'x'.

If a pre-image is denoted by x and image is denoted by y, then we can write:

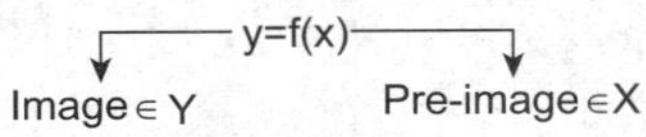

FIGURE 2.3

A function works as a machine which gets an input and produces a corresponding output as illustrated in Figure 2.4.

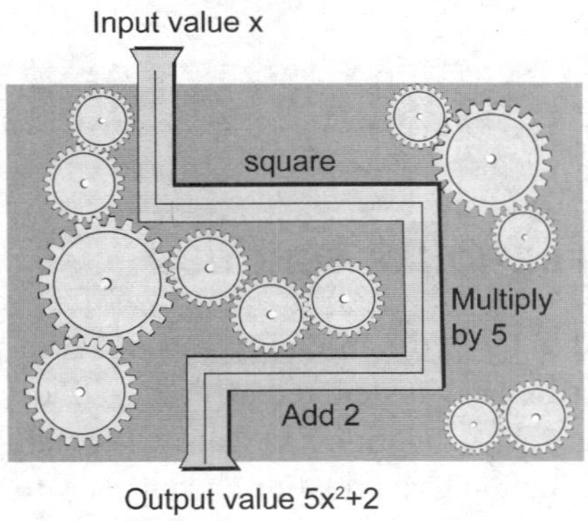

FIGURE 2.4

Notations:

$f : X \to Y$ or $X \xrightarrow{f} Y$, which reads as 'f is a function from X to Y' or 'f maps X to Y'.

Image and Pre-image: Let f be a function from set X to set Y, i.e., $f: X \to Y$ and let an element x of set X be associated to the element y of set Y through the rule 'f', then $(x, y) \in f$, i.e., $f(x) = y$, then y is called 'image of x under f' and x is called 'pre-image of y under f'.

e.g., Let $X = \{0, 1, 2, 3\}$ and $Y = \{1, 3, 5, 7, 9, 11\}$; define a function $f : X \to Y$:

$f(x) = 2x + 3$; then $f = \{(0, 3), (1, 5), (2, 7), (3, 9)\}$.
Now, $(0, 3) \in f \Rightarrow 0$ is pre-image and 3 is image,
$(1, 5) \in f \Rightarrow 1$ is pre-image and 5 is image.
$(2, 7) \in f \Rightarrow 2$ is pre-image and 7 is image.
$(3, 9) \in f \Rightarrow 3$ is pre-image and 9 is image.

ILLUSTRATION 1: If $f(x) = \dfrac{x-1}{x+1}$, then show that $\dfrac{f\left(\frac{1}{x^2}\right).\left[1+(f(x))^2\right]}{f(x)} = -2$.

SOLUTION: $f(x) = \dfrac{x-1}{x+1} \Rightarrow f\left(\dfrac{1}{x^2}\right) = \dfrac{\frac{1}{x^2}-1}{\frac{1}{x^2}+1} = \dfrac{1-x^2}{1+x^2} \Rightarrow \dfrac{f\left(\frac{1}{x^2}\right)[1+(f(x))^2]}{f(x)} = \dfrac{\left(\frac{1-x^2}{1+x^2}\right)\left[1+\left(\frac{x-1}{x+1}\right)^2\right]}{\left(\frac{x-1}{x+1}\right)}$.

$= \dfrac{(1-x^2)}{(1+x^2)} \times \dfrac{2(x^2+1)}{(x+1)^2} \times \dfrac{(x+1)}{(x-1)} = \dfrac{2(1-x)(1+x)^2}{(x+1)^2(x-1)} = -2$. Hence, proved.

ILLUSTRATION 2: Let $f: \mathbb{R} \to \mathbb{R}$ is a function satisfying $f(3) = 2$ and $f(x + 3) = f(3).f(x)$, then find $(f(-3))$.

SOLUTION: Since we are interested in finding $f(-3)$, we first put $x = -3$ in the relation, obtaining $f(0) = f(3)\ ((f(-3))$.
Thus, we must also know $f(0)$ in order to find $f(-3)$.
Letting $x = 0$ in the relation, $f(3) = f(3)\, f(0)$
$\Rightarrow f(0) = 1$ as $f(3) = 2$; Thus, $f(0) = f(3) . f(-3)$
$\Rightarrow 1 = (2) . f(-3) \qquad \Rightarrow f(-3) = \dfrac{1}{2}$.

ILLUSTRATION 3: Let $f : \mathbb{R} \to \mathbb{R}$, be a function defined as $f(x) = \dfrac{x-2}{x^2+2}$, find whether $f(0) + f(1) + f(2)$ and $f(0 + 1 + 2)$ are equal? Is there a real solution to the equation $f(x) = \dfrac{1}{x}$? Is there a real solution to the equation $f(x) = x$?

SOLUTION: $f(0) + f(1) + f(2) = \dfrac{0-2}{0^2+2} + \dfrac{1-2}{1^2+2} + \dfrac{2-2}{2^2+2} = -1 - \dfrac{1}{3} + 0 = -\dfrac{4}{3}$

Also $f(0 + 1 + 2) = f(3) = \dfrac{3-2}{3^2+2} = \dfrac{1}{11}$

Clearly, $f(0) + f(1) + f(2) \neq f(0 + 1 + 2)$

Now, $f(x) = \dfrac{1}{x}$

$\Rightarrow \dfrac{x-2}{x^2+2} = \dfrac{1}{x}$ $\qquad\qquad \Rightarrow x^2 - 2x = x^2 + 2$

$\Rightarrow x = -1$ and -1 belongs to domain of function $f(x)$.

Thus, the equation $f(x) = \dfrac{1}{x}$ has a solution $x = -1$.

Also $f(x) = x$.

$\Rightarrow \dfrac{x-2}{x^2+2} = x$ $\qquad\qquad \Rightarrow x - 2 = x^3 + 2x$

$\Rightarrow x^3 + x + 2 = 0$ $\qquad\qquad \Rightarrow (x + 1)(x^2 - x + 2) = 0$

$\Rightarrow x = -1$ is a solution. $\qquad$ [$\because$ The equation $x^2 - x + 2 = 0$ does not give real roots]

ILLUSTRATION 4: If $f(x) = \cos\{\ln(x)\}$, then prove that $f(xy) + f\left(\dfrac{x}{y}\right) = 2f(x)f(y)$.

SOLUTION: Here, we evaluate each term of the left hand side of the equation separately and then add the result.

Now, $f(x.y) = \cos\{\ln(xy)\} = \cos(\ln x + \ln y)$

and $f\left(\dfrac{x}{y}\right) = \cos\left\{\ln\left(\dfrac{x}{y}\right)\right\} = \cos(\ln x - \ln y)$ $\qquad$ ... (1)

Substituting in the LHS expression, we have:

$$\left\{f(xy) + f\left(\dfrac{x}{y}\right)\right\} = \cos(\ln x + \ln y) + \cos(\ln x - \ln y) = 2\cos(\ln x)\cos(\ln y) = 2f(x).f(y)$$

ILLUSTRATION 5: Find $f(x)$, if $f(x - 2) = (x^2 - 4)$.

SOLUTION: We have to evaluate the function $f(x)$.

We need to replace $(x - 2)$ in the given equation to find $f(x)$. The right hand side expression, however, does not contain the term $(x - 2)$. We, therefore (need to find the term), which will replace x. Clearly if x replaces $(x - 2)$, then $(x + 2)$ will replace $x - 2 + 2 = x$.

Thus, we need to replace x by $(x + 2)$.

$\Rightarrow f(x + 2 - 2) = (x + 2)^2 - 4 = x^2 + 4x + 4 - 4$

$\Rightarrow f(x) = x^2 + 4x.$

DOMAIN, CO-DOMAIN AND RANGE OF FUNCTION

If a relation f (not one–many) maps independent variables (inputs) $\in X$ to dependent variables (outputs) $\in Y$, then the subset of X containing elements x for which $f(x)$ is defined (real and finite) and $f(x) \in Y$ is called domain of f denoted by D_f.

i.e., $D_f = \{x \in X : f(x)$ is finite and real $: f(x) \in Y\}$, and hence, $f : D_f \rightarrow Y$ becomes a function.

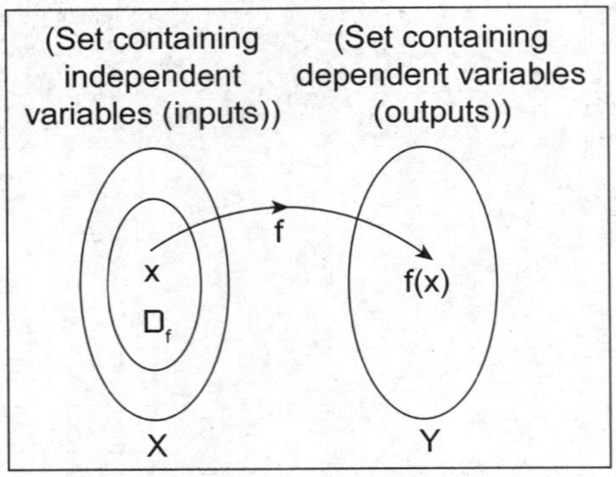

FIGURE 2.5

Natural Domain: The natural domain of a function is the largest set of real number inputs that give real number outputs of the function.

Co-domain: Set Y is called co-domain of function f.

Range of Function: If $f: D_f(\subseteq X) \to Y$ is a function with domain D_f, then the set of images y (output $\in Y$) generated corresponding to input $x \in D_f$ is called range of function, and it is denoted by R_f.

i.e., $R_f = \{f(x): x \in D_f\} \subseteq Y$.

e.g., if f is a function from set $X = \{1, 2, 3, 4\}$ to set $Y = \{1, 4, 9, 16, 25, 36\}$ defined by $f(x) = x^2$; then its range set $= R_f = \{f(1), f(2), f(3), f(4)\} = \{1, 4, 9, 16\} \subseteq Y$.

Here, the elements 25, 36 are in the co-domain but not in the range.

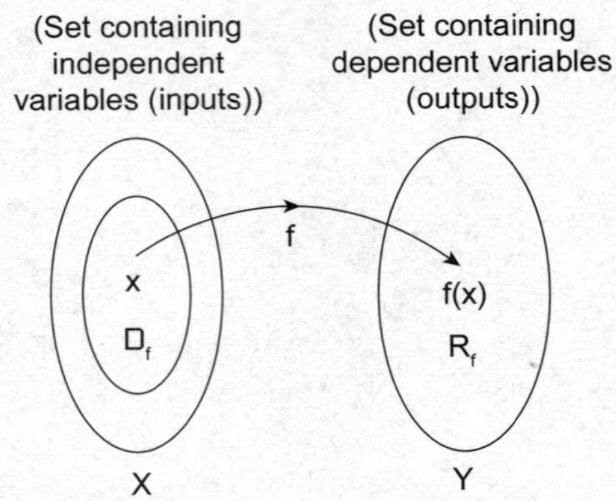

FIGURE 2.6

REMARKS

1. *To find domain of function we need to know, when does a function become undefined and when it is defined, i.e., we need to find those values of x where f(x) is finite and real and those values of x where f(x) is either infinite or imaginary.*
2. *When its value tends to infinity (∞).*

   e.g., $y = \dfrac{1}{x^2 - 1}$ *at* $x = \pm 1$; *f(x) is not defined at* $x = \pm 1$ *and defined* $\forall x \in \mathbb{R}$ *except for* ± 1; *therefore, domain of* $f(x) = \mathbb{R} \sim \{1, -1\}$.
3. *When it takes imaginary value. e.g.,* $y = \sqrt{x - 1}\ \forall x \in (-\infty, 1)$; *f(x) is not defined on* $(-\infty, 1)$ *and defined on* $[1, \infty)$; *therefore, domain of* $f(x) = [1, \infty)$.
4. *When it takes indeterminate form, i.e., becomes of the form* $\frac{0}{0}, \frac{\infty}{\infty}, 1^\infty, \infty^0, 0^0, \infty - \infty$ *etc*.

Example:

(i) $y = \dfrac{x+1}{x^2 - 1}$ takes $\dfrac{0}{0}$ form at $x = -1$, and hence, domain would not contain $x = -1$, also $f(x)$ is not defined at $x = 1$, thus, $D_f = \mathbb{R} \sim \{1, -1\}$

(ii) $y = \dfrac{1}{x^2 - 1} - \dfrac{1}{x^2 - 3x + 2}$ takes $\infty - \infty$ form at $x = 1$, and hence, domain would not contain $x = 1$. Domain for this function is given by $D_f = \mathbb{R} \sim \{1, -1, 2\}$

(iii) $y = \sec x - \tan x$ takes $\infty - \infty$ form at $x = (2n+1)\dfrac{\pi}{2}$, $n \in \mathbb{Z}$, and hence, domain would not contain odd integral multiples of $\dfrac{\pi}{2}$. Here domain of function is given by, $D_f = \mathbb{R} \sim \{(2n + 1) —; n \in \mathbb{Z}\}$

(iv) $y = (\sin x)^{\tan x}$ takes 1^∞ form at $x = (2n+1)\dfrac{\pi}{2}$, $n \in \mathbb{Z}$, and hence, domain would not contain odd integral multiples of $\frac{\pi}{2}$; $D_f = \mathbb{R} \sim \left[\left(\bigcup_{n\in\mathbb{Z}}[(2n+1)\pi,(2n+2)\pi]\right)\cup\left\{(2n+1)\frac{\pi}{2};n\in\mathbb{Z}\right\}\right]$

(v) $y = (\sin x)^{\tan x}$ takes 0^0 form at $x = n\pi$; D_f would not contain $\{n\pi;\ n \in \mathbb{Z}\}$, i.e., domain would not contain the real numbers $n\pi$, $n \in \mathbb{Z}$. Domain of the function is given in above remark.

(vi) $y = (\tan x)^{\cot x}$ takes ∞^0 form at $x = (2n+1)\frac{\pi}{2}$, and hence, domain would not contain odd integral multiples of $\frac{\pi}{2}$. Here domain of function is given by

$$D_f = \bigcup_{n\in\mathbb{Z}}\left[\left(2n\pi,(2n+1)\frac{\pi}{2}\right)\cup\left((2n+1)\pi,(4n+3)\frac{\pi}{2}\right)\right]$$

i.e., we excluded those real numbers for which $\tan x$ becomes negative and those for which $\cot x$ becomes infinite. Also at $x = (2n + 1)\pi$; $y = (0) - 1 = 1/0$, not defined. Also we excluded those real numbers for which the function takes indeterminate form ∞^0.

i.e., excluding from the set of real numbers the set

$$\left[(2n+1)\frac{\pi}{2},(2n+1)\pi\right]\cup\left[(4n+3)\frac{\pi}{2},(2n+2)\pi\right]$$

$\forall\ n \in \mathbb{Z}$

(vii) To find range of a function first of all domain D_f is determined and the range consists of images $f(x)$ for each $x \in D_f$.

ILLUSTRATION 6: Let $X = \{1, 2, 3, 4\}$ and $Y = \{2, 3, 6, 8, 10, 12\}$. Define a relation f from X to Y as $f(x) = \frac{6}{(x-1)}$. Find domain, co-domain and range of f so that it becomes a function from its domain set to set Y.

SOLUTION: $f(x) = \frac{6}{(x-1)}$

∴ $f(1)$ is not defined and $f(2) = 6$; $f(3) = 3$; $f(4) = 2$

∴ Domain set $= D_f = \{2, 3, 4\}$ and co-domain $= Y = \{2, 3, 6, 8, 10, 12\}$; $R = \{2, 3, 6\}$.

Clearly for each $x \in D_f$; $f(x)$ is real, unique and is in Y, therefore $f(x)$ is a function from D_f to Y.

ILLUSTRATION 7: Let $X = \{1, 2, 3, 4\}$ and $Y = \{0, 1, 2, 3, 4\}$, define a relation f from X to Y as $f(x) = \sqrt{x-3}$; then find domain, co-domain and range of f so that it becomes a function from its domain set to set Y.

SOLUTION: $f(x) = \sqrt{x-3}$

∴ $f(x)$ is real for $x - 3 \geq 0$ ⇒ $x \geq 3$

But $x \in X = \{1, 2, 3, 4\}$ ∴ Domain of $f = D_f = \{3, 4\}$ and co-domain of $f = Y = \{0, 1, 2, 3, 4\}$; $R_f = \{f(3), f(4)\} = \{0, 1\} \subseteq Y$.

Clearly for each $x \in D_f$, $f(x)$ is unique, real and is in Y, therefore $f(x)$ is a function from D_f to Y.

ILLUSTRATION 8: Define a function $g(x) : A \to \mathbb{R}$ defined by $g(x) = \sqrt{8x+3}$; where $A = \{x \in \mathbb{R}: 2f(x) = f(3x); f(x) = x^2 + 3x\}$. Find the domain and range of function $g(x)$.

SOLUTION: $A = \{x \in \mathbb{R}: 2f(x) = f(3x); f(x) = x^2 + 3x\}$

Now $2f(x) = f(3x)$

⇒ $2(x^2 + 3x) = (3x)^2 + 3(3x)$ ⇒ $2x^2 + 6x = 9x^2 + 9x$

⇒ $7x^2 + 3x = 0$ ⇒ $x(7x + 3) = 0$

⇒ $x = 0, -3/7$ ∴ $A = \{0, -3/7\}$

For domain of $g(x) = \sqrt{8x+3}$, $8x + 3 \geq 0$

$\Rightarrow x \geq -3/8$

$\Rightarrow$ Domain of $g(x) = D_g = \{0\}$ as $-\dfrac{3}{7} < -\dfrac{3}{8} \Rightarrow$ Range of $g(x) = R_g = \{f(0)\} = \{\sqrt{3}\}$.

ILLUSTRATION 9: Find the domain and range of $f(x) = 3 - \sqrt{x-4}$

SOLUTION: For $f(x) = 3 - \sqrt{x-4}$ to be meaningful the square root of $x - 4$ must be make sense; that means domain must consists of all real numbers x such that $x - 4 \geq 0$ or, equivalently, $x \geq 4$. That is, the domain is the interval $[4, \infty)$. As x varies from 4 to larger numbers, $f(x)$ decreases from $f(4) = 3 - \sqrt{4-4} = 3$ to arbitrarily smaller values. Thus, the range of f consists of all numbers less than or equal to 3, that is, the interval $(-\infty, 3]$.

ILLUSTRATION 10: Find the domain and range for the following functions:

(i) $f(x) = \sqrt{x-5}$ (ii) $f(x) = \sqrt{5-x}$

(iii) $f(x) = \sqrt{x^2 - 5x + 6}$ (iv) $f(x) = \sqrt{x^2 + x + 1}$

(v) $f(x) = \dfrac{x-1}{x-4}$ (vi) $f(x) = \dfrac{1}{\sqrt{(x-1)(x-2)}}$

(vii) $f(x) = \sqrt{\sin x}$ (viii) $f(x) = \sqrt{\sin(2x+3)}$

SOLUTION: (i) $f(x) = \sqrt{x-5}$; for domain $x - 5 \geq 0$

$\Rightarrow D_f = [5, \infty)$

Let $y = \sqrt{x-5}$

$\Rightarrow y^2 = x - 5$ $\Rightarrow x = y^2 + 5$

But $x \geq 5$ $\Rightarrow y^2 + 5 \geq 5$

$\Rightarrow y^2 \geq 0$ $\Rightarrow y \in \mathbb{R}$

But $f(x) = y = \sqrt{x-5} \geq 0$ (principal square root is always non-negative)

$\Rightarrow y \geq 0$ $\Rightarrow R_f = [0, \infty)$

(ii) $f(x) = \sqrt{5-x}$; for domain $5 - x \geq 0$

$\Rightarrow x \leq 5$

$\Rightarrow D_f = (-\infty, 5]$

Let $y = \sqrt{5-x}$ $\Rightarrow y^2 = 5 - x$

$\Rightarrow x = 5 - y^2$

As $x \leq 5$ $\Rightarrow 5 - y^2 \leq 5$

$\Rightarrow y^2 \geq 0$ $\Rightarrow y \in \mathbb{R}$

But $y = \sqrt{5-x} \geq 0$ (principal square root is always non-negative)

$\Rightarrow y \geq 0$ $\Rightarrow$ Range of function $= R_f = [0, \infty)$.

(iii) $f(x) = \sqrt{x^2 - 5x + 6}$; for domain $x^2 - 5x + 6 \geq 0$

$\Rightarrow (x - 2)(x - 3) \geq 0$

$\Rightarrow x \leq 2$ or $x \geq 3$ ($\because$ either both factors are positive or both non-negative)

$\Rightarrow D_f = (-\infty, 2] \cup [3, \infty)$

Also $y = f(x) = \sqrt{x^2 - 5x + 6} = \sqrt{(x-2)(x-3)}$; for $x \geq 3$: $(x - 2)(x - 3) \in [0, \infty)$; also for $x \in (-\infty, 2]$, $(x - 2)(x - 3) \in [0, \infty)$

$\Rightarrow\ y=\sqrt{(x-2)(x-3)}\in[0,\infty)$ $\qquad\Rightarrow\ R_f=[0,\infty)$

(iv) $f(x)=\sqrt{x^2+x+1}=\sqrt{x^2+x+\frac{1}{4}+\frac{3}{4}}=\sqrt{\left(x+\frac{1}{2}\right)^2+\left(\frac{\sqrt{3}}{2}\right)^2}$;

As $\left(x+\frac{1}{2}\right)^2+\left(\frac{\sqrt{3}}{2}\right)^2>0\ \forall\ x\in\mathbb{R}$

$\Rightarrow$ $f(x)$ is real for all values of x $\qquad\Rightarrow\ D_f=\mathbb{R}=(-\infty,\infty)$

Also $\left(x+\frac{1}{2}\right)^2+\left(\frac{\sqrt{3}}{2}\right)^2\geq\frac{3}{4}\ \forall\ x\in\mathbb{R}$

$\Rightarrow\ y=f(x)\geq\sqrt{\frac{3}{4}}\ \forall\ x\in\mathbb{R}$

$\Rightarrow$ Range of function $f(x)=R_f=\left[\frac{\sqrt{3}}{2},\infty\right)$

(v) $f(x)=\dfrac{x-1}{x-4}$; y is not defined for $x=4$

$\Rightarrow\ D_f=\mathbb{R}\sim\{4\}$

Now $y=\dfrac{x-1}{x-4}$

$\Rightarrow\ xy-4y=x-1$ $\qquad\Rightarrow\ x(y-1)=4y-1$

$\Rightarrow\ x=\dfrac{4y-1}{y-1}$

$\therefore$ for $x\in\mathbb{R}$, $y\neq1$ $\qquad\therefore\ R_f=\mathbb{R}\sim\{1\}$

(vi) $f(x)=\dfrac{1}{\sqrt{(x-1)(x-2)}}$; For domain $(x-1)(x-2)>0$

$\Rightarrow\ x<1$ or $x>2$

$\Rightarrow\ D_f=(-\infty,1)\cup(2,\infty)$

Now for $x>2$, $(x-1)(x-2)\in(0,\infty)$

$\Rightarrow\ \sqrt{(x-1)(x-2)}\in(0,\infty)$

$\Rightarrow\ \dfrac{1}{\sqrt{(x-1)(x-2)}}\in(0,\infty)$

$\therefore$ Range of function $R_f=(0,\infty)$

(vii) $f(x)=\sqrt{\sin x}$. For domain of function, $\sin x\geq0$

$\Rightarrow\ x\in[2n\pi,(2n+1)\pi];\ n\in\mathbb{Z}$

$\Rightarrow\ D_f=\bigcup_{n\in\mathbb{Z}}[2n\pi,(2n+1)\pi]$

Now for $y=\sqrt{\sin x}$ to be real, $\sin x\in[0,1]$

$\Rightarrow\ \sqrt{\sin x}\in[0,1]$

$\therefore$ Range of function $=R_f=[0,1]$.

(viii) $f(x)=\sqrt{\sin(2x+3)}$. For domain of function $\sin(2x+3)\geq0$

$\Rightarrow\ (2x+3)\in[2n\pi,(2n+1)\pi];\ n\in\mathbb{Z}$

$\Rightarrow 2x \in [2n\pi - 3, (2n+1)\pi - 3];\ n \in \mathbb{Z}$

$\Rightarrow\ x \in \left[n\pi - \frac{3}{2}, n\pi + \left(\frac{\pi}{2} - \frac{3}{2}\right)\right];\ n \in \mathbb{Z}$

$\therefore$ Domain $= D_f = \bigcup_{n\in\mathbb{Z}} \left[n\pi - \frac{3}{2}, n\pi + \left(\frac{\pi}{2} - \frac{3}{2}\right)\right];\ n \in \mathbb{Z}$

Clearly for $x \in D_f$, $\sin(2x + 3) \in [0, 1]$

$\Rightarrow f(x) = \sqrt{\sin(2x+3)} \in [0, 1]$

$\Rightarrow$ Range of function $= R_f = [0, 1]$.

ILLUSTRATION 11: $f(x) = \log_a x$ is defined only for $x > 0$; $a > 0$ and $a \neq 1$, and it is known that $\log_a x$ increases from $-\infty$ to ∞ as x increases from 0 onwards to ∞ for $a > 1$ and $\log_a x$ decreases from ∞ to $-\infty$ as x increases from 0 onwards to ∞ for $a \in (0, 1)$. On the basis of above information, find the domain and range of following logarithmic functions.

(a) (i) $\log_2(x - 1)$ (ii) $\log_3 \sqrt{x-4}$

(iii) $\log_{1/3}(x + 4)$ (iv) $\log_4 x^2$.

(v) $\log_e |x|$

(b) Find the domain of $f(x) = \log_{5-x}(x - 2)$

SOLUTION: (a) (i) Given that $\log_a x$ is defined only for $x > 0$, $a > 0$, $a \neq 1$

$\therefore$ For domain of $f(x) = \log_2(x - 1)$; $x - 1 > 0 \Rightarrow x > 1$

$\therefore D_f = (1, \infty)$

Since base $a = 2 > 1$, value of $\log_2(x - 1)$ increases from $-\infty$ to ∞ as $(x - 1)$ increases from 0 to ∞.

As x approaches to 1, $(x - 1)$ approaches to 0, and hence, $\log_2(x - 1)$ approaches to $-\infty$.

$\therefore$ Range of function $f(x) = R_f = (-\infty,\infty)$

(ii) $\log_3 \sqrt{x-4}$; For domain, $x - 4 > 0 \Rightarrow x > 4$ $\therefore D_f = (4, \infty)$

Here $a = 3 > 1$ $\therefore$ Range of function $= f(x) = R_f = (-\infty, \infty)$

(iii) $f(x) = \log_{1/3}(x + 4)$; For domain, $x + 4 > 0 \Rightarrow x > -4$ $\Rightarrow D_f = (-4, \infty)$

Here $a = 1/3 \in (0, 1)$, $f(x)$ decreases from ∞ to $-\infty$ as $x + 4$ increases from 0 to ∞.

$\therefore$ Range of function $= R_f = (-\infty, \infty)$

(iv) $f(x) = \log_4 x^2$

Here $x^2 \geq 0\ \forall\ x \in \mathbb{R}$. For domain $x^2 > 0$ $\Rightarrow D_f = \mathbb{R} \sim \{0\}$

As $a = 4 > 1$, $f(x)$ increases from $-\infty$ to ∞ as x increases from 0 to $\pm\infty$.

$\therefore$ Range of function $= R_f = (-\infty, \infty)$

(v) $f(x) = \log_e|x|$; $|x| > 0\ \forall\ x \in \mathbb{R} \sim \{0\}$

$\therefore D_f = \mathbb{R} \sim \{0\}$

Also range of function $= R_f = (-\infty, \infty)$

(b) $f(x) = \log_{5-x}(x - 2)$

For domain $(x - 2) > 0$; $5 - x > 0$; $5 - x \neq 1$

$\Rightarrow x \in (2, \infty)$; $x < 5$; $x \neq 4$

$\Rightarrow x \in (2, 5) \sim \{4\}$

$\therefore$ Domain of function $= D_f = (2, 5) \sim \{4\}$.

ILLUSTRATION 12: Express the length b of one-side of a right angled triangle as a function of the length a of the other with a constant hypotenuse $c = 5$. Graph this function and find its domain and range.

SOLUTION: $c = (a^2 + b^2)^{1/2}$ $\Rightarrow$ $b^2 = (c^2 - a^2)$

$\Rightarrow$ $b^2 = 25 - a^2$ $\Rightarrow$ $b = \pm(25 - a^2)^{1/2}$

$\Rightarrow$ $b = (25 - a^2)^{1/2}$ (Since b being side length is non-negative)

Thus, $b = f(a) = \sqrt{25 - a^2}$

For domain $a \in [-5, 5]$; but $0 < a < 5$ (otherwise triangle is impossible)

Also a being the length of side of triangle can never be negative, therefore $a \in (0, 5)$.

Therefore domain of f is $(0, 5)$.

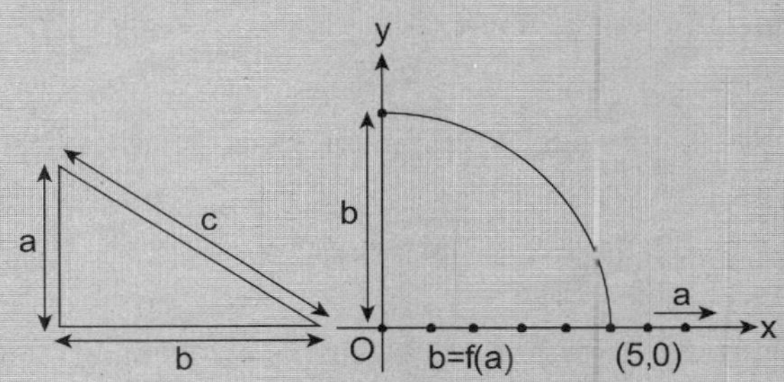

FIGURE 2.7

Also range of function consists of all values attained by b when $a \in (0, 5)$.

$\therefore$ Range of $f = R_f = (0, 5)$. Figure 2.8 represents the function $b = \sqrt{25 - a^2}$

ILLUSTRATION 13: A right circular cone is inscribed in a sphere of radius R. Find the functional relationship between the lateral surface area S of the cone and its generatrix x. Indicate the domain of definition of this function and its range.

SOLUTION: $S = \pi rl = \pi rx$ $(\because l = x)$

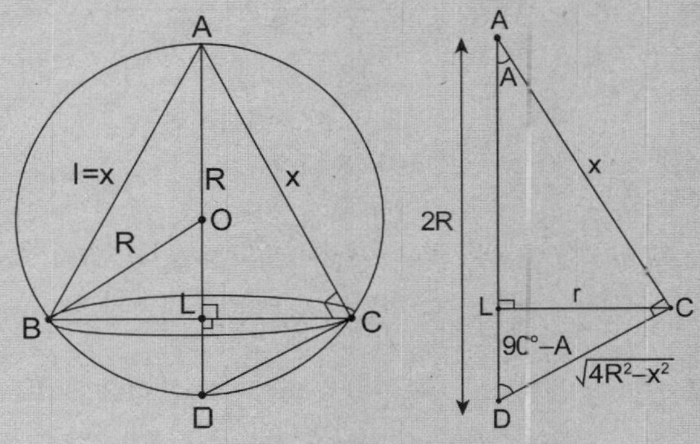

FIGURE 2.8

Now in ΔACL, $\sin A = \dfrac{r}{x}$ .... (i)

And in ΔCDL, $\operatorname{cosec}(90° - A) = \dfrac{\sqrt{4R^2 - x^2}}{r}$

$\Rightarrow$ $\sec A = \dfrac{\sqrt{4R^2 - x^2}}{r}$ .... (ii)

Now, $\cos^2 A = \dfrac{1}{\sec^2 A}$ $\Rightarrow 1 - \sin^2 A = \dfrac{r^2}{4R^2 - x^2}$

$\Rightarrow 1 - \dfrac{r^2}{x^2} = \dfrac{r^2}{4R^2 - x^2}$ $\Rightarrow r = \dfrac{x\sqrt{4R^2 - x^2}}{2R}$ (Using (i) and (ii))

$\therefore$ $S = \pi r x = \dfrac{\pi x^2}{2R}\sqrt{4R^2 - x^2}$; $0 < x < 2R \Rightarrow S = f(x) = \dfrac{\pi x^2\sqrt{4R^2 - x^2}}{2R}$

$\therefore$ Domain of function $S = f(x) = (0, 2R)$.

($\because 4R^2 - x^2 \geq 0 \Rightarrow x \in [0, 2R]$ but for $x = 0, 2R$, cone cannot be constructed)

$\therefore$ **Range of function:** As $f'(x) = \dfrac{\pi}{2R} x \dfrac{\left[8R^2 - 3x^2\right]}{\sqrt{4R^2 - x^2}} \Rightarrow f'(x) = 0$ for $x = \dfrac{2\sqrt{2}R}{\sqrt{3}}$ and $x = 0$

At $x = 0$, $f(x)$ attains minimum value 0, where as at $x = \dfrac{2\sqrt{2}R}{\sqrt{3}}$, $f(x)$ attains its maximum value $= \dfrac{\pi}{2R}\left(\dfrac{8}{3}R^2\right)\sqrt{4R^2 - \dfrac{8}{3}R^2} = \dfrac{8\pi R^2}{3\sqrt{3}}$. Thus, range $= \left(0, \dfrac{8\pi R^2}{3\sqrt{3}}\right]$.

ILLUSTRATION 14: In the Figure 2.9 express y analytically as a continuous function of x with natural domain. Also find the range of function.

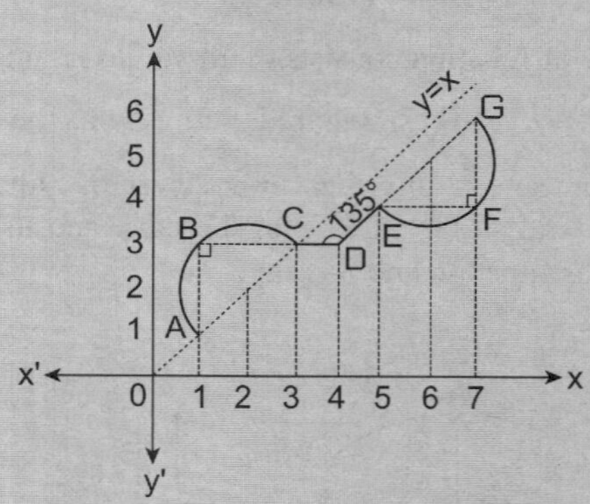

FIGURE 2.9

SOLUTION: $\widehat{ABC}$ is a semi circle with ends of diameter as (1,1) and (3,3).

$\therefore$ Equation of Arc $\widehat{ABC}$ is $(x-2)^2 + (y-2)^2 = 2$ or $y - 2 = \pm\sqrt{4x - x^2 - 2}$ ...(1)

Clearly for $x \in \left[2 - \sqrt{2}, 1\right]$ $f(x)$ is not a function as it has two output for each input given by above analytical relation in equation (1) . Therefore to convert it to function, isolating the two branches, we get $y = \begin{cases} 2 + \sqrt{4x - x^2 - 2} & ; y \geq 2 \\ 2 - \sqrt{4x - x^2 - 2} & ; y \leq 2 \end{cases}$ ...(2)

Now f to be continuous function rejecting the negative branch, i.e., for $y \leq 2$, we get

$f(x) = \begin{cases} 2 + \sqrt{4x - x^2 - 2}; 2 - \sqrt{2} \leq x \leq 3 \\ 3; 3 < x \leq 4 \end{cases}$

For $x \in [4,5]$ f is a linear polynomial given by a straight line through (4, 3) of slope 1, i.e., $f(x) = x - 1$

$$\therefore \quad f(x) = \begin{cases} 2+\sqrt{4x-x^2-2}; & 2-\sqrt{2} \le x \le 3 \\ 3 & ; 3 < x \le 4 \\ x-1 & ; 4 < x \le 5 \end{cases}$$

Similarly for the interval $x \in [5, 6+\sqrt{2}]$ $f(x)$ is given by an arc of the lower semicircle (i.e., $y \le 5$ with centre (6, 5) and radius $\sqrt{2}$).

Now equation of Arc $\widehat{EFG}$: $(x - 6)^2 + (y - 5)^2 = 2$

$$\Rightarrow \quad y = \begin{cases} 5-\sqrt{12x-x^2-34}; & y \le 5 \\ 5+\sqrt{12x-x^2-34}; & y \ge 5 \end{cases}$$

Thus, the complete analytical formula for $f(x)$ in its natural domain is given by

$$f(x) = \begin{cases} 2+\sqrt{4x-x^2-2} & ; 2-\sqrt{2} \le x \le 3 \\ 3 & ; 3 < x \le 4 \\ x-1 & ; 4 < x \le 5 \\ 5-\sqrt{12x-x^2-34} & ; 5 < x \le 6+\sqrt{2} \end{cases}$$

Domain of $f(x)$ is $[2-\sqrt{2}, 6+\sqrt{2}]$ and range of $f(x)$ is $[f(2-\sqrt{2}), f(6+\sqrt{2})]$, i.e., [2, 5].

TEXTUAL EXERCISE–1: (SUBJECTIVE)

1. If $f(x) = \sqrt{x^2-4}$, find the values of $f(1), f(2), f(-3)$, if they exist (i.e., real).

2. If $f(x) = \dfrac{(x-2)}{(x-4)(x-5)}$, find the real numbers for which $f(x)$ is not defined (not real and finite).

3. If $f(x) = \dfrac{1}{(x-1)}$; then find the real numbers for which $f(x)$ is not defined. Also find the real number(s) which the function $f(x)$ cannot attain.

4. If $f(x) = \sqrt{(x-1)(x-4)}$, then find the interval
   (i) For which $f(x)$ is not defined
   (ii) For which $\dfrac{1}{f(x)}$ is not defined
   (iii) Containing all values of $f(x)$
   (iv) Containing all values of $\dfrac{1}{f(x)}$

5. Find the set of all values of x, for which the following functions (expressions) are defined:
   (a) $\dfrac{1}{x(x-1)(x-2)}$ (b) $\dfrac{x^2-x}{x^2+x}$
   (c) $\dfrac{x+1}{x^2+x+1}$ (d) $\dfrac{1}{\sqrt{x-3}}$
   (e) $\sqrt{x-4}$ (f) $\sqrt{x-2}+\sqrt{x+2}$
   (g) $\sqrt{x-4}+\sqrt{7-x}$ (h) $\dfrac{1}{\sqrt{x-4}-\sqrt{6-x}}$
   (i) $\sqrt{x-7}-\sqrt{3-x}$

6. Find the domain of definition of the following functions:
   (a) $f(x) = \dfrac{\sqrt{x-1}}{\sqrt{6-x}}$ (b) $f(x) = \sqrt{\dfrac{x-1}{6-x}-1}$
   (c) $f(x) = \dfrac{\sqrt{x-1}}{6-x}$ (d) $\left(\sqrt{x}-1\right)\left(6-\sqrt{x}\right)$
   (e) $\left(\sqrt{x}-1\right)\sqrt{(6-x)}$

7. Find the domain of definition the following functions:
   (a) $f(x) = \sqrt{x-1}\sqrt{6-x}$ (b) $f(x) = \sqrt{(x-1)(6-x)}$
   (c) $f(x) = \sqrt{x-x^2}$

8. Find the domain of the following functions:

   (i) $\sqrt{5-x}+\sqrt{x-2}$

   (ii) $\sqrt{3-x}+\sqrt{x-5}$

9. Find the domain and range of the function $f(x)$ defined by $f(x) = \sqrt{x^2+x+1}$ from a subset of set $A = \{0, 1, 2, 3\}$ to B = set of irrational numbers.

10. Find pairs of functions from the following function(*s*) whose domain and range are same?

    (i) $f(x)=\sqrt{1-x^2}$ (ii) $g(x) = \dfrac{1}{x}$

    (iii) $h(x) = \dfrac{1}{\sqrt[3]{x}}$ (iv) $\phi(x) = \sqrt[4]{1-x^2}$

11. Find the domain and range of the function $f(x)$ from a subset of set $A = \{x : x$ is a +ve integer divisor of $36\}$ to set of real numbers ($\mathbb{R}$) defined by

    $$f(x) = \frac{x}{(x-1)(x-2)(x-3)....(x-10)}$$

12. Let $A = \{9, 10, 11, 12, 13\}$ and let $f : A \to \mathbb{N}$ be defined by $f(n)$ = the highest prime factor of n. Find the range of f.

13. A cylinder is inscribed in a sphere of radius R. Express the volume V of the cylinder as a function of its height x. Indicate the domain of definition of this function.

14. O is a fixed point on a circle of unit radius whose centre is P. A chord perpendicular to OP at a distance x from O cuts the circle at A and B. Express the area of the segment AOB as a function of x.

15. In the Figure 2.10, $BC = b$ and $AH = h$; where $AH \perp BC$. If $EF = x$, where $EF \perp BC$, then express the area and perimeter of the rectangle $DEFG$ as functions of x.

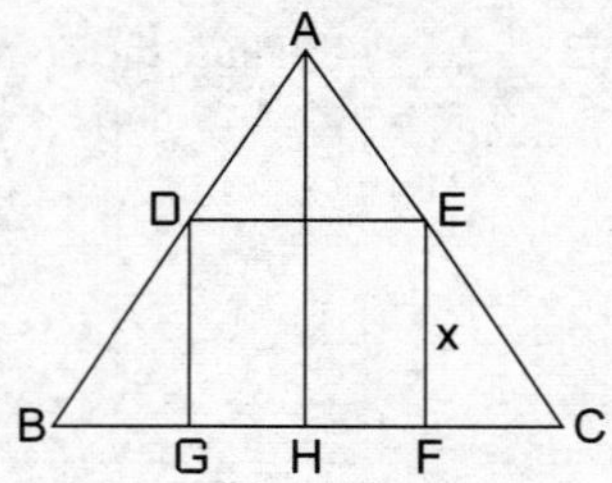

FIGURE 2.10

Answer Keys

1. $f(1)$ does not exist; $f(2) = 0$, $f(-3) = \sqrt{5}$
2. 4, 5
3. $f(x)$ is not defined for $x = 1$; $f(x)$ cannot attain 0 value.
4. (i) $(1, 4)$ (ii) $[1, 4]$ (iii) $[0, \infty)$ (iv) $(0, \infty)$
5. (a) $\mathbb{R} \sim \{0, 1, 2\}$ (b) $\mathbb{R} \sim \{0, -1\}$ (c) $\mathbb{R}$ (d) $(3, \infty)$
   (e) $[4, \infty)$ (f) $[2, \infty)$ (g) $[4, 7]$ (h) $[4, 6] \sim \{5\}$ (i) ϕ
6. (a) $[1, 6)$ (b) $[7/2, 6)$ (c) $[1, \infty) \sim \{6\}$ (d) $[0, \infty)$ (e) $[0, 6]$
7. (a) $[1, 6]$ (b) $[1, 6]$ (c) $[0, 1]$
8. (i) $[2, 5]$ (ii) ϕ
9. Domain = $\{1, 2, 3\}$ and Range = $\left\{\sqrt{3},\sqrt{7},\sqrt{13}\right\}$
10. $(g(x), h(x))$ and $(f(x), \phi(x))$
11. Domain = $\{12, 18, 36\}$; Range = $\left\{\dfrac{12}{11!},\dfrac{18\times 7!}{17!},\dfrac{36\times 25!}{35!}\right\}$
12. Range = $\{3, 5, 11, 13\}$
13. $0 < x < 2R$; $\pi x\left(R^2-\dfrac{x^2}{4}\right)$
14. $\cos^{-1}(1-x)-(1-x)\sqrt{2x-x^2}$, $0 \le x \le 1$ and $\pi - \cos^{-1}(x-1)+(x-1)\sqrt{2x-x^2}$, $1 < x \le 2$.
15. $A(x) = \dfrac{bx(h-x)}{h}$, $p(x)=2\left\{x+\dfrac{b(h-x)}{h}\right\}$

TEXTUAL EXERCISE–1: (OBJECTIVE)

1. If $f(x)=\frac{1}{1-x}$, then $f\left(\frac{1}{x}\right)$ is
   (a) $\frac{x}{x-1}$ (b) $\frac{1}{x-1}$
   (c) $\frac{1}{x+1}$ (d) None of these

2. The domain of function $f(x)=\log(1-x)+\sqrt{x^2-1}$ is
   (a) $[-1, 1]$ (b) $(1, \infty)$
   (c) $(-\infty, -1]$ (d) None of these

3. If $f(x) = ax^2 + bx + c$, then the values of a and b for which the identity $f(x + 1) - f(x) = 8x + 3$ is satisfied are
   (a) $a = 4$ and $b = -1$ (b) $a = 1$ and $b = 4$
   (c) $a = -1$ and $b = 4$ (d) None of these

4. Let $p(x) = a^2 + bx$, $q(x) = lx^2 + mx + n$. If $p(1) - q(1) = 0$, $p(2) - q(2) = 1$ and $p(3) - q(3) = 4$, then $p(4) - q(4)$ equals
   (a) 2 (b) 5
   (c) 9 (d) None of these

5. The domain of the function $f(x)=\sqrt{\log(\log x)-\log(4-\log x)-\log 3}$; (base of log is 10)
   (a) $[10^3, 10^4)$ (b) $(10^3, 10^4)$
   (c) $[10^3, \infty)$ (d) None of these

6. The domain of the function $y = f(x)$ given by $3^y+2^{x^4}=2^{4x^2-3}$ is
   (a) $(-\sqrt{3}, \sqrt{3})$ (b) $(-\sqrt{3}, -1) \cup (1, \sqrt{3})$
   (c) $(-\infty, -\sqrt{3}) \cup (\sqrt{3}, \infty)$ (d) None of these

7. The domain of definition of the function $\sqrt[3]{\frac{2x+1}{x^2-10x-11}}$ is given by
   (a) $\mathbb{R} \sim \{-1, 11\}$ (b) $\mathbb{R}$
   (c) $(0, \infty)$ (d) None of these

8. The domain of the function $f(x)=\sqrt{\log_5(\cos(\sin x))}$ is
   (a) $\mathbb{R}$ (b) $(0, \infty)$
   (c) $\{n\pi, n \in \mathbb{Z}\}$ (d) None of these

9. The domain of the function $f(x)=\frac{1}{\sqrt{x^6-13x^4+36x^2}}$ is
   (a) $(0, 2) \cup (3, \infty)$
   (b) $(-\infty, -3) \cup (-2, 0) \cup (0, 2) \cup (3, \infty)$
   (c) $\mathbb{R} \sim \{-3, -2, 0, 2, 3\}$
   (d) None of these

10. The range of the function $f(x)=x^2+\frac{1}{x^2+1}$ is
    (a) $[1, \infty)$ (b) $(0, \infty)$
    (c) $[2, \infty)$ (d) None of these

11. The domain of the function $f(x) = \log_4(\log_5(\log_3(18x - x^2 - 77)))$ is
    (a) $(8, 10)$ (b) $(-8, 10)$
    (c) $(-\infty, 8) \cup (10, \infty)$ (d) None of these

12. Let the function $f : D \to \mathbb{R}$, $f(x) = \log_5(\log_{1/3} \log_8 (2x + 1))$; where D is the natural domain of f. If S represents the sum of the absolute values of all integers from D, then the value of S is
    (a) 4 (b) 5
    (c) 6 (d) None of these

Answer Keys

1 (a) 2. (c) 3. (a) 4. (c) 5. (a) 6. (b) 7. (a) 8. (c) 9. (b) 10. (a)
11. (a) 12. (c)

■ REPRESENTATION OF FUNCTIONS

Analytical Representation: When a function is denoted as $y = f(x)$ or $f(x, y) = 0$, then it is called analytical representation.

e.g., $y = \sqrt{x^2+1}$, $f(x) = \frac{\ln x + e^x}{\sin x}$ or $f(x) = \frac{ax^2+bx+c}{e^{2x}\sin^{-1}x}$.

The advantage of analytical representation is the compactness and the possibility of evaluating $f(x)$ for any value of x in the domain. This is the most effective way of representation of a function which allows application of techniques of calculus.

Most of the functions encountered at basic level are defined by means of a single equation.

For example, $f(x) = x^2 - 2$; $f(x) = \sqrt{x+1}$. However, it is not true that a function in analytical representation always use a single equation. We may require more than one equation to represent a function analytically, depending upon its domain.

Example:

(i) $f(x) = \begin{cases} \sqrt{x-1} & \text{for } x \geq 1 \\ 2x-2 & \text{for } x < 1 \end{cases}$

(ii) $g(x) = \begin{cases} \sin x & \text{for } x < -\pi \\ x+\pi & \text{for } -\pi \leq x \leq \pi \\ \tan x & \text{for } x > \pi \end{cases}$

(iii) $h(x) = \begin{cases} x\sin\dfrac{1}{x} & \text{for } x \neq 0 \\ 0 & \text{for } x = 0 \end{cases}$ etc

The function defined above using more than one equations are called piece-wise defined function.

A piece-wise defined function has different analytical expressions (formulae) on different parts of its domain as illustrated in above examples. In a piece-wise defined function, the domain is the union of the sub-intervals. To evaluate the function at a particular value of x, we choose the appropriate formula.

For instance, for the function $f(x)$ illustrated above $f(-3) = 2(-3) - 2 = -8$ and $f(4) = \sqrt{4-1} = \sqrt{3}$.

The independent variable used in an analytical representation may be continuous or discrete. In the examples given above $f(x)$, $g(x)$ and $h(x)$ have continuous independent variable.

Now consider the function $f(x) = {}^nC_x + {}^nP_x$; where C and P are combination and permutation has discrete independent variable x and having domain $\{0, 1, 2, 3, \ldots, n\}$ consisting of first $(n + 1)$ whole numbers.

Analytical representation may use either explicit form of representation or implicit form of representation. i.e., in the form $y = f(x)$ or $f(x, y) = 0$ e.g., $y = x^2 - 1$ or $y - x^2 + 1 = 0$

Generally we deal with functions in which the dependent variable y is explicitly related to independent variable x. Such functions are called explicit function.

A function is an implicit function, if it is defined by an equation not solved for the dependent variable y. For example $y^3 - x^2 = 5x$; $2xy - 5\tan^2 y = 0$ etc.

Here, y is not directly expressed in terms of x. However, in some cases, an implicit function can be converted into an explicit function.

For example, $y^3 - x^2 = 5x$; can be expressed as $y = (x^2 + 5x)^{1/3}$. Sometimes, the conversion can change the domain. But we must consider the domain of the original expression.

e.g., $\log(x^3 - 1) + \log y - 5 = 0$

$\Rightarrow \log(x^3 - 1)y = 5$

$\Rightarrow (x^3 - 1)y = e^5$

$$\Rightarrow y = \frac{e^5}{(x^3-1)} \quad \ldots (1)$$

having its domain $\mathbb{R} \sim \{1\}$, but if we observe the original equation, for $\log y$ and $\log(x^3 - 1)$ to be defined $x^3 - 1 > 0$, $y > 0$

$\Rightarrow (x - 1)(x^2 + x + 1) > 0$

$\Rightarrow x > 1$, i.e., the domain of original function expressed in implicit form is $(1, \infty)$.

Thus, the domain is changed, so care must be taken while converting the function given in explicit form to function in implicit form and defining the domain of converted function.

REMARK

Some of the implicit equations do not represent functions. For example, the equation $9x^2 + 4y^2 = 36$ represents an ellipse and on solving it for y, we get $y^2 = \dfrac{36-9x^2}{4} \Rightarrow y = \pm\dfrac{\sqrt{36-9x^2}}{2}$

Thus, corresponding to each input x, we get two outputs $\dfrac{\sqrt{36-9x^2}}{2}$ and $-\dfrac{\sqrt{36-9x^2}}{2}$.

Thus, the given equation does not represent a function. In fact it represents a many–many relation.

However, we can define two functions here:

$\phi = \{(x, y) : y = \dfrac{\sqrt{36-9x^2}}{2}, x \in [-2, 2]\}$ *and* $y = \{(x, y) : y = -\dfrac{\sqrt{36-9x^2}}{2}, x \in [-2, 2]\}$

Such a relation is sometimes called a multi-valued function.

ILLUSTRATION 15: Consider a circle of radius r. Let $f(x)$ be the length of a chord AB of circle at a distance x from the centre of the circle. Express the function $f(x)$ analytically and find its domain of definition.

SOLUTION: Let M be the midpoint of the chord AB and let C be the centre of the circle. Note that $CM = x$ and $CB = a$. By Pythagoras theorem, from right angled ΔBCM

we have, $BM = \sqrt{a^2 - x^2}$. Hence, $AB = 2\sqrt{a^2 - x^2}$

Thus, $f(x) = 2\sqrt{a^2 - x^2}$ is the required function in algebraic form

Now $f(x)$ produces real values for $a^2 - x^2 \geq 0 \Rightarrow x \in [-a, a]$

But x being distance cannot be negative. $\Rightarrow x \in [0, a]$. For $x = a$, length of chord = 0, i.e., no chord. Hence, the domain of definition of the function f is $[0, a]$.

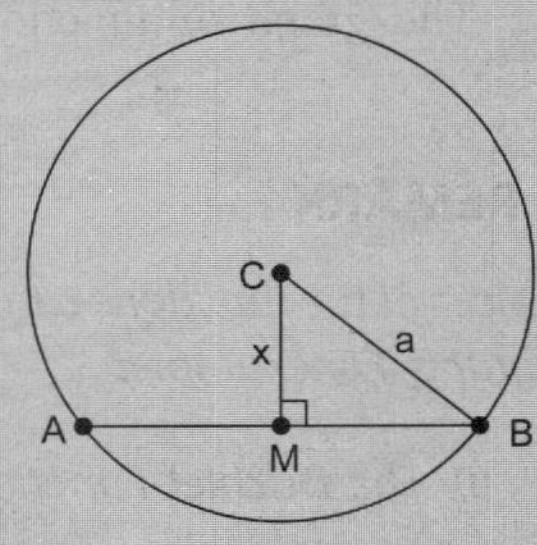

FIGURE 2.11

■ FUNCTION AS A SET OF ORDERED PAIRS

Let A and B be two non-empty sets. A relation f from A to B, i.e., a subset of

$A \times B$ is called a function (or a mapping or a map) from A to B iff

(a) For each $a \in A$ there exists $b \in B$ such that ordered pair $(a, b) \in f$,

(b) Also if $(a, b) \in f$ and $(a, c) \in f \quad \Rightarrow b = c$

Thus, a non-empty subset f of $A \times B$ is a function from A to B if each element of A appear in some ordered pair in f and no two ordered pairs in f have the same first element. If $(a, b) \in f$, then b is called the image of a under f and a is called pre-image of b under f.

Therefore, a function $y = f(x)$ can be expressed as a set of ordered pairs.

That is, if $f: A \to B$ is a function, then $f = \{(a, f(a)) : a \in A$ and $f(a) \in B\}$ is representation of function as a set of ordered pairs.

If $f: X \to Y$ is a function defined as $f(x) = 2x^2 + 1$ such that $X = \{0, 1, 2, 3\}$ and $Y = \{1, 3, 5, 7, 9, 11, 13, 15, 17, 19\}$ can be expressed as a set of ordered pairs given by $f = \{(0, 1), (1, 3), (2, 9), (3, 19)\}$.

Graphical Representation: Being a set of ordered pairs, a function can be represented graphically on (x, y) plane, where each point (x, y) on the graph represents an input x and the corresponding output y of the function. The use of graph gives a visual representation and shows the various characteristics of graph viz. concavity, convexity, monotonicity and the domain of definition of the function.

For example:

1. The graph of $f(x) = \begin{cases} \sqrt{x-1}; & \text{if } x \geq 1 \\ 2x-2; & \text{if } x < 1 \end{cases}$ is shown in Figure 2.12.

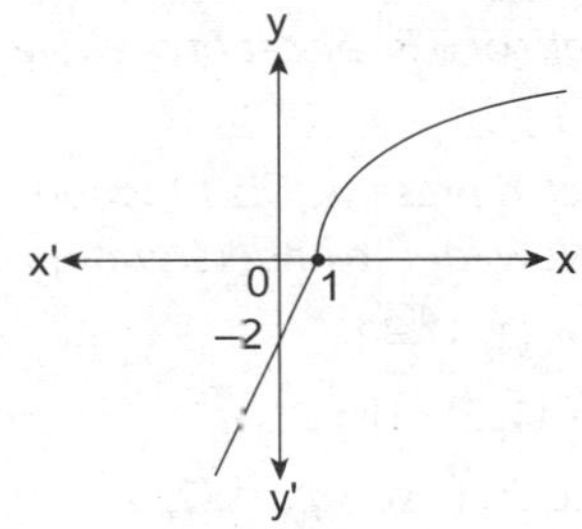

FIGURE 2.12

Corresponding to real numbers less than one the graph of function is a straight line $y = 2x - 2$ and for real numbers greater than or equal to 1, the graph of function is a portion of parabola $y^2 = x - 1$. Thus, the given function is a combination of a straight line and a parabola. Clearly the function is defined that is function takes real and finite values $\forall x \in \mathbb{R}$. Thus, the domain of function is $\mathbb{R}$. Also the function takes all real values from $-\infty$ to ∞, i.e., the range of function is $\mathbb{R}$

From the graph of given function we see that the function is monotonically increasing on $\mathbb{R}$. Also the function is concave downwards on $(1, \infty)$. The function is neither concave upwards nor concave downwards, i.e., linear for $x \in (-\infty, 1]$.

2. $f(x) = 2x^2 + 1$ can be represented graphically as shown in Figure 2.13.

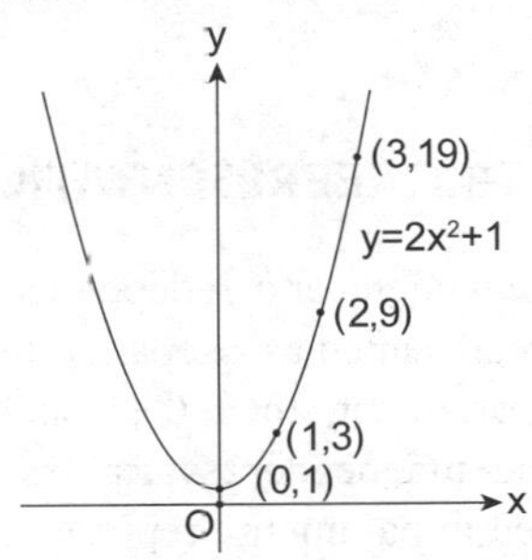

FIGURE 2.13

Observing the graph of given function we find that the domain of function is $\mathbb{R}$ and the range is $[1, \infty)$. Clearly the graph is concave upwards for all $x \in \mathbb{R}$. The graph of function is monotonically decreasing for $x \in (-\infty, 0)$ and monotonically increasing for $x \in (0, \infty)$. Also $x = 0$ is a stationary point, i.e., the point in the domain of function corresponding to which the point on the function has horizontal tangent.

REMARK

Most of the functions can be represented graphically but there are some functions which cannot be represented by a graph. For example:

(i) The Drichlet-Function which is defined as $f(x) = \begin{cases} 0, & \text{when } x \text{ is rational} \\ 1, & \text{when } x \text{ is irrational} \end{cases}$ *cannot be graphed since there exist infinite number of rationals as well as irrationals between any two real numbers.*

(ii) Consider the Euler's totient or Euler's phi function $\phi(n)$ *= Number of positive integers less than or equal to n and co-prime to n; where n is a natural number.*

The domain of ϕ *is the set of positive integers. Its range is the set of positive integers* $\{1, 2, 3, \ldots\}$.

We cannot represent this function analytically. A portion of the graph of $\phi(n)$ *is shown below for the understanding of the function.*

Since g.c.d. $(1, 1) = 1 \Rightarrow \phi(1) = 1.$

Now g.c.d. $(1, 2) = 1 \Rightarrow \phi(2) = 1$

Further g.c.d. $(1, 3) =$ *g.c.d.* $(2, 3) = 1$ *and* $1, 2 < 3 \Rightarrow \phi(3) = 2$

Similarly, g.c.d. $(4, 1) =$ *g.c.d.* $(4, 3) = 1 \Rightarrow \phi(4) = 2,$

and g.c.d. $= (1, 5) =$ *g.c.d.* $(2, 5) =$ *g.c.d.* $(3, 5) =$ *g.c.d.* $(4, 5) = 1 \Rightarrow \phi(5) = 4$

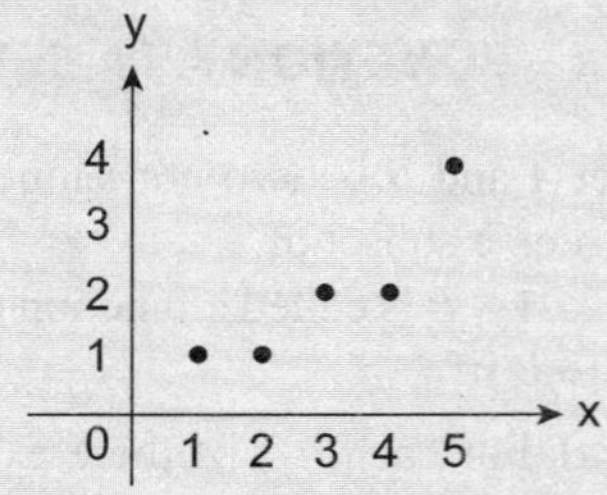

FIGURE 2.14

(iii) Consider another function called prime number function defined by f(x) = number of prime numbers less than or equal to x; where x is positive real number.

Then domain of f(x) is $(0, \infty)$ *and range is the set of non-negative integers, i.e.,* $\{0, 1, 2, 3, \ldots,\}$.

The graph of function is shown below

As x increases, the function f(x) remains constant until x reaches a prime, at which the graph of function jumps by 1. Therefore, the graph of f consists of horizontal line segments. This is an example of a class of function called step functions.

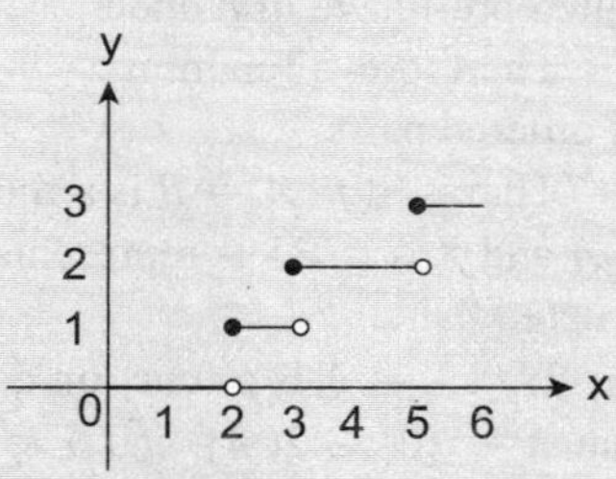

FIGURE 2.15

(iv) Another function, which is so complicated that it is impossible to draw its graph,

$$h(x) = \begin{cases} x, & \text{if } x \text{ is rational} \\ -\dfrac{x}{2}, & \text{if } x \text{ is irrational.} \end{cases}$$

As we know that between any two real numbers, there lie infinitely many rationals and irrational numbers, so it is impossible to draw its graph.

■ PARAMETRIC REPRESENTATION

If each of the dependent and independent variables of a function can be represented as a separate function of a third variable called parameter, then the function represented by dependent and independent variables as functions of parameter is called in parametric representation.

i.e., if $y = f(x)$ is a function such that

$$\left.\begin{aligned} x &= \phi(t) \\ y &= \psi(t) \end{aligned}\right\} \qquad \ldots(1)$$

where t assumes values that lies in the interval $[a, b]$. To each value of t there corresponds values of x and y (the function ϕ and ψ are assumed to be single valued). If the ordered pair (x, y) be regarded as the coordinates of a point in a coordinate xy-plane, then to each value of t there correspond a definite point in the plane. And when t varies from a to b, the point will describe a certain curve giving us the graph of function $y = f(x)$.

Equations (1) are called parametric equations of this curve, t is the parameter, and the curve is represented parametrically by equations (1).

The direct relationship between the variables x and y (not involving the parameter t) from equation (1), can be obtained by eliminating t from equations (1).

i.e., the function $x = \phi(t)$ has the inverse, $t = \phi^{-1}(x)$, then $y = \psi(t)$

$\Rightarrow\ y = \psi[\phi^{-1}(x)]$ ...(2)

Thus, equation (1) defines y as a function of x, and we say that the function y of x is represented parametrically.

For example, consider the function defined parametrically by $x = t + 2;\ y = t^2 - 1;\ t \in \mathbb{R}$

We have $t = x - 2$ and $y = t^2 - 1$

$\Rightarrow\ y = (x - 2)^2 - 1$

$\Rightarrow\ y = x^2 - 4x + 3$

which represents an upward parabola with its vertex at (2, –1) as shown in Figure 2.16..

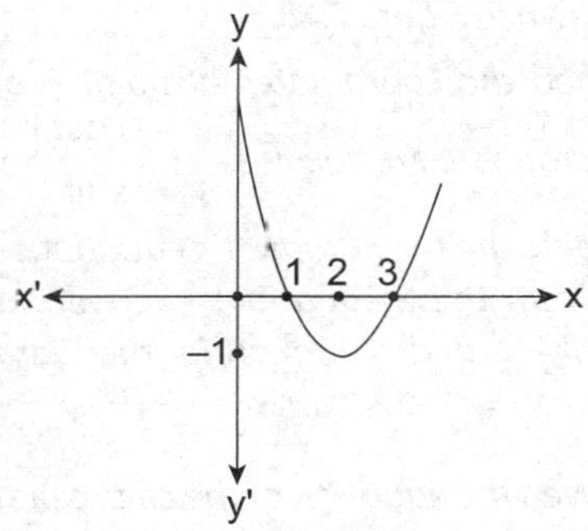

FIGURE 2.16

A parametric representation of a function (or of a curve) is sometimes more convenient than other ways of representing the function as the parametric equation may express a complicated relationship between x and y in a simpler manner.

REMARKS

(i) *If at least one of the functions of parametric equation is constant, then it is impossible to eliminate the parameter t to obtain a functional relationship y = f(x). For instance, the equations x = 2, y = cost would not provide us a functional relationship between x and y. Here they would contain the ordered pairs (2, cost); t ∈ ℝ.*

i.e., the graph is a straight line segment joining the points (2, –1) and (2, 1).

Let us consider the function represented parametrically as $x = at^2,\ y = 2at;\ t \in \mathbb{R}$

Analytically the above relation represents a right handed parabola $y^2 = 4ax$ *as shown in Figure 2.17.*

The geometric significance of the parameter t in the above equations is as follows:

When the parameter t ranges from 0 to ∞ the variable point traverses the upper half portion of parabola from the point (0, 0) to the point (∞,∞) and if t varies from 0 to –∞ it describes the lower half portion of parabola from (0, 0) to (∞, –∞). Hence, if t continuously varies from –∞ to ∞, the moving point traverse the parabola from (∞, –∞) to (∞, ∞) continuously in clockwise directions as represented by arrows on the graph of function (parabola).

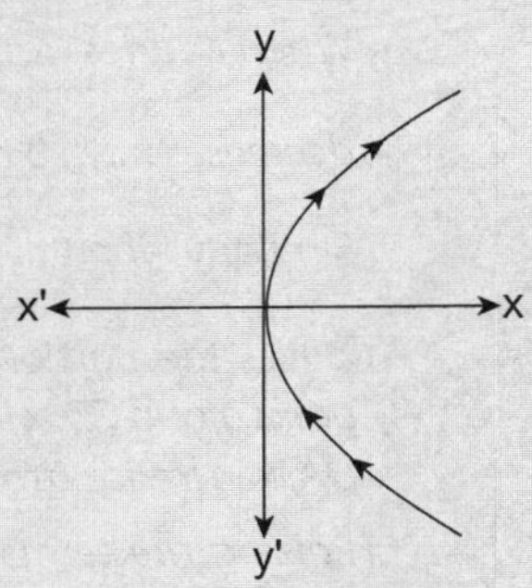

FIGURE 2.17

(ii) *Parametric representation of curves is widely used in mechanics. If in the xy-plane there is a certain object in motion and if we know its laws of motion horizontally and vertically, i.e., the relationship between distance traveled horizontally and vertically with time.*

$$\text{i.e., } \left.\begin{aligned} x &= \phi(t) \\ y &= \psi(t) \end{aligned}\right\} \qquad \text{...(3)}$$

where the parameter 't' is the time. Then equation (3) are parametric equations of the trajectory of the moving object. Eliminating from these equations the parameter t, we get the equation of the trajectory in the form y = f(x) or f(x, y) = 0.

Consider some examples of curves in parametric form.

1. *For a circle with centre at the origin and radius r. Let t denotes the positive angle between x-axis and the radius vector at some point P(x, y) of the circle as shown in Figure 2.18.*

   Then the coordinates of point P on the circle is expressed in terms of the parameter t as follows. $\left.\begin{matrix} x = r\cos t \\ y = r\sin t \end{matrix}\right\}, 0 \le t \le 2\pi$

   These are the parametric equations of the circle. If we eliminate the parameter t from these equations, we will have an equation of the circle containing only x and y. Squaring the parametric equations and adding, we get $x^2 + y^2 = r^2(\cos^2 t + \sin^2 t)$ *or* $x^2 + y^2 = r^2$.

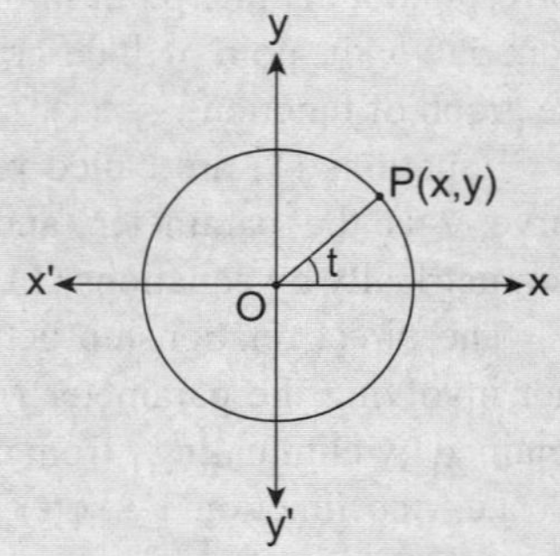

FIGURE 2.18

2. *Given the equation of the ellipse in standard form* $\frac{x^2}{a^2} + \frac{y^2}{b^2} = 1$ .... (1)

   Let $x = a\cos t$

   Putting this value of x in equation (1), we get $y = b\sin t$

   The equations $\left.\begin{matrix} x = a\cos t \\ y = b\sin t \end{matrix}\right\}; 0 \le t \le 2\pi$ *are the parametric equations of the ellipse (1).*

3. *The Asteroid is a curve which is a many–many relation and not a function as shown in Figure 2.19.*

   The parametric equations of Asteroid are $\left.\begin{matrix} x = a\cos^3 t \\ y = a\sin^3 t \end{matrix}\right\}; 0 \le t \le 2\pi$ ... (1)

   when t varies from 0 to $\frac{\pi}{2}$*, point on curve traces the portion AB, from A to B, i.e., x decreases from a to 0 where as y increases from 0 to a as is clear from the parametric equation (1)*

   When t varies from $\frac{\pi}{2}$ *to π, point on curve traces the portion BC. i.e., x decreases from 0 to –a and y also decreases from a to 0.*

   Similarly when t varies from π to $\frac{3\pi}{2}$ *and* $\frac{3\pi}{2}$ *to 2π the point on curve traces the portions CD and DA respectively. During the movement of point along CD, x increases from –a to 0 and y decreases from 0 to –a and during the movement of point along DA, x increases from 0 to a and y increases from –a to 0.*

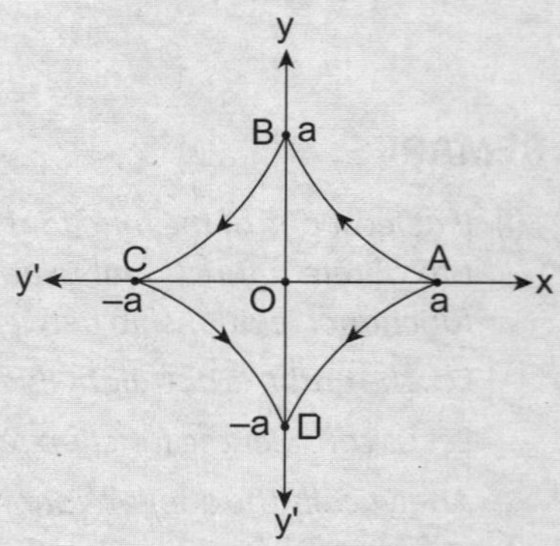

FIGURE 2.19

   Raising the terms of both equations (1) to the power 2/3 and adding, we get the following relationship between x and y: $x^{\frac{2}{3}} + y^{\frac{2}{3}} = a^{\frac{2}{3}}(\cos^2 t + \sin^2 t)$ *or* $x^{\frac{2}{3}} + y^{\frac{2}{3}} = a^{\frac{2}{3}}$

$$\Rightarrow y^{\frac{2}{3}} = a^{\frac{2}{3}} - x^{\frac{2}{3}} \quad \Rightarrow y^2 = \left(a^{\frac{2}{3}} - x^{\frac{2}{3}}\right)^3 \quad \Rightarrow y = \pm\sqrt{\left(a^{\frac{2}{3}} - x^{\frac{2}{3}}\right)^3}$$

   Thus, an asteroid is a combination of two functions $\phi = \left\{(x, y) : y = \sqrt{\left(a^{\frac{2}{3}} - x^{\frac{2}{3}}\right)^3}; x \in [-a, a]\right\}$ *and* $\psi = \left\{(x, y) : y = -\sqrt{\left(a^{\frac{2}{3}} - x^{\frac{2}{3}}\right)^3}; x \in [-a, a]\right\}$

   Here ϕ *represents upper half portion of curve, where as* ψ *represents the lower half portion of curve and* $\psi = -\phi$.

■ DIAGRAMMATIC REPRESENTATION

(By using arrow diagram): If $f: X \to Y$ is a function, then we represent X and Y by two circles or ellipses containing independent and dependent variables respectively and join the inputs with their corresponding outputs (images) by using arrows. The function $f(x) = 2x^2 + 1$ from set $X = \{0, 1, 2, 3\}$ to set $Y = \{1, 3, 5, 7, 9, 11, 13, 19\}$ is represented diagrammatically as shown below.

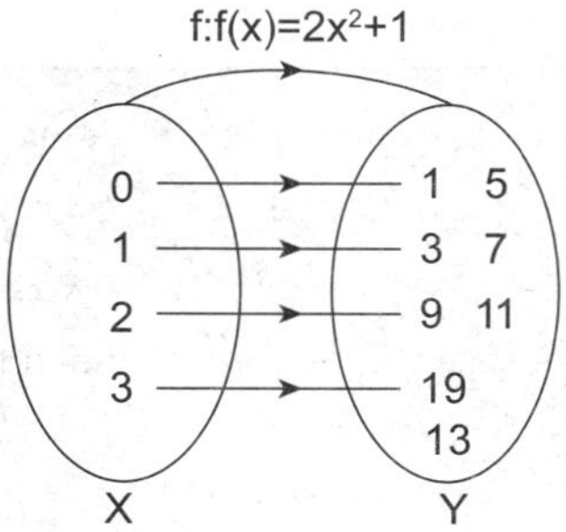

FIGURE 2.20

Methods of Testing a Relation to be a Function

Method 1: *When the relation to be tested is represented analytically*: A relation $f : X \to Y$ defined as $y = f(x)$ will be function iff $x_1 = x_2 \Rightarrow f(x_1) = f(x_2)$ since otherwise an element of X would have two different images.

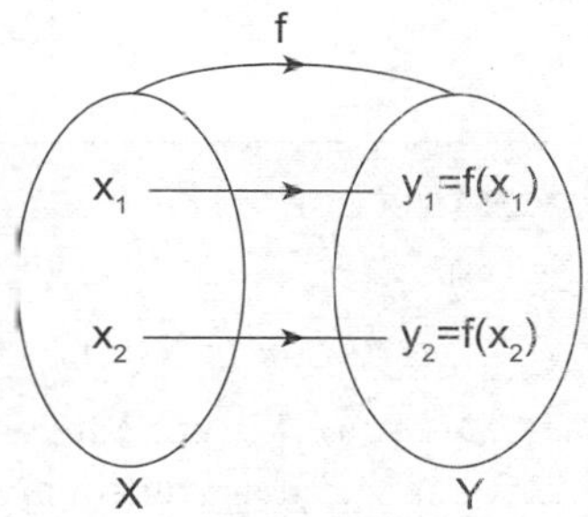

FIGURE 2.21

ILLUSTRATION 16: Test whether following relations f: $\mathbb{R} \to \mathbb{R}$ are function or not

(a) $y = x^3 + 8$ (b) $y^2 = 4x$.

SOLUTION: (a) Let $x_1 = x_2$

$\Rightarrow x_1^3 = x_2^3$ $\Rightarrow x_1^3 + 8 = x_2^3 + 8$ $\Rightarrow f(x_1) = f(x_2)$

So, $f(x) = x^3 + 8$ is a function.

(b) Let $x_1 = x_2$ $\Rightarrow 4x_1 = 4x_2$ $\Rightarrow y_1^2 = y_2^2$

$$\Rightarrow \begin{cases} y_1 = y_2 \\ \text{or} \\ y_1 = -y_2 \end{cases}$$

So, $y^2 = 4x$ is not a function but one–many relation. If the function had been $y = \sqrt{4x}$; $x \geq 0$, then it would be a function.

ILLUSTRATION 17: Which of the following correspondences can be called a function?

(i) $f_1 : \{-1, 0, 1\} \to \{0, 1, 2, 3\}; f_1(x) = x^5$.

(ii) $f_2 : \{0, 4, 9\} \to \{-3, -2, 0, 2, 3\}; f_2(x) = \pm\sqrt{x}$.

(iii) $f_3 : \{0, 1, 9\} \to \{-3, -1, 0, 1, 3\}; f_3(x) = \sqrt{x}$.

(iv) $f_4 : \{0, 4, 9\} \to \{-3, -2, 0, 2, 3\}; f_4(x) = -\sqrt{x}$.

SOLUTION: $f_3(x)$ and $f_4(x)$ are functions as definition of function is satisfied by $f_3(x)$ and $f_4(x)$.

The given correspondence $f_1(x)$ is not a function, as $f_1(-1) = -1 \notin$ co-domain.

Hence, definition of function is not satisfied.

The given relation $f_2(x)$ is not a function, as $f_2(1) = \pm 1$ and $f_2(4) = \pm 2, f_2(9) = \pm 3$

i.e., every element of domain is related with two elements of co-domain.

Hence, the definition of function is not satisfied.

Method 2: *When the relation to be tested is represented as a set of ordered pairs:* A relation $f : X \to Y$ represented as a set of ordered pairs will be function from X to Y iff

- ❑ Set of abscissa of all ordered pairs is equal to X
- ❑ No two ordered pairs should have same abscissa.

REMARK

Because f is a relation from $X \to Y$, therefore abscissa of ordered pairs must belong to X where as ordinates of ordered pairs must belong to Y.

ILLUSTRATION 18: Test whether relation f_i : $\{1,2,3,4\} \to \{2,3,4,5,6\}$ as defined below is a function or not?

(a) $f_1 = \{(1, 2), (2, 4), (4, 3), (3, 0)\}$
(b) $f_2 = \{(1, 3), (2, 4), (3, 5)\}$
(c) $f_3 = \{(1, 3), (2, 5), (3, 4), (1, 6)\}$
(d) $f_4 = \{(1, 6), (2, 5), (3, 4), (4, 2)\}$

SOLUTION: (a) f_1 is not a relation from first set to second set because 0 is not in co-domain, and hence, not a function.

(b) f_2 is not a function from first set to second set as 4 has no image under f_2, however, it is a function from set $\{1, 2, 3\}$ to set $\{2, 3, 4, 5, 6\}$.

(c) f_3 is a not a function from first set to second set as 1 has two images 3 and 6.

(d) f_4 is a function from first set to second set as each element of first set has a unique image in second set.

ILLUSTRATION 19: If $A = \{a, b, c, d, e\}$ and $B = \{p, q, r, s, t\}$, then which of the following subset(s) of $A \times B$ is/are function(s) from A to B.

(i) $f_1 = \{(a, r), (b, r), (b, s), (d, t), (e, q), (c, q)\}$
(ii) $f_2 = \{(a, r), (b, p), (c, t), (d, q)\}$
(iii) $f_3 = \{(a, p), (b, t), (c, r), (d, s), (e, q)\}$
(iv) $f_4 = \{(a, r), (b, r), (c, r), (d, r), (e, r)\}$

SOLUTION: We check for the two conditions of the functions

(i) Since b has two outputs (images) namely r and s, f_1 is not a function
(ii) Since e, an element of A, does not have any image, it is also not a function
(iii) Since every element of A has only one output, it is a function.
(iv) Even if every element's output is r, it is a function, as every element of A is participating and has a unique image r.

ILLUSTRATION 20: Decide whether or not the following are functions from A to B; where $A = \{1, 2, 3, 4, 5\}$ and $B = \{a, b, c, d, e\}$. If they are functions give the range of each. If they are not, explain why?

(i) $f_1 = \{(1, a), (2, b), (3, b), (5, e)\}$
(ii) $f_2 = \{(1, e), (5, d), (3, a), (2, b), (1, d), (4, a)\}$
(iii) $f_3 = \{(5, a), (1, e), (4, b), (3, c), (2, d)\}$

SOLUTION: (i) Since the element $4 \in A$ is not associated to any element of B, therefore, f_1 is not a function from A to B.

(ii) The element $1 \in A$ is associated to two different elements e and d of B. Therefore, f_2 is not a function from A to B.

(iii) Each element of A is associated to a unique element of B. Therefore f_3 is a function from A to B.

The range of f_3 is the set of f_3 images of all elements of A. So range of f_3 is $f_3(A) = \{a, b, c, d, e\} = B$.

ILLUSTRATION 21: Let $A = \{1, 2, 4\}$ and $B = \{1, 3\}$. Let $R = \{(x, y) : x + y$ is an even number, $x \in A, y \in B\}$. Does R represent a function?

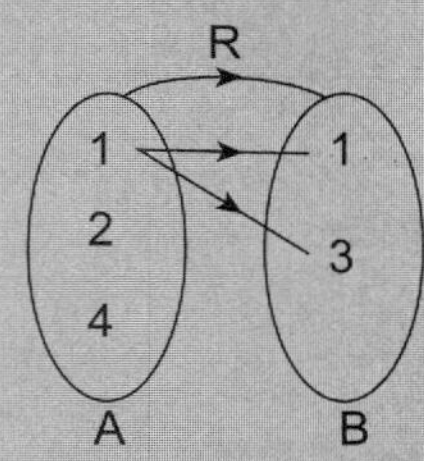

FIGURE 2.22

SOLUTION: We find all possible ordered pairs such that the sum of abscissa and ordinate is even $R = \{(1, 1), (1, 3)\}$

From the mapping it is clear that R is a relation but not a function.

ILLUSTRATION 22: If $A = \{2, 3, 4, 5\}$, then which of the following relations is a function from A to itself?

(a) $f_1 = \{(x, y) : y = x + 1\}$ (b $f_2 = \{(x, y) : x - y > 6\}$

(c) $f_3 = \{(x, y) : y < x\}$ (d) $f_4 = \{(x, y) : x - y = 7\}$

SOLUTION: Here, $f_1 = \{(2, 3), (3, 4), (4, 5)\}$

$f_2 = \{(2, 5), (3, 4), (3, 5), (4, 3), (4, 4), (4, 5), (5, 2), (5, 3), (5, 4), (5, 5)\}$

$f_3 = \{(3, 2), (4, 2), (4, 3), (5, 2), (5, 3), (5, 4)\}$

and $f_4 = \{(2, 5), (3, 4), (4, 3), (5, 2)\}$

Here, only f_4 is a function from A to itself.

Note that f_4 is a bijection.

$\left(\because D_{f_1} \neq A; f_2(3), f_2(4), f_2(5) \text{ are unique; } D_{f_3} \neq A\right)$.

Method 3: *When the relation to be tested is represented graphically*: relation $f : X \to Y$; $y = f(x)$ is function iff all the straight line $x = \alpha$; $\forall \alpha \in X$ intersect the graph of function exactly once as shown below.

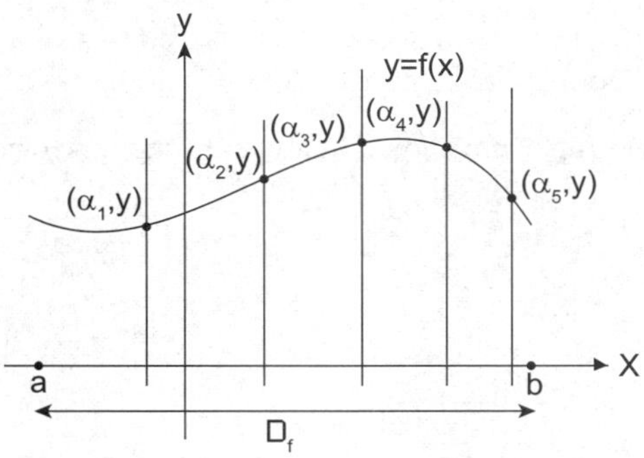

FIGURE 2.23

A relation $f : X \to Y$ will not be a function in the following two conditions.

1. If for some $\alpha \in X$, line $x = \alpha$ does not cut the curve $y = f(x)$. e.g., in the graph of function shown below the line $x = \alpha$ does not cut the graph of function and $\alpha \in X (D_f) = [a, b]$, i.e., no output for input $x = \alpha$.

$\Rightarrow f(x)$ is not a function from X to Y.

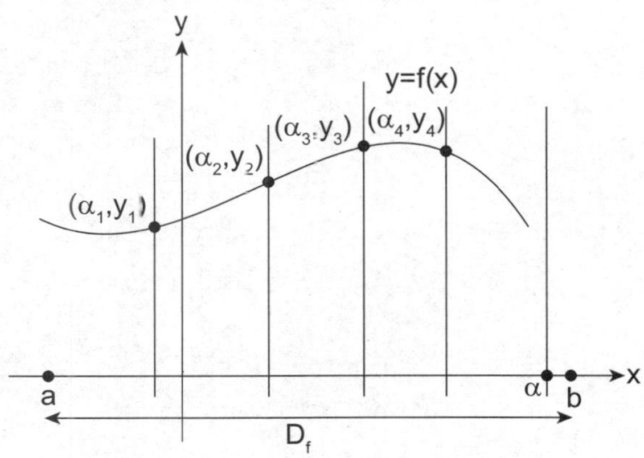

FIGURE 2.24

2. If for atleast one $\alpha \in X$, line $x = \alpha$ intersects $y = f(x)$ more than once, i.e., there exists an input having more than one output say at (α, y_1) , (α, y_2) and (α, y_3).

$\Rightarrow$ For input $x = \alpha$, $f(x)$ has three outputs y_1 , y_2 as well as y_3 as shown below

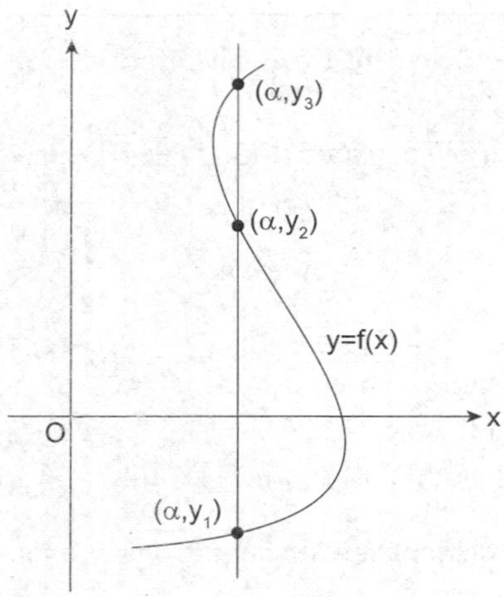

FIGURE 2.25

Hence, $f(x)$ is not function.

It is one–many relation and one–many relations are never functions.

Method 4: When the relation to be tested is represented diagrammatically: A relation $f: X \to Y$ is a function if no input has two or more outputs in Y and no $x \in X$ is un-related. e.g., define a relation from set X having fathers x_1, x_2 and x_3 to set Y having sons y_1 and y_3 and a daughter y_2. Let it be represented diagrammatically as shown.

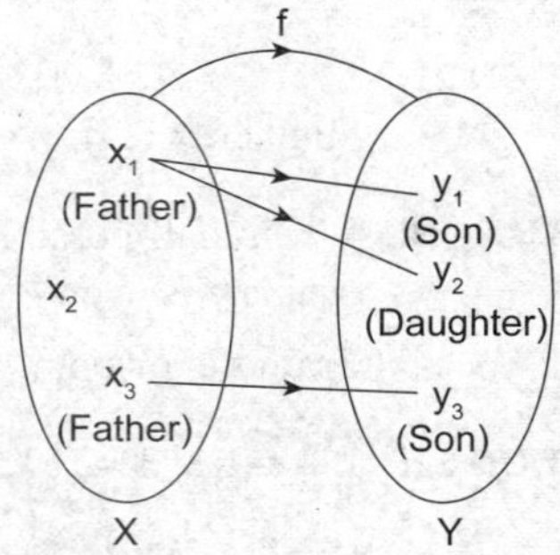

FIGURE 2.26

Because father x_1 has son y_1 and daughter y_2 i.e., input x_1 has two images i.e., f is one–many relation, and hence, not a function from set X to set Y. Moreover, x_2 has no child i.e., x_2 has no image under f, and hence, also from this point of view, f is not a function.

ILLUSTRATION 23: Check whether following sets of ordered pairs are functions or not?

(a) $\{(x, y): x$ is a person and y is an ancestor of $x\}$

(b) $\{(x, y): x$ is a person and y is the father of $x\}$

SOLUTION: (a) Because each person on this earth has more than one ancestor, therefore the given relation is one–many and hence, is not a function.

(b) The set of ordered pairs is $\{(x_1, y_1), (x_2, y_2), (x_3, y_3), ...\}$. Because each person has only one father, therefore the relation would not contain any two ordered pairs having same first element, therefore the given relation is not one–many but it can be many–one as two different persons may have same father and hence, the given relation is a function.

ILLUSTRATION 24: Check whether the following relations whose graphs are shown below are functions or not?

(a)

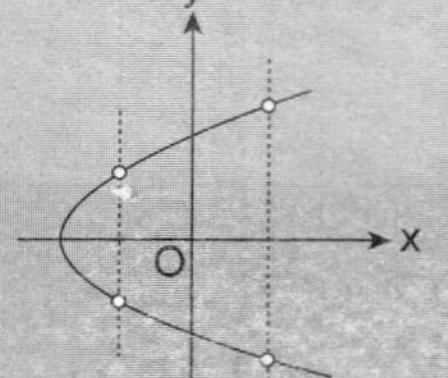

(b)

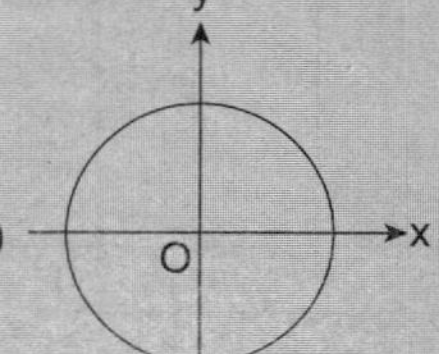

(c)

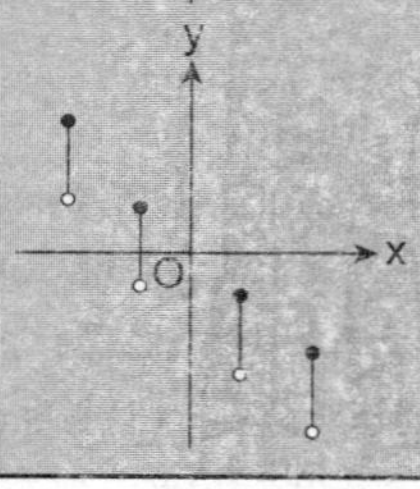

(d)

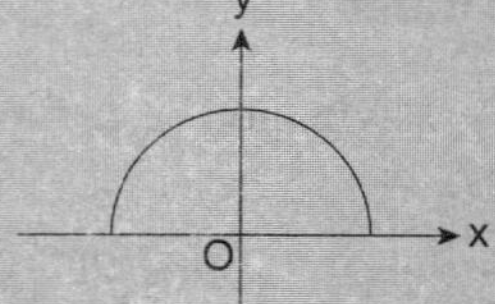

(e) 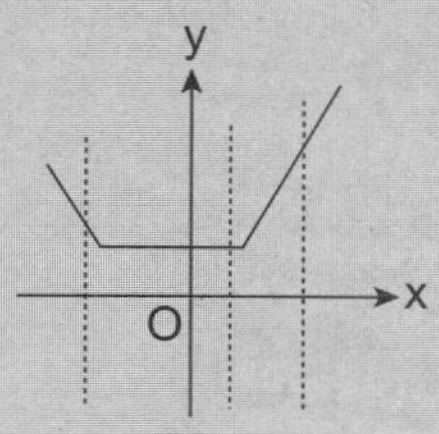

(f) 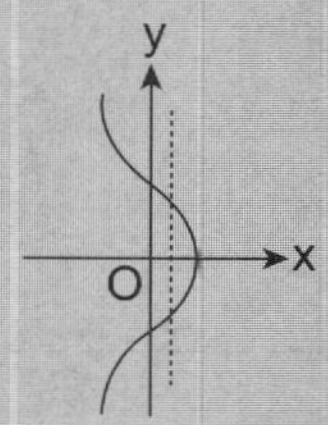

SOLUTION: For (d) and (e)

In the given domain each line drawn parallel to y-axis intersects the graph only at a single point and hence, the corresponding relations are functions in their domains.

For (a), (b), (c) and (f)

There exist lines parallel to y-axis intersecting the corresponding graphs in more than one point, and hence, the corresponding relations are not functions.

ILLUSTRATION 25: Let $A = \{x : 1 \leq x \leq 5\}$ and $B = \{y : 1 \leq y \leq 4\}$. Define $\phi = \{(x, y) : y \geq x + 1, x \in A, y \in B\}$. Plot ϕ on the $x - y$ plane and determine whether it represent a function?

SOLUTION: Here $A = \{x : 1 \leq x \leq 5\}$ and $B = \{y : 1 \leq y \leq 4\}$; $\phi = \{(x, y) : y \geq x + 1, x \in A$ and $y \in B\}$

Clearly $\phi \subseteq A \times B = [1, 5] \times [1, 4]$, i.e., the graph is entirely contained in the rectangular region R bounded by straight lines $x = 1$, $x = 5$ and $y = 1$, $y = 4$

To obtain ϕ, first of all draw the straight line $y = x + 1$ with in the above defined bounded region R shown below

Now the region above and on the line segment EF of straight line $y = x + 1$ and within the rectangle represents the region ϕ defined in the given problem. This region is shown in above diagram by shaded portion.

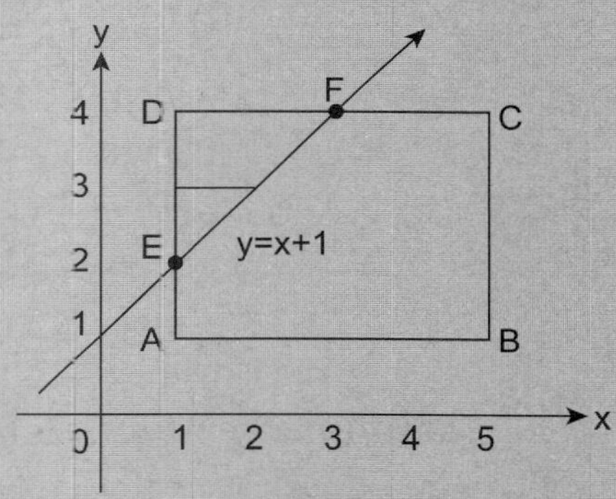

FIGURE 2.27

Clearly the above region is one–many relation.

ILLUSTRATION 26: Which of the following is not the graph of a function on set $A = [a, b]$?

(a) 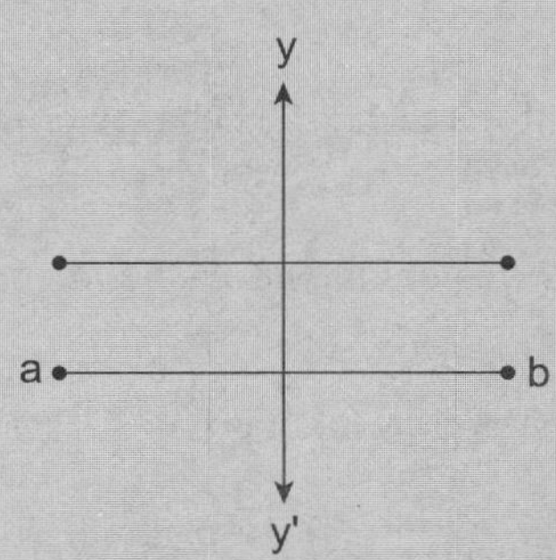

(b) 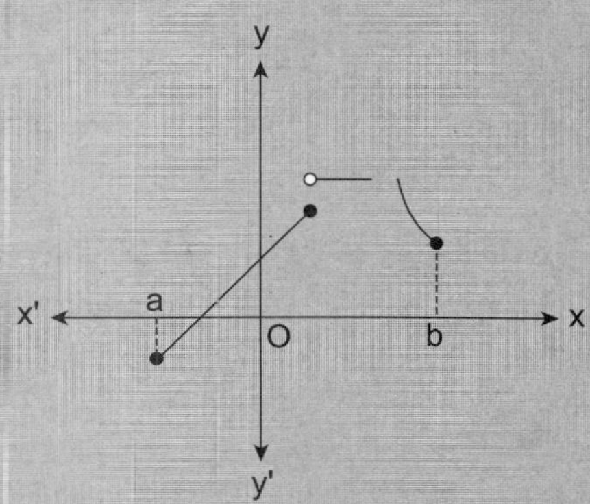

(c) 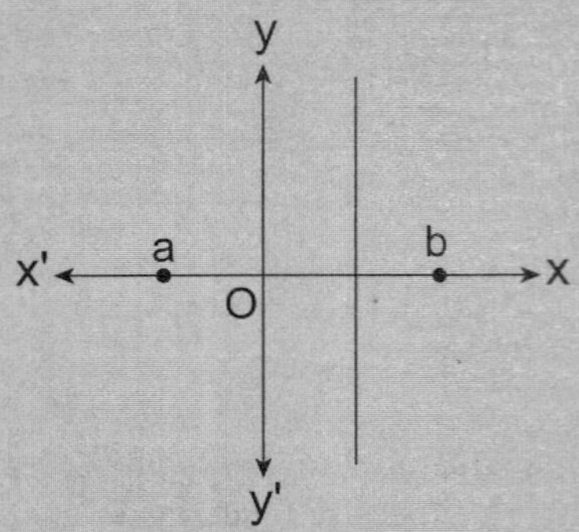

(d) 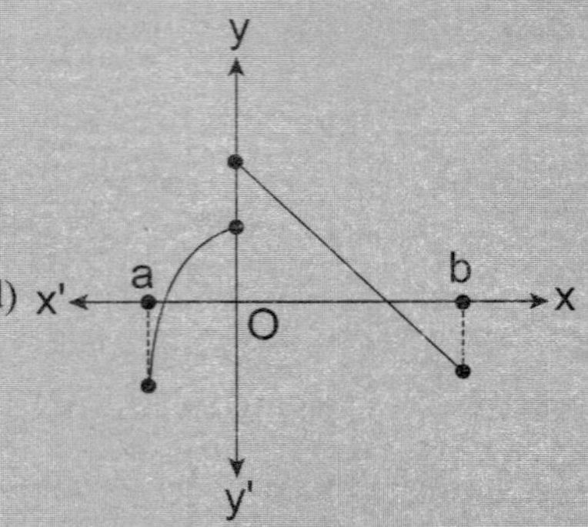

SOLUTION: No vertical line in the domain can meet the graph of a function in more than one point. In (c), the curve shown is a vertical line and in (d), y-axis is meeting the graph in two distinct points. In graph (b) there are some points in $[a, b]$ having no image under f, however except for those points graph represents the function on the remaining interval of $[a, b]$. In graph (a) each element of domain $[a, b]$ has a unique image. Thus, the relation shown in Figure (a) is a function.

ILLUSTRATION 27: Check whether the following functions expressed in analytical form are functions or not?

(i) $f_1 : [2, 7] \to \mathbb{R}$ defined by $f_1(x) = \dfrac{(x-1)}{(x-3)}$

(ii) $f_2 : [-5, 5] \to \mathbb{R}$ defined by $f_2(x) = \sqrt{x-2}$

(iii) $f_3 : [0, \infty) \to \mathbb{R}$ defined by $[f_3(x)]^2 = x$

(iv) $f_4 : [0, \infty) \to \mathbb{R}$ defined by $f_4(x) = \sqrt{x}$.

(v) $f_5 : \mathbb{R} \to \mathbb{R}$ defined by $f_5(x) = |x - 4|$.

(vi) $f_6 : \mathbb{R} \to \mathbb{R}$ defined by $f_6(x) = \sin^2 x$.

SOLUTION: (i) $\because$ $f_1(3)$ is not defined

$\therefore$ f_1 is not a function from $[2, 7]$ to $\mathbb{R}$; however, f_1 is a function from $[2, 7] \sim \{3\}$ to $\mathbb{R}$

(ii) $f_2(x)$ is real for $x - 2 \geq 0$

$\Rightarrow x \geq 2$

$\therefore$ $f_2(x)$ is not defined from $[-5, 5]$ to $\mathbb{R}$; however, $f_2(x)$ is a function from $[2, \infty)$ to $\mathbb{R}$

(iii) $[f_3(x)]^2 = x$

$\Rightarrow f_3(x) = \pm \sqrt{x}$

$\therefore$ for each $x \in [0, \infty)$, $f_3(x)$ is real but for each x, $f_3(x)$ has two images, therefore $f_3(x)$ is not a function.

(iv) $f_4(x) = \sqrt{x} \in \mathbb{R}\ \forall x \in [0, \infty)$ and $f_4(x)$ is unique for each $x \in [0, \infty)$

$\therefore$ $f_4(x)$ is a function from $[0, \infty) \to \mathbb{R}$.

(v) $f_5 : \mathbb{R} \to \mathbb{R}$ defined by $f_5(x) = |x - 4|$ is a function as $f_5(x)$ is real and unique for each $x \in \mathbb{R}$

(vi) $f_6(x) = \sin^2 x \in \mathbb{R}$ and is unique for each $x \in \mathbb{R}$

$\Rightarrow f_6(x)$ is a function from $\mathbb{R}$ to $\mathbb{R}$

TEXTUAL EXERCISE–2: (SUBJECTIVE)

1. Represent all possible functions defined from {α, β} to {1, 2} in the form of ordered pairs.

2. Find the explicit form of the following functions (or relations):
   (a) $\log_5 x + \log_5 (y + 2) = 8$
   (b) $3^{x+y} (x^2 - 3) = x^3 - 27$
   (c) $y^2 = 8x - 4y$. Also find their domain.

3. Consider the functions defined by the following equations. In each case obtain y as an explicit function of x, and state for what values of x it is defined.
   (a) $y^2 - 2y - x^2 = 0, y \geq 1$
   (b) $y^2 - 2y + x^2 = 0, y \leq 1$

4. Give three examples of algebraic functions which cannot be expressed in explicit form.

5. Test which of the following relations are functions (and also identify whether they are injective or not.) on their respective domain?
   (a) $y^{2/3} = 3x + 4$ (b) $y = 2x^2 + 1$
   (c) $y^2 = 2 \tan x + 5$ (d) $y = \sqrt{3x+2}$
   (e) $y^3 = 2x^2 - 1$ (f) $y = \dfrac{x-1}{x+1}$
   (g) $y^2 = 4x - 3$ (h) $y = ax^2 + bx + c$
   (i) $y^3 = 3x + 1$

6. Which of the following represent functions?
   (i) $y = \sqrt{x}$
   (ii) $x^2 + 2y^2 = 8$
   (iii) $x^2 + y^2 = 4, y \geq 0$
   (iv) $x^2 + y^2 = 4, x \geq 0$
   (v) $y = \begin{cases} 2x+5; & x \geq 0 \\ \dfrac{-x^2}{4}; & x < 0 \end{cases}$
   (vi) $y^3 = x$
   (vii) $y^4 = 2x$

7. (a) The relation $f : \mathbb{R} \to \mathbb{R}$ be defined by $f(x) = \begin{cases} 2x+1\ ; & x \leq 4 \\ x+4\ ; & x > 4 \end{cases}$
   (b) The relation h is defined by $h(x) = \begin{cases} x^2; & 0 \leq x \leq 3 \\ 3x; & 3 \leq x \leq 10 \end{cases}$
   (c) The relation g is defined by $g(x) = \begin{cases} x^2; & 0 \leq x \leq 2 \\ 3x; & 2 \leq x \leq 10 \end{cases}$

   Show that f and h are functions and g is not a function.

8. Give an analytical formula for the function $f(x)$ equal to length of the path from A to B and from B to C for $0 \leq x \leq 4$ as represented by the following Figure 2.28.

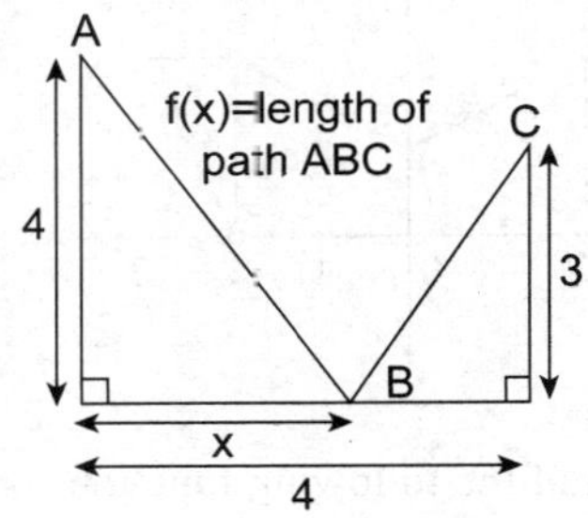

FIGURE 2.28

9. Let $A = \{x : 0 \leq x \leq 4\}$ and $B = \{y : 1 \leq y \leq 3\}$. Define $\phi = \{(x, y) : y \geq x, x \in A, y \in B\}$.
   Plot ϕ on the $x - y$ plane and determine whether it represents a function?

10. Draw the graph of the following functions:
    (i) $f(x) = \begin{cases} x^2 + 4 & \text{if } |x| > 0 \\ 3 & \text{if } x = 0 \end{cases}$
    (ii) $g(x) = \begin{cases} x^2 + 2 & \text{if } x \geq 0 \\ -x - 2 & \text{if } x < 0 \end{cases}$

11. Draw the graph of the following functions:
    (i) $f(x) = \begin{cases} 2x+2 & \text{if } x < -1 \\ x^2 - 1 & \text{if } -1 \leq x \leq 1 \\ 2x - 3 & \text{if } x > 1 \end{cases}$
    (ii) $f(x) = \begin{cases} x^2 - 1 & \text{if } x \leq -1 \\ 4x^3 & \text{if } -1 \leq x \leq 1 \\ 5 - x^2 & \text{if } 1 \leq x \leq 2 \end{cases}$

12. Define the following functions analytically:
    (a)

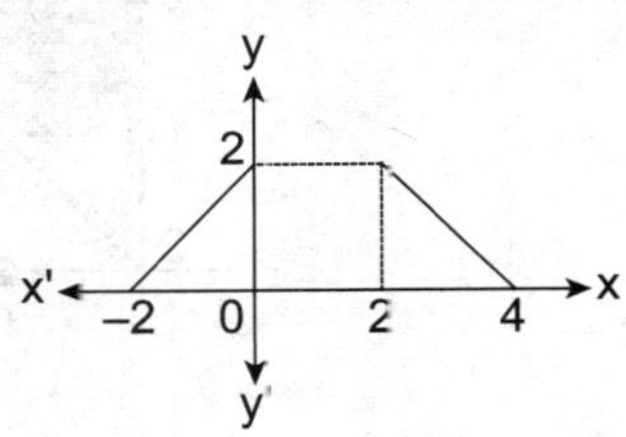

(b)

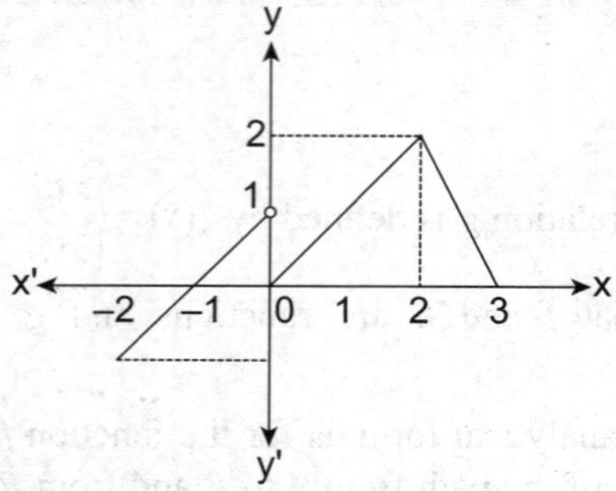

(c)

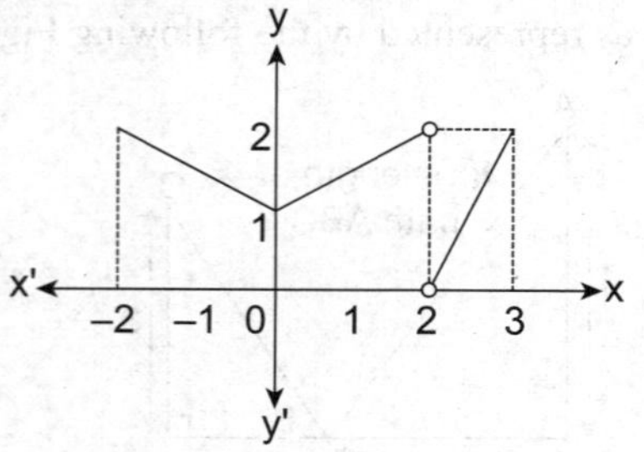

13. For which of the following functions is $f(a + b)$ equal to $f(a) + f(b)$ for all positive numbers a and b?

(a) $f(x) = x^2$ (b) $f(x) = 5x$
(c) $f(x) = -6x$ (d) $f(x) = \sqrt{x}$
(e) $f(x) = 3x + 1$ (f) $f(x) = \log x$

14. For which of the following functions is $f(ab)$ equal to $f(a)\, f(b)$ for all positive numbers a and b?

(a) $f(x) = 8x$ (b) $f(x) = x^5$
(c) $f(x) = 1/x^3$ (d) $f(x) = \sqrt{x}$
(e) $f(x) = x + 2$

15. Let f have as its domain the set of all integers. Assume that $f(x + y) = f(x) + f(y)$ for all integers x and y, and $f(1) = 3$.

(a) Show that $f(2) = 6$
(b) Show that $f(0) = 0$
(c) What can you say about $f(-1)$?
(d) Find a possible formula for f

16. Let f be the subset of $\mathbb{Z} \times \mathbb{Z}$ defined by $f = \{(ab, a + b) : a, b \in \mathbb{Z}\}$. Is f a function from $\mathbb{Z}$ to $\mathbb{Z}$? Justify your answer.

Answer Keys

1. $f_1 = \{(\alpha, 1), (\beta, 1)\}$; $f_2 = \{(\alpha, 2), (\beta, 2)\}$; $f_3 = \{(\alpha, 1), (\beta, 2)\}$; $f_4 = \{(\alpha, 2), (\beta, 1)\}$

2. (a) $y = \dfrac{(5)^8}{x} - 2$; Domain = $(0, \infty)$ (b) $y = \log_3\left(\dfrac{x^3 - 27}{x^2 - 3}\right) - x$; Domain = $(-\sqrt{3}, \sqrt{3}) \cup (3, \infty)$

(c) $y = -2 \pm \sqrt{8x + 4}$; Domain = $\left[-\dfrac{1}{2}, \infty\right)$. It represents a relation that is a combination of two functions.

3. (a) $y = 1 + \sqrt{x^2 + 1}$; $x \in \mathbb{R}$ (b) $y = 1 - \sqrt{1 - x^2}$; $x \in [-1, 1]$

4. $y^5 - y - x = 0$; $y^3 + y + 2x = 0$; $y^2 + y \sin x + 2x = 0$.

5. b, d, e, f, h, i (functions) ; d and f, i are injective.

6. (i), (iii), (v), (vi) **8.** $f(x) = \sqrt{x^2 - 8x + 25} + \sqrt{x^2 + 16}$

9. The shaded region represents ϕ. Clearly ϕ is not a function, in fact ϕ is a many–many relation.

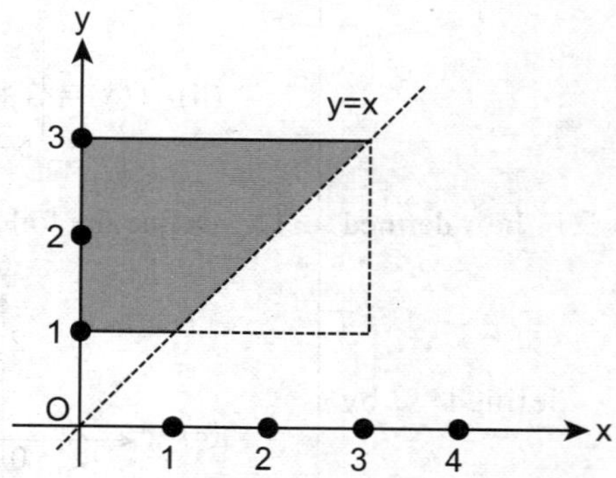

FIGURE 2.29

10. (i) 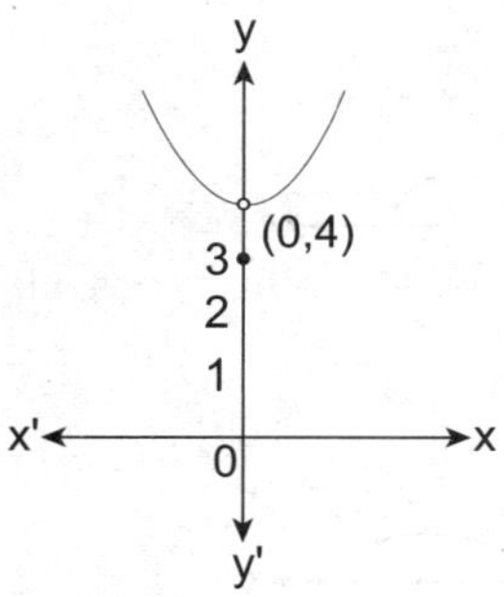

(ii) 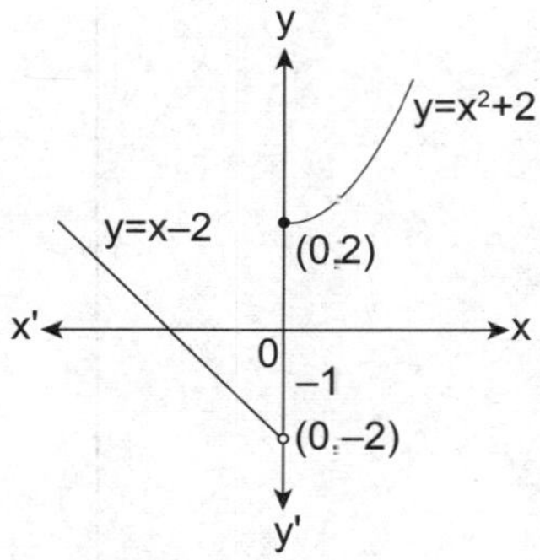

11. (i) 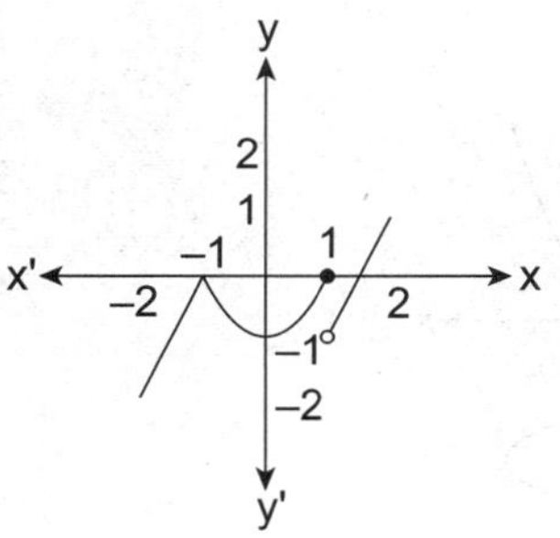

(ii) 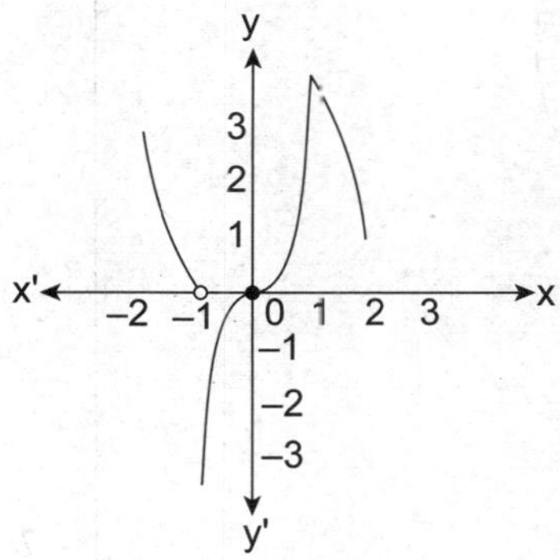

12. (a) $\begin{cases} x+2; & -2 \le x < 0 \\ 2; & 0 \le x \le 2 \\ 4-x; & 2 < x \le 4 \end{cases}$ (b) $\begin{cases} x+1; & -2 \le x < 0 \\ x; & 0 \le x \le 2 \\ 6-2x; & 2 < x \le 3 \end{cases}$ (c) $\begin{cases} 1-\dfrac{x}{2}; & -2 \le x < 0 \\ 1+\dfrac{x}{2}; & 0 \le x < 2 \\ 2x-4; & 2 < x \le 3 \end{cases}$

13. (b) and (c) 14. (b), (c) and (d) 16. No

TEXTUAL EXERCISE–2: (OBJECTIVE)

1. Which of the following relations are function from set X to Y; where $X = \{1, 3, 5, 7\}$ and set $Y = \{2, 4, 6, 8\}$?
   (a) $\{(3, 2), (3, 4), (5, 4), (7, 4), (1, 8)\}$
   (b) $\{(1, 2), (5, 8), (3, 6)\}$
   (c) $\{(1,4), (3, 8), (5, 2), (7, 6)\}$
   (d) $\{(1,4), (3,4), (5, 8), (7, 8)\}$

2. Which of the following is/are function(s) from set $\mathbb{N}$ to set W (set of whole numbers)?
   (a) $f = \{(x, y) : y = x + 2$
   (b) $f = \{(x, y) : y = x - 4\}$
   (c) $f = \{(x, y) : y^2 = x + 2; x, y \in \mathbb{N}\}$
   (d) $f = \{(x, y) : |y| = x - 1; y \in \mathbb{R}$

3. Which of the following correspondences can be called a function?
   (a) $f: \{-2, 0, 2\} \to \{0, 1, 8, 3\}; f(x) = x^3$
   (b) $f: \{0, 1, 4\} \to \{-2, -1, 0, 1, 2\}; f(x) = \pm\sqrt{x}$
   (c) $f: \{0, 1, 9\} \to \{-3, -1, 0, 1, 3\}; f(x) = \sqrt{x}$
   (d) $f: \{0, 1, 9\} \to \{-3, -1, 0, 1, 3\}; f(x) = -\sqrt{x}$

4. Which of the following are functions?
   (a) $f = \{(x, y) : y = x + 3, x \in \mathbb{N}, y \in W\}$
   (b) $f = \{(x, y) : y = x - 1, x \in \mathbb{N}, y \in W\}$
   (c) $f = \{(x, y) : y^2 = x + 1, x \in \mathbb{N}, y \in W\}$
   (d) None of these

5. Identify which of the following relations is/are function(s) from $X \to Y$?

(a) 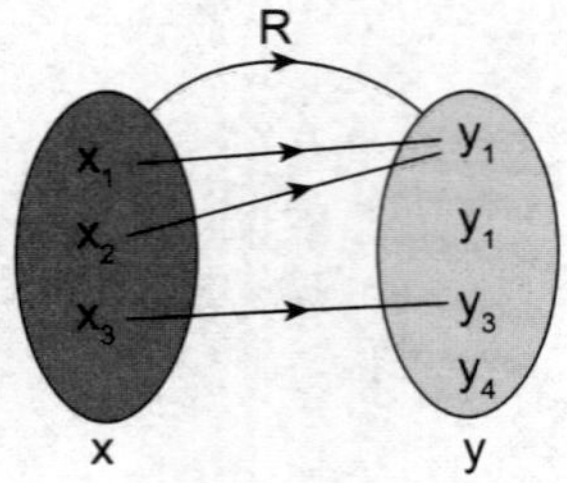

(b) 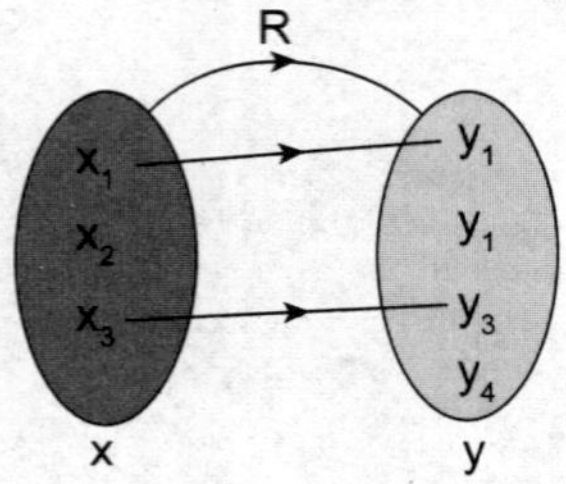

(c) 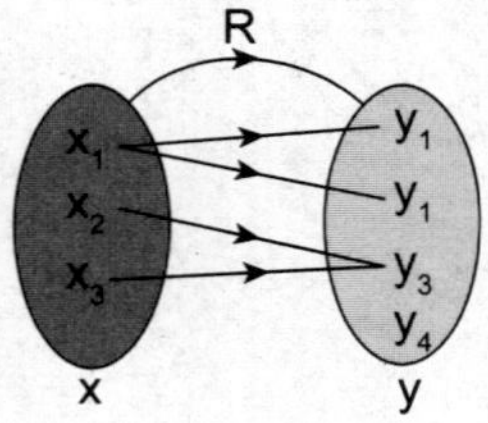

(d) 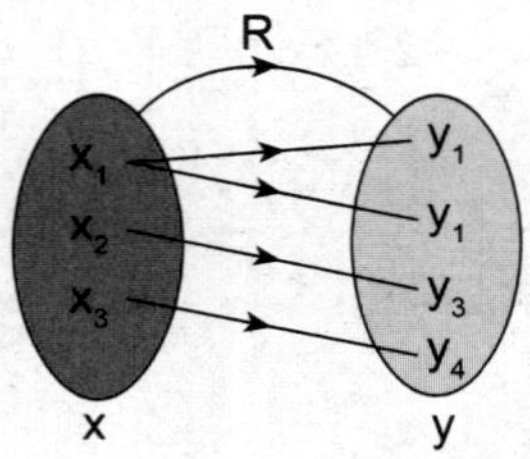

6. Which of the following graphs is/are function?

(a) 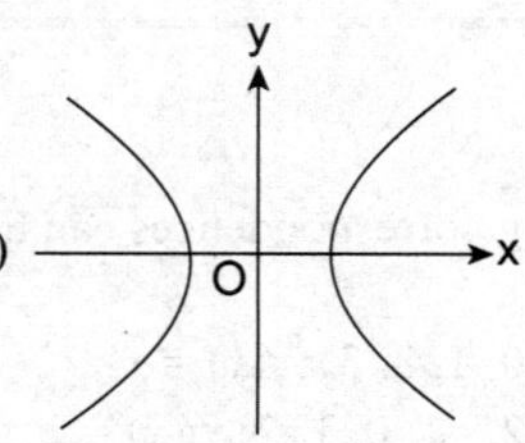

(b) 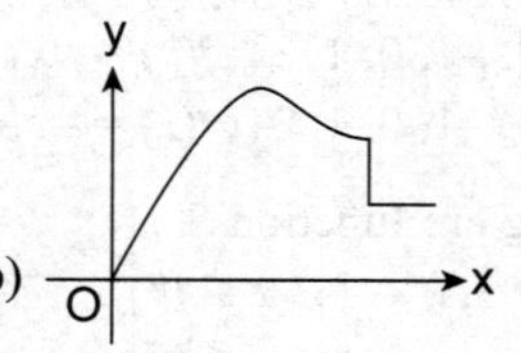

(c) 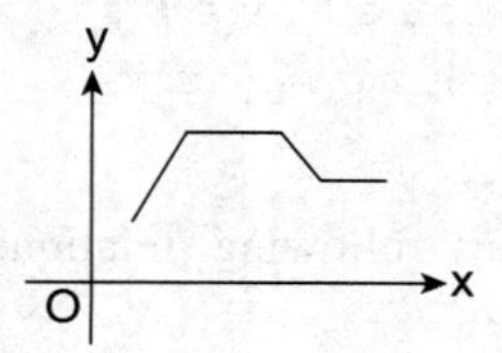

(d) 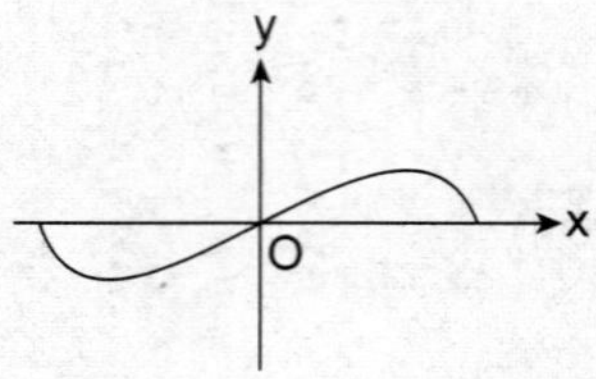

(e) 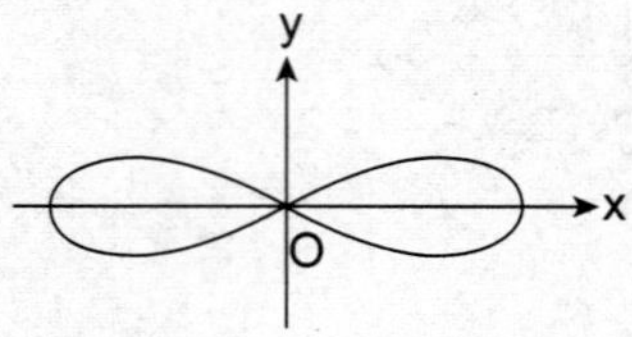

(f) 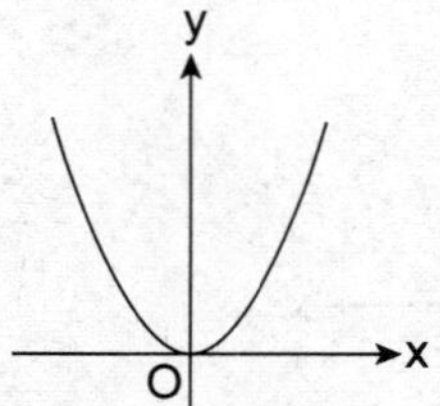

(g) 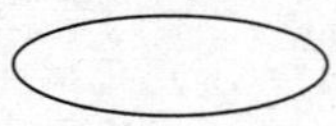

7. Which one of the following graphs represents the function $y = 1 + |x|$ for all $x \in \mathbb{R}$.

(a) 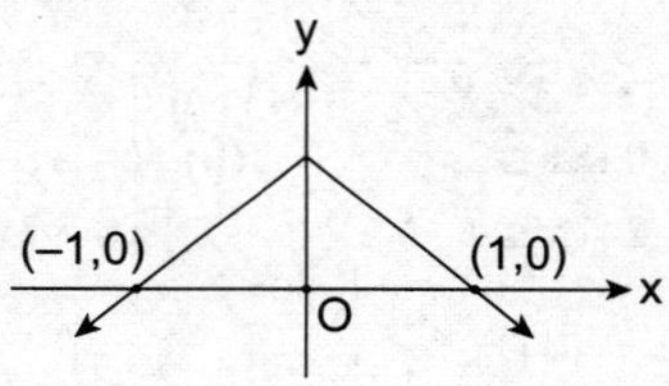

(b) 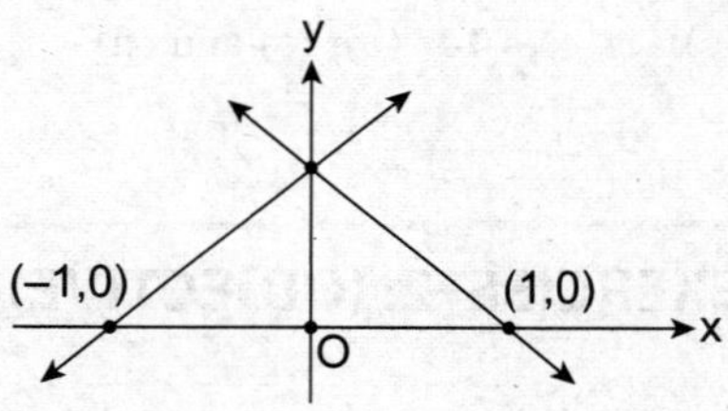

(c) 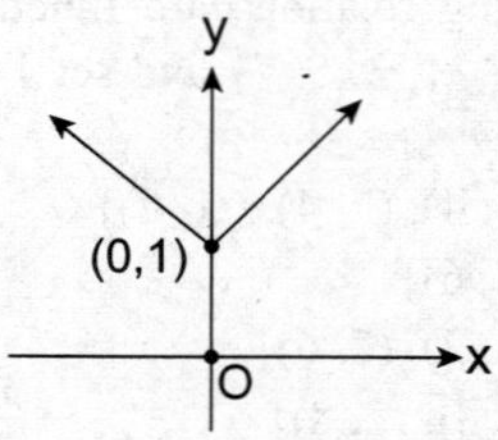

(d) 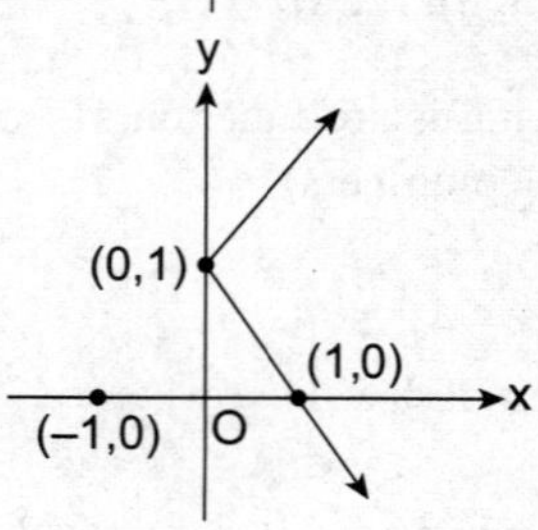

8. The graph of a relation $f(x)$ is as shown below

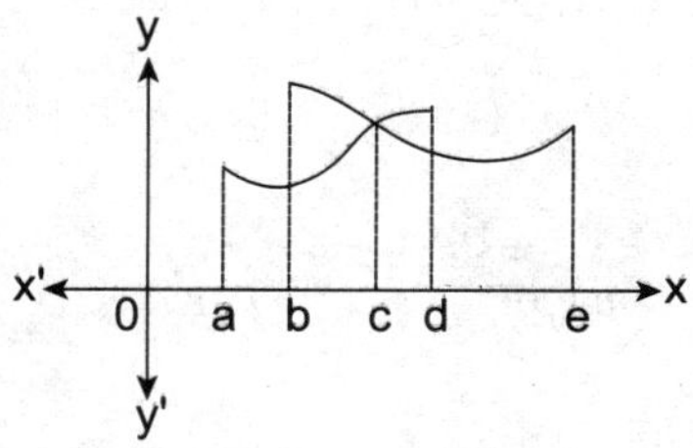

FIGURE 2.30

The domain in which the given relation represents a function is

(a) $[a, c] \cup [d, e]$ (b) $[a, b] \cup [d, e]$
(c) $[a, b) \cup (d, e]$ (d) $(a, b) \cup (d, e)$

9. The graph of a relation $f(x)$ is as shown below

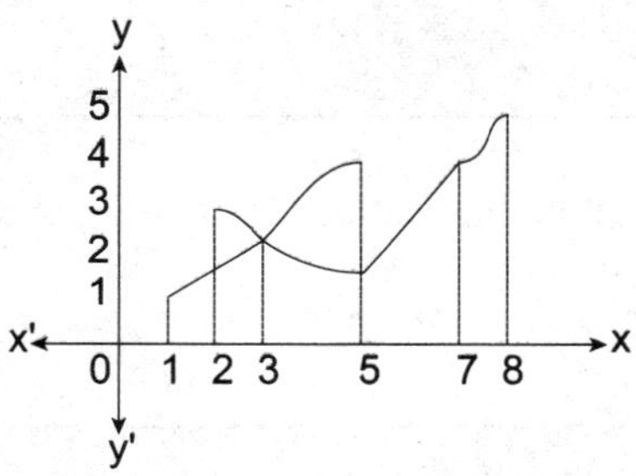

FIGURE 2.31

The domain corresponding to which the given relation represents a function with co-domain $[0.5, 3] \cup [4, 6]$ is

(a) $[1, 2) \cup (5, 8]$ (b) $[1, 2) \cup [7, 8]$
(c) $[1, 2) \cup [5, 8]$ (d) None of these

10. Which of the following equations represent a function?

(a) $|x| + |y| = 2$ (b) $|x + y| = 4$
(c) $|y| = x^2 + \sin x$ (d) $y = |x|^2 - x$

11. A is a point on the circumference of a circle. AB and AC divide the area of the circle into three equal parts. Let $\angle BAC = \alpha$, then which is/are correct?

(a) α satisfies the function $f(x) = c.\ (x + \sin x - \pi/3) = 0$

(b) α satisfies the function $f(x) = \left(x + \sin x - \frac{\pi}{3}\right)^n$ $n \in \mathbb{N}$

(c) $\alpha + \sin\alpha = \frac{\pi}{3}$

(d) None of these

12. Consider the function $f: \mathbb{R} - \{0\} \to \mathbb{R}$, defined by $f(x) = \frac{1}{x}$. Which of the following statements are always true?

(a) $f\left(\frac{a^n}{b^n}\right) = \frac{f(a^n)}{f(b^n)}$; $n \in \mathbb{N}$

(b) $f(a^n + b^n) = f(a^n) + f(b^n)$; $n \in \mathbb{N}$

(c) $f(a^n) = (f(a))^n$; $n \in \mathbb{N}$

(d) $f(a^n).f\left(\frac{1}{a^n}\right) = 1$; $n \in \mathbb{N}$

Answer Keys

1. (c,d) **2.** (a) **3.** (c, d) **4.** (a, b) **5.** (a) **6.** (c, d, f) **7.** (c) **8.** (c,d) **9.** (b)
10. (d) **11.** (a,b,c)
12. (i) True (ii) False (iii) True (d) True

■ MATHEMATICAL TOOLS USED TO FIND THE DOMAIN AND RANGE OF FUNCTIONS

Laws of Inequality

R(1): Adding same real number to both sides does not alter the nature of inequality.
i.e., $a > b \Rightarrow a + x > b + x\ \forall\ x \in \mathbb{R}$ and $a < b$
$\Rightarrow \quad a + x < b + x\ \forall\ x \in \mathbb{R}$

R(2): Transition property: $a > b$ and $b > c$ $\Rightarrow a > c$.

R(3): Multiplying by a real number k to both sides of inequality has the following effects on the nature of inequality $a > b \Rightarrow \begin{cases} ak > bk & \text{if } k > 0 \\ ak = bk & \text{if } k = 0, \\ ak < bk & \text{if } k < 0 \end{cases}$

ILLUSTRATION 28: If x is a variable described as below, then find the range of variation of $(2x + 3)$.

(i) $x \in [2, 6]$ (ii) $x \in (-3, -1)$.

SOLUTION: (i) $x \in [2, 6]$

$\Rightarrow 2 \le x \le 6$ $\Rightarrow 4 \le 2x \le 12$

$\Rightarrow 4 + 3 \le 2x + 3 \le 15$ $\Rightarrow$ Range of $2x + 3 = [7, 15]$.

(ii) $x \in (-3, -1)$ $\Rightarrow -3 < x < -1$

$\Rightarrow -6 < 2x < -2$ $\Rightarrow -6 + 3 < 2x + 3 < -2 + 3$

$\Rightarrow$ Range of $2x + 3 = (-3, 1)$.

ILLUSTRATION 29: If x is a variable described as below, then find the range of variation of $(4 - 3x)$.

(i) $x \in [3, 5]$ (ii) $x \in (-2, 3)$.

SOLUTION: (i) $x \in [3, 5]$

$\Rightarrow 3 \le x \le 5$ $\Rightarrow -9 \ge -3x \ge -15$

$\Rightarrow -9 + 4 \ge 4 - 3x \ge 4 - 15$ $\Rightarrow$ Range of $4 - 3x = [-11, -5]$.

(ii) $x \in (-2, 3)$ $\Rightarrow -2 < x < 3$

$\Rightarrow 6 > -3x > -9$ $\Rightarrow 6 + 4 > 4 - 3x > 4 - 9$

$\therefore$ Range of $(4 - 3x) = (-5, 10)$.

R(4): Law of addition: If $a_1 > b_1; a_2 > b_2; \ldots ; a_n > b_n; n \in \mathbb{N}$

$\Rightarrow (a_1 + a_2 + a_3 + \ldots.. + a_n) > (b_1 + b_2 + b_3 + \ldots. + b_n)$

R(5): Law of multiplication: If $a_1 > b_1 > 0 \ldots.; a_2 > b_2 > 0 \ldots\ldots ; a_n > b_n > 0; n \in \mathbb{N}$

$\Rightarrow (a_1.a_2.a_3. \ldots.. . a_n) > (b_1 . b_2 . b_3 \ldots\ldots b_n)$

ILLUSTRATION 30: If $x - 3 > 2 + 6x$; $y + 6 > 5 - 12x$. Then prove that $2x + y > 9$.

SOLUTION: If $x - 3 > 2 + 6x$; ... (i)

$y + 6 > 5 - 12x$ ... (ii)

from (i) $2x - 6 > 4 + 12x$ .... (iii)

(ii) + (iii) gives $2x + y > 9$, hence, proved.

ILLUSTRATION 31: If given that $x_k \ge k \; \forall \; k \in \mathbb{N}$; then show that

(i) $x_1 + x_2 + x_3 + \ldots + x_n \ge \dfrac{n(n+1)}{2}$

(ii) $x_1 . x_2 . x_3 . \ldots x_n \ge n!$

(iii) $x_1 + 2x_2 + 3x_3 + \ldots + nx_n \ge \dfrac{n(n+1)(2n+1)}{6}$

SOLUTION: (i) $x_1 \ge 1; x_2 \ge 2; x_3 \ge 3\ldots.. ; x_n \ge n$, adding above inequalities, we get

$$x_1 + x_2 + x_3 + \ldots. + x_n \ge 1 + 2 + 3 + \ldots. + n = n\left(\frac{n+1}{2}\right)$$

$$\therefore \quad x_1 + x_2 + x_3 + \ldots. + x_n \ge \frac{n(n+1)}{2}$$

(ii) $x_1 \ge 1; x_2 \ge 2; x_3 \ge 3 \ldots.. x_n \ge n$; multiplying the above inequalities, we get

$x_1 . x_2 . x_3 . \ldots.. . x_n \ge 1.2.3 \ldots.. n = n!$ $\Rightarrow x_1 .x_2 .x_3 \ldots.. .x_n \ge n!$

(iii) $x_1 \ge 1; x_2 \ge 2; x_3 \ge 3 \ldots.. x_n \ge n$;

$\Rightarrow x_1 \ge 1; 2x_2 \ge 2^2 ; 3x_3 \ge 3^2; \ldots.. nx_n \ge n^2$. Adding above inequalities, we get

$$\Rightarrow x_1 + 2x_2 + 3x_3 + ... + nx_n \geq 1^2 + 2^2 + 3^2 + ... + n^2 = \frac{n(n+1)(2n+1)}{6}$$

$$\Rightarrow x_1 + 2x_2 + 3x_3 + ... + nx_n \geq \frac{n(n+1)(2n+1)}{6}$$

ILLUSTRATION 32: Given two inequalities $x + 1 > 3 > 5 - 2x$ and $x + 1 > 5 - 2x$. Solve them separately for x and what conclusion you can draw regarding transition property of inequality?

SOLUTION: If $x + 1 > 3$ and $3 > 5 - 2x$; $x + 1 > 5 - 2x$ $\Rightarrow$ $x > 2$ and $2x > 2$; $3x > 4$

$\Rightarrow x > 2$ and $x > 1$; $x > 4/3$ $\Rightarrow x \in (2, \infty)$; $x \in (4/3, \infty)$

Conclusion: if $a > b$ and $b > c$ $\Rightarrow$ $a > c$, but the converse is not true

That is, for any three real numbers a, b, c if $a > c$, then it is not necessary that $c < b < a$.

R(6): Law of square/square root:

(a) $a > b$

$$\Rightarrow \begin{cases} a^2 > b^2 \ ; & \text{if both } a \ \& \ b \text{ are non-negative} \\ a^2 = b^2 \ ; & \text{if } |a| = |b| \\ a^2 < b^2 \ ; & \text{if } a \ \& \ b \text{ are both negative} \end{cases}$$

(b) If a and b have opposite signs and $a > b$, i.e., $a > 0$

and $b < 0$, then $\begin{cases} a^2 > b^2 \text{ iff } |a| > |b| \\ a^2 = b^2 \text{ iff } |a| = |b| \\ a^2 < b^2 \text{ iff } |a| < |b| \end{cases}$

This law can be extended for any even natural power ($2n$).

(c) If a and b both are non-negative and

$$a > b \Rightarrow \begin{cases} \sqrt{a} > \sqrt{b} \\ \sqrt[2n]{a} > \sqrt[2n]{b} \end{cases}$$

ILLUSTRATION 33: If x is a variable described as below, then find the range of variation of x^2.

(i) $x \in [2, 6]$ (ii) $x \in (-3, -1)$.

SOLUTION: (i) $x^2 \in [4, 36]$ (ii) $x^2 \in (1, 9)$

Conclusion

If x is a variable such that $a \leq x \leq b$, then to find range of variation of x^2:

Case I: If a and b are non-negative

$\Rightarrow a^2 \leq x^2 \leq b^2$ $\Rightarrow x^2 \in [a^2, b^2]$

Case II: If a and b are non-positive

$\Rightarrow a \leq x \leq b$

$\Rightarrow b^2 \leq x^2 \leq a^2$ $\Rightarrow x^2 \in [b^2, a^2]$

Case III: If $a < 0$ and $b > 0$

$\because a \leq x \leq b$

$\Rightarrow a \leq x \leq 0$ or $0 \leq x \leq b$

$\Rightarrow a^2 \geq x^2 \geq 0$ or $0 \leq x^2 \leq b^2$

$\Rightarrow x^2 \in [0, a^2] \cup [0, b^2]$

$$\Rightarrow \begin{cases} x^2 \in [0, a^2] & \text{if } |a| > |b| \\ x^2 \in [0, b^2] & \text{if } |b| > |a| \end{cases}$$

$\Rightarrow x^2 \in [0, \max\{a^2, b^2\}]$

ILLUSTRATION 34: If x is a variable described as below, then find the range of variation of x^2.

(i) $x \in [2, 6]$ (ii) $x \in (-3, -1)$

(iii) $x \in [-2,6]$ (iv) $x \in (-4, 2)$

SOLTUION: (i) $x^2 \in [4, 36]$ (ii) $x^2 \in (1, 9)$

(iii) $x^2 \in [0, 36]$ (iv) $x^2 \in [0, 16)$

R(7): Law of cube/cube root: $a > b \Rightarrow a^3 > b^3$ and $a^{1/3} > b^{1/3}\ \forall\ a, b \in \mathbb{R}$

$a < b \Rightarrow a^3 < b^3$ and $a^{1/3} < b^{1/3}\ \forall\ a, b \in \mathbb{R}$

This law can be extended for any odd natural power $(2n + 1)$ and odd root.

That is, $a > b \Leftrightarrow a^{2n+1} > b^{2n+1}$ and $a^{1/2n+1} > b^{1/2n+1}\ \forall\ a, b \in \mathbb{R}$

ILLUSTRATION 35: If x is a variable described as below, then find the range of variation of x^3.

(i) $x \in [1, 3]$ (ii) $x \in (-3, 2)$

SOLUTION: (i) $x^3 \in [1, 27]$

(ii) $x^3 \in (-27, 8)$

R(8): Law of reciprocal: Given two real numbers a and b such that $a > b$

$$\Rightarrow \begin{cases} \dfrac{1}{a} < \dfrac{1}{b} \text{ iff } a \text{ and } b \text{ have same sign} \\ \dfrac{1}{a} > \dfrac{1}{b} \text{ iff } a \text{ and } b \text{ are of opposite signs, i.e., } a > 0, b < 0 \end{cases}$$

Conclusion

Case I: Given $x \in [a, b]$: a and b are of same sign

$$\Rightarrow \frac{1}{x} \in \left[\frac{1}{b}, \frac{1}{a}\right]$$

Proof: $\because a \le x \le b$

$$\Rightarrow \frac{1}{a} \ge \frac{1}{x} \ge \frac{1}{b} \quad \Rightarrow \quad \frac{1}{b} \le \frac{1}{x} \le \frac{1}{a}$$

ILLUSTRATION 36: If x is a variable described as below, then find the range of variation of $1/x$.

(i) $x \in [3, 10]$ (ii) $x \in (-1, -1/3)$.

SOLUTION: (i) $1/x \in [1/10, 1/3]$

(ii) $1/x \in (-3, -1)$

Case II: If $x \in [a, b]$; where $a < 0$ and $b > 0$ then, $\dfrac{1}{x} \in \left(-\infty, \dfrac{1}{a}\right] \cup \left[\dfrac{1}{b}, \infty\right)$

Proof: Breaking the interval at $x = 0$, we get $x \in [a, 0) \cup [0, b]$; $x \neq 0$

(otherwise $1/x$ is not defined)

$$\Rightarrow a \le x < 0 \text{ or } 0 < x \le b$$

$$\Rightarrow \frac{1}{a} \ge \frac{1}{x} > -\infty \text{ or } \infty > \frac{1}{x} \ge \frac{1}{b}$$

$$\Rightarrow -\infty < \frac{1}{x} \le \frac{1}{a} \text{ or } \frac{1}{b} \le \frac{1}{x} < \infty$$

$$\Rightarrow \frac{1}{x} \in \left(-\infty, \frac{1}{a}\right] \cup \left[\frac{1}{b}, \infty\right)$$

ILLUSTRATION 37: If x is a variable described as below, then find the range of variation of $1/x$.

(i) $x \in (-1/3, 2)$

(ii) $x \in [-2, 2]$.

SOLUTION: (i) $1/x \in (-\infty, -3) \cup (1/2, \infty)$

(ii) $\dfrac{1}{x} \in \left(-\infty, -\dfrac{1}{2}\right] \cup \left[\dfrac{1}{2}, \infty\right)$

POLYNOMIAL EXPRESSION

An algebraic expression of type $f(x) = a_0 + a_1x + a_2x^2 + a_3x^3 + \ldots + a_nx^n$ is called polynomial in variable x, provided powers of x are whole numbers.

Terms: Quantities separated by positive or negative signs.

Coefficient: $a_0, a_1, a_2, a_3, \ldots\, a_n$, are called coefficients of polynomial.

Leading terms/leading Coefficient: The coefficient of highest power of variable x is called leading coefficient (because it governs the sign of $f(x)$ when $x \to \infty$). For example, a_nx^n is leading term and a_n is the leading coefficient.

If $f(x) = a_0 + a_1x + a_2x^n + a_3x^n + \ldots + a_nx^n$, then

$$f(x) = x^n\left(\frac{a_0}{x^n} + \frac{a_1}{x^{n-1}} + \frac{a_2}{x^{n-2}} + \ldots\ldots + \frac{a_{n-1}}{x} + a_n\right)$$

$$\text{as } x \to \infty \approx \begin{cases} \to \infty; & a_n > 0 \\ \to -\infty; & a_n < 0 \end{cases}$$

∴ Sign of polynomial expression at $x \to \infty$ is same as that of leading coefficient.

SOLVING RATIONAL INEQUALITIES

While solving rational inequalities the following facts must always be kept in mind:

(i) $\underbrace{\dfrac{f(x)}{g(x)} > 0}_{f(x) \text{ and } g(x) \text{ have same signs}} \Rightarrow f(x)\,.\,g(x) > 0;$

e.g., $\dfrac{2}{x-1} > 0 \Rightarrow 2(x-1) > 0 \Rightarrow x > 1$

(ii) $\underbrace{\dfrac{f(x)}{g(x)} < 0}_{f(x) \text{ and } g(x) \text{ have opposite signs}} \Rightarrow f(x)\,.\,g(x) < 0;$

e.g., $\dfrac{x}{x-1} - 1 < 0 \Rightarrow \dfrac{x-(x-1)}{x-1} < 0$

$\Rightarrow \dfrac{1}{x-1} < 0 \Rightarrow x - 1 < 0 \Rightarrow x < 1$

(iii) $\underbrace{\dfrac{f(x)}{g(x)} \geq 0}_{f(x) \text{ and } g(x) \text{ are of same signs or } f(x)=0} \Rightarrow \begin{cases} f(x).g(x) > 0 \\ \text{or} \\ f(x) = 0 \text{ and } g(x) \neq 0 \end{cases}$

e.g., $\dfrac{x-1}{x-2} \geq 0 \Rightarrow \dfrac{x-1}{x-2} > 0 \text{ or } x - 1 = 0$

$\Rightarrow (x-1)(x-2) > 0 \text{ or } x = 1$

$\Rightarrow x \in (-\infty, 1) \cup (2, \infty) \text{ or } x = 1$

$\Rightarrow x \in (-\infty, 1] \cup (2, \infty)$

(iv) $\underbrace{\dfrac{f(x)}{g(x)} \leq 0}_{f(x) \text{ and } g(x) \text{ are of opposite signs or } f(x)=0}$

$\Rightarrow \begin{cases} f(x).g(x) < 0 \\ or \\ f(x) = 0 \text{ and } g(x) \neq 0 \end{cases}$ e.g., $\dfrac{x-1}{x-2} \leq 0$

$\Rightarrow (x-1)(x-2) \leq 0; x \neq 2$ $\Rightarrow x \in [1, 2)$

WAVY CURVE METHOD

To find the set of solution for inequality $f(x) > 0$, $f(x) \geq 0$, $f(x) < 0$ or $f(x) \leq 0$; where $f(x)$ is a polynomial (if the given inequality is rational inequality, then convert it into polynomial inequality as discussed in previous article).

Step 1: Factorize the polynomial and find all the roots and arrange the factors in the increasing order of roots.

e.g., $f(x) = (x-\alpha)^3 (x-\beta)^2 (x-\gamma)(x-\delta)^5; \alpha < \beta < \gamma < \delta.$

Step 2: Locate the roots (with their multiplicity) on real number line.

Step 3: Keep the sign of expression in the right-most interval (same as that of leading coefficient).

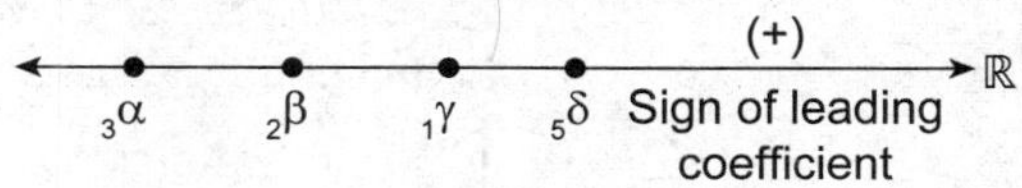

FIGURE 2.32

Step 4: Moving towards left and on changing the sign of expression across the root with multiplicity odd, and retain the same sign across the root with multiplicity even.

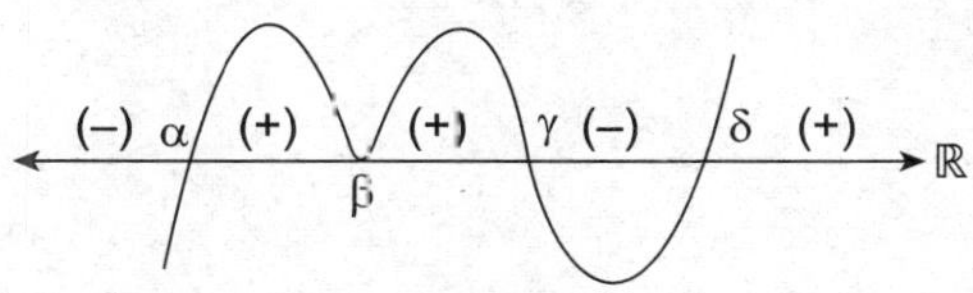

FIGURE 2.33

∵ $f(x) > 0$

$\Rightarrow x \in (\alpha, \beta) \cup (\beta, \gamma) \cup (\delta, \infty)$

Also for $f(x) \geq 0$

$\Rightarrow x \in [\alpha, \beta] \cup [\beta, \gamma] \cup [\delta, \infty)$

$\Rightarrow x \in [\alpha, \gamma] \cup [\delta, \infty)$

Similarly for $f(x) < 0$

$\Rightarrow x \in (-\infty, \alpha) \cup (\gamma, \delta) \text{ and } f(x) \leq 0$

$\Rightarrow x \in (-\infty, \alpha) \cup (\gamma, \delta) \cup (\alpha, \beta, \gamma, \delta)$

$\Rightarrow x \in (-\infty, \alpha] \cup [\gamma, \delta] \cup \{\beta\}$

ILLUSTRATION 38: Solve the following inequalities by using wavy curve method:

(i) $(x-1)^2 (x+2)^4 (x-3)^3 (x+5) > 0$

(ii) $(x-1)^3 (x+3)^4 (2x-5)^3 (5-x)^3 \geq 0$

(iii) $(2x-9)^2 (x-2)^2 (3-x) \leq 0$

(iv) $(x-5)(x-1)^2 (2x-5)^3 < 0$

SOLUTION: (i) Given inequality is $(x-1)^2(x+2)^4 (x-3)^3 (x+5) > 0$ ... (i)

Equating each factor to zero, we get $x = 1, -2, 3, -5$. Arranging the above roots along real line, as shown in Figure 2.34.

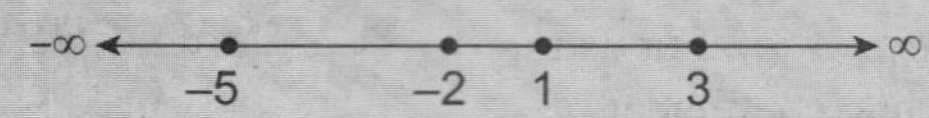

FIGURE 2.34

Sign of leading coefficient is positive and arranging the factors according to increasing order of their corresponding roots, the given inequality becomes

$(x+5)(x+2)^4 (x-1)^2 (x-3)^3 > 0$ ... (ii)

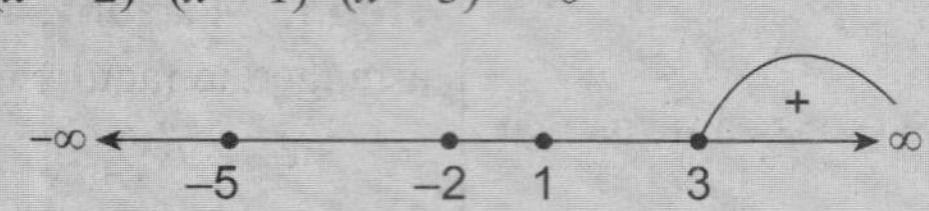

FIGURE 2.35

Now in the first interval (from right end) take the sign of leading term of inequality positive, that is, take the curve above the line and from now onwards go on changing the sign of wave for each odd powered factor of inequality observing from right of inequality (ii) and keeping same as that of previous for each even powered factor, we get the wave pattern as given in Figure 2.36.

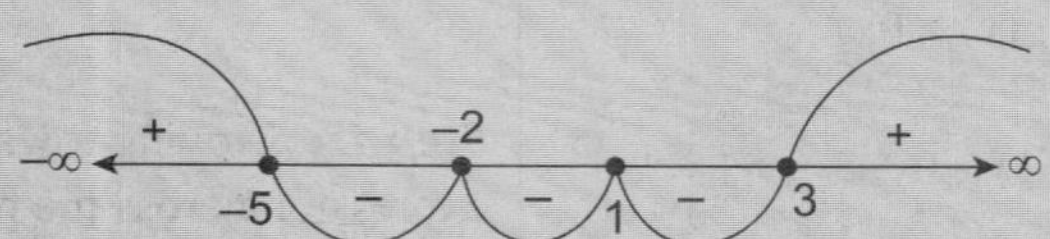

FIGURE 2.36

$\therefore \quad x \in (-\infty, -5) \cup (3, \infty)$.

Note: −5, −2, 1 and 3 are excluded, as at these points inequality vanishes.

(ii) On same steps as for part (i) the wave pattern for the inequality $(x-1)^3 (x+3)^4 (2x-5)^3 (5-x)^3 \geq 0$ will be as shown in Figure 2.37.

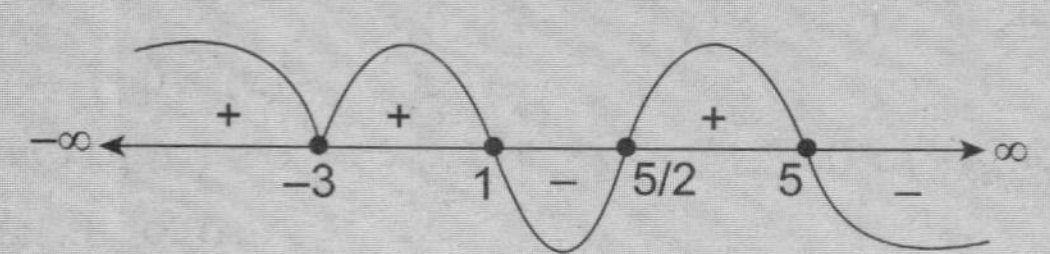

FIGURE 2.37

Ascending arrangement of factors of inequality is $(x+3)^4 (x-1)^3 (2x-5)^3 (5-x)^3 \geq 0$

$$\therefore \quad x \in (-\infty, -3] \cup [-3, 1] \cup \left[\frac{5}{2}, 5\right] \text{ or } x \in (-\infty, 1] \cup \left[\frac{5}{2}, 5\right]$$

(iii) Ascending arrangement of factors of given inequality is $(x-2)^2(3-x)(2x-9)^2 \le 0$ and the wave pattern is as shown in Figure 2.38.

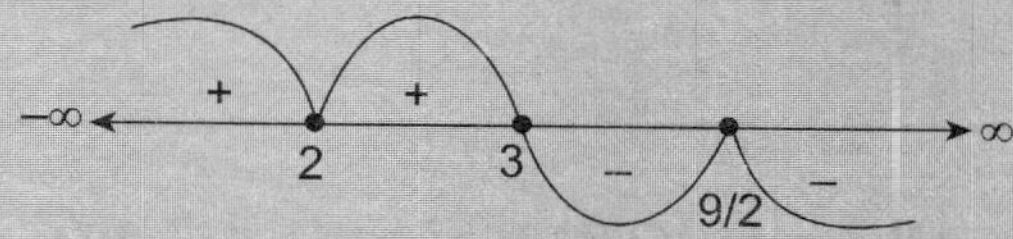

FIGURE 2.38

$$\therefore \quad x \in \left[3, \frac{9}{2}\right] \cup \left[\frac{9}{2}, \infty\right) \equiv [3, \infty)$$

(iv) Ascending arrangement of factors of given inequality is $(x-1)^2(2x-5)^3(x-5) < 0$ and the corresponding wave pattern is as shown in Figure 2.39.

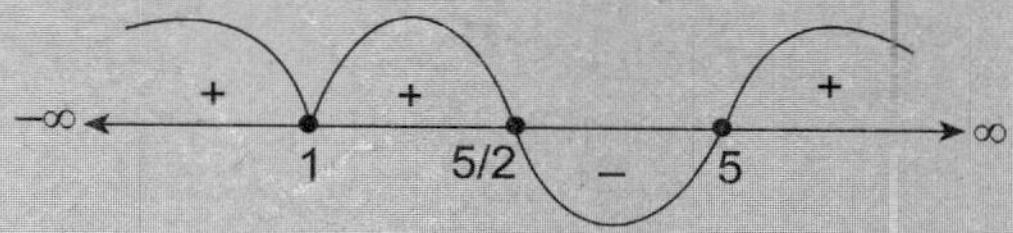

FIGURE 2.39

$$\therefore \quad x \in \left(\frac{5}{2}, 5\right)$$

TEXTUAL EXERCISE-3: (SUBJECTIVE)

1. Solve the following linear inequations and express the result in the form of intervals:
   (a) $x^3 - 6x \ge 0$ (b) $x^6 - 9x^3 + 8 > 0$
   (c) $x^4 - 2x^2 - 8 \ge 0$

2. Solve the following linear inequations and express the result in the form of intervals:
   (a) $(x^2-9)^2(x+1)(x^2-2x-3)(x-1) \ge 0$
   (b) $(x^2+3x+1)(x^2+3x-3) \ge 5$
   (c) $(x-2)^2(x-3)(x-4)^4(x-6) \ge 0$

3. Find the range of variation of y for the following functions:
   (a) $y = \dfrac{1}{3x-2}$ if $-2 < x < 4$
   (b) $y = \dfrac{x-1}{x+2}$ if $-1 < x < 3$
   (c) $y = \dfrac{1}{x^2+4}$ if $2 \le x \le 3$
   (d) $y = \dfrac{x^2-1}{x^2+1}$ if $-1 < x < 3$

4. Solve the following inequalities for x:
   (a) $\dfrac{(x+1)^5(x-1)(x+4)^2(x-3)^4}{(x+8)(2x-3)(x-6)^2} < 0$
   (b) $\dfrac{(x+1)(x-8)(x-6)^2(x-5)^4}{(x-3)^2(x-1)} < 0$
   (c) $(x^2-16)(x^2-5x+4)(x^2-1)(x+3)(x+2) \le 0.$

5. Solve the following inequality for the variable x:
   (a) $x^3 - 6x \le 0$
   (b) $x^4 - 2x^2 - 8 \ge 0$
   (c) $x^6 - 9x^3 + 8 \le 0$
   (d) $x^4 + x^3 - x - 1 > 0$
   (e) $(x^2-9)^2(x+1)(x^2-2x-3)(x-1) \le 0$
   (f) $x^2 - x - 6 \ge 0$ and $x^2 - 4x \le 0$
   (g) $4 < x^2 < 9$
   (h) $(x+1)(x-3)^2(x-5)(x-4)^2(x-2) < 0$
   (i) $(x-3)(x+1)(x+2)(x-9) \ge 0$
   (j) $x^3 - 7x^2 + 14x - 8 < 0$
   (k) $\dfrac{(x-1)(x-2)(5-x)}{(2x+5)} < 0$

6. Find the largest negative integer and smallest positive integer which satisfy:
   (a) $x^2 - 4x - 12 \ge 0$ (b) $3x^2 + 5x - 2 < 0$
   (c) $\dfrac{x^2-5x+4}{x^2-1} \le 1$

7. Find the number of positive integers satisfying $\frac{x^2-3x+2}{x-3} \le 0$

8. Find the number of integers satisfying $\frac{x^2(x+2)}{x-1} \le 0$

Answer Keys

1. (a) $(-\sqrt{6},0]\cup[\sqrt{6},\infty)$ (b) $(-\infty,1)\cup(2,\infty)$ (c) $(-\infty,-2]\cup[2,\infty)$
2. (a) $(-\infty,1]\cup[3,\infty)$ (b) $(-\infty,-4]\cup[-2-1]\cup[1,\infty)$ (c) $(-\infty,3]\cup\{4\}\cup[6,\infty)$
3. (a) $\left(-\infty,-\frac{1}{8}\right)\cup\left(\frac{1}{10},\infty\right)$ (b) $\left(-2,\frac{2}{5}\right)$ (c) $\left[\frac{1}{13},\frac{1}{8}\right]$ (d) $\left[-1,\frac{4}{5}\right)$
4. (a) $(-8,-4)\cup(-4,-1)\cup\left(1,\frac{3}{2}\right)$ (b) $(-\infty,-1)\cup(1,3)\cup(3,5)\cup(5,6)\cup(6,8)$ (c) $[-4,-3]\cup[-2,-1]$
5. (a) $(-\infty,-\sqrt{6}]\cup[0,\sqrt{6}]$ (b) $[-2,2]$ (c) $[1,2]$
   (d) $(-\infty,-1)\cup(1,\infty)$ (e) $\{-3,-1\}\cup[1,3]$ (f) $[3,4]$
   (g) $(-3,-2)\cup(2,3)$
   (h) $(-\infty,-1)\cup(2,3)\cup(3,4)\cup(4,5)$ (i) $(-\infty,-2]\cup[-1,3]\cup[9,\infty)$ (j) $x\in(-\infty,1)\cup(2,4)$
   (k) $(-\infty,-5/2)\cup(1,2)\cup(5,\infty)$
6. (a) –2, 6 (b) –1, does not exist (c) does not exist, 2 **7.** 2 **8.** 3

TEXTUAL EXERCISE–3: (OBJECTIVE)

1. Solution of the linear inequations $\frac{x}{5}<\frac{3x-2}{4}-\frac{5x-3}{5}$ expressed in the form of interval is given by
   (a) $(-\infty,2/9)$ (b) $(-\infty,2/3)$
   (c) $(-\infty,1/9)$ (d) None of these
2. Solution of the linear inequations $\frac{2x+3}{5}-2\le\frac{3(x-2)}{5}$ expressed in the form of interval is given by
   (a) $[-2,\infty)$ (b) $[2,\infty)$
   (c) $[-1,\infty)$ (d) None of these
3. Solution of the linear inequations $\frac{-x+3}{2}-2\le\frac{3(x+2)}{5}\le\frac{x}{6}$ expressed in the form of interval is given by
   (a) $[-2,\infty)$ (b) ϕ
   (c) $(3,\infty)$ (d) None of these
4. Solution of system of inequations $x+5>2(x+1)$ and $2-x<3(x+2)$ expressed in the form of intervals is given by
   (a) (–1, 3) (b) (–1, 2)
   (c) (–2, 3) (d) None of these
5. Solution of system of inequations $2(x-6)\le 3x-7$ and $11-2x\le 6-x$ expressed in the form of intervals is given by
   (a) $(-\infty,5)$ (b) $[5,\infty)$
   (c) $[-5,\infty)$ (d) None of these
6. The range of y, when $-9\le x\le 5$, $y=x^3$ is
   (a) [125, 729] (b) (–729, 125)
   (c) [–729, 125] (d) None of these
7. The range of y, when $2<x<5$, $y=\frac{1}{x}$ is
   (a) (1/5, 1/2) (b) (–1/2, 1/5)
   (c) $(1/5,\infty)$ (d) None of these
8. The range of y, when $-6<x<6$, $y=\frac{1}{x^2}$ is
   (a) (–1/36, 1/36) (b) $(1/36,\infty)$
   (c) (0, 1/36) (d) None of these
9. The range of y, when $9<x^2<25$, $y=x$ is
   (a) $(-5,-3)\cup(3,5)$ (b) (–5, – 3)
   (c) (9, 25) (d) None of these
10. Solution of the inequation $x^2-3x+2>0$ expressed in the form of intervals is given by

(a) $(-\infty, 1) \cup [2, \infty)$ (b) $(-\infty, 1) \cup (2, \infty)$
(c) $(-\infty, -1) \cup (2, \infty)$ (d) None of these

11. Solution of the inequation $x^2 - 3x - 4 \le 0$ expressed in the form of intervals is given by
(a) $[-1, 4]$ (b) $[1, 4]$
(c) $(-1, 4)$ (d) None of these

12. Solution of the inequation $x^2 - 3x + 2 < 0$ expressed in the form of intervals is given by
(a) $[1, 2]$ (b) $(1, 2)$
(c) $(-\infty, 1) \cup (2, \infty)$ (d) None of these

13. Solution of the inequation $\frac{4x+3}{2x-5} \le 6$ expressed in the form of intervals is given by
(a) $\left(-\infty, -\frac{5}{2}\right) \cup \left[\frac{33}{8}, \infty\right)$
(b) $\left(-\infty, \frac{2}{5}\right) \cup \left[\frac{33}{8}, \infty\right)$
(c) $\left(-\infty, \frac{5}{2}\right) \cup \left[\frac{33}{8}, \infty\right)$
(d) None of these

14. Solution of the inequation $\frac{x}{x-5} \ge \frac{1}{2}$ expressed in the form of intervals is given by
(a) $(-\infty, -5] \cup (5, \infty)$ (b) $(-\infty, -5]$
(c) $(-5, 5]$ (d) None of these

15. Solution of the inequality $\frac{(x-1)(x-2)(5-x)}{(2x+5)} < 0$ expressed in the form of intervals is given by
(a) $\left(-\infty, -\frac{5}{2}\right) \cup (1, 2) \cup (5, \infty)$
(b) $\left(-\infty, -\frac{5}{2}\right) \cup (5, \infty)$
(c) $\left(-\infty, -\frac{5}{2}\right) \cup (-1, 2) \cup [5, \infty)$
(d) None of these

16. Solution of the inequality $\frac{x^2 - 2x + 5}{3x^2 - 2x - 5} > \frac{1}{2}$ expressed in the form of intervals is given by
(a) $[-5, -1] \cup \left(\frac{5}{3}, 3\right)$ (b) $(-5, -1) \cup \left(\frac{5}{3}, 3\right)$
(c) $(-5, 1) \cup \left(\frac{5}{3}, 3\right)$ (d) None of these

17. Solution of the inequality $\frac{(x-1)^2(x+1)^3}{x^4(x-2)} \le 0$ expressed in the form of intervals is given by
(a) $[-1, 2)$ (b) $(-\infty, 0) \cup (0, 2)$
(c) $[-1, 0) \cup (0, 2)$ (d) None of these

18. Solution of the inequality $\frac{x(x+1)(x-3)}{(x+4)} > 0$ and $\frac{(5-x)(x+2)}{(x-8)} < 0$ expressed in the form of intervals is given by
(a) $(-1, 0) \cup (3, 5) \cup (8, \infty)$
(b) $(0, 1]$
(c) $(-\infty, 0) \cup [1, \infty)$
(d) None of these

19. The value of x satisfying the inequalities hold $\frac{(2x-1)(x-1)^4(x-2)^4}{(x-2)(x-4)^4} \le 0$
(a) $\left[\frac{1}{2}, 2\right)$ (b) R
(c) ϕ (d) $\left(\frac{1}{2}, 2\right)$

20. The set of all values of x for which $(x-2)^3(x-3) < 0$ is
(a) $(2, 3)$ (b) $[2, 3)$
(c) $(0, 3)$ (d) $(2, 3]$

21. $(x - 2)^4(x - 3)^3(x - 4)^2(1 - x) \le 0$.
(a) $(1,3)$
(b) $(-\infty, 1) \cup (3, \infty)$
(c) $(-\infty, 1] \cup [3, \infty) \cup \{2\}$
(d) None of these

22. If $c < d$, $x^2 + (c + d)x + cd < 0$
(a) $(-d, -c]$ (b) $(-d, -c)$
(c) $\mathbb{R}$ (d) ϕ

23. If $a, b, c > 0$ and $a(1 - b) > \frac{1}{4}$, $b(1 - c) > \frac{1}{4}$ and $c(1 - a) > \frac{1}{4}$, then
(a) never possible (b) always true
(c) cannot be discussed (d) None of these

Answer Keys

1. (a)	**2.** (c)	**3.** (b)	**4.** (a)	**5.** (b)	**6.** (c)	**7.** (a)	**8.** (b)	**9.** (a)	**10.** (b)
11. (a)	**12.** (b)	**13.** (c)	**14.** (a)	**15.** (a)	**16.** (b)	**17.** (c)	**18.** (a)	**19.** (a)	**20.** (a)
21. (c)	**22.** (b)	**23.** (a)							

■ INCREASING AND DECREASING FUNCTION

(i) **Increasing Function:** *A* function $y = f(x)$ is called increasing function if its output $f(x)$. (i.e., y) increases by increasing the input x (it may happen that by increasing the input x, output $f(x)$ remains same for few but not all inputs $x \in D_f$)

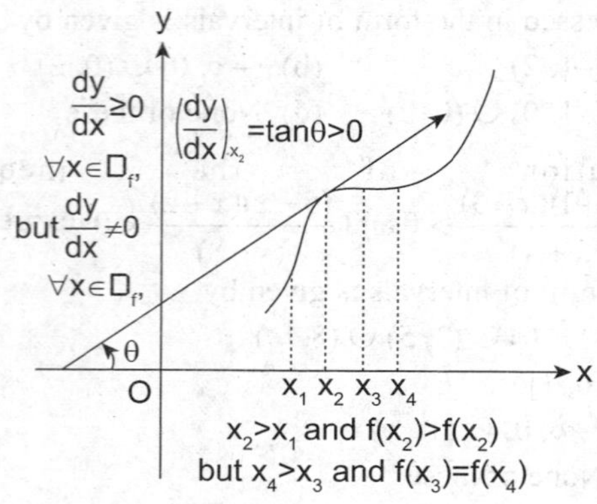

FIGURE 2.40

That is, $x_2 > x_1 \Leftrightarrow f(x_2) \geq f(x_1)$ for distinct values of x_1 and x_2.

$\therefore\ f(x_2) - f(x_1) \geq 0 \Leftrightarrow x_2 - x_1 > 0$

$\Rightarrow\ \dfrac{f(x_2) - f(x_1)}{x_2 - x_1} \geq 0$

$\Rightarrow\ \dfrac{\Delta y}{\Delta x} \geq 0$ ($\because$ when $(x_2 - x_1) = \Delta x \to 0$; $(f(x_2) - f(x_1)) = \Delta y \to 0$ or $\Delta y = 0$)

$\Rightarrow$ That is, instantaneous rate of change of $f(x)$ always remains non-negative.

(ii) **Decreasing Function:** *A* function $y = f(x)$ is called decreasing function if its output $f(x)$, (i.e., y) decreases by increasing the input x. (it may happen that by increasing the input x output $f(x)$ remains same for few but not all inputs $x \in D_f$)

That is, $x_2 > x_1 \Leftrightarrow f(x_2) \leq f(x_1)$ for distinct values of x_1 and x_2.

$\therefore\ f(x_2) - f(x_1) \leq 0 \Leftrightarrow x_2 - x_1 > 0$

$\Rightarrow\ \dfrac{f(x_2) - f(x_1)}{x_2 - x_1} \leq 0$

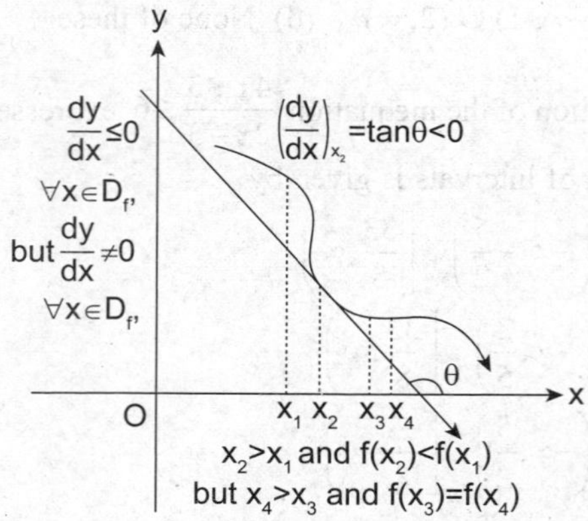

FIGURE 2.41

$\Rightarrow\ \dfrac{\Delta y}{\Delta x} \leq 0$ ($\because$ when $(x_2 - x_1) = \Delta x \to 0$; $(f(x_2) - f(x_1)) = \Delta y \to 0$ or $\Delta y = 0$)

$\Rightarrow\ \dfrac{dy}{dx} = f'(x) \leq 0$. That is, instantaneous rate of change of $f(x)$ always remains non-positive.

REMARKS

f and f^{-1} have same monotonic nature. That is, either both increasing or both decreasing.

By application of increasing function to both sides of inequality the sign of inequality remains unchanged. Same is true for removal of the function (i.e., application of its inverse function)

By application of decreasing function to both sides of inequality the sign of inequality gets reversed. Same is true for removal of the function (i.e., application of its inverse function).

ILLUSTRATION 39: Test whether the following functions are increasing or decreasing.

(i) $y = x^2$ (ii) $y = x^3$

(iii) $y = \sqrt{x}$ (iv) $y = \sqrt[3]{x}$

SOLUTION: (i) $\dfrac{dy}{dx} = 2x = \begin{cases} +; x > 0 \uparrow \\ -; x < 0 \downarrow \end{cases}$

$\therefore$ $f(x)$ is monotonically increasing for $x \geq 0$ and monotonically decreasing for $x \leq 0$.

(ii) $\dfrac{dy}{dx} = 3x^2 \geq 0 \ \forall\ x \in \mathbb{R}$

$\therefore$ $f(x)$ is monotonically increasing $\forall\ x \in \mathbb{R}$.

(iii) $\dfrac{dy}{dx} = \dfrac{1}{2\sqrt{x}} > 0 \ \forall\ x > 0$

$\therefore$ $f(x)$ is monotonically increasing $\forall\ x > 0$.

(iv) $\dfrac{dy}{dx} = \dfrac{1}{3}(x)^{-\frac{2}{3}} = \dfrac{1}{3(x^{1/3})^2} > 0;\ \forall\ x \in \mathbb{R} \sim \{0\}$

$\therefore$ $f(x)$ is monotonically increasing $\forall\ x \in \mathbb{R} \sim \{0\}$.

■ MONOTONIC FUNCTION

A function $f(x)$ is called Monotonic iff either it increases $\forall\ x \in D_f$ or decreases $\forall\ x \in D_f$ wherever it is defined.

i.e., $f(x) \geq 0\ \forall\ x \in D_f$ or $f(x) \leq 0\ \forall\ x \in D_f$

e.g., (i) $y = x$, $y = x^3$ are monotonic functions.

(ii) $y = x^2$ is not a monotonic function as it decreases for $x \leq 0$ and increases for $x \geq 0$.

■ INTERVAL OF MONOTONICITY

An interval belonging to domain of function in which function $f(x)$ is monotonic, is called interval of monotonicity.

e.g., for $y = x^2$; $f'(x) = 2x = \begin{cases} +ve & \text{for } x > 0 \\ -ve & \text{for } x < 0 \end{cases}$ and $f'(x) = 0$ only at $x = 0$;

$\Rightarrow$ $x \in [0, \infty)$ is the interval of monotonic increase and $x \in (-\infty, 0]$ is the interval of monotonic decrease.

■ TO FIND INTERVAL OF MONOTONICITY FOR $y = f(x)$

Step 1: Find the derivative of function, i.e., $f'(x)$. Let $f'(x) = (x - \alpha)(x - \beta)(x - \gamma)(x - \delta)(x - k)$.

Step 2: Find the values of $x \in D_f$ (critical points) where $f'(x) = 0$ or it is not defined.

Step 3: Locate these critical points on (number line).

Step 4: Find the sign of $\dfrac{dy}{dx}$, i.e., $f'(x)$ in these intervals obtained.

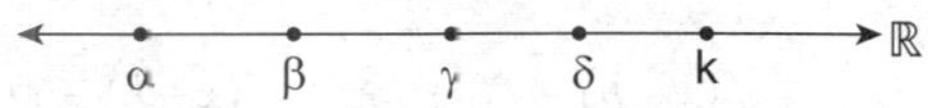

FIGURE 2.42

Suppose $f'(x) \geq 0\ \forall\ x \in (\alpha, \beta] \cup [\gamma, \delta] \cup [k, \infty)$ and $f'(x) \leq 0\ \forall\ x \in (-\infty, \alpha] \cup [\beta, \gamma] \cup [\delta, k)$, then $f(x)$ is monotonically increasing for $x \in (\alpha, \beta] \cup [\gamma, \delta] \cup [k, \infty)$ and $f(x)$ is monotonically decreasing for $x \in (-\infty, \alpha] \cup [\beta, \gamma] \cup [\delta, k)$

ILLUSTRATION 40: Find the interval of monotonicity of function $f(x) = x^4 - 2x^2 + 6$

SOLUTION: $f(x) = x^4 - 2x^2 + 6 \Rightarrow f'(x) = 4x^3 - 4x = 0 \Rightarrow x(x - 1)(x + 1) = 0$

$\Rightarrow x = 0, -1, 1$ are the critical points

$\Rightarrow f'(x) \text{ is} \begin{cases} \geq 0 & \forall\ x \in [-1, 0] \cup [1, \infty) \\ \leq 0 & \forall\ x \in (-\infty, -1] \cup [0, 1] \end{cases}$

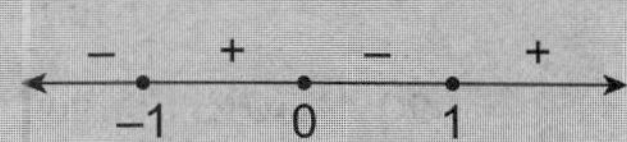

FIGURE 2.43

$\therefore$ $f(x)$ is monotonically increasing for $x \in [-1, 0] \cup [1, \infty)$ and $f(x)$ is monotonically decreasing for $x \in (-\infty, -1] \cup [0, 1]$

STRICTLY MONOTONIC FUNCTIONS

These are of two types:

(i) Strictly increasing function
(ii) Strictly decreasing function

(i) **Strictly Increasing Functions:** A function $y = f(x)$ is said to be strictly increasing on a set $S(\text{or } D_f)$ if $x_2 > x_1 \Rightarrow f(x_2) > f(x_1)$; $x_1, x_2 \in S(\text{or } D_f)$

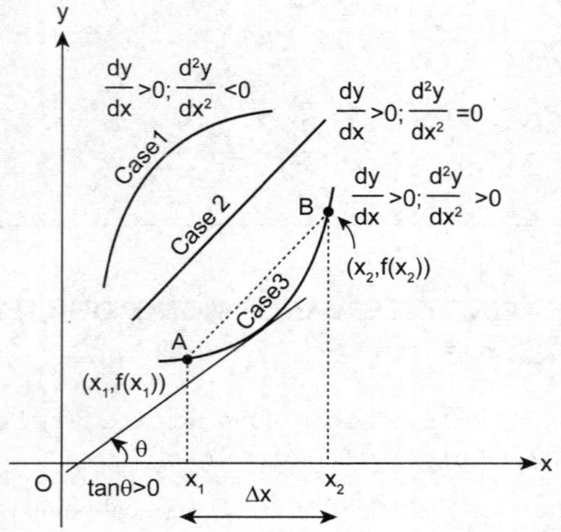

Case 1: Increases with decreasing rate of increase.
Case 2: Increases with constant rate of increase.
Case 3: Increases with increasing rate of increase.

FIGURE 2.44

i.e.,

$$f'(x) = \lim_{h\to 0^+} \frac{f(x+h)-f(x)}{h} = \lim_{h\to 0^+} \frac{f(x-h)-f(x)}{-h}.$$

$\because$ $x + h > x \Rightarrow f(x + h) > f(x)$

$\therefore$ $\frac{f(x+h)-f(x)}{h} > 0$

Also $x - h < x \Rightarrow f(x - h) < f(x)$

$\therefore$ $\frac{f(x-h)-f(x)}{-h} > 0 \Rightarrow f'(x) \geq 0$

$\therefore$ *A function* $f(x)$ is said to be strictly increasing if $f'(x) \geq 0$ and $f'(x) = 0$ occurs only at isolated points i.e., $f(x)$ does not has a line segment parallel, to x-axis as a part of its graph.

(ii) Strictly decreasing functions: *A* function $y = f(x)$ is said to be strictly decreasing on a set $S(\text{or } D_f)$ if $x_2 > x_1 \Rightarrow f(x_2) < f(x_1)$; $x_1, x_2 \in S(\text{or } D_f)$

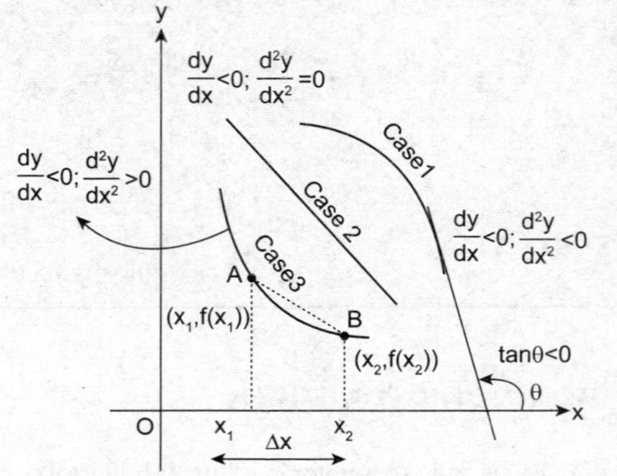

Case 1: decreases with increasing rate of decrease.
Case 2: decreases with constant rate of decrease.
Case 3: decreases with decreasing rate of decrease.

FIGURE 2.45

i.e.,

$$f'(x) = \lim_{h\to 0^+} \frac{f(x+h)-f(x)}{h} = \lim_{h\to 0^+} \frac{f(x-h)-f(x)}{-h}$$

$\because$ $x + h > x \Rightarrow f(x + h) < f(x)$

$\therefore$ $\frac{f(x+h)-f(x)}{h} < 0$

Also $x - h < x \Rightarrow f(x - h) > f(x)$

$\therefore$ $\frac{f(x-h)-f(x)}{-h} < 0 \Rightarrow f'(x) < 0$

$\therefore$ *A function* $f(x)$ is said to be strictly decreasing if $f'(x) \leq 0$ and $f'(x) = 0$ occurs only at isolated points, i.e., $f(x)$ does not has a line segment parallel to x-axis as a part of its graph.

ILLUSTRATION 41: Find the intervals in which the function $f(x) = x^3 - 7x^2 + 14x - 8$, is strictly increasing and strictly decreasing.

SOLUTION: Given function is $f(x) = x^3 - 8 - 7x^2 + 14x = (x^3 - 8) - 7x(x - 2)$

$= (x - 2)(x^2 + 4 + 2x) - 7x(x - 2) = (x - 2)[x^2 + 2x + 4 - 7x]$

$= (x - 2)(x^2 - 5x + 4) = (x - 2)(x - 1)(x - 4)$

$f'(x) = 0 \Rightarrow x = 1, 2, 4$; are the critical points

$\therefore\ f'(x) > 0 \Leftrightarrow x \in (1, 2) \cup (4, \infty)$

Also $f'(x) = 0$ at isolated points $x = 1, 2$ and 4

$\therefore\ f(x)$ is strictly increasing on $[1, 2] \cup [4, \infty)$ and $f'(x) < 0 \Leftrightarrow x \in (-\infty, 1) \cup (2, 4)$

and $f'(x) = 0$ at isolated points $x = 1, 2, 4$.

$\therefore\ f(x)$ is strictly decreasing on $(-\infty, 1] \cup [2, 4]$.

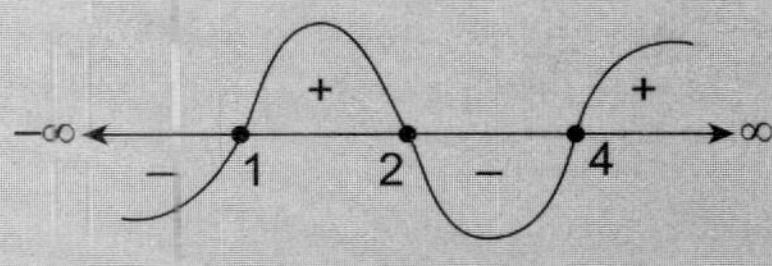

FIGURE 2.46

ILLUSTRATION 42: Find the intervals of monotonicity of the function $f(x) = \dfrac{4x}{4-x^2}$.

SOLUTION: Given function is $f(x) = \dfrac{4x}{4-x^2}$ and $f'(x) = \dfrac{(4-x^2)(4) - 4x(-2x)}{(4-x^2)^2}$

$$= \frac{4[4-x^2+2x^2]}{(4-x^2)^2} = \frac{4(4+x^2)}{(4-x^2)^2} > 0\ \forall\ x \in \mathbb{R} \sim \{-2, 2\}$$

$\therefore\ f(x)$ is strictly increasing on its domain $\mathbb{R} \sim \{-2, 2\}$. Graph of $f(x) = \dfrac{4x}{4-x^2}$ is as shown in Figure 2.47.

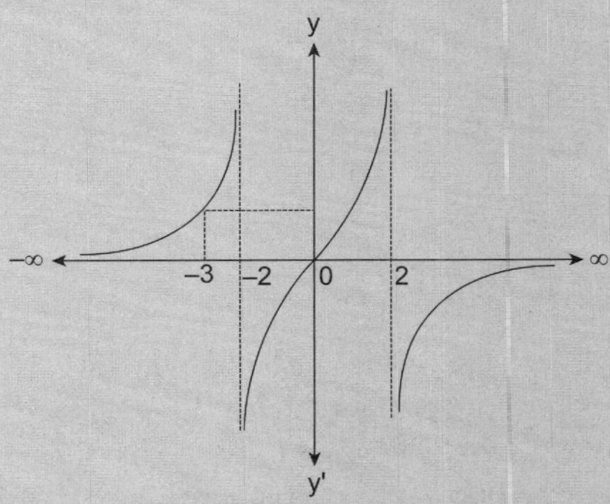

FIGURE 2.47

ILLUSTRATION 43: Find the interval of monotonicities of function $f(x) = \dfrac{x^2}{x^2-1}$

SOLUTION: Given function is $f(x) = \dfrac{x^2}{x^2-1}$

Clearly domain of $f(x) = \mathbb{R} \sim \{\pm 1\}$

Now $f'(x) = \dfrac{(x^2-1)(2x) - x^2(2x)}{(x^2-1)^2}$

$$= \frac{2x[x^2-1-x^2]}{(x^2-1)^2} = \frac{-2x}{(x^2-1)^2}$$

$\therefore\ f'(x) \geq 0$ for $x \in (-\infty, 0] \sim \{-1\}$ and $f'(x) \leq 0$ for $x \in [0, \infty) \sim \{1\}$

Thus, $f(x)$ is strictly increasing on $(-\infty, 0] \sim \{-1\}$ and is strictly decreasing on $[0, \infty) \sim \{1\}$. Graphically, it is shown in the Figure 2.48.

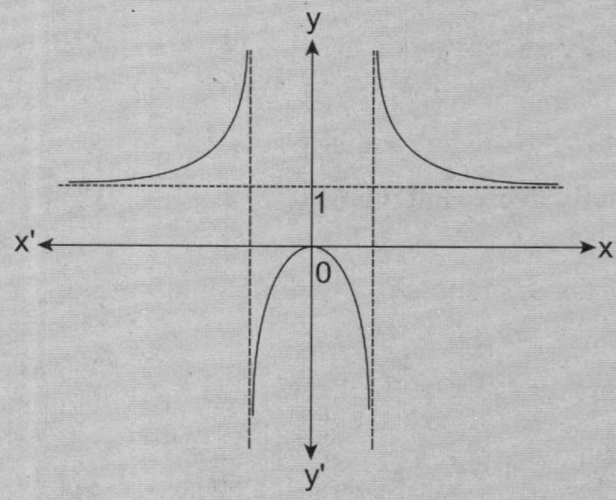

FIGURE 2.48

ILLUSTRATION 44: Find the intervals of monotonoicities of the function $f(x) = \dfrac{(x+2)}{(x-1)(x+1)}$

SOLUTION: Given function is $f(x) = \dfrac{(x+2)}{(x-1)(x+1)}$

Clearly domain of $f(x)$ is $\mathbb{R} \sim \{-1, 1\}$

$$\therefore \quad f'(x) = \frac{(x-1)(x+1)(1)-(x+2)(2x)}{[(x-1)(x+1)]^2} = \frac{x^2-1-2x^2-4x}{(x^2-1)^2} = \frac{-x^2-4x-1}{(x^2-1)^2}$$

$\therefore \quad f'(x) \geq 0 \quad \Rightarrow \quad x^2 + 4x + 1 \leq 0; x \neq \pm 1$

$$\Rightarrow \quad x = \frac{-4 \pm \sqrt{16-4}}{2} = -2 \pm \sqrt{3}$$

$\therefore \quad x^2 + 4x + 1 \leq 0 \quad \Rightarrow \quad x \in [-2 - \sqrt{3}, -2 + \sqrt{3}] \sim \{-1\}$

$\therefore \quad f(x)$ is strictly increasing on $x \in [-2 - \sqrt{3}, -2 + \sqrt{3}] \sim \{-1\}$

and $f'(x) \leq 0, x \neq \pm 1$ implies $x \in (-\infty, -2 - \sqrt{3}] \cup [-2 + \sqrt{3}, \infty) \sim \{1\}$

That is, $f(x)$ is strictly decreasing on $(-\infty, -2 - \sqrt{3}[\cup [-2 + \sqrt{3}, \infty) \sim \{1\}$

Graph of $f(x)$ is as shown in Figure 2.49.

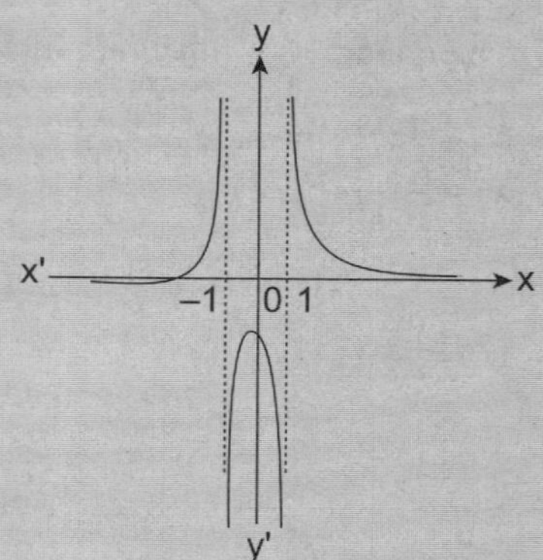

FIGURE 2.49

ILLUSTRATION 45: Find the intervals of monotonicity of the function $f(x)=\dfrac{x^2-5x+6}{x^2-16}$

SOLUTION: Given function is $f(x)=\dfrac{x^2-5x+6}{x^2-16}$; Clearly domain of function is $\mathbb{R} \sim \{4, -4\}$

and $f'(x)=\dfrac{(x^2-16)(2x-5)-(x^2-5x+6)(2x)}{(x^2-16)^2}$

$$=\frac{2x^3-5x^2-32x+80-2x^3+10x^2-12x}{(x^2-16)^2}=\frac{5x^2-44x+80}{(x^2-16)^2}$$

$\therefore\ f'(x)>0 \Rightarrow 5x^2-44x+80\ge 0$

Corresponding quadratic equation is $5x^2-44x+80=0$

$$x=\frac{44\pm\sqrt{(-44)^2-(20)(80)}}{2(5)}=\frac{44\pm\sqrt{16\times121-1600}}{10}=\frac{44\pm4\sqrt{21}}{10}$$

$$=\frac{22-2\sqrt{21}}{5},\frac{22+2\sqrt{21}}{5}$$

$\therefore\ 5x^2-44x+80\ge 0$

$$\Rightarrow x\in\left(-\infty,\frac{22-2\sqrt{21}}{5}\right]\cup\left[\frac{22+2\sqrt{21}}{5},\infty\right)\sim\{-4\}$$

That is, $f(x)$ is strictly increasing on $\left(-\infty,\dfrac{22-2\sqrt{21}}{5}\right]\cup\left[\dfrac{22+2\sqrt{21}}{5},\infty\right)\sim\{-4\}$

and $f(x)$ is strictly decreasing on $\left[\dfrac{22-2\sqrt{21}}{5},\dfrac{22+2\sqrt{21}}{5}\right]\sim\{4\}$

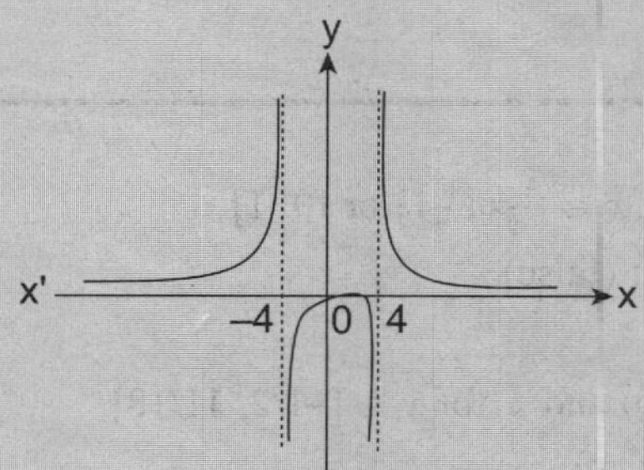

FIGURE 2.50

NOTE

Detail discussion of Derivatives and Monotonicity of Functions will be given in the chapters Methods of Derivatives and Application of Derivatives II of volume VI.

TEXTUAL EXERCISE–4: (SUBJECTIVE)

1. (a) Show that the function $y = x^3 + x$ increases every where.
   (b) Find the intervals of monotonicity of the function $y = x^4 - 2x^2 - 5$.

2. Find out the monotonic nature of the function $y = \sin x + \cos x$ in the interval $(0, \pi)$. Verify whether the inequality $(\sin 23° + \cos 23°) > (\sin 53° + \cos 53°)$ is true?

3. Find out the behaviour of the function $\frac{\sin x}{x}$ in the interval $(0, \pi)$. Verify whether $\frac{\sin\alpha}{\alpha} > \frac{\sin\beta}{\beta}$ $\forall\ 0 < \alpha < \beta < \pi$.

4. Show that the function $y = 2x^3 + 3x^2 - 12x + 1$ decreases in the interval $(-2, 1)$.

5. Show that the function $y = \sqrt{2x - x^2}$;increases in the interval (0, 1) and decreases in the interval (1, 2). Construct the rough sketch of the function.

6. Show that the function $y = \frac{x^2 - 1}{x}$ increases in any interval not containing the point $x = 0$.

7. Find the intervals of monotonicity of the given functions.
   (a) $y = (x - 2)^5 (2x + 1)^4$
   (b) $y = x - e^x$
   (c) $y = x^2 e^{-x}$
   (d) $y = \frac{x}{\ln x}$
   (e) $y = x - 2\sin x$; where $0 \le x \le 2\pi$
   (f) $y = x + \cos 2x$; where $0 \le x \le 2\pi$

8. Test whether following are increasing or decreasing.
   (i) $f(x) = 2x + 3$
   (ii) $f(x) = a^x$; $a > 1$
   (iii) $f(x) = x^3$
   (iv) $f(x) = \sqrt{x}$
   (v) $f(x) = \sqrt[3]{x}$
   (vi) $f(x) = \log_a x$; $a > 1$

9. Show that the function $f(x) = x^3 - 3x^2 + 4x$, is strictly increasing function in its domain?

10. Find the interval in which the following functions increase
    (a) $f(x) = \sin 3x : x \in \left[0, \frac{\pi}{2}\right]$
    (b) $(x + 1)^3 (x - 3)^3$
    (c) $2x^2 - 3x$

Answer Keys

1. (b) ↑ for $x \in [-1, 0]$ or $[1, \infty)$; ↓ for $x \in (-\infty, -1]$ or $[0, 1]$
2. ↑ for $x \in (0, \pi/4]$; ↓ for $x \in [\pi/4, \pi)$; (false)
3. decreasing
7. (a) ↑ for $x \in (-\infty, -1/2] \cup [11/18, \infty)$ and ↓ for $x \in [-1/2, 11/18]$
   (b) ↑ for $x \in (-\infty, 0]$ and ↓ for $x \in [0, \infty)$
   (c) ↑ for $x \in [0, 2]$ and ↓ for $x \in (-\infty, 0] \cup [2, \infty)$
   (d) ↑ for $x \in [e, \infty)$ and ↓ for $x \in (0, e] - \{1\}$
   (e) ↑ for $x \in \left[\frac{\pi}{3}, \frac{5\pi}{3}\right]$ and ↓ for $x \in \left[0, \frac{\pi}{3}\right] \cup \left[\frac{5\pi}{3}, 2\pi\right]$
   (f) ↑ for $x \in \left[0, \frac{\pi}{12}\right] \cup \left[\frac{5\pi}{12}, \frac{13\pi}{12}\right] \cup \left[\frac{17\pi}{12}, 2\pi\right]$ and ↓ for $x \in \left[\frac{\pi}{12}, \frac{5\pi}{12}\right] \cup \left[\frac{13\pi}{12}, \frac{17\pi}{12}\right]$
8. (i) increasing (ii) increasing (iii) increasing (iv) increasing
   (v) increasing (vi) increasing
10. (a) $[0, \pi/6]$ (b) $x \in [1, \infty)$ (c) $[3/4, \infty)$

TEXTUAL EXERCISE–4: (OBJECTIVE)

1. The monotonic nature of following functions:

Column I

(i) $\ln(x + \sqrt{x^2+1}\ )$

(ii) a^x, $a > 1$

(iii) $x^3 + x$

(iv) $\tan x$

(v) $x^2 - 1$

(vi) $\cot x$

Column II

(a) increasing

(b) decreasing

(c) non-increasing

(d) non-decreasing

(e) non-monotonic

(f) cannot said

Correct match is

	(i)	(ii)	(iii)	(iv)	(v)	(vi)
(a)	a	a	b	b	e	f
(b)	a	a	a	a	e	b
(c)	a	b	c	d	e	f
(d)	f	a	a	a	e	b

2. The function $f(x) = x^2 (x - 2)^2$

(a) monotonically increases

(b) decreases $\forall\ x \in (-\infty, 0) \cup (1, 2)$

(c) increasing $\forall\ x \in (0, 1) \cup (2, \infty)$

(d) None of these

3. The function $f(x) = \log(1 + x) - \dfrac{2x}{2+x}$

(a) decreases $\forall\ x \in (-1, \infty)$

(b) increasing $\forall\ x \in (-1, \infty)$

(c) increasing $\forall\ x \in (1, 2)$

(d) None of these

4. $x - \sin x$ is increasing

(a) for all real numbers

(b) for +ve real numbers only

(c) for –ve real numbers only

(d) None of these

5. $\log(\sin x)$ is

(a) decreasing in $(0, \pi/2)$ and $(\pi/2, \pi)$

(b) always increasing

(c) increasing in $(0, \pi/2)$ and decreasing in $(\pi/2, \pi)$

(d) None of these

6. $a^{kx} - a^{-kx}\ \forall\ a > 1$

(a) Increasing for $k > 0$

(b) decreasing for $k < 0$

(c) increasing for $k < 0$

(d) decreasing for $k > 0$

7. $\sin(\cos x)$ defined in $[\pi, 2\pi]$ is

(a) monotonically increasing

(b) monotonically decreasing

(c) non-monotonic

(d) None of these

8. $\cos(\sin x)$ defined for $(0, \pi/2)$ is

(a) monotonically increasing

(b) monotonically decreasing

(c) non-monotonic

(d) None of these

9. State which of the following does not represent the correct order of the functions

(a) $x < x^2 < x^3 < x^4 < \ldots$; where $x \in (1, \infty)$

(b) $x > x^2 > x^3 > x^4 > \ldots$; where $x \in (0, 1)$

(c) $x < x^3 < x^5 < \ldots$ (–ve values); $x^2 > x^4 > x^6 > \ldots$ (+ve values); where $x \in (-1, 0)$

(d) $x > x^3 > x^5 > \ldots$ (–ve values); $x^2 > x^4 > x^6 > \ldots$ (+ve values); where $x \in (-\infty, -1)$

10. State which of the following does not represent the correct order of the functions

(a) $\dfrac{1}{x} > \dfrac{1}{x^2} > \dfrac{1}{x^3} > \dfrac{1}{x^4} > \ldots$; where $x \in (1, \infty)$

(b) $\dfrac{1}{x} < \dfrac{1}{x^2} < \dfrac{1}{x^3} < \dfrac{1}{x^4} < \ldots$;where $x \in (0,1)$

(c) $\dfrac{1}{x^2} < \dfrac{1}{x^4} < \dfrac{1}{x^6} < \ldots$ (+ve values) and $\dfrac{1}{x} < \dfrac{1}{x^3} < \dfrac{1}{x^5} < \ldots$ (–ve values); where $x \in (-1, 0)$

(d) $\dfrac{1}{x^2} > \dfrac{1}{x^4} > \dfrac{1}{x^6} \ldots$ (+ve values) and $\dfrac{1}{x} < \dfrac{1}{x^3} < \dfrac{1}{x^5} \ldots$ (-ve values); where $x \in (-\infty, -1)$

11. State which of the following does not represent the correct order of the functions

(a) $x^{1/2} > x^{1/3} > x^{1/4} > x^{1/5} \ldots$; where $(1, \infty)$

(b) $x^{1/2} < x^{1/3} < x^{1/4} < x^{1/5} \ldots$; where $(0, 1)$

(c) $x^{1/3} > x^{1/5} > x^{1/7} \ldots$; where $x \in (-1, 0)$

(d) $x^{1/3} > x^{1/5} > x^{1/7} \ldots$; where $x \in (-\infty, -1)$

12. The function $\dfrac{e^{2x} - 1}{e^{2x} + 1}$ is

(a) decreasing

(b) increasing

(c) odd

(d) even

Answer Keys

1. (b) 2. (b), (c) 3. (b), (c) 4. (a) 5. (c) 6. (a), (b) 7. (a) 8. (b) 9. (d) 10. (c)
11. (d) 12. (b), (c)

SOME STANDARD FUNCTIONS AND THEIR PROPERTIES

Algebraic Function

Functions consisting of finite number of terms involving powers and roots of the independent variable and the four fundamental operations (+, –, ×, ÷) are called algebraic functions.

e.g., $x^{3/2} + 5x$, $\frac{\sqrt{x+1}}{x-1}$, $x + 1$, $3x^4 - 5x + 7$.

ILLUSTRATION 46: Which of the following functions are algebraic and find their corresponding domains.

(i) $f(x) = \frac{x^2+1}{x-1}$ (ii) $f(x) = \sqrt{\frac{x}{x^2-1}}$

(iii) $f(x) = \frac{\sqrt{\sin x + 1}}{x^2 - 1}$ (iv) $f(x) = \frac{x^2 - 5x + 6}{(x-2)}$

(v) $f(x) = x\tan x$ (vi) $f(x) = \sin x + \cos^2 x$

SOLUTION: (i), (ii), (iv) are algebraic function whereas (iii), (v) and (vi) are non-algebraic functions as they do not involve all terms contianing powers of x.

(i) $f(x) = \frac{x^2+1}{x-1}$; $D_f = \mathbb{R} \sim \{1\}$

(ii) $f(x) = \sqrt{\frac{x}{x^2-1}}$; $\frac{x}{x^2-1} \geq 0$; $x^2 - 1 \neq 0$

$\Rightarrow x(x^2 - 1) \geq 0; x \neq \pm 1$ $\Rightarrow (x + 1)(x)(x - 1) \geq 0; x \neq \pm 1$

$\Rightarrow x \in (-1, 0] \cup (1, \infty) = D_f$

(iv) $f(x) = \frac{x^2 - 5x + 6}{(x-2)} = \frac{(x-2)(x-3)}{(x-2)} = x - 3$ for $x \neq 2$; $D_f = \mathbb{R} \sim \{2\}$

(v) $f(x) = x\tan x$ is defined for all $\mathbb{R}$ except for odd integral multiples of $\frac{\pi}{2}$

Thus, domain $= \mathbb{R} \sim \{(2n + 1)\frac{\pi}{2}; n \in \mathbb{Z}\}$.

(vi) $f(x) = \sin x + \cos^2 x$ is defined for all real numbers.

$\therefore$ $D_f = \mathbb{R}$; $f(x)$ being trigonometric function is non-algebraic.

POLYNOMIAL FUNCTION

A map $f : \mathbb{R} \to \mathbb{R}$ defined by $f(x) = a_0 + a_1x + a_2x^2 + \ldots + a_nx^n$; where $x \in \mathbb{R}$ and $a_1, a_2, \ldots, a_n \in \mathbb{R}$ is said to be a polynomial function. If $a_n \neq 0$, then n is called the degree of the polynomial.

e.g., $P(x) = x^7 + 2x^5 + 4$ (a polynomial of degree 7); $Q(x) = x^2 - 3x + 2$ (a polynomial of degree 2); $R(x) = 3 = 3x^0$ (a polynomial of degree 0).

REMARKS

1. *A polynomial of degree one with no constant term is called an odd linear function, i.e., $f(x) = ax, a \neq 0$.*
2. *Every power of x occurring in polynomial function is a whole number. That is, if any power of x is not whole number then the function is not a polynomial function.*
   e.g., $f(x) = x + \frac{1}{x}$; $f(x) = 2x^2 + 5\sqrt{x} + 7$ etc.
3. *There are two polynomial functions, satisfying the relation;* $f(x)\,f\left(\frac{1}{x}\right) = f(x) + f\left(\frac{1}{x}\right)$.
   They are (i) $f(x) = x^n + 1$ and (ii) $f(x) = 1 - x^n$, where n is a positive integer. That is, $f(x) = \pm x^n + 1$.
4. *All polynomial functions are algebraic but converse is not true, i.e., there are some algebraic functions which are not polynomials* e.g., $f(x)= x + \frac{1}{x}$; $f(x) = 2x^2 + 5\sqrt{x} + 7$ etc.
5. *The function defined as $f(x) = 0 \;\forall\; x \in \mathbb{R}$ is called* ***zero function****. Domain of zero function = $\mathbb{R}$ and range of zero function = {0}.*

ILLUSTRATION 47: Which of the following functions are polynomial functions?

(i) $f(x) = x^2 - 3x + 1/5$ (ii) $f(x) = x^2 + 1/x$

(iii) $f(x) = 3x^2 + \sqrt{x} - 5$ (iv) $f(x) = \sqrt[3]{x} + \sqrt{x} + 2$

(v) $f(x) = 5x^4 - 3x^2 + 2x - 7$ (vi) $f(x) = \sqrt{5}\,x^2 + \sqrt{2}\,x + 3$

(vii) $f(x) = \tan^2 x - 5\tan x + 6$

SOLUTION: (i), (v) and (vi) are polynomial functions as they contain whole number powers of x, for (ii) $f(x) = x^2 + x^{-1}$; $-1 \notin W$

(iii) $f(x) = 3x^2 + \sqrt{x} - 5 = 3x^2 + (x)^{1/2} - 5$; $\frac{1}{2} \notin W$

(iv) $f(x) = \sqrt[3]{x} + \sqrt{x} + 2 = (x)^{1/3} + (x)^{1/2} + 2; \frac{1}{3}, \frac{1}{2} \notin W$

(vii) $f(x) = \tan^2 x - 5\tan x + 6$ is not a polynomial in x, but a polynomial in $\tan x$.

That is, substituting $\tan x = t$, we get $f(t) = t^2 - 5t + 6$; which is a polynomial in t.

ILLUSTRATION 48: If $p(x)$ is a cubic polynomial such that $p(2) = 2$, $p(3) = 3$, $p(4) = 4$ and $p(5) = 6$, then evaluate p(10)

SOLUTION: Let $g(x) = p(x) - x$, then $g(2) = p(2) - 2 = 2 - 2 = 0$,

$g(3) = p(3) - 3 = 3 - 3 = 0$ and $g(4) = p(4) - 4 = 4 - 4 = 0$

Thus, $g(x)$ has three roots 2, 3 and 4. Also $p(x)$ is cubic implies $g(x) = p(x) - x$ is also cubic.

Thus, $g(x) = k(x - 2)(x - 3)(x - 4)$ for some non-zero real number k.

Now, $g(5) = p(5) - 5 = 6 - 5 = 1$

$\Rightarrow 1 = k(3)(2)(1)$

$\Rightarrow k = 1/6$

$\therefore \quad g(x) = \frac{1}{6}(x - 2)(x - 3)(x - 4)$

$\Rightarrow p(x) = g(x) + x = \frac{1}{6}(x-2)(x-3)(x-4) + x$

$\therefore \; p(10) = \frac{1}{6}(8)(7)(6) + 10 = 66.$

ILLUSTRATION 49: Evaluate $\sqrt{(50)(51)(53)(54)+(52)^2}$ without using calculator.

SOLUTION: Let $50 = x$

$\Rightarrow \sqrt{(50)(51)(53)(54)+(52)^2} = \sqrt{x(x+1)(x+3)(x+4)+(x+2)^2}$

$= \sqrt{x(x+4)(x+1)(x+3)+(x+2)^2} = \sqrt{(x^2+4x)(x^2+4x+3)+(x+2)^2}$

$= \sqrt{(x^2+4x)^2+3(x^2+4x)+(x^2+4x)+4}$

$= \sqrt{y^2+4y+4}$; where $y = (x^2 + 4x)$

$= \sqrt{(y+2)^2} = |y + 2| = y + 2 = x^2 + 4x + 2 = (50)^2 + 4(50) + 2$

$= 2500 + 200 + 2 = 2702$

ILLUSTRATION 50: Find a cubic polynomial $p(x)$ such that $(x-1)^2$ divides $p(x) - 1$ and $(x+1)^2$ divides $p(x) - 5$.

SOLUTION: Let $p(x) = ax^3 + bx^2 + cx + d$

$\therefore \; p(x) - 1 = ax^3 + bx^2 + cx + d - 1$ ... (1)

and $p(x) - 5 = ax^3 + bx^2 + cx + d - 5$ ... (2)

Now it is given that $(x-1)^2$ divides $p(x) - 1$ and $(x+1)^2$ divides $p(x) - 5$

That is, $(x-1)^2$ and $(x+1)^2$ are factors of $p(x) - 1$ and $p(x) - 5$ respectively.

$\Rightarrow p(1) - 1 = 0$ and $p(-1) - 5 = 0$ $\Rightarrow p(1) = 1$ and $p(-1) = 5$

$\Rightarrow a + b + c + d = 1$ .... (3)

$\Rightarrow d = 1 - a - b - c$ and $-a + b - c + d = 5$ .... (4)

$\Rightarrow d = 5 + a - b + c$

$\therefore$ From (1); $p(x) - 1 = a(x^3 - 1) + b(x^2 - 1) + c(x - 1)$

and $p(x) - 5 = a(x^3 + 1) + b(x^2 - 1) + c(x + 1)$

or $p(x) - 1 = (x - 1)[a(x^2 + x + 1) + b(x + 1) + c]$

and $p(x) - 5 = (x + 1)[a(x^2 - x + 1) + b(x - 1) + c]$

Further it is given by $(x-1)^2$ divides $p(x) - 1$ and $(x+1)^2$ divides $p(x) - 5$

Thus, $(x - 1)$ divides $a(x^2 + x + 1) + b(x + 1) + c$

and $(x + 1)$ divides $a(x^2 - x + 1) + b(x - 1) + c$

$\Rightarrow 3a + 2b + c = 0$ ... (5)

and $3a - 2b + c = 0$ ... (6)

Solving (5) and (6), we get $b = 0$, $c = -3a$

Also solving (3) and (4), $b + d = 3$

$\Rightarrow d = 3$, and $a + c = -2$ $\Rightarrow a = 1, b = 0, c = -3, d = 3$

$\therefore \; p(x) = x^3 - 3x + 3$ is the required cubic polynomial.

ILLUSTRATION 51: Find that the following functions are zero functions or not.

(a) $f(x) = \tan^{-1}x + \cot^{-1}x - \frac{1}{2}\cos^{-1}(-1)$ (b) $g(x) = \sec^2x - \cos^2x - \tan^2x - \sin^2x$

(c) $h(x) = ln(\sec^2x - \tan^2x)$ (d) $\phi(x)=\begin{cases}\frac{|x|-x}{x}; & x>0\\ \frac{|x|+x}{x}; & x<0\\ 0; & x=0\end{cases}$

SOLUTION: (a) $f(x) = \tan^{-1}x + \cot^{-1}x - \frac{1}{2}\cos^{-1}(-1) = \frac{\pi}{2} - \frac{1}{2}(\pi)$

$= 0 \ \forall \ x \in \mathbb{R}$

($\because \tan^{-1}x + \cot^{-1}x = \frac{\pi}{2} \ \forall \ x \in \mathbb{R}$ and $\cos^{-1}(-1) = \pi$)

(b) $g(x) = \sec^2x - \cos^2x - \tan^2x - \sin^2x = (\sec^2x - \tan^2x) - (\sin^2x + \cos^2x) = 1 - 1 = 0$ $\forall \ x \in \mathbb{R} \sim \{(2n + 1)\ \pi/2;\ n \in \mathbb{Z}\}$.

$\therefore$ $g(x)$ is not a zero function.

(c) $h(x) = ln(\sec^2x - \tan^2x) = \ln 1 = 0 \ \forall \ x \in \mathbb{R} \sim \{(2n + 1)\ \pi/2;\ n \in \mathbb{Z}\}$.

$\therefore$ $h(x)$ is not a zero function.

(d) $\phi(x)=\begin{cases}\frac{|x|}{x}-1; & x>0\\ \frac{|x|}{x}+1; & x<0\\ 0; & x=0\end{cases} = \begin{cases}1-1=0; & x>0\\ -1+1=0; & x<0\\ 0; & x=0\end{cases}$

$\therefore$ $\phi(x) = 0 \ \forall \ x \in \mathbb{R}$. $\therefore$ $\phi(x)$ is a zero function

■ RATIONAL FUNCTION

The function which can be written as the quotient of two polynomial functions (Denominator $\neq 0$) is said to be a rational function. If $P(x) = a_0 + a_1x + a_2x^2 + \ldots + a_nx^n$;

$Q(x) = b_0 + b_1x + b_2x^2 + \ldots + b_mx^m \neq 0$ be two polynomial functions, then $\frac{P(x)}{Q(x)}$ will be a rational function of x.

ILLUSTRATION 52: Which of the following functions are rational functions of x?

(i) $f(x) = \frac{x^2 - 3x + 1}{x + 5}$ (ii) $f(x) = \frac{x^2 - 2x + 5}{\sqrt{x-5}}$

(iii) $f(x) = \sqrt[3]{x} - 5x + \frac{1}{\sqrt[3]{x}}$ (iv) $f(x) = 2x^2 - \frac{1}{x} + 5$

(v) $f(x) = \frac{\left(\sqrt{2x-1}+x\right)\left(\sqrt{2x-1}-x\right)}{(x-1)}$

SOLUTION: (i) $f(x) = \dfrac{x^2-3x+1}{x+5}$ is a rational function as both numerator and denominator are polynomial functions.

(ii) $f(x) = \dfrac{x^2-2x+5}{\sqrt{x-5}}$ is not a rational function as denominator is not a polynomial function.

(iii) $f(x)$ is not a rational function as $f(x)$ contains cube root of x.

(iv) $\dfrac{2x^3+5x-1}{x}$ is a rational function.

(v) $f(x) = \dfrac{\left(\sqrt{2x-1}+x\right)\left(\sqrt{2x-1}-x\right)}{(x-1)}$

$= \dfrac{2x-1-x^2}{(x-1)} = -\dfrac{(x^2-2x+1)}{(x-1)} = \dfrac{-(x-1)^2}{(x-1)} = -(x-1)$ for $x \neq 1$.

Therefore $f(x)$ is a rational function but with numerator polynomial on restricted domain, i.e., $\mathbb{R} \sim \{1\}$.

■ IRRATIONAL FUNCTION

The algebraic functions containing terms having rational powers of x (non-integral) are known as irrational functions.e.g., $y = \sqrt{x}$, $y = \dfrac{\sqrt{x^3+1}-\sqrt{x^{11}}}{\sqrt{x^2+x+1}}$,

$y = \dfrac{x^{17/3}+x^{103/7}-x}{\sqrt[3]{x^{17}+x^{15}-3}}$, $y = \dfrac{\sqrt{\sqrt{x^2+5}+x^{16.5}+x^{1/3}}}{\sqrt{x^2-7}-\sqrt{\sqrt{x^{2/3}-1}}}$

If such function contains $(f(x))^{\frac{2p+1}{2m}}$, $p, m \in \mathbb{Z}$, then it is undefined for $f(x) < 0$.

■ POWER FUNCTION

The function $f(x) = c.x^n$, where c, n are real constants and x is a real variable is known as power function. Usually we denote it as $f(x) = x^n$ by choosing $c = 1$. Its graph is symmetrical about y-axis if n is a rational number of the form $\dfrac{2p}{2q+1}$, where p and q are integers and symmetric about origin if n is a rational number of the form $\dfrac{2p+1}{2q+1}$, where p and q are integers. The graph of power function lies entirely in first quadrant if n is a rational number of the form $\dfrac{2p+1}{2q}$ or n is an irrational number.

Domain of power function depends on the constant n. The following cases are possible:

Case (i): If $n = \dfrac{2p+1}{2q} > 0$; where $(p, q) \in \mathbb{Z}$; $q \neq 0$, then

$f(x) = c.(x)^n = c.(x)^{\frac{2p+1}{2q}} = c.\left((x)^{2p+1}\right)^{\frac{1}{2q}}$ which is defined for non-negative values of $\left(x^{2p+1}\right)$, i.e., non-negative values of x.

∴ Domain of $f(x)$ will be $[0, \infty)$ in this case.

Case (ii): If $n = \dfrac{2p+1}{2q} < 0$; where $(p, q) \in \mathbb{Z}$; $q \neq 0$, then

$f(x) = c.(x)^n = c.(x)^{\frac{2p+1}{2q}} = c.\left((x)^{2p+1}\right)^{\frac{1}{2q}}$ which is defined for positive values of $\left(x^{2p+1}\right)$, i.e., positive values of x

∴ Domain of $f(x)$ will be $(0, \infty)$ in this case.

Case (iii) If $n = \dfrac{p}{2q+1} \geq 0$; where $p, q \in \mathbb{Z}$ and $2q+1 \neq 0$, then $f(x) = c.(x)^n = c\ (x)^{\frac{p}{2q+1}}$ is defined for all real values of x.

⇒ In this case domain of function will be $\mathbb{R}$.

Case (iv): If $n = \dfrac{p}{2q+1} < 0$, then $f(x) = c(x)^n = c(x)^{\frac{p}{2q+1}}$ is defined for all non-zero real numbers.

∴ In this case domain of function will be $\mathbb{R} \sim \{0\}$.

Case (v) If n is an irrational number (i.e., power function with irrational exponent). Let us discuss this case by using a particular power function when $n = \sqrt{2}$ and $x = 2$.

∴ $f(2) = (2)^{\sqrt{2}}$. We can find $(2)^{\sqrt{2}}$ by approximating the irrational exponent by rational exponent that are closer to the irrational one. In our example, we need to find the exponent $(2)^{\sqrt{2}}$ .We know that to one significant figure $\sqrt{2} = 1$, so the first approximation to $2^{\sqrt{2}}$ is $2^1 = 2$. To two significant figures, $\sqrt{2} = 1.4 = \dfrac{14}{10} = \dfrac{7}{5}$, so the second approximation to $(2)^{\sqrt{2}}$ is $(2)^{(7/5)}$ = the 5th root of 2^7 or the 7th power of the 5th root of 2 which is approximately 2.639. To three significant figures, $\sqrt{2} = 1.41 = \dfrac{141}{100}$, so we have to take a 100th root of 2 and then raise it to the 141st power, or else take the 100th root of 2^{141}, to get approximately 2.65737. Continuing this way, we get the sequence of approximations as given below 2, 2.639, 2.65737, 2.66475, 2.665119, 2.6651375, 2.66514310,…

The above sequence converges to a limit (this is a calculus idea), because the function 2^x is continuous (another calculus concept). That limit is what we call the value of $2^{\sqrt{2}} \approx 2.665144143$. We cannot write down all the digits in the decimal expansion. This is the way how we can find irrational exponents.

So, to find $(x)^n$; where n is an irrational real number we have to replace n by rational numbers closer and closer to n. But by doing so, we are to encounter with rational numbers of the form $\dfrac{p}{2q+1}$ as well as of the form $\dfrac{2p+1}{2q}$.

Thus, for using all these rational numbers x must be non-negative for positive irrational number n. Thus, domain for $f(x)$ will be $[0, \infty)$ in this case. Further x must be positive for negative irrational number n. Thus, domain for $f(x)$ will be $(0, \infty)$ in this case.

Thus, from above discussion we conclude that the domain of power function $f(x) = c.x^n$ is $[0, \infty)$ for positive irrational number n and it is $(0, \infty)$ for negative irrational number n.

Graphs of some power functions are as follows:

(a) When $f(x) = (x)^{2n-1}$; $n \in \mathbb{N}$; i.e., the power is an odd natural number. Domain = $\mathbb{R}$

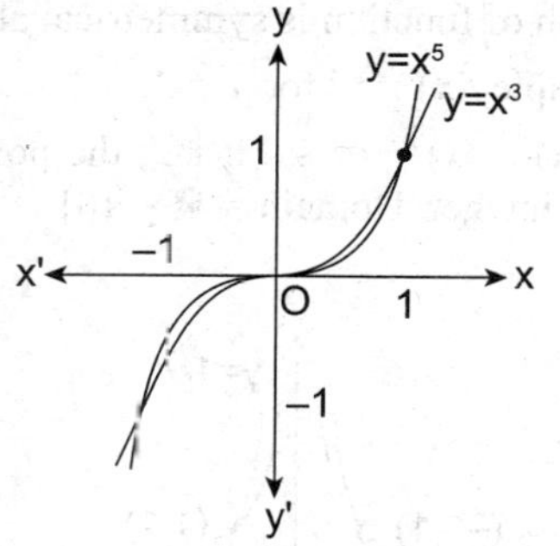

FIGURE 2.51

The graph of function is symmetrical about origin. For example, $f(x) = x^5$ for $n = 3$.

(b) When $f(x) = x^{-(2n-1)}$; $n \in \mathbb{N}$; i.e., the power is an odd negative integer. Domain = $\mathbb{R} \sim \{0\}$

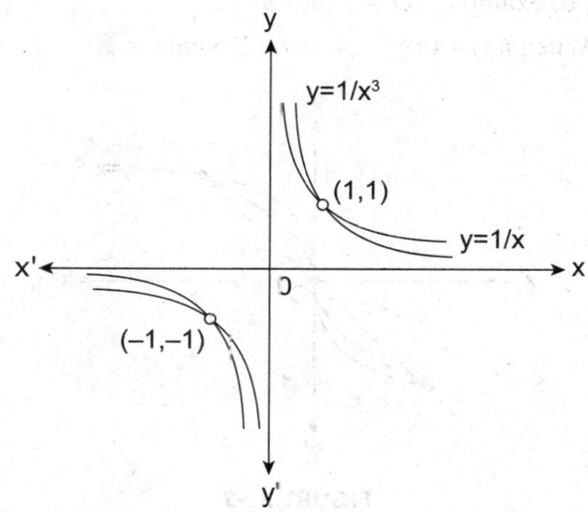

FIGURE 2.52

The graph of function is symmetrical about origin. For example, $f(x) = x^{-5}$ for $n = 3$.

(c) When $f(x) = (x)^{2n}$; $n \in \mathbb{N}$; i.e., the power is an even natural number. Domain = $\mathbb{R}$

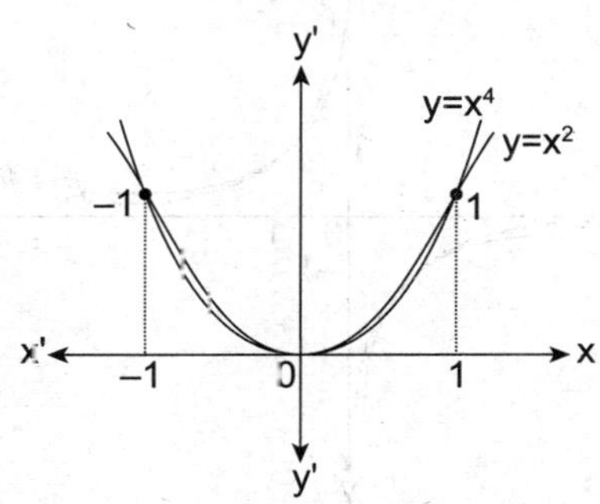

FIGURE 2.53

The graph of function is symmetrical about y-axis
For example $f(x) = x^4$ for $n = 2$.

(d) When $f(x) = (x)^{-2n}$; $n \in \mathbb{N}$; i.e., the power is an even negative integer. Domain = $\mathbb{R} \sim \{0\}$

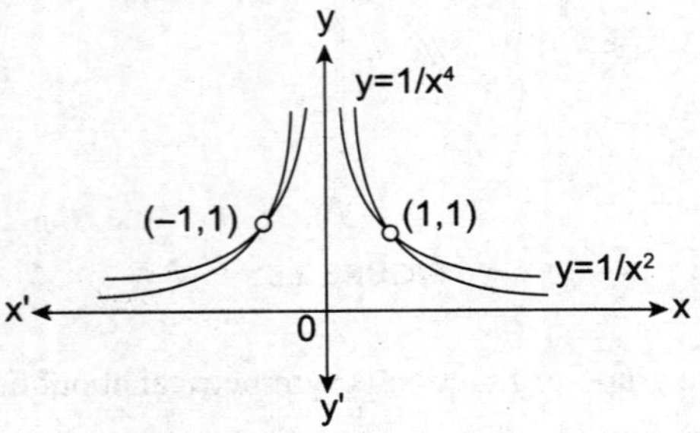

FIGURE 2.54

The graph of function is symmetrical about y-axis
For example $f(x) = x^{-4}$ for $n = 2$.

(e) When $f(x) = (x)^{1/2n-1}$; $n \in \mathbb{N}$; Domain = $\mathbb{R}$

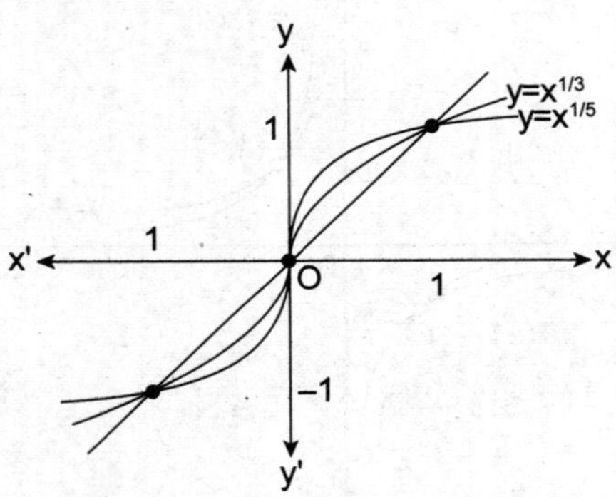

FIGURE 2.55

The graph of function is symmetrical about origin.
For example, $f(x) = x^{1/7}$ for $n = 4$.

(f) When $f(x) = (x)^{-\frac{1}{2n-1}}$; $n \in \mathbb{N}$; Domain = $\mathbb{R} \sim \{0\}$

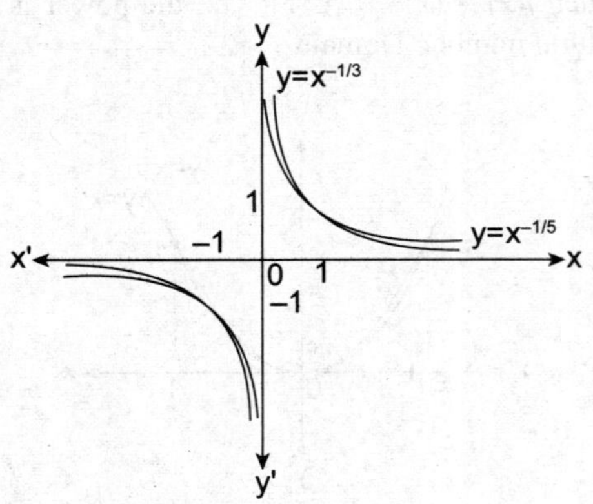

FIGURE 2.56

The graph of function is symmetrical about origin.
For example, $f(x) = x^{-1/7}$ for $n = 4$.

(g) When $f(x) = (x)^{\frac{1}{2n}}$; $n \in \mathbb{N}$; Domain = $[0, \infty)$

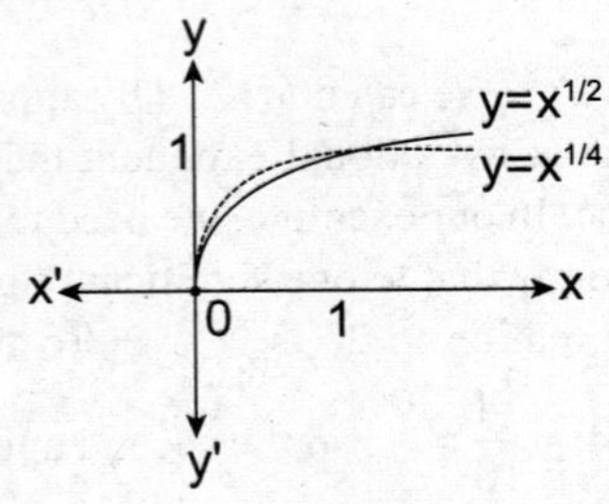

FIGURE 2.57

The graph of function lies only in first quadrant.
For example, $f(x) = x^{1/2} = \sqrt{x}$ for $n = 1$.

(h) When $f(x) = (x)^{-\frac{1}{2n}}$; $n \in \mathbb{N}$; Domain = $(0, \infty)$

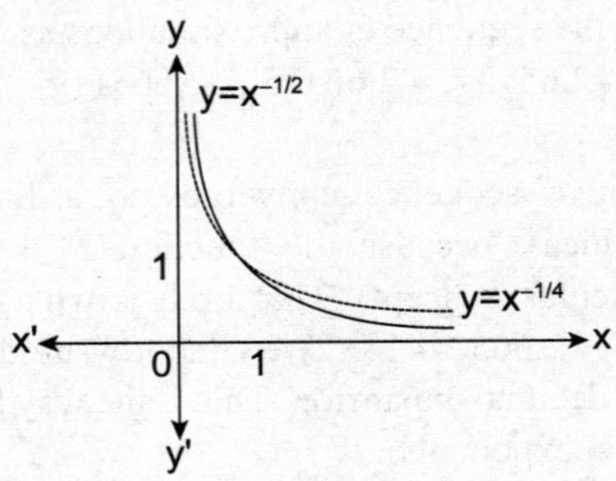

FIGURE 2.58

The graph of function lies only in first quadrant.
For example, $f(x) = x^{-1/4} = \dfrac{1}{\sqrt[4]{x}}$ for $n = 2$.

(i) When $f(x) = (x)^{\frac{2n}{2n+(2m-1)}}$; $n, m \in \mathbb{N}$. Clearly

$$0 < \frac{2n}{2n+(2m-1)} < 1 \ \forall \ n, m \in \mathbb{N}$$

Domain of function will be $\mathbb{R}$.
Its graph is as shown below as Figure 2.59.

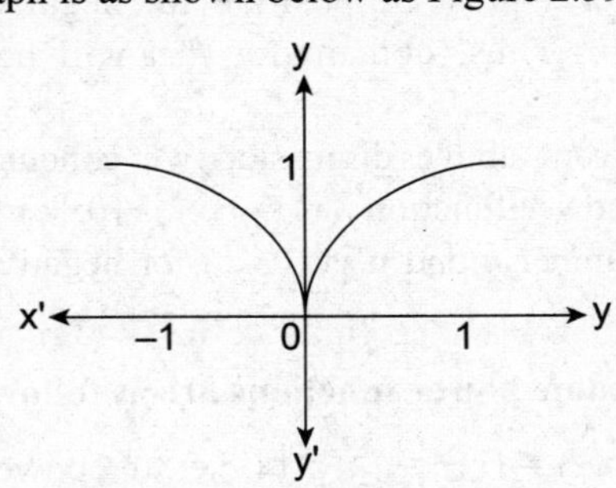

FIGURE 2.59

The graph of function is symmetrical about y-axis

For example, $y = (x)^{2/3}$ for $n = 1$, $m = 1$

(j) When $f(x) = (x)^{\frac{2n}{2n-(2m-1)}}$; $n, m \in \mathbb{N}$ and $m < \dfrac{2n+1}{2}$.

Clearly $m < \dfrac{2n+1}{2}$

$\Rightarrow 2n - (2m - 1) > 0$ and $2m - 1 \geq 1$

$\Rightarrow 2n > 2n - (2m - 1)$

$\Rightarrow \dfrac{2n}{2n-(2m-1)} > 1$

Domain of function is $\mathbb{R}$.

The graphs of such functions will be as shown in Figure 2.62.

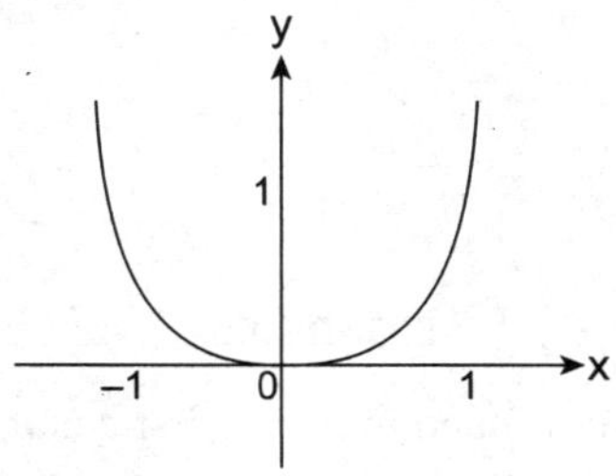

FIGURE 2.60

For example, $y = (x)^{6/5}$ for $n = 3$, $m = 1$.

(k) When $f(x) = (x)^{\frac{2n-1}{2m-1}}$; $n, m \in \mathbb{N}$; $n < m$; Domain $= \mathbb{R}$.

Clearly $n < m$

$\Rightarrow 2n - 1 < 2m - 1$

$\Rightarrow \dfrac{2n-1}{2m-1} \in (0,1)$.

The graph of function will be as shown in Figure 2.61.

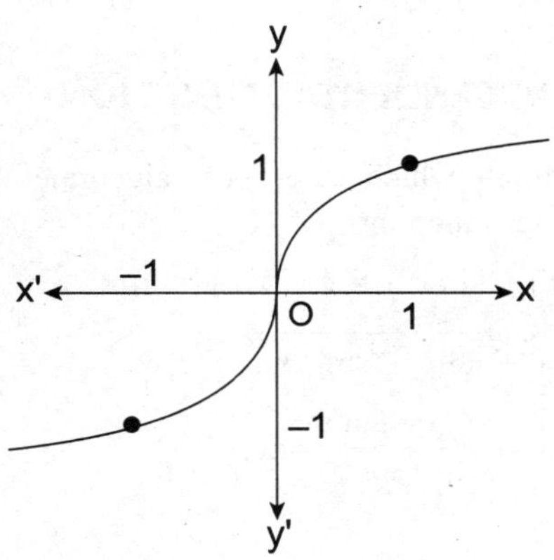

FIGURE 2.61

The graph of function is symmetrical about origin.

For example, $y = (x)^{3/5}$ for $n = 2$, $m = 3$

(l) When $f(x) = (x)^{\frac{2n-1}{2m-1}}$; $n, m \in \mathbb{N}$; $n > m$; Domain $= \mathbb{R}$.

Clearly $n > m$

$\Rightarrow 2n - 1 > 2m - 1$

$\Rightarrow \dfrac{2n-1}{2m-1} \in (1, \infty)$.

The graph of function will be as shown in Figure 2.62.

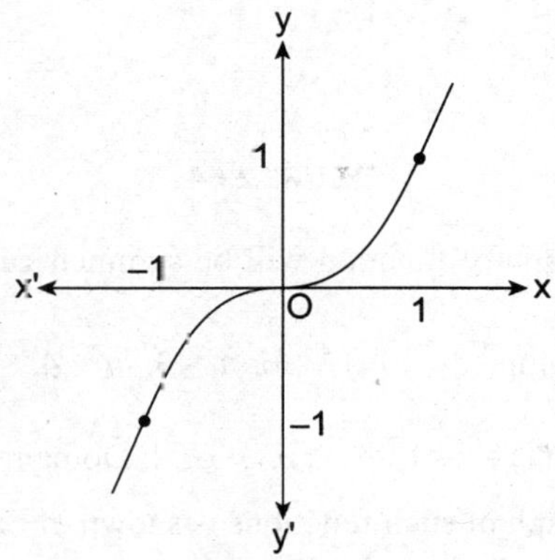

FIGURE 2.62

The graph of function is symmetrical about origin

For example, $y = (x)^{7/3}$ for $n = 4$, $m = 2$.

(m) When $y = (x)^{-\frac{(2n-1)}{2m}}$; $n, m \in \mathbb{N}$; Domain $= (0, \infty)$

The graph of such functions will be as shown below in Figure 2.63.

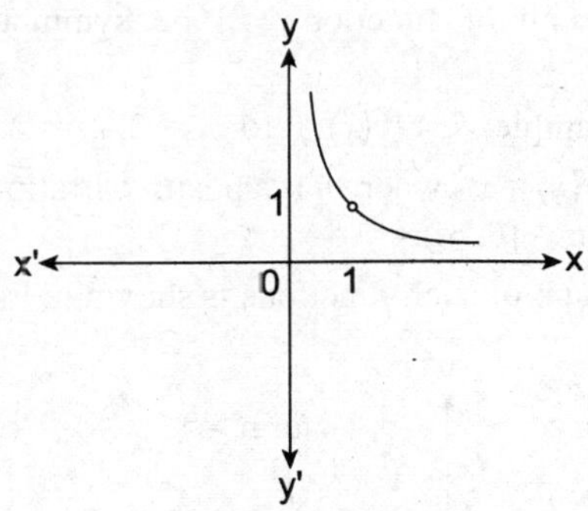

FIGURE 2.63

The graph of function will lie only in first quadrant.

For example, $y = (x)^{-5/6}$ for $n = 3$, $m = 3$.

(n) When $y = (x)^{-\frac{(2n-1)}{(2m-1)}}$; $n, m \in \mathbb{N}$; Domain $= \mathbb{R} \sim \{0\}$.

The graph of such functions will be as shown below in Figure 2.64.

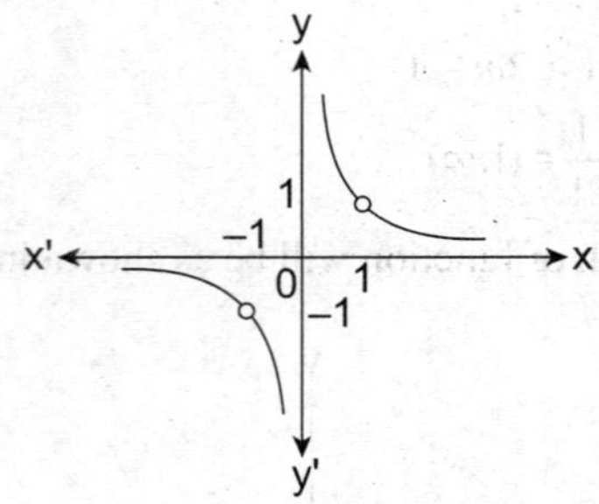

FIGURE 2.64

The graph of function will be symmetrical about origin.

For example, $y = (x)^{-5/7}$ for $n = 3$, $m = 4$.

(o) When $f(x) = (x)^{-\frac{2n}{(2m-1)}}$; $n, m \in \mathbb{N}$; Domain $= \mathbb{R} \sim \{0\}$.

The graph of such functions is shown in Figure 2.65.

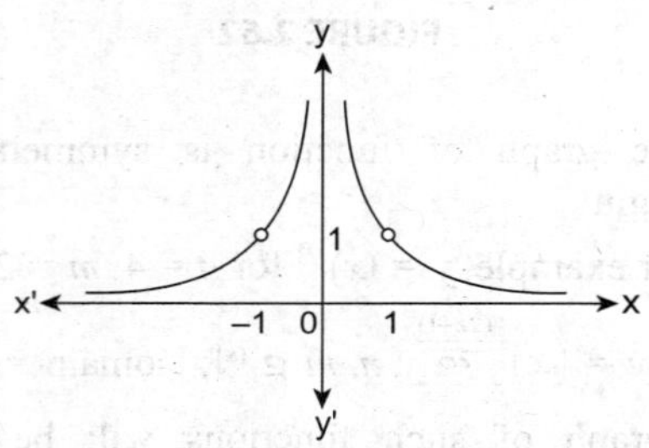

FIGURE 2.65

The graph of function will be symmetrical about y-axis.

For example, $f(x) = (x)^{-4/3}$ for $n = 2$, $m = 2$.

(p) When $f(x) = x^n$; where n is a positive irrational number. Domain $= [0, \infty)$.

The graph of such functions is shown in Figure 2.66.

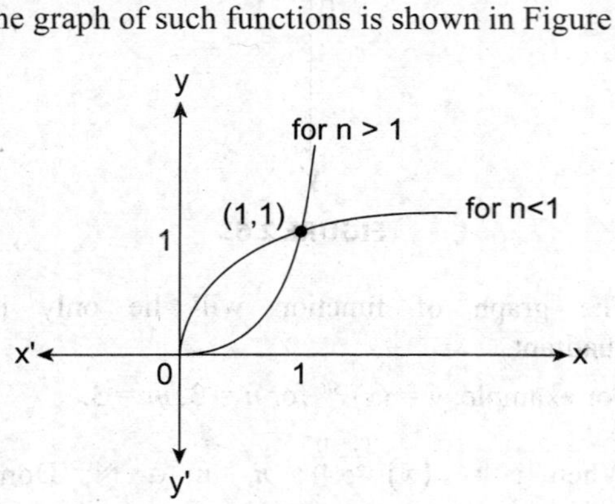

FIGURE 2.66

The graph of function lies in first quadrant.

For example, $f(x) = (x)^{\sqrt{2}}$ for $n = \sqrt{2}$ (> 1) and $f(x) = (x)^{\frac{1}{\sqrt{3}}}$ for $n = \frac{1}{\sqrt{3}}(<1)$.

(q) When $f(x) = x^n$; where n is a negative irrational number. Domain $= (0, \infty)$.

The graph of such functions wis shown in Figure 2.67.

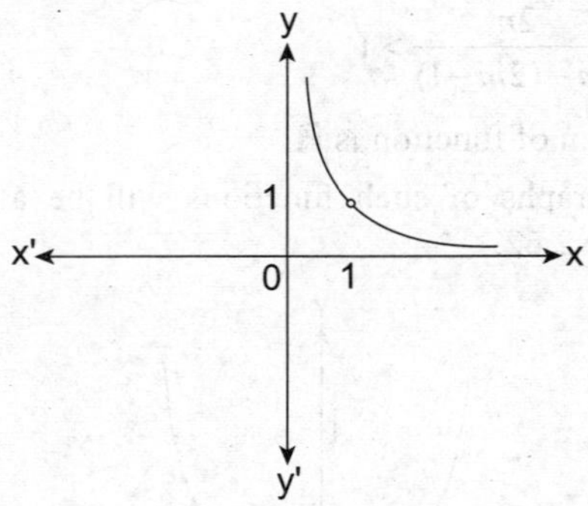

FIGURE 2.67

The graph of function lies in first quadrant.

For example, $f(x) = (x)^{-\sqrt{2}}$ for $n = -\sqrt{2}$

Comparison of the values of $x, x^2, x^3, x^4, \ldots$

For	The relative values are
$x \in (1, \infty)$	$x < x^2 < x^3 < x^4 < \ldots$
$x \in (0, 1)$	$x > x^2 > x^3 > x^4 > \ldots$
$x \in (-1, 0)$	$x < x^3 < x^5 < \ldots$ (–ve values) $x^2 > x^4 > x^6 > \ldots$ (+ve values)
$x \in (-\infty, -1)$	$x > x^3 > x^5 > \ldots$ (–ve values) $x^2 < x^4 < x^6 < \ldots$ (+ve values)

■ TRANSCENDENTAL FUNCTION

The functions which are not algebraic are called transcendental functions.

e.g., $f(x) = \sin x$, $y = \cos^{-1} x$, $y = \ln x$,

$$y = \sqrt{\ln x - \sin^{-1} x},$$

$$y = \frac{\ln x + \tan x}{\sin^{-1} x + 2^x} \text{ etc.}$$

■ MODULUS FUNCTION

The modulus function $f(x) = |x|$ is nothing but is magnitude of the real number x and it represents distance of the number

x from zero on the real number line. Since the distance is always non-negative, the modulus of a real number x is always non-negative and is defined

$$\text{as } |x| = \begin{cases} x & \text{when } x > 0 \\ 0 & \text{when } x = 0 \\ -x & \text{when } x < 0 \end{cases}$$

e.g., $|3| = 3$ and $|-6| = -(-6) = 6$.

The graph of modulus function is as shown in Figure 2.68.

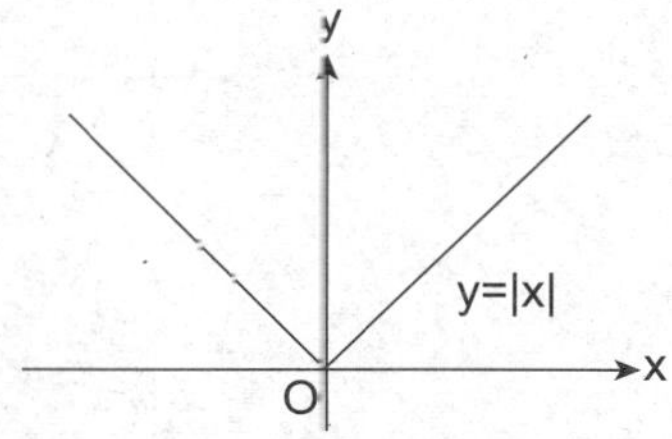

FIGURE 2.68

Clearly, the domain of modulus function is $\mathbb{R}$ and range is the set of non-negative real numbers.

ILLUSTRATION 53: Solve the equation $|x^2 - 4x| + |x - 2| = 6$

SOLUTION: $x^2 - 4x = 0 \quad \Rightarrow x = 0, 4$

and $x - 2 = 0 \quad \Rightarrow x = 2$

Thus, we divide the whole real number line into four parts. i.e., $(-\infty, 0)$; $[0, 2)$, $[2, 4)$, $[4, \infty)$.

For each part let us analyze for the solution.

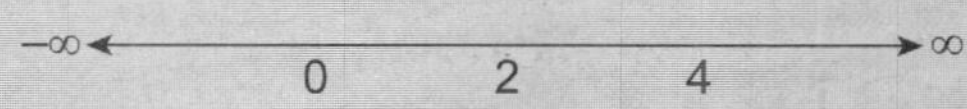

FIGURE 2.69

Case (i): For $-\infty < x < 0$; we have $x < 0$ and $x < 4$

$\Rightarrow x(x - 4) > 0 \quad \Rightarrow x^2 - 4x > 0$

$\Rightarrow |x^2 - 4x| = x^2 - 4x$

Also $x < 0 \quad \Rightarrow x < 2$

$\Rightarrow x - 2 < 0 \quad \Rightarrow |x - 2| = -(x - 2)$

$\therefore$ Given equation become $x^2 - 4x - x + 2 = 6 \quad \Rightarrow x^2 - 5x - 4 = 0$

$$\Rightarrow x = \frac{5 \pm \sqrt{25+16}}{2} = \frac{5 \pm \sqrt{41}}{2}; \text{ but } x < 0 \Rightarrow x = \frac{5 - \sqrt{41}}{2}$$

Case (ii) For $0 \le x < 2$

we have $x \ge 0$ and $x - 4 < 0$

$\Rightarrow x(x - 4) \le 0 \quad \Rightarrow |x^2 - 4x| = -(x^2 - 4x)$

Also $x < 2 \quad \Rightarrow x - 2 < 0 \Rightarrow |x - 2| = -(x - 2)$

$\therefore$ Given equation becomes $-x^2 + 4x - x + 2 = 6$

$\Rightarrow -x^2 + 3x - 4 = 0 \quad \Rightarrow x^2 - 3x + 4 = 0$; which has no real roots.

Case (iii) When $2 \le x < 4$

we have $x > 0$ and $x - 4 < 0$

$\Rightarrow x(x - 4) < 0 \quad \Rightarrow (x^2 - 4x) < 0$

$\Rightarrow |x^2 - 4x| = -(x^2 - 4x)$ and $x \ge 2 \quad \Rightarrow x - 2 \ge 0 \quad \Rightarrow |x - 2| = (x - 2)$

$\therefore$ Given equation become $-x^2 + 4x + x - 2 = 6 \Rightarrow -x^2 + 5x - 8 = 0$

$\Rightarrow x^2 - 5x + 8 = 0$ which has no real root.

Case (iv) When $x > 4$

$\Rightarrow x, x - 4 > 0 \quad \Rightarrow x^2 - 4x > 0$

$\Rightarrow |x^2 - 4x| = x^2 - 4x$ and $x > 2 \quad \Rightarrow x - 2 > 0 \quad \Rightarrow |x - 2| = x - 2$

$\therefore$ Given equation become $x^2 - 4x + x - 2 = 6 \Rightarrow x^2 - 3x - 8 = 0$

$$\Rightarrow x = \frac{3 \pm \sqrt{9+32}}{2} \Rightarrow x = \frac{3 \pm \sqrt{41}}{2}; \text{ but } x > 4 \Rightarrow x = \frac{3+\sqrt{41}}{2}$$

$\therefore \quad x = \dfrac{5-\sqrt{41}}{2}$ and $x = \dfrac{3+\sqrt{41}}{2}$ are the only solutions of the given equation.

ILLUSTRATION 54: Solve the equation $|x - |2 - x|| - 4x = 8$

SOLUTION: The given equation can be reduced to $|x - (2 - x)| - 4x = 8$ for $x \le 2$ and $|x + (2 - x)| - 4x = 8$ for $x > 2$.

i.e., $|2x - 2| - 4x = 8$ for $x \le 2$ and $2 - 4x = 8$ for $x > 2$ (impossible)

Further, it can be reduced to $2x - 2 - 4x = 8$ for $x \le 2$ and $x \ge 1$

and $-2x + 2 - 4x = 8$ for $x \le 2$ and $x < 1$

i.e., $2x = -10$ for $x \in [1, 2]$ (impossible) and $6x = -6$ for $x \in (-\infty, 1) \Rightarrow x = -1$

Thus, $x = -1$ is the only possible solution of given equation.

ILLUSTRATION 55: Find the values of x satisfying the equation $|||x^2 - 5x + 7| - 1| - 2| = x^2 - 3x - 4$

SOLUTION: $\because$ Disc. of $x^2 - 5x + 7 = 25 - 28 < 0 \Rightarrow \quad x^2 - 5x + 7 > 0\ \forall\ x \in \mathbb{R}$

So, the given equation becomes $||x^2 - 5x + 6| - 2| = x^2 - 3x - 4$

Now $x^2 - 5x + 6 \ge 0$ for $x \in (-\infty, 2] \cup [3, \infty)$ and $x^2 - 5x + 6 < 0$ for $x \in (2, 3)$

$\therefore$ We have $|x^2 - 5x + 4| = x^2 - 3x - 4$ for $x \in (-\infty, 2] \cup [3, \infty)$

and $|x^2 - 5x + 8| = x^2 - 3x - 4$ for $x \in (2, 3)$

But $x^2 - 5x + 4 \ge 0$ for $x \in (-\infty, 1] \cup [4, \infty)$

and $x^2 - 5x + 4 < 0$ for $x \in (1, 4)$ and $x^2 - 5x + 8 > 0\ \forall\ x \in \mathbb{R}$

$\therefore$ The equation reduces to $x^2 - 5x + 4 = x^2 - 3x - 4$ for $x \in (-\infty, 1] \cup [4, \infty)$

and $-(x^2 - 5x + 4) = x^2 - 3x - 4$ for $x \in (1, 2] \cup [3, 4)$

and $x^2 - 5x + 8 = x^2 - 3x - 4$ for $x \in (2, 3)$

$\Rightarrow$ $2x = 8$ for $x \in (-\infty, 1] \cup [4, \infty) \Rightarrow x = 4$ and $2x^2 - 8x = 0$ for $x \in (1, 2] \cup [3, 4)$

That is, no solution and $2x = 12$ for $x \in (2, 3)$, i.e., no solution

$\Rightarrow$ $x = 4$ is the only solution of given equation.

ILLUSTRATION 56: Find the minimum value of the expression $|x - p| + |x - 25| + |x - p - 25|$ for $x \in [p, 25]$ and $p \in [0, 25]$.

SOLUTION: Let $f(x, p) = |x - p| + |x - 25| + |x - p - 25|$ .... (1)

Now we have $0 \le p \le x \le 25$

$\Rightarrow$ $x - p \ge 0, x - 25 \le 0, x - p - 25 < 0$ as $x - 25 \le 0$ and $p \ge 0$

$\therefore$ $f(x, p) = x - p - x + 25 - (x - p - 25) \quad \therefore f(x, p) = 25 - p - x + p + 25 = 50 - x$

Which has its minimum value 25, when $x = 25$.

ILLUSTRATION 57: Draw the plane region defined by $R = \{(x, y) \in \mathbb{R}^2 : |x + 2| \le 7; |x| \ge 3; |y| \ge 2\}$

SOLUTION: Given $|x + 2| \le 7$

$\Rightarrow -7 \le x + 2 \le 7 \quad \Rightarrow -9 \le x \le 5$ .... (1)

Also $|x| \ge 3 \quad \Rightarrow x \le -3$ or $x \ge 3$ .... (2)

and $|y| \ge 2 \quad \Rightarrow y \le -2$ or $y \ge 2$ .... (3)

∴ (1), (2); and (3) hold simultaneously on region

$R = \{(x, y) \in \mathbb{R}^2 : x \in [-9, -3] \cup [3, 5]$ and $y \in (-\infty - 2] \cup [2, \infty)\}$ as shown in Figure 2.70.

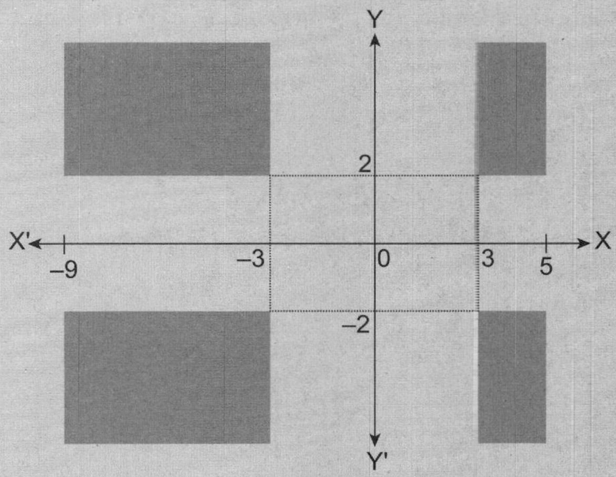

FIGURE 2.70

ILLUSTRATION 58: Solve the following inequalities graphically

(i) $4|x - 1| < (x + 2)$

(ii) $|x^2 - 4x| + |x| \geq 3$

SOLUTION: (i) Let $f(x) = |x - 1|$ and $g(x) = \frac{1}{4}(x+2)$

To solve the inequality $4|x - 1| < (x + 2)$ is equivalent to write $f(x) < g(x)$ i.e., we are to find those values of x for which the graph of $f(x)$ is below the graph of $g(x)$.

This can be done by drawing both the graphs on same $x - y$ plane and finding those points where graph of $f(x)$ is below the graph of $g(x)$ as shown in Figure 2.71.

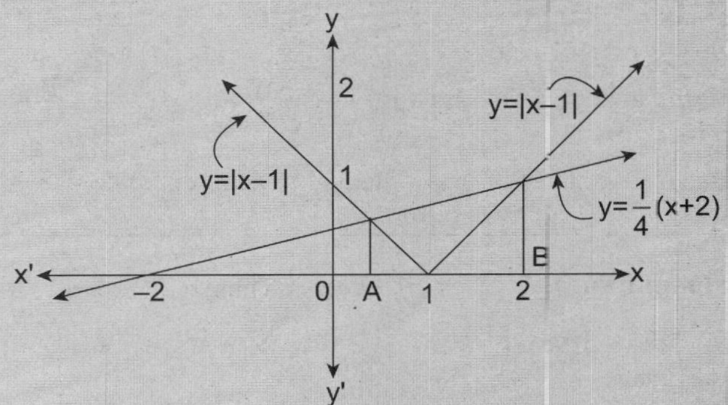

FIGURE 2.71

Clearly graph of $f(x) = |x - 1|$ is below the graph of $g(x) = \frac{1}{4}(x+2)$ for x lying on segment AB of x-axis excluding A and B. And coordinates of A and B are $\left(\frac{2}{5}, 0\right)$ and (2, 0), respectively.

Thus, solution of given inequality is given by $x \in \left(\frac{2}{5}, 2\right)$.

(ii) Given inequality is $|x^2 - 4x| + |x| \geq 3$ or equivalently $|x^2 - 4x| \geq 3 - |x|$

Let $f(x) = |x^2 - 4x|$ and $g(x) = 3 - |x|$. Thus, we are to find those points where $f(x) \geq g(x)$

The graph of $y = f(x)$ and $y = g(x)$ are as shown in Figure 2.72.

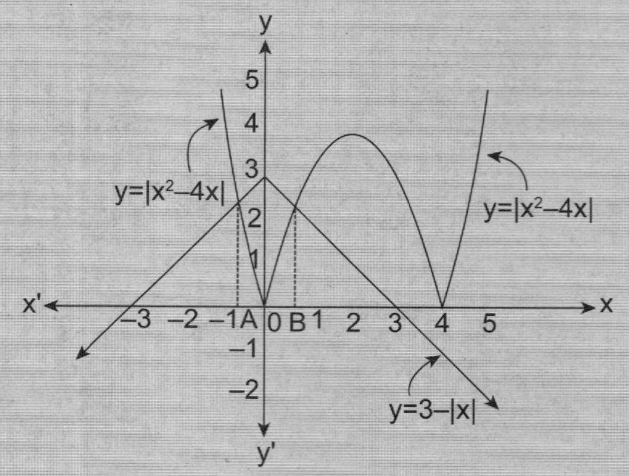

FIGURE 2.72

Clearly for x lying on segment $X'A$ and BX of x-axis, graph of $y = f(x)$ lies on or above the graph of $y = g(x)$. Coordinates of A are given by solving $x^2 - 4x = 3 + x$

$$\Rightarrow x^2 - 5x - 3 = 0 \Rightarrow x = \frac{5 \pm \sqrt{25+12}}{2} = \frac{5 \pm \sqrt{37}}{2}; \text{ But } x < 0 \quad \Rightarrow x = \frac{5-\sqrt{37}}{2}$$

$\therefore$ Coordinates of A are $\left(\frac{5-\sqrt{37}}{2}, 0\right)$

Further, coordinates of B are given by solving $-(x^2 - 4x) = 3 - x$

$$\Rightarrow x^2 - 5x + 3 = 0 \Rightarrow x = \frac{5 \pm \sqrt{25-12}}{2} = \frac{5 \pm \sqrt{13}}{2}, \text{ but } x \in (0, 4) \quad \Rightarrow x = \frac{5-\sqrt{13}}{2}$$

$\therefore$ Coordinates of B are given by $\left(\frac{5-\sqrt{13}}{2}, 0\right)$

Thus, the solution of given inequality is given by $\left(-\infty, \frac{5-\sqrt{37}}{2}\right) \cup \left(\frac{5-\sqrt{13}}{2}, \infty\right)$.

Properties of Modulus of a real number:

1. $|x_1 . x_2 . x_3 . \ldots . x_n| = |x_1| . |x_2| . |x_3| \ldots |x_n| \; \forall \, x_i \in \mathbb{R}$

Proof: Let $x_1, x_2, x_3, \ldots, x_n \in \mathbb{R}$

First of all we shall prove that $|x_1 . x_2| = |x_1| . |x_2| \ldots$ (1)

Let $x_1, x_2 \in \mathbb{R}$, then

$$|x_1 . x_2| = \begin{cases} x_1 . x_2 & \text{if } x_1 . x_2 \geq 0 \\ -(x_1 x_2) & \text{if } x_1 . x_2 < 0 \end{cases}$$

$$= \begin{cases} (x_1)(x_2) = |x_1||x_2| & \text{if } x_1 \geq 0, x_2 \geq 0 \\ (-x_1)(-x_2) = |x_1||x_2| & \text{if } x_1 < 0, x_2 < 0 \\ (-x_1).(x_2) = |x_1||x_2| & \text{if } x_1 < 0, x_2 \geq 0 \\ (x_1).(-x_2) = |x_1||x_2| & \text{if } x_1 \geq 0, x_2 < 0 \end{cases}$$

Thus, $|x_1 . x_2| = |x_1| . |x_2| \; \forall \, x_1, x_2 \in \mathbb{R}$

Now $|x_1 . x_2 . x_3 \ldots . x_n| = |x_1(x_2 . x_3 \ldots . x_n)|$

$= |x_1| . |x_2 (x_3 \ldots . x_n)|$

$\vdots \quad \vdots \quad \vdots \quad \vdots$

$= |x_1| |x_2| |x_3| \ldots . |x_n|$

2. $\left|\frac{x}{y}\right| = \frac{|x|}{|y|} \; \forall \, x, y \in \mathbb{R}$ and $y \neq 0$.

Proof: $\left|\frac{x}{y}\right| = \begin{cases} \frac{x}{y} & \text{if } \frac{x}{y} \geq 0 \\ -\frac{x}{y} & \text{if } \frac{x}{y} < 0 \end{cases}$

$$= \begin{cases} \dfrac{(x)}{(y)} & \text{if } x \ge y > 0 \text{ and } \dfrac{-x}{-y} \text{ if } x \le 0, y < 0 \\ \dfrac{(-x)}{(y)} & \text{if } x < 0, y > 0 \text{ and } \dfrac{(x)}{(-y)} \text{ if } x > 0, y < 0 \end{cases}$$

$= \dfrac{|x|}{|y|}$ in each case

Thus, $\left|\dfrac{x}{y}\right| = \dfrac{|x|}{|y|}$ $\forall\, x, y \in \mathbb{R}$ and $y \ne 0$

3. $|x^n| = |x|^n \;\forall\, n \in \mathbb{Z}$

Proof: Obviously $|x^n| = |x|^n$ holds good for $n = 1$ and $n = 0$ $(x \ne 0)$

Now let $n \in \mathbb{N}$ and $n \ge 2$, then $|x^n| = |\underbrace{x.x.x....x}_{n\text{-times}}|$

$= \underbrace{|x|.|x|.|x|....|x|}_{n\text{-times}} = |x|^n$ [by property (1)]

Next let $n = -m$; $m \in \mathbb{N}$ and $x > 0$, then

$|x^n| = |x^{-m}| = \left|\dfrac{1}{x^m}\right| = \dfrac{|1|}{|x^m|} = \dfrac{1}{|x|^m}$ (by property (2))

$= |x|^{-m} = |x|^n$.

Thus, $|x^n| = |x|^n \;\forall\, n \in \mathbb{Z}$ for all real values of x for which LHS and RHS are defined.

REMARK

$|x^t| = |x|^t \;\forall\, t \in \mathbb{Q}$ (set of rational numbers)

$$\left|x^{\frac{p}{q}}\right| = \begin{cases} (x)^{p/q} = |x|^{p/q} & \text{for } x \ge 0; \quad \dfrac{p}{q} > 0 \\ (x)^{p/q} = |x|^{p/q} & \text{for } x > 0; \quad \dfrac{p}{q} < 0 \\ (\pm x)^{p/q} = |x|^{p/q} & \text{for } p = \text{even integer}, q \text{ odd integer}, \dfrac{p}{q} > 0; \quad x \in \mathbb{R} \\ (\pm x)^{p/q} = |x|^{p/q} & \text{for } p = \text{even integer}, q = \text{odd integer}, \dfrac{p}{q} < 0; \quad x \in \mathbb{R} \sim \{0\} \\ (x)^{p/q} = |x|^{p/q} & \text{for } p = \text{odd integer}, q = \text{even integer}, \dfrac{p}{q} > 0; \quad x \in [0, \infty) \\ (x)^{p/q} = |x|^{p/q} & \text{for } p = \text{odd integer}, q = \text{even integer}, \dfrac{p}{q} < 0; \quad x > 0 \\ |x|^{p/q} & \text{for } p, q = \text{odd integer}, \dfrac{p}{q} > 0; \quad x \in \mathbb{R} \\ (-x)^{p/q} = |x|^{p/q} & \text{for } p, q = \text{odd integer}, \dfrac{p}{q} < 0; \quad x \in \mathbb{R} \sim \{0\} \end{cases}$$

$= |x|^{p/q}$ *in each case for all those values of x for which* $|x^{p/q}|$ *is defined. Hence, proved.*

4. $|-x| = |x| \;\forall\, x \in \mathbb{R}$

Proof: $|-x| = \begin{cases} -x & \text{iff } -x \ge 0 \\ -(-x) & \text{iff } -x < 0 \end{cases}$

$= \begin{cases} -x & \text{iff } x \le 0 \\ x & \text{iff } x > 0 \end{cases} = |x|$

5. $|x| = \delta \Rightarrow x = \delta$ or $x = -\delta$

Proof: Given $|x| = \delta \ge 0$

We know that there exist exactly two real numbers of opposite signs having same positive magnitude.

$\therefore\; |x| = \delta \ge 0 \quad \Rightarrow \quad x = \pm\,\delta.$

6. $|x| < \delta \;\Rightarrow\; x \in (-\delta, \delta)$ and $|x| > \delta$

$\Rightarrow x \in (-\infty, -\delta) \cup (\delta, \infty)$

Proof: Let $|x| < \delta$

$\Rightarrow$ Absolute value of x is less than δ.

$\Rightarrow$ Distance of x from origin is less than δ.

$\Rightarrow$ x will be at origin or is found either on left side of origin or on right side of origin at a distance less than δ.

$\Rightarrow x > -\delta$ or $x < \delta \Rightarrow x \in (-\delta, \delta)$; Now $|x| > \delta \Rightarrow |x| \nleq \delta$

$\Rightarrow x \notin [-\delta, \delta] \Rightarrow x \in (-\infty, -\delta) \cup (\delta, \infty)$

7. $|x-a|<\delta \Rightarrow x \in (a-\delta, a+\delta)$

Proof: $|x-a|<\delta$

$\therefore$ By above property (5)

$\Rightarrow -\delta < x-a < \delta$

$\Rightarrow a-\delta < x < a+\delta$

$\Rightarrow x \in (a-\delta, a+\delta)$

8. $|x-a| = \delta \quad \Rightarrow \quad x = a+\delta$ or $a-\delta$

Proof: Given $|x-a| = \delta$

By property (4)

$x-a = \pm\delta \quad \Rightarrow \quad x = a \pm \delta$

9. $|x-a| > \delta \quad \Rightarrow \quad x > a+\delta$ or $x < a-\delta$

Proof: Given $|x-a| > \delta$

By property (5)

$x-a < -\delta$ or $x-a > \delta$

$x < a-\delta$ or $x > a+\delta$

10. $\sqrt{x^2} = |x| \ \forall\, x \in \mathbb{R}$

Proof: $\sqrt{x^2}$ = Principal square root of x^2

$= \left|(x^2)^{1/2}\right| = |\pm x| = |x|$

11. $|x| = \max.\{-x, x\} \ \forall\, x \in \mathbb{R}$

Proof: $|x| = \begin{cases} x & \text{if } x \geq 0 \\ -x & \text{if } x < 0 \end{cases}$ .... (i)

when $x \geq 0 \quad \Rightarrow \quad -x \leq 0 \quad \Rightarrow x \geq -x$

$\Rightarrow$ maximum $\{x, -x\} = x$ ... (ii)

and when $x < 0$

$\Rightarrow -x > 0 \quad \Rightarrow -x > x \Rightarrow$ maximum $\{-x, x\} = -x$ (iii)

Thus, from (i), (ii) and (iii), we have $|x|$ = maximum $\{x, -x\}$

12. $|x| = |y| \Leftrightarrow x^2 = y^2$

Proof: Given $|x| = |y|$

$\because\ |x| = |y| \ \Rightarrow \ |x|^2 = |y|^2 \ \Rightarrow \quad x^2 = y^2$

and conversely if $|x|^2 = |y|^2$

$\Rightarrow (|x|-|y|)(|x|+|y|) = 0$

$\Rightarrow |x| = |y|$ or $|x| = -|y|$

(But $|x| = -|y|$ is possible only when $x = y = 0$)

$\Rightarrow |x| = |y| = 0$

Thus, $|x| = |y| \Leftrightarrow |x|^2 = |y|^2$

$\Leftrightarrow x^2 = y^2 \quad (\because |x|^2 = x^2\ \forall\, x \in \mathbb{R})$

13. $|x+y|$ is not always equal to $|x| + |y|$.

Proof: Given $|x+y|$

$|x+y|$

$= \begin{cases} |x|+|y| & \text{for } x>0, y>0 \text{ or } x<0, y<0 \\ \big||x|-|y|\big| < |x|+|y| & \text{for } x>0, y<0 \text{ or } x<0, y>0 \end{cases}$

Thus, $|x+y|$ is not always equal to $|x| + |y|$.

14. (Triangle inequality) $|x+y| \leq |x| + |y|$ for all real x and y, inequality holds if $x.y < 0$. That is, x and y are of opposite signs, equality holds if $x.y \geq 0$. That is, x and y are of same sign or at least one of x and y is zero.

Proof: $x \leq |x|$ and $y \leq |y|$

$\Rightarrow x+y \leq |x|+|y|$ .... (1)

Also $-x \leq |x|$ and $-y \leq |y|$

$\Rightarrow -(x+y) \leq |x|+|y|$

$\Rightarrow (x+y) \geq -(|x|+|y|)$ .... (2)

$\therefore$ from (1) and (2) we have

$-(|x|+|y|) \leq (x+y) \leq (|x|+|y|)$

$\Rightarrow |x+y| \leq |x|+|y| \quad (\because -\delta \leq x \leq \delta \Rightarrow |x| \leq \delta)$

Here $|x+y| = \begin{cases} (x+y) & \text{for } (x+y) \geq 0 \\ -(x+y) & \text{for } (x+y) < 0 \end{cases}$

$= \begin{cases} |x|+|y| & \text{for } x \geq 0,\ y \geq 0 \\ x+y < |x|+|y| & \text{for } x+y>0\ \&\ x.y<0 \\ |x|+|y| & \text{for } x<0,\ y<0 \\ -x-y < |x|+|y| & \text{for } x+y<0\ \&\ x.y<0 \end{cases}$

Thus, $|x+y| = |x| + |y|$ for x and y of same sign or at least one of x and y is zero and $|x+y| < |x| + |y|$ for x and y of opposite signs. i.e., $|x+y| = |x| + |y|$ for $x.y \geq 0$ and $|x+y| < |x| + |y|$ for $x.y < 0$

15. $|x-y| \leq |x| + |y|$ for real x and y, inequality holds if $x.y > 0$, i.e., x and y are of same sign, equality holds. If $x.y \leq 0$, That is, x and y are of opposite sign or at least one of x and y is zero.

Proof: By triangle inequality $|x+y| \leq |x| + |y|\ \forall\, x, y \in \mathbb{R}$

$\Rightarrow |x+(-y)| \leq |x| + |-y|\ \forall\, x, -y \in \mathbb{R}$

$\Rightarrow |x-y| \leq |x|+|y|\ \forall\, x, y \in \mathbb{R}$

ILLUSTRATION 59: Solve the following equations/inequations.

(i) $|x^2-4x| + |5x-10| = |x^2+x-10|$ (ii) $|x^2-3x| + |2x-6| = |x^2-5x+6|$

(iii) $|x^2-4x| + |x+6| > |x^2-5x-6|$ (iv) $|x^2-7x| + |6x-2| > |x^2-x-2|$

SOLUTION: (i) $|x^2 - 4x| + |5x - 10| = |x^2 + x - 10| = |(x^2 - 4x) + (5x - 10)|$

$\because$ $|a| + |b| = |a + b| \Leftrightarrow a.b \geq 0$

$\therefore$ $(x^2 - 4x)(5x - 10) \geq 0$

$\Rightarrow$ $x(x - 4)(x - 2) \geq 0$

$\Rightarrow$ $x \in [0, 2] \cup [4, \infty)$

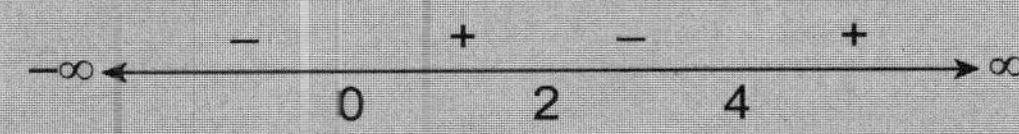

FIGURE 2.73

(ii) $|x^2 - 3x| + |2x - 6| = |x^2 - 5x + 6| = |(x^2 - 3x) - (2x - 6)|$

$\because$ $|a| + |b| = |a - b|$ $\quad \Leftrightarrow a.b \leq 0$

$\therefore$ $(x^2 - 3x)(2x - 6) \leq 0 \Rightarrow x(x - 3)(x - 3) \leq 0 \quad \Rightarrow x(x - 3)^2 \leq 0$

$\Rightarrow x \leq 0 \quad \therefore x \in (-\infty, 0]$

(iii) $|x^2 - 4x| + |x + 6| > |x^2 - 5x - 6| = |(x^2 - 4x) - (x + 6)|$

$\because$ $|a| + |b| > |a - b| \Leftrightarrow a.b > 0$

$\Rightarrow$ $(x^2 - 4x)(x + 6) > 0$

$\Rightarrow$ $x(x - 4)(x + 6) > 0$

$\Rightarrow$ $x \in (-6, 0) \cup (4, \infty)$

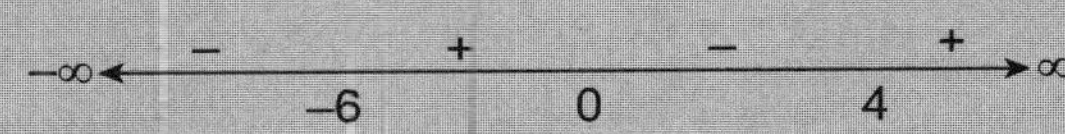

FIGURE 2.74

(iv) $|x^2 - 7x| + |6x - 2| > |x^2 - x - 2| = |(x^2 - 7x) + (6x - 2)|$

$\because$ $|a| + |b| > |a + b|$

$\Leftrightarrow$ $a.b < 0$

$\Rightarrow$ $(x^2 - 7x)(6x - 2) < 0 \quad \Rightarrow \quad x(x - 7)(3x - 1) < 0 \Rightarrow x \in (-\infty, 0) \cup (1/3, 7)$

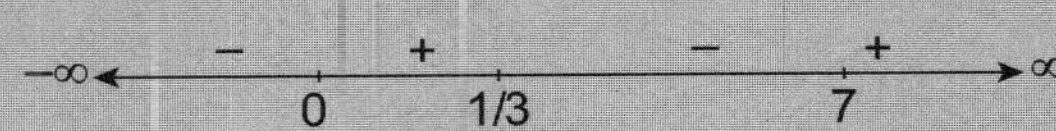

FIGURE 2.75

16. $||x| - |y|| \leq |x + y|$ for real x and y. Equality holds if x and y are of opposite signs and for same sign inequality holds.

Proof: $|x| = |(x + y) + (-y)| \leq |x + y| + |-y|$ (By triangle inequality)

$\Rightarrow$ $|x| \leq |x + y| + |y|$

$\Rightarrow$ $|x| - |y| \leq |x + y|$ $\quad \ldots (1)$

Also $|y| = |(x + y) + (-x)| \leq |x + y| + |-x|$ (By triangle inequality)

$\Rightarrow$ $|y| \leq |x + y| + |x|$

$\Rightarrow$ $|y| - |x| \leq |x + y| \quad \Rightarrow \quad -(|x| - |y|) \leq |x + y|$

or $|x| - |y| \geq -|x + y|$ $\quad \ldots . (2)$

$\therefore$ from (1) and (2)

$-|x + y| \leq |x| - |y| \leq x + y|$

$\Rightarrow$ $||x| - |y|| \leq |x + y|$ $\quad (\because -\delta \leq x \leq \delta \Rightarrow |x| \leq \delta)$

$\Rightarrow$ $|x + y| \geq ||x| - |y|| \; \forall \; x, y \in \mathbb{R}$

17. $||x| - |y|| \leq |x - y|$ for real x and y. Equality holds if x and y are of same sign and for opposite signs inequality holds.

Proof: By Property (15), $||x| - |y|| \leq |x + y|$ for real x and y. Replacing y by $-y$, we get $||x| - |-y|| \leq |x - y|$ for real x and $-y$

$\Rightarrow$ $||x| - |y|| \leq |x - y| \; \forall \; x, y \in \mathbb{R}$

ILLUSTRATION 60: Find the interval in which x can lie in order to satisfy the following inequalities:

(a) $|x - 3| < 5$ $\quad$ (b) $|x + 1/2| \geq \frac{3}{2}$

(c) $|3 - x| \leq \frac{5}{2}$ $\quad$ (d) $|x^2 - 4x + 5| = |x^2 - 3x| + |5 - x|$

SOLUTION: (a) $|x - 3| < 5 \quad \Rightarrow -5 < x - 3 < 5 \quad \Rightarrow -2 < x < 8$

(b) $|x + \frac{1}{2}| \geq \frac{3}{2} \quad \Rightarrow x + \frac{1}{2} \geq \frac{3}{2}$ or $x + \frac{1}{2} \leq -\frac{3}{2} \quad \Rightarrow x \geq 1$ or $x \leq -2$

(c) $|3-x| \le \frac{5}{2} \Rightarrow -\frac{5}{2} \le 3-x \le \frac{5}{2} \Rightarrow -\frac{5}{2} \le x-3 \le \frac{5}{2}$

$\Rightarrow 3-\frac{5}{2} \le x \le \frac{5}{2}+3 \Rightarrow \frac{1}{2} \le x \le \frac{11}{2}$

(d) $(x^2-3x)(5-x) \ge 0 \Rightarrow x(x-5)(x-3) \le 0 \Rightarrow x \in (-\infty, 0] \cup [3, 5]$

ILLUSTRATION 61: Solve the equation $x^2 - 5|x| + 6 = 0$

SOLUTION: The given equation is equivalent to $\begin{cases} x^2-5x+6=0 & \text{if } x \ge 0 \\ x^2+5x+6=0 & \text{if } x<0 \end{cases} \Rightarrow \begin{cases} (x-2)(x-3)=0 & \text{if } x \ge 0 \\ (x+2)(x+3)=0 & \text{if } x<0 \end{cases}$

Hence, the solutions of the given equation are $x_1 = 2, x_2 = 3, x_3 = -2, x_4 = -3$.

ILLUSTRATION 62: Solve $|x^2-4| + |x^2-9| = 5$.

SOLUTION: There are three cases:

Case I: When $x^2 < 4$, i.e., $-2 < x < 2$

In this case $|x^2-4| = -(x^2-4)$ and $|x^2-9| = -(x^2-9)$

So, the given equation becomes $-(x^2-4)-(x^2-9) = 5$

$\Rightarrow x^2 = 4 \qquad \Rightarrow x = \pm 2$, no solution

Case II: When $4 \le x^2 < 9$, i.e., $-3 < x \le -2$ or $2 \le x < 3$

In this case $|x^2-4| = (x^2-4)$ and $|x^2-9| = -(x^2-9)$

So, the given equation becomes $x^2-4-(x^2-9) = 5 \Rightarrow 5 = 5$

Thus, the given equation becomes an identity in this case, i.e., all values of x such that $-3 < x \le -2$ or $2 \le x < 3$ satisfy the given equation.

Case III: When $x^2 \ge 9$, i.e., $x \le -3$ or $x \ge 3$

In this case $|x^2-4| = (x^2-4)$ and $|x^2-9| = (x^2-9)$

So, the given equation becomes $(x^2-4)+(x^2-9) = 5 \Rightarrow x^2 = 9 \qquad \Rightarrow x = \pm 3$

Clearly both of these values satisfy $x \le -3$ or $x \ge 3$

$\therefore$ Solution set $= \{x : -3 \le x \le -2 \text{ or } 2 \le x \le 3\}$

■ SIGNUM FUNCTION

The function $f(x)$ defined by $f(x) = \begin{cases} \frac{|x|}{x}; & \text{if } x \ne 0 \\ 0; & \text{if } x = 0 \end{cases}$

i.e., $f(x) = \text{sgn}(x) = \begin{cases} 1 \text{ if } x > 0 \\ 0 \text{ if } x = 0 \\ -1 \text{ if } x < 0 \end{cases}$

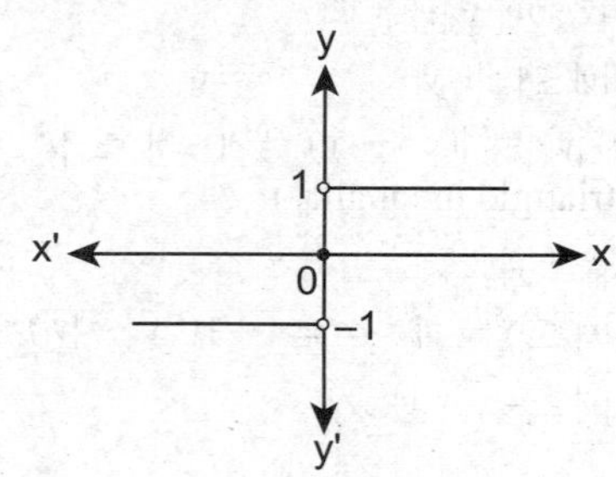

FIGURE 2.76

ILLUSTRATION 63: Solve the following equations:

(i) $(\text{sgn } x)^2 - 1 = 0$

(ii) $(\text{sgn } x) + 1 = 0$

(iii) $\frac{(\text{sgn } x - 1)(\text{sgn } x + 2)}{(\text{sgn } x - 3)} = 0$

(iv) $\text{sgn}(x-1) = -1$

(v) $\text{sgn}|x^2-1| = 0$

SOLUTION : (i) $(\text{sgn } x)^2 - 1 = 0 \Rightarrow \text{sgn}(x) = \pm 1 \Rightarrow x \in \mathbb{R} \sim \{0\}$

(ii) $\text{sgn}x + 1 = 0 \Rightarrow \text{sgn}x = -1 \Rightarrow x < 0 \Rightarrow x \in (-\infty, 0)$

(iii) $\dfrac{(\text{sgn}\, x-1)(\text{sgn}\, x+2)}{(\text{sgn}\, x-3)} = 0 \Rightarrow \text{sgn } x = 1, -2$

$\text{sgn } x = 1, -2$; but $\text{sgn} \in \{-1, 0, 1\}$ $\therefore$ $\text{sgn } x \neq -2$

$\therefore$ $\text{sgn } x = 1 \Rightarrow x > 0$ $\therefore$ $x \in (0, \infty)$

(iv) $\text{sgn } (x - 1) = -1 \Rightarrow x - 1 < 0 \Rightarrow x < 1$

(v) $\text{sgn } |x^2 - 1| = 0 \Rightarrow |x^2 - 1| = 0 \Rightarrow x^2 - 1 = 0 \Rightarrow x = \pm 1.$

■ CONSTANT FUNCTION

A function $f : A \to B$ is said to be a constant function if every element of A has the same f – image in B. That is, $f : A \to B; f(x) = c, \forall\, x \in A, c \in B$ is a constant function.

A constant function may be one–one (when domain contains only one element), many–one (when domain contains more than one elements), onto (when co-domain or range contains only single element i.e., c), into (when co-domain contains at-least one more element other than c).

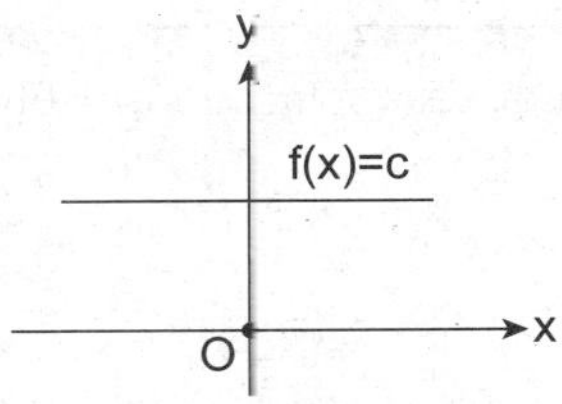

FIGURE 2.77

ILLUSTRATION 64: Which of the following are constant functions on $\mathbb{R}$?. If not on $\mathbb{R}$, then find the domain on which they are constant.

(i) $\text{sgn } x + sgn(-x)$

(ii) $\sin^2 x + \cos^2 x$

(iii) $\text{cosec}^2 x - \cot^2 x$

(iv) $\dfrac{\left(\sqrt{2x-1}+x\right)\left(\sqrt{2x-1}-x\right)}{(x-1)^2}$

(v) $\begin{cases} |x|+x & if\ x<0 \\ |x|-x & if\ x \geq 0 \end{cases}$

(vi) $\ln e^7$

(vii) $e^{ln\, 10}$

SOLUTION: (i) $f(x) = \text{sgn } x + sgn\ (-x) = -1 + 1 = 0$, for $x < 0$ and $f(x) = 0$ for $x = 0$

and $f(x) = 1 + (-1) = 0$ for $x > 0$

$\Rightarrow f(x) = 0\ \forall\ x \in \mathbb{R}$ $\Rightarrow f(x)$ is a constant function on $\mathbb{R}$

(ii) $f(x) = \sin^2 x + \cos^2 x = 1\ \forall\ x \in \mathbb{R}$

$\therefore$ $f(x)$ is a constant function on $\mathbb{R}$.

(iii) $f(x) = \text{cosec}^2 x - \cot^2 x = 1\ \forall\ x \in \mathbb{R} \sim \{n\pi : n \in \mathbb{Z}\}$

$\therefore$ $f(x)$ is not constant function on $\mathbb{R}$; but it is so on $\mathbb{R} \sim \{n\pi\ ; n \in \mathbb{Z}\}$

(iv) $f(x) = \dfrac{(\sqrt{2x-1}+x)(\sqrt{2x-1}-x)}{(x-1)^2} = \dfrac{(2x-1)-x^2}{(x-1)^2} = -\dfrac{(x-1)^2}{(x-1)^2} = -1$ for $x \in \left[\dfrac{1}{2}, \infty\right) \sim \{1\}$

Therefore $f(x)$ is not a constant function on $\mathbb{R}$, *but* $f(x)$ is constant function on $\left[\dfrac{1}{2}, \infty\right) \sim \{1\}$

(v) $f(x) = \begin{cases} |x|+x & \text{if } x<0 \\ |x|-x & \text{if } x \geq 0 \end{cases} = \begin{cases} -x+x & \text{if } x<0 \\ x-x & \text{if } x \geq 0 \end{cases}$

$\Rightarrow f(x) = 0\ \forall\ x \in \mathbb{R}$ $\Rightarrow f(x)$ is constant function $\forall\ x \in \mathbb{R}$.

■ IDENTITY FUNCTION

The function $f: A \to B$ defined by $f(x) = x;\ x \in A$; (where A is a subset of B) is called the identity function.

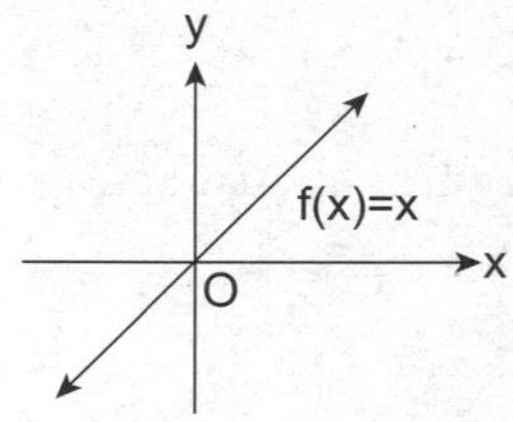

FIGURE 2.78

If $B = A$, then the function is called identity function on set A and is denoted by I_A. Identity function I_A defined on A is a bijection.

ILLUSTRATION 65: Which of the following functions is/are identity function(s) on $\mathbb{R}$?

(i) $f(x) = \frac{2}{\pi}(\sin^{-1} x + \cos^{-1} x)x$ (ii) $f(x) = \frac{2}{\pi}(\tan^{-1} x + \cot^{-1} x)x$

(iii) $f(x) = e^{\ln x}$ (iv) $f(x) = \ln e^x$

(v) $f(x) = \cos^{-1}(\cos x)$ (vi) $f(x) = \cos(\cos^{-1} x)$

(vii) $f(x) = \tan(\tan^{-1} x)$ (viii) $f(x) = \tan^{-1}(\tan x)$

SOLUTION: (i) $f(x) = \frac{2}{\pi}(\sin^{-1} x + \cos^{-1} x)x = \frac{2}{\pi}\frac{\pi}{2}.x = x\ \forall\ \in [-1,1]$

$\therefore\ f(x) = x\ \forall\ x \in [-1,1]$ but not $\forall\ x \in \mathbb{R}$

$\therefore\ f(x)$ is not identity function on $\mathbb{R}$.

(ii) $f(x) = \frac{2}{\pi}(\tan^{-1} x + \cot^{-1} x)x = \frac{2}{\pi}\frac{\pi}{2}.x = x\ \forall\ x \in \mathbb{R}$

$\therefore\ f(x) = x\ \forall\ x \in \mathbb{R}$.

$\Rightarrow f(x)$ is an identity function on $\mathbb{R}$.

(iii) $f(x) = e^{\ln x} = x$ for all positive real numbers x

$\therefore\ f(x) = x$ for all $x > 0$ but not $\forall\ x \in \mathbb{R}$

$\therefore\ f(x)$ is not an identity function on $\mathbb{R}$.

(iv) $f(x) = \ln e^x = x\ \forall\ x \in \mathbb{R}$

$\therefore\ f(x) = \ln e^x$ is an identity function on $\mathbb{R}$.

(v) $f(x) = \cos^{-1}(\cos x) = x\ \forall\ x \in [0, \pi]$ but not $\forall\ x \in \mathbb{R}$

$\therefore\ f(x)$ is not an identity function on $\mathbb{R}$.

(vi) $f(x) = \cos(\cos^{-1} x) = x\ \forall\ x \in [-1, 1]$ but not $\forall\ x \in \mathbb{R}$

$\therefore\ f(x)$ is not an identity function on $\mathbb{R}$.

(vii) $f(x) = \tan(\tan^{-1} x) = x\ \forall\ x \in \mathbb{R}$

$\therefore\ f(x)$ is an identity function on $\mathbb{R}$.

(viii) $f(x) = \tan^{-1}(\tan x) = x\ \forall x \in \left(-\frac{\pi}{2}, \frac{\pi}{2}\right)$ but not $\forall\ x \in \mathbb{R}$

$\therefore\ f(x)$ is not an identity function on $\mathbb{R}$.

■ EQUAL OR IDENTICAL FUNCTIONS

Two functions f and g are said to be equal if

1. The domain of f = the domain of g.
2. The range of f = the range of g.
3. $f(x) = g(x)$ for every x belonging to their common domain. For example, $f(x) = 1/x$ and $g(x) = x/x^2$ are identical functions.

$f(x) = \log(x^2)$ and $g(x) = 2\log(x)$ are not-identical functions as domain of $f(x) = (-\infty, \infty) \sim \{0\}$ whereas that of $g(x) = (0, \infty)$.

REMARK

Identical functions have same graph.

ILLUSTRATION 66: State whether the following pair of functions $f(x)$ and $g(x)$ are equal/identical or not. Explain your answer with proper argument.

(a) $f(x)=\dfrac{x^2-4}{x^2+3x+2};\ g(x)=\dfrac{x-2}{x+1}$ (b) $f(x)=\sqrt{x^2-2x+1};\ g(x)=|x-1|$

(c) $f(x)= \sec x.\cot x;\ g(x) = \text{cosec } x$

SOLUTION: (a) Although $f(x)=\dfrac{x^2-4}{x^2+3x+2}$ can be simplified by striking off the common factor $(x + 2)$ from numerator and denominator and one may conclude that $f(x)=\dfrac{(x-2)(x+2)}{(x+2)(x+1)}$ $=\dfrac{x-2}{x+1}=g(x)$, which is indeed not true. Because

$$f(x)=\begin{cases}\dfrac{x-2}{x+1} & \text{if } x\in\mathbb{R}\sim\{-1,-2\}\\ \text{not defined if } x=-1 \text{ or } -2\end{cases}, \text{ whereas } g(x)=\begin{cases}\dfrac{x-2}{x+1} & \forall x\in\mathbb{R}\sim\{-1\}\\ \text{not defined for } x=-1\end{cases}$$

Therefore, $f(x)$ and $g(x)$ are not identical functions because of having different natural domains, however, $f(x)$ and $g(x)$ are identical on their common domain, i.e., $\mathbb{R} \sim \{-1, -2\}$

(b) $f(x)=\sqrt{x^2-2x+1}=\sqrt{(x-1)^2}$, which is defined $\forall\ x\in\mathbb{R}$

And further $f(x)=\sqrt{(x-1)^2}=|x-1|\left(\because \sqrt{x^2}=|x|\right)$

Also $g(x) = |x - 1|$ has its domain $\mathbb{R}$

Thus, $f(x)$ and $g(x)$ have same analytical formula and having same natural domain $\mathbb{R}$.

Hence, $f(x)$ and $g(x)$ are identical functions.

(c) $f(x) = \sec x.\cot x;\ g(x) = \text{cosec } x$

Hence, $f(x)=\begin{cases}\dfrac{1}{\cos x}.\dfrac{\cos x}{\sin x}; & \sin x\neq 0, \cos x\neq 0\\ \text{not defined if either } \sin x=0 \text{ or } \cos x=0\end{cases}$

$$\Rightarrow \begin{cases}\text{cosec } x; & \sin x\neq 0, \cos x\neq 0\\ \text{not defined; otherwise}\end{cases}$$

$$\Rightarrow \begin{cases}\text{cosec } x; & x\in\mathbb{R}\sim\left\{n\pi,(2m+1)\dfrac{\pi}{2}; m,n\in\mathbb{Z}\right\}\\ \text{not defined}; & x\in\left\{n\pi,(2m+1)\dfrac{\pi}{2}; m,n\in\mathbb{Z}\right\}\end{cases}$$

Further $g(x) = \text{cosec } x;\ x \in \mathbb{R} \sim \{n\pi;\ n \in \mathbb{Z}\}$

$\therefore$ $f(x)$ and $g(x)$ are not identical due to having different natural domains, however, they are identical on their common domain, i.e., $\mathbb{R} \sim \left\{n\pi, (2m+1)\frac{\pi}{2}; n, m \in \mathbb{Z}\right\}$

TEXTUAL EXERCISE–5: (SUBJECTIVE)

1. For what set of values of x the following equations hold?
   (a) $|x| = 5$ (b) $|x| = -2$
   (c) $x + |x| = 0$ (d) $x + |x| = 2x$
   (e) $\frac{x}{|x|} = -1$ (f) $3x\sqrt{2} = \sqrt{18x^2}$
   (g) $x|x| - x^2 = 0$ (h) $|x| < -x$
2. Solve the following equations for x:
   (a) $|x| + x^2 + 1 = 0$ (b) $|5x^2 - 3| = 2$
   (c) $\left|\frac{x+4}{x+2}\right| = 3$ (d) $|x^2 - 4x| = 5$
   (e) $|x + 1| + 2 = 2$ (f) $|3x - 4| = 1/2$
   (g) $|x + 2| = 2(3 - x)$ (h) $|x| = -3x - 5$
   (i) $x^2 + |x - 1| = 1$.
3. Prove that $\sqrt{x^2-2x+1} - \sqrt{x^2+2x+1} = \begin{cases} 2 \text{ if } x \le -1 \\ -2x \text{if } x \in (-1,1) \\ -2 \text{ if } x \ge 1 \end{cases}$
4. Solve the following inequalities for x:
   (a) $|x| > 2$ (b) $|x - 1| > 3$
   (c) $|x - 2| < 1$ (d) $|x + 1| \ge 2$
   (e) $|x - 1| < 5$
5. Solve the following equations and inequalities:
   (a) $|x - 1| + |x - 3| = 2$
   (b) $|x| + |x + 5| = 5$
   (c) $|x - 1| + |x - 4| = 2$
   (d) $|x^2 - 2x| + |x - 4| = |x^2 - 3x + 4|$
   (e) $|x^2 - 2x| + |x - 4| < |x^2 - 3x + 4|$
6. Simplify the expression $\sqrt{9-6a+a^2} + \sqrt{9+6a+a^2}$ if $a < -3$
7. Which of the following functions are identical functions?
   (a) $f(x) = \text{cosec } x;\ g(x) = \frac{1}{\sin x}$
   (b) $f(x) = \tan x;\ g(x) = \frac{1}{\cot x}$
   (c) $f(x) = \ln e^x;\ g(x) = x$
   (d) $f(x) = \sec x;\ g(x) = \frac{1}{\cos x}$
8. Identify whether following pairs of functions are identical or non-identical.
   (a) $f(x) = \ln x;\ g(x) = \frac{1}{\log_x e}$
   (b) $f(x) = \sqrt{x^2-1};\ g(x) = \sqrt{x-1}\cdot\sqrt{x+1}$
   (c) $f(x) = \sqrt{1-x^2};\ g(x) = \sqrt{1-x}\cdot\sqrt{1+x}$
9. Solve the following equations.
   (i) $\text{sgn}(x^2 + 2) = 1$
   (ii) $\text{sgn}(x^2 + 2) = -1$
   (iii) $\text{sgn}(x^2 - 9) + \text{sgn}(x + 3) = 0$
   (iv) $|\text{sgn}(x - 1)| = 1$.
10. If $f(x)$ is an identity function on $\mathbb{R}$, then solve the following inequations.
    (i) $|f(x) - 5| \ge 2$
    (ii) $|\text{sgn}(f(x) - 5)| > 0$
    (iii) $\text{sgn}[f(\tan^{-1} x)] = 1$.

Answer Keys

1. (a) $\{-5, 5\}$ (b) $\{\}$ (c) $(-\infty, 0]$ (d) $[0, \infty)$ (e) $(-\infty, 0)$
   (f) $[0, \infty)$ (g) $[0, \infty)$ (h) ϕ
2. (a) $\{\}$ (b) $\left\{-\frac{1}{\sqrt{5}}, \frac{1}{\sqrt{5}}, \pm 1\right\}$ (c) $\{-1, -5/2\}$ (d) $\{-1, 5\}$ (e) $x = -1$

(f) $x = 7/6, 3/2$ (g) $x = 4/3$ (h) $x = -5/2$ (i) $x = 0, 1$

4. (a) $(-\infty,-2)\cup(2,\infty)$ (b) $(-\infty,-2)\cup(4,\infty)$ (c) $x\in(1,3)$ (d) $x\in(-\infty,-3]\cup[1,\infty)$

(e) $x\in(-4,6)$

5. (a) $[1, 3]$ (b) $[-5, 0]$ (c) $\{\}$ (d) $x\in(-\infty,0]\cup[2,4]$ (e) $x\in\{\}$

6. $-2a$

7. (a) Identical (b) Non-identical (c) Identical (d) Identical

8. (a) Non-identical (b) Non-identical (c) Identical

9. (i) $\mathbb{R}$ (ii) ϕ (iii) $(-\infty, 3)$ (iv) $\mathbb{R} - \{1\}$

10. (i) $x \in (-\infty, 3] \cup [7, \infty)$ (ii) $x \in \mathbb{R} \sim \{5\}$ (iii) $x \in (0, \infty)$

TEXTUAL EXERCISE–5: (OBJECTIVE)

1. $\sqrt{2-|x|}+\sqrt{1+|x|}$ is defined for

(a) $[-2, 2]$ (b) $(-2, 2)$

(c) $(-\infty, -1) \cup (1, 2)$ (d) None of these

2. $f(x)=\sqrt{x^2-|x|-2}$ is defined for

(a) $\mathbb{R} - (-2, 2)$ (b) $\mathbb{R} - [-2\ 2)$

(c) $\mathbb{R} - [-2, 2]$ (d) $\mathbb{R} - (-2, 2]$

3. The range of the function $f(x) = |x - 1| + |x - 2|$, $-1 \le x \le 3$, is

(a) $[1, 3]$ (b) $[1, 5]$

(c) $[3, 5]$ (d) None of these

4. Which of the following statements is incorrect?

(a) $x \text{ sgn } x = |x|$

(b) $|x| \text{ sgn } x = x$

(c) $x (\text{sgn } x) (\text{sgn } x) = x$

(d) $|x| (\text{sgn } x)^3 = |x|$

5. If $f(x)=\left\{(\text{sgn } x)^{\text{sgn } x}\right\}^n$; n is an odd integer. Then

(a) $f(x)$ is an odd function

(b) $f(x)$ is an even function

(c) $f(x) = 0$

(d) None of these

6. If $f(x)=\left(\dfrac{x}{1-|x|}\right)^{1/2001}$, then D_f is

(a) $(-\infty, -1) \cup (1, \infty)$ (b) $(-1, 1)$

(c) $\mathbb{R}$ (d) $\mathbb{R} - \{-1, 1\}$

7. If $f(x)=\left(\dfrac{x}{1-|x|}\right)^{1/2002}$ then D_f is

(a) $\mathbb{R} - \{-1, 1\}$ (b) $(-\infty, 1)$

(c) $(-\infty, -1) \cup [0, 1)$ (d) None of these

8. If $f(x)=\dfrac{\sqrt{|\tan x|+\tan x}}{\sqrt{3x}}$ is defined for

(a) $\mathbb{R}$

(b) $\mathbb{R}-\{1/3\}$

(c) $\mathbb{R}^+ -\left\{n\pi-\dfrac{\pi}{2};n\in W\right\}$

(d) None of these

9. In which of the following pairs, the functions are identical?

(a) $f(x)=\sqrt{x^2}$; $g(x)=\left(\sqrt{x}\right)^2$

(b) $f(x)=\dfrac{1}{\sqrt{x^2}}$; $g(x)=\dfrac{x}{x^2}$

(c) $f(x) = \log(x - 1) + \log(x - 2)$; $g(x) = \log(x - 1)(x - 2)$

(d) $f(x) = \sin^2 x + \cos^2 x$; $g(x) = 1$

Answer Keys

1. (a) **2.** (a) **3.** (b) **4.** (d) **5.** (a) **6.** (d) **7.** (c) **8.** (c) **9.** (d)

EXPONENTIAL FUNCTION

If a is positive real number except for 1, then a^x; where $x \in \mathbb{R}$ is always positive and it is called exponential function of x. a is called base and x is called index.

The graph of exponential functions are as shown in Figure 2.80.

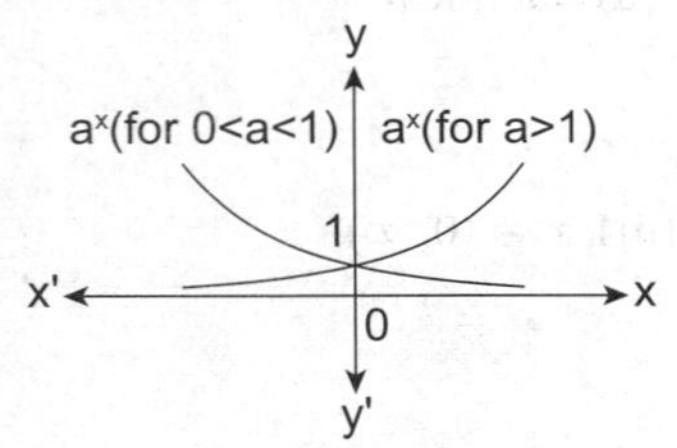

FIGURE 2.79

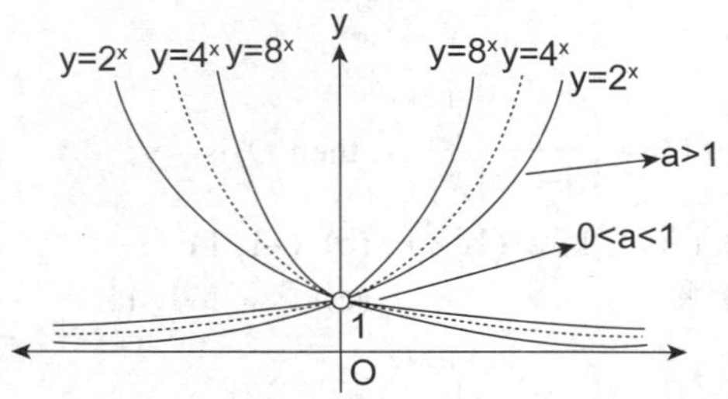

FIGURE 2.80

PROPERTIES OF EXPONENTIAL FUNCTION

(i) Domain of exponential function $y = a^x$; $D_f : (-\infty, \infty)$;
Range of exponential function $= R_f : (0, \infty)$
$\because$ a^x is defined $\forall\ x \in \mathbb{R}$ and $a^x > 0$

(ii) $\left.\begin{array}{l} f(x+y) = f(x) \cdot f(y) \\ f(x-y) = f(x)\,/\,f(y) \end{array}\right\} \forall\ x, y \in \mathbb{R}$

Proof: $f(x).f(y) = a^x.\, a^y = a^{x+y} = f(x+y)$ and

$f(x)/f(y) = \dfrac{a^x}{a^y} = a^{x-y} = f(x-y)$

(iii) $a^x \,.\, b^x = (ab)^x$ and $\dfrac{a^x}{b^x} = \left(\dfrac{a}{b}\right)^x$

(iv) $(a^x)^y = a^{xy} = (a^y)^x$

(v) a^x, where $a > 1$ (say $a = 2$) behaves as an increasing natured function as is clear from the table and graph given below for $y = 2^x$

x	−3	−2	−1	0	1	2	3	4	5
a^x	1/8	1/4	1/2	1	2	4	8	16	32

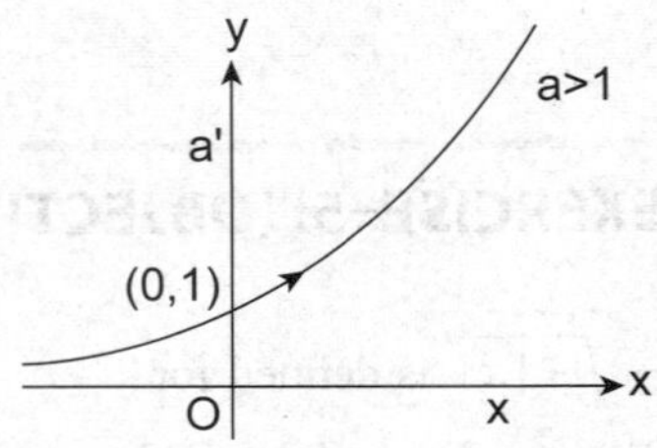

FIGURE 2.81

(vi) If $0 < a < 1$ (say $a = 1/2$) behaves like decreasing natured function as is clear from the table and graph given in Figure 2.82 for $y = (1/2)^x$

x	−5	−4	−3	−2	−1	0	1	2	3
a^x	32	16	8	4	2	1	1/2	1/4	1/8

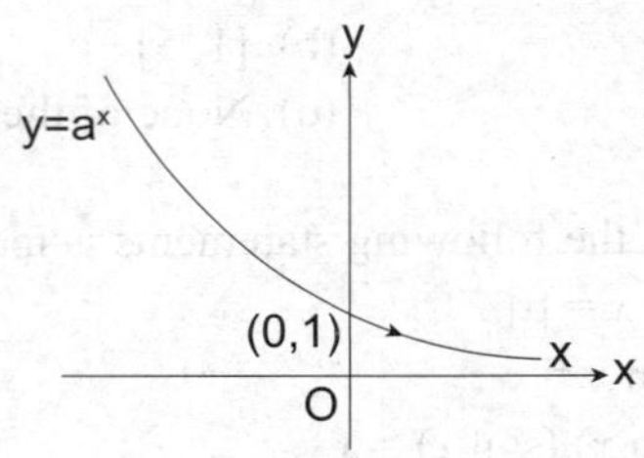

FIGURE 2.82

ILLUSTRATION 67: Find the range of the values of x for which the following functions are defined:

(a) $f(x) = \sqrt{a^x - 1}$; where $a > 1$ and what if $a < 1$

(b) $f(x) = \sqrt[2n]{2 - a^x}$; where $a < 1$

SOLUTION: (a) $f(x)$ to be defined, $a^x - 1 \geq 0$, i.e., $a^x \geq 1$

when $a > 1$: $a^x \geq 1$ $\Rightarrow x \geq 0 \Rightarrow x \in [0, \infty)$

when $a < 1$: $a^x \geq 1$ $\Rightarrow x \leq 0 \Rightarrow x \in (-\infty, 0]$

(b) $f(x)$ to be defined $2 - a^x \geq 0$ $\Rightarrow a^x \leq 2$

when $a < 1$: $a^x \leq 2$

Taking log to the base a both side: $x \geq \log_a 2 \Rightarrow x \in [\log_a 2, \infty)$.

SOLVING EXPONENTIAL EQUATIONS

To solve an exponential equation, we use the following two properties:

(i) $a^x = a^y$
$\Rightarrow$ $x = y$ or $a = 1$
(ii) $a^x = b^x$
$\Rightarrow$ either $x = 0$ or $a = b$

ILLUSTRATION 68: To solve the equation $2^{x^2-1} = 256;\ x \in \mathbb{R}$

SOLUTION: Given $2^{x^2-1} = 256 \quad \Rightarrow 2^{x^2-1} = 2^8 \quad \Rightarrow x^2 - 1 = 8 \quad \Rightarrow x^2 = 9$

$\Rightarrow x = \pm 3$. Therefore set of solution is $\{-3, 3\}$

SOLVING EXPONENTIAL INEQUALITY

To solve an exponential inequality, we use following properties of exponential functions.

1. The value of a^x increases as the value of x increases, when base $a \in (1, \infty)$.
2. The value of a^x decreases as the value of x increases, when base $a \in (0, 1)$

i.e., $a^x \ge a^y \Leftrightarrow \begin{cases} x \ge y & \text{if } a > 1 \\ x \le y & \text{if } a \in (0,1) \end{cases}$

ILLUSTRATION 69: Solve the following inequalities:

(i) $2^{x-4} \ge 8^{3x-8}$ (ii) $\left(\frac{1}{2}\right)^{2x-5} \ge (16)^{-x+5}$

(iii) $(\cos\theta)^{\frac{1}{x-4}} \le (\cos\theta)^{\frac{-x}{x+2}}$ for some fixed $\theta \in (0, \pi/2)$

SOLUTION: $2^{(x-4)} \ge 8^{(3x-8)}$

$\Rightarrow (2)^{x-4} \ge 2^{3(3x-8)} \qquad \Rightarrow (2)^{(x-4)} \ge (2)^{9x-24} \qquad (\because a = 2 > 1)$

$\Rightarrow (x-4) \ge 9x - 24 \Rightarrow 8x \le 20 \Rightarrow x \le 5/2 \Rightarrow x \in \left(-\infty, \frac{5}{2}\right]$

Thus, $(-\infty, 5/2]$ is the solution set of given inequality

(ii) $\left(\frac{1}{2}\right)^{2x-5} \ge (16)^{-x+5} \Rightarrow \left(\frac{1}{2}\right)^{2x-5} \ge \left(\frac{1}{2}\right)^{4x-20}$

$\Rightarrow (2x-5) \le 4x - 20$ [as base $a = 1/2 \in (0,1)$] $\Rightarrow 2x \ge 15$

$\Rightarrow x \ge 15/2 \Rightarrow x \in \left[\frac{15}{2}, \infty\right)$. Thus, $\left[\frac{15}{2}, \infty\right)$ is the solutions set of given inequality

(iii) $\because$ for $\theta \in (0, \pi/2)$, $\cos\theta \in (0,1)$

$\Rightarrow$ Base of exponential function belongs to $(0,1)$

$\therefore (\cos\theta)^{\frac{1}{x-4}} \le (\cos\theta)^{\frac{-x}{x+2}} \Rightarrow \frac{1}{x-4} \ge \frac{-x}{x+2} \Rightarrow \frac{1}{x-4} + \frac{x}{x+2} \ge 0$

$\Rightarrow \frac{x+2+x^2-4x}{(x-4)(x+2)} \ge 0 \Rightarrow \frac{x^2-3x+2}{(x-4)(x+2)} \ge 0 \Rightarrow \frac{(x-1)(x-2)}{(x-4)(x+2)} \ge 0$

$\Rightarrow (x+2)(x-1)(x-2)(x-4) \ge 0;\ x \ne -2, 4$

$\Rightarrow x \in (-\infty, -2) \cup [1, 2] \cup (4, \infty)$ which is the required solution set of given inequality.

■ COMPOSITE EXPONENTIAL FUNCTION

A function of the form $y = [f(x)]^{g(x)}$; i.e., a function in which both base and exponent are functions of x

e.g., $y = x^x$, $y = (\sin x)^{\tan x}$, $y = (\ln x)^x$, $y = (x)^{\ln x}$ etc.

Composite exponential function is also known as exponential power function. Composite exponential function. $y = (f(x))^{g(x)}$ is defined for those values of x for which $f(x)$ and $g(x)$ both are defined (i.e., x must be in common domain of $f(x)$ and $g(x)$) and $f(x) > 0$.

Thus, domain of $y = [f(x)]^{g(x)} = \{x \in \mathbb{R} : x \in D_f \cap D_g$ and $f(x) > 0\}$.

For example:

(i) $y = x^{\sin x}$ has its domain $= \{x \in \mathbb{R} : x > 0\} = (0, \infty)$

(ii) $y = (\sin x)^x$ has its domain $= \{x \in \mathbb{R} : \sin x > 0\}$
$= \{x \in \mathbb{R} : x \in (2n\pi, (2n+1)\pi);\ n \in \mathbb{Z}\}$
$= \bigcup\limits_{n\in\mathbb{Z}} ((2n\pi), (2n+1)\pi)$

(iii) $y = (\ln x)^x$ has its domain $= \{x \in \mathbb{R} : \ln x > 0\}$
$= \{x \in \mathbb{R} : x > 1\} = (1, \infty)$

(iv) $y = (\sin x)^{\tan x}$ has its domain $= \{x \in \mathbb{R} : \sin x > 0$ and $x \neq \left\{(2n+1)\frac{\pi}{2}; n \in \mathbb{Z}\right\}$
$= \bigcup\limits_{n\in\mathbb{Z}} \left[((2n\pi), (2n+1)\pi) \sim \left\{(2n+1)\frac{\pi}{2}\right\}\right]$

> **NOTE**
>
> *$y = \sqrt[x]{f(x)}$ is defined for $x \in \{2, 3, 4, \ldots\}$ and $f(x) > 0$ where as $y = (f(x))^{1/x}$ is defined for $x \neq 0$ and $f(x) > 0$.*
>
> ***Example:***
>
> *(i) $y = \sqrt[x]{\sin x}$ is defined for $x \in \{2, 3, 4, \ldots\}$ and $\sin x > 0$* $\Rightarrow$ *$x \in \{2, 3, 4, \ldots\}$ and $x \in \bigcup\limits_{n\in W}(2n\pi, (2n+1)\pi)$*
>
> $\Rightarrow$ *$x \in \{2, 3, 4, \ldots\}$ and $x \in (0, \pi) \cup (2\pi, 3\pi) \cup (4\pi, 5\pi)\ldots$* $\Rightarrow$ *$x \in \{2, 3, 7, 8, 9, \ldots\}$.*
>
> *(ii) Domain of $y = (\cos x)^{\frac{1}{\sin x}}$ is defined for $\cos x > 0$ and $\sin x \neq 0$* $\Rightarrow$ $x \in \bigcup\limits_{n\in\mathbb{Z}} \left[2n\pi - \frac{\pi}{2}, 2n\pi + \frac{\pi}{2}\right] \sim 2n\pi$.

■ HYPERBOLIC FUNCTIONS

There are six hyperbolic functions as discussed below:

(i) **Hyperbolic Sine:** It is denoted by $\sinh x$ and is defined as

$$\sinh x = \frac{e^x - e^{-x}}{2}$$

$$= \frac{1}{2}\left(1 + x + \frac{x^2}{2!} + \frac{x^3}{3!} + \ldots\right) - \left(1 - x + \frac{x^2}{2!} - \frac{x^3}{3!} + \ldots\right)$$

$$= \frac{1}{2}\left\{2x + \frac{2x^3}{3!} + \frac{2x^5}{5!} + \ldots\right\} = \left\{x + \frac{x^3}{3!} + \frac{x^5}{5!} + \ldots\right\}$$

Thus, $\sinh x = \dfrac{e^x - e^{-x}}{2} = x + \dfrac{x^3}{3!} + \dfrac{x^5}{5!} + \ldots$

Domain of $\sinh x = \mathbb{R}$, set of all real numbers.

Since $\dfrac{d}{dx}(\sinh x) = \left(1 + \dfrac{x^2}{2!} + \dfrac{x^4}{4!} + \ldots\right) > 0\ \forall x \in \mathbb{R}$

$\Rightarrow$ Graph of $\sinh x$ is strictly increasing $\forall x \in \mathbb{R}$

Also $\dfrac{d^2}{dx^2}(\sinh x) = \left(x + \dfrac{x^3}{3!} + \ldots\right)$ which is positive for $x > 0$ and negative for $x < 0$.

Also $\dfrac{d^2}{dx^2}(\sinh x) = 0$ for $x = 0$.

$\Rightarrow$ Graph of $\sinh x$ is concave upwards for $x > 0$ and concave downwards for $x < 0$ and has a point of inflexion at $x = 0$.

Clearly $\sinh x$ being continuous and strictly increasing and $\sinh x \to -\infty$ as $x \to -\infty$ and $\sinh x \to \infty$ as $x \to \infty$, has its range $= \mathbb{R}$.

Thus, the graph of $\sinh x$ would be as shown in Figure 2.83.

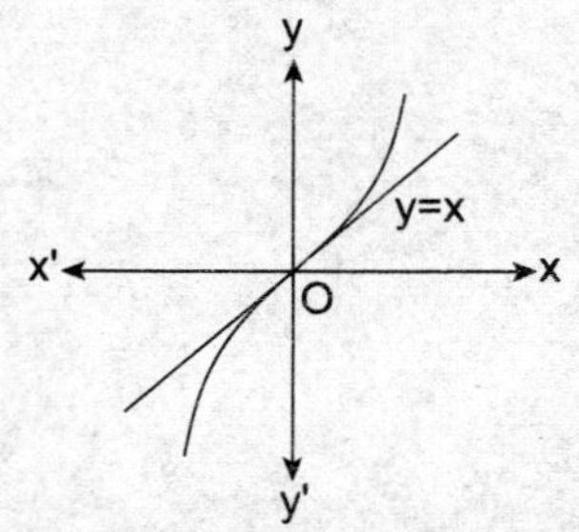

FIGURE 2.83

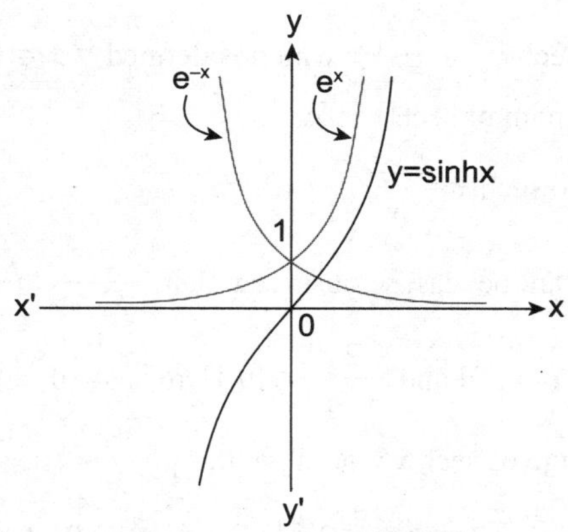

FIGURE 2.84

(ii) **Hyperbolic Cosine:** It is denoted by cosh x and is defined as $\cosh x = \dfrac{e^x + e^{-x}}{2}$

$$= \frac{1}{2}\left\{\left(1 + x + \frac{x^2}{2!} + \frac{x^3}{3!} + \ldots\right) + \left(1 - x + \frac{x^2}{2!} - \frac{x^3}{3!} + \ldots\right)\right\}$$

$$= \frac{1}{2}\left\{\left(2 + \frac{2x^2}{2!} + \frac{2x^4}{4!} + \ldots\right)\right\} = \left\{\left(1 + \frac{x^2}{2!} + \frac{x^4}{4!} + \ldots\right)\right\}$$

$\geq 1\ \forall\ x \in \mathbb{R}$ $\Rightarrow$ Range of cosh x is $[1, \infty)$

Clearly cosh x is defined $\forall\ x \in \mathbb{R}$

Also $\dfrac{d}{dx}(\cosh x) = \left(x + \dfrac{x^3}{3!} + \dfrac{x^5}{5!} + \ldots\right) > 0$

for $x > 0$ and < 0 for $x < 0$ and $= 0$ for $x = 0$.

$\Rightarrow$ cosh x is a decreasing function for $x < 0$, increasing function for $x > 0$ and has a stationary point at $x = 0$

Further $\dfrac{d^2}{dx^2}(\cosh x) = \left(1 + \dfrac{x^2}{2!} + \dfrac{x^4}{4!} + \ldots\right) > 0$

$\forall\ x \in \mathbb{R}$.

Graph of cosh x is concave upwards $\forall\ x \in \mathbb{R}$. Collecting all above conclusions, the graph of cosh x would be as shown in Figure 2.85.

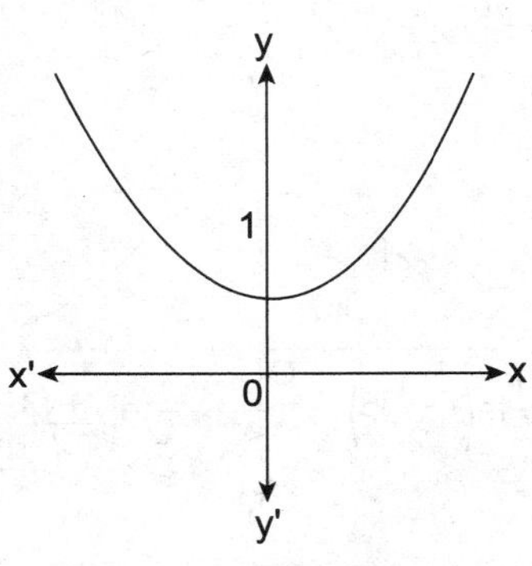

FIGURE 2.85

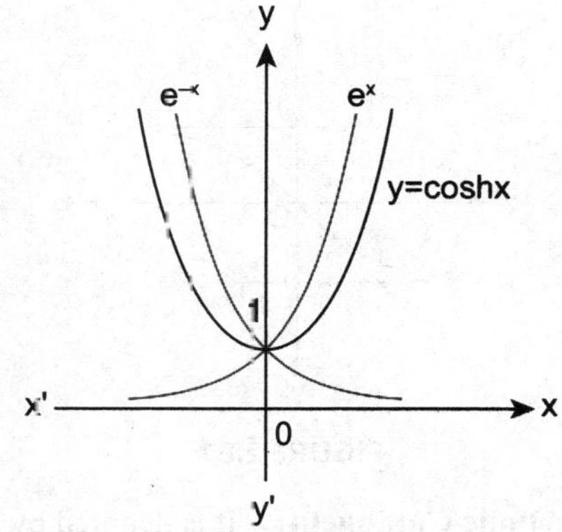

FIGURE 2.86

(iii) **Hyperbolic Tangent:** It is denoted by tanh x and is defined as $\tanh x = \dfrac{\sinh x}{\cosh x} = \dfrac{e^x - e^{-x}}{e^x + e^{-x}}$

Clearly tanh x is defined $\forall\ x \in \mathbb{R}$.

Also $\tanh x = \dfrac{e^{2x} - 1}{e^{2x} + 1} \to -1$ as $x \to -\infty$ and

$\tanh x = \dfrac{1 - e^{-2x}}{1 + e^{-2x}} \to 1$ as $x \to \infty$

Thus, range of tanh x is $(-1, 1)$.

Next $\tanh x > 0 \Leftrightarrow \dfrac{e^{2x} - 1}{e^{2x} + 1} > 0 \Leftrightarrow e^{2x} > 1$

$\Leftrightarrow$ $2x > \ln 1$ $\Leftrightarrow$ $x > 0$

Thus, $\tanh x > 0$ for $x \in (0, \infty)$

Similarly $\tanh x < 0$ for $x \in (-\infty, 0)$ and $\tanh x = 0$ for $x = 0$

$$\text{Now } \frac{d}{dx}(\tanh x) = \frac{(e^{2x} + 1)(2e^{2x}) - (e^{2x} - 1)(2e^{2x})}{(e^{2x} + 1)^2}$$

$$= \frac{4e^{2x}}{(e^{2x} + 1)^2} > 0\ \forall\ x \in \mathbb{R}$$

$\Rightarrow$ tanh x is strictly increasing $\forall\ x \in \mathbb{R}$ and

$$\frac{d^2}{dx^2}(\tanh x) = \frac{(e^{2x} + 1)^2 . 8e^{2x} - 4e^{2x} . 2(e^{2x} + 1)(2e^{2x})}{(e^{2x} + 1)^4}$$

$$= \frac{8(e^{2x} + 1)e^{2x}(1 - e^{2x})}{(e^{2x} + 1)^4} > 0 \text{ for } x < 0$$

< 0 for $x > 0$ and $= 0$ for $x = 0$

$\Rightarrow$ The graph of tanh x is concave upwards for $x < 0$, concave downwards for $x > 0$ and has a point of inflexion at $x = 0$.

Thus, from above discussion we conclude that the graph of tanh x would be as shown in Figure 2.87.

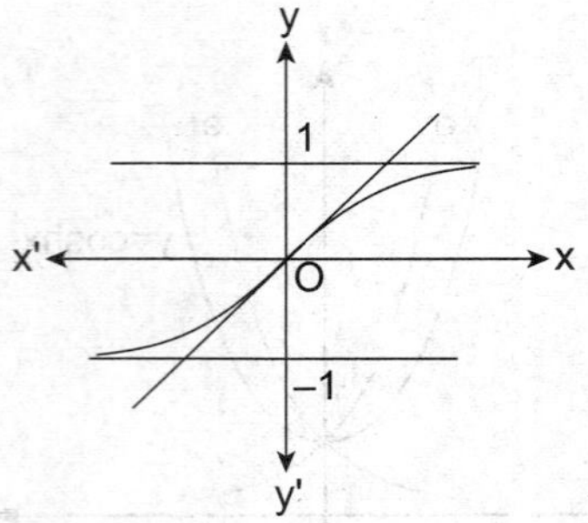

FIGURE 2.87

(iv) **Hyperbolic Cotangent:** It is denoted by $\coth x$ and is defined as $y = \coth x = \dfrac{\cosh x}{\sinh x} = \dfrac{e^x + e^{-x}}{e^x - e^{-x}} = \dfrac{e^{2x}+1}{e^{2x}-1}$ $\to -1$ as $x \to -\infty$ and $\to -\infty$ as $x \to 0$ from negative side.

Also $\coth x = \dfrac{1+e^{-2x}}{1-e^{-2x}} \to 1$ as $x \to \infty$ and $\to \infty$ as $x \to 0$ from positive side.

Thus, range of $\coth x$ is $(-\infty, -1) \cup (1, \infty)$.

Clearly domain of $\coth x$ is $\mathbb{R} \sim \{0\}$.

Now $\dfrac{dy}{dx} = \dfrac{(2e^{2x})(-2)}{(e^{2x}-1)^2} < 0 \ \forall\, x \in \mathbb{R} \sim \{0\}$

$\Rightarrow$ $\coth x$ is a strictly decreasing function $\forall\, x \in \mathbb{R} \sim \{0\}$

Next $\dfrac{d^2}{dx^2}(\coth x) = \dfrac{8e^{2x}(1+e^{2x})(e^{2x}-1)}{(e^{2x}-1)^4} > 0$ for $x > 0$

and < 0 for $x < 0$

$\Rightarrow$ The, graph of $\coth x$ is concave upwards for $x > 0$ and concave downwards for $x < 0$

Thus, the graph of $\coth x$ would be as shown below.

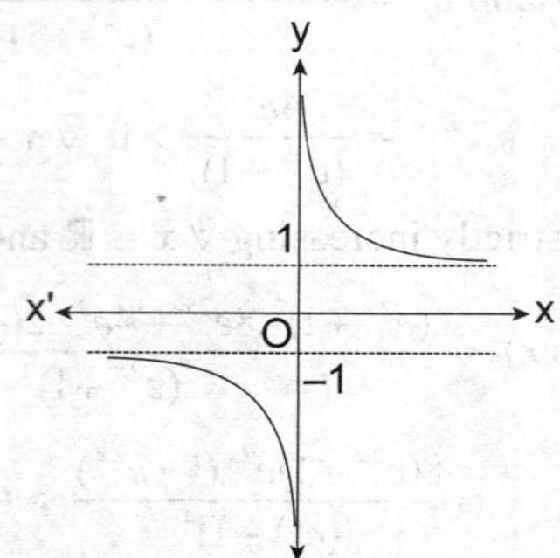

FIGURE 2.88

(v) **Hyperbolic Secant:** It is denoted by $\operatorname{sech} x$ and is defined as $\operatorname{sech} x = \dfrac{2}{e^x + e^{-x}} = \dfrac{1}{\cosh x}$

or $\operatorname{sech} x = \dfrac{2e^x}{e^{2x}+1}$ which is defined $\forall\, x \in \mathbb{R}$

$\Rightarrow$ Domain of $\operatorname{sech} x$ is $\mathbb{R}$.

Also $\operatorname{sech} x = \dfrac{2y}{y^2+1}$; where $y = e^x$

It can be easily observed that $\dfrac{2y}{y^2+1} \in [-1, 0]$ for $y \in (-\infty, 0]$ and $\dfrac{2y}{y^2+1} \in (0, 1]$ for $y \in (0, \infty)$

$\Rightarrow$ Range of $\operatorname{sech} x$ would be $(0, 1]$

Now $\dfrac{d}{dx}(\operatorname{sech} x) = 2e^x\left[\dfrac{1-e^{2x}}{(e^{2x}+1)^2}\right] < 0$ for $x > 0$, > 0 for $x < 0$ and 0 for $x = 0$.

$\Rightarrow$ $\operatorname{sech} x$ is strictly decreasing for $x > 0$, strictly increasing for $x < 0$ and $x = 0$ is a stationary point.

Further $\dfrac{d^2}{dx^2}(\operatorname{sech} x)$

$$= \frac{2e^x(e^x+1)\left[e^{2x} - \left(\dfrac{7-\sqrt{33}}{2}\right)\right]\left[e^{2x} - \left(\dfrac{7+\sqrt{33}}{2}\right)\right]}{(e^{2x}+1)^4}$$

< 0 for $x \in \left(\dfrac{1}{2}\ln\left(\dfrac{7-\sqrt{33}}{2}\right), \dfrac{1}{2}\ln\left(\dfrac{7+\sqrt{33}}{2}\right)\right)$ and > 0 for $x \in \left(-\infty, \dfrac{1}{2}\ln\left(\dfrac{7-\sqrt{33}}{2}\right)\right) \cup \left(\dfrac{1}{2}\ln\left(\dfrac{7+\sqrt{33}}{2}\right), \infty\right)$

$\Rightarrow$ $f(x)$ is concave downwards for $x \in \left(\dfrac{1}{2}\ln\left(\dfrac{7-\sqrt{33}}{2}\right), \dfrac{1}{2}\ln\left(\dfrac{7+\sqrt{33}}{2}\right)\right)$

and concave upwards for $x \in \left(-\infty, \dfrac{1}{2}\ln\left(\dfrac{7-\sqrt{33}}{2}\right)\right) \cup \left(\dfrac{1}{2}\ln\left(\dfrac{7+\sqrt{33}}{2}\right), \infty\right)$

Thus, the graph of hyperbolic secant is as shown in Figure 2.89.

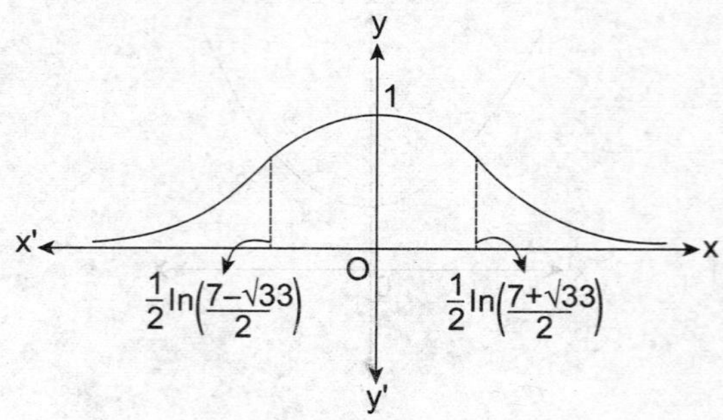

FIGURE 2.89

(vi) **Hyperbolic Cosecant:** It is denoted by cosech x and is defined as $\operatorname{cosec} hx = \frac{2}{e^x - e^{-x}} = \frac{2e^x}{e^{2x} - 1}$

Clearly domain of cosech x is $\mathbb{R} \sim \{0\}$.

It can be easily verified that function $\frac{2y}{y^2 - 1}$ decreases from 0 to $-\infty$ as y increases from 0 to 1 and decreases from ∞ to 0 as y increases from 1 to ∞ with discontinuity at $y = 1$.

Thus, range of function is $(-\infty, \infty) \sim \{0\}$ for $y \in (0, \infty)$.

Similarly cosech x takes its range $(-\infty, \infty) \sim \{0\}$ for $x \in \mathbb{R} \sim \{0\}$

Now $\frac{d}{dx}(\operatorname{cosec} hx) = 2\left[\frac{-e^x - e^{3x}}{(e^{2x} - 1)^2}\right] < 0 \ \forall x \in \mathbb{R} \sim \{0\}$

$\Rightarrow$ cosech x is a decreasing function on its domain $\mathbb{R} \sim \{0\}$.

$\Rightarrow$ Further $\frac{d^2}{dx^2}(\text{cosech } x) < 0$ for $x \in (-\infty, 0)$ and > 0 for $x \in (0, \infty)$.

Thus, the graph of cosech x is concave downwards for $x \in (-\infty, 0)$ and concave upwards for $x \in (0, \infty)$ as shown below.

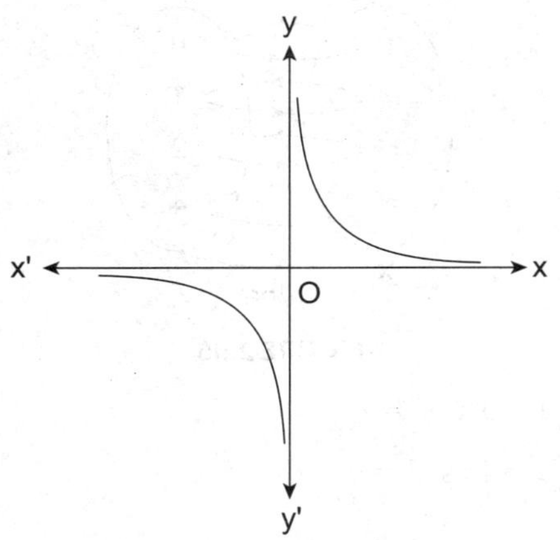

FIGURE 2.90

■ LOGARITHMIC FUNCTION

Logarithm of a positive number x to the base a is defined as a number y, which when raised to base a the resulting number becomes equal to x.

i.e., $\log_a x = y \Leftrightarrow a^y = x$, when $a > 0$ and $a \neq 1$; $x > 0$ as a^y is positive

e.g., $\log_7 49 = 2$ as $(7)^2 = 49$; $\log_3 81 = 4$ as $(3)^4 = 81$; $\log_{10} 100000 = 5$ as $(10)^5 = 100000$ etc.

Since logarithmic function $y = \log_a x$ is defined only for positive real numbers, and hence, its domain is $(0, \infty)$.

Also logarithmic function is continuous (i.e., its graph never breaks when drawn corresponding to positive real numbers x) and attains each real number, and hence, its range is $\mathbb{R}$, set of real numbers.

In general $y = \log_c x$ is an increasing function for $a > 1$ as has been illustrated below for $y = \log_{10} x$ and $y = \log_2 x$

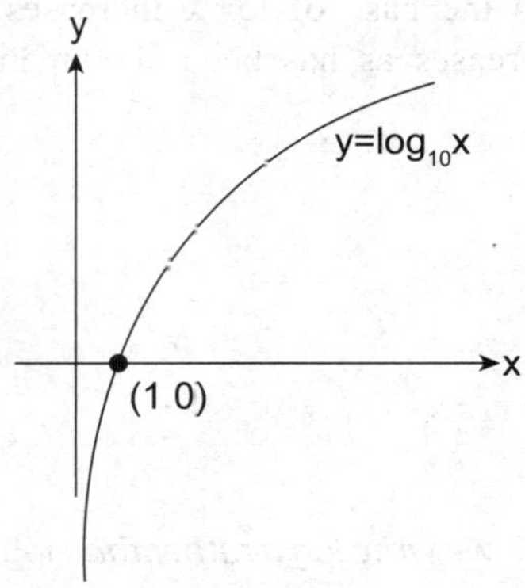

FIGURE 2.91

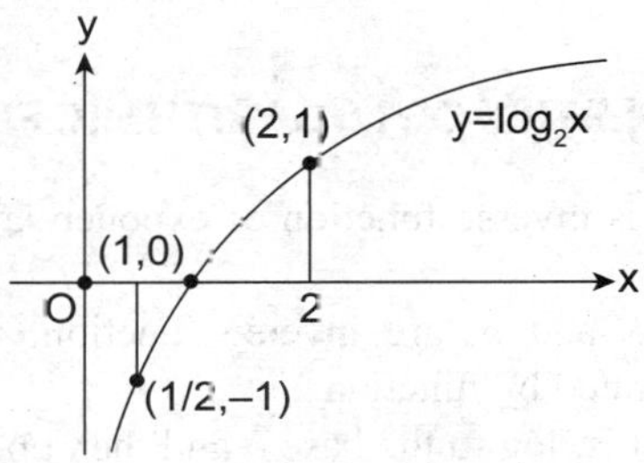

FIGURE 2.92

x	0.0001	0.001	0.01	0.1	1	10	100	1000
$\log_{10} x$	–4	–3	–2	–1	0	1	2	3

And, in general, logarithmic function is a decreasing function for $a \in (0, 1)$ as been illustrated below for $y = \log_{1/2} x$

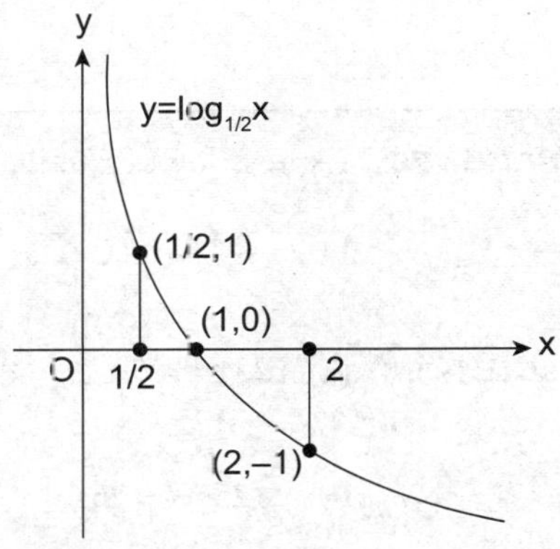

FIGURE 2.93

x	1/16	1/8	1/4	1/2	1	2	4	8
$\log_2 x$	–4	–3	–2	–1	0	1	2	3
$\log_{1/2} x$	4	3	2	1	0	–1	–2	–3

For a given $x \in (0, 1)$ as the base of $\log_a x$ increases the value of logarithm also increases and for given $x \in (1, \infty)$ as the base of $\log_a x$ increases the value of logarithm decreases as has been shown in graph given below.

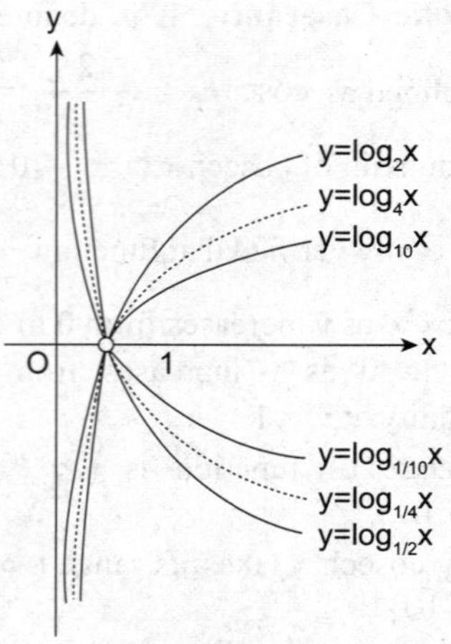

FIGURE 2.94

REMARK

If a = 10, then we write log b rather than $\log_{10} b$. If a = e, we write lnb rather than $\log_e b$.

■ PROPERTIES OF LOGARITHMIC FUNCTIONS

P.1. $\log_a x$ is inverse function of exponential function to base a

$\Rightarrow$ $\log_a x$ and a^x are inverse function, i.e., x when operated by function.
That is, log to the base a and then operated by inverse (exponential function with base a)

i.e., $a^{\log_a x}$ the result is x.

P.2 $\log_a x$ is defined iff $a > 0$, $a \neq 1$ and $x > 0$

$\Rightarrow$ Domain of function $D_f = (0, \infty)$
and Range of function $= R_f = \mathbb{R}$.

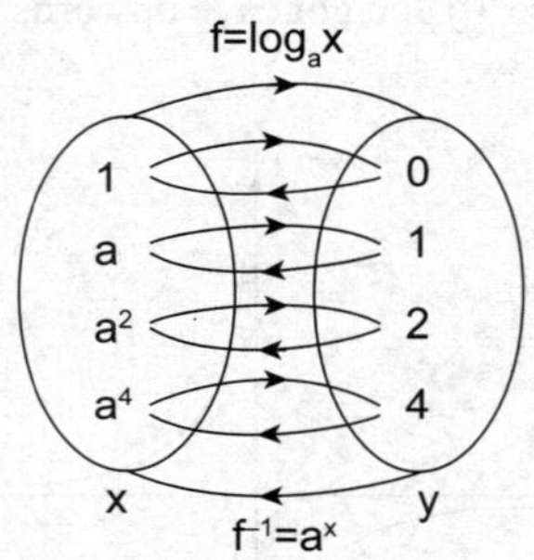

FIGURE 2.95

P.3 $\log_a 1 = 0$ as $a^0 = 1$

P.4 $\log_a a = 1$ as $a^1 = a$

ILLUSTRATION 70: Express log of x to the base 5 in each of the following case

(a) $(25)^{-\frac{1}{3}} = 5x$ (b) $(125)^{-\frac{4}{7}} = 25x$

SOLUTION: (a) $(25)^{-\frac{1}{3}} = 5x \Rightarrow \frac{(25)^{-\frac{1}{3}}}{5} = x \Rightarrow 5^{-\frac{5}{3}} = x \Rightarrow \log_5 x = -\frac{5}{3}$

(b) $(125)^{-\frac{4}{7}} = 25x \Rightarrow \frac{(125)^{-\frac{4}{7}}}{25} = x \Rightarrow 5^{-\frac{26}{7}} = x \Rightarrow \log_5 x = -\frac{26}{7}$

P.5. $\log_a|x| + \log_a|y| = \log_a|x.y|$ and $\log_a xy = \log_a|x| + \log_a|y|$

Proof: LHS $= \log_a|x| + \log_a|y|$

Let $\log_a|x| = m$ and $\log_a|y| = n$

$\Rightarrow a^m = |x|$ and $a^n = |y|$

$\Rightarrow |x.y| = a^{m+n}$

$\Rightarrow \log_a|x| + \log_a|y| = \log_a|xy|$

$[\because a^b = c \Rightarrow \log_a c = b]$ ... (1)

Now $\log_a xy$ to be defined $xy > 0$

$\Rightarrow xy = |xy|$

$\therefore \log_a xy = \log_a|xy| = \log_a|x| + \log_a|y|$ by (1)

P.6. $\log_a|x| - \log_a|y| = \log_a\left|\frac{x}{y}\right|$ and

$\log_a\frac{x}{y} = \log_a|x| - \log_a|y|$

Proof: LHS $= \log_a|x| - \log_a|y|$

Let $\log_a|x| = m$ and $\log_a|y| = n$.

$\Rightarrow a^m = |x|$ and $a^n = |y|$

$\Rightarrow \frac{|x|}{|y|} = \frac{a^m}{a^n}$

$\Rightarrow \left|\frac{x}{y}\right| = a^{m-n}$

$\Rightarrow \log_a\left|\frac{x}{y}\right| = m - n$

$\Rightarrow \log_a|x| - \log_a|y| = \log_a\left|\frac{x}{y}\right|$ ... (1)

Now $\log_a\frac{x}{y}$ to be defined $\frac{x}{y}$ should be positive

$\Rightarrow \frac{x}{y} = \left|\frac{x}{y}\right|$

$\Rightarrow \log_a\frac{x}{y} = \log\left|\frac{x}{y}\right| = \log_a|x| - \log_a|y|$ (by (1))

Therefore, $\log_a\frac{x}{y} = \log_a|x| - \log_a|y|$

Caution! $\log(x \pm y) \neq \log x \pm \log y$

$\log(x.y) \neq \log x.\log y$

$\log(x/y) \neq \frac{\log x}{\log y}$

P.7 $\log_y x = \frac{\log_a x}{\log_a y}$ [Base transformation $a > 0, a \neq 1$]

Proof: It is sufficient to prove that $\log_y x \cdot \log_a y = \log_a x$

Let $\log_y x = m$

$\Rightarrow x = y^m$ and $\log_a y = n \Rightarrow y = a^n$

$\Rightarrow x = a^{nm} \Rightarrow \log_a x = mn = \log_y x.\log_a y.$

Hence, proved.

e.g., $\log_{128} 512 = \frac{\log_2 512}{\log_2 128} = \frac{\log_4 512}{\log_4 128} = \ldots$

Further to solve $\log_{128}512$, we can proceed as follows:

$\log_{128} 512 = \frac{\log_2 512}{\log_2 128} = \frac{\log_2 2^9}{\log_2 2^7} = \frac{9}{7}$

P.8. Chain rule: $\log_a x = \log_y x.\log_z y.\log_u z.\log_a u$

Proof: RHS $= \log_y x \cdot \log_z y \cdot \log_u z \cdot \log_a u$

$= \frac{\log_b x}{\log_b y}.\frac{\log_b y}{\log_b z}.\frac{\log_b z}{\log_b u}.\frac{\log_b u}{\log_b a}$ [By property (7)]

$= \frac{\log_b x}{\log_b a} = \log_a x =$ LHS.

P.9. Reciprocal property: In a logarithm if the number and base is interchanged, then result is reciprocal of the original. i.e., $\log_y x = \frac{1}{\log_x y}$

Proof: $\log_y x.\log_x y = \frac{\log_t x}{\log_t y}\frac{\log_t y}{\log_t x} = 1$

$\Rightarrow \log_y x = \frac{1}{\log_x y}$

P.10. $\log_a(x^\alpha) = \alpha \log_a|x|$

Proof: $\log_a(x^\alpha)$ to be defined $x^\alpha > 0$

Case (i) when $x > 0$, then $\log_a(x^\alpha) = m$ (say)

$\Rightarrow x^\alpha = a^m \Rightarrow x = (a^m)^{1/\alpha} \Rightarrow x = a^{m/\alpha}$ $(\because x > 0)$

$\Rightarrow \log_a x = \frac{m}{\alpha} \Rightarrow m = \alpha\log_a x \Rightarrow m = \alpha \log_a|x|$ $(\because x > 0)$

$\Rightarrow \log_a(x^\alpha) = \alpha \log_a|x|$

Case (ii) When $x < 0$, α = an even integer, then $\log_a(x^\alpha) = m$ (say)

$\Rightarrow x^\alpha = a^m \Rightarrow x = -(a^m)^{1/\alpha} \Rightarrow |x| = a^{m/\alpha}$ $(\because x < 0)$

$\Rightarrow \log_a|x| = \frac{m}{\alpha} \Rightarrow m = \alpha \log_a|x|$

$\Rightarrow \log_a(x^\alpha) = \alpha \log_a|x|$

P.11. $\log_{a^\beta} x = \frac{1}{\beta}\log_{|a|} x$

Proof: By base condition $a^\beta > 0$ and $a^\beta \neq 1$

There arise two cases:

Case (i) When $a > 0$

Now let $\log_{a^\beta} x = m$

$\Rightarrow x = (a^\beta)^m$

$\Rightarrow x = a^{\beta m}$

$\Rightarrow \log_a x = \beta m$ $(\because a > 0)$

$\Rightarrow \log_a x = \beta \log_{a^\beta} x$

$\Rightarrow \log_{a^\beta} x = \frac{1}{\beta}\log_a x = \frac{1}{\beta}\log_{|a|} x$ $(\because a > 0)$

Case (ii) When $a < 0$; β is an even integer

Now $\log_{a^\beta} x = m$

$\Rightarrow x = (a^\beta)^m$

$\Rightarrow x = a^{\beta m}$

$\Rightarrow a = -(x)^{1/\beta m}$ $(\because a < 0)$

$\Rightarrow -a = (x)^{1/\beta m}$

$\Rightarrow |a| = (x)^{1/\beta m}$

$\Rightarrow x = |a|^{\beta m}$

$\Rightarrow \log_{|a|} x = \beta m$

$\Rightarrow m = \frac{1}{\beta}\log_{|a|} x$

Hence, $\log_{a^\beta} x = \frac{1}{\beta}\log_{|a|} x$

P.12 $a^{\log_x b} = b^{\log_x a}$

Proof: Let $a^{\log_x b} = k$; taking $\log_b$ of both sides, we get $\log_b\left(a^{\log_x b}\right) = \log_b k$

$\Rightarrow \log_x b.\log_b a = \log_b k$ $\Rightarrow \log_x a = \log_b k$

$\Rightarrow k = b^{\log_x a}$ $\Rightarrow a^{\log_x b} = b^{\log_x a}$

P.13 If a function $f: (0, \infty) \to \mathbb{R}$ satisfies

$$\left.\begin{aligned} f(x.y) &= f(x) + f(y) \\ f\left(\frac{x}{y}\right) &= f(x) - f(y) \end{aligned}\right\} \forall x, y \in (0, \infty)$$

$\Rightarrow f(x) = \log_a x$ for $a > 0, \neq 1$

Proof: Given in functional equation topic of differentiability in our volume differential calculus.

P.14 If a is a positive real number, then

(i) For $a > 1$ the logarithmic functions follows the inequality $\log_a x > \log_a y \Leftrightarrow x > y$.
and for $0 < a < 1$ the inequality $\log_a x > \log_a y \Leftrightarrow 0 < x < y$

(ii) If $0 < a < 1$, then $\log_a x > b \Leftrightarrow 0 < x < a^b$

(iii) If $a > 1$, then $\log_a x > b \Leftrightarrow x > a^b$

REMARKS

1. *The base of logarithm can be any positive number other than 1, but usually two bases are mostly used they are 10 and e ($\approx$ 2.7183).*
Logarithms of numbers to the base 10 are named as common logarithms; where as the logarithms of the numbers to the base e are called as natural or Napierian logarithms.
$\therefore$ *we find* $\log_e a = \log_{10} a.\log_e 10$ *or* $\log_{10} a = \frac{\log_e a}{\log_e 10} = 0.434 \log_e a$
$\therefore$ *To convert natural logarithm of a number to common logarithm of that number we multiply the natural logarithm by 0.434. i.e.,* $\log_{10} a = 0.434 \log_e a$
Also $\log_e a = \log_{10} a.\log_e 10 = 2.303 \log_{10} a$
Thus, to convert common logarithm of a number to natural logarithm of that number we multiply the common logarithm by 2.303, i.e., $\log_e a = 2.303 \log_{10} a$*.This result is useful in different branches of sciences. For example, chemistry where we need to find natural logarithm of a given positive real number. We find first of all common logarithm of that number with the help of logarithmic table and then multiply the result by 2.303*
e.g., $\log_{10} 2 = 0.3010$
$\Rightarrow \ln 2 = 2.303 \times 0.3010 = 0.693$
$\log_{10} 3 = 0.4771$
$\Rightarrow \ln 3 = 2.303 \times 0.4771 = 1.098$
2. *The integer part of logarithm of a number is called characteristic and the decimal part is called mantissa.*
e.g., $\log_{10} 30 = 1.4771$, *then characteristic is 1 and mantissa is 0.4771.*
3. *Detail discussion of logarithm of a function, logarithmic inequalities and logarithmic equations and their solutions has been given in our book Algebra II Fundamental of Mathematics.*

ILLUSTRATION 71: Find the characteristic and mantissa of $\log_{10}(0.12)^{15}$; given $\log_{10}2 = 0.3010$, $\log_{10}3 = 0.4771$. Hence, find the number of zeros after decimal and before first significant digit in decimal representation of $(0.12)^{15}$.

SOLUTION: $\log_{10}(0.12)^{15} = 15\log_{10}(0.12)$

$= 15\log_{10}\left[\frac{12}{100}\right] = 15\log_{10}\left[\frac{3}{25}\right] = 15[\log_{10}3 - \log_{10}25]$

$= 15\log_{10}3 - 15\log_{10}25 = 15\log_{10}3 - 30\log_{10}5 = 15\log_{10}3 - 30\log_{10}\left(\frac{10}{2}\right)$

$= 15\log_{10}3 - 30[\log_{10}10 - \log_{10}2] = 15\log_{10}3 - 30\log_{10}10 + 30\log_{10}2$

$= 15\log_{10}3 - 30 + 30\log_{10}2 = 15(0.4771) + 30(0.3010) - 30$

$= 16.1865 - 30 = 16 + 0.1865 - 30$

$= -14 + 0.1865 = \overline{14}.1865$

$\therefore$ Characteristic $= -14$, Mantissa $= 0.1865$

The number of zeros after decimal and before first significant digit in decimal representation of a number $x \in (0, 1)$ is given by $|\text{ch}(x) + 1|$.

$\therefore$ Number of such zeros in the decimal representation of $(0.12)^{15}$ will be $= |-14 + 1| = 13$

ILLUSTRATION 72: Find the domain of given logarithmic functions

(i) $f(x) = \log_4(x^2 - 1)$

(ii) $f(x) = \log_{3x}(x^2 - 4)$

(iii) $f(x) = \log_{(5-x)}\left\{\frac{(x^2-9)}{(x+1)(x+6)}\right\}$

(iv) $f(x) = \frac{\log(x-4)(x-5)}{\log(x-3)}$

(v) $f(x) = \log(x - 2) + \log(8 - x)$

SOLUTION: (i) $f(x) = \log_4(x^2 - 1)$.

For $f(x)$ to be defined $(x^2 - 1) > 0 \Rightarrow x^2 > 1$

$\Rightarrow x \in (-\infty, -1) \cup (1, \infty)$

$\therefore$ Domain of $f(x) = (-\infty, -1) \cup (1, \infty)$

(ii) $f(x) = \log_{3x}(x^2 - 4)$

By base condition, $3x > 0$; $3x \neq 1 \Rightarrow x \in (0, \infty) \sim \left\{\frac{1}{3}\right\}$ .... (1)

Also $x^2 - 4 > 0 \Rightarrow x^2 > 4 \Rightarrow x < -2$ or $x > 2$ ($\because \log f(x)$ is defined for $f(x) > 0$)

$\Rightarrow x \in (-\infty, -2) \cup (2, \infty)$ .... (2)

$\therefore$ x must satisfy (1) as well as (2) $\Rightarrow x \in (2, \infty)$

$\therefore$ Domain of function is $(2, \infty)$.

(iii) $f(x) = \log_{(5-x)}\left\{\frac{(x^2-9)}{(x+1)(x+6)}\right\}$.

For base condition $5 - x > 0; \neq 1 \Rightarrow x < 5, x \neq 4 \Rightarrow x \in (-\infty, 5) \sim \{4\}$ .... (1)

Also $\frac{x^2-9}{(x+1)(x+6)} > 0 \Rightarrow (x^2 - 9)(x + 1)(x + 6) > 0 \Rightarrow (x + 6)(x + 3)(x + 1)(x - 3) > 0$

$\therefore$ By wavy-curve method $x \in (-\infty, -6) \cup (-3, -1) \cup (3, \infty)$ ... (2)

$\therefore$ Domain is the intersection of (1) and (2), i.e., $(-\infty, -6) \cup (-3, -1) \cup (3, 5) \sim \{4\}$

(iv) $f(x)=\dfrac{\log(x-4)(x-5)}{\log(x-3)}$

Here we must have $(x-4)(x-5)>0$ and denominator $\log(x-3)\neq 0$; $(x-3)>0$

$\Rightarrow$ $x\in(-\infty,4)\cup(5,\infty)$ and $x-3\neq 1$; $x-3>0$

$\Rightarrow$ $x\in(-\infty,4)\cup(5,\infty)$ and $x\in(3,\infty)\sim\{4\}$ $\Rightarrow$ $x\in(3,4)\cup(5,\infty)=D_f$

(v) $f(x)=\log(x-2)+\log(8-x)$.

Each linear function on which log is operated, must be positive.

$\Rightarrow$ $(x-2)>0$ and $8-x>0$ $\Rightarrow$ $x>2$ and $x<8$ $\Rightarrow$ $x\in(2,8)=D_f$

ILLUSTRATION 73: Find the number of digits in $(42875)^{12}$, given $\log 2=0.3010$, $\log 7=0.8451$

SOLUTION: Here $\log(42875)^{12}=12\log(42875)=12\log(125\times 343)$

$=12\log[(5)^3\times(7)^3]=12[\log(5)^3+\log(7)^3]=12[3\log 5+3\log 7]$

$=36\log 5+36\log 7=36\log\left(\dfrac{10}{2}\right)+36\log(7)$

$=36-36\log 2+36\log 7=36-36(0.3010)+36(0.8451)$ $(\because \log 10=1)$

$=36-10.836+30.4236=55.5876$

$\Rightarrow$ Characteristic $=55$ and mantissa $=0.5876$.

As the number of digits of a positive integer is one more than the characteristic of logarithm of number $\Rightarrow$ $(42875)^{12}$ has 56 digits.

ILLUSTRATION 74: Find the domain of logarithmic functions involved in the given logarithmic equation, and hence, solve the given equations.

(a) $\log_4(x+5)=3$

(b) $\log_{(x+2)}64=2$

(c) $(0.4)^{\log^2 x+1}=(6.25)^{2-\log x^3}$

(d) $x^{0.5\log_{\sqrt{x}}(x^2-x)}=(4)^{\log_9 3}$

SOLUTION: (a) Given equation is $\log_4(x+5)=3$ .... (1)

For domain of logarithmic function on LHS of (1), $x+5>0$

$\Rightarrow$ $x\in(-5,\infty)=$ Domain of logarithmic function

Now $\log_4(x+5)=3$ $\Rightarrow$ $(x+5)=(4)^3=64$

$\Rightarrow$ $x=59$ which belongs to domain. Thus, $x=59$ is the required solution.

(b) Given equation is $\log_{(x+2)}64=2$

For domain of logarithmic function $(x+2)>0$ and $\neq 1$

$\Rightarrow$ $x>-2$ and $x\neq -1$

$\therefore$ Domain of function $=(-2,\infty)\sim\{-1\}$

Now $64=(x+2)^2$ $\Rightarrow$ $x+2=\pm 8$ $\Rightarrow$ $x=-10$ or 6

but $-10\notin(-2,\infty)\sim\{-1\}$ $\Rightarrow$ $x=6$ is the only solution.

(c) Given equation is $(0.4)^{\log^2 x+1}=(6.25)^{2-\log x^3}$ ... (1)

For domain of logarithmic function on LHS of (1), $x>0$ and for domain of logarithmic function on RHS of (1), $x^3>0$, i.e., $x>0$.

Thus, logarithmic functions involved on both sides of equation (1) are defined for $x>0$, and hence, the solution of equation (1) must lie on this common domain, i.e., $(0,\infty)$

Now, $6.25=\dfrac{25}{4}=\left(\dfrac{5}{2}\right)^2$ and $0.4=\left(\dfrac{2}{5}\right)$

$\therefore$ From equation (1), we get $\left(\dfrac{2}{5}\right)^{\log^2 x+1}=\left[\left(\dfrac{5}{2}\right)^2\right]^{(2-\log x^3)}=\left(\dfrac{2}{5}\right)^{2(\log x^3-2)}$

$\Rightarrow \log^2 x + 1 = 2(3\log x - 2)$ $\Rightarrow (\log x)^2 - 6(\log x) + 5 = 0$

$\Rightarrow \log x = 1$ or $\log x = 5$ $\Rightarrow x = (10)^1$ or $x = (10)^5$.

Both belongs to $(0, \infty)$. Thus, $x = 10, x = 10^5$ are the required solutions.

(d) Given equation is $x^{0.5\log_{\sqrt{x}}(x^2-x)} = 4^{\log_9 3}$ .... (1)

For domain of logarithmic function on L.H.S. of above equation (1), $\sqrt{x} > 0; \neq 1$ and $(x^2 - x) > 0$ $\Rightarrow x > 0; \neq 1$ and $x(x-1) > 0 \Rightarrow x > 0; \neq 1$ and $x \in (-\infty, 0) \cup (1, \infty)$.

$\Rightarrow x \in (1, \infty)$ = domain of logarithmic function on LHS of (1).

Now $x^{0.5(2)\log_x(x^2-x)} = (4)^{\log_9 3}$ $\left(\because \log_{a^N}(b) = \frac{1}{N}\log_a(b)\right)$

$\Rightarrow x^{\log_x(x^2-x)} = (4)^{\log_9 3}$

$\Rightarrow (x^2 - x) = (3)^{\log_9 4}$ $\left(\because a^{\log_a x} = x \text{ and } a^{\log_N b} = b^{\log_N a}\right)$

$\Rightarrow x^2 - x = (3)^{\log_3 (4)^{1/2}}$ $\Rightarrow x^2 - x = (4)^{1/2}$ $\Rightarrow x^2 - x = 2$

(In fact $(4)^{1/2} = \pm 2$ but $\log (4)^{1/2}$ $\Rightarrow (4)^{1/2} = 2$)

$\Rightarrow x^2 - x - 2 = 0$ $\Rightarrow (x-2)(x+1) = 0$

$\Rightarrow x = 2$ or $x = -1$, but $-1 \notin D_f = (1, \infty)$ $\Rightarrow x = 2$ is the only solution.

ILLUSTRATION 75: Solve the logarithmic inequality $\frac{1}{2}\log(2x-1) + \log\sqrt{x-9} > 1$

SOLUTION: Given inequality is $\frac{1}{2}\log(2x-1) + \log\sqrt{x-9} > 1$ .... (1)

For domain of logarithmic functions involved on LHS of inequality (1), $2x - 1 > 0$ and $x - 9 > 0 \Rightarrow x > \frac{1}{2}$ and $x > 9$.

$\Rightarrow$ Solutions of inequality (1) must belong to $(9, \infty)$

Now from equation (1), we get $\log(2x-1)^{1/2} + \log\sqrt{x-9} > 1$

$\Rightarrow \log(2x-1)^{1/2}(x-9)^{1/2} > 1$ $\Rightarrow (2x-1)^{1/2}(x-9)^{1/2} > (10)^1$

$\Rightarrow (2x-1)(x-9) > 100$ $\Rightarrow 2x^2 - 19x - 91 > 0$

$\Rightarrow (x-13)(2x+7) > 0$ $\Rightarrow x < -\frac{7}{2}$ or $x > 13$

Due to domain restriction solution set of logarithmic inequality is $(13, \infty)$.

ILLUSTRATION 76: If x is positive, then show that $\ln(1+x) < x$ and $\ln(1+x) > \frac{x}{1+x}$. Hence, show that $\ln(1+n) < 1 + \frac{1}{2} + \frac{1}{3} + \frac{1}{4} + ... + \frac{1}{n}$ for $n \in \mathbb{N}$.

SOLUTION: Given $x > 0$

$\ln(1+x) < x$

$\Leftrightarrow (1+x) < e^x$

$\Leftrightarrow (1+x) < 1 + x + \frac{x^2}{2!} + \frac{x^3}{3!} + ...$ which is true as $x > 0$

$\Leftrightarrow \ln(1+x) > \frac{x}{1+x}$ $\Leftrightarrow (1+x) > e^{\left(\frac{x}{1+x}\right)}$

$\Leftrightarrow \left(\frac{1}{\left(\frac{1}{1+x}\right)}\right) > e^{\left(\frac{x}{1+x}\right)}$ $\Leftrightarrow \left(\frac{1}{1-\frac{x}{1+x}}\right) > e^{\left(\frac{x}{1+x}\right)}$

$\Leftrightarrow \left(1-\frac{x}{1+x}\right)^{-1} > e^{\left(\frac{x}{1+x}\right)} \Leftrightarrow 1+\frac{x}{1+x}+\left(\frac{x}{1+x}\right)^2+.... > 1+\frac{x}{1+x}+\frac{1}{2!}\left(\frac{x}{1+x}\right)^2+...$

which is true.

Now $\ln(1+x) < x$ for $x > 0$ $\Rightarrow \ln\left(1+\frac{1}{y}\right) < \frac{1}{y}$ for $y > 0$

$\Rightarrow \ln\left(\frac{1+y}{y}\right) < \frac{1}{y}$ $\Rightarrow \log(1+y) - \log y < \frac{1}{y}$ .... (1)

Substituting $y = 1, 2, 3,., n$ in (1), we get $\ln 2 - \log 1 < \frac{1}{1}$

$\ln 3 - \ln 2 < \frac{1}{2}$, $\ln 4 - \ln 3 < \frac{1}{3}$, ..., $\ln(n+1) - \ln n < \frac{1}{n}$

Adding above inequalities, we get $-\log 1 + \log(n+1) < 1+\frac{1}{2}+\frac{1}{3}+...+\frac{1}{n}$

$\Rightarrow \log(n+1) < 1+\frac{1}{2}+\frac{1}{3}+...+\frac{1}{n}$

ILLUSTRATION 77: If $x \in (0, 1)$, prove that $(1+x)^{1+x}(1-x)^{1-x} > 1$. Hence, show $a^a b^b > \left(\frac{a+b}{2}\right)^{a+b}$ for $a > b > 0$.

SOLUTION: Let $y = (1+x)^{(1+x)}(1-x)^{1-x}$ .... (1)

Taking ln on both sides of (1), we get $\ln y = (1+x)\ln(1+x) + (1-x)\ln(1-x)$

$\Rightarrow \ln y = \ln(1+x) + \ln(1-x) + x[\ln(1+x) - \ln(1-x)]$ ... (2)

Now $\ln(1+x) + \ln(1-x)$

$= \left[x-\frac{x^2}{2}+\frac{x^3}{3}-\frac{x^4}{4}+...\right]+\left[-x-\frac{x^2}{2}-\frac{x^3}{3}-\frac{x^4}{4}-...\right] = -2\left[\frac{x^2}{2}+\frac{x^4}{4}+...\right]$ .... (3)

and $\ln(1+x) - \ln(1-x)$

$= \left[x-\frac{x^2}{2}+\frac{x^3}{3}-\frac{x^4}{4}+...\right]-\left[-x-\frac{x^2}{2}-\frac{x^3}{3}-\frac{x^4}{4}-...\right] = 2\left[x+\frac{x^3}{3}+\frac{x^5}{5}+...\right]$ ... (4)

Using (3) and (4) in (2), we get

$\ln y = -2\left(\frac{x^2}{2}+\frac{x^4}{4}+\frac{x^6}{6}+...\right)+2x\left[x+\frac{x^3}{3}+\frac{x^5}{5}-...\right] = \left(x^2+\frac{1}{6}x^4+\frac{1}{15}x^6+...\right) > 0$

Thus, $\ln y > 0 \Rightarrow y > 1$ $\Rightarrow (1+x)^{(1+x)}(1-x)^{(1-x)} > 1$

Thus, for $x \in (0, 1)$, $(1+x)^{(1+x)}(1-x)^{(1-x)} > 1$. ... (5)

Next, we are to show that $a^a b^b > \left(\frac{a+b}{2}\right)^{a+b}$ for $0 < b < a$ and it would hold iff $\frac{a^a b^b}{\left(\frac{a+b}{2}\right)^{a+b}} > 1$

$\Leftrightarrow \left[\frac{a}{\left(\frac{a+b}{2}\right)}\right]^a \cdot \left[\frac{b}{\left(\frac{a+b}{2}\right)}\right]^b > 1 \Leftrightarrow \left(\frac{2a}{a+b}\right)^a \cdot \left(\frac{2b}{a+b}\right)^b > 1$

$\Leftrightarrow \left(\frac{a+b+a-b}{a+b}\right)^a \cdot \left(\frac{(a+b)-(a-b)}{a+b}\right)^b > 1 \Leftrightarrow \left(1+\frac{a-b}{a+b}\right)^a \cdot \left(1-\frac{(a-b)}{a+b}\right)^b > 1$

$\Leftrightarrow (1+x)^a . (1-x)^b > 1$ for $x = \frac{a-b}{a+b}$

$\Leftrightarrow (1+x)^{\frac{2a}{a+b}} . (1-x)^{\frac{2b}{a+b}} > (1)^{\frac{2}{a+b}}$ (Raising to power $\frac{2}{a+b}$ both sides)

$\Rightarrow (1+x)^{(1+x)} . (1-x)^{(1-x)} > 1$ for $x = \frac{a-b}{a+b}$.

which is true by (5) as $x = \frac{a-b}{a+b} = \frac{a+b-2b}{a+b} = 1 - \frac{2b}{a+b} \in (0,1)$ as $a > b > 0$ (given)

ILLUSTRATION 78: Solve the equation $\log_{\cos x} 3.\log_{\cos^2 x} a + 1 = 0$.

SOLUTION: $\frac{1}{\log_3 \cos x} \cdot \frac{\log_3 a}{\log_3 \cos^2 x} + 1 = 0$; $\cos x > 0$ and $\neq 1$, $a > 0$

$\Rightarrow \frac{\log_3 a}{2(\log_3 \cos x)^2} = -1$ $\Rightarrow 2(\log_3 \cos x)^2 = -\log_3 a$ .... (1)

Clearly L.H.S. > 0 as $\cos x \neq 1$,

$\Rightarrow \log_3 a < 0$ $\Rightarrow 0 < a < 1$

$\therefore$ From equation (1), $(\log_3 \cos x)^2 = -\frac{\log_3 a}{2}$

$\Rightarrow \log_3 \cos x = \pm\sqrt{\frac{-\log_3 a}{2}}$

But $\cos x \in (0, 1)$ $\Rightarrow$ L.H.S. < 0

$\Rightarrow \log_3 \cos x = -\sqrt{\frac{-\log_3 a}{2}}$ $\Rightarrow \cos x = (3)^{-\sqrt{-\log_3 \sqrt{a}}}$

$\Rightarrow x = 2n\pi \pm (3)^{-\sqrt{-\log_3 \sqrt{a}}}$; $n \in \mathbb{Z}$

TEXTUAL EXERCISE–6: (SUBJECTIVE)

1. Simplify and compute the following expressions:

(a) $\frac{(15)^3.(21)^3}{(35)^2.(3)^4}$ (b) $(-1.4)^3.\left(3\frac{4}{7}\right)^3$

(c) $\frac{5.2^{k-2}+10.2^{k-1}}{10^{k+2}}$ (d) $\left(\frac{\sqrt[4]{ab}-\sqrt{b}}{\sqrt{a}-\sqrt[4]{ab}}\right)^{-4}$

2. Which of the given pair of numbers is greater?

(a) 2^{300} or 3^{200} (b) 54^4 or 21^{12}

(c) $(0.4)^4$ or $(0.8)^3$ (d) 10^{20} and 40^{10}

3. Perform the indicated operations and simplify the given expression:

(a) $\left(\left(x^{\frac{2}{3}}y^{-1}\right)^2\left(x^2y^{-1}\right)^{\frac{1}{2}}\left(y^{\frac{2}{3}}\right)^{\frac{3}{2}}\right)^6$

(b) $\sqrt{\frac{a}{b}\sqrt{\frac{a}{b}}.\sqrt[3]{\frac{a}{b}}}.a^{-\frac{1}{3}}.b^{\frac{1}{3}}$

4. Solve the following exponential equation for x;

(a) $4^{2x^2-1} = 2$ (b) $5^{x-1} = 10^x.2^{-x}.5^{x+1}$

(c) $5^{2x-1} + 5^{x+1} = 250$ (d) $9^x + 6^x = 2.4^x$

(e) $2^{x+1}\,5^x = 200$ (f) $6^x + 6^{x+1} = 2^x + 2^{x+1} + 2^{x+2}$

5. Solve the following exponential inequalities for x;

(a) $2^{3-8x} > 1$ (b) $16^x > 0.125$

(c) $(0.3)^{2x^2-3x+6} < 0.00243$ (d) $\left(\frac{1}{3}\right)^{\sqrt{x+2}} > 3^{-x}$

(e) $\sqrt[x+1]{3} > 9$ (f) $8^{\sqrt{8^x}} > 4096$

(g) $\left(\frac{2}{5}\right)^{\frac{6-5x}{2+5x}} < \frac{25}{4}$ (h) $2^x + 2^{-x+1} - 3 < 0$

6. Express log of x to the base 2 in each of the following cases:

(a) $32^{\frac{1}{3}} = 4x$ (b) $64^{\frac{1}{4}} = 8x$

7. Prove that $\frac{\log_a N}{\log_{ab} N} = 1 + \log_a b$ and indicate the permissible values of the letters.

8. Find the domain of following logarithmic functions:
   (a) $f(x) = \log_x 3$
   (b) $f(x) = \log_2(x - 1)$
   (c) $f(x) = \log_{2x-3}(x - 1)(x - 4)$
   (d) $f(x) = \log_2\left[\dfrac{(x-4)(x-5)}{(x-6)}\right]$

9. Find the smallest possible value of the expression $ln(x^3 - 5x^2 - 6x + 54) - ln(x + 3)$

10. Solve the logarithmic equations
   (i) $\log_{(x+3)}(x + 4) = 2$ (ii) $2^{\log_4(x+5)} = (x+5)$

11. Find the integer ordered pair solutions of equation $\log_{(x+4)}16 = (y + 2)$

12. Solve the equation $\sqrt[4]{|x-3|^{x+1}} = \sqrt[3]{|x-3|^{x-2}}$.

13. Find the solutions of the equation $\log_{\sin x} 5.\log_{\sin^2 x} a + 1 = 0$.

14. Solve the inequality $\log_{x-2} 8 + \log_{x+2} 8 > \log_{x-2} 8.\log_{x+2} 8$.

15. If $x > 0$, $y > 0$ and $z > 0$, prove that $x^{(\ln y - \ln z)} + y^{(\ln z - \ln x)} + z^{(\ln x - \ln y)} \geq 3$.

16. If $x = \dfrac{1}{2}$ satisfies the inequality $\log_a(x^2 - x + 2) - \log_a(-x^2 + 2x + 3) > 0$, then find all real solutions of the inequality.

Answer Keys

1. (a) 315 (b) –125 (c) $\dfrac{5^{-k}}{16}$ (d) $\dfrac{a}{b}$
2. (a) 3^{200} (b) 21^{12} (c) $(0.8)^3$ (d) 10^{20}
3. (a) $x^{14}.y^{-9}$ (b) $\left(\dfrac{a}{b}\right)^{\frac{1}{2}}$
4. (a) $\pm\dfrac{\sqrt{3}}{2}$ (b) {–2} (c) 2 (d) 0 (e) { 2} (f) 0
5. (a) $(-\infty, 3/8)$ (b) $(-3/4, +\infty)$ (c) $(-\infty, 1/2) \cup (1, 8)$ (d) $(2, +\infty)$
   (e) $x \in \phi$, $x \in \mathbb{N}$ (f) $(4/3, +\infty)$ (g) $(-\infty, -2) \cup (-2/5 + \infty)$ (h) (0, 1)
6. (a) –1/3 (b) –3/2
7. $a \neq 1$, $a > 0$; $b > 0$; $ab \neq 1$ $ab > 0$; $N > 0$, $N \neq 1$
8. (a) $(0, \infty) \sim \{1\}$ (b) $(1, \infty)$ (c) $(4, \infty)$ (d) (e) $(4, 5) \cup (6, \infty)$
9. ln2 **10.** (i) $\left(\dfrac{-5+\sqrt{5}}{2}\right)$ (ii) –4
11. (0, 0); (–2, 2); (12, –1) **12.** 2, 3, 4, 11
13. $x = n\pi + (-1)^n \sin^{-1} a^{\sqrt{-\log_a \sqrt{5}}}$; $n \in \mathbb{Z}$ for $a \in (0, 1)$ and $x = n\pi + (-1)^n.\sin^{-1}\left(a^{-\sqrt{-\log_a \sqrt{5}}}\right); a > 1$
14. $x \in (2, \sqrt{5}) \cup (3, \infty)$ **16.** $\left(\dfrac{3-\sqrt{17}}{4}, \dfrac{3+\sqrt{17}}{4}\right)$

TEXTUAL EXERCISE–6: (OBJECTIVE)

1. The value of $4^{2\log_9 3}$ is
   (a) 4
   (b) 2
   (c) 3
   (d) 1

2. If $\log_7 2 = n$, then $\log_{49} 28$ is equal to
   (a) $\dfrac{1+2\eta}{4}$ (b) $\dfrac{1+2\eta}{2}$
   (c) $\dfrac{1+2\eta}{3}$ (d) None of these

3. If $a^2 + 4b^2 = 12ab$, then log (a + 2b) is

(a) $\frac{1}{2}(\log a+\log b-\log 2)$

(b) $\log\frac{a}{2}+\log\frac{b}{2}+\log 2$

(c) $\frac{1}{2}(\log a+\log b+4\log 2)$

(d) $\frac{1}{2}(\log a-\log b-4\log 2)$

4. If $\log_a ab = x$, then $\log_b ab$ is equal to

(a) $\frac{1}{x}$ (b) $\frac{x}{1+x}$

(c) $\frac{x}{x-1}$ (d) $\frac{x}{1-x}$

5. If $\frac{\log_e a}{y-z}=\frac{\log_e b}{z-x}=\frac{\log_e c}{x-y}$ then $a^{y^2+yz+z^2}b^{z^2+zx+x^2}c^{x^2+xy+y^2}$ is equal to

(a) 2 (b) 0

(c) 1 (d) None of these

6. The value of $81^{\frac{1}{\log_5 3}}+27^{\log_9 36}+3^{\frac{4}{\log_7 9}}$ is equal to

(a) 49 (b) 625

(c) 216 (d) 890

7. If $f(x)=\log\left(\frac{1+x}{1-x}\right)$, then

(a) $f(x_1).f(x_2)=f(x_1+x_2)$

(b) $f(x + 2) - 2f(x + 1) + f(x) = 0$

(c) $f(x) = f(x + 1) = f(x^2 + x)$

(d) $f(x_1)+f(x_2)=f\left(\frac{x_1+x_2}{1+x_1x_2}\right)$

8. If $y=2^{\frac{1}{\log_x 4}}$, then x is equal to

(a) $\sqrt{y}$ (b) y

(c) y^2 (d) y^4

9. If $\frac{1}{\log_a x}+\frac{1}{\log_c x}=\frac{2}{\log_b x}$, then a, b, c are in

(a) A.P. (b) G.P.

(c) A.P. and G.P. both (d) None of these

10. The solution of equation $\log_{10}(x^2-x-6)-x = \log_{10}(x+2)-4$ is

(a) $x = 5$ (b) $x = 3$

(c) $x = 4$ (d) None of these

11. The number of real values of the parameter k for which $(\log_{16}x)^2 - (\log_{16}x) + (\log_{16}k) = 0$ with real coefficients will have exactly one solution is

(a) 2 (b) 1

(c) 4 (d) None of these

12. If $x+\log_{10}(1+2^x)=x\log_{10}5+\log_{10}6$, then x is equal to

(a) 4 (b) 0

(c) 1 (d) None of these

13. If $\log_{1/\sqrt{2}}\sin x>0$, $x \in [0, 4\pi)$ then the number of values of x which are integral multiples of $\pi/4$ is

(a) 6 (b) 12

(c) 3 (d) None of these

14. If $\log_{1/2}(x+1)\le\log_2(2-x)$, then x belongs to the interval

(a) $\left(0,\frac{1-\sqrt{5}}{2}\right]$ (b) $\left[\frac{1-\sqrt{5}}{2},\frac{1+\sqrt{5}}{2}\right]$

(c) $\left[\frac{1+\sqrt{5}}{2},\infty\right)$ (d) None of these

15. If $\log_{0.3}(x-1) < \log_{0.09}(x-1)$, then x lies in the interval

(a) $(2, \infty)$ (b) $(-2, -1)$

(c) $(1, 2)$ (d) None of these

16. The number of values of $x \in [0, n\pi]$, $n \in \mathbb{Z}$ that satisfy $\log_{|\sin x|}(1+\cos x)=2$ is

(a) 0 (b) n

(c) $2n$ (d) None of these

17. If $\log_{\cos x}\sin x \ge 0$ and $0 \le x \le 3\pi$, then $\sin x$ is in the interval

(a) $\left[\frac{\sqrt{5}-1}{2},1\right]$ (b) $\left(0,\frac{\sqrt{5}-1}{2}\right]$

(c) $\left[0,\frac{1}{2}\right]$ (d) None of these

18. If $\log_{\sqrt{3}}(\sin x+2\sqrt{2}\cos x)\ge 2$, $-2\pi < x \le 2\pi$, then the number of solutions of x is

(a) 0 (b) infinite

(c) 3 (d) None of these

Answer Keys

1. (a)	**2.** (b)	**3.** (c)	**4.** (c)	**5.** (c)	**6.** (d)	**7.** (d)	**8.** (c)	**9.** (b)	**10.** (c)
11. (b)	**12.** (c)	**13.** (a)	**14.** (b)	**15.** (a)	**16.** (a)	**17.** (d)	**18.** (d)		

GREATEST INTEGER FUNCTION (BRACKET FUNCTION)

Greatest integer function of x is the largest integer which does not exceed x, it is denoted as $[x]$. And also called as integral part of x

Origin: If a and b are positive integers, such that $a = qb + r,\ 0 \le r < b$

Then $\frac{a}{b} = q + \frac{r}{b}$, where $0 \le \frac{r}{b} < 1$

That is, $\left[\frac{a}{b}\right]$ is the quotient in the division of a by b.

$[x]$ = greatest integer $\le x$ = the nearest integer to left to

$$x = \begin{cases} x; & x \in \mathbb{Z} \\ x; & x \notin \mathbb{Z} \end{cases}$$

$\therefore\quad [x] = n,\ n \le x < n + 1$

$$\Rightarrow\ [x] = \begin{cases} -2; & \text{if } -2 \le x < -1 \\ -1; & \text{if } -1 \le x < 0 \\ 0; & \text{if } 0 \le x < 1 \\ 1; & \text{if } 1 \le x < 2 \end{cases}\ ;\ \text{Graph of gint } x$$

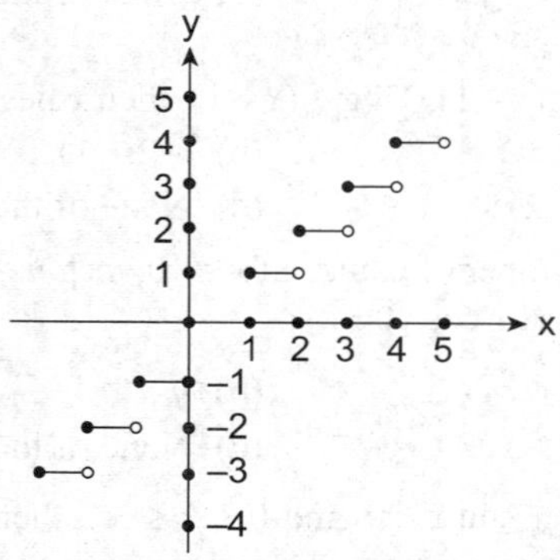

FIGURE 2.96

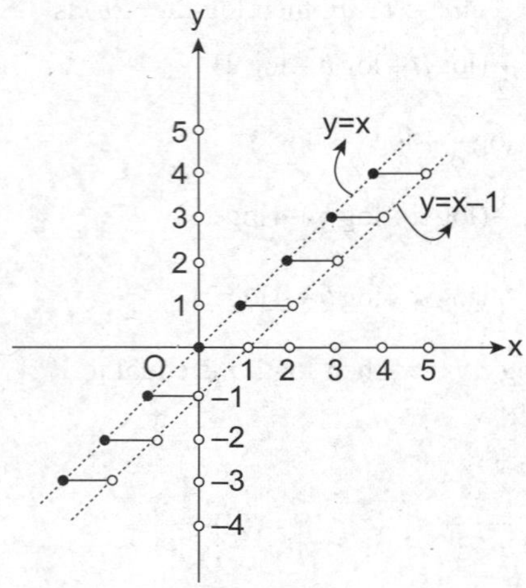

FIGURE 2.97

Graph of gint x is represented by thick horizontal unit length line segments at unit distances on, above, and below x-axis bounded between the lines $y = x$ and $y = x - 1$ as shown in Figure 2.97. The left end point of line segments is included whereas right end point is excluded in the graph.

PROPERTIES OF GREATEST INTEGER FUNCTION (BRACKET FUNCTION)

(i) Domain of $[x]$: $\mathbb{R}$; Range of $[x]$: $\mathbb{Z}$

(ii) $[[x]] = [x]$

Proof: We know that $[x] = n\ \forall\ n \in \mathbb{Z}$

Let $[x] = m$

$\Rightarrow\ [[x]] = [m] = m = [x]$

Thus, $[[x]] = [x]\ \forall\ x \in \mathbb{R}$

ILLUSTRATION 79: Find the set of all values of $[x]$ for which the function $f(x) = \frac{1}{\sqrt{6[[x]] - 5[x] - 4}}$ is defined, and hence, solve the equation $f(x) = \frac{1}{4}$ for $[x]$ showing that this equation has infinitely many solutions x.

SOLUTION: For $f(x)$ to be defined $6[[x]] - 5[x] - 4 > 0 \quad \Rightarrow 6[x] - 5[x] - 4 > 0 \quad \Rightarrow [x] > 4$

$\Rightarrow\ [x] \ge 5 \qquad \Rightarrow [x] \in \{5, 6, 7, 8, \ldots\} \qquad (\because [[x]] = [x])$

Thus, $\{5, 6, 7, 8, \ldots\}$ is the set of all values of $[x]$ for which $f(x)$ is defined

Now $f(x) = \frac{1}{4} \Rightarrow \frac{1}{\sqrt{6[[x]]-5[x]-4}} = \frac{1}{4} \Rightarrow \sqrt{6[x]-5[x]-4} = 4$

$\Rightarrow \sqrt{[x]-4} = 4 \Rightarrow [x] - 4 = 16 \Rightarrow [x] = 20$

Thus, $f(x) = \frac{1}{4}$ holds for $[x] = 20$.

Now equation $f(x) = \frac{1}{4}$ holds only when $[x] = 20$. But $[x] = 20$ holds for all real numbers which are greater than or equal to 20 but less than 21.

That is, $x \in [20, 21)$ which contains infinitely many solutions x.

(iii) $[x + m] = [x] + m$ provided $m \in \mathbb{Z}$

Proof: Let $x = n + f$, where $0 \le f < 1$ and $n \in \mathbb{Z}$

$\therefore \quad [x + m] = [(n + m) + f]$

$= n + m = [x] + m$ $\quad (\because x = n + f \Rightarrow [x] = n)$

Hence, proved.

ILLUSTRATION 80: Solve the following equations:

(a) $[x + 4] + 2[x] = 10$ (b) $2[x - 4 + [x]] = 6 - 3[x]$

SOLUTION: (a) $[x + 4] + 2[x] = 10$

$\Rightarrow [x] + 4 + 2[x] = 10$ $\quad (\because [x + m] = [x] + m$ for $x \in \mathbb{R}, m \in \mathbb{Z})$

$\Rightarrow 3[x] = 6 \Rightarrow [x] = 2 \Rightarrow x \in [2, 3)$ $\quad (\because [x] = n \Rightarrow x \in [n, n + 1))$

Thus, [2, 3) is the required solutions set.

(b) $2[x - 4 + [x]] = 6 - 3[x]$

$\Rightarrow 2([x] - 4 + [x]) = 6 - 3[x] \Rightarrow 4[x] - 8 = 6 - 3[x]$

$\Rightarrow 7[x] = 14 \Rightarrow [x] = 2 \Rightarrow x \in [2, 3)$

Thus, [2, 3) is the required solution set.

ILLUSTRATION 81: Let $S_k = \sum_{k=1}^{n} k!$, then evaluate $\sum_{n=6}^{10}\left(S_n - 6\left[\frac{S_n}{6}\right]\right)$; where [.] is gint function.

SOLUTION: Given $S_k = \sum_{k=1}^{n} k! = 1! + 2! + 3! + \ldots + n!$

For $n = 5$,

$S_5 = 1! + 2! + 3! + 4! + 5! = 1 + 2 + 6 + 24 + 120 = 153$

For $n \ge 6$,

$S_n = 1! + 2! + 3! + 4! + 5! + 6! + 7! + \ldots + n! = 153 + 6m;\ m \in \mathbb{Z} = 6m + 150 + 3$

$= 6(m + 25) + 3 = 6r + 3;\ r \in \mathbb{Z}$

$\therefore$ for $n \ge 6$, $S_n - 6\left[\frac{S_n}{6}\right] = (6r+3) - 6\left[\frac{6r+3}{6}\right]$

$= (6r+3) - 6\left[r + \frac{1}{2}\right] = (6r+3) - 6\left(r + \left[\frac{1}{2}\right]\right) = 6r + 3 - 6r = 3$

$\therefore \sum_{n=6}^{10}\left(S_n - 6\left[\frac{S_n}{6}\right]\right) = 5(3) = 15$

(iv) $[x + [y + [z]]] = [x] + [y] + [z]$

Proof: LHS $= [x + [y + [z]]] = [y + [z]] + [x]$
($\because$ By property $[x + m] = m + [x]; x \in \mathbb{Z}$)

$= [z] + [y] + [x]$

(By same property)

Thus, $[x + [y + [z]]] = [x] + [y] + [z] \ \forall\ x, y, z \in \mathbb{R}$

ILLUSTRATION 82: Solve the following equations

(a) $[[x + [x + [x]]]] = 12$ (b) $\dfrac{4[[x+2]]}{[[x+[x+[x]]]]-12} = \dfrac{1}{3}$

SOLUTION: (a) $[[x + [x + [x]]]] = 12$

$\Rightarrow [[x] + [x] + [x]] = 12$ ($\because [x + [y + [z]]] = [x] + [y] + [z]$)

$\Rightarrow 3[x] = 12 \Rightarrow [x] = 4 \Rightarrow x \in [4, 5)$ ($\because 3[x] \in \mathbb{Z}$ and $[m] = m \ \forall\ m \in \mathbb{Z}$)

(b) $\dfrac{4[[x+2]]}{[[x+[x+[x]]]]-12} = \dfrac{1}{3} \Rightarrow \dfrac{4[[x]+2]}{3[x]-12} = \dfrac{1}{3}$

($\because [x + m] = [x] + m \ \forall\ n \in \mathbb{R}, m \in \mathbb{Z}$ and by part (a))

$\Rightarrow \dfrac{4([x]+2)}{3[x]-12} = \dfrac{1}{3}$ ($\because [x] + 2 \in \mathbb{Z}$ and $[m] = m \ \forall\ m \in \mathbb{Z}$)

$\Rightarrow 12[x] + 24 = 3[x] - 12 \Rightarrow 9[x] = -36 \Rightarrow [x] = -4 \Rightarrow x \in [-4, -3)$

(v) $[x] > n; n \in \mathbb{Z}$
$\Rightarrow [x] \in \{n + 1, n + 2, n + 3, \dots\}$
$\Rightarrow x \in [n + 1, \infty)$

Proof: Given $[x] > n$
$\Rightarrow [x]$ is an integer greater than or equal to $(n + 1)$.

i.e., $[x] \geq (n + 1)$ .... (1)
but $[x] \leq x \ \forall\ x \in \mathbb{R}$ .... (2)
Thus, $(n + 1) \leq [x] \leq x$ [from (1) and (2)]
$\Rightarrow x \geq (n + 1)$
$\Rightarrow x \in [(n + 1), \infty)$.
Hence, proved

ILLUSTRATION 83: Find the domain of the functions

(a) $f(x) = \dfrac{1}{\sqrt{[x]-\sin\theta}}; \ \theta \in \left[\dfrac{-\pi}{2}, \dfrac{\pi}{2}\right]$ (b) $f(x) = \dfrac{\log([x]-1)}{\sqrt[3]{[x]-2}}$

SOLUTION: (a) $f(x) = \dfrac{1}{\sqrt{[x]-\sin\theta}}; \ \theta \in \left[\dfrac{-\pi}{2}, \dfrac{\pi}{2}\right]$

for $f(x)$ to be defined $[x] > \sin \theta$

$\Rightarrow [x] > 1 \Rightarrow [x] \in \{2, 3, 4, ..\}$ $\left(\because \theta \in \left[\dfrac{-\pi}{2}, \dfrac{\pi}{2}\right] \Rightarrow \sin\theta \in [-1, 1]\right)$

$\Rightarrow x \in [2, \infty)$ ($\because [x] > n \Rightarrow x \in [n + 1, \infty)$)

$\therefore$ Domain of given function $= D_f = [2, \infty)$

(b) $f(x) = \dfrac{\log([x]-1)}{\sqrt[3]{[x]-2}}$

For $f(x)$ to be defined, $[x] - 1 > 0$ and $[x] \neq 2$

$\Rightarrow [x] > 1$ and $[x] \neq 2 \Rightarrow [x] \in \{3, 4, \dots\} \Rightarrow x \in [3, \infty) \Rightarrow D_f = [3, \infty)$

(vi) $[x] \geq n \quad \Rightarrow \quad x \in [n, \infty)$

Proof: Given $[x] \geq n$ .... (1)

Also $[x] \leq x \;\forall\; x \in \mathbb{R}$ ..... (2)

$\therefore$ From (1) and (2)

$x \geq [x] \geq n \Rightarrow x \geq n \Rightarrow x \in [n, \infty)$

ILLUSTRATION 84: Find the domain of $f(x) = \dfrac{1}{\sqrt{[x]-2}} + \sqrt{[x]-4}$

SOLUTION: For $f(x)$ to be defined, $[x] > 2$ and $[x] \geq 4$

$\Rightarrow [x] \geq 4 \qquad \Rightarrow [x] \in [4, \infty)$

$\therefore$ Domain of function $f(x) = [4, \infty)$

ILLUSTRATION 85: Find the domain of definition of the function $f(x) = \dfrac{(\sec^{-1} x)}{\sqrt{x-[x]}}$

SOLUTION: Given function is $f(x) = \dfrac{(\sec^{-1} x)}{\sqrt{x-[x]}}$;

which is defined for $x \in (-\infty, -1] \cup [1, \infty)$ for which $x - [x] \neq 0$, i.e., $\{x\} \neq 0$

$\Rightarrow$ Domain of function is $\mathbb{R} \sim \{(-1, 1) \cup \mathbb{Z}\}$.

(vii) $[x] < n \quad \Rightarrow \quad x \in (-\infty, n)$

Proof: Let $x = [x] + f$; where $0 \leq f < 1$.

Given $[x] < n$

$\Rightarrow [x] \leq (n-1)$

$\Rightarrow x - f \leq (n-1) \qquad (\because [x] = x - f)$

$\Rightarrow x \leq n - 1 + f$

$\Rightarrow x \leq n - (1-f) < n$ as $(1-f) > 0$

$\Rightarrow x < n$

$\Rightarrow x \in (-\infty, n)$

ILLUSTRATION 86: Find the domain of following functions

(a) $f(x) = \sqrt{[x]-4} + \dfrac{1}{\sqrt{6-[x]}}$ (b) $f(x) = \sin^{-1}[x+1]$

SOLUTION: (a) $f(x) = \sqrt{[x]-4} + \dfrac{1}{\sqrt{6-[x]}}$

For $f(x)$ to be defined $[x] - 4 \geq 0$; $6 - [x] > 0 \Rightarrow x \in [4, 6)$

$\Rightarrow [x] \geq 4$ and $[x] < 6$

$\Rightarrow x \in [4, \infty)$ and $x \in (-\infty, 6) \Rightarrow x \in (-\infty, 6) \cap [4, \infty)$

(b) $f(x) = \sin^{-1}[x+1]$

For $f(x)$ to be defined $[x+1] \in [-1, 1] \Rightarrow [x+1] = -1, 0, 1$

$\Rightarrow x + 1 \in [-1, 2) \qquad \Rightarrow x \in [-2, 1)$

ILLUSTRATION 87: Find the domain of the function $f(x) = \dfrac{1}{[|x-1|]+[|x-6|]-5}$; where [] represents greatest integer function.

SOLUTION: Given $f(x)=\dfrac{1}{[|x-1|]+[|x-6|]-5}$ is defined when $[|x-1|]+[|x-6|]-5\neq 0$ .... (1)

Here we have three cases:

Case 1: When $x \le 1$

$[1-x]+[6-x]-5\neq 0,$

$\Rightarrow 1+[-x]+6+[-x]-5\neq 0,$

$\Rightarrow 2[-x]+2\neq 0 \Rightarrow [-x]\neq -1 \Rightarrow -x\notin[-1,0) \Rightarrow x\notin(0,1] \Rightarrow x\in(-\infty,0]$ .... (2)

Case II: When $1 < x \le 6$

$\Rightarrow [x-1]+[6-x]-5\neq 0$

$\Rightarrow [x]-1+6+[-x]-5\neq 0 \Rightarrow [x]+[-x]\neq 0 \Rightarrow x\notin\mathbb{Z}$

$\Rightarrow x\notin\{2,3,4,5,6\}$ .... (3)

Case III: When $x > 6$

$\Rightarrow [x-1]+[x-6]-5\neq 0$

$\Rightarrow [x]-1+[x]-6-5\neq 0 \Rightarrow 2[x]\neq 12$

$\Rightarrow [x]\neq 6 \Rightarrow x\notin[6,7) \Rightarrow x\in[7,\infty)$

Thus, for $f(x)$ to be defined $x\in(-\infty,0]\cup(1,6)\cup[7,\infty)\sim\{2,3,4,5\}$

or $x\in\mathbb{R}\sim\{(0,1]\cup[6,7)\cup\{2,3,4,5\}\}$.

(viii) $[x]\le n \Rightarrow n\in(-\infty, n+1)$

Proof: Let $x=[x]+f$; where $0\le f<1$

Given $[x]\le n$

$\Rightarrow x-f\le n \Rightarrow x\le n+f<n+1$ as $0\le f<1$

$\Rightarrow x<n+1 \Rightarrow x\in(-\infty, n+1)$

ILLUSTRATION 88: Find the domain of function $f(x)=\sqrt{([x]-2)}.\sqrt{6-[x]}$

SOLUTION: For $f(x)$ to be defined $([x]-2), (6-[x])\ge 0$

$\Rightarrow [x]\ge 2$ and $6\ge[x] \Rightarrow [x]\ge 2$ and $[x]\le 6$

$\Rightarrow x\in[2,\infty)$ and $x\in(-\infty,7) \Rightarrow x\in(-\infty,7)\cap[2,\infty)=[2,7)$

$\therefore$ Domain of function $f(x)=[2,7)$

(ix) $[-x]=\begin{cases}-[x]=-x & \text{if } x\in\mathbb{Z}\\ -1-[x] & \text{if } x\notin\mathbb{Z}\end{cases}$

Proof: We shall take two cases as given below

Case (i): If $x\in\mathbb{Z}$, then $-x\in\mathbb{Z}$

Thus, $[-x]=-x$ and $[x]=x$

$\Rightarrow [-x]=-[x]=-x$

Case (ii) If $x\notin\mathbb{Z}$

Let $x=[x]+f$; where $0<f<1$

$\because -x=-[x]-f=-[x]-1+1-f$

$=-[x]-1+f'$; where $1-f=f'\in(0,1)$

$\Rightarrow [-x]=[(-[x]-1)+f']=-[x]-1$ as $f'\in(0\ 1)$.

Hence, proved

ILLUSTRATION 89: Find the domain and range of the given the functions

(a) $f(x)=\dfrac{1}{\sqrt[3]{[x]+[-x]+1}}$ (b) $f(x)=\dfrac{\log([x]+[-x]+1)}{\sqrt{(x-2)(6-x)}}$

SOLUTION: (a) $f(x)=\dfrac{1}{\sqrt[3]{[x]+[-x]+1}}$

For $f(x)$ to be defined $[x] + [-x] + 1 \neq 0$

$\Rightarrow$ $[x] + [-x] \neq -1$

But we know that $[x]+[-x]=\begin{cases} 0 & \text{for } x \in \mathbb{Z} \\ -1 & \text{for } x \notin \mathbb{Z} \end{cases}$

$\therefore$ For $f(x)$ to be defined, $x \in \mathbb{Z}$

$\therefore$ $D_f = \mathbb{Z}$ = set of all integers. Further when $x \in D_f = \mathbb{Z}$.

$[x] + [-x] = 0 \Rightarrow f(x)=\dfrac{1}{\sqrt[3]{1}}=1$ $\therefore$ Range of $f(x) = \{1\}$

(b) $f(x)=\dfrac{\log([x]+[-x]+1)}{\sqrt{(x-2)(6-x)}}$

For $f(x)$ to be defined $[x] + [-x] + 1 > 0$; $(x - 2)(6 - x) > 0$

$[x] + [-x] = -1$, i.e., $[x] + [-x] + 1 = 0$ for $x \notin \mathbb{Z}$

and $[x] + [-x] = 0$, i.e., $[x] + [-x] + 1 = 1 > 0$ for $x \in \mathbb{Z}$

Thus, $[x] + [-x] + 1 > 0$ for $x \in \mathbb{Z}$

Also $(x - 2)(6 - x) > 0$ $\Rightarrow x \in (2, 6)$

$\therefore$ x must be an integer in $(2, 6)$ $\Rightarrow x \in \{3, 4, 5\}$

Domain of function $f(x) = D_f = \{3, 4, 5\}$ and

Range $(R_f) = \{f(3), f(4), f(5)\} = \{0\}$ $(\because f(3) = f(4) = f(5) = 0)$

(x) $x - 1 < [x] \le x$; equality holds iff $x \in \mathbb{Z}$

Proof: To prove $x - 1 < [x] \le x$

Consider two cases as given below

Case (i) If $x = n$; $n \in \mathbb{Z}$

$\therefore$ $[x] = n$

$\therefore$ $x - 1 = n - 1$; $[x] = n$ and $x = n$

$\therefore$ $(n - 1) < n = x$

$\Rightarrow$ $(x - 1) < [x] = x$

i.e., equality holds for $x \in \mathbb{Z}$.

Case (ii) If $x = n + f$, $0 < f < 1$

$\therefore$ $x - 1 = (n - 1) + f$, $[x] = n$

$\therefore$ $(n - 1) + f = n - (1 - f) < n < n + f$ as f, $(1 - f) \in (0, 1)$

Thus, $(x - 1) < [x] < x$

e.g., for $x = 2.5$

$x - 1 = 1.5$, $[x] = 2$

$\therefore$ $(x - 1) < [x] < x$

$\therefore$ inequality holds for $x \notin \mathbb{Z}$ and for $x = 5$

$(x - 1) = 4$; $[x] = 5$

$\Rightarrow$ $(x - 1) < [x] = x$

$\therefore$ equality holds for $x \equiv \mathbb{Z}$.

(xi) $[x] \le x < [x] + 1$

Proof: To prove $[x] \le x < [x] + 1$

From above property $x - 1 < [x] \le x$

$\Rightarrow$ $[x] \le x$ and $x - 1 < [x]$ ..... (1)

$\Rightarrow$ $x < [x] + 1$ ..... (2)

Combining (1) and (2), we have $[x] \le x < [x] + 1$

Hence, proved

e.g., for $x = 2.5$

$[x] = 2$, $[x] + 1 = 3$

$\therefore$ $[x] < x < [x] + 1$

$\therefore$ inequality holds for $x \notin \mathbb{Z}$

and for $x = 5$; $[x] = 5$, $[x] + 1 = 6$

$\Rightarrow$ $[x] = x < [x] + 1$

$\therefore$ equality holds for $x \equiv \mathbb{Z}$

ILLUSTRATION 90: If $\left[\sqrt{n^2+1}\right]=\left[\sqrt{n^2+\lambda}\right]$; where $n, \lambda \in \mathbb{N}$ and [.] is gint function, then show that $2n$ values of λ are possible, and hence, solve $\left[\sqrt{26}\right]=\left[\sqrt{25+\lambda}\right]$ for $\lambda \in \mathbb{N}$.

SOLUTION: Given $\left[\sqrt{n^2+1}\right]=\left[\sqrt{n^2+\lambda}\right]$; $n, \lambda \in \mathbb{N}$ ... (1)

Now $n^2 < n^2+1 < n^2+2n+1 \ \forall \ n \in \mathbb{N}$

$\Rightarrow n^2 < n^2+1 < (n+1)^2 \ \forall \ n \in \mathbb{N} \Rightarrow n<\sqrt{n^2+1}<n+1 \ \forall \ n \in \mathbb{N} \Rightarrow \left[\sqrt{n^2+1}\right]=n$.(2)

$\therefore$ From (1) and (2), we have $n=\left[\sqrt{n^2+\lambda}\right]$

$\Rightarrow n\le\sqrt{n^2+\lambda}<(n+1)$, but $\lambda \in \mathbb{N}$ $\Rightarrow \sqrt{n^2+\lambda}\ne n$

$\Rightarrow n<\sqrt{n^2+\lambda}<(n+1) \Rightarrow n^2 < n^2+\lambda < n^2+2n+1 \Rightarrow 0 < \lambda < (2n+1)$

$\Rightarrow \lambda \in \{1, 2, 3, \ldots, 2n\}$ i.e., λ can take $2n$ values

Now $\left[\sqrt{26}\right]=\left[\sqrt{25+\lambda}\right]$; $\lambda \in \mathbb{N}$ $\Rightarrow \left[\sqrt{25+1}\right]=\left[\sqrt{25+\lambda}\right]$

$\Rightarrow \left[\sqrt{(5)^2+1}\right]=\left[\sqrt{(5)^2+\lambda}\right] \Rightarrow n=5 \Rightarrow \lambda \in \{1, 2, 3, \ldots, 10\}$.

(xii) $\left[\frac{[x]}{c}\right]=\left[\frac{x}{c}\right]$ for $c \in \mathbb{N}$ and $x \in \mathbb{R}$

Proof: Let $[x] = n$

$\Rightarrow x = n + r, 0 \le r < 1$ .... (i)

Also let LHS $=\left[\frac{[x]}{c}\right]=\left[\frac{n}{c}\right]=m$ ... (ii)

RHS $=\left[\frac{x}{c}\right]=\left[\frac{n+r}{c}\right]$

$=\left[\frac{mc+cs+r}{c}\right]=\left[m+\frac{cs+r}{c}\right]$;where $0\le s<1$. (iii)

(Putting the value of n from (ii))

Now, $0 \le cs \le (c-1)$ and $0 \le r < 1 \Rightarrow 0 \le cs + r < c-1+1$

$\therefore \ 0\le\frac{cs+r}{c}<1$

$\therefore$ From (iii) RHS $=\left[m+\frac{cs+r}{c}\right]=m$

$\therefore$ LHS = RHS

ILLUSTRATION 91: Solve the following equations

(a) $\left[\frac{[x]}{4}\right]=16$ (b) $\sin\left(\frac{\pi}{\left[\frac{[x]}{4}\right]}\right)=\frac{1}{2}$

SOLUTION: (a) Given $\left[\frac{[x]}{4}\right]=16 \Rightarrow \left[\frac{x}{4}\right]=16$ $\left(\because \left[\frac{[x]}{c}\right]=\left[\frac{x}{c}\right] \text{ for } x\in\mathbb{R} \text{ and } c\in\mathbb{N}\right)$

$\Rightarrow \frac{x}{4}\in[16,17)$ $\Rightarrow x\in[64,68)$

(b) Given $\sin\left(\frac{\pi}{\left[\frac{[x]}{4}\right]}\right)=\frac{1}{2}$ .... (1)

Now $\left[\frac{[x]}{4}\right] = n \in \mathbb{Z}, n \notin 0$ and we know that $\sin\frac{\pi}{6} = \frac{1}{2}$.

$\Rightarrow \left[\frac{[x]}{4}\right] = 6$ and no other integer value of $\left[\frac{[x]}{4}\right]$ satisfies equation (1) as negative (–ve) integer values make LHS –ve whereas positive (+ve) integer values make LHS function injective.

$\therefore \left[\frac{[x]}{4}\right] = 6 \Rightarrow \left[\frac{x}{4}\right] = 6 \Rightarrow \frac{x}{4} \in [6, 7) \Rightarrow x \in [24, 28)$

(xiii) $[x] + [y] \le [x + y] \le [x] + [y] + 1$

Proof: To prove $[x] + [y] \le [x + y] \le [x] + [y] + 1$

Let us discuss three possible cases.

Case (i) When $x = n \in \mathbb{Z}$ and $y = m \in \mathbb{Z}$

$\Rightarrow [x] + [y] = n + m; [x + y] = [n + m] = n + m$

and $[x] + [y] = [x + y] < [x] + [y] + 1 = n + m + 1$

Thus, $[x] + [y] = [x + y] < [x] + [y] + 1$

Case (ii): When $x = n \in \mathbb{Z}$ and $y = m + f; 0 < f < 1$

(Without loss of generality we can assume that one of x and y is integer and other non-integer)

$\therefore [x] + [y] = n + m; [x + y] = [n + m + f] = n + m$

and $[x] + [y] + 1 = n + m + 1$

Clearly $[x] + [y] = [x + y] < [x] + [y] + 1$

Case (iii): When $x = n + f$ and $y = m + f'$, where $n, m \in \mathbb{Z}$ and $f, f' \in (0, 1)$, then

$[x] + [y] = n + m; [x + y] = [(n + m) + (f + f')]$

$$= \begin{cases} n+m & \text{if } f + f' \in (0,1) \\ n+m+1 & \text{if } f + f' \in [1,2) \end{cases}$$

and $[x] + [y] + 1 = n + m + 1$

Clearly, $[x] + [y] \le [x + y] \le [x] + [y] + 1$.

(xiv) $[x] = \left[\frac{x}{2}\right] + \left[\frac{x+1}{2}\right] \; \forall x \in \mathbb{R}$

Proof: ***Case I:*** Let $x = 2m + y$, where m is an integer and $0 \le y < 1$

$\Rightarrow [x] = 2m, \left[\frac{x}{2}\right] = m$

$\Rightarrow \left[\frac{x+1}{2}\right] = \left[\frac{2m+1+y}{2}\right] = m$

$\Rightarrow \left[\frac{x}{2}\right] + \left[\frac{x+1}{2}\right] = 2m = [x] \quad \left[\because \frac{1}{2} \le \frac{1+y}{2} < 1\right]$

Case II: Let $x = (2m + 1) + y$, where m is an integer and $0 \le y < 1$

$\Rightarrow [x] = 2m + 1$

Then, $\left[\frac{x}{2}\right] = m, \left[\frac{x+1}{2}\right] = \left[\frac{(2m+2)+y}{2}\right] = m + 1$

$\therefore \left[\frac{x}{2}\right] + \left[\frac{x+1}{2}\right] = 2m + 1 = [x]$

ILLUSTRATION 92: Solve the equation $\left[\frac{x+8}{2}\right] + \left[\frac{x+7}{2}\right] + \left[\frac{x+6}{2}\right] + \ldots\ldots + \left[\frac{x+1}{2}\right] + [x] = 21$

SOLUTION: We know that $\left[\frac{x+1}{2}\right] + \left[\frac{x}{2}\right] = [x]$

$$\therefore \text{LHS} = \left(\left[\frac{x+8}{2}\right] + \left[\frac{x+7}{2}\right]\right) + \left(\left[\frac{x+6}{2}\right] + \left[\frac{x+5}{2}\right]\right) + \left(\left[\frac{x+4}{2}\right] + \left[\frac{x+3}{2}\right]\right) + \ldots + \left(\left[\frac{x+2}{2}\right] + \left[\frac{x+1}{2}\right]\right) + [x]$$

$= [x + 7] + [x + 5] + [x + 3] + [x + 1] + [x] = 21$ (By given equation)

$= ([x] + 7) + ([x] + 5) + ([x] + 3) + ([x] + 1) + [x] = 21$

$(\because [x + m] = [x] + m \text{ for } x \in \mathbb{R}, m \in \mathbb{Z})$

$\Rightarrow 5[x] + 16 = 21 \Rightarrow 5[x] = 5 \Rightarrow [x] = 1 \Rightarrow x \in [1, 2)$

ILLUSTRATION 93: If n be any positive integer, then show that $\left[\frac{n+1}{2}\right]+\left[\frac{n+2}{4}\right]+\left[\frac{n+4}{8}\right]+\left[\frac{n+8}{16}\right]+\ldots = n$

SOLUTION: Applying the formula $[x] = \left[\frac{x}{2}\right]+\left[\frac{x+1}{2}\right]$ to $x = n, \frac{n}{2}, \frac{n}{4}, \frac{n}{8}, \frac{n}{16}, \ldots$

$$\Rightarrow [n] = \left[\frac{n}{2}\right]+\left[\frac{n+1}{2}\right]; \left[\frac{n}{2}\right] = \left[\frac{n}{4}\right]+\left[\frac{(n/2)+1}{2}\right]; \left[\frac{n}{4}\right] = \left[\frac{n}{8}\right]+\left[\frac{(n/4)+1}{2}\right] \text{ and}$$

$$\left[\frac{n}{8}\right] = \left[\frac{n}{16}\right]+\left[\frac{(n/8)+1}{2}\right], \ldots$$

Adding corresponding sides and canceling out $\left[\frac{n}{2}\right], \left[\frac{n}{4}\right], \left[\frac{n}{8}\right], \ldots$ from both sides,we get

$$[n] = \left[\frac{n+1}{2}\right]+\left[\frac{n+2}{4}\right]+\left[\frac{n+4}{8}\right]+\ldots \text{ i.e., } n = \left[\frac{n+1}{2}\right]+\left[\frac{n+2}{4}\right]+\left[\frac{n+4}{8}\right]+\ldots$$

(xv) The number of positive integers less than or equal to n and divisible by m is given by $\left[\frac{n}{m}\right]$; $m, n \in \mathbb{N}$.

Proof: Let $n, m \in \mathbb{N}$

$\therefore$ By division algorithm, there exists non-negative integers q and r such that $n = m(q) + r$; where $0 \le r < m$

$$\Rightarrow \frac{n}{m} = q + \frac{r}{m}$$

$$\Rightarrow \left[\frac{n}{m}\right] = \left[q + \frac{r}{m}\right] = q \quad \left(\because 0 \le r < m \Rightarrow 0 \le \frac{r}{m} < 1\right)$$

and we know that quotient q defines the number of possible integer multiples of m which are less than or equal to n, i.e., $1.m, 2.m, 3.m, \ldots, q.m$

Thus, there will be $\left[\frac{n}{m}\right]$ number of positive integer multiples of m less than or equal to n.

i.e., $\left[\frac{n}{m}\right]$ defines the number of positive integers less than or equal to n and divisible by m.

e.g., let $n = 29$, $m = 3$, then $\left[\frac{n}{m}\right] = \left[\frac{29}{3}\right] = [9.\bar{6}] = 9$, and hence, there are exactly 9 positive integers less than or equal to 29, divisible by 3 which are 3, 6, 9, 12, 15, 18, 21, 24, 27.

ILLUSTRATION 94: If n and k are positive integers and k is greater than 1, then $\left[\frac{n}{k}\right]+\left[\frac{n+1}{k}\right] \le \left[\frac{2n}{k}\right]$.

SOLUTION: Let $n = qk + r$, q and r are integers and $0 \le r \le k - 1$ or $0 \le r \le k$.

Then $\frac{n}{k} = q + \frac{r}{k}, \frac{n+1}{k} = q + \frac{r+1}{k}, \frac{2n}{k} = 2q + \frac{2r}{k}$.

Case I: If $r < k - 1$, then $\left[\frac{2n}{k}\right] = 2q + \left[\frac{2(k-1)}{k}\right] = 2q + 1$

$$\therefore \left[\frac{n}{k}\right] = q, \left[\frac{n+1}{k}\right] = q, \left[\frac{2n}{k}\right] = 2q + 1 \Rightarrow \left[\frac{n}{k}\right]+\left[\frac{n+1}{k}\right] < \left[\frac{2n}{k}\right].$$

Case II: If $r = k - 1$, then $\left[\frac{n}{k}\right] = q$, $\left[\frac{n+1}{k}\right] = q+1$, $\left[\frac{2n}{k}\right] = \left[2q + \frac{2(k-1)}{k}\right]$

$= \left[2q + \left(2 - \frac{2}{k}\right)\right] = 2q+1 \quad \Rightarrow \left[\frac{n}{k}\right] + \left[\frac{n+1}{k}\right] = \left[\frac{2n}{k}\right]$

Combining, the above cases, we get the desired result.

(xvi) If p is a prime number and e is the largest exponent of p such that, p^e divides $n!$, then $e = \sum_{k=1}^{\infty}\left[\frac{n}{p^k}\right]$

Proof: We know that $\left[\frac{n}{p}\right] = q$ (say) denotes the number of positive integers less than or equal to n divisible by p which are $p, 2p, 3p, \ldots, qp$ and $(q+1)\,p > n$
we are to find the highest exponent of p (say e) in $n!$ i.e., p^e divides $n!$ and p^{e+1} does not divide $n!$.

Out of first n consecutive integers the positive integers less than or equal to n divisible by p are $p, 2p, 3p, \ldots,$ $\left[\frac{n}{p}\right]p$. Their product equals $\left[\frac{n}{p}\right]!.p^{\left[\frac{n}{p}\right]}$.

Thus, the above product would contribute $\left[\frac{n}{p}\right]$ in e out of these numbers some may be again divisible by p.

Such number will be $p^2, 2p^2, 3p^2, \ldots, \left[\frac{n}{p^2}\right]p^2$.

These numbers are clearly included in $\left[\frac{n}{p}\right]$ numbers divisible by p, so they would contribute $\left[\frac{n}{p^2}\right]$ in e. Further there would be numbers among them which are divisible by p^3 and they would contribute $\left[\frac{n}{p^3}\right]$ in e.

Continuing in this way, we have

$$E_p(n!) = \left[\frac{n}{p}\right] + \left[\frac{n}{p^2}\right] + \left[\frac{n}{p^3}\right] + \ldots = \sum_{i=1}^{\infty}\left[\frac{n}{p_i}\right]$$

Alternatively $E_p(n!) = E_p(1.2.3\ldots.n)$

$= E_p\left(1.2.3\ldots p.(p+1)(p+2)\ldots 2p.(2p+1)\ldots\left[\frac{n}{p}\right]p\ldots.n\right)$

$= E_p\left(p.2p\ldots.\left[\frac{n}{p}\right]p\right)$ ($\because$ other numbers are not divisible by p)

$= E_p\left(\left[\frac{n}{p}\right]!(p)^{\left[\frac{n}{p}\right]}\right) = = E_p\left(\left[\frac{n}{p}\right]!\right) + E_p\left((p)^{\left[\frac{n}{p}\right]}\right)$

$= E_p\left(\left[\frac{n}{p}\right]!\right) + \left[\frac{n}{p}\right]$ .... (1)

Let $\left[\frac{n}{p}\right] = k$, then

$E_p(n!) = \left[\frac{n}{p}\right] + E_p(k!) = \left[\frac{n}{p}\right] + \left[\frac{k}{p}\right] + E_p\left(\left[\frac{k}{p}\right]!\right)$

(using result (1) again)

$= \left[\frac{n}{p}\right] + \left[\frac{[n/p]}{p}\right] + E_p\left(\left[\frac{k}{p}\right]!\right)$

$= \left[\frac{n}{p}\right] + \left[\frac{n/p}{p}\right] - E_p\left(\left[\frac{k}{p}\right]!\right)$

$\left(\because \left[\frac{[x]}{c}\right] = \left[\frac{x}{c}\right] \text{ for } x \in \mathbb{R} \text{ and } c \in \mathbb{N}\right)$

$= \left[\frac{n}{p}\right] + \left[\frac{n}{p^2}\right] + E_p\left(\left[\frac{k}{p}\right]!\right)$

Continuing in this way. we have

$$E_p(n!) = \left[\frac{n}{p}\right] + \left[\frac{n}{p^2}\right] + \left[\frac{n}{p^3}\right] + \ldots.. = \sum_{k=1}^{\infty}\left[\frac{n}{p^k}\right]$$

ILLUSTRATION 95: Find
(a) Exponent of 3 in 50! i.e., $E_3(50!)$
(b) Exponent of 5 in (1500)! i.e., $E_5(1500!)$

SOLUTION: (a) Exponent of 3 in 50! $= E_3(50!) = \sum_{k=1}^{\infty}\left[\frac{50}{(3)^k}\right] = \left[\frac{50}{3}\right] + \left[\frac{50}{3^2}\right] + \left[\frac{50}{3^3}\right] + \left[\frac{50}{3^4}\right] + \ldots..$

$= 16 + 5 + 1 + 0 + 0 + \ldots\ldots = 22$

$\therefore$ $E_3(50!) = 22$, i.e., $3^{22} \mid 50!$ but $3^{23} \nmid 50!$

(b) Exponent of 5 in (1500)! $= E_5(1500!) = \sum_{k=1}^{\infty}\left[\frac{1500}{(5)^k}\right]$

$= \left[\frac{1500}{5}\right]+\left[\frac{1500}{5^2}\right]+\left[\frac{1500}{5^3}\right]+\left[\frac{1500}{5^4}\right]+\left[\frac{1500}{5^5}\right]+\ldots\ldots$

$= 300 + 60 + 12 + 2 + 0 + 0 + \ldots\ldots = 374$

$\therefore$ $(5)^{374}$ divides (1500)!, but $(5)^{375}$ does not divide (1500)!.

ILLUSTRATION 96: If $f(x) = x - [x]$; $x \in \mathbb{R} \sim \{0\}$, where is [.] gint function, then show that the equation $f(x)+f\left(\frac{1}{x}\right)=1$; has infinitely many solutions.

SOLUTION: Given $f(x)+f\left(\frac{1}{x}\right)=1 \Rightarrow x-[x]+\frac{1}{x}-\left[\frac{1}{x}\right]=1 \Rightarrow x+\frac{1}{x} = [x]+\left[\frac{1}{x}\right]+1$ ... (1)

Now RHS of (1) is an integer for each $x \in \mathbb{R} \sim \{0\}$,

$\Rightarrow$ LHS. of (1) must also be an integer.

So, let $x+\frac{1}{x} = [x]+\left[\frac{1}{x}\right]+1 = k$ (an integer)

$\Rightarrow x+\frac{1}{x}=k \qquad \Rightarrow x^2 - kx + 1 = 0$

$\Rightarrow x=\frac{k\pm\sqrt{k^2-4}}{2} \Rightarrow$ For real x, $k^2 - 4 \geq 0$, i.e., $k \in (-\infty,-2] \cup [2, \infty)$

For $k = 2$; $x+\frac{1}{x}=2 \qquad \Rightarrow x = 1$

$\therefore$ From (1); $2 = 1 + 1 + 1$, which is false and for $k = -2$, $\Rightarrow x+\frac{1}{x}=-2 \Rightarrow x=-1$

$\therefore$ From (1), $-2 = -1 - 1 + 1$, which is false.

$\therefore$ Solution does not exit for $k = \pm 2$

$\therefore$ Whenever $[x]+\left[\frac{1}{x}\right]+1>2$ or <-2, there exists a real x for which

$x+\frac{1}{x} = [x]+\left[\frac{1}{x}\right]+1$ and $[x]+\left[\frac{1}{x}\right]+1>2$ or <-2 can hold for infinitely many x.

For example, if $x \in [4, 5)$, then $[x] = 4$ and $\frac{1}{x}\in\left(\frac{1}{5},\frac{1}{4}\right]$

$\Rightarrow [x]+\left[\frac{1}{x}\right]+1=5 \Rightarrow x=\frac{5\pm\sqrt{25-4}}{2}=\frac{5\pm\sqrt{21}}{2} \Rightarrow x=\frac{5-\sqrt{21}}{2}$ as $x\in[4,5)$

Similarly if $x\in\left(\frac{1}{4},\frac{1}{3}\right) \Rightarrow [x] = 0$ and $\frac{1}{x}\in(3,4) \Rightarrow \left[\frac{1}{x}\right]=3$

$\therefore [x]+\left[\frac{1}{x}\right]=3 \Rightarrow [x]+\left[\frac{1}{x}\right]+1=4 \Rightarrow x=\frac{4\pm\sqrt{16-4}}{2}=2\pm\sqrt{3}$

$\Rightarrow x=2+\sqrt{3}$ as $x\in(3,4)$

Thus, the given equation has infinitely many solutions.

■ LEAST INTEGER FUNCTION

It is also called the ceiling of x and it is represented by $\lceil x \rceil$. It is the least integer greater than or equal to the number x. Therefore $y = \lceil x \rceil = I + 1$ if $I < x \leq I + 1$

e.g., $\lceil 1.5 \rceil = 2, \lceil 2.9 \rceil = 3, \lceil -2.3 \rceil = -2, \lceil -0.6 \rceil = 0, \lceil 0.25 \rceil = 1$

Thus, $[x]$ converts $x = (I + f)$ into I while $\lceil x \rceil$ converts it into $I + 1$, but when x is an integer $[x] = x = \lceil x \rceil$

Hence, $\lceil x \rceil = -2$ for $-3 < x \leq -2$

$\lceil x \rceil = -1$ for $-2 < x \leq -1$

$\lceil x \rceil = 0$ for $-1 < x \leq 0$

$\lceil x \rceil = 1$ for $0 < x \leq 1$ and so on

It can be expressed graphically as shown in Figure 2.98.

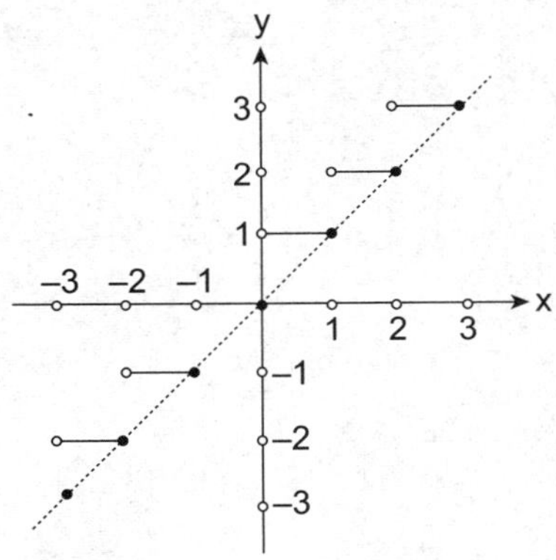

FIGURE 2.98

Properties of Least Integer Function

1. The domain of the function is: $(-\infty, +\infty)$
2. The range is the set of all integers.
3. $[x]$ converts $x = (I + f)$ into I while $\lceil x \rceil$ converts it into $I + 1$.

   e.g., If $x = 2.4$, then $2 < x < 3$

   $\Rightarrow \lceil x \rceil = 3 = I + 1$
4. When x is an integer $[x] = x = \lceil x \rceil$
5. $\lceil x + n \rceil = \lceil x \rceil + n$, where n is an integer.

Proof: Let $x \notin \mathbb{Z}$ and $x = m + f$; $m \in \mathbb{Z}$ and $f \in (0, 1)$; then $m < x < m + 1 \quad \Rightarrow \quad \lceil x \rceil = m + 1 \quad \ldots.(1)$

Now $m < x < m + 1 \quad \Rightarrow \quad m + n < x + n < m + n + 1$

$\Rightarrow \lceil x + n \rceil = m + n + 1 = n + \lceil x \rceil$ (from (1))

Thus, $\lceil x + n \rceil = n + \lceil x \rceil$, where $x \notin \mathbb{Z}$

If $x \in \mathbb{Z}$, then $\lceil x + n \rceil = x + n = \lceil x \rceil + n$

$\therefore \quad \lceil x + n \rceil = \lceil x \rceil + n \; \forall \, x \in \mathbb{R}, n \in \mathbb{Z}$.

■ FRACTIONAL PART FUNCTION

Since every real number x can be written as the sum of its integer part and fractional i.e., $x = \underbrace{I}_{\text{integer part of } x} + \underbrace{f}_{\text{fractional part}}$;

where $f \in [0, 1)$, we denote $f = \{x\}$ and is called fractional part of x.

$\Rightarrow$ Fractional part function is denoted as $\{x\}$ and defined as $\{x\} = x - [x]$

$$\Rightarrow \{x\} = \begin{cases} x+2; & -2 \leq x \leq -1 \\ x+1; & -1 \leq x < 0 \\ x; & 0 \leq x < 1 \\ x-1; & 1 \leq x < 2 \end{cases} \quad \text{and so on.}$$

Graph of fractional part function $\{x\}$ is as shown below:

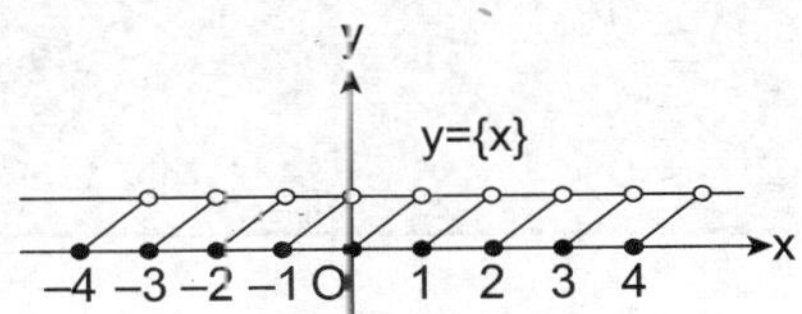

FIGURE 2.99

Properties of Fractional Part Function

(i) Domain of fractional part function $= D_f = \mathbb{R}$; Range of fractional part function $= R_f = [0, 1)$

ILLUSTRATION 97: Find the domain and range of function $f(x) = \dfrac{x - [x]}{1 - x + [x]}$

SOLUTION: $f(x) = \dfrac{x - [x]}{1 - x + [x]} = \dfrac{\{x\}}{1 - (x - [x])} = \dfrac{\{x\}}{1 - \{x\}}$

For domain of function $1 - \{x\} \neq 0 \Rightarrow \{x\} \neq 1$. Which always hold $\forall x \in \mathbb{R} \Rightarrow D_f = \mathbb{R}$

Now $f(x) = \dfrac{\{x\}}{1-\{x\}} = -\left(\dfrac{1-\{x\}-1}{1-\{x\}}\right) = -1 + \dfrac{1}{1-\{x\}}$

Now $-1 < -\{x\} \leq 0 \Rightarrow 0 < 1 - \{x\} \leq 1 \quad \Rightarrow 1 \leq \dfrac{1}{1-\{x\}} < \infty$

$\Rightarrow 0 \leq -1 + \dfrac{1}{1-\{x\}} < \infty \Rightarrow 0 \leq f(x) < \infty \quad \Rightarrow$ Range of function $f(x) = R_f = [0, \infty)$

ILLUSTRATION 98: Solve the inequality $x[x] - x^2 - 5[x] + 5x < 0$

SOLUTION: Given inequality is $x[x] - x^2 - 5[x] + 5x < 0$

$\Rightarrow x(x - \{x\}) - x^2 - 5(x - \{x\}) + 5x < 0$

$\Rightarrow x^2 - x\{x\} - x^2 - 5x + 5\{x\} + 5x < 0$

$\Rightarrow -x\{x\} + 5\{x\} < 0 \quad \Rightarrow (\{x\})(5 - x) < 0$ ...(1)

Now for $x \in \mathbb{Z}$, $\{x\} = 0$, therefore (1) would not hold, so $x \notin \mathbb{Z}$

$\Rightarrow \{x\} \in (0, 1)$, thus, from (1), we have $(5 - x) < 0 \quad \Rightarrow x > 5$

Thus, solution of given inequality is every non-integer real number greater than 5.

ILLUSTRATION 99: Prove that $[x] + \left[x + \dfrac{1}{2}\right] = [2x]$

SOLUTION: Let $x = [x] + \{x\}$

$\therefore$ LHS. of given equation becomes, $[x] + \left[[x] + \{x\} + \dfrac{1}{2}\right] = [x] + [x] + \left[\{x\} + \dfrac{1}{2}\right]$.

Let us deal with the following two cases:

Case (i): If $0 \leq \{x\} < \dfrac{1}{2} \Rightarrow \dfrac{1}{2} \leq \{x\} + \dfrac{1}{2} < 1 \Rightarrow \left[\{x\} + \dfrac{1}{2}\right] = 0$

$\therefore$ LHS $= [x] + [x] + 0 = 2[x]$ and RHS $= [2x] = [2[x] + 2\{x\}] = 2[x] + [2\{x\}] = 2[x]$

Case (ii): If $\dfrac{1}{2} \leq \{x\} < 1$, i.e., $1 \leq 2\{x\} < 2$ and $\{x\} + \dfrac{1}{2} \in \left[1, \dfrac{3}{2}\right)$

$\therefore$ LHS $= [x] + [x] + 1 = 2[x] + 1$ and RHS $= 2[x] + [2\{x\}] = 2[x] + 1$.

(ii) $\{x\}$ is periodic function with period 1.

Proof: A function $f(x)$ is periodic with period T if $f(x + T) = f(x) \ \forall x \in D_f$

Let x be any real number such that $x = n + f'$; where $n \in \mathbb{Z}$ and $0 \leq f' < 1$

Now $f(x) = \{x\} = \{n + f'\} = f'$, then $f(x + 1) = \{x + 1\}$
$= \{(n + 1) + f'\} \qquad (\because x = n + f')$
$= f' = \{x\} = f(x)$

Thus, $f(x + 1) = f(x) \ \forall x \in \mathbb{R}$ (domain of $\{x\}$)

Hence, fractional part function $\{x\}$ is periodic with period 1.

ILLUSTRATION 100: Find the domain and range of functions

(a) $f(x) = [\cos \{x\}]$ (b) $f(x) = [\tan \{x\}]$

(c) $f(x) = \{\tan x\}$

SOLUTION: (a) $\cos \theta$ is defined $\forall \theta \in \mathbb{R}$ and $\{x\} \in [0, 1) \ \forall x \in \mathbb{R}$

Thus, x can take any real value

$\Rightarrow$ Domain of function $= \mathbb{R}$

Now $0 \le \{x\} < 1$

$\Rightarrow$ $\cos 0 \ge \cos\{x\} > \cos 1$ ($\because$ for $\theta \in [0, 1]$ $\cos\theta$ decreases)

$\Rightarrow$ $1 \ge \cos\{x\} > \cos 1$

$\Rightarrow$ $[1] \ge [\cos\{x\}] \ge [\cos 1]$ ($\because$ [ ] is an increasing function)

$\Rightarrow$ $1 \ge [\cos\{x\}] \ge 0$ $\left(1 > \cos 1 > \cos\frac{\pi}{2} = 0\right)$

$\Rightarrow$ $f(x) \in [0, 1]$; but $f(x)$ can take only integer values

$\Rightarrow$ $R_f = \{0, 1\}$

(b) $\tan\theta$ is defined for $\theta \in \mathbb{R} \sim \left\{(2n+1)\frac{\pi}{2}; n \in \mathbb{Z}\right\}$

$\Rightarrow$ Range of $\{x\} = [0, 1)$ is contained in domain of $\tan\theta$

$\Rightarrow$ $\tan\{x\}$ is defined $\forall\, x \in \mathbb{R}$

$\Rightarrow$ Domain of $f(x) = [\tan\{x\}]$ is $\mathbb{R}$.

$\Rightarrow$ But $0 \le \{x\} < 1$ $\Rightarrow$ $\tan 0 \le \tan\{x\} < \tan 1$ ($\because$ $\tan\theta$ is increasing for $\theta \in [0, 1)$)

$\Rightarrow$ $0 \le \tan\{x\} < \tan 1$ $\Rightarrow$ $[0] \le [\tan\{x\}] \le [\tan 1]$ $\Rightarrow$ $0 \le f(x) \le 1$

$$\left\{\because \frac{\pi}{4} < 1 < \frac{\pi}{3} \Rightarrow \tan\frac{\pi}{4} < \tan 1 < \tan\frac{\pi}{3} \Rightarrow 1 < \tan 1 < \sqrt{3} \Rightarrow [\tan 1] = 1\right\}$$

But $f(x)$ can take only integer values $\Rightarrow$ Range of $f(x) = \{0, 1\}$.

(c) $f(x) = \{\tan x\}$, $\tan x$ is defined for $x \in \mathbb{R} \sim \left\{(2n+1)\frac{\pi}{2}; n \in \mathbb{Z}\right\}$

$\therefore$ Domain of $f(x) = \mathbb{R} \sim \left\{(2n+1)\frac{\pi}{2}; n \in \mathbb{Z}\right\}$

But $\tan x \in (-\infty, \infty)$ and $\{.\}$ is periodic with period 1 and has range $= [0, 1)$

$\Rightarrow$ $\{\tan x\} \in [0, 1) =$ Range of $f(x) = R_r$

ILLUSTRATION 101: Solve the following equations

(i) $\{\sin x\} + \{\cos x\} = 2$

(ii) $\{\sin x\} + \{\cos x\} = 0$

(iii) $\{x\} + \{\sin x\} + \{\cos x\} = 0$, where { } is fractional part function.

SOLUTION: (i) Since $\{\sin x\}, \{\cos x\} \in [0, 1)$

$\Rightarrow$ $\{\sin x\} + \{\cos x\} \in [0, 2)$ $\Rightarrow$ $\{\sin x\} + \{\cos x\} \ne 2$

$\Rightarrow$ There exists no solution for the given equation.

(ii) Again since $\{\sin x\} + \{\cos x\} \in [0, 2)$

$\therefore$ $\{\sin x\} + \{\cos x\} = 0 \Leftrightarrow$ both sinx and cosx are integers

$\Rightarrow$ $\sin x = \pm 1, \cos x = 0$ or $\sin x = 0, \cos x = \pm 1$

$\Rightarrow$ $x \in \left\{n\pi, (2n+1)\frac{\pi}{2} : n \in \mathbb{Z}\right\}$

(iii) $\{x\} + \{\sin x\} + \{\cos x\} = 0$. Each of $\{x\}, \{\sin x\}, \{\cos x\}$ is non-negative

$\Rightarrow$ $\{x\} = \{\sin x\} = \{\cos x\} = 0$ $\Rightarrow$ x, sinx as well as cosx all must be integers.

But sinx and cosx take integers values only at $x = n\pi$ or $(2n+1)\frac{\pi}{2}$ which are irrationals for $n \ne 0$, and hence, can never be integers for $n \ne 0$. So, there is only one solution for the given equation, i.e., $x = 0$.

(iii) $[\{x\}] = 0$

Proof: Let $x = n + f$; where $n \in \mathbb{Z}$ and $f \in [0, 1)$, then $\{x\} = \{n + f\} = f$

$\Rightarrow [\{x\}] = [f] = 0$ as $0 \le f < 1$.

Thus, $[\{x\}] = 0 \ \forall \ x \in \mathbb{R}$

ILLUSTRATION 102: If $f(x) = [x]$ and $g(x) = x - [x]$, then which of the following is/are the zero function(x)?

(a) $(f + g)(x)$
(b) $(f \,.\, g)(x)$
(c) $(f - g)(x)$
(d) (fog) (x)

SOLUTION: (a) $(f + g)(x) = f(x) + g(x) = [x] + x - [x] = x \ \forall \ x \in \mathbb{R}$.

$\Rightarrow (f + g)(x)$ is an identity function

(b) $(f.g)(x) = f(x) \,.\, g(x) = [x](x - [x]) \neq 0 \ \forall \ x \in \mathbb{R}$.

e.g., if $x = 2.4$; then $(f.g)(2.4) = [2.4](2.4 - [2.4]) = (2)(2.4 - 2) = 2(.4) = 0.8 \neq 0$

(c) $(f - g)(x) = f(x) - g(x) = [x] - x + [x] = 2[x] - x \neq 0 \ \forall \ x \in \mathbb{R}$.

e.g., $(f - g)(2.4) = 2(2) - 2.4 = 1.6 \neq 0$

(d) $(fog)(x) = f(g(x)) = f(x - [x]) = [x - [x]] = [\{x\}] = 0$ as $\{x\} \in [0, 1) \ \forall \ x \in \mathbb{R}$.

Thus, only $(fog)(x)$ is a zero function.

(iv) $\{[x]\} = 0$

Proof: Let $x = n + f$; where $n \in \mathbb{Z}$ and $f \in [0, 1)$, then $[x] = n$

$\Rightarrow \{[x]\} = \{n\} = 0$ as every integer has no fractional part.

Thus, $\{[x]\} = 0$

(v) $\{\{x\}\} = \{x\}$; this result is also true when fractional part function is applied on x on left hand side more than twice.

Proof: Let $x = n + f$; where $n \in \mathbb{Z}$ and $f \in [0, 1)$, then $\{x\} = \{n + f\} = f$

$\Rightarrow \{\{x\}\} = \{f\} = f$ as $0 \le f < 1$

Thus, $\{\{x\}\} = \{x\}$

The above result can be generalized to any finite number of fractional part functions applied on x.

i.e., $\{\{\{\{\ldots.\{x\}\ldots.\}\}\}\} = \{x\} \ \forall \ x \in \mathbb{R}$.

(vi) $\{-x\} = \begin{cases} 0; & x \in \mathbb{Z} \\ 1 - \{x\}; & x \notin \mathbb{Z} \end{cases}$

Proof: $\because \ -x = [-x] + \{-x\}$

$$\Rightarrow \{-x\} = -x - [-x] = \begin{cases} -x + x = 0; & \text{if } x \in \mathbb{Z} \\ -x - (-1 - [x]); & \text{if } x \notin \mathbb{Z} \end{cases}$$

$$\Rightarrow \{-x\} = \begin{cases} 0; & \text{if } x \in \mathbb{Z} \\ 1 - \{x\}; & \text{if } x \notin \mathbb{Z} \end{cases}$$

ILLUSTRATION 103: Find the domain and range of function $f(x) = \dfrac{1}{\sqrt[5]{\{x\} + \{-x\} - 1}}$

SOLUTION: For $f(x)$ to be defined $\{x\} + \{-x\} - 1 \neq 0$

$\Rightarrow \{x\} + \{-x\} \neq 1$

$$\Rightarrow \{x\} + \{-x\} = 0 \text{ as } \{x\} + \{-x\} = \begin{cases} 0 & \text{for } x \in \mathbb{Z} \\ 1 & \text{for } x \notin \mathbb{Z} \end{cases}$$

$\therefore \ f(x) = \dfrac{1}{\sqrt[5]{-1}}$ for $x \in \mathbb{Z}$ $\quad \Rightarrow f(x) = -1$ for $x \in \mathbb{Z}$

$\therefore$ Domain $= D_f = \mathbb{Z}$ and range $= \{-1\}$

(vii) $[x+y]=\begin{cases}[x]+[y]; & 0\le\{x\}+\{y\}<1\\ [x]+[y]+1; & 1\le\{x\}+\{y\}<2\end{cases}$

Proof: $\because$ $[x + y] = [[x] + [y] + \{x\} + \{y\}] = [x] + [y] + [\{x\} + \{y\}]$ $(\because [x + m] = m + [x]\ \forall\ x \in \mathbb{R})$

Now $0 \le \{x\} < 1$ and $0 \le \{y\} < 1$

$\Rightarrow$ $0 \le \{x\} + \{y\} < 2$

$\Rightarrow$ $[x+y]=\begin{cases}[x]+[y]; & 0\le\{x\}+\{y\}<1\\ [x]+[y]+1; & 1\le\{x\}+\{y\}<2\end{cases}$

ILLUSTRATION 104: Find all possible solutions of equation $[x + y] = 3$

SOLUTION: We know that $[x + y] = \begin{cases}[x]+[y]; & \text{for } \{x\}+\{y\}\in[0,1)\\ [x]+[y]+1; & \text{for } \{x\}+\{y\}\in[1,2)\end{cases}$

$\therefore$ $[x + y] = 3$

$\Rightarrow$ $[x] + [y] = 3$ for $\{x\} + \{y\} \in [0, 1)$ and $[x] + [y] + 1= 3$ for $\{x\} + \{y\} \in [1, 2)$

$\Rightarrow$ $[x] + [y] = 3$ for $\{x\} + \{y\} \in [0, 1)$ and $[x] + [y] = 2$ for $\{x\} + \{y\} \in [1, 2)$

Case 1: $\{x\} + \{y\} \in [0, 1)$

Let $[x] = m$

$\Rightarrow$ $[y] = 3 - m$ and $\{x\} + \{y\} \in [0, 1)$; $m \in \mathbb{Z}$

$\Rightarrow$ $x = m + f, y = (3 - m) + f'; f + f' \in [0, 1); m \in \mathbb{Z}$

$\Rightarrow$ $x = m + f, y = (3 - m) + f'; f' \in [0, 1 - f); f \in [0, 1)$

Case 1: $\{x\} + \{y\} = [1, 2)$, then $[x] = n$

$\Rightarrow$ $[y] = 2 - n$ and $\{x\} + \{y\} \in [1, 2)$

$\Rightarrow$ $x = n + f; y = (2 - n) + f'; 1 \le f + f' < 2$

$\Rightarrow$ $x = n + f; y = (2 - n) + f'; n \in \mathbb{Z}; f \in [0, 1); f' \in [1 - f, 2 - f)$

Thus, all possible solutions are

$x = m + f; y = (3 - m) + f'; m \in \mathbb{Z}; f \in [0, 1); f' \in [0, 1 - f)$

and $x = n + f; y = (2 - n) + f'; n \in \mathbb{Z}; f \in [0, 1); f' \in [1 - f, 2 - f)$

ILLUSTRATION 105: Solve the equation $x^2 - 6x + [x] + 7 = 0$

SOLUTION: Given equation is $x^2 - 6x + [x] + 7 = 0$ ...(1)

$\Rightarrow$ $x^2 - 6x + x - \{x\} + 7 = 0$

$\Rightarrow$ $x^2 - 5x + 7 = \{x\}$

Now RHS belongs to $[0, 1)$

$\Rightarrow$ LHS must also belong to $[0, 1)$

$\Rightarrow$ $0 \le x^2 - 5x + 7 < 1$

$\Rightarrow$ $x^2 - 5x + 7 \ge 0$ and $x^2 - 5x + 6 < 0$

First inequation always hold good as its discriminant < 0 and $x^2 - 5x + 6 < 0$

$\Rightarrow$ $(x - 2)(x - 3) < 0$

$\Rightarrow$ $x \in (2, 3)$

$\Rightarrow$ $[x] = 2$

$\therefore$ From equation (1), we have $x^2 - 6x + 9 = 0$

$\Rightarrow (x-3)^2 = 0$

$\Rightarrow x = 3$

But it does not satisfy the inequality $2 < x < 3$.

Hence, the given equation has no solution.

ILLUSTRATION 106: Solve for x, the system of simultaneous inequations $(2\{x\} - 1)(3\{x\} - 2) \leq 0$ and $(3[x] - 4)(2[x] - 8) \leq 0$; where [.] gint is function and {} is fractional part of function.

SOLUTION: Given in inequations $(2\{x\} - 1)(3\{x\} - 2) \leq 0$ ...(1)

And $(3[x] - 4)(2[x] - 8) \leq 0$ ...(2)

From (1), $\frac{1}{2} \leq \{x\} \leq \frac{2}{3}$ .... (3)

From (2), $\frac{4}{3} \leq [x] \leq 4 \Rightarrow [x] \in \{2, 3, 4\}$

$\Rightarrow x \in [2, 5)$ ... (4)

Combining (3) and (4), we note that x is a real number greater than or equal to 2 less than 5, and having its fractional part in the interval $\left[\frac{1}{2}, \frac{2}{3}\right]$.

Thus, the solution set of given simultaneous equations (1) and (2) is

$$\left[2+\frac{1}{2}, 2+\frac{2}{3}\right] \cup \left[3+\frac{1}{2}, 3+\frac{2}{3}\right] \cup \left[4+\frac{1}{2}, 4+\frac{2}{3}\right] \text{ i.e., } x \in \left[\frac{5}{2}, \frac{8}{3}\right] \cup \left[\frac{7}{2}, \frac{11}{3}\right] \cup \left[\frac{9}{2}, \frac{14}{3}\right]$$

NEAREST INTEGER FUNCTION

(x) denotes the nearest integer to x. If x is the mean of two consecutive integers, then (x) will be the greater among the two consecutive integers, i.e., $\left(\frac{n+n+1}{2}\right) = \left(\frac{2n+1}{2}\right) = n+1$

Since $(x) \geq [x] \Rightarrow (x)$ is either equal to $[x]$ or $[x] + 1$

Example:

(i) $x = 1.3829 \Rightarrow (x) = (1.3829) = 1$

(ii) $x = 5.43 \Rightarrow (x) = (5.43) = 5$

(iii) $x = 3 \Rightarrow (x) = (3) = 3$

(iv) $x = 7.82 \Rightarrow (x) = (7.82) = 8$

Thus, from definition, we have

$(x) = -2$ for $-\frac{5}{2} \leq x < -\frac{3}{2}$

$(x) = -1$ for $-\frac{3}{2} \leq x < -\frac{1}{2}$

$(x) = 0$ for $-\frac{1}{2} \leq x < \frac{1}{2}$

$(x) = 1$ for $\frac{1}{2} \leq x < \frac{3}{2}$

$(x) = 2$ for $\frac{3}{2} \leq x < \frac{5}{2}$

Graph of $f(x)$ can be expressed graphically as shown in the Figure 2.100.

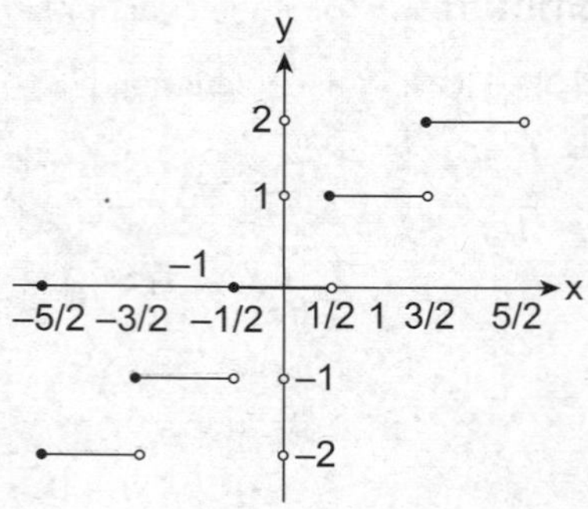

FIGURE 2.100

Properties of Nearest Integer Function

(i) $(x) = \begin{cases} [x] & \text{if } 0 \leq \{x\} < \frac{1}{2} \text{ i.e., } [x] \leq x < [x] + \frac{1}{2} \\ [x]+1 & \text{if } \frac{1}{2} \leq \{x\} < 1 \text{ i.e., } [x] + \frac{1}{2} \leq x < [x]+1 \end{cases}$

Proof: Let $x = [x] + \{x\}$

Case (i): When $0 \le \{x\} < \frac{1}{2}$

$\Rightarrow [x] \le [x] + \{x\} < [x] + \frac{1}{2}$

$\Rightarrow [x] \le x < [x] + \frac{1}{2} < [x] + 1$

$\Rightarrow$ $[x]$ is the integer nearest to x. Thus, $(x) = [x]$

Case (ii): When $\frac{1}{2} \le \{x\} < 1$

$\Rightarrow [x] + \frac{1}{2} \le [x] + \{x\} < [x] + 1$

$\Rightarrow [x] + \frac{1}{2} \le x < [x] + 1 \Rightarrow [x] < [x] + \frac{1}{2} \le x < [x] + 1$

$\Rightarrow$ $[x] + 1$ is nearest integer to x $\Rightarrow$ $(x) = [x] + 1$.

(ii) $(x + n) = (x) + n$ if $n \in \mathbb{Z}$

Proof: Let $\{x\} \in \left[0, \frac{1}{2}\right) \Rightarrow (x) = [x]$ .... (1)

$\because$ $\{x\}$ is periodic function with period 1

$\therefore$ for any positive integer n, $\{n + x\} = \{x\} \in \left[0, \frac{1}{2}\right)$

$\therefore$ By property (1), $(n + x) = [n + x] = n + [x] = n + (x)$ (By (1)) .... (2)

Again $\{x\} \in \left[\frac{1}{2}, 1\right) \Rightarrow (x) = [x] + 1$ .... (3)

By periodicity of $\{x\}$, $\{n + x\} = \{x\} \in \left[\frac{1}{2}, 1\right)$

$\Rightarrow (n + x) = [n + x] + 1 = n + [x] + 1 = n + (x)$ (By (3))

Thus, from (3) and (4), we conclude that

$(x + n) = n + (x)\ \forall\, x \in \mathbb{R},\ n \in \mathbb{Z}$

(iii) $$(-x) = \begin{cases} -(x); & \forall x \in \mathbb{R} \sim \left\{x = \left(\frac{2n+1}{2}\right); n \in \mathbb{Z}\right\} \\ -(x)+1; & \text{for } x = \left(\frac{2n+1}{2}\right); n \in \mathbb{Z} \end{cases}$$

Proof: Let $x \in \mathbb{R} \sim \left\{x = \left(\frac{2n+1}{2}\right); n \in \mathbb{Z}\right\}$

Case (i) If $x = n \in \mathbb{Z}$, then $(x) = (n) = n$ and $-x = -n \in \mathbb{Z}$

$\Rightarrow (-x) = (-n) = -n = -(x)$. Thus, $(-x) = -(x)$

Case (ii) If $x \notin \mathbb{Z}$ and $x = n + f; f \in (0,1) \sim \left\{\frac{1}{2}\right\}$

$\Rightarrow -x = -n - f \quad \Rightarrow -x = -n - 1 + 1 - f$

$\Rightarrow -x = (-n - 1) + (1 - f)$

$\therefore$ If $f \in \left(0, \frac{1}{2}\right)$, then $(1 - f) \in \left(\frac{1}{2}, 1\right)$

$\Rightarrow (x) = n$ and $(-x) = -n = -(x)$ $\therefore (-x) = -(x)$

Now if $f \in \left(\frac{1}{2}, 1\right)$, then $(1 - f) \in \left(0, \frac{1}{2}\right)$

$\Rightarrow (x) = n + 1$ and $(-x) = (-n - 1 + 1 - f) = -n - 1 = -(x)$

Thus, $(-x) = -(x)\ \forall\, x \in \mathbb{R} \sim \left\{x = \left(\frac{2n+1}{2}\right); n \in \mathbb{Z}\right\}$

Case (iii) Let $x = \left(\frac{2n+1}{2}\right)$; $n\,x \in \mathbb{Z}$. Now, $x = n + \frac{1}{2}$

$\Rightarrow (x) = (n + 1)$ and $(-x) = \left(-n - \frac{1}{2}\right) = \left(-n - 1 + \frac{1}{2}\right)$

$= (-n - 1) + 1 = n = -(n + 1) + 1 = -(x) + 1$

■ METHOD OF SOLVING INEQUALITY INVOLVING X, {X} AND [X]

e.g., $2x + [x] = 3\{x\}$ (say) .... (1)

Step (1): Replace x by $[x] + \{x\}$ in equation (1) and express $[x]$ as function of $\{x\}$.

Given, $2x + [x] = 3\{x\} \Rightarrow 3[x] + 2\{x\} = 3\{x\}$

$\Rightarrow 3[x] = \{x\}$

Step (2): Apply range of $\{x\}$ i.e., $0 \le \frac{\{x\}}{3} < \frac{1}{3}$

$\Rightarrow 0 \le [x] < \frac{1}{3}$ ...(2)

Step (3): Find all possible values of $[x]$ using (2) and corresponding values of $\{x\}$.

Using equation (2), we get $[x] = 0$ and $\{x\} = 0$

$\Rightarrow x = 0$ is the only solution.

ILLUSTRATION 107: Solve the equation $5x + 3\{x\} = 4[2x + 2] - 5$; where [.] is gint function and {} is fractional part function.

SOLUTION: Given equation is $5x + 3\{x\} = 4[2x + 2] - 5$

$\Rightarrow 5x + 3\{x\} = 4[2x] + 8 - 5$ $(\because [x + m] = [x] + m$ for $m \in \mathbb{Z})$

$\Rightarrow 5x + 3\{x\} = 4[2x] + 3$ ...(1)

Now $2x = 2([x] + \{x\})$

$\Rightarrow 2x = 2[x] + 2\{x\}$

$\Rightarrow$ $[2x] = 2[x] + [2\{x\}]$ ...(2)

Using (2) in (1) we get, $5x + 3\{x\} = 4(2[x] + [2\{x\}]) + 3$

$\Rightarrow$ $5x + 3\{x\} = 8[x] + 4[2\{x\}] + 3$ ...(3)

Let us deal with two cases:-

Case (i): When $0 \le \{x\} < \frac{1}{2}$

$\Rightarrow$ $0 \le 2\{x\} < 1$ $\Rightarrow$ $[2\{x\}] = 0$

$\therefore$ From (3), $5x + 3\{x\} = 8[x] + 3$

$\Rightarrow$ $5[x] + 5\{x\} + 3\{x\} = 8[x] + 3$ (using $x = [x] = \{x\}$)

$\Rightarrow$ $8\{x\} = 3[x] + 3$ $\Rightarrow$ $\{x\} = \frac{3[x]+3}{8}$ ...(4)

Now $\{x\} \in [0, 1/2)$ $\Rightarrow$ $\frac{3[x]+3}{8} \in \left[0, \frac{1}{2}\right)$

$\Rightarrow$ $0 \le 3[x] + 3 < 4$ $\Rightarrow$ $-3 \le 3[x] < 1$ $\Rightarrow$ $-1 \le [x] < \frac{1}{3}$

$\Rightarrow$ $[x] = -1, 0$

Using these values of $[x]$ in (4) we have,

For $[x] = -1$; $\{x\} = 0$ $\Rightarrow$ $x = -1$. For $[x] = 0$; $\{x\} = \frac{3}{8}$ $\Rightarrow$ $x = \frac{3}{8}$

$\therefore$ Solution set in this case is $\left\{-1, \frac{3}{8}\right\}$

Case (ii): When $\frac{1}{2} \le \{x\} < 1$

$\Rightarrow$ $1 \le 2\{x\} < 2$ $\Rightarrow$ $[2\{x\}] = 1$

$\therefore$ From (3), $5x + 3\{x\} = 8[x] + 7$ $\Rightarrow$ $5[x] + 5\{x\} + 3\{x\} = 8[x] + 7$

$\Rightarrow$ $8\{x\} = 3[x] + 7$ $\Rightarrow$ $\{x\} = \frac{3[x]+7}{8}$ ...(5)

Now $\{x\} \in [1/2, 1)$ $\Rightarrow$ $\frac{3[x]+7}{8} \in \left[\frac{1}{2}, 1\right)$

$\Rightarrow$ $4 \le 3[x] + 7 < 8$ $\Rightarrow$ $-3 \le 3[x] < 1$ $\Rightarrow$ $-1 \le [x] < \frac{1}{3}$ $\Rightarrow$ $[x] = -1, 0$

Using these values of $[x]$ in (5) we have,

For $[x] = -1$; $\{x\} = \frac{1}{2}$ $\Rightarrow x = -\frac{1}{2}$

For $[x] = 0$; $\{x\} = \frac{7}{8}$ $\Rightarrow x = \frac{7}{8}$

$\therefore$ Solution set in this case is $\left\{-\frac{1}{2}, \frac{7}{8}\right\}$

Thus, the complete solution set is $\left\{-1, -\frac{1}{2}, \frac{3}{8}, \frac{7}{8}\right\}$

ILLUSTRATION 108: Solve the equation $4x + 5\{x\} = 3[x] - 1$ for x; where [.] is gint function and {} is fractional part function.

SOLUTION: Given equation is $4x + 5\{x\} = 3[x] - 1$

$\Rightarrow\ 4([x] + \{x\}) + 5\{x\} = 3[x] - 1$

$\Rightarrow\ 4[x] + 9\{x\} = 3[x] - 1 \ \Rightarrow\ 9\{x\} = -[x] - 1 \ \Rightarrow\ \{x\} = \dfrac{-[x]-1}{9}$ ... (1)

But $\{x\} \in [0, 1)$ $\Rightarrow\ 0 \le -\dfrac{-[x]-1}{9} < 1$

$\Rightarrow\ 0 \le -[x] - 1 < 9$ $\Rightarrow\ 0 \ge [x] + 1 > -9$

$\Rightarrow\ -1 \ge [x] > -10$ $\Rightarrow\ -1 \ge [x] \ge -9$ ... (2)

Using values of $[x]$ from (2) in (1), we have

For $[x] = -9$; $\Rightarrow\ \{x\} = \dfrac{8}{9}$ $\Rightarrow\ x = -\dfrac{73}{9}$

For $[x] = -8$; $\Rightarrow\ \{x\} = \dfrac{7}{9}$ $\Rightarrow\ x = -\dfrac{65}{9}$

For $[x] = -7$; $\Rightarrow\ \{x\} = \dfrac{2}{3}$ $\Rightarrow\ x = -\dfrac{19}{3}$

For $[x] = -6$; $\Rightarrow\ \{x\} = \dfrac{5}{9}$ $\Rightarrow\ x = -\dfrac{49}{9}$

For $[x] = -5$; $\Rightarrow\ \{x\} = \dfrac{4}{9}$ $\Rightarrow\ x = -\dfrac{41}{9}$

For $[x] = -4$; $\Rightarrow\ \{x\} = \dfrac{1}{3}$ $\Rightarrow\ x = -\dfrac{11}{3}$

For $[x] = -3$; $\Rightarrow\ \{x\} = \dfrac{2}{9}$ $\Rightarrow\ x = -\dfrac{25}{9}$

For $[x] = -2$; $\Rightarrow\ \{x\} = \dfrac{1}{9}$ $\Rightarrow\ x = -\dfrac{17}{9}$

For $[x] = -1$; $\Rightarrow\ \{x\} = 0$ $\Rightarrow\ x = -1$

$\therefore$ The set of solutions is $\left\{-\dfrac{73}{9}, -\dfrac{65}{9}, -\dfrac{19}{3}, -\dfrac{49}{9}, -\dfrac{41}{9}, -\dfrac{11}{3}, -\dfrac{25}{9}, -\dfrac{17}{9}, -1\right\}$

ILLUSTRATION 109: Prove that $[x] + \left[x + \dfrac{1}{n}\right] + \left[x + \dfrac{2}{n}\right] + \ldots + \left[x + \dfrac{n-1}{n}\right] = [nx]\ \ \forall x \in \mathbb{R}$.

SOLUTION: Let $x = [x] + y$, where $0 \le y < 1$. We know that for a given real number, we can always find two consecutive integers, between which the number lies, so let there exists $p \in \mathbb{Z}$ such that $p - 1 \le ny < p$.

Now, $x + \dfrac{q}{n} = [x] + y + \dfrac{q}{n}$ and $p - 1 \le ny < p$

$\Rightarrow\ \dfrac{p-1}{n} \le y < \dfrac{p}{n}$

$\Rightarrow\ \dfrac{p-1}{n} + \dfrac{q}{n} \le y + \dfrac{q}{n} < \dfrac{p}{n} + \dfrac{q}{n}$

$\Rightarrow\ \dfrac{p-1+q}{n} \le y + \dfrac{q}{n} < \dfrac{p+q}{n}$

Now $y + \dfrac{q}{n}$ will be less than 1 for $\dfrac{p+q}{n} \le 1$, i.e., $q \le n - p$,

Consequently $\left[x + \dfrac{q}{n}\right] = \left[[x] + y + \dfrac{q}{n}\right] = [x] + \left[y + \dfrac{q}{n}\right] = [x] + 0 = [x]$

i.e., $\left[x + \dfrac{q}{n}\right] = [x]$ for $q = 0, 1, 2, 3, \ldots, (n - p)$

But $\left[x+\frac{q}{n}\right]=[x]+1$ for $q = n-(p-1), n-(p-2), n-(p-3), \ldots, (n-1)$

$\therefore \quad [x]+\left[x+\frac{1}{n}\right]+\ldots+\left[x+\frac{n-1}{n}\right]=\underbrace{[x]+[x]+\ldots+[x]}_{(n-p+1)\text{ times}}+\underbrace{([x]+1)+([x]+1)+\ldots+([x]+1)}_{(p-1)\text{ times}}$

$= (n-p+1)[x] + (p-1)([x]+1) = n[x] + (p-1)$ ..... (i)

Also $[nx] = [n([x]+y)] = n[x] + [ny] = n[x] + p - 1$ .... (ii)

$(\because p-1 \le ny < p)$

$\therefore$ From (i) and (ii), LHS = RHS.

TEXTUAL EXERCISE–7: (SUBJECTIVE)

1. Prove that $[\sin x + [\sin x + [\sin x]]] = 3[\sin x]$.
2. Find the value of $[\sin x + [\tan x + [\cos x + [\sin x]]]]$, when $x \in (0, \pi/4)$.
3. Find the number of solutions of equation $y=\frac{1}{3}[\sin x+[\sin x+[\sin x]]]$ and $[y + [y]] = 2\cos x$; where [ ] denotes greatest integer less than or equal to x.
4. Find the solution set of the following equations (where $[x]$, $\{x\}$ is the greatest integer $\le x$, *fractional* part of x respectively).
   (a) $4\{x\} = x + [x]$ (b) $|[x] - 2x| = 4$
5. Let $[x]$ denotes the greatest integer not larger than x (the 'integer part' of x). For every positive integer n evaluate the sum $\left[\frac{n+1}{2}\right]+\left[\frac{n+2}{2^2}\right]+\ldots+\left[\frac{n+2^k}{2^{k+1}}\right]$.

Answer Keys

2. 0 **3.** 0 **4.** (a) (0, 5/3) (b) $\left\{\pm 4, \frac{7}{2}, \frac{-9}{2}\right\}$

TEXTUAL EXERCISE–7: (OBJECTIVE)

1. The domain of definition of function $\log_{[x]} x^2$
   (a) $(2, \infty)$ (b) $[2, \infty)$
   (c) $(1, \infty)$ (d) None of these
2. The domain of definition of function $[x]\sin\left(\frac{\pi}{[x+1]}\right)$
   (a) $\mathbb{R}$ (b) $\mathbb{R} \sim [-1, 0)$
   (c) $(0, \infty)$ (d) None of these
3. The domain of definition of function $\sqrt{\frac{2-[x]}{[x]-3}}$
   (a) $[2, 3)$ (b) $(2, 3)$
   (c) $(2, \infty)$ (d) None of these
4. The domain of definition of function $\sin^{-1}[2-3x^2]$
   (a) $[-1, 1]$ (b) $[0, 1]$
   (c) $[-1, 0) \cup (0, 1]$ (d) None of these
5. The domain of definition of function $f(x) = \log\{1/([\cos x] - [\sin x])\}$
   (a) $[2n\pi, (2n+1)\pi]$ (b) $\left[(2n+1)\pi+\frac{\pi}{2}, (2n+2)\pi\right]$
   (c) $[2n\pi, (2n+2)\pi]$ (d) None of these
6. The domain of definition of function $\sqrt{([x]-1)}+\sqrt{(4-[x])}$ is

(a) (1, 5) (b) (0, 5)
(c) [1, 5) (d) None of these

7. The domain of definition of function $e^x + \sin^{-1}[(x/2) - 1] + \log\sqrt{x-[x]}$

(a) (0, 6) – {1,2,3,4,5} (b) (0, 5)
(c) (0, 6) (d) None of these

8. $f: (2, 3) \to (1, 3)$ be defined by $f(x) = x - \{-x\}$, then $f^{-1}(x)$. (where $\{y\}$ denotes fractional part of y) is

(a) $y = 3 + x$ (b) $y = \frac{3+x}{2}$
(c) $y = x - 3$ (d) None of these

9. Let $f(x) = \begin{cases} x-[x]; & \text{when } I \le x < I+0.5 \\ [x] & \text{when } I+0.5 \le x < I+1 \end{cases}$, $g(x) = \sin^4 x + \cos^4 x$, then $f\{g(x)\}$ is

(a) 1 (b) –1
(c) 0 (d) None of these

10. The range of the function ([.] denotes the greatest integer function.) $f(x) = \frac{x-[x]}{1+x-[x]}$

(a) $\left[0, \frac{1}{2}\right)$ (b) [0,1]
(c) $\left[-\frac{1}{2}, \frac{1}{2}\right]$ (d) None of these

11. The range of the function $f(x) = \frac{e^x}{1+[x]}$, $x \ge 0$ ([.] denotes the greatest integer function.)

(a) $(1, \infty)$ (b) $(-\infty, \infty)$
(c) $[1, \infty)$ as $x \ge 0$ (d) $(-\infty, -1]$ $[1, \infty)$

12. Solution of the equation $x^3 - [x] = 3$ (where $[x]$, is the greatest integer $\le x$) is

(a) $(3)^{1/4}$ (b) $(4)^{1/3}$
(c) $\sqrt{2}$ (d) None of these

13. Solution of the equation $(x)^2 + (x + 1)^2 = 25$ (where (x), is the least integer function) is

(a) (–5, 2) (b) (2, 3)
(c) $(-5, -4] \cup (2, 3]$ (d) None of these

14. Solution of the inequation $[x]^2 + (x)^2 \ge 25$ (where $[x]$, and (x), is the greatest integer $\le x$ and least integer $\ge x$, respectively) is

(a) $(-\infty, -4] \cup [4, \infty)$ (b) $(-\infty, -4]$
(c) $[4, \infty)$ (d) None of these

Answer Keys

1. (b)	2. (b)	3. (a)	4. (c)	5. (b)	6. (c)	7. (a)	8. (b)	9. (c)	10. (a)
11. (c)	12. (b)	13. (c)	14. (a)						

BINARY OPERATION

From the very beginning of school days we always come across the four fundamental operations namely addition, subtraction, multiplication, and division. By using these fundamental operations we had been associating two numbers a and b with the unique real numbers $a + b$, $a - b$, $a.b$ and a/b respectively.

If we had to add, subtract, multiply, or divide more than two elements, (say) $a_1, a_2, a_3, \ldots a_n$, first of all we operate the desired operation on two elements a_1 and a_2 and the resultant is operated by same operation with the third element a_3 and the result thus obtained is operated with the fourth element a_4 and so on till all the elements are utilised. Thus, these four fundamental operations are called binary operations as they are operated on two elements at a time, as the meaning of binary is two. To cover across all binary operations we need to give a general definition of binary operations and a set X whose elements can be operated by using these binary operations as follows.

Definition of Binary Operations

A binary operation * on a set A is a function from set $A \times A$ to A itself. Thus, * associates each pair $(a_1, a_2) \in A \times A$ to a unique element $(a_1 * a_2)$ of A. Thus, domain of a binary operation defined on set A is $A \times A$ and co-domain is A. Range is subset of A.

For example, let $A = \{-1, 0, 1\}$ and * is a function defined as $*(a_1, a_2) = a_1 . a_2$; $a_1, a_2 \in A$

Now we observe,

$*(-1, -1) = (-1) . (-1) = 1 \in A$;
$*(-1, 0) = (-1) . (0) = 0 \in A$;
$*(-1, 1) = (-1) . (1) = -1 \in A$;
$*(1, 1) = (1) . (1) = 1 \in A$;
$*(1, 0) = (1) . (0) = 0 \in A$;
$*(0, 0) = (0) . (0) = 0 \in A$;

Thus, * operated to every pair $(a_1, a_2) \in A \times A$ gives us a unique element of A.

Hence, the function * defined in the above example is a binary operation on set A.

ILLUSTRATION 110: Prove the following

(i) '+' addition is a binary operation on set of integers $\mathbb{Z}$, set of natural numbers $\mathbb{N}$, set of real numbers $\mathbb{R}$, set of rational numbers $\mathbb{Q}$, *but* not on set of irrational numbers.

(ii) '–' subtraction is a binary operation on set of integers $\mathbb{Z}$ but not on set of natural numbers.

(iii) '×' multiplication is a binary operation on set of integers $\mathbb{Z}$, set of natural numbers $\mathbb{N}$, set of rational numbers $\mathbb{Q}$ but not on set of irrational numbers.

(iv) '÷' division is a binary operation on set of non-zero rational numbers but not a binary operation on set of integers.

SOLUTION: (i) For $a, b \in \mathbb{Z}$ $\Rightarrow a + b \in \mathbb{Z}$

For $a, b \in \mathbb{N}$ $\Rightarrow a + b \in \mathbb{N}$

For $a, b \in \mathbb{Q}$ $\Rightarrow a + b \in \mathbb{Q}$

For $a, b \in \mathbb{R}$ $\Rightarrow a + b \in \mathbb{R}$

Thus, '+' is a binary operation on the set of integers, set of natural numbers, set of rational numbers and set of real numbers.

However, '+' is not a binary operation on the set of irrational numbers, e.g., $\sqrt{2}, -\sqrt{2} \in \bar{Q}$ (set of irrational numbers) but $(\sqrt{2})+\left(-\sqrt{2}\right)=0 \notin \bar{Q}$.

(ii) As difference of two integers is always an integer, it follows that subtraction '–' is a binary operation on the set of integers.

However, subtraction is not a binary operation on set of natural numbers as is clear from the following counter example: Let $a = 2$, $b = 5$, then $a - b = -3 \notin \mathbb{N}$

(iii) As the product of two integers is an integer, product of two natural number is a natural number and that of two rational numbers is a rational number, multiplication '×' is a binary operation on set of integers $\mathbb{Z}$, set of natural numbers $\mathbb{N}$ and on set of rational numbers. However, the product of two irrational numbers need not be an irrational number, e.g., if $a = \sqrt{8}$ and $b = \sqrt{2}$, then $a \times b = 4$ which is a rational number. Thus, product '×' is not a binary operation on set of irrational numbers.

(iv) Division '÷' is a binary operation on set of non-zero rational numbers as if we divide a rational number by a non-zero rational number, we always obtain a rational number. However, division is not a binary operation on set of integers $\mathbb{Z}$, as if we divide an integer by another non-zero integer, we need not obtain an integer. For example, if $a = 4$, $b = 2$, then $a/b = 2$, however, if $a = 2$, $b = 4$, then $\frac{a}{b} = \frac{1}{2} \notin \mathbb{Z}$.

ILLUSTRATION 111: Prove that the multiplication is a binary operation on set $\{-1, 1, 0, i, -i\}$; where $i = \sqrt{-1}$.

SOLUTION: For proving that 'x' is a binary operation on the given set, we take the help of composition table. It is a rectangular table containing elements of given set in first row and first column keeping the position corresponding to first row and first column for indicating binary operation '*'.

Now if $a * b = c$, then we put 'c' in the position corresponding to row containing 'a' and column containing 'b'. For * to be a binary on given set, 'c' must belong to given set for each ordered pair (a, b).

The composition table for above given set and binary operation * (x) is as given below:

$*(\times)$	-1	1	0	i	$-i$
-1	1	-1	0	$-i$	i
1	-1	1	0	i	$-i$
0	0	0	0	0	0
i	$-i$	i	0	-1	1
$-i$	i	$-i$	0	1	-1

Clearly each entry in the above composition table belongs to given set. Thus, '×' is a binary operation on given set.

ILLUSTRATION 112: Prove that the 'addition modulo 7' i.e., $a * b \pmod 7$ = least non-negative integer obtained when $a + b$ is divided by 7, is a binary operation on set $A = \{0, 1, 2, 3, 4, 5, 6\}$.

SOLUTION: We prove that * (addition modulo 7) is a binary operation on set A by using the composition table as given below:

$*\ (\oplus_7)$	0	1	2	3	4	5	6
0	0	1	2	3	4	5	6
1	1	2	3	4	5	6	0
2	2	3	4	5	6	0	1
3	3	4	5	6	0	1	2
4	4	5	6	0	1	2	3
5	5	6	0	1	2	3	4
6	6	0	1	2	3	4	5

We obtain the above composition table as described below, suppose $a = 1$, $b = 3$, then $a + b = 4$.

Now $4 = 7 \times 0 + 4$, thus, 4 is the least non-negative integer remainder obtained when $a + b(= 4)$ is divided by 7.

Thus, corresponding to row containing 1 and column containing 3, we put 4. Similarly if $a = 4$ and $b = 5$, then $a + b = 9$ and $9 = 1 \times 7 - 2$.

Thus, $a * b = 2$, the least non-negative remainder obtained when 9 is divided by 7. Thus, corresponding to row containing 4 and column-containing 5 we put 2.

From the above composition table it is clear that addition modulo 7 is a binary operation on set $\{0, 1, 2, 3, 4, 5, 6\}$. Generally addition modulo 'm' is a binary operation on set $\{0, 1, 2, 3, 4, \ldots, m - 2, m - 1\}$.

ILLUSTRATION 113: Prove that 'multiplication modulo, 11' is a binary operation on the set $A = \{0, 1, 2, 3, 4, 5, 6, 7, 8, 9, 10\}$ where multiplication modulo m is defined as $a * b = a \times_m b$ = least non-negative integer obtained when $a.\ b$ is divided by m.

SOLUTION: The composition table for the given operation is as given below.

$*\ (\otimes_{11})$	0	1	2	3	4	5	6	7	8	9	10
0	0	0	0	0	0	0	0	0	0	0	0
1	0	1	2	3	4	5	6	7	8	9	10
2	0	2	4	6	8	10	1	3	5	7	9
3	0	3	6	9	1	4	7	10	2	5	8
4	0	4	8	1	5	9	2	6	10	3	7
5	0	5	10	4	9	3	8	2	7	1	6
6	0	6	1	7	2	8	3	9	4	10	5

7	0	7	3	10	6	2	9	5	1	8	4
8	0	8	5	2	10	7	4	1	9	6	3
9	0	9	7	5	3	1	10	8	6	4	2
10	0	10	9	8	7	6	5	4	3	2	1

Clearly each entry in above composition table belongs to given set A. Thus, multiplication modulo 11 is a binary operation on set A.

ILLUSTRATION 114: Show that the following operations are binary operations on the corresponding sets.

(i) $a*b=\begin{cases}\dfrac{a+b}{2}; & \text{if } a \text{ and } b \text{ are both odd or both even}\\ \dfrac{a+b+1}{2}; & \text{if exactly one of } a \text{ and } b \text{ is odd}\end{cases}$ on $\mathbb{N}$ (set of natural numbers)

(ii) $a*b=\begin{cases}\dfrac{a.b}{2}; & \text{if at least one of } a \text{ and } b \text{ is even}\\ \dfrac{(a-1).b}{2}; & \text{otherwise}\end{cases}$ on $\mathbb{Z}$ (set of integers)

(iii) $a * b = \dfrac{a^2+a+2b}{2}$ on $\mathbb{N}$ (set of natural numbers)

(iv) $a * b = a \,.\, b$ on $A = \{1, \omega, \omega^2\}$; where 'ω' is cube root of unity.

(v) $*$ on set $A = \{\pm i, \pm j, \pm k, \pm 1\}$; where $i * i = j * j = k * k = -1$, $i * j = k = -(j * i)$, $(j * k) = i = -(k * j)$, $(k * i) = j = -(i * k)$ and $1 * a = a$, $-1 * a = -a$. $\forall\, a \in A$.

SOLUTION: (i) $a*b=\begin{cases}\dfrac{a+b}{2}; & \text{if } a \text{ and } b \text{ are both odd or both even}\\ \dfrac{a+b+1}{2}; & \text{if one of } a \text{ and } b \text{ is odd and other is even}\end{cases}$

When both a and b are odd or both even, then $(a + b)$ is even natural number ≥ 2.

$\Rightarrow$ $\dfrac{a+b}{2}$ is a natural number ≥ 1.

Again if one of a and b is odd and other is even, their sum $(a + b)$ will be odd natural number ≥ 3.

$\Rightarrow$ $(a + b + 1)$ will be an even natural number ≥ 4

$\Rightarrow$ $\dfrac{a+b+1}{2}$ will be a natural number ≥ 2. Thus, $a * b \in \mathbb{N}\ \forall\, a, b \in \mathbb{N}$

$\Rightarrow$ $*$ is a binary operation on $\mathbb{N}$.

(ii) $a * b = \begin{cases}\dfrac{a.b}{2}; & \text{if at least one of } a \text{ and } b \text{ is even}\\ \dfrac{(a-1).b}{2}; & \text{if none of } a \text{ and } b \text{ is even}\end{cases}$

$\because$ Atleast one of a and b is even $\Rightarrow \dfrac{a.b}{2} \in \mathbb{Z}$

Also if both a and b are odd, $(a - 1)$ is even $\Rightarrow \dfrac{(a-1).b}{2} \in \mathbb{Z}$.

Thus, $(a * b) \in \mathbb{Z}$; $\forall\, a, b \in \mathbb{Z}$ $\Rightarrow$ $*$ is a binary operation on $\mathbb{Z}$.

(iii) $a * b = \dfrac{a^2+a+2b}{2} = \dfrac{a(a+1)+2b}{2} = \dfrac{a(a+1)}{2} + b$

Since, a, $a + 1 \in \mathbb{N}$ and we know that the product of two consecutive integers is an even integer.

$\Rightarrow \dfrac{a(a+1)}{2} \in \mathbb{N}$; also $b \in \mathbb{N}$. $\qquad \Rightarrow \left[\dfrac{a(a+1)}{2}+b\right] \in \mathbb{N} \qquad \Rightarrow a * b \in \mathbb{N}$.

Thus, * is a binary operation on $\mathbb{N}$.

(iv) $a * b = a \,.\, b$ on $A = \{1, \omega, \omega^2\}$; ω being cube root of unity.

Clearly $1 = 1.\ \omega,\ \omega.\ \omega^2 = \omega^2.\omega = 1,\ 1.\ \omega^2 = \omega^2.1 = \omega^2$.

$\Rightarrow$ * is a binary operation on A.

(v) $A = \{\pm i, \pm j, \pm k, \pm 1\}$; $i * i = j * j = k * k = -1$; $i * j = k = -(j * i)$; $(j * k) = i = -(k * j)$; $k * i = j = -(i * k)$;

Based on above given properties of elements of A, the following composition table for * implies that * is a binary operation on set A.

*	$-i$	i	j	$-j$	k	$-k$	1	-1
$-i$	-1	1	$-k$	k	j	$-j$	$-i$	i
i	1	-1	k	$-k$	$-j$	j	i	$-i$
j	k	$-k$	-1	1	i	$-i$	j	$-j$
$-j$	$-k$	k	1	-1	$-i$	i	$-j$	j
k	$-j$	j	$-i$	i	-1	1	k	$-k$
$-k$	j	$-j$	i	$-i$	1	-1	$-k$	k
1	$-i$	i	j	$-j$	k	$-k$	1	-1
-1	i	$-i$	$-j$	j	$-k$	k	-1	1

■ PROPERTIES OF BINARY OPERATION * ON A SET A

(i) **Closure Property:** Since binary operation * on a set A is a function from $A \times A$ to A, it obeys closure law, i.e., $a * b \in A\ \forall\ a, b \in A$. Also we say that A is closed with respect to binary operation *.

(ii) **Associativity:** Binary operation * on a set A is said to be associative, if $a * (b * c) = (a * b) * c\ \forall\ a, b, c \in A$.

(iii) **Commutativity:** Binary operation * on a set A is said to be commutative if $a * b = b * a\ \forall\ a, b \in A$.

(iv) **Existence of Identity:** An element $e \in A$ is said to be an identity element of set A with respect to binary operation * if $a * e = e * a = a\ \forall\ e \in A$. For example, '+' is a binary operation on set of integer $\mathbb{Z}$. Also $0 \in \mathbb{Z}$ and $x + 0 = 0 + x = x\ \forall\ x \in \mathbb{Z} \Rightarrow 0$ is an identity element of set of integers $\mathbb{Z}$ with respect to binary operation '+' (addition). Also 0 is called additive identity of set of integers.

Similarly 1 is multiplicative identity of every subset of complex number $\mathbb{C}$.

(v) **Existence of Inverse:** An element $b \in A$ is said to be inverse of element $b \in A$ with respect to binary operation * if $a * b = e = b * a$; where e is the identity element of A with respect to binary operation *. And we denote $b = a^{-1}$.

REMARKS

1. *If a binary operation * on set A is associative and identity element exists in A and every element of A is invertible, then A is said to be a Group with respect to binary operation *.*
2. *In addition to properties given in remark (1) if * is commutative, then set A is said to be an Abelian Group with respect to binary operation *.*
3. *If $b = a^{-1}$, then $a = b^{-1}$.*

Proof: *Since $b = a^{-1}$* $\qquad \Rightarrow a * b = e = b * a$

$\Rightarrow b * a = e = a * b \qquad \Rightarrow b^{-1} = a$

4. *Identity element if exists is unique.*

Proof: *Let e and e' be two identity elements in set A with respect to binary operation **

$\Rightarrow e, e' \in A$

$\Rightarrow e.e' = e' = e'.e \qquad$ (*e is identity in A and* $e' \in A$)

and $e'.e = e = e.e' \qquad$ (*e' is identity in A and* $e \in A$)

$\Rightarrow e.e' = e' = e \qquad \Rightarrow \quad e = e'$

5. *Inverse of an element if exists is unique provided * is associative.*

Proof: *Let if possible* $a^{-1} = b$ *and* $a^{-1} = c$

$\Rightarrow a * b = e = b * a \qquad \ldots (1)$

and $a * c = e = c * a \qquad \ldots (2)$

$\therefore$ *from (1) and (2), we get* $a * b = a * c = e \Rightarrow b * (a * b) = b * (a * c) \Rightarrow (b * a) * b = (b * a) * c$ ($\because$ ** is associative*)

$\Rightarrow e * b = e * c$ (*By (1)*) $\Rightarrow b = c$ ($\because$ *e is identity element*)

Thus, a^{-1} *if exists is unique.*

6. *Number of binary operations that can be defined on a set A containing n number of elements is* $(n)^{2n}$.

Proof: *Given* $n(A) = n$

As we know that binary operation is a function from set $A \times A$ *to set A itself.*

$\therefore$ *Domain of binary operation * is* $A \times A$ *having* n^2 *elements.*

Also co-domain A consists of n elements. Now each of the n elements of co-domain A has n^2 *number of choices for its pre-image in domain* $A \times A$.

Thus, by fundamental principle of multiplication of permutations number of possible binary operations that can be defined on set $A = (n^2)^n = (n)^{2n}$.

ILLUSTRATION 115: For each operation * defined below, determine whether * is binary operation, commutative, associative, identity element that exist. Find inverse of element a if the identity exist with respect to given binary operation.

(i) on $\mathbb{Z}$, $a * b = a - b$

(ii) on $\mathbb{Q}$, $a * b = ab + 1$

(iii) on $\mathbb{Q}$, $a * b = \frac{ab}{2}$

(iv) on $\mathbb{Z}^+$, $a * b = 2^{ab}$

(v) on $\mathbb{Z}^+$, $a * b = (a)^b$

(vi) on $\mathbb{R} \sim \{-1\}$; $a * b = \frac{a}{b+1}$

SOLUTION: (i) $a * b = a - b \in \mathbb{Z}\ \forall\ a, b \in \mathbb{Z}$, as the difference of any two integers is also an integer. Thus, * is a binary operation on set $\mathbb{Z}$. Further $a * b = a - b \neq b - a = b * a$

$\Rightarrow$ * is not commutative in $\mathbb{Z}$.

Also $a * (b * c) = a - (b - c) = (a - b) + c \neq (a - b) - c = (a * b) * c$ unless $c = 0$.

Thus, for non-zero integers associativity does not hold in $\mathbb{Z}$, e.g., $a = 2$, $b = 4$, $c = 5$

$\Rightarrow a * (b * c) = 2 - (4 - 5) = 3$, whereas $(a * b) * c = (a - b) - c = (2 - 4) - 5 = -7$.

$\Rightarrow$ * is not associative in $\mathbb{Z}$.

(ii) $a * b = ab + 1 \in \mathbb{Q}\ \forall\ a, b \in \mathbb{Q}$ as the product and sum of two rational numbers is again a rational number. Thus, * is a binary operation on set $\mathbb{Q}$.

Further $a * b = ab + 1 = ba + 1 = b * a\ \forall\ a, b \in \mathbb{Q}$.

$\Rightarrow$ * is commutative on set $\mathbb{Q}$.

Now if $a, b, c \in \mathbb{Q}$, then $(a * b) * c = (ab + 1) * c$

$= (ab + 1)c + 1 = abc + c + 1$,

where as $a * (b * c) = a * (bc + 1) = a(bc + 1) + 1 = abc + a + 1$

$\therefore$ $a * (b * c) \neq (a * b) * c \neq c$ unless $a = c$

Thus, for different rational numbers a, b, c associativity does not hold.

$\Rightarrow$ * is not associative in $\mathbb{Q}$.

(iii) $a * b = \dfrac{ab}{2} \in \mathbb{Q}\ \forall\ a, b \in \mathbb{Q}$, as the product and division of two rational number ($\neq 0$) is also a rational number.

$\Rightarrow$ * is a binary operation on $\mathbb{Q}$.

Further $a * b = \dfrac{ab}{2} = \dfrac{ba}{2} = b * a\ \forall\ a, b \in \mathbb{Q}$.

$\Rightarrow$ * is commutative.

Now for $a, b, c \in \mathbb{Q}$; $a * (b * c) = a * \left(\dfrac{bc}{2}\right) = \dfrac{a\left(\dfrac{bc}{2}\right)}{2} = \dfrac{abc}{4}$

and $(a * b) * c = \left(\dfrac{ab}{2}\right) * c = \dfrac{\left(\dfrac{ab}{2}\right)(c)}{2} = \dfrac{abc}{4}$

$\Rightarrow$ * is associative on $\mathbb{Q}$.

(iv) $a * b = (2)^{ab} \in \mathbb{Z}^+$ as $a, b \in \mathbb{Z}^+$ $\Rightarrow ab \in \mathbb{Z}^+$

$\Rightarrow$ $(2)^{ab} \in \mathbb{Z}^+$ as positive integer raised to the positive integer power is always a positive integer $\Rightarrow$ * is a binary operation on the set of positive integers.

Further $a * b = (2)^{ab} = (2)^{ba} = b * a$ $\Rightarrow$ * is commutative on $\mathbb{Z}^+$.

Now for $a, b, c \in \mathbb{Z}^+$; $a * (b * c) = a * \left((2)^{bc}\right) = (2)^{a.(2)^{bc}}$ and $(a * b) * c = (2^{ab}) * c = (2)^{(2)^{ab}.c}$

Clearly in general $(2)^{a.(2)^{bc}} \neq (2)^{c.(2)^{ab}}$

For example, if we take $a = 1, b = 2, c = 3$, then $a * (b * c) = (2)^{a.(2)^{bc}} = (2)^{64}$

and $(a * b) * c = (2)^{c.(2)^{ab}} = (2)^{12}$.

(v) $a * b = (a)^b \in \mathbb{Z}^+\ \forall\ a, b \in \mathbb{Z}^+$ as the product of positive integers is always a positive integer

$\Rightarrow$ * is a binary operation on $\mathbb{Z}^+$, set of positive integers.

Further $a * b = (a)^b$, whereas $b * a = (b)^a$, but $(a)^b \neq (b)^a$ in general.

For example, if $a = 2, b = 3$, then $(a)^b = 8$ and $(b)^a = 9$ $\Rightarrow$ * is not commutative.

Now for $a, b, c \in \mathbb{Z}^+$, $a * (b * c) = a * (b)^c = (a)^{b^c}$ and $(a * b) * c = (a^b) * c = (a^b)^c = (a)^{bc}$

But in general $(a)^{b^c} \neq (a)^{bc}$ for $a, b, c \in \mathbb{Z}^+$, unless $b^c = bc$

So, * is not associative on $\mathbb{Z}^+$.

(vi) $a * b = \dfrac{a}{b+1}$ need not belong to set $\mathbb{R} \sim \{-1\}\ \forall\ a, b \in \mathbb{R} \sim \{-1\}$

For example, if we take $a = -2$ and $b = 1$, then $a * b = \dfrac{a}{b+1} = \dfrac{-2}{1+1} = -1 \notin \mathbb{R} \sim \{-1\}$

$\therefore$ * is not a binary operation on $\mathbb{R} \sim \{-1\}$.Further $a * b = \dfrac{a}{b+1}$ and $b * a = \dfrac{b}{a+1}$

$\Rightarrow a * b \neq b * a$ in general $\Rightarrow$ operation * is not commutative.

For $a, b, c \in \mathbb{R} \sim \{-1\}$; $a*(b*c) = a*\left(\dfrac{b}{c+1}\right) = \dfrac{a}{\left(\dfrac{b}{c+1}+1\right)} = \dfrac{a(c+1)}{(b+c+1)}$

And $(a*b)*c = \left(\dfrac{a}{b+1}\right)*c = \dfrac{\left(\dfrac{a}{b+1}\right)}{(c+1)} = \dfrac{a}{(b+1)(c+1)}$.

Clearly $a * (b * c) \neq (a * b) * c$ in general. Thus, operation * is not associative.

ILLUSTRATION 116: Given a non-empty set W, let $*: P(W) \times P(W) \to P(W)$ be defined as $A * B = (A - B) \cup (B - A)\ \forall\ A, B \in P(W)$. Show that the empty set ϕ is the identity for the operation * and all the elements A of $P(W)$ are invertible with $A^{-1} = A$. Here $P(W)$ is power set of set W.

SOLUTION: $A * B = (A - B) \cup (B - A)\ \forall\ A, B \in P(W)$

Let $A \in P(W)$.

Also $\phi \in P(W)$

Now $A * \phi = (A - \phi) \cup (\phi - A) = A \cup \phi = A$

$\therefore\ A * \phi = A$ ... (1)

Further $\phi * A = (\phi - A) \cup (A - \phi) = \phi \cup A = A$ ... (2)

Thus, from (1) and (2), $A * \phi = \phi * A = A$

$\Rightarrow \phi$ is an identity element of $P(W)$ with respect to binary operation *.

Now, let $A \in P(W)$, then $A * A = (A - A) \cup (A - A) = \phi \cup \phi = \phi$

$\Rightarrow A$ is the inverse of itself $\Rightarrow A^{-1} = A$.

ILLUSTRATION 117: Define a binary operation * on the set {0, 1, 2, 3, 4, 5} as $a*b = \begin{cases} a+b, & \text{if } a+b<6 \\ a+b-6, & \text{if } a+b \geq 6 \end{cases}$

Show that zero is the identity for this operation and each element $a \neq 0$ of the set is invertible with $6 - a$ being the inverse of a and inverse of 0 is 0.

SOLUTION: Given set is $A = \{0, 1, 2, 3, 4, 5\}$ and binary operation * is defined by

$$a*b = \begin{cases} a+b, & \text{if } a+b<6 \\ a+b-6, & \text{if } a+b \geq 6 \end{cases}$$

Consider the composition table as given below:

*	0	1	2	3	4	5
0	0	1	2	3	4	5
1	1	2	3	4	5	0
2	2	3	4	5	0	1
3	3	4	5	0	1	2
4	4	5	0	1	2	3
5	5	0	1	2	3	4

Clearly $a * 0 = a = 0 * a \ \forall \ a \in A$

(See row 1, row 2 and column 1 and column 2).

Further let $a \in A$, $a \neq 0$ and let the inverse of a be $b \in A$.

$\Rightarrow \ a * b = 0 = b * a$. Now there arise two cases.

Case (i): if $a + b < 6$, then $a * b = a + b = b * a$.

$\Rightarrow \ a + b = 0$ $\qquad \Rightarrow \ b = -a$

$\Rightarrow \ b = a = 0$ is the only possibility as a, $b \in A$ and A contains non-negative integers.

So, b cannot be the inverse of a when $a + b < 0$ and $a \neq 0$

Case (ii): let $a + b \geq 6$ $\qquad \Rightarrow \ a * b = 0 = b * a$

$\Rightarrow \ a + b - 6 = 0$ $\qquad \Rightarrow \ b = 6 - a$

Here $A = \{0, 1, 2, 3, 4, 5\}$

$\therefore$ for $a = 0$, $a^{-1} = 0$

for $a = 1$, $a^{-1} = 6 - 1 = 5$

for $a = 2$, $a^{-1} = 6 - 2 = 4$

for $a = 3$, $a^{-1} = 6 - 3 = 3$

for $a = 4$, $a^{-1} = 6 - 4 = 2$

for $a = 5$, $a^{-1} = 6 - 5 = 1$

Thus, inverse of 0 is 0 and inverse of non-zero element $a \in A$ is given by $6 - a$.

ILLUSTRATION 118: Show that the number of binary operations on $\{1, 3\}$ having 1 as identity and having 3 as the inverse of 3 is exactly one.

SOLUTION: A binary operation * on $\{1, 3\}$ is a function from $\{1, 3\} \times \{1, 3\}$ to $\{1, 3\}$,

i.e., a function from $\{(1, 1), (1, 3), (3, 1), (3, 3)\} \rightarrow \{1, 3\}$

Since 1 is the identity for the given binary operation *, $*(1, 1) = 1$, $*(1, 3) = 3$, $*(3, 1) = 3$ and the only choice left is for the pair (3, 3). Since 3 is the inverse of 3, i.e., $*(3, 3)$ must be equal to 1.

Thus, the number of desired binary operation is exactly one.

TEXTUAL EXERCISE–8: (SUBJECTIVE)

1. Determine whether or not each of the definition of * given below gives a binary operation. In the event that * is not a binary operation, give justification for this.

(i) On $\mathbb{N}$, define * by $a * b$ = H.C.F. (a, b)

(ii) On $\mathbb{N}$, define * by $a * b$ = LCM (a, b)

(iii) On $\mathbb{Q}$, define * by $a * b = a + b + ab$

(iv) On $\mathbb{R}$, define * by $a * b = \sqrt{ab}$

(v) On $\mathbb{R}$, define * by $a * b = \sqrt{a+b}$

(vi) On $\mathbb{R}$, define * by $a * b = \sqrt{a^2 - 3ab + 4b^2}$

(vii) On $\mathbb{Z}^+$, define * by $a * b = a - b$

(viii) On $\mathbb{Z}^+$, define * by $a * b = |a - b|$

(ix) On $\mathbb{Z}^+$, define * by $a * b = a.b$

(x) On $\mathbb{R}$, define * by $a * b = ab^2$

(xi) On $\mathbb{Z}^+$, define * by $a * b = a$

2. Let * be a binary operation on the set $\mathbb{Q}$ of rational numbers as follows:

(i) $a * b = a - b$ (ii) $a * b = a^3 + b^3$

(iii) $a * b = a + 2ab$ (iv) $a * b = (a - b)^4$

(v) $a * b = \dfrac{ab}{8}$ (vi) $a * b = 3ab^2$

Find which of the binary operations are commutative and which are associative.

3. Is * defined on the set $A = \{1, 3, 5, 7, 9\}$ by $a * b$ = LCM of a and b a binary operation? Justify your answer.

4. Let * be the binary operation on $\mathbb{N}$ defined by $a * b$ = H.C.F. of a and b. Is * commutative? Is * associative? Does there exist identity for this binary operation on $\mathbb{N}$?

5. Let * be binary operation on $\mathbb{N}$ given by $a * b$ = LCM of a and b. Find
   (i) 6 * 7, 15 * 24.
   (ii) Is * associative?
   (iii) Is * commutative?
   (iv) Find the identity element w.r.t. *
   (v) Find the invertible elements of $\mathbb{N}$ w.r.t. *?

6. Let $A = N \times N$ and * be the binary operation of A defined by $(a, b) * (c, d) = (a + c, b + d)$. Show that * is commutative as well as associative. Find the identity element if exists.

7. Consider a binary operation * on the set {1, 2, 3, 4, 5} given by the following composition table;
   (i) Find (3 * 4) * 5 and 2 * (3 * 5)
   (ii) Is * commutative?
   (iii) Find (3 * 4) * (4 * 5).

*	1	2	3	4	5
1	1	1	1	1	1
2	1	2	1	2	1
3	1	1	3	1	1
4	1	2	1	4	1
5	1	1	1	1	5

8. Consider the binary operation Δ on the set {1, 2, 3, 4, 5} defined by $a \Delta b = \min\{a, b\}$. Write the operation table of the operation Δ.

9. (a) Show that * on $\mathbb{R}$ given by $a * b = a + 2b$ is not associative.
   (b) Show that * on $\mathbb{R}$ given by $a * b = a + 2b$ is not commutative.

10. Show that $-a$ is not the inverse of a for the addition operation + on $\mathbb{N}$ and $\frac{1}{a}$ for multiplication operation × on $\mathbb{N}$, for $a \neq 1$.

11. (i) Show that $* : \mathbb{R} \times \mathbb{R} \to \mathbb{R}$ given by $(a, b) \to a + 4b^2$ is a binary operation.
    (ii) Show that the $\Delta : \mathbb{R} \times \mathbb{R} \to \mathbb{R}$ given by $\Delta(a, b) = \min\{a, b\}$ and the $\Delta : \mathbb{R} \times \mathbb{R} \to \mathbb{R}$ given by $\Delta(a, b) = max\{a, b\}$ are binary operations.
    (iii) Let P be the set of all subsets of a given set X. Show that $\cup : P \times P \to P$ given by $\cup(A, B) = A \cup B$ and $\cap : P \times P \to P$ given by $\cap(A, B) = A \cap B$ are binary operations on the set P.

12. Determine which of the following binary operations on the set $\mathbb{R}$ are associative and which are commutative.
    (a) $a * b = 4 \ \forall\ a, b \in \mathbb{R}$
    (b) $a * b = \frac{(a+b)}{4} \ \forall\ a, b \in \mathbb{R}$.

13. Given a non-empty set W, consider the binary operation $* : P(W) \times P(W) \to P(W)$ given by $A * B = A \cap B \ \forall\ A, B$ in $P(W)$ is the power set of W. Show that W is the identity element for this operation and W is the only invertible element in $P(W)$ with respect to the operation *.

14. Consider the binary operations * and o on the set of real numbers $\mathbb{R}$ defined as $a * b = |a - b|$ and $a \, o \, b = a$, $\forall\ a, b \in \mathbb{R}$. Show that * is commutative but not associative, o is associative but not commutative. Further show that $\forall\ a, b, c \in \mathbb{R}$ $a * (b \, o \, c) = (a * b) \, o \, (a * b)$. [If it is so, we say that the operation * distributes over the operation o]. Does o distribute over *? Justify your answer.

Answer Keys

1. (i) yes (ii) yes (iii) yes (iv) no (v) no (vi) yes (vii) yes (viii) no (ix) yes (x) yes (xi) yes
2. (ii), (iv), (v) are commutative; (v) is associative
3. no, $3 * 5 = 15 \notin A$
4. * is commutative and associative, identity element does not exist for *.
5. (i) 42, 120 (ii) yes (iii) yes (iv) 1 (v) 1
6. Identity element does not exist
7. (i) 1 and 1 (ii) yes (iii) 1

8.

Δ	1	2	3	4	5
1	1	1	1	1	1
2	1	2	2	2	2
3	1	2	3	3	3
4	1	2	3	4	4
5	1	2	3	4	5

12. (a) associative and commutative (b) commutative but not associative **14.** no

TEXTUAL EXERCISE–8: (OBJECTIVE)

1. Which of the following operations on set of rational numbers $\mathbb{Q}$ is/are associative?

(a) $a * b = a - b$ (b) $a * b = \dfrac{ab}{4}$

(c) $a * b = \sqrt{a^2b^2}$ (d) $a * b = a^2 - b^2$

2. Which of the following operation on set of integers is/are binary operation(s)?

(a) $a * b = \sqrt{a^2b^2 + b^2 + 2ab^2}$

(b) $a * b = g.c.d\,(a, b)$

(c) $a * b = \dfrac{a-b}{2}$

(d) $a * b = \dfrac{a^2-b^2}{4}$

3. Which of the following operations on set of integers is/are commutative?

(a) $a * b = \sqrt{a^2 + b^2 - 2ab}$

(b) $a * b = a - b$

(c) $a * b = \begin{cases} (a)^b & \text{if } b \geq 0 \\ ab & \text{if } b < 0 \end{cases}$

(d) $a * b = a^2b$

4. If $A = \{1, \omega, \omega^2\}$; where ω is cube root of unity. Define a binary operation * on A by $a * b = ab$, then

(a) ω is identity in A

(b) ω^2 is identity in A

(c) 1 is identity element in A

(d) Identity element in A does not exist

5. If $A = \{1, \omega, \omega^2\}$; ω being cube root of unity. Define a binary operation * on A by $a * b = ab$, then

(a) Inverse of ω is 1 (b) Inverse of ω^2 is 1

(c) Inverse of ω is ω^2 (d) Inverse of ω^2 is ω

6. Number of binary operations defined on set $A = \{a, b, c\}$ will be

(a) 9 (b) 81

(c) $(3)^9$ (d) None of these

7. If * is a binary operation on set $A = \{1, 3, 5\}$ defined by $a * b$ = least non-negative integer obtained when $(a.b)$ is divided by 6, then

(a) Identity in A is 1

(b) $3 * a = 3 \ \forall \ a \in A$

(c) Inverse element of 3 does not exist

(d) Inverse element of 5 is 5

8. A binary operation * is defined on set $A = \{2, 4, 6, 8, 10\}$ by the given composition table:

*	2	4	6	8	10
2	10	6	2	4	8
4	6	8	4	10	2
6	2	4	6	8	10
8	4	10	8	2	6
10	8	2	10	6	4

(a) Identity element in A is 6

(b) * is commutative in A

(c) Inverse of 8 is 10

(d) $2 * (4 * 8) \neq (2 * 4) * 8$

Answer Keys

1. (b, c) **2.** (a, b) **3.** (a) **4.** (c) **5.** (c, d) **6.** (c) **7.** (a, b, c, d) **8.** (a, b, c)

■ DOMAIN OF FUNCTIONS

Domain of Function is defined as: D_f : {x : f(x) is defined, i.e., $f(x) \in$ co-domain Y and is real and finite}.

Principal Domain: Subset of domain in which f(x) takes all its values exactly once, i.e., f(x) is one–one and on-to (Bijective) is called Principal domain. Conventionally it considered nearer to zero and preferably positive.

e.g., if we consider the function $f(x) = \frac{x^2}{4a}, a > 0$

Clearly domain of function f(x) is $\mathbb{R} = (-\infty, \infty)$ and range = $[0, \infty)$

The graph of f(x) is as given in Figure 2.101.

Clearly the function is many–one in its domain $\mathbb{R}$ and function f(x) takes all values of its range $[0, \infty)$ exactly once in $(-\infty, 0]$ as well as in $[0, \infty)$, and hence, the function f(x) is injective and onto in $(-\infty, 0]$ as well as in $[0, \infty)$.

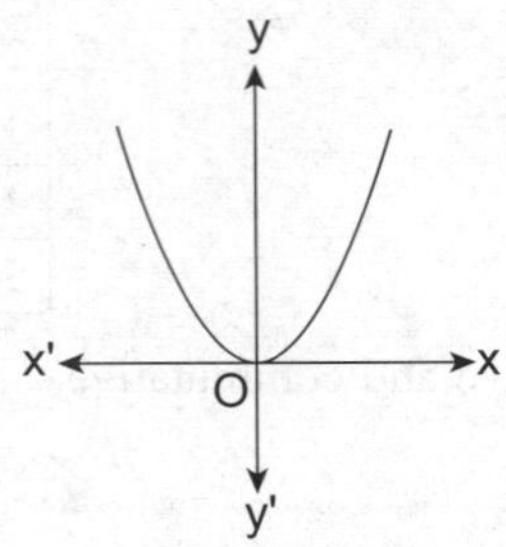

FIGURE 2.101

Among these two domains the domain containing non-negative inputs, i.e., $[0, \infty)$ is taken as its principal domain.

REMARKS

1. *Every function is bijective from its principal domain to its range. Thus, every function is invertible from its principal domain to range set.*
2. *Domain of the function $f^{-1}(x)$ is same as range of the function f(x).*
3. *Range of $f^{-1}(x)$ is same as principal domain of the function f(x).*

■ PROPERTIES OF DOMAIN

If f(x) and g(x) be two functions such that f(x) has domain D_f and g(x) has domain D_g, then following results always hold good.

Rule 1: Dom $(k \cdot f(x)) = D_f$ for all $k \in$ set of non-zero real numbers.

Rule 2: Dom$\left(\frac{1}{f(x)}\right) = D_f \sim \{x : f(x) = 0\}$

ILLUSTRATION 119: Find the domain of given functions

(a) $f(x) = \frac{3x+4}{x^2-1}$ (b) $f(x) = \frac{x^2-9}{x(x-1)(x-2)}$

SOLUTION: (a) $D_f = \mathbb{R} = \sim \{1, -1\}$ (b) $D_f = \mathbb{R} \sim \{0, 1, 2\}$

Rule 3: Dom $(f(x) \pm g(x)) = D_f \cap D_g$.

ILLUSTRATION 120: Find the domain of $f(x) = \sqrt{x-1} + \log(5-x)$

SOLUTION: $x - 1 \geq 0$ and $5 - x > 0 \Rightarrow x \geq 1$ and $x < 5 \Rightarrow D_f = [1, 5)$

Rule 4: Dom $(f(x) \cdot g(x)) = D_f \cap D_g$

ILLUSTRATION 121: Find the domain of following functions

(a) $f(x) = \sqrt{x-2}\sqrt{4-x}$ (b) $f(x) = \sqrt{(x-2)(x-4)}$

SOLUTION: (a) $x - 2 \geq 0$ and $x - 4 \geq 0 \Rightarrow x \geq 2$ and $x \geq 4 \Rightarrow D_f = [4, \infty]$

(b) $(x - 2)(x - 4) \geq 0 \Rightarrow x \in (-\infty, 2] \cup [4, \infty) \Rightarrow D_f = (-\infty, 2] \cup [4, \infty)$

Rule 5: Dom $f(g(x)) = \{x : x \in D_g \text{ and } g(x) \in D_f\} = D_g \sim \{x \mid g(x) \notin D_f\}$.

ILLUSTRATION 122: Find the domain of $f(x) = \sin^{-1}(\log_2 x)$.

SOLUTION: $x > 0$ and $\log_2 x \in [-1, 1] \Rightarrow x > 0$ and $x \in [1/2, 2] \Rightarrow x \in [1/2, 2] = D_f$

Rule 6: Domain of even root of $f(x) = \sqrt[2m]{f(x)} = D_f \sim \{x : f(x) < 0\}$

ILLUSTRATION 123: Find the domain of the following functions:

(a) $f(x) = \sqrt{x^2 - 4}$ (b) $f(x) = \sqrt[4]{\sin x}$

SOLUTION: (a) $(x^2 - 4) \geq 0 \Rightarrow x^2 \geq 4 \Rightarrow x \leq -2$ or $x \geq 2 \Rightarrow x \in (-\infty, -2] \cup [2, \infty) = D_f$

(b) $\sin x \geq 0 \Rightarrow x \in \bigcup_{n\in\mathbb{Z}} [2n\pi, (2n + 1)\pi]$

Rule 7: Domain $\sqrt[2m+1]{f(x)} = D_f$

ILLUSTRATION 124: Find the domain of the following functions:

(a) $f(x) = \sqrt[3]{x + 4}$ (b) $f(x) = \sqrt[3]{\sin x}$

SOLUTION: (a) $(x + 4) \in \mathbb{R} \Rightarrow x \in \mathbb{R} = D_f$ (b) D_f = Domain of $\sin x = \mathbb{R}$

Rule 8: Dom $(\log f(x)) = D_f \sim \{x : f(x) \leq 0\}$

ILLUSTRATION 125: Find the domain of the following functions:

(a) $\log\left(\dfrac{x^2 - 1}{27 - x^3}\right)$ (b) $\log\left(\dfrac{4 - x^2}{\sqrt{\sin x}}\right)$ (c) $\log_2(x - 1)$

SOLUTION: (a) $\left(\dfrac{x^2 - 1}{27 - x^3}\right) > 0 \Rightarrow (x^2 - 1)(27 - x^3) > 0 \Rightarrow (x^2 - 1)(x^3 - 27) < 0$

$\Rightarrow (x - 3)(x + 1)(x - 1)(x^2 + 9 + 3x) < 0 \Rightarrow (x + 1)(x - 1)(x - 3) < 0$ ($\because x^2 + 9 + 3x > 0$ as its discriminant is negative) $\Rightarrow x \in (-\infty, -1) \cup (1, 3)$

(b) $\dfrac{4 - x^2}{\sqrt{\sin x}} > 0$ and $\sin x > 0 \Rightarrow 4 - x^2 > 0$ and $x \in (2n\pi, (2n + 1)\pi)$; $n \in \mathbb{Z}$

$\Rightarrow x \in (-2, 2)$ and $x \in (2n\pi, (2n + 1)\pi)$; $n \in \mathbb{Z} \Rightarrow x \in (0, 2)$

(c) $(x - 1) > 0 \Rightarrow x \in (1, \infty)$

ILLUSTRATION 126: Find the domain of $f(x) = \log_{10} \sin x$.

SOLUTION: For existence of $f(x)$, $\sin x > 0$ and from the graph of $y = \sin x$, it is clear that $\sin x$ is positive when $2n\pi < x < (2n + 1)\pi$; $n \in \mathbb{Z}$

Hence, Domain of $f(x) = \bigcup_{n\in\mathbb{Z}} (2n\pi, (2n+1)\pi)$

ILLUSTRATION 127: Find the domain of definition of function $f(x) = \sin^{-1}(\log_2(3^{\cos x}))$

SOLUTION: This is the example for finding domain of composition function of the form, i.e., (hoφoψog) and the composition to be defined $3^{\cos x} > 0$ (always hold)

and $-1 \leq \log_2(3^{\cos x}) \leq 1 \Rightarrow 1/2 \leq 3^{\cos x} \leq 2$ ...(i)

$\Rightarrow \log_3 \frac{1}{2} \le \log_3 3^{\cos x} \le \log_3 2$ $\quad$ ($\because \log_a x$ is increasing for $a > 1$)

$\Rightarrow \log_3 \frac{1}{2} \le \cos x \le \log_3 2$ $\quad \Rightarrow -\log_3 2 \le \cos x \le \log_3 2$

$\Rightarrow x \in \bigcup_{n\in\mathbb{Z}} \{[(2n-1)\pi+\theta, (2n\pi-\theta)] \cup [(2n\pi+\theta), (2n+1)\pi-\theta]\}$

Where $\cos\theta = \log_3 2$ and $\theta \in (0, \pi/2)$

ILLUSTRATION 128: Find the domain of the function $y = \sqrt{\frac{2x-1}{2x^3+3x^2+x}}$

SOLUTION: (a) For y to be defined:

$\Rightarrow \frac{2x-1}{2x^3+3x^2+x} \ge 0 \Rightarrow \frac{2x-1}{x(2x^2+3x+1)} \ge 0 \Rightarrow \frac{2x-1}{x(2x+1)(x+1)} \ge 0$

By sign scheme, we have:

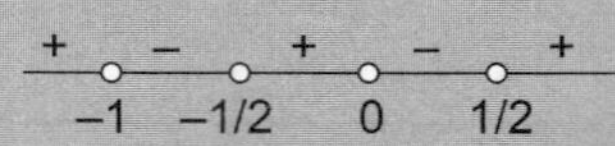

FIGURE 2.102

$\Rightarrow (2x-1)x(2x+1)(x+1) \ge 0; x \ne 0, -1/2, -1$

$\Rightarrow x \in (-\infty, -1) \cup (-1/2, 0) \cup [1/2, \infty)$.

ILLUSTRATION 129: Find the domain of the function $10^x + 10^y = 10$

SOLUTION: Given $10^x + 10^y = 10$ $\quad \Rightarrow 10^y = 10 - 10^x$

$\Rightarrow \log_{10} 10^y = \log_{10}(10 - 10^x)$ $\quad \Rightarrow y = \log_{10}(10 - 10^x)$

For y to be defined $10 - 10^x > 0$ $\quad \Rightarrow 10^x < 10$ $\quad \Rightarrow x < 1$

Hence, domain of y is $(-\infty, 1)$

ILLUSTRATION 130: Find the domain of definition of $f(x) = \sin^{-1}(|x-1| - 2)$

SOLUTION: $f(x) = \sin^{-1}(|x-1| - 2)$. For domain $-1 \le |x-1| - 2 \le 1$

$\Rightarrow 1 \le |x-1| \le 3 \Rightarrow x - 1 \in [-3, -1] \cup [1, 3] \Rightarrow x \in [-2, 0] \cup [2, 4]$

ILLUSTRATION 131: Find the domain of the function $f(x) = \sqrt[6]{4^x + 8^{(2/3)(x-2)} - 52 - 2^{2(x-1)}}$

SOLUTION: For f to be defined, we must have

$4^x + 8^{(2/3)(x-2)} - 52 - 2^{2(x-1)} \ge 0 \Leftrightarrow 2^{2x} + 2^{2(x-2)} - 2^{2(x-1)} \ge 52 \Leftrightarrow 2^{2x}[1 + 2^{-4} - 2^{-2}] \ge 52$

$\Leftrightarrow 2^{2x}\left(\frac{13}{16}\right) \ge 52 \Leftrightarrow 2^{2x} \ge 64 = 2^6$. Hence, we must have $x \ge 3$. So, the domain of f is $[3, \infty)$

ILLUSTRATION 132: Discuss the domain of definition of the function, $f(x) = \log(ax^2 + bx + c)$ for values of $a, b, c \in \mathbb{R}$.

SOLUTION: ***Case I:*** If $a = 0$, then $f(x) = \log(bx + c)$, then $f(x)$ will be defined for $bx + c > 0$

$\Rightarrow bx > -c$. if $b > 0$, then $x > -\frac{c}{b}$ and if $b < 0$, then $x < -\frac{c}{b}$

Case II: If $a = b = 0$, then $f(x) = \log(c)$ = constant function and is defined for $\forall x \in \mathbb{R}$ for which $c > 0$ and not defined for any real x if $c \le 0$.

Case III: If $a \ne 0$, then $f(x) = \log(ax^2 + bx + c)$.

Sub-case (a) If $D = b^2 - 4ac < 0$, $a > 0$, then $ax^2 + bx + c > 0\ \forall\ x \in \mathbb{R}$

$\Rightarrow$ Domain of $f(x) = \mathbb{R}$

Sub-case (b) If $D = b^2 - 4ac < 0$, $a < 0$, then $ax^2 + bx + c < 0\ \forall\ x \in \mathbb{R}$

$\Rightarrow$ Domain of $f(x) = \{\ \} = \phi$

Sub-case (c) If $D = b^2 - 4ac > 0$, $a > 0$, then $ax^2 + bx + c > 0\ \forall\ x \in (-\infty, \alpha) \cup (\beta, \infty)$; where α, β are roots of $ax^2 + bx + c = 0$ $\Rightarrow$ Domain $= (-\infty, \alpha) \cup (\beta, \infty)$.

Sub-case (d) If $D = b^2 - 4ac > 0$, $a < 0$, then $ax^2 + bx + c > 0\ \forall\ x \in (\alpha, \beta)$; where α, β are roots of $ax^2 + bx + c = 0$ $\Rightarrow$ Domain $= (\alpha, \beta)$.

Sub-case (e) If $D = b^2 - 4ac = 0$, $a > 0$, then $ax^2 + bx + c = 0$ at $x = \frac{-b}{2a}$ and $ax^2 + bx + c > 0$ $\forall x \in \mathbb{R} \sim \left\{\frac{-b}{2a}\right\}$, which is the domain in this case.

Sub-case (f) If $D = b^2 - 4ac = 0$, $a < 0$, then $ax^2 + bx + c \le 0\ \forall\ x \in \mathbb{R}$

$\Rightarrow$ $f(x)$ is not defined at any real x. $\Rightarrow$ Domain $= \{\ \} = \phi$.

Domains of Some Standard Functions:

$f(x)$	Domain : D_f	$f(x)$	Domain : D_f
Polynomial $P(x)$	$\mathbb{R}$	$\cot^{-1} x$	$\mathbb{R}$
Constant function	$\mathbb{R}$	$\sec^{-1} x$	$(-\infty, -1] \cup [1, \infty)$
$\frac{P(x)}{Q(x)}$	$\mathbb{R} - \{x : Q(x) = 0\}$	$\operatorname{cosec}^{-1} x$	$(-\infty, -1] \cup [1, \infty)$
a^x	$\mathbb{R}$	$\operatorname{sgn} x$	$\mathbb{R}$
$\log x$	$(0, \infty)$	$\sin(\sin^{-1}x)$	$[-1, 1]$
$\|x\|$	$\mathbb{R}$	$\cos(\cos^{-1}x)$	$[-1, 1]$
$\{x\}$	$\mathbb{R}$	$\tan(\tan^{-1}x)$	$\mathbb{R}$
$\sin x$	$\mathbb{R}$	$\cot(\cot^{-1}x)$	$\mathbb{R}$
$\cos x$	$\mathbb{R}$	$\sec(\sec^{-1} x)$	$(-\infty, -1] \cup [1, \infty)$
$\tan x$	$\mathbb{R} - \{(2n + 1)\frac{\pi}{2}; n \in \mathbb{Z}\}$	$\operatorname{cosec}(\operatorname{cosec}^{-1}x)$	$(-\infty, -1] \cup [1, \infty)$
$\cot x$	$\mathbb{R} - \{n\pi; n \in \mathbb{Z}\}$	$\sin^{-1}(\sin x)$	$\mathbb{R}$
$\sec x$	$\mathbb{R} - \left\{(2n+1)\frac{\pi}{2}; n \in \mathbb{Z}\right\}$	$\cos^{-1}(\cos x)$	$\mathbb{R}$
$\operatorname{cosec} x$	$\mathbb{R} - \{n\pi; n \in \mathbb{Z}\}$	$\tan^{-1}(\tan x)$	$\mathbb{R} - \left\{(2n+1)\frac{\pi}{2}; n \in \mathbb{Z}\right\}$
$\sin^{-1} x$	$[-1, 1]$	$\cot^{-1}(\cot x)$	$\mathbb{R} - \{n\pi; n \in \mathbb{Z}\}$
$\cos^{-1} x$	$[-1, 1]$	$\sec^{-1}(\sec x)$	$\mathbb{R} - \left\{(2n+1)\frac{\pi}{2}; n \in \mathbb{Z}\right\}$
$\tan^{-1} x$	$\mathbb{R}$	$\operatorname{cosec}^{-1}(\operatorname{cosec} x)$	$\mathbb{R} - \{n\pi; n \in \mathbb{Z}\}$

TEXTUAL EXERCISE-9: (SUBJECTIVE)

1 Find the domain of definition of the following functions:

(a) $f(x)=\dfrac{\sqrt{x-1}+\sqrt{6-x}}{\sqrt{1-x}+\sqrt{x-6}}$

(b) $f(x)=\dfrac{x^2+1}{x-\sqrt{(x+2)}}$

(c) $f(x)=\sqrt{\dfrac{x-2}{x+2}}+\sqrt{\dfrac{1-x}{1+x}}$

2. Find the domain of definition of the following functions:

(a) $f(x)=\sqrt{\dfrac{1-5^x}{7^{-x}-7}}$

(b) $f(x)=\dfrac{\sqrt{5-x}+\sqrt{x-2}}{\sqrt{3-x}-\sqrt{x-1}}$

3. Find the domain of definition of the following functions:

(a) $f(x)=\log_{2\{x\}-3}(x^2-5x+13)$

(b) $f(x)=\log_{10}\left(\dfrac{9-x^2}{x^2-4}\right)$

(c) $f(x)=\sqrt{\log_2\left(\dfrac{5x-x^2}{4}\right)}$

(d) $f(x)=\sqrt{\log_{\frac{1}{2}}\dfrac{5x-x^2}{4}}$

4 Find the domain of definition of the following functions:

(a) $f(x)=\dfrac{1}{\sqrt{x-|x|}}$

(b) $f(x)=\dfrac{1}{\sqrt{|x|-x}}$

(c) $f(x)=\sin^{-1}\left(\dfrac{3-|x|}{2}\right)$

(d) $f(x)=\sqrt{x^2-3|x|+2}$

5. Find the domain of definition of the following functions:

(a) $f(x)=\sqrt{\sin x}+\sqrt{16-x^2}$

(b) $\sqrt{\cos(\sin x)}+\sqrt{\sin(\cos x)}$

6. Find the domain of definition and range of the following functions:

(a) $f(x) = \cos^{-1}[x]$

(b) $f(x)=\sin^{-1}\left(x^2+1\right)$

7. Find the domain of definition of the following functions:

(a) $f(x)=\cos^{-1}\left(\dfrac{2x}{1+x^2}\right)$

(b) $f(x)=\cos^{-1}\left(\dfrac{1+x^2}{2x}\right)$

(c) $f(x)=\tan^{-1}\left(1+x^2\right)$

(d) $f(x)=\sin^{-1}\left(\dfrac{x^2-1}{2(x^2+1)}\right)$

8. Find the domain of definition of the following functions:

(a) $f(x) = \log_2(3 + 5\sin x)$

(b) $f(x) = \log_2(3 + 2\sin x)$

9. Find the domain of definition of the following functions:

(a) $f(x)=\sqrt{\log_x(\cos 2\pi x)}$

(b) $f(x)=\sqrt{\left(x^2-3x-10\right)\ln^2(x-3)}$

(c) $f(x)=\cos^{-1}\left(\dfrac{2-|x|}{4}\right)+(\ln(3-x))^{-1}$

10. Find the domain of definition of the following functions:

(a) $f(x)=\dfrac{\sqrt{\cos x-\frac{1}{2}}}{\sqrt{6+35x-6x^2}}$

(b) $f(x)=\left(\log_{\frac{x-2}{x+3}}2\right)+\sqrt{9-x^2}$

11. Find the domain of definition of the following functions:

(a) $f(x)=\dfrac{1}{[x]}+\log_{1-\{x\}}(x^2-3x+10)+\dfrac{1}{\sqrt{2-|x|}}+\dfrac{1}{\sqrt{\sec(\sin x)}}$

(b) $f(x)=\dfrac{1}{\sqrt{\sin(\cos x)}}+\sin^{-1}\left(\dfrac{2x}{\pi}\right)+\dfrac{1}{\{-x\}}+\dfrac{1}{\ln\left(1-\left[\tan\frac{x}{2}\right]\right)-\left[-\tan\frac{x}{2}\right]}$

Answer Keys

1. (a) {} (b) $(-2,-1)\cup(-1,2)\cup(2,\infty)$ (c) ϕ
2. (a) $(-\infty,-1)\cup[0,\infty)$ (b) $(2, 3]$
3. (a) ϕ (b) $(-3,-2)\cup(2,3)$ (c) $[1, 4]$ (d) $(0, 1]\cup[4, 5)$
4. (a) ϕ (b) $(-\infty, 0)$ (c) $x\in[-5,-1]\cup[1,5]$ (d) $(-\infty,-2]\cup[-1,1]\cup[2,\infty)$
5. (a) $[-4,-\pi]\cup[0,\pi]$ (b) $\bigcup_{n\in\mathbb{Z}}\left[2n\pi-\frac{\pi}{2},2n\pi+\frac{\pi}{2}\right]$
6. (a) $-1\le x<2,\left\{\pi,\frac{\pi}{2},0\right\}$ (b) $D_f=\{0\}, R_f=\left\{\frac{\pi}{2}\right\}$
7. (a) $\mathbb{R}$ (b) $\{-1, 1\}$ (c) $\mathbb{R}$ (d) $\mathbb{R}$
8. (a) $\left(2n\pi-\sin^{-1}\left(\frac{3}{5}\right),(2n+1)\pi+\sin^{-1}\left(\frac{3}{5}\right)\right);\ n\in\mathbb{Z}$ (b) $\mathbb{R}$
9. (a) $\left(0,\frac{1}{4}\right)\cup\left(\frac{3}{4},1\right)\cup\{2,3,4,.....\infty)]$ (b) $\{4\}\cup[5,\infty)$ (c) $[-6, 3)-\{2\}$
10. (a) $\left(-\frac{1}{6},\frac{\pi}{3}\right]\cup\left[\frac{5\pi}{3},6\right)$ (b) $(2, 3]$
11. (a) $(-2,-1)\cup(-1,0)\cup(1,2)$ (b) $\left(-\frac{\pi}{2},\frac{\pi}{2}\right)-\{-1,0,1\}$

TEXTUAL EXERCISE–9: (OBJECTIVE)

1. Domain of the definition of the function $\sqrt{x(x-1)}$ is
   (a) $[0, 1]$ (b) $[-1, 0]$
   (c) $(-\infty,0]\cup[1,\infty)$ (d) None of these

2. Domain of the definition of the function $(x)^{\frac{1}{\ln x}}$ is
   (a) $(0,\infty)-\{1\}$ (b) $(0, 1)$
   (c) $[0,\infty)\sim\{1\}$ (d) None of these

3. Domain of the definition of the function $\frac{1}{\sqrt{x-|x|}}$ is
   (a) { } (b) $\mathbb{R}$
   (c) $(0,\infty)$ (d) None of these

4. Domain of the definition of the function $\frac{1}{\sqrt{|x|-x}}$ is
   (a) { } (b) $(-\infty, 0)$
   (c) $(0,\infty)$ (d) None of these

5. Domain of the definition of the function $\frac{1}{2-\cos 3x}$ is
   (a) $\mathbb{R}\sim\cos^{-1}\frac{2}{3}$ (b) $\mathbb{R}$
   (c) $\mathbb{R}\sim\cos^{-1}\frac{3}{2}$ (d) None of these

6. Domain of the definition of the function $\log_{10}(1+x^3)$ is
   (a) $(-1,\infty)$ (b) $(0,\infty)$
   (c) $\mathbb{R}$ (d) None of these

7. The domain of function $\frac{1}{\sqrt{x(x-2)(x-3)}}$
   (a) $(0, 2)$ (b) $\mathbb{R}\sim\{0, 2, 3\}$
   (c) $(0,2)\cup(3,\infty)$ (d) None of these

8. The domain of function $\frac{1}{\sqrt[3]{(x-1)(x-2)(x-4)}}$
   (a) $(1,2)\cup(4,\infty)$ (b) $R-\{1, 2, 4\}$
   (c) $\mathbb{R}$ (d) None of these

9. The domain of definition of the function $y(x)$ given by the equation $2^x+2^y=2$ is
   (a) $0<x\le 1$ (b) $0\le x\le 1$
   (c) $-\infty<x\le 0$ (d) $-\infty<x<1$

10. The domain of $f(x)=\sqrt{3-x}+\cos^{-1}\left(\frac{3-2x}{5}\right)$ is equal to
    (a) $[-1, 3]$ (b) $(-1, 3]$
    (c) $[-1, 3)$ (d) None of these

11. The domain of the function $f(x)=\sin^{-1}\left(\frac{x-3}{2}\right)-\log_{10}(4-x)$ is

(a) (1, 4) (b) [1, 4]
(c) [1, 4) (d) (1, 4]

12. The domain of definition of the function $y = \frac{1}{\log_{10}(3-x)} + \sqrt{x+2}$ is

(a) [–2, 3) (b) (–2, 3)
(c) $[-2, 0) \cup (0, 3]$ (d) None of these

13. The domain of the function $f(x) = \sqrt{\frac{(x+1)(x-3)}{(x-2)}}$ is

(a) $[-1, 2) \cup [3, \infty)$
(b) $(-1, 2) \cup [3, \infty)$
(c) $[-1, 2] \cup [3, \infty)$
(d) None of these

14. The domain of definition of $f(x) = \sqrt{\frac{1-|x|}{2-|x|}}$ is

(a) $\frac{(-\infty, \infty)}{[-1, 1]}$
(b) $\frac{(-\infty, \infty)}{[-2, 2]}$
(c) $[-1, 1] \cup (-\infty, -2) \cup (2, \infty)$
(d) None of these

15. The domain of the function $f(x) = \cos^{-1}\left(\frac{3}{4+2\sin x}\right)$ is equal to

(a) $\left[-\frac{\pi}{6} + 2n\pi, \frac{\pi}{6} + 2n\pi\right]$
(b) $\left(-\frac{\pi}{6} + 2n\pi, \frac{\pi}{6} + 2n\pi\right)$
(c) $\left(-\frac{\pi}{6} + 2n\pi, \frac{\pi}{6} + 2n\pi\right]$
(d) None of these

16. If $f(x) = \frac{1}{\sqrt{\sin x}} + \sqrt[3]{\sin x}$, then D_f is

(a) $\bigcup_{k \in \mathbb{Z}} (2k\pi, (2k+1)\pi)$
(b) $(0, \pi)$
(c) $(\pi, 2\pi)$
(d) $((2k + 1)\pi, (2k + 2)\pi)$

17. The domain of $f(x) = \frac{1}{\sqrt{|\cos x| + \cos x}}$ is

(a) $\bigcup_{n \in \mathbb{Z}} [-2n\pi, 2n\pi]$
(b) $\bigcup_{n \in \mathbb{Z}} (2n\pi, (2n + 1)\pi]$
(c) $\bigcup_{n \in \mathbb{Z}} \left(\frac{(4n+1)\pi}{2}, \frac{(4n+3)\pi}{2}\right)$
(d) $\bigcup_{n \in \mathbb{Z}} \left(\frac{(4n-1)\pi}{2}, \frac{(4n+1)\pi}{2}\right)$

Answer Keys

1. (c)	**2.** (a)	**3.** (a)	**4.** (b)	**5.** (b)	**6.** (a)	**7.** (c)	**8.** (b)	**9.** (d)	**10.** (a)
11. (c)	**12.** (d)	**13.** (a)	**14.** (c)	**15.** (d)	**16.** (a)	**17.** (d)			

■ RANGE OF FUNCTIONS

Bounded and Un-bounded Functions

A function *f*(*x*) is called bounded iff there exists two real and finite numbers *m, M* such that $m \le f(x) \le M \ \forall \ x \in D_f$; *m* is called lower bound and *M* is upper bound.

Existence of single upper/lower bound means existence of infinitely many upper/lower bounds .... $m_3 < m_2 < m_1 < m < f(x) < M < M_1 < M_2 \ldots$, i.e., every real number less than a lower bound is also a lower bound and every real number greater than an upper bound is also an upper bound.

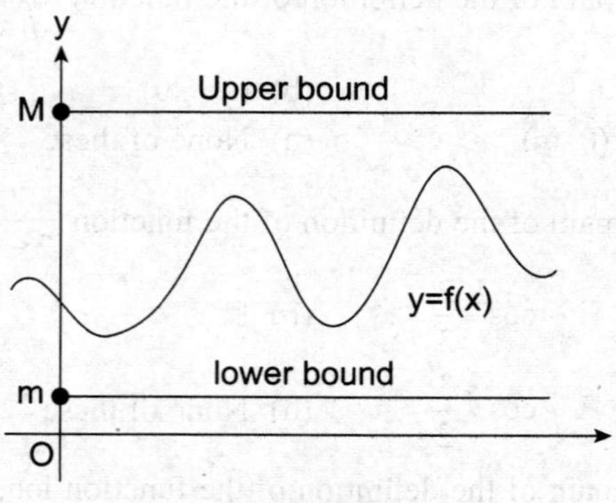

FIGURE 2.103

Greatest Lower Bound

The greatest of all lower bounds is called greatest lower bound denoted by *g.l.b.* (m_0) and if $f(x_0) = m_0$ for some $x_0 \in D_f$, then $f(x_0) = m_0$ is called minimum value of $f(x)$. However, if $f(x) > m_0 \ \forall \ x \in D_f$ but $f(x) \neq m_0$ for any $x \in D_f$, then m_0 will be the *g.l.b.* of $f(x)$ but m_0 will not be the minimum value of $f(x)$. For example, $f(x) = 1/x^2$; then $f(x) > 0 \ \forall \ x \in \mathbb{R} \sim \{0\}$, therefore *g.l.b.* of $f(x)$ is zero but it is not attained at any real number x, and hence, $f(x)$ has no minimum value.

That is, minimum value of $f(x) = 1/x^2$ does not exist but it approaches to 0.

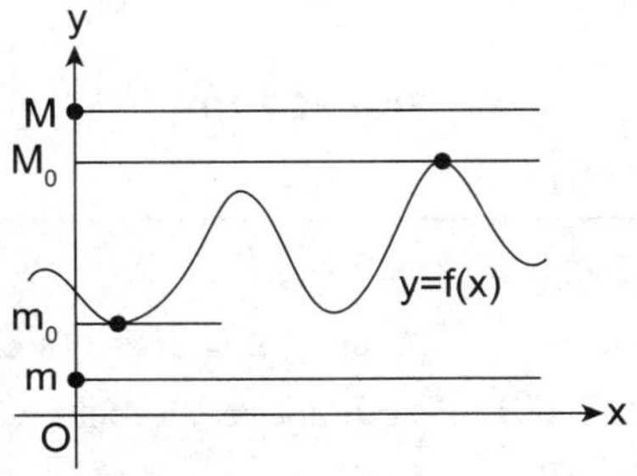

FIGURE 2.104

Conclusion

1. Greatest lower bound may or may not be the minimum value of function.
2. Minimum value of function if exists is the greatest lower bound of function
3. Every real number less than the greatest lower bound will be a lower bound of $f(x)$.
4. Every bounded function has its greatest lower bound but function may or may not attain it at any real number. If it attains its greatest lower bound, then the greatest lower bound will be the minimum value of function.
5. If the range of a function is (a, b) or $[a, b]$, then the greatest lower bound of $f(x)$ will be a. Minimum value of $f(x)$ does not exist in former case whereas minimum value of $f(x) = a$ in later case.

Least Upper Bound

The smallest of all upper bounds is called least upper bound denoted by *l.u.b.* (M_0) and if $f(x_0) = M_0$ for some x_0, then $f(x_0)$ is called maximum value of $f(x)$. However, if $f(x) < M_0 \ \forall \ x \in D_f$ but $f(x) \neq M_0$ for any $x \in D_f$, then M_0 will be the *l.u.*b. of $f(x)$ but M_0 will not be the maximum value of $f(x)$. e.g., $f(x) = 1 - \dfrac{1}{x^2}$; then $f(x) < 1 \ \forall \ x \in \mathbb{R} \sim \{0\}$, therefore, *l.u.*b. of $f(x)$ is 1, but it is not attained at any real number x, and hence, $f(x)$ has no maximum value.

That is, maximum value of $f(x) = 1 - \dfrac{1}{x^2}$ does not exist but it approaches to 1.

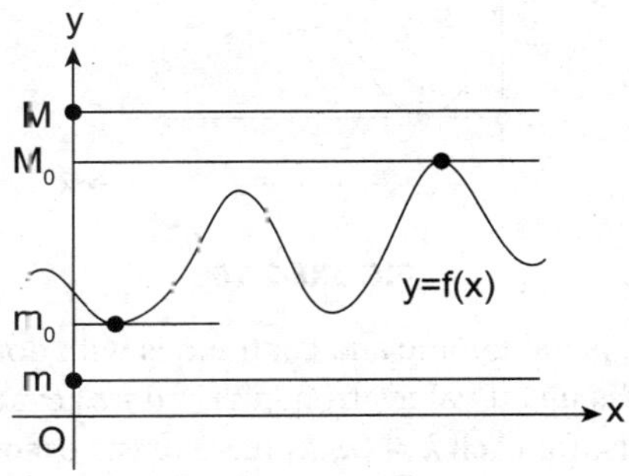

FIGURE 2.105

Conclusion

1. Least upper bound may or may not be the maximum value of function.
2. Maximum value of function if exists is the least upper bound of function.
3. Every real number greater than the least upper bound will be an upper bound of $f(x)$.
4. Every bounded function has its least upper bound but function may or may not attain it at any real number. If it attains its least upper bound, then the least upper bound will be the maximum value of function.
5. If the range of a function is (a, b) or $[a, b]$, then the least upper bound of $f(x)$ will be b. Maximum value of $f(x)$ does not exist in former case whereas maximum value of $f(x) = b$ in later case.

Intermediate Value Theorem

Every continuous and bounded function attains every real number between its bounds. That is, if a function is continuous in its domain and *g.l.b.* = a and *l.u.b.* = b, then $f(x)$ must take up all real values between a and b. That is, there exists atleast one $\alpha \in D_f$ where $f(\alpha) = k \ \forall \ k \in (a, b)$.

$\Rightarrow$ Range of

$$f(x) = \begin{cases} [a,b]; \text{ if function also attains values } a \text{ and } b. \\ (a,b); \text{ if function does not attain values} \\ a \text{ and } b. \\ [a,b); \text{ if function attains value } a \text{ but does} \\ \text{not attain } b \\ (a,b]; \text{ if function attains value } b \text{ but does} \\ \text{not attain } a. \end{cases}$$

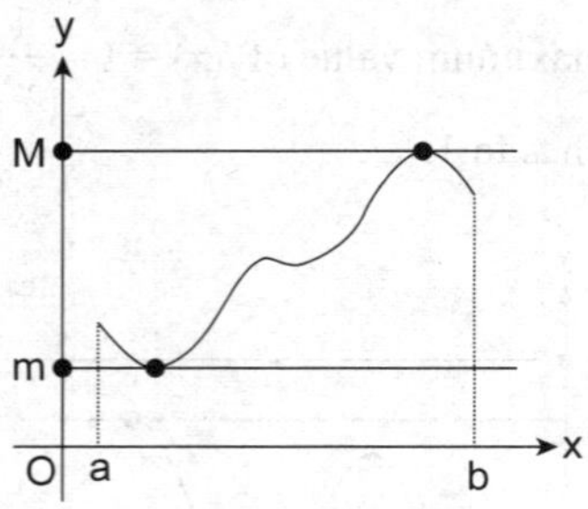

FIGURE 2.106

If $f(x)$ is monotonic and continuous with domain $[a, b]$, then it takes up all values from $f(a)$ and $f(b)$ exactly once.

That is, for each $k \in [a, b]$ there exists exactly one $\alpha \in D_f$ where $f(\alpha) = k$.

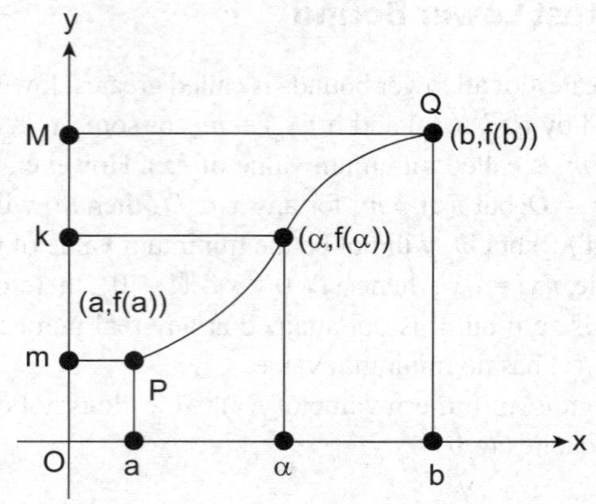

FIGURE 2.107

ILLUSTRATION 133: State whether the following statements are true or false.

(a) A function is called unbounded if at least one of its *g.l.b.* and *l.u.b.* does not exist.

(b) A function is called bounded when it is bounded from both above and below.

(c) A function may be bounded even if its *l.u.b.* and *g.l.b.* both do not exist.

(d) A function may not have its minimum value equal to its *g.l.b.*

SOLUTION: (a) True (b) True

(c) False (d) True

■ DEFINITION OF RANGE

Let f be a function from X to Y, then the range of function $= R_f = \{f(x) : x \in X\}$

Range of function $y = f(x)$ is defined as set of values of y for which x is real and finite $\forall\ x \in D_f$. It is denoted as R_f

Range is also called domain of variation and it is always a subset of co-domain (Y).

REMARK

So far, we have already discussed tools used to find the range of function, i.e., laws of inequalities, wavy curve method, monotonicity of functions, bounded ness of functions, intermediate value theorem. Now we shall use all these tools to find the range of functions as discussed further.

Methods to Find Range of Functions

Given a function $f : X \rightarrow Y$, where $y = f(x)$

Method I:

Step 1: Find domain of $f(x)$ (say) $\alpha \le x \le \beta$

Step 2: Express x in terms of y using equation of function. i.e., $x = f^{-1}(y)$

Step 3: Apply the domain restriction, i.e., $\alpha \le x \le \beta$ $\Rightarrow \alpha \le f^{-1}(y) \le \beta$

Step 4: Find the set of all possible y satisfying the above inequality.

ILLUSTRATION 134: Find the range of function $y = \cos^{-1}(x^2 + 1)$.

SOLUTION: The domain of function $f(x) = \cos^{-1}(x^2 + 1)$ *is* {0}
Therefore range of function is {$f(0)$} i.e., {0}

Method II:

For composition of continuous functions.

Step 1: Identify the function as composite function of constituent functions f, g and h (say) $\phi(x) = h(f(g(x)))$.

Step 2: Test the monotonicity of f, g and h. Let $g(\uparrow$(increasing)), $f(\downarrow$ (decreasing)), $h(\downarrow$ (decreasing))

Step 3: Find domain of $h(f(g(x)))$, (say) $\alpha \le x \le \beta$.

Step 4: $\because\ \alpha \le x \le \beta$

$\Rightarrow\ g(\alpha) \le g(x) \le g(\beta)$

$\Rightarrow\ f(g(\alpha)) \ge f(g(x)) \ge f(g(\beta))$

$\Rightarrow\ h(f(g(\alpha))) \le h(f(g(x))) \le h(f(g(\beta)))$ .... (1)

Because composition of continuous functions is also continuous, therefore, by (1) and intermediate value theorem, range of function ϕ is given by $R_\phi = [h(f(g(\alpha))), h(f(g(\beta)))]$

ILLUSTRATION 135: Find the range of function $f(x) = \dfrac{x^2 - 4}{x^2 + 4}$.

SOLUTION: Given function is $f(x) = \dfrac{x^2 - 4}{x^2 + 4} = \dfrac{x^2 + 4 - 8}{x^2 + 4} = 1 - \dfrac{8}{x^2 + 4}$

Clearly domain of function $= D_f = \mathbb{R}$

$\Rightarrow\ -\infty < x < \infty\ \Rightarrow\ 0 \le x^2 < \infty\ \Rightarrow\ 4 \le x^2 + 4 < \infty$

$\Rightarrow\ 0 < \dfrac{1}{x^2 + 4} \le \dfrac{1}{4}\ \Rightarrow\ 0 < \dfrac{8}{x^2 + 4} \le 2\ \Rightarrow\ -2 \le \dfrac{-8}{x^2 + 4} < 0\ \Rightarrow\ -1 \le 1 - \dfrac{8}{x^2 + 4} < 1$

$\Rightarrow\ f(x) \in [-1, 1)$ $\Rightarrow$ Range of function is $R_f = [-1, 1)$

ILLUSTRATION 136: Find the range of the following functions:

(i) $f(x) = \sqrt{\sin x}$ (ii) $f(x) = 3^{\sin^{-1} x}$

SOLUTION: (i) $f(x) = \sqrt{\sin x}$

For domain of function $\sin x \ge 0$, but $-1 \le \sin x \le 1$, therefore we must have $0 \le \sin x \le 1$

$\Rightarrow\ 0 \le \sqrt{\sin x} \le 1\ \Rightarrow\ f(x) \in [0, 1]$ $\therefore$ Range of $f(x) = [0, 1]$

(ii) $f(x) = 3^{\sin^{-1} x}$

For domain of function $x \in [-1, 1]$ $\Rightarrow\ -\dfrac{\pi}{2} \le \sin^{-1} x \le \dfrac{\pi}{2}$,

$\Rightarrow\ 3^{-\pi/2} \le 3^{\sin^{-1} x} \le 3^{\pi/2}$; $(\because\ a \le x \le b \Rightarrow 3^a \le 3^x \le 3^b)$

$\Rightarrow\ 3^{-\pi/2} \le f(x) \le 3^{\pi/2}$ $\therefore$ Range of $f(x) = [3^{-\pi/2}, 3^{\pi/2}]$

Some Remarks and Tips to find the Range of Functions:

1. If domain is a set having only finite number of points, then the range will be the set of corresponding values of $f(x)$.
2. If domain of $y = f(x)$ is $\mathbb{R}$ or $\mathbb{R}$ –{some finite points} or an infinite interval, then with the help of given relation, express x in terms of y and from there find the values of y for which x is defined and belongs to the domain of the function $f(x)$. The set of corresponding values of y constitute the range of function.

ILLUSTRATION 137: To find the range of $y=\dfrac{x^2-9}{x^2+9}$

SOLUTION: $\because$ Domain is $\mathbb{R}$ consider the equation $y=\dfrac{x^2-9}{x^2+9}$ $\Rightarrow$ $yx^2 + 9y = x^2 - 9$

$\Rightarrow$ $x^2=\dfrac{9(y+1)}{1-y}$ $\Rightarrow$ $x=\pm 3\sqrt{\dfrac{y+1}{1-y}}$

Thus, for x to be real $\dfrac{y+1}{1-y}\geq 0$ and $y \neq 1 \Rightarrow (y+1)(y-1) \leq 0$ and $y \neq 1$

$\Rightarrow$ $y \in [-1, 1)$. Therefore range of function = $[-1, 1)$

3. If a function is continuous, then find the least (l) and the greatest (g) values of $f(x)$ using monotonicity. Then the range of function will be $[l, g]$.

4. For the quadratic function $f(x) = ax^2 + bx + c$, domain is $\mathbb{R}$ and range is given by $R_f=\begin{cases}\left[-\dfrac{D}{4a},\infty\right) & \text{for } a>0\\ \left(-\infty,\dfrac{-D}{4a}\right] & \text{for } a<0\end{cases}$

5. For the quadratic function $f(x)=\sqrt{ax^2+bx+c}$ domain is given by $D_f=\begin{Bmatrix}\mathbb{R} \text{ for } a>0, D<0\\ \phi \text{ for } a<0, D<0\end{Bmatrix}$ and range is given by

$$R_f=\begin{cases}[0,\infty) & \text{for } D\geq 0, a>0\\ \left[\sqrt{\dfrac{-D}{4a}},\infty\right) & \text{for } D<0, a>0\\ \left[0,\sqrt{\dfrac{-D}{4a}}\right] & \text{for } D\geq 0, a<0\\ \phi & \text{for } D<0, a<0\end{cases}$$

6. For odd degree polynomial, domain and range both are $\mathbb{R}$.

7. For even degree polynomial domain is $\mathbb{R}$ and range is given by $[k, \infty)$ if the leading coefficient is positive, where k is the minimum value of polynomial occurring at one of the points of local minima, whereas range is $(-\infty, k]$ if the leading coefficient is negative where k is maximum value of polynomial occurring at one of the points of local maxima.

8. For $\dfrac{\text{Quadratic}}{\text{Quadratic}}$ or $\dfrac{\text{Linear}}{\text{Quadratic}}$ or $\dfrac{\text{Quadratic}}{\text{Linear}}$ expression, put $y=\dfrac{P(x)}{Q(x)}$;. Cross multiply, convert into a quadratic and use the knowledge of quadratic equations.

ILLUSTRATION 138: To find the range of the function : $f(x)=\dfrac{x^2-3x+4}{x^2+3x+4}$.

SOLUTION: $y=\dfrac{x^2-3x+4}{x^2+3x+4}$. Since, denominator could not be zero, therefore domain of above function is a set of real number, hence, by cross multiplying, we get $y(x^2 + 3x + 4) = (x^2 - 3x + 4)$.

$\Rightarrow (y-1)x^2 + 3(y+1)x + 4(y-1) = 0$ (is quadratic with real roots)

$\Rightarrow D \geq 0$ $\Rightarrow 9(y+1)^2 - 16(y-1)^2 \geq 0$

$\Rightarrow (7y-1)(7-y) \geq 0$ $\Rightarrow (7y-1)(y-7) \leq 0$ $\Rightarrow y \in [1/7, 7]$

9. For discontinuous functions, only method is to draw the graph and find the range known as graphical method of finding out range.

10. While determining domain and range of the functions involving trigonometric functions we need to keep in mind the following useful results.
   (i) General solution of equation $\sin\theta = k \in [-1, 1]$ is given by $\theta = n\pi + (-1)^n\alpha$; $\alpha = \sin^{-1}k$; $n \in \mathbb{Z}$
   (ii) General solution of equation $\cos\theta = k \in [-1, 1]$ is given by $\theta = 2n\pi \pm \alpha$; $\alpha = \cos^{-1}k$; $n \in \mathbb{Z}$
   (iii) General solution of equation $\tan\theta = k \in \mathbb{R}$ is given by $\theta = n\pi + \alpha$; $\alpha = \tan^{-1}k$; $n \in \mathbb{Z}$
   (iv) General solution of equation $\sin\theta = \sin\alpha$ is given by $\theta = n\pi + (-1)^n\alpha$; $n \in \mathbb{Z}$
   (v) General solution of equation $\cos\theta = \cos\alpha$ is given by $\theta = 2n\pi \pm \alpha$; $n \in \mathbb{Z}$
   (vi) General solution of equation $\tan\theta = \tan\alpha$ is given by $\theta = n\pi + \alpha$; $n \in \mathbb{Z}$
   (vii) $\sin\theta$, $\cos\theta$, $\sec\theta$, $\csc\theta$ are periodic functions with period 2π, whereas $\tan\theta$ and $\cot\theta$ are periodic functions with period π.
   (viii) (a) General solution of inequality of the form $\sin\theta \geq k$; $1 \geq k \geq 0$ is given by

$$\theta \in \bigcup_{n\in\mathbb{Z}}[2n\pi+\alpha,(2n+1)\pi-\alpha];\ \alpha = \sin^{-1}k$$

General solution of inequality of the form $\sin\theta \geq k$; $-1 \leq k < 0$ is given by

$$\theta \in \bigcup_{n\in\mathbb{Z}}[(2n\pi-\alpha),(2n+1)\pi+\alpha];\ \alpha = \sin^{-1}|k|$$

General solution of inequality of the form $\sin\theta \leq k$; $1 \geq k \geq 0$ is given by

$$\theta \in \bigcup_{n\in\mathbb{Z}}\{[2n\pi,2n\pi+\alpha]\cup[(2n+1)\pi-\alpha,(2n+2)\pi]\};$$

$\alpha = \sin^{-1}(k)$

General solution of inequality of the form $\sin\theta \leq k$; $-1 \leq k < 0$ is given by

$$\theta \in \bigcup_{n\in\mathbb{Z}}[(2n+1)\pi+\alpha,(2n+2)\pi-\alpha];\ \alpha = \sin^{-1}|k|$$

(b) General solution of inequality of the form $\cos\theta \geq k$; $1 \geq k \geq 0$ is given by

$$\theta \in \bigcup_{n\in\mathbb{Z}}[2n\pi-\alpha,2n\pi+\alpha];\ \alpha = \cos^{-1}(k)$$

General solution of inequality of the form $\cos\theta \geq k$; $-1 \leq k < 0$ is given by

$$\theta \in \bigcup_{n\in\mathbb{Z}}\left\{\begin{matrix}\left[2n\pi-\frac{\pi}{2},\alpha\right]\cup\\ \left[(2n+2)\pi-\alpha,(2n+2)\pi-\frac{\pi}{2}\right]\end{matrix}\right\};\ \alpha = \cos^{-1}(k)$$

General solution of inequality of the form $\cos\theta \leq k$; $1 \geq k \geq 0$ is given by

$$\theta \in \bigcup_{n\in\mathbb{Z}}\left\{\begin{matrix}\left[2n\pi-\frac{\pi}{2},2n\pi-\alpha\right]\cup\\ \left[2n\pi+\alpha,(2n+2)\pi-\frac{\pi}{2}\right]\end{matrix}\right\};\ \alpha = \cos^{-1}(k)$$

General solution of inequality of the form $\cos\theta \leq k$; $-1 \leq k < 0$ is given by

$$\theta \in \bigcup_{n\in\mathbb{Z}}[2n\pi+\alpha,(2n+2)\pi-\alpha];\ \alpha = \cos^{-1}(k)$$

(c) General solution of inequality of the form $\tan\theta \geq k$; $k \in \mathbb{R}$ is given by

$$\theta \in \bigcup_{n\in\mathbb{Z}}\left[2n\pi+\tan^{-1}(k),2n\pi+\frac{\pi}{2}\right)$$

General solution of inequality of the form $\tan\theta \leq k$; $k \in \mathbb{R}$ is given by

$$\theta \in \bigcup_{n\in\mathbb{Z}}\left(2n\pi-\frac{\pi}{2},2n\pi+\tan^{-1}k\right]$$

(d) General solution of inequality of the form $\cot\theta \geq k$; $k \in \mathbb{R}$ is given by

$$\theta \in \bigcup_{n\in\mathbb{Z}}(2n\pi,2n\pi+\cot^{-1}(k)]$$

General solution of inequality of the form $\cot\theta \leq k$; $k \in \mathbb{R}$ is given by

$$\theta \in \bigcup_{n\in\mathbb{Z}}[2n\pi+\cot^{-1}k,(2n+1)\pi)$$

11. Range of function $f(x) = a\sin x + b\cos x$ is $\left[-\sqrt{a^2+b^2},\sqrt{a^2-b^2}\right]$

12. Graphs of inverse circular functions and their corresponding domain and range.
   (a) Graph of $\sin^{-1}x$; Domain = $[-1, 1]$; Range = $\left[-\frac{\pi}{2},\frac{\pi}{2}\right]$

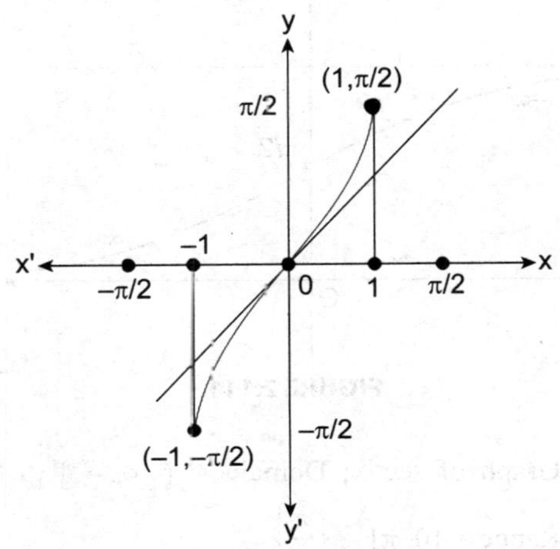

FIGURE 2.108

(b) Graph of $\cos^{-1}x$; Domain = [–1, 1]; Range = $[0, \pi]$

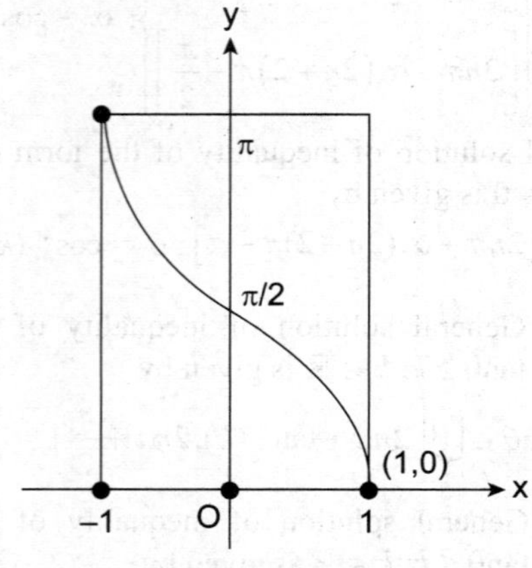

FIGURE 2.109

(c) Graph of $\tan^{-1}x$; Domain = ℝ; Range = $\left(-\dfrac{\pi}{2}, \dfrac{\pi}{2}\right)$

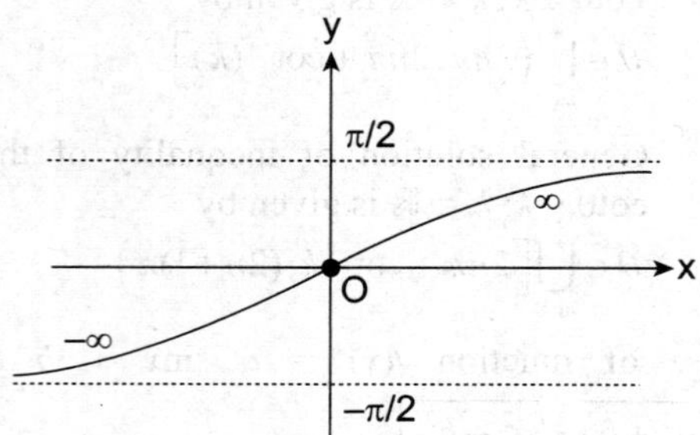

FIGURE 2.110

(d) Graph of $\cot^{-1}x$; Domain = ℝ; Range = $(0, \pi)$

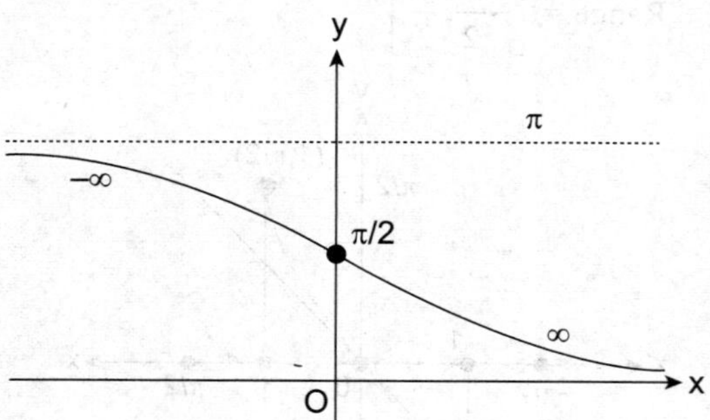

FIGURE 2.111

(e) Graph of $\sec^{-1}x$; Domain = $(-\infty, -1] \cup [1, \infty)$;

Range = $[0, \pi] \sim \left\{\dfrac{\pi}{2}\right\}$

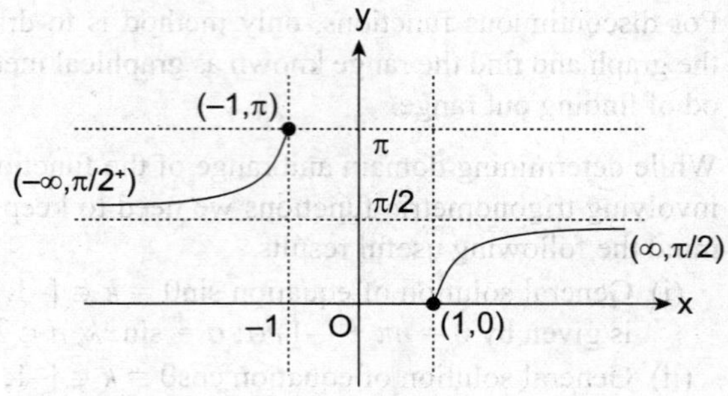

FIGURE 2.112

(f) Graph of $\operatorname{cosec}^{-1}x$; Domain = $(-\infty, -1] \cup [1, \infty)$;

Range = $\left[-\dfrac{\pi}{2}, \dfrac{\pi}{2}\right] \sim \{0\}$

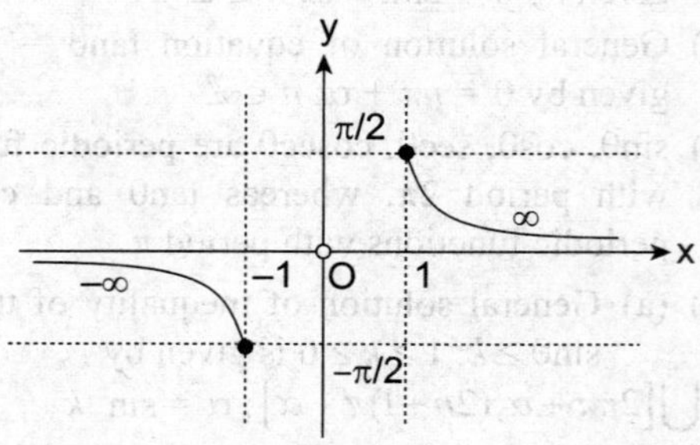

FIGURE 2.113

13. Three important identities of inverse trigonometric functions are given below

(a) $\sin^{-1}x + \cos^{-1}x = \dfrac{\pi}{2}$ (b) $\tan^{-1}x + \cot^{-1}x = \dfrac{\pi}{2}$

(c) $\sec^{-1}x + \operatorname{cosec}^{-1}x = \dfrac{\pi}{2}$

Range of Some Standard Functions:

f(x)	Range : R_f	*f(x)*	Range : R_f
Polynomial $P(x)$ of odd degree	ℝ	$\cot x$	ℝ
a^x	$(0, \infty)$	$\sec x$	$(-\infty, -1] \cup [1, \infty)$
$\log x$	ℝ	$\operatorname{cosec} x$	$(-\infty, -1] \cup [1, \infty)$
$\|x\|$	$[0, \infty)$	$\sin^{-1} x$	$[-\pi/2, \pi/2]$
$[x]$	ℤ	$\cos^{-1}x$	$[0, \pi]$
$\{x\}$	$[0, 1)$	$\tan^{-1} x$	$(-\pi/2, \pi/2)$
$\sin x$	$[-1,1]$	$\cot^{-1} x$	$(0, \pi)$
$\cos x$	$[-1,1]$	$\sec^{-1} x$	$[0, \pi] - \{\pi/2\}$
$\tan x$	ℝ	$\operatorname{cosec}^{-1} x$	$[-\pi/2, \pi/2] - \{0\}$
$\operatorname{sgn} x$	$\{-1, 0, 1\}$		

ILLUSTRATION 139: Find the range of the following functions:

(a) $y=\left(\dfrac{1}{2-\sin 3x}\right)$ (b) $y = \ln(3x^2 - 4x + 5)$

SOLUTION: (a) Given $y=\left(\dfrac{1}{2-\sin 3x}\right)$; Domain is $(-\infty, \infty)$, as $2 > \sin 3x\ \forall\ x \in \mathbb{R}$

$\Rightarrow \dfrac{1}{y}=2-\sin 3x$ $\Rightarrow \sin 3x = 2-\dfrac{1}{y}$

Since $-1 \le \sin 3x \le 1$ $\Rightarrow -1 \le 2-\dfrac{1}{y} \le 1$

$\Rightarrow -3 \le -\dfrac{1}{y} \le -1$ $\Rightarrow y \in (-\infty, 0] \cup [1/3, \infty)$ and $y \in (0, 1]$ $\Rightarrow y \in \left[\dfrac{1}{3}, 1\right]$

Hence, range is $[1/3, 1]$

(b) Given $y=\ln(3x^2-4x+5)$. For y to be defined $3x^2 - 4x + 5 > 0$

$\Rightarrow x^2-\dfrac{4}{3}x+\dfrac{5}{3}>0$ $\Rightarrow \left(x-\dfrac{2}{3}\right)^2+\dfrac{11}{9}>0$; which is true for all x

$\therefore$ Domain is $(-\infty, \infty)$. We have to find out the maximum and minimum value of y.

y is minimum, when $3x^2 - 4x + 5$ is minimum and maximum when it is $3x^2 - 4x + 5$ as $\ln x$ is an increasing function.

Now, $(3x^2 - 4x + 5)$, min $=\dfrac{11}{3}$ (when $x = 2/3$) $\Rightarrow y_{min} = \ln\dfrac{11}{3}$

For $y_{max} = (3x^2 - 4x + 5)_{max} = \infty$ $\Rightarrow y_{max} = \infty$

Hence, range $= [\ln (11/3), \infty)$.

ILLUSTRATION 140: Find the range of the values of x for which the following functions are defined:

(a) $f(x)=\sqrt{\log_{1/2}\left(\dfrac{5x-x^2}{4}\right)}$ (b) $f(x) = \log_4 \log_2 \log_{1/2}(x)$

SOLUTION: (a) y is defined if $\dfrac{5x-x^2}{4}>0 \Rightarrow$ $5x - x^2 > 0$ $\Rightarrow$ $0<x<5$ ...(i)

$\Rightarrow x \in (0, 5)$ and $\log_{1/2}\left(\dfrac{5x-x^2}{4}\right)\ge 0$ $\Rightarrow \dfrac{5x-x^2}{4}\le\left(\dfrac{1}{2}\right)^0$ $\Rightarrow x^2 - 5x + 4 \ge 0$

$\Rightarrow x \le 1$ or $x \ge 4$ ...(ii)

From (i) and (ii), we get $x \in (0, 1] \cup [4, 5)$

(b) y is defined if $\log_2 \log_{1/2}(x) > 0$ $\Rightarrow \log_{1/2}(x) > 2^0$

$\Rightarrow \log_{1/2}(x) > 1$ $\Rightarrow x < 1/2$

$\Rightarrow$ Domain $= (0, 1/2)$.

ILLUSTRATION 141: Find the domain and range of function $f(x)=\sin^{-1}x^2+\left[\left\{\ell n\sqrt{x-[x]}\right\}\right]+\cot^{-1}\left(\dfrac{1}{1+\sqrt{2x^2}}\right)$.

SOLUTION: Domain of function is $(-1, 1) - \{0\}$, because $x - [x] = 0$ for integral value of x, hence, middle term will not be defined. Also $[\{f\}] = 0$, whenever f is meaningful.

$\therefore$ Value of $f(x) = \sin^{-1} x^2 + \tan^{-1}(1 +\sqrt{2}\, x^2)$ $\left(\cot^{-1}x=\tan^{-1}\dfrac{1}{x} \text{ when } x>0\right)$

Function is continuous and is even for $x \in (-1, 1) - \{0\}$. Also $f(x)$ is ↓ an $(-1, 0)$ and ↑ on $(0, 1)$

$\therefore$ Least value of the function will occur when $x \to 0$ and is $\frac{\pi}{4}$

And maximum value = $\lim_{x\to\pm1} f(x) = \sin^{-1}1 + \tan^{-1}(1+\sqrt{2}) = \frac{\pi}{2} + \frac{3\pi}{8} = \frac{7\pi}{8}$

$\therefore$ Range of $f(x)$ is $\left(\frac{\pi}{4}, \frac{7\pi}{8}\right)$; Domain is $(-1, 1) - \{0\}$.

ILLUSTRATION 142: Find the range of $f(x) = \sqrt{\left(\frac{x-1}{2-x}\right)}$

SOLUTION: $y = \sqrt{\frac{x-1}{2-x}}$ the domain of function is $[1, 2)$

If $y = f(g(x))$ where $f(x) = \sqrt{x}$ (increasing (↑) function $\forall\ x \in [0, \infty)$)

And $g(x) = \frac{x-1}{2-x}$ (increasing (↑) function $\forall\ x \in [1, 2)$)

Now $1 \le x < 2$ $\Rightarrow g(1) \le g(x) < g(2)$ as $g(x)$ is increasing (↑)

$\Rightarrow 0 \le g(x) < \infty$ applying f

$\Rightarrow f(0) \le f(g(x)) < f(\infty)$ $\Rightarrow 0 \le \sqrt{\frac{x-1}{2-x}} < \infty$ $\Rightarrow y \in [0, \infty)$

Aliter: $y_1 = -\left(\frac{1-x}{2-x}\right) = -1 + \frac{1}{2-x}$

$\because 1 \le x < 2$ $\Rightarrow -2 \le -x \le -1$ $\Rightarrow 0 < 2 - x \le 1$

$\Rightarrow 1 \le \frac{1}{2-x} < \infty$ $\Rightarrow 0 \le -1 + \frac{1}{2-x} < \infty$ $\Rightarrow y_1 \in [0, \infty)$

$\Rightarrow y \in \sqrt{y_1} \in [0, \infty)$

ILLUSTRATION 143: Find the domain and range of the following functions:

(i) $f(x) = 3 - 4\sin x$ (ii) $f(x) = \frac{1}{2 - 5\sin x}$

(iii) $f(x) = \frac{1}{\sqrt{\sqrt{3} - \tan x}}$ (iv) $f(x) = \sqrt{2\sin x - 1}$

SOLUTION: (i) $f(x) = 3 - 4\sin x$ is defined for all those real values of x for which $\sin x$ is defined

$\Rightarrow$ Domain of function = $\mathbb{R} = (-\infty, \infty)$

Also $-1 \le \sin x \le 1$

$\Rightarrow -4 \le -4\sin x \le 4$ $\Rightarrow y\ -1 \le 3 - 4\sin x \le 7$

$\Rightarrow$ Range of $f(x) = [-1, 7]$

(ii) $f(x) = \frac{1}{2 - 5\sin x}$

For $f(x)$ to be defined $\sin x \ne \frac{2}{5}$. From the graph of $\sin x$ given below we conclude that $\sin x \ne \frac{2}{5}$

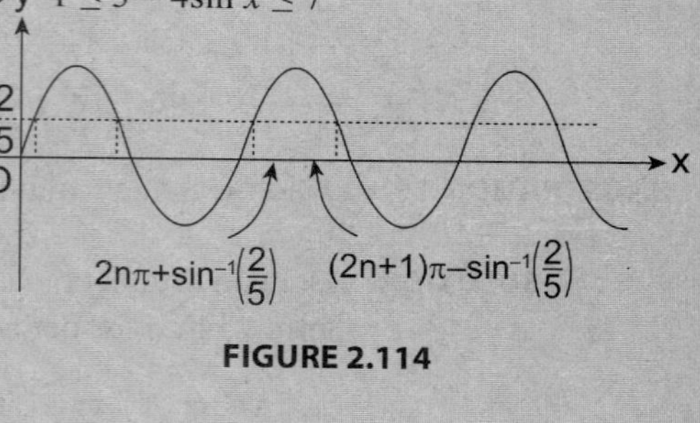

FIGURE 2.114

$\Rightarrow \quad x \neq 2n\pi + \sin^{-1}\left(\frac{2}{5}\right),\ (2n+1)\pi - \sin^{-1}\left(\frac{2}{5}\right); n \in \mathbb{Z}$

$\therefore \quad$ Domain $= \mathbb{R} \sim \left\{2n\pi + \sin^{-1}\left(\frac{2}{5}\right), (2n+1)\pi - \sin^{-1}\left(\frac{2}{5}\right); n \in \mathbb{Z}\right\}$

Clearly $-1 \le \sin x \le 1$ $\quad \Rightarrow -5 \le -5\sin x \le 5$

$\Rightarrow \quad -3 \le 2 - 5\sin x \le 7$

But $\sin x \neq \frac{2}{5}$ $\quad \Rightarrow 2 - 5\sin x \in [-3, 7] \sim \{0\}$

$\Rightarrow \quad \frac{1}{2-5\sin x} \in \left(-\infty, -\frac{1}{3}\right] \cup \left[\frac{1}{7}, \infty\right)$ $\quad \therefore$ Range $= \left(-\infty, -\frac{1}{3}\right] \cup \left[\frac{1}{7}, \infty\right)$

(iii) $f(x) = \frac{1}{\sqrt{\sqrt{3} - \tan x}}$

For $f(x)$ to be defined $\sqrt{3} - \tan x > 0$, i.e., $\tan x < \sqrt{3}$

From the graph of tan x given below

Since tan x is periodic with period π

Thus, $\tan x < \sqrt{3}$ for $x \in \left(n\pi - \frac{\pi}{2}, n\pi + \frac{\pi}{3}\right); n \in \mathbb{Z}$

Thus, domain of $f(x) = \bigcup_{n\in\mathbb{Z}} \left(n\pi - \frac{\pi}{2}, n\pi + \frac{\pi}{3}\right) = D_f$

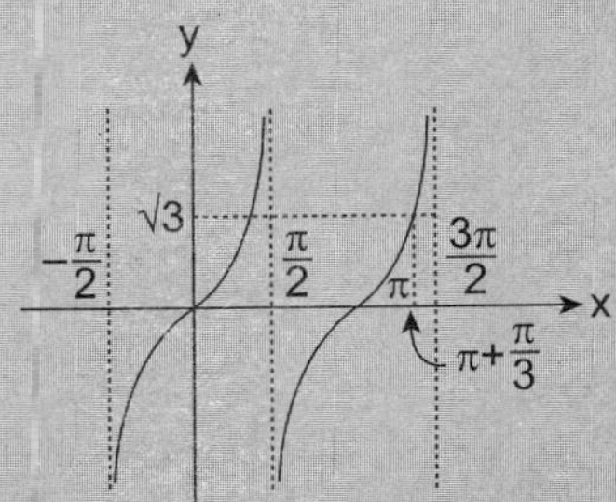

FIGURE 2.115

Also $0 < \sqrt{3} - \tan x < \infty$ for $x \in \left(n\pi - \frac{\pi}{2}, n\pi + \frac{\pi}{3}\right)$ for each $n \in \mathbb{Z}$ and $\sqrt{3} - \tan x$ is continuous function on $\left(n\pi - \frac{\pi}{2}, n\pi + \frac{\pi}{3}\right)$ for each $n \in \mathbb{Z}$

$\Rightarrow \quad (\sqrt{3} - \tan x) \in (0, \infty)$ $\quad \Rightarrow \sqrt{\sqrt{3} - \tan x} \in (0, \infty)$

$\Rightarrow \quad \frac{1}{\sqrt{\sqrt{3} - \tan x}} \in (0, \infty)$ $\quad \Rightarrow$ Range of $f(x) = (0, \infty)$

(iv) $f(x) = \sqrt{2\sin x - 1}$

For $f(x)$ to be defined $2\sin x - 1 \ge 0$ $\quad \Rightarrow \sin x \ge \frac{1}{2}$

In $[0, 2\pi]$, $\sin x \ge \frac{1}{2}$, for $x \in \left[\frac{\pi}{6}, \pi - \frac{\pi}{6}\right]$. As sin x is periodic function with period 2π

$\therefore \quad$ Domain of $f(x) = \bigcup_{n\in\mathbb{Z}} \left(2n\pi + \frac{\pi}{6}, (2n+1)\pi - \frac{\pi}{6}\right)$

Also $\frac{1}{2} \le \sin x \le 1$ $\quad \Rightarrow 1 \le 2\sin x \le 2$

$\Rightarrow \quad 0 \le 2\sin x - 1 \le 1$

$\Rightarrow \quad 0 \le \sqrt{2\sin x - 1} \le 1$ $\quad \therefore$ Range of $f(x) = [0, 1]$

ILLUSTRATION 144: Find the domain and range of the following functions

(i) $f(x) = x^2 - 6x + 10$ $\quad$ (ii) $f(x) = x^2 - 8x + 10$

(iii) $f(x) = 3x^7 - 4x^2 + 7$ $\quad$ (iv) $f(x) = 3x^4 + 8x^3 - 6x^2 - 24x + 7$

SOLUTION: (i) $f(x)$ being a polynomial function, has domain = $\mathbb{R}$ = $(-\infty, \infty)$

Now $f(x) = x^2 - 6x + 10 = x^2 - 6x + 9 + 1$

$= (x-3)^2 + 1 \geq 1 \ \forall \ x \in \mathbb{R}$

Also $f(x)$ being a polynomial function is a continuous function and as x tends to infinity, $f(x) = x^2\left(1 - \frac{6}{x} + \frac{10}{x^2}\right)$ tends to $(\infty)^2(1 - 0 + 0) = \infty$, thus, $f(x)$ would attain each and every real number from 1 onwards (intermediate value theorem).

Thus, range of $f(x) = [1, \infty)$

(ii) $f(x) = x^2 - 8x + 10$

Clearly domain = $\mathbb{R}$ and $f(x) = x^2 - 8x + 10 = x^2 - 8x + 16 - 16 + 10 = (x-4)^2 - 6 \geq -6$

$\therefore$ Range of $f(x) = [-6, \infty)$

Alternatively by theory of quadratic equations we know that range of a quadratic polynomial is given by $\left[\frac{-D}{4a}, \infty\right) = \left[\frac{-(64-40)}{4}, \infty\right) = [-6, \infty)$

(iii) $f(x) = 3x^7 - 4x^2 + 7$

Domain = $\mathbb{R}$

Also $f(x)$ being an odd degree polynomial, has its range $\mathbb{R}$, as $f(x)$ is continuous having minimum and maximum values approaching to $-\infty$ and ∞, respectively.

(iv) $f(x) = 3x^4 + 8x^3 - 6x^2 - 24x + 7$

Clearly domain = $\mathbb{R}$ and $x \to \pm\infty$, $f(x) \to \infty$.

The minimum value of $f(x)$, would exist at one of the stationary points (where $f'(x) = 0$)

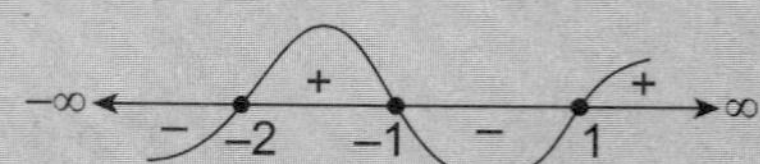

FIGURE 2.116

Now, $f'(x) = 12x^3 + 24x^2 - 12x - 24 = 12(x-1)(x+1)(x+2)$

$\therefore$ $f'(x) = 0$ $\Rightarrow x = -1, 1, -2$

By sign scheme,

$\therefore$ $f(x)$ is decreasing on interval $(-\infty, -2)$, $(-1, 1)$ and increasing on intervals $(-2, -1)$ and $(1, \infty)$

Thus, the graph of $f(x)$ would be of the form as shown below.

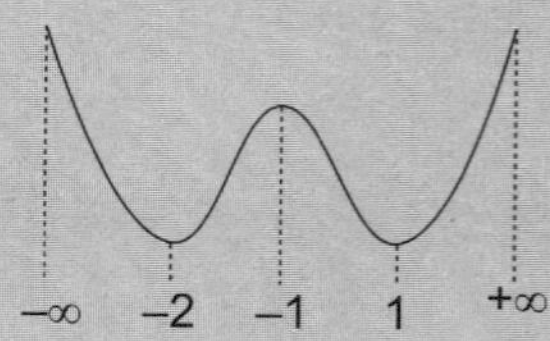

FIGURE 2.117

Thus, $f(x)$ has its minimum value at $x = -2$ or at $x = 1$

Now $f(-2) = 3(-2)^4 + 8(-2)^3 - 6(-2)^2 - 24(-2) + 7 = 15$

And $f(1) = 3(1)^4 + 8(1)^3 - 6(1)^2 - 24(1) + 7 = -12 \Rightarrow$ Range of $f(x)$ will be $= [-12, \infty)$

ILLUSTRATION 145: If $[2 \cos x] + [\sin x] = -3$, then find the range of the function, $f(x) = \sin x + \sqrt{3} \cos x$ in $[0, 2\pi]$. (where [.] denotes greatest integer function)

SOLUTION: $[2 \cos x] + [\sin x] = -3$

Now, $-2 \leq 2\cos x \leq 2 \Rightarrow [2 \cos x] \in \{-2, -1, 0, 1, 2\}$ and $-1 \leq \sin x \leq 1 \Rightarrow [\sin x] \in \{-1, 0, 1\}$

Now, equation holds true for $[2 \cos x] = -2$ and $[\sin x] = -1$

$\Rightarrow \ -1 \leq \cos x < -\frac{1}{2}$ and $-1 \leq \sin x < 0 \ \Rightarrow \ x \in \left(\frac{2\pi}{3}, \frac{4\pi}{3}\right)$ and $x \in (\pi, 2\pi) \Rightarrow \ x \in \left(\pi, \frac{4\pi}{3}\right)$

$\Rightarrow f(x) = \sin x + \sqrt{3}\cos x$

$\Rightarrow \quad f(x) = 2\sin\left(x+\frac{\pi}{3}\right)$

Now, $\frac{4\pi}{3} < x+\frac{\pi}{3} < \frac{5\pi}{3}$

$\Rightarrow \quad -1 \le \sin\left(x+\frac{\pi}{3}\right) < -\frac{\sqrt{3}}{2}$

$\Rightarrow \quad -2 \le 2\sin\left(x+\frac{\pi}{3}\right) < -\sqrt{3}$. Hence, range is $\left[-2,-\sqrt{3}\right)$

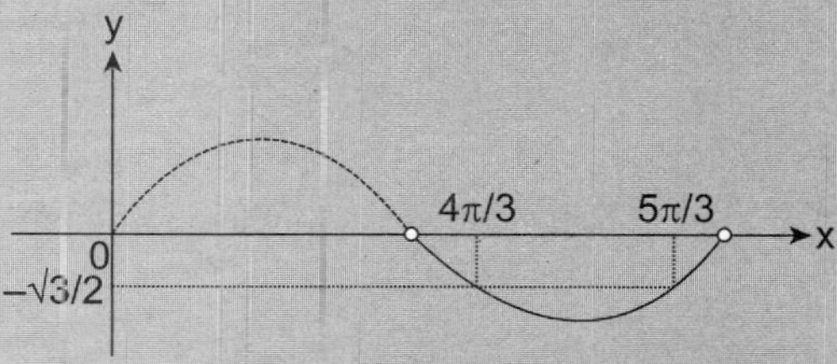

FIGURE 2.118

ILLUSTRATION 146: A function f is defined as $f(x) = x^3 - 5x^2 + 15x + \sin^{-1}\left(\frac{x}{2}\right)$, then $(f_{max.} - f_{min})$ is given by

(a) –40
(b) π – 40
(c) 76 + π
(d) None of these

SOLUTION: $f'(x) = \underbrace{3x^2 - 10x + 15}_{\substack{a>0\\D<0}} + \frac{1}{2}\frac{1}{\sqrt{1-\frac{x^2}{4}}} > 0$

$\Rightarrow f(x)$ is monotonically increasing in its domain [–2, 2]

$\therefore \quad f_{min} = f(-2) = -8 - 5(4) + 15(-2) + \left(-\frac{\pi}{2}\right) = -\left(58+\frac{\pi}{2}\right) = -\left(\frac{116+\pi}{2}\right)$

and $f_{max} = f(2) = 8 - 20 + 30 + \frac{\pi}{2} = 18+\frac{\pi}{2} = \frac{36+\pi}{2} \quad \Rightarrow f_{max} - f_{min} = 76 + \pi$

ILLUSTRATION 147: The range of $f(x) = |\sin x|^2 + 2|\sin x| - |\cos x|$ is given by

(a) [–1, 2]
(b) [–1, 1]
(c) [–1, 3]
(d) None of these

SOLUTION: $f(x)$ is periodic with period π

$$\Rightarrow \quad f(x) = \begin{cases} \sin^2 x + 2\sin x - \cos x; & \text{for } x \in \left[0,\frac{\pi}{2}\right] \\ \sin^2 x + 2\sin x + \cos x & \text{for } x \in \left[\frac{\pi}{2},\pi\right] \end{cases}$$

$\Rightarrow f(x)$ is increasing in the interval $[0, \pi/2]$ and decreasing in $\left[\frac{\pi}{2},\pi\right]$.

Thus, if $0 \le x \le \frac{\pi}{2}$ $\quad \Rightarrow f(0) \le f(x) \le f\left(\frac{\pi}{2}\right) \quad \Rightarrow \quad f(x) \in [-1,3]$

and if $\frac{\pi}{2} \le x \le \pi$ $\quad \Rightarrow f(\pi) \le f(x) \le f\left(\frac{\pi}{2}\right) \quad \Rightarrow \quad f(x) \in [-1,3]$

$\Rightarrow$ Range of f is [–1, 3]

ILLUSTRATION 148: Find the range of the expression $\frac{\tan^2\theta - 4\tan\theta - 2}{\tan^2\theta - 2\tan\theta - 5}$, for all permissible values of θ.

SOLUTION: Let $x = \tan\theta$, where $x \in \mathbb{R}$ for all permissible values of θ.

$\Rightarrow \quad y = \frac{x^2 - 4x - 2}{x^2 - 2x - 5} \quad \Rightarrow x^2y - 2xy - 5y = x^2 - 4x - 2$

$\Rightarrow (y-1)x^2 + 2x(2-y) + 2 - 5y = 0$ as $x \in \mathbb{R}$, hence, $D \geq 0$

$\Rightarrow 4(2-y)^2 - 4(y-1)(2-5y) \geq 0$ $\qquad \Rightarrow 4(4 + y^2 - 4y) - 4(-5y^2 + 7y - 2) \geq 0$

$\Rightarrow 24y^2 - 44y + 24 \geq 0$ $\qquad \Rightarrow 6y^2 - 11y + 6 \geq 0$ .... (1)

Since, coefficient of $y^2 > 0$ and $D = 121 - 144 < 0$

Hence, (1) is true for every real value of y. Therefore range of y is $(-\infty, \infty) = \mathbb{R}$.

ILLUSTRATION 149: Find the range of the function $f(\theta) = \dfrac{(\cot^2\theta + 3)(\cot^2\theta + 8)}{\cot^2\theta + 1}$ for all permissible values of θ.

SOLUTION: Let $x = \cot^2\theta + 1$; where $x \in [1, \infty)$ for all permissible values of θ.

Then $f(\theta) = \dfrac{(x+2)(x+7)}{x} = x + 9 + \dfrac{14}{x}$

$= \left(\sqrt{x}\right)^2 + \left(\sqrt{\dfrac{14}{x}}\right)^2 + 9 = \left(\sqrt{x}\right)^2 + \left(\sqrt{\dfrac{14}{x}}\right)^2 + 2\sqrt{14} + 9 - 2\sqrt{14} = \left(\sqrt{x} - \sqrt{\dfrac{14}{x}}\right)^2 + 9 + 2\sqrt{14}$

$\Rightarrow$ Range of $f(\theta) = \left[9 + 2\sqrt{14}, \infty\right)$.

ILLUSTRATION 150: Find the range of the following functions:

(i) $f(x) = \cos^{-1}\left(\dfrac{\sqrt{2x^2+1}}{x^2+1}\right)$ $\qquad$ (ii) $g(x) = \log_2(2 - \log_{\sqrt{2}}(4\cos^2 x + 1))$

SOLUTION: (i) Given $f(x) = \cos^{-1}\left(\dfrac{\sqrt{2x^2+1}}{x^2+1}\right)$

$= \sin^{-1}\left(\sqrt{1 - \dfrac{(2x^2+1)}{(x^2+1)^2}}\right) = \sin^{-1}\left(\sqrt{\dfrac{x^4}{(x^2+1)^2}}\right) = \sin^{-1}\left(\dfrac{x^2}{1+x^2}\right)$;

Now $\dfrac{x^2}{x^2+1} = 1 - \dfrac{1}{x^2+1}$ and $x^2 + 1 \geq 1$ $\Rightarrow \dfrac{1}{x^2+1} \in (0,1]$ $\Rightarrow 1 - \dfrac{1}{x^2+1} \in [0,1)$

$\Rightarrow 0 \leq \sin^{-1}\left(\dfrac{x^2}{x^2+1}\right) < \dfrac{\pi}{2}$ $\qquad \Rightarrow y \in \left[0, \dfrac{\pi}{2}\right) \Rightarrow$ The range of $f(x) = \left[0, \dfrac{\pi}{2}\right)$

(ii) Given $g(x) = \log_2(2 - \log_{\sqrt{2}}(4\cos^2 x + 1))$

Now for $g(x)$ to be well defined, $2 - \log_{\sqrt{2}}(4\cos^2 x + 1) > 0$ and $4\cos^2 x + 1 > 0$

The second inequality is true for all $x \in \mathbb{R}$.

$\Rightarrow$ $g(x)$ is well defined for $4\cos^2 x + 1 < 2$, i.e., $1 \leq 4\cos^2 x + 1 < 2$

$\Rightarrow 0 \leq \log_{\sqrt{2}}(4\cos^2 x + 1) < 2$ $\qquad \Rightarrow -2 < -\log_{\sqrt{2}}(4\cos^2 x + 1) \leq 0$

$\Rightarrow 0 < 2 - \log_{\sqrt{2}}(4\cos^2 x + 1) \leq 2$ $\qquad \Rightarrow -\infty < g(x) \leq \log_2 2$

$\Rightarrow g(x) \in (-\infty, 1]$ $\qquad \Rightarrow$ Range of $g(x)$ is $(-\infty, 1]$.

ILLUSTRATION 151: Find the range of the function $f(x) = \sin^{-1} x^4 + \left[\left\{\ln\sqrt{x - [x]}\right\}\right] + \cot^{-1}\left(\dfrac{1}{2 + \sqrt{3}x^2}\right)$; where {.} and [.] are fractional part function and greatest integer function, respectively.

SOLUTION: $\sin^{-1}x^4$ is defined for $x^4 \in [-1, 1]$ $\Rightarrow$ $x^4 \in [0, 1]$ $\Rightarrow$ $x \in [-1, 1]$

And $\cot^{-1}\left(\dfrac{1}{2 + \sqrt{3}x^2}\right)$ is defined $\forall\, x \in \mathbb{R}$, but $\ln\sqrt{x - [x]} = \ln\sqrt{\{x\}}$ is not defined for $\{x\} = 0$

i.e., $x = -1, 0, 1$ $\qquad \therefore$ Domain of given function is $(-1, 1) \sim \{0\}$

Now $\left[\left\{\ln\sqrt{x-[x]}\right\}\right]=0$, since $[\{k\}]=0$ whenever k is defined

$\therefore$ $f(x)=\sin^{-1}x^4+\cot^{-1}\left(\dfrac{1}{2+\sqrt{3}x^2}\right)$; $x\in(-1, 1)\sim\{0\}$

or $f(x)=\sin^{-1}x^4+\tan^{-1}\left(2+\sqrt{3}x^2\right)$ $\quad$ ($\because \cot^{-1}\dfrac{1}{x}=\tan^{-1}x$ for $x>0$)

Further $\sin^{-1}x^4$ and $\tan^{-1}(2+\sqrt{3}\,x^2)$ are even continuous and decreases for $x\in(-1, 0)$ and increasing for $x\in(0, 1)$.

Thus, $f(x)_{\min}\to f(0)=\sin^{-1}0+\tan^{-1}2=\tan^{-1}2$

and $f(x)_{\max}\to f(\pm 1)=\sin^{-1}1+\tan^{-1}(2+\sqrt{3})=\dfrac{\pi}{2}+\dfrac{5\pi}{12}=\dfrac{11\pi}{12}$

$\therefore$ The range of $f(x)$ is $\left(\tan^{-1}2, \dfrac{11\pi}{12}\right)$ or $\left(\tan^{-1}2, \tan^{-1}(2+\sqrt{3})\right)$

ILLUSTRATION 152: Find the range of the function $f(x)=\cos^{-1}\left(\dfrac{\sqrt{1+x^6}}{1+4x^{12}}\right)$.

SOLUTION: Clearly $\dfrac{\sqrt{1+x^6}}{1+4x^{12}}>0\ \forall\ x\in\mathbb{R}$ and as $x\to\pm\infty$, $\dfrac{\sqrt{1+x^6}}{1+4x^{12}}\to 0$ and $\dfrac{\sqrt{1+x^6}}{1+4x^{12}}=1$ for $x=0$

Also $\dfrac{\sqrt{1+x^6}}{1+4x^{12}}$ is continuous $\forall\ x\in\mathbb{R}$

$\therefore$ By extreme value theorem $\dfrac{\sqrt{1+x^6}}{1+4x^{12}}$ would attain each real number belonging to $(0, 1]$,

consequently, $f(x)=\cos^{-1}\left(\dfrac{\sqrt{1+x^6}}{1+4x^{12}}\right)$

$\therefore$ Range of $f(x)=\left[0, \dfrac{\pi}{2}\right)$

Note the function would not be defined for those values of x for which $\dfrac{\sqrt{1+x^6}}{1+4x^{12}}$ exceeds 1.

ILLUSTRATION 153: Find the domain and range of definition of the function $f(x)=\dfrac{1}{x^5-x^3+x^2-1}$

SOLUTION: Given function is $f(x)=\dfrac{1}{x^5-x^3+x^2-1}$

$$=\frac{1}{x^3(x^2-1)+1(x^2-1)}=\frac{1}{(x^2-1)(x^3+1)}=\frac{1}{(x^2-1)(x+1)(x^2-x+1)}$$

Therefore domain of $f(x)=\mathbb{R}\sim\{-1, 1\}$ as $x^2-x+1>0\ \forall\ x\in\mathbb{R}$

Also range of $x^5-x^3+x^2-1$ is $(-\infty, \infty)$, therefore range $=(-\infty, \infty)\sim\{0\}$

ILLUSTRATION 154: If $f(x)=\sin\ln\left(\dfrac{\sqrt{4-x^2}}{1-x}\right)$, then find the domain and range of $f(x)$

SOLUTION: $f(x)$ is defined for $\dfrac{\sqrt{4-x^2}}{1-x}>0 \Rightarrow 1-x>0;\ 4-x^2>0 \Rightarrow x<1;\ x^2<4 \Rightarrow x\in(-2, 1)$

Now, $f(x)=\sin\ln\left(\dfrac{\sqrt{4-x^2}}{1-x}\right)$

Let $y = \dfrac{\sqrt{4-x^2}}{1-x}$ (> 0 for $x \in (-2, 1)$); $g'(x) = \dfrac{4-x}{(1-x)^2} > 0\ \forall\ x \in (-2,1)$

$\Rightarrow$ $g(x)$ is an increasing function on $(-2, 1)$ $\Rightarrow$ $g(x) \in (0, \infty)$, also $\log_e x$ being increasing function, $\ln(g(x)) \in (-\infty, \infty)$

$\Rightarrow \sin\left(\ln\left(\dfrac{\sqrt{4-x^2}}{1-x}\right)\right)$ $\therefore$ Range of $f(x) = [-1, 1]$

$\therefore$ Domain of $f(x) = (-2, 1)$ and range $= [-1, 1]$

ILLUSTRATION 155: The domain and range of definition of the function $y(x)$ given by the equation $a^x + a^y = a (a > 1)$ is

(a) $0 < x \le 1$ (b) $0 \le x < 1$

(c) $-\infty < x < 1$ (d) $-\infty < x \le 0$

SOLUTION: Given $a^x + a^y = a$; $a > 1$ $\Rightarrow$ $a^y = a - a^x$

$\Rightarrow$ $y = \log_a(a - a^x)$ which is defined for $a - a^x > 0$ $\Rightarrow$ $a^x < a = a^1$

$\because$ $a > 1, x < 1$ $\Rightarrow$ $x \in (-\infty, 1)$

Similarly $y \in (-\infty, 1)$

$\therefore$ Domain as well as range of $y(x)$ is given by $(-\infty, 1)$

TEXTUAL EXERCISE–10: (SUBJECTIVE)

1. Find the domain of the following rational functions and find the maximum/minimum value and range of these functions:
   (a) $\sqrt{x^2+4}$ (b) $\dfrac{1}{(x-1)(x-5)}$
   (c) $\sqrt[3]{x+8}$ (d) $\dfrac{1}{x^2+4}$
2. $f(x) = {}^{x+1}C_{2x-8}$ and $g(x) = {}^{2x-8}C_{x+1}$ and $h(x) = f(x) \cdot g(x)$, then find the domain range of $h(x)$.
3. Find the range of definition of the following functions:
   (a) $f(x) = 4\tan x \cos x$ (b) $f(x) = \cos(2\sin x)$
   (c) $f(x) = \sin(\log_2 x)$
4. Find the range of definition of following functions.
   (a) $f(x) = [\{x\}]$ or $\{[x]\}$
   (b) $g(x) = \dfrac{\tan(\pi[x-\pi])}{x^2-3x+4}$
   (c) $f(x) = \cos 2x - \sin 2x$
   (d) $f(x) = \cot^2\left(x - \dfrac{\pi}{4}\right)$
5. Find the range of definition of following functions.
   (a) $f(x) = \sin^{-1}\left(\dfrac{x^2-1}{2(x^2+1)}\right)$
   (b) $f(x) = \cos^{-1}\left(\dfrac{2x}{1+x^2}\right)$
   (c) $f(x) = \cos^{-1}\left(\dfrac{1+x^2}{2x}\right)$
   (d) $f(x) = \tan^{-1}(1 + x^2)$
   (e) $f(x) = \log_2(3 + 5\sin x)$
   (f) $f(x) = \tan^{-1}\dfrac{2x}{1+x^2}$
6. Find the range of the following functions:
   (a) $f(x) = \ln(5x^2 - 8x + 4)$
   (b) $f(x) = \cot^{-1}(\log_{4/5}(5x^2 - 8x + 4))$
   (c) $f(x) = \cot^{-1}\log_{5/4}(5x^2 - 8x + 4)$
7. Find the range of the following functions:
   (a) $f(x) = \dfrac{x^2-x+1}{x^2+x+1}$ (b) $f(x) = \dfrac{x}{\ell n x}$
8. Find the domain and range of the function: $f(x) = \sin^{-1}[x^2] + \left[\left\{\ell n\sqrt{x-[x]}\right\}\right] + \cot^{-1}\left(\dfrac{1}{1+\sqrt{2}x^2}\right)$
9. Find the range of the following functions:
   (i) $\sqrt{x-1}$ (ii) $\sqrt[3]{x-2}$
   (iii) $\sqrt{(x-1)(x-4)}$ (iv) $\dfrac{1}{(x-1)(x-2)(x-3)}$

(v) $\dfrac{x-1}{x^2-4x+3}$ (vi) $\dfrac{x^2-1}{x^2+5x+4}$

(vii) $\dfrac{x^2+2x-3}{x^2-1}$ (viii) $\dfrac{x^2+2x+3}{x}$

(ix) $\dfrac{x+1}{x^2-2x+3}$ (x) $\sqrt{x-1}+\sqrt{5-x}$

(xi) $\sin^2 x - 5\sin x - 6$ (xii) ${}^{7-x}P_{x-3}$

10. Find the range of the following functions:

(i) $\log_e(3x^2-4x+5)$ (ii) $\cot^{-1}(x^2-4x+5)$

(iii) $\cot^{-1}(2x-x^2)$ (iv) $\dfrac{x}{1+|x|}$

(v) $\cos([x]\pi)$ (vi) $f(x) = 4^x - 2^x + 1$

11. Find the domain of definition of the following given function

(i) $\dfrac{1}{(|x|-1)(\cos^{-1}(2x+1))\tan 3x}$

(ii) $\log[1-\log(x^2-4x+5)]$

(iii) $\log_2\log_{1/3}\log_3(x^2-4x+3)$

(iv) $\log_2\log_3\log_{4\pi}(\tan^{-1}x)^{-1}$

(v) $\left(\dfrac{x}{1-|x|}\right)^{\frac{1}{2002}}$

12. Find the lower upper bound and greatest lower bound in each case:

(i) $\dfrac{2x}{x^2+1}$

(ii) $\dfrac{x^2-1}{x^2+1}$

(iii) $\dfrac{x^2-3x+4}{x^2+3x+4}$

(iv) $s = \dfrac{1}{2+x^2}$; $-6 \le x \le 4$

(v) $s = \dfrac{3-x}{1-x}$; $x > 0$, $x \ne 1$

(vi) $s = \{\sqrt{1-x^2} : |x| \le \sqrt{3/2}\}$

(vii) $s = \left\{\dfrac{3x+1}{2x+3} : |x-1| \le 2\right\}$

Answer Keys

1. (a) Domain $\mathbb{R}$, Minimum = 4, Maximum $\to \infty$, Range = $[4, \infty)$

(b) Domain $\mathbb{R} \sim \{1, 5)$, Minimum = –4, Maximum $\to \infty$, Range = $[-\infty, -1/4) \cup (0, \infty)$

(c) Domain $\mathbb{R}$, Minimum = $\to -\infty$, Maximum $\to \infty$, Range = $\mathbb{R}$

(d) Domain $\mathbb{R}$, Minimum = $\to 0$, Maximum $\to \dfrac{1}{4}$, Range = $\left(0, \dfrac{1}{4}\right]$

2. Domain of $h(x) = \{9\}$ and range of $h(x) = \{1\}$

3. (a) $(-4, 4)$ (b) $[\cos 2, 1]$ (c) $[-1, 1]$

4. (a) $\{0\}$ (b) $\{0\}$ (c) $[-\sqrt{2}, \sqrt{2}]$ (d) $[0, \infty)$

5. (a) $\left[-\dfrac{\pi}{6}, \dfrac{\pi}{6}\right)$ (b) $[0, \pi]$ (c) $\{0, \pi\}$ (d) $\left[\dfrac{\pi}{4}, \dfrac{\pi}{2}\right)$ (e) $(-\infty, 3]$

(f) $\left[-\dfrac{\pi}{4}, \dfrac{\pi}{4}\right]$

6. (a) $[\ln 4, \infty)$ (b) $[\cot^{-1}(\log_{4/5} 4), \pi]$ (c) $\left(0, \cot^{-1}(\log_{4/5} 4)\right]$

7. (a) $[1/3, 3]$; $f'(x) = \dfrac{2(x^2-1)}{(x^2+x+1)^2} = f(1) = \dfrac{1}{3}; f(-1) = 3$; (b) Range = $(-\infty, 0) \cup [e, \infty)]$

Domain = $\mathbb{R}$, Range = $\left[\dfrac{1}{3}, 3\right]$

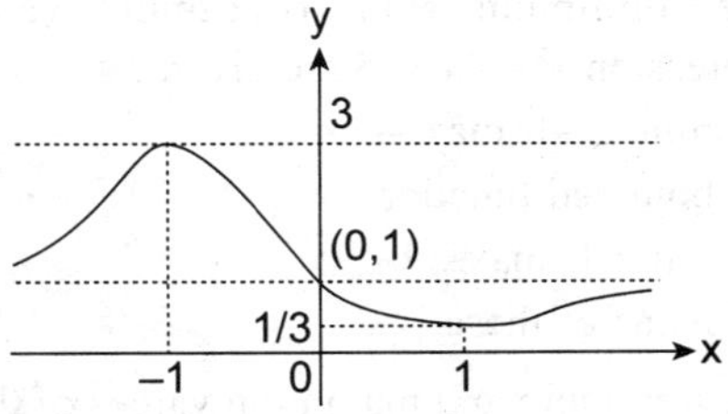

FIGURE 2.119

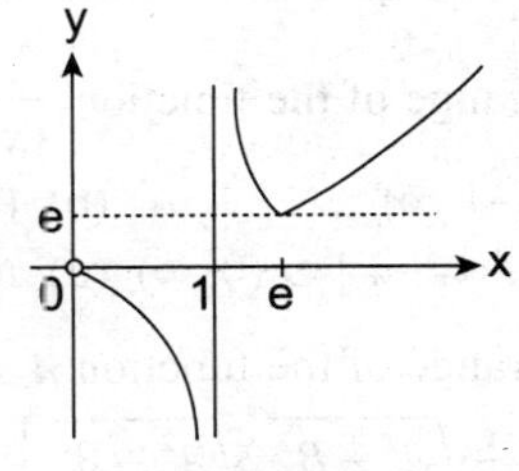

FIGURE 2.120

8. Range: $\left(\frac{\pi}{4}, \frac{7\pi}{8}\right)$; Domain is (–1, 1) – {0}

9. (i) $[0, \infty)$ (ii) $\mathbb{R}$ (iii) $[0, \infty)$ (iv) $(-\infty, \infty) \sim \{0\}$ (v) $\mathbb{R} \sim \left\{0, -\frac{1}{2}\right\}$ (vi) $\mathbb{R} \sim \left\{1, \frac{-2}{3}\right\}$

(vii) $\mathbb{R} - \{1, 2\}$ (viii) $(-\infty, 2 - 2\sqrt{3}] \cup [2\sqrt{3}, \infty)$ (ix) $\left[\frac{1}{2} - \frac{\sqrt{6}}{4}, \frac{1}{2} + \frac{\sqrt{6}}{4}\right]$ (x) $[2, 2\sqrt{2}]$

(xi) $[-10, 0]$ (xii) $\{24, 6, 1\}$.

10. (i) $\left[\log\left(\frac{11}{3}\right), \infty\right), D \in R$ (ii) $\left(0, \frac{\pi}{4}\right]$ (iii) $\left[\frac{\pi}{4}, \pi\right)$ (iv) $(-1, 1)$ (v) $\{-1, 1\}$

(vi) $\left[\frac{3}{4}, \infty\right)$

11. (i) $(-1, 0) - \left\{-\frac{\pi}{6}\right\}$ (ii) $(-1, 5)$ (iii) $(0, 2-\sqrt{2}) \cup (2+\sqrt{2}, 4)$ (iv) $(0, 1)$ (v) $(-\infty, -1) \cup [0, 1)$

12. (i) min: –1 , max: 1 (ii) min: –1, max: does not exist, *l.u.b.* = 1
(iii) min: 1/7 , max : 7 (iv) *l.u.b.*=1/8, *g.l.b.* = 1/38 (v) both *l.u.b.* and *g.l.b.* does not exist
(vi) *g.l.b.* = 0, *l.u.b.* = 1 (vii) *l.u.b.* = 10/9, *g.l.b.* = –2

TEXTUAL EXERCISE–10: (OBJECTIVE)

1. Range of the function $y = [x]$ is
(a) $\mathbb{N}$ (b) W
(c) $\mathbb{Z}$ (d) None of these

2. Range of the function $\frac{2x-1}{2x+1}$ is
(a) $\mathbb{R}$ (b) $\mathbb{R}-\{1\}$
(c) $(0, \infty)$ (d) None of these

3. Range of the function $\frac{x^2-1}{x^2+1}$ is
(a) $[-1, 1)$ (b) $(0, 1]$
(c) $[-1, 0]$ (d) None of these

4. Range of the function $\frac{2x}{1+x^2}$ is
(a) $[0, 1]$ (b) $[-1, 1]$
(c) $[-2, 2]$ (d) None of these

5. Range of the function $\frac{x^2-x+1}{x^2+x+1}$ is
(a) $[0, 3]$ (b) $[-3, 3]$
(c) $[1/3, 3]$ (d) None of these

6. The range of the function $\frac{1}{(x-1)(x-2)}$
(a) $(-4, \infty)$ (b) $(-\infty, -4) \cup (0, \infty)$
(c) $(-\infty, -4] \cup (0, \infty)$ (d) None of these

7. The range of the function $A \sin x + B \cos x$
(a) $\left[-\sqrt{A^2+B^2}, \sqrt{A^2+B^2}\right]$
(b) $\left[0, \sqrt{A^2+B^2}\right]$
(c) $[A, B]$
(d) None of these

8. The range of the function $y = \frac{x^2}{1+x^2}$ is
(a) $[0, 1)$ (b) $[1, 1]$
(c) $[0, 1]$ (d) None of these

9. The range of the function $y = \frac{1}{2-\sin 3x}$ is
(a) $(1/3, 1)$ (b) $[1/3, 1)$
(c) $[1/3, 1]$ (d) None of these

10. The minimum and maximum values of the expression $x^2 + x + 1$ are given by
(a) min: 3/4, max : ∞
(b) min: – 3/4, max : ∞
(c) max = 3/4, min $\to \infty$
(d) None of these

11. The minimum and maximum values of the expression $x^2 - 4x + 5$ are given by
(a) min = –1, max $\to \infty$
(b) bounded function
(c) min : 1, max : ∞
(d) None of these

12. The minimum and maximum values of the expression $ax^2 + bx + c$; $a > 0$ are given by

(a) min: $\frac{4ac-b^2}{4a}$, max: ∞
(b) min: $\frac{3}{4}$, max : ∞
(c) min: 1, max : ∞
(d) None of these

13. The minimum and maximum values of the expression $2 - 3x - x^2$ are given by
(a) min: , max : ∞ (b) min: $-\infty$, max :17/4
(c) min : 1, max : ∞ (d) None of these

14. The minimum and maximum values of the function $\frac{x^2-1}{x^2+1}$ are given by
(a) min: –1 , max : 1
(b) min: $-\infty$, max :1
(c) min: –1 , max : tends to 1
(d) None of these

15. The minimum and maximum values of the function $\frac{x^2-3x+4}{x^2+3x+4}$ are given by
(a) min: –1, max : 3
(b) min: 1/7, max : 7
(c) min: –7, max : tends to 1
(d) None of these

16. The *l.u.b.* and *g.l.b.* of the function $y=\frac{1}{2+x^2}$; $-6 \le x \le 4$ are given by
(a) $l.u.b. = \frac{1}{38}$, $g.l.b. = \frac{1}{2}$
(b) $l.u.b. = \frac{1}{2}$, $g.l.b. = \frac{1}{38}$
(c) $l.u.b. = \frac{1}{38}$, $g.l.b. = \frac{1}{4}$
(d) None of these

17. The *l.u.b.* and *g.l.b* of the function $y=\frac{3-x}{1-x}$; $x > 0$, $x \ne 1$ are given by
(a) *l.u.b.* = 3, *g.l.b.* = 1
(b) *l.u.b.* = 3, *g.l.b.* does not exist
(c) both *l.u.b.* and *g.l.b.* does not exist
(d) None of these

18. If $|x-5| < 1$, then the range of $\frac{x}{x+10}$ is
(a) (2/7 , 3/8) (b) [7/2, 8/3]
(c) [2/7, 3/8] (d) None of these

19. If $e^x = y+\sqrt{1+y^2}$, then y is
(a) $e^x + e^{-x}$ (b) $e^x - e^{-x}$
(c) $\frac{e^x-e^{-x}}{2}$ (d) $\frac{e^x+e^{-x}}{2}$

20. If $f(x)$ is defined on [0, 1] by the rule $f(x)=\begin{cases} x, & \text{if } x \text{ is rational} \\ 1-x, & \text{if } x \text{ is irrational}\end{cases}$, then for all $x \in [0, 1]$, $f(f(x))$ is equal to
(a) Constant (b) $1 + x$
(c) x (d) None of these

21. The range of the function $y=\frac{x}{1+x^2}$ is
(a) $\left[0, \frac{3}{2}\right]$ (b) $\left[-\frac{1}{2}, \frac{1}{2}\right]$
(c) $\left[-\frac{3}{2}, 0\right]$ (d) None of these

22. The range of functions $\frac{1}{x(x-1)(x-2)}$ is
(a) $\mathbb{R}$ (b) $(0, \infty)$
(c) $\mathbb{R} - \{0\}$ (d) None of these

23. The range of function $\log(e^x - x)$ is
(a) $\mathbb{R}$ (b) $(-\infty, 0)$
(c) $[0, \infty)$ (d) None of these

24. The range of functions $\frac{x^2}{1+x^2}$ is
(a) (0, 1) (b) [0, 1)
(c) $(0, \infty)$ (d) None of these

25. Which of the following functions are defined for all x?
(a) $\sin[x] + \cos[x]$ ($[x]$ denotes greatest integer $\le x$)
(b) $\sec^{-1}(1 + \sin^2 x)$
(c) $\tan(\log x)$
(d) $\sqrt{\frac{9}{8}+\cos x+\cos 2x}$

26. The range of the function $\sin^2 x - 5\sin x - 6$ is
(a) [–10, 0] (b) [–1, –1]
(c) $[0, \pi]$ (d) [–49/4, 0]

Answer Keys

1. (c)	**2.** (b)	**3.** (a)	**4.** (b)	**5.** (c)	**6.** (c)	**7.** (a)	**8.** (a)	**9.** (c)	**10.** (a)
11. (c)	**12.** (a)	**13.** (b)	**14.** (a)	**15.** (b)	**16.** (b)	**17.** (c)	**18.** (a)	**19.** (c)	**20.** (c)
21. (b)	**22.** (c)	**23.** (c)	**24.** (b)	**25.** (a,b,d)	**26.** (a)				

■ CLASSIFICATION OF FUNCTIONS

Based on their specific properties, functions can be classified in following ways

(i) One–one/many–one functions
(ii) Onto/Into functions
(iii) One–one and onto (Bijective) functions
(iv) Composite functions
(v) Invertible/Non-invertible functions
(v) Even/Odd/Neither even nor odd functions
(v) Periodic/Non-periodic functions

■ ONE-ONE/MANY-ONE FUNCTIONS

One–one (Injective) Function

$f: X \to Y$ is called injective, when different elements in set X are related with different elements of set Y, i.e., no two elements of domain have same image in co-domain. In other words, we can also say that no element of co-domain is related with two or more elements of domain. Consider the following mapping:

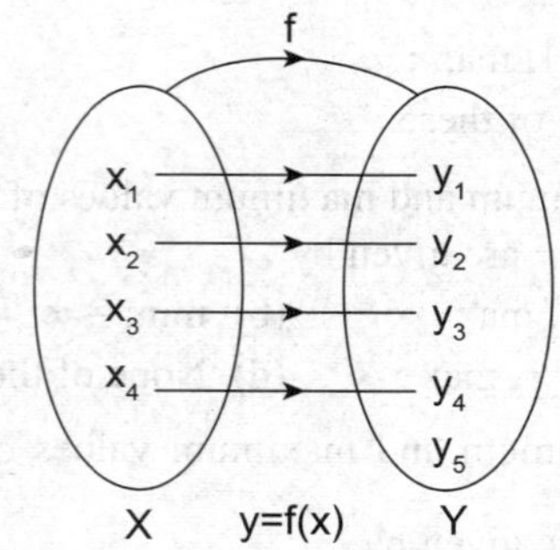

FIGURE 2.121

Clearly it is one–one because each element x_i in X is associated with a distinct element y_i in Y.

e.g., $f: \mathbb{R} \to \mathbb{R}$ such that $f(x) = x^3 + x, f(x) = 2^x - 2^{-x}$. $f(x) = mx + c, f(x) = a^x, a > 0$ and $a \neq 1; f(x) = \log_a x$, $a \neq 1, a > 0$ are injective function.

ILLUSTRATION 156: Let $A = \{1, 2, 3, 4\}$; $B = \{1, 2, 3, 4, 5, 6\}$ and $f: A \to B$ be a function defined by $f(x) = x + 2$ for all $x \in A$. Is it one–one?

SOLUTION: Using the analytical formula $f(x) = x + 2$, we get $f(1) = 3, f(2) = 4, f(3) = 5, f(4) = 6$. Therefore the function as a set of ordered pair is obtained as $f = \{(1, 3), (2, 4), (3, 5), (4, 6)\}$. It is clear that different elements in A have different images under function f. So, $f: A \to B$ is an injection.

■ MANY-ONE FUNCTIONS

$f: X \to Y$ is many–one, when there exist at least two elements in the domain set X which are related with same element of co-domain Y. For example consider a mapping.

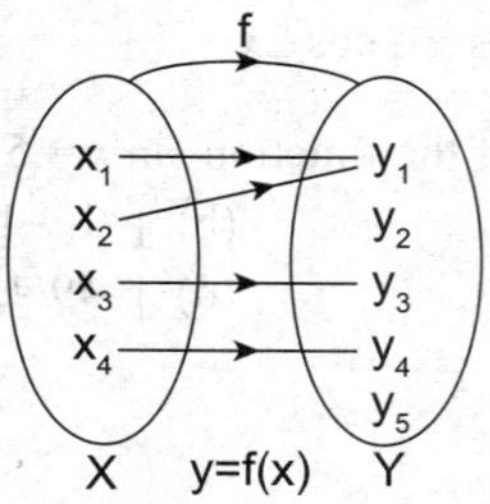

FIGURE 2.122

Clearly it is a many–one mapping as $f(x_1) = f(x_2) = y_1$ whereas x_1 and x_2 are distinct elements.

e.g., $f: \mathbb{R} \to \mathbb{R}$ given by $\sin x$, $\cos x$, $\tan x$, $x^2 + 2x$, $2^x + 2^{-x}$.

■ METHOD OF TESTING FOR INJECTIVITY

To test a given function for injectivity, we assume two different elements x_1 and x_2 in domain X and their corresponding images $f(x_1)$ and $f(x_2)$ in co-domain Y. Thus, we have to prove that for distinct pre-images x_1 and x_2 their images $f(x_1)$ and $f(x_2)$ remain different. We apply this feature to develop condition for injectivity in different ways.

(a) Analytical Method: A function $f: X \to Y$ is injective (one–one) iff whenever two images are equal then it means that they are outputs of same pre-image. i.e., $f(x_1) = f(x_2) \Leftrightarrow x_1 = x_2 \; \forall \; x_1, x_2 \in X$. Or by using contra-positive of the above condition, i.e., $x_1 \neq x_2 \Leftrightarrow f(x_1) \neq f(x_2) \; \forall \; x_1, x_2 \in X$.

NOTES

1. *If f(x) is not one–one, then it is many–one function .If we go according to definition consider $f(x_1) = f(x_2)$.*

$\Rightarrow$ *x_1 is not necessarily equal to x_2.*

i.e., If two f-images are equal, then their pre-images may or may not be equal.

2. *To test injectivity of f(x), consider $f(x_1) = f(x_2)$ and solve the equation and get x_2 in terms of x_1 .If $x_2 = x_1$ is only solution, then function f is injective, but if other real solutions also exist, then f is many–one function.*

ILLUSTRATION 157: Show that the function $f: \mathbb{Z} \to \mathbb{Z}$ defined by $f(x) = x^2 + x \ \forall \ x \in \mathbb{Z}$, is many–one function.

SOLUTION: Let $x_1, x_2 \in \mathbb{Z}$ such that $f(x_1) = f(x_2)$, then $f(x_1) = f(x_2)$

$\Rightarrow x_1^2 + x_1 = x_2^2 + x_2$ $\qquad \Rightarrow (x_1^2 - x_2^2) + (x_1 - x_2) = 0$

$\Rightarrow (x_1 - x_2)(x_1 + x_2 + 1) = 0$ $\qquad \Rightarrow x_1 = x_2$ or $x_1 + x_2 + 1 = 0$

Since, $f(x_1) = f(x_2)$ does not provide a unique solution $x_1 = x_2$ but it also provides $x_2 = -x_1 - 1$, this means there may arise a situation when $x_1 \neq x_2$, but $f(x_1) = f(x_2)$.

To verify the second situation, let us analyses the function further.

$$f(x) = x^2 + x = \left(x + \frac{1}{2}\right)^2 + \frac{3}{4} \qquad \Rightarrow f(x) = \frac{(2x+1)^2 + 3}{4}$$

it is very evident from above that $f(x)$ generates same output for $2x + 1 = \alpha$ or $-\alpha$; where $\alpha \in \mathbb{R}$

i.e., for $x = -\frac{1}{2} - \frac{\alpha}{2}$ or $\frac{-1}{2} + \frac{\alpha}{2}$. For instance when $\alpha = 1$, we get $x = -1$ or 0.

Clearly $f(0) = f(-1) = 1$. Thus, for two distinct inputs $f(x)$ generates same output. Hence, f is many–one function. Also one can make out from the above discussion that infinitely many such pairs of integer inputs are possible by choosing α from set $\{(2n + 1); n \in \mathbb{Z}\}$.

ILLUSTRATION 158: Test whether $f(x) = e^{2x^3+5}$ is an injective function or not.

SOLUTION: Consider $f(x_1) = f(x_2) \Rightarrow e^{2x_1^3+5} = e^{2x_2^3+5} \Rightarrow 2x_1^3 + 5 = 2x_2^3 + 5 \Rightarrow x_1^3 - x_2^3 = 0$

$\Rightarrow (x_1 - x_2)\left(x_1^2 + x_1x_2 + x_2^2\right) = 0$ $\qquad (\because x_1^2 + x_1x_2 + x_2^2 \geq 4)$

Consequently the only real solution is $x_1 = x_2$ .Therefore, f is one–one function.

ILLUSTRATION 159: Test the following functions for injectivity:

(*a*) $f(x) = \dfrac{x^2 - x - 2}{x^2 - 5x + 6}$ (b) $f(x) = \dfrac{2x - 3}{2x + 3}$ (c) $f(x) = \dfrac{ax^2 - 1}{ax^2 + 1}$; $(a > 0)$

SOLUTION: (a) Given function $f(x) = \dfrac{x^2 - x - 2}{x^2 - 5x + 6} = \dfrac{(x+1)(x-2)}{(x-2)(x-3)} = \dfrac{x+1}{x-3}, x \neq 2, 3$

This is clearly a rational linear fractional function and we know that it is an injective function.

(b) Given $f(x) = \dfrac{2x - 3}{2x + 3}$

$$\therefore f(x_1) = f(x_2) \Rightarrow \left(\frac{2x_1 - 3}{2x_1 + 3}\right) = \left(\frac{2x_2 - 3}{2x_2 + 3}\right)$$

Applying componendo and dividendo, we get $\dfrac{-4x_1}{6} = \dfrac{-4x_2}{6} \qquad \Rightarrow x_1 = x_2$.

$\Rightarrow$ $f(x)$ is one–one function.

(c) Given $f(x)=\dfrac{ax^2-1}{ax^2+1}$; $(a>0)$ $\therefore$ $f(x_1)=f(x_2)$ $\Rightarrow$ $\left(\dfrac{ax_1^2-1}{ax_1^2+1}\right)=\left(\dfrac{ax_2^2-1}{ax_2^2+1}\right)$

Applying componendo and dividendo, we get $-ax_1^2=-ax_2^2$ $\Rightarrow$ $x_1^2=x_2^2$

$\Rightarrow$ $x_1=x_2$ or $x_1=-x_2$ $\therefore$ $f(x)$ is many–one function.

ILLUSTRATION 160: A function $f:\mathbb{R}\to\mathbb{R}$ is defined as $f(x)=\dfrac{2x+1}{x^3+4}$. Find whether f is one–one or many–one function.

SOLUTION: Let $x_1, x_2 \in \mathbb{R}$ such that $f(x_1)=f(x_2)$ $\Rightarrow$ $\dfrac{2x_1+1}{x_1^3+4}=\dfrac{2x_2+1}{x_2^3+4}$

$\Rightarrow$ $(2x_1+1)(x_2^3+4)=(2x_2+1)(x_1^3+4)$ $\Rightarrow$ $2x_1x_2^3+8x_1+x_2^3+4=2x_2x_1^3+8x_2+x_1^3+4$

$\Rightarrow$ $2x_1x_2(x_2^2-x_1^2)+8(x_1-x_2)+(x_2^3-x_1^3)=0$

$\Rightarrow$ $(x_2-x_1)\left[2x_1x_2(x_1+x_2)+x_1^2+x_2^2+x_1x_2-8\right]=0$

$\Rightarrow$ $(x_2-x_1)\left(x_1^2+x_2^2+x_1x_2(2x_1+2x_2+1)-8\right)=0$

$\Rightarrow$ $x_2-x_1=0$ or $x_1^2+x_2^2+x_1x_2(2x_1+2x_2+1)-8=0$ ... (i)

If $x_2=0$, then $x_1^2+x_2^2+x_1x_2(2x_1+2x_2+1)-8=0$ $\Rightarrow$ $x_1^2-8=0$ $\Rightarrow$ $x_1^2=8$ $\Rightarrow$ $x_1=\pm 2\sqrt{2}$

Therefore equation (i), suggests that if $x_2=0$, then x_1 can have two values $2\sqrt{2}$ or $--2\sqrt{2}$; consequently $x_1\neq x_2$, but $f(x_1)=f(x_2)$ $\therefore$ f is a many–one function.

(b) Graphical Method:

For one–one: If every line parallel to x-axis, $y=k\in R_f$ cuts the graph of function exactly once, then the function is one–one or injective.

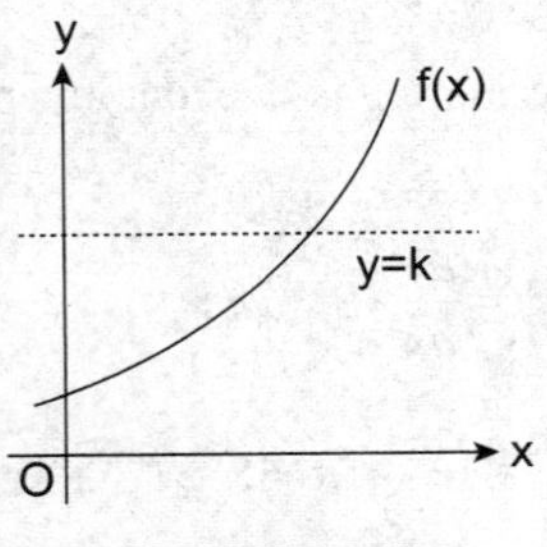

FIGURE 2.123

For Many–one: If there exists a line parallel to x-axis which cuts the graph of function at least twice, then the function is many–one.

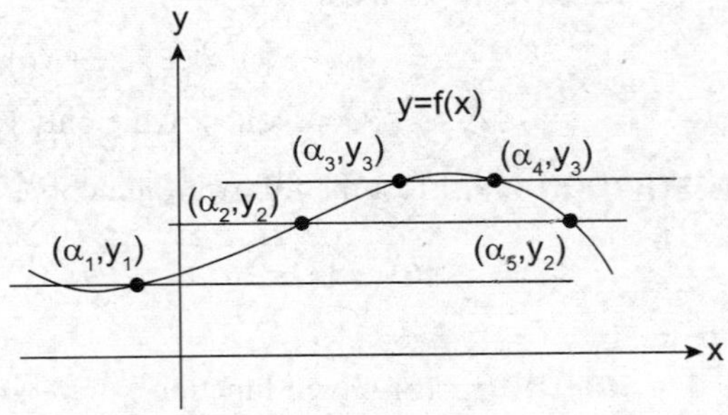

FIGURE 2.124

ILLUSTRATION 161: Function f: $[-3,\infty)\to\mathbb{R}$ is piecewise defined as $f(x)=\begin{cases}\sqrt{9-x^2}; & -3\le x\le 0\\ \dfrac{2}{3^x}+k; & 0<x<\infty\end{cases}$

Determine the range of values of k for which the function f be (a) injective (b) many–one.

SOLUTION: The function f represents quarter circle given by analytical formula $y=\sqrt{9-x^2}$, i.e., $x^2 + y^2 = 9$ for $x \in [-3, 0]$ and $y \in [0, 3]$, as shown in Figure 2.125, where as for the domain $(0,\infty)$ it is a decreasing exponential function such that $f(0) = k + 2$ and $f(\infty) \to k$, to remain injective, no horizontal line should intersect the graph more than once. Therefore

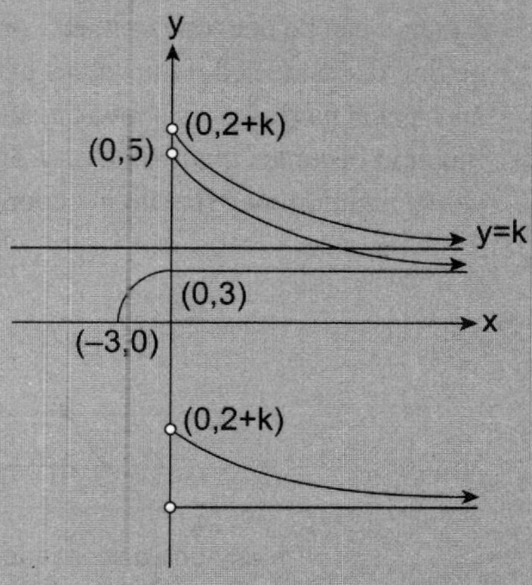

FIGURE 2.125

Case I: Either $f(x)=\dfrac{2}{3^x}+k$ above the quarter circle

$\Rightarrow k \geq 3.$

Case II: or it lies below the x-axis

$\Rightarrow 2 + k < 0$

$\Rightarrow k < -2$

Hence, if $k \in (-\infty,-2) \cup [3, \infty)$, $f(x)$ remains injective function but for $k \in [-2, 3)$, $f(x)$ becomes many–one function.

(c) Method of Monotonicity: The concept of monotonicity can be used to determine the injectivity of function conveniently for continuous functions. For discontinuous functions the study of monotonic behavior of function in the interval concerned helps to decide the injectivity / non-injectivity of function.

For one–one: If a function $f(x)$ is continuous and monotonic on an interval I, then it is always one–one on interval I because any straight line parallel to x-axis $y = k \in I$ intersects the graph of such functions exactly once.

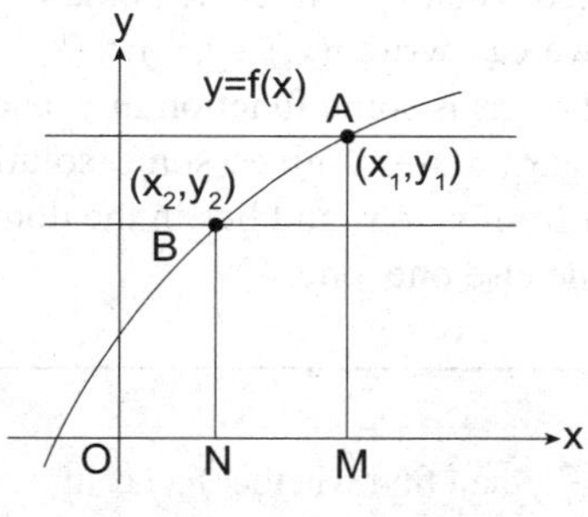

FIGURE 2.126

$f'(x) \geq 0$; $f'(x) = 0$ occurs only at isolated points or $x_2 > x_1 \Rightarrow f(x_2) > f(x_1)$

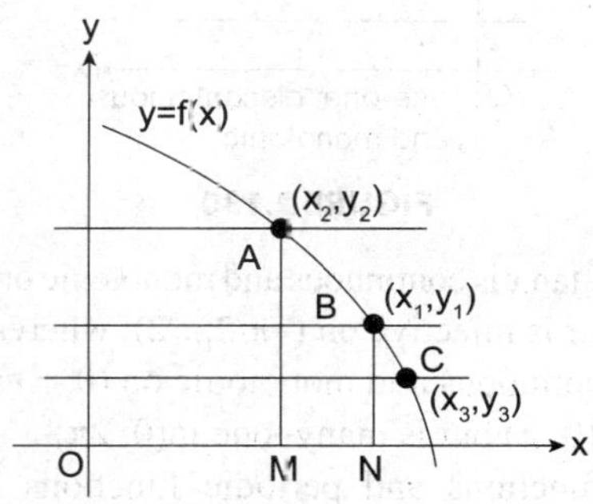

FIGURE 2.127

$f'(x) \leq 0$; $f'(x) = 0$ occurs only at isolated points or $x_2 > x_1 \Rightarrow f(x_2) < f(x_1)$

For many–one:

(i) If a function is continuous and non-monotonic on interval I, then it must be many–one on interval I.

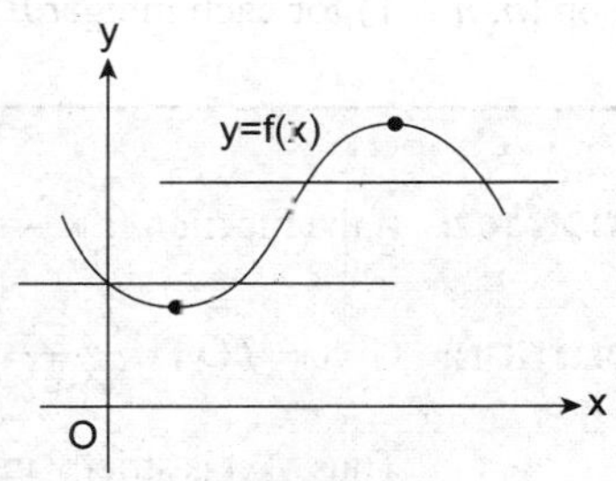

FIGURE 2.128

(ii) If a function is discontinuous and monotonic on interval I, then it can be one–one or many–one on I. Because after getting disconnected if the values of function drops down and again increases as shown in the figure below, then function becomes many–one on I. In case of jump in the value, function may remain injection on I.

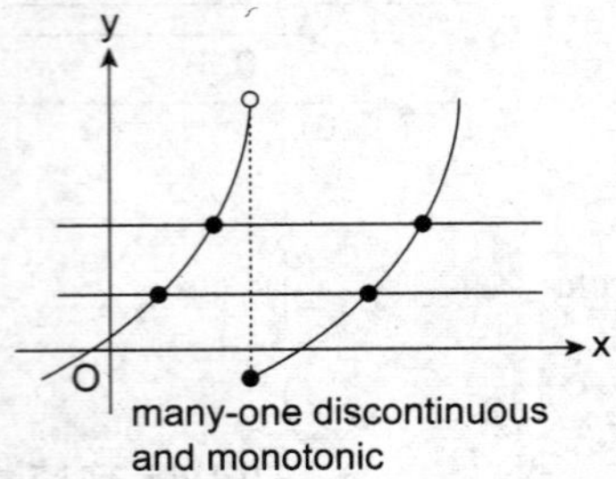

FIGURE 2.129

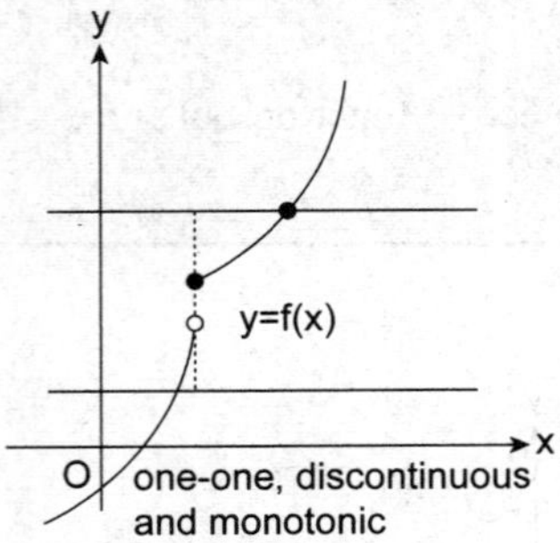

FIGURE 2.130

e.g., $y = \tan x$ is continuous and monotonic on $(-\pi/2, \pi/2)$.

$\therefore$ $y = \tan x$ is injective on $(-\pi/2, \pi/2)$; whereas $y = \tan x$ is discontinuous and monotonic on $(0, \pi)$ and is one–one in $(0, \pi)$ but is many–one in$(0, 2\pi)$.

(iii) Even functions and periodic functions are always many–one in their natural domains. Whereas they are one–one in their principal domain. They can be made one–one by restricting the domain. e.g., cos x is many–one on $\mathbb{R}$ but is one–one on $[0, \pi]$ or $\left[0, \frac{\pi}{2}\right]$.

Similarly, fractional part function $\{x\}$ is periodic function with period 1. It is many–one on $\mathbb{R}$ but one–one on $[n, n + 1)$ for each integer n.

(iv) If a function is discontinuous and non-monotonic on an interval I, then it can be one–one or many–one on I. It can be understood well by the graph shown below.

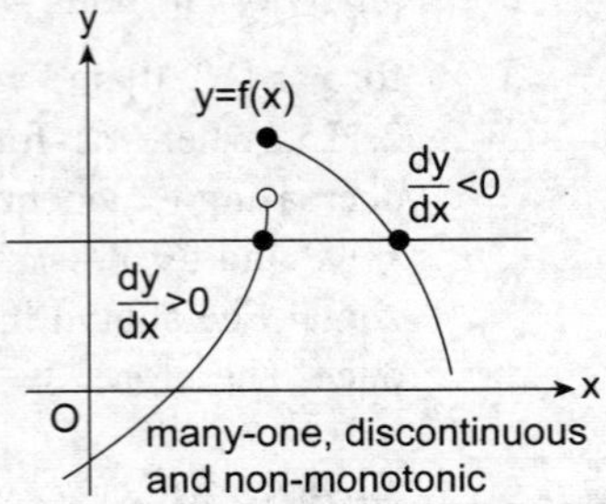

FIGURE 2.131

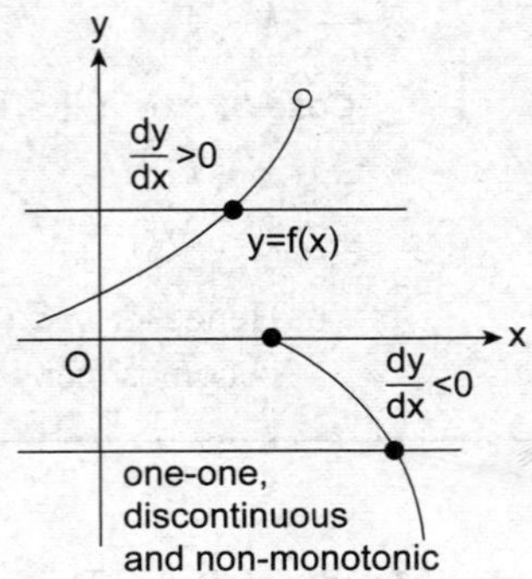

FIGURE 2.132

(v) All polynomials of even degree defined in $\mathbb{R}$ have at least one local maxima or minima and hence, are many–one in the domain $\mathbb{R}$. Polynomials of odd degree can be one–one or many–one in $\mathbb{R}$.
e.g., $f(x) = x^3 + 1$ is one–one in $\mathbb{R}$ as $f'(x) = 3x^2 \geq 0$ and $f'(x) = 0$ only at one isolated point $x = 0$; whereas $f(x) = x^3 + 4x^2 + x - 6$ is many–one in $\mathbb{R}$ as $f'(x) = 3x^2 + 8x + 1$ which changes its sign in $\mathbb{R}$. i.e., $f(x)$ is continuous and non-monotonic in $\mathbb{R}$.

(vi) If f is a rational function, then $f(x_1) = f(x_2)$ will always be satisfied when $x_1 = x_2$ in the domain.
Hence, we can write $f(x_1) - f(x_2) = (x_1 - x_2).g(x_1, x_2)$; where $g(x_1, x_2)$ is some function in x_1 and x_2.
Now if $g(x_1, x_2) = 0$ gives some solution which is different from $x_1 = x_2$ and lies in the domain, then f is many–one else one–one.

ILLUSTRATION 162: If the function f: $\mathbb{R} \to \mathbb{R}$ is defined by $f(x) = \dfrac{e^x - e^{-x}}{e^x + e^{-x}}$, then find whether $f(x)$ is injective or not.

SOLUTION: Given $f(x) = \dfrac{e^x - e^{-x}}{e^x + e^{-x}}$ $\Rightarrow$ $f'(x) = \dfrac{(e^x + e^{-x})^2 - (e^x - e^{-x})^2}{(e^x + e^{-x})^2} = \dfrac{4}{(e^x + e^{-x})^2} \geq 0 \ \forall \ x \in \mathbb{R}$.

Thus, $f(x)$ is strictly increasing and continuous function, consequently $f(x)$ is an injective function.

ILLUSTRATION 163: Find the set of all real values of parameter t for which the function $f: \mathbb{R} \to \mathbb{R}$ defined as $f(x) = 3 \sin x - 4tx + 5$ is an injective function

SOLUTION: A continuous function $f(x)$ to be one–one it should be either monotonically increasing $(f'(x) \geq 0)$ or monotonically decreasing $(f'(x) \leq 0)$ in its entire domain.

Clearly our function is continuous and $f'(x) = 3\cos x - 4t$, thus, for one–one either $f'(x) \geq 0\ \forall\ x \in \mathbb{R}$ or $f'(x) \leq 0\ \forall\ x \in \mathbb{R}$

Case (i): $f'(x) \geq 0\ \forall\ x \in \mathbb{R}$

$\Rightarrow f'(x) = 3 \cos x - 4t \geq 0\ \forall\ x \in \mathbb{R}$

$\Rightarrow\ t \leq \frac{3}{4}\cos x\ \ \forall\ x \in \mathbb{R}\ \Rightarrow\ t \leq -\frac{3}{4}\ \forall\ x \in \mathbb{R}$ as $-\frac{3}{4} \leq \frac{3}{4}\cos x\ \ \Rightarrow\ t \in \left(-\infty, -\frac{3}{4}\right]$

Case (ii): $f'(x) = 3 \cos x - 4t \leq 0\ \forall\ x \in \mathbb{R}$

$\Rightarrow\ t \geq \frac{3}{4}\cos x\ \Rightarrow\ t \geq \frac{3}{4}\ \ \because\ \frac{3}{4}\cos x \leq \frac{3}{4}\ \ \Rightarrow\ t \in \left[\frac{3}{4}, \infty\right)$

Concluding the outcome of both the above cases, we conclude that f to be one–one function

$t \in \left(-\infty, \frac{-3}{4}\right] \cup \left[\frac{3}{4}, \infty\right)$

ILLUSTRATION 164: Test whether the following functions are injective or not:

(a) $f(x) = \frac{2\sin x - 5}{2\sin x + 5}$ (b) $f(x) = \frac{a\log x^2 - 2}{a\log x^2 + 2}$; $(a, x > 0)$

SOLUTION: (a) Given function is $f(x) = \frac{2\sin x - 5}{2\sin x + 5}$

$\therefore\ f(x_1) = f(x_2)$

$\Rightarrow\ \left(\frac{2\sin x_1 - 5}{2\sin x_1 + 5}\right) = \left(\frac{2\sin x_2 - 5}{2\sin x_2 + 5}\right)$

Applying componendo and dividendo, we get

$\frac{-4\sin x_1}{10} = \frac{-4\sin x_2}{10}\ \ \Rightarrow \sin x_1 = \sin x_2$

But we know that sin x is periodic function, and hence, is many–one function. Thus, $\sin x_1 = \sin x_2$ would occur at infinitely many pairs (x_1, x_2) such that $x_1 \neq x_2$. Hence, $f(x)$ is many–one function.

(b) Given $f(x) = \frac{a\log x^2 - 2}{a\log x^2 + 2}$ $(a, x > 0)$

$\therefore\ f(x_1) = f(x_2)\ \ \Rightarrow\ \left(\frac{a\log x_1^2 - 2}{a\log x_1^2 + 2}\right) = \left(\frac{a\log x_2^2 - 2}{a\log x_2^2 + 2}\right)$

Applying componendo and dividendo, we get $\frac{-a\log x_1^2}{4} = \frac{-a\log x_2^2}{4}\ \Rightarrow\ \log x_1^2 = \log x_2^2$

But log x is a monotonic and continuous function on $(0, \infty)$, thus, log x is one–one function on $(0, \infty)$.

$\Rightarrow\ x_1^2 = x_2^2\ \Rightarrow\ (x_1 + x_2)(x_1 - x_2) = 0$

$\Rightarrow\ x_1 = x_2$ or $x_1 = -x_2$, but $x_1, x_2 > 0\ \Rightarrow\ \ x_1 \neq -x_2\ \Rightarrow\ x_1 = x_2$

$\Rightarrow\ f(x)$ is one–one function.

(d) **Hit and Trial Method to Test Many–One Functions:** Many a times by keen observation it is possible to find an element in the range of function which is f image of two or more than two elements in the domain of function thus, concluding the fact that the function being investigated is many–one function.

For instance $f(x)=\dfrac{x^2-4x+3}{x^2+4x+5}$ is clearly a many–one function since it vanishes at two different values of input x, i.e., $x = 1, 3$ (given by roots of $x^2 - 4x + 3 = 0$). But it is not necessary that to be many–one the numerator must have distinct real roots. Especially for those cases when numerator is non-vanishing we may proceed as illustrated below.

Let us try $f(x) = f(\alpha)$ (where α is some fixed real number such that $f(\alpha)$ is simple fraction, say $\alpha = 0$).

i.e., $f(x) = f(0) \Rightarrow \dfrac{x^2-4x+3}{x^2+4x+5}=\dfrac{3}{5}$

$\Rightarrow 5x^2 - 20x + 15 = 3x^2 + 12x + 15$

$\Rightarrow 2x^2 - 32x = 0 \Rightarrow 2x(x - 16) = 0$

$\Rightarrow x = 0, 16 \Rightarrow f(0) = f(16) = \dfrac{3}{5}$

Hence, $f(x)$ is many–one function while carrying out the above process it should be kept in mind that it is hit and trial method and may fail to hit the questions rightly, for instance consider $f(x)=\dfrac{x^2-3x+4}{x^2+3x+4}$

Solving $f(x) = f(0)$, we get $\dfrac{x^2-3x+4}{x^2+3x+4}=1$

$\Rightarrow 6x = 0$ i.e., $x = 0$

Thus, we can't arrive at any conclusion from the result, so f may or may not be many–one, to decide either we go by other method or try for some different real output of function say

Let $f(x) = f(1) \Rightarrow \dfrac{x^2-3x+4}{x^2+3x+4}=\dfrac{1}{4}$

$\Rightarrow 4x^2 - 12x + 16 = x^2 + 3x + 4$

$\Rightarrow 3x^2 - 15x + 12 = 0$ i.e., $x^2 - 5x + 4 = 0$ (which has $D > 0$)

$\Rightarrow x = 1, 4$

Thus, $f(1) = f(4) = 1/4$, and thus, f is many–one.

ILLUSTRATION 165: Given a function $f : \mathbb{R} \to \mathbb{R}$ defined as $f(x)=\dfrac{x^2-x+12}{x^2+x+8}$. Test whether $f(x)$ is injective function or non-injective.

SOLUTION: ***Method 1:*** **Analytically:**

Let $f(x_1) = f(x_2)$

$\Rightarrow \dfrac{x_1^2-x_1+12}{x_1^2+x_1+8}=\dfrac{x_2^2-x_2+12}{x_2^2+x_2+8}$

Applying componendo and dividendo, we get $\dfrac{4-2x_1}{2x_1^2+20}=\dfrac{4-2x_2}{2x_2^2+20}$

$\Rightarrow (2-x_1)(x_2^2+10)=(2-x_2)(x_1^2+10)$

$\Rightarrow 2x_2^2+20-x_1x_2^2-10x_1 = 2x_1^2+20-x_2x_1^2-10x_2$

$\Rightarrow 2(x_2^2-x_1^2)-x_1x_2(x_2-x_1)+10(x_2-x_1)=0 \Rightarrow (x_2-x_1)(2(x_1+x_2)-x_1x_2+10)=0$

$\Rightarrow x_1 = x_2$ or $2x_1 + 2x_2 - x_1x_2 + 10 = 0 \qquad \Rightarrow x_1 = x_2$ or $x_1=\dfrac{2(x_2+5)}{(x_2-2)}$

Thus, evidently $f(x_1) = f(x_2)$ does not necessarily implying $x_1 = x_2$. For different inputs x_1 and x_2, $f(x_1)$ and $f(x_2)$ can be equal, consequently f is many–one function.

Method 2: **Monotonically:** $f(x)$ is a continuous function because denominator is non-vanishing polynomial

Now, $f'(x)=\dfrac{(x^2+x+8)(2x-1)-(x^2-x+12)(2x+1)}{(x^2+x+8)^2}=\dfrac{2x^2-8x-20}{(x^2+x+8)^2}=\dfrac{2(x^2-4x-5)}{(x^2+x+8)^2}$

∵ Denominator is non-vanishing and perfect square, thus, always positive, whereas determinant of numerator = $D = 36 > 0$, thus, has two real roots.

$$f'(x)=\frac{2(x-5)(x+1)}{(x^2+x+8)^2}=\begin{cases}\text{positive for } x\in(-\infty,-1)\cup(5,\infty)\\ \text{negative for } x\in(-1,5)\end{cases}$$

Due to change in sign of derivative $f(x)$ is clearly continuous but non-monotonic function, so it is non-injective function.

Method 3: **Using hit and trial:**

Let $f(x) = f(0)$

$$\Rightarrow \frac{x^2-x+12}{x^2+x+8}=\frac{3}{2} \Rightarrow 2x^2-2x=3x^2+3x \Rightarrow x^2+5x=0 \Rightarrow x=0 \text{ or } -5$$

So, for distinct inputs 0 and –5; $f(0) = f(-5) = 3/2$. Thus, $f(x)$ is many–one function.

ILLUSTRATION 166: Test the injectivity of the following functions

(a) $f(x) = e^x + e^{-x}$ (b) $f(x) = e^x - e^{-x}$

SOLUTION: (a) **Analytical method:** Consider $f(x_1) = f(x_2)$ $\Rightarrow e^{x_1}+e^{-x_1}=e^{x_2}+e^{-x_2}$

$$\Rightarrow e^{x_1}-e^{x_2}=\frac{1}{e^{x_2}}-\frac{1}{e^{x_1}} \Rightarrow \left(e^{x_1}-e^{x_2}\right)-\frac{e^{x_1}-e^{x_2}}{e^{x_1+x_2}}=0 \Rightarrow \left(e^{x_1}-e^{x_2}\right)\left(1-\frac{1}{e^{x_1+x_2}}\right)=0$$

$$\Rightarrow e^{x_1}=e^{x_2} \text{ or } e^{x_1+x_2}=1 \qquad \Rightarrow x_1=x_2 \text{ or } x_1+x_2=0$$

Clearly $x_2 = x_1$ is not the only solution, $x_2 = -x_1$ is also solution. Thus, f is many–one function. The above analysis–also shows that $f(x)$ takes same values for x and $-x$, thus, being an even function, it is many–one function. Consequently, we conclude that if $f(x)$ is defined as $f: [0, \infty) \to \mathbb{R}; f(x) = e^x + e^{-x}$, it becomes an injective function.

Method of monotonicity:

$$f(x)=e^x+e^{-x} \Rightarrow f'(x)=e^x-e^{-x}=\frac{e^{2x}-1}{e^x}=\begin{cases}+ve \text{ if } x>0\\ -ve \text{ if } x<0\end{cases}$$

⇒ $f(x)$ is monotonically decreasing in $(-\infty,0)$ and increasing in $(0,\infty)$, thus, has non-monotonic nature with minima at $x = 0$, also $f(x)$ is continuous function. Consequently $f(x)$ is non-injective function.

Graphically: $f(0) = 2$

Graph of $f(x)$ is symmetric about y-axis and lines $y = k$; $k > 2$, cut the curve twice showing that function is many–one. It is also evident from the graph that restricting the domain of function either to $(-\infty, 0]$ on $[0, \infty)$ converts it to an injective function.

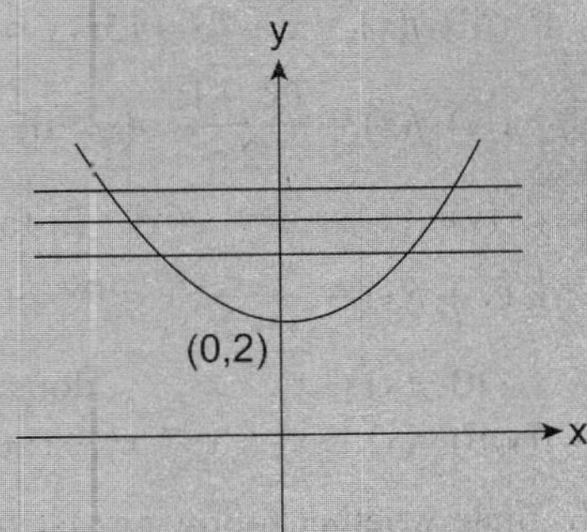

FIGURE 2.133

(b) **Analytical method:** Consider $f(x_1) = f(x_2)$

$$\Rightarrow e^{x_1}-e^{-x_1}=e^{x_2}-e^{-x_2}$$

$$\Rightarrow e^{x_1}-e^{x_2}=e^{-x_1}-e^{-x_2} \Rightarrow e^{x_1}-e^{x_2}=\frac{1}{e^{x_1}}-\frac{1}{e^{x_2}} \Rightarrow \left(e^{x_1}-e^{x_2}\right)+\frac{\left(e^{x_1}-e^{x_2}\right)}{e^{x_1+x_2}}=0$$

$$\Rightarrow \left(e^{x_1}-e^{x_2}\right)\left(1+\frac{1}{e^{x_1+x_2}}\right)=0 \Rightarrow e^{x_1}=e^{x_2} \text{ or } e^{x_1+x_2}=-1 \text{ (impossible) as } e^x>0\ \forall\ x\in\mathbb{R}$$

⇒ $x_1 = x_2$. Clearly $x_2 = x_1$ is the only solution. Thus, f is one–one, i.e., injective.

Method of monotonicity: $f(x) = e^x - e^{-x}$

$\Rightarrow f'(x) = e^x + e^{-x} = e^x + \dfrac{1}{e^x} > 0 \ \forall\, x \in \mathbb{R} \quad \Rightarrow f(x)$ is strictly increasing on $\mathbb{R}$.

Also $f(x)$ being the difference of two exponential functions is continuous on $\mathbb{R}$. Hence, $f(x)$ is injective on $\mathbb{R}$.

Graphically: $f(x) = e^x - e^{-x}$; $f(0) = 0$

$f(x) = e^x - e^{-x} \geq 0 \Leftrightarrow e^{2x} - 1 \geq 0 \Leftrightarrow e^x \leq -1$ or $e^x \geq 1 \Leftrightarrow e^x \in [1, \infty) \Leftrightarrow [0, \infty)$ and $f(x) \leq 0$ for $x \in (-\infty, 0]$. Also $f(-x) = e^{-x} - e^x = -(e^x - e^{-x}) = -f(x)$

$\Rightarrow f(x)$ is symmetric about origin

Moreover, as x increases e^x also increases, where as e^{-x} decreases

$\Rightarrow e^x - e^{-x}$ goes on increasing as x increases.

Thus, $f(x)$ increases with x as shown in Figure 2.134. Clearly $f(x)$ is injective.

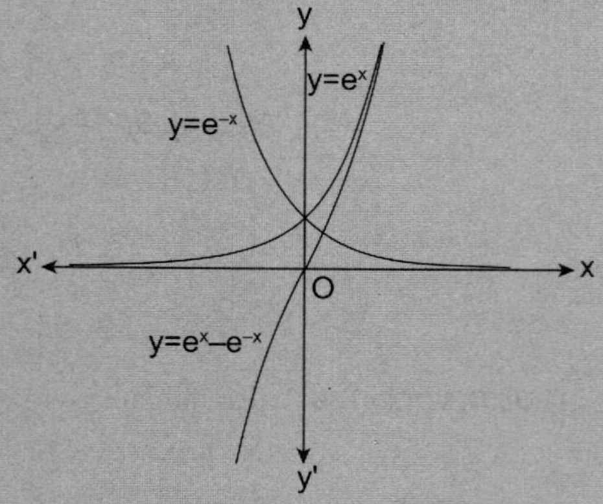

FIGURE 2.134

TEXTUAL EXERCISE–11: (SUBJECTIVE)

1. Find whether the functions defined below are injective or not?
   (i) $f(x) = 5x - 4$
   (ii) $f(x) = x - (1/x)$
   (iii) $f(x) = x^2 - 6x + 15$; $(x < 3)$
   (iv) $f(x) = \dfrac{(x^2+1)}{2x}$; $(x > 0)$
   (v) $f(x) = 2x^5 + 40x^2 + 2$; for $x \in [0, \infty)$
   (vi) $f(x) = \dfrac{x-2}{x+2}$; $x \in \mathbb{R} - \{-2\}$
   (vii) $f(x) = x^4 + x^3 + 1$; domain $\mathbb{R}$
   (viii) $f(x) = x^6 + x^4 + x^2 + 1$; domain $\mathbb{R}$

2. State whether following statements are true/false?
   (a) If f is strictly increasing function, then $[f(x)]$ is always many–one function; where [.] denotes gint function.
   (b) If f is continuous and strictly increasing function, then $[f(x)]$ is non-injective function; where [.] denotes gint function.
   (c) If f is continuous and strictly increasing function, then $\{f(x)\}$ is many–one function; where {} denotes fractional part function.
   (d) If $f(x)$ is continuous and strictly increasing function and range of f is a subset of $[0, 1)$, then $\{f(x)\}$ is injective function.
   (e) If f is continuous and strictly increasing function and range of f is superset of $[0, 1]$, then $\{f(x)\}$ is many–one function.

3. Given a set $A = \{1,2,3,4,5,6\}$. Prove that there is no injective functions $f: A \to A$ possible such that $a + f(a)$ is a perfect square for every $a \in A$. Does the above statement holds good if set A is replaced by B not containing element 1?

4. Let f: $\mathbb{R} \to \mathbb{R}$ where $f(x) = \dfrac{x^2+4x+7}{x^2+x+1}$. Is f one–one? Justify.

5. Find the values of k; if $f(x) = 2\sin x - kx + 3$, is defined from $\mathbb{R} \to \mathbb{R}$ and is one–one.

6. A function $f: D \to \mathbb{R}$ is given by $f(x) = \dfrac{5x - x^2 - 4}{5x - 4x^2 - 1}$; where D is domain of function. Is the function one–one?

7. Let f: $\mathbb{R} \to \mathbb{R}$ defined by $f(x) = \dfrac{x^2+3x+c}{x^2+x+1}$. Show that f is a many–one function for all c.

Answer Keys

1. (a) injective (ii) non-injective (iii) injective (iv) non-injective
 (v) non-injective (vi) injective (vii) non-injective (viii) non-injective
2. (a) false (b) true (c) false (d) true (e) true
3. no; only injective function $f: B \to B$ is given as {(2, 2), (3, 6), (4, 5), (5, 4), (6, 3)}
4. non-injective; $f(x)$ has one point of local maxima and one point of local minima
5. $k \in (-\infty, -2] \cup [2, \infty)$
6. yes; (since it is linear rational function)

TEXTUAL EXERCISE–11 (OBJECTIVE)

1. $f(x) = x^3 - 12x + 1$ is
 (a) non-injective on $\mathbb{R}$
 (b) injective on $(-\infty, -2]$ and on $[2, \infty)$
 (c) injective on $[-2, 2]$
 (d) non-injective on $[-2 - k, -2 + k]$ and on $[2 - k, 2 + k]$ for each $k > 0$

2. The function $f(x) = x^4 - 4x^3 + 4x^2 - 1$ is
 (a) injective on $\mathbb{R}$
 (d) non-injective on $(1 - k, 1 + k)$ for each $k > 0$
 (c) non-injective on $[2, \infty)$
 (d) non-injective on $(-\infty, 0]$

3. Let $f: \mathbb{R} \to \mathbb{R}$ be a function such that $f(x) = x^3 + x^2 + 3x + \sin x$. Then
 (a) f is injective
 (b) f is non-injective
 (c) f is increasing
 (d) decreasing

4. The function $y = 5 + e^{x^2 - 2}$ is
 (a) injective on $\mathbb{R}$
 (b) injective $[0, \infty)$
 (c) non-injective on $(-\infty, 0]$
 (d) injective on $[-k, k]$ for each real $k > 0$

5. The function $f(x) = \dfrac{x^2}{x^2 - 1}$ is
 (a) injective in $(-\infty, -1)$
 (b) non-injective in $(-1, 1)$
 (c) non-injective on $\mathbb{R}$
 (d) None of these

6. The function $f(x) = \ln(1 - \ln x)$
 (a) non-injective
 (b) injective
 (c) having range $\mathbb{R}$
 (d) decreasing function in its domain

7. The function $f(x) = \dfrac{x^3 - 2x^2 - 9x + 18}{x^2 - 4}$ is
 (a) injective on its domain
 (b) increasing at every point of its domain
 (c) non-injective on its domain
 (d) decreasing at every point of its domain

8. The function $y = [x] + \sqrt{\{x\}}$; (where [.] and {} are greatest integer function and fractional part function respectively) is
 (a) injective on $\mathbb{R}$ (d) decreasing on $\mathbb{R}$
 (c) non-injective on $\mathbb{R}$ (d) increasing on $\mathbb{R}$

9. If $A = \mathbb{R} - \{3\}$, $B = \mathbb{R} - \{1\}$ and $f: A \to B$ be defined by $f(x) = \left(\dfrac{x-2}{x-3}\right)$. Then
 (a) f is non-injective
 (b) f is one–one
 (c) f is increasing function
 (d) f is decreasing function

Answers

1. (a,b,c,d) 2. (b) 3. (a,c) 4. (b) 5. (a,b,c) 6. (b,c,d) 7. (b,c) 8. (a,d) 9. (b,d)

■ SURJECTIVE AND NON-SURJECTIVE FUNCTION

As we know that in a function all the elements of domain X must be related to some element in co-domain. When similar restriction is imposed for co-domain as well, then the function obtained is known as onto function.

Onto (Surjective) Function

A function $f: X \to Y$ is called surjective only when each element in the co-domain is f-image of at least one element in the domain, i.e., $f: X \to Y$ is onto iff $y \in Y$ there exists $x \in X$ such that $f(x) = y$, i.e., iff R_f = co-domain (Y)

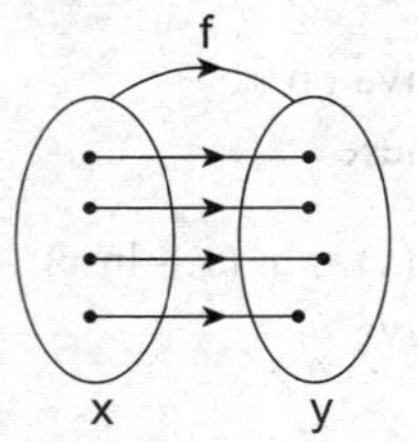

FIGURE 2.135

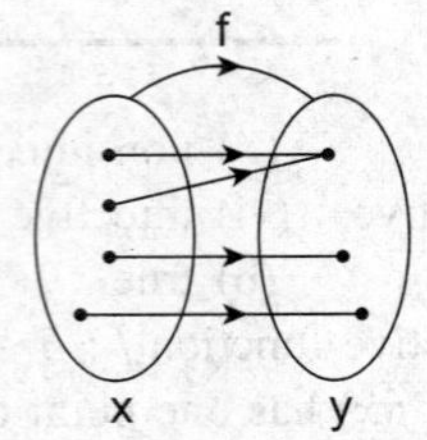

FIGURE 2.136

$\therefore$ Surjective $f: X \to Y$ reduces the co-domain set to range of function.

Example:

1. If $f(x)$ is any polynomial of odd degree, then it is surjective from $\mathbb{R} \to \mathbb{R}$
2. If $f(x) = \log_e x$ ($x > 0$), then it is surjective from $(0, \infty) \to \mathbb{R}$
3. If $f(x) = \tan x$, then it surjective from $\left(-\frac{\pi}{2}, \frac{\pi}{2}\right) \to \mathbb{R}$
4. If $f(x) = \cot x$, then $f(x)$ is surjective from $(0, \pi) \to \mathbb{R}$.

NOTE

The equality of range of function to co-domain forms the condition to test surjectivity of function. For instance to test surjectivity of f: $[0, \infty) \to [2, \infty)$ such that $f(x) = x^2 + 2$.

Using the analytic formula we obtain the rule of function for argument of x in terms of y as below:

$\because\ y = x^2 + 2$

$x^2 = y - 2$, i.e., $|x| = \sqrt{y-2}$

$\Rightarrow x = \sqrt{y-2} \qquad \because\ x \geq 0$

Now we check whether the expression of x in forms of y is valid for all elementary co-domain.

If it is so, then f is surjective otherwise it is non-surjective.

Thus, x to be real and positive RHS, i.e., $\sqrt{y-2}$ must be real and positive, thus, $y \in [2, \infty)$. Hence, the given function f is onto.

■ INTO (NON-SURJECTIVE) FUNCTION

While defining function we have mentioned that there may exist some element in the co-domain which are not related to any element in the co-domain.

$f: X \to Y$ is into iff there exists at least one $y \in Y$ which is not related with any $x \in X$.

Thus, the range of the into function is proper subset of the co-domain. That is, Range $\subset$ Co-Domain (properly).

Example:

1. If $f(x)$ is any polynomial of even degree, it is into from $\mathbb{R} \to \mathbb{R}$ as the range of function = $[k, \infty)$ where k is the minimum value of function is proper subset of $\mathbb{R}$.
2. If $f(x) = e^x$, then it is into function from $\mathbb{R} \to \mathbb{R}$ as the range of function = $(0, \infty)$ is proper subset of $\mathbb{R}$.
3. If $f(x) = \sec x$, then it is an into function from $\mathbb{R} \sim \left\{(2n+1)\frac{\pi}{2}; n \in \mathbb{Z}\right\} \to \mathbb{R}$ as its range = $(-\infty, -1] \cup [1, \infty)$ is proper subset of $\mathbb{R}$.

4. If $f(x) = \tan^2 x$, then $f(x)$ is into function from $\mathbb{R} \sim \left\{(2n+1)\frac{\pi}{2}; n \in \mathbb{Z}\right\} \rightarrow \mathbb{R}$ as its range $= [0, \infty)$ is a proper subset of $\mathbb{R}$.

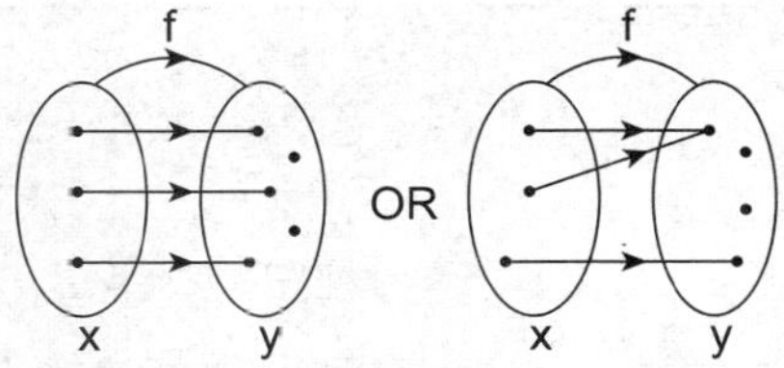

FIGURE 2.137

ILLUSTRATION 167: Find whether the following functions from $\mathbb{R} \rightarrow \mathbb{R}$ are onto or into?

(a) $f(x) = \dfrac{2x}{1+x^2}$ (b) $y = x^3$

(c) $y = x\,|x|$ (d) $y = \sin \pi x$

SOLUTION: (a) Since range of function is $[-1, 1]$, therefore, range is subset of co-domain (which is set of real number). Hence, $f(x)$ is into function.

(b) $y = x^3$ has range as set of real numbers, so it is onto function

(c) $y = x^2$ when $x \geq 0$ and $y = -x^2$ when $x < 0$

$\Rightarrow$ Range is set of real numbers. So, $f(x)$ is onto function

(d) Range of $\sin \pi x$ is $[-1, 1]$ which is a proper subset of real numbers, so it is an into function

ILLUSTRATION 168: A function $f : X \rightarrow Y$ defined as $f(x) = x + \sqrt{3 - 2x^2}$ is onto. Find the set Y if the set X is its natural domain.

SOLUTION: As $f : X \rightarrow Y$ is given as onto, therefore Y must be range of the function. Now to find range

Let $y = x + \sqrt{3 - 2x^2}$

$\Rightarrow (y - x)^2 = 3 - 2x^2$ $\Rightarrow y^2 - 2xy - x^2 = 3 - 2x^2$

$\Rightarrow 3x^2 - 2xy + y^2 - 3 = 0$. As, $x \in \mathbb{R}$, $D \geq 0 \Rightarrow y^2 - 3(y^2 - 3) \geq 0$

$\Rightarrow 2y^2 - 9 \leq 0$

$\Rightarrow y \in \left[-\dfrac{3}{\sqrt{2}}, \dfrac{3}{\sqrt{2}}\right]$. Hence, the set Y is $\left[-\dfrac{3}{\sqrt{2}}, \dfrac{3}{\sqrt{2}}\right]$.

■ HIT AND TRIAL METHOD

Sometimes we choose an element of co-domain which may not be an image of any element in domain and we test it for same. If it comes out to be true, then f is into function.

For instance $f : \mathbb{R} \rightarrow [0, \infty)$; $f(x) = \dfrac{e^x.(x^2+1)}{3+\sin x}$ is an into function, because $f(x)$ cannot attain zero value for any $x \in \mathbb{R}$, although zero is an element of co-domain.

ILLUSTRATION 169: Given $f : \mathbb{R} \rightarrow [-1, 1] : f(x) = \dfrac{3\cos x}{x^2 - 4x + 7}$, test whether $f(x)$ is a surjective function.

SOLUTION: Consider $f(x) = \dfrac{3\cos x}{x^2 - 4x + 7} = \dfrac{3\cos x}{(x-2)^2 + 3}$

Clearly values of $f(x)$ cannot be bygone the set $[-1, 1]$.

Now if we notice the element 1 or -1 in the co-domain

For $f(x) = 1$ $\Rightarrow \dfrac{3\cos x}{(x-2)^2+3} = 1$

$\Rightarrow$ $3\cos x - 3 = (x-2)^2$ $\Rightarrow -6\sin^2\dfrac{x}{2} = (x-2)^2$

LHS. $\in [-6, 0]$, where as RHS $\in [0, \infty)$. Therefore, equality may hold if LHS. = RHS = 0 for same input x, but it is never, so, as RHS vanishes at $x = 2$ but LHS is non-zero at $x = 2$.

$\Rightarrow$ $f(x) \neq 1$, neither $f(x)$ can be -1. Clearly f is an into function.

ILLUSTRATION 170: Show that $f: \mathbb{N} \to \mathbb{N}$ defined as $f(x) = 2x - 1$ is one–one function but not an onto function. Also analyse the nature of above function if it is defined from $\mathbb{R} \to \mathbb{R}$.

SOLUTION: $\because$ $f(x_1) = f(x_2)$ $\Rightarrow$ $2x_1 - 1 = 2x_2 - 1$ $\Rightarrow$ $x_1 = x_2$, thus, f is one–one

But f is not onto function as there does not exist any $x \in \mathbb{N}$ for which $f(x)$ is even.

Hence, no even natural number belonging to co-domain has its pre-image in $\mathbb{N}$.

But if f is a function: $\mathbb{R} \to \mathbb{R}$

Clearly function is one–one and being a polynomial is continuous.

Also $f'(x) = 2 > 0$, i.e., $f(x)$ is monotonic as well.

Also for any real $y \in$ co-domain $\mathbb{R}$ there exists an $x \in \mathbb{R}$ given by $x = \dfrac{y+1}{2}$ such that

$f(x) = f\left(\dfrac{y+1}{2}\right) = y$ consequently f is onto.

Concluding that $f: \mathbb{N} \to \mathbb{N}$ is injective but not surjective, whereas $f: \mathbb{R} \to \mathbb{R}$ is a bijective function.

ILLUSTRATION 171: A function $f: \mathbb{R} \to \mathbb{R}$ is given by: $f(x) = \dfrac{tx^2+3x-4}{t+3x-4x^2}$. Find the interval of values of t for which the function is onto.

SOLUTION: It is given that the co-domain of the function is $\mathbb{R}$. Since, the function is onto, the range of the function is equal to co-domain of the function, i.e., $\mathbb{R}$.

Let $y = \dfrac{tx^2+3x-4}{t+3x-4x^2}$

$\Rightarrow$ $tx^2 + 3x - 4 - ty - 3xy + 4x^2y = 0$

Representing it as a quadratic equation in variable x, we get

$\Rightarrow$ $(t + 4y)x^2 + 3(1 - y)x - (4 + ty) = 0$

Since x is real, $D \geq 0$

$\Rightarrow$ $9(1 - y)^2 + 4(t + 4y)(4 + ty) \geq 0$

$\Rightarrow$ $9(1 + y^2 - 2y) + 4(4t + t^2y + 4ty^2 + 16y) \geq 0$

$\Rightarrow$ $(9 + 16t)y^2 + (4t^2 + 46)y + (9 + 16t) \geq 0$

As the range of the given function has to be $\mathbb{R}$, implying that the above inequality holds for all real values of y

Therefore: Leading coefficient > 0 and $D \leq 0$

$\Rightarrow$ $9 + 16t > 0$ $\Rightarrow t > -9/16$ ..... (i)

$\Rightarrow$ $(4t^2 + 46)^2 - \{2(9 + 16t)\}^2 \leq 0$

$\Rightarrow$ $(4t^2 + 46 + 18 + 32t)(4t^2 + 46 - 18 - 32t) \leq 0$

$\Rightarrow$ $(t^2 + 8t + 16)(t^2 - 8t + 7) \leq 0$

$\Rightarrow (t + 4)^2 (t - 1)(t - 7) \le 0$

$\Rightarrow (t - 1)(t - 7) \le 0$ or $t = -4$

$\Rightarrow 1 \le t \le 7$ or $t = -4$ ...(ii)

Taking the intersection of the two intervals, we get $t \in [1, 7]$.

ILLUSTRATION 172: Let a function f defined from $\mathbb{R} \to \mathbb{R}$ as $f(x) = \begin{cases} 2x - 3m & \text{for } x \le 2 \\ mx - 11 & \text{for } x > 2 \end{cases}$. If the function is surjective, then find all values of m.

SOLUTION: For the function f to be surjective, its range must be the set of all real numbers, i.e., $\mathbb{R}$

For $x \le 2, f'(x) = 2$

$\Rightarrow$ Monotonically increasing for $x \le 2$

Hence, the maximum value of $f(x)$ for $x \le 2$ occurs at $x = 2$.

$\therefore$ The maximum value for $x \le 2$ is $4 - 3m$.
i.e., $f(x) \in (-\infty, 4 - 3m]$ for $x \le 2$

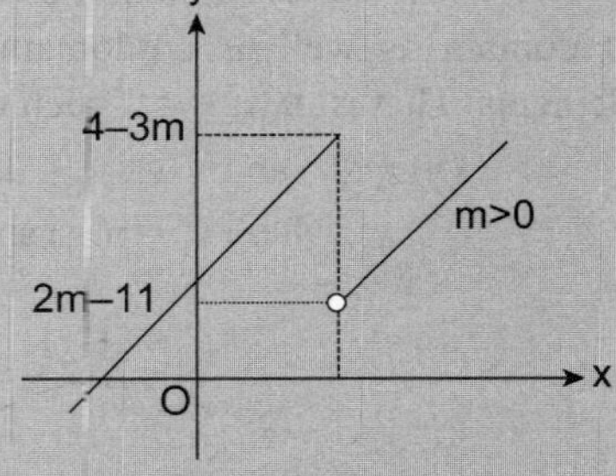

FIGURE 2.138

For range to be $\mathbb{R}$, the minimum value of $f(x)$ for $x > 2$, must be less than or equal to $4 - 3m$ and maximum must approach to infinitely.

Now for $x > 2, f'(x) = m$. Obviously $m > 0$ .... (1)

($\because$ if $m < 0, f'(x) < 0$, i.e., $f(x)$ is decreasing, then the range can't be $\mathbb{R}$ as shown in the given figure)

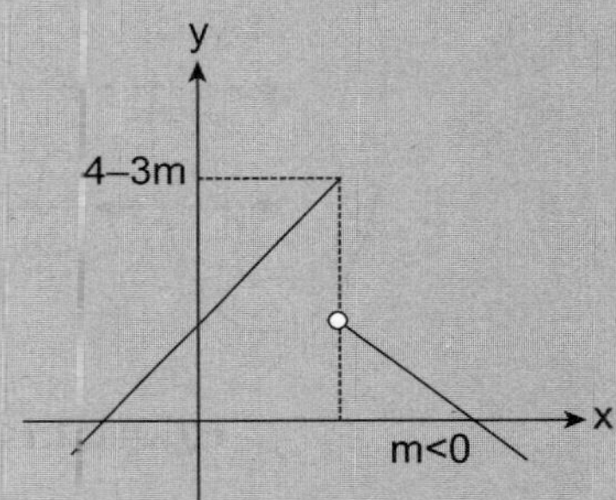

FIGURE 2.139

$\therefore$ for $x > 2$, $2m - 11 \le 4 - 3m$

$\Rightarrow 5m \le 15$

$\Rightarrow m \le 3$ ... (2)

$\therefore$ From (1) and (2), $m \in (0, 3]$

ILLUSTRATION 173: Prove that $f: \mathbb{R} - \{1\} \to \mathbb{R}$, given by $f(x) = \dfrac{x^{1/3}}{x^{1/3} - 1}$ is injective but not surjective.

SOLUTION: Let $f(a) = f(b)$ $\Rightarrow$ $\dfrac{a^{1/3}}{a^{1/3} - 1} = \dfrac{b^{1/3}}{b^{1/3} - 1}$

$\Rightarrow a^{1/3}b^{1/3} - a^{1/3} = a^{1/3}b^{1/3} - b^{1/3}$ $\Rightarrow -a^{1/3} = -b^{1/3}$ $\Rightarrow a = b$

This implies f is injective.

To prove that f is not surjective assume that $f(x) = b$; $b \in \mathbb{R}$.

Then $f(x) = b$

$$\Rightarrow \frac{x^{1/3}}{x^{1/3} - 1} = b$$

$$\Rightarrow x = \frac{b^3}{(b-1)^3}$$

The expression for x is not a real number when $b = 1$, and therefore, there is not real x such that $f(x) = 1$. Thus, $f(x)$ is not a surjective function.

■ ONE–ONE ONTO FUNCTION (BIJECTIVE FUNCTION)

If a function is both one–one as well as onto, then $f(x)$ is said to be bijective function or simply bijection. Injection means distinct $x \in X$ are related with distinct $y \in Y$ and surjective mean each $y \in Y$ is related with some $x \in X$.

Thus, taken both conditions together, bijective imposes the most strict condition for a function. It leads to invertibility of the function as all the distinct elements of domain as well as co-domain are related to distinct elements. That is, $\forall\ x, y \in X$ such that $x \neq y$.

$\Rightarrow\ f(x) \neq f(y)$ and $\forall\ y_1, y_2 \in Y$ such that $y_1 \neq y_2$

$\Rightarrow\ x_1 \neq x_2$; where $y_1 = f(x_1)$ and $y_2 = f(x_2)$

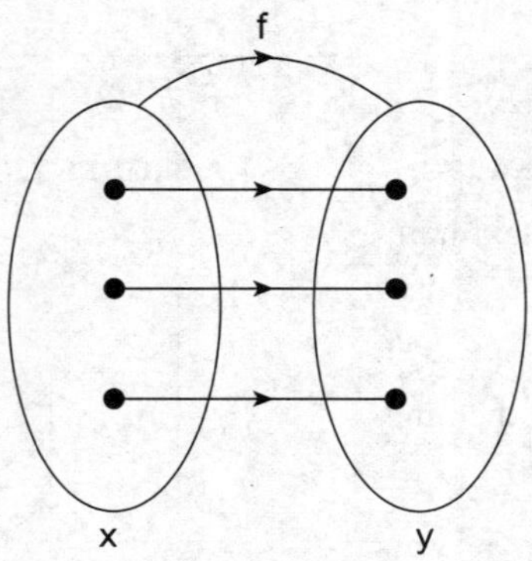

FIGURE 2.140

Thus, a function f: $X \to Y$ can be one of the given four types:

(i) one–one onto function (Injective and Surjective or Bijective):

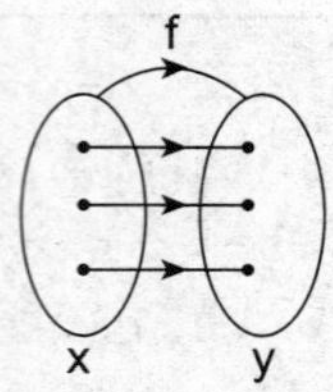

FIGURE 2.141

(ii) one–one into (injective but not surjective)

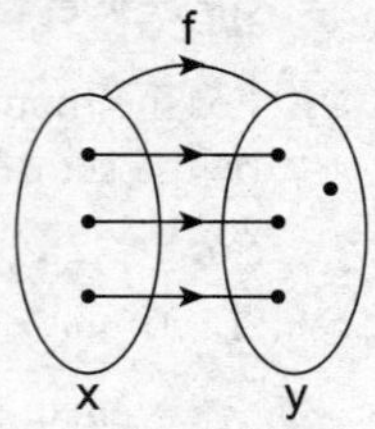

FIGURE 2.142

(iii) many–one onto (surjective but not injective)

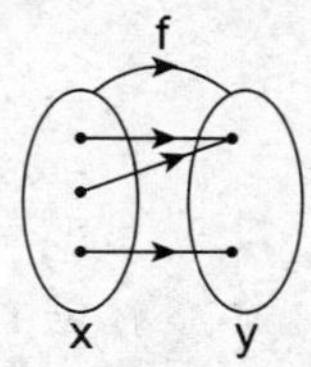

FIGURE 2.143

(iv) many–one into (neither surjective nor injective)

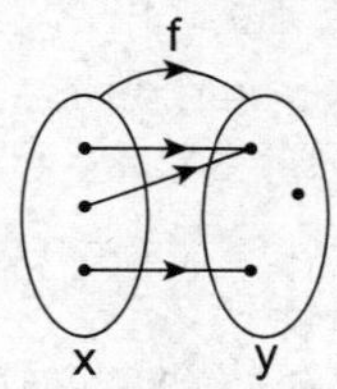

FIGURE 2.144

ILLUSTRATION 174: Show that the function $f(x) = x^2$; $f : A \to B$; where $A = \{-1, 1, 2, -2\}$; $B = \{1, 4\}$ is an onto function.

SOLUTION: $f(A) = \{(-1, 1), (1, 1), (2, 4), (-2, 4)\}$.

Thus, every element of B has a pre-image in A, thus, it is an onto function.

ILLUSTRATION 175: Show that an onto function f: $\{1, 2, 3\} \to \{1, 2, 3\}$ is always one–one.

SOLUTION: Suppose f is not one–one. Then there exists two elements, say 1 and 2 in the domain whose image in the co-domain is same. Also, the image of 3 under f can be only one element.

Therefore, the range set can have at the most two elements of the co-domain $\{1, 2, 3\}$, showing that f is not onto, a contradiction. Hence, f must be one–one.

ILLUSTRATION 176: Show that a one–one function f: {1, 2, 3} → {1, 2, 3} must be onto

SOLUTION: Since f is one–one, three elements of {1, 2, 3} must be taken to 3 different elements of the co-domain {1, 2, 3} under f. Hence, f has to be onto.

ILLUSTRATION 177: Show that f: $\mathbb{Z} \to \mathbb{Z}$, given by $f(x)=\begin{cases} x+5, \text{ if } x \text{ is odd} \\ x-5, \text{ if } x \text{ is even} \end{cases}$ is both one–one and onto.

SOLUTION: Suppose $f(x_1) = f(x_2)$. Note that if x_1 is odd and x_2 is even, then we will have $x_1 + 5 = x_2 - 5$, i.e., $x_2 - x_1 = 10$, which is impossible as the difference of an odd and even integer cannot be an even integer. Similarly, the possibility of x_1 being even and x_2 being odd can also be ruled out, using the similar argument. Therefore, both x_1 and x_2 must be either odd or even. Suppose both x_1 and x_2 are odd, then $f(x_1) = f(x_2)$

$\Rightarrow x_1 + 5 = x_2 + 5$

$\Rightarrow x_1 = x_2$

Similarly, if both x_1 and x_2 are even, then $f(x_1) = f(x_2) \Rightarrow x_1 - 5 = x_2 - 5 \Rightarrow x_1 = x_2$

Thus, f is one–one. Also any odd number $2k + 1$. ($k \in \mathbb{Z}$) in the co-domain $\mathbb{Z}$ is the image of $2k + 6$, in the domain $\mathbb{Z}$ and any even number $2r$ in the co-domain $\mathbb{Z}$ is the image of $2r - 5$ in the domain $\mathbb{Z}$. Thus, f is onto.

ILLUSTRATION 178: Investigate the function f: $(0, \infty) \to \mathbb{R}$ defined as $f(x) = e^{|\ln x|} - x^2$ for bijectivity.

SOLUTION: $f(x) = e^{|\ln x|} - x^2 = \begin{cases} e^{-\ln x} - x^2, 0 < x < 1 \\ e^{\ln x} - x^2, x \geq 1 \end{cases}$

$$= \begin{cases} \frac{1}{x} - x^2, 0 < x < 1 \\ x - x^2, x \geq 1 \end{cases}$$

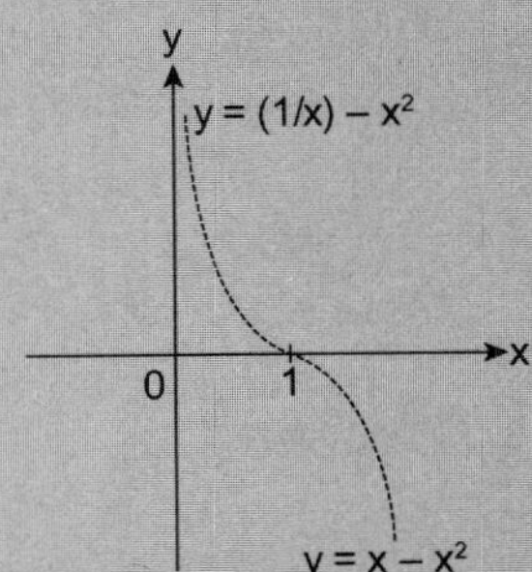

FIGURE 2.145

We obtain the graph of f in (0, 1) by graphical addition as shown below.

From the graph we can see that f is one–one and onto. Hence, f is bijective.

ILLUSTRATION 179: Let $A = \mathbb{R} - \{3\}$; $B = \mathbb{R} - \{1\}$. Let f: $A \to B$ be defined by $f(x) = \frac{x-2}{x-3}$. Is f bijective? Give reasons.

SOLUTION: For one–one (injective): Let $f(x_1) = f(x_2)$

$\Rightarrow \frac{x_1 - 2}{x_1 - 3} = \frac{x_2 - 2}{x_2 - 3} \Rightarrow x_1x_2 - 3x_1 - 2x_2 + 6 = x_1x_2 - 2x_1 - 3x_2 + 6$

$\Rightarrow x_1 = x_2$. Hence, it is one–one.

REMARK

In order to convert a function from many–one to an injective function its domain must be transformed to principle domain. In order to convert a function from into to onto, the co-domain of function must be replaced by its range.

ILLUSTRATION 180: A relation $f: \mathbb{R} \to \mathbb{R}$ such that $y = f(x)$ iff $x^2 + y^2 = 1$. Find its domain/range and convert it to

(a) Function
(b) Surjective function but not injective
(c) Injective function but not surjective
(d) Bijective function

SOLUTION: $x^2 + y^2 = 1 \Rightarrow y = \pm\sqrt{1-x^2} \Rightarrow 1 - x^2 \geq 0 \Rightarrow x^2 \leq 1 \Rightarrow x \in [-1, 1]$

$\Rightarrow D_f = [-1, 1]$. Similarly $x = \pm\sqrt{1-y^2} \Rightarrow y \in [-1, 1] \Rightarrow R_f = [-1, 1]$

Because for every value of $x \in [-1, 1]$, there are two values of y.

$\therefore$ $x^2 + y^2 = 1$ is a relation and not a function.

(a) So, to convert it into a function, redefine it as follows:

$f: [-1, 1] \to \mathbb{R}$ defined by $f(x) = \sqrt{1-x^2}$; $D_f = [-1, 1]$; $R_f = [0, 1]$

or $f: [-1, 1] \to \mathbb{R}$ defined by $f(x) = -\sqrt{1-x^2}$; $D_f = [-1, 1]$; $R_f = [-1, 0]$

The above functions represent, respectively, upper half and lower half arc of circle $x^2 + y^2 = 1$ as shown below:

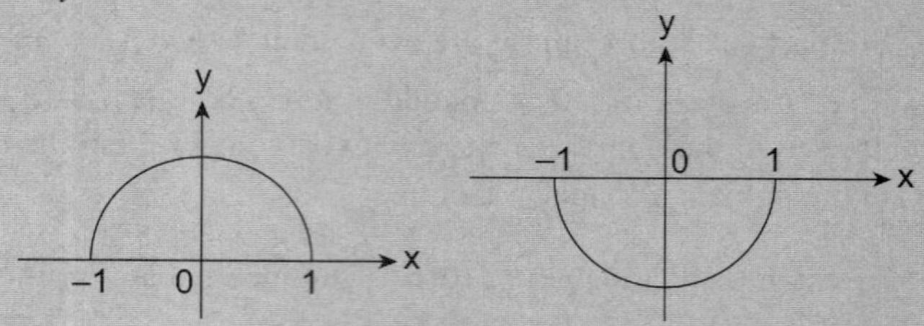

FIGURE 2.146

Clearly these functions are many–one, i.e., non-injective and non-surjective.

(b) However if we redefine the function as given below

$f: [-1, 1] \to [0, 1]$ defined by $f(x) = \sqrt{1-x^2}$; $D_f = [-1, 1]$; $R_f = [0, 1]$

or $f: [-1, 1] \to [0, 1]$ defined by $f(x) = -\sqrt{1-x^2}$; $D_f = [-1, 1]$; $R_f = [-1, 0]$

Clearly these functions represent the upper and lower half of the circle $x^2 + y^2 = 1$ and are surjective but not injective (i.e., many–one), graph of function shown in part (a).

(c) Now let $f: [0, 1] \to \mathbb{R}$ be defined by $f(x) = \sqrt{1-x^2}$; $D_f = [0, 1]$; $R_f = [0, 1]$ (fig 2.150).

or $f: [-1, 0] \to \mathbb{R}$ be defined by $f(x) = \sqrt{1-x^2}$; $D_f = [-1, 0]$; $R_f = [0, 1]$ (fig 2.151).

or $f: [-1, 0] \to \mathbb{R}$ be defined by $f(x) = -\sqrt{1-x^2}$; $D_f = [-1, 0]$; $R_f = [-1, 0]$ (fig 2.152).

or $f: [0, 1] \to \mathbb{R}$ be defined by $f(x) = -\sqrt{1-x^2}$; $D_f = [0, 1]$; $R_f = [-1, 0]$ (fig 2.153).

The above functions represent the arc of circle $x^2 + y^2 = 1$ in first, second, third, and fourth quadrant, respectively, as shown below.

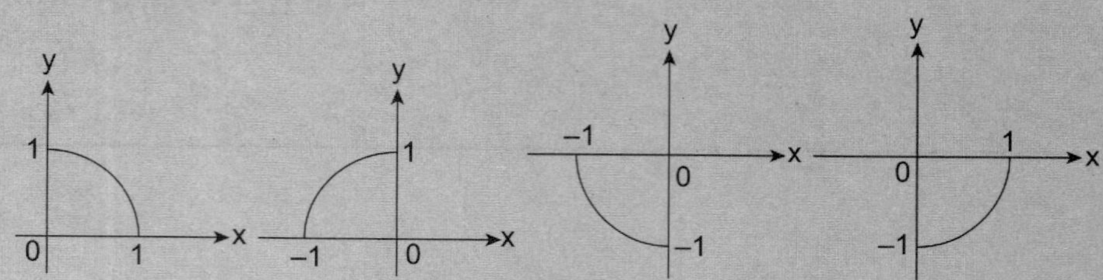

FIGURE 2.147

Clearly this function is injective but not surjective.

> **(d)** Now let $f: [0, 1] \to [0, 1]$ be defined by $f(x) = \sqrt{1-x^2}$; $D_f = [0, 1]$; $R_f = [0, 1]$.
> or $f: [-1, 0] \to [0, 1]$ be defined by $f(x) = \sqrt{1-x^2}$; $D_f = [-1, 0]$; $R_f = [0, 1]$.
> or $f: [-1, 0] \to [-1, 0]$ be defined by $f(x) = -\sqrt{1-x^2}$; $D_f = [-1, 0]$; $R_f = [-1, 0]$.
> or $f: [0, 1] \to [-1, 0]$ be defined by $f(x) = -\sqrt{1-x^2}$; $D_f = [0, 1]$; $R_f = [-1, 0]$.
> The above functions represent the arc of circle $x^2 + y^2 = 1$ in first, second, third, and fourth quadrant respectively as shown in part (c).
> Clearly these functions are injective as well as surjective. i.e., bijective functions as their Domain = principal domain and range = co-domain

■ NUMBER OF RELATIONS AND FUNCTIONS

Given two finite sets A and B having n and m elements respectively, i.e., $n(A) = n$ and $n(B) = m$.

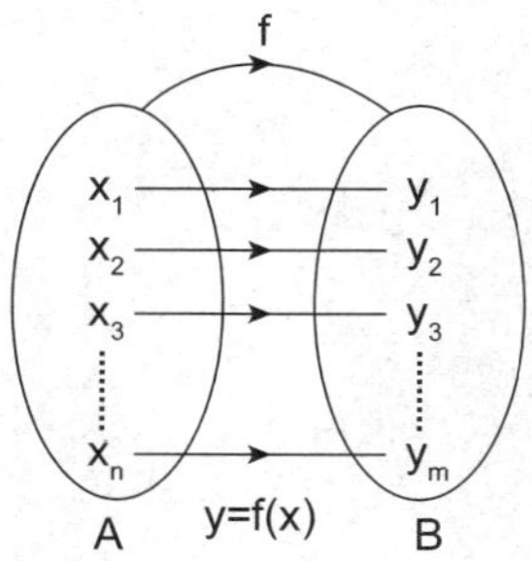

FIGURE 2.148

Number of Relations: No. of relations = Number of subsets of $A \times B = 2^{n(A\times B)} = 2^{nm}$

Number of Functions: Since each element of set A can be mapped in m ways

$\Rightarrow$ Number of ways of mapping all n elements of A

$$= \left(\underbrace{m \times m \times m \times \ldots. \times m}_{n\ times}\right) \text{ ways} = m^n \text{ ways}$$

Conclusion: $2^{nm} \geq m^n \;\forall\; m, n \in \mathbb{N}$

Number of one–one function (injective):

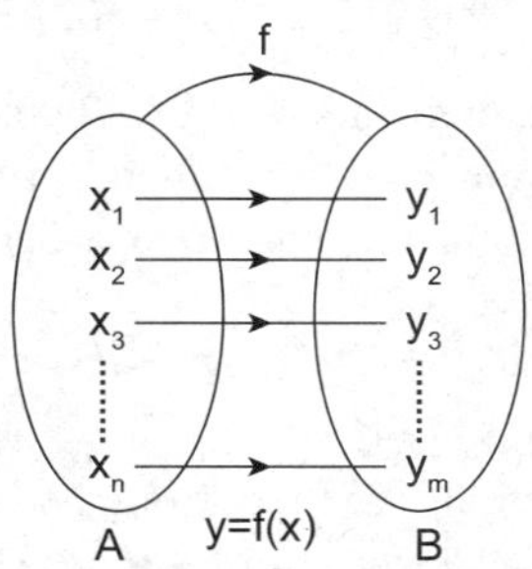

FIGURE 2.149

x_1 can be mapped in m ways

x_2 can be mapped in $(m - 1)$ ways

x_3 can be mapped in $(m - 2)$ ways

$\vdots$

x_n can be mapped in $(m - (n - 1))$ ways

$\Rightarrow$ Number of injective functions

$$= m(m-1)(m-2)\ldots.(m-n+1) = \begin{cases} {}^mP_n & m \geq n \\ 0 & m < n \end{cases}$$

Conclusion: ${}^mP_n \leq m^n$ (total number of functions).

Number of Non-surjective Functions (Into Functions)

Number of into functions (N) = Number of ways of distributing n different objects into m distinct boxes so that at least one box is empty.

$\Rightarrow$ $N = n(A_1 \cup A_2 \cup A_3 \cup \ldots \cup A_m)$; where A_i denotes the distributions when i^{th} box is empty.

$= \Sigma n(A_i) - \Sigma n(A_i \cap A_j) + \Sigma n(A_i \cap A_j \cap A_k) - \ldots.$

Now $n(A_i) = (m - 1)^n$; $n(A_i \cap A_j) = (m-2)^n$;

$n(A_i \cap A_j \cap A_k) = (m - 3)^n$

$\therefore$ ${}^mC_1(m - 1)^n - {}^mC_2(m - 2)^n + {}^mC_3\,(m - 3)^n - \ldots. + (-1)^{m-2}\,.\,{}^mC_{m-1}(1)^n.$

$$\Rightarrow N = \sum_{r=1}^{m} {}^mC_r(-1)^{r-1}(m-r)^n]$$

Number of Surjective Functions

Number of surjective functions = Total number of functions – number of into functions.

$$= m^n - \sum_{r=1}^{m} {}^mC_r(-1)^{r-1}(m-r)^n$$

$$= m^n + \sum_{r=1}^{m} {}^mC_r(-1)^r(m-r)^n = \sum_{r=0}^{m} {}^mC_r(-1)^r(m-r)^n$$

Conclusion: In case when $n(A) = n(B)$, the onto functions will be bijection

Number of onto functions = Number of one–one functions

$$\Rightarrow \sum_{r=0}^{n} {}^nC_r(-1)^r(n-r)^n = n!$$

ILLUSTRATION 181: If a function $f: X \to Y$ be such that $X = \{x, y\}$ and $Y = \{a, b, c\}$, then find :

(a) Number of relations from X to Y. **(b)** Number of functions $f: X \to Y$.

(c) Number of injective functions $f: X \to Y$. **(d)** Number of many–one functions $f: X \to Y$.

(e) Number of into functions $f: X \to Y$.

(f) Number of onto functions (surjective) $f: X \to Y$.

SOLUTION: **(a)** No. of relations from X to Y

$= Number of subsets of $X \times Y = (2)^{n(X \times Y)} = 2^{n(X) \times n(Y)} = (2)^{2\times3} = (2)^6 = 64$

(b) x can be related to a, b or c, i.e., in three ways, and corresponding to each choice of x, y can be related a, b, c in three ways. Thus, total number of functions $= 3 \times 3 = 9 = (3)^2 = [n(Y)]^{n(X)}$.

(c) Number of injective functions $= {}^{n(Y)}P_{n(X)} = {}^3P_2 = \dfrac{3!}{1!} = 3! = 6$.

Remark: If $n(X) > n(Y)$, then no injective functions can be formed from X to Y as in this case at least one element of Y has to be related to more than one element of X.

(d) Number of many–one functions

$=$ Total number of functions – number of one–one functions $= 9 - 6 = 3$.

(e) Number of into functions (non-surjective)

$\sum_{r=1}^{m} {}^mC_r(-1)^{r-1}(m-r)^n$; $n = n(X) = 2$; $m = n(Y) = 3$

$= {}^3C_1(-1)^0(3-1)^2 + {}^3C_2(-1)^1(3-2)^2 + {}^3C_3(-1)^2(3-3)^2 = 12 - 3 + 0 = 9$

(f) Number of onto functions (surjective)

$= (m)^n -$ Number of into functions $= \sum_{r=0}^{m}(-1)^r\, {}^mC_r(m-r)^n$;

where $n(X) = n$ and $n(Y) = m = (3)^2 - 9 = 0$.

REMARKS

1. *If n(X) < n(Y), then after mapping different elements of X to different elements of Y, we are left with at least one element of Y which is not related with any element of X, and hence, there will be no onto function from X to Y, i.e., all the functions from X to Y will be into.*
2. *If f from X to Y is a bijective function, then n(X) = n(Y)*

ILLUSTRATION 182: Find the number of surjections from X to Y; where $X = \{1, 2, 3, 4\}$, $Y = \{a, b\}$

SOLUTION: Every element of X can be connected to any of the two elements of Y, i.e., 2 choices. So, total number of ways $= 2^4$. But if all the elements of X get connected to a, function will not be onto. Similarly, if all the elements of A get connected to b, function will not be onto. So, number of onto functions is $2^4 - 2 = 14$ or alternatively, $\sum_{r=0}^{2}(-1)^r.{}^2C_r(2-r)^4 = {}^2C_0(2)^4 - {}^2C_1(1)^4 + {}^2C_2(0)^4 = 14$

ILLUSTRATION 183: Let $A = \{1, 2, 3\}$ and $B = \{4, 5, 6, 7\}$. How many functions are there from A to B? How many functions are there from B to A? How many injections are there from A to B? How many surjection are there from B to A.

SOLUTION: There are $(4)^3 = 64$ functions from A to B. There are 4 possibilities for the image of 1, 4 for the image of 2 and 4 for the image of 3. Similarly, there are $(3)^4 = 81$ functions from B to A. Number of surjections from B to $A = \sum_{r=0}^{3}(-1)^r.{}^3C_r(3-r)^4$

$= {}^3C_0(3)^4 - {}^3C_1(2)^4 + {}^3C_2(1)^4 = 81 - 48 + 3 = 36$

By the above result, there are 4.3.2 = 24 injections from A to B

TEXTUAL EXERCISE–12: (SUBJECTIVE)

1. Test the following functions for injectivity and surjectivity.

   (a) $y = 5x + 8$ (b) $y = \dfrac{x^2-1}{x^2+1}$

   (c) $y = \dfrac{ax+b}{ax-b}$ (d) $y = e^x + e^{-x}$

   (e) $y = e^x - e^{-x}$ (f) $y = \log\left(\dfrac{x-1}{x+1}\right)$

   (g) $y = \log(x+\sqrt{x^2+1})$ (h) $x + \dfrac{1}{x}$

2. Find number of surjection from A to B where $A = \{1, 2, 3, 4\}$, $B = \{a, b\}$

3. A function $f: X \rightarrow Y$ defined as $f(x) = \sqrt{1-2x} + x$ is from $A \rightarrow B$ and is onto. If the set A is its natural domain, then find the set B.

4. If the function $f: \mathbb{R} \rightarrow A$ given by

   (a) $f(x) = \dfrac{e^x - e^{-|x|}}{e^x + e^{-|x|}}$

   (b) $f(x) = \dfrac{e^x - e^{-|x|}}{e^x + e^{|x|}}$

   (c) $\dfrac{e^x - e^{|x|}}{e^x + e^{-|x|}}$ is surjection, then find A

5. Is the function $f: \mathbb{N} \rightarrow \mathbb{N}$ defined by $f(x) = 3x + 5$ surjective.

6. If a function $f: X \rightarrow Y$ be such that $X = \{x, y, z\}$ and $Y = \{a, b\}$. Then find :

   (a) total number of relations from X to Y.
   (b) total number of functions from X to Y.
   (c) Number of one–one functions from X to Y.
   (d) Number of many–one functions from X to Y.
   (e) Number of onto functions from X to Y.

7. Let $f(x) = ax^3 + bx^2 + cx + d \sin x$. Find the condition that $f(x)$ is always one–one function.

8. If $f: \mathbb{R} \rightarrow B$, defined by $f(x) = \sin x + \cos x - 4$, is onto, then find set B.

9. There are exactly two distinct linear functions which map $[-1, 1]$ onto $[0, 3]$, then find the point of intersection of the two functions.

10. If $f: \mathbb{R} \rightarrow \left[\dfrac{\pi}{6}, \dfrac{\pi}{2}\right)$, $f(x) = \sin^{-1}\left(\dfrac{x^2-a}{x^2+1}\right)$ is an onto function, then find the set of values of 'a'.

11. Let $f: \mathbb{R} \rightarrow \left[0, \dfrac{\pi}{2}\right)$ defined by $f(x) = \tan^{-1}(x^2 + x + a)$, then find the set of values of a for which f is onto.

12. For the following given functions $f(x) : D_f \rightarrow Y$ (D_f denotes Domain of f): find set Y for which $f(x)$ is surjective (on to) in each case.

    (a) $f(x) = \sin^6 x + \cos^6 x$
    (b) $f(x) = \log_e(|\sin x|^4 + |\cos x|^4)$
    (c) $f(x) = \sqrt{\ln|\operatorname{cosec} x|}$
    (d) $f(x) = \log_{\sqrt{2}}\left(\dfrac{\cos x + \sin x + 2\sqrt{2}}{\sqrt{2}}\right)$

13. Let $A = \{x : -k \le x \le k;\ k \in \mathbb{N}\}$ and $B_1 = \left\{\pm\dfrac{m^2}{4}; 0 \le m \le k; m \in \mathbb{Z}\right\}$; $B_2 = A$; $B_3 = \{\pm m^4;$ $0 \le m \le k;\ m \in \mathbb{R}\}$
    $B_4 = \{m^2;\ m \in \mathbb{Z};\ 0 \le m \le k\}$; $B_5 = A$. For each of the following functions from A to B_i, find whether it is surjective, injective, or bijective.

    (a) $f(x) = \dfrac{x|x|}{4}$; $f: A \rightarrow B_1$
    (b) $g(x) = \sqrt{x^2}$; $g: A \rightarrow B_2$
    (c) $h(x) = x^3|x|$; $h: A \rightarrow B_3$
    (d) $k(x) = x^2$; $k: A \rightarrow B_4$
    (e) $\phi(x) = x \cos(2x + 1)\pi x$; $\phi: A \rightarrow B_5$

14. Let $f:\mathbb{R} \to \mathbb{R}$ be a function such that $f(x) = x^3 + x^2 + 3x + \sin x$. Then check the injectivity and surjectivity of the function.

15. Which of the following functions from $\mathbb{Z}$ to itself are bijections?

(a) $f(x) = x + 3$ (b) $f(n) = x^5$

(c) $f(x) = 3x + 2$ (d) $f(x) = x^2 + x$

16. If $f : \mathbb{R} \to \mathbb{R}$ defined by $f(x) = \begin{cases} 2x & if\ x \geq 0 \\ 2x-3 & if\ x < 0 \end{cases}$.

Show that f is one–one but not onto.

17. Let $f : \mathbb{R} - \{2\} \to \mathbb{R} - \{1\}$ be defined by $f(x) = \dfrac{x-5}{x-2}$. Is f bijective? Give reasons.

18. Let $A = \mathbb{R} - \{3\}$, $B = \mathbb{R} - \{1\}$ and $f : A \to B$ defined by $f(x) = \dfrac{x-2}{x-3}$. Is f bijective? Give reason.

19. Determine the kind of mapping if $f : [1, 7] \to [2, 27]$, where $f(x) = x^2 - 4x + 6$.

20. For each of the following functions find whether it is one–one or many–one and into or onto.

(a) $f(x) = 2 \cot x$; $f : (\pi, 2\pi) \to \mathbb{R}$

(b) $f(x) = \dfrac{4}{1+x^2}$; $f : \mathbb{R} \to \mathbb{R}$

(c) $f(x) = x^4 + \ln x$; $f : (0, \infty) \to \mathbb{R}$

21. Classify the following functions $f(x)$ defined in $\mathbb{R} \to \mathbb{R}$ as injective, surjective both or none.

(a) $f(x) = \dfrac{x^2+4x+30}{x^2-8x+18}$

(b) $f(x) = x^3 - 6x^2 + 11x - 6$

(c) $f(x) = (x^2 + x + 5)(x^2 + x + 3)$

22. Find the set of values of k for which the function $f(x) = kx + 3\sin x + 5$ is one–one and onto.

23. Let $f(x) = \dfrac{x-1}{m-x^2+1}$, $x \in \mathbb{R}$. If the range of $f(x)$ does not contain the open interval $\left(-1, \dfrac{-1}{3}\right)$, then prove that $m \leq \dfrac{-1}{4}$.

24. Verify if $f(x) = \dfrac{x^2-8x+18}{x^2+4x+30}$ is an injective function.

25. Check whether $f(x) = \dfrac{x}{1+|x|}$, $x \in \mathbb{R}$ is injective or surjective or both or none.

26. Prove that $f : (-1, 1) \to \mathbb{R}$ defined by $f(x) = \begin{cases} \dfrac{x}{1+x}, & -1 < x \leq 0 \\ \dfrac{x}{1-x}, & 0 < x < 1 \end{cases}$ is a bijective function.

27. If the function $f : [2, \infty) \to X$ be bijective, where $f(x) = 5 - 4x + x^2$, then find the set X.

28. Let $f : \mathbb{N} \sim \{1\} \to \mathbb{N}$ be defined by $f(n)$ = the highest prime factor of n. Show that f is neither one–one nor onto. Find the range of f.

29. Let $f(x) = 1/(1 - x)$. If $f_2(x)$ denote $f\{f(x)\}$, $f_3(x)$ denote $f\{f\{f(x)\}\}$ and so on, then $f_{3n}(x)$ is ($n \in \mathbb{N}$).

30. Let $f(x) = \dfrac{ax+b}{cx+d}$, $x \neq -\dfrac{d}{c}$. If $d = -a$, show that $f\{f(x)\} = x$, i.e., fof is an identity function.

31. Let $f : R \to [-1, 1]$, $f(x) = \dfrac{\sin x}{x^2+1}$. Find whether f is onto

32. Show that the function $f : \mathbb{R} \to \mathbb{R}$ defined by $f(x) = \dfrac{1}{x}$ is one–one and onto, where $\mathbb{R}$ is the set of all non-zero real numbers. Is the result true, if the domain $\mathbb{R}$ is replaced by $\mathbb{N}$ with co-domain being same as $\mathbb{R}$?

33. Check the injectivity and surjectivity of the following functions:

(i) $f : \mathbb{N} \to \mathbb{N}$ given by $f(x) = x^2$

(ii) $f : \mathbb{Z} \to \mathbb{Z}$ given by $f(x) = x^2$

(iii) $f : \mathbb{R} \to \mathbb{R}$ given by $f(x) = x^2$

(iv) $f : \mathbb{N} \to \mathbb{N}$ given by $f(x) = x^3$

(v) $f : \mathbb{Z} \to \mathbb{Z}$ given by $f(x) = x^3$

Answer Keys

1. (a) (a) bijective (b) many–one into (c) one–one into (d) many–one into
(e) one–one onto (f) one–one into (g) one–one onto (h) many–one into

2. 14 **3.**

4. (a) [0, 1) (b) [0, 1/2) (c) $(-\infty, 0)$ **5.**

6. (a) 64 (b) 8 (c) 0 (d) 8 (e) 2

7. $b^2 < 3a(c - d)$; $a > 0$ and $b^2 < 3a(c + d)$; $a < a < 0$ **8.**

9. $y = \frac{3x}{2} + \frac{3}{2}, \frac{-3}{2}x + \frac{3}{2}$ **10.** $x \in \left(-1, -\frac{1}{2}\right]$ to be defined and to be onto a = -1/2

11. $x \in \left[\frac{1}{4}, \infty\right)$ to be defined and to be onto a = 1/4

12. (a) [1/4,1] (b) $[-\log_e 2, 0]$ (c) $[0, \infty)$ (d) $[0, 2\log_2 3]$

13. (a) bijective (b) non-injective, non-surjective, non-bijective
(c) non-surjective, injective, non-bijective (d) surjective, non-injective, non-bijective
(e) Injective, surjective, bijective

14. f is one–one and onto **15.** $f(x) = x + 3$

17. $f'(x) = \frac{3}{(x-2)^2} > 0\ \forall\ x \in \mathbb{R} \sim \{2\}$ $\Rightarrow$ y is injective on $\mathbb{R} \sim \{2\}$ and $y \neq 1$; $y \in \mathbb{R}$ $\Rightarrow$ y is surjective.

18. Yes, $f(x) = f(y)$ $\Rightarrow x = y$ and range = co-domain

19. non-injective, but surjective

20. (a) bijective (b) neither injective nor surjective (c) bijective

21. (a) neither surjective nor injective (b) surjective but not injective
(c) neither injective nor surjective

22. $(-\infty, -3] \cup [3, \infty)$ **24.** no **25.** one–one, not onto **27.** $[1,\infty)$

28. prime numbers **29.** x **31.** into **32.** no

33. (i) Injective but not surjective (ii) Neither injective nor surjective
(iii) Neither injective nor surjective (iv) Injective but not surjective (v) Injective but not surjective

TEXTUAL EXERCISE–12: (OBJECTIVE)

1. Function f: $(-\infty,-1) \to (0, e^5)$ defined by $f(x) = e^{x^3-3x+2}$ is

(a) many–one and onto (b) many–one and into
(c) one–one and onto (d) one–one and into

2. Given list of functions in column I and their classification in column II

Column I	Column II
(i) $e^x - e^{-x}$	(a) one–one onto
(ii) $x^3 - 1$	(b) one–one into
(iii) $\frac{2x}{1+x^2}$	(c) many–one onto
(iv) a^{x^3}	(d) many–one into
(v) $x^3\|x\|$	(e) not a function
(vi) $\frac{x^2-x+1}{x^2+x+1}$	
(vii) $\sin^3 x$	

Which of the following represents the correct match for column I and column II?

	(i)	(ii)	(iii)	(iv)	(v)	(vi)	(vii)
(a)	(a)	(c)	(d)	(b)	(a)	(d)	(d)
(b)	(c)	(a)	(d)	(b)	(d)	(a)	(d)
(c)	(a)	(c)	(b)	(d)	(a)	(a)	(d)
(d)	(b)	(a)	(c)	(a)	(d)	(b)	(c)

3. For the following given four functions if the function $f(x)\ D_f \to Y$ (D_f denotes domain of f):, then $f(x)$ is surjective (onto) for set Y.

(i) $f(x) = \sqrt{\log_e \frac{1}{|\sec x|}}$

(a) $\mathbb{R}$
(b) $[0, \infty)$
(c) $\{0\}$
(d) [0,1)

(ii) $f(x) = \dfrac{e^x - e^{-x}}{e^x + e^{-x}}$

(a) (–1, 1) (b) [–1, 1]
(c) {0} (d) None of these

(iii) $f(x) = \dfrac{x^2}{1+x^4}$

(a) [0, 1] (b) [1, 2]
(c) [3/4, 1] (d) None of these

(iv) $f(x) = \sin^4 x + \cos^2 x$

(a) [3/4, 1] (b) [1/4, 1]
(c) [0, 1] (d) None of these

4. Let $f : \mathbb{R} \to \mathbb{R}$ be a function such that $f(x) = x^3 - 6x^2 + 11x - 6$

(a) f is one–one and into
(b) f is many–one and into
(c) f is one–one and onto
(d) f is many–one and onto

5. The range of the function $f(x) = {}^{7-x}P_{x-3}$ is

(a) [1, 2, 3] (b) {3, 4, 5, 6}
(c) {1, 2, 3, 4} (d) {1, 2, 3, 4, 5}

6. Which of the following functions is not injective ?

(a) $f(x) = |x + 1|$, $x \in [-1, 0)$
(b) $f(x) = x + 1/x$, $x \in [0, \infty)$
(c) $f(x) = x^2 + 4x - 5$
(d) $f(x) = e^{-x}$, $x \in [0, \infty)$

7. A mapping f: $A \to [-1, 1]$ defined by $f(x) = \sin 3x$, is one–one and onto. Which of the following intervals can A be?

(a) $\left[-\dfrac{\pi}{6}, \dfrac{\pi}{6}\right]$ (b) $\left[-\dfrac{\pi}{3}, \dfrac{\pi}{3}\right]$

(c) $\left[\dfrac{\pi}{6}, \dfrac{\pi}{2}\right]$ (d) None of these

8. If $f : \mathbb{N} \to \mathbb{Z}$ is defined by $f(n) = \begin{cases} \dfrac{n-1}{2}, & \text{when } n \text{ is odd} \\ -\dfrac{n}{2}, & \text{when } n \text{ is even} \end{cases}$; then the type of function is

(a) injective
(b) surjective
(c) injective but not surjective
(d) surjective but not injective

9. If $f : \mathbb{R} \to \mathbb{R}$ is defined by $f(x) = \dfrac{x^2-4}{x^2+4}$, then the type of function is

(a) injective
(b) surjective
(c) injective but not surjective
(d) surjective but not injective

10. Let f: (–1, 1) $\to Y$ be a function defined by $f(x) = \tan^{-1}\dfrac{2x}{1-x^2}$, then f is bijective when Y is the set

(a) $\left[0, \dfrac{\pi}{2}\right)$ (b) $\left(0, \dfrac{\pi}{2}\right)$

(c) $\left(-\dfrac{\pi}{2}, \dfrac{\pi}{2}\right)$ (d) $\left[-\dfrac{\pi}{2}, \dfrac{\pi}{2}\right]$

11. Let g: $\mathbb{R} \to \left(0, \dfrac{\pi}{3}\right]$ is defined by $g(x) = \cos^{-1}\left(\dfrac{x^2-\alpha}{1+x^2}\right)$. Then the possible values of 'α' for which g is surjective function is/are

(a) $\left(-\dfrac{1}{2}, \dfrac{3}{4}\right]$ (b) $\left(-1, \dfrac{1}{2}\right]$

(c) $\left(-1, \dfrac{3}{4}\right]$ (d) None of these

12. If f: $\mathbb{R} \to \mathbb{R}$, is defined by $f(x) = \begin{cases} x|x| - 6, & x \in Q \\ x|x| - \sqrt{2}, & x \notin Q \end{cases}$, then the type of function is

(a) injective
(b) surjective
(c) injective but not surjective
(d) surjective but not injective

13. If $f(x) = \dfrac{\sin([x]\pi)}{x^2+x+1}$; where [.] denotes the greatest integer function, then

(a) f is one–one
(b) f is not one–one and non-constant
(c) f is a constant function
(d) None of these

14. Let $X = \{a_1, a_2, \ldots, a_6\}$ and $Y = \{b_1, b_2, b_3\}$. The number of functions f from X to Y such that it is onto and there are exactly three elements in X such that $f(a_1) = b_1$, is

(a) 75 (b) 90
(c) 100 (d) 120

15. The number of bijective functions $f : Y \to Y$, where $Y = \{4, 5, 6\}$ such that $f(4) \neq 6$, $f(5) \neq 4$, $f(6) \neq 5$, is

(a) 1 (b) 2

(c) 9 (d) None of these

16. Let f: $\mathbb{R} \to \mathbb{R}$ and g: $\mathbb{R} \to \mathbb{R}$ be two one–one and onto functions such that they are the mirror images of each other about the line $y = k$. If $\phi(x) = f(x) + g(x)$, then $\phi(x)$ is

(a) one–one and onto

(b) only one–one and not onto

(c) only onto but not one–one

(d) neither one–one nor onto

17. Let $X = \{a_1, a_3, a_3, a_4, a_5\}$, $Y = \{b_1, b_2, b_3, b_4, b_5\}$. Then the number of one–one mappings from X to Y such that $f(a_i) \neq b_i$, $\forall\, i \in \{1, 2, 3, 4, 5\}$.

(a) 40 (b) 44

(c) 24 (d) 60

Answer Keys

1. (d) **2.** (a) **3.** **(i)** (c) **(ii)** (a) **(iii)** (c) **(iv)** (b) **4.** (c) **5.** (a) **6.** (b,c)
7. (a,c) **8.** (a,b) **9.** (d) **10.** (d) **11.** (b) **12.** (c) **13.** (c) **14.** (d) **15.** (b)
16. (d) **17.** (b)

■ COMPOSITION OF FUNCTIONS

Composition of function is a process of combining two or more functions by which output of one function is applied to second function whose output in term is applied to third function and so on. For instance, consider two functions f and g such that for some input x the output $f(x)$ lies in the domain of g and therefore the function g assigns a value for the input $f(x)$ called as $g(f(x))$, the above successive operations of functions f over x and then g over $f(x)$ is called as composition and denoted by *gof*. The composition of function can be easily understood by the following machine model of composite machine $g(f(x))$.

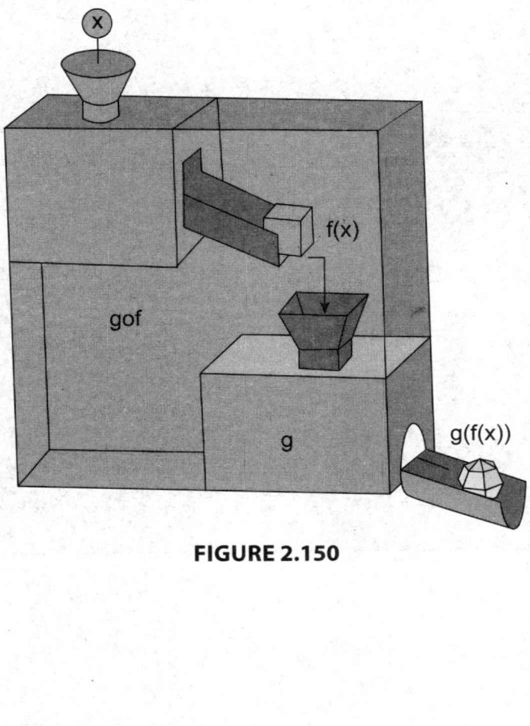

FIGURE 2.150

The output $f(x)$ of f machine is taken as input for g machine and $g(f(x))$ is the final output of composite machine *gof*.

Let us consider two functions $f : X \to Y$ and $g : Y \to Z$, such that the co-domain of f is domain of g. By composing the function g with f, we mean to define the analytical formula for a new function $h : X \to Z$, by which an element $x \in X$ is associated with an unique element $z \in Z$. The definition can be mathematically described as below.

Composite of Uniformly Defined Functions

Given two functions $f : X \to Y$ and $g : Y \to Z$, then there exists a function $h = gof : X \to Z$ such that $h(x) = (gof)(x) = g(f(x))\ \forall\, x \in X$. It is also called as 'function of function' or 'composite function of g and f' or 'g composed with f' and diagrammatically shown as

$$\xrightarrow[x \in X]{x} \boxed{f} \xrightarrow[y \in Y]{y=f(x)} \boxed{g} \longrightarrow \underbrace{z = g(f(x))}_{z \in Z}$$

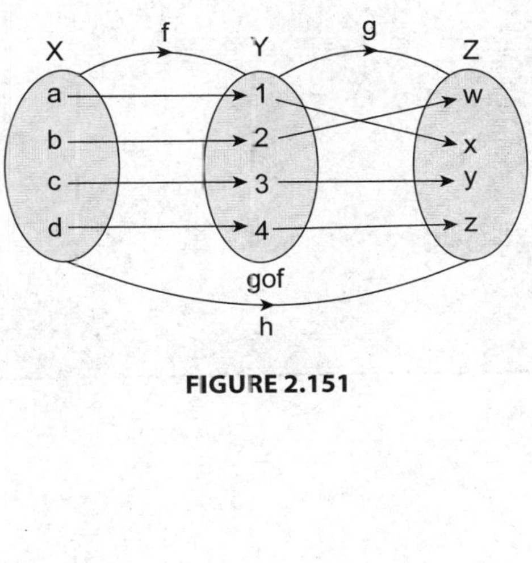

FIGURE 2.151

Thus, the image of every $x \in X$ under the function gof is the g-image of the f-image of x. gof is defined only if $\forall\ x \in X$, $f(x)$ is an element of the domain of g, so that we can take its g-image. To compute $gof(x)$, we first apply f on x, then apply g on the output $f(x)$. Figure 2.152 represents the composition function gof of functions $f: X \to Y$ and $g: Y \to Z$, where $X = \{a, b, c, d\}$; $Y = \{1, 2, 3, 4\}$; $Z = \{w, x, y, z\}$.

ILLUSTRATION 184: Let $f: \{1, 2, 3, 4\} \to \{2, 3, 5, 7, 11\}$ and $g: \{2, 3, 5, 7, 11\} \to \{5, 7, 9\}$ be functions defined as $f(1) = 2, f(2) = 3, f(3) = 5, f(4) = 7$ and $g(2) = g(3) = 5$ and $g(5) = 7$, $g(7) = 9$. Find gof.

SOLUTION: We have $gof(1) = g(f(1)) = g(2) = 5$, $gof(2) = g(f(2)) = g(3) = 5$, $gof(3) = g(f(3)) = g(5) = 7$ and $gof(4) = g(f(4)) = g(7) = 9$.

Thus, gof; $\{1, 2, 3, 4\} \to \{5, 7, 9\}$ is given by $gof = \{(1, 5), (2, 5), (3, 7), (4, 9)\}$

ILLUSTRATION 185: Given three sets $X = \{0, 1, 2, 3\}$,$Y = \{1, 2, 5, 10, 15\}$ and $Z = \{1, 3, 9, 19, 29, 31, 51, 101, 201\}$. Let $f: X \to Y$ and $g: Y \to Z$ be functions defined as $f(x) = x^2 + 1$ and $g(x) = 2x - 1$. Find $gof: X \to Z$.

SOLUTION: We have $gof(0) = g(f(0)) = g(1) = 1$, $gof(1) = g(f(1)) = g(2) = 3$, $gof(2) = g(f(2)) = g(5) = 9$ and $gof(3) = g(10) = 19$.

Thus, gof; $X \to Z$ is given by $gof = \{(0, 1), (1, 3), (2, 9), (3, 19)\}$

ILLUSTRATION 186: Let two functions be defined as $f = \{(0, 1), (1, 2), (2, 3), (3,4)\}$ and $g = \{(-1, 3), (2, 1), (3, 2), (4, 0)\}$. Define gof.

SOLUTION: Here, Domain of $f = D_1 = \{0, 1, 2, 3\}$; Range of $f = R_1 = \{1, 2, 3, 4\}$

Domain of $g = D_2 = \{-1, 2, 3, 4\}$; Range of $g = R_2 = \{0, 1, 2, 3\}$

Now domain of gof is the set A of those elements of D_1 corresponding to which the output of the function 'f' contains common elements of R_1 and D_2.

Let set $X = R_1 \cap D_2 = \{2, 3, 4\}$. Now $f(1) = 2, f(2) = 3, f(3) = 4$.

Hence, $A = \{1, 2, 3\}$. Clearly A is a subset of D_1. Now, range of gof is the set B of those elements of R_2 which are the outputs of the elements of set X under g. Now $g(2) = 1$, $g(3) = 2$ and $g(4) = 0$. Hence, $B = \{1, 2, 0\}$. Clearly B is a subset of R_2

$\therefore$ $gof: \{1, 2, 3\} \to \{1, 2, 0\}$ and $gof = \{(1, 1), (2, 2), (3, 0)\}$

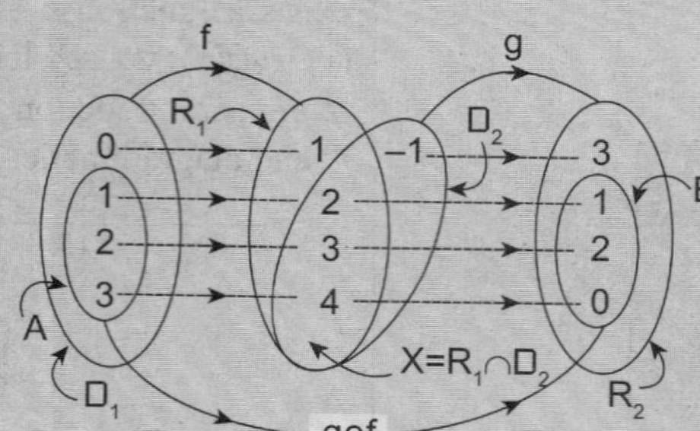

FIGURE 2.152

ILLUSTRATION 187: Show that if $f: \mathbb{R} - \left\{\frac{7}{3}\right\} \to \mathbb{R} - \left\{\frac{5}{3}\right\}$ is defined by $f(x) = \frac{5x+2}{3x-7}$ and $g: \mathbb{R} - \left\{\frac{5}{3}\right\} \to \mathbb{R} - \left\{\frac{7}{3}\right\}$ is defined by $g(x) = \frac{7x+2}{3x-5}$, then $fog = I_A$ and $gof = I_B$; where

$A = \mathbb{R} - \left\{\frac{5}{3}\right\}, B = \mathbb{R} - \left\{\frac{7}{3}\right\}; I_A(x) = x \in A, I_B(x) = x \; \forall \; x \in B$ are called identity functions on set A and B, respectively.

SOLUTION: Here we have $gof(x) = g\left(\frac{5x+2}{3x-7}\right) = \frac{7\left(\frac{5x+2}{3x-7}\right)+2}{3\left(\frac{5x+2}{3x-7}\right)-5} = \frac{35x+14+6x-14}{15x+6-15x+35} = \frac{41x}{41} = x \; \forall \; x \in B$

$\left(\because \quad g\left(\frac{5x+2}{3x-7}\right) \text{is valid for} \frac{5x+2}{3x-7} \neq \frac{5}{3} \text{ i.e., } 6 \neq -35, \text{which is true}\right)$

Similarly, $fog(x) = f\left(\frac{7x+2}{3x-5}\right) = \frac{5\left(\frac{7x+2}{3x-5}\right)+2}{3\left(\frac{7x+2}{3x-5}\right)-7} = \frac{35x+10+6x-10}{21x+6-21x+35} = \frac{41x}{41} = x \; \forall \; x \in A$

$\left(\because \quad f\left(\frac{7x+2}{3x-5}\right) \text{is valid for} \frac{7x+2}{3x-5} \neq \frac{7}{3} \text{ i.e., } 6 \neq -35, \text{which is true}\right)$

Thus, $gof(x) = x, \forall \; x \in B$ and $fog(x) = x, \forall \; x \in A$, which implies that $gof = I_B$ and $fog = I_A$.

ILLUSTRATION 188: Given two linear polynomial functions f and g such that $f(x) = mx + c$ and $g(x) = cx + m$ where m and $c \in \mathbb{N}$. If $f(g(5)) - g(f(5)) = k$, then find all possible ordered pairs (m, c) for

(a) $k = 12$ (b) $k = 35$

SOLUTION: From the definition of f and g; $f(g(x)) = m(g(x)) + c = m(cx + m) + c$

$\Rightarrow f(g(x)) = cmx + m^2 + c$ ..... (1)

Similarly; $g(f(x)) = c(mx + c) + m = cmx + c^2 + m$ .... (2)

Now $f(g(x)) - g(f(x)) = m^2 + c - c^2 - m = (m^2 - c^2) + (c - m) = (m - c)(m + c - 1)$

(a) Now since $f(g(5)) - g(f(5)) = 12$

$\Rightarrow (m - c)(m + c - 1) = 12$ .... (3)

Since $(m - c)$ and $(m + c - 1)$ are of opposite parity and $m - c < m + c - 1$ and $12 = 2^2 \times 3$

$\Rightarrow$ possible factorizations are 1×12 or 2×6 or 3×4

Case (i): $m - c = 1$ and $m + c - 1 = 12$

$\Rightarrow c = 6$ and $m = 7$

Case (ii): $m - c = 2$ and $m + c - 1 = 6$, not possible as $m - c$ and $m + c - 1$ both cannot be even as they are of opposite parity

Case (iii): $m - c = 3$ and $m + c - 1 = 4$. $\Rightarrow c = 1$ and $m = 4$

Thus, the possible ordered pairs (m, c) are (7,6);(4,1)

(b) If $f(g(5)) - g(f(5)) = 35$

$\Rightarrow (m - c)(m + c - 1) = 35$, which is never possible because product of an even and an odd integer can never be odd. Thus, there exists no ordered pair solution (m, c) for $k = 35$.

ILLUSTRATION 189: A function $f: \mathbb{R} \rightarrow \mathbb{R}$ is such that $f\left(\frac{4x-8}{x-4}\right) = x$ for all $x \neq 4$; then prove that

(i) $f(f(x)) = x \; \forall \; x \in \mathbb{R} - \{4\}$ (ii) $f(f(1/x)) = \frac{1}{x} \; \forall \; x \in \mathbb{R} - \left\{0, \frac{1}{4}\right\}$

SOLUTION: (i) If $f\left(\dfrac{4x-8}{x-4}\right)=x$ for all $x\neq 4$ .Let $y=\dfrac{4x-8}{x-4}\Rightarrow x=\dfrac{4y-8}{y-4}\Rightarrow f(y)=\dfrac{4y-8}{y-4}$

$\Rightarrow f(f(x)) = x$ (from given)

(ii) $f(1/x)=\dfrac{4(1/x)-8}{(1/x)-4}=\dfrac{4-8x}{1-4x}$ for $x\neq 0,\dfrac{1}{4}$

$$\therefore\quad f(f(1/x))=f\left(\frac{4-8x}{1-4x}\right)=\frac{4\left(\frac{4-8x}{1-4x}\right)-8}{\left(\frac{4-8x}{1-4x}\right)-4}=\frac{\left(\frac{4-8x}{1-4x}\right)-2}{\left(\frac{1-2x}{1-4x}\right)-1}=\frac{4-8x-2+8x}{1-2x-1+4x}=\frac{2}{2x}=\frac{1}{x}$$

ILLUSTRATION 190: If $f(x) = x+1;\ 0\le x\le 2$ and $g(x) = |x|;\ 0\le x\le 3$. Calculate $fog(x)$, $fof(x)$.

SOLUTION: $fog(x) = f\{g(x)\} = f(|x|);\ 0\le x\le 3$

$= |x| + 1;\ 0\le |x|\le 2$ and $0\le x\le 3$

$= |x| + 1;\ -2\le x\le 2$ and $0\le x\le 3$

$= |x| + 1;\ 0\le x\le 2$

$fof(x) = f\{f(x)\} = f(x+1);\ 0\le x\le 2$

$= (x+1)+1;\ 0\le (x+1)\le 2$ and $0\le x\le 2$

$= (x+2);\ -1\le x\le 1$ and $0\le x\le 2$

$= (x+2);\ 0\le x\le 1$

ILLUSTRATION 191: Let $f(x) = \sin x$ and $g(x)=\sqrt{|1-x|}$. Find $gof(x)$, $fog(x)$, $gog(x)$ and $fof(x)$.

SOLUTION: $gof(x) = g\{f(x)\} = g(\sin x)=\sqrt{|1-\sin x|}$

$fog(x) = f\{g(x)\} = f\left\{\sqrt{|1-x|}\right\} = \sin\sqrt{|1-x|}$

$gog(x) = g\{g(x)\} = g\left\{\sqrt{|1-x|}\right\} = \left\{\sqrt{\left|1-\sqrt{|1-x|}\right|}\right\}$

$fof(x) = f(f(x)\} = f(\sin x) = \sin(\sin x)$.

ILLUSTRATION 192: Find fog and gof, if

(i) $f(x) = |x|$; $g(x) = \sin x$ (ii) $f(x) = \sin^{-1}x$; $g(x) = x^2$

(iii) $f(x) = x^2+2$; $g(x)=1-\dfrac{1}{1-x}, x\neq 1$

SOLUTION: (i) $f(x) = |x|$ and $g(x) = \sin x$

$\Rightarrow fog(x) = f(\sin x) = |\sin x|$ and $gof(x) = g(f(x)) = g(|x|) = \sin|x|$

(ii) $f(x) = \sin^{-1}x$ and $g(x) = x^2$

$\Rightarrow fog(x) = f(g(x)) = \sin^{-1}(g(x)) = \sin^{-1}x^2$ and $gof(x) = g(f(x)) = (f(x))^2 = (\sin^{-1}x)^2$

(iii) $f(x) = x^2+2,\ g(x)=\dfrac{x}{x-1}$

$\Rightarrow fog(x) = f(g(x)) = (g(x))^2+2=\dfrac{x^2}{(x-1)^2}+2=\dfrac{3x^2-4x+2}{(x-1)^2}$

and $gof(x) = g(f(x)) = g(x^2+2)=\dfrac{x^2+2}{(x^2+2)-1}=\dfrac{x^2+2}{x^2+1}$

ILLUSTRATION 193: If $f(x) = \sin^2 x + \sin^2\left(x+\frac{\pi}{3}\right) + \cos x \cos\left(x+\frac{\pi}{3}\right)$ and $g\left(\frac{5}{4}\right)=1$, then find $(gof)(x)$.

SOLUTION: Given $f(x) = \sin^2 x + \sin^2\left(x+\frac{\pi}{3}\right) + \cos x \cos\left(x+\frac{\pi}{3}\right)$ ...(1)

and $g\left(\frac{5}{4}\right)=1$ ...(2)

We have $f(x) = \sin^2 x + \sin^2\left(x+\frac{\pi}{3}\right) + \cos x \cos\left(x+\frac{\pi}{3}\right)$

$$= \frac{1-\cos 2x}{2} + \frac{1-\cos\left(2x+\frac{2\pi}{3}\right)}{2} + \frac{1}{2}\left[2\cos x\cos\left(x+\frac{\pi}{3}\right)\right]$$

$$= \frac{1}{2}\left[1-\cos 2x+1-\cos\left(2x+\frac{2\pi}{3}\right)+\cos\left(2x+\frac{\pi}{3}\right)+\cos\frac{\pi}{3}\right]$$

$$= \frac{1}{2}\left[\frac{5}{2}-\left\{\cos 2x+\cos\left(2x+\frac{2\pi}{3}\right)\right\}+\cos\left(2x+\frac{\pi}{3}\right)\right]$$

$$= \frac{1}{2}\left[\frac{5}{2}-2\cos\left(2x+\frac{\pi}{3}\right)\cos\frac{\pi}{3}+\cos\left(2x+\frac{\pi}{3}\right)\right] = \frac{1}{2}\left[\frac{5}{2}-\cos\left(2x+\frac{\pi}{3}\right)+\cos\left(2x+\frac{\pi}{3}\right)\right]$$

or $f(x)=\frac{5}{4}$ for all x. Now, $gof(x) = g\{f(x)\} = g\left(\frac{5}{4}\right)=1$; Hence, $gof(x)=1$, for all x.

ILLUSTRATION 194: **(a)** Find the formula for the function *fogoh*, given $f(x) = \frac{x}{x+1}$; $g(x)=x^{10}$ and $h(x) = x + 3$. Find the domain of this composite function. Also compute $(fogoh)(-1)$.

(b) Given $F(x) = \cos^2(x + 9)$. Find the function f, g, h such that $F = fogoh$.

SOLUTION: **(a)** $f(x) = \frac{x}{x+1}$; $g(x) = x^{10}$; $h(x) = x + 3$

$$(fogoh)(x) = f(g(h(x))) = \frac{g(h(x))}{g(h(x))+1} = \frac{(h(x))^{10}}{(h(x))^{10}+1} = \frac{(x+3)^{10}}{(x+3)^{10}+1}$$

$$\Rightarrow (fogoh)(x) = \frac{(x+3)^{10}}{(x+3)^{10}+1} \quad \therefore f(g(h(-1))) = \frac{(-1+3)^{10}}{(-1+3)^{10}-1} = \frac{2^{10}}{2^{10}+1} = \frac{1024}{1024+1} = \frac{1024}{1025}$$

(b) $F(x) = \cos^2(x + 9)$

$\therefore F(x) = fogoh(x) \quad \Rightarrow f(x) = x^2;\ g(x) = \cos x;\ h(x) = x + 9$

ILLUSTRATION 195: Let a and b be real numbers and let $f(x) = a\sin x + b\sqrt[3]{x}+4$, $\forall\ x \in \mathbb{R}$. If $f(\log_{10}(\log_3 10)) = 5$, then find the value of $f(\log_{10}(\log_{10} 3))$

SOLUTION: Given $f(x) = a\sin x + b\sqrt[3]{x}+4$ and $f\left(\log_{10}\left(\log_3 10\right)\right) = 5$

Now, let $\log_{10}\log_3 10 = k$; then $\log_{10}\log_{10} 3$

$$= \log_{10}\left(\frac{1}{\log_3 10}\right) = (\log_{10} 1 - \log_{10}\log_3 10) = 0 - k = -k$$

Now, $\because f(k) = a\sin k + b(k)^{1/3} + 4 = 5 \Rightarrow a\sin k + b(k)^{1/3} = 1$

$\therefore f(-k) = a\sin(-k) + b(-k)^{1/3} + 4 = -(a\sin k - b(k)^{1/3}) + 4 = -1 + 4 = 3.$

PROPERTIES OF COMPOSITION OF FUNCTIONS

(a) Domain: Given two functions $f : X \to Y$ and $g : Y \to Z$. For the composition gof to be defined from set X to set Z, the range of f must be a subset of the domain of g, i.e., $R_f \subseteq Y$.

If range of f is not a subset of domain of g but has some elements common with domain of g, then domain of gof is not the set X but is given by: Domain of $g(f(x)) = \{x : x \in D_f$ and $f(x) \in D_g\}$.

ILLUSTRATION 196: Let $f(x) = \frac{2x-3}{x-4}$ and $g(x) = ln(x-1)$, then find the domain of $fog(x)$.

SOLUTION: **(i)** $fog(x)$

To find the domain of $fog(x)$, we are to find those elements of domain of $g(x)$, whose image under g belongs to the domain of function f.

i.e., domain of $fog(x) = \{x \in D_g : g(x) \in D_f\}$

Now $g(x) = ln(x-1)$; $f(x) = \frac{2x-3}{x-4}$ and domain of $g(x)$ is $(1, \infty)$ and domain of $f(x)$ is $\mathbb{R} \sim \{4\}$

$\Rightarrow$ Domain of $fog(x) = \{x \in (1, \infty): ln(x-1) \in \mathbb{R} \sim \{4\}\}$

We know that range of $ln(x-1)$ for $x \in (1, \infty)$ is $(-\infty, \infty)$.

All these values of $\ln(x-1)$ are permissible except for 4.

$\Rightarrow ln(x-1) \neq 4 \qquad \Rightarrow (x-1) \neq e^4$

$\therefore$ Domain of $fog(x) = (1, \infty) \sim \{1 + e^4\}$.

Aliter: $fog(x) = f(g(x)) = \frac{2g(x)-3}{g(x)-4} = \frac{2ln(x-1)-3}{ln(x-1)-4}$

Which is defined for $ln(x-1) - 4 \neq 0$ and $x - 1 > 0$

$\Rightarrow x - 1 \neq e^4$ and $x > 1 \qquad \Rightarrow x > 1$ and $x \neq 1 + e^4$

$\therefore$ Domain of $fog(x)$ is given by $(1, \infty) \sim \{1 + e^4\}$.

ILLUSTRATION 197: If $f(x) = \frac{1}{1-x}$ Find $f[f\{f(x)\}]$ and draw it's graph and find its domain.

SOLUTION: $f(x) = \frac{1}{1-x}$. It is defined when $x \neq 1$. Now, $f\{f(x)\} = f\left(\frac{1}{1-x}\right)$

$$\Rightarrow \frac{1}{\left(1-\frac{1}{1-x}\right)} = \frac{1}{\left(\frac{1-x-1}{1-x}\right)} = \frac{1-x}{-x}; \text{ when } x \neq 1; \text{ also } x \neq 0.$$

$$= \frac{-1+x}{x}; \text{ when } x \neq 0, 1$$

$$\therefore f[f\{f(x)\}] = \frac{1}{1-\left(\frac{x-1}{x}\right)} = \frac{x}{x-x+1} = x; \text{ when } x \neq 0, 1$$

Therefore, domain of composite function is $\mathbb{R} \sim \{0, 1\}$.

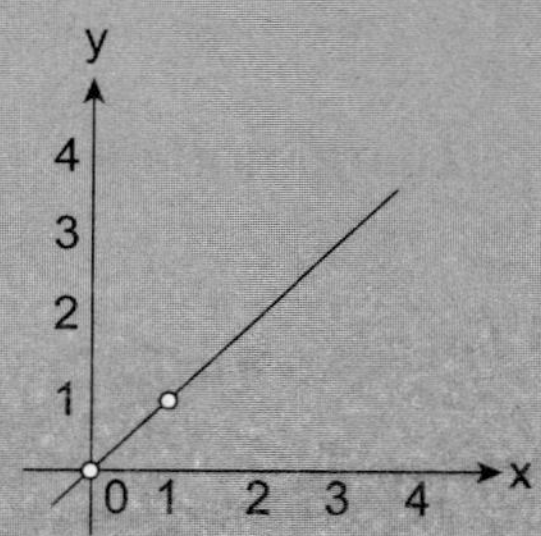

FIGURE 2.153

(b) Range: Range of $gof(x) = \{g(b): b \in R_f \cap D_g\}$ and can be obtained as given below:

(i) If $f: A \to B$ and $g: B \to C$; then $gof: A \to C$ has range $= \{gof(a_1), gof(a_2), gof(a_3), ..., gof(a_n)\}$; where $A = \{a_1, a_2, a_3, ..., a_n\}$, i.e., a finite set.

ILLUSTRATION 198: Let $A = \{2, 3, 4, 5\}$; $B = \{3, 8, 15, 24, 30, 32\}$; $C = \{3, 4/3, 15/13, 12/11, 15/14, 16/15, 17/16\}$

Consider the functions $f: A \to B$ and $g: B \to C$ defined by $f(x) = x^2 - 1$ and $g(x) = \dfrac{x}{x-2}$; find the range of composite function gof.

SOLUTION: $f(A) = \{f(2), f(3), f(4), f(5)\} = \{3, 8, 15, 24\} \subseteq B$ and $g(B) = \{g(3), g(8), g(15), g(24), g(30), g(32)\} = \{3, 4/3, 15/13, 12/11, 15/14, 16/15\} \subseteq C$

Thus, range of f is a subset of domain of g $\Rightarrow$ gof is defined from set A to set C

i.e., A is domain of gof and its range is given by $\{gof(2), gof(3), gof(4), gof(5)\}$

$= \{g(3), g(8), g(15), g(24)\} = \{3, 4/3, 15/13, 12/11\}$

(ii) If $f(x)$ and $g(x)$ are increasing functions in their respective domain, then $gof(x)$ is also an increasing function in its domain. Further, if both $f(x)$ and $g(x)$ are continuous in their respective domain, then gof is also continuous in its domain.

Now if common domain of $f(x)$ and $gof(x)$ is $[\alpha, \beta]$ or (α, β), then range of $f(x)$ is $[f(\alpha), f(\beta)]$, or $(f(\alpha), f(\beta))$ which in turn is domain of $g(x)$. Then range of $fog(x)$ will be $[g(f(\alpha)), g(f(\beta))]$ or $(g(f(\alpha)), g(f(\beta)))$.

ILLUSTRATION 199: Find the domain and range of $\log(\tan^{-1}x)$.

SOLUTION: Given function is $h(x) = \log(\tan^{-1}x)$.

If we consider $f(x) = \log x$ and $g(x) = \tan^{-1}x$, then $fog(x) = f(g(x)) = \log(g(x)) = \log(\tan^{-1}x)$

Thus, $h(x) = fog(x)$, composition of $f(x)$ and $g(x)$.

Now domain of $f(x)$ is $(0, \infty)$ and $g(x)$ is $\mathbb{R}$.

For $fog(x)$ to be defined, range of $g(x)$ must be in the domain of $f(x)$, i.e., $x \in \mathbb{R}$ such that $g(x) \in (0, \infty)$

$\Rightarrow g(x) > 0$ $\qquad$ $\Rightarrow \tan^{-1}x > 0$

$\Rightarrow \tan^{-1}x \in \left(0, \dfrac{\pi}{2}\right)$ $\qquad$ $\Rightarrow x \in (0, \infty)$.

Thus, domain of $fog(x)$ is $(0, \infty)$

Now $f(x)$ and $g(x)$ both are increasing and continuous functions, hence, $fog(x)$ is also continuous and increasing function on $(0, \infty)$. Further range of $g(x)$ for $x \in (0, \infty)$ is $(g(0), g(\infty))$, i.e., $(\tan^{-1}0, \tan^{-1}\infty)$ i.e., $\left(0, \dfrac{\pi}{2}\right)$. Hence, range of $fog(x)$ will be $\left(f(0), f\left(\dfrac{\pi}{2}\right)\right)$

i.e., $\left(\log 0, \log\left(\dfrac{\pi}{2}\right)\right)$ i.e., $\left(-\infty, \log\left(\dfrac{\pi}{2}\right)\right)$.

(iii) If $f(x)$ and $g(x)$ both are decreasing functions in their respective domain, then gof is also a decreasing function. Further if both $f(x)$ and $g(x)$ are continuous in their respective domain, then gof is continuous and increasing function in its domain. If common domain of $f(x)$ and $gof(x)$ is $[\alpha, \beta]$ or (α, β), then range of $f(x)$ is $[f(\beta), f(\alpha)]$ or $(f(\beta), f(\alpha))$ which in turn in domain of $g(x)$ which is decreasing and continuous function. Thus, range of gof will be $\left[g(f(\alpha)), g(f(\beta))\right]$ or $\left(g(f(\alpha)), g(f(\beta))\right)$.

ILLUSTRATION 200: Find the domain and range of function $e^{-\cot^{-1}x}$.

SOLUTION: Given function is $e^{-\cot^{-1}x}$

If we consider $g(x) = e^{-x}$ and $f(x) = \cot^{-1}x$, then $gof(x) = g(f(x)) = e^{-f(x)} = e^{-\cot^{-1}x}$

Thus, $h(x) = gof(x)$

Now $f(x)$ and $g(x)$ both are continuous and decreasing functions on their domain $\mathbb{R}$. Now domain of $gof(x)$ would contain those real numbers for which range of $f(x)$ is contained in domain of $g(x)$, i.e., $\mathbb{R}$, which is true for all real values of x. Hence, domain of $gof(x)$ is $\mathbb{R}$.

Further $f(x)$ is continuous and decreasing on $\mathbb{R}$ implies range of $f(x)$ is $(f(\infty), f(-\infty))$, i.e., $(0, \pi)$.

Now in $(0, \pi)$, $g(x) = e^{-x}$ is decreasing implies $gof(x)$ being continuous and decreasing has its range $(g(\pi), g(0))$, i.e., $(e^{-\pi}, e^{-0}) = (e^{-\pi}, 1)$.

Thus, range of gof is $(e^{-\pi}, 1)$.

(iv) If $f(x)$ and $g(x)$ are functions of opposite monotonicity in their respective domain, then gof is a decreasing function on its domain. Further, if $f(x)$ and $g(x)$ are continuous functions, then gof is continuous and decreasing function. If $[\alpha, \beta]$ or (α, β) is a common domain of $gof(x)$ and decreasing function $f(x)$ (say), then range of $f(x)$ is $[f(\beta), f(\alpha)]$ or $(f(\beta), f(\alpha))$ which in turn in domain of $g(x)$. $g(x)$ being continuous and increasing (say), range of $gof(x)$ will be $[g(f(\beta)), g(f(\alpha))]$ or $(g(f(\beta)), g(f(\alpha)))$. Same will be the range of $gof(x)$ if $f(x)$ is increasing and $g(x)$ is decreasing.

ILLUSTRATION 201: Find the domain and range of function $\log(\cot^{-1}x)$

SOLUTION: Given function is $h(x) = \log(\cot^{-1}x)$. Let $g(x) = \log x$ and $f(x) = \cot^{-1}x$, then $g(f(x)) = \log(f(x)) = \log(\cot^{-1}x)$

Domain of $f(x)$ is $(-\infty, \infty)$ and its range is $(0, \pi)$ and domain of $g(x)$ is $(0, \infty)$ and its range is $\mathbb{R}$.

For $gof(x)$ to be defined, range of $f(x)$ must be in domain of $g(x)$.

i.e., $(0, \pi)$ must be in domain of $g(x)$, i.e., $(0, \infty)$, which is true for all real x.

Thus, domain of $gof(x)$ is $\mathbb{R}$. Domain of $f(x)$ is $(-\infty, \infty)$ in which $f(x)$ is continuous and decreasing, and hence, having range $(f(\infty), f(-\infty))$, i.e., $(\cot^{-1}(\infty)), \cot^{-1}(-\infty))$, i.e., $(0, \pi)$.

Now range of $f(x)$ is $(0, \pi)$ in which $g(x)$ is continuous and increasing, and hence, range of $fog(x)$ is $(g(0), g(\pi))$, i.e., $(\log 0, (\log \pi))$ or $(-\infty, \log \pi)$.

(v) If $f(x)$ is an increasing and continuous function in its domain and $g(x)$ is non-monotonic having range $[\alpha, \beta]$ or (α, β), then the range of $fog(x)$ will be $[f(\alpha), f(\beta)]$ or $(f(\alpha), f(\beta))$. Similarly if $f(x)$ is decreasing and continuous function in its domain and $g(x)$ is non-monotonic having range $[\alpha, \beta]$ or (α, β), then the range of $fog(x)$ will be $[f(\beta), f(\alpha)]$ or $(f(\beta), f(\alpha))$.

ILLUSTRATION 202: Define a function $f(x) = 1 + x$ and $g(x) = (\ln x)^2$, then find the domain and range of composite functions $fog(x)$.

SOLUTION: Domain of $f(x) = \mathbb{R}$; range of $f(x) = \mathbb{R}$. Domain of $g(x) = (0, \infty)$; range of $g(x) = [0, \infty)$

Now domain of $fog(x)$ contains those elements of domain of $g(x)$ whose images under g are found in domain of f, i.e., domain of $fog(x) = \{x \in (0, \infty) : g(x) \in \mathbb{R}\} = \{x \in (0, \infty) : (\ln x)^2 \in \mathbb{R}\} = D_g$. ($\because$ $[0, \infty) \subseteq \mathbb{R}$ is true $\forall\, x \in D_g = (0, \infty)$).

Thus, domain of $fog(x)$ is also $D_g = (0, \infty)$ and $fog(x) = f(g(x)) = 1 + (g(x)) = 1 + (\ln x)^2$.

Now $fog(x) : (0, \infty) \to \mathbb{R}$ is the composition of $f(x) = 1 + x$ and $g(x) = (\ln x)^2$

Now on $(0, \infty)$, $f(x)$ is increasing function and range of $g(x)$ is $[0, \infty)$

$\Rightarrow$ range of $fog(x)$ is $[f(0), f(\infty)] = [1, \infty)$

(vi) If $f(x)$ is non-monotonic function and continuous in its domain and $g(x)$ is any function (monotonic or non-monotonic) for which the composition function fog is defined, then range of fog can be obtained by analyzing the behaviour of function $f(x)$ on the range set of function $g(x)$. i.e., by determining the intervals of monotonicity, *l.u.b.*, *g.u.b.* of $f(x)$ in range set of $g(x)$.

ILLUSTRATION 203: Let $f(x) = \sin x$ and $g(x) = \cos^{-1}x$, then find the domain and range of $fog(x)$.

SOLUTION: $fog(x) = f(g(x)) = \sin(g(x)) = \sin(\cos^{-1}x)$

Now $\sin(\cos^{-1}x)$ is defined for every value of $\cos^{-1}x$ which in turn is defined for $x \in [-1, 1]$.

$\therefore$ Domain of $fog(x)$ is $[-1, 1]$

Further range of $g(x)$ is $[0, \pi]$ in which $f(x) = \sin x$ is non-monotonic but continuous.

If we break $[0, \pi]$ into two subintervals $\left[0, \frac{\pi}{2}\right]$ and $\left[\frac{\pi}{2}, \pi\right]$, in interval $\left[0, \frac{\pi}{2}\right]$ $\sin x$ increases and belongs to $[0, 1]$. However in interval $\left[\frac{\pi}{2}, \pi\right]$ $\sin x$ decreases from 1 to 0, and hence, $\sin x$ belongs to $[0, 1]$.

Thus, the range of fog is $[0, 1]$.

ILLUSTRATION 204: Function f and g are defined by $f(x) = \sin x$, $x \in \mathbb{R}$; $g(x) = \tan x$, $x \in \mathbb{R} \sim (2n+1)\frac{\pi}{2}$; $n \in \mathbb{Z}$.

Find the range of the function fog and gof.

SOLUTION: $f(x) = \sin x$; $g(x) = \tan x$.

$\Rightarrow$ $fog(x) = f(g(x)) = \sin(\tan x)$

$\Rightarrow$ Range of $fog(x) = [-1, 1]$ ($\because$ $\tan x \in \mathbb{R}$)

Now $gof(x) = g(f(x)) = \tan(\sin x)$; $-1 \le \sin x \le 1$ and $\tan x$ is continuous and increasing in $\left(-\frac{\pi}{2}, \frac{\pi}{2}\right)$

$\Rightarrow$ $\tan(-1) \le \tan(\sin x) \le \tan 1$ $\Rightarrow$ $-\tan 1 \le \tan(\sin x) \le \tan 1$

$\therefore$ Range of $gof(x) = [-\tan 1, \tan 1]$

(vii) If $f(x)$ is monotonic and continuous in its domain and $g(x)$ is non-monotonic for which $fog(x)$ is defined and range of $g(x)$ is $[\alpha, \beta]$ or (α, β), then the range of $fog(x)$ will be $[f(\alpha), f(\beta)]$ or $(f(\alpha), f(\beta))$ if $f(x)$ is increasing and it will be $[f(\beta), f(\alpha)]$ or $(f(\beta), f(\alpha))$ if $f(x)$ is decreasing.

ILLUSTRATION 205: Let $f(x) = \sin x$ and $g(x) = \cos^{-1}x$, then find the domain and range of $gof(x)$.

SOLUTION: $gof(x) = g(f(x)) = \cos^{-1}(f(x)) = \cos^{-1}(\sin x)$

Now $\cos^{-1}(\sin x)$ is defined for $\sin x \in [-1, 1]$ which in turn attains all these values $\forall\ x \in \mathbb{R}$.

So, domain of $\cos^{-1}(\sin x)$ is $\mathbb{R}$.

Range of $\sin x$ is $[-1, 1]$ and $\cos^{-1}(x)$ is decreasing for $x \in [-1, 1]$ and decreases from π to 0.

Thus, range of $gof(x)$ is $[0, \pi]$.

(viii) If $f(x)$ and $g(x)$ both are non-monotonic and continuous, for which $fog(x)$ is defined, then the range of $f(x)$ can be obtained by analyzing the behaviour of $f(x)$ on the range set of $g(x)$ i.e., by determining the intervals of monotonicity, *l.u.b.* and *g.l.b.* of $f(x)$ in the range set of $g(x)$.

ILLUSTRATION 206: If $f(x) = \sin x$ and $g(x) = 2x^2 + 7x + 3$, then determine the domain and range of $fog(x)$ and $gof(x)$.

SOLUTION: Here both $f(x)$ and $g(x)$ are non-monotonic functions. Now $fog(x) = \sin(2x^2 + 7x + 3)$.

Now $fog(x)$ is defined for all real values of $(2x^2 + 7x + 3)$ which in turn is defined for all real values of x.

Thus, domain of $fog(x)$ is $\mathbb{R}$.

Now range of $2x^2 + 7x + 3$ is given by $\left[-\dfrac{D}{4a}, \infty\right) = \left[-\dfrac{(49-24)}{4(2)}, \infty\right)$, i.e., $\left[\dfrac{-25}{8}, \infty\right)$.

Now $\sin x$ being continuous function, when fed to inputs $\left[\dfrac{-25}{8}, \infty\right)$, by intermediate value theorem, $\sin x$ would attain each and every real number from $f\left(\dfrac{-25}{8}\right)$ to $f(\infty)$.

As $x \to \infty$ $\sin x$ attains all real values of interval $[-1, 1]$

Hence, $fog(x) = \sin(2x^2 + 7x + 3)$ would attain each value of interval $[-1, 1]$

Hence, range of fog is $[-1, 1]$

Further $gof(x) = g(f(x)) = 2(f(x))^2 + 7f(x) + 3 = 2(\sin x)^2 + 7\sin x + 3$

Now, $gof(x)$ is defined for all real values of $\sin x$ which in turn is defined for all real values of x. Hence, domain of $gof(x)$ is $\mathbb{R}$

Next, $(gof)(x) = 2\sin^2 x + 7\sin x + 3$

$$= 2\left[\sin^2 x + \frac{7}{2}\sin x\right] + 3 = 2\left[\sin^2 x + \frac{7}{2}\sin x + \frac{49}{16}\right] + 3 - \frac{49}{8} = 2\left[\sin x + \frac{7}{4}\right]^2 - \frac{25}{8}$$

Now $-1 \le \sin x \le 1$

$\Rightarrow \dfrac{3}{4} \le \sin x + \dfrac{7}{4} \le \dfrac{11}{4}$ $\qquad \Rightarrow \left(\sin x + \dfrac{7}{4}\right)^2 \in \left[\dfrac{9}{16}, \dfrac{121}{16}\right]$

$\Rightarrow 2\left(\sin x + \dfrac{7}{4}\right)^2 - \dfrac{25}{8} \in [-2, 12]$ $\qquad \Rightarrow gof(x)$ has its range $[-2, 12]$

(c) $fog(x)$ is not necessarily equal to $gof(x)$. i.e., generally not commutative. However, equality holds when f and g are functions from set A to set A itself and each is inverse of other or at least one of them is an identity function on set A.

Proof: Let $f : A \to A$ is a bijective function, then $f^{-1} = g : A \to A$ is also a bijective function.

such that $f(x) = y \Leftrightarrow g(y) = x$

Clearly $f^{-1} = g$ and $g^{-1} = (f^{-1})^{-1} = f$, i.e., f and g are inverse of each other.

Now gof and fog both are composite function from set A to set A itself.

Now for any $x \in A$, $gof(x) = g(f(x)) = g(y)$ [where $y = f(x) \Rightarrow g(y) = x$] $= x$ .... (1)

and $fog(x) = f(g(x)) = f(y')$ [where $y' = g(x) \Rightarrow f(y') = x$] $= x$ .... (2)

From (1) and (2), we have $gof(x) = fog(x) = x \ \forall\, x \in A$

$\Rightarrow gof = fog = I_A$, i.e., identity function on set A.

Next let us suppose that $f, g : A \to A$ and $g = I_A$, i.e., an identity function on set A.

$\Rightarrow g(x) = x \ \forall\, x \in A$.

Now fog, i.e., composition of f and g is a function from set A to A itself, and for each $x \in A$, $fog(x) = f(g(x)) = f(x)$ and for each $x \in A$, $gof(x) = g(f(x)) = f(x)$

Thus, $fog(x) = gof(x) = f(x) \ \forall\, x \in A$.

$\Rightarrow fog = gof = f$

Similarly, we can show that $gof = fog = g$ if f is an identity function on set A, i.e., $f = I_A$.

ILLUSTRATION 207: If $f(x) = 1 + x$ and $g(x) = \ln x$, then find the domain and range of composite functions $fog(x)$ and $gof(x)$, and hence, show that $fog \neq gof$.

SOLUTION: $fog(x) = f(g(x)) = 1 + g(x) = 1 + \ln x$, which is defined $\forall\, x > 0$

$\therefore$ Domain of $fog(x)$ is $(0, \infty)$ and $(fog)'(x) = \dfrac{1}{x} > 0 \ \forall\, x \in (0, \infty)$

$\Rightarrow$ $(fog)(x)$ is an increasing function.

Also 1 and $\ln x$ are continuous and $fog(x)$ being sum of two continuous functions is also continuous on $(0, \infty)$.

Thus, $fog(x)$ will have its range $(fog(0), fog(\infty)) = (1+ \ln(0), 1+ \ln(\infty)) = (-\infty,\infty)$

Further, $gof(x) = g(f(x)) = \ln(f(x)) = \ln(1 + x)$ which is defined for $x > -1$

$\therefore$ Domain of gof is $(-1, \infty)$ and $(gof)'(x) = \dfrac{1}{(1+x)} > 0 \ \forall\, x \in (-1, \infty)$

$\Rightarrow$ $gof(x)$ is monotonically increasing on $(-1, \infty)$

$\therefore$ Range of $gof(x)$ will be $(gof(-1), gof(\infty)) = (-\infty, \infty)$

Thus, from above discussion, we observe that range of fog and gof are same, however, they have different domains. Thus, the two functions can't be equal.

Thus, $fog \neq gof$

Aliter: Let us suppose that fog and gof have common domain A.

Now $fog = gof$ iff $fog(x) = gof(x) \ \forall\, x \in A$

Let $x = 1$, clearly fog and gof are both defined at $x = 1 \Rightarrow 1 \in A$, then $fog(1) = 1 + \ln 1 = 1$ and $gof(1) = \ln(1 + 1) = \ln 2$

Now $\ln 2 = 1 \Rightarrow 2 = e$, which is a contradiction, so we get a counter example showing that $fog(x) \neq gof(x) \ \forall\, x \in A$.

ILLUSTRATION 208: Let $f(x) = x^2 + x + 1$ and $g(x) = \sin x$. Show that $fog \neq gof$

SOLUTION: Given $f(x) = x^2 + x + 1$; $g(x) = \sin x$

$\Rightarrow fog(x) = f(g(x)) = \sin^2 x + \sin x + 1$ and $gof(x) = g(f(x)) = \sin(x^2 + x + 1)$

$\therefore fog(x) \neq gof(x)$

(d) The composition of functions is associative in nature, i.e., if f, g, h are three functions such that $fo(goh)$ and $(fog)oh$ are defined, then $fo(goh) = (fog)\,oh$.

Proof: Let $h : A \to B$; $g : B \to C$ and $f : C \to D$, then

$\Rightarrow$ $goh : A \to C$ and $fo(goh) : A \to D$.

Also $fog : B \to D$ and $(fog)oh : A \to D$

Thus, $fo(goh)$ and $(fog)oh$ has common domain A.

Let $a \in A$

$\Rightarrow$ there exists $b \in B$, $c \in C$ and $d \in D$ such that $h(a) = b$, $g(b) = c$, $f(c) = d$,

Then $[fo(goh)](a) = f[(goh(a)] = f[g(h(a))] = f[g(b)] = f(c) = d$

and $[(fog)\ oh]\ (a) = (fog)\ (h(a)) = (fog)(b) = f[g(b)] = f(c) = d$

Thus, $[fo\ (goh)]\ (a) = [(fog)oh](a)\ \forall\ a \in A$

$\Rightarrow$ $fo(goh) = (fog)oh$

ILLUSTRATION 209: Given $f : \mathbb{N} \to I_0$ (set of non-zero integers); $f(x) = 2x$ and $g : I_0 \to \mathbb{Q}$ (set of rational numbers); $g(x) = \dfrac{1}{x}$ and $h : \mathbb{Q} \to \mathbb{R}$; $h(x) = e^{1/x}$. Show that $[(hog)of](x) = [ho(gof)](x) = e^{2x}\ \forall\ x \in \mathbb{N}$.

SOLUTION: Clearly $[(hog)of](x)$ and $[ho(gof)](x)$ will be the functions from $\mathbb{N} \to \mathbb{R}$

$$\text{LHS.} = [(hog)of](x) = (hog)(f(x)) = (hog)(2x) = h(g(2x)) = h\left(\frac{1}{2x}\right) = e^{2x}$$

$$\text{RHS} = [ho(gof)](x) = ho[g(f(x))] = ho\left[\frac{1}{f(x)}\right] = h\left[\frac{1}{2x}\right] = e^{2x}.$$

Thus, $[(hog)of](x) = [ho(gof)](x) = e^{2x}\ \forall\ x \in \mathbb{N}$.

ILLUSTRATION 210: Let $f(x) = x^2$, $g(x) = \sin x$, $h(x) = \sqrt{x}$, then verify that $[fo(goh)]\ (x)$ and $[(fog)\ oh]\ (x)$ are equal

SOLUTION: Given functions are $f(x) = x^2$; $g(x) = \sin x$; $h(x) = \sqrt{x}$

Now LHS $= [fo(goh)]\ (x) = fo(goh)(x) = f(g(h(x))) = f\left(\sin\sqrt{x}\right) = \left(\sin\sqrt{x}\right)^2 = \sin^2\sqrt{x}$

and RHS $= [(fog)\ oh]\ (x) = (fog)\ oh(x) = fog(\sqrt{x}) = \sin^2\sqrt{x}$

Thus, $[fo(goh)]\ (x) = [(fog)\ oh]\ (x) = \sin^2\sqrt{x}$

(e) The composition of two bijections is a bijection.

Proof: Let $f : A \to B$ and $g : B \to C$ be two bijections such that $gof : A \to C$ exists.

Injectivity: Let $a_1, a_2 \in A$ such that $(gof)(a_1) = (gof)(a_2)$ $\Rightarrow$ $g[f(a_1)] = g\,[f(a_2)]$

$\Rightarrow$ $f(a_1) = f(a_2)$ [$\because$ g is one–one]

$\Rightarrow$ $a_1 = a_2$ [$\because$ f is one–one]

$\therefore$ gof is also one–one function.

Surjectivity: Let $c \in C$,

$\Rightarrow$ There exists $b \in B$ such that $g(b) = c$ and $b \in B$ there exists $a \in A$ such that $f(a) = b$

[$\because$ g and f are onto functions]

Therefore, we can conclude that $\forall\ c \in C$ there exists $a \in A$: $(gof)\ (a) = g(f(a)) = g(b) = c$

$\Rightarrow$ Every element of C is the gof image of some element of A.

$\Rightarrow$ gof is onto function.

$\Rightarrow$ Thus, gof being one–one and onto, is a bijection.

ILLUSTRATION 211: Define a function $f(x) = \dfrac{2x}{x^2+1}$ on $[-1, 1]$ and $g(x) = \cos^{-1}x$, then show that the composite function $gof(x)$ is a bijective function.

SOLUTION: $f(x) = \dfrac{2x}{x^2+1}$; clearly domain of function $f(x) = D_f = \mathbb{R}$

$y = \dfrac{2x}{x^2+1}$ $\Rightarrow x^2y - 2x + y = 0$

For x to be real, Disc. ≥ 0

$\Rightarrow (-2)^2 - 4y^2 \geq 0 \Rightarrow 1 - y^2 \geq 0 \Rightarrow y^2 \leq 1 \Rightarrow y \in [-1, 1]$

Thus, range of function $f(x)$ is $[-1, 1]$. Further $f(-1) = -1$ and $f(1) = 1$

Since $f(x) = \dfrac{2x}{x^2+1}$ being a rational function is continuous. Therefore by intermediate value theorem function $f(x)$ will attain each and every real number from $f(-1)$ to $f(1)$, i.e., from -1 to 1.

Now we know that domain of $g(x) = \cos^{-1}x$ is $[-1, 1]$.

Thus, range of $f(x)$ = domain of $g(x)$.

Thus, $gof(x)$ is defined from set $[-1, 1]$ to $[0, \pi]$.

Further, $f'(x) = \dfrac{2(1-x^2)}{(x^2+1)^2} \geq 0$ for $x \in [-1, 1]$.

$\Rightarrow$ $f(x)$ is strictly increasing on $[-1, 1]$.

$\Rightarrow$ $f(x)$ is a bijective function from set $[-1, 1]$ to $[-1, 1]$.

Also $g'(x) = \dfrac{-1}{\sqrt{1-x^2}} < 0$ for $x \in [-1, 1]$.

$\Rightarrow$ $g(x)$ is a bijective function from set $[-1, 1]$ to $[0, \pi]$. We shall show that $gof(x)$ is a bijective function from $[-1, 1]$ to $[0, \pi]$.

Let $gof(x_1) = gof(x_2)$ for some $x_1, x_2 \in [-1, 1]$.

$\Rightarrow g(f(x_1)) = g(f(x_2))$

$\Rightarrow \cos^{-1}\left(\dfrac{2x_1}{x_1^2+1}\right) = \cos^{-1}\left(\dfrac{2x_2}{x_2^2+1}\right); \dfrac{2x_1}{x_1^2+1}, \dfrac{2x_2}{x_2^2+1} \in [-1,1]$.

$\Rightarrow \dfrac{2x_1}{x_1^2+1} = \dfrac{2x_2}{x_2^2+1}$ as $\cos^{-1}(x)$ is a bijective function.

$\Rightarrow x_1 = x_2$ as $x_1, x_2 \in [-1, 1]$ and $f(x) = \dfrac{2x}{x^2+1}$ is a bijective function on $[-1, 1]$.

Thus, $gof(x_1) = gof(x_2)$ $\Rightarrow x_1 = x_2 \ \forall \ x_1, x_2 \in [-1, 1]$.

$\Rightarrow$ $gof(x)$ is a bijective function from set $[-1, 1]$ to $[0, \pi]$.

(f) If gof is one–one, then f is one–one and g need not be one–one.

Proof: Let $gof(x) = gof(y)$, then $x = y$

($\because$ gof is one–one) ...(1)

$\Rightarrow$ Let $f(x) = f(y)$, then $g(f(x)) = g(f(y))$ ($\because$ g is a function)

$\Rightarrow gof(x) = gof(y)$

$\Rightarrow x = y$ (by (1))

$\Rightarrow$ f is one–one, however g need not be one–one.

e.g., $y = e^{2x} = (e^x)^2$; let $g(x) = x^2$ and $f(x) = e^x$, then $gof(x) = g(e^x) = (e^x)^2 = e^{2x}$;

Clearly $gof(x)$ is monotonically increasing and hence, is one–one, also $f(x) = e^x$ is one–one but $g(x) = x^2$ is many–one.

(g) If gof is onto, then g is onto but f need not be onto.

Proof: Let $f: X \to Y$ and $g: Y \to Z$, then $gof: X \to Z$

Let $z \in Z$, then $x \in X$ such that $gof(x) = z$

$\Rightarrow g(f(x)) = z$. Let $f(x) = b \in Y$

$\Rightarrow g(b) = z$

$\Rightarrow$ g is onto, however f need not be onto.

e.g., Let $X = \{1, 2, 3, 4, 5\}$; $Y = \{-1, 1, 4, 9, 16, 25\}$ and $Z = \{0, 2\log 2, 2\log 3, 2\log 4, 2\log 5\}$;

Let $f: X \to Y$ and $g: Y \to Z$ defined as $f(x) = x^2$ and $g(x) = \log |x|$, then $gof: X \to Z$ is given by $gof(x) = 2\log|x|$ is onto. Also clearly $g(x)$ is onto but $f(x)$ is not onto as $-1 \in Y$ has no pre-image in X under f.

(h) If $f(x)$ and $g(x)$ are both continuous functions, then $g(f(x))$ is also continuous.

Proof: Let $f : X \to Y$ and $g : Y \to Z$ be two continuous functions.

Then $gof: X \to Z$ is composite function of f and g.

Let $a \in X$; such that $f(a) = b \in Y$, then $f(x)$ is continuous at $x = a$ and $g(x)$ is continuous at $x = b$

$\Rightarrow \lim\limits_{x\to a} f(x) = f(a)$ and $\lim\limits_{x\to b} g(x) = f(b)$ ....(1)

Now $\lim\limits_{x\to a} gof(x) = \lim\limits_{x\to a} g(f(x))$

$= \lim\limits_{y\to f(a)} g(y) = \lim\limits_{y\to b} g(y)$

$= g(b) = g(f(a))$

$= gof(a)$ $\left[\begin{array}{l} \because \lim\limits_{x\to a} f(x) = f(a) \\ \Rightarrow as\ x \to a; f(x) \to f(a) \\ \text{i.e. } y \to f(a) \end{array}\right]$

$\Rightarrow$ $gof(x)$ is continuous at $x = a$

$\therefore$ Composition of two continuous functions is also continuous.

ILLUSTRATION 212: Prove that

(i) $\sin(\tan^{-1}x)$ is continuous function on $\mathbb{R}$

(ii) $\ln\left(t+x^2\right)+e^{\cot^{-1}x}$ is a continuous function on $\mathbb{R}$ for each value of $t > 0$.

SOLUTION: (i) Let $f(x) = \sin x$ and $g(x) = \tan^{-1}x$, then $fog(x) = \sin(\tan^{-1}x)$ which is defined for each $x \in (-\infty, \infty)$

As for $x \in (-\infty, \infty)$, $\tan^{-1}x \in \left(-\frac{\pi}{2}, \frac{\pi}{2}\right)$ on which $\sin x$ is defined.

Thus, domain of $fog(x) = \sin(\tan^{-1}x)$ is $\mathbb{R}$

Also $\sin x$ and $\tan^{-1}x$ are continuous functions on $\mathbb{R}$.

Thus, their composition function $\sin(\tan^{-1}x)$ is also continuous function on $\mathbb{R}$.

(ii) Let $f(x) = \ln x$, $g(x) = t + x^2$; $h(x) = e^x$; $k(x) = \cot^{-1}x$, then $f(x)$ is continuous $\forall\ x > 0$.

Also $\forall\ x \in \mathbb{R}$ and $t > 0$, $g(x) > 0$

$\Rightarrow$ $f(g(x)) = \ln(t + x^2)$ is continuous on $\mathbb{R}$; Also e^x and $\cot^{-1}x$ are continuous on $\mathbb{R}$.

$\Rightarrow$ Their composition function $e^{\cot^{-1}x}$ is also continuous on $\mathbb{R}$.

Thus, $\ln(1 + x^2) + e^{\cot^{-1}x}$ being the sum of two continuous functions on $\mathbb{R}$ is also a continuous function on $\mathbb{R}$.

(i) Monotonicity of composite function: Composition of two functions having same monotonicity is a monotonically increasing function. i.e., if f is increasing (↑) and g is increasing (↑), then $f(g(x))$ is increasing (↑) and if f is decreasing (↓) and g is decreasing (↓), then $f(g(x))$ is increasing (↑).

Proof: ***Case 1:*** When f and g both are increasing functions

Let $x, y \in$ domain of fog such that $x > y$

$\Rightarrow x, y \in$ domain of $g(x)$ and $x > y$

$\Rightarrow g(x) > g(y)$ ($\because$ g is increasing)

$\Rightarrow f(g(x)) > f(g(y))$ ($\because$ f is increasing)

$\Rightarrow fog(x) > fog(y)$

$\Rightarrow$ fog is increasing function.

Case 2: When f and g both are decreasing functions

Let $x, y \in$ domain of fog such that $x > y$

$\Rightarrow x, y \in$ domain of $g(x)$ and $x > y$

$\Rightarrow g(x) < g(y)$ ($\because$ g is decreasing)

$\Rightarrow f(g(x)) > f(g(y))$ ($\because$ f is decreasing)

$\Rightarrow fog(x) > fog(y)$

$\Rightarrow$ fog is increasing function.

Aliter: $f(x)$, $g(x)$ increasing shows $f'(x) > 0$ and $g'(x) > 0$ and $\{fog(x)\}' = f'(g(x)).g'(x) > 0$

$\Rightarrow$ fog is also an increasing function

ILLUSTRATION 213: Show that the function $(\tan x)^{1/3}$ and $e^{(\tan x)^{1/3}}$ are monotonically increasing functions in their domains.

SOLUTION: Let $f(x) = (x)^{1/3}$ and $g(x) = \tan x$

$\Rightarrow$ $D_f = \mathbb{R}$ and $D_g = \mathbb{R} \sim \left\{(2n+1)\frac{\pi}{2}; n \in \mathbb{Z}\right\}$. Now, $f'(x) = \frac{1}{3(x)^{2/3}} > 0 \ \forall\ x \in \mathbb{R} \sim \{0\}$

$\Rightarrow$ $f(x)$ is monotonically increasing on $\mathbb{R}$ and $g'(x) = \sec^2 x > 0 \ \forall\ x \in \mathbb{R} \sim \left\{(2n+1)\frac{\pi}{2}; n \in \mathbb{Z}\right\}$

$\Rightarrow$ $g(x)$ is monotonically increasing on $\mathbb{R} \sim \left\{(2n+1)\frac{\pi}{2}; n \in \mathbb{Z}\right\}$

Thus, $fog(x) = (\tan x)^{1/3}$ being the composition of two increasing (same monotonicity) functions is also monotonically increasing on its domain $\mathbb{R} \sim \left\{(2n+1)\frac{\pi}{2}; n \in \mathbb{Z}\right\}$.

Next, let $h(x) = e^x$ and $k(x) = (\tan x)^{1/3}$, then $hok(x) = e^{(\tan x)^{1/3}}$ being the composition of two monotonically increasing functions $h(x)$ and $k(x)$ on their respective domains $\mathbb{R}$ and $\mathbb{R} \sim \left\{(2n+1)\frac{\pi}{2}; n \in \mathbb{Z}\right\}$ is also continuous on its domain $\mathbb{R} \sim \left\{(2n+1)\frac{\pi}{2}; n \in \mathbb{Z}\right\}$.

(j) Composition of two functions having opposite monotonicity is a decreasing function.

Proof: Let $f(x)$ be increasing and $g(x)$ be decreasing functions, then $f'(x) > 0$ and $g'(x) < 0$.

Now $\{fog(x)\}' = f'(g(x)).g'(x) < 0$

$\Rightarrow$ fog is a decreasing function.

ILLUSTRATION 214: Show that the function $3(\log_{1/2}x)^3 + 4(\log_{1/2}x)^2 + 7(\log_{1/2}x) + 11$ is a monotonically decreasing function on its domain.

SOLUTION: Let $f(x) = 3x^3 + 4x^2 + 7x + 11$ and $g(x) = \log_{1/2}x$

$\Rightarrow$ Domain of $f(x) = \mathbb{R}$; and domain of $g(x) = (0, \infty)$

Now $fog(x) = f(g(x)) = 3(g(x))^3 + 4(g(x))^2 + 7(g(x)) + 11$

$= 3(\log_{1/2}x)^3 + 4(\log_{1/2}x)^2 + 7(\log_{1/2}x) + 11$ and domain of $fog(x)$ is $(0, \infty)$.

Further $f'(x) = 9x^2 + 8x + 7$

Disc. $f'(x) = 64 - 252 = -188 < 0$ $\Rightarrow f'(x) > 0 \ \forall\ x \in \mathbb{R}$

$\Rightarrow$ $f(x)$ is monotonically increasing on $\mathbb{R}$.

Also we know that $\log_{1/2}x$ is a decreasing function on $(0, \infty)$, thus, $g(x)$ is monotonically decreasing function on $(0, \infty)$.

Thus, fog(x) being the composition of two monotonic functions of opposite monotonicity is decreasing on its domain $(0, \infty)$.

ILLUSTRATION 215: If $f(x) = \ln(x^2 - x + 2) : \mathbb{R}^+ \to \mathbb{R}$ and $g(x) = \{x\} + 1: [1, 2] \to [1, 2]$; where $\{x\}$ denotes fractional part of x. Find the domain and range of $f(g(x))$ when defined.

SOLUTION: Given $f(x) = \ln(x^2 - x + 2): \mathbb{R}^+ \to \mathbb{R}$ and $g(x) = \{x\} + 1: [1, 2] \to [1, 2]$

$\Rightarrow$ $f(g(x)) = \ln(\{x\}^2 + \{x\} + 2)$

$\Rightarrow$ Domain of $fog(x)$ contains those elements of $[1, 2]$ for which $\{x\}^2 + \{x\} + 2 > 0$ which holds $\forall\ x \in [1, 2]$ as Disc. of quadratic is negative or each term is non-negative.

$\Rightarrow$ Domain of $fog(x) = [1, 2]$, for $x \in (1, 2)$; $\{x\} = x - 1$

$\Rightarrow$ $fog(x) = \ln((x-1)^2 + (x-1) + 2) = \ln[x^2 - x + 2]$

Now since $x^2 - x + 2$ is continuous and increasing on (1, 2)

$\Rightarrow$ Range of $fog(x) = (\ln 2, \ln 4)$ for $x \in (1, 2)$ and for $x = 1$ or 2, $\{x\} = 0$

$\Rightarrow$ $fog(x) = \ln 2$ $\Rightarrow$ Range of $fog(x) = [\ln 2, \ln 4)$

■ COMPOSITION OF NON-UNIFORMLY DEFINED FUNCTIONS

Piecewise or non-uniformly defined functions are those functions whose domain is divided into two or more than two parts so that the function has different analytical formulae in different parts of its domain. We can say that a piecewise defined function is composed of branches of two or more functions.

$$\text{e.g., } f(x) = \begin{cases} 3x+1; & -\infty < x \le -\dfrac{1}{3} \\ \sin 3\pi x; & -\dfrac{1}{3} < x \le 0 \\ \tan x; & 0 < x \le \dfrac{\pi}{4} \\ x; & x > \dfrac{\pi}{4} \end{cases}$$

The domain of function $f(x)$, i.e., $(-\infty, \infty)$ is divided into four parts, i.e., $\left(-\infty, -\dfrac{1}{3}\right]$, $\left(-\dfrac{1}{3}, 0\right]$, $\left(0, \dfrac{\pi}{4}\right]$ and $\left(\dfrac{\pi}{4}, \infty\right)$. Graphically it is shown in Figure 2.154.

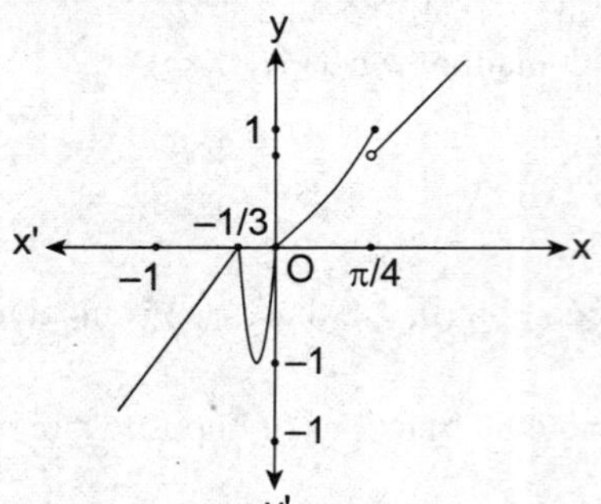

FIGURE 2.154

Now let us discuss the method to find the composition of two non-uniformly defined functions with the help of following example. Consider the functions as defined below

$$f(x) = \begin{cases} 2x-1; & 0 \le x < 2 \\ x^2+1; & 2 \le x \le 4 \end{cases} \ \& \ g(x) = \begin{cases} x+1; & -1 \le x < 1 \\ 2x; & 1 \le x \le 3 \end{cases}$$

Let us find the composite function $fog(x)$. The following steps are involved.

Step 1: Replace $g(x)$ in the place of x in the definition of $f(x)$.

$$\text{i.e., } f(g(x)) = \begin{cases} 2g(x)-1; & 0 \le g(x) < 2 \\ g(x))^2+1; & 2 \le g(x) \le 4 \end{cases}$$

Step 2: Apply the definition of $g(x)$ in the above step (1).

$$\Rightarrow f(g(x)) = \begin{cases} 2(x+1)-1; & -1 \le x < 1 \ \& \ 0 \le x+1 < 2 \\ 2(2x)-1; & 1 \le x \le 3 \ \& \ 0 \le 2x < 2 \\ (x+1)^2+1; & -1 \le x < 1 \ \& \ 2 \le x+1 \le 4 \\ (2x)^2+1; & 1 \le x \le 3 \ \& \ 2 \le 2x \le 4 \end{cases}$$

Step 3: Take the intersection of domains and find the final definition.

$$\text{i.e., } f(g(x)) = \begin{cases} 2(x+1)-1; & -1 \le x < 1 \\ 2(2x)-1; & x \in \{\} \\ (x+1)^2+1; & x \in \{\} \\ (2x)^2+1; & 1 \le x \le 2 \end{cases}$$

$$\Rightarrow \quad fog(x) = \begin{cases} 2x+1; & -1 \le x < 1 \\ 4x^2+1; & 1 \le x \le 2 \end{cases}$$

Thus, the domain of composite function $fog(x)$ is $[-1, 2]$ and graphically as shown in Figure 2.155.

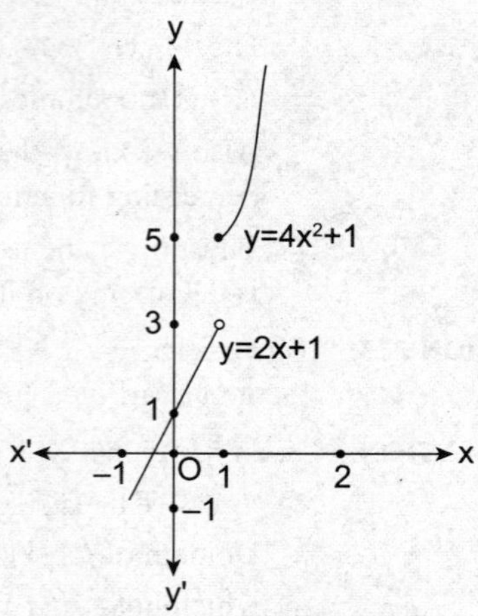

FIGURE 2.155

ILLUSTRATION 216: If $f(x) = -1 + |x-2|;\ 0 \le x \le 4$ and $g(x) = 2 - |x|;\ -1 \le x \le 3$; then find $fog(x)$ and $gof(x)$. Draw rough sketches of the graphs of $fog(x)$ and $gof(x)$.

SOLUTION: Given $f(x) = \begin{cases} -1-(x-2); & 0 \le x < 2 \\ -1+(x-2); & 2 \le x \le 4 \end{cases}$

$$\Rightarrow f(x) = \begin{cases} 1-x; & 0 \le x < 2 \\ x-3; & 2 \le x \le 4 \end{cases} \text{ and } g(x) = \begin{cases} 2+x; & -1 \le x < 0 \\ 2-x; & 0 \le x \le 3 \end{cases}$$

$$fog\,(x) = f(g(x)) = \begin{cases} 1-g(x); & 0 \le g(x) < 2 \\ g(x)-3; & 2 \le g(x) \le 4 \end{cases}$$

$$= \begin{cases} 1-(2+x); & 0 \le 2+x < 2; -1 \le x < 0 \\ 1-(2-x); & 0 \le 2-x < 2;\ 0 \le x \le 3 \\ (2+x)-3; & 2 \le 2+x \le 4; -1 \le x < 0 \\ (2-x)-3; & 2 \le 2-x \le 4;\ 0 \le x \le 3 \end{cases} = \begin{cases} -1-x; & -2 \le x < 0; -1 \le x < 0 \\ x-1; & 0 < x \le 2;\ 0 \le x \le 3 \\ x-1; & 0 \le x \le 2; -1 \le x < 0 \\ -1-x; & -2 \le x \le 0;\ 0 \le x \le 3 \end{cases}$$

$$f(g(x)) = \begin{cases} -1-x; & -1 \le x < 0 \\ x-1; & 0 \le x \le 2 \end{cases}\text{; graphically shown in Figure.}$$

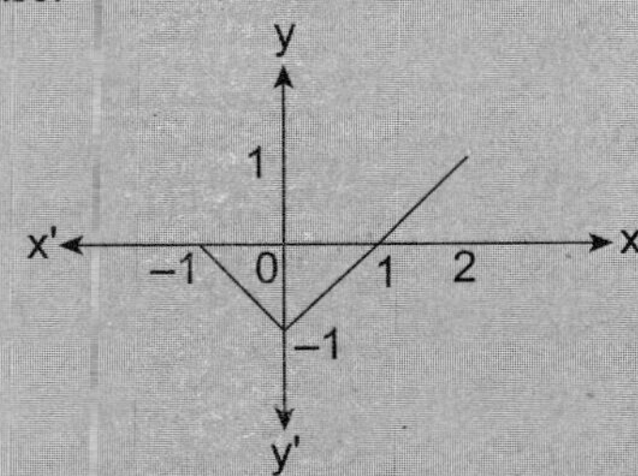

FIGURE 2.156

$$\text{Next } (gof)\,(x) = g(f(x)) = \begin{cases} 2+f(x); & -1 \le f(x) \le 0 \\ 2-f(x); & 0 \le f(x) \le 3 \end{cases}$$

$$= \begin{cases} 2-(x-3); & 0 \le (x-3) \le 3;\ 2 \le x \le 4 \\ 2-(1-x); & 0 \le (1-x) \le 3;\ 0 \le x < 2 \\ 2+(x-3); & -1 \le (x-3) \le 0;\ 2 \le x \le 4 \\ 2+(1-x); & -1 \le (1-x) \le 0;\ 0 \le x < 2 \end{cases}$$

$$= \begin{cases} 5-x; & 3 \le x \le 6;\ 2 \le x < 4 \\ 1+x; & -2 \le x \le 1;\ 0 \le x < 2 \\ x-1; & 2 \le x \le 3;\ 2 \le x \le 4 \\ 3-x; & 1 \le x \le 2;\ 0 \le x < 2 \end{cases}$$

$$(gof)(x) = \begin{cases} 1+x; & 0 \le x < 1 \\ 3-x; & 1 \le x < 2 \\ x-1; & 2 \le x < 3 \\ 5-x; & 3 \le x \le 4 \end{cases}\text{; graphically shown in Figure.}$$

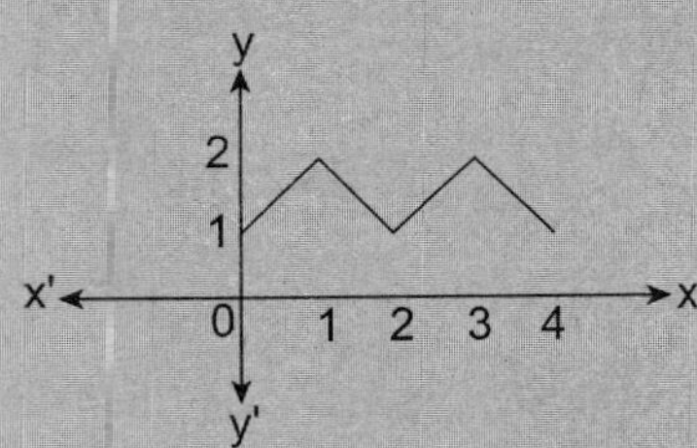

FIGURE 2.157

ILLUSTRATION 217: Composition of piecewise defined functions:
If $f(x) = |\,|x-3| - 2\,|;\ 0 \le x \le 4$
$g(x) = 4 - |2-x|;\ -1 \le x \le 3$, then find $fog(x)$ and draw rough sketch of $fog(x)$.

SOLUTION: $f(x) = |\,|x-3| - 2|;\ 0 \le x \le 4$

$$\Rightarrow f(x) = \begin{cases} |x-1|; & 0 \le x < 3 \\ |x-5|; & 3 \le x \le 4 \end{cases} = \begin{cases} 1-x; & 0 \le x < 1 \\ x-1; & 1 \le x < 3 \\ 5-x; & 3 \le x \le 4 \end{cases}$$

And $g(x) = 4 - |2-x|;\ -1 \le x \le 3$

$$= \begin{cases} 4-(2-x); & -1 \le x < 2 \\ 4-(x-2); & 2 \le x \le 3 \end{cases} = \begin{cases} 2+x; & -1 \le x < 2 \\ 6-x; & 2 \le x \le 3 \end{cases}$$

$$\therefore \quad fog(x)=\begin{cases}1-g(x);\ 0\le g(x)<1\\ g(x)-1;\ 1\le g(x)<3\\ 5-g(x);\ 3\le g(x)\le 4\end{cases}=\begin{cases}1-(2+x); & 0\le 2+x<1 & \text{and} & -1\le x<2\\ 2+x-1; & 1\le 2+x<3 & \text{and} & -1\le x<2\\ 5-(2+x); & 3\le 2+x\le 4 & \text{and} & -1\le x<2\\ 1-6+x; & 0\le 6-x<1 & \text{and} & 2\le x\le 3\\ 6-x-1; & 1\le 6-x<3 & \text{and} & 2\le x\le 3\\ 5-6+x; & 3\le 6-x\le 4 & \text{and} & 2\le x\le 3\end{cases}$$

$$=\begin{cases}-1-x; & -2\le x<-1 & \text{and} & -1\le x<2\\ 1+x; & -1\le x<1 & \text{and} & -1\le x<2\\ 3-x; & 1\le x\le 2 & \text{and} & -1\le x<2\\ x-5; & -6\le -x<-5 & \text{and} & 2\le x\le 3\\ 5-x; & -5\le -x<-3 & \text{and} & 2\le x\le 3\\ x-1; & -3\le -x\le -2 & \text{and} & 2\le x\le 3\end{cases}=\begin{cases}-1-x; & -2\le x<-1 & \text{and} & -1\le x<2\\ 1+x; & -1\le x<1 & \text{and} & -1\le x<2\\ 3-x; & 1\le x\le 2 & \text{and} & -1\le x<2\\ x-5; & 5<x\le 6 & \text{and} & 2\le x\le 3\\ 5-x; & 3<x\le 5 & \text{and} & 2\le x\le 3\\ x-1; & 2\le x\le 3 & \text{and} & 2\le x\le 3\end{cases}$$

$$=\begin{cases}1+x; & -1\le x<1\\ 3-x; & 1\le x<2\\ x-1; & 2\le x\le 3\end{cases}$$

Alternate method for finding fog: $g(x)=\begin{cases}2+x; & -1\le x<2\\ 6-x; & 2\le x\le 3\end{cases}$

Graph of $g(x)$ is

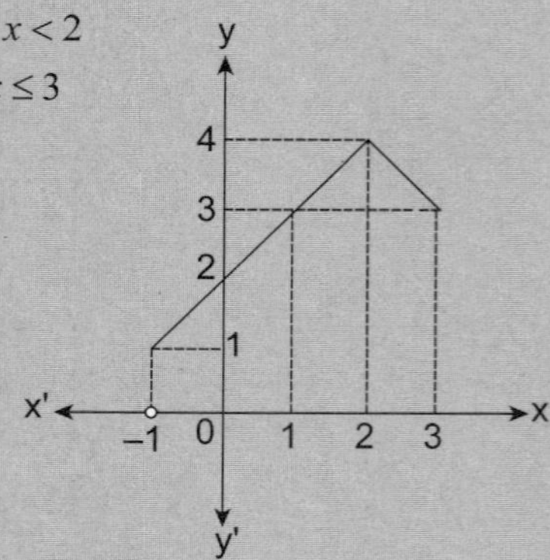

FIGURE 2.158

$$fog(x)=\begin{cases}1-g(x);\ 0\le g(x)<1\\ g(x)-1;\ 1\le g(x)<3\\ 5-g(x);\ 3\le g(x)\le 4\end{cases}$$

From the graph of $g(x)$, we note that no portion of graph of $g(x)$ lies in the interval [0, 1).

Also $g(x)\in[1, 3)$ for $x\in[-1, 1)$ and $g(x)\in[3, 4]$ for $x\in[1, 3]$

$$\therefore \quad fog(x)=\begin{cases}1-g(x); & \text{for no value}\\ g(x)-1; & -1\le x<1\\ 5-g(x); & 1\le x\le 3\end{cases} \quad \text{.... (1)}$$

Now for $x\in[-1, 1)$, $g(x)=(2+x)$; for $x\in[1, 2)$, $g(x)=(2+x)$ and for $x\in[2, 3]$, $g(x)=(6-x)$

Therefore from (1), we have

$$fog(x)=\begin{cases}2+x-1; & -1\le x<1\\ 5-(2+x); & 1\le x<2\\ 5-(6-x); & 2\le x\le 3\end{cases}$$

$$=\begin{cases}x+1; & -1\le x<1\\ 3-x; & 1\le x<2\\ x-1; & 2\le x\le 3\end{cases}$$; graphically shown in Figure.

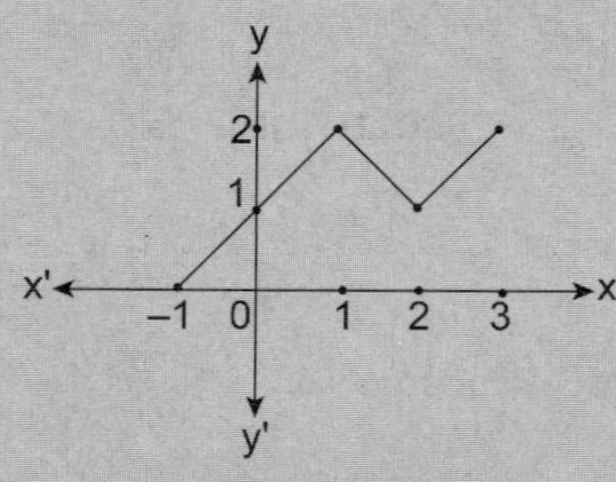

FIGURE 2.159

TEXTUAL EXERCISE–13: (SUBJECTIVE)

1. Let *f*, *g* be real valued functions defined as:

$$f(x) = \begin{cases} 7x^2+x-8; & x \le 1 \\ 4x+5; & 1 < x \le 7 \\ 8x+3; & x > 7 \end{cases} \text{ and}$$

$$g(x) = \begin{cases} |x|; & x < -3 \\ 0; & -3 \le x < 2 \\ x^2+4; & x \ge 2 \end{cases}$$

Find the values of composite functions at given points $(fog)(-3)$, $(fog)(7)$, $(fog)(9)$, $(gof)(2)$, $(gof)(0)$, $(gof)(6)$.

2. Let $f(x) = \dfrac{ax}{x+1}$ $x \ne -1$. If $(fof)(x) = x$, find the value of *a*.

3. The function *f* is defined on the interval [0, 1), then find the domain of definition of the following functions; where [ ] denotes the greatest integer function.
(i) $f(|[x-2.5]|)$
(ii) $f(\cos x)$

4. Define $fog(x)$ and $gof(x)$. Also find their domain and range.
(i) $f(x) = [x]$, $g(x) = \sin x$
(ii) $f(x) = \tan x$, $x \in \left(-\dfrac{\pi}{2}, \dfrac{\pi}{2}\right)$; $g(x) = \sqrt{1-x^2}$

5. Find the composite function $fof(x)$ for the following functions
(a) $f(x) = \begin{cases} 1+x; & 0 \le x \le 2 \\ 3-x; & 2 < x \le 3 \end{cases}$
(b) $f(x) = -1 + |x-2|$; $0 \le x \le 4$
(c) $f(x) = 2 - |x|$; $-1 \le x \le 3$
(d) $f(x) = \begin{cases} x+1; & x \le 1 \\ 5-x^2; & x > 1 \end{cases}$
(e) $f(x) = \begin{cases} -x; & x < 0 \\ x; & 0 \le x \le 1 \\ 2-x; & x > 1 \end{cases}$.

6. Find composition function $fog(x)$ for the following functions
(a) $f(x) = \begin{bmatrix} 1+x^2 & x \le 1 \\ x+1 & 1 < x \le 2 \end{bmatrix}$ and $g(x) = 1-x$; $-2 \le x \le 1$
(b) $f(x) = \begin{cases} 1+x; & x \le 1 \\ 2x+2; & 1 < x \le 2 \end{cases}$ and
$g(x) = \begin{cases} x^2; & -1 \le x < 2 \\ x+2; & 2 \le x \le 3 \end{cases}$

7. Find the composite functions $fog(x)$ and $gof(x)$ for the following functions:
(a) $f(x) = -1 + |x-2|$, $0 \le x \le 4$; $g(x) = 2 - |x|$, $-1 \le x \le 3$
Draw rough sketch of the graphs of $fog(x)$ and $gof(x)$.
(b) $f(x) = \begin{cases} x+1; & x \le 1 \\ 2x+1; & 1 < x \le 2 \end{cases}$ and
$g(x) = \begin{cases} x^2; & -1 < x \le 2 \\ x+2; & 2 < x \le 3 \end{cases}$

8. Give two function $f: \mathbb{N} \to \mathbb{N}$ and $g: \mathbb{N} \to \mathbb{N}$ such that *gof* is onto but *f* is not onto.

9. Show that if for a map $f: X \to Y$, there exists a map $g: Y \to X$ such that $(fog)(y) = y$, for every $y \in Y$, then *f* is onto.

10. Show that if for $f: X \to Y$, there exists a map $g: Y \to X$ such that $(gof)(x) = x$ for all $x \in X$, then *f* is one–one.

11. A function is defined as $f: D \to \mathbb{R}$, $f(x) = \cot^{-1}(sgn\ x) + \sin^{-1}(x - \{x\})$ where $\{x\}$ denotes the fractional part function. Find the largest domain and range of the function. State with reasons whether the function is injective or not. Also draw the graph of the function.

12. Given two functions $f(x)$ and $g(x)$ defined as below $f(x) = \begin{cases} x+2; & x \le 1 \\ 2x+1; & 1 < x \le 3 \end{cases}$ and
$g(x) = \begin{cases} x^2+1; & -1 \le x \le 4 \\ x-1; & 4 < x \le 6 \end{cases}$. Find composite functions $f(g(x))$ and $g(f(x))$ and their domain and range and also find the number of solutions of equations
(a) $f(g(x)) = 5.01$ (b) $f(g(x)) = 5$
(c) $f(g(x)) = 1$

13. Let $f(x) = \begin{cases} x+a; & \text{if } x < 0 \\ |x-1|; & \text{if } x \ge 0 \end{cases}$ and
$g(x) = \begin{cases} x+1; & \text{if } x < 0 \\ (x-1)^2+b; & \text{if } x \ge 0 \end{cases}$; where *a* and *b* are

non-negative real numbers. Determine the composite function *gof*. If (*gof*) (*x*) is continuous for all real *x*, determine the values of a and *b*. Further for these values of a and *b*, is *gof* differentiable at $x = 0$? Justify your answer.

14. Let *f* be increasing and *g* be decreasing functions from $[0, \infty)$ to $[0, \infty)$. Let $h(x) = (fog)(x)$ and $h(0) = 0$. Prove that $h(x) = 0 \ \forall\ x \in [0, \infty)$.

15. If $f : [0, 1] \to [1, 2]$, defined by $f(x) = 1 + x$ and $g : [1, 2] \to [0,1]$ defined by $g(x) = 2 - x$, determine *gof*.

16. Find domain and range of the following functions:

(i) $f(x) = \cos^{-1}\sqrt{\log_{[x]}\frac{|x|}{x}}$, where [.] denotes the greatest integer function

(ii) $f(x) = \sqrt{\ell n(\cos(\sin x))}$

Answer Keys

1. $(fog)(-3) = -8$, $(fog)(7) = 427$, $(fog)(9) = 683$, $(gof)(2) = 173$, $(gof)(0) = 8$, $(gof)(6) = 845$.

2. -1 **3.** (i) $\left[\frac{5}{2}, \frac{7}{2}\right)$ (ii) $\bigcup_{n\in\mathbb{Z}}\left[2n\pi - \frac{\pi}{2}, 2n\pi + \frac{\pi}{2}\right] \sim \{2n\pi\}$

4. (i) $gof = \sin[x]$; domain : $\mathbb{R}$; range $\{\sin a : a \in I\}$ $fog = [\sin x]$; domain : $\mathbb{R}$; range : $\{-1, 0, 1\}$

(ii) $gof = \sqrt{1-\tan^2 x}$; domain $= \left[-\frac{\pi}{4}, \frac{\pi}{4}\right]$; range : [0, 1] $fog = \tan\sqrt{1-x^2}$; domain : $[-1, 1]$; range $[0, \tan 1]$

5. (a) $\begin{cases} x+2 & 0 \le x \le 1 \\ 2-x & 1 < x \le 2 \\ 4-x & 2 < x \le 3 \end{cases}$ (b) $\begin{cases} x & ,0 \le x \le 2 \\ 4-x & ,2 < x \le 2 \end{cases}$

(c) $\begin{cases} -x & ,-1 \le x \le 0 \\ x & ,0 < x \le 2 \\ 4-x & ,2 < x \le 3 \end{cases}$ (d) $\begin{cases} x+2; & x \le 0 \\ 5-(x+1)^2; & 0 < x \le 1 \\ 5-(5-x^2)^2; & 1 < x < 2 \\ (5-x^2)+1; & x \ge 2 \end{cases}$

(e) $\begin{cases} 2+x; & x < -1 \\ -x; & -1 \le x \le 0 \\ x; & 0 \le x \le 1 \\ 2-x; & 1 < x \le 2 \\ -(2-x); & x > 2 \end{cases}$

6. (a) $\begin{cases} 2-2x+x^2; & x \le 1 \\ x+1; & -1 \le x < 0 \end{cases}$ (b) $\begin{cases} 1+x^2; & -1 \le x \le 1 \\ 2x^2+2; & 1 < x \le \sqrt{2} \end{cases}$

7. (a) $fog(x) = \begin{cases} -(1+x) & ,-1 \le x \le 0 \\ x-1 & ,0 < x \le 2 \end{cases}$; $gof(x) = \begin{cases} x+1 & ,0 \le x < 1 \\ 3-x & ,1 \le x \le 2 \\ x-1 & ,2 < x \le 3 \\ 5-x & ,3 < x \le 4 \end{cases}$

(b) $fog(x) = \begin{cases} x^2+1; & -1 \le x < 1 \\ 2x^2+1; & 1 < x \le \sqrt{2} \end{cases}$; $gof(x) = \{(x+1)^2, -2 \le x \le 1\}$.

8. $f(x) = 2x + 4$; $g(x) = \frac{x-4}{2}$; $f(x) = x^2 + 3$; $g(x) = \sqrt{x-3}$

11. $D = [-1, 2)$; $R = \left\{\frac{\pi}{4}, \frac{\pi}{2}, \frac{3\pi}{4}\right\}$; the function is neither injective nor surjective.

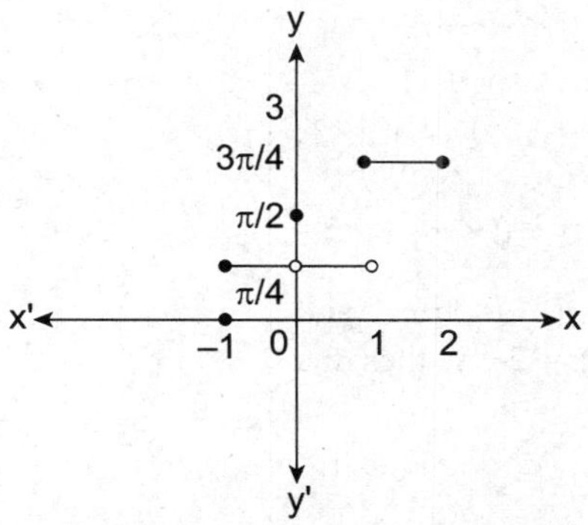

FIGURE 2.160

12. $f(g(x)) = \begin{cases} x^2+3; & x=0 \\ 2x^2+3; & -1 \le x < 0 \text{ or } 0 < x \le \sqrt{2} \end{cases}$; domain of $f(g(x)) = \left[-1, \sqrt{2}\right]$ and range [3, 7].

$gof(x) = \begin{cases} x^2+4x+5; & -3 \le x \le 1 \\ 4x^2+4x+2; & 1 < x \le 3/2 \\ 2x; & 3/2 < x \le 5/2 \end{cases}$; domain of $gof(x) = \left[-3, \dfrac{5}{2}\right]$ and range [1, 17]

(a) 1 solution (b) 2 solution (c) no solution

13. $gof(x) = \begin{cases} x+a+1; & x < -a \\ (x+a-1)^2+b; & -a \le x < 0 \\ x^2+b; & 0 \le x < 1 \\ (x-2)^2+b; & x \ge 1 \end{cases}$; $a = 1$ and $b = 0$; yes.

15. $(gof)(x) = 1 - x,\ 0 \le x \le 1$

16. (i) $D : [2, \infty)$; $R : \{\pi/2\}$ (ii) $D : n\pi,\ n \in I$; $R : \{0\}$

TEXTUAL EXERCISE–13: (OBJECTIVE)

1. If f and g are bijective functions and gof is defined then, gof must be

(a) injective (b) surjective
(c) bijective (d) into only

2. Number of functions which can be defined from $R \to R$ for which the composite function $f(f(x))$ is an identity function for every $x \in \mathbb{R}$, is

(a) zero
(b) exactly one
(c) exactly two
(d) infinite

3. Let $f(x) = \dfrac{1}{x}$ & $g(x) = \dfrac{1}{\sqrt{x}}$

(a) $f(g(x))$ and $g(f(x))$ have different domains
(b) $f(g(x))$ and $g(f(x))$ have the same range
(c) $f(g(x))$ is a bijective mapping
(d) $g(f(x))$ is neither odd nor even

4. Let f and g be two functions both being defined from $R \to R$ as follows: $f(x) = \dfrac{x+|x|}{2}$ and $g(x) = \begin{bmatrix} x \text{ for } x < 0 \\ x^2 \text{ for } x \ge 0 \end{bmatrix}$. Then

(a) fog is defined but gof is not
(b) gof is defined but fog is not
(c) both gof and fog are defined but they are unequal
(d) both gof and fog are defined and they are equal.

5. Let $f(x) = \sin x$ and $g(x) = |\ell n\, x|$ if composite functions $fog(x)$ and $gof(x)$ are defined and have ranges R_1 and R_2, respectively, then

(a) $R_1 = \{u : -1 < u < 1\}$; $R_2 = \{v : 0 < v < \infty\}$
(b) $R_1 = \{u : -\infty < u < 0\}$; $R_2 = \{v : -1 < v < 1\}$
(c) $R_1 = \{u : 0 < u < \infty\}$; $R_2 = \{v : -1 < v < 1; v \neq 0\}$
(d) $R_1 = \{u : -1 < u < 1\}$; $R_2 = \{v : 0 < v < \infty\}$

6. Let $f : [0, 1] \to [1, 2]$ defined as $f(x) = 1 + x$ and $g : [1, 2] \to [0, 1]$ defined as $g(x) = 2 - x$, then the composite function *gof* is
(a) Injective as well as surjective
(b) Surjective but not injective
(c) Injective but not surjective
(d) Neither injective nor surjective

7. If $f(x) = -1 + |x - 1|$, $-1 \le x \le 3$ and $g(x) = 2 - |x + 1|$, $-2 \le x \le 2$ then find $(fog)(3/2)$ equals
(a) 0
(b) 1
(c) 1/2
(d) None of these

8. On the interval [0, 1], $f(x)$ is defined as, $f(x)=\begin{bmatrix} x & \text{if } x \in Q \\ 1-x & \text{if } x \notin Q \end{bmatrix}$. Then for all $x \in R$ the composite function $f(f(x))$ is
(a) a constant function
(b) an identity function
(c) an odd linear polynomial
(d) $1 + x$

9. Given the graphs of the two functions, $y = f(x)$ and $y = g(x)$. In the adjacent figure from point *A* on the graph of the function $y = f(x)$ corresponding to the given value of the independent variable (say x_0), a straight line is drawn parallel to the *x*-axis to intersect the bisector of the first and the third quadrants at point *B*. From the point *B* a straight line parallel to the *y*-axis is drawn to intersect the graph of the function $y = g(x)$ at *C*. Again a straight line is drawn from the point *C* parallel to the *x*-axis, to intersect the line *NN'* at *D*. If the straight line *NN'* is parallel to *y*-axis, then the co-ordinates of the point *D* are

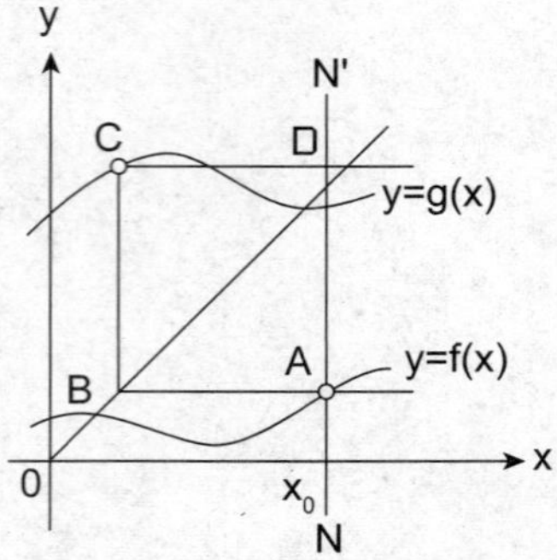

FIGURE 2.161

(a) $f(x_0), g(f(x_0))$
(b) $x_0, g(x_0)$
(c) $x_0, g(f(x_0))$
(d) $f(x_0), f(g(x_0))$

10. If $f(x) = x^2 + 2x + 1$ and $g[f(x)] = |x + 1|$ then the function $g(x)$ is
(a) $g(x) = -x\sqrt{x}$
(b) $g(x) = x\sqrt{x}$
(c) $g(x) = x^{5/2}$
(d) None of these

11. If $f(x) = x^2 + 2x + 1$ and $g[f(x)] = |x + 1|$, then the function $g(x)$ is
(a) $x\sqrt{x}$
(b) $\sqrt{x}$
(c) $\sqrt[3]{x}$
(d) None of these

12. If $f(x) = (ax^3 + b)^5$, such that $f(g(x)) = g(f(x))$, then
(a) $f(g(x)) = x$ (b) $g(x)=\left(\frac{x^{1/5}-b}{a}\right)^{1/3}$
(c) $f(g(x)) = 2x$ (d) None of these

13. If $f(x) = \sin^2 x$, $g(x) = \sqrt{x}$ x and $h(x) = \cos^{-1} x$, $0 \le x \le 1$, then:
(a) $hogof(x) = gofoh(x)$
(b) $gofoh(x) = fohog(x)$
(c) $fohog(x) = hogof(x)$
(d) None of these

Answer Keys

1. (a)	**2.** (d)	**3.** (b,c,d)	**4.** (d)	**5.** (d)	**6.** (a)	**7.** (c)	**8.** (b,d)	**9.** (c)	**10.** (b)
11. (b)	**12.** (a,b)	**13.** (d)							

■ INVERTIBLE/NON-INVERTIBLE FUNCTIONS

While studying function so far we have evolved it as a machine that picks up elements as inputs (pre-images) from domain set D_f and $\forall\ x \in D_f$ generates an output (image) in another set (co–domain) and is denoted as $f(x)$ and f is called connecting rule. *A* natural question arises, 'whether a machine exists that converts back the output (images) produced by machine f to input (pre-images)?' Of-course yes, such machines are called inverse machines and mathematically denoted as inverse function of $f(x)$, symbolized by $f^{-1}: Y \to X$ .i.e., pre-image(s) $= f^{-1}$(image)

In some case the invertibility of relation is easily conceivable, for instance the relation 'teacher of' is the inverse relation of 'student of'. On the other hand in most of the cases involving functions, the inverse relation is not so explicitly conceivable, for instance the inverse of relation '*a* is son of *b*' is not exact, as *b* may be father or mother of *a*. Therefore mathematicians needed to develop a technique (better called algorithm) to obtain inverse function (relation) for a given function.

To obtain inverse function first of all it is necessary to furnish rules by which inversion has to take place, however keeping in mind such rules, f^{1} has to be function from $Y \to X$. This clearly put a restriction that each element *y* (images under *f*) of *Y* must be related with exactly one element *x* (pre-image under *f*) of *X*.

Consequently the inverse function f^{1} so obtained is always defined from its domain (*Y*) to its co-domain (*X*). Thus, we can conclude that domain and co-domain of f is exchanged for f^{1} and there should be bidirectional restriction on $X \to Y$ that each element of one set is related with exactly one element of other set, i.e., the process of inversion can be carried out for any function $f: X \to Y$ which is bijective. For instance if f is continuous and monotonic on an interval $[a, b] \to [c, d]$, naturally it becomes invertible.

Definition of Inverse of a Function

A function $f: X \to Y$ is said to be invertible iff there exists another function $g : Y \to X$ such that $f(x) = y \Leftrightarrow g(y) = x$, $\forall$ $x \in X$ and $y \in Y$.

Then $g : Y \to X$ is called inverse of $f : X \to Y$ and is denoted by f^{-1}.

$\Rightarrow\quad g = f^{-1} = \{(f(x), x): (x, f(x)) \in f\}$

e.g., let $A = \{2, 3, 5, 7\}$; $B = \{3, 8, 24, 48\}$

Define a function $f: A \to B$ as $f(x) = x^2 - 1$

Then $f = \{(2, 3), (3, 8), (5, 24), (7, 48)\}$. Now if we define another function $g : B \to A$ as $g(x) = \sqrt{x+1}$, then $g = \{(3, 2), (8, 3), (24, 5), (48, 7)\}$. Clearly $(x, y) \in f \Leftrightarrow (y, x) \in g$ for all ordered pairs (x, y) and (y, x)

Thus, $f : A \to B$ is invertible and $f^{-1} = g$ and $g^{-1} = f$ i.e., inverse of function $f(x) = x^2 - 1$ is $g(x) = \sqrt{x+1}$ and inverse of $g(x) = \sqrt{x+1}$ is $f(x) = x^2 - 1$.

ILLUSTRATION 218: Find the inverse of $y = x^2 (x > 0)$ and draw its graph.

SOLUTION: Given function is $f(x) = x^2$, i.e., function converts x (> 0) to x^2.

Thus, $(x, x^2) \in f$ for $x > 0$, which implies $(x^2, x) \in f^{1}$ for $x > 0$

i.e., $(x, \sqrt{x}) \in f^{1}$ for $x > 0$, i.e., $y = \sqrt{x}$; $x > 0$ represents the inverse of function $y = x^2 (x > 0)$

The graphs of function $f(x) = x^2$ $(x > 0)$ and $f^{1}(x) = \sqrt{x}$ $(x > 0)$ are shown below,

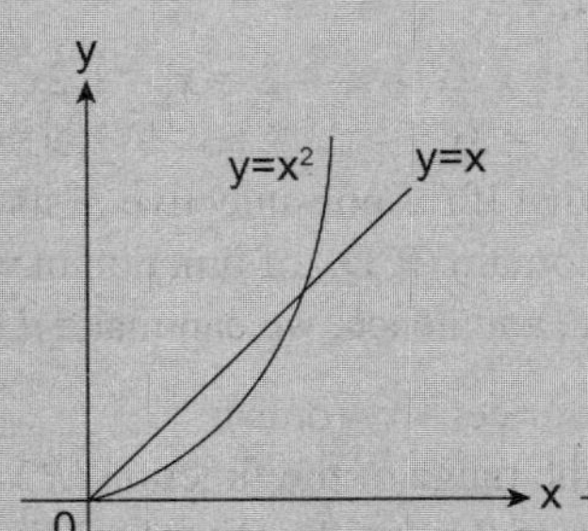

FIGURE 2.162

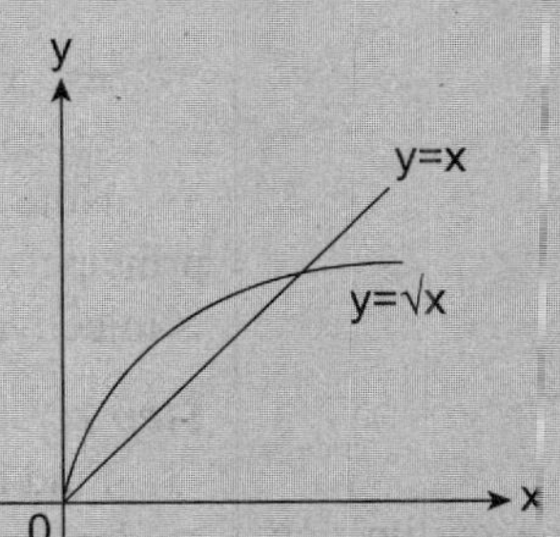

FIGURE 2.163

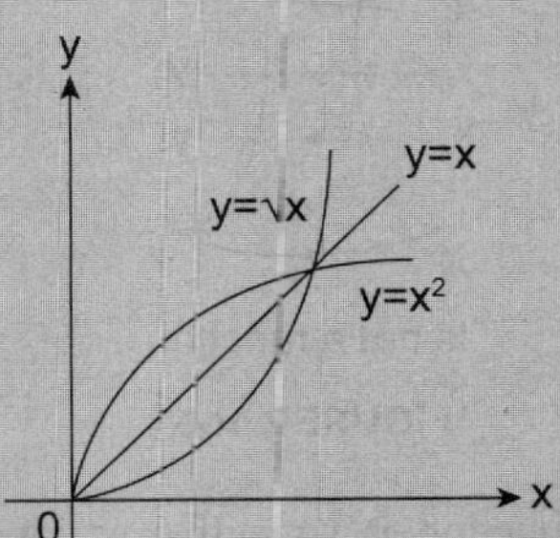

FIGURE 2.164

■ CONDITIONS OF INVERTIBILITY OF A FUNCTION

For a function to be invertible it must be a bijective function. In case the function loses at least one of the two properties i.e., surjectivity and injectivity, then the function remains no more invertible as is clear from the discussion given below.

Case I: Let f be one–one but not onto.

Consider the function $f : X \to Y$ such that $f = \{(x_1, y_1), (x_2, y_2), (x_3, y_3), (x_4, y_4)\}$ (shown in Figure 2.165), where $X = \{x_1, x_2, x_3, x_4\}$ and $Y = \{y_1, y_2, y_3, y_4, y_5\}$.

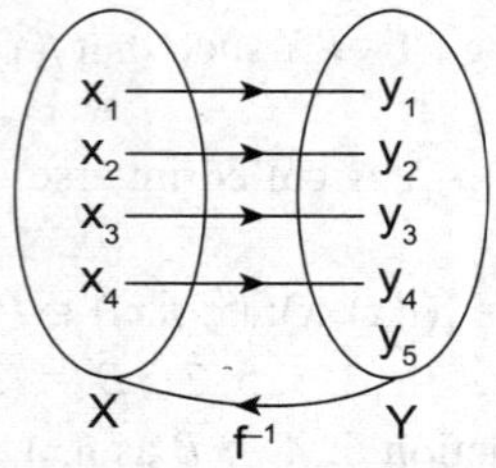

FIGURE 2.165

Clearly the function f is injective as different inputs from X are mapped to different outputs in Y. However, the function is not surjective as $y_5 \in Y$ has no pre image in X under f.

As there is no output for y_5 under the relation g from set Y to X defined by $g(y_i) = x_i \Leftrightarrow f(x_i) = y_i$.

$\Rightarrow$ $g : Y \to X$ is not a function.

$\Rightarrow$ f is not invertible from set X to set Y. Thus, for f to be invertible f should be surjective

Case II: Let f be onto but not one–one.

Consider the function f from set X to set Y such that $f = \{(x_1, y_1), (x_2, y_1), (x_3, y_2), (x_4, y_3)\}$ (shown in Figure 2.166), where $X = \{x_1, x_2, x_3, x_4\}$ and $Y = \{y_1, y_2, y_3\}$.

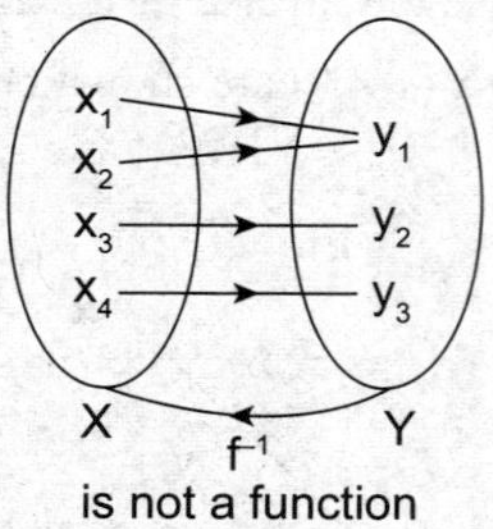

FIGURE 2.166

Clearly the function is surjective as range of function f = co-domain Y. However, the function f is not injective as there is same output y_1 corresponding to different inputs x_1, x_2.

$\Rightarrow$ the relation $g : Y \to X$ defined by $g(y_i) = x_i \Leftrightarrow f(x_i) = y_i$ is not a function h as there are two outputs x_1, x_2 corresponding to input y_1 under the relation g.

$\Rightarrow$ f is not invertible.

$\Rightarrow$ For f to be invertible it must be injective.

■ CONCLUSION

For a function to be invertible it should be one–one and onto, i.e., bijective function.

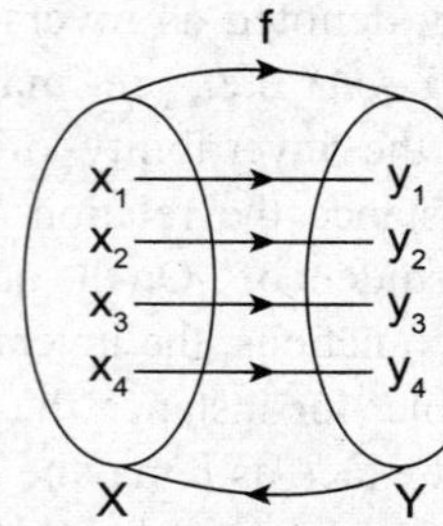

FIGURE 2.167

Method to Find Inverse of a Given Function

Before finding the inverse of a given function $f : X \to Y$ we test the function for bijectivity as if the function is bijective, only then we can find its inverse, otherwise it is not invertible.

We shall demonstrate the procedure to find the inverse of a function with the help of an illustration. Let $f(x) = \dfrac{x-1}{x+2}$ be the given function defined from $\mathbb{R} \sim \{-2\} \to \mathbb{R}$.

Step 1: Check the injectivity (one–one): Take $f(x_1) = f(x_2)$ and show that $x_1 = x_2$ or show that f is continuous and monotonic on its domain.

Here $f(x_1) = f(x_2)$

$$\Rightarrow \frac{x_1 - 1}{x_1 + 2} = \frac{x_2 - 1}{x_2 + 2}$$

$$\Rightarrow x_1x_2 + 2x_1 - x_2 - 2 = x_1x_2 + 2x_2 - x_1 - 2$$

$$\Rightarrow 3x_1 = 3x_2 \quad \Rightarrow \quad x_1 = x_2.$$

Note that if f is non-injective in its domain, then define principal domain (P. D.) of function in which every function is injective, and hence, we can make $f(x)$ injective.

Step 2: Surjectivity (onto):

Find the range of the function (R_f) and compare it with co-domain. If R_f = co-domain, then f is onto.

Here, let $y = \dfrac{x-1}{x+2}$

$\Rightarrow \quad x = \dfrac{1+2y}{1-y}$

$\Rightarrow$ Range of function is $R_f = \mathbb{R} \sim \{1\}$
So, f is an into function

$\Rightarrow f(x) = \dfrac{x-1}{x+2}$ is not invertible from set $\mathbb{R} \sim \{-2\} \to \mathbb{R}$ due to lack of surjectivity.

Note that had the function f been defined as $f: \mathbb{R} \sim \{-2\} \to \mathbb{R} \sim \{1\}$, then the function would have been invertible. If f is not onto, then to make it surjective replace co-domain by Range (R_f).

Step 3: Using equation $y = f(x)$ express x in terms of y.

$$\Rightarrow \quad x = \frac{1+2y}{1-y} \qquad \text{.... (1)}$$

Step 4: Replace x by y and y by x in the obtained relation (1) to get $y = f^{-1}(x)$.

$\Rightarrow \quad y = \dfrac{1+2x}{1-x}$ is required inverse function $f^{-1}(x)$

if $f(x)$ is defined from $\mathbb{R} \sim \{-2\} \to \mathbb{R} \sim \{1\}$ for verification, show that $f(f^{-1}(x)) = x \;\forall\, x \in Y$; where f: X $\to$ Y is bijective.

$$\text{i.e., } \frac{\dfrac{2x+1}{1-x}-1}{\dfrac{2x+1}{1-x}+2} = \frac{2x+1-1+x}{2x+1+2-2x} = \frac{3x}{3} = x$$

Hence, verified.

REMARK

Since to each $(x, y) \in f$, there exists $(y, x) \in f^{-1}$ and (y, x) and (x, y) are mirror images of each other in the line $y = x$, therefore the graph of $f^{-1}(x)$ is obtained by reflecting the graph of $f(x)$ in the line $y = x$ as shown in Figure 2.168.

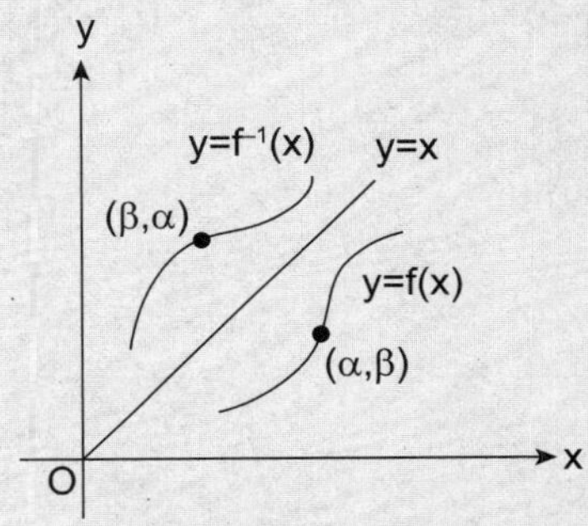

FIGURE 2.168

ILLUSTRATION 219: Find whether the function $f(x) = \dfrac{2x+5}{7}$ from $\mathbb{R} \to \mathbb{R}$ is invertible or not. If invertible, then find its inverse.

SOLUTION: Given function is $f(x) : A \to B$; where $y = \dfrac{2x+5}{7}$; $A = \mathbb{R}$; $B = \mathbb{R}$

The given function $f(x)$ will be invertible iff it is bijective, so we shall verify for the same

Injectivity: Let $x_1, x_2 \in A(=\mathbb{R})$; such that $f(x_1) = f(x_2)$

$$\Rightarrow \frac{2x_1+5}{7} = \frac{2x_2+5}{7} \Rightarrow 2x_1 + 5 = 2x_2 + 5 \Rightarrow x_1 = x_2 \Rightarrow f(x) \text{ is injective.}$$

Surjectivity: Let $y \in B\,(=\mathbb{R})$; for if possible there exists $x \in A(=\mathbb{R})$ for which $f(x) = y$

$$\Rightarrow \frac{2x+5}{7} = y \Rightarrow x = \frac{7y-5}{2} \in \mathbb{R} \text{ (being defined and finite)} \qquad \text{.... (1)}$$

$$\Rightarrow f\left(\frac{7y-5}{2}\right) = y$$

Thus, every element y of set B has its pre image $\dfrac{7y-5}{2}$ in set A

$\Rightarrow f$ is surjective

$\therefore$ f is bijective, and hence, is invertible from set A to set B.

Now from equation (1), we get $x = \dfrac{7y-5}{2} \Rightarrow f^{-1}(x) = \dfrac{7x-5}{2}$

ILLUSTRATION 220: Find whether the function $f(x) = 2x^2 - 7x + 5$ from $A = \left[\dfrac{7}{4}, \infty\right) \to B = \left[-\dfrac{9}{8}, \infty\right)$ is invertible or not. If invertible, then find its inverse.

SOLUTION: Given function is $f(x) = 2x^2 - 7x + 5$ defined from set A to B; where $A = \left[\dfrac{7}{4}, \infty\right)$; $B = \left[-\dfrac{9}{8}, \infty\right)$

We know by theory of quadratic equations, the quadratic function $f(x) = ax^2 + bx + c$ is one–one in the domain $\left[-\dfrac{b}{2a}, \infty\right)$ i.e., $\left[\dfrac{7}{4}, \infty\right)$ and its range is given by $\left[-\dfrac{D}{4a}, \infty\right)$ i.e., $\left[-\dfrac{9}{8}, \infty\right) = B$

Thus, $f(x)$ is one–one and onto, i.e., bijective from set A to set B

$\Rightarrow f(x)$ is invertible function from set A to set B

Let $y = 2x^2 - 7x + 5 \Rightarrow 2x^2 - 7x + 5 - y = 0$

$$\Rightarrow x = \frac{7 \pm \sqrt{49 - 8(5-y)}}{4} = \frac{7 \pm \sqrt{9+8y}}{4} \Rightarrow x = \frac{7 + \sqrt{9+8y}}{4} \quad \left(\because x \in \left[\frac{7}{4}, \infty\right)\right)$$

$$\Rightarrow f^{-1}(x) = \frac{7 + \sqrt{9+8x}}{4}$$

ILLUSTRATION 221: Find whether the function $f(x) = |\cos(2x)|$ from $A = \left[0, -\right] \to B = [0, 1]$ is invertible or not. If invertible, then find its inverse.

SOLUTION: Given function is $f(x) = |\cos(2x)|$ from set A to set B, where $A = \left[0, \dfrac{\pi}{2}\right]$ and $B = [0, 1]$

$$\therefore \quad x \in \left[0, \frac{\pi}{2}\right] \Rightarrow \left(\frac{\pi}{2} - x\right) \in \left[0, \frac{\pi}{2}\right]$$

Now $f(x) = |\cos(2x)|$ and $f\left(\dfrac{\pi}{2} - x\right) = |\cos(\pi - 2x)| = |-\cos(2x)| = |\cos(2x)|$

Thus, $f(x) = f\left(\dfrac{\pi}{2} - x\right) \Rightarrow$ Thus, $f(x)$ is not injective

$\Rightarrow f(x)$ is not invertible from set A to set B.

However, range of $|\cos 2x|$ for $2x \in [0, \pi]$ is $[0, 1] = B \Rightarrow f(x)$ is surjective

For making $f(x)$ invertible the domain of function should be selected $\left[0, \dfrac{\pi}{4}\right]$ for which $2x \in \left[0, \dfrac{\pi}{2}\right]$ in which function is bijective.

Now $f(x) = |\cos 2x| = \cos 2x \Rightarrow y = \cos 2x \Rightarrow x = \dfrac{1}{2}\cos^{-1} y \Rightarrow f^{-1}(x) = \dfrac{1}{2}\cos^{-1} x$

ILLUSTRATION 222: Find whether the function $f(x) = |\log x|$ from $A = (0, \infty) \to B = [0, \infty)$ is invertible or not. If invertible, then find its inverse.

SOLUTION: Given function is $f(x) = |\log x|$ from set A to set B, where set $A = (0, \infty)$ and $B = [0, \infty)$

We know that $\log x \in (-\infty, 0]$ for $x \in (0, 1]$ and $\log x \in [0, \infty)$ for $x \in [1, \infty)$

$\Rightarrow$ $|\log x| \in [0, \infty)$ twice, firstly on (0, 1] and secondly on $[1, \infty)$, graphically shown in Figure 2.169.

Thus, $f(x)$ is many–one on $(0, \infty)$ $\Rightarrow$ $f(x)$ is not bijective

$\Rightarrow$ $f(x)$ is not invertible

However, the range of function $f(x) = [0, \infty) = B =$ co-domain

$\Rightarrow$ $f(x)$ is surjective.

Now for making $f(x)$ invertible we shall take its domain as principal domain, i.e., (0, 1] in which $f(x)$ is bijective.

In $x \in (0, 1]$, $\log x \le 0 \Rightarrow f(x) = |\log x| = -\log x$

$\Rightarrow$ $y = -\log x$

$\Rightarrow$ $x = 10^{-y}$ $\Rightarrow$ $f^{-1}(x) = 10^{-x}$.

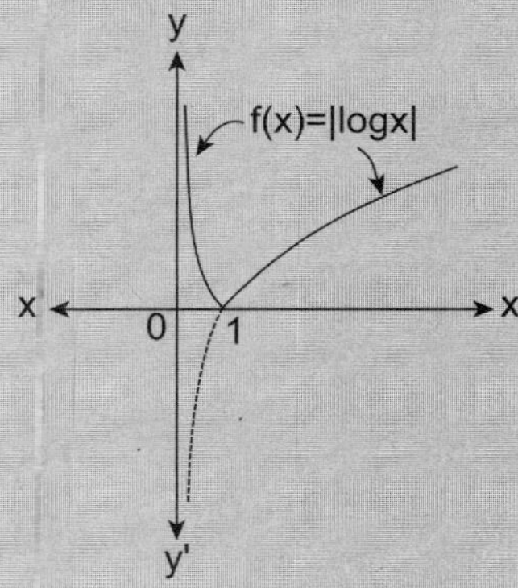

FIGURE 2.169

ILLUSTRATION 223: Test the invertibility, and hence, find the inverse function of the following.

(a) $y = \sin\left(\pi x + \frac{\pi}{4}\right)$ (b) $y = x^2 - 4x + 5$

(c) $y = \sqrt{1 - x^2}$ (d) $y = x + \frac{1}{x}$

SOLUTION: (a) For injectivity $\left(\pi x + \frac{\pi}{4}\right)$ must be in principal domain of $\sin x$, i.e., $\left[-\frac{\pi}{2}, \frac{\pi}{2}\right]$

$\Rightarrow$ $-\frac{\pi}{2} \le \left(\pi x + \frac{\pi}{4}\right) \le \frac{\pi}{2}$ $\Rightarrow$ $-\frac{3\pi}{4} \le \pi x \le \frac{\pi}{4}$

$\Rightarrow$ $x \in [-3/4, 1/4]$ and for surjectivity co-domain equals range of $\sin x$, i.e., $[-1, 1]$

i.e., $f: \left[-\frac{3}{4}, \frac{1}{4}\right] \to [-1, 1]$. Now $y = \sin\left(\pi x + \frac{\pi}{4}\right)$ $\Rightarrow$ $\sin^{-1} y = \pi x + \frac{\pi}{4}$

$\Rightarrow$ $x = \frac{1}{\pi}\left(\sin^{-1}(y) - \frac{\pi}{4}\right)$ $\Rightarrow$ $f^{-1}(x) = y = \frac{1}{\pi}\sin^{-1} x - \frac{1}{4}$ (interchanging x and y)

(b) $y = x^2 - 4x + 5$

Given function being a quadratic polynomial (even degree polynomial) is many–one on $\mathbb{R}$.

So, for injectivity the domain of function must be the principal domain, i.e., $\left[-\frac{b}{2a}, \infty\right)$

i.e., $[2, \infty)$ and for surjectivity co-domain must be equal to range, i.e., $\left[-\frac{D}{4a}, \infty\right)$ i.e., $[1, \infty)$;

Now $y = x^2 - 4x + 5$ $\Rightarrow$ $x^2 - 4x + (5 - y) = 0$

$\Rightarrow$ $x = \frac{4 \pm \sqrt{4y - 4}}{2} = 2 \pm \sqrt{y - 1}$ $\Rightarrow$ $x = 2 + \sqrt{y - 1}$ $\Rightarrow$ $f^{-1}(x) = 2 + \sqrt{x - 1}$ $(\because x \in [2, \infty))$

(c) $y=\sqrt{1-x^2}$; $D_f=[-1, 1]$

For injectivity domain should be principal domain = [0, 1] and for surjectivity co-domain should be the range of function, i.e., [0, 1]

Now $y=\sqrt{1-x^2} \Rightarrow x^2=1-y^2 \Rightarrow x=\pm\sqrt{1-y^2} \Rightarrow x=\sqrt{1-y^2}$ $(\because x\in[0, 1])$

$\Rightarrow f^{-1}(x)=\sqrt{1-x^2}$ $\therefore$ $f(x)$ is inverse of itself.

(d) $y=x+\dfrac{1}{x}$; $D_f=\mathbb{R}\sim\{0\}$; Range $=(-\infty,-2]\cup[2,\infty)$

The graph of $y = x + 1/x$ is as shown above.

For injectivity take domain as principal domain = [–1, 1] ~ {0} and

For surjectivity take co-domain = Range = $(-\infty, -2]\cup[2, \infty)$

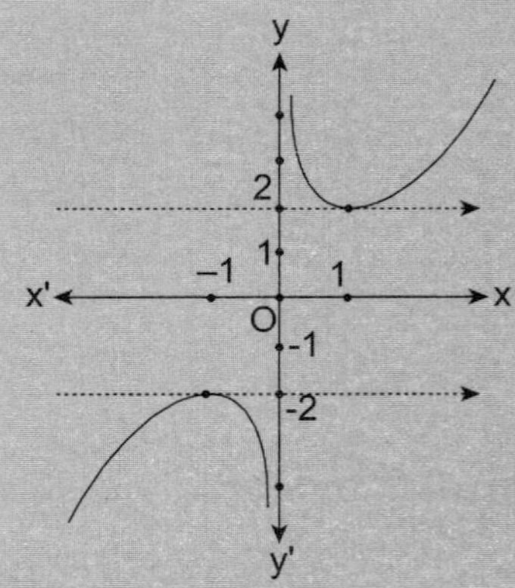

FIGURE 2.170

Now, $y=\dfrac{x^2+1}{x} \Rightarrow x^2-xy+1=0$

$\Rightarrow x=\dfrac{y\pm\sqrt{y^2-4}}{2}$

$\Rightarrow x=\dfrac{y+\sqrt{y^2-4}}{2}$ for $y\le-2$ and $x=\dfrac{y-\sqrt{y^2-4}}{2}$ for $y\ge 2$

$$\therefore f^{-1}(x)=\begin{cases}\dfrac{x+\sqrt{x^2-4}}{2}; & \text{for } x\in(-\infty,-2]\\ \dfrac{x-\sqrt{x^2-4}}{2}; & \text{for } x\in[2,\infty)\end{cases}$$

ILLUSTRATION 224: Let $f:\mathbb{R}\to\mathbb{R}$ be defined by $f(x)=\cos(5x+2)$. Is f invertible? Justify your answer.

SOLUTION: We know that any function $f: X\to Y$ is invertible iff it is bijective. Now $f:\mathbb{R}\to\mathbb{R}$, given by $f(x)=\cos(5x+2)$ is neither injective nor surjective.

For $-1\le\cos(5x+2)\le 1$

$\Rightarrow$ Range of $f\ne\mathbb{R}$ $\Rightarrow$ f is not surjective.

Also $f(x+2\pi/5)=\cos\{5(x+2\pi/5)+2\}=\cos(5x+2)=f(x)$

So, the function is periodic with period $2\pi/5$ and all periodic functions, are many–one.

$\therefore$ f is not injective. Thus, f can't be invertible.

ILLUSTRATION 225: If the function $f:[1,\infty)\to[1,\infty)$ is defined by $f(x)=a^{x(x-1)}$, then find $f^{-1}(x)$.

SOLUTION: Injectivity: $f(x)=a^{x^2-x} \Rightarrow f'(x)=a^{x^2-x}.(2x-1)$

For $f(x)$ to be one–one, it should be strictly increasing or strictly decreasing.

So, $f'(x)>0$ $\Rightarrow a^{x^2-x}.(2x-1)>0$, where $a^{x^2-x}>0$ for all x

$\Rightarrow 2x-1>0$ $\Rightarrow x>1/2$

Thus, for given domain $[1,\infty)$, $f(x)$ is always increasing, hence, one–one.

Surjectivity: As $f(x)$ is strictly increasing and being exponential function is continuous over its given domain.

$\Rightarrow$ Range $= [f(1), f(\infty)) = [1, \infty)$

$\Rightarrow$ Range of $f(x)$ = co-domain of $f(x)$, thus, $f(x)$ is onto.

To find inverse: As $f(x)$ is one–one and onto (bijective), thus, inverse of $f(x)$ can be obtained.

Let $y = f(x)$

$\Rightarrow y = a^{x^2-x} \Rightarrow x^2 - x = \log_a y \Rightarrow x^2 - x - \log_a y = 0 \Rightarrow x = \dfrac{1 \pm \sqrt{1+4\log_a y}}{2}$

$\Rightarrow x = \dfrac{1+\sqrt{1+4\log_a y}}{2}$ $(\because x \in [1, \infty))$

Hence, $f^{-1}(x) = \dfrac{1+\sqrt{1+4\log_a x}}{2}$ (replacing y by x and x by y).

PROPERTIES OF INVERSE OF A FUNCTION

(i) The inverse of a bijection is unique.

Proof: Let $f : A \to B$ be a bijection. If possible let $g : B \to A$ and $h : B \to A$ be two inverse functions of f.

Also let $a_1, a_2 \in A$ and $b \in B$ such that $g(b) = a_1$ and $h(b) = a_2$, then $g(b) = a_1$

$\Rightarrow f(a_1) = b$ and $h(b) = a_2 \Rightarrow f(a_2) = b$.

But f is one–one, therefore $f(a_1) = f(a_2)$

$\Rightarrow a_1 = a_2 \Rightarrow g(b) = h(b), \forall b \in B$

$\Rightarrow g(x) = h(x)$, i.e., inverse of f is unique

(ii) The inverse of a bijection is also a bijection.

Proof: Let $f : A \to B$ be a bijection and $g : B \to A$ be its inverse. We have to show that g is one–one and onto.

Injectivity: Let $b_1, b_2 \in B$ such that $g(b_1) = g(b_2)$... (i)

$\because b_1, b_2 \in B$ and g is a function from B to A

$\Rightarrow$ there exists $a_1, a_2 \in A$ such that $g(b_1) = a_1$ and $g(b_2) = a_2$

$\therefore$ from (i) $a_1 = a_2$ and $f : A \to B$ is a function.

$\Rightarrow f(a_1) = f(a_2)$

$\Rightarrow b_1 = b_2$

$\therefore$ g is injective.

$\left[\begin{array}{l}\because g(b_1) = a_1,\ g(b_2) = a_2 \\ \Rightarrow f(a_1) = b_1, f(a_2) = b_2 \\ \text{as } f \text{ \& } g \text{ are inverse of each other.}\end{array}\right]$

Surjectivity: Let $a \in A$

$\Rightarrow$ There exists $b \in B$ such that $f(a) = b$ (by definition of f)

$\Rightarrow a = g(b)$ $[\because f(a) = b \Rightarrow a = g(b)]$

Which proves that g is onto. Hence, g is also a surjection.

$\therefore$ If $f : A \to B$ is bijective function, then $f^{-1} : B \to A$ is also a bijective function.

(iii) If f and g are two bijections $f : A \to B$, $g : B \to C$, then the inverse of gof exists and $(gof)^{-1} = f^{-1}og^{-1}$.

Proof: Since $f : A \to B$ and $g : B \to C$ are bijections,

$\therefore gof : A \to C$ is also a bijection $\Rightarrow (gof)^{-1} : C \to A$.

Now let $a \in A$, $b \in B$, $c \in C$ such that $f(a) = b$ and $g(b) = c$

$\Rightarrow (gof)(a) = g[f(a)] = g(b) = c$

$\Rightarrow a = (gof)^{-1}(c)$ ...(1)

Now $f(a) = b \Rightarrow a = f^{-1}(b)$ ....(2)

and $g(b) = c \Rightarrow b = g^{-1}(c)$ ....(3)

$\therefore (f^{-1}og^{-1})(c) = f^{-1}(g^{-1}(c)) = f^{-1}(b)$ [by (3)]

$= a$ [by (2)]

$= (gof)^{-1}(c)$ [by (1)]

$\therefore (gof)^{-1} = f^{-1}og^{-1}$

ILLUSTRATION 226: If $f: \mathbb{R} \to \mathbb{R}$; $f(x) = e^x$ and $g : \mathbb{R} \to \mathbb{R}$: $g(x) = 3x - 2$, then show that $(fog)^{-1} = g^{-1}of^{-1}$ and $(gof)^{-1} = f^{-1}og^{-1}$. Also find domain of $(fog)^{-1}$ and $(gof)^{-1}$.

SOLUTION: Given $f(x) = e^x$

$\Rightarrow x = \ln f(x) \Rightarrow f^{-1}(x) = \ln x$ and $g(x) = 3x - 2 \Rightarrow x = \dfrac{g(x)+2}{3} \Rightarrow g^{-1}(x) = \dfrac{x+2}{3}$

Now $(fog)(x) = e^{3x-2}$; $(gof)(x) = 3e^x - 2$

$$\Rightarrow (fog)^{-1}(x) = \frac{\ln x+2}{3} \text{ and } (gof)^{-1} = \ln\left(\frac{x+2}{3}\right)$$

$$\text{Now } g^{-1}of^{-1}(x) = g^{-1}(f^{-1}(x)) = g^{-1}(\ln x) = \frac{\ln x+2}{3} \quad \text{.... (1)}$$

$$\text{and } f^{-1}og^{-1}(x) = f^{-1}(g^{-1}(x)) = f^{-1}\left(\frac{x+2}{3}\right) = \ln\left(\frac{x+2}{3}\right) \quad \text{.... (2)}$$

Therefore from equations (1) and (2), we get $(fog)^{-1} = g^{-1}of^{-1}$ and $(gof)^{-1} = f^{-1}og^{-1}$.

Domain of $(fog)^{-1} = \mathbb{R}^+ =$ range of $fog(x) =$ range of $e^{3x-2} = (0, \infty) = \mathbb{R}^+$;

Domain of $(gof)^{-1} =$ Range of $3e^x - 2 = (-2, \infty)$.

(iv) Inverse of inverse of a given function is the given function itself, i.e., $(f^{-1})^{-1} = f$

Proof: Let $f: A \to B$ is bijective, then $f^{-1}: B \to A$ is also bijective $\quad \therefore (f^{-1})^{-1}: A \to B$ exists.

Let $a \in A \Rightarrow$ there exists $b \in B$ such that $f(a) = b$

$\therefore f^{-1}(b) = a \Rightarrow (f^{-1})^{-1}(a) = b = f(a)$

$\therefore (f^{-1})^{-1}(a) = f(a)\ \forall\ a \in A \quad \Rightarrow \quad (f^{-1})^{-1} = f.$

(v) $f(x)$ and $f^{-1}(x)$ if intersect, then the point of intersection should be on the line $y = x$ or $y = -x + k$ for some real value of k.

Proof: *Case (a)* If $f(x)$ is a function such that whenever $(\alpha, \beta) \in f$, then $(\beta, \alpha) \notin f$. Now $(\alpha, \beta) \in f$

$\Rightarrow (\beta, \alpha) \in f^{-1}$, but $(\beta, \alpha) \notin f$.

Thus, there is no point common in the graph of function f and its inverse f^{-1}, i.e., function f and its inverse f^{-1} would not intersect each other at any point. i.e., the function would remain strictly on one side of the line $y = x$ as shown in Figure 2.171 and 2.172.

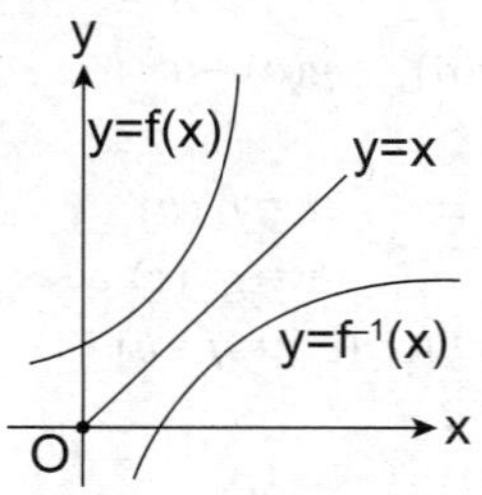

FIGURE 2.171

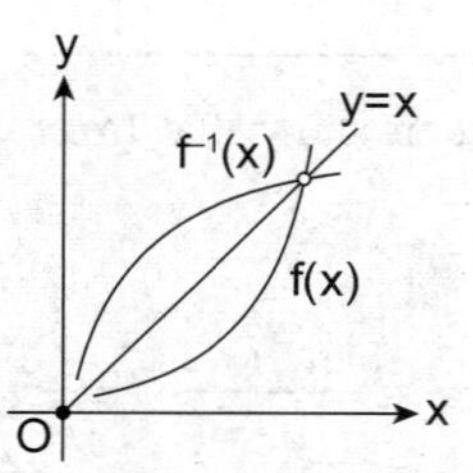

FIGURE 2.172

And if it exists on both sides of the line $y = x$, then there will be a point of discontinuity at the point across which the curve of $f(x)$ transits the line $y = x$.

Case (b) If the function $f(x)$ contains a pair (α, β) such that (β, α) belongs to function $f(x)$, then there exist two sub-cases as given below:

Sub case (i) When $\alpha = \beta$, i.e., if function is anti-symmetric

$\Rightarrow (\alpha, \beta), (\beta, \alpha) \in f \Leftrightarrow \alpha = \beta$

$\Rightarrow (\alpha, \beta) = (\beta, \alpha) = (\alpha, \alpha)$

i.e., function $f(x)$ and its inverse $f^{-1}(x)$ would intersect at the line $y = x$ as shown in Figure 2.173 and 2.174.

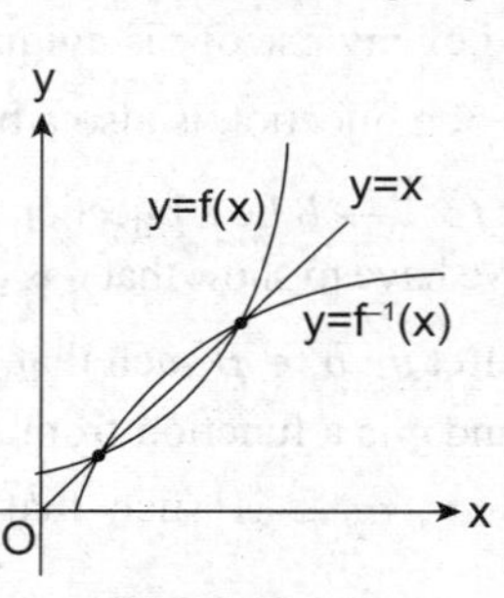

FIGURE 2.173

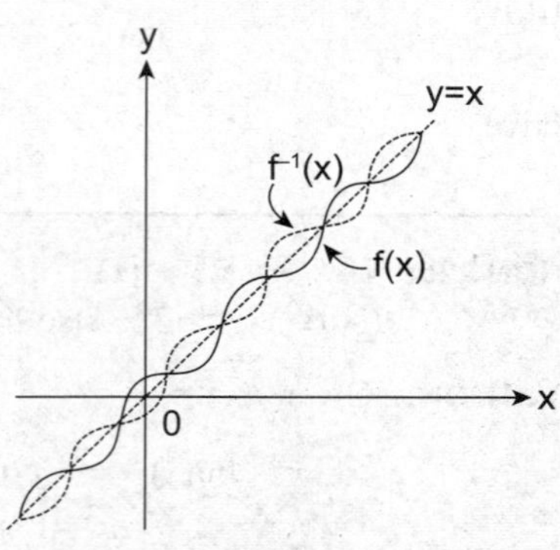

FIGURE 2.174

Sub case (ii) When $\alpha \neq \beta$.

As $f(x)$ contains two different ordered pairs (α, β) as well as (β, α).

It implies inverse function $f^{-1}(x)$ also contains the ordered pairs (β, α) and (α, β),

that means the function $f(x)$ and its inverse $f^{-1}(x)$ would intersect each other at two different points (α, β) and (β, α).

Thus, the points of intersection of $f(x)$ and its inverse $f^{-1}(x)$ would lie on the line joining the points (α, β) and (β, α) whose equation is given by

$$y-\beta=\left(\frac{\beta-\alpha}{\alpha-\beta}\right)(x-\alpha)$$

$\Rightarrow$ $y = -(x - \alpha) + \beta \Rightarrow y = -x + k$; where $k = \alpha + \beta$

i.e., $f(x)$ and $f^{-1}(x)$ intersects at line parallel to $y = -x$ as shown in Figure 2.175.

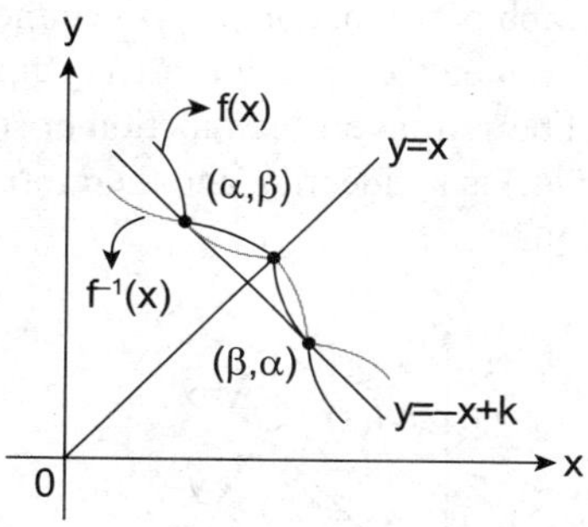

FIGURE 2.175

- If $f(x)$ has more than one points of the form (α, β) for which $(\beta, \alpha) \in f$, then if $\alpha = \beta$, then the point of intersection would lie on the line $y = x$ and if $\alpha \neq \beta$ then indeed the point of intersection would lie on the line $y = -x + k$, where $k = \alpha + \beta$ as shown in Figure 2.176.

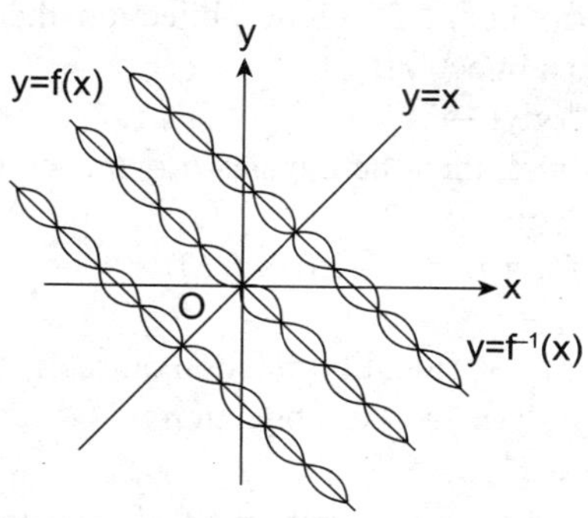

FIGURE 2.176

- If a function is symmetric about the straight line $y = x$ that is $(\alpha, \beta) \in f \Leftrightarrow (\beta, \alpha) \in f\ \forall\ (\alpha, \beta) \in f$, then the function is inverse of itself called as self invertible function graphically shown in Figure 2.177.

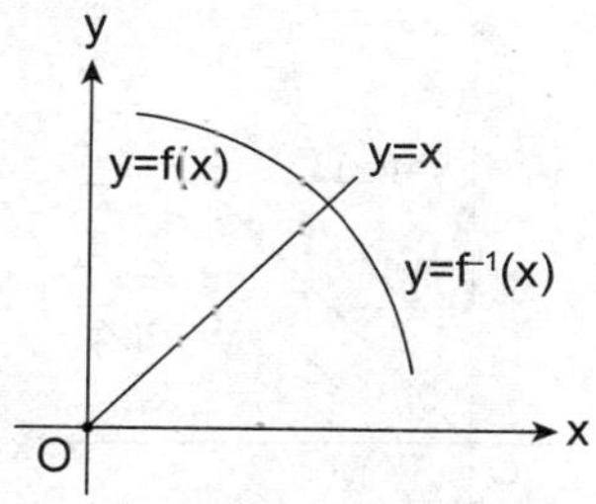

FIGURE 2.177

Further in such cases $f(x) = f^{-1}(x)$ is an identity in x, therefore infinitely many solutions.

- If a function is monotonically increasing, then $f(x)$ and $f^{-1}(x)$ cannot intersect on line $y = -x + k$ unless it is the point of intersection of $y = x$ and $y = -x + k$.

Proof: Let if possible (α, β) and $(\beta, \alpha) \in f(x)$; $\alpha < \beta$ and $f(\alpha) = \beta$ and $f(\beta) = \alpha$ .... (1)

Since $f(x)$ is monotonically increasing, it implies $f(\alpha) \leq f(\beta)$ and $f(\beta) \leq f(\alpha)$

$\Rightarrow$ $\beta \leq \alpha$ and $\alpha \leq \beta$

$\Rightarrow$ $\alpha = \beta$, which is contradiction that $\alpha < \beta$

Thus, whenever (α, β) and $(\beta, \alpha) \in f(x)$, then $\alpha = \beta$

$\Rightarrow$ $f(x)$ can't have two points (α, β) and (β, α) simultaneously for $\alpha \neq \beta$

$\Rightarrow$ $f(x)$ and $f^{-1}(x)$ cannot intersect on any line $y = -x + k$ unless it is the point of intersection of $y = x$ and $y = -x + k$

(vi) $f(x)$ and $f^{-1}(x)$ have same monotonic nature, i.e., either both increasing or both decreasing.

Proof: Let $g(x) = f^{-1}(x)$

$\Rightarrow$ $f(g(x)) = x$ $\Rightarrow$ $f'(g(x)) \cdot g'(x) = 1$

$$\Rightarrow\ g'(x)=\frac{1}{f'(g(x))}\ \Rightarrow\ g'(x)=\begin{cases}+ve & \text{if } f(x)\uparrow\\ -ve & \text{if } f(x)\downarrow\end{cases}$$

$\therefore$ If $f(x)$ is increasing, then $f^{-1}(x)$ is also increasing and if $f(x)$ is decreasing, then $f^{-1}(x)$ also decreasing

(vii) If $f(x)$ is increasing function, then $f^{-1}(x)$ is also an increasing function but $f(x)$ and $f^{-1}(x)$ have opposite curvatures, i.e., if $f(x)$ is concave upwards, then $f^{-1}(x)$ is concave downwards and if $f(x)$ is concave downwards, then $f^{-1}(x)$ is concave upwards.

Proof: ***Case (a)*** If $f(x)$ is increasing and concave upwards. From the derivative of $g(x) = f^{-1}(x)$, we have

$$g'(x)=\frac{1}{f'(g(x))}$$

$$\Rightarrow\ g'(x)=\underbrace{\frac{-1}{(f'(g(x)))^2}}_{-ve}\cdot\underbrace{f''(g(x))}_{+ve}\cdot\underbrace{g'(x)}_{+ve} \quad .... (1)$$

$\Rightarrow g'(x) < 0 \Rightarrow g(x) = f^{-1}(x)$ is concave downwards graphically shown in Figure 2.178.

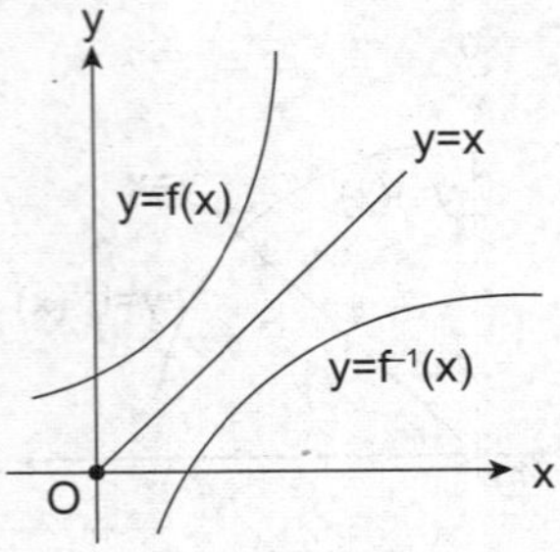

FIGURE 2.178

Case (b) Let $f(x)$ is increasing and concave downwards. From (1), first factor is negative and second factor is negative as $f(x)$ is concave downwards and third term is positive as $f(x)$ and $f^{-1}(x) = g(x)$ both are increasing functions.

$\therefore g'(x) > 0$ i.e., $g(x) = f^{-1}(x)$ is concave upwards graphically shown in Figure 2.179.

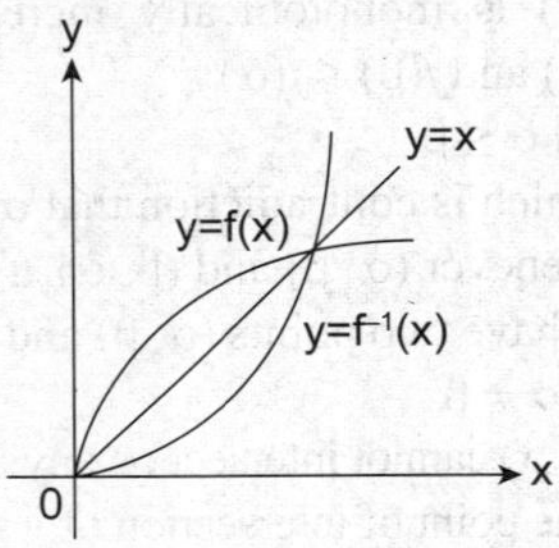

FIGURE 2.179

(viii) If $f(x)$ is a decreasing function, then $f^{-1}(x)$ is also a decreasing function, but $f(x)$ and $f^{-1}(x)$ have same curvatures.

Proof: ***Case (a)*** If $f(x)$ is decreasing and concave upwards.

$$g'(x) = \underbrace{\frac{-1}{(f'(g(x)))^2}}_{-ve} \cdot \underbrace{f''(g(x))}_{+ve} \cdot \underbrace{g'(x)}_{-ve} \quad \text{.... (i)}$$

$\Rightarrow g'(x) > 0$

$\Rightarrow g(x) = f^{-1}(x)$ is concave upwards graphically shown in Figure 2.180.

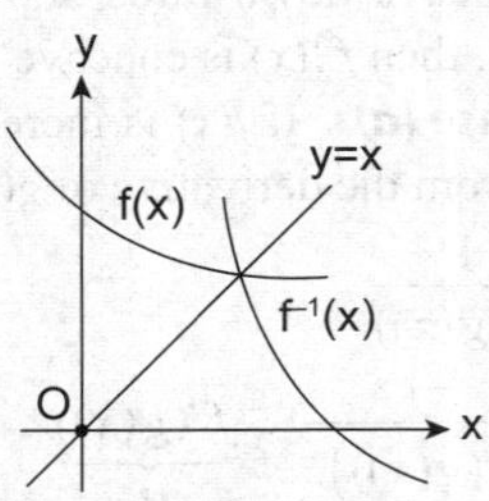

FIGURE 2.180

Case (b) If $f(x)$ is decreasing and concave downwards.

$$g'(x) = \underbrace{\frac{-1}{(f'(g(x)))^2}}_{-ve} \cdot \underbrace{f''(g(x))}_{-ve} \cdot \underbrace{g'(x)}_{-ve}$$

$\Rightarrow g(x) < 0$

$\Rightarrow g(x)$ is concave downwards, graphically shown in Figure 2.181

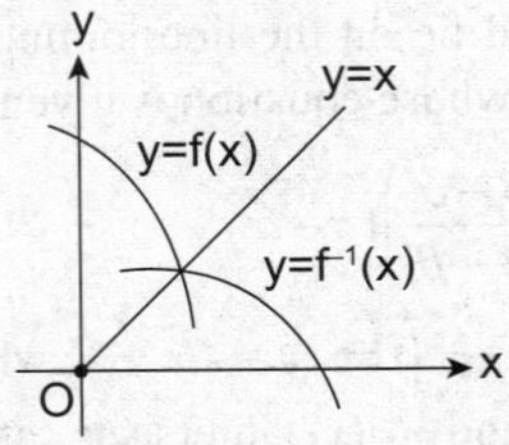

FIGURE 2.181

(ix) If the graph of a function $f(x)$ is symmetric about the line $y = x$, then $f(x)$ and $f^{-1}(x)$ are equal functions. i.e., $f(x)$ will be self invertible function or (involution).

$\Rightarrow f(x) = f^{-1}(x)$ is an identity, and therefore has infinitely many solutions.

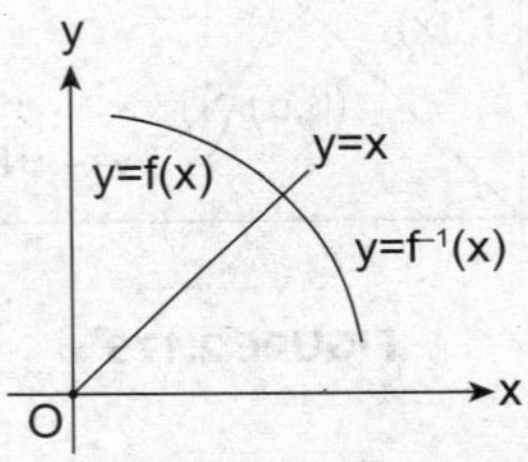

FIGURE 2.182

(x) If $f: A \to B$ is a bijection, then $f^{-1}: B \to A$ is an inverse function of f, then $f^{-1}of = I_A$ and $fof^{-1} = I_B$.

Here $\boldsymbol{I_A}$ is an identity function on set $\boldsymbol{A}$, and $\boldsymbol{I_B}$ is an identity function on set $\boldsymbol{B}$.

Proof: Let $f: A \to B$ be a bijection, then $f^{-1}: B \to A$ is also a bijection.

i.e., $f^{-1}of: A \to A$

Let $a \in A$, then there exists $b \in B$ such that $f(a) = b$ and $f^{-1}(b) = a$.

Now $f^{-1}of(a) = f^{-1}(f(a)) = f^{-1}(b) = a$

$\therefore f^{-1}of(a) = a \; \forall \; a \in A$

$\Rightarrow f^{-1}of = I_A$ i.e., identity function on set A

Also $fof^{-1}: B \to B$ is a bijection

Let $b \in B$

$\Rightarrow$ There exists $a \in A$ such that $f^{-1}(b) = a$ and $f(a) = b$

Now $fof^{-1}(b) = f(f^{-1}(b)) = f(a) = b$

$\therefore fof^{-1}(b) = b \; \forall \; b \in B$

$\therefore fof^{-1} = I_B$, i.e., identity function on set B.

ILLUSTRATION 227: If $f(x)$ is an invertible function, and $g(x) = 2f(x) + 5$, then find the value of $g^{-1}(x)$.

SOLUTION: Given equation is $g(x) = 2f(x) + 5$.

Replacing x by $g^{-1}(x)$; we get $g(g^{-1}(x)) = 2f(g^{-1}(x)) + 5$

$\Rightarrow\ x = 2f(g^{-1}(x)) + 5$

$\Rightarrow\ f(g^{-1}(x)) = \dfrac{x-5}{2}$ $\qquad \Rightarrow\ g^{-1}(x) = f^{-1}\left(\dfrac{x-5}{2}\right)$

ILLUSTRATION 228: Compute the inverse of the following functions:

(a) $f(x) = \ell n\left(x+\sqrt{x^2+1}\right)$ (b) $f(x)\quad 2$ (c) $y = \dfrac{10^x - 10^{-x}}{10^x + 10^{-x}}$

SOLUTION: (a) Given $f(x) = \ell n\left(x+\sqrt{x^2+1}\right)$

If $x \geq 0$, then $x + \sqrt{x^2+1} > 0$ and if $x < 0$, then $|x| = \sqrt{x^2} < \sqrt{x^2+1}$

Thus, magnitude of x is less than the magnitude of $\sqrt{x^2+1}$ $\Rightarrow\ x + \sqrt{x^2+1} > 0$

Thus, for every real values of x, $x + \sqrt{x^2+1} > 0$

$\Rightarrow$ Domain of $f(x)$ is $\mathbb{R}$

Also $x + \sqrt{x^2+1}$ being the sum of two continuous functions is also continuous.

Further, $f'(x) = \dfrac{1}{\sqrt{x^2+1}} > 0\ \forall\ x \in \mathbb{R}$.

$\Rightarrow$ $f(x)$ is strictly increasing function. Thus, $f(x)$ is a bijective function from $\mathbb{R} \to \mathbb{R}$ (range)

Now $y = f(x) = \ln(x+\sqrt{x^2+1})$ $\qquad \Rightarrow\ e^y = x+\sqrt{x^2+1}$ ....(1)

Again $y = \ln(x+\sqrt{x^2+1})$ $\Rightarrow\ -y = -\ln(x+\sqrt{x^2+1})$ $\Rightarrow\ -y = \ln(x+\sqrt{x^2+1})^{-1}$

$\Rightarrow\ -y = \ln\left(\dfrac{1}{x+\sqrt{x^2+1}}\right)$ $\Rightarrow\ e^{-y} = \dfrac{1}{x+\sqrt{x^2+1}} \times \dfrac{x-\sqrt{x^2+1}}{x-\sqrt{x^2+1}} = -(x-\sqrt{x^2+1})$

$\Rightarrow\ -e^{-y} = x - \sqrt{x^2+1}$ ...(2)

Adding (1) and (2), we get $e^y - e^{-y} = 2x$ or $x = \dfrac{e^y - e^{-y}}{2}$.

Thus, inverse function of $f(x)$ will be $y = \dfrac{e^x - e^{-x}}{2}$

(b) Given $f(x) = 2^{\frac{x}{x-1}}$

Domain of $f(x)$ is $\mathbb{R} - \{1\}$ and range of $\dfrac{x}{x-1}$ is $\mathbb{R} - \{1\}$

Also 2^x is continuous and increasing function, thus, range of $f(x)$ will be $(2^{-\infty}, 2^{\infty}) \sim \{2\}$.

i.e., $(0, \infty) \sim \{2\}$

Thus, $f(x)$ is a bijective function from $\mathbb{R} \sim \{1\}$ to $(0, \infty) \sim \{2\}$, and hence, is invertible when defined from set $\mathbb{R} \sim \{1\}$ to set $(0, \infty) \sim \{2\}$

Now $y = 2^{\frac{x}{x-1}}$ $\Rightarrow\ \log_2 y = \left(\dfrac{x}{x-1}\right)\log_2 2$ $\Rightarrow\ \log_2 y = \dfrac{x}{x-1}$

$\Rightarrow\ x(\log_2 y - 1) - \log_2 y = 0$ $\Rightarrow\ x = \dfrac{\log_2 y}{\log_2 y - 1}$ $\Rightarrow\ f^{-1}(x) = \dfrac{\log_2 x}{\log_2 x - 1}$

(c) Given $f(x) = \dfrac{10^x - 10^{-x}}{10^x + 10^{-x}}$. Clearly $f(x)$ is defined for all real values x, hence, domain of $f(x)$ is $\mathbb{R}$.

Further $f(x) = \dfrac{10^{2x}-1}{10^{2x}+1} = \left(1 - \dfrac{2}{10^{2x}+1}\right)$ which is continuous and having greatest lower bound –1 and least upper bound 1. Thus, range of $f(x)$ is (–1, 1).

Further $f'(x) = \dfrac{4(10)^{2x}\log 10}{(10^{2x}+1)^2} > 0 \;\forall x \in \mathbb{R}$ which implies $f(x)$ is monotonically increasing, and hence, is bijective when defined from $\mathbb{R}$ to (–1, 1).

Now $y = \dfrac{10^x - 10^{-x}}{10^x + 10^{-x}} \Rightarrow y = \dfrac{10^{2x}-1}{10^{2x}+1}$

Applying componendo and dividendo, we get $\dfrac{y+1}{y-1} = \dfrac{10^{2x}-1+10^{2x}+1}{10^{2x}-1-10^{2x}-1}$

$\Rightarrow \dfrac{y+1}{y-1} = \dfrac{2.10^{2x}}{-2} \Rightarrow y + 1 = (1 - y)\,10^{2x} \Rightarrow 10^{2x} = \dfrac{1+y}{1-y} \Rightarrow 2x = \log_{10}\left(\dfrac{1+y}{1-y}\right)$

$\Rightarrow x = \dfrac{1}{2}\log_{10}\left(\dfrac{1+y}{1-y}\right) \Rightarrow f^{-1}(x) = \dfrac{1}{2}\log_{10}\left(\dfrac{1+x}{1-x}\right)$.

ILLUSTRATION 229: Find the inverse of $f(x) = 2^{\log_{10} x} + 8$, and hence, solve the equation $f(x) = f^{-1}(x)$.

SOLUTION: Given $y = 2^{\log_{10} x} + 8$

$\log_{10}x$ is defined for $x > 0$, therefore domain of function $f(x)$ is $(0, \infty)$.

Also range of $\log_{10}x$ is $(-\infty,\infty)$ and 2^x being continuous and increasing function, $2^{\log_{10} x}$ has its range $(0, \infty)$.

Thus, range of function $f(x) = 2^{\log_{10} x} + 8$ is $(8, \infty)$. Further $f(x)$ is monotonically increasing (sum of increasing and constant function) when defined from $(0, \infty)$ to set $(8, \infty)$ is bijective, and hence, is invertible.

Now $y = 2^{\log_{10} x} + 8 \Rightarrow \log_{10}x = \log_2(y - 8) \Rightarrow x = 10^{\log_2(y-8)} \quad \therefore \quad f^{-1}(x) = 10^{\log_2(x-8)}$

Now, to solve $f(x) = f^{-1}(x)$, we solve $f(x) = x$, and $f(x) = -x + k$.

However, $f(x) = -x + k$ is taken if $f(x)$ has at least two points of symmetric about the line $y = x$, i.e., $(\alpha, \beta), (\beta, \alpha) \in f$ and $\alpha \neq \beta$.

Here, $f(x) = 2^{\log_{10} x} + 8$ is an increasing function, therefore it would not contain any two different points of symmetry. Thus, $f(x)$ and $f^{-1}(x)$ can intersect only on line $y = x$.

Thus, $f(x) = f^{-1}(x)$ is equivalent to equation $f(x) = x$.

$\therefore \quad 2^{\log_{10} x} + 8 = x \Rightarrow 2^{\log_{10} x} = x - 8 \Rightarrow \log_{10} x = \log_2(x-8) \Rightarrow \log_{x-8} x = \log_2 10$

$\Rightarrow x = 10$

ILLUSTRATION 230: Let $f : \left[-\sqrt{2}+1, \sqrt{2}+1\right] \to \left[\dfrac{-\sqrt{2}+1}{2}, \dfrac{\sqrt{2}+1}{2}\right]$ be a function defined by $f(x) = \dfrac{1-x}{1+x^2}$.

Is f invertible? If yes, then find its inverse.

SOLUTION: Domain of $f(x) = \left[-\sqrt{2}+1, \sqrt{2}+1\right]$ (given)

Here, $f(x) = \dfrac{1-x}{1+x^2} \Rightarrow f'(x) = \dfrac{x^2-2x-1}{(1+x^2)^2} \leq 0$

for $x \in \left[-\sqrt{2}+1, \sqrt{2}+1\right]$

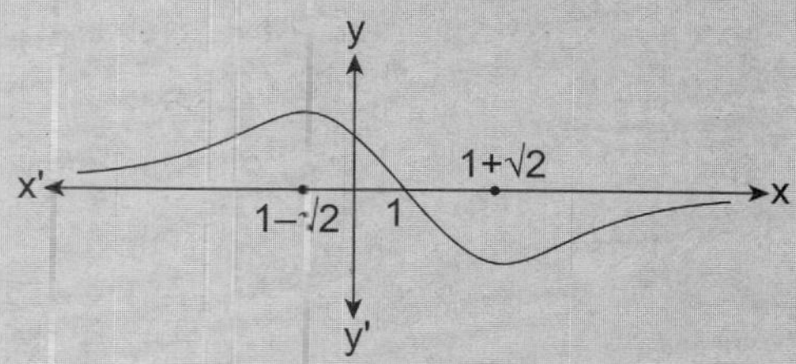

FIGURE 2.183

$\Rightarrow$ $f(x)$ is a strictly decreasing function on $\left[-\sqrt{2}+1, \sqrt{2}+1\right]$ graphically as shown in Figure 2.183.

$\Rightarrow$ $f(x)$ is injective on $[-\sqrt{2}+1, \sqrt{2}+1]$

Also $f(x)$ being a rational function is continuous on $\left[-\sqrt{2}+1, \sqrt{2}+1\right]$ as its denominator is non-vanishing.

Thus, $f(x)$ should have its range $\left[f\left(\sqrt{2}+1\right), f\left(-\sqrt{2}+1\right)\right] = \left[\dfrac{-\sqrt{2}+1}{2}, \dfrac{\sqrt{2}+1}{2}\right]$ = co-domain

$\Rightarrow$ $f(x)$ is surjective. Thus, $f(x)$ is a bijective function and hence, is invertible.

Now $y = \dfrac{1-x}{1+x^2}$ .... (1)

$\Rightarrow x^2y + y = 1 - x \qquad \Rightarrow x^2y + x + (y-1) = 0$

$$\Rightarrow x = \frac{-1 \pm \sqrt{1-4y(y-1)}}{2y} = \frac{-1 \pm \sqrt{4y-4y^2+1}}{2y} = \frac{-1 \pm \sqrt{-(4y^2-4y+1)+2}}{2y} \text{ for } y \neq 0$$

Taking negative sign, we have $x = \dfrac{-1-\sqrt{-(4y^2-4y+1)+2}}{2y}$ for $y \neq 0$

Now $\dfrac{1}{2} \in$ co-domain of f (domain of f^{-1}), substituting $y = \dfrac{1}{2}$, we have $x = -1 - \sqrt{2}$

Which does not belong to domain of f (range of f^{-1}),

Hence, rejecting negative sign, we have $x = \dfrac{-1+\sqrt{4y-4y^2+1}}{2y}$ for $y \neq 0$ and for $y = 0, x = 1$ [from (1)].

$\therefore$

$$f^{-1}(x) = \begin{cases} \dfrac{-1+\sqrt{4x-4x^2+1}}{2x} & ; x \neq 0 \\ 1 & ; x = 0 \end{cases}$$

ILLUSTRATION 231: Let $f: \mathbb{N} \to \mathbb{N}$, where $f(x) = x + (-1)^{x-1}$. Find the inverse of f.

SOLUTION: $y = f(x) = \begin{cases} x+1; & x \text{ an odd natural number} \\ x-1; & x \text{ an even natural number} \end{cases}$ ..... (1)

Injectivity: Let $x_1, x_2 \in \mathbb{N}$ such that $f(x_1) = f(x_2)$

$\Rightarrow$ $x_1 + 1 = x_2 + 1$ if x_1, x_2 are odd natural numbers $\Rightarrow$ $x_1 = x_2$ and

$\Rightarrow$ $x_1 - 1 = x_2 - 1$ if x_1, x_2 are even natural numbers $\Rightarrow$ $x_1 = x_2$

If x_1 and x_2 are opposite in nature (say) x_1 odd and x_2 even, then $f(x_1) = f(x_2)$

$\Rightarrow$ $x_1 + 1 = x_2 - 1 \Rightarrow x_2 - x_1 = 2$, which is a contradiction as difference of an odd and even integer can never be an even integer.

Similarly, x_1 even and x_2 odd is impossible. Thus, $f(x)$ is injective function.

Surjectivity: Let n be any natural number.

Now if n is odd say $n = 2m - 1$; $m \in \mathbb{N}$; then $f(2m) = 2m - 1 = n$

and if n is even say $2m$, $m \in \mathbb{N}$; then $f(2m - 1) = 2m = n$.

Thus, f is surjective function. Hence, f is an invertible function.

Now from (1), we have

$$x = \begin{cases} y-1; & \text{if } x \text{ an odd natural number} \\ y+1; & \text{if } x \text{ an even natural number} \end{cases} \quad \text{or} \quad x = \begin{cases} y-1; & \text{if } y \text{ an even natural number} \\ y+1; & \text{if } y \text{ an odd natural number} \end{cases}$$

$$\Rightarrow f^{1}(x) = \begin{cases} x \quad 1; & \text{if } x \text{ an even natural number} \\ x \quad 1; & \text{if } x \text{ an odd natural number} \end{cases} \quad \Rightarrow f^{1}(x) = (x) + (-1)^{x-1} = x + (-1)^{\pm(x \pm 1)}.$$

ILLUSTRATION 232: Let $f : D_f \to \mathbb{R}$, where D_f denotes the domain of function f. Find the inverse of f, if it exists, where (i) $f(x) = 1 - 2^{-x}$ (ii) $f(x) = [4 -(x - 7)^3]^{1/5}$

SOLUTION: (i) Given function is $f(x) = 1 - 2^{-x}$ $\Rightarrow$ $f'(x) = 2^{-x} \ln 2 > 0 \ \forall\ x \in \mathbb{R}$

$\Rightarrow$ $f(x)$ is strictly increasing and hence, is injective.

Now $2^{-x} \in (0, \infty)$ $\Rightarrow$ $-2^{-x} \in (-\infty, 0)$ $\Rightarrow$ $1 - 2^{-x} \in (-\infty, 1)$

$\therefore$ Range of function is $(-\infty, 1) \neq \mathbb{R}$

$\Rightarrow$ $f(x)$ is not surjective and hence, $f(x)$ is not bijective.

If $\mathbb{R}$ is replaced by range $(-\infty, 1)$, then $f(x)$ is invertible and for its inverse $y = 1 - 2^{-x}$

$$\Rightarrow 2^{-x} = 1 - y \Rightarrow -x = \log_2(1 - y) \Rightarrow x = \log_2\left(\frac{1}{1-y}\right) \Rightarrow f^{-1}(x) = \log_2\left(\frac{1}{1-x}\right)$$

(ii) $f(x) = [4 - (x - 7)^3]^{1/5}$

$$\Rightarrow f'(x) = \frac{1}{5}\left[4-(x-7)^3\right]^{-4/5} \cdot \left[-3(x-7)^2\right] \le 0$$

$\Rightarrow$ $f(x)$ is a decreasing function $\Rightarrow$ $f(x)$ is an injective function

Also $f(x)$ is continuous function and $\lim\limits_{x\to\infty} f(x) = -\infty$, $\lim\limits_{x\to-\infty} f(x) = \infty$

$\Rightarrow$ Domain of $f(x)$ = $\mathbb{R}$ and Range of $f(x)$ = $\mathbb{R}$ = codomain

$\Rightarrow$ $f(x)$ is a surjective function

$\therefore$ $f(x)$ is bijective function and hence, is invertible.

Now $y = [4 - (x - 7)^3]^{1/5} \Rightarrow x = 7 + (4 - y^5)^{1/3} \Rightarrow f^{1}(x) = 7 + (4 - x^5)^{1/3}$

ILLUSTRATION 233: Let $f : \left[-\frac{\pi}{3}, \frac{\pi}{6}\right] \to B$ defined by $f(x) = 2\cos^2 x + \sqrt{3}\sin 2x + 1$. Find B such that f^{1} exists. Also find $f^{1}(x)$.

SOLUTION: Given $f : \left[-\frac{\pi}{3}, \frac{\pi}{6}\right] \to B$

If f^{1} exits, then function should be one–one and onto.

Given $f(x) = 2\cos^2 x + \sqrt{3}\sin 2x + 1 = \cos 2x + 1 + \sqrt{3}\sin 2x + 1$.

$$= 2 + \cos 2x + \sqrt{3}\sin 2x = 2 + 2\left[\frac{1}{2}\cos 2x + \frac{\sqrt{3}}{2}\sin 2x\right] = 2 + 2\left(\sin\left(2x + \frac{\pi}{6}\right)\right) \quad \text{..... (1)}$$

Now for $f(x)$ to be invertible, $2x + \frac{\pi}{6} \in \left[-\frac{\pi}{2}, \frac{\pi}{2}\right]$ (principal domain of $\sin x$)

$\Rightarrow\ x \in \left[-\frac{\pi}{3}, \frac{\pi}{6}\right]$; which is true

Also $f(x) = 2 + 2\sin\left(2x + \frac{\pi}{6}\right) \in [0,4]$ = Range of $f(x)$ = co-domain (B) $\Rightarrow$ $B = [0, 4]$

Now from (1); $y - 2 = 2\sin\left(2x + \frac{\pi}{6}\right)$ $\Rightarrow$ $\sin^{-1}\left(\frac{y-2}{2}\right) = 2x + \frac{\pi}{6}$

$$\Rightarrow\ x = \frac{1}{2}\left(\sin^{-1}\left(\frac{y-2}{2}\right) - \frac{\pi}{6}\right) \quad \Rightarrow \quad f^{-1}(x) = \frac{1}{2}\left[\sin^{-1}\left(\frac{x-2}{2}\right) - \frac{\pi}{6}\right]$$

ILLUSTRATION 234: If $f(x) = \begin{cases} x; & \text{if } x < 1 \\ x^2; & \text{if } 1 \le x \le 4 \\ 8\sqrt{x}; & \text{if } x > 4 \end{cases}$; then find $f^{-1}(x)$, if $f(x)$ is invertible.

SOLUTION: $y = f(x) = \begin{cases} x; & \text{if } x < 1 \\ x^2; & \text{if } 1 \le x \le 4 \\ 8\sqrt{x}; & \text{if } x > 4 \end{cases}$ ... (1)

The graph of $f(x)$ is a shown below

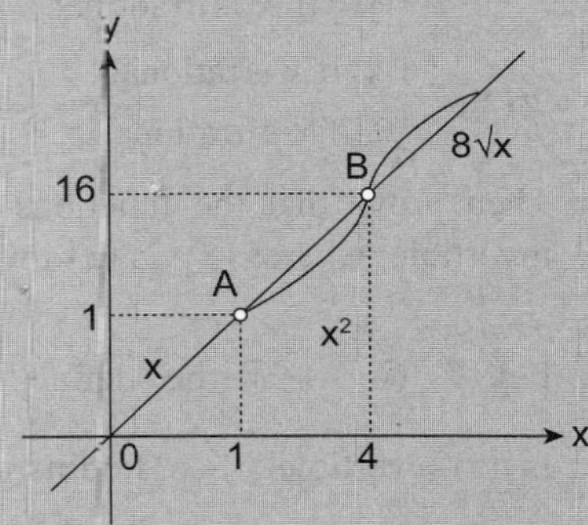

FIGURE 2.184

$$\Rightarrow\ f'(x) = \begin{cases} 1; & \text{if } x < 1 \\ 2x; & \text{if } 1 \le x \le 4 \\ \frac{4}{\sqrt{x}}; & \text{if } x > 4 \end{cases}$$

$\Rightarrow\ f'(x) > 0\ \forall\ x \in \mathbb{R}$

$\Rightarrow\ f(x)$ is strictly increasing $\forall\ x \in \mathbb{R}$

$\Rightarrow\ f(x)$ is injective function $\forall\ x \in \mathbb{R}$

$\Rightarrow\ f(x)$ is invertible from $\mathbb{R}$ to its range set.

Now from (1); $x = \begin{cases} y; & \text{if } x < 1 \\ \sqrt{y}; & \text{if } 1 \le x \le 4 \\ \frac{y^2}{64}; & \text{if } x > 4 \end{cases}$

$$\Rightarrow\ x = \begin{cases} y; & \text{if } y < 1 \\ \sqrt{y}; & \text{if } 1 \le y \le 16 \\ \frac{y^2}{64}; & \text{if } y > 16 \end{cases}$$

$$\Rightarrow\ f^{-1}(x) = \begin{cases} x & \text{if } x < 1 \\ \sqrt{x} & \text{if } 1 \le x \le 16 \\ \frac{x^2}{64} & \text{if } x > 16 \end{cases}$$

TEXTUAL EXERCISE–14: (SUBJECTIVE)

1. Determine the inverse function and its domain of definition if $f(x)=\begin{cases} x; & -\infty < x < 1 \\ x^2; & 1 \le x \le 4 \\ 2^x; & 4 < x < \infty \end{cases}$

2. Determine $f^{-1}(x)$, if given function is invertible
   (i) $f : (-\infty, -1) \to (-\infty, -2)$ defined $f(x) = -(x+1)^2 - 2$
   (ii) $f : \left[\frac{\pi}{6}, \frac{7\pi}{6}\right] \to [-1, 1]$ defined by $f(x) = \sin\left(x+\frac{\pi}{3}\right)$

3. If $f(x)=\begin{cases} x, \text{ if } x \text{ is rational} \\ 0, \text{ if } x \text{ is irrational} \end{cases}$
   $g(x)=\begin{cases} x, \text{ if } x \text{ is rational} \\ 0, \text{ if } x \text{ is irrational} \end{cases}$
   Then prove that the functions $f - g$ and $f + g$ are invertible, whereas $f.g$ is not invertible.

4. Let f: $\mathbb{R} \to \mathbb{R}$ be defined by $f(x) = \frac{e^x - e^{-x}}{2}$.
   Is $f(x)$ invertible? If so, find its inverse?

5. Find the inverse of the function (assuming it onto) $y = \log_a\left(x+\sqrt{x^2+1}\right)$; $(a > 1)$

6. If $g(x)$ be the inverse of $f(x)$ and $f'(x) = \frac{1}{1+x^3}$, then find $g'(x)$ in term of $g(x)$.

7. If $f(x) = \sin x + \cos x$; $g(x) = x^2 - 4$, then find the domain in which $g(f(x))$ is invertible.

8. If $f(x) = \sin x + \cos x$; $g(x^2) = x^2 + 7$, then find the domain in which $g(f(x))$ is invertible and also find inverse and domain of inverse function.

9. If X and Y are two non-empty sets, where $f: X \to Y$ is a function. Let $C \subseteq X$ and $D \subseteq Y$, we define $f(C) = \{f(x): x \in C\}$. Clearly $f(x) \subseteq Y$ and $f^{-1}(D) = \{x \in X; f(x) \in D\}$. Clearly $f^{-1}(D) \subseteq X$; then show that $f(f^{-1}(B)) = B$ if $B \subseteq f(x)$.

10. Let $g(x)$ be a non-negative function defined on [0, 1]. If the area of the equilateral triangle with two of its vertices at (0,0) and $(x, g(x))$ is $\frac{\sqrt{3}}{4}$; then find $g^{-1}(x)$.

11. Let f be an injective function form domain $\{1, i, \omega\}$ to range $\{5, 6, 7\}$. If it is given that exactly one of the following statements is true and other two are false $f(1) = 5$, $f(i) \ne 5$, $f(\omega) \ne 7$, then find $(f^{-1})^{2012}(6)$ $\left(\text{where } i = \sqrt{-1}; \omega = \text{cube root of unity}\right)$

12. Find the solution of equation $2x^2 - 5x - 2 = \frac{5-\sqrt{9-8x}}{4}$; where $x < \frac{5}{4}$

Answer Keys

1. $f^{-1}(x)=\begin{cases} x; & -\infty < x < 1 \\ \sqrt{x}; & 1 \le x \le 16 \\ \log_2 x; & 16 < x < \infty \end{cases}$

2. (i) $-1-\sqrt{x-2}$ (ii) $\frac{2\pi}{3}+\sin^{-1}x$

4. $\log\left(x+\sqrt{x^2+1}\right)$

5. $\frac{1}{2}(a^x - a^{-x})$

6. $1 + (g(x))^3$

7. $x \in \left[\frac{-\pi}{4}, \frac{\pi}{4}\right]$

8. $\left[-\frac{3\pi}{4}, \frac{\pi}{4}\right]$, $\sin^{-1}\left(\frac{x-7}{\sqrt{2}}\right)-\frac{\pi}{4}$, Domain of inverse function is $\left[7-\sqrt{2}, 7+\sqrt{2}\right]$

10. $\sqrt{1-x^2}$; $x \in [0, 1]$

11. ω^2.

12. $x = \frac{3-\sqrt{5}}{2}$

TEXTUAL EXERCISE–14: (OBJECITVE)

1. Find $f^{-1}(x)$ if $f : (-\infty, 1] \to (-\infty, 1]$ such that $f(x) = x(2 - x)$, then $f^{-1}(x)$ is given as
(a) $1-\sqrt{1-x}$ (b) $1+\sqrt{1-x}$
(c) $-1-\sqrt{1-x}$ (d) $-1+\sqrt{1-x}$

2. If $f(x) = 3x - 5$ and let $g(x) = f^{-1}(x)$, then $g(4)$ equals
(a) 7
(b) 3
(c) $g(x)$ does not exist as $f(x)$ is not one–one
(d) $g(x)$ does not exist as $f(x)$ is not onto

3. Suppose $f(x) = (x + 2)^2$ for $x \le -2$. If $g(x)$ is the function whose graph is the reflection of the graph of $f(x)$ with respect to the line $y = x$, then $g(x)$ is
(a) $-2-\sqrt{x}; x \ge 0$ (b) $-2+\sqrt{x}; x \ge 0$
(c) $2-\sqrt{x}; x \ge 0$ (d) $2+\sqrt{x}; x \ge 0$

4. If $y = f(x) = \dfrac{x+2}{x+1}$, then
(a) $x = f(y) + 1$
(b) $f^{-1}(4) = 2$
(c) $f^{-1}(0) = 2$
(d) y decreases with x for all $x \ne 1$.

5. If the function $f : \mathbb{R} \to \mathbb{R}$ be such that $f(x) = x = [x]$, where $[y]$ denotes the greatest integer less than or equal to y, then $f^{-1}(x)$ is
(a) $\dfrac{1}{x-[x]}$ (b) $[x] - x$
(c) not defined (d) None of these

6. Let $f : (2, 4) \to (1, 3)$ be a function defined by $f(x) = x - \left[\dfrac{x}{2}\right]$; (where [.] denotes the greatest integer function), then $f^{-1}(x)$ is equal to :
(a) $2x$ (b) $x + \left[\dfrac{x}{2}\right]$
(c) $x + 1$ (d) $x - 1$

7. If $f(x)$: $[0, \infty) \to [0,\infty)$ and $f(x) = \dfrac{x}{1+x}$, then $f(x)$ is
(a) invertible
(b) non-invertible
(c) one–one but not onto
(d) onto but not one–one

8. If f: $[1, \infty) \to [2, \infty)$ is given by $f(x) = x + \dfrac{1}{x}$, then $f^{-1}(x)$ equals
(a) $\dfrac{x+\sqrt{x^2-4}}{2}$ (b) $\dfrac{x}{1+x^2}$
(c) $\dfrac{x-\sqrt{x^2-4}}{2}$ (d) $1+\sqrt{x^2-4}$

9. If $f : [1, \infty) \to [1, \infty)$ is defined by $f(x) = 2^{x(x-1)}$, then $f^{-1}(x)$ is given as
(a) $\dfrac{1}{2}\left[1-\sqrt{1+4\log_2 x}\right]$
(b) $\dfrac{1}{2}\left[1-\sqrt{1+4\log_2 x}\right]$
(c) $\left[1-\sqrt{1+4\log_2 x}\right]$
(d) $\left[1-\sqrt{1+4\log_2 x}\right]$

10. Let $f(x) = x^x$, $x \in (0, \infty)$ and let $g(x)$ inverse of $f(x)$, then $g'(x)$ must be
(a) $x(1 + \log x)$ (b) $x(1 + \log f(x))$
(c) $\dfrac{1}{x(1+\log g(x))}$ (d) Does not exist.

11. The inverse function of the function $f(x) = \dfrac{e^x - e^{-x}}{e^x + e^{-x}}$ is
(a) $\dfrac{1}{2}\log\dfrac{1+x}{1-x}$ (b) $\dfrac{1}{2}\log\dfrac{2+x}{2-x}$
(c) $\dfrac{1}{2}\log\dfrac{1-x}{1-x}$ (d) None of these

12. If $A_1 = \{1, 2, 3, 4\}$ and $A_2 = \{5, 6, 7, 8\}$; $A_3 = \{9, 10\}$; $A_4 = \{11, 12, 13, 14\}$. Let n_{ij} = Number of invertible functions from A_i to A_j, then Σn_{ij} equals
(a) 36 (b) 576
(c) 144 (d) None of these

13. Let f be a function defined as $f(x) = \sqrt{3}\sin x - \cos x + 2$. Then $f^{-1}(x)$ is given by
(a) $\sin^{-1}\left(\dfrac{x-2}{2}\right) - \dfrac{\pi}{6}$
(b) $\sin^{-1}\left(\dfrac{x-2}{2}\right) + \dfrac{\pi}{6}$
(c) $\sin^{-1}\dfrac{2\pi}{3} + \cos^{-1}\left(\dfrac{x-2}{2}\right)$
(d) None of these

14. If $f(x) = \sqrt{\sin^{-1}(2x)+\frac{\pi}{6}}$ and $g(x) = f^{-1}(x)$, then domain of $g(x)$ is

(a) $\left[-\sqrt{\frac{2\pi}{3}}, \sqrt{\frac{2\pi}{3}}\right]$ (b) $\left[0, \sqrt{\frac{2\pi}{3}}\right]$

(c) $\left[0, \sqrt{\frac{\pi}{2}}\right]$ (d) None of these

15. If $f(x) = \sqrt{\cos^{-1}(2x)+\frac{\pi}{6}}$ and $g(x) = f^{-1}(x)$, then range of $g(x)$ is

(a) $[0,1]$ (b) $\left[-\frac{1}{2}, \frac{1}{2}\right]$

(c) $\left[\frac{1}{2}, 1\right]$ (d) None of these

16. Let $f(x) = (1 + b^2)x^2 + 2bx + 1$ and let $m(b)$ be the minimum value of $f(x)$. If b varies $m(b)$ becomes a function of b, then inverse function of $m(b)$ from its principal domain to range is given by $m^{-1}(x)$ equals

(a) $\sqrt{\frac{1-x}{x}}$ (b) $-\sqrt{\frac{1-x}{x}}$

(c) $\sqrt{\frac{x-1}{x}}$ (d) None of these

17. Let $f : (0, \infty) \rightarrow (1, \infty)$ be a function such that $F(x) = \int_0^x f(t)\,dt$. If $F(x^2) = x^2(1 + x)$, and $g(x) = f^{-1}(x)$, then g(10) equals

(a) 49 (b) 99

(c) 36 (d) None of these

18. If $f : (0, \infty) \rightarrow (1, \infty)$ be a function such that $F(x) = \int_0^x f(t)\,dt$. If $F(x^2) = x^2(1 + x)$ and $g(x) = f^{-1}(x)$, then the point where $g(x)$ and $f(x)$ intersect is

(a) $\left(\frac{1}{4}, \frac{1}{4}\right)$ (b) (4, 2)

(c) (4, 4) (d) Does not exist

Answer Keys

1. (a)	**2.** (b)	**3.** (a)	**4.** (b)	**5.** (c)	**6.** (c)	**7.** (b, c)	**8.** (a)	**9.** (b)	**10.** (c)
11. (a)	**12.** (c)	**13.** (b)	**14.** (b)	**15.** (b)	**16.** (a)	**17.** (c)	**18.** (c)		

■ EVEN AND ODD FUNCTIONS

The knowledge about the symmetry of graph of the function extends great help in study of the behaviour of function and analysis of problems involving these functions. Fundamentally functions possess two kinds of symmetry (i) symmetry about a straight line (say y-axis) (ii) symmetry about a point (say origin).

If a function has its graph symmetric about y-axis, i.e., portion of graph lying to the left of y-axis is mirror image of the portion lying to the right of y-axis, then it is known as an even function. If the graph of the function is symmetric about origin, i.e., it is symmetric in opposite quadrants, then it is known as odd function.

For instance, $f(x) = \cos x$ is symmetric about y-axis and is called an even function and $f(x) = \sin x$ is symmetric about origin and called as odd function graphically shown in the Figures.

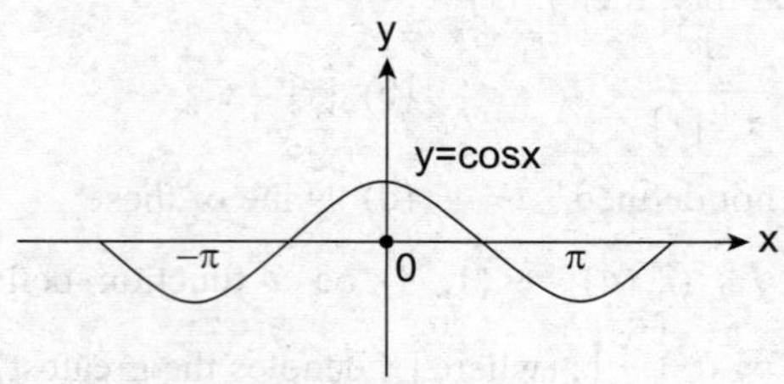

FIGURE 2.185

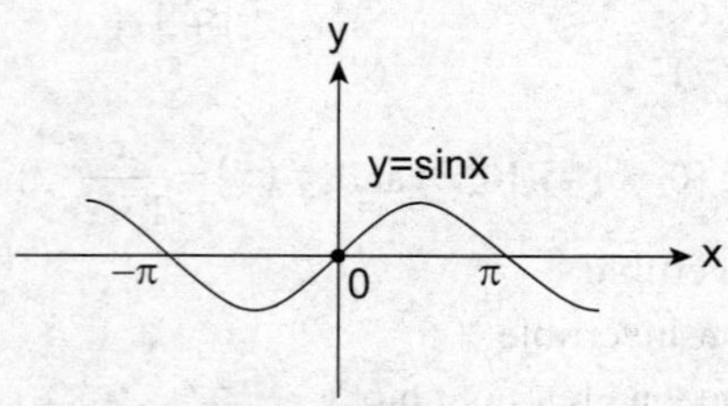

FIGURE 2.186

REMARKS

(i) The functions having no symmetry like odd/even functions are called 'neither even nor odd functions'.

(ii) Before testing the even/odd symmetry of the function it is essential to observe whether the domain of function is symmetric about y-axis, i.e., if the domain is of the type $[-x_0, x_0]$ or $[-x_2, -x_1] \cup [x_1, x_2]$ etc.

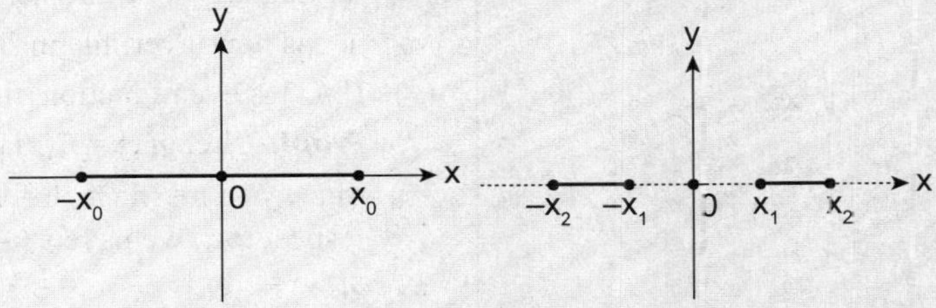

FIGURE 2.187

■ EVEN FUNCTIONS

A function $f : X \to Y$ is said to be an even function iff $f(-x) = f(x)\ \forall\ x, -x \in X$ (Domain). i.e., $f(x) - f(-x) = 0$

e.g., x^{2n}, $\sin^2 x$, $\cos x$, $\sec x$, $2^x + 2^{-x}$

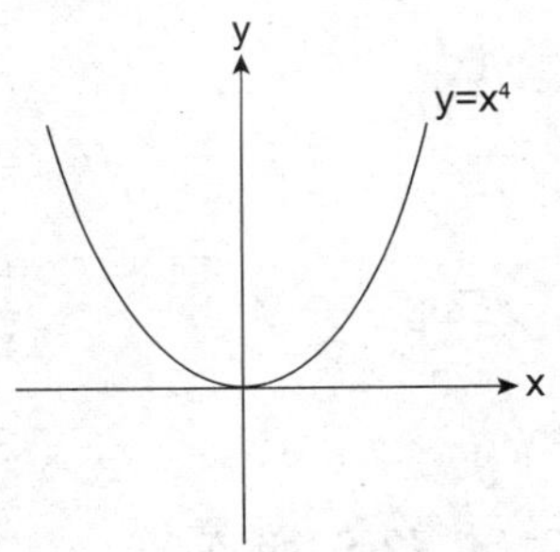

FIGURE 2.188

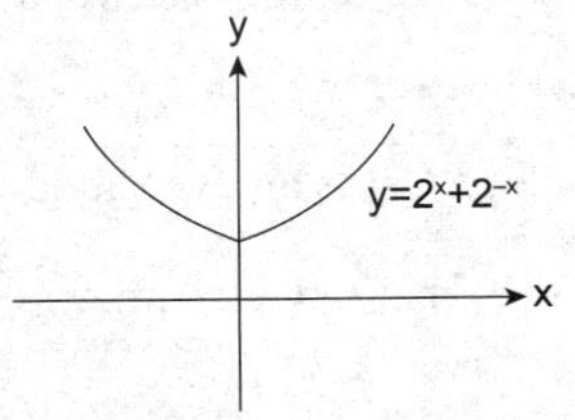

FIGURE 2.189

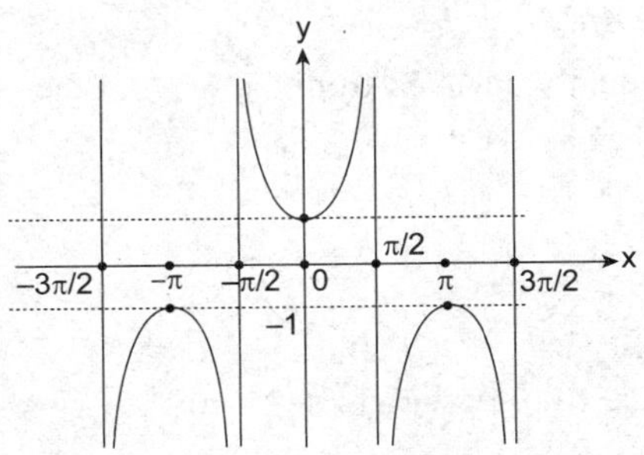

FIGURE 2.190

Properties of Even Functions:

(i) Graph of even function is symmetric about y-axis because if (x, y) lies on the curve, $(-x, y)$ also lies on the curve.

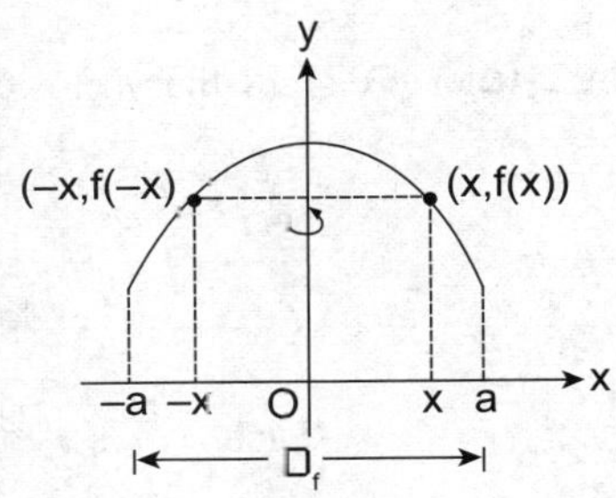

FIGURE 2.191

Proof: Since for even function $f(-x) = f(x)$ $\forall\ x, -x \in X$ (Domain), i.e., $y = f(x) \Rightarrow y = f(-x)$

Consequently $(x, y) \in f \Rightarrow (-x, y) \in f$

It is important to see that if we rotate the curve by 180° about y-axis, then the appearance of the rotated curve is same as the original curve. We can state this alternatively; if we rotate portion of the curve on the left side of y-axis by 180° about y-axis; then we get the portion of graph to the right of y-axis and vice versa.

(ii) For any function $f(x)$, if $g(x) = f(x) + f(-x)$, then $g(x)$ is always an even function.

Proof: $g(-x) = f(-x) + f(x) = g(x)\ \forall\ x, -x \in D_f$

Hence, $g(x)$ is an even function.

(iii) The domain of even function must be symmetric about zero, i.e., $D_f : [-a, a]$ or $(-a, a)$ or $(-a_2, -a_1) \cup (a_1, a_2)$; where a is some real number.

e.g., $f : [-2, 4] \to \mathbb{R}$ defined as $f(x) = x^2$ is not an even function since domain is not symmetric about zero.

However it will be an even function if we redefine the function $f:[-2,2]\to\mathbb{R}$ as $f(x)=x^2$ or . $f:[-4,4]\to\mathbb{R}$ as $f(x)=x^2$

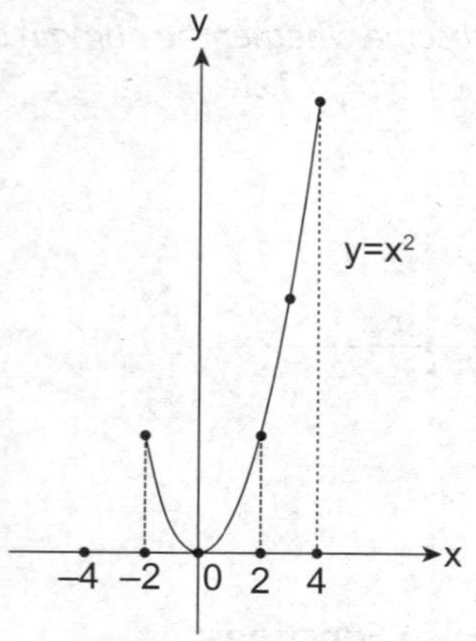

FIGURE 2.192

(iv) Even functions are non-invertible as they can't be strictly monotonic when taken in their natural domain, however, even functions can be made invertible by restricting their domains to either side of y-axis.

Proof: Since $f(-x)=f(x)\ \forall\ x, -x\in D_f$

$\Rightarrow$ $f(x)$ is many–one and hence, not bijective

$\Rightarrow$ $f(x)$ is non-invertible in D_f

(v) If $f(x)$ is even function, then $f'(x)$ is odd function.

Proof: Let $g(x)=f'(x)$, given $f(x)$ an even function. Since $f(-x)=f(x)$; differentiating both sides with respect to x, we have $f'(-x)(-1)=f'(x)$

$\Rightarrow$ $g(-x)=-g(x)$ $\Rightarrow$ $g(x)$ is an odd function.

(vi) $f(x)=c$; where c is a constant defined on symmetrical domain is an even function.

Proof: Since for $x, -x\in D_f, f(x)=f(-x)=c$

$\Rightarrow$ $f(x)$ is an even function.

ILLUSTRATION 235: Show that the function $f(x)=x^3\log\left(\frac{1-x}{1+x}\right)$ is an even function.

SOLUTION: To show that $f(x)$ is even we need to prove that $f(-x)=f(x)$.

Since we have domain of $f(x)=(-1,1)$ which is symmetric about y-axis and $f(x)=x^3\log\left(\frac{1-x}{1+x}\right)$

$$\Rightarrow\ f(-x)=(-x)^3\log\left(\frac{1-(-x)}{1+(-x)}\right)=-x^3\log\left(\frac{1+x}{1-x}\right)=-x^3\log\left(\frac{1-x}{1+x}\right)^{-1}=x^3\log\left(\frac{1-x}{1+x}\right)=f(x)$$

Thus, $f(x)$ is clearly an even function.

ILLUSTRATION 236: Test whether $f(x)=x(e^x-e^{-x})+\sqrt{\cot^{-1}(\sin(\sec^{-1}x)}$ is even function or not ?

SOLUTION: To investigate the even nature of function, we need to find the relation between $f(-x)$ and $f(x)$.

Now $f(x)=x(e^x-e^{-x})+\sqrt{\cot^{-1}(\sin(\sec^{-1}x))}$ $\Rightarrow f(-x)=-x(e^{-x}-e^x)+\sqrt{\cot^{-1}(\sin(\sec^{-1}(-x))}$

$=x(e^x-e^{-x})+\sqrt{\cot^{-1}(\sin(\sec^{-1}(x)}=f(x)$ $\Rightarrow$ Indeed $f(x)$ is an even function.

ILLUSTRATION 237: Let $f(x)=|x-4|+|x-5|+|x-6|$ and $g(x)=f(x+k)$. Find k so that $g(x)$ is an even function.

SOLUTION: Given $f(x)=|x-4|+|x-5|+|x-6|$ and $g(x)=f(x+k)$

We observe that $x-4$, $x-5$ and $x-6$ are in an $A.P.$

Since the numbers of a group of numbers are equally deviated from the $A.M.$ of the numbers of the group, so, let $y=A.M.$ of $(x-4, x-5, x-6)$ $\Rightarrow$ $y=x-5$

Replacing x by $y+5$ in $f(x)$; we get $f(y+5)=|y+1|+|y|+|y-1|$

$\Rightarrow$ $f(-y+5)=|-y+1|+|-y|+|-y-1|=|1-y|+|y|+|1+y|=f(y+5)$

$\therefore$ $g(-y)=g(y)$ for $k=5$. Hence, value of $k=5$

ILLUSTRATION 238: If $f(x)$ is a polynomial satisfying $f(x)\,.\,f(y)-f(x)-f(y)-f(x.y)+2=0;\ \forall\ x,y\in\mathbb{R}$ and $f(3)=10$, then show that $f(x)$ is an even function.

SOLUTION: Given $f(x) \,.\, f(y) - f(x) - f(y) - f(xy) + 2 = 0$ ...(1)

Putting $x = 1$ and $y = 1$ in (1), we get $f(1) \,.\, f(1) - f(1) - f(1) - f(1) + 2 = 0$

$\Rightarrow (f(1))^2 - 3(f(1)) + 2 = 0 \Rightarrow f(1) = 1$ or 2

Case I: Putting $y = 1$ and $f(1) = 1$, we get $f(x) f(1) = f(x) + f(1) + f(x) - 2$

$\Rightarrow f(x) = 1 \;\forall\, x \in \mathbb{R}$ (rejected, $\because f(3) = 10$)

Case II: Putting $y = 1$ and $f(1) = 2$, we get $f(x).f(1) = f(x) + f(1) + f(x) - 2$

$\Rightarrow 2f(x) = 2f(x) + 2 - 2$, which is identically true, hence, $f(1) = 2$

Now; given that $f(x)$ is a polynomial function, therefore putting $y = 1/x$; we get

$\Rightarrow f(x)\, f(1/x) = f(x) + f(1/x) + f(1) - 2 \Rightarrow f(x).\, f(1/x) = f(x) + f(1/x) \Rightarrow f(x) = 1 \pm x^n$

Let $f(x) = 1 + x^n$ and $f(1) = 2$; $f(3) = 10 \Rightarrow n = 2$

$\Rightarrow f(x) = 1 - x^n$ is rejected as it does not satisfy $f(1) = 2$; $f(3) = 10$ for any value of n

$\therefore f(x) = 1 + x^2$ and $f(-x) = 1 + (-x)^2 = 1 + x^2 = f(x) \Rightarrow f(x)$ is an even function

ILLUSTRATION 239: Prove that in the product $(1 - x + x^2 - x^3 + \ldots - x^{49} + x^{50})\,(1 + x + x^2 + x^3 + \ldots + x^{49} + x^{50})$, after simplification there will be no term containing odd power of x, and hence, show that the above product represents an even function.

SOLUTION: Let $f(x) = (1 - x + x^2 - x^3 + \ldots\ldots - x^{49} + x^{50})\,(1 + x + x^2 + \ldots + x^{50})$

$= [(1 + x^2 + x^4 + \ldots + x^{50}) - (x + x^3 + \ldots + x^{49})] \,.\, [(1 + x^2 + x^4 + \ldots. + x^{50}) + (x + x^3 + \ldots + x^{49})]$

$= (1 + x^2 + x^4 + \ldots + x^{50})^2 - (x + x^3 + \ldots. + x^{49})^2$

$= (1 + x^2 + x^4 + \ldots. + x^{50})^2 - x^2\,(1 + x^2 + \ldots. + x^{48})^2$

Now we can observe that the above expression does not contain any term of x having odd degree. Hence, $f(x)$ is an even function.

■ ODD FUNCTIONS

A function $f : X \to Y$ is said to be an odd function iff $f(-x) = -f(x) \;\forall\, x, -x \in X$

i.e., $f(x) + f(-x) = 0 \;\forall\, x, -x \in X$

e.g., x^3, $\sin x$, $\tan x$, $2^x - 2^{-x}$ are odd functions

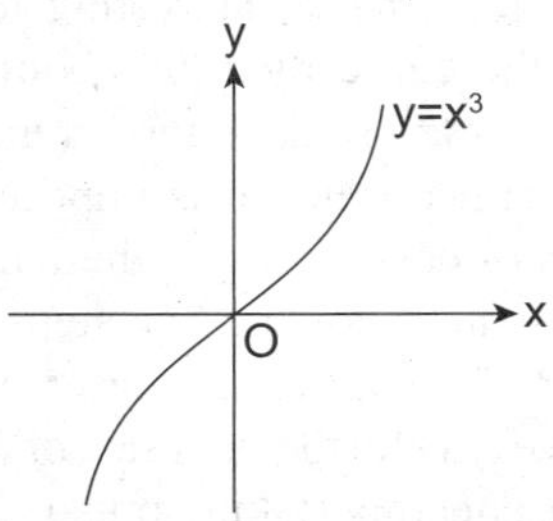

FIGURE 2.193

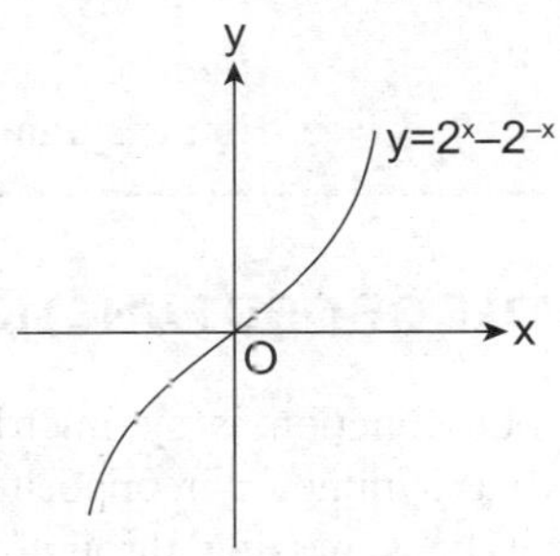

FIGURE 2.194

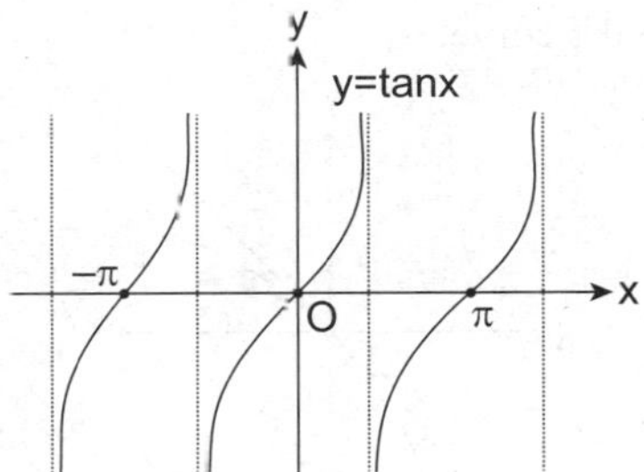

FIGURE 2.195

ILLUSTRATION 240: Prove that $f(x)=4\sqrt{1-x^3}-4\sqrt{1+x^3}$ is an odd function.

SOLUTION: Given $f(x)=4\sqrt{1-x^3}-4\sqrt{1+x^3} \Rightarrow f(-x)=4\sqrt{1-(-x)^3}-4\sqrt{1+(-x)^3}$

$= 4\sqrt{1+x^3}-4\sqrt{1-x^3} = -\left(4\sqrt{1-x^3}-4\sqrt{1+x^3}\right)=-f(x)$

Hence, $f(x)$ is an odd function.

ILLUSTRATION 241: Find whether the following functions are even or odd or none.

(a) $f(x) = \sin x + \tan x$ (b) $f(x) = x \sin^2 x - x^3$ (c) $f(x) = \sin x - \cos x$

SOLUTION: (a) Given $f(x) = \sin x + \tan x \Rightarrow f(-x) = -\sin x - \tan x = -f(x)$

$\therefore f(-x) = -f(x) \Rightarrow f(x)$ is an odd function.

(b) Given $f(x) = x \sin^2 x - x^3 \Rightarrow f(-x) = -x \sin^2 x + x^3 = -f(x)$

$\Rightarrow f(-x) = -f(x) \Rightarrow f(x)$ is an odd function

(c) Given $f(x) = \sin x - \cos x \Rightarrow f(-x) = -\sin x - \cos x \neq f(x), -f(x)$

$\therefore f(x)$ is neither odd nor even function.

ILLUSTRATION 242: Find whether the following functions are even or odd or none.

(a) $f(x)=\dfrac{(x-1)\tan x}{x-1}$ (b) $f(x)=\dfrac{x^5(x^2-1)}{x^2-1}$

SOLUTION: (a) Given function is $f(x)=\dfrac{(x-1)\tan x}{x-1}$

Domain of given function $f(x)$ is $\mathbb{R} \sim \left\{1,(2n+1)\dfrac{\pi}{2};n\in\mathbb{Z}\right\}$.

Here for $x \in D_f$, $f(x) = \tan x$ which seems to be an odd function, but actually it is not so, because the domain of function is not symmetric about the origin as $f(x)$ is defined at $x = -1$, whereas it is not defined at $x = 1$.

(b) Given function is $f(x)=\dfrac{x^5(x^2-1)}{x^2-1}$

Domain of given function $f(x)$ is $\mathbb{R} \sim \{1, -1\}$.

Here for $x \in D_f$, $f(x) = x^5$ which is an odd function since $f(-x) = -f(x)$ and domain of function is symmetric about origin. Therefore, $f(x)$ is an odd function.

■ PROPERTIES OF ODD FUNCTIONS

(i) Graph of odd function is symmetric about origin. Also known as symmetric in opposite quadrants.
i.e., straight lines passing through origin cuts the graph both sides symmetrically.
This is because if (x, y) lies on the curve, $(-x, -y)$ also lies on the curve.

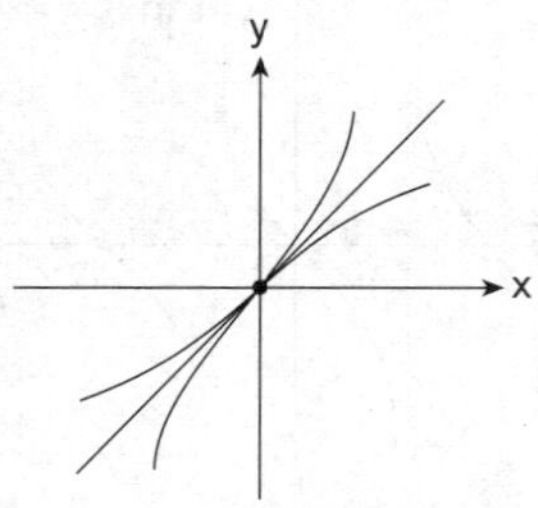

FIGURE 2.196

Proof: Since for an odd function $f(-x) = -f(x)$ $\forall\, x \in X$, i.e., $y = f(x)$

$\Rightarrow -y = f(-x)$ which clearly leads to the fact that $(x, y) \in f$

$\Rightarrow (-x, -y) \in f$

Therefore, it is really interesting to observe that if we rotate the curve by 180° about origin, then the appearance of the rotated curve remains same as the original curve. Further, it is important to notice that the portion of curve lying to the left of y-axis can be obtained by the following two steps:

Step 1: Reflecting (taking mirror image) of the portion of curve lying to the right side of y-axis about y-axis

Step 2: Reflecting (taking mirror image) of 'reflection obtained in step (1)' about x-axis.

(ii) For any function $f(x)$, if $g(x) = f(-x) - f(x)$, then $g(x)$ is always an odd function.

Proof: Since $g(x) = f(-x) - f(x)$

$\Rightarrow g(-x) = f(x) - f(-x) = -g(x)\ \forall\, x, -x \in D_f$

(iii) The domain of odd function must be symmetric about zero. i.e., D_f : $[-a, a]$ or $(-a, a)$ where a is some real number,
e.g., f: $[-\pi, 2\pi] \to \mathbb{R}$ defined as $f(x) = \sin x$ is not an odd function because its domain is not symmetric about zero.

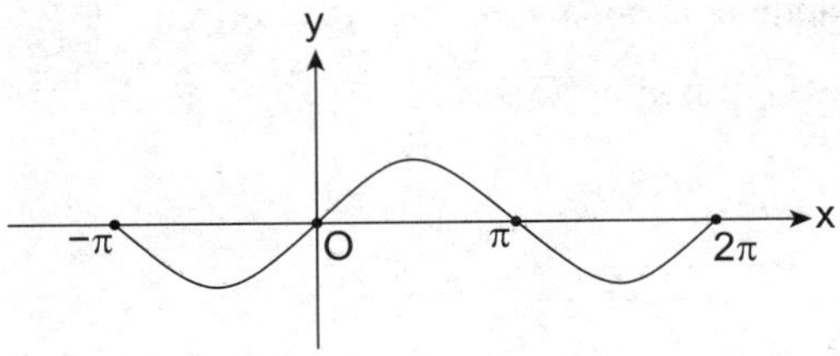

FIGURE 2.197

However $f(x) = \sin x$ is an odd function when defined on set $[-a, a]$ or $(-a, a)$ $\forall\, a \in \mathbb{R}$

(iv) If $f(x)$ is odd, then $f'(x)$ is an even function.
Proof: Let $f'(x) = g(x)$.
Since $f(-x) = -f(x)\ \forall\ x, -x \in D_f$
Differentiating with respect to x, we have $f'(x) = f'(-x)$
$\Rightarrow g(x) = g(-x)\ \ \forall\ x, -x \in D_g$
$\Rightarrow g(x) = f'(x)$ is an even function

(v) If $x = 0$ lies in the domain of an odd function, then $f(0) = 0$, i.e., the graph of an odd function must pass through origin.
Proof: Since $f(x) = -f(-x)\ \forall\ x, -x \in D_f$ and $0 \in D_f$
$\Rightarrow f(0) = -f(0) \Rightarrow\ 2f(0) = 0\ \Rightarrow f(0) = 0$
i.e., $f(x)$ passes through (0, 0) (origin)

ILLUSTRATION 243: Prove that $f(x)=\left(\sqrt{1+x}+\sqrt{1-x}\right).\left(\dfrac{a^x-1}{a^x+1}\right)$ is an odd function.

SOLUTION: Clearly the domain of $f(x)$ is $[-1, 1]$ which is symmetric about zero. Therefore, in order to prove that $f(x)$ is odd, we need to only establish that $f(-x) = -f(x)$.

Now $f(-x)=\left(\sqrt{1+(-x)}+\sqrt{1-(-x)}\right).\left(\dfrac{a^{-x}-1}{a^{-x}+1}\right) = \left(\sqrt{1-x}+\sqrt{1+x}\right)\left(\dfrac{\dfrac{1}{a^x}-1}{\dfrac{1}{a^x}+1}\right)$

$= -\left(\sqrt{1-x}+\sqrt{1+x}\right)\left(\dfrac{a^x-1}{a^x+1}\right) = -f(x)$, consequently $f(x)$ is an odd function

ILLUSTRATION 244: Identify whether the functions graphically shown below are even or odd.

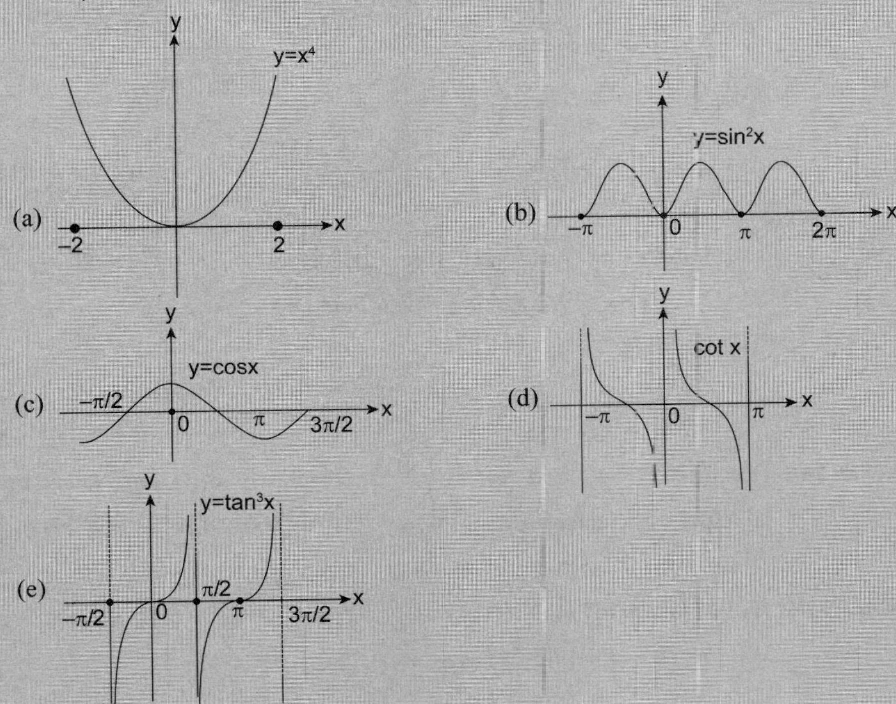

SOLUTION: (a) $f(x)$ is an even function, since the domain is symmetric about origin and the graph is symmetric about y-axis.

(b) $f(x)$ is neither even nor odd, since the domain is not symmetric about origin.

(c) $f(x)$ is neither even nor odd, since the domain is not symmetric about origin.

(d) $f(x)$ is an odd function, since the domain is symmetric about origin and the graph is symmetric in opposite quadrants.

(e) $f(x)$ is neither even nor odd, since the domain is not symmetric about origin.

ILLUSTRATION 245: Find whether the following functions are even or odd or none.

(a) $f(x)=\log(x+\sqrt{1+x^2})$ (b) $f(x)=\dfrac{x(a^x+1)}{a^x-1}$

(c) $f(x)=\dfrac{(1+2^x)^2}{2^x}$ (d) $f(x)=\dfrac{x}{e^x-1}+\dfrac{x}{2}+1$

(e) $f(x) = [(x + 1)^2]^{1/3} + [(x - 1)^2]^{1/3}$

SOLUTION: (a) Given $f(x)=\log(x+\sqrt{1+x^2})$ ...(1)

$\Rightarrow f(-x)=\log(-x+\sqrt{1+x^2})$ ...(2)

Adding (1) and (2), we have $f(-x)+f(x)=\log(\sqrt{1+x^2}+x)+\log(\sqrt{1+x^2}-x)$

$=\log[(1+x^2)-x^2] \Rightarrow f(-x)+f(x)=0 \Rightarrow f(-x)=-f(x) \Rightarrow f(x)$ is an odd function

(b) Given $f(x)=x\dfrac{(a^x+1)}{a^x-1}$

$\Rightarrow f(-x)=-\dfrac{x(a^{-x}+1)}{a^{-x}-1}=-\dfrac{x(1+a^x)}{1-a^x}=\dfrac{x(a^x+1)}{a^x-1}=f(x)$; $f(x)$ is an even function

(c) Given $f(x)=\dfrac{(1+2^x)^2}{2^x} \Rightarrow f(-x)=\dfrac{(1+2^{-x})^2}{2^{-x}}=\dfrac{\left(1+\dfrac{1}{2^x}\right)^2}{\dfrac{1}{2^x}}=\dfrac{(2^x+1)^2}{2^{2x}.\dfrac{1}{2^x}}=\dfrac{(1+2^x)^2}{2^x}=f(x)$

$\therefore$ $f(x)$ is an even function.

(d) Given $f(x)=\dfrac{x}{e^x-1}+\dfrac{x}{2}+1$ .... (1)

$\Rightarrow f(-x)=-\dfrac{x}{e^{-x}-1}-\dfrac{x}{2}+1=\dfrac{-x}{\dfrac{1-e^x}{e^x}}-\dfrac{x}{2}+1 \Rightarrow f(-x)=\dfrac{xe^x}{e^x-1}-\dfrac{x}{2}+1$ ... (2)

Subtracting equation (1) from (2), we get $f(-x)-f(x)=\dfrac{x(e^x-1)}{e^x-1}-x=0$

$\Rightarrow f(-x)=f(x)$ $\therefore$ $f(x)$ is an even function.

(e) Given $f(x) = [(x + 1)^2]^{1/3} + [(x - 1)^2]^{1/3}$

$\Rightarrow f(-x) = [(-x + 1)^2]^{1/3} + [(-x - 1)^2]^{1/3} = [(1 - x)^2]^3 + [(1 + x)^2]^{1/3}$

$= [(x - 1)^2]^{1/3} + [(1 + x)^2]^{1/3} = f(x)$ $\Rightarrow f(x)$ is an even function

ILLUSTRATION 246: Let $f(x)=e^{\{e^{|x|}\operatorname{sgn} x\}}$ and $g(x)=e^{[e^{|x|}\operatorname{sgn} x]}$, $x\in\mathbb{R}$; where { } and [ ] denotes the fractional part and integral part functions respectively. Also if $h(x)=\ln(f(x))+\ln(g(x))$ for all real x, then show that $h(x)$ is an odd function.

SOLUTION: Given $h(x)=\ln(f(x)\cdot g(x))=\ln e^{\{y\}+[y]}$; where $y=e^{|x|}\operatorname{sgn} x$

$\Rightarrow h(x)=\{y\}+[y]=y=e^{|x|}sgn\ x$

$$\therefore \quad h(x)=e^{|x|}\operatorname{sgn} x=\begin{cases} e^{x} & \text{if } x>0 \\ 0 & \text{if } x=0 \\ -e^{-x} & \text{if } x<0 \end{cases} \qquad \therefore \quad h(-x)=\begin{cases} e^{-x} & \text{if } x<0 \\ 0 & \text{if } x=0 \\ -e^{x} & \text{if } x>0 \end{cases}$$

Clearly $h(x) + h(-x) = 0$ for all $x \in \mathbb{R} \Rightarrow h(-x) = -h(x)\ \forall\ x \Rightarrow h(x)$ is an odd function.

ILLUSTRATION 247: Find whether the function $f(x)=\log\left(\frac{1+\sin x}{1-\sin x}\right)$ is odd or even or none of these.

SOLUTION: Given function is $f(x)=\log\left(\frac{1+\sin x}{1-\sin x}\right)$

$\Rightarrow f(-x)=\log\left(\frac{1-\sin x}{1+\sin x}\right)=-\log\left(\frac{1+\sin x}{1-\sin x}\right)=-f(x) \Rightarrow f(x)$ is an odd function.

ILLUSTRATION 248: Find whether the function $f(x)=[x]+\frac{1}{2}$, $x \notin \mathbb{Z}$ is odd or even or none of these.

SOLUTION: Given function is $f(x)=[x]+\frac{1}{2}, x \notin \mathbb{Z}$

$\Rightarrow f(-x)=[-x]+\frac{1}{2}=-[x]-1+\frac{1}{2}=-\left([x]+\frac{1}{2}\right)=-f(x) \quad (\because [x] + [-x] = -1 \text{ for } x \notin \mathbb{Z})$

$\therefore$ $f(x)$ is an odd function.

ILLUSTRATION 249: If the graph of the function $f(x)=\frac{a^x-1}{x^n(a^x+1)}$; $n \in \mathbb{Z}$ is symmetric about y-axis, then show that n is an odd integer.

SOLUTION: Given function is $f(x)=\frac{a^x-1}{x^n(a^x+1)}$; $D_f = \mathbb{R} - \{0\}$

Since graph of function is symmetric about y-axis, it implies that function is an even function

$\Rightarrow f(-x) = f(x)\ \forall\ x \in D_f \Rightarrow \frac{1-a^x}{(-x)^n(a^x+1)}=\frac{a^x-1}{x^n(a^x+1)} \Rightarrow -(x)^n = (-x)^n = (-1)^n x^n$

$\Rightarrow -1 = (-1)^n \Rightarrow n$ must be an odd integer.

■ ALGEBRA OF EVEN–ODD FUNCTIONS

1. $f(x) = 0$ (identically zero function) is the only function which is both, an odd and an even function, provided it is defined in a symmetric domain.

Proof: If $f(x)$ is even, then $f(-x) = f(x)$

If $f(x)$ is odd, then $f(-x) = -f(x)$

Comparing $f(-x)$, we get $f(x) = -f(x)$

$\Rightarrow f(x) = 0\ \forall\ x \in \mathbb{R}$

ILLUSTRATION 250: Prove that the function defined as $f(x)=\begin{cases} e^{-\sqrt{|\ell n\{x\}|}}-\{x\}^{\sqrt{\frac{1}{|\ell n\{x\}|}}}; & \text{whenever it exists} \\ \{x\}; & \text{otherwise} \end{cases}$; $f(x)$ is odd as well as even; where $\{x\}$ denotes fraction part of x.

SOLUTION: We have to prove that function is odd as well as even. It is possible only when $f(x) = 0$. Consider the following two cases as given below.

Case I: Whenever the expression $e^{-\sqrt{|\ell n\{x\}|}}-\{x\}^{\sqrt{\frac{1}{|\ell n\{x\}|}}}$ exists

Now, $\{x\} \in [0, 1)$ and $\ln\{x\}$ is defined for $\{x\} \in (0, 1)$. Hence, $\forall\ x \in \mathbb{R} \sim \mathbb{Z}$

Now $f(x) = \ln\{x\} < 0$ for $\{x\} \in (0, 1)$ $\Rightarrow$ $|\ln\{x\}| = -\ln\{x\}$.

$$\therefore \quad e^{-\sqrt{|\ell n\{x\}|}} - \{x\}^{\sqrt{\frac{1}{|\ell n\{x\}|}}} = e^{-(-\ln\{x\})^{1/2}} - e^{\ln\{x\}\left(\frac{1}{-\ln\{x\}}\right)^{\frac{1}{2}}} = e^{-(-\ln\{x\})^{1/2}} - e^{\frac{1}{(-\ln\{x\})^{1/2}}.\ln\{x\}}$$

$$= e^{-(-\ln\{x\})^{1/2}} - e^{-(-\ln\{x\})^{1/2}} = 0$$

Case II: $\{\text{For } x \in \mathbb{Z}\}$

$f(x) = \{x\} = 0$ ($\because$ $\{x\}$ equal to zero for x an integer). Thus, $f(x) = 0\ \forall\ x \in \mathbb{R}$

$\Rightarrow$ $f(x)$ is even as well as odd function.

ILLUSTRATION 251: It is given that $f(x)$ is an even function and satisfy the relation $f(x) = \dfrac{x\,f(x^2)}{2 + \tan^2 x . f(x^2)}$, then find the value of $f(10)$.

SOLUTION: Given $f(x) = \dfrac{xf(x^2)}{2 + \tan^2 x\, f(x^2)}$ $\Rightarrow$ $f(-x) = \dfrac{-xf(x^2)}{2 + \tan^2(x) f(x^2)}$

$\Rightarrow$ $f(-x) = -f(x)$ $\Rightarrow$ $f(x)$ is an odd function, but $f(x)$ is given to be an even function

$\Rightarrow$ $f(x)$ is odd as well as an even function $\Rightarrow$ $f(x) = 0\ \forall\ x \in \mathbb{R}$ $\Rightarrow f(10) = 0$

2. A linear combination of two or more even functions is an even function, i.e., in particular for two even functions $f(x)$ and $g(x)$, the function $(\alpha f + \beta g)$ is an even function; where $\alpha, \beta \in \mathbb{R}$.

   Proof: Since $f(x)$ and $g(x)$ are even functions, therefore $f(-x) = f(x)$ and $g(-x) = g(x)$.

   Now let $h = (\alpha f + \beta g)$; where $\alpha, \beta \in \mathbb{R}$

   $\Rightarrow h(-x) = (\alpha f + \beta g)(-x) = \alpha f(-x) + \beta g(-x)$

   $\Rightarrow h(-x) = \alpha f(x) + \beta g(x) = (\alpha f + \beta g)(x) = h(x)$

   $\Rightarrow h(-x) = h(x)$ $\Rightarrow$ $h(x)$ is an even function.

   Applying the above result for more than two functions repeatedly, we can show that linear combination of more than two even functions is also an even function.

3. A linear combination of two or more odd functions is an odd function, i.e., in particular for two odd functions $f(x)$ and $g(x)$, the function $(\alpha f + \beta g)$ is an odd function; where $\alpha, \beta \in \mathbb{R}$.

   Proof: Since $f(x)$ and $g(x)$ are odd functions, therefore $f(-x) = -f(x)$ and $g(-x) = -g(x)$.

   Let $h = \alpha f + \beta g$; where $\alpha, \beta \in \mathbb{R}$

   $\Rightarrow h(-x) = (\alpha f + \beta g)(-x) = \alpha f(-x) + \beta g(-x)$

   $\Rightarrow h(-x) = -\alpha f(x) - \beta g(x) = -(\alpha f(x) + \beta g(x))$

   $= -(\alpha f + \beta g)(x) = -h(x)$ $\Rightarrow$ $h(-x) = -h(x)$

   $\Rightarrow h(x)$ is an odd function.

   Applying the above result for more than two functions repeatedly, we can show that linear combination of more than two odd functions is also an odd function.

4. The product of two or more even functions is an even function.

   Proof: Let $f(x)$ and $g(x)$ be two even functions

   $\Rightarrow f(-x) = f(x)$ and $g(-x) = g(x)$. Let $h = f.g$

   $\Rightarrow h(x) = f(x).g(x)$

   $\Rightarrow h(-x) = (f.g)(-x) = f(-x) . g(-x)$

   $\Rightarrow h(-x) = f(x) . g(x) = (f.g)(x) = h(x)$

   $\Rightarrow h(-x) = h(x)$ $\Rightarrow$ $h = f.g$ is an even function.

   Applying the above result for more than two functions repeatedly, we can show that the product of more than two even function is again an even function.

5. The product of an odd and an even function is an odd function.

   Proof: Let $f(x)$ be an odd function and $g(x)$ be an even function

   $\Rightarrow f(-x) = -f(x)$ .... (1)

   $g(-x) = g(x)$ .... (2)

   Now let $h = f.g$ $\Rightarrow$ $h(x) = (f.g)(x) = f(x) . g(x)$

   $\therefore$ $h(-x) = f(-x) . g(-x)$

   $= [-f(x)] . [g(x)]$ (by using (1) and (2))

   $= -f(x) . g(x) = -(f.g)(x) = -h(x)$

   $\therefore$ $h(-x) = -h(x)$

   $\Rightarrow h = f.g$, i.e., the product of an odd and an even function is an odd function.

6. The quotient of two even functions (or two odd functions) is an even function.

Proof: Let $f(x)$ and $g(x)$ be two even functions

$\Rightarrow f(-x) = f(x)$ and $g(-x) = g(x)$

Let $h = \frac{f}{g}$

$$\Rightarrow h(-x) = \frac{f}{g}(-x) = \frac{f(-x)}{g(-x)} = \frac{f(x)}{g(x)} = \frac{f}{g}(x) = h(x)$$

$\Rightarrow h(-x) = h(x) \Rightarrow h(x)$ is an even function

Similarly if $f(x)$ and $g(x)$ are two odd functions, then

$$h(-x) = \frac{f}{g}(-x) = \frac{f(-x)}{g(-x)} = \frac{-f(x)}{-g(x)} = \frac{f}{g}(x) = h(x)$$

$\Rightarrow h(x)$ is an even function

7. The nature (odd or even) of product of odd functions depends upon the number of functions taken in the product. i.e., product of odd number of odd functions is an odd function and that of even number of odd functions is an even function.

Proof: ***Case I:*** If an even number of odd functions is taken, then their product will be an even function.

Let there be $2n$ number of odd functions. If we make n pairs of all the functions, then the product of functions in each pair is an even function, as the product of two odd functions is an even function.

Thus, our product is reduced to product of n even functions, which is an even function (by property (4)).

Case II: If an odd number of odd functions is taken, then their product will be an odd function.

Let there be $(2n + 1)$ number of odd functions. If we make n pairs of the functions in the product, then we are left with an unpaired odd function. The product of functions in each pair is an even function, as the product of two odd functions is an even function. Thus, our product is reduced to product of n even functions and an odd function which in turn is a product of an even and an odd function, i.e., an odd function. (by property 5).

8. Composition of several functions, $f(g(h...(p(x))...)))$ is odd iff all are odd functions.

Proof: Let $F(x) = f(g(h\ldots p(x))\ldots)))$

$\Rightarrow F(-x) = f(g(h\ldots(p(-x))\ldots))$

$= f(g(h\ldots.(-p(x))\ldots.)) = \ldots. = f(g(-(h\ldots.(p(x))\ldots)))$

$= f(-g(h\ldots.(p(x))\ldots.) = -f(g(h\ldots.(p(x))..) = -F(x)$

Thus, $F(-x) = -F(x) \Rightarrow F(x)$ is an odd function.

9. Composition of several functions is even iff atleast one function is even, provided the function composed of either even or odd functions after that even function. i.e., if $F(x) = f(g(h\ldots.(p(x))\ldots.)))$ and $g(x)$ is an even function, then $h(x), ..., p(x)$ all should be either even or odd. For example, $f(x) = e^{\log\tan(\cos\sin(x^3))}$;

then $f(-x) = e^{\log\tan\cos(\sin(-x)^3))} = e^{\log\tan(\cos(-\sin x^3))}$

$= e^{\log\tan(\cos(\sin x^3))} = f(x)$

10. Any function $f(x)$ can always be written as sum of an even function and an odd function.

i.e., $f(x) = \underbrace{\frac{f(x)+f(-x)}{2}}_{even} + \underbrace{\frac{f(x)-f(-x)}{2}}_{odd}$;

provided its domain is symmetric about origin.

Proof: Let $g(x) = \frac{f(x)+f(-x)}{2}$, then $g(-x) = g(x)$, hence, $g(x)$ is an even function.

and let $h(x) = \frac{f(x)-f(-x)}{2}$, then $h(-x) = -h(x)$, hence, $h(x)$ is an odd function.

Thus, $f(x) = g(x) - h(x)$. where $g(x)$ is even and $h(x)$ is an odd function.

NOTE

Consider $f(x) = \frac{2}{1-\tan x}$. *Suppose that we express f(x) as* $\left(\frac{1}{1-\tan x} + \frac{1}{1+\tan x}\right) + \left(\frac{1}{1-\tan x} - \frac{1}{1+\tan x}\right)$, *then the domain of the new representation is* $\mathbb{R} - \{x: \tan x = \pm 1\}$, *which is different from that of f(x) which is* $\mathbb{R} - \{x: \tan x = 1\}$, *and hence, it is a function different from f(x). This difficulty appears because the domain of f is not symmetric about* $x = 0$. *Hence, we cannot express this function as a sum of an even and an odd function*

ILLUSTRATION 252: Express $f(x) = \sin x - \cos x$ as sum of even and odd functions.

SOLUTION: Here domain of f is obviously the set of real numbers, and hence, for each x, $(-x)$ is also in the domain.

Now we can write f as $f(x) = \frac{1}{2}\{f(x) + f(-x)\} + \frac{1}{2}\{f(x) - f(-x)\}$

$= \frac{1}{2}\{(\sin x - \cos x) + (\sin(-x) - \cos(-x))\} + \frac{1}{2}\{(\sin x - \cos x) - (\sin(-x) - \cos(-x))\}$

$= -\cos x + \sin x = h(x) + g(x)$

where $h(x) = -\cos x$ is an even function and $g(x) = \sin x$ is an odd function.

Note that we have followed the standard procedure to express f as a sum of even and odd functions. The same thing could also be done without this if one could sort out all even terms together and odd terms together separately.

ILLUSTRATION 253: Test whether the following functions are even or odd

(a) $f(x) = e^x + e^{-x}$ (b) $(\tan x^5)e^{x^3 \operatorname{sgn} x^7}$

SOLUTION: (a) Given $f(x) = e^x + e^{-x} \Rightarrow f(-x) = e^{-x} + e^{-(-x)} = e^{-x} + e^x \Rightarrow f(-x) = f(x)$;

This clearly shows that the given function is even.

(b) $f(x) = (\tan x^5)e^{x^3 \operatorname{sgn} x^7}$

Since $\tan x$ and x^5 are odd functions, therefore their composition is an odd function.

And x^3, *sgn x*, x^7 are all odd functions, therefore sgn x^7 is odd function and $x^3 \times sgn\ x^7$ is an even function. Finally, the given function becomes product of an odd function and even function, so it must be an odd function.

ILLUSTRATION 254: Examine whether the following functions are even, odd or none

(i) $f(x) = \begin{cases} x|x|; & \text{if } x \le -1 \\ [1+x]+[1-x]; & \text{if } -1 < x < 1 \\ -x|x|; & \text{if } x \ge 1 \end{cases}$

(ii) $f(x) = \dfrac{2x(\sin x + \tan x)}{2\left[\dfrac{x+19\pi}{\pi}\right]-37}$, where [ ] denotes greatest integer function

SOLUTION: (i) Given function is $f(x) = \begin{cases} x|x|; & \text{if } x \le -1 \\ [1+x]+[1-x]; & \text{if } -1 < x < 1 \\ -x|x|; & \text{if } x \ge 1 \end{cases}$, graphically shown below

$\Rightarrow f(-x) = \begin{cases} -(-x)|-x|; & \text{if } x \le -1 \\ [1-x]+[1+x]; & \text{if } -1 < x < 1 \\ (-x)|-x|; & \text{if } x \ge 1 \end{cases}$

$= \begin{cases} x|x|; & \text{if } x \le -1 \\ [1-x]+[1+x]; & \text{if } -1 < x < 1 = f(x) \\ (-x)|x| & \text{if } x \ge 1 \end{cases}$

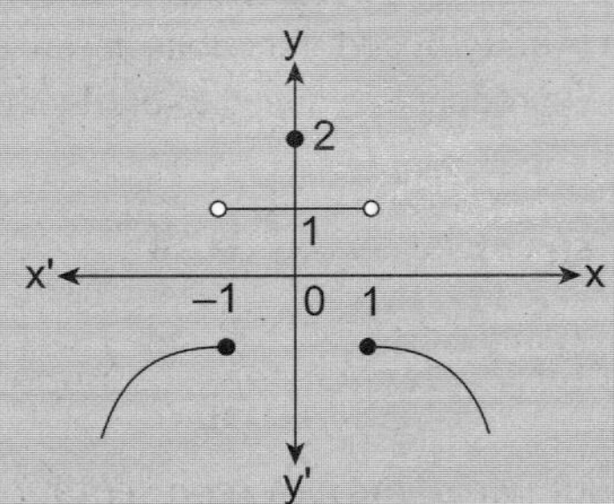

FIGURE 2.198

Hence, $f(x)$ is an even function

(ii) Given $f(x) = \dfrac{2x(\sin x + \tan x)}{2\left[\dfrac{x+19\pi}{\pi}\right]-37} = \dfrac{2x(\sin x + \tan x)}{2\left[\dfrac{x}{\pi}+19\right]-37}$

$\Rightarrow f(x) = \dfrac{2x(\sin x + \tan x)}{2\left[\dfrac{x}{\pi}\right]+1}$ ... (1)

$$\Rightarrow\ f(-x)=\frac{2(-x)[\sin(-x)+\tan(-x)]}{2\left[\frac{(-x)}{\pi}\right]+1}=\frac{2(x)[\sin(x)+\tan(x)]}{2\left[\frac{(-x)}{\pi}\right]+1}$$

Now, if $x = n\pi$, $n \in \mathbb{Z}$, then $f(x) = f(-x) = 0 \Rightarrow f(-n\pi) = -f(n\pi) = 0$

So, let $x \neq n\pi$, $n \in \mathbb{Z}$, then $-\frac{x}{\pi} \notin \mathbb{Z} \Rightarrow \left[\frac{-x}{\pi}\right]=-\left(1+\left[\frac{x}{\pi}\right]\right)$ ($\because [x]+[-x] = -1$ for $x \notin \mathbb{Z}$)

$$\Rightarrow\ f(-x)=\frac{2x(\sin x+\tan x)}{2\left\{-1-\left[\frac{x}{\pi}\right]\right\}+1}=\frac{2x(\sin x+\tan x)}{-1-2\left[\frac{x}{\pi}\right]}=-f(x)\ \Rightarrow\ f(x)\text{ is an odd function.}$$

ILLUSTRATION 255: If $f(x + y) = f(x) . f(y)$ and $f(0) \neq 0$, then prove that

(i) $g(x)=\frac{1-f(x)}{1+f(x)}$ is an odd function

(ii) $h(x)=\frac{1-f(x)+f^2(x)}{1+f(x)+f^2(x)}$ is an even function

SOLUTION: (i) Given function is $g(x)=\frac{1-f(x)}{1+f(x)}$ .... (1)

And $f(x + y) = f(x) . f(y)$ and $f(0) \neq 0$ .... (2)

Putting $x = y = 0$ in (2), we get $f(0) = (f(0))^2$

$\Rightarrow f(0) = 0$ or $f(0) = 1$

But given that $f(0) \neq 0$.

$\Rightarrow f(0) = 1$ .... (3)

Now putting $y = -x$ in (2); we get $f(x - x) = f(x) . f(-x)$

$\Rightarrow f(0) = f(x) . f(-x) \Rightarrow 1 = f(x) . f(-x) \Rightarrow f(-x)=\frac{1}{f(x)}$

Now from (1), we have $g(x)=\frac{1-f(x)}{1+f(x)}$

$$\Rightarrow\ g(-x)=\frac{1-f(-x)}{1+f(-x)}=\frac{1-1/f(x)}{1+(1/f(x))}=\frac{f(x)-1}{1+(f(x))}=-g(x)\ \Rightarrow\ g(x)\text{ is an odd function}$$

(ii) Given function is $h(x)=\frac{1-f(x)+f^2(x)}{1+f(x)+f^2(x)} \Rightarrow h(-x)=\frac{1-f(-x)+(f(-x))^2}{1+(f(-x))+(f(-x))^2}$

$$=\frac{1-\frac{1}{f(x)}+\frac{1}{(f(x))^2}}{1+\frac{1}{f(x)}+\frac{1}{(f(x))^2}}=\frac{(f(x))^2-f(x)+1}{(f(x))^2+f(x)+1}=h(x)\ \Rightarrow\ h(x)\text{ is an even function.}$$

■ EVEN AND ODD EXTENSION OF FUNCTION

If $f(x)$ is a function $f : [\alpha, \beta] \to B$ such that α and β are of same sign, then the domain of function can be extended and the function $f(x)$ can be redefined such that it becomes an even or odd function without having any change in the definition of f on $[\alpha, \beta]$.

Even Extension

Extending the domain of function $f(x)$ and redefining such that the function obtained is even.

i.e., $h(x)=\begin{cases} f(x); & \text{if } \alpha \le x \le \beta \\ f(-x); & \text{if } -\beta \le x \le -\alpha \end{cases}$

Clearly for $x \in [\alpha, \beta]$, $h(x) = f(x)$ and $-x \in [-\beta, -\alpha]$

$\Rightarrow\ h(-x) = f(x)$.

Thus, $h(-x) = h(x) = f(x)$ for $x \in [\alpha, \beta]$

Similarly for $x \in [-\beta, -\alpha]$, $h(x) = h(-x) = f(-x)$.

Thus, $h(x)$ defined above is an even function with domain $[-\beta, -\alpha] \cup [\alpha, \beta]$ called even extension of $f(x)$.

e.g., even extension of $f(x) = \begin{cases} \sqrt{x}; & \text{if } 0 \le x \le 1 \\ x; & \text{if } 1 < x \le 2 \end{cases}$ is

given by $h(x) = \begin{cases} -x; & -2 \le x < -1 \\ \sqrt{-x}; & -1 \le x \le 0 \\ \sqrt{x}; & 0 \le x \le 1 \\ x; & 1 < x \le 2 \end{cases}$

The graphical interpretation of such extension is that 'the graph of function $f(x)$ is extended by taking the mirror image of $f(x)$ in y-axis, i.e., image about y-axis'.

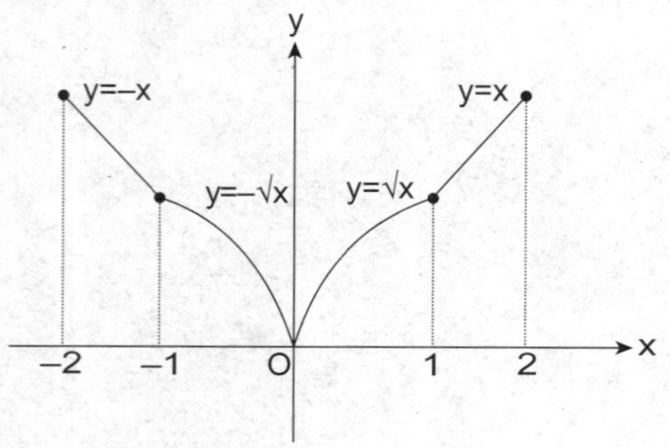

FIGURE 2.199

Odd Extension

Extending the domain of function and redefining it such that the new function obtained becomes odd.

i.e., $h(x) = \begin{cases} f(x); & \text{if } \alpha \le x \le \beta \\ -f(-x); & \text{if } -\beta \le x \le -\alpha \end{cases}$

Clearly for $x \in [\alpha, \beta]$, $h(x) = f(x)$ and $-x \in [-\beta, -\alpha]$

$\Rightarrow\ h(-x) = -f(x)$.

Thus, $h(-x) = -h(x) = -f(x)$ for $x \in [\alpha, \beta]$

Similarly for $x \in [-\beta, -\alpha]$, $h(-x) = -h(x) = -f(-x)$.

Thus, $h(x)$ defined above is an odd function with domain $[-\beta, -\alpha] \cup [\alpha, \beta]$ called odd extension of $f(x)$.

e.g., odd extension of $f(x) = \begin{cases} x^2; & 0 \le x \le 2 \\ 4; & 2 < x \le 4 \end{cases}$ is given

by $h(x) = \begin{cases} -4; & -4 \le x < -2 \\ -x^2; & -2 \le x \le 0 \\ x^2; & 0 \le x < 2 \\ 4; & 2 < x \le 4 \end{cases}$

The graphical interpretation of such extension is that 'the graph of function $f(x)$ is extended by taking the mirror image of $f(-x)$ in x-axis'.

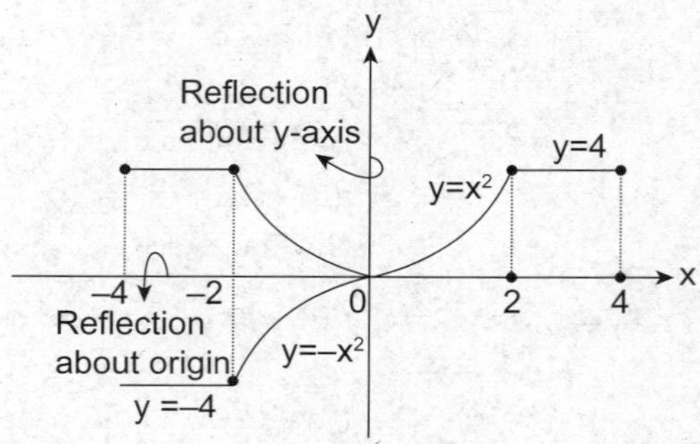

FIGURE 2.200

ILLUSTRATION 256: A function f defined for all real numbers is defined as follows $f(x) = \begin{cases} x; & \text{if } 0 \le x \le 1 \\ 1; & \text{if } x > 1 \end{cases}$

How f should be defined for $x \le 0$ so that

(a) f becomes an even function (b) f becomes an odd function

SOLUTION: (a) For making f an even function we need even extension of $f(x)$ given by $h(x) = \begin{cases} f(x); & \text{if } \alpha \le x \le \beta \\ f(-x); & \text{if } -\beta \le x \le -\alpha \end{cases}$

Thus, $h(x) = \begin{cases} x; & \text{if } 0 \le x \le 1 \\ 1; & \text{if } x > 1 \\ -x; & \text{if } -1 \le x < 0 \\ 1; & \text{if } x < -1 \end{cases}$

Thus, $f(x) = 1$ for $x < -1$ and $-x$ for $-1 \le x \le 0$

(b) For making f an odd function we need odd extension of $f(x)$ given by $h(x)=\begin{cases} f(x); & \text{if } \alpha \le x \le \beta \\ -f(-x); & \text{if } -\beta \le x \le -\alpha \end{cases}$

Thus, $h(x)=\begin{cases} x; & \text{if } 0 \le x \le 1 \\ 1; & \text{if } x > 1 \\ x; & \text{if } -1 \le x < 0 \\ -1; & \text{if } x < -1 \end{cases}$; Thus, $f(x) = -1$ for $x < -1$ and x for $-1 \le x \le 0$

ILLUSTRATION 257: Given $f(x)=\begin{cases} 1; & x \le -1 \\ -x; & -1 \le x \le 0 \end{cases}$

Find the odd and even extension of the function $f(x)$

SOLUTION: Even extension of $f(x)$ is given by $h(x)=\begin{cases} f(x); & \text{if } \alpha \le x \le \beta \\ f(-x); & \text{if } -\beta \le x \le -\alpha \end{cases}$

$$\therefore \quad h(x)=\begin{cases} 1; & x \le -1 \\ -x; & -1 \le x \le 0 \\ x; & 0 \le x \le 1 \\ 1; & 1 \le x < \infty \end{cases};$$

and odd extension of $f(x)$ is given by $h(x)=\begin{cases} f(x); & \text{if } \alpha \le x \le \beta \\ -f(-x); & \text{if } -\beta \le x \le -\alpha \end{cases}$

$$\therefore \quad h(x)=\begin{cases} 1; & x \le -1 \\ -x; & -1 \le x \le 0 \\ -x; & 0 \le x \le 1 \\ -1; & x \ge 1 \end{cases}$$

ILLUSTRATION 258: Write odd extension of the following functions:

(i) $\sin x + |\sin x|$; for $x \in [0, \infty)$ (ii) $\ln x - \dfrac{(\ln x)^2}{|\ln x|}$

SOLUTION: (i) Given $f(x) = \sin x + |\sin x|$; for $x \in [0, \infty)$

$$\Rightarrow \quad f(x)=\begin{cases} 2\sin x; & \text{if } \sin x \ge 0 \\ 0; & \text{if } \sin x < 0 \end{cases}; \text{ for } x \in [0, \infty)$$

$$\Rightarrow \text{ odd extension of function } f(x) = h(x) = \begin{cases} 2\sin x; & \text{if } \sin x \ge 0 & \text{for } x \ge 0 \\ 0; & \text{if } \sin x < 0 & \text{for } x \ge 0 \\ 2\sin x; & \text{if } \sin x \le 0 & \text{for } x \le 0 \\ 0; & \text{if } \sin x > 0 & \text{for } x \le 0 \end{cases}$$

$$= \begin{cases} 2\sin x; & \text{if } \sin x \ge 0 & \text{for } x \ge 0 \\ 0; & \text{if } \sin x < 0 & \text{for } x \ge 0 \\ \sin x - |\sin x|; & \text{if } \sin x \le 0 & \text{for } x \le 0 \\ \sin x - |\sin x|; & \text{if } \sin x > 0 & \text{for } x \le 0 \end{cases} = \begin{cases} \sin x + |\sin x|; & \text{if } x \ge 0 \\ \sin x - |\sin x|; & \text{if } x \le 0 \end{cases}$$

(ii) Given $y = \ln x - \dfrac{(\ln x)^2}{|\ln x|}$

$$\Rightarrow \quad y=\begin{cases} \ln x - \ln x; & \text{if } \ln x > 0 \\ 2\ln x; & \text{if } \ln x < 0 \end{cases} \qquad \Rightarrow \quad y=\begin{cases} 0; & \text{if } x > 1 \\ 2\ln x; & \text{if } 0 < x < 1 \end{cases}$$

$$\Rightarrow \text{ odd extension } = h(x) = \begin{cases} 0; & \text{if } x > 1 \\ 2\ln x; & \text{if } 0 < x < 1 \\ -2\ln(-x); & \text{if } -1 < x < 0 \\ 0; & \text{if } x < -1 \end{cases}$$

ILLUSTRATION 259: Let $f(x) = x^2 + 5x - 2$ defined on $A = [0, 2]$. Find even and odd extension of $f(x)$ in $[-2, 2]$.

SOLUTION: Given $f(x) = x^2 + 5x - 2$, $f(-x) = x^2 - 5x - 2$

Let g_e and f_o denote even and odd extension respectively.

$$\therefore \quad g_e(x) = \begin{cases} f(x); & x \in [0,2] \\ f(-x); & x \in [-2,0] \end{cases} \qquad [\because f(-x) = f(x) \text{ for even function } f(x)]$$

$$f_0(x) = \begin{cases} f(x); & x \in [0,2] \\ -f(-x); & x \in [-2,0] \end{cases} \qquad [\because f(-x) = f(x) \text{ for odd function } f(x)]$$

$$\therefore \quad g_e(x) = \begin{cases} x^2 + 5x - 2; & x \in [0,2] \\ x^2 - 5x - 2; & x \in [-2,0] \end{cases} \text{ and } f_0(x) = \begin{cases} x^2 + 5x - 2; & x \in [0,2] \\ -x^2 + 5x + 2; & x \in [-2,0] \end{cases}$$

ILLUSTRATION 260: If $f(x) = \begin{cases} x^3 + x^2; & \text{for } 0 \le x \le 2 \\ x + 2; & \text{for } 2 < x \le 4 \end{cases}$, then find the even and odd extension of the function $f(x)$:

SOLUTION: The even extension of $f(x)$ is given by $h(x) = \begin{cases} f(x); & \text{if } \alpha \le x \le \beta \\ f(-x); & \text{if } -\beta \le x \le -\alpha \end{cases}$

$$\text{as follows } g(x) = \begin{cases} x^3 + x^2; & \text{for } 0 \le x \le 2 \\ x + 2; & \text{for } 2 < x \le 4 \\ -x + 2; & \text{for } -4 \le x \le -2 \\ -x^3 + x^2; & \text{for } -2 \le x \le 0 \end{cases}$$

The odd extension of $f(x)$ is given by $h(x) = \begin{cases} f(x); & \text{if } \alpha \le x \le \beta \\ -f(-x); & \text{if } -\beta \le x \le -\alpha \end{cases}$

$$\text{as follows: } g(x) = \begin{cases} x^3 + x^2; & \text{for } 0 \le x \le 2 \\ x + 2; & \text{for } 2 < x \le 4 \\ x - 2; & \text{for } -4 \le x \le -2 \\ x^3 - x^2; & \text{for } -2 \le x \le 0 \end{cases}$$

TEXTUAL EXERCISE–15: (SUBJECTIVE)

1. Determine whether the following functions are even or odd or neither even nor odd:
   (i) $\tan x$
   (ii) $\cos x$
   (iii) $\sin (x^2 + 1)$
   (iv) $x + x^2$
   (v) $x - x^3$
   (vi) $f(x) = x\left(\dfrac{a^x - 1}{a^x + 1}\right)$
   (vii) $f(x) = \log\left(x + \sqrt{x^2 + 1}\right)$
   (viii) $f(x) = \sin x + \cos x$
   (ix) $f(x) = (x^2 - 1)\,|\,x\,|$

2. Check whether the following functions $f(x)$ are even/odd or neither:

(a) $2^{x^2-x^4}$

(b) $\sin x + \cos x$

(c) $x^2 - |x|$

(d) $\dfrac{x}{2^x-1}+\dfrac{x}{2}+1$

(e) $x^{10}.\log\dfrac{1+\sin x}{1-\sin x}$

(f) $|f(x)| + 1$; $f(x)$ is an odd function

(g) $\dfrac{(1+2^x)^9}{2^x}$

(h) $\sqrt{1+x+x^2}-\sqrt{1-x+x^2}$

(i) $\phi(x) = [f(x) + f(-x)]\,[g(x) - g(-x)]$

(j) $f(x)=\dfrac{\sec x+x^2-9}{x\sin x}$

3. Determine whether the function $f(x) = (-1)^{[x]}$ is even, odd or neither of the two.

4. Let $\begin{cases}4; & \text{if } x<-1\\ -4x; & \text{if } -1\le x\le 0\end{cases}$. If $f(x)$ is an even function in $\mathbb{R}$, then find the definition of $f(x)$ in $(0, \infty)$.

5. Prove that function $f(x)$ satisfying the property $f(x + y) + f(x - y) = 2f(x).f(y)$ is an even function.

6. If $f(x)$ is a real valued function, satisfying $f(x + y) + f(x - y) = 2f(x).f(y)\ \forall\ x, y \in \mathbb{R}$. Then prove that the function $f(x)$ is odd if $f(0) = 0$ and even if $f(0) = 1$.

7. Prove that $f(x)=\dfrac{2x(\sin x+\tan x)}{2\left[\dfrac{x+21\pi}{\pi}\right]-41}$ is an odd function.

8. Test whether $f(x)$ is even or odd or neither even nor odd, $f(x)=\sqrt{\cos x}$ if $x\in\left[-\dfrac{\pi}{2},\dfrac{\pi}{2}\right]$ and $\sqrt{-\cos x}$ for $x\in\left[\dfrac{\pi}{2},\dfrac{3\pi}{2}\right]$.

9. If $f : [-20, 20] \to \mathbb{R}$ defined by $f(x)=\left[\dfrac{x^2}{a}\right]\sin x+\cos x$, is an even function, then find the set of values of a.
(where [.] denotes greatest integral function)

10. A function defined for all real numbers, is defined for $x > 0$ as follows:
$f(x)=\begin{cases}x|x|, & 0\le x<1\\ 2x, & x\ge 1\end{cases}$, how should f be defined for $x < 0$? if
(i) f is an even function
(ii) f is an odd function

11. If $f(x)=\begin{cases}x^2+1; & \text{if } 0<x\le 1\\ x+1; & \text{if } 1<x\le 2\end{cases}$. Find even and odd extension of $f(x)$.

12. Extend $f(x) = x^2 - x$ defined in [0, 3] onto the interval [–3, 3] so that the extended function becomes
(i) an even function
(ii) an odd function.

13. If $f(x)=\begin{cases}x^2+\sin x; & \text{if } 0\le x<1\\ x+e^{-x}; & \text{if } x\ge 1\end{cases}$, then extend the definition of $f(x)$ for $x \in (-\infty, 0)$ such that $f(x)$ becomes
(i) an even function
(ii) an odd function

Answer Keys

1. (i) odd, (ii) even (iii) even (iv) neither even nor odd
(v) odd (vi) even (vii) odd (viii) neither even nor odd
(ix) even

2. Even: (a), (c), (f), (j); Odd: (e), (h), (i); Neither: (b) , (d), (g)

3. f is an even function when $x \in \mathbb{Z}$ and odd function when $x \notin \mathbb{Z}$

4. $f(x)=\begin{cases}4x; & \text{if } 0\le x\le 1\\ 4; & \text{if } x>1\end{cases}$

8. Neither even nor odd

9. $a\in(400,\infty)$

10. (i) $\begin{cases} x|x|; & \text{if } 0 \le x < 1 \\ 2x; & \text{if } x \ge 1 \\ -2x; & \text{if } x \le -1 \\ -x|x|; & \text{if } -1 < x \le 0 \end{cases}$ (ii) $\begin{cases} x|x|; & \text{if } 0 \le x < 1 \\ 2x; & \text{if } x \ge 1 \\ 2x; & \text{if } x \le -1 \\ x|x|; & \text{if } -1 < x \le 0 \end{cases}$

11. Even extension $= \begin{cases} x^2+1; & \text{if } 0 < x \le 1 \\ x+1; & \text{if } 1 < x \le 2 \\ x^2+1; & \text{if } -1 \le x < 0 \\ -x+1; & \text{if } -2 \le x < -1 \end{cases}$ and odd extension $= \begin{cases} x^2+1; & \text{if } 0 < x \le 1 \\ x+1; & \text{if } 1 < x \le 2 \\ -x^2-1; & \text{if } -1 \le x < 0 \\ x-1; & \text{if } -2 \le x < -1 \end{cases}$

12. (i) $\begin{cases} x^2+x; & \text{if } [0,3] \\ x^2-x; & \text{if } -3 \le x < 0 \end{cases}$ (ii) $\begin{cases} x^2+x; & \text{if } [0,3] \\ -x^2+x; & \text{if } -3 \le x < 0 \end{cases}$

13. (i) $h(x) = \begin{cases} x^2+\sin x; & \text{if } 0 \le x < 1 \\ x+e^{-x}; & \text{if } x \ge 1 \\ x^2-\sin x; & \text{if } -1 < x \le 0 \\ -x+e^{x}; & \text{if } x \le -1 \end{cases}$ (ii) $h(x) = \begin{cases} x^2+\sin x; & \text{if } 0 \le x < 1 \\ x+e^{-x}; & \text{if } x \ge 1 \\ -x^2+\sin x; & \text{if } -1 < x \le 0 \\ x-e^{x}; & \text{if } x \le -1 \end{cases}$

TEXTUAL EXERCISE–15: (OBJECTIVE)

1. Match the functions of column I with column II to correctly define their nature:

Column I

(i) $\dfrac{1-x}{1+x}$

(ii) $\dfrac{e^x-e^{-x}}{e^x+e^{-x}}$

(iii) sin (sin x)

(iv) sin (cos x)

(v) cos (cos x)

(vi) $\dfrac{\sin^4 x+\cos^4 x}{x+x^2\tan x}$

(vii) $x^{17}\left(\dfrac{a^{\sin x}-1}{a^{\sin x}+1}\right)$

Column II

(a) an odd function

(b) an even function

(c) neither odd nor even

(d) cannot be said

Which of the following represents the correct match for column I and column II?

	(i)	(ii)	(iii)	(iv)	(v)	(vi)	(vii)
(a)	C	A	A	B	B	A	B
(b)	A	A	C	B	B	A	C
(c)	C	A	A	B	B	B	C
(d)	C	A	B	A	A	B	A

2. Match the functions of column I with column II to correctly define their nature.

Column I

(i) $x^2\sin\left\{\dfrac{1}{\sin(1/x)}\right\}$

(ii) $\cos x.\log\dfrac{1+\tan x}{1-\tan x}$

(iii) $\left(\dfrac{a^{2x}+1}{a^x}\right)$

(iv) $\dfrac{(1+e^x)^2}{e^x}$

(v) $\sqrt[3]{1+x+x^2}+\sqrt[3]{1-x+x^2}$

(vi) $\sqrt{1+2x+3x^2}-\sqrt{1-2x+3x^2}$

Column II

(a) an odd function
(b) an even function
(c) neither odd nor even
(d) cannot be said

Which of the following represent the correct match for column I and column II?

	(i)	(ii)	(iii)	(iv)	(v)	(vi)
(a)	A	A	B	A	A	B
(b)	A	B	A	B	A	B
(c)	A	A	B	B	B	A
(d)	A	C	D	B	B	A

3. Which of the following functions is/are even?
(a) $f(x) = \ln |x|$
(b) $f(x) = \sin^{-1}\left(\dfrac{2x}{1+x^2}\right)$
(c) $f(x) = x\left(\dfrac{a^x - 1}{a^x + 1}\right)$
(d) $f(x) = \sin\left[\log\left(x + \sqrt{x^2+1}\right)\right]$

4. Which of the following functions is/are odd?
(a) $sgn\, x + x^{2000}$ (b) $|x| - \tan x$
(c) $x^3 \cot x$ (d) $\operatorname{cosec} x^{55}$

5. The function $f(x) = \sec\left[\log\left(x + \sqrt{1+x^2}\right)\right]$ is
(a) odd
(b) even
(c) neither odd nor even
(d) constant

6. The function $f(x) = \sin\left(\tan\left(\log\left(x + \sqrt{x^2+1}\right)\right)\right)$ is
(a) an even function
(b) an odd function
(c) a periodic function
(d) neither an even nor an odd function

7. Let $f(x) = \begin{cases} 0; & \text{for } x = 0 \\ x^2 \sin\left(\dfrac{\pi}{x}\right); & \text{for } -1 < x < 1\ (x \neq 0) \\ x|x|; & \text{for } x > 1 \text{ or } x < -1 \end{cases}$ then:
(a) $f(x)$ is an odd function
(b) $f(x)$ is an even function
(c) $f(x)$ is neither odd nor even
(d) $f'(x)$ is an even function

8. If $f(x) = 2x^6 + 3x^4 + 4x^2 + 7$, then $f'(x)$ is
(a) even function
(b) an odd function
(c) neither even nor odd
(d) None of these

9. On the interval [0, 1], $f(x)$ is defined as, $f(x) = \begin{cases} x; & \text{if } x \in \mathbb{Q} \\ 1-x; & \text{if } x \notin \mathbb{Q} \end{cases}$. Then for all $x \in \mathbb{R}$ the composite function $f(f(x))$ is:
(a) a constant function
(b) an identity function
(c) an odd linear polynomial
(d) $1 + x$

10. Let $f(x) = \begin{cases} 0; & \text{if } x \text{ is rational} \\ x; & \text{if } x \text{ is irrational} \end{cases}$ and $g(x) = \begin{cases} 0; & \text{if } x \text{ is irrational} \\ x; & \text{if } x \text{ is rational} \end{cases}$; then the function $(f - g)\, x$ is
(a) odd
(b) even
(c) neither odd nor even
(d) odd as well as even

11. If $f(x)$ is an odd function, then:
(a) $\dfrac{f(-x) + f(x)}{2}$ is an even function
(b) $\dfrac{f(x) - f(-x)}{2}$ is neither even nor odd
(c) $[\,|f(x)| + 1]$ is even; where $[x]$ = the greatest integer $\leq x$
(d) None of these

12. If $f(x) = a^{\sin x^3 \operatorname{sgn} x^9} (\tan^3 x)$; $a > 1$ is
(a) an odd function
(b) an even function
(c) neither even nor odd function
(d) None of these

13. If $f(x) = (a - x^n)^{1/n}$; $n \in \mathbb{N}$, then $f(f(x))$ is
(a) an even function
(b) an odd function
(c) neither even nor odd
(d) even as well as odd

14. If $f(x)$ is an even function and $f'(x)$ exists, then $f'(e) + f'(-e)$ is $(e \in \mathbb{R})$
(a) > 0 (b) $= 0$
(c) ≥ 0 (d) < 0

15. A function $f(x)$ not identically zero satisfy the functional equation $f(x + y) = f(x) + f(y)$, then the function $g(x) = a^{f(x)} + a^{-f(x)}$; $a > 1$ is
(a) odd function
(b) even function

(c) neither even nor odd
(d) even as well as odd

16. If $g(f(x)) = |\sin x|$ and $f(g(x)) = (\sin\sqrt{x})^2$; then
(a) $f(x)$ is even and $g(x)$ is odd
(b) $f(x)$ is odd and $g(x)$ is even
(c) $f(x)$ is even and $g(x)$ is neither even nor odd
(d) $f(x)$ is odd and $g(x)$ is neither even nor even.

17. Let $f(x)=x^3-x^2+\sin^{-1}\left(\frac{2-|x|}{3}\right)+\log(|x|+1)$, $0 \le x \le 2$, then odd extension of $f(x)$ in [–2, 2] is:
(a) $x^3-x^2-\sin^{-1}\left(\frac{2-|x|}{3}\right)-\log(|x|+1)$
(b) $x^3-x^2+\sin^{-1}\left(\frac{2-|x|}{3}\right)+\log(|x|+1)$
(c) $x^3+x^2-\sin^{-1}\left(\frac{2-|x|}{3}\right)-\log(|x|+1)$
(d) None of these

18. If $f(x) = \sin^2 x + \sin^2\left(x+\frac{\pi}{3}\right) + \cos x \cdot \cos\left(x+\frac{\pi}{3}\right)$, then $f(x)$ is
(a) an even function
(d) an odd function
(c) neither even nor odd
(d) even as well as odd

Answer Keys

1. (a)	**2.** (c)	**3.** (a, c)	**4.** (d)	**5.** (b)	**6.** (b)	**7.** (a, d)	**8.** (b)	**9.** (b, c)	**10.** (a)
11. (c)	**12.** (a)	**13.** (b)	**14.** (b)	**15.** (b)	**16.** (c)	**17.** (c)	**18.** (a)		

■ PERIODIC FUNCTIONS

In our day to day life we usually come across many man made and natural phenomenon-that repeatedly occur after a regular interval of time. For instance, rotation of planets around sun, position of needle of the clock etc. In mathematics the periodicity of functions has same notion as above, except the fact that here it can be observed with respect to any variable. Periodic functions are those who repeat their values after regular interval of values of independent variable in the entire domain. When we observe the graph of periodic functions, indeed we notice that the graph can be constructed by choosing its particular smallest periodic segment and repeating it throughout the domain. The length of such smallest periodic segment (along domain axis) is known as Fundamental Period of the function. e.g., observe the graph of $y = \{x\}$ (fraction part function), the graph can well be constructed by constructing it in an interval of 'one unit length' (say from zero to one) and repeating the same. Thus, making it very clear that we need a smallest segment (along domain axis, i.e., x-axis) of 'one unit length' to construct the entire graph.

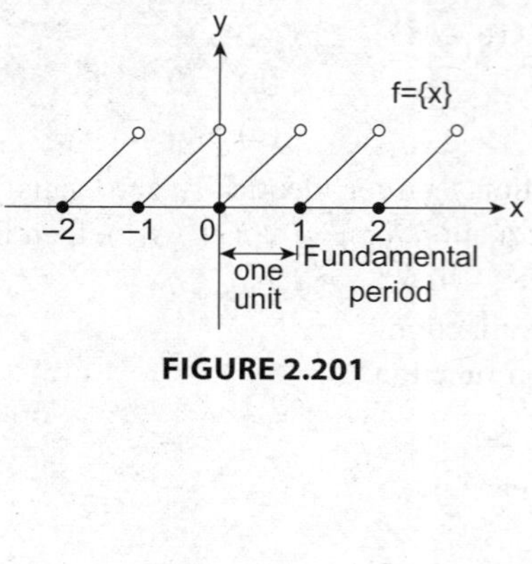

FIGURE 2.201

Observation of periodic symmetry adds further convenience in the analysis of functions due to the fact that it can be analyzed for an interval spread over one period (of length T) anywhere in its domain, as the same analysis prevails in all periods throughout their domain.

Definition of Periodic Function

A function $f(x)$ is said to be a periodic function if there exists a real positive and finite constant T independent of x such that $f(x+T) = f(x)$, $\forall\, x \in D_f$ provided, $(x+T) \in D_f$(domain). Since ... $=f(x-2T)=f(x-T)=f(x)=f(x+T)=f(x+2T)=$ ... Therefore, we conclude $f(x) = f(x+nT)$ $\forall\, n \in \mathbb{Z}$, for which $x + nT \in D_f$. Consequently if a positive constant T is period, then any natural multiple of T within the domain shall also be its period, thus, making it (period) a non-unique quantity.

The least positive value of such T (if exists), is called the *period/principal period or fundamental period* of $f(x)$. e.g., $f(x) = \tan x$, $f(x) = \sin x$ are periodic functions with period π and 2π, respectively.

The functions which are non-periodic are called as non-periodic functions.

Test of Periodicity

In order to test the periodicity of $f(x)$ put $f(x+T) = f(x)$ for all x and find all possible values of T independent of x. If no positive value of T independent of x is possible, then $f(x)$ is said to be aperiodic or non-periodic. If positive value of T independent of x is possible, then $f(x)$ is said to be periodic function and the fundamental period of $f(x)$ will be the least positive value of T.

ILLUSTRATION 261: Test the periodicity of the following functions and if periodic, find their fundamental period.

(a) $f(x) = a\cos(2x + c), a \neq 0$ **(b)** $f(x) = \sin\sqrt{x}$

(c) $f(x) = x - \cos x$ **(d)** $f(x) = \tan\left(\frac{\pi x}{3}\right)$

SOLUTION: As we check periodicity by applying the definition of periodic function, assuming its period to be T and subsequently analysing equation $f(x + T) = f(x)$

(a) Given $f(x) = a\cos(2x + c)$ and $f(x) = f(x + T)$

$\Rightarrow a\cos(2(x + T) + c) = a\cos(2x + c) \Rightarrow \cos(2(x + T) + c) - \cos(2x + c) = 0$

$$\Rightarrow 2\sin\left(\frac{2(2x+T)+2c}{2}\right)\sin\left(\frac{2(-T)}{2}\right) = 0 \Rightarrow \sin(T) = 0 \text{ or } \sin\left(2\left(x+\frac{T}{2}\right)+c\right) = 0$$

$\Rightarrow T = n\pi$ or $2x + T + c = n\pi;\ n \in \mathbb{Z}$

$\Rightarrow T = n\pi$ or $T = n\pi - 2x - c$ (rejected, as depends on x)

$\therefore\ T = n\pi\ ; n \in \mathbb{Z}$, which is constant ($\because T > 0$) $\Rightarrow T_{min} = \pi$ (fundamental period)

Therefore $f(x) = a\cos(2x + c)$ is periodic function with fundamental period π.

(b) Consider $f(x) = \sin\sqrt{x}$ be periodic with period T.

$\Rightarrow f(x) = f(x + T)$ i.e, $\sin\sqrt{(x+T)} = \sin\sqrt{x} \Rightarrow \sin\sqrt{x+T} - \sin\sqrt{x} = 0$

$$\Rightarrow 2\cos\left(\frac{\sqrt{x+T}+\sqrt{x}}{2}\right)\sin\left(\frac{\sqrt{x+T}-\sqrt{x}}{2}\right) = 0$$

$$\Rightarrow \left(\frac{\sqrt{x+T}+\sqrt{x}}{2}\right) = \frac{(2n+1)\pi}{2}, \text{ or } \left(\frac{\sqrt{x+T}-\sqrt{x}}{2}\right) = n\pi\ ;\ n \in \mathbb{Z}$$

$\Rightarrow \sqrt{x+T} + \sqrt{x} = (2n+1)\pi$, or $\sqrt{x+T} - \sqrt{x} = 2n\pi$

Therefore, T can never be made independent of x, consequently $f(x)$ is a non-periodic function.

Aliter: $\sin\sqrt{(x+T)} = \sin\sqrt{x} \Rightarrow \sqrt{(x+T)} = n\pi + (-1)^n\sqrt{x},\quad n \in \mathbb{Z}$

Squaring both sides and solving for T, we have $(x + T) = (n\pi + (-1)^n\sqrt{x})^2$

$\Rightarrow T = (n\pi + (-1)^n\sqrt{x})^2 - x$

On expanding the right hand side, we observe that the expression of T is not independent of x.

Hence, our assumption is false and therefore the given function is not a periodic function

(c) Consider $f(x) = x - \cos x$ be periodic with period T.

$\Rightarrow f(x) = f(x + T)$, i.e., $(x + T) - \cos(x + T) = x - \cos x$

$$\Rightarrow \cos(x+T) - \cos x = T \Rightarrow -2\sin\left(x+\frac{T}{2}\right)\sin\left(\frac{T}{2}\right) = T$$

Therefore, T can never be made independent of x, consequently $f(x)$ is a non-periodic function.

(d) Let $f(x) = \tan\left(\frac{\pi x}{3}\right)$ be periodic with period T.

$\Rightarrow f(x) = f(x + T) \Rightarrow \tan\left(\frac{\pi}{3}(x+T)\right) = \tan\frac{\pi x}{3}$

$$\Rightarrow \sin\frac{\pi}{3}(x+T)\cos\frac{\pi x}{3} - \cos\left(\frac{\pi}{3}(x+T)\right)\sin\frac{\pi x}{3} = 0$$

$$\Rightarrow \sin\left(\frac{\pi x}{3}+\frac{\pi T}{3}-\frac{\pi x}{3}\right) = 0 \Rightarrow \sin\left(\frac{\pi T}{3}\right) = 0 \Rightarrow \frac{\pi T}{3} = n\pi\ ;\ n \in \mathbb{Z} \Rightarrow T = 3n\ ;\ n \in \mathbb{Z}$$

Hence, $f(x)$ is a periodic function and minimum positive integer value of T, i.e., $T_{min} = 3$

Consequently fundamental period of $\tan\frac{\pi x}{3}$ is 3.

ILLUSTRATION 262: Prove that $\cos\left(\frac{1}{x}\right)$, $(x \neq 0)$ is a non-periodic function

SOLUTION: Let us assume that the function $f(x) = \cos\left(\frac{1}{x}\right)$ be periodic with periodic T, $T > 0$

$\therefore\ f(x + T) = f(x)\ \forall\ x \neq 0$

$$\Rightarrow \cos\left(\frac{1}{x+T}\right) = \cos\left(\frac{1}{x}\right) \Rightarrow \frac{1}{x+T} = 2n\pi \pm \frac{1}{x} \quad \text{... (1)}$$

Equation (1) is true for every non-zero real number. In particular, it is true for $x = T$ and $x = 2T$.

$\therefore$ Putting $x = T$ and $x = 2T$ in (1), we get $\frac{1}{2T} = 2n\pi \pm \frac{1}{T}$ ... (2)

And $\left(\frac{1}{3T}\right) = 2n\pi \pm \frac{1}{2T}$ ... (3)

Subtracting (3) from (2), we get $\frac{1}{6T} = \pm\frac{1}{2T}$ or $\frac{1}{3} = \pm 1$ which is impossible

Hence, $\cos\left(\frac{1}{x}\right)$ is a non-periodic function.

ILLUSTRATION 263: Determine whether the function $f(x) = x \sin x$ is periodic?

SOLUTION: To check periodicity, we apply the definition of the periodic functions.

Let us assume that the given function $f(x)$ is periodic with a period T $(T > 0)$, then according to the definition of the periodic functions, we have $f(x + T) = f(x)$.

$\Rightarrow (x + T) \sin (x + T) = x \sin x \Rightarrow T \sin(x + T) = x[\sin x - \sin (x + T)]$

Now, we observe that the left hand side is only a trigonometric function (apart from T, which is a constant), whereas right hand side is a product of an algebraic function and a trigonometric function.

Therefore, there is no algebraic function in x on the left which can cancel out x on the right. Thus, we conclude that T is not independent of x, and hence, our assumption is false and therefore, we conclude that the given function is not periodic.

■ SOME IMPORTANT FACTS

(a) Trigonometric Functions: The function $\sin x$, $\cos x$, $\sec x$, $\text{cosec}\, x$ are periodic with period 2π, whereas $\tan x$, $\cot x$ are periodic functions with period π.

(b) There may be Periodic Functions Which have No Fundamental Period, for example,

(i) Dirichlet Function:

$$f(x) = \begin{cases} 1, & \text{when } x \text{ is rational} \\ 0, & \text{when } x \text{ is irrational} \end{cases}$$

Let $\frac{p}{q}$: $p, q \in \mathbb{Z}$; co-prime to each other and $q \neq 0$ be period

$$\Rightarrow f\left(x + \frac{p}{q}\right) = \begin{cases} 1; & x + \frac{p}{q} \in \mathbb{Q} \\ 0; & x + \frac{p}{q} \notin \mathbb{Q} \end{cases}$$

$$\Rightarrow f\left(x + \frac{p}{q}\right) = \begin{cases} 1; & x \in \mathbb{Q} \\ 0; & x \notin \mathbb{Q} \end{cases} = f(x)$$

$\Rightarrow f(x)$ is periodic with period $\frac{p}{q}$ but has no fundamental period, as it is impossible to find a least positive rational number p/q.

(ii) Constant Function: Consider a function $f(x) = c$

Clearly $f(x + T) = f(x) = c$ holds good for all positive values of T. Therefore fulfilling the requirement of periodic function. Although any positive real number may be taken as period of constant function but indeed no such least real number can be predicted. Thus, constant function has no fundamental period.

(c) No Rational Function (except constant function) Can be a Periodic Function.

Let $F(x) = \dfrac{f(x)}{g(x)}$; where $f(x)$ and $g(x)$ are two polynomials and $g(x) \neq 0$ and $F(x)$ be periodic with period T.

$\Rightarrow F(x) = F(x + T)$ ... (1)

$\Rightarrow \dfrac{f(x+T)}{g(x+T)} = \dfrac{f(x)}{g(x)}$

$\Rightarrow f(x + T).g(x) - g(x - T)f(x) = 0$ is an identity in x therefore substituting $x = 0$, we obtain

$f(T)g(0) - g(T)f(0) = 0$ .... (2)

It is clearly a polynomial in T of degree n (here n is degree of the polynomial having larger degree out of f and g).

Now since equation (2) has degree n but can had $(n + 1)$ roots for instance $0, T, 2T, 3T, \ldots nT$.

Consequently, by fundamental theorem of algebra, $f(x)$ must be identically equal to $0\ \forall\ x \in \mathbb{R}$.

Therefore, $F(x)$ must be indeed a constant function.

(d) Algebraic Function (Except Constant Function) Can Not be a Periodic Function.

(e) A Function Can be Periodic in a Bounded Subset of Its Natural Domain.

We can discuss the periodicity of a function in an interval. For instance $f(x) = \begin{cases} \cos\sqrt{-x}; & x < 0 \\ \cos \pi x; & 0 \leq x \leq 100 \\ 101 - x; & x > 100 \end{cases}$

Is not a periodic function in its natural domain but it is clearly a periodic function in the interval [0, 98]

Because $f(x + 2) = f(x)$ holds good for all $x \in [0, 98]$.

ILLUSTRATION 264: Draw the graph of $f(x)$ defined as below in the domain [–3, 9]

$$f(x) = \begin{cases} x - 3n; & \text{if } 3n \leq x \leq 3n+1 \\ 1; & \text{if } 3n+1 \leq x \leq 3n+2 \\ 3(n+1) - x; & \text{if } 3n+2 \leq x \leq 3(n+1) \end{cases}$$ and state whether the function $f(x)$ is periodic?

If so, mention its domain of periodicity.

SOLUTION: Consider the graph of function $f(x)$ in the interval [–3, 9]

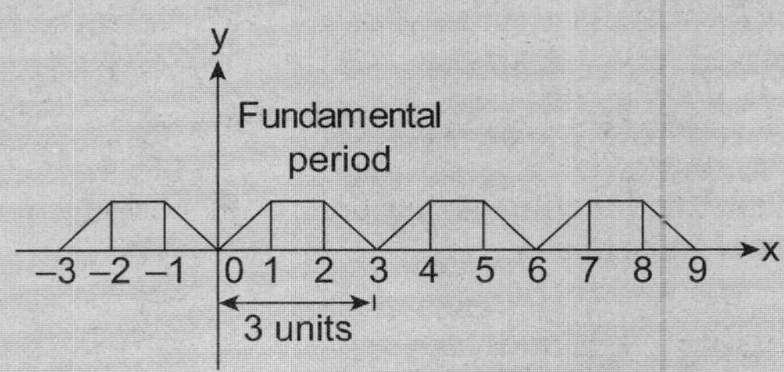

FIGURE 2.202

Clearly $f(x + 3) = f(x)$ holds $\forall\ x \in [-3, 9]$ for which $x + 3 \in [-3, 9]$.

Therefore, $f(x)$ is periodic with fundamental period 3 in the interval [–3, 6].

ILLUSTRATION 265: Let f be an even and periodic function with fundamental period 10 units and the graph of $f(x)$ is shown below for the interval [0, 5]

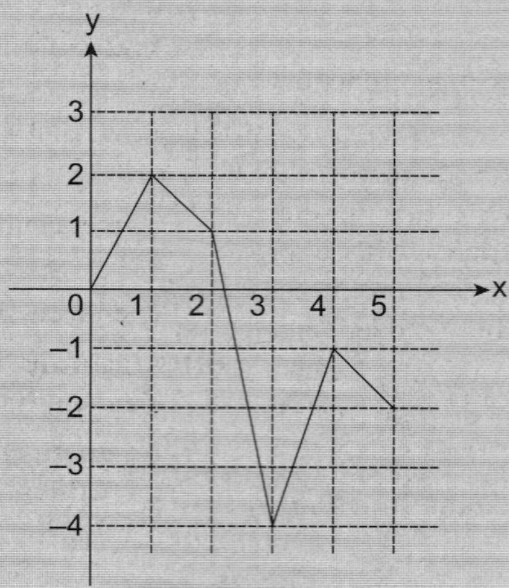

FIGURE 2.203

If [.], ⌈ ⌉ and { } represents the greatest integer/least integer/fractional part function of x; then find the value of $f\left(\frac{3}{4}\right)+3\left[f\left(\frac{-13}{2}\right)\right]+\left\{f\left(\frac{21}{4}\right)\right\}-5\left\lceil f\left(\frac{31}{2}\right)\right\rceil+\cos^{-1}\left(f\left(\frac{-1}{2}\right)\right)+\{f(-273)\}$

SOLUTION: From the graph; we can write the definition of the function for $x \in [0, 5]$

$$f(x)=\begin{cases} 2x; & \forall x \in [0,1] \\ 3-x; & \forall x \in (1,2] \\ 11-5x; & \forall x \in (2,3] \\ 3x-13; & \forall x \in (3,4] \\ 3-x; & \forall x \in (4,5] \end{cases}$$

Now given that the function is even; we can also find the function for $x \in [-5, 0)$

$$f(x)=\begin{cases} -2x; & \forall x \in [-1,0) \\ 3+x; & \forall x \in [-2,-1) \\ 11+5x; & \forall x \in [-3,-2) \\ -3x-13; & \forall x \in [-4,-3) \\ 3+x; & \forall x \in [-5,-4) \end{cases}$$

And given that the function is periodic with period equal to 10; hence, we can find the value of $f(x)\ \forall\ x \in \mathbb{R}$.

Now $f\left(\frac{3}{4}\right)=2\left(\frac{3}{4}\right)=\frac{3}{2}$ and

$$f\left(\frac{-13}{2}\right)=f\left(\frac{-13}{2}+10\right)=f\left(\frac{7}{2}\right)=3\left(\frac{7}{2}\right)-13=\frac{21}{2}-13=\frac{21-26}{2}=-\frac{5}{2}$$

$$\Rightarrow\ 3\left[f\left(\frac{-13}{2}\right)\right]=3\times(-3)=-9$$

And $f\left(\frac{21}{4}\right)=f\left(\frac{21}{4}-10\right) = f\left(\frac{-19}{4}\right)=f\left(\frac{19}{4}\right)=3-\left(\frac{19}{4}\right)=-\frac{7}{4}$

$\Rightarrow \left\{f\left(\frac{21}{4}\right)\right\}=\left\{\frac{-7}{4}\right\}=\left\{-2+\frac{1}{4}\right\}=\left\{\frac{1}{4}\right\}=\frac{1}{4}$

And $f\left(\frac{31}{2}\right)=f\left(10+\frac{11}{2}\right)=f\left(\frac{11}{2}\right) = f\left(\frac{-9}{2}\right)=f\left(\frac{9}{2}\right)=3-\frac{9}{2}=\frac{-3}{2}$

$\Rightarrow -5\left[f\left(\frac{31}{2}\right)\right]=-5\left[-\frac{3}{2}\right]=-5(-1)=5$ And $\cos^{-1}\left(f\left(\frac{-1}{2}\right)\right)=\cos^{-1}\left(f\left(\frac{1}{2}\right)\right)=\cos^{-1}1=0$

And $f(-273) = f(-270-3) = f(-3) = f(3) = -4$

$\Rightarrow \{f(-273)\} = \{-4\} = 0$

Hence, $f\left(\frac{3}{4}\right)+3\left[f\left(\frac{-13}{2}\right)\right]+\left\{f\left(\frac{21}{4}\right)\right\} - 5\left[f\left(\frac{31}{2}\right)\right]+\cos^{-1}\left(f\left(\frac{-1}{2}\right)\right)+\{f(-273)\}$

$=\left(\frac{3}{2}\right)+(-9)+\frac{1}{4}+5+0+0 = -4+\frac{3}{2}+\frac{1}{4}=\frac{-16+6+1}{4}=-\frac{9}{4}$

ILLUSTRATION 266: Using graphs, find whether the following functions are periodic, if so find the period:

(a) $y=\frac{\sin 2x}{|\sin x|}$ (b) $y = \tan x$ cct x

SOLUTION: (a) $y=\frac{\sin 2x}{|\sin x|}=\begin{cases} 2\cos x; & \sin x>0 \\ -2\cos x; & \sin x<0 \end{cases}$

Consider for $x \in (0, 2\pi) \sim \{\pi\}$; we have $y=\begin{cases} 2\cos x; & x\in(0,\pi) \\ -2\cos x; & x\in(\pi,2\pi) \end{cases}$

$\therefore$ The graph of $y=\frac{\sin 2x}{|\sin x|}$ is given by

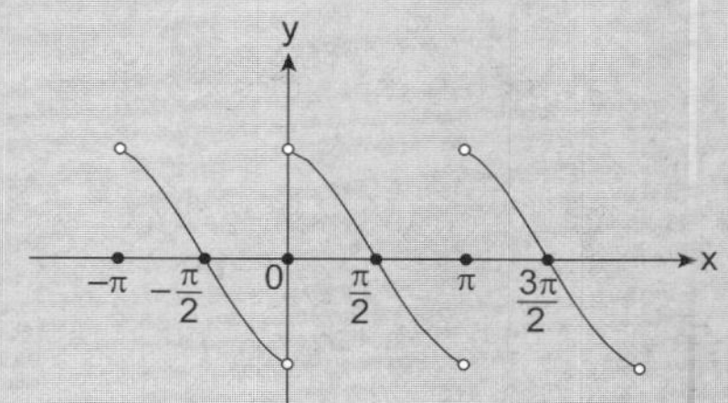

FIGURE 2.204

From the graph, we can see that the function is periodic with period $T = \pi$.

(b) $y = \tan x \,.\, \cot x \Rightarrow y = 1; x \neq \frac{n\pi}{2}$ $\therefore$ The graph of y is given below.

As is evident from the graph the period of $y = \tan x \,.\, \cot x$ is $T=\frac{\pi}{2}$

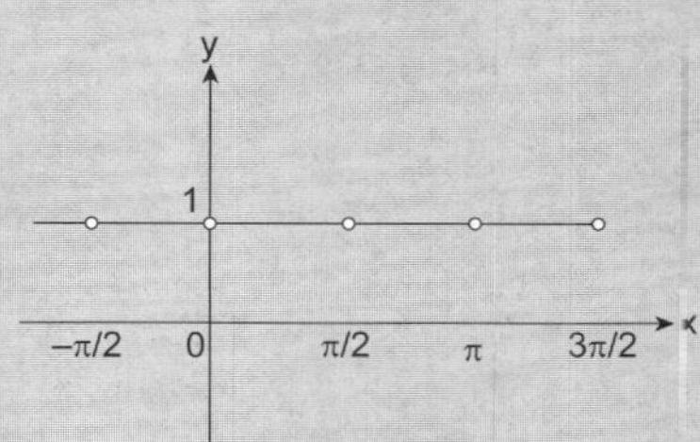

FIGURE 2.205

ILLUSTRATION 267: Check whether the function $f(x)$ defined as $f(x) = \sqrt{x-3k}$; where $3k \le x < 3(k+1)$, $k \in \mathbb{Z}$, is periodic or not.

SOLUTION: Given $f(x) = \sqrt{x-3k}$; where $3k \le x < 3(k+1)$, $k \in \mathbb{Z}$

Putting $k = 0$; we get $f(x) = \sqrt{x}$; $x \in [0, 3)$

Putting $k = 1$; we get $f(x) = \sqrt{x-3}$; $x \in [3, 6)$

Putting $k = 2$; we get $f(x) = \sqrt{x-6}$; $x \in [6, 9)$

Moving on the same pattern; we see that $f(x) = \begin{cases} \sqrt{x+3}; & x \in [-3, 0) \\ \sqrt{x}; & x \in [0, 3) \\ \sqrt{x-3}; & x \in [3, 6) \\ \sqrt{x-6}; & x \in [6, 9) \end{cases}$

$\therefore$ The graph of $f(x)$ is as shown below

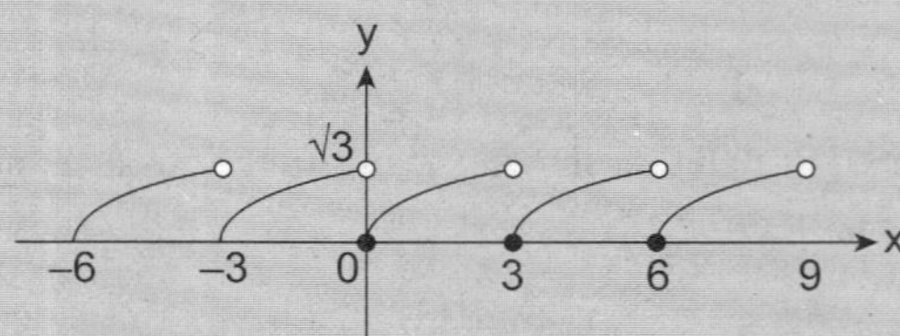

FIGURE 2.206

Now as is evident from the graph; the function is periodic with a period of $T = 3$.

ILLUSTRATION 268: Suppose that f is an even periodic function with period 2, and that $f(x) = -\sin^{-1}\sin\left(\frac{\pi x}{2}\right)$ for all x in the interval $[-1, 0]$. Find the value of $f\left(\frac{11}{3}\right)$.

SOLUTION: Given that $f(x)$ is an even function, therefore $f(x) = \sin^{-1}\sin\left(\frac{\pi x}{2}\right)$; $\forall\, x \in [0, 1]$,

$\therefore$ Graph of $f(x)$ is periodic with period 2 and is shown below

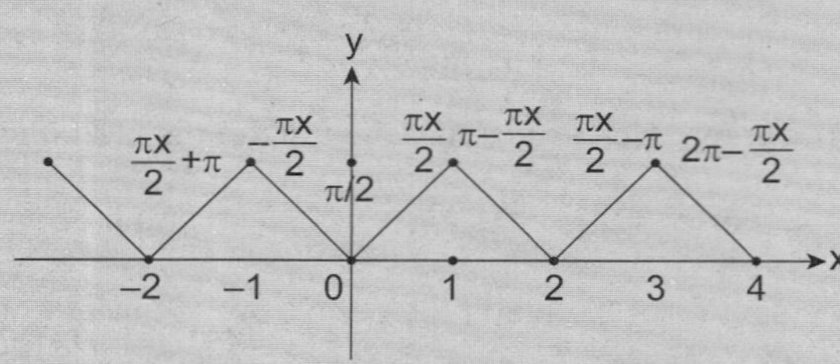

FIGURE 2.207

Now $f\left(\frac{11}{3}\right) = 2\pi - \frac{\pi}{2}\times\left(\frac{11}{3}\right) \Rightarrow f\left(\frac{11}{3}\right) = \frac{\pi}{6}$ $\left[\because 3 < \frac{11}{3} < 4 \text{ and } \forall x \in (3,4)\ \ f(x) = 2\pi - \frac{\pi}{2}x\right]$

PROPERTIES OF PERIODIC FUNCTION

(i) If $f(x)$ is periodic with period T, then $a\,f(x + k) + b$ is also periodic with same period T; where a, b are real constants and $a > 0$.

Proof: Let $g(x) = af(x + k) + b$

$\Rightarrow$ $g(x + T) = af(x + T + k) + b$ $\quad (\because f(x + T) = f(x))$

$= af(x + k) + b = g(x)$. Hence, proved.

Alternatively we may put the argument geometrically that by adding a constant (say k) to independent variable (input) the graph of function shifts as a whole horizontally either to the left or right without changing the shape and size of graph, therefore does not affect the periodicity of function.

Similarly, adding a constant to the dependent variable (output) the graph of function shifts as a whole vertically either up or to down without changing the shape and size of graph, thus, not affecting the periodicity of the function. And also it is true that the periodicity of the function is repetition of values of function after a regular interval of inputs x, therefore remains unaffected by transformations in vertical directions along y-axis.

For example, vertical stretching/compression produced in the graph of function due to multiplying $f(x)$ by a constant a also produces no change in periodicity.

(ii) If $f(x)$ is periodic with period T, then $f(kx + b)$ is periodic with period $\dfrac{T}{|k|}$ provided k is non-zero real number and $b \in \mathbb{R}$

Proof: If $f(x)$ is periodic with period T and let $g(x) = f(kx + b)$

$$\Rightarrow \quad g\left(x+\frac{T}{|k|}\right)=f\left(k\left(x+\frac{T}{|k|}\right)+b\right) = f(kx \pm T + b)$$

$= f(kx + b) = g(x)$

Converse of this property holds good.

Alternatively we may put the argument geometrically as the multiplication or division of independent variable x by a positive constant a, results in change in size with respect to origin in the horizontal direction. The graph shrinks horizontally when independent variable is multiplied by a positive constant greater than 1 by the factor which is equal to the multiplier. This mean periodicity of graph decreases by the same factor, i.e., $|a|$.

The graph stretches horizontally when the independent variable is divided by positive constant greater than 1 by the factor which is equal to the divisor. This means periodicity of graph increases by the same factor, i.e., $|a|$.

We combine these two observations by saying that period of graph decreases by a factor $|a|$.

Note that magnitude of constant a more than 1 represents multiplication and less than 1 represents division.

In the nutshell, if T is the period of $f(x)$, then period of function of the form $y = p.f(ax + b) + q$; $a \neq 0$, b, q, $p \in \mathbb{R}$. is $\dfrac{T}{|a|}$

ILLUSTRATION 269: Find the period of function $f(x) = 3 + 2\sin\left(\dfrac{\pi x+2}{3}\right)$

SOLUTION: Given function is $f(x) = 3 + 2\sin\left(\dfrac{\pi x+2}{3}\right)$

Rearranging the terms, we have $f(x) = 3 + 2\sin\left(\dfrac{\pi}{3}x+\dfrac{2}{3}\right)$ .... (1)

The period of sine function is 2π.

Comparing (1) with the function $pf(ax + b) + q$, magnitude of a

i.e., $|a|$ is $\dfrac{\pi}{3}$. Hence, period of the given function is $T'=\dfrac{T}{|a|}=\dfrac{2\pi}{\pi/3}=6$

ILLUSTRATION 270: If $f(x)=\sin\sqrt{[a]}x$; (where [.] denotes the greatest integer function) has π as its fundamental period, then find the set of the values of a.

SOLUTION: Given $f(x)=\sin\left(\sqrt{[a]}\,x\right)$; Period $=\dfrac{2\pi}{\sqrt{[a]}}=\pi$

$\Rightarrow$ $[a] = 4$ $\qquad \Rightarrow$ $a \in [4, 5)$

■ PERIOD OF COMPOSITE FUNCTIONS

While dealing with periodicity, it is important to understand the changes in the periodicity of a function $f(x)$ that may or may not occur when we compose the function with other functions like modulus or power function, exponential, logarithmic functions. If $f(x)$ is a periodic function with fundamental period T and $g(x)$ is any function for which composite function gof is defined, then gof is also periodic function with one of its period as T (not necessarily fundamental period) .

Theorem: If $f(x)$ is periodic function with fundamental period T and $g(x)$ is monotonic function, over the range of $f(x)$, then $g(f(x))$ is also periodic with fundamental period T.

For example, If $g(x)= e^x$ and $f(x) = \sin x$, then $gof(x) = e^{\sin x}$ is periodic with fundamental period 2π.

Proof: Given the period of $f(x) = T$, then $f(x + T) = f(x)\ \forall\ x \in D_f$

$\Rightarrow$ $g[f(x + T)] = g[f(x)]$

$\Rightarrow$ gof is also periodic with period T ... (1)

Let if possible $k \in \mathbb{R}^+$ and

$k < T$, be the fundamental period of gof

$\Rightarrow$ $gof\,(k + x) = gof(x)$

$\Rightarrow$ $g(f(k + x)) = g(f(x))$

$\Rightarrow$ $f(k + x) = f(x)$ as $g(x)$ is monotonic, consequently $k < T$ is fundamental period of $f(x)$, which is a contradiction to the fact that $f(x)$ has fundamental period T.

$\therefore$ gof has fundamental period T.

Corollary: If $f(x)$ is periodic with period T, then

(i) $\dfrac{1}{f(x)}$ **is also periodic with same period T.**

Proof: Since $g(x) = \dfrac{1}{x}$ is a decreasing function, therefore $gof(x) = g(f(x)) = \dfrac{1}{f(x)}$ being the composition of a monotonic function over a periodic function with period T is also periodic with same period T.

(ii) $\sqrt{f(x)}$ **is also periodic with same period T.**

Proof: Since $g(x) = \sqrt{x}$ is an increasing function, on its domain $[0, \infty)$, therefore $gof(x) = g(f(x)) = \sqrt{f(x)}$ being the composition of a monotonic function over a periodic function with period T is also periodic with same period T.

NOTE

1. *Composition of a non-monotonic function g(x) over a periodic function f(x) having period T is always a periodic function with period T. (But fundamental period may be less than T)*
   For example, if $g(x) = x^2$ and $f(x)= \cos x$, then $gof(x) = \cos^2 x$ is periodic with period 2π, but its fundamental period is π.
2. *Composition of a periodic function f(x) over a non-periodic function g(x) may be a periodic function. For example, if $g(x) = [x]$ and $f(x) = \cos \pi x$, then $fog(x) = \cos \pi[x]$ is periodic with period 2.*
3. *Composition of two non-periodic functions may be a periodic function*

   For example, Consider $g(x) = 3[x] - 2$ and $f(x) = \begin{cases} \dfrac{x^3 - 8}{x - 2}; & x \notin \mathbb{Z} \\ 3(\sin^2 x + \cos^2 x); & x \in \mathbb{Z} \end{cases}$ *we have $fog(x) = 3\ \forall\ x \in \mathbb{R}$.*

   which is a periodic function indeed.

ILLUSTRATION 271: Let $f(x) = x - \tan x$ and $g(x) = \cot x$ be two functions, then using these two functions, prove that the composite function of a periodic and a non-periodic function can be a periodic function. Also find the period of that function.

SOLUTION: Let $f(x) = x - \tan x$ and $g(x) = \cot x$

Now $f(x)$ is non-periodic, whereas $g(x)$ is periodic $g(f(x)) = \cot(x - \tan x)$

On replacing x by $x + \pi$ in $g(f(x))$; we get $g(f(x + \pi)) = \cot(x + \pi - \tan(x + \pi)) = \cot(x - \tan x) = g(f(x))$.

Hence, $g(f(x))$ is periodic with period π.

ILLUSTRATION 272: Let $f(x) = x - \cos x$ and $g(x) = \cot x$ be two functions, then using these two functions, prove that the composite function of a periodic and a non-periodic function can be a periodic function. Also find the period of that function.

SOLUTION: Let $f(x) = x - \cos x$ and $g(x) = \cot x$. Now $f(x)$ is non-periodic, whereas $g(x)$ is periodic

$\Rightarrow$ $g(f(x)) = \cot(x - \cos x)$. On replacing x by $x + 2\pi$ in $g(f(x))$; we get

$g(f(x + 2\pi)) = \cot(x + 2\pi - \cos(x + 2\pi)) = \cot(x - \cos x) = g(f(x))$

Hence, $g(f(x))$ is periodic with period 2π. Similarly $\cot(x - \cot x)$ is periodic with period π.

ILLUSTRATION 273: Using the functions $f(x) = \left[\sqrt[3]{x}\right]$; where [ ] represents the greatest integer function and $g(x) = \begin{cases} e^x; & x \notin \mathbb{Z} \\ \sin^2 x + \cos^2 x; & x \in \mathbb{Z} \end{cases}$, show that the composite function of two non-periodic functions can be periodic.

SOLUTION: Now $f(x)$ will always give an integral value. Therefore $g(f(x)) = \sin^2(f(x)) + \cos^2(f(x))$; $\forall f(x) \in \mathbb{Z} \Rightarrow g(f(x)) = 1 \ \forall x \in \mathbb{R}$

Hence, $g(f(x))$ is a constant (periodic with no fundamental period) $\forall x \in \mathbb{R}$

ILLUSTRATION 274: **(a)** If $f(x) = \tan^{-1}x$ and $g(x) = \{x\}$, then show that $fog(x)$ is a periodic function with fundamental period 1.

(b) If $f(x) = \dfrac{2x}{x^2+1}$ and $g(x) = |\sin x|$, then show that $fog(x)$ is a periodic function with period π.

SOLUTION: **(a)** $f(x) = \tan^{-1}x \Rightarrow f'(x) = \dfrac{1}{1+x^2} > 0 \ \forall x \in \mathbb{R}$

$\Rightarrow$ $f(x)$ is monotonically increasing function and $g(x) = \{x\}$.

We know that fundamental period of $\{x\}$ is 1.

Thus, $fog(x)$ represents composition of monotonic function over the periodic function with fundamental period 1

$\therefore$ By above property, $fog(x)$ is periodic function with fundamental period 1.

(b) Now $f(x) = \dfrac{2x}{1+x^2}$

$\Rightarrow$ $f'(x) = \dfrac{2(1-x^2)}{(1+x^2)^2} \geq 0$ for $x \in [-1, 1]$ and < 0 for $x \in (-\infty, -1] \cup [1, \infty)$

$\Rightarrow$ $f(x)$ is a non-monotonic function. Also $g(x) = |\sin x|$ is periodic function with period π.

$$\therefore \quad fog(x) = f(g(x)) = \frac{2|\sin x|}{1+|\sin x|^2}$$

$$\Rightarrow \quad fog(x+\pi) = \frac{2|\sin(x+\pi)|}{1+|\sin(x+\pi)|^2} = \frac{2|\sin x|}{1+|\sin x|^2} = fog(x)$$

Thus, $fog(x)$ is a periodic function with period π.

ILLUSTRATION 275: Functions f and g are defined by $f(x) = \sin x$, $x \in \mathbb{R}$; $g(x) = \tan x$, $x \in \mathbb{R} - \left(k + \dfrac{1}{2}\right)\pi$; where $k \in \mathbb{Z}$. Find periods of fog and gof.

SOLUTION: Given $f(x) = \sin x$ and $g(x) = \tan x$. Now, $fog = f(g(x)) = \sin(g(x)) = \sin(\tan x)$

Clearly period of fog is π. Also $gof = g(f(x)) = \tan(f(x)) = \tan(\sin x)$

Period $= 2\pi$ (period of $\sin x$ is 2π and $\tan x$ is an odd function)

■ PERIODICITY OF MODULUS/POWER OF A FUNCTION

(i) Period if $[f(x)]^{2n+1}$: If the fundamental period of $f(x)$ is T, then the fundamental period of $f(x)^{2n+1}$; $n \in \mathbb{Z}$ will also be T. That is, the fundamental period of function remains same on raising it to an odd integer power.
For example, we know that period of functions $\sin x$, $\cos x$, $\sec x$, $\operatorname{cosec} x$ is 2π, therefore the period of the functions $(\sin x)^{2n+1}$,$(\cos x)^{2n+1}$,$(\sec x)^{2n+1}$,$(\operatorname{cosec} x)^{2n+1}$ is also 2π.

Similarly, the period of $\tan x$, $\cot x$ is π and also the same is the period of $(\tan x)^{2n+1}$ and $(\cot x)^{2n+1}$.

Proof: If T is the period of $f(x)$, then $f(x) = f(x + T)$ ..(1)

On raising both sides of (1) to any odd degree power $(2n+1)$, we get $(f(x))^{2n+1} = (f(x + T))^{2n+1}\ \forall\ n \in \mathbb{Z}$

$\Rightarrow$ T is the period of $(f(x))^{2n+1}\ \forall\ n \in \mathbb{Z}$

Let if possible $k < T$ be the period of $(f(x))^{2n+1}$

$\Rightarrow$ $(f(x))^{2n+1} = (f(x + k))^{2n+1}\ \forall\ n \in \mathbb{Z}$

$\Rightarrow$ $f(x) = f(x + k)$ $\quad (\because a^{2n+1} = b^{2n+1} \Rightarrow a = b)$

$\Rightarrow$ $k < T$ is period of $f(x)$,which contradicts the fact that T is the fundamental period of $f(x)$.

Thus, T will be the fundamental period of $(f(x))^{2n+1}$.

ILLUSTRATION 276: Prove using graphs that the periodicity of $f(x) = \cos x$ does not change when $\cos x$ is raised to an odd power.

SOLUTION: **Graph of $\cos x$**

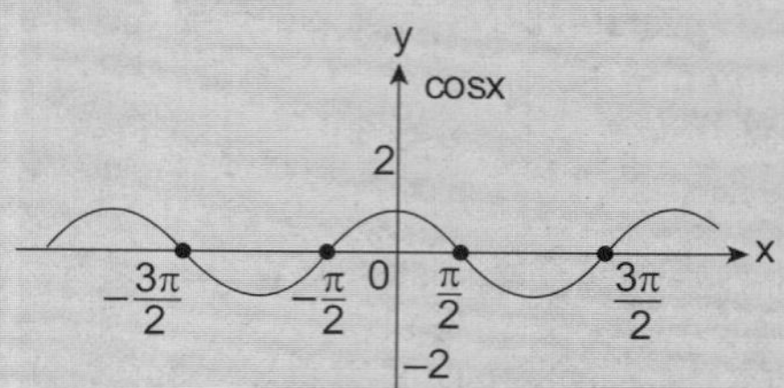

FIGURE 2.208

Graph of $(\cos x)^3$

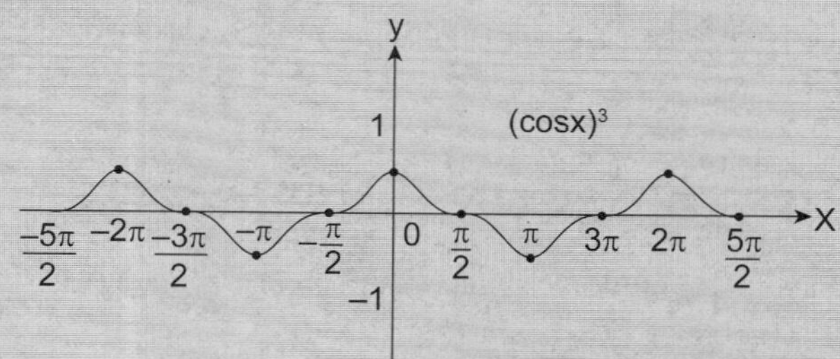

FIGURE 2.209

Graph of $(\cos x)^5$

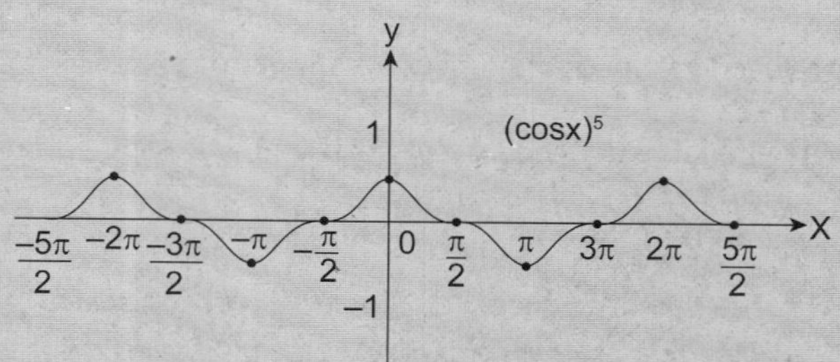

FIGURE 2.210

On generalizing, we can say that the periodicity of $\cos x$ does not change on raising its power to an odd degree.

Similarly, with the help of the graphs, we can prove that the above rule holds true for all the functions $f(x)$.

(ii) Period of $[f(x)]^{2n}$: If the fundamental period of $f(x)$ is T, then the fundamental period of $[f(x)]^{2n}$; $n \in \mathbb{Z}$ may not be T.

That is, the fundamental period of function may change on raising it to an even integer power.

For example, we know that the period of the functions $\sin x$, $\cos x$, $\sec x$, $\text{cosec } x$ is 2π and that of $\tan x$, $\cot x$ is π, whereas the period of the functions $(\sin x)^{2n}$, $(\cos x)^{2n}$, $(\sec x)^{2n}$, $(\text{cosec } x)^{2n}$, $(\tan x)^n$, $(\cot x)^n$, $|\sin x|$, $|\cos x|$, $|\tan x|$, $|\cot x|$, $|\sec x|$., $|\text{cosec } x|$ is π.

NOTE

This happens because the modulus operation on a function converts the negative quantity to a positive quantity, while keeping the magnitude same. Raising the power of a function by an even degree is the same as taking the modulus of the function and then raising the power of that function. i.e., $(f(x))^{2n} = |f(x)|^{2n} \ \forall n \in I$

ILLUSTRATION 277: Prove using graphs that the periodicity of $f(x) = \cos x$ gets changed when $\cos x$ is raised to an even power.

SOLUTION: **Graph of $\cos x$**

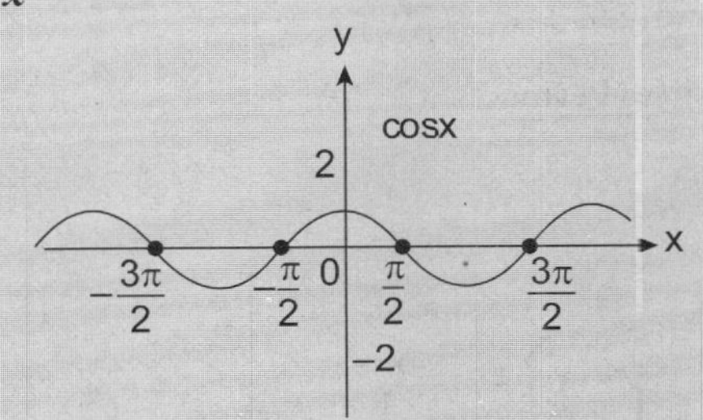

FIGURE 2.211

Graph of $|\cos x|$

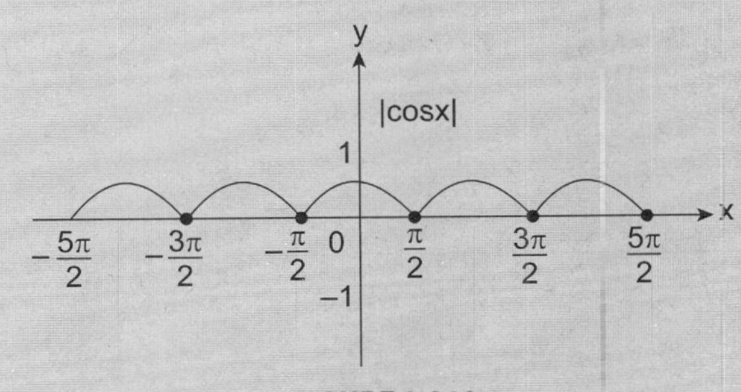

FIGURE 2.212

Graph of (cos x)2

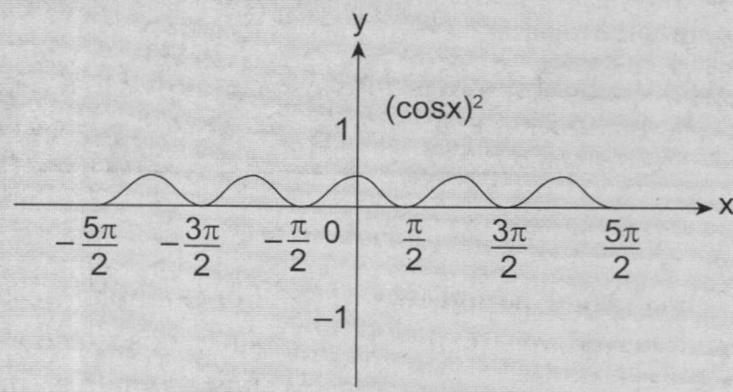

FIGURE 2.213

It is clear from above graphs that the period of cos x is 2π,whereas that of |cos x| and (cos x)2n is π.

On generalizing, we can say that the periodicity of cos x becomes p on raising its power to an even degree.

(iii) Period of [$f(x)$]p/q: where $\frac{p}{q} = \frac{2n+1}{q}$,, where p and q are co-prime, $q \neq 0$ and $n \in Z$.

For example: we know that the period of the functions sin x, cos x, sec x, cosec x is $2p$, therefore the period of the functions (sin x)p/q, (cos x)p/q, (sec x) p/q, (cosec x) p/q is also $2p$.

Similarly, the graph of tan x, cot x is p and also the same is the period of (tan x)p/q and (cot x) p/q .

ILLUSTRATION 278: Using graphs, find the periodicity of $f(x)$ = sin-1sin x, and hence, find the periodicity of (sin-1sin x)3/2 and (sin-1sin x)3/5.

SOLUTION: Graph of sin–1sinx (Periodicity = $2p$)

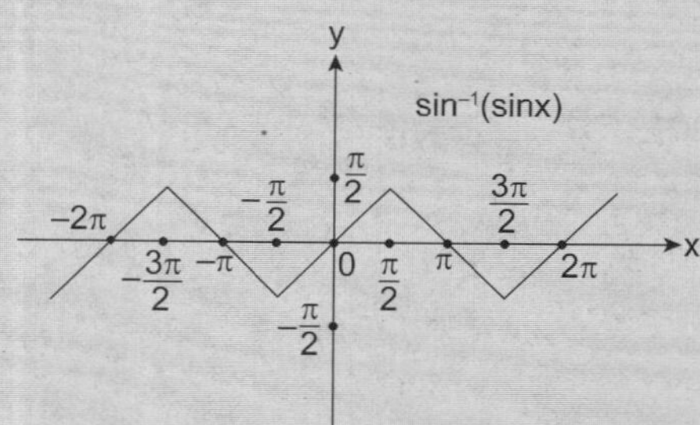

FIGURE 2.214

Graph of (sin–1 sin x)3/2 (Periodicity = $2p$)

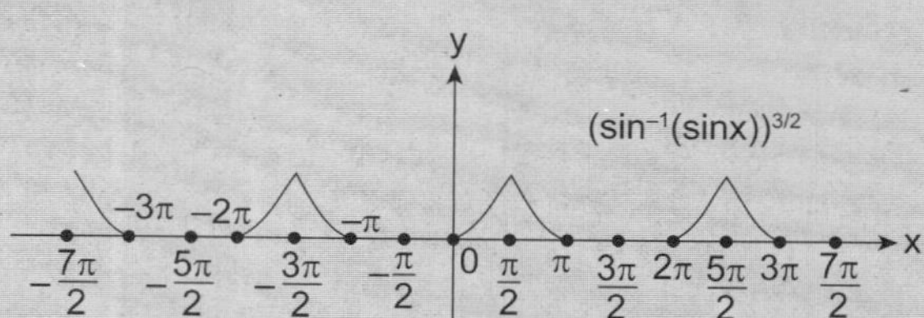

FIGURE 2.215

Graph of (sin–1 sin *x*)3/5 (Periodicity = *2p*)

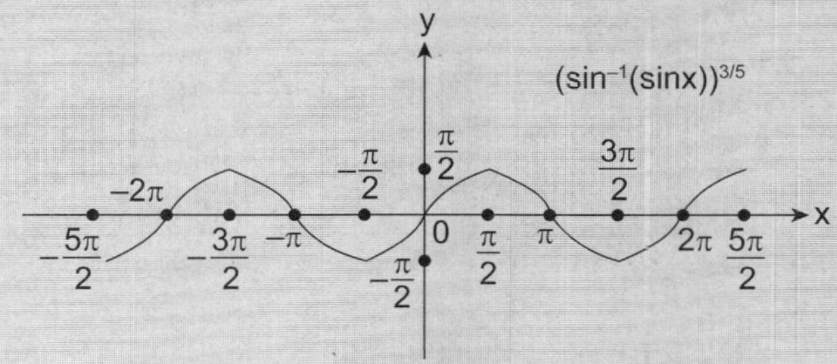

FIGURE 2.216

(iv) Period of *f*(*x*)*p*/*q*: where $\frac{p}{q} = \frac{2n}{q}$, where p and q are co-prime, $q \neq 0$ and $n \in \mathbb{Z}$.

For example, we know that the period of the functions sin x, cos x, sec x, cosec x is 2π and that of tan x, cot x is π, whereas the period of the functions $(\sin x)^{2n}$, $(\cos x)^{2n/p}$, $(\sec x)^{2n/p}$, $(\text{cosec } x)^{2n/p}$, $(\tan x)^{2n/p}$, $(\cot x)^{2n/p}$, is π.

ILLUSTRATION 279: Using graphs, find the periodicity of $f(x) = \sin^{-1}\sin x$, and hence, find the periodicity of $(\sin^{-1}\sin x)^{2/3}$ and $(\sin^{-1}\sin x)^{8/5}$.

SOLUTION: **Graph of $\sin^{-1}\sin x$ (Periodicity = 2π)**

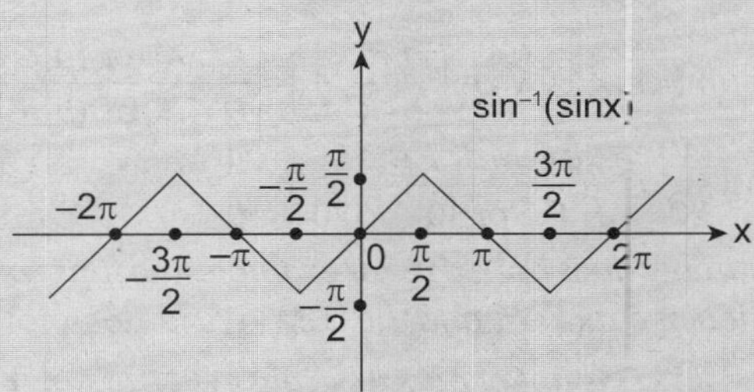

FIGURE 2.217

Graph of $(\sin^{-1}\sin x)^{2/3}$ (Periodicity = π)

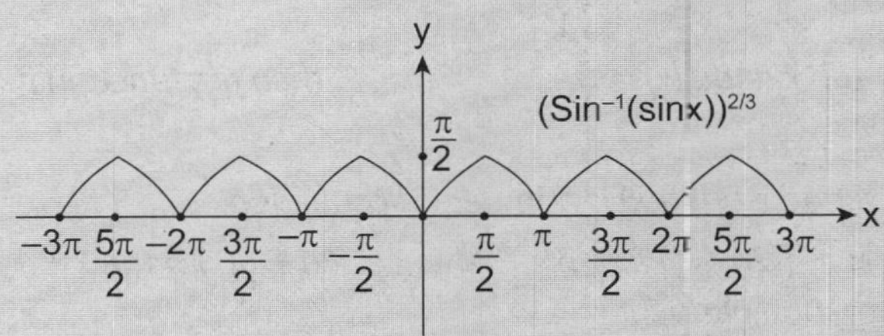

FIGURE 2.218

Graph of $(\sin^{-1}\sin x)^{8/5}$ (Periodicity = π)

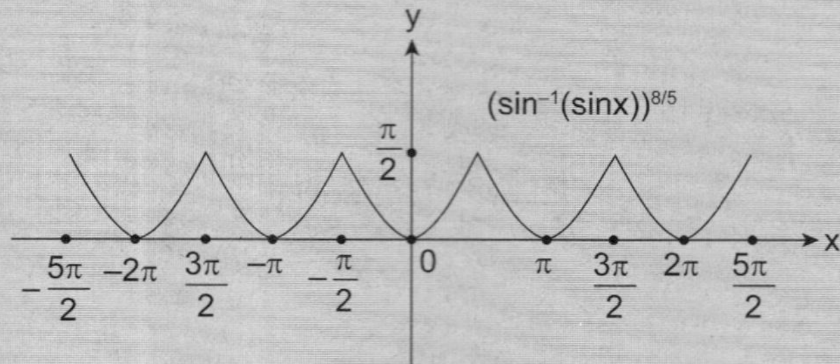

FIGURE 2.219

(v) Period of Linear Combination of Two Functions: If $f(x)$ be periodic with period T_1 and $g(x)$ with period T_2 such that LCM of T_1 and T_2 exist and is equal to T, then $a.f(x) + b.g(x)$ is a periodic function with period T (a and b are non-zeros).

Proof: Let $F(x) = a.f(x) + b.g(x)$ .... (1)

Let T_1 and T_2 be the periods of function $f(x)$ and $g(x)$, respectively.

$\Rightarrow$ $T_1, T_2 > 0$

Let $T = \text{LCM }(T_1, T_2)$

$\Rightarrow$ $T = nT_1$ and $T = mT_2$ for some positive integers n, m.

$\Rightarrow$ $F(x + T) = a.f(x + nT_1) + b.g(x + mT_2) = a.f(x) + b.g(x) = F(x)$

$(\because f(x + nT) = f(x))$

$\Rightarrow$ T is the period of $F(x)$

$\Rightarrow$ If there does not exist $0 < \lambda < T = \text{LCM }(T_1 \text{ and } T_2)$ such that $F(x + \lambda) = F(x)$, then $T = \text{LCM }(T_1 \text{ and } T_2)$ will be the fundamental period of $F(x)$. However if such a λ exists, then T will not be the fundamental period of $F(x)$.

REMARKS

(i) *LCM of two or more fractional numbers* = LCM of $\left(\frac{a}{b}, \frac{c}{d}, \frac{e}{f}\right) = \frac{\text{L.C.M. of }(a,c,e)}{\text{H.C.F. of }(b,d,f)}$

For example, The LCM of $\frac{7}{30}$ and $\frac{3}{20}$ *is* $\frac{\text{L.C.M of 7 and 3}}{\text{H.C.F of 30 and 20}} = \frac{21}{10}$.

(ii) *LCM of rational and irrational number does not exist. For example, the function {x} + cos x is non-periodic, because the period of {x} is 1 and the period of cosx is 2π and the LCM $(1, 2\pi)$ does not exist.*

Also the function sin x + tan πx + sin x/3 is not periodic; because LCM *of (2π, 1, 6π) does not exist.*

(iii) *The LCM of two irrational quantities may or may not exist. For example, the LCM of π and $\frac{\pi}{2}$ is π.*

The LCM of $\sqrt{2}$ and $\sqrt{3}$ does not exist.

Notes: **1.** *The sum / difference of a periodic and a non-periodic function can be periodic.*

For example, consider f(x) = tan x and $g(x) = \begin{cases} 1, & x \in \mathbb{R} - \frac{\pi}{2} \\ 3, & x = \frac{\pi}{2} \end{cases}$*, then the function f(x) ± g(x) is periodic*

Clearly f(x) is periodic with period π but g(x) is non-periodic function.

The domain of f(x) ± g(x) is $\mathbb{R} \sim \{(2n + 1)\,\pi/2; n \in \mathbb{Z}\}$ hence, f(x) ± g(x) = tan x ± 1 which is periodic function in its natural domain with fundamental period π.

2. *The sum/difference of two non-periodic functions can be periodic function*

e.g., consider f(x) = x + cos x and g(x) = –x + sin x, then the function f(x) + g(x) = sin x + cos x which is a periodic function with fundamental period of 2π.

ILLUSTRATION 280: Find the fundamental period of $\tan(3\pi x)+\cot\left(\frac{6\pi x}{5}\right)$

SOLUTION: The fundamental period of tan(3πx) is 1/3. And the fundamental period of $\cot\left(\frac{6\pi x}{5}\right)$ is $\frac{5}{6}$.

Therefore, the fundamental period of given function is $L.C.M\left(\frac{1}{3},\frac{5}{6}\right)=\frac{5}{3}$.

ILLUSTRATION 281: Find period of the following functions:

(i) $f(x)=\sin\frac{x}{2}+\cos\frac{x}{3}$ (ii) $f(x) = \{x\} + \sin x$

(iii) $f(x)=\sin\frac{3x}{2}-\cos\frac{x}{3}-\tan\frac{2x}{3}$

SOLUTION: (i) Period of $\sin\frac{x}{2}$ is 4π while period of $\cos\frac{x}{3}$ is 6π. Hence, period of $\sin\frac{x}{2}+\cos\frac{x}{3}$ is 12π. (LCM of 4 and 6 is 12}

(ii) Period of $\{x\}$ = 1 and that of sin x is 2π.

But LCM of 2π and 1 is not possible as their ratio is irrational number

∴ It is non-periodic

(iii) Period of $f(x)$ is LCM of $\frac{2\pi}{3/2},\frac{2\pi}{1/3},\frac{\pi}{2/3}$ = LCM of $\frac{4\pi}{3},6\pi,\frac{3\pi}{2}=12\pi$

ILLUSTRATION 282: Find period of the function $f(x)=x-[x]+|\sin\pi x|-|\sin 2\pi x|+....+|\sin n\pi x|$

SOLUTION: $x - [x]$ has period 1 and $|\sin x|$ has period π

⇒ $|\sin \pi x|$ has period $\frac{\pi}{\pi}=1$, $|\sin 2\pi x|$ has period $=\frac{\pi}{2\pi}=\frac{1}{2}$

Similarly $|\sin n\pi x|$ has period $\frac{\pi}{n\pi}=\frac{1}{n}$

⇒ period of the function $f(x)$= LCM $\left\{1,1,\frac{1}{2},\frac{1}{3},...\frac{1}{n}\right\}=1$ ∴ $f(x)$ has period 1.

ILLUSTRATION 283: Find the period of the function $f(x) = 4\sin\{3x\} + 3\cos2\{4x\}$

SOLUTION: Let $f(x) = 4\sin\{3x\} + 3\cos2\{4x\}$

Let $g(x) = 4\sin\{3x\}$ and $h(x) = 3\cos2\{4x\}$

Now period of $g(x)$ is $\frac{1}{3}$ and that of $h(x)$ is $\frac{1}{4}$

Hence, the fundamental period of $f(x)$ = LCM of $\left(\frac{1}{3},\frac{1}{4}\right)=1$

ILLUSTRATION 284: Find the fundamental period of $f(x) = |\sin x| - |\cos x|$.

SOLUTION: Given function $f(x) = |\sin x| - |\cos x|$. The period of both $|\sin x|$ and $|\cos x|$ is π.

So, LCM is π.

ILLUSTRATION 285: Find the period of $\sin\frac{\pi}{4}[x]+\cos\frac{\pi x}{2}+\cos\frac{\pi}{3}[x]$, where $[x]$ denotes the integral part of x.

SOLUTION: Given $\sin\frac{\pi}{4}[x]+\cos\frac{\pi x}{2}+\cos\frac{\pi}{3}[x]$

Let $g(x)=\sin\frac{\pi}{4}[x]$

Since $g(x) = 0, \frac{1}{\sqrt{2}}, 1, \frac{1}{\sqrt{2}}, 0, -\frac{1}{\sqrt{2}}, -1, -\frac{1}{\sqrt{2}}, 0$ when $x \in [0, 1); [1, 2), [2, 3), [3, 4), [4, 5), [5, 6), [6, 7), [7, 8)$ and $[8, 9)$. ⇒ The period of $g(x) = 8$

Similarly the period of function $p(x) = \cos\frac{\pi}{3}[x]$ is 6 and since $h(x) = \cos\frac{\pi x}{2}$, therefore the period of $h(x) = 4$

Now, according to the LCM rule, the period of $f(x)$ = LCM of 8, 4, and 6, i.e., 24.

ILLUSTRATION 286: Find the fundamental period of the function, $f(x) = x + a - [x + b] + \sin \pi x + \cos 2\pi x + \sin 3\pi x + \cos 4\pi x + \ldots\ldots + \sin (2n - 1) \pi x + \cos 2 n\pi x$ for every $a, b \in \mathbb{R}$ is: (where [ ] denotes the greatest integer function)

SOLUTION: $f(x) = x + a - [x + b] + \sin \pi x + \cos 2\pi x + \sin (3\pi x) + \cos (4\pi x) + \ldots + \sin (2n - 1)\pi x + \cos (2n\pi x)$

$\Rightarrow f(x) = \{x + b\} + a - b + \sin (\pi x) + \cos(2\pi x) + \sin(3\pi x) + \cos(4\pi x) + \ldots + \sin(2n - 1) \pi x + \cos(2n\pi x)$

Period of $f(x)$ = LCM $\left(1, 2, \frac{2}{3}, \frac{2}{4}, \ldots, \frac{2}{2n-1}, \frac{2}{2n}\right) = 2$

∴ Fundamental period of $f(x) = 2$.

■ PERIODICITY OF PRODUCT/DIVISION OF FUNCTION

Consider the function $F(x) = \frac{\prod_{k=1}^{n} f_k(x)}{\prod_{r=1}^{m} g_r(x)}$; where $f_k(x)$ and $g_r(x)$ are periodic functions with periods T_k and t_r respectively $\forall k, r \in \mathbb{N}$ and LCM of T_k and t_r exist and equals to T. Then the function $F(x)$ is periodic with period T.

However, T need not be the fundamental period of $F(x)$. To get the fundamental period, we need to check whether the fundamental period is T or not by applying either,

(a) transformation of $F(x)$ into linear combination of functions, or

(b) analyzing through graph of $F(x)$, or

(c) checking whether T/n is period of $F(x)$ for natural values of n.

NOTE

1. *The product/quotient of a periodic and a non-periodic function can be periodic.*

   For example, *consider* f(x) = *cot x and* $g(x) = \begin{cases} 1, & x \in \mathbb{R} - \{0\} \\ 3, & x = 0 \end{cases}$, *then the function* f(x) . g(x) *and* $\frac{f(x)}{g(x)}$ *are periodic*

   Clearly f(x) is periodic with period π but g(x) is non-periodic function.

   The domain of f(x) . g(x) and $\frac{f(x)}{g(x)}$ *is* $\mathbb{R} \sim \{n\pi; n \in \mathbb{Z}\}$; *hence, f(x).* $g(x) = \frac{f(x)}{g(x)} = \cot x$ *which is periodic function in its natural domain with fundamental period π.*

2. *The product/quotient of two non-periodic functions can be periodic function*

   For example, *consider* $f(x) = \begin{cases} 1; & x < 0 \\ -1; & x \geq 0 \end{cases}$ *and* $g(x) = \begin{cases} -1; & x < 0 \\ 1; & x \geq 0 \end{cases}$, *then the function f(x).g(x) and* $\frac{f(x)}{g(x)} = -1$ *which being a constant function is a periodic function with no fundamental period.*

ILLUSTRATION 287: Find the fundamental period of the following functions:

(i) $f(x) = \sin x. \tan x$

(ii) $f(x) = \left\{\frac{x}{2}\right\}.\cos\left(\frac{\pi x}{3}\right)$; ({ } is fractional part function)

SOLUTION: (i) Given $f(x) = \sin x. \tan x$; Period of $f(x)$ = LCM of $(2\pi, \pi) = 2\pi$

(ii) Given $f(x) = \left\{\frac{x}{2}\right\}.\cos\left(\frac{\pi x}{3}\right)$; Period of $f(x)$ is LCM of $(2, 3) = 6$

■ EXCEPTION TO LCM RULE

LCM Rule undoubtedly predicts the period of the function but not necessarily the fundamental period. It fails to determine the fundamental period in atleast following two situations:

Case I: If $f(x)$ be periodic with period T_1 and $g(x)$ with period T_2 such that LCM of T_1 and T_2 exists and is equal to T and $f(x)$ and $g(x)$ can be interchanged by adding a least positive constant K ($< T$).

That is, $f(x + K) = g(x)$ and $g(x + K) = f(x)$, then K is period of $f(x) + g(x)$, otherwise period will be T.

ILLUSTRATION 288: Prove that the function $f(x) = |\sin x| + |\cos x|$ does not follow the LCM rule.

SOLUTION: Let $f(x) = |\sin x| + |\cos x|$

Let $g(x) = |\sin x|$ and $h(x) = |\cos x|$ and Fundamental period of each of $g(x)$ and $h(x)$ is π

∴ According to the LCM rule; the Fundamental period of $f(x)$ should be π

But if we replace x by $x + \frac{\pi}{2}$ in $f(x)$; we get

$$f\left(x+\frac{\pi}{2}\right) = \left|\sin\left(x+\frac{\pi}{2}\right)\right| + \left|\cos\left(x+\frac{\pi}{2}\right)\right| = |\sin x| + |\cos x|; = f(x)$$

[due to the fact that $g(x)$ and $h(x)$ exchanged their values by adding a constant $\frac{\pi}{2}$ in x.]

Case II: If $f(x)$ be periodic with period T_1 and $g(x)$ with period T_2 such that LCM of T_1 and T_2 exist and is equal to T, then the period of $F(x) = f(x) \pm g(x)$ or $f(x).g(x)$ or $\frac{f(x)}{g(x)}$ is necessarily T but the fundamental period can be given by a positive constant K ($< T$) if $F(x)$ gets simplified to an equivalent function $F(x + K) = F(x)$.

ILLUSTRATION 289: Find the fundamental period of the following functions:

(i) $f(x) = \sin x. \cos x$

(ii) $f(x) = \cos^2 x \pm \sin^2 x$

(iii) $f(x) = \frac{\sin 3x}{\sin 2x.\cos x}$

(iv) $f(x) = 4\cos^3 x - 3\cos x$

(v) $f(x) = \cos x .\cos 3x$

SOLUTION: (i) Given $f(x) = \sin x. \cos x$

Now, according to the LCM rule, period of $f(x)$ = LCM of $(2\pi, 2\pi) = 2\pi$.

But $f(x) = \frac{\sin 2x}{2}$, and hence, the fundamental period of $f(x) = \pi$.

(ii) Given $f(x)=\cos^2 x \pm \sin^2 x$

Now, according to the LCM rule, period of $f(x)$ = LCM of $(\pi, \pi) = \pi$.

But for $f(x)=\cos^2 x+\sin^2 x$, the function simplifies to $f(x)=1$ which is a constant function with no fundamental period. And for $f(x)=\cos^2 x-\sin^2 x$, the function simplifies to $f(x) = \cos 2x$, and hence, the fundamental period of $f(x) = \pi$.

(iii) Given $f(x)=\dfrac{\sin 3x}{\sin 2x.\cos x}$

Now, according to the LCM Rule, period of $f(x)$ = LCM of $(2\pi, \pi, 2\pi/3) = 2\pi$.

But $f(x)=\dfrac{3\sin x-4\sin^3 x}{(\cos x)(2\sin x\cos x)}=\dfrac{3-4\sin^2 x}{2\cos^2 x}$, hence, the fundamental period of $f(x) = \pi$.

(iv) Given $f(x)=4\cos^3 x-3\cos x$

Now, according to the LCM Rule, period of $f(x)$ = LCM of $(2\pi, 2\pi) = 2\pi$.

But $f(x) = \cos 3x$, hence, the fundamental period of $f(x) = 2\pi/3$.

(v) Given $f(x) = \cos x .\cos 3x$ $\Rightarrow$ Period of $f(x)$ is LCM of $\left(2\pi, \dfrac{2\pi}{3}\right) = 2\pi$

But 2π may or may not be fundamental period, but fundamental period $=\dfrac{2\pi}{n}$, where $n \in \mathbb{N}$.

Hence, cross-checking for n = 1, 2, 3, ... we find π to be fundamental period $f(\pi + x) = (-\cos x)(-\cos 3x) = f(x)$. Hence, fundamental period of $f(x)$ is π.

ILLUSTRATION 290: Find the fundamental period of $f(x)$ defined as follows and explain as to why it does not comply with the LCM rule.

(a) $f(x) = \{x\} + \left\{x+\frac{1}{3}\right\}+\left\{x-\frac{1}{3}\right\}$

(b) $f(x) = a|\tan mx| + b|\tan nx|$

(c) $f(x) = 16(\sin^6 x + \cos^6 x) - 24(\sin^4 x + \cos^4 x) + 9$

SOLUTION: (a) Let $f(x) = \{x\} + \left\{x+\frac{1}{3}\right\}+\left\{x-\frac{1}{3}\right\}$

Let $g(x)$, $h(x)$ and $p(x)$ be $\{x\}$, $\left\{x+\frac{1}{3}\right\}$ and $\left\{x-\frac{1}{3}\right\}$ respectively.

We observe that the fundamental period of each of $g(x)$, $h(x)$ and $p(x)$ is 1

Hence, according to the LCM rule; the fundamental period of $f(x) = g(x) + h(x) + p(x)$ should be 1, but if we replace x by $x+\frac{1}{3}$ in $f(x)$,

we get $f\left(x+\frac{1}{3}\right)=\left\{x+\frac{1}{3}\right\}+\left\{x+\frac{1}{3}+\frac{1}{3}\right\}+\left\{x+\frac{1}{3}-\frac{1}{3}\right\}$

$$=\left\{x+\frac{1}{3}\right\}+\left\{x-\frac{1}{3}+1\right\}+\{x\}$$

$$=\{x\}+\left\{x+\frac{1}{3}\right\}+\left\{x-\frac{1}{3}\right\}=f(x)$$

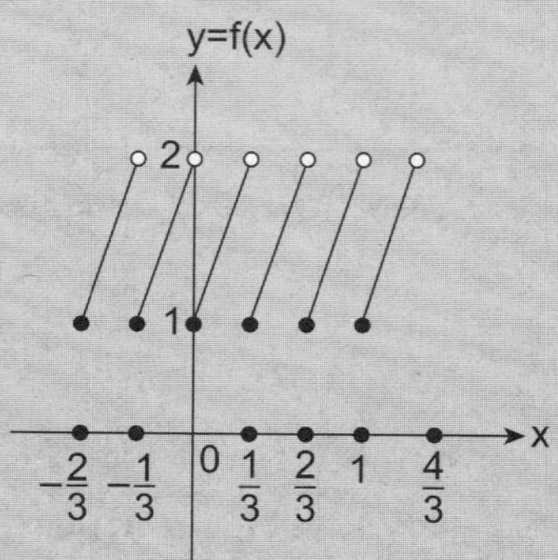

FIGURE 2.220

Hence, fundamental period of $f(x)=\frac{1}{3}$. Same can be concluded from graph.

Here $f(x) = \{x\} + \{x + 1/3\} + \{x - 1/3\}\ \forall\ x \in [0, 1/3) = x + x + 1/3 + x + 2/3 = 3x + 1$

$\therefore$ $f(x)$ is monotonic in $[0,1/3)$ $\Rightarrow$ $f(x)$ cannot have any period smaller than 1/3.

$\therefore$ The graph of $f(x)$ is given by

(b) Given $f(x) = a|\tan mx| + b|\tan nx|$

Let $g(x) = a\,|\tan mx|$ and $h(x) = b\,|\cot nx|$

Now period of $g(x)$ is $\frac{\pi}{m}$ and period of $h(x)$ is $\frac{\pi}{n}$

For $(a \neq b,\ m = n)$; $(a = b,\ m \neq n)$; $(a \neq b,\ m \neq n)$, the fundamental period of $f(x) = \text{LCM of}\left\{\frac{\pi}{m} \text{ and } \frac{\pi}{n}\right\} = \frac{\pi}{H.C.F.(m,n)}$

But when $a = b$ and $m = n$; then $g(x)$ and $h(x)$ are inter convertible, and hence, the fundamental period of $f(x) = \frac{1}{2}\left\{\text{LCM of } \frac{\pi}{m} \text{ and } \frac{\pi}{n}\right\}$ i.e., $\frac{\pi}{2m}$ or $\frac{\pi}{2n}$

(c) Given $f(x) = 16(\sin^6 x + \cos^6 x) - 24(\sin^4 x + \cos^4 x) + 9$

Let $g(x) = 16(\sin^6 x + \cos^6 x) = 16\{(\sin^2 x + \cos^2 x)^3 - 3\sin^2 x\cos^2 x\,(\sin^2 x + \cos^2 x)\}$

$= 16\left\{1-\frac{3}{4}\sin^2(2x)\right\}$ $\Rightarrow$ Fundamental period of $g(x)$ is $\frac{\pi}{2}$

Let $h(x) = -24(\sin^4 x + \cos^4 x)$

$= -24[(\sin^2 x + \cos^2 x)^2 - 2\sin^2 x\cos^2 x] = -24\left(1-\frac{1}{2}\sin^2 2x\right)$

Again Fundamental period of $h(x) = \frac{\pi}{2}$

And $p(x) = 9$, is a constant function (i.e., no fundamental period)

According to the LCM Rule; Fundamental period of $f(x) = \text{LCM of}\left(\frac{\pi}{2},\frac{\pi}{2}\right)=\frac{\pi}{2}$

But $f(x) = 16(\sin^6 x + \cos^6 x) - 24(\sin^4 x + \cos^4 x) + 9(\sin^2 x + \cos^2 x)$

$= (16\sin^6 x - 24\sin^4 x + 9\sin^2 x) + (16\cos^6 x - 24\cos^4 x + 9\cos^2 x)$

$= (4\sin^3 x - 3\sin x)^2 + (4\cos^3 x - 3\cos x)^2 = (\sin 3x)^2 + (-\cos 3x)^2 = 1$

Hence, $f(x)$ is a constant function with no fundamental period.

ILLUSTRATION 291: Find the fundamental period of $f(x) = \sec(\sin x)$.

SOLUTION: Since $\sin x$ is a periodic function with fundamental period 2π, $f(x)$ has a period 2π.

For fundamental period $f(x + \pi) = \sec(\sin(\pi + x)) = \sec(-\sin x) = \sec(\sin x) = f(x)$

$f\left(x+\frac{\pi}{2}\right) \neq f(x)$. Hence, fundamental period is π.

ILLUSTRATION 292: Find the fundamental period of $f(x)$ defined as follows and explain as to why it does not comply with the LCM rule.

(a) $f(x) = \frac{|\cos x| + |\sin x|}{\cot x - \tan x}$ (b) $f(x) = \frac{\cos x - \cos 3x}{\sin x - \sin 3x}$

(c) $\tan\left(\frac{\pi}{3}-x\right).\tan x.\tan\left(\frac{\pi}{3}+x\right)$ (d) $\frac{9\tan\theta - 84\tan^3\theta + 126\tan^5\theta - 36\tan^7\theta + \tan^9\theta}{1 - 36\tan^2\theta + 126\tan^4\theta - 8\tan^6\theta + 9\tan^8\theta}$

SOLUTION: **(a)** Given $f(x) = \dfrac{|\cos x| + |\sin x|}{\cot x - \tan x}$

Now let $g(x) = |\cos x| + |\sin x|$ and $h(x) = \cot x - \tan x$

And the fundamental period of each of $g(x)$ and $h(x)$ is π

$\therefore$ The fundamental period of $f(x)$ should be π

But if we replace x by $x + \dfrac{\pi}{2}$ in $f(x)$; we get $f\left(x + \dfrac{\pi}{2}\right) = \dfrac{\left|\cos\left(x + \dfrac{\pi}{2}\right)\right| + \left|\sin\left(x + \dfrac{\pi}{2}\right)\right|}{\cot\left(x + \dfrac{\pi}{2}\right) - \tan\left(x + \dfrac{\pi}{2}\right)}$

$= \dfrac{|\cos x| + |\sin x|}{\cot x - \tan x}$. Hence, fundamental period of $f(x)$ is $\dfrac{\pi}{2}$

(b) Given $f(x) = \dfrac{\cos x - \cos 3x}{\sin x - \sin 3x}$

Let $g(x) = \cos x - \cos 3x$ and $h(x) = \sin x - \sin 3x$

Fundamental period of each of $g(x)$ and $h(x)$ is 2π

$\therefore$ According to the LCM rule, the fundamental period of $f(x)$ should be 2π.

But $f(x) = \dfrac{-2\sin 2x \sin(-x)}{-2\sin x \cos 2x} = -\tan 2x$; $\sin x \neq 0$ and the period of $\tan 2x$ is $\dfrac{\pi}{2}$

But as explained earlier, we need to be careful while dealing with domain.

$\sin x \neq 0 \Rightarrow x \neq n\pi \ \forall\ n \in \mathbb{Z}$

Thus, the period of discontinuity of function is π.

$\therefore$ The fundamental period of $f(x)$ will be LCM of π and $\dfrac{\pi}{2}$, i.e., π.

(c) Given $f(x) = \tan\left(\dfrac{\pi}{3} - x\right).\tan x.\tan\left(\dfrac{\pi}{3} + x\right)$

Let $g(x) = \tan\left(\dfrac{\pi}{3} - x\right)$; $h(x) = \tan x$ and $p(x) = \tan\left(\dfrac{\pi}{3} + x\right)$, respectively.

Fundamental period of each of $g(x)$, $h(x)$ and $p(x)$ is π

$\therefore$ According to the LCM rule, the Fundamental period of $f(x)$ should be π.

But $f(x) = \tan\left(\dfrac{\pi}{3} - x\right).\tan x.\tan\left(\dfrac{\pi}{3} + x\right) = \tan 3x$

$\therefore$ Fundamental period of $f(x) = \dfrac{\pi}{3}$.

(d) Given $f(x) = \dfrac{9\tan\theta - 84\tan^3\theta + 126\tan^5\theta - 36\tan^7\theta + \tan^9\theta}{1 - 36\tan^2\theta + 126\tan^4\theta - 84\tan^6\theta + 9\tan^8\theta}$

Let $g(x) = 9\tan\theta - 84\tan^3\theta + 126\tan^5\theta - 36\tan^7\theta + \tan^9\theta$

and $h(x) = 1 - 36\tan^2\theta + 126\tan^4\theta - 84\tan^6\theta + 9\tan^8\theta$

Now Fundamental period of each of $g(x)$ and $h(x) = \pi$

$\therefore$ According to LCM rule; Fundamental period of $f(x) = \pi$

But $f(x) = \dfrac{9\tan\theta - 84\tan^3\theta + 126\tan^5\theta - 36\tan^7\theta + \tan^9\theta}{1 - 36\tan^2\theta + 126\tan^4\theta - 8\tan^6\theta + 9\tan^8\theta} = \tan 9\theta$.

Hence, fundamental period of $f(x) = \dfrac{\pi}{9}$

PERIODICITY OF FUNCTIONS EXPRESSED BY FUNCTIONAL EQUATIONS

Many a times we encounter a problem to determine period of a function $f(x)$ which is not defined directly but expressed in the form of equation/equations called as functional equation. In these situations, we often need to manipulate the given relation in such a way that leads to generate an equation of type $f(x+T) = \pm f(x)$ or $f(x+T) = \pm\frac{1}{f(x)}$.

Usually it is achieved by carrying out some suitable substitution in place of independent variable to obtain desired objective.

The process does not involves well defined algorithm (skilled based), thus, can be better understood only by working out on some examples.

(i) If a function $f(x)$ is defined such that $f(x+T) = -f(x)$; where T is a positive constant, then f is periodic with period $2T$. (Converse is not true)

Proof: Given $f(x+T) = -f(x)$

Replacing x by $x+T$, we have $f(x+2T) = -f(x+T)$

$\Rightarrow f(x+2T) = -(-f(x))$

$\Rightarrow f(x+2T) = f(x)\ \forall\ x \in D_f$

e.g., $f(x) = \sin x, \cos x, \sec x, \text{cosec}\, x$

(ii) If a function $f(x)$ is defined such that $f(x+T) = \frac{1}{f(x)}$ or $f(x+T) = \frac{-1}{f(x)}$; where T is a positive constant, then f is periodic with period $2T$. (Converse is not true)

Proof: Given $f(x+T) = \pm\frac{1}{f(x)}$

Replacing x by $x+T$, we have

$$f(x+2T) = \pm\frac{1}{f(x+T)} = \frac{\pm 1}{\pm(f(x))^{-1}} = f(x)$$

e.g., $f(x) = \tan x, \cot x$

As $f\left(x+\frac{\pi}{2}\right) = \tan\left(\frac{\pi}{2}+x\right) = -\frac{1}{\tan x}$

$\Rightarrow$ Period of $\tan x = 2\left(\frac{\pi}{2}\right) = \pi$.

(iii) If $f(x+\lambda) = g(f(x))$ such that $\underbrace{g(g(g(\ldots(g(x))\ldots)))}_{\text{composed } n \text{ times}} = x$, then prove that $f(x)$ is periodic with period $n\lambda$ (where λ is fixed positive real constant)

Proof: Given $f(x+2\lambda) = g(f(x+\lambda)) = g(g(f(x))) = g^2(f(x))$

Proceeding similarly $f(x+3\lambda) = g(f(x+2\lambda)) = g^2(f(x+\lambda)) = g^2(g(f(x))) = g^3(f(x))$ and $f(x+n\lambda) = g^{n-1}(f(x+\lambda)) = g^{n-1}(g(f(x)) = g^n(f(x)) = f(x)$

$\Rightarrow$ Period of $f(x)$ is $n\lambda$

ILLUSTRATION 293: Let $f: \mathbb{R} \to \mathbb{R} - \{x\}$ be a function such that there exists $T > 0$ for which $f(x+T) = \frac{f(x)-5}{f(x)-3}$ for every $x \in \mathbb{R}$. Prove that $f(x)$ is periodic.

SOLUTION: Given $f(x+T) = \frac{f(x)-5}{f(x)-3}$;

Replacing x by $x+T$, we have $f(x+2T) = \frac{f(x+T)-5}{f(x+T)-3} = \frac{\frac{f(x)-5}{f(x)-3}-5}{\frac{f(x)-5}{f(x)-3}-3} = \frac{f(x)-5-5f(x)+15}{f(x)-5-3f(x)+9}$

$$\Rightarrow f(x+2T) = \frac{-4f(x)+10}{-2f(x)+4} = \frac{2f(x)-5}{f(x)-2};$$

Replacing x by $x+2T$, we have $f(x+4T) = \frac{2f(x+2T)-5}{f(x+2T)-2} = \frac{2\left(\frac{2f(x)-5}{f(x)-2}\right)-5}{\frac{2f(x)-5}{f(x)-2}-2}$

$$= \frac{4f(x)-10-5f(x)+10}{2f(x)-5-2f(x)+4} = \frac{-f(x)}{-1} = f(x) \Rightarrow f(x+4T) = f(x)$$

Hence, $f(x)$ is a periodic function with a fundamental period of $4T$.

ILLUSTRATION 294: Find the period of $f(x)$ satisfying the condition:

(i) $f(x + p) = 1 + \{1 - 3f(x) + 3f^2(x) - f^3(x)\}^{1/3}$

(ii) $f(x - 1) + f(x + 3) = f(x + 1) + f(x + 5)$

SOLUTION: (i) Given $f(x + p) = 1 + \{1 - 3f(x) + 3f^2(x) - f^3(x)\}^{1/3} = 1 + (1 - f(x))$

$\Rightarrow f(x + p) + f(x) = 2$ ...(1)

$\Rightarrow f(x + 2p) + f(x + p) = 2$ ...(2)

From (1) and (2), we get $f(x) = f(x + 2p) \Rightarrow$ Period $= 2p$

(ii) Given $f(x - 1) + f(x + 3) = f(x + 1) + f(x + 5)$ .....(1)

Replacing x by $x + 2$, we have $f(x + 1) + f(x + 5) = f(x + 3) + f(x + 7)$ ......(2)

(1) + (2) gives, $f(x - 1) = f(x + 7) \quad \Rightarrow f(x + 8) = f(x) \quad \Rightarrow$ period = 8

ILLUSTRATION 295: Let f be a function that satisfies $f(x + 6) + f(x - 6) = f(x)$ for all real x. Prove that any such function is periodic with a common positive period p for all of them. Also, find the value of the period p.

SOLUTION: Given $f(x + 6) + f(x - 6) = f(x)$ .... (1)

Replacing x by $x + 6$ in equation (1), we get $f(x + 12) + f(x) = f(x + 6)$ ...(2)

Substituting the value of $f(x + 6)$ from (1) in (2), we get $f(x + 12) + f(x) = f(x) - f(x - 6)$ ...(3)

Again replacing x by $x + 6$ in equation (3), we get $f(x + 18) = -f(x)$

Now, replacing x by $x + 18$, we get $f(x + 36) = -f(x + 18)$

$\Rightarrow f(x + 36) = f(x) \Rightarrow f(x)$ is periodic with period 36.

ILLUSTRATION 296: Let $y = f(x)$, $x \in \mathbb{R}$ be a function such that the graph of $f(x)$ is symmetrical about the lines $x = \alpha$ and $x = \beta$; where $\alpha < \beta$. Prove that $f(x)$ is periodic, also find the period of $f(x)$.

SOLUTION: We have $f(\alpha - x) = f(\alpha + x)$ ...(1)

and $f(\beta - x) = f(\beta + x)$ ...(2)

[Since the function $f(x)$ is symmetrical about lines $x = \alpha$ and $x = \beta$]

Replacing x by $\alpha - x$ in equation (1), we have $f(x) = f(2\alpha - x)$ ...(3)

Replacing x by $(\beta - x)$ in equation (2), we have $f(x) = f(2\beta - x)$ ...(4)

From equation (3), we have $f(x) = f(2\alpha - x) = f\{2\beta - (2\alpha - x)\} = f\{x + 2(\beta - \alpha)\}$ (from (4))

Hence, $f(x)$ is periodic, having a period $2(\beta - \alpha)$

ILLUSTRATION 297: Let f be real valued function defined for all real numbers x such that for some positive constant a, the equation $f(x+a) = \frac{1}{2} + \sqrt{f(x) - f(x))^2}$ holds for all x. Prove that the function f is periodic.

SOLUTION: Given $f(x+a) = \frac{1}{2} + \sqrt{f(x) - f(x))^2}$ or $f^2(x + a) + \frac{1}{4} - f(x + a) = f(x) - f^2(x)$

or $f^2(x) + f^2(x + a) + \frac{1}{4} = f(x) + f(x + a)$ ....(1)

Replacing x by $x + a$, we have $f^2(x + a) + f^2(x + 2a) + \frac{1}{4} = f(x + a) + f(x + 2a)$ ...(2)

(1) − (2), gives $f^2(x) - f^2(x + 2a) = f(x) - f(x + 2a)$

$\Rightarrow \{f(x) - f(x + 2a)\}\ \{f(x) + f(x + 2a)\} = 0$

$\Rightarrow f(x) = f(x + 2a)$ or $f(x) = -f(x + 2a)$ (rejected, as by given equation, $f(x)$ is positive)

$\Rightarrow$ Period of $f(x) = 2a$

ILLUSTRATION 298: Find the period of the following functions:

(i) $f(x) = sgn\ (e^{-x}) - \sin x + |\sin x| + \min\ (\sin x, |x|)$

(ii) $\left[x+\frac{1}{2}\right]+\left[x-\frac{1}{2}\right]+2\ [-x]$, where $[x]$ denotes the greatest integer function

SOLUTION: (i) Given $\text{sgn}(x) = \begin{cases} 1, & x > 0 \\ 0, & x = 0 \\ -1, & x < 0 \end{cases}$

$\because\ e^{-x} > 0 \Rightarrow sgn\ (e^{-x}) = 1$

$\therefore\ sgn\ (e^{-x})$ is constant function which is periodic with no fundamental period.

$\therefore\ f(x) = 1 - \sin x + |\sin x| + \sin x$

$\min\ (\sin x, |x|) = \sin x\ (\because\ \sin x \le |x|)$

$\therefore\ f(x) = 1 - \sin x + |\sin x| + \sin x$

Hence, $f(x) = 1 + |\sin x|$ which is periodic with period π.

(ii) Given $f(x)=\left[x+\frac{1}{2}\right]+\left[x-\frac{1}{2}\right]+2[-x]$

Case I: If $x \in \mathbb{Z}$; then $f(x) = [x]+\left[\frac{1}{2}\right]+[x]+\left[\frac{-1}{2}\right] + 2\ (-[x]) = 0 -1 = -1$

Case II: If $x \notin \mathbb{Z}$

Sub-case (i): $x = k + \lambda$; where k is an integer and $\lambda \in (0,1/2)$

Hence, $\left[k+\lambda+\frac{1}{2}\right]=k\left[\lambda+\frac{1}{2}\right]$ and $k < k + \lambda + 1/2 < k + 1 \Rightarrow [x + 1/2] = k$

Also $[x - 1/2] = [k + \lambda - 1/2]$ and $k - 1 < k + \lambda - 1/2 < k$

$\therefore\ [x - 1/2] = k - 1$ and $[-x] = -[x] - 1 = -k - 1$

$\therefore\ \left[x+\frac{1}{2}\right]+\left[x-\frac{1}{2}\right]+2[-x] = (k) + (k - 1) + 2(-k - 1) = -3$

Sub-case (ii): If $x = k + \lambda$; where k is an integer and $1/2 \le \lambda < 1$

Hence, $x + 1/2 = k + \lambda + 1/2$ and $k + 1 \le k + \lambda + 1/2 < k + 2$

$\therefore\ [x + 1/2] = k + 1$

Also $(x - 1/2) = k + \lambda - 1/2$ and $k \le k + \lambda - 1/2 < k + 1$

$\therefore\ [x - 1/2] = k$ and $[-x] = -[x] - 1 = -k - 1$

$\therefore\ [x + 1/2] + [x - 1/2] + 2\ [-x] = (k + 1) + k + 2(-k - 1) = -1$

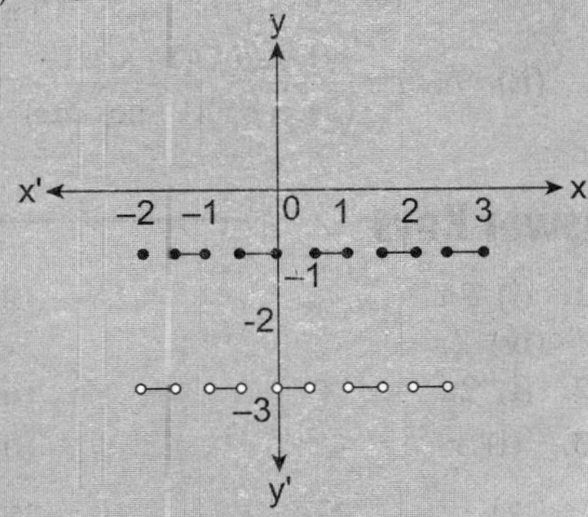

FIGURE 2.221

$\therefore$ The graph of $f(x)$ is as shown in Figure.

Clearly, we can see that the function is periodic with a fundamental period 1.

TEXTUAL EXERCISE–16: (SUBJECTIVE)

1. Find the fundamental period of the following functions:
   (i) $f(x) = 2 + 3\cos(x - 2)$
   (ii) $f(x) = \cos\frac{3}{5}x - \sin\frac{2}{7}x$
   (iii) $f(x) = \sin\frac{\pi x}{4} + \sin\frac{\pi x}{3}$
   (iv) $f(x) = \frac{1}{1-\cos x}$
   (v) $f(x) = \sin(2x + \cos x)$
2. Find the fundamental period of the following functions:
   (i) $f(x) = \sin 3x + \cos 2x + |\tan x|$
   (ii) $f(x) = [\sin 3x] + |\cos 6x|$
   (iii) $f(x) = \frac{\sin 12x}{1+\cos^2 6x}$
   (iv) $f(x) = \sec^3 x + \text{cosec}^3 x$
3. Find the period of the following functions:
   (i) $f(x) = \frac{\sin x + \sin 3x}{\cos x + \cos 3x}$
   (ii) $f(x) = 1 - \frac{\sin^2 x}{1+\cot x} - \frac{\cos^2 x}{1+\tan x}$
   (iii) $f(x) = \tan\frac{\pi}{2}[x]$, where [.] denotes greatest integer function
   (iv) $f(x) = \ln(2 + \cos 3x)$
   (v) $f(x) = e^{\ln \sin x} + \tan^3 x - \text{cosec}(3x - 5)$
   (vi) $f(x) = \sin x + \tan\frac{x}{2} + \sin\frac{x}{2^2} + \tan\frac{x}{2^3} + \ldots + \sin\frac{x}{2^{n-1}} + \tan\frac{x}{2^n}$
4. Find period of the following functions:
   (i) $f(x) = \cos\frac{4x}{5} + \sin\frac{4x}{3} + \tan\frac{8x}{3}$
   (ii) $f(x) = \frac{(1+sinx)(1+\sec x)}{(1+\cos x)(1+\cos ecx)}$
   (iii) $f(x) = \sin\left(2\pi x + \frac{\pi}{3}\right) + 2\sin\left(3\pi x + \frac{\pi}{4}\right) + 3\sin(5\pi x)$
5. Find the period of the following functions:
   (i) $f(x) = \left|\cos^5\left(\frac{2x}{3}\right)\right|$
   (ii) $f(x) = \sin(\pi x) + [x] + 2 - x$
   (iii) $f(x) = x - [x - b]$
6. Prove that the function $f(x) = \begin{cases} 1 & \text{if } x \text{ is rational} \\ 0 & \text{if } x \text{ is irrational} \end{cases}$ is a periodic function with indeterminate period.
7. Find the period of the following functions:
   (i) $f(x) = \frac{1}{2}\left\{\frac{|\sin x|}{\cos x} + \frac{|\cos x|}{\sin x}\right\}$
   (ii) $f(x) = \sin\frac{\pi x}{n!} - \cos\frac{\pi x}{(n+1)!}$
8. Find the period of function $f(x)$ if for a fixed positive real number λ exactly one of the following relations hold.
   (a) $f(x + \lambda) = -f(x)$
   (b) $f(x + \lambda) = \pm\frac{1}{f(x)}$
9. Prove that the function satisfying the following functional equations $f(x+a) = \frac{1+f(x)}{1-f(x)}$ $\forall x \in \mathbb{R}$ and a fixed a is periodic function, where a is fixed positive real number.
10. Let $f(x) = \sin x + \cos\left(\sqrt{4-a^2}\right)x$, then find the set of all integer values of a for which $f(x)$ is a periodic function.

Answer Keys

1. (i) 2π (ii) 70π (iii) 24
   (iv) 2π (v) 2π
2. (i) 2π (ii) $2\pi/3$ (iii) $\pi/6$ (iv) 2π
3. (i) π (ii) π (iii) 2
   (iv) $\frac{2\pi}{3}$ (v) 2π (vi) $2^n\pi$
4. (i) $\frac{15\pi}{2}$ (ii) π (iii) 2
5. (i) $\frac{3\pi}{2}$ (ii) 2 (iii) 1

7. (i) 2π (ii) $2((n+1)!)$
8. (a) 2λ (b) 2λ
9. $4a$
10. $\{-2, 0, 2\}$

TEXTUAL EXERCISE–16: (OBJECTIVE)

1. The period of the function $f(x) = \sin 2\pi x + \sin\left(\frac{\pi x}{3}\right) + \sin\left(\frac{\pi x}{5}\right)$ is
(a) 2 (b) 6
(c) 15 (d) 30

2. The function $f(x) = sgnx \,.\, \sin x$ is
(a) discontinuous no where
(b) an even function
(c) non-periodic
(d) differentiable for all x

3. Which of the following function(s) is/are periodic with period π?
(a) $f(x) = |\sin x|$ (b) $f(x) = [x + \pi]$
(c) $f(x) = \cos(\sin x)$ (d) $f(x) = \cos^2 x$
(where [.] denotes the greatest integer function)

4. Period of $f(x) = nx + n - [nx + n]$; ($n \in \mathbb{N}$; where [ ] denotes the greatest integer function is)
(a) 1 (b) 1/n
(c) n (d) None of these

5. The period of the function $f(x) = \sin(x + 3 - [x + 3])$, where [ ] denotes the greatest integer function is
(a) $2\pi + 3$ (b) 2π
(c) 1 (d) 3

6. Minimum period of the function $f(x) = |\sin^3 2x| + |\cos^3 2x|$ is
(a) π (b) $\frac{\pi}{2}$
(c) $\frac{\pi}{4}$ (d) $\frac{3\pi}{4}$

7. The period of the function $f(x) = \frac{|\sin x| + |\cos x|}{|\sin x - \cos x|}$ is
(a) $\pi/2$ (b) $\pi/4$
(c) π (d) 2π

8. Which one is not periodic?
(a) $|\sin 3x| + \sin^2 x$ (b) $\cos\sqrt{x} + \cos^2 x$
(c) $\cos 4x + \tan^2 x$ (d) $\cos^2 x + \sin x$

9. Which of the following function(s) is/are periodic?
(a) $f(x) = x - [x]$
(b) $g(x) = \sin(1/x)$, $x \neq 0$ and $g(0) = 0$
(c) $h(x) = x \cos x$
(d) $w(x) = \sin^{-1}(\sin x)$

10. If $f(x) = e^{\sin(x - [x]) \cos \pi x}$, then $f(x)$ is ([x] denotes the greatest integer function)
(a) non-periodic
(b) periodic with no fundamental period
(c) periodic with period 2
(d) periodic with period π

11. If $f(x) = 2\tan 3x + 5\sqrt{1 - \cos 6x}$; $g(x)$ is a function having the same time period as that of $f(x)$, then which of the following can be $g(x)$?
(a) $(\sec^2 3x + \text{cosec}^2 3x)\tan^2 3x$
(b) $2\sin 3x + 3\cos 3x$
(c) $2\sqrt{1 - \cos^2 3x} + \text{cosec } 3x$
(d) $3\,\text{cosec } 3x + 2\tan 3x$

12. If $n \in \mathbb{N}$, and the period of $\frac{\cos nx}{\sin\left(\frac{x}{n}\right)}$ is 4π, then n is equal to
(a) 4 (b) 3
(c) 2 (d) 1

13. Which one of the following statements is NOT CORRECT?
(a) The derivative of a differentiable periodic function is a periodic function with the same period.
(b) If $f(x)$ and $g(x)$ both are defined on the entire number line and are non-periodic then the function $F(x) = f(x) \,.\, g(x)$ can not be periodic.
(c) Derivative of an even differentiable function is an odd function and derivative of an odd differentiable function is an even function.
(d) Every function $f(x)$ can be represented as the sum of an even and an odd function

14. If $f(x)$ is an odd periodic function with period 2, then $f(4)$ equals

(a) 0

(b) 2

(c) 4

(d) –4

15. The period of the function $f(x) = \dfrac{\sin 8x \cos x - \sin 6x \cos 3x}{\cos 2x \cos x - \sin 3x \sin 4x}$ is

(a) π (b) 2π

(c) $\dfrac{\pi}{2}$ (d) None of these

16. Suppose that f is a periodic function with period $\dfrac{1}{2}$ and that $f(2) = 5$ and $f\left(\dfrac{9}{4}\right) = 2$ then $f(-3) - f\left(\dfrac{1}{4}\right)$ has the value equal to

(a) 2 (b) 3

(c) 5 (d) 7

Answer Keys

1. (d)	**2.** (a,b,c)	**3.** (a,c,d)	**4.** (b)	**5.** (c)	**6.** (c)	**7.** (c)	**8.** (b)	**9.** (a,d)	**10.** (c)
11. (a)	**12.** (c)	**13.** (b)	**14.** (a)	**15.** (c)	**16.** (b)				

MULTIPLE-CHOICE QUESTIONS

SECTION-I

OBJECTIVE-TYPE SOLVED EXAMPLES

1. Let $f(x)=\dfrac{ax+b}{cx+d}$. Then $fof(x) = x$; provided that

(a) $d = -a$ (b) $d = a$
(c) $a = b = c = d = 1$ (d) $a = b = 1$

Solution: **(a)** We have $f(x)=\dfrac{ax+b}{cx+d}$.

Therefore, $fof(x) = x \Leftrightarrow f(f(x)) = x$

$$\Leftrightarrow f\left(\frac{ax+b}{cx+d}\right)=x \quad \Leftrightarrow \frac{a\left(\dfrac{ax+b}{cx+d}\right)+b}{c\left(\dfrac{ax+b}{cx+d}\right)+d}=x$$

$$\Leftrightarrow \frac{x(a^2+bc)+ab+bd}{x(ac+cd)+bc+d^2}=x \ \forall x \in \mathbb{R}$$

Clearly, $d = -a$ satisfies this relation.

2. Let $g(x) = 1 + x - [x]$ and $f(x)=\begin{cases}-1, & x<0\\ 0, & x=0\\ 1, & x>0\end{cases}$. Then for all x, $f(g(x))$ is equal to; (where [] denotes the greatest integer function)

(a) x (b) 1
(c) $f(x)$ (d) $g(x)$

Solution: (b) $g(x) = 1 + x - [x]$ is greater than 1, since $x - [x] > 0$
$f[g(x)] = 1$, since $f(x) = 1$ for all $x > 0$

3. The set of all values of x for which $|f(x) + g(x)| < |f(x)| + |g(x)|$ is true if $f(x) = x - 3$ and $g(x) = 4 - x$ is given by

(a) $\mathbb{R}$ (b) $\mathbb{R}$ –]3, 4[or $\mathbb{R} - (3, 4)$
(c) $\mathbb{R} - [3, 4]$ (d) None of these

Solution: **(c)** The given inequality is equivalent to $1 < |x - 3| + |4 - x|$
i.e., $1 < |x - 3| + |x - 4|$ ....(1)
For $x < 3$, we have $3 - x + 4 - x = 7 - 2x > 1$ ....(2)
i.e., $x < 3$, which is true in the domain
For $3 \le x < 4$ (1), gives $x - 3 + 4 - x = 1 > 1$,
Which is not true ...(3)
For $4 \le x$, we have from (1) $2x - 7 > 1$
$\Rightarrow x > 4$. which holds in case domain ...(4)
From (2) and (4), we have the solution of the inequality as $x < 3$ or $x > 4$
$\therefore$ i.e., $x \in \mathbb{R} - [3, 4]$.

4. The domain of $f(x)=\sqrt{\log_{1/4}\left(\dfrac{5x-x^2}{4}\right)}+{}^{10}C_x$ is

(a) $(0, 1] \cup [4, 5)$ (b) $(0, 5)$
(c) $\{1, 4\}$ (d) None of these

Solution: (c) Let $f_1=\sqrt{\log_{1/4}\left(\dfrac{5x-x^2}{4}\right)}$ and $f_2={}^{10}C_x$

Clearly f_1 is defined for $\log_{1/4}\left(\dfrac{5x-x^2}{4}\right)\ge 0$ and

$\dfrac{5x-x^2}{4}>0 \quad \Rightarrow 0<\left(\dfrac{5x-x^2}{4}\right)\le 1$

$\Rightarrow \dfrac{5x-x^2}{4}>0$ and $\dfrac{5x-x^2}{4}\le 1$

$\Rightarrow x(x-5) < 0$ and $x^2 - 5x + 4 \ge 0$

$\Rightarrow x \in (0, 5)$ and $x \in (-\infty, 1] \cup [4, \infty)$

$\Rightarrow f_1$ is defined for $x \in (0, 1] \cup [4, 5) = D_{f_1}$ (say)

f_2 is defined for $x \in \{0, 1, 2, 3, 4, 5, 6, 7, 8, 9, 10\} = D_{f_2}$ (say)

$f(x)$ is defined for $x \in D_{f_1} \cap D_{f_2} = \{1, 4\}$

5. The number of one–one functions $f : \{1, 2, 3, \ldots, 10\} \to \{1, 2, 3, \ldots, 10\}$ such that $f(i) \ne i$ but $f(f(i)) = i$ for each $i = 1, 2, 3, \ldots, 10$ is

(a) 945 (b) 256
(c) 2560 (d) None of these

Solution **(a)** $f(i) \ne i$ and $f(f(i)) = i \Rightarrow f^{-1} = f$
$\Rightarrow$ Functions will be self invertible
$\Rightarrow$ Functions are symmetric, i.e., $(\alpha, \beta) \in f$
$\Rightarrow (\beta, \alpha) \notin f^{1} \quad \Rightarrow (\beta, \alpha) \in f$ and $\alpha \ne \beta$
Which can be formed by selecting five pairs of 10 in $\dfrac{{}^{10}C_2 \times {}^8C_2 \times {}^6C_2 \times {}^4C_2 \times {}^2C_2}{5!}$ ways, i.e., 945 ways.

6. The number of functions f from {1, 2, ..., 25} onto {1, 2, ..., 25} such that $f(k)$ is a multiple of 3 whenever k is a multiple of 4 is

(a) $(8)^6$. 19! (b) 6!.19!

(c) $\frac{8!}{2!}\times 19!$ (d) None of these

Solution: (c) A = {1, 2, 3,...,25} contains 6 multiples of 4, i.e., k = 4, 8, 12, 16, 20, 24 and there are 8 multiples of 3

Now out of 8, we can select any 6 in $^8C_6$ ways and can be associated with 6 k's in $^8C_6 \times 6!$ ways and the remaining 19 elements can associated in 19! ways.

∴ Total number of required functions

$= {}^8C_6\times 6!\times 19! = \frac{8!}{2!}\times 19!$

7. The number of bijective functions $f: A \to A$ where A = {1, 2, 3, 4}; such that $f(1) \neq 3, f(2) \neq 1. f(3) \neq 4, f(4) \neq 2$ is

(a) 11 (b) 23

(c) 12 (d) 9

Solution: (d) The number of bijections is equal to number of ways of distributing 4 letters into envelops so that no letter goes to its correct address

$= 4!\left(1-\frac{1}{1!}+\frac{1}{2!}-\frac{1}{3!}+\frac{1}{4!}\right)=9.$

8. Let f be a function defined on [–1, 3], then the function $g(x) = f(2x^2 - 1)$ has domain

(a) [0, 2] (b) $(-\infty, -2] \cup [2, \infty)$

(c) [–2, 2] (d) None of these

Solution: (c) For the validity of given equation $g(x) = f(2x^2 - 1)$; $-1 \leq 2x^2 - 1 \leq 3$

$\Rightarrow 0 \leq 2x^2 \leq 4 \qquad \Rightarrow 0 \leq x^2 \leq 2$

$\Rightarrow x \in [-2, 2]$

9. The largest interval lying in $\left(-\frac{\pi}{2},\frac{\pi}{2}\right)$ for which the function $f(x)=3^{-x^2}+\cos^{-1}\left(\frac{1}{2}x-1\right)+\log.\cos x$ is defined, is

(a) $[0, \pi]$ (b) $\left[-\frac{\pi}{2},\frac{\pi}{2}\right]$

(c) $[0, \pi/2)$ (d) None of these

Solution: (c) 3^{-x^2} is defined for all $x \in \mathbb{R}$

$\cos^{-1}\left(\frac{1}{2}x-1\right)$ is defined for $-1\leq\left(\frac{x}{2}-1\right)\leq 1$

i.e., $0 \leq x \leq 4$ and log cos x is defined (real) for $\cos x > 0$, i.e., $2n\pi-\frac{\pi}{2}<x<2n\pi+\frac{\pi}{2}$

Hence, the largest interval lying in $\left(-\frac{\pi}{2},\frac{\pi}{2}\right)$ is $\left[0,\frac{\pi}{2}\right)$.

10. Let $f(x)=\sqrt{[\sin 2x]-[\cos 2x]}$ (where [.] denotes the greatest integer function), then range of $f(x)$ will be

(a) {0} (b) {1}

(c) {0, 1} (d) {0, 1, √2}

Solution: (c) We should have $[\sin 2x] \geq [\cos 2x]$

we can have $[\sin 2x] = 1, [\cos 2x] = 1, 0, -1$

$[\sin 2x] = 0, [\cos 2x] = 0, -1$

$[\sin 2x] = -1, [\cos 2x] = -1$ but $[\sin 2x] = 1$,

$[\cos 2x] = 1$ and $[\sin 2x] = 1, [\cos 2x] = -1$ are impossible

So, range = {0, 1}

11. Range of the function $f(x)=\sin^{-1}\left(\left[x^2-\frac{1}{3}\right]-1\right)+\cos^{-1}\left[x^2+\frac{2}{3}\right]$ is ([.] denotes the greatest integer function)

(a) $\left[-\frac{\pi}{2}+\frac{3\pi}{2}\right]$ (b) $\left\{-\frac{\pi}{2}\right\}$

(c) $\left\{-\frac{\pi}{2}, 0, \frac{\pi}{2}, \pi, \frac{3\pi}{2}\right\}$ (d) None of these

Solution: (b)

$f(x)=\sin^{-1}\left(\left[x^2-\frac{1}{3}\right]-1\right)+\cos^{-1}\left[x^2+\frac{2}{3}\right]$

Since $\cos^{-1}y$ is defined for $-1 \leq y \leq 1$

So, $\left[x^2+\frac{2}{3}\right]=-1, 0, 1$ but $\left[x^2+\frac{2}{3}\right]=-1$ is impossible

$\Rightarrow \left[x^2+\frac{2}{3}\right]=0, x^2+\frac{2}{3}\in\left[\frac{2}{3},1\right)$

$\Rightarrow x^2\in\left[0,\frac{1}{3}\right)\Rightarrow\left[x^2-\frac{1}{3}\right]$

$\Rightarrow \sin^{-1}\left(\left[x^2-\frac{1}{3}\right]-1\right)$ is not defined.

$\therefore \left[x^2+\frac{2}{3}\right]=1\Rightarrow\left[x^2-\frac{1}{3}\right]-1=-1$

$\Rightarrow f(x) = \sin^{-1}(-1) + \cos^{-1}(1)$

$\Rightarrow -\frac{\pi}{2}+0=-\frac{\pi}{2}$

12. Least value of the expression $\dfrac{1}{2bx-(x^2+b^2+\sin^2 x)}$, $x \in [-1, 0]$, $b \in [2, 3]$ is

(a) $\dfrac{1}{4}$ (b) $-\dfrac{1}{4}$

(c) $\dfrac{-1}{8+\sin^2 1}$ (d) None of these

Solution: (b) Given expression $= \dfrac{1}{-f(x)}$; where

$f(x) = x^2 + b^2 + \sin^2 x - 2bx = (x - b)^2 + \sin^2 x$

Now, $x \in [-1, 0]$ and $b \in [2, 3]$

$\Rightarrow |x - b| \in [2, 4] \Rightarrow (x - b)^2 \in [4, 16]$ and $\sin^2 x \in [0, \sin^2 1]$. As x increases from -1 to 0; $\sin^2 x$ and $(x - b)^2$ both decreases from $\sin^2 1$ to 0 and $(1 + b)^2$ to b^2 respectively and $b \in [2, 3]$.

$\Rightarrow f(x) \in [4, 16 + \sin^2 1]$

$$\Rightarrow \frac{1}{f(x)} \in \left[\frac{1}{16+\sin^2 1}, \frac{1}{4}\right]$$

$$\Rightarrow \frac{1}{-f(x)} \in \left[-\frac{1}{4}, -\frac{1}{16+\sin^2 1}\right]$$

So, least value of expression is $\dfrac{-1}{4}$.

13. If $f(x) = |x - 1|$, $f: \mathbb{R}^+ \to \mathbb{R}$, $g(x) = e^x$, $g: [-1, \infty) \to \mathbb{R}$. If the function $fog\ (x)$ is defined, then its domain and range respectively are:

(a) $(0, \infty)$ and $[0, \infty)$

(b) $[-1, \infty)$ and $[0, \infty)$

(c) $[-1, \infty)$ and $\left[1-\dfrac{1}{e}, \infty\right)$

(d) $[-1, \infty)$ and $\left[\dfrac{1}{e}-1, \infty\right)$

Solution: (b) Given function is $f(x) = |x - 1|$;

$f: \mathbb{R}^+ \to \mathbb{R}$ and $g(x) = e^x$, $g: [-1, \infty) \to \mathbb{R}$

Now $fog(x) = f[g(x)] = |e^x - 1|$

Now $x \in [-1, \infty)$ $\Rightarrow g(x) \in [e^{-1}, \infty)$

$\Rightarrow (e^x - 1) \in \left[\dfrac{1}{e}-1, \infty\right) \Rightarrow |e^x - 1| \in [0, \infty)$

$\therefore$ Range of $fog(x)$ is $[0, \infty)$ and domain $[-1, \infty)$.

14. If $f(x) = \cot^{-1} x : \mathbb{R} \to \left(0, \dfrac{\pi}{2}\right)$ and $g(x) = 2x - x^2$: $\mathbb{R} \to \mathbb{R}$. Then the range of the function $f(g(x))$ wherever defined is

(a) $\left(0, \dfrac{\pi}{2}\right)$ (b) $\left(0, \dfrac{\pi}{4}\right)$

(c) $\left[\dfrac{\pi}{4}, \dfrac{\pi}{2}\right)$ (d) $\left(\dfrac{\pi}{4}\right)$

Solution: (c) Given $f(x) = \cot^{-1} x : \mathbb{R} \to \left(0, \dfrac{\pi}{2}\right)$;

$g(x) = 2x - x^2 : \mathbb{R} \to \mathbb{R} \Rightarrow f(g(x)) = \cot^{-1}(2x - x^2)$

Now $2x - x^2$ is continuous and has its range $(-\infty, 1]$ and $\cot^{-1}(x)$ is defined from $\mathbb{R} \to \left(0, \dfrac{\pi}{2}\right)$ and is continuous and decreasing function.

$\Rightarrow \cot^{-1}(2x - x^2)$ has its range

$$[\cot^{-1}1, \cot^{-1}(-\infty)] = \left[\frac{\pi}{4}, \pi\right) \cap \left(0, \frac{\pi}{2}\right) = \left[\frac{\pi}{4}, \frac{\pi}{2}\right)$$

15. Let $f(x) = 1 + \dfrac{1}{\sqrt[4]{x}}$ and $g(x, y) = \log_x y$, then the domain of $g\left(\dfrac{1}{2}, -g(2, f(x)) - 1\right)$ is

(a) $0 < x < 1$ (b) $0 < x \le 1$

(c) $x \ge 1$ (d) Null set

Solution: (d) $-g(2, f(x)) = -\log_2\left(1 + \dfrac{1}{\sqrt[4]{x}}\right)$

$$\Rightarrow -g(2, f(x)) - 1 = -\log_2\left(1 + \frac{1}{\sqrt[4]{x}}\right) - 1$$

$$\therefore\ g\left(\frac{1}{2}, -g(2, f(x)) - 1\right) = \log_{1/2}\left(-\log_2\left(1 + \frac{1}{\sqrt[4]{x}}\right) - 1\right)$$

$$\Rightarrow \log_2\left(1 + \frac{1}{\sqrt[4]{x}}\right) + 1 < 0 \quad \Rightarrow 0 < 1 + \frac{1}{\sqrt[4]{x}} < 2^{-1}$$

$$\Rightarrow -1 < \frac{1}{\sqrt[4]{x}} < -\frac{1}{2} \quad \Rightarrow x \in \phi \text{ (null set)}$$

16. Let $f(x) = \sin x - \cos x$ and $g(x) = \log_{\sqrt{5}} x$; then the range of $g\left(\sqrt{2} f(x) + 3\right)$ is

(a) $[0, 1]$ (b) $[0, 2]$

(c) $\left[0, -\right]$ (d) None of these

Solution: (b) $g(\sqrt{2} f(x) + 3)$

$= \log_{\sqrt{5}}\left(\sqrt{2}(\sin x - \cos x) + 3\right)$.

We know that $-\sqrt{2} \le (\sin x - \cos x) \le \sqrt{2}$, $\forall\ x \in \mathbb{R}$

$\left[\because -\sqrt{a^2+b^2} \le a\sin x + b\cos x \le \sqrt{a^2+b^2}\right]$

$\Rightarrow -2 \le \sqrt{2}(\sin x - \cos x) \le 2$

$\Rightarrow 1 \le \sqrt{2}(\sin x - \cos x) + 3 \le 5$

$\Rightarrow 0 \le \log_{\sqrt{5}}\left(\sqrt{2}(\sin x - \cos x) + 3\right) \le 2$

($\because \log_a x$ is increasing function for $a > 1$)

Hence, range of $g(\sqrt{2} f(x) + 3)$ is $[0, 2]$.

17. Let $f(x) = 16 \sin^2 x + 1$ and $g(x, y) = \log_x y$, then the range of $h(x) = g\left(\sqrt{2}, (2 - g(2, f(x)))\right)$ is

(a) $(-\infty, 1)$ (b) $(-\infty, 2)$

(c) $(-\infty, 1]$ (d) $(-\infty, 2]$

Solution: (d) $h(x) = g\left[\sqrt{2}, (2 - g(2, f(x)))\right]$

$= \log_{\sqrt{2}}[2 - g(2, f(x))] = \log_{\sqrt{2}}[2 - \log_2 f(x)]$

$\Rightarrow 0 < 16 \sin^2 x + 1 < 4 \quad \Rightarrow 1 < 16 \sin^2 x + 1 < 4$

$\Rightarrow 0 \le \sin^2 x < \dfrac{3}{16} \quad \Rightarrow 1 \le 16 \sin^2 x + 1 < 4$

$\Rightarrow 0 \le \log_2 (16 \sin^2 x + 1) < 2$

$\Rightarrow 2 \ge 2 - \log_2 (16 \sin^2 x + 1) > 0$

$\Rightarrow \log_{\sqrt{2}} 2 \ge \log_{\sqrt{2}}\left(2 - \log_2\left(16\sin^2 x + 1\right)\right) > -\infty$

$\Rightarrow h(x) = (-\infty, 2]$.

18. Domain (D) and Range (R) of $f(x) = \sin^{-1}(\cos^{-1}[x])$ is respectively; where [.] greatest integer function.

(a) $D \equiv x \in [1, 2),\ R \equiv \{0\}$

(b) $D \equiv x \in [0, 1],\ R \equiv \{-1, 0, 1\}$

(c) $D \equiv x \in [-1, 1],\ R \equiv \left\{0, \sin^{-1}\left(\dfrac{\pi}{2}\right), \sin^{-1}(\pi)\right\}$

(d) $D \equiv x \in [-1, 1],\ R \equiv \left\{\dfrac{\pi}{2}, 0, \dfrac{\pi}{2}\right\}$

Solution: (a) $f(x) = \sin^{-1}(\cos^{-1}[x])$

$\Rightarrow f(x)$ is defined when $\cos^{-1}[x] \in [-1, 1]$.

But $\cos^{-1}[x] \in [0, \pi] \Rightarrow \cos^{-1}[x] \in [0, 1]$

$\Rightarrow [\cos 1, 1] \quad \Rightarrow [x] = 1$

$\Rightarrow f(x) = \sin^{-1}\left(\cos^{-1} 1\right)$ or $\sin^{-1} 0 = 0$

$\Rightarrow$ Range $= \{0\}$ and domain $\{x: [x] = 1\}$

$\Rightarrow x \in [1, 2) \therefore$ Domain $= [1, 2)$ and Range $= \{0\}$

19. The range of the function $f(x) = \sin^{-1}\left[x^2 + \dfrac{1}{2}\right]$ $+ \cos^{-1}\left[x^2 - \dfrac{1}{2}\right]$, where [.] is the greatest integer function is

(a) $\left\{\dfrac{\pi}{2}, \pi\right\}$ (b) $\left\{0, \dfrac{\pi}{2}\right\}$

(c) $\{\pi\}$ (d) $\left(0, \dfrac{\pi}{2}\right)$

Solution: (c) Given function is $f(x) = \sin^{-1}\left[x^2 + \dfrac{1}{2}\right]$ $+ \cos^{-1}\left[x^2 - \dfrac{1}{2}\right]$

$= \sin^{-1}\left[x^2 + \dfrac{1}{2}\right] + \cos^{-1}\left[x^2 + \dfrac{1}{2} - 1\right]$

$= \sin^{-1}\left[x^2 + \dfrac{1}{2}\right] + \cos^{-1}\left(\left[x^2 + \dfrac{1}{2}\right] - 1\right)$

Since $x^2 + \dfrac{1}{2} \ge \dfrac{1}{2}$, $\left[x^2 + \dfrac{1}{2}\right] = 0$ or 1,

$\sin^{-1}\left[x^2 + \dfrac{1}{2}\right]$ is defined only for these two values.

$\therefore$ When $\left[x^2 + \dfrac{1}{2}\right] = 0$

$\Rightarrow f(x) = \sin^{-1} 0 + \cos^{-1}(-1) = \pi$

and when $\left[x^2 + \dfrac{1}{2}\right] = 1$

$\Rightarrow f(x) = \sin^{-1} 1 + \cos^{-1} 0 = \pi$. Therefore range of $f(x) = \{\pi\}$.

20. The range of $f(x) = \cos\left(\sin\left(\ln \dfrac{x^2 + e}{x^2 + 1}\right)\right)$ $+ \sin\left(\cos\left(\ln\left(\dfrac{x^2 + e}{x^2 + 1}\right)\right)\right)$ is

(a) $[-\sqrt{2}, \sqrt{2}]$

(b) $[-2, 2]$

(c) $[\cos(\sin 1) + \sin \cos 1, 1 + \sin 1]$

(d) $[-1, 1]$

Solution: (c) The function $g(x) = \dfrac{x^2 + e}{x^2 + 1}$ is continuous with range $(1, e]$.

Since $\ln x$ increases for all $x > 0$.

So, $0 < \ln g(x) \le 1$; again $\sin \theta$ is increasing for $\theta \in \left(0, \dfrac{\pi}{2}\right]$

So, $\sin(\ln(g(x)))$ increases for $\ln(g(x)) \in (0, 1]$

Thus, $\cos(\sin 1) \le \cos(\sin \ln g(x)) < 1$ ($\cos x$ decreases on $[0, 1]$.

Thus, $\cos\left(\sin\left(\ln\left(\dfrac{x^2 + e}{x^2 + 1}\right)\right)\right)$ is a decreasing function with domain $\mathbb{R}$.

Similarly, $0 < \ln(g(x)) \le 1$

$\Rightarrow \cos 1 \le \cos(\ln(g(x))) < 1$

$\Rightarrow \sin(\cos 1) \le \sin(\cos(\ln(g(x)))) < \sin 1.$

Now as x increases, $\ln x$ increases

$\Rightarrow \cos(\ln x)$ decreases

$\Rightarrow \sin(\cos(\ln x))$ also decreases

Thus, $\sin\left(\cos\left(\ln\left(\frac{x^2+e}{x^2+1}\right)\right)\right)$ is also a decreasing function on $\mathbb{R}$.

Thus, both constituent functions of $f(x)$ are decreasing.

$\Rightarrow$ range of $f(x)$

$\Rightarrow [\cos(\sin 1) + \sin(\cos 1), 1 + \sin 1]$

21. If $f\left(x+\frac{y}{8}, x-\frac{y}{8}\right) = xy$, then $f(m, n) + f(n, m) = 0$

(a) only when $m = n$ (b) only when $m \ne n$
(c) only when $m = -n$ (d) for all m and n

Solution: (d) Given function is $f\left(x+\frac{y}{8}, x-\frac{y}{8}\right) = xy$,

Putting $\frac{y}{8} = k$; we have $f(x + k, x - k) = 8xk$ ... (1)

Putting $x + k = A$ and $x - k = B$

or $x = \frac{A+B}{2}$ and $k = \frac{A-B}{2}$ in (1), we have

$f(A, B) = 8\left(\frac{A+B}{2}\right)\left(\frac{A-B}{2}\right) = 2(A^2 - B^2)$

$\Rightarrow f(m, n) + f(n, m) = 2(m^2 - n^2) + 2(n^2 - m^2) = 0 \;\forall\; m, n$

22. If $f(x + 1) + f(x - 1) = 2f(x)$ and $f(0) = 0$, therefore, $n \in \mathbb{N}$, $f(n)$ equals

(a) $nf(1)$ (b) $(f(1))^n$
(c) 0 (d) None of these

Solution: (a) Putting $x = 1, f(2) + f(0) = 2f(1)$

$\Rightarrow f(2) = 2f(1)$ and $f(3) = 3f(1)$

Let us assume $f(n) = nf(1)$; for $n = 1, 2, \ldots\ldots, n$.

Now, $f(n + 1) + f(n - 1) = 2f(n)$

$\Rightarrow f(n + 1) + (n - 1)f(1) = 2nf(1)$

$\Rightarrow f(n + 1) = (n + 1)f(1)$

$\therefore$ By principle of mathematical induction, $f(n) = nf(1)$ for all $n \in \mathbb{N}$.

23. Let $f(1) = 1$ and $f(n) = 2.\sum_{r=1}^{n-1} f(r)$. Then $\sum_{n=1}^{m} f(n)$ is equal to

(a) $3^m - 1$ (b) 3^{m-1}
(c) $3^m + 1$ (d) None of these

Solution: (b) Given $f(1) = 1$ and $f(n) = 2.\sum_{r=1}^{n-1} f(r)$

Now $f(n) = 2\{f(1) + f(2) + \ldots\ldots. + f(n-1)\}$

and $f(n + 1) = 2\{f(1) + f(2) + \ldots. + f(n)\}$

$\Rightarrow f(n - 1) = 3f(n)$ for $n \ge 2$

$\Rightarrow f(n - 1) - f(n) = 2f(n)$

Also $f(2) = 2f(1) = 2$

$\therefore f(3) = 3f(2) = (3.2)$ and

$f(4) = 3.f(3) = 3.(3.2) = 2.(3)^2$ and so on.

$\therefore \sum_{n=1}^{m} f(n) = f(1) + f(2) + \ldots\ldots + f(m)$

$= 1 + 2 + 2.3 + 2.3^2 + \ldots + 2.3^{m-2}$

$= 1 + 2(1 + 3 - 3^2 + \ldots. + 3^{m-2}) = 3^{m-1}$

24. If $f(x) = 9.4^x - 24.2^x$ and $g(x) = \cos 2x - 4\sin^2 x - 5\cos^2 x$, then the value of x and y for which $f(x) + 12 = g(y)$ are

(a) $x = 3, y = 2n\pi;\; n \in \mathbb{Z}$

(b) $x = \log_2 \frac{4}{3};\; y = n\pi;\; n \in \mathbb{Z}$

(c) $x = \log_2 \frac{4}{3};\; y = \frac{2n\pi}{3};\; n \in \mathbb{Z}$

(d) $x = 2 - \log_4 9,\; y = n\pi;\; n \in \mathbb{Z}$

Solution: (b) $9.4^x - 24.2^x + 12 = \cos 2y - 4\sin^2 y - 5\cos^2 y$. Putting $2^x = t$ we have

$\Rightarrow 9t^2 - 24t + 12 = 1 - 2\sin^2 y - 4\sin^2 y - 5\cos^2 y$

Now $9t^2 - 24t + 12$

$= 9\left\{\left(t-\frac{4}{3}\right)^2 - \frac{4}{9}\right\} = 9\left(t-\frac{4}{3}\right)^2 - 4 \ge -4$ and

$1 - 6\sin^2 y - 5\cos^2 y = -4 - \sin^2 y \le -4.$

$\therefore$ Equality holds, i.e., both LHS and RHS are -4 and for this $t - \frac{4}{3} = 0$ and $\sin^2 y = 0$

$\Rightarrow y = n\pi, n \in \mathbb{Z}$ and $t = \frac{4}{3} \Rightarrow x = \log_2 \frac{4}{3}$.

25. Let $f(x) = a^x (a > 0)$ be written as $f(x) = g(x) + h(x)$, where $g(x)$ is an even function and $h(x)$ is an odd function. Then the value of $g(x + y) + g(x - y)$ is

(a) $2g(x)\,g(y)$ (b) $2g(x + y)\,g(x - y)$
(c) $2g(x)$ (d) None of these

Solution: (a) Clearly, $g(x) = \frac{1}{2}(a^x + a^{-x})$ and

$h(x) = \frac{1}{2}(a^x - a^{-x})$

Now $g(x+y)+g(x-y)=\frac{1}{2}(a^{x+y} + a^{-(x+y)}) + \frac{1}{2}(a^{x-y} + a^{-x+y})$

$= \frac{1}{2}(a^x a^y + a^x a^{-y} + a^{-x} a^y + a^{-x} a^{-y})$

$= \frac{1}{2}(a^x (a^y + a^{-y}) + a^{-x} (a^y + a^{-y}))$

$= 2\left(\frac{1}{2}(a^x + a^{-x})\right)\left(\frac{1}{2}(a^y + a^{-y})\right) = 2g(x)\,g(y)$

26. Let $f(x) = ([a]^2 - 5[a] + 4)x^3 - (6\{a\}^2 - 5\{a\} + 1)x - (\tan x)\, sgn\, x$, be an even function for all $x \in \mathbb{R} - \left\{(2n+1)\frac{\pi}{2}; n \in \mathbb{Z}\right\}$, then sum of all possible values of a is (where [] and { } denotes greatest integer function and fractional part functions, respectively)

(a) $\frac{17}{6}$ (b) $\frac{53}{6}$

(c) $\frac{35}{3}$ (d) None of these

Solution: (c) ∵ $f(x)$ is an even function

$\Rightarrow f(x) = f(-x)\ \forall\, x \in \mathbb{R} - \left\{(2n+1)\frac{\pi}{2}; n \in \mathbb{Z}\right\}$

$\Rightarrow ([a]^2 - 5[a] + 4)x^3 - (6\{a\}^2 - 5\{a\} + 1)x - (\tan x)\, sgn(x)$
$= -([a]^2 - 5[a] + 4)x^3 + (6\{a\}^2 - 5\{a\} + 1)x + \tan x\, sgn(-x)$

$\Rightarrow 2([a]^2 - 5[a] + 4)x^3 - 2(6\{a\}^2 - 5\{a\} + 1)x - \tan x\, (sgn(x) + sgn(-x)) = 0\ \forall\, x \in \mathbb{R} - \left\{(2n+1)\frac{\pi}{2}; n \in \mathbb{Z}\right\}$

But $sgn\, x + sgn\,(-x) = 0\ \forall\, x \in \mathbb{R}$

$\Rightarrow ([a]^2 - 5[a] + 4)x^3 - (6\{a\}^2 - 5\{a\} + 1)x = 0\ \forall\, x \in \mathbb{R} - \left\{(2n+1)\frac{\pi}{2}; n \in \mathbb{Z}\right\}$

$\Rightarrow [a]^2 - 5[a] + 4 = 0$ and $6\{a\}^2 - 5\{a\} + 1 = 0$

$\Rightarrow ([a] - 1)([a] - 4) = 0$ and $(3\{a\} - 1)(2\{a\} - 1) = 0$

$\Rightarrow [a] = 1$ or $[a] = 4$ and $\{a\} = \frac{1}{3}$ or $\{a\} = \frac{1}{2}$

$\therefore\ [a] = 1, \{a\} = \frac{1}{3} \Rightarrow a = \frac{4}{3}$

$[a] = 1, \{a\} = \frac{1}{2} \Rightarrow a = \frac{3}{2}$

$[a] = 4, \{a\} = \frac{1}{3} \Rightarrow a = \frac{13}{3}$

$[a] = 4, \{a\} = \frac{1}{2} \Rightarrow a = \frac{9}{2}$

∴ Sum of all possible values of

$a = \frac{4}{3} + \frac{3}{2} + \frac{13}{3} + \frac{9}{2} = \frac{8+9+26+27}{6} = \frac{35}{3}$

27. If $f(x)$ and $g(x)$ be periodic and non-periodic functions respectively, then $f(g(x))$ is

(a) always periodic
(b) never periodic
(c) periodic, when $g(x)$ is a linear function of x
(d) can't say

Solution: (c) Since we know if $f(x)$ is periodic, then $f(ax + b)$ is also periodic function with period $\frac{T}{|a|}$

Hence, $g(x)$ should be a linear function of x.

28. Consider the following statements:

S_1: A function can never be odd and even simultaneously
S_2: Domain of the function $f(x) = \log x^2$ is $\mathbb{R}$
S_3: Period of $\sin^{99} x$ is 2π
S_4: $\sin(e^x)$ is a periodic function.

Which of the following sequences of answers is correct about the above given statements?
(T = true, F = false).

(a) FFTF (b) TFTTT
(c) FTTF (d) TFTF

Solution: (a) S_1 is incorrect as zero function, i.e., $f(x) = 0$; $\mathbb{R} \to \mathbb{R}$ is both odd and even simultaneously. S_2 is incorrect as domain of $f(x)$ is $\mathbb{R} \sim \{0\}$; $x = 0$ is not in domain. S_3 is correct as $f(x) = \sin^{99}x$

$\Rightarrow f(x + 2\pi) = \sin^{99}(x + 2\pi) = \sin^{99}x = f(x)$

∴ Period of $\sin^{99}x$ is 2π.

S_4 is false.

∵ Composition of a periodic function, over a non-periodic and non-linear function is non-periodic.

29. Let f be a real valued function such that for any real x, $f(\lambda + x) = f(\lambda - x)$ and $f(2\lambda + x) = -f(2\lambda - x)$ for some $\lambda > 0$. Then

(a) f is even and non-periodic
(b) f is odd and periodic
(c) f is odd and non-periodic
(d) f is even and periodic

Solution: (b) Given $f(\lambda + x) = f(\lambda - x)$ ... (1)

$f(2\lambda + x) = -f(2\lambda - x)$ ... (2)

for $\lambda > 0$

Replacing x by $\lambda - x$ in $\lambda - x$ in (1), we get

$f(2\lambda - x) = f(x)$ .... (3)

$\therefore$ From (2) and (3), $f(x) = -f(2\lambda + x)$

$\Rightarrow f(x) = -[-f(2\lambda + 2\lambda + x)]$

$\Rightarrow f(x) = f(x + 4\lambda)$ ... (4)

$\Rightarrow f(x)$ is periodic with period 4λ.

Further from (3), replacing x by $-x$, we get

$f(2\lambda + x) = f(-x)$ .... (5)

From (2), (3) and (5), we have

$f(-x) = f(2\lambda + x) = -f(2\lambda - x) = -f(x)$

i.e., $f(-x) = -f(x)$

$\Rightarrow f(x)$ is odd function

Thus, f is odd and periodic function.

30. Consider the following statements:

S_1: If $f(x)$ is an even function and $g(x)$ is an odd function, then fog and gof are even functions

S_2: (odd function) × (even function) = odd function

S_3: Any function can be expressed as a sum of an even function and an odd function

S_4: If f is decreasing odd function, then f^{-1} is also odd and decreasing

Which of the following sequences of answers is correct? (T = true, F = False)

(a) TTFT (b) TTTT

(c) FTTF (d) TTFF

Solution: (a) $\because f(g(-x)) = f(-g(x)) = f(g(x))$ and $g(f(-x)) = g(f(x))$

$\Rightarrow$ fog and gof both are even functions

$\therefore$ S_1 is true.

S_2 is obviously true since $(fg)(-x) = f(-x)\,g(-x) = -f(x)\,g(x) = -(fg)(x)$

S_3 holds if domain is symmetric about origin, then we can express

$$f(x) = \left(\frac{f(x)+f(-x)}{2}\right)+\left(\frac{f(x)-f(-x)}{2}\right)$$

$$= \underbrace{h(x)}_{\text{even}} + \underbrace{g(x)}_{\text{odd}}$$

Let f be an odd and decreasing function with its domain D_f symmetric about origin, i.e., $x, -x \in D_f$ and $f(-x) = -f(x)$ $\Rightarrow f(x), -f(x) \in R_f$, i.e., range is also symmetric about origin.

Now $f^{-1}(f(x)) = x$ for $x \in$ principal domain of $f(x)$

$\Rightarrow f^{-1}(f(-x)) = -x \in$ Principal domain of $f(x)$

$\Rightarrow f^{-1}(f(-x)) = -f^{-1}(f(x))$, but f is odd

$\Rightarrow f(-x) = -f(x)$ $\therefore$ $f^{-1}(-f(x)) = -f^{-1}(f(x))$

$\Rightarrow f^{-1}(-y) = -f^{-1}(y)$; where $y = f(x)$, $-y = -f(x) \in R_f$

$\Rightarrow f^{-1}$ is an odd function. Also f^{-1} is decreasing.

31. Solution set of $f^{-1}(x) = x$ is a proper subset of the solution set of $f(x) = f^{-1}(x)$; then

(a) Solution set of $f^{-1}(x) = x$, is identical to solution set of $f(x) = x$

(b) $f(x) = f^{-1}(x)$ is identical to solution set of $f(x) = x$

(c) $f(x)$ and $f^{-1}(x)$ would intersect at a point perpendicular to $y = x$, but not lying on $y = x$.

(d) all of the above

Solution: (c) Curves of $y = f(x)$ and $y = f^{-1}(x)$ either intersect on $y = x$ line or intersect on a line perpendicular to $y = x$.

Since solution set of $f^{-1}(x) = x$ is a proper subset of solution set of $f(x) = f^{-1}(x)$, thus, $f(x)$ and $f^{-1}(x)$ must intersect at a line perpendicular to line $y = x$ and point of intersection not lying on line $y = x$.

32. Consider the following statements:

S_1: If $f(x)$ is increasing, then $f^{-1}(x)$ is also increasing.

S_2: If $f(x)$ is a constant function, then $f^{-1}(x)$ is also a constant function.

S_3: If graph of $f(x)$ and $f^{-1}(x)$ are intersecting, then they always intersect on $y = x$ line.

S_4: The inverse of $f(x) = \dfrac{x}{1+|x|}$ is $\dfrac{x}{1-|x|}$.

Which of the following sequences of answers is correct about the statements? (T = true, F = false).

(a) TTTF (b) TFFT

(c) FFFT (d) TFTT

Solution: (b) S_1: Obviously true as

$$(f^{-1}(x)) = \frac{1}{f'(f^{-}(x))} > 0 \text{ as } f'(x) > 0\ \forall\ x \in D_f$$

S_2: Since constant function is non-invertible, hence, its inverse does not exist.

$\therefore$ Statement S_2 is invalid, and hence, stands false.

S_3: $f(x)$ and $f^{-1}(x)$ can intersect not only on $y = x$ but also they can intersect on a line perpendicular to $y = x$ and not lying on $y = x$.

Hence, the given statement is false.

$$S_4:\ f(x) = \begin{cases} \dfrac{x}{1+x} : & x \ge 0 \\[2mm] \dfrac{x}{1-x} : & x < 0 \end{cases}$$

$$\Rightarrow\ f^{-1}(x) = \begin{cases} \dfrac{x}{1-x} : & x \ge 0 \\[2mm] \dfrac{x}{1+x} : & x < 0 \end{cases} = \frac{x}{1-|x|}$$

Hence, S_4 is true.

33. Let $f:\left[\frac{1}{2},1\right]\to[-1,1]$ is given by $f(x) = 4x^3 - 3x$, then $f^{-1}(x)$ is given by

(a) $\cos\left(\frac{1}{3}\cos^{-1}x\right)$ (b) $3\cos(\sin^{-1}x)$

(c) $3\sin^{-1}(\cos x)$ (d) None of these

Solution: (a) $f'(x) = 12x^2 - 3 = 3(4x^2 - 1)$
$= 3(2x + 1)(2x - 1) \geq 0$,

for $x\in\left(-\infty,\frac{-1}{2}\right]\cup\left[\frac{1}{2},\infty\right)$

$\Rightarrow f(x)$ is strictly increasing on $\left[\frac{1}{2},1\right]$, i.e., injective

Also range of function on $\left[\frac{1}{2},1\right]$ is $[-1, 1]$ = co-domain.

Thus, $f(x)$ is invertible

Let $g(x)$ be the inverse of f, so $f(g(x)) = x\ \forall\ x \in [-1, 1]$

$\Rightarrow 4(g(x))^3 - 3g(x) = x$

Let $g(x) = \cos\theta$ and $g(x)\in\left[\frac{1}{2},1\right]\Rightarrow\theta\in\left[0,\frac{\pi}{3}\right]$

$\Rightarrow \cos3\theta = x$ and $3\theta\in[0,\pi]\Rightarrow\cos^{-1}(\cos3\theta)=3\theta$

$\Rightarrow\ \theta=\frac{1}{3}\cos^{-1}x$, so $g(x)=\cos\left(\frac{1}{3}\cos^{-1}x\right)$

34. If f: $[1, \infty) \to [2, \infty)$ is given by, $f(x)=x+\frac{1}{x}$, then $f^{-1}(x)$ equals

(a) $\frac{x+\sqrt{x^2-4}}{2}$ (b) $\frac{x}{1+x^2}$

(c) $\frac{x-\sqrt{x^2-4}}{2}$ (d) $1-\sqrt{x^2-4}$

Solution: (a) Let $y=x+\frac{1}{x}\ \Rightarrow\ y=\frac{x^2+1}{x}$

$\Rightarrow xy = x^2 + 1 \ \Rightarrow\ x^2 - xy + 1 = 0$

$\Rightarrow\ x=\frac{y\pm\sqrt{y^2-4}}{2}\ \Rightarrow\ f^{-1}(x)=\frac{x\pm\sqrt{x^2-4}}{2}$

Since, the range of the inverse function is $[1, \infty)$,

then we take $f^{-1}(x)=\frac{x+\sqrt{x^2-4}}{2}$

$\because$ If we consider $f^{-1}(x)=\frac{x-\sqrt{x^2-4}}{2}$. Then $f^{-1}(x)>1$

$\Rightarrow\ \frac{x-\sqrt{x^2-4}}{2}>1\ \Rightarrow\ x-2>\sqrt{x^2-4}$ which is possible only if $(x - 2)^2 > x^2 - 4$.

i.e., $x^2 + 4 - 4x > x^2 - 4$.

i.e., if $8 > 4x$ or $x < 2$, whereas in domain of $f^{-1}(x)$; $x \in [2, \infty)$.

Thus, $f^{-1}(x)=\frac{x+\sqrt{x^2-4}}{2}$

35. Suppose $f(x) = (x + 2)^2$ for $x \geq -2$. If $h(x)$ is the function whose graph is the reflection of the graph of $f(x)$ with respect to the line $y = x$ and $g(x)$ is the function whose graph is obtained by shifting 4 units to the left the graph of $h(x)$, then $g(x)$ equals.

(a) $\sqrt{x-4}-2, x\geq4$ (b) $\frac{1}{(x+4)^2}, x\neq-4$

(c) $\sqrt{x-4}, x\geq4$ (d) $\sqrt{x+4}-2, x\geq-4$

Solution: (d) Given $h(x) = f^{-1}(x)$

But $y = f(x) = (x + 2)^2 \ \Rightarrow\ x + 2 = \pm\sqrt{y}; x + 2 \geq 0$

$\Rightarrow\ x = \sqrt{y} - 2 \qquad \Rightarrow\ f^{-1}(x) = h(x) = \sqrt{x} - 2$

Now $g(x) = h(x + 4)$ (given)

$= \sqrt{x+4}-2; x\geq-4$.

36. If $f(x)$ is defined on $[0, 1]$ by $f(x)=\begin{cases}x; & \text{if } x \text{ is rational}\\ 1-x; & \text{if } x \text{ is irrational}\end{cases}$, then for all $x \in [0, 1]$, $f(f(x))$ is

(a) real (b) $1 - x$

(c) x (d) None of these

Solution: (a, c) If x is rational, then $f(x) = x$

$\Rightarrow f(f(x)) = f(x) = x$

If x is irrational, then $f(x) = 1 - x$ = irrational

($\because$ rational-irrational = irrational)

$\Rightarrow f(f(x)) = f(1 - x) = 1 - (1 - x) = x$

Thus, $f(f(x)) = x$ for all x in $[0, 1]$

$\Rightarrow f(f(x)) = x$ (real)

37. The number of functions f from the set $A = \{2, 3, 5\}$ into the set $B = \{1, 3, 5, 7, 9, 11, 13\}$ such that $f(i) \leq f(j)$ for $i < j$ and $i, j \in A$.

(a) ${}^9C_3$ (b) ${}^9C_3 + 2({}^9C_2)$

(c) ${}^8C_3 + {}^8C_2$ (d) None of these

Solution: (a,c) A function $f : A \to B$ such that $f(2) \leq f(3) \leq f(5)$ can be generated in the following four cases.

Case i: $f(2) < f(3) < f(5)$

There are ${}^7C_3$ functions in this case.

Case ii: $f(2) = f(3) < f(5)$
There are ${}^7C_2$ functions in this case.
Case iii: $f(2) < f(3) = f(5)$
There are ${}^7C_2$ functions in this case.
Case iv: $f(2) = f(3) = f(5)$
There are ${}^7C_1$ functions in this case.
Thus, the number of desired functions is ${}^7C_3 + {}^7C_2 + {}^7C_2 + {}^7C_1 = {}^8C_3 + {}^8C_2 = {}^9C_3$.
Thus, (a) and (c) will be the correct options.

38. Let $f(x) = \cos(\pi/x)$ and $D^+ = \{x : f(x) > 0\}$. Then D^+ contains

(a) $\left(\frac{2}{5}, \frac{2}{3}\right)$ (b) $\left(\frac{2}{9}, \frac{2}{7}\right)$
(c) $\left(\frac{-2}{3}, \frac{-2}{5}\right)$ (d) $\left(\frac{1}{2}, \frac{2}{3}\right)$

Solution: (a, b, c, d)

Given $D^+ = \{x : f(x) > 0\} = \left\{x : \cos\left(\frac{\pi}{x}\right) > 0\right\}$

$$= \left\{x : \frac{\pi}{x} \in \mathbb{Z} \bigcup_{n\in\mathbb{Z}} \left(2n\pi - \frac{\pi}{2}, 2n\pi + \frac{\pi}{2}\right)\right\}$$

$$= \left\{x : x \in \bigcup_{n\in\mathbb{Z}-\{0\}} \left(\frac{2}{4n+1}, \frac{2}{4n-1}\right)\right\} \cup (-\infty, -2) \cup (2, \infty)$$

$\Rightarrow$ D^+ contains $\left(\frac{2}{5}, \frac{2}{3}\right)$ for $n = 1$

D^+ contains $\left(\frac{2}{9}, \frac{2}{7}\right)$ for $n = 2$

D^+ contains $\left(-\frac{2}{3}, -\frac{2}{5}\right)$ for $n = -1$

Also D^+ contains $\left(\frac{2}{5}, \frac{2}{3}\right) \supset \left(\frac{1}{2}, \frac{2}{3}\right)$

D^+ also contains $\left(\frac{1}{2}, \frac{2}{3}\right)$

39. Let $f(x) = 2 + \sqrt{x}$ and $g(x) = \frac{2x}{x^2+1}$, then

(a) Domain $(f + g + 2) = (-1, \infty)$
(b) Domain $(f + g + 2) = [0, \infty)$
(c) Range $f \cap$ range $(g + 2) = [2, 3]$
(d) Range $f \cup$ range $(g + 2) = [1, \infty)$

Solution: (b, c, d) Domain of $f(x) = [0, \infty)$
Domain of $g(x) = (-\infty, \infty)$
$\Rightarrow$ Domain of $(g + 2)(x) = (-\infty, \infty)$
$\therefore$ Domain of $(f + g + 2)(x) = [0, \infty) \cap (-\infty, \infty) = [0, \infty)$

Further range of $f(x) = [2, \infty)$ as $f'(x) = \frac{1}{2\sqrt{x}} > 0 \, \forall x \in (0, \infty)$.

$\Rightarrow$ $f(x)$ is an increasing and continuous function on $[0, \infty)$.
$\therefore$ $f(x)$ has its minimum value $f(0) = 2 + \sqrt{0} = 2$ and maximum tending to infinite.

Now $f(x) = \frac{2x}{1+x^2}$. Graph of $g(x)$ is as shown below

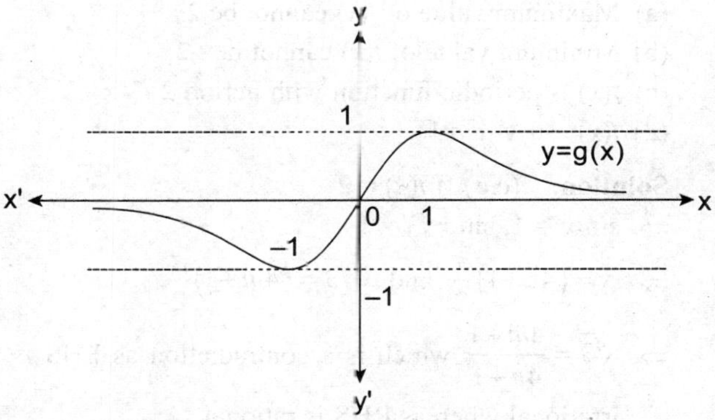

Clearly $g(x)$ has its range $[-1, 1]$
$\Rightarrow$ $(g + 2)(x)$ can be obtained by shifting the graph of $g(x)$ by 2 units above x-axis as shown below

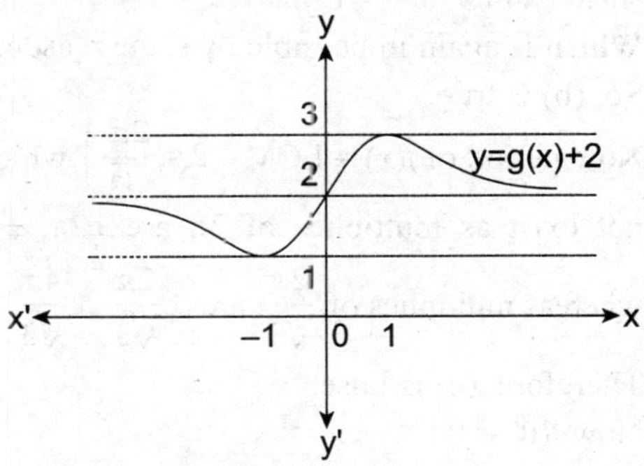

$\therefore$ Range of $(g + 2)(x)$ is $[1, 3]$
$\therefore$ Range of $f(x) \cap$ Range of $(g + 2)(x) = [1, 3] \cap [2, \infty) = [2, 3]$
and range of $f(x) \cup$ range of $(g + 2)(x) = [1, 3] \cup [2, \infty) = [1, \infty)$

40. Which of the following functions have range which is a proper subset of $(-\infty, \infty)$?

(a) $\tan x$ (b) $\cot x$
(c) $\log \sin x$ (d) $\tan x + \cot x$

Solution: (c, d) (a), (b) are false since $\cot x$, $\tan x$ have range as $(-\infty, \infty)$

(c) is true since, $\sin x \in (0, 1]$

$\Rightarrow$ $\log \sin x \in (-\infty, 0]$ which is a proper subset of $(-\infty, \infty)$.

(d) is true since $\tan x + \cot x = \dfrac{\sin x}{\cos x} + \dfrac{\cos x}{\sin x}$

$= \dfrac{1}{\sin x \cos x} = 2 \operatorname{cosec} 2x$; $\sin x, \cos x \neq 0$

$\Rightarrow$ Range of function is $(-\infty, -2] \cup [2, \infty)$ which is a proper subset of $(-\infty, \infty)$

41. Let $f(x) = \sin x + \sin(x\sqrt{3})$. Then, which of the following are false?

(a) Maximum value of $f(x)$ cannot be 2

(b) Minimum value of $f(x)$ cannot be -2

(c) $f(x)$ is periodic function with period $2\sqrt{3}\pi$

(d) $f(x) > 0\ \forall\ x \in \mathbb{R}$.

Solution: (c,d) If $f(x) = 2$

$\Rightarrow$ $\sin x = 1$, $\sin x\sqrt{3} = 1$

$\Rightarrow$ $x = (4n+1)\dfrac{\pi}{2}$ and $x\sqrt{3} = (4m+1)\dfrac{\pi}{2}$

$\Rightarrow$ $\sqrt{3} = \dfrac{4m+1}{4n+1}$ which is a contradiction as LHS is irrational whereas RHS is rational.

$\therefore$ $f(x)$ cannot attain value 2.

$\therefore$ 2 cannot be the maximum value of $f(x)$.

Similarly $f(x) = -2$.

$\Rightarrow$ $\sin x = \sin x\sqrt{3} = -1$.

Which is again impossible by same reason.

So, (b) is true.

Now period of $f(x) = \text{LCM}\left(2\pi, \dfrac{2\pi}{\sqrt{3}}\right)$ which does not exist as multiplies of 2π are $\pm 2\pi, \pm 4\pi, \ldots$ whereas multiplies of $\dfrac{2\pi}{\sqrt{3}}$ are $\pm\dfrac{2\pi}{\sqrt{3}}, \pm\dfrac{4\pi}{\sqrt{3}}, \pm\dfrac{6\pi}{\sqrt{3}}$.

Therefore, (c) is false.

Now $f(0) = 0$

$\therefore$ $f(x) > 0\ \forall\ x \in \mathbb{R}$ is false, i.e., (d) is false.

42. If $f(x) = \sin x + \tan x + sgn\,(x^2 - 6x + 10)$, then it is

(a) periodic with period 2π

(b) periodic with period π

(c) non-periodic

(d) periodic with period 4π

Solution: (a, d) Given $f(x) = \sin x + \tan x + sgn\,(x^2 - 6x + 10)$

$= \sin x + \tan x + sgn\,((x-3)^2 + 1)$

$= \sin x + \tan x + 1$

$(\because (x-3)^2 + 1 \geq 1 \Rightarrow sgn\,[(x-3)^2 + 1] = 1)$

$\Rightarrow$ Period of $f(x) = \text{LCM}\,(2\pi, \pi) = 2\pi$, as period of $\sin x$ is 2π and period of $\tan x$ is π, and the period of function is also 4π

43. Let $f(x)$ and $g(x)$ be two real valued functions given by $f(x) = -\ln x$ and $g(x) = e^{-x}$. Let $h(x) = f(x) - x$ and $m(x) = g(x) - x$. Further let the number of solutions of $h(x) = 0$ and $m(x) = 0$ be a and b, then

(a) $f(x)$ and $g(x)$ intersect at $y = x$

(b) $a = b$

(c) $a = 1$ and $b = 1$

(d) $a \neq b$

Solution: (a, b, c) First we can see that $h(x) = f(x) - x = 0$.

$\Rightarrow$ $f(x) = x$ equation will have only one root

$\because$ We have only one intersection point, and hence, only one solution is possible as is clear from the figure given below.

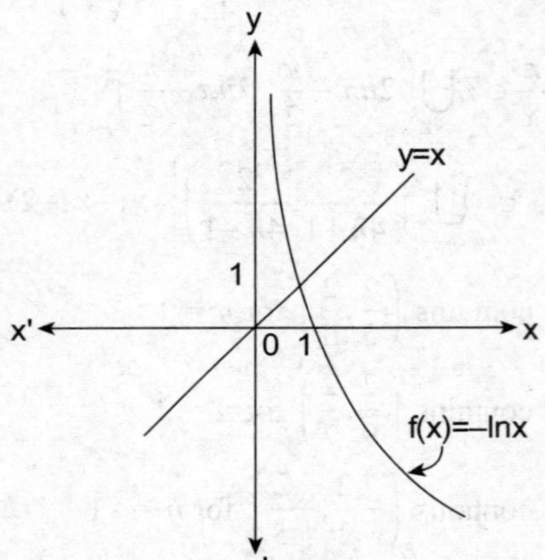

Similarly for $m(x) = 0$

$\Rightarrow$ $g(x) = x$, we have only one solution as shown in the figure that follows

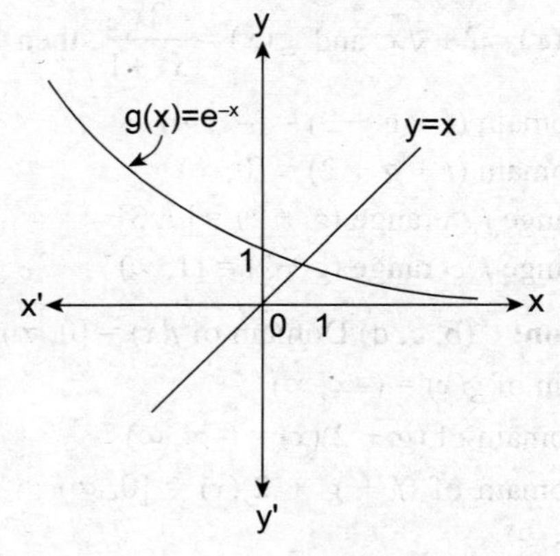

$\therefore$ $a = 1$ and $b = 1$. Moreover one can see that $f(x)$ and $g(x)$ are inverse of each other and are continuous and cross the line $y = x$

Thus, $y = f(x)$ and $y = g(x) = f^{-1}(x)$ will intersect on line $y = x$.

44. The function $\dfrac{x^2+ax+b}{x^2+cx+d}$ is

(a) defined for all x if $c^2 < 4d$

(b) not invertible for any values of a, b, c, d

(c) invertible if $b = 0, d = 0, a \neq c$

(d) invertible if $a = 0, c = 0, bd \neq c$

Solution: (a, c) (a) is true since if $c^2 < 4d$, then $x^2 + cx + d > 0$ for all x and the function is defined.

(b) is not true since $b = 0, d = 0, a \neq c$

$$\Rightarrow f(x) = \frac{x^2+ax}{x^2+cx} = \frac{x+a}{x+c}$$

which is invertible if defined from $\mathbb{R} - \{0, -c\}$ to $\mathbb{R} - \{1\}$

(c) is true (sec (b))

(d) is not true since $\dfrac{x^2+b}{x^2+d}$ is not one–one.

45. Let $f: \left[-\dfrac{\pi}{3}, \dfrac{2\pi}{3}\right] \to [0, 4]$, be a function defined as $f(x) = \sqrt{3}\sin x - \cos x + 2$. Then $f^{-1}(x)$ is given by

(a) $\sin^{-1}\left(\dfrac{x-2}{2}\right) - \dfrac{\pi}{6}$ (b) $\sin^{-1}\left(\dfrac{x-2}{2}\right) + \dfrac{\pi}{6}$

(c) $\dfrac{2\pi}{3} - \cos^{-1}\left(\dfrac{x-2}{2}\right)$ (d) None of these

Solution: (b, c) Given $f(x) = \sqrt{3}\sin x - \cos x + 2 = 2\sin\left(x - \dfrac{\pi}{6}\right) + 2$ ..... (1)

For $x \in \left[-\dfrac{\pi}{3}, \dfrac{2\pi}{3}\right]$; $\left(x - \dfrac{\pi}{6}\right) \in \left[-\dfrac{\pi}{2}, \dfrac{\pi}{2}\right]$ and range of $f(x) = [0, 4] =$ co-domain.

$\Rightarrow f(x)$ in one–one and onto, f is invertible

$\Rightarrow f^{-1}$ exists

Now from (1)

$$y = 2\sin\left(x - \frac{\pi}{6}\right) + 2 \Rightarrow \frac{y-2}{2} = \sin\left(x - \frac{\pi}{6}\right)$$

$$\Rightarrow x = \frac{\pi}{6} + \sin^{-1}\left(\frac{y-2}{2}\right)$$

$$\Rightarrow f^{-1}(x) = \sin^{-1}\left(\frac{x-2}{2}\right) + \frac{\pi}{6}$$

Also $f^{-1}(x) = \dfrac{\pi}{2} - \cos^{-1}\left(\dfrac{x-2}{2}\right) + \dfrac{\pi}{6}$

$= \dfrac{2\pi}{3} - \cos^{-1}\left(\dfrac{x-2}{2}\right)$

46. Let $f(x) = e^x$; $\mathbb{R}^+ \to \mathbb{R}$ and $g(x) = \sin^{-1} x$; $[-1, 1] \to \left[-\dfrac{\pi}{2}, \dfrac{\pi}{2}\right]$, then

(a) Domain of $fog(x)$ is $[-1, 1]$

(b) Range of $fog(x)$ is $\left(1, e^{\frac{\pi}{2}}\right]$

(c) Domain of $fog(x)$ is $(0, 1]$

(d) Range of $fog(x)$ is $\left[e^{-\frac{\pi}{2}}, e^{\frac{\pi}{2}}\right]$

Solution: (b,c) $fog(x) = e^{\sin^{-1} x}$

Now domain of $fog(x)$ would contain those elements of domain of $\sin^{-1} x$, i.e., $[-1, 1]$ for which $\sin^{-1} x$ belongs to domain of $f(x)$, i.e., $\mathbb{R}^+$

$\Rightarrow$ Domain of $fog(x) = (0, 1]$ and Range of

$$fog(x) = \left(e^{\sin^{-1} 0}, e^{\sin^{-1} 1}\right] = \left(1, e^{\frac{\pi}{2}}\right]$$

47. If $f(x) = \dfrac{\sin \pi[x]}{\{x\}}$, where $\{x\}$ denotes fractional part function and [.] denotes greatest integer function, then $f(x)$ is:

(a) periodic with fundamental period 1

(b) even

(c) range of $f(x)$ is a singleton set

(d) $f(x)$ is identical to $g(x) = \text{sgn}\left(\text{sgn}\dfrac{\{x\}}{\sqrt{\{x\}}}\right) - 1.$

Solution: (a, b, c, d) Given function is $f(x) = \dfrac{\sin \pi[x]}{\{x\}}$, $x \notin \mathbb{Z}$; as otherwise denominator becomes, zero, i.e., $f(x)$ is not defined for $x \in \mathbb{Z}$;

But $\dfrac{\sin \pi[x]}{\{x\}} = 0 \ \forall\ x \notin \mathbb{Z}$;

$$f(x) = \begin{cases} 0; & x \notin \mathbb{Z} \\ \text{not defined}; & x \in \mathbb{Z} \end{cases}$$

$\therefore$ The graph of $f(x)$ is as shown below

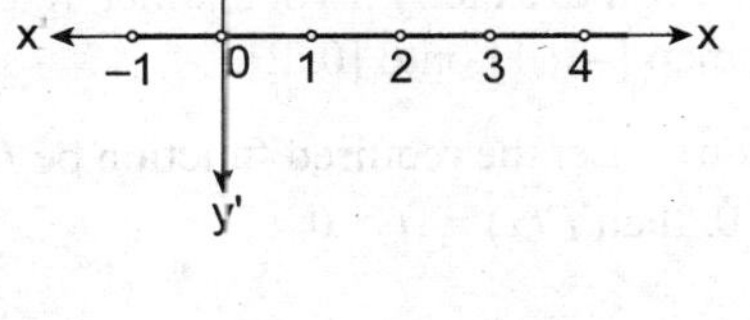

(a) It is clear from the above graph that the fundamental period of given function is one

(b) Also $f(-x) = 0 = f(x)\ \forall\ x \notin \mathbb{Z}$

$\Rightarrow f(x)$ is an even function

(c) Range of $f(x) = \{0\}$, which is a singleton set

(d) Now $g(x) = \text{sgn}\left(\text{sgn}\dfrac{\{x\}}{\sqrt{\{x\}}}\right) - 1;\ x \notin \mathbb{Z}$

$\because\ \dfrac{\{x\}}{\sqrt{\{x\}}} = \sqrt{\{x\}} > 0$ for $x \notin \mathbb{Z}$;

$\Rightarrow \left(\text{sgn}\dfrac{\{x\}}{\sqrt{\{x\}}}\right) = 1$

$\Rightarrow g(x) = sgn\ (1) - 1 \Rightarrow g(x) = 1 - 1 = 0$

$\Rightarrow g(x) = 0,\ x \notin \mathbb{Z}$

$\Rightarrow f(x)$ and $g(x)$ have same domain $x \notin \mathbb{Z}$ and $f(x) = g(x) = 0$ for $x \notin \mathbb{Z}$;

$\Rightarrow f(x)$ and $g(x)$ are identical.

48. Let $g(x) = f(x - 1) + f(x + 1)$; where $f(x) = \begin{cases} 1-|x|; & |x| \le 1 \\ 0; & |x| > 1 \end{cases}$. The number of points of intersections with $y = \sin\alpha$; where α is constant

(a) 0; $(\pi < \alpha < 2\pi)$

(b) 4; $(0 < \alpha < \pi)$

(c) infinitely many; $(\alpha = 2\pi)$

(d) None of these

Solution: (a, b, c) $f(x) = \begin{cases} 1-|x|; & |x| \le 1 \\ 0; & |x| > 1 \end{cases}$

$$= \begin{cases} 1-|x|; & -1 \le x \le 1 \\ 0; & x < -1 \text{ or } x > 1 \end{cases} = \begin{cases} 1+x; & -1 \le x < 0 \\ 1-x; & 0 \le x \le 1 \\ 0; & x < -1 \text{ or } x > 1 \end{cases}$$

$$\therefore\ f(x-1) = \begin{cases} 1+(x-1); & -1 \le x-1 < 0 \\ 1-(x-1); & 0 \le x-1 \le 1 \\ 0; & x-1 < -1 \text{ or } x-1 > 1 \end{cases}$$

$$\Rightarrow\ f(x-1) = \begin{cases} x; & 0 \le x < 1 \\ 2-x; & 1 \le x \le 2 \\ 0; & x < 0 \text{ or } x > 2 \end{cases} \quad \dots (1)$$

$$\Rightarrow\ f(x+1) = \begin{cases} 1+(x+1); & -1 \le x+1 < 0 \\ 1-(x+1); & 0 \le x+1 \le 1 \\ 0; & x+1 < -1 \text{ or } x+1 > 1 \end{cases}$$

$$\Rightarrow\ f(x+1) = \begin{cases} 2+x; & -2 \le x < -1 \\ -x; & -1 \le x \le 0 \\ 0; & x < -2 \text{ or } x > 0 \end{cases} \quad \dots (2)$$

$$\therefore\ f(x-1)+f(x+1) = \begin{cases} 0; & \text{for } x < -2 \text{ or } x > 2 \\ 2+x; & \text{for } -2 \le x < -1 \\ -x; & \text{for } -1 \le x \le 0 \\ x; & \text{for } 0 < x < 1 \\ 2-x; & \text{for } 1 \le x \le 2 \end{cases}$$

The graph of $g(x) = f(x - 1) + f(x + 1)$ is as shown below

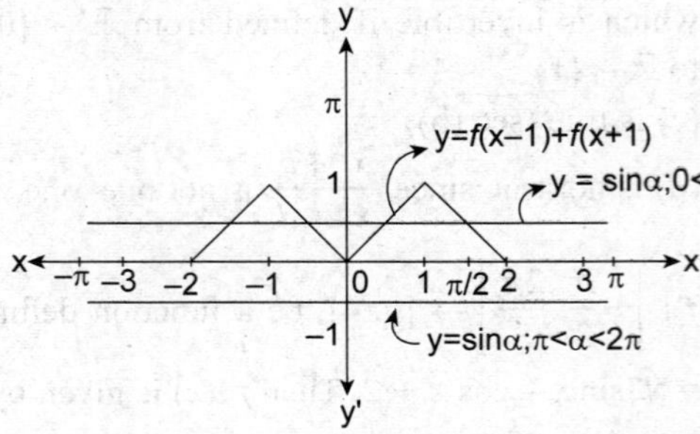

Clearly $g(x)$ and $\sin\alpha$ do not intersect for $\pi < \alpha < 2\pi$ as $\sin\alpha < 0$ for $\pi < \alpha < 2\pi$, i.e., $y = \sin\alpha$ lies below x-axis. So, (a) is correct Also $g(x)$ and $\sin x$ intersect at four points for $0 < \alpha < \pi$, as $\sin\alpha \in (0, 1)$, and hence, $y = \sin\alpha$ is a horizontal line between, $y = 0$ and $y = 1$, so (b) is also correct. Clearly $g(x)$ and $\sin x$ intersect at infinitely many points for $\alpha = 2\pi$ as for $\alpha = 2\pi$, $\sin\alpha = 0$

$\therefore\ y = \sin\alpha$ is equivalent to x-axis which intersect the function $g(x)$ at infinitely many points.

SECTION–II

SUBJECTIVE-TYPE SOLVED EXAMPLES

1. Determine the exactly two distinct linear functions which map $[-1, 1]$ onto $[0, 2]$.

Solution: Let the required function be $f(x) = ax + b$. If $a > 0$, then $f'(x) = a > 0$

$\Rightarrow f(x)$ is monotonically increasing in $[-1, 1]$

$\Rightarrow f(-1) = 0$ and $f(1) = 2$

That is $-a + b = 0$ and $a + b = 2$ so that $b = 1$ and $a = 1$.

$\Rightarrow f(x) = x + 1$

If $a < 0$, then $f'(x) = a < 0$

$\Rightarrow f(x)$ is monotonically decreasing on $[-1, 1]$

$\Rightarrow f(-1) = 2$ and $f(1) = 0$

That is $-a + b = 2$ and $a + b = 0$ so that $b = 1$ and $a = -1$.

$\Rightarrow f(x) = -x + 1$

Hence, $f(x) = x + 1$ or $f(x) = -x + 1$.

2. Let $f: \{x, y, z\} \to \{a, b, c\}$ be a one–one function. It is known that only one of the following statements is true,

(a) $f(x) \neq b$ (b) $f(y) = b$

(c) $f(z) \neq a$

Determine $f^{-1}(b)$.

Solution: As only one of the given statements is true we have the following possibilities:

	$f(x) \neq b$	$f(y) = b$	$f(z) \neq a$
Case i:	T	F	F
Case ii:	F	T	F
Case iii:	F	F	T

(where T, F stand for True, False respectively)

Case i: In this case we would have $f(x) = a$ (or c); $f(y) = c$ (or a); $f(z) = a$

This possibility is clearly ruled out as f is one–one.

Case ii: In this case we would have $f(x) = b$; $f(y) = b$; $f(z) = a$

Once again this possibility is ruled out as image of x and y are identical.

Case iii: In this case we would have $f(x) = b$; $f(y) = a$ or c; $f(z) = c$ or b

Thus, $f(x) = b$; $f(y) = a$; $f(z) = c$

Hence, $f^{-1}(b) = x$

3. Solve $(x)^2 = [x]^2 + 2x$; where $[x]$ represents greatest integer less than or equal to x and (x) represents integer just greater than or equal to x.

Solution: ***Method 1:***

Case i: Let $x = n \in \mathbb{Z}$

Given equation becomes: $n^2 = n^2 + 2n \Rightarrow n = 0$

Case ii: Let $x \notin \mathbb{Z}$; i.e., $n < x < n + 1$

Given equation becomes: $(n + 1)^2 = n^2 + 2x$

$$\Rightarrow x = n + \frac{1}{2}, n \in \mathbb{Z}$$

$$\therefore x = 0 \text{ or } x = n + \frac{1}{2}; n \in \mathbb{Z}$$

Method 2: ***Case i:*** For $x = n \notin \mathbb{Z}$, the equation holds for $n + \frac{1}{2}$; $x = 0$ as proved in case (I)

So, let $x \notin \mathbb{Z}$

Let $x = [x] + \{x\}$; where $\{x\}$ represents fractional part of x.

But $(x) = [x] + 1 \Rightarrow [x] = (x) - 1$

$\Rightarrow x = (x) - 1 + \{x\} \Rightarrow (x) = x + 1 - \{x\}$

$\therefore$ Using it in given equation we have, $((x + 1) - \{x\})^2 = (x - \{x\})^2 + 2x$ (using the given equation)

$\Rightarrow (x - \{x\})^2 + 1 + 2(x - \{x\}) = (x - \{x\})^2 + 2x$

$$\Rightarrow 1 - 2\{x\} = 0 \Rightarrow \{x\} = \frac{1}{2}$$

$$\Rightarrow x = n - \frac{1}{2}; n \in \mathbb{Z}$$

Thus, $x = 0$, $x = n + \frac{1}{2}$; $n \in \mathbb{Z}$ are required solutions.

4. Let $f : \mathbb{R} \sim \{2\} \to \mathbb{R}$ be a function satisfying the following functional equation:

If $2f(x) + 3f\left(\frac{2x+29}{x-2}\right) = 100x + 80$; $\forall x \in \mathbb{R} \sim \{2\}$,

Determine $f(x)$.

Solution: Here, $f(x) = -\frac{3}{2}f\left(\frac{2x+29}{x-2}\right) + 50x + 40$.(1)

Replacing x by $\frac{2x+29}{x-2}$ in the given equation (1), we get $f\left(\frac{2x+29}{x-2}\right)$

$$= -\frac{3}{2}f\left(\frac{2\left(\frac{2x+29}{x-2}\right)+29}{\left(\frac{2x+29}{x-2}\right)-2}\right) + 50\left(\frac{2x+29}{x-2}\right) + 40$$

$$= -\frac{3}{2}f(x) + 50\left(\frac{2x+29}{x-2}\right) + 40 \quad \text{.... (2)}$$

Substituting the values of $f\left(\frac{2x+29}{x-2}\right)$ from (2) in (1), we get $f(x) = 136 - 40x + \frac{1980}{x-2}$

5. Let $[x]$ denotes greatest integer less than or equal to x. If all the values of x such that the product $\left[x - \frac{1}{3}\right]\left[x + \frac{1}{3}\right]$ is prime, belongs to the set $[\alpha, \beta) \cup [\gamma, \delta)$; (where $\alpha, \beta, \gamma, \delta$ being in lowest form), find the value of (i) $\alpha + \beta + \gamma + \delta$ (ii) $9(\alpha^2 + \beta^2 + \gamma^2 + \delta^2)$

Solution: $\because a \times b =$ a prime number

$$\text{implies} \begin{cases} a = 1, b = \text{prime number} \\ b = 1, a = \text{prime number} \\ a = -1, b = -(\text{prime number}) \\ b = -1, a = -(\text{prime number}) \end{cases}$$

Given $\left[x-\frac{1}{3}\right].\left[x+\frac{1}{3}\right]$ is prime, thus, there arise following four cases.

Case i: $\left[x-\frac{1}{3}\right]=1$; $\left[x+\frac{1}{3}\right]$ = prime number

$\Rightarrow x-\frac{1}{3}\in[1,2)$; $x\in\left[\frac{4}{3},\frac{7}{3}\right)$; $x+\frac{1}{3}\in\left[\frac{5}{3},\frac{8}{3}\right)$

Here $\left[x+\frac{1}{3}\right]$ must be a prime number, but only prime number in $\left[\frac{5}{3},\frac{8}{3}\right)$ is 2

$\Rightarrow \left[x+\frac{1}{3}\right]=2 \Rightarrow \left(x+\frac{1}{3}\right)\in\left[2,\frac{8}{3}\right) \Rightarrow x\in\left[\frac{5}{3},\frac{7}{3}\right)$

Case ii: $\left[x-\frac{1}{3}\right]$ = prime number and $\left[x+\frac{1}{3}\right]=1$

$\Rightarrow x+\frac{1}{3}\in[1,2) \Rightarrow x\in\left[\frac{2}{3},\frac{5}{3}\right) \Rightarrow x-\frac{1}{3}\in\left[\frac{1}{3},\frac{4}{3}\right)$

$\Rightarrow \left[x-\frac{1}{3}\right]=0,1$ which are not a prime number.

So, in this case we have no solution.

Case iii $\left[x-\frac{1}{3}\right]$ = –prime number and $\left[x+\frac{1}{3}\right]=-1$

$\Rightarrow x+\frac{1}{3}\in[-1,0) \Rightarrow x\in\left[-\frac{4}{3},-\frac{1}{3}\right)$

$\Rightarrow x-\frac{1}{3}\in\left[-\frac{5}{3},-\frac{2}{3}\right) \Rightarrow \left[x-\frac{1}{3}\right]=-2$, which is possible for $\left(x-\frac{1}{3}\right)\in\left[-\frac{5}{3},-1\right)$, i.e, $x\in\left[-\frac{4}{3},-\frac{2}{3}\right)$

Case iv: $\left[x-\frac{1}{3}\right]=-1$ and $\left[x+\frac{1}{3}\right]$ = –prime number

Now $\left[x-\frac{1}{3}\right]=-1$

$\Rightarrow x-\frac{1}{3}\in[-1,0) \Rightarrow x\in\left[-\frac{2}{3},\frac{1}{3}\right)$

$\Rightarrow x+\frac{1}{3}\in\left[-\frac{1}{3},\frac{2}{3}\right) \Rightarrow \left[x+\frac{1}{3}\right]=-1$ or 0. i.e., we get no –ve prime number.

So, in this case we get no solution.

Thus, from above case analysis we see that the product $\left[x-\frac{1}{3}\right]\left[x+\frac{1}{3}\right]$ is prime number for

$x\in\left[-\frac{4}{3},-\frac{2}{3}\right)\cup\left[\frac{5}{3},\frac{7}{3}\right)$

∴ Without loss of generality, we can take

$$\alpha=-\frac{4}{3},\beta=-\frac{2}{3},\gamma=\frac{5}{3} \text{ and } \delta=\frac{7}{3}$$

$\Rightarrow \alpha+\beta+\gamma+\delta=-2+4=2$

and $\alpha^2+\beta^2+\gamma^2+\delta^2=\frac{16+4+25+49}{9}=\frac{94}{9}$

$\Rightarrow 9(\alpha^2+\beta^2+\gamma^2+\delta^2)=94$

6. Show that there exists no polynomial $f(x)$ with integral coefficients which satisfy $f(a) = b$, $f(b) = c$, $f(c) = a$, where a, b, c are distinct integers.

Solution: Let $f(x) = a_0 + a_1x + a_2x^2 + \ldots + a_nx^n$; where $a_i \in$ integer ($i = 0, 1, 2, \ldots, n$)

Now $f(a) = a_0 + a_1a + a_2a^2 + \ldots + a_na^n = b$ ....(1)

$f(b) = a_0 + a_1b + a_2b^2 + \ldots + a_nb^n = c$ .... (2)

$f(c) = a_0 + a_1c + a_2c^2 + \ldots + a_nc^n = a$ .... (3)

$\Rightarrow f(a), f(b), f(c)$ are integers

∴ $f(a) - f(b) = (a - b).[a$, function in terms of a and $b]$

$= (a - b).\ f_1(a, b) = b - c$; where $f_1(a, b)$ is an integer .... (4)

Similarly $(b - c).f_1(b, c) = c - a$ ....(5)

and $(c - a).f_1(c, a) = a - b$ ....(6)

Multiplying (4), (5) and (6), we get

$f_1(a, b) . f_1(b, c) . f_1(c, a) = 1$

$\Rightarrow f_1(a, b) = 1, f_1(b, c) = 1, f_1(c, a)$; [as product of integers is 1, if each is one]

$\Rightarrow a - b = b - c = c - a$

$\Rightarrow a = b = c$ which is not possible [as a, b, c are distinct]

Hence, there exists no polynomial of such type.

7. Determine all values of c so that $f(x)=\frac{x-1}{c-x^2+1}$ does not take any value in the interval $\left[-1,-\frac{1}{3}\right]$

Solution: Given $f(x)=\frac{x-1}{c-x^2+1}$ i.e., $y=\frac{x-1}{c-x^2+1}$

Take $y = -t$, where $t\in\left[1,\frac{1}{3}\right]$ and given function assume the values $(-t)$ at some $x = x_0$, then $f(x_0) = -t$

$\Rightarrow -t=\frac{x_0-1}{c-x_0^2+1} \Rightarrow x_0^2-c-1=\frac{x_0-1}{t}$

Now, we have to just make sure that this quadratic in x does not give any real value of x for $t\in\left[1,\frac{1}{3}\right]$

$\Rightarrow$ Discriminant of the quadratic must be negative.

$$\frac{1}{t^2}-4\left(\frac{1}{t}-c-1\right)<0$$

$$\Rightarrow \frac{1}{t^2}-\frac{4}{t}+4<-4c \quad \Rightarrow \quad c+\frac{1}{4}\left(\frac{1}{t}-2\right)^2<0$$

$$\Rightarrow c<-\frac{1}{4}\left(\frac{1}{t}-2\right)^2$$

Now $t\in\left[1,\frac{1}{3}\right]; -1\le\frac{1}{t}-2\le 1$

$$\Rightarrow 0\le\frac{1}{4}\left(\frac{1}{t}-2\right)^2\le\frac{1}{4} \Rightarrow -\frac{1}{4}\le-\frac{1}{4}\left(\frac{1}{t}-2\right)^2\le 0$$

Hence, $c\in\left(-\infty,-\frac{1}{4}\right)$

8. Find the domain of the following functions and sketch their corresponding graphs, and hence, find their range

(a) $f(x) = x^4 - 2x^2 + 3$ (b) $f(x)=\dfrac{2x}{1+x^2}$

(c) $f(x) = \sin^2 x - 2\sin x$

Solution: (a) Given $f(x) = x^4 - 2x^2 + 3$

(i) Domain of $f(x)$ is $\mathbb{R}$

(ii) $f(x)$ is even so graph will be symmetrical about y-axis.

(iii) $y = x^4 - 2x^2 + 3 = (x^2 - 1)^2 + 2$

So, minimum value of y is 2 at $x^2 = 1$, Further $f'(x) = 2(x^2 - 1)(2x) \ge 0$ for $x \in [-1, 0] \cup [1, \infty)$

Thus, $f(x)$ is increasing $\forall\ x \in [-1, 0] \cup [1, \infty)$

(iv) Further $f'(x) = 0$ at $x = 0, \pm 1$

(v) When $x = 0$ the value of $y = 3$ and at $x = \pm 1$, $f(x) = 2$

$\therefore$ Graph of $f(x)$ would be as shown below

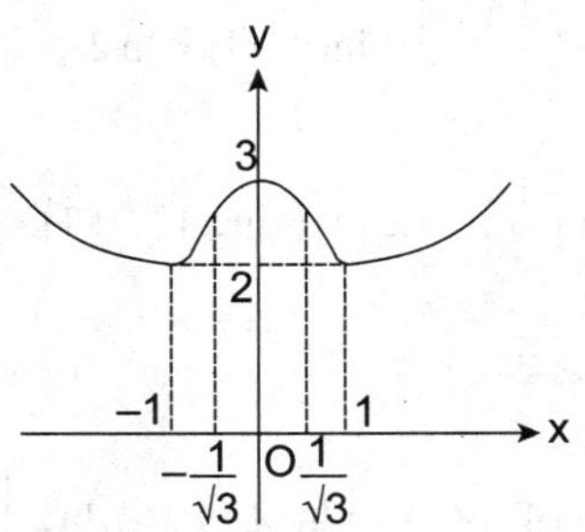

Clearly the range of function is $[2, \infty)$

(b) $y=f(x)=\dfrac{2x}{1+x^2}$

(i) Domain = $\mathbb{R}$

(ii) $f(x) = -f(x)$, so function is odd the graph is not symmetric about any axis but symmetric about origin.

So, it is sufficient to consider only, $x \ge 0$.

(iii) $y = 0$ when $x = 0$ there is no other point of intersection with coordinate axes

$\Rightarrow x^2 + 1 \ge 2x$

So, $\dfrac{2x}{x^2+1}\le 1$ and equality holds at $x = 1$.

Also from 0 to 1 the function increases and from 1 to ∞ it decreases.

So, graph is as shown in Figure below.

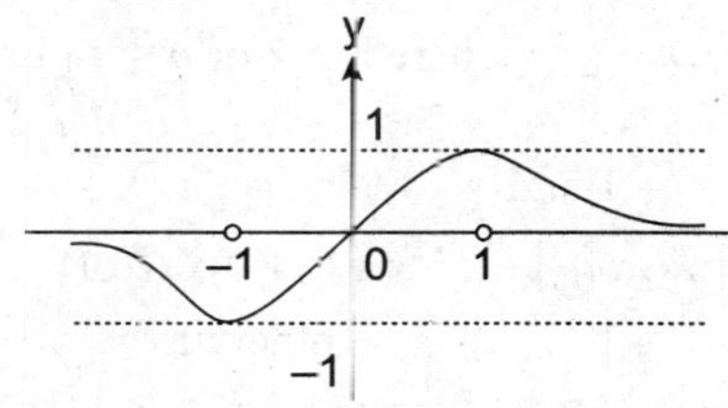

Clearly the range of function is $[-1, 1]$

(c) $y = f(x) = \sin^2 x - 2 \sin x$

(i) Domain of y is $\mathbb{R}$

(ii) $0 \le (\sin x - 1)^2 \le 4$

$\Rightarrow 0 \le \sin^2 x - 2\sin x + 1 \le 4$

$\Rightarrow -1 \le \sin^2 x - 2\sin x \le 3$

(iii) $f(x)$ has period 2π, so it is sufficient to draw the graph for domain $[0, 2\pi]$

(iv) $y = 0$ for all $x \in n\pi$

Graph is shown in the figure

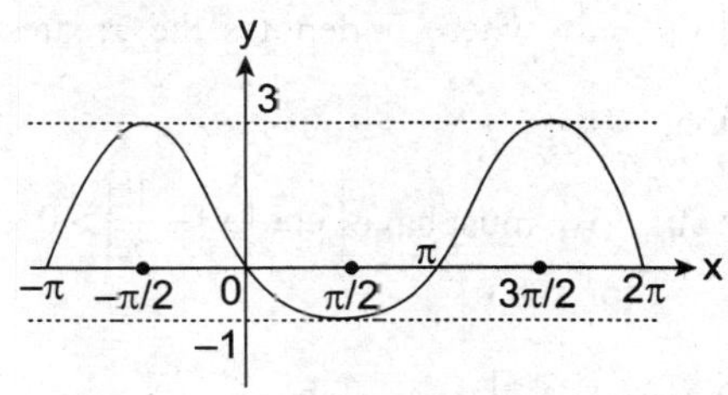

Clearly the range of function is $[-1, 3]$

9. Find the domain of definition of the function, $f(x)=[2\tan\pi x]^{\left\{\log_{[2\tan\pi x]}\left(\frac{x^2+2x-3}{4x^2-4x-3}\right)\right\}}$; where [.] denotes the greatest integer function.

Solution: $\because a^{\log_a b}=b$

$$\Rightarrow f(x)=\left(\frac{x^2+2x-3}{4x^2-4x-3}\right) \text{ and } [2\tan \pi x] > 0, \ne 1$$

and $\dfrac{x^2+2x-3}{4x^2-4x-3}>0 \quad \Rightarrow \quad [2\tan \pi x] \ge 2$

$\Rightarrow \tan \pi x \ge 1$ i.e., $\dfrac{(x+3)(x-1)}{(2x-3)(2x+1)}>0$

$\Rightarrow x \in (-\infty, -3) \cup (-1/2, 1) \cup (3/2, \infty)$ ...(1)

Also $\tan \pi x \ge 1$

$\Rightarrow n\pi+\frac{\pi}{4}\le \pi x< n\pi+\frac{\pi}{2}$; $n\in\mathbb{Z}$

$\Rightarrow n+\frac{1}{4}\le x< n+\frac{1}{2}$; .... (2)

$\therefore$ From (1) and (2), we get

$x\in\left[n+\frac{1}{4},n+\frac{1}{2}\right);n\in\mathbb{Z}-\{-3,-2,-1,1\}$

Thus, common solutions to (1) and (2) is $\left[n+\frac{1}{4},n+\frac{1}{2}\right)$; where $n\ge 2$ or $n\le -4$ or $n=0$.

10. Let $f(x)=x^2-1$ and

$$g(x)=\begin{cases}[|f(|x|)|]+1; & x\in(-1,0)\cup(0,1)\\ 1; & \text{otherwise}\end{cases}.$$

Then find the range of $\ln([|g(x)|])$; where [.] denotes the greatest integer function.

Solution: $|f(|x|)|=1-x^2$; $x\in(-1,0)\cup(0,1)$

$\Rightarrow [|f(|x|)|]=0$; $x\in(-1,0)\cup(0,1)$ and $g(x)=1$; otherwise

Hence, $g(x)=1, x\in(-1,0)\cup(0,1)$ and 1, otherwise

$\Rightarrow g(x)=1\ \forall\ x\in\mathbb{R} \Rightarrow [|g(x)|]=1$

$\Rightarrow \ln[|g(x)|]=0\ \forall\ x\in\mathbb{R} \Rightarrow$ Range of $\ln[|g(x)|]$ is $\{0\}$.

11. Find the domain and range of $f(x)=\log\left[\cos|x|+\frac{1}{2}\right]$; where [] denotes the greatest integer function.

Solution: We must have $\left[\cos|x|+\frac{1}{2}\right]>0$; {as $\log x$ is defined for $x>0$}

$\Rightarrow \cos|x|+\frac{1}{2}\ge 1$ ...(1)

But we know; $-1\le\cos\theta\le 1$; (for $\theta\in\mathbb{R}$}

$\therefore -1\le\cos|x|\le 1$

or $-1+\frac{1}{2}\le\cos|x|+\frac{1}{2}\le 1+\frac{1}{2}$

or $-\frac{1}{2}\le\cos|x|+\frac{1}{2}\le\frac{3}{2}$ ...(2)

$\therefore$ From (1) and (2), we require those values of x which satisfy, $1\le\cos|x|+\frac{1}{2}\le\frac{3}{2}$

$\Rightarrow \left[\cos|x|+\frac{1}{2}\right]=1$ and $\frac{1}{2}\le\cos|x|\le 1$;

Thus, $f(x)$ is defined for $\frac{1}{2}\le\cos x\le 1$

($\because \cos|x|=\cos x\ \forall\ x\in\mathbb{R}$)

$\therefore$ Domain is $x\in\bigcup_{n=\mathbb{Z}}\left[\left(2n\pi-\frac{\pi}{3}\right),\left(2n\pi+\frac{\pi}{3}\right)\right]$ and range for $f(x)$ is $f(x)=\log(1)$

i.e., $f(x)=0$ $\therefore$ Range of $f(x)$ is $\{0\}$

12. Find the range of the following functions:

(i) $f(x)=\ln(\sin x^{\sin x}+1)$; where $0<x<\pi/2$

(ii) $f(x)=\ln(2\sin x+\tan x-3x+1)$; where $\frac{\pi}{6}\le x\le\frac{\pi}{3}$

Solution: (i) $0<x<\pi/2$

$\Rightarrow 0<\sin x<1$

$\therefore$ Range of $\ln(\sin x^{\sin x}+1)$ for $0<x<\pi/2$

= Range of $\ln(t^t+1)$ for $0<t<1$

Let $h(t)=t^t+1=e^{t\ln t}+1$

$\therefore h'(t)=e^{t\ln t}(1+\ln t)$

$\Rightarrow h'(t)>0$ for $t>1/e$ and $h'(t)<0$ for $t<1/e$

$\therefore h(t)$ has a minima at $t=\frac{1}{e}$ and $h\left(\frac{1}{e}\right)=\left(\frac{1}{e}\right)^{\frac{1}{e}}+1$

Also $\lim_{t\to 0^+}h(t)=1+e^{\lim_{t\to 0}\left(\frac{\ln t}{1/t}\right)}=1+e^{\lim_{t\to 0}\left(\frac{1/t}{-1/t^2}\right)}$

$=1+e^0=2$ and $\lim_{t\to 1^-}h(t)=2$

$\therefore h(t)$ has its minimum value $=\left(\frac{1}{e}\right)^{\frac{1}{e}}+1$ and maximum value less than 2

$\therefore$ for $0<t<1$

$\Rightarrow 1+\left(\frac{1}{e}\right)^{\frac{1}{e}}\le(t^t+1)<2$

$\Rightarrow \ln\left(1+\left(\frac{1}{e}\right)^{1/e}\right)\le\ln(t^t+1)<\ln 2$

$\Rightarrow \ln\left(1+\left(\frac{1}{e}\right)^{1/e}\right)\le\ln\left((\sin x)^{\sin x}+1\right)<\ln 2$ for $0<x<\frac{\pi}{2}$

$\therefore$ Range of $f(x)=\left[\ln\left(1+e^{\frac{-1}{e}}\right),\ln 2\right)$

(ii) Let $h(x)=(2\sin x+\tan x-3x+1)$

$\Rightarrow h'(x)=(2\cos x+\sec^2 x-3)$

$=\frac{2\cos^3 x-3\cos^2 x+1}{\cos^2 x}$

$\therefore h'(x)\ge 0$

$\Rightarrow 2\cos^3 x-3\cos^2 x+1\ge 0$ and $\cos^2 x\ne 0$

$\Rightarrow\ (\cos x-1)^2(2\cos x+1)\geq 0$

$\Rightarrow\ 2\cos x+1\geq 0; \cos^2 x\neq 0$, which holds $\forall\, x\in\left[\frac{\pi}{6},\frac{\pi}{3}\right]$

$\Rightarrow$ $h(x)$ is an increasing function of x

$\Rightarrow\ h\left(\frac{\pi}{6}\right)\leq h(x)\leq h\left(\frac{\pi}{3}\right)$

$\Rightarrow\ \ln h\left(\frac{\pi}{6}\right)\leq \ln h(x)\leq \ln h\left(\frac{\pi}{3}\right)$

$\Rightarrow\ \ln\left(1+\frac{1}{\sqrt{3}}-\frac{\pi}{2}+1\right)\leq f(x)\leq \ln\left(\sqrt{3}+\sqrt{3}-\pi+1\right)$

$\Rightarrow$ Range of $f(x)$ is $\left[\ln\left(2+\frac{1}{\sqrt{3}}-\frac{\pi}{2}\right), \ln(1+2\sqrt{3}-\pi)\right]$

13. Functions $f(x)$ and $g(x)$ are defined in $[a, b]$ such that $f(x)$ is continuous and monotonically increasing while $g(x)$ is continuous and monotonically decreasing. It is given that the range of $f(x)$ as well as that of $g(x)$ is a subset of $[a, b]$. Find the range and domain of $h(x) = fog(x) + gof(x)$.

Solution: Domain of the increasing function $f(x)$ is $[a, b]$ $\quad\Rightarrow f'(x) > 0$ in $[a, b]$

Domain of the decreasing function $g(x)$ is $[a, b]$

$\Rightarrow g'(x) < 0$ in $[a, b]$

Now $h'(x) = f(g(x)) + g(f(x))$

$\Rightarrow\ h(x) = \underbrace{g'(x)f'(g(x))}_{-ve}+\underbrace{f'(x)g'(f(x))}_{-ve}<0$

($\because$ $g(x) \in [a, b] \Rightarrow f'(g(x)) > 0$ and $g'(x) < 0$ in $[a, b]$. Similarly $f'(x) > 0$; $g'(f(x)) < 0$)

Hence, $h(x)$ is decreasing function.

Also range of $g(x)$ is subset of $[a, b]$

$\Rightarrow$ Domain of $fog(x)$ is $[a, b]$

Similarly, domain of $gof(x)$ is $[a, b]$. Hence, the domain of $h(x)$ is $[a, b]$.

Since $h(x)$ is bijective and sum of two continuous functions (composition of continuous functions) is also continuous and monotonically decreasing on domain $[a, b]$.

Therefore, range of $h(x) = [h(b), h(a)]$.

14. Let $f : [0, 1] \to [0, 1]$ defined by $f(x)=\frac{1-x}{1+x}$; $0 \leq x \leq 1$ and let $g : [0, 1] \to [0, 1]$ defined by $g(x) = 4x(1 - x) \leq 1$; $0 \leq x \leq 1$. Determine the composition fog and gof.

Solution: $(fog)(x) = f(g(x)) = f[4x(1 - x)]$; $0 \leq 4x(1 - x) \leq 1$; $0 \leq x \leq 1$

$=\frac{1-4x(1-x)}{1+4x(1-x)}$; $0\leq x\leq 1$ and $0\leq 4x-4x^2\leq 1$

$=\frac{1+4x^2-4x}{1-4x^2+4x}$; $0\leq x\leq 1$ and $0\leq (4x-4x^2)\leq 1$

when $0 \leq 4x - 4x^2$

$\Rightarrow 4x(1 - x) \geq 0 \qquad \Rightarrow 0 \leq x \leq 1$ and $4x - 4x^2 \leq 1$

$\Rightarrow 4x^2 - 4x + 1 \geq 0$

$\Rightarrow (2x - 1)^2 \geq 0$; which is true for all x

Hence, $(fog)(x)=\frac{1+4x^2-4x}{1-4x^2+4x}; 0\leq x\leq 1$

$(gof)(x)=g(f(x))=g\left(\frac{1-x}{1+x}\right); 0\leq x\leq 1$

$=4\left(\frac{1-x}{1+x}\right)\left(1-\frac{1-x}{1+x}\right); 0\leq x\leq 1$ and $0\leq\frac{1-x}{1+x}\leq 1$

$=\frac{8x(1-x)}{(1+x)^2}; 0\leq x\leq 1$ and $0\leq 1-x\leq 1+x$

$=\frac{8x(1-x)}{(1+x)^2}; 0\leq x\leq 1$ and $0\leq x\leq 1$

Hence, $(gof)(x)=\frac{8x(1-x)}{(1+x)^2}; 0\leq x\leq 1$

15. Find the domain and range of $h(x) = g(f(x))$, where $f(x)=\begin{cases}[x], & -2\leq x\leq -1\\ |x|+1, & -1<x\leq 2\end{cases}$ and $g(x)=\begin{cases}[x], & -\pi\leq x\leq 0\\ \sin x & 0<x\leq\pi\end{cases}$; and [.] denotes the greatest integer function.

Solution:

$$h(x)=g(f(x))=\begin{cases}[f(x)]; & -\pi\leq f(x)\leq 0\\ \sin(f(x)); & 0<f(x)\leq\pi\end{cases}$$

$$=\begin{cases}[[x]]; & -\pi\leq[x]\leq 0; & -2\leq x\leq -1\\ [|x|+1]; & -\pi\leq|x|+1\leq 0; & -1<x\leq 2\\ \sin[x]; & 0<[x]\leq\pi; & -2\leq x\leq -1\\ \sin(|x|+1); & 0<|x|+1\leq\pi; & -1<x\leq 2\end{cases}$$

$$=\begin{cases}[x]; & x\in[-3,1)\cap[-2,-1]\\ [|x|+1]; & \text{no value of } x\\ \sin[x]; & x\in[1,4)\cap[-2,-1]\\ \sin(|x|+1); & x\in[-\pi+1,\pi-1]\cap(-1,2]\end{cases}$$

$$=\begin{cases}[x]; & x\in[-2,-1]\\ \sin(|x|+1); & x\in(-1,2]\end{cases}$$

$$=\begin{cases}-2; & x\in[-2,-1)\\ -1; & x=-1\\ [\sin 3,1]; & x\in(-1,2]\end{cases}$$

$\Rightarrow$ Domain of $h(x)$ is $[-2, 2]$ and range of $h(x)$ is $\{-2, -1\} \cup [\sin 3, 1]$

16. If $f(x) = 1 + x$, when $0 \le x \le 2$ and $f(x) = 3 - x$, when $2 < x \le 3$, then determine the following (where [] represents the greatest integer function):

(a) $f(x) = f(f(x))$ (b) $f(f(f(x)))$
(c) $f([x])$ (d) $[f(x)]$

Solution: (a) $f(f(x)) = \begin{Bmatrix} 1+f(x); & 0 \le f(x) \le 2 \\ 3-f(x); & 2 < f(x) \le 3 \end{Bmatrix}$

First consider the case $f(x) = 1 + x$, $0 \le x \le 2$.

$$f(f(x)) = \begin{Bmatrix} 1+1+x; & 0 \le 1+x \le 2 \\ 3-1-x; & 2 < 1+x \le 3 \end{Bmatrix}$$

$$= \begin{Bmatrix} 2+x; & -1 \le x \le 1 \\ 2-x; & 1 < x \le 2 \end{Bmatrix}$$

Since our considered domain is $0 \le x \le 2$,

so, $f(f(x)) = \begin{Bmatrix} 2+x; & 0 \le x \le 1 \\ 2-x; & 1 < x \le 2 \end{Bmatrix}$

Next let us consider the case when $f(x) = 3 - x$, $2 < x \le 3$

$$f(f(x)) = \begin{Bmatrix} 1+3-x; & 0 \le 3-x \le 2 \\ 3-3+x; & 2 < 3-x \le 3 \end{Bmatrix}$$

$$= \begin{Bmatrix} 4-x; & -3 \le -x \le -1 \\ x; & -1 < -x \le 0 \end{Bmatrix} = \begin{Bmatrix} 4-x; & 1 \le x \le 3 \\ x; & 0 \le x < 1 \end{Bmatrix}$$

Since our considered domain is $2 < x \le 3$, therefore $f(f(x)) = 4 - x$

$$\therefore \quad f(f(x)) = \begin{Bmatrix} 2+x; & 0 \le x \le 1 \\ 2-x; & 1 < x \le 2 \\ 4-x; & 2 < x \le 3 \end{Bmatrix}$$

Graph of $f(f(x))$ is as shown below

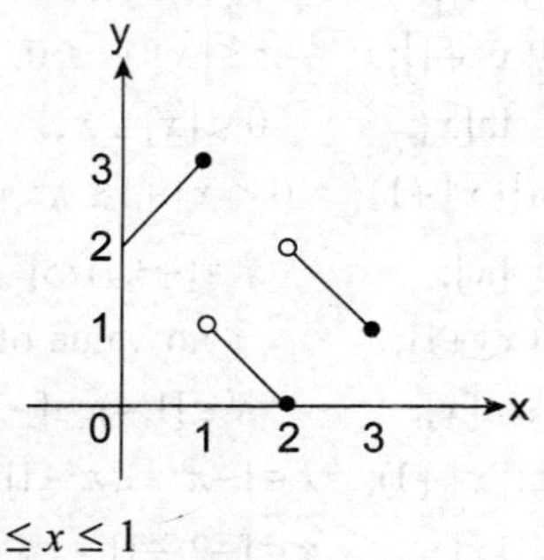

(b) Let $0 \le x \le 1$

$\Rightarrow f(f(f(x))) = f(2 + x)$ where $2 \le 2 + x \le 3$

But we observe that there is no single definition of $f(f(x))$ for this interval.

Therefore, we reduce the interval $0 \le x \le 1$ to $x = 0$ and $0 < x \le 1$ at $x = 0$, $2 + x = 2$

$\therefore$ $f(2 + x) = f(2) = 1 + 2 = 3$

For $0 < x \le 1$; $x + 2 \in (2, 3]$

$\Rightarrow f(x + 2) = 3 - (x + 2) = 1 - x$

Next let $1 < x \le 2$

$\Rightarrow f(f(f(x))) = f(2 - x);\ 0 \le 2 - x < 1$

$= 1 + 2 - x = 3 - x$

Now, let $2 < x \le 3 = f(f(f(x))) = f(4 - x);\ 1 \le 4 - x < 2$

$= 1 + (4 - x) = 5 - x$

$$\therefore \quad f(f(f(x))) = \begin{cases} 3; & x = 0 \\ 1-x; & 0 < x \le 1 \\ 3-x; & 1 < x \le 2 \\ 5-x; & 2 < x \le 3 \end{cases}$$

Graph of $f(f(f(x)))$ is as shown below

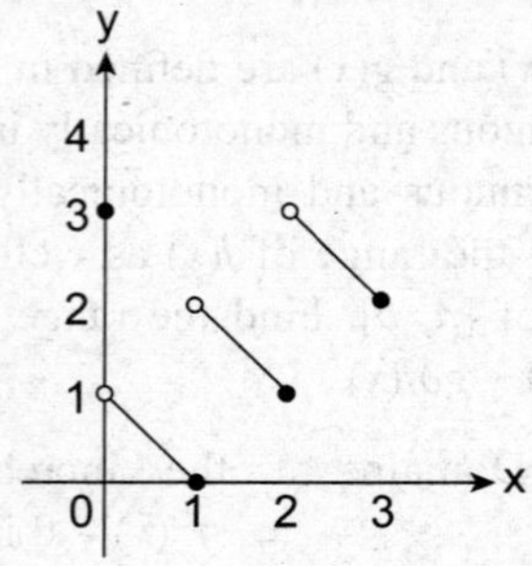

(c) $f([x])$

Now for $0 \le x < 1$

$\Rightarrow [x] = 0 \qquad \Rightarrow f[x] = f(0) = 1;$

for $1 \le x < 2$

$\Rightarrow [x] = 1 \qquad \Rightarrow f[x] = f(1) = 2;$

for $2 \le x < 3$

$\Rightarrow [x] = 2 \qquad \Rightarrow f([x]) = f(2) = 3;$

for $x = 3$

$\Rightarrow [x] = 3 \qquad \Rightarrow f([x]) = f(3) = 0$

$$\therefore \quad f[x] = \begin{cases} 1; & 0 \le x < 1 \\ 2, & 1 \le x < 2 \\ 3, & 2 \le x < 3 \\ 0, & x = 3 \end{cases}$$

Graph of $f[x]$ is as follows

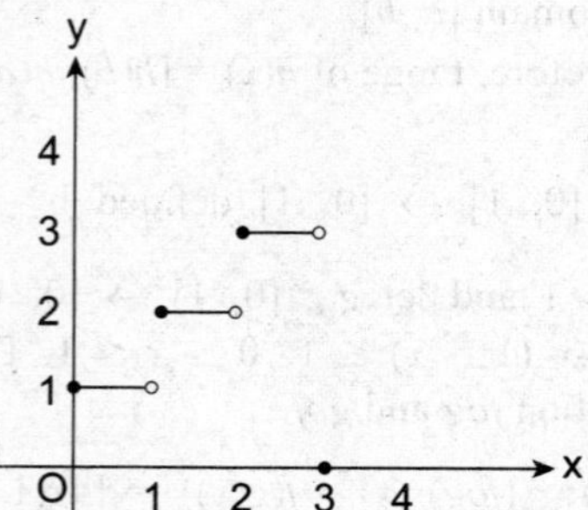

(d) $y = [f(x)]$, we have for $0 \le x < 1$; $f(x) = x + 1$

$\Rightarrow 1 \le f(x) < 2 \quad \Rightarrow [f(x)] = 1;$

for $1 \le x < 2$; $f(x) = x + 1$

$\Rightarrow 2 \le f(x) < 3 \quad \Rightarrow [f(x)] = 2;$

for $x = 2$

$\Rightarrow f(x) = 3 \quad \Rightarrow [f(x)] = 3;$

For $2 < x \le 3$; $f(x) = 3 - x$

$\Rightarrow 0 \le f(x) < 1 \quad \Rightarrow [f(x)] = 0$

$$\therefore \ [f(x)] = \begin{cases} 1, & 0 \le x < 1 \\ 2, & 1 \le x < 2 \\ 3, & x = 2 \\ 0, & 2 < x \le 3 \end{cases}$$

Graph of $[f(x)]$ is as shown below

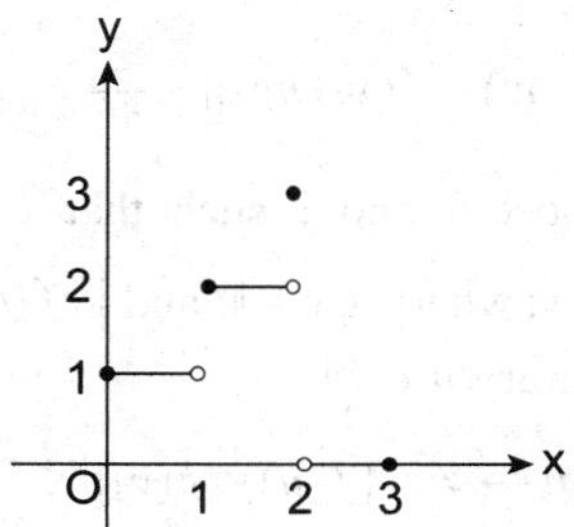

17. Consider $f(x) = (1 - x^n)^{1/n}$ and $g(x) = x^2 + px + q$; ($p, q \in \mathbb{R}$). Let $g(x) = kx$; ($k > 0$) has imaginary roots, then show that $g(g(g(x))) = k^3 f(f(f(f(x))))$ has no real solution.

Solution: Given $f(x) = (1 - x^n)^{1/n}$

$$\Rightarrow f(f(x)) = \left[1 - \{(1 - x^n)^{1/n}\}^n\right]^{1/n} = x$$

$\Rightarrow f(f(f(f(x)))) = f(f(x)) = x$

Now as, $g(x) = kx$ has no real roots

It means, $x^2 + px + q - kx > 0$ i.e., $g(x) > k(x)$

So $g(g(x)) > kg(x) > k^2x$

$\Rightarrow g(g(g(x))) > kg(g(x)) > k.k^2x$

$\Rightarrow g(g(g(x))) > k^3(x)$

Hence, $g(g(g(x))) = k^3 f(f(f(f(x))))$ has no real solution.

18. Describe fog and gof wherever is possible for the following functions:

(i) $f(x) = \sqrt{x+3}, g(x) = 1 + x^2$

(ii) $f(x) = \sqrt{x}, g(x) = x^2 - 1$

Solution: (i) Domain of f is $[-3, \infty)$, range of f is $[0, \infty)$.

Domain of g is R, range of g is $[1, \infty)$ for $gof(x)$

Since range of f is a subset of domain of g,

$\therefore$ Domain of gof is $[-3, \infty)$ {equal to the domain of f}

$gof(x) = g\{f(x)\} = g(\sqrt{x+3}) = 1 + (x + 3) = x + 4$. Range of gof is $[1, \infty)$

For $fog(x)$

Since range of g is a subset of domain of f,

$\therefore$ Domain of fog is $\mathbb{R}$ {equal to the domain of g}

$\therefore$ $fog(x) = f\{g(x)\} = f(1 + x^2) = \sqrt{x^2 + 4}$; Range of fog is $[2, \infty)$.

(ii) $f(x) = \sqrt{x}$, $g(x) = x^2 - 1$

Domain of f is $[0, \infty)$, range of f is $[0, \infty)$.

Domain of g is $\mathbb{R}$, range of g is $[-1, \infty)$.

For $gof(x)$

Since range of f is a subset of the domain of g.

$\therefore$ domain of gof is $[0, \infty)$ and $g\{f(x)\} = g(\sqrt{x}) = x - 1$.

Range of gof is $[-1, \infty)$.

For $fog(x)$

Since range of g is not a subset of the domain of f.

i.e., $[-1, \infty) \not\subset [0, \infty)$.

$\therefore$ fog is not defined on whole of the domain of g.

Domain of fog is $\{x \in R$, the domain of g: $g(x) \in [0, \infty)$, the range of $f\}$.

Thus, the domain of fog is $D = \{x \in R: 0 \le g(x) < \infty\}$

i.e., $D = \{x \in R: 0 \le x^2 - 1\} = \{x \in R: x \le -1$ or $x \ge 1\} = (-\infty, -1] \cup [1, \infty)$

$fog(x) = f\{g(x)\} = f(x^2 - 1) = \sqrt{x^2 - 1}$.

Its range is $[0, \infty)$.

19. Let $f(x) = x^2 + 3x - 3$; If n points $x_1, x_2, x_3, \ldots, x_n$ are chosen on positive x-axis such that

(a) $\frac{1}{n}\sum_{i=1}^{n} f^{-1}(x_i) = f\left(\frac{1}{n}\sum_{i=1}^{n}(x_i)\right)$

(b) $\sum_{i=1}^{n} f^{-1}(x_i) = \sum_{i=1}^{n}(x_i)$; where f^{-1} denotes the inverse of f. Find the A.M. of x_i, s

Solution: Given $\frac{f^{-1}(x_1) + f^{-1}(x_2) + \ldots\ldots + f^{-1}(x_n)}{n}$

$$= f\left(\frac{x_1 + x_2 + \ldots. + x_n}{n}\right) \quad \ldots. (1)$$

and $f^{-1}(x_1) + f^{-1}(x_2) + \ldots. + f^{-1}(x_n) = (x_1 + x_2 + \ldots + x_n)$ ... (2)

Using (2) in (1), we get

$$\frac{x_1 + x_2 + x_3 + \ldots + x_n}{n} = f\left(\frac{x_1 + x_2 + x_3 + \ldots + x_n}{n}\right)$$

$\Rightarrow\ f(\bar{x}) = \bar{x}$; where $\dfrac{x_1 + x_2 + ... + x_n}{n} = \bar{x}$

$\Rightarrow\ \bar{x}^2 + 3\bar{x} - 3 = \bar{x}$ $\quad \Rightarrow\ \bar{x}^2 + 2\bar{x} - 3 = 0$

$\Rightarrow\ \bar{x} = -3, 1$ $\quad \Rightarrow\ \bar{x} = 1$ as $\bar{x} > 0$ $(\because x_i > 0)$

20. Let f be a real valued function satisfying $f(x) + f(x + 4) = f(x + 2) + f(x + 6)$. Prove that $\int_x^{x+8} f(t)\,dt$ is a constant function.

Solution: Given that $f(x) + f(x + 4) = f(x + 2) + f(x + 6)$ ....(1)

Replacing x by $x + 2$, we get

$f(x + 2) + f(x + 6) = f(x + 4) + f(x + 8)$ ....(2)

From (1) and (2), we have $f(x) = f(x + 8)$ .....(3)

Now let $g(x) = \int_x^{x+8} f(t)\,dt$

$\Rightarrow\ g'(x) = f(x + 8) - f(x) = 0$ (from (3))

$\Rightarrow\ g$ is a constant function

21. If $f(r) = 1 + \dfrac{1}{2} + \dfrac{1}{3} + ... + \dfrac{1}{r}$ and $f(0) = 0$, then find $\sum_{r=1}^{n} (2r+1)\,f(r)$

Solution: Since $\sum_{r=1}^{n} (2r+1)\,f(r)$

$= \sum_{r=1}^{n} (r^2 + 2r + 1 - r^2)\,f(r)$

$= \sum_{r=1}^{n} \{(r+1)^2 f(r) - (r+1)^2 f(r+1) +$
$(r+1)^2 f(r+1) - r^2\, f(r)\}$

$= \sum_{r=1}^{n} \{(r+1)^2 \{f(r) - f(r+1)\} +$
$\sum_{r=1}^{n} \{(r+1)^2\ f(r+1) - r^2 f(r)\}$

$= -\sum_{r=1}^{n} \dfrac{(r+1)^2}{r+1} + \sum_{r=1}^{n-1} \{(r+1)^2\ f(r+1) + (n+1)^2 f(n+1)$
$- \sum_{r=1}^{n} r^2 f(r)$

$= -\sum_{r=1}^{n} r + 1 + \{2^2 f(2) + 3^2 f(3) + ...n^2 f(n)\} + (n+1)^2$
$f(n + 1) - \{1^2 f(1) + 2^2 f(2) + \ldots + n^2 f(n)\}$

$= -\sum_{r=1}^{n} r - \sum_{r=1}^{n} 1 + (n+1)^2 f(n+1) - 1^2 f(1)$

$= -\dfrac{n(n+1)}{2} - n + (n+1)^2\ f(n+1) - f(1)$ $(\because f(1) = 1)$

$= (n+1)^2\ f(n+1) - \dfrac{n(n+3n+2)}{2}$.

22. Suppose that function $f: \mathbb{R} \to \mathbb{R}$ satisfies the inequality $\left|\sum_{k=1}^{n} 3^k \{f(x+ky) - f(x-ky)\}\right| \le 1$; for every positive integer n and k, $\forall\ x, y \in \mathbb{R}$. Prove that f is a constant function.

Solution: Given

$\left|\sum_{k=1}^{n} 3^k \{f(x+ky) - f(x-ky)\}\right| \le 1$ ...(1)

Replacing n by $(n - 1)$, we get

$\left|\sum_{k=1}^{n-1} 3^k \{f(x+ky) - f(x-ky)\}\right| \le 1$ ...(2)

Solving inequations (1) and (2), we get

$\left|3^n \{f(x+ny) - f(x-ny)\}\right| \le 2$

$\Rightarrow\ \left|\{f(x+ny) - f(x-ny)\}\right| \le \dfrac{2}{3^n}$

We choose x and y such that $x + ny = u$ and $x - ny = v$; where $u, v \in \mathbb{R}$ and $\left|\{f(u) - f(v)\}\right| \le \dfrac{2}{3^n}$ for arbitrary $n \in \mathbb{N}$

i.e., as $n \to \infty$, $\left|\{f(u) - f(v)\}\right| \le \lim_{n\to\infty} \dfrac{2}{3^n}$

$\Rightarrow\ |f(u) - f(v)| \le 0$ $\quad \Rightarrow\ f(u) = f(v)$

$\Rightarrow f$ is a constant function.

23. Show that the inverse of a linear fraction function is always a linear fraction function (except where it is not defined).

Solution: Let, $f(x) = \dfrac{a+bx}{c+dx}$ be the said linear fraction function.

Let at some x it attains value y, so $\dfrac{a+bx}{c+dx} = y$

$\Rightarrow\ a + bx - cy - dxy = 0$

$\Rightarrow\ a - cy + x(b - dy) = 0$

$\Rightarrow\ x = \dfrac{cy - a}{b - dy}$; which is again a linear fraction function defined in R except at $y = \dfrac{b}{d}$ and inverse of the given function is, $y = \dfrac{cx - a}{b - dx}$

24. Find the value of a so that $f(x) = \dfrac{ax+2}{x+4}$ is identical to $f^{-1}(x)$.

Solution: If $f(x) = f^{-1}(x)$, then $fof^{-1}(x) = x$

$\Rightarrow\ fof(x) = x$ $\quad \Rightarrow\ \dfrac{af(x)+2}{f(x)+4} = x$

$$\Rightarrow \frac{a\left(\frac{ax+2}{x+4}\right)+2}{\frac{ax+2}{x+4}+4} = x$$

$\Rightarrow a^2x + 2a + 2x + 8 \equiv x(ax + 2 + 4x + 16)$

$\Rightarrow (a^2 + 2)x + 2a + 8 = (a + 4)x^2 + 18x$

$\Rightarrow a + 4 = 0$ and $a^2 + 2 = 18$ and $2a + 8 = 0$

$\Rightarrow a = -4$ and $a = \pm 4, a = -4 \Rightarrow a = -4$

25. If the function $f(x) = ax + b$ is self invertible, then find the all possible ordered pairs (a, b).

Solution: Let $y = f(x)$

$\Rightarrow x = f^{-1}(y)$ and $y = ax + b$

$\Rightarrow x = \frac{y}{a} - \frac{b}{a} \qquad \Rightarrow f^{-1}(y) = \frac{y}{a} - \frac{b}{a}$

$\Rightarrow f^{-1}(x) = \frac{x}{a} - \frac{b}{a}$ and $f(x) = ax + b$

Now in order that (1) and (2), coincide $a = \frac{1}{a}$ and $b = \frac{-b}{a}$

$\Rightarrow a^2 = 1 \qquad \Rightarrow a = 1$ or -1

if $a = -1$, then $b \in \mathbb{R}$

if $a = 1$, then $2b = 0 \quad \Rightarrow b = 0$

Hence, the ordered pairs (a, b) are $(-1, b)$, $(1, 0)$; where $b \in \mathbb{R}$.

26. Check the invertibility of the function $f(x) = (e^x - e^{-x})$ and then find its inverse.

Solution: We have $f(x) = (e^x - e^{-x})$; $x \in \mathbb{R}$

$\lim_{x\to\infty} f(x) = \infty$ and $\lim_{x\to-\infty} f(x) = -\infty$

$f'(x) = e^x + e^{-x} > 0$; $\forall x \in \mathbb{R}$

$\therefore f(x)$ is invertible when defined from $\mathbb{R}$ to $\mathbb{R}$.

Now, $f(x) = y = t - \frac{1}{t}$; [where $t = e^x > 0$]

$\Rightarrow t^2 - 1 = ty \qquad \Rightarrow t^2 - ty - 1 = 0$

$\Rightarrow t = \frac{y + \sqrt{y^2 + 4}}{2}$ [$\because$ t can't be negative]

Now, $t = e^x$

$\Rightarrow e^x = \frac{y+\sqrt{y^2+4}}{2} \qquad \Rightarrow x = \ln\left(\frac{y+\sqrt{y^2+4}}{2}\right)$

Interchanging x and y, we get,

Inverse of $f(x)$ is $f^{-1}(x) = \ln\left(\frac{x+\sqrt{x^2+4}}{2}\right)$

27. Find the set X if the function $f: [2, \infty) \to X$; where $f(x) = 5 - 4x + x^2$ is bijective, and hence, find its inverse.

Solution: $y = x^2 - 4x + 5 = (x - 2)^2 + 1$; when $x = 2, y = 1$

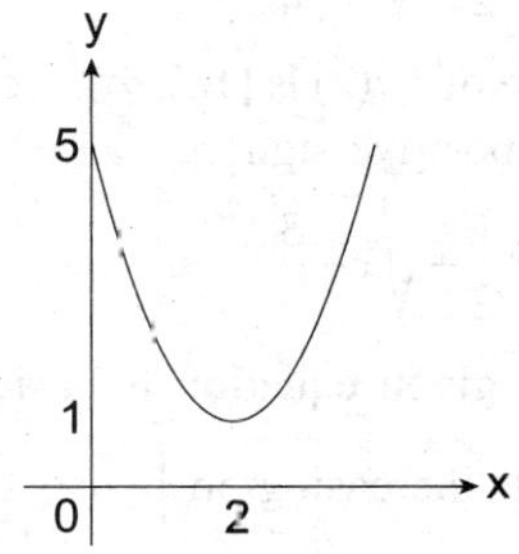

As $x \in [2, \infty)$, then $y \in [1, \infty)$.

$\therefore$ i.e., range of function is $[1, \infty)$.

(It is clear from the figure)

$\therefore$ For $f(x)$ to be invertible, range = co-domain

$\Rightarrow$ Set $X \equiv [1, \infty)$

To find the inverse: (using the given rule of function)

$y = 5 - 4x + x^2$

$\Rightarrow x^2 - 4x + 5 - y = 0$

$\Rightarrow x = \frac{4 \pm \sqrt{16 - 4(5-y)}}{2} = 2 \pm \sqrt{y-1}$

$\because x \geq 2$. So, ignoring positive sign, we have $x = 2 + \sqrt{y-1}$

Interchanging x and y, we get $y = 2 + \sqrt{x-1}$

$\Rightarrow f^{-1}(x) = 2 + \sqrt{x-1}$

28. Let $f: \left[\frac{1}{2}, \infty\right) \to \left[\frac{3}{4}, \infty\right)$; where $f(x) = x^2 - x + 1$.

Find the inverse of $f(x)$. Hence, or otherwise solve the equation $x^2 - x + 1 = \frac{1}{2} + \sqrt{x - \frac{3}{4}}$.

Solution: $f(x) = x^2 - x + 1 = (x - 1/2)^2 + 3/4$

$\Rightarrow$ Principal domain of $f(x) = \left[\frac{1}{2}, \infty\right)$

and range $= \left[\frac{3}{4}, \infty\right)$

Thus, it is clear that the given function is one–one and onto in the given domain and co-domain.

Thus, its inverse can be obtained.

Clearly $f(f^{-1}(x)) = (f^{-1}(x))^2 - f^{-1}(x) + 1$

$\Rightarrow x = (f^{-1}(x))^2 - (f^{-1}(x)) + 1$

$\Rightarrow (f^{-1}(x))^2 - f^{-1}(x) + (1 - x) = 0$

$\Rightarrow\ f^{-1}(x) = \frac{1 \pm \sqrt{1-4(1-x)}}{2} = \frac{1}{2} \pm \sqrt{x - \frac{3}{4}}$

$\Rightarrow\ f^{-1}(x) = \frac{1}{2} + \sqrt{x - \frac{3}{4}}$

[As range of $f^{-1}(x)$ is $[1/2, \infty)$, we have to consider only the positive sign]

$\Rightarrow\ f^{-1}(x) = \frac{1}{2} + \sqrt{x - \frac{3}{4}}$

Now the given equation is basically $f(x) = f^{-1}(x)$ and $f(x)$ is increasing on $\left[\frac{1}{2}, \infty\right)$.

We know that increasing function $f(x)$ and $f^{-1}(x)$ meet on the line $y = x$.

Hence, solution of the given equation will also be solution of $f(x) = x$.

$\Rightarrow x^2 - x + 1 = x \quad \Rightarrow x^2 - 2x + 1 = 0$

$\Rightarrow (x-1)^2 = 0 \quad \Rightarrow x = 1$

29. Consider a function $f(x) = \frac{x+\lambda}{x-1}$, $x \in \mathbb{R} - \{1\}$; where λ is a real constant. If f is not a constant function, then find the following.

(i) f^{1}, if it exists (ii) the range of f

(iii) $f\left(\frac{1}{f(f(x))}\right) - f\left(f\left(f\left(\frac{1}{x}\right)\right)\right)$

Solution: (i) Given function is

$y = f(x) = \frac{x+\lambda}{x-1}, (x \neq 1)$

$\Rightarrow\ f'(x) = \frac{(x-1)-(x+\lambda)}{(x-1)^2} = \frac{-(\lambda+1)}{(x-1)^2}$

Since f is not constant here $\lambda \neq -1$ for $\lambda < -1$, $\lambda + 1 < 0$

$\Rightarrow f'(x) > 0\ \forall\ x \in \mathbb{R} \sim \{1\}$ and for $\lambda > -1$, $\lambda + 1 > 0$

$\Rightarrow f'(x) < 0\ \forall\ x \in \mathbb{R} \sim \{1\}$

$\therefore$ $f(x)$ strictly increasing for $\lambda < -1$ and strictly decreasing for $\lambda > -1$

Hence, $f'(x)$ is either always increasing or decreasing functions.

Therefore f^{1} is defined $\forall\ \lambda \neq -1$

Now, $y = \frac{x+\lambda}{x-1}$

$\Rightarrow yx - y = x + \lambda \quad \Rightarrow x(y-1) = y + \lambda$

$\Rightarrow\ x = f^{-1}(y) = \frac{y+\lambda}{y-1} \Rightarrow\ f^{-1}(x) = \frac{x+\lambda}{x-1}$

$\Rightarrow$ $f(x)$ is self invertible function for $\lambda \neq -1$

(ii) The graph of f (for $\lambda \neq -1$) is as shown

(a) 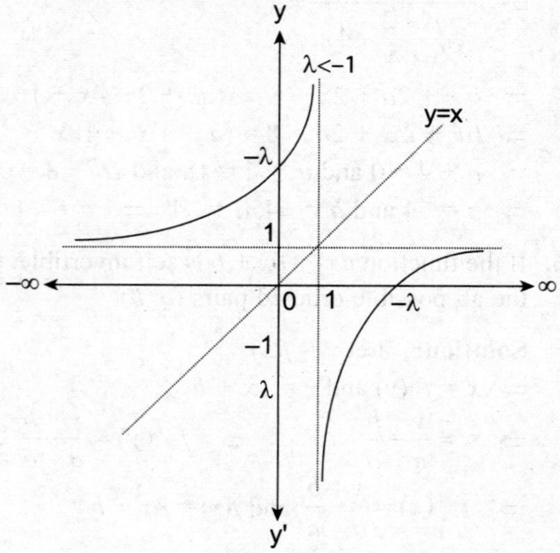

(b) 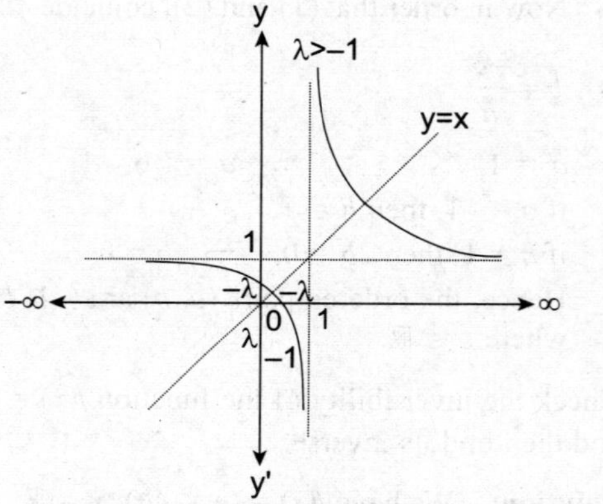

Hence, the range of function is $\mathbb{R} - \{1\}$

(iii) Again $f(x) = \frac{x+\lambda}{x-1}$

Since $f^{1}(x) = f(x)$ and $f(f^{1}(x)) = x$

$\Rightarrow f(f(x)) = x \quad \Rightarrow \frac{1}{(fof)(x)} = \frac{1}{x}$

$$\Rightarrow\ f\left(\frac{1}{f(f(x))}\right) = f\left(\frac{1}{x}\right) \quad \text{.... (1)}$$

Similarly $f\left(f\left(\frac{1}{x}\right)\right) = \frac{1}{x}$

$$\Rightarrow\ f\left(f\left(f\left(\frac{1}{x}\right)\right)\right) = f\left(\frac{1}{x}\right) \quad \text{.... (2)}$$

Hence, from (1) and (2),

$$f\left(\frac{1}{f(f(x))}\right) - f\left(f\left(f\left(\frac{1}{x}\right)\right)\right) = 0.$$

30. If a function $f(x)$ satisfies the equation $2f(x)+xf\left(\frac{1}{x}\right)$ $-\ 2f\left(\left|\sqrt{2}\cos\left(\pi\left(x+\frac{1}{4}\right)\right)\right|\right) = 4\cos^2\frac{\pi x}{2}+x\cos\frac{\pi}{x}$, then show that

(i) $f(2)+f\left(\frac{1}{2}\right)=1$ (ii) $f(1) + f(2) = 0$

Solution: Given $2f(x)+xf\left(\frac{1}{x}\right)$ –

$$2f\left(\left|\sqrt{2}\cos\left(\pi\left(x+\frac{1}{4}\right)\right)\right|\right)=4\cos^2\frac{\pi x}{2}+x\cos\frac{\pi}{x} \quad (1)$$

Putting $x = 1$ in (1), we have $3f(1)– 2f(1) = – 1$

$\Rightarrow f(1) = -1$

Putting $x = 2$ in (1), we have

$$2f(2)+2f\left(\frac{1}{2}\right)-2f(1)=4$$

$$\Rightarrow f(2)+f\left(\frac{1}{2}\right)=1 \quad (\because f(1)=-1) \quad \text{... (2)}$$

Now substituting $x=\frac{1}{2}$ in (1) we get

$$2f\left(\frac{1}{2}\right)+\frac{1}{2}f(2)-2f(1)=2+\frac{1}{2}$$

$$\Rightarrow 2f\left(\frac{1}{2}\right)+\frac{1}{2}f(2)=\frac{1}{2}\Rightarrow 4f\left(\frac{1}{2}\right)+f(2)=1 \quad \text{...(3)}$$

Solving (2) and (3), we get

$f\left(\frac{1}{2}\right)=0; f(2)=1$, then $f(2)+f\left(\frac{1}{2}\right)=1$ which proves part (i) and $f(1) + f(2) = 0$, which proves part (ii).

Solved Assertion and Reason

31. A: Let f: $\mathbb{R}$ – {1, 2, 3} → $\mathbb{R}$ be a function defined by $f(x)=\frac{1}{x-1}+\frac{2}{x-2}+\frac{3}{x-3}$. Then f is many–one function.

R: If either $f'(x) > 0\ \forall\ x \in D_f$ or $f'(x) < 0$, $\forall\ x \in D_f$, then $y = f(x)$ is one–one function.

Solution: (c) The graph of given function $f(x)$ is as shown below

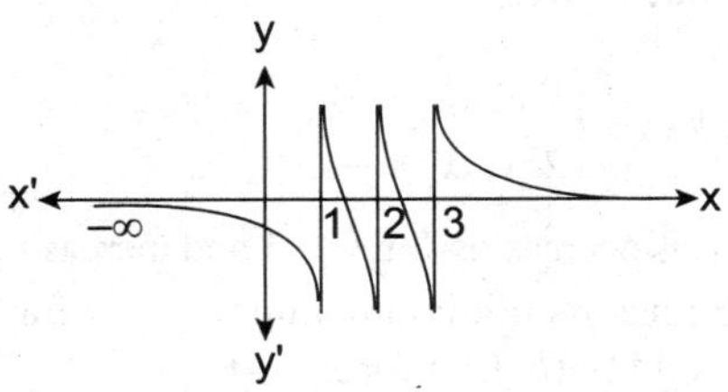

From the graph it is clear that $f(x)$ is not one–one. That is, many–one. Therefore, assertion is true.

Also $f'(x) < 0$, $\forall\ x \in D_f$, but the function is not one–one. so the reason is false.

Infact the reason is true if the function $f(x)$ is continuous.

32. A: Domain of definition of function $f(x)=e^x+\cos^{-1}\left(\frac{x}{2}-1\right)$ + $\log\sqrt{x-[x]}$ is (0, 4) – {1, 2, 3}.

R: Domain of $\cos^{-1}\left(\frac{x}{2}-1\right)$ is (0, 4).

Solution: (c) Given function is

$f(x)=e^x+\cos^{-1}\left(\frac{x}{2}-1\right)$ + $\log\sqrt{x-[x]}$

Now e^x is defined $\forall\ x \in \mathbb{R}$ ... (1)

$\cos^{-1}\left(\frac{x}{2}-1\right)$ is defined for $-1\le\frac{x}{2}-1\le 1$

i.e., $0\le\frac{x}{2}\le 2$ $\Rightarrow x \in [0, 4]$ ... (2)

Also $\log\sqrt{x-[x]}=\log\sqrt{\{x\}}$ is defined for $x \notin \mathbb{Z}$ as otherwise $\{x\} = 0$ ... (3)

∴ From (1), (2) and (3) domain must be (0, 4) – {1, 2, 3}

∴ Assertion is true, but reason is false.

∴ Thus, (c) must be the correct option.

33. A: The range of the function $f(x) = \sin^2 x + p \sin x + q$, where $|p| > 2$, will be the set of real numbers between $q-\frac{p^2}{4}$ and $q + p + 1$.

R: The function $g(t) = t^2 + pt + 1$, where $t \in [-1, 1]$ and $|p| > 2$, will attain minimum and maximum value at –1 and 1.

Solution: (d) Given $f(x)=\left(\sin x+\frac{p}{2}\right)^2+q-\frac{p^2}{4}$

If $|p| > 2$, the perfect square term can't vanish, therefore $f(x)$ will be minimum or maximum when $\sin x = 1$ or –1, i.e., $f(x)$ lies between $(-p + q + 1)$ and $(1 - p + q)$.

$\Rightarrow$ Assertion (A) is false (Assertion (A) will be true if $|p| < 2$)

$$g(t)=t^2+pt+\frac{p^2}{4}+1-\frac{p^2}{4} = \left(t+\frac{p}{2}\right)^2+1-\frac{p^2}{4}$$

for $|p| > 2$, $t \in [-1, 1]$

$\Rightarrow |t|\ne\left|\frac{p}{2}\right|$ $\Rightarrow \left(t+\frac{p}{2}\right)^2$ can't vanish

⇒ minimum/maximum value of $g(t)$ occurs at –1 and 1

∴ Reason is true.

34. **A:** Let A and B be two sets each with a finite number of elements. Assume that there is an injective mapping from A to B and that there is an injective mapping from B to A. Then there is a bijective mapping A to B.

R: An onto function is not necessarily one–one.

Solution: (b) ∵ Three is an injective map from A to B

⇒ Number of elements of $A \le$ Number of elements of B .... (1)

Similarly, there is an injective map from B to A

⇒ Number of elements of $B \le$ Number of elements of A .... (2)

∴ From (1) and (2), we have $n(A) = n(B)$

⇒ $f : A \to B$ and $g : B \to A$ are bijective.

Clearly reason is correct but does not support the assertion.

35. **A:** The function defined by $f(x) = x^3 + ax^2 + bx + c$ is invertible if and only if $a^2 \le 3b$.

R: A function is invertible if and only if it is bijective

Solution: (a) $f(x)$ will be invertible if $f'(x) \ge 0$ for all x as $f(-\infty) = -\infty$ and $f(\infty) = \infty$

or $3x^2 + 2ax + b \ge 0$; which is true, if $4a^2 - 12b \le 0$ or $a^2 \le 3b$ ⇒ (a) is true.

36. **A:** The function $f(x) = \dfrac{2x+a}{bx-2}$ coincides with its inverse if $ab = -4$.

R: $\dfrac{ax+b}{cx+d}$ reduces to a constant if $ad - bc \ne 0$.

Solution: (b) Given $y = \dfrac{2x+a}{bx-2}$

⇒ $bxy - 2y = 2x + a$ ⇒ $x(by - 2) = 2y + a$

⇒ $x = \dfrac{2y+a}{by-2}$ ⇒ $f^{-1}(x) = \dfrac{2x+a}{bx-2}$

⇒ $f(x)$ is self invertible and $f'(x) = \dfrac{-4-ab}{(bx-2)^2} > 0$

or < 0 for $ab \ne -4$. For $ab = -4$, $f(x)$ is constant

Thus, $f(x)$ is self invertible for $ab \ne -4$.

⇒ Assertion is true and reason is also true, but does not explain assertion completely.

37. A function $y = f(x)$ is represented by equation $y^2 - 2 + \log_3(x-1) = 0$; where $f(x) \ge 0\ \forall\ x \in D_f$.

A: The domain of $f(x)$ is (1, 10]

R: The domain of inverse of $f(x)$ is $\mathbb{R}$

Solution: (c) The given equation is valid if $x > 1$.

Now $y = \sqrt{2 - \log_3(x-1)}$ is defined if $2 \ge \log_3(x-1)$

$\Leftrightarrow 9 \ge x - 1$ $\Leftrightarrow x \le 10$

Hence, the domain of $f(x)$ is (1, 10].

Also $2 - y^2 = \log_3(x-1)$ ⇒ $x = 1 + 3^{2-y^2}$; $y \ge 0$

Hence, the inverse of the function is defined by

$f^{-1}(x) = 1 + 3^{2-x^2}$ whose domain is $[0, \infty)$.

38. **A:** There are exactly two values of n for which the function $f(x) = x^n$ coincides with its inverse.

R: Both the functions x and $1/x$ are inverse of themselves.

Solution: (a) $y = x^n$, $x = y^{1/n}$

⇒ Inverse is $y = x^{1/n}$

At the point of intersection $x^n = x^{1/n}$

⇒ $x^{n-\frac{1}{n}} = 1$ ⇒ $n^2 - 1 = 0$ ⇒ $n = \pm 1$

∴ Reason is clearly true and explains the assertion.

Solved Comprehension Passage

A: Consider the functions $f(x) = \begin{cases} 2x+a; & x \ge -1 \\ bx^2+3; & x < -1 \end{cases}$

and $g(x) = \begin{cases} x+4; & 0 \le x \le 8 \\ -3x-2; & -2 \le x < 0 \end{cases}$; $b > 0$. Based on the given functions answer the following questions:

39. $g(f(x))$ is not defined if

(a) $a \in (10, \infty)$; $b \in (5, \infty)$

(b) $a \in (4, 10)$; $b \in (5, \infty)$

(c) $a\ (\in 10, \infty)$; $b \in (1, 5)$

(d) $a \in (4, 10)$; $b \in (1, 5)$

40. If the natural domain of $g(f(x))$ is [–1, 4], then

(a) $a = 2$; $b > 7$ (b) $a = 0$; $b > 5$

(c) $a = 2$; $b > 10$ (d) $a = 0$; $b \in \mathbb{R}$

41. If $a = 2$ and $b = 3$, then range of $g(f(x))$ is

(a) (–2, 8] (b) (0, 8]

(c) [4, 12] (d) None of these

Solution: Given $f(x) = \begin{cases} 2x+a; & x \ge -1 \\ bx^2+3; & x < -1 \end{cases}$; $b > 0$

⇒ $f'(x) = \begin{cases} 2; & x > -1 \\ 2bx; & x < -1 \end{cases}$

⇒ $f(x)$ is decreasing for $x < -1$ and increasing for $x > -1$

⇒ $f(x)$ has its minimum value $-2 + a$ for $x \ge -1$ and has g.l.b. $(b + 3)$ for $x \le -1$

∴ Graph of $f(x)$ would be as shown below

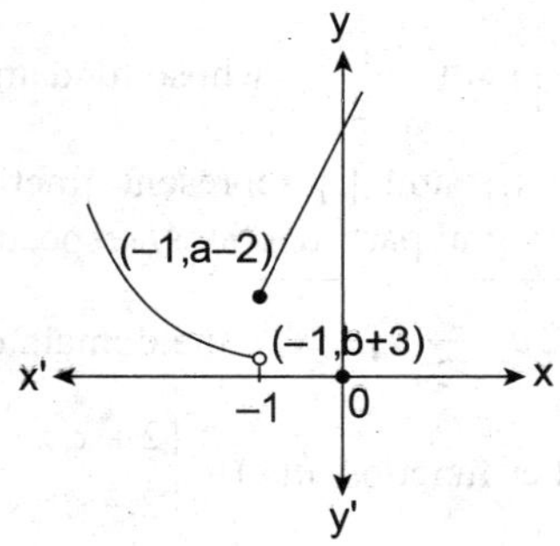

or

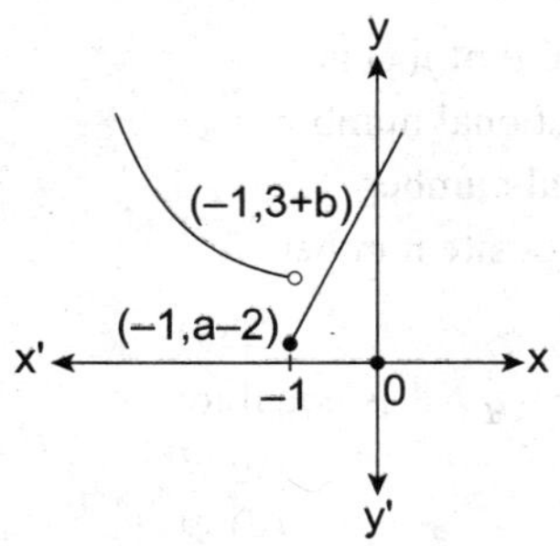

39. (a) For $g(f(x))$ to be undefined range of $f(x)$ should be disjoint from the domain of $g(x)$ which is $(-2, 8]$

$\Rightarrow$ The graph of $f(x)$ must be above the line $y = 8$

$\Rightarrow a - 2 > 8$ and $b + 3 > 8$

$\Rightarrow a > 10$ and $b > 5$ $\Rightarrow a \in (10, \infty), b \in (5, \infty)$

40. (b) Given natural domain of $g(f(x))$ is $[-1, 4]$, i.e., $g(f(x))$ is defined only for $x \in [-1, 4]$ and for $x \in [-1, 4]$; range of $f(x)$ must be entirely contained in the domain of $g(x)$ i.e., situation graphically shown below

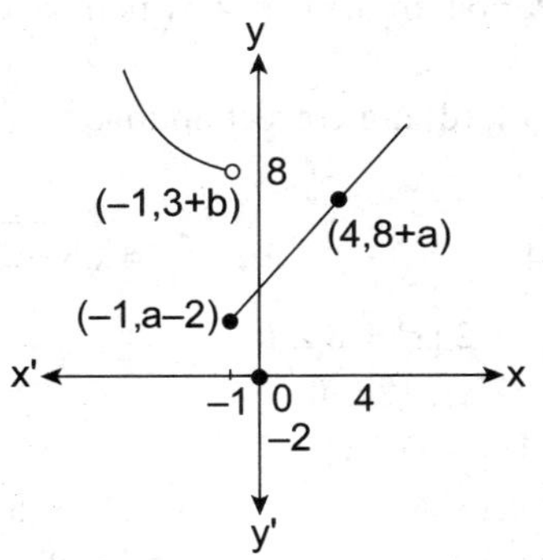

$\Rightarrow -2 \le a - 2 \le 8$ and $-2 \le a + 8 \le 8$; $b + 3 > 8$

$\Rightarrow 0 \le a \le 10$ and $-10 \le a \le 0$; $b > 5$

$\Rightarrow a = 0, b > 5$

41. (c) If $a = 2$, $b = 3$, then $f(x) = \begin{cases} 2x+2; & x \ge -1 \\ 3x^2+3; & x < -1 \end{cases}$ and

$$g(x) = \begin{cases} x+4; & 0 \le x \le 8 \\ -3x-2; & -2 \le x < 0 \end{cases}$$

$$\Rightarrow g(f(x)) = \begin{cases} f(x)+4; & 0 \le f(x) \le 8 \\ -3f(x)-2; & -2 \le f(x) < 0 \end{cases}$$

$$= \begin{cases} 2x+6; & 0 \le 2x+2 \le 8; \quad x \ge -1 \\ 3x^2+7; & 0 \le 3x^2+3 \le 8; \quad x < -1 \\ -3(2x+2)-2 = -6x-8; & -2 \le 2x+2 < 0; \quad x \ge -1 \\ -3(3x^2+3)-2 = -9x^2-11; & -2 \le 3x^2+3 < 0; \quad x < -1 \end{cases}$$

$$= \begin{cases} 2x+6; & -1 \le x \le 3 \\ 3x^2+7; & -\sqrt{\dfrac{5}{3}} \le x < -1 \end{cases}$$

$\Rightarrow$ Range of $g(f(x)) = [4, 12]$

Alternatively: Range of $f(x)$ is $[0, \infty)$ which when fed to function $g(x)$, then range of resulting composition function $gof(x)$ would be $[4, 12]$.

B: If $f(x) = \text{Mid}\{g(x), h(x), p(x)\}$ means the function which will be second in order when values of the three functions at a particular x are arranged in ascending or descending order.

Consider the function:

$$f(x) = \text{Mid}\left\{x-1, (x-3)^2, 3 - \frac{(x-3)^2}{2}\right\}; \ x \in [1, 4].$$

Now answer the following questions based on above defined function $f(x)$.

42. The value of $fof(2.5))$ is

(a) 2.25 (b) 1.50

(c) 1.875 (d) None of these

43. The greatest value of $f(x)$ in $[1, 4]$ will be

(a) $1 + \sqrt{3}$ (b) $2 + \sqrt{3}$

(c) $3 + \sqrt{3}$ (d) None of these

44. Range of $f(x)$ for $x \in [1, 4]$ is

(a) $[\sqrt{3} - 1, 1]$ (b) $[1 + \sqrt{2}, 1 + \sqrt{3}]$

(c) $[1, 1 + \sqrt{3}]$ (d) None of these

Solution:

The graphs of functions $y = x - 1$, $y = (x - 3)^2$, $y = 3 - \dfrac{(x-3)^2}{2}$ for $x \in [1, 4]$ represented w.r.t. same coordinate axes are shown below.

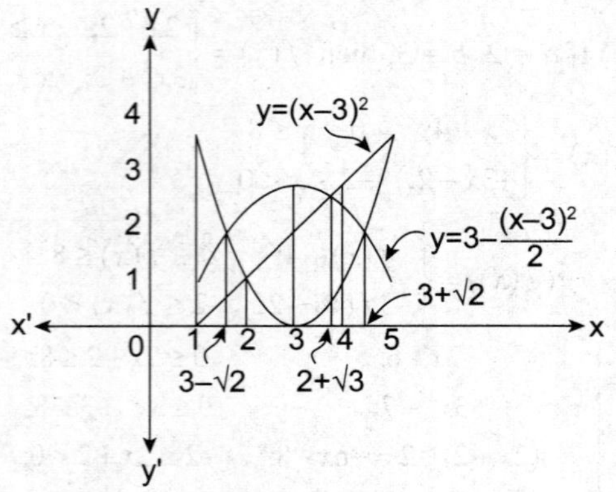

Now $f(x) = \text{Mid}\left\{x-1, (x-3)^2, 3-\frac{(x-3)^2}{2}\right\}; x \in [1, 4]$

can be represented as shown below.

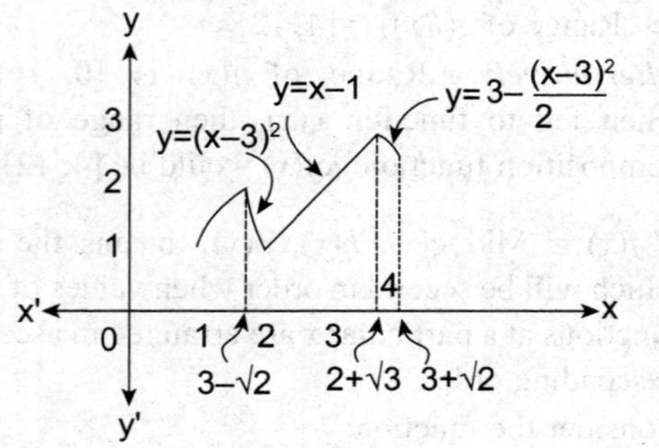

42. (c) At $x = 2.5$, $(x-3)^2 < x-1 < 3-\frac{(x-3)^2}{2}$

$\Rightarrow f(2.5) = 2.5 - 1 = 1.5$

$\therefore fof(2.5) = f(f(2.5)) = f(1.5);$

Further at $x = 1.5$, $x - 1 < 3 - \frac{(x-3)^2}{2} < (x-3)^2$

$\Rightarrow f(1.5) = 3 - \frac{(1.5-3)^2}{2} = 3 - \frac{2.25}{2} = \frac{3.75}{2} = 1.875$

43. (a) Clearly from graph of $f(x)$; $f(x)$ is maximum when

$x - 1 = 3 - \frac{(x-3)^2}{2} \Rightarrow x + \frac{(x-3)^2}{2} = 4$

$\Rightarrow x = \frac{4 \pm \sqrt{16-4}}{2} = \frac{4 \pm 2\sqrt{3}}{2} = 2 \pm \sqrt{3}$

$\Rightarrow$ Clearly $f(x)$ has greatest value at $x > 3$.

$\therefore f(x)$ has greatest value at $x = 2 + \sqrt{3}$ and is $x - 1 = 2 + \sqrt{3} - 1 = 1 + \sqrt{3}$.

44. (c) Maximum of $f(x) = 1 + \sqrt{3}$ and minimum of $f(x) = 1$ for $x \in [1, 4]$

$\therefore$ Range of $f(x)$ is $[1, 1 + \sqrt{3}]$

C: Given a function $f(x) = e^{\tan\left\{\frac{x}{4}\right\}} + \cos \pi \left(\frac{1+2[x]}{2}\right) + \sin\left(\frac{\pi[x]}{2}\right)$ whose fundamental period is p (where {.} and [.] represent fractional part and greatest integral part functions, respectively) and

$g(x) = \sqrt{2p + \frac{p}{2}[x] - [x]^2}$ the domain of y is $[q, r)$

One another function $h(x) = \begin{cases} 2+x, x \geq 0 \\ 2-x, x < 0 \end{cases}$.

Then on the basis of above information answer the following questions:

45. The period p of $f(x)$ is

(a) an irrational number
(b) rational number
(c) a composite number
(d) 4

46. Value of $r - q - 1$ is equal to

(a) 6 (b) 7
(c) 8 (d) 9

47. Range of $hoh(x)$ in terms of p, q, r is:

(a) $[p, \infty)$ (b) $[q, \infty)$
(c) $[r, \infty)$ (d) $(-\infty, -r) \cup (p, \infty)$

Solution: Period of $e^{\tan\left\{\frac{x}{4}\right\}}$ is 4

$\cos \pi\left(\frac{(1+2[x])}{2}\right) = 0 \forall x \in \mathbb{R}$

Period of $\sin\left(\frac{\pi[x]}{2}\right)$ is 4

45. (c) $\therefore$ Period of $f(x)$ is 4 which is composite and rational.

$\therefore$ (b), (c), (d) are correct options.

46. (a)

$\therefore p = 4 \qquad \Rightarrow y = \sqrt{8 + 2[x] - [x]^2}$

$\Rightarrow -[x]^2 + 2[x] + 8 \geq 0$

$\Rightarrow [x]^2 - 2[x] - 8 \leq 0$

i.e., $([x] - 4)([x] + 2) \leq 0$

$\therefore -2 \leq [x] \leq 4 \qquad \therefore -2 \leq x < 5$

$\Rightarrow$ Domain of $g(x) = [-2, 5) = [q, r)$

$\Rightarrow q = -2, r = 5$

$\therefore r - q - 1 = 5 + 2 - 1 = 6$

$\Rightarrow$ (a) is the correct option

47. (a) $h(x)=\begin{cases}x+2; & x\ge 0\\ 2-x; & x<0\end{cases}$

$\Rightarrow\ hoh(x))=\begin{cases}2+h(x); & h(x)\ge 0\\ 2-h(x); & h(x)<0\end{cases}$

$=\begin{cases}2+x+2; & x+2\ge 0 \text{ and } x\ge 0\\ 2-(x+2); & x+2<0 \text{ and } x\ge 0\\ 2+2-x\ ; & 2-x\ge 0 \text{ and } x<0\\ 2-(2-x); & 2-x<0 \text{ and } x<0\end{cases}$

$=\begin{cases}4+x; & x\ge 0\\ 4-x; & x<0\end{cases}$

Range of $hoh(x)$ is $[4, \infty) \cup (4, \infty) = [4, \infty) = [p, \infty)$

$\Rightarrow$ (a) is the correct option

D: Let $y = f(x)$: $A \to B$ is one–one and onto, then $y = f(x)$ is invertible and its inverse $y = f^{-1}(x)$: $B \to A$ exists. If point (α, β) lies on $y = f(x)$, then the point (β, α) lies on $y = f^{-1}(x)$. Let m be the minimum number of points of intersection of $y = f(x)$ and $y = f^{-1}(x)$.

Now answer the following questions:

48. If (2, 3), (3, 2) lie on $y = f^{-1}(x)$ and $y = f(x)$ is continuous, then

(a) $m = 3$ (b) $m = 4$
(c) $m = 6$ (d) $f(x) = f^{-1}(x)\ \forall\ x \in A$

49. If (α, β) $\forall$ α ∈ A lies on $y = f(x)$ but not on $y = f^{-1}(x)$ (where α ≠ β), then

(a) $y = f(x)$ and $y = f^{-1}(x)$ do not intersect
(b) either $y = f(x)$ and $y = f^{-1}(x)$ do not intersect or $y = f(x)$ and $y = f^{-1}(x)$ intersect on $y = x$.
(c) $y = f(x)$ and $y = f^{-1}(x)$ intersect on $y = x$
(d) $y = f(x)$ and $y = f^{-1}(x)$ can not intersect on $y = x$

50. If $f(x) = -x + \sin x$, then

(a) All point of intersection of $y = f(x)$ and $y = f^{-1}(x)$ lies on $y = x$
(b) All point of intersection of $y = f(x)$ and $y = f^{-1}(x)$ lies on $y = -x$
(c) $y = f(x)$ and $y = f^{-1}(x)$ never intersect except at origin
(d) $f(x) = f^{-1}(x)\ \forall\ x \in \mathbb{R}$

Solutions:

48. (a) If (2, 3), (3, 2) lie on $y = f^{-1}(x)$, then both lie on $y = f(x)$ also.

Further since $y = f(x)$ is continuous

Therefore, the graph must cross the line $y = x$

∴ there are at least 3 points of intersection.

49. (b) Suppose $y = f(x)$ and $y = f^{-1}(x)$ intersect each other at some point (α, β) not lying on $y = x$, then α ≠ β

∴ (α, β) lies on both $y = f(x)$ and $y = f^{-1}(x)$ which is contrary to the given hypothesis

∴ the curves either do not intersect or they intersect on $y = x$

50. (b) To solve the equation $f(x) = f^{-1}(x)$, we first draw the graphs of both the functions to observe their points of intersection.

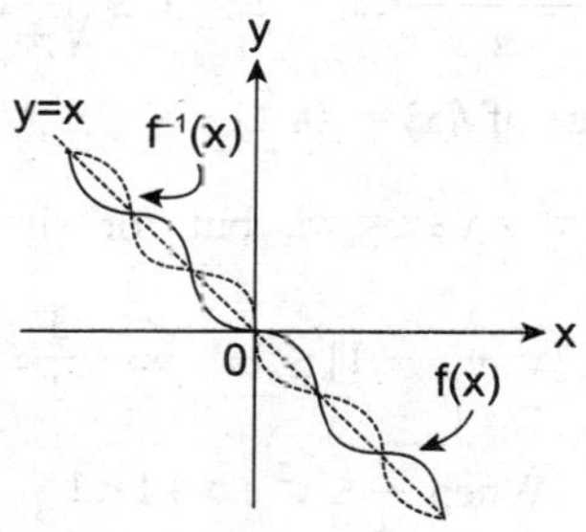

From, the graph, we realize that only the point (0, 0) lies on the line $y = x$. There are other points of intersection $(n\pi, n\pi)$, $n \in \mathbb{Z}$ which lies on the line $y = -x$. Hence, the solution set is $\{n\pi, n \in \mathbb{Z}\}$.

Thus, all the points of intersection lie on $y = -x$.

Solved Column Matching

51. Match the following columns.

Column I

(i) Range of $sgn\ \{x\}$ is (where {.} represents fractional part function)
(ii) Domain of $\sin^{-1}x - \sin^{-1}(1-x)$ is
(iii) Range of $\sqrt{\dfrac{2\tan^{-1}x}{\pi}}$ is
(iv) Range of $\dfrac{2}{\pi}\sin^{-1}[x^2 + x + 1]$ is (where [.] represent greatest integer function)

Column II

(a) {1}
(b) [0, 1)
(c) {0, 1}
(d) [0, 1]

Ans. (i) → (c), (ii) → (d), (iii) → (b), (iv) → (c)

Solution: (i) When $\{x\} = 0$, then $sgn\{x\} = 0$ and when $0 < \{x\} < 1$, then $sgn\ \{x\} = 1$

$\Rightarrow$ Range of $sgn\{x\} = \{0, 1\}$

(ii) For domain $-1 \le x \le 1$ and $-1 \le 1 - x \le 1$

$\Rightarrow -1 \le x \le 1$ and $0 \le x \le 2 \Rightarrow 0 \le x \le 1$

$\Rightarrow$ Domain of function = [0, 1]

(iii) $-\dfrac{\pi}{2} < \tan^{-1} x < \dfrac{\pi}{2}\ \forall x \in \mathbb{R}$

$\Rightarrow -1 < \dfrac{2}{\pi}\tan^{-1} x < 1;$

for $f(x) = \sqrt{\dfrac{2\tan^{-1} x}{\pi}}$; $\dfrac{2\tan^{-1} x}{\pi} \ge 0$

$\Rightarrow 0 \le \dfrac{2\tan^{-1} x}{\pi} < 1 \quad \Rightarrow \quad 0 \le \sqrt{\dfrac{2}{\pi}\tan^{-1} x} < 1$

$\Rightarrow$ Range of $f(x) = [0, 1)$

(iv) $\dfrac{3}{4} \le x^2 + x + 1 < \infty$, but for $\sin^{-1}[x^2 + x + 1]$;

$-1 \le [x^2 + x + 1] \le 1 \quad \Rightarrow \quad \dfrac{3}{4} \le x^2 + x + 1 < 2$

Case I: When $\dfrac{3}{4} \le x^2 + x + 1 < 1$

$\Rightarrow [x^2 + x + 1] = 0 \quad \Rightarrow \sin^{-1}[x^2 + x + 1] = 0$

$\Rightarrow f(x) = \dfrac{2}{\pi}\sin^{-1}[x^2 + x + 1] = 0$

Case II: When $1 \le x^2 + x + 1 < 2$,

$\Rightarrow [x^2 + x + 1] = 1$

$\Rightarrow \sin^{-1}\left[x^2 + x + 1\right] = \dfrac{\pi}{2} \quad \Rightarrow \quad f(x) = \dfrac{2}{\pi}\cdot\dfrac{\pi}{2} = 1$

$\therefore$ Range of given function is {0, 1}.

52. Let $f(x) = \ln x$ and $g(x) = x^2 - 1$. Column-I contains composite functions and column-II contains their domain. Match the entries of column-I with their corresponding answer is column-II.

Column-I

(i) *fog*
(ii) *gof*
(iii) *fof*
(iv) *gog*

Column-II

(a) $(1, \infty)$
(b) $(-\infty, \infty)$
(c) $(-\infty, -1) \cup (1, \infty)$
(d) $(0, \infty)$

Ans. (i) → (c) (ii) → (d)
(iii) → (a) (iv) → (b)

Solution: Given $f(x) = \ln x$ and $g(x) = x^2 - 1$

(i) $fog(x) = f(g(x)) = \ln(x^2 - 1)$ which is defined for $x^2 - 1 > 0$

$\Rightarrow (x - 1)(x + 1) > 0 \Rightarrow x \in (-\infty, -1) \cup (1, \infty)$

$\Rightarrow$ (i) → (c)

(ii) $gof(x) = g[f(x)] = (\ln x)^2 - 1$ which is defined for $x > 0$

$\Rightarrow$ domain of $gof(x)$ is $(0, \infty)$

$\Rightarrow$ (ii) → (d)

(iii) $fof(x) = f[f(x)] = \ln(\ln x)$ which is defined for $\ln x > 0$ and $x > 0$

$\Rightarrow x > 1$

$\therefore$ Domain of $fof(x)$ is $(1, \infty)$

$\Rightarrow$ (iii) → (a)

(iv) $gog(x) = g[g(x)] = (g(x))^2 - 1 = (x^2 - 1)^2 - 1$, which is defined for all $x \in \mathbb{R}$

$\Rightarrow$ Domain of $gog(x)$ is $\mathbb{R} \Rightarrow$ (iv) → (b)

53. If [.] and {.} represent the greatest integer and fractional part functions respectively, then match the columns given below.

Column I

(i) Number of solutions of $[x] = \cos^{-1} x$
(ii) Number of solution of $\sin^{-1}x = sgn(x)$
(iii) Number of solutions of $\{x\} = e^{x^2}$
(iv) Number of solutions of $= \dfrac{\sin^{-1} x + \cos^{-1} x}{2} = \{x\}$

Column II

(a) 3
(b) 2
(c) 1
(d) 0

Ans. (i) → (d) (ii) → (a)
(iii) → (d) (iv) → (b)

Solution: (i) The graph of $\cos^{-1}(x)$ and $[x]$ represented with respect to the same coordinate axes as shown in the graph below.

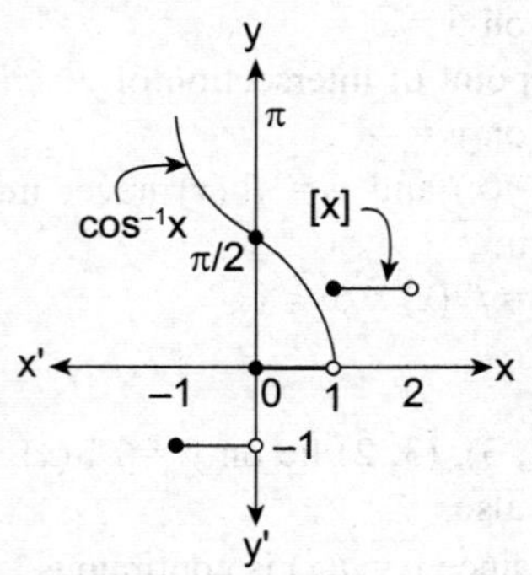

Clearly $[x] = \cos^{-1} x$, has no solution as $f(x) = [x]$ and $g(x) = \cos^{-1} x$ never intersects.

(ii) The graph of $sgn(x)$ and $\sin^{-1}(x)$ represented with respect to the same coordinate axes as shown below.

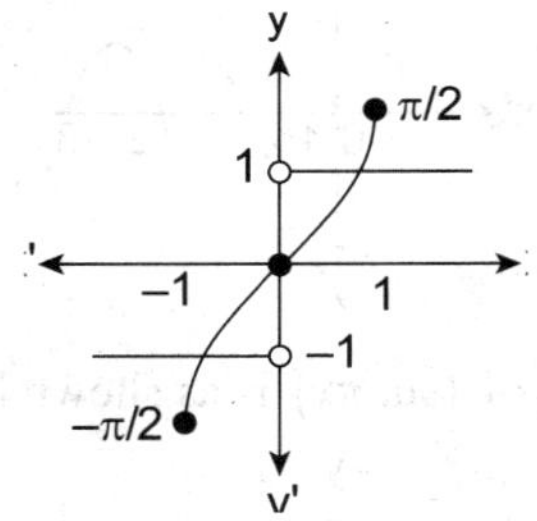

Clearly $sgn(x) = \sin^{-1} x$ has 3 solutions, as $sgn(x)$ and $\sin^{-1} x$ intersect at three points once in $x \in (-1, 0)$. Secondly at $x = 0$ and finally in $x \in (0, 1)$.

(iii) $\{x\} = e^{x^2}$ has no solution.

$\because\ 0 \le \{x\} < 1$ and $e^{x^2} \ge 1$ for all $x \in \mathbb{R}$

$\Rightarrow \{x\}$ and e^{x^2} never intersect.

(iv) The graph of $\dfrac{\sin^{-1} x + \cos^{-1} x}{2} = \dfrac{\pi}{4}$ and $\{x\}$ represented with respect to the same coordinate as shown below

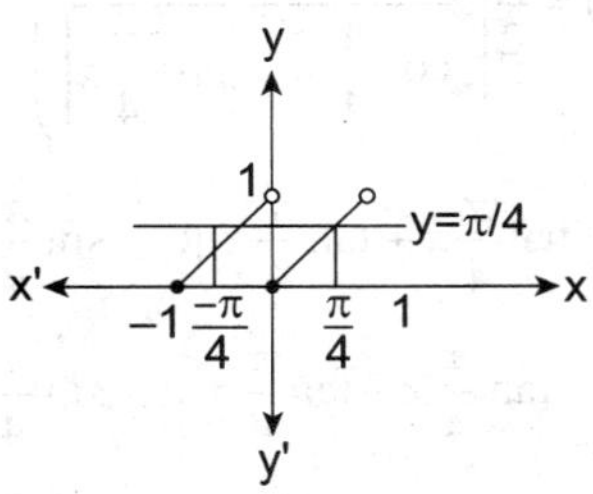

Clearly $\dfrac{\sin^{-1} x + \cos^{-1} x}{2} = \dfrac{\pi}{4}$ and $\{x\}$ intersect at two points, and hence, the equation

$\dfrac{\sin^{-1} x + \cos^{-1} x}{2} = \{x\}$ has exactly two solutions.

Also $\dfrac{\sin^{-1} x + \cos^{-1} x}{2} = \{x\}$

$\Rightarrow \{x\} = \dfrac{\pi}{4}$; where $-1 \le x \le 1$

$\left(\because \sin^{-1} x + \cos^{-1} x = \dfrac{\pi}{2}\right)$

$\Rightarrow x = -1 + \dfrac{\pi}{4}, \dfrac{\pi}{4}$, i.e., $x = \dfrac{\pi - 4}{4}, \dfrac{\pi}{4}$ are only two solutions.

54. Match the following columns

Column I

(i) Let $X = \{a_1, a_2, ..., a_7\}$ and $Y = \{b_1, b_2, b_3\}$. The number of functions f from X to Y such that it is onto and there are exactly three elements x in X such that $f(x) = b_1$ is

(ii) The number of real solutions for x, y if $y = |\sin x|$ and $y = \sin^{-1}(\sin x)$; where $x \in [-2\pi, 2\pi]$ is

(iii) If a, b and c are distinct positive real numbers such that $a + b + c = 1$, then $\dfrac{(1+a)(1+b)(1+c)}{(1-a)(1-b)(1-c)}$ is greater than

(iv) Period of the function $[8x + 7] + \cos \pi x - 8x$, where [.] denotes the greatest integer function is

Column II

(a) 2

(b) 5

(c) 490

(d) 8

Ans. (i) → (c); (ii) → (b); (iii) → (d) (iv) → (a)

Solution: (i) Since any 3 elements out of 7 can be chosen in ${}^7C_3$ ways which are two be associated with b_1 and each of remaining 4 elements has two choices that is, b_2 and b_3, but there are two functions in which all the four elements will be associated to b_2 or b_3 and other remains unassociated.

So, required number of functions $= {}^7C_3\,(2^4 - 2) = 490$.

(ii) The graph of $|\sin x|$ and $\sin^{-1}(\sin x)$ in $x \in [-2\pi, 2\pi]$ is as that follows:

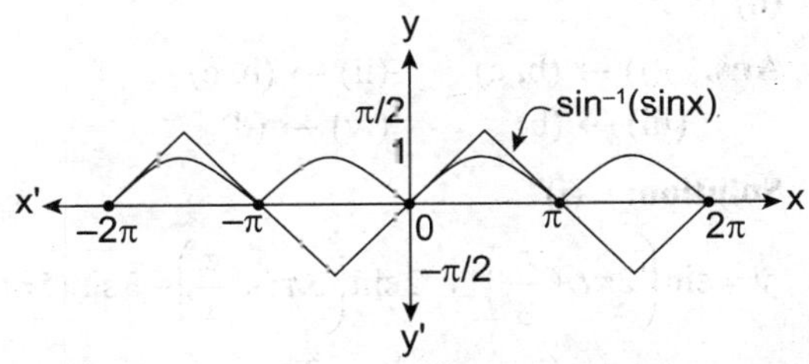

$\therefore$ From figure it is clear that the two graphs would intersect at five points $x = -2\pi, -\pi, 0, \pi, 2\pi$, and hence, number of solutions is 5.

(iii) $a = 1 - b - c$

$\Rightarrow 1 + a = (1 - b) + (1 - c) > 2\sqrt{(1-b)(1-c)}$ ...(1)

$(\because (1 - b) = a + c > 0 \Rightarrow 1 - b > 0.)$

Similarly, $1 - a$, $1 - c > 0$ and $AM > GM$ for positive real numbers) $1 + b > 2\sqrt{(1-c)(1-a)}$ (2)

and $1 + c > 2\sqrt{(1-a)(1-b)}$ .... (3)

$\therefore$ From (1), (2) and (3), we have

$\therefore$ $(1 + a)(1 + b)(1 + c) > 8(1 - a)(1 - b)(1 - c)$

$\Rightarrow \dfrac{(1+a)(1+b)(1+c)}{(1-a)(1-b)(1-c)} > 8$

$\therefore$ Required expression > 8.

(iv) $[8x] + 7 + \cos \pi x - 8x = -\{8x\} + \cos \pi x + 7$

Now fundamental period of $\{8x\}$ is $\dfrac{1}{8}$ and that of $\cos \pi x$ is 2.

Hence, fundamental period of given function

$= \text{LCM}\left(\dfrac{1}{8}, 2\right) = 2.$

55. Column-I

(i) The period of the function $y = \sin(2\pi t + \pi/3) + 2\sin(3\pi t + \pi/4) + 3\sin 5\pi t$ is

(ii) $y = \{\sin(\pi x)\}$ is a many–one function for $x \in (0, a)$; where a may be

(iii) The fundamental period of the function $y = \dfrac{1}{2}\left(\dfrac{|\sin(\pi/4)x|}{\cos(\pi/4)x} + \dfrac{\sin(\pi/4)x}{|\cos(\pi/4)x|}\right)$ is

(iv) If $f: [0, 2] \to [0, 2]$ is bijective function defined by $f(x) = ax^2 + bx + c$, where a, b, c are non-zero real numbers, then $f(2)$ is equal to

Column II

(a) 1/2

(b) 8

(c) 2

(d) 0

Ans. (i) → (b, c) (ii) → (b, c)
(iii) → (b) (iv) → (d)

Solution: (i)

$y = \sin\left(2\pi t + \dfrac{\pi}{3}\right) + 2\sin\left(3\pi t + \dfrac{\pi}{4}\right) + 3\sin(5\pi t)$

Period of $\sin\left(2\pi t + \dfrac{\pi}{3}\right)$ is $\dfrac{2\pi}{2\pi} = 1$;

Period of $\sin\left(3\pi t + \dfrac{\pi}{4}\right)$ is $\dfrac{2\pi}{3\pi} = \dfrac{2}{3}$ and period of $\sin(5\pi t)$ is $\dfrac{2\pi}{5\pi} = \dfrac{2}{5}$

$\therefore$ Period of given function $= \text{LCM}\left(1, \dfrac{2}{3}, \dfrac{2}{5}\right)$

$= \dfrac{\text{L.C.M.}(1,2,2)}{\text{H.C.F.}(1,3,5)} = \dfrac{2}{1} = 2$

$\Rightarrow$ 8 is also period of given function

$\therefore$ (i) → (b, c)

(ii) Graph of $\sin \pi x$ is as shown below

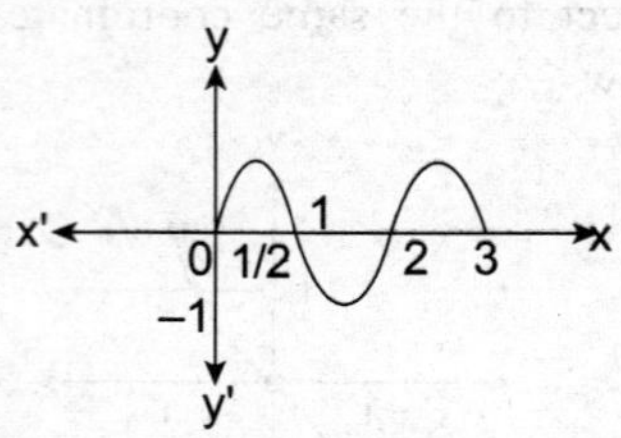

Graph of $\{\sin \pi x\}$ is as shown below

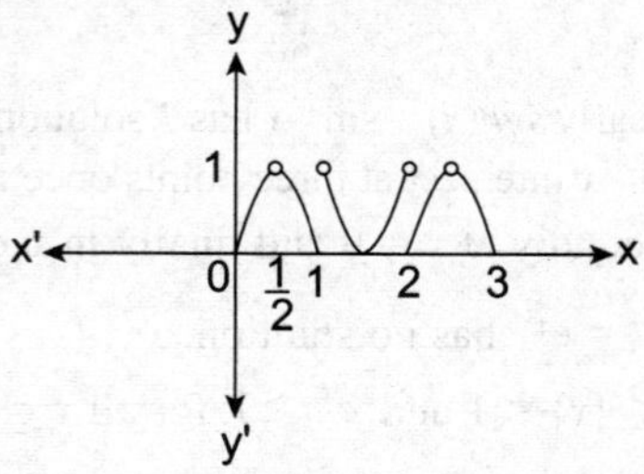

Clearly, $\{\sin \pi x\}$ is periodic with period 2 and 8.

$\therefore$ (ii) → (b, c)

(iii) $f(x) = \dfrac{1}{2}\left(\dfrac{\left|\sin\dfrac{\pi}{4}x\right|}{\cos\dfrac{\pi}{4}x} + \dfrac{\sin\dfrac{\pi}{4}x}{\left|\cos\dfrac{\pi}{4}x\right|}\right)$

$$= \begin{cases} \dfrac{1}{2}\left(\tan\dfrac{\pi}{4}x + \tan\dfrac{\pi}{4}x\right); & \sin\dfrac{\pi}{4}x, \cos\dfrac{\pi}{4}x > 0 \\ \dfrac{1}{2}\left(-\tan\dfrac{\pi}{4}x - \tan\dfrac{\pi}{4}x\right); & \sin\dfrac{\pi}{4}x, \cos\dfrac{\pi}{4}x < 0 \\ 0; & \sin\dfrac{\pi}{4}x.\cos\dfrac{\pi}{4}x \le 0, \text{ and } \cos\dfrac{\pi}{4}x \ne 0 \\ \text{not defined}; & \cos\dfrac{\pi}{4}x = 0 \end{cases}$$

Let us consider $\dfrac{\pi}{4}x \in [0, 2\pi]$.

$$\Rightarrow f(x) = \begin{cases} \tan\dfrac{\pi}{4}x; & 0 \le \dfrac{\pi}{4}x < \dfrac{\pi}{2} \\ -\tan\dfrac{\pi}{4}x; & \pi \le \dfrac{\pi}{4}x < \dfrac{3\pi}{2} \\ 0; & \dfrac{\pi}{2} < \dfrac{\pi}{4}x \le \pi \text{ and } \dfrac{3\pi}{2} < \dfrac{\pi}{4}x \le 2\pi \\ \text{not defined}; & \dfrac{\pi}{4}x = \dfrac{\pi}{2}, \dfrac{3\pi}{2} \end{cases}$$

$$\Rightarrow f(x) = \begin{cases} \tan\frac{\pi}{4}x; & 0 \le x < 2 \\ -\tan\frac{\pi}{4}x; & 4 \le x < 6 \\ 0; & 2 < x \le 4 \text{ and } 6 < x \le 8 \\ \text{not defined if } x = 2, 6 \end{cases}$$

and so on.

$\therefore$ Graph of $f(x)$ would be as shown below

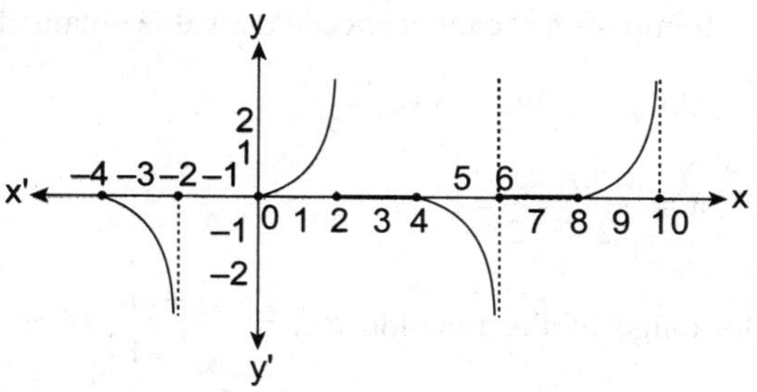

Clearly, the function is periodic with period 8.

$\therefore$ (iii) $\to$ (b)

(iv) Since $f(x)$ is bijective,

$\therefore$ $f(0) = 0$ or 2 but $f(0) = 0$

$\Rightarrow$ $c = 0$ (which is not true)

$\therefore$ $f(0) = 2$.

We know that a quadratic function is of opposite monotonicity on intervals $\left(-\infty, \frac{-b}{2a}\right]$ and $\left[\frac{-b}{2a}, \infty\right)$

$\therefore$ $f(0) = 2$ if $f(x)$ is increasing on [0, 2], then $f(x) > 2$ for $x > 0$.

But range of $f(x) = [0, 2]$

$\Rightarrow$ $f(x)$ must be decreasing on [0, 2]

$\Rightarrow$ $f(2) = 0$

$\therefore$ (iv) $\to$ (d)

Solved Integer-type Questions

56. Let $f(x) = \frac{9^x}{9^x + 3}$, then if the value of the sum $f\left(\frac{1}{2006}\right) + f\left(\frac{2}{2006}\right) + f\left(\frac{3}{2006}\right) + \ldots + f\left(\frac{2005}{2006}\right) = S$, then find $2S$.

Solution: Observe the argument of 1st and last term. If argument of 1st term is x, then the argument of the last is $1 - x$ and similar relation exists for each pair of terms that are equidistant from the both ends.

Consider, $f(x) + f(1 - x)$, i.e., $\frac{9^x}{9^x + 3} + \frac{9^{1-x}}{9^{1-x} + 3}$

$$= \frac{9^x}{9^x + 3} + \frac{9}{9 + 3\cdot 9^x} = \frac{9^x}{9^x + 3} + \frac{3}{3 + 9^x} = 1$$

Now since $f(x) + f(1 - x) = 1$

$\therefore$ Sum S becomes $\left[f\left(\frac{1}{2006}\right) + f\left(\frac{2005}{2006}\right)\right] + \left[f\left(\frac{2}{2006}\right) + f\left(\frac{2004}{2006}\right)\right] + \ldots + f\left(\frac{1003}{2006}\right)$

Clearly it contains 2005 terms

$\therefore$ 1002 pairs (each summed up as 1) and an isolated term $f\left(\frac{1003}{2006}\right)$

$$\Rightarrow S = 1002 + f\left(\frac{1003}{2006}\right) = 1002 + f\left(\frac{1}{2}\right)$$

$$\Rightarrow S = 1002 + \frac{1}{2} = 1002 + 0.5 = 1002.5.$$

$$\Rightarrow 2S = 2 \times \frac{2005}{2} = 2005$$

57. The set of real values of x satisfying the equality $\left[\frac{3}{x}\right] + \left[\frac{4}{x}\right] = 5$; (where [] denotes the greatest integer function) belongs to the interval $\left(a_1, \frac{a_2}{a_3}\right]$; where a_1, $a_2, a_3 \in \mathbb{N}$ and $\frac{a_2}{a_3}$ is in its lowest form. Find the value of $\sum a_i + \sum_{i \ne j} a_i a_j + \sum_{i \ne j \ne k} a_i a_j a_k$.

Solution: *Case i:* If $x < 0$, then $\left[\frac{3}{x}\right]$ and $\left[\frac{4}{x}\right]$ is negative; hence, $\left[\frac{3}{x}\right] + \left[\frac{4}{x}\right]$ can never be equal to 5

Case ii: If $x > 0$; we have $\frac{3}{x} < \frac{4}{x}$

$\therefore$ $\left[\frac{3}{x}\right] \le \left[\frac{4}{x}\right]$

Since each of $\left[\frac{3}{x}\right]$ and $\left[\frac{4}{x}\right]$ is a non-negative integer

$\therefore$ 3 possibilities are there (sub-cases)

Sub-case i: $\left[\frac{3}{x}\right] = 0$ and $\left[\frac{4}{x}\right] = 5$

Sub-case ii: $\left[\frac{3}{x}\right] = 1$ and $\left[\frac{4}{x}\right] = 4$

Sub-case iii: $\left[\frac{3}{x}\right]=2$ and $\left[\frac{4}{x}\right]=3$

As $\left[\frac{3}{x}\right]+\left[\frac{4}{x}\right]=5$. Now, If $\left[\frac{3}{x}\right]=0$

$\Rightarrow\ 0\le\frac{3}{x}<1 \quad \Rightarrow\ 0\le 3<x\sim$ ...(i)

$\Rightarrow$ Further $\left[\frac{4}{x}\right]=5 \quad \Rightarrow\ 5\le\frac{4}{x}<6$

$\Rightarrow \frac{1}{6}<\frac{x}{4}\le\frac{1}{5} \Rightarrow \frac{2}{3}<x\le\frac{4}{5}$ ...(ii)

These two inequations (i) and (ii) are impossible simultaneously. Hence, no solutions in sub-case (i)

Sub case (ii): Now, $\left[\frac{3}{x}\right]=1$

$\Rightarrow\ 1\le\frac{3}{x}<2 \quad \Rightarrow \frac{1}{2}<\frac{x}{3}\le 1 \quad \Rightarrow \frac{3}{2}<x\le 3$ ...(iii)

Further $\left[\frac{4}{x}\right]=4 \Rightarrow\ 4\le\frac{4}{x}<5 \quad \Rightarrow \frac{1}{5}<\frac{x}{4}\le\frac{1}{4}$

$\Rightarrow\ \frac{4}{5}<x\le 1$ ...(iv)

(iii) and (iv) are impossible, hence, no solution in sub-case (ii)

Sub case (iii): Again if $\left[\frac{3}{x}\right]=2 \Rightarrow\ 2\le\frac{3}{x}<3$

$\Rightarrow\ \frac{1}{3}<\frac{x}{3}\le\frac{1}{2} \quad \Rightarrow\ 1<x\le\frac{3}{2}$ ...(v)

Further $\left[\frac{4}{x}\right]=3 \quad \Rightarrow\ 3\le\frac{4}{x}<4$

$\Rightarrow\ \frac{1}{4}<\frac{x}{4}\le\frac{1}{3} \quad \Rightarrow\ 1<x\le\frac{4}{3}$ ...(vi)

Common solution $1<x\le\frac{4}{3}$

Hence $x\in\left(1,\frac{4}{3}\right]$

$\therefore\ a_1=1,\ a_2=4,\ a_3=3;$

$\therefore\ \sum a_i+\sum_{i\ne j}a_ia_j+\sum_{i\ne j\ne k}a_ia_ja_k$

$=a_1+a_2+a_3+a_1a_2+a_2a_3+a_3a_1+a_1a_2a_3$

$=1+4+3+4+12+3+12=39$

58. If a, b, are positive real numbers such that $a-b=4$, then find the smallest value of the constant λ for which $\sqrt{x^2+ax}-\sqrt{x^2+bx}<\lambda$ for all $x>0$.

Solution: Given $f(x)=\sqrt{x^2+ax}-\sqrt{x^2+bx}$

$\Rightarrow\ f(x)=\frac{x^2+ax-x^2-bx}{\sqrt{x^2+ax}+\sqrt{x^2+bx}}$

$=\frac{(a-b)x}{\sqrt{x^2+ax}+\sqrt{x^2+bx}}=\frac{a-b}{\sqrt{1+a/x}+\sqrt{1+b/x}}$

$\because\ x>0$, as x increases $\frac{1}{x}$ decreases, and denominator of above fraction decreases, and hence, $f(x)$ goes on increasing.

It implies $f(x)$ cannot exceed the value obtained by taking the $\lim_{x\to\infty}f(x)=\frac{a-b}{2}$

$\therefore\ \lambda=\frac{a-b}{2}=\frac{4}{2}=2$

59. The range of the function $f(x)=\frac{x+m}{x^2+1}$, $(m\in\mathbb{R})$ contains the interval [0, 1]. If $m\ge\frac{3}{k}$, then find k

Solution: Given function is $y=\frac{x+m}{x^2+1}$

$\Rightarrow\ yx^2-x+(y-m)=0$

we must have $D\ge 0$ for $y\in[0,1]$

$\Rightarrow 1-4y(y-m)\ge 0$ for $y\in[0,1]$

$\Rightarrow g(y)=4y^2-4my-1\le 0$ for $y\in[0,1]$

$\Rightarrow g(y)\le 0$, for $y\in[0,1] \Rightarrow\ g(0)\le 0, g(1)\le 0$

$\Rightarrow -1\le 0$ and $3-4m\le 0 \Rightarrow\ m\ge\frac{3}{4} \quad\Rightarrow\ k=4$

60. Let $f(x)=(x+1)(x+2)(x+3)(x+4)+5$; where $x\in[-6,6]$. If the range of the function is $[a,b]$; where $a,b\in\mathbb{N}$, then find the value of $(a+b)$.

Solution: Given $f(x)=(x^2+5x+4)(x^2+5x+6)+5$

$=[(x^2+5x+5)-1]\,[(x^2+5x+5)+1]+5$

$=(x^2+5x+5)^2-1+5$

$\Rightarrow f(x)=(x^2+5x+5)^2+4$

Hence, $f(x)$ has a minimum value 4 when $x^2+5x+5=0$, i.e., $x=\frac{-5\pm\sqrt{5}}{2}\in[-6,6]$

Also maximum occurs at $x=6$.

$\Rightarrow f(x)_{max}=(36+30+5)^2+4=(71)^2+4=5041+4=5045$

Range is $[4, 5045]\equiv[a,b]$ (given)

$\Rightarrow a=4;\ b=5045 \quad\Rightarrow\ a+b=5049$

61. Suppose $p(x)$ is a polynomial with integer coefficients. The remainder when $p(x)$ is divided by $x-1$ is 2 and remainder when $p(x)$ is divided by $x - 4$ is 11. If $r(x)$ is the remainder when $p(x)$ is divided by $(x - 1)(x - 4)$, find the value of $r(2013)$.

Solution: Given $p(x) = (x - 1)\, g(x) + 2$

$\Rightarrow p(1) = 2$ and $p(x) = (x - 4)\, h(x) + 11$

$\Rightarrow p(4) = 11$

Further let $s(x)$ and $r(x)$ be the quotient and remainder when $p(x)$ is divided by $(x - 1)(x - 4)$ and let $r(x) = ax + b$

$\Rightarrow p(x) = (x - 1)(x - 4)\, s(x) + r(x)$

$\Rightarrow p(1) = a + b = 2$ ...(1)

and $p(4) = 4a + b = 11$ ...(2)

Using (1) and (2), we get $a = 3$, $b = -1$

$\therefore\ r(x) = ax + b$

$\Rightarrow r(x) = 3x - 1$

$\therefore\ r(2013) = 3(2013) - 1 = 6039 - 1 = 6038.$

62. Find the minimum number of roots of $f(x) = f\left(\dfrac{x+4}{x-2}\right)$.

Solution: Given $f(x) = f\left(\dfrac{x+4}{x-2}\right)$

One of the possibilities is $x = \dfrac{x+4}{x-2}$

$\Rightarrow x^2 - 2x - x - 4 = 0 \Rightarrow x^2 - 3x - 4 = 0$

Disc. $= 9 + 16 = 25 > 0$

$\therefore$ Minimum number of roots = 2.

63. If $f(2x + 1) = 4x^2 + 14x$, then find the sum of the squares of roots of the equation $f(x) = 0$

Solution: Given $f(2x + 1) = 4x^2 + 14x$ ...(1)

we are to find the sum of squares of roots of equation $f(x) = 0$. Putting $2x + 1 = y$

$\Rightarrow x = \dfrac{y-1}{2}$ in (1), we have $f(y) = 4\left(\dfrac{y-1}{2}\right)^2 + 14\left(\dfrac{y-1}{2}\right)$

$\Rightarrow f(y) = y^2 + 1 - 2y + 7y - 7$

$\Rightarrow f(y) = y^2 + 5y - 6$

$\therefore\ f(x) = 0$

$\Rightarrow x^2 + 5x - 6 = 0 \quad \Rightarrow (x + 6)(x - 1) = 0$

$\Rightarrow x = -6$ or $x = 1 \quad \therefore\ \alpha^2 + \beta^2 = 36 + 1 = 37$

64. If $\alpha = e^{\frac{2\pi i}{13}}$ and $f(x) = 7 + \sum_{k=1}^{50} A_k x^k$, then find the value of $\left(\dfrac{1}{13}\right)\sum_{r=0}^{12} f(\alpha^r x)$.

Solution: Clearly α is a non-real complex root of equation $x^{13} = 1$.

But α is non-real complex, α is a root of $1 + x + x^2 + \dots + x^{12} = 0$

Now $\sum_{r=0}^{12} f(\alpha^r x) = f(x) + f(\alpha x) + f(\alpha^2 x) + \dots + f(\alpha^{12} x)$

$$= \left(7 + \sum_{k=1}^{50} A_k x^k\right) + \left(7 + \sum_{k=1}^{50} A_k \alpha^k x^k\right) + \dots + \left(7 + \sum_{k=1}^{50} A_k \alpha^{12k} x^k\right)$$

$$= 91 + \sum_{k=1}^{50} A_k x^k [1 + \alpha^k + \dots + \alpha^{12k}]$$

$$= 91 + \sum_{k=1}^{50} A_k x^k \frac{1 - (\alpha^k)^{13}}{1 - \alpha^k} = 91 + \sum_{k=1}^{50} A_k x^k \frac{(1 - \alpha^{13k})}{(1 - \alpha^k)}$$

$= 91 + 0$ ($\because \alpha$ is a root of $x^{13} = 1 \Rightarrow \alpha^{13} = 1 \Rightarrow \alpha^{13k} - 1 = 0$)

$\therefore\ \dfrac{1}{13}\sum_{r=0}^{12} f(\alpha^r x) = 7$

65. If $f(x)$ is a function such that $\dfrac{f(x-1) + f(x+1)}{2f(x)} = \sin 60°$ and $f(5) = 100$, find $\sum_{r=0}^{99} f(5 + 12r)$

Solution: Given $f(x - 1) + f(x + 1) = 2f(x) \sin 60°$

$\Rightarrow f(x-1) + f(x+1) = \sqrt{3}\, f(x)$ .....(1)

From equation (1)

$f(x + 3) + f(x + 1) = \sqrt{3}\, f(x + 2)$ (replacing x by $x + 2$) ...(2)

Adding equations (1) and (2), we get

$f(x - 1) + f(x + 3) + 2f(x + 1) = \sqrt{3}\,\{f(x) + f(x + 2)\}$

$= \sqrt{3} \times \sqrt{3}\, f(x + 1)$; (from (1) putting $(x + 1)$ in place of x)

$= 3 f(x + 1)$

$\therefore\ f(x - 1) + f(x + 3) = f(x + 1)$ ....(3)

and $f(x + 1) + f(x + 5) = f(x + 3)$ ...(4)

Adding (3) and (4), we get

$f(x - 1) + f(x + 1) + f(x + 3) + f(x + 5) = f(x + 1) + f(x + 3)$

$\Rightarrow f(x - 1) + f(x + 5) = 0 \Rightarrow f(x - 1) = -f(x + 5)$

$\Rightarrow f(x) = -f(x + 6)$ ....(5)

From equation (5) $f(x) = -[-f(x + 12)]$

$\Rightarrow f(x + 12) = f(x)$

Hence, $f(x)$ is a periodic function with period 12

Now, $\sum_{r=0}^{99} f(5+12r) = f(5) + f(5+12) + f(5+2.12) + \ldots + f(5+99.12)$
$= f(5) + f(5) + f(5) + \ldots$ to 100 terms
$= 100f(5) = 100 \times 100 = 10000.$

66. Find the natural number a for which $\sum_{k=1}^{n} f(a+k) = 2n(33+n)$; where the function f satisfies the relation $f(x+y) = f(x) + f(y)$ for all natural numbers x, y and further $f(1) = 4$.

Solution: Since given $f(x+y) = f(x) + f(y)$ for all natural numbers x, y and $f(1) = 4$,
Therefore $f(n) = f(\underbrace{1+\ldots+1}_{n \text{ times}})$

$= \underbrace{f(1)+f(1)+\ldots+f(1)}_{n \text{ times}} = 4n$, for every natural number n.

$\Rightarrow f(n) = 4n$ for $n \in \mathbb{N}$

The given relation can be written as $\sum_{k=1}^{n} 4(a+k) = 2n(33+n)$

$\Rightarrow 4an + 2n(n+1) = 2n(33+n)$

$\Rightarrow 4an + 2n^2 + 2n = 66n + 2n^2 \Rightarrow 4an = 64n$

$\Rightarrow a = 16$

67. Find the natural number a for which $\sum_{k=1}^{n} f(a+k) = 16(2^n - 1)$; where the function f satisfies the relation $f(x+y) = f(x).f(y)$ for all natural numbers x, y and further $f(1) = 2$

Solution: $\sum_{k=1}^{n} f(a+k) = 16(2^n - 1)$

$\Rightarrow f(a+1) + f(a+2) + \ldots + f(a+n) = 16(2^n - 1).$

Now $f(x+y) = f(x).f(y)$ and $f(1) = 2$ (given)

$\Rightarrow f(2) = f(1+1) = f(1).f(1) = (f(1))^2 = (2)^2$; $f(3) = f(2+1) = f(2).f(1) = (2)^2(2) = (2)^3$.

$\Rightarrow f(n) = 2^n \ \forall \ n \in \mathbb{N}$.

Now, $f(a+1) + f(a+2) + \ldots + f(a+n)$
$= 2^a[2 + 4 + \ldots + 2^n] = 2^a.2(2^n - 1) = 16(2^n - 1)$

$\Rightarrow 16 = 2^{a+1} \qquad \Rightarrow a = 3$

68. $f(x)$ and $g(x)$ are linear functions such that for all x, $f(g(x))$ and $g(f(x))$ are identity functions. If $f(0) = 9$ and $g(5) = 8$, then compute $f(-2012)$.

Solution: Given $f(g(x))$ and $g(f(x))$ are identity functions. Therefore, $f(x)$ and $g(x)$ are inverse to each other. Let $y = f(x) = ax + b$ be the linear function.

$\Rightarrow y = ax + b \Rightarrow x = \frac{y-b}{a} \Rightarrow f^{-1}(x) = \frac{x-b}{a}$

$\Rightarrow g(x) = \frac{x-b}{a}$

Now $f(0) = 9 \Rightarrow b = 9$ and $g(5) = 8 \Rightarrow a = \frac{-1}{2}$

$\therefore f(x) = -\frac{1}{2}x + 9 \Rightarrow f(-2012) = 606 + 9 = 615.$

69. Let $f(x, y)$ be a periodic function satisfying $f(x, y) = f(2x + 2y, 2y - 2x)$ for all x, y. Define $g(x) = f(2^x, 0)$, then find the period of function g.

Solution: Given $g(x) = f(2^x, 0) = f(2.2^x + 2.0, 2.0 - 2.2^x)$
$= f(2^{x+1}, -2^{x+1})$
$= f(2.2^{x+1} + 2(-2^{x+1}), 2(-2^{x+1}) - 2.2^{x+1})$
$= f(0, -2^{x+3}) = f(-2^{x+4}, -2^{x+4}) = f(-2^{x+6}, 0)$
$= f(-2^{x+7}, 2^{x+7}) = f(0, 2^{x+9}) = f(2^{x+10}, 2^{x+10})$
$= f(2^{x+12}, 0) = g(x + 12) \Rightarrow$ Period of g is 12.

70. Let $g(x) = \frac{e^x - e^{-x}}{2}$ and $g(f(x)) = x$, then evaluate $f\left(\frac{e^{22}-1}{2e^{11}}\right)$.

Solution: Let $y = g(x) = \frac{e^x - e^{-x}}{2}$

$\Rightarrow e^{2x} - 1 = 2ye^x$

Substituting $e^x = t$, we have $t^2 - 2yt - 1 = 0$

$\Rightarrow t = \frac{2y \pm \sqrt{4y^2+4}}{2} = y \pm \sqrt{y^2+1}$

$\Rightarrow e^x = y + \sqrt{y^2+1} \qquad (\because e^x > 0)$

$\Rightarrow x = \ln\left(y + \sqrt{y^2+1}\right)$

$\Rightarrow g^{-1}(y) = \ln\left(y + \sqrt{y^2+1}\right)$

$\therefore g^{-1}(x) = f(x) = \ln\left(x + \sqrt{x^2+1}\right)$

$(\because g(f(x)) = x \Rightarrow g^{-1}(x) = f(x))$

$\therefore f\left(\frac{e^{22}-1}{2e^{11}}\right) = \ln\left(\frac{e^{22}-1}{2e^{11}} + \sqrt{\left(\frac{e^{22}-1}{2e^{11}}\right)^2 + 1}\right)$

$= \ln\left(\frac{e^{22}-1}{2e^{11}} + \sqrt{\left(\frac{e^{22}+1}{2e^{11}}\right)^2}\right) = \ln[e^{11}] = 11$

71. All the values of m for which the function $f(x) = (m+2)x^3 - 3mx^2 + 9mx - 1$ is invertible lies in the interval $(-\infty, -(\lambda + 1)] \cup [-\lambda + 2, \infty)$, then find the value of λ.

Solution: Given $f(x) = (m + 2)x^3 - 3mx^2 + 9mx - 1$

$\Rightarrow f'(x) = 3(m + 2)x^2 - 6mx + 9m$

$\Rightarrow f(x)$ will be monotonically increasing for all x if $m + 2 > 0$, $36m^2 - 108m(m + 2) \le 0$

or $m + 2 > 0$, $m(m + 3) \ge 0$

$\Rightarrow m \in (-2, \infty)$ and $m \in (-\infty, -3] \cup [0, \infty)$

$\Rightarrow m \in [0, \infty)$

Again $f(x)$ will be monotonically decreasing for all x if $m + 2 < 0$ and $36m^2 - 108m(m + 2) \le 0$

$\Rightarrow m \in (-\infty, -2)$ and $m \in (-\infty, -3] \cup [0, \infty)$

$\Rightarrow m \in (-\infty, -3]$

$\therefore$ $f(x)$ is monotonically increasing for all x or monotonically decreasing for all x (i.e., invertible) if $m \in (-\infty, -3] \cup [0, \infty)$.

$\Rightarrow \lambda = 2$

72. Let $A = \{1, 2, 3, 4, 5, \ldots, 10\}$ and $B = \{1, 2, 3, 4, \ldots, 10\}$, then find the number of functions f from A to B such $f(f(i)) = i \ \forall \ i \in A$

Solution: $f(f(i)) = i \ \forall \ i \in A$

Let $(i, j) \notin f$

$\Rightarrow f(i) = j$

$\Rightarrow f(f(i)) = f(j)$ but $f(f(i)) = i$ (given)

$\Rightarrow f(j) = i \qquad \Rightarrow (i, j)) \in f$

$\Rightarrow f$ is a self invertible function.

Let us deal with two cases as given below.

Case i: When $(i, j) \in f \Leftrightarrow (j, i) \in f$ and $i \ne j$ for every pair $(i, j) \in f$

Case ii: When $(i, j) \in f \Leftrightarrow (j, i) \in f$ and f contains pairs of the form (i, i).

Case i: When $(i, j) \in f \Leftrightarrow (j, i) \in f$ and $i \ne j$ for every pair $(i, j) \in f$

We can generate such functions by making five ordered pairs (i, j) having elements from set A such that $i \ne j$ and if (i, j), (k, l) are any two of the five ordered pairs then $i \ne k$ and $i \ne j$, which is equivalent to distribution of 10 different objects into 5 unnamed groups each group containing 2 objects

$= ({}^{10}C_2 \times {}^8C_2 \times {}^6C_2 \times {}^4C_2 \times {}^2C_2) \div (5!)$

$$= \frac{10 \times 9 \times 8 \times 7 \times 6 \times 5 \times 4 \times 3 \times 2 \times 1}{2 \times 2 \times 2 \times 2 \times 2 \times 5!} = 945$$

Now each of the above 945 ways of forming five ordered pairs when taken with the same five pair with their elements interchanged would represent a symmetric function.

A self invertible function not intersecting the line $y = x$. We get 945 functions one of which is {(2, 3), (4, 5), (7, 8), (6, 9), (1, 10), (3, 2), (5, 4), (8, 7), (9, 6), (10, 1)}

Case ii: When $(i, j) \in f \Leftrightarrow (j, i) \in f$ and f contains pairs of the form (i, i).

If the collection contains only one pair (i, i) and rest of the type (i, j), (j, i); $i \ne j$, then we can't have such function, as leaving 1 element i, we are left with 9 elements (odd) and it is impossible to distribute all of then into graphs each containing two elements similarly we can't have functions having 3 pairs of the form (i, i).

Thus, we can form functions having exactly 2 or 4 or 6 or 8 or 10 pairs of the form (i, i).

Sub-case (a) When functions have exactly two pairs of the form (i, i). Two such pairs can be selected in ${}^{10}C_2$ ways and the remaining 8 elements can be distributed among 4 pairs in $\left\{\frac{1}{4!}\left({}^8C_2 \times {}^6C_2 \times {}^4C_2 \times {}^2C_2\right)\right\}$ ways, so total number of functions in this case would be

$$= \frac{{}^{10}C_2 \times {}^8C_2 \times {}^6C_2 \times {}^4C_2 \times {}^2C_2}{4!}$$

$$= \frac{10 \times 9 \times 8 \times 7 \times 6 \times 5 \times 4 \times 3 \times 2 \times 1}{2 \times 2 \times 2 \times 2 \times 2 \times 4!} = 4725.$$

Sub-case (b) When functions contains 4 pairs of the form (i, i). The number of function in this case would be ${}^{10}C_4 \times \frac{{}^6C_2 \times {}^4C_2 \times {}^2C_2}{3!}$

$$= \frac{10 \times 9 \times 8 \times 7}{4!} \times \frac{6 \times 5 \times 4 \times 3 \times 2 \times 1}{2 \times 2 \times 2 \times 3!} = 3150$$

Sub-case (c) When functions contain 6 pairs of the form (i, i). The number of function in this case would be

$$= {}^{10}C_6 \times \frac{{}^4C_2 \times {}^2C_2}{2!} = {}^{10}C_4 \times 3$$

$$= \frac{10 \times 9 \times 8 \times 7}{4 \times 3 \times 2 \times 1} \times 3 = 630$$

Sub-case (d) When functions contain 8 pairs of the form (i, i). The number of function in this case would be ${}^{10}C_8 \times {}^2C_2 = {}^{10}C_2 = 45$

Sub-case (e) When functions contains 10 pairs of the form (i, i). There will be only one function, i.e., identity function.

Thus, total number of possible self invertible functions from A to B

$= 945 + 4725 + 3150 + 630 + 45 + 1 = 9496$

TUTORIAL EXERCISE

SECTION-III

(ONY ONE CORRECT ANSWER)

1. If $2f(x^2)+3f\left(\frac{1}{x^2}\right)=x^2-1$ for all $x \in \mathbb{R} \sim \{0\}$. Then $f(x^2)$ is equal to.
(a) $\frac{1-x^4}{5x^2}$ (b) $\frac{(1-x^2)(3+2x^2)}{5x^2}$
(c) $\frac{(1-x^2)(3+2x^2)}{3x^2}$ (d) None of these

2. The domain of definition of the function $f(x)=\sqrt{\frac{2-[x]}{[x]-3}}$ is equal to
(a) [2, 3) (b) (2, 3)
(c) $(2, \infty)$ (d) None of these

3. The domain of definition of the function $f(x) = \sin^{-1}[2-3x^2]$ is equal to
(a) [–1, 1] (b) [0, 1]
(c) $[-1, 0) \cup (0, 1]$ (d) None of these

4. The real function $f(x) = \cos^{-1}\sqrt{x^2+3x+1}+\cos^{-1}\sqrt{x^2+3x}$ is defined on the set.
(a) {0, 3} (b) interval (0, 3)
(c) {0, –3} (d) interval [–3, 0]

5. Find which of the following statements is/are true $f(x)=\sin^{-1}x+\sqrt{2x-x^2} - \frac{1}{\sqrt{8x-4x^2-3}}$.
(a) Domain is [0, 2] (b) Domain is $\left[-1,\frac{1}{2}\right]$
(c) Domain is $\left(\frac{1}{2},1\right]$ (d) None of these

6. The domain of the function $f(x)=\frac{1}{\sqrt{1-\sqrt{1-\sqrt{1-x^2}}}}$ is
(a) $\{x: x < 1\}$ (b) (–1, 1)
(c) [–1, 1] (d) None of these

7. The domain of the function $f(x)=\sqrt{3-2^x-2^{1-x}}+\sqrt{\sin^{-1}x}$ is given by.
(a) $\left[0,\frac{1}{2}\right]$ (b) $\left(\frac{1}{2},1\right]$
(c) [0, 1] (d) None of these

8. The domain of definition of $f(x) = \cos^{-1}x + \sqrt{1-\log_3(2x^2+6x-5)}$ is equal to
(a) (0, 1] (b) $\left(\frac{1}{2},1\right]$
(c) $\left(\frac{\sqrt{19}-3}{2},1\right]$ (d) None of these

9. The domain of the function $f(x)=\cos^{-1}\left(\frac{3}{4+2\sin x}\right)$ is equal to.
(a) $\bigcup_{n\in\mathbb{Z}}\left((2n+1)\pi+\frac{\pi}{6},(2n+2)\pi-\frac{\pi}{6}\right)$
(b) $\left(-\frac{\pi}{6}+2n\pi,\frac{\pi}{6}+2n\pi\right)$
(c) $\left(-\frac{\pi}{6}+2n\pi,\frac{\pi}{6}+2n\pi\right]$
(d) None of these

10. The domain of definition of function $\frac{1}{\sqrt{x^2-x-2}}+\frac{\sin^{-1}\left(\log_2\left(\frac{x^2}{2}\right)\right)}{\sqrt{5|x|-x^2-6}}$ is
(a) [–2, –1) (b) $[-2, 1) \cup [1, 2]$
(c) ϕ (d) None of these

11. The domain of definition of the function $f(x)=e^x+\sin^{-1}\left[\left(\frac{x}{2}\right)-1\right]+\log\sqrt{x-[x]}$ is equal to;
[] is gint function in 2nd and 3rd term.
(a) $(0, 6) \sim \{1, 2, 3, 4, 5\}$
(b) (0, 5)
(c) (0, 6)
(d) None of these

12. The domain of definition of the function $f(x) = \log\left\{\dfrac{1}{([\cos x]-[\sin x])}\right\}$ is equal to

(a) $\bigcup_{n\in\mathbb{Z}} [2n\pi, (2n + 1)\pi]$

(b) $\bigcup_{n\in\mathbb{Z}}\left[(2n+1)\pi+\dfrac{\pi}{2},(2n+2)\pi\right]$

(c) $\bigcup_{n\in\mathbb{Z}} [(2n + 1)\pi, (2n + 2)\pi]$

(d) None of these

13. The set of all real numbers x for which $\log_{2004}(\log_4(\log_{2002}(\log_{2001} x)))$ is defined as $\{x|x > c\}$. The value of c is

(a) 0 (b) $(2001)^{2002}$

(c) $(2003)^{2004}$ (d) None of these

14. The domain of the function $f(x)$ $\sqrt{\sin(\log x)} + \sqrt{\cos(\sin x)} + \sin^{-1}\left(\dfrac{1+x^2}{2x}\right)$

(a) $\{x : 1 \le x \le 2\}$

(b) $\{1\}$

(c) not defined for any value of x

(d) $\{-1, 1\}$

15. The domain of the function $f(x) = \sin^{-1}\left(\dfrac{2-|x|}{4}\right) + \cos^{-1}\left(\dfrac{2-|x|}{4}\right) + \tan^{-1}\left(\dfrac{2-|x|}{4}\right)$ is.

(a) [0, 3] (b) [–6, 6]

(c) [–1, 1] (d) [–3, 3]

16. The least value of x for which $f(x) = \dfrac{\sqrt{x^2-4}}{\sin^{-1}(2-x)}$ is defined is

(a) $x = 1$ (b) $x = 2$

(c) $x = 3$ (d) Does not exist

17. If P is a point on a circle of radius a and centre O (origin) the distance of chord AB from P lying along OP is x, then $\angle AOB \le \pi$ written as a function of x has which of the following property?

(a) $2\cos^{-1}\left(\dfrac{1}{a}|x|\right); 0 < x < 2a$

(b) $2\sin^{-1}\left(\dfrac{1}{a}|x-a|\right); 0 < x < 2a$

(c) $2\cos^{-1}\left(\dfrac{1}{a}|x-a|\right); 0 < x < 2a$

(d) None of these

18. Let S be the set of all triangles and $\mathbb{R}^+$ be the set of positive real numbers. Then the function $f: S \to \mathbb{R}^+$, $f(\Delta)$ = area of the Δ, where $\Delta \in S$ is

(a) Injective but not surjective

(b) Surjective but not injective

(c) Injective as well as surjective

(d) Neither injective nor surjective

19. The domain of the real valued function $f(x)$ for which $4^{f(x)} + 4^{1-f(x)} = 4^x$ is

(a) $(-1, 1]$ (b) $[1, \infty)$

(c) $(-\infty, 1]$ (d) $(-\infty, -1]$

20. Let $f(x) = (x^{12} - x^9 + x^4 - x + 1)^{-1/2}$. The domain of the function is

(a) $(-\infty, -1)$ (b) $(-1, 1)$

(c) $(1, \infty)$ (d) $(-\infty, \infty)$

21. Domain of $\sin^{-1}[\sec x]$ ([.] is greatest integer less than or equal to x) is

(a) $\{(2n + 1)\pi, (2n + 9)\pi\} \cup \{[(2m - 1)\pi, 2m\pi - \pi/3), m \in \mathbb{Z}\}$

(b) $(2n\pi, n \in \mathbb{Z}\} \cup \{[2m\pi, (2m + 1)\pi, m \in \mathbb{Z}\}$

(c) $\{(2n + 1)\pi, n \in \mathbb{Z}\} \cup \{(2m\pi - \pi/3, 2m\pi + \pi/3], m \in \mathbb{Z}\}$

(d) none of these

22. The range of function $f : \mathbb{R} \to \mathbb{R}$ defined by $f(x) = 2x^3 - 50000x^2 + 0.1x + \sin x$ is

(a) $\mathbb{R}$ (b) $[-1, 1]$

(c) $[0, \infty)$ (d) None of these

23. The range of the function $f(x) = \log_{\sqrt{2}}(2 - \log_2(16\sin^2 x - 1))$ is

(a) $(-\infty, 1)$ (b) $(-\infty, 2)$

(c) $(-\infty, 1]$ (d) $(-\infty, 2]$

24. Range of $f(x) = \dfrac{1}{\sqrt{\cos(\sin x)}}$ is

(a) $[1, \sqrt{\sec 1}]$ (b) $\left[\sqrt{\cos 1}, \sqrt{\sec 1}\right]$

(c) $\mathbb{R} - \{0\}$ (d) None of these

25. Let $f(x) = [9^x - 3^x + 1]\ \forall\ x \in (-\infty, 1)$, then range of $f(x)$ is ([.] denotes the greatest integer function.)

(a) {0, 1, 2, 3, 4, 5, 6} (b) {0, 1, 2, 3, 4, 5, 6, 7}

(c) {1, 2, 3, 4, 5, 6} (d) {1, 2, 3, 4, 5, 6, 7}

26. The range of the function $f(x) = 6^x + 3^x + 6^{-x} + 3^{-x} + 2$ is

(a) $[-2, \infty)$ (b) $(-2, \infty)$

(c) $(6, \infty)$ (d) $[6, \infty)$

27. The image of interval [–1, 2] under the mapping $f: \mathbb{R} \to \mathbb{R}$ defined by $f(x) = 2x^3 - 6x$ is
(a) [-4, 4) (b) (-4, 4)
(c) [-4, 4] (d) (-4, 4]

28. If $2 < x^2 < 3$, then the number of positive roots of $\{x^2\} = \left\{\frac{1}{x}\right\}$, (where $\{x\}$ denotes the fractional part of x) is
(a) 0 (b) 1
(c) 2 (d) 3

29. The minimum value of the function $f(x) = \frac{\sin x}{\sqrt{1-\cos^2 x}} + \frac{\cos x}{\sqrt{1-\sin^2 x}} + \frac{\tan x}{\sqrt{\sec^2 x - 1}} + \frac{\cot x}{\sqrt{\operatorname{cosec}^2 x - 1}}$ is
(a) 4 (b) –2
(c) 0 (d) 2

30. Solution of the equation $x^3 - [x] = 3$ is (where $[x]$, is the greatest integer $\leq x$)
(a) $x = (3)^{1/4}$ (b) $x = (4)^{1/3}$
(c) $x = \sqrt{2}$ (d) None of these

31. Solution set of the equation $(x)^2 + (x + 1)^2 = 25$ is (where (x) represent least integer $\geq x$)
(a) (–5, 2) (b) (2, 3)
(c) (–5, –4] ∪ (2, 3] (d) None of these

32. Solution set of the inequation $[x]^2 + (x)^2 > 25$ is (where $[x]$, (x),} is the greatest integer $\leq x$, least integer $\geq x$, respectively)
(a) (–∞, –4] ∪ [4, ∞) (b) (–∞, –4]
(c) [4, ∞) (d) None of these

33. If the function $f(x) = [3.5 + b \sin x]$ (where [.] denotes the greatest integer function) is an even function, then complete set of values of b is:
(a) (– 0.5, 0.5) (b) [–0.5, 0.5]
(c) (0, 1) (d) [–1, 1]

34. The domain of definition of the function $f(x) = \log\sqrt{(10.3^{x-2} - 9^{x-1} - 1)} + \sqrt{\cos^{-1}(2-x)}$ is
(a) [1, 2] (b) [1, 2)
(c) (0, 2) (d) None of these

35. Let

$$f(x) = \sqrt{\sqrt{\cot(5+3x)(\cot(5)+\cot(3x))} - \sqrt{\cot 3x + 1}},$$

then the domain of function $f(x)$ is

(a) $\mathbb{R} - \bigcup_{n\in\mathbb{Z}}\left[\frac{n\pi}{3} + \frac{1}{3}\cot^{-1}\left(\frac{2}{\cot 5 - 1}\right), \frac{1}{3}\left(n + \frac{3}{4}\right)\pi\right]$

(b) $\bigcup_{n\in\mathbb{Z}}\left[\frac{n\pi}{3} + \frac{1}{3}\cot^{-1}\left(\frac{2}{\cot 5 - 1}\right), \frac{1}{3}\left(n + \frac{3}{4}\right)\pi\right)$

(c) $\mathbb{R} - \left\{\frac{n\pi}{3}, \frac{n\pi - 5}{3}\right\}, n \in \mathbb{Z}$

(b) None of these

36. If $f(x) = \log_{100x}\left(\frac{2\log_{10} x + 2}{-x}\right)$; $g(x) = \{x\}$; where $\{x\}$ denotes the fractional part of x. If the function $(fog)(x)$ exists, then the maximum possible range of $g(x)$ is
(a) $(0, 10^{-1})$
(b) $(0, 10^{-2})$
(c) $(0, 10^{-2}) \cup (10^{-2}, 10^{-1})$
(d) None of these

37. If $f(x) \,.\, f(y) = f(x) + f(y) + f(xy) - 2 \;\forall\; x, y \in \mathbb{R}$ and if $f(x)$ is not a constant function, then the value of $f(1)$ is
(a) 1 (b) 2
(c) 0 (d) –1

38. If a function $f(x)$ is such that $f\left(\frac{2\tan x}{1+\tan^2 x}\right) = \frac{(\cos 2x + 1)(\sec^2 x + 2\tan x)}{2}$, then the value of $f\left(\frac{1}{3}\right)$ equals
(a) $\frac{1}{3}$ (b) $\frac{4}{3}$
(c) $\frac{4}{9}$ (d) None of these

39. Let f and g be two functions defined from $\mathbb{R} \to \mathbb{R}$ as follows:

$$f(x) = \begin{cases} 0 \text{ if } x \text{ is rational} \\ x \text{ if } x \text{ is irrational} \end{cases} \text{ and}$$

$$g(x) = \begin{cases} 0 \text{ if } x \text{ is irrational} \\ x \text{ if } x \text{ is rational} \end{cases}, \text{ then the function } f - g$$

(a) one–one but not onto
(b) onto–but not one–one
(c) both one–one and onto
(d) neither one–one nor onto

40. Let T be the set of all 2 × 2 matrices with entries from the set of real numbers $\mathbb{R}$. Then the function $f: T \to \mathbb{R}$ defined $f(A) = |A|$, i.e., (det. A) for every $A \in T$, is

(a) one–one and onto
(b) neither one–one nor onto
(c) one–one but not onto
(d) onto but not one–one

41. Let $n(A) = 4$ and $n(B) = 6$. Then the number of one–one functions from $A \to B$, and number of onto functions from $B \to A$ can be given as
(a) 120, 1020 (b) 360, 1560
(c) 24, 120 (d) None of these

42. Let $A = \{1, 2, 3, 4, 5, 6\}$. If f be a bijective function from A to A, then the number of such functions for which $f(\lambda) \neq \lambda, \forall \lambda \in A$ is
(a) 44 (b) 265
(c) 325 (d) 4585

43. Let $f: \mathbb{R} \to \mathbb{R}$ be given by $f(x) = (x + 1)^2 - 1, x \geq -1$. The set $S = \{x : f(x) = f^{-1}(x)\}$ is given by
(a) $\{0, 1\}$ (b) $\{0, -1\}$
(c) $\{-1, 1\}$ (d) None of these

44. Let $h(x) = |kx + 5|$ and domain of $f(x)$ and $f(h(x))$ are $[-5, 7]$ and $[-6, 1]$ respectively, then value of k is
(a) 1/3 (b) 4/5
(c) 1 (d) None of these

45. If $f(x) = \sin^2 x + \sin^2\left(x + \frac{\pi}{3}\right) + \cos x.\cos\left(x + \frac{\pi}{3}\right)$ and $g\left(\frac{5}{4}\right) = 1298$, then 4 $gof(x)$ is equal to
(a) 1298 (b) 2596
(c) 5192 (d) Not defined

46. Let $f(x) = 1 + x^2$ and g be a function such that $f(g(x)) = 1 + x^2 - 2x^3 + x^4$. The value of $g(18)$ is
(a) ±306 (b) 304
(c) –304 (d) None of these

47. The functions $f(x) = \cos^{-1}\sqrt{1-x^2}$ and $g(x) = -\sin^{-1} x$ are identical for x belonging to
(a) $[-1, 1]$ (b) $[0, 1]$
(c) $[-1, 0]$ (d) None of these

48. Let the function $f(x) = x^2 + x + \sin x - \cos x + \log(1 + |x|)$ be defined on the interval $[0, 1]$. The function $g(x)$ on $[-1, 1]$ satisfying $g(-x) = -f(x)$ is
(a) $x^2 + x + \sin x + \cos x - \log(1 + |x|)$
(b) $-x^2 + x + \sin x + \cos x - \log(1 + |x|)$
(c) $-x^2 + x + \sin x + \cos x + \log(1 + |x|)$
(d) None of these

49. If $f[x]$ and $\{x\}$ represent integral and fractional part of x, then the function defined by $f(x) = [x] + \sum_{r=1}^{1000} \frac{\{x+r\}}{1000}$ equal to.
(a) $2[x] + \{x\}$ (b) $4x$
(c) x (d) $4[x] + 100\{x\}$

50. Let X and Y be two non-empty sets. Let $f: X \to Y$ be a function. For $A \subset X$ and $B \subset Y$, define $f(A) = \{f(x) : x \in A\}$; $f^{-1}(B) = \{x \in X\ f(x) \in B\}$, then
(a) $f(f^{-1}(B)) = B$ (b) $f(f^{-1}(B)) \subset B$
(c) $f^{-1}(f(A)) = A$ (d) $f^{-1}(f(A)) \subset A$

51. If $f: \mathbb{R} \to \mathbb{R}$ is defined by $f(x) = x^2 + 1$, then the number of elements in $\{f^{-1}(17)\} \cup \{f^{-1}(3)\}$ is
(a) 2 (b) 4
(c) 6 (d) None of these

52. The set of all integer values of n for which the function $f(x) = \cos nx.\sin\frac{5x}{n}$ is periodic with period 2π is
(a) $\{1, 5, 10\}$ (b) $\{1, 5\}$
(c) $(\pm 1, \pm 5\}$ (d) None of these

53. If $f(x) = 1 - x^3 - x^4 - 2x^5 = g(x) + h(x)$, where g is an even function and h is an odd function. Then $h(-5)$ is equal to
(a) 6375 (b) 3250
(c) 6125 (d) None of these

54. Let $f : \mathbb{R} \to \mathbb{R}$; where $f(x) = \left(\frac{ax+5}{x^2+2}\right)$, then the values of a for which the function is invertible is.
(a) $(0, \infty)$ (b) $(1, \infty)$
(c) $(0, 1)$ (d) None of these

55. The period of the function $f(x) = \frac{1}{2}[\cos(\sin 4x) + \cos(\cos 4x)]$ is
(a) π (b) $\frac{\pi}{2}$
(c) $\frac{\pi}{4}$ (d) $\frac{\pi}{8}$

56. Let $f(x) = \cos\sqrt{k}\,x$; where $k = [m]$ = the greatest integer $\leq m$, if the period of $f(x)$ is π, then
(a) $m \in [4, 5)$
(b) $m = 4, 5$
(c) $m = [4, 5]$
(d) None of these

57. If $f(x)$ and $g(x)$ are periodic functions with periods 7 and 11 respectively, then the period of $F(x)=f(x)g\left(\frac{x}{5}\right)-g(x)f\left(\frac{x}{3}\right)$ is

(a) 177 (b) 222
(c) 433 (d) 1155

58. The period of $\sin(x + 4x + 9x + \ldots + (n+1)^2x)$ is $\frac{\pi}{7}$, then $n \in \mathbb{N}$ is equal to

(a) 2 (b) 3
(c) 4 (d) None of these

59. The function $f(x) = 2(x - [x]) + \sin 2\pi(x - [x])$ is (where [] denotes greatest integer function)

(a) non-periodic
(b) periodic with period 1
(c) periodic with period 2
(d) None of these

60. If $f(x)=2\cot 3x+5\sqrt{1-\cos 6x}$ and $g(x)$ is a function having the same period as that of $f(x)$, then which of the following can be $g(x)$?

(a) $(\sec^2 3x + \operatorname{cosec}^2 3x)$
(b) $2\sin 3x + 3\cos 3x$
(c) $2\sqrt{1-\cos^2 3x}+\operatorname{cosec}6x$
(d) None of these

61. Let $f(x) = x(1 - x)$, $0 \le x \le 1$, and $f(x)$ is extended for $x \in \mathbb{R}$ by $f(x + 1) = f(x)$, then f is periodic with period

(a) 1/2 (b) 1
(c) π (d) None of these

62. If $f(x)=\begin{cases} x^2\sin\left(\frac{\pi x}{2}\right); & \text{when } |x|<1 \\ x|x|; & \text{when } |x|\ge 1\end{cases}$, then $f(x)$ is

(a) an even function
(b) an odd function
(c) a periodic function
(d) None of these

63. Let the function $f(x) = x^2 - 1$ and $g(x) = x^3 - 7x^2 + 5x + 6$ be two curves, then number of pairs of points (P, Q) where P lies on $f(x)$ and Q on $g(x)$, such that tangent at P and Q are parallel to each other is equal to

(a) one (b) two
(c) zero (d) infinite

64. Let $f''(x) > 0\ \forall\ x \in \mathbb{R}$ and $g(x) = f(x^2) - f(x^2 + 3)$, then $g(x)$ is

(a) increasing in $(0, \infty)$
(b) decreasing in $(0, \infty)$
(c) increasing in $\mathbb{R}$
(d) decreasing $[-1, 2]$

65. The domain of the function $f(x)=\frac{x^3-3x^2+3x-7}{\sqrt{(x^{14}-x^{11}+x^{10}-x^7+x^6-x^3+x^2+1)}}$ is

(a) $x \in (-\infty, \infty)$
(b) $x \in (-\infty, 0] \cup [1, \infty)$
(c) $(0, \infty)$
(d) None of these

66. The domain of the function $f(x)=\log_{(x^2+x+1)}(3x^2-4x+5)$ is

(a) $\mathbb{R}$
(b) $\mathbb{R} - \{0, -1\}$
(c) $[0, 1]$
(d) None of these

67. The domain of the function: $f(x)=\sqrt{8-3^{x+1}-3^{1-x}}+\sqrt{\sin^{-1}(2x+1)}$ is

(a) $[0, 1]$
(b) $(-1/2, 1)$
(c) $[-1/2, 0]$
(d) None of these

68. If the range of the function $f(x)=\frac{3\cos^2 x+3\cos x+4}{\cos^2 x+\cos x+1}$ is $[\lambda, \mu]$, then the value of $6\lambda + 9\mu + 2$ is

(a) 23 (b) 20
(c) 61 (d) None of these

69. The quadratic polynomial $f(x) \equiv x^2 - px + q$ has prime zeroes (roots). If $p + q = 11$ and $a = q - p$, then $f(a)$ equals

(a) 3 (b) 2
(c) 7 (d) None of these

70. The maximum vertical distance d between the parabola $y = -x^2 + 5x + 7$ and line $y = 2x + 3$ throughout the region bounded between two curves is

(a) $\frac{5}{2}$ (b) $\frac{25}{9}$
(c) $\frac{25}{4}$ (d) None of these

SECTION–IV

(MORE THAN ONE CORRECT ANSWER)

1. Which of the following functions are periodic?
   (a) $sgn(e^{-x})$
   (b) $f(x) = \begin{cases} 1 \text{ if } x \text{ is a rational number} \\ 0 \text{ if } x \text{ is an irrational number} \end{cases}$
   (c) $f(x) = \sqrt{\dfrac{8}{1+\cos x} + \dfrac{8}{1-\cos x}}$
   (d) $\left[x + \dfrac{1}{2}\right] + \left[x - \dfrac{1}{2}\right] + 2[-x]$; (where [] denotes greatest integer function)

2. Let $f(x) = [x]^2 + [x + 1] - 3$, (where $[x]$ = greatest integer $\le x$), then
   (a) $f(x)$ is a many–one and into function
   (b) $f(x) = 0$ for infinite number of values of x
   (c) $f(x) = 0$ for only two real values of x
   (d) None of these

3. Which of the following is true about the function $f(x) = \dfrac{x^2 - 3x + 2}{x^2 + x - 6}$?
   (a) Domain is $\mathbb{R} - \{2, -3\}$
   (b) Domain is $\mathbb{R} - \{-3\}$
   (c) Range is $\mathbb{R} - \{1\}$
   (d) Range is $\mathbb{R} - \left\{\dfrac{1}{5}, 1\right\}$

4. Which of the statements given below is/are true about $f(x) = \sqrt{2-x} + \sqrt{1+x}$?
   (a) Domain is (–1, 2)
   (b) Range is $[\sqrt{3}, \sqrt{6})$
   (c) Domain is [–1, 2]
   (d) Range is $[\sqrt{3}, \sqrt{6}]$

5. Which of the following is true regarding the relation $\log_x y . \log_{xy} y . \log_{x^2y} y = \dfrac{1}{6}$?
   (a) It can be written in explicit form as $(x^2 - y^2)(x^2 + y^2 + xy) = 0$
   (b) It can be written explicitly as $y = x$
   (c) Its domain is $(0, 1) \cup (1, \infty)$
   (d) Its domain is $(1, \infty)$

6. If $f(x) = (1 + \tan x)\left\{1 + \tan\left(\dfrac{\pi}{4} - x\right)\right\}$ and let $g(x)$ be defined for all real x, then which of the following statements is/are true for $gof(x)$?
   (a) domain of $gof(x)$ is $\mathbb{R}$
   (b) $gof(x)$ is constant $\forall\, x \in D_f$
   (c) $gof(x)$ is monotonically increasing function
   (d) $gof(x)$ is non-surjective function

7. The function $f(x) = \sqrt{x}\sqrt{x-1}$ and $g(x) = \sqrt{x(x-1)}$ are
   (a) equal function $\forall\, x \in \mathbb{R}$
   (b) identical function in their common domain
   (c) identical functions for $x \in [1, \infty)$
   (d) None of these

8. Let $g(x)$ be a function defined on [–1, 1]. If the area of the equilateral triangle with two of its vertices at (0, 0) and $\{x, g(x)\}$ is $\dfrac{\sqrt{3}}{4}$, then the function $g(x)$ is
   (a) $\pm\sqrt{1+x^2}$ (b) $\sqrt{1-x^2}$
   (c) $-\sqrt{1-x^2}$ (d) $\sqrt{1+x^2}$

9. Let $f(x) = \sec^{-1}[1 + \cos^2 x]$, where [.] denotes the greatest integer function, then
   (a) the domain of f is $\mathbb{R}$
   (b) the domain of f is [1, 2]
   (c) the range of f is [1, 2]
   (d) the range of f is $\{0, \pi/3\}$.

10. If the function $f(x) = \sin^{-1}\dfrac{2x}{1+x^2}$ and $g(x) = \cos^{-1}\dfrac{1-x^2}{1+x^2}$ are identical functions, then domain D_f and range R_f are given by
    (a) $D_f = [0, 1]$ (b) $R_f = \left[0, \dfrac{\pi}{4}\right]$
    (c) $D_f = \left[0, \dfrac{1}{2}\right]$ (d) $R_f = \left[0, \dfrac{\pi}{2}\right]$

11. Let X_1 be the set of values of x satisfying the equation $\sin\left(\dfrac{\cos^{-1} x}{y}\right) = 1$; for $y \in Y_1 \subseteq \mathbb{Z} - \{0\}$, then

(a) $X_1 = \{-1, 1\}$ (b) $X_1 = \{-1, 0\}$
(c) $Y_1 = \{2, 1\}$ (d) $Y_1 = \{-1, 1\}$

12. Let X_2 be the set of values of x satisfying the equation $\cos\left(\frac{\sin^{-1} x}{y}\right) = 0$; for $y \in Y_2 \subseteq \mathbb{Z} - \{0\}$, then

(a) $X_2 = \{-1, 1\}$
(b) $X_2 = \{-1, 0, 1\}$
(c) $Y_2 = \{-1, 1\}$
(d) $Y_2 = \{-1, 1, 0\}$

13. Number of functions from set $\{1, 2, 3, \ldots, n\}$ to set $\{-1, 1\}$ that are one-to-one is
(a) 2 for $n = 1$
(b) 2 for $n = 2$
(c) ${}^nP_2$ for $n \geq 3$
(d) 0 for $n \geq 3$

14. Number of functions from set $\{1, 2, 3, \ldots, n\}$ to set $\{-1, 1\}$ that assign -1 to both 1 and n is
(a) 1 for $n = 1$
(b) $(2)^{n-2}$ for $n \geq 2$
(c) 1 for $n \geq 2$
(d) None of these

15. Number of functions from set $\{1, 2, 3, \ldots, n\}$ to set $\{-1, 1\}$ that assign 1 to exactly one of the positive integer less than n, is
(a) 0 for $n = 1$
(b) $2(n - 1)$ for $n \geq 2$
(c) 2 for $n = 2$
(d) $(n - 1)$ for $n \geq 1$

16. For the function $f(x) = \sqrt{\log_{1/2}(\log_5([x^2]-3))}$; ([.] denotes greatest integer function)

(a) $[x^2] \in \{5, 6, 7, 8\}$
(b) $x \in (-3, -\sqrt{5}] \cup [\sqrt{5}, 3)$
(c) $[x] \in \{-3, 2\}$
(d) Range of $f(x)$ = $\{\sqrt{\log_{1/2}(\log_5 2)}, \sqrt{\log_{1/2}(\log_5 3)}, \sqrt{\log_{1/2}(\log_5 4)}, 0\}$

17. If $f(x)$ and $g(x)$ are two functions of x such that $f(x) + g(x) = e^x$ and $f(x) - g(x) = e^{-x}$, then
(a) $f(x)$ is an odd function
(b) $g(x)$ is an odd function
(c) $f(x)$ is an even function
(d) $g(x)$ is an even function

18. Let $f(x) = 2x + \cos x$ and $g(x) = \sqrt[3]{x}$, then
(a) range of *gof* is R
(b) *gof* is one–one
(c) both f and g are one–one
(d) both f and g are onto

19. Which of the following functions (is) are/are injective map (s)?
(a) $f(x) = |x + 1|, x \in [-1, \infty)$
(b) $g(x) = x + \frac{1}{x}; x \in (0, \infty)$
(c) $h(x) = x^2 + 4x - 5, x \in (0, \infty)$
(d) $k(x) = e^{-x}, x \in [0, \infty)$

20. If $f(x) = \cos[\pi^2]x + \cos[-\pi^2]x$; where $[x]$ stands for the greatest integer function, then
(a) $f(\pi/2) = -1$
(b) $f(\pi) = 1$
(c) $f(-\pi) = 0$
(d) None of these

SECTION–V

ASSERTION AND REASON-TYPE QUESTIONS

1. A: Exponential functions are defined as $y = k^x$; where $k \in \mathbb{R}^+$ and $k \neq 1$

R: The restriction that the base k for exponential functions be greater than zero is a matter of convention; we could have allowed $k < 0$ without affecting the domain or range of the function.

2. A: The inverse of a strictly increasing exponential function is a logarithmic function that is strictly decreasing

R: ℓnx is inverse of e^x

3. A: Fundamental period of $\sin x + \tan x$ is 2π

R: If the period of $f(x)$ is T_1 and the period of $g(x)$ is T_2, then the fundamental period of $f(x) + g(x)$ is the LCM of T_1 and T_2.

4. A: $y = -x + \sin x$ and its inverse intersect on the line $y = -x$.

R: Let $f(x)$ be an invertible function and $f^{-1}(x)$ be the inverse of $f(x)$. Then $y = f(x)$ and $y = f^{-1}(x)$ intersect either on $y = x$ or on $y = -x + c$; where $c \in \mathbb{R}$.

5. A: $f(x) = \sin x$ is periodic and $g(x) = \cos x$ is also periodic.

R: If the derivative of a function is periodic, then the function will also be periodic.

6. A: function $f(x) = \sin(x + 3\sin x)$ is periodic.

R: $f(g(x))$ is periodic if $g(x)$ is periodic.

7. A: There is no continuous onto function $f(x)$ defined on $[0, 2]$ and whose co-domain is $(1, 3)$.

R: A function defined on a closed interval attains its greatest and least values.

8. A: If $y = f(x)$ is increasing in $[\alpha, \beta]$, then its range is $[f(\alpha), f(\beta)]$.

R: Every increasing function need not to be continuous.

9. A: The greatest value of function $f(x) = \cos(x\, e^{[x]} + 2x^2 - x)$; $x \in (-1, \infty)$ is 1.

R: $\cos\theta$ has its maximum value 1 if $\theta \in (k, \infty)$ for some finite real number k.

10. A: If $f(x) = \begin{cases} \sin x; & x \neq n\pi;\ n \in \mathbb{Z} \\ 2; & \text{otherwise} \end{cases}$ and

$g(x) = \begin{cases} x^2 + 1; & x \neq 0, 2 \\ 4; & x = 0 \\ 5; & x = 2 \end{cases}$, then $\lim_{x \to 0} gof(x)$ is 1.

R: $g(f(x)) = \begin{cases} 1; & \text{for } x \neq n\pi;\ n \in \mathbb{Z} \\ 5; & \text{for } x = n\pi;\ n \in \mathbb{Z} \end{cases}$.

11. A: If $y + \cos x = \sin x$ has a real solution for given value of y, then range of y is $[-\sqrt{2}, \sqrt{2}]$

R: Range of $f(x) = a\cos x + b\sin x$ is $\left[-\sqrt{a^2+b^2}, \sqrt{a^2+b^2}\right]$.

12. A: Range of $4^x + 2^x + 4^{-x} + 2^{-x} + 3$ is $\left[\frac{3}{4}, \infty\right)$.

R: The given equation reduces to $f(z) = z^2 + z + 1$, $z = 2^x + \frac{1}{2^x}$.

13. A: The function $f(x) = x^6 + 4x^4 + 3x + 7$ defined from $\mathbb{R} \to \mathbb{R}$ is non-injective.

R: Every polynomial of even degree is an even function, and hence, is non-injective.

14. A: The function $f(x) = x^4 + 5x^2 + 3x + 1$ defined from $\mathbb{R} \to \mathbb{R}$ is non-invertible.

R: Every polynomial of even degree is many-one, that is, non-injective, and hence, non-invertible.

15. A: If $f: \mathbb{R} \to \mathbb{R}$ is a function such that $f(x) = x^3 + x^2 f'(1) + x f''(2) + f'''(3)\ \forall\, x \in \mathbb{R}$, then $f(2) - f(1) = -6$

R: $f(0) = -6$ and $f(2) - f(1) = f(0)$.

16. A: If $A = \{1, 2, 3, \ldots, 2n\}$, then the number of self invertible functions f from $A \to A$ such that $f(i) \neq i$ is equal to $({}^{2n}C_2 \times {}^{2n-2}C_2 \times {}^{2n-4}C_2 \times \ldots \times {}^{4}C_2 \times {}^{2}C_2)/n!$.

R: Number of ways of distributing $(2n)$ different objects into n unnamed groups each having 2 elements $= \frac{(2n)!}{(2)^n . n!}$.

17. A: If f, g and h are even, odd and odd functions, respectively and each one is a polynomial such that

$f(-7) = 9, f(-3) = 0, g(4) = 7, g(-12) = 9, g(2) = 3, h(-2) = -4, h(9) = 12$, then

$f(g(h(2))) + g(h(f(7))) + h(f(g(2))) = 0$.

R: For every even continuous function $p(x)$ on $\mathbb{R}$, $p(0) \neq 0$, i.e., there exist even continuous functions $p(x)$ on $\mathbb{R}$ for which $p(0) \neq 0$.

18. A: There are exactly 3 integers in the range of the function $f(x) = \frac{7}{2 + 9a^x}; a > 0 \neq 1$.

R: If the range of a function is (α, β), then the number of integers in the range is $[\beta - \alpha]$; where [.] is the greatest integer function.

19. A: If a function f satisfies $f(x) + f(5x + y) + 6xy = f(6x - y) + 2x^2 - 1\ \forall\, x, y \in \mathbb{R}$, then $f(5) = -24$.

R: By substituting $y = \frac{x}{2}$, in the given equation, we can get analytical formula for $f(x)$ which gives us the value of $f(5)$.

SECTION–VI

LINKED COMPREHENSION-TYPE QUESTIONS

A: In the given figure, triangle ABC with base $BC = b$ and altitude $AH = h(AH \perp BC)$. If $EF = x$, where $EF \perp BC$, then the area and perimeter of the rectangle $DEFG$ can be expressed as function of x. H is mid point of BC.

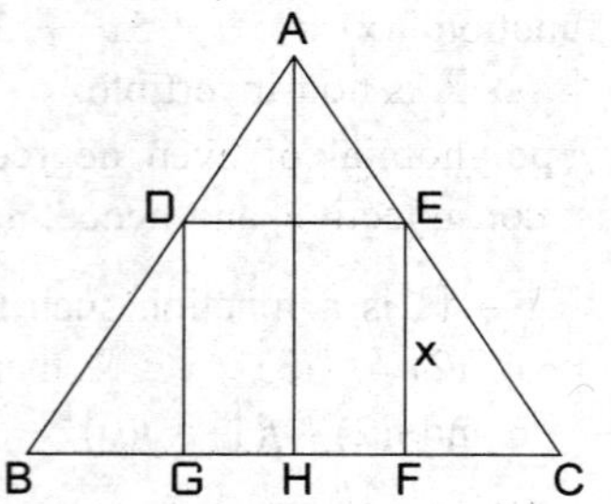

1. The perimeter of rectangle $DEFG$ as function of x is given as

(a) $\dfrac{x(h-b)+bh}{x}$ (b) $2\left\{x+\dfrac{b(h-x)}{h}\right\}$

(c) $\dfrac{2b(h-x)}{x}$ (d) None of these

2. Area of rectangle $DEFG$ as function of x is given are

(a) $\dfrac{bx(h+x)}{h}$ (b) $\dfrac{bx^2}{2h}$

(c) $\dfrac{bx(h-x)}{h}$ (d) None of these

3. Values of x for which perimeter and area are numerically equal given that $b = 2$, $h = 4$

(a) $x = 4$ (b) $x = 1, 3$

(c) no real value of x (d) None of these

B: If $f : [0, 2] \to [0, 2]$ is a bijective function defined by $f(x) = ax^2 + bx + c$; where a, b, c are non-zero real numbers, then

4. $f(2)$ is equal to

(a) 2 (b) α where $a \in (0, 2)$

(c) 0 (d) cannot be determined

5. Which of the following is one of the roots of $f(x) = 0$?

(a) $\dfrac{1}{a}$ (b) $\dfrac{1}{b}$

(c) $\dfrac{1}{c}$ (d) $\dfrac{1}{a}+\dfrac{1}{b}+\dfrac{1}{c}$

6. Which of the following is not a value of a?

(a) $a = -\dfrac{1}{4}$ (b) $a = \dfrac{1}{2}$

(c) $a = -\dfrac{1}{2}$ (d) $a = 1$

C: Let $f : \mathbb{R} \to \mathbb{R}$ is a function satisfying $f(2 - x) = f(2 + x)$ and $f(20 - x) = f(x)$, $\forall\ x \in \mathbb{R}$. For this function f answer the following questions.

7. If $f(0) = 5$, then minimum possible number of values of x satisfying $f(x) = 5$, for $x \in [0, 170]$, is

(a) 21 (b) 12

(c) 11 (d) 22

8. Graph of $y = f(x)$ is

(a) symmetrical about $x = 18$

(b) symmetrical about $x = 5$

(c) symmetrical about $x = 8$

(d) symmetrical about $x = 20$

9. If $f(2) \neq f(6)$, then

(a) fundamental period of $f(x)$ is 4

(b) fundamental period cannot be 16

(c) period of $f(x)$ cannot be 8

(d) fundamental period of $f(x)$ is 8

D: A tower has the following shape: a truncated right circular cone (one with radii $2R$(the lower base) and R(the upper base), and the height R, bears a right circular cylinder whose radius is R, the height being $2R$. Finally, a hemisphere of radius R is mounted on the cylinder. Suppose that the cross-sectional area S of the tower is given by $f(x)$, where x is the distance of the cross section from the lower base of cone.

10. The domain of the function $f(x)$ is

(a) $(-\infty, \infty)$ (b) $[0, 4R]$

(c) $[0, R]$ (d) $[R, 4R]$

11. For $0 \le x \le R$, the function $f(x)$ is given by

(a) $\pi(2R - x)^2$ (b) $\pi(R - x)^2$

(c) πR^2 (d) $4\pi x^2$

12. The range of $f(x)$ is

(a) $[0, 4\pi R^2]$ (b) $[\pi R^2, 4\pi R^2]$

(c) $[0, \pi R^2]$ (d) $\pi R^2\cdot$ 0, $3\pi R^2$

13. The function $f(x)$ is
(a) one–one on $[R, 2R]$
(b) one–one on $[R, 3R]$
(c) one–one on $[0, 4R]$
(d) one–one on $[0, R] \cup [3R, 4R]$

E: The accompanying figure shows the graph of a function $f(x)$ with domain [0, 2] and range [0, 1]. Now answer the following questions:

(i)
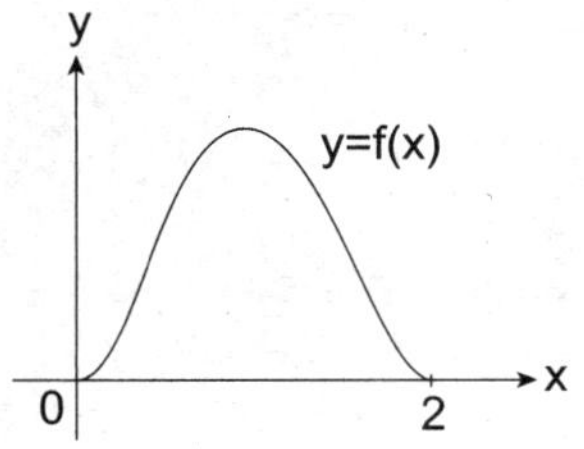

(ii)
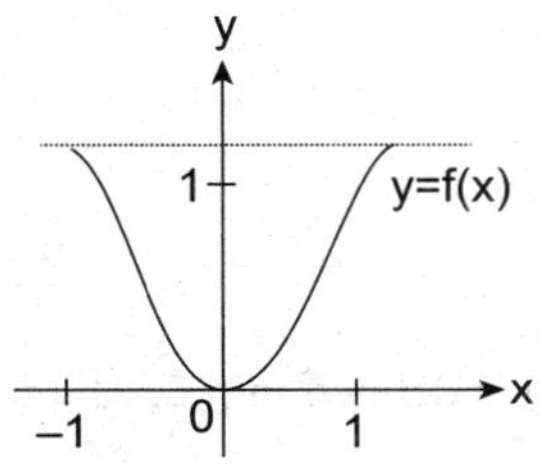

(iii)
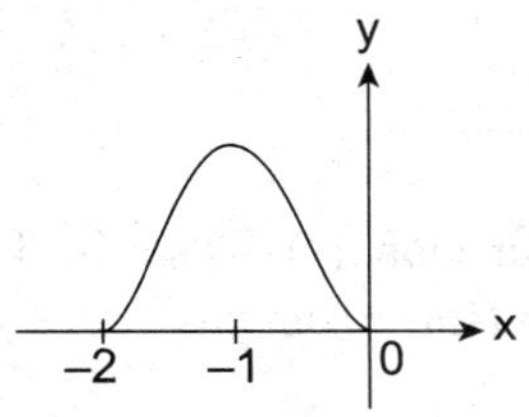

14. Figure-(ii) represents the graph of the function
(a) $-f(x)$ (b) $-f(x-1)+1$
(c) $-f(x+1)-1$ (d) $-f(x+1)+1$

15. [1, 3] and [0,1] are the domain and range (respectively) of the function in (figure-i)
(a) $-f(x)$ (b) $f(x-1)$
(c) $-f(x+1)+1$ (d) $-f(x+1)$

16. Figure-(iii) represents the graph of function
(a) $2f(x)$ (b) $f(x-2)$
(c) $f(x+2)$ (d) $f(x-2)+1$

17. The domain and range (respectively) of
(a) $f(-x)$ are $[-2, 0]$ and $[-1, 0]$
(b) $f(x)-1$ are $[0,2]$ and $[0, 1]$
(c) $f(x)+2$ are $[0, 2]$ and $[1, 2]$
(d) $-f(x+1)+1$ are $[-1,1]$ and $[0, 1]$

F: If C_1 is a set of sets and * is an operator which can be operated on each pair of elements of C_1, then we say that.
(i) C_1 is closed w.r.t. (*) if $A * B \in C_1\ \forall A, B \in C_1$
(ii) (*) is associative in C_1 if $(A * B) * C = A * (B * C)\ \forall A, B, C \in C_1$.
(iii) (*) is commutative in C_1 if $(A * B) = (B * A)\ \forall A, B \equiv C_1$
(iv) C_1 has an identity element, if there exists $I \in C_1$ such that $A * I = A = I * A\ \forall A \in C_1$
(v) * is said to be invertible in C_1, if for each $A \in C_1$, there exists $B \in C_1$ such that $A * B = I = B * A$. Then, choose the most appropriate alternative in the following

If $C = \{(a, b, c): a, b, c$ are three consecutive even whole number$\}$
Consider the operation * on C defined by $(a, b, c) * (d, e, f) = (a + d, b + e - 2, c + f - 4)$, then answer the following questions:

18. Which of the following statement is correct?
(a) C is closed w.r.t *
(b) C is not closed w.r.t. *
(c) C is closed w.r.t. * but * is not commutative in C
(d) C is closed w.r.t. * as well as * is commutative in C

19. Which of the following statement is correct?
(a) * is associative in C
(b) * is invertible in C
(c) C does not have an identity element
(d) None of these

20. Which of the following statement is correct
(a) C does not have an identity element
(b) C has an identity element
(c) * is not associative in C
(d) All of these

21. Which of the following statement is correct
(a) * is not commutative in C
(b) * is not associative in C
(c) * is not invertible in C
(d) * is not closed in C

G: Let $A = \{2, 4, 6, 8, 10, 12\}$ and $B = \{3, 7, 11\}$ be two sets. Then answer the following questions

22. Number of functions defined from set A to B is
(a) $(6)^3$ (b) $(3)^6$
(c) ${}^6C_3$ (d) ${}^6P_3$

23. Number of functions defined from A to B, such that element 3 in B has exactly 2 pre-images in A is
(a) 80 (b) 160
(c) 240 (d) None of these

24. Number of functions from A to B, such that range does not contain the element 7 is
(a) $(2)^6$ (b) $(6)^2$
(c) $^6C_2$ (d) $^6P_2$

25. Number of functions such that element 3 of B has two, 7 of B has three and 11 of B has one pre-image in B is
(a) 90 (b) 60
(c) 120 (d) None of these

26. Number of functions such that $f(2) = 7$ is
(a) $(2)^5$ (b) $^5C_2$
(c) $(3)^5$ (d) None of these

SECTION–VII

COLUMN MATCHING-TYPE QUESTIONS

1. Match the column

Column I

(i) The number of possible values of k if fundamental period of $\sin^{-1}(\sin kx)$ is $\dfrac{\pi}{2}$

(ii) Number of points in the domain of $f(x) = \tan^{-1}x + \sin^{-1}x + \sec^{-1}x$

(iii) $f(x) = \sin\left(\dfrac{\pi x}{2}\right).\operatorname{cosec}\left(\dfrac{\pi x}{2}\right)$ is periodic with period

(iv) If range of the function $f(x) = \cos^{-1}[5x]$, where [.] denotes greatest integer, is $\{a, b, c\}$, then $a + b + c = k\pi/2$, then k is

Column II

(a) 1
(b) 2
(c) 3
(d) 4

2. Match the column

Column I

(i) Smallest positive integral value of x for which $x^2 - 3x + \sin^{-1}(\sin 2) > 0$ is

(ii) Number of solution of $2[x] = x + 2\{x\}$ is {where $[x]$, $\{x\}$ are greatest integer and fractional part functions respectively}

(iii) If $x^2 + y^2 = 1$, then maximum value of $(x + y)^2$ is

(iv) $f\left(x+\dfrac{1}{2}\right)+f\left(x-\dfrac{1}{2}\right)=f(x)$ for all $x \in \mathbb{R}$, then period of $f(x)$ is

Column II

(a) $3\pi/2$
(b) 3
(c) 1
(d) 2

3. **Column I**

(i) If function $f(x)$ is defined in $[-2, 2]$, then domain of $f(|x| + 1)$ is

(ii) Range of the function $f(x)=\dfrac{\sin^{-1}x+\cos^{-1}x+\tan^{-1}x}{\pi}$ is

(iii) Range of the function $f(x) = 3|\sin x| - 4|\cos x|$ is

(iv) Range of $f(x) = (\sin^{-1}x)\sin x$ is

Column II

(a) $\left[\dfrac{1}{4},\dfrac{3}{4}\right]$
(b) $[-1, 1]$
(c) $[-4, 3]$
(d) $\left[0,\dfrac{\pi}{2}\sin 1\right]$

4. Let $f(x) = \sin^{-1}x$, $g(x) = \cos^{-1}x$ and $h(x) = \tan^{-1}x$. For what interval of variation of x the following are true?

Column I

(i) $f(\sqrt{x}) + g(\sqrt{x}) = \pi/2$

(ii) $f(x)+g\left(\sqrt{1-x^2}\right)=0$

(iii) $g\left(\dfrac{1-x^2}{1+x^2}\right)=2h(x)$

(iv) $h(x)+h(1)=h\left(\dfrac{1+x}{1-x}\right)$

Column II

(a) $[0, \infty)$
(b) $[0, 1]$
(c) $(-\infty, 1)$
(d) $[-1, 0]$

5. **Column I**

(i) Number of solutions of the equation $sgn(\{x\}) = |1 - x|$ is

(ii) Number of elements in the domain of the function is $f(x) = \sin^{-1}\left(\frac{x^2 - 2x}{3}\right) + \sqrt{[x] + [-x]}$ is

(iii) Let $f(x)$ be a function defined on $\mathbb{R}$ such that $f(x + 2) = f(x - 2)\ \forall\ x \in \mathbb{R}$. If $f(x) = 0$ has exactly three roots in the interval [4, 8] and 8 is one of the three roots, then the number of roots of $f(x) = 0$ in the interval [–8, 12] will be $(k + 7)$, then k equals.

(iv) If $f(x) = \frac{1}{x-1}$, then $f\left(\frac{1}{x-1}\right)$ is not defined at x equal to; {where [.] and{.} represents greatest integer and fractional part functions respectively}.

Column II

(a) 2
(b) 4
(c) 5
(d) 1

6. **Column I**

(i) $f(x) = \sqrt{-2\sqrt{2}(\cos \pi x) - \sqrt{3} - 1}$ is defined if x lies in

(ii) $\lim\limits_{x \to 1^-} \frac{3}{4}[x] + \frac{7}{8}\{x\} = L_1$ lies in; {where [.] and {.} represent greatest integer and fractional part function respectively}

(iii) If $\sqrt{\log_x (0.75)} < 1$, then x lies in

(iv) If $\frac{|x-1|}{x+2} > 1$, then x lies in

Column II

(a) $(0, 1)$
(b) $(0, 3/4)$
(c) $\left[\frac{11}{12}, \frac{13}{12}\right]$
(d) $\left(-2, -\frac{1}{2}\right)$

SECTION–VIII

INTEGER TYPE QUESTIONS

1. If q is the absolute difference of $\sqrt{x^2 + x + 3}$ $(= y \text{ say})$ and x, for which both x and $\sqrt{x^2 + x + 3}$ are rationals, then x and y are given by $\frac{q^2 - a}{1 - bq}$ and $\frac{q^2 - q + c}{|1 - bq|}$; $\left(q \neq \frac{1}{b}\right)$, then find the number of positive integer divisors of $(a.b.c)$.

2. Find the maximum numerical value of $f(x)$; $f(x) = {}^{15-x}C_{3x-1} + {}^{20-4x}C_{5x-7}$.

3. Let $f(x) = x^{99} + x^{79} - x^{69} + x^9 + 1$. If $f(x)$ is divided by $x^3 - x$, then the remainder is some function of x say $g(x)$. Find the value of $g(20)$.

4. If $f\left(x + \frac{1}{x}\right) = x^3 + x^{-3}$, then find $f(7)$.

5. If $f(x)$ is an even function, then find the number of distinct real numbers x such that $f(x) = f\left(\frac{x+1}{x+2}\right)$.

6. If $f(x + y) = f(x).f(y)\ \forall\ x, y \in \mathbb{N}$ and $f(1) = 2$, then find $\sum\limits_{n=1}^{10} f(n)$.

7. If $g(x) = \left(4\cos^4 x - 2\cos 2x - \frac{1}{2}\cos 4x - x^9\right)^{\frac{1}{9}}$, then find the value of $g(g(2016))$.

8. The fundamental period of the function $\frac{\sin x + \sin 3x + \sin 5x + \sin 7x}{\cos x + \cos 3x + \cos 5x + \cos 7x}$ is $\frac{\pi}{k}$, then find k.

9. If the function $\sin^{-1}(\sin 4\pi x)$ is periodic with period k, then evaluate $4k$.

10. If the period of $f(x)$ satisfying the condition: $f(x + p) = 1 + \{1 - 3f(x) + 3f^2(x) - f^3(x)\}^{1/3}$ is λp, then evaluate λ.

11. Find the period of $f(x)$ satisfying the condition $f(x - 1) + f(x + 3) = f(x + 1) + f(x + 5)$.

12. The function $f(x) = \frac{x^3}{3} + (m-1)x^2 + (m+5)x + 11$ is invertible only for k integer values of m. Then find k.

13. Let $f(x, y)$ be a function satisfying the functional equation: $f(x, y) = f(2x + 2y, 2y - 2x)$ for all real numbers x, y. Define $g(x)$ by $g(x) = f(2^x, 0)$. Also given that $g(x)$ is a periodic function with period k, then find value of k.

14. If the function $f: \mathbb{R} \to \mathbb{R}$ defined by $f(x) = \frac{ax^2 + 6x - 8}{a + 6x - 8x^2}$ is onto for $a \in [m, n]$, then evaluate $\sqrt{mn - 3}$.

15. Given the function $y = \frac{x-4}{16-\lambda^2}$ and the initial value of the independent variable $x_1 = 4 - \lambda$. At what terminal value x_2 of the independent variable x, the increment Δy equal to $\frac{1}{4-\lambda}$.

16. If $f(x) = \cos^2 x + \cos^2\left(\frac{\pi}{3} + x\right) - \cos x \cos\left(\frac{\pi}{3} + x\right)$ and $g(3/4) = 2$, then find the value of $(gof)(1)$.

17. Find the number of maps f from the set $\{1, 2, 3, 4\}$ into the set $\{1, 2, 3, 4, 5\}$ such that $f(i) \le f(j)$, when ever $i < j$ and $i, j \in \{1, 2, 3\}$.

18. The quadratic polynomial $p(x)$ is such that $p(x) \ge 0$ $\forall\, x \in \mathbb{R}$ and $p(1) = 0$, $p(2) = 2$. Find the value of $p(0) + p(3)$.

19. Let p be the product of non-real roots of the equation $x^4 - 4x^3 + 6x^2 - 4x = 2008$, where [.] denotes the greatest integer function, then find $[p]$.

20. Find the maximum number of points of intersection of the function $f(x) = ax^2 + bx + c$, $a > 0$ and $g(x) = \frac{1}{x^2 - 4}$.

Answer Keys

SECTION–III

1. (b)	2. (a)	3. (c)	4. (c)	5. (c)	6. (b)	7. (c)	8. (c)	9. (a)	10. (c)
11. (a)	12. (b)	13. (b)	14. (b)	15. (b)	16. (d)	17. (c)	18. (b)	19. (b)	20. (d)
21. (c)	22. (d)	23. (d)	24. (a)	25. (a)	26. (d)	27. (c)	28. (a)	29. (b)	30. (b)
31. (c)	32. (a)	33. (a)	34. (b)	35. (b)	36. (c)	37. (b)	38. (b)	39. (c)	40. (d)
41. (b)	42. (b)	43. (b)	44. (d)	45. (c)	46. (a)	47. (c)	48. (b)	49. (c)	50. (b)
51. (b)	52. (c)	53. (a)	54. (d)	55. (d)	56. (a)	57. (d)	58. (a)	59. (b)	60. (c)
61. (b)	62. (b)	63. (d)	64. (b)	65. (a)	66. (b)	67. (c)	68. (c)	69. (b)	70. (c)

SECTION–IV

1. (a,b,c,d) 2. (a,b) 3. (a,d) 4. (c,d) 5. (b,c) 6. (b,d) 7. (b,c) 8. (b),(c)
9. (a,d) 10. (a,d) 11. (b,c) 12. (a,c) 13. (a,b,d) 14. (a,b) 15. (a,b,c) 16. (a,b,c,d)
17. (b,c) 18. (a,b,c,d) 19. (a,c,d) 20. (a,c)

SECTION–V

1. (c)	2. (d)	3. (c)	4. (a)	5. (c)	6. (b)	7. (c)	8. (d)	9. (b)	10. (c)
11. (a)	12. (d)	13. (c)	14. (a)	15. (c)	16. (a)	17. (b)	18. (c)	19. (a)	

SECTION–VI

1. (b)	2. (c)	3. (c)	4. (c)	5. (a)	6. (c)	7. (b)	8. (a)	9. (c)	10. (b)
11. (a)	12. (a)	13. (b)	14. (d)	15. (b)	16. (c)	17. (d)	18. (a,d)	19. (a)	20. (b)
21. (c)	22. (b)	23. (c)	24. (a)	25. (b)	26. (c)				

SECTION–VII

1. (i) → (b), (ii) → (b), (iii) → (b), (iv) → (c)
2. (i) → (b), (ii) → (b), (iii) → (d), (iv) → (b)
3. (i) → (b), (ii) → (a), (iii) → (c), (iv) → (d)
4. (i) → (b) (ii) → (d) (iii) → (a) (iv) → (c), (d)
5. (i) → (d) (ii) → (c) (iii) → (b) (iv) → (a), (d)
6. (i) → (c) (ii) → (a) (iii) → (a), (b) (iv) → (d)

SECTION–VIII

1. 6	**2.** 1507	**3.** 41	**4.** 322	**5.** 4	**6.** 2046	**7.** 2016	**8.** 4	**9.** 2	**10.** 2
11. 8	**12.** 6	**13.** 12	**14.** 5	**15.** 8	**16.** 2	**17.** 175	**18.** 10	**19.** 45	**20.** 4

HINTS AND SOLUTIONS

TEXTUAL EXERCISE–1: (SUBJECTIVE)

1. $f(x)=\sqrt{x^2-4}$; $f(1)$ doesn't exist

$f(2)=\sqrt{2^2-4}=\sqrt{4-4}=0$

$f(-3)=\sqrt{(-3)^2-4}=\sqrt{9-4}=\sqrt{5}$

2. $f(x)=\dfrac{x-2}{(x-4)(x-5)}$, when $x\to 4$, $f(x)\to\pm\infty$

And when $x\to 5$ side $f(x)\to\pm\infty$

Therefore, $f(x)$ is not defined at $x=4$ and $x=5$.

3. $f(x)=\dfrac{1}{x-1}$; $x=1$

$\Rightarrow\ f(1)=\dfrac{1}{1-1}=\dfrac{1}{0}$ i.e., not defined, therefore, $f(x)$ is not defined at $x=1$.

As the numerator is never zero, therefore, $f(x)$ cannot attain the value 0.

4. $f(x)=\sqrt{(x-1)(x-4)}$

(i) For $f(x)$ to be undefined, the quantity inside the square root should be negative, therefore, $(x-1)(x-4)<0$.

$\Rightarrow x\in(1,4)$

(ii) $\dfrac{1}{f(x)}=\dfrac{1}{\sqrt{(x-1)(x-4)}}$

For $\dfrac{1}{f(x)}$ to be undefined, the quantity inside the square root should be negative or 0, therefore, $(x-1)(x-4)\le 0$.

$\Rightarrow x\in[1,4]$

(iii) $f(x)=\sqrt{(x-1)(x-4)}=\sqrt{x^2-5x+4}=\sqrt{\left(x-\dfrac{5}{2}\right)^2-\dfrac{9}{4}}$

$\Rightarrow\ \left(x-\dfrac{5}{2}\right)^2-\dfrac{9}{4}\ge-\dfrac{9}{4}$, but for $f(x)$ to be defined

$\left(x-\dfrac{5}{2}\right)^2-\dfrac{9}{4}\ge 0$

$\Rightarrow\ \sqrt{\left(x-\dfrac{5}{2}\right)^2-\dfrac{9}{4}}\ge 0$

$\Rightarrow f(x)\ge 0 \qquad \Rightarrow f(x)\in[0,\infty)$

(iv) $\dfrac{1}{f(x)}=\dfrac{1}{\sqrt{(x-1)(x-4)}}$

$\Rightarrow (x-1)(x-4)=x^2-5x+4=\left(x-\dfrac{5}{2}\right)^2-\dfrac{9}{4}$

$\Rightarrow\ \left(x-\dfrac{5}{2}\right)^2-\dfrac{9}{4}\ge-\dfrac{9}{4}$

$\Rightarrow\ \left(x-\dfrac{5}{2}\right)^2-\dfrac{9}{4}\in\left[-\dfrac{9}{4},\infty\right)$

For $\dfrac{1}{\sqrt{(x-1)(x-4)}}$ to be defined $\dfrac{1}{\left(x-\dfrac{5}{2}\right)^2-\dfrac{9}{4}}\in(0,\infty)$

$\Rightarrow\ \dfrac{1}{\sqrt{\left(x-\dfrac{5}{2}\right)^2-\dfrac{9}{4}}}\in(0,\infty)$

$\Rightarrow\ \dfrac{1}{f(x)}\in(0,\infty)$

5. (a) $f(x)=\dfrac{1}{x(x-1)(x-2)}$; for $f(x)$ to be defined the denominator should never be zero.

$\Rightarrow x(x-1)(x-2)\ne 0 \ \Rightarrow x\ne 0,1,2$

$\Rightarrow x\in\mathbb{R}\sim\{0,1,2\}$

(b) $f(x)=\dfrac{x^2-x}{x^2+x}$; for $f(x)$ to be defined the denominator should never be zero.

$\Rightarrow x^2+x\ne 0 \qquad \Rightarrow x(x+1)\ne 0$

$\Rightarrow x\ne 0,-1 \qquad \Rightarrow x\in\mathbb{R}\sim\{0,-1\}$

(c) $f(x)=\dfrac{x+1}{x^2+x+1}$; for $f(x)$ to be defined $x^2+x+1\ne 0$

As the discriminate of the quadratic in denominator is $1-4=-3$ is negative, hence, the above quadratic expression has no roots, i.e., $x^2+x+1\ne 0$. Hence, $D_f=\mathbb{R}$.

(d) $f(x)=\dfrac{1}{\sqrt{x-3}}$; for $f(x)$ to be defined $x-3>0$

$\Rightarrow x>3 \qquad \Rightarrow x\in(3,\infty)$

(e) $f(x)=\sqrt{x-4}$; for $f(x)$ to be defined $x-4\ge 0$

$\Rightarrow x\ge 4 \qquad \Rightarrow x\in[4,\infty)$

(f) $f(x)=\sqrt{x-2}+\sqrt{x+2}$; for $f(x)$ to be defined $x-2\ge 0$ and $x+2\ge 0$

$\Rightarrow x\ge 2$ and $x\ge -2 \qquad \Rightarrow x\in[2,\infty)$ and $x\in[-2,\infty)$

$\Rightarrow x\in[2,\infty)$

(g) $f(x)=\sqrt{x-4}+\sqrt{7-x}$; for $f(x)$ to be defined $x-4\ge 0$ and $7-x\ge 0$

$\Rightarrow x\ge 4$ and $7\ge x \qquad \Rightarrow x\in[4,\infty)$ and $x\in[-\infty,7]$

$\Rightarrow x\in[4,7]$

(h) $f(x)=\dfrac{1}{\sqrt{x-4}-\sqrt{6-x}}$; for $f(x)$ to be defined $x-4\ge 0$ and $6-x\ge 0$ and $\sqrt{x-4}-\sqrt{6-4}\ne 0$

$\Rightarrow x\ge 4$ and $6\ge x$ and $\sqrt{x-4}\ne\sqrt{6-x}$

$\Rightarrow x\in[4,\infty)$ and $x\in(-\infty,6]$ and $x-4\ne 6-x$

$\Rightarrow x\in[4,6]$ and $x\ne 5 \ \Rightarrow x\in[4,6]\sim\{5\}$

(i) $f(x)=\sqrt{x-7}-\sqrt{3-x}$; $x-7\ge 0$ and $3-x\ge 0$

$\Rightarrow x\in[7,\infty)$ and $x\in(-\infty,3]$

$\Rightarrow x\in\phi$

6. (a) $f(x)=\dfrac{\sqrt{x-1}}{\sqrt{6-x}}$; $x-1\ge 0$ and $6-x>0$

$\Rightarrow x\ge 1$ and $x<6 \qquad \Rightarrow x\in[1,\infty)$ and $x\in(-\infty,6)$

$\Rightarrow x\in[1,6)$

(b) $f(x)=\sqrt{\frac{x-1}{6-x}-1}=\sqrt{\frac{2x-7}{6-x}}$

$\Rightarrow$ $2x-7=0$ or $(2x-7)(6-x)>0$

$\Rightarrow$ $x=\frac{7}{2}$ or $x\in\left(\frac{7}{2},6\right)$ $\Rightarrow$ $x\in\left[\frac{7}{2},6\right)$

(c) $f(x)=\frac{\sqrt{x-1}}{6-x}$; $x-1\geq 0$ and $6-x\neq 0$

$\Rightarrow$ $x\in[1,\infty)$ and $x\neq 6$ $\Rightarrow$ $x\in[1,\infty)\sim\{6\}$

(d) $f(x)=(\sqrt{x}-1)(6-\sqrt{x})$; $x\geq 0$

$\Rightarrow$ $x\in[0,\infty)$

(e) $f(x)=(\sqrt{x}-1)\sqrt{(6-x)}$

$\Rightarrow$ $x\geq 0$ and $6-x\geq 0$ $\Rightarrow$ $x\geq 0$ and $x\leq 6$

$\Rightarrow$ $x\in[0,\infty)$ and $x\in(-\infty,6]$

$\Rightarrow$ $x\in[0,6]$

7. (a) $f(x)=\sqrt{x-1}\sqrt{6-x}$

$\Rightarrow$ $x-1\geq 0$ and $6-x\geq 0$

$\Rightarrow$ $x\geq 1$ and $6\geq x$

$\Rightarrow$ $x\in[1,\infty)$ and $x\in(-\infty,6]$

$\Rightarrow$ $x\in[1,6]$

(b) $f(x)=\sqrt{(x-1)(6-x)}$; $(x-1)(6-x)\geq 0$

$\Rightarrow$ $x\in[1,6]$

(c) $f(x)=\sqrt{x-x^2}$ $\Rightarrow$ $x-x^2\geq 0$

$\Rightarrow$ $x(1-x)\geq 0$ $\Rightarrow$ $x\in[0,1]$

8. (i) $f(x)=\sqrt{5-x}+\sqrt{x-2}$

$\Rightarrow$ $5-x\geq 0$ and $x-2\geq 0$

$\Rightarrow$ $x\in(-\infty,5]$ and $x\in[2,\infty)$

$\Rightarrow$ $x\in[2,5]$

(ii) $f(x)=\sqrt{3-x}+\sqrt{x-5}$

$\Rightarrow$ $3-x\geq 0$ and $x-5\geq 0$

$\Rightarrow$ $x\leq 3$ and $x\geq 5$ $\Rightarrow$ $x\in(-\infty,3]$ and $x\in[5,\infty)$

$\Rightarrow$ $x\in\phi$

9. $f(x)=\sqrt{x^2+x+1}$; $f: A\to B$; where A = {0, 1, 2, 3} and B = set of irrational numbers

$f(0)=\sqrt{0^2+0+1}=\sqrt{1}=1$; Which is not irrational number, hence, the output doesn't lie in co-domain, therefore, 0 do, not lie in the domain of f.

$f(2)=\sqrt{2^2+2+1}=\sqrt{4+2+1}=\sqrt{7}$; which is irrational and lie in co-domain, therefore, 2 lies in the domain of f.

$f(3)=\sqrt{3^2+3+1}=\sqrt{13}$; which is irrational and lie in co-domain, therefore, 3 lies in the domain of f.

Hence, D_f = {1, 2, 3} and $R_f=\{\sqrt{3},\sqrt{7},\sqrt{13}\}$

10. (i) $f(x)=\sqrt{1-x^2}$ $\Rightarrow$ $1-x^2\geq 0$

$\Rightarrow$ $(1-x)(1+x)\geq 0$

$x\in[-1,1]$ $\Rightarrow$ $D_f=[-1,1]$

$\Rightarrow$ $x^2\geq 0$ $\Rightarrow$ $-x^2\leq 0$

$\Rightarrow$ $1-x^2\leq 1$

$\Rightarrow$ $\sqrt{1-x^2}\in[0,1]$ $\Rightarrow$ $R_f=[0,1]$

(ii) $g(x)=\frac{1}{x}$ $\Rightarrow$ $D_f=\mathbb{R}-\{0\}$

$\Rightarrow$ $x\in(-\infty,0)\cup(0,\infty)$ $\Rightarrow$ $\frac{1}{x}\in(-\infty,0)\cup(0,\infty)$

$\Rightarrow$ $R_f=\mathbb{R}-\{0\}$

(iii) $h(x)=\frac{1}{\sqrt[3]{x}}$ $\Rightarrow$ $D_f=R-\{0\}$

$\Rightarrow$ $x\in(-\infty,0)\cup(0,\infty)$ $\Rightarrow$ $\sqrt[3]{x}\in(-\infty,0)\cup(0,\infty)$

$\Rightarrow$ $\frac{1}{\sqrt[3]{x}}\in(-\infty,0)\cup(0,\infty)$

$\Rightarrow$ $D_f=R-\{0\}$

(iv) $\phi(x)=\sqrt[4]{1-x^2}$ $\Rightarrow$ $1-x^2\geq 0$

$\Rightarrow$ $(1-x)(1+x)\geq 0$ $\Rightarrow$ $D_f=[-1,1]$

$\Rightarrow$ $x\in[-1,1]$

$\Rightarrow$ $x^2\geq 0$ $\Rightarrow$ $-x^2\leq 0$

$\Rightarrow$ $1-x^2\leq 1$

$\Rightarrow$ $\sqrt[4]{1-x^2}\in[0,1]$ $\Rightarrow$ $R_f=[0,1]$

Hence, ($f(x)$, $\phi(x)$) and ($h(x)$, $g(x)$) are the pairs of functions having same range and domain.

11. A = {x: x is a positive integer divisor of 36} = {1, 2, 3, 4, 6, 9, 12, 18, 36}

$f(x)=\frac{x}{(x-1)(x-2)(x-3)....(x-10)}$

$f(x)$ is not defined when $x\in$ {1, 2, 3, 4, 6, 9}, but $f(x)$ is defined when $x\in$ {12, 18, 36}

Hence, D_f = {12, 18, 36}

$f(12)=\frac{12}{11\times 10\times 9\times 8\times 7\times 6\times 5\times 4\times 3\times 2}=\frac{12}{11!}$

$f(18)=\frac{18}{17\times 16\times 15\times 14\times 13\times...\times 8}=\frac{18\times 7!}{17!}$

$f(36)=\frac{36}{35\times 34\times 33\times....\times 26}=\frac{36\times 25!}{35!}$

12. A = {9, 10, 11, 12, 13}; $f: A\to\mathbb{N}$

$f(x)$ = The highest prime factor of n

$f(9)=3$; $f(10)=5$; $f(11)=11$; $f(12)=3$; $f(13)=13$

$\therefore$ R_f = {3, 5, 11, 13}

13. In ΔABC; $AB=\frac{x}{2}$ (half of the height of cylinder)

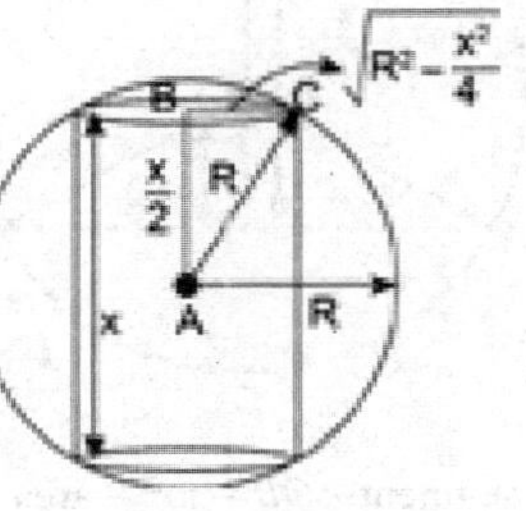

$AC=R$

$BC=\sqrt{R^2-\frac{x^2}{4}}$ (Pythagoras theorem)

Volume of cylinder $= \pi \times (BC)^2 \times x = \pi \times \left(R^2 - \frac{x^2}{4}\right) \times x$

$= \pi x\left(R^2 - \frac{x^2}{4}\right)$

As volume of cylinder can never be negative or 0 and height of cylinder can never be negative or 0

$\pi \times x\left(R - \frac{x}{2}\right)\left(R + \frac{x}{2}\right) > 0$ and $x > 0$

$\Rightarrow \quad x\left(R - \frac{x}{2}\right)\left(R + \frac{x}{2}\right) > 0$ and $x > 0$

$\Rightarrow x(2R - x)(2R + x) > 0$ and $x > 0$

$\Rightarrow x \in (-\infty, -2R) \cup (0, 2R)$ and $x > 0$

$\Rightarrow x \in (0, 2R)$

$\Rightarrow 0 < x < 2R$

14. **Case I:** $x \in (0, 1]$

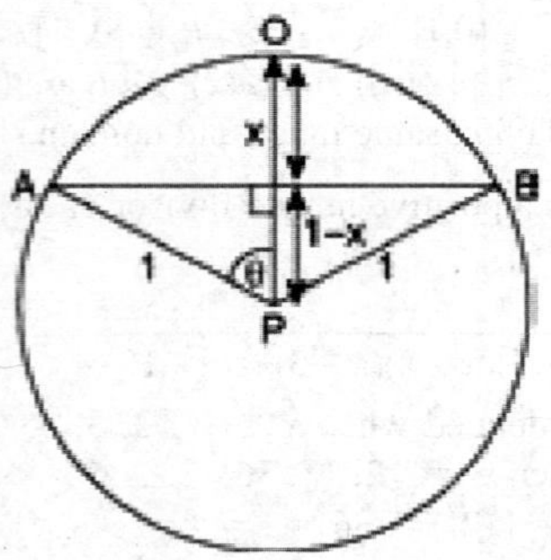

Area of sector $AOB = r^2\theta = 1^2 \times \cos^{-1}(1 - x) = \cos^{-1}(1 - x)$

Area of $\Delta ABP = \frac{1}{2} \times (1 - x) \times 2 \times \sqrt{1 - (1 - x)^2}$

$= (1 - x)\sqrt{1 - 1 - x^2 + 2x} = (1 - x)\sqrt{2x - x^2}$

Area of segment $AOB = \cos^{-1}(1 - x) - (1 - x)\sqrt{2x - x^2}$

Case II: $x \in (1, 2)$

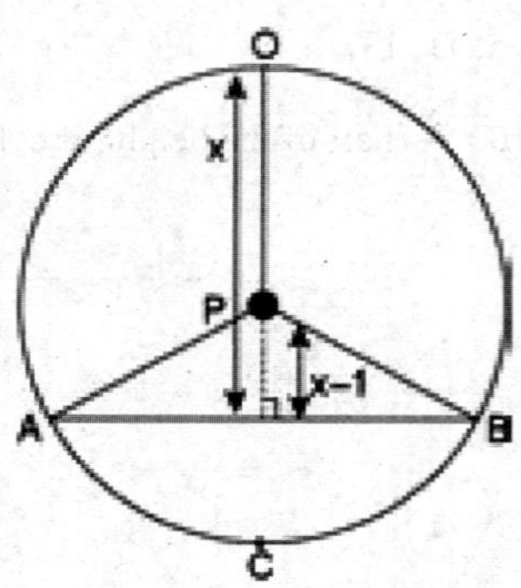

Area of segment $AOB = \pi r^2$ – area of segment ACB

$= \pi(1)^2 - [\cos^{-1}(1 - x) - (1 - x)\sqrt{2x - x^2}]$

$= \pi - \cos^{-1}(1 - x) + (1 - x)\sqrt{2x - x^2}$

15. $HC = \frac{b}{2}$; $\tan C = \frac{AH}{HC} = \frac{EF}{FC}$

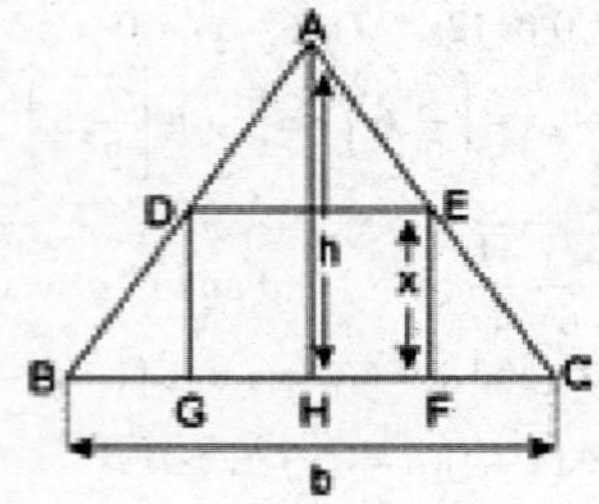

$\Rightarrow \frac{h}{\frac{b}{2}} = \frac{x}{FC} \qquad \Rightarrow FC = \frac{bx}{2h}$

$\Rightarrow HF = HC - FC = \frac{b}{2} - \frac{b\,x}{2\,h} = \frac{b}{2}\left(1 - \frac{x}{h}\right)$

$\Rightarrow GF = 2HF = 2 \times \frac{b}{2}\left(1 - \frac{x}{h}\right) = b\left(1 - \frac{x}{h}\right)$

Perimeter of rectangle $DEFG = 2\left(x + b\left(1 - \frac{x}{h}\right)\right)$

Area of rectangle $DEFG = x \times b\left(1 - \frac{x}{h}\right) = bx\left(1 - \frac{x}{h}\right)$

TEXTUAL EXERCISE–1: (OBJECTIVE)

1. **(a)** $f(x) = \frac{1}{1 - x} \quad \Rightarrow \quad f\left(\frac{1}{x}\right) = \frac{1}{1 - \frac{1}{x}} = \frac{x}{x - 1}$

2. **(c)** $f(x) = \log(1 - x) + \sqrt{x^2 - 1}$

$1 - x > 0$ and $x^2 - 1 \geq 0$

$x < 1$ and $(x - 1)(x + 1) \geq 0$

$\Rightarrow x \in (-\infty, 1)$ and $x\ (-\infty, -1] \cup [1, \infty)$

$\Rightarrow x \in (-\infty, -1]$

3. **(a)** $f(x) = ax^2 + bx + c$

$f(x + 1) = a(x^2 + 2x + 1) + bx + b + c = ax^2 + (2a + b)x + a + b + c$

$f(x + 1) - f(x) = 8x + 3$

$ax^2 + (2a + b)x + a + b + c - ax^2 - bx - c = 8x + 3$

$2ax + a + b = 8x + 3$

$2a = 8 \quad \Rightarrow \quad a = 4$ and $a + b = 3$

$\Rightarrow b = -1$

4. **(c)** $p(x) = a^2 + bx$

$q(x) = lx^2 + mx + x$

$\therefore \ p(1) - q(1) = 0$

$\Rightarrow (a^2 + b - l - m - n) = 0$ ......(i)

$\Rightarrow p(2) - q(2) = 1$

$\Rightarrow (a^2 + 2b) - (4l + 2m + n) = 0$ ......(ii)

And $p(3) - q(3) = 4$

$\Rightarrow (a^2 + 3b) - (9l + 3m + n) = 4$ ......(iii)

Solving (i), (ii) and (iii), we get
$l = -1, b - m = -2, a^2 - n = 1$

$\therefore\ p(x) - q(x) = (a^2 - n) + (b - m)x - lx^2 = 1 - 2x + x^2 = (x - 1)^2$

$\Rightarrow\ p(4) - q(4) = (4 - 1)^2 = 9$

5. **(a)** $f(x) = \sqrt{\log(\log x) - \log(4 - \log x) - \log 3}$

$= \sqrt{\log\left(\dfrac{\log x}{3(4 - \log x)}\right)} \Rightarrow \dfrac{\log x}{3(4 \log x)} \ge 1$

$\Rightarrow \dfrac{\log x}{4 - \log x} - 3 \ge 0 \quad \Rightarrow \dfrac{4\log x - 12}{4 - \log x} \ge 0$

$\Rightarrow \dfrac{\log x - 3}{4 - \log x} \ge 0$

$\Rightarrow \log x = 3$ or $\dfrac{\log x - 3}{4 - \log x} > 0$

$\Rightarrow x = 10^3$ or $\log x \in (3, 4)$

$\Rightarrow x = 10^3$ or $x \in (10^3, 10^4)$

$\Rightarrow x \in [10^3, 10^4)$

6. **(b)** $3^y = 2^{4x^2 - 3} - 2^{x^4}$; y to be real $3^y > 0$

$\Rightarrow 2^{4x^2-3} - 2^{x^4} > 0$

$\Rightarrow 4x^2 - 3 > x^4$

$\Rightarrow x^4 - 4x^2 + 3 < 0$

$\Rightarrow (x^2 - 1)(x^2 - 3) < 0$

$\Rightarrow (x - 1)(x + 1)(x - \sqrt{3})(x + \sqrt{3}) < 0$

$\Rightarrow x \in (-\sqrt{3} - 1) \cup (1, \sqrt{3})$

7. **(a)** $f(x) = \sqrt[3]{\dfrac{2x+1}{x^2 - 10x - 11}} = \sqrt[3]{\dfrac{2x+1}{(x-11)(x+1)}}$

$\Rightarrow x \in \mathbb{R} - \{11, -1\} \quad \Rightarrow \mathbb{R} - \{-1, 11\}$

8. $f(x) = \sqrt{\log_5(\cos(\sin x))}$

$\cos(\sin x) \ge 1$ but $\cos(\sin x) \in [-1, 1]$

$\Rightarrow \cos(\sin x) = 1$

$\Rightarrow \sin x = 0, 2\pi, 4\pi$ but $\sin x \in [-1, 1]$

$\Rightarrow \sin x = 0 \quad \Rightarrow x = n\pi$, where $n \in \mathbb{Z}$

9. **(b)** $f(x) = \dfrac{1}{\sqrt{x^6 - 13x^4 + 36x^2}} = \dfrac{1}{\sqrt{(x^4 - 13x^2 + 36)x^2}}$

$= \dfrac{1}{\sqrt{(x^2 - 9)(x^2 - 4)x^2}}$

$\Rightarrow x^2(x - 3)(x + 3)(x - 2)(x + 2) > 0$

$\Rightarrow (x - 3)(x + 3)(x - 2)(x + 2) > 0, x \ne 0$

$\Rightarrow x\ (-\infty, -3) \cup (-2, 0) \cup (0, 2) \cup (3, \infty)$

10. **(a)** $f(x) = x^2 + \dfrac{1}{x^2 + 1} = y; y \ge 0$

$\Rightarrow y = \dfrac{x^4 + x^2 + 1}{x^2 + 1} \quad \Rightarrow x^4 + (1 - y)x^2 + (1 - y) = 0$

Equation to have real roots, $D \ge 0$

$\Rightarrow (1 - y)^2 - 4(1 - y) \ge 0$

$\Rightarrow (1 - y)(1 - y - 4) \ge 0$

$\Rightarrow (y - 1)(y + 3) \ge 0 \quad \Rightarrow y \ge 0$

$\Rightarrow y + 3 \ge 3 \quad \Rightarrow y - 1 \ge 0$

$\Rightarrow y \ge 1 \quad \Rightarrow y \in [1, \infty)$

11. **(a)** $f(x) = \log_4(\log_5(\log_3(18x - x^2 - 77)))$

$\Rightarrow \log_5(\log_3(18x - x^2 - 77)) > 0$

$\Rightarrow 18x - x^2 - 77 > 3 \quad \Rightarrow x^2 - 18x + 80 < 0$

$\Rightarrow (x - 10)(x - 8) < 0 \quad \Rightarrow x \in (8, 10)$

12. **(c)** $\log_5(\log_{1/3}(\log_8(2x + 1)) = f(x)$

$f(x)$ to be defined

$2x + 1 > 0$ and $\log_{1/3}(\log_8(2x + 1)) > 0$

$\Rightarrow x > -\dfrac{1}{2}$ and $\log_8(2x + 1) < 1$

$\Rightarrow x \in \left(-\dfrac{1}{2}, \infty\right)$ and $2x + 1 < 8$

$\Rightarrow x \in \left(-\dfrac{1}{2}, \infty\right)$ and $x \in \left(-\infty, \dfrac{7}{2}\right)$

$x \in \left(-\dfrac{1}{2}, \dfrac{7}{2}\right)$

$D = \left(-\dfrac{1}{2}, \dfrac{7}{2}\right)$; integers belonging to D are 0, 1, 2, 3

$S = 0 + 1 + 2 + 3 = 6$

TEXTUAL EXERCISE–2: (SUBJECTIVE)

1. $f_1 = \{(\alpha, 1), (\beta, 1)\}; f_2 = \{(\alpha, 2), (\beta, 2)\}; f_3 = \{(\alpha, 1), (\beta, 2);$
$f_4 = \{(\alpha, 2), (\beta, 1)\}$

2. **(a)** $\log_5 x + \log_5(y + 2) = 8$

$\Rightarrow \log_5 x(y + 2) = 8 \quad \Rightarrow x(y + 2) = 5^8$

Domain: for $\log_5 x$ to be defined, $x > 0$ and $y = \dfrac{5^8}{x} - 2$

$\Rightarrow x \in (0, \infty)$ and $y + 2 > 0$

$\Rightarrow \dfrac{5^8}{x} > 0 \quad \Rightarrow x > 0$

$\Rightarrow x \in (0, \infty)$

(b) $3^{x+y}(x^2 - 3) = x^3 - 27$

$\Rightarrow 3^{x+y} = \dfrac{x^3 - 27}{x^2 - 3} \quad \Rightarrow x + y = \log_3\left(\dfrac{x^3 - 27}{x^2 - 3}\right)$

$\Rightarrow y = \log_3\left(\dfrac{x^3 - 27}{x^2 - 3}\right) - x$

Domain: $\dfrac{x^3 - 27}{x^2 - 3} > 0$

$\Rightarrow \dfrac{(x - 3)(x^2 + 9 + 3x)}{(x - \sqrt{3})(x + \sqrt{3})} > 0$

$\Rightarrow \dfrac{(x - 3)}{(x - \sqrt{3})(x + \sqrt{3})} > 0$

[$x^2 + 9 + 3x$ is always positive as $D < 0$ and leading coefficient > 0]

$\Rightarrow x \in (-\sqrt{3}, \sqrt{3}) \cup (3, \infty)$

(c) $\Rightarrow y^2 = 8x - 4y \quad \Rightarrow y^2 + 4y + 4 = 8x + 4$

$\Rightarrow (y + 2)^2 = 8\left(x + \dfrac{1}{2}\right)$

$\Rightarrow \quad y = \pm\sqrt{8\left(x+\frac{1}{2}\right)} - 2$

Domain: $\left(x+\frac{1}{2}\right) \geq 0 \quad \Rightarrow \quad x \geq -\frac{1}{2} \Rightarrow x \in \left[-\frac{1}{2}, \infty\right)$

3. **(a)** $y^2 - 2y - x^2 = 0; y \geq 1$

$\Rightarrow y^2 - 2y + 1 = x^2 + 1$

$\Rightarrow (y-1)^2 = x^2 + 1 \quad \Rightarrow \quad y - 1 = \sqrt{x^2+1}$

$\Rightarrow [y - 1 \geq 0 \Rightarrow y - 1 = \sqrt{x^2+1}]$

$\Rightarrow y = 1 + \sqrt{x^2+1} \quad \Rightarrow x^2 + 1 \geq 0$ true for all $x \in \mathbb{R}$

$\Rightarrow D_f = \mathbb{R}$

(b) $y^2 - 2y + x^2 = 0; y \leq 1$

$\Rightarrow (y-1)^2 = 1 - x^2$

$\Rightarrow y - 1 = -\sqrt{1-x^2} \quad \Rightarrow \quad y = 1 - \sqrt{1-x^2}$; $[y - 1 \leq 0]$

$\Rightarrow 1 - x^2 \geq 0$

$\Rightarrow x \in [-1, 1] \quad \Rightarrow \quad D_f = [-1, 1]$

5. **(a)** $y^{2/3} = 3x + 4 \quad \Rightarrow y^2 = (3x+4)^3$

$\Rightarrow y = \pm(3x+4)^{3/2}$

Hence, it is a one–many relation, so, it is not a function.

(b) $y = 2x^2 + 1$

If $x_1 = x_2 \quad \Rightarrow \quad 2x_1^2 = 2x_2^2$

$\Rightarrow 2x_1^2 + 1 = 2x_2^2 + 1 \quad \Rightarrow \quad y_1 = y_2$

Hence, it is a function.

If $y_1 = y_2$

$\Rightarrow 2x_1^2 + 1 = 2x_2^2 + 1 \quad \Rightarrow \quad x_1^2 = x_2^2$

$\Rightarrow x_1 = x_2$ or $x_1 = -x_2$

Since it is a many–one function, it is not injective.

(c) $y^2 = 2\tan x + 5 \quad \Rightarrow \quad y = \pm\sqrt{2\tan x + 5}$

It is a one–many relation.

Hence, it is not a function.

(d) $y = \sqrt{3x+2}$

If $x_1 = x_2 \quad \Rightarrow \quad 3x_1 + 2 = 3x_2 + 2$

$\Rightarrow \sqrt{3x_1+2} = \sqrt{3x_2+2} \Rightarrow y_1 = y_2$

Hence, it is a function

If $y_1 = y_2 \quad \Rightarrow \quad \sqrt{3x_1+5} = \sqrt{3x_2+5}$

$\Rightarrow 3x_1 + 5 = 3x_2 + 5$

$\Rightarrow x_1 = x_2$

Hence, it is a one–one function, i.e., injective.

(e) $y^3 = 2x^2 - 1$

Let $x_1 = x_2 \quad \Rightarrow \quad 2x_1^2 - 1 = 2x_2^2 - 1$

$\Rightarrow y_1^3 = y_2^3 \quad \Rightarrow \quad y_1^3 - y_2^3 = 0$

$\Rightarrow (y_1 - y_2)(y_1^2 + y_2 y_1 + y_2^2)$

$\Rightarrow y_1 = y_2$

Hence, it is a function.

Let $y_1 = y_2$

$\Rightarrow (2x_1^2 - 1)^{\frac{1}{3}} = (2x_2^2 - 1)^{\frac{1}{3}}$

$\Rightarrow 2x_1^2 - 1 = 2x_2^2 - 1$

$\Rightarrow x_1^2 - x_2^2 = 0 \quad \Rightarrow \quad (x_1 - x_2)(x_1 + x_2) = 0$

$\Rightarrow x_1 = x_2$ or $x_1 = -x_2$

Hence, it is a many–one function, so it is not injective.

(f) $y = \frac{x-1}{x+1}$

Let $x_1 = x_2 \quad \Rightarrow \quad x_1 + 1 = x_2 + 1$

$\Rightarrow \frac{1}{x_1+1} = \frac{1}{x_2+1} \quad \Rightarrow \quad \frac{-2}{x_1+1} = \frac{-2}{x_2+1}$

$\Rightarrow 1 - \frac{2}{x_1+1} = 1 - \frac{2}{x_2+1} \quad \Rightarrow \quad \frac{x_1-1}{x_1+1} = \frac{x_2-1}{x_2+1} \Rightarrow y_1 = y_2$

Hence, it is a function.

Let $y_1 = y_2$

$\Rightarrow \frac{x_1-1}{x_1+1} = \frac{x_2-1}{x_2+1} \quad \Rightarrow \quad 1 - \frac{2}{x_1+1} = 1 - \frac{2}{x_2+1}$

$\Rightarrow \frac{-2}{x_1+1} = \frac{-2}{x_2+1} \quad \Rightarrow \quad \frac{1}{x_1+1} = \frac{1}{x_1+1} \Rightarrow x_1 = x_2$

Hence, it is an injective function.

(g) $y^2 = 4x - 3$

Let $x_1 = x_2 \quad \Rightarrow \quad 4x_1 - 3 = 4x_2 - 3$

$\Rightarrow y_1^2 = y_2^2$

$\Rightarrow y_1 = y_2$ or $y_1 = -y_2$

Hence, it is a one–many relation, so, it is not a function.

(h) $y = ax^2 + bx + c$

Let $x_1 = x_2 \quad \Rightarrow \quad x_1 + \frac{b}{2a} = x_2 + \frac{b}{2a}$

$\Rightarrow \left(x_1 + \frac{b}{2a}\right)^2 = \left(x_2 + \frac{b}{2a}\right)^2$

$\Rightarrow a\left(x_1 + \frac{b}{2a}\right)^2 - \left(\frac{b^2-4ac}{4a}\right)$

$= a\left(x_2 + \frac{b}{2a}\right)^2 - \left(\frac{b^2-4ac}{4a}\right)$

$\Rightarrow y_1 = y_2$

Hence, it is a function.

Let $y_1 = y_2$

$\Rightarrow ax_1^2 + bx_1 + c = ax_2^2 + bx_2 + c$

$\Rightarrow a\left(x_1 + \frac{b}{2a}\right)^2 - \left(\frac{b^2-4ac}{4a}\right)$

$= a\left(x_2 + \frac{b}{2a}\right)^2 - \left(\frac{b^2-4ac}{4a}\right)$

$\Rightarrow \left(x_1 + \frac{b}{2a}\right)^2 = \left(x_2 + \frac{b}{2a}\right)^2$

$\Rightarrow x_1 = x_2$ or $x_1 = -x_2 - \frac{b}{a}$

Hence, it is a many–one function, and therefore, it is not injective function.

(i) $y^3 = 3x + 1$

Let $x_1 = x_2 \quad \Rightarrow \quad 3x_1 + 1 = 3x_2 + 1$

$\Rightarrow y_1^3 = y_2^3$

$\Rightarrow (y_1 - y_2)(y_1^2 + y_2^2 + y_1 y_2) = 0$

$\Rightarrow y_1 = y_2$

Hence, it is a function.

Let $y_1 = y_2 \quad \Rightarrow \quad (3x + 1)^{1/3} = (3x_2 + 1)^{1/3}$

$\Rightarrow\ 3x_1 + 1 = 3x_2 + 1$
$\Rightarrow\ x_1 = x_2$
Hence, it is injective.

6. (i) $y = \sqrt{x}$
Let $x_1 = x_2 \quad\Rightarrow\quad \sqrt{x_1} = \sqrt{x_2} \Rightarrow y_1 = y_2$
Hence, it is a function.

(ii) $x^2 + 2y^2 = 8 \quad\Rightarrow\quad 2y^2 = 8 - x^2$
$\Rightarrow\ y^2 = \dfrac{8 - x^2}{2}$
Let $x_1 = x_2 \quad\Rightarrow\quad -x_1^2 = -x_2^2$
$\Rightarrow\ \dfrac{8 - x_1^2}{2} = \dfrac{8 - x_2^2}{2}$
$\Rightarrow\ y_1^2 = y_2^2 \quad\Rightarrow\quad y_1 = y_2$ or $y_1 = -y_2$
$\Rightarrow$ Hence, it is not a function.

(iii) $x^2 + y^2 = 4;\ y \geq 0$
$y^2 = 4 - x^2$
Let $x_1 = x_2$
$\Rightarrow\ -x_1^2 = -x_2^2 \quad\Rightarrow\quad 4 - x_1^2 = 4 - x_2^2$
$\Rightarrow\ y_1^2 = y_2^2$
$\Rightarrow\ (y_1 - y_2)(y_1 + y_2) = 0 \Rightarrow y_1 = y_2$ or
$\Rightarrow\ y_1 = y_2 = 0$
Hence, it is a function.

(iv) $x^2 + y^2 = 4;\ x \geq 0 \quad\Rightarrow\quad y^2 = 4 - x^2$
$\Rightarrow$ let $x_1 = x_2 \quad\Rightarrow\quad -x_1^2 = -x_2^2$
$\Rightarrow\ 4 - x_1^2 = 4 - x_2^2$
$\Rightarrow\ y_1^2 = y_2^2 \quad\Rightarrow\quad (y_1 - y_2)(y_1 + y_2) = 0$
$\Rightarrow\ y_1 = y_2$ or $y_1 = -y_2$
Hence, it is not a function.

(v) $y = \begin{cases} 2x + 5\ ;\ x \geq 0 \\ \dfrac{-x^2}{4}\ ;\ x < 0 \end{cases}$

For $x \geq 0$; let $x_1 = x_2 \Rightarrow 2x_1 + 5 = 2x_2 + 5$
$\Rightarrow\ y_1 = y_2$
For $x < 0$; let $x_1 = x_2 \Rightarrow -\dfrac{x_1^2}{4} = \dfrac{-x_2^2}{4} \Rightarrow y_1 = y_2$
Hence, it is function.

(vi) $y^3 = x$;
Let $x_1 = x_2 \quad\Rightarrow\quad y_1^3 = y_2^3$
$\Rightarrow\ (y_1 - y_2)(y_1^2 + y_2^2 + y_1y_2) = 0$
$\Rightarrow\ y_1 = y_2$
Hence, it is a function.

(vii) $y^4 = 2x$
let $x_1 = x_2 \quad\Rightarrow\quad 2x_1 = 2x_2$
$\Rightarrow\ y_1^4 = y_2^4$
$\Rightarrow\ (y_1^2 - y_2^2)(y_1^2 + y_2^2) = 0$
$\Rightarrow\ y_1 = y_2$ or $y_1 = -y_2$ or $y_1 = y_2 = 0$
Hence, it is not a function.

7. (a) $f: R \to R;\ f(x) = \begin{cases} 2x + 1; & x \leq 4 \\ x + 4; & x > 4 \end{cases}$
For $x \leq 4$
Let $x_1 = x_2 \quad\Rightarrow\quad 2x_1 + 1 = 2x_2 + 1$
$\Rightarrow\ f(x_1) = f(x_2)$
For $x > 4$
Let $x_1 = x_2 \quad\Rightarrow\quad x_1 + 4 = x_2 + 4$
$\Rightarrow\ f(x_1) = f(x_2)$
$\Rightarrow\ f(x)$ is *a* function.

(b) $f(x) = \begin{cases} x^2; & 0 \leq x \leq 3 \\ 3x; & 3 \leq x \leq 10 \end{cases}$

For $0 \leq x \leq 3$
Let $x_1 = x_2 \quad\Rightarrow\quad x_1^2 = x_2^2$
$\Rightarrow\ f(x_1) = f(x_2)$
For $3 \leq x \leq 10$
Let $x_1 = x_2 \quad\Rightarrow\quad 3x_1 = 3x_2$
Hence, $h(x_1) = h(x_2)$
At $x = 3$
$\Rightarrow\ f(x) = x^2 = 3^2 = 9 \quad\Rightarrow\quad f(x) = 3x = 3 \times 3 = 9$
Hence, $h(x)$ is a function.

(c) $g(x) = \begin{cases} x^2\ ;0 \leq x \leq 2 \\ 3x\ ;2 \leq x \leq 10 \end{cases}$

For $0 \leq x \leq 2$
Let $x_1 = x_2 \quad\Rightarrow\quad x_1^2 = x_2^2$
$\Rightarrow\ g(x_1) = g(x_2)$
For $2 \leq x \leq 10$
Let $x_1 = x_2 \quad\Rightarrow\quad 3x_1 = 3x_2$
$\Rightarrow\ g(x_1) = g(x_2)$
At $x = 2$
$g(x) = x^2 = 4$ and $g(x) = 3x = 6$
Hence, at $x = 2$ the relation has two values, hence, it is not a function.

8. Length $AB = \sqrt{4^2 + x^2}$ and length $BC = \sqrt{3^2 + (4 - x)^2}$
From Pythagoras theorem

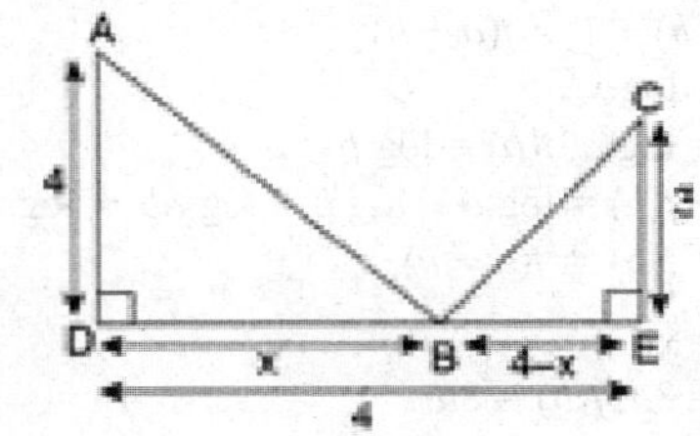

Hence, $f(x) = \sqrt{16 + x^2} + \sqrt{25 + x^2 - 8x}$; for $x \in [0, 4]$

9. See the answer

10. (i) $f(x) = \begin{cases} x^2 + 4; & |x| > 0 \\ 3; & x = 0 \end{cases}$

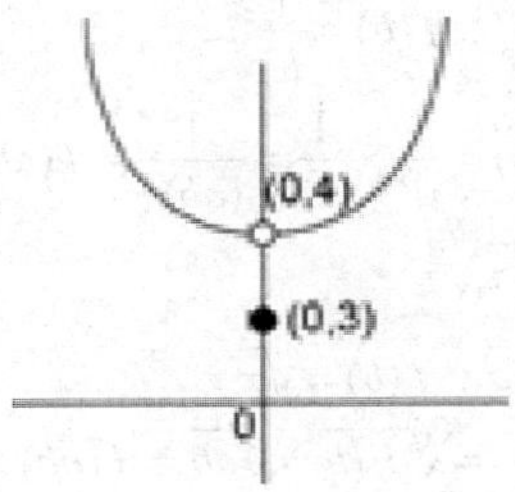

(ii) $g(x)=\begin{cases} x^2+2; & \text{if } x\geq 0 \\ -x-2; & \text{if } x<0 \end{cases}$

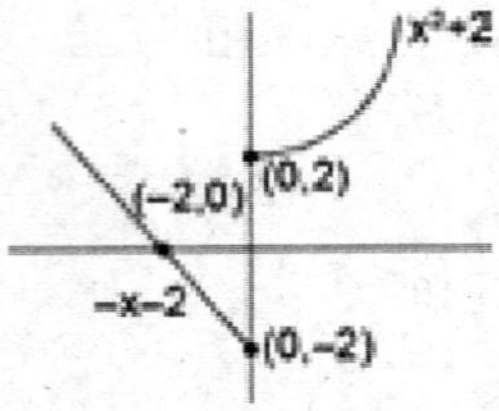

11. See the answer

12. See the answer

13. **(a)** $f(x) = x^2$
$\Rightarrow f(a) = a^2; f(b) = b^2$
$\Rightarrow f(a + b) = (a + b)^2 = a^2 + b^2 + 2ab \neq f(a) + f(b)$
(b) $f(x) = 5x$
$\Rightarrow f(a) = 5a;\ f(b) = 5b$
$\Rightarrow f(a) + f(b) = 5a + 5b = 5(a + b) = f(a + b)$
(c) $f(x) = -6x$
$\Rightarrow f(a) = -6a; f(b) = -6b$
$\Rightarrow f(a) + f(b) = -6a - 6b = -6(a + b) = -f(a + b)$
(d) $f(x)=\sqrt{x}$
$\Rightarrow f(a)=\sqrt{a}\,;\ f(b)=\sqrt{b}$
$\Rightarrow f(a)+f(b)=\sqrt{a}+\sqrt{b}\neq\sqrt{a+b}$
$\Rightarrow f(a) + f(b) \neq f(a + b)$
(e) $f(x) = 3x + 1$
$\Rightarrow f(a) = 3a + 1; f(b) = 3b + 1$
$\Rightarrow f(a) + f(b) = 3a + 1 + 3b + 1 = 3(a + b) + 1 + 1$
$\Rightarrow f(a + b) + 1 \neq f(a + b)$
(f) $f(x) = \log x$
$\Rightarrow f(a) = \log a; f(b) = \log b$
$\Rightarrow f(a) + f(b) = \log a + \log b = \log ab \neq \log (a + b)$
$\Rightarrow f(a) + f(b) \neq f(a + b)$

14. **(a)** $f(x) = 8x$
$\Rightarrow f(a) = 8a; f(b) = 8b$
$\Rightarrow f(a) . f(b) = 8a \times 8b = 64ab \neq 8ab$
$\Rightarrow f(a) . f(b) \neq f(ab)$
(b) $f(x) = x^5$
$\Rightarrow f(a) = a^5; f(b) = b^5$
$\Rightarrow f(a) . f(b) = a^5b^5 = (ab)^5 = f(ab)$
(c) $f(x)=\frac{1}{x^3}$
$\Rightarrow f(a)=\frac{1}{a^3};\ f(b)=\frac{1}{b^3}$
$\Rightarrow f(a).f(b)=\frac{1}{a^3}\times\frac{1}{b^3}=\frac{1}{(ab)^3}=f(ab)$
(d) $f(x)=\sqrt{x}$
$\Rightarrow f(a)=\sqrt{a}\,;\ f(b)=\sqrt{x}$
$\Rightarrow f(a).f(b)=\sqrt{a}\sqrt{b}=\sqrt{ab}=f(ab)$
(e) $f(x) = x + 2$
$\Rightarrow f(a) = a + 2; f(b) = b + 2$
$\Rightarrow f(a) . f(b) = (a + 2) (b + 2) = ab + 4 + 2(a + b) \neq ab + 2$
$\Rightarrow f(a) . f(b) \neq f(ab)$

15. $f(x + y) = f(x) + f(y); f(1) = 3$ for all integers x and y
(a) $f(x + y) = f(x) + f(y)$
Let $x = y = 1$
$\Rightarrow f(1 + 1) = f(1) + f(1)$
$\Rightarrow f(2) = 3 + 3 = 6$
$\Rightarrow f(2) = 6$
(b) Let $x = 1; y = 0$
$\Rightarrow f(1 + 0) = f(1) + f(0) \Rightarrow f(0) = 0$
(c) Let $x = -1; y = 0$
$\Rightarrow f(-1 + 1) = f(1) + f(-1)$
$\Rightarrow f(0) = f(1) + f(-1)$
$\Rightarrow 0 = f(1) + f(-1)$
$\Rightarrow f(-1) = -f(1) = -3$

16. $\because f(6) = f(2 \times 3) = 2 + 3 = 5$; Also $f(6) = f(1 \times 6) = 1 + 6 = 7$
$\Rightarrow f(6)$ does not have a unique image
$\Rightarrow f(x)$ is not a function

TEXTUAL EXERCISE–2: (OBJECTIVE)

1. **(c), (d)**
(a) one–many relation as 3 has two images in Y, i.e., 2 and 4.
(b) Not a function as 7 has no image in Y.
(c) is a function as every element $\in X$ has only one image in Y.
(d) is a function as every element $\in X$ has only one image in Y.

2. **(a)** (a) $\because$ For every $x \in \mathbb{N}, y \geq 3$ and $y \in W$
$\Rightarrow f$ is a function.
(b) $\because$ For $f(2) = -2 \notin W$
$\Rightarrow f$ is not a function.
(c) $\because\ y = \pm(x + 2)$
$\Rightarrow y$ is one–many, and hence, it is not a function.
(d) $\because\ y = \pm(x - 1)$
$\Rightarrow y$ is one–many relation (not a function).

3. **(c), (d)**
(a) f: $\{-2, 0, 2\} \rightarrow \{0, 1, 8, 3\}; f(x) = x^3$
If $x = -2$, then $f(x) = -8$; which is not present in co-domain, hence, it is not a function.
(b) f: $\{0, 1, 4\} \rightarrow \{-2, 1, 0, 1, 2\}; f(x)=\pm\sqrt{x}$
If $x = 1$, then $f(x)=\pm\sqrt{x}=\pm 1$
Hence, for one input there are two output, hence, it is not a function.
(c) f: $\{0, 1, 9\} \rightarrow \{-3, -1, 0, 1, 3\};\ f(x)=\sqrt{x}$
If $x = 0$; $f(x)=\sqrt{x}=0$; if $x = 1$, $f(x)=\sqrt{x}=\sqrt{1}=1$
If $x = 9$; $f(x)=\sqrt{x}=\sqrt{9}=3$
Hence, for every input, there is only one output and all of which are present in the co-domain, hence, it is a function.

(d) f: {0, 1, 9} → {–3, –1, 0, 1, 3}; $f(x) = -\sqrt{x}$

If $x = 0$; $f(0) = -\sqrt{0} = 0$, if $x = 1$, $f(1) = -\sqrt{1} = -1$

If $n = 9$; $f(9) = -\sqrt{9} = -3$

Hence, for every input, there is unique output and all of which are present in the co-domain. Hence, it is a function.

4. (a), (b) (a) For every $x \in \mathbb{N}, y \in W$

$\Rightarrow$ y is a function.

(b) For every $x \in \mathbb{N}, y \geq 0$ and $y \in W$

$\Rightarrow$ y is a function.

(c) $y = \pm\sqrt{x+1}$

$\Rightarrow$ y is a relation not a function.

5. (a) (a) Every element of domain has a unique image in co-domain, hence, it is a function.

(b) x_2 do not have an image

(c) x_1 has two images

(d) x_1 has two images

6. (c), (d), (f)

(a) many–many relation

(b) one–many relation

(e) many–many relation

(g) many–many relation

7. (c) ∵ Output is obtained by increasing the magnitude of input by 1 unit.

8. (c), (d)

(a) From $[b, c]$, the relation is a one–many relation, hence, it not a function.

(b) At $x = b$, the relation has two images.

9. (b) ∵ On $[1, 2) \cup [7, 8]$, $f(x)$ is one–one and $f(x) \in [1, 2) \cup [4, 5]$, i.e., $f(x)$ is in co-domain.

(a) From (5, 7], the function generates values which are not an image in co-domain.

(b) At $x = 5$, the relation has two values, hence, it is not a function.

10. (d)

(a) $|y| = 2 - |x|$

$\Rightarrow y = \pm(2 - |x|) = \begin{cases} \pm(2+x) \text{ for } x < 0 \\ \pm(2-x) \text{ for } x \geq 0 \end{cases}$

$\Rightarrow$ Relation represents one–many relation, and hence, not a function.

(b) $x + y = \pm 4$ $\quad\Rightarrow y = -x \pm 4$

$\Rightarrow$ Relation is one–many.

(c) $|y| = x^2 + \sin x$ $\quad\Rightarrow y = \pm(x^2 + \sin x)$

$\Rightarrow$ Relation is one–many.

(d) $|y| = |x|^2 - x = x^2 - x = \left(x - \frac{1}{2}\right)^2 - \frac{1}{4}$

$\because x^1 = x^2 \quad \Rightarrow \left(x_1 - \frac{1}{2}\right) = \left(x_2 - \frac{1}{2}\right)$

$\Rightarrow \left(x_1 - \frac{1}{2}\right)^2 = \left(x_2 - \frac{1}{2}\right)^2$

$\Rightarrow \left(x_1 - \frac{1}{2}\right)^2 - \frac{1}{4} = \left(x_2 - \frac{1}{2}\right)^2 - \frac{1}{4}$

$\Rightarrow y_1 = y_2 \quad\quad \Rightarrow$ It is a function

11. (a), (b), (c)

AB and AC must be symmetric about AO

Area $(ABDC)$ = 2(area of ΔOAB) + (area of sector $OBDC$)

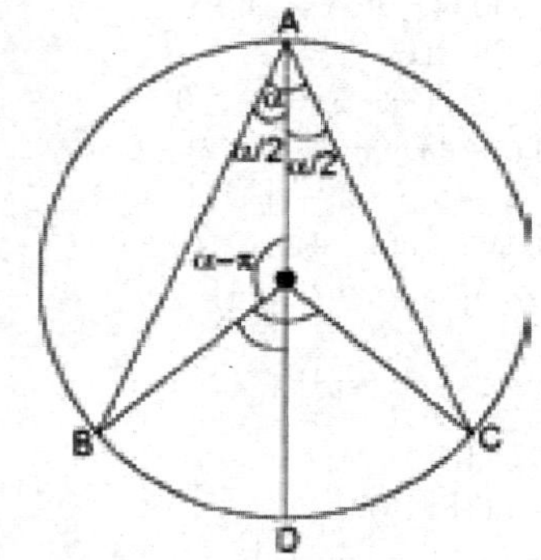

$= 2\left[\frac{1}{2}r^2 \sin(\pi - \alpha)\right] + \frac{2\alpha}{2\pi}(\pi r^2) = \frac{\pi r^2}{3}$

$\Rightarrow \sin\alpha + \alpha = \frac{\pi}{3}$

∴ α satisfies the function

∴ $f(x) = c\left(x + \sin x - \frac{\pi}{3}\right)^n \forall c \in \mathbb{R}, n \in \mathbb{R}$

12. f: $\mathbb{R} - \{0\} \to \mathbb{R}$; $f(x) = \frac{1}{x}$

(a) $f\left(\frac{a^n}{b^n}\right) = \frac{b^n}{a^n} = \frac{\frac{1}{a^n}}{\frac{1}{b^n}} = \frac{f(a^n)}{f(b^n)}; n \in \mathbb{N}$ (True)

(b) $f(a^n + b^n) = \frac{1}{a^n - b^n} \neq \frac{1}{a^n} + \frac{1}{b^n}$

$\Rightarrow f(a^n + b^n) \neq f(a^n) + f(b^n)\ n \in \mathbb{N}$ (False)

(c) $f(a^n) = \frac{1}{a^n} = \left(\frac{1}{a}\right)^n = (f(a))^n; n \in \mathbb{N}$ (True)

(d) $f(a^n).f\left(\frac{1}{a^n}\right) = \frac{1}{a^n} \times a^n = 1;\ n \in \mathbb{N}$ (True)

TEXTUAL EXERCISE-3: (SUBJECTIVE)

1. (a) $x^3 - 6x \geq 0$ $x(x - \sqrt{6})(x + \sqrt{6}) \geq 0$

$\Rightarrow x \in [-\sqrt{6}, 0] \cup [\sqrt{6}, \infty)$

(b) $x^6 - 9x^3 + 8 > 0 \quad \Rightarrow (x^3 - 1)(x^3 - 8) > 0$

$\Rightarrow (x - 1)(x - 2)(x^2 + 1 + x)(x^2 + 4 + 2x) > 0$

$\Rightarrow (x - 1)(x - 2) > 0$

[∵ $(x^2 + x + 1)$ and $(x^2 + 4 + 2x)$ are always positive as $D < 0$ and leading co-efficient > 0]

$\Rightarrow x \in (-\infty, 1) \cup (2, \infty)$

(c) $x^4 - 2x^2 - 8 \geq 0 \quad \Rightarrow (x^2 + 2)(x^2 - 4) \geq 0$
$\Rightarrow (x^2 + 2)(x - 2)(x + 2) \geq 0$
$\Rightarrow x \in (-\infty, -2] \cup [2, \infty)$

2. (a) $(x^2 - 9)^2 (x + 1)(x^2 - 2x - 3)(x - 1) \geq 0$
$\Rightarrow (x - 3)^2 (x + 3)^2 (x + 1)(x - 1)(x - 3)(x + 1) \geq 0$
$\Rightarrow (x - 3)^3 (x + 3)^2 (x + 1)^2 (x - 1) \geq 0$
$\Rightarrow x \in (-\infty, 1] \cup [3, \infty)$

(b) $(x^2 + 3x + 1)(x^2 + 3x - 3) \geq 5$
$\Rightarrow (x^2 + 3x)^2 - 2(x^2 + 3x) - 8 \geq 0$
$\Rightarrow (x^2 + 3x - 4)(x^2 + 3x + 2) \geq 0$
$\Rightarrow (x + 4)(x - 1)(x + 1)(x + 2) \geq 0$
$\Rightarrow x \in (-\infty, -4] \cup [-2, -1] \cup [1, \infty)$

(c) $(x - 2)^2 (x - 3)(x - 4)^4 (x - 6) \geq 0$
$\Rightarrow x \in (-\infty, 3] \cup [6, \infty) \cup \{4\}$

3. (a) $y = \dfrac{1}{3x - 2}; x \in (-2, 4)$

$3x \in (-6, 12)$
$3x - 2 \in (-8, 10)$

$\Rightarrow \dfrac{1}{3x-2} \in \left(-\infty, -\dfrac{1}{8}\right) \cup \left(\dfrac{1}{10}, \infty\right)$

$y \in \left(-\infty, -\dfrac{1}{8}\right) \cup \left(\dfrac{1}{10}, \infty\right)$

(b) $y = \dfrac{x-1}{x+2}; -1 < x < 3$

$y = \dfrac{x+2-3}{x+2} = 1 - \dfrac{3}{x+2}$

$\because x \in (-1, 3)$

$\Rightarrow x + 2 \in (1, 5) \quad \Rightarrow \dfrac{1}{x+2} \in \left(\dfrac{1}{5}, 1\right)$

$\Rightarrow \dfrac{-3}{x+2} \in \left(-3, -\dfrac{3}{5}\right) \quad \Rightarrow 1 - \dfrac{3}{x+2} \in \left(-2, \dfrac{2}{5}\right)$

$\Rightarrow \dfrac{x-1}{x+2} \in \left(-2, \dfrac{2}{5}\right) \quad \Rightarrow y \in \left(-2, \dfrac{2}{5}\right)$

(c) $y = \dfrac{1}{x^2 + 4}; x \in [2, 3]$

$\Rightarrow x^2 \in [4, 9] \quad \Rightarrow x^2 + 4 \in [8, 13]$

$\Rightarrow \dfrac{1}{x^2+4} \in \left[\dfrac{1}{13}, \dfrac{1}{8}\right] \quad \Rightarrow y \in \left[\dfrac{1}{13}, \dfrac{1}{8}\right]$

(d) $y = \dfrac{x^2 - 1}{x^2 + 1}; -1 < x < 3$

$\Rightarrow y = \dfrac{x^2 + 1 - 2}{x^2 + 1} = 1 - \dfrac{2}{x^2 + 1}$

$\Rightarrow x = (-1, 3) \quad \Rightarrow x^2 \in [0, 9]$

$\Rightarrow x^2 + 1 \in [1, 10] \quad \Rightarrow \dfrac{1}{x^2+1} \in \left(\dfrac{1}{10}, 1\right]$

$\Rightarrow \dfrac{-2}{x^2+1} \in \left[-2, -\dfrac{1}{5}\right) \quad \Rightarrow 1 - \dfrac{2}{x^2+1} \in \left[-1, \dfrac{4}{5}\right)$

$\Rightarrow y \in \left[-1, \dfrac{4}{5}\right)$

4. (a) $\dfrac{(x+1)^5 (x-1)(x+4)^2 (x-3)^4}{(x+8)(2x-3)(x-6)^2} < 0$

$\Rightarrow (x + 8)(x + 4)^2 (x + 1)^5 (x - 1)(2x - 3)(x - 3)^4 (x - 6)^2 < 0$

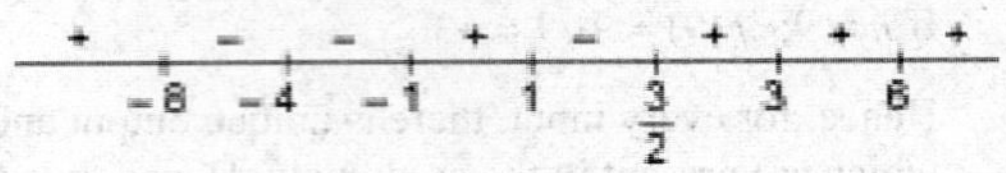

$\Rightarrow x \in (-8, -4) \cup (-4, -1) \cup \left(1, \dfrac{3}{2}\right)$

(b) $\dfrac{(x+1)(x-8)(x-6)^2 (x-5)^4}{(x-3)^2 (x-1)} < 0$

$\Rightarrow (x + 1)(x - 1)(x - 3)^2 (x - 5)^4 (x - 6)^2 (x - 8) < 0$

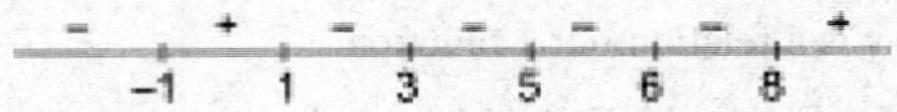

$\Rightarrow x \in (-\infty, -1) \cup (1, 3) \cup (3, 5) \cup (5, 6) \cup (6, 8)$

(c) $(x^2 - 16)(x^2 - 5x + 4)(x^2 - 1)(x + 3)(x + 2) \leq 0$
$\Rightarrow (x - 4)(x + 4)(x - 1)(x - 4)(x - 1)(x + 1)(x + 3)(x + 2) \leq 0$
$\Rightarrow (x + 4)(x + 3)(x + 2)(x + 1)(x - 1)^2 (x - 4)^2 \leq 0$

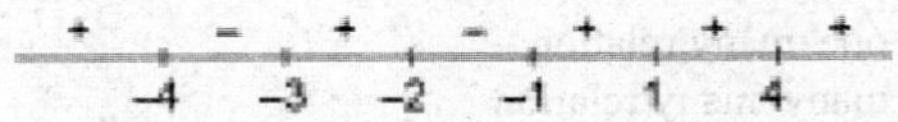

$\Rightarrow x \in [-4, -3] \cup [-2, -1]$

5. (a) $x^3 - 6x \leq 0 \Rightarrow x(x^2 - 6) \leq 0$
$\Rightarrow (x + \sqrt{6})x(x - \sqrt{6}) \leq 0$
$\Rightarrow (-\infty, -\sqrt{6}] \cup [0, \sqrt{6}]$

(b) $x^4 - 2x^2 - 8 \leq 0 \quad \Rightarrow (x^2 - 4)(x^2 + 2) \leq 0$
$\Rightarrow x \in [-2, 2]$

(c) $x^6 - 9x^3 + 8 \leq 0 \quad \Rightarrow (x^3 - 8)(x^3 - 1) \leq 0$
$\Rightarrow x \in [1, 2]$

(d) $x^4 + x^3 - x - 1 > 0 \quad \Rightarrow x^3 (x + 1) - 1 (x + 1) > 0$
$\Rightarrow (x - 1)(x^2 + x + 1)(x + 1) > 0$
$\Rightarrow x \in (-\infty, -1) \cup (1, \infty)$

(e) $(x^2 - 9)^2 (x + 1)(x^2 - 2x - 3)(x - 1) \leq 0$
$\Rightarrow x = \pm 3, (x - 1)(x - 3)(x + 1)^2 \leq 0$
$\Rightarrow x = 3, -1, (x - 1)(x - 3) \leq 0$
$\Rightarrow x \in [1, 3] \cup \{-1, -3\}$

(f) $x^2 - x - 6 \geq 0 \quad \Rightarrow (x - 3)(x + 2) \geq 0$
$\Rightarrow x \leq -2$ or $x \geq 3$; $(x^2 - 4x) \leq 0$
$\Rightarrow x \in [0, 4]$
$\Rightarrow x \in [3, 4]$

(g) $4 < x^2 < 9 \quad \Rightarrow x^2 \in (4, 9)$
$\Rightarrow x \in (-3, -2) \cup (2, 3)$

(h) $(x + 1)(x - 3)^2 (x - 5)(x - 4)^2 (x - 2) < 0$
$\Rightarrow (x + 1)(x - 2)(x - 3)^2 (x - 4)^2 (x - 5) < 0$

$\Rightarrow x \in (-\infty, -1) \cup (2, 3) \cup (3, 4) \cup (4, 5)$

(i) $(x - 3)(x + 1)(x + 2)(x - 9) \geq 0$
$\Rightarrow (x + 2)(x + 1)(x - 3)(x - 9) \geq 0$

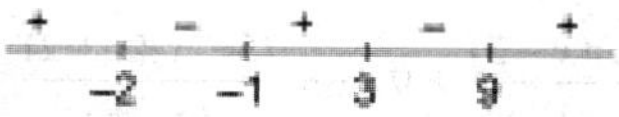

$\Rightarrow x \in (-\infty, -2) \cup [-1, 3] \cup (9, \infty)$

(j) $x^3 - 7x^2 + 14x - 8 < 0$

$\Rightarrow (x-2)(x^2 + 2x + 4) - 7x(x-2) < 0$

$\Rightarrow (x-2)(x^2 - 5x + 4) < 0$

$\Rightarrow (x-2)(x-1)(x-4) < 0$

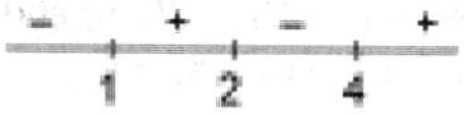

$\Rightarrow x \in (-\infty, 1) \cup (2, 4)$

(k) $\dfrac{(x-1)(x-2)(5-x)}{(2x+5)} < 0$

$\Rightarrow -(2x+5)(x-1)(x-2)(x-5) < 0$

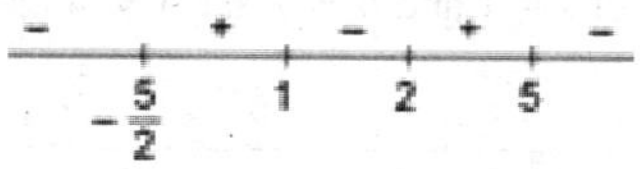

$\Rightarrow x \in \left(-\infty, -\dfrac{5}{2}\right) \cup (1,2) \cup (5,\infty)$

6. (a) $x^2 - 4x - 12 \geq 0 \Rightarrow (x-6)(x+2) \geq 0$

$\Rightarrow x \in (-\infty, -2] \cup [6, \infty)$

Largest negative integer = −2

Smallest positive integer = 6

(b) $3x^2 + 5x - 2 < 0 \Rightarrow 3x^2 + 6x - x - 2 < 0$

$\Rightarrow (3x-1)(x+2) < 0$

$\Rightarrow x \in \left(-2, \dfrac{1}{3}\right)$

Largest negative integer = −1

Smallest positive integer does not exist.

(c) $\dfrac{x^2 - 5x + 4}{x^2 - 1} \leq 1 \Rightarrow \dfrac{x^2 - 5x + 4 - x^2 + 1}{x^2 - 1} \leq 0$

$\Rightarrow \dfrac{-5(x-1)}{(x^2-1)} \leq 0 \Rightarrow \dfrac{(x-1)}{x^2-1} \geq 0$

$\Rightarrow x \in (-1, \infty) - \{1\}$

Largest negative integer does not exist.

Smallest positive integer = 2.

7. $\dfrac{x^2 - 3x + 2}{x - 3} \leq 0 \Rightarrow \dfrac{(x-1)(x-2)}{x-3} \leq 0$

$\Rightarrow x \in (-\infty, 1] \cup [2, 3)$

$\Rightarrow$ Number of positive integers satisfying the above condition = 2, i.e., 1 and 2

8. $\dfrac{x^2(x+2)}{x-1} \leq 0 \Rightarrow x = 0, -2$ or $(x-1)(x+2) < 0$

$\Rightarrow x = 0, -2$ or $x \in (-2, 1)$

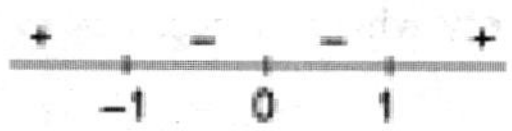

$\Rightarrow x \in [-2, 1)$

$\Rightarrow$ Number of integers satisfying the above inequality → 3

TEXTUAL EXERCISE–3: (OBJECTIVE)

1. (a) $\dfrac{x}{5} < \dfrac{3x-2}{4} - \dfrac{5x-3}{5}$

$\Rightarrow 0 < \dfrac{3x-2}{4} - \dfrac{(5x-3+x)}{5}$

$\Rightarrow \dfrac{3x-2}{4} - \dfrac{(6x-3)}{5} > 0$

$\Rightarrow \dfrac{15x - 10 - 24x + 12}{20} > 0$

$\Rightarrow \dfrac{-9x+2}{20} > 0 \Rightarrow x \in \left(-\infty, \dfrac{2}{9}\right)$

2. (c) $\dfrac{2x+3}{5} - 2 \leq \dfrac{3x-6}{5}$

$\Rightarrow 2x + 3 - 10 \leq 3x - 6 \Rightarrow x + 1 \geq 0$

$\Rightarrow x \in [-1, \infty)$

3. (b) $\dfrac{-x+3}{2} - 2 \leq \dfrac{3(x+2)}{5} \leq \dfrac{x}{6}$

$\Rightarrow \dfrac{-x+3}{2} - 2 \leq \dfrac{3x+6}{5}$ and $\dfrac{3x+6}{5} \leq \dfrac{x}{6}$

$\Rightarrow -5x + 15 - 20 \leq 6x + 12$ and $18x + 36 \leq 5x$

$\Rightarrow 11x + 17 \geq 0$ and $13x - 36 \leq 0$

$\Rightarrow x \in \left[-\dfrac{17}{11}, \infty\right)$ and $x \in \left(-\infty, -\dfrac{36}{13}\right]$

$\Rightarrow x \in \left[-\dfrac{17}{11}, \infty\right) \cap \left(-\infty, -\dfrac{36}{13}\right]$

$\Rightarrow x \in \phi$

4. (a) $x + 5 > 2x + 2$ and $2 - x < 3x + 6$

$\Rightarrow x - 3 < 0$ and $4x + 4 > 0$

$\Rightarrow x \in (-\infty, 3)$ and $x \in (-1, \infty)$

$\Rightarrow x \in (-\infty, 3) \cap (-1, \infty) \Rightarrow x \in (-1, 3)$

5. (b) $2x - 12 \leq 3x - 7$ and $11 - 2x \leq 6 - x$

$\Rightarrow x + 5 \geq 0$ and $x - 5 \geq 0$

$\Rightarrow x \in [-5, \infty)$ and $x \in [5, \infty)$

$\Rightarrow x \in [5, \infty)$

6. (c) $-9 \leq x \leq 5; y = x^3 \Rightarrow x^3 \in [-729, 125]$

7. (a) $2 < x < 5,\ y = \dfrac{1}{x} \Rightarrow \dfrac{1}{5} < \dfrac{1}{x} < \dfrac{1}{2}$

$\Rightarrow y \in \left(\dfrac{1}{5}, \dfrac{1}{2}\right)$

8. (b) $y = \dfrac{1}{x^2}; x \in (-6, 6) \Rightarrow x \in (-6, 6)\ ;\ x^2 \in (0, 36)$

$\Rightarrow \dfrac{1}{x^2} \in \left(\dfrac{1}{36}, \infty\right) \Rightarrow y \in \left(\dfrac{1}{36}, \infty\right)$

9. (a) $x^2 \in (9, 25) \Rightarrow x \in (-5, -3) \cup (3, 5)$

$\Rightarrow y \in (-5, -3) \cup (3, 5)$

10. (b) $x^2 - 3x + 2 > 0 \Rightarrow (x-1)(x-2) > 0$

$\Rightarrow x \in (-\infty, 1) \cup (2, \infty)$

11. (a) $x^2 - 3x - 4 \leq 0 \Rightarrow (x-4)(x+1) \leq 0$

$\Rightarrow x \in [-1, 4]$

12. **(b)** $x^2 - 3x + 2 < 0 \Rightarrow (x-1)(x-2) < 0$

$\Rightarrow x\ (1, 2)$

13. **(c)** $\frac{4x+3}{2x-5} \le 6 \quad \Rightarrow \quad \frac{4x+3-12x+30}{2x-5} \le 0$

$\Rightarrow \frac{-8x+33}{2x-5} \le 0$

$\Rightarrow -8x + 33 = 0$ or $(-8x + 33)(2x - 5) < 0$

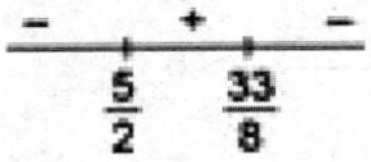

$\Rightarrow x \in \left(-\infty, \frac{5}{2}\right) \cup \left(\frac{33}{8}, \infty\right) \cup \left\{\frac{33}{8}\right\}$

$\Rightarrow x \in \left(-\infty, \frac{5}{2}\right] \cup \left[\frac{33}{8}, \infty\right)$

14. **(a)** $\frac{x}{x-5} \ge \frac{1}{2} \quad \Rightarrow \quad \frac{2x-x+5}{2(x-5)} \ge 0$

$\Rightarrow \frac{}{2(\quad 5)}$ or $x = -5$

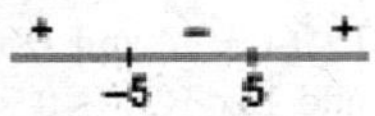

$\Rightarrow x \in (-\infty, -5) \cup (5, \infty) \cup \{-5\}$

$\Rightarrow x \in (-\infty, -5] \cup (5, \infty)$

15. **(a)** $\frac{(x-1)(x-2)(5-x)}{(2x+5)} < 0$

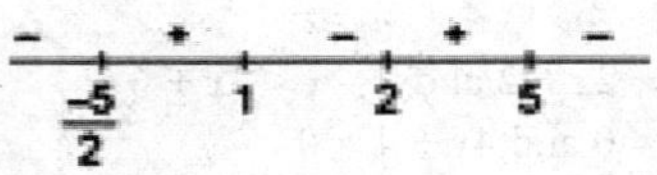

$\Rightarrow x \in \left(-\infty, -\frac{5}{2}\right) \cup (1,2) \cup (5,\infty)$

16. **(b)** $\frac{x^2-2x+5}{3x^2-2x-5} > \frac{1}{2}$

$\Rightarrow \frac{2x^2-4x+10-3x^2+2x+5}{3x^2-2x-5} > 0$

$\Rightarrow \frac{-x^2-2x+15}{3x^2-5x+3x-5} > 0$

$\Rightarrow \frac{(x+5)(x-3)}{(x+1)(3x-5)} < 0$

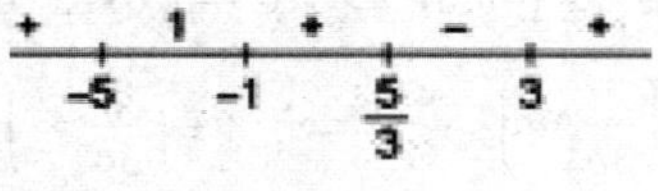

$\Rightarrow x \in (-5,-1) \cup \left(\frac{5}{3}, 3\right)$

17. **(c)** $\frac{(x-1)^2(x+1)^3}{x^4(x-2)} < 0 \quad$ or $\quad \frac{(x-1)^2(x+1)^3}{x^4(x-2)} = 0$

$\Rightarrow (x + 1)^3(x - 2) < 0$ or $x = \pm 1;\ x \ne 0, 2$

$\Rightarrow x \in (-1, 2)$ or $x = \pm 1 \Rightarrow x \in [-1, 0) \cup (0, 2)$

18. **(a)** $\frac{x(x+1)(x-3)}{(x+4)} > 0$ and $\frac{(5-x)(x+2)}{(x-8)} < 0$

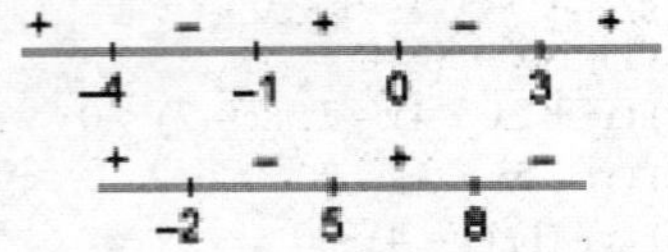

$\Rightarrow x \in (-\infty, -4) \cup (-1, 0) \cup (3, \infty)$ and $x \in (-2, 5) \cup (8, \infty)$

$\Rightarrow x \in (-1, 0) \cup (3, 5) \cup (8, \infty)$

19. **(a)** $\frac{(2x-1)(x-1)^4(x-2)^4}{(x-2)(x-4)^4} \le 0$

$\Rightarrow \frac{(2x-1)(x-1)^4(x-2)^4}{(x-2)(x-4)^4} < 0$

$\Rightarrow x = \frac{1}{2}$ or $x = 1$ and $n \ne 2$ and $x \ne 4$ or $\frac{(2x-1)}{(x-2)} < 0$

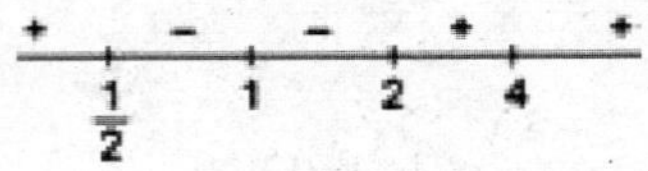

$\Rightarrow x \in \left(\frac{1}{2}, 1\right) \cup (1,2)$ or $x \in \left\{\frac{1}{2}, 1\right\}$

$\Rightarrow x \in \left[\frac{1}{2}, 2\right)$

20. **(a)** $(x - 2)^3 (x - 3) < 0 \Rightarrow \quad x \in (2, 3)$

21. **(c)** $(x - 2)^4(x - 3)^3(x - 4)^2(1 - x) < 0$ or $x \in \{2, 3, 4, 1\}$

$\Rightarrow (x - 3)^3(x - 1) > 0$ or $x \in \{1, 2, 3, 4\}$

$\Rightarrow x \in (-\infty, 1] \cup \{2\} \cup [3, \infty)$

22. **(b)** $c < d,\ x^2 + (c + d)x + cd < 0$

$\Rightarrow x(x + c) + d(x + c) < 0$

$\Rightarrow (x + c)(x + d) < 0 \quad \Rightarrow x \in (-d, -c)$

23. **(a)** $a, b, c > 0$, and $a(1 - b) > 1/4$

$\Rightarrow 0 < b < 1$

Similarly $0 < a < 1,\ 0 < c < 1$

$\Rightarrow a,\ 1 - b > 0$

By AM-GM inequality, $\frac{a+1-b}{2} \ge \sqrt{a(1-b)} > \sqrt{\frac{1}{4}}$

$\Rightarrow a + 1 - b > 1 \quad \Rightarrow a > b$

Similarly, $b > c$ and $c > a$

$\Rightarrow a > b > c > a \quad \Rightarrow a > a$, which is impossible

TEXTUAL EXERCISE–4: (SUBJECTIVE)

1. **(a)** $y = x^3 + x$

$\Rightarrow \frac{dy}{dx} = 3x^2 + 1 \ge 0\ \forall x \in \mathbb{R}$

$\therefore \frac{dy}{dx} > 0$ every where, hence, $y = x^3 + x$ increases every where.

(b) $y = x^4 - 2x^2 - 5$

$\Rightarrow \frac{dy}{dx} = 4x^3 - 4x$

$\Rightarrow\ f'(x) = 4x(x^2 - 1) = 4x\,(x - 1)\,(x + 1)$

– + – +
–1 0 1

$\Rightarrow\ f'(x) \geq 0$, i.e., $f(x)\uparrow$, when $x \in [-1, 0]$ or $[1, \infty)$ and $f'(x) \leq 0$, i.e., $f(x)\downarrow$, when $x \in (-\infty, -1]$ or $[0, 1]$.

2. $y = \sin x + \cos x;\ x \in (0, \pi)$

$$\Rightarrow\ \frac{dy}{dx} = \cos x - \sin x = \begin{cases} +ve; & x \in \left(0, \dfrac{\pi}{4}\right) \\ -ve; & x \in \left(\dfrac{\pi}{4}, \pi\right) \end{cases}$$

Hence, $f(x)\uparrow$, when $x \in \left(0, \dfrac{\pi}{4}\right)$ and $\downarrow$ when $x \in \left[\dfrac{\pi}{4}, \pi\right)$

For $x \in \left(0, \dfrac{\pi}{4}\right]$; $f(x)$ is increasing

$\Rightarrow\ f(27°) > f(23°)$

$\Rightarrow\ \sin 27° + \cos 27° > \sin 23° + \cos 23°$

$\Rightarrow\ \sin 53° + \cos 53° > \sin 23° + \cos 23°$

Hence, the given result is false.

3. $y = \dfrac{\sin x}{x}$

$$\Rightarrow\ \frac{dy}{dx} = \frac{x\cos x - \sin x}{x^2} = \frac{x\cos x\left(1 - \dfrac{\tan x}{x}\right)}{x^2}$$

$$= \frac{\cos x\left(1 - \dfrac{\tan x}{x}\right)}{x}$$

For $\left(0, \dfrac{\pi}{2}\right)$

$\Rightarrow\ \left(1 - \dfrac{\tan x}{x}\right)$ is –ve, x is +ve and $\cos x$ is +ve and

$\dfrac{dy}{dx} = -\dfrac{4}{\pi^2} < 0$

$\Rightarrow\ \dfrac{dy}{dx}$ is –ve in $\left(0, \dfrac{\pi}{2}\right]$

From $\left(\dfrac{\pi}{2}, \pi\right)$

$\Rightarrow\ 1 - \dfrac{\tan x}{x}$ is +ve, x is +ve and $\cos x$ is –ve

$\Rightarrow\ \dfrac{dy}{dx}$ is –ve over the interval $(0, \pi)$, hence, y is always decreasing

$\Rightarrow\ 0 < \alpha < \beta < \pi$

$\Rightarrow\ \dfrac{\sin\alpha}{\alpha} > \dfrac{\sin\beta}{\beta}$, hence, verified.

4. $y = 2x^3 + 3x^2 - 12x + 1$

$\Rightarrow\ \dfrac{dy}{dx} = 6x^2 + 6x - 12 = 6(x^2 + x - 2) = 6\,(x + 2)\,(x - 1)$

+ – +
–2 1

$$\Rightarrow\ \frac{dy}{dx} = \begin{cases} -ve \text{ when } x \in (-2, 1) \\ +ve \text{ when } x \in (-\infty, -2) \cup (1, \infty) \end{cases}$$

Hence, function decreases in the interval (–2, 1)

5. $y = \sqrt{2x - x^2}\ \Rightarrow\ \dfrac{dy}{dx} = \dfrac{2 - 2x}{2\sqrt{2x - x^2}} = \dfrac{1 - x}{\sqrt{2x - x^2}} > 0$ for

$x - 1 \leq 0$ and $(2 - x)x > 0$, i.e., $x \leq 1$ and $x\ (0, 2)$

$\Rightarrow\ x \in (0, 1]$

$\therefore\ f(x)\uparrow$ on (0, 1) and $\downarrow$ on (1, 2).

6. $y = \dfrac{x^2 - 1}{x}$

$$\Rightarrow\ \frac{dy}{dx} = \frac{x(2x) - (x^2 - 1)}{x^2} = \frac{2x^2 - x^2 + 1}{x^2} = \frac{x^2 + 1}{x^2} = 1 + \frac{1}{x^2}$$

$\Rightarrow\ \dfrac{dy}{dx}$ is always +ve $\forall\ x \in (-\infty, \infty) - \{0\}$, i.e., increasing on every interval not containing 0.

7. (a) $y = (x - 2)^5\,(2x + 1)^4$

$y' = 5(x - 2)^4\,(2x + 1)^4 + 8(2x + 1)^3\,(x - 2)^5$

$= (x - 2)^4\,(2x + 1)^3\,[5(2x + 1) + 8(x - 2)]$

$= (x - 2)^4\,(2x + 1)^3\,(18x - 11)$

+ – + +
$-\frac{1}{2}$ $\frac{11}{18}$ 2

$\therefore\ y\uparrow$ when $x \in \left(-\infty, -\dfrac{1}{2}\right)$ or $\left(\dfrac{11}{8}, \infty\right)$ and $y\downarrow$ when $x \in \left[-\dfrac{1}{2}, \dfrac{11}{18}\right]$

(b) $y = x - e^x \qquad \Rightarrow\ y' = 1 - e^x$

$\Rightarrow\ y\uparrow$ when $x \in (-\infty, 0]$ and $y\downarrow$ when $x \in [0, \infty)$

+ –
0

(c) $y = x^2 e^{-x}$

$\Rightarrow\ y' = 2xe^{-x} - x^2e^{-x} = xe^{-x}\,(2 - x) = x(2 - x)\,e^{-x}$

$\because\ e^{-x}$ is always +ve

$\Rightarrow$ sign of y' depends on $x(2 - x)$

– + –
0 2

$\Rightarrow\ y\uparrow$ when $x \in [0, 2]$ and $y\downarrow$ when $x \in (-\infty, 0]$ or $[2, \infty)$

(d) $y = \dfrac{x}{\ln x} \qquad \Rightarrow\ y' = \dfrac{\ln x - \dfrac{1}{x} \times x}{(\ln x)^2} = \dfrac{\ln x - 1}{(\ln x)^2}$

– – +
0 e

$\Rightarrow\ y$ when $x \in [e, \infty)$ and $y\downarrow$ when $x \in (0, e] - \{1\}$

(e) $y = x - 2\sin x;\ x \in [0, 2\pi]$

$$\Rightarrow\ y' = 1 - 2\cos x = \begin{cases} +ve & \left(\dfrac{\pi}{3}, \dfrac{5\pi}{3}\right) \\ -ve & \left(\dfrac{5\pi}{3}, 2\pi\right) \cup \left(0, \dfrac{\pi}{3}\right) \end{cases}$$

$\Rightarrow \; y\uparrow \forall x\in\left[\frac{\pi}{3},\frac{5\pi}{3}\right]$ and $y\downarrow \forall x\in\left[0,\frac{\pi}{3}\right]$ or $\left[\frac{5\pi}{3},2\pi\right]$

(f) $y = x + \cos 2x;\ x \in [0, 2\pi]$

$$\Rightarrow \quad y' = 1 - 2\sin 2x = \begin{cases} \le \text{ for } x\in\left[\frac{\pi}{12},\frac{5\pi}{12}\right] \text{ or } \left[\frac{13\pi}{12},\frac{17\pi}{12}\right]; y\downarrow \\ \ge \text{ for } x\in\left[0,\frac{\pi}{12}\right] \text{ or } \left[\frac{5\pi}{12},\frac{13\pi}{12}\right]\cup\left[\frac{17\pi}{12},2\pi\right]; y\uparrow \end{cases}$$

8. **(i)** $f(x) = 2x + 3 \quad \Rightarrow f'(x) = 2$

$\Rightarrow f(x)$ is always $\uparrow$

(ii) $f(x) = a^x \quad \Rightarrow a > 1$

$\Rightarrow f'(x) = (\ln a)\, a^x \to +\text{ve}$

$\Rightarrow f(x)$ is always $\uparrow$

(iii) $f(x) = x^3 \quad \Rightarrow f'(x) = 3x^2 \ge 0$

$\Rightarrow f(x)$ is always $\uparrow$

(iv) $f(x) = \sqrt{x} \quad \Rightarrow f'(x) = \frac{1}{2\sqrt{x}} > 0$

$\Rightarrow f(x)$ is always $\uparrow$

(v) $f(x) = \sqrt[3]{x} \Rightarrow f'(x) = \frac{1}{3(x)^{\frac{2}{3}}} > 0$. Hence, $f(x)$ is always $\uparrow$

(vi) $f(x) = \log_a x$ and $a > 1 \Rightarrow \quad f'(x) = \frac{1}{x\log_e a} > 0$

$\Rightarrow f(x)$ is always $\uparrow$

9. $f(x) = x^3 - 3x^2 + 4x \Rightarrow f'(x) = 3x^2 - 6x + 4$

$D = 36 - 48 = -12 < 0$

Since $D < 0$ and leading coefficient is +ve, and hence, $f'(x)$ is always +ve.

Hence, $f(x)$ is strictly increasing in its domain.

10. **(a)** $f(x) = \sin 3x;\ x\in\left[0,\frac{\pi}{2}\right]$

$\Rightarrow f'(x) = 3\cos 3x \ge 0$ for $x\in\left[0,\frac{\pi}{6}\right]$

(b) $f(x) = (x + 1)^3(x - 3)^3 = (x^2 - 2x - 3)^3$

$\Rightarrow f(x) = 3(2x - 2)(x^2 - 2x - 3)^3$

$\therefore \; f'(x) \ge 0$ for $(x - 1) \ge 0$ or $x = -1, 3$

$\Rightarrow f(x)\uparrow$ for $x \in [1, \infty)$

(c) $f(x) = 2x^2 - 3x$

$\Rightarrow f'(x) = 4x - 3 \ge 0$ for $x\in\left[\frac{3}{4},\infty\right)$

TEXTUAL EXERCISE–4: (OBJECTIVE)

1. **(b)** **(i)** $f(x) = \ln(x + \sqrt{x^2+1})$

$\Rightarrow \quad f'(x) = \frac{1}{\sqrt{x^2+1}} > 0 \forall x\in\mathbb{R}$

$\Rightarrow$ (i)$\to$(a)

(ii) $f(x) = a^x,\ a > 1 \quad \Rightarrow f'(x) = a^x \ln a > 0\ \forall\ a > 1$

$\Rightarrow$ (ii)$\to$(a)

(iii) $f(x) = x^3 + x \quad \Rightarrow f'(x) = 3x^2 + 1 > 0$

$\Rightarrow$ (iii)$\to$(a)

(iv) $f(x) = \tan x \quad \Rightarrow f'(x) = \sec^2 x > 0$

$\Rightarrow$ (iv)$\to$(a)

(v) $f(x) = x^2 - 1 \quad \Rightarrow f'(x) = 2x$

$\Rightarrow f(x)\uparrow$ for $x > 0$ and $f(x)\downarrow$ for $x < 0$

$\Rightarrow$ Non-monotonic $\quad \Rightarrow$ (v)$\to$(e)

(vi) $f(x) = \cot x \quad \Rightarrow f'(x) = -\text{cosec}^2 x < 0$

$\Rightarrow f(x)\downarrow \quad \Rightarrow$ (vi)$\to$(b)

2. **(b), (c)** $f(x) = x^2 (x - 2)^2$

$\Rightarrow f'(x) = 2x (x - 2)^2 + 2x^2 (x - 2) = 2x (x - 2) (x - 2 + x)$

$= 4x (x - 2) (x - 1)$

$\Rightarrow f(x)\uparrow$ when $x \in (0, 1) \cup (2, \infty)$ and $f(x)\downarrow$ when $x \in (-\infty, 0) \cup (1, 2)$

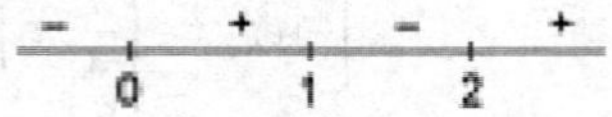

3. **(b), (c)** $f(x) = \ln(1+x) - \frac{2x}{2+x}$

$D_f = (-1,\infty)$ and $f'(x) = \frac{1}{(1+x)} - \frac{[(2+x)(2)-2x]}{(2+x)^2}$

$= \frac{1}{(1+x)} - \frac{2}{(x+2)^2} = \frac{x^2+2x+2}{(x+1)(x+2)^2} > 0$ on $(-1, \infty)$

$\Rightarrow f(x)$ is M.I. on its domain.

4. **(a)** $x - \sin x = y \quad \Rightarrow \quad \frac{dy}{dx} = 1 - \cos x$

$\Rightarrow \quad \frac{dy}{dx} \ge 0\ \forall x\in\mathbb{R}$

$\Rightarrow$ $x - \sin x$ is increasing for all real numbers.

5. **(c)** $y = \log \sin x \quad \Rightarrow \quad \frac{dy}{dx} = \frac{1}{\sin x}\times\cos x = \cot x$

$\Rightarrow \quad \frac{dy}{dx}$ is +ve when $x\in\left(0,\frac{\pi}{2}\right)$ and is –ve when $x\in\left(\frac{\pi}{2},\pi\right)$

Therefore, log sin x is increasing in $\left(0,\frac{\pi}{2}\right)$ and decreasing in $\left(\frac{\pi}{2},\pi\right)$

6. **(a), (b)** $y = a^{kx} - a^{-kx}\ \forall\ a > 1$

$\Rightarrow f'(x) = ka^{kx}\ln a + ka^{-kx}\ln a = (k \ln a)\,(a^{kx} + a^{-kx})$

$\Rightarrow f'(x) \ge 0$ for $k \ln a \ge 0$ for $k \ge 0$ and $f'(x) \le 0$ for $k \le 0$

$\Rightarrow f(x)\uparrow$ for $k > 0$ and $\downarrow$ for $k < 0$

7. **(a)** $y = \sin(\cos x);\ x\in [\pi, 2\pi]$

$\frac{dy}{dx} = \cos(\cos x)\times(-\sin x) = -\sin x\cos(\cos x)$

In $[\pi, 2\pi]$, $\sin x < 0$ and $\cos x \in [-1, 1]$

Therefore, $\cos(\cos x) > 0$.

$\Rightarrow \quad \frac{dy}{dx} > 0$

Therefore, sin (cos x) is increasing in $[\pi, 2\pi]$

8. **(b)** $f(x) = \cos(\sin x)$

$\Rightarrow f'(x) = -\cos x.\sin(\sin x) < 0$ for $x\ (0, /2)$

9. **(d)** (a) $\because f(x) = a^x$ for $a > 1$ is an increasing function

$\Rightarrow x^1 < x^2 < x^3 < x^4 < \ldots$ for $x \in(1, \infty)$

$\Rightarrow$ correct order given.

(b) ∵ $f(x) = a^x$ for $0 < a < 1$ is a decreasing function.
⇒ $x > x^2 > x^3 > x^4 > ....$ for $x \in (0, 1)$
⇒ correct order given
(c) ∵ for $x \in (0, 1)$
⇒ $x > x^2 > x^3 > x^4 > x^5 > .....$
⇒ $x > x^3 > x^5 > ......$
⇒ $-x < -x^3 < -x^5 < ......$
⇒ $y < y^3 < y^5....$ for $y \in (-1, 0)$; $y = -x$
Also, for $x \in (0, 1)$, $x^2 > x^4 > x^6 > ......$
⇒ $(-x)^2 > (-x)^4 > (-x)^6 > ......$
⇒ $y^2 > y^4 > y^6 > ...$ for $y \in (-1, 0)$
⇒ correct order given
(d) ∵ for $x \in (1, \infty)$
⇒ $x < x^2 < x^3 < x^4 < .....$
⇒ $x < x^3 < x^5 < ......$
⇒ $-x > -x^3 > -x^5 > ......$
⇒ $y > y^3 > y^5 > ....$ for $y \in (-\infty, -1)$
Also, for $x \in (1, \infty)$, $x^2 < x^4 < x^6 < ......$
⇒ $(-x)^2 < (-x)^4 < (-x)^6 < ......$
⇒ $y^2 < y^4 < y^6 < ...$ for $y \in (-\infty, -1)$
⇒ Incorrect order given

10. **(c)** (a) For a $\in (0, 1)$, $a^x \downarrow$
⇒ $x > x^2 > x^3 > .....$ for $x \in (0, 1)$
⇒ $\left(\frac{1}{x}\right) > \left(\frac{1}{x}\right)^2 > \left(\frac{1}{x}\right)^3 > ....$ for $x \in (1, \infty)$
⇒ Correct sequence.
(b) For $a \in (1, \infty)$, $a^x \uparrow$
⇒ $x < x^2 < x^3 < ....$ for $x \in (0, 1)$
⇒ $\left(\frac{1}{x}\right) < \left(\frac{1}{x}\right)^2 < \left(\frac{1}{x}\right)^3 < ....$ for $x \in (0, 1)$
⇒ Correct sequence.
(c) For $x \in (0, 1)$
$\frac{1}{x} < \frac{1}{x^2} < \frac{1}{x^3} < ....$(By part(b))
⇒ $\frac{1}{x^2} < \frac{1}{x^4} < \frac{1}{x^6} < ....$ for $x \in (0, 1)$
⇒ $\left(\frac{-1}{x}\right)^2 < \left(\frac{-1}{x}\right)^4 < \left(\frac{-1}{x}\right)^6 < ....$ for $x \in (-1, 0)$
⇒ $\frac{1}{x^2} < \frac{1}{x^4} < \frac{1}{x^6} < ....$ for $x \in (-1, 0)$
Also $\frac{1}{x} < \frac{1}{x^3} < \frac{1}{x^5} < ...$ for $x \in (0, 1)$
⇒ $\left(\frac{-1}{x}\right) < \left(\frac{-1}{x^3}\right) < \left(\frac{-1}{x^5}\right) < ...$ for $x \in (-1, 0)$
⇒ $\frac{1}{x} > \frac{1}{x^3} > \frac{1}{x^5} > .....$ for $x \in (-1, 0)$
⇒ In correct sequence.
(d) for $x \in (1, \infty)$,
$\frac{1}{x} > \frac{1}{x^2} > \frac{1}{x^3} > ......$ (By) part(a))
⇒ $\frac{1}{x^2} > \frac{1}{x^4} > \frac{1}{x^6} > .....$ for $x \in (1, \infty)$
⇒ $\left(\frac{1}{-x}\right)^2 > \left(\frac{1}{-x}\right)^4 > \left(\frac{1}{-x}\right)^6 > ....$ for $x \in (-, -1)$
⇒ $\frac{1}{x^2} > \frac{1}{x^4} > \frac{1}{x^6} > .....$ for $x \in (-\infty, -1)$
Also $\frac{1}{x} > \frac{1}{x^3} > \frac{1}{x^5} > ...$ for $x \in (1, \infty)$
⇒ $\frac{1}{-x} > \frac{1}{(-x)^3} > \frac{1}{(-x)^5} > .....$ for $x \in (-\infty, -1)$
⇒ $\frac{1}{x} < \frac{1}{x^3} < \frac{1}{x^5} < ......$ for $x \in (-\infty, -1)$
⇒ Correct sequence

11. **(d)** (a) ∵ for $a \in (1, \infty)$, $a^x \uparrow$
⇒ $x^{1/2} > x^{1/3} > x^{1/4} ...$ for $x \in (1, \infty)$
⇒ Correct sequence.
(b) ∵ for $a \in (0, 1)$, $a^x \downarrow$
$x^{1/2} < x^{1/3} < x^{1/4} < ...$ for $x \in (0, 1)$
⇒ Correct sequence.
(c) By part (b), $x^{1/2} < x^{1/3}$, $x^{1/4} < x^{1/5} < ...$ for $x \in (0, 1)$
⇒ $x^{1/3} < x^{1/5} < x^{1/7} < .....$ for $x \in (0, 1)$
⇒ $(-x)^{1/3} < (-x)^{1/5} < (-x)^{1/7} < ...$ for $x \in (-1, 0)$
⇒ $x^{1/3} > x^{1/5} > x^{1/7} > ...$ for $x \in (-1, 0)$
⇒ Correct sequence.
(d) By part(a), $x^{1/2} > x^{1/3} > x^{1/4} > ....$ for $x \in (1, \infty)$
$x^{1/3} > x^{1/5} > x^{1/7} > ...$ for $x \in (1, \infty)$
⇒ $(-x)^{1/3} > (-x)^{1/5} > (-x)^{1/7} > ....$ for $x \in (-\infty, -1)$
⇒ $x^{1/3} < x^{1/5} < x^{1/7} < .....$ for $x \in (-\infty, -1)$
⇒ In correct sequence.

12. **(b), (c)** $y = \frac{e^{2x}-1}{e^{2x}+1}$
⇒ $\frac{dy}{dx} = \frac{2(e^{2x}+1)e^{2x} - 2e^{2x}(e^{2x}-1)}{(e^{2x}+1)^2}$
$= \frac{4e^{2x}}{(e^{2x}+1)^2} > 0 \ \forall x \in \mathbb{R}$
⇒ $\frac{e^{2x}-1}{e^{2x}+1}$ is increasing $\forall x \in \mathbb{R}$
⇒ $f(x) = \frac{e^{2x}-1}{e^{2x}+1}$
⇒ $f(-x) = \frac{e^{-2x}-1}{e^{-2x}+1} = \frac{1-e^{2x}}{1-e^{2x}} = -\left(\frac{e^{2x}-1}{e^{2x}+1}\right) = -f(x)$
Hence, $\frac{e^{2x}-1}{e^{2x}+1}$ is odd

TEXTUAL EXERCISE-5: (SUBJECTIVE)

1. **(a)** $|x| = 5$ ⇒ $x = 5$ or $x = -5$. Hence, $x \in \{5, -5\}$
(b) $|x| = -2$ never possible as modulus of a number cannot be –ve. Hence, $x \in \{\}$.
(c) $x + |x| = 0$ ⇒ $|x| = -x$
As modulus of a number is always non-negative, hence, x is always –non positive, hence, $x \in (-\infty, 0]$.

(d) $x + |x| = 2x \Rightarrow |x| = x$
$\Rightarrow x \in [0, \infty)$

(e) $\frac{x}{|x|} = -1 \Rightarrow x \neq 0$
$\Rightarrow x = -|x| \Rightarrow |x| = -x$
$\Rightarrow x \in (-\infty, 0]$ and $x \neq 0$
$\Rightarrow x \in (-\infty, 0)$

(f) $3x\sqrt{2} = \sqrt{18x^2} = 3\sqrt{2}\,|x|$
$\Rightarrow x = |x| \Rightarrow x \in [0, \infty)$

(g) $x|x| - x^2 = 0 \Rightarrow x(|x| - x) = 0$
$\Rightarrow x = 0$ or $|x| = x \Rightarrow x \in [0, \infty)$

(h) $|x| < -x$, never possible
$\Rightarrow x \in \phi$

2. (a) $|x| + x^2 + 1 = 0; \quad \because |x| \geq 0, x^2 \geq 0$
$\Rightarrow x^2 + |x| \geq 0$
$\Rightarrow x^2 + |x| \neq -1$, hence, $x \in \{\}$

(b) $|5x^2 - 3| = 2 \Rightarrow 5x^2 - 3 = 2$ or $5x^2 - 3 = -2$
$\Rightarrow 5x^2 = 5$ or $5x^2 = 1 \Rightarrow x^2 = 1$ or $x^2 = \frac{1}{5}$
$\Rightarrow x = \pm 1$ or $x = \pm\frac{1}{\sqrt{5}} \Rightarrow x \in \left\{\frac{1}{\sqrt{5}}, \frac{-1}{\sqrt{5}}, 1, -1\right\}$

(c) $\left|\frac{x+4}{x+2}\right| = 3 \Rightarrow \frac{x+4}{x+2} = 3$ or $\frac{x+4}{x+2} = -3$
$\Rightarrow \frac{x+4-3x-6}{x+2} = 0$ or $\frac{x+4+3x+6}{x+2} = 0$
$\Rightarrow \frac{-2x-2}{x+2} = 0$ or $\frac{4x+10}{x+2} = 0$
$\Rightarrow x = -1$ or $x = -\frac{5}{2}$
$\Rightarrow x \in \left\{-1, -\frac{5}{2}\right\}$

(d) $|x^2 - 4x| = 5 \Rightarrow x^2 - 4x = 5$ or $x^2 - 4x = -5$
$\Rightarrow x^2 - 4x - 5 = 0$ or $x^2 - 4x + 5 = 0$
$\Rightarrow (x - 5)(x + 1) = 0$ or $x^2 - 4x + 5 = 0$
$\Rightarrow x = 5$ or $x = -1$ or $x^2 - 4x + 5 = 0$
$\Rightarrow D = 16 - 20 = -4$.
Hence, no real roots, $x \in \{5, -1\}$

(e) $|x + 1| + 2 = 2 \Rightarrow |x + 1| = 0$
$\Rightarrow x = -1$

(f) $|3x - 4| = \frac{1}{2} \Rightarrow 3x - 4 = \frac{1}{2}$ or $3x - 4 = -\frac{1}{2}$
$\Rightarrow x = \frac{3}{2}$ or $x = \frac{7}{6} \Rightarrow x \in \left\{\frac{3}{2}, \frac{7}{6}\right\}$

(g) $|x + 2| = 2(3 - x)$ and $3 - x > 0$
$\Rightarrow x < 3$
$\Rightarrow x + 2 = 2(3 - x)$ or $-x - 2 = 2(3 - x)$
$\Rightarrow x + 2 = 6 - 2x$ or $-x - 2 = 6 - 2x$
$\Rightarrow x = \frac{4}{3}$ or $\Rightarrow x = 8$ but $x < 3$
$\Rightarrow x = \frac{4}{3}$

(h) $|x| = -3x - 5 \Rightarrow -3x - 5 \geq 0$
$\Rightarrow -5 \geq 3x$
$\Rightarrow -\frac{5}{3} \geq x \Rightarrow x \in \left(-\infty, -\frac{5}{3}\right]$
$\Rightarrow |x| = -x \quad (\because x < 0)$
$\Rightarrow -x = -3x - 5 \Rightarrow 2x = -5$
$\Rightarrow x = -\frac{5}{2}$

(i) $x^2 + |x - 1| = 1; |x - 1| = 1 - x^2; 1 - x^2 \geq 0$
$\Rightarrow x \in [-1, 1] \Rightarrow x - 1 \leq 0$
$\Rightarrow -x + 1 = 1 - x^2 \Rightarrow x^2 - x = 0$
$\Rightarrow x(x - 1) = 0 \Rightarrow x = 0$ or $x = 1$
$\Rightarrow x \in \{0, 1\}$

3. $\sqrt{x^2 - 2x + 1} - \sqrt{x^2 + 2x + 1} = \sqrt{(x-1)^2} - \sqrt{(x+1)^2}$
$= |x - 1| - |x + 1|$

Case (i): $x \leq -1 \Rightarrow x - 1 \leq -2$ and $x + 1 \leq 0$
$\Rightarrow |x - 1| = -(x - 1)$ and $|x + 1| = -(x + 1)$
$\Rightarrow \sqrt{x^2 - 2x + 1} - \sqrt{x^2 + 2x + 1} = |x - 1| - |x + 1| = -x + 1 + x + 1 = 2$

Case (ii): $x \in (-1, 1)$; $x - 1 \in (-2, 0)$ and $x + 1 \in (0, 2)$
$\Rightarrow |x - 1| = 1 - x$ and $|x + 1| = x + 1$
$\Rightarrow \sqrt{x^2 - 2x + 1} - \sqrt{x^2 + 2x + 1} = |x - 1| - |x + 1| = 1 - x - x - 1 = -2x$

Case (iii): $x \geq 1 \Rightarrow x - 1 \geq 0$ and $x + 1 \geq 2$
$\Rightarrow |x - 1| = x - 1$ and $|x + 1| = x + 1$
$\Rightarrow \sqrt{x^2 - 2x + 1} - \sqrt{x^2 + 2x + 1} = x - 1 - (x + 1) = -2$

4. (a) $|x| > 2 \Rightarrow x > 2$ or $-x > 2$
$\Rightarrow x \in (2, \infty)$ or $x \in (-\infty, -2)$
$\Rightarrow x \in (-\infty, -2) \cup (2, \infty)$

(b) $|x - 1| > 3 \Rightarrow x - 1 > 3$ or $-x + 1 > 3$
$\Rightarrow x > 4$ or $-2 > x \Rightarrow x \in (-\infty, -2) \cup (4, \infty)$

(c) $|x - 2| < 1 \Rightarrow 0 \leq x - 2 < 1$ or $0 \leq -x + 2 < 1$
$\Rightarrow x \in [2, 3)$ or $x \in (1, 2]$
$\Rightarrow x \in (1, 3)$

(d) $|x + 1| \geq 2 \Rightarrow x + 1 \geq 2$ or $-x - 1 \geq 2$
$\Rightarrow x \geq 1$ or $x \leq -3 \Rightarrow x \in (-\infty, -3] \cup [1, \infty)$

(e) $|x - 1| < 5 \Rightarrow 0 \leq x - 1 < 5$ or $0 \leq 1 - x < 5$
$\Rightarrow x \in [1, 6)$ or $x \in (-4, 1]$
$\Rightarrow x \in (-4, 6)$

5. (a) $|x - 1| + |x - 3| = 2$

Case: (i) Let $x \in (-\infty, 1]$, then $1 - x + 3 - x = 2$
$\Rightarrow 2 = 2x \Rightarrow x = 1$

Case: (ii) Let $x \in (1, 3]$, then $x - 1 + 3 - x = 2$
$\Rightarrow 2 = 2$ true for all $x \in (1, 3]$

Case: (iii) Let $x \in (3, \infty)$, then $x - 1 + x - 3 = 2$
$\Rightarrow x = 3$, but $x \in (3, \infty)$, hence, no $x \in (3, \infty)$ satisfies the equation.

Hence, solution of equation is $x \in [1, 3]$

(b) $|x| + |x + 5| = 5$. Let $y = |x| + |x + 5| = f(x)$, then $ABOC$ represents the graph of $y = f(x)$ as shown below:

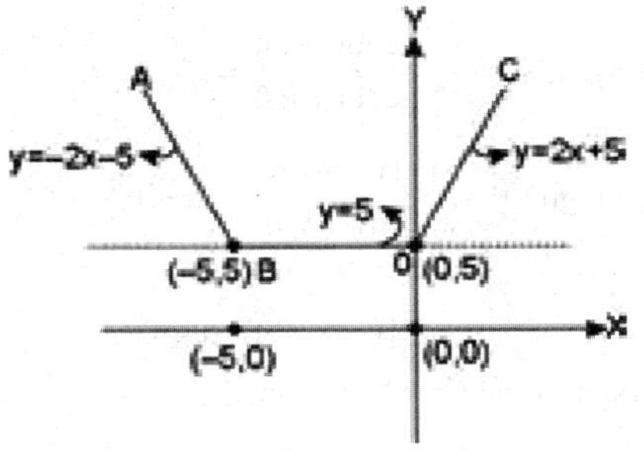

$\therefore$ $y = 5$ holds from B to 0

$\Rightarrow$ $x \in [-5, 0]$

Hence, solution of equation is $x \in [-5, 0]$

(c) $|x - 1| + |x - 4| = 2$

Case: (i) Let $x \in (-\infty, 1]$

$\Rightarrow$ $|x - 1| + |x - 4| = 1 - x + 4 - x = 5 - 2x$

$\Rightarrow$ $5 - 2x = 2$ $\Rightarrow$ $\frac{3}{2} = x$, but $\frac{3}{2} \notin (-\infty, 1]$

$\Rightarrow$ No solution in this case.

Case: (ii) Let $x \in (1, 4]$

$\Rightarrow$ $|x - 1| + |x - 4| = x - 1 + 4 - x = 3 \neq 2$

Hence, no $x \in (1, 4]$ satisfies the equation.

Case: (iii) Let $x \in [4, \infty)$

$\Rightarrow$ $|x - 1| + |x - 4| = 2x - 5$

$\Rightarrow$ $2x - 5 = 2$ $\Rightarrow$ $x = \frac{7}{2}$, but $\frac{7}{2} \notin [4, \infty)$

$\Rightarrow$ No solution in this case.

Hence, there is no solution to the equation.

$\Rightarrow$ $x \in \phi$

(d) $|x^2 - 2x| + |x - 4| = |x^2 - 3x + 4|$

$\Rightarrow$ $|x(x - 2)| + |x - 4| = x^2 - 3x + 4$

($|x^2 - 3x + 4| = x^2 - 3x + 4$ as leading coefficient is +ve and $D < 0$, so, the value of quadratic will always be +ve)

Case: (i) Let $x \in (-\infty, 0]$

$\Rightarrow$ $x^2 - 2x + 4 - x = x^2 - 3x + 4$

$\Rightarrow$ $4 = 4$

Hence, true $\forall\, x \in (-\infty, 0]$

Case: (ii) Let $x \in (0, 2]$

$\Rightarrow$ $2x - x^2 + 4 - x = x^2 - 3x + 4$

$\Rightarrow$ $4x = 2x^2$

$\Rightarrow$ $x = 0$ or $x = 2$

$\Rightarrow$ $x = 2$ (By case condition)

Case: (iii) Let $x \in (2, 4]$

$\Rightarrow$ $x^2 - 2x + 4 - x = x^2 - 3x + 4$

$\Rightarrow$ $4 = 4$

$\Rightarrow$ True for all $x \in (2, 4]$.

Case: (iv) Let $x \in (4, \infty)$

$\Rightarrow$ $x^2 - 2x + x - 4 = x^2 - 3x + 4$

$\Rightarrow$ $x = 4 \notin (4, \infty)$

Hence, solution of the equation is $x \in (-\infty, 0] \cup [2, 4]$

(e) $|x^2 - 2x| + |x - 4| < |(x^2 - 2x) - (x - 4)|$

$$\begin{bmatrix} \because & |a \pm b| \le |a| + |b| \\ \Rightarrow & |a| + |b| \not\le |a \pm b| \end{bmatrix}$$

6. $\sqrt{9 - 6a + a^2} + \sqrt{9 + 6a + a^2} = \sqrt{(a-3)^2} + \sqrt{(a+3)^2}$

$= |a - 3| + |a + 3|$; $a < -3$

$\Rightarrow$ $|a - 3| = 3 - a$ and $|a + 3| = -3 - a$

$\Rightarrow$ $\sqrt{9 - 6a + a^2} + \sqrt{9 + 6a + a^2} = |a - 3| + |a + 3| = 3 - a - 3 - a = -2a$

7. (a) $f(x) = \operatorname{cosec} x$; $D_f = \mathbb{R} - \{n\pi;\, n \in \mathbb{Z}\}$; $R_f = (-\infty, -1] \cup [1, \infty)$

$g(x) = \frac{1}{\sin x}$; $D_f = \mathbb{R} - \{n\pi;\, n \in \mathbb{Z}\}$; $R_f = (-\infty, -1] \cup [1, \infty)$

$\Rightarrow$ $f(x)$ and $g(x)$ are identical

(b) $f(x) = \tan x$; $D_f = \mathbb{R} - \{(2n + 1)\frac{\pi}{2}\}$; $R_f = (-\infty, \infty)$

$g(x) = \frac{1}{\cot x}$; $D_f = \mathbb{R} - \{n\pi, (2n + 1)\frac{\pi}{2};\, n \in \mathbb{Z}\}$; $R_f = (-\infty, \infty)$

$\Rightarrow$ $f(x)$ and $g(x)$ are non-identical.

(c) $f(x) = \ln e^x$; $D_f = \mathbb{R}$ and $R_f = (-\infty, \infty)$; $g(x) = x$; $D_f = \mathbb{R}$ and $R_f = (-\infty, \infty)$ and $f(x) = g(x)$

$\Rightarrow$ Identical.

(d) $f(x) = \sec x$

$= \frac{1}{\cos x} = g(x)$ and $D_f = D_g = 1$

$= \mathbb{R} - \{(2n + 1)\frac{\pi}{2};\, n \in \mathbb{Z}\}$ and $R_f = R_g = \mathbb{R} - (-1, 1)$

8. (a) $f(x) = \ln x$ and $g(x) = \frac{1}{\log_x e}$

$$\Rightarrow \quad f(x) = \begin{cases} \ln x & \forall x \in (0, \infty) \\ \text{not deifined} & \forall x \in (-\infty, 0] \end{cases}$$

$$\Rightarrow \quad g(x) = \begin{cases} \ln x & x \in (0, \infty) \sim (1) \\ \text{not defined} & \forall x \in (-\infty, 0] \cup \{1\} \end{cases}$$

Hence, $f(x)$ and $g(x)$ are not identical as they don't have common natural domain.

(b) $f(x) = \sqrt{x^2 - 1}$ and $g(x) = \sqrt{x - 1}\sqrt{x + 1}$

$$\Rightarrow \quad f(x) = \begin{cases} \sqrt{x^2 - 1} & \text{if } x \in (-\infty, -1] \cup [1, \infty) \\ \text{not defined} & \text{if } x \in (-1, 1) \end{cases}$$

$$\Rightarrow \quad g(x) = \begin{cases} \sqrt{x - 1}\,\sqrt{x + 1} & \text{if } x \in [1, \infty) \\ \text{not defined} & \text{if } x \in (-\infty, 1) \end{cases}$$

Hence, $f(x)$ and $g(x)$ are not identical as they don't have common natural domain.

(c) $f(x) = \sqrt{1 - x^2}$ and $g(x) = \sqrt{1 - x}\sqrt{1 + x}$

$$\Rightarrow \quad f(x) = \begin{cases} \sqrt{1 - x^2} & \text{if } x \in [-1, 1] \\ \text{not defined} & \text{if } x \in (-\infty, -1) \cup (1, \infty) \end{cases}$$

$$\Rightarrow \quad g(x) = \begin{cases} \sqrt{1 - x}\sqrt{1 + x} & \text{if } x \in [-1, 1] \\ \text{not defined} & \text{if } x \in (-\infty, -1) \cup (1, \infty) \end{cases}$$

$\Rightarrow$ $f(x)$ and $g(x)$ have same analytical formula and hence, same natural domain $[-1, 1]$, hence, are identical.

9. (i) $\operatorname{sgn}(x^2 + 2) = 1$ $\Rightarrow$ $x^2 + 2 > 0$, true $\forall\, x \in \mathbb{R}$

(ii) $\operatorname{sgn}(x^2 + 2) = -1$

$\Rightarrow$ $x^2 + 2 < 0$, not true for any $x \in \mathbb{R}$

Hence, $x \in \phi$

(iii) sgn $(x^2 - 9)$ + sgn $(x + 3) = 0$

Case: (a) $x^2 - 9 = 0$ and $x + 3 = 0$

$\Rightarrow$ $(x - 3)(x + 3) = 0$ and $x = -3$

$\Rightarrow$ $x = 3, -3$ and $x = -3$

$\Rightarrow$ $x = -3$

Case: (b) $x^2 - 9 > 0$ and $x + 3 < 0$

$\Rightarrow$ $x \in (-\infty, -3) \cup (3, \infty)$ and $x \in (-\infty, -3)$

$\Rightarrow$ $x \in (-\infty, -3)$

Case: (c) $x^2 - 9 < 0$ and $x + 3 > 0$

$\Rightarrow$ $x \in (-3, 3)$ and $x \in (-3, \infty)$

$\Rightarrow$ $x \in (-3, 3)$

Therefore, all $x \in (-\infty, 3)$ satisfies above equation.

(iv) $|\text{sgn}(x - 1)| = 1$

Case: (a) sgn $(x - 1) = 1$

$\Rightarrow$ $x - 1 > 0 \Rightarrow x \in (1, \infty)$

Case: (b) sgn $(x - 1) = -1$

$\Rightarrow$ $x - 1 < 0$ $\Rightarrow$ $x \in (-\infty, 1)$

$\Rightarrow$ $x \in \mathbb{R} \sim \{1\}$

10. (i) $|x - 5| \geq 2 \Rightarrow x - 5 \leq -2$ or $x - 5 \geq 2$

$\Rightarrow$ $x \leq 3$ or $x \geq 7$ $\Rightarrow$ $x \in (-\infty, 3] \cup [7, \infty)$

(ii) $|\text{sgn}(x - 5)| > 0$ $\Rightarrow$ $(x - 5) \neq 0$

$\Rightarrow$ $x \neq 5$ $\Rightarrow$ $x \in \mathbb{R} - \{5\}$

(iii) sgn $[\tan^{-1} x] = 1$ $\Rightarrow$ $\tan^{-1} x > 0$

$\Rightarrow$ $x \in (0, \infty)$

TEXTUAL EXERCISE–5: (OBJECTIVE)

1. (a) $\sqrt{2-|x|} + \sqrt{1+|x|}$ is defined when $2 - |x| > 0$ and $1 + |x| > 0$

$\Rightarrow$ $|x| \leq 2$ and $|x| \geq -1$ $\Rightarrow$ $x \in [-2, 2]$ and $x \in \mathbb{R}$

$\Rightarrow$ $x \in [-2, 2]$

2. (a) $f(x) = \sqrt{x^2 - |x| - 2}$ is defined when $|x|^2 - |x| - 2 \geq 0$

$(|x|^2 - |x| - 2) \geq 0$ $\Rightarrow$ $(|x| - 2)(|x| + 1) \geq 0$

$\Rightarrow$ $|x| \in (-\infty, -1] \cup [2, \infty)$

But $|x| \geq 0$

$\Rightarrow$ $|x| \in [2, \infty)$ $\Rightarrow$ $x \in (-\infty, -2] \cup [2, \infty)$

$\Rightarrow$ $x \in \mathbb{R} \sim (-2, 2)$

3. (b) $f(x) = |x - 1| + |x - 2|$; $-1 \leq x \leq 3$

Case: (i) when $x \in [-1, 1]$, then $f(x) = 1 - x + 2 - x = 3 - 2x$

$\Rightarrow$ $x \in [-1, 1]$ $\Rightarrow$ $-2x \in [-2, 2]$

$\Rightarrow$ $3 - 2x \in [1, 5]$

Case: (ii) when $x \in (1, 2]$, then $f(x) = x - 1 + 2 - x = 1$

Case: (iii) when $x \in (2, 3]$, then $f(x) = x - 1 + x - 2 = 2x - 3$

$\Rightarrow$ $x \in (2, 3]$

$\Rightarrow$ $2x - 3 \in (1, 3]$

$\Rightarrow$ Range of $f(x)$ when $x \in [-1, 3]$ is $[1, 5]$

4. (d) (a) $x \text{ sgn } x = \begin{cases} -x \text{ for } x < 0 \\ x \text{ for } x \geq 0 \end{cases} = |x|$

(b) $|x| \text{ sgn} = \begin{cases} -|x| \text{ for } x < 0 \\ |x| \text{ for } x \geq 0 \end{cases} = \{x \forall x \in \mathbb{R}$

(c) $x(\text{sgn})(\text{sgn}) = \begin{cases} x \text{ for } x < 0 \\ x \text{ for } x \geq 0 \end{cases} = x \forall x \in \mathbb{R}$

(d) $|x| (\text{sgn } x)^3 = \begin{cases} -|x| \text{ for } x < 0 \\ |x| \text{ for } x \geq 0 \end{cases} = x \neq |x|$

5. (a) $\{(\text{sgn } x)^{\text{sgn } x}\}^n = \begin{cases} \left((-1)^{-1}\right)^n \text{ for } x < 0 \\ \text{Not defined at } x = 0 \\ \left((1)^1\right)^n \text{ for } x > 0 \end{cases}$

$= \begin{cases} -1 \text{ for } x < 0 \\ \text{Not defined at } x = 0 \\ 1 \text{ for } x > 0 \end{cases}$

$\Rightarrow$ $f(x)$ is an odd function

6. (d) $f(x) = \left(\dfrac{x}{1-|x|}\right)^{\frac{1}{2001}}$ $\Rightarrow$ $|x| \neq 1$

$\Rightarrow$ $x \neq 1, -1$ $\Rightarrow$ $x \in \mathbb{R} \sim \{1, -1\}$

7. (c) $f(x) = \left(\dfrac{x}{1-|x|}\right)^{\frac{1}{2002}}$ $\Rightarrow$ $|x| \neq 1$

and $\dfrac{x}{1-|x|} \geq 0$

Case (i): $x \geq 0$

$\Rightarrow$ $\dfrac{x}{1-x} \geq 0$

$\Rightarrow$ $x(1 - x) \geq 0$; $x \neq 1$

$\Rightarrow$ $x \in [0, 1]$

Case (ii): $x < 0$

$\Rightarrow$ $\dfrac{x}{1+x} \geq 0$ $\Rightarrow$ $x(1 + x) > 0$

$\Rightarrow$ $x \in (-\infty, -1)$

$\therefore$ $D_f = (-\infty, -1) \cup [0, 1)$

8. (c) $f(x) = \dfrac{\sqrt{|\tan x| + \tan x}}{\sqrt{3x}} \Rightarrow x > 0, x \neq (2n+1)\dfrac{\pi}{2}$ and $|\tan x| + \tan x \geq 0$

$\Rightarrow$ $x > 0$, $x \neq (2n + 1)\dfrac{\pi}{2}$; $|\tan x| \geq -\tan x$

$\Rightarrow$ $D_f = \mathbb{R}^+ - \left\{n\pi - \dfrac{\pi}{2}; n \in \mathbb{N}\right\} = \mathbb{R}^+ - \left\{n\pi - \dfrac{\pi}{2}; n \in W\right\}$

9. (d) (a) $f(x) = \sqrt{x^2} = |x|; g(x) = \left(\sqrt{x}\right)^2 = x$

$\Rightarrow$ $f(x) \neq g(x)$, i.e., not identical.

(b) $f(x) = \dfrac{1}{\sqrt{x^2}} = \dfrac{1}{|x|}$ and $x \in \mathbb{R} - \{0\}$ and $g(x) = \dfrac{x}{x^2} = \dfrac{1}{x}$ for $x \in \mathbb{R} - \{0\}$

$\Rightarrow$ $f(x)$ and $g(x)$ are not identical.

(c) $f(x) = \log(x - 1) + \log(x - 2)$; $x > 2$

$= \log(x - 1)(x - 2)$; $x \in (2, \infty)$

$g(x) = \log(x - 1)(x - 2))$; $x \in (-\infty, 1) \cup (2, \infty)$

$\Rightarrow$ $f(x)$ and $g(x)$ are not identical.

(d) $f(x) = \sin^2 x + \cos^2 x = 1\ \forall\ x \in \mathbb{R}$ and $g(x) = 1\ \forall\ x \in \mathbb{R}$.

$\Rightarrow$ $f(x)$ and $g(x)$ are identical.

TEXTUAL EXERCISE-6: (SUBJECTIVE)

1. (a) $\dfrac{(15)^3.(21)^3}{(35)^2.(3)^4} = \dfrac{3^6 \times 5^3 \times 7^3}{5^2 \times 7^2 \times 3^4} = 9 \times 5 \times 7 = 315$

(b) $(-1.4)^3\left(\dfrac{25}{7}\right)^3 = -\dfrac{7^3}{5^3} \times \dfrac{5^6}{7^3} = -125$

(c) $\dfrac{5.2^{k-2} + 10.2^{k-1}}{10^{k+2}} = \dfrac{5.2^{k-2} + 5.2^k}{10^{k+2}}$

$= \dfrac{5^2.2^{k-2}}{5^{k+2}.2^{k+2}} = \dfrac{1}{5^k.16} = \dfrac{5^{-k}}{16}$

(d) $\left(\dfrac{\sqrt[4]{ab} - \sqrt{b}}{\sqrt{a} - \sqrt[4]{ab}}\right)^{-4} = \left(\dfrac{\sqrt{a} - \sqrt[4]{ab}}{\sqrt[4]{ab} - \sqrt{b}}\right)^4$

$= \left(\dfrac{\sqrt[4]{a}}{\sqrt[4]{b}}\left(\dfrac{\sqrt[4]{a} - \sqrt[4]{b}}{\sqrt[4]{a} - \sqrt[4]{b}}\right)\right)^4 = \dfrac{a}{b}$

2. (a) 2^{300} or 3^{200}

Let $2^{300} > 3^{200}$; taking log on both sides 300.

$\ln 2 > 200 \ln 3$

$\Rightarrow$ $\ln 8 > \ln 9$; which is false.

Hence, 3^{200} is greater.

(b) 54^4 or 21^{12}

Let $54^4 > 21^{12}$

$\Rightarrow$ $3^{12}.\ 2^4 > 3^{12}.\ 7^{12}$

$\Rightarrow$ $3^{12}\ (2^4 - 7^{12}) > 0$; which is false.

$\Rightarrow$ Hence, 21^{12} is greater.

(c) $(0.4)^4$ or $(0.8)^3$ $\Rightarrow$ $(0.\ 8)^3 > (0.\ 8)^4$ and $(0.\ 8)^4 > (0.\ 4)^4$ $[\because a^x \downarrow$ for $a \in (0, 1)]$

$\Rightarrow$ $(0.\ 8)^3 > (0.\ 4)^4$

(d) 10^{20} or 40^{10}

$10^{20} = (10^2)^{10} = (100)^{10} > (40)^{10}$

$\Rightarrow$ 10^{20} is greater

3. (a) $\left(\left(\dfrac{x^{\frac{2}{3}}}{y}\right)^2\left(\dfrac{x^2}{y}\right)^{\frac{1}{2}}\left(y^{\frac{2}{3}}\right)^{\frac{3}{2}}\right)^6 = \left(\dfrac{x^{\frac{4}{3}}}{y^2}\dfrac{x}{y^{\frac{1}{2}}}y\right)^6$

$= \left(\dfrac{x^{\frac{7}{3}}}{y^{\frac{3}{2}}}\right)^6 = \dfrac{x^{14}}{y^9} = x^{14}y^{-9}$

(b) $\sqrt{\dfrac{a}{b}\sqrt{\dfrac{a}{b} \times \dfrac{a^{\frac{1}{3}}}{b^{\frac{1}{3}}}}}\ .a^{-\frac{1}{3}}.b^{\frac{1}{3}} = \sqrt{\dfrac{a}{b}.\dfrac{a^{\frac{2}{3}}}{b^{\frac{2}{3}}}}\ a^{-\frac{1}{3}}.b^{\frac{1}{3}}$

$= \dfrac{a^{\frac{5}{6}}}{b^{\frac{5}{6}}}a^{-\frac{1}{3}}.b^{\frac{1}{3}} = a^{\frac{3}{6}}b^{-\frac{1}{2}} = \left(\dfrac{a}{b}\right)^{1/2}$

4. (a) $4^{2x^2-1} = 2 \Rightarrow 2^{4x^2-2} = 2$

$\Rightarrow$ $4x^2 - 2 = 1$ $\Rightarrow$ $x^2 = \dfrac{3}{4}$

$\Rightarrow$ $x = \pm\dfrac{\sqrt{3}}{2}$

(b) $5^{x-1} = 5^x 2^x.\ 2^{-x}.5^{x+1}$

$\Rightarrow$ $5^{x-1} = 5^{2x+1}$ $\Rightarrow$ $x - 1 = 2x + 1$

$\Rightarrow$ $-2 = x$

(c) $5^{2x-1} + 5^{x+1} = 250$ $\Rightarrow$ $5^{2x-1} + 5^{x+1} = 2.5^3$

$\Rightarrow$ $5.(5^{x-1})^2 + 25.(5^{x-1}) - 250 = 0$

$\Rightarrow$ $(5^{x-1})^2 + 5(5^{x-1}) - 50 = 0$

$\Rightarrow$ $(5^{x-1} + 10)\ (5^{x-1} - 5) = 0$

$\Rightarrow$ $5^{x-1} = 5$ or $5^{x-1} = -10$ (not possible)

$\Rightarrow$ $5^{x-1} = 5$ $\Rightarrow$ $x - 1 = 1$

$\Rightarrow$ $x = 2$

(d) $9^x + 6^x = 2.4^x$

$\Rightarrow$ $3^{2x} + 2^x\ 3^x = 2^{2x+1}$ $\Rightarrow$ $(3^x)^2 + 2^x\ 3^x - 2\ (2^x)^2 = 0$

$\Rightarrow$ $(3^x - 2^x)(3^x + 2.2^x) = 0$

$\Rightarrow$ $3^x = 2^x$ $\Rightarrow$ $x = 0$

(e) $2^{x+1}.\ 5^x = 200$ $\Rightarrow$ $10^x = 100$

$\Rightarrow$ $x = 2$

(f) $6^x + 6^{x+1} = 2^x + 2^{x+1} + 2^{x+2}$

$\Rightarrow$ $7.6^x = 2^x.\ 7$ $\Rightarrow$ $6^x = 2^x$

$\Rightarrow$ $x = 0$

5. (a) $2^{3-8x} > 1$ $\Rightarrow$ $2^{3-8x} > 2^0$

$\Rightarrow$ $3 - 8x > 0$ $\Rightarrow$ $3 > 8x$

$\Rightarrow$ $x \in \left(-\infty, \dfrac{3}{8}\right)$

(b) $16^x > 0.125$ $\Rightarrow$ $2^{4x} > 2^{-3}$

$\Rightarrow$ $4x > -3$ $\Rightarrow$ $x \in \left(-\dfrac{3}{4}, \infty\right)$

(c) $(0.3)^{2x^2-3x+6} < 0.00243$

$\Rightarrow$ $(0.3)^{2x^2-3x+6} < (0.3)^5$

$\Rightarrow$ $2x^2 - 3x + 6 > 5$ $\Rightarrow$ $2x^2 - 3x + 1 > 0$

$\Rightarrow$ $2x^2 - 2x - x + 1 > 0$

$\Rightarrow$ $(2x - 1)\ (x - 1) > 0$ $\Rightarrow$ $x \in \mathbb{R} - \left(\dfrac{1}{2}, 1\right)$

$\Rightarrow$ $x \in \left(-\infty, \dfrac{1}{2}\right) \cup (1, \infty)$

(d) $\left(\dfrac{1}{3}\right)^{\sqrt{x+2}} > 3^{-x}$ $\Rightarrow$ $3^{-\sqrt{x+2}} > 3^{-x}$

$\Rightarrow$ $-\sqrt{x+2} > -x$

$\Rightarrow$ $\sqrt{x+2} < x$

$\Rightarrow$ $x > 0$ as $\sqrt{x+2}$ is always +ve

$\Rightarrow$ $x + 2 < x^2$ $\Rightarrow$ $x^2 - x - 2 > 0$

$\Rightarrow$ $(x - 2)\ (x + 1) > 0$

$\Rightarrow$ $x \in (-\infty, -1) \cup (2, \infty)$ but $x > 0$

$\Rightarrow$ $x \in (2, \infty)$

(e) $\sqrt[x+1]{3} > 9$ $\Rightarrow$ $(3)^{1/x+1} > (3)^2$

$\Rightarrow$ $\dfrac{1}{x+1} > 2$

$\Rightarrow\ x+1<\frac{1}{2}$ ($\because x+1 \geq 2$ and $x+2$ ℕ)

$\Rightarrow\ x<\frac{1}{2}$ but $x \geq 1$ $\quad \Rightarrow\ x \in \phi$

(f) $8^{\sqrt{8^x}}>4096$ $\quad \Rightarrow\ 2^{3.2^{\frac{3x}{2}}}>2^{12}$

$\Rightarrow\ 3.2^{\frac{3x}{2}}>12$ $\quad \Rightarrow\ 2^{\frac{3x}{2}}>4$

$\Rightarrow\ \frac{3x}{2}>2$ $\quad \Rightarrow\ x>\frac{4}{3}$

$\Rightarrow\ x \in\left(\frac{4}{3}, \infty\right)$

(g) $\left(\frac{2}{5}\right)^{\frac{6-5x}{2+5x}}<\left(\frac{2}{5}\right)^{-2}$ $\quad \Rightarrow\ \frac{6-5x}{2+5x}>-2$

$\Rightarrow\ \frac{6-5x+4+10x}{2+5x}>0$

$\Rightarrow\ \frac{5(x+2)}{5x+2}>0$ $\quad \Rightarrow\ (x+2)(5x+2)>0$

$\Rightarrow\ x \in(-\infty,-2) \cup\left(-\frac{2}{5}, \infty\right)$

(h) $2^x+2^{-x+1}-3<0$ $\quad \Rightarrow\ 2^x+\frac{2}{2^x}-3<0$

$\Rightarrow\ \frac{2^{2x}-3.2^x+2}{2^x}<0$

$\Rightarrow\ (2^x)^2-2^x-2.2^x+2<0$

$\Rightarrow\ (2^x-2)(2^x-1)<0$

$\Rightarrow\ 2^x-2>0$ and $2^x-1<0$ or $2^x-2<0$ and $2^x-1>0$

$\Rightarrow\ 2^x>2$ and $2^x<1$ or $2^x<2$ and $2^x>1$

$\Rightarrow\ x>1$ and $x<0$ or $x<1$ and $x>0$

$\Rightarrow\ x \in \phi$ or $x \leftarrow (0, 1)$

$\Rightarrow\ x \in (0, 1)$

6. (a) $32^{\frac{1}{3}}=4x \Rightarrow\ 2^{\frac{5}{3}}=4x$

Taking $\log_2$ on both sides, we get $\frac{5}{3}=\log_2 x+2$

$\Rightarrow\ \log_2 x=-\frac{1}{3}$

(b) $64^{\frac{1}{4}}=8x$ $\quad \Rightarrow\ 2^{\frac{3}{2}}=8x$

Taking $\log_2$ on both sides, we get $\frac{3}{2}=3+\log_2 x$

$\Rightarrow\ \log_2 x=-\frac{3}{2}$

7. $\frac{\log_a N}{\log_{ab} N}=1+\log_a b$

$\Rightarrow\ \frac{\log_a N}{\log_{ab} N}=\frac{\frac{1}{\log_N a}}{\frac{1}{\log_N ab}}=\frac{\log_N ab}{\log_N a}$

$=\log_a ab=1+\log_a b$

$\Rightarrow\ a>0$ and $a \neq 1$; $b>0$

$\Rightarrow\ ab \neq 1$ and $ab>0$; $N>0$ and $N \neq 1$

8. (a) $f(x)=\log_x 3$; $D_f=(0, \infty)-\{1\}$

(b) $f(x)=\log_2(x-1)$; $D_f=(1, \infty)$

(c) $f(x)=\log_{2x-3}(x-1)(x-4)$; $2x-3>0, 1$ and $(x-1)(x-4)>0$

$\Rightarrow\ x>\frac{3}{2}$, $x \neq 2$ and $x \in(-\infty, 1) \cup(4, \infty)$

$\Rightarrow\ x \in(4, \infty)$

(d) $f(x)=\log_2\left[\frac{(x-4)(x-5)}{(x-6)}\right]$

$\Rightarrow\ (x-4)(x-5)(x-6)>0$

$\Rightarrow\ x \in(4,5) \cup(6, \infty)$

9. $f(x)=\ell n\left(\frac{x^3-5x^2-6x+54}{x+3}\right)$

$=\ell n\left[\frac{(x^2-8x+18)(x+3)}{(x+3)}\right]$

$\because\ x^2-8x+18>0\ \forall\ x \in \mathbb{R}$.

$\Rightarrow\ x+3 \in 0$

$\therefore\ D_f=\mathbb{R}-\{-3\}$.

$\Rightarrow\ f(x)=\ell n(x^2-8x+18)$; $x \in \mathbb{R}-\{3\}=\ell n[(x-4)^2+2]$; $x \in \mathbb{R}-\{3\}$

$\Rightarrow\ f(x) \in[\ell n 2, \infty)$

$\Rightarrow$ Smallest possible value $=\ell n 2$ at $x=4$

10. (i) $\log_{(x+3)}(x+4)=2$

For log to be defined $x+4>0$

$\Rightarrow\ x \in(-4, \infty)$

$\Rightarrow$ And $x+3>0$ and $x+3 \neq 1$

$\Rightarrow\ x>-3$ and $x \neq-2$

$\Rightarrow\ x \in(-3,-2) \cup(-2, \infty)$

Taking anti log on both sides, we get $x+4=(x+3)^2$

$\Rightarrow\ x+4=x^2+6x+9$

$\Rightarrow\ x^2+5x+5=0$

$\Rightarrow\ x=\frac{-5 \pm \sqrt{25-20}}{2}=\frac{-5 \pm \sqrt{5}}{2}$

$\Rightarrow\ x=\frac{-5+\sqrt{5}}{2}$ by applying domain restriction

(ii) $2^{\log_4(x+5)}=x+5$

$\Rightarrow\ x+5>0$ $\quad \Rightarrow\ x \in(-5, \infty)$

$\Rightarrow\ 2^{\frac{1}{2}\log_2(x+5)}=x+5$ $\quad \Rightarrow\ (x+5)^{\frac{1}{2}}=x+5$

$\Rightarrow\ x^2+10x+25=x+5$

$\Rightarrow\ x^2+9x+20=0$ $\quad \Rightarrow\ (x+4)(x+5)=0$

$\Rightarrow\ x=-4$ or $x=-5$

Applying domain restrictions $x=-4$

11. $x+4>0$; $x+4 \neq 1$

$\Rightarrow\ x>-4$; $x \neq-3$

$\Rightarrow\ x \in(-4,-3) \cup(-3, \infty)$

Also $(x+4)^{y+2}=16$ as, $x, y \in \mathbb{Z}$, $x+4$, $y+2 \in \mathbb{Z}$

$\Rightarrow\ (x+4)^{y+2}=(-4)^2,(-2)^4,(2)^4$, and $(4)^2,(16)^1$

$\Rightarrow\ (x, y) \in\{(-8,0),(-6,2),(-2,2),(0,0),(12,-1)\}$

But, by domain restrictions $(x, y) \in\{(-2,2),(0,0),(12,-1)\}$

12. $\sqrt[4]{|x-3|^{x+1}} = \sqrt[3]{|x-3|^{x-2}}$

$\Rightarrow$ $(|x-3|^{(x+1)})^3 = (|x-3|^{(x-2)})^4$

$\Rightarrow$ $|x-3|^{(3x+3)} = |x-3|^{(4x-8)}$

$\Rightarrow$ $|x-3|^{x-11} = 1$ $\quad\Rightarrow$ $x - 11 = 0$ or $|x-3| = 1$

$\Rightarrow$ $x = 11$ or $x = 4$ or 2

Also $x = 3$ satisfies the equation

$\Rightarrow$ $x \in \{2, 3, 4, 11\}$

13. $\log_{\sin x} 5 . \log_{\sin^2 x} a + 1 = 0$; $a > 0$ and no solution for $a = 1$

$\Rightarrow$ $a > 0, \neq 1$

$\Rightarrow$ $\dfrac{\log_a 5}{\log_a \sin x} . \dfrac{1}{\log_a \sin^2 x} = -1$

$\Rightarrow$ $\log_a 5 = -2(\log_a \sin x)^2$

$\Rightarrow$ $(\log_a \sin x) = \pm\sqrt{\dfrac{\log_a 5}{-2}}$

Case (i): $0 < a < 1$; L.H.S > 0

$\Rightarrow$ $\log_a \sin x = \sqrt{-\log_a \sqrt{5}} \Rightarrow \sin x = a^{\sqrt{-\log_a \sqrt{5}}}$

$\Rightarrow$ $x = n\pi + (-1)^n . \sin^{-1}\left(a^{\sqrt{-\log_a \sqrt{5}}}\right)$

Case (ii): $a > 1$; L.H.S < 0

$\Rightarrow$ $\log_a \sin x = -\sqrt{-\log_a \sqrt{5}} \Rightarrow \sin x = a^{-\sqrt{-\log_a \sqrt{5}}}$

$\Rightarrow$ $x = n\pi + (-1)^n . \sin^{-1}\left(a^{-\sqrt{-\log_a \sqrt{5}}}\right)$

14. $\log_{x-2} + \log_{x+2} 8 > \log_{x-2} 8 . \log_{x+2} 8$

Here $x - 2 > 0, \neq 1$ and $x + 2 > 0, \neq 1$

$\Rightarrow$ $x > 2,\ 3, x > -2 \neq -1$

$\Rightarrow$ $x \in (2, \infty) - \{3\}$

Case (i): $x > 3$; $\log_{x-2} 8 . \log_{x+2} 8 > 0$

$\Rightarrow$ $\dfrac{1}{\log_{x+2} 8} + \dfrac{1}{\log_{x-2} 8} > 0$

$\Rightarrow$ $\log_8 (x + 2)(x - 2) > 0$

$\Rightarrow$ $(x + 2)(x - 2) > 0$ $\quad\Rightarrow$ $x^2 - 5 > 0$

$\Rightarrow$ $x \in \left(-\infty, -\sqrt{5}\right) \cup \left(\sqrt{5}, \infty\right)$

Due to case restriction, $x \in (3, \infty)$

Case (ii): $2 < x < 3$; $\log_{x-2} 8 . \log_{x+2} 8 < 0$

$\Rightarrow$ $\log_8 (x + 2)(x - 2) < 0$

$\Rightarrow$ $0 < x^2 - 4 < 1$ $\quad\Rightarrow$ $4 < x^2 < 5$

$\Rightarrow$ $x \in \left(2, \sqrt{5}\right)$ [Due to base restriction]

$\therefore$ $x\ \left(2, \sqrt{5}\right) \cup (3, \infty)$

15. $x > 0, y > 0, z > 0,$

L.H.S. $= x^{\ell n\left(\frac{y}{z}\right)} + y^{\ell n\left(\frac{z}{x}\right)} + z^{\ell n\left(\frac{x}{y}\right)}$

By A.M $\geq$ G.M for non-negative reals.

L.H.S $\geq 3\sqrt[3]{x^{\ell n \frac{y}{z}} . y^{\ell n \frac{z}{x}} . z^{\ell n \frac{x}{y}}} = 3\sqrt[3]{\left(\dfrac{y}{z}\right)^{\ell nx} . \left(\dfrac{z}{x}\right)^{\ell ny} . \left(\dfrac{x}{y}\right)^{\ell nz}}$

$= 3\sqrt[3]{\dfrac{y^{\ell nx}}{z^{\ell nx}} . \dfrac{z^{\ell ny}}{x^{\ell ny}} . \dfrac{x^{\ell nz}}{y^{\ell nz}}} = 3\sqrt[3]{\dfrac{x^{\ell ny} y^{\ell nz} . z^{\ell nx}}{z^{\ell nx} . x^{\ell ny} . y^{\ell nz}}}$

$= 3\ \left[\because a^{\log_N b} = b^{\log_N c}\right]$

$\therefore$ L.H.S 3

16. $\log_a\left(\dfrac{x^2 - x + 2}{-x^2 + 2x + 3}\right) > 0$. At $x = \dfrac{1}{2}, \dfrac{x^2 - x + 2}{-x^2 + 2x + 3} = \dfrac{\frac{1}{4} - \frac{1}{2} + 2}{-\frac{1}{2} + 1 + 3}$

$= \dfrac{\frac{3}{2} + \frac{1}{4}}{\frac{7}{2}} = \dfrac{\left(\frac{6+1}{4}\right)}{\left(\frac{7}{2}\right)} = \dfrac{7}{4} \times \dfrac{2}{7} = \dfrac{1}{2} < 1$

$\Rightarrow$ $0 < a < 1$ $\quad\Rightarrow$ $0 < \dfrac{x^2 - x + 2}{-x^2 + 2x + 3} < 1$

$\Rightarrow$ $-x^2 + 2x + 3 > 0$; $\dfrac{x^2 - x + 2 + x^2 - 2x - 3}{-x^2 + 2x + 3} < 0$

$\Rightarrow$ $-x^2 + 2x + 3 > 0$; $\dfrac{2x^2 - 3x - 1}{-x^2 + 2x + 3} < 0$

$\Rightarrow$ $(2x^2 - 3x - 1) < 0$

$\Rightarrow$ $\left(x - \left(\dfrac{3 - \sqrt{17}}{4}\right)\right)\left(x + \left(\dfrac{3 + \sqrt{17}}{4}\right)\right) < 0$

$\Rightarrow$ $x \in \left(\dfrac{3 - \sqrt{17}}{4}, \dfrac{3 + \sqrt{17}}{4}\right)$

TEXTUAL EXERCISE-6: (OBJECTIVE)

1. (a) $4^{2\log_9 3} = 4^{\frac{2}{2}\log_3 3} = 4^1 = 4$

2. (b) $\log_7 2 = n$

$\Rightarrow$ $\log_{49} 28 = \dfrac{1}{2}\log_7 28 = \dfrac{1}{2}[2\log_7 2 + 1] = \eta + \dfrac{1}{2} = \dfrac{2\eta + 1}{2}$

3. (c) $a^2 + 4b^2 = 12ab$ $\quad\Rightarrow$ $\log(a + 2ab)$

$\Rightarrow$ $a^2 + 4b^2 + 4ab = 16ab$

$\Rightarrow$ $(a + 2b)^2 = 16ab$

Taking log on both sides, we get $2\log(a + 2b) = \log 16 + \log a + \log b$

$\Rightarrow$ $\log(a + 2b) = \dfrac{1}{2}(4\log 2 + \log a + \log b)$

4. (c) $\log_a ab = x$ $\quad\Rightarrow$ $1 + \log_a b = x$

$\Rightarrow$ $x - 1 = \log_a b$

$\Rightarrow$ $\dfrac{1}{x - 1} = \log_b a$ $\quad\Rightarrow$ $1 + \dfrac{1}{x - 1} = 1 + \log_b a$

$\Rightarrow$ $\dfrac{x}{x - 1} = \log_b ab$

5. (c) Let $\dfrac{\ln a}{y - z} = \dfrac{\ln b}{z - x} = \dfrac{\ln c}{x - y} = m$

Let $a^{y^2 + yz + z^2} . b^{z^2 - zx + x^2} . c^{x^2 + xy + y^2} = t$

Taking log on both sides, we get $(y^2 + yz + z^2)\ln a + (z^2 + zx + x^2)\ln b + (x^2 - xy + y^2)\ln c = \ln t$

$\Rightarrow$ $\dfrac{(y^3 - z^3)}{(y - z)}\ln a + \dfrac{(z^3 - x^3)}{(z - x)}\ln b + \dfrac{\ln c}{x - y}(x^3 - y^3) = \ln t$

$\Rightarrow$ $m(y^3 - z^3 + z^3 - x^3 + x^3 - y^3) = \ln t$

$\Rightarrow$ $m(0) = \ln t$ $\quad\Rightarrow$ $0 = \ln t$

$\Rightarrow$ $t = 1$

6. **(d)** $81^{\log_3 5} + 27^{\frac{1}{2}\log_3 36} + 3^{4\times\frac{1}{2}\log_3 7} = 5^4 + 6^3 + 7^2 = 625 + 216 + 49 = 890$

7. **(d)** $f(x) = \log\left(\frac{1+x}{1-x}\right)$

(a) $f(x_1).f(x_2) = \log\left(\frac{1+x_1}{1-x_1}\right)\log\left(\frac{1+x_2}{1-x_2}\right) \neq \log\left(\frac{1+x_1+x_2}{1-x_1-x_2}\right)$,

(b) $f(x + 2) - 2f(x + 1) + f(x)$

$= \log\left(\frac{3+x}{-x-1}\right) - 2\log\left(\frac{2+x}{-x}\right) + \log\left(\frac{1+x}{1-x}\right)$

$\Rightarrow \log\left(\frac{3+x}{-x-1}\right)\left(\frac{1+x}{1-x}\right)\left(\frac{x^2}{(x+2)^2}\right)$

$= \log\frac{(x+3)x^2}{(x-1)(x+2)^2} \neq 0$

(c) $f(x) = \log\left(\frac{1+x}{1-x}\right)$ and $f(x+1) = \log\left(\frac{2+x}{-x}\right)$

$\Rightarrow f(x) \neq f(x + 1)$

(d) $f(x_1) + f(x_2) = \log\left(\frac{1+x_1}{1-x_1}\right) + \log\left(\frac{1+x_2}{1-x_2}\right)$

$= \log\left(\frac{1+x_1+x_2+x_1x_2}{1-x_1-x_2+x_1x_2}\right)$

$= \log\left(\frac{1+\frac{x_1+x_2}{1+x_1x_2}}{1-\frac{(x_1+x_2)}{1+x_1x_2}}\right) = f\left(\frac{x_1+x_2}{1+x_1x_2}\right)$

8. **(c)** $y = 2^{\frac{1}{\log_x 4}} = 2^{\frac{1}{2}\log_2 x} = \sqrt{x}$

$\Rightarrow x = y^2$

9. **(b)** $\frac{1}{\log_a x} + \frac{1}{\log_c x} = \frac{2}{\log_b x}$

$\Rightarrow \log_x ac = \log_x b^2 \quad \Rightarrow b^2 = ac$

$\Rightarrow$ a, b, c are in G.P.

10. **(c)** $\log_{10}(x^2 - x - 6) - x = \log_{10}(x + 2) - 4$

$\Rightarrow \log_{10}\left(\frac{x^2-x-6}{x+2}\right) = x - 4$

$\Rightarrow \log_{10}(x - 3) = x - 4$

$\Rightarrow x - 3 = 10^{x-4}$

if $x = 5$, $\Rightarrow 2 = 10$ which is not true

Hence, $x \neq 5$

If $x = 3$, $\Rightarrow 0 = 10^{-1}$ which is not true

$\Rightarrow x \neq 3$

If $x = 4$, $\Rightarrow 1 = 10^0$

$\Rightarrow$ true

Hence, $x = 4$

11. **(b)** $(\log_{16}x)^2 - (\log_{16} x) + \log_{16} k = 0;\ k > 0;\ x > 0$

For exactly one solution, $D = 0$

$\Rightarrow 1 - 4\log_{16} k = 0 \quad \Rightarrow 1 - \frac{4}{4}\log_2 k = 0$

$\Rightarrow 1 = \log_2 k \quad \Rightarrow k = 2$

So, number of values of k is 1.

12. **(c)** $x + \log_{10}(1 + 2^x) = x\log_{10} 5 + \log_{10} 6$

$\Rightarrow 10^x = \frac{6.5^x}{1+2^x} \quad \Rightarrow (2^x)^2 + 2^x = 6$

$\Rightarrow (2^x)^2 + 2^x - 6 = 0$

$\Rightarrow (2^x + 3)(2^x - 2) = 0 \Rightarrow 2^x = 2$

$\Rightarrow x = 1$

13. **(a)** $\log_{1/\sqrt{2}} \sin x \geq 0 \quad \Rightarrow \quad 0 < \sin x \leq 1$

$\Rightarrow x \in (0, \pi)$ and $(2\pi, 3\pi)$

$\Rightarrow$ Integer multiples of $\pi/4 \in \left\{\frac{\pi}{4}, \frac{\pi}{2}, \frac{3\pi}{4}, \frac{9\pi}{4}, \frac{5\pi}{2}, \frac{11\pi}{4}\right\}$

That is, 6 solutions.

14. **(b)** $\log_{1/2}(x + 1) \leq \log_2(2 - x)$

$\Rightarrow 2 - x > 0$ and $x + 1 > 0$

$\Rightarrow x \in (-1, \infty)$ and $x < 2$

$\Rightarrow x \in (-1, 2) - \log_2(x + 1) \leq \log_2(2 - x)$

$\Rightarrow \log_2(2 - x)(x + 1) \geq 0$

$\Rightarrow (2 - x)(x + 1) \geq 1$

$\Rightarrow x^2 - x - 1 \leq 0 \quad \Rightarrow x \in \left[\frac{1-\sqrt{5}}{2}, \frac{1+\sqrt{5}}{2}\right]$

15. **(a)** $\log_{0.3}(x - 1) < \log_{0.09}(x - 1)$

$\Rightarrow (x - 1) > 0$ and $\log_{0.3}(x - 1) < \frac{1}{2}\log_{0.3}(x - 1)$

$\Rightarrow (x - 1) > \sqrt{x-1};\ x > 1$

$\Rightarrow (x - 1)^2 > (x - 1);\ x > 1$

$\Rightarrow x^2 - 3x + 2 > 0;\ x > 1$

$\Rightarrow (x - 1)(x - 2) > 0;\ x > 1$

$\Rightarrow x < 1$ or $x > 2$ and $x > 1$

$\Rightarrow x \in (2, \infty)$

16. **(a)** $\log_{|\sin x|}(1 + \cos x) = 2;\ x \in [0, n\pi];\ n \in \mathbb{Z}$

$\Rightarrow 1 + \cos x > 0 \quad \Rightarrow \cos x > -1$

$\Rightarrow x \neq (\text{odd})\pi$

$\Rightarrow$ Also $|\sin x| \in (0, 1) \Rightarrow x \neq \frac{n\pi}{2}$

$\therefore$ Domain of equation $[0, n\pi] - \left\{\frac{n\pi}{2}; n \in \mathbb{Z}\right\}$

$\Rightarrow$ By given equation, $(1 + \cos x) = |\sin x|^2$

$\Rightarrow 1 + \cos x = \sin^2 x$

$\Rightarrow \cos^2 x + \cos x = 0$

$\Rightarrow \cos x(1 + \cos x) = 0$ but $1 + \cos x > 0$

$\Rightarrow \cos x = 0$

$\Rightarrow$ But $x \neq \frac{n\pi}{2} \quad \Rightarrow \cos x \neq 0$

$\Rightarrow$ No real $x \in [0, n\pi]$ satisfy, i.e., $x \in \{\}$

17. **(d)** $\log_{\cos x} \sin x \geq 0;\ x \in [0, 3\pi]$

$\Rightarrow$ Here $\sin x > 0$, $\cos x > 0, \neq 1$

$\Rightarrow x \in \left(0, \frac{\pi}{2}\right) \cup \left(2\pi, \frac{5\pi}{2}\right)$

$\Rightarrow$ Also by given inequality, $0 < \sin x \leq 1$ which holds $\forall\ x \in \left(0, \frac{\pi}{2}\right) \cup \left(2\pi, \frac{5\pi}{2}\right)$

18. **(d)** $\log_{\sqrt{3}}\left(\sin x + 2\sqrt{2}\cos x\right) \geq 2;\ -2\pi < x \leq 2\pi$

$\Rightarrow$ Here $\sin x + 2\sqrt{2}\cos x \geq 3$ ....(1)

$\Rightarrow$ Also $-3 \leq \sin x + 2\sqrt{2}\cos x \leq 3$ ....(2)

$\Rightarrow$ From (1) and (2), we get 1 $\sin x + 2\sqrt{2}\cos x = 3$

Let 1 = r cos

$\Rightarrow$ $r = 3$; $\tan\theta = 2\sqrt{2}$

$\Rightarrow$ $3\sin x\cos\theta + 3\sin\theta\cos x = 3$

$\Rightarrow$ $\sin(x+\theta) = 1;\ \theta = \tan^{-1}\left(2\sqrt{2}\right) = \cos^{-1}(1/3) \in \left(\frac{\pi}{3}, \frac{\pi}{2}\right)$

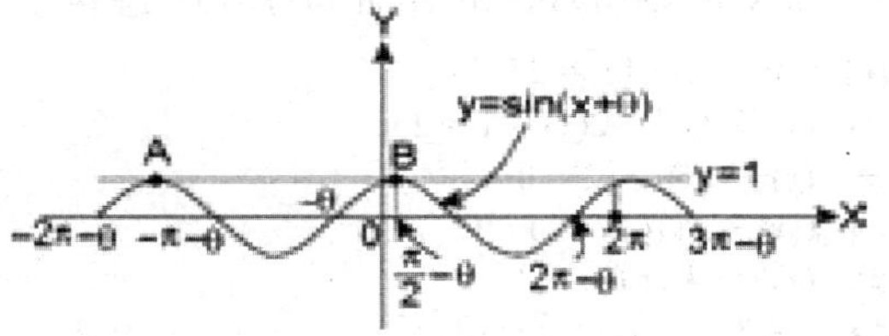

$\Rightarrow$ There will be exactly 2 solutions.

TEXTUAL EXERCISE–7: (SUBJECTIVE)

1. L.H.S. = $[\sin x + [\sin x + [\sin x + [\sin x]]]$

$= [\sin x] + [\sin x + [\sin x]]$

$(\because [x + m] = m + [x];\ m \in \mathbb{Z})$

$= [\sin x] + [\sin x] + [\sin x] = 3[\sin x]$ = R. H.S.

2. $f(x) = [\sin x] + [\tan x + [\cos x + [\sin x]]]$

$= [\sin x] + [\tan x] + [\cos x + [\sin x]]$

$= [\sin x] + [\tan x] + [\sin x] + [\cos x]$

$\because\ x \in (0, \pi/4)$

$\Rightarrow \sin x \in \left(0, \frac{1}{\sqrt{2}}\right)$

$\tan x \in (0, 1)$, $\cos x \in \left(\frac{1}{\sqrt{2}}, 1\right)$

$\Rightarrow [\sin x] = 0,\ [\tan x] = 0,\ [\cos x] = 0$

$\therefore f(x) = 0 + 0 + 0 = 0$

3. $y = \frac{1}{3}[\sin x + [\sin x + [\sin x]]] = \frac{1}{3}[3[\sin x]] = [\sin x]$

$\Rightarrow [y + [y]] = 2\cos x \quad \Rightarrow 2[y] = 2\cos x$

$\Rightarrow [y] = \cos x \quad \Rightarrow [[\sin x]] = \cos x$

$\Rightarrow [\sin x] = \cos x \quad \Rightarrow$ $\cos x$ has to be integer

$\Rightarrow \cos x \in \{1, 0, -1\}$

If $\cos x = 1$, then $\sin x = 0$

$\Rightarrow [\sin x] = 0, \neq 1$, hence, not possible

If $\cos x = 0$, then $\sin x = 1$

$\Rightarrow [\sin x] = 1, \neq 0$, hence, not possible

If $\cos x = -1$, then $\sin x = -1$

$\Rightarrow [\sin x] = 0, \neq 1$, hence, not possible

$\therefore$ No solution

4. **(a)** $4\{x\} = x + [x] \Rightarrow 4\{x\} = \{x\} + 2[x]$

$\Rightarrow \frac{3}{2}\{x\} = [x]$

But, $\{x\} \in [0, 1) \quad \Rightarrow \frac{3}{2}\{x\} \in \left[0, \frac{3}{2}\right)$

$\Rightarrow [x] = 0$ or 1

If $[x] = 0 \quad \Rightarrow \{x\} = 0$

$\Rightarrow x = [x] + \{x\} = 0$

If $[x] = 1 \quad \Rightarrow \{x\} = \frac{2}{3}$

$\Rightarrow x = [x] + \{x\} = 1 + \frac{2}{3} = \frac{5}{3}$

$\therefore$ 0, 5/3

(b) $[x] - 2x| = 4$

$\Rightarrow [x] - 2x = 4$ or $[x] - 2x = -4$

$\Rightarrow -[x] - 2\{x\} = 4$ or $-[x] - 2\{x\} = -4$

$\Rightarrow 2\{x\} = -[x] - 4$ or $2\{x\} = 4 - [x]$

$\{x\} \in [0, 1)$

$\Rightarrow 2\{x\} \in [0, 2) \quad -[x] - 4,\ 4 - [x] \in \{0, 1\}$

Case (i): $-[x] - 4 = 0$

$\Rightarrow [x] = -4 \quad \Rightarrow \{x\} = 0$

$\Rightarrow x = -4 + 0 = -4$

Case (ii): $\quad -[x] - 4 = 1$

$\Rightarrow [x] = -5 \quad \Rightarrow \{x\} = 1/2$

$\Rightarrow x = 5 + \frac{1}{2} = -\frac{9}{2}$

Case (iii): $4 - [x] = 1 \quad \Rightarrow [x] = 3$

$\Rightarrow \{x\} = 1/2$

$\Rightarrow x = 3 + 1/2 = 7/2$

Case (iv): $4 - [x] = 0 \quad \Rightarrow [x] = 4$

$\Rightarrow \{x\} = 0$

$\Rightarrow x = 4 + 0 = 4 \quad \Rightarrow \left\{\pm 4, \frac{7}{2}, \frac{-9}{2}\right\}$

5. Follow the steps given Illustration No. 93

TEXTUAL EXERCISE–7: (OBJECTIVE)

1. **(b)** $\log_{[x]} x^2 \quad \Rightarrow [x] > 0$ and $[x] \neq 1$

$\Rightarrow [x] > 1 \quad \Rightarrow [x] \geq 2$

$\Rightarrow x \in [2, \infty)$

2. **(b)** $[x]\sin\left(\frac{\pi}{[x+1]}\right) \quad \Rightarrow [x + 1] \neq 0$

$\Rightarrow x + 1 \notin [0, 1) \quad \Rightarrow x \notin [-1, 0)$

$\Rightarrow x \in \mathbb{R} - [-1, 0)$

3. **(a)** $\sqrt{\frac{2-[x]}{[x]-3}} \Rightarrow \frac{2-[x]}{[x]-3} > 0$ or $2 - [x] = 0$ and $[x] \in \mathbb{Z}$

$\Rightarrow [x] \in (2, 3)$ and $[x] \in \mathbb{Z}$ or $[x] = 2$

$\Rightarrow x \in [2, 3)$

4. **(c)** $\sin^{-1}[2 - 3x^2]$

$[2 - 3x^2] \in [-1, 1]$

$\Rightarrow (2 - 3x^2) \in [-1, 2) \quad \Rightarrow -3x^2 \in [-3, 0)$

$\Rightarrow x^2 \in (0, 1]$

$\Rightarrow x \in [-1, 0) \cup (0, 1]$

5. **(b)** $f(x) = \log\left\{\frac{1}{([\cos x] - [\sin x])}\right\}$; $[\cos x] - [\sin x] > 0$

$\Rightarrow [\cos x] > [\sin x]$

$\because$ [cos x] – [sin x] is periodic with period 2π, we shall work only for $x \in [0, 2\pi]$.

$\therefore$ [cos x] > [sin x} at $x = 0$ and $x \in \left[\frac{3\pi}{2}, 2\pi\right]$

$\Rightarrow x \in \left[2n\pi + \frac{3\pi}{2}, 2n\pi + 2\pi\right]$, i.e., x

$\in \left[(2n+1)\pi + \frac{\pi}{2}, (2n+2)\pi\right]$

6. (c) $\sqrt{[x]-1} + \sqrt{4-[x]}$

$\Rightarrow [x] - 1 \geq 0$ and $4 - [x] \geq 0$

$\Rightarrow [x] \geq 1$ and $4 \geq [x]$

$\Rightarrow x \in [1, \infty)$ and $x \in (-\infty, 5)$

$\Rightarrow x \in [1, 5)$

7. (a) $e^x + \sin^{-1}\left[\left(\frac{x}{2} - 1\right)\right] + \log\sqrt{x - [x]}$

$= e^x + \sin^{-1}\left[\left(\frac{x}{2}\right) - 1\right] + \log\sqrt{\{x\}}$

$\left[\frac{x}{2} - 1\right] \in [-1, 1] \quad \Rightarrow \quad \frac{x}{2} - 1 \in [-1, 2)$ and $\{x\} \neq 0$

$\Rightarrow x \in [0, 6)$ and $x \notin \mathbb{Z} \Rightarrow x \in (0, 6) - \{1, 2, 3, 4, 5\}$

8. (b) $f : (2, 3) \to (1, 3); f(x) = x - \{-x\} = x - (1 - \{x\})$

$= x + \{x\} - 1 = [x] + 2\{x\} - 1$

$\Rightarrow f(x) = \begin{cases} = 2 + 2(x-2) - 1 \\ = 2x - 3 \end{cases}$

$\Rightarrow y = 2x - 3 \quad \Rightarrow x = \frac{y+3}{2}$

$\Rightarrow f^{1}(x) = \frac{x+3}{2}$

9. (c) $f(x) = \begin{cases} x - [x]; I \leq x \leq I + 0.5 \\ [x]; I + 0.5 \leq I + 1 \end{cases} = \begin{cases} x - I; I \leq x \leq I + 0.5 \\ I; I + 0.5 \leq x < I + 1 \end{cases}$

$f(g(x)) = f(\sin^4 x + \cos^4 x)$

$= f\left[1 - \frac{1}{2}\sin^2 2x\right]; k = 1 - \frac{1}{2}\sin^2 2x$

$= f\left[\frac{1}{2} \leq k \leq 1\right] = \left\{\text{for} \frac{1}{2} \leq k \leq 1\right.$

10. (a) $f(x) = \frac{x - [x]}{1 + x - [x]} = \frac{\{x\}}{1 + \{x\}} = 1 - \frac{1}{1 + \{x\}}$

$\Rightarrow \{x\} \in [0, 1) \quad \Rightarrow \{x\} + 1 \in [1, 2)$

$-\frac{1}{\{x\}+1} \in \left[-1, -\frac{1}{2}\right) \Rightarrow 1 - \frac{1}{\{x\}+1} \in \left[0, \frac{1}{2}\right)$

$\Rightarrow R_f \to \left[0, \frac{1}{2}\right)$

11. (c) $f(x) = \frac{e^x}{1+[x]}; x \geq 0 = \begin{cases} e^x \text{ for } 0 \leq x < 1 \\ \frac{e^x}{2} \text{ for } 1 \leq x < 2 \\ \frac{e^x}{3} \text{ for } 2 \leq x < 3 \end{cases}$ and so on.

$\Rightarrow f(x) \in [1, e)$ for $x \in [0, 1)$

$\Rightarrow f(x) \in \left[\frac{e}{2}, \frac{e^2}{2}\right)$ for $x \in [1, 2)$

$\Rightarrow f(x) \in \left[\frac{e^2}{3}, \frac{e^3}{3}\right)$ for $x \in [2, 3)$ and so on.

$\Rightarrow f(x) \in [1, \infty)$

12 (b) $x^3 - [x] = 3 \quad \Rightarrow x^3 - 3 = [x]$

$\Rightarrow x^3$ should be integer

$\Rightarrow$ only $4^{\frac{1}{3}}$ satisfy the equation $(4^{\frac{1}{3}})^3 - 3 = 1 = [4^{\frac{1}{3}}]$

13. (c) $(x)^2 + (x + 1)^2 = 25$

$\Rightarrow (x)^2 + (x)^2 + 2(x) + 1 = 25$

$\Rightarrow (x)^2 + (x) - 12 = 0$

$\Rightarrow ((x) + 4)((x) - 3) = 0$

$\Rightarrow (x) = -4$ or $(x) = 3$

$\Rightarrow x \in (-5, -4]$ or $x \in (2, 3]$

$\Rightarrow x \in (-5, -4] \cup (2, 3]$

14. (a) Case (i): $x \notin \mathbb{Z}$

$[x]^2 + (x)^2 > 25$

$[x]^2 + ([x] + 1)^2 > 25$

$2[x]^2 + 2[x] + 1 - 25 > 0$

$\Rightarrow [x]^2 + [x] - 12 > 0$

$\Rightarrow ([x] + 4)([x] - 3) > 0$

$\Rightarrow [x] < -4$ or $[x] > 3$

$\Rightarrow [x] \leq -5$ or $[x] \geq 4$

$\Rightarrow x < -4$ or $x \geq 4$

$\Rightarrow x \in (-\infty, -4) \cup [4, \infty)$ ......(i)

Case (ii): $x \in \mathbb{Z}$

$\Rightarrow [x] = (x) = x$

$\Rightarrow 2x^2 > 25$

$\Rightarrow x^2 > 12.5$

$\Rightarrow x > \sqrt{12.5}$ or $x < -\sqrt{12.5}$

$\Rightarrow x \in [4, \infty)$ or $x \in (-\infty, -4]$ .....(ii)

$\therefore$ Combing (i) and (ii), we get $x \in (-\infty, -4] \cup [4, \infty)$

TEXTUAL EXERCISE-8: (SUBJECTIVE)

1. (i) $a * b = HCF(a, b)$ is a binary operation as HCF of two natural number is always another natural number.

(ii) $\because$ LCM$(a, b) \in \mathbb{N}$ for $a, b \in \mathbb{N}$

$\Rightarrow$ Binary operation

(iii) $a + b = ab \in \mathbb{Q} \ \forall \ a, b \in \mathbb{Q}$

$\Rightarrow a + b + ab \in \mathbb{Q} \quad \Rightarrow$ Binary operation

(iv) $a * b = \sqrt{ab}$ is not a binary operation on $\mathbb{R}$.

e.g., $a = 2, b = -2 \quad \Rightarrow \sqrt{-4} \notin \mathbb{R}$

(v) $a * b = \sqrt{a+b}$ is not a binary operation on $\mathbb{R}$.

e.g., $a = 2$ $b = -3 \quad \Rightarrow a + b = -1$

$\Rightarrow \sqrt{a+b} \notin \mathbb{R}$

Hence, not *a* binary operation.

(vi) $\because$ For $b, a \in \mathbb{R}$, Disc. $= (-3b)^2 - 4(1)(4b)^2 = -7b^2 < 0$

$\Rightarrow a^2 - 3ab + 4b^2 > 0 \ \forall \ a, b \in \mathbb{R}$

$\Rightarrow \sqrt{a^2 - 3ab + 4b^2} \in \mathbb{R}$ Binary operation

(vii) $a * b = (a - b)$ on $\mathbb{Z}^+$

Put $a = 2, b = 3$ $\Rightarrow$ $a - b = -1 \notin \mathbb{Z}^+$

Not a binary operation.

(viii) If $a = b$, then $a * b = |a - b| = 0 \in \mathbb{Z}^+$

$\Rightarrow$ Not a binary operation

(ix) $\because$ $a, b \in \mathbb{Z}^+$ $\Rightarrow$ $a.b \in \mathbb{Z}^+$

$\Rightarrow$ Binary operation

$\Rightarrow$ (x) $a, b \in \mathbb{R}$ $\Rightarrow$ $a, b^2 \in \mathbb{R}$

$\Rightarrow$ $a. b^2 \in \mathbb{R}$ $\Rightarrow$ Binary operation.

(xi) $\because a, b \in \mathbb{Z}^+$ $\Rightarrow$ $a * b = a \in \mathbb{Z}^+$

$\Rightarrow$ Binary operation

2. (i) $a * b = a - b$

Neither commutative nor associative as subtraction of real numbers is so.

(ii) $a * b = a^3 + b^3$

$\Rightarrow$ Commutative as $a * b = b * a$, i.e., $a^3 + b^3 = b^3 + a^3$

Not associative as $a * (b * c) = a * (b^3 + c^3) = a^3 + (b^3 + c^3)^3$ and $(a * b) * c = (a^3 + b^3) * c = (a^3 + b^3) + c^3$

(iii) $a * b = a + 2ab$

$\Rightarrow$ Not commutative, as $b * a = b + 2ab$

$\Rightarrow$ Not associative, as $(a * b) * c = (a + 2ab) * c = (a + 2ab) + 2(a + 2ab)c$ and $a * (b * c) = a + 2a(b * c) = a + 2a(b + 2bc)$

(iv) $a * b = (a - b)^4$

$\Rightarrow$ Commutative, $a * b = b * a$ as $(a - b)^4 = (b - a)^4$

$\Rightarrow$ Not associative, as $a * (b * c) = a * (b - c)^4 = [a - (b - c)^4]^4$ and $(a * b) * c = (a - b)^4 * c = [(a - b)^4 - c]^4$

(v) $a * b = ab/8$ $\because$ $ab/8 = ba/8$

$\Rightarrow$ Commutative as well as associative as $(a * b) * c = \left(\frac{ab}{8}\right) * c = \frac{abc}{64}$ and $(a * (b * c) = a * \left(\frac{bc}{8}\right) = \frac{abc}{64}$

(vi) $a * b = 3ab^2$ and $(b * a) = 3ba^2$

$\Rightarrow$ Not commutative

Also, $(a * b) * c = 3ab^2 * c = 3(3ab^2)c^2 = 9ab^2c^2$

and $a * (b * c) = a * (3bc^2) = 3a(3bc^2)^2 = 27ab^2c^4$

$\Rightarrow$ Not associative

3. LCM of $(a, b) = a * b$ is not a binary operation on A as $3 * 5 = 15 \notin A$ and $5 * 7 = 35 \notin A$

4. Yes, $a * b$ is a binary operation of N

HCF (a, b) = HCF (b, a)

$\Rightarrow$ * is commutative

Also * is associative.

No identity element exists for * as $\exists$ no $e \in \mathbb{N}$ such that HCF $(a, e) = a$

5. (i) $6 * 7 = 42$

$15 * 24 = 120$

(ii) $(a * b) * c = a * (b * c)$

$\Rightarrow$ * is associative

(iii) LCM (a, b) = LCM (b, a)

$\Rightarrow$ * is a commutative

(iv) LCM $(1, a) = a$

$\Rightarrow$ 1 is the identity elements of *

(v) 1 is the only inventible element

6. $(a, b) * (c, d) = (a + c, b + d) = (c + a, d + b) = (c, d) * (a, b)$

$\Rightarrow$ * is commutative

Let $(a, b), (c, d), (e, f) \equiv \mathbb{N} \times \mathbb{N}$, then $(a, b) * [(c, d) * (e, f)]$

$= (a, b) * [(c + e, d + f)] = (a + (c + e), b + (d + f)) = ((a + c), e, (b + d) + f) = ((a + c), (b + d)) * (e, f) = ((a, b) * (c, d)) * (e, f)$

$\Rightarrow$ * is associative on $\mathbb{N} \times \mathbb{N}$.

7. (i) $(3 * 4) * 5 = (1 * 5) = 1$

(ii) Yes it is commutative

(iii) $(3 * 4) * (4 * 5) = (1) * (1) = 1$

8. See the Answer.

9. (a) $a * b = a + 2b$

$(a * b) * c = (a + 2b) * c = a + 2b + 2c$

$a * (b * c) = a * (b + 2c) = a + 2b + 4c$

$\Rightarrow$ Not associative

(b) $a * b = a + 2b$

$b * a = b + 2a$

$\Rightarrow$ $a * b \neq b * a$ $\Rightarrow$ Not commutative

10. $\because$ for $a \in \mathbb{N}, -a \notin \mathbb{N}$

$\Rightarrow$ $-a$ can't be inverse of 'a' moreover the identity element '0' does not exist in $\mathbb{N}$

Also for $a \in \mathbb{N} - \{1\}$, $\frac{1}{a} \in \mathbb{N}$, and hence, $\frac{1}{a}$ can't be the multiplicative inverse of a on $\mathbb{N}$.

11. (i) $(a * b) = a + 4b^2$ ($\because$ Product and sum of two real numbers is real)

$\Rightarrow a + 4b^2 \in \mathbb{R}$ $\Rightarrow$ $a * b$ is a binary operation.

(ii) $\Delta(a, b) = \min\{a, b\}$.

If a, b are reals.

$\Rightarrow$ $a * b = \min\{a, b\}$ is also real.

Similarly $a * b = \max\{a, b\}$ is also binary operations.

(iii) $\cup: P \times P \to P$

$\cup(A, B) = A \cup B$

If $A \in P, B \in P$ $\Rightarrow$ $A \cup B \in P$

$\Rightarrow$ $\cup$ is binary operation on P

Also, $\cap : P * P \to P$, defined by $\cap(A, B) = (A \cap B)$

Similar as explained above if $A \in P$

$\Rightarrow$ $B \in P$ $\Rightarrow$ $A \cap B \in P$

$\Rightarrow$ $\cap$ is a binary operation on P

12. (a) $a * b = 4$ is commutative as $a * b = b * a = 4$

Also $a * (b * c) = a * 4 = 4$ and $(a * b) * c = 4 * c = 4$

$\Rightarrow$ * is associative.

(b) $a * b = \frac{a + b}{4} = b * a$

$\Rightarrow$ * is commutative

Also, $(a * b) * c = \left(\frac{a + b}{4}\right) * c = \frac{\frac{a + b}{4} + c}{4} = \frac{a + b + 4c}{16}$

$a * (b * c) = a * \left(\frac{b + c}{4}\right) = \frac{a + \frac{b + c}{4}}{4} = \frac{4a + b + c}{16}$

$\Rightarrow$ * is not associative

13. $A * B = A \cap B \;\forall\; A, B \in P(W)$

$\therefore$ $W \cap$ (any element $P(W)$) = that element of $P(W)$, as $P(W)$ is the collection of all subsets of W

$\Rightarrow$ W is the identity element with respect to *.

$\because$ $A * B = W$ $\Rightarrow$ $A \cap B = W \Leftrightarrow A = B = W$

$\Rightarrow$ W is the only invertible element and self invertible.

14. $a * b = |a - b|$

$a \text{ o } b = a$

$a * b = |a - b| = b * a = |b - a|$

$\Rightarrow$ * is commutative.

Next, $(a * b) * c = |a - b| * c = ||a - b| - c|$ and $a * (b * c) = a * |b - c| = |a - |b - c||$

$\Rightarrow$ * is not associative.

Now, $aob = a$ but $boa = b$

$\Rightarrow$ o is not commutative.

Next, $ao(boc) = aob = a$

Also, $(aob)oc = aoc = a$

$\Rightarrow$ o is associative .

We have $a * (boc) = |a - b|$ and $(a * b)o(a * b) = |a - b|o|a - b| = |a - b|$

$\Rightarrow$ Yes * distributes over o

Next, $ao(b * c) = ao(|b - c|) = a$ and $(aob) * (aoc) = a * a = |a - a| = 0$

$\Rightarrow$ No 'o' does not distribute over *

TEXTUAL EXERCISE–8: (OBJECTIVE)

1. **(b), (c)** An operation * is associative on set A

$\Leftrightarrow$ $(x * y) * z = x * (y * z) \;\forall\; x, y, z \in A$

(a) $(a * b) * c = (a - b) - c = a - b - c$ and $a * (b * c) = a * (b - c) = a - b + c$

$\Rightarrow$ * is not associative

(b) $(a * b) * c = \left(\frac{ab}{4}\right) * c = \frac{abc}{16}$ and $a * (b * c)$

$= a * \left(\frac{bc}{4}\right) = \frac{abc}{16}$

$\Rightarrow$ * is associative

(c) $(a * b) * c = \left(\sqrt{a^2b^2}\right) * c = \sqrt{a^2b^2c^2} = abc$

$\Rightarrow$ $a * (b * c) = a + \left(\sqrt{b^2c^2}\right) = \sqrt{a^2b^2c^2} = abc$

$\Rightarrow$ * is associative

(d) $(a * b) * c = (a^2 - b^2) * c$

$= (a^2 - b^2) - c^2$

$= (a^2 - b^2 + c)(a^2 - b^2 - c)$

Also, $a * (b * c) = a * (b^2 - c^2)$

$= a^2 - (b^2 - c^2)^2$

$= (a - b^2 + c^2)(a + b^2 - c^2)$

$\Rightarrow$ * is not associative

2. **(a), (b)** Precisely, a binary operation * on a sets is a map which sends elements of the cartesian products $S \times S$ to S.

$* \; S \times S \rightarrow S$

(a) $a * b = \sqrt{a^2b^2 + b^2 + 2ab^2}$; where $a, b \in \mathbb{Z}$

$\Rightarrow$ $a * b = \sqrt{(ab + b)^2} = |b(a + 1)| \in \mathbb{Z}$

$\Rightarrow$ * is *a* binary operation

(b) $a * b = \gcd(a, b) \in \mathbb{Z}$

$\Rightarrow$ * is a binary operation

(c) $a * b = \frac{a - b}{2}$ need not be an integer, e.g., if $a = 7$, $b = 2$, then $a * b = \frac{7 - 2}{2} = \frac{5}{2} \notin \mathbb{Z}$

$\Rightarrow$ * is not *a* binary operation on $\mathbb{Z}$.

(d) $a * b = \frac{a^2 - b^2}{4}$ need not be an integer, e.g., if $a = 4$, $b = 3$, then $a * b = \frac{16 - 9}{4} = \frac{7}{4} \notin \mathbb{Z}$

$\Rightarrow$ * is not a binary operation on $\mathbb{Z}$.

3. **(a)** A binary operation $f: A \times A \rightarrow B$ is commutative it $f(x, y) = f(y, x) \;\forall\; x, y \in A$

(a) is commutative

$a * b = \sqrt{a^2 + b^2 - 2ab}$

$b * a = \sqrt{b^2 + a^2 - 2ab}$

(b) $a * b = a - b$

$b * a = b - a$

$\Rightarrow$ Not commutative.

(c) $a * b = \begin{cases} (a)^b & \text{if } b \geq 0 \\ ab & \text{if } b < 0 \end{cases}$

Let a = 2, b = 3

$\Rightarrow$ $a * b = (2)^3 = 8$ and $b * a = (3)^2 = 9$

$\Rightarrow$ * is not commutative.

if $a = 2, b = -4$

$\Rightarrow$ $a * b = a. b = -8$ and $b * a = (-4)^2 = 16$

$\Rightarrow$ $a * b \neq b * a$

$\Rightarrow$ * is not commutative.

(d) $a * b = a^2 b$ and $b * a = b^2 a$

$\Rightarrow$ * is not commutative

4. **(c)** $A = \{1, \omega, \omega^2\}$; = ω cube root of unity

$a * b = ab$

$\therefore$ $1. 1 = 1, 1. \omega = \omega$ and $1. \omega^2 = \omega^2$

$\Rightarrow$ 1 is an identity element in A.

5. **(c), (d)** $A = \{1, \omega, \omega^2\}$

$\therefore$ $a*b = ab$

$\therefore$ $\omega\omega^2 = \omega^3 = 1$

$\Rightarrow$ Inverse of ω^2 is ω and inverse of ω is ω^2

6. **(c)** $* : A \times A \rightarrow A$

$n(A \times A) = 9$ $\because$ $A \times A$ has 9 elements and each element has 3 choices.

$\Rightarrow$ Total number of binary operations defined on set $A = (3)^9$

7. **(a), (b), (c), (d)**

(a) $a * b$ = least non- negative integer obtained when $(a.b)$ is divided by 6

$\Rightarrow$ 1 is the identity elements in A

Clearly, $1 * 3 = 3$ and $1 * 5 = 5$

$\Rightarrow$ (a) is true

(b) $3 * a$ $\Rightarrow$ $3 * 1 = 3$

$\Rightarrow$ 3 * 5 = 3 $\quad\Rightarrow$ 3 * 3 = 3

$\Rightarrow$ (b) is true

(c) No elements of A can give 3 * a = 1

$\Rightarrow$ (c) is true

(d) Clearly, 5 * 5 = 1 $\quad\Rightarrow$ (d) is true

8. (a), (b), (c)

$A = \{2, 4, 6, 8, 10\}$

Option (a) is correct as $\forall\ a \in A$

6 * a = a

(b) * is commutative as $\forall\ a, b \in A$

$a * b = b * a$ by the table

(c) Since 8 * 10 = 6, 10 * 8 = 6

Where 6 is the identity elements of * as proved above

$\Rightarrow$ Inverse of 8 is 10

(d) 2 * (4 * 8) = 2 * 10 = 8 and (2 * 4) * 8 = (6 * 8) = 8

$\Rightarrow$ (d) is false

TEXTUAL EXERCISE–9: (SUBJECTIVE)

1. (a) $f(x) = \dfrac{\sqrt{x-1}+\sqrt{6-x}}{\sqrt{1-x}+\sqrt{x-6}}$

$x - 1 \geq 0$ and $6 - x \geq 0$ and $1 - x \geq 0$ and $x - 6 \geq 0$ and $\sqrt{1-x}+\sqrt{x-6} \neq 0$

$\Rightarrow x \geq 1$ and $x \leq 6$ and $x \leq 1$ and $x \geq 6$ and $1 - x \neq x - 6$ (never possible simultaneously)

$x \in \phi$

(b) $f(x) = \dfrac{x^2+1}{x-\sqrt{x+2}}$

$\Rightarrow x - \sqrt{x+2} \neq 0$ and $x + 2 \geq 0$

$\Rightarrow x^2 - x - 2 \neq 0$ and $x \in [-2, \infty)$

$\Rightarrow x \neq 2, -1$ and $x \in [-2, \infty)$

$\Rightarrow x \in [-2, \infty) - \{2, -1\}$

(c) $f(x) = \sqrt{\dfrac{x-2}{x+2}} + \sqrt{\dfrac{1-x}{1+x}}$

$\Rightarrow \dfrac{x-2}{x+2} > 0$ or $x = 2$ and $\dfrac{1-x}{1+x} > 0$ or $x = 1$

$\Rightarrow x \in (-\infty, -2) \cup (2, \infty)$ or $x = 2$ and $x \in (-1, 1)$ or $x = 1$

$\Rightarrow x \in (-\infty, -2)\ [2, \infty)$ and $x \in (-1, 1]$

$\Rightarrow x \in \phi$

2. (a) $f(x) = \sqrt{\dfrac{1-5^x}{7^{-x}-7}} = \sqrt{7^x\left(\dfrac{1-5^x}{1-7^{x+1}}\right)}$

$\Rightarrow 7^x > 0 \quad\Rightarrow \dfrac{1-5^x}{1-7^{x+1}} \geq 0$

$\Rightarrow \dfrac{5^x-1}{7^{x+1}-1} > 0$ or $x = 0$

$5^x - 1 > 0$ and $7^{x+1} - 1 > 0$ or $5^x - 1 < 0$ and $7^{x+1} - 1 < 0$ or $x = 0$

$\Rightarrow x > 0$ and $x + 1 > 0$ or $x < 0$ and $x + 1 < 0$ or $x = 0$

$\Rightarrow x \in (0, \infty)$ or $x \in (-\infty, -1)$ or $x = 0$

$x \in (-\infty, -1) \cup [0, \infty)$

(b) $f(x) = \dfrac{\sqrt{5-x}+\sqrt{x-2}}{\sqrt{3-x}-\sqrt{x-1}}$

$x \leq 5$ and $x \geq 2$ and $x \leq 3$ and $x \geq 1$ and $3 - x \neq x - 1$

$x \in [2, 3]$ and $x \neq 2 \Rightarrow x \in (2, 3]$

3. (a) $f(x) = \log_{2\{x\}-3}(x^2 - 5x + 13)$

$x^2 - 5x + 13 > 0$ and $2\{x\} - 3 > 0$ and $2\{x\} - 3 \neq 1$

$\Rightarrow x^2 - 5x + 13 > 0$ is true for all $x \in \mathbb{R}$ as $D < 0$ and leading coefficient is +ve and

$\{x\} > \dfrac{3}{2}$ is not possible for any value of x and $\{x\} \neq$ is 2 true for all x.

Hence, $x \in \phi$.

(b) $f(x) = \log_{10}\left(\dfrac{9-x^2}{x^2-4}\right)$

$\Rightarrow \dfrac{9-x^2}{x^2-4} > 0$

$\Rightarrow (3 - x)(3 + x)(x - 2)(x + 2) > 0$

$\Rightarrow x \in (-3, -2) \cup (2, 3)$

(c) $f(x) = \sqrt{\log_2\left(\dfrac{5x-x^2}{4}\right)}$

$\Rightarrow \dfrac{5x-x^2}{4} > 0$ and $\log_2\left(\dfrac{5x-x^2}{4}\right) \geq 0$

$\Rightarrow x(5 - x) > 0$ and $\dfrac{x(5-x)}{4} \geq 1$

$\Rightarrow x \in (0, 5)$ and $x^2 - 5x - 4 \leq 0$

$\Rightarrow x \in (0, 5)$ and $x \in [1, 4]$

$\Rightarrow x \in [1, 4]$

(d) $f(x) = \sqrt{\log_{\frac{1}{2}}\left(\dfrac{5x-x^2}{4}\right)}$

$\dfrac{x(5-x)}{4} > 0$ and $\log_{\frac{1}{2}}\left(\dfrac{5x-x^2}{4}\right) \geq 0$

$x \in (0, 5)$ and $x(5 - x) \leq 4$

$\Rightarrow x \in (0, 5)$ and $x \in (-\infty, 1]\ [4, \infty)$

$\Rightarrow x \in (0, 1] \cup [4, 5)$

4. (a) $f(x) = \dfrac{1}{\sqrt{x-|x|}} \quad\Rightarrow x - |x| > 0$

$\Rightarrow x > |x| \quad\Rightarrow x \in \phi$

(b) $f(x) = \dfrac{1}{\sqrt{|x|-x}} \quad\Rightarrow |x| > x$

$\Rightarrow x \in (-\infty, 0)$

(c) $f(x) = \sin^{-1}\left(\dfrac{3-|x|}{2}\right)$

$\Rightarrow \dfrac{3-|x|}{2} \in [-1, 1] \quad\Rightarrow 3 - |x| \in [-2, 2]$

$\Rightarrow -|x| \in [-5, -1]$

$\Rightarrow |x| \in [1, 5] \quad\Rightarrow x\ [-5, -1] \cup [1, 5]$

(d) $f(x) = \sqrt{x^2 - 3|x| + 2}$

$\Rightarrow x^2 - 3|x| + 2 \geq 0 \quad\Rightarrow |x|^2 - 3|x| + 2 \geq 0$

$\Rightarrow (|x| - 1)(|x| - 2) \geq 0$

$\Rightarrow$ $|x| \in (-\infty, 1] \cup [2, \infty)$ but $|x| \geq 0$

$\Rightarrow$ $|x| \in [0, 1] \cup [2, \infty)$

$\Rightarrow$ $x \in (-\infty, -2] \cup [-1, 1] \cup [2, \infty)$

5. **(a)** $f(x) = \sqrt{\sin x} + \sqrt{16 - x^2}$

$\sin x \geq 0$ and $16 - x^2 \geq 0$

$\Rightarrow$ $x \in \bigcup_{n \in \mathbb{Z}} [2n\pi, (2n+1)\pi]$ and $x \in [-4, 4]$

$\Rightarrow$ $x \in [-4, -\pi] \cup [0, \pi]$

(b) $f(x) = \sqrt{\cos(\sin x)} + \sqrt{\sin(\cos x)}$

$\Rightarrow$ $\cos(\sin x) \geq 0$ and $\sin(\cos x) \geq 0$

$\Rightarrow$ $x \in \mathbb{R}$ and $\cos x \in [0, 1]$

$\Rightarrow$ $x \in \bigcup_{n \in \mathbb{Z}} \left[(4n-1)\frac{\pi}{2}, (4n+1)\frac{\pi}{2}\right]$

6. **(a)** $f(x) = \cos^{-1}[x] \Rightarrow [x] \in [-1, 1]$

$\Rightarrow$ $x \in [-1, 2)$

$\Rightarrow$ $R_f = \{\cos^{-1}(-1), \cos^{-1}(0), \cos^{-1}(1)\} = \{\pi, \pi/2, 0\}$

(b) $f(x) = \sin^{-1}(x^2 + 1) \quad \Rightarrow \quad x^2 + 1 \in [-1, 1]$

$\Rightarrow$ $x^2 \in [-2, 0]$ but $x^2 \geq 0$

$\Rightarrow$ $x^2 = 0$

$\Rightarrow$ $x = 0$; $x \in \{0\}$ and $R_f = \{\sin^{-1}\} = \{\pi/2\}$

7. **(a)** $f(x) = \cos^{-1}\left(\frac{2x}{1+x^2}\right)$

$$\Rightarrow \frac{2x}{1+x^2} \in [-1, 1] \quad \Rightarrow -1 \leq \frac{2x}{1+x^2} \leq 1$$

$$\Rightarrow \frac{(x+1)^2}{1+x^2} \geq 0 \text{ and } \frac{(x-1)^2}{1+x^2} \geq 0$$

$x = -1$ or $\frac{(x+1)^2}{1+x^2} > 0$ true $\forall x \in \mathbb{R}$ and $x = 1$ or $\frac{(x-1)^2}{1+x^2} > 0$ true $\forall x \in \mathbb{R}$

Hence, $x \in \mathbb{R}$

(b) $f(x) = \cos^{-1}\left(\frac{1+x^2}{2x}\right)$

$$\Rightarrow \frac{1+x^2}{2x} \in [-1, 1] \quad \Rightarrow -1 \leq \frac{1+x^2}{2x} \leq 1$$

$$\Rightarrow \frac{(x+1)^2}{2x} \geq 0 \text{ and } \frac{(x-1)^2}{2x} \leq 0$$

$\Rightarrow$ $x = -1$ or $x > 0$ and $x = 1$ or $x < 0$

$\Rightarrow$ $x \in (0, \infty) \cup \{-1\}$ and $x \in (-\infty, 0) \cup \{1\}$

$\Rightarrow$ $x \in \{-1\} \cup \{1\} \quad \Rightarrow \quad x \in \{-1, 1\}$

(c) $f(x) = \tan^{-1}(1 + x^2) \quad \Rightarrow \quad 1 + x^2 \in (-\infty, \infty)$

$\Rightarrow$ $x^2 \in (-\infty, \infty)$ but $x^2 \geq 0$

$\Rightarrow$ $x^2 \in [0, \infty) \quad \Rightarrow \quad x \in (-\infty, \infty)$

$\Rightarrow$ $x \in \mathbb{R}$

(d) $f(x) = \sin^{-1}\left(\frac{x^2 - 1}{2(x^2+1)}\right)$

$$\Rightarrow -1 \leq \frac{x^2-1}{2(x^2+1)} \leq 1$$

$$\frac{x^2 - 1 + 2x^2 + 2}{2(x^2+1)} \geq 0 \text{ and } \frac{x^2 - 1 - 2x^2 - 2}{2(x^2+1)} \leq 0$$

$$\Rightarrow \frac{3x^2+1}{2(x^2+1)} \geq 0 \text{ and } \frac{x^2+3}{2(x^2+1)} \leq 0$$

$\Rightarrow$ $x \in \mathbb{R}$

8. **(a)** $f(x) = \log_2(3 + 5\sin x)$

$\Rightarrow$ $3 + 5\sin x > 0$

$\Rightarrow$ $\sin x > -\frac{3}{5}$ and $\sin x \in [-1, 1]$

$\Rightarrow$ $\sin x \in \left(-\frac{3}{5}, 1\right]$

$\Rightarrow$ $x \in \bigcup_{n \in \mathbb{Z}} \left(2n\pi - \sin^{-1}\frac{3}{5}, (2n+1)\pi + \sin^{-1}\frac{3}{5}\right)$

(b) $f(x) = \log_2(3 + 2\sin x) \quad \Rightarrow 3 + 2\sin x \geq 0$

$\Rightarrow$ $\sin x \geq -\frac{3}{2} \quad \Rightarrow x \in \mathbb{R}$

9. **(a)** $f(x) = \sqrt{\log_x(\cos 2\pi x)}$

$\Rightarrow$ $x > 0, \neq 1$, $\log_x(\cos 2\pi x) \geq 0$, $\cos 2\pi x > 0$

Case (i): $0 < x < 1$

$\Rightarrow$ $0 < \cos 2\pi x \leq 1$

For $0 < x < 1$, $0 < 2\pi x < 2$

$\Rightarrow$ $2\pi x \in \left(0, \frac{\pi}{2}\right)$ or $\left(\frac{3\pi}{2}, 2\pi\right)$

$\Rightarrow$ $x \in \left(0, \frac{1}{4}\right) \cup \left(\frac{3}{4}, 1\right)$

Case (ii): $x > 1$; $\cos 2\pi x \;\, 1$

$\Rightarrow$ $\cos 2\pi x = 1$

$\Rightarrow$ $x \in \{2, 3, 4, \ldots\}$

$\therefore$ $D_f = \left(0, \frac{1}{4}\right) \cup \left(\frac{3}{4}, 1\right) \cup \{2, 3, 4, \ldots\ldots\infty\}$

(b) $f(x) = \sqrt{(x^2 - 3x - 10)\ln^2(x-3)}$

$\Rightarrow$ $x^2 - 3x - 10 \geq 0$ or $x - 3 = 1$ and $x - 3 > 0$

$\Rightarrow$ $x \in (-\infty, -2]\ [5, \infty)$ or $x > 3$ and $x = 4$

$\Rightarrow$ $x \in \{4\} \cup [5, \infty)$

(c) $f(x) = \cos^{-1}\left(\frac{2-|x|}{4}\right) + (\ln(3-x))^{-1}$

$\Rightarrow$ $\frac{2-|x|}{4} \in [-1, 1]$ and $3 - x \neq 1$ and $3 - x > 0$

$\Rightarrow$ $-|x| \in [-6, 2]$ and $x \neq 2$ and $x < 3$

$\Rightarrow$ $|x| \in [-2, 6]$ and $x \neq 2$ and $x < 3$

$|x| \in [0, 6]$ and $x \in (-\infty, 3) - \{2\}$

$\Rightarrow$ $x \in [-6, 6]$ and $x \in (-\infty, 3) - \{2\}$

$\Rightarrow$ $x \in [-6, 3) - \{2\}$

10. **(a)** $f(x) = \frac{\sqrt{\cos x - \frac{1}{2}}}{\sqrt{6 + 35x - 6x^2}}$

$\Rightarrow$ $\cos x - \frac{1}{2} \geq 0$ and $6 + 35x - 6x^2 > 0$

$\Rightarrow$ $\cos x \geq \frac{1}{2}$ and $6x^2 - 35x - 6 < 0$

$\Rightarrow \cos x \in \left[\frac{1}{2},1\right]$ and $(6x+1)(x-6)<0$

$\Rightarrow x \in \bigcup_{n\in\mathbb{Z}}\left[2n\pi-\frac{\pi}{3},2n\pi+\frac{\pi}{3}\right]$ and $x\in\left(-\frac{1}{6},6\right)$

$\Rightarrow x\in\bigcup\left[-\frac{\pi}{3},\frac{\pi}{3}\right]\cup\left[\frac{5\pi}{3},\frac{7\pi}{3}\right]\cup....$ and $x\in\left(-\frac{1}{6},6\right)$

$\Rightarrow x\in\left(-\frac{1}{6},\frac{\pi}{3}\right]\cup\left[\frac{5\pi}{3},6\right)$

(b) $f(x)=\left(\log_{\left(\frac{x-2}{x+3}\right)}2\right)+\sqrt{9-x^2}$

$\Rightarrow 9-x^2\geq 0$ and $\frac{x-2}{x+3}\neq 1$ (always hold) and $\frac{x-2}{x+3}>0$

$\Rightarrow x\in[-3,3]$ and $(x-2)(x+3)>0$

$\Rightarrow x\in[-3,3]$ and $x\in(-\infty,-3)\cup(2,\infty)$

$\Rightarrow x\in(2,3]$

11. (a) $f(x)=\frac{1}{[x]}+\log_{1-\{x\}}(x^2-3x+10)$

$+\frac{1}{\sqrt{2-|x|}}+\frac{1}{\sqrt{\sec(\sin x)}}$

$\Rightarrow [x]\neq 0$ and $1-\{x\}>0$ and $1-\{x\}\neq 1$ and $x^2-3x+10>0$ and $2-|x|>0$ and $\sec(\sin x)>0$

$\Rightarrow x\notin[0,1)$ and $x\in\mathbb{R}$ and $x\notin\mathbb{Z}$ and $x\in\mathbb{R}$ and $x\in(-2,2)$ and $x\in\mathbb{R}$

$\Rightarrow x\in(-2,-1)\cup(-1,0)\cup(1,2)$

(b) $f(x)=\frac{1}{\sqrt{\sin(\cos x)}}+\sin^{-1}\left(\frac{2x}{\pi}\right)$

$+\frac{1}{\{-x\}}+\frac{1}{\ln\left(\left(1-\left[\tan\frac{x}{2}\right]\right)-\left[-\tan\frac{x}{2}\right]\right)}$

$\sin(\cos x)>0$ and $\frac{2x}{\pi}\in(-1,1)$ and $x\notin\mathbb{Z}$ and

$\ln\left(1-\left[\tan\frac{x}{2}\right]\right)-\left[-\tan\frac{x}{2}\right]\neq 0$ and $1-\left[\tan\frac{x}{2}\right]>0$

$\cos x\in(0,1]$ and $x\in\left(-\frac{\pi}{2},\frac{\pi}{2}\right)$ and $x\notin\mathbb{Z}$ and

$\ln\left(1-\left[\tan\frac{x}{2}\right]\right)-\left[-\tan\frac{x}{2}\right]\neq 0$ and $\tan\frac{x}{2}\in(-\infty,1)$

$\Rightarrow x\in\left(-\frac{\pi}{2},\frac{\pi}{2}\right)$ and $x\notin\mathbb{Z}$ and

$\ln\left(1-\left[\tan\frac{x}{2}\right]\right)+\left[-\tan\frac{x}{2}\right]\neq 0$, $\tan\frac{x}{2}\in(-\infty,1)$

$\Rightarrow x\in\left(\frac{-\pi}{2},-1\right)\cup(-1,0)\cup(0,1)\cup\left(1,\frac{\pi}{2}\right)$ and ln

$\left(1-\left[\tan\frac{x}{2}\right]\right)+\left[-\tan\frac{x}{2}\right]\neq 0$

$\because$ If $x\in\left(-\frac{\pi}{2},\frac{\pi}{2}\right) \Rightarrow \frac{x}{2}\in\left(-\frac{\pi}{4},\frac{\pi}{4}\right)$

$\Rightarrow \tan\frac{x}{2}\in(-1,1)$

$\because \tan\frac{x}{2}\in(-1,1)\Rightarrow\left[\tan\frac{x}{2}\right]\in\{-1,0\}$

Case (i): $\frac{-\pi}{2}<x<-1$

$\Rightarrow \frac{-\pi}{4}<\frac{x}{2}<\frac{-1}{2}$

$\Rightarrow -1<\tan\frac{x}{2}<\tan\left(\frac{-1}{2}\right)$

$\Rightarrow \left[\tan\frac{x}{2}\right]=-1$ and $\left[-\tan\frac{x}{2}\right]=0$

$\Rightarrow \ln\left(1-\left[\tan\frac{x}{2}\right]\right)+\left[-\tan\frac{x}{2}\right]=\ln 2\neq 0$

Case (ii): $-1<x<0$

$\Rightarrow \ln\left(1-\left[\tan\frac{x}{2}\right]\right)+\left[-\tan\frac{x}{2}\right]=\ln 2$

Case (iii): $0<x<1$

$\Rightarrow \ln\left(1-\left[\tan\frac{x}{2}\right]\right)+\left[-\tan\frac{x}{2}\right]=-1\neq 0$

Case (iv): $1<x<\pi/2$

$\Rightarrow \ln\left(1-\left[\tan\frac{x}{2}\right]\right)+\left[-\tan\frac{x}{2}\right]=-1\neq 0$

$D_f=\left(\frac{-\pi}{2},-1\right)\cup(-1,0)\cup(0,1)\cup\left(1,\frac{\pi}{2}\right)$

TEXTUAL EXERCISE-9: (OBJECTIVE)

1. (c) $\sqrt{x(x-1)} \quad\Rightarrow x(x-1)\geq 0$

$\Rightarrow x\in(-\infty,0]\cup[1,\infty)$

2. (a) $x^{\frac{1}{\ln x}} \quad\Rightarrow x>0$ and $x\neq 1$

$\Rightarrow x\in(0,\infty)\sim\{1\}$

3. (a) $\frac{1}{\sqrt{x-|x|}} \quad\Rightarrow x-|x|>0$

$\Rightarrow x>|x| \quad\Rightarrow x\in\phi$

4. (b) $\frac{1}{\sqrt{|x|-x}} \quad\Rightarrow |x|-x>0$

$\Rightarrow |x|>x \quad\Rightarrow x\in(-\infty,0)$

5. (b) $\frac{1}{2-\cos 3x} \quad\Rightarrow 2-\cos 3x\neq 0$

$\Rightarrow \cos 3x\neq 2 \quad\Rightarrow x\in\mathbb{R}$

6. (a) $\log_{10}(1+x^3) \quad\Rightarrow 1+x^3>0$

$\Rightarrow x^3>-1 \quad\Rightarrow x\in(-1,\infty)$

7. (c) $\frac{1}{\sqrt{x(x-2)(x-3)}} \quad\Rightarrow x(x-2)(x-3)>0$

$\Rightarrow x\in(0,2)\cup(3,\infty)$

8. **(b)** $\dfrac{1}{\sqrt[3]{(x-1)(x-2)(x-4)}}$

$\Rightarrow$ $(x-1)(x-2)(x-4) \neq 0$

$\Rightarrow$ $x \neq 1, 2, 4$ $\Rightarrow$ $x \in \mathbb{R} \sim \{(1, 2, 4)\}$

9. **(d)** $2^x + 2^y = 2$ $\Rightarrow$ $2^y = 2 - 2^x$

$\Rightarrow$ $2^y > 0$ $\Rightarrow$ $2 - 2^x > 0$

$\Rightarrow$ $2 > 2^x$ $\Rightarrow$ $x < 1$

$\Rightarrow$ $x \in (-\infty, 1)$

10. **(a)** $f(x) = \sqrt{3-x} + \cos^{-1}\left(\dfrac{3-2x}{5}\right)$

$\Rightarrow$ $3 - x \geq 0$ and $\dfrac{3-2x}{5} \in [-1, 1]$

$\Rightarrow$ $x \in (-\infty, 3]$ and $x \in [-1, 4]$

$\Rightarrow$ $x \in [-1, 3]$

11. **(c)** $f(x) = \sin^{-1}\left(\dfrac{x-3}{2}\right) - \log_{10}(4-x)$

$\Rightarrow$ $\dfrac{x-3}{2} \in [-1, 1]$ and $4 - x > 0$

$\Rightarrow$ $x \in [1, 5]$ and $x < 4$ $\Rightarrow$ $x \in [1, 4)$

12. **(d)** $y = \dfrac{1}{\log_{10}(3-x)} + \sqrt{x+2}$

$\Rightarrow$ $x > -2$ and $3 - x \neq 1$ and $3 - x > 0$

$\Rightarrow$ $x > -2$ and $x \neq 2$ and $x < 3$

$\Rightarrow$ $x \in (-2, 3) - \{2\}$

13. **(a)** $f(x) = \sqrt{\dfrac{(x+1)(x-3)}{x-2}}$

$\Rightarrow$ $\dfrac{(x+1)(x-3)}{(x-2)} > 0$ or $x = -1, 3$

$\Rightarrow$ $x \in (-1, 2) \cup (3, \infty)$ or $x = -1, 3$

$\Rightarrow$ $x \in [-1, 2) \cup [3, \infty)$

14. **(c)** $f(x) = \sqrt{\dfrac{1-|x|}{2-|x|}}$

$\Rightarrow$ $1 - |x| = 0$ or $\dfrac{1-|x|}{2-|x|} > 0$

$\Rightarrow$ $x = -1, 1$ or $|x| \in (-\infty, 1) \cup (2, \infty)$ and $|x| \geq 0$

$\Rightarrow$ $x = -1, 1$ or $|x| \in [0, 1) \cup (2, \infty)$

$\Rightarrow$ $x = -1, 1$ or $x \in (-\infty, -2) \cup (-1, 1) \cup (2, \infty)$

$\Rightarrow$ $x \in (-\infty, -2) \cup [-1, 1] \cup (2, \infty)$

15. **(d)** $f(x) = \cos^{-1}\left(\dfrac{3}{4+2\sin x}\right)$

$\Rightarrow$ $\dfrac{3}{4+2\sin x} \in [-1, 1]$ $\Rightarrow$ $\dfrac{1}{4+2\sin x} \in \left[-\dfrac{1}{3}, \dfrac{1}{3}\right]$

$\Rightarrow$ $4 + 2\sin x \in (-\infty, -3] \cup [3, \infty)$

$\Rightarrow$ $2\sin x \in (-\infty, -7] \cup [-1, \infty)$

$\Rightarrow$ $\sin x \in \left(-\infty, -\dfrac{7}{2}\right] \cup \left[-\dfrac{1}{2}, \infty\right)$, but $\sin x \in [-1, 1]$

$\Rightarrow$ $\sin x \in \left[-\dfrac{1}{2}, 1\right]$

$\Rightarrow$ $x \in \bigcup_{n\in\mathbb{Z}} \left[2n\pi - \dfrac{\pi}{6}, (2n+1)\pi + \dfrac{\pi}{6}\right]$

16. **(a)** $f(x) = \dfrac{1}{\sqrt{\sin x}} + \sqrt[3]{\sin x}$

$\Rightarrow$ $\sin x > 0$ $\Rightarrow$ $x \in \bigcup_{k\in\mathbb{Z}} (2k\pi, (2k+1)\pi)$

17. **(d)** $f(x) = \dfrac{1}{\sqrt{|\cos x| + \cos x}}$

$\Rightarrow$ $|\cos x| + \cos x > 0$

$\Rightarrow$ $|\cos x| > -\cos x$ $\Rightarrow$ $\cos x > 0$

$\Rightarrow$ $x \in \left(2n\pi - \dfrac{\pi}{2}, 2n\pi + \dfrac{\pi}{2}\right)$

$\Rightarrow$ $x \in \bigcup_{n\in\mathbb{Z}} \left((4n-1)\dfrac{\pi}{2}, (4n+1)\dfrac{\pi}{2}\right)$

TEXTUAL EXERCISE–10: (SUBJECTIVE)

1. **(a)** $\sqrt{x^2+4}$ $\Rightarrow$ $x^2 + 4 \geq 0$ true $\forall x \in \mathbb{R}$

$\Rightarrow$ $x \in (-\infty, \infty)$ $\Rightarrow$ $x^2 \in [0, \infty)$

$\Rightarrow$ $x^2 + 4 \in [4, \infty)$

(b) $\dfrac{1}{(x-1)(x-5)}$ $\Rightarrow$ $x \neq 1, 5$

$\Rightarrow$ $x \in \mathbb{R} \sim \{1, 5\}$ is the domain

$\dfrac{1}{(x-1)(x-5)} = \dfrac{1}{x^2-6x+5} = \dfrac{1}{(x-3)^2-4}$

$x \in (-\infty, 1) \cup (1, 5) \cup (5, \infty)$

$x - 3 \in (-\infty, -2) \cup (-2, 2) \cup (2, \infty)$

$\Rightarrow$ $(x-3)^2 \in [0, 4) \cup (4, \infty)$

$\Rightarrow$ $(x-3)^2 - 4 \in [-4, 0)\ (0, \infty)$

$\Rightarrow$ $\dfrac{1}{(x-3)^2-4} \in \left(-\infty, -\dfrac{1}{4}\right] \cup (0, \infty)$

(c) $\sqrt[3]{x+8}; x \in \mathbb{R}$

$x + 8 \in \mathbb{R}$ $\Rightarrow$ $x + 8\ (-\infty, \infty)$

$\sqrt[3]{x+8} \in (-\infty, \infty)$ $\therefore$ Range is $\mathbb{R}$

(d) $y = \dfrac{1}{x^2+4}$; $x^2 + 4 \neq 0$ true $\forall x \in \mathbb{R}$

Now as $x \in (-\infty, \infty)$ $\Rightarrow$ $x^2 \in [0, \infty)$

$\Rightarrow$ $x^2 + 4 \in [4, \infty)$ $\Rightarrow$ $\dfrac{1}{x^2+4} \in \left(0, \dfrac{1}{4}\right]$

$\therefore$ Range is $\left(0, \dfrac{1}{4}\right]$

2. $f(x) = {}^{x+1}C_{2x-8}$; $g(x) = {}^{2x-8}C_{x+1}$

$\Rightarrow$ $h(x) = f(x).g(x) = {}^{x+1}C_{2x-8}.{}^{2x-8}C_{x+1}$

$\Rightarrow$ $x + 1 > 0$ and $2x - 8 > 0$ and $x + 1 \geq 2x - 8$ and $2x - 8 \geq x + 1$

$\Rightarrow$ $x \in (4, \infty)$ and $x = 9$ $\Rightarrow$ $x = 9$

$\therefore$ $D_f(h(x)) = \{9\}$; $R_f = \{1\}$

3. (a) $f(x) = 4\tan x \cos x = 4\dfrac{\sin x}{\cos x}\cos x$

$= \begin{cases} 4\sin x & x \in \mathbb{R} \sim \bigcup_{n\in\mathbb{Z}} (2n+1)\dfrac{\pi}{2} \\ \text{undefined} & \text{otherwise} \end{cases}$

Hence, $D_f = \mathbb{R} \sim \bigcup_{n\in\mathbb{Z}} \left\{(2n+1)\dfrac{\pi}{2}\right\}$

$\Rightarrow$ $x \in \mathbb{R} \sim \bigcup_{n\in\mathbb{Z}} \left\{(2n+1)\dfrac{\pi}{2}\right\}$

$\Rightarrow$ $\sin x \in (-1, 1)$

$\Rightarrow$ $4 \sin x \in (-4, 4)$

$\Rightarrow$ $R_f = (-4, 4)$

(b) $\cos (2 \sin x)$

$\sin x \in [-1, 1]$

$\Rightarrow$ $2 \sin x \in [-2, 2]$

$2 \sin x \in [-2, 0]$ or $2 \sin x \in [0, 2]$

$\cos (2 \sin x) \in [\cos (-2), 1]$ or $\cos (2 \sin x \in [\cos 2, 1])$

$\cos (2 \sin x) \in [\cos 2, 1] \cup [\cos 2, 1]$

$\cos (2 \sin x) \in [\cos 2, 1]$

(c) $\sin (\log_2 x)$ for $\log_2 x$ to be defined, $x > 0$

$\Rightarrow$ $x \in (0, \infty)$ $\Rightarrow$ $\log_2 x \in (-\infty, \infty)$

$\Rightarrow$ $\sin (\log_2 x) \in [-1, 1]$

4. (a) $f(x) = [\{x\}]$ or $\{[x]\}$

$\{x\} \in [0, 1)$ $\Rightarrow$ $[\{x\}] \in \{0\}$

Also, $[x] \in \mathbb{Z}$ $\Rightarrow$ $\{[x]\} \in \{0\}$

(b) $g(x) = \dfrac{\tan(\pi[x-\pi])}{x^2 - 3x + 4}$

$x^2 - 3x + 4 \neq 0$ true $\forall\ x \in \mathbb{R}$ as $D < 0$, hence, no real roots

$\tan (\pi [x - \pi])$

$\Rightarrow$ The numerator will always be the tangent of multiple of π, hence, it is 0.

$\Rightarrow$ $R_f \in \{0\}$

(c) $f(x) = \cos 2x - \sin 2x = \sqrt{2}\left(\dfrac{1}{\sqrt{2}}\cos 2x - \dfrac{1}{\sqrt{2}}\sin 2x\right)$

$= \sqrt{2}\left(\cos\left(2x + \dfrac{\pi}{4}\right)\right)$

$\cos\left(2x + \dfrac{\pi}{4}\right) \in [-1, 1]$

$\Rightarrow$ $\sqrt{2}\cos\left(2x + \dfrac{\pi}{4}\right) \in [-\sqrt{2}, \sqrt{2}]$

(d) $f(x) = \cot^2\left(x - \dfrac{\pi}{4}\right)$; $x - \dfrac{\pi}{4} \in (-\infty, \infty)$

$\cot\left(x - \dfrac{\pi}{4}\right) \in (-\infty, \infty)$

$\Rightarrow$ $\cot^2\left(x - \dfrac{\pi}{4}\right) \in [0, \infty)$

5. (a) $f(x) = \sin^{-1}\left(\dfrac{x^2 - 1}{2(x^2+1)}\right)$

$\dfrac{x^2 - 1}{2(x^2+1)} = \dfrac{1}{2} - \dfrac{1}{x^2+1}$

$-1 \le \dfrac{1}{2} - \dfrac{1}{x^2+1} \le 1$

$\Rightarrow$ $-\dfrac{3}{2} \le -\dfrac{1}{x^2+1} \le \dfrac{1}{2}$

$\Rightarrow$ $-\dfrac{1}{2} \le \dfrac{1}{x^2+1} \le \dfrac{3}{2}$, but $\dfrac{1}{x^2+1} > 0$

$\Rightarrow$ $0 < \dfrac{1}{x^2+1} \le \dfrac{3}{2}$ $\Rightarrow$ $\dfrac{2}{3} \le x^2 + 1 < \infty$

$\Rightarrow$ $-\dfrac{1}{3} \le x^2 < \infty$ true $\forall\ x \in \mathbb{R}$

Now as $x \in (-\infty, \infty)$ $\Rightarrow$ $x^2 + 1 \in [1, \infty)$

$\dfrac{1}{x^2+1} \in (0,1]$ $\Rightarrow$ $-\dfrac{1}{x^2+1} \in [-1, 0)$

$\Rightarrow$ $\dfrac{1}{2} - \dfrac{1}{x^2+1} \in \left[-\dfrac{1}{2}, \dfrac{1}{2}\right)$

$\Rightarrow$ $\sin^{-1}\left(\dfrac{x^2-1}{2(x^2+1)}\right) \in \left[-\dfrac{\pi}{6}, \dfrac{\pi}{6}\right)$

(b) $f(x) = \cos^{-1}\left(\dfrac{2x}{1+x^2}\right)$

$-1 \le \dfrac{2x}{1+x^2} \le 1$ $\Rightarrow$ $\dfrac{(x+1)^2}{x^2+1} \ge 0$ or $\dfrac{(x-1)^2}{(x^2+1)} \ge 0$

$\Rightarrow$ $x \in \mathbb{R}$

$\dfrac{2x}{1+x^2} = \dfrac{2}{x + \dfrac{1}{x}}$ if $x \in \mathbb{R} \sim \{0\}$

$\Rightarrow$ $x + \dfrac{1}{x} \in (-\infty, -2] \cup [2, \infty)$

$\Rightarrow$ $\dfrac{1}{x + \dfrac{1}{x}} \in \left[-\dfrac{1}{2}, 0\right) \cup \left(0, \dfrac{1}{2}\right]$

$\dfrac{2}{x + \dfrac{1}{x}} \in [-1, 0) \cup (0, 1]$

$\Rightarrow$ $\cos^{-1}\left(\dfrac{2x}{1+x^2}\right) \in [0, \pi] \sim \left\{\dfrac{\pi}{2}\right\}$

If $x = 0$, then $\dfrac{2x}{1+x^2} = 0$

$\Rightarrow$ $\cos^{-1} 0 = \dfrac{\pi}{2}$ $\Rightarrow$ $R_f \rightarrow [0, \pi]$

(c) $f(x) = \cos^{-1}\left(\dfrac{1+x^2}{2x}\right)$

$-1 \le \dfrac{1+x^2}{2x} \le 1$

$-1 \le \dfrac{1+x^2}{2x}$

$$0 \le \frac{x^2+2x+1}{2x}$$

$\Rightarrow \dfrac{(x+1)^2}{2x} \ge 0 \quad \Rightarrow x > 0$ or $x = -1$

Also, $\dfrac{1+x^2}{2x} - 1 \le 0$

$\Rightarrow \dfrac{x^2+1-2x}{2x} \le 0 \quad \Rightarrow \dfrac{(x-1)^2}{2x} \le 0$

$\Rightarrow x < 0$ or $x = 1$

$\Rightarrow x \in \{-1, 1\}$

$\Rightarrow f(x) = \cos^{-1}(-1)$ or $\cos^{-1}(1)$, i.e., π or 0

$\Rightarrow R_f = \{0, \}$

(d) $f(x) = \tan^{-1}(1 + x^2)$

$x^2 + 1 \in [1, \infty) \quad \Rightarrow \tan^{-1}(x^2+1) \in \left[\dfrac{\pi}{4}, \dfrac{\pi}{2}\right)$

(e) $f(x) = \log_2(3 + 5\sin x)$

Now as $3 + 5\sin x > 0$

$\Rightarrow \sin x > -\dfrac{3}{5}$ and $\sin x \in [-1, 1]$

$\Rightarrow \sin x \in \left(-\dfrac{3}{5}, 1\right] \quad \Rightarrow 5\sin x \in (-3, 5]$

$\Rightarrow 3 + 5\sin x \in (0, 8]$

$\Rightarrow \log_2(3 + 5\sin x)\ (-\infty, 3]$

(f) $f(x) = \tan^{-1}\dfrac{2x}{1+x^2}$

If $x \ne 0$, then $\dfrac{2x}{1+x^2} = \dfrac{2}{x+\dfrac{1}{x}}$

$\Rightarrow x + \dfrac{1}{x} \in (-\infty, -2] \cup [2, \infty)$

$\dfrac{2}{x+\dfrac{1}{x}} \in [-1, 0) \cup (0, 1]$

If $x = 0$, then $\dfrac{2x}{1+x^2} = 0$

$\Rightarrow \dfrac{2x}{1+x^2} \in [-1, 1]$

$\Rightarrow \tan^{-1}\dfrac{2x}{1+x^2} \in \left[-\dfrac{\pi}{4}, \dfrac{\pi}{4}\right]$

6. (a) $5x^2 - 8x + 4 = 5\left[\left(x^2 - \dfrac{8}{5}x\right) + \dfrac{4}{5}\right]$

$= 5\left(x^2 - 2\times\dfrac{4}{5}x + \dfrac{16}{25}\right) + 4 - \dfrac{16}{5} = 5\left(x - \dfrac{4}{5}\right)^2 + \dfrac{4}{5}$

Now, $5\left(x - \dfrac{4}{5}\right)^2 \in [0, \infty)$

$\Rightarrow 5\left(x - \dfrac{4}{5}\right)^2 + \dfrac{4}{5} \in \left[\dfrac{4}{5}, \infty\right)$

$\Rightarrow \ln(5x^2 - 8x + 4) \in \left[\ln\dfrac{4}{5}, \infty\right)$

(b) $\cot^{-1}\left[\log_{\frac{4}{5}}(5x^2 - 8x + 4)\right)$

$5x^2 - 8x + 4 \in \left[\dfrac{4}{5}, \infty\right)$

$\log_{4/5}(5x^2 - 8x + 4) \in (0, 1]$

$\cot^{-1}(\log_{4/5}(5x^2 - 8x + 4)) \in \left[\dfrac{\pi}{4}, \dfrac{\pi}{2}\right)$

(c) $5x^2 - 8x + 4 \in \left[\dfrac{4}{5}, \infty\right)$

$\log_{5/4}(5x^2 - 8x + 4) \in [-1, \infty)$

$\cot^{-1}\log_{\frac{5}{4}}(5x^2 - 8x + 4) \in \left(0, \dfrac{3\pi}{4}\right]$

7. (a) $f(x) = \dfrac{x^2 - x + 1}{x^2 + x + 1} = 1 - \dfrac{2x}{x^2 + x + 1}$

If $x \ne 0$, then $\dfrac{2x}{x^2+x+1} = \dfrac{2}{x + \dfrac{1}{x} + 1}$;

$x + \dfrac{1}{x} \in (-\infty, -2] \cup [2, \infty)$

$x + \dfrac{1}{x} + 1 \in (-\infty, -1] \cup [3, \infty)$

$\Rightarrow \dfrac{1}{x + \dfrac{1}{x} + 1} \in \left(0, \dfrac{1}{3}\right] \cup [-1, 0)$

$\Rightarrow \dfrac{2}{x + \dfrac{1}{x} + 1} \in \left(0, \dfrac{2}{3}\right] \cup [-2, 0)$

$\Rightarrow 1 + \left(\dfrac{-2}{x + \dfrac{1}{x} + 1}\right) \in \left[\dfrac{1}{3}, 1\right) \cup (1, 3]$

If $x = 0$, then $\dfrac{x^2 - x + 1}{x^2 + x + 1} = 1$

$\Rightarrow \dfrac{x^2 - x + 1}{x^2 + x + 1} \in \left[\dfrac{1}{3}, 3\right]$

(b) $f(x) = \dfrac{x}{\ln x}$; $x \in (0, \infty) \sim \{1\}$

$f'(x) = \dfrac{\ln x - 1}{(\ln x)^2}$; $f'(x) = 0$ when $\ln x = 1$

$\Rightarrow x = e$

If $x > e$, then $f'(x) > 0$ and if $x < e$, then $f'(x) < 0$

$\therefore$ On $(0, 1)$, $f(x) < 0$

$\Rightarrow \lim\limits_{x \to 0^+} f(x) = \lim\limits_{x \to 0} \dfrac{x}{\ln x} = 0$

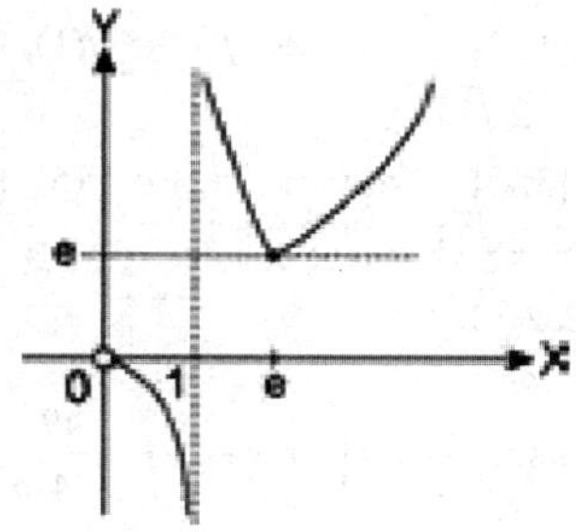

Also, $\lim\limits_{x\to 1^-} f(x) = \lim\limits_{h\to 0}\frac{1-h}{\ln(1-h)} = -\infty$

On $(1, e)$; $f'(x) < 0$ and $\lim\limits_{x\to 1^+} f(x) = \lim\limits_{h\to 0}\frac{1+h}{\ln(1+h)} = \infty$

$f(e) = e$

On (e, ∞); $f'(x) > 0$; $\lim\limits_{x\to\infty} f(x) = \lim\limits_{x\to\infty}\frac{x}{\ln x}$

Applying L-H rule $\lim\limits_{x\to\infty} f(x) = \lim\limits_{x\to\infty}\frac{x}{\ln x} = \lim\limits_{x\to\infty}\frac{1}{\frac{1}{x}} = \lim\limits_{x\to\infty} x = \infty$

$\therefore$ Range is $(-\infty, 0) \cup [e, \infty)$

8. $f(x) = \sin^{-1} x^2 + [\{\ln\sqrt{x-[x]}\}] + \cot^{-1}\left(\frac{1}{1+\sqrt{2}x^2}\right)$

$= \sin^{-1} x^2 + [\{\ln\sqrt{\{x\}}\}] + \cot^{-1}\left(\frac{1}{1+\sqrt{2}x^2}\right)$

If $x \notin \mathbb{Z}$, then $f(x) = \sin^{-1} x^2 + 0 + \cot^{-1}\left(\frac{1}{1+\sqrt{2}x^2}\right)$

$= \sin^{-1} x^2 + \cot^{-1}\left(\frac{1}{1+\sqrt{2}x^2}\right)$

$\Rightarrow x \notin \mathbb{Z}$ and $x^2 \in [-1, 1]$ and $x^2 \in [0, \infty)$ and $\frac{1}{1+\sqrt{2}x^2} \in (-\infty, \infty)$

$\Rightarrow$ $x \notin \mathbb{Z}$ and $x^2 \in [0, 1]$ and $1+\sqrt{2}x^2 \in (-\infty, 0) \cup (0, \infty)$

$\Rightarrow$ $x \notin \mathbb{Z}$ and $x \in [-1, 1]$ and $x^2 \in \left(-\infty, -\frac{1}{\sqrt{2}}\right) \cup \left(-\frac{1}{\sqrt{2}}, \infty\right)$

but $x^2 \geq 0$

$\Rightarrow$ $x \in [-1, 1]$ and $x^2 \in [0, \infty)$ and $x \notin \mathbb{Z}$

$\Rightarrow$ $x \in [-1, 1]$ and $x \in \mathbb{R}$ and $x \notin \mathbb{Z}$

$\Rightarrow$ $x \in [-1, 1]$ and $x \notin \mathbb{Z}$

$\Rightarrow$ $x \in (-1, 1) \sim \{0\}$

If $x \in \mathbb{Z}$, then function $f(x)$ will be undefined as ln 0 is not defined. For the respective domain $(-1, 1) \sim \{0\}$

$f(x) = \sin^{-1} x^2 + [\{\ln\sqrt{x-\{x\}}\}] + \cot^{-1}\left(\frac{1}{1+\sqrt{2}x^2}\right)$

$= \sin^{-1} x^2 + \cot^{-1}\left(\frac{1}{1+\sqrt{2}x^2}\right)$

$\Rightarrow$ Range of $f(x) = \left(\frac{\pi}{4}, \frac{7\pi}{8}\right)$

9. **(i)** For $\sqrt{x-1}$ to be defined $x - 1 \geq 0$

$\Rightarrow x \geq 1$ $\qquad \Rightarrow x \in [1, \infty)$

$\Rightarrow x - 1 \in [0, \infty)$ $\qquad \Rightarrow \sqrt{x-1} \in [0, \infty)$

(ii) $\sqrt[3]{x-2}$; $x \in \mathbb{R}$ $\qquad \Rightarrow x - 2 \in (-\infty, \infty)$

$\Rightarrow \sqrt[3]{x-2} \in (-\infty, \infty)$ $\qquad \Rightarrow \sqrt[3]{x-2} \in \mathbb{R}$

(iii) $\sqrt{(x-1)(x-4)}$ for square root to be defined $(x-1)(x-4) \geq 0$

$\Rightarrow x \in (-\infty, 1] \cup [4, \infty)$

Now, $(x-1)(x-4) = x^2 - 5x + 4 = \left(x-\frac{5}{2}\right)^2 - \frac{9}{4}$

$\Rightarrow x \in (-\infty, 1] \cup [4, \infty)$

$\Rightarrow \left(x-\frac{5}{2}\right) \in \left(-\infty, -\frac{3}{2}\right] \cup \left[\frac{3}{2}, \infty\right)$

Now, $\left(x-\frac{5}{2}\right)^2 - \frac{9}{4} \in [0, \infty)$

$\Rightarrow \sqrt{(x-1)(x-4)} \in [0, \infty)$

(iv) $\frac{1}{(x-1)(x-2)(x-3)}$; $x \in \mathbb{R} \sim \{1, 2, 3\}$

The expression is the denominator is cubic in x it will take all values from $(-\infty, \infty)$ and its reciprocal will take all values except 0.

Hence, $R_f = (-\infty, \infty) \sim \{0\}$

(v) $\frac{x-1}{x^2-4x+3} = \frac{(x-1)}{(x-1)(x-3)}$; $D_f \to \mathbb{R} \sim \{1, 3\}$

If $x = 1$, then $\frac{x-1}{x^2-4x+3}$ is not defined

If $x \neq 1$, then $\frac{x-1}{x^2-4x+3} = \frac{1}{x-3}$

$\Rightarrow x - 3 \in (-\infty, \infty) \sim \{-2\}$

$\Rightarrow x - 3 \in (-\infty, -2) \cup (-2, \infty)$

$\Rightarrow \frac{1}{x-3} \in \left(-\frac{1}{2}, 0\right) \cup \left(-\infty, -\frac{1}{2}\right) \cup (0, \infty)$

$\Rightarrow R_f \to \mathbb{R} \sim \left\{0, -\frac{1}{2}\right\}$

(vi) $\frac{x^2-1}{x^2+5x+4} = \frac{(x-1)(x+1)}{(x+4)(x+1)}$; $x \in \mathbb{R} \sim \{-1, -4\}$

If $x = -1, -4$, then $\frac{x^2-1}{x^2+5x+4}$ is not defined

If $x \neq -1, -4$, then $\frac{x^2-1}{x^2+5x+4} = \frac{x-1}{x+4} = 1 - \frac{5}{x+4}$

$x \in (-\infty, -4) \cup (-4, -1) \cup (-1, \infty)$

$x + 4 \in (-\infty, 0) \cup (0, 3) \cup (3, \infty)$

$\frac{1}{x+4} \in (-\infty, 0) \cup \left(0, \frac{1}{3}\right) \cup \left(\frac{1}{3}, \infty\right)$

$1 - \frac{5}{x+4} \in \left(-\infty, -\frac{2}{3}\right) \cup \left(-\frac{2}{3}, 1\right) \cup (1, \infty)$

$\Rightarrow\ R_f \to \mathbb{R} \sim \left\{1, -\dfrac{2}{3}\right\}$.

(vii) $\dfrac{x^2+2x-3}{x^2-1} = \dfrac{(x+3)(x-1)}{(x-1)(x+1)}; x \in \mathbb{R} \sim \{1, -1\}$

If $x \neq 1, -1$, then $\dfrac{x^2+2x-3}{x^2-1} = \dfrac{x+3}{x+1} = 1 + \dfrac{2}{x+1}$

$x \in (-\infty, -1) \cup (-1, 1) \cup (1, \infty)$

$\Rightarrow\ x + 1 \in (-\infty, 0) \cup (0, 2)\ (2, \infty)$

$\Rightarrow\ \dfrac{1}{x+1} \in (-\infty, 0) \cup \left(0, \dfrac{1}{2}\right) \cup \left(\dfrac{1}{2}, \infty\right)$

$\Rightarrow\ 1 + \dfrac{2}{x+1} \in (-\infty, 1) \cup (1, 2) \cup (2, \infty)$

$\Rightarrow\ R_f \to \mathbb{R} \sim \{1, 2\}$

(viii) $\dfrac{x^2+2x+3}{x}$; $D_f \to \mathbb{R} \sim \{0\}$

If $x \neq 0$, then $\dfrac{x^2+2x+3}{x} = x + \dfrac{3}{x} + 2$

$\Rightarrow\ x + \dfrac{3}{x} \in (-\infty, -2\sqrt{3}] \cup [2\sqrt{3}, \infty)$

$x + \dfrac{3}{x} + 2 \in (-\infty, 2 - 2\sqrt{3}] \cup [2 + 2\sqrt{3}, \infty)$

(ix) $f(x) = \dfrac{x+1}{x^2-2x+3} = \dfrac{x+1}{(x+3)(x-1)} = \dfrac{A}{x+3} + \dfrac{B}{x-1}$

$\Rightarrow\ B = 1/2, A = 1/2$

Let $y = \dfrac{x+1}{x^2-2x+3} \Rightarrow x^2y - 2xy + 3y = x + 1$

$\Rightarrow\ x^2y - (2y+1)x + 3y - 1 = 0$

For $y \in \mathbb{R}$ and $y \neq 0$, i.e., $x \neq -1$

Disc. ≥ 0 $\Rightarrow\ (2y+1)^2 - 4y(3y-1) \geq 0$

$\Rightarrow\ 4y^2 + 4y + 1 - 12y^2 + 4y \geq 0$

$\Rightarrow\ -8y^2 + 8y + 1 \geq 0$

$\Rightarrow\ 8y^2 - 8y + 1 \geq 0$

$\Rightarrow\ y \in \left[\dfrac{1}{2} - \dfrac{\sqrt{6}}{4}, \dfrac{1}{2} + \dfrac{\sqrt{6}}{4}\right]$

For $x = -1$, $y = 0$

$\Rightarrow\ R_f = \left[\dfrac{1}{2} - \dfrac{\sqrt{6}}{4}, \dfrac{1}{2} + \dfrac{\sqrt{6}}{4}\right]$

(x) $y = \sqrt{x-1} + \sqrt{5-x}; x \in [1, 5]$

$\Rightarrow\ \dfrac{dy}{dx} = \dfrac{\sqrt{5-x} - \sqrt{x-1}}{2\sqrt{x-1}\sqrt{5-x}}$ if $\sqrt{5-x} > \sqrt{x-1}$

$\Rightarrow\ \dfrac{dy}{dx} > 0$

If $x < 3$, then $\dfrac{dy}{dx} > 0$

If $x > 3$, then $\dfrac{dy}{dx} < 0$

If $x = 3$, then $\dfrac{dy}{dx} = 0$

For $x \in [1, 3]$ $\Rightarrow\ f(x) \in [f(1), f(3)]$

$\Rightarrow\ f(x) \in [2, 2\sqrt{2}]$

For $x \in [3, 5]$ $\Rightarrow\ f(x) \in [f(5), f(3)]$

$\Rightarrow\ f(x) \in [2, 2\sqrt{2}]$

$\Rightarrow\ R_f \to [2, 2\sqrt{2}]$

(xi) $\sin^2 x - 5\sin x - 6 = \left(\sin x - \dfrac{5}{2}\right)^2 - \dfrac{49}{4}$

$\sin x \in [-1, 1]; \left(\sin x - \dfrac{5}{2}\right)^2 \in \left[\dfrac{9}{4}, \dfrac{49}{4}\right]$

$\left(\sin x - \dfrac{5}{2}\right)^2 - \dfrac{49}{4} \in [-10, 0]$

(xii) ${}^{7-x}P_{x-3}$

$\Rightarrow\ x \in \mathbb{Z}$ and $7 - x \geq 0$ and $x - 3 \geq 0$ and $7 - x \geq x - 3$

$\Rightarrow\ x \in \mathbb{Z}$ and $x \in [3, 7]$ and $x \in (-\infty, 5]$

$\Rightarrow\ x \in \mathbb{Z}$ and $x \in [3, 5]$ $\Rightarrow\ x \in \{3, 4, 5\}$

$f(3) = {}^{7-3}P_{3-3} = {}^4P_0 = 24; f(4) = {}^{7-4}P_{4-3} = {}^3P_1 = 6$

$f(5) = {}^{7-5}P_{5-3} = {}^2P_2 = 1$

$R_f = \{1, 24, 6\}$

10. (i) $\log_e(3x^2 - 4x + 5) = \ln(3x^2 - 4x + 5) = 3\left[\left(x^2 - \dfrac{4}{3}x\right) + \dfrac{5}{3}\right]$

$= 3\left[\left(x^2 - 2.\left(\dfrac{2}{3}\right).x + \dfrac{4}{9}\right) - \dfrac{4}{9} + \dfrac{15}{9}\right]$

$\Rightarrow\ 3\left[\left(x - \dfrac{2}{3}\right)^2 + \dfrac{11}{9}\right]$

$\Rightarrow\ 3(x - 2/3)^2 \in (0, \infty)$

$\Rightarrow\ 3(x - 2/3)^2 + 11/3 \in [11/3, \infty)$

$\Rightarrow\ \ln(3x^2 - 4x + 5) \in [\ln(11/3), \infty)$

(ii) $f(x) = \cot^{-1}(x^2 - 4x + 5)$; $D_f \in \mathbb{R}$

$(x^2 - 4x + 5) = (x^2 - 4x + 4) + 1$

$= (x-2)^2 + 1 \in [1, \infty)$

$\Rightarrow\ R_f = (0, /4]$

(iii) $\cot^{-1}(-x^2 + 2x) = \cot^{-1}(-x(x-2))$

Domain of $\cot^{-1}(x) = \mathbb{R}$ and $-x(x-2) \in (-\infty, 1)$

$\Rightarrow\ \cot^{-1}(-x(x-2))\ [\cot^{-1}(1), \cot^{-1}(\infty)]$

$\Rightarrow\ R_f = [\pi/4, \pi)$

(iv) $f(x) = \dfrac{x}{1+|x|}$

For $x > 0$; $y = \dfrac{x}{1+x}$

$\Rightarrow\ xy + y = x$ $\Rightarrow\ x(y-1) = -y$

$\Rightarrow\ x = \dfrac{-y}{y-1} > 0$

$\Rightarrow\ y(y-1) < 0$ $\Rightarrow\ y \in (0, 1)$

For $x < 0$; $y = \dfrac{x}{1-x}$

$\Rightarrow\ y - xy = x$ $\Rightarrow\ x(1+y) = y$

$\Rightarrow\ x = \dfrac{y}{1+y} < 0$ $\Rightarrow\ y \in (-1, 0)$

For $x = 0$; $y = 0$ $\Rightarrow\ y \in (-1, 1) = R_f$

(v) $\cos([x]\,\pi)$

$[x]$ is always an integer, i.e., positive or negative

$\Rightarrow$ cos[[x] π] = cosine of a negative integer or a positive integer.

$\Rightarrow \cos[[x]\pi] = \{-1, 1\}$

(vi) $f(x) = 4^x - 2^x + 1$

Let $2^x = y$

$f(y) = y^2 - y + 1 \quad \Rightarrow \quad y^2 - 2\left(\frac{1}{2}\right)y + \frac{1}{4} + \frac{3}{4}$

$\Rightarrow \left(y - \frac{1}{2}\right)^2 + \frac{3}{4} \quad \Rightarrow \quad f(y) \in [3/4, \infty)$

Hence, range of $f(x)$ as $2^x \in (0, \infty)$

$\Rightarrow f(x) \in [3/4, \infty)$

11. (i) $\dfrac{1}{(|x|-1)(\cos^{-1}(2x+1))\tan 3x}$

$|x| - 1 \neq 0$ and $2x + 1 \in [-1, 1]$ and $\cos^{-1}(2x + 1) \neq 0$

and $3x \in \mathbb{R} \sim \{0\}$ and $3x \neq (2n+1)\frac{\pi}{2}, n \in \mathbb{Z}$

$\Rightarrow x \neq 1, -1$ and $x \in [-1, 0]$ and $x \neq 0$ and $x \in \mathbb{R} \sim \{0\}$

and $3x \neq (2n+1)\frac{\pi}{2}; n \in \mathbb{Z}$

$\Rightarrow x \in (-1, 0)$ and $x \neq -\frac{\pi}{6}$

$\Rightarrow x \in (-1, 0) - \left\{-\frac{\pi}{6}\right\}$

(iii) $\log_2 \log_{1/3} \log_3 (x^2 - 4x + 3)$

$x^2 - 4x + 3 > 0$ and $\log_{1/3} \log_3 (x^2 - 4x + 3) > 0$

$\Rightarrow x \in (-\infty, 1) \cup (3, \infty)$ and $x^2 - 4x + 3 < 3$

$\Rightarrow x \in (-\infty, 1) \cup (3, \infty)$ and $x \in (0, 4)$

$\Rightarrow x \in (0, 1) \cup (3, 4)$

(iv) $\log_2 \log_3 \log_{4/\pi} (\tan^{-1} x)^{-1}$

$\Rightarrow (\tan^{-1} x)^{-1} > 0$ and $\log_3 \log_{4/\pi} (\tan^{-1} x)^{-1} > 0$

$\Rightarrow (\tan^{-1} x)^{-1} > \frac{4}{\pi}$ and $(\tan^{-1} x)^{-1} > 0$

$\Rightarrow \tan^{-1} x < \frac{\pi}{4}$ and $(0, \infty)$

$\Rightarrow x \in (0, 1)$

(v) $f(x) = \left(\dfrac{x}{1-|x|}\right)^{1/2002}$ for $x \geq 0$

$\Rightarrow f(x) = \left(\dfrac{x}{1-x}\right)^{1/2002} \quad \Rightarrow \quad f(x) = \left(\dfrac{-1}{1-x} + 1\right)^{1/2002}$

Similarly for $x < 0$

$\Rightarrow f(x) = \left(\dfrac{1}{x+1} - 1\right)^{1/2002}$

$\Rightarrow R_f \in (-\infty, -1) \cup [0, 1)$

12. (i) $\dfrac{2x}{x^2+1}$

This can be written as $\dfrac{2}{x + \frac{1}{x}}$

$\therefore \; x + 1/x \in (-\infty, -2] \cup [2, \infty)$

$\Rightarrow \dfrac{1}{\frac{1}{x} + x} \in [-1/2, 0) \cup (0, 1/2]$

$\Rightarrow \dfrac{2}{x + \frac{1}{x}} \in [-1, 0)\ (0, 1]$

$\Rightarrow$ Minimum = – 1

$\Rightarrow$ Maximum = 1

(ii) $f(x) = \dfrac{x^2-1}{x^2+1} = \left(1 - \dfrac{2}{x^2+1}\right)$

$\Rightarrow x^2 \in [0, \infty)$

$\Rightarrow x^2 + 1 \in [1, \infty)$

$\Rightarrow 1/(x^2 + 1) \in (0, 1]$

$\Rightarrow 2/(x^2 + 1) \in (0, 2] \quad \Rightarrow \quad f(x) \in [-1, 1)$

$\Rightarrow$ Min. $f(x) = -1$, Max $f(x)$ does not exist, but lub = 1

(iii) $\dfrac{x \;\; - 3x + 4}{x \;\; + 3x + 4}$

$\Rightarrow y(x^2 + 3x + 4) = x^2 - 3x + 4$

$\Rightarrow (y - 1)x^2 + 3(y + 1)x + 4(y - 1) = 0$

$D \geq 0$

$\Rightarrow 9(y + 1)^2 - 16(y - 1)^2 \geq 0$

$\Rightarrow (7y - 1)(7 - y) \geq 0$

$\Rightarrow y \in [1/7, 7] \quad \Rightarrow \quad y_{\min} = \frac{1}{7}, y_{\max} = 7$

(iv) $y = \dfrac{1}{2 + x^2}$

$\Rightarrow x^2 \in [0, 36]$

$\Rightarrow x^2 + 2 \in [2, 38]$

$\Rightarrow \dfrac{1}{x^2+2} \in \left[\dfrac{1}{38}, \dfrac{1}{2}\right]$

$\Rightarrow$ Lower bound = 1/38

$\Rightarrow$ Upper bound = 1/2

(v) $S = \dfrac{3-x}{1-x} = \left(\dfrac{2}{1-x} + 1\right); x > 0, x \neq 1$

$\Rightarrow -x < 0; -x \neq -1$

$\Rightarrow 1 - x < 1; 1 - x \neq 0 \quad \Rightarrow \quad \dfrac{1}{1-x} \in (-\infty, 0) \cup (1, \infty)$

$\Rightarrow \dfrac{2}{1-x} + 1 \in (-\infty, 1) \cup (3, \infty)$

$\Rightarrow$ Upper and lower does not exist.

(vi) $|x| \leq \sqrt{\frac{3}{2}} \Rightarrow -\sqrt{\frac{3}{2}} \leq x \leq \sqrt{\frac{3}{2}}$

$\Rightarrow 0 \leq x^2 \leq 3/2 \quad \Rightarrow \quad -x^2 \geq -\frac{3}{2}$

$\Rightarrow 1 \geq 1 - x^2 \geq -\frac{1}{2}$

$\Rightarrow 1 \geq \sqrt{1 - x^2} \geq 0$

$\Rightarrow$ *glb* = 0 and least upper bond = 1

(vii) $|x - 1| \leq 2$

$\Rightarrow -2 \leq x - 1 \leq 2 \quad \Rightarrow \quad -1 \leq x \leq 3$

$\Rightarrow -2 \leq 2x \leq 6$

$\Rightarrow 1 \leq 2x + 3 \leq 9 \quad \Rightarrow \quad \frac{1}{9} \leq \dfrac{1}{2x+3} \leq 1$

$y = \dfrac{3x+1}{2x+3} = \dfrac{3}{2} + \left(\dfrac{-7/2}{2x+3}\right)$

$\Rightarrow\ -\dfrac{7}{18} \ge \dfrac{-7/2}{2x+3} \ge -\dfrac{7}{2}$

$\Rightarrow\ \dfrac{3}{2}-\dfrac{7}{18} \ge \dfrac{3}{2}+\left(\dfrac{-7/2}{2x+3}\right) \ge \dfrac{3}{2}-\dfrac{7}{2}$

$\Rightarrow\ \dfrac{10}{9} \ge y \ge -2$ $\Rightarrow$ glb = –2 and lub = 10/9

TEXTUAL EXERCISE–10: (OBJECTIVE)

1. (c) $y = [x]$ $\Rightarrow R_f = \mathbb{Z}$

2. (b) $\dfrac{2x-1}{2x+1}$ $\Rightarrow x \in \mathbb{R} - \left\{-\dfrac{1}{2}\right\}$

$\dfrac{2x-1}{2x+1} = 1 - \dfrac{2}{2x+1}$; $x \in \left(-\infty, -\dfrac{1}{2}\right) \cup \left(-\dfrac{1}{2}, \infty\right)$

$\Rightarrow 2x + 1 \in (-\infty, 0) \cup (0, \infty)$

$\Rightarrow \dfrac{1}{2x+1} \in (-\infty, 0) \cup (0, \infty)$

$\Rightarrow 1 - \dfrac{2}{2x+1} \in (-\infty, 1) \cup (1, \infty)$

$\Rightarrow R_f \to \mathbb{R} \sim \{1\}$

3. (a) $\dfrac{x^2-1}{x^2+1} = 1 - \dfrac{2}{x^2+1}; x^2 \ge 0$

$\Rightarrow 1 + x^2 \ge 1$ $\Rightarrow \dfrac{1}{x^2+1} \in (0, 1]$

$\Rightarrow 1 - \dfrac{2}{x^2+1} \in [-1, 1)$

4. (b) $\dfrac{2x}{1+x^2} = y$

$\Rightarrow yx^2 + y - 2x = 0$

For real x; $D \ge 0$ $\Rightarrow 4 - 4y^2 \ge 0 = 1 - y^2 \ge 0$

$\Rightarrow (1 + y)(1 - y) \ge 0$ $\Rightarrow (y + 1)(y - 1) \le 0$

$\Rightarrow y \in [-1, 1]$

5. (c) $y = \dfrac{x^2-x+1}{x^2+x+1}$

$\Rightarrow yx^2 + yx + y = x^2 - x + 1$

$\Rightarrow x^2(y - 1) + x(y + 1) + y - 1 = 0$

For real roots = $(y + 1)^2 - 4(y - 1)^2 \ge 0$

$\Rightarrow y^2 + 1 + 2y - 4(y^2 + 1 - 2y) \ge 0$

$\Rightarrow -3y^2 + 10y - 3 \ge 0$

$\Rightarrow -3y^2 + 9y + y - 3 \ge 0$

$\Rightarrow -3y(y - 3) + (y - 3) > 0$

$\Rightarrow (y - 3)(-3y + 1) \ge 0$

$\Rightarrow (y - 3)(y - 1/3) \le 0$

$\Rightarrow y \in [1/3, 3]$

6. (c) $y = \dfrac{1}{(x-1)(x-2)}$

$\Rightarrow y = \dfrac{1}{x^2-3x+2}; y \ne 0, x \ne 1, 2$

$\Rightarrow yx^2 - 3yx + 2y - 1 = 0$

$\Rightarrow 9y^2 - 4y(2y - 1) \ge 0$ and $y \ne 0$

$\Rightarrow 9y^2 - 8y^2 + 4y \ge 0$ $\Rightarrow y^2 + 4y \ge 0, y \ne 0$

$\Rightarrow y(y + 4) \ge 0, y \ne 0$ $\Rightarrow y \in (-\infty, -4] \cup (0, \infty)$

7. (a) $y = A \sin x + B \cos x$

Which can be written as

$y = \left(\dfrac{A\sin x}{\sqrt{A^2+B^2}} + \dfrac{B\cos x}{\sqrt{A^2+B^2}}\right)\sqrt{A^2+B^2}$

Let $\cos u = \dfrac{A}{\sqrt{A^2+B^2}}$

$\Rightarrow y = (\cos u \sin x + \sin u . \cos x)\sqrt{A^2+B^2}$

$\Rightarrow y = \sin(x + u)\sqrt{A^2+B^2}$

$\Rightarrow y \in \left[-\sqrt{A^2+B^2}, \sqrt{A^2+B^2}\right]$

8. (a) $y = \dfrac{x^2}{1+x^2}; y \ne 1$

$\Rightarrow y + yx^2 = x^2$ $\Rightarrow yx^2 - x^2 + y = 0$

$\Rightarrow x^2(y - 1) + y = 0, y \ne 1$

$\Rightarrow -4y(y - 1) \ge 0, y\ 1$ $\Rightarrow y(y - 1) \le 0, y \ne 1$

$\Rightarrow y \in [0, 1)$

9. (c) $y = \dfrac{1}{2-\sin 3x}$; $\sin 3x \in [-1, 1]$; $2 - \sin 3x \in [1, 3]$

$\Rightarrow \dfrac{1}{2-\sin 3x} \in \left[\dfrac{1}{3}, 1\right]$

10. (a) $x^2 + x + 1 = \left(x+\dfrac{1}{2}\right)^2 + \dfrac{3}{4}$ $\Rightarrow x^2 + x + 1 \ge \dfrac{3}{4}$

Hence, min = $\dfrac{3}{4}$; max $\to \infty$

11. (c) $x^2 - 4x + 5 = (x - 2)^2 + 1$

$x^2 - 4x + 5 \ge 1$ $\Rightarrow$ min = 1; max $\to \infty$

12. (a) $ax^2 + bx + c = a\left(x^2 + 2\times\dfrac{b}{2a}x\right) + c; a > 0$

$= a\left(x+\dfrac{b}{2a}\right)^2 + c - \dfrac{b^2}{4a} = a\left(x+\dfrac{b}{2a}\right)^2 + \dfrac{4ac-b^2}{4a}$

$\Rightarrow ax^2 + bx + c \in \left[\dfrac{4ac-b^2}{4a}, \infty\right)$

13. (b) $2 - 3x - x^2 = -(x^2 + 3x) + 2 = -\left(x^2+3x+\dfrac{9}{4}\right)+\dfrac{9}{4}+2$

$= -\left(x+\dfrac{3}{2}\right)^2 + \dfrac{17}{4}$

$\because \left(x+\dfrac{3}{2}\right)^2 \le 0$ $\Rightarrow -\left(x+\dfrac{3}{2}\right)^2 + \dfrac{17}{4} \le \dfrac{17}{4}$

$\Rightarrow$ min $\to -\infty$ and max = $\dfrac{17}{4}$

14. (a) $\dfrac{x^2-1}{x^2+1} = 1 - \dfrac{2}{x^2+1}$

Now as $x^2 + 1 \ge 1$ $\Rightarrow 0 \ge -\dfrac{1}{x^2+1} \ge -1$

$\Rightarrow 1 \ge 1 - \dfrac{2}{x^2+1} \ge -1$

$\Rightarrow \dfrac{x^2-1}{x^2+1} \in [-1, 1]$

15. (b) $\frac{x-3x+4}{x^2+3x+4} = -\frac{6x}{x^2+3x+4}$

If $x = 0$, then $\frac{x^2-3x+4}{x^2+3x+4}=1$

If $x \neq 0$, then $\frac{x^2-3x+4}{x^2+3x+4}=1-\frac{6x}{x^2+3x+4}=1-\frac{6}{x+\frac{4}{x}+3}$

$\Rightarrow \quad x+\frac{4}{x}\in(-\infty,-4]\cup[4,\infty)$

$\Rightarrow \quad x+\frac{4}{x}+3\in(-\infty,-1]\cup[7,\infty)$

$\Rightarrow \quad \frac{1}{x+\frac{4}{x}+3}\in[-1,0)\cup\left(0,\frac{1}{7}\right]$

$\Rightarrow \quad 1-\frac{6}{x+\frac{4}{x}+3}\in\left[\frac{1}{7},1\right)\cup(1,7]$

$\Rightarrow \quad \frac{x^2-3x+4}{x^2+3x+4}\in\left[\frac{1}{7},7\right]$

16. (b) $y=\frac{1}{2+x^2}; -6\le x\le 4$

$\Rightarrow x^2 \in [0, 36] \qquad \Rightarrow x^2+2\in[2,38]$

$\Rightarrow \quad \frac{1}{x^2+2}\in\left[\frac{1}{38},\frac{1}{2}\right]$

$\therefore \quad g.l.b.=\frac{1}{38};\ l.u.b.=\frac{1}{2}$

17. (c) $y=\frac{3-x}{1-x}; x>0$

$\Rightarrow y-yx=3-x \qquad \Rightarrow x(1-y)=3-y$

$\Rightarrow x=\frac{3-y}{1-y}; x>0$

$\Rightarrow (3-y)(1-y)>0 \qquad \Rightarrow (y-1)(y-3)>0$

$\Rightarrow y\in(-\infty,1)\cup(3,\infty)$

$\Rightarrow$ *glb*, *lub* does not exist.

18. (a) $|x-5|<1 \qquad \Rightarrow x\in(4,6)$

Now as $\frac{x}{x+10}=\frac{1}{1+\frac{10}{x}}$

$\Rightarrow \frac{1}{x}\in\left(\frac{1}{6},\frac{1}{4}\right) \qquad \Rightarrow \frac{10}{x}+1\in\left(\frac{16}{6},\frac{14}{4}\right)$

$\Rightarrow \frac{1}{\frac{10}{x}+1}\in\left(\frac{2}{7},\frac{3}{8}\right)$

19. (c) $e^x=y+\sqrt{1+y^2} \qquad \Rightarrow (e^x-y)^2=1+y^2$

$\Rightarrow e^{2x}+y^2-2e^xy=1+y^2$

$\Rightarrow \frac{e^{2x}-1}{2e^x}=y \qquad \Rightarrow y=\frac{e^x-e^{-x}}{2}$

20. (c) $f(x)=\begin{cases}x & x\in\mathbb{Q}\\ 1-x & x\notin\mathbb{Q}\end{cases}\ \forall x\in[0,1]$

If $x\in\mathbb{Q}$

$f(x)=x \qquad \Rightarrow f(f(x))=x;\ x\in\mathbb{Q}$

If $x\notin\mathbb{Q} \qquad \Rightarrow f(x)=1-x$

Since $1-x$ is also irrational.

$\Rightarrow f(f(x))=(1-(1-x))=x$

21. (b) $y=\frac{x}{1+x^2} \qquad \Rightarrow y=0$ for $x=0$

$\Rightarrow y+yx^2=x \qquad \Rightarrow yx^2-x+y=0$

$\Rightarrow 1-4y^2\ge 0$ for $y\neq 0$

$\Rightarrow (1-2y)(1+2y)\ge 0; y\neq 0$

$\Rightarrow (y-1/2)(y+1/2)\le 0$

$\Rightarrow y\in\left[-\frac{1}{2},\frac{1}{2}\right]-\{0\}$

But y = 0 at $x=0 \qquad \Rightarrow R_f=\left[-\frac{1}{2},\frac{1}{2}\right]$

22. (c) $y=\frac{1}{x(x-1)(x-2)}$

$\Rightarrow y=\frac{1}{x(x^2-3x+2)} \qquad \Rightarrow y=\frac{1}{x^3-3x^2+2x}$

Consider $f(x)=x^3-3x^2+2x$

$\Rightarrow f'(x)=3x^2-6x+2$

$\Rightarrow x=\frac{6\pm\sqrt{36-24}}{6}=1\pm\frac{\sqrt{12}}{6}=1\pm\frac{\sqrt{3}}{3}$

$\Rightarrow x=1\pm\frac{1}{\sqrt{3}}$

$\Rightarrow$ Range of function $\mathbb{R}-\{0\}$

23. (c) Consider $e^x-x=g(x)$

$\Rightarrow g'(x)=e^x-1 \qquad \Rightarrow g'(x)=0$ at $x=0$

$\Rightarrow g'(x)>0 \qquad \Rightarrow x>0$

$\Rightarrow g'(x)<0 \qquad \Rightarrow x<0$

$\Rightarrow$ Range of function $=[0,\infty)$

24. (b) $y=\frac{x^2}{1+x^2}\ y+yx^2-x^2=0$

$\Rightarrow x^2(y-1)+y=0$

$\Rightarrow -4(y)(y-1)\ge 0 \qquad \Rightarrow y(y-1)\le 0$

$\Rightarrow y\in[0,1)$

25. (a), (b), (d)

Functions (a), (b), (d) are defined for all x.

While tan(log x) is not defined for x. It has the restriction $x>0$

26. (a) $y=\sin^2 x-5\sin x-6$

Replace $\sin x=k \qquad \Rightarrow y=k^2-5k-6$

$\Rightarrow y'=2k-5$

$\Rightarrow y=0$

$\Rightarrow k=5/2=2.5$ which is not position.

$\Rightarrow y<0\ \forall\ k<5/2$, which is always possible. Hence, y is decreasing.

$\Rightarrow$ Range $=[f(k=1),f(k=-1)]=[-10,0]$

TEXTUAL EXERCISE-11: (SUBJECTIVE)

1. (i) $f(x) = 5x - 4$

$\Rightarrow f'(x) = 5 > 0 \quad \Rightarrow f(x)$ is injective

(ii) $f(x) = x - (1/x) \quad \Rightarrow f'(x) = 1 + \frac{1}{x^2} > 0\ \forall\ x\ 0$

Also $\lim_{x\to-\infty} f(x) = -\infty$, $\lim_{x\to0^-} f(x) = \infty$, $\lim_{x\to0^+} = -\infty$, $\lim_{x\to\infty} f(x) = \infty$

$\Rightarrow f(x)$ is many–one, i.e., non-injective.

(iii) $f(x) = x^2 - 6x + 15$; $(x < 3)$

$f(x)$ is injective when defined on subset of $(-\infty, 3]$ or on subset of $[3, \infty)$

$\Rightarrow f(x)$ is injective

(iv) $f(x) = \frac{(x^2+1)}{2x}$; $(x > 0) = \frac{1}{2}\left(x + \frac{1}{x}\right)$

$\Rightarrow f'(x) = \frac{1}{2}\left(1 - \frac{1}{x^2}\right) = \frac{1}{2}\left(\frac{x^2-1}{x^2}\right)$

$\Rightarrow f(x) \downarrow$ on $(0, 1]$ and $\uparrow$ on $[1, \infty)$

$\Rightarrow f(x)$ is non-injective.

(v) $f(x) = 2x^5 + 40x^2 + 2$; for $x \in [0, \infty)$

$\Rightarrow f'(x) = 10x^4 + 80x\ \forall\ x \in [0, \infty)$

$\Rightarrow f(x) \uparrow \forall\ x \in [0, \infty)$ and being polynomial is continuous, and hence, it is injective.

(vi) $f(x) = \frac{x-2}{x+2}$; $x \in \mathbb{R} - \{-2\}$

$\Rightarrow f(x) = 1 - \frac{4}{x+2}$

$\Rightarrow f'(x) = \frac{4}{(x+2)^2} > 0\ \forall\ x \in \mathbb{R} - \{-2\}$

$\lim_{x\to-2^-} f(x) = \infty$, $\lim_{x\to-2^+} f(x) = -\infty$,

$\lim_{x\to-\infty} f(x) = 1^+$; $\lim_{x\to\infty} f(x) = 1^-$, i.e., $f(x) \in (1, \infty)$ for $x < -2$ and $f(x) \in (-\infty, 1)$ for $x > -2$

$\Rightarrow f(x)$ is injective.

(vii) $f(x) = x^4 + x^3 + 1$; domain $= \mathbb{R}$

$\Rightarrow f'(x) = 4x^3 + 3x^2 = x^2(4x + 3)$

$\Rightarrow f'(x) < 0$ for $x < -3/4$ and $f'(x) \geq 0$ for $x > -3/4$ and $f(x)$ being polynomial is continuous.

$\Rightarrow f(x)$ is non-injective.

(viii) $f(x) = x^6 + x^4 + x^2 + 1$

$\Rightarrow f(x)$ is an even function domain $\mathbb{R}$ (symmetric about origin)

$\Rightarrow f(x)$ is non-injective.

2. (a) False, it will be true if $f(x)$ is continuous.

(b) It is true as $f(x)$ is continuous, hence, $f(x) \in (k, k+1)$ for some $k \in \mathbb{Z}$ and for some set A.

$\Rightarrow [f(x)] = k\ \forall\ x \in A \quad \Rightarrow [f(x)]$ is non-injective.

(c) False, as if $f(x)$ is strictly increasing with range $(k, k+1)$ for some $k \in \mathbb{Z}$, then $\{f(x)\} = x - k\ \forall\ x \in D_f$

$\Rightarrow \{f(x)\}$ is injective .

(d) True, as for such function $\{f(x)\} = f(x) - [f(x)] = f(x) - 0 = f(x)$, which is continuous and strictly increasing, hence, $\{f(x)\}$ is injective.

(e) Since range of $f(x) \supseteq [0, 1]$

$\Rightarrow \{f(x)\} = \begin{cases} f(x)+1 \text{ for } f(x)\in[-1,0) \\ f(x) \text{ for } f(x)\in[0,1) \\ f(x)-1 \text{ for } f(x)\in[1,2) \end{cases}$

$\Rightarrow \{f(x)\} \in [0, 1)$ for $f(x)$ $[-1, 0)$

Again $\in [0, 1)$ for $f(x)$ $[0, 1)$ and again $\in [0, 1)$ for $f(x) \in [0, 1)$

$\Rightarrow \{(f(x)\}$ is many–one function

3. $A = \{1, 2, 3, 4, 5, 6\}$

Let $a + f(a) = k^2$; then $a, f(a)$

$\Rightarrow a + f(a) \in \{2, 3, 4, \ldots, 12\}$

$\Rightarrow k^2 \in \{4, 9\}$

$\Rightarrow a + f(a) = 4$ or $9\ \forall\ a \in A$

$\Rightarrow f(1) = 3, f(2) = 2, f(3) = 1$ or $6, f(4) = 5, f(5) = 4, f(6) = 3$

$\Rightarrow f(x)$ is non-injective.

Now, let $B = \{2, 3, 4, 5, 6\}$ and $f: B \to B$; $a, f(a) \in B$

$\Rightarrow a + f(a) \in \{4, 5, 6, 12\}$

$\Rightarrow k^2 \in \{4, 5, 6, \ldots, 12\} \Rightarrow k^2 \in \{4, 9\}$

$\Rightarrow f(2) = 2, f(3) = 6, f(4) = 5, f(5) = 4, f(6) = 3$

$\Rightarrow f(x)$ is injective. Thus, when A is replaced by B, then the statement is no more holds good.

4. $f: \mathbb{R} \to \mathbb{R}$; $f(x) = \frac{x^2+4x+7}{x^2+x+1}$

$\Rightarrow f(x) = \frac{(x^2+x+1)+(3x+6)}{(x^2+x+1)}$

$\Rightarrow f(x) = 1 + \frac{3(x+2)}{(x^2+x+1)}$

$\Rightarrow f'(x) = ..$, which is not having a unique sign as discriminant of $(x^2 + 4x + 1)$ is possible.

Also $x^2 + x + 1 > 0\ \forall\ x \in \mathbb{R}$, implies $f(x)$ is continuous; hence, $f(x)$ is non-injective.

5. $f(x) = 2\sin x - kx + 3$, $f'(x) = 2\cos x - k$

Clearly $f(x)$ is continuous and will be injective if either $f'(x) \geq 0\ \forall\ x \in \mathbb{R}$ or $f'(x) \leq 0\ \forall\ x \in \mathbb{R}$.

Now $f'(x) \geq 0\ \forall\ x \in \mathbb{R}$

$\Rightarrow k \leq 2\cos x\ \forall\ x \in \mathbb{R} \Rightarrow k \leq -2$

Also for $f'(x) \leq 0\ \forall\ x \in \mathbb{R}$

$\Rightarrow k \geq 2\cos x\ \forall\ x \in \mathbb{R} \Rightarrow k \geq 2$

Thus, $k \in (-\infty, -2]$ $[2, \infty)$

6. $f: D \to \mathbb{R}$; $f(x) = \frac{5x - x^2 - 4}{5x - 4x^2 - 1} = \frac{(x-1)(x-4)}{(4x-1)(x-1)}$

$\Rightarrow D = \mathbb{R} - \left\{\frac{1}{4}, 1\right\}$

$\Rightarrow f(x) = \frac{(x-4)}{(4x-1)}$; $x \in \mathbb{R} - \left\{\frac{1}{4}, 1\right\} = D$

$\Rightarrow f'(x) = \frac{15}{(4x-1)^2} > 0\ \forall\ x \in D$

$\lim_{x\to-\infty} f(x) = \left(\frac{1}{4}\right)^+$, $\lim_{x\to\left(\frac{1}{4}\right)^-} f(x) = \infty$,

$\lim\limits_{x\to\left(\frac{1}{4}\right)} f(x) = -\infty, \lim\limits_{x\to 1^-} = -1, \lim\limits_{x\to 1^+} f(x) = -1, \lim\limits_{x\to\infty} f(x) = \left(\frac{1}{4}\right)^-$

$\therefore\ f(x) \in \left(-\infty, \frac{1}{4}\right) - \{-1\}$ for $x \in \left(\frac{1}{4}, \infty\right)$ and $f(x)\ \left(\frac{1}{4}, \infty\right)$

for $x \in \left(-\infty, \frac{1}{4}\right)$ and $f(x) \uparrow$ on D

$\Rightarrow$ $f(x)$ is injective.

7. $f: \mathbb{R} \to \mathbb{R}; f(x) = \frac{x^2+3x+c}{x^2+x+1} = \frac{-2x^2+2(1-c)x+(3-c)}{(x^2+x+1)^2}$

Disc. $-2x^2 + 2(1-c)x + (3-c)$
$= 4(1-c)^2 + 8(3-c) = 4[c^2 + 1 - 2c + 6 - 2c] = 4[c^2 - 4c + 7] = 4[c^2 - 4c + 4 + 3] = 4[(c-2)^2 + 3] \geq 12\ \forall\ c\ \mathbb{R}$

$\Rightarrow$ $-2x^2 + 2(1-c)x + (3-c)$ changes its sign $\forall\ c \in \mathbb{R}$

$\Rightarrow$ $f'(x)$ changes its sign for each $c \in \mathbb{R}$ and $x^2 + x + 1 > 0\ \forall\ x \in \mathbb{R}$

$\Rightarrow$ $f(x)$ is continuous. Hence, $f(x)$ is many–one $\forall\ c \in \mathbb{R}$.

TEXTUAL EXERCISE–11: (OBJECTIVE)

1. **(a), (b), (c), (d)** $f(x) = x^3 - 12x + 1$

$\Rightarrow$ $f'(x) = 3x^2 - 12 = 3(x^2 - 4) > 0$ for $x \in (-\infty, -2) \cup (2, \infty)$ and ≤ 0 for $x \in [-2, 2]$

$\Rightarrow$ $f(x)$ is non-injective on $\mathbb{R}$.

2. **(b)** $f(x) = x^4 - 4x^3 + 4x^2 - 1$

$\Rightarrow$ $f(x) = (x-1)^2(x^2 - 2x - 1)$

$f(x)$ will be of the form

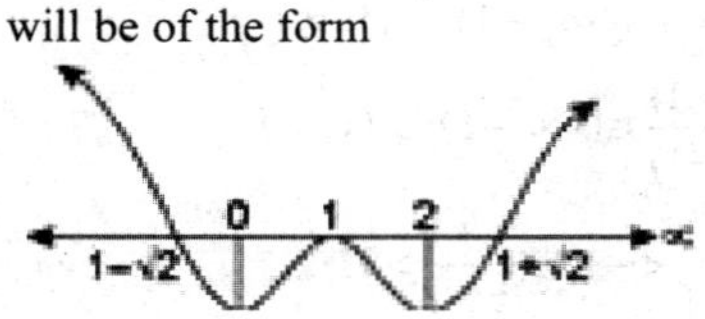

Also $f'(x) = 0 \qquad \Rightarrow\ x = 1, 0, 2$

$\Rightarrow$ $f(x)$ is non-injective on $(1-k, 1+k)$ for each $k > 0$, injective on $[2, \infty)$ and on $(-\infty, 0)$.

3. **(a), (c)** $f(x) = x^3 + x^2 + 3x + \sin x$

$\Rightarrow$ $f'(x) = 3x^2 + 2x + 3 + \cos x$

Now, $3x^2 + 2x + 3 \geq \frac{8}{3}\left(\because\ \geq \frac{-D}{4a}\right)$

$\Rightarrow$ $f'(x) \geq \frac{8}{3} - 1 = \frac{5}{3} > 0$

$\Rightarrow$ $f(x)$ is increasing and being continuous (polynomial) is injective function.

4. **(b)** $f(x) = 5 + e^{x^2-2}$

$\Rightarrow$ $f'(x) = \left(e^{x^2-2}\right)(2x) = 2x \,.\, e^{x^2-2} \geq 0\ \forall\ x \in [0, \infty)$ and $\leq 0\ \forall\ x \in (-\infty, 0)$

$\Rightarrow$ $f(x)$ is injective on $[0, \infty)$, $(-\infty, 0)$ and non-injective on $[-k, k]\ \forall\ k > 0$

5. **(a), (b), (c)**

$f(x) = \frac{x^2}{x^2-1} = 1 + \frac{1}{x^2-1}$

$\Rightarrow$ $f'(x) = \frac{-2x}{\left(x^2-1\right)^2} \geq 0$ for $x \leq 0, -1$ and $\leq 0\ \forall\ x \geq 0, 1$

$f(-\infty) = 1^+, f(-1^-) = \infty, f(-1^+) = -\infty, f(-1^-) = -\infty, f(1^+) = \infty, f(\infty) = 1^+$

Graph of $f(x)$ would be as shown below:

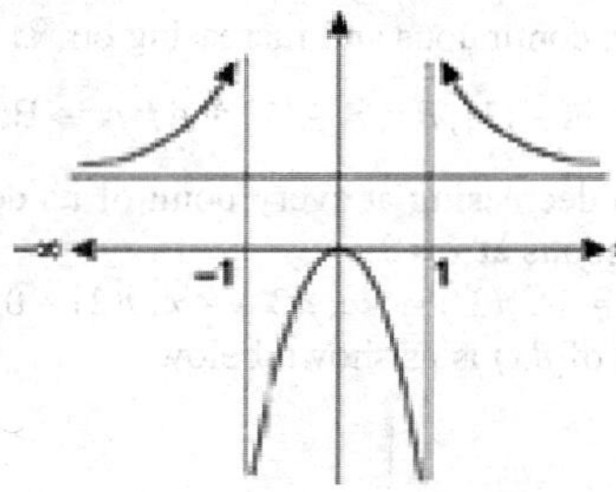

$\Rightarrow$ $f(x)$ is injective in $(-\infty, -1)$, non-injective in $(-1, 1)$, non-injective on $\mathbb{R}$

6. **(b), (c), (d)** $f(x) = \ln(1 - \ln x)$

$D_f = \{x: 1 - \ln x > 0; x > 0\} = (0, e)$

$f'(x) = \frac{1}{1-\ell nx}.\left(\frac{-1}{x}\right) = \frac{-1}{x(1-\ell nx)}$

$\Rightarrow$ $f'(x) < 0$ as $x > 0$, $1 - \ln x > 0$

$\Rightarrow$ $f(x)$ is a decreasing function with domain $(0, e)$ on $(0, e)$, $\ln x \in (-\infty, 1)$

$\Rightarrow$ $-\ln x \in (-1, \infty) \qquad \Rightarrow \qquad 1 - \ln x \in (0, \infty)$

$\Rightarrow$ $\ln(1 - \ln x) \in (-\infty, \infty) = \mathbb{R}$

7. **(b), (c)** $f(x) = \frac{x^3 - 2x^2 - 9x + 18}{x^2 - 4} = \frac{(x-2)(x^2-9)}{(x^2-4)}$

$D_f = \mathbb{R} - \{\pm 2\}$

$\Rightarrow$ $f(x) = \frac{x^2-9}{x+2}\ ; x \in \mathbb{R} - \{\pm 2\}$

$\Rightarrow$ $f'(x) = \frac{x^2+4x+9}{(x+2)^2} > 0\ \forall\ x - 2$

$\Rightarrow$ $f(x)$ is an increasing function, but discontinuous.

$f(-\infty) = -\infty, f(-3) = 0, f(-2^-) = \infty, f(-2^+) = -\infty, f(2^-) = \frac{-5}{4}, f(2^+) = \frac{-5}{4}, f(3) = 0, f(\infty) = \infty$

The graph of $f(x)$ will be as shown below:

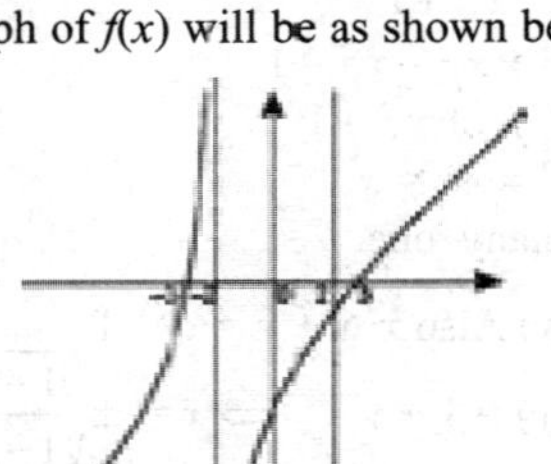

Clearly $f(x)$ is non-injective on its domain, also $f(x)$ is increasing at every point of its domain.

8. **(a), (d)** $y = [x] + \sqrt{\{x\}}$ for $x \in (k, k+1); k \in \mathbb{Z}$

$y = k + \sqrt{x-k} < k + 1$

$\Rightarrow f'(x) = \dfrac{1}{2\sqrt{x-k}} > 0 \ \forall \ x \in (k, k+1)$

$\Rightarrow f(k) = k, f(k+1) = k+1$

Thus, $f(k) = k, f(x) = k + \sqrt{x-k} \in (k, k+1)$

$f(k+1) = k+1$ and $f'(x) > 0 \ \forall \ x \ (k, k+1)$

$\Rightarrow f(x)$ is continuous and increasing on $\mathbb{R}$.

9. **(b), (d)** $A = \mathbb{R} - \{3\}, B = \mathbb{R} - \{1\}$ and $f: A \to B; f(x) = \left(\dfrac{x-2}{x-3}\right)$

$\Rightarrow f(x)$ is decreasing at every point of its domain, but discontinuous at $x = 3$.

$f(-\infty) = 1^-, f(3^-) = -\infty, f(3^+) = \infty, f(2) = 0, f(\infty) = 1^+$. The graph of $f(x)$ is as shown below.

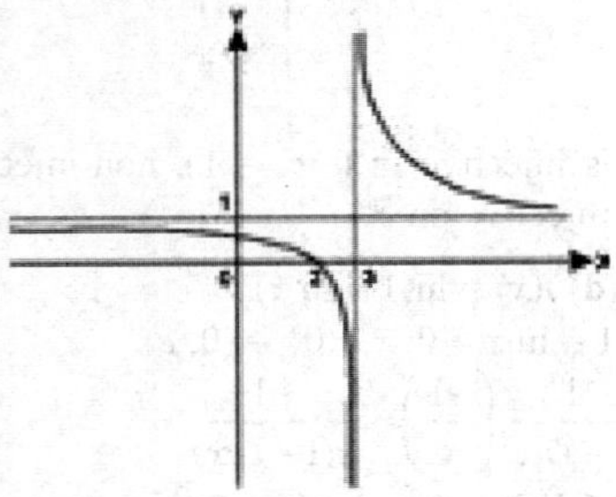

Thus, $f(x) < 1$ for $x \in (-\infty, 3)$ and $f(x) > 1$ for $x \in (3, \infty)$ and $f(x)$ is decreasing in each of these intervals.

Thus, $f(x)$ is injective function.

TEXTUAL EXERCISE–12: (SUBJECTIVE)

1. **(a)** $y = 5x + 8$

Injectivity: $f(x_1) = f(x_2) \Rightarrow 5x_1 + 8 = 5x_2 + 8$

$\Rightarrow x_1 = x_2$

Subjectivity: $f(x) = y \Rightarrow x = \dfrac{y-8}{5} \Rightarrow f\left(\dfrac{y-8}{5}\right) = y$

$\Rightarrow f(x)$ is onto

(b) $y = \dfrac{x^2-1}{x^2+1}$

Intectivity: $f(x_1) = f(x_2)$

$\Rightarrow \dfrac{x_1^2-1}{x_1^2+1} = \dfrac{x_2^2-1}{x_2^2+1}$

$\Rightarrow x_1^2 + x_2^2 + x_1^2 - x_2^2 - 1$

$\Rightarrow x_1^2 x_2^2 - x_1^2 + x_2^2 - 1$

$\Rightarrow x_1^2 = x_2^2 \not\Rightarrow x_1 = x_2$

$\Rightarrow f(x)$ is many–one.

Subjectivity: Also $x^2 y + y = x^2 - 1$

$\Rightarrow x^2(1-y) = 1 + y \quad \Rightarrow x = \pm\sqrt{\dfrac{1+y}{1-y}}$

$\Rightarrow y \in [-1, 1) \quad \Rightarrow f(x)$ is into

(c) $y = \dfrac{ax+b}{ax-b}$

Injectivity: $f(x_1) = f(x_2) \Rightarrow \dfrac{ax_1+b}{ax_1-b} = \dfrac{ax_2+b}{ax_2-b}$

$\Rightarrow a^2 x_1 x_2 - abx_1 + abx_2 - b^2$

$= a^2 x_1 x_2 + abx_1 - abx_2 - b^2$

$\Rightarrow 2ab\, x_1 = 2\, ab\, x_2 \quad \Rightarrow x_1 = x_2$

Subjectivity: $axy - by = ax + b$

$\Rightarrow x(ay - a) = b(1 + y) \quad \Rightarrow x = \dfrac{b(y+1)}{a(y-1)}$

$\Rightarrow y\ 1 \quad \Rightarrow f(x)$ is into

(d) $f(x) = e^x + e^{-x}$, clearly $f(x)$ is continuous

$f'(x) = e^x - e^{-x} = \dfrac{e^{2x}-1}{e^x} > 0$

$\Rightarrow e^{2x} > 1 \quad \Rightarrow 2x > 0$

$\Rightarrow x > 0$ and $f'(x) \le 0 \quad \Rightarrow x \le 0$

$\Rightarrow f(x)$ decrease for $x \le 0$ and increase for $x > 0$

$\Rightarrow f(x)$ is many–one function.

Also $f(x) = e^x + \dfrac{1}{e^x} \ge 2 \ \forall \ x \in \mathbb{R}$

$\Rightarrow f(x)$ is into

(e) $y = e^x - e^{-x}$

$\Rightarrow f'(x) = e^x + e^{-x} > 0 \ \forall \ x \in \mathbb{R}$

$\Rightarrow f(x)$ is increasing function.

$\Rightarrow f(x)$ is one–one. Clearly, $f(x)$ is continuous function, $f(-\infty) = 0 - \infty$ and $f(\infty) = \infty - 0 = \infty$

$\Rightarrow f(x)$ has its range $= (-\infty,)$

$\Rightarrow f(x)$ is onto

(f) $y = \log\left(\dfrac{x-1}{x+1}\right)$

$D_f = (-\infty, -1) \cup (1, \infty)$

Let $y = \dfrac{x-1}{x+1} \quad \Rightarrow x = \dfrac{-(z+1)}{(z-1)}$

$\Rightarrow$ As $x \in (-\infty, -1) \cup (1, \infty)$

$\Rightarrow \dfrac{(z+1)}{(z-1)} \in (-\infty, -1) \cup (1, \infty)$

$\Rightarrow \dfrac{z+1}{z-1} < -1$ or $\dfrac{z+1}{z-1} > 1$

$\Rightarrow \dfrac{2z}{(z-1)} < 0$ or $\dfrac{2}{z-1} > 0$

$\Rightarrow z \in (0, 1)$ or $z > 1$

$\Rightarrow z \in (0, \infty) - \{1\}$

$\therefore \ y = \log(z); z \in (0,) - \{1\}$

$\Rightarrow y \in (-\infty, \infty) - \{0\}$ and $y = \log(z)$ in increasing on $(0, \infty) - \{1\}$

$\Rightarrow f(x)$ is one–one and into.

(g) $y = \log\left(x + \sqrt{x^2+1}\right)$

$f'(x) = \dfrac{1}{\left(x + \sqrt{x^2+1}\right)}\left(\dfrac{\sqrt{x^2+1}+x}{\sqrt{x^2+1}}\right)$

$\Rightarrow f'(x) = \dfrac{1}{\sqrt{x^2+1}} > 0 \ \forall \ x \in D_f$

$\Rightarrow f(x)$ is injective (one–one) and also $\left(x + \sqrt{x^2+1}\right) > 0 \ \forall \ x \in \mathbb{R}$.

$\Rightarrow y = \log\left(x + \sqrt{x^2+1}\right) \in (-\infty, \infty)$

$\Rightarrow f(x)$ is onto.

(h) $f(x) = x + \frac{1}{x}$

$f'(x) = 1 - \frac{1}{x^2} = \left(\frac{x^2-1}{x_2}\right)$

$\therefore\ f'(x) > 0 \quad \Rightarrow \frac{x^2-1}{x^2} > 0$

$\Rightarrow x^2 - 1 > 0$

$\Rightarrow x \in (-\infty, -1) \cup (1,)$ and $f'(x) < 0$

$\Rightarrow \frac{x^2-1}{x^2} < 0 \quad \Rightarrow x^2 - 1 < 0$

$\Rightarrow x \in (-1, 1) - \{0\}$

Thus, $f(x)$ is many–one, also $f(x) \in (-\infty, -2] \cup [2,)$

$\Rightarrow f(x)$ is into.

2. $A = \{1, 2, 3, 4\}$; $B = \{a, b\}$

Each element of A has two choice a or b.

$\therefore$ Total number of onto functions $= (2)^4 - (2) = 14$

3. $f: X \to Y; f(x) = \sqrt{1-2x} + x$

$A = \{x: 1 - 2x \geq 0\} = \left(-\infty, \frac{1}{2}\right]$. Let $y = \sqrt{1+2x} + x$

$\Rightarrow y - x = \sqrt{1-2x} \quad \Rightarrow x^2 - 2x(y-1) + y^2 - 1 = 0$

$\therefore$ For $x \in \mathbb{R}$; Disc. 0 $\quad \Rightarrow (y-1)^2 - 4(y^2-1) \geq 0$

$\Rightarrow 3y^2 + 2y - 5 \leq 0$

$\Rightarrow (3y+5)(y-1) \leq 0 \Rightarrow \frac{-3}{5} \leq y \leq 1 \Rightarrow y \in \left[\frac{-5}{3}, 1\right]$

$\Rightarrow B = \left[\frac{-5}{3}, 1\right]$

4. $f: \mathbb{R} \to A$

(a) $f(x) = \frac{e^x - e^{-|x|}}{e^x + e^{-|x|}} = \begin{cases} \frac{e^x - e^{-x}}{e^x + e^{-|x|}}; x \geq 0 & ; x \geq 0 \\ 0 & ; x < 0 \end{cases}$

Let $y = \frac{e^{2x}-1}{e^{2x}+1}$ for $x \geq 0$

$\Rightarrow y' = \frac{4e^{2x}}{\left(e^{2x}+1\right)} > 0\ \forall\ x \in \mathbb{R}$

$\Rightarrow f(x)$ is an increasing function, also $f(x)$ is continuous.

$\Rightarrow A = [f(0), f(\infty) \cup \{0\}] = [0, 1) \cup \{0\} = [0, 1)$

(b) $f(x) = \frac{e^x - e^{-|x|}}{e^x + e^{|x|}} = \begin{cases} 0 \text{ if } x \leq 0 \\ \frac{e^x - e^{-x}}{2e^x}; x \geq 0 \end{cases}$

Let $y = \frac{e^x - e^{-x}}{2e^x}; x \geq 0$

$\Rightarrow y' = \frac{1}{e^{2x}} > 0\ \forall\ x \geq 0$

$\Rightarrow f(x)$ has range $= A = \left[0, \frac{1}{2}\right)$

(c) $f(x) = \frac{e^x - e^{|x|}}{e^x + e^{-|x|}} = \begin{cases} 0 \text{ if } x \geq 0 \\ \frac{e^x - e^{-x}}{2e^x} \text{ if } x \leq 0 \end{cases}$

Let $y = \frac{e^x - e^{-x}}{2e^x} = \frac{1}{2} - \frac{1}{2}e^{-2x}$

$\Rightarrow y' = e^{-2x} > 0\ x \leq 0$

$\Rightarrow$ Range $f(x) = A = (f(-\infty), f(0)] = (-\infty, 0]$

5. $f: \mathbb{N} \to \mathbb{N}; f(x) = 3x + 5$

Let $y \in \mathbb{N}$ and $f(x) = y$ (suppose)

$\Rightarrow 3x + 5 = y \quad \Rightarrow x = \frac{y-5}{3}$

$\therefore$ For $x \in \mathbb{N}$, $3|(y-5)\ \forall\ y\ \mathbb{N}$ and $y \geq 6$

$\Rightarrow$ Range of $f(x) = \{8, 11, 14, 17, \ldots\}$

$\Rightarrow f(x)$ is not subjective from $\mathbb{N}$ to $\mathbb{N}$.

6. $f: X \to Y$; $X = \{x, y, z$ and $Y = \{a, b\}$

(a) Total number of relations from X to $Y = 2^{n(X) \times n(Y)} = 2^6 = 64$

(b) Total number of functions from X to $Y = (2)^3 = 8$

(c) Number of one–one functions from X to $Y = 0$ as $n(Y) < n(X)$

(d) All functions are many–one

$\Rightarrow$ 8 in numbers.

(e) Number of onto functions $= (2)^3 - {}^2C_1 (1)^3 = 8 - 2 = 6$

7. $f(x) = ax^3 + bx^2 + cx + d \sin x$

$f'(x) = 3ax^2 + 2bx + c + d \cos x$ for $f(x)$ to be injective, $f'(x) \geq 0$

$\Rightarrow 3ax^2 + 2bx + c + d \cos x \geq 0$

$\Rightarrow a > 0, 4b^2 - 4(3a)(c + d\cos x) \leq 0\ \forall\ \cos x$

$\Rightarrow a > 0, b^2 - 3a(c + d \cos x) \leq 0$

$\Rightarrow b^2 \leq 3a(c + d\cos x)$

$\Rightarrow b^2 \leq 3a(c-d)$ if $d \geq 0$ or $b^2 \leq 3a(c+d)$ if $d \leq 0$

8. $f: \mathbb{R} \to B$: $f(x) = \sin x + \cos x - 4$

Range $f(x) = \left[-\sqrt{2}-4, \sqrt{2}-4\right]$

9. $f: [-1, 1] \to [0, 3]$ such that $f(x) = ax + b$

$\Rightarrow f'(x) = a$

Case: (i) If $a > 0, f(x) \uparrow \quad \Rightarrow f(-1) = 0, f(1) = 3$

$\Rightarrow -a + b = 0, a + b = 3$

$\Rightarrow a = b = 3/2 \quad \Rightarrow f_1(x) = \frac{3}{2}x + \frac{3}{2}$

Case: (ii) If $a < 0, f(x) \quad \Rightarrow f(-1) = 3, f(1) = 0$

$\Rightarrow -a + b = 3, a + b = 0 \Rightarrow b = \frac{3}{2} = -a$

$\Rightarrow f_2(x) = \frac{-3}{2}x + \frac{3}{2}$

$\Rightarrow$ Point of intersection of $f_1(x)$ and $f_2(x)$ is $\left(0, \frac{3}{2}\right)$

10. $f: \mathbb{R} \to \left[\frac{\pi}{6}, \frac{\pi}{2}\right); f(x) = \sin^{-1}\left(\frac{x^2-a}{x^2+1}\right)$

For onto function, $\frac{\pi}{6} \leq \sin^{-1}\left(\frac{x^2-a}{x^2+1}\right) < \frac{\pi}{2}$

$\Rightarrow \frac{1}{2} \leq \frac{x^2-a}{x^2+1} < 1$

$\Rightarrow x^2 + 1 \leq 2x^2 - 2a < 2x^2 + 2$

$\Rightarrow x^2 \geq 2a + 1; a > -1$

$\Rightarrow 2a + 1 \leq 0; a > -1 \quad \Rightarrow a \in \left(-1, \frac{-1}{2}\right]$

Now $f(x) = \frac{x^2-a}{x^2+1} = 1 - \frac{(a+1)}{x^2+1}$

As $a > -1 \quad \Rightarrow \quad a + 1 > 0$

$\Rightarrow f(x) < 1$ and $f(x) \downarrow$ for $x < 0$ and $\uparrow$ for $x > 0$

$\therefore \quad f(0) = \frac{1}{2}$ for onto functions

$\Rightarrow -a = \frac{1}{2} \Rightarrow a = \frac{-1}{2}$

11. $f: \mathbb{R} \to \left[0, \frac{\pi}{2}\right)$

$f(x) = \tan^{-1}(x^2 + x + a)$

For onto function, $0 \le \tan^{-1}(x^2 + x + a) < \frac{\pi}{2}$

$\Rightarrow 0 \le (x^2 + x + a) < \infty$

$\Rightarrow x^2 + x + a \ge 0$

$\Rightarrow 1 - 4a \le 0 \quad \Rightarrow a \ge \frac{1}{4}$

Let $f(x) = x^2 + x + a = \left(x + \frac{1}{2}\right)^2 + \left(a - \frac{1}{4}\right)$ and $f(x) \in [0, \infty)$

$\Rightarrow f(x) = 0$, at $x = \frac{-1}{2}, a = \frac{1}{4}$

$\therefore$ For onto function $a = \frac{1}{4}$

12. $f(x): D_f \to Y$

(a) $f(x) = \sin^6 x + \cos^6 x$

$= (\sin^2 x + \cos^2 x)^3 - 3\sin^2 x \cos^2 x$

$= 1 - \frac{3}{4}\sin^2 2x \in \left[\frac{1}{4}, 1\right] = Y$

(b) $f(x) = \ln(|\sin x|^4 + |\cos x|^4)$

$(\sin x)^4 + (\cos x)^4 + 1 - 2\sin^2 x \cos^2 x$

$= 1 - \frac{1}{2}\sin^2 2x \in \left[\frac{1}{2}, 1\right]$

$\Rightarrow f(x) \in \left[\ln\frac{1}{2}, \ln 1\right] = [-\ln 2, 0] = Y$

(c) $f(x) = \sqrt{\ln|\text{cosec}\, x|} \quad \because \quad |\text{cosec}\, x| \in [1, \infty)$

$\Rightarrow \ln|\text{cosec}\, x| \in [0, \infty)$

$\Rightarrow f(x) \in [0, \infty) = Y$

(d) $f(x) = \log_{\sqrt{2}}\left(\frac{\cos x + \sin x + 2\sqrt{2}}{\sqrt{2}}\right)$

$\because \quad (\cos x + \sin x + 2\sqrt{2}) \in [\sqrt{2}, 3\sqrt{2}]$

$\Rightarrow \left(\frac{\cos x + \sin x + 2\sqrt{2}}{\sqrt{2}}\right) \in [1, 3]$

$\Rightarrow f(x) \in [\log_{\sqrt{2}} 1, \log_{\sqrt{2}} 3] = [0, 2\log_2 3] = Y$

13. $A = \{x: -k \le x \le k, k \in \mathbb{N}\}$ and $B_1 = \left\{\pm\frac{m^2}{4}; 0 \le m \le k; n \in \mathbb{Z}\right\}$

$B_2 = A$, $B_3 = \{\pm m^4; 0 \le m \le k; m \in \mathbb{R}\}$

$B_4 = \{m^2; m \in \mathbb{Z}; 0 \le m \le k\}$; $B_5 = A$

(a) $f(x) = \frac{x|x|}{4}$; $f: AB = \begin{cases} \frac{-x^2}{4}; x \in [-k, 0); k \in \mathbb{N} \\ \frac{x^2}{4}; x \in [0, k]; k \in \mathbb{N} \end{cases}$

$\Rightarrow f'(x) = \begin{cases} \frac{-x}{2}; x \in (-k, 0); k \in \mathbb{N} \\ \frac{x}{2}; x \in (0, k); k \in \mathbb{N} \end{cases}$

$\Rightarrow f'(x) \ge 0 \; \forall x \in (-k, 0); k \in \mathbb{N}$

$\Rightarrow f(x) \uparrow \forall x \in [-k, k]$

$\Rightarrow f(x)$ is injective

Let $y \in B_1 \quad \Rightarrow y = \frac{m^2}{4}$ or $\frac{-m^2}{4}$; $m \in \mathbb{Z}$

$\Rightarrow y = f(m) = \frac{m^2}{4}$; $m \in \mathbb{N}$ and $m \in [0, k]$ and

$y = f(-m) = \frac{-m^2}{4}$, $-m \in [-k, 0)$

$\Rightarrow f(x)$ is surjective $\quad \Rightarrow f(x)$ is bijective.

(b) $f(x) = \sqrt{x^2}$; $g: A \to B_2$

$\Rightarrow f(x) = |x|$; $g: [-k, k] \to [-k, k]$; $k \in \mathbb{N}$

Clearly, $f(x)$ is many–one as $f(t) = |t|$

$\Rightarrow f(x)$ is not injective.

Thus, $f(x)$ is neither injective nor subjective

(c) $h(x) = x^3|x|$; $h[-k, k] \to \{\pm m^4, 0 \le m \le k; m \le \in \mathbb{R}\}$

$= \begin{cases} x^4; x \ge 0, \text{ i.e.}, x \in [0, k] \\ -x^4; x < 0, \text{ i.e.}, x \in [-k, 0] \end{cases}$

$\Rightarrow h'(x) = \begin{cases} 4x^3; x \in (0, k) \\ -4x^3; x \in (-k, 0) \end{cases}$

$\Rightarrow h'(x) \ge 0 \; \forall x \in [-k, k]$

$\Rightarrow h(x)$ is injective

Also, $m^4 = h(m)$; $m \in [0, k]$ and $-m^4 = h(-m)$;

$-m \in [-k, 0]$

$\Rightarrow h(x)$ is bijetive.

(d) $k(x) = x^2: [-k, k]$; $k \in \mathbb{N} \to \{m^2; m \in 0 \le m \le k\}$

Clearly, $k(x)$ as many–one as $f(-t) = f(t) \; \forall t \in [-k, k]$

Also range of $k(x) = [0, k^2] \ne \{m^2; m \in \mathbb{Z}; 0 \le m \le k\}$

$\Rightarrow k(x)$ is non-surjective, non-bijective

(e) $\phi(x) = x\cos(2n + 1)\pi x$; $:[-k, k] \to [-k, k]$; $\pi x\,[-k\pi, k]$

$\Rightarrow (2n + 1)\pi x\,[-(2n + 1)k\pi, (2n + 1)k\pi]$

14. $f: \mathbb{R} \to \mathbb{R}$; $f(x) = x^3 + x^2 + 3x + \sin x$

$f'(x) = 3x^2 + 2x + 3 + (\cos x)$

Now Discrioninant of $f'(x) = (2)^2 - 4(3)(3 + \cos x)$

$= 4[1 - 9 - 3\cos x] = 4[-8 - 3\cos x]$

$\because \quad -3 \le -3\cos x \le 3$

$\Rightarrow 4(-8 - 3\cos x)\,[-44, -20]$

$\Rightarrow D < 0 \quad \Rightarrow f'(x) > 0 \; \forall x \, \mathbb{R}$

$\Rightarrow f(x)$ is an increasing function

$\Rightarrow f(x)$ is injective.

Also $(x^3 + x^2 + 3x)\,(-\infty, \infty)$ and $\sin x\,[-1, 1]$

$\Rightarrow f(x)\,(-\infty, \infty)\, f(x)$ is surjective .

15. $f: \mathbb{Z} \to \mathbb{Z}$

(a) $f(x) = x + 3$, which being an increasing function is injective. Also $f(y - 3) = y \; \forall \mathbb{Z}$

$\Rightarrow f(x)$ is surjective. Hence, a bijection.

(b) $f(x) = x^5$

$\Rightarrow f'(x) = 5x^4 \ge 0 \quad \Rightarrow f(x)$ is increasing function

$\Rightarrow$ Injective.

Also $f(x) = y$ $\Rightarrow$ $y = x^5$

$\Rightarrow$ $x = (y)^{1/5} \notin \mathbb{Z}$ for every y $\mathbb{Z}$, e.g., if $y = 6$, then $f((6)^{1/5}) = 6$ but $(6)^{1/5} \notin \mathbb{Z}$

$\Rightarrow$ $f(x)$ is not surjective.

(c) $f(x) = 3x + 2$

$f'(x) = 3 > 0$ $\Rightarrow$ $f(x)$ is injective .

If y $\mathbb{Z}$, then $y = f(x)$

$\Rightarrow$ $y = 3x + 2$

$\Rightarrow$ $x = \dfrac{y-2}{3}$, which need not necessary an integer

$\Rightarrow$ $f(x)$ is not surjective, and hence, not bijection.

(d) $f(x) = x^2 + x$

$\Rightarrow$ $f'(x) = 2x + 1 > 0$ for $x > -\dfrac{1}{2}$ and < 0 for $x < -\dfrac{1}{2}$

$\Rightarrow$ $f(x)$ is many–one, i.e., not injective and hence, not bijection.

16. $f: \mathbb{R} \to \mathbb{R}$

$\Rightarrow$ $f(x) = \begin{cases} 2x; \text{if } x \ge 0 \\ 2x - 3; \text{if } x < 0 \end{cases}$

$\Rightarrow$ $f'(x) = \{2\ \forall\ x\ 0$ and $f(0) = -3$ and $f(0^+) = 0$

$\Rightarrow$ $f(x)$ is injective. Also range $f(x) = (-\infty, -3) \cup [0, \infty)$ $\mathbb{R}$

$\Rightarrow$ $f(x)$ is not onto.

17. $f: \mathbb{R} - \{2\} \to \mathbb{R} - \{1\}$

$f(x) = \dfrac{x-5}{x-2}$

$D_f = \mathbb{R} - \{2\}$

Let $f(x_1) = f(x_2)$ $\Rightarrow$ $\dfrac{x_1 - 5}{x_1 - 2} = \dfrac{x_2 - 5}{x_2 - 2}$

$\Rightarrow$ $x_1x_2 - 2x_1 - 5x_2 + 10 = x_1x_2 - 5x_1 - 2x_2 + 10$

$\Rightarrow$ $3x_1 = 3x_2$ $\Rightarrow$ $x_1 = x_2$

$\Rightarrow$ $f(x)$ is injective.

Let $y = \dfrac{x-5}{x-2}$ $\Rightarrow$ $xy - 2y = x - 5$

$\Rightarrow$ $x(y - 1) = 2y - 5$ $\Rightarrow$ $x = \dfrac{2y-5}{y-1}$

$\Rightarrow$ $y \ne 1$

$\Rightarrow$ $R_f = \mathbb{R} - \{1\}$ $\Rightarrow$ $f(x)$ is surjective

$\therefore$ $f(x)$ is bijective

18. $A: \mathbb{R} - \{3\} \to \mathbb{R} - \{1\}$

$f(x) = \dfrac{x-2}{x-3}$ $\Rightarrow$ $f'(x) = \dfrac{-1}{(x-3)^2} < 0\ \forall\ x\ 3$

$\Rightarrow$ $f(x)$ is injective function. Also $y = \dfrac{x-2}{x-3}$

$\Rightarrow$ $xy - 3y = x - 2$

$\Rightarrow$ $x(y - 1) = 3y - 2$ $\Rightarrow$ $x = \dfrac{3y-2}{y-1}$

$\Rightarrow$ $y \ne 1$

$\Rightarrow$ $R_f = \mathbb{R} - \{1\}$ $\Rightarrow$ Surjective

Thus, $f(x)$ is bijective function.

19. $f: [1, 7] \to [2, 27]$;

$f(x) = x^2 - 4x + 6$

$f'(x) = 2x - 4 < 0$ for x $[1, 2)$ and $f'(x) \ge 0$ for x $[2, 7]$

$\Rightarrow$ $f(x)$ is not injective.

Range of $f(x) = \left[\dfrac{-(16-24)}{4}, \infty\right) = [2, \infty)$

$\therefore$ $f(x)$: $[1, 7] \to [2, 27]$ is not surjective.

20. **(a)** $f(x) = 2 \cot x$; $f: (\pi, 2\pi) \to \mathbb{R}$

$f'(x) = -2 \operatorname{cosec}^2 x < 0\ \forall\ x\ (\pi, 2)$

$\Rightarrow$ $f(x)$ is injective function. Also range $f(x) = (2 \cot (2\pi^-), 2 \cot (\pi^+)) = (-\infty, \infty) = \mathbb{R}$

$\Rightarrow$ $f(x)$ is surjective (onto).

(b) $f(x) = \dfrac{4}{1+x^2}$; $f: \mathbb{R} \to \mathbb{R}$

$\Rightarrow$ $f'(x) = \dfrac{-8}{1+x^2} \le 0$ for $x \ge 0$ and > 0 for $x < 0$

$\Rightarrow$ $f(x) \downarrow$ for $x \ge 0$ and $\uparrow$ for $x < 0$ and continuous.

$\Rightarrow$ $f(x)$ is not surjective and range $= (f(-\infty), f(0))$ as $f(x)$ is even

$\Rightarrow$ $R_f \equiv (0, 4)$ $\mathbb{R}$ $\Rightarrow$ $f(x)$ is not surjective.

(c) $f(x) = x^4 + \ln x$; $f: (0,) \to \mathbb{R}$

$\Rightarrow$ $f'(x) = 4x^3 + \dfrac{1}{x} < 0$ for $x < 0$ and > 0 for $x > 0$.

$\Rightarrow$ $f(x) \uparrow$ and continuous for x $(0, \infty)$

$\Rightarrow$ $f(x)$ is injectivite

$\Rightarrow$ Range of $f(x) = (f(0), f(\infty)) \equiv (-\infty, \infty) = \mathbb{R}$

$\Rightarrow$ $f(x)$ is surjective.

21. **(a)** $f(x) = \dfrac{x^2 + 4x + 30}{x^2 - 8x + 18}$

$\Rightarrow$ $f'(x) = \dfrac{-12(x^2 + 2x - 26)}{(x^2 - 8x + 18)^2}$

$\because$ Disc. of $x^2 + 2x - 26 = 108 > 0$

$\Rightarrow$ $f'(x) < 0$ for x $(-\infty, \alpha) \cup (\beta, \infty)$ and > 0 for x (α, β) where α, β are roots of $x^2 + 2x - 26 = 0$

$\Rightarrow$ $f(x)$ is not injective.

Let $y = \dfrac{x^2 + 4x + 30}{x^2 - 8x + 18}$

$\Rightarrow$ $x^2(1 - y) + (4 + 8y)x + (30 - 18y) = 0$

$\Rightarrow$ If $y = 1$, then $x = -1$ and if y 1, then for x $\mathbb{R}$, Disc. ≥ 0

$\Rightarrow$ $y^2 - 32y + 13 \le 0$

$\Rightarrow$ $R_f = \left[16 - \sqrt{243}, 16 + \sqrt{243}\right]$

$\Rightarrow$ $f(x)$ is not surjective.

(b) $f(x) = x^3 - 6x^2 + 11x - 6$

$\Rightarrow$ $f'(x) = 3x^2 - 12x + 11$ having disc. $= 12$

$\Rightarrow$ $f'(x)$ would change its sign.

$\Rightarrow$ $f(x)$ is not injective, however, being a cubic polynomial its range $= (-\infty, \infty)$ $\Rightarrow$ $f(x)$ is surjective.

(c) $f(x) = (x^2 + x + 5)(x^2 + x + 3) = x^4 + 2x^3 + 9x^2 + 8x + 15$

$\Rightarrow$ $f'(x) = 4x^3 + 6x^2 + 18x + 8$

$\Rightarrow$ $f'(x)$ $(-\infty, \infty)$ $\Rightarrow$ $f'(x)$ changes its sign

$\Rightarrow$ $f(x)$ is not injective.

Also $x^2 + x + 5 > 0$ as disc. $= -19 < 0$ and $x^2 + x + 3 > 0$ as disc. $= -11 < 0$

$\Rightarrow$ $f(x) > 0$ x $\mathbb{R}$ $\Rightarrow$ $f(x)$ is not surjective.

22. $f(x) = k_x + 3 \sin x + 5$ $\Rightarrow$ $f'(x) = k + 3 \cos x$

$\Rightarrow$ $k - 3 \le f'(x) \le k + 3$

$\Rightarrow$ $f'(x) \le 0$ for $k \le -3$ and $f'(x) \ge 0$ for $k \ge +3$

Also $f(x)$ being a linear function for k 0 would have its range $(-\infty, \infty)$.

$\therefore$ For one–one and onto function k $(-\infty, -3] \cup [3, \infty)$

23. $f(x) = \dfrac{x-1}{m-x^2+1}; x \in \mathbb{R}$

By given condition, $f(x) \le -1$ or $f(x) \ge \dfrac{-1}{3}$ or

$$m \in \left(\mathbb{R} - \left\{m : f(x) \in \left(-1, \frac{-1}{3}\right)\right\}\right)$$

$\Rightarrow \dfrac{(x-1)}{m-x^2+1} > -1$ and $\dfrac{(x-1)}{m-x^2+1} < -\dfrac{1}{3}\ \forall x \in \mathbb{R}$

$\Rightarrow \dfrac{(x-1)+m-x^2+1}{m-x^2+1} > 0$ and $\dfrac{3x-3+m-x^2+1}{m-x^2+1} < 0$

$\Rightarrow \dfrac{-x^2+x+m}{m-x^2+1} > 0$ and $\dfrac{-x^2+3x-2+m}{m-x^2+1} < 0$

$\Rightarrow (x^2 - x - m)(x^2 - m - 1) > 0$ and $(x^2 - 3x + 2 - m)(x^2 - m - 1) < 0\ \forall x \in \mathbb{R}$; which is impossible

So, either $f(x) > -1\ \forall x \in \mathbb{R}$ or $f(x) < -\dfrac{1}{3}\ \forall x \in \mathbb{R}$

24. $f(x) = \dfrac{x^2-8x+18}{x^2+4x+30}$

$\Rightarrow f'(x) = \dfrac{12(x^2+2x-26)}{(x^2+4x+30)^2}$

$\Rightarrow$ Disc. of $x^2 + 2x - 26$ is $108 > 0$

$\Rightarrow f'(x)$ changes its sign and $x^2 + 4x + 30 > 0\ \forall x \in \mathbb{R}$

Thus, $f(x)$ is non-monotomic and continuous.

$\Rightarrow f(x)$ is many–one, function, i.e., non-injective.

25. $f(x) = \dfrac{x}{1+|x|}; x \in \mathbb{R}$

$\Rightarrow f(x) = \begin{cases} \dfrac{x}{1+x}; x \ge 0 \\ \dfrac{x}{1-x}; x < 0 \end{cases} \quad \Rightarrow f'(x) = \begin{cases} \dfrac{1}{(1+x)^2}; x > 0 \\ \dfrac{1}{(1-x)^2}; x < 0 \end{cases}$

$\Rightarrow f'(x) > 0\ \forall x \in \mathbb{R} - \{1, 1\}$

$\Rightarrow f(x)$ is continuous and increasing function

$\Rightarrow f(x)$ is injective

Also $f(-\infty) = -1$ and $f(\infty) = 1$

$\Rightarrow$ Range of $f(x) = (-1, 1)$

$\Rightarrow f(x)$ is injective, not surjective.

26. $f(-1, 1) \to \mathbb{R}$

$\Rightarrow f(x) = \begin{cases} \dfrac{x}{1+x}, -1 < x \le 0 \\ \dfrac{x}{1-x}; 0 < x < 1 \end{cases}$

$\Rightarrow f'(x) = \begin{cases} \dfrac{1}{(1+x)^2}, -1 < x \le 0 \\ \dfrac{1}{(1-x)^2}; 0 < x < 1 \end{cases}$

$\Rightarrow f'(x) > 0\ \forall x \in \mathbb{R}$ and $f(x)$ is continuous on $(-1, 1)$

$\Rightarrow f(-1^+) = -\infty, f(1^-) = \infty$

$\Rightarrow f(x)$ is injective and surjective, i.e., bijective.

27. $f: [2, \infty) \to X; f(x) = 5 - 4x + x^2$

Principal domain of $f(x) = [2, \infty)$

$\therefore$ For bijective function, $X = [f(2), f(\infty)) \equiv [1, \infty)$

28. $f: \mathbb{N} \to \mathbb{N}; f(x) =$ highest prime factor of n

$\because f(3) = 3 = f(6)$

$\Rightarrow f(x)$ is many–one, i.e., not injective.

Also $\exists$ no $n \in \mathbb{N} - \{1\}$ for which $f(n) = 1$

$\Rightarrow f(x)$ is not onto.

29. $f(x) = 1/(1-x)$

$f_2(x) = f\{f(x)\}; f_3(x) = f\{f\{f(x)\}\}$……..,

$f_{3n}(x) = ?$

$\Rightarrow f_2(x) = f\left(\dfrac{1}{1-x}\right) = \dfrac{1}{1-\left(\dfrac{1}{1-x}\right)} = \dfrac{1-x}{-x}$

$\Rightarrow f_3(x) = \dfrac{1}{1-\left(\dfrac{x-1}{x}\right)} = \dfrac{x}{1} = x$

$\Rightarrow f_4(x) = f(f_3(x) = f(x)$

$\Rightarrow f_3(x) = f_6(x) = f_9(x) = \ldots = f_{3n}(x) = x$

30. $f(x) = \dfrac{ax+b}{cx+d}, x \ne \dfrac{-d}{c}$ for $d = -a$, $f(x) = \dfrac{ax+b}{cx-a}$

$f(f(x)) = \dfrac{a\left(\dfrac{ax+b}{cx-a}\right)+b}{c\left(\dfrac{ax+b}{cx-a}\right)-a} = \dfrac{a^2x+bcx}{cb+a^2} = x$

$\Rightarrow$ fof is an identity function.

31. $f: \mathbb{R} \to [-1, 1]$; $f(x) = \dfrac{\sin x}{x^2+1}$, clearly $f(x)$ is continuous

Let $f(x) = 1 \quad \Rightarrow \dfrac{\sin x}{x^2+1} = 1$

$\Rightarrow \sin x = x^2 + 1$ but $\sin x \le 1$ and $x^2 + 1 \ge 1$

$\Rightarrow \sin x = x^2 + 1 = 1$

$\Rightarrow \sin x = 1, x^2 = 0$, i.e., $x = 0$, which is impossible.

$\therefore f(x)$ is into.

32. $f: \mathbb{R} - \{0\} \to \mathbb{R} - \{0\}; f(x) = \dfrac{1}{x}$

$\Rightarrow f'(x) = \dfrac{-1}{x^2} < 0\ \forall x \in \mathbb{R} - \{0\}$ and $f(x) < 0$ for $x < 0$, $f(x) >$ 0 for $x > 0$

$\Rightarrow f(x)$ is an injective function.

Also for $y \in \mathbb{R} - \{0\}, f\left(\dfrac{1}{y}\right) = y$ and $\dfrac{1}{y} \in \mathbb{R} - \{0\}$

$\Rightarrow f(x)$ is onto.

If domain $\mathbb{R} - \{0\}$ is replaced by $\mathbb{N}$ keeping the co-domain same, i.e., $f: \mathbb{N} \to \mathbb{R} - \{0\}, f(x) = \dfrac{1}{x}$

$f(x) = \dfrac{1}{x}$ being a decreasing function and continuous for $x > 0$ is injective.

However, $2 \in \mathbb{R} - \{0\}$ and $f\left(\dfrac{1}{2}\right) = 2$ but $\dfrac{1}{2} \notin \mathbb{N}$

$\Rightarrow f(x)$ is not onto.

33. **(i)** $f: \mathbb{N} \to \mathbb{N}; f(x) = x^2$

$f'(x) = 2x > 0\ \forall x > 0$

$\Rightarrow f(x)$ is injective on $\mathbb{N}$

Clearly, $f(x)$ is not surjective, e.g., $f(\sqrt{2}) = 2$ but $\sqrt{2} \notin \mathbb{N}$

(ii) $f: \mathbb{Z} \to \mathbb{Z}$; for $f(x) = x^2$

$\because\ f(-k) = f(k) = k^2\ \forall\ k\ \mathbb{Z}$

$\Rightarrow$ $f(x)$ is not injective. Also $f(x)$ is not surjective, e.g., $f(\sqrt{3}) = 3\ \mathbb{Z}$ but $\sqrt{3} \notin \mathbb{Z}$

(iii) $f: \mathbb{R} \to \mathbb{R}; f(x) = x^2$

Clearly $f(-k) = f(k) = k^2\ \forall\ k\ \mathbb{R}$

$\Rightarrow$ $f(x)$ is not injective and $f(x) \geq 0\ \forall\ x\ \mathbb{R}$

$\Rightarrow$ $f(x)$ is not surjective.

(iv) $f: \mathbb{N} \to \mathbb{N}; f(x) = x^3$

$f'(x) = 3x^2 > 0\ \forall\ x > 0$

$\Rightarrow$ $f(x)$ is increasing, and hence, injective function on $\mathbb{N}$.

However, $f(x)$ is not surjective e.g., $f(3\sqrt{5}) = 5\ \mathbb{N}$ but $3\sqrt{5} \notin \mathbb{N}$.

(v) $f: \mathbb{Z} \to \mathbb{Z}; f(x) = x^3$

Let $f(x_1) = f(x_2)$

$\Rightarrow x_1^3 - x_2^3 = 0 \qquad \Rightarrow (x_1 - x_2)(x_1^2 + x_1x_2 + x_2^2) = 0$

$\Rightarrow x_1 = x_2$ or $x_1^2 + x_1x_2 + x_2^2 = 0$

But $x_1^2 + x_1x_2 + x_2^2 = 0$ gives imaginary roots x_1 for each real x_2.

$\Rightarrow x_1 = x_2 \qquad \Rightarrow$ $f(x)$ is injective .

Also clearly $f(x)$ is not subjective as $f(3\sqrt{5}) = 5\ \mathbb{Z}$ but $3\sqrt{5} \notin \mathbb{Z}$.

TEXTUAL EXERCISE–12: (OBJECTIVE)

1. (d) $f: (-\infty, -1) \to (0, e^5); f(x) = e^{x^3-3x+2}$

$\Rightarrow f'(x) = (3x^2 - 3) . e^{x^3-3x+2} = 3(x^2 - 1). e^{x^3-3x+2}$

$\Rightarrow f'(x) > 0$ for $x\ (-\infty, -1) \cup (1, \infty)$ and $< 0\ \forall\ x\ (-1, 1)$

$\Rightarrow f(x) \uparrow$ for $x\ (-\infty, -1) \Rightarrow f(x)$ is injective.

$\Rightarrow$ Range of $f(x) \equiv (f(-\infty), f(-1)) \equiv (0, e^4) \subset (0, e^5)$

$\Rightarrow f(x)$ is not subjective.

2. (a) (i) $f(x) = e^x - e^{-x}$

$\Rightarrow f'(x) = e^x + e^{-x} > 0\ \forall\ x\ \mathbb{R}$, also being continuous and $f(-\infty) = -\infty, f(\infty) = \infty$

$\therefore$ (i) $\to$ (p)

(ii) $f(x) = x^3 - 1$

$\Rightarrow f'(x) = 3x^2 > 0\ \forall\ x\ \mathbb{R}$ and $f(x)$ is continuous

$\Rightarrow$ one–one

Also Range = $(-\infty,)$ $\Rightarrow$ onto

$\therefore$ (ii) $\to$ (p)

(iii) $f(x) = \dfrac{2x}{1+x^2} \Rightarrow f'(x) = \dfrac{2(1-x^2)}{(1+x^2)^2}$

$\Rightarrow f'(x) < 0$ for $x\ (-\infty, -1) \cup (1, \infty)$ and $f'(x) > 0$ for $x\ (-1, 1)$, graphically shown below.

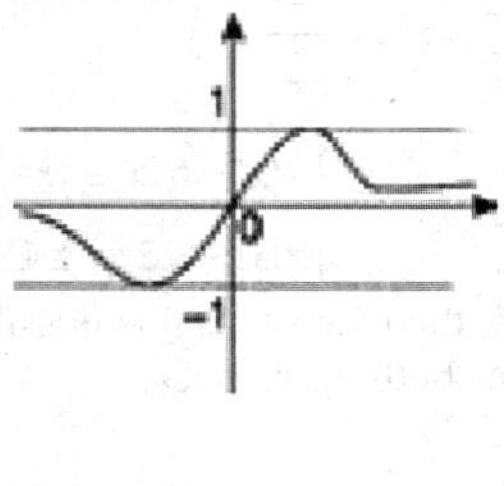

$\Rightarrow f(x)$ is many–one and having range $[-1, 1]$ is into

$\therefore$ (iii) $\to$ (s)

(iv) $f(x) = a^{x^3} \qquad \because\ f'(x) = \left(a^{x^3} \ell na\right)(3x^2)$

$\Rightarrow f'(x)$: $\begin{cases} > 0 \forall x \in \mathbb{R}, a > 1 \\ < 0 \forall x \in \mathbb{R}, a \in (0,1) \end{cases}$

$\Rightarrow f(x) \uparrow$ for $a > 1$ and $\downarrow$ for $a\ (0, 1)$

$\Rightarrow f(x)$ is injective function as continuous. Also $f(x) > 0\ \forall\ x\ \mathbb{R}$ and $\forall$ a > 0

$\Rightarrow R_f\ \mathbb{R} \qquad \Rightarrow f(x)$ is into

$\therefore$ (iv) $\to$ (q)

(v) $f(x) = x^3\ |x| = \begin{cases} x^4; x \geq 0 \\ -x^4; x < 0 \end{cases}$

$\Rightarrow f'(x) = \begin{cases} 4x^3; x > 0 \\ -4x^3; x < 0 \end{cases}$

$\Rightarrow f(x) \uparrow \forall\ x \in \mathbb{R}$ and is continuous. Also $f(-\infty) = -\infty$ and $f(\infty) = \infty$

$\therefore$ (v) $\to$ (p)

(vi) $f(x) = \dfrac{x^2 - x + 1}{x^2 + x + 1}$

$\Rightarrow f'(x) = \dfrac{2(x^2-1)}{(x^2+x+1)} < 0$ for $x\ (-1, 1) > 0$ for $x < -1$ or $x > 1$

Also $x^2 + x + 1\ 0\ \forall\ x\ \mathbb{R}$

$\Rightarrow f(x)$ is continuous function.

$\Rightarrow f(x)$ is many–one function and $x^2 - x + 1 > 0$, $x^2 + x + 1 > 0\ \forall\ x\ \mathbb{R}$

$\Rightarrow f(x) > 0\ \forall\ x\ \mathbb{R} \qquad \Rightarrow f(x)$ is into

$\therefore$ (vi) $\to$ (s)

(vii) $f(x) = \sin^3 x$

$\Rightarrow f'(x) = 3 \sin^2 x \cos x \geq 0\ \forall\ x \left[2n\pi - \dfrac{\pi}{2}, 2n\pi + \dfrac{\pi}{2}\right]$

$\Rightarrow f(x)$ is not injective.

Also $f(x)\ [-1, 1] \qquad \Rightarrow f(x)$ is into

$\therefore$ (viii)$\to$ (s)

3. (i) (c) $f(x) = \sqrt{\ell n \dfrac{1}{|\sec x|}}$

For domain, $\ell n \dfrac{1}{|\sec x|} \geq 0$

$\Rightarrow \dfrac{1}{|\sec x|} \geq 1 \qquad \Rightarrow |\sec x| \leq 1$

$\Rightarrow |\sec x| = 1 \qquad \Rightarrow R_f = \{0\}$

(ii) (a) $f(x) = \dfrac{e^x - e^{-x}}{e^x + e^{-x}} = \dfrac{e^{2x} - 1}{e^{2x} + 1}$

$\Rightarrow -1$ for $x \to -\infty$ and $\to 1$ for $x \to \infty$

Also $f'(x) = \dfrac{4}{(e^x + e^{-x})^2} > 0\ \forall\ x \in \mathbb{R}$

$\Rightarrow f(x)$ is increasing, and hence, injective with range $(-1, 1)$

(iii) (c) $f(x) = \dfrac{x^2}{1+x^4} = \dfrac{1}{\left(x^2 + \dfrac{1}{x_2}\right)}$; $x\ 0$

$\because\ x^2 + \frac{1}{x^2}\ [2, \infty)$ for $x\ 0$

$\Rightarrow f(x)\ \left(0, \frac{1}{2}\right]$ for $x\ 0$

Also $f(0) = 0 \quad \Rightarrow R_f = \left[0, \frac{1}{2}\right]$

(iv) (a) $f(x) = \sin^4 x + \cos^2 x = \sin^4 x + 1 - \sin^2 x = \sin^4 x - \sin^2 x + \frac{1}{4} + \frac{3}{4} = \left(\sin^2 x - \frac{1}{2}\right)^2 + \frac{3}{4}$

$\because\ 0 \le \left(\sin^2 x - \frac{1}{2}\right)^2 \le \frac{1}{4}$

$\Rightarrow f(x) \in \left[\frac{3}{4}, 1\right]$

4. (d) $f: \mathbb{R} \to \mathbb{R}; f(x) = x^3 - 6x^2 + 11x - 6$

$\Rightarrow f'(x) = 3x^2 - 12x + 11$, Disc. $= 12 > 0$

$\Rightarrow f'(x)$ would change its sign and $f(x)$ is continuous

$\Rightarrow f(x)$ is many–one.

Also being a cubic polynomial range $= (-\infty, \infty)$.

$\Rightarrow f(x)$ is many–one onto.

5. (a) $f(x) = {}^{7-x}P_{x-3}$

$\Rightarrow 7 - x \ge x - 3 \quad \Rightarrow x \le 5$ and $x - 3 \ge 0$

$\Rightarrow x\ [3, 5]$ but $x\ \mathbb{Z} \quad \Rightarrow x\ \{3, 4, 5\}$

$\Rightarrow R_f = \{{}^4P_0, {}^3P_1, {}^2P_2\} = \{1, 3, 2\}$

6. (b), (c) $f(x) = |x + 1|; x\ [-1, 0)$

$\Rightarrow f(x) = x + 1$ and $f'(x) = 1 > 0$

$\Rightarrow f(x)$ is injective.

$\Rightarrow f(x) = x + \frac{1}{x}; x\ (0, \infty)$

$\Rightarrow g'(x) = 1 - \frac{1}{x^2}$

$\Rightarrow g'(x) < 0$ for $x\ (0, 1)$ and > 0 for $x\ (1, \infty)$

$\Rightarrow$ non-injective.

$h(x) = x^2 + 4x - 5$, being quadratic polynomial is many–one, i.e., non-injective.

$k(x) = e^{-x}; x\ [0, \infty)$

$\Rightarrow k'(x) = -e^{-x} < 0$ and continuous

$\Rightarrow k(x)$ is injective.

7. (a), (c) $f: A \to [-1, 1]; f(x) = \sin 3x$

For one–one and onto function, $3x \left[\frac{-\pi}{2}, \frac{\pi}{2}\right] \Rightarrow x \in \left[\frac{-\pi}{6}, \frac{\pi}{6}\right]$

Also for one–one and onto function, $3x \left[\frac{\pi}{2}, \frac{3\pi}{2}\right] \Rightarrow x \in \left[\frac{\pi}{6}, \frac{\pi}{2}\right]$

8. (a), (b) $f: \mathbb{N} \to \mathbb{Z}; f(n) = \begin{cases} \frac{n-1}{2}; n = \text{odd} \\ -\frac{n}{2}; n = \text{even} \end{cases}$

Let $n_1, n_2\ \mathbb{N}$

Case (i): n_1, n_2 odd or n_1, n_2 even, $f(n_1) = f(n_2)$

$\Rightarrow n_1 = n_2$

Case (ii): n_1 = odd, n_2 = even, then $f(n_1) = f(n_2)$

$\Rightarrow \frac{n_1 - 1}{2} = \frac{-n_2}{2}$

$\Rightarrow n_1 + n_2 = 1$, which is impossible.

$\Rightarrow f(x)$ is injective. Also if $n \in \mathbb{N}$, then

n = odd + ve $\quad \Rightarrow (2n + 1) = n$,

n = odd – ve $\quad \Rightarrow f(-2n) = n$,

n = even + ve $\quad \Rightarrow f(2n + 1) = n$,

n = even – ve $\quad \Rightarrow f(-2n) = n$ and $f(1) = 0$

$\Rightarrow f(x)$ is surjective.

9. (d) $f: \mathbb{R} \to [-1, 1); f(x) = \frac{x^2 - 4}{x^2 + 4}$, clearly $f(-x) = f(x)$

$\Rightarrow f(x)$ is not injective. Also $f(x) = 1 - \frac{8}{x^2 + 4} \in [-1, 1)$

$\Rightarrow f(x)$ is surjective.

10. (c) $f: (-1, 1) \to Y, f(x) = \tan^{-1}\left(\frac{2x}{1 - x^2}\right)$

$\because\ \frac{d}{dx}\left(\frac{2x}{1 - x^2}\right) = \frac{1 + 2x^2}{(1 - x^2)^2} > 0\ \forall\ x\ (-1, 1)$

$\Rightarrow f(x)$ is $\uparrow \forall\ x\ (-1, 1)$ and continuous

$\Rightarrow Y = (f(-1), f(1)) = (\tan^{-1}(-\infty), \tan^{-1}(\infty)) = \left(\frac{-\pi}{2}, \frac{\pi}{2}\right)$

11. (b) $g: \mathbb{R} \to \left(0, \frac{\pi}{3}\right]; g(x) = \cos^{-1}\left(\frac{x^2 - \alpha}{1 + x^2}\right)$

Here $0 < \cos^{-1}\left(\frac{x^2 - \alpha}{1 + x^2}\right) \le \frac{\pi}{3} \forall x \in \mathbb{R}$

$\Rightarrow \cos\frac{\pi}{3} \le \frac{x^2 - \alpha}{1 + x^2} < \cos 0$

$\Rightarrow \frac{1}{2} \le \left(\frac{x^2 - \alpha}{1 + x^2}\right) < 1\ \forall\ x\ \mathbb{R}$ ...(1)

Now $\frac{x^2 - \alpha}{1 + x^2} = \frac{x^2 + 1 - (\alpha + 1)}{1 + x^2} = 1 - \frac{(\alpha + 1)}{(x^2 + 1)}$ .....(2)

From (1), we get $1 + x^2 \le 2x^2 - 2\alpha < 2 + 2x^2\ \forall\ x\ \mathbb{R}$

$\Rightarrow 2\alpha + 1 \le x^2; \alpha > -1\ \forall\ x\ \mathbb{R}$

$\Rightarrow 2\alpha + 1 \le 0; \alpha > -1$

$\Rightarrow \alpha \left(-1, \frac{-1}{2}\right]$ ...... (3)

From (2) and (3), clearly $\frac{x^2 - \alpha}{1 + x^2} < 1\ \forall\ x\ \mathbb{R}$

Let $h(x) = \frac{x^2 - \alpha}{1 + x^2} \Rightarrow h'(x) = \frac{2(1 + \alpha)x}{1 + x^2}$

$\Rightarrow h(x) \downarrow$ for $x < 0$ and $h(x) \uparrow$ for $x > 0$

$\Rightarrow h(x)$ has its minimum value $= \frac{1}{2}$ at $x = 0$

$\Rightarrow \frac{0 - \alpha}{1 + 0} = \frac{1}{2} \Rightarrow \alpha = \frac{-1}{2}$

12. (c) $f: \mathbb{R} \to \mathbb{R}; f(x) = \begin{cases} x|x| - 6; x \in \mathbb{Q} \\ x|x| - \sqrt{2}; x \notin \mathbb{Q} \end{cases}$

If $x_1, x_2\ \mathbb{R}$, then $f(x_1) = f(x_2)$ is possible when either both $x_1, x_2\ \mathbb{Q}$ or both $x_1, x_2 \in \mathbb{Q}$

If x_1, x_2 Q, then $x_1\,|x_1| - 6 = x_2\,|x_2| - 6$

$\Rightarrow x_1|x_1| = x_2\,|x_2|$

$\Rightarrow x_1^2 = x_2^2$ for $x_1, x_2 \geq 0$ and $-x_1^2 = -x_2^2$ for $x_1, x_2 < 0$

$\Rightarrow (x_1 - x_2)(x_1 + x_2) = 0$

$\Rightarrow x_1 = x_2$ $\quad (\because x_1, x_2 \geq 0$ or $x_1, x_2 < 0)$

$\Rightarrow f(x)$ is injective.

For $y = -\sqrt{2}$

If $x|x| - 6 = -\sqrt{2}$

$\Rightarrow x|x| = 6 - \sqrt{2}$ $\quad \Rightarrow x = \sqrt{6-\sqrt{2}} \notin \mathbb{Q}$

If $x\,|x| - \sqrt{2} = -\sqrt{2}$ $\quad \Rightarrow x\,|x| = 0$

$\Rightarrow x = 0 \in \mathbb{Q}$

$\Rightarrow$ no value of x satisfy $f(x) = -\sqrt{2}$

$\Rightarrow f(x)$ is not surjective.

13. (c) $\because \sin\,[x]\,\pi = 0$

$\Rightarrow f(x) = 0\ \forall\ x\ \mathbb{R}$

$\Rightarrow f(x)$ is many–one function and a constant function.

14. (d) $f: X \xrightarrow{onto} Y$;

$X = \{a_1, a_2, a_3, \ldots a_6\}$; $Y = \{b_1, b_2, b_3\}$

Let $f(a_1) = f(a_2) = f(a_3) = b_1$, choose a_i, a_j, a_k in ${}^6C_3$ ways.

Each of a_4, a_5, a_6 has two choice b_2 and b_3, but there are two cases when each of a_4, a_5, a_6 is associated with b_2 or b_3 in this case b_3 or b_2 remains unassociated.

Thus, number of such onto functions $= {}^6C_3\,((2)^3 - 2)$

$= 20(6) = 120$

15. (b) $f: Y \rightarrow$ Y; $Y = \{4, 5, 6\}$; $f(4)$ 6, $f(5)$ 4, $f(6)$ 5

$\therefore$ $f(4)$ 6 $\quad \Rightarrow f(4) = 4$ or 5,

$f(5)$ 4 $\quad \Rightarrow f(5) = 5$ or 6,

$f(6)$ 5 $\quad \Rightarrow f(6) = 4$ or 6

$\therefore$ If $f(4) = 4$ $\quad \Rightarrow f(6) = 6, f(5) = 5$

If $f(4) = 5$ $\quad \Rightarrow f(5) = 6, f(6) = 4$

$\Rightarrow f_1 = \{(4, 4), (5, 5), (6, 6)\}$ and $f_2 = \{(4, 5), (5, 6), (6, 4)\}$ are two possible bijective functions.

16. (d) By given condition of mirror image about $y = $ k, $f(x) - k = k - f(x)$

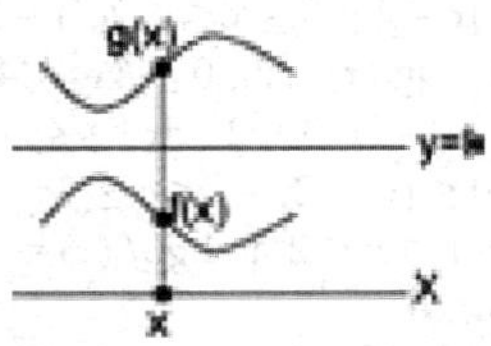

$\Rightarrow f(x) + f(x) = 2k$ $\quad \therefore \phi(x) = f(x) + f(x)$

$\Rightarrow \phi(x) = 2k\ \forall\ k\ \mathbb{R}$ $\quad \Rightarrow \phi$ is a constant function.

$\Rightarrow$ Many–one and into

17. (b) $X = \{a_1, a_2, a_3, a_4, a_5\}$; $Y = \{b_1, b_2, b_3, b_4, b_5\}$

$f: X \rightarrow Y$ such that, $f(x)$ is bijective and $f(a_i)$ b_i, then number of such functions will be equal to the number of ways of placing 5 letters into five envelops, so that no letter goes to its corresponding addressed envelope.

$$= 5!\left[1 - \frac{1}{1!} + \frac{1}{2!} - \frac{1}{3!} + \frac{1}{4!} - \frac{1}{5!}\right]$$

$$= 5!\left[\frac{1}{2} - \frac{1}{6} + \frac{1}{24} - \frac{1}{120}\right] = 60 - 20 + 5 - 1 = 44$$

TEXTUAL EXERCISE–13: (SUBJECTIVE)

1. $fof(-3) = f(f(-3)) = f(0) = -8$, $fof(7) = f(f(7)) = f(53) = 427$, fog $(9) = f(f(9)) = f(85) = 683$, $gof\,(2) = f(f(2)) = f(13) = 173$, $gof\,(0) = f(f\,(0)) = f(-8) = |-8| = 8$, $gof\,(6) = f(f(6)) = f(29)$ $= 845$

2. $f(x) = \dfrac{ax}{x+1}$, x –1, $fof\,(x) = \dfrac{a\,f(x)}{f(x)+1} = \dfrac{a\left(\dfrac{ax}{x+1}\right)}{\dfrac{ax}{x+1}+1}$

$$= \frac{a^2x}{ax+x+1} = \frac{a^2x}{(a+1)x+1} = x$$

$\Rightarrow a^2\,x = (a + 1)x^2 + x$ $\quad \Rightarrow (a + 1)x^2 + (1 - a^2)x = 0$

$\Rightarrow (a + 1)\,[x^2 + (1 - a)\,x] = 0$

$\Rightarrow (a + 1)x\,(x + 1 - a) = 0\ \forall\ x$ –1

$\Rightarrow a = -1$

3. $D_f\,[0, 1)$

(i) $f(|[x - 2.5]|)$ $\quad \Rightarrow |[x - 2.5]|\ [0, 1)$

$\Rightarrow |[x - 2.5]|\ (-1, 1)$

$\Rightarrow [x - 2.5] = 0$ $\quad \Rightarrow (x - 2.5)\ [0, 1)$

$\Rightarrow x\ [2.5, 3.5)$

$\Rightarrow x\ \left[\dfrac{5}{2}, \dfrac{7}{2}\right)$

(ii) $f(\cos x)$ $\quad \Rightarrow \cos x\ [0, 1)$

$$\Rightarrow x \in \bigcup_{n\in\mathbb{Z}}\left\{\left[2n\pi - \frac{\pi}{2}, 2n\pi + \frac{\pi}{2}\right] - \{2n\pi\}\right\}$$

4. (i) $f(x) = [x]$, $f(x) = \sin x$

$\Rightarrow fof(x) = [\sin x]$

$\Rightarrow$ Domain of fog $(x) = \mathbb{R}$ and range of $fog\,(x) = \{-1, 0, 1\}$; gof $(x) = \sin\,[x]$

$\Rightarrow$ Domain of gof $(x) = \mathbb{R}$; Range of $gof\,(x) = \{\sin x;\ a\ \mathbb{Z}\}$

(ii) $f(x) = \tan x$, x $\left(\dfrac{-\pi}{2}, \dfrac{\pi}{2}\right)$; $f(x) = \sqrt{1-x^2}$

$\Rightarrow fog\,(x) = \tan\,\sqrt{1-x^2}$

$\Rightarrow x\,[-1, 1]$ $\quad \Rightarrow$ Domain of $fog\,(x) = [-1, 1]$

$\Rightarrow$ Range of $fog\,(x) = [0, \tan 1]$

$\Rightarrow gof\,(x) = \sqrt{1-\tan^2 x}$

$\Rightarrow \tan x\ [-1, 1]$

$\Rightarrow$ Domain of $gof\,(x) = \left[\dfrac{-\pi}{4}, \dfrac{\pi}{4}\right]$ and range of $gof\,(x) = [0, 1]$

5. (a) $f(x) = \begin{cases} 1+x;\ 0 \leq x \leq 2 \\ 3-x;\ 2 < x \leq 3 \end{cases}$

$$\Rightarrow fof(x) = \begin{cases} 1+f(x);\ 0 \leq f(x) \leq 2 \\ 3-f(x);\ 2 < f(x) \leq 3 \end{cases}$$

$$= \begin{cases} 1+(1+x);\ 0 \leq 1+x \leq 2;\ 0 \leq x \leq 2 \\ 1+(3-x);\ 0 \leq 3-x \leq 2;\ 2 < x \leq 3 \\ 3-(1+x);\ 2 < 1+x \leq 3;\ 0 \leq x \leq 2 \\ 3-(3-x);\ 2 < 3-x \leq 3;\ 2 < x \leq 3 \end{cases}$$

$$= \begin{cases} 2+x;\ 0 \leq x \leq 1 \\ 4-x;\ 2 < x \leq 3 \\ 2-x;\ 1 < x \leq 2 \end{cases} = \begin{cases} 2+x;\ 0 \leq x \leq 1 \\ 2-x;\ 1 < x \leq 2 \\ 4-x;\ 2 < x \leq 3 \end{cases}$$

(b) $f(x) = -1 + |x-2|;\ 0 \le x \le 4$

$$\Rightarrow f(x) = \begin{cases} 1-x; 0 \le x < 2 \\ x-3; 2 \le x \le 4 \end{cases}$$

$$\Rightarrow fof(x) = \begin{cases} 1-f(x); 0 \le f(x) < 2 \\ f(x)-3; 2 \le f(x) \le 4 \end{cases}$$

$$= \begin{cases} 1-(1-x); 0 \le 1-x < 2; 0 \le x < 2 \\ 1-(x-3); 0 \le x-3 < 2; 2 \le x \le 4 \\ (1-x)-3; 2 \le 1-x \le 4; 0 \le x < 2 \\ (x-3)-3; 2 \le x-3 \le 4; 2 \le x \le 4 \end{cases}$$

$$= \begin{cases} x; 0 \le x \le 1 \\ 4-x; 3 \le x \le 4 \end{cases}$$

$$\therefore\ fof(x) = \begin{cases} x; 0 \le x \le 1 \\ \text{Not defined for } 1 < x < 3 \\ 4-x; 3 \le x \le 4 \end{cases}$$

(c) $f(x) = 2 - |x|;\ -1 \le x \le 3$

$$\Rightarrow f(x) = \begin{cases} 2+x; x < 0 \\ 2-x; x \ge 0 \end{cases}$$

$$\Rightarrow f(f(x)) = \begin{cases} 2+f(x); -1 \le f(x) < 0 \\ 2-f(x); 0 \le f(x) \le 3 \end{cases}$$

$$= \begin{cases} 2+(2+x); -1 \le 2+x < 0, x < 0 \\ 2+(2-x); -1 \le 2-x < 0, x \ge 0 \\ 2-(2+x); 0 \le 2+x \le 3, x < 0 \\ 2-(2-x); 0 \le 2-x \le 3, x \ge 0 \end{cases} = \begin{cases} 4-x; 2 < x \le 3 \\ -x; -1 \le x \le 0 \\ x; 0 < x \le 2 \end{cases}$$

(d) $f(x) = \begin{cases} x+1; x \le 1 \\ 5-x^2; x > 1 \end{cases}$

$$\Rightarrow fof(x) = \begin{cases} f(x)+1; f(x) \le 1 \\ 5-(f(x))\ ; f(x) > 1 \end{cases}$$

$$= \begin{cases} (x+1)+1; x+1 \le 1; x \le 1 \\ (5-x)^2+1; (5-x^2) \le 1; x > 1 \\ 5-(x+1)^2; (x+1) > 1; x \le 1 \\ 5-(5-x^2)^2; 5-x^2 > 1; x > 1 \end{cases}$$

$$= \begin{cases} x+2; x \le 0 \\ 6-x^2; x \ge 2 \\ 5-(x+1)^2; 0 < x \le 1 \\ 5-(5-x^2)^2; 1 < x < 2 \end{cases}$$

(e) $f(x) = \begin{cases} -x; & x < 0 \\ x; & 0 \le x \le 1 \\ 2-x; & x > 1 \end{cases}$

$$\Rightarrow f(f(x)) = \begin{cases} -f(x); f(x) < 0 \\ f(x); 0 \le f(x) \le 1 \\ 2-f(x); f(x) > 1 \end{cases}$$

$$= \begin{cases} -(-x); -x < 0; x < 0 \\ -(x); x < 0; 0 \le x \le 1 \\ -(2-x); 2-x < 0; x > 1 \\ -x, 0 \le -x \le 1; x < 0 \\ x; 0 \le x \le 1; 0 \le x \le 1 \\ 2-x; 0 \le 2-x \le 1; x > 1 \\ 2-(-x); -x > 1; x < 0 \\ 2-x; x > 1; 0 \le x \le 1 \\ 2-(2-x); 2-x > 1; x > 1 \end{cases} = \begin{cases} 2+x; x < -1 \\ x-2; x > 2 \\ -x;\ -1 \le x < 0 \\ x; 0 \le x \le 1 \\ 2-x; 1 < x \le 2 \end{cases}$$

6. (a) $f(x) = \begin{cases} 1+x^2; x \le 1 \\ x+1; 1 < x \le 2 \end{cases}$ and $f(x) = \{1-x; -2 \le x \le 1$

$$\text{fog}(x) = \begin{cases} 1+(g(x))^2; g(x) \le 1 \\ g(x)+1; 1 < g(x) \le 2 \end{cases}$$

$$= \begin{cases} 1+(1-x)^2; (1-x) \le 1, -2 \le x \le 1 \\ (1-x)+1; 1 < 1-x \le 2; -2 \le x \le 1 \end{cases}$$

$$= \begin{cases} 2-2x+x^2; 0 \le x \le 1 \\ 2-x; -1 \le x < 0 \end{cases}$$

(b) $f(x) = \begin{cases} 1+x; x \le 1 \\ 2x+2; 1 < x \le 2 \end{cases}$ and $f(x) = \begin{cases} x^2; -1 \le x < 2 \\ x+2; 2 \le x \le 3 \end{cases}$

$$\Rightarrow \text{fog}(x) = \begin{cases} 1+g(x); g(x) \le 1 \\ 2.g(x)+2; 1 < g(x) \le 2 \end{cases}$$

$$= \begin{cases} 1+x^2; x^2 \le 1; -1 \le x \le 2 \\ 1+(x+2); x+2 \le 1; 2 \le x \le 3 \\ 2x^2+2; 1 < x^2 \le 2; -1 \le x < 2 \\ 2(x+2)+2; 1 < x+2 \le 2; 2 \le x \le 3 \end{cases}$$

$$= \begin{cases} 1+x^2; -1 \le x \le 1 \\ 2x^2+2; 1 < x \le \sqrt{2} \end{cases}$$

7. (a) $f(x) = -1 + |x-2|;\ 0 \le x \le 4;\ f(x) = 2 - |x|;\ -1 \le x \le 3$

$fog(x) = -1 + |g(x) - 2|;\ 0 \le f(x) \le 4;\ -1 \le x \le 3$

$= -1 + |2 - |x| - 2|;\ 0 \le 2 - |x| \le 4;\ -1 \le x \le 3$

$= -1 + |x|;\ 0 \le |x| \le 2,\ -1 \le x \le 3$

$= -1 + |x|;\ -1 \le x \le 2$ and $gof(x) = 2 - |f(x)|;\ -1 \le f(x) \le 3;\ 0 \le x \le 4$

$= 2 - |-1 + |x-2||;\ -1 \le -1 + |x-2| \le 3;\ 0 \le x \le 4$

$$= \begin{cases} 2+(-1+|x-2|); 0 \le |x-2| \le 1; 0 \le x \le 4 \\ 2-(-1+|x-2|); 1 \le |x-2| \le 4; 0 \le x \le 4 \end{cases}$$

$$= \begin{cases} 1+|x-2|; 1 \le x \le 3 \\ 3-|x-2|; 0 \le x \le 1, 3 \le x \le 4 \end{cases}$$

The graphs of fog (x) and gof (x) are as given below.

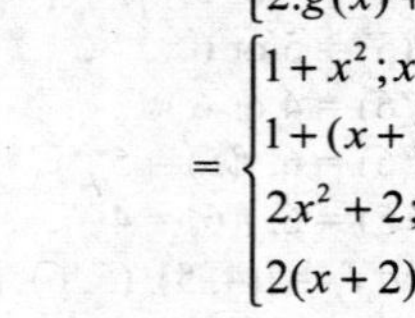

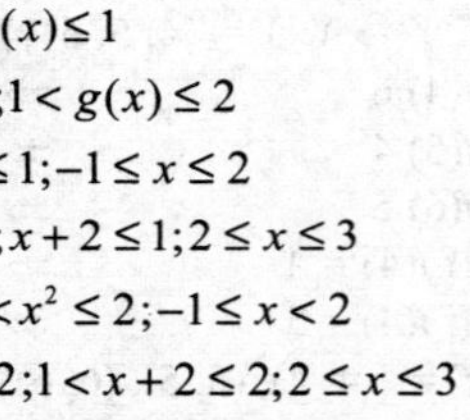

(b) $f(x) = \begin{cases} x+1; x \le 1 \\ 2x+1; 1 < x \le 2 \end{cases}$ and $f(x) = \begin{cases} x^2; -1 < x \le 2 \\ x+2; 2 < x \le 3 \end{cases}$

$$\text{fog}(x) = \begin{cases} g(x)1; g(x) \le 1; -1 < x \le 3 \\ 2g(x)+1; 1 < g(x) \le 2; -1 < x \le 3 \end{cases}$$

$$= \begin{cases} x^2+1; x^2 \le 1; -1 < x \le 2 \\ (x+2)+1; (x+2) \le 1; 2 < x \le 3 \\ 2x^2+1; 1 < x^2 \le 2; -1 < x \le 2 \\ 2(x+2)+1; 1 < (x+2) \le 2; 2 < x \le 3 \end{cases}$$

$$= \begin{cases} x^2+1; -1 < x \le 1 \\ 2x^2+1; 1 < x \le \sqrt{2} \end{cases} \text{ and gof}(x)$$

$$= \begin{cases} (f(x))^2; -1 < f(x) \le 2, x \le 2 \\ f(x)+2; 2 < f(x) \le 3; x \le 2 \end{cases}$$

$$= \begin{cases} (x+1)^2; -1 < (x+1) \le 2; x \le 1 \\ (2x+1)^2; -1 < (2x+1) \le 2; 1 < x \le 2 \\ (x+1)+2; 2 < x+1 \le 3; x \le 1 \\ (2x+1)+2; 2 < 2x+1 \le 3; 1 < x \le 2 \end{cases}$$

$= \{(x+1)^2; -2 < x \le 1$

The graphs of fof(x) and gof (x) are as given below.

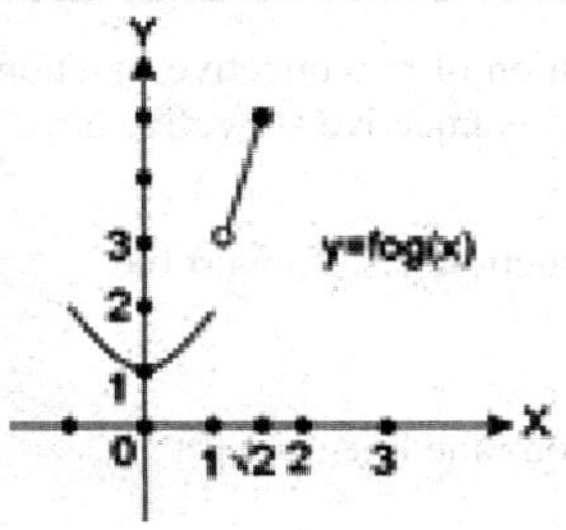

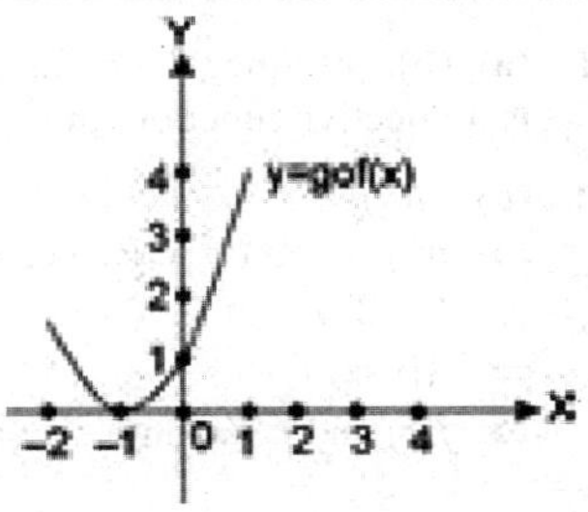

8. Example1: $f(x) = 2x + 4$; $f(x) = \dfrac{x-4}{2}$

Clearly $f(x)$ is not onto as gives even images only and gof(x) = x which is onto.

Example 2: $f(x) = x^2 + 3$; $g(x) = \sqrt{x-3}$

$f(x)$ 5 as $x^2 + 3 = 5$ $\Rightarrow x^2 = 2$

$\Rightarrow x = \pm\sqrt{2}$; x N

$\Rightarrow f(x)$ is not onto

Now, gof (x) = $|x| = x$ as x N

$\Rightarrow$ gof (x) is onto.

9. Let $y \in Y$ $\Rightarrow$ fog (y) = y

$\Rightarrow f(f(y)) = y$ but $f(y)$ X

$\Rightarrow f(y) = x$ for some $x \in x$

$\Rightarrow f(x) = y$ for some $x \in x$

$\Rightarrow f(x)$ is onto.

10. Let $f(x_1) = f(x_2)$ for some x_1, x_2 X

$\Rightarrow f(x_1), f(x_2)$ Y and g is a function from $Y \to X$

$\Rightarrow f(f(x_1)) = f(f(x_2)))$ (unique image)

$\Rightarrow x_1 = x_2$ $(\because \text{gof}(x) = x \ \forall \ X)$

$\Rightarrow f(x)$ is one–one.

11. $f(x) = \cot^{-1}(\text{sgn}(x)) + \sin^{-1}(x - \{x\}) = \cot^{-1}(\text{sgn}(x)) + \sin^{-1}[x]$

$\Rightarrow [x]\ \{-1, 0, 1\}$

$\Rightarrow x\ [-1, 2)$. which is the largest domain.

Also $f([-1, 2)) = \{\cot^{-1}(-1) + \sin^{-1}(-1), \cot^{-1} 1 + \sin^{-1} 0,$ $\cot^{-1}(0) + \sin^{-1}(0), \cot^{-1}(1) + \sin^{-1} 1\} = \left\{\dfrac{\pi}{4}, \dfrac{\pi}{2}, \dfrac{3\pi}{4}\right\}$

$$\because f(x) = \begin{cases} \dfrac{\pi}{4} \text{ for } x \in [-1,0) \cup (0,1) \\ \dfrac{\pi}{2} \text{ for } x = 0 \\ \dfrac{3\pi}{4} \text{ for } x \in [1,2) \end{cases}$$

$\Rightarrow f(x)$ is not injective function.

12. $f(x) = \begin{cases} x+2; x \le 1 \\ 2x+1; 1 < x \le 3 \end{cases}$ and $f(x) = \begin{cases} x^2+1; -1 \le x \le 4 \\ x-1; 4 < x \le 6 \end{cases}$

$$\therefore f(f(x)) = \begin{cases} g(x)+2; g(x) \le 1; -1 \le x \le 6 \\ 2g(x)+1; 1 < g(x) \le 3; -1 \le x \le 6 \end{cases}$$

$$= \begin{cases} (x^2+1)+2; (x^2+1) \le 1; -1 \le x \le 4 \\ (x-1)+2; (x-1) \le 1; 4 < x \le 6 \\ 2(x^2+1)+1; 1 < x^2+1 \le 3; -1 \le x \le 4 \\ 2(x-1)+1; 1 < x-1 \le 3; 4 < x \le 6 \end{cases}$$

$$= \begin{cases} 3; x = 0 \\ 2x^2+3; -1 \le x <, 0 \text{ or } 0 < x \le \sqrt{2} \end{cases}$$

$= 2x^2 - 3; x \in [-1, \sqrt{2}]$

$\therefore$ Domain = $[-1, \sqrt{2}\,]$, Range = [3, 7]

$$\therefore f(f(x)) = \begin{cases} (f(x))^2+1; -1 \le f(x) \le 4; x \le 3 \\ f(x)-1; 4 < f(x) \le 6 \end{cases}$$

$$= \begin{cases} (x+2)^2+1; -1 \le x+2 \le 4; x \le 1 \\ (2x+1)^2+1; -1 \le 2x+1 \le 4; 1 < x \le 3 \\ (x+2)-1; 4 < x+2 \le 6; x \le 1 \\ (2x+1)-1; 4 < 2x+1 \le 6; 1 < x \le 3 \end{cases}$$

$$= \begin{cases} x^2+4x+5; -3 \le x \le 1 \\ 4x^2+4x+2; 1 < x \le \dfrac{3}{2} \\ 2x; \dfrac{3}{2} < x \le \dfrac{5}{2} \end{cases}$$

$\Rightarrow$ Domain = $\left[-3, \dfrac{5}{2}\right]$ and range = [1, 17]

(a) $f(f(x)) = 5.01$

$\Rightarrow 2x^2 + 3 = 5.01$

For x [–1, 0); fog (x) decrease from 5 to 3 and for x $[0, \sqrt{2}]$, fog (x) increase from 3 to 7.

$\Rightarrow f(f(x)) = 5.01$ has only one solution.

(b) $f(f(x)) = 5$ has solution.
(c) $f(f(x)) = 1$ has no solution.

13. $f(x)=\begin{cases}x+a; \text{if } x<0\\ |x-1|; \text{if } x\geq 0\end{cases}$ and $f(x)=\begin{cases}(x+1); \text{if } x<0\\ (x-1)^2+b \text{ if } x\geq 0\end{cases}$; $a, b \geq 0$

$\Rightarrow$ (gof)(x) = $\begin{cases}f(x)+1; f(x)<0\\ (f(x)-1)^2+b; f(x)\geq 0\end{cases}$

$= \begin{cases}(x+a)+1; (x+a)<0; x<0\\ |x-1|+1; |x-1|<0; x\geq 0\\ (x+a-1)^2+b; (x+a)\geq 0; x<0\\ (|x-1|)^2+b; |x-1|\geq 0; x\geq 0\end{cases}$

$= \begin{cases}x+a+1; x<-a\\ (x+a-1)^2+b; -a\leq x<0\\ (|x-1|-1)^2+b; x\geq 0\end{cases}$

$= \begin{cases}(x+a+1); x<-a\\ (x+a-1)^2+b; -a\leq x<0\\ (x)^2+b; 0\leq x\leq 1\\ (x-2)^2+b; x\geq 1\end{cases}$

$\because$ gof (x) is continuous.

$\Rightarrow \lim_{x\to -a^-} gof(x) = gof(-a) = 1+b$

$\Rightarrow 1 = 1 + b \qquad \Rightarrow b = 0$

Also $\lim_{x\to 0^-} gof(x) = gof(0)$

$\Rightarrow (a-1)^2 + b = b$

$\Rightarrow a = 1$

$\Rightarrow$ (gof)′ (x) = $\begin{cases}1; x<-1\\ 2(x); -1<x<0\\ 2x; 0\leq x<1\\ 2(x-2); x>1\end{cases}$

$\therefore$ L.H.D of gof (x) at $x = 0$ equals 0 and R.H.D of gof (x) at $x = 0$ equals 0.

$\Rightarrow$ gof(x) is differentiable at $x = 0$.

14. $h'(x) = (fog)'(x) = f'(f(x)).g'(x) \leq 0$ as $f'(x) \geq 0\ \forall\ x\ [0, \infty)$, $g'(x) \leq 0\ \forall\ x\ [0, \infty)$

$\Rightarrow$ $h(x)$ is a decreasing function from $[0, \infty)$ to $[\infty, 0)$. Also $h(0) = 0$

$\Rightarrow h(x) = 0\ \forall\ x\ [0, \infty)$

15. f: $[0, 1] \to [1, 2]$; $f(x) = (1 + x)$ and g: $[1, 2] \to [0, 1]$; $f(x) = (2 - x)$ $gof(x) = 2 - f(x)$; $x\ [0, 1] = 2 - (1 + x)$; $x\ [0, 1]$

$\Rightarrow gof(x) = 1 - x$; $x\ [0, 1]$

16. **(i)** $f(x) = \cos^{-1}\sqrt{\log_{[x]}\frac{|x|}{x}}$

For domain, $\sqrt{\log_{|x|}\frac{|x|}{x}} \in [0,1]$

$\Rightarrow \log_{|x|}\frac{|x|}{x}\ [0, 1]$; $[x] > 0\ 1$

$\Rightarrow \log_{|x|}\frac{|x|}{x}\ [0, 1]$; $[x] \geq 2$

$\Rightarrow 1 \leq \frac{|x|}{x} \leq [x]$; $x \geq 2$

$\Rightarrow x \leq |x| \leq x\,[x]$; $x \geq 2 \quad \because \quad x \geq 2$

$\Rightarrow |x| = x$

$\Rightarrow x \leq x\,[x]$

$\Rightarrow 1 \leq [x]$; $x \geq 2$; which is true $\forall\ x \geq 2$

$\therefore$ Domain of $f(x) = [2, \infty)$

$f(x) = \cos^{-1}\sqrt{\log_{[x]}1}$ $(\because x > 0 \Rightarrow |x| = x)$

$\Rightarrow f(x) = \cos^{-1}(0) = \frac{\pi}{2}$

$\Rightarrow$ Range = $\left\{\frac{\pi}{2}\right\}$

(ii) $f(x) = \sqrt{\ell n(\cos(\sin x))}$

For domain ln (cos (sin x)) ≥ 0

$\Rightarrow \cos(\sin x) \geq 1$

$\Rightarrow \cos(\sin x) = 1$

$\Rightarrow \sin x = 2n\pi$; n $\mathbb{Z}$

$\Rightarrow \sin x = 0$

$\Rightarrow$ Domain = $\{n\}$; n $\mathbb{Z}$ and range = $\{0\}$

TEXTUAL EXERCISE–13: (OBJECTIVE)

1. **(a), (b), (c)** Since the composition of two bijective function is a bijective function, then gof is injective surjective also.

2. **(d)** $f(f(x)) = x\ \forall\ x\ \mathbb{R}$

$\Rightarrow f(x) = f^{-1}(x)\ \forall\ x\ \mathbb{R}$, i.e., function is self invertible.

$\therefore$ $(\alpha, \beta) f$

$\Rightarrow$ $(\beta, \alpha) f$

$\Rightarrow$ $f(x)$ and $f^{-1}(x)$ intersect along the line, $(y - \beta)$

$= \frac{\alpha-\beta}{\beta-\alpha}(x-\alpha)$

$\Rightarrow (y - \beta) = -(x - \alpha)$

$\Rightarrow y = -x + (\alpha - \beta)$

$\Rightarrow$ Such functions are infinitely many.

3. **(b), (d)** $f(x)$ = – and $f(x) = \frac{1}{\sqrt{x}}$

$\Rightarrow D_f = \mathbb{R} - \{0\}$; $D_g = (0, \infty)$

Now, $f(f(x)) = \frac{1}{g(x)} = \sqrt{x}$ with its domain $(0, \infty) = D_g$ and range of $f(x)$.

$f(f(x)) = \frac{1}{\sqrt{f(x)}} = \sqrt{x}$ with its domain $(0, \infty) = D_g$ and range = $(0, \infty)$

4. **(d)** f, g: $\mathbb{R} \to \mathbb{R}$

$f(x) = \frac{x+|x|}{2}$ and $f(x) = \begin{cases}x \text{ for } x<0\\ x^2 \text{ for } x\geq 0\end{cases}$

fog (x) = $\frac{g(x)+|g(x)|}{2}$

$= \begin{cases} 0 \text{ if } g(x)<0 \\ g(x) \text{ if } g(x)\ge 0 \end{cases} = \begin{cases} 0 \text{ if } x<0 \\ x^2 \text{ if } x\ge 0 \end{cases}$ and gof (x)

$= \begin{cases} f(x) \text{for } f(x) \quad 0 \\ (f(x) \ \text{for } f(x)\ge 0 \end{cases} = \begin{cases} x^2 \text{ for } x\ge 0 \\ 0 \text{ for } x<0 \end{cases}$

$\Rightarrow$ fog (x) = gof (x) $\forall$ x $\mathbb{R}$

5. (d) $f(x) = \sin x$, $f(x) = |\ln x|$

$\Rightarrow$ fog $(x) = \sin |\ln x|$ with its domain $= (0, \infty)$ and range $= [-1, 1] = R_1$

And gof $(x) = |\ln (\sin x)|$ with its domain

$= \bigcup_{n\in\mathbb{Z}} (2n\pi,(2n+1)\pi)$ and range $= [0, \infty) = R_2$

7. (c) $f(x) = -1 + |x - 1|$; $-1 \le x \le 3$ and $f(x) = 2 - |x + 1|$; $-2 \le x \le 2$

fog $(3/2) = f(f(3/2)) = f\left(2-\left|\frac{5}{2}\right|\right) = f\left(-\frac{1}{2}\right)$

$= -1 + \left|-\frac{1}{2}-1\right| = \frac{1}{2}$

8. (b), (c) $f(x) = \begin{cases} x; x\in\mathbb{Q} \\ 1-x; x\notin\mathbb{Q} \end{cases}$

$\Rightarrow f(f(x)) = \begin{cases} f(x); f(x)\in\mathbb{Q} \\ 1-f(x); f(x)\notin\mathbb{Q} \end{cases}$

$= \begin{cases} x; x\in\mathbb{Q}; x\in\mathbb{Q} \\ 1-x; 1-x\in\mathbb{Q}; x\notin\mathbb{Q} \\ 1-x; x\notin\mathbb{Q}, x\in\mathbb{Q} \\ 1-(1-x); 1-x\notin\mathbb{Q}, x\in\mathbb{Q} \end{cases}$

$= \begin{cases} x; x\in\mathbb{Q} \\ x; x\notin\mathbb{Q}\ \forall x\in\mathbb{R} \end{cases} \Rightarrow f(f(x)) = x$

$\Rightarrow$ An identity function an odd linear as polynomial.

9. (c) Clearly, abscissa of $D = x_0$ and ordinate of D = ordinate of C.

$= g$ (abscissa of B) $= g$ (ordinate of B as $y = x$)

$= g$ (ordinate of A) $= f(f(x_0))$

$\Rightarrow D = (x_0, f(f(x_0)))$

11. (b) $f(x) = x^2 + 2x + 1 = (x + 1)^2 \Rightarrow g[f(x)] = |x + 1|$

$\Rightarrow f((x + 1)^2) = |x + 1| = \sqrt{(x+1)^2}$

$\Rightarrow f(x) = \sqrt{x}$

12. (a), (b) $f(x) = (ax^3 + b)^5$; $f(f(x)) = f(f(x))$

$\Rightarrow f(x) = (f(x))^{-1} = \left(\frac{x^{1/5}-b}{a}\right)^{1/3}$

Also $f(f(x)) = f(f(x)) = x$

TEXTUAL EXERCISE-14: (SUBJECTIVE)

1. $f(x) = \begin{cases} x; -\infty<x<1 \\ x^2; 1\le x\le 4 \\ 2^x; 4<x<\infty \end{cases}$

$\Rightarrow x = \begin{cases} y; -\infty<x<1; -\infty<y<1 \\ \sqrt{y}; 1\le x\le 4; 1\le y\le 16 \\ \log_2 y; 4<x<\infty; 16<y<\infty \end{cases}$

$\Rightarrow f^{-1}(x) = \begin{cases} x; -\infty<x<1 \\ \sqrt{x};\ 1\le x\le 16 \\ \log_2 x: 16<x<\infty \end{cases}$

2. (i) $f: (-\infty, -1) \to (-\infty, -2)$; $f(x) = -(x + 1)^2 - 2$

$\Rightarrow f'(x) = -2(x + 1) \ge 0$ as $x \le -1$ and $y + 2 = -(x + 1)^2$

$\Rightarrow (x + 1)^2 = -(y + 2)$

$\Rightarrow x + 1 = \pm\sqrt{-(y+2)}$ but $x + 1 \le 0$ and $y + 2 \le 0$

$\Rightarrow x + 1 = -\sqrt{-(y+2)} \Rightarrow f^{-1}(x) = -1 - \sqrt{-(x+2)}$

(ii) $f: \left[\frac{\pi}{6}, \frac{7\pi}{6}\right] \to [-1, 1]$; $f(x) = \sin\left(x+\frac{\pi}{3}\right)$

$\Rightarrow f'(x) = \cos\left(x+\frac{\pi}{3}\right) \le 0$ for $x \in \left[\frac{\pi}{6}, \frac{7\pi}{6}\right]$

$\Rightarrow f(x)$ is decreasing function and $y = \sin\left(x+\frac{\pi}{3}\right)$

$\Rightarrow \sin^{-1} y = \sin^{-1}\left(\sin\left(x+\frac{\pi}{3}\right)\right)$

$\Rightarrow \sin^{-1} y = \sin^{-1}\left[\sin\left(\pi-\left(x+\frac{\pi}{3}\right)\right)\right]$

$= \sin^{-1}\left[\sin\left(\frac{2\pi}{3}-x\right)\right] \quad \left(\because \frac{-\pi}{2} \le \pi-\left(x+\frac{\pi}{3}\right) \le \frac{\pi}{2}\right)$

$\Rightarrow \sin^{-1}(y) = \frac{2\pi}{3} - x$

$\Rightarrow x = \frac{2\pi}{3} - \sin^{-1}(y)$

$\Rightarrow f^{-1}(x) = \frac{2\pi}{3} - \sin^{-1} x; x \in [-1,1]$.

3. $f(x) = \begin{cases} 0, \text{ if } x \text{ is rational} \\ x, \text{if } x \text{ is irrational} \end{cases}$ and $f(x) = \begin{cases} x, \text{ if } x \text{ is rational} \\ 0, \text{if } x \text{ is irrational} \end{cases}$

$\Rightarrow (f-g)(x) = \begin{cases} -x, \text{ if } x\in\mathbb{Q} \\ x, \text{ if } x\in\overline{\mathbb{Q}} \end{cases}$

We claim that $h = (f - g)$ is one–one and onto

Injectivity: Let $h(x_1) = h(x_2)$

$\Rightarrow \begin{cases} -x_1 = -x_2 \text{ if } x_1, x_2 \in\mathbb{Q} \\ x_1 = x_2 \text{ if } x_1, x_2\in\overline{\mathbb{Q}} \\ -x_1 = x_2 \text{ if } x_1\in\mathbb{Q}, x_2\in\overline{\mathbb{Q}} \end{cases}$

$\Rightarrow x_1 = x_2 \qquad \Rightarrow$ Injectivity

Subjectivity: Also if y $\mathbb{R}$, then h$(-y)$ if y $\mathbb{Q}$ and $h(y) = y$ if y $\mathbb{Q}$

$\Rightarrow h(x) = (f - g)(x)$ is subjective.

Hence, $(f - g)(x)$ is bijective, i.e., invertible.

Also $(f + g)(x) = x \ \forall \ \mathbb{R}$, which is clearly bijective, and hence, invertible.

Now $(f.g)\ (x) = 0\ \forall\ x\ \mathbb{R}$, which being constant, and hence, many–one.

$\Rightarrow$ Not invertible.

4. $f: \mathbb{R} \to \mathbb{R};\ f(x) = \dfrac{e^x - e^{-x}}{2}$

$\Rightarrow f'(x) = \dfrac{e^x + e^{-x}}{2} > 0\ \forall\ x\ \mathbb{R}$

$\Rightarrow f(x)$ is increasing and continuous function.

Also $f(-\infty) = \dfrac{e^{-\infty} - e^{\infty}}{2} = -\infty$ and $f(\infty) = \dfrac{e^{\infty} + e^{-\infty}}{2} = \infty$

$\Rightarrow f: \mathbb{R} \to \mathbb{R}$ is invertible. Now, $y = \dfrac{e^x - e^{-x}}{2} = \dfrac{e^{2x} - 1}{2e^x}$

$\Rightarrow (e^x)^2 - 2y\, e^x - 1 = 0$

$\Rightarrow e^x = \dfrac{2y \pm \sqrt{4y^2 + 4}}{2} \Rightarrow e^x = y \pm \sqrt{y^2 + 1}$

$\Rightarrow e^x = y + \sqrt{y^2 + 1}$ as $e^x > 0\ \forall\ x\ \mathbb{R}$

$\Rightarrow x = \ln\left(y + \sqrt{y^2 + 1}\right) \Rightarrow f^{-1}(x) = \ln\left(x + \sqrt{x^2 + 1}\right)$

5. $y = \log_a\left(x + \sqrt{x^2 + 1}\right);\ a > 1$

$\Rightarrow a^y = x + \sqrt{x^2 + 1} \Rightarrow a^y - x = \sqrt{x^2 + 1}$

$\Rightarrow a^{2y} + x^2 - 2a^y.x = x^2 + 1$

$\Rightarrow a^{2y} - 2\,x.a^y - 1 = 0 \Rightarrow x = \dfrac{a^{2y} - 1}{2a^y} = \dfrac{a^y - a^{-y}}{2}$

$\Rightarrow f^{-1}(x) = \dfrac{(a^x - a^{-x})}{2}$

6. $f(x) = f^{-1}(x)$ and $f'(x) = \dfrac{1}{1 + x^3}$

Let $y = f(x) = f^{-1}(x)$

$\Rightarrow f(y) = x$

$\Rightarrow f'(y) = \dfrac{dx}{dy}$ (Diff. w.r.t y)

$\Rightarrow \dfrac{dy}{dx} = \dfrac{1}{f'(y)} = 1 + y^3 = 1 + (f(x))^3$

$\Rightarrow \dfrac{d}{dx}(g(x)) = 1 + (g(x))^3$

7. $f(x) = \sin x + \cos x;\ f(x) = x^2 - 4$

$\Rightarrow f(x) = \sqrt{2}\sin\left(x + \dfrac{\pi}{4}\right);\ g(x) = x^2 - 4$

$\Rightarrow f(f(x)) = (f(x))^2 - 4 = 2\sin^2\left(x + \dfrac{\pi}{4}\right) - 4 = 1 - \cos\left(2x + \dfrac{\pi}{2}\right) - 4 = -3 + \sin 2x$

$\therefore f(x) = \sin 2x - 3$

$\Rightarrow f(x)$ is invertible for $2x \in \left[\dfrac{-\pi}{2}, \dfrac{\pi}{2}\right]$

$\Rightarrow x \in \left[\dfrac{-\pi}{4}, \dfrac{\pi}{4}\right]$

8. $f(x) = \sqrt{2}\sin\left(x + \dfrac{\pi}{4}\right);\ f(x) = x^2 + 7$

$\Rightarrow f(x) = x + 7$

$\Rightarrow f(f(x)) = (f(x)) + 7 = \sqrt{2}\sin\left(x + \dfrac{\pi}{4}\right) + 7$, which is invertible for $x + \dfrac{\pi}{4} \in \left[\dfrac{-\pi}{2}, \dfrac{\pi}{2}\right]$

$\Rightarrow x \in \left[\dfrac{-3\pi}{4}, \dfrac{\pi}{4}\right]$

Also $y = \sqrt{2}\sin\left(x + \dfrac{\pi}{4}\right) + 7$

$\Rightarrow \dfrac{y - 7}{\sqrt{2}} = \sin\left(x + \dfrac{\pi}{4}\right)$

$\Rightarrow \sin^{-1}\left(\dfrac{y - 7}{\sqrt{2}}\right) = \sin^{-1}\left(\sin\left(x + \dfrac{\pi}{4}\right)\right) = x + \dfrac{\pi}{4}$

For $x + \dfrac{\pi}{4} \in \left[\dfrac{-\pi}{2}, \dfrac{\pi}{2}\right]$ and $\dfrac{y - 7}{\sqrt{2}} \in [-1, 1]$

$\Rightarrow x = \sin^{-1}\left(\dfrac{y - 7}{\sqrt{2}}\right) - \dfrac{\pi}{4}$

$\Rightarrow f^{-1}(x) = \sin^{-1}\left(\dfrac{x - 7}{\sqrt{2}}\right) - \dfrac{\pi}{4}$ with domain

$x \in \left[7 - \sqrt{2}, 7 + \sqrt{2}\right]$

9. $f(C) = \{f(x) : x\ C\}$

$F^{-1}(D) = \{x \in x : f(x)\ D\}$

Let $y \in f(f^{-1}(B))$

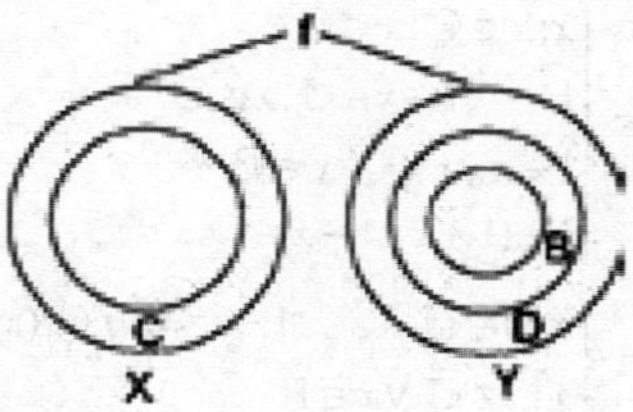

$\Rightarrow y = f(x)$ for some $x\ f^{-1}(B)$

$\Rightarrow f(x)\ B \qquad \Rightarrow y \in B \subseteq f(X)$

$\Rightarrow f(f^{-1}(B)) \subseteq B$ ....(i)

Conversely, let $y \in B \subseteq f(X)$

As $y \in f(X)$

$\Rightarrow \exists\ x \in X$ such that $y = f(x) \in B$

$\Rightarrow x \in f^{-1}(B) \subseteq X$

$\Rightarrow f(x) \in f(f^{-1}(B))$

$\Rightarrow y \in f(f^{-1}(B))$

$\Rightarrow B \subseteq f(f^{-1}(B))$ ....(iii)

$\therefore$ From (i) and (ii), $f(f^{-1}(B)) = B$

10. Area of $\Delta = \dfrac{\sqrt{3}}{4}a^2 = \dfrac{\sqrt{3}}{4}[x^2 + (f(x))^2] = \dfrac{\sqrt{3}}{4}$ (given)

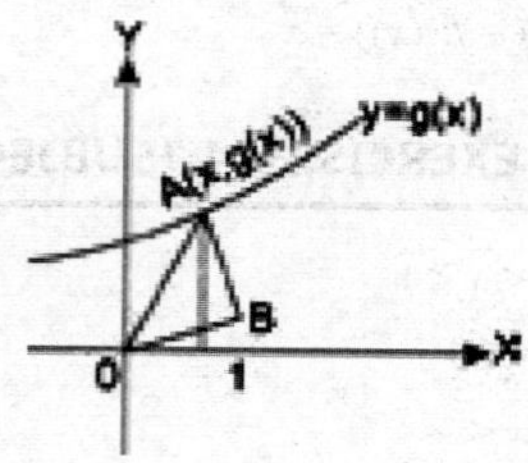

$\Rightarrow x^2 + (f(x))^2 = 1$ $\Rightarrow x = \pm\sqrt{1-y^2}; y \geq 0$

$\Rightarrow x = \sqrt{1-y^2}$ $\Rightarrow g^{-1}(x) = \sqrt{1-x^2}; x \in [0, 1]$

11. f: {1, i, w} → {5, 6, 7}

Case (i) : $f(1) = 5$ (true) , $f(i)$ 5 (false), $f(w)$ 7 (false).

$\Rightarrow f(1) = 5, f(i) = 5, f(w) = 7$ but it is many–one.

Case (ii): $f(1) = 5$ (false), $f(i)$ 5

$\Rightarrow f(w) = 7, f(1)$ 5, f(i) 5

$\Rightarrow f(x)$ is not onto.

Case (iii): $f(1) = 5$ (false), $f(i)$ 5 (false), $f(w)$ 7 (true)

$\Rightarrow f(1)$ 5, f(i) = 5, $f(w)$ 7

$\Rightarrow f(1) = 7, f(i) = 5, f(w) = 6$

$\Rightarrow f^{-1}(6) = w$

$\Rightarrow (f^{-1})^{2012}(6) = w^{2012} = (w^3)^{670}.w^2 = w^2$

12. $2x^2 - 5x + 2 = \dfrac{5-\sqrt{9+8x}}{4}; x < \dfrac{5}{4}$ ...(i)

Let $y = 2x^2 - 5x + 2$

$\Rightarrow 2x^2 - 5x + (2 - y) = 0 \Rightarrow x = \dfrac{5 \pm \sqrt{25-4(2)(2-y)}}{4}$

$\Rightarrow x = \dfrac{5\pm\sqrt{9+8y}}{4}$ $\Rightarrow x = \dfrac{5+\sqrt{9+8y}}{4} > \dfrac{5}{4}$

But $x < 5/4$

$\Rightarrow x = \dfrac{5-\sqrt{9+8y}}{4}$

$\Rightarrow f^{-1}(x) = \dfrac{5-\sqrt{9+8x}}{4}$ .....(ii)

From (i) and (ii), $f(x) = f^{-1}(x)$

$\Rightarrow f(x) = x$ $\Rightarrow 2x^2 - 5x + 2 = x$

$\Rightarrow 2x^2 - 6x + 2 = 0$ $\Rightarrow x^2 - 3x + 1 = 0$

$\Rightarrow x = \dfrac{3\pm\sqrt{9-4}}{2} = \dfrac{3\pm\sqrt{5}}{2}$ but $x < 5/4$

$\Rightarrow x = \dfrac{3-\sqrt{5}}{2}$

TEXTUAL EXERCISE-14: (OBJECTIVE)

1. (a) $f: (-\infty, 1] \to (-\infty, 1]$

$f(x) = x(2 - x)$

$\Rightarrow y = -x^2 + 2x$ $\Rightarrow x^2 - 2x + y = 0$

$\Rightarrow x = \dfrac{2\pm\sqrt{4-4y}}{2}$ $\Rightarrow x = 1 \pm\sqrt{1-y}; x \leq 1; y \leq 1$

$\Rightarrow x = 1-\sqrt{1-y}$ $\Rightarrow f^{-1}(x) = 1-\sqrt{1-x}$

2. (b) $f(x) = 3x - 5$ $\Rightarrow f^{-1}(x) = \dfrac{x+5}{3}$

$\Rightarrow f(x) = \dfrac{x+5}{3}$ $\Rightarrow f(4) = 3$

3. (a) $f(x) = (x + 2)^2$ for $x \leq -2$

$\Rightarrow y = (x + 2)^2$ $\Rightarrow x = -2\pm\sqrt{y}$

But $x \leq -2$ $\Rightarrow x = -2-\sqrt{y}$

$\Rightarrow f(x) = f^{-1}(x) = -2-\sqrt{x}; x \geq 0$

4. (d) $y = f(x) = \dfrac{x+2}{x+1}$

$\Rightarrow xy + y = x + 2$ $\Rightarrow x(y - 1) = 2 - y$

$\Rightarrow x = \dfrac{2-y}{y-1}$ $\Rightarrow f^{-1}(x) = \dfrac{2-x}{x-1}$

$\Rightarrow f^{-1}(4) = \dfrac{-2}{3}; f^{-1}(0) = -2$, also $f(y) + 1 = \dfrac{y+2}{y+1} + 1 = \dfrac{2y+3}{y+1}$

$\Rightarrow x f(y) + 1$ $\Rightarrow f'(x) = \dfrac{-1}{(x+1)^2}$

$\Rightarrow f(x)$ decrease for x –1

5. (c) $f: \mathbb{R} \to \mathbb{R}; f(x) = x - [x]$

$\Rightarrow f(x) = \{x\}$, which is many–one

$\Rightarrow f^{-1}(x)$ is not defined on $\mathbb{R}$.

6. (c) $f: (2, 4) \to (1, 3); f(x) = x - \left[\dfrac{x}{2}\right]$

$\therefore \dfrac{x}{2} \in (1,2) \Rightarrow \left[\dfrac{x}{2}\right] = 1$

$\Rightarrow f(x) = x - 1$ $\Rightarrow x = y + 1$

$\Rightarrow f^{-1}(x) = x + 1$

7. (b), (c) $f(x)$: $[0, \infty) \to [0,)$

$f(x) = \dfrac{x}{1+x}$ $\Rightarrow y + xy = x$

$\Rightarrow x(y - 1) = -y$ $\Rightarrow x = \dfrac{y}{1-y}$

$\Rightarrow f'(x) = \frac{1}{(1+x)^2} \to 0$

$\Rightarrow f(0) = 0, f(\infty) = 1, f(x)$ is continuous on $[0, \infty)$

$\Rightarrow f(x)$ has its range $[0, 1)$

$\Rightarrow f(x)$ is one–one but not onto, and hence, is non-invertible on $[0, \infty)$

8. (a) $f: [1, \infty) \to [2, \infty); f(x) = x + \dfrac{1}{x}$

$\Rightarrow xy = x^2 + 1$ $\Rightarrow x^2 - xy + 1 = 0$

$\Rightarrow x = \dfrac{y\pm\sqrt{y^2-4}}{2}; x \geq 1$

$\Rightarrow f^{-1}(x) = \dfrac{x+\sqrt{x^2-4}}{2}$

9. (b) $f:[1, \infty) \to [1, \infty); f(x) = 2^{x(x-1)}$

$\Rightarrow y = 2^{x(x-1)}$ $\Rightarrow \log_2 y = x^2 - x$

$\Rightarrow x = \dfrac{1\pm\sqrt{1+4\log_2 y}}{2}$

But $x \geq 1$ $\Rightarrow x = \dfrac{1+\sqrt{1+4\log_2 y}}{2}$

$\Rightarrow f^{-1}(x) = \dfrac{1+\sqrt{1+4\log_2 x}}{2}$

10. (c) Let $f(x) = f^{-1}(x); f(x) = x^x$

$\Rightarrow f(f(x)) = x$ $\Rightarrow f'(f(x)).g'(x) = 1$

$\Rightarrow g'(x) = \dfrac{1}{f'(g(x))} = \dfrac{1}{(g(x)^{g(x)}(1+\log g(x))}$

$= \dfrac{1}{x(1+\log_e g(x))} \begin{pmatrix} \therefore (g(x)^{g(x)} \\ = f(g(x)) = x \end{pmatrix}$

11. (a) $f(x) = \dfrac{e^x - e^{-x}}{e^x + e^{-x}} \Rightarrow y = \dfrac{e^{2x}-1}{e^{2x}+1}$

$\Rightarrow e^{2x}.y + y = e^{2x} - 1$

$\Rightarrow e^{2x}(y-1) = -y-1 \quad \Rightarrow e^{2x} = \dfrac{y+1}{1-y}$

$\Rightarrow 2x = \ell n\left(\dfrac{y+1}{1-y}\right)$

$\Rightarrow x = \dfrac{1}{2}\ell n\left(\dfrac{1+y}{1-y}\right) \quad \Rightarrow f^1(x) = \dfrac{1}{2}\ell n\left(\dfrac{1+x}{1-x}\right)$

12. (c) $A_1 = \{1, 2, 3, 4\}$; $A_2 = \{5, 6, 7, 8\}$; $A_3 = \{9, 10\}$; $A_4 = \{11, 12, 13, 14\}$

$n_{12} = 4!, n_{13} = 0, n_{14} = 4!, n_{21} = 4!, n_{23} = 0, n_{24} = 4!, n_{31} = 0, n_{32} = 0, n_{34} = 0, n_{41} = 4!, n_{42} = 4!, n_{43} = 0$

$\Rightarrow \sum n_{ij} = 6(4!) = 6(24) = 144$

13. (b) $f(x) = \sqrt{3}\sin x - \cos x + 2$

$= 2\left(\dfrac{\sqrt{3}}{2}\sin x - \dfrac{1}{2}\cos x\right) + 2 = 2\sin\left(x - \dfrac{\pi}{6}\right) + 2$

$\Rightarrow \dfrac{y-2}{2} = \sin\left(x - \dfrac{\pi}{6}\right) \quad \Rightarrow x - \dfrac{\pi}{6} = \sin^{-1}\left(\dfrac{y-2}{2}\right)$

$\Rightarrow f^1(x) = \dfrac{\pi}{6} + \sin^{-1}\left(\dfrac{x-2}{2}\right)$

14. (b) $f(x) = \sqrt{\sin^{-1}(2x) + \dfrac{\pi}{6}}$ ....(1)

$\Rightarrow y^2 = \sin^{-1}(2x) + \pi/6$

$\Rightarrow \left(y^2 - \dfrac{\pi}{6}\right) = \sin^{-1}(2x)$

$\Rightarrow x = \dfrac{1}{2}\sin\left(y^2 - \dfrac{\pi}{6}\right)$

$\Rightarrow f^1(x) = \dfrac{1}{2}\sin\left(x^2 - \dfrac{\pi}{6}\right) = f(x)$ (say)

From (i), $\sin^{-1}(2x)$

$\in \left[\dfrac{-\pi}{2}, \dfrac{\pi}{2}\right] \Rightarrow \sin^{-1}(2x) + \dfrac{\pi}{6} \in \left[\dfrac{-\pi}{3}, \dfrac{2\pi}{3}\right]$

$\Rightarrow y \in \left[0, \sqrt{\dfrac{2\pi}{3}}\right]$

$\Rightarrow$ Domain of $f^1(x)$ is $\left[0, \sqrt{\dfrac{2\pi}{3}}\right]$

15. (b) $f(x) = \sqrt{\cos^{-1}(2x) + \dfrac{\pi}{6}}$

Range of $f(x) = f^1(x)$ means domain of $f(x)$

$\Rightarrow \cos^{-1}(2x) + \dfrac{\pi}{6} \geq 0$

$\Rightarrow \cos^{-1}(2x) \geq \dfrac{-\pi}{6}$, which is true $\forall x \in \left[\dfrac{-1}{2}, \dfrac{1}{2}\right]$

$\Rightarrow$ Range $f(x)$ is $\left[\dfrac{-1}{2}, \dfrac{1}{2}\right]$

16. (a) $f(x) = (1 + b)x^2 + 2bx + 1$

$\Rightarrow m(b) = \dfrac{-\left[(2b)^2 - 4(1+b^2)\right]}{4(1+b^2)} = \dfrac{1}{4(1+b^2)}$

Which has principle domain $[0, \infty)$ and range $(0, 1]$

Let $y = \dfrac{1}{1+b^2} \Rightarrow 1 + b^2 = \dfrac{1}{y} \Rightarrow b^2 = \dfrac{1}{y} - 1$

$\Rightarrow b = \pm\sqrt{\dfrac{1}{y} - 1}$; $b \in [0, \infty)$

$\Rightarrow b = \sqrt{\dfrac{1}{y} - 1} \Rightarrow m^{-1}(x) = \sqrt{\dfrac{1}{x} - 1}$

17. (c) $f: (0, \infty) \to (1, \infty)$

$F(x) = \int_0^x f(t)dt$

$\Rightarrow F'(x) = f(x)$ ......(i)

Now $F(x^2) = x^2(1 + x)$

$\Rightarrow F(x) = x(1 + \sqrt{x})$

$\Rightarrow F'(x) = 1 + \dfrac{3}{2}\sqrt{x}$ ....(ii)

$\therefore$ From (i) and (ii), we get $f(x) = 1 + \dfrac{3}{2}\sqrt{x}$

$\Rightarrow x = \left[\dfrac{2}{3}(y-1)\right]^2 \quad \Rightarrow f^1(x) = \dfrac{4}{9}(x-1)^2 = f(x)$

$\Rightarrow g(10) = 36$

18. (c) From above, $f(x) = f(x)$

$\Rightarrow f(x) = x$

$\Rightarrow 1 + \dfrac{3}{2}\sqrt{x} = x \quad \Rightarrow \dfrac{3}{2}\sqrt{x} = x - 1$

$\Rightarrow 2x - 3\sqrt{x} - 2 = 0$

$\Rightarrow (2\sqrt{x}+1)(\sqrt{x}-2) = 0$

$\Rightarrow \sqrt{x} = 2 \quad \Rightarrow x = 4$

$\Rightarrow$ Required points are (4, 4)

TEXTUAL EXERCISE-15: (SUBJECTIVE)

1. (i) Domain of $\tan x$ is symmetric about origin and $\tan(-x) = -\tan x$

$\Rightarrow$ odd function

(ii) Domain of $\cos x$ is symmetric about origin and $\cos(-x) = \cos x$

$\Rightarrow$ even function

(iii) Domain of $\sin(x^2 + 1)$ is $\mathbb{R}$ and $\sin((-x)^2 + 1) = \sin(x^2 + 1)$

$\Rightarrow$ even function

(iv) Domain of $x + x^2$ is $\mathbb{R}$ and $f(-x) = -x + x^2 f(x), -f(x)$

$\Rightarrow f(x)$ is neither even nor odd

(v) Domain of $x - x^3$ is $\mathbb{R}$ and $f(-x) = -f(x)$

$\Rightarrow$ odd function

(vi) $f(x) = x\left(\dfrac{a^x - 1}{a^x + 1}\right)$; $D_f = \mathbb{R}$ and $f(-x) = -x\left(\dfrac{a^{-x}-1}{a^{-x}+1}\right) = x\left(\dfrac{a^x-1}{a^x+1}\right) = f(x)$

$\Rightarrow$ even function

(vii) $f(x) = \log\left(x+\sqrt{x^2+1}\right)$

$\because \quad \sqrt{x^2+1} > |x| \geq \pm x \quad \Rightarrow \quad x + \sqrt{x^2+1} > 0$

$\Rightarrow \quad D_f = \mathbb{R}$ and $f(-x) = \log\left(-x+\sqrt{x^2+1}\right)$

$= \log\left(\dfrac{-x+\sqrt{x^2+1}}{-x-\sqrt{x^2+1}} \times \dfrac{-x-\sqrt{x^2+1}}{1}\right)$

$= \log\left(\dfrac{x^2-x^2-1}{-x-\sqrt{x^2+1}}\right) = -\log\left(x+\sqrt{x^2+1}\right) = -f(x)$

$\Rightarrow$ $f(x)$ is an odd function

(viii) $f(x) = \sin x + \cos x$

$f(-x) = -\sin x + \cos x\, f(x), -f(x)$

$\Rightarrow$ $f(x)$ is neither odd nor even.

(ix) $f(x) = (x^2 - 1)\,|x|$

$\Rightarrow f(-x) = (x^2-1)\,|-x| = (x^2-1) = f(x)$

$\Rightarrow$ $f(x)$ is an even function

2. (a) $f(x) = 2^{x^2-x^4} \quad \Rightarrow D_f = \mathbb{R}$ and

$f(-x) = 2^{x^2-x^4} \quad \Rightarrow f(x) = f(-x)$

$\Rightarrow$ $f(x)$ is an even function.

(b) $f(x) = \sin x + \cos x;\ D_f = \mathbb{R}$

$\Rightarrow f(-x) = -\sin x + \cos x\, f(x), -f(x)$

$\Rightarrow$ $f(x)$ is neither even nor odd .

(c) $f(x) = x^2 - |x|$

$\Rightarrow f(-x) = x^2 - |-x| = x^2 - |x| = f(x)$

$\Rightarrow$ $f(x)$ is an even function

(d) $f(x) = \dfrac{x}{2^x-1} + \dfrac{x}{2} + 1$

$\Rightarrow f(-x) = \dfrac{-x}{2^{-x}-1} - \dfrac{x}{2} + 1 = \dfrac{x.2^x}{2^x-1} - \dfrac{x}{2} + 1$

$= x\left(\dfrac{2^x-1+1}{2^x-1}\right) - \dfrac{x}{2} + 1 = x + \dfrac{x}{2^x-1} - \dfrac{x}{2} + 1$

$= \dfrac{x}{2} + \dfrac{x}{2^x-1} + 1 = f(x)$

$\Rightarrow$ $f(x)$ is an even function

(e) $f(x) = x^{10}.\log\left(\dfrac{1+\sin x}{1-\sin x}\right)$

$\Rightarrow f(-x) = x^{10}.\log\left(\dfrac{1-\sin x}{1+\sin x}\right) = -x^{10}\log\left(\dfrac{1+\sin x}{1-\sin x}\right) = -f(x)$

$\Rightarrow$ $f(x)$ is an odd function.

(f) $|f(x)| + 1$; $f(x)$ is and odd function

Let $f(x) = |f(x)| + 1$

$\Rightarrow g(-x) = |f(-x)| + 1 = |-f(x)| + 1 = |f(x)| + 1 = f(x)$

$\Rightarrow$ even function

(g) $f(x) = \dfrac{(1+2^x)^9}{2^x}$

$\Rightarrow f(-x) = \dfrac{(1+2^{-x})^9}{2^{-x}} = \dfrac{(1+2^x)^9}{2^{8x}} \in f(x), -f(x)$

$\Rightarrow$ $f(x)$ is neither odd nor even.

(h) $f(x) = \sqrt{1+x+x^2} - \sqrt{1-x+x^2}$

$\Rightarrow f(-x) = \sqrt{1-x+x^2} - \sqrt{1+x+x^2} = -f(x)$

$\Rightarrow$ odd function

(i) $\phi(x) = [f(x) + f(-x)].[f(x) - g(-x)]$

$\Rightarrow \phi(-x) = [(-x) + f(x)].[f(-x) - f(x)] = -\phi(x)$

$\Rightarrow$ odd function

(j) $f(x) = \dfrac{\sec x + x^2 - 9}{x \sin x}$

$f(-x) = \dfrac{\sec x + x^2 - 9}{(-x)(-\sin x)} = f(x)$

$\Rightarrow$ even function

3. $f(x) = (-1)^{[x]}$

$\Rightarrow f(-x) = (-1)^{[-x]} = \begin{cases} (-1)^{-[x]} \text{ for } x \in \mathbb{Z} \\ (-1)^{-1-[x]} \text{ for } x \notin \mathbb{Z} \end{cases}$

$\Rightarrow f(-x) = \begin{cases} \dfrac{1}{(-1)^{[x]}} \text{ for } x \in \mathbb{Z} \\ (-1)^{-1}.(-1)^{-[x]} \text{ for } x \notin \mathbb{Z} \end{cases}$

$\Rightarrow$ $f(x)$ is even function for $x \in \mathbb{Z}$ and odd function for $x \notin \mathbb{Z}$

$\Rightarrow$ $f(x)$ is neither even nor odd

4. $f(x) = \begin{cases} 4; \text{if } x < -1 \\ -4x; \text{if } -1 \leq x \leq 0 \end{cases}$ .....(i)

$\because$ $f(x)$ is an even function, $f(-x) = f(x)$, $\forall x \in \mathbb{R}$ and $f(-x)$

$= \begin{cases} 4 \text{ if } x > 1 \\ -4(-x); \text{ if } 0 \leq x \leq 1 \end{cases} = f(x)$ .....(ii)

$\therefore$ From (i) and (ii), we get $f(x) = \begin{cases} 4;\ x < -1 \text{ or } > 1 \\ -4x;\ -1 \leq x \leq 0 \\ 4x;\ 0 \leq x \leq 1 \end{cases}$

$\Rightarrow f(x) = \begin{cases} 4x;\ 0 < x \leq 1 \\ 4;\ x > 1 \end{cases}$

5. $f(x+y) + f(x-y) = 2f(x).f(y)$

For $x = y = 0$, we have $2f(0) = 2[f(0)]^2$

$\Rightarrow f(0) = 0$ or $f(0) = 1$

For $y = 0$, we have $f(x) + f(x) = 2f(x).f(0)$

$\Rightarrow 2f(x)\,(f(0) - 1) = 0$

$\Rightarrow f(x) = 0\ \forall\, x \in \mathbb{R}$ or $f(0) = 1$ if $f(x) = 0\ \forall\, x \in \mathbb{R}$, then $f(x)$ is an even function.

If $f(0) = 1$; then $f(y) + f(-y) = 2f(y)$

$\Rightarrow f(-y) = f(y)\ \forall\, y \in \mathbb{R}$

$\Rightarrow$ $f(x)$ is an even function. Thus $f(x)$ is an even function.

7. $f(x) = \dfrac{2x(\sin x + \tan x)}{2\left[\dfrac{x+21\pi}{\pi}\right]-41} = \dfrac{2x(\sin x + \tan x)}{2\left[\dfrac{x}{\pi}+21\right]-41}$

$= \dfrac{2x(\sin x + \tan x)}{2\left[\dfrac{x}{\pi}\right]+1}$ and $f(-x) = \dfrac{2(-x)(-\sin x - \tan x)}{2\left[\dfrac{-x}{\pi}\right]+1}$

$= \dfrac{2x(\sin x + \tan x)}{2\left(-1-\left[\dfrac{x}{\pi}\right]\right)+1}$ if $x\ n\pi$; $x \in \mathbb{Z}$

$$= \frac{2x(\sin x + \tan x)}{-1-2\left[\frac{x}{\pi}\right]} = -\frac{2x(\sin x + \tan x)}{2\left[\frac{x}{\pi}\right]+1} = -f(x) \text{ if } x\ n\pi;\ n \in \mathbb{Z}$$

If $x = n\pi$; then $f(x) = f(-x) = 0$

$\Rightarrow$ $f(x)$ is an odd function .

8. $f(x) = \begin{cases} \sqrt{\cos x}\ ; x \in \left[\frac{-\pi}{2}, \frac{\pi}{2}\right] \\ \sqrt{1-\cos x}\ ; x \in \left[\frac{\pi}{2}, \frac{3\pi}{2}\right] \end{cases}$

$\because$ Domain of $f(x)$ is not symmetric about origin.

$\Rightarrow$ $f(x)$ is neither even nor odd.

9. $f: [-20, 20] \to \mathbb{R}, f(x) = \left[\frac{x^2}{a}\right] \sin x + \cos x$

$\Rightarrow f(-x) = -\left[\frac{x^2}{a}\right]\sin x + \cos x$

$\because$ $f(x)$ is an even function.

$\Rightarrow \left[\frac{x^2}{a}\right] = 0\ \forall\ x \in [-20, 20]$

$\Rightarrow \left[\frac{x^2}{a}\right] = 0\ \forall\ x^2 \in [0, 400]$

$\Rightarrow 0 \le \frac{x^2}{a} < 1\ \forall\ x^2 \in [0, 400]$

$\Rightarrow a \in (400, \infty)$

10. $f(x) = \begin{cases} x|x|; 0 \le x < 1 \\ 2x\ ; x \ge 1 \end{cases}$

(i) For $f(x)$ to be even, $f(-x) = f(x)$

$\Rightarrow f(-x) = \begin{cases} -x|x|; 0 \le -x < 1 \\ -2x;\ -x \ge 1 \end{cases}$

$\Rightarrow \begin{cases} -x|x|; -1 < x \le 0 \\ -2x\ ; x \le -1 \end{cases} \quad \Rightarrow f(x) = \begin{cases} -2x;\ x \le -1 \\ -x|x|; -1 < x \le 0 \\ x|x|; 0 \le x < 1 \\ 2x;\ x \ge 1 \end{cases}$

(ii) For $f(x)$ to be odd, $f(-x) = -f(x)$

$\Rightarrow f(x) = \begin{cases} 2x;\ x \le -1 \text{ or } x \ge 1 \\ x|x|;\ -1 < x < 1 \end{cases}$

11. $f(x) = \begin{cases} x^2+1; 0 < x \le 1 \\ x+1\ ; 1 < x \le 2 \end{cases}$

$\Rightarrow f(-x) = \begin{cases} x^2+1; 0 < -x \le 1 \\ -x+1\ ;\ 1 < -x \le 2 \end{cases} = \begin{cases} x^2+1\ ; -1 \le x < 0 \\ -x+1\ ; -2 \le x < -1 \end{cases}$

(i) For even extension: $f(-x) = f(x)$

$\Rightarrow f(x) = \begin{cases} -x+1; -2 \le x < -1 \\ x^2+1; -1 \le x < 0 \\ x^2+1; 0 < x \le 1 \\ x+1;\ 1 < x \le 2 \end{cases}$

(ii) For odd Extension: $f(-x) = -f(x)$

$\Rightarrow f(x) = \begin{cases} x-1; -2 \le x < -1 \\ -x^2-1; -1 \le x < 0 \\ x^2+1; 0 < x \le 1 \\ x+1; 1 < x \le 2 \end{cases}$

12. $f(x) = x^2 + x$ for x $[0, 3]$

$\Rightarrow f(-x) = x^2 - x$ for $-x \in [0, 3]$

$\Rightarrow f(-x) = x^2 - x$ for $x \in [-3, 0]$

(i) For even function: $f(-x) = f(x)$

$\Rightarrow f(x) = \begin{cases} x^2 - x \text{ for } x \in [-3, 0] \\ x^2 + x \text{ for } x \in [0, 3] \end{cases}$

(ii) For odd function: $f(-x) = -f(x)$

$\Rightarrow f(x) = \begin{cases} -x^2 + x \text{ for } x \in [-3, 0] \\ x^2 + x \text{ for } x \in [0, 3] \end{cases}$

13. $f(x) = \begin{cases} x^2 + \sin x;\ 0 \le x < 1 \\ -x + e^{-x};\ x \ge 1 \end{cases}$

$\Rightarrow f(-x) = \begin{cases} x^2 - \sin x\ ; 0 \le -x < 1 \\ -x + e^x\ ; -x \ge 1 \end{cases}$

$\Rightarrow f(-x) = \begin{cases} x^2 - \sin x; -1 < x \le 0 \\ -x + e^x\ ; x \le -1 \end{cases}$

(i) For even function, $f(-x) = f(x)$

$\Rightarrow f(x) = \begin{cases} -x + e^x\ ; x \le -1 \\ x^2 - \sin x\ ; -1 < x \le 0 \\ x^2 + \sin x;\ 0 \le x < 1 \\ x + e^{-x}\ ; x \ge 1 \end{cases}$

(ii) For odd function, $f(-x) = -f(x)$

$\Rightarrow f(x) = \begin{cases} x - e^x\ ; x \le -1 \\ -x^2 + \sin x : -1 < x \le 0 \\ x^2 + \sin x\ ; 0 \le x < 1 \\ x + e^{-x}\ ; x \ge 1 \end{cases}$

TEXTUAL EXERCISE-15: (OBJECTIVE)

1. (i) $f(x) = \frac{1-x}{1+x} \Rightarrow f(-x) = \frac{1+x}{1-x} \ne f(x), -f(x)$

$\Rightarrow$ Neither odd nor even

(ii) $f(x) = \frac{e^x - e^{-x}}{e^x + e^{-x}}$

$\Rightarrow f(-x) = \frac{e^{-x} - e^x}{e^{-x} + e^x} = -\left(\frac{e^x - e^{-x}}{e^x + e^{-x}}\right) = -f(x)$

$\Rightarrow$ $f(x)$ is an odd function.

(iii) $f(x) = \sin(\sin x)$

$\Rightarrow$ $f(-x) = \sin(\sin(-x)) = \sin(-\sin x) = -\sin(\sin x) = -f(x)$

$\Rightarrow$ $f(x)$ is an odd function.

(iv) $f(x) = \sin(\cos x)$ $\quad\Rightarrow f(-x) = \sin(\cos(-x)) = f(x)$

$\Rightarrow$ $f(x)$ is an even function.

(v) $f(x) = \cos(\cos x)$

$\Rightarrow f(-x) = \cos(\cos(-x)) = \cos(\cos x) = f(x)$

$\Rightarrow f(x)$ is an even function.

(vi) $f(x) = \dfrac{\sin^4 x + \cos^4 x}{x + x^2 \tan x}$

$\Rightarrow f(-x) = \dfrac{\sin^4 x + \cos^4 x}{-x - x^2 \tan x} = -f(x)$

$\Rightarrow f(x)$ is an odd function.

(vii) $f(x) = x^{17} = \left(\dfrac{a^{\sin x} - 1}{a^{\sin x} + 1}\right)$

$\Rightarrow \quad f(-x) = -x^{17}\left(\dfrac{a^{-\sin x} - 1}{a^{-\sin x} + 1}\right) = x^{17}\left(\dfrac{a^{\sin x} - 1}{a^{\sin x} + 1}\right) = f(x)$

$\Rightarrow \quad f(x)$ is an even function.

2. (i) $f(x) = x^2 \sin\left\{\dfrac{1}{\sin\left(\dfrac{1}{x}\right)}\right\}$

$\Rightarrow f(-x) = x^2 \sin\left(\dfrac{1}{-\sin\left(\dfrac{1}{x}\right)}\right)$

$\Rightarrow f(-x) = -x^2 \sin\left\{\dfrac{1}{\sin\left(\dfrac{1}{x}\right)}\right\} = -f(x)$

$\Rightarrow f(x)$ is an odd function.

(ii) $f(x) = \cos x.\log\left(\dfrac{1+\tan x}{1-\tan x}\right)$

$\Rightarrow f(-x) = \cos x.\log\left(\dfrac{1-\tan x}{1+\tan x}\right) = -\cos x.\log\left(\dfrac{1+\tan x}{1-\tan x}\right)$

$= -f(x)$

$\Rightarrow$ odd function.

(iii) $f(x) = \left(\dfrac{a^{2x}+1}{a^x}\right) \Rightarrow f(-x) = \dfrac{a^{-2x}+1}{a^{-x}} = \dfrac{1+a^{2x}}{a^x} = f(x)$

$\Rightarrow$ even function.

(iv) $f(x) = \dfrac{(1+e^x)^2}{e^x}$

$\Rightarrow f(-x) = \dfrac{(1+e^{-x})^2}{e^{-x}} = \dfrac{(1+e^x)^2}{e^x} = f(x)$

$\Rightarrow$ even function.

(v) $f(x) = \sqrt[3]{1+x+x^2} + \sqrt[3]{1-x+x^2}$

$\Rightarrow f(-x) = \sqrt[3]{1-x+x^2} + \sqrt[3]{1+x+x^2} = f(x)$

$\Rightarrow$ even function.

(vi) $f(x) = \sqrt{1+2x+3x^2} - \sqrt{1-2x+3x^2}$

$\Rightarrow f(-x) = \sqrt{1-2x+3x^2} - \sqrt{1+2x+3x^2} = -f(x)$

$\Rightarrow$ odd function

3. (a), (c) (a) $f(x) = \ln|x|$

$\Rightarrow f(-x) = \ln|-x| = \ln|x| = f(x)$

$\Rightarrow$ even function.

(b) $f(x) = \sin^{-1}\left(\dfrac{2x}{1+x^2}\right) \Rightarrow f(-x) = \sin^{-1}\left(\dfrac{-2x}{1+x^2}\right) = -\sin^{-1}\left(\dfrac{2x}{1+x^2}\right)$

$\Rightarrow$ odd function

(c) $f(x) = x\left(\dfrac{a^x-1}{a^x+1}\right)$

$\Rightarrow f(-x) = -x\left(\dfrac{a^{-x}-1}{a^{-x}+1}\right) = x\left(\dfrac{a^x-1}{a^x+1}\right)$

$\Rightarrow$ even function.

(d) $f(x) = \sin\left[\log\left(x+\sqrt{x^2+1}\right)\right]$

$\Rightarrow f(-x) = \sin\left[\log\left(-x+\sqrt{x^2+1}\right)\right]$

$= \sin\left[\log\left(\dfrac{-1}{-x-\sqrt{x^2-1}}\right)\right] = -\sin\left[\log\left(x+\sqrt{x^2+1}\right)\right]$

$= -f(x)$

$\Rightarrow$ odd function.

4. (d) (a) $f(x) = \text{sgn } x + x^{2000}$

$\Rightarrow f(-x) = \text{sgn}(-x) - (-x)^{2000} = -\text{sgn } x + x^{2000}$

$\Rightarrow$ Neither even nor odd.

(b) $f(x) = |x| - \tan x \quad \Rightarrow f(-x) = |x| + \tan x\, f(x), -f(x)$

$\Rightarrow$ Neither even nor odd.

(c) $f(x) = x^3 \cot x \quad \Rightarrow f(-x) = x^3 \cot x = f(x)$

$\Rightarrow$ even function

(d) $f(x) = \text{cosec } x^{55}$

$\Rightarrow f(-x) = \text{cosec } (-x)^{55} = -\text{cosec } x^{55}$

$\Rightarrow$ odd function.

5. (b) $f(x) = \sec\left[\log\left(x+\sqrt{1+x^2}\right)\right]$

$\Rightarrow f(-x) = \sec\left[\log\left(-x+\sqrt{1+x^2}\right)\right]$

$= \sec\left[\log\left(\dfrac{\qquad}{-x-\sqrt{\quad}+x}\right)\right]$

$= \sec\left[\log\left(x+\sqrt{1+x^2}\right)\right] = f(x)$

$\Rightarrow$ even function.

6. (b) $f(x) = \sin\left(\tan\left(\log\left(x+\sqrt{x^2+1}\right)\right)\right)$

$\Rightarrow f(-x) = \sin\left(\tan\left(\log\left(-x+\sqrt{x^2+1}\right)\right)\right)$

$\Rightarrow f(-x) = \sin\left(\tan\left(\log\left(x+\sqrt{x^2+1}\right)^{-1}\right)\right) = -\sin$

$\left(\tan\left(\log\left(x+\sqrt{x^2+1}\right)\right)\right) = -f(x)\; f(x)$ is an odd function

7. (a) $f(x)=\begin{cases}0\,;\text{for } x=0\\ x^2\sin\left(\dfrac{\pi}{x}\right);\text{for}-1<x<1(x\neq 0)\\ x|x|;\text{for } x>1 \text{ or } x<-1\end{cases}$

For $x<-1; f(x)=x|x|=-x^2, f(-x)=(-x)|-x|=(-x)(-x)=x^2$

For $-1<x<1; f(x)=x^2\sin\left(\dfrac{\pi}{x}\right), f(-x)=x^2\sin\left(\dfrac{-\pi}{x}\right)=-x^2\sin\dfrac{\pi}{x}$

For $x>1; f(x)=x|x|=x^2, f(-x)=(-x)|-x|=(-x)(x)=-x^2$

Clearly, $f(-x)=-f(x)\ \forall\ x\in\mathbb{R}$.

$\Rightarrow$ odd function.

8. (b) $f(x)=2x^6+3x^4+4x^2+7, f'(x)=12x^5+12x^3+8x$

$\Rightarrow f'(-x)=12(-x)^5+12(-x)^3+8(-x)$

$\Rightarrow -(12x^5+12x^3+8x)=-f'(x)$

$\Rightarrow f'(x)$ is an odd function.

9. (b), (c) $f(x)=\begin{cases}x\,;\text{if } x\in\mathbb{Q}\\ 1-x\,;\text{if } x\notin\mathbb{Q}\end{cases}$

$\Rightarrow f(f(x))=\begin{cases}f(x)\text{if } f(x)\in\mathbb{Q}\\ 1-f(x)\text{if } f(x)\notin\mathbb{Q}\end{cases}=\begin{cases}x;\text{if } x\in\mathbb{Q}\\ 1-(1-x)\,;\text{if } x\notin\mathbb{Q}\end{cases}$

$\Rightarrow f(f(x))=x\ \forall\ x\in\mathbb{R}$

$\Rightarrow f(f(x))$ is an odd function and is an identity function and clearly a linear polynomial.

10. (c) $f(x)=\begin{cases}0\,;\text{if } x \text{ is rational}\\ x;\text{if } x \text{ is irrational}\end{cases}$ and $f(x)=\begin{cases}0\,;\text{ if } x \text{ is irrational}\\ x\,;\text{if } x \text{ is rational}\end{cases}$

$\Rightarrow (f-g)(x)=f(x)-f(x)=\begin{cases}0-x\text{ if } x\in\mathbb{Q}\\ x-0\text{ if } x\notin\mathbb{Q}\end{cases}=\begin{cases}-x\text{ if } x\in\mathbb{Q}\\ x\text{ if } x\notin\mathbb{Q}\end{cases}$

$\because$ If $x\in\mathbb{Q}$, then $-x\in\mathbb{Q}$

$\Rightarrow f(-x)=-(-x)=x=f(x)$ and if $x\notin\mathbb{Q}$, then $-x\notin\mathbb{Q}$

$\Rightarrow f(-x)=-x=-f(x)$

$\Rightarrow (f-g)(x)$ is neither even nor odd.

11. (a), (c) (a) Let $f(x)=\dfrac{f(-x)+f(x)}{2}=\dfrac{-f(x)+f(x)}{2}=0$ as $f(x)$ is an function

$\Rightarrow f(x)$ is an even function

(b) $f(x)=\dfrac{f(x)-f(-x)}{2}=\dfrac{f(x)+f(x)}{2}$

$\Rightarrow f(x)=f(x)$ $\quad\Rightarrow$ an odd function.

(c) $h(x)=[|f(x)|+1]$

$\Rightarrow h(-x)=[|f(-x)|+1]=[|-f(x)|+1]=[|f(x)|+1]=h(x)$

$\Rightarrow$ an even function

12. (a) $f(x)=a^{\sin x^3\,\text{sgn}\,x^9}(\tan^3 x)$; $a<1$

$\Rightarrow f(-x)=a^{(-\sin x^3)(-\text{sgn}\,x^9)}.\tan^3 x$

$\Rightarrow f(-x)=-a^{(\sin x^3)(\text{sgn}\,x^9)}.\tan^3 x=-f(x)$

$\Rightarrow f(x)$ is an odd function.

13. (b) $f(x)=(a-x^n)^{1/n}; n\in\mathbb{N}$,

$f(f(x))=(a-(f(x))^n)^{1/n}; n\in\mathbb{N}$

$=(a-(a-x^n))^{1/n}; n\in\mathbb{N}$

$=x\ \forall\ x\in\mathbb{R}, n\in\mathbb{N}$, which is an odd function.

14. (b) $f(-x)=f(x)$ $\quad(\because f(x)$ is even)

$\Rightarrow -f'(-x)=f'(x)$

$\Rightarrow f'(x)$ is an odd function.

$\Rightarrow f'(e)+f'(-e)=f'(e)=-f'(e)=0$.

15. (b) $f(x)$ is not identically zero and $f(x+y)=f(x)+f(y)$ (given)

Replacing y by 0, we get $f(x)=f(x)+f(0)$

$\Rightarrow f(0)=0$

Again, replacing y by $-x$, we get $f(x-x)=f(x)+f(-x)$

$\Rightarrow 0=f(x)+f(-x)$

$\Rightarrow f(-x)=-f(x)$ $\qquad\Rightarrow f(x)$ and odd function.

$\therefore f(-x)=a^{f(-x)}+a^{-f(-x)}=a^{-f(x)}+a^{f(x)}=f(x); a>1$

$\Rightarrow f(x)$ is an even function.

16. (c) $f(f(x))=|\sin x|; f(f(x))=\left(\sin\sqrt{x}\right)^2$

Clearly, $f(x)=\sqrt{x}, f(x)=\sin^2 x$

Domain of $f(x)$ is $[0,\infty)$, which is not symmetric about origin.

$\Rightarrow f(x)$ is neither even nor odd and $f(-x)=f(x)=\sin^2 x$

$\Rightarrow f(x)$ is even.

17. (c) $f(x)=x^3-x^2+\sin^{-1}\left(\dfrac{2-|x|}{3}\right)+\log(|x|+1), 0\le x\le 2$

$f(-x)=-x^3-x^2+\sin^{-1}\left(\dfrac{2-|x|}{3}\right)+\log(|x|+1); 0\le -x\le 2$

$\Rightarrow f(-x)=-x^3-x^2+\sin^{-1}\left(\dfrac{2-|x|}{3}\right)+\log(|x|+1); -2\le x\le 0\backslash$

For odd extension $f(-x)=-f(x)$, i.e., $f(x)=-f(-x)$

$\therefore f(x)=\begin{cases}x^3+x^2-\sin^{-1}\left(\dfrac{2-|x|}{3}\right)+\log(|x|+1); -2\le x\le 0\\ x^3-x^2+\sin^{-1}\left(\dfrac{2-|x|}{3}\right)+\log(|x|+1); 0\le x\le 2\end{cases}$

18. (a) $f(x)=\sin^2 x+\sin^2\left(x+\dfrac{\pi}{3}\right)+\cos x.\cos\left(x+\dfrac{\pi}{3}\right)$

$=\dfrac{1-\cos 2x}{2}+\dfrac{1-\cos\left(2x+\dfrac{2\pi}{3}\right)}{2}+\dfrac{1}{2}\left[\cos\left(2x+\dfrac{\pi}{3}\right)+\cos\dfrac{\pi}{3}\right]$

$=\dfrac{5}{4}-\dfrac{1}{2}\cos 2x-\dfrac{1}{2}\cos\left(2x+\dfrac{2\pi}{3}\right)+\dfrac{1}{2}\cos\left(2x+\dfrac{\pi}{3}\right)$

$=\dfrac{5}{4}-\dfrac{1}{2}\cos 2x+\dfrac{1}{4}\cos 2x+(\sin 2x)\dfrac{\sqrt{3}}{4}$

$+\dfrac{1}{4}\cos 2x-\dfrac{\sqrt{3}}{4}\sin 2x=\dfrac{5}{4}$

$\Rightarrow f(x)=\dfrac{5}{4}\ \forall\ x\in\mathbb{R}$ $\quad\Rightarrow$ even function

TEXTUAL EXERCISE–16: (SUBJECTIVE)

1. (i) $f(x)=2+3\cos(x-2)$

Fundamental period $=2\pi$ as it is same for $f(x)$ and $(x\pm k)$ and $\alpha\pm f(x\pm k)$; $\alpha, k\in\mathbb{R}$.

(ii) $f(x) = \cos\frac{3}{5}x - \sin\frac{2}{7}x$

Fundamental period of $\cos\frac{3}{5}x = \frac{2\pi}{\frac{3}{5}} = \frac{10\pi}{3}$

Fundamental period of $\sin\frac{2}{7}x = \frac{2\pi}{\frac{2}{7}} = 7\pi$

$\therefore$ Period $\left(\cos\frac{3}{5}x - \sin\frac{2}{7}x\right) = \text{L.C.M}\left(\frac{10\pi}{3}, 7\pi\right) = \text{L.C.M}$ $\left(\frac{10}{3}, 7\right)\pi = \frac{70}{1}\pi$

= 70 π which is also fundamental period.

(iii) $f(x) = \sin\frac{\pi x}{4} + \sin\frac{\pi x}{3}$

Fundamental period of $\sin\frac{\pi x}{4} = \frac{2\pi}{\frac{\pi}{4}} = 8$

Fundamental period of $\sin\left(\frac{\pi x}{3}\right) = \frac{2\pi}{\frac{\pi}{3}} = 6$

Fundamental period of $\sin\left(\frac{\pi x}{4}\right) + \sin\left(\frac{\pi x}{3}\right)$ = L.C.M (8, 6) = 24

(iv) $f(x) = \frac{1}{1 - \cos x}$

$\Rightarrow f(x) = \frac{1}{2\sin^2\frac{x}{2}} = \frac{1}{2}\text{cosec}^2 x\frac{x}{2} = \frac{1}{2}\left(1 + \cot^2\frac{x}{2}\right)$

Which has its fundamental period $= \frac{\pi}{\frac{1}{2}} = 2\pi$

(v) $f(x) = \sin(2x + \cos x)$

$\because f(2\pi + x) = \sin[2(2\pi + x)) + \cos(2\pi + x)]$

$= \sin(4\pi + 2x + \cos x) = \sin(2x + \cos x)$

$\Rightarrow f(x)$ has fundamental period 2π.

2. (i) $f(x) = \sin 3x + \cos x + |\tan x|$

Fundamental period $= \text{L.C.M}\left(\frac{2\pi}{3}, \pi, \pi\right) = 2\pi$

(ii) $f(x) = [\sin 3x] + |\cos 6x|$

Fundamental period of $[\sin 3x] = \frac{2\pi}{3}$ and fundamental period of $|\cos 6x| = \pi/6$

Fundamental period of $[\sin 3x] + |\cos 6x|$

$= \text{L.C.M}\left(\frac{2\pi}{3}, \pi\right) = 2\pi$

(iii) $f(x) = \frac{\sin 12x}{1 + \cos^2 6x} = \frac{\sin 12x}{1 + \frac{1}{2}(1 + \cos 12x)}$

$\Rightarrow f(x) = \frac{2\sin 12x}{3 + \cos 12x}$ having fundamental period $\frac{2\pi}{12} = \frac{\pi}{6}$

(iv) $f(x) = \sec^3 x + \text{cosec}^3 x$ which has fundamental period 2π.

3. (i) $f(x) = \frac{\sin x + \sin 3x}{\cos x + \cos 3x} = \frac{2\sin 2x \cos x}{2\cos 2x \cos x} = \tan 2x$ having fundamental period $\frac{\pi}{2}$.

(ii) $f(x) = 1 - \frac{\sin^2 x}{1 + \cot x} - \frac{\cos^2 x}{1 + \tan x}$

$= 1 - \frac{\sin^3 x}{\sin x + \cos x} - \frac{\cos^3 x}{\cos x + \sin x}$

$= 1 - \frac{(\sin x + \cos x)(1 + \sin x \cos x)}{(\sin x + \cos x)}$

$= 1 - 1 - \sin x \cos x = -\frac{1}{2}\sin 2x$ having fundamental period $= \frac{2\pi}{2} = \pi$

(iii) $f(x) = \tan\frac{\pi}{2}[x]$ $\quad\because f(x + 2) = \tan\frac{\pi}{2}[x + 2]$

$= \tan\frac{\pi}{2}(2 + [x]) = \tan\left(\pi + \frac{\pi}{2}[x]\right) = \tan\frac{\pi}{2}[x] = f(x)$

$\Rightarrow f(x)$ is periodic with period 2.

(iv) $f(x) = \ln(2 + \cos 3x) = \ln\left(1 + 2\cos^2\frac{3}{2}x\right)$ which is periodic with period $\frac{2\pi}{3}$.

(v) $f(x) = e^{\ln \sin x} + \tan^3 x - \text{cosec}(3x - 5)$

$= \sin x + \tan^3 x - \text{cosec}(3x - 5)$

$\Rightarrow$ Period of $f(x) = \text{L.C.M}\left(2\pi, \pi, \frac{2\pi}{3}\right) = 2\pi$

(vi) $f(x) = \sin x + \tan\frac{x}{2} + \sin\frac{x}{2^2} + \frac{x}{2^3} + \ldots\ldots$

$+ \sin\frac{x}{2^{n-1}} + \tan\frac{x}{2^n}$

Period of $f(x) = \text{L.C.M.}\{2\pi, 2\pi, 8\pi, 8\pi, \ldots\ldots, 2^n\pi, 2^n\pi$

$= \text{L.C.M.}\{(2, 2^3, \ldots. 2^n)\}.\pi = 2^n\pi$

4. (i) $f(x) = \cos\frac{4x}{5} + \sin\frac{4x}{3} + \tan\frac{8x}{3}$

$\Rightarrow$ Period $= \text{L.C.M}\left(\frac{2\pi}{\frac{4}{5}}, \frac{2\pi}{\frac{4}{3}}, \frac{\pi}{\frac{8}{3}}\right)$

$\Rightarrow \text{L.C.M.}\left(\frac{5\pi}{2}, \frac{3\pi}{2}, \frac{3\pi}{8}\right)$

$\Rightarrow \text{L.C.M.}\left(\frac{5}{2}, \frac{3}{2}, \frac{3}{8}\right)\pi = \frac{15}{2}\pi$

(ii) $f(x) = \frac{(1 + \sin x)(1 + \sec x)}{(1 + \cos x)(1 + \text{cosec} x)} = \frac{\sin x}{\cos x}$ for $\sin x \neq -1, 0$ and $\cos x \neq -1, 0$

$= \tan x,\ x \neq \frac{n\pi}{2}, n \in \mathbb{Z}$

$\Rightarrow$ Period of $f(x)$ = L.C.M. $\left(\frac{\pi}{2}, \pi\right) = \pi$. Hence, $\pi/2$ is the period of discontinuity.

(iii) $f(x) = \sin\left(2\pi x + \frac{\pi}{3}\right) + 2\sin\left(3\pi x + \frac{\pi}{4}\right) + 3\sin(5\pi x)$

Period of $f(x)$ = L.C.M $\left(\frac{2\pi}{2\pi}, \frac{2\pi}{3\pi}, \frac{2\pi}{5\pi}\right)$

$= \text{L.C.M}\left(1, \frac{2}{3}, \frac{2}{5}\right)$

$= \frac{\text{L.C.M.}(1,2,2)}{\text{L.C.F.}(1,3,5)} = \frac{2}{1} = 2$

5. (i) $f(x) = \left|\cos^5\left(\frac{2x}{3}\right)\right|$ $\quad\because$ Period of $|\cos^5 x| = \pi$

$\Rightarrow$ Period of $\left|\cos^5\left(\frac{2x}{3}\right)\right| = \frac{\pi}{\frac{2}{3}} = \frac{3\pi}{2}$

(ii) $f(x) = \sin(\pi x) + [x] = 2 - x$
$= \sin(\pi x) + x - \{x\} + 2 - x$
$= \sin(\pi x) + 2 - \{x\}$

$\Rightarrow$ Period of $f(x)$ = L.C.M. $\left(\frac{2\pi}{\pi}, 1\right)$ = L.C.M $(2, 1) = 2$

(iii) $f(x) = x - [x - b] = x - (x - b - \{x - b\}) = b + \{x - b\}$
$\Rightarrow$ Period of $f(x) = 1$

6. $f(x) = \begin{cases} 1 \text{ if } x \text{ is rational} \\ 0 \text{ if } x \text{ is irrational} \end{cases}$

Let if possible $T > 0$ be the fundamental period $f(x)$
$\Rightarrow f(x + T) = f(x)\ \forall\ x \in \mathbb{R}$
If $x \in \mathbb{Q}$ and $T \in \mathbb{Q}$, then $f(x + T) = f(x) = 1$
Also $T/2 \in \mathbb{Q}$
$\Rightarrow f(x + T/2) = f(x) = 1$
Similarly $f(x + T/2^n) = f(x) = 1\ \forall\ x \in \mathbb{N}$
$\Rightarrow$ There is no fundamental period of $f(x)$. Hence, $f(x)$ is a periodic function period.

7. (i) $f(x) = \frac{1}{2}\left\{\frac{|\sin x|}{\cos x} + \frac{|\cos x|}{\sin x}\right\}$

$= \frac{1}{2}\left\{\frac{\sin x|\sin x| + \cos x|\cos x|}{\sin x \cos x}\right\}$

$$= \frac{1}{2}\begin{cases} \sec x.\operatorname{cosec} x; x \in \left[0, \frac{\pi}{2}\right) \\ \frac{\sin^2 x - \cos^2 x}{\sin x.\cos x}; x \in \left(\frac{\pi}{2}, \pi\right) \\ -\sec x.\operatorname{cosec} x; x \in \left(\pi, \frac{3\pi}{2}\right) \\ \frac{\cos^2 x - \sin^2 x}{\sin x.\cos x}; x \in \left(\frac{3\pi}{2}, 2\pi\right) \end{cases}$$

$$= \begin{cases} \operatorname{cosec} 2x; x \in \left(0, \frac{\pi}{2}\right) \\ -\cot 2x; x \in \left(\frac{\pi}{2}, \pi\right) \\ -\operatorname{cosec} 2x; x \in \left(\pi, \frac{3\pi}{2}\right) \\ \cot 2x; x \in \left(\frac{3\pi}{2}, 2\pi\right) \end{cases}$$

$\Rightarrow$ Period of $f(x)$ = L.C.M. $\left\{\pi, \frac{\pi}{2}, 2\pi\right\} = 2\pi$

(ii) $f(x) = \sin\frac{\pi x}{n!} - \cos\frac{\pi x}{(n+1)!}$

Period of $f(x)$ = L. C. M $\left\{\frac{2\pi}{\frac{\pi}{n!}}, \frac{2\pi}{\frac{\pi}{(n+1)!}}\right\}$

= L.C.M $\{2n!, 2(n + 1)!\} = 2((n + 1)!)$

8. (a) $f(x + \lambda) = -f(x)$
$\Rightarrow f(x) = -f(x + \lambda) = -[-f(x + 2\lambda)]$
$\Rightarrow f(x) = f(x + 2\lambda)$
$\Rightarrow f(x)$ is periodic with period 2λ.

(b) $f(x + \lambda) = \pm\frac{1}{f(x)}$

$\Rightarrow f(x) = \pm\frac{1}{f(x+\lambda)} = \frac{\pm 1}{\left[\pm\frac{1}{f(x+2\lambda)}\right]}$

$\Rightarrow f(x) = f(x + 2\lambda)$
$\Rightarrow f(x)$ is periodic with period 2λ.

9. Given, $f(x + a) = \frac{1 + f(x)}{1 - f(x)}\ \forall x \in \mathbb{R}$

$\Rightarrow \frac{f(x+a)+1}{f(x+a)-1} = \frac{2}{2f(x)}$

$\Rightarrow f(x) = \frac{f(x+a)-1}{f(x+a)+1}$

$\Rightarrow f(x) = \frac{\frac{f(x+2a)-1}{f(x+2a)+1} - 1}{\frac{f(x+2a)-1}{f(x+2a)+1} + 1} = \frac{-2}{2f(x+2a)} = \frac{-1}{f(x+2a)}$

$\Rightarrow f(x) = \frac{-1}{\left(\frac{-1}{f(x+4a)}\right)} = f(x + 4a)$

$\Rightarrow f(x)$ is periodic with period '$4a$'.

10. $f(x) = \sin x + \cos\left(\sqrt{4 - a^2}\right)x$, Period of $\sin x = 2\pi$

Period of $\cos\left(\sqrt{4 - a^2}\right)x = \frac{2\pi}{\sqrt{4 - a^2}}$

$\Rightarrow$ Period of $f(x)$ = L.C.M. $\left(2\pi, \frac{2\pi}{\sqrt{4-a^2}}\right) = 2\pi$

$\Rightarrow$ L.C.M $\left(1, \frac{1}{\sqrt{4-a^2}}\right)$, which exists if $\sqrt{4-a^2}$ is equal

$\Rightarrow$ $4 - a^2$ is a perfect square

$\Rightarrow$ $4 - a^2 = k^2;\ k \in \mathbb{Q}$

$\Rightarrow$ $a = \pm\sqrt{4-k^2}$ for $a \in \mathbb{Z}$, $4 - k^2 \geq 0$ and must be a perfect square.

$\Rightarrow$ $k^2 = 0$ or 4 $\Rightarrow$ $k = 0, \pm 2$

$\Rightarrow$ $a = 0, \pm 2$ $\Rightarrow$ $a \in \{-2, 0, 2\}$

TEXTUAL EXERCISE–16: (OBJECTIVE)

1. (d) $f(x) = \sin(2\pi x) + \left(\frac{\pi x}{3}\right) + \sin\left(\frac{\pi x}{5}\right)$

$\Rightarrow$ Period of $f(x)$ = L.C.M. $\left\{1, \frac{2\pi}{\frac{\pi}{3}}, \frac{2\pi}{\frac{\pi}{5}}\right\}$

= L.C.M $\{1, 6, 10\} = 30$

2. **(a), (b), (c)** $f(x) = \text{sgn } x.\sin x$

$$= \begin{cases} -\sin x & \text{for } x < 0 \\ 0 & \text{for } x = 0 \\ \sin x & \text{for } x > 0 \end{cases}$$

$\Rightarrow$ $f(x + 2\pi) = -f(x)$ for $x \in (-\infty, -2\pi]$ and for $x \in [0, \infty)$ and $f(x + 2\pi) = -f(x)$ for $x \in (-2\pi, 0)$

$\Rightarrow$ $f(x)$ is non-periodic but clearly $f(x)$ is a continuous function.

Also $f'(x) = \begin{cases} -\cos x & \text{for } x < 0 \\ \cos x & \text{for } x > 0 \end{cases}$

$\Rightarrow$ $f'(0^-) = -1, f'(0^+) = 1$

$\Rightarrow$ $f(x)$ is non-differentiable at $x = 0$.

Also $f(-x) = -\sin(-x)$ for $x > 0$

$= \sin x = f(x)$

And $f(-x) = \sin(-x)$ for $x < 0$

$= -\sin x = f(x)$

And $f(-0) = f(0) = 0$

$\Rightarrow$ $f(x)$ is an even function.

3. **(a), (c), (d)**

(a) Period of $f(x) = |\sin x|$ is π

(b) $f(x) = [x + \pi]$; which being an increasing function is non-periodic

(c) $f(x) = \cos(\sin x)$

$\Rightarrow$ $f(x + \pi) = \cos(\sin(x + \pi)) = \cos(-\sin x) = \cos(\sin x)$

$\Rightarrow$ $f(x)$ is periodic with period π.

(d) $f(x) = \cos^2 x$ is periodic with period π.

4. (b) $f(x) = (nx + n) - [nx + n]$

$= nx + n - [nx] - n$

$= nx - [nx] = \{nx\}$

which is periodic with period $\frac{1}{n}$

5. (c) $f(x) = \sin(x + 3 - [x + 3]) = \sin(x + 3 - [x] - 3) = \sin(\{x\})$

$\Rightarrow$ $f(x + 1) = \sin(\{x + 1\}) = \sin(\{x\}) = f(x)$

$\Rightarrow$ $f(x)$ is periodic with period 1

6. (c) $f(x) = |\sin^3 2x| + |\cos^3 2x| = |\sin 2x|^3 + |\cos 2x|^3$

Fundamental period of $|\sin x|^3 + |\cos x|^3$ is $\frac{\pi}{2}$

Fundamental period of $|\sin 2x|^3 + |\cos 2x|^3$ is $\frac{\pi}{4}$

Verification:- f

$$f\left(x + \frac{\pi}{4}\right) = \left|\sin 2\left(x + \frac{\pi}{4}\right)\right|^3 + \left|\cos 2\left(x + \frac{\pi}{4}\right)\right|^3$$

$$= \left|\sin\left(2x + \frac{\pi}{2}\right)\right|^3 + \left|\cos\left(2x + \frac{\pi}{2}\right)\right|^3$$

$$= |\cos 2x|^3 + |\sin 2x|^3 = f(x)$$

7. (c) $f(x) = \frac{|\sin x| + |\cos x|}{|\sin x - \cos x|}$

Clearly, $f\left(x + \frac{\pi}{2}\right) = \frac{|\cos x| + |\sin x|}{\cos x + \sin x|} \neq f(x)$ and $f(x + \pi)$

$$= \frac{|-\sin x| + |-\cos x|}{|-\sin x + \cos x|} = \frac{|\sin x| + |\cos x|}{|\sin x - \cos x|} = f(x)$$

$\Rightarrow$ $f(x)$ is periodic with period π

8. (b) Functions given in options (a), (c) and (d) being the sum of periodic functions are periodic . Also $\cos\sqrt{x}$ being non-periodic function, $f(x) = \cos\sqrt{x} + \cos^2 x$ is non-periodic.

9. (a), (d) (a) $f(x) = x - [x] = \{x\}$ which is periodic with period 1.

(b) $f(x) = \begin{cases} \sin\frac{1}{x}; x \neq 0 \\ 0;\ x = 0 \end{cases}$

Graph of $f(x)$ is shown below.

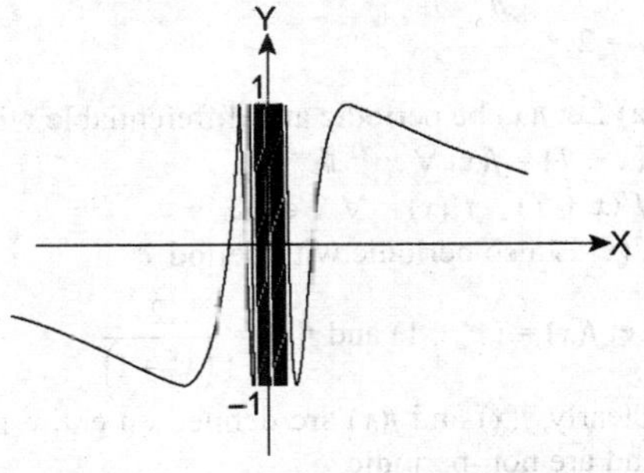

Clearly $f(x)$ is non-periodic as $x \to 0$, $\frac{1}{x} \to \infty$ and $\sin\frac{1}{x}$ oscillates in between –1 and 1 with increasing frequency.

(c) $h(x) = x \cos x$ is non-periodic.

(d) $w(x) = \sin^{-1}(\sin x)$ is periodic with period 2π.

10. **(c)** If $f(x) = e^{\sin(x-[x]\cos\pi x}$

$\Rightarrow f(x) = e^{\sin\{x\}.\cos\pi x}$

$\sin\{x\}$ has period 1 and $\cos\pi x$ has period 2

$\Rightarrow$ Period of $f(x)$ = L.C.M.(1, 2) = 2

Also $f(x+2) = e^{\sin\{x+2\}.\cos\pi(x+2)} = e^{\sin\{x\}.\cos\pi x} = f(x)$

11. **(a)** $f(x) = 2\tan 3x + 5\sqrt{1-\cos 6x}$

$\Rightarrow f(x) = 2\tan 3x + 5\sqrt{2\sin^2 3x}$

$\Rightarrow f(x) = 2\tan 3x + 5\sqrt{2}|\sin 3x|$

$\Rightarrow$ Period of $f(x)$ = L.C.M $\left(\frac{\pi}{3},\frac{\pi}{3}\right) = \frac{\pi}{3}$

(a) $f(x) = (\sec^2 3x + \operatorname{cosec}^2 3x)\tan^2 3x$

$= \left(\frac{1}{\cos^2 3x\sin^2 3x}\right).\tan^2 3x$

$= \frac{1}{\cos^4 3x} = \sec^4 3x$ having period $\frac{\pi}{3}$

(b) $h(x) = 2\sin 3x + 3\cos 3x$

$\Rightarrow$ Period of $h(x) = \frac{2\pi}{3}$

(c) $k(x) = 2\sqrt{1-\cos^2 3x} + \operatorname{cosec} 3x$

$= 2\sqrt{\sin^2 3x} + \operatorname{cosec} 3x$

$= 2|\sin 3x| + \operatorname{cosec} 3x$

$\Rightarrow$ Period of $k(x)$ = L.C.M $\left(\frac{\pi}{3},\frac{2\pi}{3}\right) = \frac{2\pi}{3}$

(d) $p(x) = 3\operatorname{cosec} 3x + 2\tan 3x$

$\Rightarrow$ Period of $p(x)$ = L.C.M. $\left(\frac{2\pi}{3},\frac{\pi}{3}\right) = \frac{2\pi}{3}$

12. **(c)** $n \in \mathbb{N}, f(x) = \dfrac{\cos nx}{\sin\left(\frac{x}{n}\right)}$

$\Rightarrow$ Period of $f(x)$ = L.C.M. $\left(\frac{2\pi}{n}, 2n\pi\right) = 2\pi$

L.C.M. $\left(\frac{1}{n}, n\right) = 2n\pi = 4\pi$ (given)

$\Rightarrow n = 2$

13. **(b)** **(a)** Let $f(x)$ be periodic and differentiable with period T.

$\Rightarrow f(x+T) = f(x)\ \forall x \in \mathbb{R}$

$\Rightarrow f'(x+T) = f'(x) = \forall x \in \mathbb{R}$

$\Rightarrow f'(x)$ is also periodic with period T

(b) Let $f(x) = (x^2+1)$ and $f(x) = \dfrac{2}{(x^2+1)}$

Clearly, $f(x)$ and $f(x)$ are defined on entire number line and are non-periodic.

However, $f(x).f(x) = 2$, which is periodic function.

(c) Let $f(x)$ is an even differential function, then $f(-x) = f(x)$

$\Rightarrow -f'(-x) = f'(x)$

$\Rightarrow f'(-x) = -f'(x)$

$\Rightarrow f'(x)$ is an odd function.

Similarly derivative of an odd differentiable function is even.

(d) $f(x) = \underbrace{\frac{f(x)+f(-x)}{2}}_{\text{even function}} + \underbrace{\frac{f(x)-f(-x)}{2}}_{\text{odd function}}$

14. **(a)** $f(-x) = -f(x)\ \forall x \in \mathbb{R}$ and $f(x+2) = f(x)\ \forall x \in \mathbb{R}$

$f(4) = -f(-4)$ ....(1)

But $f(-4) = f(-4+2) = f(-2+2) = f(0+2)$

$= f(2+2) = f(4)$ ....(2)

From (1) and (2), we get $f(4) = 0$

15. **(c)** $f(x) = \dfrac{\sin 8x\cos x - \sin 6x\cos 3x}{\cos 2x\cos x - \sin 3x\sin 4x}$

$= \dfrac{(\sin 9x + \sin 7x) - (\sin 9x + \sin 3x)}{(\cos 3x + \cos x) - (\cos x - \cos 7x)}$

$= \dfrac{\sin 7x - \sin 3x}{\cos 3x + \cos 7x}$

$= \dfrac{2\cos 5x\sin 2x}{2\cos 5x\cos 2x} = \tan 2x$

which is periodic with period $\frac{\pi}{2}$

16. **(b)** $f\left(x+\frac{1}{2}\right) = f(x); f(2) = 5; f\left(\frac{9}{4}\right) = 2, f(-3) - f\left(\frac{1}{4}\right) = ?$

$\because f(x)$ is periodic with period $\frac{1}{2}$

$\Rightarrow f(x) = f\left(x+\frac{n}{2}\right)\forall x \in \mathbb{N}$

$\Rightarrow f(-3) = f\left(-3+\frac{10}{2}\right) = f(2) = 5$ and

$f\left(\frac{1}{4}\right) = f\left(\frac{1}{4}+4\left(\frac{1}{2}\right)\right) = f\left(\frac{9}{4}\right) = 2$

$\therefore f(-3) - f\left(\frac{1}{4}\right) = 5 - 2 = 3$

SECTION–III (SINGLE ANSWER CORRECT)

1. **(b)** If $2f(x^2) + 3f\left(\frac{1}{x^2}\right) = x^2 - 1\quad \forall x \in \mathbb{R} \sim \{0\}$. ....(i)

Replacing x^2 by $\frac{1}{x^2}$,

we get $2f\left(\frac{1}{x^2}\right) + 3f(x^2) = \frac{1}{x^2} - 1$ ....(ii)

Solving (i) and (ii), we get $-5f(x^2) = 2x^2 - \frac{3}{x^2} + 1$

$\Rightarrow f(x^2) = \frac{-2}{5}x^2 + \frac{3}{5x^2} - \frac{1}{5} = \frac{-2x^4+3-x^2}{5x^2}$

$= \dfrac{(1-x^2)(2x^2+3)}{5x^2}$

2. **(a)** $f(x) = \sqrt{\dfrac{2-[x]}{[x]-3}}$; for domain of function, $\dfrac{2-[x]}{[x]-3} \geq 0$

$\Rightarrow (2-[x])([x]-3) \geq 0;\ [x]-3 \neq 0$

$\Rightarrow$ $([x]-2)([x]-3) \le 0;\ [x] \ne 3$

$\Rightarrow$ $[x] \in [2, 3];\ [x] \ne 3$

$\Rightarrow$ $x \in [2, 4);\ [x] \ne 3$

$\Rightarrow$ $x \in [2, 3)$

3. (c) $f(x) = \sin^{-1}[2 - 3x^2]$; for domain $[2 - 3x^2] \in [-1, 1]$

$\Rightarrow$ $2 - 3x^2 \in [-1, 2);\ -2 < 3x^2 - 2 \le 1$

$\Rightarrow$ $3x^2 > 0$ and $x^2 \le 1$

$\Rightarrow$ $x \ne 0$ and $x \in [-1, 1]$

$\therefore$ Domain = $[-1, 0] \cup (0, 1]$

4. (c) $f(x) = \cos^{-1}\sqrt{x^2+3x+1} + \cos^{-1}\sqrt{x^2+3x}$; for domain $0 \le \sqrt{x^2+3x+1} \le 1$ and $0 \le \sqrt{x^2+3x} \le 1$

$\Rightarrow$ $0 \le x^2 + 3x + 1 \le 1$ and $0 \le x^2 + 3x \le 1$

$\Rightarrow$ $x^2 + 3x + 1 \ge 0;\ x^2 + 3x \le 0$ and $x^2 + 3x \ge 0;\ x^2 + 3x - 1 \le 0$

$\Rightarrow$ $x^2 + 3x = 0$ $\Rightarrow$ $x(x + 3) = 0$

$\Rightarrow$ $x = 0$ or $x = -3$

$\therefore$ Domain = $\{0, -3\}$

5. (c) $f(x) = \sin^{-1} x + \sqrt{2x - x^2} - \dfrac{1}{\sqrt{8x - 4x^2 - 3}}$; for domain $x \in [-1, 1]$

$\Rightarrow$ $2x - x^2 \ge 0$ and $-4x^2 + 8x - 3 > 0$, i.e., $x \in [-1, 1]$; $x \in [0, 2]$ and $x \in \left(\dfrac{1}{2}, \dfrac{3}{2}\right)$ $x \in \left(\dfrac{1}{2}, 1\right]$

6. (b) $f(x) = \dfrac{1}{\sqrt{1-\sqrt{1-\sqrt{1-x^2}}}}$; for domain $1 - \sqrt{1-\sqrt{1-x^2}} > 0$

$\Rightarrow$ $\sqrt{1-\sqrt{1-x^2}} \in [0, 1)$ $\Rightarrow$ $0 \le 1 - \sqrt{1-x^2} < 1$

$\Rightarrow$ $0 < \sqrt{1-x^2} \le 1$

$\Rightarrow$ $0 < 1 - x^2 \le 1$ $\Rightarrow$ $0 \le x^2 < 1$

$\Rightarrow$ $x \in (-1, 1)$

7. (c) $f(x) = \sqrt{3 - 2^x - 2^{1-x}} - 2^{1-x} + \sqrt{\sin^{-1} x}$; for domain $3 - 2^x - 2^{1-x} \ge 0$; $\sin^{-1} x \in \left[0, \dfrac{\pi}{2}\right]$

$\Rightarrow$ $3 - 2^x - \dfrac{2}{2^x} \ge 0;\ x \in [0, 1]$

$-(2^x)^2 + 3(2^x) - 2 \ge 0;\ x \in [0, 1]$

$\Rightarrow$ $(2^x)^2 - 3(2^x) + 2 \le 0;\ x \in [0, 1]$

$\Rightarrow$ $(2^x - 1)(2^x - 2) \le 0;\ x \in [0, 1]$

$\Rightarrow$ $1 \le 2^x \le 2$ and $x \in [0, 1]$

$\Rightarrow$ $x \in [0, 1]$

8. (c) $f(x) = \cos^{-1} x + \sqrt{1 - \log_3(2x^2 + 6x - 5)}$; for domain $x \in [-1, 1]$ and $\log_3(2x^2 + 6x - 5) \le 1$

$\Rightarrow$ $x \in [-1, 1]$ and $2x^2 + 6x - 5 \in (0, 3]$

$\Rightarrow$ $x \in [-1, 1]$ and $2x^2 + 6x - 5 > 0$ and $2x^2 + 6x - 8 \le 0$

$\Rightarrow$ $x \in [-1, 1]$ and $x \in \left(-\infty, \dfrac{-6-\sqrt{76}}{4}\right) \cup \left(\dfrac{-6+\sqrt{76}}{4}, \infty\right)$ and $x \in [-4, 1]$

$\Rightarrow$ $x \in \left(\dfrac{-3+\sqrt{19}}{2}, 1\right]$

9. (a) $f(x) = \cos^{-1}\left(\dfrac{3}{4 + 2\sin x}\right)$; for domain $-1 \le \dfrac{3}{4 + 2\sin x} \le 1$

$\Rightarrow$ $-4 - 2\sin x \le 3 \le 4 + 2\sin x$

$\Rightarrow$ $2\sin x \ge -7$ and $2\sin x \ge -1$

$\Rightarrow$ $\sin x \ge \dfrac{-1}{2}$

$\Rightarrow$ $x \in \mathbb{R} - \bigcup_{n\in\mathbb{Z}}\left((2n+1)\pi + \dfrac{\pi}{6}, (2n+2)\pi - \dfrac{\pi}{6}\right)$

10. (c) $f(x) = \dfrac{1}{\sqrt{x^2 - x - 2}} + \dfrac{\sin^{-1}\left(\log_2\left(\dfrac{x^2}{2}\right)\right)}{\sqrt{5|x| - x^2 - 6}}$; for domain $x^2 - x - 2 > 0$; $\log_2\left(\dfrac{x^2}{2}\right) \in [-1, 1]$ and $x^2 - 5|x| + 6 < 0$

$\Rightarrow$ $x \in (-\infty, -1) \cup (2, \infty)$ and $x \in [-2, -1] \cup [1, 2]$ and $2 < |x| < 3$ (i.e., $x \in (-3, -2)$ $(2, 3)$)

$\Rightarrow$ $x \in \phi$

11. (a) $f(x) = e^x + \sin^{-1}\left[\left(\dfrac{x}{2}\right) - 1\right] + \log\sqrt{x - [x]}$; for domain $\left[\dfrac{x}{2} - 1\right] \in [-1, 1]$ and $x - [x] > 0$

$\Rightarrow$ $x \in (0, 6)$ and $\{x\} > 0$

$\Rightarrow$ $x \in (0, 6)$ and $x \notin \mathbb{Z}$

$\Rightarrow$ $x \in (0, 6) - \{1, 2, 3, 4, 5\}$

12. (b) $f(x) = \log\left\{\dfrac{1}{([\cos x] - [\sin x])}\right\}$; for domain $[\cos x] - [\sin x] > 0$

$\cos x$ and $\sin x$ are periodic with period 2π.

$\Rightarrow$ $x = 0, \left[\dfrac{3\pi}{2}, 2\pi\right]$

$\Rightarrow$ $x \in \left[2n\pi - \dfrac{\pi}{2}, 2n\pi\right];\ n \in \mathbb{Z}$

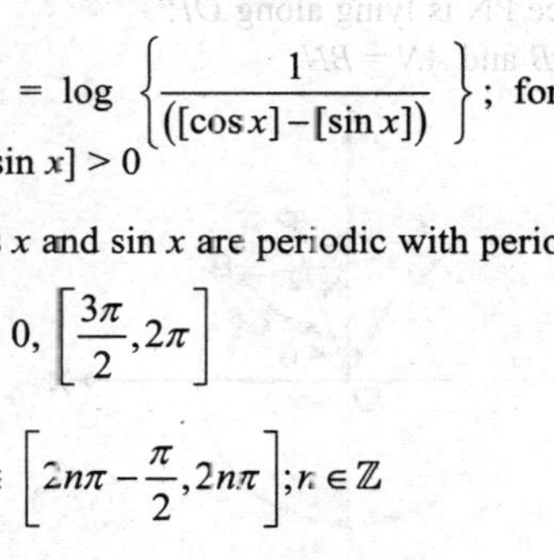

Equivalently, $x \equiv \left[(2n+1)\pi + \dfrac{\pi}{2}, (2n+1)\pi\right]$

13. (b) $\log_{2004}(\log_4(\log_{2002}(\log_{2001} x)))$

$\Rightarrow$ $\log_4(\log_{2002}(\log_{2001} x)) > 0$

$\Rightarrow$ $\log_{2002}(\log_{2001} x) > 1$

$\Rightarrow$ $\log_{2001}(x) > 2002$

$\Rightarrow$ $x > (2001)^{2002}$

14. (b) $f(x)=\sqrt{\sin^{-1}(\log_2 x)}+\sqrt{\cos(\sin x)}+\sin^{-1}\left(\frac{1+x^2}{2x}\right)$; for domain $\sin^{-1}(\log_2 x)\in\left[0,\frac{\pi}{2}\right]$ and $\cos(\sin x)\geq 0$; and $\left(\frac{1+x^2}{2x}\right)\in[-1,1]$

$\Rightarrow \log_2 x\in[0,1]$ and $\frac{1+x^2}{2x}=-1,1$

$\Rightarrow x\in[1,2]$ and $x=\pm 1 \Rightarrow x\in\{1\}$

15. (b) $f(x)=\sin^{-1}\left(\frac{2-|x|}{4}\right)+\cos^{-1}\left(\frac{2-|x|}{4}\right)+\tan^{-1}\left(\frac{2-|x|}{4}\right)$;

for domain $\left(\frac{2-|x|}{4}\right)\in[-1,1]$

$\Rightarrow 2-|x|\in[-4,4]$ $\qquad\Rightarrow -|x|\in[-6,2]$

$\Rightarrow |x|\in[-2,6]$ $\qquad\Rightarrow x\in[-6,6]$

16. (d) $f(x)=\frac{\sqrt{x^2-4}}{\sin^{-1}(2-x)}$

Here $x^2-4\geq 0$ and $(2-x)\in[-1,1]-\{0\}$

$\Rightarrow x\in(-\infty,-2]\cup[2,\infty)$ and $x\in(1,3)$

$\Rightarrow x\in[2,3)-\{x\}$, i.e., $x\in(2,3)$

$\therefore$ Least value of x does not exist.

17. (c) $PN=x \quad\Rightarrow ON=(a-x)$

Since distance PN is lying along *OP*.

$\Rightarrow ON\perp AB$ and $AN=BN$

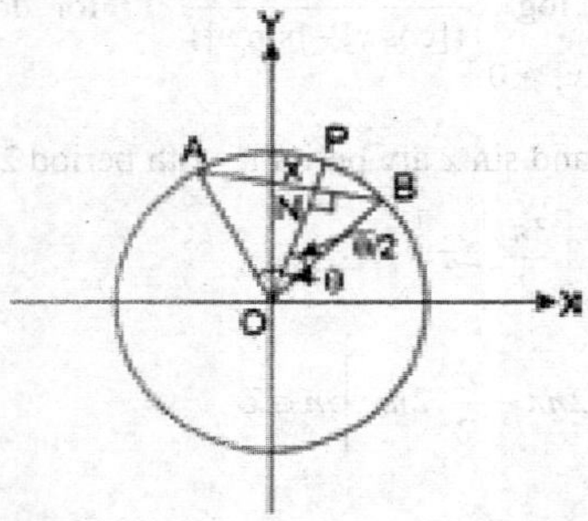

$\Rightarrow$ *ONP* is $\perp$ bisector of chord *AB*

$\Rightarrow$ In ΔOBN, $\angle BON=\frac{\theta}{2}$

$\therefore \quad \cos\frac{\theta}{2}=\frac{ON}{OB}=\frac{|a-x|}{a}$

$\Rightarrow \quad 2\cos\left(\left|a \quad x\right|\right)$; $0<x<2a$

18. (b) $\because$ There exist more than one Δ's of given area

$\Rightarrow f: S\to\mathbb{R}^+$ *is* many–one, and hence, not injective .

Let $k\in\mathbb{R}^+$, then $f(\Delta)=k=\frac{1}{2}(a)\times(b)$

$\Rightarrow b=\frac{2k}{a}$

$\therefore$ If $k\in\mathbb{R}^+$ and $a\in\mathbb{R}^+$, then we can find $b=\frac{2k}{a}$; such that $k=\frac{1}{2}(a)(b)$, e.g., $k=4$, $a=3$, $b=\frac{8}{3}$

$\therefore$ We can form a Δ having base length 3 and altitude $\frac{8}{3}$

$\therefore$ f is subjective.

19. (b) $4^{f(x)}+4^{1-f(x)}=4^x$

$\Rightarrow 4^{f(x)}+\frac{4}{4^{f(x)}}=4^x$

$\Rightarrow (4^{f(x)})^2-(4^x)(4^{f(x)})+4=0$

$\Rightarrow$ Disc. ≥ 0 $\qquad\Rightarrow 16^x\geq 16$

$\Rightarrow x\geq 1$ $\qquad\Rightarrow x\in[1,\infty)$

20. (d) $f(x)=(x^{12}-x^9+x^4-x+1)^{-1/2}$

For $x<0$, $x^{12}-x^9+x^4-x+1>0$,

For $x=0$, $x^{12}-x^9+x^4-x+1=1$,

For $x\in(0,1)$; $x^{12}>0$, $x^4>x^9$, $1>x$,

$\Rightarrow x^{12}-x^9+x^4-x+1>0$

For $x\in(1,\infty)$, $x^{12}>x^9$ and $x^4>x$

$\Rightarrow x^{12}-x^9+x^4-x+1>0$

$\therefore x^{12}-x^9+x^4-x+1>0\ \forall\ x\in\mathbb{R}$

$\Rightarrow (x^{12}-x^9+x^4-x+1)^{-1/2}\in\mathbb{R}\ \forall\ x\in\mathbb{R}$

$\therefore$ Domain $=(-\infty,\infty)$ or $\mathbb{R}$

21. (c) $f(x)=\sin^{-1}$ [sec x], [.] = gint function); for domain [sec x] $\in[-1,1]$

$\Rightarrow \sec x\in[-1,2)$ $\qquad\Rightarrow \sec x=-1$ or $\sec x\in[1,2)$

$\Rightarrow x=(2n+1)\pi$; $n\in\mathbb{Z}$ and $\sec x\in[1,2)$

$\Rightarrow x\in\left(2m\pi-\frac{\pi}{3},2m\pi+\frac{\pi}{3}\right)$; $m\in\mathbb{Z}$

$\therefore$ Domain $=\{(2n+1)\pi;\ n\in\mathbb{Z}\}$

$\cup\left\{\left(2m\pi-\frac{\pi}{3},2m\pi+\frac{\pi}{3}\right);m\in\mathbb{Z}\right\}$

22. (d) $f:\mathbb{R}\to\mathbb{R}$; $f(x)=2x^3-50000x^2+0.1x+\sin x$

$\therefore$ $f(x)=2x^3-50000x^2+0.1x$ being a cubic polynomial has its range $(-\infty,\infty)$.

Also $h(x)=\sin x$ has its range $[-1,1]$. Thus $f(x)$ has its range $(-\infty,\infty)$

23. (d) $f(x)=\log_{\sqrt{2}}\left(2-\log_2\left(16\sin^2 x+1\right)\right)$; for domain $2-\log_2(16\sin^2 x+1)>0$

$\Rightarrow \log_2(16\sin^2 x+1)<2$

$\Rightarrow 16\sin^2 x+1<4$

Also $16\sin^2 x+1\geq 1$ $\therefore$ $1\leq 16\sin^2 x+1<4$

$\Rightarrow \log_2 1\leq\log_2(16\sin^2 x+1)<\log_2 4$

$\Rightarrow 0\leq\log_2(16\sin^2 x+1)<2$

$\Rightarrow -2<-\log_2(16\sin^2 x+1)\leq 2$

$\Rightarrow 0<2-\log_2(16\sin^2 x+1)\leq 2$

$\Rightarrow -\infty<\log_{\sqrt{2}}(2-\log_2(16\sin^2 x+1))\leq 2$

$\Rightarrow$ Range $=(-\infty,2]$

24. (a) $f(x)=\frac{1}{\sqrt{\cos(\sin x)}}$ ($\because \sin x\in[-1,1]$)

$\Rightarrow \cos(\sin x)\in[\cos 1,1]$

$\Rightarrow \sqrt{\cos(\sin x)}\in\left[\sqrt{\cos 1},1\right]$ ($\because f(x)=(x)^{1/2}$ is increasing)

$\Rightarrow \dfrac{1}{\sqrt{\cos(\sin x)}} \in \left[1, \dfrac{1}{\sqrt{\cos 1}}\right]$

$\Rightarrow$ Range $= \left[1, \sqrt{\sec 1}\right]$

25. (a) $f(x) = [9^x - 3^x + 1]\ x\ \forall \in (-\infty, 1)$

Let $3^x = t$

$\therefore\ 9^x - 3^x + 1 = t^2 - t + 1 = \left(t - \dfrac{1}{2}\right)^2 + \dfrac{3}{4}$ for $x\ (-\infty, 1)$,

$3^x \in (0, 3)\ t \in (0, 3)$

$\Rightarrow \left(t - \dfrac{1}{2}\right)^2 + \dfrac{3}{4} \in \left[\dfrac{3}{4}, 7\right)$

$\Rightarrow 9^x - 3^x + 1 \in \left[\dfrac{3}{4}, 7\right)$

$\Rightarrow f(x) = [9^x - 3^x + 1] \in \{0, 1, 2, 3, 4, 5, 6\}$

26. (d) $f(x) = 6^x + 3^x + 6^{-x} + 3^{-x} + 2$

$= \left(6^x + \dfrac{1}{6^x}\right) + \left(3^x + \dfrac{1}{3^x}\right) + 2$

$\because\ 6^x, 3^x > 0\ \forall\ x \in \mathbb{R}$

$\therefore$ By A.M. $\geq$ G.M. $6^x + \dfrac{1}{6^x} \in [2, \infty)$; $3^x + \dfrac{1}{3^x} [2, \infty)$

Also for $x < 0$; both $6^x + \dfrac{1}{6^x}$ and $3^x + \dfrac{1}{3^x}$ are decreasing functions and continuous functions having their range $[2, \infty)$ and both are even functions.

Thus range of $f(x) = [2 + 2 + 2, \infty) = [6, \infty)$

27. (c) $f: \mathbb{R} \to \mathbb{R}; f(x) = 2x^3 - 6x$

$f'(x) = 6x^2 - 6$

$f'(x) > 0$

$\Rightarrow x \in (-\infty, -1) \cup (1, \infty)$ and $f'(x) < 0$

$\Rightarrow x \in (-1, 1)$

$\therefore\ f(x)$ decrease from $[-1, 1]$ and $f(x)$ increase from $[1, 2]$

$\Rightarrow$ Range of $f(x) = [f(1), f(-1)] \cup [f(1), f(2)] = [-4, 4] \cup [-4, 4] = [-4, 4]$

28. (a) If $2 < x^2 < 3 \quad \Rightarrow \{x^2\} = x^2 - 2$ .....(i)

$\because 2 < x^2 < 3$

$\Rightarrow x \in \left(-\sqrt{3}, -\sqrt{2}\right) \cup \left(\sqrt{2}, \sqrt{3}\right)$

$\Rightarrow \dfrac{1}{x} \in \left(\dfrac{-1}{\sqrt{2}}, \dfrac{-1}{\sqrt{3}}\right) \cup \left(\dfrac{1}{\sqrt{3}}, \dfrac{1}{\sqrt{2}}\right)$

$\Rightarrow \left\{\dfrac{1}{x}\right\} = \dfrac{1}{x} - (-1)$ for $x \in \left(-\sqrt{3}, -\sqrt{2}\right)$ and

$\left\{\dfrac{1}{x}\right\} = \dfrac{1}{x} - (0)$ for $x \in \left(\sqrt{2}, \sqrt{3}\right)$

For positive roots, $x \in \left(\sqrt{2}, \sqrt{3}\right)$

Given equation becomes, $x^2 - 2 = \dfrac{1}{x}$

$\Rightarrow x^3 - 2x = 0 \qquad \Rightarrow x(x^2 - 2) = 0$

$\Rightarrow x = 0$ or $x = \sqrt{2}$, but $x \in \left(\sqrt{2}, \sqrt{3}\right)$

$\Rightarrow$ There is no positive root.

29. (b) $f(x) = \dfrac{\sin x}{\sqrt{1 - \cos^2 x}} - \dfrac{\text{ccs}\, x}{\sqrt{1 - \sin^2 x}} + \dfrac{\tan x}{\sqrt{\sec^2 x - 1}} + \dfrac{\cot x}{\sqrt{\text{cosec}^2 x - 1}}$

$\therefore\ \sqrt{1 - \cos^2 x} = \pm \sin x,\ \sqrt{1 - \sin^2 x} = \pm \cos x,$

$\sqrt{\sec^2 x - 1} = \pm \tan x$ and $\sqrt{\text{cosec}^2 x - 1} = \pm \cot x$

In I^st quadrant: $f(x) = 1 + 1 + 1 + 1 = 4$

In IInd quadrant: $f(x) = 1 - 1 - 1 - 1 = -2$

In IIIrd quadrant: $f(x) = -1 - 1 + 1 + 1 = 0$

In IVth quadrant: $f(x) = -1 + 1 - 1 - 1 = -2$

$\therefore$ Minimum value of $f(x) = -2$

30. (b) $x^3 - [x] = 3$

$\Rightarrow x^3 - 3 = [x]$ .....(i)

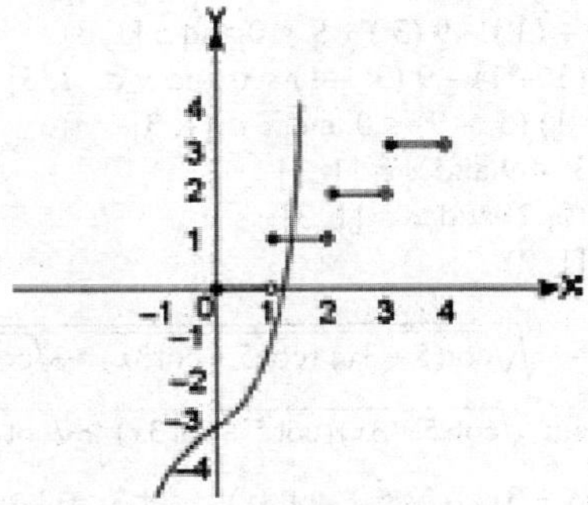

Clearly, $y = [x]$ and $y = x^3 - 3$ intersect each other, where $[x] = 1$

$\Rightarrow x^3 - 3 = 1 \qquad \Rightarrow x^3 = 4$

$\Rightarrow x = (4)^{1/3}$

31. (c) $(x)^2 + (x + 1)^2 = 25$ .....(i)

Let $k < x \leq (k + 1) \quad \Rightarrow (x) = (k + 1); k \in \mathbb{Z}$

$\Rightarrow k + 1 < (x + 1) \leq k + 2$

$\Rightarrow (x + 1) = (k + 2)$

$\therefore$ (i) becomes, $(k + 1)^2 + (k + 2)^2 = 25$

$\Rightarrow 2k^2 + 6k + 5 - 25 = 0 \Rightarrow 2k^2 + 6k - 20 = 0$

$\Rightarrow k^2 + 3k - 10 = 0$

$\Rightarrow (k + 5)(k - 2) = 0 \quad \Rightarrow k = -5$ or $k = 2$

$\Rightarrow x \in (-5, -4] \cup (2, 3]$

32. (a) Let $k < x < (k + 1); k \in \mathbb{Z}$

$\Rightarrow [x] = k; (x) = (k + 1)$

$\therefore\ [x]^2 + (x)^2 > 25 \quad \Rightarrow k^2 + (k + 1)^2 > 25$

$\Rightarrow 2k^2 + 2k - 24 > 0$

$\Rightarrow k^2 + k - 12 > 0 \quad \Rightarrow (k + 4)(k - 3) > 0$

$\Rightarrow k \in (-\infty, -4) \cup (3, \infty)$

$\Rightarrow k \in (-\infty, -3] \cup [4, \infty)$ .....(i)

If $x = k \in \mathbb{Z}$, then $[x] = (x) = k$

$\therefore\ [x]^2 + (x)^2 > 25 \quad \Rightarrow 2k^2 > 25$

$\Rightarrow k \in \left(-\infty, \dfrac{-5}{\sqrt{2}}\right) \cup \left(\dfrac{5}{\sqrt{2}}, \infty\right)$

$\Rightarrow k \in \{\ldots\ldots, -6, -5, -4, 4, 5, 6, \ldots.\}$ .....(ii)

Combing (i) and (ii), we observe that $x\ (-\infty, -4] \cup [4, \infty)$

33. **(a)** $\because f(x)$ is an even function, $f(-x) = f(x)$

$\Rightarrow$ $[3.5 - b \sin x] = [3.5 + b \sin x]\ \forall\ x \in \mathbb{R}$

$\Rightarrow$ $[3.5 - k] = [3.5 + k]$; $k = b \sin x$

$\Rightarrow$ $\frac{-1}{2} < k < \frac{1}{2} \Rightarrow \frac{-1}{2} < b \sin x < \frac{1}{2}$

$\therefore$ $-1 < \sin x < 1$; for $b > 0$, $-b \sin x < b$ and for $b < 0$; $-b > b \sin x > b$

$\Rightarrow$ $b \in \left(\frac{-1}{2}, \frac{1}{2}\right)$

34. **(b)** $f(x) = \log\sqrt{10.3^{x-2} - 9^{x-1} - 1} + \sqrt{\cos^{-1}(2-x)}$; for domain $\frac{10.(3)^x}{9} - \frac{(3^x)^2}{9} - 1 > 0$ and $(2-x) \in [-1, 1]$

$\Rightarrow$ $10\,(3)^x - (3^x)^2 - 9 > 0$ and $x \in [1, 3]$

$\Rightarrow$ $-10\,(3)^x + (3^x)^2 + 9 < 0$ and $x \in [1, 3]$

$\Rightarrow$ $(3^x)^2 - (3^x) - 9\,(3^x) + 9 < 0$ and $x\,[1, 3]$

$\Rightarrow$ $(3^x)(3^x - 1) - 9\,(3^x - 1) < 0$ and $x \in [1, 3]$

$\Rightarrow$ $(3^x - 1)(3^x - 9) < 0$ and $x \in [1, 3]$

$\Rightarrow$ $1 < 3^x < 9$ and $x \in [1, 3]$

$\Rightarrow$ $x \in (0, 2)$ and $x \in [1, 3]$

$\Rightarrow$ $x \in [1, 2)$

35. **(b)** $f(x) = \sqrt{\sqrt{\cot(5+3x)\,(\cot 5 + \cot 3x)} - \sqrt{\cot 3x + 1}}$; for domain $\sqrt{\cot(5+3x)(\cot 5 + \cot 3x)} \geq \sqrt{\cot 3x + 1}$

$\Rightarrow$ $\cot(5 + 3x)(\cot 5 + \cot 3x) \geq \cot 3x + 1 \geq 0$

$\Rightarrow$ $\cot(5+3x)\left[\frac{\sin 3x \cos 5 \quad \cos 3x.\sin 5}{\sin 5.\sin 3}\right] \geq \cot(3\ \ ) + 1 \geq 0$

$\Rightarrow$ $\cot(5 + 3x)\,.\left[\frac{\sin(3x+5)}{\sin 5.\sin 3x}\right] \geq \cot 3x + 1 \geq 0$

$\Rightarrow$ $\frac{\cos(5+3x)}{\sin 5.\sin 3x} \geq \cot 3x + 1 \geq 0$

$\Rightarrow$ $\frac{\cos 5.\cos 3x - \sin 5.\sin 3x}{\sin 5 \sin 3x} \geq \cot 3x + 1 \geq 0$

$\Rightarrow$ $(\cot 5).\cot 3x - 1 \geq \cot 3x + 1 \geq 0$

$\Rightarrow$ $(\cot(5) - 1)\cot 3x \geq 2$; $\cot 3x \geq -1$

$\because$ $5 \in \left(\frac{3\pi}{2}, 2\pi\right) \Rightarrow \cot 5 < 0$

$\Rightarrow$ $(\cot 5 - 1) < 0$

$\Rightarrow$ $\cot 3x \leq \frac{2}{(\cot 5 - 1)}$ and $\cot 3x \geq -1$

$\Rightarrow$ $-1 \leq \cot 3x \leq \frac{2}{(\cot 5 - 1)}$

$\Rightarrow$ $n\pi + \cot^{-1}\left(\frac{2}{\cot 5 - 1}\right) \leq 3x \leq (n+1)\pi - \frac{\pi}{4}$

$\Rightarrow$ $\frac{n\pi}{3} + \frac{1}{3}\cot^{-1}\left(\frac{2}{\cot 5 - 1}\right) \leq x \leq \frac{1}{3}\left(n + \frac{3}{4}\right)\pi; x \in \mathbb{Z}$

$\Rightarrow$ Domain $= \bigcup_{x \in \mathbb{Z}}\left[\frac{n\pi}{3} + \frac{1}{3}\cot^{-1}\left(\frac{2}{\cot 5 - 1}\right), \frac{1}{3}\left(n + \frac{3}{4}\right)\pi\right]$

36. **(c)** $f(x) = \log_{100x}\left(\frac{2\log_{10} x + 2}{-x}\right)$; $g(x) = \{x\}$;

For fog (x) to exist

Range of $f(x)$ must be subset of domain of $f(x)$.

Now, range $f(x) = [0, 1)$

For domain of $f(x)$: $100\,x > 0, \neq 1$ and $\frac{2\log_{10} x + 2}{-x} > 0$

$\Rightarrow$ $x > 0$; $x \neq \frac{1}{100}$ and $\frac{\log_{10} x + 1}{x} < 0$

$\Rightarrow$ $x > 0$; $x \neq \frac{1}{100} \log_{10} x < -1$

$\Rightarrow$ $x > 0$; $x \neq \frac{1}{100}; x < \frac{1}{10}$

$\Rightarrow$ $x \in \left(0, \frac{1}{10}\right) - \left\{\frac{1}{100}\right\}$

$\therefore$ Maximum possible range of

$f(x) = \left(0, \frac{1}{10}\right) - \left\{\frac{1}{100}\right\} = \left(0, \frac{1}{100}\right) \cup \left(\frac{1}{100}, \frac{1}{10}\right)$

i.e., $(0, 10^{-2}) \cup (10^{-2}, 10^{-1})$

37. **(b)** $f(x).f(y) = f(x) + f(y) + f(xy) - 2\ \forall\ x, y \in \mathbb{R}$ ....(i)

Put $x = 1$, $y = 1$

$\Rightarrow$ $[f(1)]^2 = f(1) + f(1) + f(1) - 2$

$\Rightarrow$ $[f(1)]^2 = 3f(1) - 2$

$\Rightarrow$ $(f(1) - 1)(f(1) - 2) = 0$

$\Rightarrow$ $f(1) = 1$ or $f(1) = 2$

Now, put $x = x$, $y = 1$ in (i), we get $f(x).f(1) = f(x) + f(1) + f(x) - 2\ \forall\ x \in \mathbb{R}$

If $f(1) = 1$, then $f(x) = f(x) + 1 + f(x) - 2\ \forall\ x \in \mathbb{R}$

$\Rightarrow$ $f(x) = 1\ \forall\ x \in \mathbb{R}$

$\Rightarrow$ $f(x)$ is a constant function, which contradicts the given hypothesis that $f(x)$ is not a constant function.

Thus, $f(1) = 2$

38. **(b)** $f\left(\frac{2\tan x}{1+\tan^2 x}\right) = \frac{(\cos 2x + 1)(\sec^2 x + 2\tan x)}{2}$

$\Rightarrow$ $f(\sin 2x) = \frac{(\cos 2x + 1)(\sec^2 x + 2\tan x)}{2}$

$= \frac{2\cos^2 x}{2}\left[\frac{1+\sin^2 x}{\cos^2 x}\right] = (1 + \sin 2x)$

Put $\sin 2x = \frac{1}{3}$

$\Rightarrow$ $f\left(\frac{1}{3}\right) = 1 + \frac{1}{3} = \frac{4}{3}$

39. **(c)** $f(x) = \begin{cases} 0 \text{ if } x \text{ is rational} \\ x \text{ if } x \text{ is irrational} \end{cases}$ and $g(x) = \begin{cases} 0 \text{ if } x \text{ is irrational} \\ x \text{ if } x \text{ is rational} \end{cases}$

$\therefore$ $(f - g)\,x = \begin{cases} -x \text{ if } x \text{ is rational} \\ x \text{ if } x \text{ is irrational} \end{cases} = h(x)$ (say)

Let $x_1, x_2 \in \mathbb{R}$ and $x_1, x_2 \in \mathbb{Q}$, then $h(x_1) = h(x_2)$

$\Rightarrow -x_1 = -x_2 \qquad \Rightarrow x_1 = x_2$

Similarly $x_1, x_2 \in \overline{\mathbb{Q}}$ such that $h(x_1) = h(x_2)$

$\Rightarrow x_1 = x_2$

Further if $x_1 \in \mathbb{Q}, x_2 \in \overline{\mathbb{Q}}$ such that $h(x_1) = h(x_2)$

$\Rightarrow -x_1 = x_2$

which is false as in this case either both x_1, x_2 are rational or both irrational.

$\Rightarrow (f-g)(x)$ is injective (one–one)

Also for each $x \in \mathbb{R}$.

If $x \in \mathbb{Q}$, then $(f-g)(-x) = x$ and If $x \in \overline{\mathbb{Q}}$, then $(f-g)(x) = x$

$\Rightarrow (f-g)(x)$ is subjective (onto).

40. (d) $T = \left\{\begin{bmatrix} a & b \\ c & d \end{bmatrix}; a,b,c,d \in \mathbb{R}\right\}; f: T \to \mathbb{R}$ such that $f(A) = |A| \ \forall A \in T$

Clearly f can't be injective as for every real number k, there exist at least two matrices having same determinant k.

e.g., $A = \begin{bmatrix} 7 & 4 \\ 6 & 8 \end{bmatrix}; B = \begin{bmatrix} 5 & 2 \\ 4 & 8 \end{bmatrix}$; then $f(A) = |A| = 32$ and $f(B) = |B| = 32$

For every real number k, there is a matrix having determinant k, e.g., $A = \begin{bmatrix} k & 1 \\ 0 & 1 \end{bmatrix}$

$\Rightarrow |A| = k$

$\Rightarrow f$ is subjective.

41. (b) $n(A) = 4$; $n(B) = 6$

Number of one–one functions $= {}^6P_4 = \dfrac{6!}{2!} = 360$ (from A to B)

Number of onto functions from B to A.

= Number of ways of putting 6 balls into 4 boxes, so that no box remains empty.

$= (4)^6 - [{}^4C_1 (3)^6 - {}^4C_2 (2)^6 + {}^4C_3 (1)^6] = 1560$

42. (b) $A = \{1, 2, 3, 4, 5, 6\}$

$f: A \to A$ is an injective function such that $f(\lambda) \neq \lambda$. Then number of such functions is equal to the number of ways of putting 6 letters into 6 envelopes, so that no letter goes to its correct addressed envelope.

$= 6!\left[1 - \dfrac{1}{1!} + \dfrac{1}{2!} - \dfrac{1}{3!} + \dfrac{1}{41} - \dfrac{1}{51} + \dfrac{1}{6!}\right] = 360 - 120 + 30 - 6 + 1 = 265$

43. (b) $f: \mathbb{R} \to \mathbb{R}$ is given by $f(x) = (x+1)^2 - 1, x \geq -1$

$y = (x+1)^2 - 1$

$\Rightarrow (x+1)^2 = y + 1$

$\Rightarrow x + 1 = \pm\sqrt{y+1}$

But $x \geq -1 \qquad \Rightarrow x + 1 \geq 0$

$\Rightarrow x + 1 = \sqrt{y+1} \Rightarrow x = \sqrt{y+1} - 1$

$\Rightarrow f^1(y) = \sqrt{y+1} - 1$

$\Rightarrow f^1(x) = \sqrt{x+1} - 1$

$\therefore f^1(x) = f(x) \qquad \Rightarrow \sqrt{x+1} - 1 = (x+1)^2 - 1$

$\Rightarrow \sqrt{x+1} = (x+1)^2 \qquad \Rightarrow (x+1)[(x+1)^3 - 1] = 0$

$\Rightarrow x = -1$ or $x = 0 \qquad \Rightarrow S = \{0, -1\}$

44. (d) $h(x) = |kx + 5|$

Domain of $f(x) = [-5, 7]$ and domain $f(h(x)) = [-6, 1]$

$\Rightarrow -5 \leq h(x) \leq 7 \ \forall x \in [-6, 1]$

$\Rightarrow -5 \leq |kx + 5| \leq 7 \ \forall x \in [-6, 1]$

$\Rightarrow 0 \leq |kx + 5| \leq 7 \ \forall x \in [-6, 1]$

$\Rightarrow -7 \leq (kx + 5) \leq 7 \ \forall x \in [-6, 1]$

Case (i): If $k > 0$, then $(kx + 5)$ is increasing.

$\Rightarrow k(-6) + 5 = -7$ and $k(1) + 5 = 7$

$\Rightarrow k = 2$

Case (ii): If $k < 0$, then $(kx + 5)$ is decreasing.

$\Rightarrow k(-6) + 5 = 7$ and $k(1) + 5 = -7$

$\Rightarrow k = -\dfrac{1}{3}$ and $k = -12$, which can't hold simultaneously.

$\therefore k = 2$

45. (c) $f(x) = \sin^2 x + \left[\dfrac{1 - \cos\left(2x + \frac{2\pi}{3}\right)}{2}\right] + \cos x \cos\left(x + \dfrac{\pi}{3}\right)$

$= \dfrac{1}{2}\left[1 - \cos 2x + 1 - \cos\left(2x + \dfrac{2\pi}{3}\right) + 2\cos x \cos\left(x + \dfrac{\pi}{3}\right)\right]$

$= \dfrac{1}{2}\left[2 - \cos 2x - \cos\left(2x + \dfrac{2\pi}{3}\right) + \cos\left(2x + \dfrac{\pi}{3}\right) + \cos\left(\dfrac{\pi}{3}\right)\right]$

$= \dfrac{1}{2}\left[2 - \cos 2x - \cos\left(2x - \dfrac{\pi}{3}\right) + \cos\left(2x + \dfrac{\pi}{3}\right) + \dfrac{1}{2}\right]$

$= \dfrac{1}{2}\left[2 - \cos 2x + 2\cos 2x \cos\dfrac{\pi}{3} + \dfrac{1}{2}\right] = \dfrac{1}{2}\left[\dfrac{5}{2}\right] = \dfrac{5}{4}$

$\therefore \ 4 \text{ gof}(x) = 4g\left(\dfrac{5}{4}\right) = 4.(1298) = 5192$

46. (a) $f(x) = 1 + x^2$; $f(f(x)) = 1 + x^2 - 2x^3 + x^4$

$\Rightarrow 1 + (f(x))^2 = 1 + x^2 - 2x^3 + x^4$

$\Rightarrow (f(x))^2 = x^4 - 2x^3 + x^2$

$\Rightarrow f(x) = \pm\sqrt{x^4 - 2x^3 + x^2}$

$\Rightarrow f(18) = \pm\sqrt{(18)^4 - 2(18)^3 + (18)^2}$

$= \pm 18\sqrt{(18)^2 - 2(18) + 1} = \pm 18\sqrt{(18-1)^2} = \pm 18\,(17)$

$= \pm 06$

47. (c) $f(x) = \cos^{-1}\sqrt{1-x^2}$ and $f(x) = -\sin^{-1} x$; $f(x) = f(x)$

$\Rightarrow \cos^{-1}\sqrt{1-x^2} = -\sin^{-1} x$

$\Rightarrow \sin^{-1} x = -\cos^{-1}\sqrt{1-x^2}$

$\Rightarrow x \in [-1, 0]$

48. (b) $f(x) = x^2 + x + \sin x - \cos x + \log(1 + |x|)$, $f(-x) = -f(x)$

$\Rightarrow f(x) = -f(-x)$

$= -x^2 + x + \sin x + \cos x - \log(1 + |x|)$

49. (c) $f(x) = [x] + \sum\limits_{r=1}^{1000} \dfrac{\{x + r\}}{1000} = [x] + \sum\limits_{r=1}^{1000} \dfrac{\{x\}}{1000} = [x] + 1000 \dfrac{\{x\}}{1000} = [x] + \{x\} = x$

50. (b) $f(f^{-1}(B)) = \{f(x): x \in f^{-1}(B)\} = \{f(x): f(x) \in B\}$

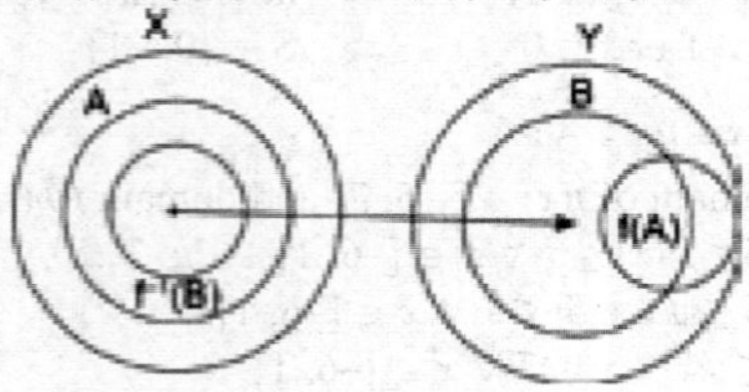

$\Rightarrow f(f^{-1}(B)) \subset B$

Now if $x \in B \subset Y \quad \Rightarrow \quad x \in Y$

It may happen that $f^{-1}(x)$ does not Exist in x as function is not given to be subjective.

$\therefore \quad f(f^{-1}(B)) \neq B$

Also, $f^{-1}(f(A)) = \{x \in X: f(x) \in f(A)\}$ but $f(A) = \{f(x): x \in A\}$

From above, we can't conclude $f^{-1}(f(A) \subset A$.

If the function is non-injective, then it may happen that $x \notin A$ and $f(x) \in f(A)$.

$\Rightarrow f^{-1}(f(A) \not\subset A \quad \Rightarrow \quad f^{-1}(f(A)) \neq A$

51. (b) $f: \mathbb{R} \to \mathbb{R}; f(x) = x^2 + 1$

Here it is not given that $f^{-1}(x)$ is a function, so, let us treat $f^{-1}(x)$ as a relation given by $f^{-1}(x) = \pm\sqrt{x-1}$

$\therefore \quad f^{-1}(17) = \pm 4$ and $f^{-1}(3) = \pm\sqrt{2}$

$\Rightarrow \quad \{f^{-1}(17)\} \cup \{f^{-1}(3)\} = \{\pm 4, \pm\sqrt{2}\}$

52. (c) $f(x) = \cos nx.\sin\left(\frac{5x}{n}\right)$

Period of $\cos nx = \frac{2\pi}{|n|}$

Period of $\sin\frac{5x}{n} = \frac{2\pi}{\left|\frac{5}{n}\right|} = \frac{2|n|\pi}{5}$

$\therefore \quad$ Period of $f(x) = \text{L.C.M}\left(\frac{2\pi}{|n|}, \frac{2|n|\pi}{5}\right) = 2\pi$ (given).

$\Rightarrow \text{L.C.M}\left(\frac{1}{|n|}, \frac{|n|}{5}\right) = 1 = \frac{\text{L.C.M}(1, |n|)}{\text{H.C.F}(|n|, 5)} = 1$

$\Rightarrow \quad \frac{|n|}{\text{H.C.F}(|n|, 5)} = 1$

$\Rightarrow$ H.C.F $(|n|, 5) = |n|$

If g.c.d $(|n|, 5) = 1 \quad \Rightarrow \quad |n| = 1$

$\Rightarrow n = 1$

If g.c.d $(|n|, 5) \neq 1 \quad \Rightarrow \quad |n| = 5m;\ m \in \mathbb{N}$

$\Rightarrow$ g.c.d $(5m, 5) = 5$

$\Rightarrow |n| = 5 \qquad \Rightarrow \quad n = \pm 5$

$\therefore \quad n \in \{\pm 1, \pm 5\}$

53. (a) $f(x) = 1 - x^3 - x^4 - 2x^5 = f(x) + h(x)$, where $f(x)$ = even function and $h(x)$ is an odd function

$\Rightarrow h(x) = \frac{f(x) - f(x)}{2} \quad \Rightarrow \quad h(-5) = \frac{f(-5) - f(5)}{2}$

$= \left[\frac{1 + 125 - 625 + 6250 - 1 + 125 + 625 + 6250}{2}\right]$

$= 125 + 6250 = 6375$

54. (d) $f: \mathbb{R} \to \mathbb{R}; f(x) = \left(\frac{ax}{\quad}\right)$

$$f'(x) = \frac{(x^2+2)(a) - (ax+5)(2x)}{(x^2+2)^2}$$

$$= \frac{ax^2 + 2a - 2ax^2 - 10x}{(x^2+2)^2} = \frac{2a - 10x - ax^2}{(x^2+2)^2}$$

For a continuous function $f(x)$ to be invertible, $f(x) > 0$ or $f'(x) < 0$; where the or used is exclusive.

$\Rightarrow \quad ax^2 + 10x - 2a < 0$ or exclusive $> 0\ \forall x \in \mathbb{R}$

$\therefore \quad$ Disc. $= 100 + 8a^2 > 0$

$\therefore$ For no real value of a, $f(x)$ is invertible. Thus, $a \in \{\}$

55. (d) $f(x) = \frac{1}{2}[\cos(\sin 4x) + \cos(\cos 4x)]$

Period of $\cos(\sin x) + \cos(\cos x) = g(x)$, (say) is $\frac{\pi}{2}$ as

$$g\left(\frac{\pi}{2} + x\right) = \cos\left(\sin\left(\frac{\pi}{2} + x\right)\right) + \cos\left(\cos\left(\frac{\pi}{2} + x\right)\right)$$

$= \cos(\cos x) + \cos(-\sin x)$

$= \cos(\cos x) + \cos(\sin x) = g(x)$

$\therefore \quad f(x) = \frac{1}{2}[\cos(\sin 4x) + \cos(\cos 4x)]$ has period $= \frac{\frac{\pi}{2}}{4} = \frac{\pi}{8}$

56. (a) $f(x) = \cos\sqrt{k}\,x;\ k = [m]$; Period of $f(x) = \frac{2\pi}{\sqrt{k}} = \pi$

$\Rightarrow \quad \sqrt{k} = 2 \qquad \Rightarrow \quad k = 4$

$\Rightarrow \quad [m] = 4 \qquad \Rightarrow \quad m \in [4, 5)$

57. (d) $F(x) = f(x).\,g\left(\frac{x}{5}\right) - g(x).f\left(\frac{x}{3}\right)$

Period of $f(x).g\left(\frac{x}{5}\right) = \text{L.C.M}(7, 55) = 385$

Period $f(x).f\left(\frac{x}{3}\right) = \text{L.C.M}(11, 21) = 231$

$\therefore \quad$ Period of $F(x) = \text{L.C.M}(385, 231) = 1155$

58. (a) $\sin[x + 4x + 9x + \ldots\ldots + (n+1)^2 x]$

$= \sin\left[\frac{(n+1)(n+2)(2n+3)}{6}\right]x$

Its period $= \frac{12\pi}{(n+1)(n+2)(2n+3)} = \frac{\pi}{4}$ (given)

$\Rightarrow \quad (n+1)(n+2)(2n+3) = 3 \times 4 \times 7$

$\Rightarrow \quad n = 2$

59. (b) $f(x) = 2\{x\} + \sin 2\pi\{x\}$

$\because \quad f(x+1) = 2\{x+1\} + \sin 2\pi\{x+1\}$

$= 2\{x\} + \sin 2\pi\{x\} = f(x)$

$\Rightarrow f(x)$ is periodic with period 1.

60. (c) $f(x) = 2\cot 3x + 5\sqrt{1 - \cos 6x}$

$f(x) = 2\cot 3x + 5\sqrt{2}\,|\sin 3x|$

Period = L.C.M $\left(\frac{\pi}{3}, \frac{\pi}{3}\right) = \frac{\pi}{3}$

Now, $\sec^2 3x + \text{cosec}^2 3x = \frac{4}{\sin^2 6x} = 4\,\text{cosec}^2 6x$, having period $\frac{\pi}{6}$

$2 \sin 3x + 3 \cos 3x$ has period L.C.M $\left(\frac{2\pi}{3}, \frac{2\pi}{3}\right) = \frac{2\pi}{3}$

$2\sqrt{1-\cos^2 3x} + \text{cosec}\, 6x = 2\,|\sin 3x| + \text{cosec}\, 6x$ has period = L.C.M $\left(\frac{\pi}{3}, \frac{2\pi}{6}\right) = \frac{\pi}{3}$

$\therefore$ $f(x)$ can be $2\sqrt{1-\cos^2 3x} + \text{cosec}\, 6x$

61. (b) $f(x) = x(1 - x);\ 0 \le x \le 1;$

Graph of $f(x)$ for $x \in [0, 1]$ is as shown below.

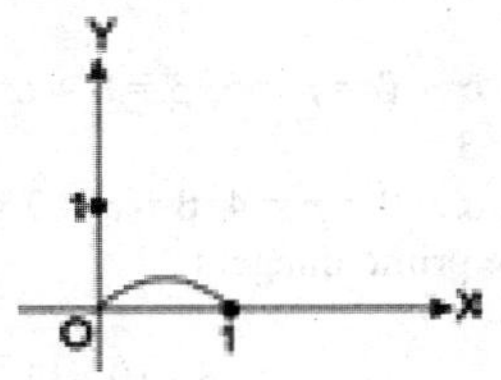

If $f(x)$ is extended by $f(x + 1) = f(x)$, then the new function will be represented as shown below.

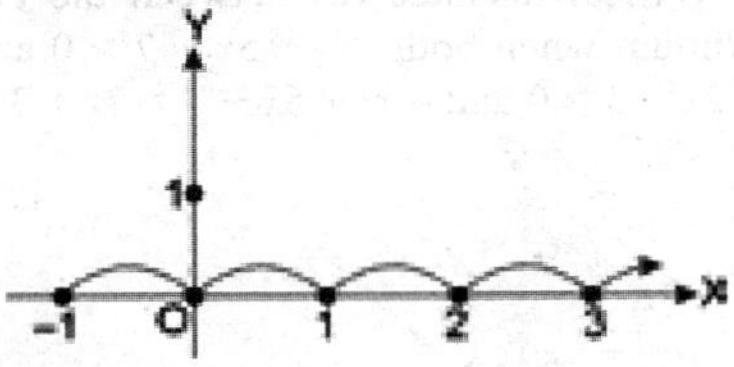

$\Rightarrow$ The new function will be a periodic function with period 1.

62. (b) $f(x) = \begin{cases} x^2 \sin\left(\frac{\pi x}{2}\right); |x| < 1 \\ x|x|; \quad |x| \ge 1 \end{cases} = \begin{cases} x^2 \sin\left(\frac{\pi x}{2}\right); -1 < x < 1 \\ -x^2 \quad ; \ x \le -1 \\ x^2 \quad ; \ x \ge 1 \end{cases}$

$\Rightarrow f(-x) = \begin{cases} x^2 \sin\left(\frac{\pi x}{2}\right); 0 \le x < 1 \\ x^2 \ ; \ x \ge 1 \end{cases}$ and $f(-x)$

$= \begin{cases} -x^2 \sin\left(\frac{\pi x}{2}\right); 0 \le x \le 1 \\ -x^2 \ ; \ x \ge 1 \end{cases}$

$\therefore f(x) = -f(-x)\ \forall\ x \in [1, \infty)$

$\Rightarrow f(x)$ is an odd function

63. (d) $f(x) = x^2 - 1$ and $f(x) = x^3 - 7x^2 + 5x + 6$

$\Rightarrow f'(x) = 2x$ and $g'(x) = 3x^2 - 14x + 5$

Let $P \equiv (h, k)$ and $Q \equiv (u, v)$

Since tangent at P to $f(x)$ is parallel to tangent at Q to $f(x)$

$\Rightarrow 2h = 3u^2 - 14u + 5$

$\Rightarrow 3u^2 - 14u + (5 - 2h) = 0$

Disc. $= (-14)^2 - 4(3)(5 - 2h)$

$= 196 - 60 + 24h$

$= 136 + 24h > 0$, for $h > -\frac{136}{24}$ or $h > -\frac{17}{3}$

$\therefore$ For $h > -\frac{17}{3}$; u has two real values given by

$u = \frac{14 \pm \sqrt{136 + 24h}}{6}$ or $u = \frac{7 \pm \sqrt{34 + 6h}}{3}$

$\therefore$ Corresponding to each point $p(h, k)$ on $f(x)$; $h > \frac{-17}{3}$; there will be two points $Q(u, v)$ on $g(x)$ such that at tangent at P is to the Q.

Thus, there will be the infinitely many pairs (P, Q).

64. (b) $f''(x) > 0\ \forall\ x \in \mathbb{R}$ and $g(x) = f(x^2) - f(x^2 + 3)$

$\Rightarrow g'(x) = f'(x^2).(2x) - f'(x^2 + 3)(2x) = (2x)\,[f'(x^2) - f'(x^2 + 3)]$ ....(1)

$\because f'(x) > 0\ \forall\ x \in \mathbb{R}$

$\Rightarrow f'(x)$ is an increasing function $x \in \mathbb{R}$,

$\Rightarrow f'(x^2) - f'(x^2 + 3) < 0.$ ......(2)

$\therefore$ From (1) and (2), we note that $g'(x) < 0$ for $x > 0$ and $g'(x) > 0$ for $x < 0$

$\Rightarrow g(x)$ is decreasing in $(0, \infty)$.

65. (a) $f(x) = \frac{(x^3 - 3x^2 + 3x - 7)}{\sqrt{x^{14} - x^{11} - x^{10} - x^7 + x^6 - x^3 + x^2 + 1}}$

$\Rightarrow$ For domain, $f(x) = (x^{14} - x^{11} + x^{10} - x^7 + x^6 - x^3 + x^2 + 1) > 0$

For $x \le 0$, $f(x) > 0$

For x $(0, 1)$, $x^{10} > x^{11}$, $x^6 > x^7$, $x^2 > x^3$

$\Rightarrow f(x) > 0$

For $x \in [1, \infty)$, $x^{14} \ge x^{11}$, $x^{10} \ge x^7$, $x^6 \ge x^3$

$\Rightarrow f(x) > 0$ $\quad\therefore\ f(x) > 0\ \forall\ x \in \mathbb{R}$

$\Rightarrow$ Domain $f(x) = (-\infty, \infty)$

66. (b) $f(x) = \log_{(x^2 + x + 1)}(3x^2 - 4x + 5)$

$\Rightarrow$ For domain, $x^2 + x + 1 > 0$ and $\ne 1$, disc. of $x^2 + x + 1 = -3 < 0$

$\Rightarrow x^2 + x + 1 = 1 > 0\ \forall\ x \in \mathbb{R}$ and $x^2 + x + 1 = 1$ for $x = 0$ or -1

$\therefore$ For base, $x \in \mathbb{R} - \{0, -1\}$ ....(i)

Also for $3x^2 - 4x + 5 > 0$ which holds $\forall\ x \in \mathbb{R}$ as its disc $= -44 < 0$

$\Rightarrow$ Domain of $f(x) = \mathbb{R} - \{0, -1\}$

67. (c) $f(x) = \sqrt{8 - 3^{x+1} - 3^{1-x}} + \sqrt{\sin^{-1}(2x + 1)}$

For domain of $f(x)$, $8 - 3(3^x) - \frac{3}{(3^x)} \ge 0$ and $\sin^{-1}(2x + 1) \ge 0$

$\Rightarrow 8(3^x) - 3(3^x)^2 - 3 \ge 0$ and $(2x + 1) \in [0, 1]$

$\Rightarrow 3(t^2) - 8t + 3 \le 0$ and $x \in \left[\frac{-1}{2}, 0\right]$; where $t = 3^x$

$\Rightarrow t \in \left[\frac{4 - \sqrt{7}}{3}, \frac{4 + \sqrt{7}}{3}\right]$ and $x \in \left[\frac{-1}{2}, 0\right]$

$$\Rightarrow\ 3^x \in \left[\frac{4-\sqrt{7}}{3}, \frac{4+\sqrt{7}}{3}\right] \text{and}\ x \in \left[\frac{-1}{2}, 0\right]$$

$$\Rightarrow\ x \in \left[\log_3\left(\frac{4-\sqrt{7}}{3}\right), \log_3\left(\frac{4+\sqrt{7}}{3}\right)\right] \text{ and } x \in \left[\frac{-1}{2}, 0\right]$$

$$\because\ \frac{4+\sqrt{7}}{3} > 1 \Rightarrow \log_3\left(\frac{4+\sqrt{7}}{3}\right) > 0 \text{ and}$$

$$\frac{4-\sqrt{7}}{3} = \frac{9}{3(4+\sqrt{7})} = \frac{3}{4+\sqrt{7}} < \frac{3}{\sqrt{12}+\sqrt{3}} = \frac{1}{\sqrt{3}}$$

$$\Rightarrow\ \log_3\left(\frac{4-\sqrt{7}}{3}\right) < \log_2\left(\frac{1}{\sqrt{3}}\right) = \frac{-1}{2}$$

$$\Rightarrow\ \left[\frac{-1}{2}, 0\right] \subset \left[\log_3\left(\frac{4-\sqrt{7}}{3}\right), \log_3\left(\frac{4+\sqrt{7}}{3}\right)\right]$$

$$\Rightarrow\ \text{Domain of } f(x) = \left[-\frac{1}{2}, 0\right]$$

68. (c) $f(x) = \dfrac{3\cos^2 x + 3\cos x + 4}{\cos^2 x + \cos x + 1} = \dfrac{3\left[\cos^2 x + \cos x + 1\right] + 1}{\cos^2 x + \cos x + 1}$

$$= 3 + \frac{1}{(\cos^2 x + \cos x + 1)} = 3 + \frac{1}{\left\{\left(\cos x + \frac{1}{2}\right)^2 + \frac{3}{4}\right\}}$$

as $\cos x \in [-1, 1]$

$$\Rightarrow\ \left(\cos x + \frac{1}{2}\right) \in \left[\frac{-1}{2}, \frac{3}{2}\right]$$

$$\Rightarrow\ \left(\cos x + \frac{1}{2}\right)^2 \in \left[0, \frac{9}{4}\right]$$

$$\Rightarrow\ \left\{\left(\cos x + \frac{1}{2}\right)^2 + \frac{3}{4}\right\} \in \left[\frac{3}{4}, 3\right]$$

$$\Rightarrow\ \frac{1}{\left\{\left(\cos x + \frac{1}{2}\right)^2 + \frac{3}{4}\right\}} \in \left[\frac{1}{3}, \frac{4}{3}\right]$$

$$\Rightarrow\ 3 + \frac{1}{\left\{\left(\cos x + \frac{1}{2}\right)^2 + \frac{3}{4}\right\}} \in \left[\frac{10}{3}, \frac{13}{3}\right] = [\lambda, \mu]$$

$$\Rightarrow\ \lambda = \frac{10}{3}, \mu = \frac{13}{3}$$

$\therefore\ 6\lambda + 9\mu + 2 = 20 + 39 + 2 = 61$

69. (b) $f(x) = x^2 - px + q$ ....(i)

Given, $q + p = 11$ and $q - p = a$

$$\Rightarrow\ q = \frac{11+a}{2} \text{ and } p = \frac{11-a}{2}$$

$$\Rightarrow\ f(x) = x^2 - \left(\frac{11-a}{2}\right)x + \left(\frac{11+a}{2}\right)$$

$$\Rightarrow\ f(a) = a^2 - \left(\frac{11-a}{2}\right)a + \left(\frac{11+a}{2}\right)$$

$$\Rightarrow\ f(a) = \frac{2a^2 - 11a + a^2 + 11 + a}{2}$$

$$\Rightarrow\ f(a) = \frac{3a^2 - 10a + 11}{2} \quad \text{........(2)}$$

If α, β are prime roots of (1), then $\alpha + \beta = p$

$$= \frac{11-a}{2}, \alpha\beta = q = \frac{11+a}{2}$$

$\because\ p, q \in \mathbb{N}$ (as α, β are prime integers)

$\Rightarrow\ 2/(11 - a)$ and $2/(11 + a)$ as $11 - a > 0$

$\Rightarrow\ a \in \{1, 3, 5, 7, 9\}$

Also $\alpha + \beta = p = \dfrac{11-a}{2}$ and α, β are prime

$\Rightarrow\ \alpha + \beta \geq 4 \quad \Rightarrow\ \dfrac{11-a}{2} \geq 4$

$\Rightarrow\ 11 - a \geq 8 \quad \Rightarrow\ a \leq 3$

$\Rightarrow\ a = 1$ or 3

For $a = 1$, $\alpha + \beta = p = 5$, $\beta = q = 6$

$\Rightarrow\ \alpha = 2, \beta = 3$

For $a = 3$, $\alpha + \beta = p = 4$, $\beta = q = 7$ which is impossible as α, β are prime integers .

$\Rightarrow\ a = 1$

$\therefore$ From (2), we get $f(a) = \dfrac{3 - 10 + 11}{2} = 2$

70. (c) The vertical distance (d) between the curves will be maximum when both $-x^2 + 5x + 7 > 0$ and $2x + 3 > 0$ and $2x + 3 > 0$ and $-x^2 + 5x + 7 > 2x + 3$

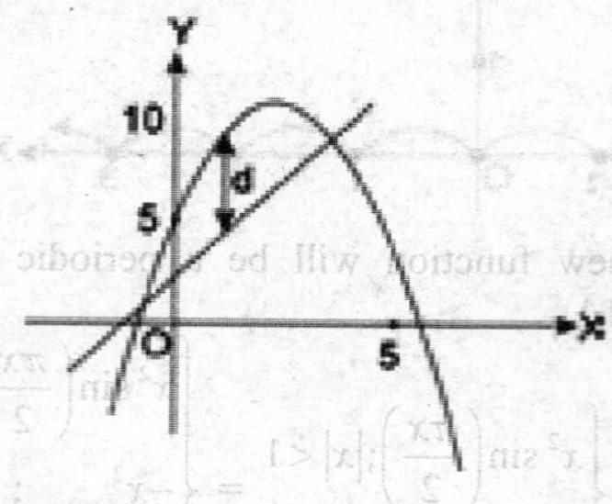

Further (d) is given by $|(-x^2 + 5x + 7) - (2x + 3)|$

$= -x^2 + 5x + 7 - 2x - 3$

$d(x) = -x^2 + 3x + 4$

$$\Rightarrow\ \text{Maximum } d(x) = \frac{-\left[(3)^2 - 4(-1)(4)\right]}{4(-1)} = \frac{-[9+16]}{-4} = \frac{25}{4}$$

SECTION–IV (MORE THAN ONE ANSWER CORRECT)

1. (a), (b), (c), (d)

(a) $\text{sgn}(e^{-x}) = 1$ as $e^{-x} > 0\ \forall\ x \in \mathbb{R}$

$\Rightarrow$ It is a constant function, and hence, is a periodic function with no fundamental period.

(b) $f(x) = \begin{cases} 1 \text{ if } x \text{ is a rational no.} \\ 0 \text{ if } x \text{ is an irrational no.} \end{cases}$

There exists infinitely many 'h' for which $f(x + h) = f(x)$ $\forall\ x \in \mathbb{R}$.

e.g., if $h = 2$, then $f(x + h) = f(x) = 1$ if $x \in \mathbb{Q}$ and $f(x + h) = f(x) = 0$ if $x \in \overline{\mathbb{Q}}$

$\Rightarrow f(x+h)=f(x)\ \forall\ x\in\mathbb{R}$, but we can't find smallest positive real 'h' for which $f(x+h)=f(x)\ \forall\ x\in\mathbb{R}$

$\Rightarrow f(x)$ is periodic with no fundamental period.

(c) $f(x)=\sqrt{\dfrac{8}{1+\cos}+\dfrac{8}{1-\cos x}}=4\,|\text{cosec } x|$, which is periodic function with period π.

(d) $\left[x+\frac{1}{2}\right]+\left[x-\frac{1}{2}\right]+2[-x]$

$$=\left[x+\frac{1}{2}\right]+\left[\left(x+\frac{1}{2}\right)-1\right]+2([-x])=2\left[x+\frac{1}{2}\right]+2[-x]-1$$

$$=\begin{cases}2x-2x-1=-1 \text{ if } x\in\mathbb{Z}\\ 2n+2+2(-n-1)-1=-1 \text{ if } x=n+\frac{1}{2}\\ 2n-2n-2-1=-3; n<x<n+\frac{1}{2}\\ 2n+2-2n-2-1=-1; n+\frac{1}{2}<x<n+1\end{cases}$$

The graph of $f(x)$ will be as shown below

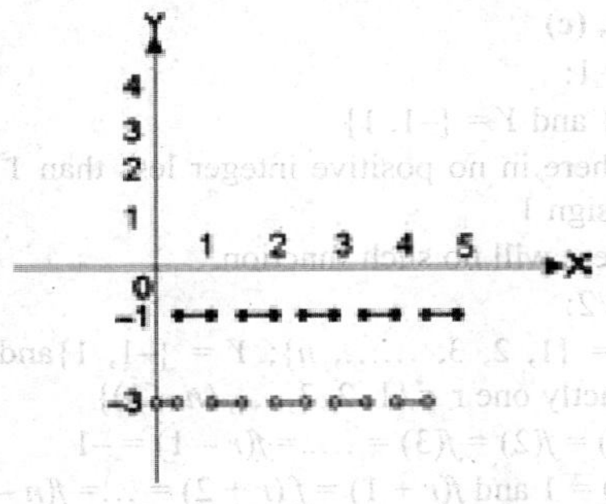

Clearly, the period of $f(x)$ is 1

$$f(x+1)=\left[x+1+\frac{1}{2}\right]+\left[x+1-\frac{1}{2}\right]+2[-x-1]$$

$$=1+\left[x+\frac{1}{2}\right]+1+\left[x-\frac{1}{2}\right]+2[-x]-2$$

$$=\left[x+\frac{1}{2}\right]+\left[x-\frac{1}{2}\right]+2[-x]=f(x)$$

2. (a), (b) $f(x)=[x]^2+[x+1]-3$

$\Rightarrow f(x)=[x]^2+[x]-2$

$\Rightarrow f(x)=([x]+2)([x]-1)$

$\therefore f(x)=0 \quad \Rightarrow [x]=-2$ or $[x]=1$

$\Rightarrow f(x)=0$ for $x\in[-2,-1)\cup[1,2)$

$\Rightarrow f(x)$ is many–one function, $f(x)=0$ for infinite number of values of x.

Also range of $f(x)$ consists of only integer values, and hence, $f(x)$ is into.

3. (a), (d) $f(x)=\dfrac{x^2-3x+2}{x^2+x-6}=\dfrac{(x-1)(x-2)}{(x+3)(x-2)}=\dfrac{(x-1)}{(x+3)}$ for x 2

$\therefore$ Domain of $f(x)=\mathbb{R}-\{2,-3\}$

Now, $y=\dfrac{x-1}{x+3} \quad \Rightarrow xy+3y=x-1$

$\Rightarrow x(y-1)=-3y-1 \quad \Rightarrow x=\dfrac{3y+1}{1-y}$

$\therefore\ x\in\mathbb{R}$ for $y\neq 1$ also $x\neq 2$

$\Rightarrow 2\neq\dfrac{3y+1}{1-y}$

$\Rightarrow 2-2y\neq 3y+1 \quad \Rightarrow y\neq 1/5$

$\Rightarrow$ Range $=\mathbb{R}-\left\{1,\frac{1}{5}\right\}$

4. (c), (d) $f(x)=\sqrt{2-x}+\sqrt{1+x}$

For domain $2-x\geq 0$ and $1+x\geq 0$

$\Rightarrow x\leq 2$ and $x\geq -1$

Domain $=[-1,2]$

Now, $y^2=3+2\sqrt{(2-x)(1+x)}$

$\Rightarrow y^2=3+2\sqrt{-x^2+x+2}$

In domain, $[-1,2]$, $-x^2+x+2\in\left[0,\frac{9}{4}\right]$

$\Rightarrow y^2\in[3,6]$ and $y>0 \Rightarrow y\in\left[\sqrt{3},\sqrt{6}\right]$

$\Rightarrow$ Range $=\left[\sqrt{3},\sqrt{6}\right]$

5. (b), (c) $\log_x y.\log_{xy} y.\log_{x^2y} y=\dfrac{1}{6}$ ....(i)

For domain $x>0, y>0, x\neq 1, xy\neq 1, x^2y\neq 1$

Further (i) can be written as $\dfrac{\log y}{\log x}.\dfrac{\log y}{(\log xy)}.\dfrac{\log y}{\log x^2 y}=\dfrac{1}{6}$

$\Rightarrow \dfrac{(\log y)^3}{(\log x)(\log x+\log y).(2\log x+\log y)}=\dfrac{1}{6}$

$\Rightarrow 6(\log y)^3=(\log y)^2(\log x)+3(\log x)^2(\log y)+2(\log x)^3$

Put $\log y=t$, $\log x=u$

$\Rightarrow 6t^3-ut^2-3u^2t-2u^3=0$

Clearly $t=u$ satisfy it $(t-u)$ is its factor.

$\Rightarrow (t-u)(6t^2+5ut+2u^2)=0$

Disc. of $6t^2+5ut+2u^2$ is $-23u^2<0$

$\Rightarrow t=u$ is the only possible root.

$\Rightarrow \log y=\log x \quad \Rightarrow y=x$

$\therefore$ In Explicit form (i) can be written as $y=x$ for domain $x>0, x\neq 1$

6. (b), (d) $f(x)=(1+\tan x)\left\{1+\tan\left(\dfrac{\pi}{4}-x\right)\right\}=(1+\tan x)\left\{1+\dfrac{1-\tan x}{1+\tan x}\right\}=2$ for $\tan x\neq -1$

Also $g(x)$ is given to be defined for every real x.

$\text{gof}(x)=f(2)$ for $x\neq n\pi+\left(\dfrac{-\pi}{4}\right):n\in\mathbb{Z}$

$\Rightarrow$ gof (x) is constant $\forall\ x\in D_f$

$\Rightarrow$ gof (x) is non-subjective function.

7. (b), (c) $f(x)=\sqrt{x}\sqrt{x-1}$ and $g(x)=\sqrt{x(x-1)}$

Domain of $f(x)=[1,\infty)$ and Domain of $f(x)=(-\infty,0]\ [1,\infty)$

Since Domain of $f(x)\neq$ domain of $f(x)$

$\Rightarrow f(x)$ and $f(x)$ are not equal functions $\forall\ x\in\mathbb{R}$.

Also $f(x) = f(x)\ \forall\ x \in [1, \infty)$, i.e., they are identical in their common domain.

8. (b), (c) Area of Equilateral $\Delta = \frac{\sqrt{3}}{4}a^2 = \frac{\sqrt{3}}{4}$

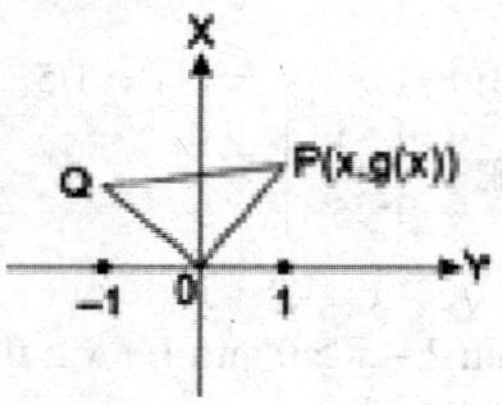

$\Rightarrow\ a = 1 \qquad \Rightarrow\ OP = 1$

$\Rightarrow\ x^2 + (f(x))^2 = 1$

$\Rightarrow\ x^2 + y^2 = 1 \qquad \Rightarrow\ y^2 = 1 - x^2$

$\Rightarrow\ y = \pm\sqrt{1-x^2}$

For y to be defined $x^2 - 1 \le 0$

$\Rightarrow\ x \in [-1, 1]$

9. (a), (d) $f(x) = \sec^{-1}[1 + \cos^2 x]$

$1 + \cos^2 x \in [1, 2]$

$\Rightarrow\ [1 + \cos^2 x] \in \{1, 2\}$

$\Rightarrow\ f(x) = \{\sec^{-1} 1, \sec^{-1} 2\} = \left\{0, \frac{\pi}{3}\right\}$

Domain of $f(x) = \mathbb{R}$ and Range of $f(x) = \left\{0, \frac{\pi}{3}\right\}$

10. (a), (d) $f(x) = \sin^{-1}\left(\frac{2x}{1+x^2}\right)$ and $f(x) = \cos^{-1}\left(\frac{1-x^2}{1+x^2}\right)$

$\therefore\ 2\tan^{-1}x = \begin{cases} \sin^{-1}\left(\frac{2x}{1+x^2}\right) \\ \text{for } x \in [-1, 1] \end{cases}$ and $2\tan^{-1}x = \begin{cases} \cos^{-1}\left(\frac{1-x^2}{1+x^2}\right) \\ \text{for } x \in [0, \infty) \end{cases}$

$\Rightarrow\ \sin^{-1}\left(\frac{2x}{1+x^2}\right) = \cos^{-1}\left(\frac{1-x^2}{1+x^2}\right)$ for x [0, 1]

$\Rightarrow$ Domain of $f(x) = [0, 1] = D_f$

Hence, range of $f(x) = \left[0, \frac{\pi}{2}\right] = R_f$

11. (b), (c) $\sin\left(\frac{\cos^{-1}x}{y}\right) = 1$

$\Rightarrow\ \frac{\cos^{-1}x}{y} = 2n\pi + \frac{\pi}{2}; n \in \mathbb{Z}$

Also $y \in Y \subseteq \mathbb{Z} - \{0\}$

$\Rightarrow\ \frac{\cos^{-1}x}{y} = (4n+1)\frac{\pi}{2} \Rightarrow x = 0,\ y = 1,\ n = 0$ or $\cos^{-1} x =$ $(4n + 1)k\pi;\ y = 2k;\ k \in \mathbb{Z} - \{0\}$

$\Rightarrow\ \cos^{-1} x = 0$ or π

$\Rightarrow\ (4n + 1)k = 0$ or 1

$\Rightarrow\ n = 0, k = 0, 1 \qquad \Rightarrow\ y = 0, 2$

$\therefore\ x \in \{-1, 1\}$ and $y \in \{0, 2\}$

Since $y \in Y_1 \subseteq \mathbb{Z} - \{0\}, y \ne 0, x \ne 1$

$\Rightarrow\ Y_1 = \{2, 1\}$ and $x \in X_1 = \{-1, 0\}$

12. (a), (c) $\cos\left(\frac{\sin^{-1}x}{y}\right) = 0;\ y\ Y_2 \subseteq \mathbb{Z} - \{0\}$

$\Rightarrow\ \frac{\sin^{-1}x}{y} = (2n+1)\frac{\pi}{2}; x \in \mathbb{Z}$

$\Rightarrow\ x = \pm 1, y = \pm 1$ or $\sin^{-1} x = k(2n + 1)\pi;\ y = 2k;\ k \in \mathbb{Z} - \{0\}$

$\Rightarrow\ (2n + 1)k = 0 \qquad \Rightarrow\ n = 0, k = 0$

$\Rightarrow\ x = 0, y = 0$

$\Rightarrow$ No more solution expect for $x = \pm 1, y = \pm 1$

$\Rightarrow\ X_2 = \{1, -1\}$ and $Y_2 = \{1, -1\}$

13. (a), (b), (d) Clearly for $n \ge 3$, there is no one–one function. For $n = 1$, there will be two functions namely, $f_1(1) = -1$ and $f_2(1) = 1$

For $n = 2$, there will be two functions namely, $f_1 = \{(1, -1), (2, 1)\}$ and $f_2 = \{(1, 1), (2, -1)\}$

14. (a), (b) $f(1) = -1, f(x) = -1$

Now each one of 2, 3, 4 …..$(n - 1)$ has 2 choice, i.e., –1 and 1

$\Rightarrow$ Total number of possible functions $(2)^{n-2}$ for $n \ge 3$ and It is 1 for $n = 2$ and 1 for $n = 1$

$\Rightarrow\ (2)^{n-2}$ for $n \ge 2$ and 1 for $n = 1$

15. (a), (b), (c)

For $n = 1$:

$X = \{1\}$ and $Y = \{-1, 1\}$

Since there in no positive integer less than 1 (= n), which is to assign 1

$\therefore$ There will no such function.

For $n \ge 2$:

$X = \{1, 2, 3, \ldots\ldots, n\}$; $Y = \{-1, 1\}$ and $f(r) = 1$ for exactly one r $\in \{1, 2, 3, \ldots, (n - 1)\}$

$\Rightarrow\ f(1) = f(2) = f(3) = \ldots\ldots = f(r - 1) = -1$

$f(r) = 1$ and $f(r + 1) = f(r + 2) = \ldots = f(n - 1) = -1$

$f(n)$ has two choice, i.e., – 1 and 1

Now, for r we have choice, 1, 2, 3, ….., $(n - 1)$

$\therefore$ Total number of functions = (number of ways of choosing r) × (number of ways for $f(n)$)

$= (n - 1) \times 2 = 2(n - 1)$

16. (a), (b), (c), (d)

$f(x) = \sqrt{\log_{\frac{1}{2}}\left(\log_5\left([x^2] - 3\right)\right)}$;

for domain $\log_{\frac{1}{2}}(\log_5([x^2] - 3)) \ge 0$

$\Rightarrow\ 0 < \log_5([x^2] - 3) \le 1 \Rightarrow\ 10 < [x^2] - 3 \le 5$

$\Rightarrow\ 4 < [x^2] \le 8$

$\Rightarrow\ 5 \le [x^2] \le 8 \qquad \Rightarrow\ [x^2] \in \{5, 6, 7, 8\}$

$\Rightarrow$ option (a) is correct,

$\Rightarrow\ x^2 \in [5, 9) \qquad \Rightarrow\ x \in \left(-3, -\sqrt{5}\right] \cup \left[\sqrt{5}, 3\right)$

option (b) is correct.

$\Rightarrow\ [x] \in [-3, 2) \qquad \Rightarrow$ option (c) is correct

$\because\ [x^2] \in \{5, 6, 7, 8\}$

$\Rightarrow$ Range of $f(x)$

$= \left\{\sqrt{\log_{\frac{1}{2}}(\log_5(2))}, \sqrt{\log_{\frac{1}{2}}\log_5(3)}, \sqrt{\log_{\frac{1}{2}}(\log_5(4))}, 0\right\}$

option (d) is correct.

17. (b), (c) $f(x) + g(x) = e^x$ ....(i)

$f(x) - f(x) = e^{-x}$ ....(ii)

Adding (i) and (ii), we get $f(x) = \dfrac{e^x + e^{-x}}{2}$

$\Rightarrow f(-x) = f(x)$

Subtracting, we get $f(x) = \dfrac{e^x - e^{-x}}{2}$

$\Rightarrow f(-x) = \dfrac{e^{-x} - e^x}{2} = -f(x)$

$\Rightarrow$ $f(x)$ is an even function and $f(x)$ is an odd function.

18. (a), (b), (c), (d)

$f(x) = 2x + \cos x$ and $f(x) = \sqrt[3]{x}$, gof $(x) = f(f(x)) = (2x + \cos x)^{1/3}$

Clearly, domain of gof(x) is $\mathbb{R}$, $2x + \cos x \in (-\infty, \infty)$ and $(x)^{1/3}$ is an increasing function.

$\Rightarrow$ gof (x) has range $\mathbb{R}$ and (gof $)'(x) = \dfrac{1}{3}(2x + \cos x)^{-\frac{2}{3}}$

$(2 - \sin x) = \dfrac{(2 - \sin x)}{3(2x + \cos)^{\frac{2}{3}}} > 0 \ \forall\, x \in \mathbb{R} - \left\{\dfrac{-1}{2}\cos x\right\}$

$\Rightarrow$ gof is an injective function.

Further, $f'(x) = 2 - \sin x > 0 \ \forall\, x \in \mathbb{R}$ and $g'(x) = \dfrac{1}{3(x)^{\frac{2}{3}}}$

$> 0 \ \forall\, x \in \mathbb{R} - \{0\}$

$\Rightarrow$ $f(x)$ and $f(x)$ are injective.

Range of $f(x) = (-\infty, \infty)$

$\Rightarrow$ $f(x)$ is onto.

Also range of $f(x) = (-\infty, \infty)$

$\Rightarrow$ $g(x)$ is onto

19. (a), (c), (d) $f(x) = |x + 1|, x \in [-1, \infty)$

$\Rightarrow f(x) = x + 1$; which is injective,

$f(x) = x + \dfrac{1}{2}; x \in (0, \infty)$

$f(x) \in (\infty, 2]$ for $x \in (0, 1]$ and $f(x) \in [2, \infty)$ for x $[1, \infty)$

$\Rightarrow$ $g(x)$ is non- injective

$\Rightarrow h(x) = x^2 + 4x - 5, x \in (0, \infty)$

$\Rightarrow h'(x) = 2x + 4 > 0$ for $x \in (-2, \infty)$

$\Rightarrow$ $h(x)$ is injective.

$\Rightarrow k(x) = e^{-x}$

$\Rightarrow k'(x) = -e^{-x} < 0 \ \forall\, x \in \mathbb{R}$

20. (a), (c) $f(x) = \cos[\pi^2]\, x + \cos[-\pi^2]\, x = \cos 9x + \cos 10x$

$\Rightarrow f\left(\dfrac{\pi}{2}\right) = \cos\dfrac{9\pi}{2} + \cos 5 = 0 - 1 = -1$

$\Rightarrow f(\pi) = \cos 9\pi + \cos 10\pi = -1 + 1 = 0$

$\Rightarrow f(-\pi) = \cos(-9\pi) + \cos(-10\pi) = -1 + 1 = 0$

SECTION–V (ASSERTION / REASON)

1. (c) Obviously the assertion is correct, but reason is incorrect as when $k < 0$, then $y = k^x$ becomes non-real for x of the form

$\dfrac{(2m+1)}{2n}$, $m, n \in \mathbb{Z}, n \neq 0$.

$\Rightarrow$ In this case domain $= \mathbb{R} - \left\{x : x = \dfrac{2m+1}{2n}, m, n \in \mathbb{Z}, n \neq 0\right\}$

and range $= \{k^x; x \in D_f\}$

$\therefore$ Domain and range will be changed.

For $k = 1$, $y = k^x$ $\Rightarrow y = 1 \ \forall x \in \mathbb{R}$

$\Rightarrow$ Function becomes a constant function, which is not desirable here, as if we want to find its inverse , then it will be impossible as inverse exists for one–one functions.

2. (d) $y = k^x$ is strictly increasing for $k > 1$. Its inverse is $y = \log k^x$ and which is strictly increasing as $k > 1$

$\Rightarrow$ Assertion is incorrect, however, reason is correct.

3. (c) Fundamental period of $\sin x = 2\pi$,

Fundamental period of $\tan x = \pi$

Fundamental period of $\sin x + \tan x$

$=$ L.C.M $(2, \pi) = 2\pi$

$\Rightarrow$ Assertion is correct.

But L.C.M (T_1, T_2) is period of $f(x) + f(x)$, but not necessary its fundamental period.

e.g., fundamental period of $|\sin x| + |\cos x|$ is $\dfrac{\pi}{2}$ inspite fundamental period of $|\sin x|$ and $|\cos x|$ is π and L.C.M $(\pi, \pi) = \pi$

$\therefore$ Assertion is correct reason incorrect

4. (a) Graph of $y = -x + \sin x$ and its inverse are as shown below.

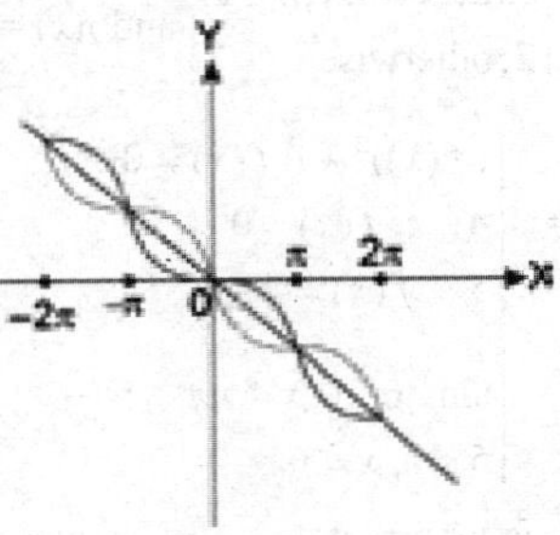

Clearly reason is correct.

By reason, if $f(x)$ and $f^{-1}(x)$ intersect at $y = x$, then $x = -x + \sin x$

$\Rightarrow 2x = \sin x$ $\Rightarrow x = 0$ is the only solution.

If $f(x)$ and $f^{-1}(x)$ intersect at $y = -x + \sin x$

$\Rightarrow \sin x = 0$ $\Rightarrow x = n\pi; n \in \mathbb{Z}$

$\therefore$ $f(x)$ and $f^{-1}(x)$ intersect at $y = -x$ at each $x = n\pi; n \in \mathbb{Z}$

$\Rightarrow$ Assertion is also correct and decided by reason.

5. (c) If we consider a function $f(x) = x + \sin x$

$f'(x) = 1 + \cos x$, which is periodic with period 2π, but $f(x)$ is not periodic .

Thus, reason is incorrect, however, assertion is correct.

6. (b) $\because f(f(x + T)) = f(f(x))$, if T is period of $f(x)$.

$\Rightarrow$ fog (x) is also periodic with period T

$\Rightarrow$ Reason is correct.

If $f(x) = x + 3\sin x$, then it is non-periodic and $\sin x$ is periodic, and $\sin[(2\pi + x) + 3\sin(2\pi + x)] = \sin[2\pi + x + 3\sin x] = \sin(x + 3\sin x)$

$\Rightarrow$ sin $(x + 3 \sin x)$ is periodic with period 2 .
$\Rightarrow$ Assertion is correct, but it is not concluded from reason.

7. (c) If a function is defined on a closed interval, and then it attains its greatest and least values only when it is continuous, e.g., $y = \begin{cases} \tan x; x\in[0,2) \\ 0; x=0 \end{cases}$ is defined on $\left[0,\frac{\pi}{2}\right]$, but does not attains its greatest value as it discontinuous. Thus reason is in correct. Also if a function is continuous and defined on a closed interval, then its range = co-domain will be a closed interval. Thus assertion is correct.

8. (d) Clearly, reason is correct.
e.g., $y = \tan x$ is increasing but not continuous, however, assertion is incorrect as it true only when $f(x)$ is continuous.

9. (b) Clearly, reason is correct as cos θ is a periodic function, and hence, repeats its maximum value 1 infinitely many times in (k, ∞).
i.e., in continuous domain.
Let $f(x) = xe^{[x]} + 2x^2 - x$ for $x \in (-1, \infty)$
Clearly, $g(0) = 0$
$\Rightarrow \cos(f(0)) = \cos 0 = 1 \Rightarrow \cos(xe^{[x]} + 2x^2 - x)$ attains its maximum value 1 in $(-1, \infty)$.
But in reason cos θ is continuous for $\theta \in (k, \infty)$, where as $f(x) = \cos(xe^{[x]} + 2x^2 - x)$ is discontinuous in $x \in (-1, \infty)$

10. (c) $f(x) = \begin{cases} \sin x; x \neq n\pi; n\in\mathbb{Z} \\ 2; \text{otherwise} \end{cases}$ and $f(x) = \begin{cases} x^2+1; x\neq 0,2 \\ 4; x=0 \\ 5; x=2 \end{cases}$

$$\Rightarrow f(f(x)) = \begin{cases} (f(x))^2+1; f(x)\neq 0,2 \\ 4 \quad ; f(x)=0 \\ 5; \ f(x)=2 \end{cases}$$

$$\Rightarrow f(f(x)) = \begin{cases} \sin^2 x+1; x\neq n\pi \\ 5 \quad ; x=n\pi \end{cases}$$

$\Rightarrow$ Reason is incorrect.
Now, $\lim\limits_{x\to 0} gof(x) = \lim\limits_{x\to 0}\left(\sin^2 x+1\right) = 1$
$\Rightarrow$ Assertion is correct

11. (a) $y + \cos x = \sin x$
$\Rightarrow y = \sin x - \cos x$

$$\Rightarrow y = \sqrt{2}\left[\sin x.\frac{1}{\sqrt{2}} - \cos x.\frac{1}{\sqrt{2}}\right]$$

$$\Rightarrow y = \sqrt{2}\left[\sin\left(x-\frac{\pi}{4}\right)\right]$$

$\therefore$ Range of $y = \left[-\sqrt{2}, \sqrt{2}\right]$, Also reason is correct and Explains the assertion.

12. (d) $f(x) = 4^x + 2^x + 4^{-x} + 2^{-x} + 3 = \left(2^x + \frac{1}{2^x}\right) + \left(4^x + \frac{1}{4^x}\right) + 3$
$= y + y^2 - 2 + 3 = y^2 + y + 1$
Now $y = 2^x + \frac{1}{2^x} \in [2, \infty)\ \forall\ x \in \mathbb{R}$

$$\Rightarrow y^2 + y + 1 = \left(y+\frac{1}{2}\right)^2 + \frac{3}{4} \geq \left(2+\frac{1}{2}\right)^2 + \frac{3}{4} \geq \frac{28}{4} = 7$$

$\Rightarrow$ Range $f(x) = [7, \infty)$.
$\Rightarrow$ Assertion is incorrect, also is correct.

13. (c) Reason is incorrect, even degree polynomial is even only when each term contains even power of x, however, assertion is correct as for even degree polynomial.
$f(x) = a_0 x^n + a_1 x^{n-1} + a_2 x^{n-2} + \ldots + a_{n-1} x + a_n$
$f(-\infty) = f(\infty) = \pm\infty$ is finite and $f(0) = a_n$
$\Rightarrow f(x)$ is non-injective.

14. (a) If $f(x) = a_0 x^n + a_1 x^{n-1} + a_2 x^{n-2} + \ldots + a_{n-1} x + a_n$ is an even degree polynomial, then $f(-\infty) = f(\infty) = \pm\infty$ and $f(0)$ is finite
$\Rightarrow f(x)$ is non-injective $\Rightarrow f(x)$ is non-invertible

15. (c) $f(x) = x^3 + x^2 f'(1) + xf''(2) + f'''(3)\ \forall\ x \in \mathbb{R}$ ...(i)
$\Rightarrow f'(x) = 3x^2 + 2xf'(1) + f''(2)$ ...(ii)
$\Rightarrow f''(x) = 6x + 2f'(1)$ ...(iii)
$\Rightarrow f'''(x) = 6 \quad \Rightarrow f'''(3) = 6$ ...(iv)
And from (iii), $f'''(2) = 12 + 2f'(1)$ ...(v)
Using (iv) and (v) in (i), we have $f(x) = x^3 + x^2 f'(1) + 12x + 2f'(1)x + 6$
$\Rightarrow f'(x) = 3x^2 + 2xf'(1) + 12 + 2f'(1)$
$\Rightarrow f'(1) = 3 + 2f'(1) + 12 + 2f'(1)$
$\Rightarrow f'(1) = -5$
$\therefore f(x) = x^3 - 5x^2 + 12x - 10x + 6$
$\Rightarrow f(0) = 6$
$\Rightarrow f(2) - f(1) = [7 - 5(3) + 12(1) + 10(1)]$
$\Rightarrow f(2) - f(1) = -6, f(0) = 6$
$\Rightarrow$ Assertion is correct, reason is incorrect.

16. (a) $A = \{1, 2, 3, \ldots, 2n\}$, then the self invertible functions have pairs of the form (a, b) and (b, a) and not of the for (a, a) {According to question $f(i) \neq i$}, then such ordered pairs can't be selected $\left[{}^{2n}C_2 \times {}^{2n-2}C_2 \times \ldots \times {}^2C_2\right] \times \frac{1}{n!}$
Also the reason is correct and explains the assertion correctly.

17. (b) $f(x)$, $f(x)$ and $h(x)$ are even and odd functions respectively.
$f(f(h(2)) + f(h(f(7))) + h(f(f(2))$
$= f(g)(4)) + f(h(9)) + h(f(3))$
$= f(7) + f(12) + h(0)$
$= 9 - 9 = 0$
$\Rightarrow$ Assertion is correct. Also reason is correct, but does not explain the assertion.

18. (c) $f(x) = \frac{7}{2+9a^x}; a > 0 \neq 1, a^x \in (0, \infty)$
$\Rightarrow 9a^x \in (0, \infty)$
$\Rightarrow 2 + 9a^x \in (2, \infty) \quad \Rightarrow \frac{1}{2+9a^x} \in \left(0, \frac{1}{2}\right)$
$\Rightarrow \frac{7}{2+9a^x} \in \left(0, \frac{7}{2}\right)$
which contains exactly 3 integer solutions 1, 2 and 3.
$\Rightarrow$ Assertion is correct.

If the end point of range are α, $\beta \in \mathbb{Z}$ and range is (α, β), then the number of integer solutions will be $(\beta - 1) - \alpha]$.

$\therefore$ Reason is incorrect.

19. (a) $f(x) + f(5x + y) + 6xy = f(6x - y) + 2x^2 + 1 \; \forall \; x, y \in \mathbb{R}$

Replacing y by $\frac{x}{2}$, we get $f(x) + f\left(\frac{11}{2}x\right) + 3x^2 = f\left(\frac{11}{2}x\right) + 2x^2 + 1$

$\Rightarrow f(x) = -x^2 + 1 \qquad \Rightarrow f(5) = -24$

$\Rightarrow$ Assertion as well as reason both are correct and reason explain the assertion correctly.

SECTION–VI (COMPREHENSION TYPE)

A:

1. (b) Perimeter of rectangle $DEFG = 2x + 2DE$ ...(i)

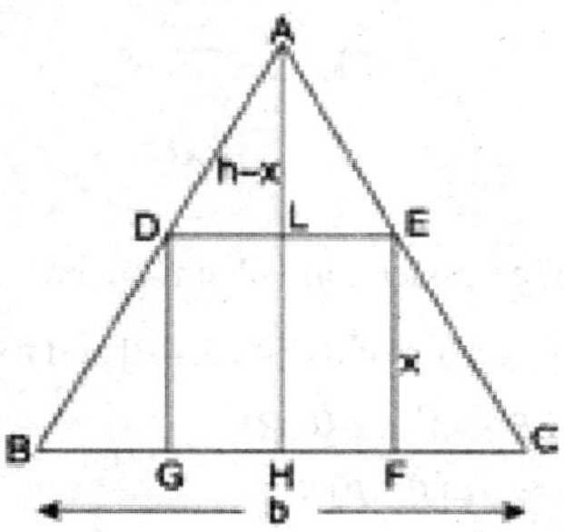

In similar Δ's ADL and ABH, $\frac{AL}{AH} = \frac{DL}{BH} \Rightarrow \frac{h-x}{h} = \frac{DL}{\frac{b}{2}}$

$\Rightarrow DL = \frac{b(h-x)}{2h} \qquad DE = 2DL = \frac{b(h-x)}{h}$ ...(ii)

Using (ii) in (i), we get perimeter of rectangle $= 2x + \frac{2b(h-x)}{h} = 2\left\{x + \frac{b(h-x)}{h}\right\}$

2. (c) Area of rectangle $DEFG = x.DE = x\left\{\frac{b(h-x)}{h}\right\}$

3. (c) Perimeter = Area (numerically)

$\Rightarrow 2\left|x + \frac{b(h-x)}{h}\right| = \left|\frac{xb}{h}(h-x)\right|$

$\Rightarrow 2\left|x + \frac{b(h-x)}{h}\right| = \frac{xb}{h}(h-x) \qquad (\because h > x)$

Given, $b = 2$, $h = 4$

$\Rightarrow 2\left|x + \frac{2(4-x)}{4}\right| = \frac{2x}{4}(4-x)$

$\Rightarrow \left|x + 2 - \frac{x}{2}\right| = \frac{x}{4}(4-x) \Rightarrow \left|\frac{x}{2} + 2\right| = \frac{x}{4}(4-x)$

$\Rightarrow (x + 4) = \pm\frac{x}{2}(4 - x)$

$\Rightarrow x^2 - 2x + 8 = 0$ or $x^2 - 6x - 8 = 0$

First quadratic equation has no real root, while second one has roots $\frac{6 \pm \sqrt{68}}{2} = 3 \pm \frac{\sqrt{68}}{2}$ among which one is negative and other is greater than h (= 4).

$\therefore$ No real value of x is possible

B:

4. (c) $f: [0, 2] \to [0, 2]$ is a bijective function, given by $f(x) = ax^2 + bx + c$, which is continuous, and hence, either $f(0) = 2, f(2) = 0$ or

$f(0) = 0, f(2) = 2$

For later case, $c = 0$ which is against the given condition that a, b, c are non-zero.

Thus, $f(2) = 0$

5. (a) From above, $f(0) = 2, f(2) = 0$

$\Rightarrow c = 2, 4a + 2b + 2 = 0$

$\Rightarrow 2a + b = -1, \alpha\beta = -\frac{\ }{a} \; \alpha + \beta = \frac{\ }{a}$

$\Rightarrow \alpha + \beta = \frac{2a+1}{a} = 2 + \frac{1}{a} \Rightarrow \alpha = 2, \beta = \frac{1}{a}$

6. (c) $ax^2 + bx + c = 0$

$\Rightarrow a(x-2)\left(x - \frac{1}{a}\right) = 0$

$\Rightarrow ax^2 - (2a + 1)x + 2 = 0$

$\therefore f(2) = 0$ and $f(0) = 2$

$\Rightarrow f(x)$ is a decreasing function $\forall \; x \in [0, 2]$

$\Rightarrow f'(x) = 2ax - (2a + 1) \le 0 \; \forall \; x \in [0, 2]$

$\Rightarrow 2a(x - 1) \le 1 \; \forall \; x \in [0, 2]$

Now, $x \in [0, 2] \qquad \Rightarrow -1 \le x - 1 \le 1$

$\Rightarrow - | \le 2a < 0$ or $| \le 2a$

$\Rightarrow a \in \left[\frac{-1}{2}, 0\right)$ or $a \in \left[\frac{1}{2}, \infty\right)$

$\Rightarrow a \ne -\frac{7}{2}$

C:

$f(2 - x) = f(2 + x)$ ......(i)

$f(20 - x) = f(x) = \forall \; x \in \mathbb{R}$ ..... (ii)

$f(2 - x) = f(2 + x)$

$f(x)$ is symmetric about the line $x = 2$

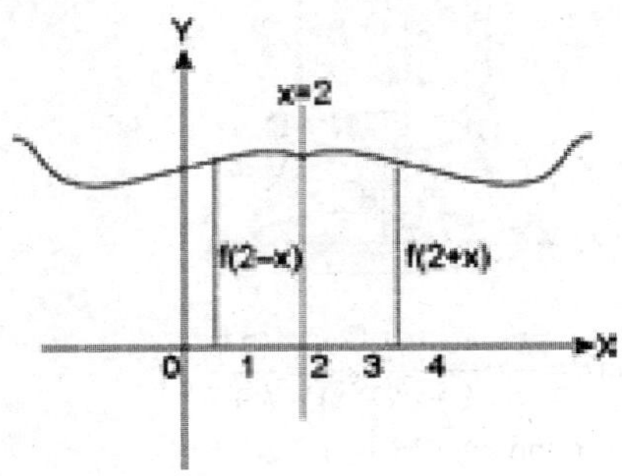

$f(2-x) = f(20-(2-x))$ ..[using (ii)]

$= f(18+x)$

$f(2+x) = f(18+x)$ …. [Using (i)]

$\Rightarrow f(x) = f(x+16)$

$\Rightarrow f(x)$ is a function periodic with period 16.

Also $f(2-x) = f(2+x) = f(0) = f(4)$ and the period of $f(x)$ is 16

$\Rightarrow f(0) = f(4) = f(20) = f(36)$

$= \ldots\ldots = f(4+(n-1)(16))$ where $4+(n-1)(16) \le 170$

$\Rightarrow 16n - 12 \le 170$

$\Rightarrow 16n \le 182$

$\Rightarrow n \le 11\frac{3}{8}$

$\therefore f(x) = 5$ for $x \in \{0, 4, 20, \ldots, 176\}$, i.e., 12 value of x.

7. (b)

8. (a) $\because f(x)$ is symmetrical about $x = 2$ and and $f(x)$ is periodic with period 16.

$\Rightarrow f(2) = f(2+16) = f(18)$

$\Rightarrow f(x)$ is also symmetrical about $x = 18$

Also $f(x-2) = f(2-x)$

$\Rightarrow f((20-x)-2) = f(2-(20-x))$

$\Rightarrow f(18-x) = f(x-18)$

9. (c) $f(-2) \ne f(6)$

$\Rightarrow f(-2+8) \ne f(-2)$

$\Rightarrow$ 8 can't be the periodic with period $f(x)$.

$\Rightarrow f(x)$ can't be periodic with fundamental period of $f(x)$.

D:

Clearly, $f(x) =$

$$\begin{cases} \text{Area of cross section of frustum for } x \in [0, R] \\ \text{Area of cross-section of cylinder for } x \in [R, 3R] \\ \text{Area of cross-section of hemi-sperial cross-section for } x \in [3R, 4R] \end{cases}$$

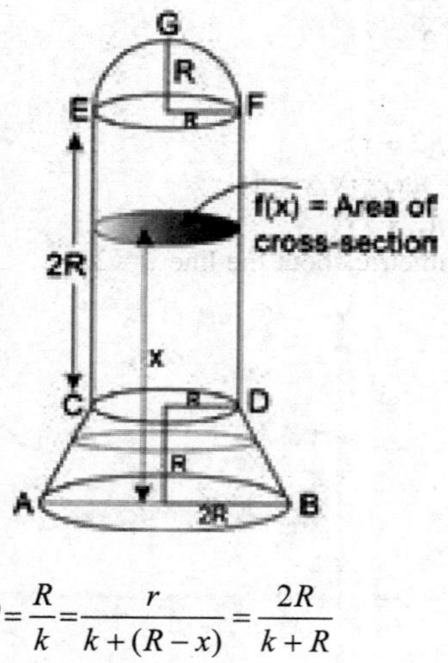

$\Rightarrow \tan\theta = \frac{R}{k} = \frac{r}{k+(R-x)} = \frac{2R}{k+R}$

$\Rightarrow k = R$ and $r = (2R-x)$

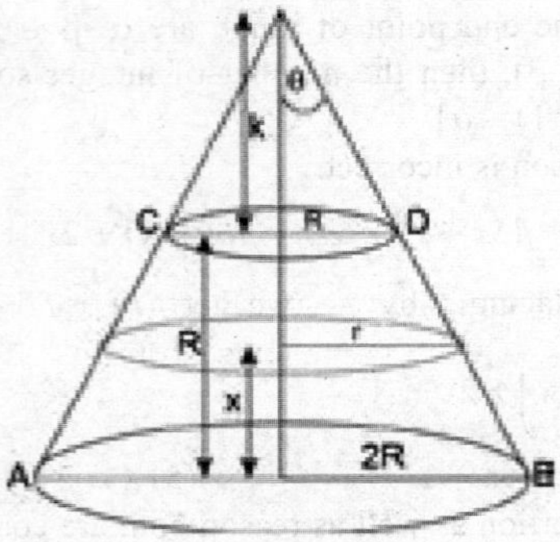

$\therefore$ Area of cross-section of frustum $= \pi r^2 = \pi(2R-x)^2$

For hemi-sphere $r = \sqrt{R^2 - \lambda^2}$;

$\Rightarrow r = \sqrt{R^2 - (x-3R)^2}$

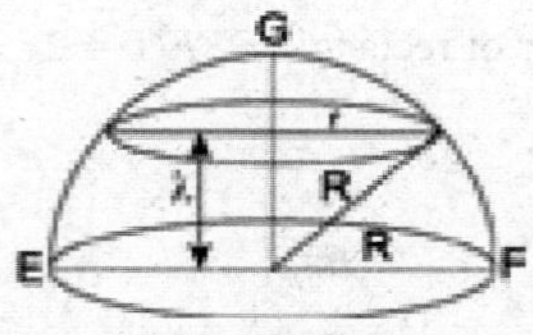

$\therefore$ Area of cross-section of hemi-sphere $= \pi[R^2 - (x-3R)^2]$

Clearly domain of $f(x) = [0, 4R]$ and $f(x)$ is given by $f(x)$

$$= \begin{cases} \pi(2R-x)^2; x \in [0, R] \\ \pi R^2; x \in [R, 3R] \\ \pi[R^2 - (x-3R)^2]; x \in [3R, 4R] \end{cases}$$

$\therefore f(x)$ is a decreasing and continuous function on $[0, 4R]$

$\Rightarrow$ Range of $f(x) = [f(4R), f(0)] = [0, 4\pi R^2]$

Clearly $f(x)$ is one–one on the intervals $[0, R] \cup [3R, 4R]$

10. (b)

11. (a)

12. (a)

13. (d)

E:

14. (d) Clearly, figure (ii) can be obtained in the following steps.

Step 1: By replacing the function $f(x)$ on x-axis, i.e., $y = f(x)$ changes to $y = -f(x)$.

Step 2: Now lifting the function obtained by 1 unit above the x-axis, i.e., $y = 1 - f(x)$.

Step 3: Shifting the function obtained in step (2) by 1 unit towards left side, i.e., $y = 1 - f(x+1)$.

15. (b) If $f(x)$ is made such that its domain is [1, 3] and range is [0, 1] that is as shown below.

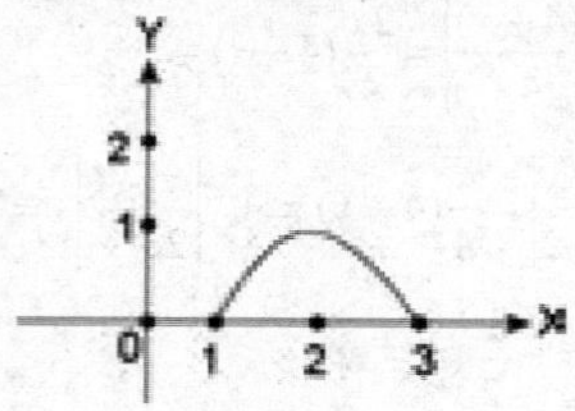

The above graph can be obtained by shifting $f(x)$ by 1 unit towards right side to obtain $y = f(x - 1)$

16. **(c)** Figure (iii) can be obtained by shifting the graph of $y = f(x)$ towards left side by 2 units to obtained the function $y = f(x + 2)$.

17. **(d)** **(i)** For domain of $f(-x)$; $-x \in [0, 2]$

$\Rightarrow$ $x \in [-2, 0]$

$\therefore$ Domain $f(-x) = [-2, 0]$ and Range is same, i.e., $[0, 1]$

(ii) For $y = f(x) - 1$; Domain $= [0, 2]$ and Range $= [-1, 0]$

(iii) For $y = f(x) + 2$; Domain $= [0, 2]$ and Range $= [2, 3]$

(iv) For $y = -f(x + 1) + 1$; $(x + 1) \in [0, 2]$

$\Rightarrow$ $x \in [-1, 1]$ and Range $= [0, 1]$

F:

$C = \{(a, b, c)$: a, b, c are three consecutive even whole numbers$\}$

$= \{(2n - 2, 2n, 2n + 2); n \in \mathbb{N}\}$

$*$: $C \times C \rightarrow C$ is given by $(a, b, c) * (d, e, f) = (a + d, b + e - 2, c + f - 4)$

Closureness: Let $(a, b, c) \equiv (2n - 2, 2n, 2n + 2)$ and $(d, e, f) = (2m - 2, 2m, 2m + 2)$

$\therefore$ $(a, b, c) * (d, e, f) = (2(m + n) - 4, 2(n + m) - 2, 2(m + n))$

$= [2(m + n - 1) - 2, 2(m + n - 1), 2(m + n - 1) + 2] \in C$

$\Rightarrow$ C is closed w.r.t. *

Commutative: $(a, b, c) * (d, e, f) = (a + d, b + e - 2, c + f - 4)$ and $(d, e, f) * (a, b, c)$

$= (d + a, e + b - 2, f + c - 4)$

Clearly $(a, b, c) * (d, e, f) = (d, e, f) * (a, b, c)$

$\therefore$ (*) is commutative in C

Associativity: Let $(a, b, c), (d, e, f), (g, h, i) \in C$, then $(a, b, c) * ((d, e, f) * (g, h, i))$

$= (a, b, c) * (d + g, e + h - 2, f + i - 4)$

$= (a + d + g, b + e + h - 4, c + f + i - 8)$ and $[(a, b, c) * (d, e, f)] * (g, h, i)$

$= (a + d, b + e - 2, c + f - 4) * (g, h, i)$

$= (a + d + g, b + e + h - 4, c + f + i - 8)$

$\Rightarrow$ * is associative in C.

Existence of identity: Clearly $(0, 2, 4) \in C$ and let $(a, b, c) \in C$, then $(a, b, c) * (0, 2, 4)$

$= (0, 2, 4) * (a, b, c)$

$= (a + 0, b + 2 - 2, c + 4 - 4)$

$= (a, b, c)$

$\Rightarrow$ $(0, 2, 4)$ is an identity element in C w.r.t. *

Existence of inverse: Let $(a, b, c) \in C$, then it is not necessary that for some (d, e, f).

$(a, b, c) * (d, e, f) = (0, 2, 4)$ as if it holds, then $(a + d, b + e - 2, c + f - 4) = (0, 2, 4)$

$\Rightarrow$ $a + d = 0, b + e = 4, c + f = 8$

$\Rightarrow$ $a = d = 0, b = e = 2, c = f = 4$, i.e., $(0, 2, 4)$ is the only element which is the inverse of itself.

18. **(a), (d)**

19. **(a)**

20. **(b)**

21. **(c)**

G: $A = \{2, 4, 6, 8, 12\}$ and $B = \{3, 7, 11\}$

22. **(b)** Each element of A has three options, i.e., 3, 7 and 11.

$\therefore$ Total number of functions $= (3)^6$.

23. **(c)** Pre-image of 3 can be defined ${}^6C_2$ ways and remaining 4 elements can be associated with 7 or 11, i.e., in two ways.

$\therefore$ Total number of possible functions $= {}^6C_2 \times (2)^4 = 15 \times 16 = 240$.

24. **(a)** Each of the elements of A has two possible images, i.e., 3 and 11.

$\therefore$ No. of possible functions $= (2)^6$

25. **(b)** x_1, x_2 can be selected in ${}^6C_2$ ways x_3, x_4, x_5 can be selected in ${}^4C_3$ ways.

x_6 can be selected in ${}^1C_1$ way.

$\therefore$ Number of possible functions $= {}^6C_2 \times {}^4C_3 \times {}^1C_1 = 15 \times 4 \times 1 = 60$.

26. **(c)** $\because f(2) = 7$ and each of 4, 6, 8, 10, 12 has three possibilities of association, i.e., 2, 3, or 11.

$\therefore$ Number of functions $= (3)^5$.

SECTION–VII (COLUMN MATCHING TYPE)

1. **(i) → (b); (ii) → (b); (iii) → (b); (iv) → (c)**

(i) Fundamental period of $\sin^{-1}(\sin x)$ is 2π

$\therefore$ Fundamental period of $\sin^{-1}(\sin k_x) = \dfrac{2\pi}{|k|} = \dfrac{\pi}{2}$ (given)

$\Rightarrow$ $|k| = 4$ $\qquad \Rightarrow$ $k = \pm 4$

$\therefore$ $(i) \rightarrow (b)$

(ii) $f(x) = \tan^{-1} x + \sin^{-1} x + \sec^{-1} x$

Domain of $f(x) = (-\infty, \infty) \cap [-1, 1] \cap \{(-\infty, -1] \cup [1, \infty)\} = \{-1, 1\}$; which contains exactly two points

$\therefore$ (ii) → (b)

(iii) $f(x) = \sin\left(\dfrac{\pi x}{2}\right).\text{ccsec}\left(\dfrac{\pi x}{2}\right)$

$\Rightarrow$ $f(x) = \begin{cases} 1 \text{ for } \text{—} \neq \\ \text{Not defined at —} \end{cases}$

$\Rightarrow$ $f(x) = \begin{cases} 1 \text{ at } x \neq 2n; x \in \mathbb{Z} \\ \text{Not defined at } x = 2n; n \in \mathbb{Z} \end{cases}$

$\Rightarrow$ $f(x)$ is periodic with period 2

$\therefore$ (iii) → (b)

(iv) $f(x) = \cos^{-1}[5x]$

For function to be defined $[5x] \in \{-1, 0, 1\}$

$\therefore$ Range of $f(x) = \{\cos^{-1}(-1), \cos^{-1}(0), \cos^{-1}(1)\}$

$= \left\{\pi, \dfrac{\pi}{2}, 0\right\} = \{a, b, c\}$

$\Rightarrow$ $a + b + c = \dfrac{3\pi}{2}$ $\qquad \Rightarrow$ $k = 3$

$\therefore$ (iv) → (c)

2. (i) → (b); (ii) → (b); (iii) → (d); (iv) → (b)

(i) $x^2 - 3x + \sin^{-1}(\sin 2) > 0$

Let $2 = \pi - \theta;\ \theta \in \left(0, \frac{\pi}{2}\right)$

$\Rightarrow x^2 - 3x + \sin^{-1}(\sin(\pi - \theta)) > 0$

$\Rightarrow x^2 - 3x + \sin^{-1}(\sin \theta) > 0$

$\Rightarrow x^2 - 3x + \theta > 0$ as $\theta \in \left(0, \frac{\pi}{2}\right)$

$\Rightarrow x^2 - 3x + (\pi - 2) > 0$

$\Rightarrow x \in \mathbb{R} - \left(\frac{3-\sqrt{17-4\pi}}{2}, \frac{3+\sqrt{17-4\pi}}{2}\right)$

⇒ Positive integer values of x satisfying the given inequality are belonging to set {3, 4, 5, 6,….,}.

⇒ Smallest positive integer value of $x = 3$

∴ (i) → (b)

(ii) $2[x] = x + 2\{x\}$

$\Rightarrow 2[x] = [x] + \{x\} + 2\{x\}$

$\Rightarrow [x] = 3\{xy\} \qquad \Rightarrow \{x\} = \frac{[x]}{3}$

$\Rightarrow [x] \in \{0, 1, 2\}$

$\Rightarrow x \in \left\{0, \frac{4}{3}, \frac{8}{3}\right\} \qquad$ ⇒ There are 3 solutions

(ii) → (b)

(iii) $x^2 + y^2 = 1$

Let $x = \cos\theta$, $y = \sin\theta$, then $x + y = (\sin\theta + \cos\theta)$ having its maximum value $= \sqrt{2}$

⇒ Maximum value of $(x + y)^2 = 2$.

∴ (iii) → (d)

(iv) $f\left(x+\frac{1}{2}\right) + f\left(x-\frac{1}{2}\right) = f(x)\ \forall \in \mathbb{R}$ ……(i)

Replacing x by $x + \frac{1}{2}$, we get $f(x + 1) + f(x)$

$= f\left(x+\frac{1}{2}\right)$ …. (2)

Equation (1) + (2) given, $f(x + 1) + f\left(x-\frac{1}{2}\right) = 0$

$\Rightarrow f\left(x-\frac{1}{2}\right) = -f(x+1) \Rightarrow f(x) = -f\left(x+\frac{3}{2}\right)$

$\Rightarrow f(x) = -\left[-f\left(x+\frac{3}{2}+\frac{3}{2}\right)\right]$

$\Rightarrow f(x) = f(x + 3)$

⇒ $f(x)$ is periodic with period 3.

∴ (iv) → (b)

3. (i) → (b); (ii) → (a); (iii) → (c); (iv) → (d)

(i) Domain of $f(x)$ is $[-2, 2]$ for domain of $f(|x| + 1)$, $-2 \le |x| + 1 \le 2$

$\Rightarrow -3 \le |x| \le 1 \qquad \Rightarrow x \in [-1, 1]$

∴ (i) (b)

(ii) $f(x) = \dfrac{\sin^{-1}x + \cos^{-1}x + \tan^{-1}x}{\pi}$

Domain of $f(x) = [-1, 1]$

$f(x) = \dfrac{\frac{\pi}{2} + \tan^{-1}x}{\pi} = \frac{1}{2} + \frac{1}{\pi}\tan^{-1}x$, which is an increasing function.

⇒ Range of $f(x) = [f(-1), f(1)]$

$= \left[\frac{1}{2} + \frac{1}{\pi}\tan^{-1}(-1), \frac{1}{2} + \frac{1}{\pi}\tan^{-1}(1)\right] = \left[\frac{1}{4}, \frac{3}{4}\right]$

(ii) → (a)

(iii) $f(x) = 3|\sin x| - 4|\cos x|$

Clearly, $f(x)$ is periodic with period π, so, it is sufficient to find the range for $x \in [0, \pi]$

$$\Rightarrow f(x) = \begin{cases} 3\sin x - 4\cos x; 0 \le x \le \frac{\pi}{2} \\ 3\sin x + 4\cos x; \frac{\pi}{2} < x \le \pi \end{cases}$$

$$\Rightarrow f(x) = \begin{cases} 5\sin(x-\theta); x \in \left[0, \frac{\pi}{2}\right] \\ 5\sin(x+\theta); x \in \left[\frac{\pi}{2}, \pi\right] \end{cases}; \text{ where}$$

$\theta = \tan^{-1}\left(\frac{4}{3}\right)$ and $\theta \in \left(\frac{\pi}{4}, \frac{\pi}{2}\right)$

$$\Rightarrow f(x) = \begin{cases} 5\sin(x-\theta); x \in \left[0, \frac{\pi}{2}\right] \\ 5\sin(x+\theta); x \in \left[\frac{\pi}{2}, \pi\right] \end{cases}$$

Now $\frac{-\pi}{2} < -\theta < (x-\theta) < \frac{\pi}{2} - \theta < \frac{\pi}{4}$ for $x \in \left[0, \frac{\pi}{2}\right]$

and $\frac{3\pi}{4} < \frac{\pi}{2} + \theta < (x+\theta) < \pi + \theta < \frac{3\pi}{2}$ for $x \in \left[\frac{\pi}{2}, \pi\right]$

⇒ $5\sin(x - \theta)$ ↑ for $x \in \left[0, \frac{\pi}{2}\right]$ and $5\sin(x + \theta)$ ↓ for $x \in \left[\frac{\pi}{2}, \pi\right]$

$$\Rightarrow f(x) \in \begin{cases} \left[-5\sin\theta, 5\sin\left(\frac{\pi}{2}-\theta\right)\right] \text{ for } x \in \left[0, \frac{\pi}{2}\right] \\ \left[5\sin(\pi+\theta), 5\sin\left(\frac{\pi}{2}+\theta\right)\right] \text{ for } x \in \left[\frac{\pi}{2}, \pi\right] \end{cases}$$

$$\Rightarrow f(x) \in \begin{cases} [-4, 3] \text{ for } x \in \left[0, \frac{\pi}{2}\right] \\ [-4, -3] \text{ for } x \in \left[\frac{\pi}{2}, \pi\right] \end{cases}$$

⇒ Range of $f(x) = [-4, 3]$

∴ (iii) → (c)

(iv) $f(x) = (\sin^{-1}x).\sin x$

$f(x)$ is defined for $x \in [-1, 1]$

$$f'(x) = \begin{cases} (\sin^{-1})\cos x + \dfrac{\sin x}{\sqrt{1-x^2}} \text{ for } x \in (-1, 1) \end{cases}$$

In (–1, 1), cos x, $\frac{1}{\sqrt{1-x^2}} > 0$ and in (–1, 0], sin x, $\sin^{-1} x \le 0$ and in [0, 1), sin x, $\sin^{-1} x \ge 0$

$\Rightarrow f'(x) \le 0$ for $x \in (-1, 0]$ and $f'(x) \ge 0$ for $x \in [0, 1)$

$\Rightarrow f(x) \in \left[0, \frac{\pi}{2}\sin 1\right]$ for x [–1, 0] and $f(x) \in \left[0, \frac{\pi}{2}\sin 1\right]$ for $x \in [0, 1)$

$\Rightarrow$ Range of $f(x) = \left[0, \frac{\pi}{2}\sin 1\right]$

(iv) → (d)

4. (i) → (b); (ii) → (d); (iii) → (a); (iv) → (c) , (d)

$f(x) = \sin^{-1} x$, $f(x) = \cos^{-1} x$, $h(x) = \tan^{-1} x$

(i) $f(\sqrt{x}) + g(\sqrt{x}) = \frac{\pi}{2}$

$\Rightarrow \sin^{-1}\sqrt{x} + \cos^{-1}\sqrt{x} = \frac{\pi}{2}$ holds for $\sqrt{x} \in [-1, 1]$ but $\sqrt{x} \ge 0$

$\Rightarrow \sqrt{x} \in [0, 1] \quad \Rightarrow x \in [0, 1]$

∴ (i) → (b)

(ii) $f(x) + g\left(\sqrt{1-x^2}\right) = 0$

$\Rightarrow \sin^{-1} x + \cos^{-1}\sqrt{1-x^2} = 0$; x [–1, 1]

$\Rightarrow \sin^{-1} x = -\cos^{-1}\sqrt{1-x^2}$

$\Rightarrow x \in [-1, 0] \quad$ ∴ (ii) → (d)

(iii) $g\left(\frac{1-x^2}{1+x^2}\right) = 2h(x) \Rightarrow \cos^{-1}\left(\frac{1-x^2}{1+x^2}\right) = 2\tan^{-1} x$

$$\Rightarrow x \ge 0, \text{i.e.,} x \in [0, \infty) \text{ as } 2\tan^{-1} x = \begin{cases} \cos^{-1}\left(\frac{1-x^2}{1+x^2}\right); x \ge 0 \\ -\cos^{-1}\left(\frac{1-x^2}{1+x^2}\right); x < 0 \end{cases}$$

∴ (iii) → (a)

(iv) $h(x) + h(1) = h\left(\frac{1+x}{1-x}\right)$

$\Rightarrow \tan^{-1} x + \frac{\pi}{4} = \tan^{-1}\left(\frac{1+x}{1-x}\right)$

$\Rightarrow \tan\left(\frac{\pi}{4} + \tan^{-1} x\right) = \frac{1+x}{1-x}$

$\Rightarrow \frac{1+x}{1-x} \; \frac{1+x}{1-x}$; which is true $\forall x \in \mathbb{R} - \{1\}$

$\Rightarrow$ Then equation holds for $x \in (-\infty, 1)$ as well as for $x \in [-1, 0]$

∴ (iv) → (c), (d)

5. (i) → (d); (ii) → (c); (iii) → (b); (iv) → (a), (d)

(i) $sgn(\{x\}) = |1 - x| \quad \Rightarrow |1-x| = \begin{cases} 0 \text{ for } \{x\} = 0 \\ 1 \text{ for } \{x\} \in (0,1) \end{cases}$

$\Rightarrow |1-x| = \begin{cases} 0 \text{ for } x \in \mathbb{Z} \\ 1 \text{ for } x \notin \mathbb{Z} \end{cases}$

$\Rightarrow |1-x| = \begin{cases} 0 \text{ for } x = 1 \\ \text{No solution for } x \ne 1 \end{cases}$

$\Rightarrow x = 1$ is the only solution

∴ (i) → (d)

(ii) $f(x) = \sin^{-1}\left(\frac{x^2-2x}{3}\right) + \sqrt{[x]+[-x]}$

For domain, $\frac{x^2-2x}{3} \in [-1, 1]$

$\Rightarrow x^2 - 2x \in [-3, 3]$

$\Rightarrow x^2 - 2x - 3 \ge 0$ and $x^2 - 2x - 3 \le 0$

$\Rightarrow x \in \mathbb{R} \cap [-1, 3] = [-1, 3]$ .....(i)

Also $[x] + [-x] \ge 0$ but $[x] + [-x] = \begin{cases} -1 \text{ for } x \notin \mathbb{Z} \\ 0 \text{ for } x \in \mathbb{Z} \end{cases}$

$\Rightarrow x \in \mathbb{Z}$ .....(ii)

∴ From (i) and (ii), domain of $f(x) = \{-1, 0, 2, 3\}$, which contains 5 elements.

∴ (ii) → (c)

(iii) $f(x + 2) = f(x - 2) \; \forall x \in \mathbb{R}$

$\Rightarrow f(x + 4) = f(x) \; \forall x \in \mathbb{R}$

$\Rightarrow f(x)$ is periodic with period 4

∴ $f(8) = 0 \quad \Rightarrow f(4) = 0$

But $f(x)$ has exactly 3 roots in the interval [4, 8], implies $f(x)$ also has a root at $x = 4 + a$, for some $a \in (0, 4)$ as shown below.

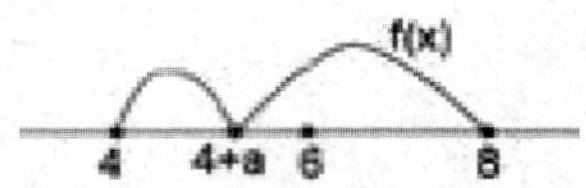

Since, $f(x)$ is periodic with period 4.

$\Rightarrow$ In [–8, 12], $f(x) = 0$, would have roots given by the set $\{-8, -8 + a, -4, -4 + a, 0, a, 4, 4 + a, 8, 8 + a, 12\}$ i.e., $11 = k + 7$ (given)

$\Rightarrow k = 4$

∴ (iii) → (b)

(iv) $f(x) = \frac{1}{x-1}$ and $f\left(\frac{1}{x-1}\right)$

$f(x)$ is not defined at $x = 1$

$\Rightarrow f\left(\frac{1}{x-1}\right)$ is not defined at $x = 1$ and where $\frac{1}{x-1} = 1$ i.e., at $x = 2$

∴ $f\left(\frac{1}{x-1}\right)$ is not defined at $x = 1$ and $x = 2$

∴ (iv) → (a), (d)

6. (i) → (c); (ii) → (a); (iii) → (a), (b); (iv) → (d)

(i) $f(x) = \sqrt{-2\sqrt{2}(\cos\pi x) - \sqrt{3} - 1}$ is defined for $2\sqrt{2}\cos\pi x + \sqrt{3} + 1 \le 0$

$\Rightarrow \cos\pi x \le -\frac{(\sqrt{3}+1)}{2\sqrt{2}} = -\left[\frac{\sqrt{3}}{2}.\frac{1}{\sqrt{2}} + \frac{1}{2}.\frac{1}{\sqrt{2}}\right]$

$= -\left[\cos\left(\frac{\pi}{4} - \frac{\pi}{6}\right)\right]$

$\Rightarrow \cos \pi x \le -\cos\dfrac{\pi}{12} = \cos\dfrac{11\pi}{12}$

$\Rightarrow \pi x \in \left[(2n+1)\pi - \dfrac{\pi}{12}, (2n+1)\pi + \dfrac{\pi}{12}\right]$

$\Rightarrow x \in \left[(2n+1) - \dfrac{1}{2}, (2n+1) + \dfrac{1}{12}\right]; x \in \mathbb{Z}$

In particular, for n = 0, $x \in \left[\dfrac{11}{2}, \dfrac{13}{12}\right]$

$\therefore$ (i) → (c)

(ii) $\lim\limits_{x\to 1^-} \dfrac{3}{4}[x] + \dfrac{7}{8}\{x\} = L_1$

$\Rightarrow L_1 = \dfrac{3}{4}(0) + \dfrac{7}{8}\left(\lim\limits_{x\to 1^-}(x-0)\right) = \dfrac{7}{8}(1) = \dfrac{7}{8} > \dfrac{3}{4}$ but $< \dfrac{11}{12}, 1$

$\Rightarrow L_1 \in (0, 1)$

$\therefore$ (ii) → (a)

(iii) $\sqrt{\log_x(0.75)} < 1$ for domain, $x \in (0, 1)$ and $\log_x(0.75) < 1$

$\Rightarrow 0.75 > x$

$\Rightarrow x \in \left(0, \dfrac{3}{4}\right) \subset (0, 1)$ $\quad \therefore$ (iii) → (a), (b)

(iv) $\dfrac{|x-1|}{x+2} > 1$

For $x < -2$, $-(x-1) < (x+2)$

$\Rightarrow 2x > -1$

$\Rightarrow x > \dfrac{-1}{2}$; which is against the case condition.

For $-2 < x < 1$, $-(x-1) > x+2$

$\Rightarrow 2x < -1 \qquad \Rightarrow x < \dfrac{-1}{2}$

$\Rightarrow x \in \left(-2, \dfrac{-1}{2}\right)$ in this case. For $x \ge 1$; $x - 1 > x + 2$

$\Rightarrow -1 > 2$; which is an absurd

$\Rightarrow x \ngeq 1$

$\therefore$ If the given inequality holds, then x lies in $\left(-2, \dfrac{-1}{2}\right)$

$\therefore$ (iv) → (d)

SECTION–VIII (INTEGER TYPE)

1. $\left|\sqrt{x^2+x+3} - x\right| = q$ ......(i)

Case (i): If $x \le 0$, then $\sqrt{x^2+x+3} > x$

$\Rightarrow \left|\sqrt{x^2+x+3} - x\right| = \sqrt{x^2+x+3} - x$

Case (ii): If $x > 0$, then $\sqrt{x^2+x+3} > x$

If $x^2 + x + 3 > x^2$, i.e., if $x + 3 > 0$ which is true.

$\therefore \left|\sqrt{x^2+x+3} - x\right| = \sqrt{x^2+x+3} - x$

Thus equation (1) becomes, $\sqrt{x^2+x+3} - x = q$

$\Rightarrow \sqrt{x^2+x+3} = x + q \Rightarrow x^2 + x + 3 = x^2 + 2qx + q^2$

$\Rightarrow x = \dfrac{q^3-3}{1-2q} = \dfrac{q^2-a}{1-bq}\left(b \ne \dfrac{1}{q}\text{given}\right)$

$\Rightarrow a = 3, b = 2$

Also $y = \sqrt{x^2+x+3} = x + q = |x + q|$

$\left(\because \sqrt{x^2+x+3} > 0\right)$

$= \left|\dfrac{q^2-3}{1-2q} + q\right| = \left|\dfrac{q^2-q+3}{1-2q}\right| = \dfrac{q^2-q+3}{|1-2q|}$

$(\because q^2 - q + 3 > 0 \ \forall\ q)$

$= \dfrac{q^2-q+c}{|1-bq|}$ (given) $\Rightarrow c = 3$

$\therefore$ abc = (3)(2)(3) = $2(3)^2$

$\Rightarrow$ Number of positive integer divisors of (abc) = 2 × 3 = 6

2. $f(x) = {}^{15-x}C_{3x-1} + {}^{20-4x}C_{5x-7}$ .....(i)

$15 - x \ge 3x - 1 \ge 0$; $15 - x \ne 0$ ...(ii)

And $20 - 4x \ge 5x - 7 \ge 0$; $20 - 4x \ne 0$ ....(iii)

From (ii), $x \in \left[\dfrac{1}{3}, 4\right] \cap \left[\dfrac{7}{5}, 3\right]; x \in \mathbb{Z}$

$\Rightarrow x \in \left[\dfrac{7}{5}, 3\right]; x \in \mathbb{Z} \quad \Rightarrow x \in \{2, 3\}$

$\Rightarrow f(x) \in \{{}^{13}C_5 + {}^{12}C_3, {}^{12}C_8 + {}^{8}C_8\} = \{1507, 496\}$

$\Rightarrow$ Maximum value of $f(x) = 1507$

3. $f(x) = x^{99} + x^{79} - x^{69} + x^9 + 1$

When $f(x)$ is divided by $(x^3 - x)$, the remainder will be a quadratic polynomial $(ax^2 + bx + c)$ (say) = $f(x)$.

$\therefore f(x) = (x^3 - x).q(x) + (ax^2 + bx + c)$

$\Rightarrow f(0) = c = 1; f(1) = a + b + 1 = 3$

$\Rightarrow a + b = 2$ and $f(-1) = a - b + 1 = -1$

$\Rightarrow a - b = -2$

$\Rightarrow a = 0, b = 2, c = 1 \quad \Rightarrow f(x) = 2x + 1$

$\Rightarrow f(20) = 41$

4. $f\left(x + \dfrac{1}{x}\right) = x^3 + x^{-3} = x^3 + \dfrac{1}{x^3}$

$\because \left(x + \dfrac{1}{x}\right)^3 = x^3 + \dfrac{1}{x^3} + 3\left(x + \dfrac{1}{x}\right)$ for $x + \dfrac{1}{x} = 7$; 343

$= \left(x^3 + \dfrac{1}{x^3}\right) + 21$

$\Rightarrow x^3 + \dfrac{1}{x^3} = 322 \qquad \therefore f(7) = 322$

5. $\because f(x)$ is an even function

$\Rightarrow f(-x) = f(x) \qquad \therefore f(x) = f\left(\dfrac{x+1}{x+2}\right)$

$\Rightarrow$ Either $x = \dfrac{x+1}{x+2}$ or $\dfrac{x+1}{x+2} = -x$

$\Rightarrow (x + 1) = \pm (x^2 + 2x)$

$\Rightarrow x^2 + x - 1 = 0$ or $x = \dfrac{-3 \pm \sqrt{5}}{2}$

$\Rightarrow$ There are 4 distinct real values.

6. $f(x+y) = f(x).f(y)\ \forall\ x \in \mathbb{N}$ and $f(1) = 2$.
$\Rightarrow f(x+1) = f(x).f(1) \quad \Rightarrow f(x+1) = 2f(x)$ given
$\Rightarrow f(x+1) = 2f(x)\ \forall\ x \in \mathbb{N}$
$\therefore \sum_{n=1}^{10} f(x) = f(1) + f(2) + f(3) + ...+ f(10) = 2 + 2(2) + 2(2)^2 + 2(2)^3 + ...+ 2(2)^9 = 2 + (2)^2 + (2)^3 + (2)^4 + ...+ (2)^{10}$

$$= 2\left[\frac{(2)^{10}-1}{(2-1)}\right] = 2046$$

7. $f(x) = \left(4\cos^4 x - 2\cos 2x - \frac{1}{2}\cos 4x - x^9\right)^{\frac{1}{9}}$

$$= \left[4\cos^4 x - 2\left(2\cos^2 x - 1\right) - \frac{1}{2}\left(2\cos^2 2x - 1\right) - x^9\right]^{\frac{1}{9}}$$

$$= \left[4\cos^4 x - 4\cos^2 x + 2 + \left(-\right) - \left(4\cos^4 x + 1 - 4\cos^2 x\right) - x^9\right]$$

$$= \left[\frac{3}{2} - x^9\right]^{\frac{1}{9}}$$

$$\Rightarrow g(g(x)) = \left[\frac{3}{2} - (g(x))^9\right]^{\frac{1}{9}} = \left[\frac{3}{2} - \left(\frac{3}{2} - x^9\right)^9\right]^{\frac{1}{9}} = x$$

$\therefore f(f(2016)) = 2016$

8. $\dfrac{\sin x + \sin 3x + \sin 5x + \sin 7x}{\cos x + \cos 3x + \cos 5x + \cos 7x}$

$= \dfrac{2\sin 4x \cos x + 2\sin 4x \cos 3x}{2\cos 4x \cos x + 2\cos 4x \cos 3x} = \tan 4x$, which has period

$\dfrac{\pi}{4} = \dfrac{\pi}{k}$ (given)

$\Rightarrow k = 4$

9. Period of $\sin^{-1}(\sin x)$ is 2π
$\Rightarrow$ Period of $\sin^{-1}(\sin 4\pi x)$ is $\dfrac{2\pi}{4\pi} = \dfrac{1}{2} = k$
$\Rightarrow 4k = 2$

10. $f(x+p) = 1 + \{1 - 3f(x) + 3f^2(x) - f^3(x)\}^{1/3}$
$\Rightarrow f(x+p) = 1 + (1 - f(x)) = 2 - f(x)$
$\Rightarrow f(x+p) = 2 - [2 - f(x-p)]$
$\Rightarrow f(x+p) = f(x-p)$
$\Rightarrow f(x) = f(x+2p)$
$\Rightarrow$ Period of $f(x) = 2p = \lambda p$ (given)
$\Rightarrow \lambda = 2$

11. $f(x-1) + f(x+3) = f(x+1) + f(x+5)$
Replacing x by $x+2$, we get $f(x+1) + f(x+5) = f(x+3) + f(x+7)$
Adding above two equations, we get $f(x-1) = f(x+7)$
$\Rightarrow f(x) = f(x+8)$
$\Rightarrow$ Period of $f(x) = 8$

12. $f(x) = \dfrac{x^3}{3} + (m-1)x^2 + (m+5) + 11$ and $f^{-1}(x)$ exists only for k integer values of m.

$f'(x) = x^2 + 2(m-1)x + (m+5)$
Disc. $= 4(m-1)^2 - 4(m+5) = 4[m^2 + 1 - 2m - m - 5]$
$= 4[m^2 - 3m - 4] = 4(m-4)(m+1) \leq 0$ for $m \in [-1, 4]$
$\Rightarrow f'(x) \geq 0\ \forall\ x \in \mathbb{R}$ if $m \in (-1, 4)$
$\Rightarrow f(x)$ is invertible for integer values of $m \in \{-1, 0, 2, 3, 4\}$
$\Rightarrow k = 6$

13. Given $f(x, y) = f(2x + 2y, 2y - 2x)\ \forall\ x, y \in \mathbb{R}, f(x) = f(2^x, 0)$ and $f(x)$ is periodic with period k.
$\Rightarrow f(x) = f(2^x, 0) = f(2.2^x + 2(0), 2(0) - 2.2^x) = f(2^{x+1}, -2^{x+1})$
$= f(2.2^{x+1} - 2.2^{x+1}, -2.2^{x+1} - 2.2^{x+1}) = f(0, -2^{x+3})$
$= f(2.(-2^{x+3}), -2.2^{x+3}) = f(-2^{x+4}, -2^{x+4}) = f(-2^{x+6}, 0)$
$= f(-2^{x+7}, 2^{x+7}) = f(0, 2^{x+9}) = f(2^{x+10}, 20^{x+10}) = f(2^{x+12}, 0)$
$= f(x+12)$
$\Rightarrow f(x)$ is periodic with period 12.
$\Rightarrow k = 12$

14. Let $y = \dfrac{ax^2 + 6x - 8}{a + 6x - 8x^2}$; We want y to be real for every real x
$\Rightarrow (8y + a)x^2 - 6yx + 6x - 8 - ay = 0$ for $x, y \in \mathbb{R}$ ......(i)
If $8y + a = 0$, i.e., $y = -\dfrac{a}{8}$

$$\Rightarrow -6\left(\frac{-a}{8}\right)x + 6x - 8 - a\left(\frac{-a}{8}\right) = 0$$

$$\Rightarrow \frac{3a}{4}x + 6x - 8 + \frac{a^2}{8} = 0$$

$$\Rightarrow x\left(\frac{3a}{4} + 6\right) = 8 - \frac{a^2}{8}$$

$$\Rightarrow x = \frac{64 - a^2}{8} \times \frac{4}{3a + 24} = \frac{64 - a^2}{6a + 12} \in \mathbb{R} \text{ for a} \neq -2$$

$\therefore$ If $a \neq -2$ and $y = -\dfrac{a}{8}$, then $x \in \mathbb{R}$

$\Rightarrow$ For $a = -2$ and $y = \dfrac{1}{4}$; $x \in \mathbb{R}$

$\Rightarrow a \neq -2$ ......(ii)
If $(8y + a) \neq 0$, then for real roots 'x' of (i); Disc. $\geq 0\ \forall\ y \in \mathbb{R}$
$\Rightarrow (6 - 6y)^2 + 4(8y + a)(8 + ay) \geq 0\ \forall\ y \in \mathbb{R}$
$\Rightarrow (9 + 8a)y^2 + (a^2 + 46)y + (9 + 8a) \geq 0\ \forall\ y \in \mathbb{R}$
If $9 + 8a = 0$, then $y \geq 0\ \forall\ y \in \mathbb{R}$, which is false, so,
$a \neq -\dfrac{9}{8}$ ...(iii)
Now for $9a + 8a \neq 0$
$\Rightarrow (a^2 + 46)^2 - 4(9 + 8a)(9 + 8a) \leq 0$
$\Rightarrow (a^2 + 46)^2 - [2(9 + 8a)]^2 \leq 0$
$\Rightarrow -2(9 + 8a) \leq (a^2 + 46) \leq 2(9 + 8a)$
$\Rightarrow a^2 + 16a + 64\ 0$ and $a^2 - 16a + 28 \leq 0$
$\Rightarrow (a + 8)^2\ 0$ and $(a - 2)(a - 14) \leq 0$
$\Rightarrow a \in [2, 14]$ ....(iv)
$\therefore$ From (ii), (iii) and (iv), we have $a \in [2, 14] = [m, n]$ (given)
$\Rightarrow m = 2, n = 14$
$\Rightarrow \sqrt{mn - 3} = 5$

15. $y = \dfrac{x-4}{16-\lambda^2}$; $x \in [x_1, x_2]$; where $x_1 = 4 - \lambda$; $x = x_2$ such that

$\Delta y = \dfrac{1}{4-\lambda}$

$\Delta y = y_2 - y_1 = f(x_2) - f(x_1)$

$\Rightarrow \dfrac{1}{4-\lambda} = \dfrac{x_2-4}{16-\lambda^2} - \dfrac{x_1-4}{16-\lambda^2}$

$\Rightarrow \dfrac{1}{4-\lambda} = \dfrac{x_2-4}{16-\lambda^2} - \dfrac{(4-\lambda)-4}{16-\lambda^2}$

$\Rightarrow \dfrac{1}{4-\lambda} = \dfrac{x_2-4-4+\lambda+4}{16-\lambda^2}$

$\Rightarrow 4 + \lambda = x_2 + \lambda - 4 \quad \Rightarrow x_2 = 8$

16. $f(x) = \cos^2 x + \cos^2\left(\dfrac{\pi}{3}+x\right) - \cos x . \cos\left(\dfrac{\pi}{3}+x\right)$; $g\left(\dfrac{3}{4}\right) = 2$;

$gof(x) = ?$

$f(1) = \cos^2 1 + \cos^2\left(\dfrac{\pi}{3}+1\right) - \cos 1 \cos\left(\dfrac{\pi}{3}+1\right)$

$\Rightarrow f(1) = \cos^2 1 + \cos\left(\dfrac{\pi}{3}+1\right).\left[\cos\left(\dfrac{\pi}{3}+1\right) - \cos 1\right]$

$\Rightarrow f(1) = \cos^2 1 + \cos\left(\dfrac{\pi}{3}+1\right).\left[-2\sin\left(\dfrac{\pi}{6}+1\right)\sin\dfrac{\pi}{6}\right]$

$\Rightarrow f(1) = \cos^2 1 - \cos\left(\dfrac{\pi}{3}+1\right)\sin\left(\dfrac{\pi}{6}+1\right)$

$\Rightarrow f(1) = \cos^2 1 - \dfrac{1}{2}\left[\sin\left(\dfrac{\pi}{2}+2\right) + \sin\left(-\dfrac{\pi}{6}\right)\right]$

$\Rightarrow f(1) = \cos^2 1 - \dfrac{1}{2}\left[\cos 2 - \dfrac{1}{2}\right]$

$= \cos^2 1 - \dfrac{1}{2}\left(2\cos^2 1 - 1\right) + \dfrac{1}{4} = \dfrac{3}{4}$

$\therefore \; gof(1) = f(f(1)) = f(3/4) = 2$

17. f: {1, 2, 3} → {1, 2, 3, 4, 5} such that $f(i) \le f(j)$ whenever $i < j$ and $i, j \in$ {1, 2, 3}

Case (i): $f(1) = f(2) < f(3)$

Now select any 2 numbers out of 1, 2, 3, 4, 5 and arrange them in ascending order, the smallest will be the value $f(1)$ and $f(2)$ and greatest of 5 values $f(4)$ can take any of 5 values.

$\therefore$ Number of functions = ${}^5C_2 \times 5 = 50$

Case (ii): $f(1) < f(2) = f(3)$

$\Rightarrow$ Number of functions = ${}^5C_2 \times 5 = 50$

Case (iii): $f(1) = f(2) = f(3)$

$\Rightarrow$ Number of functions = ${}^5C_1 \times 5 = 25$

Case (iv): $f(1) < f(2) < f(3)$

$\Rightarrow$ Number of functions = ${}^5C_3 \times 5 = 50$

$\therefore$ Total number of possible functions = 50 + 50 + 25 + 50 = 175

18. Let $p(x) = ax^2 + bx + c$ then, $p(x) \ge 0 \; \forall \; x \in \mathbb{R}$

$\Rightarrow a > 0, \; b^2 - 4ac \le 0$ ...(i)

Also $p(1) = 0$ and $p(2) = 2$ ...(ii)

$\because \; p(1) = 0$

$\Rightarrow$ 1 is a root

$\Rightarrow p(x)$ must have repeated root 1

$\Rightarrow \dfrac{p(x)}{a} = x^2 + \dfrac{b}{a}x + \dfrac{c}{a} = (x-1)^2$

$\Rightarrow \dfrac{b}{a} = -2, \dfrac{c}{a} = 1$

$\Rightarrow b = -2a, \; c = a$

$\therefore \; p(x) = ax^2 - 2ax + a = a(x-1)^2$

$\because \; p(2) = 2$

$\Rightarrow a = 2$

$\Rightarrow p(x) = 2(x-1)^2$

$\Rightarrow p(0) + p(3) = 2(1) + 2(2)^2 = 10$

19. $x^4 - 4x^3 + 6x^2 - 4x = 2008$

$\Rightarrow (x-1)^4 = 2008$

$\Rightarrow (x-1)^2 = \pm\sqrt{2008}$

$\therefore$ Imaginary roots are given by $(x-1)^2 = -\sqrt{2008} = \sqrt{2008}i^2$

$\Rightarrow x - 1 = \pm (2008)^{1/4}\, i$

$\Rightarrow x = 1 \pm i(2008)^{1/4}$

$\Rightarrow x_1x_2 = p = 1 + (2008)^{1/2}$

$\Rightarrow p \in (1 + 44.8, 1 + 44.9)$

$\Rightarrow p \in (45.8, 45.9)$

$\Rightarrow [p] = 45$

20. $f(x) = ax^2 + bx + c$, $a > 0$ and $f(x) = \dfrac{1}{x^2-4}$

Graph of $y = f(x)$ and $y = ax^2 + bx + c$ drawn on same frame of reference the maximum number of point of intersection is as shown below.

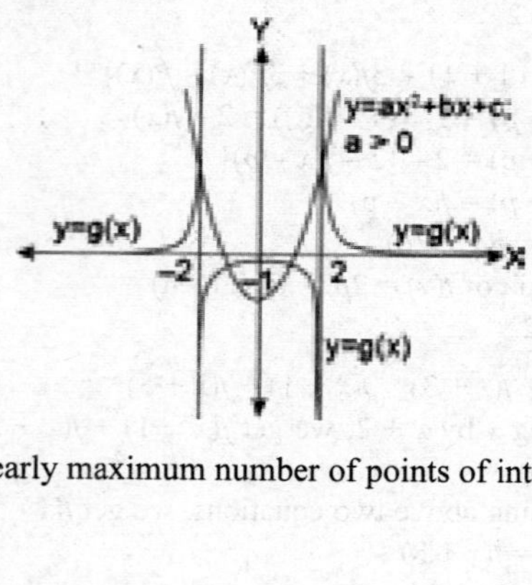

Clearly maximum number of points of intersection is 4.

CHAPTER 3

Graph Theory

■ INTRODUCTION

The word Graph originated from the Greek word 'GRAPHO' which means to write. One may define it as 'Things written or drawn in a specified way, e.g., photograph, painting etc. You may also call it as a diagram showing the relation between variable quantities'. In discrete mathematics a graph is a representation of a set of 'points or nodes' (objects) where some pairs of points are connected by links (straight or curved). The interconnected point objects are called as vertices and the connecting links are known as edges.

It is better to say that drawing 'Graph' is a visual or descriptive art, which is vividly descriptive and easily understandable. It provides maximum information in a minimum space about the function (thing which it represents) and being a visual representation always leaves an impression lasting longer than that of any other manner of representation like mathematical, analytical etc. As the photograph of a person conveys his identity better than any amount of description of his physical measurement, color etc. Similarly the graph of a function provides us better understanding of the nature and behavior of a function. Graphs not only provide information about functions but also help in solving many problems related to number of solution of some equations and area enclosed by curves.

So, we are going to analyze the graphical approach of understanding the function and we will try to graph a function with the help of properties of function like domain, range, limits, continuity, differentiability derivative, mono-tonicity, maxima/minima of functions. Thus, to sketch the graph of some unknown function, the complete knowledge of differential calculus is required along with the understanding of some very basic functions and their curves. And with the above tools available to us we will try to portray the graph in the best possible way with the added application of our individual logical skills.

■ GRAPHS OF FUNCTION

Graph of a function means the curve obtained by plotting all the ordered pairs (x, y) which satisfy the equation of the given function, $y = f(x)$. Let us classify the basic curves function wise.

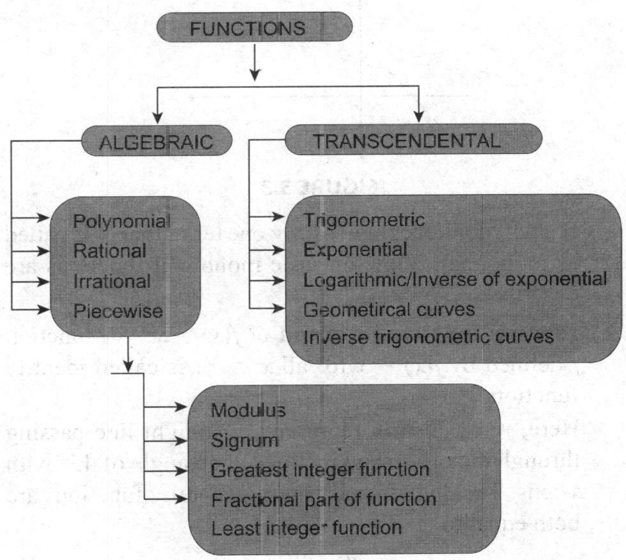

FIGURE 3.1

■ ALGEBRAIC FUNCTIONS

Polynomial Function

A function of the form: $f(x) = a_0 + a_1x + a_2x^2 + ... + a_nx^n$; where $n \in \mathbb{N}$ and $a_0, a_1, a_2, ..., a_n \in \mathbb{R}$ is known as polynomial function in x. The natural number n is called as degree of polynomial. Depending on the value of n these are classified into different categories, e.g., linear ($n = 1$), quadratic ($n = 2$), cubic ($n = 3$), biquadratic ($n = 4$).

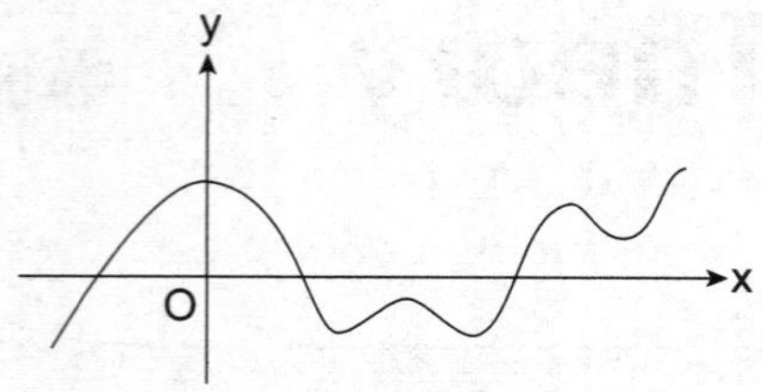

FIGURE 3.2

(a) **Straight line (linear polynomial):** Every first degree equation in *x, y* represents a straight line. So, the general equation of a line is $ax + by + c = 0$. To draw a straight line, find the points where it meets with the coordinate axes by putting $y = 0$ and $x = 0$ respectively in its equation. By joining these two points, we get the sketch of the line

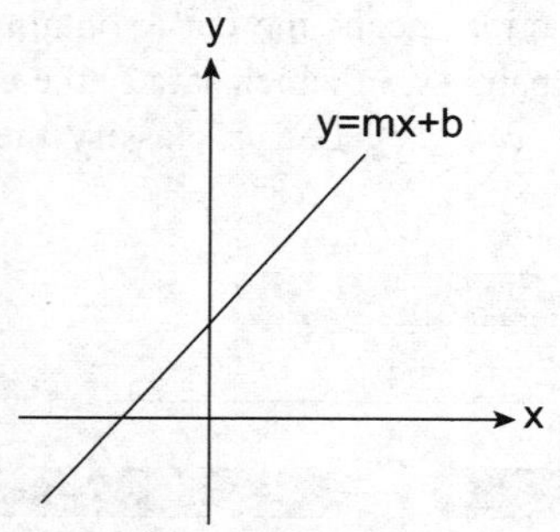

FIGURE 3.3

If a polynomial contains only one term, then it is called as monomial. Some of basic monomial functions are described below:

(b) **Identity function or graph of $f(x) = x$:** A function f defined by $f(x) = x$ for all $x \in \mathbb{R}$, is called identity function.

Here, $y = x$ clearly represents a straight line passing through the origin and inclined at an angle of 45° with *x*-axis. The domain and range of identity functions are both equal to $\mathbb{R}$.

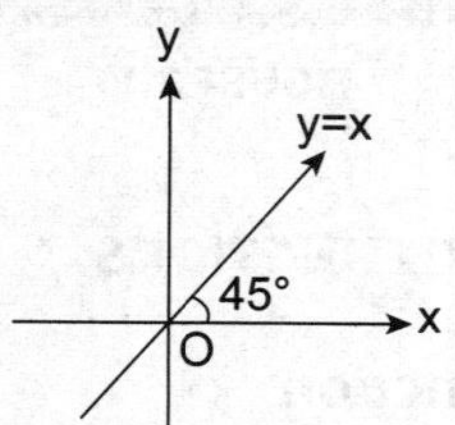

FIGURE 3.4

(c) **Graph of $f(x) = x^2$:** A function given by $f(x) = x^2$ is a pure quadratic monomial called as 'square function'.

The domain of square function is $\mathbb{R}$ and its range is $\mathbb{R}^+ \cup \{0\}$ or $[0, \infty)$. Since $y = x^2$ is an even function, so, its graph is clearly a parabola symmetrical about *y*-axis with vertex at origin (0, 0) as shown below.

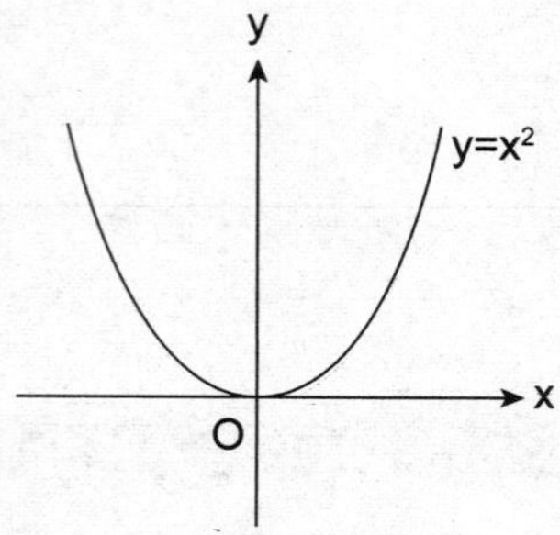

FIGURE 3.5

(d) **Graph of $f(x) = x^3$:** A function given by $f(x) = x^3$ is called a cubic monomial function with the domain and range both equal to $\mathbb{R}$. The following table represents few inputs and corresponding outputs of the above function.

x	.....	–3	–2	–1	0	1	2	3	.....
y	.....	–27	–8	–1	0	1	8	27	.....

It is clearly an odd continuous function, thus, its graph must be symmetric about origin as shown below.

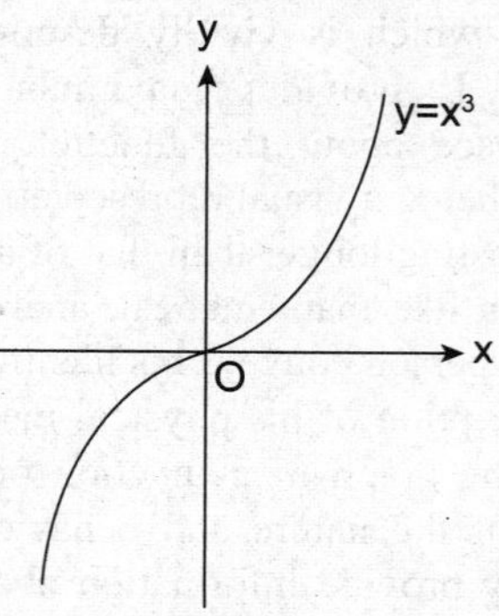

FIGURE 3.6

(e) **Power functions:**

(i) Graph of $f(x) = x^{2n}$; $n \in \mathbb{N}$: If $n \in \mathbb{N}$, then function f given by $f(x) = x^{2n}$ is an even function.

So, its graph is always symmetrical about *y*-axis. To sketch these curves for various possible *n* and to know the relative position it is required to analyze and understand the following facts.

The value of x^{2n} decreases by increasing the exponent (power) in the domain $x \in (-1, 1)$, whereas it increases by increasing the power for all $x \in (-\infty, -1] \cup (1, \infty)$.

i.e., $x^2 > x^4 > x^6 > x^8 > \ldots\ \forall\ x \in (-1, 1)$ and $x^2 < x^4 < x^6 < x^8 < \ldots 1\ \forall\ x \in (-\infty, -1] \cup (1, \infty)$.
The relative graphs of $y = x^2$, $y = x^4$, $y = x^6$,...etc. are drawn as shown in the following diagram:

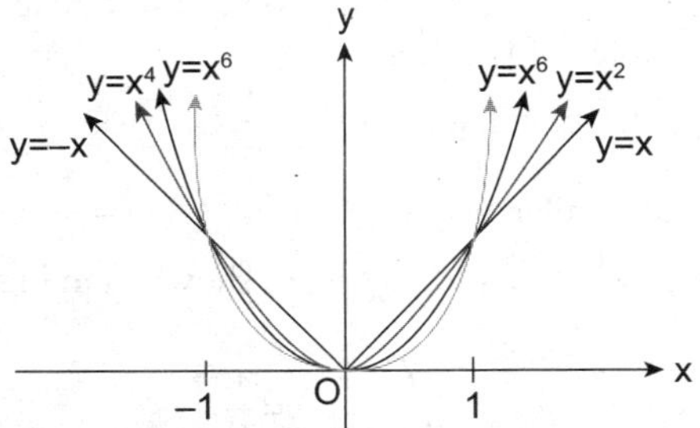

FIGURE 3.7

Rectify the GRAPH

(ii) Graph of $\boldsymbol{f(x) = x^{2n-1}}$; $n \in \mathbb{N}$: If $n \in \mathbb{N}$, then function f given by $f(x) = x^{2n-1}$ is an odd function. So, its graph is always symmetrical about origin or in opposite quadrants. To study the relative positioning of these graphs for different values of $n \in \mathbb{N}$, we need to compare the values of x, x^3, x^5,..... etc.

For instance $\forall\ x \in (1, \infty)$; $x < x^3 < x^5 < \ldots$.whereas for $x \in (0, 1)$ $x > x^3 > x^5 > \ldots$.

But when $x \in (-1, 0)$, then $x < x^3 < x^5 < \ldots$.

And for $x \in (-\infty, -1)$ we find that $x > x^3 > x^5 > \ldots$.

Then put a point mirror at the origin and you will find that for every point (x_1, x_1^3) on the curve, there is an image point $(-x_1, -x_1^3)$. i.e., the curve $y = x^3$, i.e., symmetrical about origin. In the light of the above facts we get the graphs of $f(x) = x$, $f(x) = x^3$, $f(x) = x^5$,.. etc. as shown below.

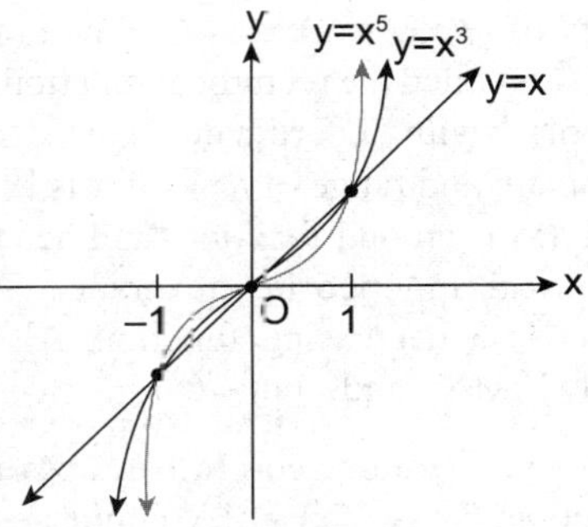

FIGURE 3.8

ILLUSTRATION 1: Find the area of the region enclosed by $f(x) = x^5$ and the semi-circular arc of the circle $x^2 + y^2 = 2$, lying below the straight line $y = x$.

SOLUTION: The semi-circular arc described in the problem is drawn as shown in Figure 3.9. The graph of $f(x) = x^5$ passes through $A(-1, -1)$, $O(0, 0)$, $B(1, 1)$ as drawn in Figure 3.10.

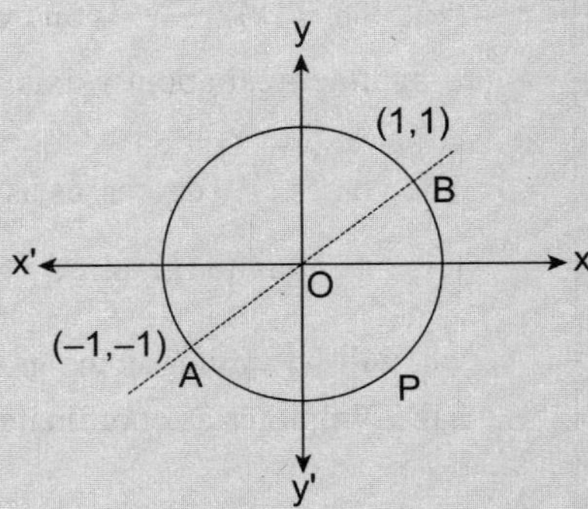

FIGURE 3.9

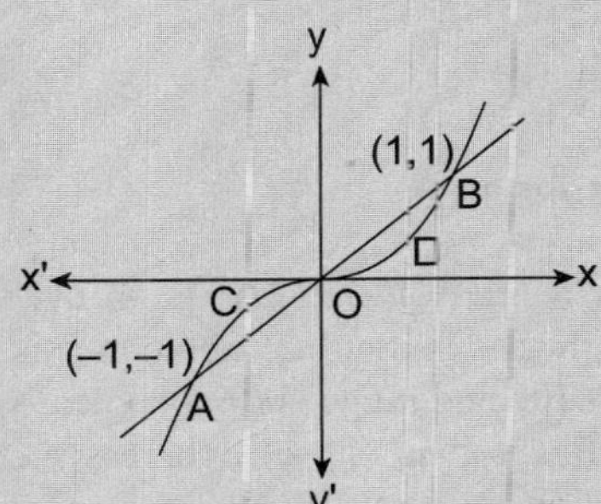

FIGURE 3.10

Clearly, the area $\widehat{ACOA}$ is equal to area $\widehat{ODBO}$ (say Δ) because $f(x) = x$ and $f(x) = x^3$ both the curves are symmetric about origin.

Thus, the required area is shaded in Figure 3.11 must be equal to

Area of semicircle – Δ + Δ = Area of semicircle $= \pi(\sqrt{2})^2 = 2\pi$ square unit.

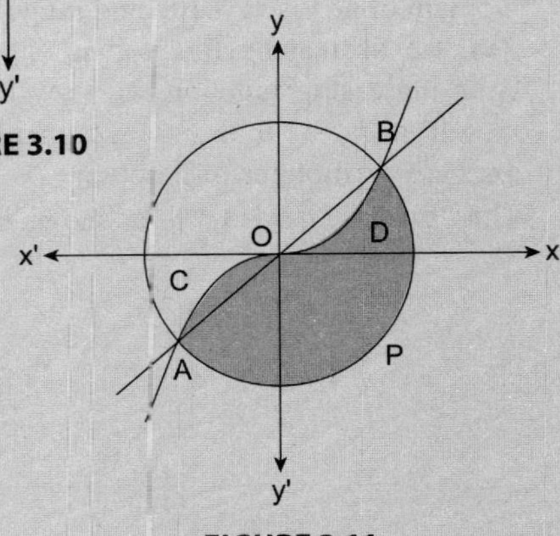

FIGURE 3.11

■ RATIONAL FUNCTIONS

The function, written as the quotient of two polynomial functions is known as a rational function. Given two polynomial functions $P(x) = a_0 + a_1x + a_2x^2 + ... + a_n x^n$ and $Q(x) = b_0 + b_1x + b_2x^0 + ... + b_m x^m$, the function $f(x) = \frac{P(x)}{Q(x)}$ is a rational function of x. Domain $= \mathbb{R} - \{x : Q(x) \neq 0\}$. i.e., domain $= \mathbb{R}$, except for those points for which denominator $= 0$. Graphs of the some basic rational functions are discussed as below:

(a) **Graph of $f(x) = 1/x$:** A function defined by $f(x) = 1/x$ is called the reciprocal function or rectangular hyperbola, with coordinate axes as asymptotes. The domain and range of $f(x) = 1/x$ is $\mathbb{R} - \{0\}$.
Indeed $f(x)$ is an odd function, and hence, its graph is symmetrical in opposite quadrants. The reciprocal function is a decreasing function. Also we observe $\lim_{x\to 0^+} f(x) = +\infty$ and $\lim_{x\to 0^-} f(x) = -\infty$. As $x \to \pm\infty$ $\Rightarrow f(x) \to 0$. Therefore, co-ordinate axes are asymptotes of function. Thus, $f(x) = 1/x$ could be shown in the graph shown below.

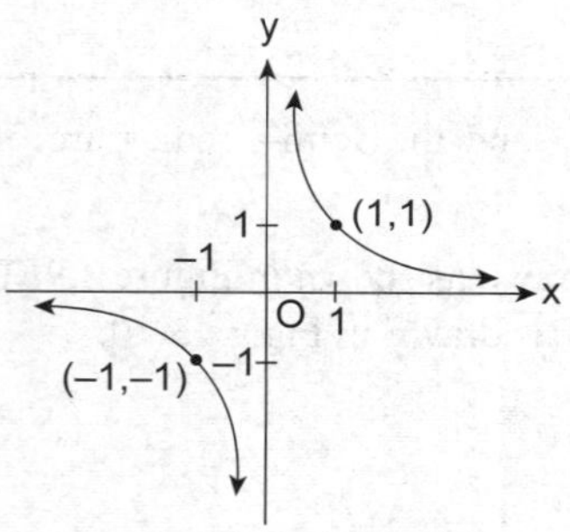

FIGURE 3.12

(b) **Graph of $f(x) = 1/x^2$:** Here $f(x) = 1/x^2$ is an even function, so, its graph is symmetrical about y-axis. Domain of $f(x)$ is $\mathbb{R} - \{0\}$ and range is $(0, \infty)$. Clearly $f(x)$ is a decreasing function in $(0, \infty)$, whereas $f(x)$ is an increasing function in $(-\infty, 0)$. Also $y \to \infty$ as $x \to 0^{\pm}$ and $y \to 0$ as $x \to \pm\infty$, therefore, co-ordinate axes are asymptotes of function.
Thus, graph of $f(x) = 1/x^2$ is as shown in the Figure 3.13.

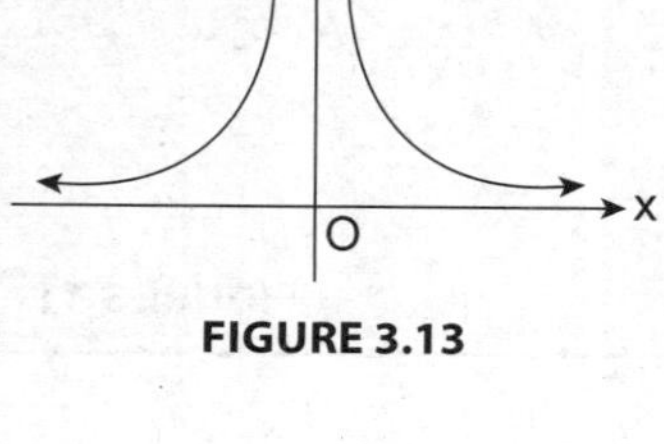

FIGURE 3.13

(c) **Graph of $f(x) = \frac{1}{x^{2n-1}}$; $n \in \mathbb{N}$:** Here, $f(x) = \frac{1}{x^{2n-1}}$ is an odd function, so, its graph is symmetrical in opposite quadrants. Also, $y \to \infty$ when $x \to 0^+$ and $y \to -\infty$ as $x \to 0^-$. Therefore, co-ordinate axes are asymptotes of function.
Thus, the graph for $f(x) = \frac{1}{x^3}$; $f(x) = \frac{1}{x^5}$, ..., etc., will be similar to the graph of $f(x) = \frac{1}{x}$ which has asymptotes as coordinate axes, shown as in Figure 3.14.

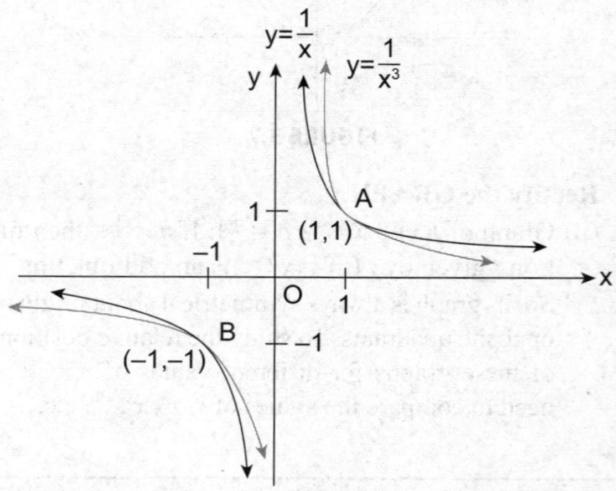

FIGURE 3.14

(d) **Graph of $f(x) = \frac{1}{x^{2n}}$; $n \in \mathbb{N}$:** We observe that the function $f(x) = \frac{1}{x^{2n}}$ is an even function, so, its graph is symmetrical about y-axis. Also, $y \to \infty$ as $x \to 0^{\pm}$ and $y \to 0$ as $x \to \pm\infty$.
The values of y decreases as the values of x increases for $x > 0$. Thus, the graph of $f(x) = \frac{1}{x^4}$; $f(x) = \frac{1}{x^6}$,....., etc. will be similar as the graph of $f(x) = \frac{1}{x^2}$, which has asymptotes as coordinate axis, as shown in Figure 3.15.

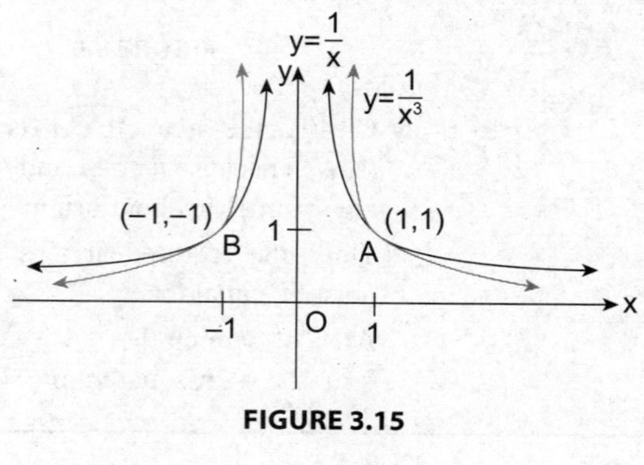

FIGURE 3.15

ILLUSTRATION 2: Find the number of solution of equation $x^3.\{ x \} = 1$, lying in the interval $[-2, 5]$. Here $\{.\}$ denotes fractional part function.

SOLUTION: Given equation $x^3.\{ x \} = 1 \Rightarrow \{ x \} = 1/x^3$

Therefore, by drawing both the curves $y = \{ x \}$ and $y = 1/x^3$ as shown below in Figure 3.16

we can count the number of points of intersections as four. Consequently the given equation has only four real solutions lying in the interval $[-2, 5]$.

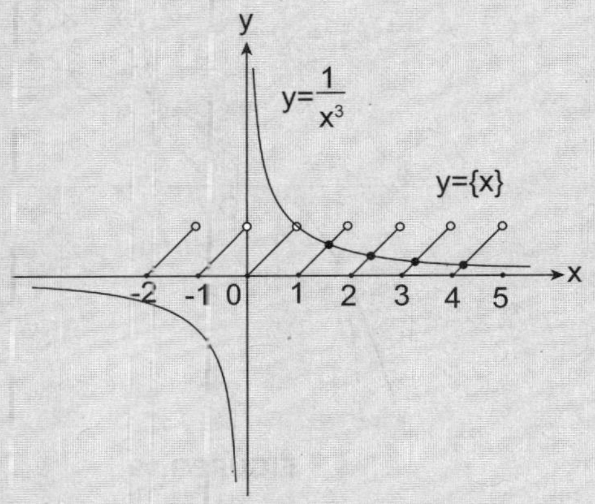

FIGURE 3.16

■ IRRATIONAL FUNCTION

The algebraic functions having at least one term containing non-integer rational power of x are termed as irrational functions of x.

Graph of Some Basic Irrational Function

(a) **Graph of $f(x) = x^{1/2n}$; $n \in \mathbb{N}$:** Since, $f(x) = x^{1/2n}$ is defined for all $x \in [0, \infty)$ and generates positive values only, therefore, both the domain and range of $f(x)$ must be $[0, \infty)$.

Also being inverse function of the function $f(x) = x^{2n}$, the graph of $f(x) = x^{1/2n}$ is the mirror image of the graph of $f(x) = x^{2n}$ about the line $y = x$; $\forall\, x \in [0, \infty)$.

Thus, the graphs of $f(x) = x^{1/2}$, $f(x) = x^{1/4}$,.... are as shown in the Figure 3.17.

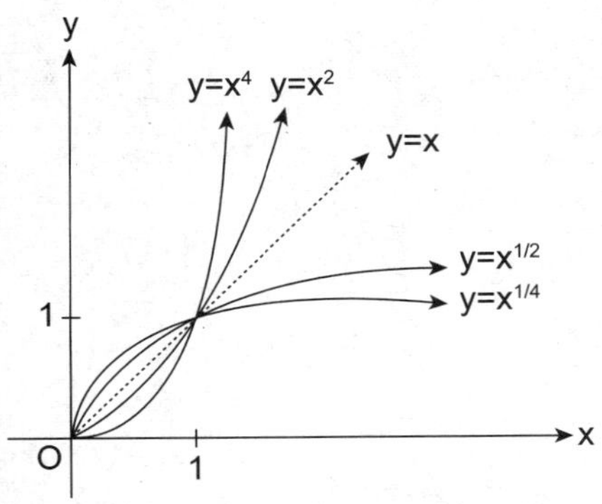

FIGURE 3.17

For instance; the graph of $f(x) = \sqrt{x}$, i.e., $x^{1/2}$ is the portion of the parabola $y^2 = x$, which lies above x-axis. its domain and range both are given as $[0, \infty)$. It is shown below

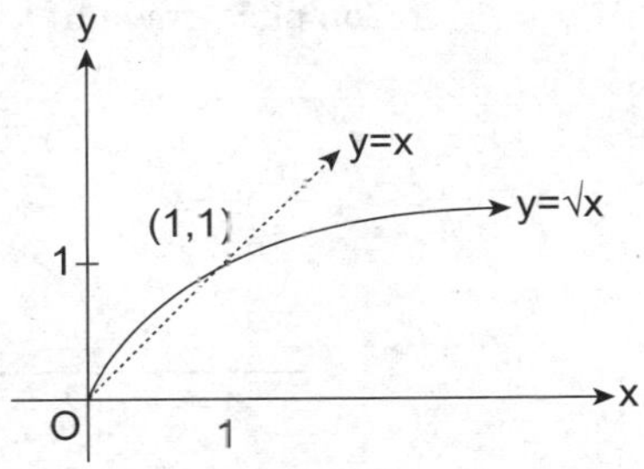

FIGURE 3.18

(b) **Graph of $f(x) = x^{1/2n-1}$**; when $n \in \mathbb{N}$

The function $f(x) = x^{1/2n-1}$ is defined for all $x \in \mathbb{R}$ as the odd root of every real number is defined as real number. Also we can see that $f(x)$ returns positive values for positive input and negative values corresponding to negative inputs. Thus, the domain as well and range of $f(x)$ is $\mathbb{R}$.

Also $f(x) = x^{1/2n-1}$ being the inverse function of $f(x) = x^{2n-1}$, the graph of $f(x) = x^{1/2n-1}$ is the mirror image of the graph of $f(x) = x^{2n-1}$ about the line $y = x\ \forall\ x \in \mathbb{R}$. Consequently the graph of, $f(x) = x^{1/3}$, $f(x) = x^{1/5}$,..., shall be as shown in the following Figure 3.19.

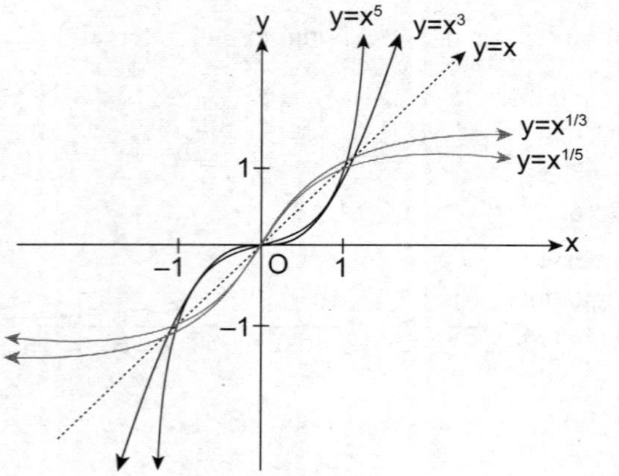

FIGURE 3.19

e.g., Graph of $f(x) = x^{1/3}$. As discussed above, is inverse of $g(x) = x^3$. Therefore, the graph of $f(x) = x^{1/3}$ is image of $g(x)$ about $y = x$. where domain and and range of $f(x)$ is $\mathbb{R}$. Thus, the graph of $f(x) = x^{1/3}$ is as shown in the Figure 3.20.

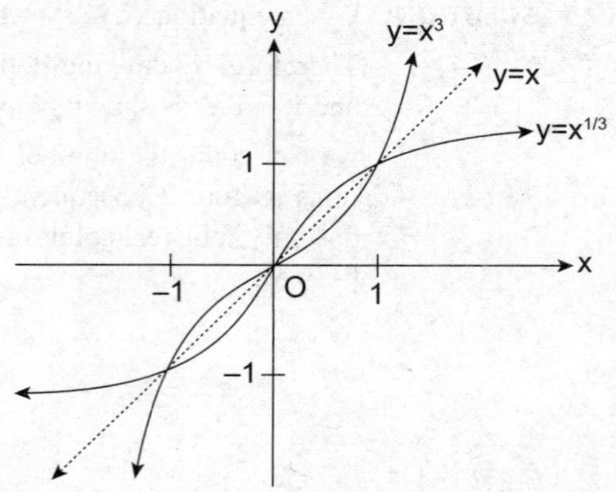

FIGURE 3.20

ILLUSTRATION 3: A function $f(x)$ is defined as $f(x) = \begin{cases} x^{1/3}; & x \geq 0 \\ -x^{1/3}; & x < 0 \end{cases}$, whereas $g(x)$ is given by $g(x) = \begin{cases} -\dfrac{1}{x}; & x < 0 \\ x(x-1); & x \geq 0 \end{cases}$. Find the number of points of intersections of $f(x)$ and $g(x)$.

SOLUTION: Clearly for $x \in [0, \infty)$; $f(x)$ is reflection of x^3 in $y = x$ and then taking its even extension . Complete graph of $f(x)$ and $g(x)$ are shown below in Figure 3.21 and 3.22 respectively.

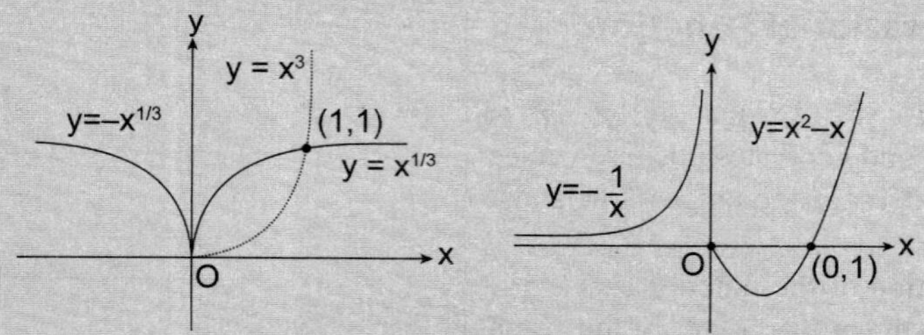

FIGURE 3.21

Clearly, sketching both functions together as drawn below, we observe that they have three points of intersections.

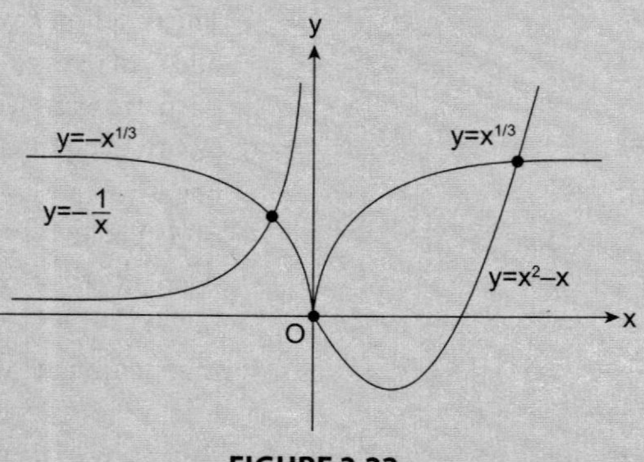

FIGURE 3.22

■ PIECE-WISE DEFINED FUNCTIONS

(a) **Modulus function or absolute value function:**
The function $f: \mathbb{R} \to \mathbb{R}$ is said to be modulus function or absolute value function if

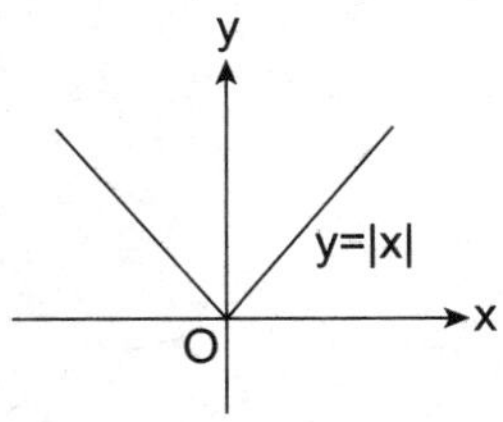

FIGURE 3.23

$f(x) = |x| = \begin{cases} x, & \text{if } x \geq 0 \\ 0, & \text{if } x = 0 \\ -x, & \text{if } x < 0 \end{cases}$; $|x|$ is pronounced as modulus of x or in brief mod x.

Note: $|x|$ is also defined as $\sqrt{x^2}$ and max $\{x, -x\}$.

(b) **Signum function:** The function $f(x) = \begin{cases} \dfrac{|x|}{x}, & x \neq 0 \\ 0, & x = 0 \end{cases}$ is called a signum function and is denoted by *sgn* (x). Graph of signum function, i.e., $y = sgn(x)$ is shown. Hence, *sgn* $(f(x))$ is:

$$f(x) = \begin{cases} \dfrac{|f(x)|}{f(x)} = 1 \ ; & f(x) > 0 \\ -\dfrac{f(x)}{f(x)} = -1; & f(x) < 0 \\ 0 \qquad ; & f(x) = 0 \end{cases}$$

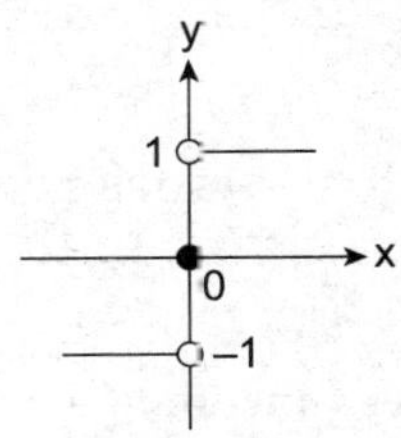

FIGURE 3.24

ILLUSTRATION 4: Draw the graph of *sgn* (sin x)

SOLUTION: $sgn\,(\sin x) = \begin{cases} 1, & \text{when } \sin x > 0 \\ -1, & \text{when } \sin x < 0 \\ 0, & \text{when } \sin x = 0 \end{cases}$

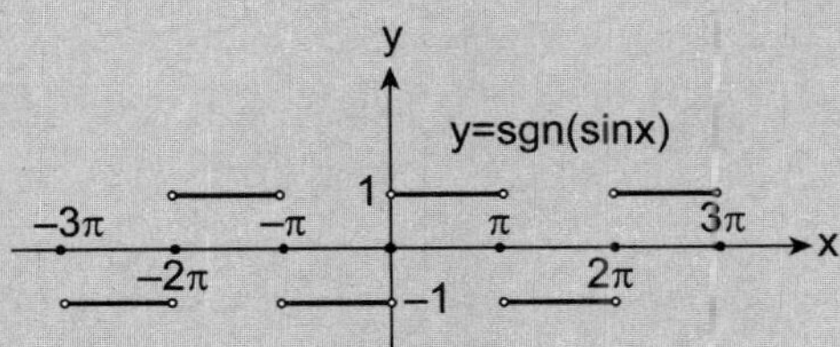

FIGURE 3.25

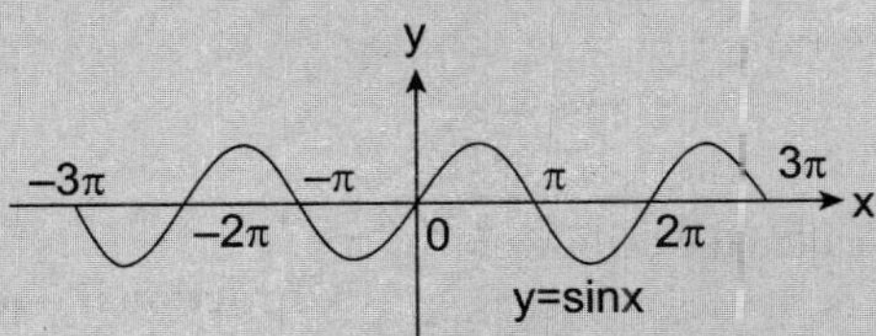

FIGURE 3.26

ILLUSTRATION 5: Find the number of real solutions of equation $f(x) = g(x)$ where f and g are functions defined as $f(x) = \begin{cases} |x+1|; & x \leq 0 \\ \sqrt{1-x^2}; & x > 0 \end{cases}$; $g(x) = \begin{cases} -x^{1/5}; & x < 0 \\ x^2; & x \geq 0 \end{cases}$

SOLUTION: The function $f(x)$ can be defined as $f(x)=\begin{cases}-(1+x); & x<-1\\ x+1; & -1\le x\le 0\\ \sqrt{1-x^2}; & 0<x\le 1\end{cases}$

Thus, its graph is given below.

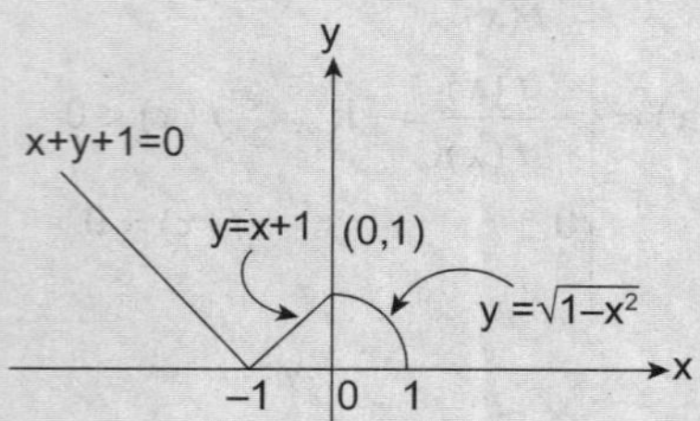

FIGURE 3.27

The graph of $g(x)$ is as shown below

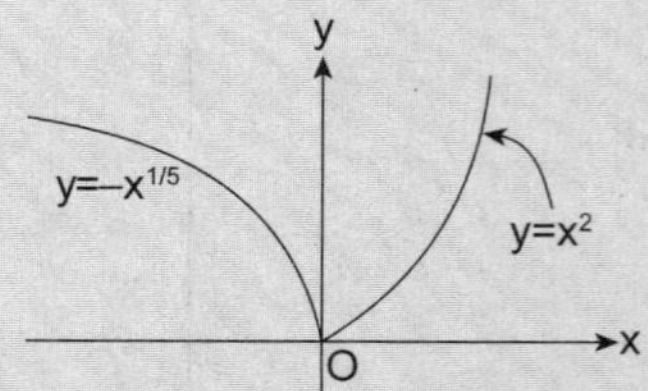

FIGURE 3.28

Sketching them together or superimposing $g(x)$ on $f(x)$, we get $f(x) = g(x)$ has three solutions

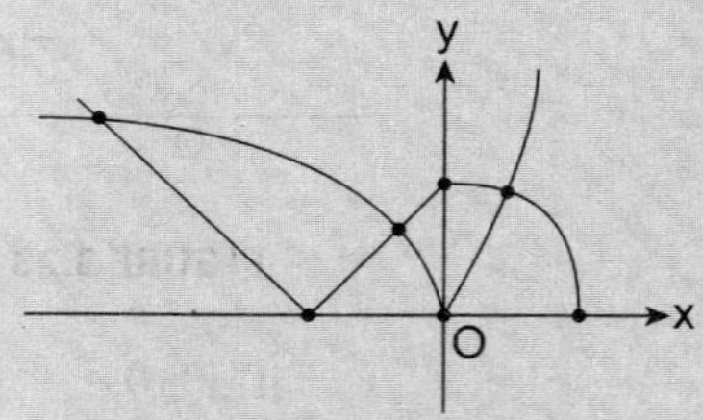

FIGURE 3.29

(c) **Greatest integer function:** For any real number x, we denote $[x]$, the greatest integer less than or equal to x, it is also known as integral part of the number x.

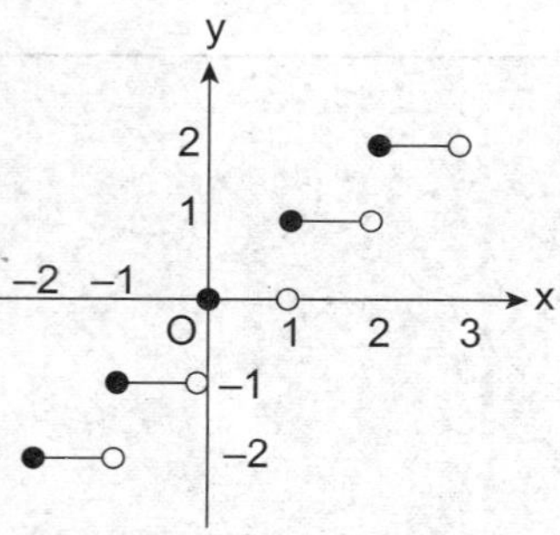

FIGURE 3.30

i.e., $f(x) = [x] = -1$ for $-1 \le x < -2$
$[x] = 0$ for $0 \le x < 1$
$[x] = 1$ for $1 \le x < 2$
$[x] = 2$ for $2 \le x < 3$

The domain of the function is: $(-\infty, +\infty)$ and the range is : set of *all integers*.

(d) **Least integer function:** It is also called the ceiling of x and it is represented by $\lceil x \rceil$. It is the least integer greater than or equal to the number. Therefore, $y = \lceil x \rceil = I + 1$ if $I < x \le I + 1$

e.g., $\lceil 1.5 \rceil = 2, \lceil 2.9 \rceil = 3, \lceil -2.3 \rceil = -2$, $\lceil -0.6 \rceil = 0, \lceil 0.25 \rceil = 1$, thus, $[x]$ converts $x = (I + f)$ into I while $\lceil x \rceil$ converts it into $I + 1$. But when x is an integer $[x] = x = \lceil x \rceil$. Thus,

$\lceil x \rceil = -2$ for $-3 < x \le -2$
$\lceil x \rceil = -1$ for $-2 < x \le -1$
$\lceil x \rceil = 0$ for $-1 < x \le 0$
$\Rightarrow \lceil x \rceil = 1$ for $0 < x \le 1$
$\lceil x \rceil = 2$ for $1 < x \le 2$
$\lceil x \rceil = 3$ for $2 < x \le 3$

and can be expressed graphically as shown in Figure 3.31.

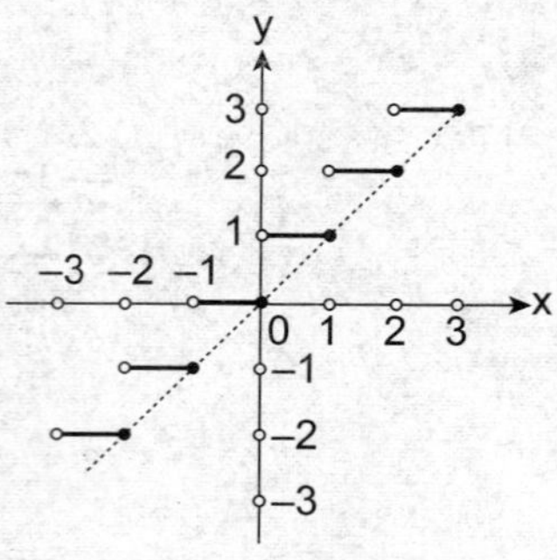

FIGURE 3.31

(e) **Fractional—part function:** Since we know that $x \ge [x]$. the difference between the number x and it's integral value $[x]$ is called the fractional part of x and is symbolically denoted as $\{x\}$.

Thus, $\{x\} = x - [x]$

e.g., $\{2.5\} = 0.5$, $\{-1.9\} = -1.9 - [-1.9] = -1.9 + 2 = 0.1 = 1 - (0.9) = 1 - \{1.9\}$

Since $f(x) = \{x\}$,

$\{x\} = x$ for $0 \le x < 1$

$$\begin{aligned} &\{x\} = x - 1 && \text{for} && 1 \le x < 2 \\ \Rightarrow\ &\{x\} = x - 2 && \text{for} && 2 \le x < 3 \\ &\{x\} = x + 1 && \text{for} && -1 \le x < 0 \\ &\{x\} = x + 2 && \text{for} && -2 \le x < -1 \end{aligned}$$

and can be expressed graphically as shown in Figure 3.32:

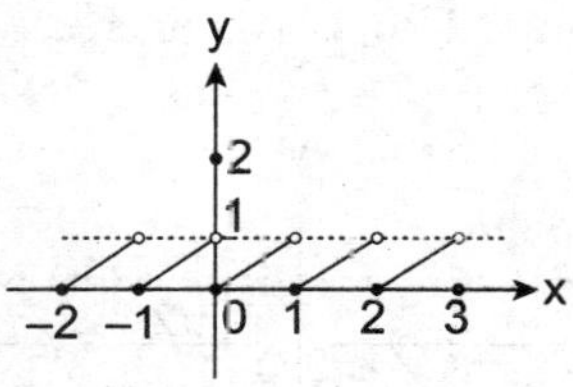

FIGURE 3.32

ILLUSTRATION 6: Obtain the number of real solution of the equation $\left[\frac{x}{2}\right] = \log x$, where [.] denotes the integer function of x.

SOLUTION: Consider $f(x) = \left[\frac{x}{2}\right] = \begin{cases} -1; -2 \le x < 0 \\ 0;\ 0 \le x < 2 \\ 1;\ 2 \le x < 4 \end{cases}$

and $g(x) = \log x$

Superimposing both the curves together, clearly the equation has only one solution, Figure 3.32. i.e., $x = 1$.

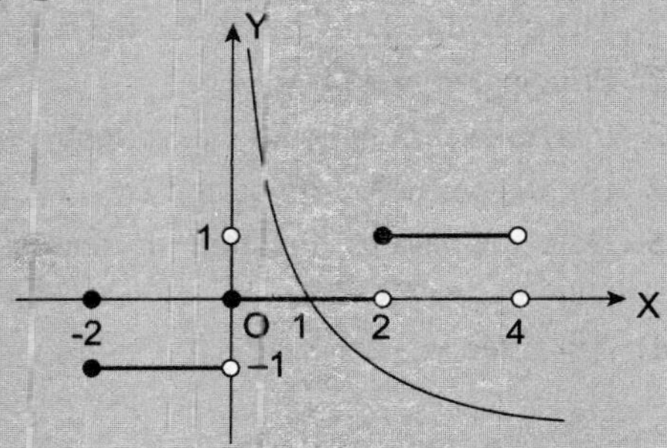

FIGURE 3.33

■ TRANSCENDENTAL FUNCTIONS

Trigonometric Curves

sin$x$, cos x, tan x, cot x, sec x, cosec x are trigonometric curves. Their graphs are as follows:

(a) $f(x) = \sin x$: Let $f(x) = \sin x$, increases strictly from – 1 to 1 as x increases from – $\pi/2$ to $\pi/2$, decreases for x changing from $\pi/2$ to $3\pi/2$ and so on, so, the graph of sin x and cosec x will be as shown in the Figure 3.34.

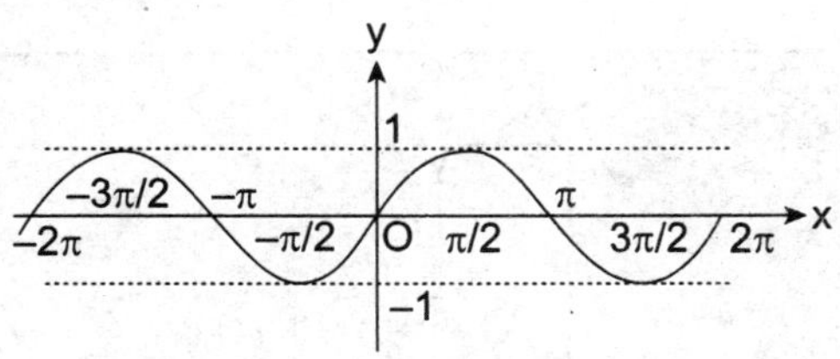

FIGURE 3.34

Properties:

1. Domain of sin x is $\mathbb{R}$ and range is [–1, 1].
2. It is an odd function.
3. sin x is periodic function with period 2π.
4. Principal domain is [– $\pi/2$, $\pi/2$].
5. It is a continuous function and increases in first and fourth quadrants while decreases in second and third quadrants.

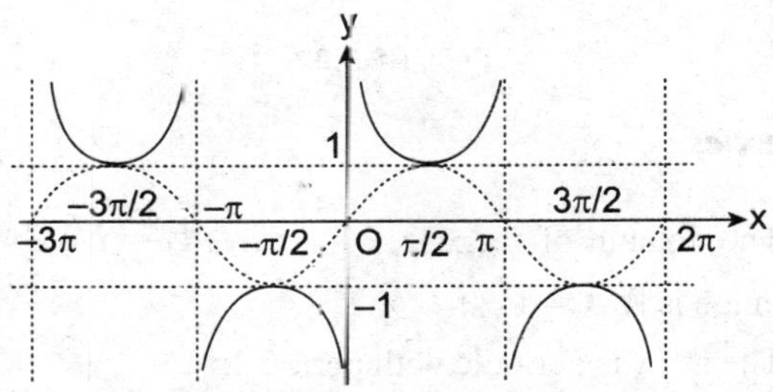

FIGURE 3.35

(b) $f(x)$ = cosec x: cosec x is reciprocal of sin x.

Properties:

1. The domain is $\mathbb{R} - \{n\pi \mid n \in \mathbb{Z}\}$.
2. Range of cosec$x$ is $\mathbb{R}$ – (–1, 1).
3. Principal domain is: $[-\pi/2, \pi/2] - \{0\}$
4. The cosec x is periodic with period 2π; $n \in \mathbb{Z}$
5. It is odd function discontinuous at $x = n\pi$
6. It decreases in first and fourth quadrants while increases in second and third quadrants.

(c) $f(x)$ = cos x: As discussed, cos$x$ decreases strictly from 1 to – 1 as x increases from 0 to π, increases strictly from – 1 to 1 as x increases from π to 2π and so on.

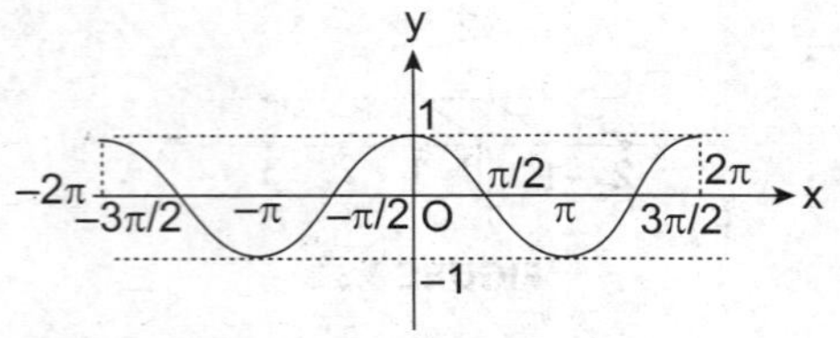

FIGURE 3.36

Properties:

1. The domain of cos x is ℝ and the range is [–1, 1].
2. Principal domain is [0, π].
3. It is an even function, i.e., symmetric about y-axis.
4. cos x is periodic with period 2π.
5. It is continuous function decreases in I[st] and IInd quadrant increases in IIIrd and IVth quadrant.

(d) $f(x)$ = sec x: sec x is reciprocal of cos$x$.

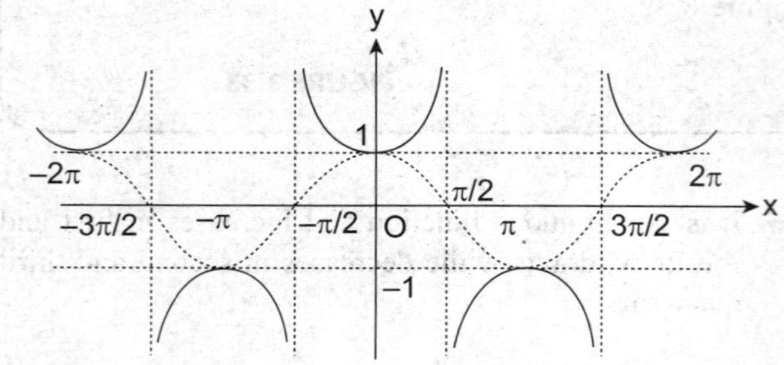

FIGURE 3.37

Properties:

1. The domain of sec x is $\mathbb{R} - \left\{(2n+1)\frac{\pi}{2} \middle| n \in Z\right\}$ and range is ℝ – (– 1, 1).
2. The sec x is periodic with period 2π.
3. Principal domain is [0, π] – {π/2}
4. It is discontinuous at x = (2n +1) π/2; n ∈ ℤ.

(e) y = tan x:

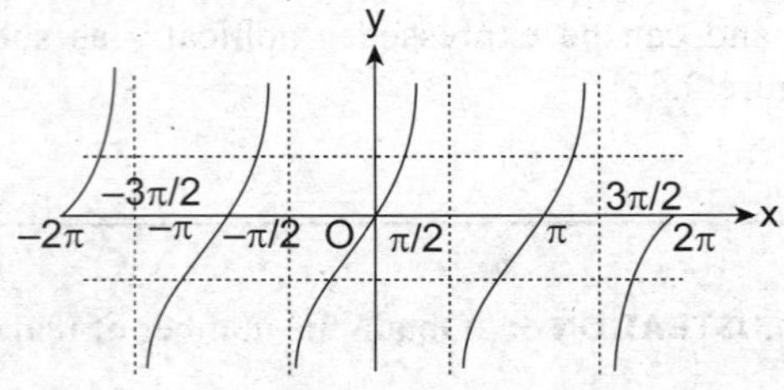

FIGURE 3.38

1. The domain of tan x is $\mathbb{R}-\{(2n+1)\pi/2\}$ and range ℝ or (– ∞, ∞). Principal domain is (– π/2, π/2).
2. It is periodic with period π.
3. It is discontinuous at x = $\mathbb{R}-\{(2n+1)\pi/2\}$ and it is strictly increasing function in its domain.

(f) y = cot x: cot x is reciprocal of tan x.

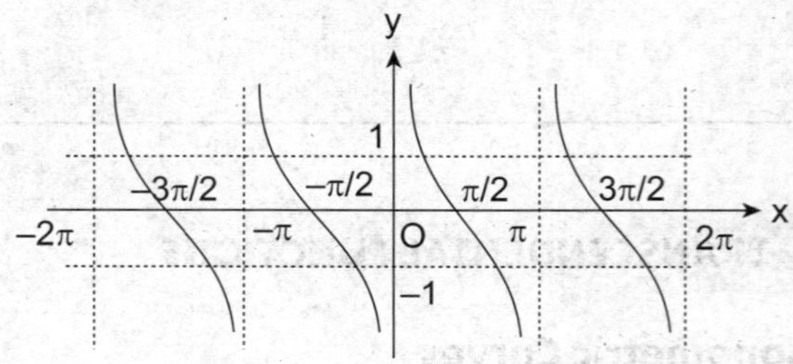

FIGURE 3.39

1. The domain of $f(x)$ = cot x = ℝ ~ {nπ}; Range = ℝ.
2. It is periodic with period π and x = nπ, n ∈ ℤ as asymptotes.
3. Principal domain is (0, π).
4. It is discontinuous at x = nπ; n ∈ ℤ.
5. It is strictly decreasing function in its domain

ILLUSTRATION 7: Determine the number of solutions of the equation tan x = log x lying in the interval [0, 3π].

SOLUTION: Sketching both the graph on same set of axes, we get clearly four real solutions of the given equation.

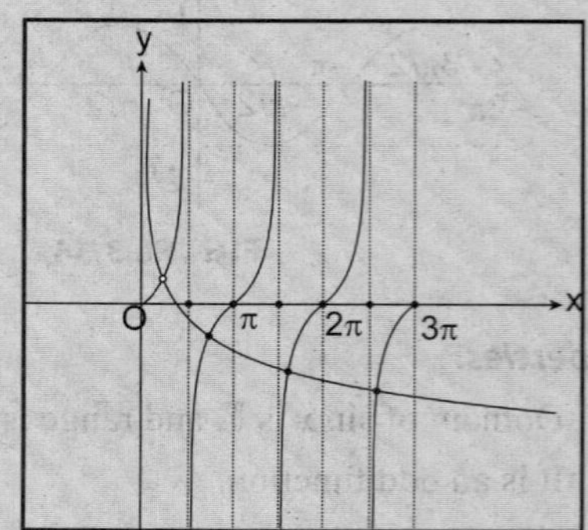

FIGURE 3.40

ILLUSTRATION 8: Find the number of real values of x satisfying the equation $\sin x - x^3 = 0$.

SOLUTION: $f(x) = x^3$ is an increasing function and $f(x) = x^3 \in [-1, 1]$ when $x \in [-1, 1]$.

Thus, solution exist only in the interval [–1, 1] and represented by number of point of intersection of the graph $y = x^3$ and $y = \sin x$.

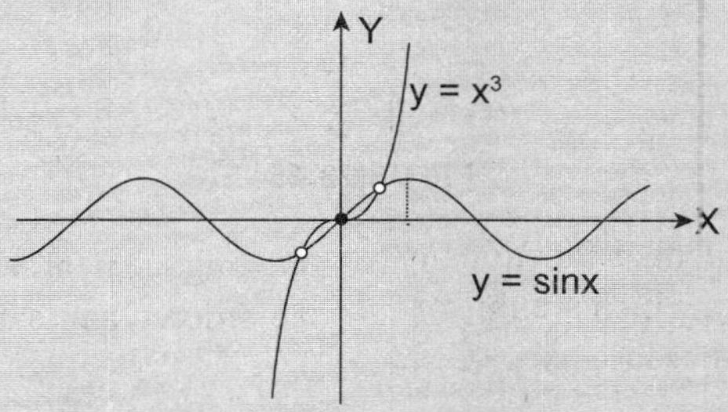

FIGURE 3.41

Clearly, from the graph we can see the three real solutions.

■ Exponential Function

Here, $f(x) = a^x$, $a > 0$, $a \neq 1$, and $x \in \mathbb{R}$, where domain = $\mathbb{R}$, range = $(0, \infty)$.

Case I. **$a > 1$:** Here, $f(x) = y = a^x$ increases with the increase in x,

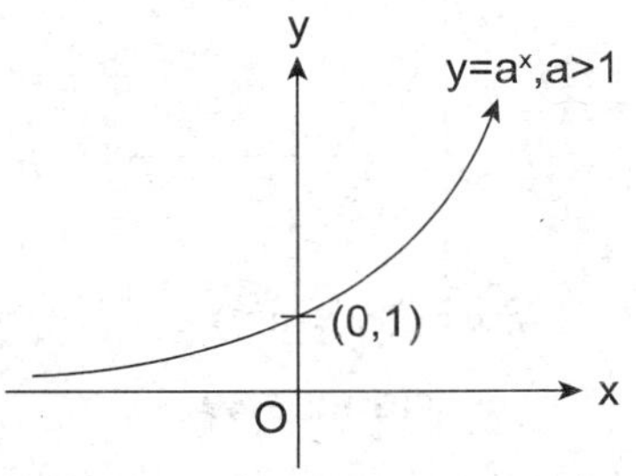

FIGURE 3.42

That is, $f(x)$ is increasing function on $\mathbb{R}$.

For example, $y = 2^x$, $y = 3^x$, $y = 4^x$,.... We have; $2^x < 3^x < 4^x <$.... for $x > 1$ and $2^x > 3^x > 4^x >$.... for $0 < x < 1$.

and they can be shown as shown in Figure 3.43..

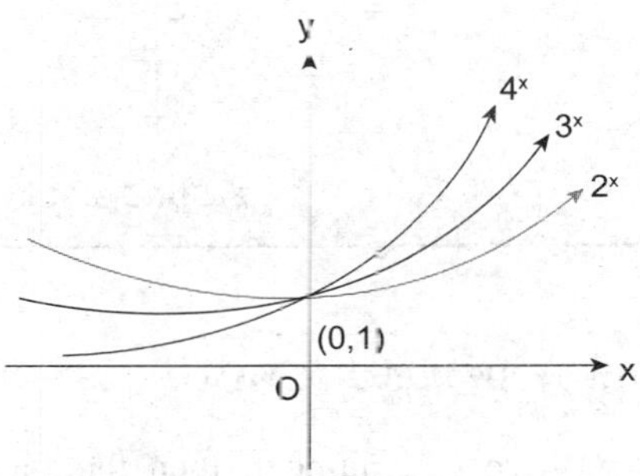

FIGURE 3.43

Case II. **$0 < a < 1$:** Here, $f(x) = a^x$ decrease with the increase in x, i.e., $f(x)$ is decreasing function on $\mathbb{R}$.

'In general, exponential function increases or decreases as $(a > 1)$ or $(0 < a < 1)$ respectively'.

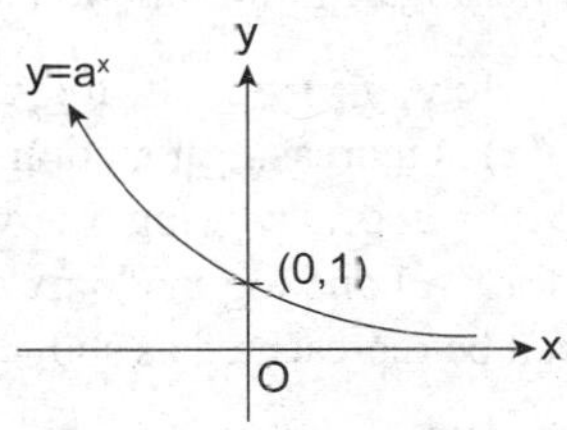

FIGURE 3.44

ILLUSTRATION 9: Find the number of ordered pairs (x, y); $x, y \in \mathbb{R}$ satisfying the equation $y = x^{1/3}$; and $y^2 = 4^{-x}$ simultaneously.

SOLUTION: Graph of $x^{1/3}$ is shown below in Figure 3.45.

The other curve given is $y^2 = 4^{-x}$

$\Rightarrow y = \pm\sqrt{4^{-x}} = \pm\, 2^{-x}$

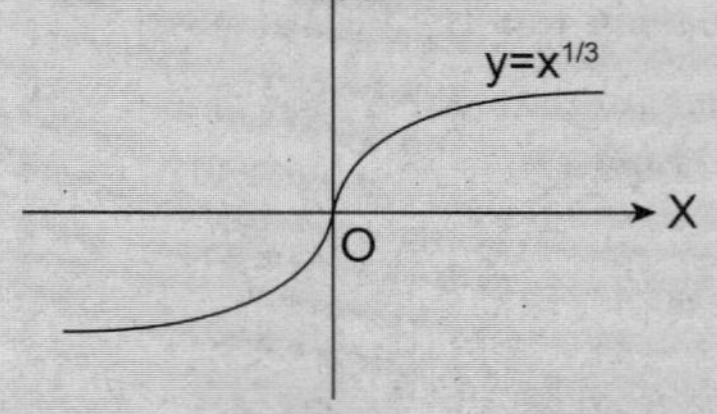

FIGURE 3.45

is a pair of exponential functions $y = 2^{-x}$ and $y = -2^{-x}$ which are mirror image of each other in x-axis.

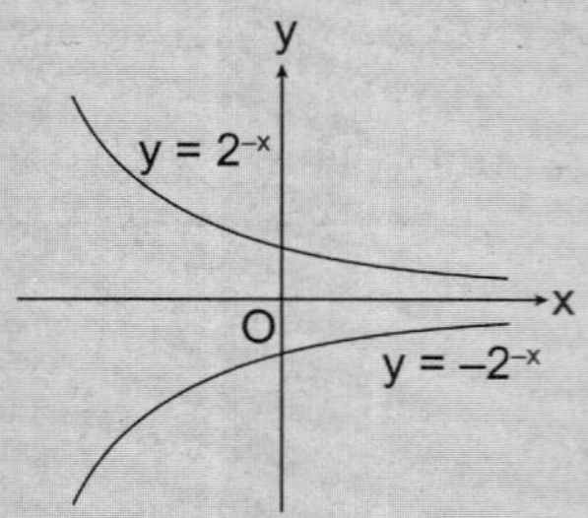

FIGURE 3.46

Drawing them on same axes exactly one ordered pair satisfies both.

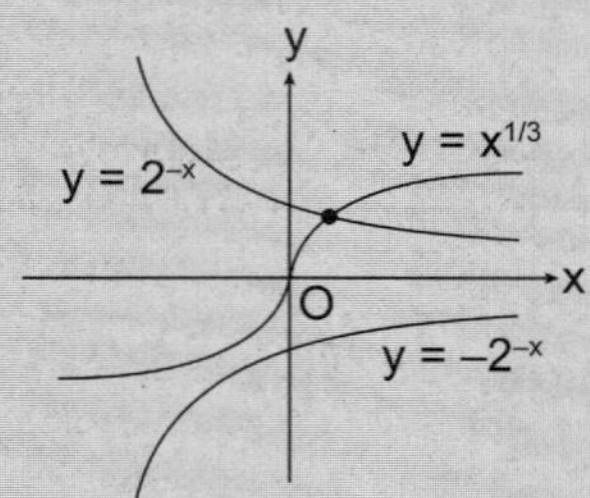

FIGURE 3.47

■ LOGARITHMIC FUNCTION

If 'a' is a positive real number, then the function that associates every positive real number to $\log_a x$. That is, $y = \log_a x$ is called the logarithmic function and it is defined as the inverse of exponential function to the same base.

e.g., $y = \log_{10}(x^2 + x + 1)$

The domain of the logarithmic function is $(0, \infty)$

The range of the logarithmic function is : $(-\infty, +\infty)$

Case I. $\mathbf{a > 1}$**:** Here, $f(x) = y = \log_a x$ increases with increase in x, i.e., $f(x)$ is increasing function on $\mathbb{R}$.

e.g., $y = \log_2 x$, $y = \log_3 x$, $y = \log_4 x, \ldots$ we have; $\log_2 x > \log_3 x > \log_4 x > \ldots$ for $x > 1$ and $\log_2 x < \log_3 x < \log_4 x < \ldots$ for $0 < x < 1$ and they can be represented as shown in Figure 3.48.

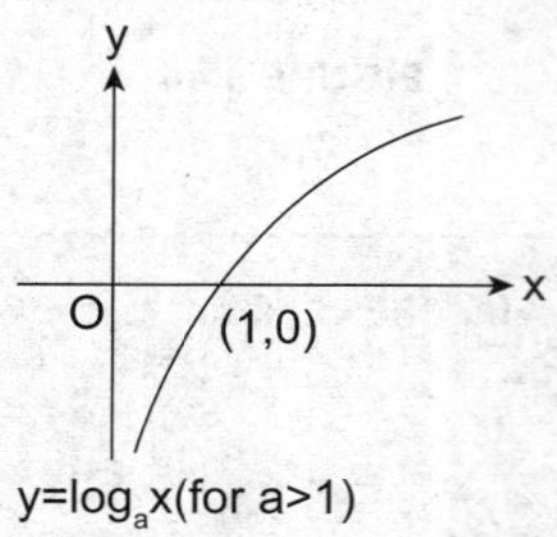

FIGURE 3.48

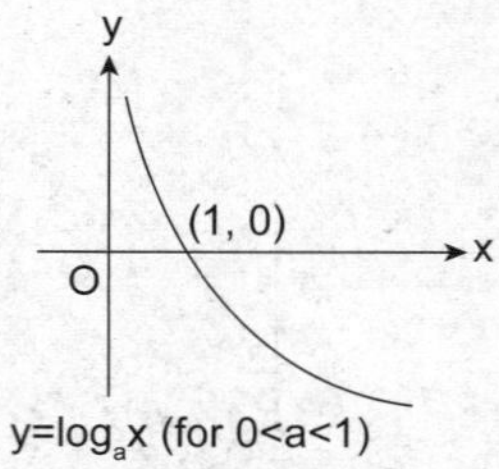

FIGURE 3.49

Case II. $\mathbf{0 < a < 1}$**:** Here, $f(x) = \log_a x$ decreases with increase in x, i.e., $f(x)$ is a decreasing function on $\mathbb{R}$.

"In general, logarithmic function increases or decreases as $(a > 1)$ or $(0 < a < 1)$ respectively" as shown in Figure 3.50.

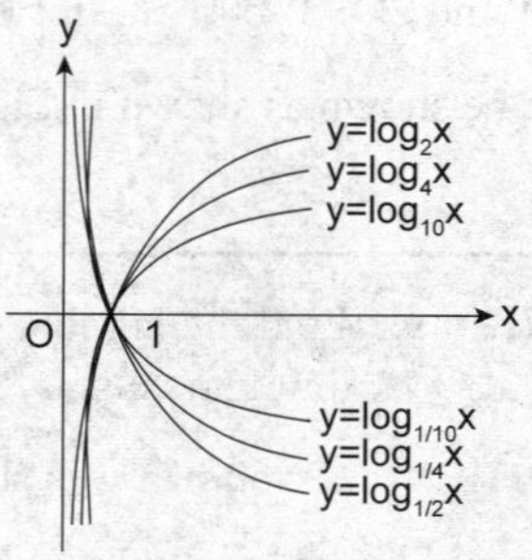

FIGURE 3.50

ILLUSTRATION 10: Find the number of real solutions of the equation $x^3 - 4x = \log_2 x$.

SOLUTION: Sketching the graph of cubic polynomial $f(x) = x^3 - 4x$ as it has 3 real roots $x = 0, -2, 2$ and $g(x) = \log_2 x$ on the same reference frame, we get

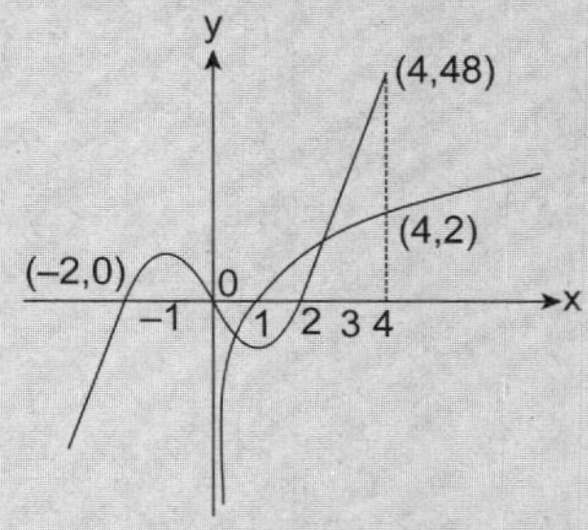

FIGURE 3.51

$\because\ f(4) = x^3 - 16 = 48$ and $g(4) = 2 \qquad \Rightarrow f(4) > g(4)$

Thus, from the graph, we can see that curves intersect twice. Thus, given equation has exactly two real roots.

■ INVERSE CIRCULAR FUNCTIONS

(a) **$\sin^{-1} x$:** Its domain is $[-1, 1]$. Its range is $[-\pi/2, \pi/2]$. It is an increasing function.
It is an odd function, i.e., $\sin^{-1}(-x) = -\sin^{-1}x\ \forall\ x \in [-1, 1]$

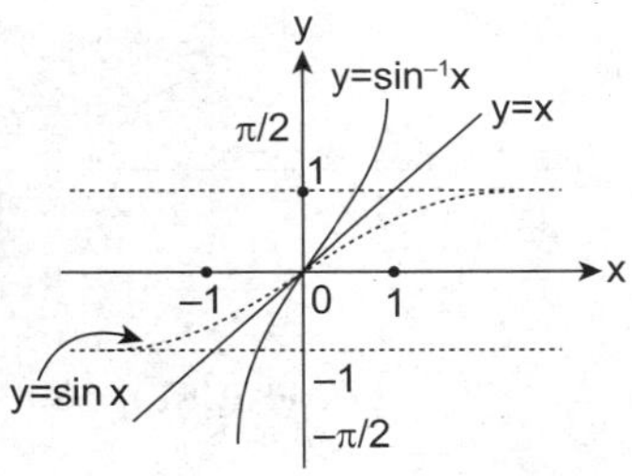

FIGURE 3.52

(b) **$\cos^{-1} x$:** Its domain is $[-1, 1]$. Its range is $[0, \pi]$. It is a decreasing function. It neither an even function nor odd function $\cos^{-1}(-x) = \pi - \cos^{-1}x$.

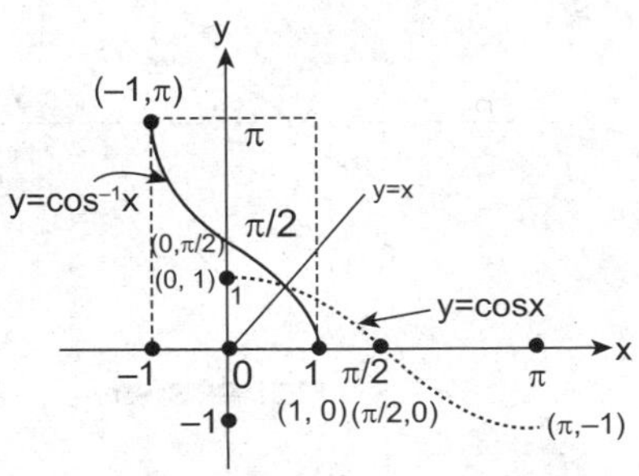

FIGURE 3.53

(c) **$\tan^{-1} x$:** Its domain is $\mathbb{R}$. Its range is $(-\pi/2, \pi/2)$. It is an increasing function.
It is an odd function. $\tan^{-1}(-x) = -\tan^{-1}x\ \forall\ x \in \mathbb{R}$.

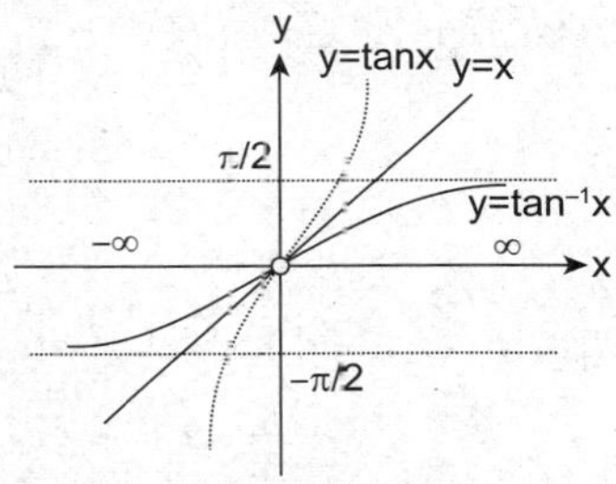

FIGURE 3.54

(d) **$\cot^{-1} x$:** Its domain is $\mathbb{R}$. Its range is $(0, \pi)$. It is a decreasing function. It is neither an even function nor odd function $\cot^{-1}(-x) = \pi - \cot^{-1}x$.

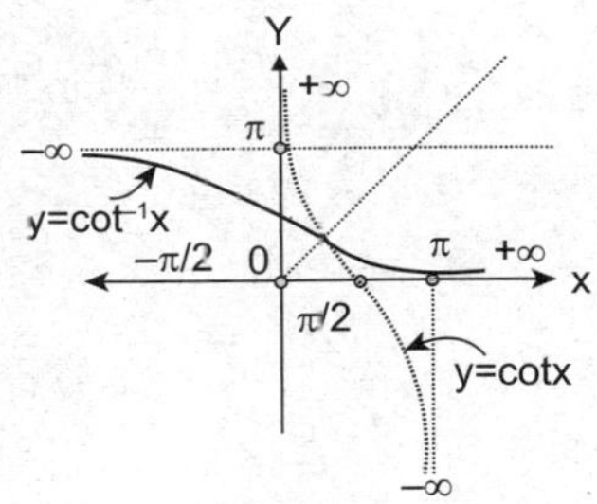

FIGURE 3.55

(e) **$\sec^{-1} x$:** Its domain is $\mathbb{R} - (-1, 1)$. Its range is $[0, \pi] - \{\pi/2\}$. It is an increasing function. It neither an even function nor odd function $\sec^{-1}(-x) = \pi - \cot^{-1}x$.

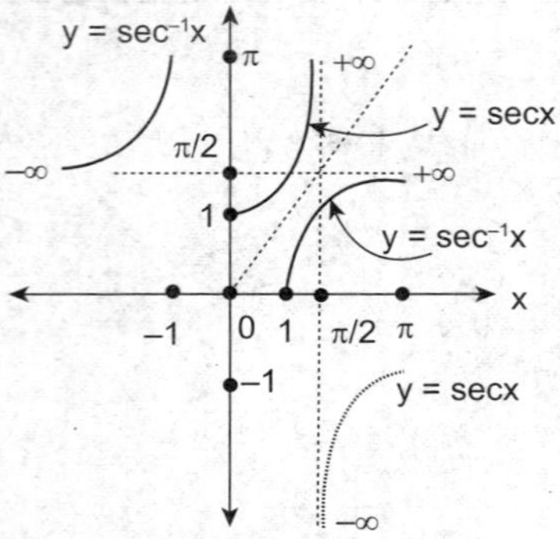

FIGURE 3.56

(f) cosec^{-1}x: Its domain is $\mathbb{R}$ – (–1, 1). Its range is [– π/2, π/2] ~ {0}. It is an decreasing function. It is an odd function cosec^{-1}(–x) = – cosec^{-1}x.

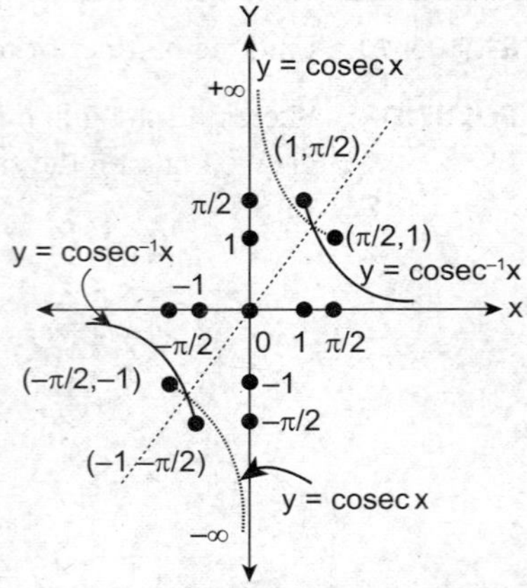

FIGURE 3.57

ILLUSTRATION 11: Given f and g as two functions defined as $f(x)=\begin{cases}|x| & \text{if } x<0 \\ \sin^{-1}x & \text{if } x\ge 0\end{cases}$ and $g(x)=\cot^{-1}x$.

Find the number of real roots of equation $f(x) = g(x)$.

SOLUTION: Clearly $f(x)=\begin{cases}-x; & x<0 \\ \sin^{-1}x; & x\ge 0\end{cases}$ and $g(x) = \cot^{-1}x$

Sketching both curves on same x-y plane and counting the point of intersection, we get two solutions.

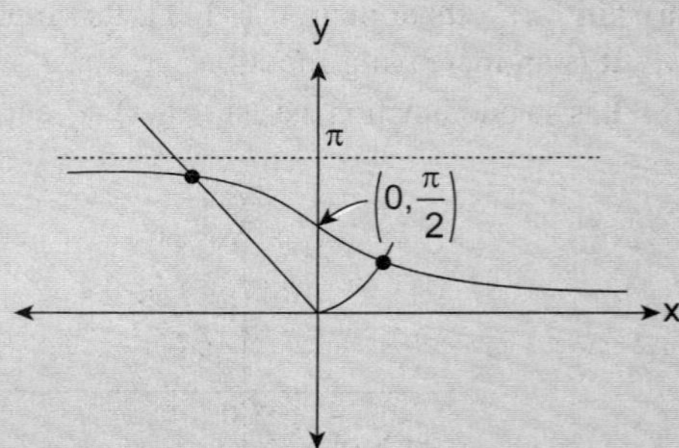

FIGURE 3.58

ILLUSTRATION 12: Find the set of common solutions satisfying the inequality $x^2 - 8|x| + 7 > 0$ and

$$\frac{\pi^2}{4}+\frac{\pi}{2}\tan^{-1}x-6(\tan^{-1}x)^2\ge 0$$

SOLUTION: Given $|x|^2 - 8|x| + 7 > 0$

$\Rightarrow (|x| - 1)(|x| - 7) > 0 \qquad \Rightarrow |x| < 1$ or $|x| > 7$

$\Rightarrow x \in (-1, 1) \cup (-\infty, -7) \cup (7, \infty)$ and

$$\frac{\pi^2}{4}+\frac{\pi}{2}\left(\tan^{-1}x\right)-6\left(\tan^{-1}x\right)^2\ge 0$$

$\Rightarrow 24(\tan^{-1}x)^2 - 2\pi\tan^{-1}x - \pi^2 \le 0$

$\Rightarrow (6\tan^{-1}x + \pi)(4\tan^{-1}x - \pi) \le 0$

$$\Rightarrow -\frac{\pi}{6}\le\tan^{-1}x\le\frac{\pi}{4}\Rightarrow -\frac{1}{\sqrt{3}}\le x\le 1$$

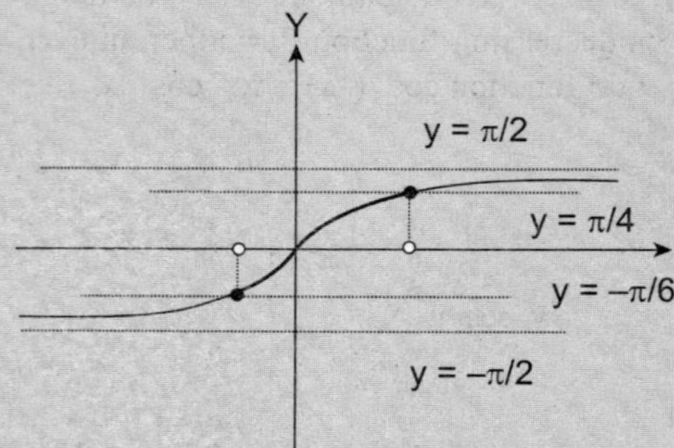

FIGURE 3.59

ILLUSTRATION 13: Solve the inequality $\tan^{-1}x\le\cot^{-1}x<\frac{3\pi}{4}$.

SOLUTION: **Method 1:** $\because\ \tan^{-1}x+\cot^{-1}x=\frac{\pi}{2}$

Thus, the inequality $\tan^{-1}x \le \cot^{-1}x < \frac{3\pi}{4}$

$\Rightarrow \quad \tan^{-1}x \le \frac{\pi}{2} - \tan^{-1}x < \frac{3\pi}{4} \quad \Rightarrow \quad \tan^{-1}x \le \frac{\pi}{4} \;\&\; \tan^{-1}x > \frac{-\pi}{4} \quad \Rightarrow \quad -\frac{\pi}{4} < \tan^{-1}x \le \frac{\pi}{4}$

$\because$ tan x is an increasing function in the interval $\left(-\frac{\pi}{2}, \frac{\pi}{2}\right)$

$\therefore \quad \tan\left(\frac{-\pi}{4}\right) < x \le \tan\frac{\pi}{4} \quad \Rightarrow \quad -1 < x \le 1$. Consequently the solut on set is (–1, 1]

Method II: Graphically

Drawing the graph $y = \frac{3\pi}{4}$, $y = \tan^{-1}x$ and $y = \cot^{-1}x$ on the same x-y plane as shown in the Figure 3.60.

Clearly, the values of x satisfying the given inequality are $x \in (-1, 1]$.

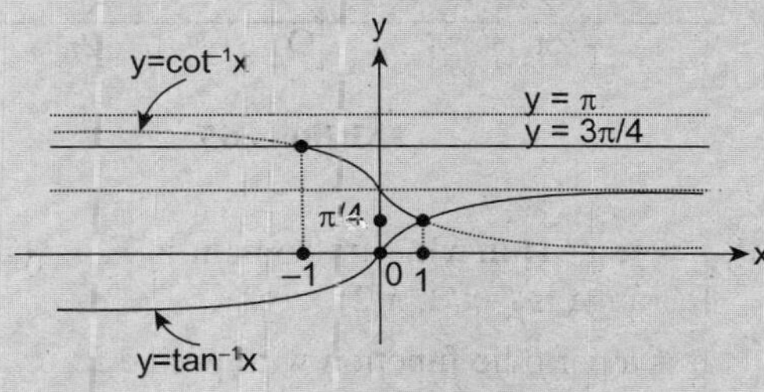

FIGURE 3.60

(g) $y = \sin(\sin^{-1}x) = \cos(\cos^{-1}x) = x$
Its domain is [–1, 1]. Its range is [–1, 1]. It is a non-periodic, monotonically increasing, odd function

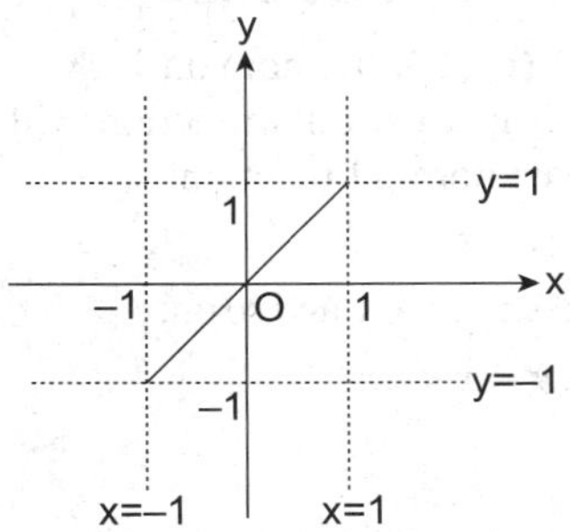

FIGURE 3.61

(h) $y = \text{cosec}(\text{cosec}^{-1}x) = \sec(\sec^{-1}x) = x$: Its domain is $\mathbb{R} - (-1, 1)$. Its range is $\mathbb{R} - (-1, 1)$.
It is a non-periodic, monotonically increasing, odd function.

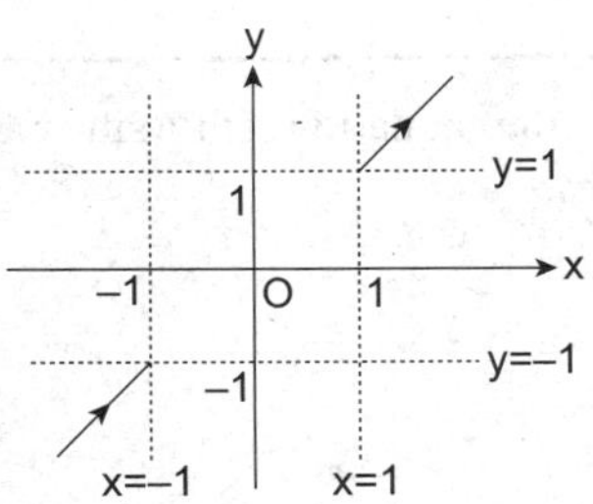

FIGURE 3.62

(i) $y = \tan(\tan^{-1}x) = \cot(\cot^{-1}x) = x$
Its domain is R. Its range is $\mathbb{R}$. It is a non-periodic, monotonically increasing, odd function.

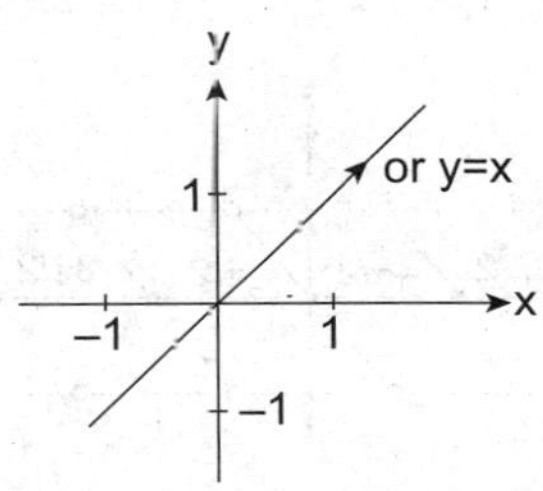

FIGURE 3.63

(j) $y = \sin^{-1}(\sin x)$: Its domain is $\mathbb{R}$ and its range is $[-\pi/2, \pi/2]$.
It is a periodic function with period 2π. It is an odd function.

$$= \begin{cases} x; & -\frac{\pi}{2} \le x \le \frac{\pi}{2} \\ -\pi - x; & -\frac{3\pi}{2} \le x \le -\frac{\pi}{2} \\ \pi - x; & \text{when } \frac{\pi}{2} \le x \le \frac{3\pi}{2} \end{cases}$$

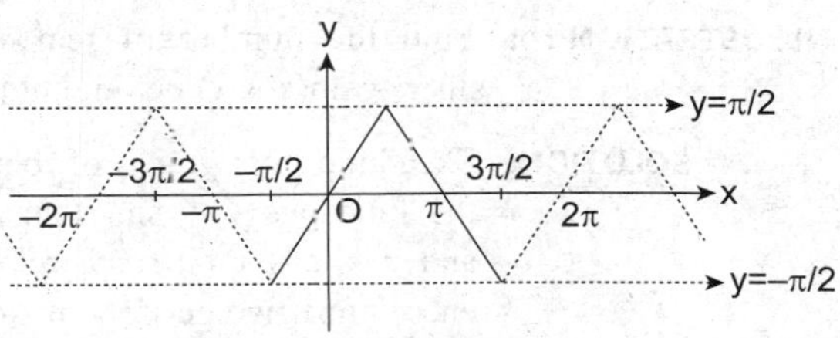

FIGURE 3.64

(k) $y = \cos^{-1}(\cos x)$: Its domain is $\mathbb{R}$. Its range is $[0, \pi]$.
It is a periodic function with period 2π. It is an even function

$$= \begin{cases} x; & 0 \le x \le \pi \\ 2\pi - x; & 0 \le 2\pi - x \le \pi \text{ or } \pi \le x \le 2\pi \end{cases}$$

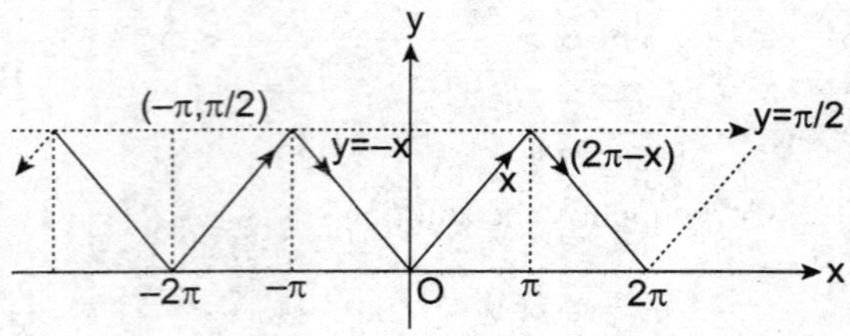

FIGURE 3.65

(l) $y = \tan^{-1}(\tan x)$: Its domain is $\mathbb{R} - \{(2n + 1)\pi/2\}$. Its range is $(-\pi/2, \pi/2)$

It is a periodic function with period π.

It is an odd function and monotonically increasing function and $\left\{x;\ -\frac{\pi}{2} < x < \frac{\pi}{2}\right\}$

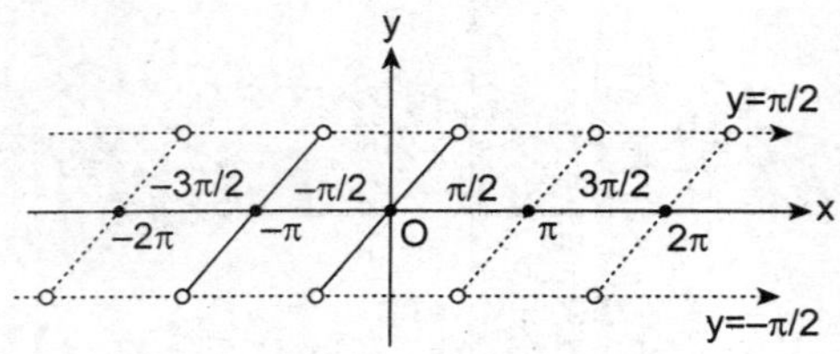

FIGURE 3.66

(m) $y = \sec^{-1}(\sec x)$: Its domain is $\mathbb{R} - \{(2n + 1)\pi/2\}$

Its range is $[0, \pi] - \{\pi/2\}$. It is a periodic function with period 2π. It is an even function.

$$= \begin{cases} x; & x \in \left[0, \frac{\pi}{2}\right) \cup \left(\frac{\pi}{2}, \pi\right] \\ 2\pi - x; & 2\pi - x \in \left[0, \frac{\pi}{2}\right) \cup \left(\frac{\pi}{2}, \pi\right] \text{or} [\pi, 2\pi] - \left\{\frac{3\pi}{2}\right\} \end{cases}$$

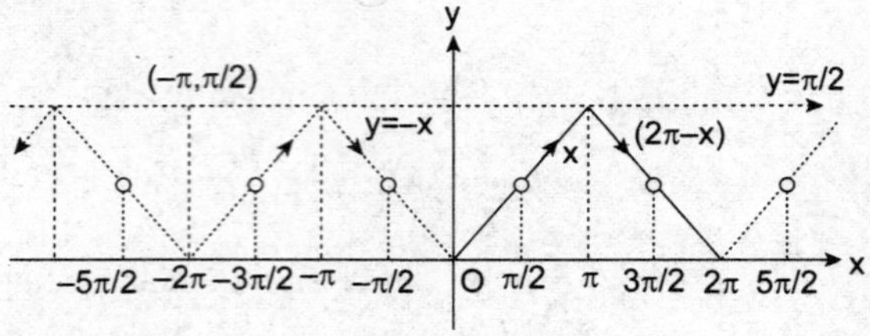

FIGURE 3.67

(n) $y = \text{cosec}^{-1}(\text{cosec}\, x)$: Its domain is $\mathbb{R} - \{n\pi: n \in \mathbb{Z}\}$ Its range is $[-\pi/2, \pi/2] - \{0\}$. It is a periodic function with period 2π. It is an odd function.

$$= \begin{cases} x & -\frac{\pi}{2} \le x < 0 \ \cup\ 0 < x \le \frac{\pi}{2} \\ \pi - x & -\frac{\pi}{2} \le \pi - x < 0 \ \cup\ 0 \le \pi - x \le \frac{\pi}{2} \end{cases}$$

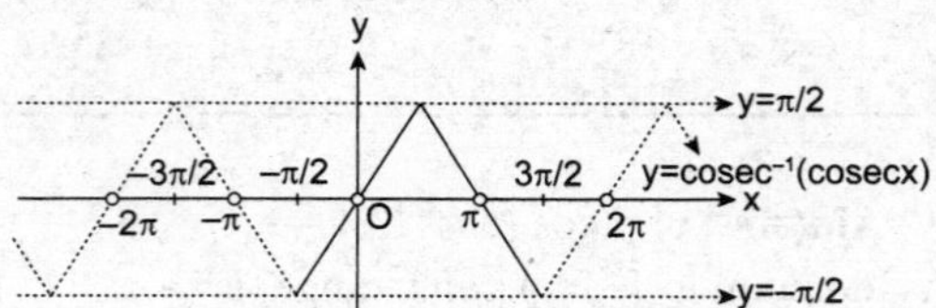

FIGURE 3.68

(o) $y = \cot^{-1}(\cot x)$. Its domain is $\mathbb{R} - \{n\pi\}$. Its range is $(0, \pi)$. It is a periodic function with period π. It is neither even nor odd function.

$$= \begin{cases} x;\ 0 < x < \pi \\ x + \pi;\ -\pi < x < 0 \text{ and so on.} \\ x - \pi;\ \pi < x < 2\pi \end{cases}$$

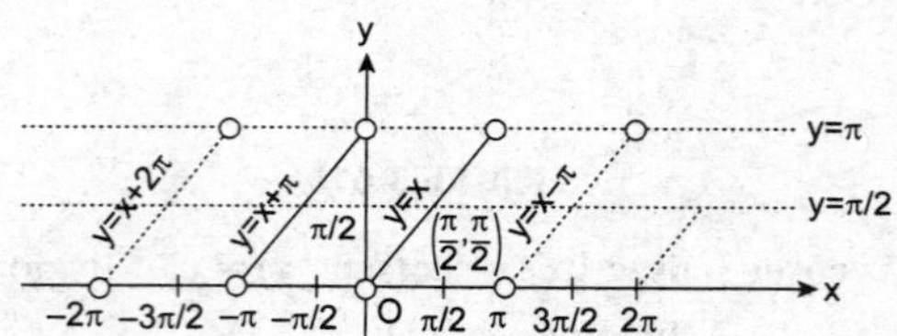

FIGURE 3.69

ILLUSTRATION 14: Find the number of real values of x satisfying the equation $\sin^{-1}(\sin x) = \cos x$ or $\sin x = \sin(\cos x)$ belonging to the interval $[-2\pi, 3\pi]$.

SOLUTION: Sketching the graph of both the functions $y = \sin^{-1}(\sin x)$ and $y = \cos x$ on same reference frame, we get 5 points of intersection in the interval $[-2\pi, 3\pi]$ as obvious from the Figure 3.70, Thus, the given equation has 5 real solutions $\in [-2\pi, 3\pi]$

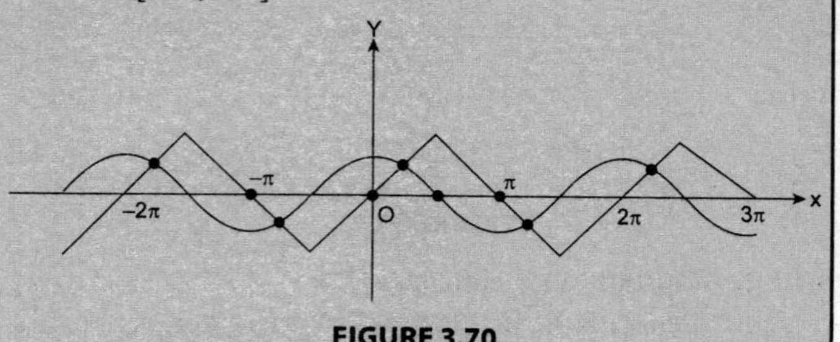

FIGURE 3.70

STANDARD CONIC SECTIONS

Circle

The general equation of a circle is $x^2 + y^2 + 2gx + 2fy + c = 0$

To draw a sketch of a circle, we write the equation in the standard form $(x + g)^2 + (y + f)^2 = \left(\sqrt{g^2 + f^2 - c}\right)^2$, whose centre is $(-g, -f)$; and radius $r = \sqrt{g^2 + f^2 - c}$.

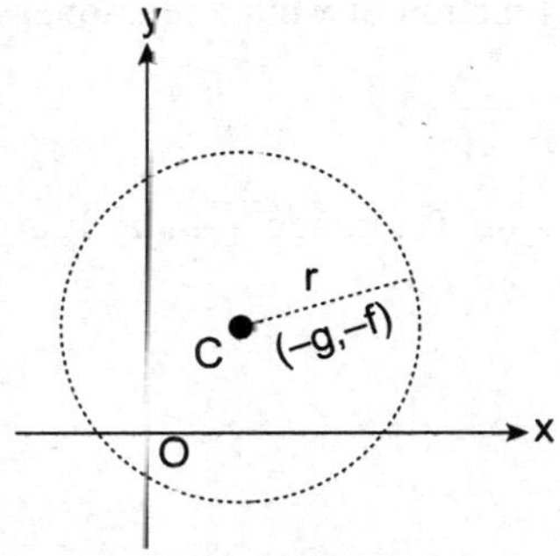

FIGURE 3.71

NOTE

(i) *If centre is origin and radius is a, then the equation of circle is $x^2 + y^2 = a^2$.*
It is not function in x but it is a relation in x and symmetric in all four quadrants.

(ii) *If the end points of diameter are (x_1, y_1) and (x_2, y_2), then the equation of circle is $(x - x_1)(x - x_2) + (y - y_1)(y - y_2) = 0$;.*

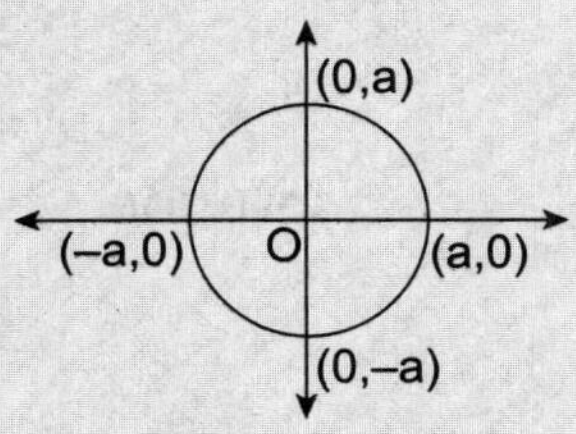

FIGURE 3.72

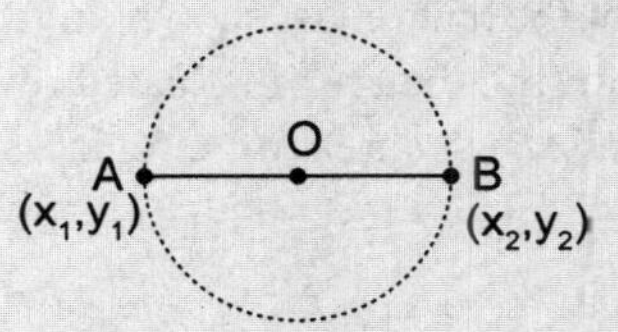

FIGURE 3.73

REPRESENTATION AS A FUNCTION

Clearly, the above equation of circle are not functions rather are many–many relations. After converting them in to functions following cases arise that may be worth noticing.

(i) $y = \sqrt{a^2 - x^2}$

Domain: $[-a, a]$; Range: $[0, a]$. Even function in x, Symmetrical about y-axis.

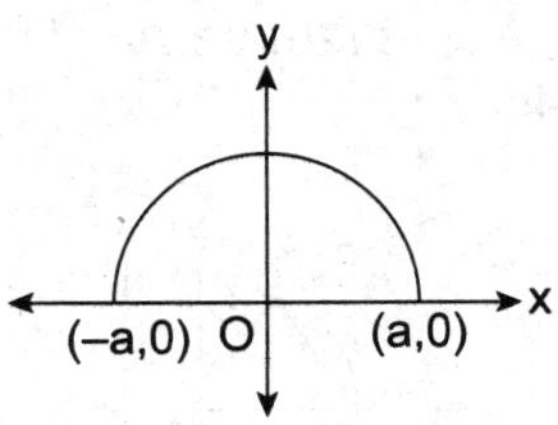

FIGURE 3.74

(ii) $y = -\sqrt{a^2 - x^2}$

Domain: $[-a, a]$, Range: $[-a, 0]$
Even function in x, Symmetrical about y-axis.

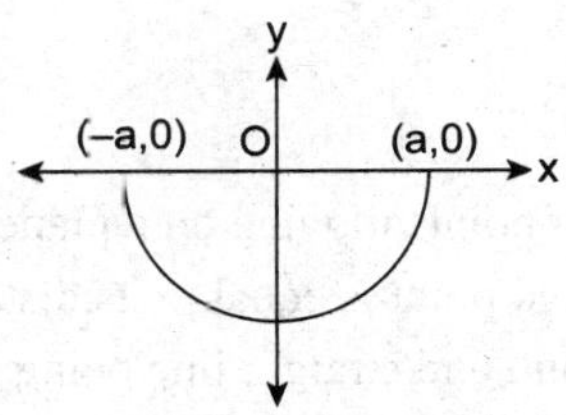

FIGURE 3.75

(iii) $x = \sqrt{a^2 - y^2}$

Domain: $[0, a]$, Range: $[-a, a]$

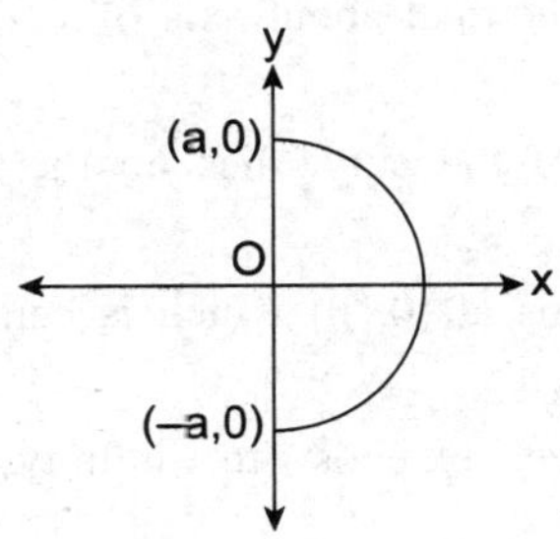

FIGURE 3.76

It is not function of x but a relation, symmetric about x-axis.

(iv) $x = -\sqrt{a^2 - y^2}$

Domain: $[-a, 0]$; Range: $[-a, a]$. It is a relation, symmetric about x-axis.

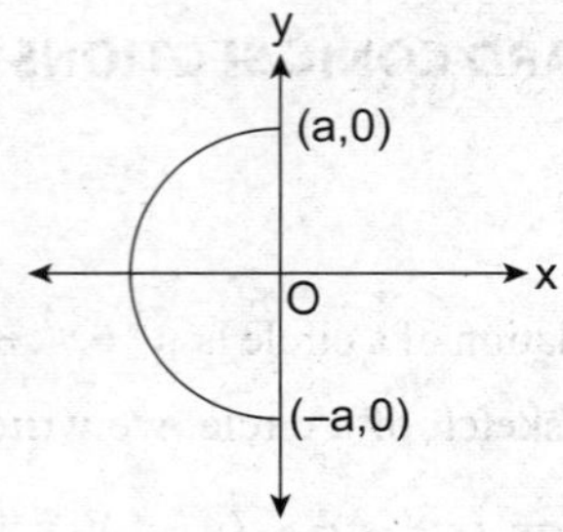

FIGURE 3.77

ILLUSTRATION 15: Find the area of region lying above the curve $y = \begin{cases} -x\sqrt{3}; & x < 0 \\ x\sqrt{3}; & x > 0 \end{cases}$ and inside the circle $x^2 + y^2 - 4y = 0$.

SOLUTION: $\because\ x^2 + y^2 - 4y = 0 \Rightarrow \quad (x-0)^2 + (y-2)^2 = 4$

Clearly $x^2 + y^2 - 4y = 0$ represents circle with centre (0, 2) and radius 2.

Sketching both the curve as shown in Figure 3.78, we need to find the area of shaded region $= 2(\text{area of } \Delta OAB) + \text{area of circular sector } \Delta\widehat{BDC}$

$$= \frac{1}{2}(2)(2)\sin\left(\frac{2\pi}{3}\right) + \frac{1}{2}(2)^2\frac{2\pi}{3} = \left(\sqrt{3} + \frac{4\pi}{3}\right)$$

Square units.

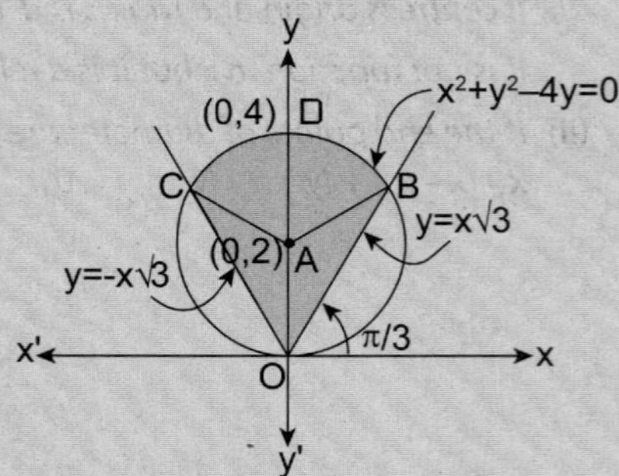

FIGURE 3.78

Parabola

It is the locus of points moving on a plane such that its distance from a fixed point is equal to its distance from a fixed straight line, point and straight line being on plane of moving point. Taking the fixed straight line $x = -a$, $a > 0$ and fixed point $(a, 0)$, we get the equation of parabola $y^2 = 4ax$.

Nature of curve:

(a) It passes through (0, 0)

(b) It is symmetrical about axis of x. (called as axis of parabola)

(c) No part of the curve lies on the negative side of axis of x.

(d) Curve turns at (0, 0) which is called the vertex of the curve.

(e) The curve extends to infinity. It is not a close curve.

(i) $y^2 = 4ax$

Shape

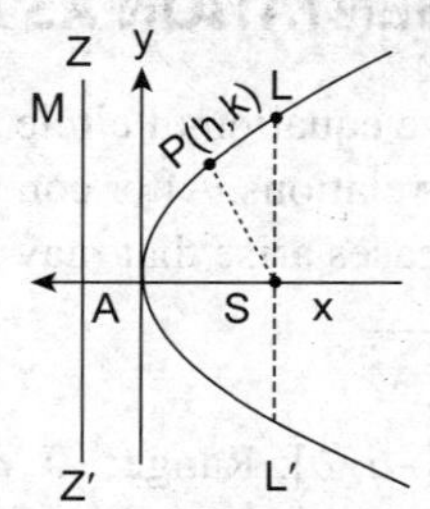

(Right handed parabola)

FIGURE 3.79

(ii) $y^2 = -4ax$

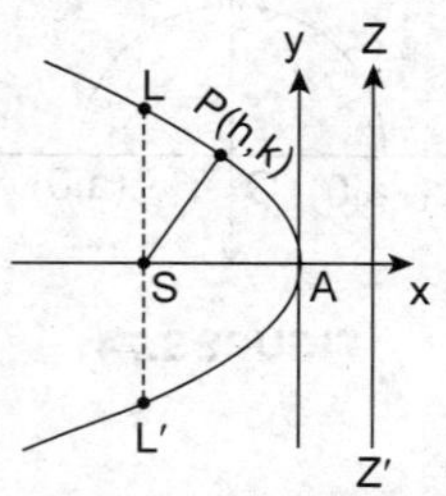

(Left handed parabola)

FIGURE 3.80

(iii) $x^2 = 4ay$

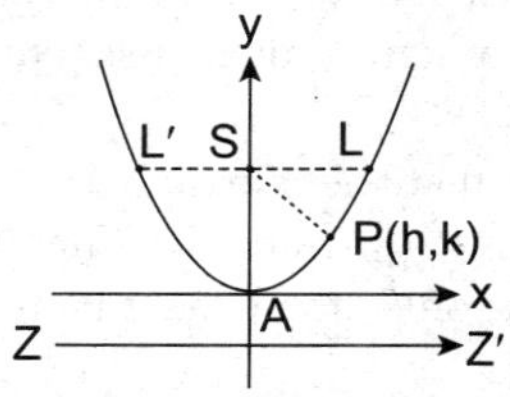

(Upwards parabola)

FIGURE 3.81

(iv) $x^2 = -4ay$

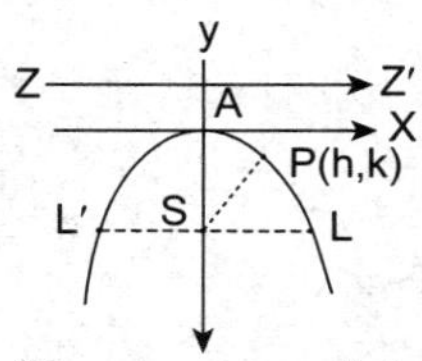

(Downwards parabola)

FIGURE 3.82

(v) $(y-k)^2 = 4a(x-h)$; $a > 0, h, k > 0$

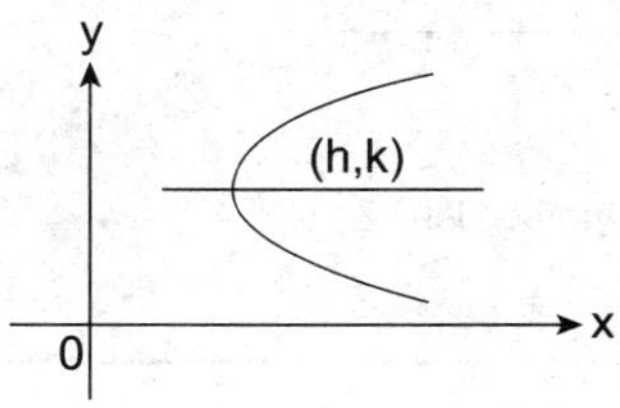

FIGURE 3.83

2. $y^2 = 4a(x-h)$; $a > 0$, $h > 0$

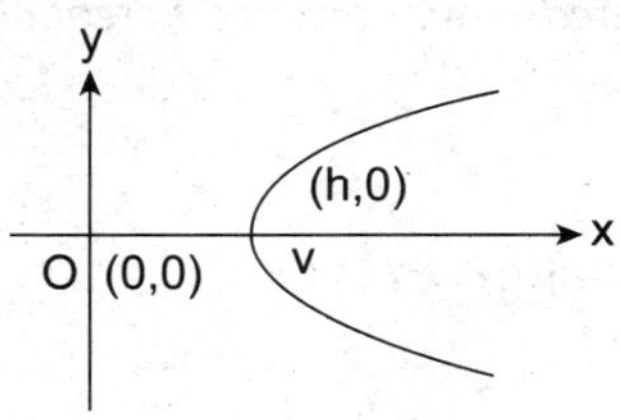

FIGURE 3.84

3. $y^2 = 4a(x+h)$; a and h are positive

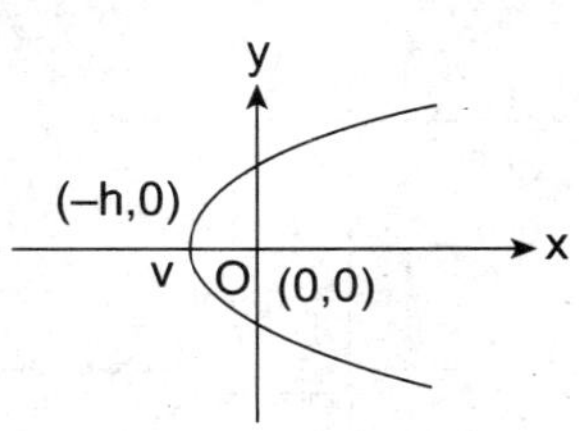

FIGURE 3.85

4. $y^2 = -4a(x-h)$; $a, h > 0$

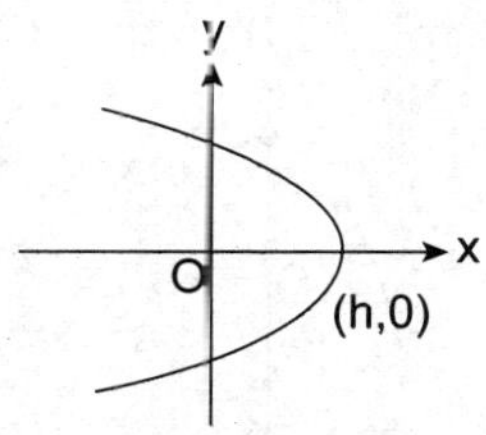

FIGURE 3.86

5. $y^2 = -4a(x+h)$; $a, h > 0$; where $a, h > 0$

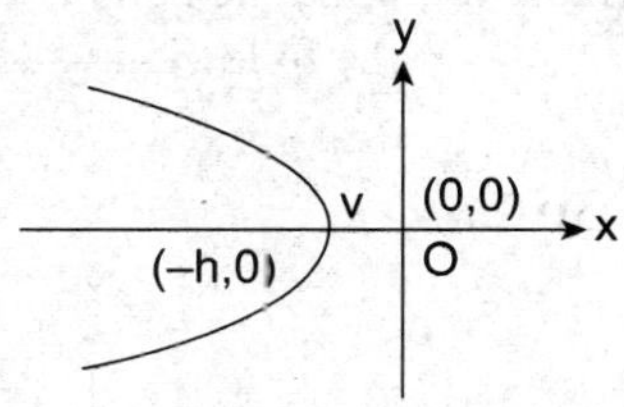

FIGURE 3.87

6. $x^2 = 4a(y+k)$; $a > 0, k > 0$

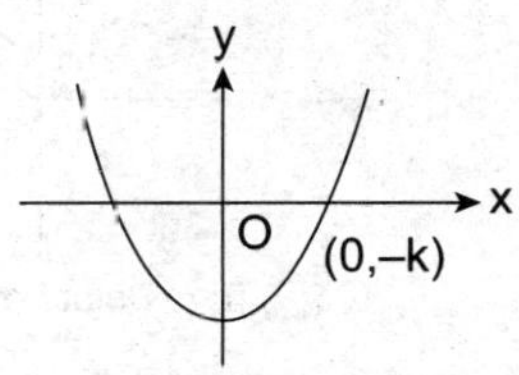

FIGURE 3.88

7. $x^2 = 4a(y-k)$; $a, k > 0$

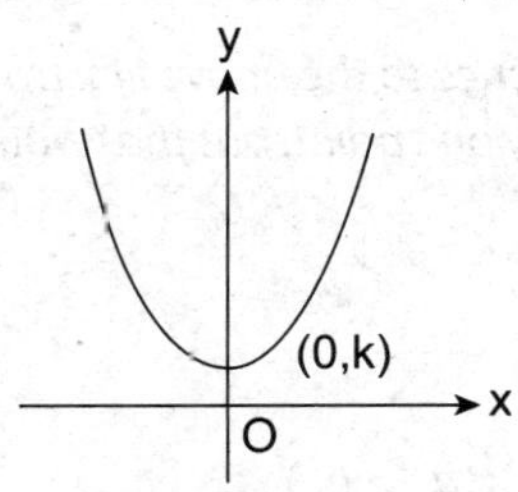

FIGURE 3.89

8. $x^2 = -4a(y+k)$; $a, k > 0$

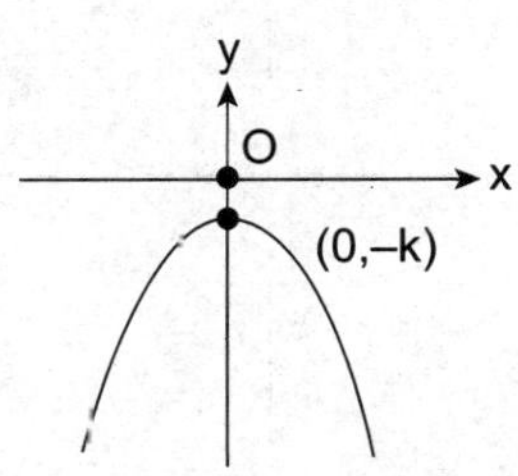

FIGURE 3.90

9. $x^2 = -4a(y-k)$; $a, k > 0$

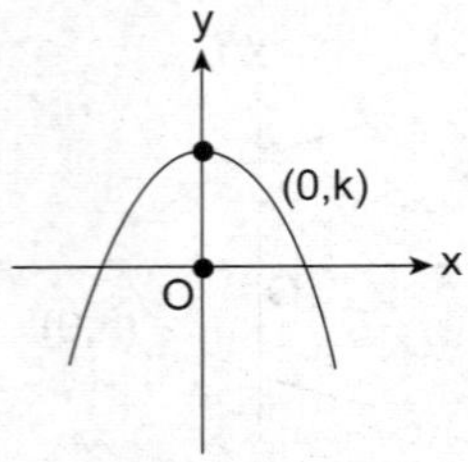

FIGURE 3.91

We observe that the function $y = x^2$ is symmetrical about y-axis. As a rule, if $f(x)$ contains even powers of x only, then the curve is symmetric about y-axis.

We observe that the function $y^2 = x$ is symmetrical about x-axis. As a rule, if a function contains even powers of y only, then the function is symmetrical about x-axis.

ILLUSTRATION 16: Find the number of points at which the two curves given by $y^2 = 4x$ and $y = x^2 + k$ meet for the following values of 'k'.

(a) $k = 0$ (b) $k = 4$

SOLUTION: (a) (b)

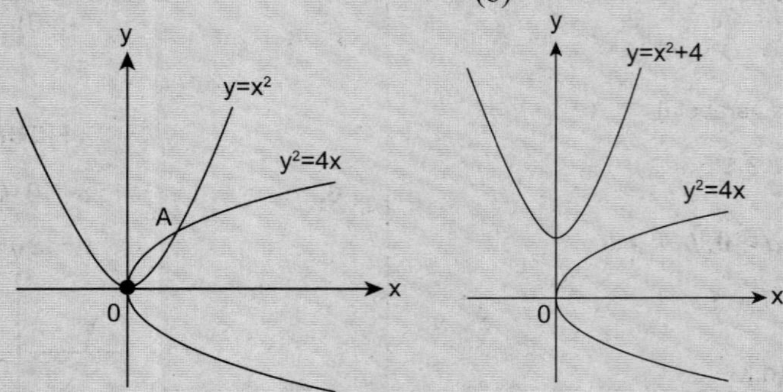

Two points of intersection 0 and A No point of intersection

FIGURE 3.92

NOTE

In fact, in reference to the above illustration, we can also find out the value of 'k' for which the two curves touch each other at exactly one point, but that would require use of calculus and is covered in our book of differential calculus.

Ellipse

(i) $\dfrac{x^2}{a^2} + \dfrac{y^2}{b^2} = 1; (a^2 > b^2)$

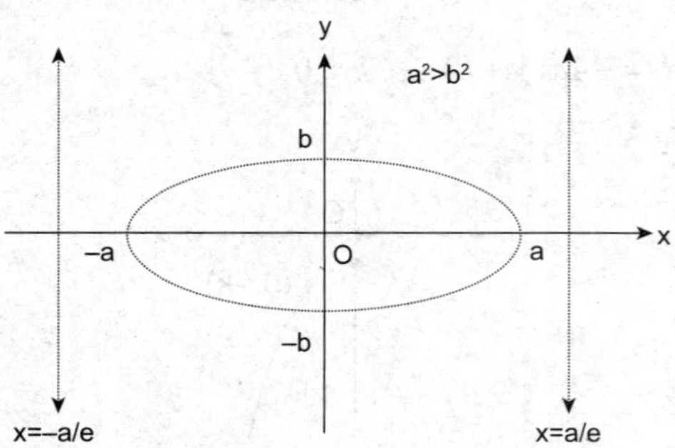

FIGURE 3.93

(ii) $\dfrac{x^2}{a^2} + \dfrac{y^2}{b^2} = 1; (a^2 < b^2)$

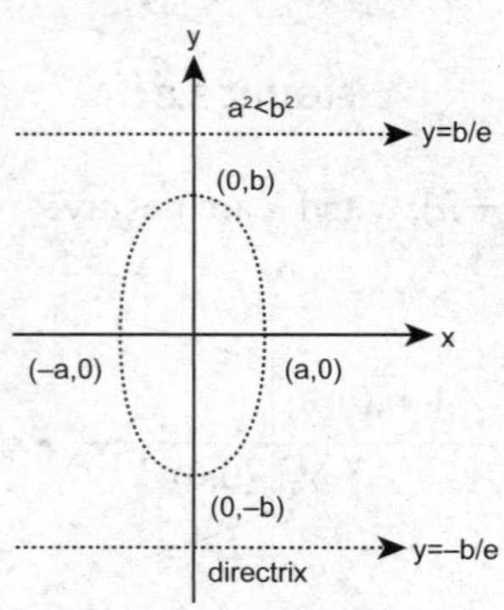

FIGURE 3.94

(iii) $\dfrac{(x-h)^2}{a^2}+\dfrac{(y-k)^2}{b^2}=1;(a^2>b^2)$

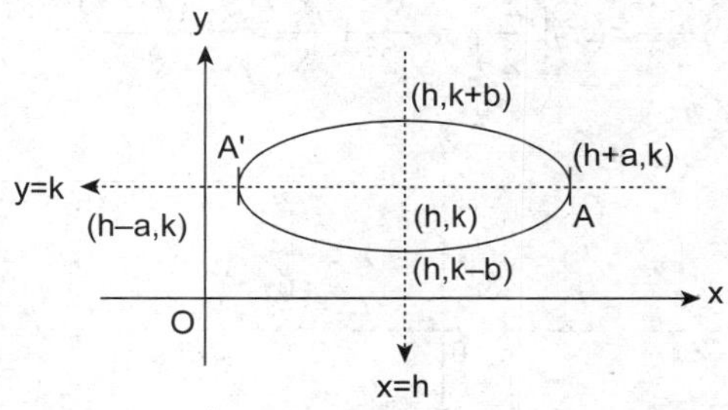

FIGURE 3.95

ILLUSTRATION 17: Compute the area enclosed by curves $3y=2\sqrt{9-x^2}$ and $y=\sqrt{9-x^2}$

SOLUTION: Indeed $y=\sqrt{9-x^2}$ is semicircle of radius 3 unit centered at origin lying above x-axis. Whereas $y=\frac{2}{3}\sqrt{9-x^2}$ is semi ellipse above x-axis with centre as origin and major axis as x-axis of length 6 and minor axis as y-axis of length 4. Therefore, the required area is given by shaded region in the Figure 3.96.

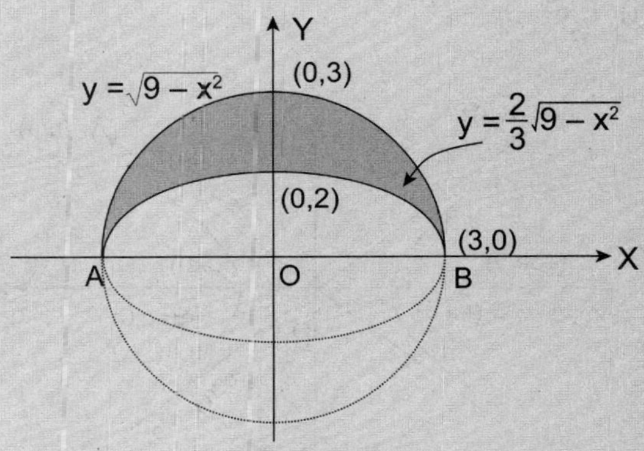

FIGURE 3.96

The area of shaded region = (area of semi-circle) – (area of semi ellipse)

$=\dfrac{\pi a^2}{2}-\dfrac{\pi ab}{2}=\dfrac{\pi a}{2}(a-b)=\dfrac{3\pi}{2}(3-2)$

$=\dfrac{3\pi}{2}$ Square unit.

ILLUSTRATION 18: Compute the area enclosed by the boundaries formed by the curves $f(x)$ defined as $f(x)=\begin{cases}\cos^{-1}\cos x; & 0\le x\le\pi\\ \sqrt{8\pi x-3\pi^2-4x^2}; & \pi<x\le\dfrac{3\pi}{2}\end{cases}$ and x-axis.

SOLUTION: Given function can be defined as $f(x)=\begin{cases}\cos^{-1}(\cos x); & 0\le x\le\pi\\ \sqrt{8\pi x-3\pi^2-4x^2}; & \pi<x\le\dfrac{3\pi}{2}\end{cases}$

$\Rightarrow\ f(x)=\begin{cases}x; & 0\le x\le\pi\\ \sqrt{8\pi x-3\pi^2-4x^2}; & \pi<x\le\dfrac{3\pi}{2}\end{cases}$. For $x\in\left(\pi,\dfrac{3\pi}{2}\right]$; $f(x)$ is quarter ellipse whose complete equation is given by $\dfrac{(x-\pi)^2}{(\pi/2)^2}+\dfrac{y^2}{\pi^2}=1$ with major axis $x=\pi$ of length 2π and minor axis $y=0$ of length π and centre $(\pi, 0)$. Therefore, the area of shaded region is as shown in the Figure 3.97.

$= \text{Area of } \Delta OAB + \text{Area of quarter ellipse } (BCAB)$

$$= \frac{1}{2}(\pi)(\pi) + \frac{1}{4}\pi(\pi)\left(\frac{\pi}{2}\right) = \frac{\pi^2}{2} + \frac{\pi^3}{8} = \frac{\pi^2(4+\pi)}{8}$$

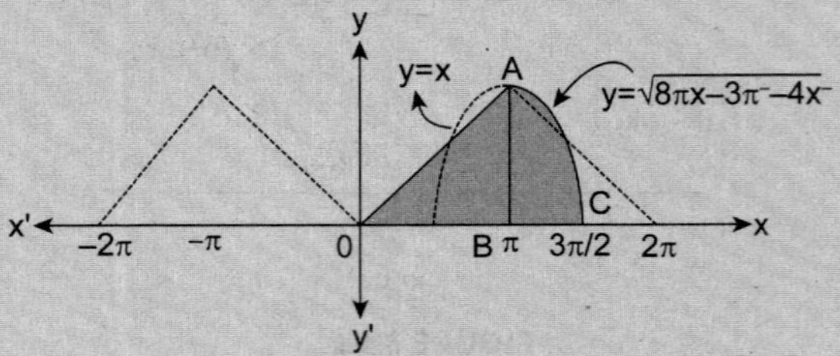

FIGURE 3.97

Hyperbola

(i) $\frac{x^2}{a^2} - \frac{y^2}{b^2} = 1$

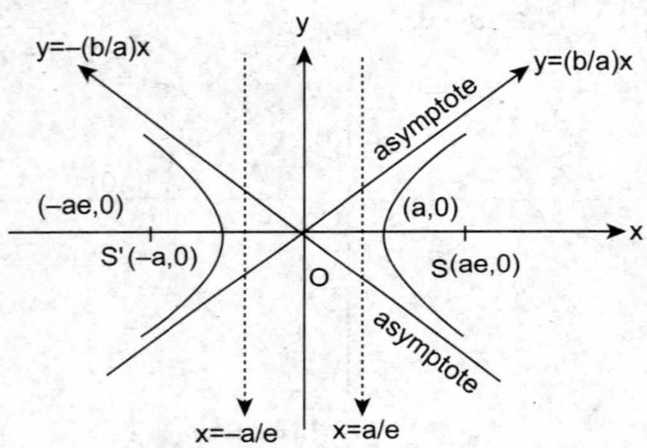

FIGURE 3.98

(ii) $-\frac{x^2}{a^2} + \frac{y^2}{b^2} = 1$

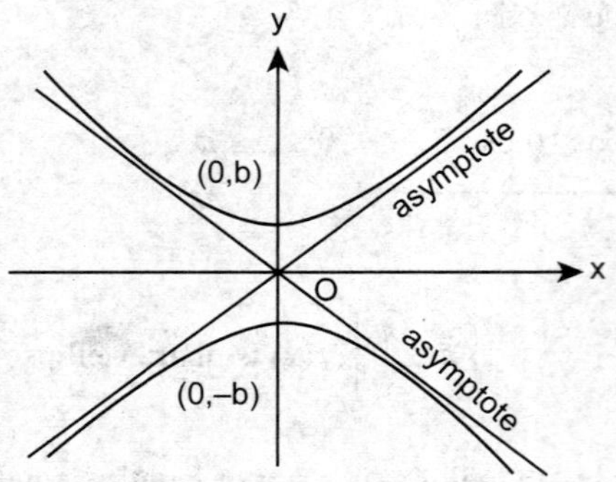

FIGURE 3.99

(iii) $\frac{(x-h)^2}{a^2} - \frac{(y-k)^2}{b^2} = 1$

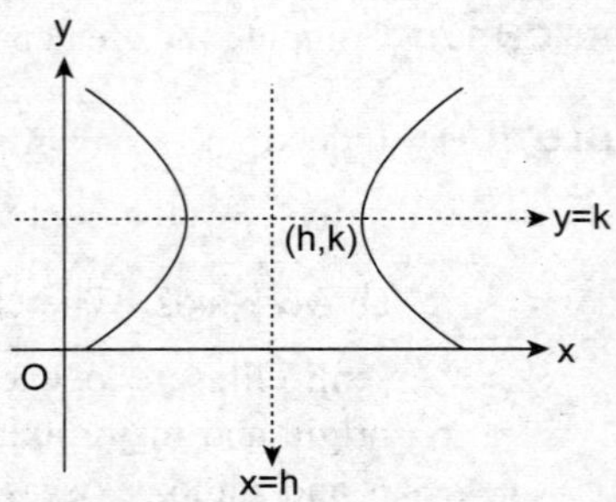

FIGURE 3.100

(iv) $x^2 - y^2 = a^2$
(Rectangular hyperbola)

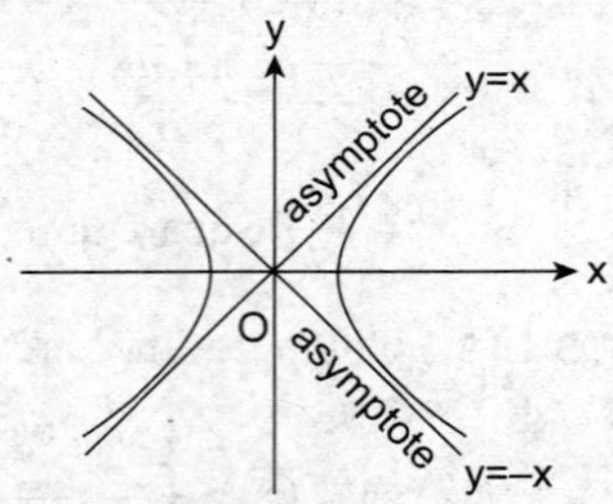

FIGURE 3.101

(v) $xy = c^2$

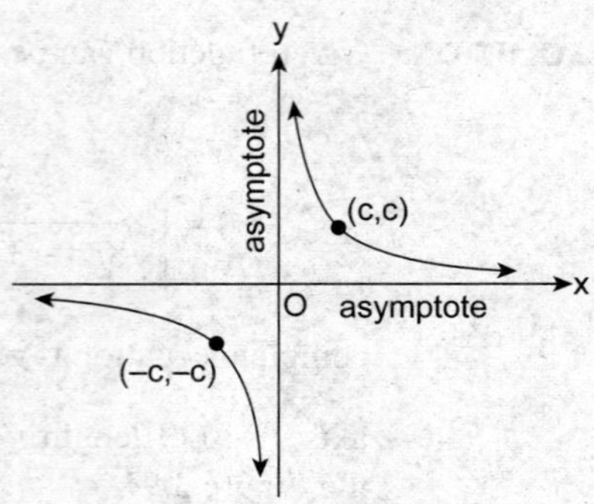

FIGURE 3.102

ILLUSTRATION 19: Find the number of points where the curves $x^2 + y^2 = 9$ and $x^2y^2 = 1$ intersect.

SOLUTION: Clearly, $x^2 + y^2 = 9$ is a circle with centre (0, 0) and radius 3 units, whereas equation $x^2y^2 = 1$

$\Rightarrow$ $y = \pm\frac{1}{x}$ or $xy = \pm 1$ is a pair of conjugate rectangular hyperbola with co-ordinate axes as asymptotes graphing them together on same x-y plane as shown below.

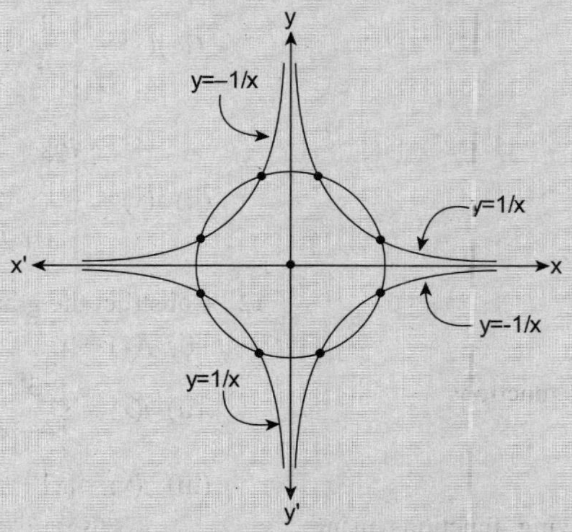

FIGURE 3.103

Clearly both curves have 8 points of intersections.

Aliter: $x^2 + \frac{1}{x^2} = 9$

$\Rightarrow x^4 - 9x^2 + 1 = 0$

$x^2 = \frac{9 \pm \sqrt{81-4}}{2}$ $\Rightarrow x^2 = \frac{9 \pm \sqrt{77}}{2}$

both values are positive. Thus, x has four real roots. For each x, we get two corresponding points, thus, eight points of intersection.

TEXTUAL EXERCISE–1: (SUBJECTIVE)

1. Sketch the following curves and show their relative nature on same graph sheet:
   (a) $y = x$ (b) $y = x^2$
   (c) $y = |x|$ (d) $y = \sqrt{x}$
   (e) $y = x^{1/3}$

2. Sketch the curve of the following functions:
   (a) $y = -\sqrt{9-x^2}$, $x \in [-3, 0)$
   (b) $y = -\sqrt{9-x^2}$, $x \in [0, 3]$
   (c) $y = \sqrt{9-x^2}$, $x \in [-3, 0)$
   (d) $y = \sqrt{9-x^2}$, $x \in x \in [0, 3]$

3. Sketch the curve of the following functions:
   (a) $y = -4\sqrt{x-3} + 5$, $x \geq 3$
   (b) $y = 4\sqrt{x-3} + 5$, $x \geq 3$
   (c) $y = -4\sqrt{3-x} + 5$, $x \leq 3$
   (d) $y = 4\sqrt{3-x} + 5$, $x \leq 3$

4. Sketch the curve of the following functions:
   (a) $\sqrt{-\frac{x^2}{16} + 1} = \frac{y}{3}$, $x \in [-4, 0)$
   (b) $-\sqrt{-\frac{x^2}{16} + 1} = \frac{y}{3}$, $x \in [-4, 0)$

(c) $\sqrt{-\frac{x^2}{16}+1}=\frac{y}{3},\quad x\in[0,4]$

(d) $-\sqrt{-\frac{x^2}{16}-1}=\frac{y}{3},\quad x\in[0,4]$

5. Sketch the curve of the following functions:

(a) $\sqrt{\frac{x^2}{16}-1}=\frac{y}{3},\quad x\geq 4$

(b) $-\sqrt{\frac{x^2}{16}-1}=\frac{y}{3},\quad x\geq 4$

(c) $\sqrt{\frac{x^2}{16}-1}=\frac{y}{3},\quad x\leq -4$

(d) $-\sqrt{\frac{x^2}{16}-1}=\frac{y}{3},\quad x\leq -4$

6. Draw the graph of the following functions:

(i) $y = |x-3| + |x+1| + 2x$

(ii) $y = x|x| - 2x - 3$

7. Sketch the graph of the following functions using transformation:

(a) $y = \cos x + |\cos x|$

(b) $y = 1+\log_x \sqrt{x}$

(c) $y = \log_{10}x + |\log_{10}x|$

8. Draw the graph of the following functions:

(a) $y = x^2 - 2|x+1| - 1$

(b) $y = |2x^2 - 3x + |x-1||$

(c) $y = -|x^2 - 2x|$

9. Draw the graph of the following functions:

(a) $y = 4^{(|x|+x)/2x}$

(b) $y=\dfrac{\cos\left(|x|-\frac{3\pi}{2}\right)}{2\sin x}$

(c) $y = (2-x)|x+3|$

10. Draw the graph of following functions:

(a) $f(x) = \log|x| - \log x^2$

(b) $f(x)=\frac{1}{2}\left(\frac{|\sin x|}{\cos x}+\frac{|\cos x|}{\sin x}\right)$

11. Construct the graph for:

(i) $f(x)=\begin{cases} x-1; & x<0 \\ \frac{1}{4}; & x=0 \\ x^2; & x>0 \end{cases}$

(ii) $f(x)=\begin{cases} 2x+3; & -3\leq x<-2 \\ x+1; & -2\leq x<0 \\ x+2 & 0\leq x\leq 1 \end{cases}$

12. Construct the graph of the function:

(i) $f(x) = |x-1| + |x+1|$

(ii) $f(x)=\begin{cases} 3^x; & -1\leq x\leq 1 \\ 4-x; & 1\leq x<4 \end{cases}$

(iii) $f(x) = [x] + |x-1|;\ -1\leq x\leq 3$ (where [.] denotes greatest integer function).

(iv) $f(x)=\begin{cases} x^4; & x^2<1 \\ x; & x^2\geq 1 \end{cases}$

13. Draw the following curves given by implicit relations:

(a) $16x^2 + 24xy + 9y^2 - 5x - 10y + 1 = 0$

(b) $4x^2 - 4xy + y^2 - 12x + 6y + 9 = 0$

(c) $x^2 - xy - 6y^2 = 6$

(d) $xy = a(x+y)$

(e) $x^2 + xy + y^2 + x + y = 1$

14. Draw the following graphs and find out what will be the graph of

(i) $y = \sin^4 x$,

(ii) $y = \sin^5 x$

(ii) $y = \sin^{2n} x$ as $n\to\infty\ n\in I$

(iii) $y = \sin^{(2n+1)} x$ as $n\to\infty\ n\in I$

Answer Keys

1.

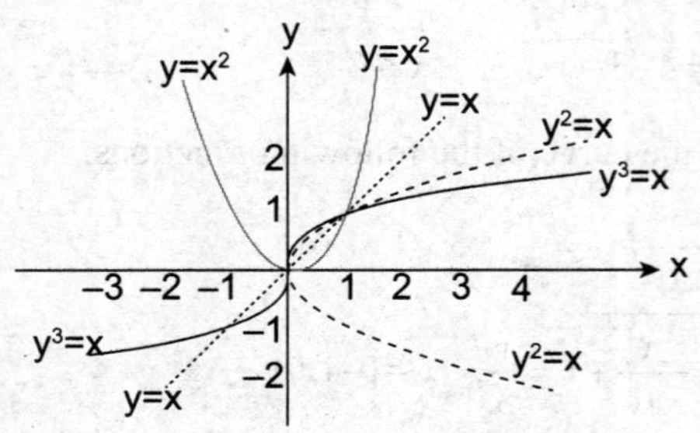

2. (a) 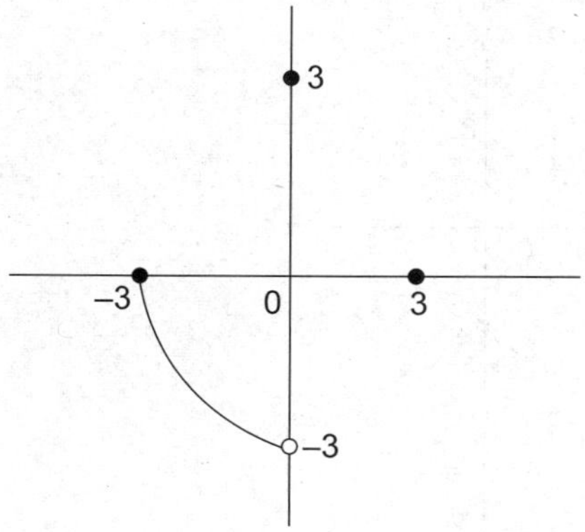

(b) 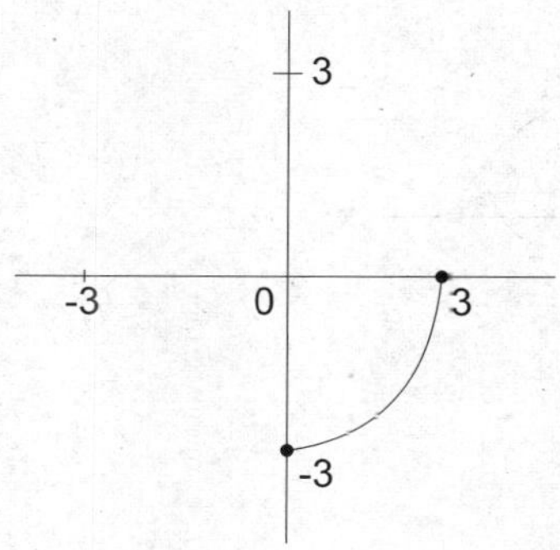

(c) 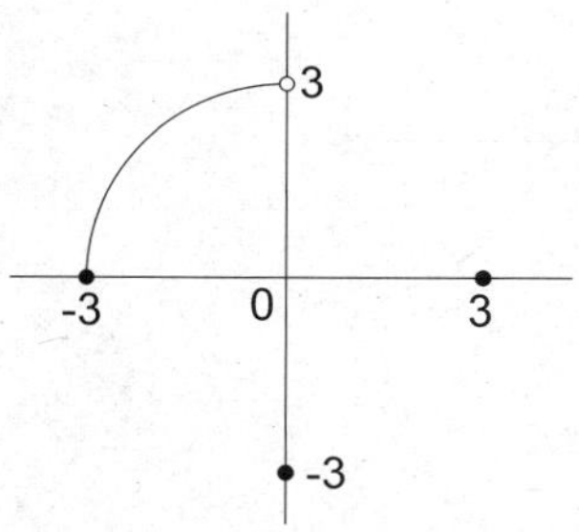

(d) 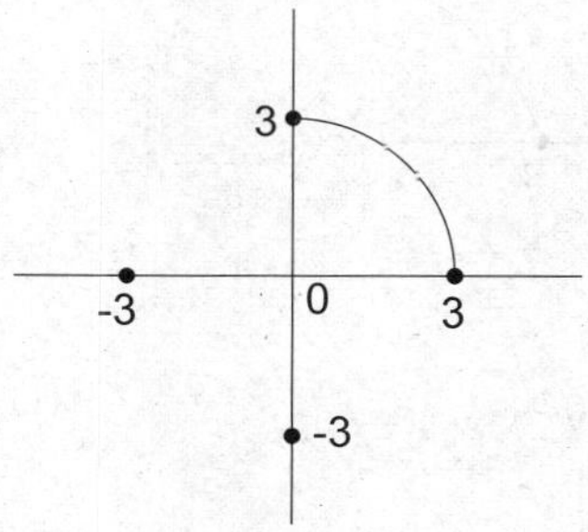

3. (a) 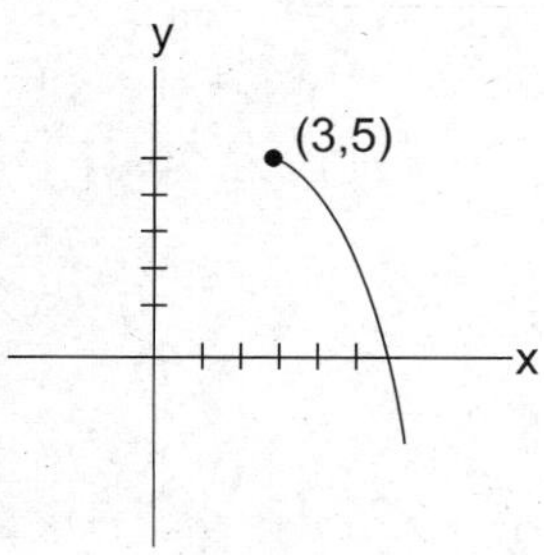

(b) 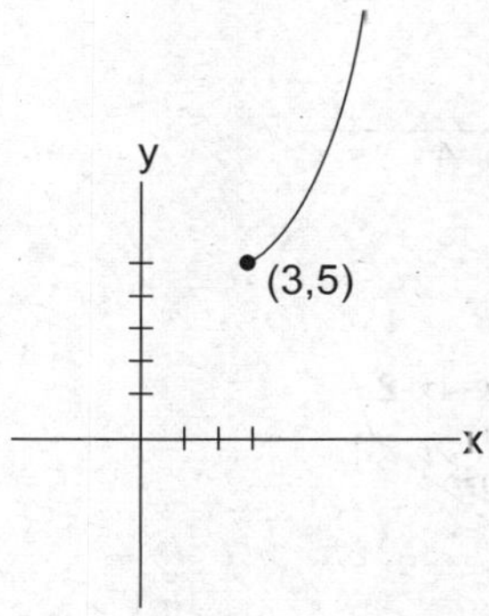

(c) 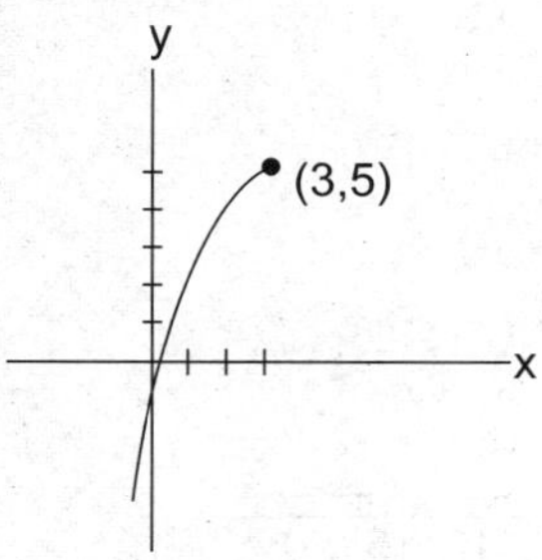

(d) 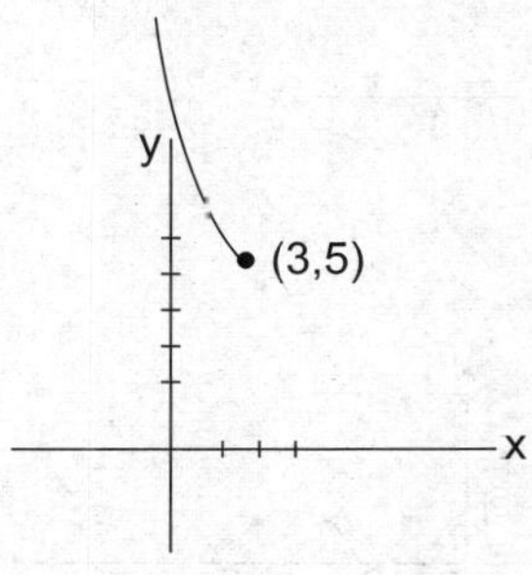

4. (a) 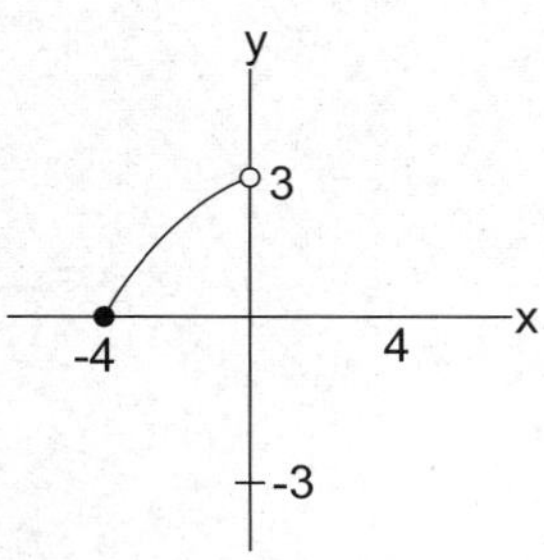

(b) 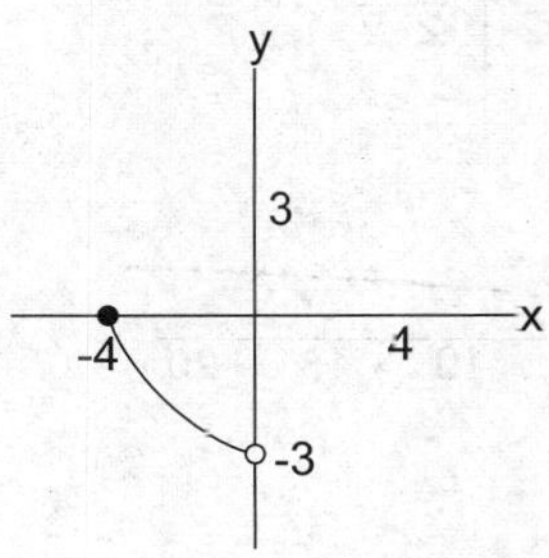

(c)

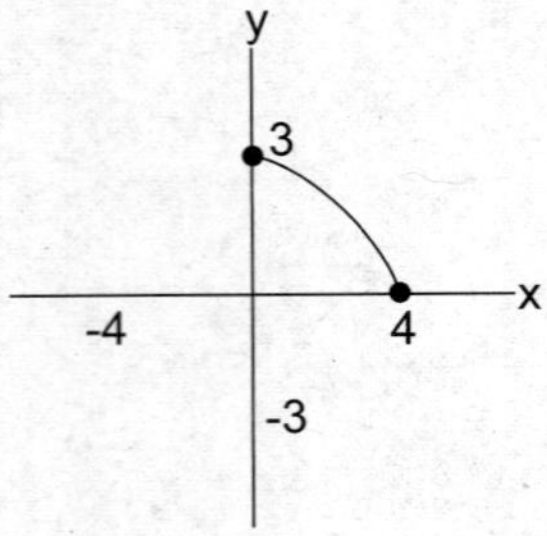

(d)

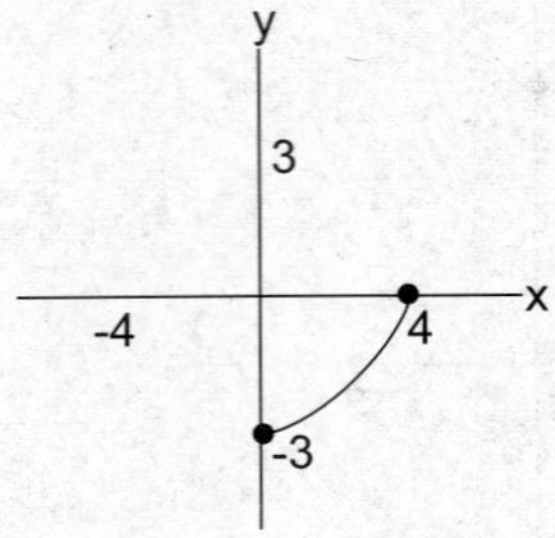

5. (a)

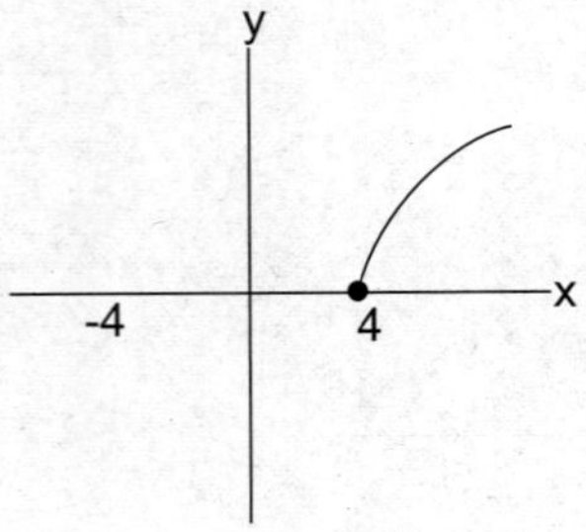

(b)

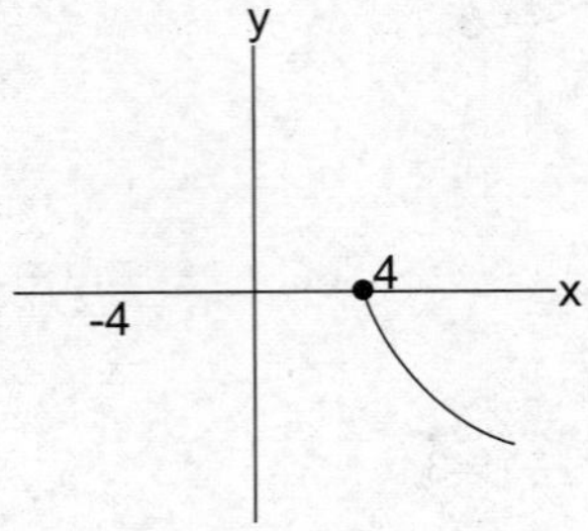

(c)

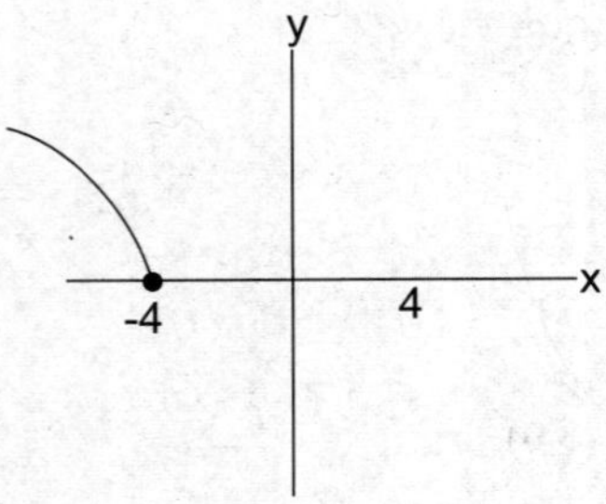

(d)

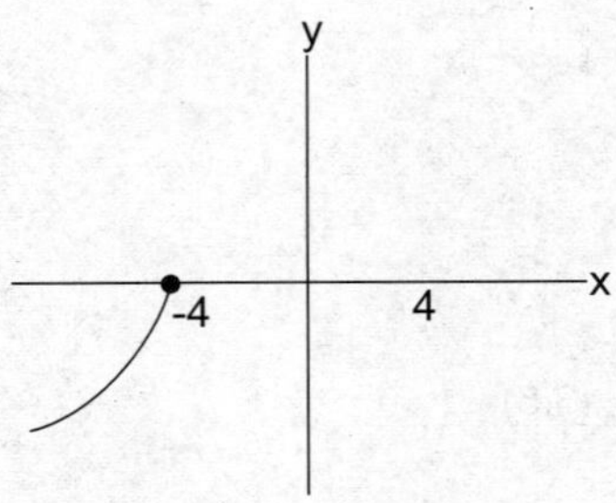

6. (i)

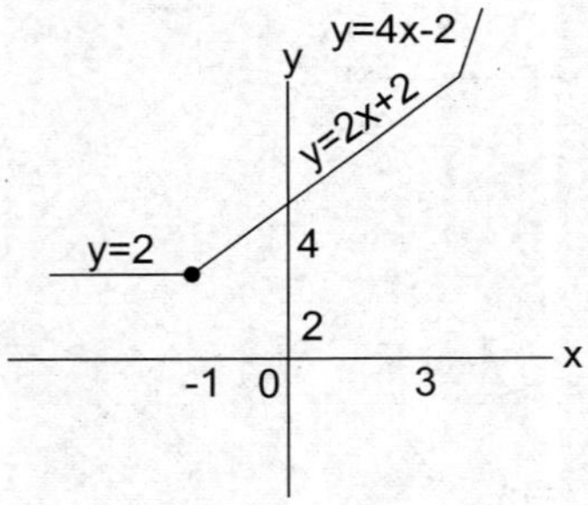

(ii)

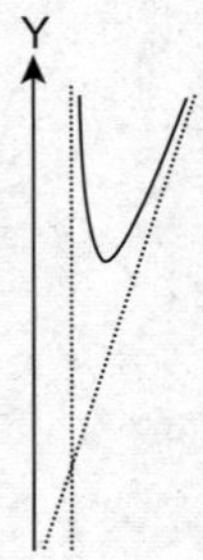

7. (a)

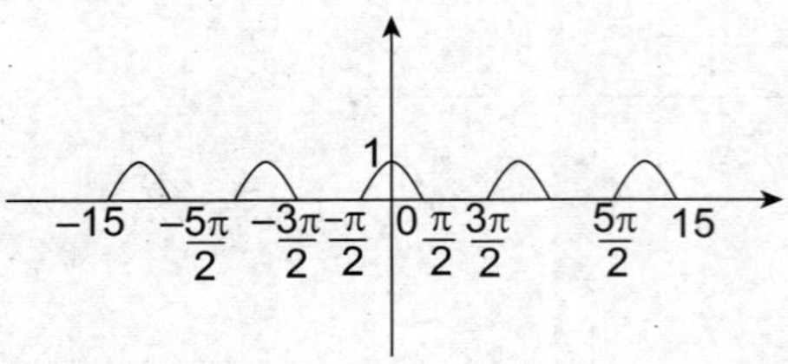

(b)

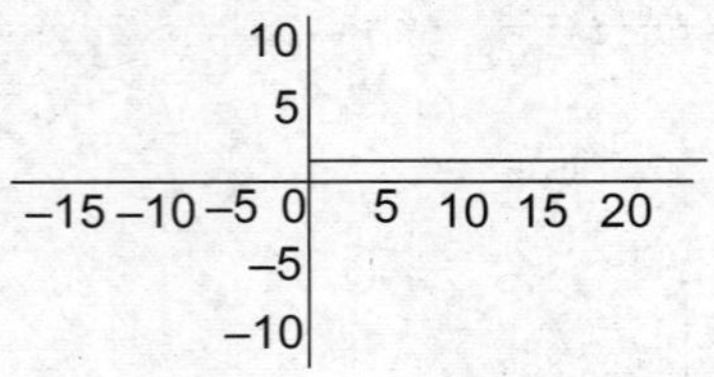

(c)

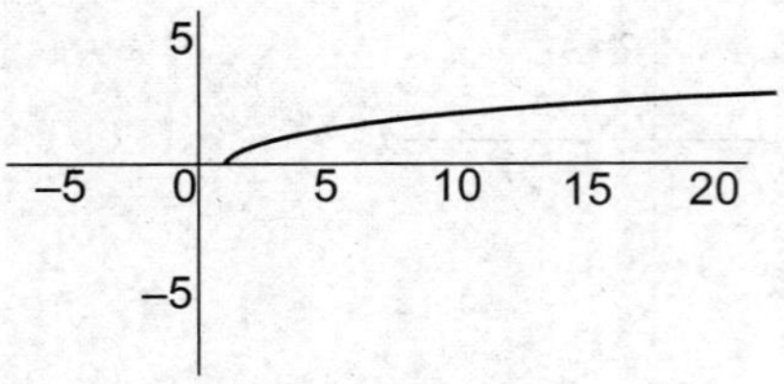

8. (a) 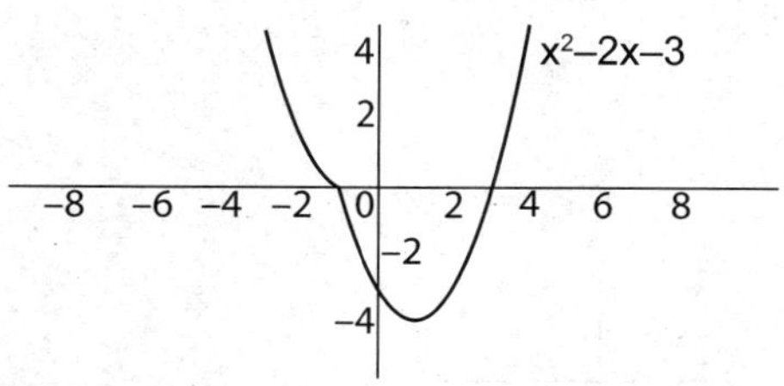

(b) 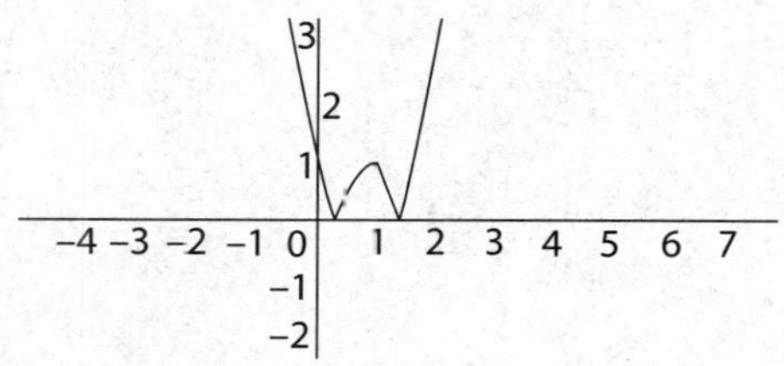

(c) 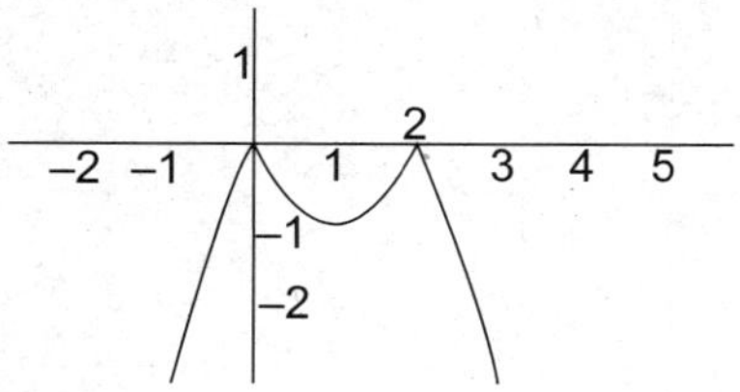

9. (a) 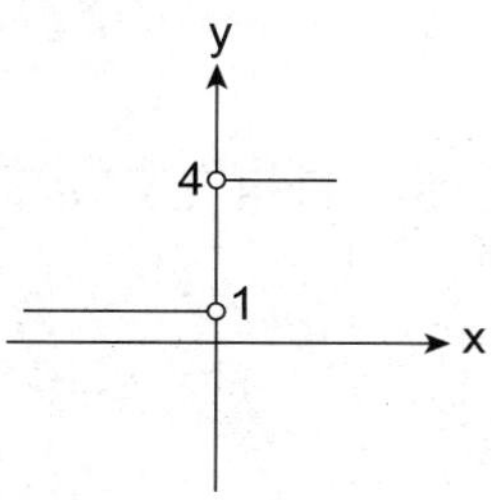

(b) 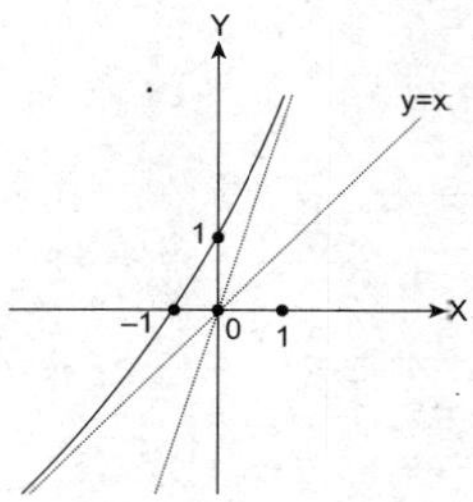

(c) 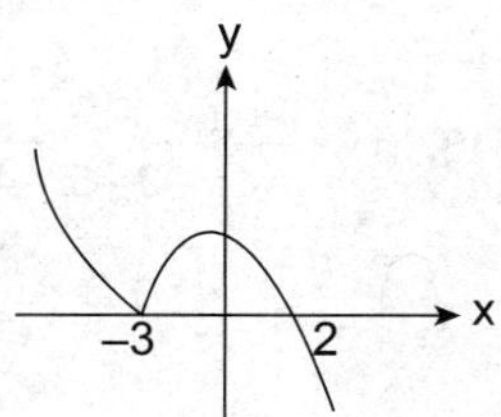

10. (a) 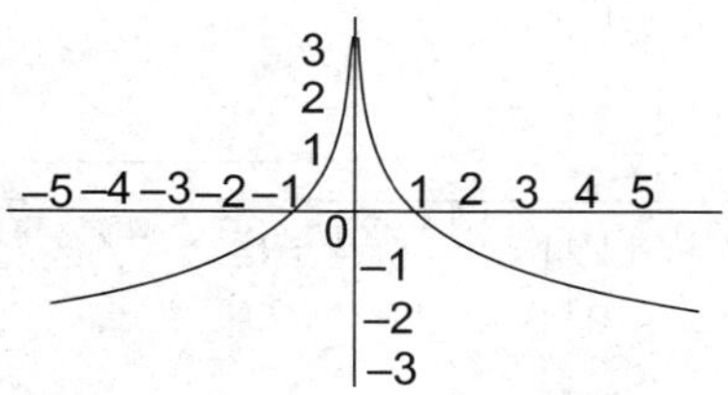

(b) 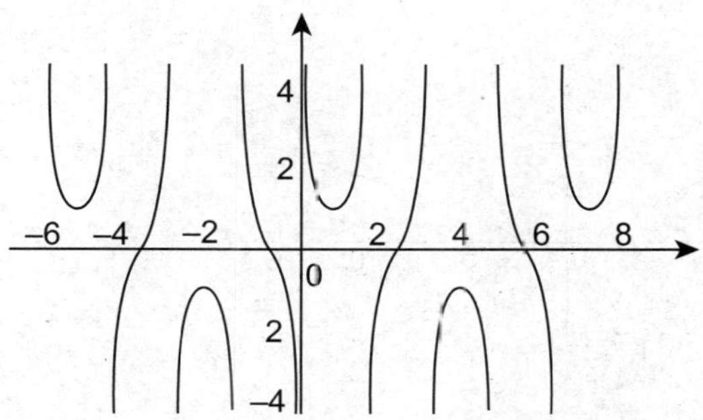

11. (a) 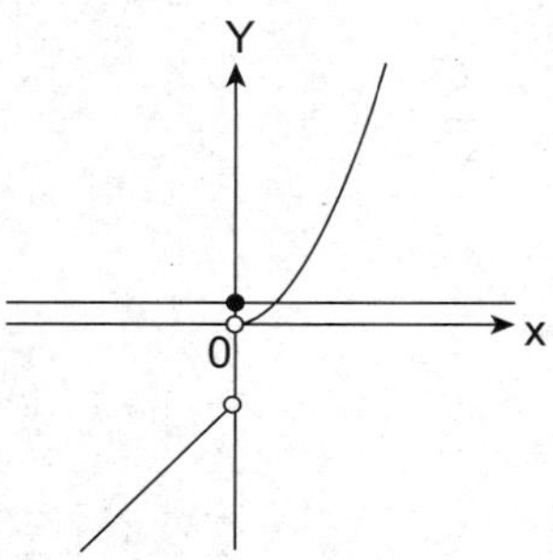

(b) 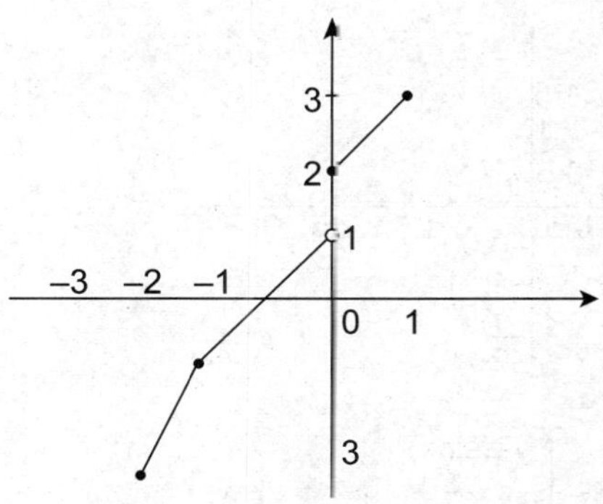

12. (i) 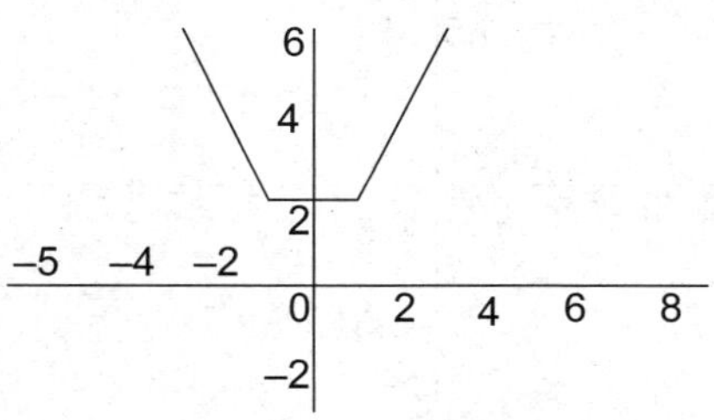

(ii) 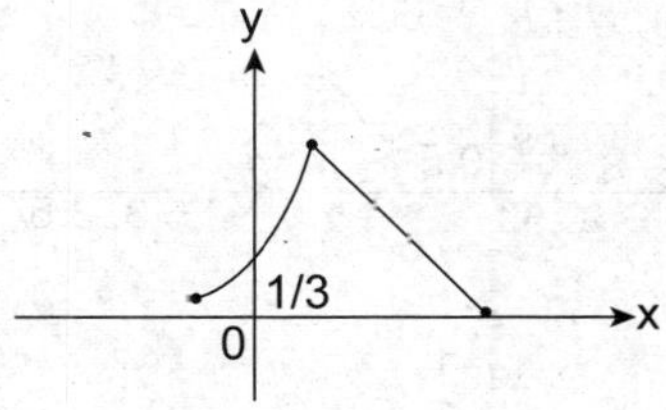

(iii) 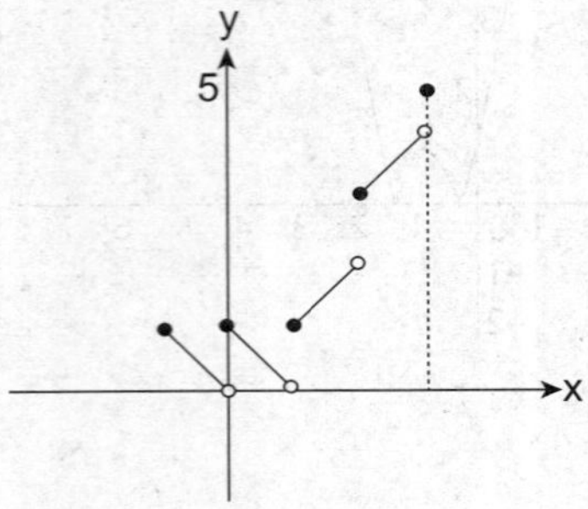

(iv) 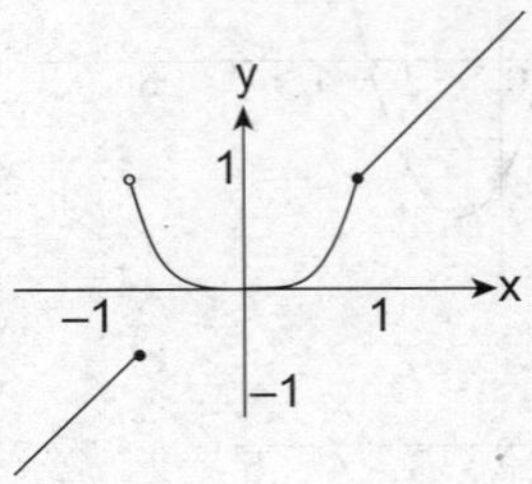

13. (i) 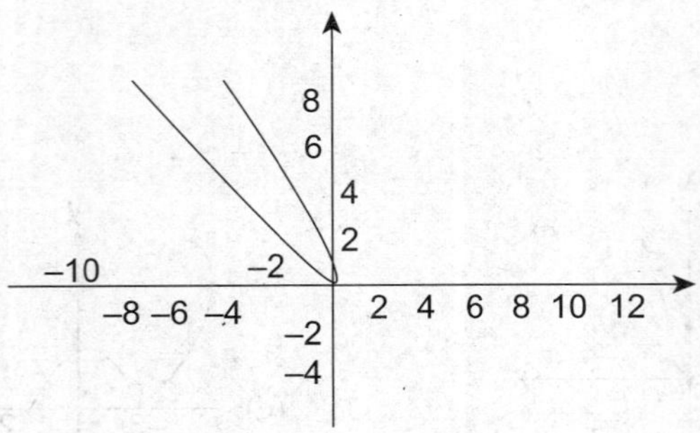

(ii) 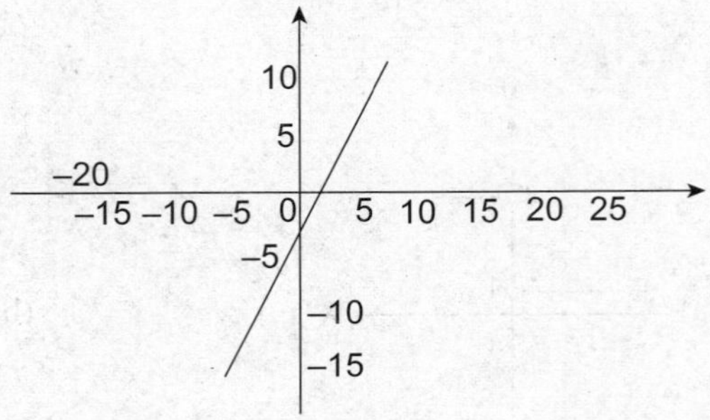

(iii) 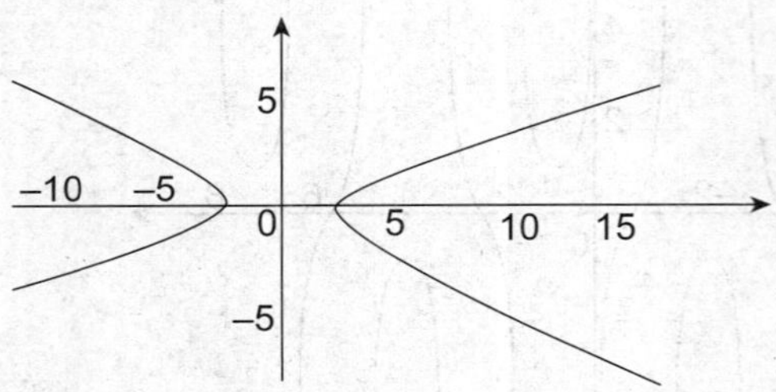

(iv) 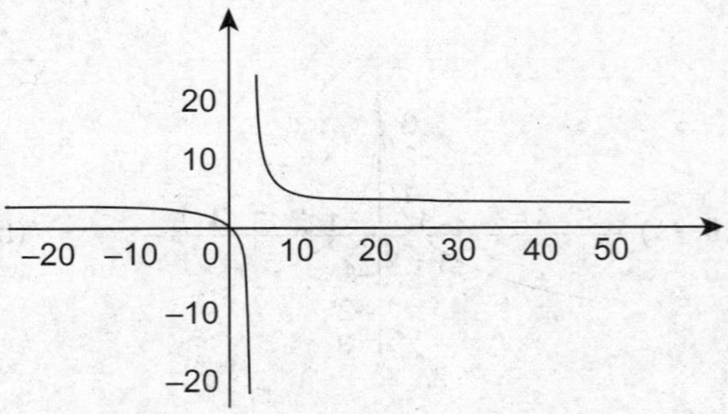

(v) 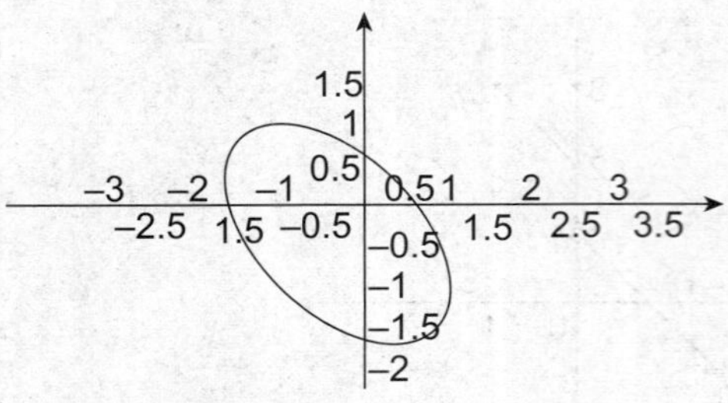

14. (i) 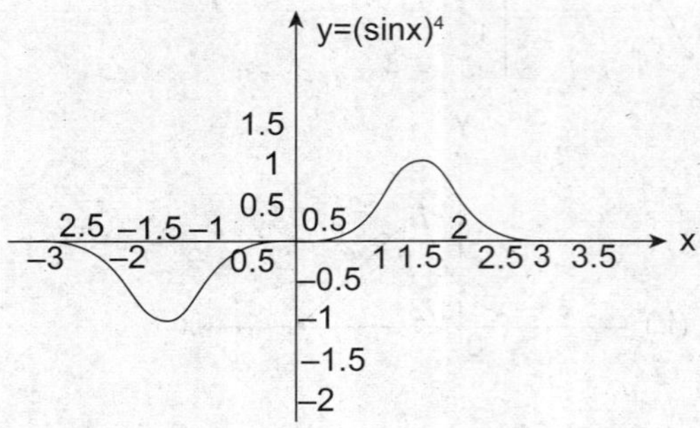

(ii) 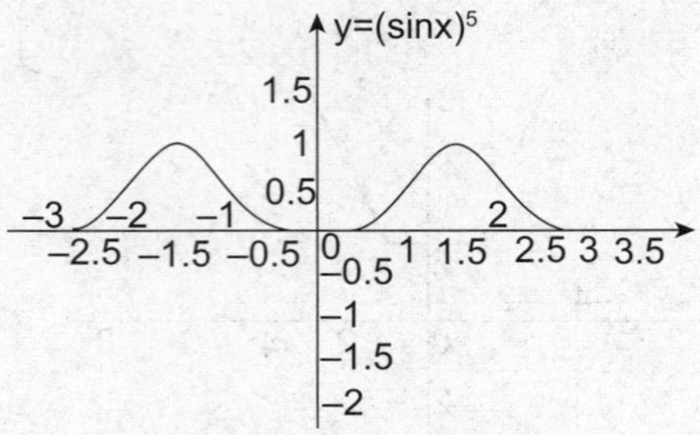

(iii)

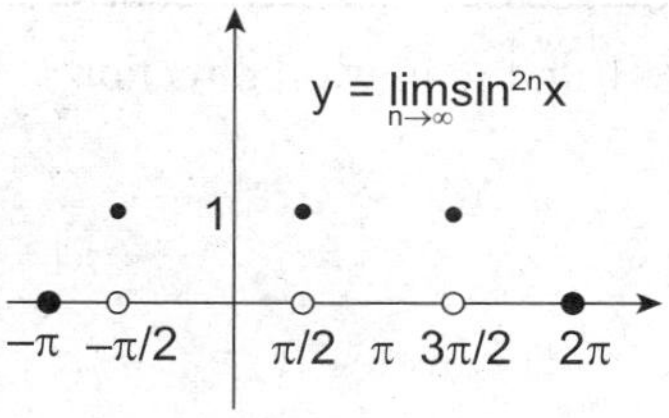

(iv)

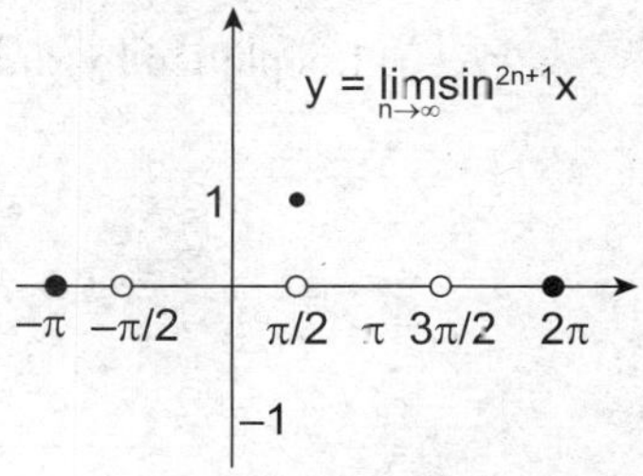

■ TRANSFORMATION OF GRAPHS

In this chapter, we shall study the change in the nature of graph of the function going through different standard transformations. These transformations are very helpful in solving questions geometrically. For this purpose we shall take the help of graph of a function as shown below.

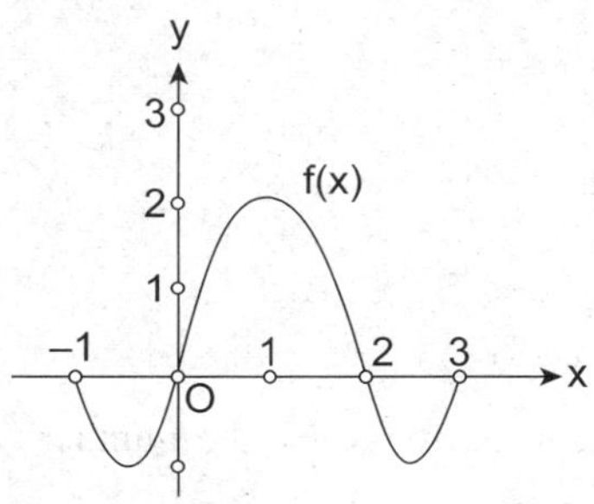

FIGURE 3.104

1. **Graph of $y = f(x) + k$:** Graph of $y = f(x) + k$ can be obtained by translating graph of $f(x)$ by $|k|$ unit along y-axis in the direction same as sign of k, i.e., upward when $k > 0$ and downward when $k < 0$.
   This is because each out put of the function is added by k. Therefore, each point of graph shifts vertically by k unit.

For example, graph of $y = f(x) + 1$ is as shown in the Figure 3.105 and graph of $y = f(x) - 1$ is shown in Figure 3.106.

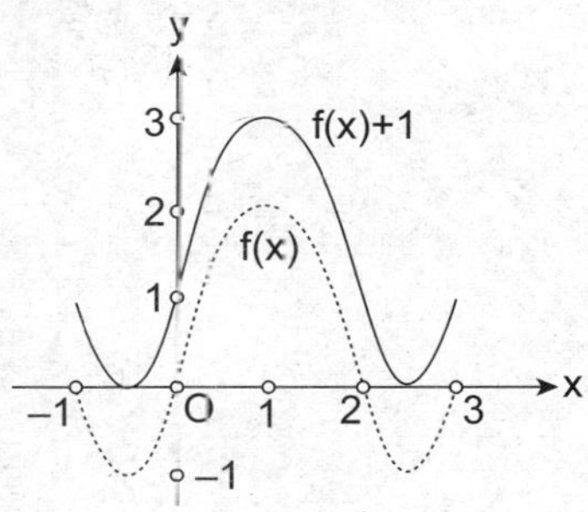

FIGURE 3.105

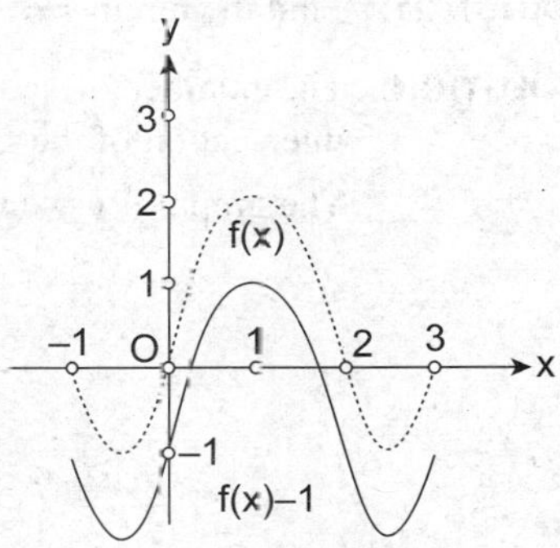

FIGURE 3.106

ILLUSTRATION 20: Draw the graph of $y = e^x$, and hence, draw the graph of $y = e^x + 1$ and $y = e^x - 1$

SOLUTION: We know, $y = e^x$ could be plotted as shown below:

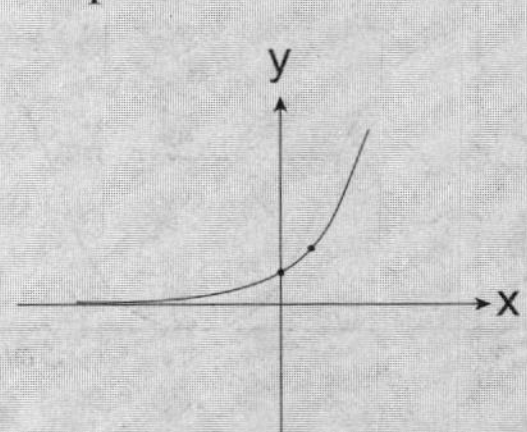

FIGURE 3.107

$y = e^x + 1$ is plotted by shifting the graph of $y = e^x$ by 1 unit in upward direction.

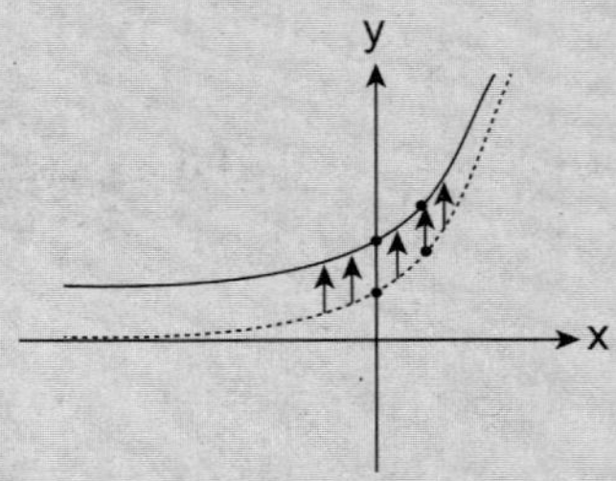

FIGURE 3.108

Also $y = e^x - 1$ can be plotted by shifting the graph of $y = e^x$ downwards by 1 unit.

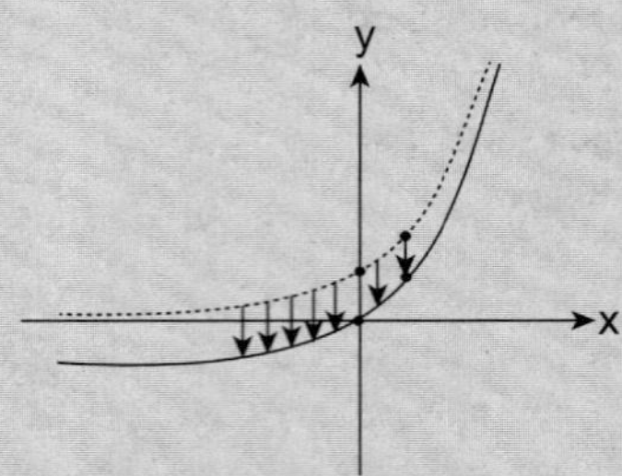

FIGURE 3.109

ILLUSTRATION 21: Find the number of solutions of equation $1 + \cos x = \log_2 x$

SOLUTION: The number of solutions of the above equation can be found by the number of points of intersection of the graphs $y = 1 + \cos x$ and $y = \log_2 x$

The graph of $y = \cos x$ is shown in Figure 3.110.

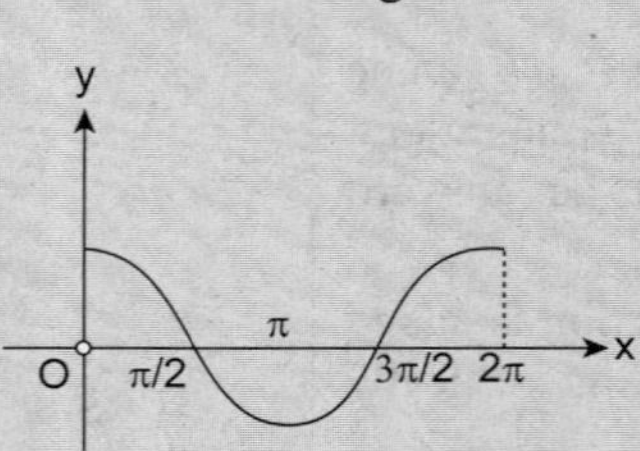

FIGURE 3.110

The graph of $y = 1 + \cos x$ can be obtained by shifting the curve of $y = \cos x$ by 1 unit in the upward direction.

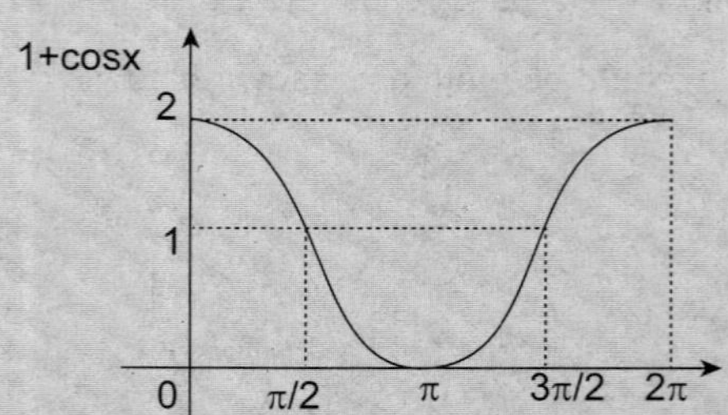

FIGURE 3.111

The graph of $y = \log_2 x$ is shown in Figure 3.112.

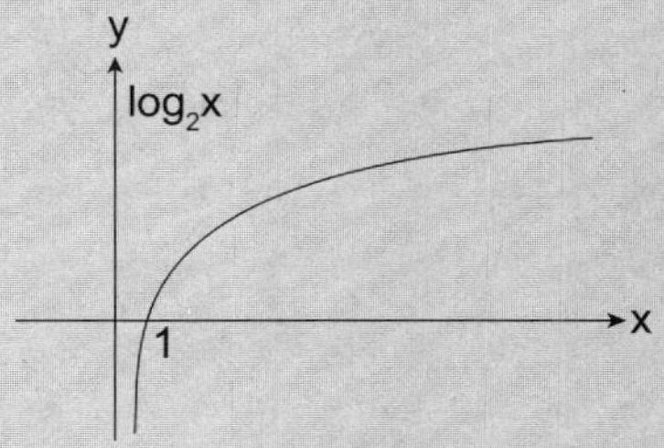

FIGURE 3.112

Now; maximum of $1 + \cos x = 2$

Now $\log_2 x \leq 2 \Rightarrow x \leq 4$

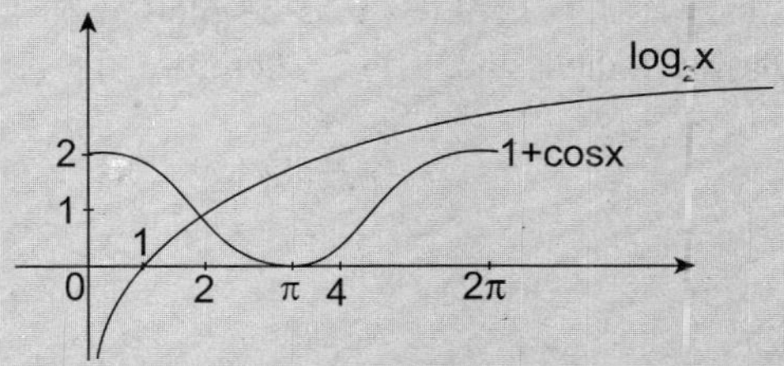

FIGURE 3.113

Clearly, only one solution is possible.

2. **Graph of $y = f(x + k)$:** Graph of $y = f(x + k)$ can be obtained by translating graph of $y = f(x)$ by $|k|$ units in the direction opposite to the sign of k along x-axis. That is, a addition and subtraction to independent variable leads to horizontal shift because each output $f(x)$ of the original function is obtained by the transformed function $f(x + k)$ at the input $x - k$.

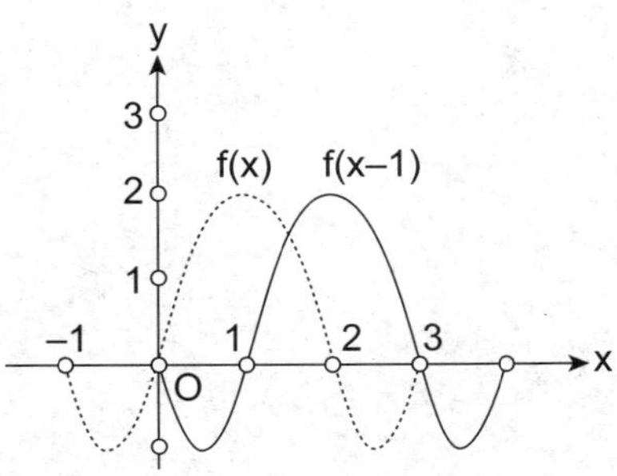

FIGURE 3.114

For example, graph of $f(x - 1)$ is as shown in the Figure 3.114 and that of $f(x + 1)$ is shown in Figure 3.115. Because if the origin is shifted to (1, 0). And in new system of axes, $f(x+ k)$ behaves as $f(x)$.

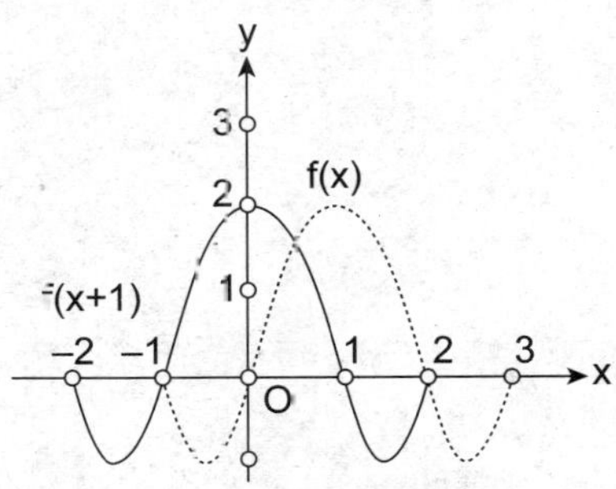

FIGURE 3.115

ILLUSTRATION 22: Draw the graph of $y = x^2$, and hence, draw the graph of $y = x^2 + 2x + 1$ and also the graph of $y = x^2 - 2x + 1$, and therefore, predict the co-ordinates of vertex of the parabola $y = x^2 + 2x + 1$ and $y = x^2 - 2x + 1$.

SOLUTION: We know; $y = x^2$ could be plotted as

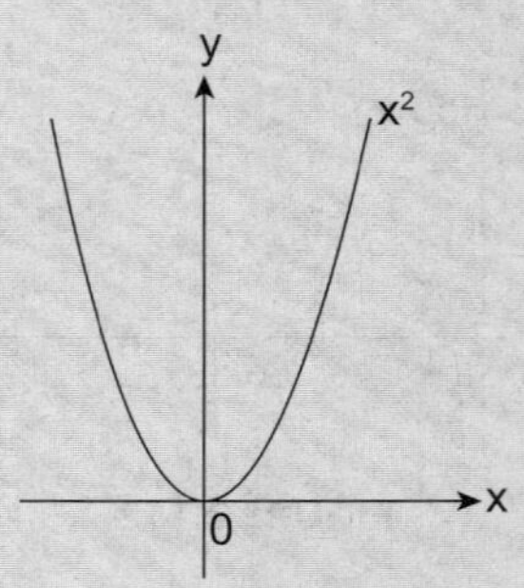

FIGURE 3.116

Now $y = x^2 + 2x + 1 = (x+1)^2$ would be plotted by shifting $y = x^2$ by 1 unit in the left direction as shown in the Figure 3.117. Therefore, the vertex of the parabola would be (–1, 0).

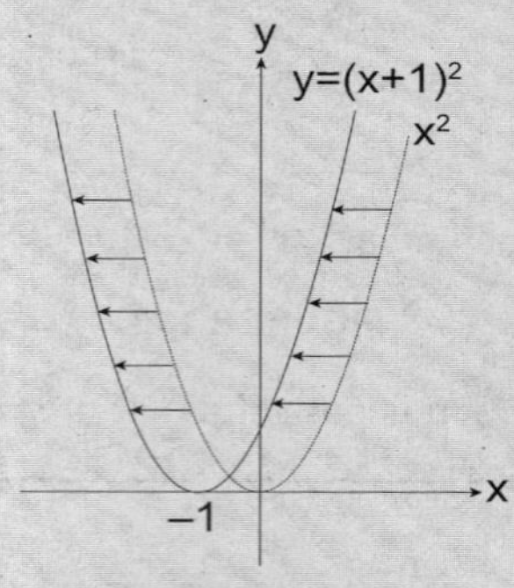

FIGURE 3.117

Now $y = x^2 - 2x + 1 = (x - 1)^2$ would be plotted by shifting $y = x^2$ by 1 unit in the right direction, and hence, the vertex of new parabola lies at (1, 0).

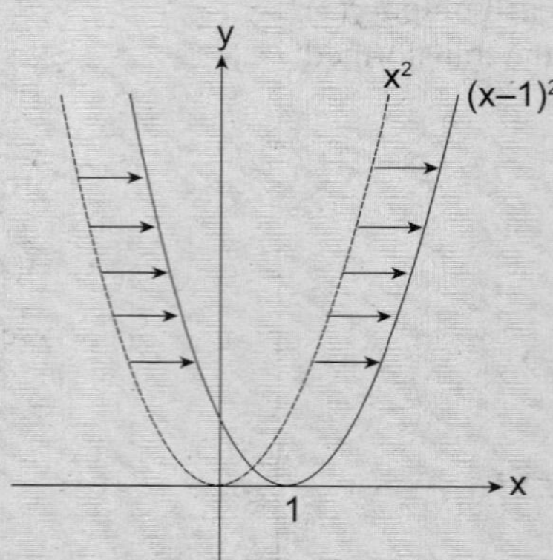

FIGURE 3.118

3. **Graph of $y = k(f(x))$:** Graph of $y = k(f(x))$ can be obtained by vertically stretching or contracting the graph of $f(x)$ depending on the value of k. It is because each output of the obtained function becomes k times that of the original function. Hence, due to this transformation no stretching/compression is produce along x-axis. There are few important facts that are worth noticing in this case.

(i) no change in the domain of the function.

(ii) the behaviour of the function at $y = 0$ (i.e., x intersect/roots) remains same as the original function.

(iii) the range of the function may be change.

The detail of the transformation can be understood by considering the following two cases as described below.

Case I: When $0 < |k| < 1$, compressing the graph of $f(x)$, i.e., $f(x)$ is transformed to k times $f(x)$ along y-axis towards x-axis.

e.g., graph of $y = \frac{1}{2} f(x)$ is shown in the Figure 3.119 and graph of $y = -\frac{1}{2} f(x)$ is shown in Figure 3.120.

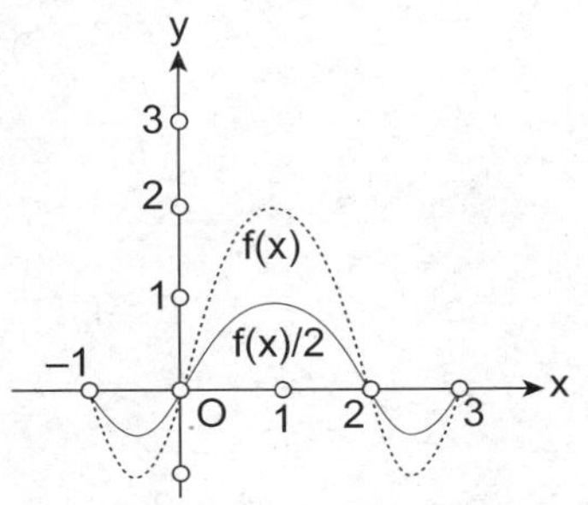

FIGURE 3.119

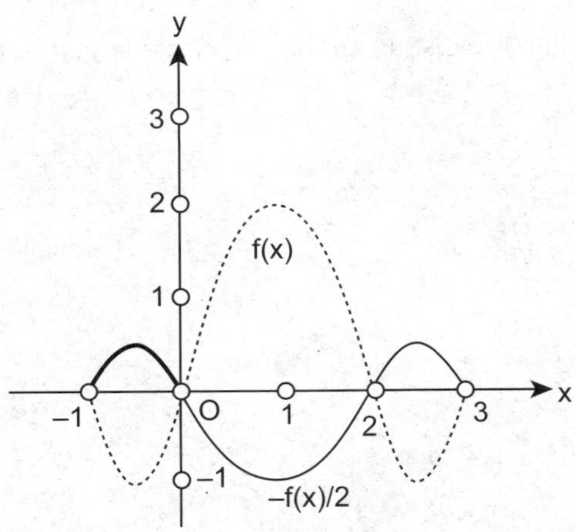

FIGURE 3.120

Case II: When $|k| > 1$, stretching the graph of $f(x)$, along y-axis away from x-axis.

That is, $f(x)$ is transformed to k times $f(x)$.

For example, graph of $y = 2 f(x)$ is as shown in the Figure 3.121 and graph of $y = -2 f(x)$ is as shown in Figure 3.122.

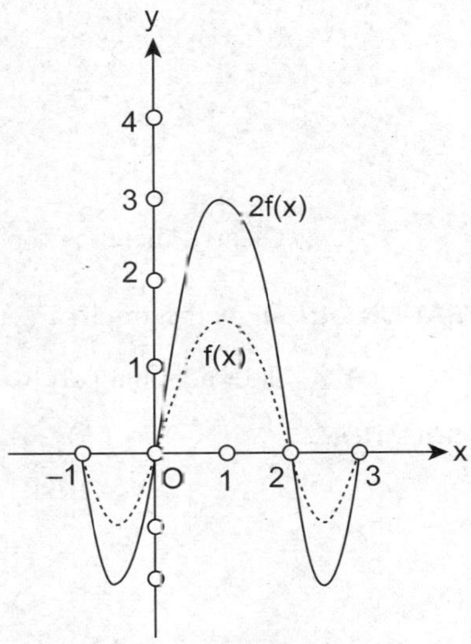

FIGURE 3.121

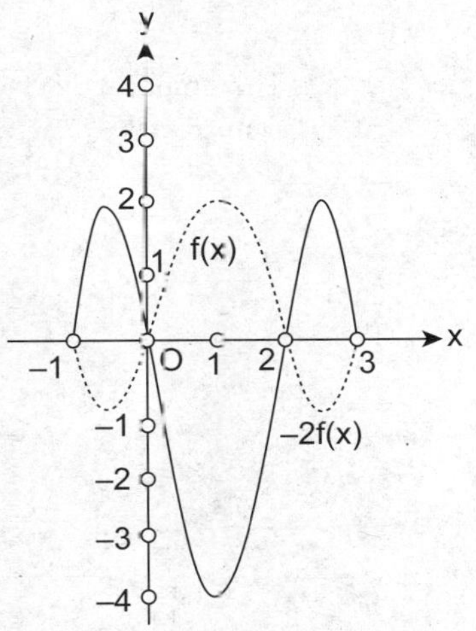

FIGURE 3.122

ILLUSTRATION 23: Find the number of solutions of $(x + 3)^2 = 2\ln x$.

SOLUTION: The number of solutions of the above equation can be found by the number of point of intersection of the graphs $y = (x + 3)^2$ and $y = 2\ln x$.

Clearly, $x > 0$ (Domain)

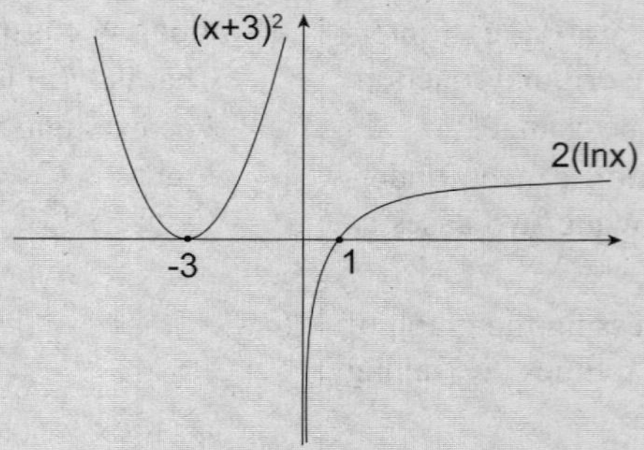

FIGURE 3.123

Clearly, there is no point of intersection, and hence, no solution.

ILLUSTRATION 24: Draw the graph of $\{x\}$, and hence, draw the graphs of 3 $\{x\}$ and also $\frac{1}{2}\{x\}$, where $\{x\}$ denotes the fractional part of x.

SOLUTION:

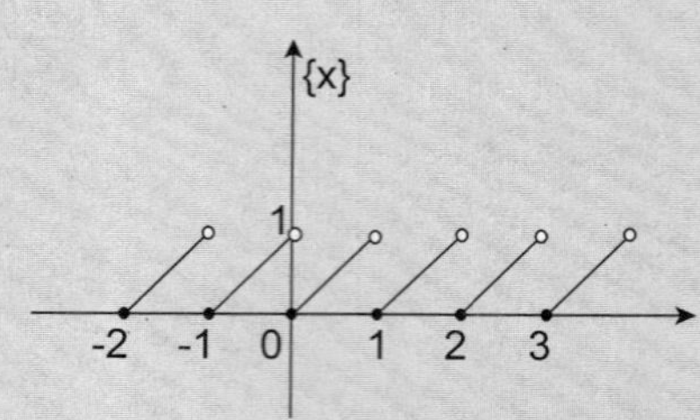

FIGURE 3.124

The graph of $3\{x\}$ can be drawn by stretching 3 times, the graph of $\{x\}$ along y-axis, away from x-axis.

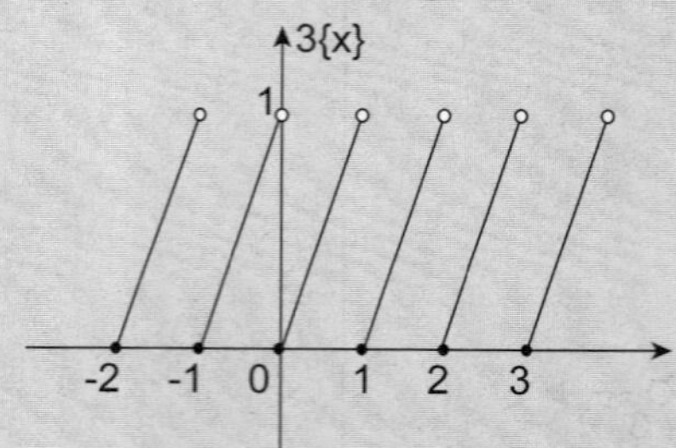

FIGURE 3.125

The graph of $\frac{1}{2}\{x\}$ can be drawn by compressing to 1/2 times the graph of $\{x\}$ along y-axis, towards x-axis.

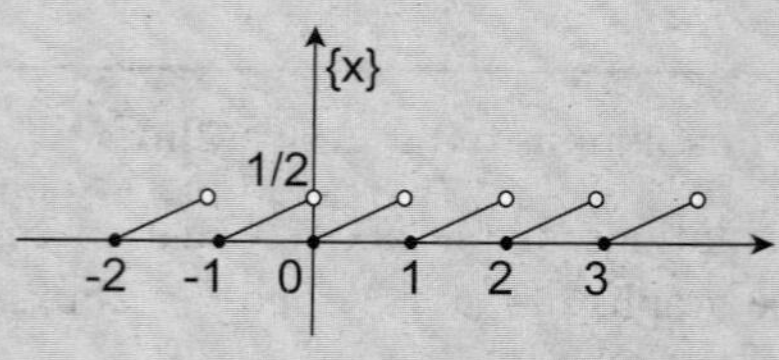

FIGURE 3.126

4. Graph of $y = f(kx)$: Graph of $y = f(kx)$ can be obtained by compressing or stretching the graph of $y = f(x)$ along x-axis towards y-axis or away from y-axis depending on the value of k as described below.

Case I: When $|k| > 1$, compressing the graph of $f(x)$ horizontally towards y-axis. For example, graph of $f(2x)$ is shown in Figure 3.127 and graph of $f(-2x)$ is shown in Figure 3.128.

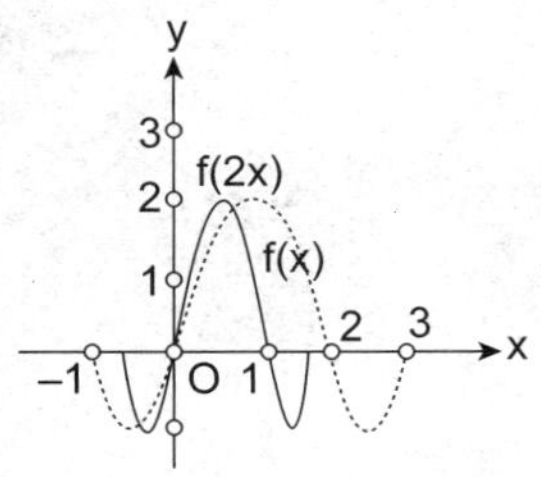

FIGURE 3.127

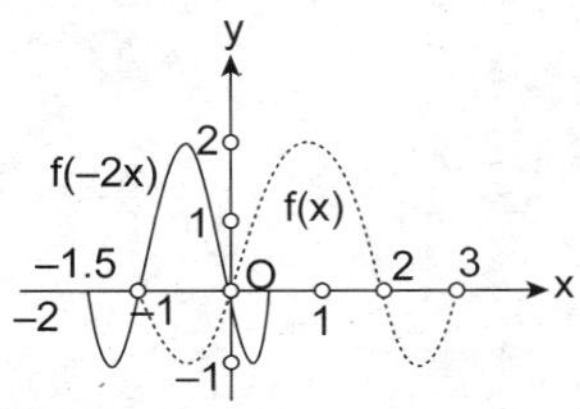

FIGURE 3.128

Case II: When $0 < |k| < 1$, stretching the graph of $y = f(x)$ along x-axis away from y-axis.

e.g., graph of $f(x/2)$ is shown in Figure 3.129 and graph of $f(-x/2)$ is shown in Figure 3.130.

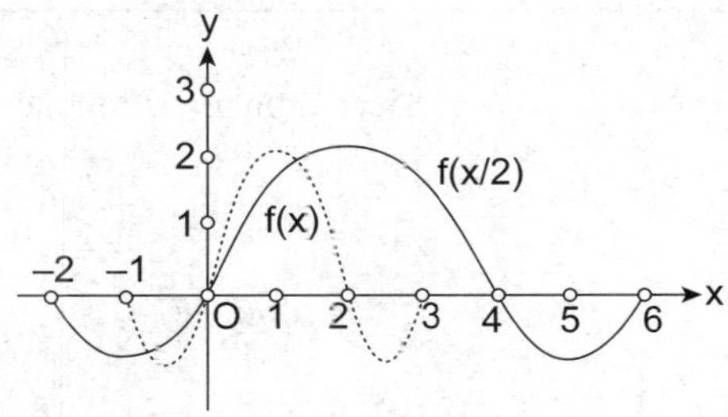

FIGURE 3.129

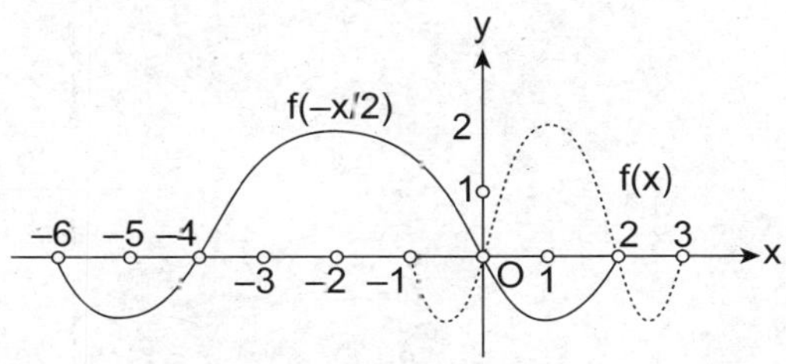

FIGURE 3.130

The above effect of horizontal stretching and compression towards y-axis is due to the fact that the transformed function takes up the same values for the input x/k, as the original function takes up for input x. that is why the domain of function is either stretched or compressed as may be the case, whereas the range of the function remains unchanged in this transformation. This transformation also explains why the period of the periodic function $f(kx)$ becomes $1/|k|$ times the period of $f(x)$.

ILLUSTRATION 25: A function $f:\left(\frac{\pi}{2},\frac{3\pi}{2}\right)\to\mathbb{R}$ such that $f(x) = \tan x$. Now draw $f(2x)$, $f(-2x)$ and $f\left(\frac{-x}{2}\right)$

SOLUTION: The graph of tan x for $x \in \left(\frac{\pi}{2},\frac{3\pi}{2}\right)$ is as shown below.

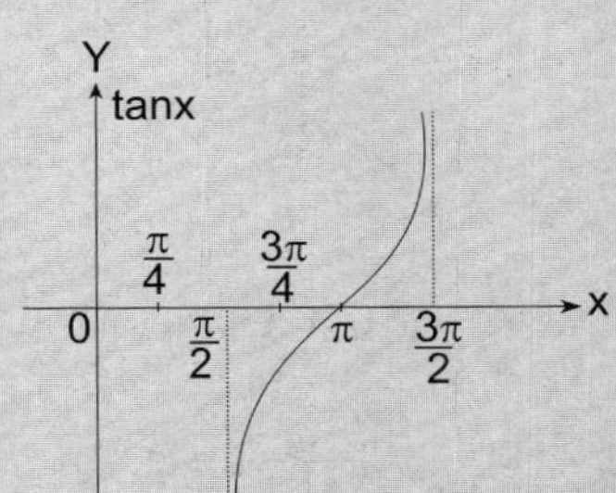

FIGURE 3.131

Since domain of function f is $\left(\frac{\pi}{2}, \frac{3\pi}{2}\right)$

$\therefore \quad f(2x) \Rightarrow 2x \in \left(\frac{\pi}{2}, \frac{3\pi}{2}\right)$

$\Rightarrow \quad x \in \left(\frac{\pi}{4}, \frac{3\pi}{4}\right)$

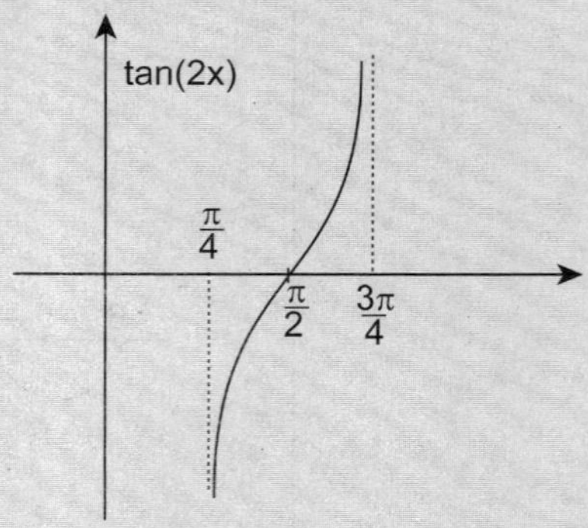

FIGURE 3.132

Since domain of function f is $\left(\frac{\pi}{2}, \frac{3\pi}{2}\right)$

$\therefore \quad f(-2x) \Rightarrow -2x \in \left(\frac{\pi}{2}, \frac{3\pi}{2}\right)$

$\Rightarrow \quad x \in \left(\frac{-3\pi}{4}, \frac{-\pi}{4}\right)$

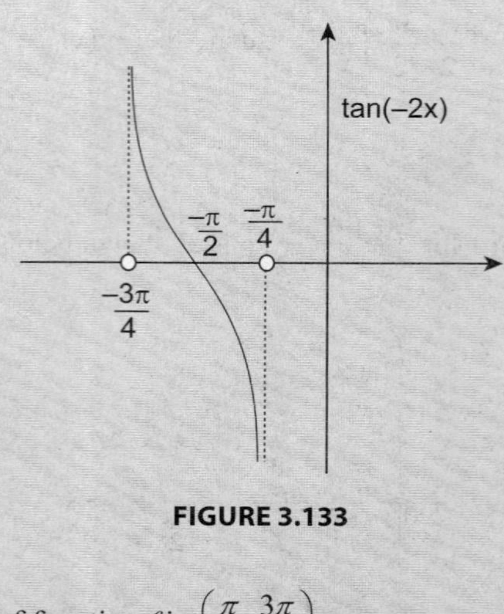

FIGURE 3.133

Since domain of function f is $\left(\frac{\pi}{2}, \frac{3\pi}{2}\right)$

$$f\left(\frac{x}{2}\right) \Rightarrow \frac{x}{2} \in \left(\frac{\pi}{2}, \frac{3\pi}{2}\right) \Rightarrow x \in (\pi, 3\pi)$$

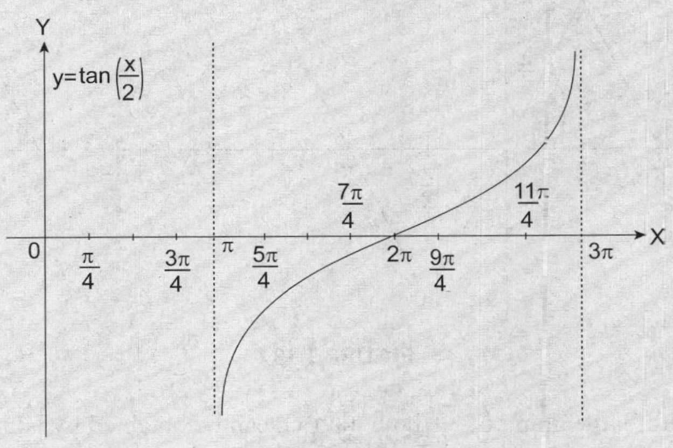

FIGURE 3.134

For $f\left(\frac{-x}{2}\right); -\frac{x}{2} \in \left(\frac{\pi}{2}, \frac{3\pi}{2}\right) \Rightarrow x \in (-3\pi, -\pi)$

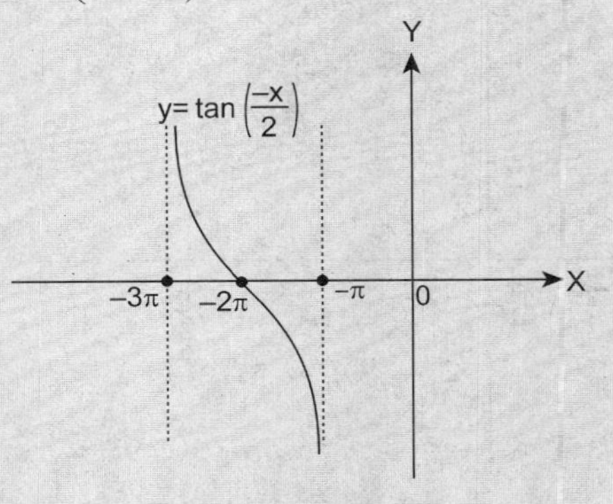

FIGURE 3.135

ILLUSTRATION 26: Draw the graph of $\sin^{-1}(\sin x)$, and hence, draw the graphs of $-2(\sin^{-1}(\sin x))$ and $\frac{-1}{2}(\sin^{-1}(\sin x))$.

SOLUTION: The graph of $\sin^{-1}(\sin x)$ is given by

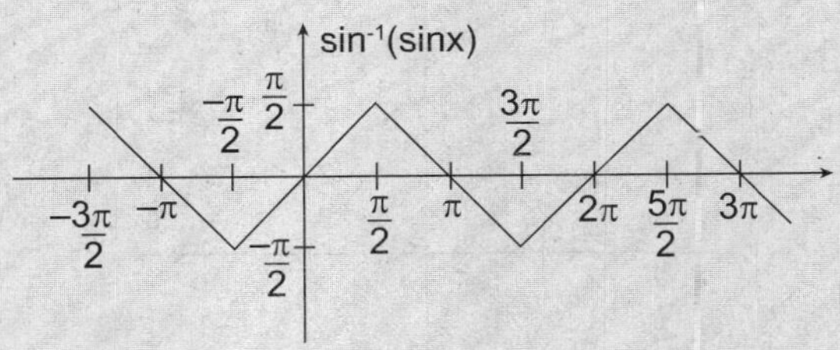

FIGURE 3.136

Therefore, the graph of $-2(\sin^{-1}(\sin x))$ can be obtained by taking mirror image of the graph of $\sin^{-1}(\sin x)$ about x-axis, and there by, stretching the resulting graph 2 times along y-axis, away from the x-axis.

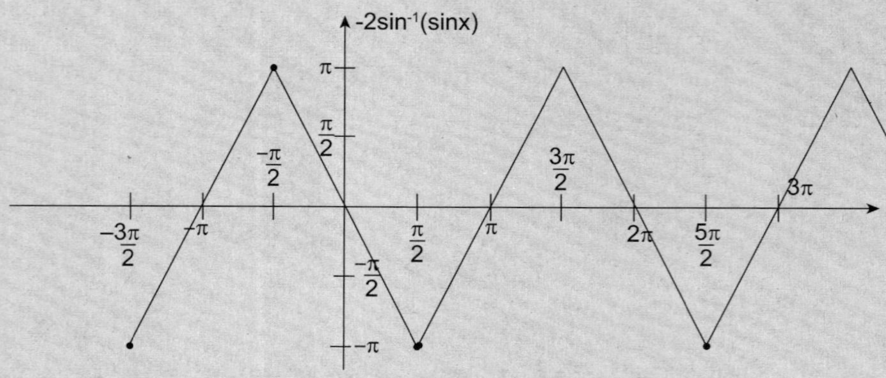

FIGURE 3.137

Therefore, the graph of $\frac{-1}{2}(\sin^{-1}(\sin x))$ can be obtained by taking mirror image of the graph of $\sin^{-1}(\sin x)$ about x-axis and thereby compressing the resulting graph 2 times along y-axis, towards the x-axis.

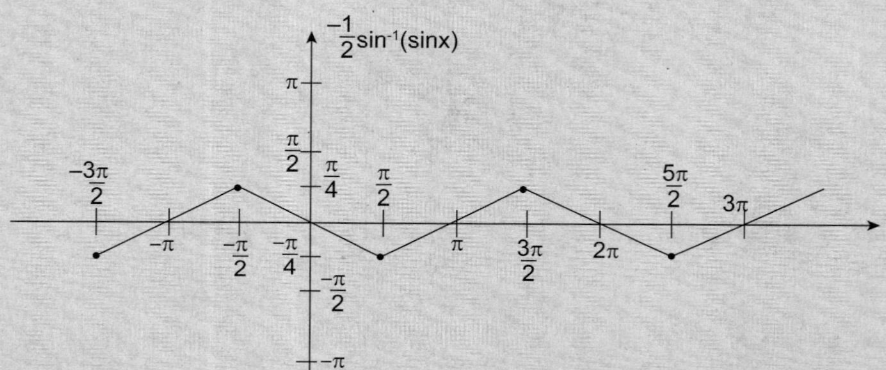

FIGURE 3.138

ILLUSTRATION 27: Find the number of solutions of $\sin^{-1}(-x-1) = \cos^{-1}x$

SOLUTION: Graph of $\sin^{-1}x$

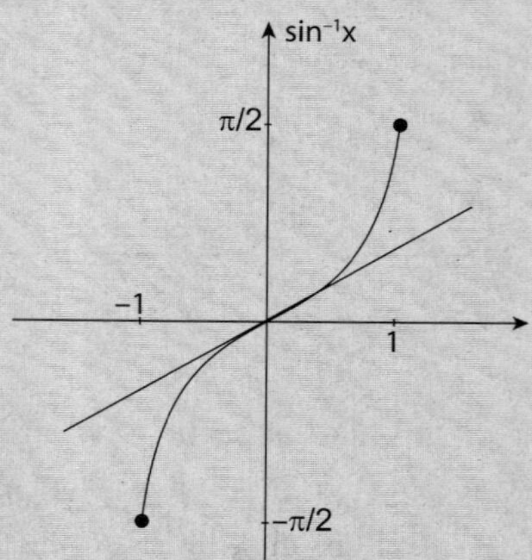

FIGURE 3.139

Graph of $\sin^{-1}(-x)$

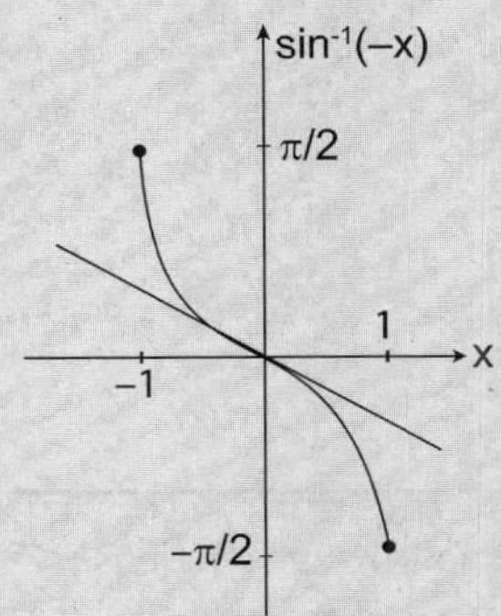

FIGURE 3.140

Graph of $\sin^{-1}(-x-1)$

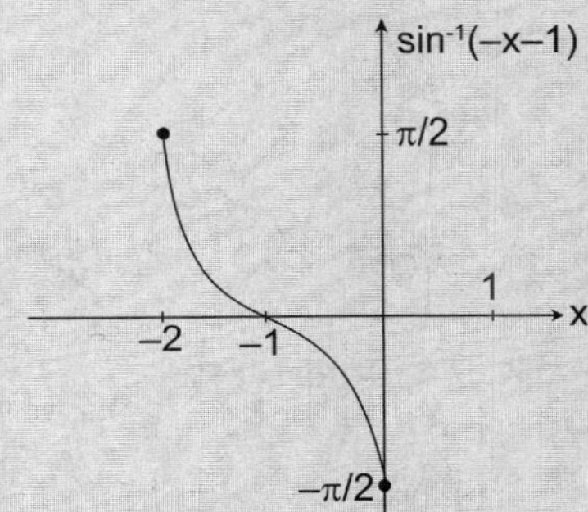

FIGURE 3.141

Graph of $\cos^{-1} x$

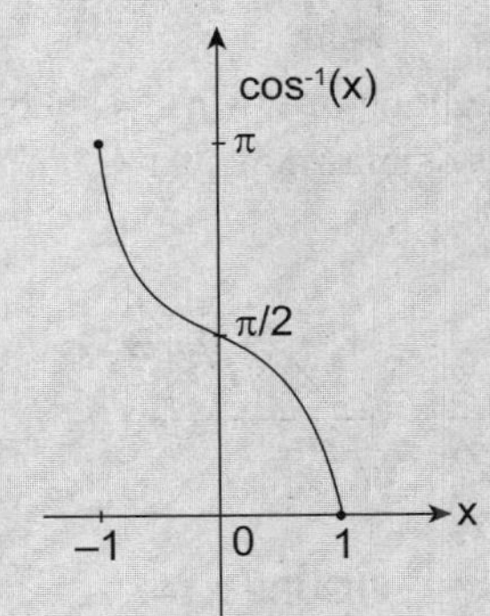

FIGURE 3.142

Clearly, the two graphs do not have a point of intersection, and hence, no solution.

5. **Graph of $y = |f(x)|$:** Graph of $y = |f(x)|$ can be obtained by reflecting the portion of the graph of $f(x)$ lying below x-axis on x-axis as a mirror and keeping the portion of graph above x-axis as it is. Since $y = f(x)$ when $f(x) \geq 0$ and $y = -f(x)$ when $f(x) < 0$. Hence, the graph of $y = |f(x)|$ is as shown in Figure 3.143 and 3.144.

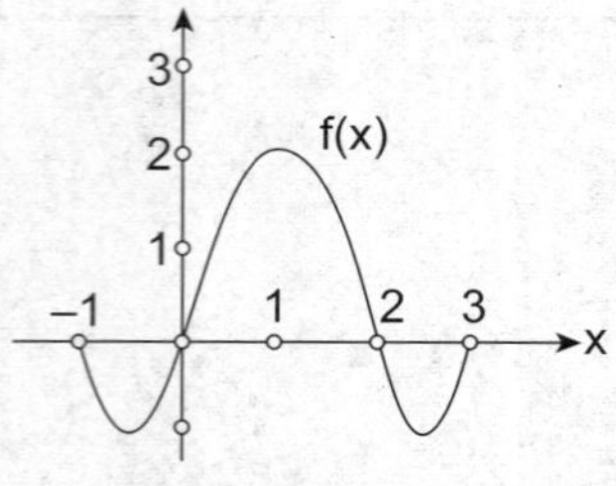

FIGURE 3.143

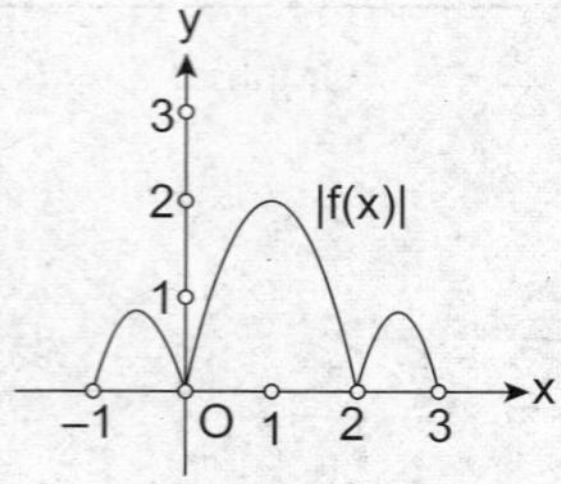

FIGURE 3.144

ILLUSTRATION 28: Draw the graphs of the following functions.

(i) $y = |\sin x|$ (ii) $y = |\ln x|$ (iii) $y = |[x]|$

SOLUTION: (i) Graph of $y = |\sin x|$. Graph of $y = |f(x)|$ is obtained by reflecting the portion of graph of $f(x)$ below x-axis, taking x-axis as mirror. So, graph of $y = |\sin x|$ would be as shown below.

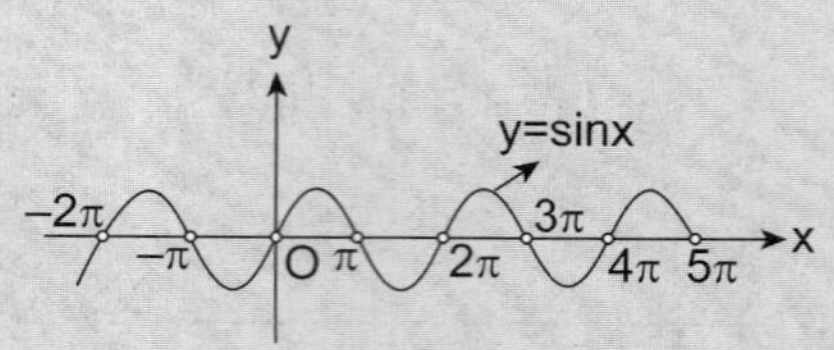

FIGURE 3.145

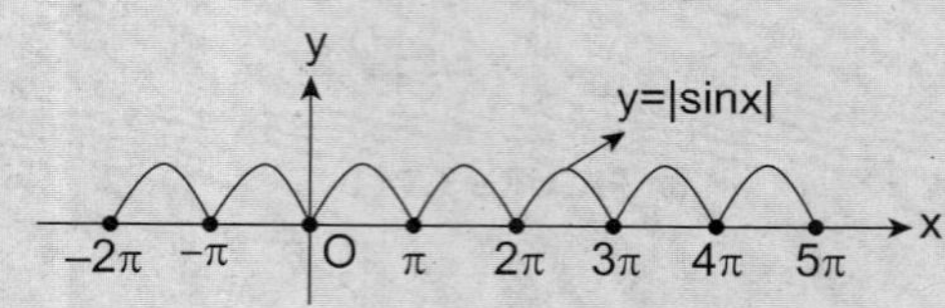

FIGURE 3.146

(ii) Graph of $y = |\ln x|$: Graph of $y = |f(x)|$ is obtained by reflecting the portion of graph below x-axis taking x-axis as mirror.

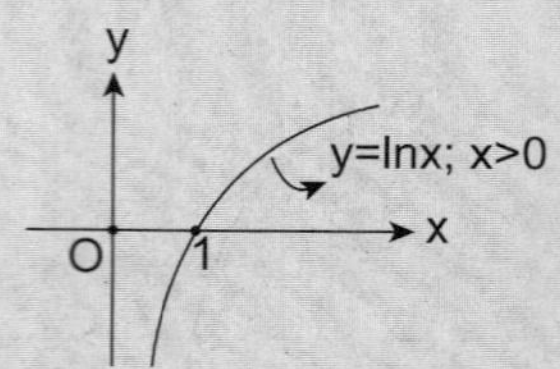

FIGURE 3.147

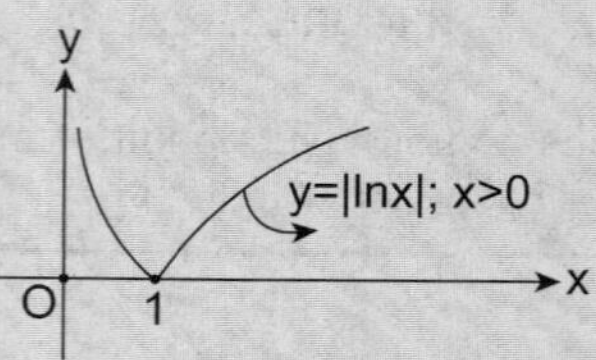

FIGURE 3.148

(iii) Graph of $y = |[x]|$

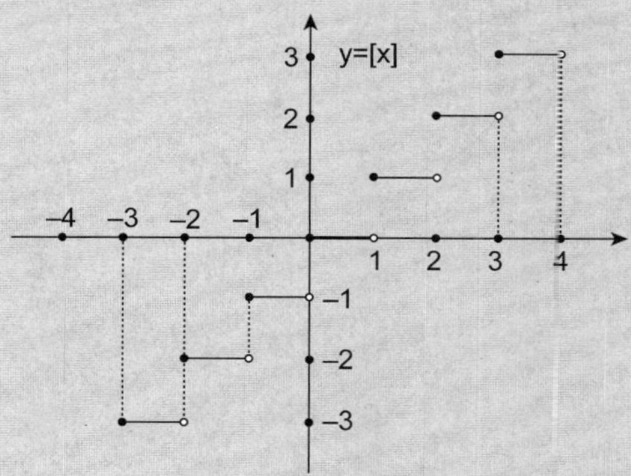

FIGURE 3.149

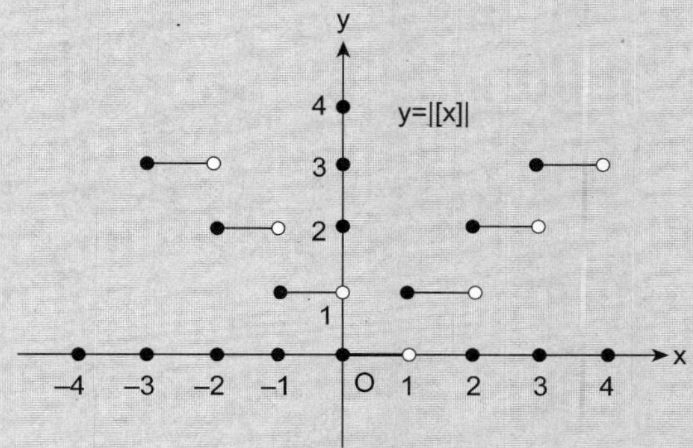

FIGURE 3.150

ILLUSTRATION 29: Draw the graph of $f(x) = ||||x| - 1| - 2| - 3|$, and hence, find value of 'k' (where k is a constant) so that the number of solutions of $f(x) = k$ is maximum.

SOLUTION: Graph of $y = x$

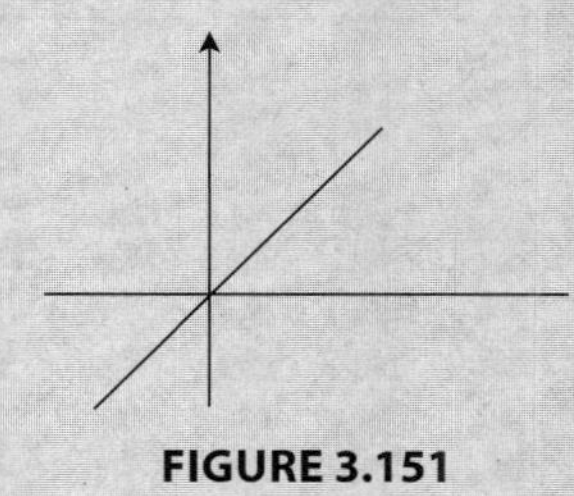

FIGURE 3.151

Graph of $y = |x|$

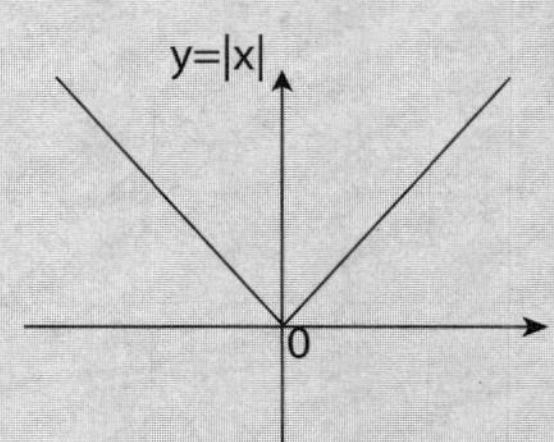

FIGURE 3.152

Graph of $y = |x| - 1$

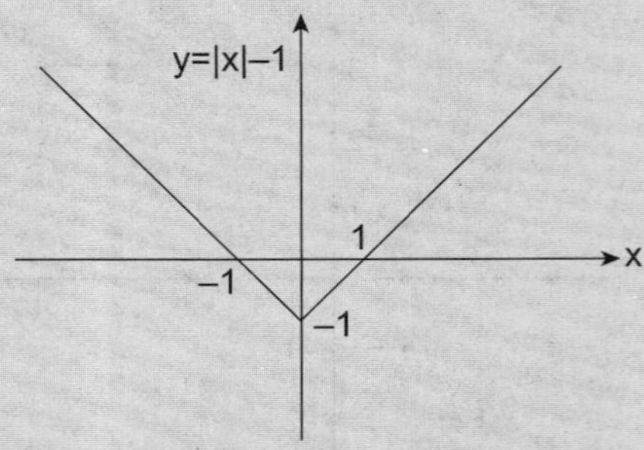

FIGURE 3.153

Graph of $y = ||x| - 1|$

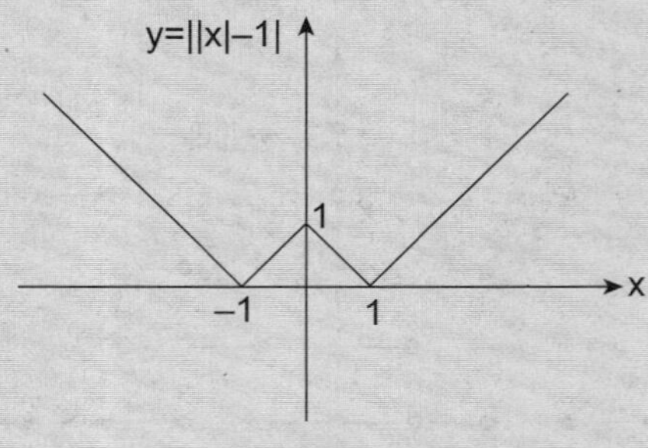

FIGURE 3.154

Graph of $y = ||x| - 1| - 2$

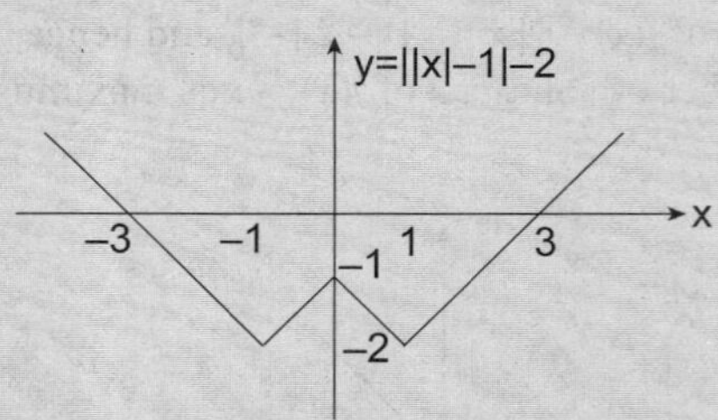

FIGURE 3.155

Graph of $y = ||x| - 1| - 2|$

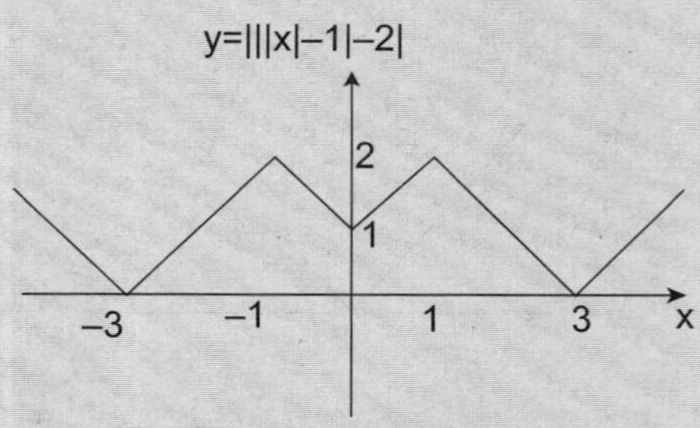

FIGURE 3.156

Graph of $y = |||x| - 1| - 2| - 3$

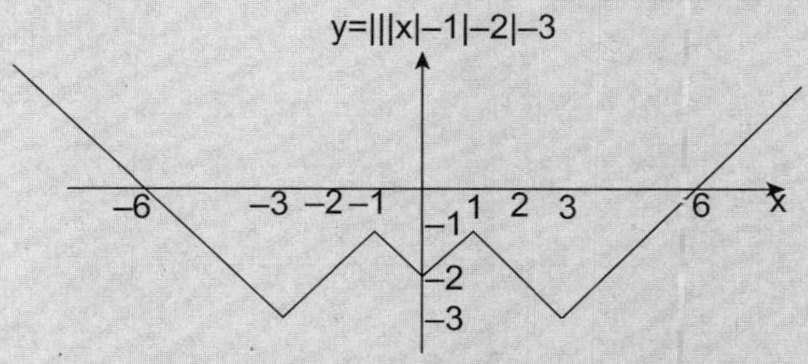

FIGURE 3.157

Graph of $y = ||||x|-1|-2|-3|$

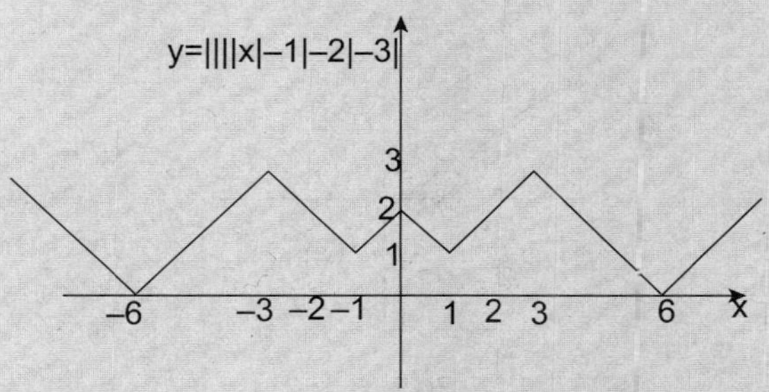

FIGURE 3.158

Now, clearly $f(x) = k$ will have maximum (8) solutions for $k \in (1,2)$.

6. **Graph of $y = f(|x|)$:** Graph of $y = f(|x|)$ can be obtained by keeping the portion of graph of $f(x)$ on right side of y-axis and replacing the portion of the graph of $y = f(x)$ on left side of y-axis by the reflection of right graph on y-axis. Graph of $y = f(|x|)$ is as shown in Figure 3.59 and 3.160.

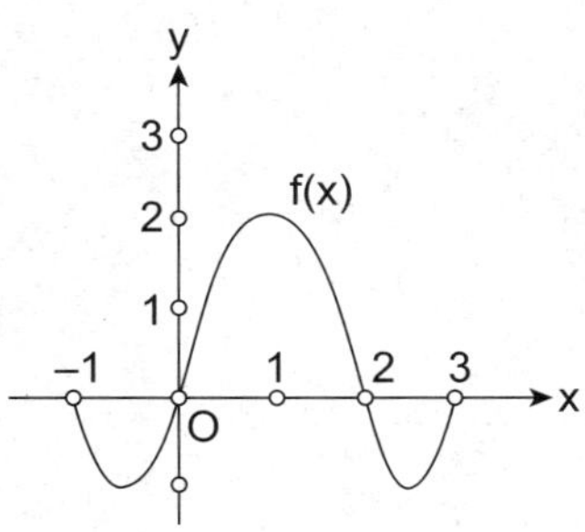

FIGURE 3.159

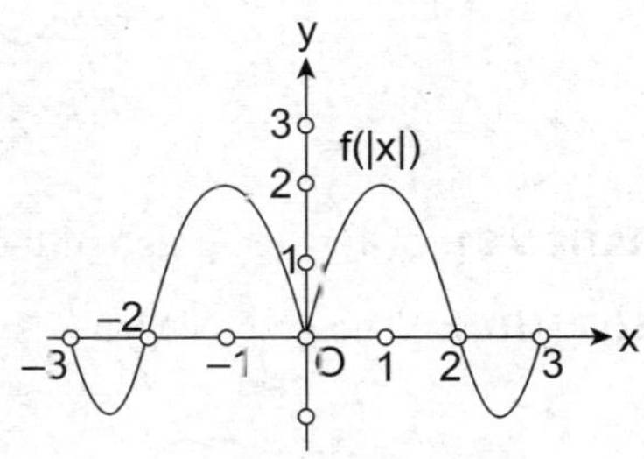

FIGURE 3.160

ILLUSTRATION 30: Draw the graph of the following functions:

(i) $y = \ln |x|$ (ii) $y = \sin |x|$

SOLUTION: **Graph of $y = \ln |x|$:** Graph of $y = f(|x|)$ is obtained by reflecting the right side graph of $y = f(x)$ on y-axis.

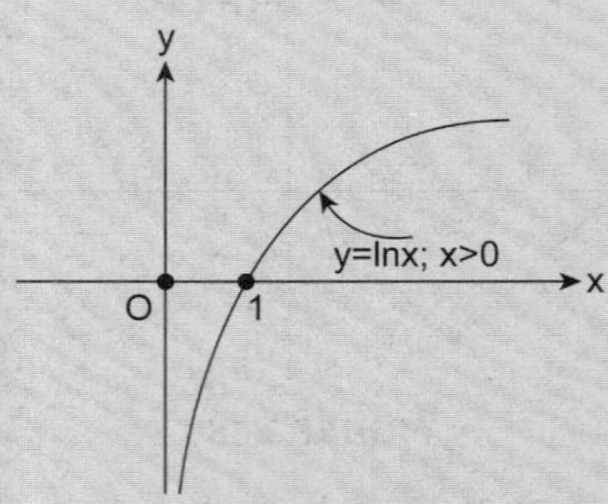

FIGURE 3.161

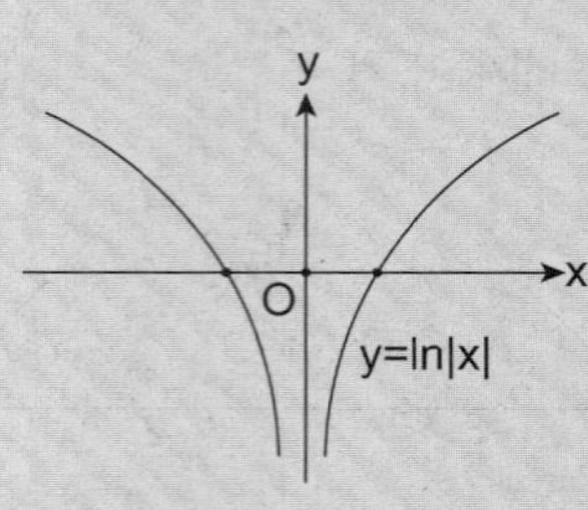

FIGURE 3.162

Graph of sin |x|:

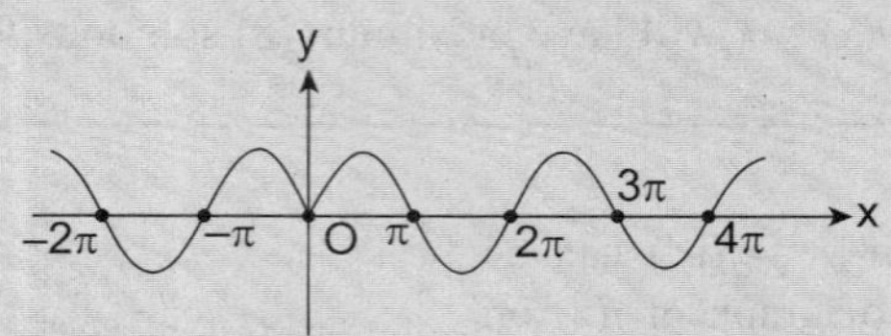

FIGURE 3.163

ILLUSTRATION 31: Draw the graph of the function $f(x) = \tan |x|$ and show that it is non-periodic in its domain.

SOLUTION: The graph of $\tan x$ is as shown below.

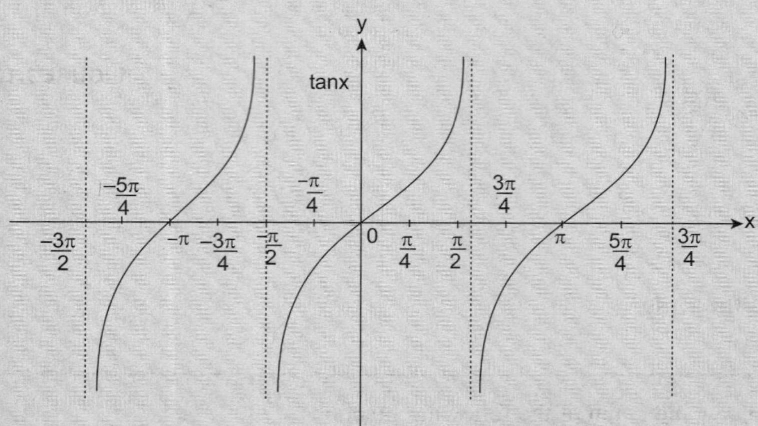

FIGURE 3.164

The graph of tan x for $x > 0$ is as shown in Figure 3.165.

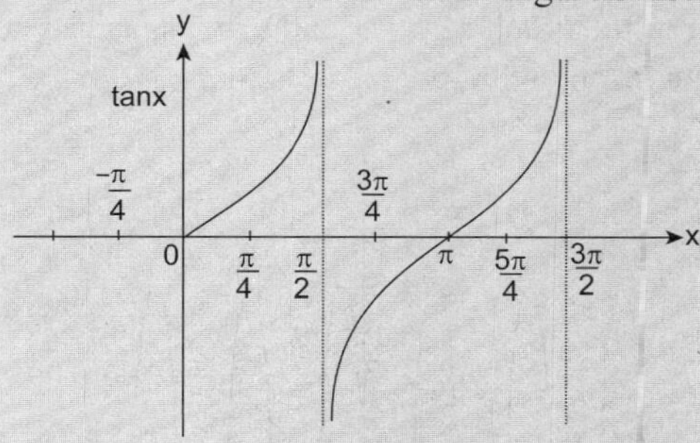

FIGURE 3.165

The graph of tan $|x|$ can be obtained by taking the mirror image of the graph of tan x for $x > 0$ about the y-axis, and hence, the resulting graph of tan $|x|$ is as shown in Figure 3.166.

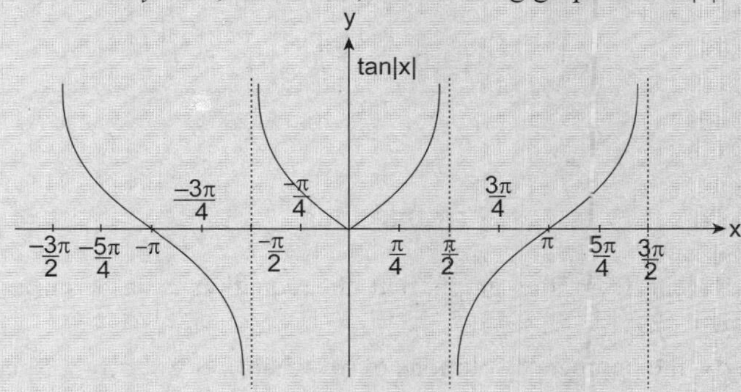

FIGURE 3.166

As is seen in the graph; tan $|x|$ is not a periodic function.

ILLUSTRATION 32: Find the number of solutions of $x = 5\sin(\pi x)$. Also find the number of solutions of $|x| = 5 \sin \pi x$. Hence, or otherwise, prove that the number of solutions of $x = 5\sin(\pi x)$ and $|x| = 5 \sin\pi x$ are not equal.

SOLUTION: The graph of $y = 5\sin(\pi x)$ $\forall$ $x \in [-5, 5]$ is as shown in Figure 3.167.

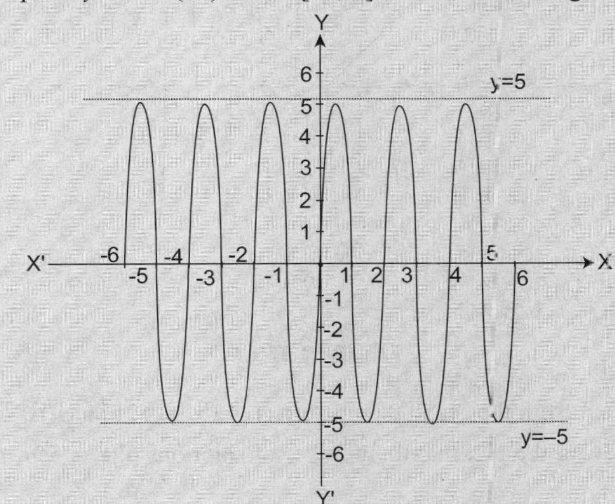

FIGURE 3.167

Therefore, the number of solutions of $x = 5\sin(\pi x)\ \forall\ x \in [-5, 5]$ can be observed as the point of intersection of the graph of $y = x$ and $y = 5\ \sin(\pi x)\ \forall\ x \in [-5, 5]$ drawn in same reference frame as shown in Figure 3.168.

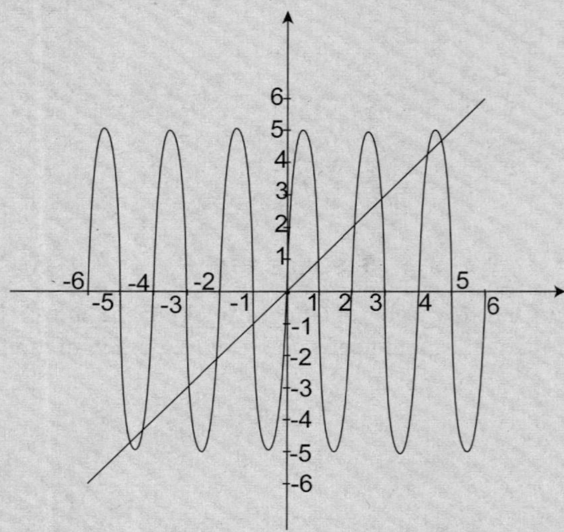

FIGURE 3.168

It is evident from the graph that the equation $x = 5\ \sin(\pi x)\ \forall\ x \in [-5, 5]$ has 11 solutions.

Similarly, the number of solutions of $|x| = 5\sin(\pi x)\ \forall\ x \in [-5, 5]$ can be observed as the point of intersection of the graph of $y = |x|$ and $y = 5\ \sin(\pi x)$ simultaneously.

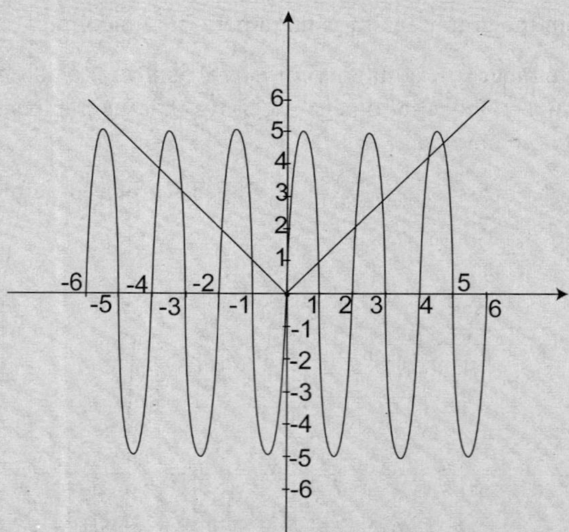

FIGURE 3.169

It is evident from the graph $|x| = 5\sin(\pi x)\ \forall\ x \in [-5, 5]$ has 10 solutions.

Thus, proving the fact that the number of solutions of $x = 5\sin(\pi x)$ and $|x| = 5\ \sin\ \pi x$ are not equal.

7. Graph of $y = |f|x||$ can be obtained in two steps:

Step 1: Using graph of $y = f(x)$, draw the graph of $f|x|$.

Step 2: Using graph of $y = f|x|$, draw the graph of $y = |f|x||$.

ILLUSTRATION 33: Draw the graph of $y = |\ln|x||$

SOLUTION: **Graph of $y = |\ln|x||$:** Is obtained by reflecting the portion of graph of $y = \ln|x|$ below x-axis on x-axis as shown in Figure 3.170.

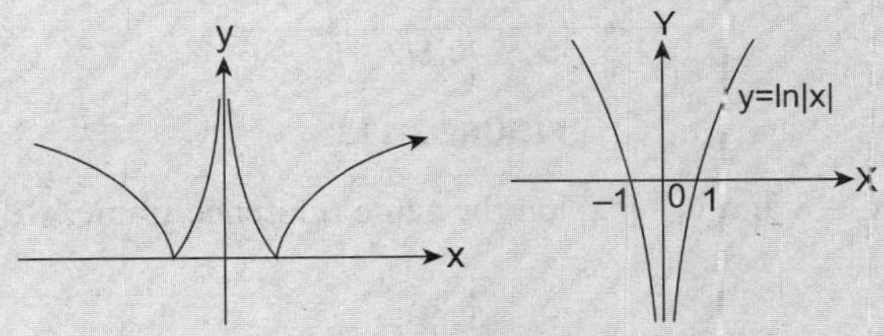

FIGURE 3.170

ILLUSTRATION 34: Sketch the graph of $y = |x^2 - 5|x| - 6|$, and hence, find the number of solutions of $|x^2 - 5|x| - 6| = 8$.

SOLUTION: Let $f(x) = x^2 - 5x - 6$

Graph of $f(x)$

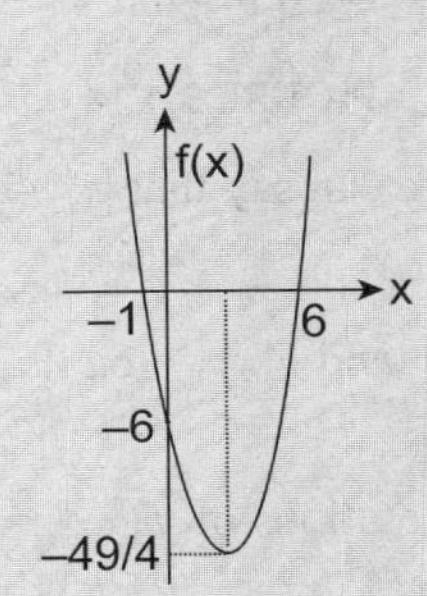

FIGURE 3.171

Graph of $f|x|$

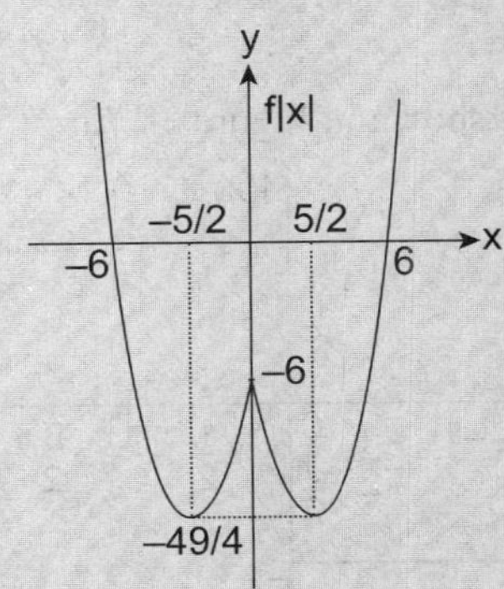

FIGURE 3.172

Graph of $|f|x||$

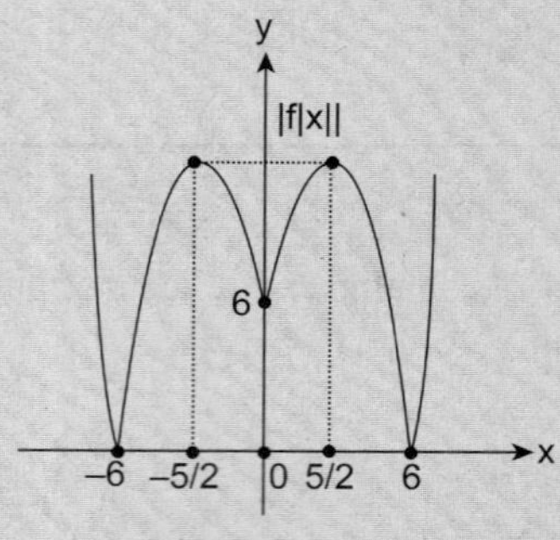

FIGURE 3.173

Drawing $y = 8$ and $y = |f|x||$ on the same reference frame, we get

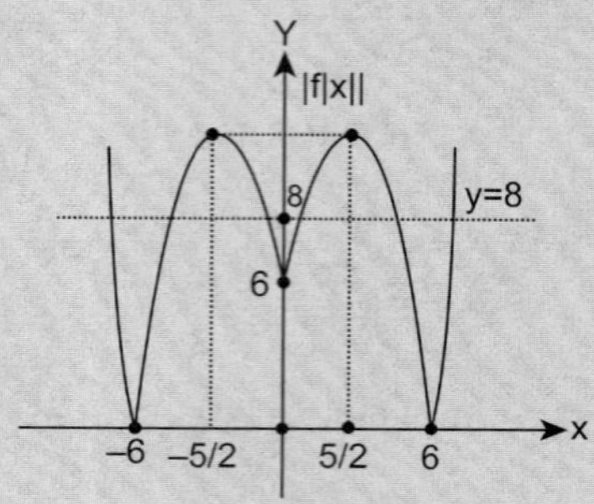

FIGURE 3.174

Clearly from the graph, we can say that $|x^2 - 5|x| - 6| = 8$ has 6 solutions.

ILLUSTRATION 35: If $f(x) = \begin{cases} 1; x \geq 1 \\ 2x - 1; 0 < x < 1 \\ -1; x \leq 0 \end{cases}$ and $g(x) = \log_b |ax|$ and $h(x) = g|x|$

Then find the number of solutions of $|f(x)|| = g(x)$ when (a, b) is given by

(i) $(1, e)$ (ii) $(1, 1/e)$ (iii) $\left(10, \dfrac{1}{10}\right)$

Also, find the points of intersection, if possible.

Also find the number of solutions of $|f|x|| = |h(x)|$ when (a, b) is given by

(iv) (1/10, 1/10) (v) (10, 1/10)

SOLUTION: The graph of $f(x)$ is as shown in Figure 3.175.

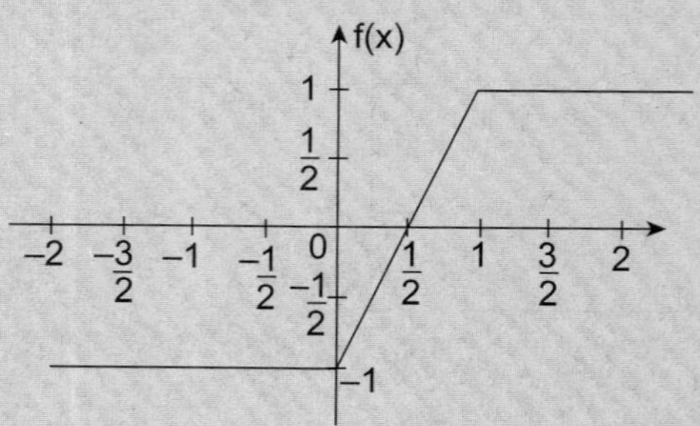

FIGURE 3.175

Now, the graph of $f|x|$ can be obtained by erasing the graph of $f(x)$ on the left hand side of the y-axis and taking the mirror image of the graph of the right hand side of the y-axis about y-axis.

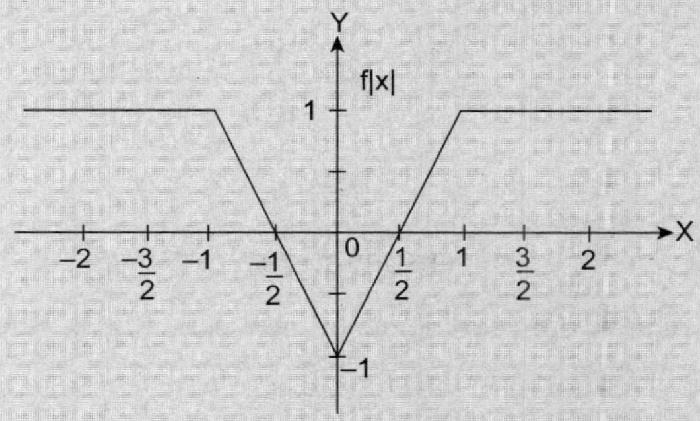

FIGURE 3.176

Now, the graph of $|f|x||$ can be obtained by taking the modulus of the graph of $f|x|$, i.e., reflecting the portion below x-axis on x-axis.

Hence, the graph of $|f|x||$ is as shown in Figure 3.177.

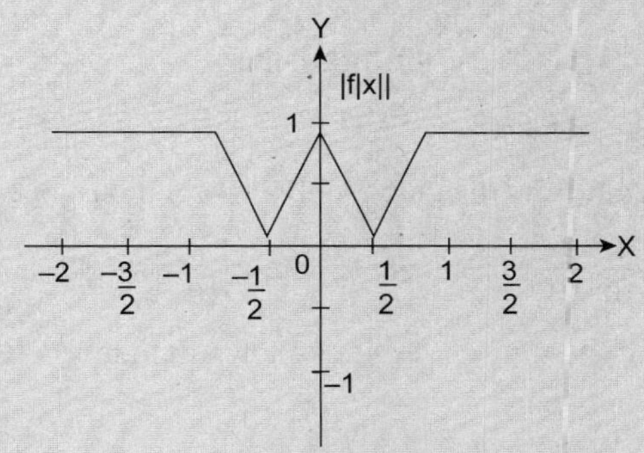

FIGURE 3.177

(i) The number of solutions of $|f|x|| = g(x)$, where $g(x) = \log_b |ax|$ and (a, b) is given by $(1, e)$. Hence, the function $g(x) = \log_e|x|$

The number of solutions of $|f|x|| = g(x)$ can be seen by drawing both the graphs on the same reference plane.

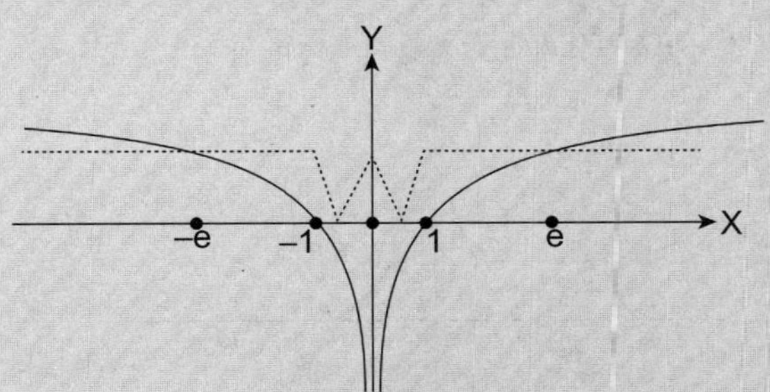

FIGURE 3.178

Hence, points of the intersection are $x = \pm e$

(ii) $(a, b) = (1, 1/e)$ $\Rightarrow$ $g(x) = \log_{1/e}|x|$ and to find the solution of $|f|x|| = \log_{1/e}|x|$

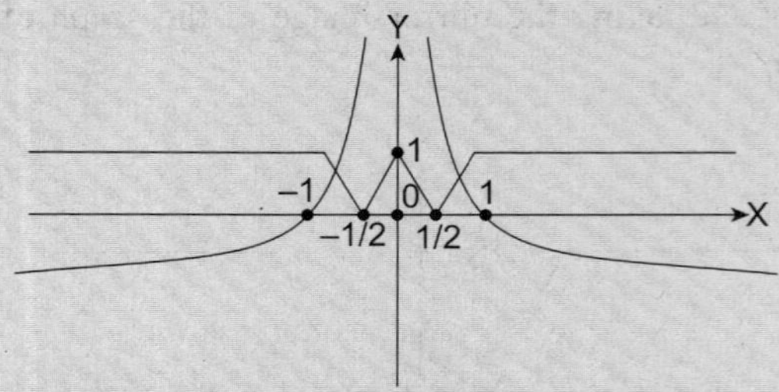

FIGURE 3.179

Here, we have only two points of intersection lying between (–1, –1/2) and (1/2, 1)

(iii) $(a, b) = (10, 1/10)$ $\Rightarrow$ $g(x) = \log_{(1/10)}|10\,x|$

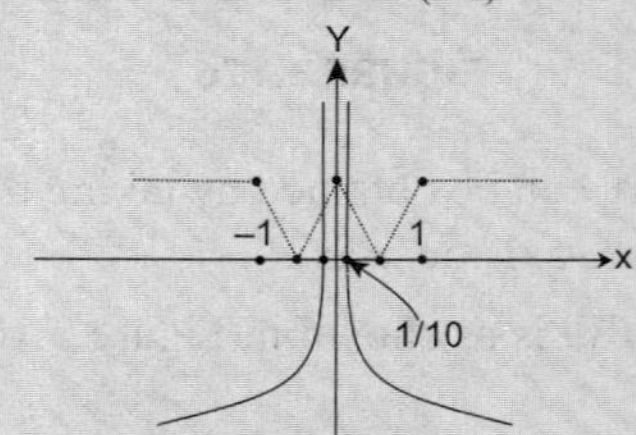

FIGURE 3.180

$\Rightarrow$ $g(x) = \log_{1/10}|10x|$

As is evident from the graph, only two solutions, one each in (–1/10, 0) and (0, 1/10)

(iv) $(a,b) = \left(\frac{1}{10}, \frac{1}{10}\right)$ $\Rightarrow$ $g(x) = \log_{1/10}\left|\frac{1}{10}x\right|$

$\Rightarrow$ Graph of $g(x)$ or $g|x|$ or $h|x|$ is as shown in Figure 3.181.

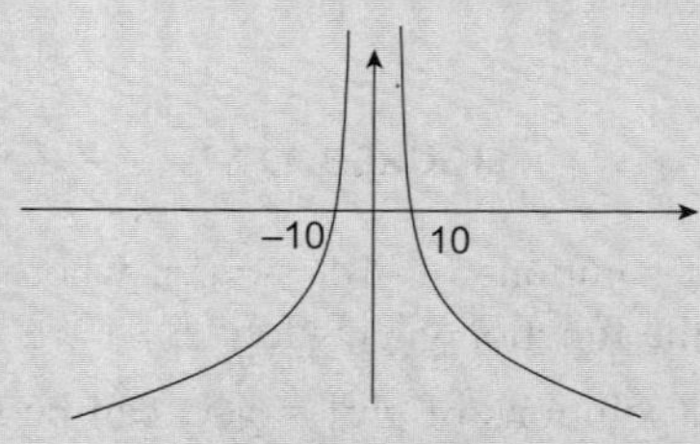

FIGURE 3.181

Graph of $|h(x)|$ and $|f|x||$

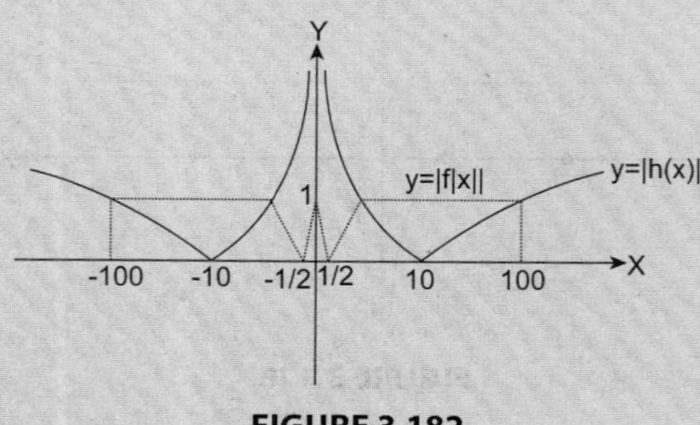

FIGURE 3.182

$\therefore\ |h(x)| = |f|x|| \Rightarrow \left|\log_{1/10}\left|\frac{1}{10}x\right|\right| = 1$

$\Rightarrow \log_{1/10}\left|\frac{1}{10}x\right| = \pm 1$

$\Rightarrow \left|\frac{1}{10}x\right| = \left(\frac{1}{10}\right)^{\pm 1} = 10 \text{ or } \frac{1}{10}$ $\Rightarrow |x| = 100 \text{ or } 1$ $\Rightarrow x = \pm 100 \text{ or } \pm 1$

Hence, 4 solutions $x = \pm 100$ and $x = \pm 1$

(v) $(a, b) = (10, 1/10)$

$\Rightarrow g(x) = \log_{1/10}|10\,x|$ $\therefore\ |h(x)| = |g|x|| = |g(x)|$

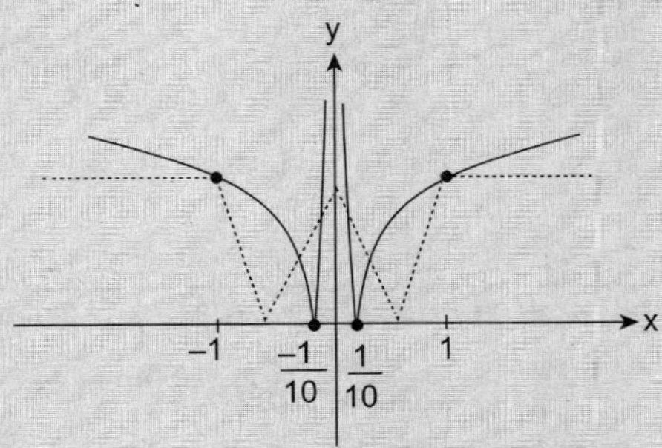

FIGURE 3.183

Hence, 4 solutions $x = \pm 1$, one each in $(-1/10, 0)$ and $(0, 1/10)$

ILLUSTRATION 36: Sketch the graph of $y = |e^{-|x|} - 1/4|$

SOLUTION: We know, the graph of $y = e^{-x}$

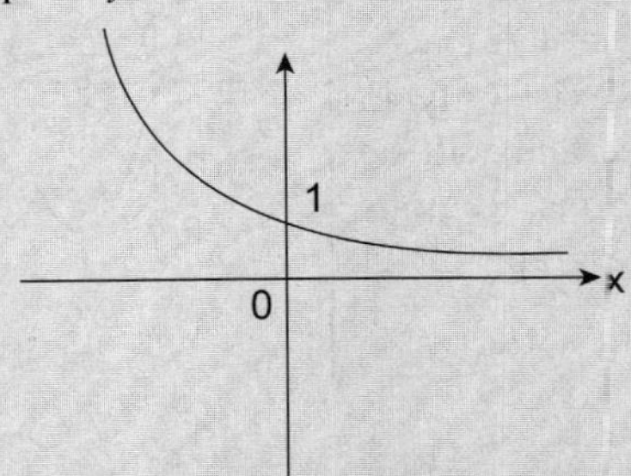

FIGURE 3.184

Now graph of $y = e^{-|x|}$

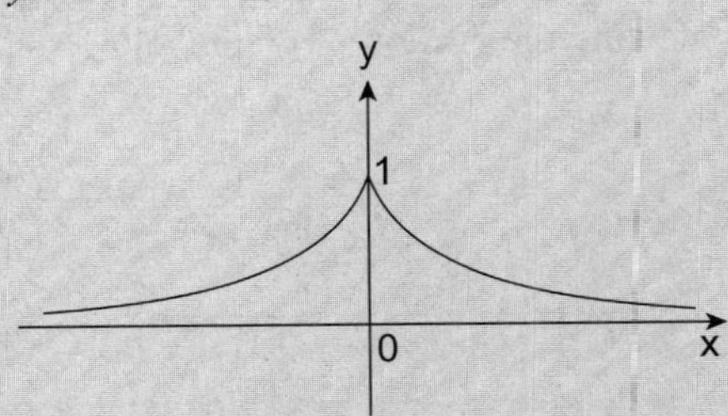

FIGURE 3.185

Graph of $y = e^{-|x|} - 1/4$

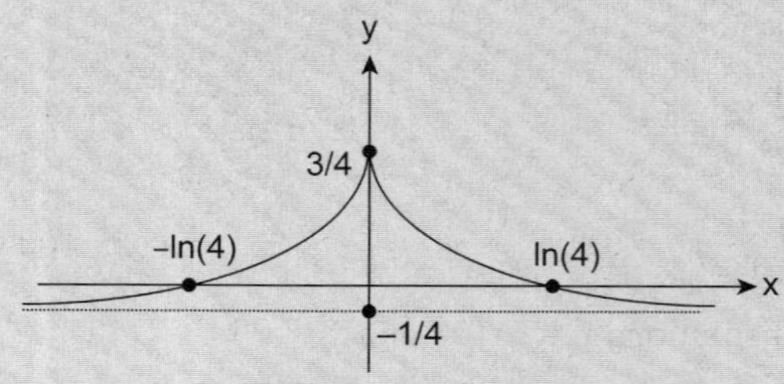

FIGURE 3.186

Hence, graph of $y = |e^{-|x|} - 1/4|$

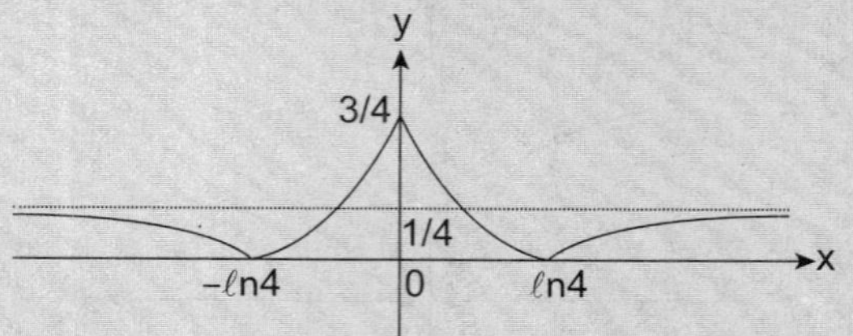

FIGURE 3.187

8. Graph of $|y| = f(x)$: Graph of $|y| = f(x)$ is obtained by discarding the portion of graph of $f(x)$ below x-axis ($\because |y| \geq 0$) and reflecting the portion of graph of $f(x)$ above x-axis on x-axis.
If $f(x) < 0$, graph of $|y| = f(x)$ would not exist.
And if $f(x) \geq 0$, $|y| = f(x)$ would give $y = \pm f(x)$.
Hence, graph of $|y| = f(x)$ would exist only in the regions where $f(x)$ is non-negative and will be reflected about x-axis only in those regions. Regions where $f(x) < 0$ will be neglected. The graph of $|y| = f(x)$ is shown in Figure 3.188

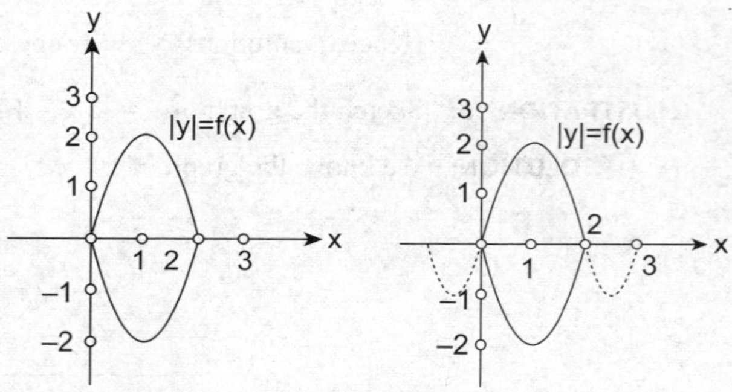

FIGURE 3.188

ILLUSTRATION 37: Draw the graph of the following functions: (i) $|y| = \ln|x|$ (ii) $|y| = \tan x$

SOLUTION: Graph of $|y| = f(x)$ is obtained by reflecting the portion of graph above x-axis taking x-axis is as mirror and neglecting the portion of graph below x-axis. (i) graph of $|y| = \ln|x|$

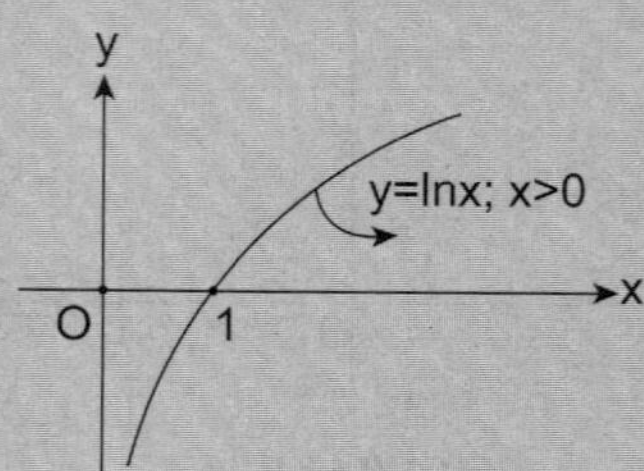

FIGURE 3.189

Graph of $|y| = \ln|x|$: It can be obtained by reflecting the graph of $|y| = \ln x;\ x > 0$ on y-axis.

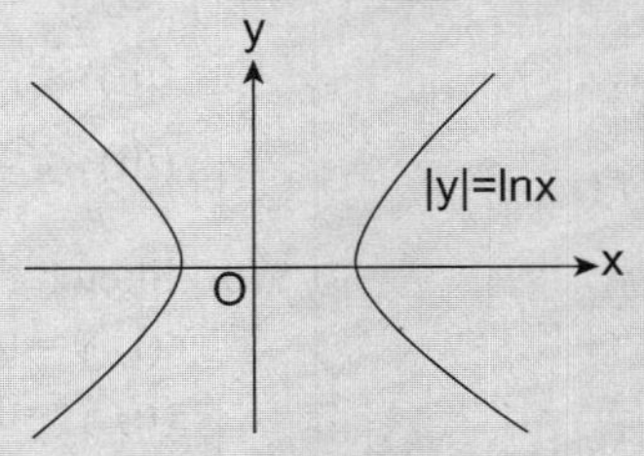

FIGURE 3.190

(ii) Graph of $|y| = \tan x$

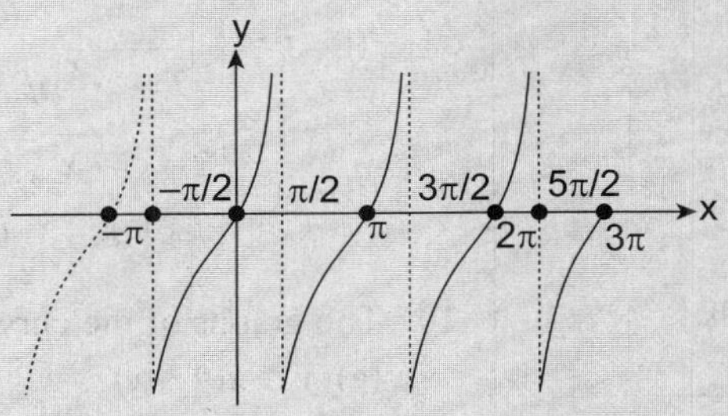

FIGURE 3.191

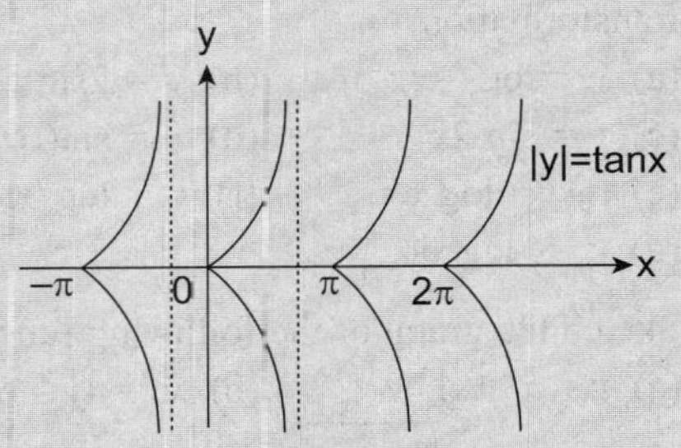

FIGURE 3.192

9. **Graph of $|y| = |f(x)|$:** Graph of $|y| = |f(x)|$ can be obtained by the following two steps:

(i) Using graph of $f(x)$, plot the graph of $|f(x)|$.

(ii) Now, take the mirror image of the graph of $y = |f(x)|$ on x-axis, and hence, we obtain the graph of $|y| = |f(x)|$.

ILLUSTRATION 38: Draw the graph of the following functions:

SOLUITON: Graph of $|y| = |\ln|x||$ is obtained by reflecting the graph of $y = |\ln|x||$ on x-axis as shown in Figure 3.193.

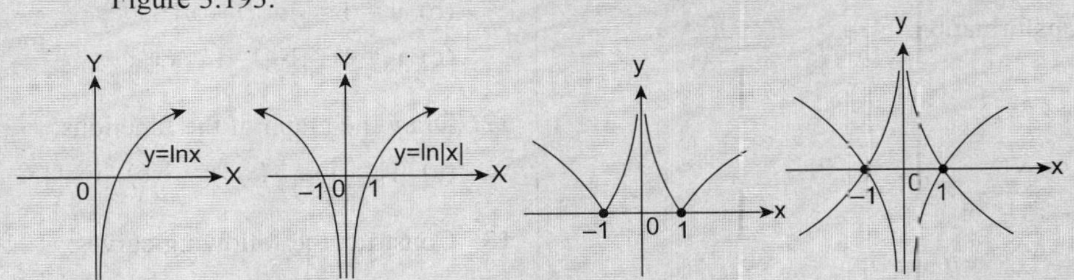

FIGURE 3.193

TEXTUAL EXERCISE–2: (SUBJECTIVE)

1. If a function is defined as $f(x) = \begin{cases} x & ; \quad 0 \le x \le 1 \\ 2-x & ; \quad 1 < x \le 2 \\ (x-2)(x-4); & \quad 2 \le x \le 4 \end{cases}$ then sketch the graph of $y = f(x)$, and hence, sketch the curves of the following functions:

(a) $y = f(-x)$ (b) $y = -f(x)$

(c) $y = -f(-x)$ (d) $y = f(x+2)$

(e) $y = f(x) + 3$ (f) $y = f(x+2) + 3$
(g) $y = 2f(x)$ (h) $y = f(2x)$
(i) $y = 2f(3x)$ (j) $y = |f(x)|$
(k) $y = f(|x|)$ (l) $y = |f(|x|)|$
(m) $y = f(x) + |f(x)|$ (n) $y = f(x) - |f(x)|$
(o) $y = \frac{|f(x)|}{f(x)}$ (p) $y = sgn(f(x))$
(q) $y = f^2(x)$ (r) $y^2 = f(x)$
(s) $y = (f(x))^{1/2}$

2. Sketch the graph of the following functions using transformation:
(a) $y = \log_e(-x)$ (b) $y = 2\sin x$
(c) $y = \sin 2x$ (d) $y = \sin(|x|)$
(e) $|y| = \log x$ (f) $y = \log |x|$
(g) $y = |\log x|$

3. Sketch the graph of the following functions:
(a) $y = x^2 + 4$ (b) $x^2 = 4y - 6$
(c) $x = 1 + \sqrt{4y - y^2}$ (d) $y = 3 + \sqrt{4x - x^2 + 5}$
(e) $y = \sqrt{x^2 - 16}$ (f) $x = 1 - \sqrt{y^2 - 4x + 8}$
(g) $y = \sin x + \cos x$ (h) $y = \frac{2}{3}\sqrt{9 - x^2}$

4. Sketch the graph of the following functions:
(a) $f(x) = 4\sin(3x)$
(b) $f(x) = \ln(4x - 5)$
(c) $f(x) = 3\log_2(-2x) - 5$

5 Sketch the graph of each of the following functions starting with the graph of $y = \sqrt{x}$ using suitable graphical transformation.
(a) $y = 2\sqrt{x} - 3$
(b) $y = 2\sqrt{x + 5}$
(c) $f(x) = 2 + \sqrt{x - 3}$
(d) $f(x) = -\sqrt{3 - 2x}$
(e) $y = \begin{cases} 3^x - 1, & if\ x < 0 \\ \sqrt{2x - x^2}, & if\ x \geq 0 \end{cases}$

6. Sketch the graph of each of the following functions starting with the graph of $y = \sqrt{1 - x^2}$, using suitable graphical transformation.
(a) $f(x) = \sqrt{1 - (x/2)^2}$
(b) $f(x) = 1 + 3\sqrt{1 - (x - 2)^2 / 9}$
(c) $f(x) = -3 + \sqrt{4 - (x - 1)^2}$

7. Sketch the graph of the following functions:
(i) $y = (x - 1)^{2/3}$
(iii) $y = \sqrt[3]{x - 8}$
(iii) $y = \sqrt[3]{2x + 8} - 5$

8. Sketch the graph of the following functions:
(i) $y = \log_3(4 - x)$
(ii) $y = \log_{1/2}(4 - 2x)$

9. Sketch the graph of the following functions:
(i) $y = \begin{cases} 3^x - 1, & if\ x < 0 \\ \sqrt{2x - x^2}, & if\ x \geq 0 \end{cases}$
(ii) $y = \begin{cases} 2 - \sqrt{1 - x^2}, & if\ x \leq 1 \\ 2 + \log_{1/2} x, & if\ x > 1 \end{cases}$

10. The graphs of the curves
(a) $y = x(4 - x)$
(b) $y = 3x - 5$
(c) $y = |x + 1| - 2$
Through the following successive transformations, Find the resulting equations of each curve after the transformation T_3 have been exerted.
(T_1) A vertical translation of 2 units up.
(T_2) A reflection about the y-axis.
(T_3) A horizontal translation of 3 unit to the left.

11. Draw the following graphs in succession
(a) $y = |1 - |1 - x||$
(b) $y = 1 - |1 - |1 - x||$
(c) $y = 1 - |1 - |1 - |1 - x|||$

12. Draw the graph of the functions:
(a) $|y| = |\log_{1/3}(x/3)|$ (b) $|y| = |3 - |x - 2||$

13. Construct the following curves:
(i) $\frac{y}{x + 2} = -1$
(ii) $|y| + x = -4$
(iii) $|x| + |y| = 5$
(iv) $|y - 4| = |x - 1|$

14. Sketch the graph of the following functions:
(a) $y = \cos(x - 1)$ (b) $y = \sin^2 x - 2\sin x$
(c) $y = 2^{\sin x}$ (d) $y = |2 - |x - 1||$
(e) $y = x^2 - 2|x|$

Answer Keys

1. 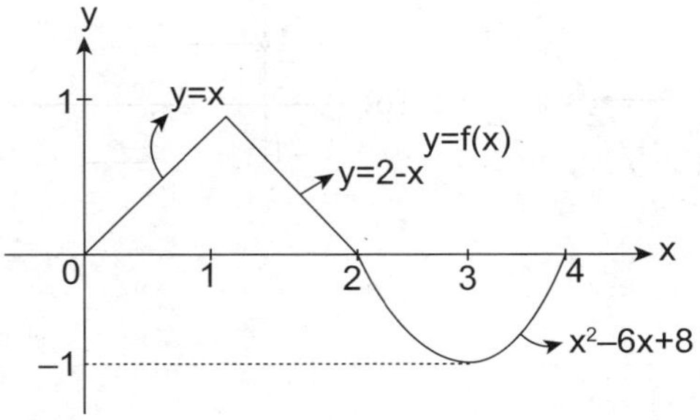

(a) 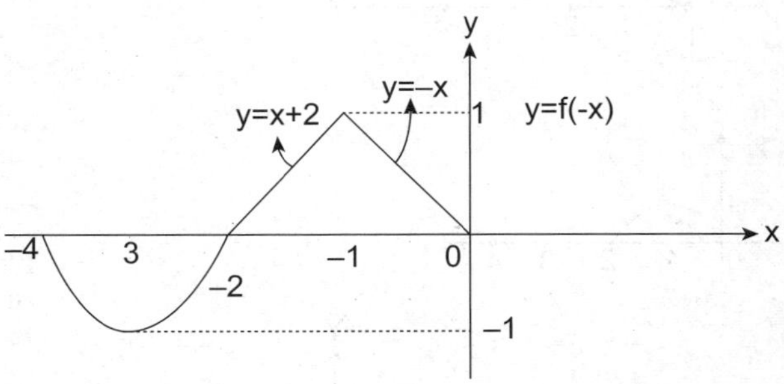

(b) 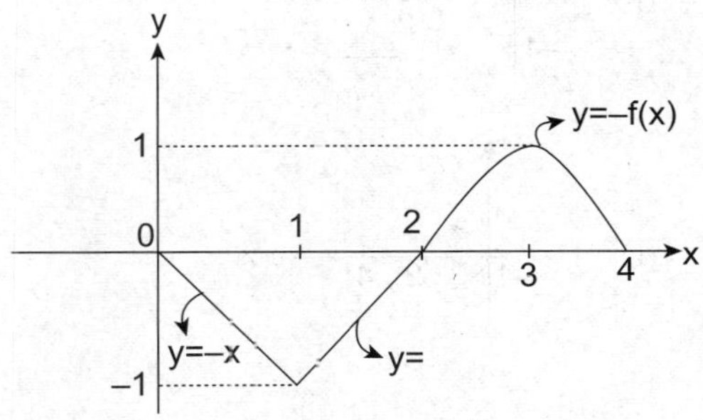

(c) 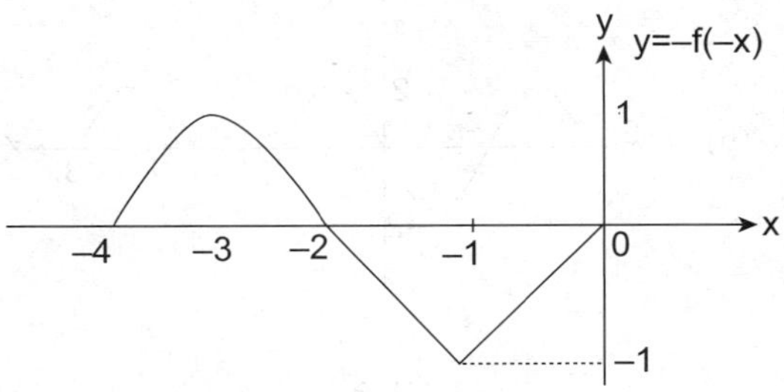

(d) 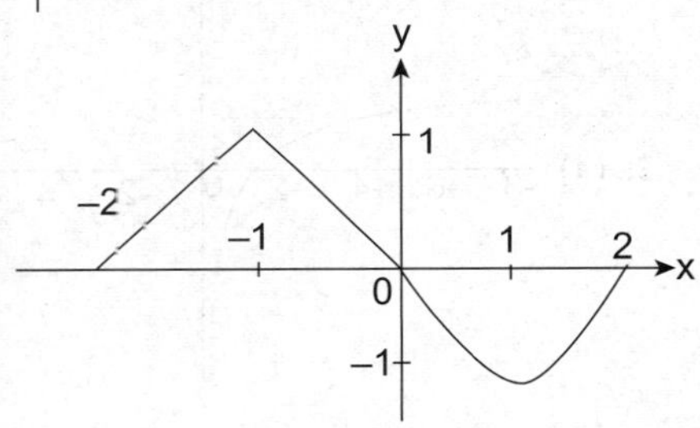

(e) 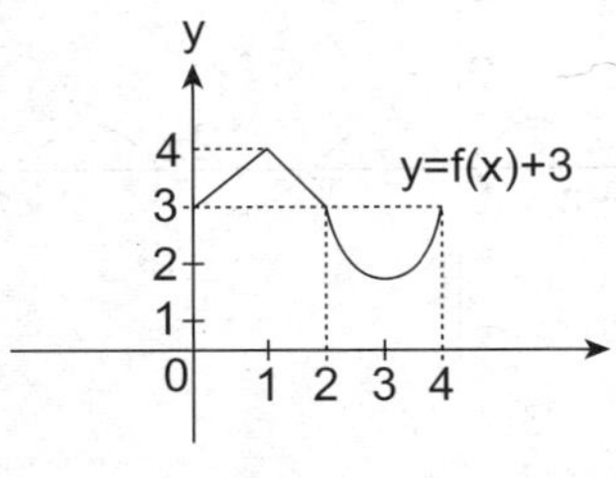

(f) 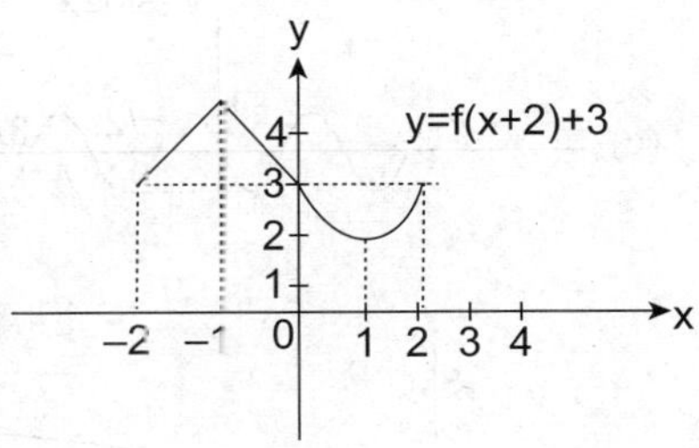

(g) 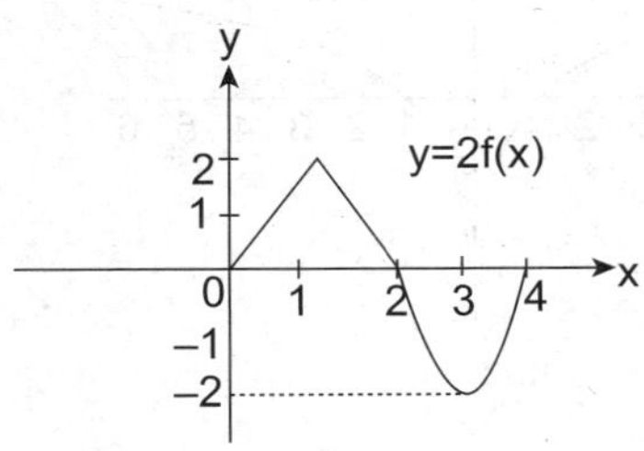

(h) 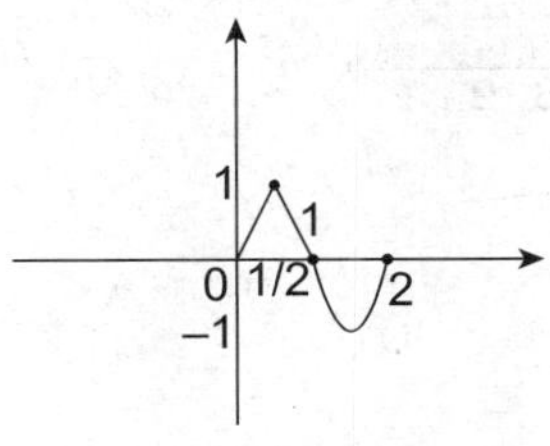

(i) 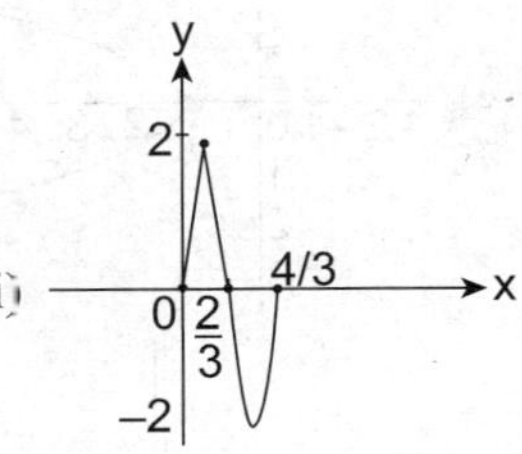

(j) 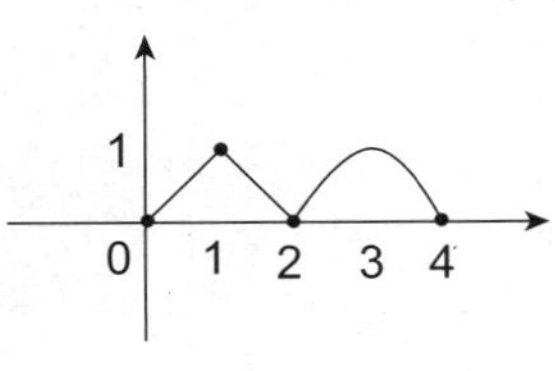

(k) 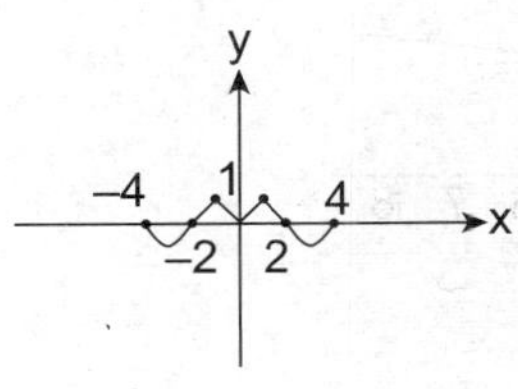

(l) 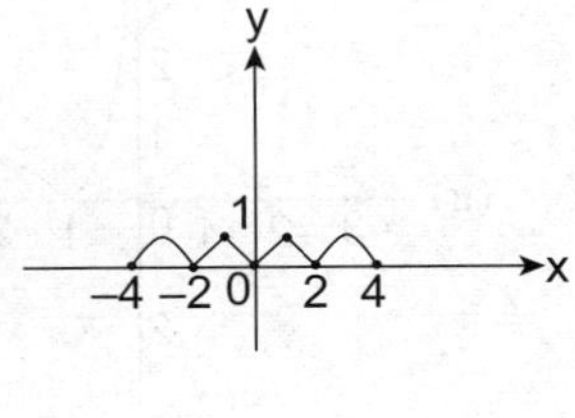

(m) 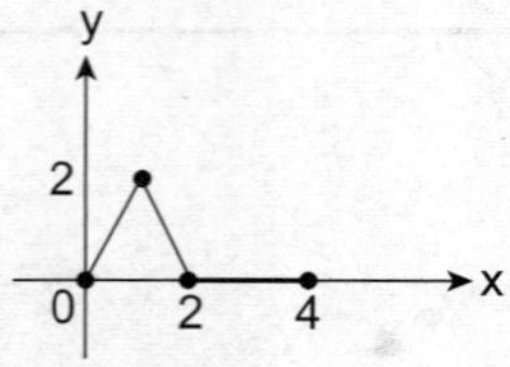

(n) 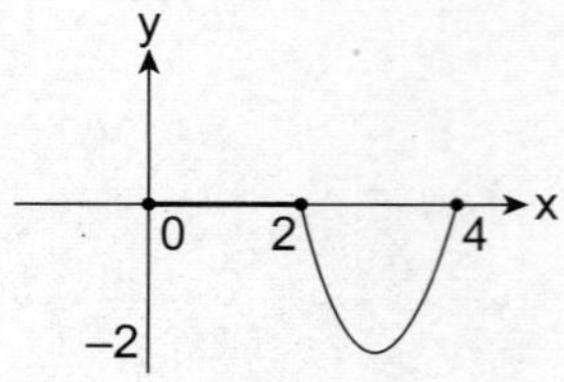

(o) 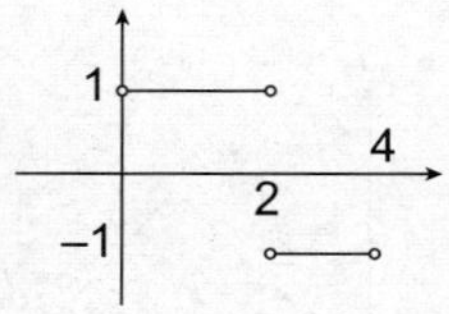

(p) 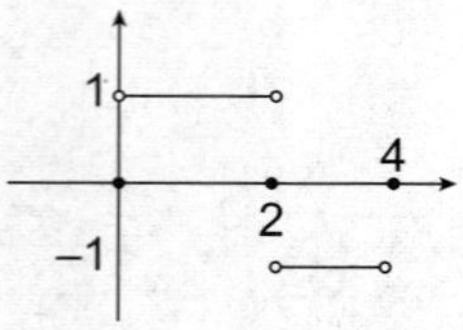

(q) 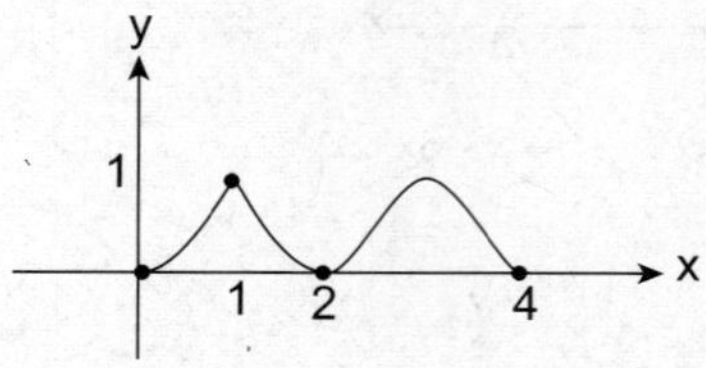

(r) 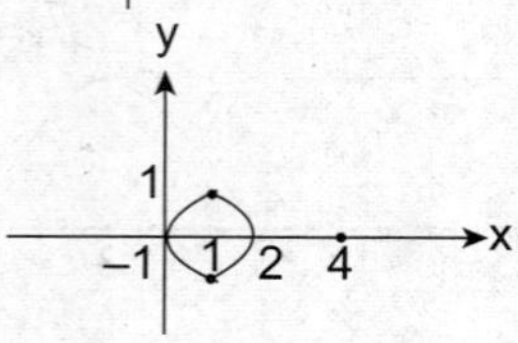

(s) 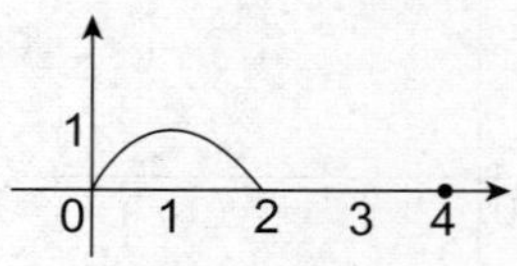

2. (a) 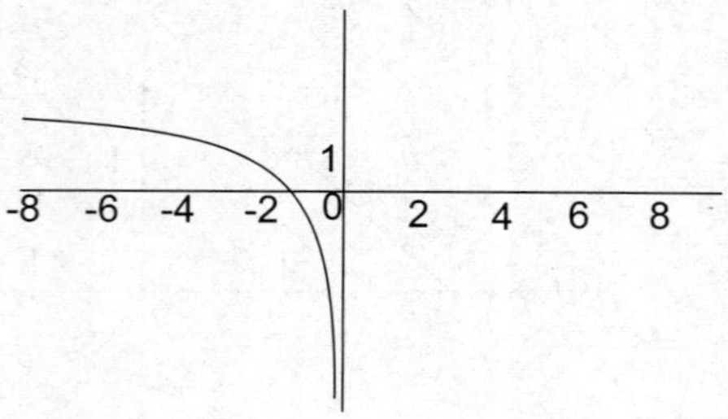

(b) 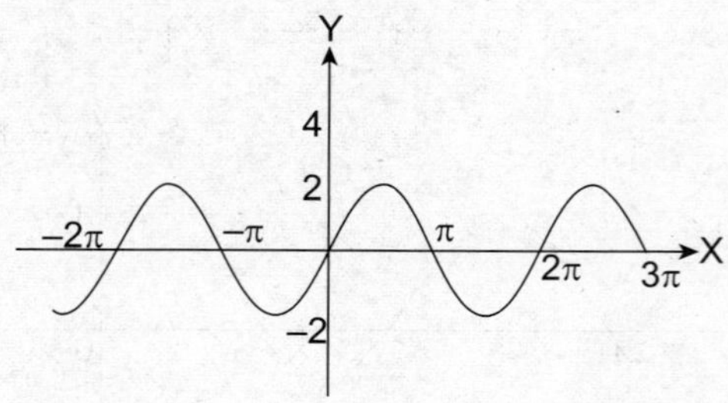

(c) 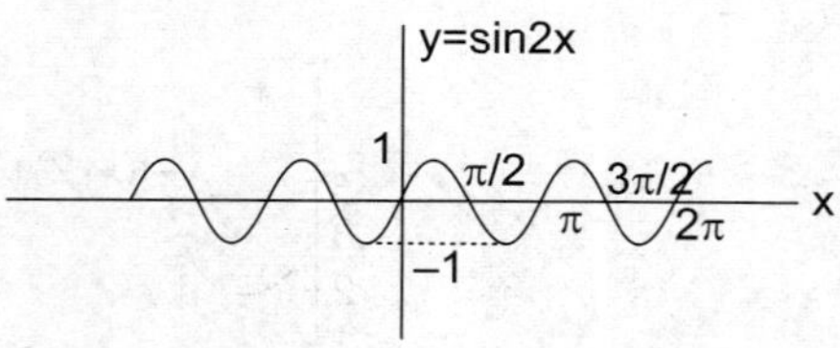

(d) 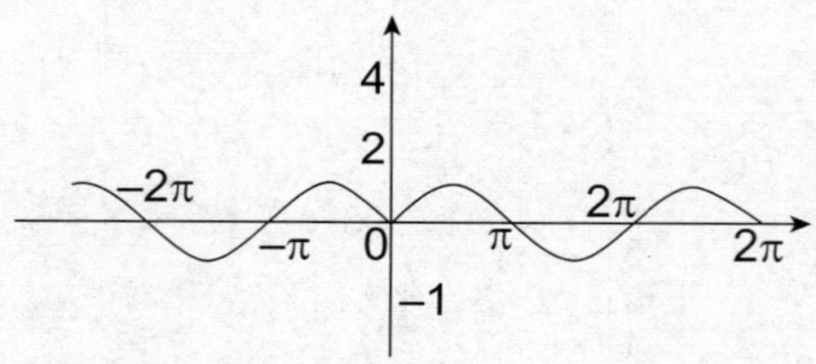

(e) 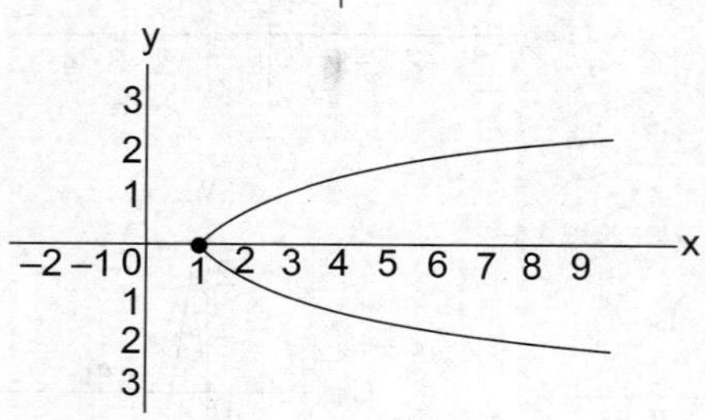

(f) 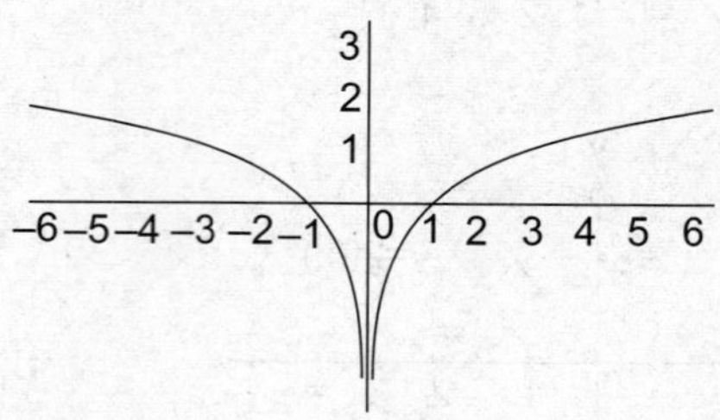

(g) 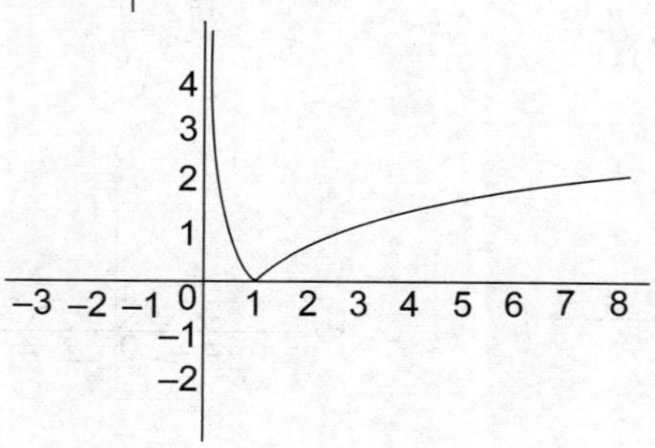

3. (a)

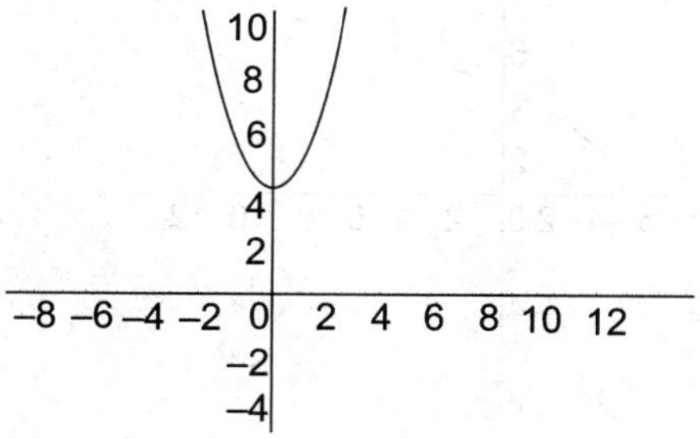

(b)

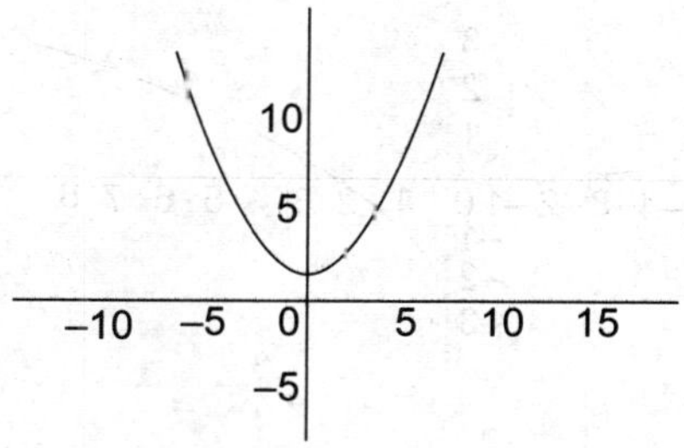

(c)

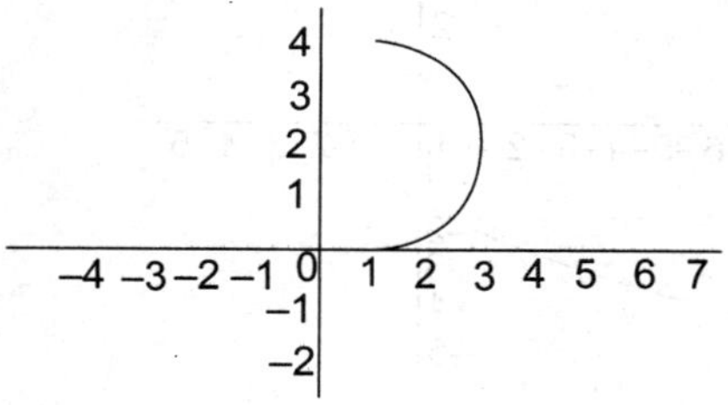

(d)

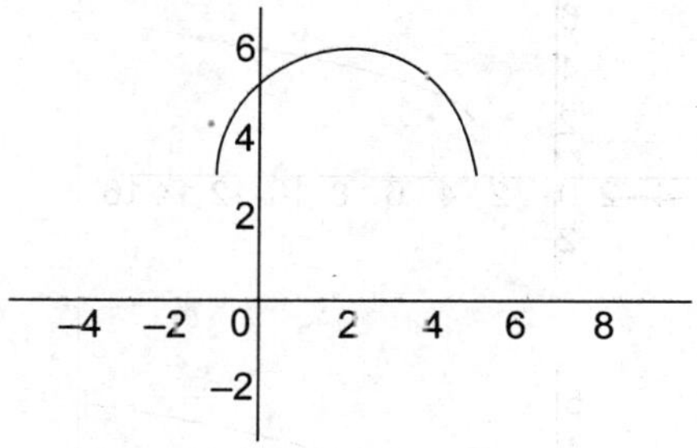

(e)

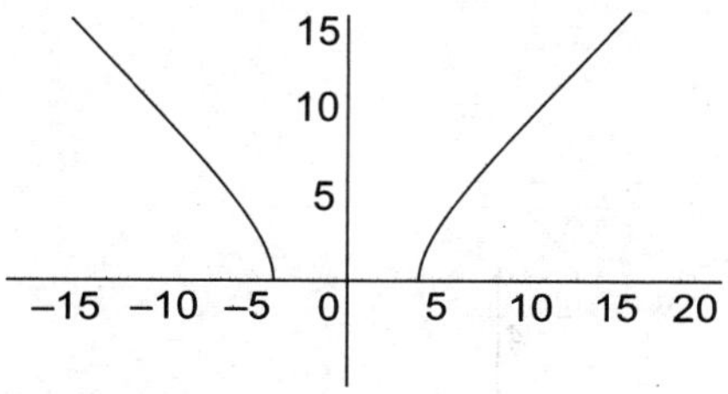

(f)

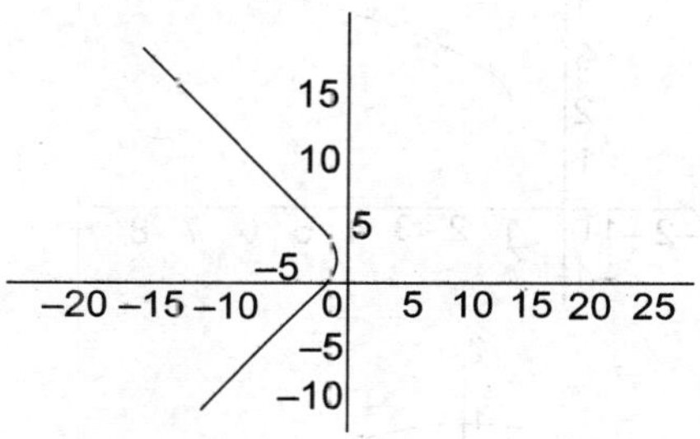

(g)

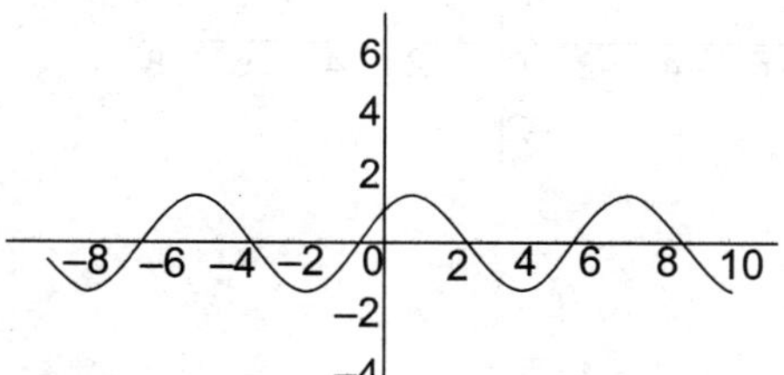

(h)

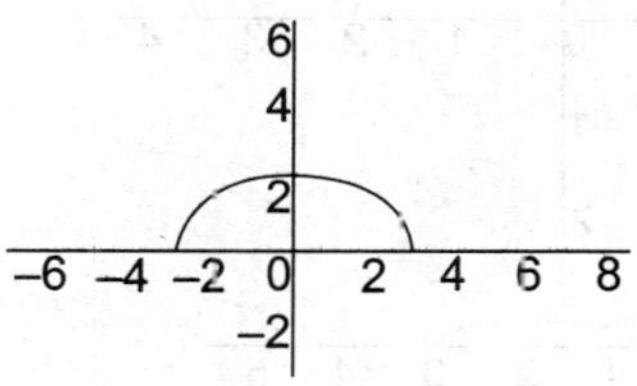

4. (a)

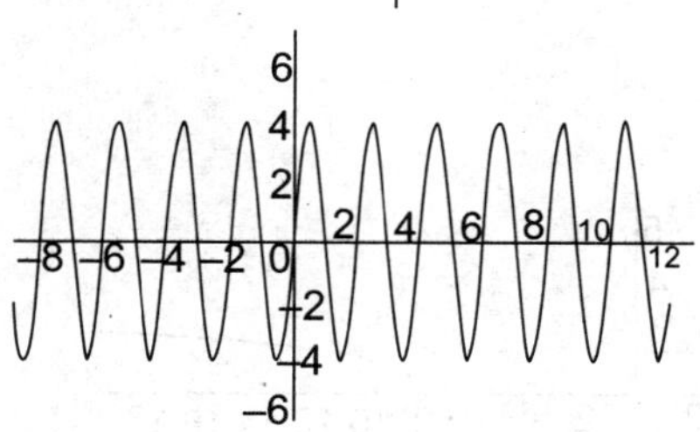

(b)

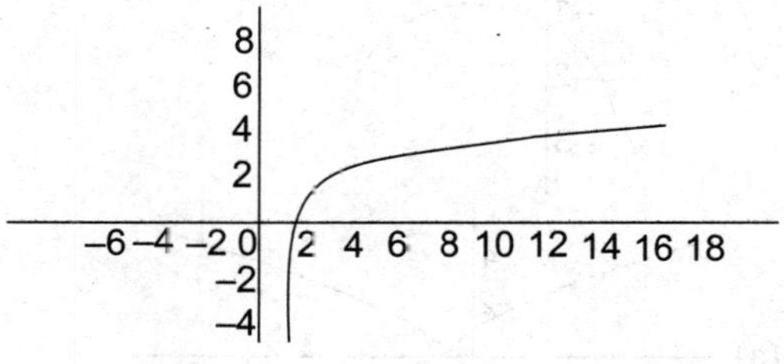

(c)

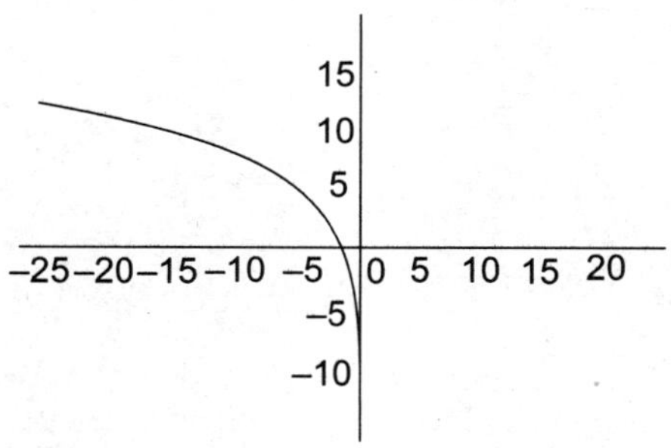

5. (a)

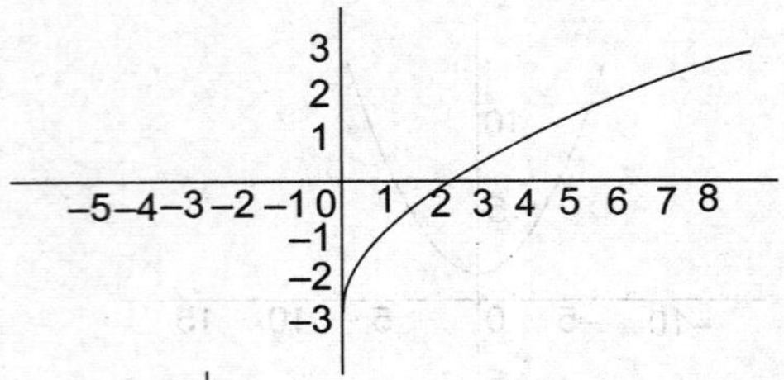

(b)

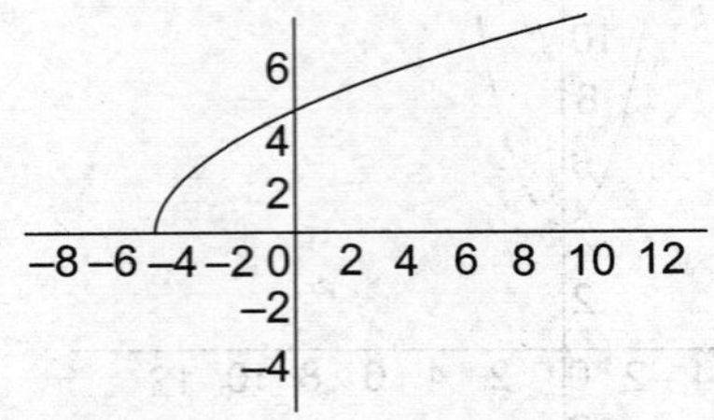

(c)

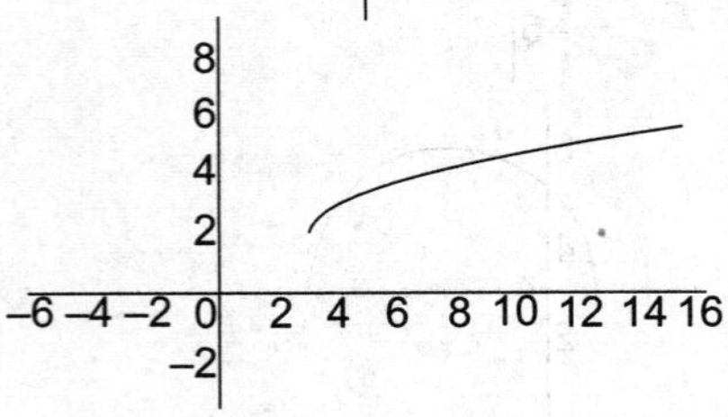

(d)

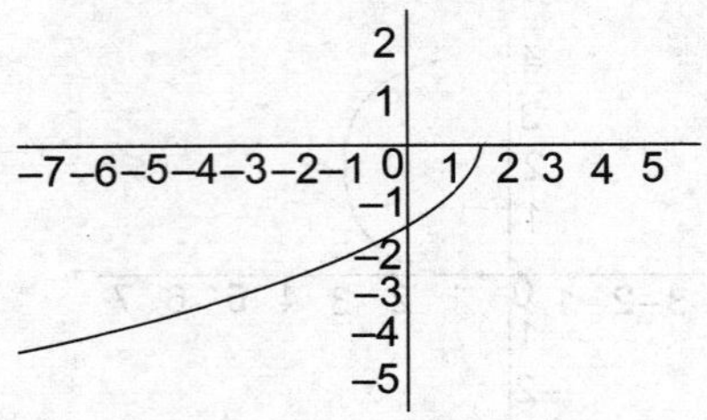

(e)

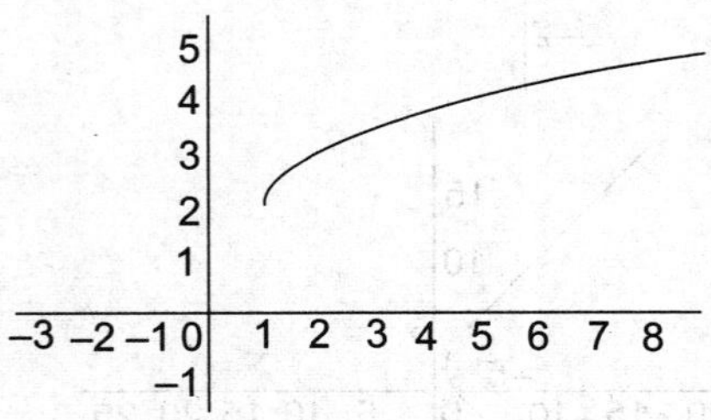

6. (a)

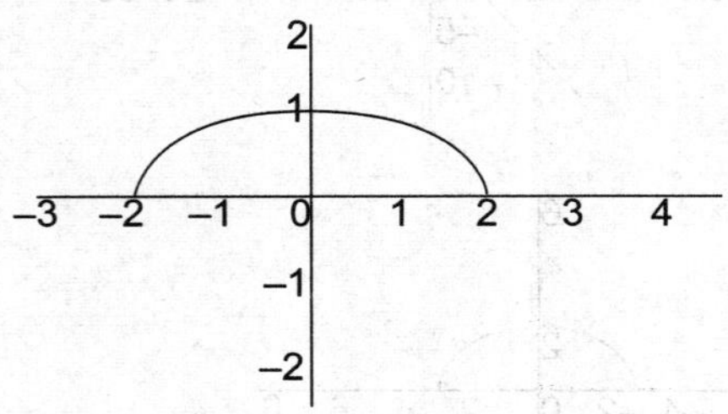

(b)

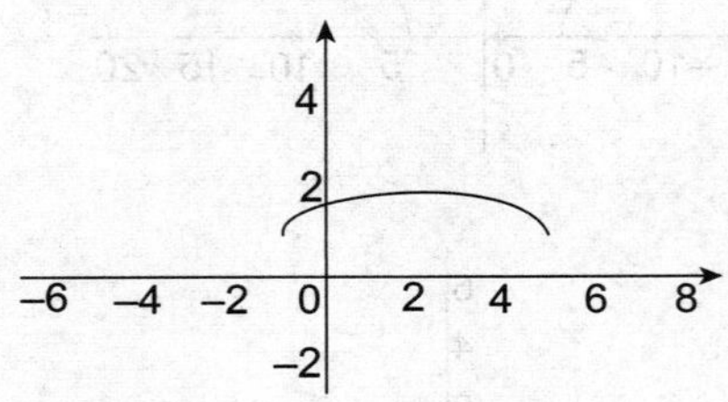

(c)

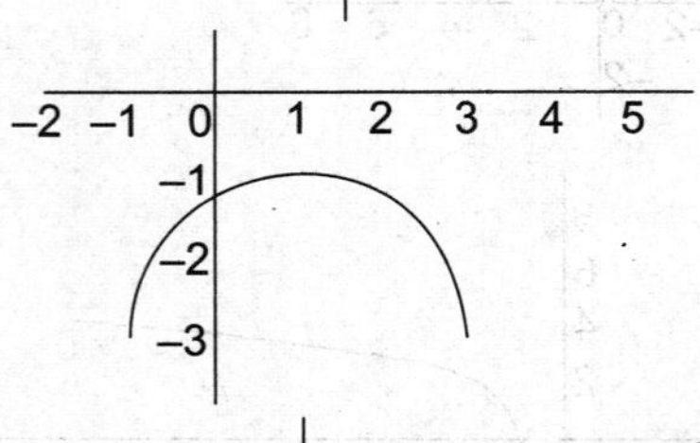

7. (a)

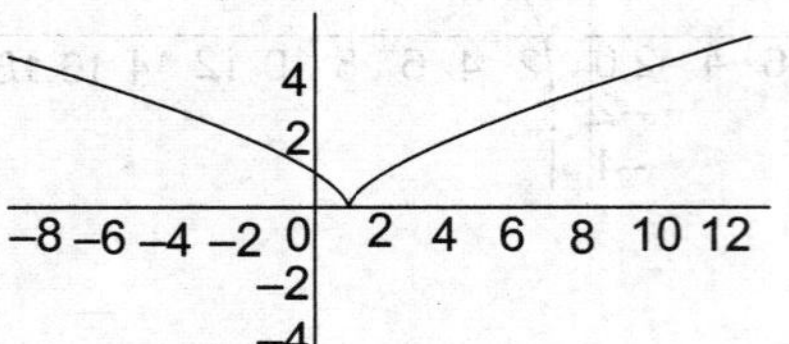

(b)

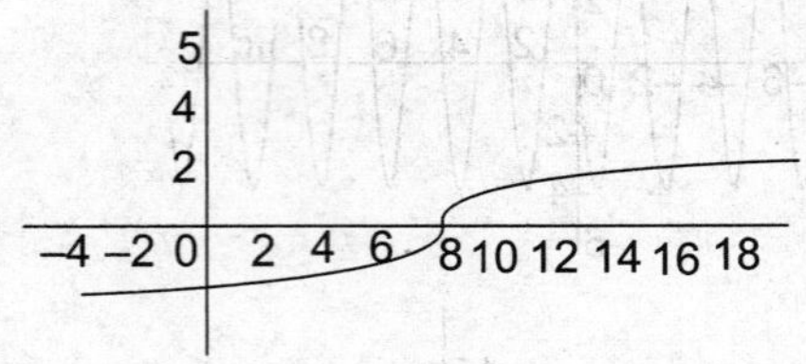

(c)

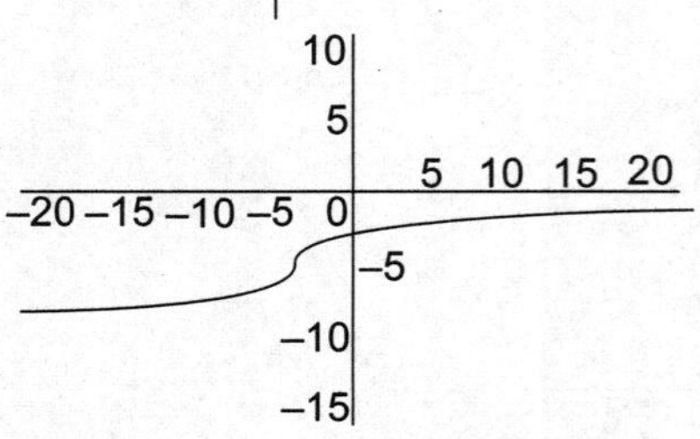

8. (a)

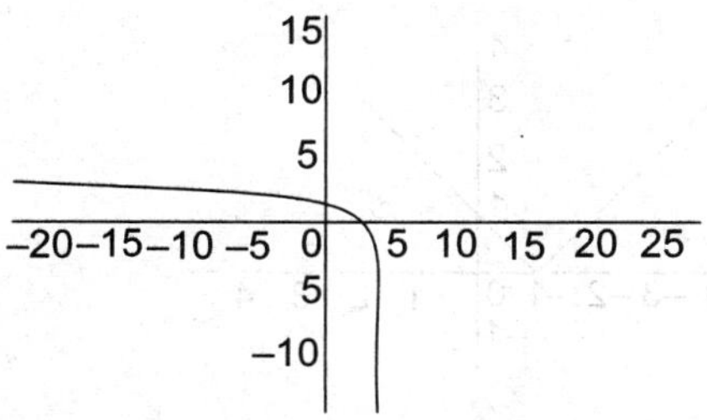

(b)

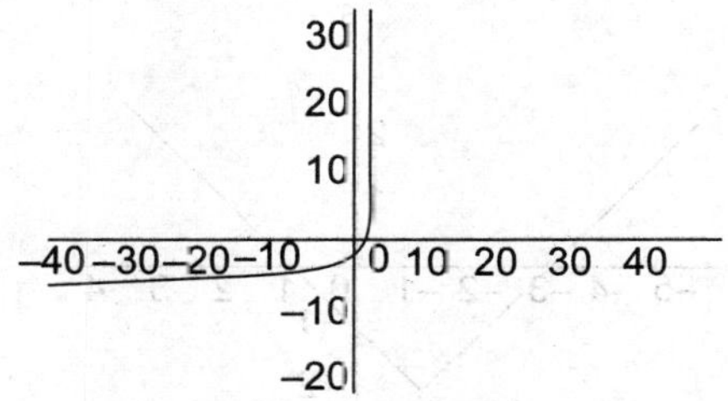

9. (i)

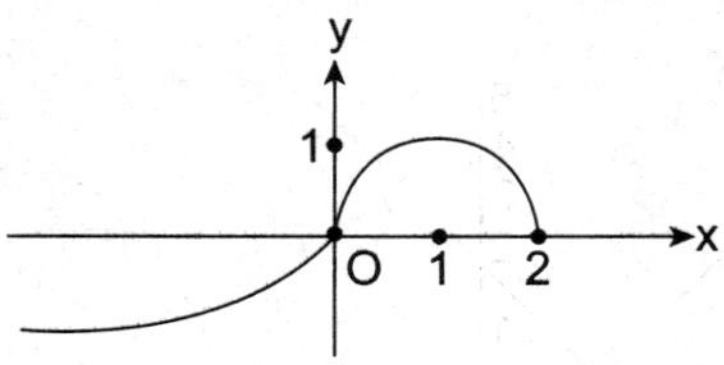

(ii)

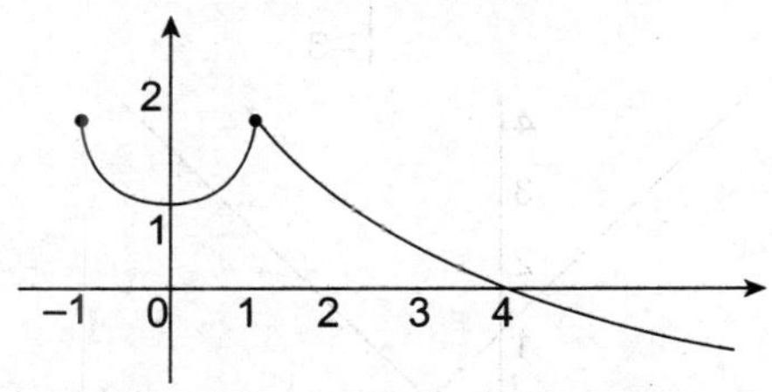

10. (a) (i)

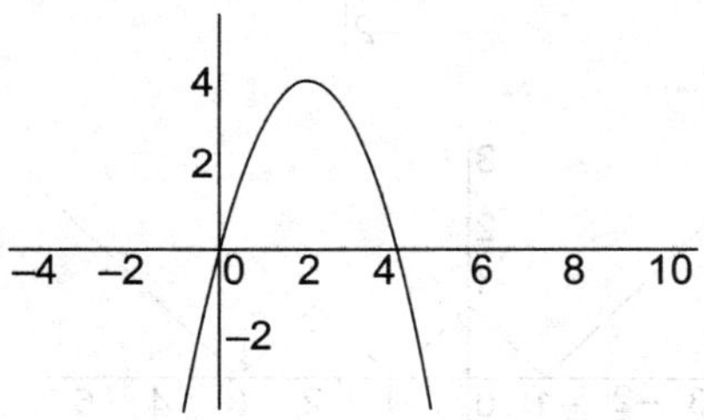

(ii)

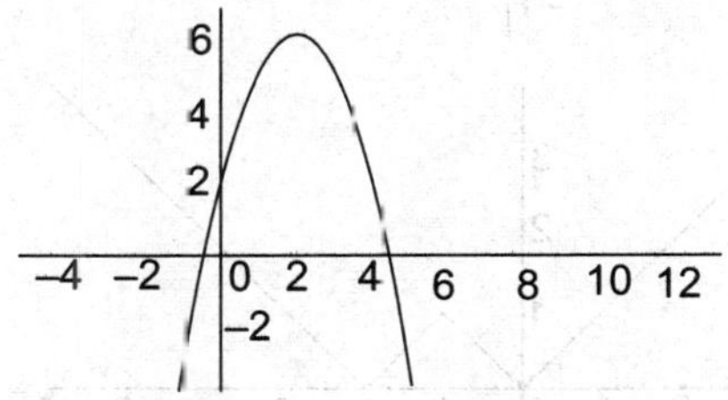

(iii)

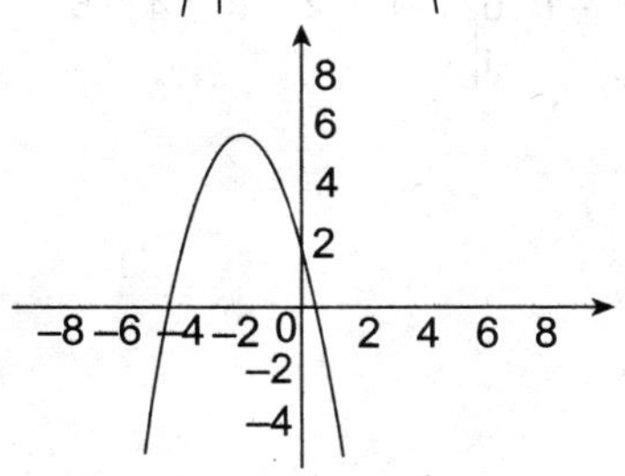

(iv)

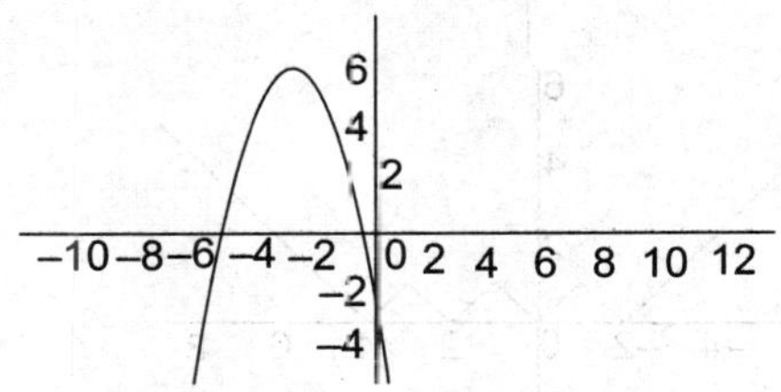

(b) (i)

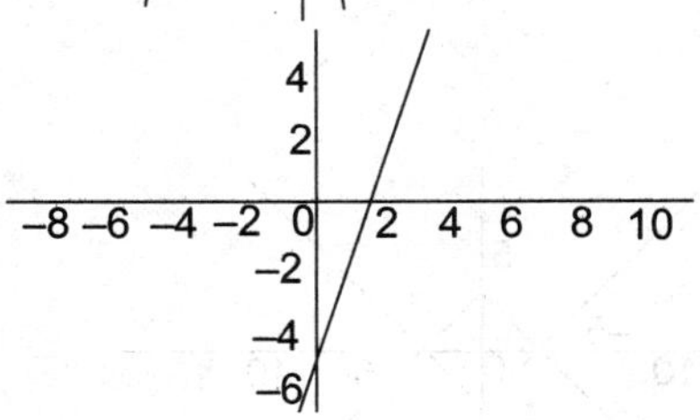

(ii)

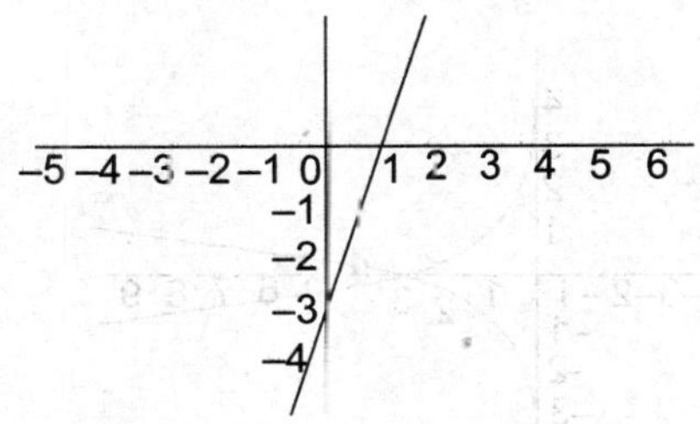

(iii)

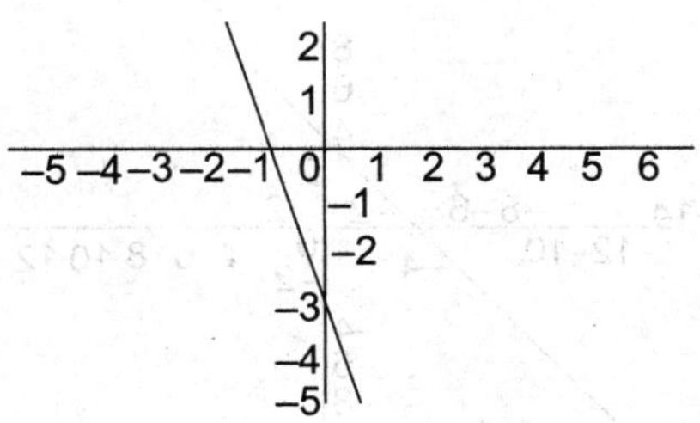

(iv)

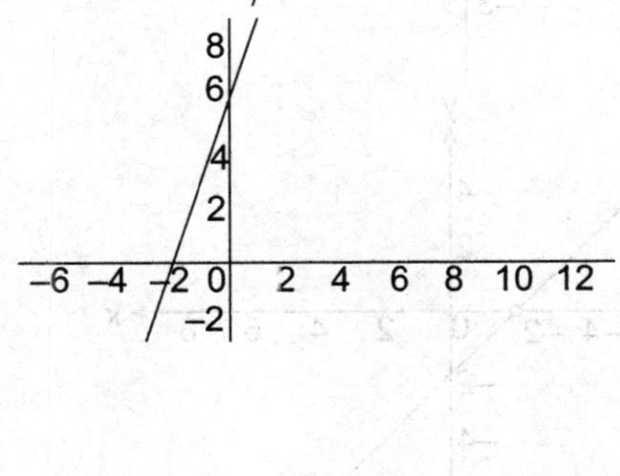

(c) (i)

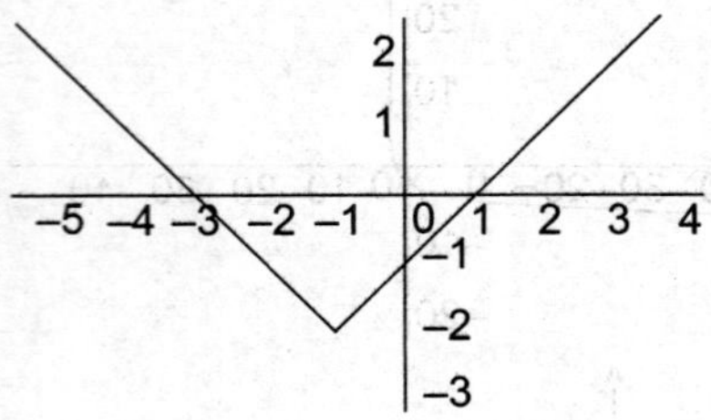

(ii)

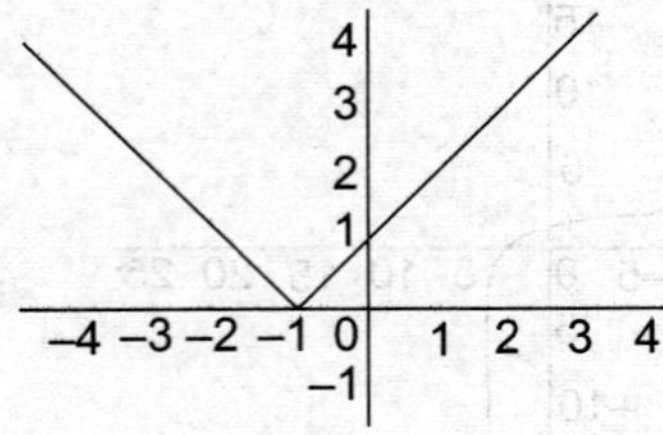

(iii)

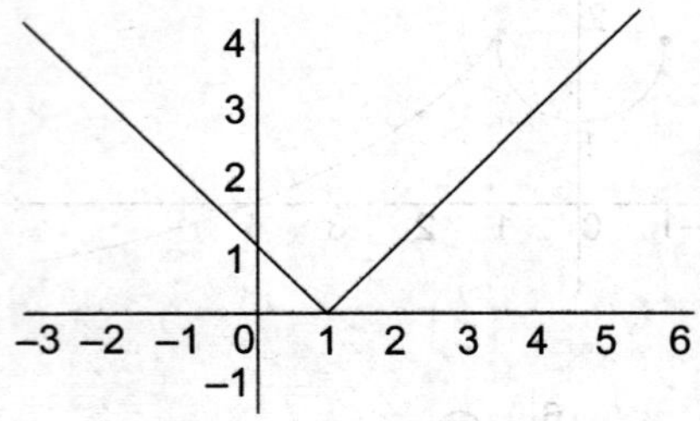

(iv)

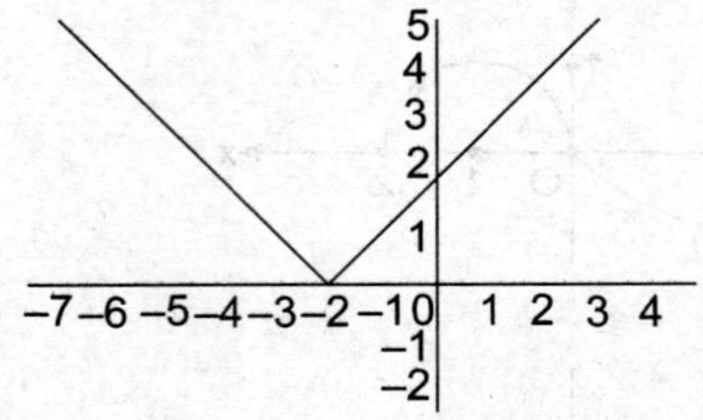

11. (a)

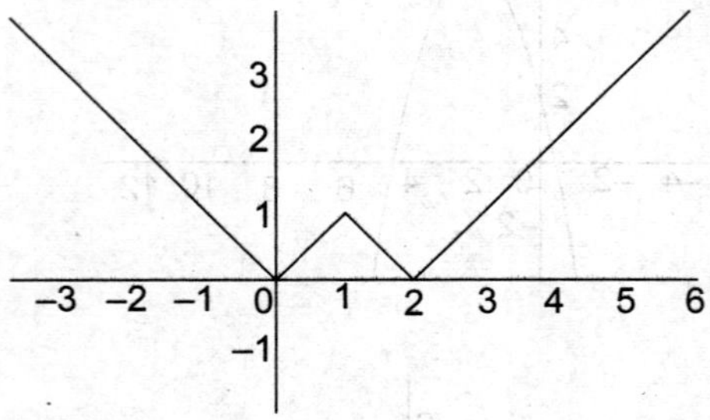

(b)

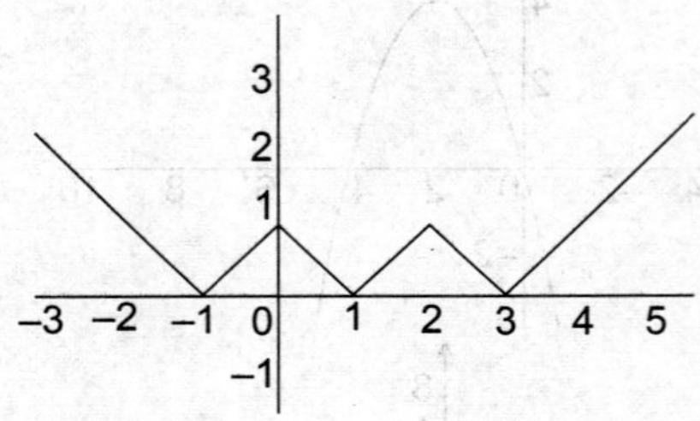

(c)

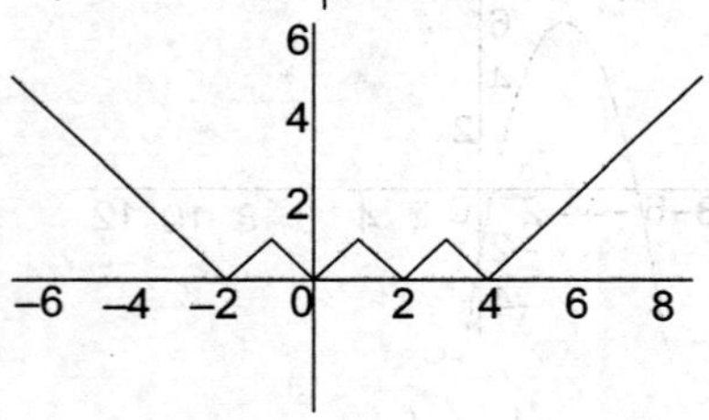

12. (a)

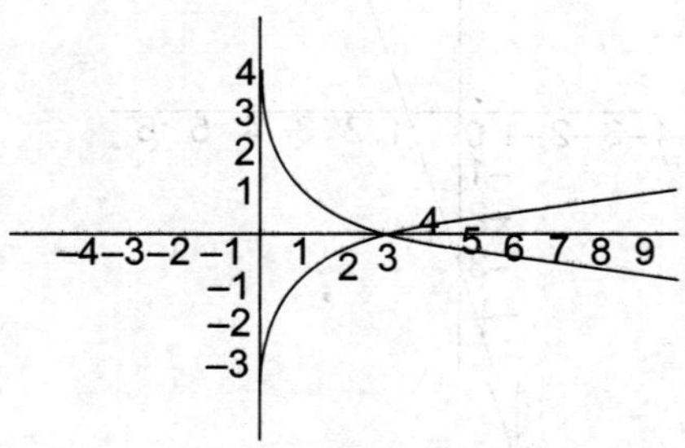

(b)

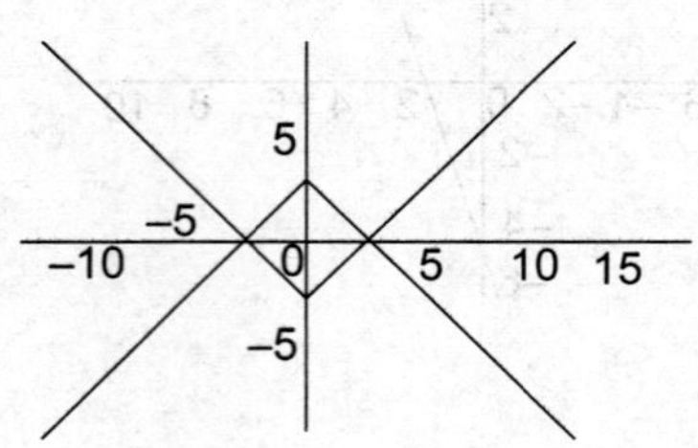

13. (i)

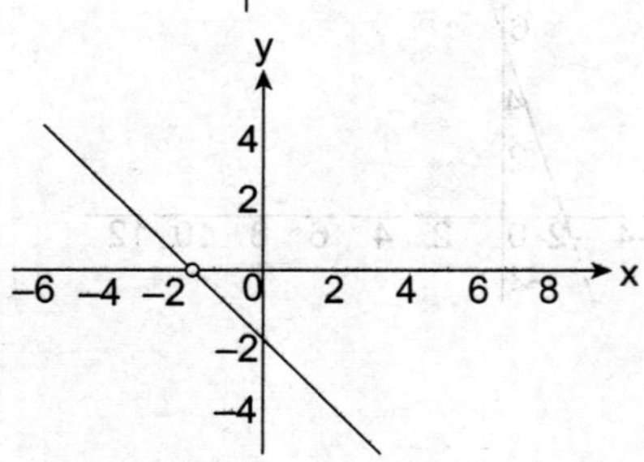

(ii)

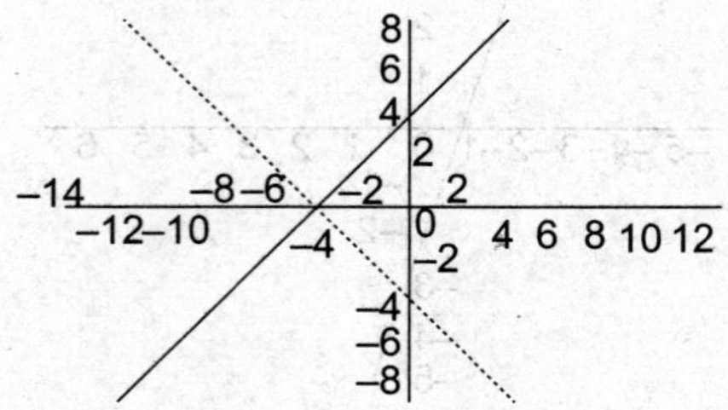

(iii) 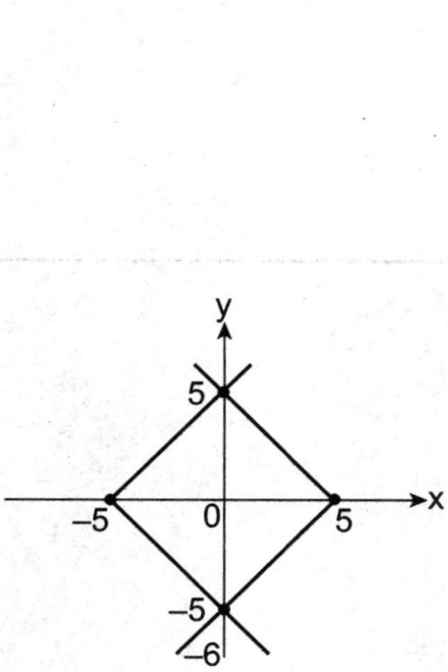

(iv) 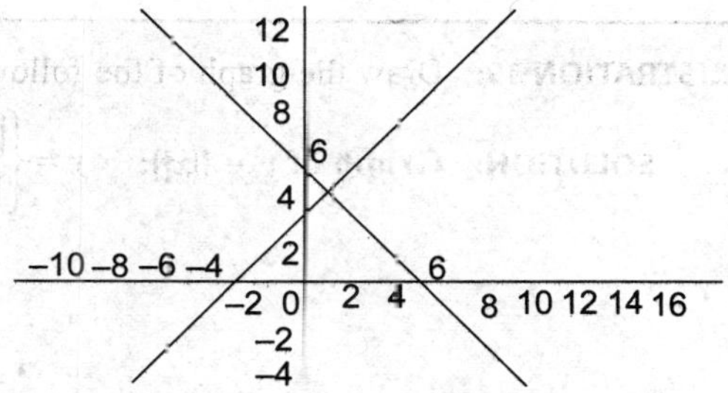

14. (a) 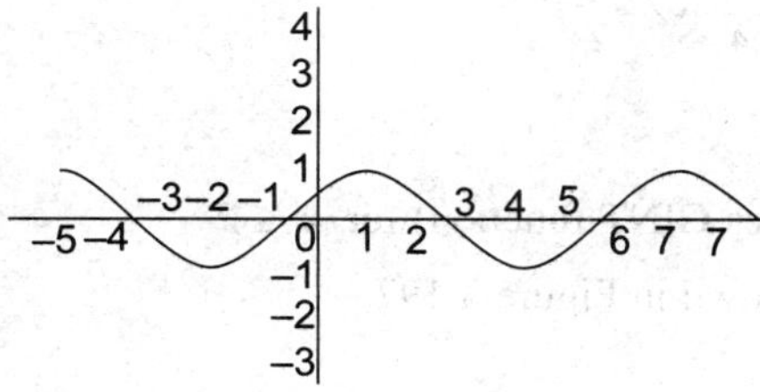

(b) 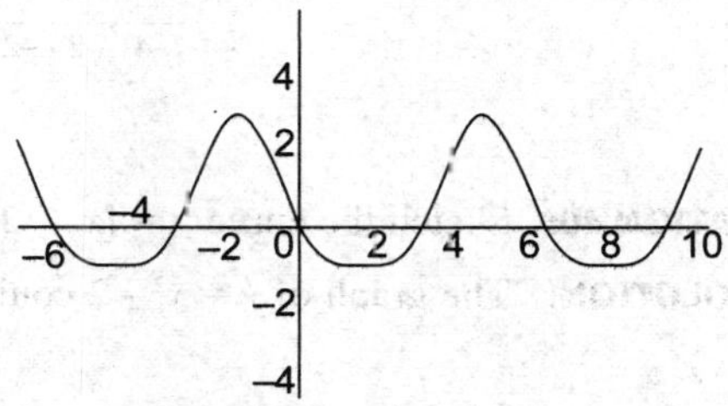

(c) 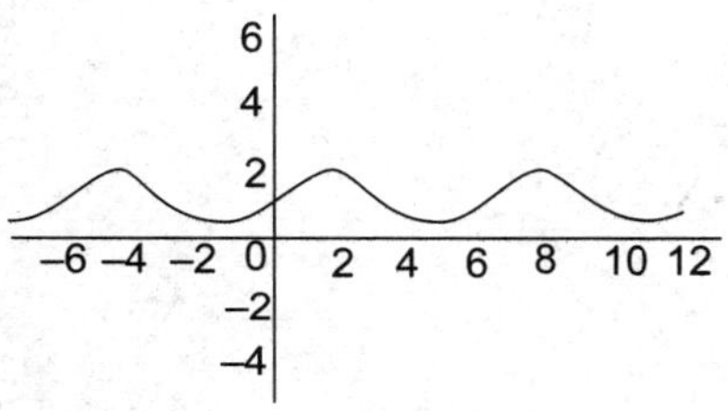

(d) 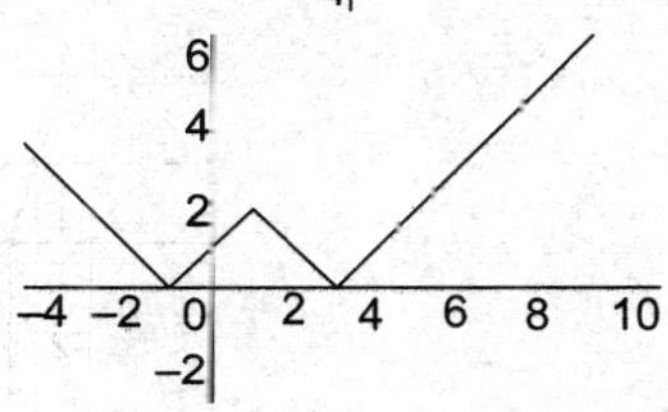

(e) 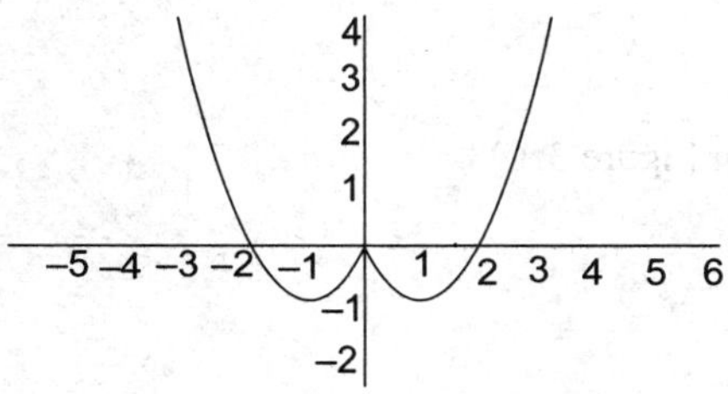

Transformation of Graph Continued

10. Graph of $y = [f(x)]$ where [] denotes the GINT function: It is clear that if $n \leq f(x) < n + 1, n \in \mathbb{Z}$, then $[f(x)] = n$. Thus, we would first locate all points on the graph having integer ordinates and then draw lines parallel to the x-axis in the direction of increasing ordinate from each such point upto the ordinate of next such points. And this process is to be done for all the portion on the curve where $f(x)$ lies between two successive integers. (see in Figures 3.194 and 3.195).

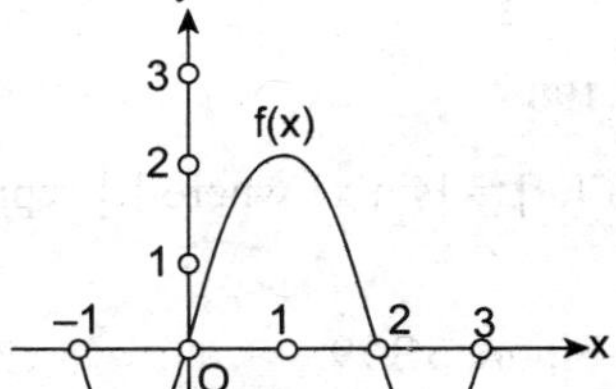

FIGURE 3.194

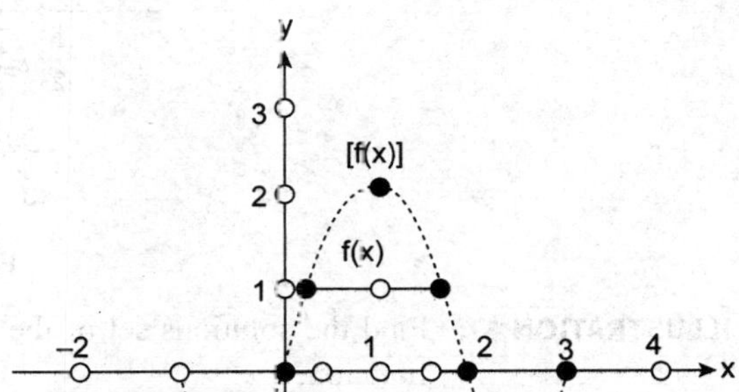

FIGURE 3.195

Clearly, it is evident that if at any such point the ordinate (output) of the curve decreases on both sides, then no projection is drawn from that point in either direction. Thus, that point remains an isolated point on the transformed curve.

ILLUSTRATION 39: Draw the graph of the following functions:

SOLUTION: **Graph of $y = [|x|]$:** $y = \begin{cases} [x] & for\ x \geq 0 \\ [-x] & for\ x < 0 \end{cases}$

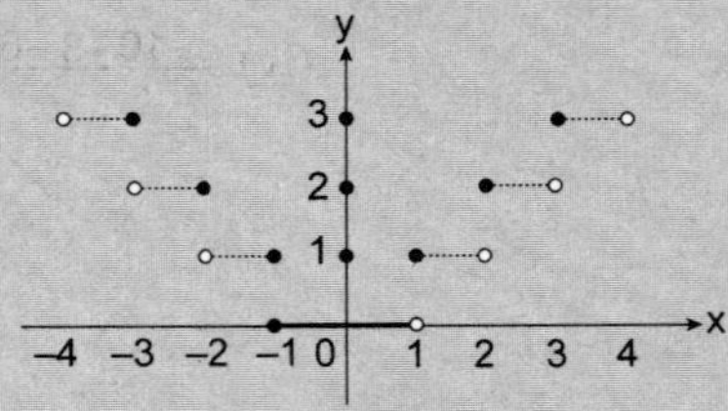

FIGURE 3.196

ILLUSTRATION 40: Sketch the curve $y = [x^2 - 2]$ (where [.] denotes GINT function) for $|x| \leq 2$

SOLUTION: The graph of $y = x^2 - 2$ could be plotted as shown in Figure 3.197.

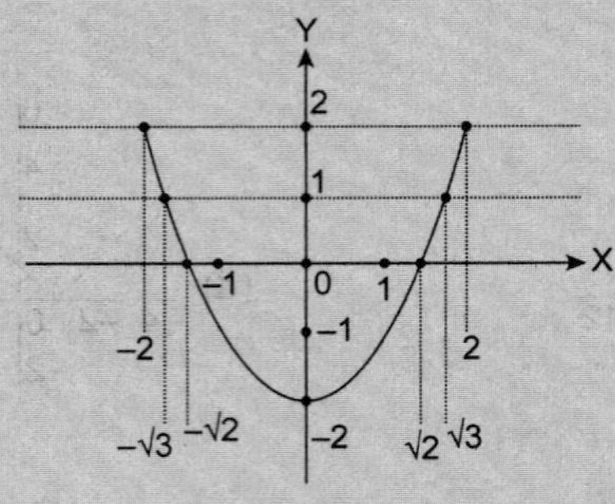

FIGURE 3.197

Hence, the graph of $y = [x^2 - 2]$ is as shown in Figure 3.198.

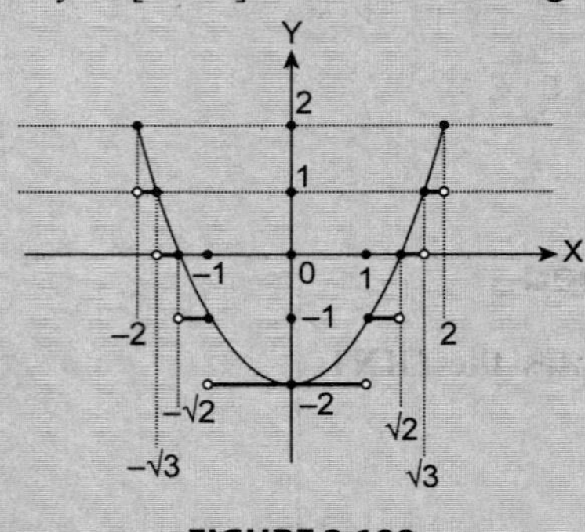

FIGURE 3.198

ILLUSTRATION 41: Find the solutions set of the equation $[e^x] = [\sin x]$ where [.] represents the greatest integer function.

SOLUTION: The graph of $y = \sin x$ is as shown in Figure 3.199.

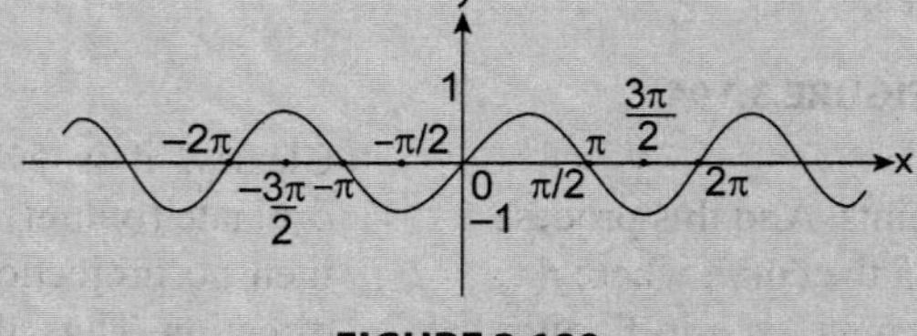

FIGURE 3.199

Hence, the graph of $y = [\sin x]$ is as shown in Figure 3.200.

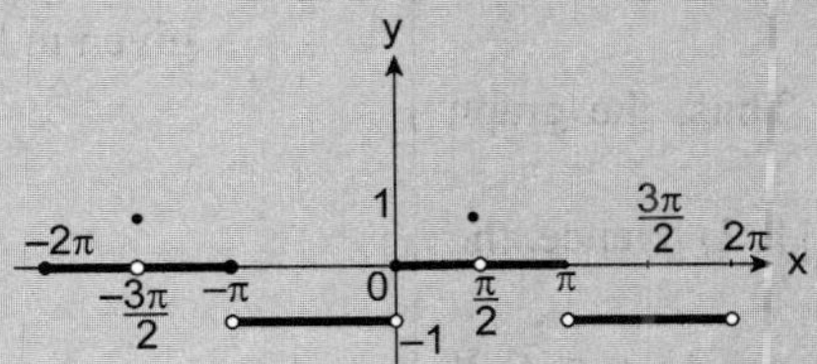

FIGURE 3.200

Now, graph of $y = e^x$ is as shown in Figure 3.201.

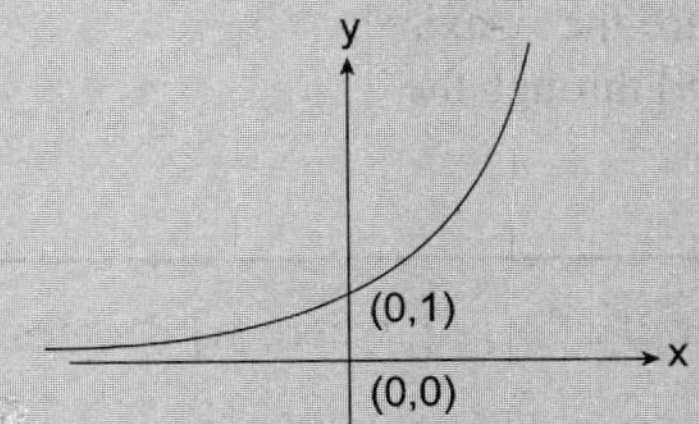

FIGURE 3.201

Hence, the graph of $y = [e^x]$ is shown in Figure 3.202.

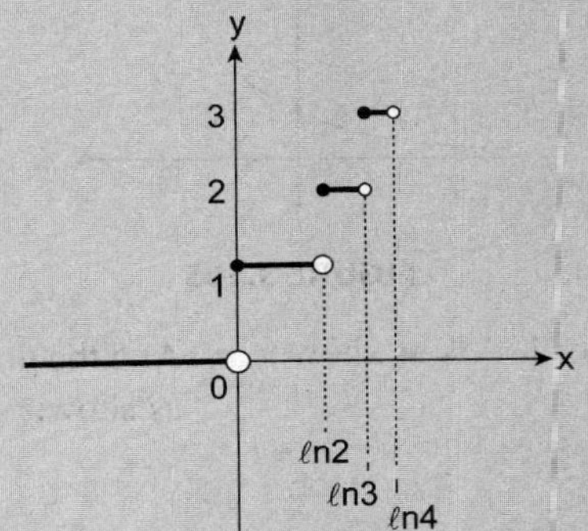

FIGURE 3.202

Now, plotting the two curves together, we infer that the solutions set of $[e^x] = [\sin x]$ can be pictorially seen as the points of intersection of $y = [e^x]$ and $y = [\sin x]$.

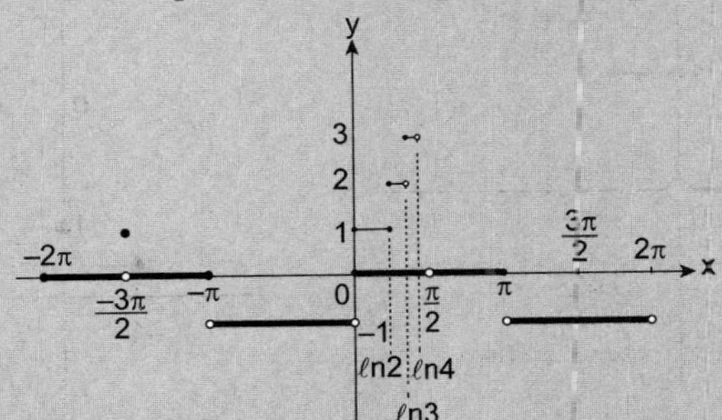

FIGURE 3.203

Clearly; the graphs have no point of intersection for $x \geq 0$.
And for $x < 0$; the two graphs; intersect for $[-2n\pi, -2n\pi - \pi] - \{-2n\pi + \pi/2\}$; where $n \in \mathbb{N}$

11. Graph of $y = f([x])$: To obtain the graph of $y = f([x])$, it is necessary to observe the following facts.
When $x \in [0, 1)$ the value of $[x] = 0$.
$\Rightarrow f([x]) = f(0)$ for all $x \in [0, 1)$. Thus, the graph becomes $y = f(0)\ \forall\ x \in [0, 1)$.
Similarly $f([x]) = f(1)$ for all $x \in [1, 2)$. Hence, the graph becomes $y = f(1)\ \forall\ x \in [1, 2)$.
In general, $f([x]) = f(n)\ \forall\ x \in [n, n + 1), n \in \mathbb{Z}$. It implies that first of all we should locate all such points on the graph of $y = f(x)$ having integer x-coordinates say $(n, f(n))$ and then draw a line segments of unit length parallel to the x-axis projecting rightwards given by $y = f(n)$ through the points $(n, f(n))$ excluding right end point, for all n lying in the domain of the function. Illustrated given in Figure 3.204.

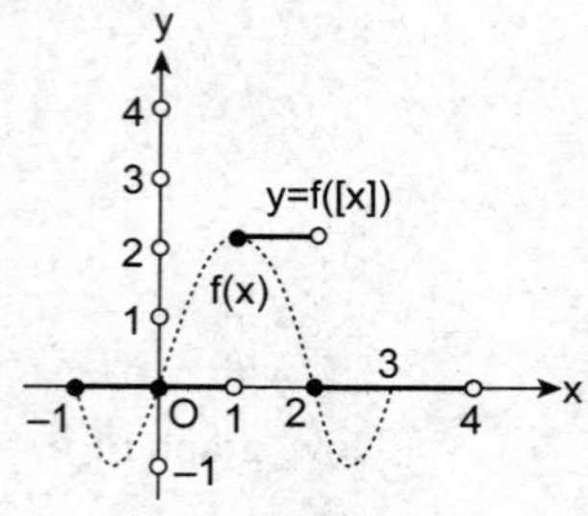

FIGURE 3.204

ILLUSTRATION 42: Find the solution set of $e^{[x]} = [e^x]$, where $[x]$ denotes the greatest integer function.

SOLUTION: Graph of e^x is as shown in Figure 3.205.

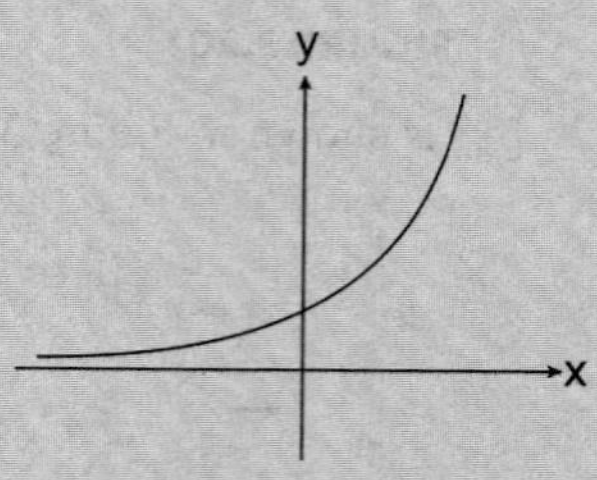

FIGURE 3.205

Hence, the graph of $[e^x]$ is as shown in Figure 3.206.

And the graph of $e^{[x]}$ will be given by as shown in Figure 3.207.

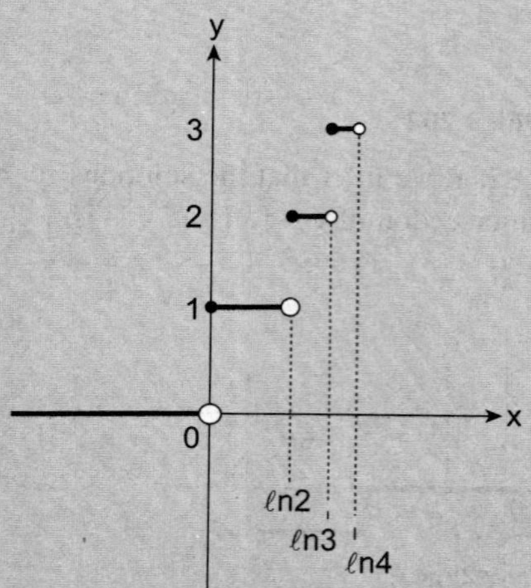

FIGURE 3.206

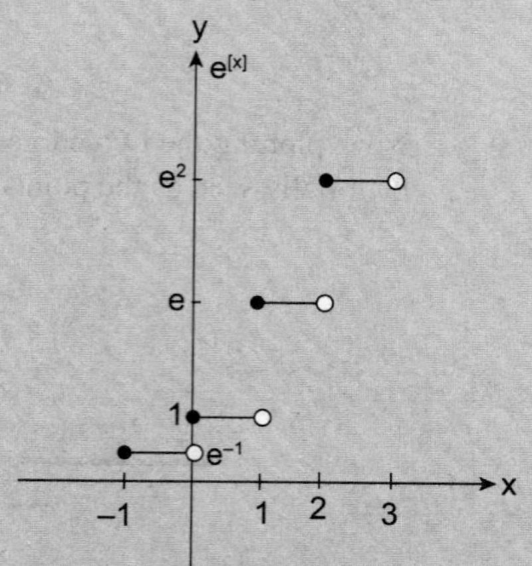

FIGURE 3.207

Now, plotting the two graphs together, we can see that

For $x < 0$; $e^{[x]} > 0$ and $[e^x] = 0$, and hence, no solution is possible.

For $x \in [0, \ln 2)$; $e^{[x]} = e^0 = 1$ and $[e^x] = 1 \quad \Rightarrow e^{[x]} = [e^x] = 1\ \forall\ x \in [0, \ln 2)$

Hence $x \in [0, \ln 2)$ is a solution set.

For $x \in [\ln 2, 1)$; $e^{[x]} = 1$, where as $[e^x] = 2$ and $x \geq 1$: $[e^x] \in \mathbb{Z}$ and $e^{[x]} \notin \mathbb{Z}$ and is irrational.

$\therefore$ No more point of intersection.

Hence, the solution is $x \in [0, \ln 2)$

ILLUSTRATION 43: Sketch the curve $y = \sin [x]$; where [] denotes the GINT function and also, suggest whether $\sin [x]$ is a periodic function or not?

SOLUTION: The curve for $y = \sin [x]$; could be plotted as shown in Figure 3.208.

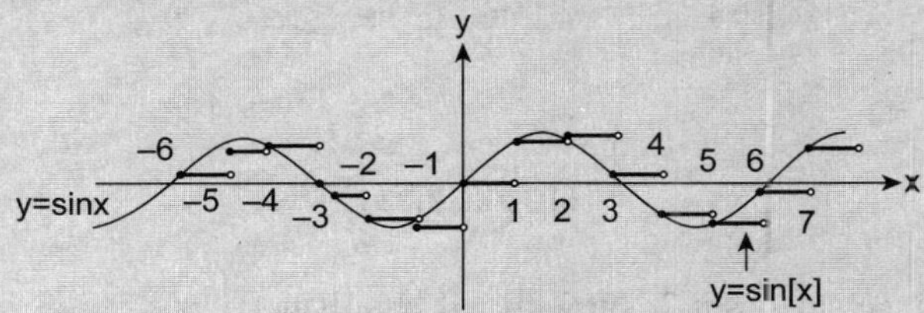

FIGURE 3.208

We know, that $\sin x$ is periodic with a period of π, but $[x]$ only takes integral values, hence, $[x]$ can never be a multiple of π, hence, $\sin [x]$ is not a periodic function.

ILLUSTRATION 44: Sketch the curve for $y = \cos[x]$ and $y = [x]^2$, and hence, find the number of solutions to the equation $\cos[x] = [x]^2$ where [] denotes the GINT function.

SOLUTION: The curve $y = \cos[x]$ could be plotted as,

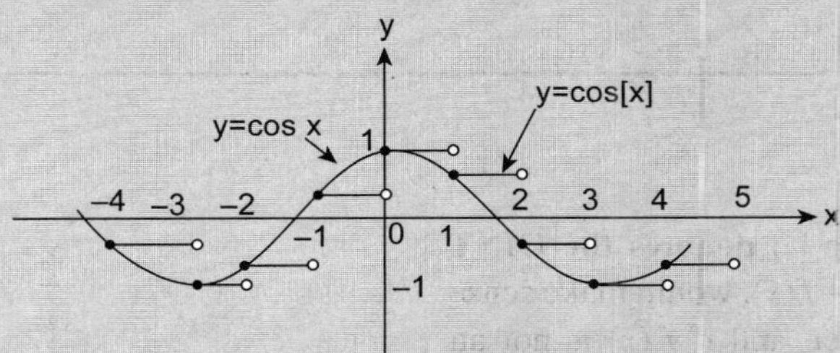

FIGURE 3.209

And the curve $y = [x]^2$ for $x \in [-2, 2]$ is given by

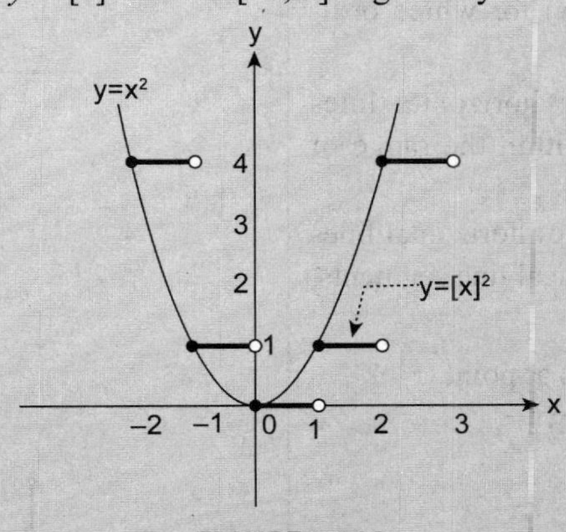

FIGURE 3.210

Plotting the two graphs together, we can see that the two graphs never intersect each other, and hence, the equation $\cos[x] = [x]^2$ does not have any solution.

ILLUSTRATION 45: Sketch the curve $y = [\sin [x]]$; where [] denotes the GINT function when $x \in [0, 2\pi]$.

SOLUTION: The graph of the function $y = \sin[x]$; where [] denotes the GINT function when $x \in [0, 2\pi]$ is as shown in Figure 3.211.

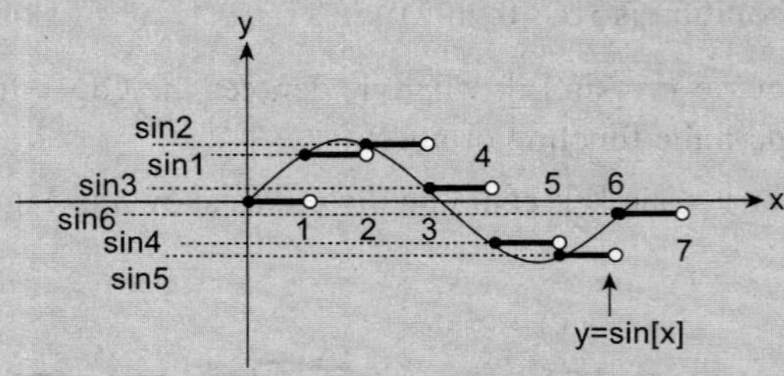

FIGURE 3.211

Now, since sin 1, sin 2, sin 3 are all less than 1 and greater than 0, therefore, $y = [\sin[x]] = 0$ for $x \in [0, 4)$.

Also, since sin 4, sin 5, sin 6 are all greater than –1 and less than 0, therefore, $y = [\sin[x]] = -1$ for $x \in [4, 2\pi]$.

Hence, the graph of $y = [\sin[x]]$ for $x \in [0, 2\pi]$ is given in Figure 3.212.

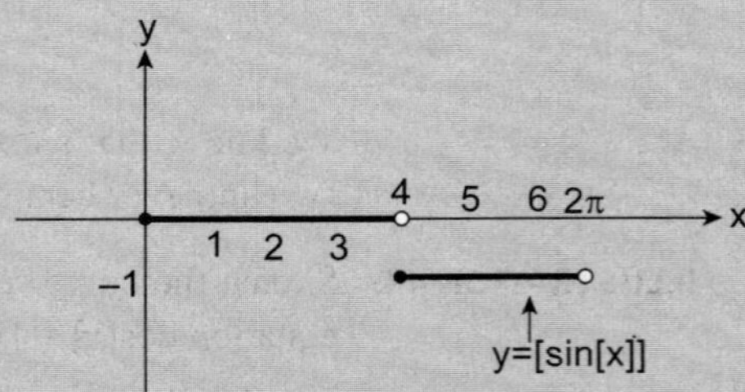

FIGURE 3.212

12. Graph of [y] = f(x), where [ ] denotes the GINT function: It is clear that $[y] = f(x)$, would make sense only when $f(x)$ is an integer, and if $f(x)$ is not an integer graph of $[y] = f(x)$ would not exist. As such to obtain the graph of $[y] = f(x)$ first of all we would locate those points on graph of $f(x)$ for which ordinate is integer.

This can be done by considering horizontal lines through every integer on y-axis within the range of function.

Now from the point of intersection of horizontal lines and the curve we draw one unit vertical line segments, excluding the top end point.

Suppose $f(x_0) = 2$, then for $[y] = f(x)$ at point $(x_0, 2)$, we get $[y] = 2$ consequently $y \in [2, 3)$,

That is, $\{x_0, y): y \in [2, 3)\}$

i.e., we draw a line segment $x = x_0$ for $y \in [2, 3)$ and so on. Therefore, the graph of $y = f(x)$ and $[y] = f(x)$ are as shown in Figures 3.213 and 3.214, respectively.

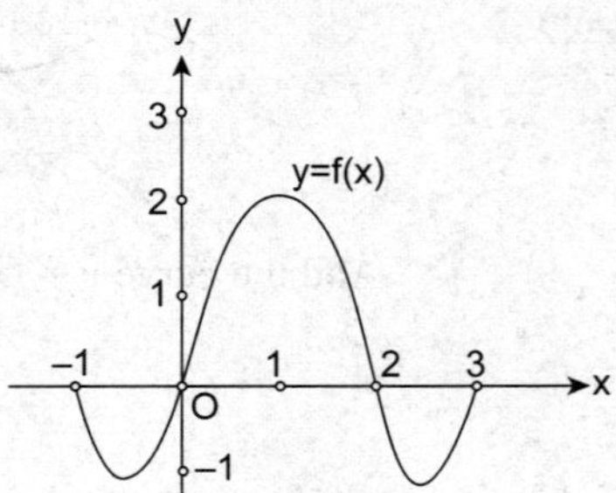

FIGURE 3.213

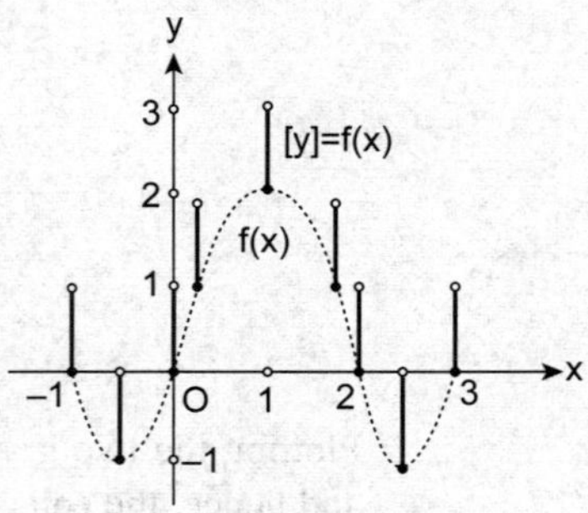

FIGURE 3.214

ILLUSTRATION 46: Draw the graph of $[y] = \sin^{-1}x$.

SOLUTION: The graph of $y = \sin^{-1}x$ is as shown in Figure 3.215.

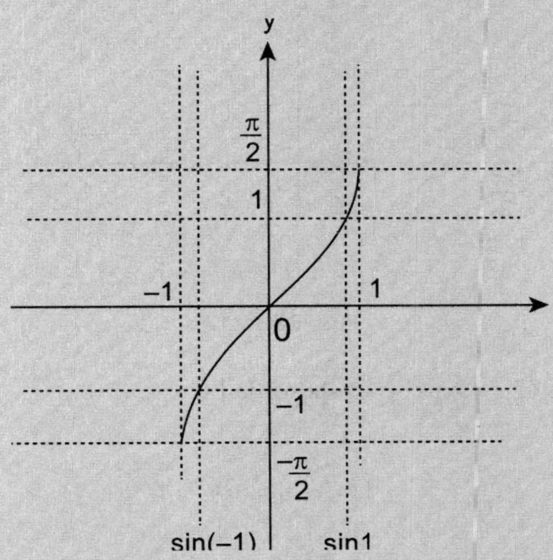

FIGURE 3.215

Hence, the graph of $[y] = \sin^{-1}x$ is as shown in Figure 3.216.

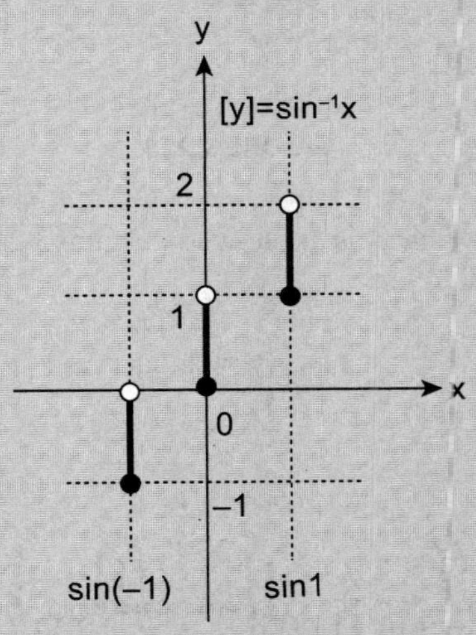

FIGURE 3.216

13. Graph of $[y] = [f(x)]$, where [] denotes the GINT function: The graph of $[y] = [f(x)]$ can be plotted by the following two simple steps.

Step I. Draw the graph of $y = [f(x)]$ as discussed earlier.

Step II. Apply [] on y.

ILLUSTRATION 47: Draw the curve $[y] = [\sin x]$ where [] represents the GINT function.

SOLUTION: The graph of $y = \sin x$ is as shown in Figure 3.217.

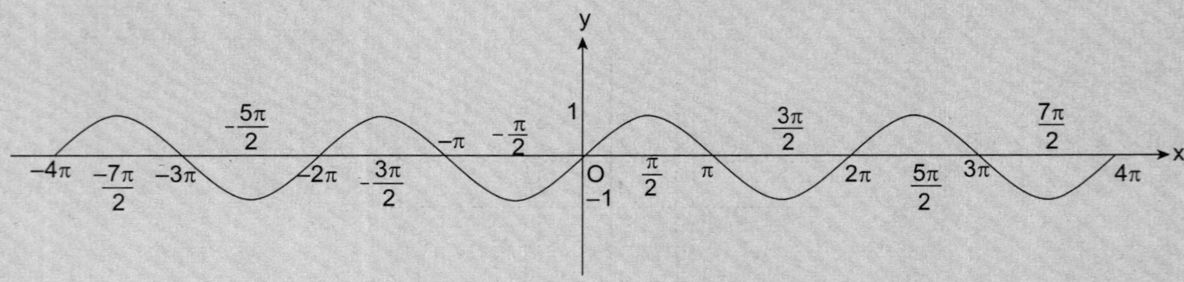

FIGURE 3.217

The graph of $y = [\sin x]$ is as shown in Figure 3.218.

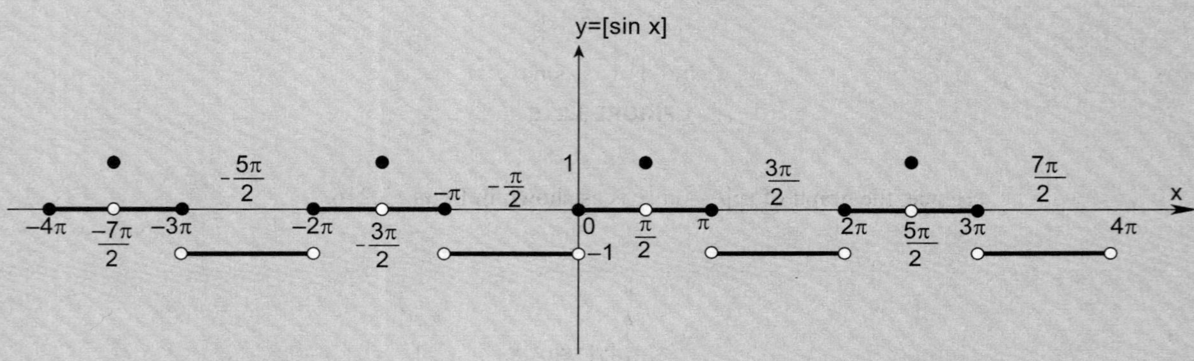

FIGURE 3.218

The graph of $[y] = [\sin x]$ is as shown in Figure 3.219.

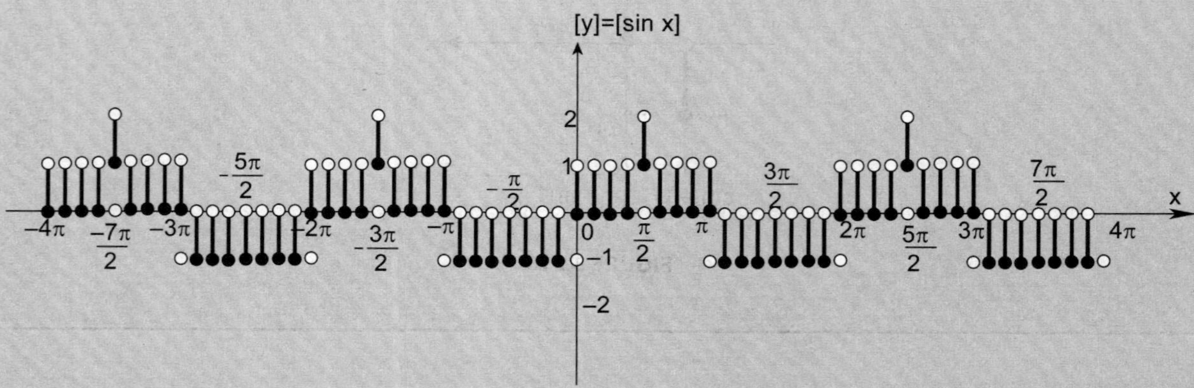

FIGURE 3.219

ILLUSTRATION 48: Draw the curve for $[y] = [2^x]$

SOLUTION: The graph of $y = 2^x$ is as shown in Figure 3.220.

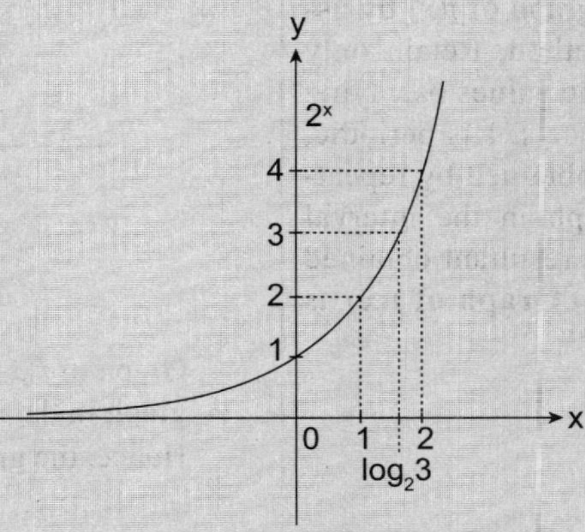

FIGURE 3.220

Therefore, the graph of $y = [2^x]$ must be as shown in Figure 3.221.

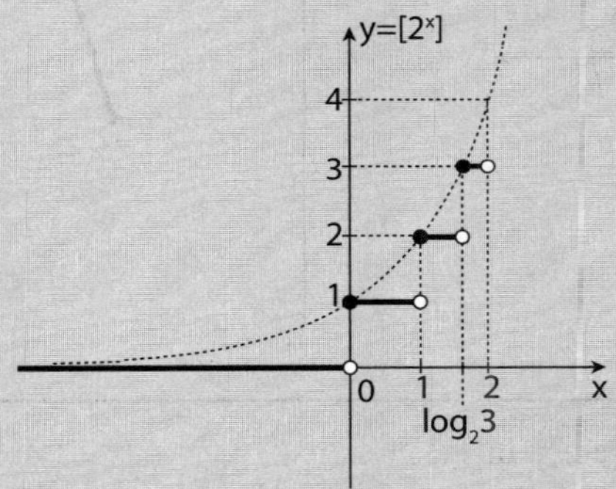

FIGURE 3.221

When $x < 0$	$\Rightarrow [y] = 0$	$\Rightarrow y \in [0,1)$
When $x \in [0,1)$	$\Rightarrow [y] = 1$	$\Rightarrow y \in [1,2)$
When $x \in [1, \log_2 3)$	$\Rightarrow [y] = 2$	$\Rightarrow y \in [2,3)$
$x \in [\log_2 3, 2)$	$\Rightarrow [y] = 3$	$\Rightarrow y \in [3,4)$

consequently the graph of $[y] = [2^x]$ should be as shown in Figure 3.222.

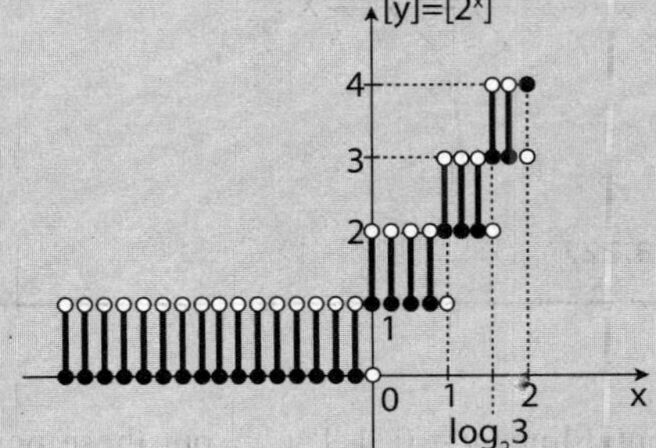

FIGURE 3.222

14. Graph of $y = f(\{x\})$; where $\{x\}$ represents the fractional part of x: We are well aware of the fact that $\{x\}$ is a periodic function with a fundamental period of 1. Therefore, the graph of $f(x - [x])$ or $f(\{x\})$ can be obtained from the graph of $f(x)$ by using the following mentioned method, Retain only the part of the graph of $f(x)$ for the values of x lying between interval [0, 1). Now, since $\{x\}$ is periodic, hence, the graph of $f\{x\}$ can be obtained by repeating the retained portion of graph in the interval [0, 1) (taking periodicity 1). The resultant obtained function is a graph for $y = f(\{x\})$.**Graph of $f(x)$** as in Figure 3.223.

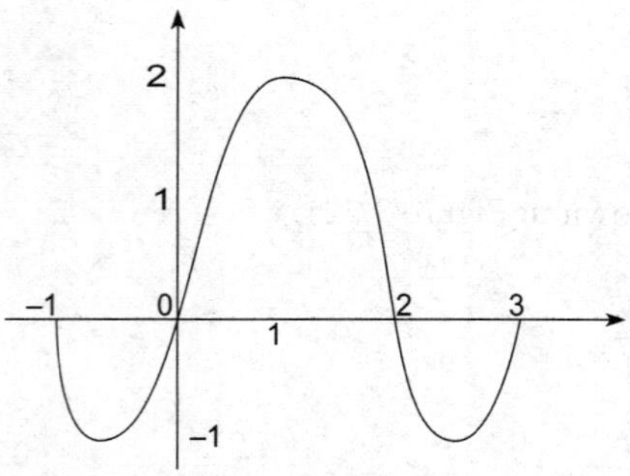

FIGURE 3.223

Graph of $f(x)$ from [0,1) as in Figure 3.224.

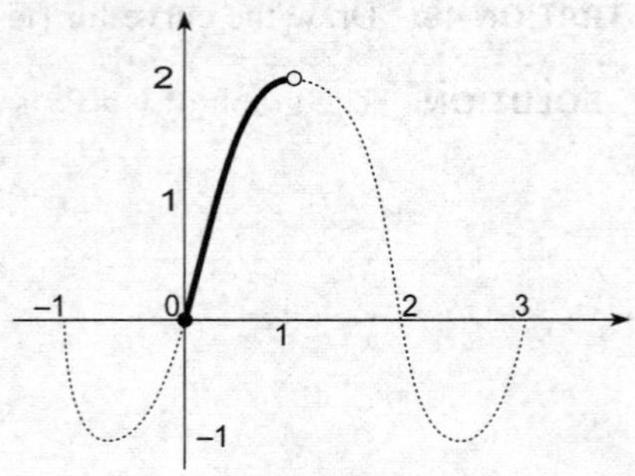

FIGURE 3.224

Graph of $f\{x\}$ can be obtained by repeating the part of graph in the interval [0, 1) (taking periodicity 1). Hence, the graph of $f\{x\}$ is as shown in Figure 3.225.

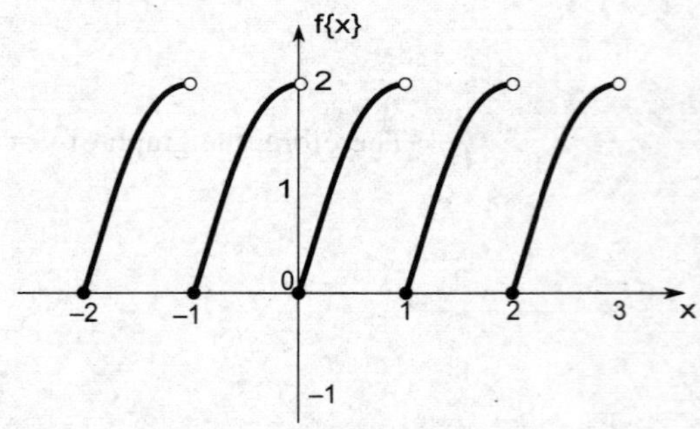

FIGURE 3.225

ILLUSTRATION 49: Sketch the curve $y = \ln\{x\}$

SOLUTION: The graph of $\ln x$ is given as:

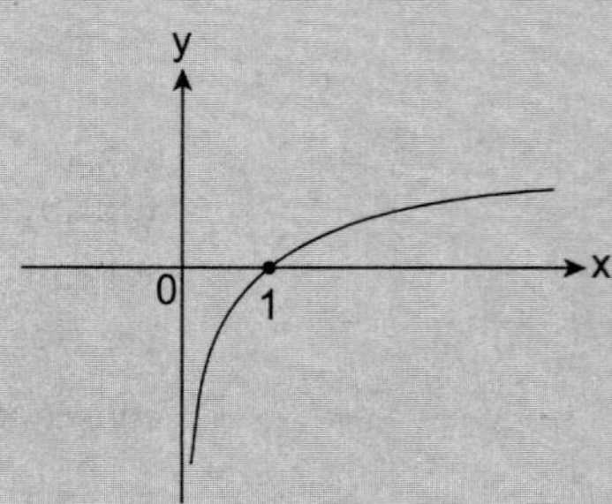

FIGURE 3.226

The graph of $\ln\{x\}$ can be obtained by repeating the part of graph in the interval [0,1) (taking periodicity 1).

Hence, the graph of $f\{x\}$ is as shown below.

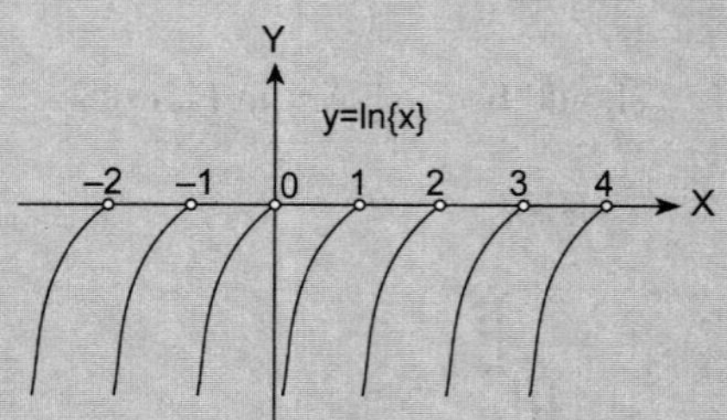

FIGURE 3.227

15. Graph of $y = \{f(x)\}$: Plot the horizontal lines $y = 0, 1$ and for all the integral values of y. Now cut the points of graphs for which $f(x) \in [n, n + 1)$; $n \in W - \{0\}$, put these portions on x-axis transforming them vertically. We need to do the above mentioned step because $\{f(x)\}$ must lie in [0, 1).

NOTE

Graph of {y} = {f(x)}
We know that, the range of graph of y= {f(x)} is [0, 1), and hence, there is no difference between the graphs of {y} ={f(x)} and the graph of y = {f(x)}.

ILLUSTRATION 50: Draw the graph of $y = f(x)$ where $f(x) = x^2$.
Also draw the graph of $y = \{f(x)\} = \{x^2\}$.

SOLUTION: The graph of $y = x^2$ for $x \in [-2, 2]$ is given as in Figure 3.228.

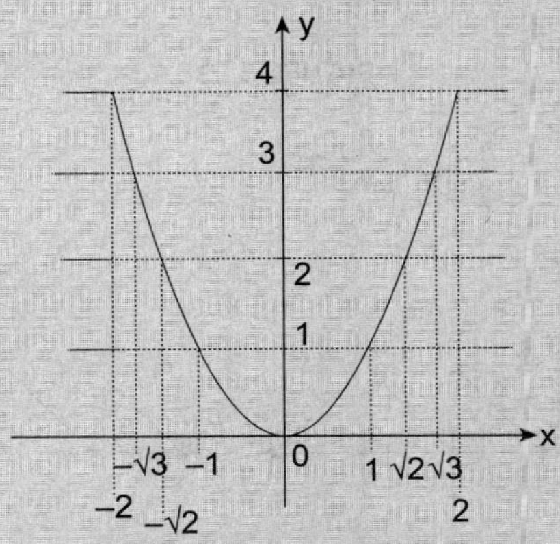

FIGURE 3.228

The graph of $y = \{x^2\}$ for $x \in [-2, 2]$ is given as in Figure 3.229.

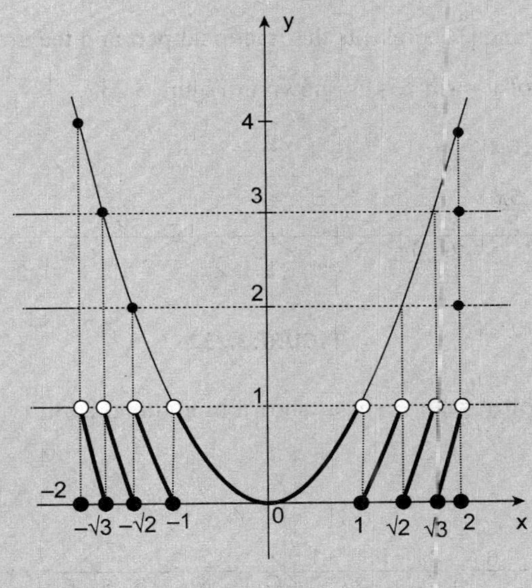

FIGURE 3.229

ILLUSTRATION 51: Draw the graph of $y = f(x)$ where $f(x) = \dfrac{2}{\pi}\sin^{-1}\sin\left(\dfrac{\pi x}{2}\right)$.

Also draw the graph of $y = \{f(x)\}$.

SOLUTION:

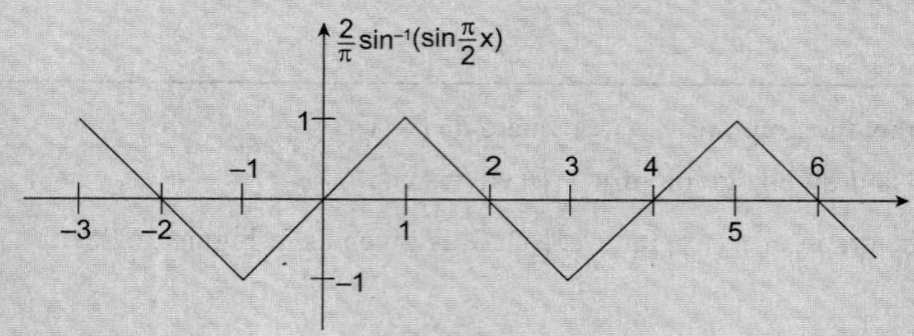

FIGURE 3.230

The graph of $y = \left\{\dfrac{2}{\pi}\sin^{-1}\sin\left(\dfrac{\pi x}{2}\right)\right\}$.

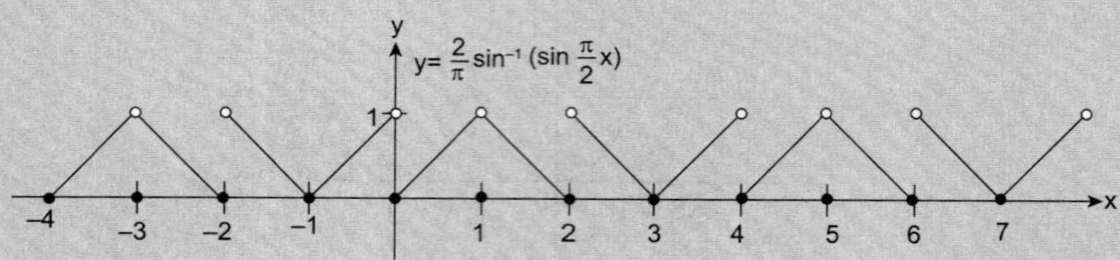

FIGURE 3.231

ILLUSTRATION 52: Find the number of solutions of $\left\{\sin\dfrac{\pi x}{2}\right\} = \dfrac{2^x}{2^{[x]}}$.

Where $\{x\}$ and [] represents the fractional part and the greatest integer function respectively

SOLUTION: The graph of $y = \sin x$ is as shown in Figure 3.232.

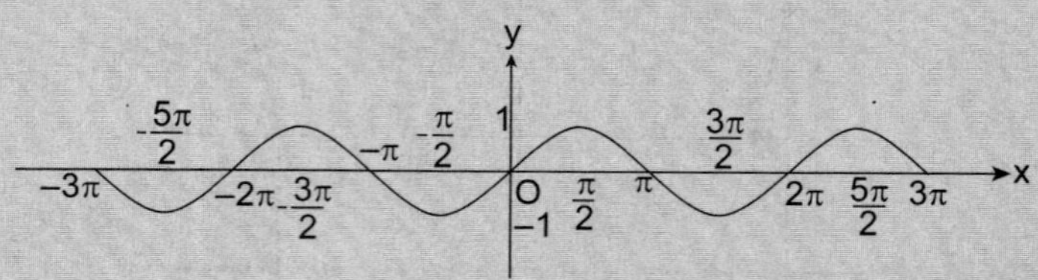

FIGURE 3.232

The graph of $y = \sin\dfrac{\pi x}{2}$ is as shown in Figure 3.233.

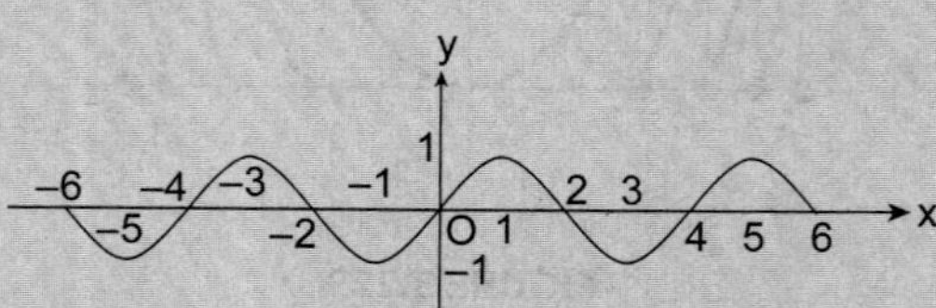

FIGURE 3.233

The graph of $y = \left\{\sin\dfrac{\pi x}{2}\right\}$ is as shown in Figure 3.234.

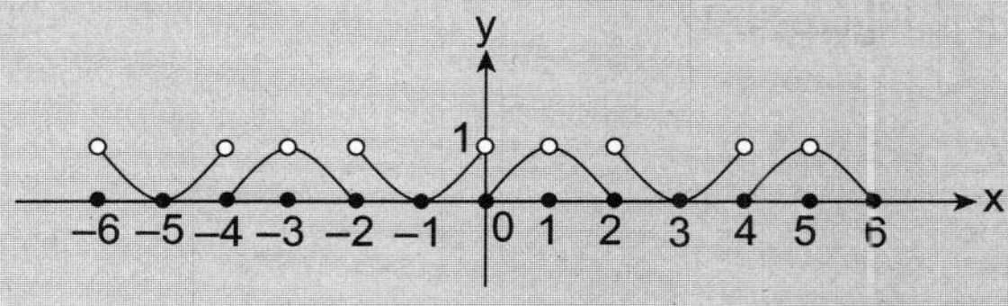

FIGURE 3.234

The graph of $y = 2^x$ is as shown in Figure 3.235.

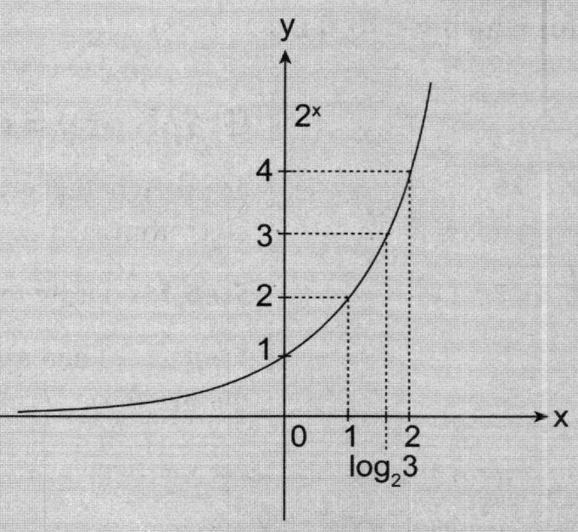

FIGURE 3.235

Now, $y = \dfrac{2^x}{2^{[x]}} = 2^{\{x\}}$ for all real values of *x*, which is a periodic function with a fundamental period of 1.

Its graph can be plotted using the graph of $y = 2^{\{x\}}$ for $x \in [0, 1)$.

Hence, the graph of $y = 2^{\{x\}}$ is as shown in Figure 3.236.

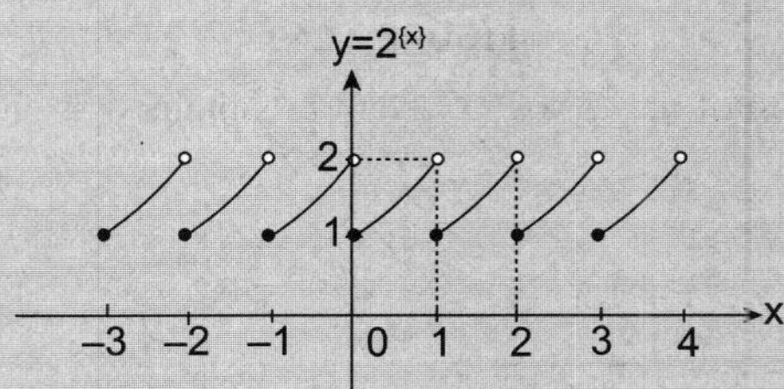

FIGURE 3.236

As is evident from the graphs $y = \dfrac{2^x}{2^{[x]}}$ is always greater than or equal to 1 whereas $y = \left\{\sin\dfrac{\pi}{2}x\right\}$ is always less than 1. Hence, the two graphs never intersect each other and thereby, number of solutions is zero.

16. Graph of $\{y\} = f(x)$ where $\{x\}$ represents the fractional part: To obtain the graph of $\{y\} = f(x)$, retain only the portion of the graph for which $y \in [0, 1)$ and ignore all the parts of the curve for which y obtains other values of $f(x)$. Graph of $y = f(x)$ as shown in Figure 3.237.

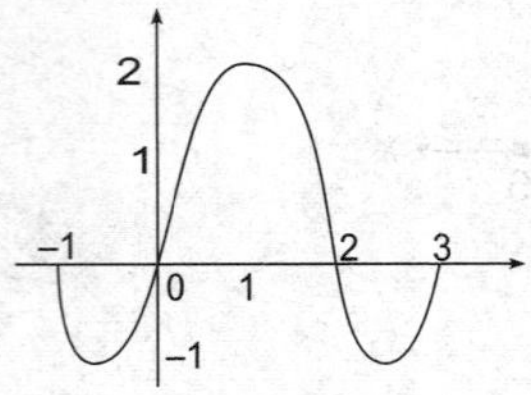

FIGURE 3.237

Highlighting the graph of $y = f(x)$ for which $y \in [0, 1)$.

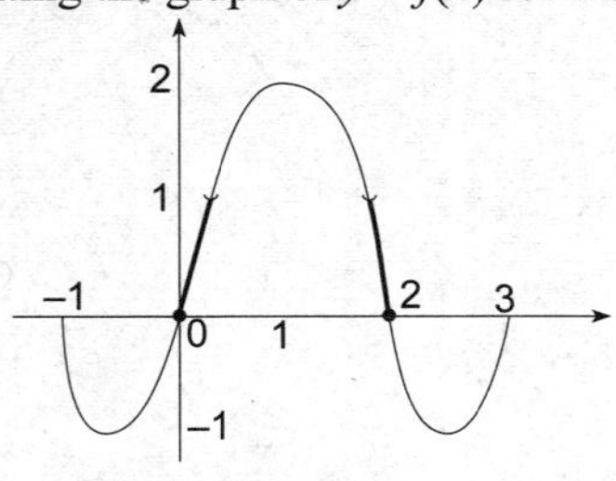

FIGURE 3.238

Retaining only that part of the graph and deleting the rest of the graph, we obtain the graph of $\{y\} = f(x)$ as shown in Figure 3.239.

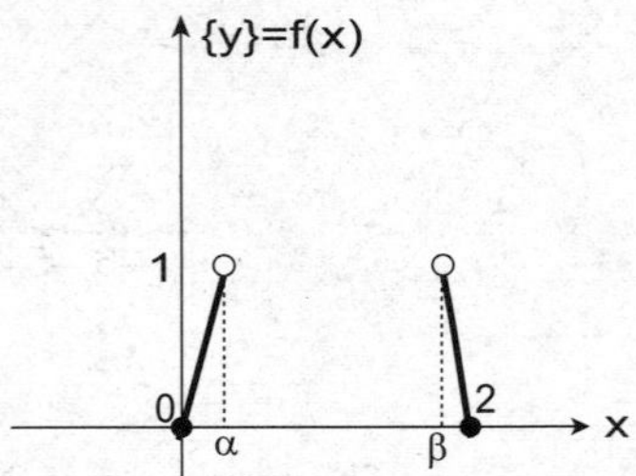

FIGURE 3.239

Graph of y = {f{x}}

To sketch the graph of $y = \{f\{x\}\}$, we follow the given algorithm.

Step 1: Draw the graph of $y = f\{x\}$

Step 2: Then apply the { } on $f\{x\}$, and hence, we obtain the graph of $\{f\{x\}\}$

ILLUSTRATION 53: Sketch the graph of $y = \{2 \cos \{x\}\}$

SOLUTION: The graph of $y = 2 \cos x$ is shown as in Figure 3.240.

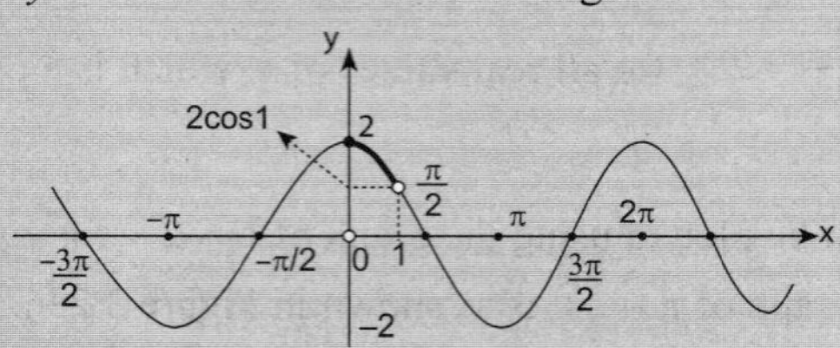

FIGURE 3.240

Thus, the graph of $y = 2 \cos \{x\}$ shall be obtained as shown in Figure 3.241.

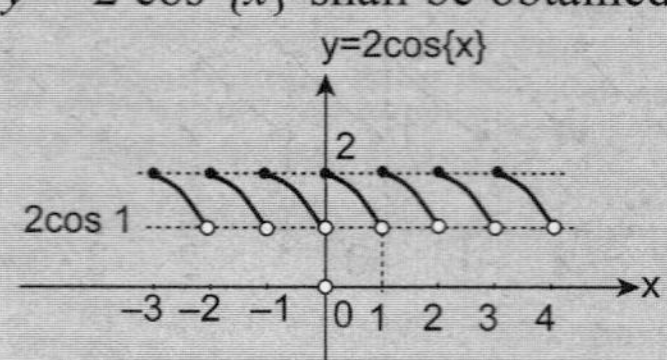

FIGURE 3.241

Now since $\cos 1 > \cos \pi/3$ [Since $1 < \pi/3$ and $\cos x$ is a decreasing function in $[0, \pi/2)$].

$\Rightarrow \cos 1 > 1/2 \Rightarrow 2 \cos 1 > 1$

Alone when $x = 0$; $\cos 0 = 1 \Rightarrow 2 \cos 0 = 2$

Therefore, the graph of $y = \{2\cos\{x\}\}$ can be plotted by applying the { } on $y = 2 \cos\{x\}$ and it is shown as in Figure 3.242.

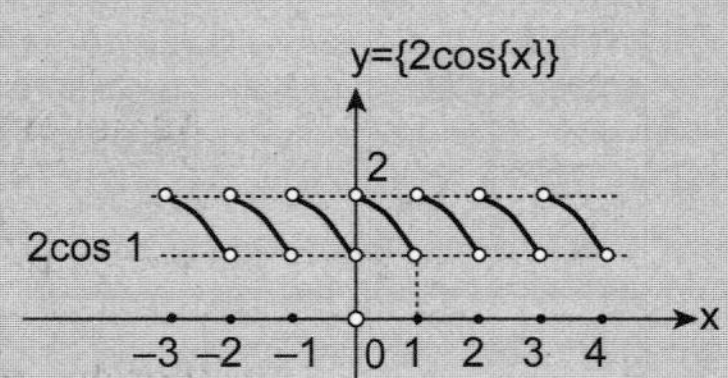

FIGURE 3.242

TEXTUAL EXERCISE–3: (SUBJECTIVE)

1. Draw the graphs of the following functions involving greatest integer functions:
   (i) $y = [x/2] - (x/2)$
   (ii) $y = [2x]$
   (iii) $y = 2[|x|]$
   (iv) $y = \{2x\}$
   (v) $y\ \{x\}^2$
   (vi) $y = [1/[|x|]]$
   (vii) $y = [e^{-x}] \ln x$

2. If a function is defined as $y(x) = \begin{cases} x & 0 \le x \le 1 \\ 2-x & 1 < x \le 2 \\ (x-2)(x-4) & 2 \le x \le 4 \end{cases}$ then sketch the following functions:
   (a) $y = [f(x)]$
   (b) $y = f([x])$
   (c) $[y] = f(x)$
   (d) $y = f\{x\}$
   (e) $y = \{f(x)\}$
   (f) $y = \{f\{x\}\}$
   (g) $\{y\} = f(x)$

3. Draw the graph of the following functions
   (i) $y = 2\{x\}^2 - 5\{x\} + 3$
   (ii) $y = [\sin x - \cos x]$
   (iii) $y = [\sin x + \cos x]$
   (iv) $y = \cot\left(\dfrac{\pi}{2} - \pi\{x\}\right)$

4. Draw the graphs of following functions involving greatest integer functions:
   (a) $y = \sin(x - [x])$
   (b) $y = sgn\ (x - [x])$
   (c) $y = [x] + [-x]$
   (d) $y = [|\sin x|]$
   (e) $y = [\sin |x|]$
   (f) $y = |[\sin x]|$
   (g) $y = \sin[x] - \cos[x]$

Answer Keys

1. (i)

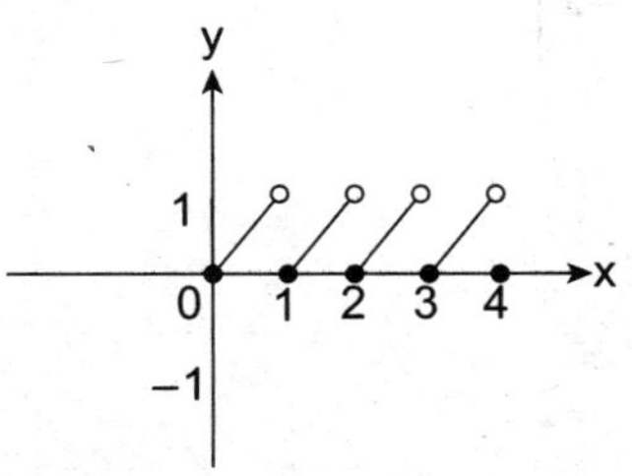

(ii)

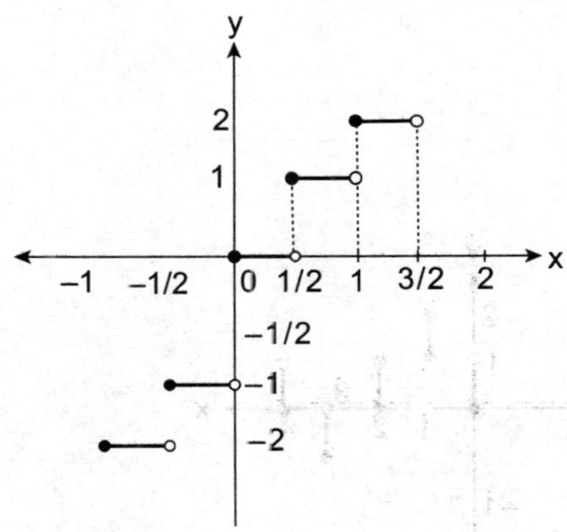

(iii)

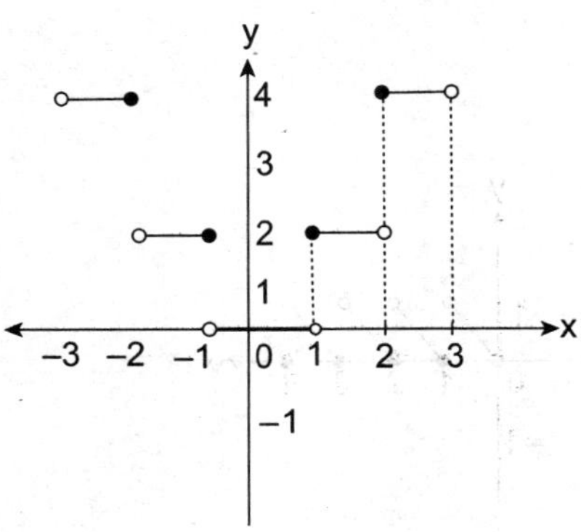

(iv)

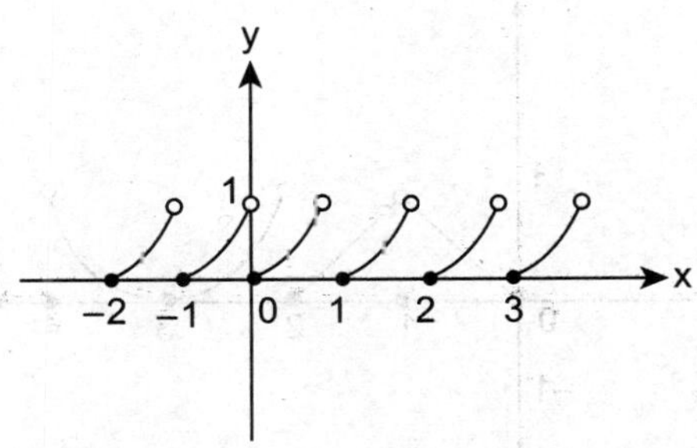

(v)
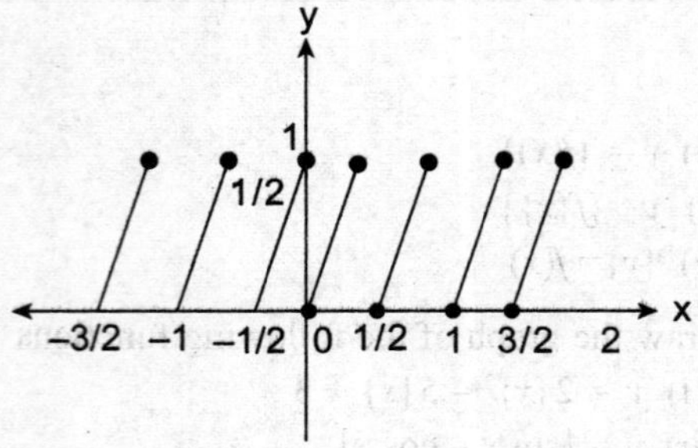

(vi)
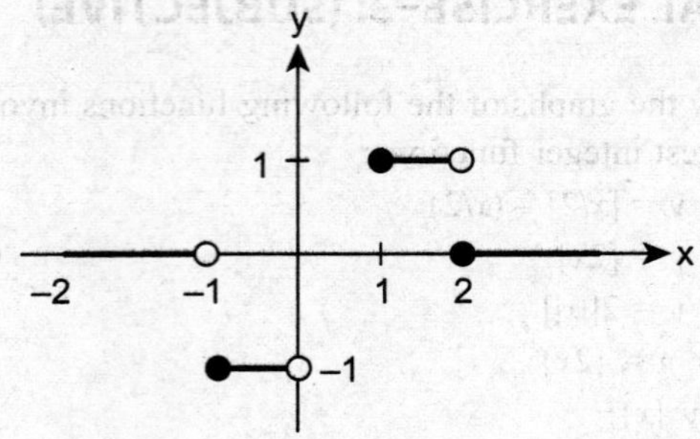

(vii)
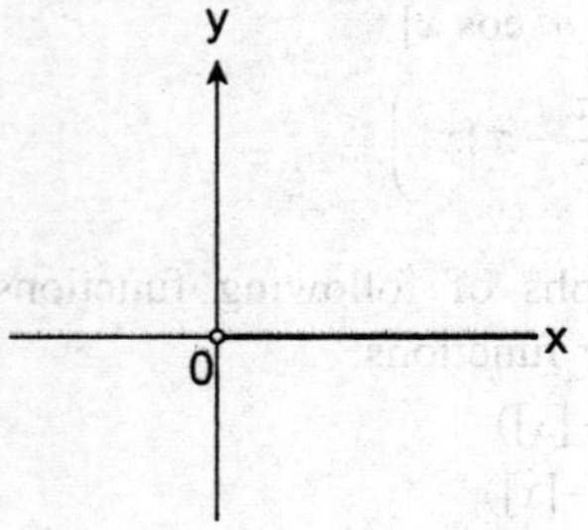

2. (a)
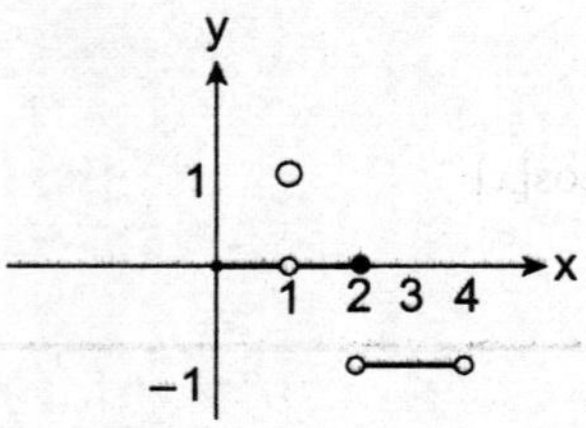

(b)
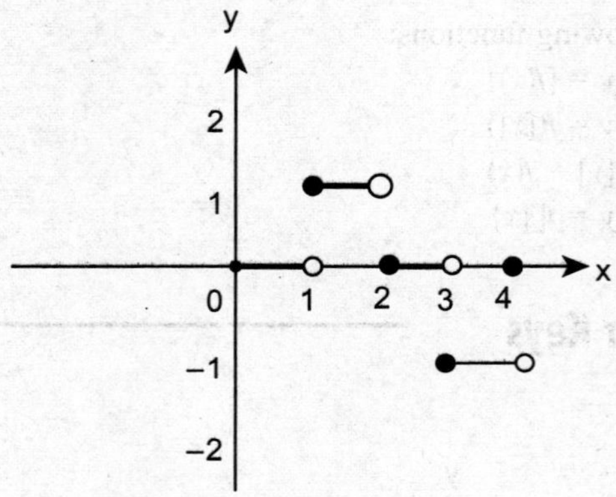

(c)
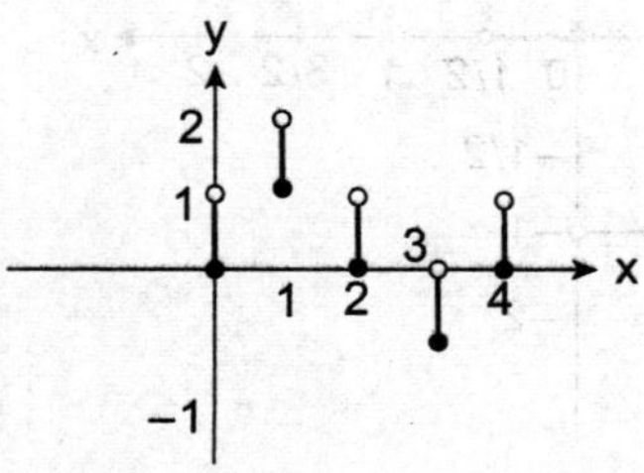

(d)
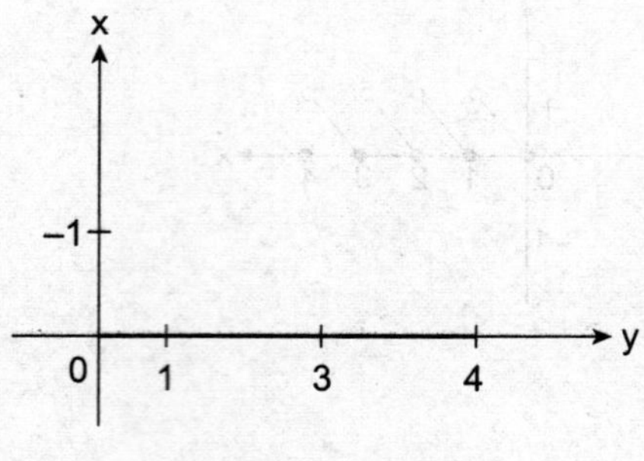

(e)
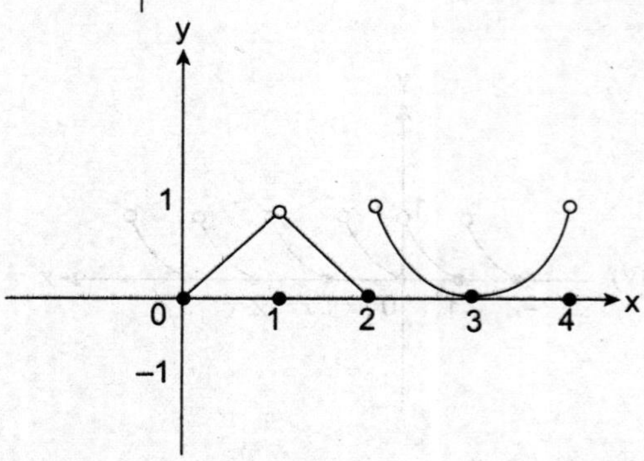

(f)
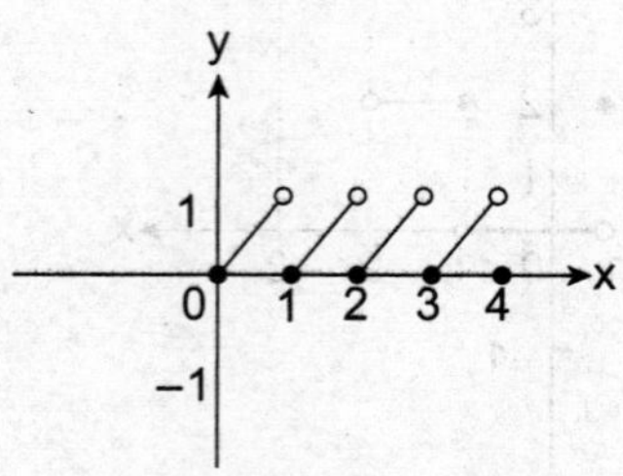

(g)
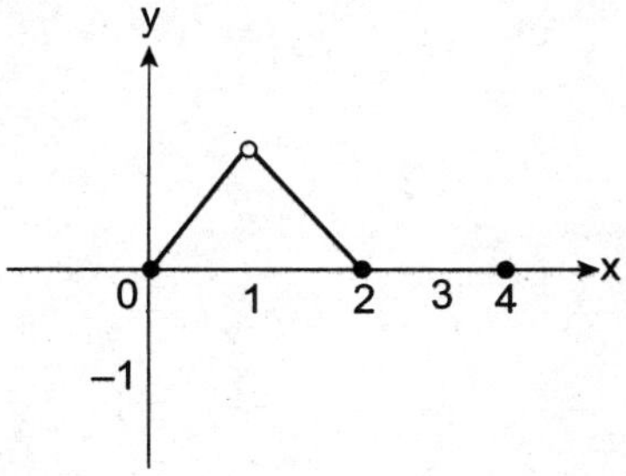

3. (i)
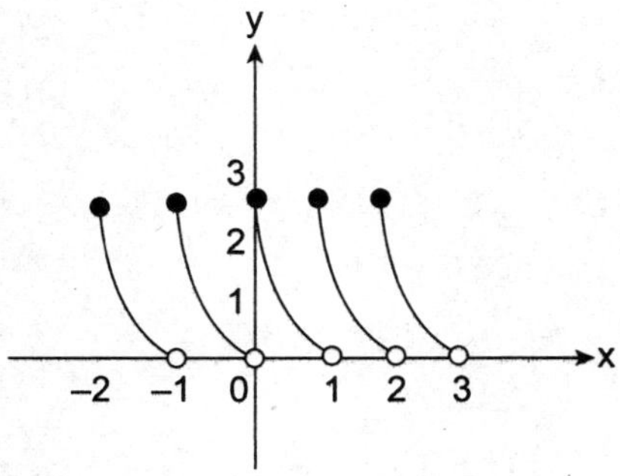

(ii)
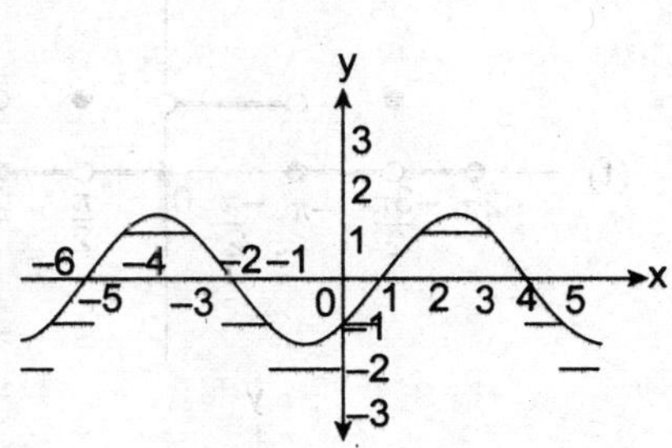

(iii)
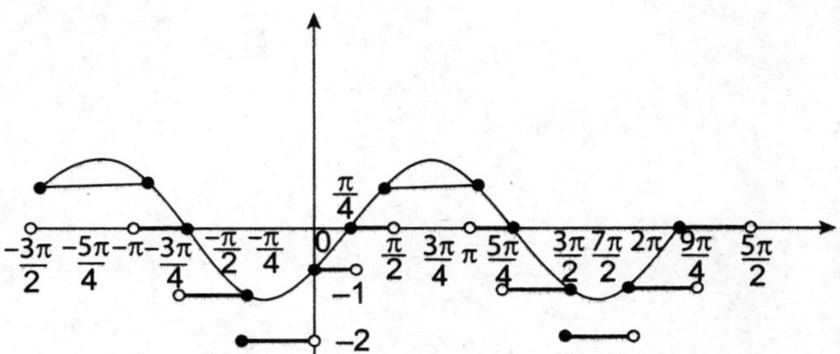

(iv)
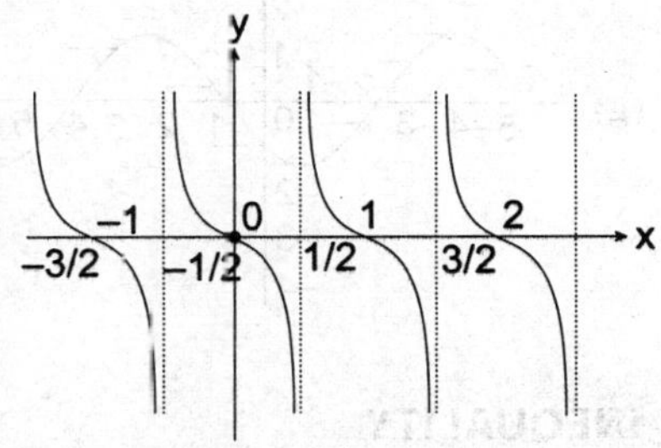

4. (a)
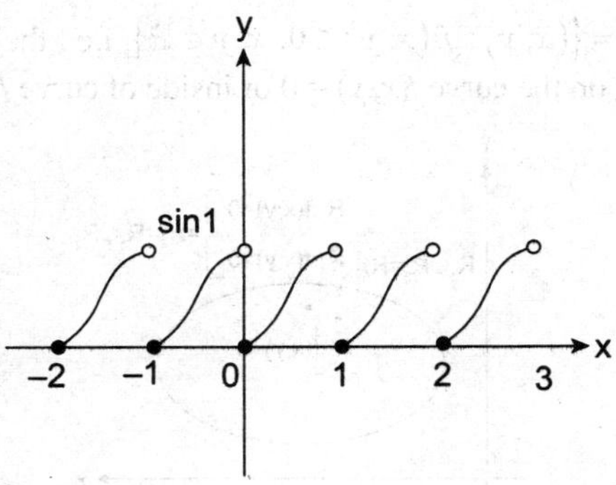

(b)
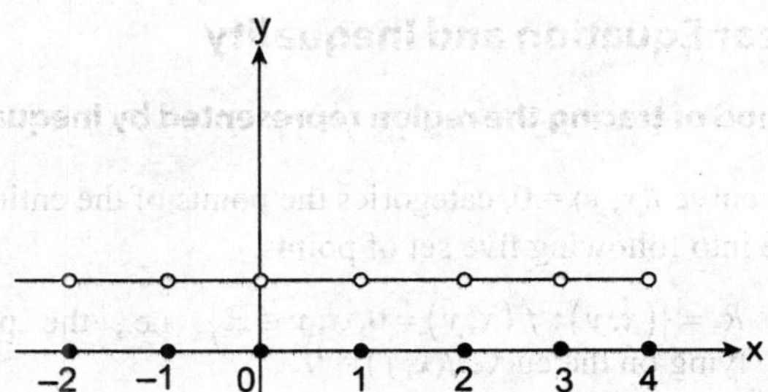

(c)
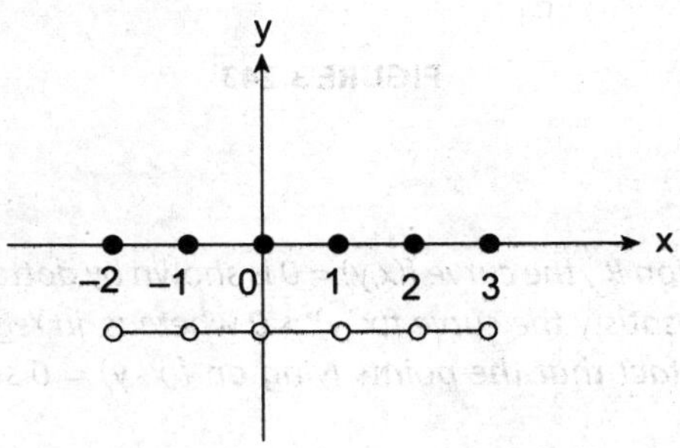

(d)
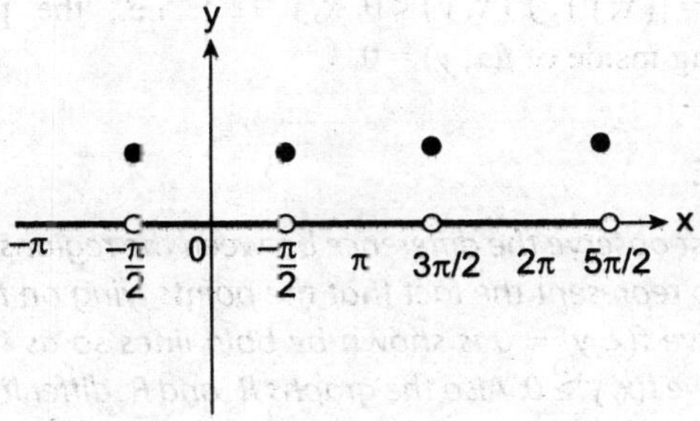

(e)
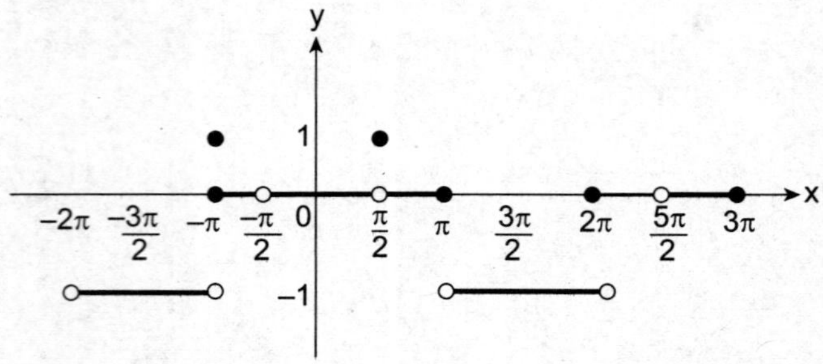

(f)
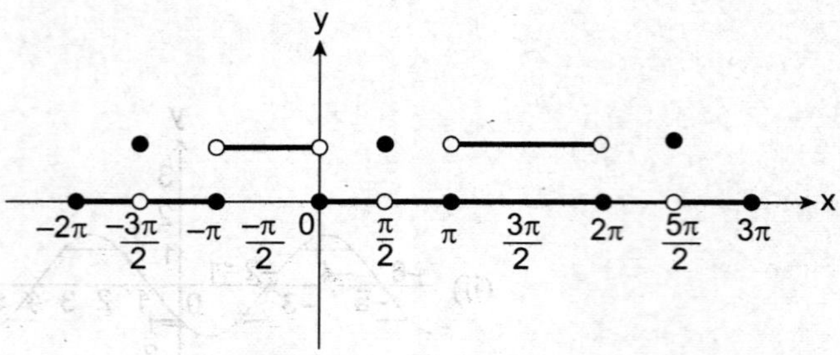

(g)
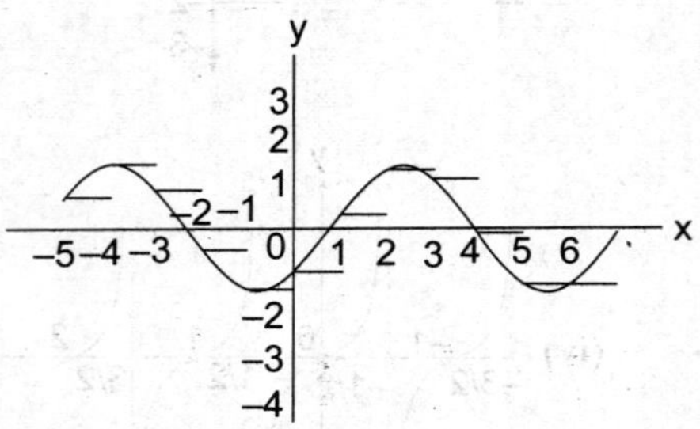

■ INEQUALITY

Linear Equation and Inequality

Method of tracing the region represented by inequality

Each curve $f(x, y) = 0$, categories the points of the entire x-y plane into following five set of points.

(i) $R = \{(x, y) : f(x, y) = 0,\ x, y \in \mathbb{R}\}$, i.e., the points lying on the curve $f(x, y) = 0$

(ii) $R_2 = \{(x, y) : f(x, y) > 0,\ x, y \in \mathbb{R}\}$, i.e., the points lying outside of curve $f(x, y) = 0$.

(iii) $R_3 = \{(x, y) : f(x, y) < 0,\ x, y \in \mathbb{R}\}$, i.e., the points lying inside of $f(x, y) = 0$.

(iv) $R_4 = \{(x, y) : f(x, y) \geq 0,\ x, y \in \mathbb{R}\}$, i.e., the points lying on the curve $f(x, y) = 0$ or outside of curve $f(x, y) = 0$.

(v) $R_5 = \{(x, y) : f(x, y) \leq 0,\ x, y \in \mathbb{R}\}$, i.e., the points lying on the curve $f(x, y) = 0$ or inside of curve $f(x, y) = 0$.

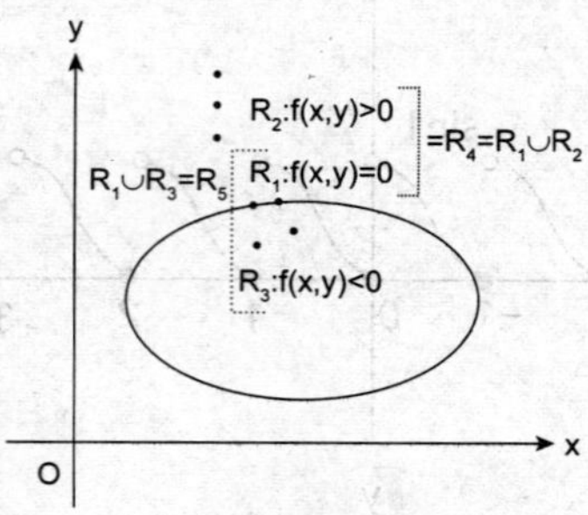

FIGURE 3.243

NOTE

We must observe the difference between the regions R_2 and R_4. In region R_2, the curve f(x,y) = 0 is shown by dotted lines so as to represent the fact that the points lying on f(x, y) = 0 do not satisfy the curve f(x, y) > 0 whereas, in region R_4, the curve f(x, y) = 0 is shown by bold lines so as to represent the fact that the points lying on f(x, y) = 0 satisfies the curve f(x, y)≥ 0. Also the graphs R_3 and R_5 differ in the same way.

■ ALGORITHM

To identify the region represented by a given inequality $f(x, y) \geq 0$.

Step I: Consider the equality and draw the curve using the symmetry and other concepts of curve sketching and transformation of graphs.

Step II: Consider any points (α, β) not lying on the curve preferably (0, 0) {or point on coordinate axis} and determine the sign of $f(\alpha, \beta)$.

Step III: If $f(\alpha, \beta) > 0$, then $f(x, y) \geq 0$ represents the region containing (α, β). If $f(\alpha, \beta) < 0$, then the region which does not contain point (α, β) will be represented by inequality $f(x, y) > 0$.

Similarly, we can identify the region represented by a given inequality $f(x, y) \leq 0$. For example, The inequality $(x-a)^2 + (y-b)^2 < r^2$ represents the interior or a circle.

The inequality $(x-a)^2 + (y-b)^2 > r^2$ represents the exterior of a circle. (i.e., region lying outside the circle).

We take the independent variables along x-axis and dependent variables along the y-axis in the cartesian coordinate system.

ILLUSTRATION 54: Mark the region represented by $3x + 4y < 12$.

SOLUTION: Converting the inequality into equation, we get $3x + 4y = 12$. This line meets the coordinate axes at (4, 0) and (0, 3), respectively.

Join these points to obtain straight line represented by $3x + 4y = 12$

This straight line divides the plane in two parts besides from itself. One part contains the origin and the other does not contain the origin. Clearly (0, 0) satisfy the inequality $3x + 4y < 12$. So, the region represented by $3x + 4y < 12$ is region containing the origin containing the origin, i.e., the half plane below the line $3x + 4y = 12$.

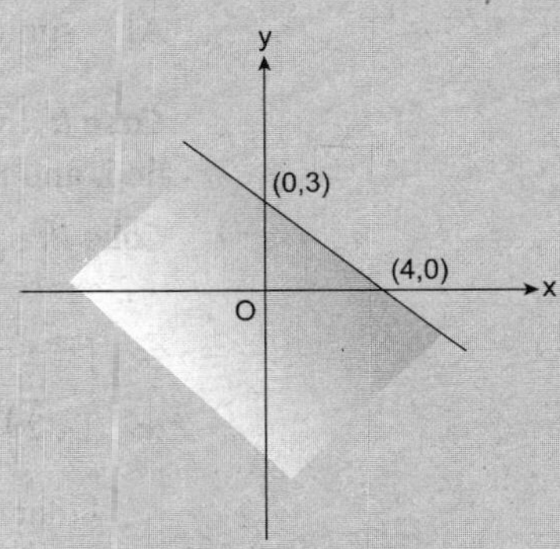

FIGURE 3.244

ILLUSTRATION 55: Sketch the region represented by the following inequalities:

(a) $y > x$ (b) $y < -x$ (c) $y \geq |x - 1|$ (d) $x - 3y + 15 \leq 0$, $y + 5 \leq 5x$ and $4y + 28 \geq 7x$

(e) $(x^2 - x) < (y - xy)$

SOLUTION: (a)

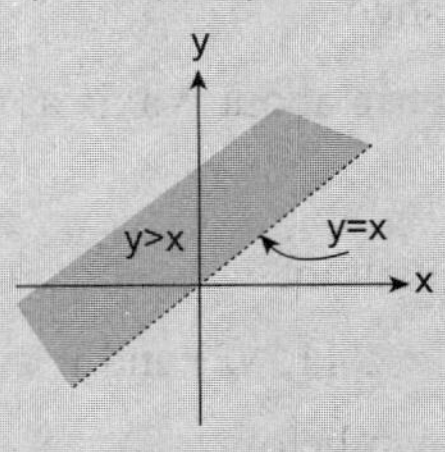

(b)

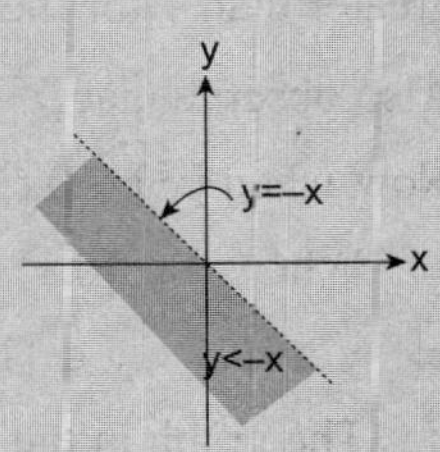

(c)

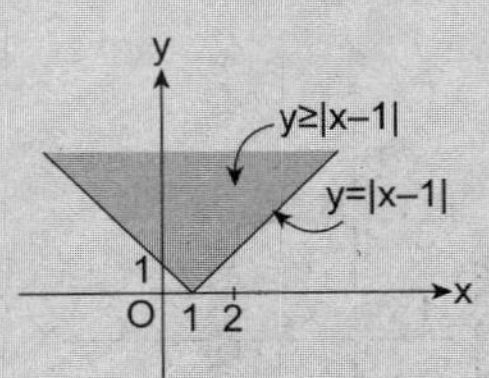

(d)

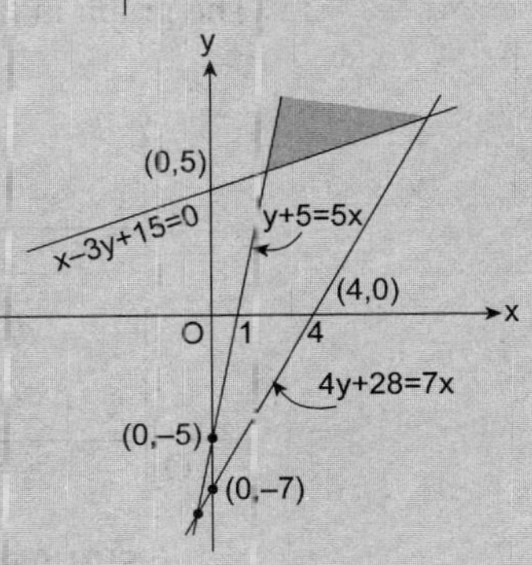

(e)

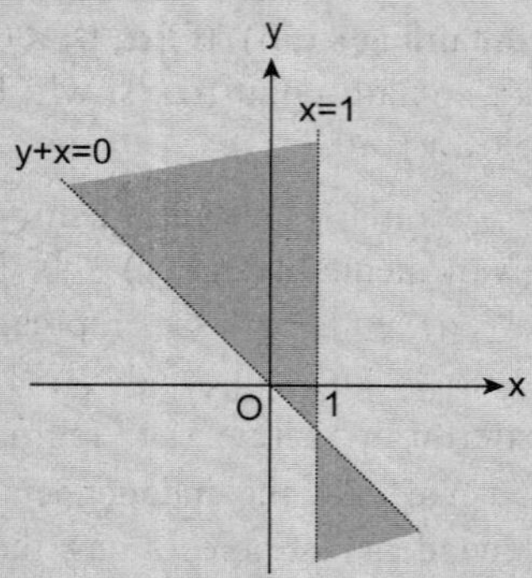

ILLUSTRATION 56: Plot the region which satisfies the equation $[x^2 + y^2] - 2\ \text{sgn}\ (x^2 + y^2) = 0$.

SOLUTION: As is obvious from the expression $[x^2 + y^2] - 2\ \text{sgn}\ (x^2 + y^2)$, we understand that the required graph will be symmetric about x-axis as well as y-axis.

Also $\text{sgn}\ (x^2 + y^2) = \begin{cases} 0;\ x = y = 0 \\ 1;\text{otherwise} \end{cases}$

Case I: when $x = y = 0$, then the above equation is satisfied, and hence, (0,0) is a point on the required graph.

Case II: When x, y are not simultaneously zero $[x^2 + y^2] - 2\ \text{sgn}(x^2 + y^2) = 0$.

$\Rightarrow\ [x^2 + y^2] = 2 \qquad \Rightarrow\ (x^2 + y^2) \in [2, 3)$

$\Rightarrow\ \left(\sqrt{2}\right)^2 \le x^2 + y^2 < \left(\sqrt{3}\right)^2$; which will represent a circular ring.

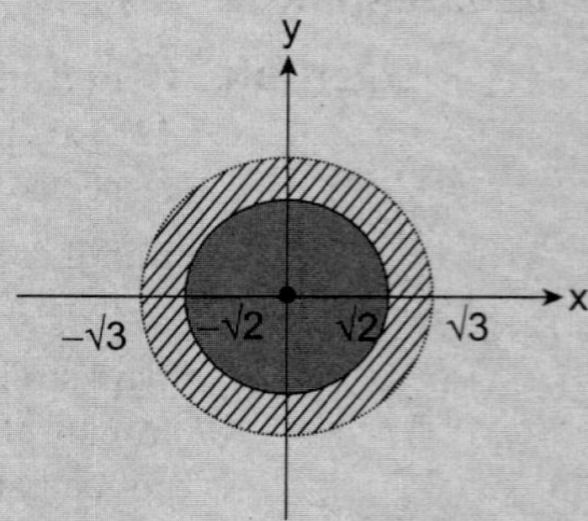

FIGURE 3.245

Hence, the overall graph will be as shown in Figure 3.245.

ILLUSTRATION 57: Plot the region which satisfies the equation $[x^2] + [y^2] = 1$

SOLUTION: Obviously $[x^2]$ or $[y^2]$ can never be negative, and hence, $[x^2]$ or $[y^2]$ can never take value greater than 1 for the given equation to be satisfied.

Also observe that $[x^2] + [y^2] = 1$ will be symmetric about x-axis as well as about y-axis,

Now when $[x^2] = 0$; $[y^2] = 1$

$\Rightarrow$ When $x^2 \in [0,1)$; $y^2 \in [1, 2)$. In the first quadrant.

$\Rightarrow\ x \in [0,1)$; $y \in [1, \sqrt{2})$ and vice-versa, i.e., $x \in [1, \sqrt{2})$ and $y \in [0, 1)$

$\therefore$ The graph in the I[st] quadrant will be as shown below.

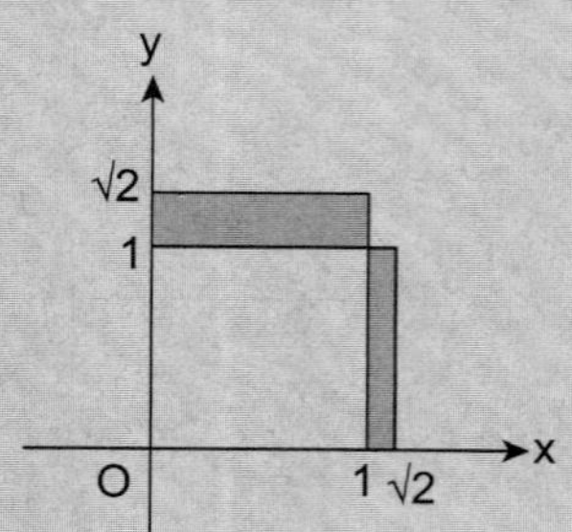

FIGURE 3.246

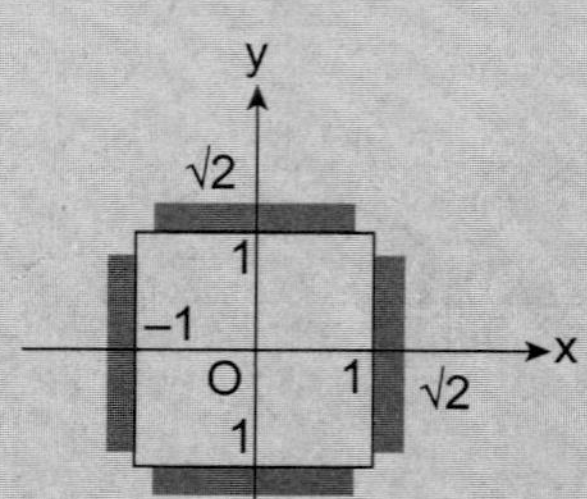

FIGURE 3.247

ILLUSTRATION 58: Plot the region which satisfies the equation $(|x| - |y|)(x - y) \leq 4$

SOLUTION: ***Case I:*** $x, y \geq 0$ $\therefore$ $(x - y)^2 \leq 4$ $-2 \leq x - y \leq 2$

and the graphs can be plotted as shown in Figure 3.248.

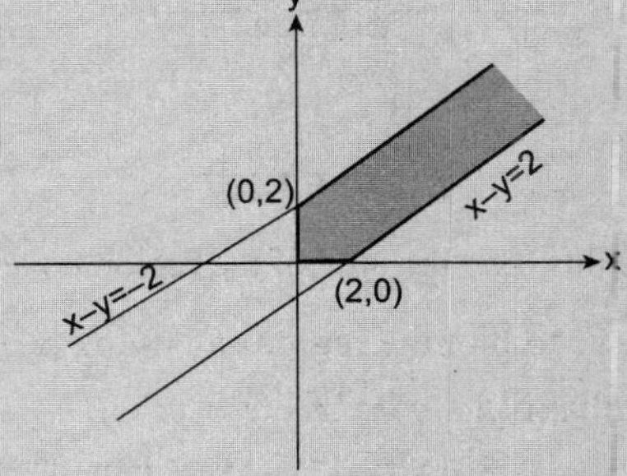

FIGURE 3.248

Case II: $x, y \leq 0$ $\therefore$ $((-x) - (-y))\ (x - y) \leq 4$

$\Rightarrow$ $(y - x)\ (x - y) \leq 4$ $\Rightarrow$ $(x - y)^2 \geq -4$ which is true $\forall\ x, y \leq 0$

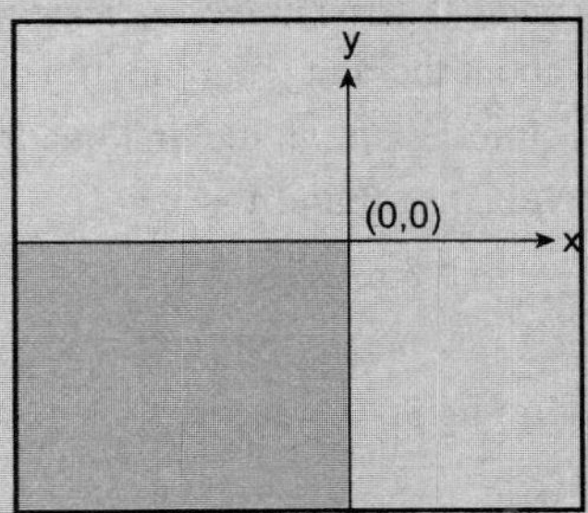

FIGURE 3.249

Case III: If $x \leq 0$ and $y \geq 0$; then we get $((-x) - (y))\ (x - y) \leq 4 \Rightarrow y^2 - x^2 \leq 4$

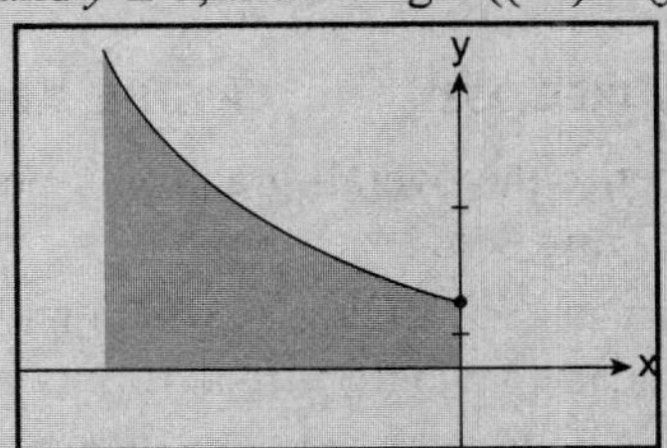

FIGURE 3.250

Case Iv: If $x \geq 0$ and $y \leq 0$; then we get $(x - (-y))\ (x - y) \leq 4 \Rightarrow x^2 - y^2 \leq 4$

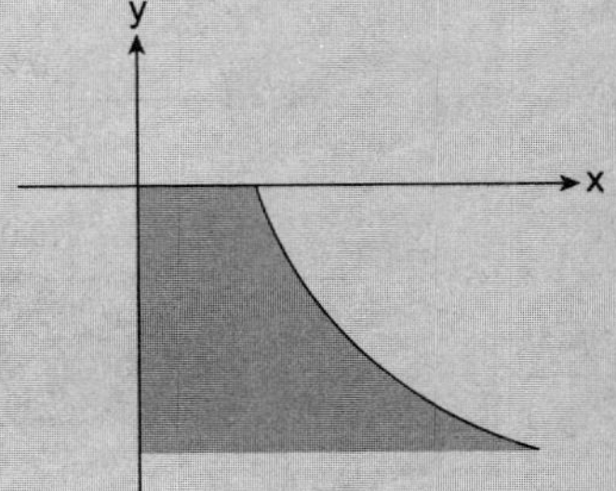

FIGURE 3.251

Hence, the graph of $(|x| - |y|)(x - y) \le 4$ will be given as in Figure 3.252.

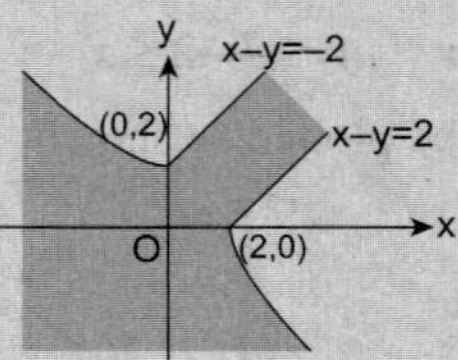

FIGURE 3.252

ILLUSTRATION 59: Without using calculus, find the area of the region covered by $|x + y| + |x - y| \le 4$ and $x^2 + y^2 \ge 4y$.

SOLUTION: First of all, let us try to plot the region satisfying $|x + y| + |x - y| \le 4$

Now; we observe that if $f(x, y) = |x + y| + |x - y|$

Then $f(-x, -y) = |-x - y| + |-x + y| = |x + y| + |x - y| = f(x, y)$ ....(1)

Also $f(y, x) = |y + x| + |y - x| = f(x, y)$ ....(2)

And $f(-x, y) = |-x + y| + |-x - y| = f(x, y)$ ...(3)

And $f(x, -y) = |x - y| + |x + y| = f(x, y)$ ...(4)

Equations (1), (2), (3) and (4) respectively indicates the symmetry of the graph of $f(x, y) = |x + y| + |x - y|$ about origin, about the line $y = x$, about y-axis and about x-axis, respectively.

Hence, we draw the required graph in the first quadrant only and that too below, the line $y = x$;

In this region ; we have $x, y \ge 0$ and $y \le x$

$\Rightarrow\ |x + y| + |x - y| = 2x \le 4 \Rightarrow x \le 2$

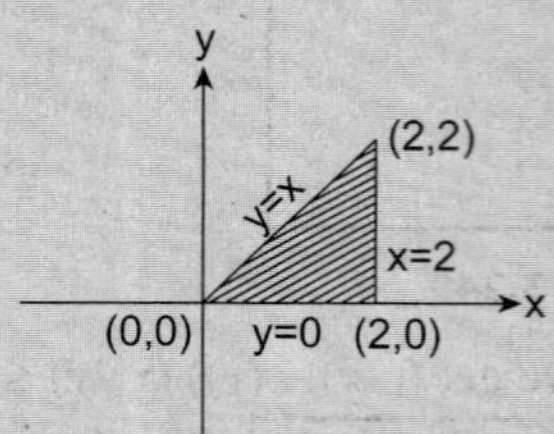

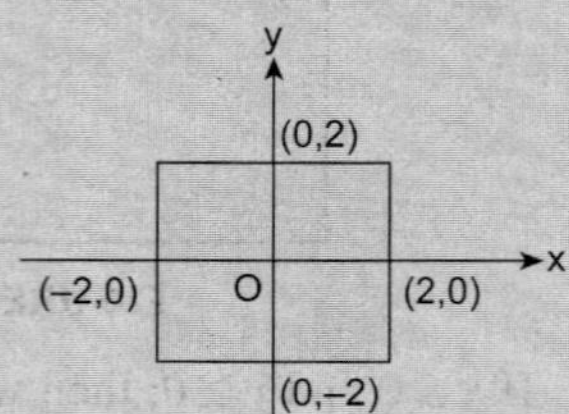

FIGURE 3.253 **FIGURE 3.254**

Hence, using symmetry, the overall graph will be a square of length 4 units with centre at origin as shown in Figure 3.254.

Now; $x^2 + y^2 \ge 4y\ \Rightarrow\ x^2 + (y - 2)^2 \ge 4$, which will represent the outside area of the circle of radius 2 and its boundary having centre at (0,2).

∴ The common area bounded by the two inequalities will be shown by the shaded region in the Figure 3.255.

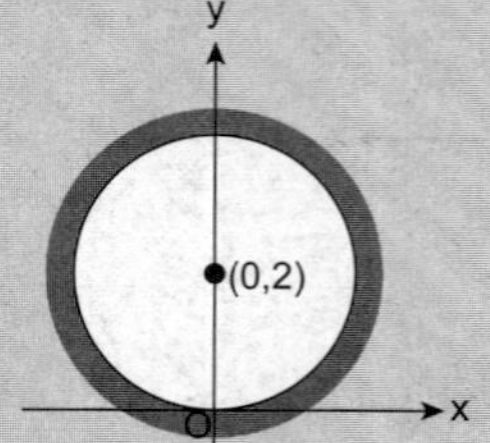

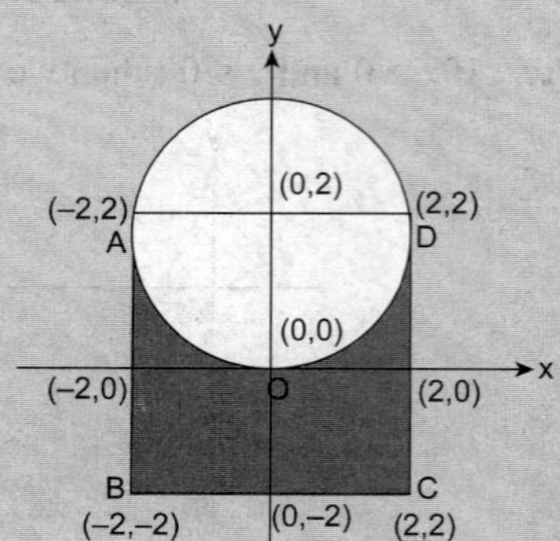

FIGURE 3.255 **FIGURE 3.256**

∴ Required area (area of region $ABCD\ O$) = (area of square $ABCD$) – (area of semi-circle AOD) = $(16 - 2\pi)$ square units.

ILLUSTRATION 60: Sketch the region bounded by $9 \le x^2 + y^2 \le 3\,(|x| + |y|)$

SOLUTION: The graph of $x^2 + y^2 \ge 9$ will be as shown below.

We observe the graph is a circle with centre at origin and hence, symmetric about both the axes.

Now consider $x^2 + y^2 \le (|x| + |y|)$

Here, also we observe that $f(x, y) = f(-x, -y) = f(x, -y) = f(-x, y) = f(y, x)$

Hence, the graph is symmetric about both the axes first of all we plot the curve $x^2 + y^2 \le 3\,(|x| + |y|)$ only in first quadrant.

$\Rightarrow$ $(x^2 - 3x + 9/4) + (y^2 - 3y + 9/4) \le 9/2$

$\Rightarrow$ $(x - 3/2)^2 + (y - 3/2)^2 \le (3/\sqrt{2})^2$ which is a circle with centre at (3/2, 3/2) and radius $\dfrac{3}{\sqrt{2}}$

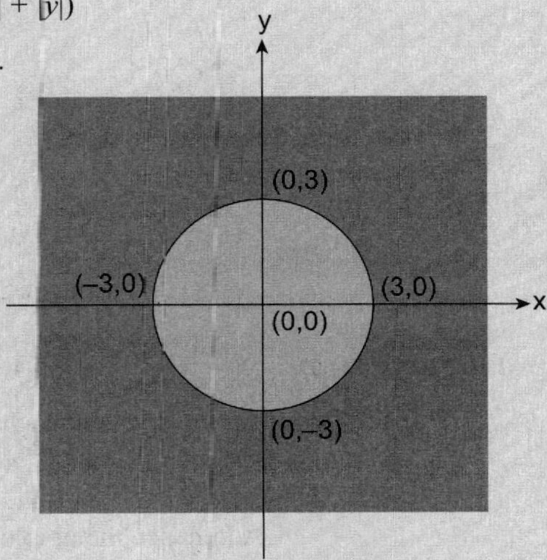

FIGURE 3.257

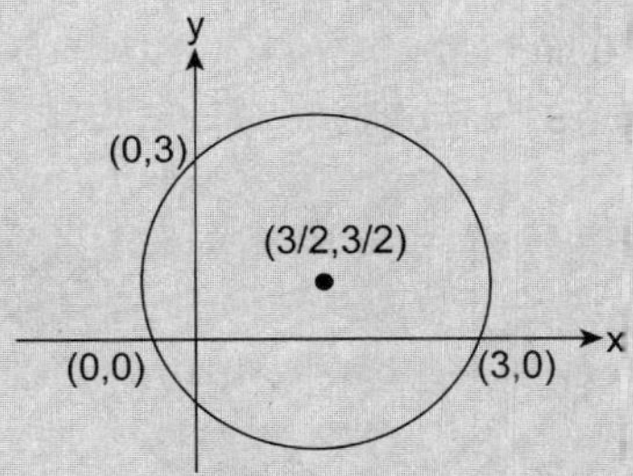

FIGURE 3.258

Therefore, the curve $x^2 + y^2 \le 3\,(|x| + |y|)$ for $x, y \in \mathbb{R}$ will be as shown in Figure 3.259.

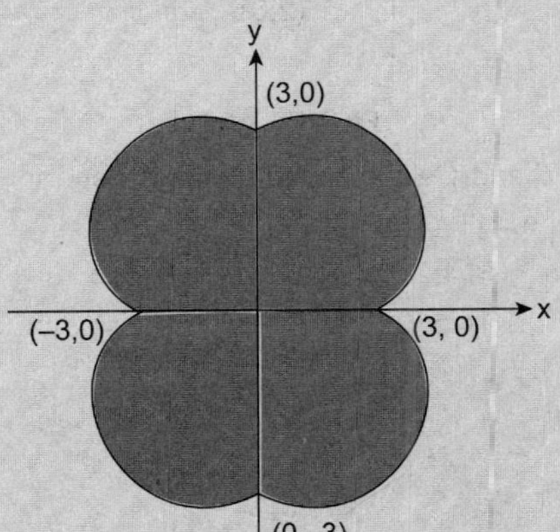

FIGURE 3.259

Now plotting the two curves together on the same reference plane, we shade the region satisfying $9 \le x^2 + y^2 \le 3\,(|x| + |y|)$.

Now; to find the area, we find the shaded area in the first quadrant only

Area of curve ($ADBCA$) = (area of semi-circle $ABCA$) – (area of arc $ABDA$)

$= \dfrac{\pi\left(\dfrac{3}{\sqrt{2}}\right)^2}{2}$ – (area of quarter circle $OADBO$ – area of ΔOAB)

$= \dfrac{9\pi}{4} - \left(\dfrac{\pi}{4}\times(3)^2 - \dfrac{1}{2}\times 9\right) = \dfrac{9}{2}$. Hence, total shaded area

$= 4\times\dfrac{9}{2} = 18$ square units.

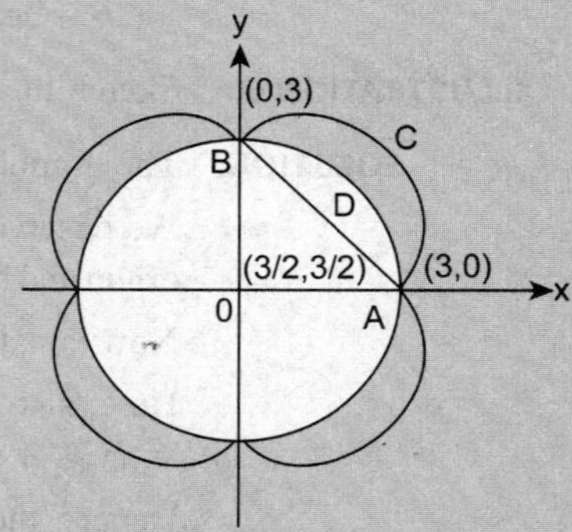

FIGURE 3.260

ILLUSTRATION 61: $||x| - |y|| + |x - y| \le 4$

SOLUTION: We observe that $f(x, y) = f(y, x)$

Hence, the graph is symmetric about $y = x$

Also, $f(-x, -y) = f(x, y)$

And hence the graph is symmetric about origin. Hence, we need to plot the curve in the first quadrant (below $y = x$) and also in the second quadrant and using that, we can plot the complete graph.

Case I: For $x, y \ge 0$ and $y \le x$

$|x - y| + |x - y| \le 4 \Rightarrow x - y \le 2$

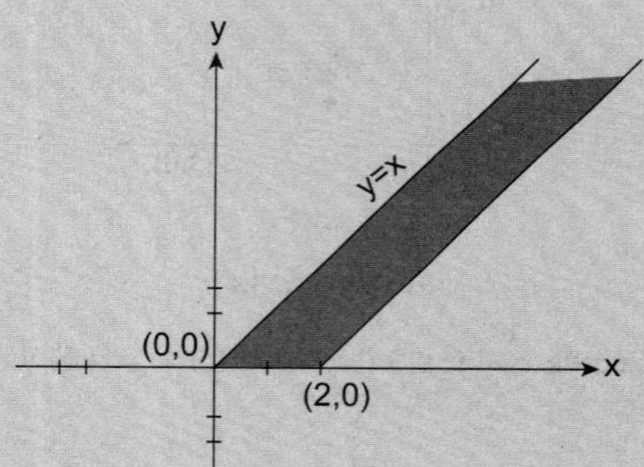

FIGURE 3.261

Case II: If $x \le 0$ and $y \ge 0$ (second quadrant) and $y + x \ge 0$, i.e., $y \ge -x$

Then $|x| - |y|| + |x - y| \le 4$

$\Rightarrow |-x - y| + |x - y| \le 4$ $\Rightarrow |x + y| + |y - x| \le 4$

$\Rightarrow x + y + y - x \le 4 \Rightarrow 2y \le 4$ $\Rightarrow y \le 2$

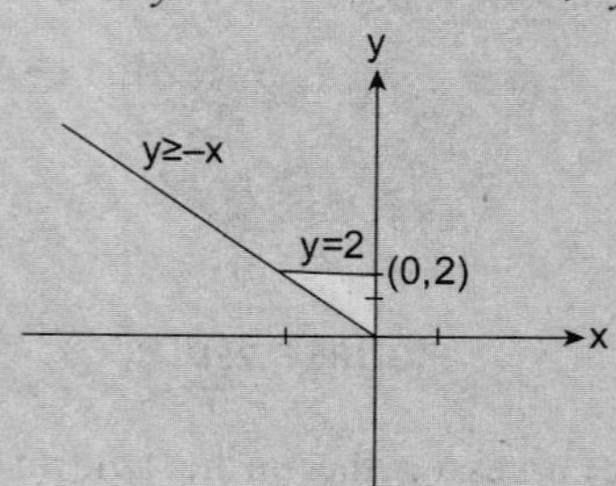

FIGURE 3.262

Case III: If $x \le 0$ and $y \ge 0$ and $y + x \le 0$, i.e., $y \le -x$ then $||x| - |y|| + |x - y| \le 4$

$\Rightarrow |-x - y| + |y - x| \le 4 \qquad \Rightarrow |x + y| + |y - x| \le 4$

$\Rightarrow -x - y + y - x \le 4 \qquad \Rightarrow -2x \le 4 \Rightarrow x \ge -2$

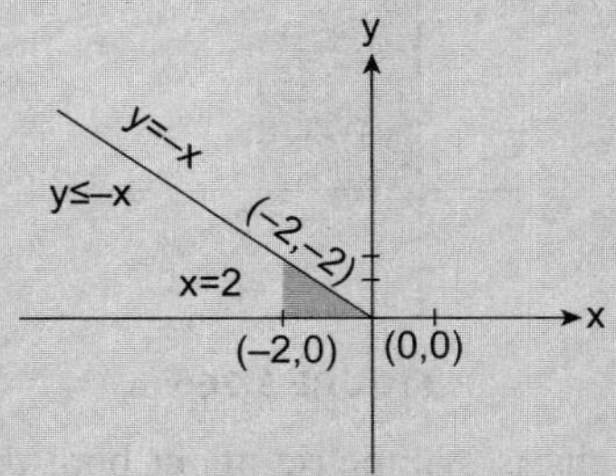

FIGURE 3.263

And using the above three figures, we can draw the required region

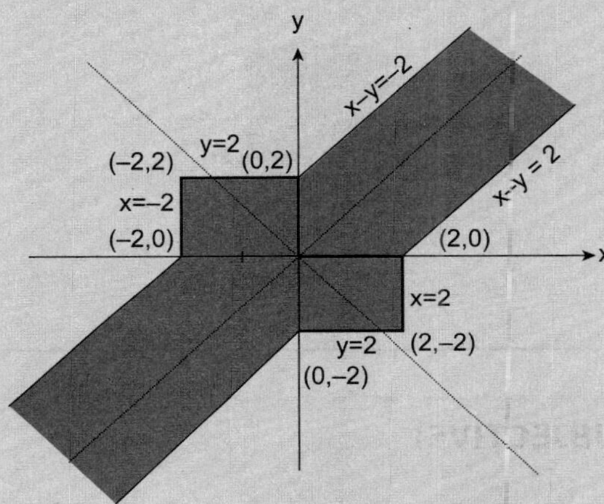

FIGURE 3.264

ILLUSTRATION 62: $3^{|x|}\,|y| + 3^{|x|-1} \le 1$; $3|x| \le 1$;

SOLUTION: Now $3^{|x|}\,|y| + \dfrac{3^{|x|}}{3} \le 1 \;\Rightarrow\; 3^{|x|}\left(|y| + \dfrac{1}{3}\right) \le 1 \;\Rightarrow\; |y| + \dfrac{1}{3} \le 3^{-|x|}$

As we observe, $f(x, y) = f(-x, -y) = f(x, -y) = f(-x, y)$

Hence, the graph is symmetric about both the axis.

For $x, y \ge 0$; we have $y + \dfrac{1}{3} \le 3^{-x} \;\Rightarrow\; y \le 3^{-x} - (1/3)$

Graph of $y = 3^{-x}$ and $y = 3^{-x} - (1/3)$ are shown in Figure 3.265.

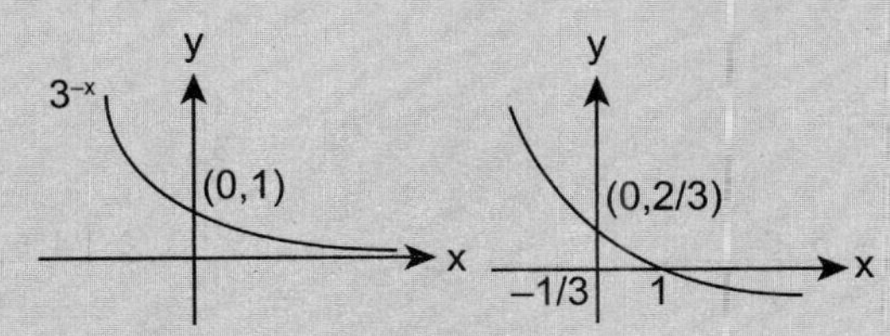

FIGURE 3.265

For $x \in [0, 1/3]$; we represent $y \le 3^{-x} - 1/3$ by the shaded region.

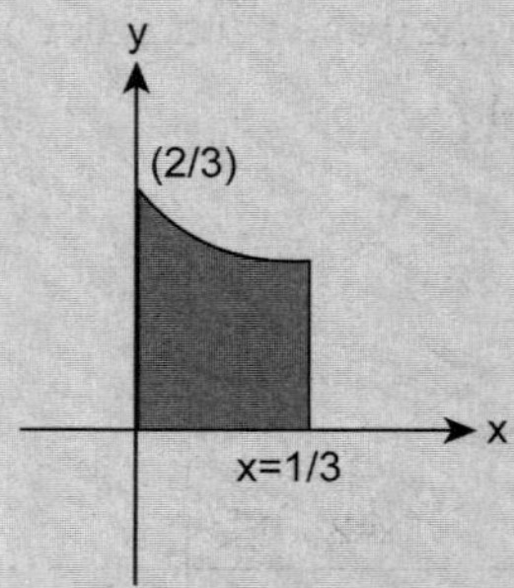

FIGURE 3.266

Now since the graphs is symmetric about both the axes; hence, the required graph will as shown in Figure 3.267.

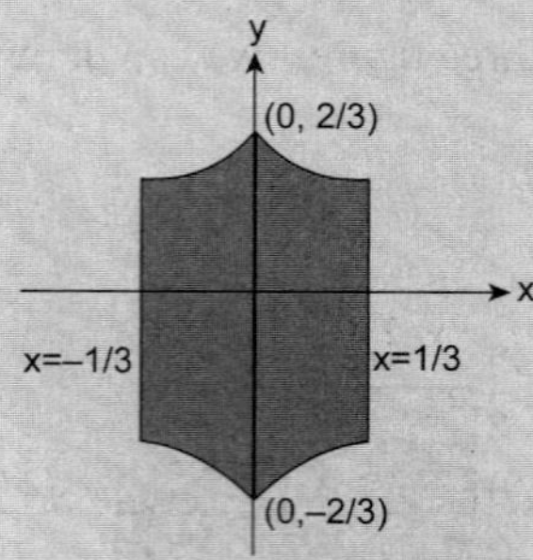

FIGURE 3.267

TEXTUAL EXERCISE–4: (SUBJECTIVE)

1. Sketch the region represented by following linear inequations:

   (a) $y > x$ (b) $y < -x$
   (c) $y \geq |x-1|$ (d) $x > |y-1|$
   (e) $|x-y| \leq 2$ (f) $|x+y| \geq 3$
   (g) $|x|-|y| \geq 1$ (h) $|x|+|y| \leq 2$
   (i) $|x-2|+|y+1| \geq 3$

2. Sketch the curve of $y = [x+y]^2$. Hence, find the area of the region represented by $[x+y]^2 = 4$ and lying in the first quadrant.

3. Sketch the following graphs:

   (i) $y \leq [x]-[x-(1/2)]$ (ii) $[x]+[y]=1$
   (iii) $[x]-[y]=1$ (iv) $[x][y]=1$
   (v) $[y]=[x]$ (vi) $[x+1]=[y+2]$

4. Sketch on $x-y$ plane: $[|x^2-2|]^2 + [|y+1|]^2 = 0$

Answer Keys

1. (a)

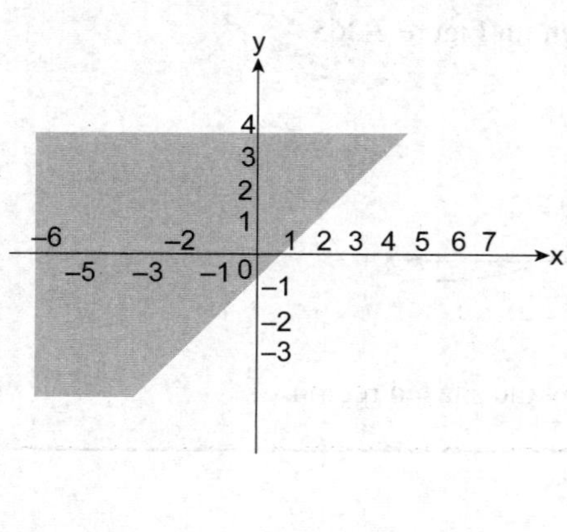

(b)

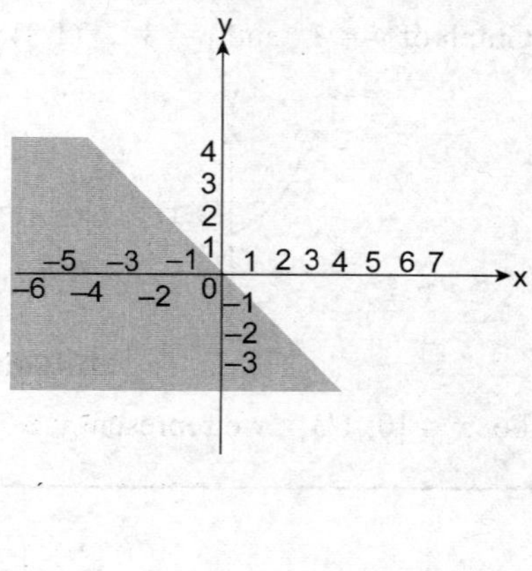

(c) 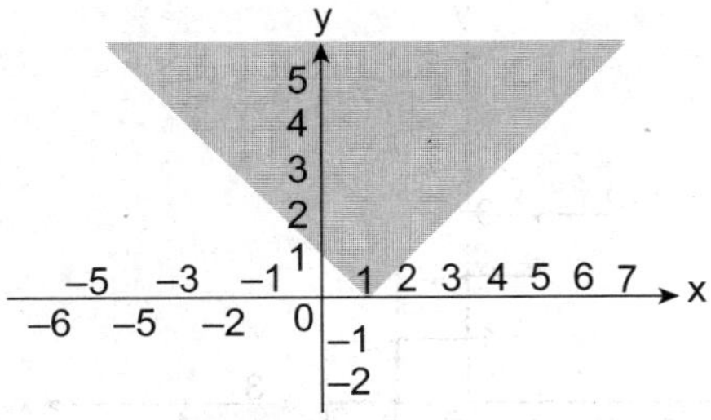

(d) 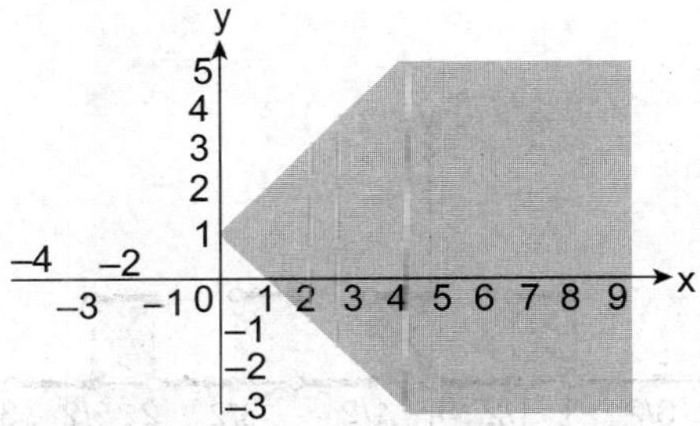

(e) 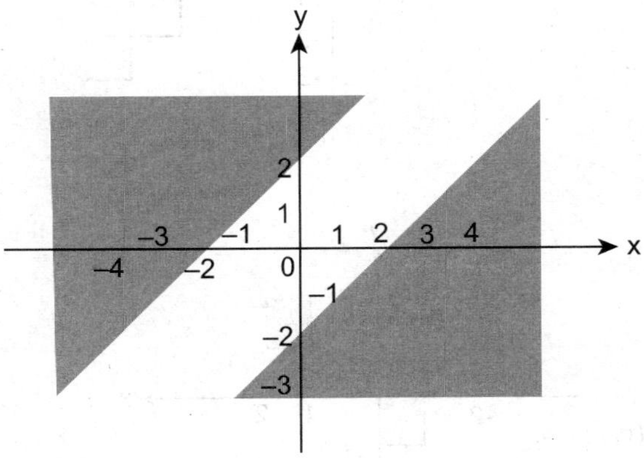

(f) 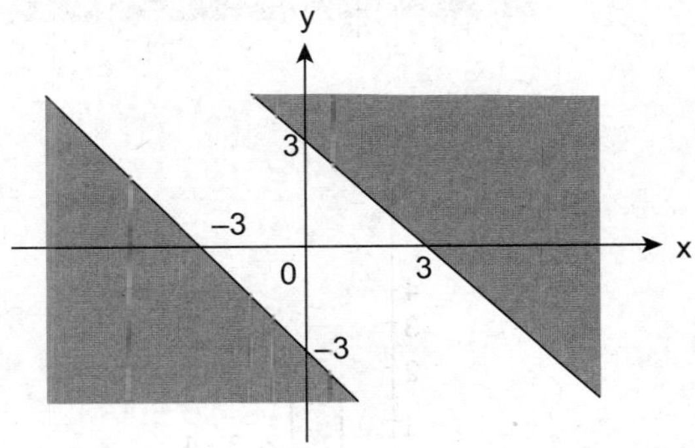

(g) 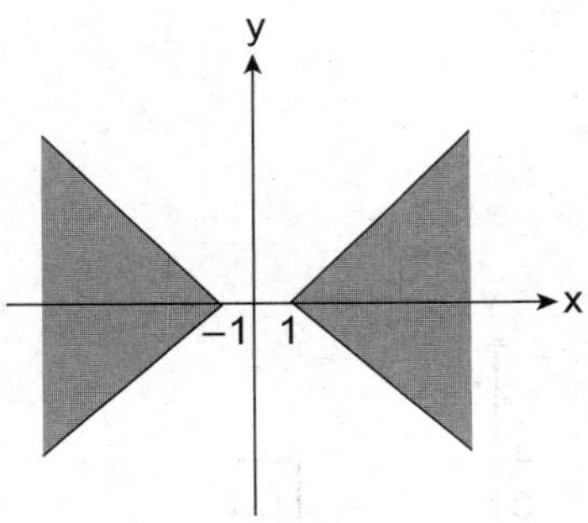

(h) 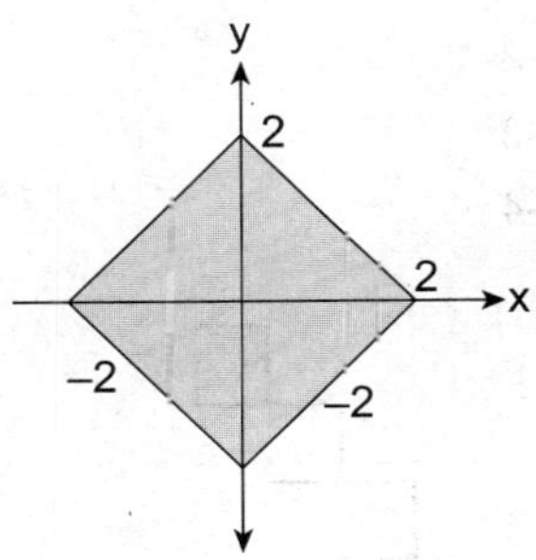

(i) 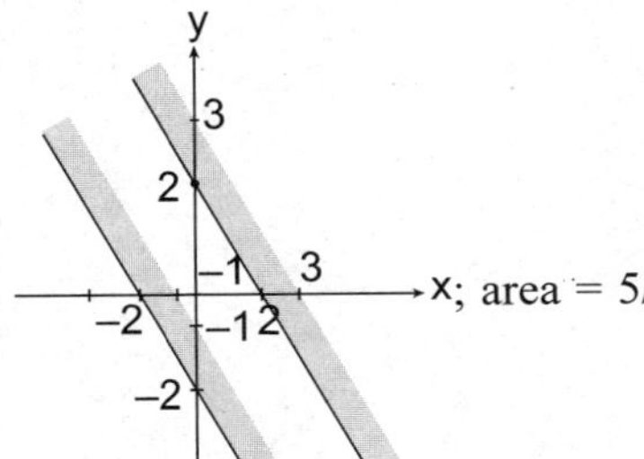

2. 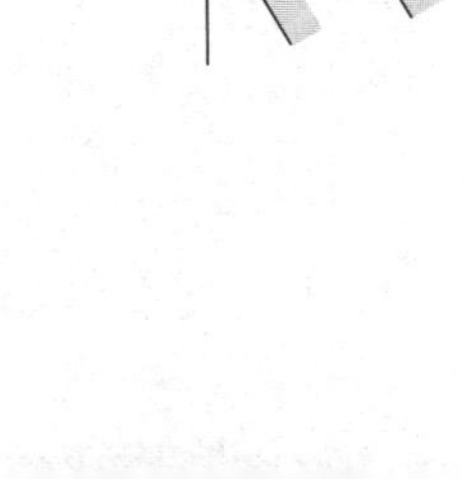

x; area = 5/2

3. (i)

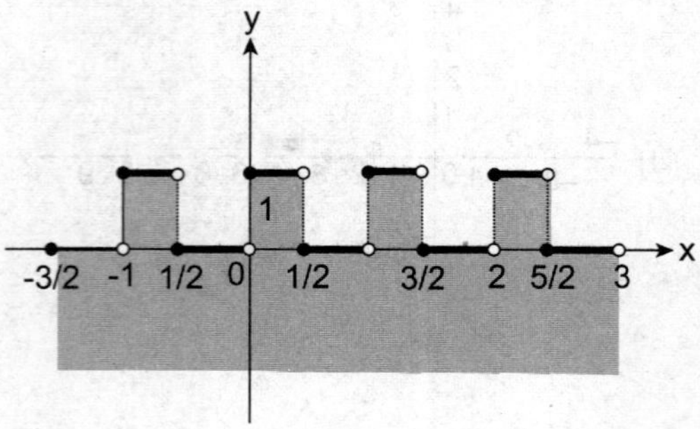

(ii)

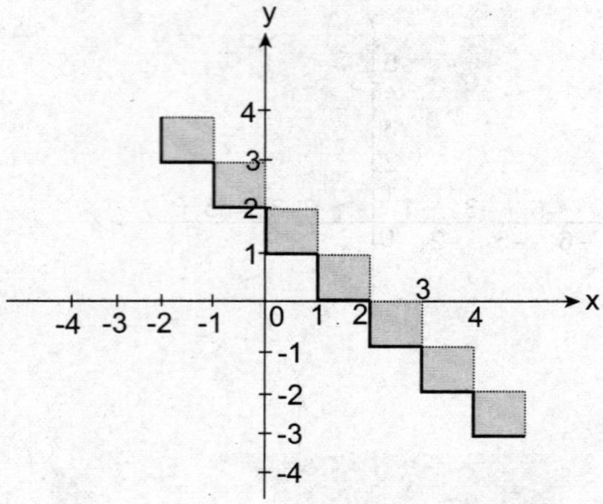

(iii)

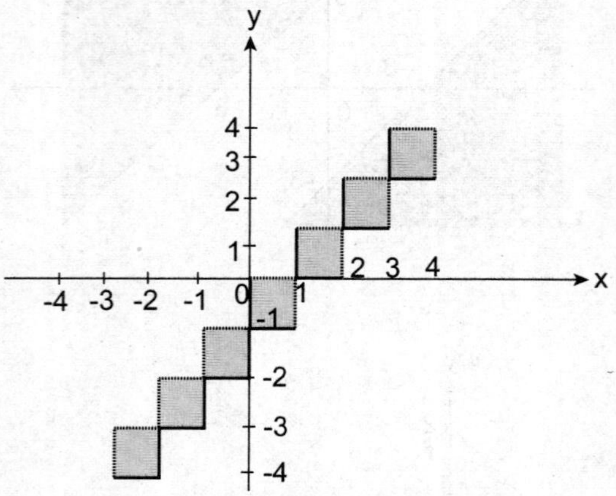

(iv)

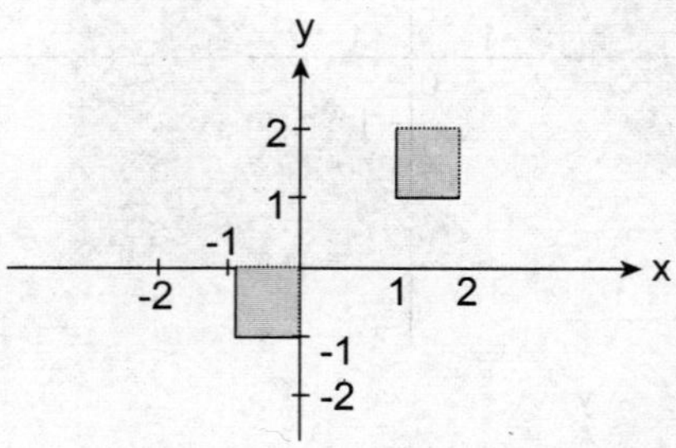

(v)

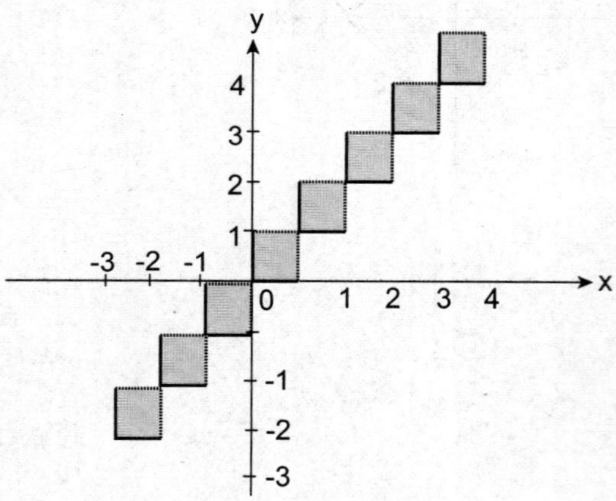

(vi)

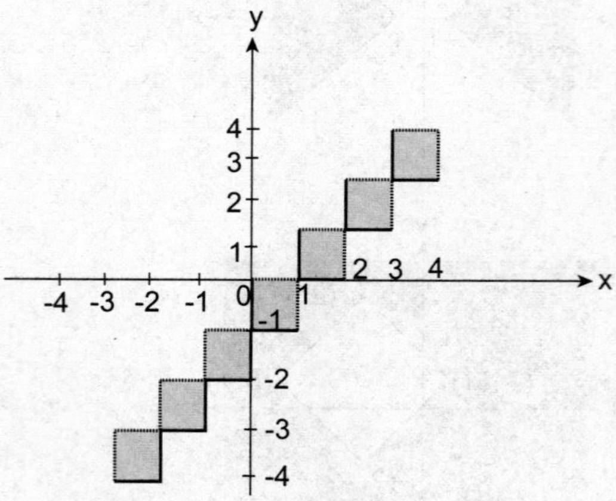

4.

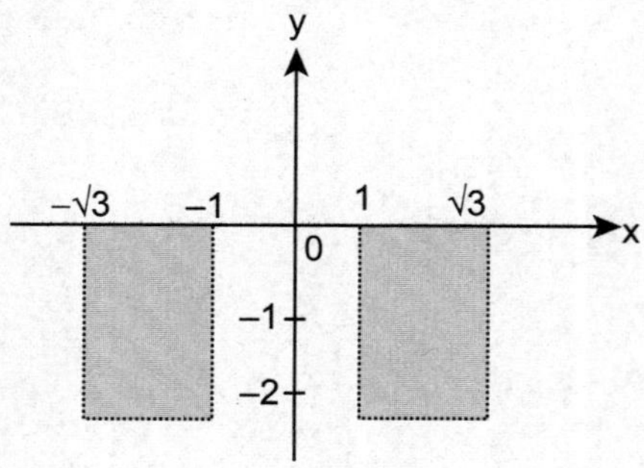

■ GRAPHS OF RECIPROCAL FUNCTION

In order to draw the graph of reciprocal of a function $f(x)$, it is necessary to keep in mind the following facts relating the output $f(x)$ and $\frac{1}{f(x)}$.

1. $\frac{1}{f(x)}$ is not defined when $f(x) = 0$. As it tends to $\pm\infty$ whenever $f(x)$ approaches to 0 respectively from positive/negative side.
   Therefore, the lines $x = \alpha$, where $f(\alpha) = 0$ (i.e., α is root of $f(x)$) are tangents to the curve $\frac{1}{f(x)}$ at $\pm\infty$ known as vertical asymptote of the function $\frac{1}{f(x)}$.
2. If $\lim_{x\to\pm\infty} f(x) = k$, then $y = 1/k$ will be the horizontal asymptote of the function $1/f(x)$.
3. $f(x)$ and $\frac{1}{f(x)}$ meet each other whenever $f(x) = \pm 1$.
4. The output of the function $f(x)$ and $\frac{1}{f(x)}$ have same sign, i.e., if $f(x)$ is positive/negative in an interval I; then $1/f(x)$ is also positive/negative in that interval.
5. As the function $f(x)$ and $1/f(x)$ have opposite monotonicity, therefore, as and when $f(x)$ increases/decreases, the reciprocal function $1/f(x)$ decreases/increases, respectively. Therefore, if $f(x)$ is small/big in magnitude at a point x_1, then $\frac{1}{f(x)}$ is big/small in magnitude at that point.
   Therefore, to obtain an approximate sketch of the function $1/f(x)$, we should follow the algorithm given below:

Step 1: Draw the graph of $f(x)$ and locate its roots (say α, β etc.) as well as the points where it takes the value ± 1 (say γ, δ etc.).

Step 2: Draw the vertical asymptotes $x = \alpha$, $x = \beta$ etc.

Step 3: From the points on $f(x)$ (say $(\gamma, 1)$), draw the curve $1/f(x)$, taking care of its monotonicity, so that it approaches to the neighbouring asymptotes.

Step 4: Find the $\lim_{x\to\pm\infty} \frac{1}{f(x)}$, (say it is '$k$'). Then $y = 1/k$ will be the horizontal asymptote of the function $1/f(x)$.

ILLUSTRATION 63: Sketch the graph of $y = 1/x$

SOLUTION: Graph of $y = x$ Graph of $y = 1/x$

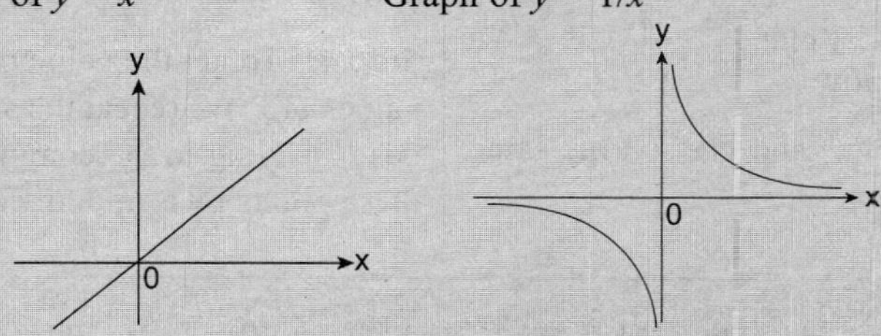

FIGURE 3.268

ILLUSTRATION 64: Sketch the graph of $y = \frac{1}{(x+1)(x)(x-2)}$.

SOLUTION: The graph of $y = (x + 1)(x)(x - 2)$ is as shown is in Figure 3.269.

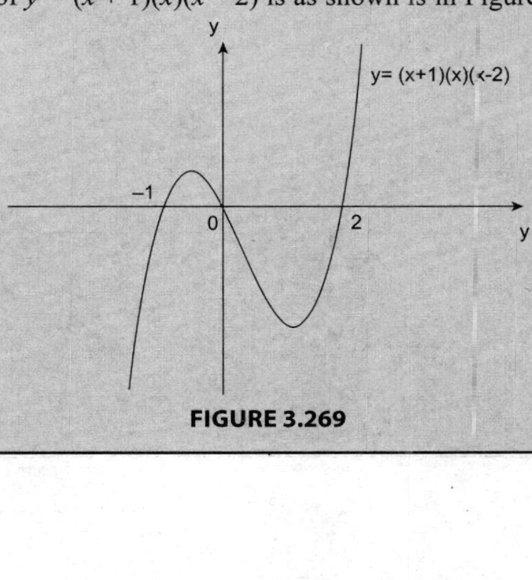

FIGURE 3.269

Hence, the graph of $y=\dfrac{1}{(x+1)(x)(x-2)}$ is as given in Figure 3.270.

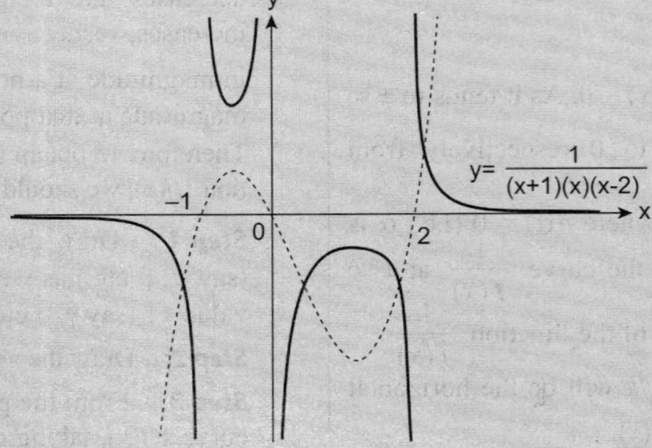

FIGURE 3.270

■ ADDITION OF GRAPHS

As we already know that the addition of two functions, $f(x)$ and $g(x)$, i.e., $y = f(x) + g(x)$ is defined for those values of x which lie in the domain of both the functions.

For the construction of the graph $y = f(x) + g(x)$, we follow the algorithm given below.

Step 1: We draw the graph of $f(x)$ and $g(x)$ on the same axes.

Step 2: At any x_0 lying in the common domain, we draw vertical arrows on the two functions, hence, getting the values of $f(x_0)$ and $g(x_0)$.

Step 3: We now draw a vertical arrow at the same x_0 with a height equal to $f(x_0) + g(x_0)$.

Step 4: To get the value of $y = f(x) + g(x)$ at several other values of x, we repeat the steps (2) and (3) for different values of x lying in the common domain, and thereby, joining these points by a smooth curve, we get the desired curve.

ILLUSTRATION 65: Construct the graph of $y = [x] + \{x\}$ using addition of graphs.

SOLUTION: Let us consider $y_1 = [x]$ and $y_2 = \{x\}$

Let us consider $y_1 = [x]$ and $y_2 = \{x\}$

Graph of $y_1 = [x]$

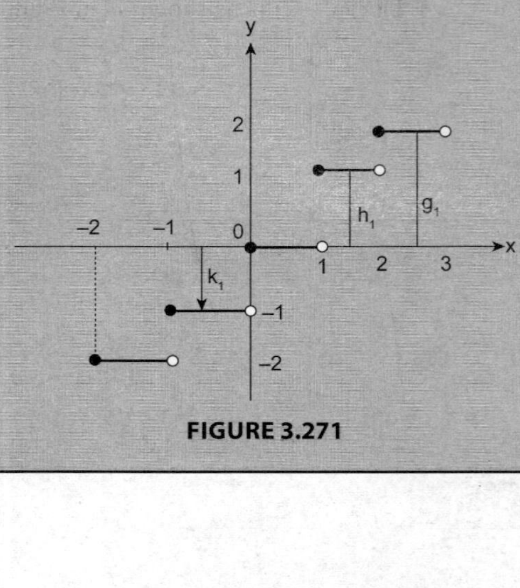

FIGURE 3.271

Graph of $y_2 = \{x\}$

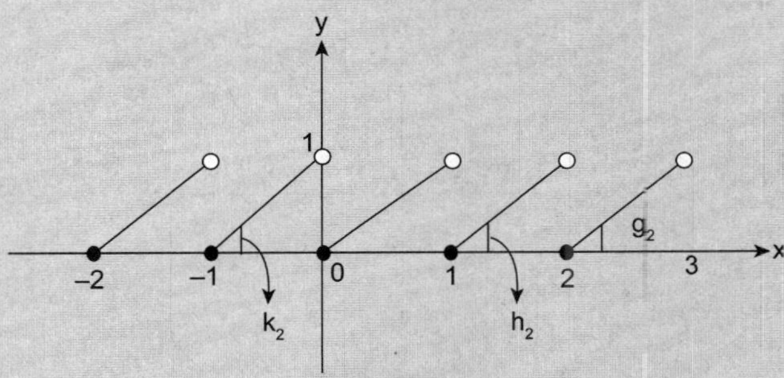

FIGURE 3.272

Adding the heights h_1 and h_2; g_1 and g_2; k_1 and k_2 obtained on the two different graphs, for some point x in the common domain, we get

Graph of $y = [x] + \{x\}$

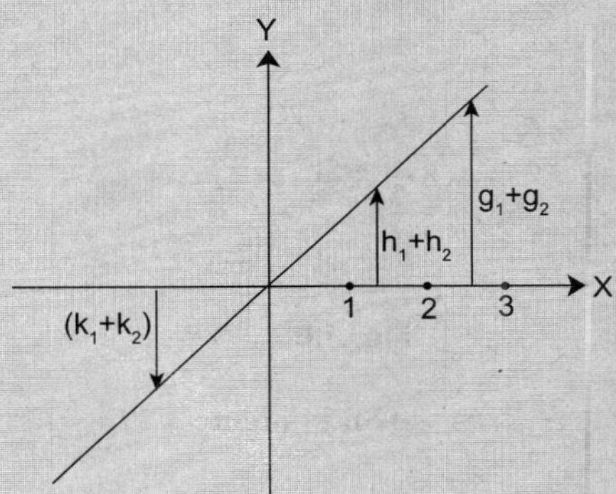

FIGURE 3.273

ILLUSTRATION 66: Using addition of graphs, draw the graphs of $y = x + \sin x$.

SOLUTION: The graph of $y = x$ is as shown in Figure 3.274.

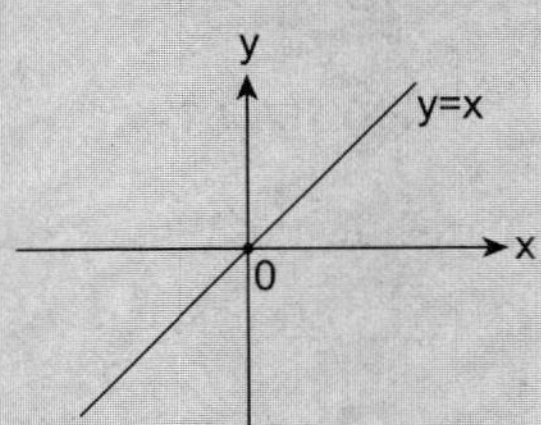

FIGURE 3.274

The graph of $y = \sin x$ is as shown in Figure 3.275.

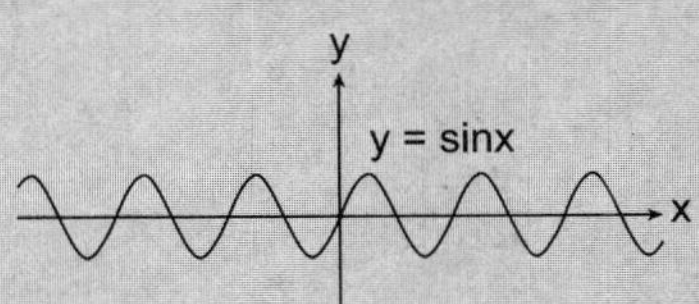

FIGURE 3.275

Hence, the graph of $y = x + \sin x$ is as shown in Figure 3.276.

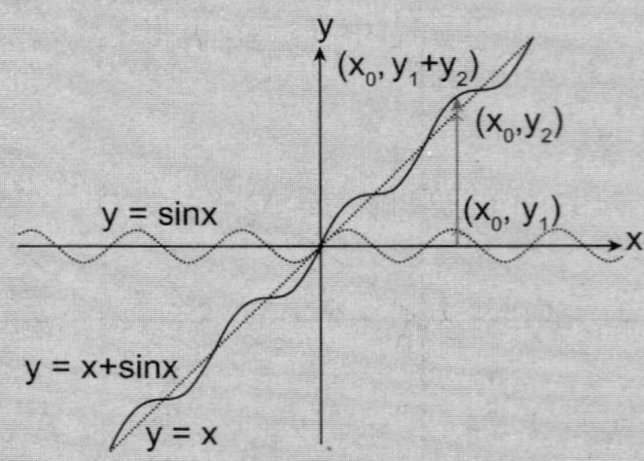

FIGURE 3.276

ILLUSTRATION 67: Draw the graphs of $y = e^x$ and $y = e^{-x}$, and hence, draw the graph of $y = e^x + e^{-x}$ and also the graph of $y = e^x - e^{-x}$.

SOLUTION: The graph of $y = e^x$ is as shown in Figure 3.277.

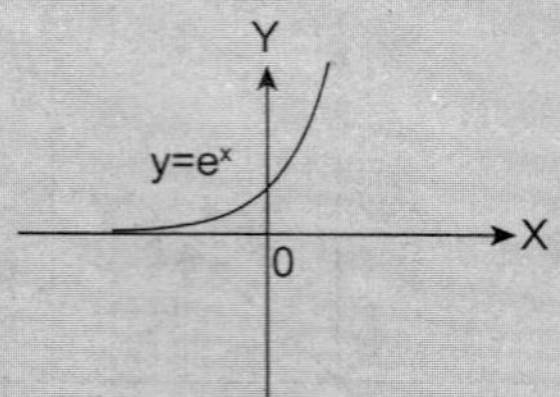

FIGURE 3.277

The graph of $y = e^{-x}$ is as shown in Figure 3.278.

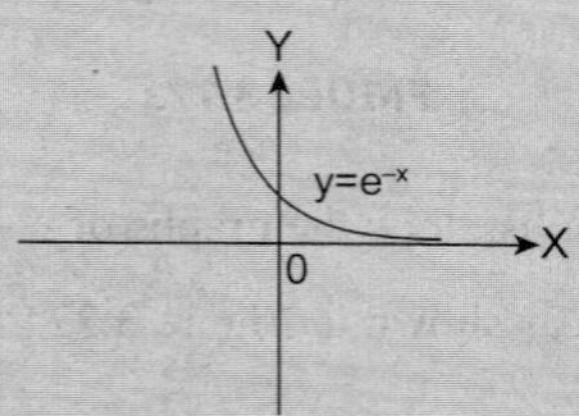

FIGURE 3.278

The graph of $y = -e^{-x}$ is as shown in Figure 3.279.

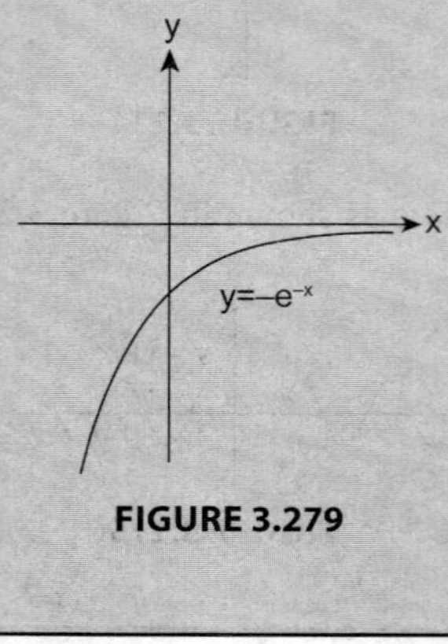

FIGURE 3.279

The graph of $y = e^x + e^{-x}$ is as shown in Figure 3.280.

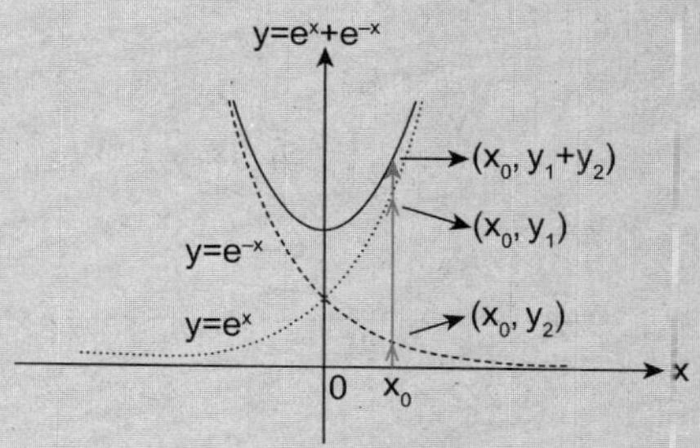

FIGURE 3.280

The graph of $y = e^x - e^{-x}$ is as shown in Figure 3.281.

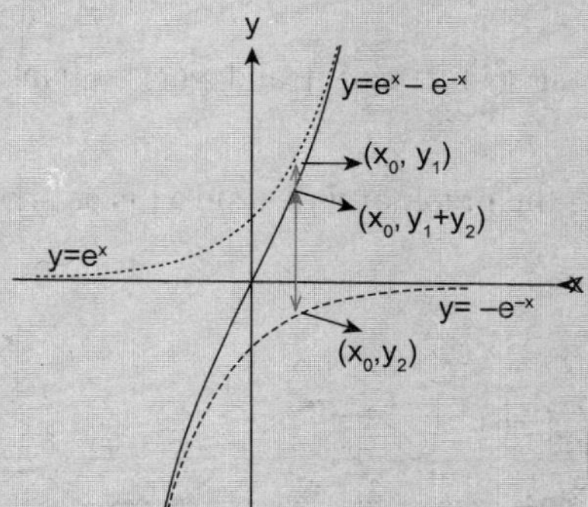

FIGURE 3.281

ILLUSTRATION 68: Draw the graph of $f(x) = x^2$ and $g(x) = 1/x$, and hence, $h(x) = f(x) + g(x)$.

SOLUTION: The graph of $y = x^2$ is as shown in Figure 3.282.

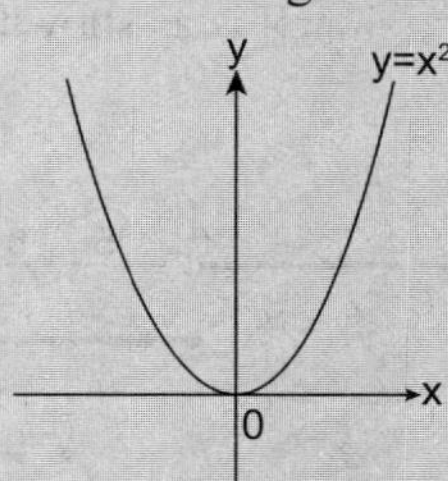

FIGURE 3.282

The graph of $y = 1/x$ is as shown in Figure 3.283.

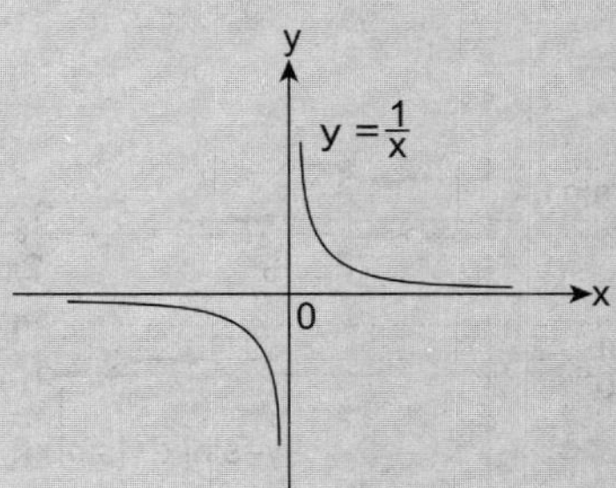

FIGURE 3.283

The graph of $y = x^2 + 1/x$ is as shown in Figure 3.284.

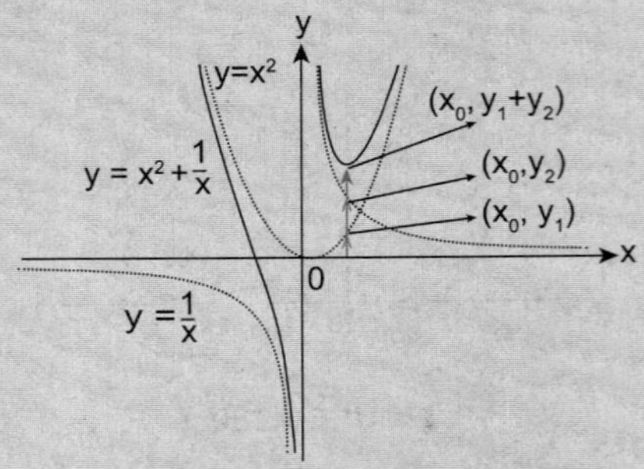

FIGURE 3.284

ILLUSTRATION 69: Draw the graph of $f(x) = \sin[x]$ and $g(x) = [\sin[x]]$, and hence, $h(x) = f(x) + g(x)$ for $x \in [0, 2\pi]$.

SOLUTION: We already know, the graph of $f(x) = \sin[x]$ is as shown in Figure 3.285.

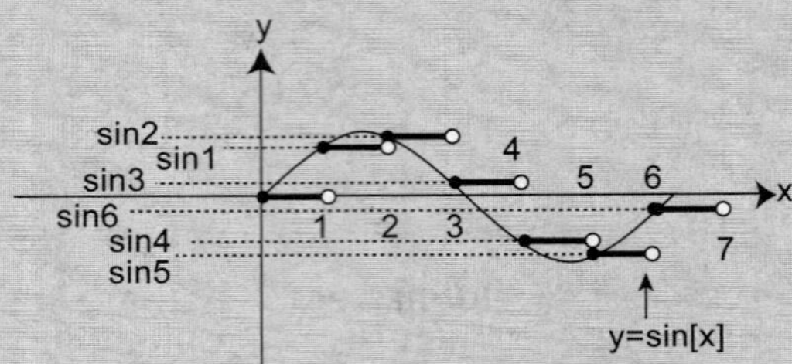

FIGURE 3.285

Also, the graph of $g(x) = [\sin[x]]$ is as shown in Figure 3.286.

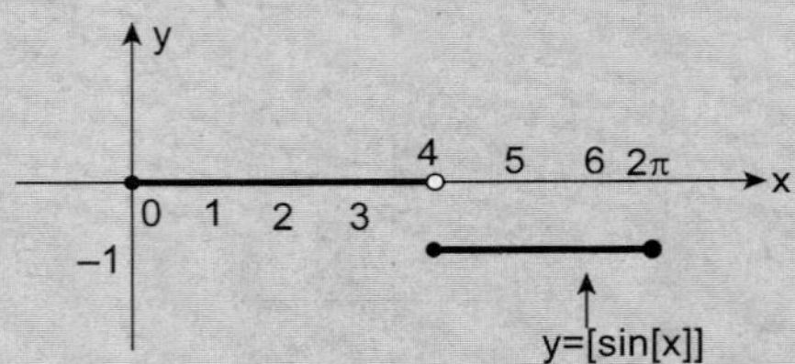

FIGURE 3.286

Now, the function $h(x) = f(x) + g(x) = \sin[x] + [\sin[x]]$ and its graph is as shown in Figure 3.287.

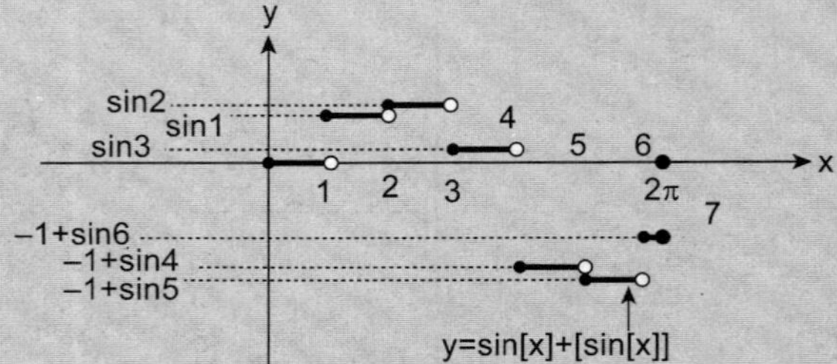

FIGURE 3.287

■ MULTIPLICATION OF GRAPHS

As we already know that the multiplication of two functions, $f(x)$ and $g(x)$, i.e., $y = f(x).\ g(x)$ is defined for those values of x which lie in the domain of both the functions. For the construction of the graph $y = f(x).\ g(x)$, we follow the algorithm given below.

Step 1: We draw the graph of $f(x)$ and $g(x)$ on the same axes.

Step 2: At any x_0 lying in the common domain, we draw vertical arrows on the two functions, hence, getting the values of $f(x_0)$ and $g(x_0)$.

Step 3: We now draw a vertical arrow at the same x_0 with a height equal to $f(x_0).\ g(x_0)$.

Step 4: To get the value of $y = f(x).\ g(x)$ at several other values of x, we repeat the steps (2) and (3) for different values of x lying in the common domain and thereby, joining these points by a smooth curve. we get the desired curve.

NOTE

As such it is not very easy to plot these graphs.

■ SPECIAL CASE OF ENVELOPED GRAPHS

When one of the functions is a trigonometric function like $\sin x$, $\cos x$, $|\sin x|$, etc.

That is, we wish to draw functions like $y = f(x) \sin x$, $y = f(x) \cos x$, $y = f(x)\,|\sin x|$, etc.

ILLUSTRATION 70: Construct the graph of the functions $y = x \sin x$

SOLUTION: We know that $-1 \le \sin x \le 1$ or we can say that $|\sin x| \le 1$.

Hence, $|x \sin x| \le |x|$.

It is obvious that $y = 0$ for the values $x = k\pi$, $k = 0, \pm 1, \pm 2, \ldots$ for which $\sin x = 0$. and so the graph of the function y crosses the positive x-axis at the point $x = k\pi$, $k \in 0, 2\ \forall\ k \in \mathbb{Z}$

Also, for $x > 0$, $|x \sin x| \le |x| \Rightarrow -x \le x \sin x \le x$.

Hence, for positive values of the independent variable 'x', the amplitude of the graph of the function y does not extend above the straight line $y = x$ or below the straight line $y = -x$, In this case, the points of the graph of the function y that correspond to the values of $x > 0$ for which $\sin x = \pm 1$, i.e., the graph $y = x.\ \sin x$ touches the graph $y = \pm\, x$ at the points where

$y = \sin x = \pm 1$, i.e., at $x = (4n+1)\dfrac{\pi}{2}, n \in W$.

Also, for $x < 0$, $|x \sin x| \le |x| \Rightarrow x \le x \sin x \le -x$.

Hence, for negative values of the independent variable 'x', the amplitude of the graph of the function y does not extend above the straight line $y = -x$ or below the straight line $y = x$. In this case, the points of the graph of the function y that correspond to the values of $x < 0$ for which $\sin x = \pm 1$ i.e., the graph $y = x.\ \sin x$ touches the graph $y = \pm\, x$ at the points where

$y = \sin x = \pm 1$ i.e., at $x = (4n+1)\dfrac{\pi}{2}, n \in \mathbb{Z} - W$.

The graph of $y = x$ is given as in Figure 3.288.

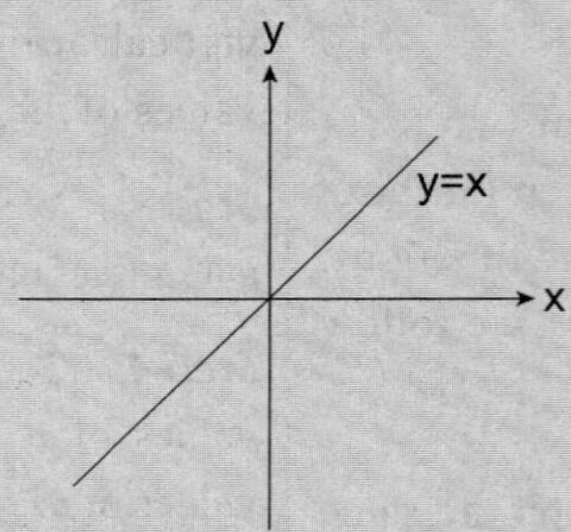

FIGURE 3.288

Now, creating an envelope whose boundaries are given by $y = \pm x$, we get the envelope as

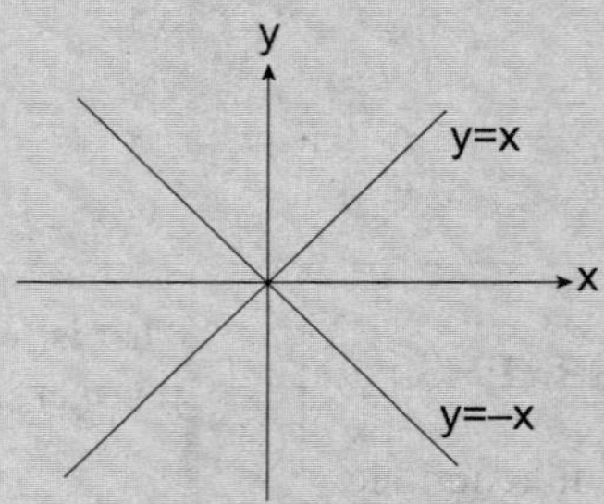

FIGURE 3.289

Now, as discussed earlier, the graph of $y = x \sin x$ will be contained in/on the graph $y = \pm x$. Hence, the graph of $y = x \sin x$ will be as shown in Figure 3.290.

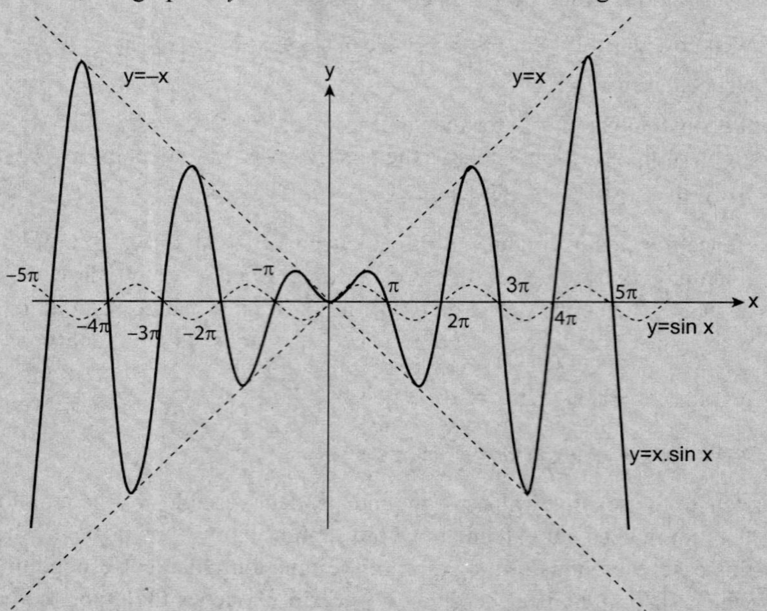

FIGURE 3.290

ILLUSTRATION 71: Construct the graph of the functions $y = (1.1)^x \sin x$.

SOLUTION: The graph of $y = (1.1)^x$ is as shown in Figure 3.291

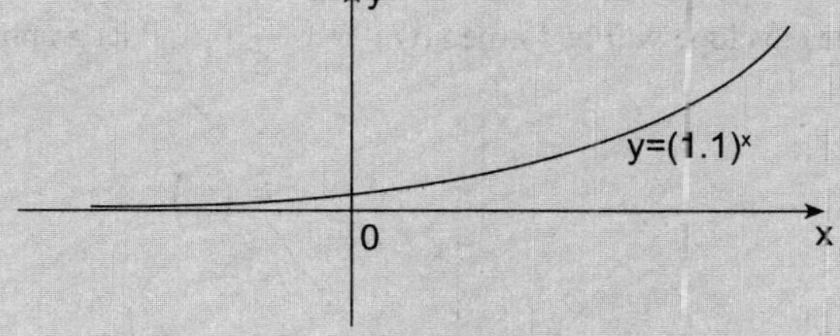

FIGURE 3.291

Hence, the envelope will be formed by $y = \pm\,(1.1)^x$, and its graph will be shown in Figure 3.292.

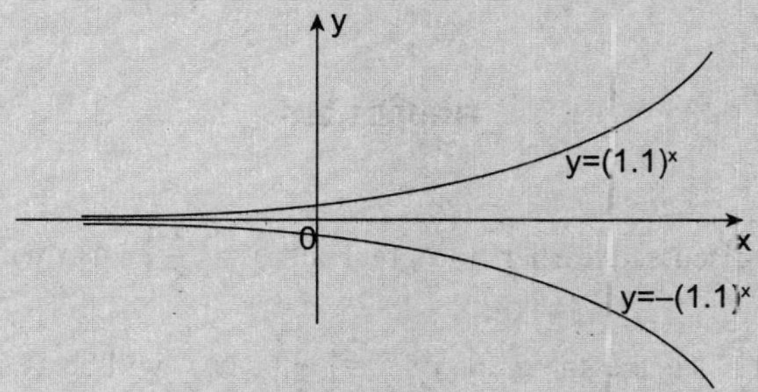

FIGURE 3.292

Now, as discussed earlier, the graph of $y = (1.1)^x \sin x$ will be contained in/on the graph $y = \pm\,(1.1)^x$. Hence, the graph of $y = (1.1)^x \sin x$ is as shown in Figure 3.293.

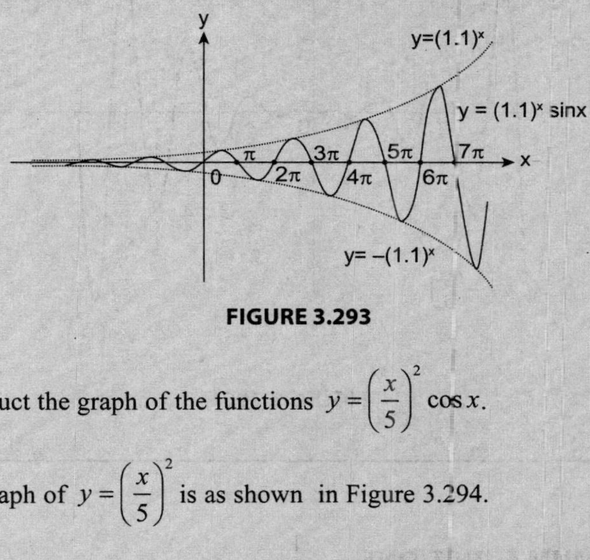

FIGURE 3.293

ILLUSTRATION 72: Construct the graph of the functions $y = \left(\frac{x}{5}\right)^2 \cos x$.

SOLUTION: The graph of $y = \left(\frac{x}{5}\right)^2$ is as shown in Figure 3.294.

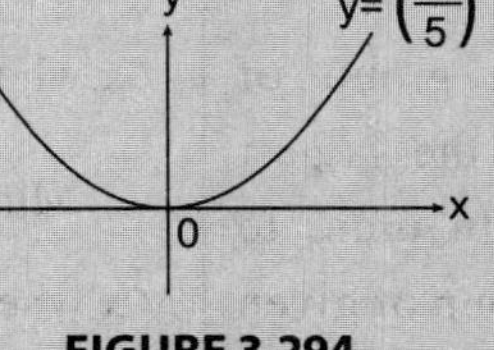

FIGURE 3.294

Hence, the envelope will be formed by $y = \pm\left(\frac{x}{5}\right)^2$, and its graph will be as shown in Figure 3.295.

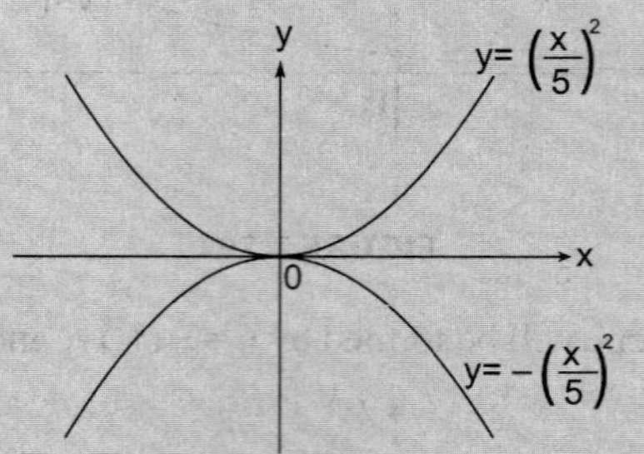

FIGURE 3.295

Now, as discussed earlier, the graph of $y = \left(\frac{x}{5}\right)^2 \cos x$ will be contained in/on the graph $y = \pm\left(\frac{x}{5}\right)^2$. Hence, the graph of $y = \left(\frac{x}{5}\right)^2 \cos x$ will be as shown in Figure 3.296.

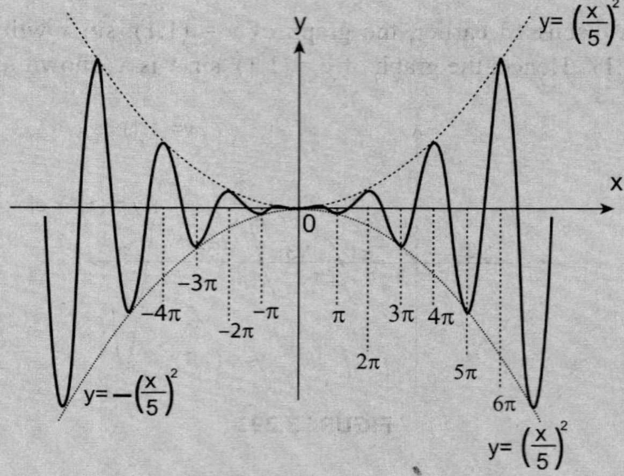

FIGURE 3.296

■ MAXIMUM AND MINIMUM FUNCTIONS

Maximum/minimum function of a given group of functions is that function which takes up the largest value/least value in the common domain. In order to select maxima/minimum function out of a group of given functions we can use the following definition:

$$\text{Max}\ \{f(x), g(x)\} = \frac{f(x)+g(x)+|f(x)-g(x)|}{2} = f(x)$$

$\forall\ x$ where $f(x) \geq g(x)$ and $g(x)\ \forall\ x$ where $f(x) \leq g(x)$

$$\text{Min.}\ \{f(x), g(x)\} = \frac{f(x)+g(x)-|f(x)-g(x)|}{2} = g(x)$$

$\forall\ x$ where $f(x) \geq g(x)$ and $f(x)\ \forall\ x$ where $f(x) \leq g(x)$

Above definition can also be extended to group of more than two functions.

ILLUSTRATION 73: Let $h(x)$ = max. $\{x, x^2\}$. Then write the equivalent definition of $f(x)$.

SOLUTION: Given $f(x) = x$ and $g(x) = x^2$ and sketching their graphs as shown in Figure 3.297.

In order to find the maximum value of two functions

$f(x)$ and $g(x)$, we get $h(x) = \begin{cases} x^2; x \le 0 \text{ or } x \ge 1 \\ x\ ;\ 0 \le x \le 1 \end{cases}$

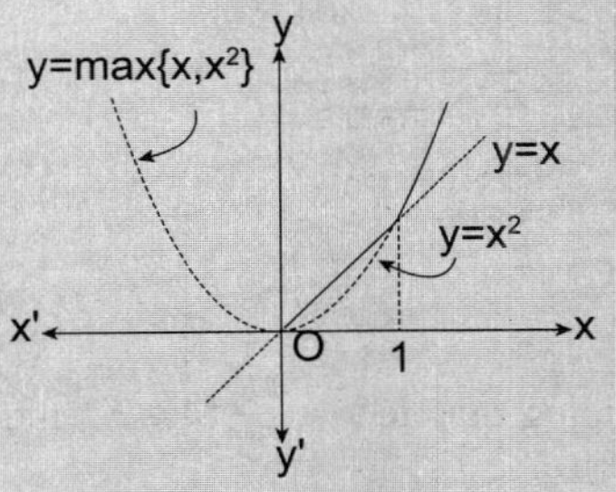

FIGURE 3.297

ILLUSTRATION 74: Sketch the graph of the following functions:

(a) y = max.$(\sin x, \cos x)$; $\forall x \in \left[-\pi, \frac{3\pi}{2}\right]$ (b) y = max. $\{\tan x, \cot x\}$

SOLUTION: (a) To sketch the graph of y = max $\{\sin x, \cos x\}$ $\forall x \in \left[-\pi, \frac{3\pi}{2}\right]$ draw the graph of $y = \sin x$ and $y = \cos x$ in described domain and obtaining their points of intersections, i.e., $x = \frac{-3\pi}{4}, \frac{\pi}{4}, \frac{5\pi}{4}$ and considering the upper boundary for maximum function, we get

$$y = \begin{cases} \sin x; & x \in \left[-\pi, -\frac{3\pi}{4}\right) \\ \cos x; & x \in \left[-\frac{3\pi}{4}, \frac{\pi}{4}\right) \\ \sin x; & x \in \left[\frac{\pi}{4}, \frac{5\pi}{4}\right) \\ \cos x; & x \in \left[\frac{5\pi}{4}, \frac{3\pi}{2}\right] \end{cases}$$

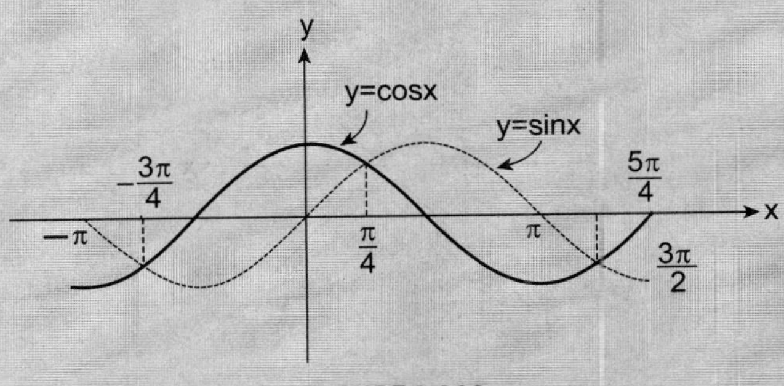

FIGURE 3.298

(b) $y = \max\{\tan x, \cot x\}$. Of course the given function is periodic with period π as both $\tan x$ and $\cot x$ are periodic with period π.

Thus, sketching $y = \tan x$ and $y = \cot x$ both, we get

$$y = \begin{cases} \cot x; & x \in \left(0 < x < \dfrac{\pi}{4}\right) \\ \tan x; & x \in \left[\dfrac{\pi}{4} < x < \dfrac{\pi}{2}\right) \\ \cot x; & x \in \left(\dfrac{\pi}{2} < x < \dfrac{3\pi}{4}\right) \\ \tan x; & x \in \left[\dfrac{3\pi}{4} < x < \pi\right) \end{cases}$$ and then it repeats periodically with period π.

It is worth noticing that at $x = \dfrac{n\pi}{2}; n \in \mathbb{Z}$, the given function is not defined.

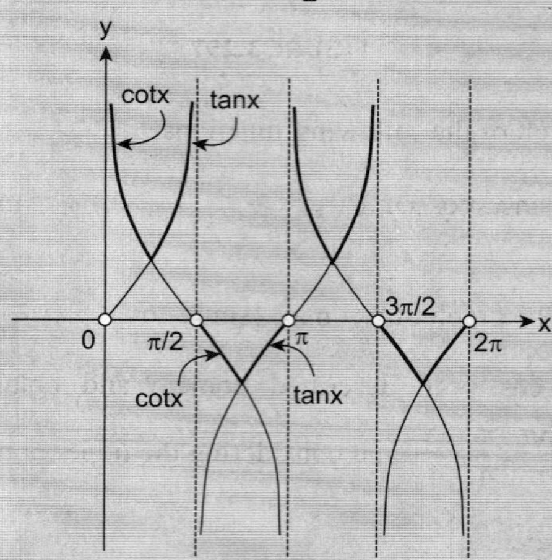

FIGURE 3.299

ILLUSTRATION 75: Plot the curve $y = \max\{|x| + |y|, 3|x| - |y|\}$

SOLUTION: ***Case I:*** If $|x| + |y| \geq 3|x| - |y|$, then $2|y| \geq 2|x|$

$\Rightarrow$ $|y| \geq |x|$ and the corresponding region could be plotted as shown in Figure 3.300.

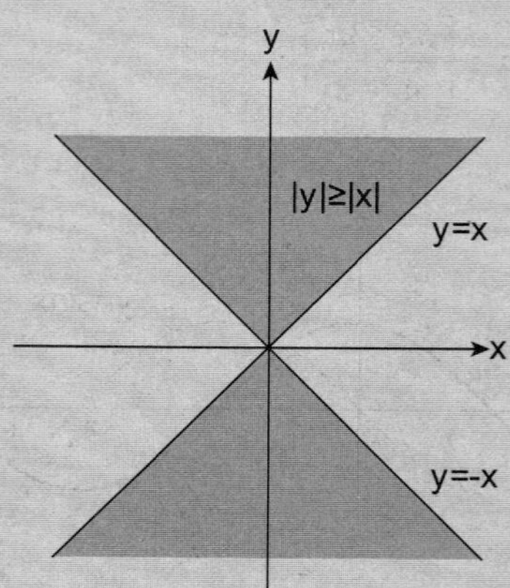

FIGURE 3.300

And in that region, we have $y = |x| + |y|$

Case I: $y \geq 0$

$\Rightarrow y = |x| + y \Rightarrow |x| = 0 \Rightarrow x = 0$

Case II: $y < 0 \Rightarrow |y| = -y \Rightarrow y = |x| - y$

$\Rightarrow y = \frac{|x|}{2}$ not possible in the given region.

$\therefore$ The curve $y = |x| + |y|$ is non-negative infinite segment of y-axis.

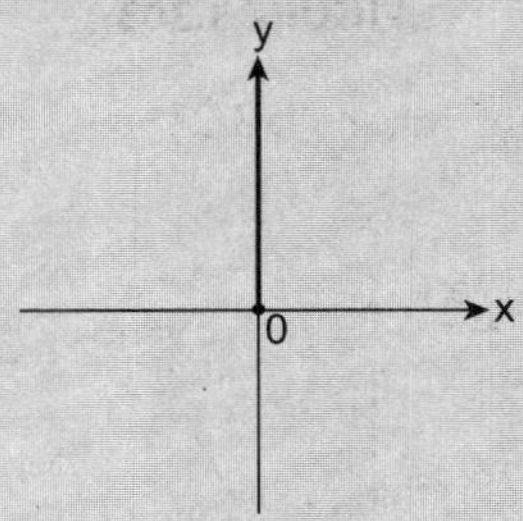

FIGURE 3.301

Case II: When $|x| + |y| \leq 3|x| - |y| \Rightarrow 2|y| \leq 2|x| \Rightarrow |y| \leq |x|$

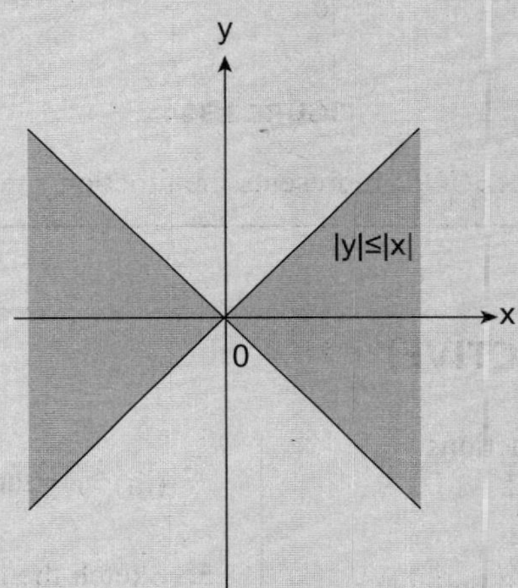

FIGURE 3.302

And in this region, we must equate $y = 3|x| - |y|$.

Case II: ***(a)*** when $y \geq 0 \Rightarrow y = 3|x| - y \Rightarrow 2y = 3|x| \Rightarrow y = \frac{3|x|}{2}$

Which is impossible for $|x| > 0$ as $|y| \leq |x|$

Thus, the only point satisfying $y = 3|x| - |y|$ and $y \geq 0$ is $(0, 0)$

Case II (b) When $y < 0 \Rightarrow y = 3|x| - (-y) \Rightarrow 3|x| = 0 \Rightarrow x = 0$

$\Rightarrow |x| = 0$, but $|y| \leq |x| \Rightarrow |y| \leq 0$, impossible as $y < 0 \Rightarrow |y| > 0$

$\therefore$ Thus, the given shaded region could have no point satisfying the inequalities

Hence,the graph of $y = \max\{|x| + |y|, 3|x| - |y|\}$ is shown in Figure 3.300, i.e., non-negative infinite segment of y-axis.

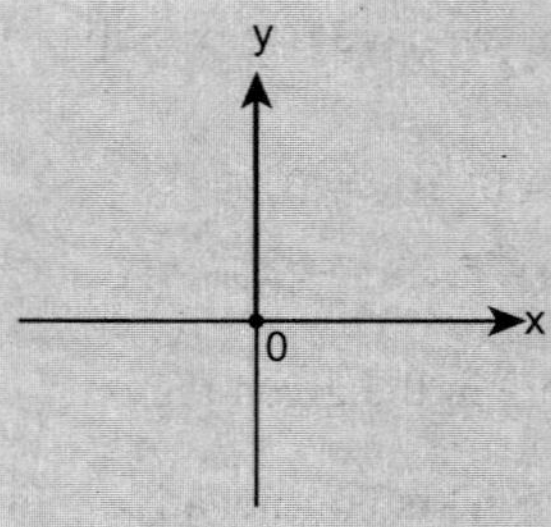

FIGURE 3.303

ILLUSTRATION 76: Draw the curve $y = \min.\ \{e^x, e^{-x+1}, 3/2\}$

SOLUTION:

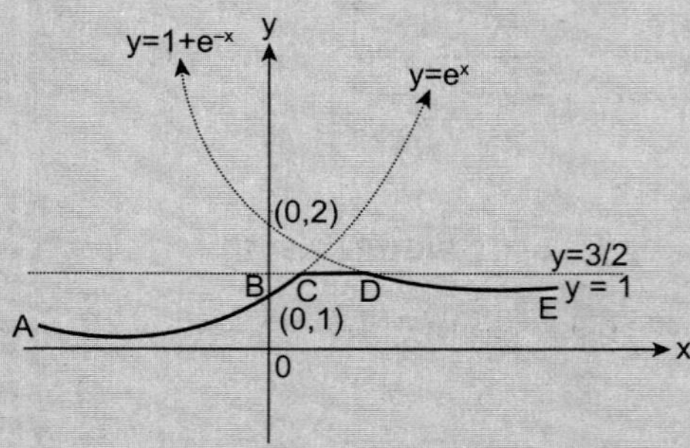

FIGURE 3.304

The dark curve ($ABCDE$) represents the function $y = \min.\ \{e^x, 1 + e^{-x}, 3/2\}$

TEXTUAL EXERCISE–5: (SUBJECTIVE)

1. Sketch the graph of the following functions:
   (i) $y = \dfrac{x-5}{x+3}$ (ii) $y = \dfrac{3x-1}{x+2}$

2. Construct the graph of the following functions:
   (i) $y = \dfrac{2}{|x-1|-2}$ (ii) $y = \dfrac{|x-2|}{|x|-2}$
   (iii) $y = 2 - \dfrac{4}{|x-1|}$

3. Draw the graph of following functions:
   (i) $y = \max\ \{2 - x, 2 + x, 5\}$
   (ii) $y = max\ \{|x|, |x - 4|, 2 - |x - 2|\}$
   (iii) $y = min\left\{e^{2x}, \dfrac{1}{2}, \left(\dfrac{1}{7} + e^{-x}\right)\right\}$

4. Construct the graph of the following functions:
   (i) $y = \dfrac{x^4+4}{x^2}$
   (ii) $y = \sec x + \dfrac{1}{x^2}, -\dfrac{\pi}{2} < x < \dfrac{\pi}{2}$
   (iii) $y = \tan x + \dfrac{1}{x}, -\dfrac{\pi}{2} < x < \dfrac{\pi}{2}$

5. Sketch the graph of the following function:
   (a) $y = |x|\ \cos^2 x$
   (b) $y = \dfrac{3\sin \pi x}{2x}$
   (c) $y = \sqrt{-x}\ \sin\left(\dfrac{1}{x}\right)$

6. Sketch the following curves and show their relative nature on same graph sheet:
   (i) $y = \dfrac{1}{x}$ and $y = \dfrac{1}{x^2}$
   (ii) $y = \dfrac{1}{(x-1)(x-3)}$ and $y = \dfrac{1}{x(x+2)}$
   (iii) $y = \dfrac{1}{x^2+1}$ and $y = \dfrac{x-1}{x+1}$

7. Using general concept of curve sketching draw the following curves:

(a) $y = \dfrac{x^2 - 1}{x^2 + 1}$ (b) $y = \dfrac{2x}{x^2 + 1}$

(c) $y = \dfrac{x^2 - 1}{x^2 + 2}$

8. Sketch the following:

(i) $y = \max(x, 1 - x)$
(ii) $y = \max(|x|, |x - 1|)$
(iii) $y = \max(x, x^3)$
(iv) $y = \max(\sin x, \cos x)$
(v) $y = \min(\sin x, \cos x)$
(vi) $y = \max(x, x^2)$
(vii) $y = \min(x, x^2)$
(xiii) $y = \max(|x - 1|, |x|, |x + 1|)$
(xiv) $y = \min(|x - 1|, |x|, |x + 1|)$
(xv) $y = \min(|\sin x|, |\cos x|, 1/2)$
(xvi) $y = \max(\sin x, \cos x, 1/2)$
(xvii) $y = \max(x - [x], -x - [-x])$
(xviii) $f(x) = \min(x - [x], -x - [-x])$
(xix) $y = \min(|x| + |y|, |x| - |y|)$
(xx) $y = \max(|x| + |y|, |x| - |y|)$
(xxi) $y = \max(|x|, |y|)$
(xxii) $\min(|x|, |y|) = 1$

Answer Keys

1. (i)

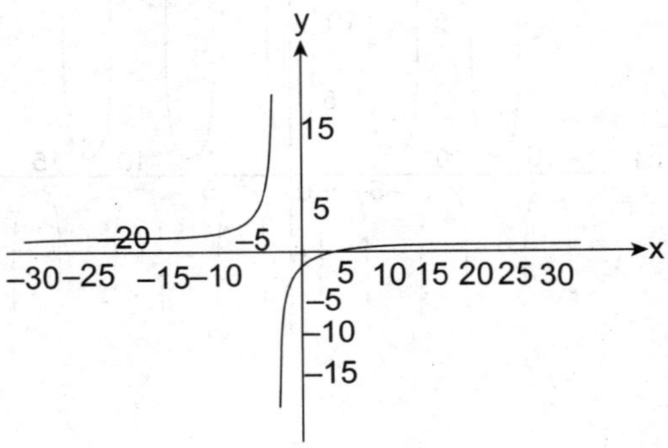

(ii)

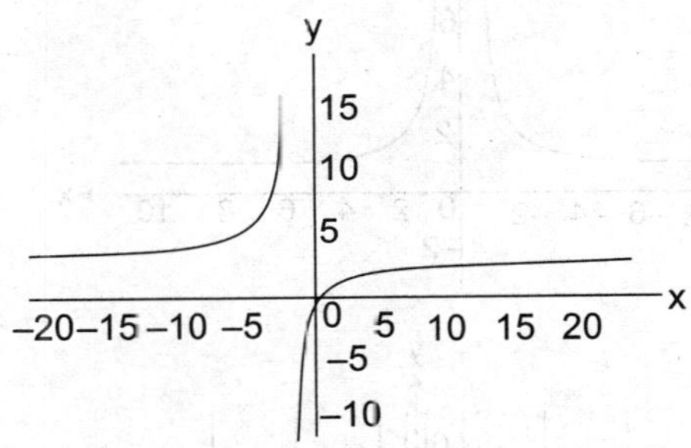

2. (i)

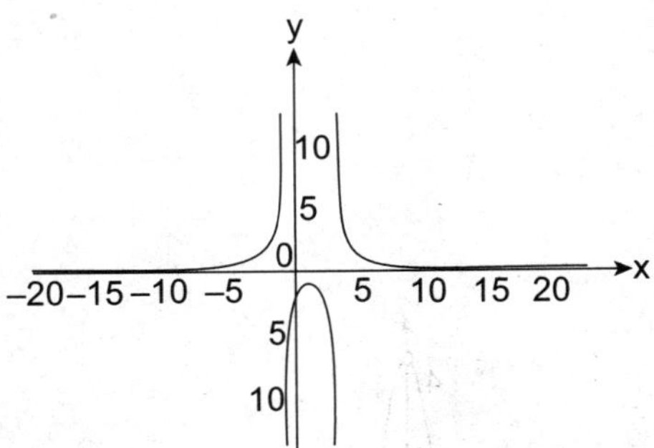

(ii)

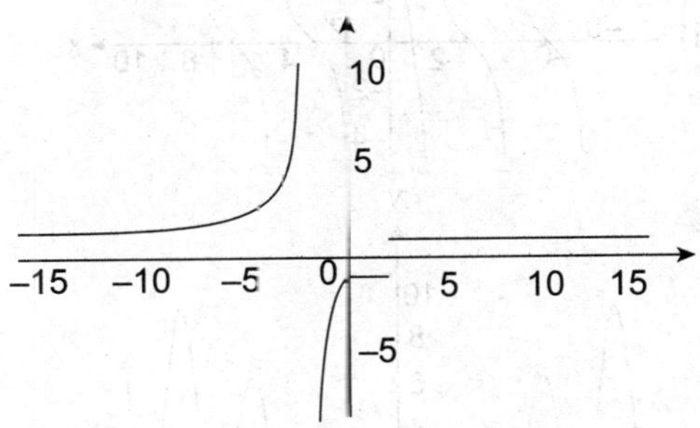

(iii)

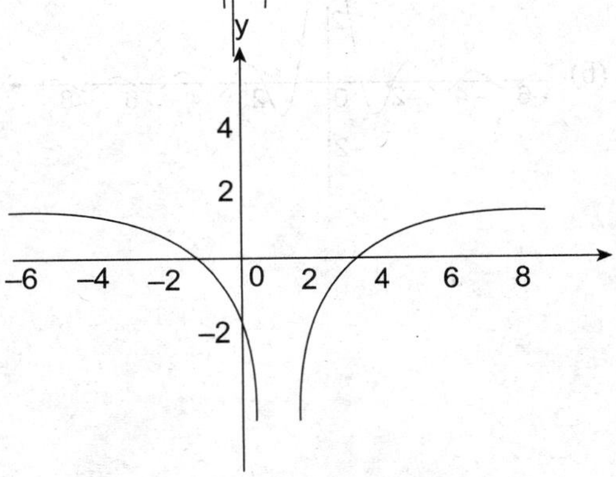

3. (i)

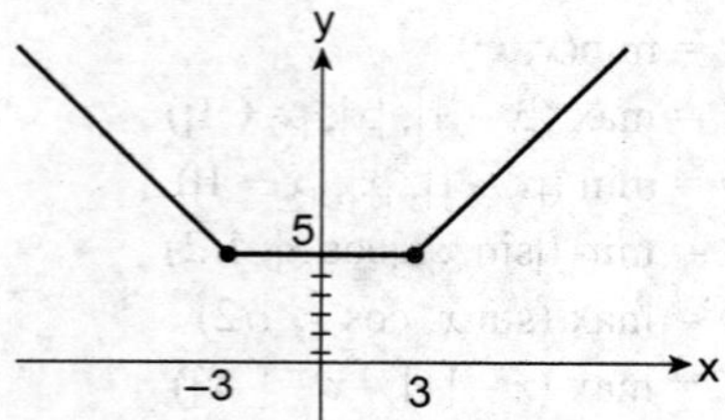

(ii)

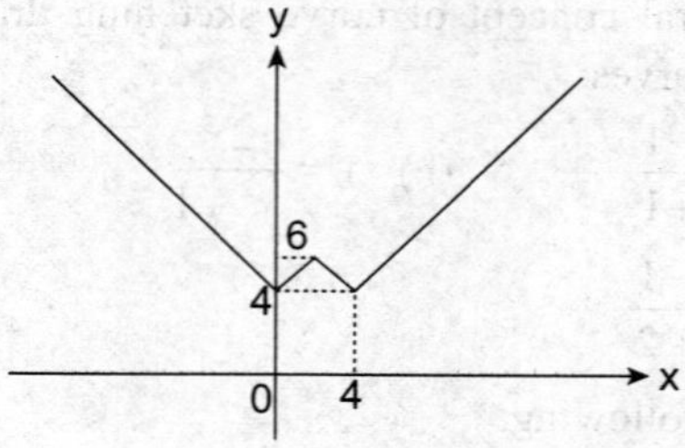

(iii)

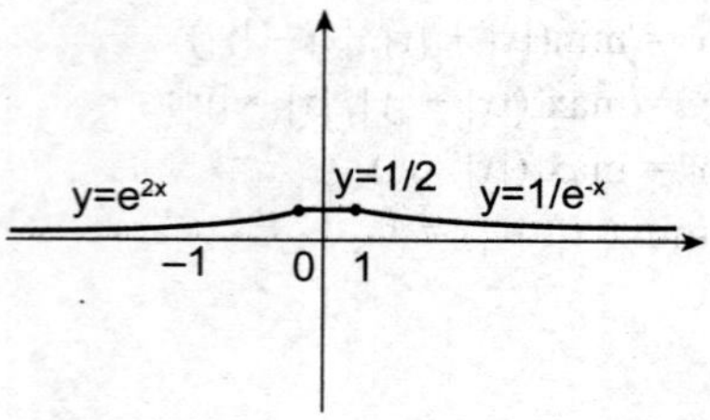

4. (i)

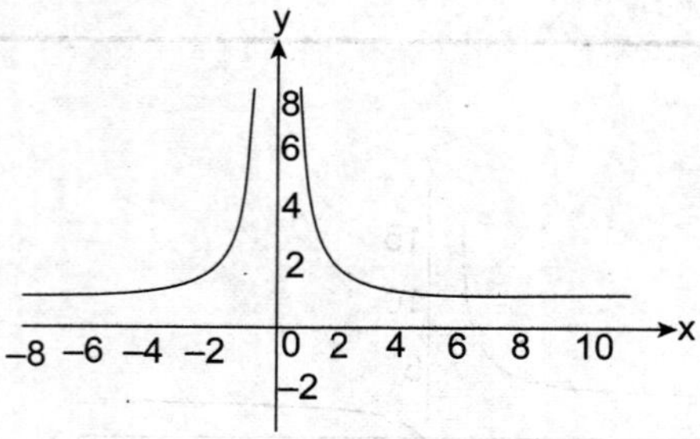

(ii)

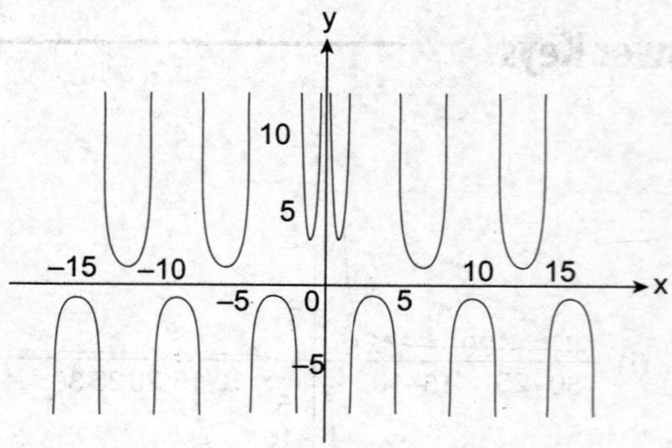

(iii)

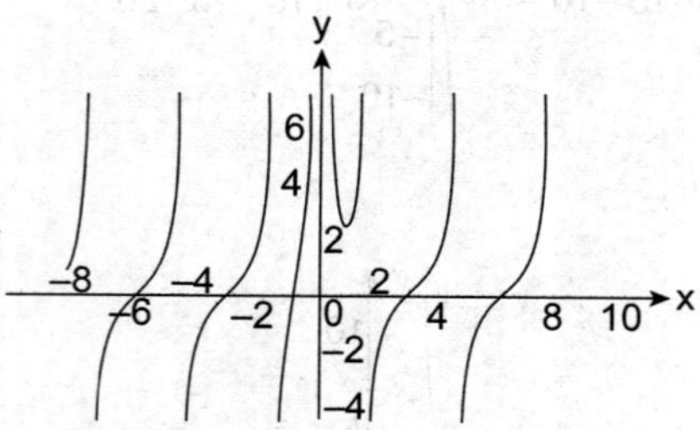

5. (a)

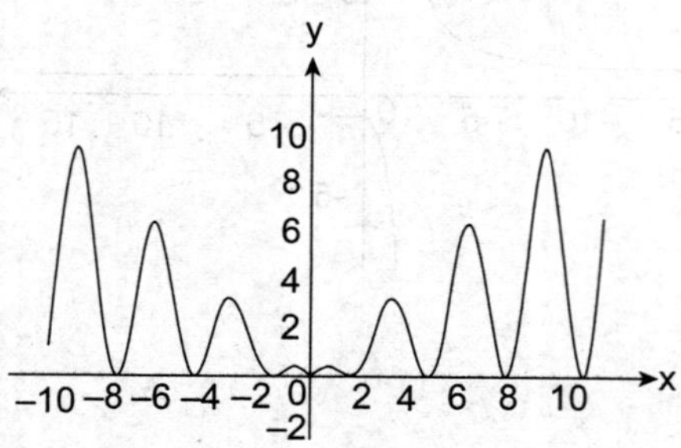

(b)

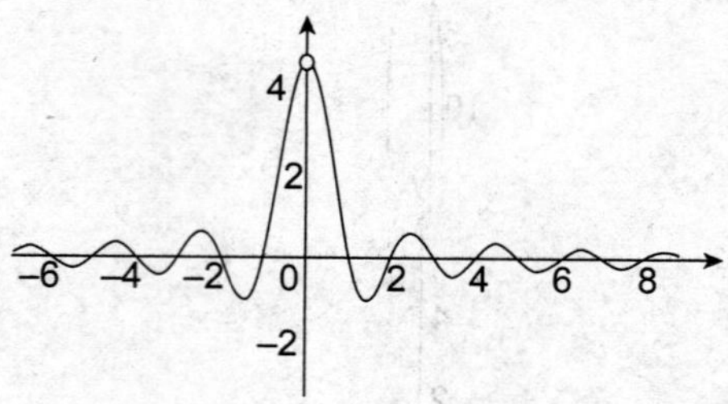

(c)

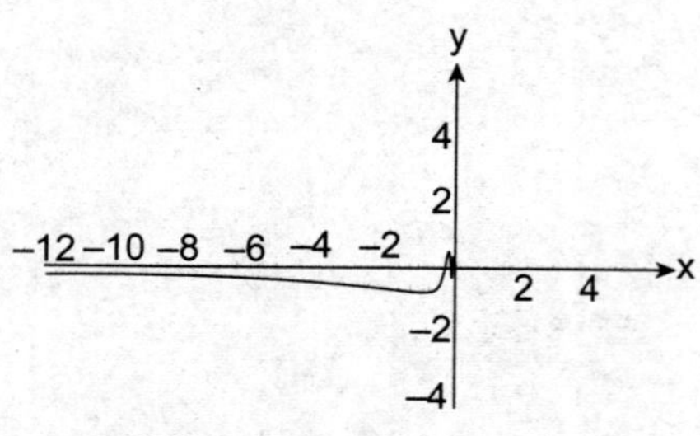

6. (i)

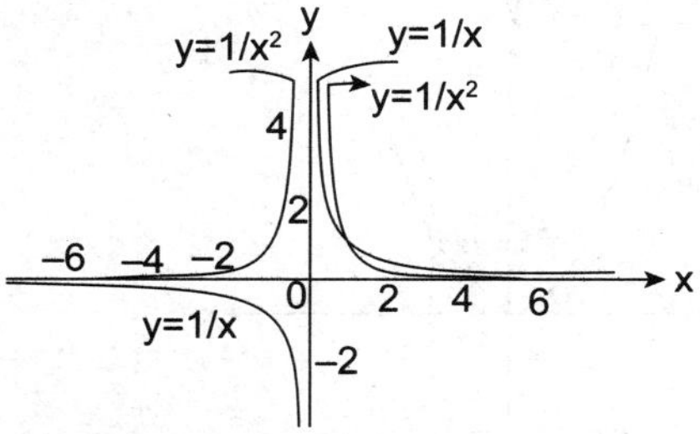

(ii)

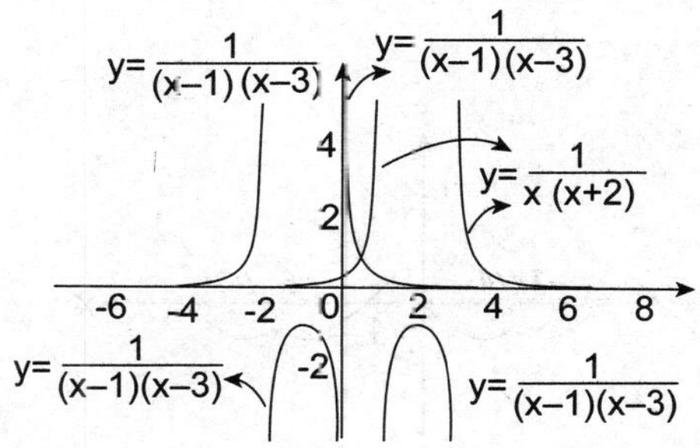

(iii)

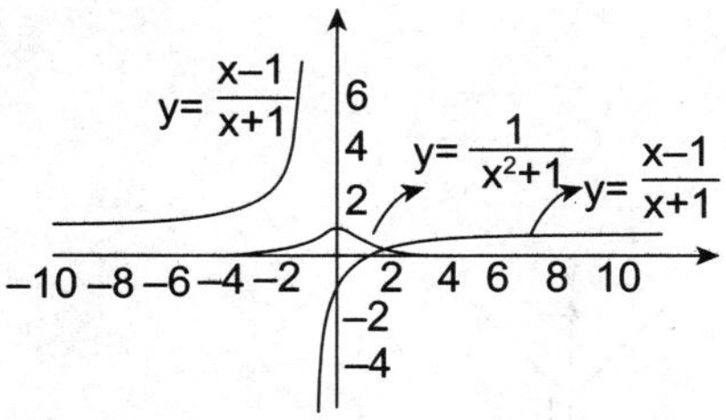

7. (a)

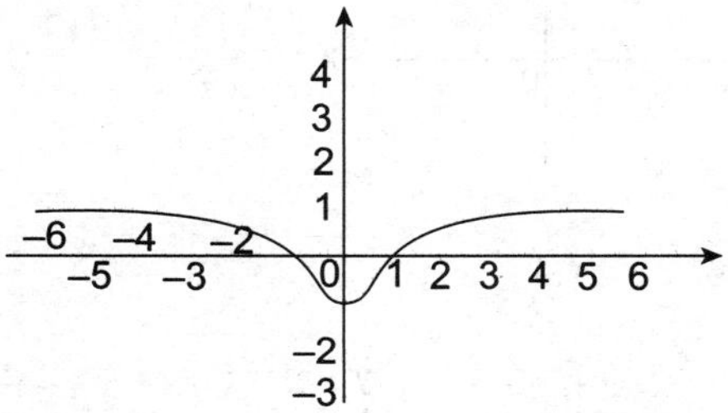

(b)

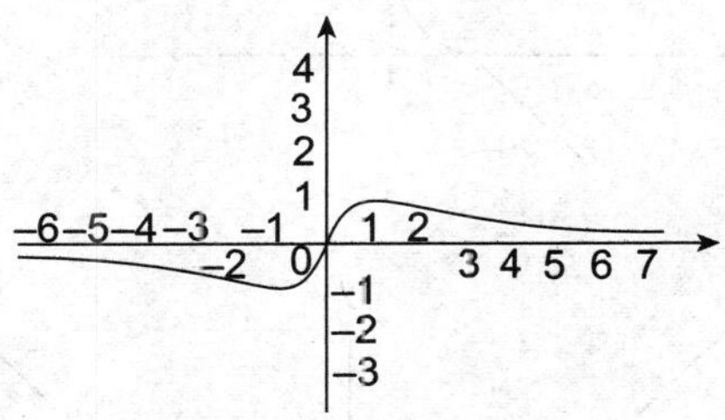

(c)

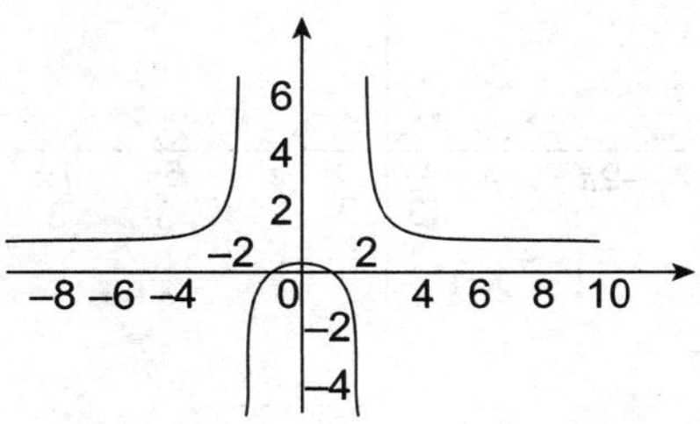

8. (i)

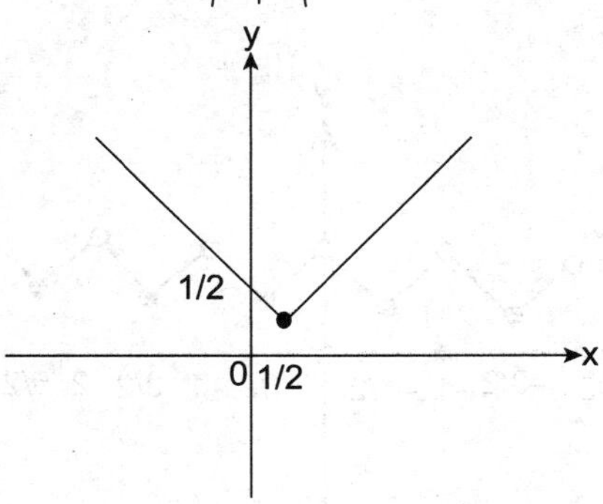

(ii)

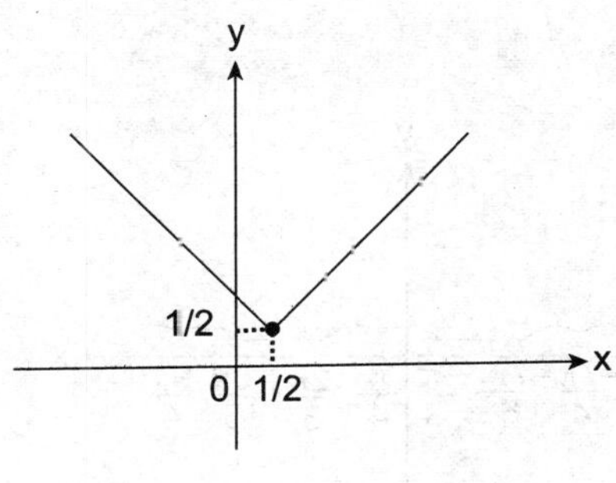

(iii)

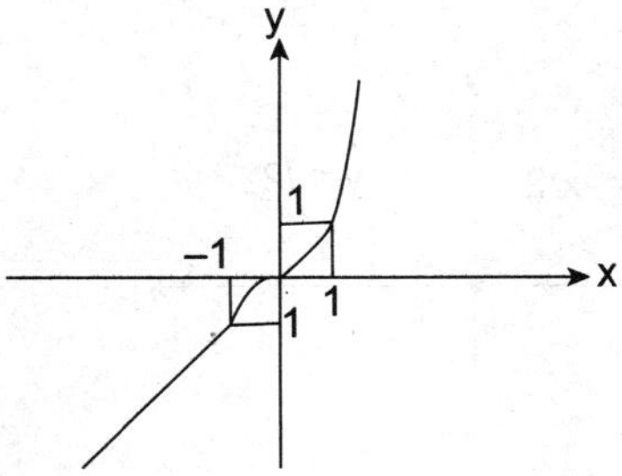

(iv)

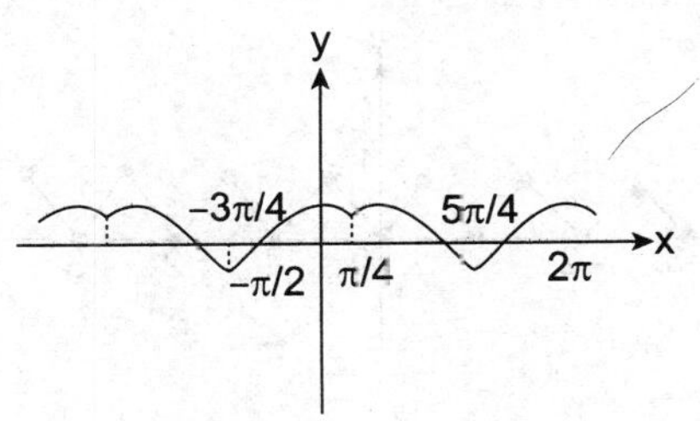

(v)
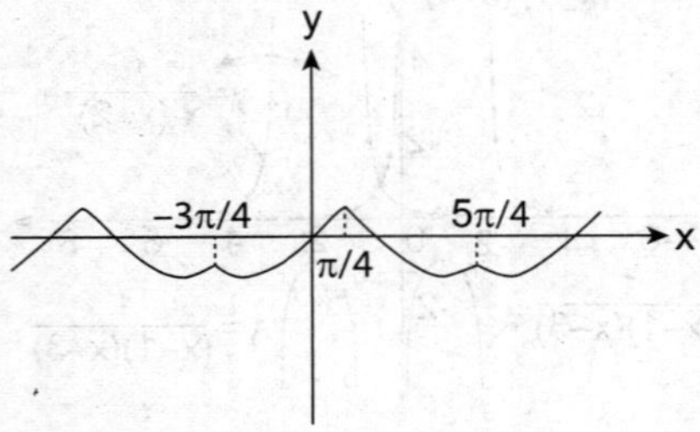

(vi)
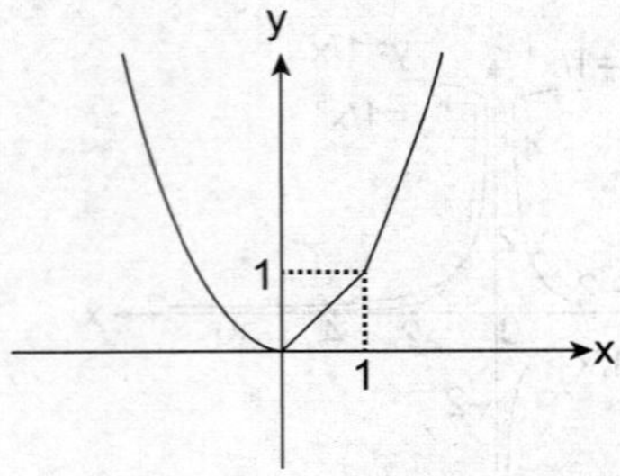

(vii)
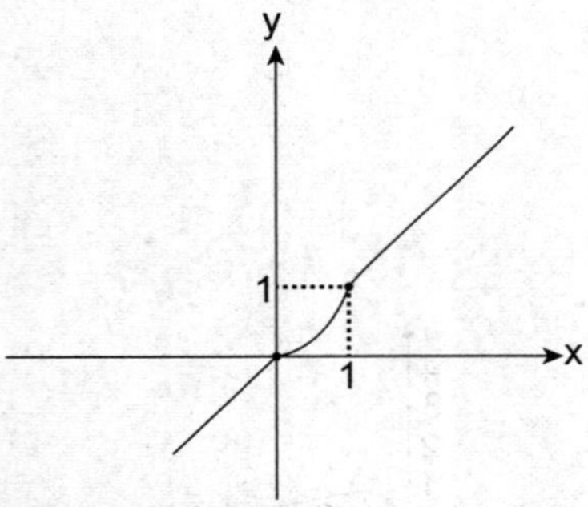

(viii)
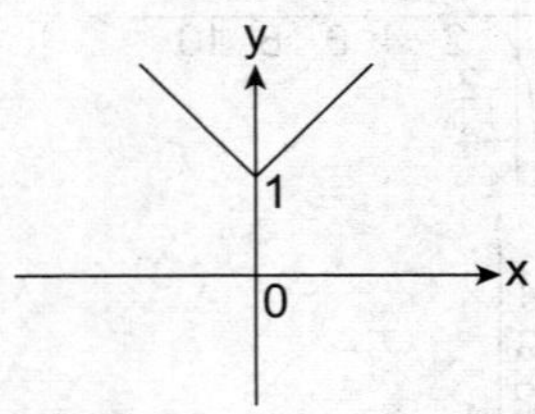

(ix)
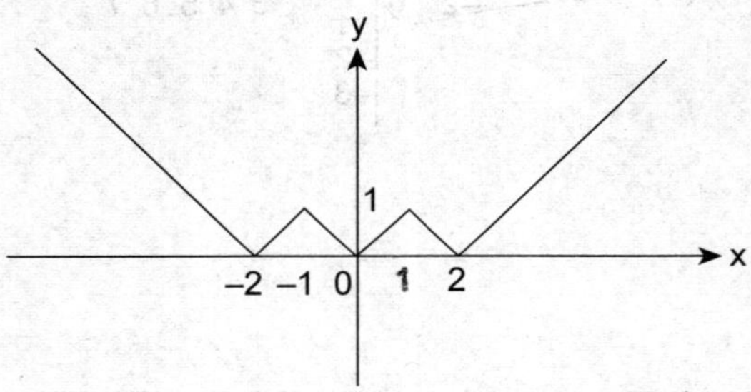

(x)
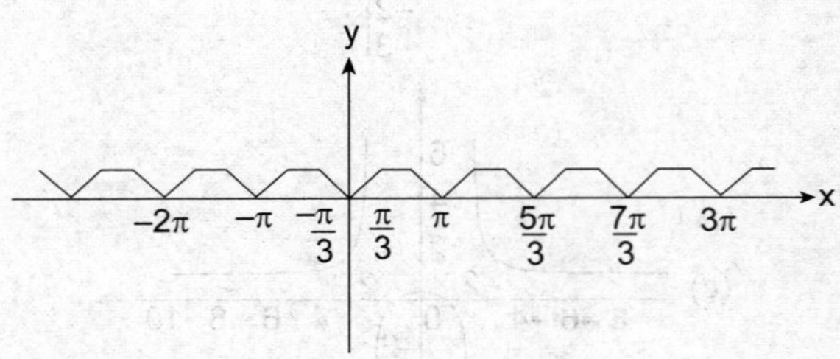

(xi)
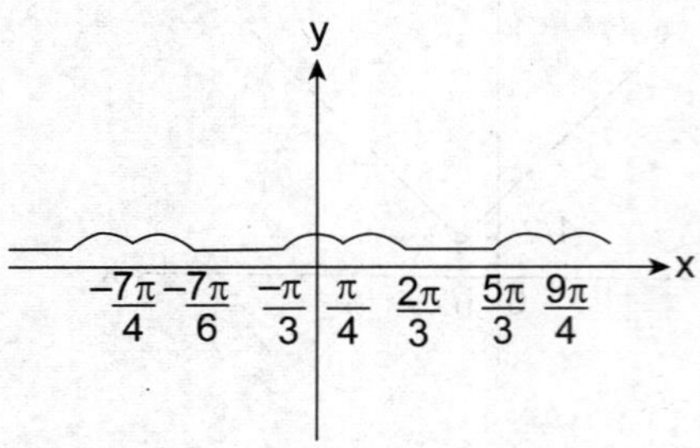

(xii)
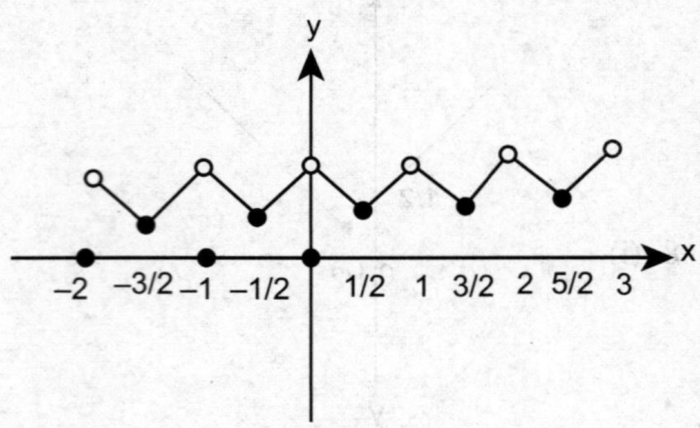

(xiii)
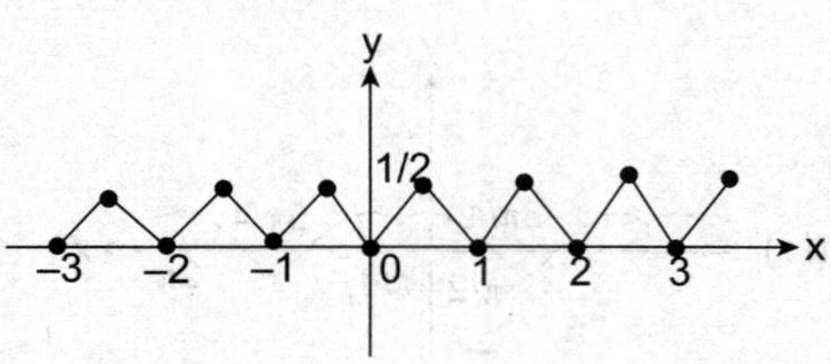

(xiv)
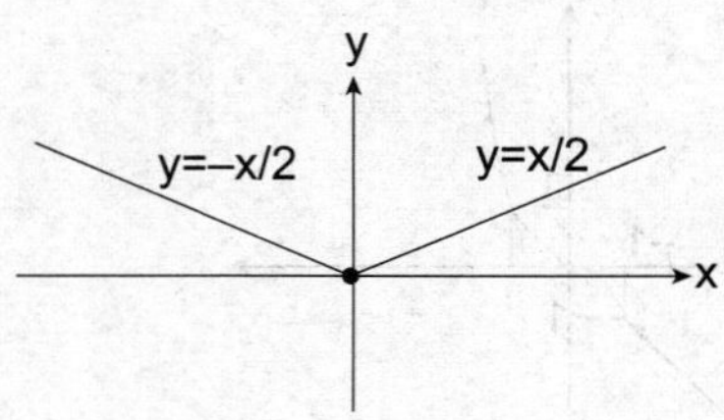

(xv) 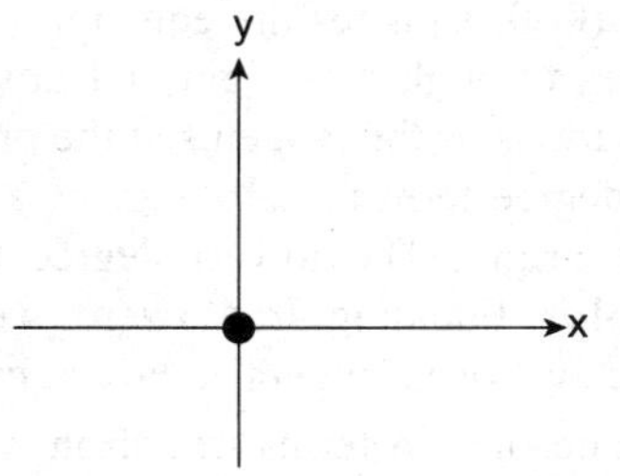

(xvi) 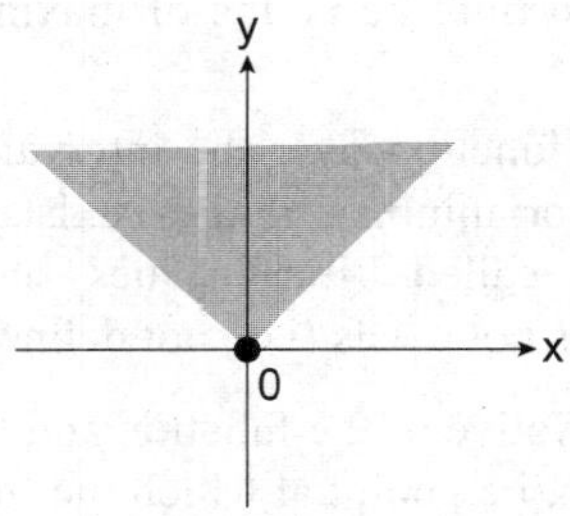

(xvii) 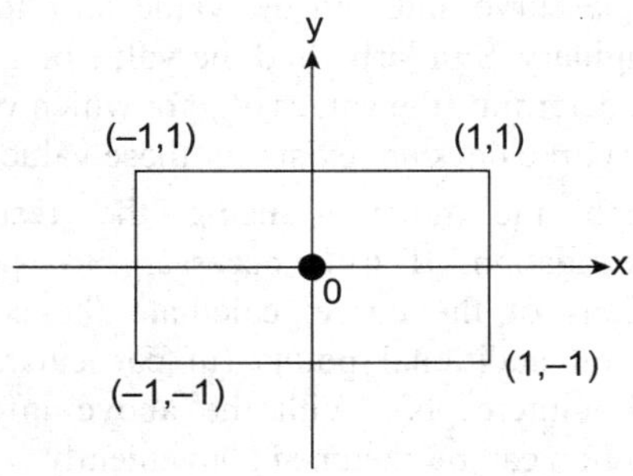

SKETCHING OF NON-STANDARD CURVES

The analysis and sketching of functions by elementary methods and transformation of standard curves has been already considered in chapter functions. Now we will carry out more profound and comprehensive study of various properties of function using the knowledge of differential calculus and explain the shape of its graph with the help of monotonicity convexity, concavity and extrema of the function.

To plot unknown curves the following investigations will be of immense help:

1. Find the domain of the function and if possible range of the function.
2. By putting $y = 0$ in the equation of the given curve, find points where the curve crosses the x-axis. Similarly by putting $x = 0$ in the equation of the given curve we can find points where the curve crosses the y-axis. i.e., the roots of the function are abscissa of point of intersection with x-axis and the value of function at $x = 0$ is the point of intersection with y-axis.
3. Test the periodicity of the function, if the function is periodic. i.e., if $f(x + T) = f(x)$ for real and finite positive constant T, then graph of $f(x)$ is repeated throughout the domain after interval of length T.

SYMMETRY/MONOTONICITY/CURVATURE OF FUNCTION

(a) $f(-x, y) = f(x, y)$, i.e., even w.r.t x, so, symmetric about y-axis. If all the powers of x in equation of the given curve are even, then it is symmetric about y-axis, e.g., $x^2 = 4ay$ is symmetric about y-axis.

(b) $f(x, -y) = f(x, y)$, i.e., even w.r.t y, so, symmetric about x-axis. If all the powers of y in equation of the given curve are even, then it is symmetric about x-axis. That is, the shape of the curve above x-axis, is exactly identical to its shape below x-axis e.g., $y^2 = 4ax$ is symmetric about x-axis.

(c) $f(-x, -y) = f(x, y)$, i.e., symmetry about origin. If by putting $-x$ for x and $-y$ for y the equation of curve remains same, then it is symmetric in opposite quadrants. e.g., $xy = c^2$, $x^2 + y^2 = a^2$.

(d) $f(x, y) = f(y, x)$ i.e., symmetry about line $y = x$. If the equation of a given curve remains unaltered by interchanging x and y then it is symmetric about the line $y = x$ which passes through the origin and makes an angle of 45° with positive direction of x-axis.

(e) $f(a - x) = f(a + x) \Rightarrow$ symmetry about line $x = a$.

(f) $f(x) = f(2a - x) \Rightarrow$ symmetry about line $x = a$.

5. Test the function for continuity, find out the discontinuities and their character.
6. Test the monotonicity of the function, i.e., find the points at which $\frac{dy}{dx} = 0$. At these points the tangent to the curve is parallel to x-axis. Find the interval in which $\frac{dy}{dx} > 0$. In this interval, the function is monotonically increasing and the interval in which $\frac{dy}{dx} < 0$. In this interval, the function is monotonically decreasing. Put $\frac{dy}{dx^2} = 0$ and check the sign of $\frac{d^2y}{dx^2}$ at the

points so obtained to find the points of maxima and minima.

If f is a continuous function over the interval (a, b) then local maxima or minima, if they exists, must occur at values of x, called critical values, such that $f'(x) = 0$ or $f'(x)$ does not exists (i.e., not defined).

7. Find the second derivative of the function and test the curvature of function, i.e., point at which the function is concave up $\frac{d^2y}{dx^2} > 0$ and concave down $\frac{d^2y}{dx^2} < 0$.
8. Find the points of inflexion on its graph of the function, compute the values of the function and of its derivative at these points. Find the intervals of convexity/concavity of the graph of the function.
9. Find the limit of function at the end point of the domain (if domain is open interval) and find the asymptotes of the function.
10. If the point (0, 0) satisfies the equation of the curve, then it passes through the origin and in such case to find the equations of the tangents at the origin, equate the lowest degree term to zero. e.g., $y^2 = 4ax$ passes through the origin. The lowest degree term in the equation is $4ax$. Equating $4ax$ to zero, we get $x = 0$. So, $x = 0$, i.e., y-axis is tangent at the origin to $y^2 = 4ax$.
11. Find the value of y in terms of x from the equation of the curve and find the value of x for which y is imaginary. Similarly, find the value of x in terms of y and determine the values of y for which x is imaginary. The curve does not exists for these values of x and y.
12. Graph the function using the results of this investigation. If it is necessary to specify certain regions of the curve, calculate the coordinates of several additional points (in particular, x-intercepts and y-intercepts). With the above information the function can be sketched conveniently.

ILLUSTRATION 77: Graph the function: $y = x^3 - 5x^2 + 4x$

SOLUTION: **Step 1: Factories the function, if possible.**

$y \neq x^3 - 5x^2 + 4x = x(x^2 - 5x + 4) = x(x^2 - x + 4 - 4x) = x(x - 1)(x - 4)$

Step 2: $y = 0 \Rightarrow x(x-1)(x-4) = 0 \Rightarrow x = 0$ or $x = 1$ or $x = 4$

$\Rightarrow$ The function intersects the x-axis at three points, i.e., $x = 0$, $x = 1$ and $x = 4$.

Step 3: Find points of local maxima/minima $y' = 3x^2 - 10x + 4$.

$y' = 0$ for points of local maxima/minima

$\Rightarrow 3x^2 - 10x + 4 = 0$

$\Rightarrow x = \frac{10 \pm \sqrt{100-48}}{6} = \frac{10 \pm 7.2}{6}$

$\Rightarrow$ 2.86 or 0.47

$\Rightarrow \frac{d^2y}{dx^2} = 6x - 10$

$\Rightarrow f''(2.86) = +\text{ve}$

$\Rightarrow x = 2.86$ is point of local minima and local minimum value is $f(2.86) = -5.86$

$\Rightarrow f''(0.47) = -\text{ve}$

$\Rightarrow x = 0.47$ is a point of local maxima and local maximum value is $f(0.47) = 0.88$

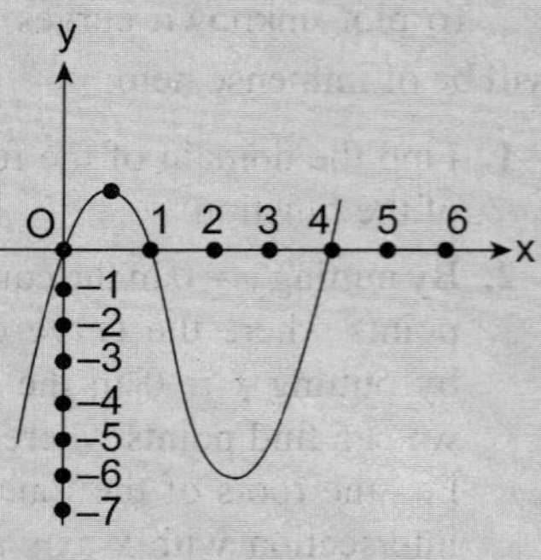

FIGURE 3.305

Step 4: $\lim_{x \to -\infty} y = \lim_{x \to \pm\infty} x^3 \left(1 - \frac{1}{x}\right)\left(\frac{1-4}{x}\right) = \pm\infty$. Thus, from the above information the graph of the function can be drawn as follows:

ILLUSTRATION 78: Sketch $y = (x - 1)(x - 2)$

SOLUTION: Here $y = (x - 1)(x - 2)$

(i) Put $y = 0 \Rightarrow x = 1, 2$

(ii) $y = x^2 - 3x + 2$

$\Rightarrow \dfrac{dy}{dx} = 2x - 3$ and $\dfrac{d^2y}{dx^2} = 2$ $\therefore$ minimum at $x = 3/2$ (as $\dfrac{d^2y}{dx^2} > 0$)

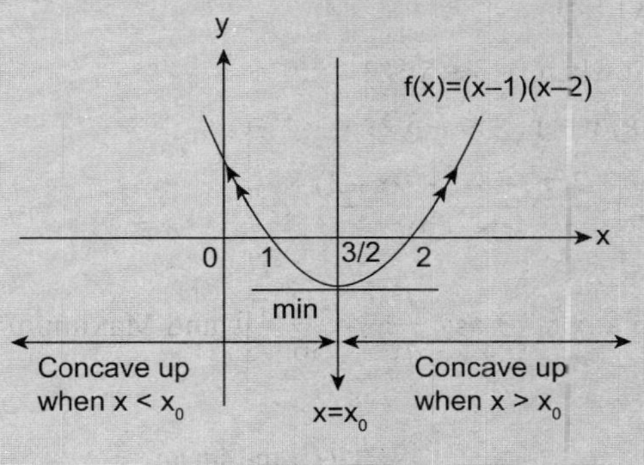

FIGURE 3.306

(iii) Increase when $x > 3/2$ and decreases when $x < 3/2$

(iv) Concave upwards for $x > 3/2$ or $x < 3/2$

ILLUSTRATION 79: Sketch the graph for the function: $y = |x + 3|\,(x + 1)$.

SOLUTION: Here, $y = |x + 3|\,(x + 1) = \begin{cases} (x+3)(x+1); & x \geq -3 \\ -(x+3)(x+1); & x < -3 \end{cases}$

$\Rightarrow x = -1, -3$ when $y = 0$ ...(i)

Also $\dfrac{dy}{dx} = \begin{cases} 2x+4; & x \geq -3 \\ -2x-4; & x < -3 \end{cases}$ and $\dfrac{d^2y}{dx^2} = \begin{cases} 2; & x \geq -3 \\ -2; & x < -3 \end{cases}$

Increasing when $x < -3$ or $x > -2$ and Decreasing when $-3 < x < -2$

Local maximum at $x = -3$ and local minimum at $x = -2$

Concave down when $x < -3$ and concave up when $x > -3$

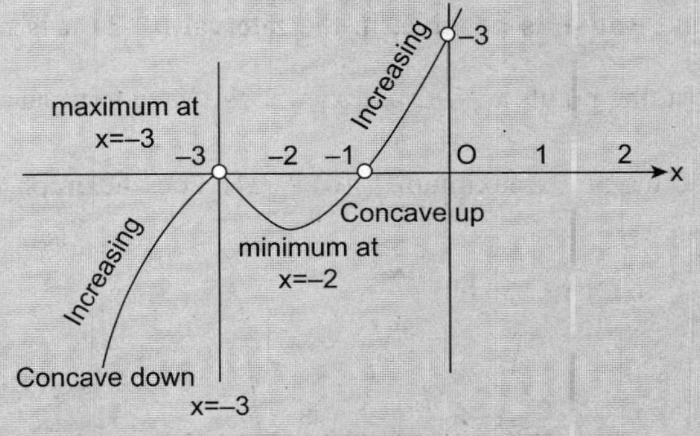

FIGURE 3.307

ILLUSTRATION 80: Sketch the graph for $f(x) = \dfrac{x+1}{x^2+3}$

SOLUTION: Here $y = \dfrac{x+1}{x^2+3}$

$\Rightarrow x = -1$, when $y = 0$

$y = 1/3$, when $x = 0$

$$\frac{dy}{dx} = \frac{-x^2 - 2x + 3}{(x^2+3)^2} = \frac{-(x+3)(x-1)}{(x^2+3)^2}$$

$\Rightarrow$ Increasing when, $-3 < x < 1$

Decreasing when, $x < -3$ or $x > 1$

Also $\dfrac{d^2y}{dx^2} = \dfrac{2(x^3 + 3x^2 - 9x - 3)}{(x^2+3)^3}$

Minimum at $x = -3$ as; $\dfrac{d^2y}{dx^2} = \dfrac{1}{36} > 0$ and Maximum at $x = 1$ as; $\dfrac{d^2y}{dx^2} = -\dfrac{1}{4} < 0$

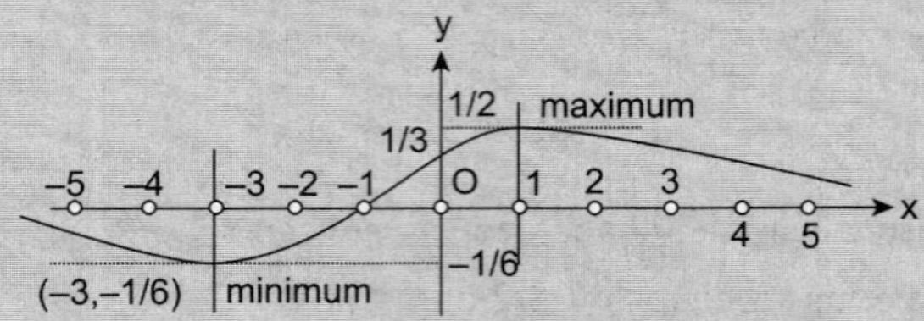

FIGURE 3.308

ILLUSTRATION 81: Plot the curves of the following functions and also indicate their extrema.

(a) $f(x) = \frac{3}{4}x^4 - x^3 - 9x^2 + 7$ (b) $f(x) = x(x + 1)^3 (x - 3)^2$

SOLUTION: (a) The given function is a polynomial function, and hence, it is defined and differentiable over the entire number scale. Therefore, the critical points can be obtained by equating the derivative $f'(x) = 3x^3 - 3x^2 - 18x = 3x(x + 2)(x - 3)$ to zero. We find the critical points to be $x_1 = -2$, $x_2 = 0$, $x_3 = 3$ (they should always be arranged in an increasing order). Let us now investigate the sign of the derivative in the neighbourhood of each of these points. Since there are no critical points to the left of the point $x = -2$, the derivative at all the points $x < -2$ has one and the same sign; it is negative. Analogously, in the interval (–2, 0) the derivative is positive, in the interval (0, 3) it is negative, at $x > 3$ it is positive. Hence, at the points $x_1 = -2$ and $x_3 = 3$. We have minima $f(-2) = -9$ and $f(3) = -40\frac{1}{4}$, and at the point $x_2 = 0$, maximum $= f(0) = 7$. Hence, the graph will be as given in Figure 3.309.

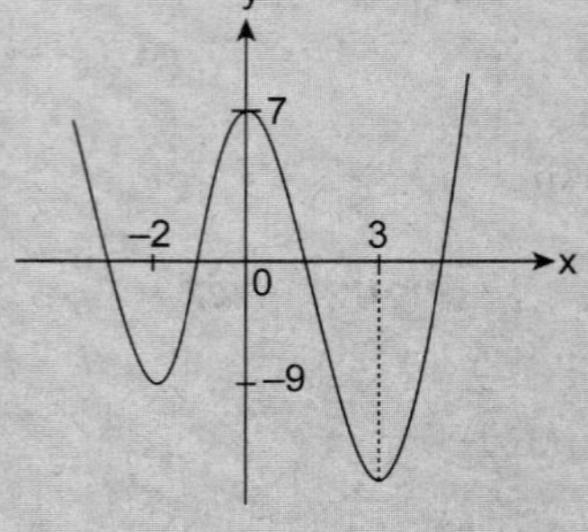

FIGURE 3.309

(b) The critical points are the roots of the derivative $f'(x)$, since the function is defined and differentiable throughout the number scale.

$$f'(x) = (x+1)^3(x-3)^2 + 3x(x+1)^2(x-3)^2 + 2x(x+1)^3(x-3)$$
$$= 3(x+1)^2(x-3)(2x^2-3x-1)$$

Equating this expression to zero, we find the critical points.

$$x_1 = -1,\ x_2 = \frac{(3-\sqrt{17})}{4},\ x_3 = \frac{(3+\sqrt{17})}{4},\ x_4 = 3$$

Let us tabulate the signs of the derivative in the intervals between the critical points.

Intervals	$x < x_1$	$x_1 < x < x_2$	$x_2 < x < x_3$	$x_3 < x < x_4$	$x_4 < x$
Sign of $f'(x)$	–	–	+	–	+

As is seen from the table, there is no extremum at the point $x_1 = -1$, there is a minimum at the point $x = \frac{3-\sqrt{17}}{4}$, a maximum at the point $x = \frac{3+\sqrt{17}}{4}$ and a minimum at the point $x = 3$.

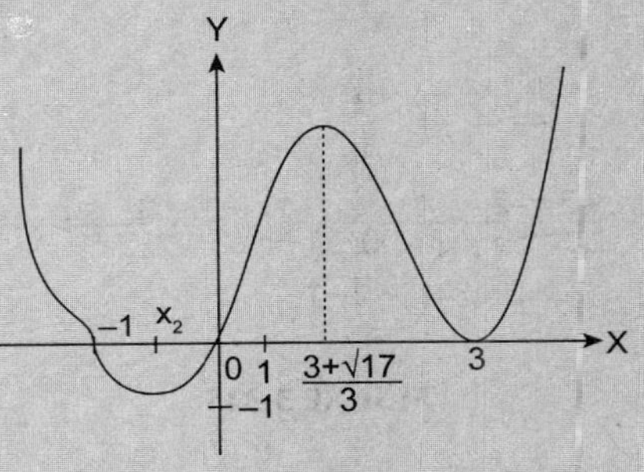

FIGURE 3.310

ILLUSTRATION 82: Investigate and graph the following functions $y = \sqrt[3]{x} - \sqrt[3]{x+1}$.

SOLUTION: The function is defined and continuous over the entire number scale and is negative everywhere, since $\sqrt[3]{x} < \sqrt[3]{x+1}$.

The graph has neither vertical, nor inclined asymptotes, since the order of magnitude of y is less than unity as $x \to \infty$. Determine the horizontal asymptote:

$$\lim_{x\to\pm\infty} y = \lim_{x\to\pm\infty}\left(\sqrt[3]{x} - \sqrt[3]{x+1}\right) = \lim_{x\to\pm\infty} \frac{-1}{\sqrt[3]{x^2} + \sqrt[3]{x(x+1)} + \sqrt[3]{(x+1)^2}} = 0$$

Hence, the straight line $y = 0$ is the horizontal asymptote of the graph.

The first derivative $y' = \frac{1}{3\sqrt[3]{x^2}} - \frac{1}{3\sqrt[3]{(x+1)^2}} = \frac{\sqrt[3]{(x+1)^2} - \sqrt[3]{x^2}}{3\sqrt[3]{x^2(x+1)^2}}$ becomes zero at the point $x_1 = -\frac{1}{2}$ and infinite at the points $x_2 = -1, x_3 = 0$.

The second derivative $y'' = \frac{1}{3}\left(-\frac{2}{3}\right)\frac{1}{\sqrt[3]{x^5}} - \frac{1}{3}\left(-\frac{2}{3}\right)\frac{1}{\sqrt[3]{(x+1)^5}} = \frac{-2\left[\sqrt[3]{(x+1)^5} - \sqrt[3]{x^5}\right]}{9\sqrt[3]{[x(x+1)]^5}}$ does not vanish and is infinite at the same points $x_2 = -1, x_3 = 0$. Compile a table

x	-1	$\left(-1, -\frac{1}{2}\right)$	$-\frac{1}{2}$	$\left(-\frac{1}{2}, 0\right)$	0	$(0, \infty)$	1
y'	$-\infty$	$-$	0	$+$	∞	$+$	
y''	∞	$+$	$+\frac{16}{9\sqrt[3]{2}}$	$+$	∞	$-$	
	vertical tangent		point of minima		vertical tangent		
y	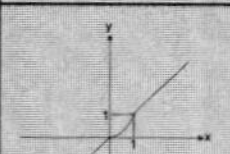						-0.26

With the aid of this table, and of the asymptote $y = 0$, construct the graph of the function as shown below.

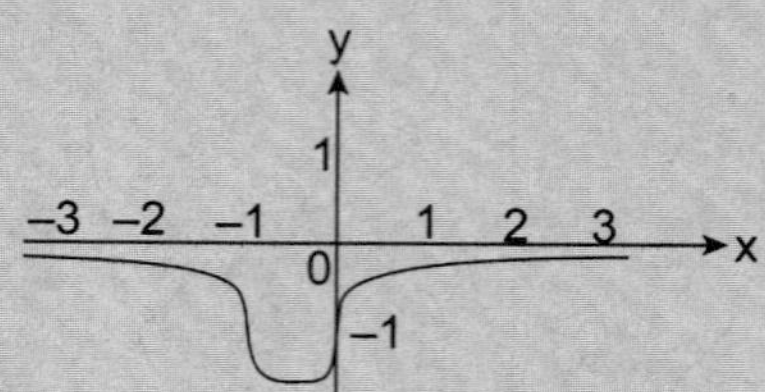

FIGURE 3.311

ILLUSTRATION 83: Investigate and graph the following functions $y = x^2 e^{1/x}$:

SOLUTION: The function is defined positive and continuous on each of the intervals $(-\infty, 0)$ and $(0, \infty)$. The point $x = 0$ is a discontinuity.

Since $\lim\limits_{x\to 0^+} y = \lim\limits_{x\to 0^+} x^2 e^{\frac{1}{x}} = \lim\limits_{t\to +\infty} \frac{e^t}{t^2} = \infty$ where $\left(t = \frac{1}{x}\right)$,

The straight line $x = 0$ is a vertical asymptote. But $\lim\limits_{x\to 0^-} y = \lim\limits_{x\to 0^-} x^2 e^{\frac{1}{x}} = 0$.

There are no inclined asymptotes since the function $y = x^2 e^{1/x}$ has the second order of smallness with respect to x as $x \to \pm\infty$.

Let us find the extrema of the function, for which purpose we evaluate the derivative

$y' = 2xe^{1/x} - e^{1/x} = 2e^{1/x}(x - 1/2)$; whence we find the only critical point $x = 1/2$

Since for $x \neq 0$

$$y''(x) = 2e^{1/x} - \frac{2}{x}e^{1/x} + \frac{1}{x^2}e^{1/x} = \frac{1}{x^2}e^{1/x}\left(2x^2 - 2x + 1\right) > 0$$

On each of the intervals of the domain of definition, the graph of the function is concave upwards, and at the point $x = 1/2$ the function has a minimum.

$= y\left(\frac{1}{2}\right) = \frac{1}{4}e^2 \approx 1.84; f(-1) = e^{-1} = 0.37, f(1) = e \approx 2.72.$

From the information obtained we can sketch the graph as Figure 3.312.

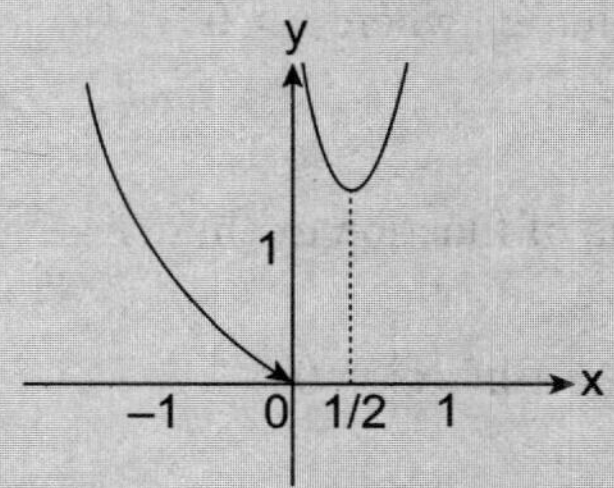

FIGURE 3.312

ILLUSTRATION 84: Investigate and graph the following functions $y = arc\ \sin\dfrac{1-x^2}{1+x^2}$.

SOLUTION: The function is defined and continuous throughout the number scale, since at any x; $\left|\dfrac{1-x^2}{1+x^2}\right| \le 1$.

Since the function is even, we may confine ourselves to the investigation of the function at $x \ge 0$.

As the function is continuous, the graph has no vertical asymptotes, but it has a horizontal asymptote.

$\lim\limits_{x\to+\infty} y = \arcsin(-1) = -\dfrac{\pi}{2}$

The first derivative $y' = \dfrac{1}{\sqrt{1-\dfrac{(1-x^2)^2}{(1+x^2)^2}}} \times \dfrac{-2x(1+x^2)-2x(1-x^2)}{(1+x^2)^2} = -\dfrac{1}{2|x|} \times \dfrac{4x}{(1+x^2)^2}$ is negative for $x > 0$, therefore, the function decreases. The derivative is non-existent at the point $x = 0$. By virtue of the symmetry of the graph about the y-axis, there will be a maximum at the point $y(0) = \dfrac{\pi}{2}$.

Notice that at the point $x = 0$ the right derivative is equal to -1, and the left one is $+1$

The second derivative = $y''(x) = \dfrac{4x}{(1+x^2)^2} > 0$ for all $x > 0$ and $\dfrac{-4x}{(1+x^2)^2} > 0 \,\forall\, x < 0$.

Hence, in the interval $(-\infty, 0)$ and $(0, \infty)$ the graph of the function is concave upwards. Also note that the curve intersects with the x-axis at the points $x = \pm 1$.

Taking into consideration the results of the investigation, construct the graph of the function as is shown in Figure 3.313.

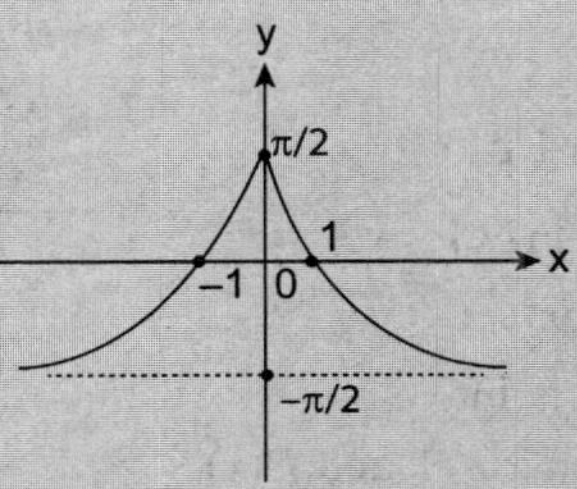

FIGURE 3.313

ILLUSTRATION 85: Draw the graph of ex ln (ex),where $x > 0$

SOLUTION: **Step 1:** $y = ex \ln ex = 0$

$\Rightarrow \quad x = \frac{1}{e}$ is the roots of function ex (ln ex)

Step 2: $y' = e\left\{x \frac{1}{ex}.e + \ln ex\right\} = 0$

$\Rightarrow \; e(1 + \ln ex) = 0 \;\Rightarrow\; \ln ex = -1 \;\Rightarrow\; ex = e^{-1} \Rightarrow\; x = \frac{1}{e^2}$

Next, $y'' = \frac{e}{ex}.e = \frac{e}{x} \;\Rightarrow\; y'' > 0 \;\forall\, x > 0$

$\Rightarrow f(x)$ has minima at $x = \frac{1}{e^2}$ and $y_{min} = e.\frac{1}{e^2}\ln e\frac{1}{e^2} = \frac{1}{e}(-1) = -\frac{1}{e}$

Further $y' > 0 \;\forall\, x > \frac{1}{e^2} \;\Rightarrow f(x)$ increases and $y' < 0 \;\forall\, 0 < x < \frac{1}{e^2} \;\Rightarrow f(x)$ decreases.

Step 3: (a) $\lim\limits_{x\to\infty} ex \ln ex = \infty$

(b) $\lim\limits_{x\to 0} ex \ln ex = \lim\limits_{x\to 0} e\left[\frac{1+\ln x}{\frac{1}{x}}\right]\left(\frac{\infty}{\infty}\text{form}\right) = 0 = \lim\limits_{x\to\infty}\frac{\left(\frac{h}{x}\right)}{\left(-\frac{1}{x^2}\right)} = 0$

With these information we can draw the graph of ex ln (ex) as follows:

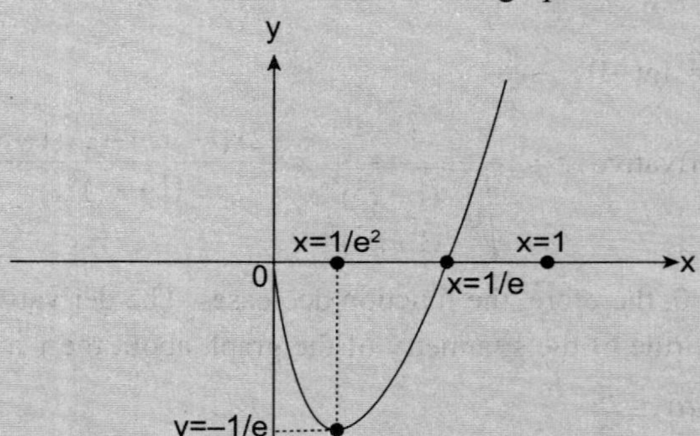

FIGURE 3.314

ILLUSTRATION 86: Draw the graph of $f(x) = \frac{\ln(ex)}{ex}$, where $x > 0$

SOLUTION: **Step 1:** Domain of the $f(x)$ is $(0, \infty)$

$f(x) = 0 = \frac{\ln ex}{ex}$

$\Rightarrow$ Root of equation is $1/e$

Step 2: $f'(x) = \frac{(1 - \ln ex)}{ex^2} = 0$

$\Rightarrow x = 1$ is the critical point.

Clearly, $f'(x) > 0$ when $x < 1$ and $f'(x) < 0$ when $x > 1$

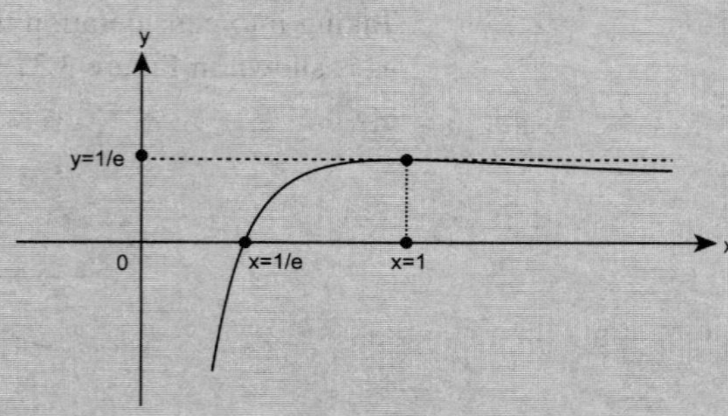

FIGURE 3.315

So, the graph of $f(x)$ will be as shown figure:

Hence, $x = 1$ is point of maxima and the maximum value of $f(x) = \frac{1}{e}$

Step 3: $\lim_{x\to\infty} \frac{\ln ex}{ex} = \lim_{x\to\infty} \frac{\frac{e}{ex}}{e} = 0$ and $\lim_{x\to 0^+} f(x) = \lim_{x\to 0^+} \frac{\ln ex}{ex} = -\infty$

TEXTUAL EXERCISE–6: (SUBJECTIVE)

1. Draw the graph of the following functions:

(a) $y = \frac{2}{x^2+1}$ (b) $y = \frac{2}{x^2-4}$

(c) $y = \frac{2x}{x^2-1}$ (d) $y = \frac{x^2+2}{x^2-4}$

2. Sketch the curve

(a) $y = (1 - x^{2/3})^{3/2}$

(b) $y = (x - 1)\, x^{2/3}$

(c) $x^{2/3} + y^{2/3} = a^{2/3}$

3. Sketch the curves

(i) $y = \frac{e^x + e^{-x}}{2}$ (ii) $y = \frac{e^x - e^{-x}}{2}$

(iii) $y = \frac{e^x - e^{-x}}{e^x + e^{-x}}$ (iv) $y = \frac{e^x + e^{-x}}{e^x - e^{-x}}$

4. Sketch the curves

(a) $y = 2 \sin x + \cos 2x$

(b) $y = e^{-x^2}$ (Gaussian curve)

(c) $y^2 = x^3$ (Semi-cubical curve)

(d) $y = x^4 - x^6$

(e) $y = \frac{\sin 2x}{2} + \cos x.$

5. Sketch the curves

(a) $y^2 = (x - 1)(x - 2)(x - 3).$

(b) $y = 1 + x^2 - \frac{1}{2} x^4$

(c) $y = (x + 1)(x - 2)^2$

(d) $y = \frac{a^2 x}{a^2 + x^2}$

(e) $y = ex \log ex$

(f) $y = \frac{\log ex}{ex}$

(g) $y = x^x$

(h) $y^2 x^2 = (x - 1)(x - 2)(x - 3)$

Answer Keys

1. (a)

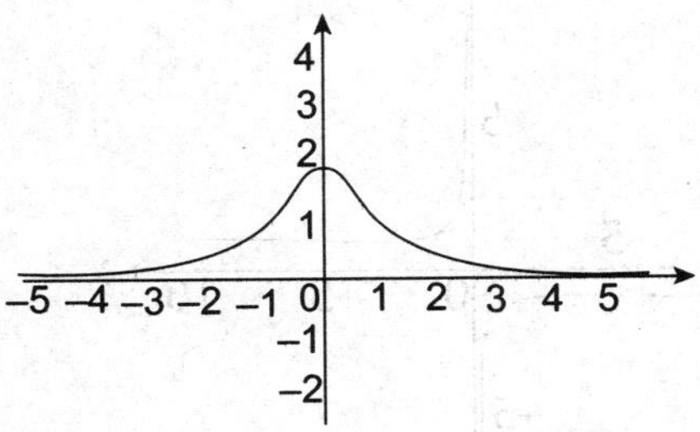

(b)

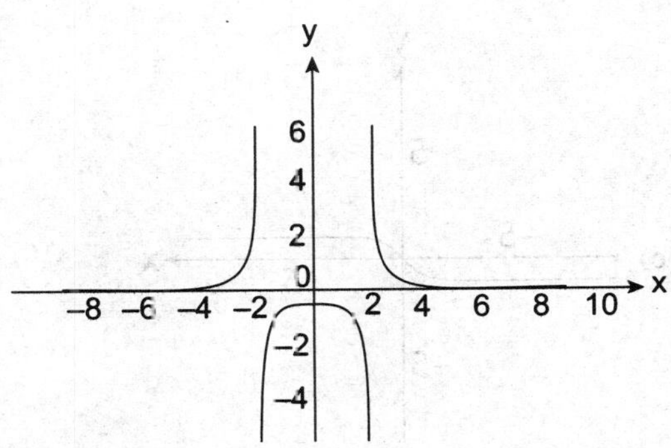

(c)

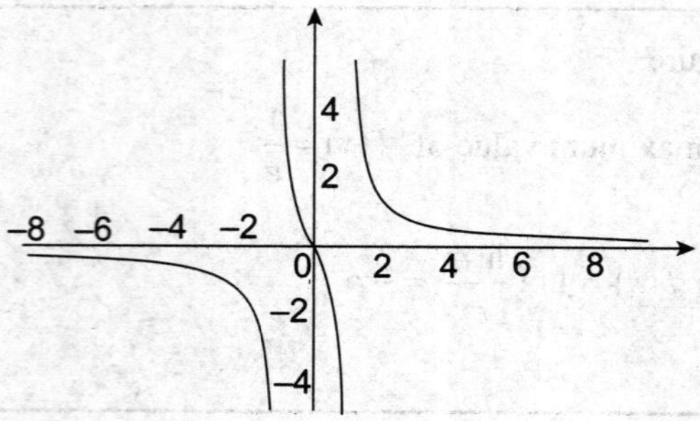

(d)

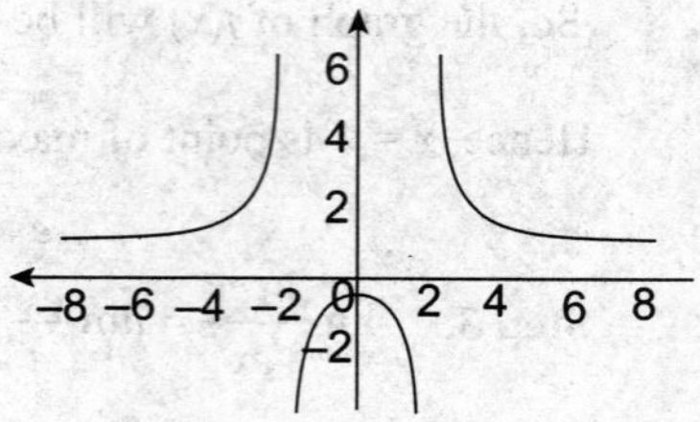

2. (a)

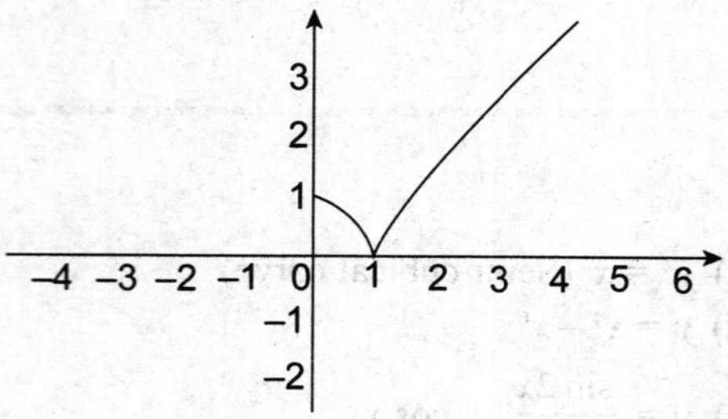

(b)

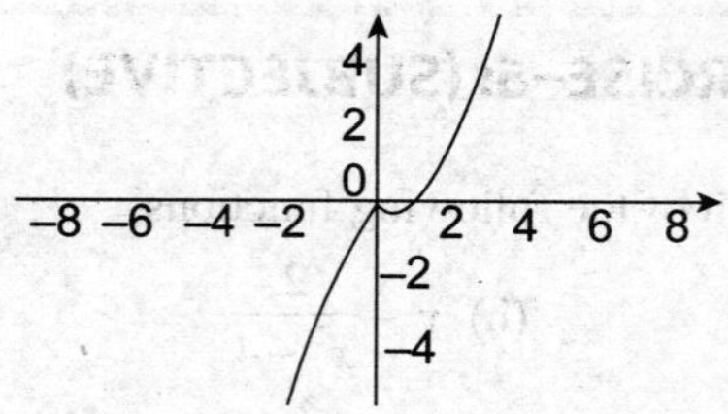

(c)

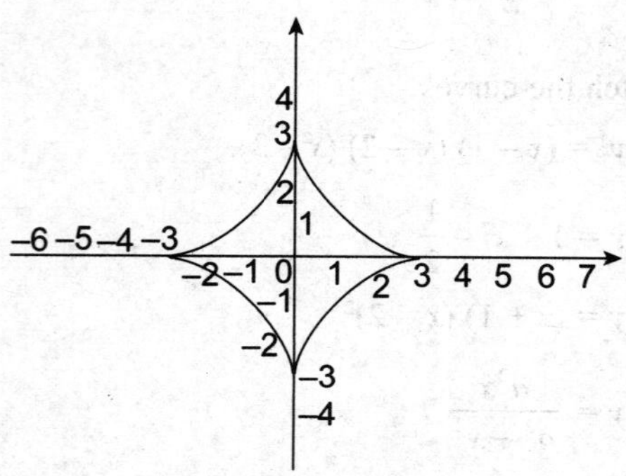

3. (a)

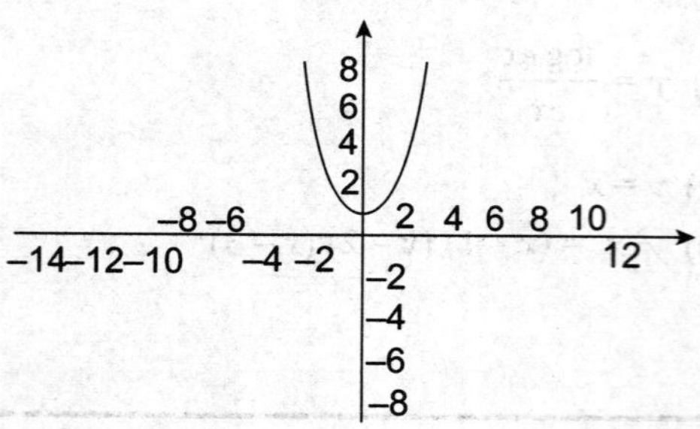

(b)

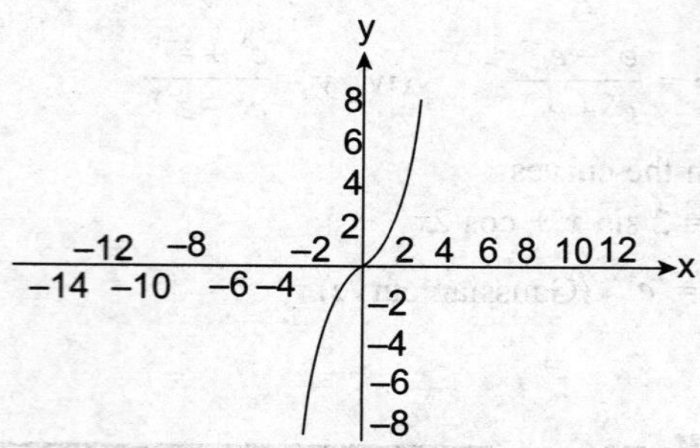

(c)

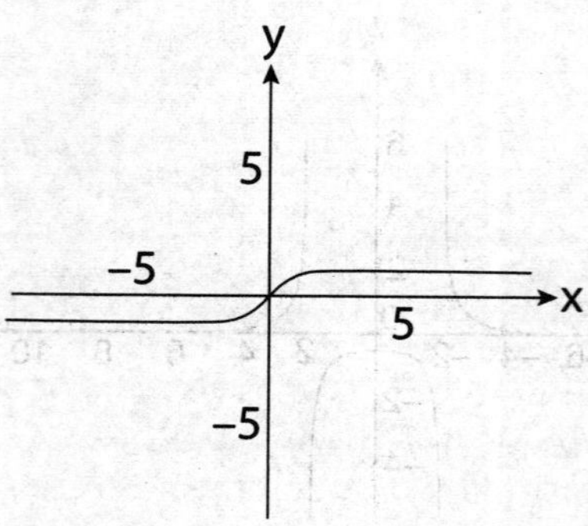

(d)

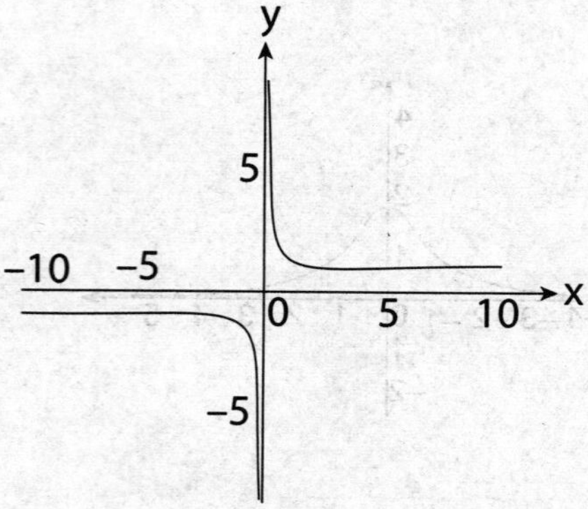

4. (a)

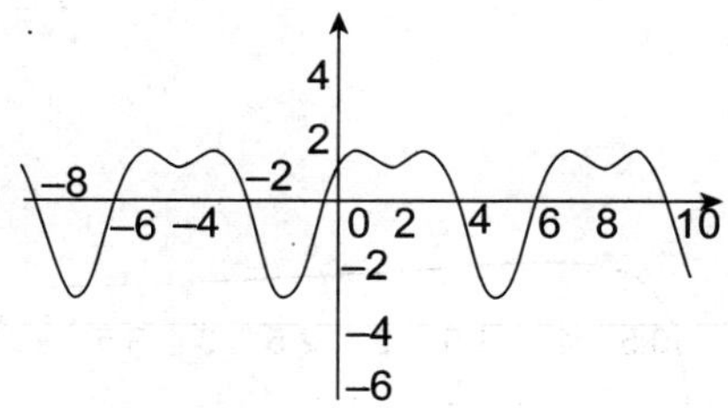

(b)

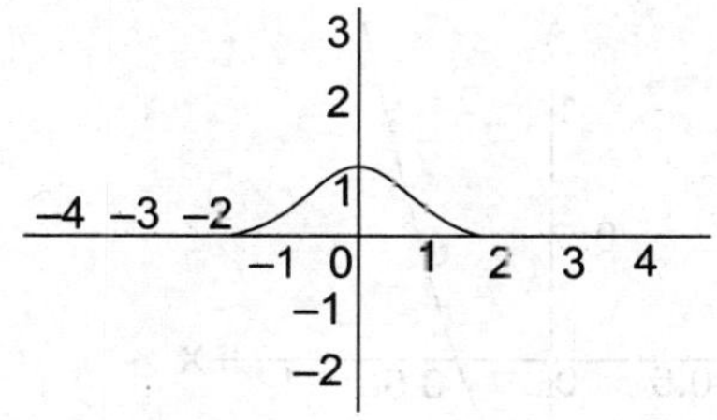

(c)

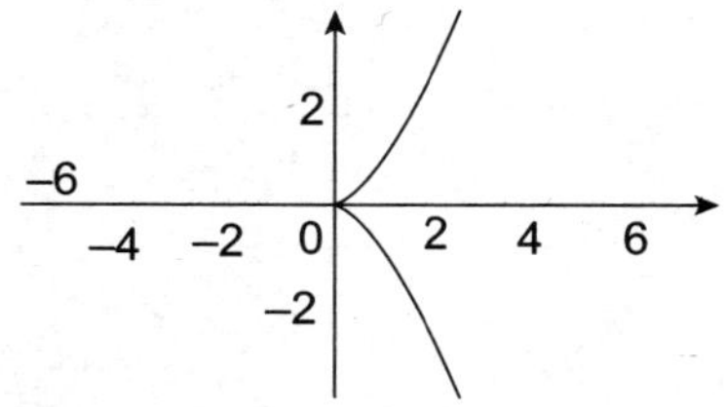

(d)

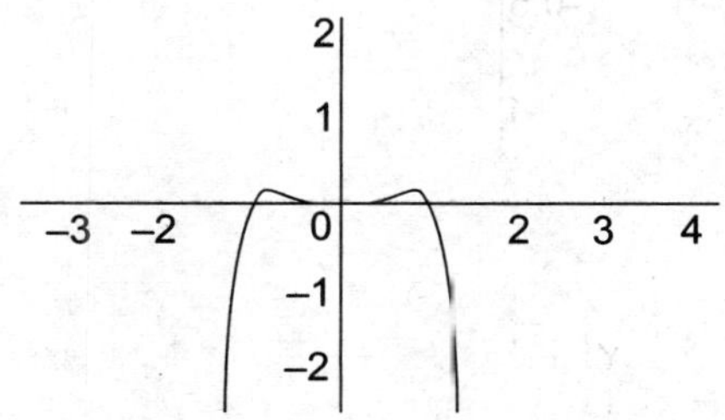

(e)

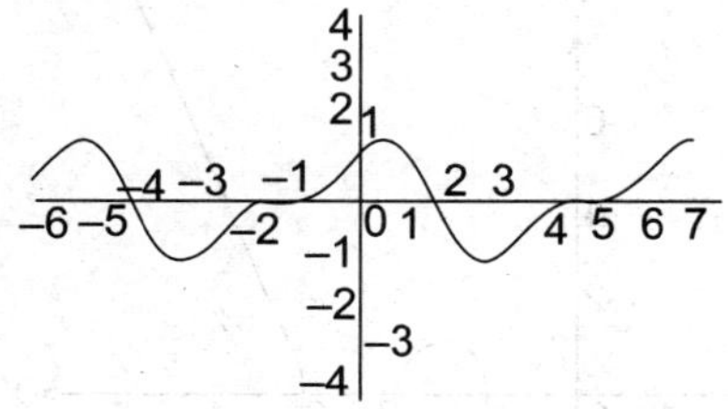

5. (a)

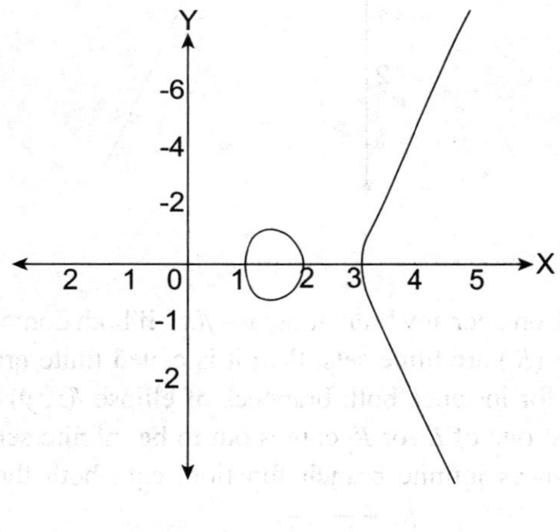

(b)

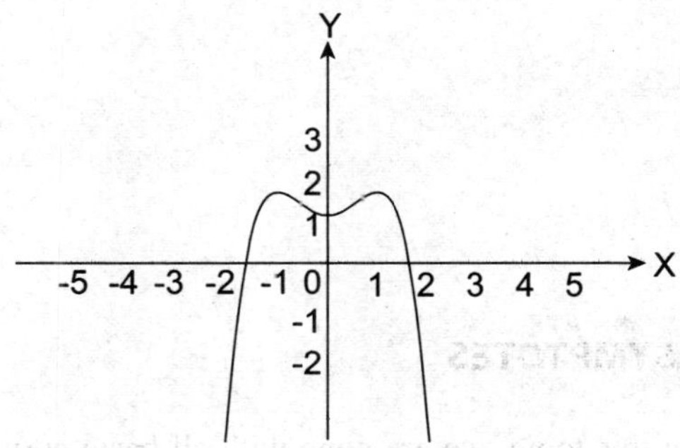

(c)

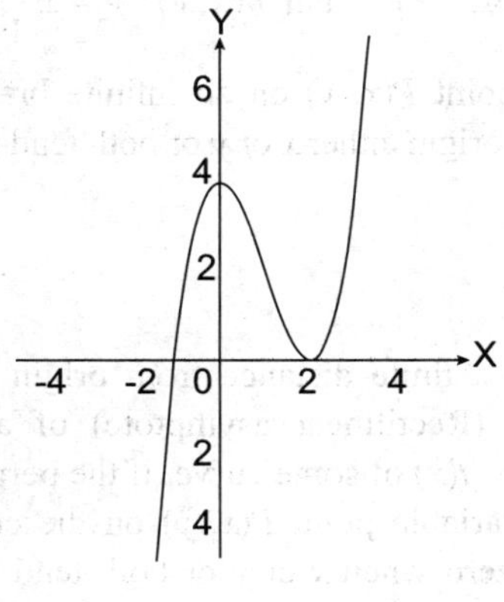

(d)

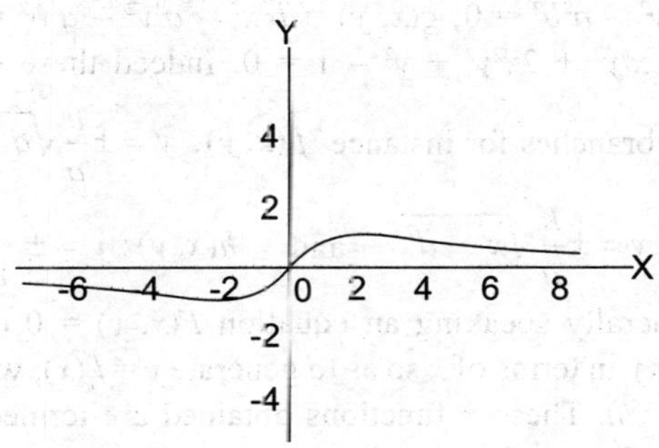

(e) 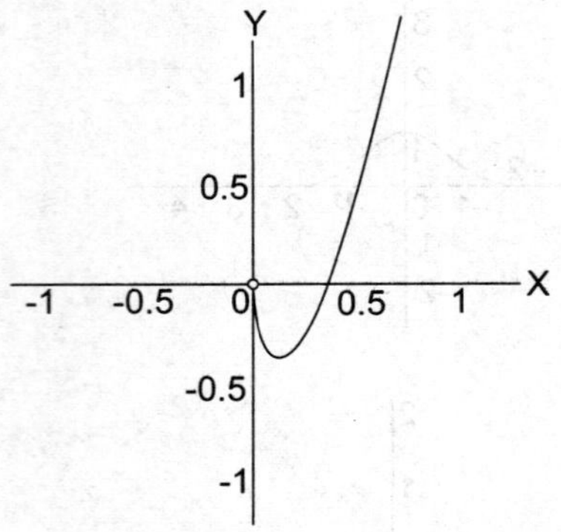

(f) 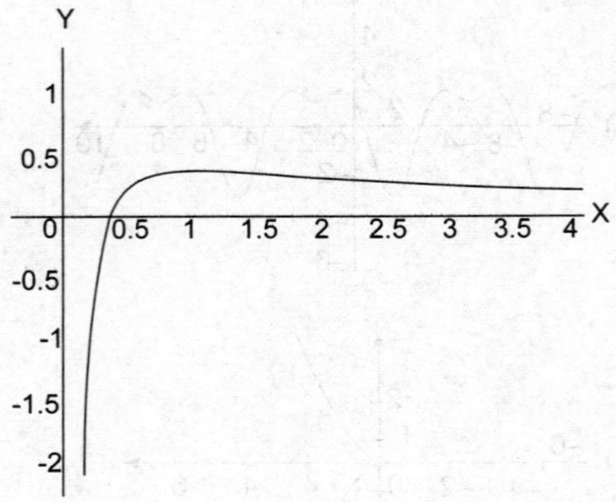

(g) 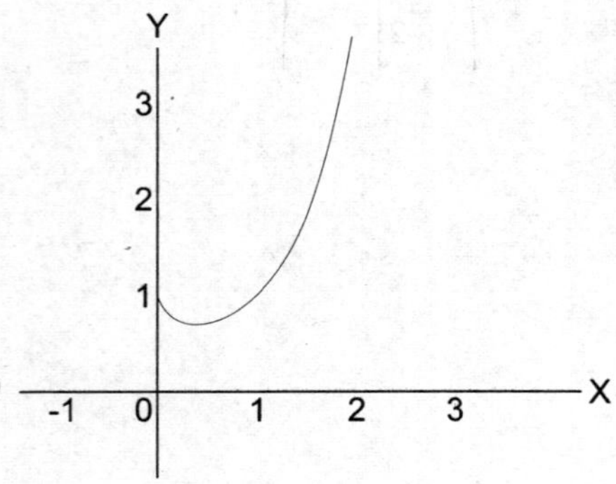

(h) 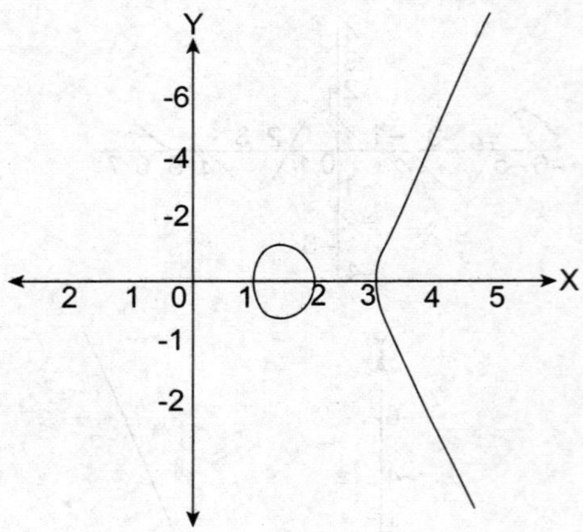

■ ASYMPTOTES

So far in this topic, we are done with all basic curves and various geometric transformations over them. As of now we have also learned tracing of simple curves having expression as an explicit function of x. But there are some known curves $f(x, y) = 0$, with implicit nature as well, e.g., $f(x, y) = b^2x^2 + a^2y^2 - a^2b^2 = 0$; $g(x, y) = b^2x^2 - a^2y^2 - a^2b^2 = 0$ or $h(x, y) = x^4y^2 + 2x^2y^2 + y^2 - 1 = 0$. Indeed these curves have two branches for instance $f(x,y)\colon\ y = \pm\frac{b}{a}\sqrt{a^2 - x^2}$,

$$g(x,y)\colon\ y = \pm\frac{b}{a}\sqrt{x^2 - a^2} \quad \text{and} \quad h(x,y): y = \pm\frac{1}{1+x^2}.$$

More generally speaking an equation $F(x, y) = 0$ can be solved for y in terms of x so as to generate $y = f_k(x)$; where $k = 1, 2, \ldots, n$. These n functions obtained are termed as n branches of curve $F(x, y) = 0$.

Consider any branch say $y = f(x)$, if both domain (D_f) and range (R_f) are finite sets, then it is called finite branch function, for instance both branches of ellipse $f(x, y) = 0$ and if atleast one of D_f or R_f comes out to be infinite set, then it is known as infinite branch function, e.g., both the branches

$$g(x,y)\colon\ y = \pm\frac{b}{a}\sqrt{x^2 - a^2} \text{ and } h(x,y): y = \pm\frac{1}{1+x^2}.$$ It is

so because as a point $P(x, y)$ on an infinite branch curve moves away from origin either x or y or both tend to infinity.

Definition

A straight line at a finite distance from origin is said to be an asymptote (Rectilinear asymptote) of an infinite branch function $y = f(x)$ of some curve, if the perpendicular distance of any variable point $P(x, y)$ on the curve from the line tends to zero when x or y or both tend to infinity (i.e., it tends to meet the given curve at infinity) as shown in Figures 3.316 and 3.317.

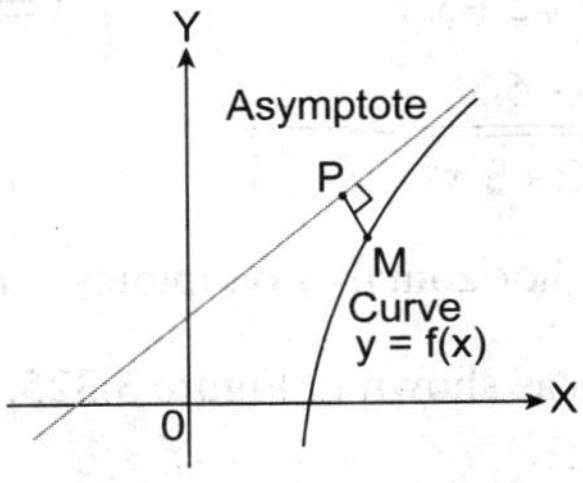

FIGURE 3.316

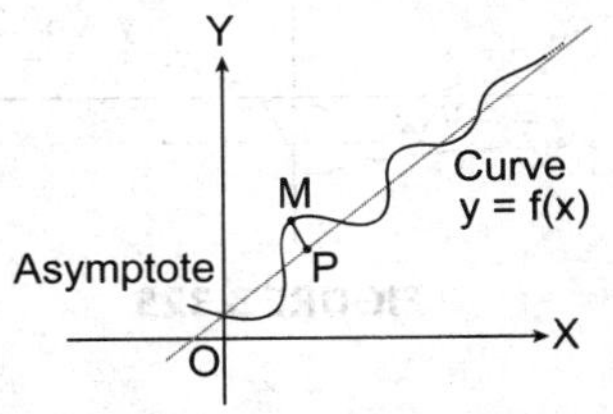

FIGURE 3.317

Mathematically

Let $y = f(x)$ be a curve and let (x, y) be a point on it.

Tangent at (x, y) is given by $Y - y = \frac{dy}{dx}(X - x)$

$$\Rightarrow \quad Y = \frac{dy}{dx}.X + \left(y - x\frac{dy}{dx}\right) \qquad \text{...(i)}$$

Now, if asymptotes exists, then $x \to \infty$

$$\Rightarrow \quad \frac{dy}{dx} \text{ and } \left(y - x\frac{dy}{dx}\right) \to \text{finite limit say } m \text{ and } c.$$

Say, $\frac{dy}{dx} \to m$ and $y - x\frac{dy}{dx} \to c$

$\therefore$ Equation (i) reduces to $y = mx + c$ is an asymptote of equation.

In Figure (3.318) asymptote is parallel to x-axis and is called a horizontal asymptote

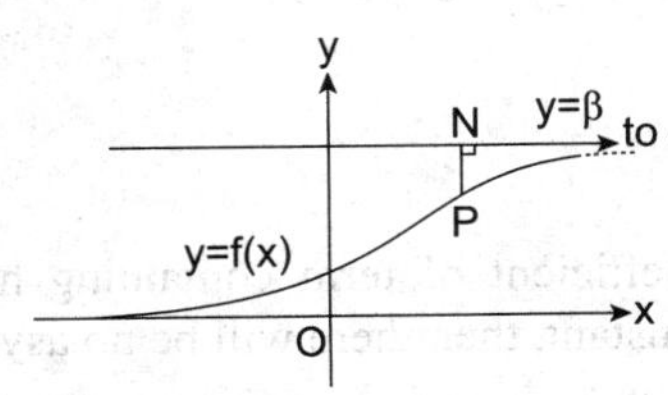

FIGURE 3.318

In Figure (3.319) asymptote is parallel to y-axis and is called a vertical asymptote.

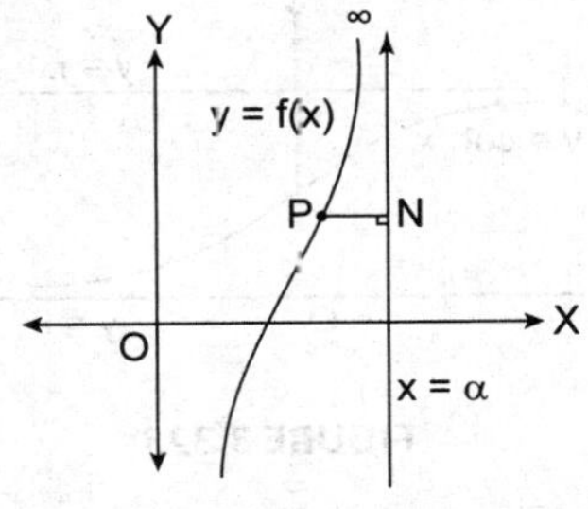

FIGURE 3.319

If it is neither parallel to x-axis nor to y-axis, then it is called as oblique asymptote.

For instance the straight line $y = 0$ is a horizontal asymptote to the curve $y = \frac{1}{1+x^2}$

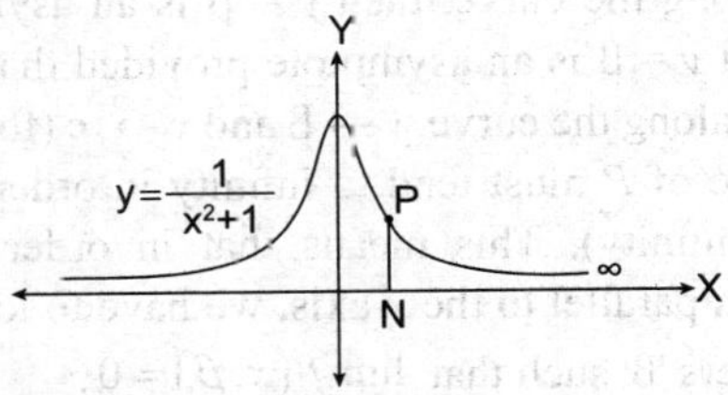

FIGURE 3.320

The lines $y = \pm\frac{b}{a}x$ are pair of asymptotes of hyperbola $\frac{x^2}{a^2} - \frac{y^2}{b^2} = 1$

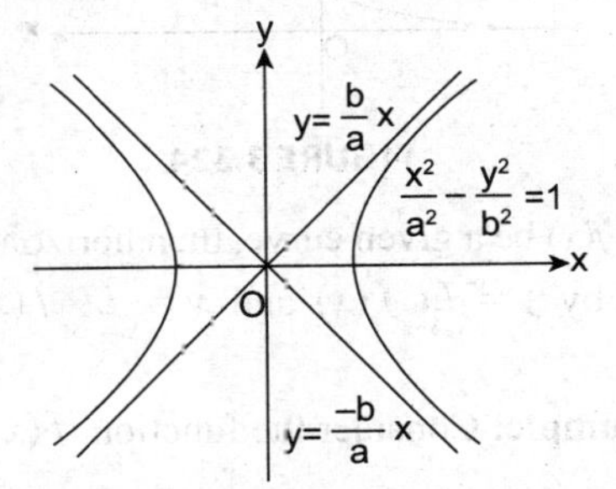

FIGURE 3.321

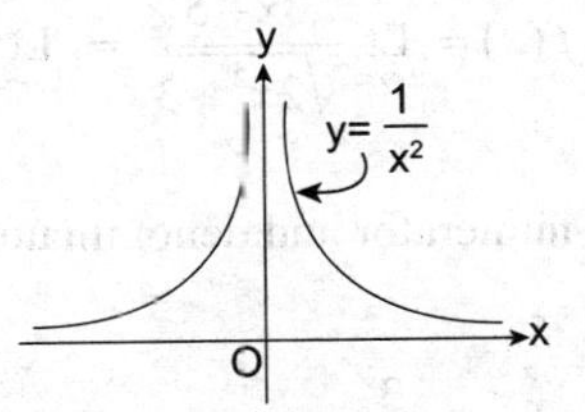

FIGURE 3.322

The line $x = 0$ is vertical asymptote and $y = 0$ is horizontal asymptote of $y = \frac{1}{x^2}$ $y = 0$; π are asymptotes of $y = \cot^{-1}x$.

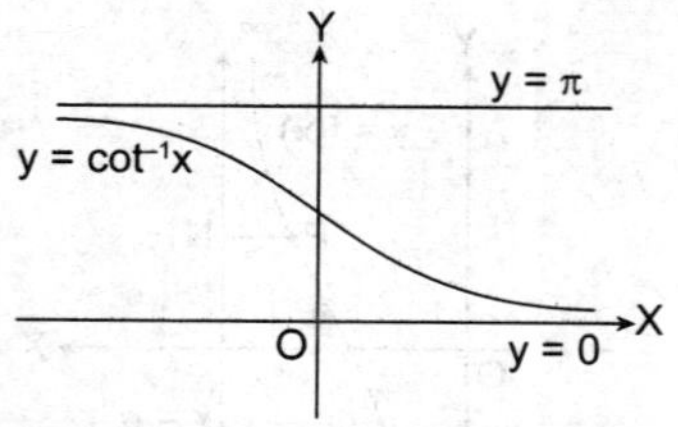

FIGURE 3.323

HORIZONTAL ASYMPTOTE (ASYMPTOTES PARALLEL TO X-AXIS)

Consider $y = \beta$ be a line parallel to the x-axis, and P be any point on the curve $f(x, y) = 0$, also PN be the perpendicular from P on $y = \beta$. Then $PN = |y - \beta|$. If $PN \to 0$ as P tends to infinity along the curve, then $y = \beta$ is an asymptote. This means that $y = \beta$ is an asymptote provided that, as P tends to infinity along the curve, $y \to \beta$ and $x \to \infty$ (for at least one co-ordinate of P must tend to infinity in order that P may tends to infinity). This means that in order to find the asymptotes parallel to the x-axis, we have to look for those real numbers 'β' such that $\lim_{x\to\infty} f(x,\beta) = 0$.

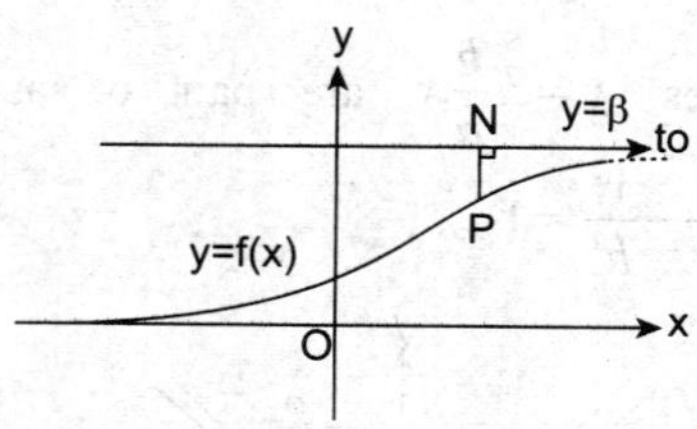

FIGURE 3.324

Let $y = f(x)$ be a given curve, then horizontal asymptote is/are given by $y = \underset{x\to\infty}{Lt} f(x)$ and $y = \underset{x\to-\infty}{Lt} f(x)$.

For example: Consider the function $f(x) = \dfrac{3x-5}{\sqrt{2x^2+3}}$

Then $\underset{x\to\infty}{\text{Lt}} f(x) = \underset{x\to\infty}{\text{Lt}} \dfrac{3x-5}{\sqrt{2x^2+3}} = \underset{x\to\infty}{\text{Lt}} \dfrac{\frac{3x}{x} - \frac{5}{x}}{\sqrt{2 + \frac{3}{x^2}}}$

(dividing each numerator and denominator by x)

$$= \underset{x\to\infty}{\text{Lt}} \frac{3 - \frac{5}{x}}{\sqrt{2 + \frac{3}{x^2}}} = \frac{3}{\sqrt{2}} \text{ and } \underset{x\to-\infty}{\text{Lt}} f(x) = \underset{x\to-\infty}{\text{Lt}} \frac{3x-5}{\sqrt{2x^2+3}}$$

$$= \underset{x\to-\infty}{\text{Lt}} \frac{3x-5}{\sqrt{x^2}\sqrt{2+3/x^2}}.$$

$$= \underset{x\to-\infty}{\text{Lt}} \frac{3x-5}{|x|\sqrt{2+3/x^2}} \qquad \left(\because x<0 \Rightarrow \sqrt{x^2} = |x| = -x\right)$$

$$= \underset{x\to-\infty}{Lt} \frac{3-5/x}{-\sqrt{2+3/x^2}} = -\frac{3}{\sqrt{2}}$$

The two horizontal asymptotes are $y = \dfrac{3}{\sqrt{2}}$ and $y = -\dfrac{3}{\sqrt{2}}$. It is as shown in Figure 3.325.

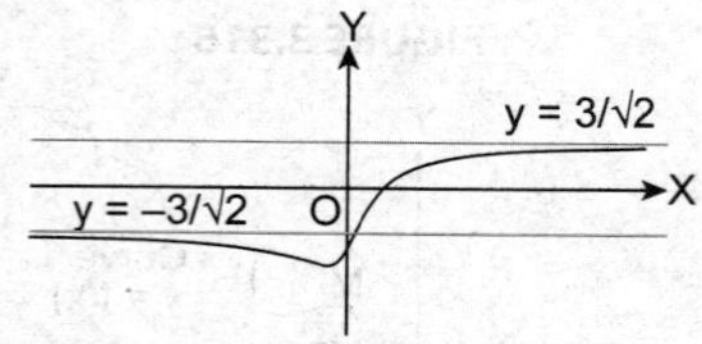

FIGURE 3.325

PROCEDURE TO FIND HORIZONTAL ASYMPTOTE TO ALGEBRAIC CURVE

Let $F(x, y) = 0$ be a rational algebraic curve of degree n. Arranging $F(x, y)$ in descending powers of x, the equation $F(x, y) = 0$ can be written as

$$x^p g_0(y) + x^{p-1} g_1(y) + x^{p-2} g_2(y) + \ldots = 0 \qquad \ldots(1)$$

where $p \le n$, and $g_0(y), g_1(y), g_2(y), \ldots$ are polynomials in y.

Dividing (1) throughout by x^p, i.e., highest power term of x, the equation can be re-written as

$$g_0(y) + (1/x)g_1(y) + (1/x^2)g_2(y) + \ldots = 0 \qquad \ldots(2)$$

Taking limits as $x \to \infty$, and replacing $\lim y = \beta$, yields $g_0(\beta) = 0$ so that β is a root of $g_0(\beta) = 0$

If $\beta_1, \beta_2, \beta_3, \ldots$ are the roots of $g_0(\beta) = 0$, then $y = \beta_1$, $y = \beta_2$, $y = \beta_3$, ... are the asymptotes parallel to the x-axis. Therefore, the joint equation of the asymptotes parallel to the x-axis is

$(y - \beta_1)(y - \beta_2)(y - \beta_3) \ldots = 0$

i.e., $g_0(y) = 0$. Consequently since $g_0(y)$ is the coefficient of the highest power of x in $F(x, y)$, we have the following rule for finding asymptotes parallel to the x-axis.

Algorithm

1. If the coefficient of term containing highest power of x is constant, then there will be no asymptote parallel to x-axis.
2. For finding the asymptotes parallel to x-axis put the coefficient of term containing highest power of x equal to zero.

ILLUSTRATION 87: Find the horizontal asymptotes to curves

(i) $x^2y^2 + xy - 4x^2 = 0$ (ii) $x^3y^2 - x^2y^3 - 3yx^3 + 2x^3 = 0$

SOLUTION: (i) Given equation is $x^2y^2 + xy - 4x^2 = 0$ or $x^2 (y^2 - 4) + xy = 0$

Term containing the highest power of x is $x^2 (y^2 - 4)$ and coefficient of x^2 is $y^2 - 4$

Putting $y^2 - 4 = 0$, we get, $y + 2 = 0$ and $y - 2 = 0$

$\therefore$ $y = -2$ and $y = 2$ are two horizontal asymptotes to given curve.

(ii) Given equation is $x^3y^2 - x^2y^3 - 3yx^3 + 2x^3 = 0$ or $x^3 (y^2 - 3y + 2) - x^2y^3 = 0$

Equating the coefficient of term containing the highest power of x, i.e., of x^3 equal to zero, we get $y^2 - 3y + 2 = 0$ or $(y - 2)(y - 1) = 0$

$\Rightarrow$ $y = 2$ and $y = 1$ are two horizontal asymptotes to the given curve.

■ VERTICAL ASYMPTOTES (ASYMPTOTES PARALLEL TO Y-AXIS)

Consider $x = \alpha$ be a line parallel to the y-axis, and P be any point on the curve $F(x, y) = 0$, also PN be the perpendicular from P on $x = \alpha$. Then $PN = |x - \alpha|$. If $PN \to 0$ as P tends to infinity along the curve, then $x = \alpha$ is an asymptote. This means that $x = \alpha$ is an asymptote provided that as P tends to infinity along the curve, $x \to \alpha$, and $y \to \infty$ (for at least one co-ordinate of P must tend to infinity in order that P may tends to infinity). This means that in order to find the asymptotes parallel to the y-axis, we have to look for those real numbers α which are such that $\lim\limits_{\to\infty} F(\ ,y)\ \ 0$.

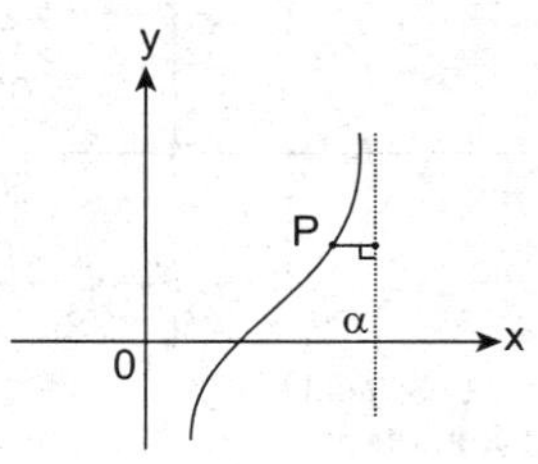

FIGURE 3.326

To find the vertical asymptotes of the infinite branch function $y = f(x)$ of the curve $F(x, y) = 0$, express x in terms of y, i.e., $x = g(y)$ and vertical asymptotes can be obtained by applying limit $y \to \infty$ and $y \to -\infty$ on $g(y)$, i.e., $x = \underset{y\to-\infty}{\text{Lt}}\, g(y)$ and $x = \underset{y\to\infty}{\text{Lt}}\, g(y)$ give us vertical asymptotes. Any curve $y = f(x)$ can have any number (or infinite number) of vertical asymptotes, as a function can be many one, and hence, $y \to \pm\infty$ can occur at infinitely many inputs x.

e.g., $y = \tan x$ has infinitely many vertical asymptotes at $x = (2n+1)\frac{\pi}{2}$; $n \in \mathbb{Z}$ as shown Figure 3.327.

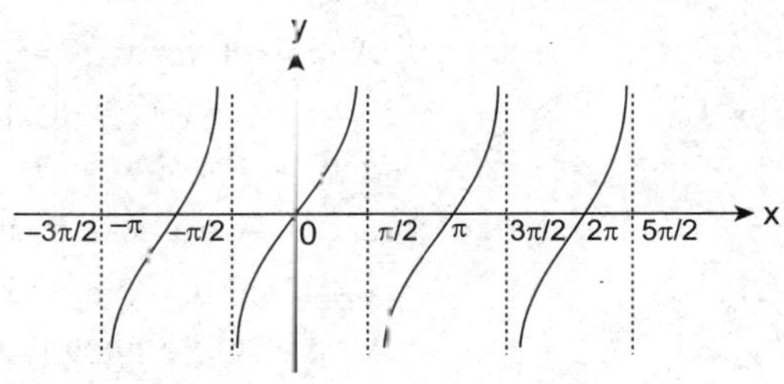

FIGURE 3.327

ILLUSTRATION 88: Find the horizontal and vertical asymptotes to curve.

(i) $y = \dfrac{1}{x-5}$ (ii) $y = \dfrac{3x-4}{x+2}$ (iii) $y = \dfrac{1}{x(x-2)}$

SOLUTION: (i) $y = \dfrac{1}{(x-5)}$; clearly $y = \underset{x\to\pm\infty}{\text{Lt}}\left(\dfrac{1}{x-5}\right) = 0$ is the only horizontal asymptote, and $y > 0$ for $x > 5$ and $y < 0$ for $x < 5$.

Now, $x - 5 = \dfrac{1}{y} \Rightarrow x = 5 + \dfrac{1}{y}$

$\therefore$ Vertical asymptotes are given by $x = \underset{y\to\infty}{\text{Lt}}\left(5+\frac{1}{y}\right)$ and $x = \underset{y\to-\infty}{\text{Lt}}\left(5+\frac{1}{y}\right)$.

i.e., $x = 5$ and $x > 5$ when $y \to \infty$; $x < 5$ when $y \to -\infty$. Graphically as shown in Figure 3.328.

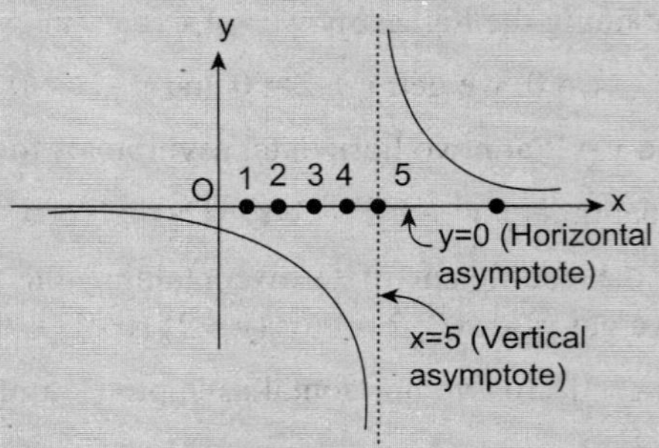

FIGURE 3.328

(ii) $y = \frac{3x-4}{x+2}$, horizontal asymptotes are given by $y = \underset{x\to\pm\infty}{\text{Lt}}\left(\frac{3x-4}{x+2}\right) = \underset{x\to\pm\infty}{\text{Lt}}\left(\frac{3-4/x}{1+2/x}\right) = 3$

$\Rightarrow$ $y = 3$ is the only horizontal asymptote and $y > 0 \Rightarrow (3x-4)(x+2) > 0$

$\Rightarrow$ $x \in (-\infty, -2) \cup \left(\frac{4}{3}, \infty\right)$ and $y < 0 \Rightarrow x \in \left(-2, \frac{4}{3}\right)$

Now, $y \to \infty$ for $x + 2 \to 0 \Rightarrow x \to -2$

$\therefore$ $x = -2$ is the only vertical asymptote, when $x \to -2^-$; $y \to +\infty$ and when $x \to -2^+$; $y \to -\infty$

Graphically shown in Figure 3.329.

(iii) $y = \frac{1}{x(x-2)}$. For horizontal asymptotes, $y = \underset{x\to\pm\infty}{\text{Lt}}\frac{1}{x(x-2)} = 0$

$\therefore$ $y = 0$ is the only horizontal asymptote and $y < 0$ for $x \in (0, 2)$.

And $y > 0$ for $x \in (-\infty, 0) \cup (2, \infty)$.

$\therefore$ $y \to 0^+$ for $x \to \pm\infty$. Also $y \to -\infty$ as $x \to 0^+$ and $y \to \infty$ as $x \to 0^-$

and $y \to \infty$ as $x \to 2^+$ and $y \to -\infty$ as $x \to 2^-$

$\therefore$ $x = 0$ and $x = 2$ are to vertical asymptotes. Graphically shown in Figure 3.330.

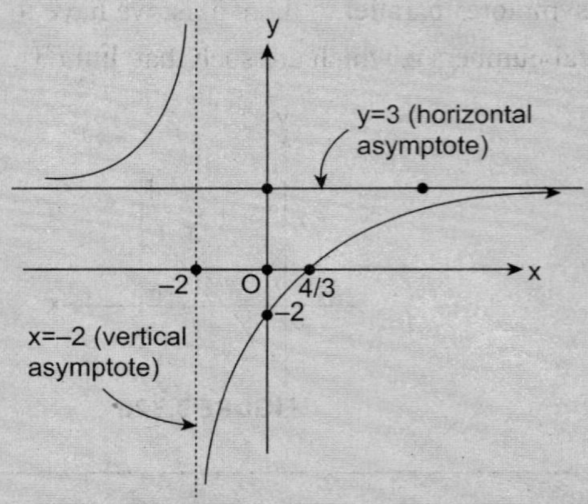

FIGURE 3.329

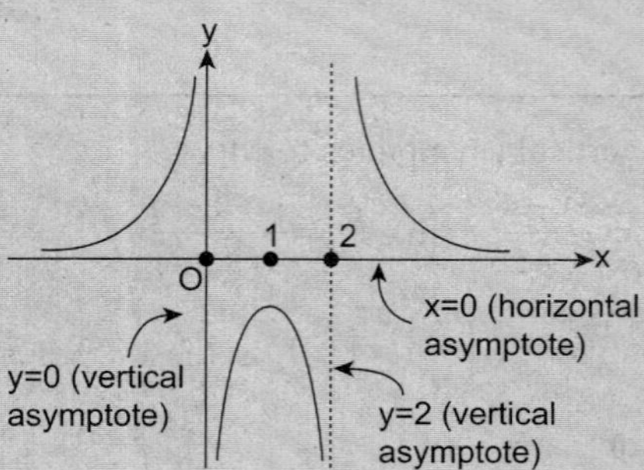

FIGURE 3.330

PROCEDURE TO FIND VERTICAL ASYMPTOTE

Let $f(x, y) = 0$ be a rational algebraic curve of degree n. Arranging $F(x, y)$ in descending powers of y, the equation $F(x, y) = 0$ can be written as

$$y^p f_0(x) + y^{p-1} f_1(x) + y^{p-2} f_2(x) + ... = 0 \qquad ...(1)$$

where $p \le n$ and $f_0(x), f_1(x), f_2(x), ...$ are polynomials in x.

Dividing (1) throughout by y^p, i.e., highest power term of y, the equation can be re-written as

$$f_0(x) + (1/y) f_1(x) + (1/y^2) f_2(x) + ... = 0 \qquad ...(2)$$

Taking limits as $y \to \infty$, and replacing lim $x = \alpha$, yields $f_0(\alpha) = 0$ so that α is a root of $f_0(x) = 0$.

If $\alpha_1, \alpha_2, \alpha_3, ...$ are the root of $f_0(x) = 0$, then $x = \alpha_1, x = \alpha_2, x = \alpha_3 ......$ are the asymptotes parallel to the x-axis, Therefore, the joint equation of the asymptotes parallel to the x-axis is

$$(x - \alpha_1)(x - \alpha_2)(x - \alpha_3) .... = 0$$

i.e., $f_0(x) = 0$. Consequently since $f_0(x)$ is the co-efficient of the highest power of y in $F(y, x)$, we have the following rule for finding asymptotes parallel to the y-axis.

(i) If the coefficient of term containing highest power of y is non-zero, then there will be no asymptote parallel to y-axis.

(ii) Equating the coefficient of term containing highest power of y equal to zero gives us vertical asymptotes.

ILLUSTRATION 89: Find the vertical asymptotes to the curves

(i) $x^2y^2 - 5xy + 6y = 0$ (ii) $3y^2 - 5xy + 2y = 0$ (iii) $x^3y^2 + 3xy - y^2x = 0$

SOLUTION: (i) Given curve is $x^2y^2 - 5xy + 6y = 0$. Coefficient of highest power of y, i.e., of y^2 is x^2

$\therefore$ Vertical asymptotes are given by $x^2 = 0 \Rightarrow x = 0$ (y-axis)

(ii) Given curve is $3y^2 - 5xy + 2y = 0$. Coefficient of highest power of y (i.e., y^2) is 3, which is constant. Thus, there is no asymptote parallel to y-axis.

(iii) Given curve is $x^3y^2 + 3xy - y^2x = 0$ or $y^2(x^3 - x) + 3xy = 0$

Coefficient of highest power of y (i.e., y^2) is $x^3 - x$

$\therefore$ Vertical asymptotes are given by $x^3 - x = 0$

$\Rightarrow x(x^2 - 1) = 0 \qquad \Rightarrow x = 0, x = -1, x = 1$

$\therefore$ There are three vertical asymptotes, namely $x = 0$, $x = -1$ and $x = 1$.

OBLIQUE ASYMPTOTES

Let $y = f(x)$ be a given infinite branch function of some curve $F(x, y) = 0$ and $P(x, y)$ be any variable point on it, then equation of tangent to curve at point $P(x, y)$ will be

$$Y - y = \frac{dy}{dx}(X - x) \quad \text{or} \quad Y = y + \frac{dy}{dx}(X - x)$$

$$\text{or} \quad Y = \frac{dy}{dx} X + \left(y - x\frac{dy}{dx} \right) \qquad .....(1)$$

$\because$ There exists an oblique asymptote for the given curve, as $x, y \to \infty$, slope of tangent (m) should be finite and also y-intercept should be finite

$$\Rightarrow \quad m = \underset{\substack{x\to\infty \\ y\to\infty}}{\text{Lt}} \left(\frac{dy}{dx} \right) \quad \text{and} \quad c = \underset{\substack{x\to\infty \\ y\to\infty}}{\text{Lt}} \left(y - x\frac{dy}{dx} \right)$$

$\therefore$ the straight line $y = mx + c$ obtained is indeed the required oblique asymptote.

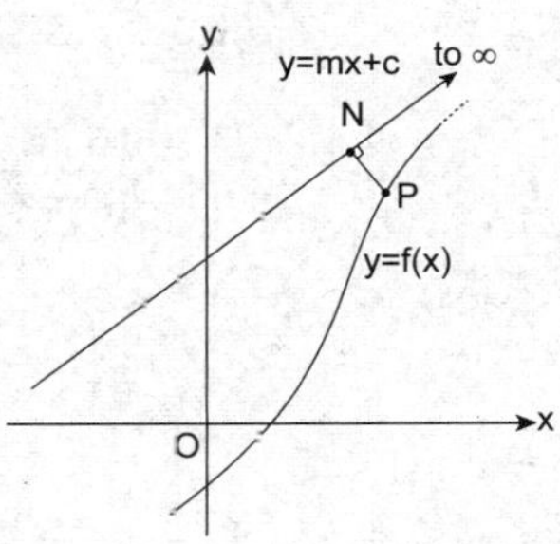

FIGURE 3.331

Procedure to Find Oblique Asymptotes

Step 1: Obtain $\frac{dy}{dx}$ and find $m = \underset{\substack{x\to\infty \\ y\to\infty}}{\text{Lt}} \left(\frac{dy}{dx} \right)$

Step 2: Also find $c = \underset{\substack{x\to\infty \\ y\to\infty}}{\text{Lt}} \left(y - x\frac{dy}{dx} \right)$

Step 3: Consequently $y = mx + c$ gives us oblique asymptote.

ILLUSTRATION 90: Find the asymptotes to the given curves:

(i) $y = 5x - \dfrac{2}{x}$ (ii) $2y = 3\sqrt{x^2 + 4}$

SOLUTION: (i) Equation of curve is $y = 5x - \dfrac{2}{x}$ or $xy = 5x^2 - 2$

For horizontal asymptote:

Since the coefficient of x^2, i.e., 5 is a non-zero constant, so, there is no asymptote parallel to x-axis.

For vertical asymptote:

Put coefficient of y, i.e., x equals to zero, i.e., $x = 0$ (y-axis) is the only vertical asymptote.

For oblique Asymptote:

$$y = 5x - \frac{2}{x} \quad \Rightarrow \quad \frac{dy}{dx} = 5 + \frac{2}{x^2}$$

$$\therefore \quad m = \underset{\substack{x\to\infty \\ y\to\infty}}{\text{Lt}} \left(\frac{dy}{dx}\right) = \underset{\substack{x\to\infty \\ y\to\infty}}{\text{Lt}} \left(5 + \frac{2}{x^2}\right) = 5 \text{ and } c = \underset{\substack{x\to\infty \\ y\to\infty}}{\text{Lt}} \left(y - x\frac{dy}{dx}\right) = \underset{\substack{x\to\infty \\ y\to\infty}}{\text{Lt}} \left(y - x\left(5 + \frac{2}{x^2}\right)\right)$$

$$\Rightarrow c = \underset{\substack{x\to\infty \\ y\to\infty}}{\text{Lt}} \left(y - 5x - \frac{2}{x}\right) = \underset{x\to\infty}{\text{Lt}} -\left(\frac{2}{x} + \frac{2}{x}\right) = \underset{x\to\infty}{\text{Lt}} \left(-\frac{4}{x}\right) = 0$$

$\therefore$ $y = 5x + 0$ or $y = 5x$

$\therefore$ The straight lines $x = 0$, $y = 5x$ are the asymptotes to the curve.

(ii) Given curve $2y = 3\sqrt{x^2 + 4}$ or $4y^2 = 9(x^2 + 4)$ $\Rightarrow$ $4y^2 = 9x^2 + 36$

$\Rightarrow$ There is no asymptote parallel to coordinate axis as coefficient of x^2 and y^2 are non-zero constant.

$$\text{Now, } y = \frac{3}{2}\sqrt{x^2 + 4} \quad \Rightarrow \quad \frac{dy}{dx} = \frac{3}{2}\left(\frac{1}{2}\right) \cdot \frac{1}{\sqrt{x^2 + 4}}(2x) \quad \Rightarrow \quad \frac{dy}{dx} = \frac{3x}{2\sqrt{x^2 + 4}}$$

$$\therefore \quad \text{As } x \to \infty \; m = \underset{x\to\infty}{\text{Lt}} \frac{3x}{2\sqrt{x^2 + 4}} = \underset{x\to\infty}{\text{Lt}} \frac{3}{2} \frac{x}{|x|\sqrt{1 + 4/x^2}} = \underset{x\to\infty}{\text{Lt}} \frac{3}{2} \frac{1}{\sqrt{1 + 4/x^2}} = \frac{3}{2}$$

$$\text{and As } x \to \infty \; m = \underset{x\to-\infty}{\text{Lt}} \frac{3}{2} \frac{x}{|x|\sqrt{1 + 4/x^2}} = \underset{x\to-\infty}{\text{Lt}} \frac{3}{2} \frac{x}{(-x)\sqrt{1 + 4/x^2}} = -\frac{3}{2} \text{ and}$$

$$c = \underset{\substack{y\to\infty \\ x\to\infty}}{\text{Lt}} \left(y - x\frac{dy}{dx}\right) = \underset{\substack{x\to\infty \\ y\to\infty}}{\text{Lt}} \frac{3}{2}\left(\sqrt{x^2 + 4} - x^2 \cdot \frac{1}{\sqrt{x^2 + 4}}\right) = \underset{x\to\infty}{\text{Lt}} \frac{6}{\sqrt{x^2 + 4}} = 0$$

$\therefore$ $y = -\dfrac{3}{2}x + 0$ and $y = \dfrac{3}{2}x + 0$, i.e., $y = \pm\dfrac{3}{2}x$ are the only asymptotes to the given curve.

■ ANOTHER METHOD TO FIND OBLIQUE ASYMPTOTE FOR SECOND DEGREE CURVE

Let $F(x, y) = 0$ be the given curve, and the straight line $y = mx + c$ be the oblique asymptote(s). Put $y = mx + c$ in $F(x, y) = 0$ to obtain a polynomial in x. Substituting the highest power of x equal to zero gives us the possible slopes and second highest power of x equal to zero gives us the possible values of y-intercept 'c'.

ILLUSTRATION 91: Find the asymptotes of the curve $y=\dfrac{3x^2-2x+4}{x}$.

SOLUTION: Given equation is $xy = 3x^2 - 2x + 4$ or $3x^2 - xy - 2x + 4 = 0$

Horizontal asymptote: As coefficient of $x^2 = 3$ (non-zero constant) there is no asymptote parallel to x-axis.

Vertical asymptote: Coefficient of y is $x = 0$ (y-axis) is only vertical asymptote.

Oblique asymptote: Let $y = mx + c$ be the oblique asymptote.

$\therefore$ $3x^2 - x(mx + c) - 2x + 4 = 0$

$\Rightarrow$ $x^2(3 - m) - (2 + c)x + 4 = 0$

$\therefore$ slope of asymptote is given by $3 - m = 0$ and y-intercept is given by $2 + c = 0$

$\Rightarrow$ $m = 3,\ c = -2$

$\therefore$ $y = 3x - 2$ is the only oblique asymptote to the given curve.

REMARKS

1. *A curve of n-degree in x and y can't have more than n-asymptotes.*
2. *For a given value of x, the values of y for different branches of the curve f(x, y) = 0 will be different. Therefore, we may get several different values of m and correspondingly several different values of* $\lim_{x\to\infty}(y-mx)$. *This shows that a curve may have more than one asymptote.*
3. *The above method determines not only oblique asymptotes but also horizontal asymptotes. It does not, however, determine the vertical asymptote.*

■ METHOD TO FIND OBLIQUE ASYMPTOTES FOR ALGEBRAIC CURVES OF ANY DEGREE

Let the equation of a rational algebraic curve of degree 'n' in x and y be of the form

$(a_0x^n + a_1x^{n-1}y + a_2x^{n-2}y^2 + \ldots. + a_ny^n) + (b_1x^{n-1} + b_2x^{n-2}y + b_3x^{n-3}y^2 + \ldots. + b_ny^{n-1}) + (c_2x^{n-2} + c_3x^{n-3}y + \ldots. + c_ny^{n-2}) + \ldots. + = 0$

i.e., $H_n + H_{n-1} + H_{n-2} + \ldots.. + H_2 + H_1 + H_0 = 0$ ......(1)

Where H_r is a homogeneous polynomial of degree r in x, y

Therefore, we can write $H_r = x^r\,\phi_r\,(y/x)$, where ϕ_r is a polynomial of degree at the most r in y/x.

Consequently equation (1) can be written in the form

$$x^n\phi_n\left(\frac{y}{x}\right)+x^{n-1}\phi_{n-1}\left(\frac{y}{x}\right)+x^{n-2}\phi_{n-2}\left(\frac{y}{x}\right)+\ldots+$$
$$x\phi_1\left(\frac{y}{x}\right)+\phi_0\left(\frac{y}{x}\right)=0 \qquad \ldots.(2)$$

Dividing (2) throughout by x^n, we have

$$\phi_n\left(\frac{y}{x}\right)+\left(\frac{1}{x}\right)\phi_{n-1}\left(\frac{y}{x}\right)+\left(\frac{1}{x^2}\right)\phi_{n-2}\left(\frac{y}{x}\right)+\ldots+$$
$$\left(\frac{1}{x^n}\right)\phi_0\left(\frac{y}{x}\right)=0 \qquad \ldots..(3)$$

On taking limits of both sides of (3) as $x \to \infty$, $\dfrac{y}{x}\to m$, we have equation

$(a_0 + a_1m + a_2m^2 + \ldots. + a_nm^n) +$
$1/x(b_1 + b_2m + b_3m^2 - \ldots + b_nm^{n-1}) +$
$1/x^2(c_2 + c_3m + \ldots + c_nm^{n-2}) + \ldots. + = 0$

i.e., $\phi_n(m) = 0$ ... (4)

Here, $\phi_n\,(m)$ denotes the polynomial of degree n in 'm' by which we determines the (possible) slopes of the asymptotes .

If we determine the polynomial of degree $n-1$ in m by $\phi_{n-1}(m)$, the polynomial of degree $n-2$ in 'm' by $\phi_{n-2}\,(m)$ and so on. Following algorithm helps to determine asymptotes of an algebraic curve.

Step I: Putting $\phi_n(m) = 0$, gives us at most n real roots m_1, m_2, m_3, ... m_n, i.e., slope of asymptotes.

Step II: Now to find y-intercept 'c' corresponding to a given slope $m_i (= m)$ we use

$c\phi_n'(m) + \phi_{n-1}(m) = 0$, if m is a non-repeated root, $\frac{c^2}{2!}\phi_n''(m) + \frac{c}{1!}\phi_{n-1}'(m) + \phi_{n-2}(m) = 0$, if m is a root twice repeated $\frac{c^3}{3!}\phi_n'''(m) + \frac{c^2}{2!}\phi''_{n-1}(m) + \frac{c}{1!}\phi'_{n-2}(m) + \phi_{n-3}(m) = 0$, if m is a root thrice repeated and so on.

Step III: Asymptotes are given by $y = mx + c$

ILLUSTRATION 92: Find all the asymptotes to the curve $(x^3y - x^2y^2) + (4x^2y + 2xy^2) - 8xy + 12x + 10 = 0$

SOLUTION: Given curve is $(x^3y - x^2y^2) + (4x^2y + 2xy^2) - 8xy + 12x + 10 = 0$

$$\Rightarrow x^4\left(\frac{y}{x} - \left(\frac{y}{x}\right)^2\right) + 2x^3\left(2\left(\frac{y}{x}\right) + \left(\frac{y}{x}\right)^2\right) - 8x^2\left(\frac{y}{x}\right) + (12x+10)\left(\frac{y}{x}\right)^0 = 0$$

Asymptotes || to x-axis are given by $y = 0$ (equating the coefficient of, highest power of x, i.e., x^3 equal to 0).

Asymptotes || to y-axis are given by $2x - x^2 = 0$ (equating the coefficient of $y^2 = 0$)

$\Rightarrow$ $x(2 - x) = 0$

$\Rightarrow$ $x = 0$ and $x = 2$ are two asymptotes parallel to y-axis

$\phi_4(m) = m - m^2$

and $\phi_3(m) = 4m + 2m^2$, $\phi_2(m) = -8m$, $\phi_1(m) = 12$, $\phi_0(m) = 10$

Now slopes of oblique asymptotes are given by $\phi_4(m) = 0$

i.e., $m - m^2 = 0 \Rightarrow$ m $(1 - m) = 0$

$\Rightarrow$ $m = 0$ and $m = 1$

But $m = 0$ corresponds to asymptote parallel to x-axis, i.e., $y = 0$

$\therefore$ $m = 1$ corresponds to oblique asymptote not parallel to x-axis, corresponding y-intercept 'c' is given by $c\phi_4'(m) + \phi_3(m) = 0$

$\Rightarrow$ $c(1 - 2m) + (4m + 2m^2) = 0$

$\Rightarrow$ $c(1 - 2) + (4 + 2) = 0$ $\quad\Rightarrow$ $c = 6$

$\therefore$ $y = x + 6$ is the oblique asymptote

Thus, $y = 0$, $x = 0$, $x = 2$, $y = x + 6$ are asymptotes to given curve.

■ ASYMPTOTE BY EXPANSION

If the equation of the curve is of the form $y = mx + c + \frac{A}{x} + \frac{B}{x^2} + \frac{C}{x^3} + \ldots\ldots\ldots\ldots$, then $y = mx + c$ will be an asymptote of the given curve.

ILLUSTRATION 93: Find the asymptote for $y = 2x + 5 + 3/x$.

SOLUTION: Here, $y = 2x + 5 + 3/x$ is of the form, $y = mx + c + \frac{A}{x} + \frac{B}{x^2} + \ldots..$

$\Rightarrow$ $y = 2x + 5$ is an asymptote of the curve $y = 2x + 5 + 3/x$.

ILLUSTRATION 94: Find the asymptotes to the curve $y^3 = 8x^3 + 24x^2 + 16x$.

SOLUTION : Given the curve $y^3 = 8x^3 + 24x^2 + 16x$.

$$\Rightarrow y^3 = 8x^3\left(1+\frac{3}{x}+\frac{2}{x^2}\right) \Rightarrow y = 2x\left(1+\frac{3}{x}+\frac{2}{x^2}\right)^{1/3}$$

$$\Rightarrow y = 2x\left[1+\frac{1}{3}\left(\frac{3}{x}+\frac{2}{x^2}\right)+\frac{\left(\frac{1}{3}\right)\left(\frac{-2}{3}\right)\left(\frac{3}{x}+\frac{2}{x^2}\right)^2}{2!}+....\right]$$

$$\Rightarrow y = 2x\left[1+\frac{1}{3}\left(\frac{3}{x}+\frac{2}{x^2}\right)-\frac{1}{9}\left(\frac{3}{x}+\frac{2}{x^2}\right)^2+....\right]$$

$$\Rightarrow y = 2x\left(1+\frac{1}{x}+\frac{5}{3x^2}+.....\right)$$

$\therefore$ $y = 2(x+1)$ is the oblique asymptote to the given curve .

■ THE POSITION OF THE CURVE WITH RESPECT TO AN ASYMPTOTE

Let the equation of the curve be of the form:

$$y = mx + c + \frac{A}{x}+\frac{B}{x^2}+\frac{C}{x^3}+....., \text{ then,}$$

(a) The curve lies above the asymptote if

(i) $A \neq 0$ and A and x have same signs.

(ii) $A \neq 0, B > 0$

(iii) $A = 0, B = 0, C \neq 0$ and C and x have same signs.

(b) The curve lies below the asymptote if

(i) $A \neq 0$ and A and x have opposite signs.

(ii) $A = 0, B < 0$

(iii) $A = 0,\ B = 0,\ C \neq 0$ and C and x have opposite signs.

ILLUSTRATION 95: For the curve $y^4 - x^4 + 3x^3 = 0$

(i) show that the curve lie above asymptote $y = x - 1/2$ for $x < 0$

(ii) show that the curve lie below asymptote $y = x - 1/2$ for $x > 0$

SOLUTION: Given equation of curve is $y^4 - x^4 + 2x^3 = 0$

$$\Rightarrow y^4 = x^4 - 2x^3 \Rightarrow y^4 = x^4\left(1-\frac{2}{x}\right) \Rightarrow y = x\left[1-\frac{2}{x}\right]^{1/4}$$

$$\Rightarrow y = x\left(1+\frac{1}{4}\left(\frac{-2}{x}\right)+\frac{\frac{1}{4}\left(\frac{1}{4}-1\right)\left(\frac{-2}{x}\right)^2}{2!}+\frac{\left(\frac{1}{4}\right)\left(\frac{1}{4}-1\right)\left(\frac{1}{4}-2\right)\left(-\frac{2}{x}\right)^3}{3!}+....\right)$$

$$\Rightarrow y = x\left(1-\frac{1}{2x}-\frac{3}{8x^2}-\frac{7}{16x^3}-...\right) \qquad \Rightarrow y = \left(x-\frac{1}{2}-\frac{3}{8x}-\frac{7}{16x^2}-...\right)$$

Comparing with $y = mx + c + \frac{A}{x}+\frac{B}{x^2}+...$, we get

the oblique asymptote given by $y = \left(x-\frac{1}{2}\right)$, $A = -3/8$, $B = -7/16$

Since both A and B are negative.

$\therefore$ The curve lies above the asymptote for $x < 0$ because x and A are of same sign.

And the curve lies below the asymptote for $x > 0$ since x and A are opposite sign.

$\therefore$ The curve lies above asymptote $y = \left(x - \frac{1}{2}\right)$ for $x < 0$

and the curve lies below asymptote $y = \left(x - \frac{1}{2}\right)$ for $x > 0$.

■ SINGULAR POINTS (MULTIPLE POINTS)

Introduction

We know that there are many relations which are multiple valued (one–many) that is why their equations are of the form $F(x, y) = 0$ (and not of the form $y = f(x)$. An equation of the form $F(x, y) = 0$ may sometimes be not solvable so as to yield $y = f(x)$, for it may give rise to several values of y corresponding to a single value of x, and these different values of y give rise to different branches of the curve.

Definition

A point on a curve is said to be a multiple point of order r, if r branches of the curve pass through this point. If P is the multiple point of order r, then there will be r tangents at P, one of each of the r branches. These r tangents may be real, imaginary, distinct, coincident.

■ DOUBLE POINTS

A point on a curve is said to be a double point of the curve, if two branches of the curve pass through this point. Double points have two tangents, they may be real, imaginary, distinct or coincident.

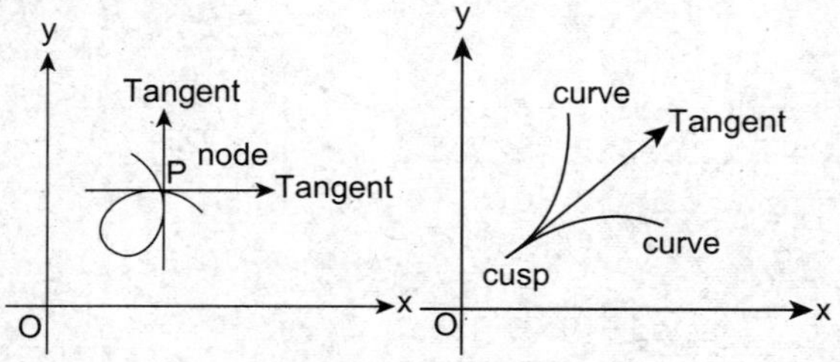

FIGURE 3.332

Types of Double Points

(a) Node: If the two branches of a curve through the double point and the tangents to them at the point are real and distinct, then the double point is called a node. For instance, $y^2 = (x - 2)(x - 5)^2$. The curve has two branches given by analytic equation $y = \pm|x - 5|\sqrt{x-2}$. The point (2, 0) and (5, 0) is common to both. The graph of this curve is as shown in figure 3.333 indeed the two branches have different tangents at the point (5, 0), therefore, this point shall be called as Node.

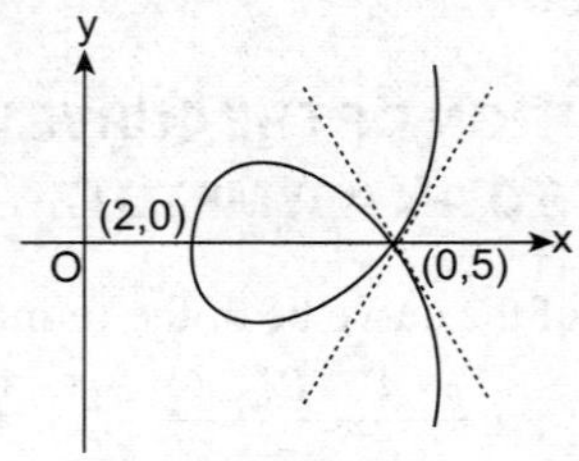

FIGURE 3.333

(b) Cusp: If the two branches of the curve pass through the double point and the tangent to them at the point are real and coincident, then the double point is called cusp.
The graph of a continuous function $y = f(x)$ has a cusp at a point $x = c$ if the concavity is same on the both side of c and either

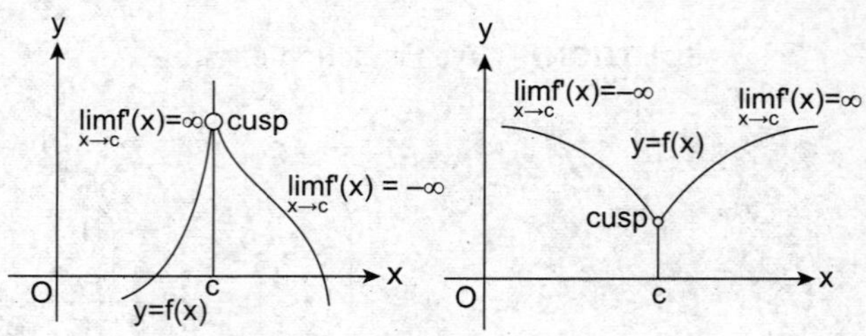

FIGURE 3.334

1. $\lim\limits_{x \to c^-} f'(x) = \infty$ and $\lim\limits_{x \to c^+} f'(x) = -\infty$
2. $\lim\limits_{x \to c^-} f'(x) = -\infty$ and $\lim\limits_{x \to c^+} f'(x) = \infty$

A cusp can either be local maximum (1) or a local minima as in (2).

For instance, the curves described by equation $y^2(2a - x) = x^3$, also has two functional branches given by functional formulae $y=\pm|x|\sqrt{\dfrac{x}{2a-x}}$; having origin as common point to both the branches. The graph of this curve is as shown in the figure given below. Clearly, both the branches of the curve have a common tangent there, namely $y = 0$. Thus, the origin is a cusp here.

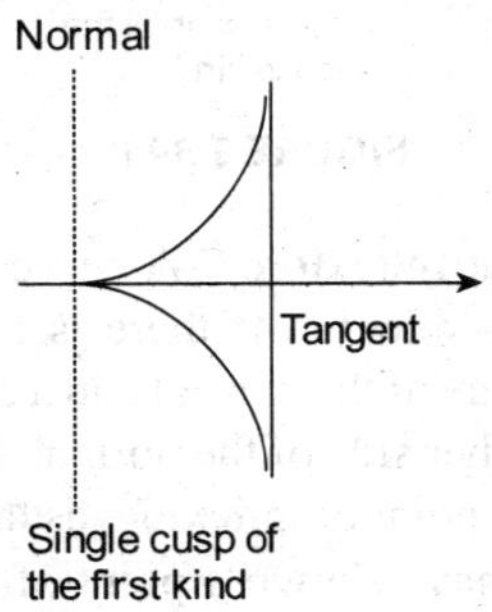

FIGURE 3.335

(c) Isolated point: If there are no real point on the curve in the neighborhood of a point P, then it is called an isolated or a conjugate point. e.g., $y^2 = x(x + a)^2$, $a > 0$ has two functional branches given by functional formulae $y=\pm|x+a|.\sqrt{x}$; The graph of this curve is as shown in figure. Here the points $(-a, 0)$ and $(0,0)$ are common to both the branches. Tangent at $(-a, 0)$ is imaginary with joint equation as $y^2 + (x + a)^2 = 0)$ since there is no other point on the curve in a any neighborhood of $(-a, 0)$.Whereas the tangents to both the branches at $(0, 0)$ are vertical (the slope of tangent at this point does not exits finitely).

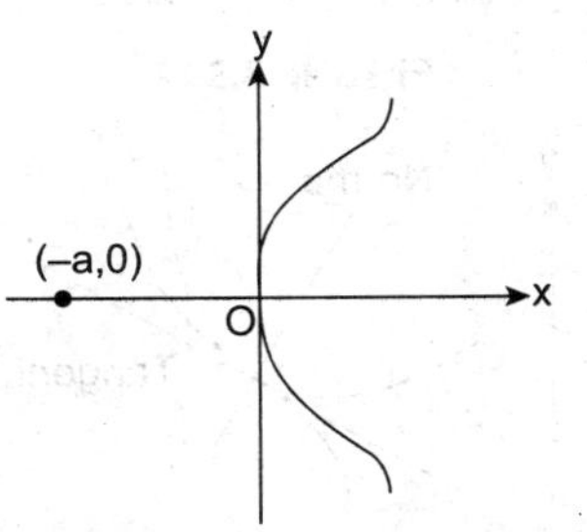

FIGURE 3.336

NECESSARY CONDITIONS FOR THE EXISTENCE OF DOUBLE POINTS

Let (x, y) be a point on the given curve $f(x, y) = 0$. The necessary and sufficient conditions for (x, y) to be double points are $f = 0, \dfrac{\partial f}{\partial x} = 0, \dfrac{\partial f}{\partial y} = 0$ at (x, y).

Now , if $\dfrac{\partial^2 f}{\partial x\,\partial y}$, i.e., $f^2{}_{xy}$; $\dfrac{\partial^2 f}{\partial x^2}$, i.e., f_{xx} and $\dfrac{\partial^2 f}{\partial y^2}$, i.e., f_{yy} are not all zero then,

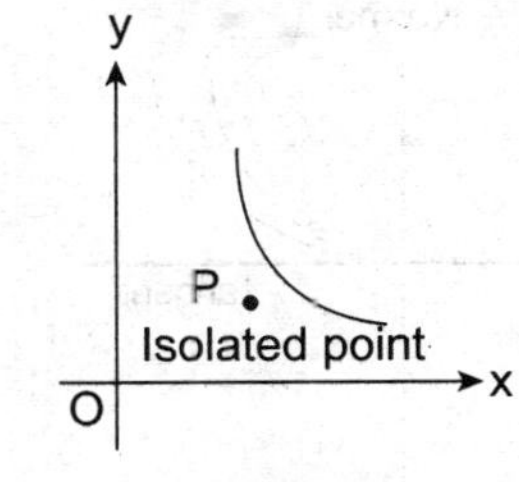

FIGURE 3.337

(i) Double point will be a node if $\left(\dfrac{\partial^2 f}{\partial x\,\partial y}\right)^2 = \left(\dfrac{\partial^2 f}{\partial x^2}\right)\left(\dfrac{\partial^2 f}{\partial y^2}\right) > 0$

or $f_{xy}^2 - f_{xx}f_{yy} > 0$

(ii) The double point will be an isolated point if $f_{xy}^2 - f_{xx}f_{yy} < 0$

(iii) The double point will be a cusp if $f_{xy}^2 - f_{xx}f_{yy} = 0$
Here , $f_{xx} = f_{xy} = f_{yy} = 0$ if at (x, y) then it will be a multiple point of order greater than 2.

TYPES OF CUSPS

As we have understood that if two branches of a curve pass through a point and the tangents are coincident it is known as cusp. Therefore, normal to the branches at a cusp would also be coincident. Cusp can be classified as below.

(a) Single cusp of first species: If the branches of the curve lie on the same side of the common normal, then the cusp is called a single cusp. But if the branches of the curve lie on the both sides of common tangents, then the cusp is called as single cusp of first kind.

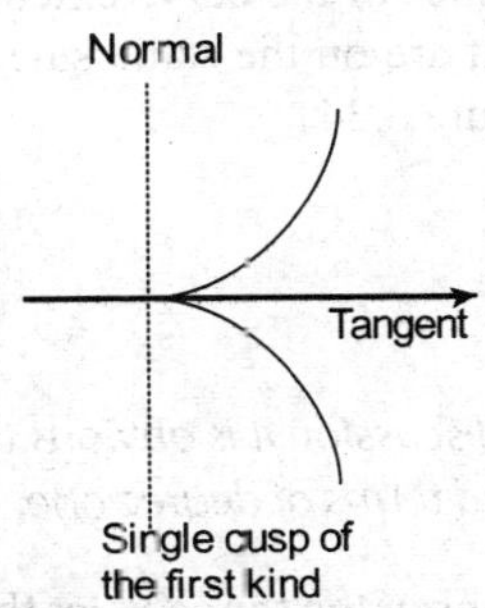

FIGURE 3.338

(b) Single cusp of second species: If the branches of the curve lie on the same side of the common normal, but the branches of the curve also lie on the same sides of common tangents, then the cusp is known as single cusp of second kind.

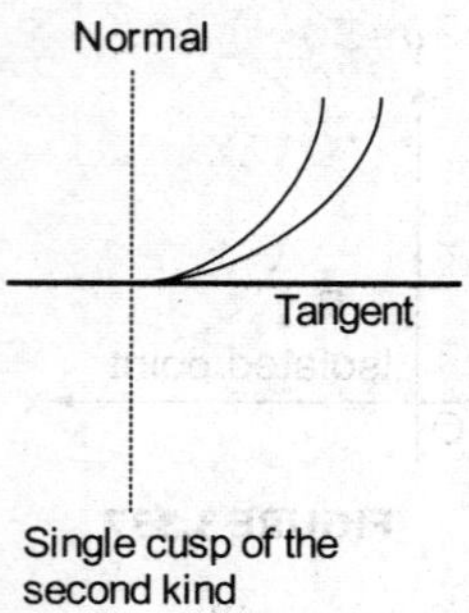

FIGURE 3.339

(c) Double cusp of first species: A curve is said to have a double cusp of the first kind at a point if both the branches of the curve extend to both the sides of the normal at the point and lie on opposite sides of the tangent at that point as shown in Figure 3.340.

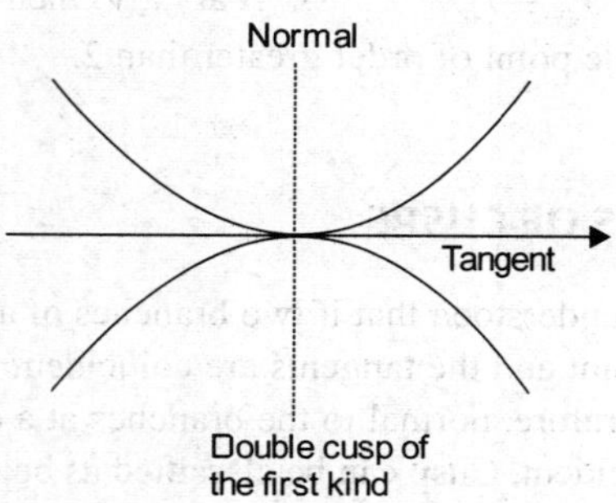

FIGURE 3.340

(b) Double cusp of second species: A curve is said to have a double cusp of the second kind at a point if both the branches of the curve extend to both sides of the normal but are on the same side of the tangent as shown in Figure 3.341.

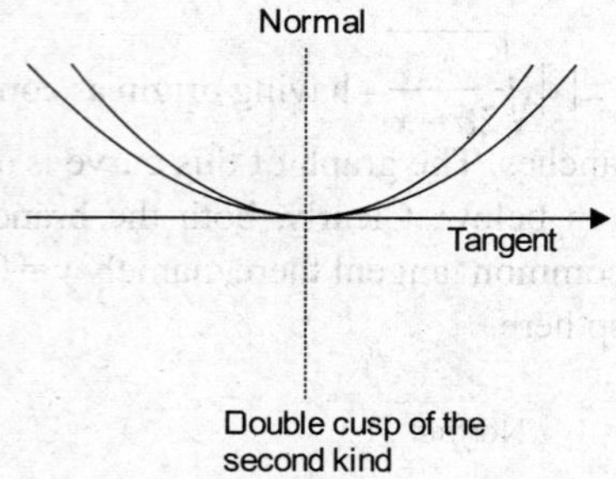

FIGURE 3.341

(c) Point of Oscu-inflexion: A curve is said to have a point of oscu-inflexion if there is a cusp of the first kind on one side of the normal and a cusp of the second kind on the other side of the normal. In such a case the point is also a point of inflexion, as the name suggests. In figure we have shown a point of oscu-inflexion in which the curve has a cusp of the first kind on the right of the normal and a cusp of the second species on the left of the normal. We can also have a point of oscu-inflexion in which there is a cusp of the first species on the left of the normal and a cusp of the second species on the right of the normal see Figures 3.342 and 3.343.

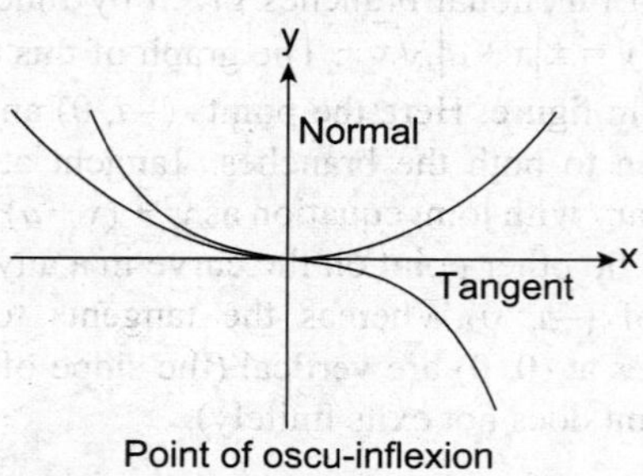

FIGURE 3.342

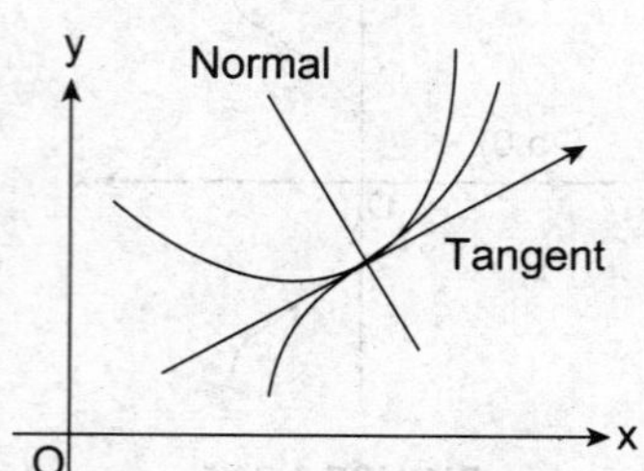

FIGURE 3.343

REMARKS

From the above discussion it is obvious that the origin is a multiple point if and only if f(x, y) does not contain any constant term and terms of degree one.

1. *The equations of the tangents at the origin to the curve $x^4 + y^4 = a^2xy$ are $x = 0, y = 0$, so that the origin is a node.*

2. *The equation of the tangents at the origin to the curve $x^4 + y^4 + 2x^3 = x^2 + 2xy + y^2$ is $x^2 + 2xy + y^2 = 0$, i.e., $(x + y)^2 = 0$. Since the tangents are coincident, the origin is a cusp.*
3. *The equation of the tangents at the origin to the curve $(x^2 + y^2)(x - a) + b^2x^3 = 0$. Since the tangents are imaginary ($y = \pm ix$), therefore, the origin is a conjugate point on the curve.*
4. *The equation of the tangents at the origin to the curve $3x^4 + y^4 + 3y(x^2 - y^2) = 0$ is $y(x^2 - y^2) = 0$. Since there are three tangents at the origin, namely $y = 0, x \pm y = 0$, therefore, the origin is a triple point on the curve.*

ILLUSTRATION 96: Show that the origin is a single cusp of the first species on the curve $(y - 2x^2)^2 = x^3$.

SOLUTION: It is obvious that (0, 0) is a point on the curve. The equation of the tangents at (0, 0) are given by $y^2 = 0$, showing that (0, 0) is a cusp.
Since the left hand side can never be negative, it follows that x can never be negative, i.e., the curve lies entirely to the right of the normal at the cusp (i.e., $x = 0$). This implies that the origin is a single cusp.
Writing the equation of the curve as $y = 2x^2 \pm x^{3/2}$.
We find that for every positive value of x there are two values of y. Since $x^{3/2} > x^2$ for small positive values of x, therefore, for every small positive value of x, the two values of y are of opposite sign. Hence, the cusp is of first species.

ILLUSTRATION 97: Find the position and nature of the cusp on the curve $y^2 + 3x^4 = 4x^2y + x^5$.

SOLUTION: Writing the equation of the curve as $f(x, y) = y^2 + 3x^4 - 4x^2y - x^5 = 0$
We have $f_x = 12x^3 - 8xy - 5x^4$.
$f_y = 2y - 4x^2$
Solving the equations $f(x, y) = 0, f_x = 0, f_y = 0$ together, we find that (0, 0) is the only multiple point.
Equating to zero the lowest degree terms, we find that $y = 0$ is a cuspidal tangent.
Solving $f(x, y) = 0$, as a quadratic in y, we have $y = 2x^2 \pm x^2\sqrt{(1 + x)}$. ... (1)
From (1), we find that for each small positive value of x, there are two values of y which are both positive (because $2x^2 > x^2\sqrt{(1 + x)}$)
Again, for every numerically small but negative value of x, there are two values of y which are both positive.
Thus, in the neighborhood of the origin, the curve lies on both sides of the y-axis, but entirely above the x-axis (which is the cuspidal tangent).
Hence, the origin is a double cusp of the second species.

ILLUSTRATION 98: Compute the area of this figure contained between the curve, $xy^2 = 8 - 4x$ and its asymptote.

SOLUTION: $x = \dfrac{8}{4 + y^2}$

$$\Rightarrow A = 2\int_0^\infty \frac{8}{4 + y^2}dy = \frac{2.8}{2}.\tan^{-1}\frac{y}{2}\Big]_0^\infty = 4\pi$$

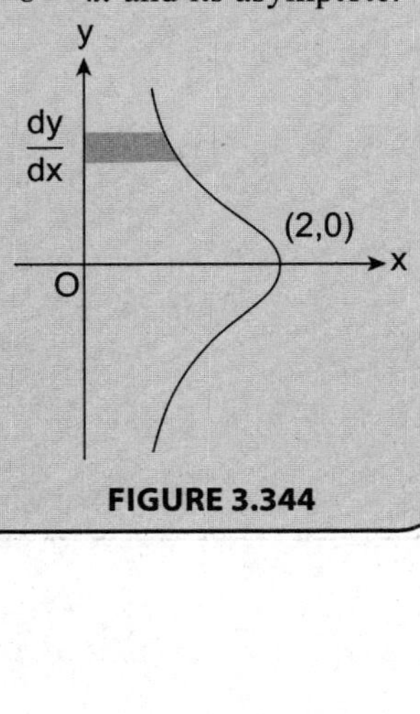

FIGURE 3.344

ILLUSTRATION 99: Sketch the graph of the following functions:

(a) $y = \dfrac{2}{x^2 + 1}$ (b) $y = x + \dfrac{1}{x}$, $x \in \mathbb{R} - \{0\}$

(c) $y = 2x^2 - \log|x|$, $x \neq 0$

SOLUTION: (a) Given function is $y = \dfrac{2}{x^2+1}$

Clearly the domain of the function is $(-\infty.\ \infty)$ and the range is $(0, \infty)$.

It has no roots and at $x = 0$, $y = 2$ which means intersects the y-axis at (0, 2). Since it is even function w.r.t x, therefore, the graph will be symmetric about y-axis. As we know that $f(x) = x^2 + 1$ is a parabola opening upwards with vertex (0, 2) and it increases for $x > 0$ and decreases for all $x < 0$.

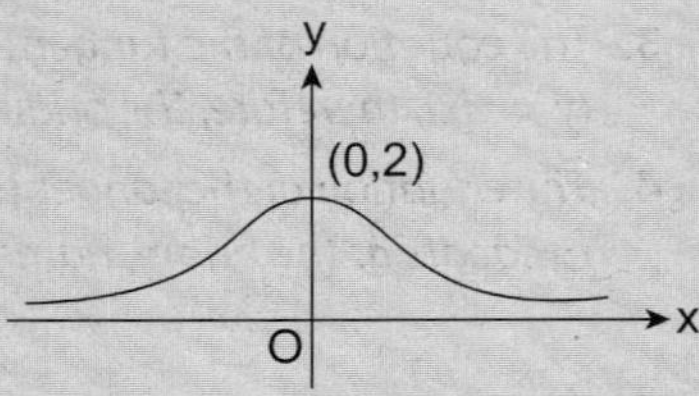

FIGURE 3.345

So, the given function $y = \dfrac{2}{x^2+1}$ will increase for all $x < 0$ and decrease for $x > 0$. Also $\lim\limits_{x\to\infty} f(x) = 0$, so, x-axis is the horizontal asymptote.

(b) Clearly the function does not exist at $x = 0$, and therefore, discontinuous at $x = 0$.

$y' = 1 - \dfrac{1}{x^2} = \dfrac{x^2-1}{x^2} \Rightarrow \quad ' \quad \Rightarrow x = -1, 1$

Also is undefined at $x = 0$. But y at $x = 0$ is also undefined, therefore, $x = 0$ is not a critical point. Therefore, only critical points are the stationary points $x = -1, 1$.

We now use the second derivative test to decide the nature of extrema if they exist.

$y'' = \dfrac{2}{x^3} \Rightarrow y''$ at $x = -1$ is $-2 < 0$ and y'' at $x = 1$ is $2 > 0$

Clearly y'' is positive for $x > 0$ (so, function is concave up) and negative for $x < 0$ (so function is concave down).

Hence, $x = -1$ is a point of local maximum and $x = 1$ is a point of local minimum . Now there are two consecutive extrema , maximum at $x = -1$ and minimum at $x = 1$. Also, y at $x = -1$ is -2 and at $x = 1$ is 2.

The value of y at a point of local maximum is less than the value of y at a point of local minimum.

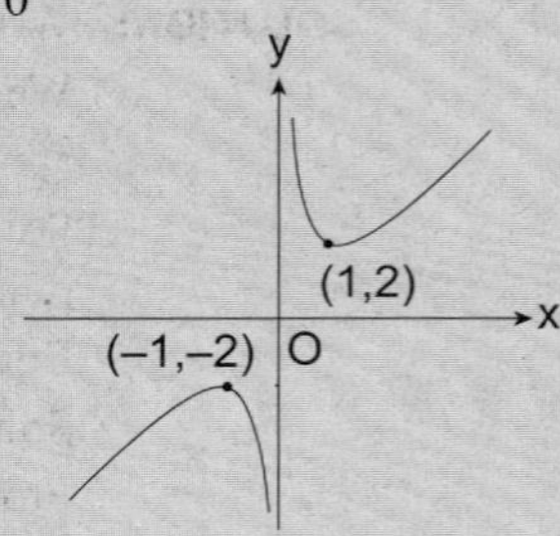

FIGURE 3.346

If minimum value > maximum value at two consecutive extrema, there must be a discontinuity between them.

(c) Clearly y is not defined at $x = 0$ as log 0 is undefined

$\dfrac{dy}{dx} = 4x - \dfrac{1}{x} = \dfrac{4x^2-1}{x} = \dfrac{4(x-1/2)(x+1/2)}{x}$. $\quad \left[\because \dfrac{d}{dx}\log|x| = \dfrac{1}{x}\right]$

Since, y is not defined at $x = 0$, $x = 0$ is not a critical point though $\dfrac{dy}{dx}$ is undefined at $x = 0$. The only critical points are $x = -1/2$ and $1/2$ where $\dfrac{dy}{dx} = 0$.

Now $\dfrac{d^2y}{dx^2} = 4 + \dfrac{1}{x^2} > 0$ at $x = -1/2$ and $1/2$

$\therefore$ y has local minima at both points $x = -1/2$ and $x = 1/2$ shows an illusion that two minima occur consecutively but note that there is a discontinuity at $x = 0$ between them.

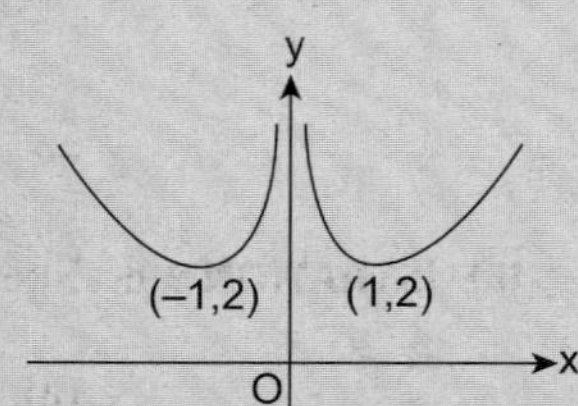

FIGURE 3.347

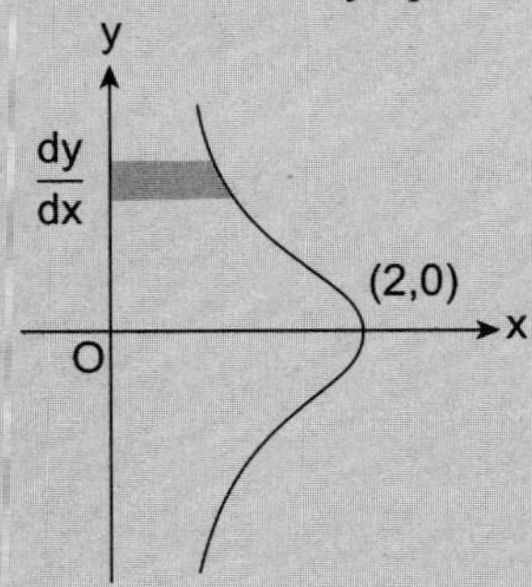

ILLUSTRATION 100: Find the asymptotes of the following curves $y=\dfrac{3x}{x-1}+3x$.

SOLUTION: The curve has a vertical asymptote $x = 1$

since $\lim\limits_{x\to 1^-} y = \lim\limits_{x\to 1^-}\left(\dfrac{3x}{x-1}+3x\right) = -\infty$

$$\lim_{x\to 1^+} y = \lim_{x\to 1^+}\left(\frac{3x}{x-1}+3x\right) = \infty$$

Find the inclined asymptotes:

$$m = \lim_{x\to\pm\infty}\frac{y}{x} = \lim_{x\to\pm\infty}\left(\frac{3}{x-1}+3\right) = 3$$

$$c = \lim_{x\to\pm\infty}(y-mx) = \lim_{x\to\pm\infty}\left(\frac{3x}{x-1}+3x-3x\right) = 3$$

Thus, the straight line $y = 3x + 3$ is an inclined asymptote as shown in the figure.

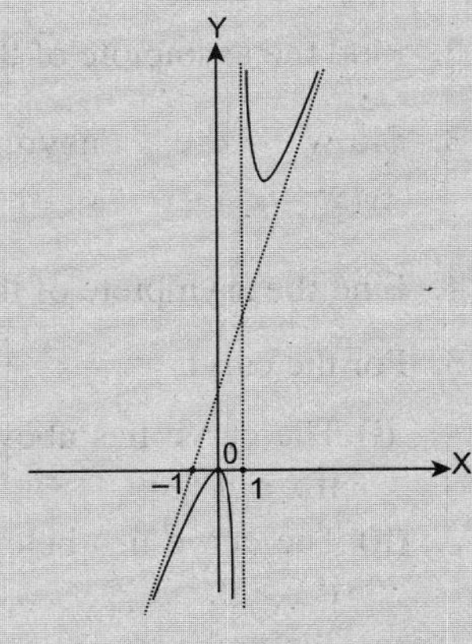

FIGURE 3.348

ILLUSTRATION 101: Find the asymptotes of the following curves $y=\sqrt{1+x^2}+2x$.

SOLUTION: The curve has no vertical asymptotes, since the function is continuous everywhere. Let us look for inclined asymptotes. The limits will be different as $x \to +\infty$ and $x \to +\infty$, therefore, we have to consider two cases separately.

Find the right asymptote (as $x \to +\infty$):

$$k_1 = \lim_{x\to+\infty}\frac{\sqrt{1+x^2}+2x}{x} = \lim_{x\to+\infty}\frac{\sqrt{\dfrac{1}{x^2}+1}+2}{1} = 3$$

$$b_1 = \lim_{x\to+\infty}\left(\sqrt{1+x^2}+2x-3x\right) = \lim_{x\to+\infty}\left|\sqrt{1+x^2}-x\right|$$

$$= \lim_{x\to+\infty}\frac{1+x^2-x^2}{\sqrt{1+x^2}+x} = 0.$$

Thus, as $x \to +\infty$ the curve has an asymptote $y = 3x$.

Find the left asymptote (as $x \to +\infty$):

$$k_2 = \lim_{x\to-\infty}\frac{\sqrt{1+x^2}+2x}{x} = \lim_{x\to-\infty}\frac{|x|\sqrt{\dfrac{1}{x^2}+1+2x}}{x} = 1$$

$$b_2 = \lim_{x\to-\infty}\left|\sqrt{1+x^2}+2x-x\right| = \lim_{x\to-\infty}\frac{1}{\sqrt{1+x^2}-x} = 0$$

Since both summands $\left(\sqrt{1+x^2}\text{ and }(-x)\right)$ in the denominator are positive at $x < 0$, and so, the curve has an asymptote $y = x$, as $x \to -\infty$.

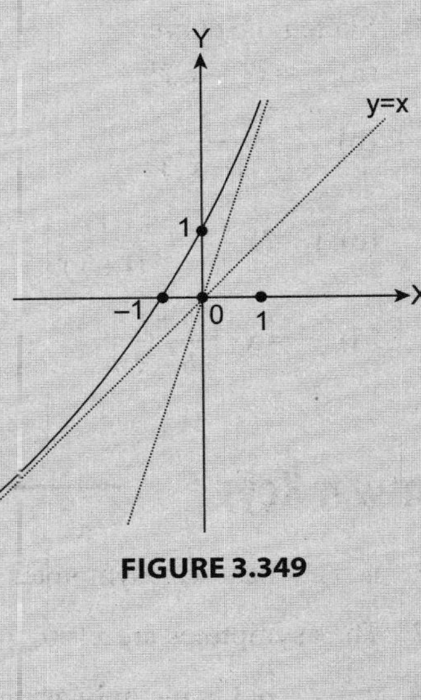

FIGURE 3.349

TEXTUAL EXERCISE–7: (SUBJECTIVE)

1. Show the curve $y = e^{1/x}$ has a vertical and horizontal asymptote.

2. Find the asymptote of the curve $x^2y + xy^2 = a^3$.

3. Show the asymptote of the curve $xy(x^2 - y^2) + x^2 + y^2 - 1 = 0$ cut at 8 points.

4. Find the asymptote of the curve $y^3 = x^2(x - a)$.

5. For the curve $y^5 = x^5 + 2x^4$; show
   (i) The curve lies above the asymptote $y = x + 2/5$ if $x < 0$.
   (ii) The curve lies below the asymptote $y = x + 2/5$ if $x > 0$.

6. Show the curve $y = e^{1/x}$ has a vertical and horizontal asymptote.

7. Find the asymptote to the curve $y = x + 1/x$ and then sketch.

8. Sketch the curve
   (a) $y^2 (a + x) = x^2 (a - x)$
   (b) $y^2x^2 = x^2 - a^2$
   (c) $y^2(x^2 - 1) = (2x - 1)$
   (d) $x^3 + y^3 = 3ax^2$ $(a > 0)$.
   (e) $y^2 (x^2 - 1) = x^2 - 4$
   (f) $(y^2 - 1)(x^2 - 1) = x$
   (g) $(y^2 - 1)(x^2 - 1) = y^2 + x^2$
   (h) $(y^2 - 1)(x^2 + 1) = y^2 + x^2$

9. Sketch the curve
   (a) $y = (1 - x^2)^{-1}$
   (b) $y = \dfrac{x}{(1-x^2)^2}$
   (c) $y = 2x - 1 + \dfrac{1}{(1+x)}$
   (d) $y^2 = x^2\left(\dfrac{a+x}{b-x}\right)$
   (e) $y = \dfrac{8a^3}{x^2 + 4a^2}$
   (f) $y = \dfrac{\cos x}{\cos 2x}$
   (g) $y^2 = 8x^2 - x^4$
   (h) $y^2 = \dfrac{x-1}{x+1}$

10. Sketch the graph of the following functions:
    (a) $y = x^{2/3}$
    (b) $y = \dfrac{2x}{x^2 + 1}$
    (c) $y = \dfrac{x^2 - 1}{x^2 + 1}$
    (d) $y = \dfrac{x^2 + x - 1}{x^2 + x + 1}$
    (h) $y = x^{1/x}$

11. Investigate and graph the following functions:
    (a) $y = x^6 - 3x^4 + 3x^2 - 5$
    (b) $y = \dfrac{2x^3}{x^2 - 4}$
    (c) $y = \dfrac{1 - x^3}{x^2}$
    (d) $y = x + \ln(x^2 - 1)$
    (e) $y = x^2 e^{1/x}$
    (f) $y = 1 + x^2 - \dfrac{x^4}{2}$
    (g) $y = \dfrac{1}{x} + 4x^2$
    (h) $y = \dfrac{x^3}{x^2 - 1}$
    (i) $y = \sqrt[3]{x^2} - \sqrt[3]{x^2 - 4}$
    (j) $y = x^2 \ln(x + 2)$; $y = x^3 e^{-4x}$

Answer Keys

1. $y = e^{1/x}$ has two asymptotes $x = 0$ and $y = 1$.

2. The asymptotes are $x = 0$, $y = 0$, $x + y = 0$

4. $y = x - a/3$ is the only asymptote of the given curve.

6.

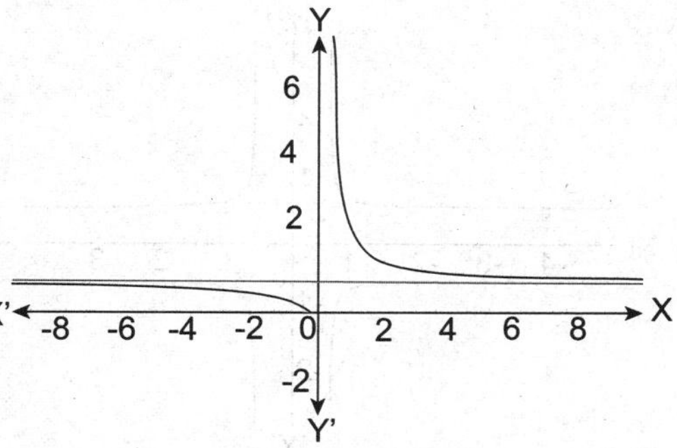
Y
6
4
2
X'
-8 -6 -4 -2 0 2 4 6 8
X
-2
Y'

7.

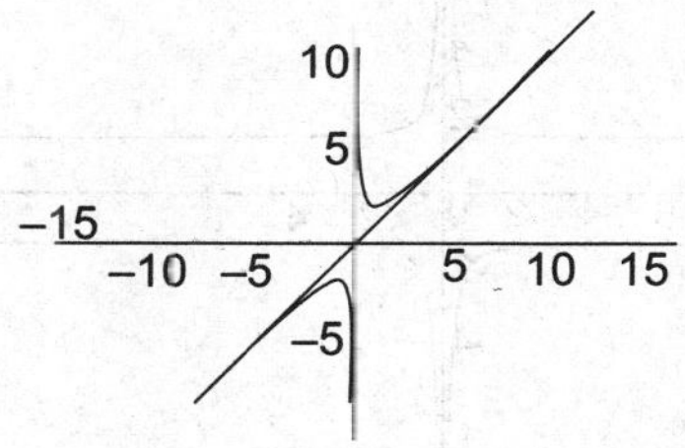
10
5
−15
−10 −5
5 10 15
−5

8. (a)

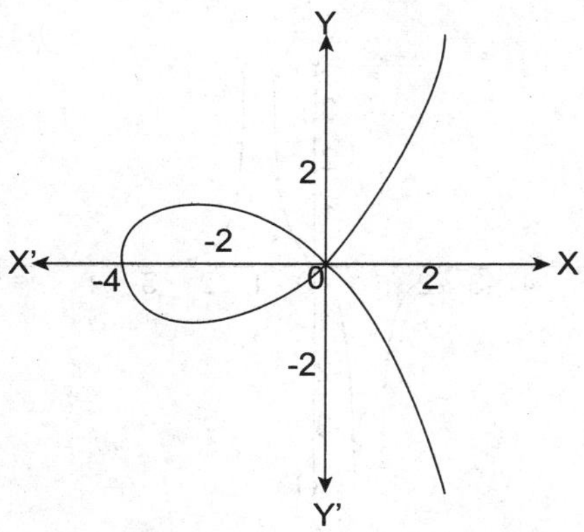
Y
2
-2
X'
-4
0
2
X
-2
Y'

(c)

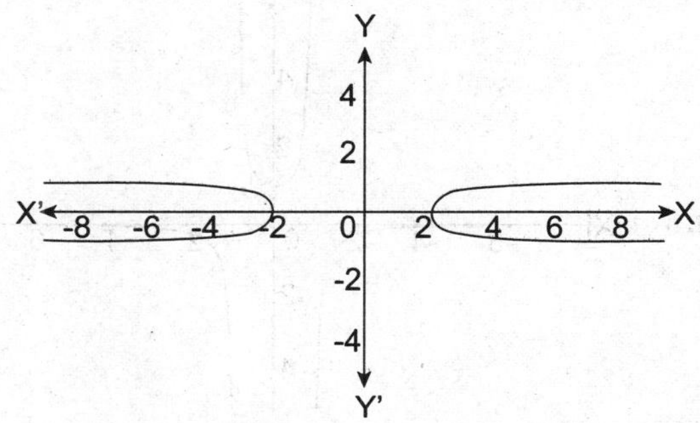
Y
4
2
X'
-8 -6 -4 -2 0 2 4 6 8
X
-2
-4
Y'

(d)

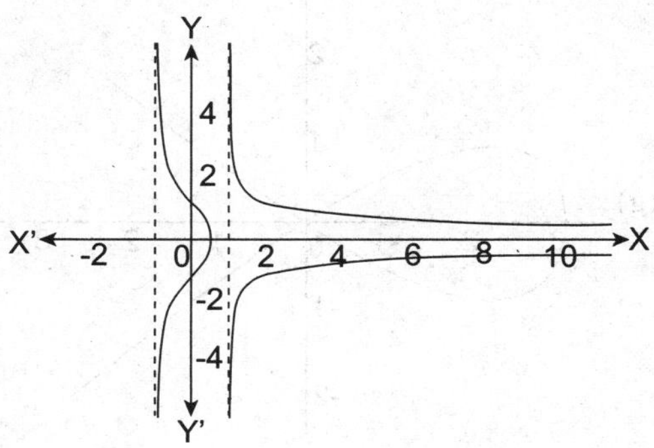
Y
4
2
X'
-2 0 2 4 6 8 10
X
-2
-4
Y'

(e)

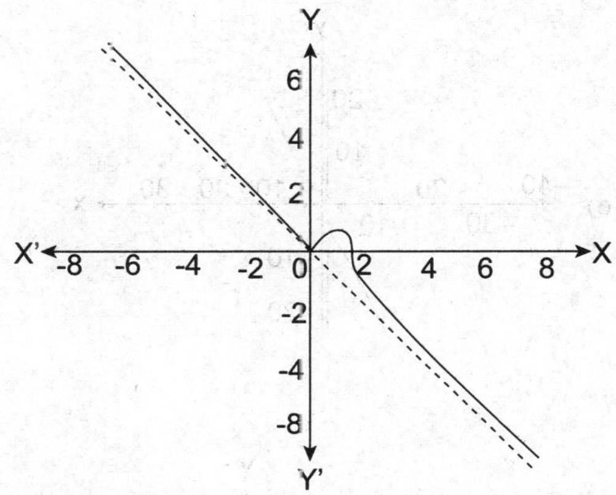
Y
6
4
2
X'
-8 -6 -4 -2 0 2 4 6 8
X
-2
-4
-8
Y'

(g)

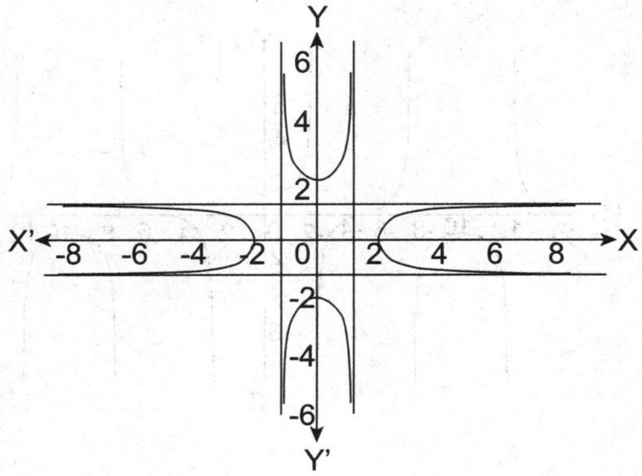
Y
6
4
2
X'
-8 -6 -4 -2 0 2 4 6 8
X
-2
-4
-6
Y'

(h)

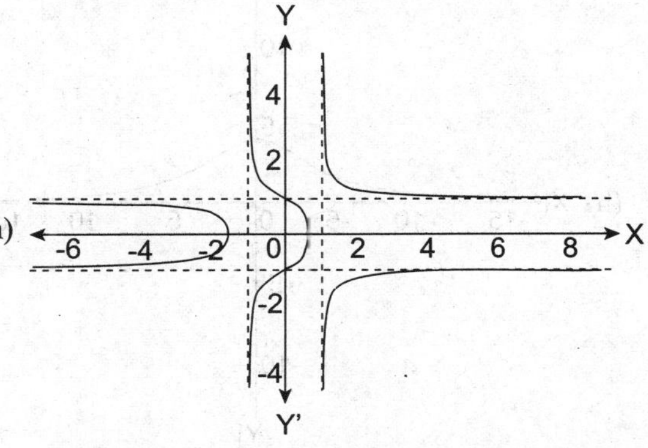
Y
4
2
-6 -4 -2 0 2 4 6 8
X
-2
-4
Y'

(i) 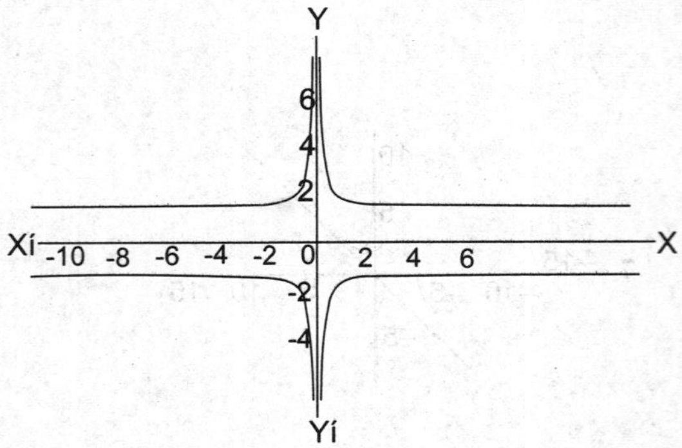
Y
6
4
2
Xí
-10 -8 -6 -4 -2 0 2 4 6
X
-2
-4
Yí

(j) 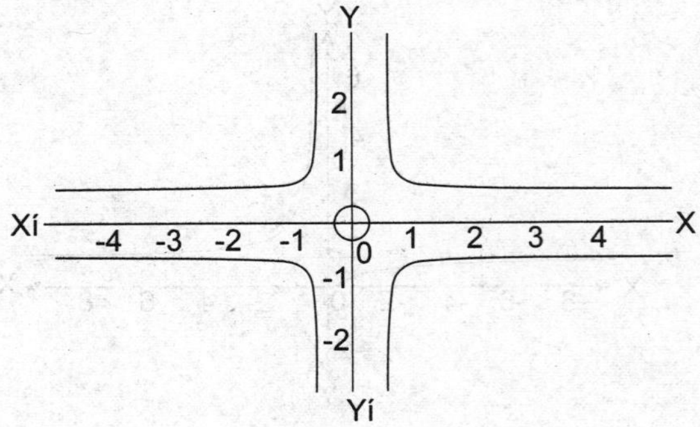
Y
2
1
Xí
-4 -3 -2 -1 0 1 2 3 4
X
-1
-2
Yí

9. (c) 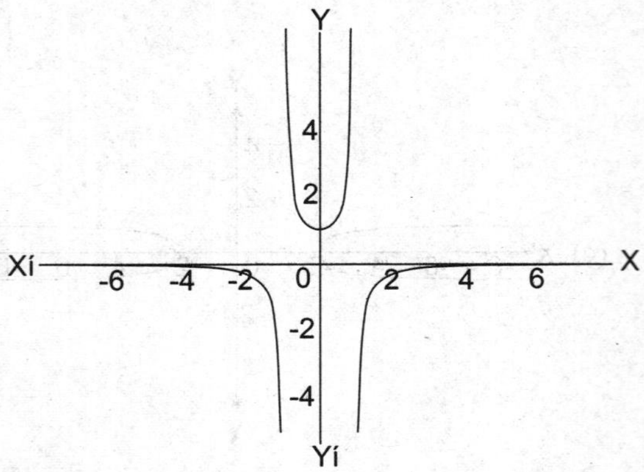
Y
4
2
Xí
-6 -4 -2 0 2 4 6
X
-2
-4
Yí

(d) 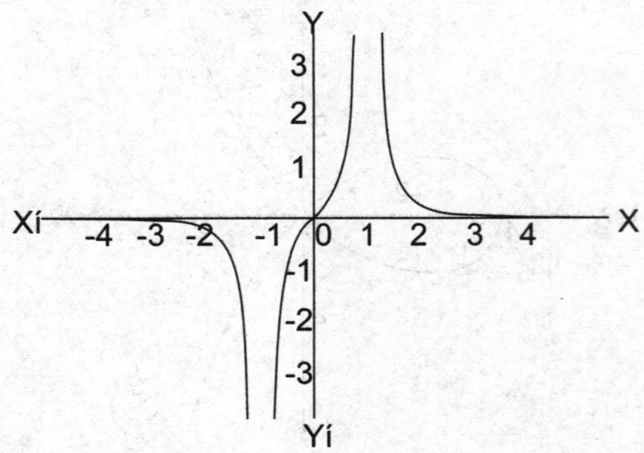
Y
3
2
1
Xí
-4 -3 -2 -1 0 1 2 3 4
X
-1
-2
-3
Yí

(e) 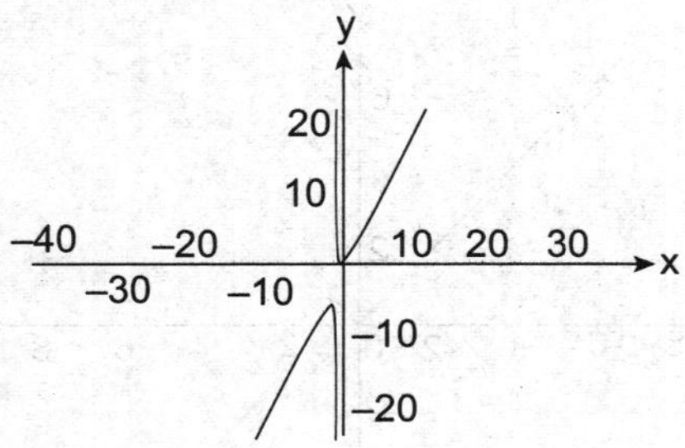
y
20
10
–40 –20 10 20 30
–30 –10
x
–10
–20

(g) 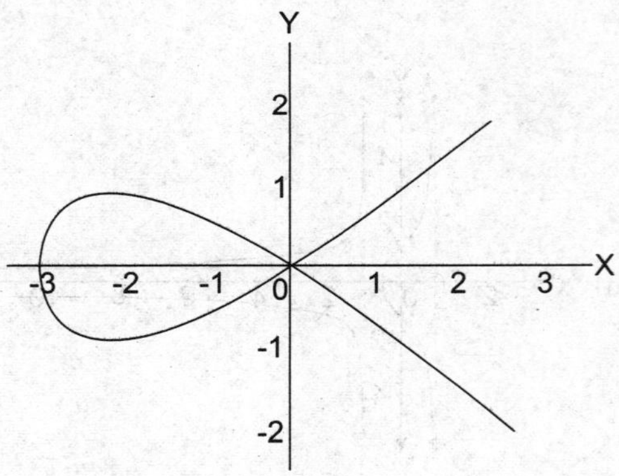
Y
2
1
-3 -2 -1 0 1 2 3
X
-1
-2

(h) 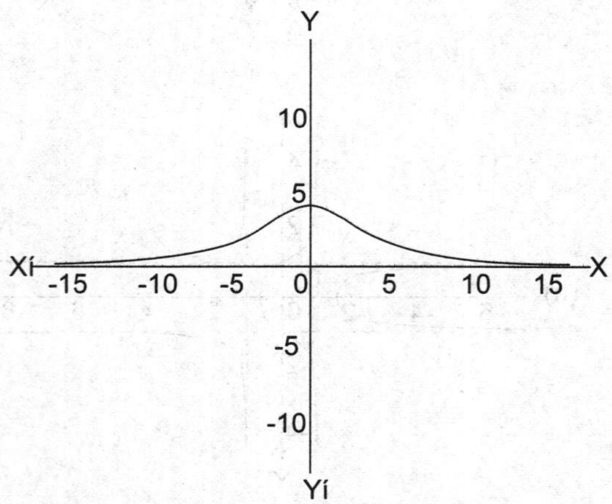
Y
10
5
Xí
-15 -10 -5 0 5 10 15
X
-5
-10
Yí

(i) 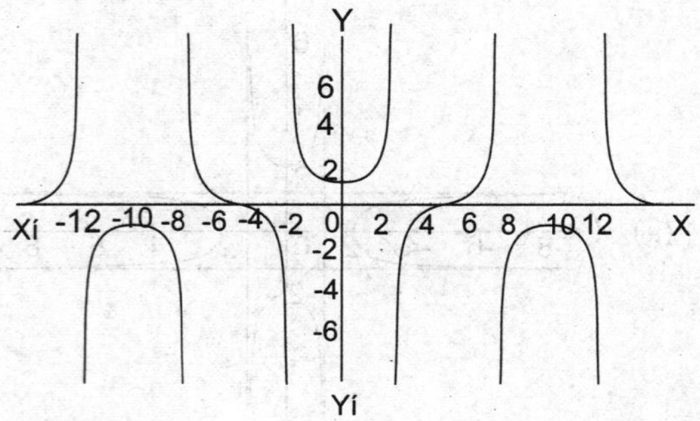
Y
6
4
2
Xí -12 -10 -8 -6 -4 -2 0 2 4 6 8 10 12
X
-2
-4
-6
Yí

(j) 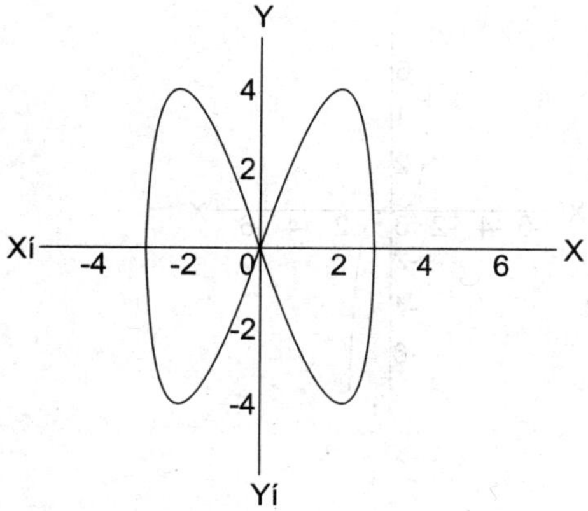

(k) 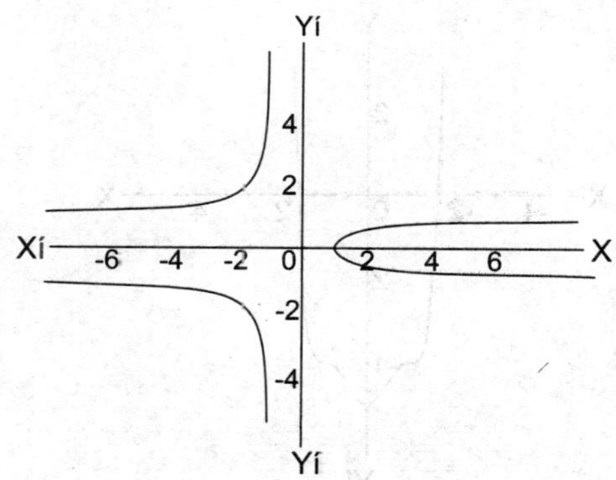

10. (a) 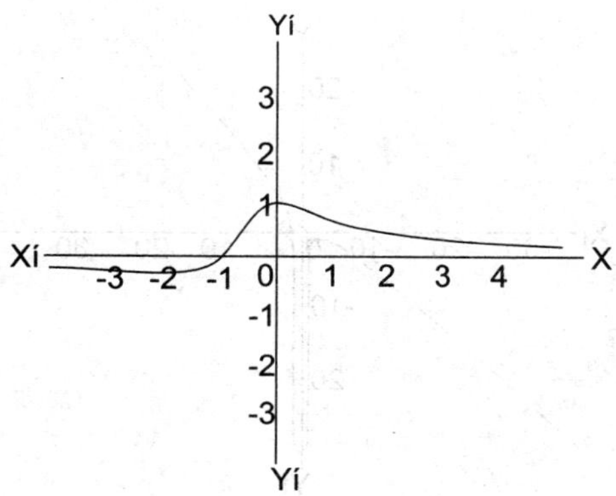

(b) 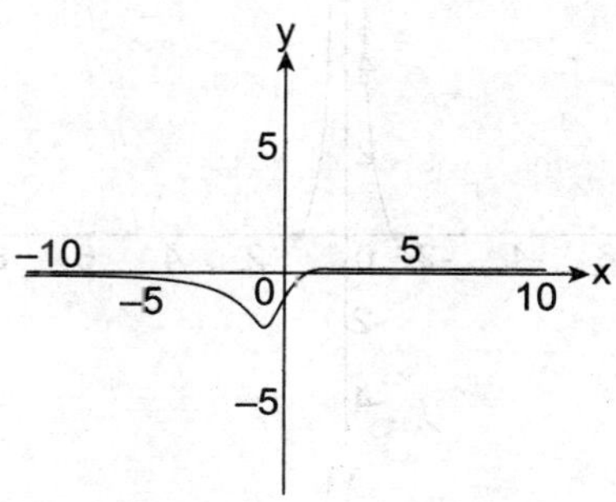

(c) 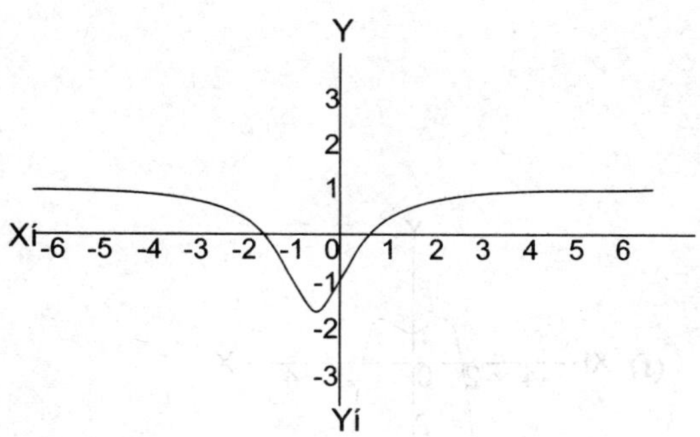

(d) 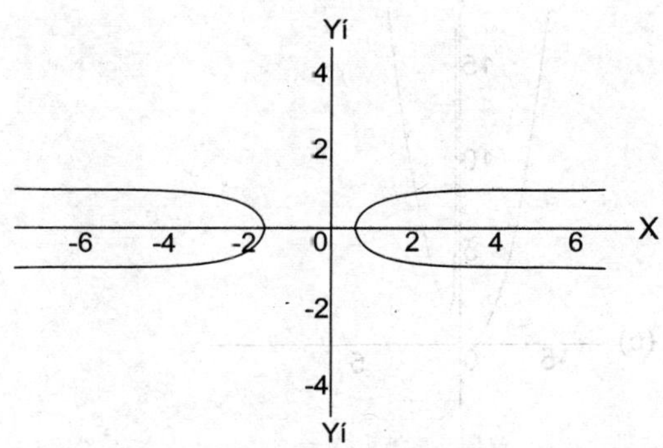

(h) 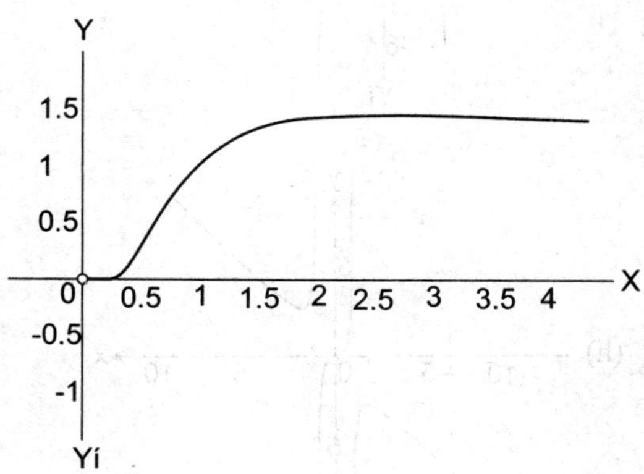

11. (a)
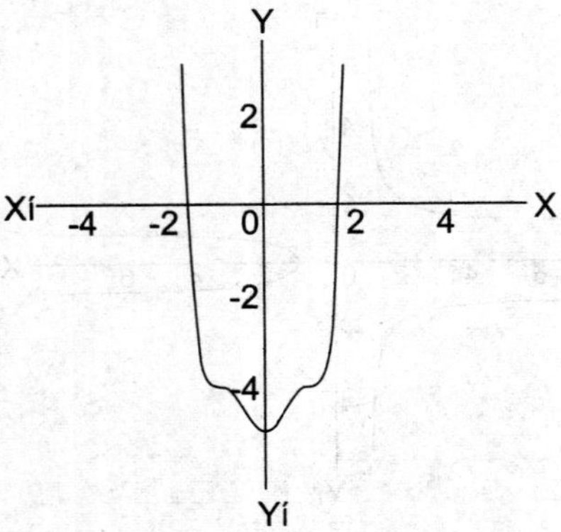
Y
2
Xí
-4
-2
0
2
4
X
-2
-4
Yí

(b)
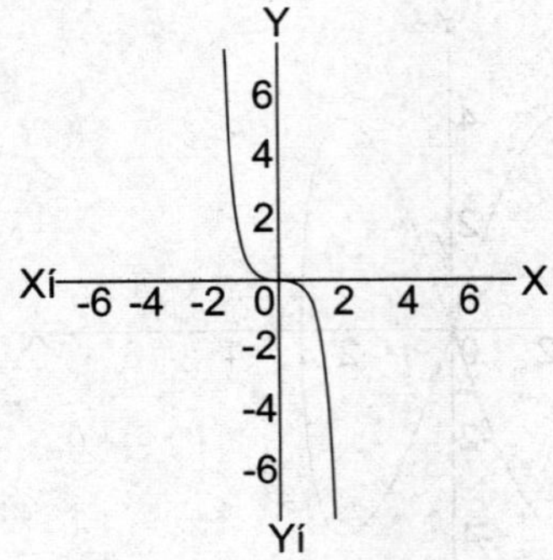
Y
6
4
2
Xí
-6 -4 -2 0
2 4 6
X
-2
-4
-6
Yí

(c)
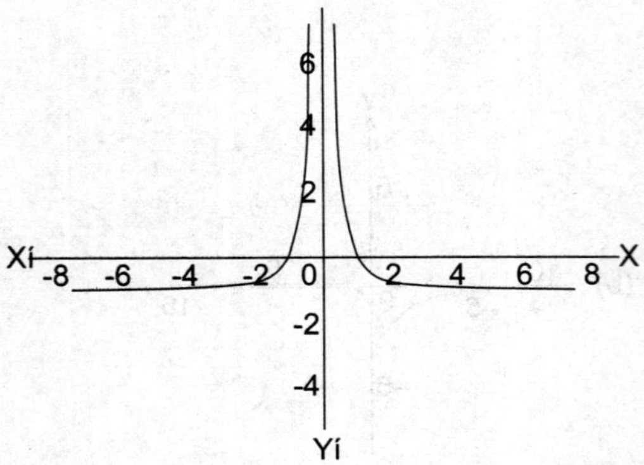
6
4
2
Xí
-8 -6 -4 -2 0
2 4 6 8
X
-2
-4
Yí

(d)
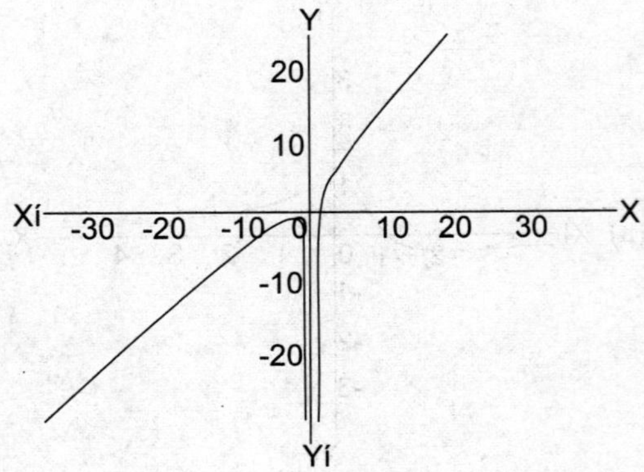
Y
20
10
Xí
-30 -20 -10 0
10 20 30
X
-10
-20
Yí

(e)
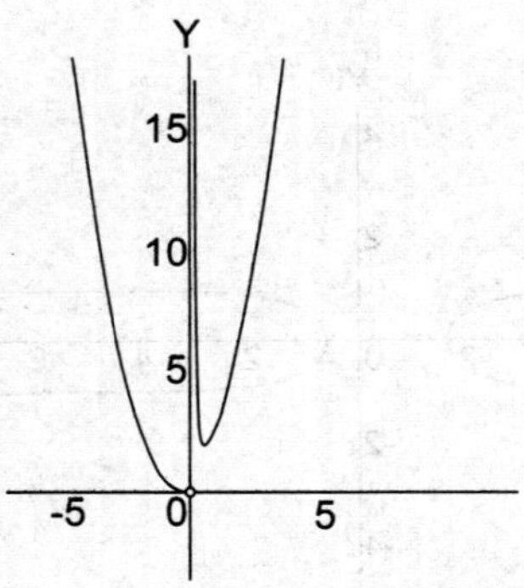
Y
15
10
5
-5
0
5

(f)
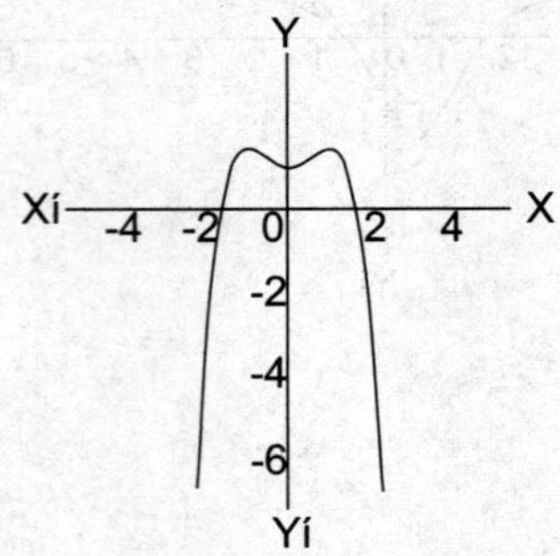
Y
Xí
-4 -2 0
2 4
X
-2
-4
-6
Yí

(g)
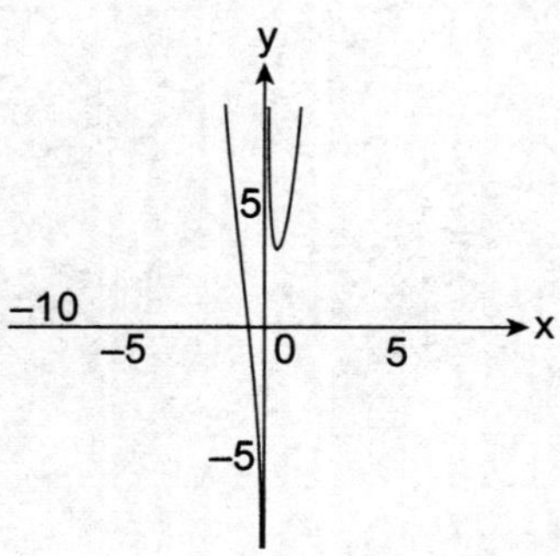
y
5
–10
–5
0
5
x
–5

(h)
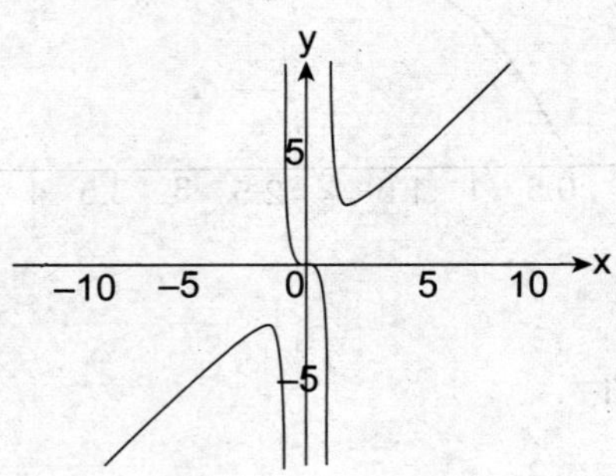
y
5
–10 –5
0
5 10
x
–5

(i) 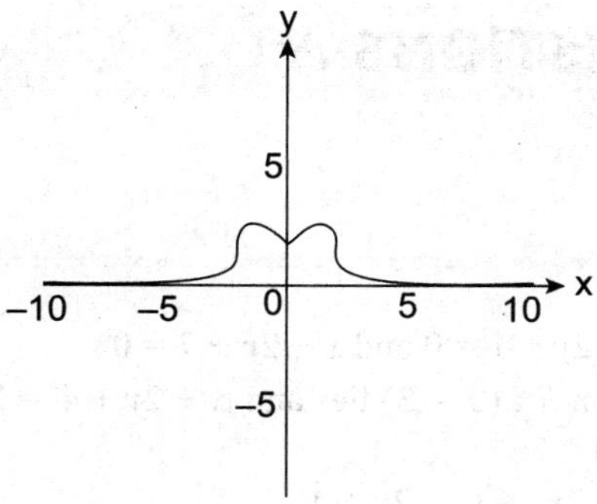

(j) 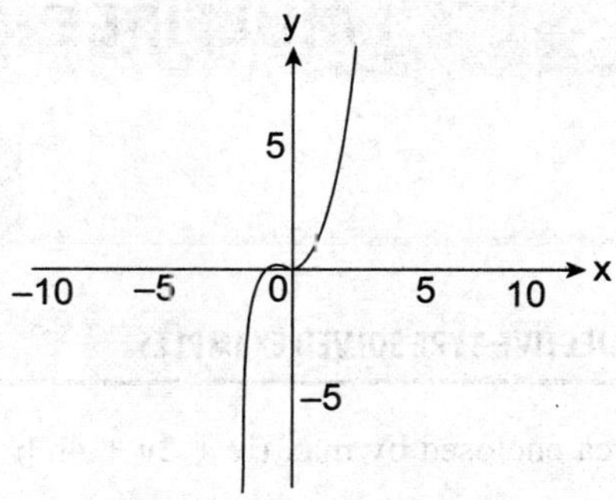

(k) 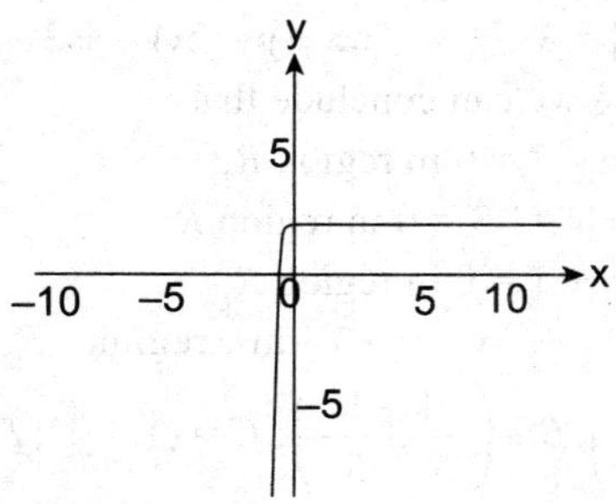

MULTIPLE-CHOICE QUESTIONS

SECTION–I

OBJECTIVE-TYPE SOLVED EXAMPLES

1. Find the area enclosed by max $(|x + 2y + 4|, |y - 2x|) = 3$

(a) 42 sq units (b) 7.2 sq units

(c) 33 sq units (d) None of these

Solution: (b)

To find the area enclosed by max $\{|x + 2y + 4|, |y - 2x|\} = 3$, first of all let us observe where

$|x + 2y + 4| = |y - 2x|$

$\Rightarrow x + 2y + 4 = \pm (y - 2x)$

$\Rightarrow 3x + 2y + 4 = 0$ ....(i)

$\Rightarrow x - 3y - 4 = 0$ ....(ii)

Lines (i) and (ii) are perpendicular to each other with their point of intersection at $\left(\frac{-4}{5}, \frac{-8}{5}\right)$ as shown below.

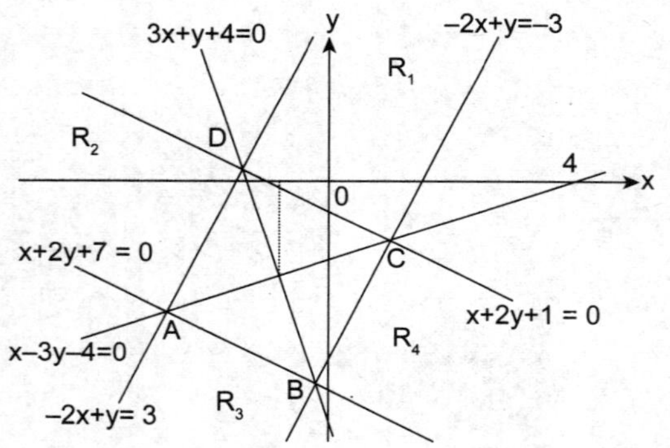

In region R_1; (0, 0) lies and $|x + 2y + 4| = 4$ at (0, 0); $|y - 2x| = 0$ at (0, 0)

$\Rightarrow |x + 2y + 4| > |y - 2x|$

$\Rightarrow |x + 2y + 4| = 3$

$\Rightarrow x + 2y + 4 = \pm 3$

$\Rightarrow x + 2y + 7 = 0$ and $x + 2y + 1 = 0$

In region R_2: (– 2, 0) lies, $|x + 2y + 4| = 2$ at (– 2, 0) and $|y - 2x| = 4$ at (–2, 0)

$\Rightarrow |y - 2x| = 3$ $\Rightarrow y - 2x = \pm 3$

In region R_3: (0, 5) lies and $|x + 2y + 4| = |-6| = 6$; $|y - 2x| = 5$

$\Rightarrow |x + 2y + 4| > |y - 2x|$ $\Rightarrow |x + 2y + 4| = 3$

$\Rightarrow x + 2y + 4 = \pm 3$

$\Rightarrow x + 2y + 1 = 0$ and $x + 2y + 7 = 0$

In region R_4: (0, – 3) lies and $|x + 2y + 4| = 2$; $|y - 2x| = 3$

$\Rightarrow |y - 2x| > |x + 2y + 4|$

$\Rightarrow |y - 2x| = 3$ $\Rightarrow (y - 2x) = \pm 3$

From above we can conclude that

AB: $x + 2y + 7 = 0$ in region R_3

BC: $-2x + y = -3 = 0$ in region R_4

CD: $x + 2y + 1 = 0$ in region R_1

DA: $-2x + y = 3$ in region R_2 and $A\left(\frac{-13}{5}, \frac{-11}{5}\right)$; $B \equiv \left(\frac{-1}{5}, \frac{-17}{5}\right)$; $C = (1, -1)$; $D\left(\frac{-7}{5}, \frac{1}{5}\right)$

Clearly, $AB \perp BC$; $CD \perp DA$; $BC \perp CD$

$\Rightarrow ABCD$ is a rectangle.

Now $BC = \sqrt{\left(\frac{-1}{5} - 1\right)^2 + \left(\frac{-17}{5} + 1\right)^2} = \frac{6}{\sqrt{5}}$;

$AB = \sqrt{\left(\frac{-13}{5} + \frac{1}{5}\right)^2 + \left(\frac{-11}{5} + \frac{17}{5}\right)^2} = \frac{6}{\sqrt{5}}$

$\Rightarrow ABCD$ is a rectangle having its area $= \left(\frac{6}{\sqrt{5}}\right)^2 = \frac{36}{5}$ sq. units = 7.2 units.

2. Find two values of θ in the interval (0, π) satisfying the equation $(1 - \cot\theta)(1 + \cot\theta)\,\text{cosec}^2\theta + 2^{\cot^2\theta} = 0$. Also, find the total number of roots of the equation

(a) π/6, 5π/6, 4 (b) π/3, 2π/3, 4

(c) π/6, 5π/6, 6 (d) None of these

Solution: (a) Here $(1 - \cot^2\theta)(1 + \cot^2\theta) + 2^{\cos^2\theta} = 0$

Putting $\cot^2\theta = x$; we get, $(1 - x)(1 + x) + 2^x = 0$

$\Rightarrow 1 - x^2 + 2^x = 0$ $\Rightarrow 2^x = x^2 - 1$

By observation, we can get $x = 3$ as one of the roots of the above equation.

($\because 2^3 = 8$ and $3^2 - 1 = 8$)

Now we have been asked two values of θ in the interval.

$\Rightarrow \cot^2\theta = 3 \Rightarrow \cot\theta = \pm\sqrt{3}$

$\Rightarrow \theta = \pi/6$ or $5\pi/6$

Now, sketching the curves $y = 2^x$ and $y = x^2 - 1$ on the same axis, we get

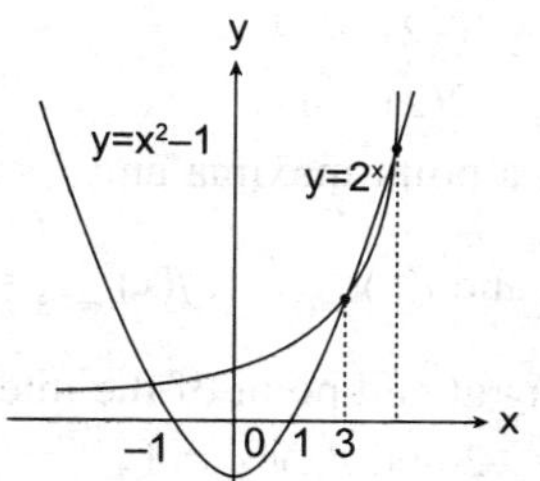

Here, we see that one value of x is negative whereas the other two are positive.

Now $\cot^2\theta = x$ will not be satisfied for any values of θ for negative value of x.

Whereas $\cot^2\theta = x$ will have two value of θ lying between $(0,\pi)$ for every positive value of x.

Hence, total 4 solutions.

3. Find the number of points of intersection of the graphs of $(x-1)^2 + y^2 - 9 = 0$ and $|y| = |\ln(|x| - 1)|$

(a) 4 (b) 6

(c) 7 (d) None of these

Solution: (c) The graph of $y = \ln|x|$ is as shown below.

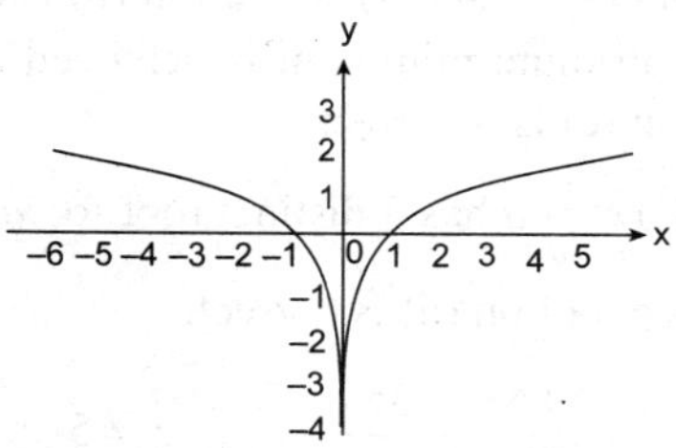

The graph of $y = \ln(|x| - 1)$ is as shown below.

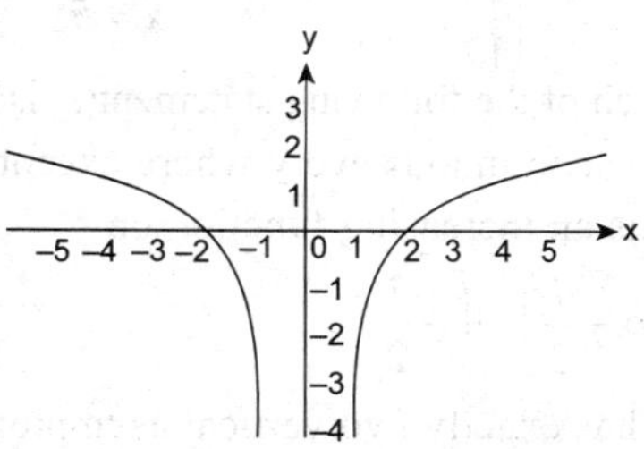

The graph of $|y| = |\ln(|x| - 1)|$ is as shown below.

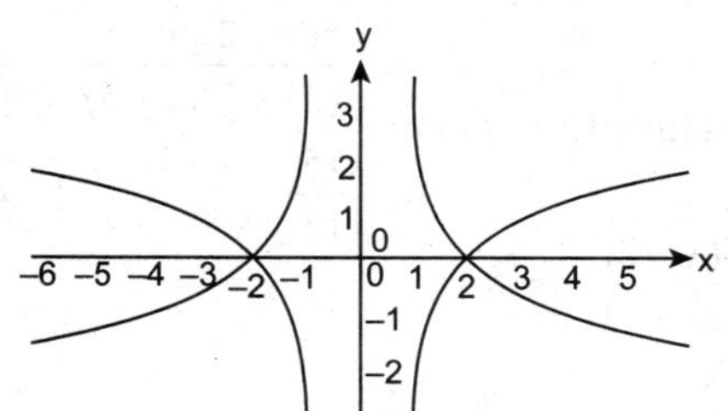

Now $(x-1)^2 + y^2 = 9$ will be a circle with centre at $(1,0)$ and radius $= 3$.

Plotting the two curves on the same axis, we get

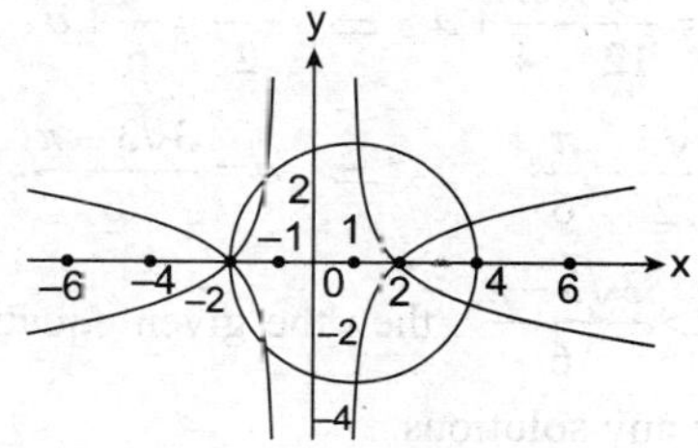

Hence, with the help of the diagram, we can see that the number of points of intersection of the two curves is 7.

4. Find the all possible value of 'a' for which $|\cos 2x| = |x - \pi/4| + a$ does not have any real solution.

(a) $\left(0, \dfrac{3\sqrt{3}-\pi}{6}\right)$ (b) $\left(0, \dfrac{3\sqrt{3}+\pi}{6}\right)$

(c) $\left(\dfrac{3\sqrt{3}-\pi}{6}, \infty\right)$ (d) $\left(\dfrac{3\sqrt{3}+\pi}{6}, \infty\right)$

Solution: (c) We would need to consider the limiting case when the graphs of $y = |\cos 2x|$ and $y = |x - \pi/4| + a$ touch each other.

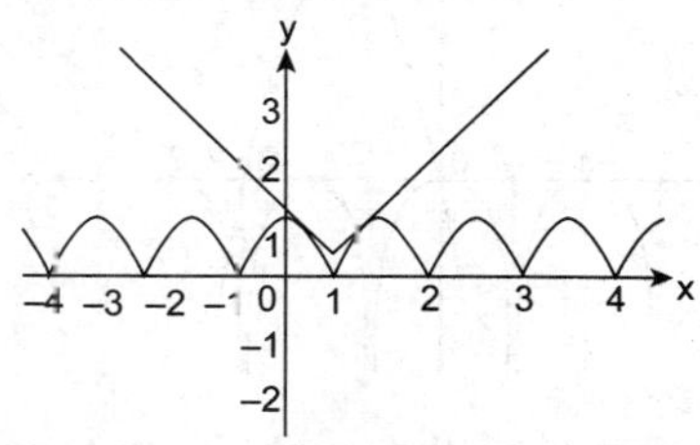

If A is the point of contact, then at point A, the slopes of the two curves are the same.

Hence, $\dfrac{d}{dx}(|\cos 2x|) = \dfrac{d}{dx}\left(\left|x - \dfrac{\pi}{4}\right| + a\right)$

Considering the case when $x > \pi/4$ and $x < \pi/2$, then $|\cos 2x| = -\cos 2x$ and $|x - \pi/4| = x - \pi/4$

$\Rightarrow \dfrac{d}{dx}(-(\cos 2x)) = \dfrac{d}{dx}\left(\left(x - \dfrac{\pi}{4}\right) + a\right)$

$\Rightarrow 2\sin 2x = 1 \Rightarrow \sin 2x = 1/2$

$\Rightarrow \sin 2x = \sin \pi/6 \Rightarrow 2x = n\pi + (-1)^n \pi/6$

Now $x \in (\pi/4, \pi/2)$

$\Rightarrow 2x \in \left(\dfrac{\pi}{2}, \pi\right)$ $\Rightarrow 2x = \pi - \pi/6 = 5\pi/6$

$\Rightarrow x = 5\pi/12$

Now since the point A also lies on $y = x - \pi/4 + a$; hence, we have

$\Rightarrow \left|\cos\frac{5\pi}{6}\right| = x - \frac{\pi}{4} + a$

$\Rightarrow \frac{\sqrt{3}}{2} = \frac{5\pi}{12} - \frac{\pi}{4} + a \Rightarrow \frac{\sqrt{3}}{2} = \frac{\pi}{6} + a$

$\Rightarrow a = \frac{\sqrt{3}}{2} - \frac{\pi}{6} \Rightarrow a = \frac{3\sqrt{3}-\pi}{6}$

If $a > \frac{3\sqrt{3}-\pi}{6}$, then the given equation will not have any solutions.

Thus, the required set of value of 'a' is given by $\left(\frac{3\sqrt{3}-\pi}{6}, \infty\right)$.

5. Find the number of points of intersection of the curves given by $y = \ln|\cos x|$ and $y = -x(x - 3\pi/2)$ in $(-3, 6)$

(a) 2 (b) 3

(c) 4 (d) None of these

Solution: (c) The number of points of intersection can be found out by drawing the two curves simultaneously.

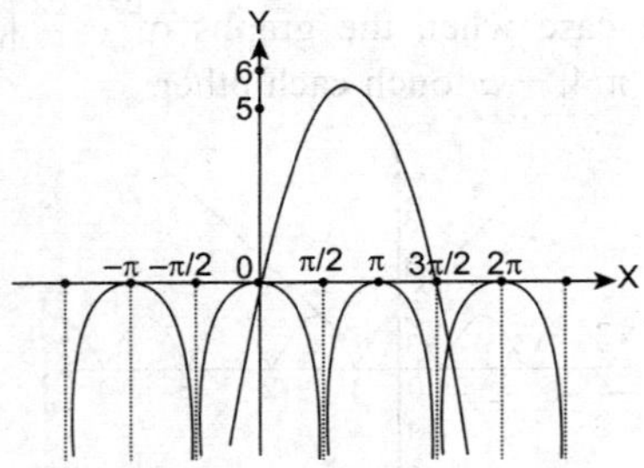

As is evident from the graph the two curve intersect at 4 points.

6. Which of the following statement*(s)* is/are true for the function $f(x) = (x - 1)^2(x - 3) + 1$ defined on the interval [0, 3].

(a) Range of $f(x)$ is $[-2, 0]$

(b) The absolute maximum is achieved at two different points.

(c) The absolute minimum is not achieved.

(d) The values of 'a' for which $f(x) = a$ has 3 distinct roots is given by $\left(-\frac{5}{27}, 1\right)$.

Solution: (b, d) $f(x) = (x - 1)^2(x - 3) + 1$

$f'(x) = 2(x - 1)(x - 3) + (x - 1)^2$

$\therefore f'(x) = 0 \Rightarrow x = 1$ or $7/3$

$f''(x) = (3x - 7) + 3(x - 1) = 6x - 10 = 2(3x - 5)$

$f''(x)|_{x=1} = 2(-2) = -4$

$f''(x)|_{x=7/3} = 2(2) = 4$

$\therefore$ $x = 1$ is a point maxima and $x = 7/3$ is a point of minima and $f(x)|_{x=1} = 1, f(x)|_{x=7/3} = 7/3 = \frac{-5}{27}$

Checking at end point of the interval, we have $f(x)|_{x=0} = -2$ and $f(x)|_{x=3} = 1$

Hence, the graph of $y = f(x)$ will be given as shown below.

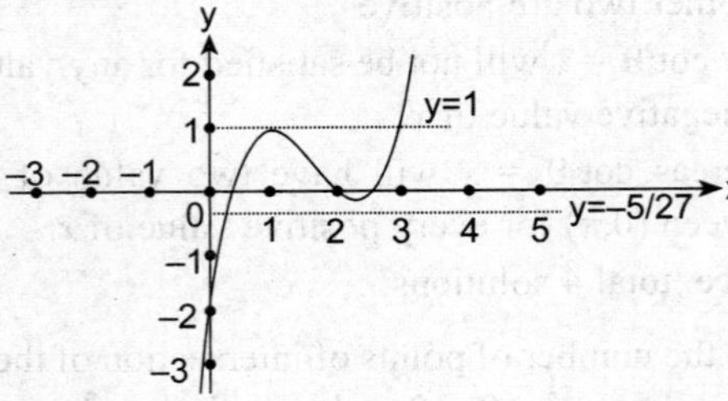

From the diagram we can see that range of $f(x)$ is $[-2, 1]$

Hence, option (a) is incorrect.

The absolute maximum is achieved at two different point ($x = 1$, and 3) so, option (b) is correct.

The absolute minimum is achieved at $x = 0$, so, option (c) is incorrect.

And $f(x) = a$ has 3 distinct root for $a \in \left(-\frac{5}{27}, 1\right)$.

Hence, option (d) is correct.

7. Given $f(x) = \begin{cases} \frac{5x^2 - 35x + 50}{2x^2 - 3x - 35}; & x \neq 5 \\ \frac{15}{17}; & x = 5 \end{cases}$ be a function,

then which of the following statement(s) is/are correct ?

(a) $f(x)$ is continuous every where except for $x = 5$

(b) $f(x)$ is an increasing function on $\left(-\infty, -\frac{7}{2}\right) \cup \left(-\frac{7}{2}, \infty\right)$

(c) $f(x)$ has exactly two vertical asymptotes

(d) $f(x)$ has only one horizontal asymptote

Solution: (d): $f(x) = \begin{cases} \frac{5(x-2)(x-5)}{(2x+7)(x-5)}; & x \neq 5 \\ \frac{15}{17}; & x = 5 \end{cases}$

$= \begin{cases} \frac{5(x-2)}{(2x+7)}; x \neq 5 \\ \frac{15}{17} \quad ; x = 5 \end{cases}$

Obviously $f(x)$ is not defined for $x = -7/2$. Hence $x = -7/2$ will be a vertical asymptote. Also $x = -7/2$ will be a point of discontinuity. Hence, option (a) is incorrect. The graph of $f(x)$ is as shown below

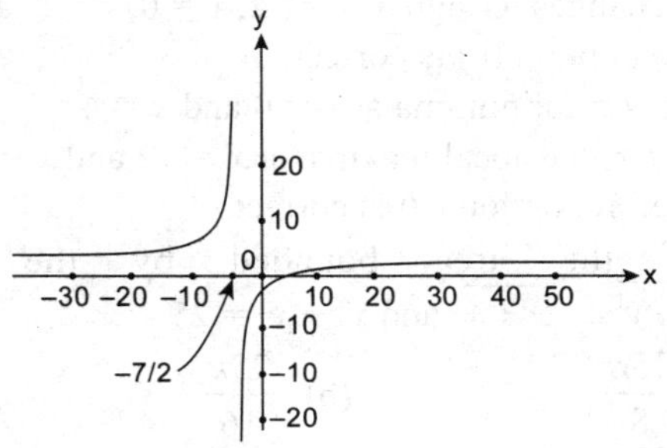

As is evident from the graph $f(x)$ is an increasing function at every point in $\left(-\infty, -\frac{7}{2}\right)$ and at every point $\left(-\frac{7}{2}, \infty\right)$, but for $x_1 \in \left(-\infty, -\frac{7}{2}\right)$ & $x_2 \in \left(-\frac{7}{2}, \infty\right)$

$\Rightarrow f(x_1) > f(x_2)$ for $x_1 < x_2$

$\Rightarrow f(x)$ is an increasing function on

$$\left(-\infty, -\frac{7}{2}\right) \cup \left(-\frac{7}{2}, \infty\right)$$

Hence option (b) is incorrect.

Also $x = -7/2$ is the only vertical asymptote, hence, option (c) is incorrect

Let $y = \dfrac{5(x-2)}{2x+7} \quad \Rightarrow \quad 2xy + 7y = 5x - 10$

$\Rightarrow 2xy - 5x = -7y - 10 \Rightarrow x(5 - 2y) = 7y + 10$

$\Rightarrow x = \dfrac{7y+10}{5-2y} \quad \Rightarrow \quad f^{-1}(x) = \dfrac{7x+10}{5-2x}$

So, $f^{-1}(x)$ is not defined on $x = 5/2$

$\Rightarrow f(x)$ does not achieve 5/2

Hence, $x = 5/2$ is the only horizontal asymptote.

Hence, option (d) is correct.

8. If the graph of $y = f(x)$ is shown as below

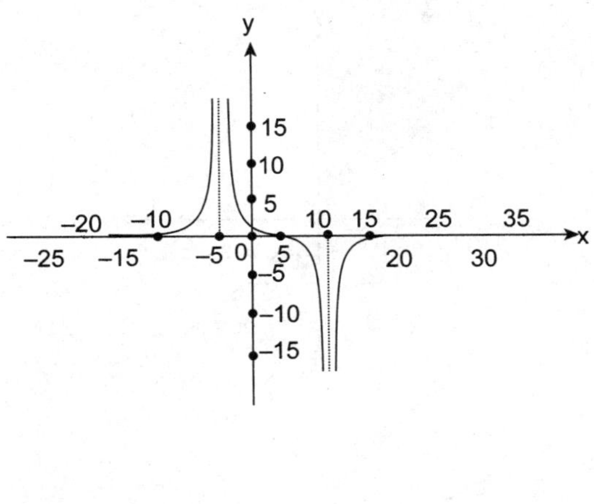

Given $f(x) = \dfrac{p(x)}{q(x)}$; where $p(x)$ and $q(x)$ are quadratic expressions. Also known that $f(x)$ is a rational function with $f(2) = f(5) = 0$; then which of the following represents the approximate graph of $y = f(x)$.

(a)

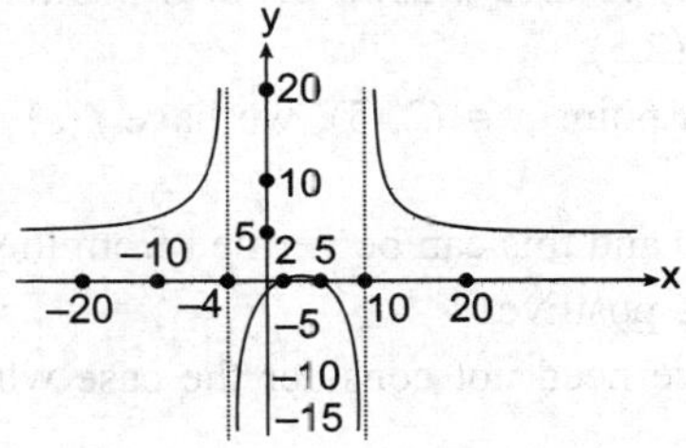

(b)

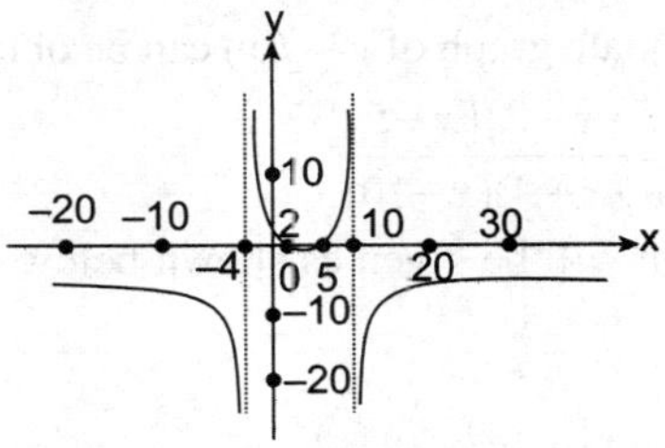

(c)

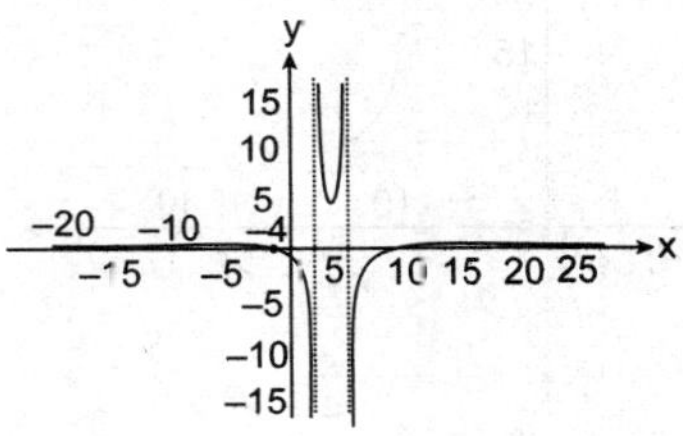

(d)

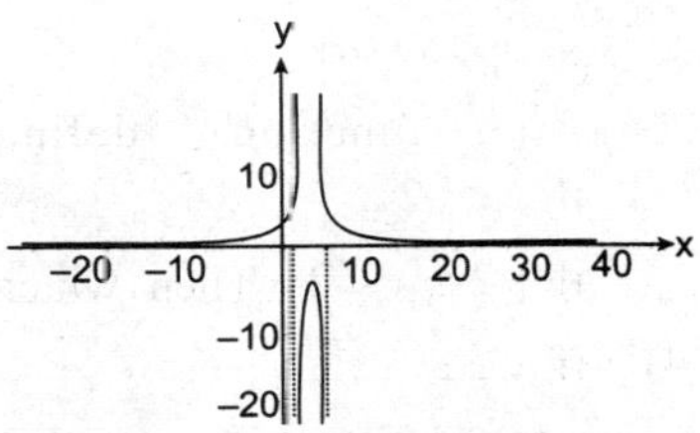

Solution: (a) As is evident from the graph of $y = f'(x)$ The graph of $f'(x)$ has vertical asymptote at $x = -4$ and $x = 10$

Hence, the graph of $f(x)$ is not defined at $x = -4$ and at $x = 10$.

Hence, $q(x) = a(x + 4)(x - 10)$; $a \in \mathbb{R} \sim \{0\}$

Also given $f(2) = f(5) = 0$

$\Rightarrow p(x) = b(x - 2)(x - 5)\ \forall\ b \in \mathbb{R} \sim \{0\}$

Hence, $f(x) = \dfrac{p(x)}{q(x)} = \dfrac{b}{a}\dfrac{(x-2)(x-5)}{(x+4)(x-10)}$

Now, using the graph of $y = f'(x)$, we need to find the sign of $\dfrac{b}{a}$

If b/a is positive, then Wavy curve of $f(x)$ will be shown as below.

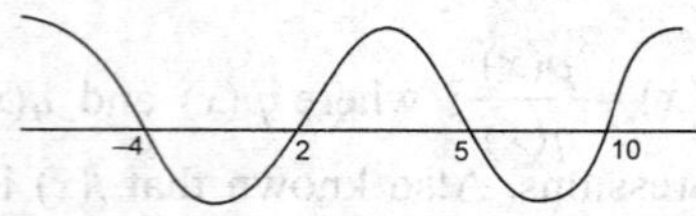

Also $x \to \pm\infty \Rightarrow f(x) \to 1$

Clearly $f(x)$ will have a point of local maxima in the interval $x = (2,5)$

Hence, for a point $c \in (2, 5)$; we have $f'(c) = 0$ and $f'(c^-) > 0$.

and $f'(c^+) < 0$ and this can be verified from the graph.

Hence, b/a is positive.

Therefore, we need not consider the case when 'b/a' is negative.

Now approximate graph of $y = f(x)$ can be obtained by taking $f(x) = \dfrac{(x-2)(x-5)}{(x+4)(x-10)}$.

And the graph will be given as shown below.

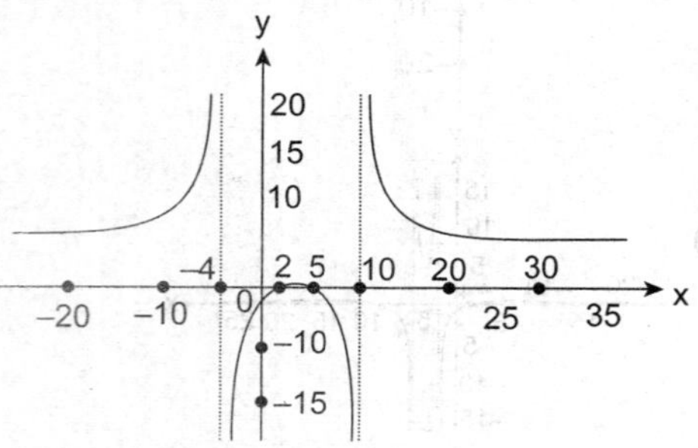

Which is same as in option (a).

9. If $f(x)$ is a function defined as

$$f(x) = \begin{cases} x+6 & \text{if } x < -2 \\ x^2 & \text{if } -2 \le x < 2 \\ (x-4)^2 & \text{if } x \ge 2 \end{cases}$$

. Then which of the following statement(s) is/are correct:

(a) $f(x)$ is continuous at $x \in \mathbb{R}$.

(b) The function is non-differentiable at exactly 3 points.

(c) $f'(x)$ changes its sign exactly 4 times.

(d) $f(x)$ has exactly two local minima and two local maxima.

Solution: (a, c, d) The graph of $y = f(x)$ is as shown below

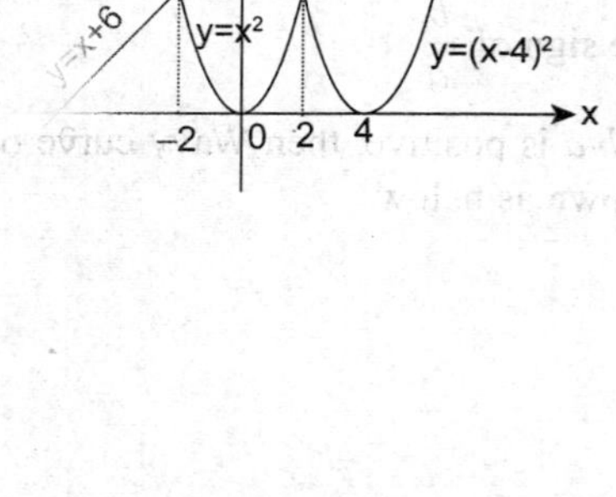

As is evident from the graph $f(x)$ is continuous at each $x \in \mathbb{R}$, so, option (a) is correct.

The function $f(x)$ is non-differentiable at $x = -2, 2$.

Hence, option (b) is incorrect.

$f'(x)$ changes its sign at $x = -2, x = 0, x = 2$, and $x = 4$

Hence, option (c) is correct.

$f(x)$ has local minima at $x = 0$ and $x = 4$

Also $f(x)$ has local maxima at $x = -2$ and $x = 2$

Therefore, option (d) is correct.

10. Find the area bounded by the curves $\sqrt{|x-y|} \ge \sqrt{x+y}$ and $x^2 + y^2 = 25$

(a) $\dfrac{25\pi}{8}$ (b) $\dfrac{25\pi}{16}$

(c) $\dfrac{25\pi}{4}$ (d) $\dfrac{25\pi}{2}$

Solution: (c) From the inequality we have $x + y \ge 0$

$\Rightarrow y \ge -x$

Case I. $y \ge x$

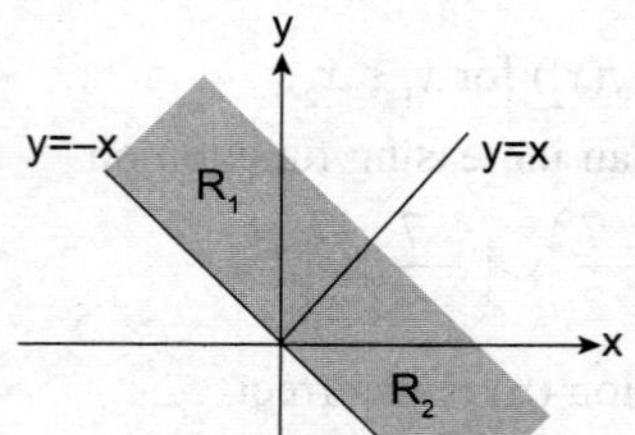

Considering region R_1; we have $|x - y| = y - x$

Now the inequality $\sqrt{|x-y|} \ge \sqrt{x+y}$

$\Rightarrow \sqrt{y-x} \ge \sqrt{x+y}$

$\Rightarrow y - x \ge x + y \quad \Rightarrow -2x \ge 0 \Rightarrow x \le 0$

Case II: $x > y$

Considering Region R_2; we have $|x - y| = x - y$

$\therefore$ we have $\sqrt{x-y} \ge \sqrt{x+y}$

$\Rightarrow x - y \ge x + y \quad \Rightarrow y \le 0$

$\therefore$ The region that satisfy $\sqrt{|x-y|} \ge \sqrt{x+y}$ is shown as below

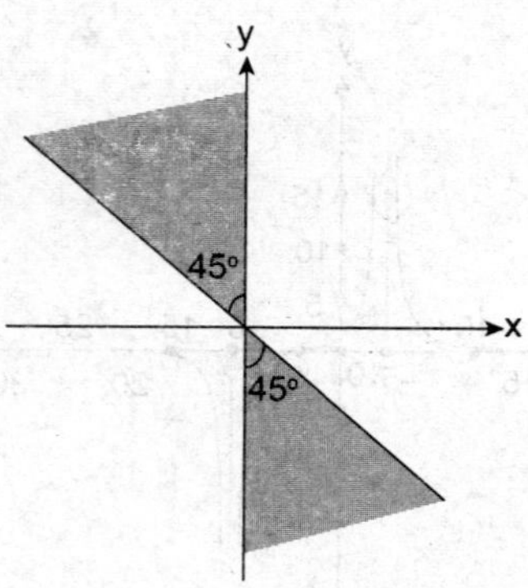

The area bounded by the two curves is as shown below.

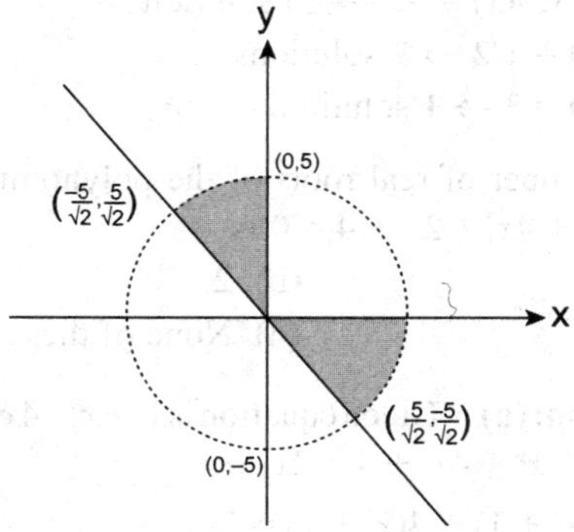

$$\text{Shaded area} = \frac{\pi \times 5^2}{4} = \frac{25\pi}{4}$$

11. Find the region on the *x-y* plane which satisfies exactly 3 out of the 4 following inequalities:
(i) $|x + y| + |x - y| \le 3$ (ii) $|x| \le 2$
(iii) $y \ge \sqrt{x^2 - 2x + 1}$ (iv) $|y| \le 2$

(a) 8 (b) 9
(c) 7 (d) None of these

Solution: (b) As already known the inequality $|x + y| + |x - y| \le 3$ is plotted as shown below.

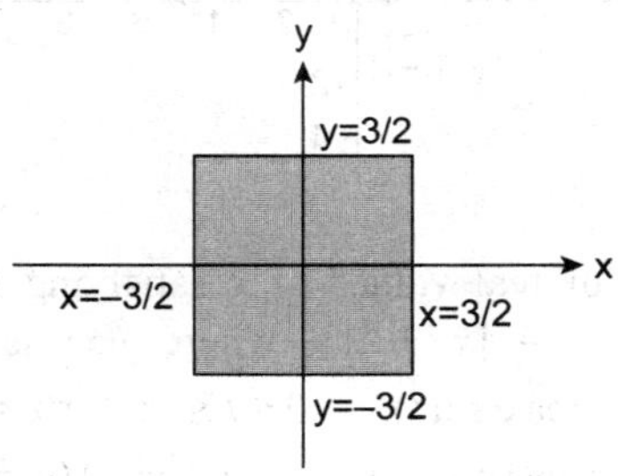

and the graph of $|x| \le 2$ is plotted as shown below.

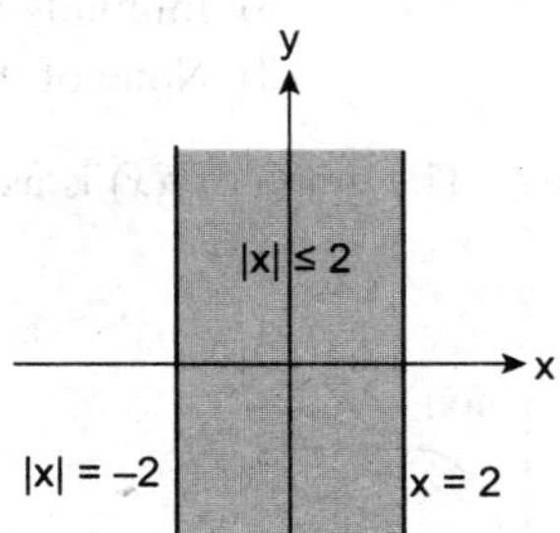

Also $y \ge \sqrt{x^2 - 2x + 1} \Rightarrow y \ge |x - 1|$ and its graph is shown as below.

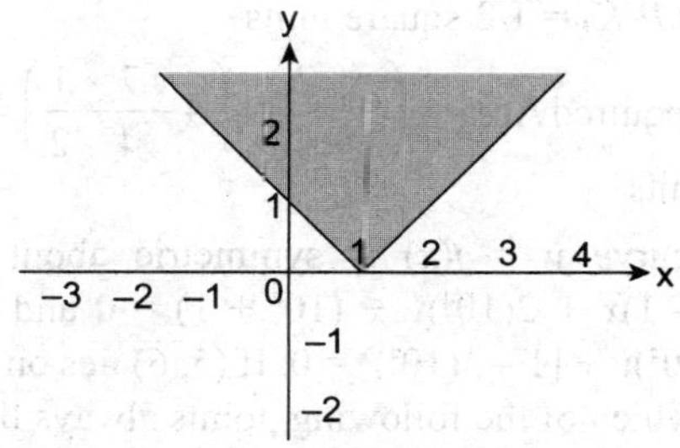

Similarly, the graph of $|y| \le 2$ is as shown below.

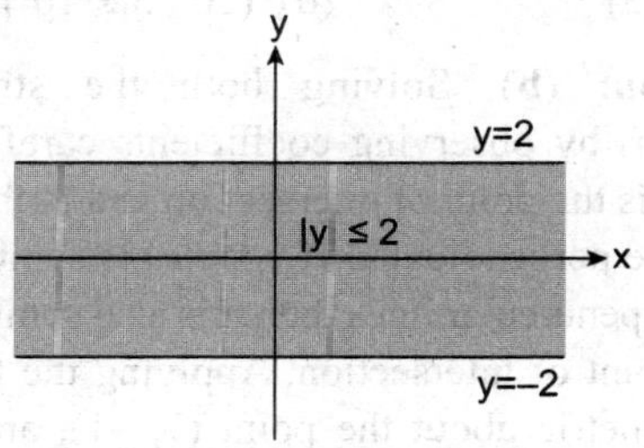

Hence, the region satisfying exactly 3 out of the 4 above mentioned inequalities is shown in figure below.

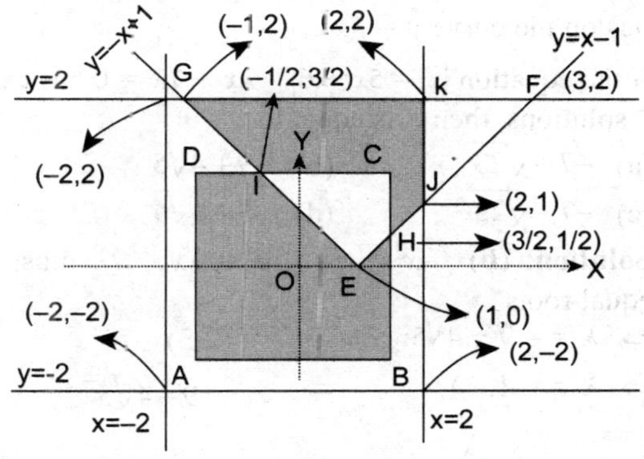

Now, we need to find the area of the shaded region in the figure shown above.

Area = area (*ABHEID*) + area (*HJKGICH*)
= [area (*ABCD*) – area (*EHCI*)] + [area (*EFG*) – area (*EHCI*) – area (*JFK*)]

Now area (*ABCD*) = 9 square units

$$\text{Area } (EHCI) = \frac{1}{2}\begin{vmatrix} 1 & 0 \\ 3/2 & 1/2 \\ 3/2 & 3/2 \\ -1/2 & 3/2 \\ 1 & 0 \end{vmatrix} = \frac{7}{4} \text{ square units}$$

$$\text{Area } (EFG) = \frac{1}{2}\begin{vmatrix} 1 & 0 \\ 3 & 2 \\ -1 & 2 \\ 1 & 0 \end{vmatrix} = \frac{1}{2} \times 8 = 4$$

Area (JFK) = 1/2 square units

$\therefore$ Required Area $= \left(9-\dfrac{7}{4}\right)+\left(4-\dfrac{7}{4}-\dfrac{1}{2}\right)=9$ square units

12. The curve $y = f(x)$ is symmetric about the lines $(10^4 - 1)x + 2(10^4)y + (10^4 + 1) = 0$ and $2(10^4)x + (1 - 10^4)y + [1 - 3(10^4)) = 0$. If (5, 6) lies on the curve, then which of the following points always lies on $f(x)$:

(a) (11, –11) (b) (–3, –8)
(c) (6, 5) (d) $(10^5, 3 \times 10^5)$

Solution: (b) Solving both the straight lines together, by observing coefficients carefully, we get (1, –1) is the point of intersection and both the straight lines are perpendicular. If $y = f(x)$ is symmetric about two perpendicular lines then it is also symmetric about their point of intersection. Applying the fact $y = f(x)$ is symmetric about the point (1, –1), and therefore, image of (5, 6) in (1, –1) say (α,β) also lies on $y = f(x)$. Thus, $\alpha + 5 = 2$ and $\beta + 6 = -2$
$\Rightarrow \alpha = -3$ and $\beta = -8$. Consequently (–3, –8) always lies on the curve $y = f(x)$.

13. If the equation $|x^2 - 5x + 6| - \lambda x + 7\lambda = 0$ has exactly 3 solutions, then λ is equal to

(a) $-7+\sqrt{23}$ (b) $-9+4\sqrt{5}$
(c) $-7-\sqrt{23}$ (d) $-9-4\sqrt{5}$

Solution: (b) $-x^2 + 5x - 6 = \lambda x - 7\lambda$ must have equal roots

$\Rightarrow \lambda = -9 \pm 4\sqrt{5};\ x=\dfrac{5-\lambda}{2}\in(2,3)$

$\Rightarrow \lambda \in (-1, 1) \quad \Rightarrow \lambda=-9+4\sqrt{5}$

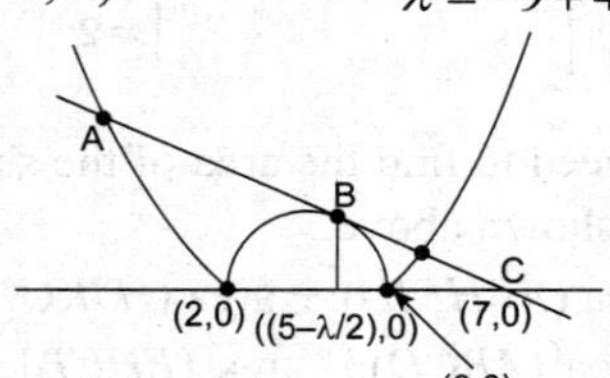

14. The graph of $y = f(x)$ is shown, then the number of solutions of $f(f(x)) = 2$ will be

(a) 1 (b) 2
(c) 3 (d) 4

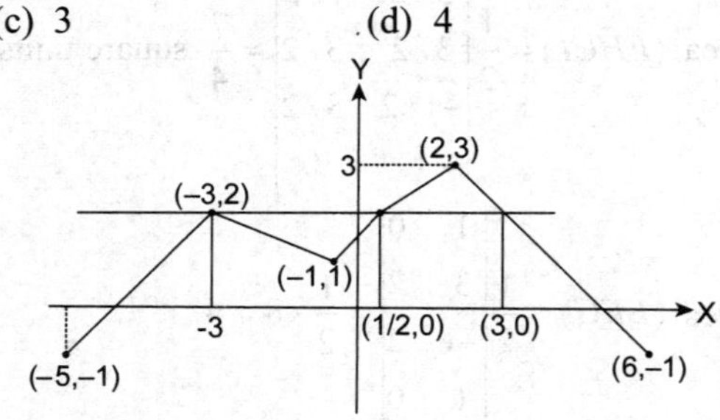

Solution: (c) Let $f(x) = t$

$\Rightarrow f(t) = 2$, so, $t = -3, 1/2, 3$

Now, $f(x) = -3 \rightarrow$ no solution

$f(x) = 1/2 \rightarrow 2$ solutions

$f(x) = 3 \rightarrow 1$ solution.

15. The number of real roots of the polynomial equation $x^8 + x^6 + 4x^2 - 2x + 4 = 0$ is

(a) 0 (b) 2
(c) 4 (d) None of these

Solution: (a) Given equation is $x^8+x^6+4x^2-2x+4=0$

$\Rightarrow x^8 + x^6 + 4x^2 + 4 = 2x$

$\Rightarrow x^6(x^2 + 1) + 4(x^2 + 1) = 2x$

$\Rightarrow (x^2 + 1)(x^6 + 4) = 2x$

$\Rightarrow x^6+4=\dfrac{2x}{x^2+1}$

Now range of L.H.S. $[4, \infty)$ whereas range of R.H.S. [–1, 1].

Clearly, no real solutions

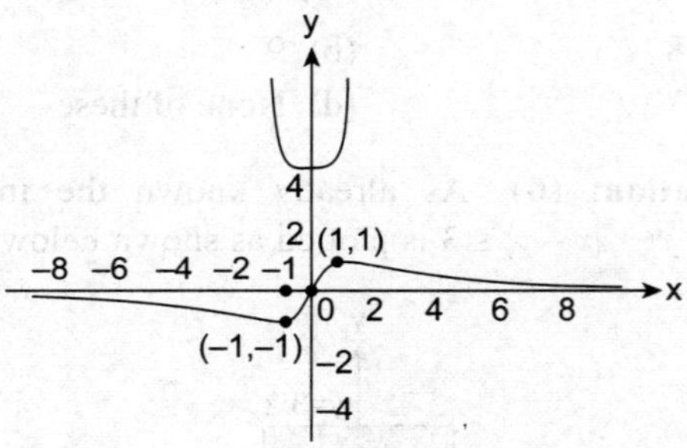

16. Number of real values of x satisfying the equation $f(|x|) = x - [x + 1]$; where $f(x)$ is defined as

$$f(x)=\begin{cases}\max(\sin t); & 0\le t\le x;\quad \forall x\in[0,\pi]\\ \min(1+\sin t); & \pi<t\le x;\quad \forall x\in[\pi,2\pi]\end{cases}$$

is equal to ([] is greatest integer function)

(a) 3 (b) Infinitely many
(c) 2 (d) None of these

Solution: (d) The graph of $f(x)$ is as shown below

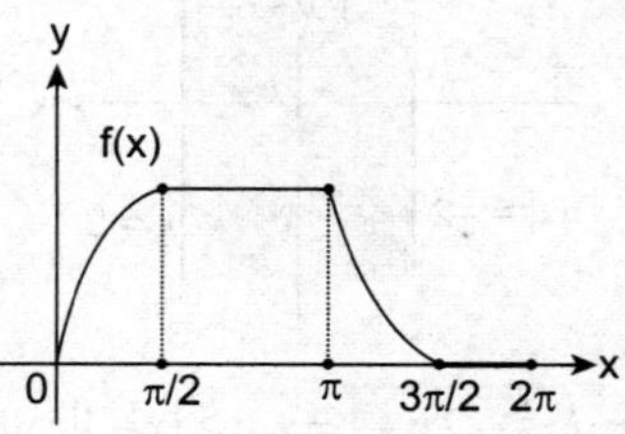

Hence, the graph of $f|x|$ will be as shown below.

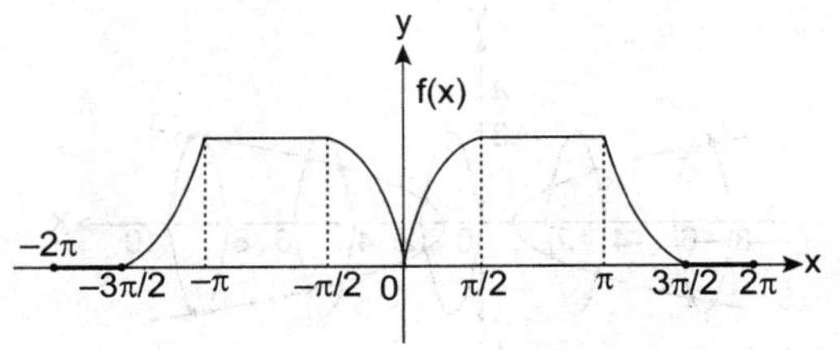

Now let $g(x) = x - [x + 1] = x - [x] - 1 = \{x\} - 1$

Graph of $\{x\}$ is as shown below.

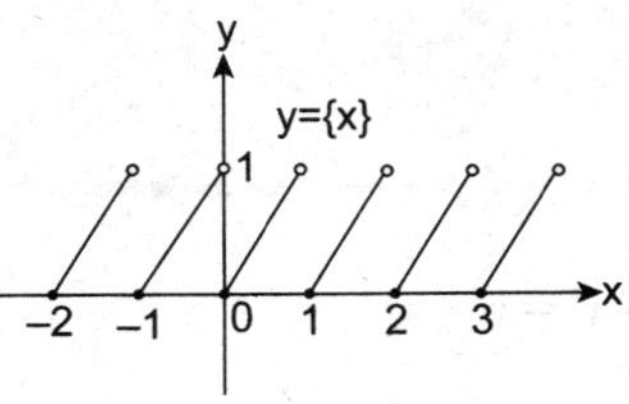

Graph of $g(x) = \{x\} - 1$ is shown as below.

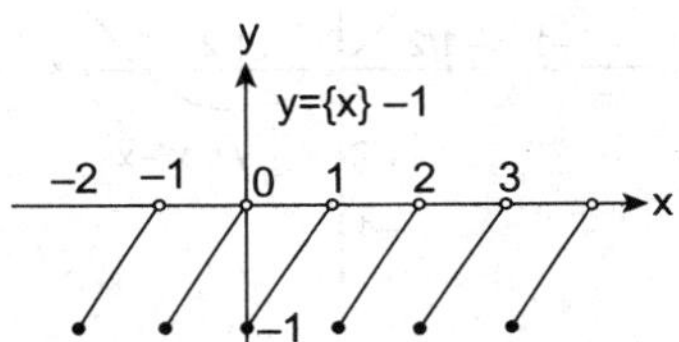

Now as is evident from the graph $y = f(|x|)$ is always greater than or equal to 0, whereas $g(x)$ is always less than 0.

Hence, the two graphs never intersect each other, and hence, no real value of x satisfies $f(|x|) = x - [x + 1]$

17. If $\{x\}$ denotes the fractional part of x, then find the number of real solutions of the equation $(x - 3)\{x\} = \{x\} - 1 \ \forall\, x > -4$

(a) 16 solutions (b) ∞ solutions

(c) 5 solutions (d) None of these

Solution: (c) The graph of $y = \{x\} - 1$ is as given below.

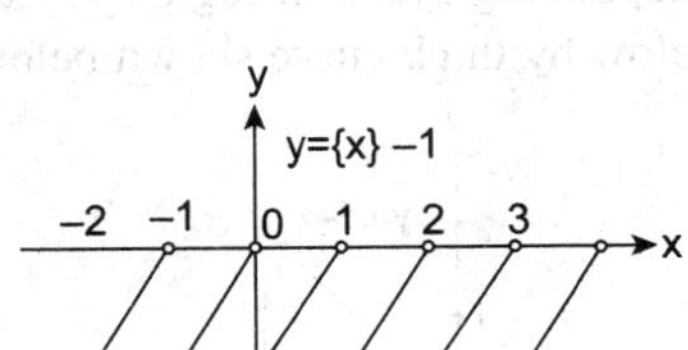

The graph of $y = (x - 3)\{x\}$ is as given below.

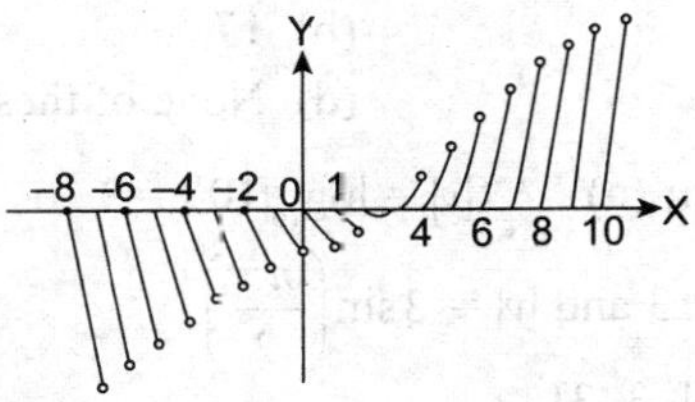

Sketching the two curves in the same frame of reference, we get

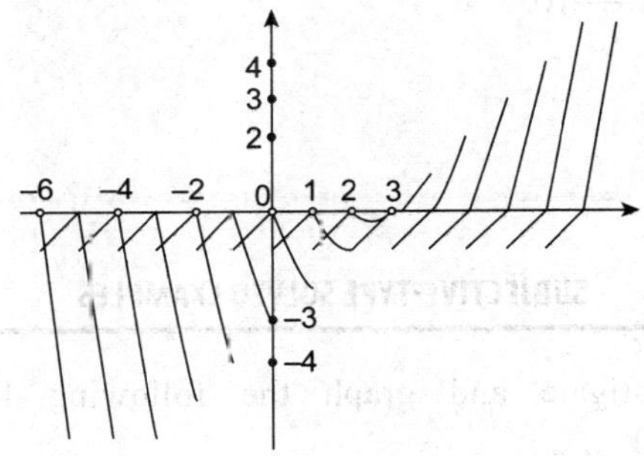

As is evident from the graph, we have 6 solutions.

18. A function $f : \mathbb{R} \to \mathbb{R}$ is defined such that

$$f(x) = \begin{cases} 2\sin^2\left(\dfrac{2}{\pi}x\right); & 0 < x \le 1 \\ 3\{x\}; & 1 < x \le \dfrac{4}{3} \\ x^2 - 8x + 15; & x \ge \dfrac{4}{3} \end{cases}$$

and $2f(0) = 1$, the number of real solution of equation $2f(|x|) = 1$ is

(a) 9 (b) 8

(c) 11 (d) None of these

Solution: (c) Graph of $y = f|x|$ is as shown in the figure. We can see that $f(0) = \dfrac{1}{2}$, and therefore, line $y = \dfrac{1}{2}$ cuts the graph at 11 distinct, points therefore, the equation $2f(|x|) = 1$ has 11 distinct solutions.

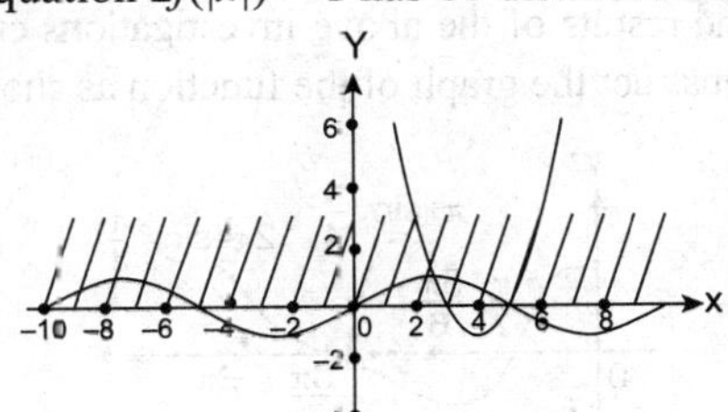

19. The number of ordered pairs (x, y) satisfying the following two curves simultaneously $|y| = 3\sin\left(\dfrac{\pi x}{2}\right)$ and $|y| = \log_{10}|x^3|$ is equal to

(a) 18 (b) 17

(c) 16 (d) None of these

Solution: (a) $\because |y| = \log_{10}|10^3| = 3$

$\Rightarrow y = \pm 3$ and $|y| = 3\sin\left(\frac{\pi x}{2}\right)$

$\Rightarrow y \in [-3, 3]$

$\Rightarrow$ No point of intersection after $x = 10$ and before $x = -10$.

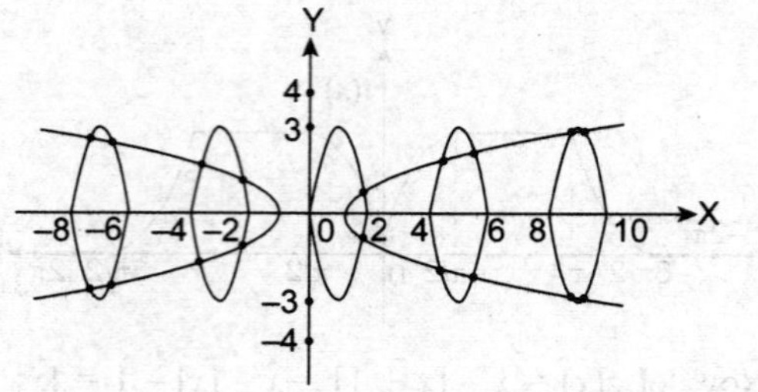

SECTION–II

SUBJECTIVE-TYPE SOLVED EXAMPLES

1. Investigate and graph the following functions $y = \frac{1}{2}\sin 2x + \cos x$:

Solution: The function is defined and continuous throughout the number scale and has a period 2π. Therefore, in investigating we may confine ourselves to the interval $[0, 2\pi)$. The graph of the function has no asymptote by virtue of continuity and periodicity.

Find the first derivative $y' = \cos 2x - \sin x$.

Now, $y' = 0$

$$\Rightarrow x_1 = \frac{\pi}{6},\ x_2 = \frac{5\pi}{6},\ x_3 = \frac{3\pi}{2}$$

Evaluate the second derivative; $y'' = -2\sin 2x - \cos x$.

On the interval $[0, 2\pi]$, it has four roots

$$x_1 = \frac{\pi}{2},\ x_2 = \pi + \text{arc}\sin\left(\frac{1}{4}\right),\ x_3 = \frac{3\pi}{2},$$

$$x_4 = 2\pi - \text{arc}\sin\left(\frac{1}{4}\right)$$

The results of the above investigations enable us to construct the graph of the function as shown below.

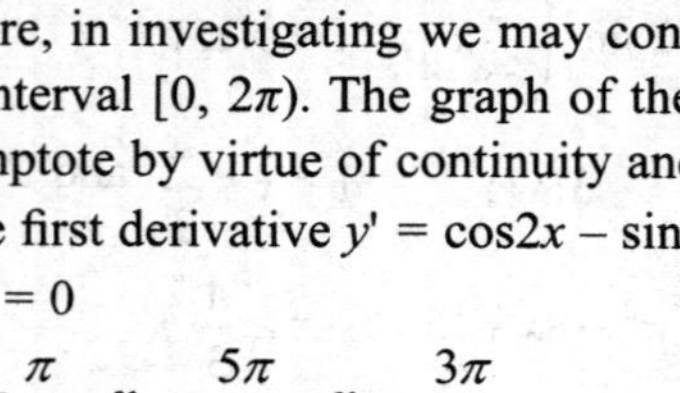

2. Plot the curve $y = \max\{x^2 - y, x\}$

Solution: when $x^2 - y \geq x$

i.e., for $y \leq x^2 - x$

Now $y = x^2 - x$

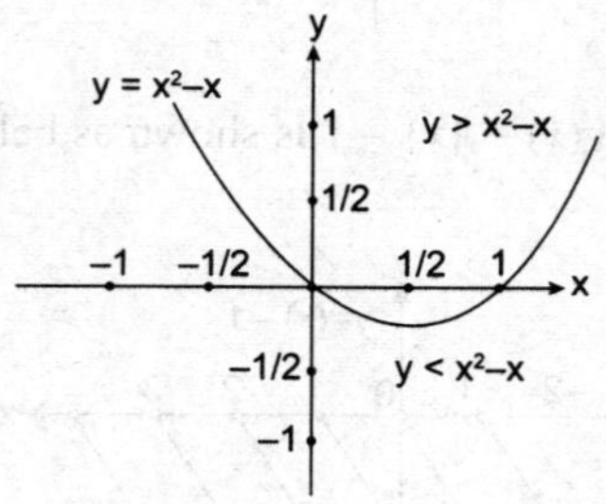

Now for the region representing $y \leq x^2 - x$, max

$\{x^2 - y, x\} = x^2 - y \quad \Rightarrow y = x^2 - y \Rightarrow y = \frac{x^2}{2}$

$\Rightarrow \frac{x^2}{2} \leq x^2 - x \quad \Rightarrow x \in (-\infty, 0] \cup [2, \infty)$

$\therefore$ In region $y \leq (x^2 - x)$

$\Rightarrow y = \frac{x^2}{2}$ will be as shown below.

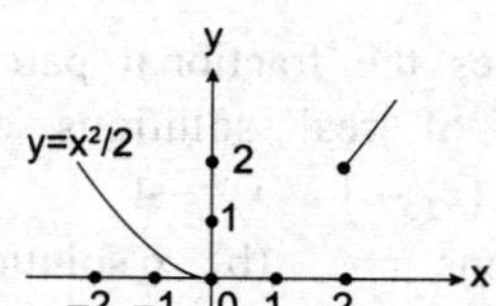

$\therefore y > x^2 - x \quad \Rightarrow x > x^2 - x$

$\Rightarrow x^2 - 2x < 0 \quad \Rightarrow x \in (0, 2)$

The corresponding graph in region $y > x^2 - x$, will be shown below by thick curve shown below.

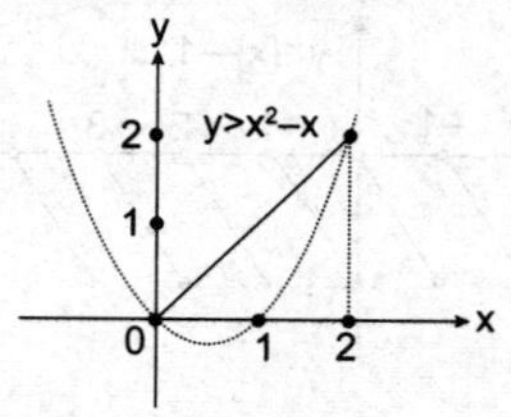

And for the region satisfying $y > x^2 - x$

$\Rightarrow$ max $\{x^2 - y, x\} = x$, then $y = x$

Hence, the graph of $y = \max\{x^2 - y, x\}$ will be as shown by thick curve given below.

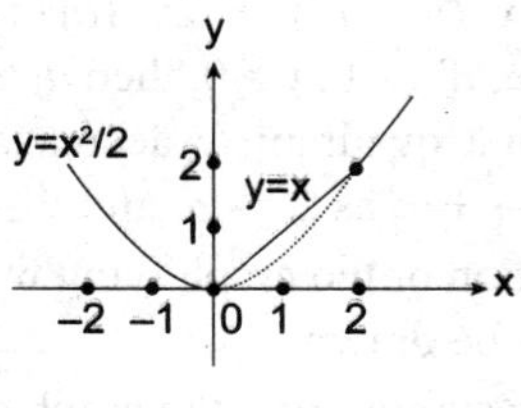

3. Find the number of point of intersection of the graphs $|y| = ||x|^2 - 2|x| - 3|$ and $|y| = \pi \cos x/2$

Solution: $y = \pi \cos\left(\dfrac{x}{2}\right)$

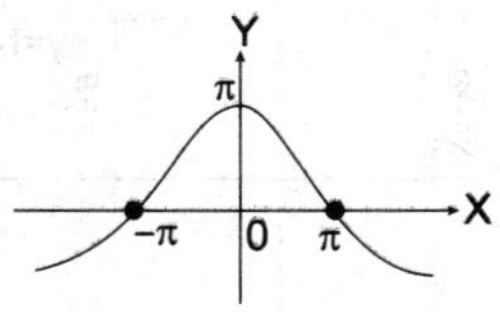

$|y| = \pi \cos x/2$

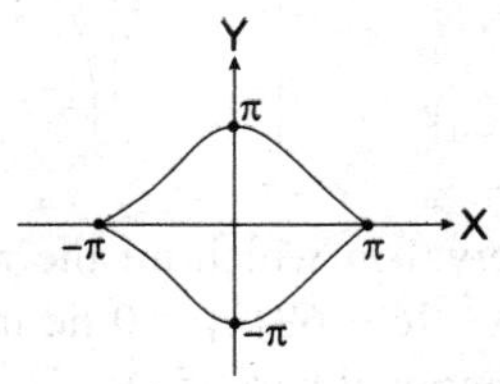

Now sketching the two curves together, we get

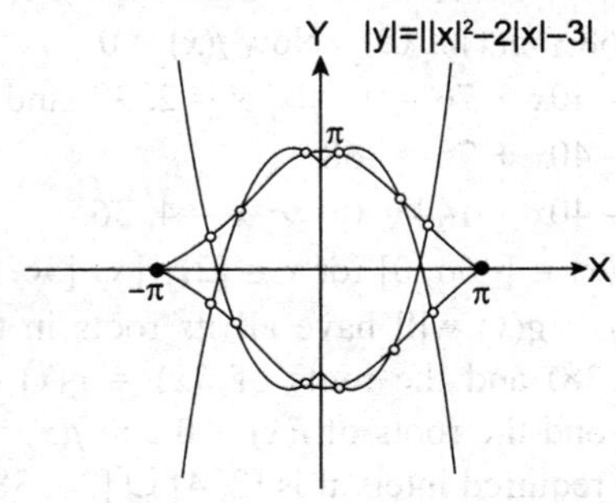

Clearly, the two curves intersect at 12 points

4. Find the number of solutions of $\dfrac{[x]}{\{x\}} = 7$; where $[x]$ denotes the greatest integer function and $\{x\}$ denotes the fractional part of x

Solution: Clearly, x can't be an integer

$(\because \{x\} = 0 \ \forall\, x \in \mathbb{Z})$

$\Rightarrow [x] = 7\{x\}$

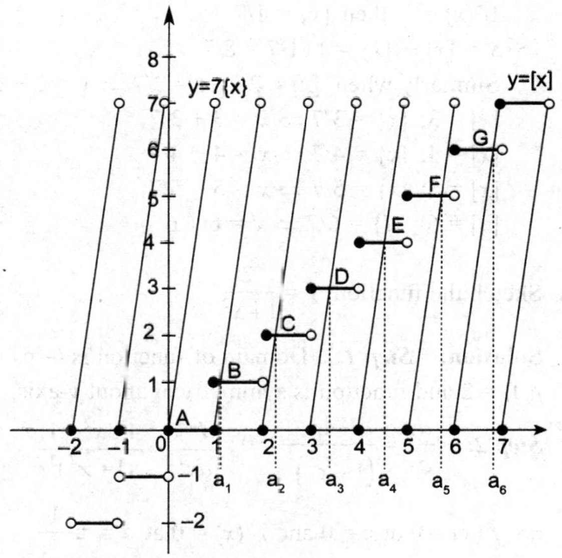

Now, clearly there are only 6 point of intersection, and hence, only 6 values of x which satisfy the above equation, as A(0, 0) corresponds to $x = 0 \in \mathbb{Z}$.

Now, these solutions can be found out diagram magically

$a_1 = 1 + 1/7$, $a_4 = 4 + 4/7$

$a_2 = 2 + 2/7$, $a_5 = 5 + 5/7$

$a_3 = 3 + 3/7$, $a_6 = 6 + 6/7$

Aliter, $[x] = x - \{x\}$, then $[x] = 7\{x\}$

$\Rightarrow x - \{x\} = 7\{x\}$

$\Rightarrow x = 8\{x\}$

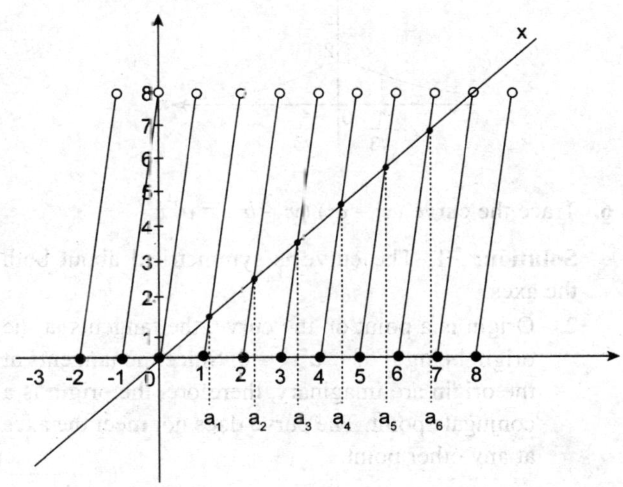

As shown in the diagram above, there are 6 number of solutions.

Since, $0 < \{x\} < 1$

Now, $[x] = 7\{x\} \in (0, 7)$

$\Rightarrow 0 < [x] < 7$

If $[x] = 1$, then $\{x\} = 1/7$

$\Rightarrow x = [x] + \{x\} = 1+1/7 = 8/7$

Similarly when $[x] = 2$; $\{x\} = 2/7 \Rightarrow x = 2 + 2/7$

$[x] = 3$; $\{x\} = 3/7 \Rightarrow x = 3 + 3/7$

$[x] = 4$; $\{x\} = 4/7 \Rightarrow x = 4 + 4/7$

$[x] = 5$; $\{x\} = 5/7 \Rightarrow x = 5 + 5/7$

$[x] = 6$; $\{I\} = 6/7 \Rightarrow x = 6 + 6/7$

5. Sketch the function $y = \dfrac{2}{1+x^2}$

Solution: ***Step 1:*** Domain of function is $(-\infty, \infty)$ $f(0) = 2$ and function is symmetrical about y-axis.

Step 2: $\dfrac{dy}{dx} = \dfrac{-4x}{(1+x^2)^2} = 0$; $\dfrac{d^2y}{dx^2} = \dfrac{4(3x^2-1)}{(1+x^2)^3}$

$\Rightarrow f'(x) = 0$ at $x = 0$ and $f''(x) = 0$ at $x = \pm\dfrac{1}{\sqrt{3}}$

$\Rightarrow f'(x)$ is concave downwards for $x \in \left(-\dfrac{1}{\sqrt{3}}, \dfrac{1}{\sqrt{3}}\right)$

and $\dfrac{dy}{dx} > 0$ *where* $x < 0$ (y increasing),

$\dfrac{dy}{dx} < 0$ when $x > 0$ (y decreasing) and

Point $x = 0$ is point of maxima.

Step 3: $\lim\limits_{x\to\pm\infty} y = 0$, so, graph of the function is

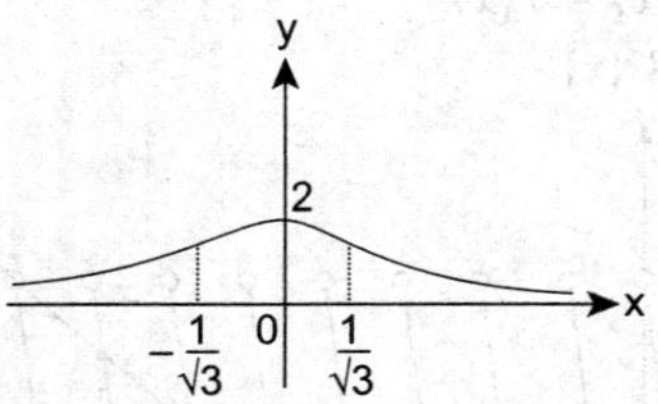

6. Trace the curve $(x^2 - a^2)(y^2 - b^2) = a^2 b^2$

Solution: 1. The curve is symmetrical about both the axes.

2. Origin is a point on the curve, the tangents at the origin being $b^2x^2 + a^2y^2 = 0$. Since the tangents at the origin are imaginary, therefore, the origin is a conjugate point. The curve does not meet the axes at any other point.

3. Re-writing the equation in the form $y = \pm\sqrt{\dfrac{b^2x^2}{x^2-a^2}}$ we find that $|x| > a$. Similarly it can be seen that $|y| > b$. Therefore, no portion of the graph (except the conjugate point (0, 0)) lies in the region bounded by the lines $x = \pm a$, $y = \pm b$.

4. The lines $x = \pm a$, $y = \pm b$ are the asymptotes of the curve. The portion of the curve lying in the first quadrant is above the asymptote $y = b$, and on the right of the asymptote $x = a$.

5. Since $2x(y^2 - b^2) + 2y(dy/dx)(x^2 - a^2) = 0$, therefore, if $x > 0, y > 0$, then $dy/dx < 0$. Therefore, in the first quadrant, y decreases as x increases. Also $y \to +\infty$ as $x \to a$, and $y \to b$ as $x \to +\infty$.

6. The portion or the graph lying in the first quadrant can now be drawn.

By using symmetries, the graph can be completed. The graph is as shown in the figure given below.

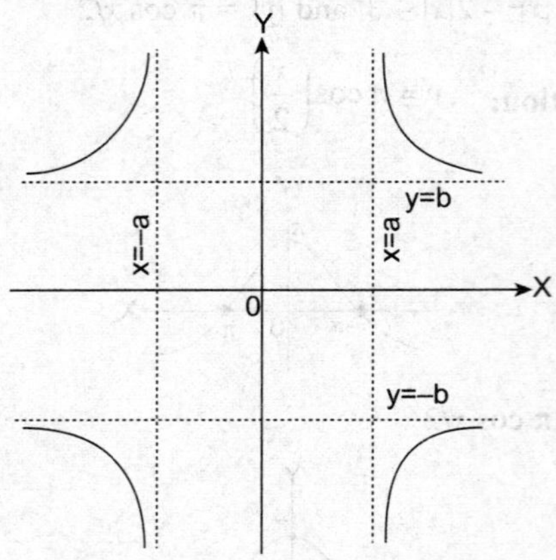

7. Find the interval in which all the roots of the equation $x^2 - 40x + 76 + 68\{x\} = 0$ lie in the interval ($\{x\}$ represents fractional part of x).

Solution: Let $f(x) = x^2 - 40x + 76$ and $g(x) = -68\{x\}$

Now $-68 < g(x) \le 0$. Now $f(x) = 0$

$\Rightarrow x^2 - 40x + 76 = 0 \Rightarrow x = 2, 38$; and $f(x) = -68$

$\Rightarrow x^2 - 40x + 76 = -68$

$\Rightarrow x^2 - 40x + 144 = 0 \Rightarrow x = 4, 36$.

Thus, $f(x) \in [-68, 0]$ for $x \in [2, 4] \cup [36, 38)$

$\therefore$ $f(x) = g(x)$ will have all its roots in the interval $[2, 38)$ and the roots of $f(x) = g(x)$ can not lie beyond the roots of $f(x) = 0$ and $f(x) = 68$. Thus, the required interval is $[2, 4] \cup [36, 38)$.

8. Using the first derivative, find the extrema of the following functions $f(x) = 3\sqrt[3]{x^2} - x^2$

Solution: The function is defined and continuous throughout the number scale.

Let us find the derivative: $f'(x) = 2\left(\dfrac{1}{\sqrt[3]{x}} - x\right)$

From the equation $f'(x) = 0$, we find the roots of the derivative $x = \pm 1$.

Furthermore, the derivative goes to infinity at the point $x = 0$. Thus, the critical points are $x_1 = -1, x_2 = 0$, $x_3 = 1$. The results of investigating the sign neighborhood of these points are given in figure.

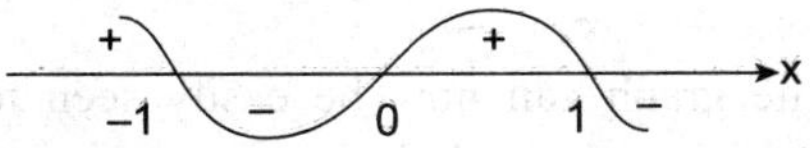

The investigation shows that the function has two maxima: $f(-1) = 2, f(1) = 2$ and a minimum $f(0) = 0$.

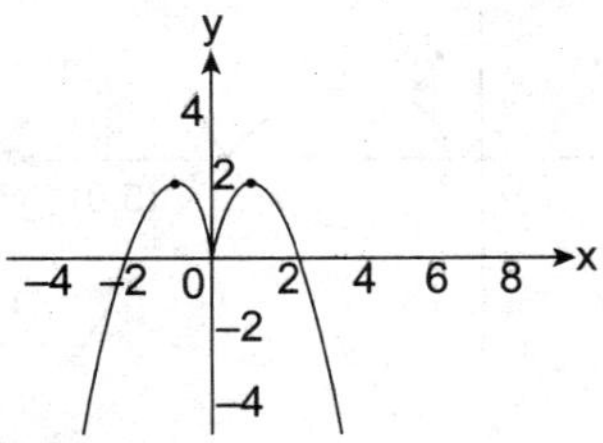

9. Using the second derivative, find out the character of the extrema of the following functions $y = 2\sin x + \cos 2x$

Solution: Since the function is a periodic one, we may confine ourselves to the interval $[0, 2\pi]$. Find the first and second derivatives: $y' = 2\cos x - 2\sin 2x = 2\cos x\,(1 - 2\sin x)$; $y'' = -2\sin x - 4\cos 2x$.

From the equation $2\cos x(1 - 2\sin x) = 0$, determine the critical points on the interval $[0, 2\pi]$; $x_1 = \pi/6$, $x_2 = \pi/2, x_3 = 5\pi/6, x_4 = 3\pi/2$

Now, find the sign of the second derivative at each critical point:

$y''(\pi/6) = -3 < 0$; hence, we have a maximum $y(\pi/6) = 3/2$ at the point $x_1 = \pi/6$

$y''(\pi/2) = 2 > 0$; hence, we have a minimum $y(\pi/2) = 1$ at the point $x_2 = \pi/2$

$y''(5\pi/6) = -3 < 0$; hence, we have a maximum $y(5\pi/6) = 3/2$ at the point $x_3 = 5\pi/6$

$y''(3\pi/2) = 6 > 0$; hence, we have a minimum $y(3\pi/2) = -3$ at the point $x_4 = 3\pi/2$ as shown in the figure given below.

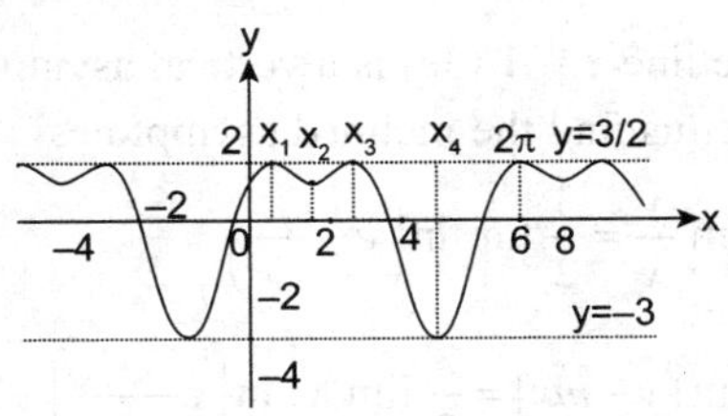

10. Find the asymptotes of the following curves $y = xe^{\frac{1}{x}}$:

Solution: The curve has a vertical asymptote $x = 0$,

since $\lim\limits_{x\to 0^+} y = \lim\limits_{x\to 0^+} xe^{\frac{1}{x}} = \lim\limits_{t=\frac{1}{x}\to +\infty} \dfrac{e^t}{t} = +\infty$

Find the inclined asymptotes:

$$m = \lim_{x\to\pm\infty} \frac{y}{x} = \lim_{x\to\pm\infty} e^{\frac{1}{x}} = e^0 = 1 \text{ and}$$

$$c = \lim_{x\to\pm\infty}\left(xe^{\frac{1}{x}} - x\right) = \lim_{x\to\pm\infty} \frac{e^{\frac{1}{x}}-1}{1/x} = \lim_{1/x=z\to 0} \frac{e^z-1}{z} = 1$$

Thus, the straight line $y = x + 1$ will be an inclined asymptote of the curve as shown in the figure

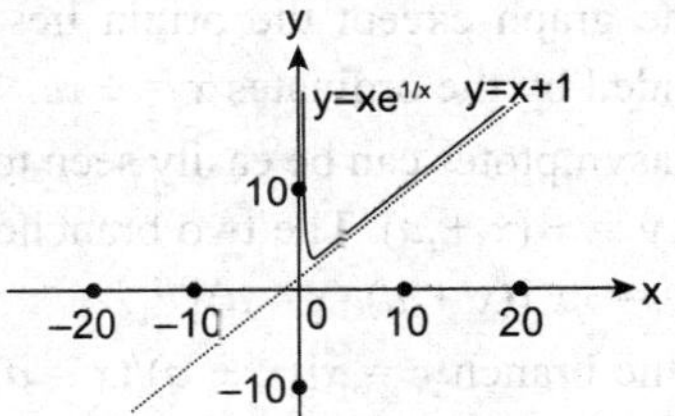

11. Find the asymptotes of the following curves $y = \sqrt{1+x^2}\,\sin\dfrac{1}{x}$:

Solution: The curve has no vertical asymptotes; since it is continuous at $x \neq 0$ and in the neighbourhood of the point $x = 0$ the function is bounded.

Let us find the inclined asymptotes. We have

$$m = \lim_{x\to+\infty} \frac{y}{x} = \lim_{x\to+\infty} \frac{|x|\sqrt{1+\frac{1}{x^2}}\,\sin\frac{1}{x}}{x} = \pm 1.0 = 0$$

Then $c = \lim\limits_{x\to+\infty}(y - mx) = \lim\limits_{x\to+\infty} |x|\sqrt{1+\dfrac{1}{x^2}}\,\sin\dfrac{1}{x}$

$$= \begin{cases} 1; & \text{as } x \to +\infty \\ -1; & \text{as } x \to -\infty \end{cases}$$

Thus, the curve has two horizontal asymptotes: $y = +1$ and $y = -1$ (as shown in the figure). The same result can be obtained proceeding from symmetry about the origin and keeping in mind that the function y is odd.

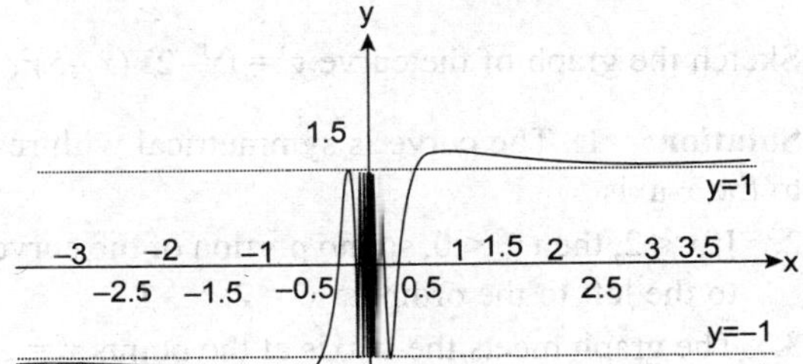

12. Trace the curve $y^2(x - a) = x^2(x + a), a > 0$.

Solution: 1. The curve is symmetrical with respect to the x-axis.

2. The curve meets the x-axis at the points given by $x = 0$, and $x = -a$, i.e., at (0, 0) and $(-a, 0)$. It does not meet the y-axis except at the origin. The tangents at (0, 0) are given by $x^2 + y^2 = 0$. Since the tangents at (0, 0) are imaginary, therefore, (0, 0) is a conjugate point. The tangent at $(-a, 0)$ can be easily seen to be the line $x + a = 0$.
3. If $-a < x < a$ and $x \neq 0$, then $y^2 < 0$, so that no part of the graph except the origin lies in the region bounded by the ordinates $x = \pm a$.
4. The asymptotes can be easily seen to be the lines $x = a$, $y = \pm (x + a)$. The two branches of the curve are $y = \pm x\,[(x + a)/(x - a)]^{1/2}$.

   For the branch $y = x[(x + a)/(x - a)]^{1/2}$, we have $y = x + a + a^2/2x + \ldots$

   So that if $x > 0$, then the curve is above the line $y = x + a$, and if $x < 0$, then the curve is below $y = x + a$. Similarly, it can be seen that if $x > 0$, then the curve is below $y = -x - a$, and if $x < 0$, then the curve is above $y = -x - a$. Also, if $x > 0$, then the curve is to the right of $x = a$

   The graph of the curve can now be easily seen to be as is shown in the figure given below.

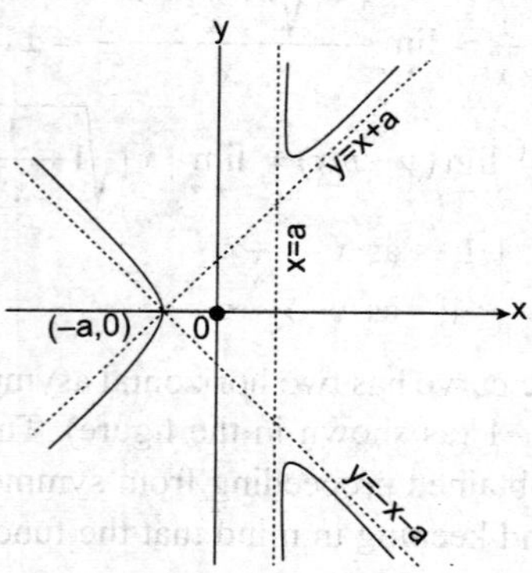

13. Sketch the graph of the curve $y^2 = (x - 2)(x - 5)^2$.

Solution: 1. The curve is symmetrical with respect to the x-axis

2. If $x < 2$, then $y^2 < 0$, so, no portion of the curve lies to the left to the ordinate $x = 2$.
3. The graph meets the x-axis at the points $x = 2$ and $x = 5$. It does not meet the y-axis. The tangents at (2, 0) is the line $x = 2$. The tangents at (5, 0) are the lines $y = \pm\sqrt{3}(x - 5)$. This can be seen by shifting the origin to (5,0) by the transformation $x = X + 5$, $y = Y$. The equation of the curve transforms to $Y^2 = X^2(X + 3)$. Equating to zero the lowest degree terms, the tangents are given by $Y^2 = 3X^2$, i.e., $y^2 = 3(x - 5)^2$]. Since there are two distinct tangents at (5, 0), therefore, it is a node.
4. There are no asymptotes.
5. As $x \to +\infty$, $y^2 \to +\infty$

   The graph can now be easily seen to be as in the figure shown below:

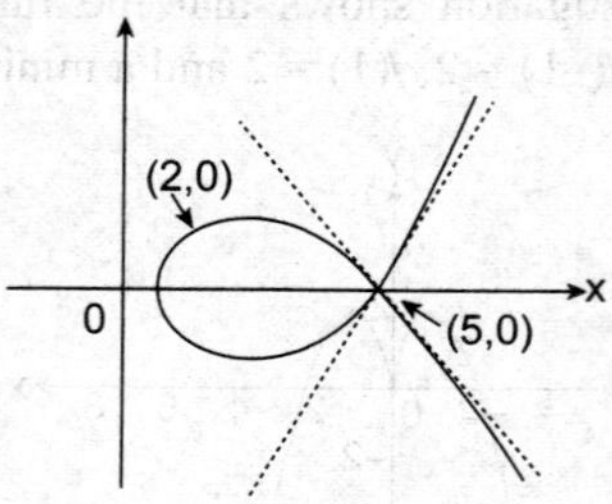

14. Find the asymptotes of the following curves $y = \dfrac{3x}{2}\ln\left(e - \dfrac{1}{3x}\right)$:

Solution: The function is defined and continuous at $e - \dfrac{1}{3x} > 0$. i.e., at $x < 0$ and $x > \dfrac{1}{3e}$.

Since the function is continuous at every point of the domain of definition, vertical asymptotes can exist only on finite boundaries of the domain of definition.

As $x \to 0^-$, we have $\lim\limits_{x\to 0^-} y = \lim\limits_{x\to 0-} \dfrac{3x}{2}\ln\left(e - \dfrac{1}{3x}\right)$

$$= -\frac{1}{2}\lim_{z\to\infty}\frac{\ln(e + z)}{z} = 0\text{; Putting } \left(z = -\frac{1}{3x}\right)$$

i.e., the straight line $x = 0$ is not a vertical asymptote.

As $x \to \left(\dfrac{1}{3e}\right)^+$, we have

$$\lim_{x\to\left(\frac{1}{3e}\right)^+} y = \frac{3}{2}\lim_{x\to\left(\frac{1}{3e}\right)^+} x\ln\left(e - \frac{1}{3x}\right) = -\infty$$

i.e., the line $x = 1/(3e)$ is a vertical asymptote.

Now let us find the inclined asymptotes

$$m = \lim_{x\to\pm\infty}\frac{y}{x} = \frac{3}{2}\lim_{x\to\pm\infty}\ln\left(e - \frac{1}{3x}\right) = \frac{3}{2}$$

$$c = \lim_{x\to\pm\infty}[y - mx] = \frac{3}{2}\lim_{x\to\pm\infty} x\left[\ln\left(e - \frac{1}{3x}\right) - 1\right]$$

$$= \frac{-1}{2e}\lim_{x\to\pm\infty}\frac{\ln\left(1 - \dfrac{1}{3xe}\right)}{\left(1 - \dfrac{1}{3xe}\right)} = -\frac{1}{2e}$$

Hence, the straight line $y=\frac{3x}{2}-\frac{1}{2e}$ is an inclined asymptote as shown in the figure given below:

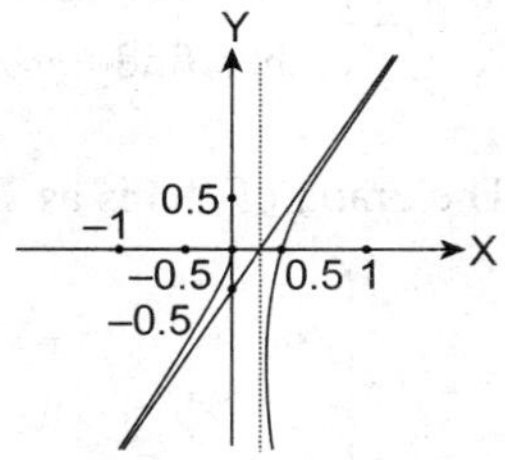

15. Investigate and graph the following functions $y = x^6 - 3x^4 + 3x^2 - 5$:

Solution: The function is defined and continuous throughout the number scale, therefore, the curve has no vertical asymptote. The function is even, since $f(-x) = f(x)$. Consequently, its graph is symmetric about the y-axis, and therefore, it is sufficient to investigate the function only on the interval $[0, \infty)$.

There are no inclined asymptotes, since as $x \to \infty$ the quantity y turns out to be an infinitely large quantity of the sixth order with respect to x.

Investigate the first derivatives $y' = 6x^5 - 12x^3 + 6x = 6x(x^4 - 2x^2 + 1) = 6x(x^2 - 1)^2$; the critical points are:

$$x_1 = -1, \qquad x_2 = 0, \qquad x_3 = 1$$

Since in the interval $[0, \infty)$ the derivative $y' \geq 0$, the function increases.

Investigate the second derivative $y'' = 30x^4 - 36x^2 + 6 = 6(5x^4 - 6x^2 + 1)$

The positive roots of the second derivative $x_1 = \frac{1}{\sqrt{5}}, x_2 = 1.$

Using the results of the investigation and taking into consideration the symmetry principle, we construct the graph of the function. As is seen from the graph, the function has roots $x = \pm\, a$, where $a \approx 1.6$

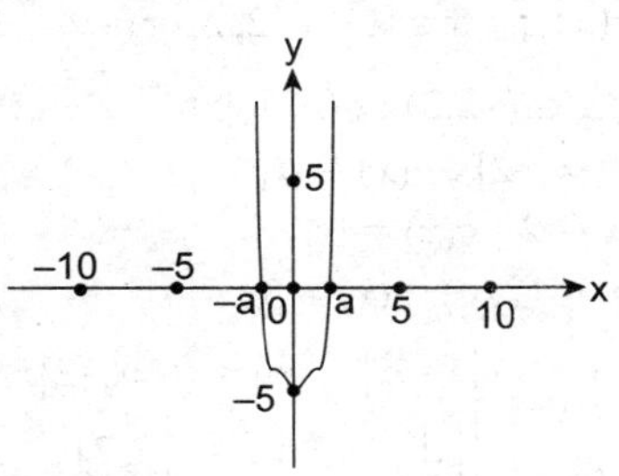

16. Investigate and graph the following functions $y = x + \ln(x^2 - 1)$

Solution: The function is defined and continuous at all values of x for which $x^2 - 1 > 0$ or $|x| > 1$, i.e., on two intervals $(-\infty, -1)$ and $(1, +\infty)$

We seek the vertical asymptotes:

$$\lim_{x\to-1^-} y = \lim_{x\to-1^-}\left[x+\ln(x^2-1)\right] = -\infty$$

$$\lim_{x\to1^+} y = \lim_{x\to1^+}\left[x+\ln(x^2-1)\right] = -\infty$$

Thus, the curve has two vertical asymptotes: $x = -1$ and $x = +1$.

Find inclined asymptotes:

$$m = \lim_{x\to\pm\infty}\frac{y}{x} = \lim_{x\to\pm\infty}\frac{x+\ell n(x^2-1)}{x}$$

$$= \lim_{x\to\pm\infty}\left[1+\frac{\ell n(x^2-1)}{x}\right] = 1 \text{ and}$$

$$c = \lim_{x\to\pm\infty}[y-x] = \lim_{x\to\pm\infty}\ln\left(x^2-1\right) = \infty$$

Hence, the curve has neither inclined nor horizontal asymptotes.

Since the derivative $y' = 1+\frac{2x}{x^2-1}$ exists and is finite at all points of the domain of definition of the function, only the zeros of the derivative. $x_1 = -1 - \sqrt{2}$; $x_2 = -1 + \sqrt{2}$ can be critical points. At the point $x_2 = -1 + \sqrt{2}$ the function is not defined; hence, there is only one critical point $x_1 = -1 - \sqrt{2}$ belonging to the interval $(-\infty, -1)$. In the interval $(1, \infty)$ derivative $y' > 0$, and hence, the function increases. The second derivative $y'' = -\frac{2(x^2+1)}{(x^2-1)^2} < 0$, hence, the curve is convex upwards everywhere, and at the point $x_1 = -1 - \sqrt{2} \approx -2.41$ the function has a maximum $y(-1 - \sqrt{2}) \approx -1 - \sqrt{2} + \ln(2 + 2\sqrt{2}) \approx -0.84$.

To plot the graph in the interval $(1, \infty)$, where there are no characteristics points, we choose the following additional points $x = 2$; $y = 2 + \ln 3 \approx 3.10$ and $x = 1.2$; $y = 1.2 + \ln 0.44 \approx 0.38$.

The graph of the function is shown below.

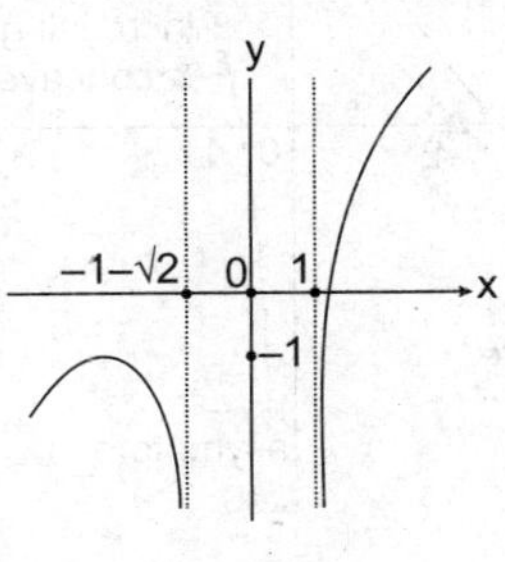

17. Find the asymptotes of the curve $y = \frac{x^2+2x-1}{x}$ and hence, sketch.

Solution: Here, the curve $y = \frac{x^2+2x-1}{x}$ could be written as $x^2 + 2x - yx - 1 = 0$

(i) No asymptote parallel to x-axis

(ii) Asymptote parallel to y-axis $\Rightarrow x = 0$

(iii) Oblique asymptote

Let $y = mx + c$ be oblique asymptote

$\therefore \quad x^2 + 2x - x(mx + c) - 1 = 0$

$x^2 - mx^2 + 2x - cx - 1 = 0$

$\Rightarrow \quad x^2(1-m) + x(2-c) - 1 = 0$

For oblique asymptote equate the highest power and second highest power of x to zero.

i.e., Coefficient of $x^2 = 0 \Rightarrow m = 1$

Coefficient of $x = 0$

$\Rightarrow c = 2$

$y = x + 2$ is oblique asymptote to $y = x - 1/x + 2$

(iv) Neither symmetric about axis nor about origin

(v) Domain is $\mathbb{R} - \{0\}$

(vi) Range is $\mathbb{R}$

(vii) $\frac{dy}{dx} = 1 + \frac{1}{x^2} \quad \Rightarrow \quad \frac{dy}{dx} > 0$ for all $x \in \mathbb{R} - \{0\}$

(viii) $\frac{d^2y}{dx^2} = -\frac{2}{x^3} > 0$ for $x < 0$ and < 0 for $x > 0$

$\Rightarrow$ when $x > 0$, curve is concave down.

when $x < 0$, curve is concave up.

From the above information, we can plot the curve $y = x - 1/x + 2$ as shown below:

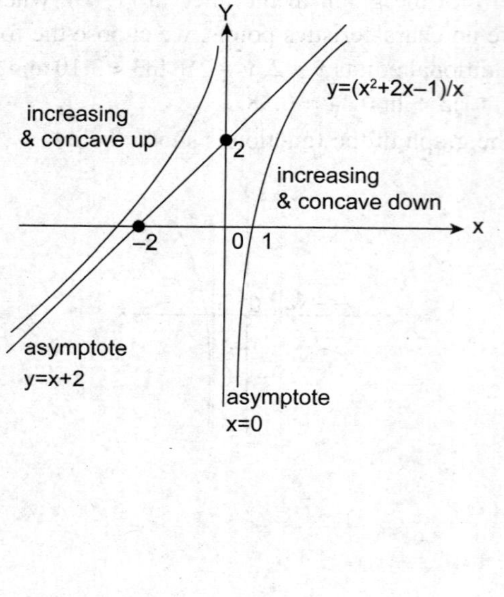

18. Let $f(x) = \begin{cases} x & ; x < -1 \\ x+1 & ; -1 \le x < 2 \\ 1-x & ; x \ge 2 \end{cases}$ and $g(x) = \begin{cases} |x| & ; x \le 2 \\ 3x & ; x > 2 \end{cases}$, then find $fog(x)$ and $gof(x)$

Solution: The graph of $f(x)$ is as shown below.

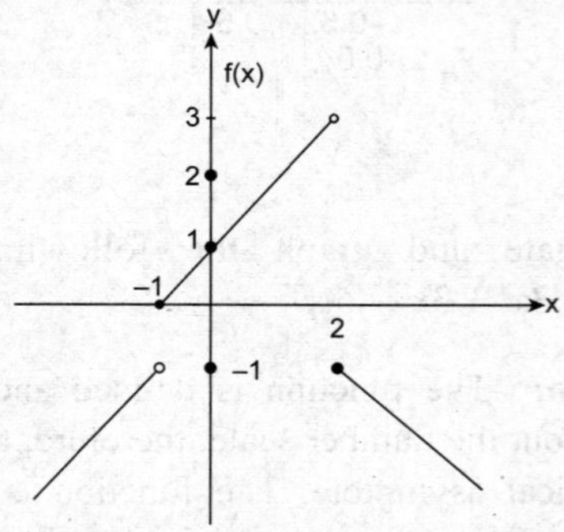

Clearly; $f(x) \le 2 \; \forall \; x \in R \sim (1,2)$ and $f(x) > 2 \; \forall \; x \in (1, 2)$

The graph of g(x) is as shown below.

Clearly $g(x) < 0$ is not satisfied for any value of (x)

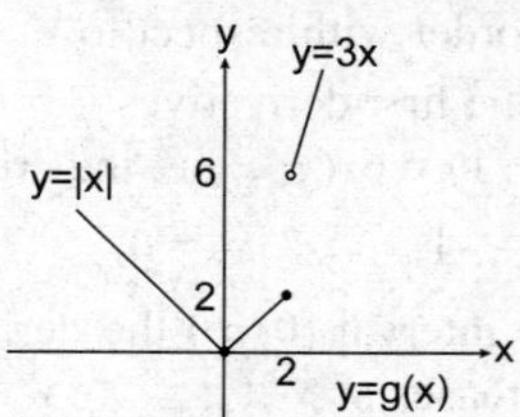

Now $0 \le g(x) < 2 \Rightarrow x \in [0, 2)$ and $g(x) \ge 2$

$\Rightarrow x \in \mathbb{R} \sim (-2, 2)$

To find fog (x), i.e., $f(g(x))$

$$= \begin{cases} g(x); & g(x) < -1 \\ g(x)+1; & -1 \le g(x) < 2 \text{ or } 0 \le g(x) < 2 \\ 1-g(x); & g(x) \ge 2 \end{cases}$$

$$= \begin{cases} g(x)+1 \; ; & x \in (-2,2) \\ 1-g(x) \; ; & x \in \mathbb{R} \sim (-2,2) \text{ or } (-\infty,-2] \cup [2,\infty) \end{cases}$$

Also for $x \in (-2,2)$; $g(x) = |x|$

for $x \in (-\infty,-2]$; $g(x) = |x|$

and for $x = 2$; $g(x) = |x|$

and for $x \in (2,\infty)$; $g(x) = 3x$

$$\Rightarrow \quad f(g(x)) = \begin{cases} 1-|x| & ; x \in (-\infty,-2] \\ |x|+1 & ; x \in (-2,2) \\ 1-|x| & ; x = 2 \\ 1-3x & ; x \in (2,\infty) \end{cases}$$

∴ The graph of $f(g(x))$ will be as shown below

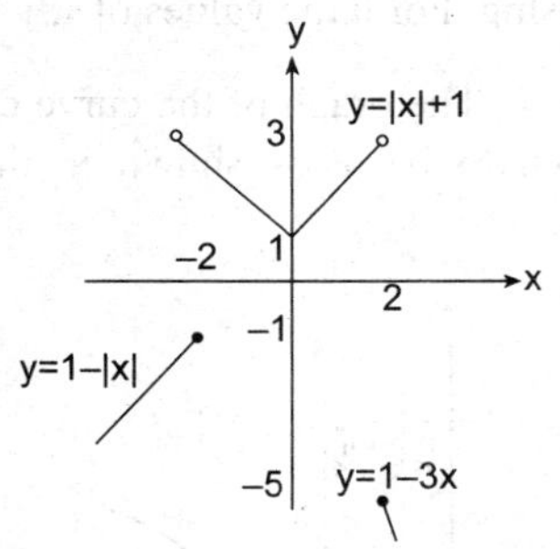

To find $gof(x)$

$$g(f(x))=\begin{cases}f|(x)|; & f(x)\le 2\\ 3f(x); & f(x)>2\end{cases}=\begin{cases}|f(x)|; x\in\mathbb{R}\sim(1,2)\\ 3f(x); x\in(1,2)\end{cases}$$

Also for $x < -1$; $f(x) = x$

for $x \in [-1, 1]$; $f(x) = x + 1$

for $x \in (1, 2)$; $f(x) = x + 1$

and for $x \ge 2$; $f(x) = 1 - x$

$$\therefore \begin{cases}|x| & ; x<-1\\ |x+1| & ; x\in[-1,1]\\ 3(x+1) & ; x\in(1,2)\\ |1-x| & ; x\ge 2\end{cases}$$

∴ The graph of $g(f(x))$ will be as shown below

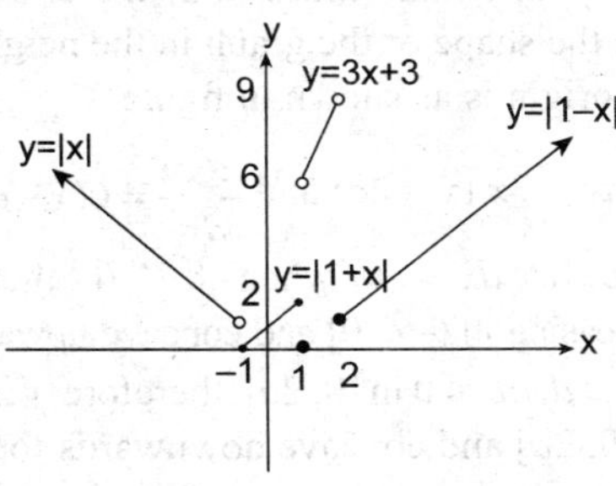

19. Graph the function $y = x^3 - 5x^2 + 4x$

Solution: ***Step 1:*** Factorize the function, if possible, $y = x^3 - 5x^2 + 4x$

$= x(x^2 - 5x + 4)$

$= x(x^2 - x + 4 - 4x)$

$= x(x - 1)(x - 4)$

Step 2: $y = 0 \Rightarrow x(x - 1)(x - 4) = 0$

$\Rightarrow x = 0$ or $x = 1$ or $x = 4$

⇒ The function intersects the x-axis at the three point

i.e., $x = 0$ or $x = 1$ or $x = 4$.

Step 3: Find points of local maximum/minima

$y' = 3x^2 - 10x + 4$

$y' = 0$ for points of local maximum/minima.

$\Rightarrow 3x^2 - 10x + 4 = 0$

$$\Rightarrow x=\frac{10\pm\sqrt{100-48}}{6}=\frac{10\pm 7.2}{6}=2.86 \text{ or } 0.47$$

$$\Rightarrow \frac{d^2y}{dx^2}=6x-10 \quad \Rightarrow f''(2.86) = +\text{ ve}$$

⇒ $x = 2.86$ is a point of local minima and local minimum value is $f(2.86) = -6.06$ and $f''(0.47) = -\text{ve}$

⇒ $x = 0.47$ is a point of local maxima and local maximum value is $f(0.47) = 0.88$

Step 4: $\lim\limits_{x\to\infty} y = \lim\limits_{x\to\infty} x^3\left(1-\frac{1}{x}\right)\left(1-\frac{4}{x}\right)=\infty$

and $\lim\limits_{x\to-\infty} y = \lim\limits_{x\to-\infty}(x)^3\left(1-\frac{1}{x}\right)\left(1-\frac{4}{x}\right)=-\infty$

Thus, from the above information, the graph of the function can be drawn as follow:

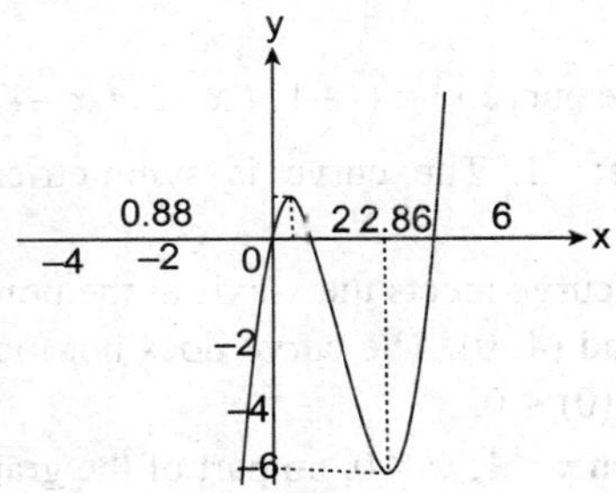

20. Graph $y = (x - 1)(x - 3)^2$

Solution: ***Step 1:*** $y = 0$

⇒ $x = 1, x = 3$ are roots of function where graphs cuts x-axis, $f(0) = (-1)(-3)^2 = -9$

⇒ graph cuts y-axis at pt $(0,-9)$

Step 2: $\frac{dy}{dx} = 2(x-1)(x-3)+(x-3)^2 = 0$

$\Rightarrow (x - 3)(2x - 2 + x - 3) = 0$

$\Rightarrow (x - 3)(3x - 5) = 0$

⇒ Critical points are $x = 3, \frac{5}{3}$

$$\Rightarrow \frac{d^2y}{dx^2}=3(x-3)+(3x-5)=6x-14$$

Now, $\left(\frac{d^2y}{dx^2}\right)_{x=3} = +ve$; hence, local minima at $x = 3$

and $y_{min} = 0$

Also, $\left(\frac{d^2y}{dx^2}\right)_{x=\frac{5}{3}} = -ve$, hence, local maxima at $x=\frac{5}{3}$

and $(y_{max}) = \frac{2}{3}\times\frac{16}{9} = \left(\frac{32}{27}\right)$

Step 3: $\lim_{x\to\infty}(x-1)(x-3)^2 = +\infty$

and $\lim_{x\to-\infty}(x-1)(x-3)^2 = -\infty$

From the above informations, we can easily draw the graph as shown below.

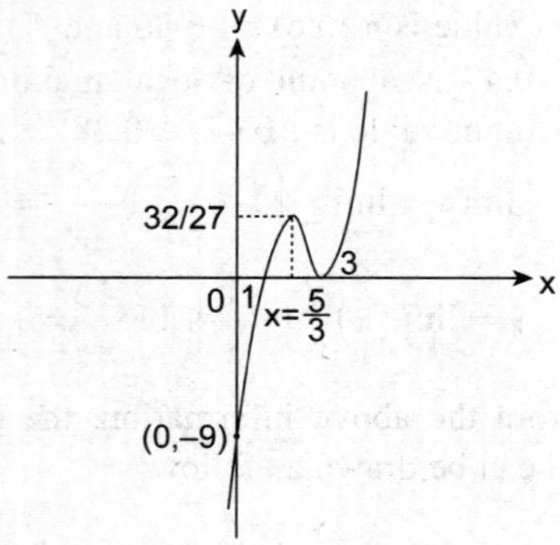

21. Trace the curve $y^2 = (x-1)(x-2)(x-4)$

Solution: **1.** The curve is symmetrical about the x-axis

2. The curve meets the x-axis at the points (1, 0), (2, 0) and (4, 0). The curve does not meet the y-axis as $y^2(0) < 0$.

3. When $x < 1$, $y^2 < 0$, no part of the graph lies to the left of the line $x = 1$. In particular, no part of the graph lies in the second and the third quadrants. Also, If $2 < x < 4$, $y^2 < 0$, so, no part of the graph lies in the region bounded by the lines $x = 2$ and $x = 4$.

4. The equations of the tangents at the points (1, 0), (2, 0) and (4, 0) are $x = 1$, $x = 2$ and $x = 4$, respectively.

5. There are no multiple points.

6. There are no asymptotes.

7. Since y vanishes at $x = 1$ and $x = 2$, therefore, y^2 must have a maximum for some values of x lying between 1 and 2.

In fact, $\frac{d(y^2)}{dx} = 3x^2 - 14x + 14$, so that

$\frac{d(y^2)}{dx} = 0$ when $x = \frac{1}{3}(7\pm\sqrt{7})$

Let $x_1 = \frac{1}{3}(7-\sqrt{7}), x_2 = \frac{1}{3}(7+\sqrt{7})$

Then $1 < x_1 < 2$, and $2 < x_2 > 4$

Also y^2 is a maximum when $x = x_1$

The portion of graph between $x = 1$ and $x = 2$ is, therefore, an oval.

8. When x takes values greater than 4, y^2 keeps on increasing. For large values of x, $y^2 \approx x^3$, and $\lim_{x\to\infty} y \to \pm\infty$. The graph of the curve can now be easily seen to be as is shown in the figure given below.

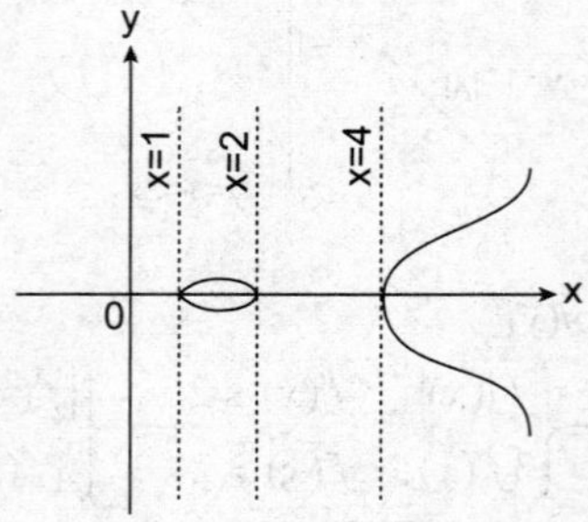

22. Trace the curve $y = x^2(x-3a)$, $a > 0$

Solution: **1.** The curve does not possess any symmetry

2. If $x < 3a$, then $y < 0$ In particular, no portion of the graph lies in the second quadrant

3. The curve meets the x-axis at points given by $x = 0, 3a$, i.e., at (0, 0), $(3a, 0)$.It meets the y-axis only at the origin

4. The tangents at the origin is the line $y = 0$. Since $y < 0$ for small values of x, therefore, it follows that the shape of the graph in the neighborhood of the origin is as shown in figure

5. $dy/dx = 3x(x-2a)$ and $\frac{d^2y}{dx^2} = 6(x-a)$

Since $dy/dx > 0$ when $x < 0$, therefore, y is increasing in $(-\infty, 0]$ and concave upwards for $x > a$

Since $dy/dx < 0$ in $[0, 2a]$, therefore, y is decreasing in $[0, 2a]$ and concave downwards for $x < a$

Again, since $dy/dx > 0$ if $x > 2a$, therefore, y is increasing in $(2a, \infty)$.

Also, y has a maximum at (0, 0) and a minimum at $(2a, -4a^3)$ and $x = a$ is a point of inflexion.

6. $y \to -\infty$ as $x \to -\infty$ and $y \to +\infty$ as $x \to +\infty$

7. There are no asymptotes

The graph of the curve can now be seen to be as shown in figure.

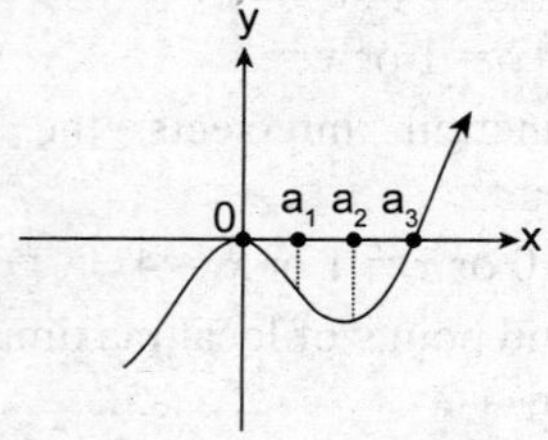

23. Sketch the graph of $y^2 = x^2(4 - x^2)$

Solution: ***Step 1:*** (a) Domain of given relation is $(-\infty,\infty)$

(b) Roots of equation $x^2(4 - x^2) = 0$ are $x = 0$ and $x = \pm 2$

(c) We can observe that since $f(x)$ contains only even power terms of x and y, hence, graph will be symmetrical about x as well as y-axis.

$\therefore\ f(-x) = f(x)$

Step 2: $2y.\dfrac{dy}{dx} = x^2(-2x) + (4 - x^2)2x$

$= 2x(-x^2 + 4 - x^2) = 2x(4 - 2x^2)$

$$\frac{dy}{dx} = \frac{2x(2-x^2)}{\sqrt{x^2(4-x^2)}} \text{ for } y > 0 \text{ and } \frac{-2x(2-x^2)}{\sqrt{x^2(4-x^2)}} \text{ for } y < 0$$

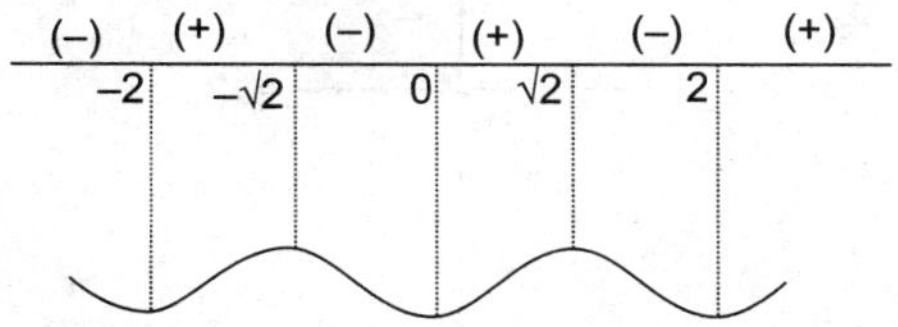

So, critical points are $x = \pm\sqrt{2}$, $x = 0$, $x = \pm 2$

Curve has local minima at $x = -2, 0, 2$ for $y > 0$

$(y)_{x=-2} = 0;\ (y)_{x=0} = 0;\ (y)_{x=2} = 0$

Curve has maxima at $x = \pm\sqrt{2}$ for $y > 0$

and $(y)_{x=-\sqrt{2}} = 4$, $(y)_{x=+\sqrt{2}} = 4$

Step 3: $\lim\limits_{x\to\infty} f(x) = \infty$

So, the graph of $f(x)$ will be as shown below:

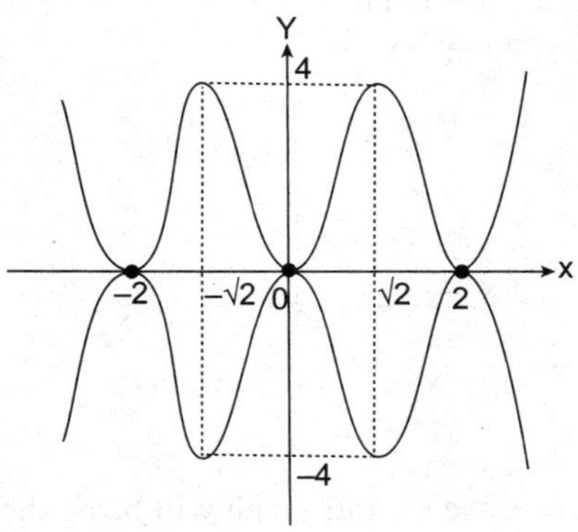

24. Draw the graph of $y^2 = x^3 - x$

Solution: ***Step 1:*** $y^2 = x^3 - x = x(x^2 - 1)$

$y^2 = x(x-1)(x+1)$

$\Rightarrow$ Roots of this equation are $x = 0$, $x = 1$, $x = -1$

Step 2: $2y\dfrac{dy}{dx} = 3x^2 - 1$; $y = \pm\sqrt{x^3 - x}$

$\Rightarrow \dfrac{dy}{dx} = \dfrac{\pm(3x^2-1)}{2\sqrt{x^3-x}}$. Critical points are $x = \pm\dfrac{1}{\sqrt{3}}, 1$

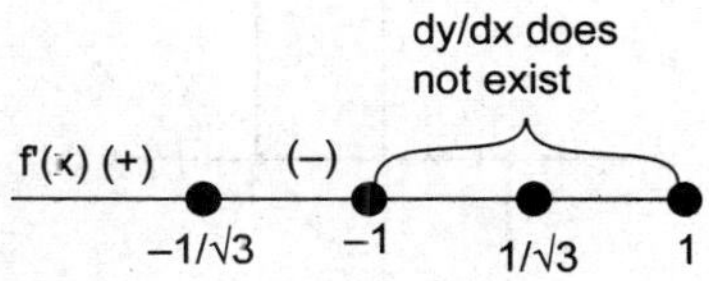

Domain of relation is $[-1, 0] \cup [1, \infty)$

$$\frac{dy}{dx} = \pm\frac{3}{2}\frac{\left(x^2 - \frac{1}{3}\right)}{\sqrt{x(x-1)(x+1)}}$$

Point $x = -\dfrac{1}{\sqrt{3}}$ is of maxima and $y = \sqrt{x^3 - x}$

increasing in $x \in \left[-1, -\dfrac{1}{\sqrt{3}}\right] \cup [1,\infty)$ and decreasing in $x \in \left(-\dfrac{1}{\sqrt{3}}, 0\right)$

$$(y)_{x=-\frac{1}{\sqrt{3}}} = -\frac{1}{3\sqrt{3}} + \frac{1}{\sqrt{3}} = \frac{2}{3\sqrt{3}} \text{ for } y = \sqrt{x^3 - x};$$

$$(y)_{x=0} = (y)_{x=1} = (y)_{x=-1} = 0 \text{ for } y = \pm\sqrt{x^3 - x}$$

Step 3: $\lim\limits_{x\to+\infty} \sqrt{x^3 - x} = \infty$

So, graph of $y^2 = x^3 - x$ will be as shown below.

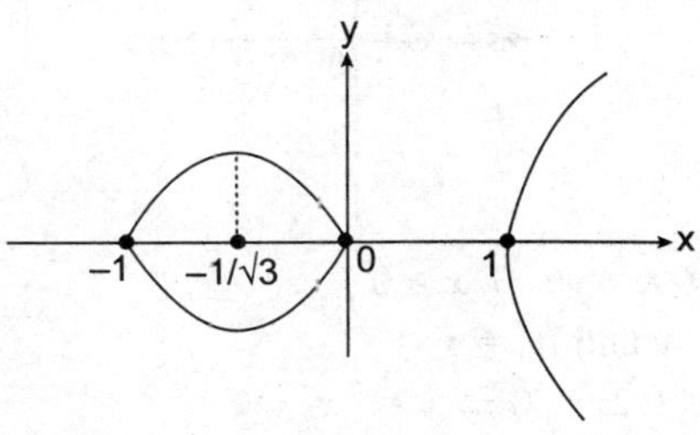

25. Plot the points on x-y plane which satisfy the following equations.

(i) $y = x|y|$ (ii) $y - |y| + x + |x| = 0$

(iii) $x - |x| = y - |y|$ (iv) $|2x + 3y| + |2x - 3y| = 10$

Solution: (i) $y = x|y|$

Case I: $y = 0$

$\Rightarrow x \in \mathbb{R}$ $\Rightarrow$ Entire x-axis

Case II: $y > 0$

$\Rightarrow xy = y \Rightarrow x = 1$

Case III: $y < 0$

$x(-y) = y \Rightarrow x = -1$

Thus, the graph of $y = x|y|$ is as shown below:

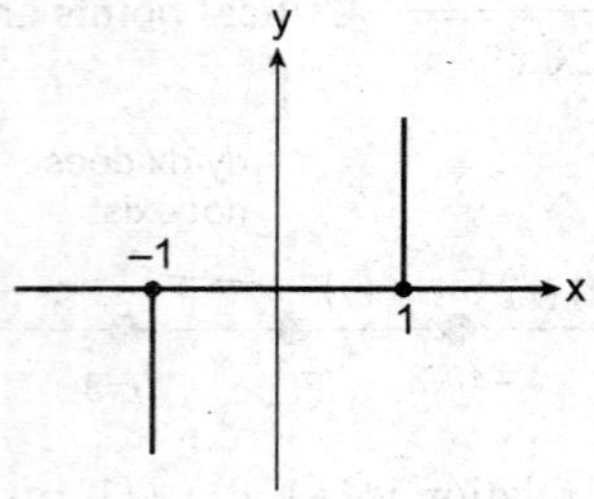

(ii) $y - |y| + x + |x| = 0$

Case I: $y \geq 0\ ;\ x \geq 0$

$\Rightarrow\ |y| = y$ and $|x| = -x \Rightarrow\ 2x = 0 \Rightarrow x = 0$

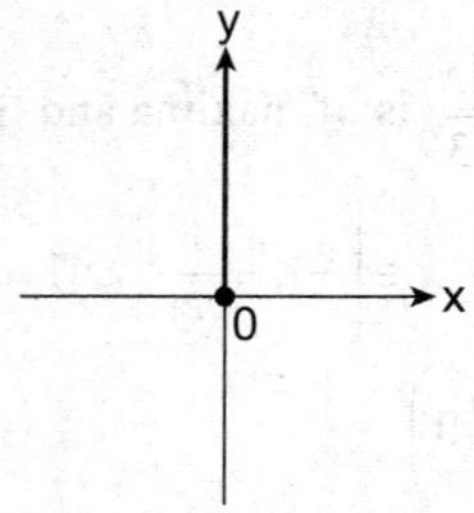

Case II: $y \geq 0\ ;\ x < 0$

$\Rightarrow\ |y| = y$ and $|x| = -x$

$\Rightarrow\ 0 = 0$

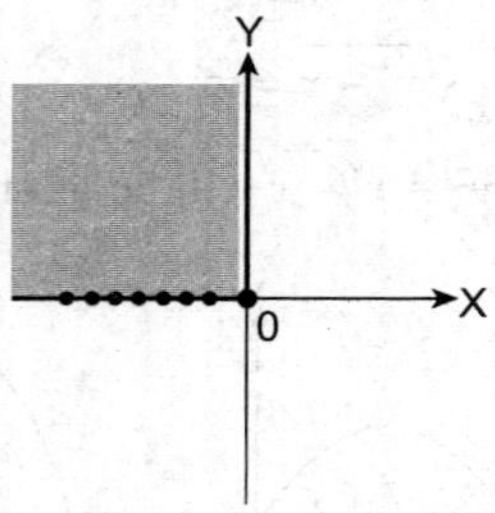

Case III: $y < 0;\ x \geq 0$

$|y| = -y$ and $|x| = x$

$\Rightarrow\ 2y + 2x = 0 \Rightarrow y = -x$

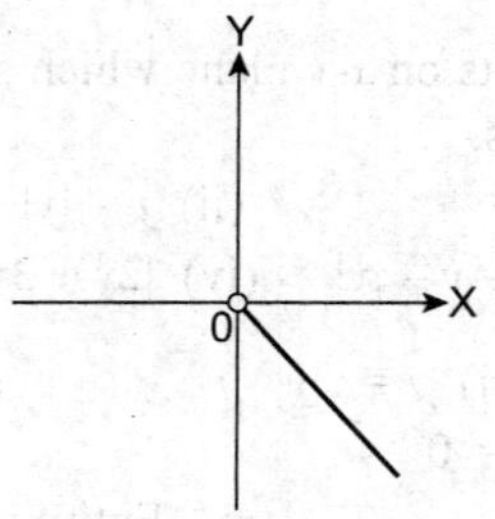

Case IV: $y < 0\ ;\ x < 0$

$\Rightarrow\ |y| = -y$ and $|x| = -x$

$\Rightarrow\ 2y = 0 \Rightarrow y = 0 \qquad \Rightarrow$ No reason

Hence, the overall graph is as shown figure:

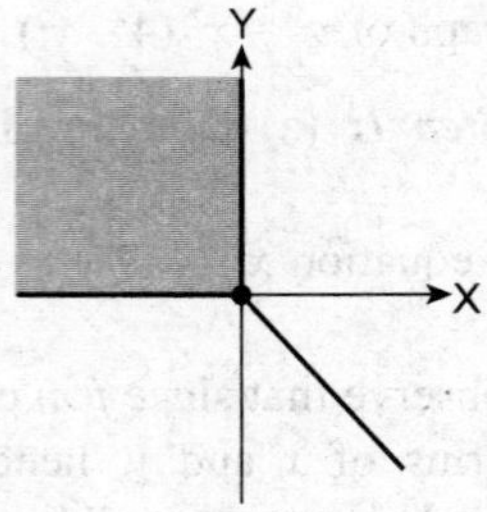

(iii) $x - |x| = y - |y|$

Case I: $x \geq 0$ and $y \geq 0$

$\Rightarrow\ 0 = 0$

$\Rightarrow$ Entire Ist quadrant including positive x and y-axis.

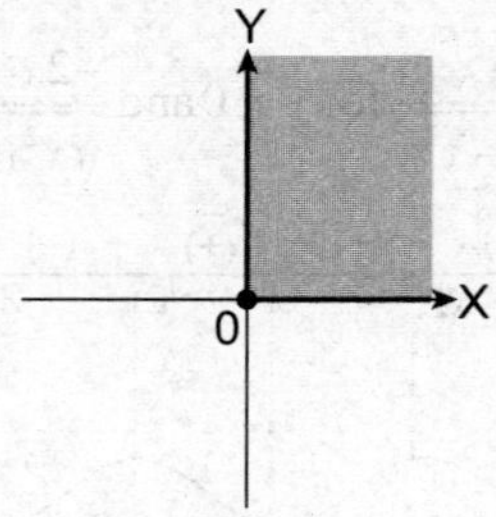

Case II: $x \geq 0$ and $y < 0$

$\Rightarrow\ 0 = 2y$

$\Rightarrow y = 0$

$\Rightarrow$ No region

Case III: $x < 0$ and $y \geq 0$

$\Rightarrow\ 2x = 0$

$\Rightarrow x = 0$

$\Rightarrow$ No region

Case IV: $x < 0$ and $y < 0$

$\Rightarrow\ 2x = 2y \Rightarrow x = y$

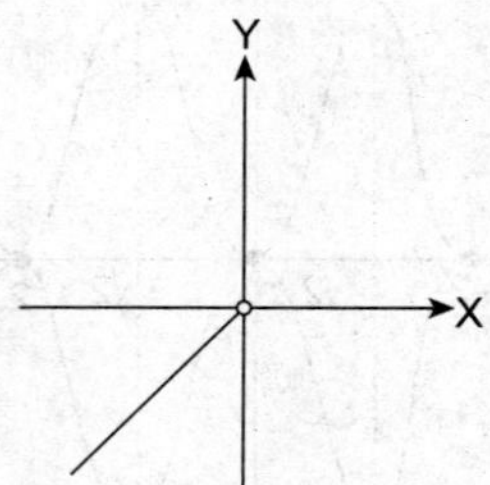

Hence, the overall graph will be as shown below

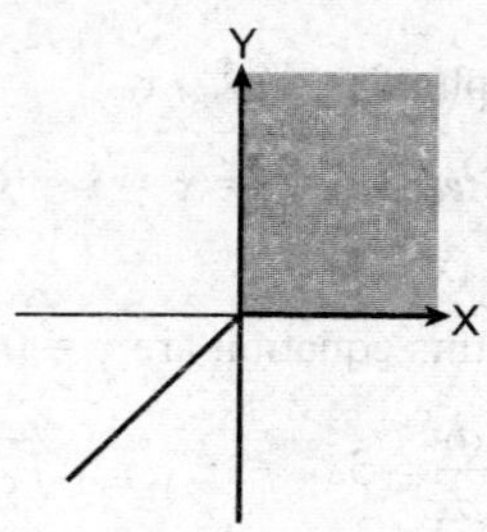

(iv) $|2x + 3y| + |2x - 3y| = 10$

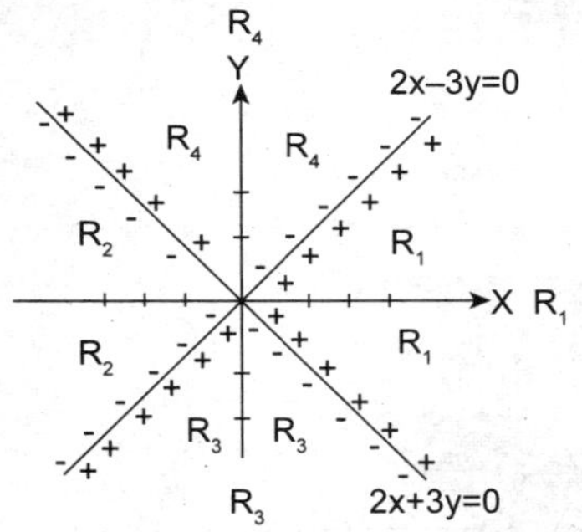

Let R_1 be the region defined by $2x + 3y \geq 0$ and $2x - 3y \geq 0$

Similarly $R_2 : 2x + 3y < 0$ and $2x - 3y < 0$

$R_3 : 2x + 3y < 0$ and $2x - 3y \geq 0$

$R_4 : 2x + 3y \geq 0$ and $2x - 3y < 0$

Case I: Considering region R_1; we have

$2x + 3y + 2x - 3y = 10$

$\Rightarrow 4x = 10 \qquad \Rightarrow x = 5/2$

Case II: Considering region R_2; we have

$-2x - 3y - 2x + 3y = 10$

$\Rightarrow -4x = 10 \qquad \Rightarrow x = -5/2$

Case III: Considering region R_3; we have

$-2x - 3y + 2x - 3y = 10$

$\Rightarrow -6y = 10 \qquad \Rightarrow y = -5/3$

Case III: Considering region R_4; we get $2x + 3y - 2x + 3y = 10 \qquad \Rightarrow y = 5/3$

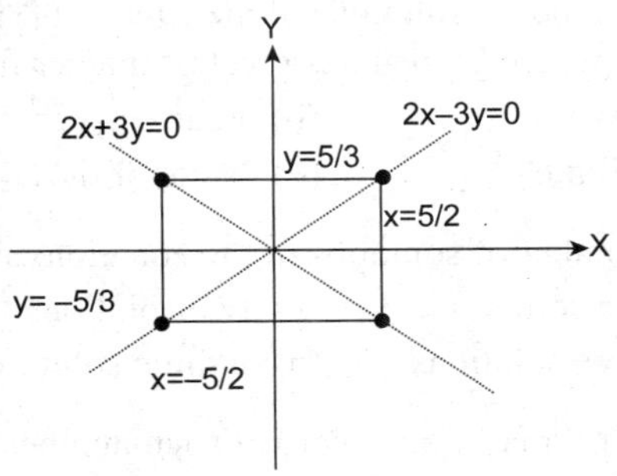

Assertions and reason

26. A: The number of real roots of the equation $5^{1+\cos\pi x} + 4^{1-|x|} = 2$ is 2.

R: If $k > 1$ and f, g be real valued functions such that $f(x) + g(x) \geq 0$, then $k^{f(x)} + k^{g(x)} = 2$ will have $x = \alpha$ as solution if $f(\alpha) = g(\alpha)$

(a) A is true, R is a correct explanation for A

(b) A is true, R is true but R is not a correct explanation for A

(c) A is true, R is false

(d) A is false, R is true

Solution: (a) $\dfrac{k^{f(x)} + k^{g(x)}}{2} \geq \left(k^{f(x)+g(x)}\right) \geq 1$

$\Rightarrow k^{f(x)} + k^{g(x)} \geq 2$. Equally holds when $f(x) = g(x) = 0$.

By above reason, $1 - \cos\pi x = 1 - |x| = 0$

$\Rightarrow \cos\pi x = -1, |x| = 1 \Rightarrow x = \pm 1$ are two solutions

Comprehension Passage

A: Let the lines represented by the equation $x^2y^2 - x^2 - y^2 + 1 = 0$ form a square $ABCD$. A point 'P' is taken on the same plane of square such that atleast two sides of all the triangles PAB, PBC, PCD and PDA are equal.

27. The number of possible positions of the point 'P' is.

(a) 7 (b) 5

(c) 17 (d) 9

Solution: (d) $x^2y^2 - x^2 - y^2 + 1 = 0$

$\Rightarrow x^2(y^2 - 1) - 1(y^2 - 1) = 0$

$\Rightarrow (y^2 - 1)(x^2 - 1) = 0 \Rightarrow y = \pm 1, x = \pm 1$

$\Rightarrow ABCD$ square is obtained bounded by $x = \pm 1$ and $y = \pm 1$.

Clearly 8 possible points will be the intersection of the circle (with centre at vertex and radius as side of the square) and the line which is perpendicular bisector of the sides. Centre of square will be one such point. Thus, total 9 such points will be there.

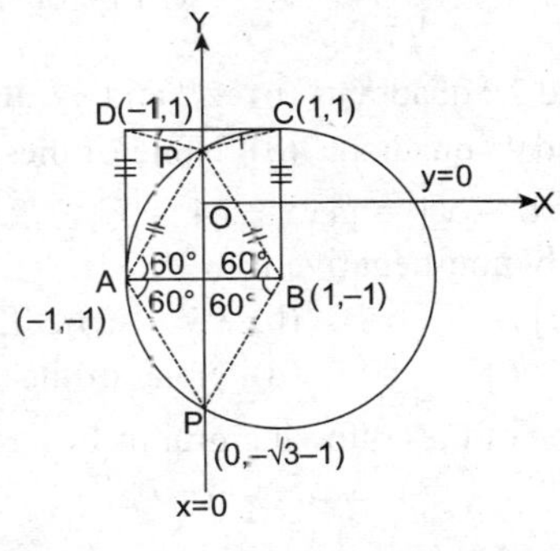

28. For all the possible position of point 'P'. How many of the given triangles have all the three sides equals

(a) 0 (b) 4

(c) 8 (d) 5

Solution: (c) Clearly for all the different position of 'P' except origin there will be one equilateral triangle.

29. One of the possible position of the 'P' such that atleast one of the given triangle is equilateral is given by

(a) $(0, 0)$ (b) $(-\sqrt{3} + 1, 0)$

(c) $(0, \sqrt{3} - 2)$ (d) $(\sqrt{3} + 1, \sqrt{3} - 1)$

Solution: (b) Different positions of P except origin will be $(0, -\sqrt{3} - 1)$, $(0, \sqrt{3} - 1)$, $(\sqrt{3} - 1, 0)$, $(-\sqrt{3} - 1, 0)$, $(0, \sqrt{3} + 1)$, $(0, -\sqrt{3} + 1)$, $(\sqrt{3} + 1, 0)$ and $(-\sqrt{3} + 1, 0)$

TUTORIAL EXERCISE

SECTION–III

ONLY ONE CORRECT ANSWER

1. The number of real solutions of the equation $e^x + x = 0$ is:

(a) 2 (b) 1

(c) 3 (d) None of these

2. The number of real solutions of the equation $\log_a x = |x|$, $0 < a < 1$, is

(a) 1 (b) 2

(c) 3 (d) None of these

3. If high voltage (440 V) current is applied on the field which is given by the graph $y + |y| - x - |x| = 0$. On which of the following curve Mr. Calculus can move so that he remains safe?

(a) x^2 (b) $sgn\ (-e^x)$

(c) $\log_{1/3} x$ (d) $|m + |x||\ (m > 3)$

4. The graph of the function $f(x) = -\left(\dfrac{|x|^3 + |x|^2 + |x|}{1+x^2}\right)$ will lie on

(a) 1st and 2nd quadrant (b) 2nd and 3rd quadrant

(c) 3rd and 4th quadrant (d) None of these

5. If $|f(x) + 6 - x^2| = |f(x)| + |4 - x^2| + 2$, then $f(x)$ is necessarily non-negative in

(a) $[-2, 2]$ (b) $(-\infty, -2) \cup (2, \infty)$

(c) $[-\sqrt{6}, \sqrt{6}]$ (d) None of these

6. Which one of the following graphs best represents the $\{(x, y) \in R^2: x^2 + y^2 \le 25, y \ge -x\}$?

(a)
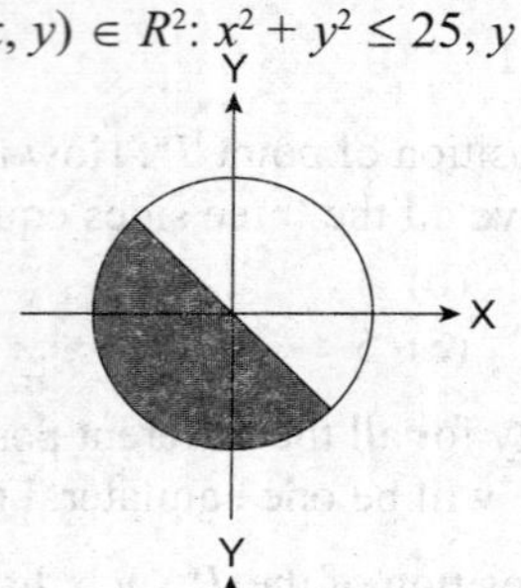

(b)
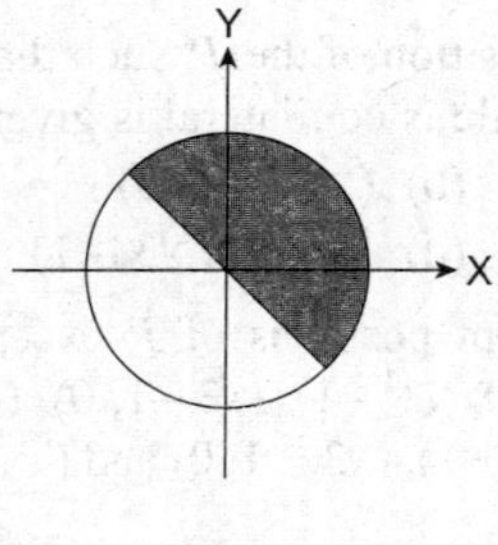

(c)
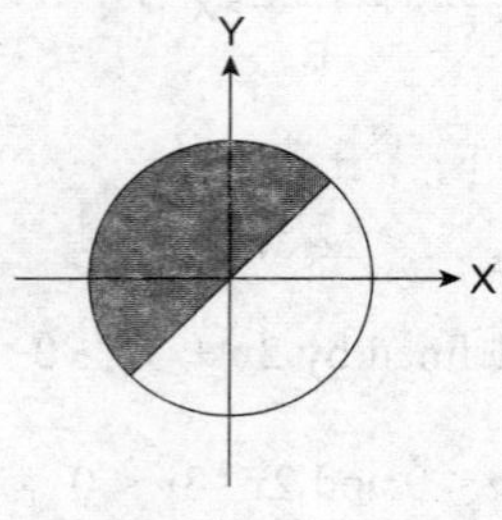

(d)
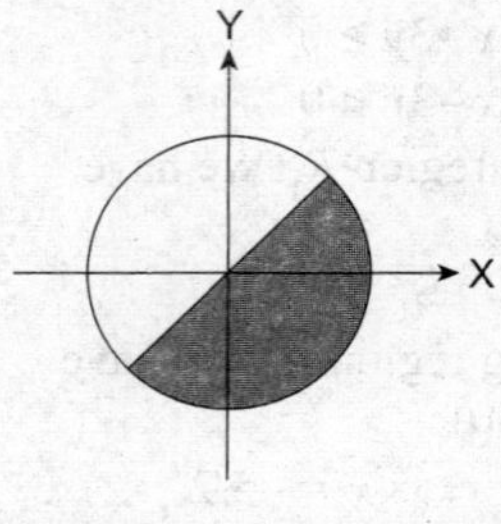

7. The graph of the relation $x^4 + y^3 = 1$ is symmetric with respect to

(a) the x-axis (b) the y-axis

(c) the origin (d) the line $y = x$

8. The number of solutions of the equation $[x]^2 + [x + 3] = 4$ is: where $[x]$ denotes greatest integer function

(a) Two (b) Four

(c) Infinite (d) None of these

9. The number of solutions of the equation; $\sin x = e^{-x}$:

(a) one solution (b) two solutions

(c) three solutions (d) infinite solution

10. Let $f(x) = \max\{\tan x, \cot x\}$. Then number of roots of the equation $f(x) = \sqrt{3}$ in $(0, 2\pi)$ is

(a) 2 (b) 4

(c) 0 (d) None of these

11. The number of solutions of the equation, $\sin x = \dfrac{x}{10}$ are

(a) 3 (b) 6

(c) 7 (d) 10

12. Number of solutions of $5^{|x|} = |3 - |x||$ is

(a) 0 (b) 2

(c) 4 (d) infinite

13. How many roots does the following equation posses, $x^2 - 2x - \log_2 |1 - x| = 3$?

(a) 2 (b) 3
(c) 4 (d) 5

14. The equation $e^{2x} + e^x - 2e = 0$ has

(a) no real root in the interval [0, 1]
(b) at least one real root in [0, 1]
(c) two real roots in [0, 1]
(d) none of these

15. The set of real value(s) of p for which the equation, $|2x + 3| + |2x - 3| = px + 6$ has more than two solutions is:

(a) $[0, 4\}$ (b) $(-4, 4)$
(c) $R - \{4, -4, 0\}$ (d) $\{0\}$

16. Number of solutions of $\sin x/2 + 2\pi x = x^2 + \pi^2$ is

(a) 0 (b) 1
(c) 2 (d) None of these

17. The number of solutions of the equation $2 \cos (e^x) = 5^x + 5^{-x}$ are

(a) no solutions (b) one solution
(c) two solution (d) infinitely many solutions

18. The graph of the curve $y = \dfrac{1}{x}$ and $y = px$ intersects at

(a) one point for any value of p
(b) two points for any values of p
(c) two points for $p \geq 0$
(d) None of these

19. The general solution of $|\sin x| = \cos x$; $n \in \mathbb{Z}$ is given by

(a) $n\pi + \dfrac{\pi}{4}$ (b) $2n\pi \pm \dfrac{\pi}{4}$
(c) $n\pi \pm \dfrac{\pi}{4}$ (d) $n\pi - \dfrac{\pi}{4}$

20. The equation $||x - 2| + a| = 4$ can have four distinct real solutions for x if a belongs to the interval

(a) $(-\infty, -4)$ (b) $(-\infty, 0)$
(c) $[4, \infty)$ (d) None of these

21. Let $f_1(x) = \begin{cases} x & \text{for } 0 \leq x \leq 1 \\ 1 & \text{for } x > 1 \\ 0 & \text{for otherwise} \end{cases}$ and $f_2(x) = f_1(-x)$ for all x $f_3(x) = -f_2(x)$ for all x $f_4(x) = f_3(-x)$ for all x

Which of the following is necessarily true?

(a) $f_4(x) = f_1(x)$; for all x
(b) $f_1(x) = -f_3(-x)$; for all x
(c) $f_2(-x) = f_4(x)$; for all x
(d) $f_1(x) + f_3(x) = 0$; for all x

22. The number of solutions of the equation $x^2 - 2[x] = 0$ ([.] denotes greatest integer function) is

(a) one (b) two
(c) four (d) infinity

23. Which of the following represents the graph $f(x) = sgn([x + 1])$ where [ ] denotes the GINT function.

(a) 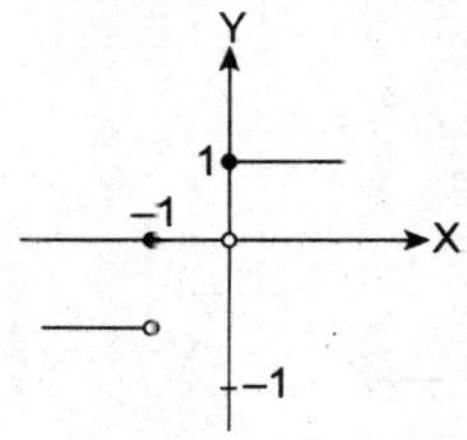

(b) 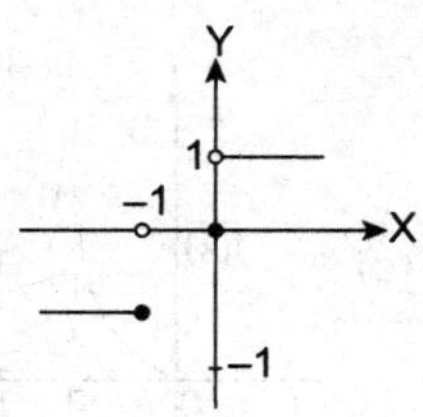

(c) 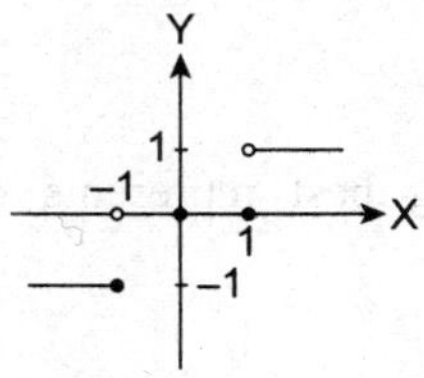

(d) 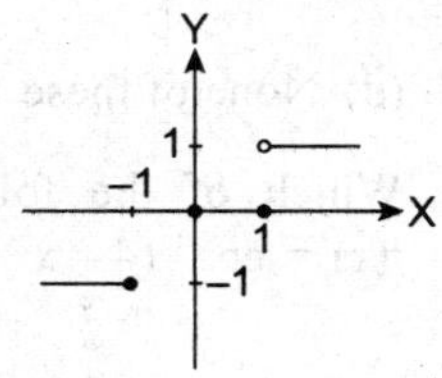

24. Suppose f is defined from $R \to [-1,1]$ as $f(x) = \dfrac{x^2 - 1}{x^2 + 1}$; where R is the set of real number. Then the statement which does not hold is

(a) f is many–one and onto
(b) f increase for $x < 0$ and decrease for $x < 0$
(c) minimum value is attained
(d) maximum value is not attained even though f is bounded

25. The graph of function $y = f(x)$ is as shown in the figure given below.

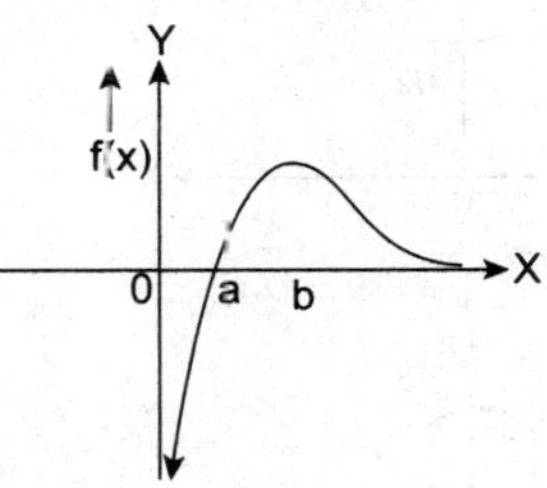

Then the graph of the function $\dfrac{1}{f(x)}$ will be best represented by

(a) 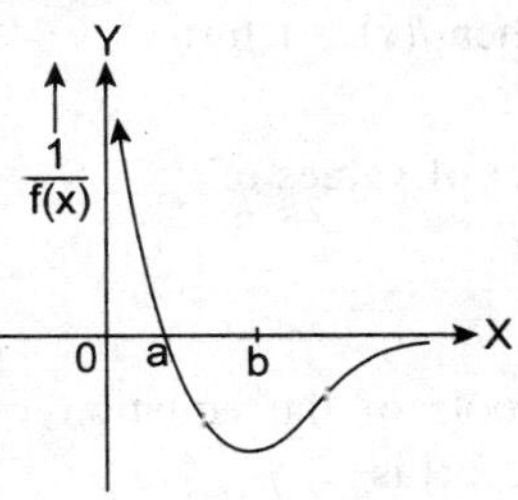

(b) 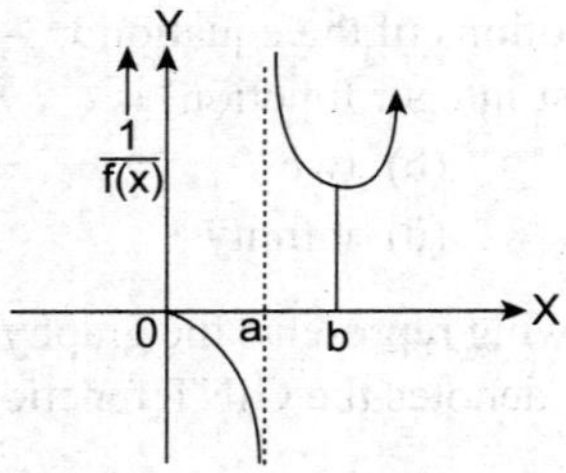

(c) 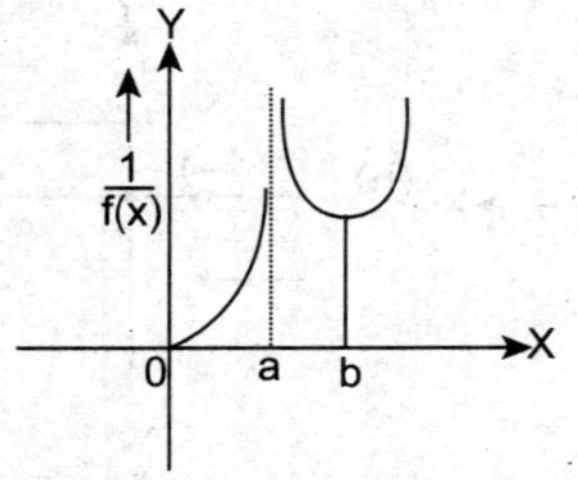

(d) None of these

26. Which of the following best represents graph of $f(x) = \cot^{-1}(4 - x^2)$?

(a) 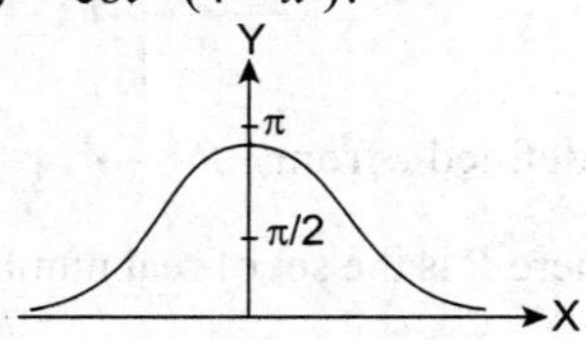

(b) 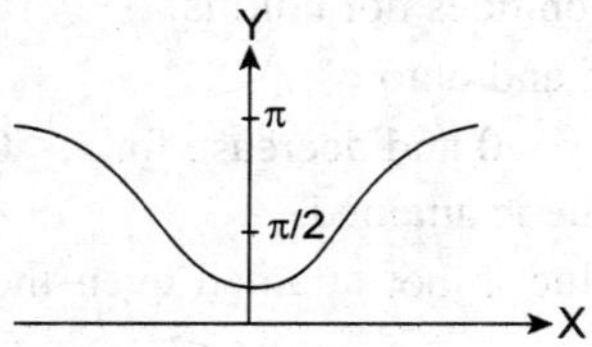

(c) 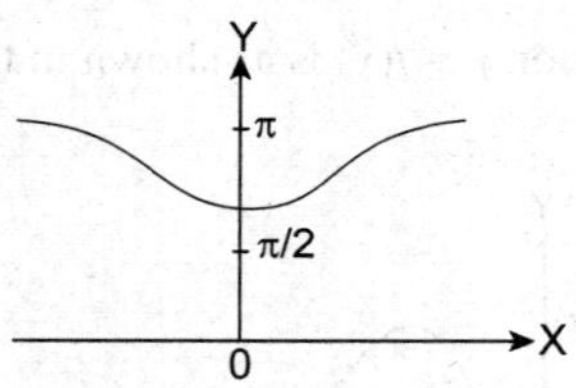

(d) 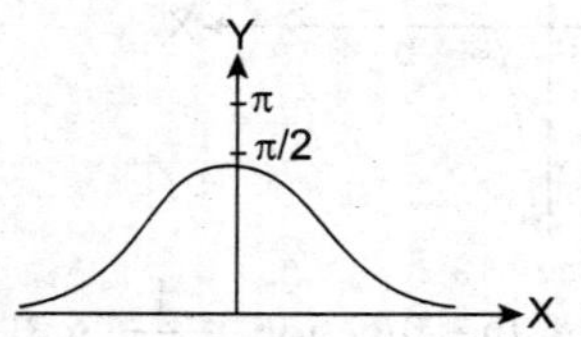

27. Let $[x]$ = greatest integer $\le x$ and $\{x\} = x - [x]$. If $f(x) = \{x\}[x]$, then $f(x) = 1$ for:

(a) no value of x
(b) infinite number of values of x
(c) one value of x
(d) None of these

28. The number of roots of the equation $x \sin x = 1$, $x \in [-2\pi, 0) \cup (0, 2\pi]$ is

(a) 2 (b) 3
(c) 4 (d) 0

29. The number of points (x, y), where the curves $|y| = \ln|x|$ and $(x-1)^2 + y^2 - 4 = 0$ cut each other is

(a) 2 (b) 3
(c) 1 (d) 6

30. The number of solutions of equation $2^{\cos x} = |\sin x|$, when $x \in [0, 2\pi]$ is

(a) 4 (b) 3
(c) 0 (d) 2

31. The number of solutions of the equation $\sin \pi x = |\ln|x||$ is

(a) infinite (b) 8
(c) 6 (d) 0

32. The number of roots of the equation $1 + \log_2(1 - x) = 2^{-x}$ is

(a) 0 (b) 1
(c) 2 (d) infinitely many

33. Number of roots of $|\sin|x|| = x + |x|$ in $[-4\pi, 2\pi]$ is

(a) 2 (b) 3
(c) 4 (d) 5

34. The equation $3^{x-1} + 5^{x-1} = 12$ has

(a) No solution (b) one solution
(c) two solution (d) None of these

35. The number of solution of the equation $\cos[x] = 2^{4x-1}$, $x \in [0, 2\pi]$

(a) 1 (b) 2
(c) 3 (d) 4

36. The number of real roots of the equation $x^2 + x + 3 + 2\sin x = 0$, $x \in [-\pi, \pi]$

(a) 2 (b) 4
(c) 6 (d) None of these

37. The total number of real roots of the equation $|x - x^2 - 1| = |2x - 3 - x^2|$ is

(a) 0 (b) 1
(c) 2 (d) infinitely many

38. The equation $\dfrac{x^2}{1-|x-2|} = 1$ has

(a) one real solution (b) two real solution
(c) three real solutions (d) no real solution

39. The graph of the function $f: \mathbb{R} \to \mathbb{R}$ defined by $f(x) = \dfrac{|x|^3 + |x|}{1 - x^2}$ may lie in

(a) 1st quadrant (b) 2nd quadrant
(c) 3rd quadrant (d) Each of 4th quadrant

40. The number of solutions of the equation $\tan 4x = \cos x$; for $0 < x < \pi$ is

(a) 1 (b) 2

(c) 5 (d) 8

41. The number of real solutions of the equation $\log_{0.5} |x| = 2|x|$ is

(a) 1 (b) 2

(c) 0 (d) None of these

42. Let $f(x) = \max \{1 + \sin x, 1, 1 - \cos x\}, x \in [0, 2\pi]$ and $g(x) = \max \{1, |x - 1|\}; x \in \mathbb{R}$, then

(a) $g(f(0)) = 1$ (b) $f(f(1)) = 1$

(c) $f(g(1)) = 1$ (d) $f(g(0)) = \sin 1$

43. If f: $\mathbb{R} \to \mathbb{R}$, g: $\mathbb{R} \to \mathbb{R}$ be two given functions, then $2 \min\{f(x) - g(x), 0\}$ equals

(a) $f(x) + g(x) - |g(x) - f(x)|$

(b) $f(x) + g(x) + |g(x) - f(x)|$

(c) $f(x) - g(x) + |g(x) - f(x)|$

(d) $f(x) - g(x) - |g(x) - f(x)|$

44. If the graph of $y = f(x)$ is as shown in the figure below, then answer the questions that follow:

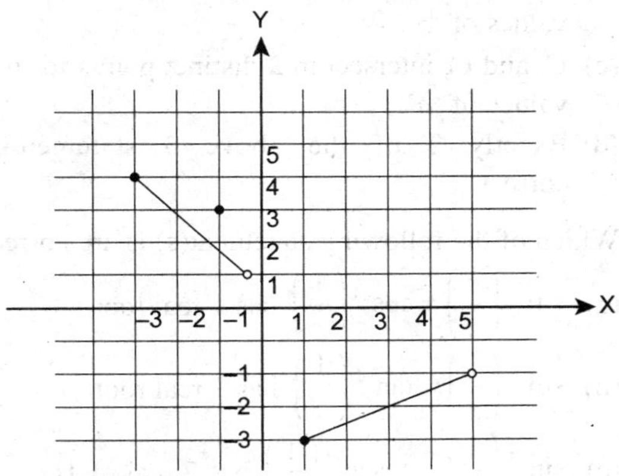

(i) Find $f(-2)$

(a) 5/2 (b) 7/2

(c) 3 (d) None of these

(ii) The domain of the function $f(x)$

(a) $[-3, -1] \cup [1, 5)$ (b) $[-3, -1) \cup [1, 5)$

(c) $[-3, -1] \cup [1, 5]$ (d) None of these

(iii) The range of the function $f(x)$

(a) $[-3, -1] \cup [1, 4]$ (b) $[-3, -1] \cup [1, -4)$

(c) $[-3, -1) \cup (1, 4]$ (d) None of these

45. Find the area bounded by the following inequalities:

(i) $x - 2y \le 4$, $2x + y > 5$, $y \ge x$, $x < 6$, $y < 8$

(a) $\frac{313}{12}$ (b) $\frac{337}{12}$

(c) ∞ (d) None of these

(ii) $4x + y \le 5$; $x - 4y > 9$; $y < -x + 1$; $xy \ge 0$; $|x| \le 3$, $|y| \le 3$

(a) $\frac{7}{8}$ (b) $\frac{9}{8}$

(c) 1 (d) None of these

46. The number of solutions of the equation $[x]^2 + [x + 3] = 4$ is (where $[x]$ denotes greatest integer function)

(a) two (b) four

(c) infinite (d) None of these

47. The number of solutions of the equation $x^2 - 2 - [x] = 0$ ([.] denotes greatest integer function) is

(a) one (b) two

(c) three (d) infinity

48. The number of real solutions of equation $\max (x^2 - 4x) = 1$ is

(a) 1 (b) 2

(c) 3 (d) infinitely many solution

SECTION–IV

MORE THAN ONE ANSWER CORRECT

1. The graph of the function $y = f(x)$ is as shown in the figure. Then which one of the following graphs is correct?

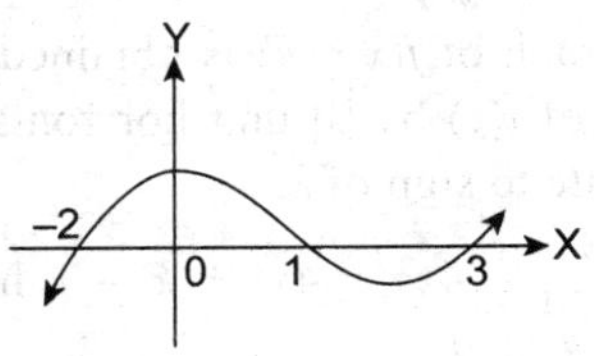

(a) $|y| = sgn\,(f(x))$

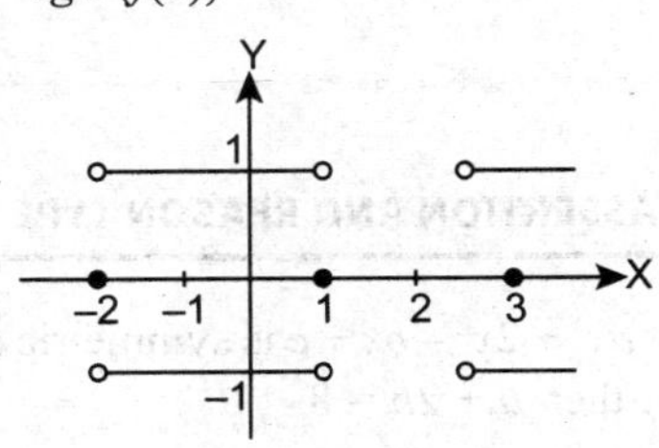

(b) $|y| = sgn\,(-f(|x|))$

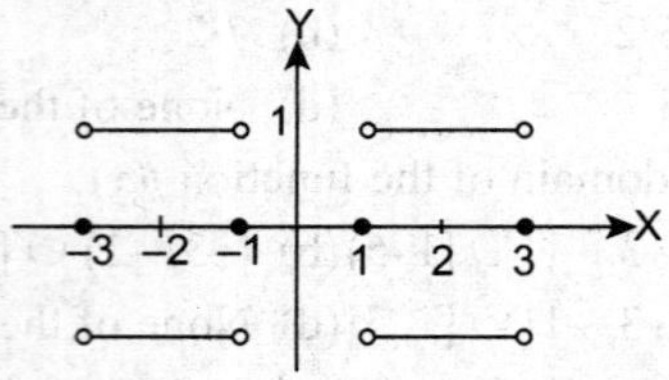

(c) $|y| = |f|x||$

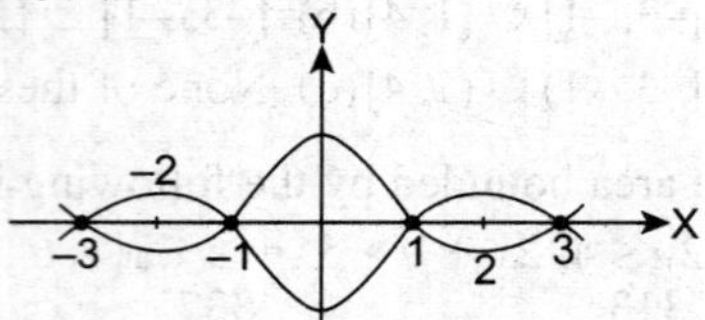

(d) $y = x\, sgn\,(f(x))$

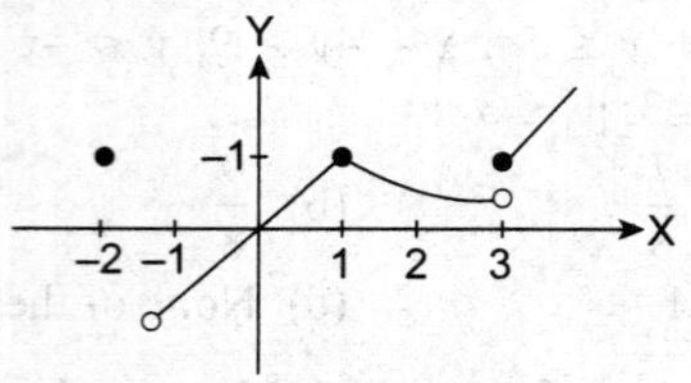

2. The equation $2|x| - 1 = 3|\sin \pi x|$ has

(a) 4 solutions

(b) no solution lies in $[2, \infty)$

(c) 6 solutions

(d) two solution lies in $(0, 1/2)$

3. Let $f(x) = x^2 + 3x + 5$ and $g(x) = |x - k|$, then which of the following statements is/are correct?

(a) $f(x) = g(x)$ has exactly one root for exactly two distinct values of 'k'.

(b) $f(x) = g(x)$ has no real root for $k \in (-3, 1)$.

(c) $f(x) = g(x)$ has two real roots for $k > 5$.

(d) None of these

4. Let $f(x) = ||x - 1| - 2|$ and $g(x) = x + |x - 1| + \dfrac{|x-2|}{x-2}$; then which of the following statements is/are correct

(a) $f(x) = g(x)$ has exactly 3 real roots

(b) $f(x) = g(x)$ has exactly 2 real roots

(c) $y = g(x)$ has one point of discontinuity

(d) $y = f(x)$ has 3 points of non-differentiability

5. Let $(x^2 + y^2)y - ax^2 = 0$ and $(x^2 + y^2) = a^2(x^2 - y^2)$; $a \neq 1$ be two curves; then which of the following statements is/are correct?

(a) The two curves intersect at atmost two distinct points.

(b) The two curves intersect at 3 distinct points for exactly one particular value of 'a'.

(c) The two curves intersect at 3 distinct points for $a \in \mathbb{R} \sim [-1, 1]$.

(d) The curves $(x^2 + y^2)y - ax^2 = 0$ has exactly 1 cusp.

6. Consider two curves

C_1: $100(x^2 + y^2) = a^2x^2y^2$ and C_2: $y = (a^3 - x^3)^{1/3}$

Which of the following statements is/are correct?

(a) C_1 and C_2 intersect in 3 distinct points for exactly 2 values of 'a'.

(b) C_1 and C_2 intersect in 4 distinct points for infinite values of 'a'.

(c) C_1 and C_2 intersect in 2 distinct points for infinite values of 'a'.

(d) Exactly 2 of the above 3 statements are correct.

7. Which of the following statement(s) is/are correct?

(a) $\sin^{-1}\left(\dfrac{1}{x}\right) = \cos^{-1}\left(\dfrac{1}{x}\right)$ has 1 real root

(b) $\sin^{-1}\left(\dfrac{1}{x}\right) = \tan^{-1}\left(\dfrac{1}{x}\right)$ has 1 real root

(c) $\sin^{-1}\left(\dfrac{1}{x}\right) = \text{cosec}^{-1}\left(\dfrac{1}{x}\right)$ has 2 real roots

(d) $\sin^{-1}\left(\dfrac{1}{x}\right) = \cot^{-1}\left(\dfrac{1}{x}\right)$ has 1 real root

SECTION–V

ASSERTION AND REASON TYPE

1. A: $f(x) = ax^3 + 2x^2 - bx + c$ is symmetric about the line $x = 1$, then $a + 2b = 8$

R: An odd degree polynomial can never be symmetric about any vertical line every quadratic polynomial is symmetric about its axis.

2. A: $y = f(x)$ is a +ve valued function $x \in \mathbb{R}$; $\int_a^b f(x)x = \int_{a-k}^{b-k} f(x+k)dx$

R: The graph of $f(x + k)$ is obtained by shifting the graph of $f(x)$ by $|k|$ unit horizontally in direction opposite to sign of k.

3. A: $f(x) = x^4 - 4x^3 + 4x^2 + k - 1$ has no real root $k \in (1, \infty)$.

R: graph of $y = g(x) + c$ can be obtained by vertical scaling of graph of $y = g(x)$ by $|c|$ unit upwards if $c > 0$ and downward if $c < 0$.

4. Let $f: \mathbb{R} \to \mathbb{R}$ defined by $f(x) = \cos \pi[x]$, where $tx]$ denotes the greatest integer function less than or equal to x.
A: $f(x)$ is a periodic function.
R: $[x]$ is a periodic function.

5. Let $g: \mathbb{R} \to \mathbb{R}$ defined by $g(x) = \{e^x\}$, where $\{x\}$ denotes fractional part function.
A: $g(x)$ is periodic function.
R: $\{x\}$ is periodic function.

6. A: The function $f(x) = \tan\left(\frac{3\pi}{2}[x]\right)$ where $[x]$ is the greatest integer function, is a periodic.
R: $g(x) = [x]$ is a periodic.

SECTION–VI

COMPREHENSION PASSAGE

A: The diagram given below represents graph of a function $f(x)$. Observe its properties carefully and based on it answer the following questions:

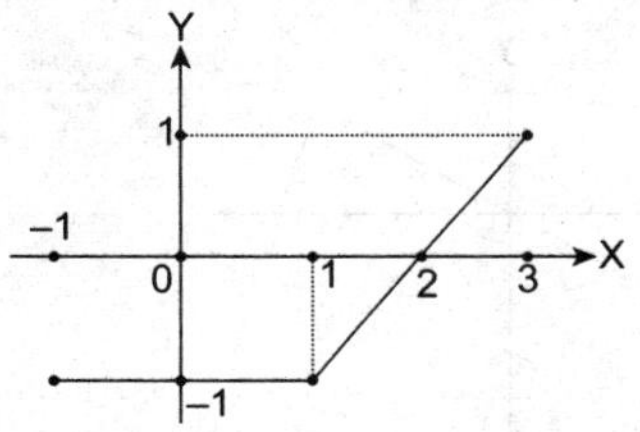

1. $|f(x)|$ is an increasing function in the interval
(a) (2, 3) (b) (1, 3)
(c) (0, 2) (d) None of these

2. $-|f(x)|$ is non-differentiable at x = (in the interval (–1, 3))
(a) 3 and 2 (b) 1 and 2
(c) 0 and 2 (d) None of these

3. $f(-|x|)$ is
(a) increasing function
(b) a decreasing function
(c) a constant function
(d) positive $\forall\, x \in$ Domain

4. $g(x) = \frac{1}{2}(|f(x)| + f(x)))$ is a constant function in the interval
(a) [–1, 3] (b) [0, 3]
(c) [–1, 2] (d) None of these

5. $h(x) = \frac{1}{2}(|f(x)| - f(x))$ is a constant function in the interval
(a) [–1, 2] (b) $[-1, 1] \cup [2, 3)$
(c) [1, 3) (d) None of these

6. $g(x) = f\left(\frac{|x|}{x}\right)$ is
(a) an increasing function
(b) a decreasing function
(c) a constant function
(d) None of these

B: Consider a rational function $f(x)$ by $f(x) = \frac{(x^2-1)(x-3)}{x^2(x+2)}$.

7. Which of the following is a horizontal asymptote of $y = f(x)$?
(a) $y = 2$ (b) $y = 1$
(c) $y = -1$ (d) None of these

8. Which of the following is/are vertical asymptote(s) on $y = f(x)$?
(a) $x = 0$ (b) $x = 2$
(c) $x = -2$ (d) All of these

9. The approximate graph of $y = f(x)$ is given by

(a) 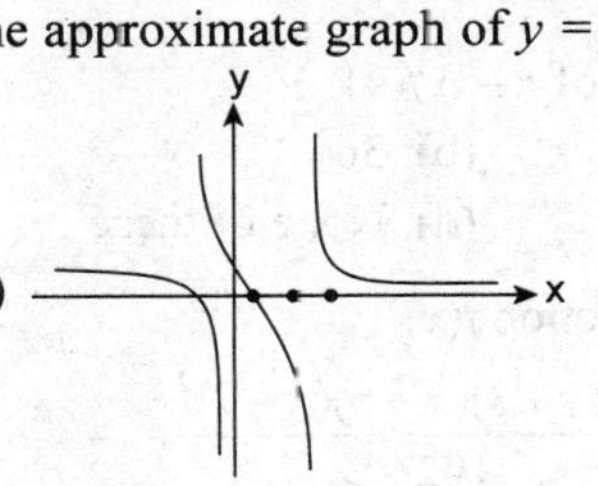

(b) 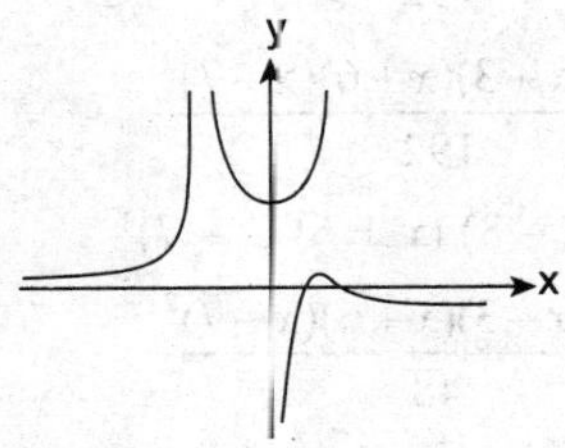

(c) 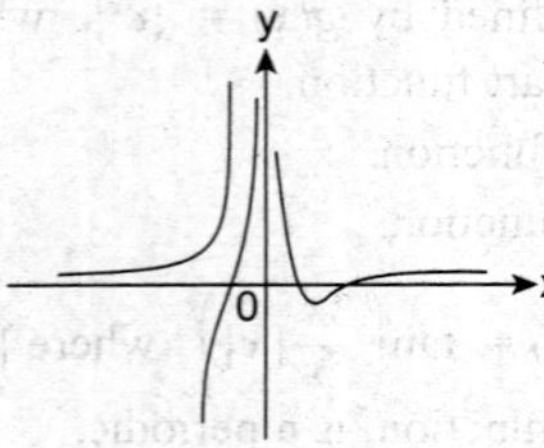

(d) 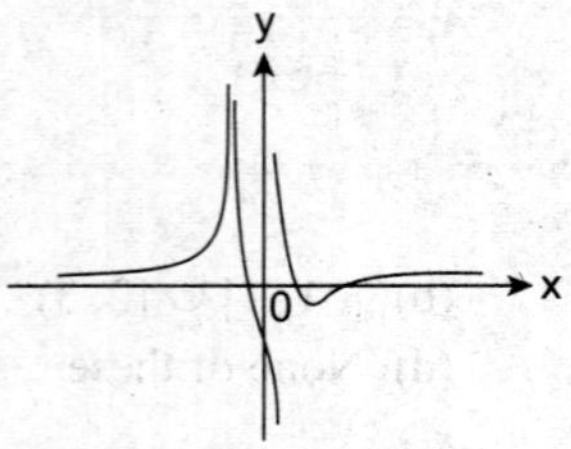

C: Consider the function as shown in the figure given below. The shown figure is a polynomial of degree 5. The points marked with black dots have integral coordinates.

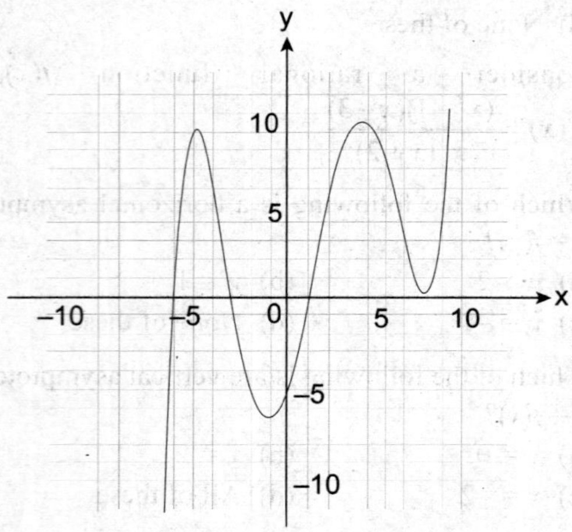

10. What is the value of $f(-5).f(4)$

(a) 0 (b) 36

(c) 81 (d) None of these

11. Determine the function $f(x)$

(a) $f(x)=\dfrac{(x-1)(x+3)(x+6)(x-7)^2}{192}$

(b) $f(x)=\dfrac{(x-1)(x+3)(x+6)(x-7)^2}{192}$

(c) $f(x) = (x - 1)(x - 3)(x + 6)(x - 7)^2$

(d) $f(x)=\dfrac{(x-1)(x-3)(x+6)(x-7)^2}{48}$

12. Determine the values of $f(f(-5))$

(a) 12 (b) 15

(c) 30 (d) None of these

D: Let us consider a function given by

$$f(x)=\begin{cases}(x-3)^3+3; & \text{if } x\in(3,5]\\ x; & \text{if } x\in[-3,3]\\ -(x+3)^2-3; & \text{if } x\in[-5,-3)\end{cases}$$

Then on the basis of the information given above answer the questions that follow.

13. Which of the following gives an approximate graph of $f(x)$?

(a) 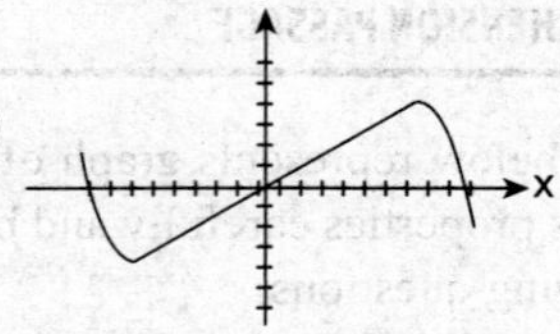

(b) 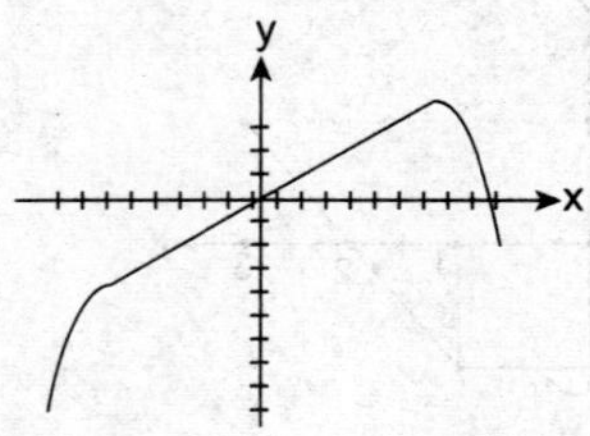

(c) 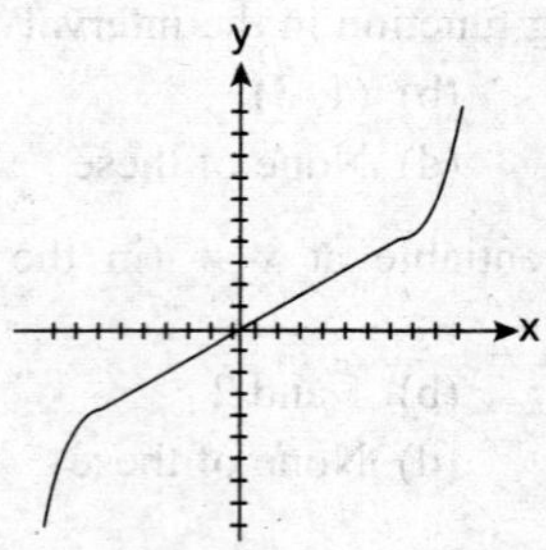

(d) 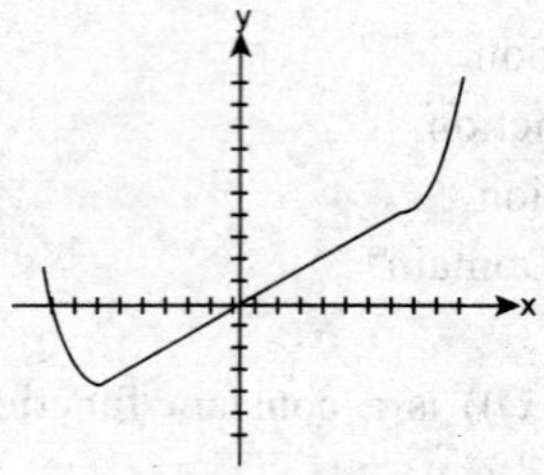

14. Let $g(x)$ be a function such that $g(x)=\underbrace{f.f.f....f}_{n\ \text{compositions}}(x)$; where $n \in \mathbb{N}$, then $g(x)$ can never achieve which of the following values?

(a) 0 (b) 4

(c) 8 (d) None of these

15. Which of the following gives as approximate graph of $f^{-1}(x)$?

(a) 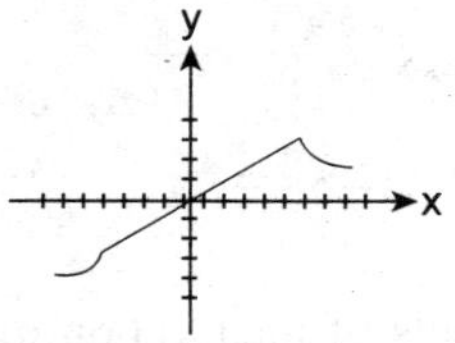

(b) 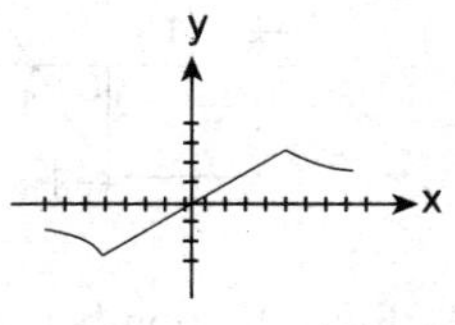

(c) 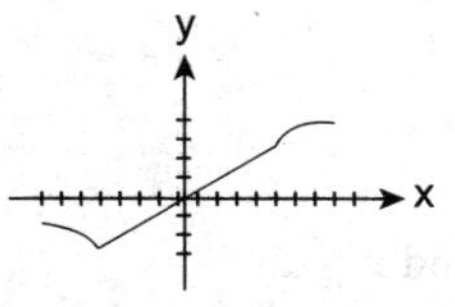

(d) 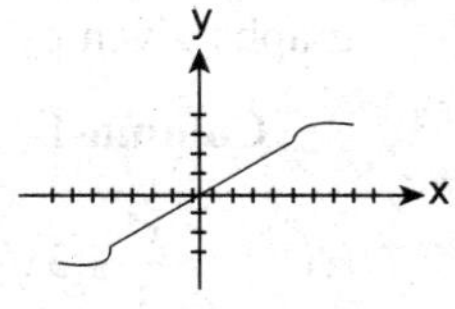

E: For $x, y \in \mathbb{R}$ the functions are defined here under; $f_1(x, y) = |x| + |y|$, $f_2(x, y) = \min(x + y, x - y)$, $f_3(x, y) = [x] + [y]$ (where [.] denotes the greatest integer function).

16. Which of the following is always true?
(a) $f_1(x, y) < f_2(x, y); x, y \in \mathbb{R}$
(b) $f_2(x, y) < f_3(x, y); x, y \in \mathbb{Z}^+$ (set of +ve integers)
(c) $f_1(x, y) = -f_3(x, y); x, y \in \mathbb{Z}^-$ (set of –ve integers)
(d) None of these

17. In $h_1(x) = f_1(\sin\{x\}, \sin \pi x)\ \forall x \in \mathbb{R}$ (where {.} represents fractional part function). $h_2(x) = f_2(x, \sin x)\ \forall\ 0 < x < 1$, $h_3(x) = f_3(x, -x)\ \forall x \in \mathbb{R}$, then
(a) h_1: (x) is non-periodic function
(b) h_2: $(0, 1) \to (0, 1)$ then h_2 is bijective
(c) h_3 : (x) is periodic function
(d) None of these

18. Which of the following can never be true?
(a) $f_1(x, y) > f_3(x, y); x, y \in \mathbb{R}$
(b) $f_2(x, y) = x + y;\ x, y < 0$
(c) $f_3(x, y) = f_3(-x, -y); x, y \in \mathbb{R}$
(d) $f_1(x, y) = f_3(x, y); x, y \in \mathbb{R} - \mathbb{Z}$

F: Let H_1: $x^2 - 4y^2 + 4$ and $H_2 : x^2 - 9y^2 - \frac{1-a}{1+a}$ then answer the following questions

19. The exhaustive set of values of a for which there exist at least one ordered pair (x, y) which satisfy the inequality $H_1 \leq 0$ and $H_2 \leq 0$ satisfy simultaneously is
(a) $a \in (-\infty, \infty)$
(b) $a \in [-5/4, -1) \cup (-1, 1)$
(c) $a \in (-1, 1)$
(d) $a \in (-\infty, -1) \cup (-1, \infty)$

20. The exhaustive set of values of a for which $H_1 \leq 0$ and $H_2 \geq 0$ satisfy simultaneously is
(a) $a \in \mathbb{R} \sim \{-1\}$
(b) $a \in \left(\frac{5}{4}, -1\right)$
(c) $a \in \left(-\frac{5}{4}, -1\right)$
(d) None of these

21. Number of integral values of a for which $H_1 \geq 0$ and $H_2 \geq 0$ does not possess a common solution is
(a) 0
(b) 1
(c) infinitely many
(d) 2

G: $f(x)$ is a continuous function satisfying $x^4 - 4x^2 \leq f(x) \leq 2x^2 - x^3\ \forall x \in [0, 2]$ such that the area bounded by $y = f(x)$, $y = x^4 - 4x^2$ and the line $x = t$, $(0 \leq t \leq 2)$ is n times the area bounded by $y = f(x)$, $y = 2x^2 - x^3$ and the line $x = t$, $(0 \leq t \leq 2)$, then

22. At what point $f(x)$ attains a local minima, when $n = 1$?
(a) 2
(b) $\frac{3+\sqrt{73}}{8}$
(c) $\frac{-3-\sqrt{73}}{8}$
(d) 2

23. For $n = 2$, $f(x)$ attains a point of inflexion at $x =$
(a) $\sqrt{2}$
(b) 3/2
(c) 1
(d) None of these

24. The value of $\int_{-1}^{1} f(x)dx$ is
(a) $\frac{2}{15(n+1)}(23-10n)$
(b) $\frac{2}{15(n+1)}(10n-17)$
(c) $\frac{2}{15(n+1)}(23+10n)$
(d) $\frac{2}{15(n+1)}(10n+17)$

SECTION–VII

COLUMN MATCHING

1. Match the column

[.] and {.} represent the greatest integer and fractional part functions respectively

Column-I
(i) Number of solutions of $[x] = \cos^{-1}x$
(ii) Number of solution of $\sin^{-1}x = sgn(x)$
(iii) Number of solutions of $\{x\} = e^{x^2}$
(iv) Number of solutions of $1 - x = \{x\}$

Column-II

(a) 3
(b) 2
(c) 1
(d) 0

2. The graph of the function $y = f(x)$ is as follows.

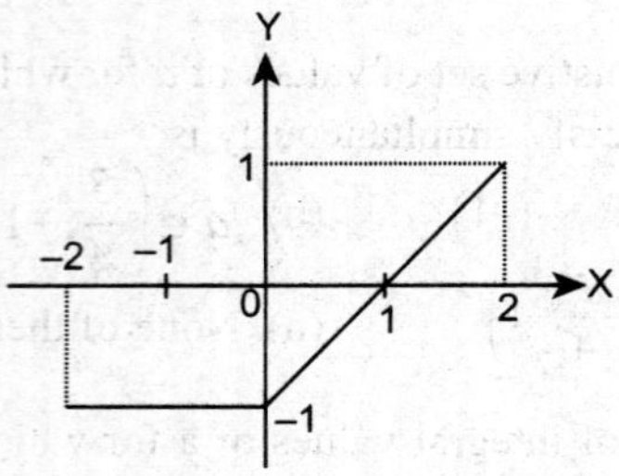

Match the *function* mentioned in Column-I with the respective *graph* given in Column-II.

Column-I

(i) $y = |f(x)|$
(ii) $y = f(|x|)$
(iii) $y = f(-|x|)$
(iv) $y = \frac{1}{2}(|f(x)| - f(x))$

Column-II

(a) 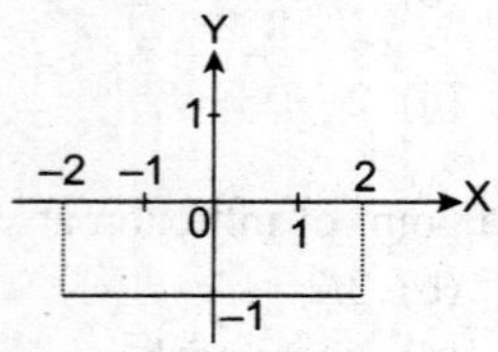

(b) 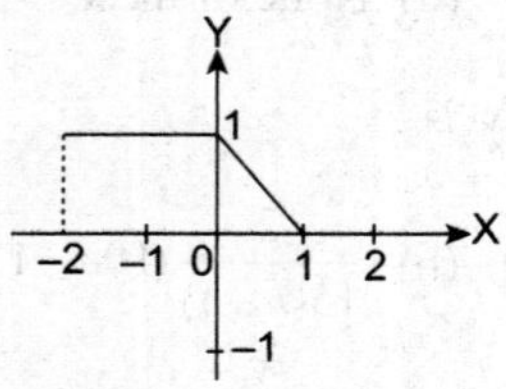

(c) 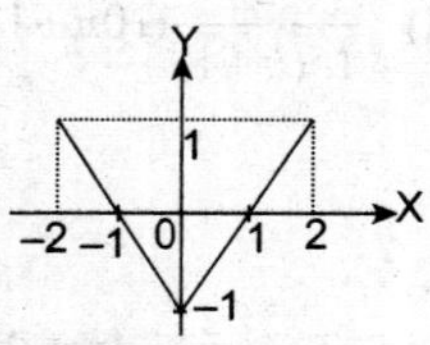

(d) 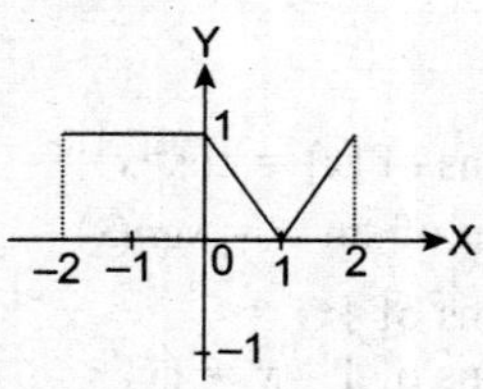

(e) 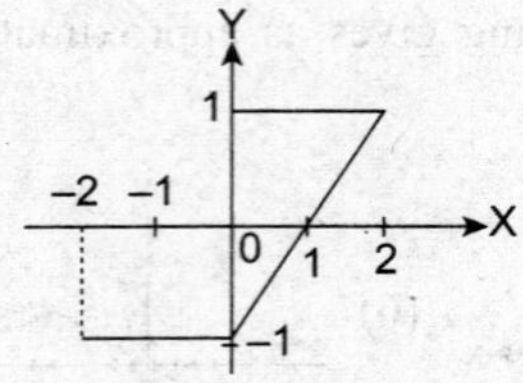

3. Find the number of points of intersection of the two graphs given by

Column-I

(i) $y = \frac{x^3}{3} + 3x^2 + 5x$ and $x = 2y - y^2$
(ii) $|y| = x^3 - 3x + 2$ and $|y| = \cos(\sin x)$
(iii) $y = |\ln|x^2 - x||$ and $y = \left|\left|\frac{1}{x}\right| - 2\right|$
(iv) $y = \cos e^x$ and $y = \tan e^x$ $\forall x \in \left(-\infty, \frac{\pi}{2}\right)$
(v) $y = \sin e^x$ and $y = \sec e^x$ $\forall x \in (-\infty, 2)$

Column-II

(a) 8
(b) 6
(c) 2
(d) 0
(e) 6

4. If $f(x) = x^4 - 5x^2 + 7$ be a function and $|y| = x^4 - 5x^2 + 7$; then find the values of 'k' for which the number of point of intersection; of $|y| = x^4 - 5x^2 + 7$ and $y = k$ is given by 'n'. Then match the entries in column I (value of n) to the entire in column II (all possible values of 'k' corresponding to a particular 'n').

Column-I

(i) $n = 0$
(ii) $n = 1$
(iii) $n = 2$
(iv) $n = 3$
(v) $n = 4$

Column-II

(a) $(-\infty, -7) \cup (7, \infty) \cup \{\pm 3/4\}$
(b) $\{\pm 7\}$
(c) ϕ
(d) $\left(-\frac{3}{4}, \frac{3}{4}\right)$
(e) $\left(-7, -\frac{3}{4}\right) \cup \left(\frac{3}{4}, 7\right)$

SECTION–VIII

INTEGER TYPE

1. If $y = f(x)$ is continuous on $[0, \infty)$ and differentiable on $(0, \infty)$ except for 4 points of non-differentiability and $f'(0^+) > 0$, then find the number of points of non-differentiability of the graph $y = f(|x|)$; $x \in \mathbb{R}$.

2. Let $f(x)$: $[2, 10] \to \mathbb{R}$ be a continuous function having points of non-differentiability at $x = 3, 4, 5, 6, 7, 8, 9$, then find the number of points of non-differentiability of $y = f(x-2) = g(x)$ (say) in $[2, 10)$, assuming that $f(x)$ is non-oscillating.

3. In the graph shown below,

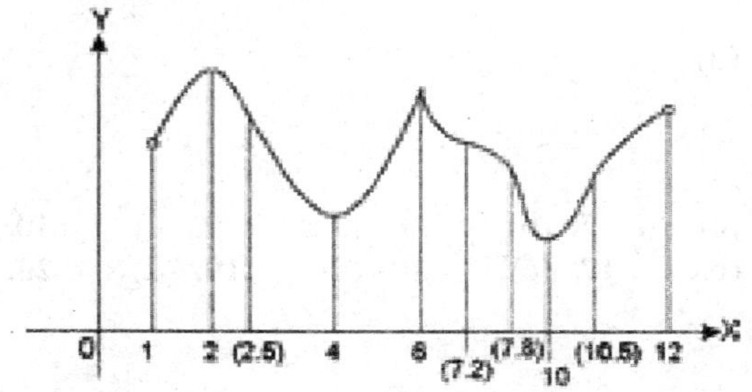

$x = x_1, x_2$ are points of local maxima, $x = y_1, y_2$ are points local minima, $x = z_1, z_2, z_3, z_4$ are points of inflexion and $x = u_1$ is points of non-differentiability, then evaluate $\sum x_i + \sum y_i - \sum z_i + u_1$.

4. Let $y = f(x)$ has the graphs as shown below.

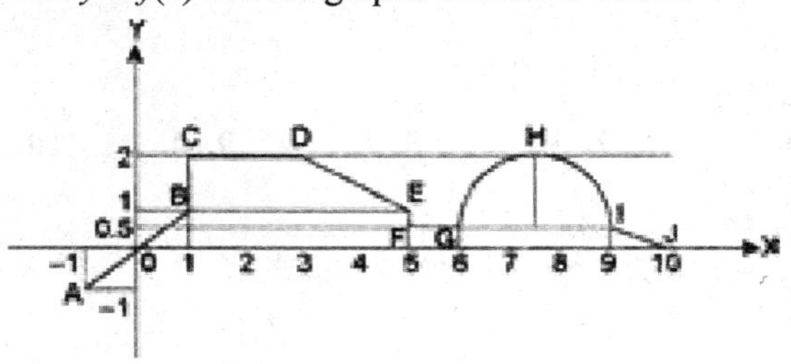

Find the area enclosed by the graph of $|y| = |f(|x|)|$ with x-axis is $\left(a + \frac{b\pi}{c}\right)$ square units, where $g.c.d.(b, c) = 1$, then find $a + c - 4b$.

5. Let $f(x) = \begin{cases} |x-1| \text{ for } 0 \le x < 2 \\ e^{x-2} \text{ for } 2 \le x < 2 + ln6 \\ x \text{ for } x \ge 2 + ln6 \end{cases}$ and $g(x) = \begin{cases} \left|\sin\frac{x\pi}{4}\right| \text{ for } 0 \le x < 2 \\ 2x-3 \text{ for } 2 \le x < 4 \\ \log_2 x \text{ for } x \ge 4 \end{cases}$; then find the number of points where $f(x) = g(x)$.

6. $f(x) = \begin{cases} -x - \frac{\pi}{2}; & x \le \frac{-\pi}{2} \\ -\cos x, & \frac{-\pi}{2} < x \le 0 \\ x - 1, & 0 < x \le 1 \\ \ln x, & x > 1 \end{cases}$ and $g(x) = \begin{cases} 1-x; & x < 1 \\ (1-x)(2-x); & 1 \le x \le 2 \\ 3-x; & x > 2 \end{cases}$; then the number of solutions of equation of $f(x) = g(x) + \ln 2$ is k_1, k_2 = number of points of non-differentiability of $y = f(x)$, k_3 = number of points of non-differentiability of $y = g(x)$, then find $\left(\frac{k_1 + k_2}{k_3}\right)$.

7. Let $f(x) = |x^2 - 9| - |x - a|$. Find the number of integers in the range of a so that $f(x) = 0$ has 4 distinct real root.

8. If f: $\mathbb{R} \to \mathbb{R}$ be an injective mapping and p, q, r are non-zero distinct real quantities satisfying $f\left(\frac{p}{r}\right) = f\left(\frac{p-q}{q-r}\right)$ and $f\left(\frac{q}{r}\right) = f\left(\frac{r}{p}\right)$.
If the graph of $g(x) = px^2 + qx + r$ passes through M (1, 6), then find the value of q.

9. Let f: $\mathbb{R} \to \mathbb{R}$ defined by $f(x) = \min.(|x|, 1 - |x|)$, then find the number of solution of equation $3f(x) - 1 = 0$.

10. If the function $f(x) = ax + b$ has its own inverse and passing through the point (2, 3), then evaluate $(2a + b)$.

11. Let $f(x) = \text{sgn}(arc \cot x) + \tan\left(\frac{\pi}{2}[x]\right)$, where $[x]$ is the greatest integer function less than or equal to x. Then find the number of solutions of equation $2f(x) = 1 + 2\{x\}$; where $\{x\}$ denotes fractional parts of x in $[-4, 5]$.

Answer Keys

SECTION–III

1. (b)	**2.** (a)	**3.** (d)	**4.** (c)	**5.** (a)	**6.** (b)	**7.** (b)	**8.** (d)	**9.** (d)	**10.** (b)
11. (c)	**12.** (b)	**13.** (c)	**14.** (b)	**15.** (d)	**16.** (c)	**17.** (a)	**18.** (d)	**19.** (b)	**20.** (a)
21. (b)	**22.** (c)	**23.** (a)	**24.** (b)	**25.** (b)	**26.** (b)	**27.** (b)	**28.** (c)	**29.** (b)	**30.** (a)
31. (c)	**32.** (b)	**33.** (d)	**34.** (b)	**35.** (a)	**36.** (d)	**37.** (b)	**38.** (d)	**39.** (d)	**40.** (c)
41. (b)	**42.** (a)	**43.** (d)	**44.** (i) (a)	(ii) (a)	(iii) (c)				
45. (i) (b)	(ii) (b)	**46.** (d)	**47.** (c)	**48.** (d)					

SECTION–IV

1. (a,b,c) **2.** (b,c) **3.** (a,b,c) **4.** (b,c,d) **5.** (c,d) **6.** (a,b,c) **7.** (a,c,d)

SECTION–V

1. (a) **2.** (a) **3.** (a) **4.** (d) **5.** (d) **6.** (d)

SECTION–VI

1. (a)	**2.** (b)	**3.** (c)	**4.** (c)	**5.** (b)	**6.** (c)	**7.** (b)	**8.** (a,c)	**9.** (c)	**10.** (c)
11. (b)	**12.** (c)	**13.** (c)	**14.** (d)	**15.** (d)	**16.** (b,c)	**17.** (c)	**18.** (a)	**19.** (d)	**20.** (a)
21. (d)	**22.** (c)	**23.** (c)	**24.** (b)						

SECTION–VII

1.	(i) → (d),	(ii) → (a),	(iii) → (d),	(iv) → (b)	
2.	(i) → (d)	(ii) → (c)	(iii) → (a)	(iv) → (b)	
3.	(i) → (b)	(ii) → (b)	(iii) → (b)	(iv) → (c)	(v) → (d)
4.	(i) → (d)	(ii) → (c)	(iii) → (a)	(iv) → (b)	(v) – (3)

SECTION–VIII

1. 9	**2.** 5	**3.** 0	**4.** 5	**5.** 3	**6.** 4	**7.** 17	**8.** 8	**9.** 4	**10.** 3
11. 5									

HINTS AND SOLUTIONS

TUTORIAL EXERCISE: (SECTION III)

1. (b) $e^x + x = 0$

$\Rightarrow$ $e^x = -x$

$\Rightarrow$ The solution will be the abscissa of points of intersection of $y = e^x$ and $y = -x$.

The two graphs drawn on same frame of reference will be as shown below.

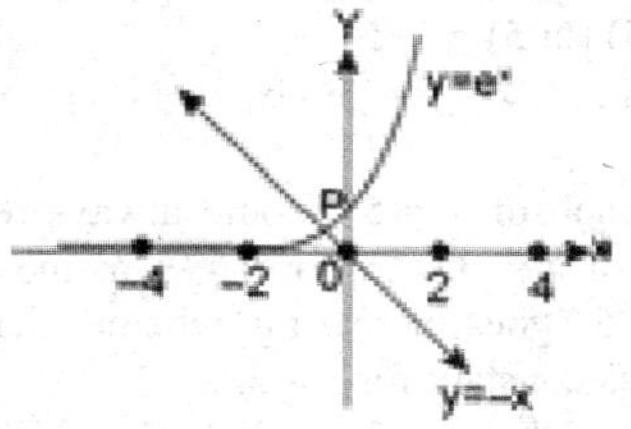

Clearly, only one point of intersection 'P', and hence, only one solution.

2. (a) $\text{Log}_a x = |x|$, $0 < a < 1$

Graph of $y = \log_a (x)$ and $y = |x|$ for $0 < a < 1$ drawn on same frame of reference will be as shown below.

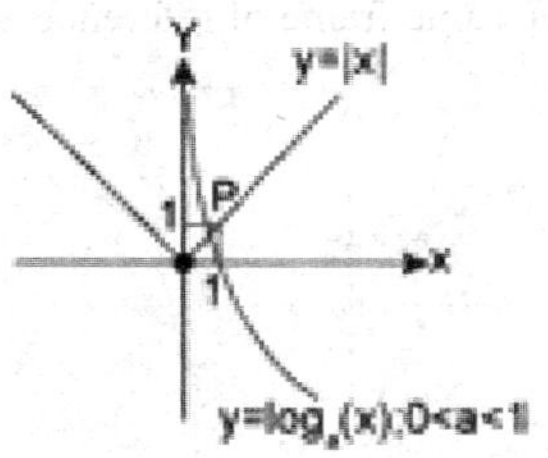

Clearly, there is only one point of intersection 'P' and, hence, only one solution.

3. (d) $y + |y| - x - |x|$

$\Rightarrow$ $y + |y| = x + |x|$ ....(i)

Case (i): $y \geq 0, x \geq 0$ $\Rightarrow$ $y = x$

Case (ii): $y \geq 0, x \leq 0$ $\Rightarrow$ $y = 0$

$\Rightarrow$ + *ve* x-axis

Case (iii): $y \leq 0, x \leq 0$ $\Rightarrow$ $0 = 0$

$\Rightarrow$ whole IIIrd quadrant

Case (iv): $y \leq 0, x \geq 0$ $\Rightarrow$ $x = 0$

$\Rightarrow$ –ve y-axis

The complete graph represented by (1) will be as shown below.

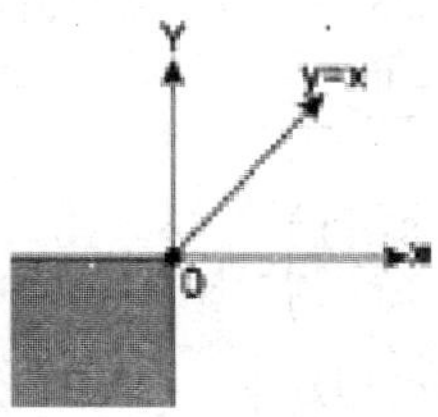

The graphs of $y = x^2$ and $y = \log_{1/3} x$ interests the line $y = x$ which has current.

Also $y = \text{sgn}(-e^x) = -1 \ \forall \ x \in \mathbb{R}$, as $e^x > 0 \ \forall \ x \in \mathbb{R}$

$\Rightarrow$ $-e^x < 0 \ \forall \ x \in \mathbb{R}$

$\Rightarrow$ $\text{sgn}(-e^x) = -1 \ \forall \ x \in \mathbb{R}$

$\Rightarrow$ $\text{sgn}(-e^x) = -1$ is $y = -1$, which intersect the third quadrant having current.

Now $y = |m + |x||$ $(m > 3)$

$\Rightarrow$ $y = (m + |x|)$ as $m > 3$, $|x| \geq 0$

$\Rightarrow$ $m + |x| > 0$

Its graphs are as shown below

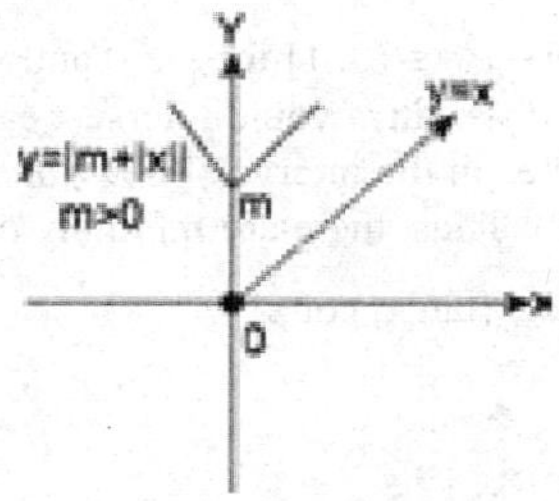

Thus, the curve $y = |m + |x||$ is disjoint from the current carrying curve, and hence, safer for Mr. calculus .

4. (c) $f(x) = -\left(\dfrac{|x|^3 + |x|^2 + |x|}{1 - x^2}\right)$

Clearly, $f(x) \leq 0 \ \forall \ x \in D_f$ and $D_f = \mathbb{R}$

$\Rightarrow$ $f(x) \leq 0 \ \forall \ x \in \mathbb{R}$

$\Rightarrow$ Graph of $f(x)$ would lie in IIIrd and IVth quadrants.

5. (a) $|f(x) + 6 - x^2| = |f(x)| + |4 - x^2| + 2$

By triangle inequality, $|f(x) + 6x - x^2| \leq |f(x)| + |6 - x^2|$ $= |f(x)| + |(4 - x^2) + 2| \leq |f(x)| + |4 - x^2| + 2$

Given, $|f(x) + 6 - x^2| = |f(x)| + |4 - x^2| + 2$

$\Rightarrow$ $2(4 - x^2) \geq 0$ and $f(x).(6 - x^2) \geq 0$

$\left(\begin{array}{l} \because |a+b| \leq |a| + |b| \\ \text{and equality holds } a.b \geq 0 \end{array}\right)$

$\Rightarrow$ $4 - x^2 \geq 0$ and $f(x).[4 - x^2 + 2] \geq 0$

$\Rightarrow$ $4 - x^2 \geq 0$ and $f(x) \geq 0$

$\Rightarrow$ $f(x) \geq 0$ for $x \in [-2, 2]$

6. (b) $\{(x, y) \in R^2 : x^2 + y^2 \leq 25, y \geq -x\}$ represents the point on and in interior of circle $x^2 + y^2 = 25$, which are above the line $y = -x$.

7. (b) $x^4 + y^3 + 1$; contains even power of x

$\Rightarrow$ $f(x, y) = f(-x, y)$

$\Rightarrow$ Curve is symmetric about y-axis

8. (d) $[x]^2 + [x + 3] = 4$ ...(i)

$\Rightarrow$ $[x]^2 + [x] + 3 = 4$

$\Rightarrow$ $[x]^2 - [x] - 1 = 0$

$\Rightarrow$ $[x] = ..$

$\Rightarrow$ $[x] = \dfrac{-1 \pm \sqrt{5}}{2}$, which is impossible as L.H.S is an integer, whereas R.H.S is non-integer.

$\Rightarrow$ No solution.

9. (d) Graphs of $y = \sin x$ and $y = e^{-x}$ drawn on same frame of reference are as shown below.

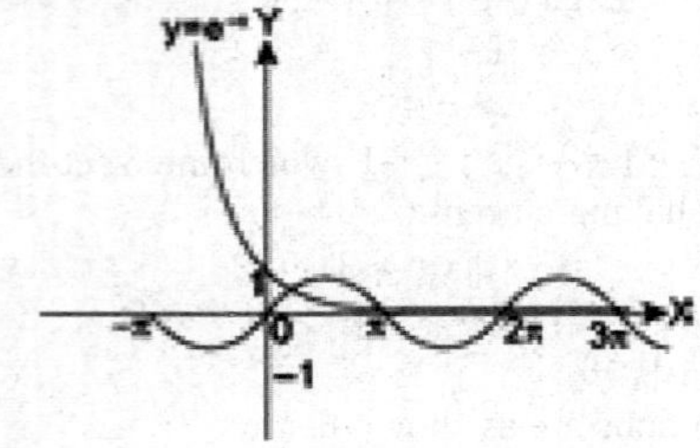

Clearly $y = e^{-x} \in (0, 1]$ for $x \geq 0$ and $\in (1, \infty)$ for $x < 0$

$\Rightarrow$ $y = e^{-x}$ and $y = \sin x$ would intersect each other infinitely many times in the intervals $(0, \infty)$ and do not intersects in $(-\infty, 0)$. Thus, there are infinitely many solutions.

10. (b) $f(x) = \max. \{\tan x, \cot x\}$

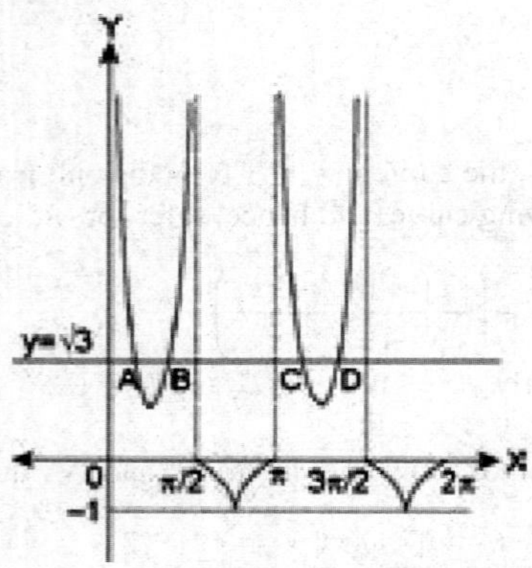

Clearly, $f(x) = \max.\{\tan x, \cot x\}$ and $y = \sqrt{3}$ intersect each other at four points A, B, C and D.

Hence, there will be four solutions in $(0, 2\pi)$.

11. (c) $\sin x = .\dfrac{x}{10}$ ...(i)

$\because$ $\sin x \in [-1, 1]$; for (1) to hold $\dfrac{x}{10} \in [-1, 1]$, i.e., $x \in [-10, 10]$

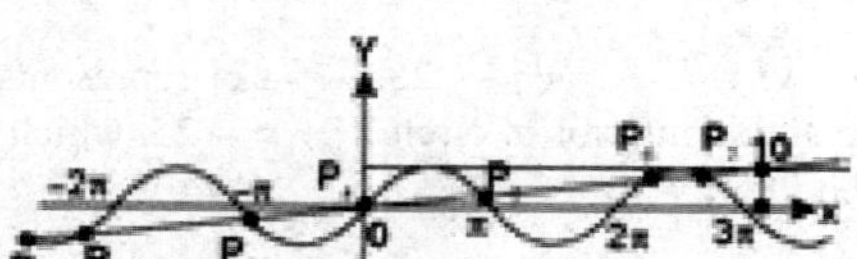

Clearly, there will be 7 points of intersection 3 on each side of y-axis along with origin.

12. (b) $5^{|x|} = |3 - |x||$

$y = 5^{|x|}$ and $y = |3 - |x||$ drawn on same reference plane are as shown below.

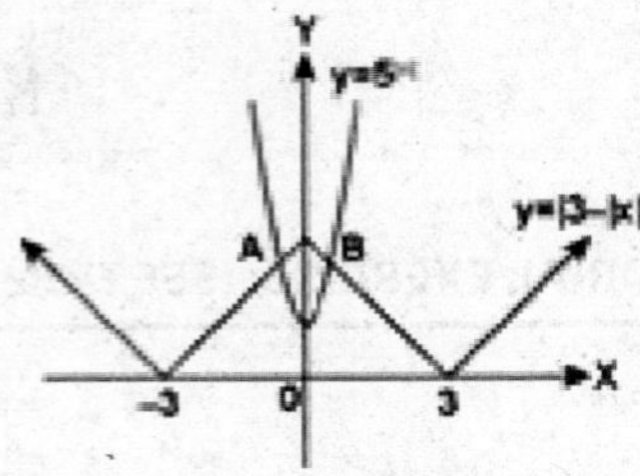

The graphs of functions $y = 5^{|x|}$ and $y = |3 - |x||$ would intersect each other at A and B.

In (3,), $y = 5^{|x|} = 5^x$ $\Rightarrow$ $y' = 5^x \ln 5 > 0$

$\Rightarrow$ $y = 5^x$ is an increasing function and $y'(3) = (5)^3 \ln 5 = (125)(\ln 5) > 125$.

Also, in $(3, \infty)$, $y = |3 - |x|| = |3 - x| = x - 3$

$\Rightarrow$ $y' = 1$

$\Rightarrow$ The graph of $y = 5^{|x|}$ would always remain above the graph of $y = |3 - |x||$ for $x > 3$, as the slope of tangent to $y = 5^{|x|}$ goes increasing, whereas that of $y = |3 - |x||$ remains constant for $x > 3$.

Similar is the case for $x < -3$. Thus, there will be only 2 solutions .

13. (c) $x^2 - 2x - \log_2 |1 - x| = 3$

$\Rightarrow$ $x^2 - 2x - 3 = \log_2 |1 - x|$

$\Rightarrow$ $(x - 3)(x + 1) = \log_2 |1 - x|$

The graphs of $f(x) = (x - 3)(x + 1)$ and $g(x) = \log_2 |1 - x|$ drawn on same frame of reference are given below.

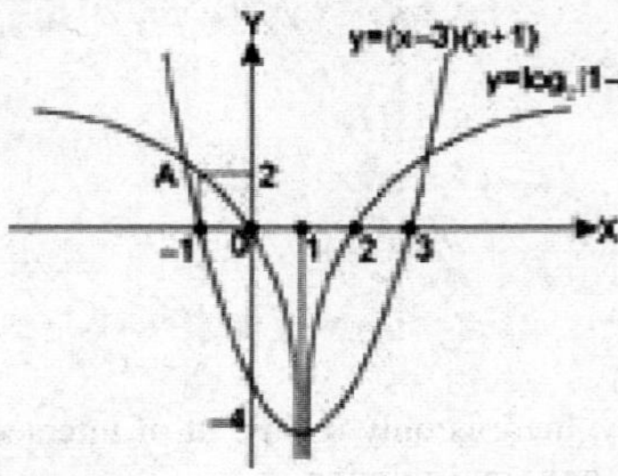

Clearly, there will be 4 points of intersection, and hence, 4 solutions.

14. (b) Given equation is $e^{2x} + e^x - 2e = 0$ $e^x = \dfrac{-1 \pm \sqrt{1+8e}}{2(1)}$ but $e^x > 0$

$\Rightarrow$ $e^x = \dfrac{\sqrt{1+8e} - 1}{2}$

$\Rightarrow$ $x = ln\left(\dfrac{\sqrt{1+8e} - 1}{2}\right)$ is the only solution.

Now, $1 < e < 3$

$\Rightarrow$ $9 < 1 + 8e < 25$ $\Rightarrow$ $3 < \sqrt{1+8e} < 5$

$\Rightarrow$ $1 < \dfrac{\sqrt{1+8e} - 1}{2} < 2$

$\Rightarrow$ $0 < \ln\left(\dfrac{\sqrt{1+8e} - 1}{2}\right) < \ln 2 < 1$

$(\because \ln 2 < \ln e = 1)$

$\Rightarrow$ $x \in (0, 1)$. Thus, only one solution in (0, 1) or [0, 1]
The statement that equation has at least one root in [0, 1] is also true.

15. (d) $|2x + 3| + |2x - 3| = px + 6$. Let $f(x) = |2x + 3| + |2x - 3|$ and $g(x) = px + 6$
Graph of $f(x) = |2x + 3| + |2x - 3|$ will be as shown below.

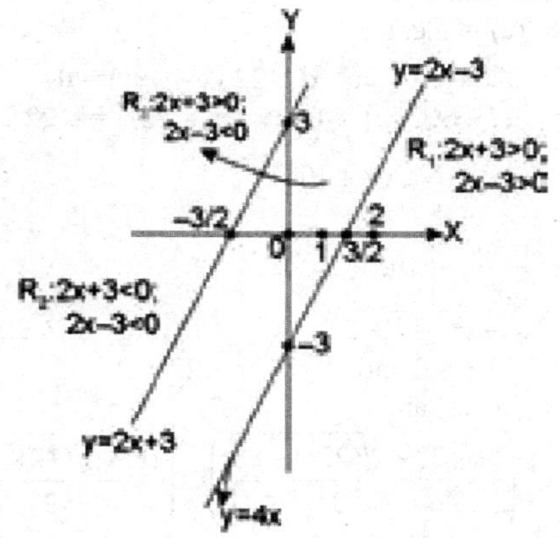

In Region R_1: Thus, $2x + 3 \geq 0$ and $2x - 3 \geq 0$ for $x \in \left[\frac{3}{2}, \infty\right)$

$\therefore$ In intervals $\left[\frac{3}{2}, \infty\right)$; $y = |2x + 3| + |2x - 3| = 2x + 3 + 2x - 3$

$\Rightarrow$ $y = 4x$

In Region R_2: $2x + 3 \leq 0$; $2x - 3 \leq 0$ for $x \in \left(-\infty, \frac{-3}{2}\right]$

$\therefore$ In interval $\left(-\infty, \frac{-3}{2}\right)$; $y = -2x - 3 - 2x + 3$

$\Rightarrow$ $y = -4x$

In Region R_3: $2x + 3 \geq 0$; $2x - 3 \leq 0$ for $x \in \left[\frac{-3}{2}, \frac{3}{2}\right]$

$\therefore$ In interval $\left[\frac{-3}{2}, \frac{3}{2}\right]$, $y = 2x + 3 - 2x + 3$

$\Rightarrow$ $y = 6$

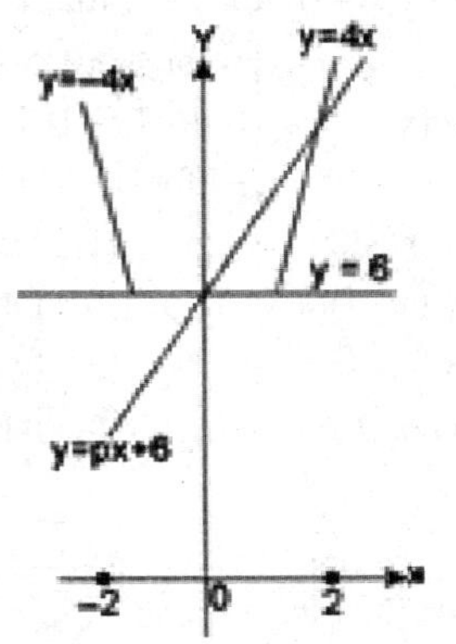

Clearly $y = px + 6$ and $y = |2x + 3| + |2x - 3|$ would intersect each other at more than two points (infinitely many points).

If $y = px + 6$ coincide with $y = 6$
$\Rightarrow$ $p = 0$, i.e., $p \in \{0\}$

16. (c) $\sin\left(\frac{x}{2}\right) + 2x = x^2 + \pi^2$

$\Rightarrow$ $\sin\left(\frac{x}{2}\right) = x^2 - 2\pi x + \pi^2$

$\Rightarrow$ $\sin\left(\frac{x}{2}\right) = (x - \pi)^2$

Let $f(x) = \sin\left(\frac{x}{2}\right)$ and $g(x) = (x - \pi)^2$

The graphs of $f(x)$ and $g(x)$ drawn on same reference plane are as shown below.

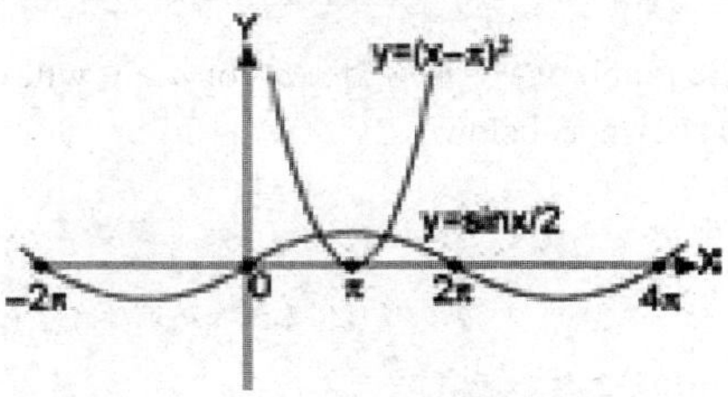

Clearly, there will be two solutions only.

17. (a) $2 \cos (e^x) = 5^x + 5^{-x}$ ...(i)
$\because$ $5^x, 5^{-x} > 0\ \forall\ x \in \mathbb{R}$,

By A.M. ≥ G.M., $5^x + 5^{-x}\ 2\sqrt{5^x.5^{-x}}$, i.e., $5^x + 5^{-x} \geq 2$, whereas $2 \cos (e^x) \leq 2$

$\therefore$ Equation (1) is satisfied when both sides are equal to 2
$\Rightarrow$ $\cos (e^x) = 1$ $\Rightarrow$ $e^x = 2n\pi$; $n \in \mathbb{N}$
$\Rightarrow$ $x = \ln (2n\pi)$; $n \in \mathbb{N}$, but $5^x + 5^{-x} = 2$ for $x = 0$
$\therefore$ (1) does not hold for any $x \in \mathbb{R}$
$\Rightarrow$ No solution.

18. (d) The graphs of $y = \frac{1}{x}$ and $y = px$ drawn on same reference frame are shown below.

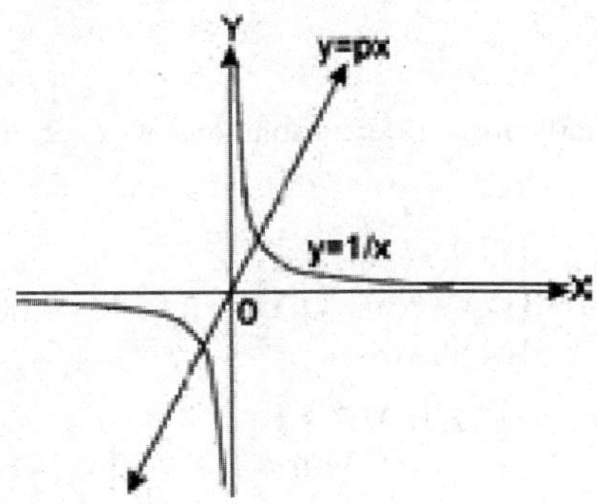

For very value of $p > 0$, $y = px$ and $y = \frac{1}{x}$ intersect each other exactly at two points. As for $p = 0$, x-axis is asymptote and for $p < 0$, $y = px$ completely lie in *I*, IInd and IIIrd quadrant in which no portion of $y = \frac{1}{x}$ lies.

19. (b) $|\sin x| = \cos x$ ...(1)

Let $f(x) = |\sin x|$ and $g(x) = \cos x$

The graphs of $y = |\sin x|$ and $y = \cos x$ drawn on same reference plane are as shown below.

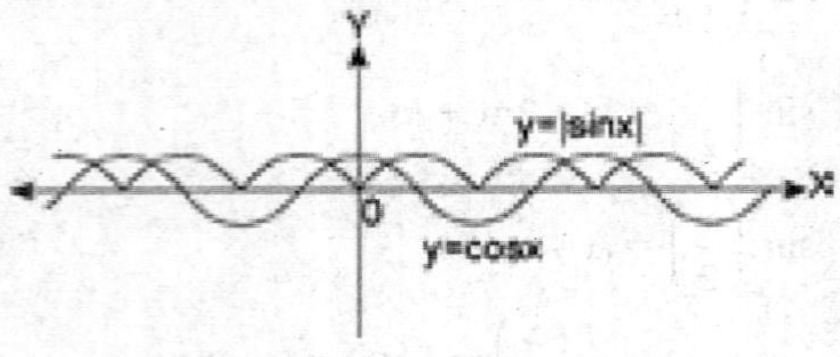

Clearly, the two graphs intersect at $x = 2n\pi \pm \dfrac{\pi}{4}$; for each $n \in \mathbb{Z}$.

20. (a) The graph of $y = ||x - 2| + a|$ for $a \geq 0$ will of the form as shown as below.

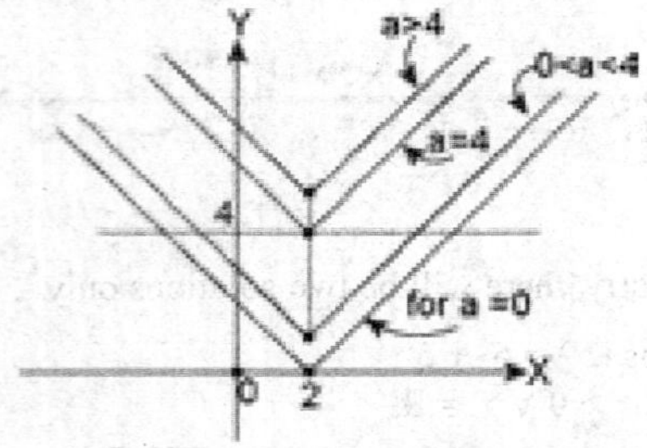

Clearly, for $a \geq 0$, we get at most two solutions of equation $||x - 2| + a| = 4$

$\Rightarrow$ For more than two solutions $a < 0$.

The graphs of $y = ||x - 2| + a|$ for $a < 0$ are as shown below.

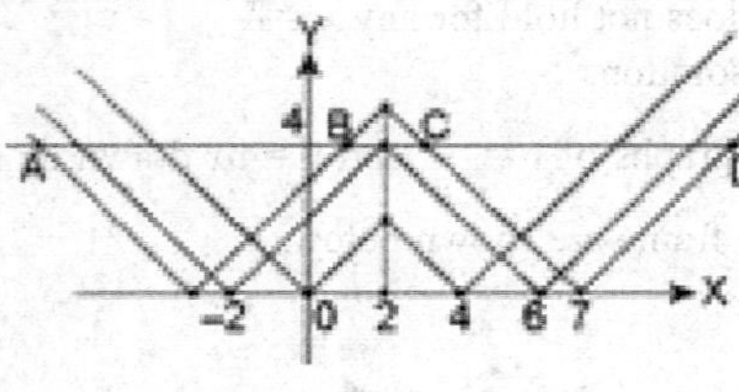

Clearly, for 4 different solutions of $||x - 2| + a| = 4$; $a \in (-\infty, -4)$.

21. (b) $f_1(x) = \begin{cases} x\,;\ 0 \leq x \leq 1 \\ 1\,;\ x > 1 \\ 0\,;\text{otherwise} \end{cases}$; $f_2(x) = f_1(-x)\ \forall\ x$; $f_3(x) = -f_2(x)$

$\forall\ x$; $f_4(x) = f_3(-x)\ \forall\ x$

$$f_2(x) = f_1(-x) = \begin{cases} -x;\ 0 \leq -x \leq 1 \\ 1;\ -x > 1 \\ 0;\ \text{otherwise} \end{cases} = \begin{cases} -x; -1 \leq x \leq 0 \\ 1;\ x < -1 \\ 0\ ;\text{otherwise.} \end{cases}$$

$$f_3(x) = -f_2(x) = \begin{cases} x;\ -1 \leq x \leq 0 \\ -1\,;\ x < -1 \\ 0\ ;\text{otherwise} \end{cases}$$

$$f_4(x) = f_3(-x) = \begin{cases} -x; -1 \leq -x \leq 0 \\ 1\ ;\ -x < -1 \\ 0\ ;\text{otherwise} \end{cases} = \begin{cases} -x\ ;\ 0 \leq x \leq 1 \\ -1\ ;\ x > 1 \\ 0\ ;\text{otherwise} \end{cases} = -f_1(x)$$

Thus, $f_1(x) = -f_4(x) \Rightarrow$ (a) is incorrect

$f_1(x) = -f_3(-x)$

$\Rightarrow$ (b) is correct and (d) is incorrect.

Also $f_4(x) = f_3(-x) = -f_2(-x)$

$\Rightarrow$ (c) is incorrect.

22. (c) $x^2 - 22[x] = 0 \Rightarrow x^2 - 22(x - \{x\}) = 0$

$\Rightarrow x^2 - 22x + 22\{x\} = 0 \Rightarrow x^2 - 22x = -22\{x\}$

$\Rightarrow \dfrac{22x - x^2}{22} = \{x\} \in [0, 1)$

$\Rightarrow \dfrac{22x - x^2}{22} \in [0, 1)$

$\Rightarrow (22x - x^2) \in [0, 22) \Rightarrow 0 \leq 22x - x^2 < 22$

$\Rightarrow x^2 - 22x \leq 0$ and $x^2 - 22x + 22 > 0$

$\Rightarrow x \in [0, 22]$ and

$x \in \left(-\infty, \dfrac{22 - \sqrt{(22)^2 - 88}}{2}\right) \cup \left(\dfrac{22 + \sqrt{(22)^2 - 88}}{2}, \infty\right)$

$\Rightarrow x \in [0, 22]$ and $x \in \left(-\infty, \dfrac{22 - 19}{2}\right) \cup \left(\dfrac{22 + 19}{2}, \infty\right)$

$\Rightarrow x \in [0, 1.5) \cup (20.5, 22]$ (consider super set for more accuracy)

For $x \in [0, 1)$; $[x] = 0$

$\therefore x^2 = 22[x] = 0 \Rightarrow x = 0$

For $x \in [1, 1.5)$; $[x] = 1$

$\therefore x^2 = 22[x] = 22 \Rightarrow x = \sqrt{22}$

$\Rightarrow [x] \neq 1 \quad \therefore$ No solution

For $x \in (20.5, 21)$; $[x] = 20$

$\therefore x^2 = 22[x] = 440 \Rightarrow x = \sqrt{440} \simeq 20.9$

$\Rightarrow [x] = 21$

For $x \in [21, 22)$; $[x] = 21$

$\therefore x^2 = 22[x] = 462 \Rightarrow x = \sqrt{462} \simeq 21.4$

$\Rightarrow [x] = 21$

For $x = 22$; $[x] = 22$

$\therefore x^2 = 22[x] = (22)^2 \Rightarrow x = 22$; $[x] = 22$

Thus, $x = 0$, $x = \sqrt{440}$, $x = \sqrt{462}$, $x = 22$ are four solutions .

23. (a) $f(x) = \text{sgn}[x + 1] = \begin{cases} 1 \text{ for } [x+1] > 0 \\ 0 \text{ for } [x+1] = 0 \\ -1 \text{ for } [x+1] < 0 \end{cases}$

$$= \begin{cases} 1 \text{ for } x + 1 \geq 1 \\ 0 \text{ for } (x+1) \in [0,1) \\ -1 \text{ for } (x+1) \in (-\infty, 0) \end{cases} = \begin{cases} 1 \text{ for } x \geq 0 \\ 0 \text{ for } x \in [-1, 0) \\ -1 \text{ for } x \in (-\infty, -1) \end{cases}$$

$\therefore$ The graph of $f(x) = \text{sgn}[x + 1]$ will be as shown below.

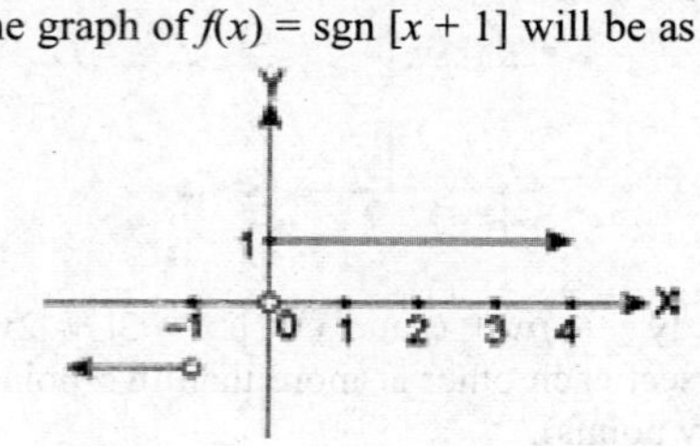

24. **(b)** $f: \mathbb{R} \to [-1, 1]$ defined as $f(x) = \dfrac{x^2 - 1}{x^2 + 1}$

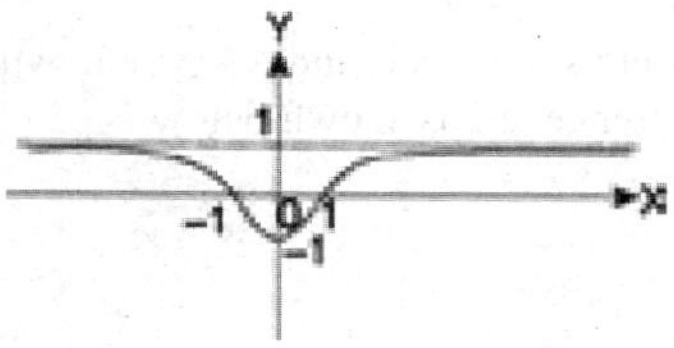

Clearly $f(\pm 1) = 0$ $\Rightarrow$ ± 1 are roots of $f(x) = 0$

$\Rightarrow f(x) = 1 - \dfrac{2}{x^2+1} \Rightarrow f'(x) = -2\left(\dfrac{-1}{(x^2+1)^2}\right)(2x)$

$= \dfrac{4x}{(x^2+1)^2} > 0$ for $x > 0$ and < 0 for $x < 0$;

$f''(x) = \dfrac{-4(3x^2-1)}{(x^2+1)^3} < 0$ for $x < \dfrac{-1}{\sqrt{3}}$ or $x > \dfrac{1}{\sqrt{3}}$ and > 0

for $x \in \left(\dfrac{-1}{\sqrt{3}}, \dfrac{1}{\sqrt{3}}\right)$

Also as $x \pm \infty$, $f(x)$ 1

$\Rightarrow$ $y = 1$ is a horizontal asymptotes.

$\Rightarrow$ Thus, the graph of $f(x)$ will be as shown above. Clearly $f(x)$ is many–one and onto from $\mathbb{R}$ to $[-1, 1]$

$f(x)$ is bounded, but if does not attain its maximum value.

However, $f(x)$ decrease for $x < 0$ and increase for $x > 0$

25. **(b)** From, the graph we can observe , that

(i) $\lim\limits_{x \to 0^+} f(x) = -\infty$

$\Rightarrow$ $\lim\limits_{x \to 0^+}\left(\dfrac{1}{f}(x)\right) = 0^-$

(ii) $f(a) = 0$ and $f(x) < 0$ for $x \in (0, a)$; $f(x) > 0$ for $x \in (a, \infty)$

$\Rightarrow$ $\dfrac{1}{f(x)} < 0$ for $x \in (0, a)$; $\dfrac{1}{f(x)} > 0$ for $x \in (a, \infty)$;

$\lim\limits_{x \to a^-} \dfrac{1}{f(x)} = -\infty$ and $\lim\limits_{x \to a^+} \dfrac{1}{f(x)} = \infty$

(iii) $f(x) \to 0^+$ as $x \to \infty$

$\Rightarrow$ $\dfrac{1}{f(x)} \to +\infty$ $x \to \infty$

(iv) $\dfrac{d}{dx}\left(\dfrac{1}{f(x)}\right) = \dfrac{-1}{[f(x)]^2} \cdot f'(x)$

$\Rightarrow$ $\dfrac{1}{f(x)}$ decrease for $x \in (0, a)$ and (a, b) increase for $x \in (b, \infty)$

Collecting information from above we conclude that the rough graph of $1/f(x)$ would be as represents below.

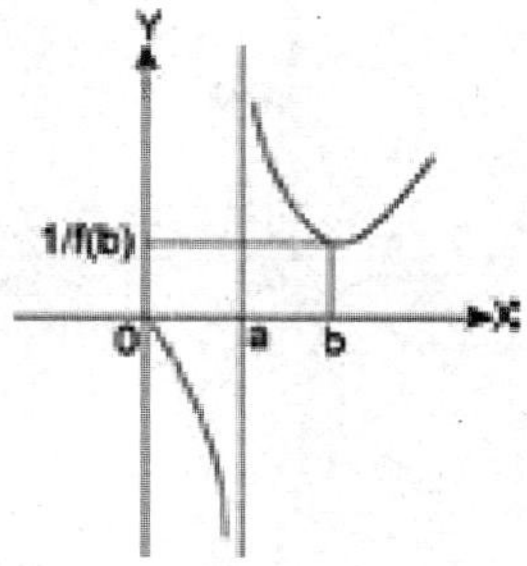

26. **(b)** $f(x) = \cot^{-1}(4 - x^2) \in (0, \pi)$

We observe the following:

(i) $f(x)$ is symmetric about y-axis

(ii) $\cot^{-1}(4 - x^2) \in \left(0, \dfrac{\pi}{2}\right)$ for $4 - x^2 > 0$, i.e., $x \in (-2, 2)$

(iii) $\cot^{-1}(4 - x^2) \in \left(\dfrac{\pi}{2}, \pi\right)$ for $4 - x^2 < 0$, i.e., $x \in (-\infty, -2) \cup (2, \infty)$

(iv) $\cot^{-1}(4 - x^2) = \dfrac{\pi}{2}$ for $4 - x^2 = 0$ i.e., $x = \pm 2$

(v) $f'(x) = \dfrac{-1}{1+(4-x^2)^2}.(-2x) = \dfrac{2x}{1+(4-x^2)^2} > 0$ for $x > 0$

and < 0 for $x > 0$

$\Rightarrow$ $x = 0$ is a critical point and is a point of local minima, and the local minimum value of $f(x)$ is

$\text{Cot}^{-1}(4) < \cot^{-1}(0) = \dfrac{\pi}{2}$

(vi) $\cot^{-1}(4 - x^2) \to \pi$ for $4 - x^2 \to -\infty$

$\Rightarrow$ $x^2 \to \infty$ $\Rightarrow$ $x \to \pm\infty$

$\Rightarrow$ $y = \pi$ is a horizontal asymptote.

Thus, the graph of $f(x)$ will be as shown below.

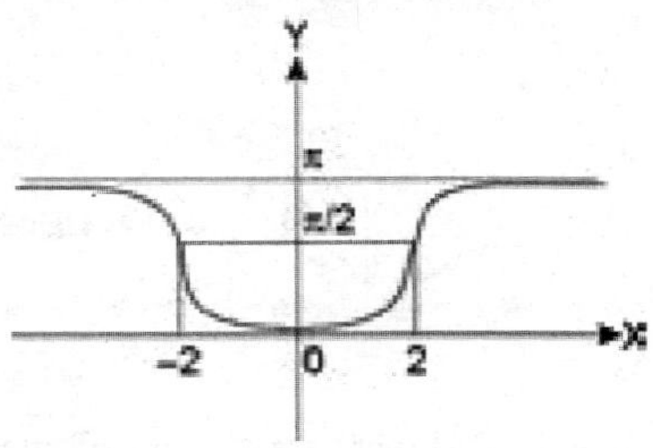

27. **(b)** $f(x) = \{x\}.[x]$

$\therefore$ $f(x) = 1$ $\Rightarrow$ $\{x\}[x] = 1$

$\Rightarrow$ $[x] > 0$ $\Rightarrow$ $[x] \geq 1$

$\Rightarrow$ $x \in [1, \infty)$ and $x \notin \mathbb{Z}$ as otherwise $\{x\} = 0$

Now $\{x\} = \dfrac{1}{[x]}$ and $[x] > 1$; $x \notin \mathbb{Z}$

$\Rightarrow$ $x = 2 + \dfrac{1}{2}; 3 + \dfrac{1}{3}, 4 + \dfrac{1}{4}, 5 + \dfrac{1}{5}, \ldots\ldots$

$\Rightarrow$ There will be infinitely many solutions.

28. **(c)** Given equation is $x \sin x = 1$ or $\sin x = \dfrac{1}{x}$

Draw the graph of $f(x) = \sin x$ and $g(x) = \dfrac{1}{x}$ on same frame of reference as shown below.

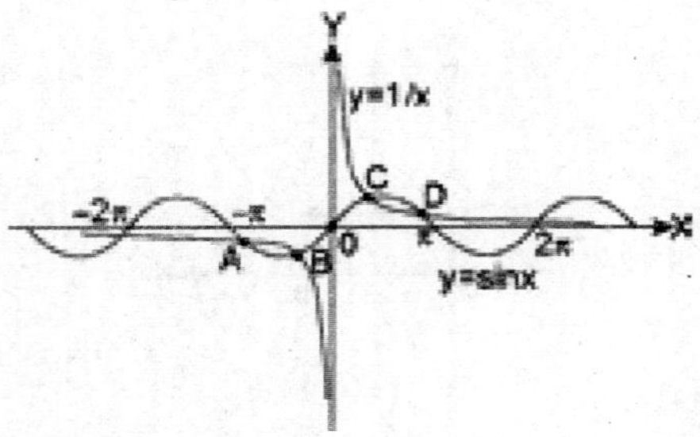

Clearly, there will be infinitely many points of intersection of $f(x) = \sin x$ and $g(x) = 1/x$.
In fact all points of intersection belong to $(-\infty, -1) \cup (1, \infty)$ and in $[-2\pi, 0) \cup (0, 2\pi]$, there lie exactly 4 points of intersection, and hence, 4 roots.

29. (b) The graphs of $|y| = \ln|x|$ and $(x-1)^2 + y^2 - 4 = 0$ are as shown below.

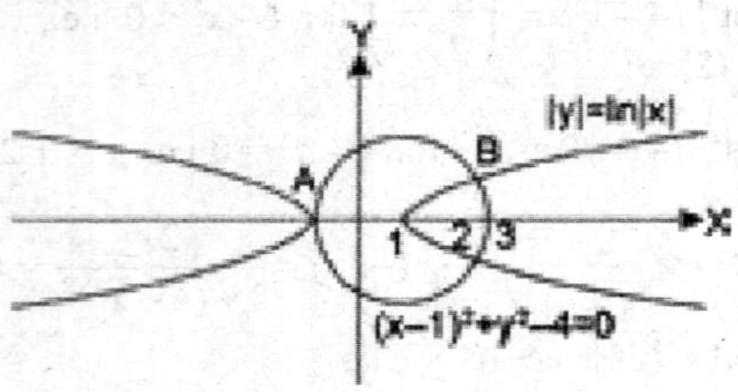

Clearly there will be 3 points of intersection, and hence, 3 solutions, i.e., 3 points (x, y)

30. (a) Given equation is $2^{\cos x} = |\sin x|$
$y = |\sin x|$ and $y = 2^{\cos x}$ are periodic functions with period π and 2 respectively.
$\therefore$ $2^{\cos x} = |\sin x|$ will also be periodic with period 2π. Thus, it is sufficient to drawn the graph in $[0, 2\pi]$ as shown below.

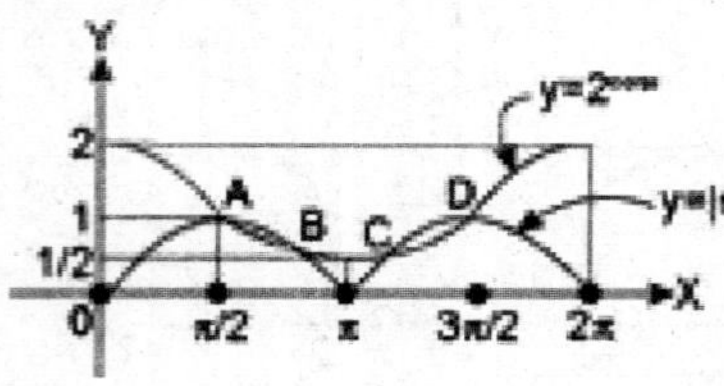

Clearly in $[0, 2\pi]$ there are 4 points of intersection, and hence, 4 solutions.

31. (c) $\sin \pi x = |\ln|x||$
Graph of $y = \sin \pi x$ and $y = |\ln|x||$ are as shown below.

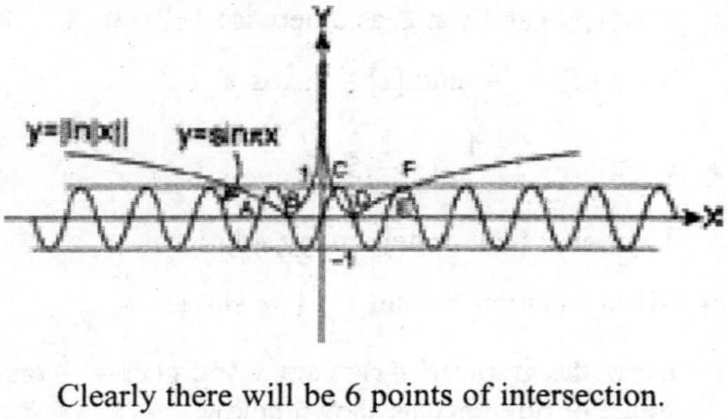

Clearly there will be 6 points of intersection.

32. (b) Given equation is $1 + \log_2(1-x) = 2^{-x}$
$\Rightarrow$ $\log_2(1-x) = 2^{-x} - 1$ ...(1)
Let $f(x) = \log_2(1-x)$; $(1-x) > 0$, i.e., $x \in (-\infty, 1)$
and $g(x) = 2^{-x} - 1$ ...(2)
The graphs of $y = f(x)$ and $y = g(x)$ drawn on same frame of reference are as shown below.

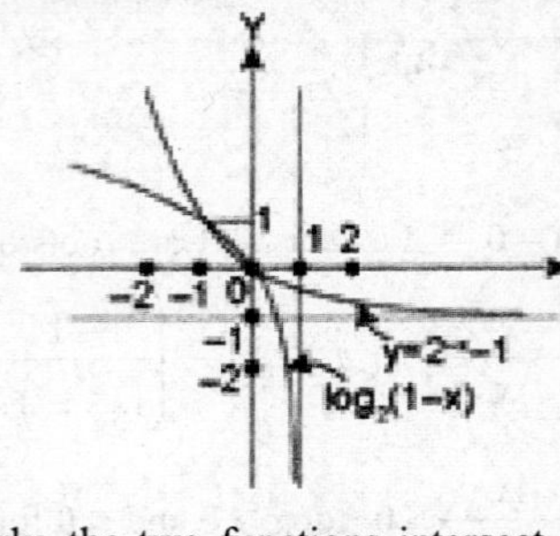

Clearly, the two functions intersect each other at two points.
Thus, there will be 2 solutions.

33. (d) Let $f(x) = |\sin|x||$ and $g(x) = x + |x|$; $x \in [-4\pi, 2\pi]$
The graphs of $f(x)$ and $g(x)$ drawn on same frame of reference are as shown below.

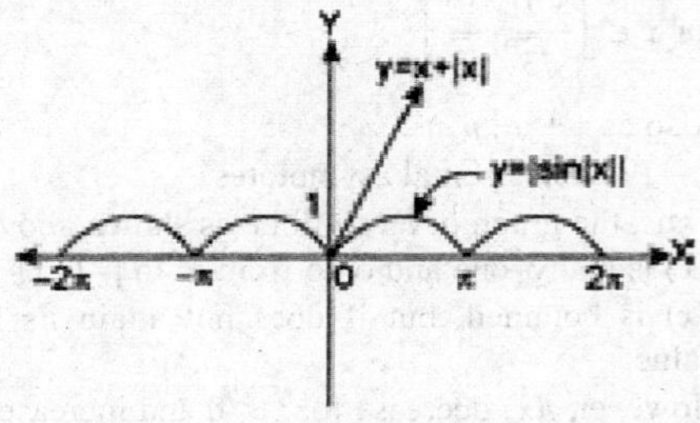

Hence, $f(x) = |\sin|x|| = \begin{cases} |\sin x|; x \geq 0 \\ |-\sin x|; x < 0 \end{cases}$ and $g(x)$

$= \begin{cases} 2x \text{ for } x \geq 0 \\ 0 \text{ for } x < 0 \end{cases}$

Clearly $f(x) = g(x)$ at $x = -4\pi, -3, -2\pi, -\pi, 0$
$\therefore$ There will be total 5 solutions.

34. (b) $\because$ $3^{x-1} + 5^{x-1}$ is a continuous and increasing function with range $(0, \infty)$.
Thus, $3^{x-1} + 5^{x-1}$ takes every real numbers > 0 exactly once. Hence, the equation $(3)^{x-1} + (5)^{x-1} = 12$ has Exactly one solution.

35. (a) $\cos[x] = 2^{4x-1}$; $x \in [0, 2\pi]$
$\cos[x] \leq 1$ and $2^{4x-1} > 1 = 2^0$ for $x > \frac{1}{4}$
$\therefore$ $\cos[x] = 2^{4x-1}$ can hold in $\left[0, \frac{1}{4}\right]$ but in $\left[0, \frac{1}{4}\right]$; $[x] = 0$
$\Rightarrow$ $\cos 0 = 2^{4x-1}$ for $x \in \left[0, \frac{1}{4}\right]$
$\Rightarrow$ $1 = 2^{4x-1}$ for $x \in \left[0, \frac{1}{4}\right]$
$\Rightarrow$ $x = \frac{1}{4}$ is the only solution.

36. **(d)** Let $f(x) = x^2 + x + 3$ and $g(x) = -2\sin x$; $x \in [-\pi, \pi]$

$\because$ $f(x) \in \left[\frac{11}{4}, \infty\right)$ $\Rightarrow f(x) > 2$, whereas $g(x) \in [-2, 2]$

$\Rightarrow$ $f(x) \neq g(x)$ for any $x \in \mathbb{R}$

$\Rightarrow$ There is no real root of given equation.

37. **(b)** Given equation is $|x - x^2 - 1| = |2x - 3 - x^2|$ ......(i)

$\Rightarrow$ $(-x^2 + x - 1) \in \left(-\infty, -\frac{3}{4}\right]$

$\Rightarrow$ $|x - x^2 - 1| \in \left[\frac{3}{4}, \infty\right)$

Also $(-x^2 + 2x - 3) \in (-\infty, -2]$

$\Rightarrow$ $|2x - 3 - x^2| \in [2, \infty)$

Also $-x^2 + x - 1 < 0$, $-x^2 - 2x - 3 < 0$

$\therefore$ (1) becomes, $x^2 - x + 1 = x^2 - 2x + 3$

$\Rightarrow$ $x = 2$ is the only solution.

38.(d) $\frac{x^2}{1-|x-2|} = 1 \quad \Rightarrow \quad x^2 = 1 - |x - 2|$

$$\Rightarrow x^2 = \begin{cases} 3-x \text{ for } x \geq 2 & x^2+x-3=0 \text{ for } x \geq 2 \\ x-1 \text{ for } x < 2 & \text{and } x^2-x+1=0 \text{ for } x < 2 \end{cases}$$

But $x^2 + x - 3$ for $x \geq 2$ and $x^2 - x + 1 \geq \frac{3}{4}$ for $x \in \mathbb{R}$,

Hence, for $x < 2$

$\therefore$ (1) is not satisfied for any real value x.

39. **(d)** $f(x) = \frac{|x|\quad|x|}{}$ $D_f = \mathbb{R} - \{-1, 1\}$

$$\Rightarrow f(x) = \frac{|x|\left(|x|^2+1\right)}{1-x^2} = \frac{|x|\left(1+x^2\right)}{\left(1-x^2\right)}$$

$$\Rightarrow f(x) = \begin{cases} +\text{ve for } x \in (-1,1)-\{0\} \\ 0 \text{ at } x = 0 \\ -\text{ve for } x \in (-\infty,-1) \cup (1,\infty) \end{cases}$$

$\Rightarrow$ $f(x)$ lie in each of 4 quadrants.

40. **(c)** $\tan 4x = \cos x$; $0 < x < \pi$.

The graph of $y = \tan 4x$ and $y = \cos x$ for $x \in (0, \pi)$ drawn on same frame of reference is as shown below.

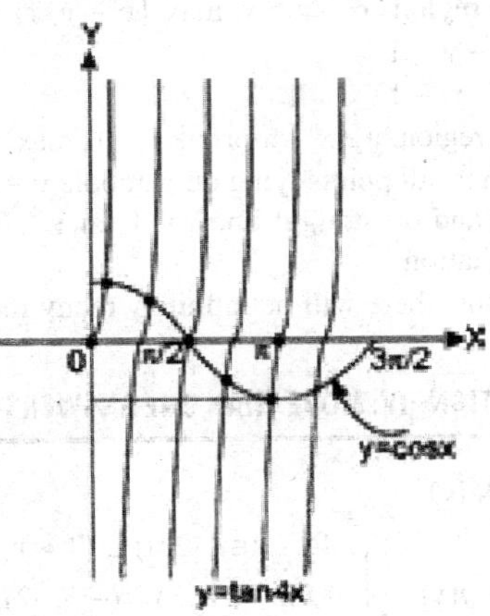

Clearly, there are 5 points of intersection of $y = \tan 4x$ and $y = \cos x$ in $(0, \pi)$.

41. **(b)** $\log_{0.5}|x| = 2|x|$ $\Rightarrow \log_2 -1^{|x|} = 2|x|$

$\Rightarrow$ $-\log_2|x| = 2|x|$ $\Rightarrow \log_2|x| = -2|x|$

Graphs of $y = \log_2|x|$ and $y = -2|x|$ drawn on same frame are as shown below.

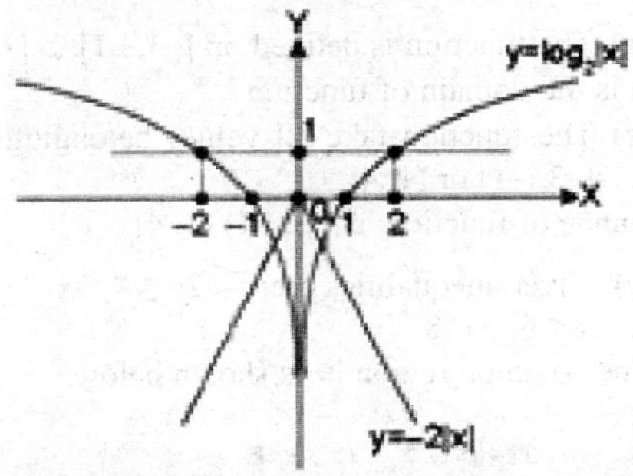

Clearly, there are two points of intersection, and hence, 2 solutions.

42. **(a)** $f(x) = \max.\{1 + \sin x, 1, 1 - \cos x\}$; $x \in [0, 2\pi]$

$g(x) = \max.\{1, |x - 1|\}$; $x \in \mathbb{R}$

Clearly, $g(x) = \begin{cases} |x-1| \text{ for } x \in (-\infty, 0] \cup [2, \infty) \\ 1 \text{ for } x \in (0, 2) \end{cases}$

For $f(x)$, let us draw its graph as shown below.

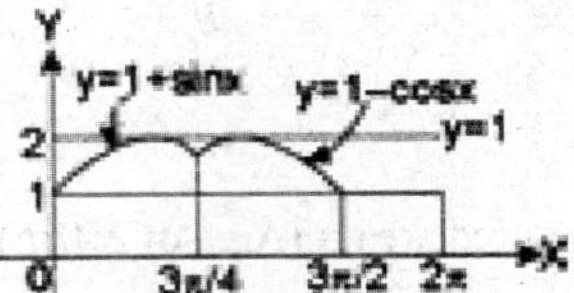

$$\therefore f(x) = \begin{cases} 1+\sin x;\ 0 \leq x \leq \frac{3\pi}{4} \\ 1-\cos x;\ \frac{3\pi}{4} < x \leq \frac{3\pi}{2} \\ 1;\ \frac{3\pi}{2} < x \leq 2\pi \end{cases}$$

$\therefore$ $g(f(0)) = g(1) = 1$ $\Rightarrow$ (a) is correct

$f(f(1)) = f(1 + \sin 1)$

$\left(\because \frac{3\pi}{4} > 2, 1+\sin 1 < 2 \Rightarrow 1+\sin 1 < \frac{3\pi}{4}\right)$

$= 1 + \sin(1 + \sin 1)$

Also $f(g(1)) = f(1) = 1 + \sin 1$

$\Rightarrow$ (c) is incorrect

Further $f(g(0)) = f(1) = 1 + \sin 1$

$\Rightarrow$ (d) is incorrect.

43. **(d)** $f: \mathbb{R} \to \mathbb{R}$; $g: \mathbb{R} \to \mathbb{R}$

We know that min. $\{f_1(x), f_2(x)\}$

$$= \frac{(f_1(x)+f_2(x)) - |f_1(x)-f_2(x)|}{2}$$

$\therefore$ min $\{f(x) - g(x), 0\}$

$$= \frac{(f(x)-g(x)+0) - |f(x)-g(x)-0|}{2}$$

$$= \frac{(f(x)-g(x)) - |f(x)-g(x)|}{2}$$

44. **(i)** **(a)** Clearly, $f(-2) = \frac{5}{2}$ as on line joining (–3, 4) and (–1, 1), i.e., $y - 1 = \frac{-3}{2}(x + 1)$

(ii) **(a)** The function is defined on $[-3, -1] \cup [1, 5)$

$\Rightarrow$ It is the domain of function.

(iii) **(c)** The function take all values belonging to interval $[-3, -1)$ or $(1, 4]$

$\therefore$ Range of function is $[-3, -1)$ $(1, 4]$

45. **(i)** **(b)** Given inequalities are $x - 2y \le 4$, $2x + y > 5$, $y \ge x$, $x < 6$, $y < 8$

The common region is as shown below.

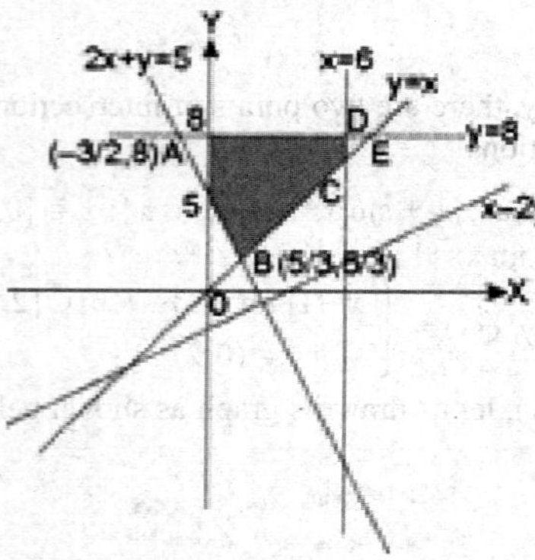

The required area = (Area of ΔABE) – (Area of ΔCDE)

$= \frac{1}{12}(361) - \frac{1}{2}(2)(2) = \frac{361-24}{12} = \frac{337}{12}$ square units.

(ii) **(b)** Given inequalities are $4x + y \le 5$; $x - 4y > 9$; $y < -x + 1$; $xy \ge 0$; $|x| \le 3$; $|y| \le 3$.

The common bounded region is as shown below.

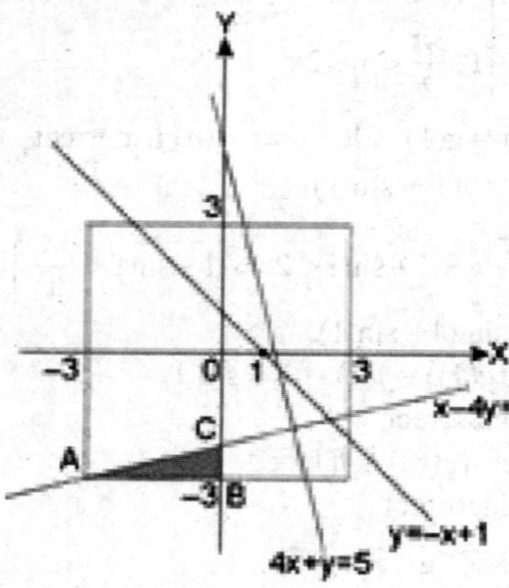

$\therefore$ The Required area = area of ΔABC

$= \frac{1}{2}(AB)\times(BC) = \frac{1}{2}\times 3 \times \left|\left(3 - \frac{9}{4}\right)\right|$

$= \frac{1}{2}\times(3)\times\left(\frac{3}{4}\right) = \frac{8}{9}$ sq. units

46. **(d)** Given Equation is $[x]^2 + [x + 3] = 4$

$\Rightarrow [x]^2 + [x] - 1 = 0$; Let $[x] = y$

$\Rightarrow y^2 + y - 1 = 0 \quad \Rightarrow y = \frac{-1 \pm \sqrt{(1)^2 + 4}}{2} = \frac{1 - \pm\sqrt{5}}{2}$

But $y \in \mathbb{Z} \quad \Rightarrow$ There exists no solution.

47. **(c)** $x^2 - 2 - [x] = 0 \Rightarrow x^2 - 2 - (x - \{x\}) = 0$

$\Rightarrow x^2 - x - 2 = -\{x\} \quad \Rightarrow (x - 2)(x + 1) = -\{x\}$

The graphs of function $y = (x - 2)(x + 1)$ and $y = -\{x\}$ drawn on same reference plane are as shown below.

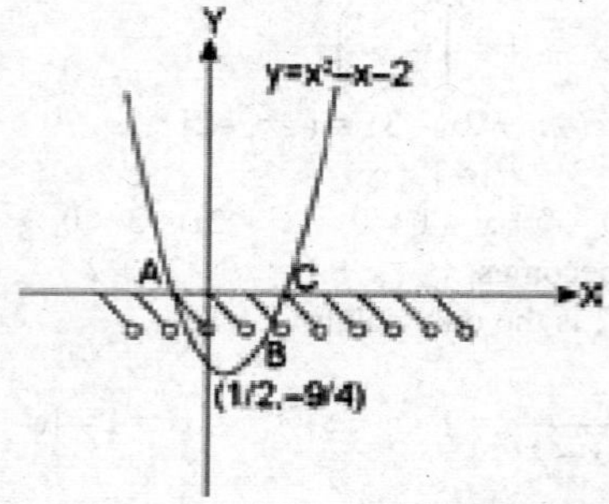

Clearly, the two graphs $y = x^2 - x - 2$ and $y = -\{x\}$ intersect each other at 3 points, hence, there will be 3 solutions.

48. **(d)** max. $\{x^2 - y, x\} = 1$

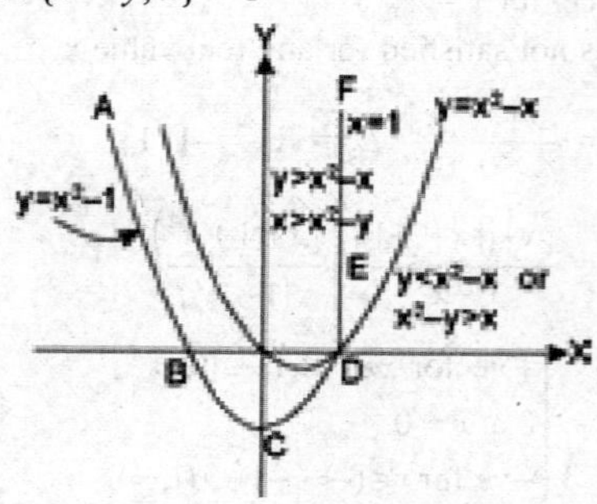

$x^2 - y = x$

$\Rightarrow y = x^2 - x$

Now $x^2 - y \ge x$

$\Rightarrow y \le x^2 - x$

In region, $x^2 - y > x$, max $\{x^2 - y, x\} = 1$

$\Rightarrow x^2 - y = 1$

$\Rightarrow y = x^2 - 1$

In region, $y \ge x^2 - x$ or $x \ge x^2 - y$, max $\{x^2 - y, x\} = x = 1$

Thus, all points lying on parabola $y = x^2 - 1$ on $x \in (-\infty, 1)$ and on straight line $x = 1$ for $y \ge 0$ satisfy the given equation.

Thus, there will be infinitely many real solutions (x, y).

SECTION–IV: MORE THAN ONE ANSWERS CORRECT

1. **(a), (b), (c)**

(a) $\text{sgn} f(x) = \begin{cases} 1 \text{ for } x \in (-2, 1) \cup (3, \infty) \\ -1 \text{ for } x \in (1, 3) \cup (-\infty, -2) \\ 0 \text{ for } x = -2, 1, 3 \end{cases}$

$\Rightarrow |y| = \text{sgn} f(x)$ will be as shown below.

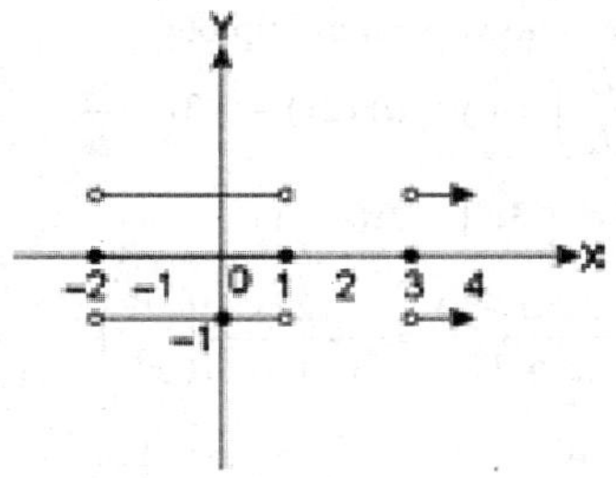

(b) $y = f(|x|)$ is as shown below.

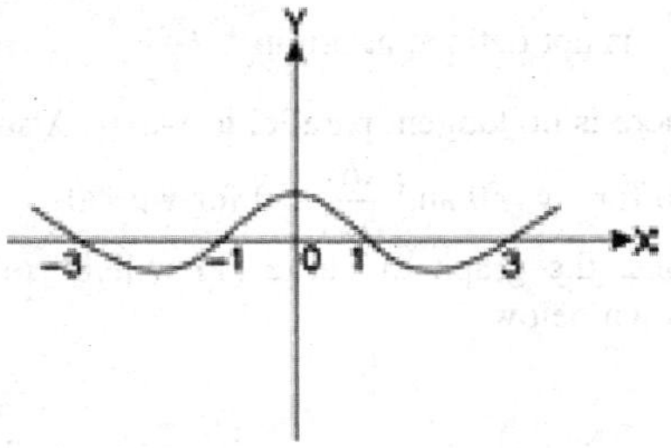

$\Rightarrow$ $y = (-f(|x|))$ will be as shown below.

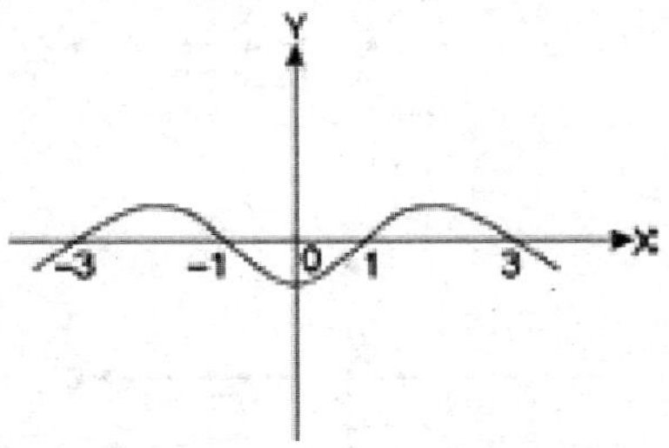

$$\Rightarrow \text{sgn}\,(-f(|x|)) = \begin{cases} -1 \text{ for } x \in (-\infty,-3) \cup (-1,1) \cup (3,\infty) \\ 0 \text{ for } x = -3,-1,3 \\ 1 \text{ for } x \in (-3,-1) \cup (1,3) \end{cases}$$

Thus, the graph of $|y| = \text{sgn}\,(-f\,(|x|))$ will be as shown below.

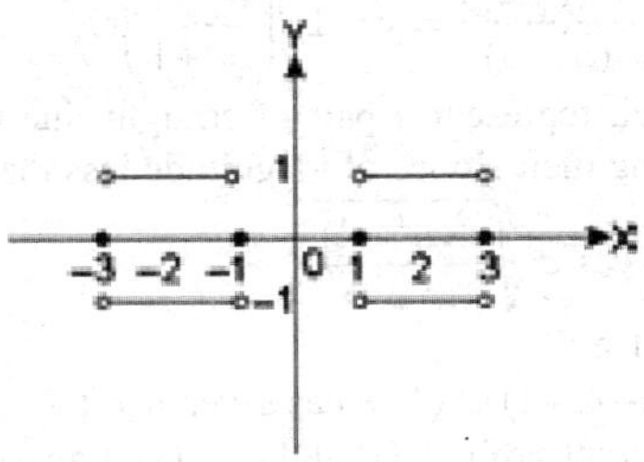

(c) Graph of $|y| = |f(|x|)|$ will be as shown below.

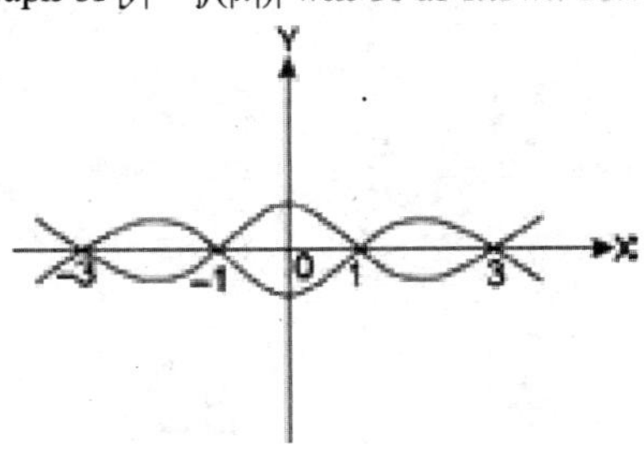

$$\text{(d)}\ \ y = x^{\text{sgn}\,f(x)} = \begin{cases} x \text{ for } x \in (-2,1) \cup (3,\infty) \\ x^{-1} \text{ for } x \equiv (-\infty,-2) \cup (1,3) \\ 1 \text{ for } x = -2,1,3 \end{cases}$$

$\therefore$ The graph of $y = x^{\text{sgn}\,f(x)}$ will be as shown below.

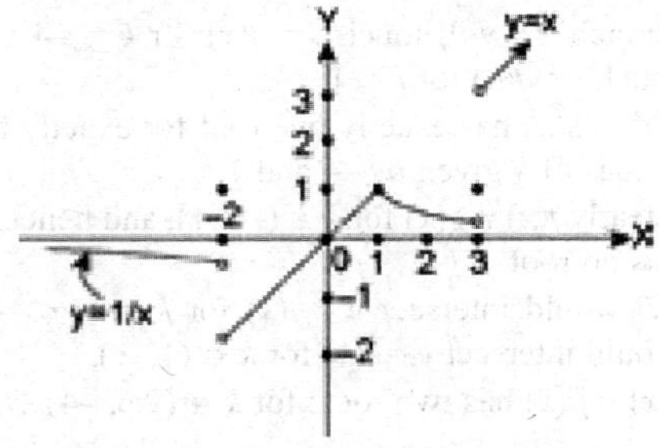

Clearly, option (d) is incorrect.

2. (b), (c) Given equation is $2|x| - 1 = 3|\sin \pi x|$

Period of $y = 3|\sin \pi x|$ is $\frac{\pi}{\pi} = 1$

Draw graphs of $y = 2|x| - 1$ and $y = 3|\sin x|$ for $x \in [0, 1]$ as shown below.

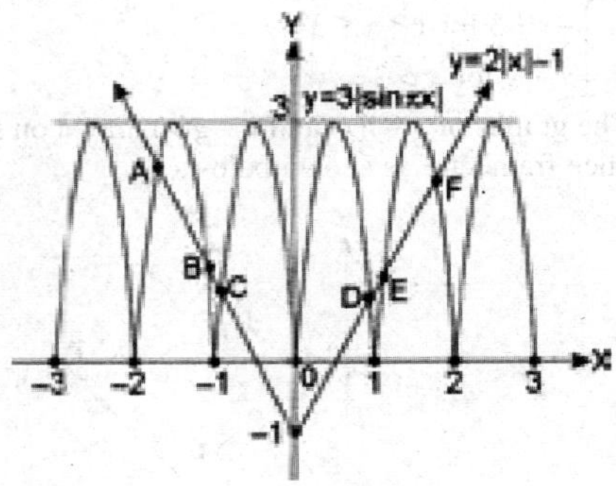

Clearly, there are 6 points of intersection, and hence, 6 solutions in (–2, 2) and no solution in $[2, \infty)$.

Also no solution in $\left(0, \frac{1}{2}\right)$.

3. (a), (b), (c) $f(x) = x^2 + 3x + 5$; $g(x) = |x - k|$

Graph of $y = f(x)$ and $y = g(x)$ drawn on same reference plane are as shown below.

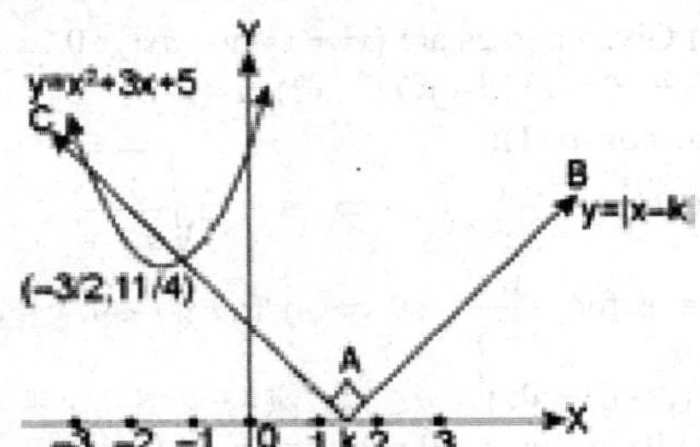

$f'(x) = 2x + 3 = \pm 1$

$\Rightarrow 2x = -3 \pm 1 \qquad \Rightarrow x = \frac{-3 \pm 1}{2} = -1, -2$

Equation of tangent to parabola $y = x^2 + 3x + 5$ with slope 1 and –1 will be at (–1, 3) and (–2, 3), respectively and are given by $(y - 3) = 1\ (x + 1)$ and $(y - 3) = -1(x + 2)$, i.e., $y = x + 4$ and $y = -x + 1$

They will intersect x-axis at (–4, 0) and (1, 0) respectively.

$\therefore$ Branch AB will touch $y = f(x)$ for $k = -4$ and AC will touch $y = f(x)$ for $k = 1$

$\Rightarrow$ $f(x) = g(x)$ has exactly one root for exactly two distinct values of k given by –4 and 1.

Clearly $f(x) \neq g(x)$ for $k \in (-4, 1)$, and hence, $f(x) = g(x)$ has no root in (–3, 1).

AB would intersect $y = f(x)$ for $k \in (-\infty, -4)$ and AC would intersect $y = f(x)$ for $k \in (1, \infty)$.

$\therefore$ $f(x) = g(x)$ has two roots for $k \in (-\infty, -4) \cup (1, \infty)$

4. (b), (c), (d) $f(x) = ||x - 1| - 2|$ and $g(x) = x + |x - 1| + \dfrac{|x-2|}{(x-2)}$;

$$g(x) = \begin{cases} 2x \text{ for } x > 2 \\ 2x - 2 \text{ for } 1 < x < 2 \text{ and } f(x) \\ 0 \text{ for } x < 1 \end{cases}$$

$$= \begin{cases} -x - 1 \text{ for } x \leq -1 \\ x + 1 \text{ for } -1 < x \leq 1 \\ -x + 3 \text{ for } 1 < x \leq 3 \\ x - 3 \text{ for } x > 3 \end{cases}$$

The graphs of $y = f(x)$ and $y = g(x)$ drawn on same reference frame are as shown below.

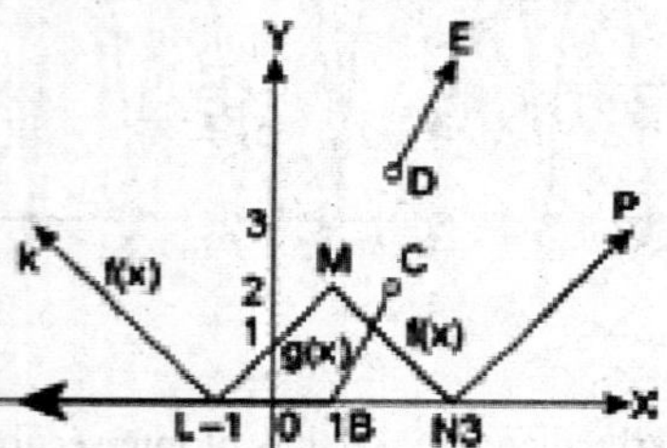

Clearly, $f(x) = g(x)$ holds at L, Q has exactly 2 solutions. Also clearly, $y = g(x)$ has a point of discontinuity at $x = 2$.

Further we observe that $y = f(x)$ has 3 points of non-differentiability, i.e., L, M and N.

5. (c), (d) Given curves are $(x^2 + y^2)y - ax^2 = 0$ ……(i) and $(x^2 + y^2) = a^2(x^2 - y^2)$ …..(2), a $\neq 1$

For curve (1):

(i) $x^2(y - a) = -y^3$ $\quad\Rightarrow\quad x = \pm\sqrt{\dfrac{y^3}{a-y}}$

$\Rightarrow$ $x \in \mathbb{R}$ for $\dfrac{y^3}{a-y} \geq 0 \Rightarrow y^3(a - y) \geq 0; y \neq a$

$\Rightarrow$ $y^3\ (y - a) \leq 0; y \neq a \quad\Rightarrow\quad y(y - a) \leq 0; y \neq a$

$\Rightarrow$ $y \in [0, a)$ for $a > 0$ and $y \in (a, 0]$ for $a < 0$

(ii) Also, the curve is symmetric about y-axis.

(iii) Curve intersect x-axis, where $y = 0$

$\Rightarrow$ $x = 0$, i.e., at origin

(iv) Horizontal asymptote is given by $y - a = 0$

(v) There is no vertical asymptote.

(vi) $x^2\left(\dfrac{dy}{dx}\right) + (y - a)(2x) = -3y^2\dfrac{dy}{dx}$

$\Rightarrow$ $\dfrac{dy}{dx}[x^2 + 3y^2] = 2x(a - y)$

$\Rightarrow$ $\dfrac{dy}{dx} = \dfrac{2x(a-y)}{x^2+3y^2} = \dfrac{(2x)}{(x^2+3y^2)}\left(\dfrac{y^3}{x^2}\right) = \dfrac{2y^3}{x(x^2+3y^2)}$

$\therefore$ $\dfrac{dy}{dx} = 0 \qquad\Rightarrow\ x = 0$ or $y = a$; but $y \neq a$

$\Rightarrow$ $x = 0 \qquad\Rightarrow\ y = 0$

$\Rightarrow$ $\dfrac{dy}{dx}$ is not defined at origin.

There is no tangent parallel to x-axis. Also, clearly $\dfrac{dy}{dx} > 0$ for $x.y > 0$ and $\dfrac{dy}{dx} < 0$ for $x.y < 0$

Thus, the graph of curve (1) will be of the type as shown below.

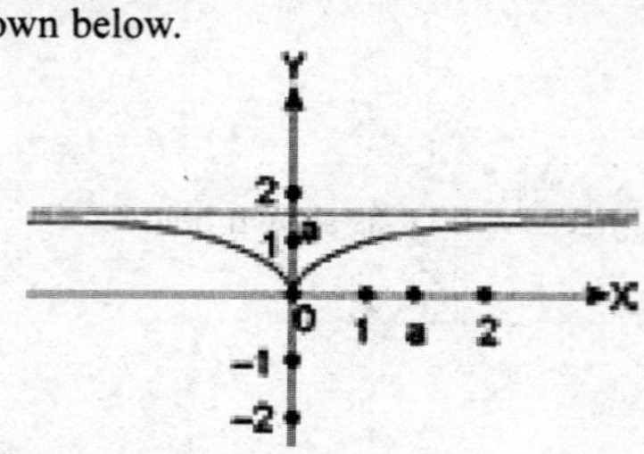

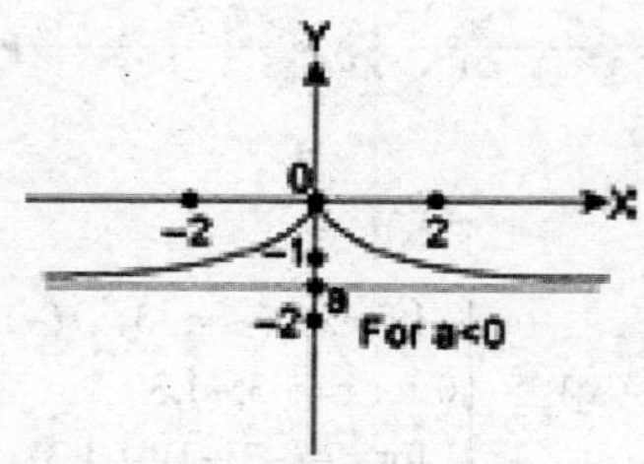

For curve (2):

(i) $x^2(1 - a^2) = -y^2(1 + a^2)$

$x^2 = \dfrac{y^2(1+a^2)}{(a^2-1)} \Rightarrow y = \pm\sqrt{\left(\dfrac{a^2-1}{a^2+1}\right)}x$

Which represent a pair of straight line through origin having their slopes of magnitude less than 1.

Also $y = \pm\sqrt{\dfrac{x^2(a^2-1)}{(a^2+1)}}$

$\Rightarrow$ $a^2 - 1 \geq 0$

$\Rightarrow$ $a \in (-\infty, -1) \cup (1, \infty)$ as given a $\neq 1$

$\therefore$ The graphs of $y = f(x)$ and $y = g(x)$ drawn on same frame of reference will be as shown below (for $a > 1$)

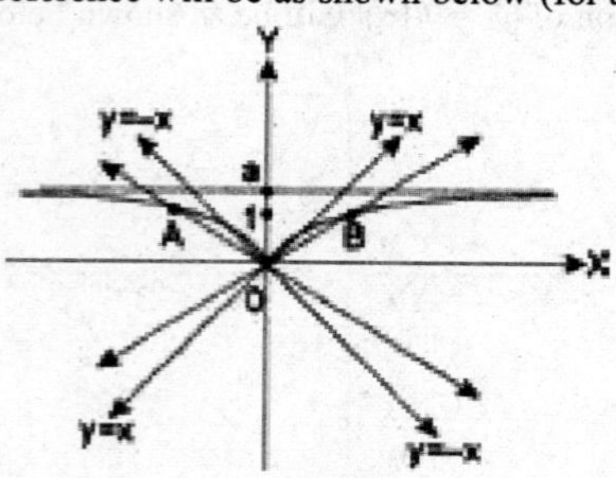

Clearly, $y = f(x)$ and $y = g(x)$ intersect each other at exactly 3 points for $a \in (-\infty, -1) \cup (1, \infty)$.
Also $(x^2 + y^2).y - ax^2 = 0$ has exactly one cusp.

6. (a), (b), (c)

C_1: $100(x^2 + y^2) = a^2 x^2 y^2$ ...(1)

C_2: $y = (a^3 - x^3)^{1/3}$ ...(2)

For C_1 :

(i) $x^2(100 - a^2 y^2) + 100 y^2 = 0$ or $y^2(100 - a^2 x^2) + 100 x^2 = 0$

$\Rightarrow$ Horizontal asymptotes are given by $y = \pm \dfrac{10}{a}$ and vertical asymptotes are $x = \pm \dfrac{10}{a}$

(ii) C_1 passes through origin.

(iii) C_1 is symmetric about x-axis and y-axis.

(iv) C_1: $\dfrac{1}{y^2} + \dfrac{1}{x^2} = \dfrac{a^2}{100} \quad \Rightarrow \quad \dfrac{1}{y^2} = \dfrac{a^2}{100} - \dfrac{1}{x^2}$

$$\Rightarrow y^2 = \frac{100x^2}{(a^2x^2 - 100)}$$

$$\Rightarrow y = \pm\frac{10x}{\sqrt{a^2x^2 - 100}} \Rightarrow x < \frac{-10}{a} \text{ or } > \frac{10}{a} \text{ at } x$$

$$= \frac{15}{a}, y = \frac{\pm\frac{150}{a}}{\sqrt{225 - 100}}$$

$$\Rightarrow y = \pm\frac{150}{a(5\sqrt{5})} = \pm\frac{30}{\sqrt{5}a} \qquad y = \pm\frac{6\sqrt{5}}{a}$$

(v) C_1 is symmetric about $y = x$

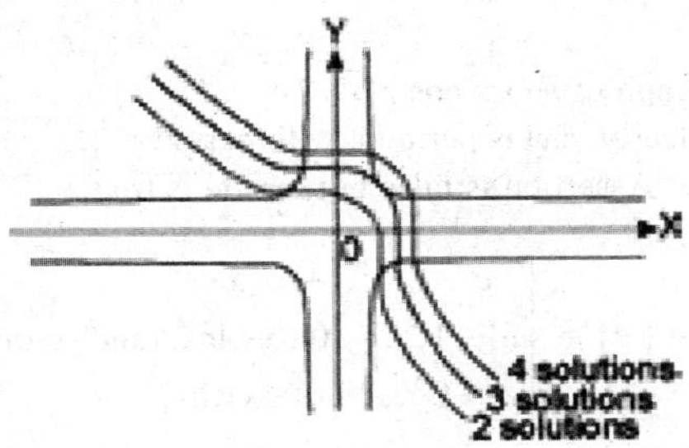

For C_2: $y^3 = a^3 - x^3$

$\Rightarrow$ Intersect x-axis, where $x = a$ and intersect y-axis, where $y = a$;

Also C_2 is symmetric about $y = x$ and also $3y^2 \dfrac{dy}{dx} = -3x^2$

$$\Rightarrow \frac{dy}{dx} = \frac{-x^2}{y^2} < 0$$

$$\Rightarrow \frac{dy}{dx} = 0 \text{ at } x = (0, a)$$

$$\Rightarrow \frac{dy}{dx} \to \infty \text{ at } (a, 0)$$

Graphs of $y = f(x)$ and $y = g(x)$ drawn on same reference frame are as shown below.

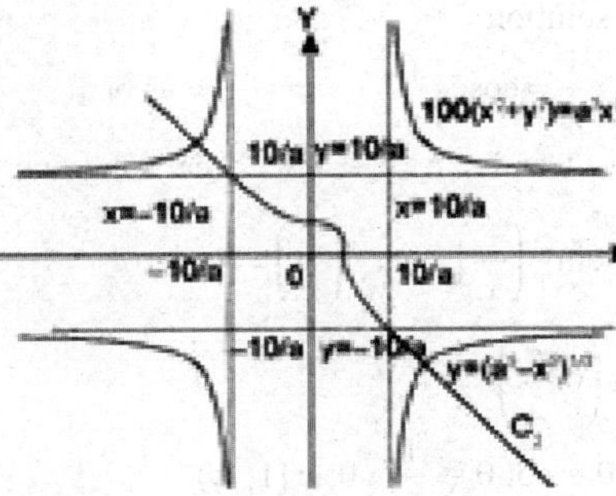

At $x = y$ for C_1: $200 y^2 = a^2 y^4$

$$\Rightarrow \frac{200}{a^2} = y^2 \Rightarrow y = \frac{\sqrt{200}}{a}$$

For C_2: $y^3 = a^3 - y^3 \Rightarrow y^3 = \dfrac{a^3}{2}$

$$\Rightarrow y = \frac{a}{3\sqrt{2}}$$

Clearly, there will be 4 points of intersection for ${}^yC_2 > {}^yC_1$, i.e., $\dfrac{a}{3\sqrt{2}} > \dfrac{\sqrt{200}}{a}$

$\Rightarrow a^2 > 3\sqrt{2}\sqrt{200} = k$ (say)

$\Rightarrow a \in (-\infty, -\sqrt{k}) \cup (\sqrt{k}, \infty)$

i.e., there will be infinitely many values of 'a'

Also for 3 points of intersection, ${}^yC_2 = {}^yC_1$

$\Rightarrow \dfrac{a}{3\sqrt{2}} = \dfrac{\sqrt{200}}{a} \Rightarrow a \pm \sqrt{3\sqrt{2}.\sqrt{200}}$, i.e., exactly two real value of 'a'.

Also there will be two points of intersection for ${}^yC_2 < {}^yC_1$

$\Rightarrow \dfrac{a}{3\sqrt{2}} < \dfrac{\sqrt{200}}{a} \Rightarrow a^2 < 3\sqrt{2}.\sqrt{200} = k$ (say)

$\Rightarrow a \in (-\sqrt{k}, \sqrt{k})$

$\Rightarrow$ There will be 2 points of intersection for infinitely many values 'a'.

7. (a), (c), (d)

(a) $\sin^{-1}\dfrac{1}{x} = \cos^{-1}\dfrac{1}{x} \Rightarrow \dfrac{1}{x} \in (0, 1]$

$$\Rightarrow \sin^{-1}\frac{1}{x} + \sin^{-1}\frac{1}{x} = \frac{\pi}{2} \Rightarrow 2\sin^{-1}\frac{1}{x} = \frac{\pi}{2} \Rightarrow \sin^{-1}\frac{1}{x} = \frac{\pi}{4}$$

$$\Rightarrow \frac{1}{x} = \frac{1}{\sqrt{2}} \Rightarrow x = \frac{1}{\sqrt{2}} \Rightarrow \text{ only one solution}$$

(b) Let $\sin^{-1}\dfrac{1}{x} = \tan^{-1}\dfrac{1}{x} = \theta$; where $\theta \in \left(\dfrac{-\pi}{2}, \dfrac{\pi}{2}\right)$

$$\Rightarrow \sin\theta = \frac{1}{x} = \tan\theta \neq 0$$

$$\Rightarrow \cos\theta = 1 \Rightarrow \theta = \frac{\pi}{2} \notin \left(\frac{-\pi}{2}, \frac{\pi}{2}\right)$$

$\therefore$ No solution

(c) $\sin^{-1}\dfrac{1}{x} = \text{cosec}^{-1}\dfrac{1}{x} \Rightarrow \dfrac{1}{x} = -1 \text{ or } 1$

$\Rightarrow x = -1 \text{ or } 1 \quad \Rightarrow$ 2 real solutions.

(d) Let $\sin^{-1}\left(\dfrac{1}{x}\right) = \cot^{-1}\left(\dfrac{1}{x}\right) = \theta$

$\Rightarrow \theta \in \left(0, \dfrac{\pi}{2}\right)$

$\Rightarrow \sin\theta = \cot\theta = \dfrac{1}{x} > 0;\ x\ [1, \infty)$

$\sin^2\theta = \cos\theta \quad \Rightarrow \cos^2\theta + \cos\theta - 1 = 0$

$\Rightarrow \cos\theta = \dfrac{-1 \pm \sqrt{1+4}}{2} \quad \Rightarrow \cos\theta = \dfrac{-1-\sqrt{5}}{2}, \dfrac{\sqrt{5}-1}{2}$ but

$\dfrac{-1-\sqrt{5}}{2} < -1 \Rightarrow \cos\theta = \dfrac{\sqrt{5}-1}{2}$

$\Rightarrow \sin\theta = \sqrt{1 - \left(\dfrac{\sqrt{5}-1}{2}\right)^2}$

$\Rightarrow \sqrt{\dfrac{4-(6-2\sqrt{5})}{4}} = \sqrt{\dfrac{2\sqrt{5}-2}{4}} = \dfrac{\sqrt{\sqrt{5}-1}}{\sqrt{2}}$

$\Rightarrow \cot\theta = \dfrac{\cos\theta}{\sin\theta} = \dfrac{\sqrt{\sqrt{5}-1}}{\sqrt{2}} = \dfrac{1}{x}$

$\Rightarrow x = \dfrac{\sqrt{2}}{\sqrt{5}-1} > 1 \text{ as } 2 > \sqrt{5}-1 \text{ as } 3 > \sqrt{5}$

$\therefore \sin^{-1}\left(\dfrac{1}{x}\right) = \cot^{-1}\left(\dfrac{1}{x}\right)$ has only one solution $x = \dfrac{\sqrt{2}}{\sqrt{\sqrt{5}-1}}$

SECTION–V: ASSERTION AND REASON TYPE

1. (a) Reason is clearly true.

$\therefore$ a = 0 and $y = 2x^2 - bx + c$ should have $x = 1$ as its axis.

$\Rightarrow \dfrac{b}{4} = 1 \quad \Rightarrow b = 4$

$\Rightarrow a + 2b = 8$

2. (a) Clearly Assertion is true, and therefore, area enclosed by $y = f(x)$ and x-axis between ordinate $x = a$ and $x = b$ is same as that of enclosed by $y = f(x + k)$ and x-axis between ordinates $x = a - k$ and $x = b - k$.

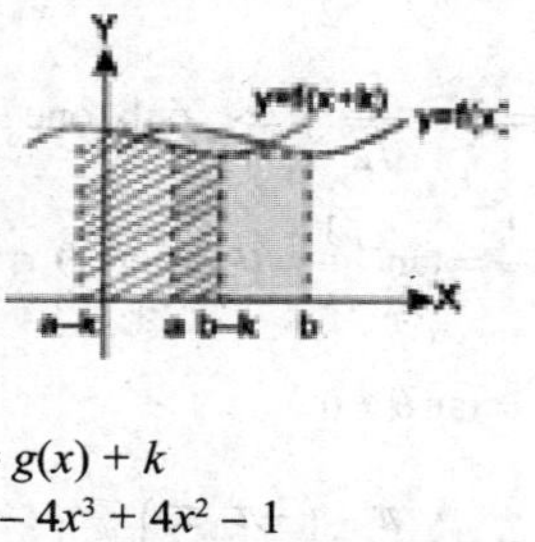

3. (a) Let $f(x) = g(x) + k$

$g(x) = x^4 - 4x^3 + 4x^2 - 1$

$g'(x) = 4x^3 - 12x^2 + 8x = 4x(x^2 - 3x + 2) = 4x(x-1)(x-2)$

Clearly $x = 1$ is local maxima and $x = 0, 2$ are local minima and the graph is shown in the figure.

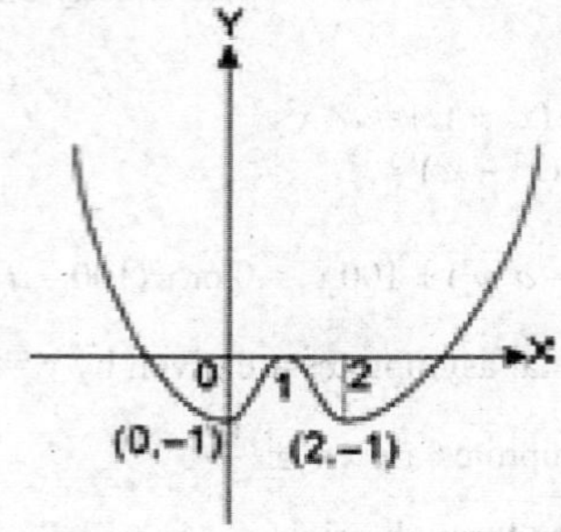

$f(1) = 1$ and $f(0) = f(2) = -1$

$g(x)$ if shifted upwards by k where $k > 1$ lies above x-axis.

$\therefore f(x) = g(x) + k$ has no real roof if $k > 1$

4. (d) We have $f(x) = \cos\pi[x] = \begin{cases} 1, x \in [2n, 2n+1) \\ -1, x \in [2n+1, 2n+2) \end{cases}$ where $n \in \mathbb{Z}$

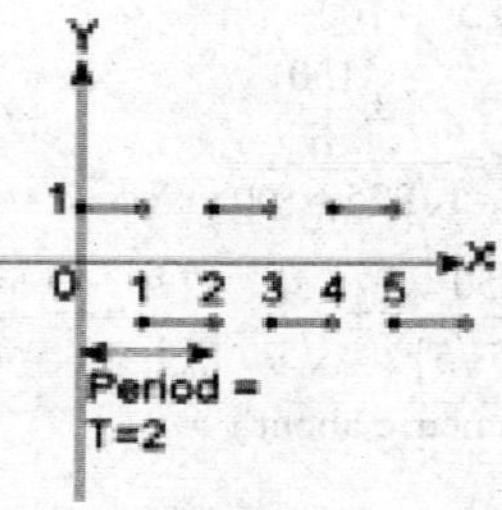

Graph of $f(x) = \cos\pi[x]$

Clearly, $f(x)$ is periodic with period = 2.

$\Rightarrow$ Assertion is false but reason is true.

5. (d) $y = \{e^x\} = \begin{cases} e^x & ; \quad -\infty < x < 0 \\ e^x - 1 & ; \quad 0 \le x < \ln 2 \\ e^x - 2 & ; \quad \ln 2 \le x < \ln 3 \end{cases}$ and so on

Clearly $f(x)$ is a periodic on R.

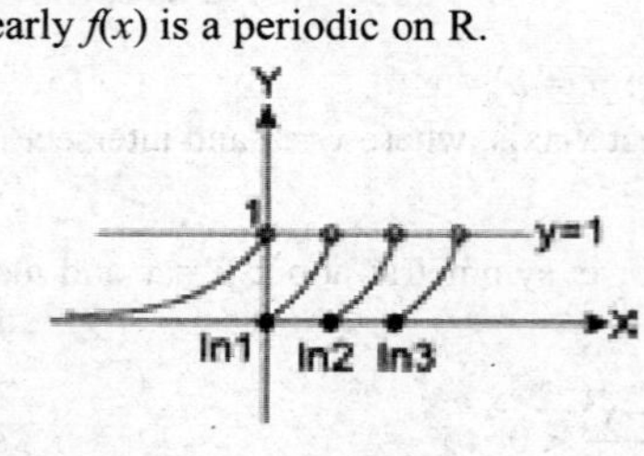

$\Rightarrow$ Assertion is false but reason is true.

6. (d) A is false as it has a period equal to 2 and R is true

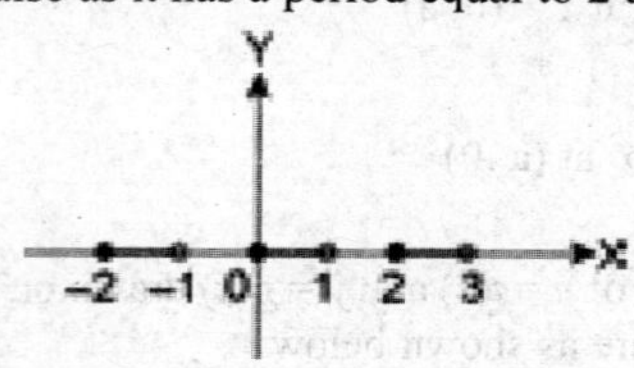

$$f(x)=\begin{cases}0; & -2\le x<-1\\ \text{N.D}; & -1\le x<0\\ 0 & 0\le x<1\\ \text{N.D}; & 1\le x<2\\ 0 & 2\le x<3\end{cases}$$

⇒ period 2

SECTION-VI: COMPREHENSION PASSAGE

Passage A:

1. **(a)** $y = |f(x)|$

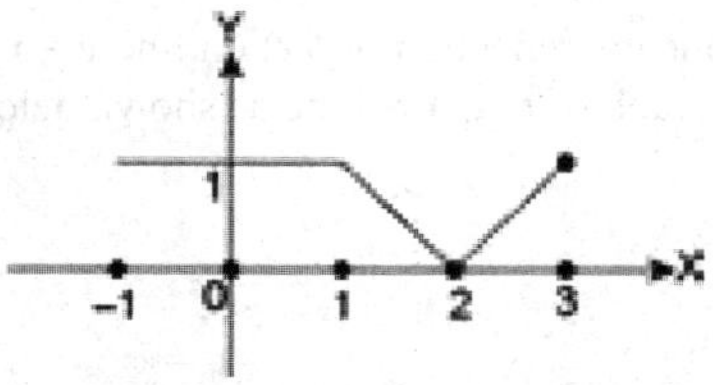

Clearly, $|f(x)|$ increases in (2, 3)

2. **(b)** $y = -|f(x)|$ has following graph in the interval (–1, 3), $f(x)$ has sharp turns at P and Q, having abscissa $x = 1$ and $x = 2$ respectively.

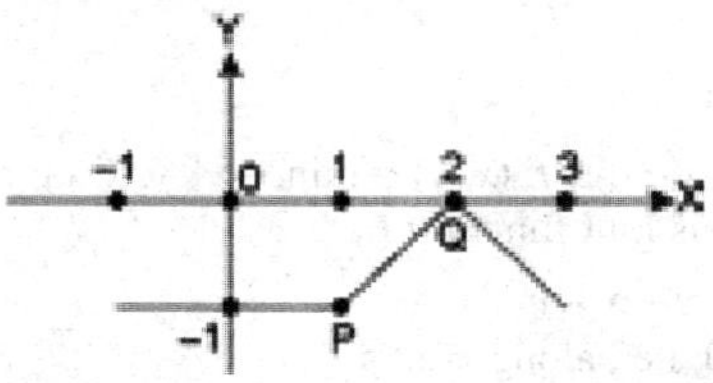

Thus, $x = 1$ and $x = 2$ are the points of non-differentiability.

3. **(c)** $y = f(-|x|)$ is as shown below.

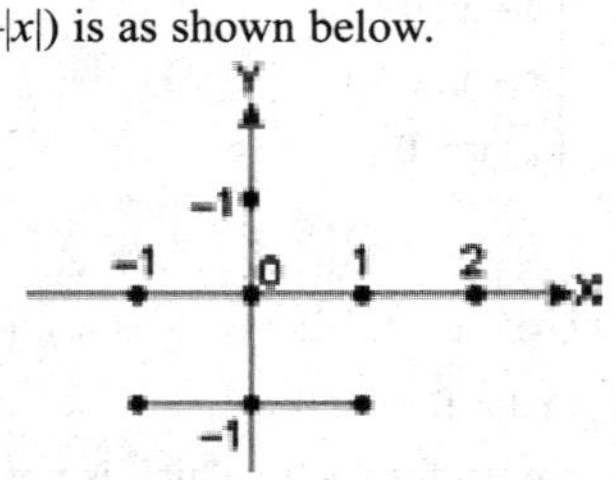

Clearly $y = f(-|x|) = -1\ \forall\ x \in [-1, 1]$
⇒ It is a constant function.

4. **(c)** $g(x) = \frac{1}{2}(|f(x)| + f(x))$

$$=\begin{cases}\frac{1}{2}(1+(-1));-1\le x\le 1\\ \frac{1}{2}((2-x)+(x-2));1\le x\le 2\\ \frac{1}{2}(f(x)+f(x))=(x-2);2\le x\le 3\end{cases}\quad \text{or } g(x)$$

$$=\begin{cases}0;-1\le x\le 2\\ (x-2);2\le x\le 3\end{cases}$$

⇒ $g(x)$ is a constant function in [–1, 2]

5. **(b)** $h(x) = \frac{1}{2}(|f(x)| - f(x)) = \begin{cases}1;-1\le x\le 1\\ 2-x;1\le x\le 2\\ 0;2\le x\le 3\end{cases}$

⇒ $h(x)$ is a constant function in $[-1, 1] \cup [2, 3]$

6. **(c)** $g(x) = f\left(\frac{|x|}{x}\right) = \begin{cases}f(1)\text{ for } x>0\\ f(-1)\text{ for } x<0\\ \text{Not defined for } x=0\end{cases}\quad g(x)$

$$=\begin{cases}-1\text{ for } x>0 \text{ and } x<0\\ \text{Not defined at } x=0\end{cases}$$

⇒ $g(x)$ is a constant function on domain $(-, \infty) - \{0\}$

Passage B:

$$f(x)=\frac{(x^2-1)(x-3)}{x^2(x+2)}$$

7. **(b)** $y=\frac{(x^2-1)(x-3)}{x^2(x+2)}$

Horizontal asymptotes are given by $y = c$; where $C = \lim\limits_{x\to\infty}\frac{(x^2-1)(x-3)}{x^2(x+2)}, \lim\limits_{x\to-\infty}\frac{(x^2-1)(x-3)}{x^2(x+2)}$

$$\therefore\ C=\lim_{x\to\infty}\frac{\left(1-\frac{1}{x^2}\right)\left(1-\frac{3}{x}\right)}{\left(1+\frac{2}{x}\right)}=1$$

∴ $y = 1$ is a horizontal asymptote

8. **(a), (c)** Vertical asymptote(s) are given by $x = c$; where $c = \lim\limits_{x\to\pm\infty} x$

Now $y \pm \infty$ ⇒ $x^2(x + 2) \to 0$
⇒ $x = 0$ or $x = -2$
⇒ $x = 0$ and $x = -2$ are two vertical asymptotes to $y = f(x)$

9. **(c)** **(i)** $f(x) = 0$ has roots, $x = \neq 1$ and $x = 3$
(ii) Horizontal asymptote is $y = 1$
(iii) Vertical asymptotes are $x = 0, x = -2$
(iv) $f(x) = \frac{(x^2-1)(x-3)}{x^2(x+2)}$
⇒ $f(x) > 0$ for $x \in (-\infty, -2) \cup (-1, 1) \cup (3, \infty)$ and $f(x) < 0$ for $x \in (-2, -1) \cup (1, 3)$.
From above, we conclude that the graph of $y = f(x)$ will be as shown below.

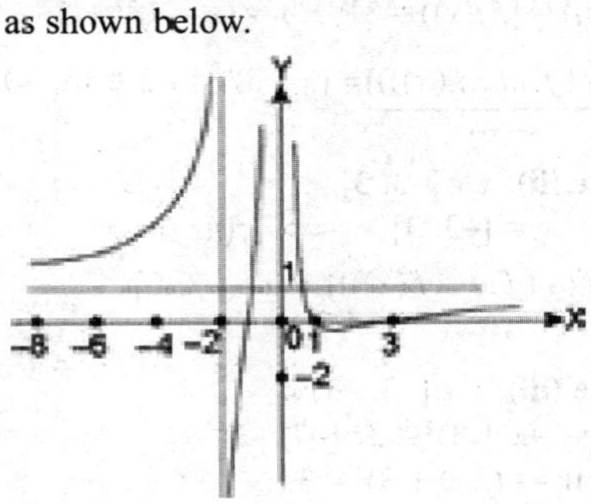

Passage C:

10. (c) From the graph, $f(-5) = 9$ and $f(4) = 9$

$\Rightarrow f(-5).f(4) = 81$

11. (b) Clearly $x = -6, -3, 1, 7, 7$ are roots of $f(x) = 0$.

$\therefore$ Let $f(x) = a(x + 6)(x + 3)(x - 1)(x - 7)^2$

Now $f(-5) = 9 \Rightarrow a(1)(-2)(-6)(-12)^2 = 9$

$$\Rightarrow a = \frac{9}{144 \times 12} = \frac{1}{192}$$

$$\Rightarrow f(x) = \frac{(x-1)(x+3)(x+6)(x-7)^2}{192}$$

12. (c) $f(f(-5)) = f(9) = \dfrac{(8)(12)(15)(14)}{192} = 30$

Passage D:

$$f(x) = \begin{cases} (x-3)^3 + 3; \text{if } x \in (3,5] \\ x; \text{if } x \in [-3,3] \\ -(x+3)^2 - 3; \text{if } x \in [-5,3) \end{cases}$$

13. (c) $f'(x) = \begin{cases} 3(x-3)^2 \text{ if } x \in (3,5) \\ 1 \text{ if } x \in (-3,3) \\ -2(x+3) \text{ if } x \in (-5,3) \end{cases}$

$\Rightarrow f(x)$ is increasing function on $\mathbb{R}$

Also $f''(x) = \begin{cases} 6(x-3) \text{ if } x \in (3,5) \\ 0 \text{ if } x \in (-3,3) \\ -2 \text{ if } x \in (-5,-3) \end{cases}$

$\Rightarrow f(x)$ is concave upwards on (3, 5) concave downwards on (–5, –3) linear on (–3, 3).

Thus, the graph of $f(x)$ would be as shown below.

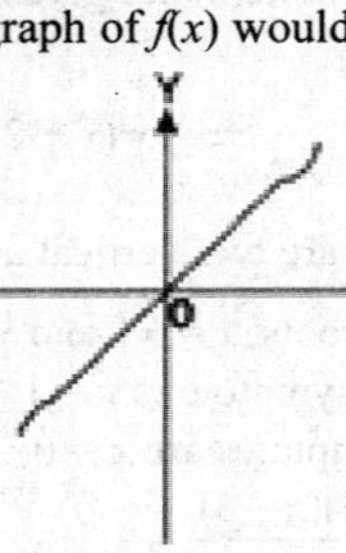

14. (d) Case (i): $x \in (3, 5]$

$\Rightarrow f(x) = (x - 3)^3 + 3 \quad \Rightarrow f(x) \in (3, 11]$

$\Rightarrow f(f(x)) = (f(x) - 3)^3 + 3 = (x - 3)^9 + 3$

$\Rightarrow f(f(x)) = [f(f(x)) - 3]^3 + 3 = (x - 3)^{27} + 3$

$\Rightarrow \underbrace{f(f(f.......f(x))))}_{n-times} = (x-3)^{(3^n)} + 3 \in (3, \infty)$

Case (ii): $x \in [-3, 3]$

$\Rightarrow f(x) = x \in [-3, 3] \quad \Rightarrow f(f(x)) = x$

$\Rightarrow \underbrace{f(f(f(f.......f(x)))))}_{n-times} = x \in [-3,3]$

Case (iii): $x \in [-3, -3)$

$\Rightarrow f(x) = -(x + 3)^2 - 3 \in [-7, -3)$

$\Rightarrow f(f(x)) = -(f(x) + 3)^2 - 3$

$\Rightarrow f(f(x)) = -[-(x + 3)^2]^2 - 3 = -(x + 3)^4 - 3 < -3$

$\Rightarrow f(f(f(x))) = -(f(f(x)) + 3)^2 - 3 = -[-(x + 3)^4]^2 - 3 = -(x + 3)^8 - 3 < -3$

$\Rightarrow \underbrace{f(f(f(......(f(x)))).......}_{n-times} = -(x+3)^{(2^n)} - 3 < -3$

$\therefore$ From above, we observe that the composition of n – $f(x)$'s takes value $\in (-\infty, 3) \cup (3, \infty)$

$\Rightarrow$ Can take all 0, 4 and 8 values.

15. (d) $y = \begin{cases} (x-3)^3 + 3; \text{if } x \in (3,5] \\ x; \text{if } x \in [-3,3] \\ -(x+3)^2 - 3; \text{if } x \in [-5,-3) \end{cases}$

$\therefore f^{-1}(x)$ is the reflection of $f(x)$ on line $y = x$

$\therefore$ The graph of $f^{-1}(x)$ will be as shown below.

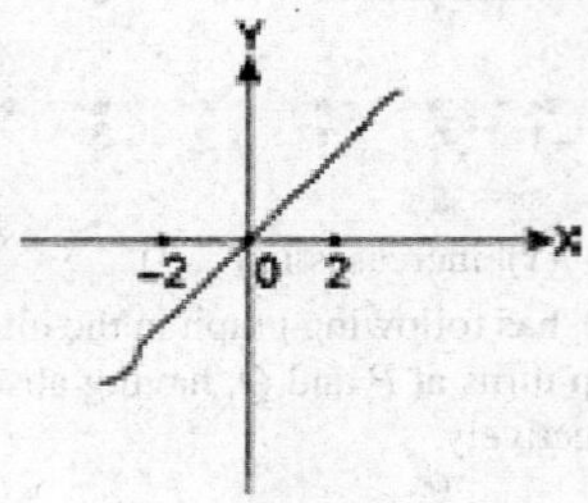

Passage E:

$f_1(x, y) = |x| + |y|$; $f_2(x, y) = \min.(x + y, x - y)$; $f_3(x, y) = [x] + [y]$; $[x]$ is gint function.

Now, $x + y = x - y$

$\Rightarrow y = 0$, i.e., along x-axis

Now, $x + y > x - y \Rightarrow y > 0$ and $x + y < x - y$

$\Rightarrow y < 0$

$\therefore f_2(x, y) = \begin{cases} x + y; y < 0 \\ x - y; y > 0 \\ x; y = 0 \end{cases}$

16. (b), (c)

(a) $f_1(x, y) < f_2(x, y) \Rightarrow |x| + |y| < f_2(x, y)$

$\Rightarrow \begin{cases} |x| - y < x + y \text{ for } y < 0; \\ |x| + y < x + y \text{ for } y > 0; \\ |x| < x \text{ for } y = 0 \end{cases}$ which is not always true for instance for $y > 0$

$|x| + y < x - y$, for $x > 0$;

$\Rightarrow x + y < x - y \quad \Rightarrow y < -y$

$\Rightarrow y < 0$; which is false.

(b) $f_2(x, y) < f_3(x, y)$

$\Rightarrow \begin{cases} x + y < [x] + [y] \text{ for } y < 0 \\ x - y < [x] + [y] \text{ for } y > 0 \\ x < [x] + [y] \text{ for } y = 0 \end{cases}$ but for $x, y \in \mathbb{Z}^+$

$\Rightarrow x - y < [x] + [y]$ for $x, y \in \mathbb{Z}^+$

$\Rightarrow x - [x] < y + [y]$ for $x, y \in \mathbb{Z}^+$

$\Rightarrow \{x\} < y + [y]$

$\Rightarrow \{x\} < 2y$; as $y \in \mathbb{Z}^+ \Rightarrow [y] = y$

$\Rightarrow$ $0 < 2y$ as $x \in \mathbb{Z}^+$ $\Rightarrow$ $\{x\} = 0$

$\Rightarrow$ $0 < y$ which is true as $y \in \mathbb{Z}^+$

(c) $x, y \in \mathbb{Z}^-$

$\therefore$ $f_1(x, y) = -f_3(x, y)$

$\Rightarrow$ $|x| + |y| = -([x] + [y])$

$\Rightarrow$ $-x - y = -x - y$, which is true

17. (c) $h_1(x) = f_1(\sin\{x\}, \sin \pi x)\ \forall\ x \in \mathbb{R}$,
$h_2(x) = f_2(x, \sin x)\ \forall\ 0 < x < 1$,
$h_3(x) = f_3(x, -x)\ \forall\ x \in \mathbb{R}$

$\Rightarrow$ $h_1(x) = |\sin\{x\}| + |\sin \pi x|$

$\because$ $|\sin\{1 + x\}| = |\sin\{y\}| \Rightarrow$ period is 1 and $|\sin \pi x|$ has period $\dfrac{\pi}{\pi} = 1$

$\therefore$ $h_1(x)$ is periodic with period 1.
Clearly, $h_1(1 + x) = |\sin\{1 + x\}| + |\sin \pi(1 + x)| = |\sin\{x\}| + |-\sin \pi x| = |\sin\{x\}| + |\sin \pi x| = h_1(x)$

(b) $h_2(x) = f_2(x, \sin x) = \min.\{x + \sin x, x - \sin x\}$
Now h_2: $(0, 1) \to (0, 1)$

$\Rightarrow$ $x \in (0, 1)$ $\Rightarrow$ $\sin x > 0$

$\Rightarrow$ $\sin x > -\sin x$ $\Rightarrow$ $x + \sin x > x - \sin x$

$\Rightarrow$ $h_2(x) = x - \sin x$ $\Rightarrow$ $h'_2(x) = 1 - \cos x = 2\sin^2\dfrac{x}{2} > 0$

$\Rightarrow$ $h_2(x)$ is increasing function

$\Rightarrow$ $h_2(x)$ is injective
Also $h_2(x)$ is continuous and injective

$\Rightarrow$ Range of $h_2(x) = (h_2(0), h_2(1)) = (0, |-\sin|) \subset (0, 1)$ (property)

$\Rightarrow$ h_2: $(0, 1) \to (0, 1)$ is not subjective

$\Rightarrow$ h_2 is not bijective

(c) $h_3(x) = f_3(x, -x) = [x] + [-x] = -1$

$\Rightarrow$ $h_3(x) = -1$

$\Rightarrow$ $h_3(x)$ is a constant function, and hence is periodic.

18. (a) $f_1(x, y) > f_3(x, y)$

$\Rightarrow$ $|x| + |y| > [x] + [y]$
It is true for $x, y < 0$

(b) $f_2(x, y) = x + y$; $x, y < 0$

$\Rightarrow$ $\min.\{x + y, x - y\} = x + y$; $x, y < 0$

$\because$ $y < -y$ as $y < 0$

$\Rightarrow$ $x + y < x - y$ $\Rightarrow$ $\min\{x + y, x - y\} = (x + y)$

(c) $f_3(x, y) = f_3(-x, -y)$ $\Rightarrow$ $[x] + [y] = [-x] + [-y]$

$\Rightarrow$ $[x] + [y] = (-1 - [x]) + [-1 - [y])$ for $x, y \notin \mathbb{Z}$

$\Rightarrow$ $2[x] + 2[y] = -2$ for $x, y \notin \mathbb{Z}$

$\Rightarrow$ $[x] + [y] = -1$ for $x, y \notin \mathbb{Z}$

$\Rightarrow$ $[y] = -1 - [x]$ $\Rightarrow$ $[y] = [-x]$

$\Rightarrow$ $y = -x$

$\Rightarrow$ (c) can hold for $y = -x$ and $x, y \notin \mathbb{Z}$

(d) $f_1(x, y) = f_3(x, y)$; $x, y \in \mathbb{R} - \mathbb{Z}$

$\Rightarrow$ $|x| + |y| = [x] + [y]$; $x, y \in \mathbb{R} - \mathbb{Z}$

Case (i): If $x > 0, y > 0$

$\Rightarrow$ $x + y = [x] + [y]$ $\Rightarrow$ $(x - [x]) + (y - [y]) = 0$

$\Rightarrow$ $\{x\} + \{y\} = 0$ $\Rightarrow$ $\{y\} = \{y\} = 0$

$\Rightarrow$ $x, y, \in \mathbb{Z}$ but here $x, y \in \mathbb{R} - \mathbb{Z}$

$\therefore$ Equality does not hold.

Case (ii): If $x > 0, y < 0$

$\Rightarrow$ $x - y = [x] + [y]$

$\Rightarrow$ $\{x\} = y + [y]$ impossible, as L.H.S > 0 and R.H.S < 0

Case (iii): If $x < 0, y < 0$

$\Rightarrow$ $-x - y = [x] + [y]$ impossible as L.H.S > 0 and R.H.S < 0

Case (iv): if $x < 0, y > 0$ $\Rightarrow$ $-x + y = [x] + [y]$

$\Rightarrow$ $y - [y] = x + [x]$

$\Rightarrow$ $\{y\} = x + [x]$ impossible as L.H.S > 0; R.H.S < 0

Passage F:

H_1: $x^2 - 4y^2 + 4$; H_2: $x^2 - 9y^2 - \dfrac{(1-a)}{(1+a)}$

$H_1 = 0$ $\Rightarrow$ $x^2 - 4y^2 = -4$

$\Rightarrow$ $\dfrac{y^2}{(1)} - \dfrac{x^2}{4} = 1$ ...(i)

Which is a hyperbola of the form $\dfrac{y^2}{a^2} - \dfrac{x^2}{b^2} = 1$, having asymptotes given by $y = \dfrac{\pm a}{b}x$, i.e., $y = \pm\dfrac{1}{2}x$

$H_2 = 0$ $\Rightarrow$ $x^2 - 9y^2 = \dfrac{(1-a)}{(1+a)}$ ...(ii)

Case (i): when $\dfrac{1-a}{1+a} > 0$, i.e., $a \in (-1, 1)$

In this case (2) will be a hyperbola of the form $\dfrac{x^2}{\left(\sqrt{\dfrac{1-a}{1+a}}\right)^2} - \dfrac{y^2}{\left(\dfrac{1}{3}\sqrt{\dfrac{1-a}{1+a}}\right)^2} = 1$ having its asymptotes,

$y = \pm\dfrac{b}{a}x$ i.e., $y = \pm\dfrac{1}{3}x$

Thus, $H_1 = 0$ and $H_2 = 0$ will be hyperbolas as shown below

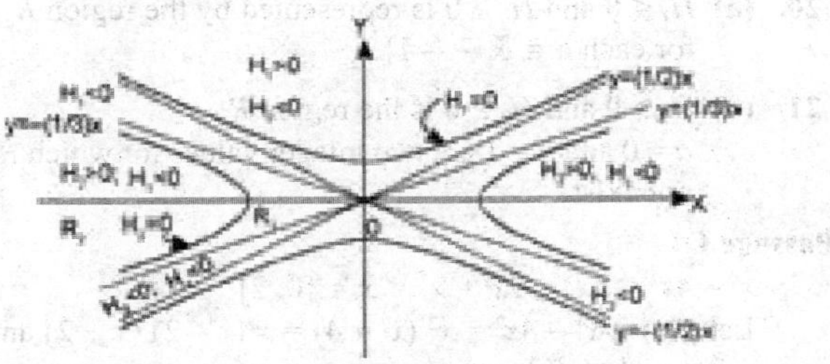

Case (ii): When $\dfrac{1-a}{1+a} < 0$, i.e., $a \in (-\infty, -1) \cup (1, \infty)$

In this case (2) will be a hyperbolas of the form $ay^2 - x^2 = \dfrac{(a-1)}{(a+1)}$ or $\dfrac{y^2}{\left(\dfrac{1}{3}\sqrt{\dfrac{a-1}{a+1}}\right)^2} - \dfrac{x^2}{\left(\sqrt{\dfrac{a-1}{a+1}}\right)^2} = 1$ with its asymptotes given by $y = \pm\dfrac{1}{3}x$

Thus, $H_1 = 0$ and $H_2 = 0$ will be hyperbola as shown below.

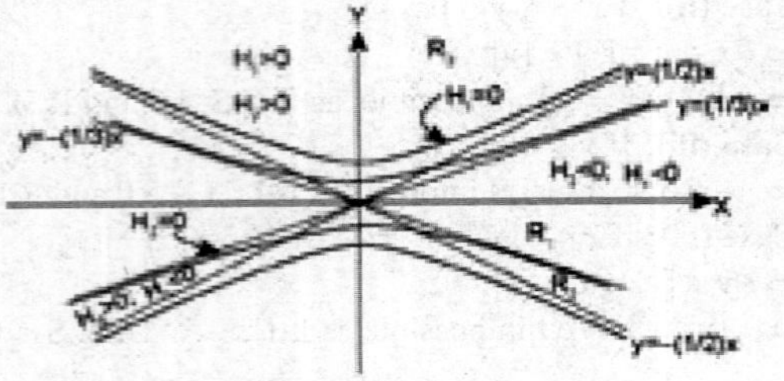

or

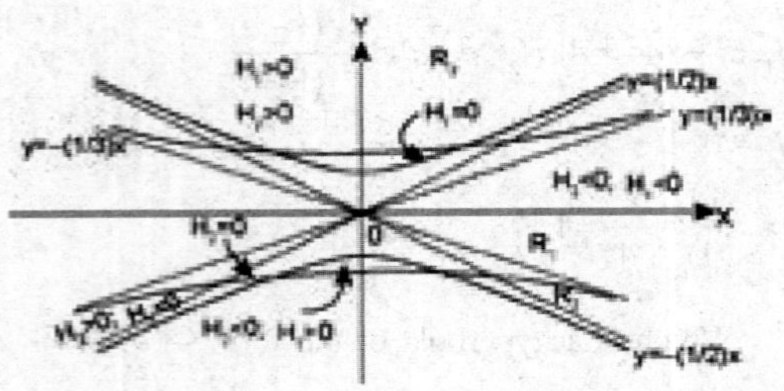

Case (iii): a = 1, In this case (2) becomes, H_2: $x^2 - 9y^2$

$\therefore$ $H_2 = 0$ is a pair of straight lines given by $y = \pm\frac{1}{3}x$

$\therefore$ $H_1 = 0$ and $H_2 = 0$ will be represented as shown below.

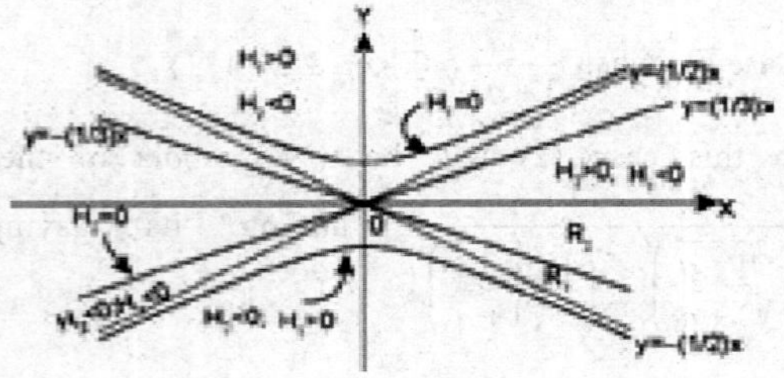

19. (d) From above we conclude that, $H_1 \le 0$ and $H_2 \le 0$ is the region R_1 exists for each a $\in \mathbb{R} - \{-1\}$.

20. (a) $H_1 \le 0$ and $H_2 \ge 0$ is represented by the region R_2 exists for each a $\in \mathbb{R} - \{-1\}$.

21. (d) $H_1 \ge 0$ and $H_2 \ge 0$ is the region R_3.

$\therefore$ $a = 0$ and $a = 1$ are two integer values for which R_3 does not exist.

Passage G:

$x^4 - 4x^2 \le f(x) \le 2x^2 - x^3 \;\forall\; x \in [0, 2]$

Let $g(x) = x^4 - 4x^2 = x^2(x^2 - 4) = x^2(x - 2)(x + 2)$ and $h(x) = 2x^2 - x^3 = x^2(2 - x)$

The graphs of $y = g(x)$ and $y = h(x)$ are as shown below.

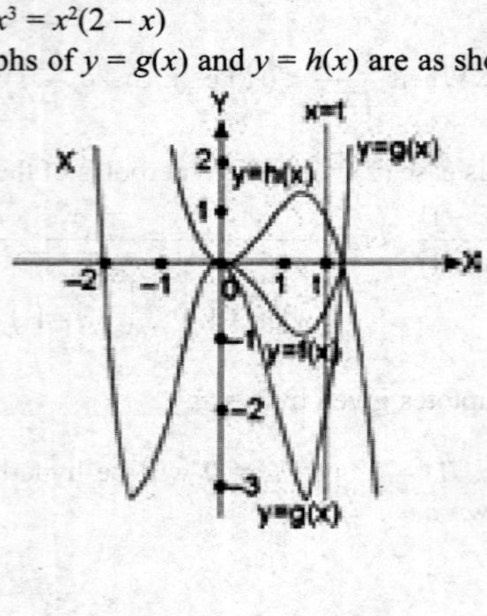

Now, $g(x) \le f(x) \le h(x) \;\forall\; x \in [0, 2]$

A.T.Q. $\int_0^t (f(x) - [x^4 - 4x^2]dx = n\int_0^t [(2x^2 - x^3) - f(x)]dx;$

$0 \le t \le 2$

$\Rightarrow \int_0^t f(x)\,dx -$

$$\left[\frac{t^5}{5} - \frac{4t^3}{3}\right] = n\left[\frac{2t^3}{3} - \frac{t^4}{4}\right] - n\int_0^t f(x)dx; 0 \le t \le 2$$

$$\Rightarrow (n+1)\int_0^t f(x)dx = n\left(\frac{2t^3}{3} - \frac{t^4}{4}\right) + \left(\frac{t^5}{5} - \frac{4t^3}{3}\right);\; 0 \le t \le 2$$

$$\Rightarrow \int_0^t f(x)dx = \left(\frac{n}{n+1}\right)\left[\frac{2t^3}{3} - \frac{t^4}{4}\right] + \frac{1}{(n+1)}\left[\frac{t^5}{5} - \frac{4t^3}{3}\right]$$

$$\Rightarrow f(t) = \frac{n}{(n+1)}\left[\frac{2}{3}(3t^2) - \frac{1}{4}(4t^3)\right] + \frac{1}{(n+1)}\left[t^4 - 4t^2\right]$$

$$\Rightarrow f(t) = \frac{n}{(n+1)}(2t^2 - t^3) + \frac{1}{(n+1)}(t^4 - 4t^2)$$

$$\Rightarrow f' = \frac{n}{(n+1)}\left[4t - 3t^2\right] + \frac{1}{(n+1)}(4t^3 - 8t)$$

22. (c) for $n = 1$; $f'(t)$

$$= 2t^2 - \frac{3t^2}{2} - 2t \Rightarrow f'(x) = 0 \Rightarrow \left(\frac{4t^3 - 3t^2 - 4t}{2}\right) = 0$$

$\Rightarrow t(4t^2 - 3t - 4) = 0$

$\Rightarrow t = 0$ or $t = \frac{3 \pm \sqrt{73}}{2}$

Now $f''(t) = \frac{1}{2}(12t^2 - 6t - 4) = 6t^2 - 3t - 2$

$f''(0) = -2$

$\Rightarrow$ $t = 0$ is a point local maxima and $\frac{3 + \sqrt{73}}{2} > 2$

$\therefore$ $f(x)$ has a local minima at $x = t = \frac{3 - \sqrt{73}}{2}$

23. (c) $f(x) = \frac{n}{(n+1)}(2x^2 - x^3) + \frac{1}{(n+1)}(x^4 - 4x^2)$

$$\Rightarrow f'(x) = \frac{n}{(n+1)}(4x - 3x^2) + \frac{1}{(n+1)}(4x^3 - 8x)$$

$$\Rightarrow f''(x) = \frac{n}{(n+1)}(4 - 6x) + \frac{1}{n+1}(12x^2 - 8)$$

At point of inflexion, $f''(x) = 0$

$\Rightarrow$ $n(4 - 6x) + (12x^2 - 8) = 0$

$\Rightarrow$ $n(2 - 3x) + (6x^2 - 4) = 0$

For $n = 2$, $4 - 6x + 6x^2 - 4 = 0$

$\Rightarrow$ $6x^2 - 6x = 0$

$\Rightarrow$ $x(x - 1) = 0$

$\Rightarrow$ $x = 0$ or $x = 1$

$\therefore$ $f(x)$ attains a point of inflexion at $x = 0$ as $x = 1$

24. (b) $\int_{-1}^{1} f(x)dx = \int_{-1}^{1}\left[\frac{n}{n+1}(2x^2 - x^3) + \frac{1}{(n+1)}(x^4 - 4x^2)\right]dx$

$$= 4\int_0^1 \frac{n}{(n+1)}(x^2)dx + \frac{2}{(n+1)}\int_0^1 x^4 dx - \frac{8}{(n+1)}\int_0^1 x^2 dx$$

$$= \frac{4n}{(n+1)}\cdot\left[\frac{x^3}{3}\right]_0^1 + \frac{2}{(n+1)}\left[\frac{x^5}{5}\right]_0^1 - \frac{8}{(n+1)}\left[\frac{x^3}{3}\right]_0^1$$

$$= \frac{4n}{3(n+1)} + \frac{2}{5(n+1)} - \frac{8}{3(n+1)}$$

$$= \frac{4n}{3(n+1)} + \frac{2}{5(n+1)} - \frac{8}{3(n+1)}$$

$$= \frac{20n + 6 - 40}{15(n+1)} = \frac{20n - 34}{15(n+1)} = \frac{2}{15(n+1)}(10n - 17)$$

SECTION–VII: COLUMN MATCHING

1. (i) → (d); (ii) →(a); (iii) →(d); (iv) →(b)

(i) $[x] = \cos^{-1} x$ ...(i)

$[x] \in \{0, \pm1, \pm2, \pm3, \ldots\}$ and $\cos^{-1} x \in [0, \pi]$

∴ (i) can holds for $\cos^{-1} x \in \{0, 1, 2, 3\}$

⇒ $[x] \in \{0, 1, 2, 3\}$

⇒ $x \in [0, 4)$

But for $y = \cos^{-1} x$; $x \in [-1, 1]$

∴ $x \in [-1, 1] \cap [0, 4]$

⇒ $x \in [0, 1]$

⇒ $[x] = 0$ or 1

If $[x] = 0$

⇒ $\cos^{-1}x = 0$

⇒ $x = 1$

But it $[x] = 1$ which is false.

If $[x] = 1$ $\cos^{-1} x = \cos 1 \Rightarrow [x] = 0$, which is false.

⇒ (i) has no solution.

(ii) $\sin^{-1} x = \text{sgn}(x)$ ...(i)

$\sin^{-1} x \in \left[\frac{-\pi}{2}, \frac{\pi}{2}\right]$; sgn (x) $\{-1, 0, 1\}$

case (i): If sgn $(x) = -1$ ⇒ $\sin^{-1} x = -1$

⇒ $x = -\frac{\pi}{2}$, which satisfy (i)

case (ii): If sgn $(x) = 0$ $\sin^{-1} x = 0$

⇒ $x = 0$, which satisfy (i)

case (iii): If sgn $(x) = 1$

⇒ $\sin^{-1} x = 1$

⇒ $x = \frac{\pi}{2}$, which also satisfy (i)

∴ $x = \frac{-\pi}{2}, 0 \frac{\pi}{2}$, i.e., 3 solutions.

(iii) $\{x\} = e^{x^2}$

Drawing the graphs of $y = \{x\}$ and $\{y\}$ and $y = e^{x^2}$ on same reference frame as given below.

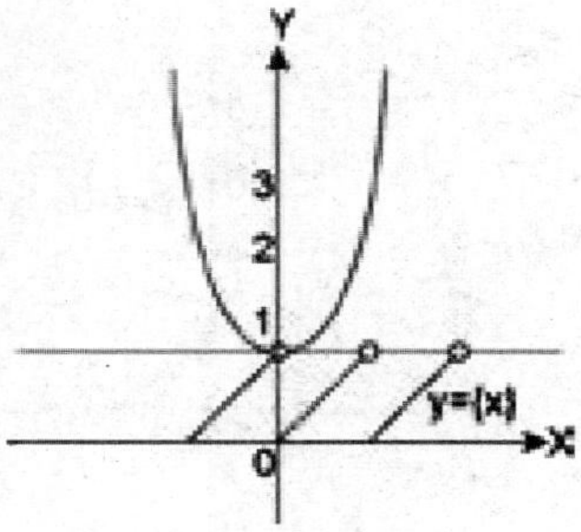

∴ There is no point of intersection, i.e., no solution.

(iv) $1 - x = \{x\}$

Draw the graph of $y = 1 - x$ and $y = \{x\}$ on same frame of reference as given below.

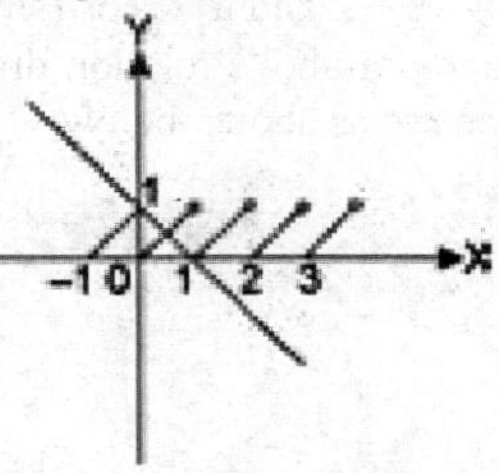

∴ There are two points of intersection, and hence, two solutions.

2. (i) →(d); (ii) →(c); (iii) →(a); (iv) →(b)

(i) $y = |f(x)| = \begin{cases} 1 \text{ for } -2 \le x \le 0 \\ 1 - x \text{ for } 0 \le x \le 1 \\ x - 1 \text{ for } 1 \le x \le 2 \end{cases}$

∴ (i) → (s)

(ii) $y = f(|x|) = \begin{cases} -x - 1 \text{ for } x \le 0 \\ x - 1 \text{ for } x > 0 \end{cases}$

∴ (b)→(r)

(iii) $y = f(-|x|) = \begin{cases} f(-x); x \ge 0 \\ f(x); x < 0 \end{cases} = \{-1\ \forall x \in \mathbb{R}$

∴ (iii)→ (p)

(iv) $y = \frac{1}{2}(|f(x)| - f(x)) = \begin{cases} 0 \text{ for } f(x) \ge 0 \\ -f(x) \text{ for } f(x) < 0 \end{cases}$

$$= \begin{cases} 1 \text{ for } -2 \le x \le 0 \\ 1 - x \text{ for } 0 < x \le 1 \\ 0 \text{ for } x > 1 \end{cases}$$

∴ (iv)→ (b)

3. (i) → (b); (ii) →(b); (iii) →(b); (iv) →(c);(v) →(d)

(i) $y = \frac{x^3}{3} + 3x^2 + 5x$ ...(i)

$x = 2y - y^2$ ...(ii)

Draw the graphs of $y = \frac{x^3}{3} + 3x^2 + 5x$ and $(x - 1) = -(y - 1)^2$ same frame of reference as shown below.

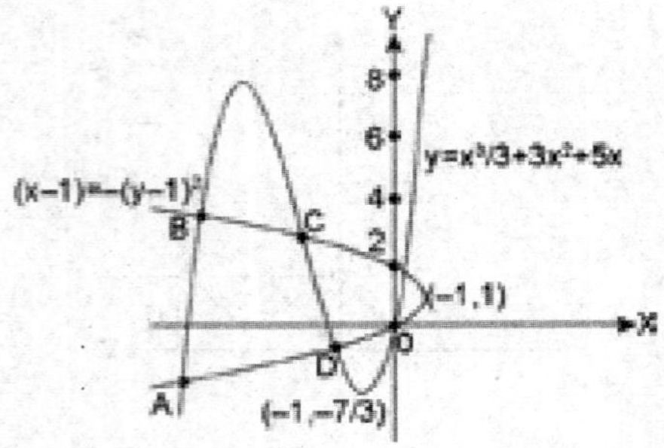

Clearly, the two graphs intersect each other at 6 points A, B, C, D, E and O.

$\therefore$ **(i)→ (b)**

(ii) $|y| = x^3 - 3x + 2$ and $|y| = \cos(\sin x)$.

The graphs of above relation drawn on same frame of reference are as shown below.

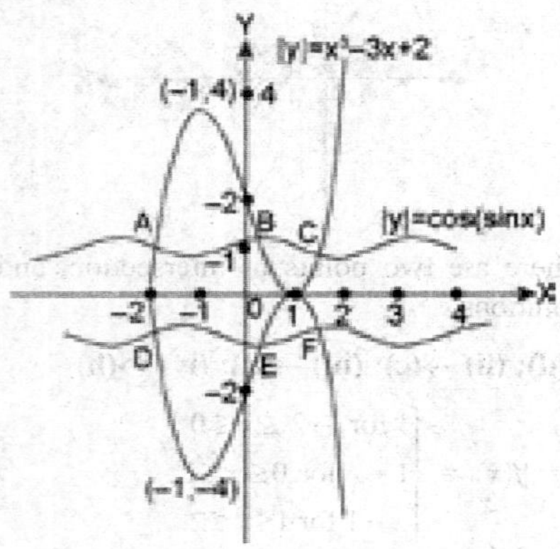

Clearly, there will be 6 point of intersection.

$\therefore$ **(ii)→ (b)**

(iii) $y = |\ln|x^2 - x||$ and $y = \left|\left\|\frac{1}{|x|}\right\| - 2\right|$

$|x^2 - x| \geq 1 \quad \Rightarrow \quad x^2 - x \leq -1$ or $x^2 - x \geq 1$

$\Rightarrow x^2 - x + 1 \leq 0$ or $x^2 - x - 1 \geq 0$

Disc. of $x^2 - x + 1 = -3 < 0$

$\Rightarrow x^2 - x + 1 > 0 \ \forall x \in \mathbb{R}$ and $x^2 - x - 1 \geq 0$

$$\Rightarrow x \in \left(-\infty, \frac{1-\sqrt{5}}{2}\right] \cup \left[\frac{1+\sqrt{5}}{2}, \infty\right)$$

$$\therefore \ y = \ln|x^2 - x| \text{ for } x \in \left(-\infty, \frac{1-\sqrt{5}}{2}, \infty\right] \cup \left[\frac{1+\sqrt{5}}{2}, \infty\right)$$

Similarly, $|x^2 - x| \in (0, 1)$

$\Rightarrow -1 < x^2 - x < 1;\ x^2 - x \neq 0$

$\Rightarrow x^2 - x - 1 < 0$ and $x^2 - x + 1 > 0$

$$\Rightarrow x \in \left(\frac{1-\sqrt{5}}{2}, \frac{1+\sqrt{5}}{2}\right)$$

$$\therefore y = \begin{cases} \ln|x^2 - x|; x \in \left(-\infty, \frac{1-\sqrt{5}}{2}\right] \cup \left[\frac{1+\sqrt{5}}{2}, \infty\right) \\ -\ln|x^2 - x|; x \in \left(\frac{1-\sqrt{5}}{2}, \frac{1+\sqrt{1+5}}{2}\right) \end{cases}$$

$$\Rightarrow y = \begin{cases} \ln(x^2 - x); x \in \left(-\infty, \frac{1-\sqrt{5}}{2}\right] \cup \left[\frac{1+\sqrt{5}}{2}, \infty\right) \\ -\ln(x^2 - x); x \in \left(\frac{1-\sqrt{5}}{2}, 0\right] \cup \left[1, \frac{1+\sqrt{5}}{2}\right) \\ -\ln(x - x^2);\ x \in (0,1) \end{cases}$$

The graph of $y = |\ln|x^2 - x||$ and $y = \left|\left\|\frac{1}{|x|}\right\| - 2\right|$ will be as shown below.

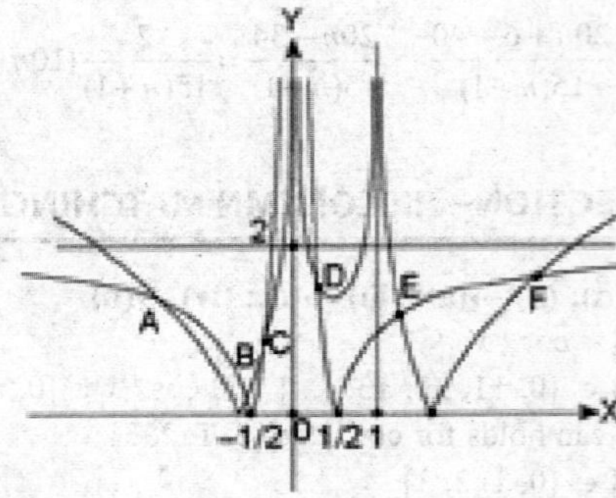

Clearly, the two graphs intersect each at 6 points, i.e., A, B, C, D, E and F.

$\therefore$ (iii) → (b)

(iv) $y = \cos e^x$ and $y = \tan e^x \ \forall x \in \left(-\infty, \frac{\pi}{2}\right)$

For $x \in \left(-\infty, \frac{\pi}{2}\right)$, $e^x \in \left(e^{-\infty}, e^{\frac{\pi}{2}}\right)$, i.e.,

$$\left(0, e^{\frac{\pi}{2}}\right) = \left(0, \frac{\pi}{2}\right) \cup \left(\frac{\pi}{2}, \pi\right] \cup \left(\pi, e^{\frac{\pi}{2}}\right)$$

$$\Rightarrow \cos e^x = \begin{cases} \text{decrease from 1 to 0 for } e^x \in \left(0, \frac{\pi}{2}\right] \\ \text{decrease from 0 to} -1 \text{ for } e^x \in \left(\frac{\pi}{2}, \pi\right] \\ \text{increase from } -1, \cos\left(e^{\frac{\pi}{2}}\right) \text{ for } e^x \in \left(\pi, e^{\frac{\pi}{2}}\right) \end{cases}$$

$$\text{and } \tan e^x = \begin{cases} \text{increase from 0 to } \infty \text{ for } e^x \in \left(0, \frac{\pi}{2}\right) \\ \text{increase from } -\infty \text{ to 0 for } e^x \in \left(\frac{\pi}{2}, \pi\right] \\ \text{increase from 0 to tan for } e^x \in \left(\pi, e^{\frac{\pi}{2}}\right) \end{cases}$$

Thus, the graphs of $y = \cos e^x$ and $y = \tan e^x \ \forall x \in \left(-\infty, \frac{\pi}{2}\right)$ will be as shown below.

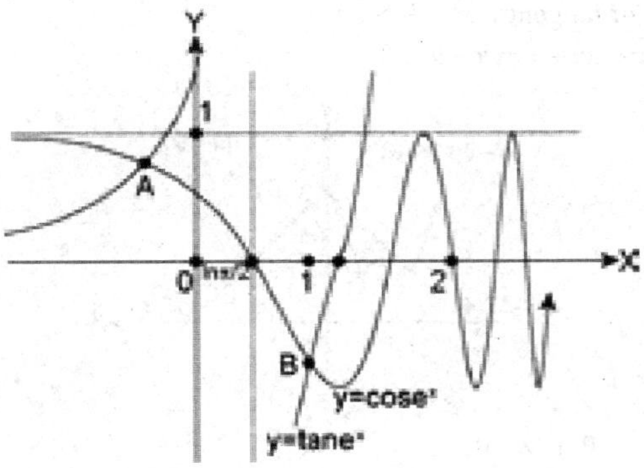

Clearly, the two functions intersect each other only at two points and B in $\left(-\infty, \frac{\pi}{2}\right)$ as shown above.

$\therefore$ There will be only 2 solutions.

$\therefore$ (iv) → (c)

(e) $y = \sin e^x$ and $y = \sec e^x$ $\forall$ $x \in (-\infty, 2)$

For $x \in (-\infty, 2)$, $e^x \in (0, e^x) \subset \left(0, \frac{5\pi}{2}\right)$ and $(0, e^2) \supset (0, 2\pi)$

$y = \sin e^x$ and $y = \sec e^x$ drawn as shown below.

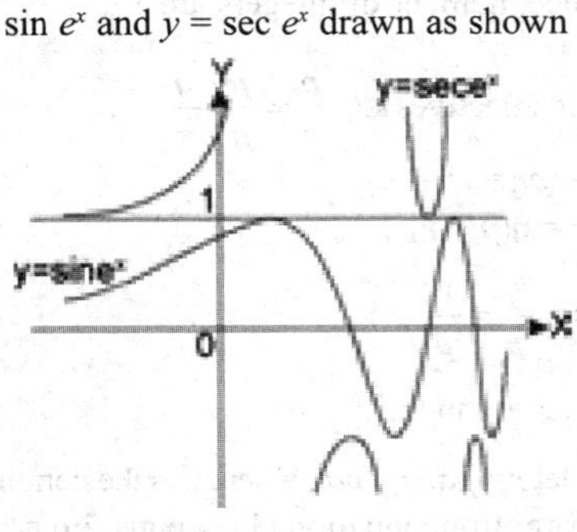

Clearly, there is no point of intersection.

$\therefore$ **(v)→ (d)**

4. (i) →(d); (ii) →(c); (iii) →(a); (iv) →(b); (v) →(e)

$f(x) = x^4 - 5x^2 + 7$

$|y| = x^4 - 5x^2 + 7$; Clearly, Disc. of $(x^4 - 5x^2 + 7) < 0$

$\Rightarrow$ $x^4 - 5x^2 + 7 > 0$ $\forall$ $x \in \mathbb{R}$

The graph of $y = x^4 - 5x^2 + 7$ and $|y| = x^4 - 5x^2 + 7$ drawn on same reference frame are as shown below.

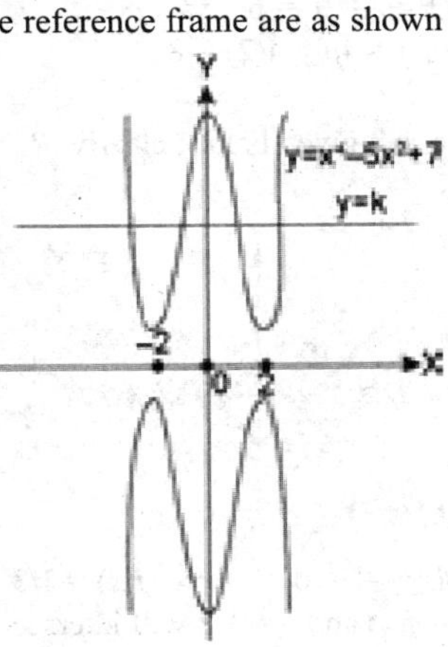

(i) Clearly for $n = 0$, i.e., no point of intersection $k \in \left(\frac{-3}{4}, \frac{3}{4}\right)$ $\therefore$ **(i)→ (d)**

(ii) Clearly for $n = 1$, i.e., only one point of intersection is impossible $\therefore$ **(ii)→ (c)**

(iii) For $n = 2$, i.e., two point of intersection, $k \in (-\infty, -7) \cup (7, \infty) \cup \left\{\pm\frac{3}{4}\right\}$ $\therefore$ **(iii)→ (a)**

(iv) For $n = 3$, i.e., three points of intersection, $k \in \{-7, 7\}$ $\therefore$ **(iv)→ (b)**

(v) For $n = 4$, i.e., four points of intersection, $k \in \left(-7, \frac{-3}{4}\right) \cup \left(\frac{3}{4}, 7\right)$ ∴ **(v)→ (e)**

SECTION–VIII: INTEGER TYPE

1. since $y = f(x)$ has 4 points of non-differentiability x_1, x_2, x_3, x_4 (say)

$y = f(|x|)$ being reflection of $y = f(x)$ on y-axis along with $y = f(x)$ has $-x_1, -x_2, -x_3, -x_4$ points of non-differentiability as well .

Also $f'(0^+) = k(\neq 0)$ $\Rightarrow$ $f(0^-) = -k(\neq 0)$

$\Rightarrow$ $x = 0$ is also a point of non-differentiability, hence, total 9 points of differentiability are there.

2. Since $y = f(x - 2)$ $\Rightarrow$ $2 \le x - 2 \le 10$

$\Rightarrow$ $4 \le x \le 12$

$\Rightarrow$ $y = g(x)$ would be having points of non-differentiability at $x = 5, 6, 7, 8$ and 9, i.e., 5 points in [2, 10), i.e., 5 points.

3. Clearly $x_1 = 2$, $x_2 = 6$, $y_1 = 4$, $y_2 = 10$, $z_1 = 2.5$, $z_2 = 7.2$, $z_3 = 7.8$, $z_4 = 10.5$ and $u_1 = 6$

$\therefore$ Required sum $= (2 + 6) + (4 + 10) - (2.5 + 7.2 + 7.8 + 10.5) + 6 = (22 + 6) - (28) = 0$

4. $y = f(|x|)$ is obtained by reflecting the graph of $y = f(x)$ on y-axis and $y = |f(|x|)$ will be obtained by reflecting the negative portion of $y = f(|x|)$ on x-axis and finally $|y| = |f(|x|)|$ is obtained by reflecting the + *ve* portion of $y = |f(|x|)|$ on x-axis. Thus, the required area = 4(Area bounded by $y = f(x)$ with x-axis for $x \in [0, 10]$).

$$= 4\left[\frac{1}{2}(1)(1) + (2)(2) + \frac{1}{2}(2+1)(2) + 1\times\left(\frac{1}{2}\right) + 3\times\frac{1}{2} + \frac{1}{2}\pi\left(\frac{3}{2}\right)^2 + \frac{1}{2}\times\left(1\times\frac{1}{2}\right)\right]$$

$$= 4\left[\frac{1}{2} + 4 + 3 + \frac{1}{2} + \frac{3}{2} + \frac{9\pi}{8} + \frac{1}{4}\right] = 4\left[9.75 + \frac{9\pi}{8}\right] = 39 + \frac{9\pi}{2}$$

$$= a + \frac{b\pi}{c} \quad a = 39, b = 9, c = 2$$

$\Rightarrow$ $a + c - 4b = 41 - 36 = 5$

5. Graph of $y = f(x)$ is as shown below.

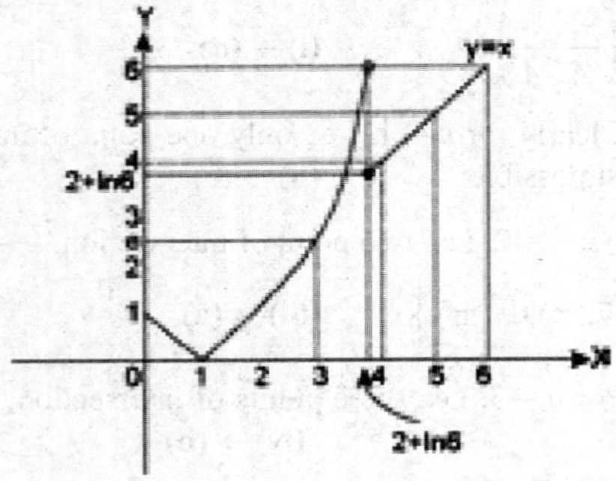

The graph of $y = g(x)$ is as shown below.

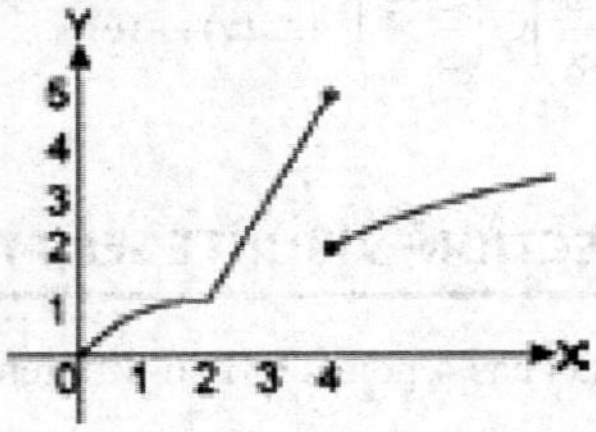

Let's draw the graph of $y = f(x)$ and $y = g(x)$ on same co- ordinate plane as shown below.

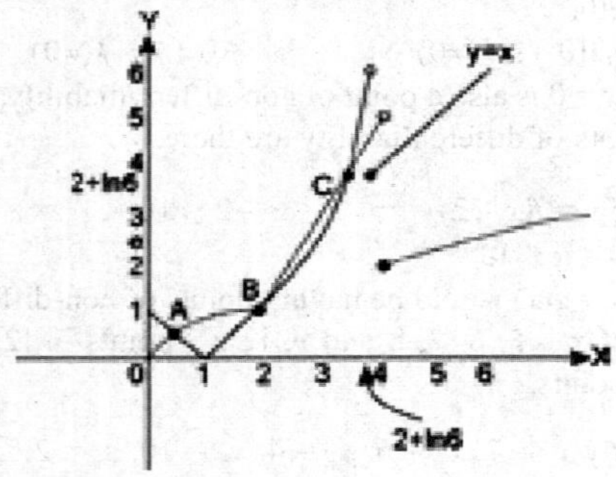

Clearly the two graphs intersect each other at 3 points A, B and C.

6. Clearly, $f(x) = g(x) + ln\,(2)$ has 3 points of intersection (by vertical transformation)

$\Rightarrow k_1 = 3$

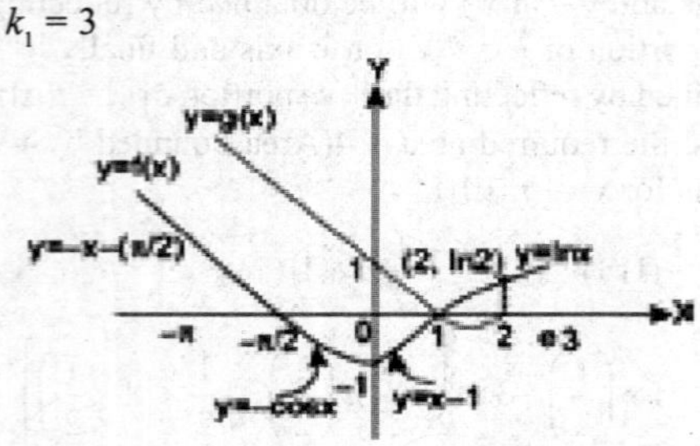

$x = 0$ is the only point of non-differentiability of $y = f(x)$

$\Rightarrow k_2 = 1$ and $x = 2$ is the only point of non-differentiability of $y = g(x)$

$\Rightarrow k_3 = 1$

$\therefore \quad \dfrac{k_1 + k_2}{k_3} = \dfrac{3+1}{1} = 4$

7. For tangency, $x^2 - 9 = x - a$

$\Rightarrow x^2 - x + a - 9 = 0$

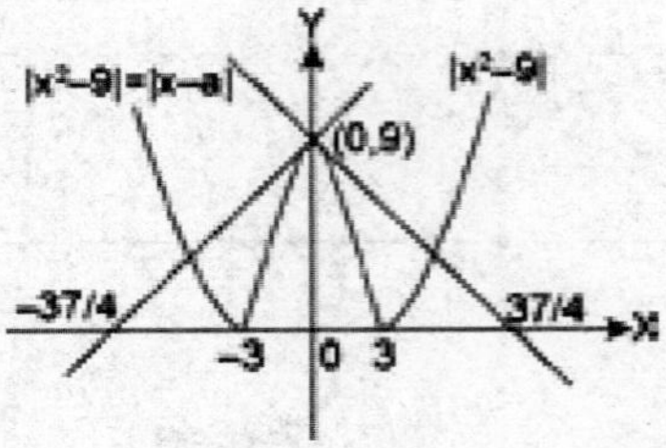

Put $D = 0$

$\Rightarrow 1 - 4a + 36 = 0$

$\Rightarrow a = \dfrac{37}{4}$

Similarly, $a = \dfrac{-37}{4}$

$\therefore$ For 4 distinct solution,

$a \in \left(\dfrac{-37}{4}, -3\right) \cup (-3, 3) \cup \left(3, \dfrac{37}{4}\right)$

Hence, number of integers are 17.

8. Since f is injective, so, $\dfrac{p}{r} = \dfrac{p-q}{q-r}$

$\Rightarrow pq - pr = rp - rq$

$\Rightarrow 2pr = q(p + r)$ ......(1)

Also, $\dfrac{q}{r} = \dfrac{r}{p}$

$\Rightarrow p, r, q$ are in G.P.

So, let $r = pa$, $q = pa^2$, where a is the common ratio of G.P.

Therefore, from equation (1), we get $2{\cdot}p{\cdot}pa = pa^2\,(p + pa)$

$\Rightarrow 2 = a^2 + a \quad \Rightarrow a^2 + a - 2 = 0$

$\Rightarrow (a + 2)\,(a - 1) = 0 \quad \Rightarrow a = -2, 1$

So, $(p, -2p, 4p)$ and (p, p, p)

(But common ratio $= a = 1$ is not possible as p, q, r are non-zero distinct quantities.)

Also, $p + q + r = 6$ [As $g(x) = px^2 + qx + r$ passes through $M\,(1, 6)$]

$\Rightarrow p + 4p - 2p = 6 \quad \Rightarrow p = 2$

Hence, $q = 4p = 4(2) = 8$

9. From the graph given below, clearly $R_f = \left(-\infty, -\dfrac{1}{2}\right]$

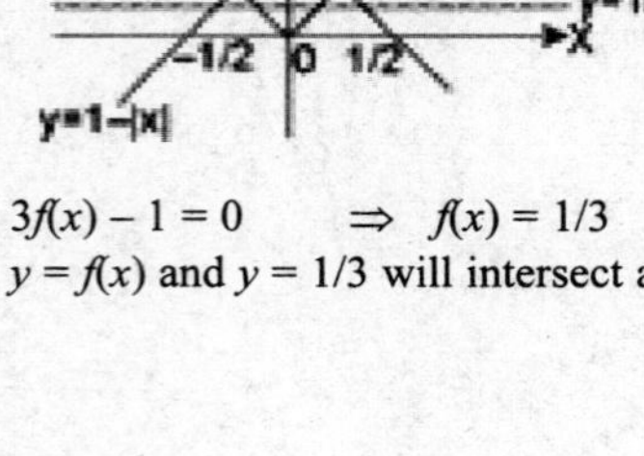

$\therefore \; 3f(x) - 1 = 0 \quad \Rightarrow f(x) = 1/3$

$\Rightarrow y = f(x)$ and $y = 1/3$ will intersect at 4 points.

10. $y = ax + b$ is inverse of itself. $\Rightarrow a = \pm 1$

For $a = -1$, $y = -x + b$ is its own inverse $\forall\ b \in \mathbb{R}$

For $a = 1$, $y = x + b$ will be inverse of itself for $b = 0$, i.e., $y = x$

Given that it is passing through (2, 3)

$\Rightarrow\ 3 = -2 + b$

$\Rightarrow\ b = 5$ and $a = -1$, i.e., $y = -x + 5$

$\Rightarrow\ 2a + b = -2 + 5 = 3$

11. Clearly domain of $f(x) = \bigcup_{n \in \mathbb{Z}} [2n, 2n + 1)$

$\Rightarrow\ f(x) = 1,\ \forall\, x \in D_f$

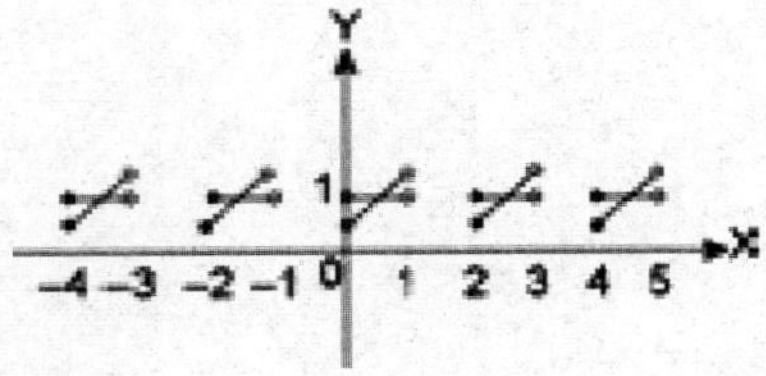

Now, $2f(x) = 1 + 2\{x\} \Rightarrow f(x) = \frac{1}{2} + \{x\}$

Clearly, the two graphs $y = f(x)$ and $y = \frac{1}{2} + \{x\}$ intersect at 5 points. Thus, there will be 5 solutions.

ANCIENT INDIAN TRADITION AND MYTHOLOGY

Translated by
BOARD OF SCHOLARS

Edited by
PROF. J.L. SHASTRI

VOLUME 10

ANCIENT INDIAN TRADITION AND MYTHOLOGY

Mahāpurāṇas *Translated into English*

Gen. Ed. DR. G.C. TRIPATHI

Founder Eds. LATE J.L. SHASTRI and LATE G.P. BHATT

PUBLISHED VOLUMES

Vols. 1-4	ŚIVA PURĀṆA *Tr.* J.L. Shastri
Vol. 5-6	LIṄGA PURĀṆA *Tr.* J.L. Shastri
Vol. 7-11	BHĀGAVATA PURĀṆA *Tr.* G.V. Tagare
Vol. 12-14	GARUḌA PURĀṆA *Tr.* J.L. Shastri
Vol. 15-19	NĀRADA PURĀṆA *Tr.* G.V. Tagare
Vol. 20-21	KŪRMA PURĀṆA *Tr.* G.V. Tagare
Vol. 22-26	BRAHMAṆḌA PURĀṆA *Tr.* G.V. Tagare
Vol. 27-30	AGNI PURĀṆA *Tr.* N. Gangadharan
Vol. 31-32	VARĀHA PURĀṆA *Tr.* S. Venkitasubramonia Iyer
Vol. 33-36	BRAHMA PURĀṆA *Tr.* J.L. Shastri
Vol. 37-38	VĀYU PURĀṆA *Tr.* G.V. Tagare
Vol. 39-48	PADMA PURĀṆA *Tr.* N.A. Deshpande
Vol. 49-71	SKANDA PURĀṆA *Ed.* G.P. Bhatt, *Tr. & Annot.* Shridhar Balooni & Pratosh Panda
Vol. 72-73	VĀMANA PURĀṆA *Tr. & Annot.* R.S. Shiva Ganesha Murthy
Vol. 74-76	GAṆEŚA PURĀṆA *Tr. & Annot.* Greg Bailey
Vol. 77-80	BRAHMAVAIVARTA PURĀṆA *Tr. & Annot.* G.P. Bhatt
Vol. 81-82	ŚRĪ VIṢṆU PURĀṆA *Tr. & Annot.* T.K. Narsimhan
Vol. 86	MĀRKAṆḌEYA PURĀṆA *Tr. & Annot.* I.S. Madugula

PURĀṆA*S* UNDER PREPARATION

Harivamśa Purāṇa • Bhavisya Purāṇa • Matsya Purāṇa

Devi Bhāgavata Purāṇa • Kālikā Purāṇa • Viṣṇudharmottara Purāṇa

THE BHĀGAVATA PURĀṆA

Translated and Annotated by
DR. G.V. TAGARE

PART IV

MOTILAL BANARSIDASS
PUBLISHING HOUSE • DELHI
Email: naraina@mlbd.in • *Website: www.mlbd.in*
@mlbdofficial

*5th Reprint: Delhi, **2023***
First Edition: Delhi, 1978

UNESCO COLLECTION OF REPRESENTATIVE WORKS—*Indian Series*
This book has been accepted in the Indian Translation Series of the UNESCO Collection of Representative Works, jointly sponsored by the United Nations Educational, Scientific and Cultural Organization (UNESCO) and the Government of India

ISBN: 978-93-5676-110-0 (Hardcover)
ISBN: 978-93-5676-111-7 (Paperback)

Printed & Published by
Rajendra P Jain *for*
Motilal Banarsidass Publishing House
A-44, Naraina Industrial Area, Phase I,
New Delhi–110 028 (INDIA)
Email: naraina@mlbd.in Website: www.mlbd.in
Tel.: (+91-11)4751 1592
Showroom:
4637/20, F-2, Hari Sadan, First Floor, Ansari Road, Daryaganj
Delhi–110 002 (Opp. Fire Station) ***Tel.*** : (+91-11)4559 7999

PUBLISHER'S NOTE

The purest gems lie hidden in the bottom of the ocean or in the depth of rocks. One has to dive into the ocean or delve into the rocks to find them out. Similarly, truth lies concealed in the language which with the lapse of time has become obsolete. Man has to learn that language before he discovers that truth.

But he has neither the means nor the leisure to embark on that course. We have, therefore, planned to help him acquire knowledge by an easier course. We have started the series of *Ancient Indian Tradition and Mythology* in English Translation. Our goal is to universalize knowledge through the most popular international medium of expression. The publication of the Purāṇas in English translation is a step towards that goal.

PREFACE

The present Volume contains the *Bhāgavata Purāṇa* Part IV (Skandha X) in English translation. It is the tenth in the series of fifty Volumes on *Ancient Indian Tradition and Mythology*.

The project of the series was envisaged and financed in 1970 by Shri Sundarlal Jain, the Veteran enterprizer in the field of Oriental Publication and the leading partner Messrs Motilal Banarsidass. Hitherto ten Volumes of the Series, including the present one, (that is, four Vols. of the *Śiva Purāṇa*, two Vols. of the *Liṅga Purāṇa* and four Vols. of the *Bhāgavata Purāṇa*, Skandhas 1-10) have been published and released for sale.

The present translation is based on the Sanskrit text of the *Bhāgavata Purāṇa* published by Messrs Kṣemarāja Śrīkṛṣṇadāsa Veṅkaṭeśvara Press, Bombay. This text, constructed on the Collation of Mss. and supported by the oldest Commentator Śrīdhara Svāmin, is fairly accurate. But we have also recorded the translation of all the additional verses accepted as genuine in the authoritative commentaries of Rāmānuja and Madhva Schools, that are not found in the text of Śrīdhara Svāmin.

The *Bhāgavata Purāṇa* deals with a variety of subjects—geographical, historical, philosophical, religious and the like which need elucidation. This task could not be accomplished by a mere translation. We have, therefore, provided footnotes on the topics. On the philosophical verses, especially, we have recorded different interpretations of the commentators belonging to different schools of thought, viz. those of Śaṅkara, Rāmānuja, Madhva, Nimbārka, Vallabha and Caitanya (Gauḍīya School of Vaiṣṇavism) and also two eminent Marathi Commentators—Kṛṣṇa Dayārṇava and Ekanātha. In the accomplishment of this task we have also utilized the commentaries published in the Bhāgavata Vidyā Peeth, Ahmedabad Edition and the Vrindavana edition of this Purāṇa.

In order to help the reader understand the background of the subject matter we have prefixed to part I of the Purāṇa a critical and comparative introduction which discusses, among other topics, the date, authorship, philosophy, religion, general characteristics and the commentators of this Purāṇa. A List of Abbreviations prefixed to Part I of the Purāṇa is also repeated here for the convenience of the reader, while a general index is thought to be included in the last part of this work.

Before closing, it is our pleasant duty to put on record our sincere gratitude to Dr. S.K. Chatterjee, Dr. V. Raghavan, Dr. R.N. Dandekar, Shri K.R. Kripalani, and the authorities of the UNESCO for their kind encouragement and valuable help which render this work more valuable to scholars than it would otherwise have been. We must also thank the learned translator and annotator Dr. G.V. Tagare for his untiring zeal and sustained efforts in bringing out this Volume within scheduled time, in spite of untold obstacles.

Finally, we avail of this opportunity to state that any critical suggestion and advice for improvement are welcome and will receive proper consideration from us.

—Editor

ABBREVIATIONS

Common and self-evident abbreviations such as Ch. (s)—Chapter (s), P.—Page, PP.—(Pages), V.—Verse, VV.—Verses, Ft. n—Foot-note, *Hist. of Ind. Phil.*—*History of Indian Philosophy* are not included in the list below.

The abbreviated form of the commentator's name is used for his commentary on the *Bhāgavata Purāṇa*.

ABORI.	*Annals of the Bhandarkar Oriental Research Institute*, Poona.
Agni P.	*Agni Purāṇa.*
AIHT.	*Ancient Indian Historical Tradition* by F. E. Pargiter.
ASD.	Apte's *Sanskrit-English Dictionary* (Motilal Banarsidass, 1963). "P" after ASD means the page No. of the dictionary.
BDCRI.	*Bulletin of the Deccan College Research Institute*, Poona.
BG.	*The Bhagavad Gītā.*
Bh. P.	*The Bhāgavata Purāṇa.* Bhāgavata Vidyā Peeṭha Ahmedabad edition, 1965-1975 and the Veṅkaṭeśvara Edition used.
BM.	*The Bhāgavata Māhātmya* (*Padma Purāṇa Uttara Khaṇḍa*) Editor : Krishna Shankar Shastri, Ahmedabad, 1965.
BP.	Bhagavata Prasāda's *Bhakta-manorañjani* (A com. on the Bh. P., Ahmedabad edition).
BPK.	*Bhāratiya Paurāṇika Kośa* (Marathi), Pub.: D.S, Yande and Co., Bombay, 1929.
CHI.	*Cambridge History of India* (Ed. E.J. Rapson).
Com.	Commentary.
DHM.	*A Classical Dictionary of Hindu Mythology* by John Dowson, Kegan Paul, London, 1928.
ERE.	*Encyclopaedia of Religion and Ethics* Ed. by Hastings.

Garuḍa P.	*Garuḍa Purāṇa* Ed. by Ramashankar Bhattacarya, Chowkhamba Varanasi 1964.
GD.	Gosvāmī Giridhara-lāl's *Bāla-prabodhinī*, a com. on the Bh.P. (*Śuddhādvaita* School).
GDAMI	*The Geographical Dictionary of Ancient and Medieval India* by Nundo Lal De, Luzac and Co, London, 1927.
GS	Gaṅgā Sahāya's *Anvitārtha-prakāśikā* : A com. on the Bh. P. (*Advaita* School).*
HDS	*History of Dharma Śāstra* by P. V. Kane, G.O.S. Class B., 6 : BORI Poona, 1930 onwards. (References are to Volumes and pages).
HIL	*History of Indian Literature*, by M. Winternitz, 2nd Edn.. Oriental Books Reprint Corporation, New Delhi, 1972.
IA	*Indian Antiquary*, Bombay.
IHQ	*Indian Historical Quarterly*, Calcutta.
JG	Jīva Gosvami's *Krama-sandarbha* a Com. on the Bh. P. It represents the Bengal School of Vaiṣṇavism.
Kūrma P.	*Kūrma Purāṇa* Edt. by Ramashankar Bhattacarya, Indological Book House, Varanasi.
MBH.	*Mahābhārata* (Gita Press, Gorakhpur). References show the Parva No. or name (e.g. Vana, Mausala) the Ch. in that *parvan* and the verse No.
MNK.	Mahābhārata Nāmānukramaṇikā (Gita Press Gorakhpur).
Matsya P.	*Matsya Purāṇa* (Guru Mandal Grantha Mālā, Calcutta. Unless mentioned otherwise, the Purāṇas mentioned here belong to that Grantha Mālā).

* With the exception of Skandha X of the Bh. P. I have used the text of the Comm. as published in the Bhāgavata Vidyā-Peeth Ahmedabad's edition of the Bh. P. For Skandha X I have followed the text of the Comm. as found in the Vrindavan Edition of the Bh. P.

PCK	*Bhāratavarṣiya Prācina Caritra Kośa*, by M.M. Siddheshvara Shastri Chitrav, Poona, 1968.
PG.	Puruṣottama Gosvāmi's *Subodhini-prakāśa* a Com. on the Bh. P. *Śuddhādvaita* School).
PI	*Purāṇa Index*, by V.R. Ramchandra Dikshitar, (References are to Volumes and Pages) Madras.
PSB.	*The Philosophy of the Śrimad Bhāgavata*, by Siddheshvara Bhattacarya, Visva Bharati, Santiniketana, 1960 and 1962.
PSK.	*Prācina Bhāratiya sthala Kośa* by M. M. Siddheshvar Shastri Chitrav, Poona, 1969.
PYP.	*Pātañjala Yoga Pradipa* (Gita Press, Gorakhpur).
RN	*Ṛju-nāmni* Com. on the B.M. by Ramapratāp, Son of Brajalāl of Vijayapur (Śekhāvat).
RR.	Rādhā Ramaṇa Gosvāmī's *Dipini*, a Com. on the Bh. P. (*Advaita* School).
RV	*Ṛg Veda Saṁhitā* (Both Aundha and Poona editions used).
SD.	Śuka Deva's *Siddhānta-pradipa*, a com. on the Bh P. (It represents the Nimbārka School of Vedānta).
SGAMI	*Studies in the Geography of Ancient and Medieval India by* D. C. Sircar (Motilal Banarsidass, 1971).
Śiva P.	*Śiva Purāṇa*, Pandit Pustakalaya, Kaśi, Samvat 2020.
ŚR.	Śrīdhara Svāmī's *Bhāvāratha Dipikā*, the oldest Com. on the Bh. P. (*Advaita* School).
Vāyu P.	*Vāyu Purāṇa*.
VB.	Vallabhācārya's *Subodhinī*, a Com. on the Bh. P. (*Śuddhādvaita* School).
VC.	Viśvanātha Cakravarti's *Sārārtha-darśini*, a Com. on the Bh. P. (Bengal school of Vaiṣṇavism).

VD.	Vaṁśīdhara's *Bhāvārtha-dīpikā-prakāśa*, a Com. on the Bh. P. (*Advaita* School).
Viṣṇu P. also VP.	*Viṣṇu Purāṇa* (Gita Press, Gorakhpur).
VJ.	Vijayadhvaja's *Padaratnāvalī*, a Com. on the Bh. P. (*Dvaita* School).
v.l.	A varient; a different reading.
VR.	Vīra-rāghava's *Bhāgavata Candrikā*, a Com. on Bh. P. (*Viśiṣṭādvaita* school).
YSP.	*The Yoga Sūtras of Patañjali*, By J. H. Woods (Harvard Oriental Series).

Self-evident abbreviations, e.g. *Hist. of Ind. Civilization* by R.K. Mukerjee are not included.

CONTENTS

SKANDHA X

SKANDHA TENTH

CHAPTER ONE

Introduction : Kaṁsa kills Devakī's Sons

The King (Parīkṣit) said :

1. Your worship has been pleased to narrate the detailed account of the Lunar and Solar dynasties and also the extremely wonderful exploits of kings, born in both these families.

2. (You have also described) especially the race of Yadu, of extremely pious nature. Oh the best of Sages ! Do you now be pleased to describe to us the great deeds of Lord Viṣṇu who incarnated in his family, along with his part-manifestation (*aṁśa* viz. Balarāma).

3. Please recount to us in details all those deeds that the Almighty Lord, the Maker (Protector) and the Soul of all beings, performed after incarnating in Yadu's race.

4. What man other than a slaughterer will desist from (listening to) the recital of the excellent attributes of Lord Kṛṣṇa, of auspicious glory—glory constantly sung by those who are freed from the influence of desires (and are liberated), a specific remedy for (release from) *saṁsāra*, and extremely pleasant to the ears and the mind.

5. Using Him (Kṛṣṇa) as a raft, my grandfathers (i.e. grandfather Arjuna and granduncles such as Yudhiṣṭhira), crossed the ocean in the form of the Kaurava army, so difficult to tide over, due to its being infested with monstrous whales in the form of unrivalled (chariot-riding) warriors like Bhīṣma and others, the vanquishers of even celestials in battles, contemptuously treating it (the ocean-like army) like a (shallow) depression caused by a calf's hoof.

6. And armed with a discus (*Sudarśana*), He entered the womb of my mother (Uttarā) who sought his refuge and protected this body of mine—the seed for the continuity of the races of Kurus and Pāṇḍavas—while it (my body) was being scorched by the missile (*Brahmāstra*) discharged by Aśvatthāman, Droṇā's son.

7. Oh learned sage, be pleased to recount to me (for my benefit), the glorious exploits of him (Kṛṣṇa) who has assumed human form through his Māyā-power, and who pervades all embodied beings internally and externally, and who, as an Inner Controller and as a Destroyer (Time-Spirit)—severally dispenses Liberation to the spiritually-minded ("inner-seers") and death, i.e. *saṁsāra*, to those with worldly propensities.

8. Balarāma alias Saṅkarṣaṇa was (first) stated by you to be the son of Rohiṇī (vide *supra* 9.24.46). How could he be connected with the womb of Devakī (vide *supra* 9.24.54) without assuming another body ?

9. Why for did glorious Mukunda (Lord Kṛṣṇa) migrate from his father's residence to Vraja ? Where (in what places) did the Lord of Sātvatas (gods or a clan of Yadus) settle down with his kinsmen ?

10. What were the activities (lit. did he do) of Keśava while residing at Vraja, as well as in Mathurā, the city founded by demon Madhu ? Why did he personally kill Kaṁsa, his mother's brother who, as such, did not deserve it.

11. After assuming human body, for how many years did he stay at Dvārakā along with Vṛṣṇis (Yādavas)? How many were the consorts of the Lord ?

12. Oh Omniscient Sage ! It behoves you to describe in details to me, a faithful devotee, this and every other deed performed by Kṛṣṇa.

13. Though I have given up even drinking of water in this (life-long) fast, this extremely unbearable hunger does not torment me, as I drink the nectar of Hari's stories flowing from the moon-lotus in the form of your mouth.

Sūta said :

14. Oh Śaunaka, having listened to the laudable inquiry, the worshipful son of Vyāsa (Śuka) who was the foremost among the votaries of viṣṇu, complimented king Parīkṣit (one protected by Viṣṇu) and commenced to extol the life and episodes of Lord Kṛṣṇa, which destroy the sins and impurities of Kali (Or which remove the miseries of *saṁsāra*.)

Śrī Śuka said :

15. Oh foremost among saintly kings! Your mind has been properly directed, inasmuch as the utmost and firmest devotion to the stories of Vāsudeva has been engendered in you.

16. Inquiries about the stories of Vāsudeva certainly purify all the three persons concerned, namely, the reciter, the inquirer and the members of the audience, just as water washing his feet i.e. the Gaṅgā (Or the water washing Śālagrāma) purifies all.

17. Mother Earth which was overburdened with the crushing weight of millions and millions of the hosts of Daityas who assumed the guise of arrogant kings, sought refuge to god Brahmā.

18. Taking the form of a depressed and piteously lowing cow and with her face overflowing with tears, she approached god Brahmā's presence and represented to him her grievous plight.

19. Realizing the piteous condition of the earth, god Brahmā accompanied by the three-eyed god Śiva and other gods, came to the shore of the milky ocean, along with her.

20. After reaching there, he with perfect concentration of mind, praised in terms of the Puruṣa-Sūkta the Supreme Person, the Lord of the world, the god of gods, the absolutely blissful Enjoyer of sacrifices.

21. Listening to the voice uttered in the sky while he was meditating (upon the Lord), god Brahmā spoke out to the celestials, "Oh immortals, hear from me the words of the Supreme Person and comply immediately with them. Let there be no delay."

22. The affliction of Mother Earth was already understood by the Supreme Person before we appealed to him. You should now take birth in the Yadu Clan, in your part-manifestation, while the Lord of gods will walk over the earth, reducing its burden through his potency called Time.

23. The glorious Supreme Lord will directly manifest Himself in the house of Vasudeva. Let the heavenly damsels be born (on the earth) to minister to his pleasures.

23—A. VR's text adds :

As commanded by him, let the sages be made to assume the form of cattle for the purpose of propitiating Lord Viṣṇu by yielding him milk, Oh gods.

24. The self-effulgent thousand-faced Lord Śeṣa imbued with a part of Vāsudeva, will be born as the elder brother, with a view to catering to his pleasures.

25. The divine Yoga-Māyā of Viṣṇu who has deluded the world, has been commanded to take birth in part-manifestation for fulfilling his mission."

Śrī Śuka said :

26. Having directed the hosts of gods in this way, and consoling the Earth in reassuring words, god Brahmā, the Ruler of Prajāpatis, repaired to his exalted region.

27. In former times, Śūrasena, the chief of the Yadu clan, ruled over the territories of Mathurā and Śūrasena, while residing in the city of Mathurā.

28. Thenceforth, Mathurā became the metropolis of all kings of the Yādava dynasty. In that city, the glorious Lord Hari ever exhibits his presence in a special way.

29. In that city, on one occasion, Vasudeva, son of Śūra, whose marriage with Devakī was celebrated, ascended the chariot with his newly wedded wife, to proceed to his place after marriage.

30. Kaṁsa, the son of Ugrasena, being desirous of pleasing his sister (cousin), took over the reins of the horses, surrounded by hundreds of gold-plated chariots.

31-32. At the time of departure, Devaka who was fond of his daughter, gave, as wedding presents, four hundred elephants caparisoned with gold chains, fifteen thousand horses, eighteen hundred chariots and two hundred comely maidservants, adorned with gold ornaments.

33. As the procession of the bride and the bridegroom started, conchs, clarionets, drums and kettle-drums were sounded simultaneously in the most auspicious manner.

34. On the way, an incorporeal voice from the sky addressed Kaṁsa who was holding the reins: "Oh foolish fellow, the eighth son from the womb of her whom you are conducting, shall slay you".

35. Being thus warned, the wicked sinful fellow, who was a disgrace to the Bhoja family, with a sword in hand, seized his sister by her braids of hair and proceeded to kill her.

36. The great-souled Vasudeva pleaded in conciliatory terms with the cruel, shameless perpetrator of disgraceful deeds.

Vasudeva urged :

37. You possess virtues extolled by the brave and are the glory to the Bhoja family. As such how is it that you (attempt to) kill your sister on the festive occasion of her marriage.

38. (If you say that you are doing so as a precautionary measure), death is born along with the body of all creatures, Oh warrior ! Death is inevitable to all creatures, whether it may be today or at the end of hundred years.

39. When the body is on the point of dissolving in five component-Elements (i.e. at the time of death), the Soul residing in it automatically, under the force of his *karmas* (as good as) obtains another body and quits his previous frame.

40. Just as a man while walking, stands with his one foot established on the earth, while the other paces forward, or just as a caterpillar leaves the (previous) blade of grass only when it catches the hold of another, similarly does an embodied being, caught in the current of *karmas*.

41. Just as a person whose mind is obsessed with a strong desire, and who is mentally brooding over the objects of his desires, with his mind deeply impressed by what he has seen or heard, seems to realize it in dreams, and identifies himself with it, for getting himself (his body in the waking state). So does the soul attain his new body quitting the old one.

42. To whatever modification of five *bhūtas* created by *Māyā* that the mind consisting of various emotions and passions feels impelled by destiny, and flows to it, and is attached at the time of death, the soul abiding in the body identifies itself with it and passes into that form along with the mind.

42a. Being impelled by Destiny, the mind, consisting of emotions and passions, feels impelled to, flows to and is attached to (at the time of death) whatever modifications of the five *Bhūtas* created by Māyā, the soul abiding in the body identifies itself with that form, and passes into it along with the mind.

43. Just as a luminous body (e.g. the Sun or the Moon) which, when reflected in water in an earthen container, appears to move or change according to the speed of the wind that ruffles the liquid reflecting medium (though actually—the original luminary—does not shake), so does the embodied soul, through attachment, enter the bodies or forms created by his own Māyā and is overcome with delusion.

44. Therefore, a person being so conditioned but seeking his own welfare, should not do wrong to anyone. For there is fear to the wrong-doers from others (such as god of death, the person wronged etc.).

45. This poor girl, your younger sister, is just like a daughter to you (or a lifeless doll). It does not become you who are kind to the helpless, to kill her who has just completed the marriage rites.

Śrī Śuka continued :

46. Oh descendant of Kuru ! Even though admonished with conciliatory words and words inspiring fear (of dire consequences), the relentless Kaṁsa, following the ways of demons, did not desist (from his determination).

47. Observing his firm determination (to kill Devakī), Vasudeva thought for a while how to avert this imminent danger for the time being, and devised the following expedient for it.

48. (He thought to himself :) "An intelligent person should try to avert death to the utmost limit of his intellectual and physical abilities. So if, despite these, it could not be warded off, no blame will be attached to him.

49. I shall rescue this helpless girl by promising in exchange handing over of her sons to Death (viz. Kaṁsa who is going to kill them), provided the sons are born or he (Kaṁsa) does not die in the meanwhile.

50. Or might not the contrary take place (i.e. my son might kill him), unscrutable are the ways of the Providence; for the imminent may be averted and what is averted may happen again.

51. Just as, in a forest conflagrations, there is no apparent cause (except Fate) for its coming in contact with a parti-

cular tree or remaining aloof from another, so also in the case of a created being, the cause of its being—associated or dissociated with a particular body is very difficult to be comprehended."

52. Having carefully considered (this problem) to the best of his intellectual capacity, Vasudeva respectfully addressed the wicked fellow, with (apparently) great esteem.

53. Simulating a blooming lotus-like (cheerful) countenance, in spite of his heart full of pain, he smilingly spoke to that hard-hearted and shameless fellow.

Vasudeva said:

54. Oh gentle-natured Kaṁsa! There is certainly no fear to you from this girl as has been intimated to you by the incorporeal voice from the sky. I shall handover to you her sons from whom you apprehend danger.

Śrī Śuka said:

55. Kaṁsa, who properly understood the significance of Vasudeva's words, desisted from killing his sister (Devakī). Even Vasudeva who was pleased, extolled him and entered his palace.

56. After a lapse of time, in due course, Devakī who was devoted to the Lord who is the soul of all deities and was permeated with the divinities, gave birth to eight sons and a daughter, one every year.

57. Vasudeva who (by nature) was intensely agitated to act falsely, handed over with great pains his first born son, Kīrtimān, to Kaṁsa.

58. What is there which a truthful person (like Vasudeva) cannot endure? Is there anything which the knowers of the truth (that the Lord alone is the reality) long for? (Did Vasudeva think that Kaṁsa would spare his child when handed over personally? No.). There is nothing which the wicked would not do. (How is it that Devakī parted with the child?) What thing would they not sacrifice who cherish Hari in their hearts?

59. Seeing the equanimity and firmness in truth of Vasudeva Kaṁsa was highly pleased with him and spoke to him smilingly: Oh King.

60. "Let this boy return (to his mother) as there is no danger from him to me, as my death has been ordained from your eighth child."

61. Taking back his son in compliance of Kaṁsa's words, Vasudeva returned home. He was however not happy over the words of that wicked Kaṁsa of uncontrolled mind.

61A. Additional verse in VJ.'s text :

Then the divine sage Nārada, the son of Brahmā, called upon Kaṁsa, and conferring with him privately spoke as follows.

62-63. "Whatever cowherds of whom Nanda is the chief, there are in Vraja and again all their women and all Vṛṣṇis headed by Vasudeva and Yādava women of whom Devakī is the foremost—all the kinsmen, relations and friends of both Nanda and Vasudeva who are loyal to Kaṁsa—are mostly gods. : (while) those who are the followers of Kaṁsa.

63—A. VR.'s text adds :

Are verily all *asuras* who trouble the world."

64. (Considering that the Lord would not incarnate earlier by Kaṁsa's such peaceful attitude) Nārada approached Kaṁsa and advised him as above, apprising him of the endeavours made (by god Brahmā and others) for the annihilation of Daityas who became a burden to the earth.

65. On the departure of the sage, Kaṁsa looked upon all Yadus as gods and every child born of Devakī as Viṣṇu intent upon slaying himself.

66. Fettering Devakī and Vasudeva in chains, he imprisoned them in their house and killed every new-born child, fearing him to be god Viṣṇu.

67. Generally, the kings on the earth who are covetous and thirsty after the lives of others, kill their mother, father, brothers and all friends as well.

68. Realising himself to be the great *asura* Kālanemi whom Viṣṇu had formerly killed, born here again, he commenced hostilities with Yādavas.

69. Being endowed with enormous power, he arrested his father Ugrasena, the king of Yādavas, Bhojas and Andhakas and took over the government of the Śūrasena region.

CHAPTER TWO

The Lord's descent in Devakī's womb

Śrī Śuka continued :

1-2. Aided by *asuras* like Pralamba, Baka, Cāṇūra, Tṛṇāvarta, Agha (the great devourer), Muṣṭika, Ariṣṭa, Dvivida, Pūtanā, Keśī, Dhenuka and forming an alliance with other *asura* kings like Bāṇa and Bhauma, and with the support of Jarāsandha, the king of Magadha, the mighty Kaṁsa began to harass Yadus.

3. Hard pressed by him, they migrated in disguise to different countries, viz. Kurus, Pāñcālas, Kekayas, Śālvas, Vidarbhas, Niṣadhas, Videhas and Kosalas as well.

4-5. Some of his relatives, however, continued to serve him obediently. When Kaṁsa, the son of Ugrasena, killed six sons of Devakī, a part of the lustre of Lord Viṣṇu, known as Ananta, became the seventh child entering Devakī's womb who enhanced her joy and grief at the same time.

6. Being cognisant of the fear caused by Kaṁsa to Yadus, his proteges, he commanded his Yoga-Māyā (as follows) :

7. "Oh auspicious goddess ! Do you go to Vraja adorned with residence of cowherds and cows (by their affluence)? There, in the settlement of cowherds headed by Nanda dwells Rohiṇī, the wife of Vāsudeva. His other wives too being apprehensive of Kaṁsa have gone underground (stay in secret places).

8. In the womb of Devakī lies my part-manifestation known as Śeṣa. Taking him from her womb, transfer him to Rohiṇīs womb.

9. I shall then become her son by my part-manifestation (with my full powers[1]) while you will be born of Yaśodā, the wife of Nanda.

10. Recognizing you as the supreme dispenser of boons to persons desirous of progeny and bestower of boons granting all

1. To substantiate the statement *Kṛṣṇastu bhagavān svayam* (Kṛṣṇa is the Almighty Lord himself) ŚR. gives different explanations of *aṁśa-bhāga*. VT. and others endorse ŚR. but Brahma Purāṇa accepts Kṛṣṇa as 'part-manifestation'.

desires, people will worship you with incense, offerings of food and other presents.

11-12. People will erect temples for you on the earth and will designate you with various names such as Durgā, Bhadrakālī, Vijayā, Vaiṣṇavī, Kumudā, Caṇḍikā, Kṛṣṇā, Mādhavī, Kanyakā, Māyā, Nārāyaṇī, Īśānī, Śāradā and Ambikā.

13. Due to his being taken out of the womb of Devakī (and transfer to that of Rohiṇī), he will be known as Saṅkarṣaṇa. As he would give delight to the world, he would be called Rāma, and Bala on account of his eminence among the mighty people.

14. When commanded by the Lord thus, she accepted it with the words, 'Yes ! That will be done'. After circumambulating him, she went down to the earth, and executed his orders.

15. When the child from the womb of Devakī was transferred to that of Rohiṇī by the goddess *Yoga-nidrā*, citizens of Mathurā sorrowfully talked about the miscarriage of Devakī.

16. And the Almighty Lord, who is the soul of the universe, and gives assurance of safety to his votaries, entered the mind of Vasudeva[1], with all his divine potencies in their fullness.

17. Being surcharged with (lit. bearing) the glorious presence of the Supreme Person (Lord Viṣṇu), Vasudeva resplendent like unto the Sun, became unapproachable and unassailable to all created beings.

18. Thereupon, like unto the (eastern) direction bearing the moon, the delighter of all, queen Devakī, refulgent with pure *sattva* conceived in her mind—when conveyed through psychological process (*vedha-dīkṣā*) by Vasudeva—the Lord, the auspiciousness of the world incarnate[2], whose potencies are undiminishing, and who as the indwelling Soul of all, was already present in her.

1. And not through usual physiological process—ŚR.

2. Or : The Lord who, though omnipresent, assumes a limited body for showing His grace to His devotees—ŚR.

19. Like unto the flame of a lamp enclosed by an earthen pot, or like deep scholarship of a narrow-minded person who refuses to impart it (to others), Devakī, though now the abiding place of the Lord who is the abode of all the universe, did not shine superbly (failed to give delight to the world at large, though she herself enjoyed the ecstasy of the presence of the Lord), as she was (then) imprisoned in the palace of Kaṁsa, the king of Bhojas.

20. When Kaṁsa perceived that Devakī, bearing in her womb the invincible Lord Viṣṇu and beaming with pure smiles, illuminated the whole (prison-) house with her effulgence, he said (to himself), "This is Hari who, intent on robbing me of my life, has certainly entered her (Devakī's) womb, like a lion entering a den, for never before did she appear so brilliant.

21. "What immediate remedy should I now adopt in this matter today? For determined as he is on accomplishing his purpose (viz. serving the interest of gods), he would not desist from his prowess (in killing me, when he is born. Should I finish with Devakī just now, before he is born?—But even a selfish person does not wreck his reputation and prowess by such a deed). For this murder of a woman, my own sister in pregnancy, will forthwith spoil my reputation, prosperity for all time to come and (will affect even) my life as well.

22. He who lives by perpetrating extreme atrocities is as good as dead even during his life-time. People at large pronounce curses upon him while alive. When his body falls dead, he will surely go to the hell of blinding darkness, the destination of those who identify their Souls with their bodies.[1]

23. Reasoning with himself thus, the mighty Kaṁsa desisted (of his own accord) from his darkest design (of killing Devakī). Cherishing inveterate enmity to Lord Hari, he continued to await his birth.

1. VJ.'s text reads :
dehe mṛte tam anu hyartha-kāmau
Yaśomalaṁ gaur abhimānino dhruvam /
When the body of the man who identifies with his Soul becomes defunct his objectives viz. *artha*, *kāma*, his pure reputation, knowledge and emancipation (*mokṣa*) are surely lost to him.

24. Pondering over Lord Kṛṣṇa, the Lord of the senses, (suspecting that he may manifest himself at any moment and kill him) while sitting, lying, standing, eating, moving about and drinking, Kaṁsa saw that the whole world was pervaded by Him.[1]

25. Gods Brahmā and Śiva accompanied by sages like Nārada and others (such as Sanaka, Sanandana) and gods along with their attendants arrived at that place, and glorified the Lord who showers all desired boons.

The gods said :

26.* We resort as a shelter to you who are of true resolve; to attain to whom, truthfulness is the only highest means; who exist and are the reality in the past, present and future (before the creation, during the subsistence and after the destruction of the universe); the cause and the source of the three elements—the earth, water and fire (aggregatively known as *sat*—) and the wind and the ether (collectively called *tyat* in Tait. Upa 2.6.1); who reside in them as *antaryāmin*; who are the truth of the truth (the highest Reality even after the dissolution of the universe); who are the promulgator of truthful speech and impartially equable vision (towards all) and the embodiment of truthfulness.

1. Kaṁsa was made to think of Him by Kṛṣṇa, the Lord of senses, in all states and actions in life for manifesting himself to Kaṁsa who thus perceived that the world is full of Kṛṣṇa—VB.

* VR. : We have sought shelter in You Who carry out what is avowed by you and are hence of real resolve; Who are distinct from the real world consisting of the sentient (*cid*) and non-sentient (*acid*); Whose body consists of three real entities--Prakṛti, Puruṣa and Time (*kāla*) ; Whose wish is carried out as you are the controller of the whole world comprising of Prakṛti (Puruṣa etc); Who are the source of the real *prapañca* consisting of the intelligent and non-intelligent (*cid* and *acid*) ; Who abide in the highest part of the sky; Who are the real of the reals; Who are the director of the Moon (the path of righteousness) and the Sun (truthfulness) ; Who are the embodiment of the unmodifiable reality.

VJ. : We sought refuge in You Who are the embodiment of perfect Bliss and Knowledge; absolutely distinct from the Earth and other elements; Who are the main gist of the three Vedas; the source of Prapañca which is a reality; abiding as *antaryāmin* in the world, a reality; the director and donor of the spiritual wisdom and happiness to the world—a reality; Whose blissful essential nature is unaffected.

27.* The primeval tree in the form of (visible) universe has on one base (viz. *Prakṛti*), two fruits (viz. pleasure and pain), three roots (viz. the *guṇas, sattva, rajas* and *tamas*), four kinds of secretions (viz. the objectives of human life, religion, property and wealth, sensual desires and liberation), five attributes (the sense organs), six folds or states (viz. birth, existence, growth, ripeness, decay and destruction or natural affections viz. hunger and thirst, grief and delusion, old age and death), seven kinds of barks (the constituents of the body viz skin, blood, flesh, albumen, bone, marrow and semen), eight branches (the five elements—*bhūtas*, the mind, the reason and the ego), nine hollows (the 'gates' of the body, viz. two sockets of eyes, two cavities of ears, two nostrils, the mouth, the organs of urination and defecation), ten leaves (the vital airs—*prāṇas*), two birds (the individual Soul and the Indwelling Supreme Soul).

28. You alone are the cause of the (above-mentioned tree in the from of) phenomenal universe; You are its resting place (after its dissolution), and You are its protector. Those whose minds (knowledge or wisdom) are clouded by Your Māyā (the deluding potency), look upon you as many, but not so those who possess spiritual wisdom.

29. You are essentially knowledge and consciousness (the internal controller of all). Repeatedly You assume forms for conferring happiness on the mobile and immobile creation. Your forms are purely *sāttvic* (unadulterated with *rajas* and *tamas*). They bring happiness to the righteous and mete out destruction to the wicked.

30. Oh lotus-eyed god, some persons who have fixed their minds through concentration on you, the embodiment of

* (1) VR. interprets *ādi-vṛkṣa* as 'the corporeal body' and its eight branches are hands, feet, neck, chest and stomach and the 'leaves' are ten objects of senses.

(2) VJ. regards the universe as 'the eternal' tree which has Hari as its one (the sole) support, two fruits (viz. *puṇya* and *pāpa*—merit and sin); the three roots are *vyāhṛtis, vedas* or states); four results are heaven, hell, darkness (*tamas*) and emancipation; five special roots are vital airs (*prāṇas*). The rest of details are like ŚR. Hari destroys this tree. Hence Hari's supremacy.

pure *sattva*, easily cross the ocean of *saṁsāra* (as is done by the great) by the raft in the form of your feet as if it (*saṁsāra*) were as insignificant as the shallow footprint of a calf.

31. Oh self-effulgent Lord ! Having themselves crossed the extremely impassable, terrible ocean of *saṁsāra*, those devotees of unbounded friendliness to all creatures have (however) gone to the other side (of *saṁsāra*) leaving behind them the boat in the form of your lotus-like feet (i.e. the path of devotion); for you are gracious unto the righteous.

32. Oh lotus-eyed god ! Those others who follow the path of knowledge and regard themselves as emancipated, get their minds and intellect corrupted due to their lack of devotion to you (or whose mind is clouded, though they are clever in disputations). These persons, attaining with great difficulty to a high state (e.g. birth in a noble family), fall down therefrom, as they feel no respect for your feet.

33. Never do your devotees who have cherished deep affection to you, deviate from the right path that way, Oh Lord of Lakṣmī ! Protected on every side by you, they dauntlessly move about trading over the heads of the commanders of armies of obstacles and impediment, Oh Lord.

34. For the sake of preservation of the world you assume an absolutely pure—*sāttvic*—body which bestows the desired boons (*puruṣārthas*) to embodied beings, and wherewith people (belonging to different *āśramas*—stages in life) worship you by studying the Vedas, performance of religious rituals, Yogic practices, austere penance and deep meditation (worship of the Lord is impossible in the absence of a corporeal form).

35. Oh creator of the universe ! Had you not assumed this absolutely pure *sāttvic* form of yours, the Supreme direct knowledge which thoroughly annihilates ignorance and the notion of difference resulting from it, could not be engendered at all. Your worship can only be inferred (and not realized directly) by the light shed by *guṇas* (or the cognitive senses) as a particular *guṇa* can become in a special way and with a particular person, a source of light or knowledge. (When you are worshipped through your pure *sāttvic* form and the mind becomes one with you, God realization takes place through your grace).

36. Your name and form along with your excellences, deeds and births cannot be comprehended fully and described (as they are divine and super-natural). You are the direct witness of everything, but your nature can only be inferred (and not directly perceived) by the mind and the Vedic words. But Oh self-effulgent Lord ! Your votaries, however, do realize you directly while they are engaged in their acts (of worship and meditation).

37. He who during the performance of his activities has his mind concentrated on your lotus-like feet by hearing, singing, reminding others and contemplating on your auspicious names and forms, does not deserve to be born again (in *saṁsāra*).

38. Fortunately, On Hari ! The heavy burden of this earth which represents your foot, has been removed by the birth (*avatāra*) of Your Lordship. It is our good luck that we shall now see the earth impressed with your auspiciously-marked beautiful foot-prints and the heavens showered with Your mercy.

39. Oh Lord ! Verily we cannot conceive any other reason, except your own pleasure, of assuming a form (birth) that You, the unborn are born. Oh Lord You are eternally free and a shelter from fear. Birth, continuation in life and death in the case of individual Souls are brought through *avidyā* (ignorance about you).

40. Oh Lord ! Now be pleased to protect us and the three worlds and relieve the earth of her heavy burden as you did (in the past) by incarnating Yourself in the form of a fish, a horse (*Hayagriva*), a tortoise, a man-lion (Nṛsiṁha), a boar (Varāha), a swan, a Kṣattriya (Rāma), a Brāhmaṇa (Paraśurāma) and a god (Vāmana). Our salutations to You, Oh the best and foremost of Yadus.

41. (Addressing Devakī) :

"Oh mother (Devakī) ! It is really a good luck that the Supreme Person, the veritable Almighty Lord himself has entered your womb with his *aṁśa* (divine powers which are his parts), for the sake of our welfare. Let there be no more fear from Kaṁsa, the king of Bhojas whose death is imminent. Your son will be the protector of Yadus".

Śri Śuka said :

42. Having thus eulogized the Supreme Person whose nature is distinct from the visible universe, the gods headed by Brahmā and Śiva returned to heaven.

CHAPTER THREE

Description of the Birth of Śrīkṛṣṇa

Śri Śuka continued :

1. Now came the most auspicious time full of all blessings when the constellation Rohiṇī presided over by god Brahmā, the son of Viṣṇu, was at the ascendant and all constellations of stars (like *Aśvini* and others), planets and stars assumed peaceful aspects.

2. All the directions became clear and propitious (despite the continuation of the rainy season in the month of Śrāvaṇa) the sky became illumined with innumerable clusters of stars shining unobscured; the earth with its towns, villages, settlements of cowherds and mines revelled in auspicious festivities.

3. The waters of the rivers became crystal clear; the lakes were blooming with lotuses; the rows of forest trees laden with bunches of flowers were resounded with swarms of the sweetly humming bees and cooing of birds.

4 A pure, cool breeze wafting sweet fragrance blew delighting in its touch; the sacred fires maintained in the houses of the twice-borns (automatically) burst into flames.

5. With the exception of demons like Kaṁsa, the minds of all the creatures and those of gods became filled with delight. When the birthless (Lord Viṣṇu) was about to incarnate, kettle-drums were being sounded in the celestial region.

6. At that time Kinnaras and Gandharvas burst forth singing, Siddhas and Cāraṇas sang prayers; ladies of the Vidyādhara clan danced along with celestial damsels.

7. Overwhelmed with joy the gods and sages showered (heaps of) flowers; following the roaring of the seas, clouds gave forth a low rumbling sound.

8. At midnight when the darkness tormenting the people was thickening, Lord Viṣṇu, the Indweller of the hearts of all, manifested himself in his own complete divine form, like the full moon rising in the East, through Devakī who was like unto a goddess.

9-10. Vasudeva saw that wonderful child of lotus-like eyes, endowed with four arms, bearing a conch and wielding aloft a mace and a discus (and a lotus); having (on his chest) the Śrīvatsa mark (of curl of golden hair), with the Kaustubha gem (hanging from his neck but) beautified by his neck; clad in yellow silken garments, possessing the charming complexion of rain-bearing cloud; his profuse locks of hair bathed in the lustre of his crown and ear-rings studded with invaluable *vaidūrya*-gems (lapis lazuli); resplendent with his exquisite and valuable zone, armlets, bracelets and other ornaments.

11. With eyes blooming wide open with amazement, Vasudeva beheld Lord Hari (born as) his son. With his mind confused with rapture on that happy and auspicious occasion of Kṛṣṇa's incarnation, he (Vasudeva) was overcome with (lit. bathed in) delight, and gave ten thousand cows as gift to Brāhmaṇas.

12. Now realizing the child who illuminated the lying-in-chamber with his splendour, was Lord Viṣṇu, the Supreme Person, Vasudeva of pure heart, who, due to his awareness of Viṣṇu's prowess completely lost his fear, began to praise him with folded palms, and body bent low in humility, Oh scion of Bharata.

(Having first embraced the Lord as his son)

Vasudeva said :

13. How blessed I am that I have seen you directly —you the Supreme Person, transcendental to and distinct from *Prakṛti*, absolute wisdom and supreme bliss incarnate, and (as inner controller) the witness of all minds and intellects.

14. (As a matter of fact you never entered the womb of Devakī for) you are factually of such absolute nature as is

described above. Having evolved this universe consisting of three *guṇas* through your creative potency called Māyā, at the beginning of creation, you have not really entered into it (for the Lord is infinite and the universe is limited); you are, however, presumed to have entered it (as a *Puruṣa* and the omnipresent Inner Controller).

15. Just as these unmodified elementary principles (such as *mahat*, *Ahaṁkāra*) are in existence at the beginning of the creation, and are severally incapable of creation though endowed with different properties and powers, they give rise to the universe after combining with their evolutes.

16. Having come together (synthesizing) with their (sixteen) evolutes, they create the universe and appear to have entered into it; but due to their existence prior to the creation (as its cause), their (later) entry is an impossibility. (Similarly, the Lord existed before Devakī and his appearance to have entered her womb is not a reality).

17.* In this way, even though your revered self exists along with the objects which are cognisable through senses (the true nature of which is) inferrable through perception of sense-objects you are not perceived along with those objects, directly (as the senses can perceive only their specific objects and God is not such an object); (for you, being unconditioned and all-pervading, the distinction of being inside or outside is inapplicable to you. You are everything and the indwelling Soul of all, the self-abiding real essence. (Hence your entry in the womb of Devakī is not a reality).

* (1) VR. : Though you abide in all creatures like gods, men—the products of *guṇas*—you are not affected by their limitations. You are above modifications, essentially of unlimited knowledge and blissful nature. You are un-enveloped i.e. of unlimited knowledge. Being all-pervading and the cause of all the distinction of being 'in' and 'out' is not applicable to you. As you are the independent Inner Controller, *antaryāmin*, the limitations of the body do not affect you.

(2) SD. emphasizes that the direct vision of God is due to His grace and He is beyond the ken of senses.

(3) VT. : As you are always loving to your devotees, you have come to us as a son which is the highest reward (of our devotion).

18.* He who presumes real independent existence—as distinct from the Soul—in the case of objects perceived by him (or by the Soul) is an ignorant person. For when these objects (i.e. the world) are subjected to investigation, they are (found to be) of verbal nature and essentially unreal. He who acknowledges the unreality as a distinct reality is (certainly) a dullard.

19. Oh all-pervading Lord ! They say that the creation, preservation and destruction of the universe proceeds from you who are above all *guṇas*, (and hence) desireless (and performing no acts), and subject to no modification. As you are both Brahman and the Supreme Ruler, there is no contradiction in transcendence to modifications and the creation etc. of the universe. For though the activity is carried out by *guṇas*, it is ascribed to you as *guṇas* (ultimately depend on you only).

20. You who are of such a nature (as described above) verily assume, through your Māyā potency, pure white complexion (Brahmā form) full of the principle of *rajas* for the creation of these worlds, and a dark complexion (Rudra form) through *tamas* for the destruction of the universe.

21. Oh all-pervading Lord, the supreme Ruler of all ! (how gracious of you it is that though Your *avatāra* is an impossibility in the real sense of the term), You have incarnated yourself in my house (despite its being a prison-cell), with a desire to protect this world. You will annihilate the hordes led by millions of Asura chiefs passing under the name of Kṣatriyas.

22. Oh Lord of gods ! Hearing (the prediction) of Your birth in our house, this villainous fellow (Kaṁsa) has (cold-bloodedly) killed your elder brothers. Learning your incarnation directly through the reports of his servants, he will just now rush here with uplifted weapons."

* VJ. : In the absence of the support of Vedic texts, it is untenable to admit the conclusion of the ignorant that you are identical with the body or the senses simply because of Your presence in them. For the Supreme Man (Lord Viṣṇu) has accepted (or revealed) the super-human faultless Vedic texts which dispel all doubts.

Śrī Śuka said :

23. Now, seeing that this son of hers bore the characteristics of the supreme person (Lord Viṣṇu), Devakī who was (erstwhile) afraid of Kaṁsa, (now) smiled happily and began to pray him :

Devakī said :

24. (How can there be any danger to you) who are verily the Lord Viṣṇu himself, the Illuminator of the aggregate of intelligence, senses and other psycho-physical organisms: and who are that indescribable Reality whom the Vedas declare as the unmanifest primordial cause, the Supreme Brahman, pure consciousness transcending all *guṇas* and modifications, absolute existence attributeless, and devoid of activity.

25. When at the end of the period of two *parārdhas* (which terminates the life-time of Brahmā), by the velocity of time, the universe dissolves and all the gross elements (*Mahābhūtas*) are absorbed into their primordial subtle form (viz. *ahaṁkāra* which in its turn is absorbed into the principle called *mahat*) and the principle *mahat* is merged in the unmanifest (*pradhāna* which is absorbed in you), You alone remain behind (remaining cognisant that the *Pradhāna* lying merged in You is to be re-awakened) and hence you are designated as the Residue (*Śeṣa*) or the complete whole (*aśeṣa*).

26. The wise say that this mighty time as described above which begins with a *nimeṣa* (twinkling of the eye) and extends (through cycle of years) to the end of *dviparārdha* (Brahmā's life) and which controls the cyclic course of the universe, is your own sportful activity, Oh Director of the *Prakṛti* ! I seek your protection—You who are the Supreme Ruler and the abode of security.

27. A mortal, being apprehensive of the serpent (in the form) of death, and running about all the world (for security against death), failed to find a place free from fear. Today having attained to your lotus-like feet through an unexpected stroke of good luck (and through your grace), he reposes in peace and security. It is (now) Death that runs away from him.

28. Of such nature as You are, protect us (your devotees) who are afraid of the terrible son of Ugrasena; for you are the rescuer of your devotees (servants) from fear. Let not this divine form of yours which is worthy of being the object of meditation, be manifest to the gross physical eyes of human beings.

29. Let not that wicked Kaṁsa know of your birth from me, Oh Madhusūdana (slayer of the demon Madhu). Being naturally timid, I am terribly afraid of Kaṁsa, for your sake.

30. Oh soul of the universe ! May you withdraw this Superhuman form with four arms furnished with the superb splendour of conch, discus, mace and lotus.

31. That your Lordship, the Supreme Person who contains within yourself all this universe *in extenso* at the end of the cosmic night (during *Pralaya*), should get himself accommodated in my womb is certainly a wonderful imitation of the human (ways of the) world."

The Lord said :

32. "Oh chaste lady ! In your previous birth in the age of Svāyambhuva Manu, you were Pṛśni and this sinless Vasudeva your husband, was then a Prajāpati named Sutapas.

33. When both of you were directed by god Brahmā to create progeny, you subdued all your senses and performed a very austere penance.

34. Enduring in due course, all the inclemencies of the seasons such as rains, storms, solar rays, snow-fall and heat, you completely washed off the impurities of the mind by breath-control.

35. Subsisting on withered leaves and merely on air and actuated with the desire to obtain your cherished objects from me, you were determined to propitiate Me with a serene mind.

36. Thus rolled by twelve thousand divine years, while both of you, with your heart fixed on Me, were performing a very difficult and austere penance.

37-38. Being continuously contemplated upon in the heart with faith, devotion and asceticism, I was highly pleased with you and manifested myself before you in this very form with a desire to fulfil your cherished objects, Oh sinless one,

When I, the foremost bestower of boons, told you to ask Me for a boon, the boon for having a son like Me was sought by you.

39. Though both of you had not tasted the conjugal and other pleasures of ordinary sensual objects and were childless, you did not seek for Emancipation (from the world) as you were deluded by My divine Māyā.

40. When I disappeared from your view and you, having secured the boon of getting a son like Me and thus accomplishing your cherished desire, you indulged in enjoying sensual pleasures.

41. Finding that nobody else in this world is comparable to Me in goodness of nature, generosity and other virtues in this world, I Myself was born as your son and became known as *Pṛśni-garbha*.

42. And again of you both (as Aditi and Kaśyapa) I was born of Aditi from Kaśyapa and was famous as Upendra and also as Vāmana due to shortness of stature.

43. Now even in this third incarnation, I aṁ verily born with that very form again of you both (who are former Aditi and Kaśyapa). In this way, my word has been kept, Oh pious lady.

44. I have revealed this form of Mine to you in order to remind you of my previous births (from you); otherwise the knowledge about my real being is not possible through the semblance of human form. (Now as desired by you, I shall assume the form of a human baby).

45. Thinking of Me constantly as your son as well as contemplating upon Me as Supreme Brahman and loving me affectionately, both of you will attain to the highest state in relation to Me.

45-A. (*Vṛndāvana edition adds*)

If you are still afraid of Kaṁsa, quickly take me to Gokula and bring (as substitute) My Māyā who has been born from (the womb of) Yaśodā."

Śrī Śuka said :

46. Having spoken thus, Hari became silent. With his Māyā power, the Lord immediately became an ordinary

human babe, while the parents were simply looking on (with wonder).

47. Thereupon, when Vasudeva, the son of Śūra desired to go out of the lying-in-chamber taking his son with him (and was about to start) as directed by the Lord, Yoga-Māyā, though (herself) birthless, was born of Nanda's wife.

48-49. By Yoga-Māyā the gate-keepers were deprived of all their consciousness and functioning of their senses and even the citizens were steeped in deep sleep; all the gates (of the palace prison) which were closed by huge doors secured with iron chains and bolts automatically flung open at the approach of Vasudeva carrying Kṛṣṇa (on his head) like darkness dispersing at the appearance of the Sun. The rain cloud showered with a gentle rumbling and the serpent Śesa (closely) followed him, warding off the rain-water with his hoods spread over his head (like an umbrella).

50. While Indra, the god of rains, continuously poured showers of rain (and even though) the river Yamunā (the presiding deity of which was Yamunā, the younger sister of Yama—the god of death) covered with foam created by waves set up by the velocity of the swiftly-moving deep flood and was full of hundreds of fearful whirlpools, afforded passage (to Vasudeva and Kṛṣṇa) as the Sea did to the Lord of Lakṣmī (Lord Śrī Rāma) formerly.

51. Arriving at Nanda's Vraja, Vasudeva found that all the cowherds were deeply buried in sleep. Placing his son on the bed of Yaśodā, taking up her daughter (in exchange), Vasudeva returned home (his palace-prison).

52. Placing the daughter on the bed of Devakī, Vasudeva put the iron fetters on his feet and remained confined as before.

53. And Yaśodā, Nanda's wife was vaguely conscious of having delivered a child, but she was so exhausted and had her memory (so much) clouded under delusion, that she did not discern the sex of the baby.

CHAPTER FOUR

Yoga-Māyā's Prophecy and Kaṁsa's Order to Slaughter all Children

Śrī Śuka said :

1. (After the return of Vasudeva) all the gates of the outer and inner apartments became closed as before. Hearing the cry of the baby, the palace guards became wide-awake.

2. They, on their part, (promptly and) hastily approached Kaṁsa, the King of Bhojas, and reported (to him) Devakī's delivery of that (eighth) child which he was expecting anxiously.

3. Springing up hurriedly from the bed and bewildered at the thought that that (child) was his (veritable god of) death, he, with tottering steps and dishevelled hair, rushed hastily to (Devakī's) lying-in-room.

4. To her brother (Kaṁsa), the pious, divine, (yet) miserable lady piteously addressed. "This is your daughter-in-law, Oh blessed brother. She may be the eighth child (but) it is not proper that you should kill a female (child).

5. Dear Brother ! Impelled as you were by Destiny, a number of my children brilliant like fire, were killed by you. Be pleased to give (spare) this one daughter to me.

6. Oh mighty king ! Am I not your miserable younger sister who am bereaved of all my sons ? Unfortunate as I am, it behoves you, Oh dear brother, to spare this last child for me".

Śrī Śuka said :

7. (Although) he was thus implored by Devakī while hugging the child to her bosom and weeping piteously like a most helpless woman, the wicked fellow sternly rebuked her and snatched away the baby from her.

8. His affection (for the sister and niece) being uprooted (superseded) by his (vile) self-interest, he seized the new-born daughter of his sister by her feet and dashed her against the surface of a slab.

9. Flying off from (the grip of) of hands, she rose up to the sky and (stationing herself in the sky), the younger sister of Kṛṣṇa manifested herself as a goddess with eight mighty arms wielding weapons.

10. She was adorned with heavenly garlands, garments, pigments, jewelled ornaments and wielded (in her arms) a bow, a spear, an arrow, a shield, a sword, a conch, a discus and a mace.

11. She was being praised by Siddhas, Cāraṇas, Gandharvas, Apsaras (divine damsels), Kinnaras and serpents who offered her rich, sumptuous presents. She spoke :

12. "You dunce ! What have you gained by killing me ? Your destroyer, your adversary in the former birth, is born somewhere (in an unknown place). Do not unnecessarily kill helpless, innocent children."

13. Having warned him thus, the goddess (disappeared). The venerable goddess Māyā is known under many names and is worshipped in many shrines, bearing different names.

14. Kaṁsa was extremely flabbergasted to hear her pronouncement. He set Vasudeva and Devakī at liberty and apologised in humility :

15. "Alas ! My sister ! Oh my brother-in-law ! Like a cannibal preying on his own child, many a son of yours has been killed by me, a wicked sinner.

16. For being so, (a sinner) bereft of mercy, for disowning my friends and relatives, for being virtually dead though breathing (merely alive), I do not know to what infernal region I shall be taken as in the case of a slayer of Brāhmaṇas.

17. Not only mortals but even the celestials also speak untruth. Putting faith in them, I, a wicked sinner, killed my sister's children.

18. Oh high-souled ones ! Do not lament for your sons who reaped the fruit of their previous deeds. Creatures are at the mercy of the Providence. They do not live or are not together (at the same place) for ever.

19. Just as in this world earthen articles are created out of and (after destruction) become one with the earth, but the earth itself persists (unmodified), similarly in the process of

creation and destruction of physical bodies the Soul undergoes no modifications.

20. Misapprehension about the nature of the Soul arises in him who does not understand the Reality as it is. That leads to the notion of difference (contrary to the real nature of the Soul). Thus there is no end to *saṁsāra* and to the union and separation from the body (i.e. the cycle of births and deaths).

21. Inasmuch as every creature has inevitably and helplessly to reap the fruit of his actions, Oh blessed sister, do not grieve over (the death of) your sons, even though they were killed by me.

22. So long as a person does not cognize the real nature of his Self and identifies his body with the Soul, and (wrongly) regards himself as being killed or being the killer, that ignorant fellow is subject to the role of being the subject or object of suffering.

23. Saintly persons are compassionate to the afflicted and the poor. Please do forgive me for my wickedness." With these words and with his face overflowing with tears, he clasped the feet of his sister and her husband.

24. Being reassured by the words of the daughter of Devakī, Kaṁsa, as a testimony of his personal affection to them, released Vasudeva and Devakī from chains (prison).

25. Due to the (sincere) regrets and repentance of her brother, the wrath of Devakī was pacified, and she gave him leave (to go). Vasudeva smiled and spoke to him :

26. "Oh highly fortunate Kaṁsa ! It is exactly as you say. The notion of creatures that they are identical with the body is born of ignorance, and that is the cause of the difference in regarding this as one's own and that as another's.

27. Persons possessing differentiating outlook and sense of distinction and suffering from grief, joy, fear, malice, covetousness, delusion and pride do not perceive the self-existent Reality (God) who brings about the destruction of beings through their mutual action (against each other), caused by their passions."

Śrī Śuka said :

28. Thus sincerely addressed by kindly disposed Devakī and Vasudeva, Kaṁsa took leave of them and returned to his palace.

29. When the night was over, Kaṁsa summoned his ministers and reported to them everything that had been said by *Yoganidrā* (the trance—sleep of Lord Viṣṇu).

30. Hearing the narration of their master, the demons (sons of Diti), the (sworn) enemies of gods, who cherished deep anger against the celestials, but were not foresighted spoke to him.

31. "If this be the case, Oh Lord of Bhojas, we shall verily massacre today all children of ten days or less (dwelling) in cities, towns, cowherds' camps and (such) other places.

32. What can the gods do with all their endeavours. They are cowards on the battlefield. They live in perpetual terror of the twanging of your bow-string.

33. Being beaten on all sides with volleys of arrows discharged by you, they, being anxious to save their lives, deserted the battlefield and took to their heels.

34. Some gods in their wretched plight laid down their arms and stood with folded palms, while others with their loin-cloth untucked and hair on the head untied and dishevelled announced, "We are afraid."

35. You do not strike at those (enemies) who have forgotten their arms and missiles or have lost their chariots or are terror-stricken or are attending to something else or have turned away (from the battlefield) or have their bows broken or have given up fighting.

36. What can gods, the warriors in peace times and boastful outside the battlefield, do (to harm us)? Of what account is Hari who lies in concealment or Śiva who dwells in a forest? Why care for Indra of poor strength or Brahmā (always) absorbed in penance?

37. We, however, think that gods due to their (inborn) enmity, should not be ignored. Therefore, deploy us, your obedient servants to dig out and destroy even their roots.

38. Just as a disease in the body, if neglected, strikes deep roots and becomes impossible to be cured or the senses if

uncontrolled and ignored (become unmanageable), so the enemy, if ignored, grows in strength and cannot be dislodged.

39. Viṣṇu is the root (the main stay) of all gods. Where there is Viṣṇu, there abides the eternal righteousness (*dharma*). The roots of the *dharma* are the Vedas, cows, Brāhmaṇas, asceticism and sacrifices with donation of liberal gifts.

40. Therefore, Oh King, we shall kill by all (possible) means Brāhmaṇas, the reciters of the Vedas, the ascetics performing penance and those continually engaged in sacrificial acts, and cows yielding all the materials for sacrificial oblations.

41. Brāhmaṇas, cows, the Vedas, penance, truthfulness, control of senses, serenity of mind, faith, mercy, endurance and the sacrifices constitute the body of Hari.

42. For he is the Supreme Ruler of all gods, the enemy of Asuras, the indweller in the hearts of all. All divinities including Lord Śiva and the four-faced god Brahmā depend on him as their support (root). Hence extirpation (through persecution) of sages is really the only means of killing him."

Śrī Śuka said :

43. Having thus conferred with his wicked ministers, the evil-minded Kaṁsa who was enmeshed in the snare of Death, considered massacre of Brāhmaṇas as conducive to his good.

44. Having commissioned Dānavas who were naturally disposed to persecute others and who could assume any form at will, for harassing the good people in all directions, Kaṁsa entered his palace.

45. Constituted as they were by predominantly *rājasic* nature, and with their minds deluded by *tamas*, they started their campaign of hatred of the good as their death was imminent.

46. Serious violations of the great destroy one's span of life, prosperity, glory, righteousness, (attainment of) heavenly regions, and all other blessings.

CHAPTER FIVE

Celebration of Kṛṣṇa's Birth : Meeting of Nanda and Vasudeva

Śrī Śuka said :

1-2. Delighted at the birth of a son, the noble-minded Nanda too took a bath, got purified and adorned himself. He sent for Brāhmaṇas well versed in astrology and made them recite the *Svastyayana* (prescribed benedictory Vedic hymns) and got the *jāta-karma* ceremony of his child, as well as the worship of his forebears (*pitṛs*)and gods duly performed according to precepts.

3. As a gift (on this joyous occasion), he presented to Brāhmaṇas two-hundred thousands of richly adorned cows, and seven mountain-like heaps[1] of sesamum seeds covered with streams (large quantities) of precious stones and gold-cloth.

4.* Some material things become purified by passage of time (e.g. the earth), some by ablution (e.g. our body), or washing (e.g. things covered with dirt), some by special rites (e.g. the foetus), some by penance (e.g. senses), some by sacrificial performance (e.g. Brāhmaṇas), some by charitable gifts (wealth), some by contentment (mind), while the soul is purified by (meditation and) knowledge of the Self.

5. Brāhmaṇas, Sūtas[2], Māgadhas and Vandins uttered auspicious blessings; musicians sang; drums and kettle-drums were frequently sounded.

6. All the entrances, enclosures, and interiors of the houses of *Vraja* were well-swept and properly besprinkled (with

1. VC. quotes the *Bhaviṣyottara Purāṇa* and states the best 'Sesamum mountain' consists of ten *droṇas*, medium of five, and the lowest of three *droṇas*.

* Examples in the bracket are supplied by ŚR.

2. Normally *sūtas* are the reciters of Purāṇas; Māgadhas are bards reciting the glories of royal dynasties; Vandins are clearheaded persons making observations suitable for the occasion.

sūtāḥ paurāṇikāḥ proktā, Māgadhā vaṁśa-śaṁsakāḥ |
Vandinas tvamala-prajñāḥ prastāva-sadṛśoktayaḥ ||

But VJ. states : *Sūtas* sing the eulogies composed by themselves, Māgadhas sing compositions of others, while Vandins read panygerics from books.

water). It (the *Vraja*) was decorated with flags and buntings of different colours, banners, wreaths, arches of (silken) raiments, and tender leaves.

7. The oxen, cows and heifers (grown up calves) were smeared with oil mixed with turmeric power. They were painted with various colours, and adorned with peacock feathers, wreaths, cloths and gold chains (round the neck).

8. Adorned with valuable garments, costly ornaments, coats and turbans, the cowherds came to visit (Nanda) with various kinds of presents in their hands.

9. On hearing the news of the birth of a son to Yaśodā, the cowherd women were delighted, and they beautified themselves with costly garments, ornaments and (the make-up of) collyrium etc.

10. The beauty of their lotus-like faces was enhanced with the decoration of saffron-paste like unto filaments heightening the beauty of a lotus. In spite of their heavy buttocks, they hastily went with presents (to Yaśodā) heaving their heavy breasts (while going).

11. Wearing ear-rings set with well-polished jewels, necklaces of gold-coins about their necks, and clad in wonderfully wrought garments of various colours the *gopa* damsels proceeded to the palace of Nanda showering on the way flowers dropped from the braids of their hair. They appeared (lit. shone) most beautiful with bangles round their wrists, their swaying ear-rings and dangling necklaces on heaving breasts.

12. Invoking blessings (of God) on the child, "May you protect the child for a long time"[1] they sprayed the (assembled) people with water mixed with oil and turmeric power and sang lustily. (Or : they sang in a high pitch the praise of the Unborn—Kṛṣṇa).

13. On the great festive occasion of the coming of Lord Kṛṣṇa, the Infinite, the Supreme Lord of the universe, a variety of musical instruments were played on.

1. Or : May you protect us forever—VR and others.
This interpretation is obviously illogical and out of context with the sentence, "Invoking blessings on the child".

14. The merry cowherds joyously sprayed and besmeared one another with curds, milk, ghee and water and they threw (balls of) butter at each other.[1]

15-16* For the propitiation of Lord Viṣṇu and for the well-being of his son, the noble-minded Nanda presented to the cowherds garments, ornaments and wealth in the form of cows (or kine, gold and silver). The generous-hearted Nanda respectfully worshipped Sūtas, Māgadhas, Vandins and others who lived by their arts, skills or crafts (e.g. astrologers, dancers etc.), and conferred upon them their (respective) desired objects.

17. Welcomed by Nanda, the chief of cowherds, Rohiṇī, who was highly fortunate (as she was to be witness to the sportive activities of Lord Kṛṣṇa from his childhood) was adorned with very costly (heavenly-type) Lower garment and other clothes, garland and necklace and was moving about in Nanda's palace (particularly in that reception).

18. Thence forward the *Vraja* of Nanda became blessed with prosperity in every respect as it was turned into a pleasure garden for the sporting of goddess Lakṣmī due to its becoming the abode of Hari, Oh King.

19. Having instructed the cowherds to take care of and protect the Gokula, Nanda went to Mathurā to pay his annual tribute to Kaṁsa, Oh Parīkṣit (the best of Kurus).

20. Having learnt (from the public) that his brotherly Nanda had come and having (reliably) known that Nanda's (official) work of payment of tributes was over, Vasudeva repaired to his lodging place (the parking ground of wagons).

21. Seeing him (Vasudeva) come, he promptly sprang to his feet as a body (in an unconscious stage) does on the return of life (or consciousness). Being overjoyed and over-

1. Or : Thickly besmearing one another with butter, they tried to throw each other on (the slippery) ground.—VT.

* ŚR : The nobleminded Nanda presented to cowherds as also to Sūtas, Māgadhas, Vandins and others who lived by their skill in arts, crafts, etc., garments, ornaments, kine and wealth.

For the propitiation of Lord Viṣṇu and the well-being of the child, the generous-minded Nanda honoured others (visitors, guests etc.) by bestowing on them their desired objects.

whelmed with affection, he flung his arms round his dearest friend to embrace him.

22. Oh Protector of the People ! When Vasudeva was respectfully received, comfortably seated and was honoured with the enquiry about his health, he, with his mind deeply attached to both of his sons, courteously addressed Nanda as follows :

23. "Brother ! It is indeed fortunate that a darling child has been born to you who were childless till this advanced age and had lost hopes of getting an issue.

24. It is due to sheer good luck that you have met me today like one born again in this whirling cycle of Saṁsāra. For the sight of dear ones is very rare.

25. Oh dear friend ! The staying together of intimate friends (howsoever dear but) following varied professions, is not possible like unto the coming together of floating logs of wood (etc.) in a stream of water but which are swept away by the current.

26. Is the Gokula (Vṛndāvana) where you are now dwelling accompanied (lit. surrounded) by your friends and relatives favourable to the cattle ? Does it abound in plenty of water, grass and plants ? Is it free from disease and epidemics ?

27. Oh brother ! Does my son (Balarāma) who regards you to be his father and is dearly fondled by you and your wife, doing well along with his mother, in your *Vraja* ?

28. For, the threefold objective of human life (viz. *dharma, artha* and *kāma*) is prescribed (as beneficial) insofar as they are shared with one's kith and kin. But if they suffer distress, that threefold purpose of life does not contribute to happiness."

Nanda said :

29. "Alas ! Many of your sons born of Devakī have been killed by Kaṁsa. And only the youngest daughter survived—even she flew to heaven.

30.* It is definite that people in this world have their end in the unseen (according to their destiny. When good

* VR : All people definitely find their end in the unseen (as destined along with happiness and misery). The destiny is the ultimate supreme controller. He who realises that pleasure and pain are always due to his destiny, is always equable and serene in prosperity and adversity.

fortune, blessing one with the pleasure of having sons etc., ceases to smile, one is bereaved of them). The destiny is supreme. (If one is separated from one's sons, the destiny reunites them). He who knows that the destiny is the reality about Ātman (and as such is the ever constant cause of pleasure and pain) does not get bewildered."

Vasudeva said :

31. "The annual tribute has been paid by you to the king, and we have seen (each other). You should not stay here any longer, for omens indicating calamities are seen at Gokula."

Śrī Śuka said :

32. Thus advised by Vasudeva, Nanda and other cowherds, taking leave of him, mounted on carts drawn by bullocks and returned to Gokula.

CHAPTER SIX

Pūtanā emancipated

Śrī Śuka said :

1. On his way (back to Gokula), Nanda pondered that the words of Vasudeva might not be untrue. Being apprehensive of impending calamities, (mentally) he sought refuge in Lord Hari.

2. Deputed by Kaṁsa, the terrible, infant-killer Pūtanā moved about, killing babes and infants in cities, towns, cowherd-settlements (on her way).

3. Wherever, people, while attending to their duties, do not listen to (recite etc.) the names and deeds of the Lord of Sātvatas (Kṛṣṇa) which are capable of annihilating demons, there and there only, ogresses (and other evil spirits) prevail.

4. One day, that Pūtanā who was capable of coursing through the sky, flew (through the sky) to the Gokula ruled by Nanda. Assuming the form of a young beautiful woman

through her witchcraft, she entered the Gokula as the wantonness was capable of assuming any guise, and moving into any house she pleased.

5-6. On seeing that beautiful damsel the braids of whose hair were adorned with jasmine flowers (interwoven therein), whose slender waist was (as if) crushed between her big buttocks and heavy breasts, who was clad in rich garments, whose face was beautified with the locks of hair lustrous with the radiance of the brilliant swaying ear-rings, who with her charming smiles and sidelong glances captivated the hearts of the inhabitants of Vraja (who hence failed to extern her), and whom, due to her wearing a blooming lotus in hand, the Gopa women thought to be goddess Lakṣmī incarnate, who had come to see her Lord (and they kept silent in awe and respect, instead of barring her entrance).

7. Pūtanā, that infant-killer evil spirit, roving in search for babies, came by chance to the house of Nanda, and saw the child Kṛṣṇa who was the exterminator of the wicked, but was lying in bed with his immeasurable innate glory veiled, like fire covered under ashes.

8. Recognizing her to be the evil spirit which kills infants, the Lord of the mobile and immobile creation lay quiet with his eyes closed[1]. And she placed the Infinite Lord, her very death, on her lap, as a stupid person would do to a sleeping serpent, mistaking it for a rope.

8A. Even though he was the Supreme Ruler of the universe the Lord, playing the part of a child, spoke nothing. But the fiendess was unaware that he was the lord Hari who by his very nature knows directly all the activities of the world.

9. Finding suddenly within their house that superb accomplished lady behaving (externally) most affectionately and in a charming way, even though her heart was sharp (cruel like sword encased in a charming scabbard, both the mothers (Yaśodā and Rohiṇī) were stupefied with her effulgence and stood agazing (instead of preventing her).

10. The terrible demoness placed the child Kṛṣṇa on her lap and suckled him at her breast full of indigestible virulent

1. VJ.'s text intersperses one verse here.

poison. Thereupon, with indignation, the Lord squeezed hard her breast with his hands and sucked it along with her life.

11. Being crushed in all her vital parts, she cried out "Let me go, enough of it, leave me". With her body drenched in perspiration and with her hands and feet thrown in convulsions and with distended eyes, she wailed loudly.

12. By her extremely loud and deep cry, the earth along with the mountains, and the heavens along with the planets, were shaken. The netherworld and all the cardinal points were reverberated with the Sound. People being afraid of the discharge of Vajra, fell down on the ground.

13. Oh King, the demoness who, being excruciatingly afflicted at the breast, thus fell dead, reverting to her original form with her mouth agape and her hair, hands and feet stretched near the cowpen even as Vṛtra fell when struck down with *Vajra* (thunderbolt).

14. Even while it fell, her (giant) body crushed to powder trees within an area of twelve miles. It was the most astonishing sight, Oh king of kings.

15-17. The cowherds—men and women—whose hearts, ears and heads were already rent asunder with the terrible roars and yells of the demoness, were struck with terror to see her fearful body with a mouth raged with a terrible set of tusks long like the poles of ploughs, with nostrils resembling mountain caverns; breasts huge like (a pair of hillocks, her reddish hair terribly dishevelled, her eyes deep like dark wells, her buttock terrifically big like sand dunes, her arms, legs and thighs resembling dams (around) her belly looking like a dried up, waterless pool.

18. Seeing the child playing fearlessly on her bosom, the cowherd-women, in their bewilderment, quickly came to him and picked him up.

19. They, also with Yaśodā and Rohiṇī ensured the (future) safety of the child on all sides, against evil spirits (and such other mishaps) by performing the ceremony of waving of the cow's tail round the child and other rites.

20. They bathed the child with the urine of a cow and besmeared it with dust raised by her hoofs. And by applying

cowdungs to twelve (different) parts of his body[1] pronouncing simultaneously twelve (different) names of the Lord, they ensured his safety (by this spiritual talisman).

21. (The *Gopa* women, being bewildered, forgot that they have to get themselves so consecrated before applying the talisman to the child. When they recovered....)

They performed the *ācamana* (sipping of water uttering the names of God for self-purification), made the *bija-nyāsa* (assignment of the various parts of the body to deities accompanied with the uttering of some 'seed-letters' and corresponding gesticulations) first on both of their hands and parts of their body, and then followed the same procedure of the 'placement of seed-letters' on the body of the child (as follows :).

(The Gopa women said)

22. "May Aja (the birthless Lord) protect your feet! May Maṇiman[2] (the Indweller of the *jīva*.) guard your knees;

1. VB. enumerates the parts of the body to be so daubed with cowdung, as follows :

Lalāṭam bāhumūle ca hṛdayam nābhi-pārśvakam /
kaṇṭhaḥ skandhau kaṭir mūrdhā stanau ceti vidur budhāḥ //

Forehead, arms, chest, navel, throat, shoulders, waist, head and the nipples on the chest. And names of god Viṣṇu to be uttered are the first twelve names out of the twenty-four names uttered at the beginning of *Sandhyā vandana*.

VT. quotes from the *Padma Purāṇa* the procedure which is as follows : The particular aspect of the Lord is visualized as consecrating and abiding in that particular part of the body.

Part of the body to be daubed.	*Name of the Lord to be uttered at this time*
Forehead	Keśava
Abdomen (but KD. : Navel)	Nārāyāṇa
Chest	Mādhava
Throat	Govinda
Right side (but KD. : right arm-pit)	Viṣṇu
Right arm	Madhusūdana
Neck (but KD. : right ear-bottom)	Trivikrama
Left side (but KD. : Left arm-pit)	Vāmana
Left arm	Śrīdhara
Neck (but KD. : Left ear bottom)	Hṛṣikeśa
Back	Padmanābha
Waist (but KD. : near the neck)	Dāmodara

2. v.l. *maṇiman*—the wearer of the Kaustubha gem—KD.

Yajña, your thighs; Acyuta, your loins; Hayagrīva (horse-necked Lord), your abdomen; Keśava, your heart; Īśa (the Supreme Ruler), your bosom; Ina (The Lord), your throat; Viṣṇu, your arms; Urukrama, your mouth; and Īśvara (the Supreme Lord), your head.

23. May the wielder of (Sudarśana) discus protect you at the front, and the Bearer of the (Kaumodakī) mace, at the back; May the slayer of Madhu and Ajana (the birthless Lord) each bearing a bow and a sword, protect you on both the sides; May *Urugāya* (the Lord sung by many) bearing the conch (Pāñcajanya), at the four corners (points intervening between quarters); Upendra (Vāmana), overhead; Tārkṣya, on the ground and the Spreme Man wielding a plough, on all sides.

24. May Hṛṣīkeśa protect your senses; Nārāyaṇa, your vital breaths; the Lord of Śvetadvīpa, your heart (the seat of intellect); the Lord of Yoga, your mind.

25. May the son of Pṛśni protect Your understanding; the Supreme Lord, Your *ahaṁkāra* (ego); may Govinda protect You while You are playing; Mādhava, while sleeping.

26. May Vaikuṇṭha guard You while walking; the Lord of Śrī, while sitting. The enjoyer of sacrifices, the terror to all evil spirits, while (You are) eating.

27-29. (All evil spirits like) *Dākinī, Yātudhānī, Kūṣmāṇḍas,* the wicked spirits troubling young infants, *Bhūtas, Pretas, Piśācas, Yakṣas, Rākṣasas* and *Vināyakas, Koṭarā, Revatī, Jyeṣṭhā, Pūtanā, Mātṛkās* and others; *Unmādas* (spirits causing insanity,) and *Apasmāras* which trouble the body, senses and vital breaths; the evil spirits that frighten in dreams, the great calamitous portents, and those wicked spirits that seize the old and the young all these which are terrified at the mention of Viṣṇu's name—may all these wicked spirits be destroyed."

Śrī Śuka said :

30. When the safety of the child was secured in this way (by performing the above-mentioned rites) by the Gopa women, bound to him with ties of affection, the mother suckled him and put him to bed.

31. In the meanwhile, Nanda and other Gopas (cowherds) reached Vraja from Mathurā. They became extremely astonished to see the (enormous) body of Pūtanā.

32. (They said to each other) "How wonderful! Certainly a veritable seer or a master of Yoga (in his previous incarnation) must have been born (in the form of Vasudeva). For that very calamity has been seen by us as was predicted by Vasudeva.

33. (Then) the inhabitants of Vraja hacked down that (Pūtanā's) body with axes and threw the pieces at a distance and burnt it limb by limb on pyres of logs of wood.

34. There arose (a column of) smoke fragrant like that of *aguru* sandle wood, out of that burning body, the sins of which were instantaneously annihilated, the moment Kṛṣṇa sucked (the life out of) it.

35. (How wonderful!) Pūtanā, the blood-sucking demoness, the infant-killer in this world attained to *Mokṣa* by giving suck to him, despite her intention of killing him.

36. How much more would they who dedicate with faith and devotion their most beloved objects to Kṛṣṇa, the Supreme Lord, attain to *Mokṣa* as did his deeply attached mothers.[1]

37-38. When the Lord traversed Pūtanā's body with his feet which are enshrined in the hearts of his devotees, and are adorable to those (gods like Śiva and Brahmā) who are themselves worshipped by people, and sucked her breast, she, in spite of her being a demoness, attained to heaven, the destination (after death) of his mothers. What more need be said of those cows and mothers (Gopa women) the milk from whose breasts and udders was sucked (so fondly) by Kṛṣṇa? They must definitely attain to his abode.

1. ŚR. explains the plural form 'mothers' when Kṛṣṇa had actually two mothers—Yaśodā and Rohiṇī—by referring to Ch. 13 *infra* in which Kṛṣṇa is said to have assumed the forms of cowherd boys and calves when god Brahmā stole them away for one year and Kṛṣṇa in these forms was sucked by the *Gopa* women (the mothers of his abducted companions) and by cows (of those stolen calves). Thus those innumerable Gopa-women and cows became *ipso facto* his mothers.

39. For the glorious Lord, the son of Devakī, the dispenser of Final Emancipation and all other blessings, drank to his heart's content the milk flowing (out of their breasts) through maternal affection.

40. They who have incessantly looked upon (and thus meditated upon) him as their own son, shall never revert to *Saṁsāra,* the cause of which is ignorance.

41. Having smelt the fragrance of the smoke issuing from the funeral pyre (of Pūtanā), the inhabitants of Vraja (who were then away from home) returned to Vraja enquiring, "What it is this (fragrance) due to ? Whence is it coming ?"

42. Hearing from the cowherds the account of the arrival of Pūtanā etc., her death and the safety of the child, they were extremely wonderstruck.

43. Taking up the child (in his arms) as if he had returned from the jaws of death, the noble-minded Nanda smelt him on the crown of his head, and was overwhelmed with joy, Oh best of Kurus.

44. A man who will listen with faith this wonderful account of the liberation of Pūtanā, a sportive achievement of Lord Kṛṣṇa in his childhood, will develop love and devotion to Govinda.

CHAPTER SEVEN

Destruction of the Cart and Tṛṇāvarta

Śrī Śuka said :

*0.A In this way, achieving a number of feats (like the liberation of Pūtanā, by way of sportive activities as a child) which brought joy and happiness to Gopas and their wives, Viṣṇu, the exterminator of the wicked, grew up in the house of Nanda.

*0.B Thus (as narrated in the previous chapters) grew up in Nanda's house Kṛṣṇa (Viṣṇu), the destroyer of the wick-

** The Vṛndāvana edition includes the above verses from the texts of VR. and VJ.

ed people, giving delight day and night to the cowherds and their wives.

The King (Parikṣit) urged :

1. whatever (sportive) acts the glorious Lord Hari, the Supreme Ruler, does in whatever incarnation (like the Fish, the Tortoise etc. the accounts of which are narrated by you) they are pleasing to the ear and fascinating to our minds, Oh Master.

2. May it please you to favour us by narrating that very fascinating account (of Lord Hari's deeds), by listening to which (the feeling of) despondency and the various cravings (which generate it) fade away (leaving no trace behind), the mind gets purified in a short time, and devotion unto Lord Hari and friendly feelings towards his votaries are engendered.

3. Do you describe to us any other marvellous deed of Kṛṣṇa as a child who, after his descent in the human (form and) world, enacted (imitated) the ways of human beings.

3A. (VJ.'s text and Vṛndāvana edition)

Oh Master ! You are gracious unto us. So out of mercy towards me, be pleased to describe in details (Kṛṣṇa's sportive acts in childhood) which (completely) annihilate all sins, Oh past-master in Dharma !

Śrī Śuka said :

4. One day (at the end of the third month), when the constellation (Rohiṇī) that presided at the birth of Kṛṣṇa was in ascendance, and coincided with the ceremonial festive ablution to celebrate the infant's (Kṛṣṇa's) turning in the bed was to take place, the chaste lady Yaśodā performed the rite of auspicious bathing of the child in the assemblage of Gopa women (who visited her house for this occasion), while musical instruments were played, songs were sung and benedictory *Mantras* were being chanted (by Brāhmaṇas).

5. When the infant's bath and toilet were over, and Brāhmaṇas who were duly honoured with liberal gifts of (sumptuous) food, garments, garlands and cows of their choice, pronounced the auspicious benediction (with Vedic *Mantras*), Yośodā (the generous wife of liberal Nanda) seeing her child's

eyes closing in sleep, gently put him to bed (in a cradle under a cart).

6. With her mind full of enthusiasm on the festive occasion of Kṛṣṇa's turning in bed, the noble-minded lady, who was busy in receiving with honour the inhabitants of Vraja who came to (congratulate her) on that occasion, did not hear the crying of her child who, wishing to suck his mother, kicked up his tiny feet.

7. Being hit by the small feet, delicate like tender shoots of the baby that was lying beneath, the cart was overturned with its upside down, and all the pots of bell-metal containing various liquid delicacies (and other sweets) were crushed and the wheels, the axle tree were overturned and its yoke shattered.

8. Noticing it (the overturned position of the cart) Yaśodā and other women of Vraja who assembled there for the festive occasion (of Kṛṣṇa's turning in the bed) and Nanda and other cowherds as well, were perplexed at that marvellous sight and wondered, "How this cart could automatically be overturned?"

8A. (VR. and VJ.'s text and VN Edn.)

Speaking thus and arguing about its cause in a perplexed manner, the people of Vraja surrounded the cart in a distressed mood, as it were.

9. Childern (playing nearby) told the Gopas and their wives whose minds were confused and uncertain (about the cause of overturning of the cart)—

"There is absolutely no doubt that it was upturned with the foot (kick) by this (Kṛṣṇa) while crying".

10. But the Gopas disbelieved it as mere prattle of children, as they did not know the immeasurable might of that baby.

11. Taking up her son, Yaśodā who suspected the trouble of evil spirits, made Brāhmaṇas to recite the benedictory Vedic hymns (to drive out the spirits), and to bless the child, and gave him suck.

12. Brāhmaṇas offered oblations to fire (to propitiate the presiding deities of planets).[1] When powerful *Gopas* assembled (the parts of) the cart as before along with the metal pots

1. Or : the offerings of *bali* (cooked rice) were distributed to eight irections—ŚR.

of dairy products etc., they worshipped it with curds, unbroken rice-grains, Kuśa grass and water[1] (as that was the symbol of their calling and the abode of Lakṣmī).

13. "The benedictions uttered by those who are truthful by nature and completely free from jealousy, falsehood, hypocrisy, intolerance, violence and pride, never become fruitless."

14-15. With this conviction, the cowherd Nanda took up the child and got it sprinkled with water sanctified with sacred *mantras* from the *Sāma*, *Ṛg* and *Yajur*-Vedas, by the best of Brāhmaṇas. Making the Brāhmaṇas pronounce the prescribed benedictory hymns (*Svastyayana*) and offering oblations to fire, Nanda with a serene mind, gave them a heavy feast (of rich, delicious articles of food).

16. For the all-round prosperity of the child, Nanda donated to them cows possessing all good (and auspicious) qualities, adorned them with cloth, garlands and necklaces of gold coins. And Brāhmaṇas, on their part, pronounced blessings to the child.

17. It is obvious that whatever benedictions are pronounced by Brāhmaṇas who are well-versed in Vedas and devoted to God shall never turn out to be fruitless.

18. On one day, the pious lady seated the child in her lap and was fondling him. But (suddenly) she was not able to bear the weight of the Baby, as if it was heavy like a mountain peak.

19. The cowherdess being oppressed with the burden (of the child), was astonished and placed him on the ground. She contemplated on the Supreme Lord not knowing that the whole universe is contained in his body and set about her work.

20. A demon called Tṛṇāvarta in the service of Kaṁsa was specially detailed and deputed (to kill Kṛṣṇa). Assuming the form of a whirl-wind, he carried away the child that was sitting.

21. He enveloped the whole of Gokula with a cloud of dust and blinded the eyes (of the inhabitants). He made the quarters and intermediate points tremble with his extremely terrible roar.

1. Or : with unbroken rice mixed with curds and sprinkling water with Kuśa grass (VT.)

22. For an hour or so the whole of Gokula was covered with (a cloud of) dust and darkness. Yaśodā could not see her son at the place where she kept him.

23. Being assailed by sand particles wafted by Tṛṇāvarta, nobody could see himself or another person in that blinding confusion.

24. Thus not being able to find the trace of her son in the heavy downpour of dust caused by the whirlwind of vehement velocity, the helpless mother (Yaśodā), brooding over him, tenderly began to bewail in the most pitiable manner, and dropped down to the ground like unto a cow bereaved of her calf.

25. When the vehemence of the stormy wind and of the dust-shower abated, the Gopīs (cowherd-women) heard the lamentations of Yaśodā. Not finding Nanda's son there, they were extremely tormented at heart, and broke out crying with their faces flooded with tears.

26. Having assumed the form of a whirlwind, Tṛṇāvarta carried away Kṛṣṇa to the skies. But in consequence of his having been compelled to bear the (unbearably) stupendous weight of Kṛṣṇa, he could not proceed further (beyond a certain height) and his velocity abated (to a stand-still).

27. Due to his extraordinary weight, the Asura thought him to be a mountain. As he was tightly gripped at the throat by him, he could not disengage himself from that wonderful (superhuman) child.

28. Being tightly clasped at the throat with extraordinary pressure, he was rendered motionless. His eyes came out of their sockets. With an indistinct groan he fell dead on the ground at Vraja, with the child dangling from his neck.

29. The bewailing women who assembled there saw the terrible demon falling from the sky on a rock, getting all his limbs shattered like the city (Tripura) cleft by the arrow of Rudra.

30. Astonished to see Kṛṣṇa dangling on the chest of the demon, they picked him up and restored him to his mother. Finding him safe and sound in body though carried away through the sky by the demon, and getting him back unscath-

ed from the jaws of death, Gopīs and Gopas headed by Nanda were verily filled with rapturous delight.

31. "Oh ! How miraculous ! This child, carried by the demon, and (practically) brought to its end (death), has come back safe ! While the blood-thirsty wicked (demon) was killed under the weight of his own sins, and a pious soul is saved from fear due to his even-ness of attitude (towards all).

32. Oh ! What austere penance, what adoration to Lord Viṣṇu, what charitable acts in public interest (like building of temples or tanks), what sacrificial performances, what deeds benevolent to living beings have been done by us that (by virtue of which) the child which was as good as dead, has been fortunately restored to us, bringing delight to us, his kinsfolk."

33. Amazed at the frequent recurrence of such miracles in that big forest (Gokula), Nanda highly esteemed the (parting) words of Vasudeva.

34. One day the beautiful lady (Yaśodā) placed the child on her lap, and being overcome with motherly affection made him suck her breast overflowing with milk.

35-36. When his sucking was almost over, she was caressing his face which was beaming with graceful smile. And Lo ! Oh King ! When he yawned she saw the following in his mouth :

The sky, the firmament above and the earth below, host of luminaries, the cardinal points, the Sun, the Moon, the fire-god, the wind-god, oceans, continents, mountains and their daughters (i.e. rivers), forests and the mobile and immobile creation.

37. Perceiving suddenly the whole of the universe (in his mouth) she was seized with tremor. The lady with eyes resembling those of fawns, closed her eyes, and stayed greatly astonished.

CHAPTER EIGHT

Kṛṣṇa's Sports—Display of Viśvarūpa

Śrī Śuka continued :

1. At the request of Vasudeva, Garga, the family priest of Yadus, noted for rigid asceticism, visited Nanda's Vraja, Oh king.

2. He (Nanda) was highly pleased to see Garga. He stood up to show respect to him and folded his palms. He worshipped him, lying prostrate before him, regarded him to be Lord Viṣṇu.

3. When the sage was properly received and comfortably seated, Nanda, pleasing him with sweet words, asked, "Oh Brāhmaṇa, what service should I render to you who are self-accomplished (and want nothing).

4. Oh venerable sage ! Visits of great people like you contribute to the supreme good to persons who are attached to their households and are distressed in their minds. They never turn out to the contrary.

5. You have directly compiled a treatise on the science of astrology (lit. the movements of luminaries) which is beyond the range of senses. It is by that that a man knows his past and future.

6. You are foremost among the knowers of the Vedas. You should, therefore, perform the purificatory rites of these two boys; for a Brāhmaṇa is the preceptor of all people, by his very birth."

Garga said :

7. "I am the family priest of the Yadus and I am known over the world as such. If I were to consecrate your son with religious rites, they will regard him as the son of Devakī.

8-9. Kaṁsa is wicked by nature. The friendship between you and Vasudeva (is also well known). Kaṁsa has heard the words of Devakī's daughter that the eighth born (womb) of Devakī cannot be a female. If taking into account all these, he (Kaṁsa) gets suspicious, and if he were to kill (your son), it will be our blunder."

Nanda replied :

10. "Please perform the purificatory rites proper for members of the twice-born castes, invoking heavenly blessings with benedictory hymns. Please do so secretly at Gokula, without being noticed even by my own people."

Śrī Śuka said :

11. Thus requested (by Nanda), the Brāhmaṇa who himself was desirous of it performed the naming ceremony of the two boys (the sons of Rohiṇī and Yaśodā) secretly, remaining himself unnoticed.

Garga said :

12. "This son of Rohiṇī will be called Rāma as he will delight his friends with his amiable excellent qualities, and he will be known as *Bala* due to his superiority in strength. They will call him Saṅkarṣaṇa due to his capacity to draw together and unite dissenting Yadus (Garga does not want to disclose the transfer of Balarāma from the womb of Devakī to Rohiṇī due to which he was really called Saṅkarṣaṇa).

13. As to this (second son), he assumed human forms in every Yuga with three different complexions, viz., white, red and yellow for each, successively. Now he has assumed the dark complexion. (Hence he will be known as Kṛṣṇa).

14. Formerly, this son of yours was sometime born in the house of Vasudeva. Hence the wise (knowers of this fact) will designate him as Vāsudeva, the glorious.

15. Numerous are the names and forms of this son of yours suitable to excellent qualities and marvellous deeds. I know them (all), but not the common people.

16. This delight of Gopas and Gokula (i.e. Kṛṣṇa) will bring prosperity to you all, and you will easily surmount all calamities with his help.

17. In times of yore, while anarchy prevailed, he protected pious people who were harassed by rogues and robbers, and when strengthened by him, they (righteous people) vanquished the miscreants.

18. Just as those who side with Viṣṇu are not vanquished

by Asuras, those fortunate persons who (passionately) love him are not overpowered by enemies.

19. Therefore, Oh Nanda, this son of yours is a compeer of Lord Nārāyaṇa[1] in excellent qualities, splendour, glory and prowess. Therefore, please take care of him with very minute attention."

20. When Garga returned home after instructing Nanda thus (or addressing Lord Kṛṣṇa), Nanda was so highly delighted that he considered himself blessed with all well-beings.

21. In a short while, Rāma and Keśava began to creep on their hands and knees and sportfully went round Gokula.

22. While they crawled speedily even in the moist places of Vraja, dragging the pair of their legs (behind them), there arose a sweet tinkling sound of the tiny bells of their girdles and anklets. Their minds being delighted with the jingling sound, they followed the passers-by (a few steps) only to return to their mothers, as if in bewilderment and fright.

23. Their two mothers with their breasts spontaneously overflowing with milk due to motherly affection, embraced in their arms their sons who looked charming with their bodies besmeared with mud. They enjoyed ecstatic delight while gazing at their (sons') countenances beaming with bewitching smiles and tiny tender teeth when they were sucking the breasts.

24. When they attained to the age when the sports of boys become attractive to women to see, the damsels of Vraja witnessed how both of them, holding the tails of calves were dragged behind them hither and thither. Forgetting their household duties, they burst out laughing and were transported with joy.

25. When their mothers found it impossible to restrain their extremely active and playful sons from horned beasts, fire, animals of sharp teeth, sharp lethal weapons, water, (carnivorous, cruel) birds and thorns or even to attend to their household duties, they experienced a great mental (strain of) distraction.[2]

26. After a short time, Oh royal sage, Rāma and Kṛṣṇa

1. To whom Nārāyaṇa bears resemblance by his attributes—JG.

2. ŚR. regards this as the highest point of their domestic happiness.

began to move about easily on feet, in Gokul, without rubbing their knees (against the floor).

27. Then, in course of time, the glorious Lord Kṛṣṇa accompanied by Balarāma began to play with boys of his own age, enhancing the joys of the women of Vraja.

28. Observing the charming boyish pranks of Kṛṣṇa, the cowherd-women came in a body (to his house) and actually spoke (complained) as follows within the hearing of his mother.

29. "Sometimes he untethers the calves untimely (before the milking time of cows allowing the calves to drink up all the milk). If scolded, he (derisively) laughs. Inventing novel ways of stealing, he drinks up the sweet and tasty curds and milk stolen by him. Sometimes he distributes it to the monkeys. If the monkey does not partake of it, he smashes the jar (or milk or curds). If he gets no material (to eat), he gets angry with the infants (people in the) house and goes away setting the infants (in the house) crying.

30. If the jar (of milk, curds or butter) is (kept hanging) beyond the reach of his hands, he constructs contrivance with the help of wooden seats and mortars. Knowing the contents of the pots suspended in slings, he strikes holes into the pots. In a dark room he uses like a lamp his own person, decorated profusely with jewels—he does all this at a time when the Gopa women have their minds fully engrossed in performing their household duties.

31. In this way, he commits acts of nuisance such as passing urine and leaving excretions in our cleansed houses. Having perpetrated such mischiefs and using all devices of stealing, he sits near you like an innocent boy of good behaviour".

Even though such complaints were lodged by women who gazed at his beautiful face with terrified eyes, Yaśodā full of smiles did not feel inclined to chastise him.

32. On one occasion, while cowherd-boys headed by Balarāma were playing, they complained to the mother (Yaśodā) that Kṛṣṇa had eaten earth.

33. Thereupon, Yaśodā who was anxious about his wellbeing and health), caught Kṛṣṇa by his hand and rebuking him, while his eyes assumed bewildering look (as if) through fear, she spoke :

34. 'You naughty boy! Why did you eat earth secretly? These your playmates tell me and this your elder brother also says the same.'

35. 'No mother, I did not eat earth. All these are liars. If (you still think that) they tell the truth, you look into my mouth personally.'

36. 'If that be the case, open your mouth.' Thus ordered, the glorious Lord Hari of unlimited supreme powers, and who, out of sport, had assumed the form of a human child, opened his mouth.

37-38. She (Yaśodā) beheld therein the universe consisting of mobiles and immobiles, the ethereal dome, the cardinal points, the sphere of the earth along with the mountains, continents and oceans, the wind, the fire (of lightning), the moon, the stars, the (whole of the) planetary system, (elements like) water, fire, wind and the sky, (the presiding deities of) the senses and the mind, subtle elements and the three *guṇas*.

39. Seeing in the body, nay in the gaping mouth of her child, this marvellous universe consisting of a variety of organisms produced by (factors like Souls, Time, Nature, Destiny and Mind as well as the whole of Vraja including herself, she was seized with terror.

40. (She bemused) "Is this a dream or an illusion created by the Lord? Or is it a fantasy—a delusion of my own mind? Or is it the innate divine power of this very child of mine?

41. Hence I bow down to the feet of the Supreme Lord, which are extremely difficult to comprehend and the real nature of which cannot be grasped easily by the intellect, mind, deeds and words; which are the basis of the universe and through the instrumentality of which and from out of which the universe is manifested.

42. He (that Supreme Lord) is my refuge by whose deluding potency (Māyā) arise perverse notions such as 'I am (Yaśodā)', 'This is my husband', 'This (Kṛṣṇa) is my son', 'I am that chaste lady who protect the whole property of Nanda (the Lord of Vraja)', 'All the cowherds—men and women along with the wealth of cattle—are mine'."

43. The Omnipotent Supreme Lord cast over the Gopa-lady who had thus realized the truth, his deluding *Vaiṣṇava*

(divine) charm which filled her with maternal affection for (her) son.

44. Instantly the Gopa-lady lost her memory (regarding the real nature of the Lord). She placed her son on her lap. Her heart overflowed with intense affection as before.

45. She began to look upon Hari as her own son—Hari whose glory is being sung by the three Vedas, Upaniṣads, Sāṅkhya and Yoga systems and by Sātvatas (or votaries of the Lord).

The King said :

46. Oh Brāhmaṇa Sage! What highly meritorious act did Nanda perform so as to deserve such great fortune? What did the highly fortunate Yośodā do that Lord Hari sucked her breasts?

47. While the (real) parents of Kṛṣṇa could not witness the childly sports of Kṛṣṇa which wipe out the sins of the world and which are still extolled by the wise and learned people.

Śuka replied :

48. When Droṇa, the foremost of Vasus, along with his wife Dharā was intent upon executing the orders of god Brahmā, he requested that divinity.

49. "When we are born on the earth, may we entertain the highest devotion to Hari, the Supreme God, and the Lord of the universe—devotion through which a person easily and certainly overcomes evil destiny in this world."

50. 'Let it be so', replied the glorious god (granting his prayer). The illustrious Droṇa was born in Vraja and became well-known as Nanda. And the above-mentioned Dharā (his wife) became 'Yaśodā'.

51. Hence, out of all Gopa men and women, that couple entertained the most intense and passionate devotion to the glorious Lord Viṣṇu (Janārdana) who became their son, Oh descendant of Bharata.

52. In order to carry out (and fulfil) Brahmā's boon (to them), the Omnipresent Lord Kṛṣṇa along with Balarāma lived at Vraja and brought delight to them all, by his sportive activities.

CHAPTER NINE

Grace upon the Gopī (Yaśodā)

(Kṛṣṇa tied to the mortar)

Śrī Śuka continued :

1. One day, when the female servants were directed to do some other work, Yaśodā, the wife of Nanda, began to churn the curds personally.

2. At the time of churning the curds, she recalled whatever acts of her child were sung there in Vraja and she herself sang them.

3. Wearing round her big waist (loins) a silk garment fastened with a zone, and with her pair of shaking breasts that were overflowing with milk from maternal affection for her son, with her ear-rings set in motion as well as her bangles moving about her forearms, fatigued with pulling the churning rope to and fro and her face bedewed with drops of perspiration, the handsome lady went on churning while jasmine flowers continued to drop from the braids of her hair.

4. Approaching his mother who was engaged in churning (the curds), Śrī Hari, desiring to suck her, caught hold of the churning rod, and awakening her maternal affection for him (by is gestures etc.), he stopped her churning.

5. On his climbing up to her lap, she began to suckle him at her bosom overflowing with milk, through affection, and to gaze at his countenance which was beaming with smiles. But when the milk placed on the oven (for boiling) was about to overflow, she went in haste, leaving him alone, still unsatisfied.

6. Flared up with indignation, he bit his quivering ruddy lips with his teeth and smashed the pot for churning curds with a piece of stone (used for grinding condiments etc. on a slab of stone). Shedding false tears, he entered the interior of the house and began to eat butter clandestinely.

7. After getting down the (pot of) well-boiled milk, the Gopa-lady re-entered (the churning-room) only to find that pot of curds smashed. Knowing that to be the act of her son and failing to see him there, she just laughed (it away).

8. Observing that her son was standing firmly on the base of an overturned mortar, giving freely to a monkey the butter kept on a swing, and looking about with his eyes through caution and fear, lest somebody should detect the theft, she stealthily approached him from behind.

9. Seeing his mother clearly with a rod in her hand, he hastily got down from the mortar and ran away as if in fear. The Gopa-lady pursued him, but failed to overtake him whom even the minds of yogins impelled and attuned through the force of penance (and concentration) do not reach (even though they are capable to do so.)

10. Running after him, the beautiful mother (lit. mother of beautiful waist) whose speed was impeded by her bulky, moving hips and who was, as it were, followed by the flowers dropping from her braid of hair loosened by the speed (of her running), ultimately caught hold of him.

11. Holding by the hand, she threatened to beat Kṛṣṇa, who was crying for having committed that offence, and was rubbing his eyes with his hand whereby the collyrium (applied to his eyes) got spread all over and who was looking up (to his mother) with eyes bewildered and agitated with fear.

12. Perceiving that her son was terrified, Yaśodā, who was extremely affectionate to her child, threw away the stick. It is traditionally reported that being unable to comprehend the prowess of Kṛṣṇa, Yaśodā wished to bind him with a rope.

13*-14. In relation with him there is neither inside nor outside, neither before nor behind; but he is in front and at the back, outside and inside the universe; (nay) he is the universe itself. Presuming such unmanifest supra-sensuous Lord who had assumed a human form, to be her child, the cowherd-woman tried to bind him with a rope to the mortar, as one would tie down an ordinary human child.

15. While binding her child with a rope for his mischief, the cowherd lady found that it was short by two-fingers

* VJ. : There is nothing self-existent and self-dependent as he is everywhere. Since he exists from eternity to eternity nothing pre-exists him or outlasts him. He exists before and after the universe, and is immanent and transcendent to the world. He is the universe as everything is within his power.

(about an inch or so). So she added to it another piece (of rope).

16. When that (additional) string fell short, she tied yet another piece. In this way, whatever additional piece (of string) she brought, it too fell short by two fingers (about an inch).

17. While Yaśodā was putting together all the ropes in her house (and still it fell short by two fingers), all the Gopa-women laughed; and she too joined them smiling, but felt amazed at it.

18. Noticing the over-exhaustion of his mother whose body was bathed in perspiration, and the wreaths of flowers from whose loosened braids of hair were falling down, Kṛṣṇa, out of compassion for her, allowed himself to be tied.

19. In this way, dear Parīkṣit! was demonstrated his subjection to the control of his votaries by Hari, even though Kṛṣṇa is absolutely self-dependent and has the whole of the universe along with its rulers, under his control.

20. Neither (his son) god Brahmā nor (his very Soul) Lord Śiva nor the goddess Lakṣmī who clings to his person, was recipient of such grace as was enjoyed by the Gopī (Yaśodā) at the hands of that bestower of *Mokṣa* (Liberation).

21. The glorious Lord Kṛṣṇa who is (i.e. has assumed the form of) the son of Yaśodā is not so easily attainable to the ascetics who identify themselves with their bodies and to those who possess spiritual wisdom, as to those who are devoted to him and identify themselves with him.[1]

22. While his mother Yaśodā was engrossed in carrying out her household duties, Lord Kṛṣṇa noticed that the pair of Arjuna trees were in their former birth, two *Guhyakas*, the sons of Kubera, the bestower of wealth.

23. They were known as Nala Kūbara and Maṇigrīva. Endowed with great splendour as they were, they were reduced to the state of trees, through the curse imprecated by Nārada due to their pride.

1. vl. *ātma-potānām* / Who make him their only raft to cross *Saṁsāra* —VR., VJ.

CHAPTER TEN

(Uprooting of Arjuna Trees—Redemption of Nalakūbara and Maṇigrīva)

The King (Parīkṣit) enquired :

1. Worshipful Sage ! Be pleased to narrate (to us) the reason of the pronouncement of imprecation on them (viz. Nalakūbara and Maṇigrīva by (Nārada). What was their reproachful act which aroused the ire[1] of that divine sage.[2]

Śrī Śuka replied :

2-3. On becoming the attendants of god Rudra, those two sons of Kubera, grew puffed up with vain gloriousness. Dead drunk with the liquor called Vāruṇī, thoroughly inebriated with their eyes rolling through intoxication, they, in company of singing women, were strolling through a pleasure-garden in the vicinity of mount Kailāsa, and through woodlands full of blossom, on the banks of the Mandākinī (the Gaṅgā in heaven).

4. Entering the waters of the Gaṅgā which were beautified by blossoming lotus-beds, they sported amorously[3] with young damsels, like unto a pair of he-elephants with she-elephants.[4]

5. By the will of the Providence, the worshipful divine sage Nārada happened to see the pair of gods there, and perceived them to be intoxicated (and speaking vulgarly), Oh descendant of Kurus.

1. *tamas*—(i) Ignorance which is the cause of anger—SS. (Sudarśan Sūri)

(ii) aroused the *Tamo-guṇa* (in Nārada), the effect of which is anger —VJ.

2. v.l. in VR. : *yena vā devarṣiḥ kupitaḥ* 'which enraged the divine sage'.

3. KD. being a born poet gives a graphic description of various love-sports indulged in by them.

4. VB. enumerates a series of sinful mistakes and grievous offences committed by Nalakūbara and Maṇigrīva in VV. 2-4, and shows that the curse by Nārada was inevitable and a perfectly just punishment meted out to them.

6. Seeing him, the celestial damsels felt ashamed at their nudity, and were afraid of being cursed. Instantly and quickly they put on their garments. But not so the two Yakṣas (whose godliness disappeared due to their being drunk), and they stayed on stark naked (despite the persistent requests of the celestial nymphs).

7. Observing that those two sons of god Kubera were inebriated with wine, and blind with arrogance of affluence, he (Nārada) with a view of showering grace on them, intended to pronounce an imprecation, and spoke (lit. sang) as follows :

Nārada said :

8. In the case of a person who indulges in the enjoyment of objects of pleasure, no other effect of *rajo-guṇa* (such as the pride of heredity or of scholarship) is powerful enough to cloud his understanding and good sense as the pride of one's affluence. For wherever this form of vanity predominates, women, wine and gambling are found associated with it.

9. Where such pride of wealth is dominant, animals are ruthlessly slaughtered by such merciless persons of uncontrolled mind who (wrongly) regard this transient perishable body as immune from decrepitude of old age and above mortality.

10. Though this body is designated as god (among men—*naradeva* or on the earth—*bhūdeva*), it is ultimately reduced to what are called worms, excretion and ashes. Does the person who harms living beings[1] for the sake of his body, know his own interest ? Does he know that such violence leads to hell ?

11. Does this body belong to the employer (who gives food or money for its maintenance), or to the procreator (or father), or to the mother (who conceives it and nourishes it during childhood), or the maternal grand-father (who adopts it by *putrikā dharma* stipulations), or to the mighty (who compels forced labour), or to the purchaser (in the slave-market when presented for sale), or to fire (which consumes it when cremated), or to the dog (when it lies unclaimed and uncremated) ?

1. VJ takes *bhūta-dhṛk* as 'a person acting against Brahman by indulging in talk of being identical with Brahman, but SS., VR., VB. etc. follow ŚR in interpreting *bhūta* as 'a living being'.

12. Knowing that this body is the common property (of all as stated above), and that it comes out of and vanishes into something unmanifest, what wise person other than an ignorant fool, regard it as his real self, and would kill living beings (for its sake).

12A. *VJ.'s text adds* here, again a verse composed of 9b and 10a above.

13. Poverty is the best (sight-recovering) collyrium to wicked persons blinded with the pride of affluence. A poverty-stricken person correctly realizes that all others are like himself (experiencing the same pleasures or pangs of life).

14. Just as a person, part of whose body is pricked with a thorn, does not wish similar pain to other creatures, as he realizes the equality of other creatures by their gestures expressing pain. But such understanding sympathy is not found in those who have no experience of being pricked.

15. Being devoid of obdurate egotism, a poor person becomes free from all forms of pride here. The severe hardships that come to his lot, by the will of the Providence, serve as a great austere penance (Hence poverty is conducive to final Liberation).

16. The senses and organs of a poverty-stricken person whose body gets over-emaciated with starvation, and who longs to have food (sufficient to keep body and soul together), become too much dried up and feeble to commit injury (and consequently the desire for violence also disappears[1]).

17. Saintly persons who regard all as equals (with impartiality) associate themselves only with the poor. It is in the company of the righteous that he destroys all his thirst (passion for having worldly objects), and in a short while becomes absolutely pure.[2]

18. What interest have the righteous saints who possess equanimity and equal regard to all, and yearn for the attainment of the feet of Lord Viṣṇu, in the wicked people who are

1. Cf. *viṣayā vinivartante nirāhārasya dehinaḥ* /

—BG. 2.59

2. v.l. *ārād hi siddhyati*, 'attains final Liberation within a short time'

—VJ.

arrogantly proud of their wealth, and who resort to sinful company and hence deserve to be ignored ?

19. I shall, therefore, relieve the pride born of ignorance of these two woman-addicts of uncontrollable mind, blinded with the pride of wealth, and now inebriated with the sweet liquor Vāruṇī.

20-21. Inasmuch as, these two, though the sons of an (exalted) protector of the sphere (Kubera) are too steeped in *tamas* (arrogance begotten of ignorance) to be conscious of their nudity, and are haughtily vainglorious (to remain so even in my presence), these deserve to be (nude, unbending) immobile trees so that they won't behave so again. They will, however, through my grace and favour, retain the memory (and consciousness of their guilt and punishment) even in that immobile stage.

22. After one hundred celestial years, they, who had by then acquired devotion (unto Vāsudeva), will attain to the presence of Lord Vāsudeva, and shall be restored to the celestial status.

Śrī Śuka said :

23. After pronouncing the imprecation thus, the divine sage went to the hermitage of Nārāyaṇa, while Nalakūbara and Maṇigrīva were transformed into the twin-Arjuna trees.

24. To make good the veracity of the words of the sage (Nārada) who is the prominent one among his devotees, Lord Kṛṣṇa slowly went to the spot where the twin Arjuna trees grew together.

25. "The divine sage Nārada is the most beloved of me. These (twin-Arjuna trees) are the sons of Kubera. I shall now accomplish what has been sung (prophesied) by the noble-souled sage".

26. With this aim in view, Kṛṣṇa crawled in between the twin-Arjuna trees. By the mere entry of his person between them, the mortar fell crosswise.

27. The trees were vehemently uprooted by the child, with a rope tied round its belly, while it was dragging the mortar after him. They fell down with a terrific crash, their

trunks, leaves and branches were heavily shaken by the forcible pull exerted by the Supreme Lord.

28. Irradiating all direction with their dazzling lustre, emerged the two Siddhas like fire emanating from trees. Bowing down with their heads to Kṛṣṇa, the Lord and protector of the entire universe, they, now absolutely free from egotism, praised him with folded palms.

29.* "Oh Kṛṣṇa! Oh Supreme Brahman in human form! Oh great *yogin* (whose infinite power is unimaginable), you are the primordial 'Supreme Person'. Brāhmaṇas (i.e. persons who have realized the Brahman or are experts in the Vedas) know that the universe both manifest and un-manifest is your form.

30.** You are the One, the controller of the body, vital breaths, the 'I-ness', senses and organs of all beings. You are the glorious Lord Viṣṇu, whose form (sport) is the time-spirit, and who is the imperishable Absolute Ruler.

31. You are the Subtle Prakṛti constituted of the three *guṇas*—*sattva*, *rajas* and *tamas*. You are the (evolute of Prakṛti called) *Mahat-tattva*. You are the witness, the Puruṣa—the Inner controller of all beings who know all the modifications and changes in all beings.

* (i) VR: Your subtle body (composed of both *cit* and *acit* (is the cause of which your gross body (consisting of *cit and acit*) is the effect.

(ii) VJ: The universe is full of your presence, but does not limit your power or nature. You are the Supreme Brahman who pervade the universe.

KD: You are the First Cause as both Prakṛti and Puruṣa were evolved (lit. brought to light) from you.

** (i) VR.:— You are not only the material cause (*upādāna-kāraṇa*), but also the instrumental or efficient cause (*nimittakāraṇa*) of the universe. As the Controller of bodies of all beings, you are the cause of subsistence of the world, and as the Time-spirit you are the destroyer of the world—but though a cause, you undergo, no change or modification.

(ii) VB. This verse describes how the Lord pervades all forms from the *adhi-daivika* point of view.

The time spirit on which depends rulership, affluence (*aiśvarya*) is not merely the sport or activity of the Lord, but the Lord himself.

32.* It is not possible that you can be perceived through the modifications of Prakṛti (e.g. intelligence, 'I'-ness, cognitive and conative senses), or through the *guṇas* (modes of Prakṛti) which lie within the ken of perception. What being in this world, enveloped as he is in the product of *guṇas* (viz. his physical body), is capable of realizing you who were already in existence before the creation (of the Universe).

33.** Obeisance to you glorious Lord Vāsudeva, the Creator (of the Universe), the perfect Brahman who have concealed your great glory by means of *guṇas* which are illumined by your own effulgence.

34. You are (really) incorporal. But your incarnations in corporal frames are perceived by their various heroic feats which are too unparallel or unequalled and of too supreme excellence to be found in those associated with and conditioned by corporal forms.

35. You, the Lord of all auspicious blessings[1], are such (as described above). At present your Lordship has descended in this incarnation with a part of your divineself[2], for the prosperity and emancipation of the entire world.

*(i) (VJ) : Hari alone is capable of perceiving himself. He cannot be seen by Brahmā and other deities or Jīvas presiding over the evolutes of Prakṛti like *mahat ahaṁkāra* etc. Deities who are always near him like Śrī, Durgā etc. can perceive him to some extent. Products of Prakṛti (e.g. things in the world) are perceptible to senses, but are incapable of seeing the Brahman.

(ii) VT : You are endowed with natural qualities like mercifulness etc. which undergo no change or modifications, as can be actually experienced. You cannot, however, be realized as you actually are. Who though properly possessed of qualities like *bhakti* (devotion) and though your actions have taken place in Nanda's Gokula and as such are famous, is capable of realizing you and your *līlās* adequately ?

(iii) VC : It is through your Grace that you can be visualized, otherwise you are always invisible.

** VT : regards this as salutation to the deities in the two manifestations (*Vyūhas*) of the *Pañcarātrins*. Thus the 1st manifestation is Vāsudeva, *Vedhas* is Saṅkarṣaṇa, the creator of the world.

1. : VT. The Lord who confers whatever is desired by the devotees.

2. *aṁśa-bhāgena* etc, :

(i) VR : You have incarnated along with your part (or ray) Balarāma for the creation and prosperity of the world.

36. Salutation to you The Supreme bliss ! Hail to you the supremely auspicious Lord, the son of Vasudeva, the blemishless happiness incarnate, the Lord and protector of Yādavas and Gopas.

37. Be pleased to allow us, the two servants of your follower (Rudra), to go, Oh Perfect Lord ! It is through the Grace of the Sage Nārada, that we had the good fortune of (being blest with) the sight of your glorious Lordship.

38. (May our previous nature not reappear). May our speech be engaged in extolling your excellent qualities and actions; our ears in listening to your stories; our hands be devoted to do your work, and our mind in musing over and remembering your feet; our head bowing to the world which is your abode, and our sight in seeing saintly persons who are but your form.

Śrī Śuka said :

39. The glorious Lord Kṛṣṇa, the ruler of Gokula who remained tied down to the mortar with a rope, laughingly spoke to the two Guhyakas who had glorified him thus.

The Lord replied :

40. It was already known to me that the sage Nārada of a compassionate heart had favoured you with his grace, in degrading you (to the status of trees), by uttering an imprecation on you, who were blind with the arrogance of affluence.

41. Just as no obstruction (from darkness etc.) to the sight of man can remain when the sun appears, no bondage (of sin or *saṁsāra*) can exist at the sight of righteous Souls who

(ii) VB : incarnated with a part of your (original self) : *aṁśena bhāgena ca . . . avatīrṇaḥ*

(iii) VJ : *bhāgena-aṁśena* VJ. insists that Kṛṣṇa is an incarnation of Nārāyaṇa, the Supreme Lord.

(iv) VT : The dogma of Gauḍīya Vaiṣṇavas is that Kṛṣṇa is not a part-incarnation, but the Lord (*bhagavān*) Himself, as stated in V. 33 above: *tasmai . . . Kṛṣṇas tu bhagavān svayam! ityādau prasiddhyā*

The same is implied here though VT. is silent on these words in the texts.

(v) KD : takes *aṁśa* as 'Kṛtsnāṁśa'—entirety.

have realized the *ātman* (and possess equanimity of mind), and have thoroughly devoted their hearts to me.

42. Oh Nalakūbara (and Maṇigrīva)! Now that unswerving devotion toward me is enkindled in you, do you proceed to your own abode. The most covetable supreme devotion unto me which terminates the *saṁsāra*, has now been generated in you.

Śrī Śuka said :

43. Being thus addressed, they both circumambulated the Lord tied to the wooden mortar. They repeatedly prostrated themselves before him (to show respect), and with his leave, proceeded towards the North.

CHAPTER ELEVEN

Exodus from Gokula—Destruction of demons Vatsa and Baka

Śrī Śuka said :

1. Hearing the crashing sound of the falling (Arjuna) trees, cowherds headed by Nanda (thinking it to be a roar of thunder) rushed to the spot, afraid as they were of a thunderbolt, Oh prominent Kuru.

2. They saw the twin Arjuna trees fallen to the ground. They were bewildered as they could not guess the cause of that fall which was quite obvious.

3. It was the child who was dragging the wooden mortar tied to it with a cord. (But not believing in it) they got distressed as to who did it, what could be the cause of that wonder or whether it is an evil portent.

4. The boys (who were present there) reported, "It (the uprooting of the trees) has been done by him (Kṛṣṇa) who going between the trees dragged the mortar, which lay athwart the trees. We also saw two divine figures (rising from the fallen trees)."

5. They did not believe in the report of the boys. The sceptics reasoned with themselves the impossibility of uprooting the two big trees by the child, while a few others had some reservations in their minds (as they remembered Kṛṣṇa's previous feats).

6. It is traditionally reported that seeing his own child tethered with a cord and dragging the mortar, Nanda with his countenance beaming with a smile, set him free.

7. Glorious Lord (of the Universe) though he was, he sometime danced like a child, sometimes sang loudly and behaved like a wooden doll under the control of the Gopīs (cowherd women), when they encouraged him with their clapping of hands and coaxings.

8. Commanded by them, sometimes he would bring articles like a wooden stool, a measure or a pair of wooden sandals, and sometimes he would swing up his arms bringing delight and affection to his own people (his devotees).

9. To the people who recognize him (as God), he, thereby demonstrates his subservience to (the will of) his servants. The glorious Lord thus brought great joy to (i.e. in the life of) people in Vraja through his child-like playful activities.

10*. Hearing the vendor's cry, "Oh people, purchase fruits", Kṛṣṇa rushed to him quickly with food grains (in the hollow of his palms to give in exchange of fruit), desirous of

*Verses 10-20, both inclusive, are not commented upon by ŚR and VB. (as they obviously do not recognize them as a part of the text), but VR., VJ., VT., JG., VC. have recognized them as an integral part of the Bh. P. and have annotated on them. VT. notes that though there are variations in the order of these verses, the Gauḍīya Sampradāya text is followed.

Though it is not possible to present a concordance of the various text-traditions of the Bh. P., the complexity of the problem can be indicated by comparing ŚR. and VJ.'s text here. Ch. XI in ŚR. is Ch. XII in VJ. In this Chapter after the 9th verse, the order of vv in VJ. is as follows :

I. Vv 10-18.

21-29 (in ŚR.) : From *Gopa-vṛddhā mahot-pātān*...upto *bhavatāṁ yadi rocate* /

getting the fruits, though he himself is the bestower of fruits (of actions, prayers, etc.) to all.

11. The fruit-seller-woman filled with fruits (the hollow of the) palms of his hands from which grains were slipping down (through the gap between them) and the basket of fruits was filled with precious stones.

12. On one occasion, queen Rohiṇī called (Bala-) Rāma and Kṛṣṇa, the uprooter of the Arjuna trees, who were engrossed in playing with children on the bank of the river.

13. When both the sons being deeply interested in play did not come back despite her calling, Rohiṇī sent Yaśodā who was so much affectionate to her child.

14. Yaśodā, with her breasts overflowing with affection for her child, repeatedly shouted for her child who along with his elder brother was playing with the children beyond the (usual) time-limit.

15. "Oh Kṛṣṇa, Kṛṣṇa of lotus-eyes ! Child ! Come up and suck at my bosom. Enough of playing. You must be feeling fatigued with hunger and exhausted with exertions in playing, my sonny.

16. Oh Rāma ! Come quickly with your younger brother. Oh child. It is very early in the morning that you had a breakfast. You must take food now, Oh delight of the family.

17. Oh Dāśārha ! Nanda, the head of this Vraja who is about to take his meals is waiting for you. Do come and bring joy to us both. Oh boys ! You return to your houses.

18. Your body has been covered with dust, Oh child !

II. 19A (extra verse) *tac chrutvaika-dhiyo gopāḥ sarve Nanda purogamāḥ /*
Upa-nanda-vaco rājan pratinandya gṛhān yayuḥ // 19.

Vs. 20-28
III. 12-20 (in ŚR) :

Sarit-tīragatam Kṛṣṇaṁ kṛtavatyathodayam (?)

IV 29A
(Additional verse) :

atha Śandaḥ samāhūya gopānidam abhāṣata /
Śveto Vṛndāvanaṁ yāmo yattā bhavatha māciraṁ /

V The remaining 30 verses from *tac chrutvaikadhiyā gopāḥ sādhu sādhviti vādinaḥ/* etc. are common to ŚR. & VJ. This is the XII ch. in VJ.

Go and take your bath. The star, presiding over your birth, is in the ascent. Get purified by bath, and give cows to Brāhmaṇas.

19. Behold your play-mates. They have been washed and well-adorned by their mothers. You also take your bath, have your meals, and after getting well-adorned, go to play."

20. In this way, Yaśodā whose mind was bound with the ties of maternal affection, regarded, Kṛṣṇa, the crown of all as her child. She took both Rāma and Kṛṣṇa by hand, and brought them to her house, and made them perform the auspicious rites.

Śuka said :

21. Observing extremely ominous portents in the Bṛhadvana (Gokula), elderly Gopas (cowherds) like Nanda and others met in a conference and deliberated the measures to be adopted in the interest of Vraja.

22. Out of them, a cowherd called Upananda, who was senior to others in wisdom and age, and who was endowed with a penetrating insight into the exigencies of the time, place and things (situation), and a well-wisher of Balarāma and Kṛṣṇa advised as follows :

23. "We, the well-wishers of Gokula should now migrate from this place; for, terrible portents of an evil nature forboding destruction of our children are visiting this place.

24. This child Kṛṣṇa certainly had a miraculous escape with great difficulty from the ogress (Pūtanā), the slayer of children. It was surely through the grace of Lord Hari, that the cart did not fall on Kṛṣṇa.

25. He was carried away to the skies, the region of birds, by a demon in the form of a whirlwind. He fell on a rock, but was protected by great gods (our deities).

26. It is sheerly due to the protection afforded by Lord Acyuta that this child or any other boy should not die on getting in between the (Arjuna) trees (as they crashed).

27. Before Vraja is not overtaken by any calamity indicated by these evil portents, let us repair to some other place along with our children and followers and attendants.

28. There is a virgin forest tract called Vṛndāvana which along with its sacred hills, pasturage, trees and plants, is suitable to our cattle and fit to be a happy settlement to our milkmen, women and cattle.

29. Let us, therefore, shift there, this very day. Get our carts and vehicles ready. Be quick (No delay please). If you so approve of it, let our wealth, the herds of cattle, go ahead in advance."

29A. *VJ.'s text adds* :

Having heard the speech of Upananda with concentration of mind (and attentively), all the cowherds of which Nanda was the leader, approved of it, and repaired to their houses, Oh King.

29B. Then Nanda summoned together all the Gopas and directed (spoke) as follows:

"Tomorrow we shall go from this place to Vṛndāvana. Be prepared. Don't delay."

30. Unanimously approving his speech, all Gopas exclaimed "That's right ! Very good". They got their respective conveyances ready with their effects, packed and loaded.

31. Having put into their carriages the aged persons, young children and their women-folk along with utensils and other accessories, the Gopas who were all alert carried bows already strung, in their hands.

32. Keeping their wealth of cattle in their front in advance, accompanied by their family priests, they started on their journey with a flourish of blowing horns and sounding trumpets on all sides.

33. Mounted on chariots, the Gopa women of lovely complexion, with fresh application of saffron-paint to their breasts, wore strings of gold coins round their necks, and put on excellent garments, they felt supremely happy and sang the sportive acts of Kṛṣṇa.

34. So also Yaśodā and Rohiṇī occupied the same carriage, and were eager to hear the sportive acts of their dear children, shone (brightly) with Kṛṣṇa and Rāma (on their laps).

35. Entering Vṛndāvana which was pleasant in all seasons, they, with a crescent-shaped formation of their

vehicles, set up the habitation (for them and the cattle), semicircular like unto the half disc of the moon.

36. Beholding the forest of Vṛndāvana, the Govardhana hill (nearby), and the sand-banks of the Yamunā, the hearts of Rāma and Kṛṣṇa surged with great joy.

37. In this way, giving delight to the inhabitants of Vraja with their child-like sportive activities and sweet lisping, they, in due course, began to tend calves.

38. In the vicinity of their habitation, and in the company of cowherd boys, they tended the calves, taking with them various articles of play.

39-40. Sometimes they played on flutes. Sometimes they used fruits of the Bilva tree or of the Emblic Myrobalan (*āmalaka*) for throwing as balls; sometimes they played kicking those with their feet, making a tinkling noise of small bells (of the anklets); sometimes they imitated the cattle with two-three boys as the tender of cattle, sometime they played the part of bellowing and fighting bulls. Sometimes they imitated the cries of birds like swans and peacocks. In this way they roved simulating ordinary children.

41. On one occasion, while both Rāma and Kṛṣṇa were pasturing the calves along with their friends, a demon came there, with the intention of killing Kṛṣṇa and Balarāma.

42. On seeing him assume the form of a calf and mix with the herd of calves, he (Kṛṣṇa) pointed him out to Balarāma, and slowly approached the demon, posing as if he knew nothing about him.

43. Catching hold of him by his hind legs and tail, and whirling him round, he hurled him lifeless to the top of the wood-apple (*Kapittha*) tree. The huge-bodied demon (who assumed his demonic form at the time of death) fell down along with wood-apples which were made to fall (with the impact of the huge dead body).

44. Astonished to see him fall, all children cried out, "Bravo! Well-done!" Gods being highly delighted, showered flowers.

45. The sole protectors of all the worlds became the two tenders of calves, and with the breakfast in their wallet, roamed about leading the calves in their charge to pasture.

46. On one occasion, all the cowherd boys wanted to take their respective herd of calves to water. They went to a tank[1] of water, made the calves to drink and they also drank of it.

47. The boys saw there standing a monstrous creature like unto a peak of a mountain sundered by (Indra's) thunderbolt, and slipped (of the mountain) and they got terrified.

48. It was verily a powerful demon called Baka who assumed the form of a stork. Swooping down suddenly, the powerful monster with a sharp beak, swallowed up Kṛṣṇa.

49. Perceiving Kṛṣṇa swallowed up by a big crane, children like Balarāma (but not Balarāma) became stupefied like organs and senses of the body in the absence of the vital breath.

50. But Baka had to vomit out Kṛṣṇa, the son of a cowherd (Nanda), but (as a matter of fact) the father of god Brahmā, the creator of the world, as Kṛṣṇa burnt like fire the root of his palate. Finding him unhurt, Baka again attacked Kṛṣṇa with his bill, to kill him.

51. As Baka, the friend of Kaṁsa, rushed at him, Kṛṣṇa, the protector of the righteous[2], caught hold of him by the two halves of the bill, and while the children were looking on, tore him up like a blade of grass in a sportive way, and brought delight to residents of the celestial world.

52. The denizens of heaven then showered the slayer of the demon Baka with jasmine and other flowers from the celestial garden Nandana, and praised him, expressing delight by blowing of conchs, and sounding of drums, beholding which the cowherd boys stood agape with amazement.

53. On finding Kṛṣṇa safely released from the mouth of Baka and return to the playground, children like Balarāma and others, like unto senses would do to the vital breath, embraced him and felt relieved and happy. Collecting their calves together, they returned to Vraja and reported (sang) that exploit (of Kṛṣṇa).

1. VT. locates it to the east of the Nandīśvara hill, near the spot now known as *baka-sthala*.

2. v.l. *satāṁ gatiḥ* 'The final abode of the righteous'—VT.

54. Astonished to hear it, Gopa men and women, who had an intensely loving regard for him, gazed him with eager (lit. thirsty) eyes, as if he had returned from the land of the dead.

55. They said, "how wonderful yet pitiable that this child should have so many mortal enemies. However, it is they who suffered the evil consequences, as they spelt terror to others previously.

56. Howsoever terrible-looking the demons be, they dare not and cannot overpower him at all. Approaching him with a desire to kill, they themselves get destroyed like moths in fire.

57. Oh ! The words of those who are conversant with the Brahman, never prove to be untrue. What the worshipful Garga predicted has been exactly found to be true (by experience)."

58. In this way, recounting with joys the stories of Kṛṣṇa and Rāma, Nanda and other cowherds passed their time happily and did not experience the agonies of *saṁsāra*.

59. In this way, they (Kṛṣṇa and Rāma) passed their childhood at Vraja in child-like sports such as hide-and-seek, constructing dams in play, jumping like monkeys and the like.

CHAPTER TWELVE[1]

Slaying of Aghāsura

Śrī Śuka said :

1. One day, intending to have his break-fast (first meal) in the woods, Hari got up early in the morning and woke up his fellow cowherd boys (tending the calves) by the charming sound of his horn, and proceeded from Vraja with calves going in front.

1. VJ.'s text omits this and the next two chapters. The omission is noted and the chapters are annotated by SS., VR., VB., JG., and VC. who express their disapproval of this omission. But VT.'s tirade against this omission is vehement.

2. Immediately, at that clarion-call rushed forth joyfully thousands[1] of affectionate young boys simultaneously, equipping themselves with slings, sticks, horns and flutes, each driving his own herd of thousands of calves.

3. It is traditionally reported that making their own calves join the herd of innumerable calves of Kṛṣṇa, and grazing them, they diverted themselves in children's games at various places.

4. Although they were already adorned (by their mothers) with glass-beads, Guñjā seeds, precious stones and gold ornaments, they decorated themselves with fruits, tender foliage, bunches of flowers, feathers and coloured earths.

5. They stole the slings and other objects belonging to each other, and when detected, they threw them at a distance. Boys who were sitting there threw them still further laughing all the while, returning them (to the respective owners when they were on the point of shedding tears).

6. If Kṛṣṇa had gone to a distance to observe the beauty of the forest, they vied with each other in touching Kṛṣṇa first and enjoyed themselves (in this competition).

7. Some played on the flutes; some blew their horns, some sang humming (hummed) in tune with black-bees, some imitated the sweet notes of the cuckoo.

8. Some ran with the shadows of the (flying) birds; some walked beautifully like royal swans; some sat down with the cranes, while others danced with peacocks.

9. Some pulled monkey's tails dangling down from branches of trees, while others climbed trees along with the tails in hand. Some were making wry faces at monkeys while others were jumping from one branch to another (like monkeys).

10. Hopping with frogs, some became drenched with the waters of the streams and waterfalls; some were laughing at their own shadows (while making faces at one's own reflection), while others cursed their own echoes.

11. In this way, the cowherd boys who amassed a vast fund of merits (in the past), played with Kṛṣṇa who was to the knowers the veritable Brahman, with all the realization of the

1. Innumerable—*vatsānāṁ bālānāṁ ca asaṅkhyeyatvam uktam*—VT., VC.

absolute bliss, the Supreme Deity to the devotees who dedicated themselves to his service, and a human child to those who are under the influence of Māyā or Ignorance.

12. Is it possible to describe the blessedness and good fortune of the inhabitants of Vraja unto whose ken of perception he presented himself in person? The Lord, the dust of whose feet cannot be obtained (and attained to) by the self-controlled *yogis* who have performed austerities for many past lives.

13. Now (on one occasion), a powerful demon named Agha who could not tolerate the sight of their happy games, attacked the demon whose vulnerable point i.e. death was eagerly watched over even by immortals who had been anxious to safeguard their lives (from him), even though they assimilated (drunk) nectar (and hence had no fear from death).[1]

14. Seeing the Gopa children of whom Kṛṣṇa was the leader, the demon Agha, the younger brother of Bakī (Pūtanā) and Baka (the demon killed by Kṛṣṇa), who was deputed by Kaṁsa (to kill Kṛṣṇa) said to himself, "This is the slayer of my brother and sister. To avenge them both I shall now kill Kṛṣṇa along with his army (of cowherd boys).

15. When these (Kṛṣṇa and his cowherd companions) are killed (and thus are made as if propitiatory libations of sesamum seeds and water to my departed brother and sister), all the residents of Vraja are as good as dead. Why worry

1. *Or* ŚR.: The sight of their happy games which even gods who have drunk nectar are anxious to realize in their hearts, to sustain their life thereby.

Life is not really fruitful by drinking nectar but by drinking the ambrosia of the Lord's name and by remembering and contemplating the sports of the glorious Lord.

KD.: Gods who attained immortality by drinking nectar wish to take a birth as mortals on the earth, and participate in singing the eulogy of Kṛṣṇa's exploits.

VT. takes *amara* as 'Liberated beings who, being free from gross and subtle bodies, are immortal'. Though they have imbibed *amṛta* or *Mokṣa*, they desire to take a *Līlāvigraha* (sportive body) to participate in Hari's sport.

According to Gauḍīya Vaiṣṇavism, a soul does not lose his individuality in the Mokṣa stage.

about the Physical body when the vital breath (life) is departed ? And all those who live (as human beings) have (i.e. consider) their children as their very life."

16. Having made up his mind thus, wicked demon assumed a gigantic body of a boa-constrictor one *yojana* (eight miles) in length and stout like a big mountain, and with a desire to swallow them all, he lay motionless on their path, with his flabbergasting cavelike mouth kept wide open.

17. His lower lip lay on the earth, while the upper lip touched the clouds; the mouth between them appeared like a vale; his fangs were like summits of mountains, and the interior Part of his mouth was full of darkness; his tongue was like a broad road; his breath was like a tempestuous blast, while his enraged red hot eyes were (scorching) like a forest-conflagration.

18. Beholding him in that form, all regarded it as a beautiful landscape of Vṛndāvana. And in a sportive mood they fancied its semblance to the open mouth of a boa-constrictor.

19. (The children began to talk about it as follows : "Ah ! How wonderful ! Tell us friends, if this animal like formation (living mountain) standing before us, does or does not resemble the open mouth of a gigantic wicked serpent anxious to devour us all ?"

20. (Another boy) "Really ! The cloud reddened with rays of the sun looks like his upper lip, while the earth grown red through the reflection (of the cloud) looks like the lower lip."

21. (The third boy) "Look here ! The mountain Caverns on its right as well as on the left are as if competing with the jaws; and the rows of lofty mountain-summits as it were vie with its fangs.

22. The broad and long road is vying with its tongue, while the darkness pent up in between the peaks, emulates the darkness in the internal part of its mouth.

23. Look here ! The fierce blast of wind heated by forest fire feels like its breath, and the bad odour of animals burnt in that forest fire stinks like the flesh of animals in the stomach of a serpent.

24. "Will he swallow us all if we enter his mouth ?[1] In that case, like Bakāsura, he will meet his death in a moment at the hands of Kṛṣṇa". Saying so, and looking at the fascinating face of Kṛṣṇa, the slayer of Baka, they all entered (that mouth) laughing loudly and clapping their hands.

25. Hearing the mutual discussion—which was far removed from reality—of his friends who were ignorant of the factual state of things, Kṛṣṇa knew that that was really a demon simulating the form of a serpent, as the Lord is present in the hearts of all creatures. The Lord made up his mind to prevent his companions from entering the demon's mouth.

26. In the meanwhile, the children along with the calves entered into the bowels of that demon. But they were not swallowed up by that ogre who remembered the slaying of his dear ones, and was expecting the entry of the slayer of Baka viz. Kṛṣṇa.

27. Lord Kṛṣṇa, who affords protection to all, was moved with compassion to see the helpless children and calves who had no other saviour, and who having slipped out of (the protective control of) his hands, had become the victims of the gastric fire of the demon. He was surprised[2] at the working of the Providence.

28. "What should be done now ? How both the objects viz. the termination of the life of this wicked (demon) and averting the death of these pious innocents, can be achieved ?" Pondering over this problem, and knowing the expedient, the omniscient Hari entered his (Aghāsura's) mouth.

29. At that instant, gods who were behind the curtain of clouds, shrieked in terror bewailing 'Alas ! Alas', while the demonic friends of Aghāsura of whom Kaṁsa was prominent, exulted in joy.

30. Hearing those (cries and shouts of joy), the Imperishable glorious Lord Kṛṣṇa instantly increased himself in huge

1. v.l. *viśantu sarve grasitāḥ kim asmān*:

Let us all enter it. Let us see if he can devour us—VR.

2. VT. states that Kṛṣṇa was surprised at the powerful working of Providence, as it exercised its effect even in the presence of himself, in the case of his devotees who entered the mouth of Aghāsura despite his attempts to prevent them.

dimensions into the throat of that demon who desired to crush to powder Kṛṣṇa along with children and calves.

31. All the passage of breath of that huge-bodied monster was choked, and his eyes shot out of their sockets. He was writhing on all sides. His breath being completely obstructed in his lungs, forced its way out through an aperture in the crown of its head called *Brahma randhra*.

32. When all the vital breaths of the demon passed out that way, Lord Kṛṣṇa revived to life with his nectarine look, all his friends and calves who were as good as dead, and came out of the mouth of the demon again, along with them.

33. A mysterious and powerful light setting ablaze (as it were) all the ten directions, with its brilliant effulgence, rose from the huge body of the serpent. It waited in the firmament for the coming out of the Lord (from the serpent's mouth) and (immediately) entered his person while all the residents of the celestial world simply looked on in amazement.

34. Overjoyed at the accomplishment of their purpose by Kṛṣṇa, the jubilant gods offered their worship by showering flowers, the celestial damsels, through dancing, Gandharvas, experts in vocal music, with singing, those well-versed in instrumental music, by playing on their instruments, Brāhmaṇas (like Nārada) through singing hymns of praise, and his attendants and followers (like Garuḍa and others) with shouts of victory.

35. Hearing in the vicinity of his abode (*Satya Loka*) the auspicious and joyous sounds of wonderful hymns of praise, instrumental and vocal music and shouts of victory, god Brahmā, immediately came to the spot and was wonder-struck at the glorious feat of the Lord.

36. Oh King! When the hide of that weird boa-constrictor became dry, it served for a long time as a hiding place in playing (like a big cave) to the residents of Vraja.

37. Witnessing the exploit of Hari, as a child of five years, in rescuing them from death (from Aghāsura) and the demon-serpent from death (involved in rebirth in *Saṃsāra*), the cowherd boys of Vraja told to each other of it in his sixth year with equal astonishment.

38. That even a demon like Agha should get his sins absolved by his touch, and should get absorbed in him—an attainment extremely difficult for the unrighteous, is not to be wondered at in the case of Hari who has assumed through his Māyā, the form of a human child, but who is (really) the Creator of all beings, great and small.

39. Even if the semblance of the personality of the Lord is once installed in one's heart in meditation, it leads to the attainment of divine position. What indeed would he not give to Aghāsura in whom he had actually entered, as he had warded off Māyā by the eternal realization of the bliss of his Divine self.[1]

Sūta said :

40. Oh Śaunaka and other Brāhmaṇas ! Having heard this wonderful story of his saviour, king Parīkṣit, who was a gift (whose life was protected in womb) by Kṛṣṇa, the Lord of Yādavas, found his heart fascinated with it, and again requested Śuka, the Son of Vyāsa, to narrate the same sacred story about him.

The King (Parikṣit) submitted[2]

41. Oh Brāhmaṇa Sage! You said just now that what was done by Hari in his childhood stage of five years, was sung by the cowherd boys in the sixth year (in the *paugaṇḍa* stage)[3]. Now could an act done at a distant time, can be regarded as done in the present time.

42. Be pleased to narrate to me, Oh Great Yogin, as I feel great curiosity about it. How can it be possible unless it is due to the deluding power (*Māyā*) of Hari, Oh preceptor.

43. Though we are (after all) ordinary Kṣatriyas we are the blessed-most persons in this world, inasmuch as we can

1. Here ends the XIII Chapter in VR.

2. Ch. XIII in VR. begins here.

3. The following are names of different stages in life : childhood *Kaumāra* to the end of the 5th year, boyhood (*Paugaṇḍa*) to the end of the 10th year Adolescence (*Kiśora*. to the end of the 15th year. Youth after the 15th year (*Yauvana*).

repeatedly drink the hallowing nectar in the form of stories of Lord Kṛṣṇa from you.

Sūta said :

44. Oh the most excellent devotee of the Lord ! When thus queried, Śuka, the son of Bādarāyaṇa who lost his senses (i.e. consciousness), due to his immersion in contemplation about Kṛṣṇa when reminded of the Lord by Parīkṣit's question, slowly regained his consciousness of the external world (with difficulty), and began to narrate.

CHAPTER THIRTEEN

Infatuation of God Brahmā

Śrī Śuka said :

1. A good query has been made by you, Oh highly fortunate king. By listening to the stories of the Lord again and again, you bring new charm to them (by your intelligent questions), Oh best of Hari's votaries.

2. It is the nature of the righteous persons who assimilate only the essentials, that, just as the topic of young damsels is ever fresh and fascinating to gallants[1], the auspicious stories of Lord Acyuta (who never slips from *rasa* appear with fresh sweetness every moment to them, though their speech, ears and minds are devoted to them).

3. Listen to me attentively, Oh king, for I am disclosing to you a secret; for preceptors confide what is even confidential and most hidden, to their loving disciples.

4. Having saved the cowherd boys from death in the mouth of the demon Agha in the aforesaid manner, the Lord brought them to the sandy bank of the river, and spoke as follows:

1. If an extremely disgustible object like a woman can become an object of ever fresh sweetness and love, what need be said about the glorious Lord—VT.

5. "Extremely beautiful is this bank of soft, clean, stainless sand, so spacious and suitable for our sports, oh friends ! It is encircled by beautiful trees, rendered fascinating by the echoing notes and humming of bees attracted here by the sweet smell of blooming lotuses.

6. Let us have our meal here. It is high time now as the day is considerably advanced and we are oppressed with hunger. Let the calves drink water and leisurely graze the grass nearby."

7. Approving of his proposal, (lit. saying 'so be it'), they led the calves to drink water and set them to graze in the green pasture. Untying their slings (and opening their tiffin-boxes), they enjoyed the lunch with the Lord in great delight.

8. Sitting together closely round Kṛṣṇa in a number of circular rows, and all of them facing him[1] with their eyes blooming fully, the boys of Vraja shone (looked brilliant) like lotus-petals grown round the pericarp (of that lotus).

9. Some improvised flowers and leaves as dining plates, some tender leaves and shoots, some fruits, some their wallet-slings, some barks and slabs of stones (for plates), and they enjoyed their meals.

10. (Even though each boy participated something of the dishes, others had brought) each boy severally showed (by gestures etc.) the special taste of his own dish, laughing himself and making all others laugh. (In this way) all took their meals with the Lord (who also tasted something of the dish brought by each of them).

11. The presiding Deity and the Enjoyer of sacrifices as he was, he indulged in child-like sports, and with his flute between his belly and his *pitāmbara* (silken loin cloth[2]) and his horn and cane under the left arm (pit), and holding a soft morsel of boiled rice mixed with curds and (choice eatable) fruits held in between his fingers of his left hand, he occupied a

1. VC. explains that it was Kṛṣṇa who, being 'possessed of hands, feet, eyes, heads and faces in all directions' (*sarvataḥ pāṇi-pādam tat sarvato'kṣi-śiro-mukham*) faced each of them, making each elated to feel that he alone had the privilege of facing him directly—a blessing denied to others.

KD. : The boys lost their individuality in Kṛṣṇa (13.24-28).

2. Belt-like garment round the waist. (KD).

central position in the circle of his friends, and made them to laugh by cracking jokes—And gods from the celestial regions simply looked on (envious that they are not lucky enough to participate).

12. As the cowherd boys whose minds were absorbed in Lord Kṛṣṇa were having their repast, the calves, being allured by luxuriantly grown pasture, strayed away deep into the woods, oh scion of Bharata.

13. Perceiving that they were overwhelmed with fear (at the straying away of calves), Kṛṣṇa, the terror to the terrors of the world, reassured them, saying, "Friends, (Don't worry—lit. cast aside all your fears). Please do not disturb your meal. I shall fetch all the calves here".

14. With these words, while the morsel of boiled rice mixed with curds was in his hand, Kṛṣṇa went in search of his calves over the mountains, in caverns, in bushes and thick jungle.

15. God Brahmā (the lotus-born god)[1] who formerly stood in heaven to witness the release (of the cowherd boys and calves) from Aghāsura and was greatly astonished, desired to see another sweet feat of the Lord who assumed the form of a child through his Māyā power, and he lifted up the calves and abducted the cowherd boys, and carried them to some place and vanished himself.

16. Not being able to find the calves, and failing to see the cowherd boys on the sandy bank, Kṛṣṇa searched for both of them all round.

17. Not finding either the calves or their protectors (cowherd boys) anywhere within that forest, Kṛṣṇa who knows everything in the Universe, understood it to be the work of god Brahmā.

18. Thereupon, with a view to bring joy to the mothers of the cowherd-boys (by restoring their children and calves), as well as to god Brahmā (by allowing the boys and calves to

1. VC. suggests a pun on *jala*(*ḍa*) due to the interchangeability of -d- and -l-. A lotus is born out of *Jala* (water) which is *jaḍa* (wanting in intelligence) and god Brahmā is born out of that knowledgeless inert being called lotus. Hence his own intelligence shares the stupidity of its heredity.

remain in his charge), Kṛṣṇa, the Maker and the Controller of the Universe, converted himself both (into the cowherd boys and the calves).

19. Having exactly changed him into the same size and number of small bodies of the cowherd boys and calves, with same proportion and size of their limbs like hand, feet etc.. taking with them the same (number and size of) sticks, horns, flutes, decorative leaves on the head, slings and wearing the same clothes and ornaments, and assuming the same goodness of nature (or character), accomplishments, name, form and age as well as their ways of sporting etc. (of each individual), the birthless Lord Kṛṣṇa, being thus identical with all forms, shone there as a concrete illustration, proving the veracity of the Vedic text : "Everything in the universe is pervaded by Viṣṇu."

20. Having converted himself into the form of calves which were tended back by his ownself in the form of cowherd boys, and playing with his own forms, Kṛṣṇa, the self and the self of all, entered Vraja.

21. Having taken the respective calves separately to their own houses, and tying them into their respective stalls, he entered the respective houses of the cowherd boys and stayed there in their form, oh King.

22. Rising hurriedly at the sound of the flutes, the mothers (of the cowherd boys) raised them up and hugged them fast in their arms. With their breasts overflowing with milk of motherly affection which was sweet like nectar and inebriating, they suckled the *Para Brahman* mistaking him for their children.

23. Observing the time-schedule of games etc., during different parts of the day, and returning in time in the evening at the usual time, Kṛṣṇa (the consort of Lakṣmī) in the form of a cowherd boy) was fondled and treated with shampooing, bathing, anointing (with sandal paste, pigments etc.), decorating (with ornaments), evil-warding rites, applying the decorative mark (*tilaka*) on the forehead, feeding (with dishes) etc. (by the Gopīs). He also filled them with great joy by his sportive winsome ways.

24. Thereupon the cows returned hurriedly to their own pens, and inviting their respective calves by their specific

lowing-calls, suckled them with milk overflowing from their udders, licking the calves (all over), every now and then.

25. The maternal affection of the kine and the Gopīs towards him (in the form of calves and cowherd boys), was the same as before, except that their affection grew more ardent, and Hari's behaviour towards them as (their) child was the same as before, but there was no delusion (in Kṛṣṇa's relation with them, as was in the case of their real children).

26. (In this way) for one year, the affection of the residents of Vraja towards their children grew gradually every day (as they were the parts *aṁśas* of the Lord), but in the case of Kṛṣṇa it developed in an unprecedent way and became unlimited (as he was the *aṁśin*—the Lord himself).

27. In this way, protecting and being tended himself in the form of calves, by himself, in the capacity of cowherd boys, he sported himself for one year, in the forest, as well as in Vraja.

28. One day, while it was some five or six days to complete the period of a year, Kṛṣṇa, alongwith Balarāma entered the forest, while they were tending the calves.

29. The cows which were grazing grass on the top of the Govardhana hill saw from afar their calves pasturing near Vraja.

30. As soon as the herd of cows saw them, they being overpowered with affection for the calves, forgot themselves. They rushed by a path difficult to be followed by their protectors (cowherds). Like bipeds (due to fast running on all fours), with their necks contracted towards their humps and with tails raised up, they dashed on speedily bellowing (all the while), and with milk oozing out of their udders, all the way.

31. Coming down to the foot of the Govardhana hill, the cows, though they had their own calves, suckled them with the milk from their udders, licking the bodies of the calves (with such intense eagerness) as if they wanted to swallow them.

32. Being extremely angry at their disgrace and inability in restraining and controlling the cows, and making their way with great difficulty through the inaccessible hilly track, they saw their sons, along with the calves.

33. With their hearts submerged in (i.e. overwhelmed with) affection at the sight of their children and with filial love

surging in them, they forgot their anger, and raising their children with their arms and embracing them, they smelt on the crowns of their heads and were enraptured.

34. Then the grown-up Gopas who felt extremely happy at the embrace of their children, withdrew slowly with a heavy heart from that place with tears gushing out at their memory.

35. Observing the intense longing and love growing every moment in the heart of Vraja (people and the cows) for their children (and calves), though weaned away from their mother's breast, Balarāma failed to understand its reason and began to think :

36. "It is really wonderful that the affection of the people of Vraja—and I am no exception to it—towards their children is increasing in intensity by leaps and bounds as never before, as it did in the case of Vāsudeva, the soul of the whole of the universe.

37. What infatuation is this ? Whence has it emerged ? Is this delusion caused by gods, men or demons ? Most probably it must be the deluding potency of my Lord and of none else, as it enchants even me (No other Māyā has this power of deluding me)".

38. Giving deep thought to the matter, Balarāma, of the Dāśārha clan, saw through his spiritual eye (lit. the eye of knowledge) that all the calves and his cowherd friends were the Lord Kṛṣṇa himself.

39.* (Balarāma asked Kṛṣṇa)—"These (cowherd boys) are not the rulers of gods. Nor are these (cows) the sages (as I know them to be). It is you who appear in these different forms. Be pleased to tell me, how all this took place." The Lord briefly explained which Balarāma could grasp correctly.

39A. *VR.'s text adds* :

(When Brahmā returned after hiding the cows and cowherd boys to *Satya loka*) Even Brahmā was disallowed by

*(1) *SS.* Balarama wanted to know how the Lord though one became many. Here SS. quotes *Tait-Up.* 2.5 *vijñānaṁ cāvijñānaṁ ca Satyaṁ cānṛtaṁ ca satyam abhavat.*

(2) *VR.* 'Be pleased to tell how you who are the one, came to be many.' Kṛṣṇa explained that as stated in the Vedas, He accomplished it through His Will. Balarāma came to understand it now.

his own doorkeepers who were deluded by Kṛṣṇa who assumed the four-faced form and occupied his (Brahmā's) seat in the *satyaloka*, and he had to go back.

40. When the self-born god (Brahmā) returned in a quarter of a moment or half (the time of winking of eyes) according to his measure of time which amounted to one human year, he saw Hari playing as before with all his companions, even at the end of the year.

41. "Whatever number of children there was in Gokula along with the calves—all of them are stupefied and lying in the bed of my Māyā-power and none of them has awakened.

42. Who are these and whence have they come as they are other than those who are under the spell of my deluding power ? They are the same in number and have been playing with Kṛṣṇa (Viṣṇu—the all-pervading Lord) for a period of one year.

43. Pondering for a long time on these differences (between children under his spell and those playing with Kṛṣṇa), the self-born god Brahmā could not, even with difficulty, distinguish between those (children and calves) who were real and who were not.

44. Thus in his attempt to delude Viṣṇu (Kṛṣṇa) who transcends all delusion, yet is deluding the whole universe, god Brahmā found himself enchanted by his own deluding capacity.

45. Just as the darkness caused by a drop of mist (becomes absorbed in the darkness of night, and like the light emitted by the fire-fly gets merged in the broad day-light, similarly lower type of *māyā* (deluding power) when used against a superior person loses its effectiveness and is lost to the user.

46. And Lo ! While god Brahmā was looking on, in a moment all the cowherds appeared dark as cloud in complexion and wearing silken yellow garments.

47. (They were) endowed with four arms wielding in each hand a conch, a discus, a mace and a lotus; (they were) wearing crowns, ear-rings. pearl-necklace and wreaths of sylvain flowers.

48. (They were) adorned with Śrī-vatsa (a curl of golden hair on the right bosom), armlets (*aṅgada*) and a pair of

bejeweled bracelets marked with three lines like conchs, on their wrists.

48A. *VR.'s text* :

With their chest beautified by *Śrī-vatsa* and with *kaustubha* gem-pendant round the neck, they appeared shining with anklets, bangles, girdles and rings.

49. All over their persons, from head to foot, they were beautified with wreaths of tender, fresh *Tulasi* offered to them by highly meritorious (devotees).

50. With their smiles bright like the moon-light (the whiteness of which represents the *sattva-guṇa*, whose function is the protection and preservation of the world) and with their side-long glances from their reddish eyes (the reddishness of which stands for the *rajo-guṇa* the function of which is the creation of the world), they looked like the creators and protectors of the desires of their votaries (they fulfilled whatever desire aroused in the heart of their devotees) with the help of *sattva* and *rajas*.[1]

51. They were adored severally by means of dancing, singing and offering many other courses of worship by all embodied beings, mobile and immobile, from Brahmā's own self to a clump of grass, all endowed with a corporeal form.

52. They were waited upon all around by mystic powers like *aṇimā* (power of becoming atomic in size) and by potencies such as Māyā, Vidyā and by twentyfour principles (enumerated by *Sāṅkhyas*) beginning with *Mahat* (—all assuming the forms of persons).

53. They were also attended upon by the Time-spirit[2] (which sets in motion the process of creation by disturbing the balance of the *guṇas* of *Prakṛti*), Nature, Saṁskāras (latent desires or proclivities), Desire (for enjoyment), Activity, the three *guṇas*—all assuming corporal forms, with their glories eclipsed by the Lord.

54. All of them were embodiments of the one absolute essence consisting of reality, knowledge and infinite bliss. Their

1. They appeared like Protectors with their white *sattva*-like smiles and shone with their reddish side-glances like creators by the reddish-*rajas guṇa*—ŚR.

2. C. *Kālaḥ svabhāvo niyatir yaddṛcchā* etc.—*ŚV. Up.* 1.2

greatness and glory were incomprehensible even to those who have obtained the vision of *Upaniṣadic* knowledge.

55. It was only once that Brahmā espied that all those forms were identical with the Supreme Brahman by whose light the universe both mobile and immobile, animate and inanimate stands revealed.[1]

56. Thereupon, when god Brahmā, out of great curiosity and wonder, directed his eyes elsewhere (towards himself or to his seat on the swan, he was so over-whelmed by the spiritual effulgence of the Lord that all his eleven sense-organs (five conative, five cognitive senses and the mind) became dazed and motionless; And he stood still and silent like a statuette of a secondary deity by the side of the presiding deity of that settlement (*Vraja*).

57. When Brahmā, the Lord of Sarasvatī (the goddess of learning) who was incapable of comprehending Lord Kṛṣṇa's (or the Supreme Brahman's) special glory and greatness, became confused about Brahman which is beyond the reach of logical reasoning, and is thus incomprehensible—Brahman which stands resplendent in its perfect bliss; is far above and beyond Māyā, and is unborn, and can be known only through the *Vedāntic* (*Upaniṣadic*) texts which describe It in the negative terms (*neti, neti*—'It is not so, It is not such'), and he could not even perceive the manifestation at all, Kṛṣṇa, the Supreme Unborn Lord immediately understood god Brahmā's perplexity, and drew off the curtain of his Māyā.

58. Thereupon god Brahmā whose vision to view the outside world was restored, opened his eyes with difficulties like a person brought back to life from death, and verily saw again this whole universe along with himself.

59. Immediately he cast his eyes around in all directions and found stretched before him the (vista of) Vṛndāvana forest abounding in trees providing the means of subsistence to people, and with desirable objects[2] (necessities of life) in plenty.

1. *tasya bhāsā sarvam idaṁ vibhāti—Muṇḍ. Up.* 2.2.10, *Śv. Up.* 6.14.

2. SS., VT. interpret 'samapriya' as :

(i) Vṛndāvana, Govardhana etc. Liked by Lord Kṛṣṇa or (ii) along with Lord Kṛṣṇa who was dear to goddess Lakṣmī (mā).

60. In that forest, men, deer and other animals who are (normally) inimical by nature, lived together as friends, and from which hatred, covetiouness (and other passions) had disappeared due to the presence of Kṛṣṇa.

61. (ŚR.) brings out the full significance of every attribute of Kṛṣṇa thus):

And Brahmā, the highest deity in the Universe, perceived the Lord acting before him the part of a child born in the family of cowherd—The Lord who, though without a second, was searching for calves, though absolutely one, was (trying to find) his friends (cowherd boys), though endowed with unfathomable knowledge, was attempting to search them (as if he did not know); though he was Infinite and omnipresent, he was looking around; though he was the Supreme Lord, he was behaving like a child, and though the Brahman himself, he held a morsel of food in his hand.

62. As soon as he beheld it, Brahmā hastily alighted from his mount (swan) and lay prostrate before him like a stuff of gold on the ground. Touching his pair of feet with the crest of his four crowns, he paid respects to him and bathed his feet with his holy tears of joy.

63. And repeatedly remembering the great glory of the Lord witnessed by him uptill now, he rose again and again to lay prostrate at his feet for a long time.

64. Thereupon, rising up gradually, he rubbed his eyes. Looking up intently at Hari but with a bent head, he folded his palms and with great humility and concentration of mind, he, with his body trembling with emotions and in a faltering voice, chanted the praise of the Lord.

CHAPTER FOURTEEN

God Brahmā eulogizes Kṛṣṇa

Brahmā said :

1. I submit my eulogium unto you, Oh praiseworthy Lord (in the form of) the child of the cowherd Nanda—The Lord whose personality is dark-blue like a rainy cloud, in complexion; (who is) clad in silken garments refulgent like lightning; whose sublimely charming face appears glorious with ornaments of *Guñjā* seeds and a crest of peacock feathers; (who is) adorned with wreaths of sylvain foliage and flowers; whose splendid beauty is enhanced with a morsel of food (in the left hand), a cane and a horn (under left arm-pit) and flute and other emblems and whose feet are soft and tender.

2. Even though I am (god) Brahmā (the creator of the world), I am not really competent to comprehend even with my mind concentrated (inwardly) this corporeal form of yours which you have revealed to me for showering your Grace on me[1]—a form you assumed at your sweet will (or as desired by your devotees) but is not composed of elements[2] (gross or subtle). Much less can I comprehend directly you who (being transcendental to *guṇas*) are absolute bliss of The Self.[3]

3. Oh Lord! Unconquerable as you are in the three

1. *SS*. It is impossible for me to comprehend any form you assume in your incarnations, and the greatness of your attributes, unless you, who are the absolute truth, bliss and consciousness condescend to enable me to do so, out of grace.

2. *ŚN*. (Śrinivāsa-Sūri)—A follower of Rāmānuja :—The personality of the Supreme Self (God) is never composed of elements :

na bhūta-saṅgha-saṁsthāno dehosya paramātmanaḥ / quotes Śrinivāsa-Sūri (ŚN). It is through His Grace that His all-pervading sentient-cum-nonsentient personality can be grasped with pure mind.

3. *VB and GD*. : Eulogy is the description of greatness. But even though you, out of grace unto me, have assumed this form, it is impossible for me to comprehend even this, with all the capacity of pure mind concentrated within. Need it be told that it is impossible for me to comprehend the greatness of your self of absolute existence, consciousness and bliss.

worlds, you appear conquered by those (devotees) who giving up all efforts in attaining knowledge, lead their life reverentially paying their respects with their body, speech and mind, to your stories (spontaneously recounted by the righteous), as they come to their ears without leaving their homes (but by remaining in the company of those pious devotees). (What is the propriety in exerting for knowledge ?)

4*. Nothing else but sheer exertions only like those who engage themselves in pounding merely the outer husk of grains (which contains no grains and as such yield no food-grains at all by this labour of pounding), is the resultant lot of those who, neglecting the path of devotion which is the fountain head of all blessings in the form of material prosperity here and liberation from *Saṁsāra* hereafter, undergo troubles to attain mere knowledge only, Oh Omnipresent Lord !

5. Oh Infinite Lord ! In days of old, in this (very) world, a number of *yogins* (who failed to attain spiritual wisdom by the path of *yoga*) dedicated all their desires and activities unto you, and obtained the knowledge of their self only through Devotion awakened in them by the resignation of their activities and desires (to you), and by virtue of listening to your stories, and thus they easily attained to your Supreme Nature (God-head), Oh Acyuta.

6. It is, however, possible, Oh Almighty Lord, to comprehend your glory properly by the pure-souled ones (who have thoroughly controlled their senses) through their personal realization of the self, who is above modifications and

* (i) *SS.*, *VR.*, *SN.* The pursuit of the Self by following the path of knowledge (brushing aside the path of devotion) results in nothing but more afflictions as stated in BG 12.5:

Kleśo'dhika-taras teṣām avyaktāsakta-cetasām /

(ii) *VB.* : Bhakti (Devotion) is like the Wish-yielding-gem (*Cintāmaṇi*). It confers knowledge of the self as well. But mere pursuit of self-knowledge is sheer affliction and does not bear any fruit (*Kleśayuktaḥ, na tu phalayuktaḥ*). It does not yield secondary or unessential fruit or even incidental (*prāsaṅgika*) fruit.

(iii) KD. interprets *bhakti* (devotion) as *abheda bhakti* (in which the distinction between the devotee and God disappears). *Bhakti* itself is the essential knowledge (*Bhakti ceci mukhya Jñāna*), and people reached *nirvāṇa* (Liberation) through *bhakti* only (14.4.31-89)

transcends all forms, for it is self-illuminating (and as such is beyond objective perception in 'this—that relation') and not by any other way.

7. Has anyone ever been able even to calculate (and estimate) your attributes when you are verily their actual support and controller—especially when you have incarnated for the well-being of the universe by manifesting innumerable qualities? Nobody, even if he be so exceptionally competent and clever as to count minutely all the particles of the (dust on the) earth, or the dew-drops in the sky, or the luminous particles in the rays of the sun, in a span of many births.[1]

8. He who, eagerly and anxiously waiting for your compassion and grace, experiences (in a detached manner), the fruits of his (past) actions and leads a life of complete reverential submission unto you, in thought word and deed, becomes a partner in the State of Liberation[2] (as if it is his ancestral property).

9. Oh Almighty Lord! Look at this wicked foolhardiness of mine. Extremely insignificant as I am (before you of whom I am born) like a flame of fire emanating from (the universe consuming) conflagration, I, with a view to see the exhibition of my magnificent grandeur, tried to cover (delude) even you with my *māyā* when you are the Infinite, Eternal, Supreme Self, the Deluder of the deluders.

10. Hence, Oh Imperishable Lord, be pleased to forgive me who am born of *rajas* and therefore steeped in ignorance. Under the false notion that I am the real Supreme Ruler independent of you, I became blind by my arrogant ignorance of being the real birthless creator of the universe. Therefore this person (I, Brahmā) may please be regarded as deserving your grace (pity) as he (I) has a protector in you.

11. What am I after all, but an insignificant being invested with a body of seven spans (according to my humble

1. Cf. *Yo vā Anantasya guṇān anantān /*
anu-kramiṣyan sa tu bāla-buddhiḥ//
rajāṁsi bhūmer gaṇayet kathañcit /
Kālena naivākhila-śakti-dhāmnaḥ //

KD—*Sukalpa*—Span of life extending over innumerable births.
14.7.264

2. J.G.B. (*JG.'s Bṛhatkrama-sandarbha*):
Become an attendant (*pārṣada*) of Viṣṇu in this very life.

measure), and confined in a momentary perishable small pot-like egg called the world, covered with the sheaths of *tamas* i.e. *Prakṛti* (Primordial matter), *mahat* (cosmic intelligence), *ahaṁkāra* (cosmic ego), elements like the ether, air, fire, water and earth? How infinitely great is your glory?[1] The pores (of the skin) of whose body are like ventilators through which innumerable egg-like universes (each as big as mine) flow in and out like atoms. How can I stand any comparison with you? (Being extremely insignificant, compassion may kindly be shown to me of your own accord (Sanātana Gosvāmī's *Bṛhat Toṣaṇi*).

12. Oh Lord, transcendental to sense perception![1] Does the raising of feet by the foetus become an offence against the mother? (No. On the contrary the mother is happy to feel that the child in her is alive and kicking. Hence whatever has been committed by me, does not constitute an offence). Is there anything described as being existent or non-existent outside your bowels?[2] (It behoves you to forgive all my offences with a motherly affection, as you have announced yourself (in BG.9.17) to be the father, mother and protector of the universe).

13. The traditional scriptural statement that Brahmā, the unborn god, was verily born of (lit. sprang from) the stalk of the lotus forming the umbilical cord of the navel of Nārāyaṇa lying on the cosmic waters of the deluge, caused by commingling all the seas, at the end of the three worlds, is not false. Am I not thus born of you Oh Lord?

14* Are you not Nārāyaṇa? Yes, you are Nārāyaṇa inasmuch as you are the soul of all embodied creatures, who

1. *Adhokṣaja*: As I owe all the power of my senses etc. to you, no act committed by me be taken as an offence—VT.

2. All the sentient and non-sentient universe born of you and ultimately is being absorbed in you, is insignificant like an atom and is within you—SS.

*This verse gives or rather implies different popular etymologies of 'Nārāyaṇa'. ŚR gives them as follows

Nāraṁ Jīvasamūhaḥ, ayanam āśrayaḥ—

thus form your dwelling place (and *nāra* means the aggregate of living beings). You are Nārāyaṇa as you are the Lord who preside over and promote life in all beings, and being the witness to the entire universe, you alone know them all. You are the Nārāyaṇa—the Deity that abide in (and thus are the basis) of all the twenty-four principles evolved out of Nara, as well as waters—your abode for reposing, which is the evolute of Nara who is also your part. Even your reposing on water is also not true, but your *māyā*, as your form is indiscernible.

15. (Your form is beyond accurate determination or ascertainment, for) If your form which is the basic support of the world, reposed on cosmic waters in reality, how is it that I could not see it at that time when I tried for one hundred years to explore through the lotus-stalk out of which I came, (the source of my birth), Oh Lord of inconceivable power. Or why

(i) *Nāra*—aggregate of all beings; *ayanam*—abode. Hence one who dwells in all bodies as their soul.

(ii) *Nārasya ayanam pravṛttiḥ*—The source of the Promoter of all the aggregate of *jīvas*.

(iii) *Nāram ayase*—You know the aggregate of all beings. ay—to know.

(iv) Nāra—that which is produced from Nara.
Nāra—water. Nārāyaṇa is one who dwells in or reposes on water.

The above etymologies are supported by SS., VR. etc. SN. quotes the following verses in support of the above etymologies.

nārāṇām ayanatvācca Nārāyaṇa iti smṛtaḥ /
nāra-śabdena jīvānāṁ samūhaḥ procyate budhaiḥ//
teṣām ayana-bhūtatvān Nārāyaṇa iti smṛtaḥ /
nāro narāṇāṁ saṅghātas tasyāham ayanaṁ gatiḥ /
tenāsmi munibhir nityaṁ Nārāyaṇa iti smṛtaḥ //
cetanā'cetanaṁ sarvaṁ Viṣṇor yad vyatiricyate /
nāraṁ tadayanaṁ cedaṁ yasya Nārāyaṇas tu saḥ //

VT. states that God's reposing on cosmic water is not illusory (*māyika*), because it, being a sportive act (*līlā*) of God, is real.

SG. explains, god Brahmā was so over-whelmed with the spiritual feat (of assuming the form of calves, cowherd boys etc.) that he regarded Lord Kṛṣṇa as greater than Nārāyaṇa, "Oh Kṛṣṇa you are not Nārāyaṇa, Oh Lord of the totality of Brahmāṇḍas (all the universe) is only your part or a ray ?"

According to SG. Kṛṣṇa is the real, complete Supreme Person (*Kṛṣṇas tu pūrṇa puruṣottamaḥ*)

was it that it became clearly visible to me in my heart when I performed severe penance and why was it that it instantly disappeared.[1]

16. It is here only in this your incarnation (as Kṛṣṇa) that you have clearly demonstrated the illusory nature of this entire external universe to your mother, by manifesting it completely in your abdomen, Oh dispeller of Māyā.

17. Just as this entire universe including yourself appears present in your bowels, it is also manifested the same way even outside your bowels. Is this (double manifestation) possible except through your deluding potency.

18. Has not the illusive nature of this universe with the exception of your own self, been demonstrated to me by you even today?—At first (before I stole away the calves and the cowherd boys from Vraja) you were one. Then you assumed the forms of all your friends and calves from Vraja. You then revealed yourself in as many four-armed forms which were worshipped by all as well as by me. Then you became as many universes. You still remain the sole same Infinite Brahman without any second.[2]

19. To persons who are ignorant of your real nature,[3] you, the all-pervading Lord abide in *Prakṛti* and you spread your Māyā at your free will, and appear (though one as many) as if you are myself (i.e. god Brahmā) at the creation of the Universe,

1. VB : As I am your son the parental relation requires mutual sights. How is it that I could not see you often ?

2. V.B. In the ultimate analysis nothing but Brahman without a second remains and nothing else.

SG. The forms of calves and cowherd boys assumed by you were not illusory. Although whatever forms you manifested were discernible as separate, you are the second-less Brahman who baffle (all attempts at) discernment. What remains is your own self, the Brahman characterised by Truth, Knowledge, infinite Bliss.

3. JG.—Those who do not comprehend your greatness call this all as Māyā and not the working of your yogic power which is indescribable. The process of creation, protection or destruction of the world or assumption of the forms of calves and cowherds is not jugglery or *Māyā*, but your real sport at your free will.

Padavī—The path of devotion (SG., VC.) and *anātmani*—'In the body.'

as yourself i.e. Viṣṇu for its protection, and as the three-eyed god Śiva, at the time of the dissolution of the universe.

20. Oh Creator and Controller of the Universe ! Unborn as you are, you incarnate among gods (e.g. Vāmana), sages (e.g. Vyāsa), as well as among men (e.g. Rāma and Kṛṣṇa), sub-human beings (e.g. beasts as in the Boar incarnation) and acquatic animals (the Fish and Tortoise incarnations) for subduing the pride of the wicked, and showering grace on the righteous and saintly people[1], Oh Lord !

21. Oh Supreme Lord ! The receptacle of infinite powers (like knowledge, power, energy etc.) ! The In-dweller in the hearts of all ! Who knows (or is capable of knowing) the nature, time, place, extent of your sportive acts in which you indulge, after spreading out (exhibiting) your Yogic (deluding) Potency, in these three worlds, Oh Master of Yoga.

22. Hence, though this entire world which is of unreal nature like dream-experience, devoid of intelligence and full of endless, innumerable miseries, appears and disappears in You who are infinite, eternal bliss and knowledge *incarnate*, and through Māyā it seems to be real and possessing your characteristics.

23. You are the only one Self (*ātman*) abiding in the bodies of living beings, the ancient-most, real, self-refulgent, infinite, first and foremost, eternal, imperishable person of unobstructed blissfulness, untainted (by any blemish or Māyā), perfect, without any second, free from limitations and immortal.

24. Those who, through correct *upaniṣadic* mystic vision obtained from the sun-like spiritual preceptors, properly comprehend you as being of the above description, as the self-abiding in all beings, and as their own soul, easily cross this ocean of *Saṁsāra* (metem-psychosis) which is (as a matter of fact) unreal.

25. In the case of those who do not comprehend the *ātman* (The Self) in its essential nature, the entire world or *Saṁsāra* is created due to this lack of understanding. But

1. *Pari-trāṇāya sādhūnāṃ vināśāya ca duṣkṛtām |*
dharma-saṁsthāpanārthāya sambhavāmi yuge yuge ||

—BG.4.8

through realization and enlightenment (about his nature) the *saṁsāra* disappears again, as the appearance and disappearance of the body of a serpent (super-imposed through ignorance) on a rope (does before and after realization of the real nature of the rope).

26. The bondage of *saṁsāra* and Liberation from it, are terms which, as a matter of fact, are instituted through ignorance. They are not separate entities distinct from the reality characterised by truth and knowledge. When considered against the background of the absolute transcendental *Paramātman* of eternal consciousness, they cease to have separate existence, as do the day and night in the (sphere of the) sun.

27. How pitiable is the ignorance of these ignorant people that they consider you, their real self, as other (different from themselves), and their body as their very self. And thus they think that their real self is to be searched for outside in external objects.

28. Oh Infinite Lord ! Righteous people really seek you within the body (which is composed of matter and the spirit), by discarding that which is 'Not-that' (non-self). Can pious men of accurate judgement arrive at that correct conclusion, that the rope lying near (which was mistaken for a serpent) is certainly a rope, unless they have negated the wrong super-imposition of a serpent over that rope (through ignorance).

29. It is, however, he (your devotee) who is blest with the slightest grace of the pair of your lotus-like feet, who understands the real nature of the glory and power of the Lord, and not a person who is searching for it for a long time (but has not been favoured with your Grace), Oh Lord !

30. Oh Protector (of the universe) ! May I be blessed with that great luck, whereby in this very life (of Brahmā) or in any other birth, even in sub-human beings, I shall be one of your devotees, and serve your foliage-like tender feet ?

31. Oh ! How highly blessed are the cows and women of Vraja, the nectarine milk from whose udders and breasts is sucked with extreme delight (and satisfaction) by you in the form of calves and (cowherd) boys, Oh ! Omnipresent Lord, to whom even sacred sacrifices have not been able to give gratification (to that extent) even till today.

32. How surprisingly admirable (and enviable) is the good luck of Nanda and the cowherds of Vraja, that they have a friend in you, the eternal perfect Brahman, the embodiment of the highest bliss.

33. (As it is simply beyond the capacity of anyone to describe it) let the greatness of the fortune of these cowherds be kept aside for the time being. But we eleven[1]-god Śiva and others (the presiding deities of sense-organs) are exceptionally fortunate, for, through the *cups* in the form of the sense-organs (of these cowherds), we constantly drink the exhilarating and inebriating sweet nectar-like honey of your lotus-feet, (How much more blessed are the cowherds of Vraja who can enjoy your personal charms through all their senses, if our single organ medium is so enchanting !).

34. It will be an exceedingly high fortune to be born in any species (even as humble grass) here, in this forest (of Vṛndāvana), especially in Gokula, where one may have the (good luck) of bathing (from head to foot, all over the body) in the dust of the feet of any one (of the devoted inhabitants) from Gokula; for their entire life is the Lord Mukunda Himself, the dust of whose feet is still sought after by the Vedas.

35. As Pūtanā merely through her assumption of the guise of the good (pretending motherly affection to you) was brought to your region along with the members of her family, our mind is baffled in trying to guess what fruit other than yourself, the highest possible reward in the world, you can confer on these residents of Vraja whose homes, wealth, friends, beloved relatives, their selves, sons, life and mind are completely dedicated to you (and are meant for you), Oh Lord.

36. Oh Lord Kṛṣṇa ! So long as people do not become yours (your votaries), passions like desire, hatred etc. act as

1. ŚR gives the following list of organs presided over by deities. The mind (the moon god), *buddhi*—intellect (Brahmā), *ahaṁkāra*—ego (Śiva), the auditory sense (*dig-devatā*—deities presiding over the cardinal points), the tactile sense (Vāyu—the wind god). the sight (the sun gods) the sense of taste (Varuṇa—the Lord of waters), the olfactory sense (Aśvinī Kumāras), organ of speech (Agni—the fire god), hands (Indra), feet (Upendra). The organs of excretion and urination seem to have been excluded in the *Bhāgavata* verse and the inclusion of god Brahmā and Śiva are substituted to make up the number eleven.

thieves (to deprive them of their merits or spiritual wealth) and the house serves as a prison and infatuation works as fetters.

37. Oh Lord! Even though you are transcendental to the world and as such have nothing to do with the worldly life, you play your role in this (worldly) life for enhancing the rapturous joy of people who have submitted to you for resort.

38. I have nothing to say about those who (pose that they) know you. Let them. (In fact, they are deluded in thinking that way). But as far as I am concerned, your glory is beyond the ken of my mind, body (senses) and speech.

39. Oh Kṛṣṇa! Be pleased to grant me leave (to depart). You know everything, Oh Omniscient Lord. You are the protector of the world. This world and this person (both of which I wrongly regarded as mine) are now offered to you.

40. My respectful obeisance to the end of this Kalpa (the duration of my life) to you; Oh Lord Kṛṣṇa who cause delight to the lotus (in the form) of Vṛṣṇi clan, who bring flow-tide to the sea in the form (i.e. enhance the prosperity) of the earth, gods, Brāhmaṇas and the cows; the dispeller of the darkness of the pseudo-religious hypocrites, the destroyer of the demons on the earth and adorable to gods (right) from the sun.

Śrī Śuka said :

41.* After offering his hymn in praise of the Supreme Lord in this way, god Brahmā (the creator of the Universe) circumambulated him thrice (out of respect), and bowing down to his feet, he returned to his region which is adorable to and desired by all.

42. The Lord granted permission to god Brahmā who was born of him (and was therefore, pardoned his audacity to test the Lord). He brought back the (original) calves to the sandy bank of his choice (for the common dinner with the cowherd boys in that picnic) where his companions were (already waiting) as before.

*VT. notes that Kṛṣṇa by his silence, refused god Brahmā's request to stay in his vicinity and indicated that one must execute one's prescribed duties during the tenure of his office—

yāvad adhikāram avasthitir adhikāriṇām

43. Though the children were separated from Kṛṣṇa, the very lord of their life, for one complete year, they thought it to be only half a moment due to the effect of the illusive power of Kṛṣṇa, Oh king.

44. What do they not forget in this world when the mind is infatuated with the Māyā Potency of the Lord ? The whole world under its deluding influence often forgets itself.

45. His companions greeted Kṛṣṇa, "Welcome for your speedy return. Not a single morsel has been eaten by us (during your absence). Have a hearty meal."

46. Laughing (loudly at the welcome) Kṛṣṇa, the Lord of sense organs, had his meal with the cowherd boys. He showed them the skin of the boa-constrictor, and returned to Vraja from the forest.

47. With person attractively decorated with peacock feathers, flowers and variegated mineral colours and exultant at the fanfare of the transporting sounds of flutes whistles of leaves and horns that were loudly blown, and shouting at the calves while tending them, Kṛṣṇa whose looks brought delight to the eyes of the cowherd women,[1] entered Vraja, while his companions singing his hallowing glory, followed him.

48. The children sang in Vraja : "By this child, the delight of Yośodā, a big serpent was killed today and we were saved from it".

King Parīkṣit enquired :

49. Oh Brahman sage ! Be pleased to explain to me how was this unbounded abundance of love which was never before exhibited (by the inhabitants of Vraja) even to the children born to them, was possible in the case of Kṛṣṇa who was born of another.[2]

1. SG., as an alternate explanation, introduces Rādhā here. *yad vā Śrī-Kṛṣṇaika-priyāyā bhagavatyāḥ Śrī Rādhādevyāḥ tan netrāṇām eva viśeṣatas taddarśanotsavasiddheḥ/*

2. vide Supra 13.26.

Śrī Śuka explained :

50.* Oh King ! One's own self (*ātman*)[1] is the most beloved to all created beings. Others such as children, wealth etc. are dear, because they are beloved to the self.

51** One does not cherish that much love to one's progeny, wealth, house etc. which (being dependent on their feeling of mine-ness) is called their own, as one has for one's body (which is identified with the self), by all embodied beings, Oh Great King.

52. To persons who believe in the identity of the body and the (indwelling) Soul, their own body is the dearest to them and not so much the children etc. which come after it (or are connected with it), Oh best of Kṣattriyas.

53. (If, instead of believing in the one-ness of the body with the soul) this body shares the feeling of 'mine-ness' (is regarded as different from the soul yet 'mine') it would not be so intensely loved as the soul itself. For when this body is being worn out, the desire to live grows stronger.[2]

54. Hence one's own self is the most beloved to all embodied beings. It is for the sake of the Self that all this world mobile and immobile, exists.

55. Do you know that this Kṛṣṇa is the soul of all embodied beings. It is for the good of the world that he, through his Māyā power, appears to have assumed a corporal form.

56. To those who know the Reality, everything mobile and immobile in this world, is Kṛṣṇa.[3] Everything is the

1. VR. *ātman*=The Supreme Self.

* For vv. 50-54 cf. *na vā are patyuḥ Kāmāya patiḥ priyo bhavati / ātmanas tu kāmāya patiḥ priyo bhavati/* etc.—*Bṛhad. Upa.* 2.4.5.

** *VB*. The feeling of love for one's own body, due to the 'I'ness attributed to it by these who identify the body with the soul, is stronger than that (which one feels) for one's progeny or wealth with which 'mine-ness' is associated.

2. SG. and VT. read: *jivitāśā abalīyasī*: The desire to live is not so strong as the person's ego is eliminated through discriminatory (philosophical) thinking.

3. SS. quotes *tad-ananyatvam-ārambhaṇa-śabdādibhyaḥ* BR. S.2.1.15) (0.14 according to Śaṅkara) in support of Kṛṣṇa's person comprising everything sentient and non-sentient in the universe.

Also cf. Infra 11.2.41.

manifestation of the the Almighty Lord and there is nothing else (than he).

57. Of all things that exist, their essence lies in their cause and Lord Kṛṣṇa is the ultimate cause of all these causes. Hence, tell me if there is anything apart from him.

58. To those who resort to the boat in the form of the foliage like tender feet of Kṛṣṇa, (the slayer of demon Mura) of hallowing reputation—the final abode of the great (sages) (saints etc.)—the ocean of *saṁsāra* is as shallow as the footprint of a calf. They attain to the highest region (vaikuṇṭha) from which they never revert to the Saṁsāra, the region of miseries.

59. Whatever I have been asked by you here as to show what was done by Hari in his stage as a child was proclaimed broadcast in his boyhood, has been completely narrated to you.

60. By listening to or by glorifying how Lord Kṛṣṇa (The Slayer of demon Mura) played with his chums, his slaying of the demon Agha, his repast on the meadow, his assumption of non-phenomenal forms and the sublime hymn of praise sung by god Brahmā, a person attains everything that he desires.

61. In this way, they both (Kṛṣṇa and Balarāma) passed their childhood at Vraja, in child-like sports such as hide-and-seek, playful construction of dams, jumping like monkey (from one branch of a tree to another).

CHAPTER FIFTEEN

Slaying the demon Dhenuka

Śrī Śuka continued :

1. And after attaining the *paugaṇḍa* stage (boyhood from the age of six to nine), those two brothers (Balarāma and Kṛṣṇa) were approved (by Nanda and others) as suitable for the job of tending the cows[1]. While grazing the cows and their

1. VT. quotes *Padma P.* which states that during their childhood, Kṛṣṇa and Balarāma tended calves. On their attainment of the sixth year, from the 8th day of the bright half of Kārttika, they became *bona fide* cow tenders. Hence that day is now known as *Gopāṣṭamī*.

calves in company of their friends, they rendered the region of Vṛndāvana extremely sacred, by their foot-prints.[1]

2. On one occasion, playing on his own flute, accompanied by Balarāma and surrounded by cowherds singing his glory, Mādhava (Kṛṣṇa, 'the Lord of Lakṣmī as well as the spring) tending his herd of kine in front of him, and desirous of indulging in sports, entered a forest blossoming with flowers and affording a good pasture suitable to the cattle.

3. Observing that the (Vṛndāvana) forest was resounded with the sweet notes, sound and humming of birds, beasts (or deer) and bees, and was wafted with a breeze cool due to its contact with pools with waters translucent like (the pure) minds of the great, and fragrant with lotuses, the Lord set his heart to play there.

4. Perceiving at every place, trees glowing with the beauty of reddish foliage and touching their feet with their heads—top branches—heavy with a burden of fruits and flowers, Kṛṣṇa, the Primeval Person, slightly smiled out of delight, and addressed his elder brother.

The glorious Lord said :

5. Oh ! How wonderful ! Carrying the presents of fruits and flowers on their heads (top branches), these trees bow down their heads (branches) laden heavily with fruits to your lotus-feet which are adored by the immortals, with a view to absolve themselves of the sin or ignorance (*tamas*)[2] which caused their birth as trees, Oh prominent God.

6. These (humming) bees, singing your glory that purifies all the world, are resorting to you at every step—you the Ancientmost Person. Most probably, these are the hosts of sages who

Śuklāṣṭamī Kārttikasya smṛtā Gopāṣṭamī budhaiḥ |
taddinād Vāsudevo' bhūd gopaḥ purvaṁ tu vatsapaḥ ||

1. Cowherds used to go bare-footed. Hence the imprints of Kṛṣṇa's feet on the soil of Vṛndāvana—VT.

2. VT. argues that it was ignorance but they deliberately accepted birth as a tree in Vṛndāvana forest, as god Brahmā made a similar request in his prayer (Supra 14.34)

VB. regards these three verses 5, 6 and 7 as if prayers from the trees, bees, birds and beasts.

are prominent among devotees, and they do not let you miss—their personal Deity—even though you lie concealed in the (Vṛndāvana) forest, Oh sinless one!

7. On your arrival at their home, the peacocks are dancing joyously; the female deer, overwhelmed with joy are giving you delight with their oglings like unto cowherd women (of Vraja), and the flocks of cuckoos welcome you with their sweet cooing. Blessed are these forest-dwellers.[1] For such is the nature of the saintly persons.

8.* Blessed is the earth today; and also the blades of grass and plants touching your feet, and the trees and creepers gently pricked by your nails (to pluck leaves or flowers), and the rivers, hills, birds and beasts that have been viewed at with kind looks, and the Gopa girls who are hugged to your bosom (between your arms) for which even the goddess of beauty, (Lakṣmī) longs.

9. Being delighted at least at the sight of Vṛndāvana (the beauty of which is described above), Lord Kṛṣṇa enjoyed himself along with his companions, while grazing the cows in the pastures on the river bank, in the vicinity of the (Govardhana) mount.

10. Adorned with garlands and accompanied by Balarāma (Saṅkarṣaṇa)[2], he used to burst out into singing in imitation of the sweet humming of bees intoxicated with the honey sucked by them, while his followers were extolling his feats in song.

11. Sometimes he imitated the rapturous notes of swans, and sometimes he danced mimicking the dancing peacocks, provoking his companions to laughter.

11-A. *Vṛndāvana edition adds*[3]

Sometimes he imitated the chattering of the parrots in

1. VJ. regards that words *śikhi & Kokila* also mean 'sages—one with matted hair', and the gods Brahmā (ka) Śiva (*u*) and others.

*This verse is No. 19 in VJ's Text (in which this ch. is No 13) and is spoken by Śrī Śuka.

2. *Saṅkarṣaṇa* is used to indicate that Balarāma being non-different from Kṛṣṇa, joined him in singing—VT.

3. P. 565 Footnote. Source not given but VT's text comments on this verse and not on V. 11 above.

sweet indistinct words. Sometimes he sweetly cooed in imitation of the warbling and cooing of cuckoos.

12. Sometimes, in a voice deep and sonorous like the rumbling of clouds, and extremely fascinating to the cows and cowherds (alike), he would affectionately call out (by names) cows that have strayed away to distant pastures.

13. He used to imitate the notes and cries of birds like *Cakora* (a fabulous bird subsisting on lunar rays), *Krauñca* (a curlew or heron), *cakravāka* (the ruddy goose), *Bhāradvāja* (a sky-lark) and also peacocks, and sometimes behaved or shrieked like animals terrified at tigers and lions.

14. Sometimes by shampooing his feet and rendering other services (like fanning), Kṛṣṇa would remove the fatigue of his elder brother, Balarāma, exhausted with playing, and lying with his head on the cushion-like lap of a cowherd boy.

15. Sometimes holding each other by hands, they (Balarāma and Kṛṣṇa) laughingly applauded the cowherd boys who were dancing, capering, singing, prattling and wrestling with each other.

16. At times, being exhausted with (physical) exertions in wrestling, he used to lie on different beds[1] of tender leaves (prepared by his companions) at the foot of trees, placing his head on the cushion-like laps of (elderly) cowherd-boys.

17. Some cowherd boys kneaded the feet of the great-souled Lord while other sinless ones fanned him with fans made of tender leaves.

18. Others whose hearts (lit. intellect) were steeped in love and devotion for him, sang gently and in sweet low tone beautiful songs suitable for the occasion, and pleasing to him (or songs pertaining to his feats), Oh Great King!

19. In this way, Kṛṣṇa, by his Māyā, had concealed his course (i.e. real divine nature) and played his *role* as a cowherd

1. VT. states that by His Māyā power, Kṛṣṇa lay on all the beds leading each group to believe that Kṛṣṇa was honouring the bed prepared by them.

VB. explains that Kṛṣṇa did so for the sages who were occupying the feet of trees and his beds were the heart of *yogins* where he lay and he showed his preference and respect to cowherd boys by placing his head on their laps.

boy by his acts (sports and behaviour). The Lord whose foliage-like tender feet were caressed by goddess Lakṣmī played like a rustic boy with rustics, though occasionally he behaved like the Almighty Lord.

20. A certain cowherd called Śrīdāman was a bosom friend of Rāma and Kṛṣṇa and so were other cowherd boys like Subala, Stoka. Kṛṣṇa spoke to them with friendly affection.

(VJ. reads : Śrīdāman spoke to Subala, Aśoka, Kṛṣṇa and other cowherds out of friendliness).

21. "Oh Rāma ! Balarāma of mighty arms ! Oh Kṛṣṇa, the destroyer of the wicked ! Not far from this place, there is a great dense forest thick with rows of palmyra trees.[1]

22. Abundant fruits lie fallen and have been falling there, but they are all monopolised by Dhenuka of wicked soul.

23. He is a demon of mighty prowess[2], Oh Rāma ! Oh Kṛṣṇa ! Assuming the form of a donkey, he lives surrounded by members of his tribe (donkeys), all of whom are equal in strength to him.

24. Being afraid of that cannibal who feeds on human beings, the tract of forest is not visited by men and is also avoided by herds of beasts and flocks of birds.

25. Very delicious and sweet smelling fruits untasted by us lie there. And it is the sweet fragrance of those fruits that has filled the air all around, and we perceive that here also.

26. Oh Kṛṣṇa ! Be pleased to give those to us whose hearts are enamoured of their odour. A very strong yearning urges us, Oh Rāma. We make a move if you approve of it.

27. Hearing the request of his friend and with a desire to accomplish their wishes, those two mighty gods laughed heartily, and proceeded to the Palm forest accompanied by the cowherds.

28. Balarāma entered the forest and by violently shaking the palm trees with his arms like a young elephant, he made the fruit drop down by his physical power.

1. VT. locates it with 'Tālasi' or 'Tāraphara'. It is to the southwest of Mathura at a distance of 8 miles from Govardhana.

2. v.l. *atitīvra*—of extremely ferocious nature—VJ

29. Hearing the sound of the falling of fruits, the Asura in the form of a donkey, rushed to the place making the earth along with mountains tremble and quake.

30. Rushing at Balarāma, the powerful demon kicked with his hind legs on the chest of Balarāma, and braying loudly the wicked fellow ran away to some distance. (moved hither and thither around Balarāma).

31. Approaching Balarāma again, the donkey stayed with its face away from Balarāma, and in violent wrath, he flung his hind legs (struck with his hind hoofs) Balarāma, Oh King !

32. Catching hold of both his legs with one hand, Balarāma violently whirled him and when the demon died due to that terrible whirling, he hurled him to the top of a tall palm tree.

33. Being struck (with the carcass of that donkey), the big palm tree with heavy (palm-fruit laden) head crashed, and shook heavily the adjoining tree which fell down, despatching its neighbouring tree to the same fate.

34. Being struck down by the impact of the dead body of the donkey which was sportively hurled by Balarāma, all the palm trees shook heavily, as if swept down by a violent hurricane.

35. This is not miraculous in the case of the glorious Lord Śeṣa (who incarnated as Balarāma) the Ruler of the universe, in whom the universe is woven warp and woof, like a piece of cloth into the threads, Oh dear child !

36. The whole tribe of Dhenuka, the donkeys which flung in rage due to the killing of their brother, dashed at Rāma and Kṛṣṇa.

37. As they attacked, both Rāma and Kṛṣṇa held them by their hind legs, and flung them easily to the tops of the tall palm trees, as if in sport.

38. Littered over with heaps of palm fruits, the tops of the palm trees, and the dead bodies of the demons, the surface of the earth looked like the sky overcast with clouds (red, white and blue in colours).

39. Hearing of their marvellous feat, gods and others (such as demigods, celestial damsels etc.) let down showers of

flowers on them, played on the divine musical instruments, and praised them highly.

40. Then the forest being thus rid of Dhenuka, people being free from fear, enjoyed (ate) to the full, fruits of those palm trees, and the cattle grazed in the pasture fearlessly.

41. Kṛṣṇa whose eyes were large like lotus-petals, and the hearing and singing of whose glory is hallowing and meritorious, entered Vraja along with his elder brother Balarāma, in company of his cowherd followers who were glorifying and praising him.

42. The cowherd women rushed out in crowds to welcome and see with eager eyes, Lord Kṛṣṇa, looking charming with sylvain flowers and peacock feathers adorning his curly locks of hair, overlaid with dust raised by (the hoofs of) cows, of beautiful eyes and bewitching smiles, and who was playing on his flute while followed by cowherds singing his glory.

43. Drinking with their black-bee-like eyes the honey (i.e. charm) in the lotus-like countenance of Mukunda (Kṛṣṇa), the damsels of Vṛaja got subsided their fever of separation from him during the day time. Kṛṣṇa, on his part, entered the cow-pen after duly receiving their worship, welcome (consisting) of bashful smiles, ogling with side glances and modesty.

44. Yaśodā and Rohiṇī who were very fond and affectionate to their sons, poured their benedictions suitable to the occasion to their heart's content.

45. They whose fatigue of journey (while tending the cows) was removed by bath, massage etc. in the forest, were dressed in beautiful clothes, and were adorned with excellent garlands, perfumes (sandal paste) etc.

46. They partook of the sweet dish served to them by their mother, and after being caressed by them, they went to sleep in excellent beds, and enjoyed sweet, happy sleep at Vraja.

47. In this way, Lord Kṛṣṇa used to move in the Vṛndāvana. On one occasion, unaccompanied by Balarāma, but in company of (lit. surrounded by) his friends, he went to the Yamunā.

48. There, being tormented with the heat of the summer and oppressed with thirst, the cows as well as cowherds drank the river water polluted due to the contamination of poison.

49. Being deprived of their discretion and judgement by the Providence,[1] immediately after sipping the poisonous water, they all fell dead, by the side of the water[2], Oh best of Kurus.

50. Finding them verily reduced to that condition, Kṛṣṇa, the Lord of the masters of Yoga, restored his *proteges* to life by his glance that (as if) showered nectar.

51. Recovering their consciousness immediately, all of them rose up from the brink of the water and gazed at each other with amazement.

52. They came to understand that their restoration to life after death by drinking poison was the result of the gracious look of Kṛṣṇa (Govinda), Oh King Parīkṣit.

CHAPTER SIXTEEN

Expulsion of Kāliya

Śrī Śuka said :

1. Perceiving that the (waters of the) Kṛṣṇā (i.e. Yamunā) had been poisoned by a black serpent (Kāliya), the Almighty Kṛṣṇa, desirous of purifying it, expelled him (from that place).

The King (*Parīkṣit*) *asked* :

2. May it be kindly narrated to me as to how Lord Kṛṣṇa caught hold of (and subdued) the serpent in the interior of the unfathomable waters (of the Yamunā), and (secondly)

1. Those whose knowledge was affected by the power of the sportive activities of the glorious Lord—VT.

2. Jīva Gosvāmī, in *ṣaṭ-sandarbha* (in *Kṛṣṇa-sandarbha*) explains that Gopas being attendants of the Lord did not die by the poisonous water. This is simply to show that they are human beings as the Lord behaved as a human incarnation.

tad bhāgavata iva nara-līlaupāyikatayā prapañcitam iti mantavyam

For details vide De—*Vaiṣṇava Faith and Movement*. pp. 55-56. VJ. regards this a bit allegorical indicating that the poison of *saṁsāra* does not affect the devotees of Hari (vide Intro. to ch. 16).

a serpent is not an acquatic animal; how could he make his abode in the interior part of water for ages together, Oh learned Brāhmaṇa.[1]

3. Who will feel satiated while drinking the nectar of the noble deeds of the glorious omnipotent Lord of absolute free will, while he was acting his role as a cowherd, Oh Brāhmaṇa Sage ?

Śrī Śuka said :

4. In the Yamunā, there was a certain pool, the haunt of Kāliya, the waters whereof were boiling with the serpent's fiery poison and even the birds flying over it, fell dead (due to poisonous vapours).

5. Beings, mobile and immobile, on the banks of that river, succumbed to death at the touch of the wind charged with the poisonous spray, while blowing over the ripples of that deadly water.

6. Kṛṣṇa, whose incarnation was for the subjugation of the wicked, considered how the real power of the snake lay in its virulent venom and that it had polluted the river with its contamination. Climbing up a very tall *Kadamba* tree (on the bank of the Yamunā[2]), he tightened his girdle and striking his arms (as if challenging Kāliya to fight) jumped down into the poisonous water.

7. The pool of the serpent, the voluminous waters of which were swelled with venom discharged by the serpent, extremely agitated by the vehemence of the plunge of the Supreme Man, dashed up overflowing on all sides to a distance of hundred bows (i.e. four hundred *hastas* or cubits) in terrible

1. VT. supports this meaning of 'Vipra' by quoting Yājñavalkya—
janmanā, Brāhmaṇo jñeyaḥ, saṁskārair dvija ucyate |
vidyayā yāti vipratvaṁ tribhiḥ śrotriya-lakṣaṇam ||

2. ŚR. & VR. explain that that Kadamba tree did not get dry by Kāliya's poison due to contact of nectar while Garuḍa was carrying it away from the custody of gods (Mbh. Adi. 33) VB. states that Garuḍa used to perch on it, waiting for Kāliya to come out so that he would kill it. The tree was thus preserved for Kṛṣṇa. VT. states it was Lord Kṛṣṇa's tree—as if identical with him (*Śrī-Kṛṣṇa-vṛkṣatvāt*) and was protected by Lord Kṛṣṇa for his sports.

waves saturated and bitter with poison. But there is nothing miraculous in this in the case of the Almighty Lord (of infinite strength).

8. Hearing the thunderous sound of water agitated by the strokes of the mighty arms (of the Lord) who was sporting with the prowess of a supreme powerful elephant, and perceiving it as an attack on his abode, and unable to tolerate it, the serpent (whose eyes functioned also as ears) advanced rustling against Kṛṣṇa, Oh dear King!

9. Biting him in all tender parts, twisting himself, he enclosed completely in his coils the Lord who looked extremely beautiful, delicate and effulgent like a cloud; (who) was adorned with *Śrīvatsa* mark and was dressed in raiment of bright golden hue; who, with a bewitching, smiling face and with feet tender like the pericarp of a lotus, was sporting (in the water) with absolute fearlessness.

10. On seeing Kṛṣṇa caught in the coils of the serpent and no movement of his being visible, his dearest chums, the cowherds, who had dedicated to him their own selves, their belongings, family and even desires, became extremely distressed, and dropped down with their minds maddened with grief, sorrow and fear in succession.

11. Fixing their gaze at Kṛṣṇa and extremely distressed cows, bulls and heifers began to bellow; they stood there as if weeping through fear.

12. And at Vraja, very ominous and terrible portents of three-fold character indicating imminent danger appeared on the earth (e.g. seismic disturbance), in the sky (e.g. raining of meteors or blood), and to persons (throbbing of the left-side in the case of men and right side in the case of women).

13. Noticing the evil omens and learning that Kṛṣṇa unaccompanied by Balarāma had left for grazing the cattle, the cowherds of whom Nanda was prominent, were overwhelmed with fear.

14. Being ignorant of the real (omnipotent) nature of Kṛṣṇa, they concluded from the omens, the death (or fatal calamity) of Kṛṣṇa. As they regarded him as their very life, and had set their hearts on him, they became submerged in grief, sorrow and fear.

15. Young and old, men and women who followed the vocation of cowherds (or were extremely affectionate) being eager to have a look at Kṛṣṇa, proceeded from Gokula in a sad melancholy mood.

16. Perceiving them so nervous and terrified, the glorious Lord Balarāma who knew the prowess of the younger brother, laughed heartily, but spoke nothing.

17. In search of their beloved Kṛṣṇa, they followed the track indicated by his foot-prints bearing the special marks of being the supreme Lord, and they reached the bank of the Yamunā.

18. On the way, and in between the foot-prints of cows and others, they carefully observed the foot-prints of the Lord characterised by the marks of a lotus, a barley seed, a goad, the thunder bolt and a banner, and they proceeded quickly, dear Parīkṣit.

19. Noticing from a distance Kṛṣṇa entwined in the coils of the serpent, and being merged motionless in water in the interior of the pool, and the cow-herds fallen in a swoon on the bank and the piteously lowing all around, they became sorely distressed, and lost their consciousness.

20. With their hearts deeply attached to the infinite Glorious Lord Kṛṣṇa, and cherishing the memory of his warm-hearted friendship, charming smile, meaningful glances and pleasing words, the Gopīs (cowherdesses) were extremely tormented with grief to find their most beloved (Kṛṣṇa) trapped in the coils of the serpent, and looked upon the three worlds bereft of their beloved, as totally desolate and interestless.

21. Shedding profusely tears of grief, the cowherdesses who were equally grieved like Yaśodā, closely held her back (from following Kṛṣṇa in the Pool as her heart followed her child. They were recounting the stories of Kṛṣṇa so beloved in Vraja. With their eyes riveted on the face of Kṛṣṇa, they stood there like lifeless bodies.

22. Noticing that Nanda and others whose very life was Kṛṣṇa, entering the pool of water, glorious Lord Balarāma who knew the prowess of Kṛṣṇa, prevented them from doing so.

23. Observing that the whole of his Gokula including women and children entirely depended on him for shelter and

was extremely grieved for his sake, Kṛṣṇa who followed the role of mortals, stayed for about a *muhūrta* a short while (about 48 minutes) in that entrapped condition, and emerged out of the coils of the serpent.

24. His body being oppressed by the (internal) pressure of the expanding dimensions of Kṛṣṇa's body, the enraged serpent freed Kṛṣṇa from his coils, and raised his hoods breathing out violently poison from his hissing nostrils, and was staring at him with eyes motionless yet hot like a frying pan, and mouth emitting flames of fire.

25. Like Garuḍa, the king of birds, watching for an opportunity (to pounce on his prey), Lord Kṛṣṇa sported with the serpent which was constantly licking the corners of its mouth with its forked tongue, and whose eyes sending forth extremely virulent poisonous (flames of) fire, and wheeling round the serpent, he made it whirl around itself.

26. When all the energy (and prowess) of the serpent became exhausted in whirling round itself, Kṛṣṇa, the First (Eternal) Person bent down its raised shoulders (i.e. neck, with his hands[1]), and mounted on its broad hood.[2] With his lotus feet extremely red and refulgent with their contact with the heaps of jewels on the heads of the serpent, the First Teacher of all arts[3] began to dance.

27. Observing that the Lord intends to dance and is about to commence it, all his (servants—celestial artists like) Gandharvas, Siddhas, gods, Cāraṇas, heavenly damsels (*apsarās*)[4] suddenly, promptly and with loving devotion presented them-

1. *Śiraḥ sa Kṛṣṇo jagrāha*
Svahastenā'vanamya ca—Harivaṁśa, quoted by VT., VC also VB.

2. VB. raises the question how the Holy Lord rode on an inauspicious reptile and replies that firstly, being the creator of all, the problem of inauspiciousness does not arise, and secondly, He is habituated to sleep on a serpent (Śeṣa) as (*Śeṣa-śāyi*)

3. v.l.—*amṛta-Kalādhi-guruḥ*—VJ. who is the Supreme Master of the moon of nectarine rays.

4. VB.—The following are the functions of the celestials on such occasions : *Gandharvas*, to sing; *Siddhas*, to shower flowers; sages, to compose hymns of praise; *Cāraṇas*, to play on musical instruments and *apsarās* celestial damsels to dance. But the procedure of dancing viz. *Nāndī*, followed by scattering of flowers etc. was upset by the suddenness of the Lord's decision to dance.

selves there with drums, tabors and musical instruments, flowers, singing the songs of his praise.

28. Dear Parīkṣit! During the course of dancing (at every beat), the Lord who wields a rod to punish the wicked, struck down and scalped with the stroke[1] (so that the next kick in the dancing beat should be more painful) the unbending hood of the hundred and one hooded serpent which was whirling round and round, and was on the point of death. Profusely vomitting blood through his nostrils and mouths, the serpent became utterly depressed in spirits.

29. During the course of his dance, Kṛṣṇa kicked and bent down whatever head (hood of the serpent) was raised by the serpent that was profusely emitting poison through its eyes, and was hissing (through nostrils) with rage, and thus subdued it. Looking upon him as the Most Ancient Person (Lord Nārāyaṇa on the bed of the coiled body of Śeṣa), he was devoutly worshipped with (the showers of) flowers (by Gandharvas).

30. With its umbrella-like hoods being crushed and wounded by the violent and unearthly dance, and vomitting blood profusely out of its mouth, the serpent, all the limbs of whose body were shattered[2], remembered the Ancient Person Nārāyaṇa, the Father (Creator) of the mobile and immobile creation, and mentally resorted to him for refuge.

31. Finding their serpent-husband collapsing under the infinite weight of Kṛṣṇa carrying (innumerable) worlds in his abdomen, and his umbrella-like hoods crushed and shattered under the strokes of his heels, its distressed wives with dishevelled hair and clothes and ornaments in disorder approached him.

32. Being overwhelmed with anxiety (for their husband) the wives of Kāliya, holding their babies[3] in their hands in

1. V.B. *Kiṁcana prahāra-mātraṁ karoti, Kiṁ tu mamarda —pādena mardanam api karoti, yathoparatāni tvag gacchati, dvitīyaprahāre adhikavyathā—jananāsthaṁ/*

2. VB : crushing of hoods etc. is the expiation of external sins and vomitting blood is absolving of internal sins. When both types of sins were purged, Kāliya remembered God.

3. v.l. *puraskṛtārhāḥ*—Who have already worshipped him (*agre kṛta-pūjanāḥ*)—VJ.

front of them, prostrated themselves on the ground[1] before the Lord, the Creator of all beings. With an earnest desire to absolve their husband from sin, and to secure the deliverance of their sinning husband from the hands of the Supreme Lord (also), the pious ladies folded their palms, and sought asylum in him who affords protection to all.

The serpent's wives submitted :*

33. "As your incarnation is intended for the chastisement of the wicked (and for showering Grace on the righteous[2]), the punishment meted out to this (Kāliya) who has committed sinful acts, is quite just. You entertain equal impartial outlook and attitude towards your enemy as well as to your sons. It is with a view to confer good fruit (or your Grace, or Eternal Happiness) that you inflict punishment[3] (proportionate to the nature of the offence.)

34. As a matter of fact, the punishment inflicted (on Kāliya) is a blessing and a favour (in disguise), conferred on us all, for your chastisement of the wicked absolves them of their sins. Your wrath is regarded (by us) as a blessing and a favour bestowed (by you), as it destroyed all the sins of this embodied being (Kāliya) whose state of being a serpent was due to those sins.

35. (We really marvel) how great austere penance (as per correct procedure) must have been practised in former life by Kāliya, himself remaining free from pride, and giving due respect to others, or what righteous acts out of compassion to

1. VT. states that there was a small island in the middle of Kāliya's pool in the Yamunā.

*ŚR states the analysis of this panegyric as follows:

(1) Acquiescence in the punishment meted out to Kāliya (6 verses).

(2) Hari's praise (10 verses), (3) Prayer to Lord Hari (5 verses). VB's analysis is slightly different.

KD. shows that five characteristics of peaceful negotiations (*sāma*) are seen in the appeal of Kāliya's wives as follows (1) Relation of Just punishment proportionate to offence (*sambandha*) V. 34; (2) Benefit:*lābha* v. 35; (3) obligation—*upakṛti*, v. 36; (4) Non-difference v. 37-8; (5) Praise of virtues—*guṇakīrtana* Vv. 39ff.

2. Otherwise your incarnation will be of a negative character—VT.

3. *SS.*—Even your wrath is a form of your Grace.

all beings, must have been performed by him then, that you, who support the life of all, have been pleased with him.

36. We simply cannot understand what meritorious acts entitled him to the privilege of touching the dust of your feet, with a desire to receive which, the most charming goddess Lakṣmī, giving up all pleasures, performed austere penance for a long time, observing strict vows, Oh Gracious Lord!

37. Those who have attained the dust at his (the Lord's) feet, do not covet for (a life in) the celestial regions, or the position of the sovereignty over the whole of this world, or the post of god Brahmā, or the rulership of the subterranean regions, or mastery over the mystic powers secured through *yoga*, or the Liberation from *saṁsāra* whence there is no return (to *saṁsāra*).

38* Oh Lord! Though this serpent-king is born of *tamas* (viz. of the ignorant race of serpents), and is of wrathful nature, he could attain ('the bliss of being favoured with the dust of your feet' 'the touch of your feet' 'the direct visualization of your person') that which is attainable to others only with great difficulty and by desiring to secure which, corporeal beings whirling on the wheel of *saṁsāra*, realize all desirable prosperity including liberation from *saṁsāra*.

39** Salutations to You, the Almighty Lord of incomprehensible excellences, the dweller in the bodies of all beings (as Their Inner Controller), yet undiscernible (or All-pervader). You are the support of all elements like the sky (the wind, water etc.), or the abode of all beings. You are eternally existent as cause of all, but are transcendental to causal relation[1].

40. As the treasure house (or the source) of all knowledge and consciousness, you are perfectly full of them. You are the *Brahman* of infinite power, devoid of (and transcendental to) all attributes and immutable, the regulator and motivator of

*KD. : By riding over the heads of our husband, you became his crest-jewel and in a way both of you became one. Nay, our husband became in a way superior to the Lord who became a head-ornament of Kāliya. This is the *abheda*—(identity) stage in *sāman* (pacific measures or negotiations)

—10.16.499-504.

**The next ten verses form the *guṇa-kīrtana* (eulogy of excellences), the next stage is *sāman* (peaceful negotiations)—KD.

1. *Kāraṇātītāya* (ŚR)

Prakṛti (or possessor of Supernatural Potencies). We bow to you.

41. (We pay obeisance to) you who are the (very embodiment of) Time-Spirit[1], the support of (the potencies of) Time, the witness to different divisions of Time; you are the universe itself as well as its Director[2], creator as well as its (material and instrumental) cause.

42. Hail to you who constitute all the elements[3] (both gross and subtle), all the (ten) cognitive and conative sense-organs, the (five) vital breaths, the mind, the intellect and the heart. You keep yourself shrouded from the *jivas* due to their ego (*ahaṁkāra*) comprising of three *guṇas*.[4]

43. We bow to you who are infinite, subtle (and hence beyond the ken of perception and therefore) not subject to changes or modifications, and the Omniscient. (Due to your Māyā) You are the subject of various theories[5] (such as you exist, do not exist, are Omniscient, non-omniscient, bound in *saṁsāra*, absolutely free, one, many). You are the power that is described in the words as also the power of description inherent in words.[6]

1. *Kālāya*—One who is like a Wish-yielding cow to his devotees—VJ

2. Due to 'difference-cum-non-difference', and 'Duality-cum-non duality relations', this is explanable—SD.

3. *bhūtātmane*—

(i) VR. To him who enters in and controls all the beings (*Brahman* as *niyantā*). This verse brings out the causal relation between the subtle and gross sentient-cum-non-sentient aspects of Brahman as well as body-cum-soul relation. (*evaṃ sūkṣma-cidācid-viśiṣṭa-Brahmaṇaḥ sthūlāvasthā cidacid-viśiṣṭabhede tayoḥ kārya-kāraṇa-bhāvaḥ...śarīrātmabhāvaśceti nibandhanadvayam uktam*/

(ii) VT.—to him who inspires consciousness i.e. gives knowledge of beings (*Jñāna-pradāya*)

4. VJ. reads v.l. *nirguṇenābhimānena*

You, whose glory remains concealed through ignorance (*ajñānena*) which is not born of *guṇas* like *sattva* (*sattvādi-guṇa-janmarahitena*).

5. *nānāvādānurodhāya*—(i) Established despite various theories—SS.

(ii) Common to all theories—VJ.

(iii) God appears according to one's views (*yathā nirūpyate tathā Bhagavān bhavati*—VB

6. *Vācyavācaka-śaktaye*—Both meaning and word derive their power from you.—VT.

44. Salutations to you who are the Source of the means or instruments to arrive at correct knowledge[1]; Absolute Wisdom[2] (independent of any source of knowledge); the source of Scriptures (i.e. whose breath are the Vedas).[3] We salute again and again to you who are both participation in and withdrawal from the worldly activities, and the Veda itself[4] (which prescribes both types of injunctions).

45. We bow to you Kṛṣṇa, the embodiment of the highest bliss, whose nature is to draw away (i.e. to absolve) the sins of his devotees, whose fourfold forms or manifestations (*vyūhas*) are Rāma i.e, Saṅkarṣaṇa, Vāsudeva (of pure *sattva*), Pradyumna, of the highest splendour (and possessor of Supreme affluence), and Aniruddha, comprehensible only to the wise—you who protect your votaries bestowing them with grades of liberation such as *Sāyujyatā* etc.

46.* Obeisance to you who illuminate the internal organ by presiding over its four aspects—mind, reason, the intel-

1. *Pramāṇa-mūlāya* (i) The source of perception or cognition (lit. the eye of the eye etc.)—ŚR.

(ii) The source and support of the Vedas, the authority of which rests on you.—VB.

2. *Kavaye* : (i) The knower of the past, (present) and the Future —VJ.

(ii) Whose form is the Word or the material cause of the Word—VB.

3. *Śāstra-yonaye* : cf.:(i) *Śāstra-yonitvāt* ! *Brahma Sūtra* 1.1.3

(ii) *are'sya mahato bhūtasya niśvasitam etad yad Ṛgvedo Yajur vedaḥ sāma vedo'tharvāṅgirasaḥ.* —*Bṛha. Up.* 4.5.11

(i) Knowable through *śāstras* i.e. The Vedas—VJ.

(ii) Hence whose testimony are the *śāstras* or the accurate conception about whom is found in *śāstras*—VT., SD.

4. *nigamāya*—The promulgator of *Upaniṣadic* knowledge—SS., VR.

* (i) VR: Salutations to you who enhance the attributive intelligence (*dharma-bhūta-jñāna*) of your devotees and reduce or diminish the knowledge of your non-devotees by shrouding them (as it were) with Māyā constituted of three *guṇas* who are indicated through the function of the mental faculties comprising of *guṇas*; the witness of the hearts of all beings simultaneously; the eternal self-illuminating light of knowledge.

(ii) VJ : We bow to you who shed light on *sattva* and other *guṇas*, as also on knowledge, devotion etc. (of the devotees) ; who dwell in the *Prakṛti* constituted of *guṇas*; whose existence is deduced through knowledge received through sense-organs; the self-knowing witness to all *guṇas*.

lect and the ego, in the form of four manifestations—*vyūhas*—(mentioned above); who shroud yourself under those *guṇas* and shine forth as many; who are indicated and perceived through the functions of the internal organ (mentioned above), who are merely the witness to the mental faculties or aspects (referred to above), yourself remaining self-knowing yet beyond the ken of perception.

47. Oh Lord ! The Prompter of Senses ! May our obeisance be paid to you whose greatness and working are beyond the comprehension (of our intellectual capacity), but are implicit as the cause of every phenomenon.[1] You are the silent sage[2] revelling in your own blissful self.

48.* We bow to you who are conversant with the ways (courses) of the high and low (or the gross and the subtle) and preside over them all; who are both transcendental to and immanent in the Universe, and its witness as well as the cause.[3]

49. (Beings are under your control. How can you hold them responsible for their nature or behaviour) Oh Lord ! Though perfectly detached, you wield the eternal power called

1. *Sarva-vyākṛta-siddhaye*—(i) You are the source of everything and everyone such as gods etc. that are manifested and the controller of senses —VR.

(ii) The source of the manifestation of the world of name and form (*nāma-rūpātmakaṁ jagat sarvaṁ vyākṛtam, tasya siddhir utpattir yena*)—VJ.

2. *munaye* etc. (*i*) You observe complete silence inspite of your mercifulness in protecting *jīvas* (creatures) from three types of miseries, and your superiority to the world from god Brahmā to a clump of grass—VR.

(ii) The All-knower who never speaks anything irrelevant or false —VJ.

*Salutations to you who know the state or condition of both the cause and the effect; who stand above them all; who are different from *jīvas* yet are called *viśva* due to your presence in them—VJ.

(ii) We bow to you who know the causes of the gross and the subtle. You are the basis of the Universe which is superimposed on you. You are free from the conditions known as *viśva, taijasa* etc. Knowing that Kṛṣṇa was pleased with the fiftyfive epithets given to him in praise, the serpent's wives argue that the nature of a being is created as such by the Lord and hence Kāliya is not guilty as he acted according to his nature for which the Lord is responsible.—KD 16.46. 607-622.

3. Who are above the states called *Viśva, taijasa* etc. but still appear to be a part and parcel of it through Māyā—ŚR.

Time, and bring about the creation, preservation and destruction of this universe by means of *guṇas* (of *Prakṛti*). You carry on your fruitful sportive activity by awakening with your glance the various (latent) propensities in the nature of all creatures.

50* All these forms of quiet, turbulent and stupid natures found in all the three worlds, are the toys in your sports. Now the gentle-natured are dear to you, as you have incarnated for the establishment of righteousness, and you are present here to protect the saintly, righteous people (*or* your forms which desire to protect the righteous are gentle and dear).

51. The first offence of one's child (or subject) deserves to be condoned (and tolerated) by the Lord. Oh tranquil-minded Lord ! Be pleased to pardon this stupid creature who has not recognised you (your divine nature).

52. Be gracious to him, Oh Lord. The serpent is on the point of death. We, women, deserve to be pitied by the good and the righteous. Be pleased to grant unto us our life in the form of our husband.

53. May you be pleased to ordain us, your maid-servants, what we should do for you ; for one who faithfully abides by your command, becomes free from fear of all kinds (or attains to liberation from *saṁsāra*)."

Śrī Śuka said :

54. The glorious Lord who was thus fervidly appealed to and praised by the wives of the serpent, left the swooning serpent whose hoods were badly smashed with his kicking (with heels).

55. Regaining gradually his senses and vitality, Kāliya began to breathe slowly with difficulty. The miserable creature folded its palms, addressed to Lord Kṛṣṇa (as follows).

Kāliya said :

56. Dominated as we are by *tamas*, we are wicked-mind-

* It behoves you to be gracious unto all gentle-natured (*Sāttvika*), ferocious-tempered (*rājasic*) and dull-natured (*tāmasika*) forms, teeming in the three worlds. You have, however, incarnated for the protection of righteousness. Hence the protection to the gentle is dear to you and equally so are those who wish to renounce their offensive nature —VR.

ed since our very birth, and entertain wrath for a long time. It is difficult, Oh Lord, to relinquish one's natural disposition (whereby one identifies one's body with the soul and feels attachment to body and its belongings), as it exercises a powerful hold on people like an evil spirit.

57*. By you has been created this universe as the outcome of the three *guṇas* and is replete with various natures, prowess, energy, hereditary or class differences (seeds), latent desires and bodily shapes of forms, Oh Creator of the Universe.

58. Oh glorious Lord ! In this world, we, serpents, are by nature deeply wrathful. Deluded by nature as we are, how can we escape from (the clutches of) your Māyā which is so difficult to shake off.

59. You, Omniscient Lord of the world, are the cause of relieving us from the influence of Māyā; therefore, be pleased to confer your grace or punishment on us as you deem it proper.

Śri Śuka said :

60. Hearing his speech, the Lord who assumed the human form for a specific purpose (of helping gods) ordered : "You must not stay here, Oh serpent. Hurry up and go to the sea along with your wives, children and kinsmen. Let this river be used by cows and men.

61. Whatever mortal being remembers this command of mine to you, and recites it both in the morning and in the evening, shall have no fear from you (serpents).

62. Whoever, after taking bath in this pool, the scene of my sport, propitiates gods (and *manes*) by offering water-libations, and observing a fast, worships Me meditating on Me all the while, is absolved of all sins.

63. That Garuḍa of beautiful wings, in terror of whom, you fled (abandoned) the island Ramaṇaka and resorted to this pool, shall not now devour you, as you bear my foot-prints."

Śri Śuka said :

64. Thus addressed by Lord Kṛṣṇa of miraculous feats,

* VJ. Although Viṣṇu is the creator of the Universe, god Brahmā created the different varieties of *guṇas* or natural characteristics. They are due to the variety in the proportions and combinations of *svabhāva* (in-born nature), *vīrya* (prowess), *ojas* (virility, vitality) etc.

Kāliya and his wives devoutly worshipped him with delight (at the assurance of safety from Garuḍa).

65-66. They worshipped the Lord of the Universe with celestial clothes, necklaces and gems and ornaments of superb quality, with heavenly perfumes and ointments and a grand wreath of blue lotuses. Having propitiated the Lord whose banner is Garuḍa, they, with great pleasure, circumambulated him and bowed to him and were duly permitted by the Lord.

67. Accompanied by his wives, friends and children, Kāliya went to the Ramaṇaka island in the sea. The Yamunā of nectar-like water became instantly rid of poison through the grace of the Lord, who out of sport has assumed a human form.

CHAPTER SEVENTEEN

Rescue from the Forest Conflagration

King Parikṣit enquired :

1. Why did Kāliya migrate from Ramaṇaka, the home of the Nāgas ? Or what specific offence did he commit against Garuḍa ?

Śrī Śuka replied :

2-3. Oh King of mighty arms ! It was formerly agreed[1] that whatever share of offerings was received by the Nāgas, every month, from the serpent-worshippers, was to be dedicated to the noble-souled Garuḍa, and to be deposited on every New Moon day at the foot of a particular tree (in Ramaṇaka) by serpents who were the prey of Garuḍa. All Nāgas thus contributed their share for self-protection.

1. V.B. : quotes the following agreement brought about by Brahmā between Garuḍa and the serpents :

amāyāṁ vṛkṣa-mūle tu Nāga-lokeṣu yad bhavet /
ekasmin divase tāvad ekatra sthāpayantu hi //
tato hi Garuḍas tasmins tad bhuktvā naiva pīḍayet/
iti vyavasthayā sarpā māsi māsi baliṁ daduḥ//

SS. states that they offered one serpent per month to Garuḍa.

4. Being elated with pride for its power and virulence of its poison, Kāliya, the son of Kadru, slighted Garuḍa, and ate up the offerings intended for him.

5. On learning this, the glorious Garuḍa, beloved of the Lord, got enraged, and with a desire to kill Kāliya, swooped down on it with terrific speed, Oh King.

6. Raising up its numerous heads (hoods), the serpent whose weapon is poison, advanced against Garuḍa who was vehemently rushing at it, and bit him with fangs as its weapons, and looked terrific with its dreadful tongues, poisonous hissing and cruel eyes.

7. Brushing it aside with the terrific vehemence of his speed, the wrathful Garuḍa, the son of Tārkṣya (the sage Kāśyapa), the carrier of Lord Viṣṇu and possessed of terrific prowess, struck it down with its left wing[1] brilliant like gold.

8. Struck down with the wing of Garuḍa, Kāliya became overwhelmed with fear and agitated. It entered the pool of the Yamunā that was out of bounds for Garuḍa, and hence unapproachable.

9. On one occasion Garuḍa, being extremely hungry carried away by force his favourite prey—an acquatic creature, though he was prohibited from doing so by the Sage Śaubhari.[2]

10. Seeing that the fish were greatly over-whelmed with grief and felt miserable due to the death of that fish king, Śaubhari, out of compassion for the acquatic creatures in that pool, and for the safety of the creatures living in that pool declared;

11. "If ever Garuḍa enters this pool and eats the fish hereof, he will instantly meet death. I utter the truth."

12. Only Kāliya knew this (Śaubhari's) curse but no other serpent knew it. So it resided in that pool out of the fear of Garuḍa. It was expelled out of it by Kṛṣṇa.

13-14. Finding Kṛṣṇa come out of the pool, decorated with heavenly garlands, sandal pigment and rich dress and

1. VT. notes that it was to express his contempt for Kāliya that Garuḍa used his left wing.

2. Probably the same sage who married all the fifty daughters of Māndhātā. It might be during his stay in the pool of the Yamunā for performing the penance, that the above incident took place. (*vide Supra*) 9.6. 39-55, also VP. 4.2.69-131)

beautified with numerous costly big diamonds, gems and gold ornaments all over his Person, all cowherds leapt to their feet like sense-organs on return of life (or 'creatures after the return of the vital Principle'), and with their hearts overwhelmed with rapturous joy, embraced him with deep affection.

15. Regaining their consciousness, Yaśodā, Rohiṇī, Nanda and other cowherds and cowherdesses got their desires fulfilled by meeting Kṛṣṇa.

16. Balarāma clasped Kṛṣṇa in the arms and laughed, as he knew the prowess of Kṛṣṇa.

16A. *VR's text adds this half-verse*:

He seated him on his lap and looked at him again and again in great affection. The trees, cows, bullocks, calves all were filled with extreme joy.

17. The Brāhmaṇa preceptors (of Nanda) along with their wives (who had already come there along with all the inhabitants of Vraja), now approached Nanda and congratulated him, "Thank God ! How fortunate it is that your son seized by Kāliya is liberated from its clutches.

18. Confer some gifts on Brāhmaṇas, on account of the deliverance of Kṛṣṇa (from Kāliya)". Delighted at heart Nanda immediately gave cows and gold as gifts.

19. The highly fortunate Yaśodā who got restored to her child, which was as good as lost, hugged him. Seating him on her lap, he again and again shed tears of joy.

19-A *VR's text adds* :

In the meanwhile, when the sun set, Kṛṣṇa along with Rāma camped there along with their parents, cowherds and their wealth—the herds of cattle.

20. The inhabitants of Vraja and cows, oppressed as they were by hunger, thirst and physical exhaustion, passed that night near the bank of the Yamunā, oh King of Kings !

20-A *VJ.'s text adds* : (a half verse)

At that time, in Vraja, Oh best of Kurus !

21. In the jungle dried up with summer, a great forest conflagration broke out at midnight, and surrounding the Vraja lying fast asleep, it began to scorch them.

22. Touched by the fire, the inhabitants of Vraja woke up and in their bewilderment sought resort to Lord Kṛṣṇa, the Supreme Lord who had assumed a human form through his Māyā.

23. "Oh Kṛṣṇa ! Oh highly fortunate Kṛṣṇa ! Oh Rāma ! Oh Rāma of infinite prowess ! This extremely terrific fire is now consuming us who are yours (your devotees).

24. Oh Lord ! Protect us who are your well-wishers and friends, from this death-like (deadly) fire from which it is extremely difficult to escape. We cannot give up your feet (resorting to which) there is no fear from any quarter".

25. Perceiving this helplessness and danger of his people (devotees), the Supreme Ruler of the earth, the Infinite Lord of unfathomable powers, swallowed up that terrible fire.

CHAPTER EIGHTEEN

Slaying of the Demon Pralamba

Śrī Śuka said :

1. Surrounded by his kinsmen whose hearts were full of delight, Kṛṣṇa, whose glories were sung (by them), entered Vraja (looking) beautiful with herds of cows.

2. While they (Balarāma and Kṛṣṇa) assuming through their Māyā power, the guise of cowherds, were indulging in various sports, there was the advent of the season called the Summer which is not much pleasant to embodied beings.

3. It, however, appeared like the spring due to the special (environmental) characteristics of Vṛndāvana where the glorious Lord Keśava (Kṛṣṇa) was personally staying along with Balarāma.

4. It resounded with the sound of cascades that drowned the jingling of the crickets. It looked beautiful with clusters of trees constantly sprayed with the particles of water from the waterfalls.

5. Due to the pleasant breeze blowing over the waves of the rivers and the pools (and the cascades) and moistened with spray and carrying the fragrant pollen of white lilies, blue lotuses and other flowers, the inhabitants of that forest (Vṛndāvana) which, covered with meadows richly overgrown with green grass, did not experience the scorching heat radiating from the sun and forest fires in the summer.

6. At the place, the scorching rays of the sun, fierce like virulent poison, were not able to dry up the moisture and verdant nature of the soil wherein the mixture of sand and mire on all sides of the bank remained always wet by the waves that used to beat against the banks of rivers with unfathomable water.

7. The resplendently beautiful forest was in full blossom and was resounded with the cries and notes of various birds and beasts, with singing peacocks and humming bees and warbling cuckoos and waterfowls.

8. With a desire to enjoy sports, the glorious Lord Kṛṣṇa, accompanied by Balarāma and surrounded with cows and cowherds, entered the forest playing upon his flute.

9. With their persons decorated with tender foliage, peacock feathers, clusters of flowers and coloured earth, Balarāma, Kṛṣṇa and other cowherds indulged in dancing, wrestling and singing.

10. While Kṛṣṇa was dancing, some cowherds sang, some clapped their hands, some played on flutes or blew their horns, while others applauded and cheered up.

11. Gods who had assumed the forms of cowherds[1] and thus completely concealed their god-head, eulogised in applause both Kṛṣṇa and Balarāma, as actors do to cheer up another actor (in spite of their master-servant relation).

12. The two brothers wearing side-locks, sometimes, sported by running in circles, long-jumps, shot-putting, striking of arms, tug-of-war and wrestling.

1. VR. reads *gopa-jāti-praticchannau* as adj. qualifying 'Kṛṣṇa-Rāmau' and interprets : 'Gods who assumed the forms of cowherds glorified Kṛṣṇa and Balarāma who had completely concealed their divinity in the guise of cowherds.'

13. Sometimes while other cowherds were dancing both (Kṛṣṇa and Balarâma) sang personally, and played on instruments and applauded (with words) "well-done! Buck up", Oh great king.

14-16. Some time they would play with a *Bilva* fruit, sometime with *Kumbha* fruit, and now with a handful of *Āmalaka* fruits (myrobalans). Sometimes (in a running race or with swift movements in an arena) they would playfully not allow themselves to be touched, while at times they would play hide-and-seek after shutting the eyes of a cowherd boy—or by blindfolding and such other games. Sometimes they would divert themselves by mimicking the sounds and notes of beasts, birds. Now they would indulge in jumping like frogs, and now they would cut jokes of various kinds; now by swinging with the help of branches of trees and sometimes by playing the role of kings.

Indulging in such sports well known among the people, they rambled all over the area in the rivers, on the mountains, in the valleys, bowers, in woods and lakes.

17. While Balarāma and Kṛṣṇa were grazing their cattle in the meadows of that forest, a demon called Pralamba assumed the guise of a cowherd and entered his followers with a view to kidnapping them.

18. Even though Kṛṣṇa, the omniscient (All-perceiving) Lord of the Yadu clan, knew it (his real intention), he agreed to be his playmate and friend, with an intention of finishing with him.

19. Kṛṣṇa, a past-master in games, summoned all the cowherds and proposed, "Oh comrade-cowherds! Now let us play by dividing ourselves into two suitable parties."

20. In that game, the cowherds selected Balarāma and Kṛṣṇa as their captains—some (one party) accepted Kṛṣṇa's side, while the rest (the other party) Balarāma's side.

21. They indulged in various sports characterised by one party members to carry as mounts the members of the other party—the winners being the riders and the defeated party-members, the carriers.

22. In this way, some boys riding and some carrying and

simultaneously grazing the cattle—they went near a banyan tree called Bhāṇḍīraka.

23. When cowherds like Śrīdāmā, Vṛṣabha and others belonging to the party of Rāma, became victorious in the game, Kṛṣṇa and others carried them on their backs, Oh King.

24. Being defeated, Lord Kṛṣṇa bore Śrīdāman, Bhadra carried Vṛṣabha and Pralamba took Balarāma, the son of Rohiṇī on his back.

25. Considering that Kṛṣṇa was irresistible, the prominent demon Pralamba swiftly carried away Balarāma far beyond the limit for dismounting.

26. When his progress was stopped by carrying Balarāma who grew weighty as the mount Meru (the king of all mountains), the demon who assumed his original (demonic) form adorned with gold ornaments and clothes, looked like a cloud illuminated with flashes of lightning carrying the Moon (the Lord of Stars) on his back.

27. Balarāma (the wielder of a plough as a weapon) was a bit disturbed to see the demon's body soaring with crashing speed in the sky, and with burning eyes, terrific (frowning) brows, terrible jaws and teeth, hair like flames of blazing fire, weirdly dazzling with the splendour of gold wristlets, crown and ear-rings.

28. The very next moment, Balarāma regained his consciousness (of his divine nature) and grew fearless. And like Indra striking vehemently a mountain with his Vajra, in great rage, he dealt a heavy blow with his fist on the head of his enemy who was carrying him away from his group of cowherd friends.

29. The moment the blow descended on his head, it was shattered to pieces; vomitting blood profusely (from his mouth), he lost his consciousness. Giving out a terrific roar, the demon fell dead, like a mountain struck down by Indra's weapon (thunderbolt).

30. Seeing the demon Pralamba killed by the mighty Balarāma, the cowherds were extremely astonished and shouted, "Bravo ! well done !".

31. Pronouncing benedictions on him, they highly praised him. And he deserved it. With their hearts overwhelmed with

affection, they embraced him as one returned from the realm of death.

32. When the sinful demon Pralamba was killed, gods felt highly gratified and happy. They showered on Balarāma wreaths of flowers and applauded him with their approbations "well done ! Well done !"

CHAPTER NINETEEN

Swallowing up of a Forest-conflagration

Śrī Śuka continued :

1. While the cowherds were deeply engrossed in playing, their cows roamed to a great distance, grazing at will, and lured by green pasture, strayed into an inaccessible part of the dense jungle.

2. Entering from one forest (-area) to another, the she-goats, cows and she-buffaloes became thirsty while wandering in the forest, began to cry loudly and got into a thicket of reeds.

3. Not finding the cattle, cowherds, of whom Kṛṣṇa and Balarāma were prominent, felt repentance (for their dereliction of duty). Despite their search for the cows, they were at a loss to know where they could have gone.

4. Having thus lost their means of livelihood, the cowherds got perplexed not knowing what to do. Then all of them followed the track of the cows marked with their footprints and blades of grass cut by their hoofs.

5. Finding their wealth of cattle strayed from its path in the jungle of Muñja-grass and lowing helplessly, they directed their herds back and were overwhelmed with fatigue and thirst.

5-A. *VR's text adds*:

Climbing up to the top of a tall tree and showing his personality dark like a cloud in complexion, Kṛṣṇa loudly called out those distressed cows by their individual names.

6. Being called by their names by the glorious Lord in a tone deep like the thundering of clouds, the cows became overwhelmed with joy to hear the sound of their names, and responded with lowing loudly.

7. Thereafter, as the Fate would have it, there broke out, on all side, a forest conflagration causing havoc in all the inhabitants of the forest. And helped by its assistant, the strong wind, the great fire appeared desirous of lapping up all the mobile and immobile creatures with its tongues of dreadful flames.

8. Observing the advance of the forest-fire on all sides, the cowherds and cows got horrified. Just as people afflicted with the fear of death seek asylum with Lord Hari, they resorted to Kṛṣṇa along with Balarām, for shelter and prayed to Him.

9. "Oh Kṛṣṇa ! Oh Kṛṣṇa of infinite prowess ! Oh Balarāma ! Balarāma of immeasurable power ! It now behoves you to protect us who are being burnt by fire, and have approached you for asylum.

10. We are really your kinsmen and as such, should not be destroyed thus. You are the knower of all that is righteousness. We are all devoted to you and have in you our saviour."

Śrī Śuka said :

11. Hearing the pitiful appeal of his cowherd-comrades, Lord Hari assured them, "Don't be afraid. Please close your eyes."

12. With the words 'Be it so', they closed their eyes when, in the meanwhile, Kṛṣṇa, the Supreme Master of Yoga swallowed up that menacing conflagration and completely saved them from that calamity.

13. Then, on opening their eyes, they were extremely surprised to find themselves and their cows safe from danger, and brought over to Bhāṇḍīra[1].

1. From the details given in VT. about the bunyan tree called Bhāṇḍira, it appears that at the time of Jīva Gosvāmī, they located it to the Northwest of the Śiva temple called 'Spāro' (?) near Vṛndāvana, and the jungle of muñja grass where the conflagration was swallowed up by Kṛṣṇa was ten miles to the south of the bunyan tree.

—Bh.P. 10.19.13 (*Vrindabana Edn* Vol. I P. 673)

14. Observing that it was due to the yogic power of Kṛṣṇa and the manifestation of his Yogic Potency (yogamāyā) that they were delivered from (death from) the forest fire, they came to believe in his divine nature.

15. Tending homewards the cows in the evening, Kṛṣṇa along with Balarāma, returned to Vraja, playing on his flute, while the cowherd boys were singing his praise.

16. The very sight of Kṛṣṇa (Govinda) filled the Gopīs (cowherd-women) with Supreme delight, as every moment of separation from him was felt by them as a hundred ages (*yugas*).

CHAPTER TWENTY

Description of the Rainy Season and the Autumn

*Śrī Śuka said**:

1. The cowherd-boys related to their mothers and other women-folk (particularizing the special points) in details, the miraculous feats of them both (*viz.* of Kṛṣṇa and Balarāma) as to how Kṛṣṇa rescued them from a forest-conflagration, and how Balarāma killed the demon Pralamba.

2. Listening to the account, elderly cowherds and cowherd women were astonished. They (thenceforth) looked upon Kṛṣṇa and Balarāma as the most prominent gods who have come down to stay in Vraja.

3.** Then (after the summer), there was the advent of the rainy season which is favourable to the regeneration of all be-

* In VJ.'s text verses 1 and 2 form a part of the last i.e. VJ's 17th chapter. VJ's new (18th) chapter begins from the 3rd verse of this (20th) chapter.

** Note : VV. 3-24 give a spiritually suggestive, beautiful description of the rainy season in the epic style. Annotators have tried to find some 'hidden meaning' convenient to their school of thought in these verses.

VJ. regards this description as an illustration (*dṛṣṭānta*) of the deep or superficial (of pure and not so pure) devotion to god Nārāyaṇa. (*Nārāyaṇa-bhakti-vaiśadyāvaiśadya-dṛṣṭāntatvena Prāvid ṛtum varṇayati* /

ings, and during which, the sky appears beautiful with refulgent circles (round the Sun and the Moon), and is resounded with thunders.

4. Being overspread with thick dark blue clouds (heavy with water), attended with lightning and thunder, and with its light (of the Sun or the Moon) being obscured and dimmed, the sky looked like Brahman modified by the conditioning *guṇas* of *Prakṛti*[1] (or the individual soul whose spiritual wisdom is obscured by *sattva, rajas* and *tamas* each corresponding to the lightning, thunder and clouds which overcast the sky)[2].

5. (Like a king redistributing his wealth for public welfare to his subjects, from whom he collected it in the form of land revenue and other taxes). At the proper time (in the rainy season), the Sun-god or the Rainy season[3] began to release the wealth in the form of water to the earth from which he absorbed it with his rays, during the (last) eight months.

6. Mighty clouds charged with lightning (with which they viewed the earth parched with the summer heat) and violently tossed by tempestuous winds (as if they were overwhelmed with compassion for the world afflicted with the summer) showered down the life-giving[4] water (resuscitating the world) which brought delight to all, just as merciful persons[5] lay down their lives out of compassion for the harassed and tormented people.

1. *Saguṇa Brahman*—(1) Individual soul conditioned by *guṇas* but capable of expanding by *guṇas* and not physically—VR (2) Four-faced god Brahmā—VJ

2. (i) VR : By nature, the sky is clear, pure and bright but gets darkened by clouds etc. So also though knowledge is inherent in the *Jīva*, the cognitive power remains ineffective till the *Jīva* attains Liberation or *mukti*. Hence one should try for Liberation.

(ii) The Sun: the brightest luminary is shrouded with clouds like god Brahmā with the three *guṇas*.—VJ.

3. *Parjanya*—The sun-god who presides over the thundering clouds —VJ.

4. v.l. *prāṇinām*—The very life of living beings—VR.

5. Just as the glances of Lord Kṛṣṇa shower the water in the form of Spiritual Knowledge on his earnest devotees—VJ.

7.* Just as the shrivelled and emaciated body of a person undergoing severe austerities for the attainment of some desired object, regains its normal health and plumpness after the realization of that object, the earth that was parched and shrivelled through the heat of the sun (in the summer), now swelled up (and became green) when drenched with water by the rain-god.

8. At the nightfall (when the sky is overcast with clouds) it is the fire-flies and not the planets that shine through darkness even as the heretical scriptures dazzle in their sins, in the Kali age and not the *Vedas*.

9. Just as young Brāhmaṇa pupils break their silence at the end of their daily religious routine, and begin their recitation of the *Vedas* on hearing the voice of their preceptor, the hibernating frogs which were lying silent, broke out croaking on hearing the sound of rains (or the thunder of the rainy clouds).

10. Rivulets that dry up in the summer, now overflow their banks and flowed into the wrong channel, like the body and riches of persons with unrestrained mind (and enslaved by their senses) and misdirected to the wrong track.

11. Like the army (camp) of a king, the earth appeared green with verdant grass (at some places), crimson-coloured by (the crowds of) *Indragopa* insects, and at some places, it became covered with the growth of umbrella-shaped mushrooms.

12.** Fields with their rich crop brought delight to the farmers and heart-burning[1] to the rich (feeling jealousy towards

* This verse shows the *pravṛtti mārga* of worldly prosperity—VJ.

** SR & KD. : Fields caused joy or grief to the farmers according to the richness or failure of harvests as they did not know that everything depends on destiny.

VT. takes *kṣetra* as 'a body'.

VR: The verse teaches that one should feel joy at the prosperity of others.

VJ. interprets *kṣetra* as 'a sacred place' and explains: Due to the vision of the great glory of the Lord, holy places bring joy. But to those who are proud and materialistic and think about the cost of pilgrimage find that the same holy places are full of misery and anxiety. One who is keen on getting *Mokṣa* (Liberation) should devote himself to the lotus feet of Hari.'

1. VB. : To the proud kings who are bent on conquering the enemies, the rains and fields covered with crops, cause obstruction and troubles, as they do not know that victory or defeat depends on the Will of the Lord.

the farmers) as they did not know that everything depends on the luck.

13.* Being drenched with the fresh rain-waters,[1] all beings living on the land and in water assumed a beautiful, winsome appearance immediately, even as persons attain to attractive divine form[2] through the service (worship and contemplation) of Hari (due to its being the highest form of religion and of supremely blissful nature).

14. The sea, the waters of which are already tossed into high waves by stormy winds, becomes more violently agitated at the confluences with rivers, even as the heart of an immature *yogi*, still influenced with passions, becomes highly perturbed by contacts with worldly objects.[3]

15. Though continuously subjected to the down-pour of rains, the mountains were not agitated at all, like the devotees of Hari whose minds are absorbed in the meditation of the Lord and are not perturbed even under overwhelming calamities (of threefold nature).

16. Being unused (or unrepaired for a long time) and hence overgrown and covered with grass, the tracks and paths become doubtful (unrecognizable) like the *Vedas* which are not properly studied (and repeatedly recited), get consigned to oblivion by the force (passage) of time.

17. Just as pleasure-seeking women bear no constancy to men of virtue and merit (if devoid of money), the fickle-hearted

* VT. endorses ŚR. and states that both the process and attainment (*sādhanāvasthā* and *sādhyāvasthā*) of the service of Hari are supremely blissful.

VR. : No Grace can be attained except through the service of Hari.

1. VJ. interprets *vāri* as 'knowledge' that removes the misery of *saṁsāra* of the denizens of the nether-world (*pātāla*), inhabitants of the terrestrial globe and residents of the higher (celestial) world. To these inhabitants, pure spiritual knowledge leading to gracious divine forms, is attainable through the service of Hari.

2. VB. : Just as devotees assume the four-armed divinely refulgent Hari-like form etc. 'The inhabitants of land etc.' stand for persons characterised by *sattva*, *rajas* and *tamas*.

3. *guṇa*—(i) *rajo-guṇa*—VJ.

(ii) Natural propensities creating agitation in the mind for sensual pleasure. These are to be controlled by meditating on Hari.—VR.

flashes of lightning did not remain constant (and faithful) to clouds which are the friends of the world.

18. Just as the attributeless Supreme Person manifests himself in the world which is a product or conglomeration of *guṇas*, (viz. *sattva*, *rajas* and *tamas*), the rain-bow (Indra's bow) though devoid of a *guṇa* (a string), shone forth in the sky, the special quality (*guṇa*) of which is sound.

19. Veiled over by clouds shining with her own beams of light, the moon did not shine forth like the individual soul, enveloped and shrouded in its ego-sense, illumined by its own light.

20. Just as persons sorely distressed and (hence) disgusted with the miseries of household life (*saṁsāra*) feel delighted at the arrival of the devotees of Lord Kṛṣṇa, peacocks to which the advent of the rainy season (*lit.* the appearance of the clouds) is itself an occasion of joy, become exulted with their hair (feathers) standing on their end (while dancing with their feathers spread out).

21.* Just as persons, at first grown emaciated and exhausted through asceticism, become stout and robust on attaining the fruition of their desires, the trees shrunk and dried up through the heat of the summer, sucked water through their feet (i.e. roots) and assumed many new (rich) forms (putting forth luxuriantly new branches, foliage, fresh blossoms, fruits etc.).

22. (This verse shows the characteristics of persons permanently indulging in saṁsāra—*nitya-saṁsāri*).

The cranes continue to stay even in sliding, miry and thorny banks of lakes, Oh Parīkṣit, like unto wicked-minded persons given to low pleasures, continue to live in houses wherein they carry on their detestable cruel (*lit.* of non-pacific nature) jobs.

* VR. Persons performing penance with some material end in view grow emaciated through penance, but after realizing the fruition of their desire, become multiplied in the form of sons, grandsons etc., and persons who, with no ulterior motive except the propitiation of the Lord, perform penance, attain Liberation, and are endowed with various supernatural forms and life similar to the Lord.

VJ. interprets *pādapa* as 'ascetics' and explains: As ascetics performing penance, drink the ambrosia of *Śāstric* knowledge and controlling their senses and minds realize the Supreme Soul (*paramātman*) Himself.

23. While the god of rains poured down showers of rains, dams and bridges got damaged and breached by floods, just as the paths[1] (of religious duties prescribed for different classes of society (*varṇas*) and stages of life (*āśramas*) in the Vedas, are breached by attacks of false heretical theories in the *Kali* Age.

24. Clouds impelled by winds showered their nectar-like waters to creatures below, just as rulers of the earth or merchant kings advised by Brāhmaṇas at opportune times, distribute their blessed wealth among the subjects (or carry out works of social welfare).

25. When the forest was thus abounding in trees richly laden with ripe dates and rose apples, Kṛṣṇa, surrounded by cows and cowherds, and accompanied by Balarāma, entered in it for sporting.

26. At the call of Kṛṣṇa, cows which (normally) proceeded in slow gait owing to the weight of heavy udders, hastened with quick steps, showering with joy the milk from their udders on the way.

27. On the way, Lord Kṛṣṇa saw the inhabitants of the forest (men, birds and beasts) exulted with joy, rows of trees dripping with honey, streams of waters cascading from hills, and their echoing sound in the hills and the caves that were at hand.

28. Sometimes when it rained, the Lord took shelter under a tree or entered a cave, and sported Himself joyously eating bulbs, roots and fruits.

29. Accompanied by Balarāma, he sat on a slab of stone near water, and ate the rice mixed with curds (brought from home), sharing it with cowherds who were to sit with him for the meal.[2]

30-31. Beholding the bulls and calves lying on the lush green grass ruminating in great satisfaction, with their eyes

1. Due to the heretical arguments advanced by the Buddha and his followers the Vedic paths of action (*Karma*), of Knowledge and of Devotion are broken down—VB. Bhakti, however, has a place in non-vedic religions in India.

KD. includes the followers of *āgamas* and *tantras* under heretics.

2. Some other cowherds made their own arrangement at different places—VB.

closed, and cows fatigued with the heavy weight of their udders (also resting and chewing the cud in satisfaction), and the splendid beauty of the rainy season enhanced by his own enchanting powers, bringing delight to all creatures, the Lord felt gratified (with them all).

32. While Balarāma and Kṛṣṇa were dwelling at that Vraja in this way, the autumn characterised by cloudless skies crystal-like waters and gentle breezes, set in.

33. (Originally waters are crystal clear, but they become turbid due to rainy season). Now due to the autumnal season which makes the lotus-plants blossom forth, waters have regained their original translucent nature, just as the minds of persons who have fallen from the path of *yoga*, regain their mental serenity by resuming their *yogic* practices.

34. Just as devotion to Kṛṣṇa removes all the evils setting upon persons belonging to different stages of life (*āśramas*)[1], the Autumn dispelled all the clouds from the sky and prevented the contacts of the elements or the congestion of created beings, dried up the mire on the earth, and cleansed the turbidity from water.

35. Having discharged (and thus renounced) all their possessions (in the form of the waters in them), the clouds shone forth in their spotless white splendour, as quiescent sages who have absolved themselves of all sins do, after renouncing all their three-fold desires (about progeny, property and celebrity).

36. Just as people with spiritual wisdom impart their nectar-like knowledge on some occasions, and refuse to do so on others, the mountains also at some places allowed the streams of pure water to flow, while at others they withheld them.

37. Just as ignorant persons immersed in their household matters are not cognisant of the daily shortening of the span of their life, so the creatures in shallow waters did not perceive the diminishing water level every day.

38. Just as a poverty-stricken, wretched man burdened with family responsibilities but of uncontrolled senses, undergoes

1. SR. enumerates the evils : The trouble of physical work during studenthood, the pangs of separation in married state, and sexual passions etc in *sannyāsins*.

miseries, the creatures in shallow waters suffered from the heat of the autumnal sun.

39. Marshy tracts of land gradually gave up their marshiness, and the plants their unripeness, just as (spiritually) wise men slowly (step by step) discard their notions of 'I' and 'mine' with respect to their bodies and belongings which are distinctly different from their self.

40. When the season of autumn set in, the waters of the ocean grew calm and still, even as a meditative sage established in his self, gives up ritualistic performances and recitation of the Vedas.

41. Cultivators secured the supply of water to their fields by strengthening the bunds (and thus stopping the breaches and leakages), just as *Yogins*, by control of senses, preserve their spiritual knowledge which otherwise gets dissipated (through unsubdued senses)[1].

42. The moon relieved the sufferings of creatures caused by the rays (heat) of the autumnal sun, just as the (revelation of) spiritual knowledge alleviates the troubles caused by the (false) identification of the body with the soul, or Lord Kṛṣṇa removes the pangs of separation of (cowherd) women of Vraja.

43. The cloudless sky shone forth beautifully with bright stars twinkling clearly in autumnal nights, as the mind with the predominance of *Sattva*, correctly comprehends the import of the *Vedas* (*Śabda-Brahman*) as decided by the *Pūrva* and *Uttara Mimāṁsās*.

44. The full moon, surrounded by stars, shone resplendent in the heavens, just as Kṛṣṇa, the Lord of Yadus, did in his circle of Vṛṣṇi clansmen, on the earth.

45. People, embraced by the (cooling) temperate breeze which has blown over blossoming forests, felt relieved of the heat (of the sun) but not so the Gopa women whose heart was stolen (captivated) by Kṛṣṇa (whom they embraced in their hearts) as the pangs of actual separation were enhanced thereby.

46. Due to the (fecundating influence of the) Autumn, and through the insistent courting of their mates, cows, female deer

1. VB. aptly quotes :
ūrdhvendriyais tu vikṣepo jñānasyā'dho vināśanam |
nirodhe puñja-bhāvena svakāryaṁ sādhayed dhruvam ||

(or beasts), she-birds and women, conceived (irrespective of their willingness), just as the acts for propitiating the Lord are followed by the concomitant fruit (automatically).

47. At the sunrise all lotuses (except moon-lotuses) bloomed forth, just as all subjects except criminals (or robbers) become fearless on the installation of a king (i.e. restoration of good government).

48. The earth, rich with ripe cornfields, shone bright and beautiful, especially due to the incarnation of the two rays (*āṃśas*) of Lord Hari (viz. Kṛṣṇa and Balarāma) and also with the performance of Vedic sacrifices of harvest season (wherein new corn is offered), and with festivities and grand celebrations gratifying the senses, which were carried on in cities and villages.

49. Just as *Siddhas* (the masters of *yoga* and *mantras*—mystic incantations), detained (in their present bodies) by their ordained span of life, attain their respective desired heavenly bodies, when the appropriate time arrives, merchants, sages, kings and *snātakas* (life-long bachelor-students) shut up in their places due to the rainy-season, (and were impeded from undertaking an expedition or journey) now set out to achieve their respective objects.

CHAPTER TWENTYONE*

The Song of Gopīs (cowherd-women)

Śrī Śuka continued:

1. In this beautiful forest, with its waters made crystal-clear by the Autumn, and caressed by a breeze surcharged with the fragrance of beds of lotuses, Lord Kṛṣṇa entered deep, along with his cows and cowherds.

* Ch. XIX according to VJ.'s text. He thinks that the object of this chapter is to emphasize that everyone should perform devotion, the means of spiritual knowledge, according to his capacity—

sva-yogyatānusāreṇa Harau jñāna-sādhanaṁ bhaktiḥ kartavyā |

2. While grazing the cattle, Kṛṣṇa, in company of cowherds and Balarāma, entered deep into the forests, the lakes, rivers and mountains wherein were resonant with the warbling of flocks of enraptured birds and hummings of bees; through the glades of trees adorned with their floral wealth; and he played[1] charmingly on his flute.

3. When the damsels of Vraja heard from a distance that enchanting music of the flute exciting erotic sentiments,[2] some of them sung unto their friends the excellences of Kṛṣṇa,[3] in his absence.

4. Hardly did they begin to describe when, remembering his dalliance with them, they could not proceed, as their mind was distracted by the vehement force of passion, Oh King.

5. (The cowherd women depict their mental vision of Kṛṣṇa as he entered Vṛndāvana. This visualization of Kṛṣṇa distracted the Gopīs as mentioned in the above verse.)

Possessed of a charming personality like an accomplished actor,[4] graced with a crown of peacock feathers,[5] his ears

1. *cukūja*—(i) played on, sounded—ŚR., VR., SD.
(ii) conveying an erotic invitation to Gopīs—VJ., VB.

2. VB. says that it was a divine music. Hence it could be heard from such a long distance.

3. SG. & VT. carefully exclude elderly ladies like Yaśodā and Rohiṇī from this effect. In them, motherly affection was awakened. While Rādhā being deeply moved conveyed her feelings to her friends like Lalitā. The text of the Bh. P., however, is silent about names of erotically excited *gopīs*, including Rādhā.

4. v.l. *naṭa-vara-vapuḥ*—(i) The most beautiful among all the forms assumed so far by the Lord.—VT.
(ii) Just as an actor puts on a special dress for playing a particular part on the stage, the Lord assumed this human form with this special dress on the stage of the world.—SG.
(iii) By looking at which (form), all beings dance with joy—SG.

5. MR. (Miśra Rāmakṛṣṇa in his com. *Prema-mañjarī*) quotes from *Kṛṣṇa-yāmala*.

Rādhā-priya-mayūrasya patraṁ Rādhekṣaṇa-prabham /
bibharti śirasā Kṛṣṇas tasyāś cūḍānibhaṁ yataḥ //

A poetic explanation that Kṛṣṇa wore the feathers of a peacock due to the similarity of the 'eye' (eye-like bright bluish coloured centre) of the feather to Radhā's eye.

decorated by *karṇikāra* flowers, clad in garments (brilliant) yellow like molten gold, wearing the Vaijayantī wreath made of flowers of five different colours, (consisting of *tulasī, kunda, mandāra, pārijāta* and *lotuses*[1]) filling the holes of his flute with the nectar of his lips[2] and accompanied by the cowherds[3] singing his glory, Kṛṣṇa entered the Vṛndāvana forest, beautified with his foot-prints.

5A. *VJ's text adds* :

Kṛṣṇa wore a crest of peacock's feathers and appeared as a forest-dweller with Karṇikāra flowers adorning his ears. He rested his face on his left arm (his face was turned to the left). Breathing through the flute with appropriate histrionic movements of eye-brows and fingers, he made all the hosts of cowherds sing classical music (the *Gāndharva Veda* as compiled by Bharata), and gave delight to all the creatures in the world.

6. Listening to the music of the flute which bewitched and transported the hearts of all beings, all the women of Vraja embraced him mentally, as they were (each) engaged in describing it.

The cowherd women sang* :

7. "This is the highest reward of being blessed with eyes; we do not know if there can be any greater felicity than this, Oh friends. Those only have enjoyed the fruit who have drunk to their hearts' content (*ni-pītam*) (the charm) of the counte-

1. MR. in his com. (mentioned above) quotes a verse giving names of flowers woven in the Vaijayantī wreath :

Tulasī-kunda-mandāra-pārijāta-saroruhaiḥ /
pañcabhiḥ kusumair etair vanamālā prakīrtitā //

2. The musical notes issuing from the flute were sweet like nectar to the ear, but this sweetness is transferred poetically to the breath that issued from Kṛṣṇa's lips (mouth)—VB.

3. Balarāma is implied in Kṛṣṇa as that was the inseparable pair.

* It is presumed that the *gopīs*, one after another sing these verses. The names of *gopīs* given in SG or VT are not mentioned in the Text of the Bh. P. The *gopīs* express their eagerness to be with Lord Kṛṣṇa to enjoy his company personally, and each regards herself as unfortunate as compared even with inanimate objects like rivers and Govardhana hill which are supposed to enjoy Kṛṣṇa's melodious music on the flute.

nance of the sons of Nanda as they played on the flute, casting around their loving side-glances at the time of tending their cattle to the forest, along with their cowherd-companions.

8. Picturesquely clad in garments intertwined with tender mango-leaves, with tufts of peacock feathers, and bunches of flowers (decorating the head), and wearing wreaths of lilies and lotuses, and singing[1] and dancing freely sometimes in the midst of the group of cowherds, they (Kṛṣṇa and Balarāma) appeared exceedingly beautiful like actors on the stage.

9. Oh Gopīs! What infinitely great meritorious acts must have been performed by this flute, in consequence of which it can freely enjoy to its heart's content, the nectar flowing from the lips of Dāmodara (Kṛṣṇa)—which is the legitimate monopoly of *Gopīs*—and leaves but little to others; the rivers (which like mothers nourished with their waters the life of the bamboo of which the flute is made) which enjoyed a part of it, expressed their ecstasy with the blooming of lotuses (like hair standing on their ends with joy). The bamboos (the parent of the flute) like righteous elderly people shedding tears of joy to find a great devotee of the Lord born in their family, shed drops of dew.

10. Oh friend! Vṛndāvana which has attained the splendid beauty of bearing the imprints of the lotus-feet of Lord Kṛṣṇa,[2] has enhanced the glory of the earth (far above

1. *gāyamānau*—Some times when exhausted they invited other cowherd boys to sing at intervals and exhibited their superiority. The cowherd boys are blessed as they could fully enjoy the singing and dancing of Balarāma and Kṛṣṇa who felt shy to do so at Vraja among elderly people. Hence the Gopīs felt that they are extremely unfortunate, as they missed the free exhibition of dancing and singing of Kṛṣṇa—SG.

VT. repeats SG. VB. explains how this Lord's act was full of all *rasas*. His *rasa* theory is beyond the scope of a footnote.

2. The epithet is *Devakī-suta* 'the son of Devakī', and not *Yaśodā-suta* 'the son of Yaśodā'. In fact, the *gopīs* did not know that Kṛṣṇa was Devakī's son, and they presumed that he was Yaśodā's son. The narrator Śuka and members of the audience, knew that Kṛṣṇa was Devakī's son, and hence the author of the Bh. P. who represented that it was Śuka

that of the heaven). While seeing the rapturous dance of peacocks on hearing the music of Kṛṣṇa's flute, which they felt to be deep and low rumbling of clouds, all other animals on the hills stood motionless.[1]

11. Blessed are the female deer which though lacking in reasoning, capacity (due to their birth in animal species) offer, along with their mates, the black-antelopes, their worship to him with their loving glances, on hearing the music of flute played by the picturesquely dressed Kṛṣṇa, the son (or delight) of Nanda (while our cowherd-husbands are too petty-minded to tolerate it, if we do the same).

12. Beholding Kṛṣṇa, whose handsome appearance and amiable disposition were enhancing the delight of women, and listening to the enchanting music played upon by him, celestial damsels moving in the aerial cars (seated on the laps of their heavenly husbands) became infatuated under the spell of the god of love, and had the chaplets of flowers drop down from the braids of their hair, and the folds of their garments slip down and unsettled.

13. And the cows quaffed, with goblets in the form of their ears raised erect, the nectar-like melodious music of the flute flowing from the mouth (i.e. the breath) of Kṛṣṇa, and the calves stood entranced and motion-less[2], holding in their mouth the mouthful of milk sucked from the flowing udders.

who reported even this speech of *Gopīs*, used the term *Devakī-suta*, without being aware of the slip. SG., VT., VC defend it by quoting from *Bṛhad-Viṣṇu Purāṇa* that 'Yaśodā' and 'Devaki' are two names of Nanda's wife.

dve nāmnī Nanda-bhāryāyā Yaśodā Devakītyapi /

But the quotation is not found in my (*Gita Press*, Gorakhpur) edition of VP. Other annotators accept the epithet *Devakī-Suta* as Kṛṣṇa, and have just ignored the textual slip. SG.'s defence that Devakī merely gave birth to Kṛṣṇa, but he was really brought up by Yaśodā (*suta-śabdena kevalaṁ tayā prasūta eva, putras tu Yaśodāyā eva iti bhāvaḥ*) is merely a cover-up.

1. SJ. interprets the motionlessness as 'swoon due to the impact of divine love' (*Prema-mūrcchā*). This blessed state is not enjoyed even in Vaikuṇṭha. The *gopīs* regret their misfortune of not being transported to that swoon-like state. This shows the unsatiable nature of Divine Love.

2. This is the manifestation of *Sāttvika-vikāra*—SG.

(of their mothers).[1] Through (the medium of) their eyes, they embraced Govinda (Lord Kṛṣṇa), with tears of joy trickling from their eyes.

14. How wonderful! Oh mother! The birds in this forest must most probably be considered as sages, for (just as sages desirous of visualizing Kṛṣṇa follow different branches of the Veda, and perform the duties prescribed therein, without any desire for the fruits accruing from them), the birds are perching on the branches of trees covered with charming fresh foliage (without flowers and fruit obstructing Kṛṣṇa's sight) in order to have complete (unobstructed) view of Kṛṣṇa with un-winking eyes,[2] and to listen to the melodious music of the flute (with full absorbing attention), remaining speechless and oblivious to the external world (like sages happily absorbed in Kṛṣṇa's music or praise).

15. Listening to the music of Kṛṣṇa with wrapt attention, even the (inanimate) rivers exhibited their passion for him, by the whirlpools which thereby diminished the rapidity of their currents (flowing to the sea, their Lord), and (under the pretext of) offering him the present of lotuses, they, with the arms in the form of waves, clasped the pair of his feet, as if to camouflage their act of embracing.

16*. Perceiving[3] that in the heat of the sun, Kṛṣṇa pasturing the cattle of Vraja in company of Balarāma and cowherds, and himself following them playing on the flute, the rain-cloud (due to Kṛṣṇa's being similar to it in complexion and dispel-

1. VJ. (and as an alternative explanation SG. & VT.) regard *snuta-stana-payaḥ-kavalāḥ* an adj. qualifying *gāvaḥ* (cows), and interpret: "With milk flowing from their udders and a mouthful of grass in their mouth". I think the music of the flute enchanted both the cows and the calves, and they forgot even to swallow the mouthful of milk. Hence my translation as above.

2. v.l. *Sṛṇvanti mīlitadṛśaḥ* 'Listening with half-closed eyes'—SG. "Listen with closed eyes without looking at anything else"—SD.

* VT. states that noticing the effect of the heat of the Sun on the cattle and cowherds, Kṛṣṇa played the musical mode called *mallāra rāga*) (*Megha-malhāra rāga*) on his flute, which effected a shower. It is believed that if this *rāga* (musical mode) is scientifically sung, it brings rain-showers immediately.

3. With its eyes of lightning—VT.

ling heat-like distress of the people) arose and out of overflowing friendliness to him, spread out his body as an umbrella over them, and showered him with flowers[1] (i.e. flower-like showers).

17. Perfectly accomplished of purpose are the Pulinda (including aboriginal and backward class) women who, after being overcome and distressed with passion at the sight of the saffron (colour) sticking to the blades of grass (as well as rocks and other places)—the saffron-paste originally applied to the breast of the Divine Consort[2] (of Kṛṣṇa) and rendered still more charming by its contact with the reddish, lotus-like feet of the Lord of high renown (or whose glory is sung in the *Vedas*)—got cured of those pangs (of having a vision of Kṛṣṇa) by smearing their faces and breasts with that paste.

18. "Alas! Oh friends! Even this mount Govardhana is the foremost among the servants (devotees) of Lord Hari, inasmuch as it derives extremely high delight from the touch of the feet of Balarāma and Kṛṣṇa, and it receives them with respect, catering to their needs and to those of their (cowherd) friends and cattle, by offering fresh water, good grazing ground, caverns for shelter and edible bulbs and roots.

19. Oh friend! Of Kṛṣṇa and Balarāma who tend their cattle from one forest to another along with their young cowherd friends, and characterised by carrying ropes[3] (for tying hind-legs of cows when milking), and string-nooses (for controlling unruly cows), it is, however, wonderful that the sublimely sweet and melodious notes of their flutes cause motionlessness in mobile corporeal beings, and induce bristling with joy (which is a form of motion) among the (immobile) trees."

20. While describing to each other such (fascinating) sports of the Lord who ranged over the forest called Vṛndāvana, the cowherd-ladies became completely absorbed in them (or in him).

1. The flowers of the clouds are the rain-drops— *megha-puṣpaṁ ghana-rasam* quote SG. and VT.

2. VT. insists that she is no other than Rādhā.

3. *niryoga-pāśa* etc.—Extremely powerful bonds or ties created by *yoga*—VJ.

CHAPTER TWENTYTWO*

Cowherd-maids Pray to Kātyāyanī—Kṛṣṇa's carrying away their garments

Śrī Śuka said :

1. In the first month (Mārgaśīrṣa), in the season of Hemanta,[1] maids in the Vraja (cowherd-settlement of Nanda), observed the vow of adoring goddess Kātyāyanī, eating only pure food fit for being offered to sacrificial fire.

2-3. Having taken bath in the waters of the Yamunā at day-break, they made an image in sand of the goddess, just near the river water, on the bank, and worshipped her with sandal-paste, fragrant flowers, offering her propitiatory oblations, burning frank-incense, waving lights before her, and presenting other miscellaneous gifts of varying costs, along with tender shoots, fruits and unbroken grains of rice.

4. Those virgins performed the worship of the goddess, each repeating the prayer (as a *mantra* or incantation) : "Oh goddess Kātyāyanī ! Oh great deluding potency of the Lord ! Oh great *yoginī* (of great Super-human powers) ! Oh absolute ruler of the universe ! Be pleased to grant the son of cowherd Nanda (i.e. Kṛṣṇa) as my husband ![2]

5. The maidens who have set their heart on Kṛṣṇa, observed the vow for the period of a month, worshipping goddess Bhadrakālī with the prayer, "May Nanda's son be our husband".

6. Getting up early in the morning, and calling others by their names (to wake them up), they sang in loud chorus

* It is significant that this episode is not given in the *HVP* and *VP*. The object of this chapter is to demonstrate that devotion alone 'generates' (brings about) the Lord's grace.

bhaktir eva bhagavat-prasāda-jananīti darśayitum—VJ.

1. This season consists of the following months of the Hindu calendar—Mārgaśīrṣa and Pauṣa.

2. This Sanskrit verse is regarded as a *mantra* and it is to be repeated 1,600 times a day, during the period of *Kātyāyanī-vrata*—KD.22.52.

VT and VC. quote *Nārada-pañcarātra* to show that every *mantra* about Kṛṣṇa has goddess Durgā as the presiding deity. Hence the justification of this *vrata* and *japa* for getting Kṛṣṇa as a husband.

the glory of Lord Kṛṣṇa, as they went to bathe in the Yamunā clasping each other's hand.

7. On one occasion (on the last day of that vow which was a full-moon day), they, as usual, left their garments on the bank, and singing the glory of Kṛṣṇa, they sported in the water merrily (as that was the concluding day of their vow). Thus they concentrated on him in mind, word and deed).[1]

8. Understanding their intention, the glorious Lord Kṛṣṇa, the Supreme Master of all other experts in *yoga*,[2] surrounded by his companions,[3] went there to grant them the fruit of their vow.[4]

9. It is traditionally reported that he collected all their garments and quickly climbed a *Kadamba* tree (nearby). Laughing loudly, he spoke to them in fun, while (other) boys also kept a-laughing.

10. "Oh delicate girls! As you are exhausted by observing a religious vow, I am not joking. Earnestly I tell you. Let each of you come here at will, and receive her respective garments.

11. As these (cowherd) boys know it, I have never spoken a lie up till now. Oh girls with beautiful waist (Oh girls of pure hearts)! You may come here one by one or all together, and take your own clothes.[5]

1. *evaṁ mānasa-vācika-kāyikaikatānatvaṁ darśitam*—VT. The poet-annotator KD. says that the maidens imagined the bluish water of Yamunā as the person of Kṛṣṇa and embraced Him (in the form of water) and kissed it etc.—KD.22.84-87.

2. The epithets *bhagavān yogeśvareśvaraḥ* shows that it is the 'eternal metaphysical Lord—the third aspect of the Reality' which is implied here and not the human Vāsudeva Kṛṣṇa (vide Intro. XLVIII-XLIX Bh.P. vol. I). KD. underscores the same, "He became many to satisfy them." —KD. 22.99.

3. VT. quotes *Gautamī Tantra* and shows that these companions are 'Intellect, ego, mind, heart'.

4. VB. thinks that the maidens have committed the following faults: nude bath, breaking of silence and playing while observing a vow. To purge them of these, Lord Kṛṣṇa came there and by his look did it.

5. It is the erotically tinged devotion of Gauḍīya Vaiṣṇavas which makes VT. state that Kṛṣṇa was desirous of seeing the central part of their

12. Perceiving (the implications of) his joke, the cowherd girls were overcome with love. Bashfully they looked at each other and smiled, but none came out of the water.

13. When Kṛṣṇa was speaking to them jocularly, the girls got confused in their mind. Keeping themselves immersed in the cold water upto the neck, they requested him, while shivering with cold.

14. "Oh dear Kṛṣṇa ! Pray, do not be unjust to us. Darling ! We know that you, the son of Nanda, are our beloved, whom the whole of Vraja praises. Pray, do return our clothes to us, as we are shivering (with biting cold).

15. Oh beautiful Kṛṣṇa of charmingly bluish complexion ! We are your servants. We all shall carry out your behests. You are a knower of *dharma*[1] (righteous conduct). Pray return our clothes, else we shall (be constrained to) report the matter to the king (Nanda)" (threatened the elderly gopī's).

The glorious Lord said :

16. "If you are my servants (as you say), and undertake to abide by my biddings, come here and take back each your (respective) clothes, have a countenance beaming with a smile.

16A. *VJ. and VT. record a half-verse*

Otherwise, I will not return the garments. What will the angry chief do to me ?".

bodies (*yuṣmākam madhyabhāgādisaundaryam eva draṣṭum iṣyate, na ca vastrair etair matprayojanam iti nigūḍho bhāvaḥ*/) It is on the background of Tantricism that this Vaiṣṇavism was developed. Hence the commentator's words should not be superficially understood at their face value in view of note on page 1396. VB. says Kṛṣṇa wanted to see their hearts, interpreting *madhya* as 'heart'. Other annotators have just passed it over. As Kṛṣṇa's physical age was *only six years and four months* at this time, the girls wishing to marry him must have been presumably *less than six years* of age and as such this episode appears allegorical.

1. VB. quotes a *smṛti* text which prohibits the seeing of the secret parts of a girl, sexual act of beasts, a naked woman or one whose breasts are exposed to view :

17. At this, all the girls shivering with cold and covering their private parts with the palms of their hands, came out of the water, frozen (lit. shrunk) with cold.

18. Perceiving their virginity,[1] the glorious Lord who was propitiated with the purity of their hearts, placed their clothes on the branch of the tree and smilingly addressed them, with great pleasure.

19. "It is a positive offence against gods, that you entered water in a nude state,[2] after undertaking the observance of a religious vow. For the expiation of this sin, you bow raising up your folded palms to your heads, and lay prostrate (on the ground) after which you accept your (respective) clothings."

Additional verses in the Texts of VR and VJ.

19-A. Hearing this command full of religious significance, from the great Soul (Lord Kṛṣṇa), the damsels paid obeisance to him with one hand, covering their private part with the other.

19-B. Seeing them (violate the proper way of bowing to the Lord), the glorious Lord uttered this observation full of righteousness (and concerning religious formality), "Those who are experts in Vedas know it (and have laid it down) that he who bows to god Acyuta (Kṛṣṇa or Viṣṇu) with one hand only, should be punished by cutting off the other hand (not used in bowing).

19-C. Hence, a person should pay respects to his Lord by both of his hands. You, therefore, comply that way, and that will please me the better".

20. Considering what was explained to them by Lord Kṛṣṇa (Acyuta), the maids of Vraja realized that taking a plunge (bath) in a nude state is a transgression in the observation of their vow. Being desirous of completely fulfilling the vow, with all the related rites and formalities, they

Kanyā-yoniṁ paśu-krīḍām nagna-strīṁ prakaṭa-stanīṁ nāvalokayet/
Hence as a knower of *dharma*, Kṛṣṇa should return the clothes.

1. On seeing them arrived—VT.

2. Cf. *na nagnaḥ karhicit snāyāt l*

—*MBH. Anu.* 104.51

bowed to Lord Kṛṣṇa, the very embodiment of the fruit and religious rites, directly present before them. And it was he who washes off all sins, flaws and transgressions.

21. Seeing them bowing down humbly before him, the merciful Lord Kṛṣṇa, the son of Devakī, was pleased with them, and returned to them all their clothes.

22. Though they were badly deceived by the criticism of their nudity (in verse 19), were compelled to give up bashfulness, were ridiculed (by saying that he was not joking (verse 10), were treated like puppets and robbed of their clothings, they were so much satisfied with the company of their beloved that they bore no displeasure towards him.

23. They put on their clothes. So charmed were they with the company of the Lord, and their hearts were so much attracted, that they did not stir away from that place but continued to cast their bashful glances at him.

24. Understanding that their motive of undertaking the observance (of Kātyāyanī) vow was the longing to touch his feet, the glorious Lord Dāmodara (Kṛṣṇa) addressed the maidens :

25. "Oh chaste ladies! Your object (in observing the Kātyāyanī vow) viz. to worship me, is already known to me. It is approved of by me, and it shall be realized.

26. Your desire for my company is not censurable, for your longing to have enjoyment with me will not again lead to a birth in Saṁsāra. A seed once fried or boiled does not sprout.

27. Return to Vraja, Oh girls, as your object is accomplished. You will spend the autumnal nights in enjoyment with me—the object for which you, good ladies, have observed the vow of the worship of Kātyāyanī."

Śrī Śuka said :

28. Thus commanded by the Lord, the maidens whose object was accomplished, continued to contemplate in their minds the lotus-feet of the Lord, and returned to Vraja most grudgingly (lit. with great difficulty).

29. The glorious Lord, the son of Devakī, accompanied by Balarāma and surrounded by cowherds, went to a great distance from Vṛndāvana, grazing the cattle.

30. Perceiving that the trees served as umbrellas by spreading their shade in the scorching heat of the summer sun, Kṛṣṇa addressed to his cowherd friends, the residents of Vraja:

31. "Oh little Kṛṣṇa, Oh Aṁśu, Oh Śrīdāman, Subala, Arjuna, Viśāla, Ṛṣabha, Tejasvin, Devaprastha and Varūthapa !

32. Have a look at these great blessed souls who live only for the welfare of others, and themselves undergo (for others) the severity of stormy winds, heavy showers, summer heat and snow, and save them off from us.

33. The birth of the trees is verily the most blessed in the world, as it contributes to the well-being of all creatures. Just as no needy person returns disappointed from benevolent persons, so is the case with a person who approaches these for shelter.

34. They fulfil the desires (needs) of others by means of their leaves, flowers, fruits, shade, roots, bark, wood, fragrance, gums or exudations, ashes, coals and tender leaves.

35. That a person should sacrifice his life, wealth, intellect and speech for doing what is beneficial to others, is the farthest limit of the usefulness of embodied beings for their fellow creatures."

36. Praising them (the trees) thus, the Lord proceeded to the Yamunā passing through the avenue of trees whose branches were bent low with clusters of young leaves, foliage, bunches of fruits and flowers and other leaves.

37. Having made their cattle drink that very sweet, cool and healthy water of the Yamunā (to their fill), the cowherds themselves drank that sweet water to their heart's content, Oh king.

38. The cowherd pastured their cattle in the groves on the bank of the Yamunā. Being oppressed with hunger they approached Balarāma and Kṛṣṇa and addressed as follows :

CHAPTER TWENTYTHREE*

Spiritual Emancipation of the Wives of Brāhmaṇa Sacrificers

The cowherd boys urged :

1. Oh Balarāma ! Oh Rāma[1] of extra-ordinary prowess ! Oh Kṛṣṇa, the annihilator of the wicked ! This hunger is sorely troubling us, indeed. It behoves you both to appease it.

Śrī Śuka said :

2. When the glorious Lord Kṛṣṇa, the son of Devakī, was thus requested by the cowherd boys, he spoke to them with the intention of showering his grace on some Brāhmaṇa women[2] who were devoted to him.

3. "Go to the sacrificial hall where Brāhmaṇas who are reciters of the Vedas (but who do not know the meaning and implications of the Vedic text recited) are engaged in conducting a sacrificial session, called Āṅgirasa, with a desire to attain the celestial region, (after death).

4. After arriving there, tell them the names of my elder brother and of mine, and that you are deputed by us, and request them (to give you some) cooked rice, Oh Gopas !"

5. Being thus commanded by the Lord, they went there, folded the palms of their hands, and lay prostrate on the ground like a staff before the Brāhmaṇas (by way of paying them obeisance), and begged of them :

* This is the XXI chapter in VJ.'s text. The object of this chapter is to emphasize that it is the internal capability and faith that is more powerful and effective in the devotion of Lord Kṛṣṇa and not the scholarship or knowledge of the Śāstras—VJ.

1. The Supreme Brahman—VB. He is so called as *yogins* find spiritual delight in that infinite Supreme Soul characterised by Reality, Bliss and Consciousness. He quotes :

ramante yogino'nante satyānande cidātmani /
iti Rāma-padenāsau param brahmābhidhīyate //

2. The singular *bhāryāyāḥ* is used in the sense of the plural or a class, meaning "wives"—VR. VJ.

6. "Oh Brāhmaṇas (the veritable gods on the earth)! Be pleased to listen. We are the cowherds, the servants of Lord Kṛṣṇa. We have arrived here under instructions from Balarāma. May God bless you.

7. Not far from this place, Balarāma and Kṛṣṇa are grazing their cows. They are hungry and hence they desire to have food from you. If you have real faith in them, supply them the cooked rice which they seek from you, Oh Brāhmaṇas, the best knowers of *dharma*.

8. Oh excellent-most people, (as you know it), it has been decided in the *dharma-śāstra* that it does not involve any violation (of *dharma*), if food from a person who has been consecrated for sacrifices is eaten, the exception being his consecration for a sacrifice requiring animal slaughter or a *sautrāmaṇi*[1] sacrifice, (when such eating is prohibited)."

9. Cherishing petty longings (viz. life in heaven whence down-fall is certain) yet engaged in elaborate and toilsome acts (of sacrificial procedure), ignorant yet considering themselves as learned and vainglorious of their wisdom, (as they knew not that by the path of devotion which is easier than the path of *Karma* the *summum bonum* is attained) the Brāhmaṇas, though they heard the solicitations of the Lord (who out of Grace sent his friends for food to them), did not care to heed it.

10-11. Looking upon their bodies as their souls (and in their caste-pride), and being of perverted mentality, they looked upon Kṛṣṇa, that Supreme Brahman, the veritable glorious Lord, (the possessor of six excellences), that suprasensuous Being, as merely an ordinary mortal being, though

1. It is not a *soma* sacrifice but a combination of an *iṣṭi* with an animal sacrifice (*Śatapatha Br.* XII. 7.2.10). Its chief characteristic is offering of *surā* (wine). This is performed at the end of *Rājasūya* sacrifice or *cayana*. This sacrifice frees a son from debt due to his mother. The peculiar thing about *Sautrāmaṇi* is that here wine is offered and the remnants of it are drunk by a Brāhmaṇa hired for that purpose or are poured on an ant-hill.

(*Brāhmaṇam parikrīṇīyād uccheṣaṇasya pātāram* / *Āpastamba XIX*, 33)
(*Brāhmaṇaṁ parikrīṇīte grahoccheṣaṇasya pātāraṁ* ... *valmīkavapāyām avanamet* /—*Satyāṣāḍha* XIII-8.28-31)

he really constituted the time and place (of the performance of sacrifices), the substances to be oblated, the *mantras* (for invoking deities), the procedure (prescribed for performing sacrifices), the priests (officiating over the performance), the sacrificial fires, the deities invoked, the performer of the sacrifice, the actual act of sacrificing itself and the religious merits accruing from that sacrifice.

12. As they said neither 'Yes' nor 'No', the cowherds became disappointed, and returning to Kṛṣṇa and Balarāma, reported accordingly, Oh repressor of enemies.

13. On hearing their words, the Almighty Lord of the Universe burst out laughing, and in order to acquaint the cowherds with the ways of the world, (that beggars are not choosers and that one should try till achieving success), he spoke to them again :

14. "Inform the wives (of those sacrificers—Brāhmaṇas) that I, along with Balarāma, have arrived here. They are affectionate and (with their hearts engrossed in contemplating upon me), they live in me mentally. They will give you (abundant) food, to your heart's content".

15. Thereupon, the cowherds went to the apartment reserved for the consecrated wives of the sacrificers, and saw them decked with ornaments, and seated comfortably there. Paying respects to those chaste Brāhmaṇa ladies, the cowherds respectfully submitted :

16. "Salutations to you Brāhmaṇa ladies! Kindly listen to us. We are deputed here by Kṛṣṇa who, while wandering, has arrived (here) not far from this place.

17. While grazing the cows, he along with Balarāma and cowherds, has come far afar (from his house). May food be served to him, hungry as he is, along with his companions.

18. The Brāhmaṇa ladies who, due to their hearing (and contemplating over) the stories of Kṛṣṇa, were ever eager and anxious to see him, found themselves in a flurry, when they listened to the (news of his) arrival so near.

19-20. Like rivers flowing towards the ocean, all of them hastened to the beloved Lord Kṛṣṇa, taking with them in vessels, large quantity of sumptuous food of four kinds,[1] even though they were prohibited by their husbands, fathers, brothers and relatives, for they, having heard of him for a long time, had fixed their hearts on the glorious Lord of hallowing renown.

21-22. There in a grove beautified with the new tender foliage of Aśoka[2] trees, on the bank of the Yamunā, the women (wives of sages) beheld Kṛṣṇa strolling leisurely, surrounded by cowherds, along with his elder brother (Balarāma)—Kṛṣṇa of dark blue complexion, wearing silken garment of golden colour (or a girdle of gold), dressed like an actor decorated with a wreath of sylvan flowers, peacock-feathers and tender shoots, beautified with mineral paints; who rested one of his hands on the shoulders of his trusted companions, and playfully dangling a lotus in the other hand; with lilies gracing his ears and locks of curly hair hanging against his cheeks, he wore a face beaming with smile.

23. They had their minds completely absorbed in him, their most beloved one, the frequent audition of whose excellent glories have rendered completely fruitful the very function (and existence) of the ears, and adorned them like ornaments. Welcoming his arrival through the gates of their eyes into their hearts, they embraced him there for a pretty long time, and got rid of all their anguish and misery (of separation from him), just as the egoistic propensities get submerged after embracing the *prājña*,[3] (the soul, that is ever awake as a witness of sleep) and forget all afflictions.

1. The kinds of food mentioned are :
(1) *bhakṣya*—easily gulpable
(2) *bhojya* —requiring mastication before swallowing
(3) *Lehya* —which is to be licked
(4) *coṣya* —which is to be sucked

2. The pun on *a-śoka* suggests that their grief for their inability to see Lord Kṛṣṇa is now removed.

3. The soul that is ever awake as a witness of sleep.

Kd. : Just as the out-going propensities return and embrace the *prājña* and forgetting all worldly afflictions, merge themselves into sleep. 23.245.

24. The Lord, being the witness of the mind and intellect of all had come to know that they had arrived there solely with the earnest desire of seeing him and had given up all hopes and longings for their husbands etc. (as they came in defiance of the orders of their men-folk) addressed to them with a smiling face.

The glorious Lord Said :

25. Welcome—very auspicious is your arrival, Oh highly blessed ladies. Be seated comfortably. What can we do for you? That you have come with a desire of seeing us (despite the opposition of your men) is really worthy of you.

26. Discerning persons who really understand their self-interest and object in life, engage themselves directly in constant uninterrupted devotion unto me without any ulterior motive, as I am the most beloved Self.

27. Who else can be more beloved than one's own Soul through contact with whom life, vital breath, intellect, mind, body, wives, children, wealth etc. have endeared themselves to us.

28. Now that you have achieved your object in life (of seeing me), please return to the sacrificial hall, where the Brāhmaṇas, your husbands who will successfully complete their sacrificial session with your presence, and their status of being householders depends on you, your being with them.

The wives of the sages said :

29. Oh all-pervading Lord (who know everything about us)! It does not behove you to utter such harsh words. We beseech you to fulfil your own promise (in *Vedas* viz. He, who approaches the Lord does not revert to Saṁsāra,

VR. Just as after realization of the Supreme Soul the urges and curiosities of seeing him shake off all types of anguishes and eagerness of seeing Him.

VJ. : Just as all the absorption of all sense-activities into Prājña, the knowers shake off all their affliction.

The basic *upaniṣadic* concept of Prājña is as follows : Prājña is the enjoyer of bliss (*Maṇḍ*. 4.1) of dreamless sleep.

(*Chāndogya Up*. 8. 15.1). We have approached your feet in defiance of and transgressing the wishes of our relatives and shall wear in our hair the wreaths of *Tulasī* leaves indifferently kicked off at us by you (i.e. have come to serve you even as slaves)."

30. Neither our husbands, nor our parents, sons, brothers, relatives, friends will now accept us (back), not to speak of others. Oh Subduer of the internal foes like passion, avarice etc. !

Now that we have laid ourselves prostrate at the feet of your glorious self, may you be pleased to confer or ordain that state of life (your absolute service or slavery) whereby we shall have no other go to heaven or any other world."

The Lord said :

31. Now that you have been commanded to return by me, neither your husbands, nor parents, brothers, sons and others, nor even the public shall scorn you or get angry with you. Even the gods shall approve of it (your act of coming to me).

32. (If you still feel unable to leave me, please note that) Bodily contact among men does not contribute to happiness or love in this world. If you concentrate your mind on me, you will attain to me before long.

VR. adds

32-A. Devotion unto me is engendered by listening to my attributes, by visualizing me, by contemplating on me and not so much by physical proximity. Therefore, return to your homes.

Śrī Śuka said :

33. Therefore, as directed (by the Lord) the wives of the sages returned to the sacrificial hall. Not only did the sages not expostulate them, but they carried the sacrificial session to a successful conclusion with their help.

34. One lady out of them, who was detained per force by her husband, embraced in her heart the Lord as pictured by

her through what she heard about him, and gave up her body that came to her lot by her *karma* (deeds) in past life.

35. Lord Govinda first made the cowherds feast on the four kinds of that food. The Lord partook of it only afterwards.

36. In this way, the Lord who, out of sports, had assumed a human body and imitated the ways of the world led a sportive life giving joy to cows, cowherds and cowherdessess by his charming personality, sweet words and deeds.

37.* Then remembering (their disgraceful behaviour), the Brāhmaṇas who committed that offence repented, "Alas ! We have disregarded the entreaty of the Lords of the Universe who are imitating the behaviour of human beings.

38. Perceiving the extra-ordinarily supreme devotion of their women in Kṛṣṇa and realizing that they were wanting in it, they were extremely tormented and censured themselves.

39. "Fie upon our three-fold birth,[1] our mastery of Vedic lore ! Fie upon our observance of vows (of continence during sacrificial sessions) ! Fie upon our extensive versatility of knowledge ! Fie upon our spotless pedigree ! Fie upon our expertise in ritualistic technicalities in sacrifice, when we are averse to (*lit.* have turned away our face from) the supra-sensuous Lord Kṛṣṇa !

40. Verily the *Māyā* of the Lord is capable of infatuating even experts in *yoga*. Hence we, Brāhmaṇas, the spiritual preceptors of men, are deluded with regard to our real interests.

41. Oh ! Look at the unfathomable[2] devotion even of

* Here the doubt in Parīkṣita's mind about the goodness of the Brāhmaṇas is cleared up in this verse. The Brāhmaṇas were auspicious by nature, for they were filled with remorse at the offence they committed, when they remembered, "Alas We have scornfully treated the request of the Lords of the Universe who (outwardly) imitate human behaviour."

1. According to ŚR the threefold birth is as follows :

i) Purity of heredity and family (*Śaukla*)

ii) Investiture of the sacred thread and initiation into Gāyatrī Mantra (Sāvitra),

iii) Consecration for Vedic sacrifices (*daikṣa*).

2. Ignorant, weaker sex as explained in the next verse
duranta-bhāva—Bond of devotion that brooks no separation—SS.

our women in Kṛṣṇa, the father and preceptor of the world, which cut asunder the bonds of death called the ties of the household.

42. These have not undergone the purificatory rite (known as the investiture of the sacred thread) which is regarded as the second birth (for Vedic and other studies). Nor have they stayed in the preceptor's house (for Vedic studies or Śāstric learning). They have not performed any austerities and have no grounding in the *śāstric* enquiry about the Soul. They are not characterised by any special (spiritual or external) purity or any auspicious or meritorious (sacrificial, or other rites or) acts.

43. Despite these, they entertain such firm and unflinching devotion unto Kṛṣṇa of hallowing renown, the Lord of the experts of *yoga*, a devotion not engendered in us even though we have undergone the purificatory rites (such as the investiture of thread) and have other qualifications (mentioned above).

44. Oh! How gracious of him it was that although he himself was the goal to be achieved through sacrificial and other activities prescribed by the Vedas,[1] he, through the message sent with the cowherds reminded us[2] (of the futility of all acts if devoid of devotion to God)—who were too stupid to understand our real self interest and were negligent due to household activities.

45. To request food from us who are absolutely under his control, was a mere pretext of the Ruler of the universe who has all his desires fulfilled, and is the master who confers all blessing like bestowing Liberation from Saṁsāra.

46. His solicitation for food was merely a ruse to delude the world, as the Goddess of Affluence, giving up her proverbial fault of fickleness or inconstancy, discards others and seeks permanent resort in him, with the hope of touching his feet at least once.

47-48. He is verily that self-same glorious Lord Viṣṇu who constitutes the time, the place of sacrifice, the substances

1. *or* The refuge or main-stay of the pious saints.
2. *or* : that he has now incarnated for the protection of the good —VR.

to be oblated to fire (e.g. *caru*), the *mantras* (mystical formulae for invoking the deities), the technicalities of sacrificial procedure, the priests (engaged in carrying out various duties in sacrifice) deities to be invoked, the sacrificial fire, the sacrificer, the performance of the sacrifice and the merit accruing therefrom. We have heard that he was born in the Yadu clan. But stupid and deluded as we are, we do not recognize him.

49. How blessed-most we are in having such women as our wives due to whose devotion in him, we too have our minds firmly fixed on Lord Hari.

50. Salutations to You, Oh glorious Lord Kṛṣṇa of unobstructed (all-penetrating) intelligence! As we have our minds deluded by your Māyā, we are wandering in the paths of *Karma*.

51. May that Ancient-most Person be pleased to condone and forgive our transgression, as we, due to our minds being infatuated with your Māyā, the deluding potency, have not been able to realize your prowess and glory.

52. Having thus recollected the sinful offence given by them to Lord Kṛṣṇa by their behaviour of disregarding him, the Brāhmaṇas, though desirous and eager to see the two Acyuta brothers (Kṛṣṇa and Balarāma) did not dare to stir out due to the fear of Kaṁsa.

CHAPTER TWENTY-FOUR

Prevention of Sacrifice to Indra[1]

Śrī Śuka continued :

1. While living in that very locality (viz. Vṛndāvana, Vraja) in the company of Balarāma, even the glorious Lord

1. The story of Kṛṣṇa's opposition to Gopas' offering a sacrifice to Indra and his advice to offer it to mount Govardhana instead, is recorded in *VP*. 5. ch. 10 and *HV*. 2, ch. 15. These stories show that Kṛṣṇa directly

Kṛṣṇa feigned as if he did not notice the cowherds engaged in preparation for the *Indra-yāga* (worship of the rain-god Indra).[1]

2. Despite his thorough knowledge of it, the omniscient glorious Lord who was the indwelling Soul of all beings, with great humility, enquired of elderly Gopas of whom Nanda was prominent.

3. "May it be told to me, Oh father, what occasion for your hurry and flurry has arrived? (If it be a sacrifice) what is the fruit or purpose of it? Who is regarded as competent to perform it? And with what materials is it to be performed?

4-5. I am desirous of hearing it, Oh father! Please do tell it to me who am eager to learn. For there is nothing worth concealing in the case of the righteous who look upon the self-same soul as abiding in all beings also in the case of those who do not discriminate between people (or things) as their own or as of others (and are of impartial outlook), have no friends, aliens or enemies, and have nothing to hide from others. But to those who retain this discrimination, the neutrals may be avoided as enemies, but a friend or a well-wisher has been

over-rode the older Vedic gods, especially Indra, and that the Kṛṣṇa cult superseded local and contemporaneous divinities including the great god Indra of the Vedic period. Indra's attempt to punish the cowherds by downpour of heavy rains and his final discomfiture by Kṛṣṇa who protected the cowherds with their cattle and other belongings under the umbrella of mount Govardhana lifted by him, show the recession of the Vedic religion and the positive advance of the Kṛṣṇa cult.

The roots of rivalry between Indra and Kṛṣṇa cults go back to the Vedic period, if we are to accept Nīlakaṇṭha Caturdhara's interpretation of *RV.* 5.48.3 given at the beginning of his com. on *HV*, 2. ch.15. It is as follows:

āgrāvabhir ahanyebhir aktabhir variṣṭhaṁ
vajram ājigharti māyini /
śataṁ vā yasya pracaran sve dame saṁvartayanto vivartayannahaḥ //

RV. 5.48.3 (as quoted by Nīlakaṇṭha)

"For (seven) nights, Indra sent down heavy showers like his most powerful weapon *Vajra* on *māyin* i.e. Kṛṣṇa, who had assumed a human form through His *Māyā* Potency, and who made the Gopas to use the materials (collected) for Indra's sacrifice to the sacrifice of mount Govardhana".

1. Cf. *PV.* 5.10.26.

called as one's own self[1] (and as such, nothing should be kept secret from him. I, being such, should be confided with this sacrifice affair).

6. People perform actions with or without understanding the purpose or the fruit of the act. The ignorant persons do not accomplish the fruit of that action (to that extent) as people with full knowledge achieve.

7. May it be clearly explained to me who am inquisitive about it, as to whether your present course of action (viz. performance of sacrifice to Indra) has been undertaken after enquiring into the *Śāstras* or in consultation with friends or is it a mere blind traditional function in the ways of the world.

Nanda explained :

8.* The great god Indra is (the presiding deity of) the rainfall itself and clouds are his loving manifestations. They shower water which is the very source of delight[2] and life of all beings.

9. Oh child! We and other people like us, worship[3] Indra, the ruler of clouds and controller of the world, by performing sacrifices with materials produced with his seminal discharge viz. rain-water.

10. It is on the remnants of the sacrifice that people subsist for achieving their three purposes in life (viz. *dharma*—

1. VJ. explains : one should not keep everything secret from everybody. One should avoid a neutral party as an enemy, but not do so in the case of a friend or a well-wisher who is as good as one's own-self.

* VR. quotes the famous verse which identifies the sun-god with the rain :

aṣṭau māsān nipītaṁ yad bhūmyāś codamayaṁ vasu /
sva-gobhir moktum ārebhe parjanyaḥ kālam āgate //

But he is under Indra's control and as such, the presiding deity of rain and Indra are identified. The clouds are like so many bodies of Indra. They shower water which is so vital to the life of the people and are a source of strength and happiness to them.

2. v.l.—*prāṇanaṁ* (VJ) "infusing life and activity".

3. VT explains—Otherwise it will be ungratefulness. The 3 P. pl. *yajante* instead of *Vayaṁ yajāmaḥ* is used as Nanda felt abashed before Kṛṣṇa.

righteousness, *artha*—affluence and worldly prosperity and *kāma*—enjoyment of pleasures). The rain-god is the real bestower of fruits to persons who exert in agriculture, industry etc.

11. He who, out of passion, greed, fear or hatred, gives up the customary religious rites handed down by tradition, does not attain his real good.

Śrī Śuka said :

12. Hearing the explanatory speech of Nanda as well as that of other residents of Vraja, Keśava (Kṛṣṇa) addressed his father with a view to provoking Indra's wrath (and finally to discomfit him).[1]

The glorious Lord said :

13. A being comes into existence only by its own past deeds (*karma*),[2] and passes away through the force of its own *karmas*. It is only through the instrumentality of one's past actions, that the being experiences worldly pleasures, pain, fear or blessings (hereafter). (The favour or disfavour of a divinity is immaterial and irrelevant).

14. If there be any authority like the Supreme Ruler to dispense fruits of actions of others, and if he were to resort to confer fruits of the deeds on the doer of the actions, and he will have no control over him who abstains from committing any act.[3]

15. What power can Indra exercise on beings who follow the course of their actions (and experience the resulting fruit)? He is incapable of modifying its destined course of action of human beings according to their own individual nature. (It is the Almighty God and not Indra who can do it.)

1. Cf. *VP*. 5.10.25.

2. VJ. Here *karma* means Nārāyaṇa as He is the agent of all activities (*Nārāyaṇa eva sarvasya kartetyabhiprekṣya sarvasya kāraṇaṁ karmaivetyāha* /)

3. ŚR. : explains that this is a refutation of those who regard God as dependent on *karmas*. God is untouched by and above all *karmas*. He is the bestower of the fruit of an action to its doer.

VJ. : If it is presumed that there is a Supreme Controller to dispense weal or woe as a result of the *karma* of a person, He will be a mere helper (*sahāyabhūtaḥ*) with no independence of His own.

16. People are the slaves of their Nature and follow their own individual natural disposition and proclivities. The whole world of gods, *asuras* and human-beings thus has their being established in nature and follow it.[1]

17. It is through the force of past actions (*karma*) that a being comes by and casts off corporeal forms of a high or low order. It is (nothing but one's Karma that assumes the role of) an enemy, a friend, an indifferent person, a preceptor or the Supreme Controller.

18.* Hence abiding in one's own nature (i.e. following one's natural disposition) one should do one's duty (according to one's own class or position in life), and thus respect (lit. adore) it (one's prescribed *karma*). That deed whereby one can lead a happy (and a successful) life is verily his deity.

19.† A person who, entertaining faith in one god offers services to another, does not attain happiness and welfare, just as an unchaste woman gratifying her paramour, (fails to get prosperity or happiness).

20. A Brāhmaṇa should maintain his livelihood by the study and the teachings of the Vedas; the Kṣattriya by the protection of the earth; a person from the Vaiśya community, by means of *vārtā* (as explained in the next verse); and a Śūdra by rendering service to the twice-born castes (mentioned above).[2]

21. *Vārtā* is four-fold: viz. agriculture, commerce, rearing of cattle and the fourth, usury. As far as we are concerned, cows (the cattle) have been the means of our subsistence.

1. VJ identifies Nature with Nārāyaṇa. The above verses refuse the power to secondary divinities like Indra who are mistaken for the Supreme Lord. It is Nārāyaṇa who is designated by the term *svabhāva*.

* VJ interprets *karma* as Nārāyaṇa and states: One should perform his duty prescribed as such by his *Varṇa* (caste) and *āśrama* (stage in life), and dedicate every thing to Nature i.e. God Nārāyaṇa who is the creator and supporter of the world and is involved in every religious rite. The name of any god whom a being worships (e.g. god Gaṇeśa), denotes as a matter of fact Lord Nārāyaṇa Himself.

† Verse No. 24 in VJ's Text.

2. Cf. *VP* 5.10. 16-31.

22. The attributes called *sattva*, *rajas*, and *tamas* are causes of the maintenance, creation and dissolution of the Universe. It is through *rajas* that the universe of various kinds of things is created by the mutual union of man and woman.

23. It is after being impelled by *rajas* that the clouds shower water all round. By means of these waters people accomplish their purpose (of growing food etc.). What has the great Indra to do with this ?

24. Father ! We have no towns, no countries or territories, no villages or no houses to dwell. We are forever forest-dwellers, living in jungles and on mountains.

25. Therefore, let a sacrifice dedicated for the propitiation of cows, Brāhmaṇas and the mount (*Govardhana*) be instituted. And let this sacrifice be accomplished with the materials collected for the worship to Indra.

26. Let different varieties of sweet dishes from rice, boiled in milk with sugar, down to boiled pulses and various puddings and cakes be prepared and all the milk collected from all the cows be brought together.

27. Let sacrificial fires be properly fed with oblations by Brāhmaṇas who are well versed in the Vedas, and let various food preparations be given to them along with cows, as sacrificial fees.

28. Food should also be distributed to all others upto the *cāṇḍāla*, the low castes and dogs as may be deemed proper. Cows should be supplied with grass and the above mentioned articles of food be offered as *bali* to the mount Govardhana.

29. After taking your meals you put on your ornaments and painting yourselves with sandal-pastes etc. and putting on excellent clothes, circumambulate by the right side to cow, Brāhmaṇas, sacrificial fires and the Govardhana mountain.

30. This is my view and religious belief, Oh father. It may be adopted if it is approved of by you. This type of worship and sacrifice will be liked by cows, Brāhmaṇas, the mountain (Govardhana) itself and by me as well.

Śrī Śuka said :

31. Hearing the exposition of (the creed as elucidated

by) the glorious Lord who, as the Time-Spirit was desirous of crushing the pride of Indra, the Gopas headed by Nanda approved of it with words, "Correct, very nice".

32-33. And they carried out everything as Kṛṣṇa, the slayer of the demon Madhu, instructed them. Having got recited the benedictory hymns (and the expiatory rites to avert evil) known as *Svastyayana*, they propitiated with great respect, the mountain (Govardhana) and Brāhmaṇas with those very materials (collected for *Indra-yāga*, the worship of and sacrifice to Indra) and offered grass to the kine. With their wealth of cattle in front of them, they circumambulated the mount (Govardhana) by keeping that mount always on their right.

34. With the gracefully adorned Gopa women singing the exploits of Kṛṣṇa, and with Brāhmaṇas pronouncing benedictions, the cowherds who also wore excellent ornaments, rode their carts with bullocks yoked to them, and went round the mountain keeping it ever to their right.

35. In order so inspire confidence and belief in the Gopas, Kṛṣṇa, on his part assumed a totally different personality. Announcing that he is the mountain Govardhana itself, he with his gigantic body, consumed the enormous quantity of the food offered.[1]

36. Thereupon, along with the inhabitants of Vraja Kṛṣṇa presented salutation to his own other form and exclaimed, "How wonderful! Lo! This mountain has manifested himself.

37. This mountain is capable of taking any form he likes, at will. He kills the forest-dwellers who showed disrespect to him. To him let us bow for the welfare of us as well as of our cattle."

38. The Gopas thus carried out the worship of the mountain, the cows and the Brāhmaṇas according to the directions of Lord Vāsudeva and they returned to Vraja along with Kṛṣṇa.

1. Cf. VP. 5.10.47.

CHAPTER TWENTY-FIVE

Lifting up of Mount Govardhana[1]

Śrī Śuka said :

1. Then perceiving that his worship had been stopped, Indra got enraged upon the cowherds headed by Nanda who regarded Kṛṣṇa as their Protector.

2. Being incensed, Indra directed the host of clouds called *Saṁvartaka* which bring about the destruction of the universe. Priding himself as the Supreme Ruler of the Universe he commanded :

3. "Oh ! Look at the astounding audacity and arrogance due to wealth and prosperity of those cowherds who are after all forest-dwellers, but depending on a mortal (called) Kṛṣṇa, have set at nought a deity.

4. Giving up the path of knowledge involving the meditation of the Self or self-realization, they expect to cross the ocean of Saṁsāra or worldly existence with the help of the

1. The hill called 'mountain Govardhana' is 18 miles from Vṛndāvana, in Mathura district. In the village "Paitho", Kṛṣṇa is believed to have held up the mountain on his little finger. This episode is narrated in *VP*. 5 ch. 11 and in *HV*. 2 ch. 18, the latter seems to be an enlarged version. The common verses and repetition of similar expressions in these three works indicate that these three works have used a common traditional bardic source.

Nīlakaṇṭha in his com. on *HV*. 2. 18 quotes the following *Ṛc*. :

tamasya rājā Varuṇas tam Aśvinau |
kratuṁ sacanta Mārutasya Vedhasaḥ ||
dādhāra dakṣam uttamam aharvidam |
Vrajaṁ ca Viṣṇuḥ sakhivā aporṇute||

—*RV* 1.156.4 (also *Ait. Br*. 1.30 and *Kauṣītaki Br*. 9.6)

Aundh Ed. of RV. reads *Aśvinā* for *Aśvinau*. Nīlakaṇṭha interprets : "Varuṇa and the twin Aśvinikumāras gave their consent to the sacrifice offered to the mountain (Govardhana) at his behest by Viṣṇu. When Indra got angry at the destruction of the sacrifice to be offered to him, to the Wind god and god Brahmā, Viṣṇu held up the mountain that was the recipient of the sacrifice but was capable of offering excellent protection from showers. A friend of all the inhabitants of Vraja as he was, he covered the Vraja with the mountain.

so-called unreliable boats in the form of sacrifices consisting of rituals.

5*. Similarly, taking resort to that garrulous, foolish, arrogant, ignorant mortal Kṛṣṇa who (out of pedantry) regards himself as a great scholar, the cowherds have dared to offend me.

6. Shatter down (lit. shake off) the arrogance of affluence of the cowherds who are puffed with pride of wealth and prosperity and have their minds filled with insolence through the influence of Kṛṣṇa. Destroy all of their cattle."

7**. With a view to annihilate the camp (the cattle-wealth) of Nanda, I shall follow you riding my elephant *Airāvata* and accompanied with the troop of *maruts* of enormous prowess."

Śrī Śuka said :

8. Thus commanded and freed (from their bonds) by Indra, the (*saṁvarta*) clouds vehemently harassed Nanda's *Gokula* with heavy showers.

9. Dazzling with flashes of lightning and thundering with the roar of thunderbolts and impelled by tempestuous winds, they showered hail-stones.

10. When the clouds let loose incessant downpour of showers as big as columns (in volume), the earth was inundated with torrential floods of water, and the elevations and the depressions of the ground became invisible.

11. The cattle which were shivering (with cold) under excessively driving showers and tempestuous winds, and the cowherds and their women who were afflicted with severe cold, sought refuge in Lord Kṛṣṇa.

12. Covering their heads and their children (and calves) with their bodies and acutely suffering from the torrential downpour, they approached shivering, to the feet of the Lord.

*. VT.—tries to explain the implied glorification of Kṛṣṇa e.g. *vācālam*—whose word is effective or powerful. *Paṇḍita-māninaṁ*—respected by persons who are *paṇḍitas* or knowers of *Brahman*.

VJ. Kṛṣṇa who is *vācāla* i.e. speaks what is censured by the scriptures and who regards himself as an authority (*Paṇḍitamāninam*).

** Cf. *VP*. 5.11.5 and *HV*. 2.18.5

13. "Oh Kṛṣṇa ! Oh highly glorious Kṛṣṇa ! The whole of *Gokula* has none else but you as its protector, Oh Lord ! You are affectionate to your devotees. It behoves you to protect us from the enraged divinity (Indra)".

14. Observing that due to the beating of the volley of the hail-stones, the Gokula had fallen senseless, the glorious Lord Hari came to know that it was the working of indignant Indra.

15. "As the sacrifice to be offered to him has been obstructed by us, Indra is pouring down for our destruction tremendously heavy showers full of hail-stones, accompanied by terrific stormy winds, out of season.

16. Now I shall employ an effective counter-measure through my *yogic* power and remove the *tamas* (darkness) in the form of the arrogance of affluence of the divinities who, through their foolishness, regard themselves as the supreme ruler of the world.

17. It is not desirable that celestials, who are endowed with the quality of *Sattva* (goodness) or devotion to me to a special degree, should be puffed up with the vain pride of being the (Supreme) ruler of the world. The humiliation of these wicked divinities at my hand will work as Grace unto them.[1]

18. With all the *yogic* power at my command, I will, therefore, protect this *Gokula* which has sought shelter in me and has accepted me as their Master and which now entirely depends on me. This is the eternal vow taken by me."

19. Observing thus (to himself), Kṛṣṇa, though a child, uprooted with ease the mount Govardhana with one of his hands[2] and held it up sportively as if it were a mushroom.

20. And quoth the glorious Lord to cowherds "Oh mother ! Oh father ! Oh residents of Vraja. Enter comfortably

1. (i) *anugraha eva*—ŚR
(ii) Will lead to deeper devotion to me—VJ.
2. with left hand—VT. He quotes *HV* 2.18.31.
sa dhṛtaḥ saṅgato meghair giriḥ savyena pāṇinā

VT.'s graphic description and dramatic narration of this episode deserves perusal in the original.

into the cavity beneath the mountain along with your wealth of cattle.

21. You need not entertain any fear that the mountain will slip down from my hand. Dispel all the fear about storms or (driving) showers, for protection (against them) has been already securely devised."

22. With their minds thus reassured by Kṛṣṇa, they entered into the cavity (beneath Govardhana) along with their wealth, herds of cattle, their dependants (like priests etc.) food-grains etc. according to the accommodation (which was sufficiently available).

23. Being gazed at by those inhabitants of Vraja who disregarded their pangs of hunger and thirst and thus neglected their personal comforts, Kṛṣṇa up-held the mountain for seven days and did not move from his position.

24. Observing the yogic power of Kṛṣṇa, Indra was extremely astounded. Being shorn of pride and thwarted of his design, he restrained his saṁvartaka clouds.

25. Noticing the sky cleared of clouds, the sun already risen and the terrific tempestuous winds and the downpour of hails had ceased altogether, Kṛṣṇa, the bearer of Govardhana, told the cowherds.

26. "Oh cowherds! Now that the stormy winds and showers have stopped and the waters of the flooded rivers have almost receded, you dismiss all your apprehension and go out into the open with your women, children and property (cattle)."

27. Taking with them their respective wealth (viz. herds of cattle) and all the cart-loads of their belongings, the cowherds slowly came out (of the cavity) along with their wives, children and elders.

28. The glorious Lord on his part sportfully placed the mountain on its previous position while all beings stood a-gazing.

29. Overflowing with a flood of affection the inhabitants of Vraja approached him embracing (blessing, smelling the crown of his head and doing such acts expressive of love), according to their position and relations. The cowherd women overwhelmed with affection and joy worshipped him

with curds and unbroken rice (*akṣatas*)[1] and expressed their choicest blessings profusely (out of grateful affection and not out of a sense of seniority as they knew his divine nature).

30. Yaśodā, Rohiṇī, Nanda and Balarāma, the mighty among the mightiest, were overwhelmed with affection and impatience and embracing Kṛṣṇa, they showered him with benedictions.

31. In the heavens, hosts of celestials, Sādhyas, Siddhas, Gandharvas and Cāraṇas sang his glory and out of joy showered flowers on him, Oh king.

32. Commanded by the celestials, conchs and kettle-drums were sounded in the sky and leaders of Gandharvas (celestial *artistes*) headed by *Tumbaru* participated in singing.

33. Oh king! Surrounded by his affectionate cowherd-friends and accompanied by Balarāma, Kṛṣṇa proceeded to Gokula from that place. And young cowherd women, delighted at heart, returned to their respective homes singing all the while such miraculous exploits of Kṛṣṇa (like lifting up of Govardhana) who has captivated their hearts.

CHAPTER TWENTYSIX

Conversation between Nanda and Cowherds

Śrī Śuka said :

1. Witnessing Kṛṣṇa's miraculous feats of this type (such as lifting up of mount Govardhana) the cowherds, being unaware of his prowess, were extremely astonished and coming to Nanda, they spoke unto him (as follows):

2. "Verily the exploits of this child are extremely marvellous. How does he deserve to be born among rustic people like us—a birth really unworthy and censurable to him.

1. VB. : The cowherd women made a circular mark of curds on his forehead on which some unbroken rice were applied and water was waved round his face and sipped.

3. How is it that a child of seven years as he is, he could hold up with ease (as if in sport) a big mountain on one hand, as an elephant king would do to a lotus (with its trunk) ?

4. Even as the god of death takes life out of the body of a living organism, he, as a babe, with half closed eyes, sucked the breast of the mighty giantess Pūtanā along with her life.

5. While a baby of only one month,[1] when he was made to sleep (and was placed) under a cart, he, while crying and kicking up his feet, turned the cart topsy-turvy by the touch of the fore-part of his foot.

6. While he was an infant of one year and was being carried away through the sky by a demon called Tṛṇāvarta, he killed the demon who was strangled to death on account of being caught by the neck by Kṛṣṇa.

7. On one occasion, when he was tied to a mortar by his mother for stealing butter, he, while crawling on his hands and feet (along with mortar) between two Arjuna trees, made them fall down uprooted.

8. While grazing calves in the forest, he, accompanied by Balarāma and surrounded by cowherd boys, tore open with his hands the bill of the enemy, a demon called Baka (who assumed the form of a heron) with the intention of killing him.

9. He killed the demon Dhenuka who, assuming the form of a calf, was entering the herd of calves with the desire of killing, and *hurling* with ease the (demon's) carcass against a Kapittha tree, caused Kapittha fruits fall down in great number.

10. Accompanied with Balarāma (and possessed of supreme power), he killed the demon in the form of a donkey along with his brethren, he made the forest of palm trees which were laden with abundant ripened fruit, free from fear.

11. Having made the mighty Balarāma kill the ferocious Pralamba, he rescued the cattle and cowherds in the Vraja from forest conflagration.

12. Having subdued the great serpent Kāliya of the

1. *Māsyasya*—some annotators interpret this as 'three months old'.

most virulent poison, he humiliated his pride and expelled him per force from the deep pool (in the Yamunā) and made the waters of the Yamunā free from poisonous pollution.

13. Oh Nanda, all of us, the inhabitants of Vraja cherish for this son of yours undissociable affection. And even he bears towards us all a deep love since his birth.

14. A child of seven and the feat of uplifting and holding up a great mountain ! How inconceivable it is ! Hence we entertain a suspicion (and a fear too) about (the real nature of) your son."

Nanda replied :

15. "Oh cowherds ! Hear from me what the sage Garga predicted to me with reference to this boy. And that will dispel all your doubts or fears.

16. 'Assuming different bodies in different *yugas*, He has manifested himself in bodies of three colours viz. white, red and yellow. Now he has adopted a dark-complexioned body.

17. As this son of yours was at first born of Vasudeva in some place (Mathurā), the knowers will call him distinctly as the son of Vasudeva, the Lord of the goddess Śrī.

18. Your son has got so many names and forms suitably designating his excellences and deeds that I do not know them all nor do these people at large.

19. A delight to cowherds and Gokula, he will bring about your weal. And you will easily cross over all difficulties and calamities with his help.

20. Oh Lord of Vraja ! Formerly when anarchy prevailed he protected righteous people who were troubled by the miscreant. Through his protection they prospered and subdued the bandits.

21. Those extremely fortunate persons who cherish affection to him shall not be defeated by enemies even as the partisans of Viṣṇu at the hands of Asuras.

22. Therefore, Oh Nanda, this boy is similar to Lord Nārāyaṇa in excellences, majesty or affluence, glory and prowess. Hence no amazement need be felt at his exploits.'[1]

1. VP.5.13 states that the Gopas directly asked Kṛṣṇa about his feat of lifting up Govardhana, but Kṛṣṇa out of modesty told them that he was one of them and not a superior being.

23. Exhorting me thus directly, the sage Garga returned home. Since then I took upon Kṛṣṇa, the remover of all afflictions, as an *aṁśa* (part manifestation) of Nārāyaṇa."

24. Hearing from Nanda's speech the report of the account given by Garga about Kṛṣṇa's glory and having witnessed and heard personally the great prowess of Kṛṣṇa of infinite energy and power, the inhabitants of Vraja became delighted. They respectfully honoured Nanda and ceased to feel any amazement about Kṛṣṇa's feats.

25. May that Lord of cows be gracious unto us—the Lord who finding that the Gokula with all the cowherds, cows, and women had resorted to him for shelter as they were afflicted by the driving showers of rain, hail-stones, thunderbolts and tempestuous winds let loose by the deity Indra, wrathful at the destruction of the sacrifice (to be offered to him), took compassion on them, and smilingly uprooted the mountain sportively as one would pluck up a mushroom and holding it up on one hand protected the Gokula and thus crushed pride of Indra.

CHAPTER TWENTYSEVEN

Indra coronates Kṛṣṇa

Śrī Śuka continued :

1. When Kṛṣṇa held up the mount Govardhana and protected Vraja (Gokula) from heavy showers, Surabhi, the wishyielding heavenly cow, came down from Go-loka[1] to Kṛṣṇa, and Indra too approached him.

nāhaṁ devo na gandharvo na yakṣo na ca dānavaḥ |
ahaṁ vo bāndhavo jāto naitaccintyam ito'nyathā || —VP. 5.13.12

1. A special heaven for cows. It is above Brahmaloka. Surabhi, daughter of Dakṣa or the divine cow, Rādhā, Kṛṣṇa's companion at Gokula and other eminent devotees of Kṛṣṇa have a place there. This divine world was granted to Surabhi by god Brahmā (MBH *Anu* 83. 29-39). It is described in glorious terms in the same chapter (*Anu* 83. 37-44).

2. Indra who felt abashed at his humiliation (by Kṛṣṇa) met him in privacy (in a solitary place) and touched his feet by his crown brilliant like the sun.

3. Having witnessed and heard the prowess of Kṛṣṇa of immeasurable lustre, energy and power, Indra with his pride of being the ruler of three worlds, subdued, spoke to him with folded palms.

Indra said :

4.* Your essential nature consists of absolutely pure *sattva* and as such it is one uniform quiescent existence full of (spiritual) knowledge untainted by *rajas* and *tamas*. This saṁsāra consisting of the stream of *guṇas* which is the product of Māyā has no place in you.

5. Oh Controller of the *Māyā* ! How could greed and other passions which characterise the ignorant and which are both the product as well as the cause of *Māyā*[1] possibly affect you (lit. have a place in you) ? It is, however, for the protec-

*(1) VR. Your abode constitutes of absolutely pure *sattva*, untinged by *rajas* and *tamas* and hence quiescent (free from love, hate etc.). It is attainable through your meditation and worship. This phenomenal existence which is the current of three *guṇas* and their products originates in your will; the causes of the assumption of a corporeal form have no place in You.

(2) VJ. I seek shelter in your Abode (which is verily yourself). In it even absolutely pure *sattva* has no place, what of *rajas* and *tamas*. It is auspicious, constituted of knowledge. The stream of three *guṇas* which is controlled by your will has no place there as it has in *jīvas* due to their attachment. *Māyā* the cause of *guṇa*-current has no place in you.

1. *tad-hetava...tat-kṛtāḥ* :

VR. : Greed and others which are the consequences after assuming the body and the causes leading to other future births.

VJ. : How can the *guṇas* which cause *saṁsāra* be imagined in the Lord.

VJ. further states that the Lord disciplines both the good and the wicked and quotes *Agni P.*

asatāṁ ca satāṁ caiva Harir evānuśāsakaḥ /
satāṁ tu śreyase saiva hyanuśāstir bhaviṣyati //

tion of righteousness and the control of the wicked (in their interest and out of grace unto them) that you exercise authority (lit. bear the sceptre for punishing the wicked).

6. You are the progenitor, preceptor and Supreme controller of the worlds. You are the undefiable Time-spirit who hold the rod of punishment.[1] It is for the welfare of the world that you act, manifesting yourself at will, your (sportive) forms and crushing down the pride of those who fancy themselves to be the masters of the world.

7.* Noticing your fearlessness and formidability in times of stress and peril, ignorant fools like me who prided themselves to be the rulers of the world, immediately shed off their arrogance, and getting rid of their egotism, betake themselves to the path of righteousness. In this way your sportive acts are meant for the punishment and discipline of the wicked as well.

8. Oh Ruler of the world! It behoves you to pardon me—your offender, who was puffed up with the pride of my affluence and was totally ignorant of your prowess. Oh Lord! May not the intellect (and mind) of a stupid fellow like me become so wicked (and perverse) again.[2]

9. This incarnation of yours in this world is for the destruction of those powerful army-leaders who are themselves a burden to the earth and whose birth has become a source of troubles to others, and for the prosperity of the followers of the feet of your Lordship. (As such, I, being your servant, deserve pardon and mercy even though I have committed a grave offence against you, Oh Adhokṣaja—Lord beyond the ken of sense-perception).

1. VB. By assuming forms of a father, preceptor and god of death you inflict punishment for the good of the people. VB. enumerates the incarnations e.g. the Fish, Tortoise etc. as representing the father, the preceptor etc. but does not completely illustrate it.

* When, at the end of our lives, we see your fearful form, we shed off our pride immediately and take to the noble path of *bhakti* consisting of remembering the name of the Lord, applying *gopīcandana*, wearing a wreath of *Tulasī* etc.—VB.

2. VT. cautions us that Indra did not pray this with a sincere and pure heart and he behaved the same way at the time of taking away the *pārijāta* tree.

10. Obeisance to you, a glorious God, who reside in the hearts of all and who are still too great-souled to be discerned;[1] you Kṛṣṇa, the son of Vasudeva and the Lord of Sātvatas.

11. Salutations to you who assume a form to comply with the wishes of your devotees; who are the embodiment of absolutely pure knowledge; who are all-pervading, the seed (the primary cause) of everything and the indwelling[2] soul of all beings.[3]

12. Oh Lord ! Flying in blind rage at the interruption of the sacrifice offered to me, I did this for destroying the Gokula, with heavy showers and stormy winds.

13. With my pride crushed and efforts to destroy Gokula frustrated, I have been favoured by you, Oh Lord. I have sought shelter in you, Oh Supreme Ruler, Preceptor, nay, my own soul itself.

Śrī Śuka said :

14. Thus extolled highly by Indra, the glorious Lord Kṛṣṇa, replied to him laughingly, in a voice deep like the rumbling of clouds, as follows :

The Lord said :

15. Oh Indra ! Highly intoxicated as you were with the pride of the majesty of Indra-hood (kingship of the celestials), it was out of grace unto you that I interrupted the sacrificial worship to be offered to you, so that you should ever remember me.

16. Out of those who have grown blind with the arrogance of supreme power and affluence and do not recognise me as the wielder of the rod of punishment, I deprive that person of his position and wealth unto whom I condescend to show grace.

1. *antaḥsthe' pyaparicchinnāya*—ŚR.

2. You are the cause and controller of everything but are not identical as a Substance—VR.

3. Here God's being embodiment of *sat* (Existence), *cit* (Consciousness) and *ānanda* (bliss), bestower of the wishes of the devotees and having a form constituted of pure knowledge are emphasized—VB.

17. You may now return, Oh Indra! May all be well with you. Carry out my commandments. All of you should continue in your respective offices (and execute your duties) diligently without being puffed up with pride or haughtiness.

18. Paying respects, along with her progeny (cows), to Kṛṣṇa, the Supreme Lord in the guise of a cowherd, the noble-minded Surabhi (the celestial cow) submitted to him:

Surabhi said:

19. Oh Kṛṣṇa! Oh great *yogin*! Oh Inner controller of the Universe! Oh Creator of the world! Oh Immortal Lord! We are now blessed with a Lord in you as the protector of the world.

20. Oh Protector of the World! You are the only Supreme Deity to us. Hence for the prosperity and success of cows, Brāhmaṇas and gods as well as of saintly persons, you be our Ruler (Indra).

21. As per directions of god Brahmā, we are going to crown (lit. give coronatory ablution to) you as our Supreme Ruler (Indra). You have incarnated for lightning the burden of the earth, Oh Inner Soul of the Universe.

Śrī Śuka said:

22-23. Praying Kṛṣṇa with these words, Surabhi, the celestial cow, consecrated him by sprinkling her milk on him, while Indra, accompanied by gods and sages and instructed by (Aditi and other) mothers of gods crowned him, bathing him with waters of the heavenly Gaṅgā brought by the celestial king-elephant Airāvata, with his trunk. He proclaimed Kṛṣṇa, the descendant of Daśārha as 'Govinda'.

Indra said:

23A*. I am the Indra of gods. You have attained the Indrahood of the cows (cattle). People will sing of you as 'Govinda' in this world.

* Yande's Bombay edition adds this verse in the footnote *Bh. P* vol. 7 p. 397.

24. Gandharvas, Vidyādharas, Siddhas and Cāraṇas headed by Tumbaru, Nārada and others arrived there. They sang of Hari's glory that washes off all the sins of the world. Overwhelmed with joy, celestial damsels danced beautifully.

25. The prominent ones among gods glorified him and showered him profusely with wonderful flowers. At that time, all the three worlds attained the Zenith of felicity while the cows drenched the earth with their milk.

26. Rivers flowed with various kinds of delicious drinks; the trees exuded sweet honey profusely. Bumper crops were harvested from unploughed lands and mountains exhibited precious stones (on their outward parts instead of concealing them in mines).

27. When Kṛṣṇa was crowned, all animals, though cruel and ferocious by nature, shed off their enmity.

28. Having thus coronated Lord Govinda (Kṛṣṇa) as the Protector of cows and *Gokulas*, Indra, with the permission of Kṛṣṇa, went to the celestial world in the company of gods.

CHAPTER TWENTYEIGHT

Nanda rescued from Varuṇa

Śrī Śuka said :

1. On the *Ekādaśī* day (the eleventh day of the lunar fortnight, so sacred to devotees of Viṣṇu) Nanda observed complete fast and worshipped Lord Viṣṇu (Janārdana). On the twelfth day, Nanda entered the waters of the Yamunā for performing ablution.

2. Nanda, being ignorant of the time reserved for the demons, entered the waters during night time. A demon (*asura*) servant of Varuṇa seized Nanda and produced him before Varuṇa.

3. Not seeing Nanda, the cowherds cried out, "Oh Kṛṣṇa, Oh Balarāma". Hearing the cry and knowing that his father had been carried off to Varuṇa, the Omnipresent Lord, who affords protection to his devotees, approached Varuṇa.

4. Seeing that Lord Kṛṣṇa (the Ruler of senses) had arrived, Varuṇa, the protector of the world, was highly enraptured and worshipping him respectfully submitted :

Varuṇa said :

5. "Today (the object of assuming) my body has been fulfilled. Though I am the Lord of ocean, which is a mine of precious stones, never before such a treasure-trove was found by me as today.

[*VR. adds* :

By the very sight of you, Oh omnipresent Lord, the (purpose of my) eyes and tongue have become fulfilled.] Those who resort to your feet achieve the end of their journey (of *saṁsāra*).

6. I salute you Oh glorious Lord, the Brahman himself and the Supreme Soul wherein the very name of the Māyā, the cause of creation of the various worlds, is not even heard of.

7. Your father has been brought here by my ignorant servant who did not know the limits and nature of his duty. It behoves your Lordship to pardon him.

8. Oh Kṛṣṇa ! The witness of everything in the Universe ! Be pleased to shower your grace on me. Oh Govinda, full of filial love ! This is your father. He may be taken back."

[*VR. adds* :

We have been fortunate to see you as your father has been brought here. We are your progeny (or subjects). It behoves you to be gracious unto us, despite our offences.]"

Śrī Śuka said :

9. Thus propitiated by Varuṇa, the glorious Lord Kṛṣṇa, the Supreme Ruler of rulers, took his father with him and returned, thereby bringing delight to his kith and kin.

10. Nanda was struck with wonder at the affluence and grandeur of the protectors of the world which he had never witnessed so far, and also the submissiveness of the Lokapālas to Kṛṣṇa—with amazement he related everything to his relatives.

11. Thinking him to be the Almighty Lord himself, the cowherds whose minds were still more overwhelmed with eagerness and wonder, thought (to themselves) : "Would that the Supreme Lord grant unto us his imperceptible state (called Brahman) and take us to his eternal region ?"

12. Knowing the wish (cherished at heart) by his own people, the all-perceiving glorious Lord, out of his own accord, and out of grace, began to think with a view to accomplishing their desires.

13. "While wandering in this world in higher and lower forms of existence due to the force of the Nescience, desire and actions (*karma*), people verily do not know their own fate."

14-15. Considering this, the highly compassionate, glorious Lord Hari manifested to the cowherds his own realm which is beyond the range of *tamas* and his essential nature which is absolutely real, not subject to modification or destruction but is pure consciousness, infinite, self-luminous, eternal and perfect stage which is realized by the sages after transcending the trinity of *guṇas* (when the bondage of *guṇas* is severed).

16. They were at first transported to *Brahmahrada*[1]—pool-like deeply absorbed state in Brahman—and were made to plunge into it and were eventually taken out of it (i.e. were awakened from that *samādhi* or trance). There they beheld the divine region of Brahman by the Grace of

1. ŚR.'s 1st explanation : *Para-Brahman* is the pool in which the cowherds were made to remain immersed in a trance and again roused from the *samādhi* by Kṛṣṇa.

Lord Kṛṣṇa through which formerly[1] Akrūra also saw the divine abode.

17. Beholding in that realm Kṛṣṇa being extolled by personified Vedas in different hymns, Nanda and others were filled with supremely ecstatic delight and were greatly amazed as well.

CHAPTER TWENTYNINE

Lord Kṛṣṇa's Rāsa[2] *with Gopīs*

Śrī Śuka said :

1. Perceiving that those (indescribably beautiful and hence proper for indulging in delightful sports[3]) nights were

ŚR.'s 2nd explanation: The pool in the Yamunā wherein the Akrūra beheld the *Brahma-loka* (vide infra chs. 39.40-55) is also called *Brahma-hrada*. Although ŚR gives this alternative explanation that they were taken to this pool in the Yamunā by Kṛṣṇa and were shown *Brahma-loka* that is not complementary to the Almighty Lord Kṛṣṇa. Hence ŚR.'s first explanation is accepted.

1. ŚR. explains : "The word *purā* is used as the incident took place before the dialogue between Śuka and Parīkṣit took place."

2. *Rāsa* or *hallīsaka* is a dance in which one male dancer plays his part with a number of female dancers moving in a circle. Jīva Goswāmī quotes in BKS.

nartakībhir anekābhir maṇḍale vicariṣṇubhiḥ /
yatraiko nṛtyati naṭas tad vai hallīsakaṁ viduḥ //

Ch. 20 in HV. 2 is titled *hallīsaka-krīḍanam* in stead of *rāsa*. This *rāsa-krīḍā* forms a part of VP 5.13, but the *rāsa-pañcādhyāyī* which begins from this chapter is poetically superb. SG. calls these "five vital breaths"-*pañca-prāṇa-tulya-pañcā'dhyāyī*. These five chapters form the corner-stone of the warm, sensuous *madhurā bhakti*. Commentators of Bengal school of Vaiṣṇavism such as Sanātana Gosvāmī, Jīva Gosvāmī have grown ecstatically lyrical and have given full play to their poetic imagination. Vallabha also is at his best while annotating these chapters. These annotators have written so exhaustively (over and above the implication of the actual wording of the text) that it cannot be compressed here, as it will be an independent book by itself to include them all.

For the significance of *Rāsa-līlā vide* Intro. pp. XLIX-LIV.

3. *tā anirvacanīyāḥ sarva-kālataḥ śreṣṭha-tarāḥ paramānanda-rasamayīs tat-krīḍāyogyā ityarthaḥ /*

beautified with full-blown jasmines of the autumnal (*śarad*) season, even the glorious Lord, in exercise of his Supreme *yogic Māyā* potency[1] made up his mind to play (*rāsa*).

2. Like a lover, returning after a long absence (would make the face of his beloved blush into crimson-red by the touch of his hand as if he) painted the face of his beloved with

1. *Yogamāyā upāśritaḥ* : in the company of Rādhā—SG. equates Rādhā with *yogamāyā* as follows:

> *yogasya sambhogasya māyo mānam paryāptir yasyāṁ sā yoga-māyā śrī Rādhā—SG*

"Rādhā in whom was the highest accomplishment of enjoyment"
—SG

VJ : exercising his own essential powers.

Various conjectures are expressed by annotators why Lord Kṛṣṇa exercised his yogic Māyā Potency. He used it (i) to hypnotize the minds of people in Vraja, (2) to devise a flute capable of attracting Gopa woman (Vaiṣṇava-Śaraṇa's *Siddhāntārthadīpikā*), (3) to supply the necessities of such a dance in a forest (SD., also Rāmanārāyaṇa's *Bhāvābhāva-vibhāvikā* etc.

KD : Kandarpa, the god of love, who subdued all gods like Hari, Hara and Brahmā was elated with pride. His pride was humiliated by Kṛṣṇa in this *rāsa krīḍā* (29.57-59). KD. raises the usual moral problem of playing with women married to others and explains the words *yogamāyām upāśritaḥ* as "without touching the wife of another man, he enjoyed himself in his natural essential bliss", and quotes *ātmārāmo pyarīramat* The Lord was the subduer of the god of love (*Manmatha mathana*) and under the pretext of eroticism, these five chapters lead to the stage of spiritual renunciation (29.63-68). Dhanapati-Sūri in *Bhāgavatagūḍhārthadīpikā* endorses ŚR's view that this *Pañcādhyāyī* leads to renunciation from *saṁsāra*.

Here two currents of interpretations become obvious in the various annotations in the Vrindavana edition, one endorsing *madhurā bhakti* and the other (including ŚR., VJ.) advocating the usual non-erotic *bhakti*.

SG : As soon as the desire to play with Gopīs arose in the mind of Kṛṣṇa, the moon (the hero) was actuated with the same desire towards the Orient (the heroine), the stars being their attendants. By his balmy beams he removed the distress not only of the Orient but also of other people of the trouble caused by the autumnal sun's heat.

VJ : *carṣaṇī*—The plant-world.

BKS : Although he loved all the Gopīs of Vraja and removed their distress, he daubed the face of Rādhā with saffron paste even though he was ever present with her (*priyayā saha dīrghaṁ sārvakālīnaṁ darśanaṁ yasya svādhīna-bhartṛkatvāt*)

saffron-paste by his extremely soothing hands, the lord of stars—the moon—arose presently making the face of the orient blush into crimson-red by his balmy beams, (simultaneously) mitigating the distress of the people caused by the scorching heat of the sun.

3.* Beholding the moon, the friend of lilies (which blossom at the touch of his rays) in full orb, reddish like fresh saffron, superbly resplendent like the countenance of goddess Lakṣmī and seeing the groves (of Vṛndāvana) lit up with its soft rays, he breathed forth such melodious music through his flute as to captivate the hearts of the beautiful-eyed Gopīs.

4. Hearing that music which increased their love for him (or rather "which enhanced their forgetfulness about their own person"[1]), the damsels of Vraja whose hearts were

Or: *dīrgha-darśana*—of large eyes. Dhanapati in *Gūḍhārtha dīpikā* : The moon was the predecessor of Kṛṣṇa. He painted the face of the Orient (which is legally Indra's direction) with his soft balmy beams and advised (by his example) Kṛṣṇa to do the same with Rādhā who was another man's wife and remain above sin like himself.

VB. : The moon is the presiding deity of the mind and he naturally emulates whatever arose in Kṛṣṇa's mind. *carṣaṇī*—Faculties. These were concentrated in highest bliss.

* VT. informs that the place where the *rāsa* play took place is known as *Rāsaulī*. SG. and VT. emphasize that all adjectives or adjectival phrases used in this verse show that the time, place etc. were quite proper and opportune for love-making.

VB. The moon, the presiding deity of the mind, was the brother of Lakṣmī and as such had facial similarity with her. And he appeared reddish like Lakṣmī's countenance at the time of her marriage awakening eroticism. He quotes a śruti text : "Women love a singer" and states that Kṛṣṇa invited all beautiful maidens of Vraja by the sweet notes of the flute.

1. *anaṅga-vardhanam*—The usual translation following annotators will be "Increasing the feeling of love of Gopīs for Kṛṣṇa is not complimentary to Gopīs or Kṛṣṇa. The word *anaṅga*—means 'bodiless'. The Gopīs were so much engrossed in Kṛṣṇa's devotion that they practically forgot themselves. This forgetfulness about their person was so much enhanced by listening to the flute-call that they left their work then and there and ran to him. Even an exponent of *madhurā bhakti* like SG., warns that the word *anaṅga* is not used in a vulgar sense : *grāmya-dharma-hetu-prākṛta-kāmāṁśābhāva-vivakṣayā.*

captivated by Kṛṣṇa, unmindful of what the other was doing, arrived hastily with their (gold) ear-rings dangling through their fast gait, at the spot where their Lover was waiting.

5. (Even hearing the name of Kṛṣṇa instantaneously makes his devotees renounce all other activities and hence the Gopīs left their work half-done as follows :)

Being extremely eager (to join the Lord), some who were milking cows, went away leaving the milking half-done; others started, placing the milk (for heating) on the oven to boil (without removing it from the oven), while others flew to Kṛṣṇa without removing the dressed dish (of wheat flour) from the hearths.

6. Some who were serving food (to the members of their family) left off without serving (any further); some others suckling their babies set them aside and fled; some others who were waiting upon their husbands suddenly stopped and departed; while others who were taking their meals, set aside their food and started.

7. Some were painting their bodies (with pigments, sandal paste), while others were cleansing their person, still others were applying collyrium to their eyes, while others were bedecking themselves with clothes and ornaments in a disorderly[1] way—All hastened to the presence of Kṛṣṇa (leaving their work half-done in the middle).

8. Though prevented and obstructed by their husbands, fathers, brothers and relatives, their hearts being lured away and robbed by Lord Kṛṣṇa, the Gopīs were hypnotised and they did not return.

VB. understands the destruction of the gross body and the creation of a new one by the word *anaṅga*—

aṅgaṁ tu nāśayatyeva ato nūtana utpannaḥ /

1. This is technically known as *vibhrama*. SG and VT quote the famous characteristic :

Vallabha-prāpti-velāyāṁ madanāveśa-sambhramāt /
Vibhramo hāra-mālyādi-bhūṣāsthāna-viparyayaḥ //

When the time of arrival of the Lover approaches and the mind is overwhelmed and confused with the passion of love, the wrong or disorderly way of wearing clothes and ornaments is the characteristic of *Vibhrama* (confusion).

9. Some being shut up in the inner apartment, could not manage to get out. They closed their eyes and meditated upon Lord Kṛṣṇa with their minds absorbed in his devotion.

10-11.* Their inauspicious *karmas* being consumed by the fire-like intense agony of unbearable separation from their dearest Lord, and with their auspicious *karmas* being exhausted by the ecstatic bliss of the embrace of the Immortal Lord enjoyed in their meditation on him, the cowherd women who became united with[1] that Supreme Soul, even as a beloved would do with her paramour,[2] and with all the *karmic* bonds of mundane existence being instantaneously sundered off, they cast off their mortal coil constituted of three *guṇas*.

*. VJ. explains that even *sañcita karma* (Potential *karma* which did not begin to give its effect) is destroyed by the knowledge and realization of God.

SG. The Gopīs lost all the bonds of hopes of participating in the *rāsa* by retaining their bodies (as pointed out in the *Bhāgavatāmṛta*). There is more intense joy in separation from a lover as it gives rise to more fervent love.

Alternately SG. explains: By their attachment (*saṅgam āsaktim*) to the Supreme Lord as their paramour, they, by their suffering intense agony at the unbearable separation from their dearest Lord, destroyed the inauspicious sufferings of three types (physical: elemental etc.) of the world and had enhanced the auspiciousness of the world (*akṣiṇamaṅgalaḥ—akṣiṇaṁ puṣṭaṁ vṛddhiṁ gatam, jagatāṁ maṅgalam*) by their bliss of the happy embrace of Lord Kṛṣṇa attained by them in their meditation, gave up the various states of mind (*Bhāva*).

SG concludes : Liberation (*mokṣa*) is attained by knowledge, attainment of the region of Vaikuṇṭha, by loving devotion of the Lord; the Lord is won over by *sakhya prema* (friendly affection); by intensity of love and always regarding him as the dearest Lord, leads to union with him at Vraja.

1 *Saṅgata*—Who properly realized Nārāyaṇa, the Supreme Lord —VJ.

2 VT. raises the point whether the Gopīs united with the Lord as a paramour (in illicit sexual relations) and ably refutes the moral charge. It is the intensity of passion of a beloved for the paramour which is implied here.

12.* They (the damsels of Vraja) knew him only as a Supreme Lover and could not recognize him as the *Brahman* himself. How did the cessation of the flow of *guṇas* (in the form of continuity of the cycle of birth and death, take place in the case of those women whose minds were under the influence of *guṇas*.

Śrī Śuka explained :

13. It has been previously[1] explained to you that as Śiśupāla, the king of Cedis, attained the *summum bonum* (absorption in the person of Lord Kṛṣṇa), there is no problem at all how the beloveds of the Supra-sensuous Lord should do so.

14. Even though the Lord is not subject to any modification or change; is beyond the ken of intellect, and infinite; transcends all the *guṇas* yet controls them; he manifests himself for the good (Final beatitude) of people.

15. Persons who always cherish love, anger, fear, affection, identity and friendliness unto Lord Hari, ultimately attain one-ness with him.[2]

*ŚR correctly explains the nature of Parīkṣit's doubt. The husbands or sons of those Gopīs were, as a matter of fact, *Brahman* himself. But as they had no knowledge or capacity to recognize that *Brahman* in them, they could not attain Liberation (*Mokṣa*). Similarly they did not look upon Kṛṣṇa as the *Brahman* but only as a Lover. Hence how could their association with him be the cause of *Mokṣa* ?

SG. endorses the question raised above by ŚR. but adds : To the Gopīs or devotees, *Mokṣa* (Liberation) is quite insignificant as they were more interested in the excellences such as superb beauty, sweetness, love etc. of the Lord. He, however, clarifies that King Parīkṣit had personally no such doubt, but it is for the knowledge of others that he asked this question.

VJ. explains in the next verse that Liberation (*Mukti*) is attained by direct realization through uninterrupted devotion, but not due to *Kāma* (desire, sexual or otherwise). If *kāma* is amalgamated with *Bhakti* (devotion), it brings in the Grace of the Lord. But this love of the Supreme Being cannot be regarded as the paramour-beloved relation. (It seems VJ. treats Vr. 11-13 as a unit and explains the *api* in v. 11 as implying this explanation.

1. Vide Supra 7. 1-30.

2. VR and VJ reject the notion of *Mokṣa* as absorption of the

16. It does not behove your Majesty to entertain such feeling of wonder in the case of the birthless glorious Lord Kṛṣṇa, the Ruler of all the masters of *yoga*, through whose Grace, the entire (mobile and immobile) creation gets emancipated (from *saṃsāra*).

17. Seeing that all the damsels of Vraja[1] have approached him, the Lord who was the foremost among the eloquents, addressed them, hypnotising them with the most fascinating or loving expressions.

The glorious Lord said[2] :

18. Hail to you, Oh highly blessed ladies ! You are welcome. What pleasant services can I render to you ?[3] Is everything well with Vraja ? Please explain to me the cause of your hasty arrival.

19.* Oh ladies with beautiful waists ! This night is of frightful appearance. It is infested with ferocious beasts (and demons). Please do return to Vraja. This place is not fit for women to stay out at night.

individual soul with the Supreme Soul. Naturally VR interprets *tanmayatāṁ yānti* as "attain similarity to Him"—*tat-prakāratāṁ tat-sādharmyaṁ yānti*

VJ. states that due to cherishing Love etc. for the Lord, the souls of such persons become saturated with those very feelings even in the final stage, but they do not become identical with Hari.

Harau kāmādikaṁ vidadhata upāsate te tan-mayatāṁ yānti kāmādyātmatāṁ āpnuvanti, na tu bhagavan-mayatām.

1. All women of Vraja young and old who should have stayed at Vraja instead of coming into the forest—SG.

2. SR : Noticing that all the damsels of Vraja have hastened there in an agitated state of mind, Kṛṣṇa expresses anxiety and asks.

SG. : Kṛṣṇa pretends indifference.

VB. : In the following ten verses Kṛṣṇa wards off the *tāmasa*, *rājasa* and *sāttvika* categories of characters in the following order : *tāmasa*-cum-*sāttvika*, *tāmasa*-cum-*rājasa* and *tāmasa*-cum-*tāmasa*.

3. By serving the cause pious ladies like you, I shall attain special merit—SG.

* SG. explains the *double entendre* thus :

This full-moon-night is delightful to people (*janān rañjayati ti rajanī*). (Due to absence of darkness) it is quiet and beautiful in appearance (*aghora-rūpa*). It is inhabited (and visited) by beautiful creatures (*a-ghora-*

20. Not seeing you in Vraja, your mothers, fathers, sons, brothers and husbands must be searching for you. Do not create fear and anxiety in your relatives.

21. You have now seen how the forest is adorned with floral beauty and illuminated with the silvery beams of the full moon, and beautified with the tender foliage of trees dancing sportively with the gentle breeze blowing from the Yamunā.

22. Oh ye virtuous ladies! Please return to Gokula without delay. Wait upon your husbands as ideal wives. Your children and calves are crying, suckle them and milk the cows.

23. Or if you have come as your heart is attached to me out of deep affection to me, it is quite natural (that you should have done so) for all creatures are affectionate to me.

24. But it is the supreme duty of women to wait upon and render service to husbands with sincerity of hearts, to look after the well-being of relatives and to nourish children.

25. The husband may be ill-natured or quarrelsome unfortunate, decrepit with age, dull-witted, sickly or penniless but women desirous of the heavenly world should not desert him if he be morally not fallen.

26. Resorting to illicit intercourse with a paramour by women of noble families, is a hindrance to the attainment of the heavenly world; it is scandalous, base, fraught with miseries and dangers, and it is abhorred everywhere.

27. Devotion to me is truly engendered by hearing about me, by looking at me, by meditating upon me and glorifying my sportive and noble deeds, and not by physical proximity. Therefore, please return home.

sattva-niṣevitā) like deer and peacocks (which awaken erotic sentiment), or it is being enjoyed by a person like me who am quiescent and pleasant by nature (*aghoraṁ sukhadaṁ śāntam svobhāvaḥ yasya tena mayā niṣevitā*) Therefore, please do not go back to Vraja (*pratiyāta Vrajaṁ na*). As you are beautiful women, you please stay on here (*ihāstheyam*).

SD : As you have by chance come here, please return. It is night time, it is not desirable that women should stay with me now.

Śrī Śuka said :

28. Having heard that unpleasant speech of Kṛṣṇa, the cowherd women grew despondent as their expectations were frustrated, and they were immersed in deep anxiety out of which they could not extricate.

29. With their faces down-cast (in disappointment), and their *Bimba*-like red lips parched with hot breaths of grief, scratching the ground with their toe-nails and washing the saffron-painting on their breasts with tears mixed with collyrium, they stood silent, heavily burdened with distress.

30. The Gopīs who discarded all their cherished desires for his sake, and who were still deeply attached to him, wiped out their eyes sore with weeping, and with their voice chocked up with anger resulting from frustration, and in faltering accents, they addressed to their dearest Kṛṣṇa who talked to them as if he bore no love to them.

Gopīs urged :

31. "It does not behove, you, Oh Omnipresent Lord, to speak so harsh to us, your devotees, who have renounced all objects of enjoyment and have resorted to the soles of your feet. Pray do not abandon us your earnest devotees but accept us as does the Deity (Viṣṇu), the most ancient person, accept his devotees desirous of Liberation from Saṁsāra.

32. Knower of the principles of righteousness as you are, it may be as you say it, that the natural duty of women is to attend upon and render service to their husbands, children and friends or well-wishers. May this be so in the case of you, Oh dear Lord, who are the origin and object of such precepts. For, you being the Soul, the most beloved relative of all embodied beings, are dearest to all.[1]

1. KD. explains that just as a coin of the highest denomination contains within it the coins of lower denomination (e.g. a rupee consists of one hundred paise. When you possess a rupee you have with you one hundred paise, similarly) when you, who are the soul of all creatures, are served well, other beings like husbands, sons etc. are automatically served properly. You form the basis of our desired objects as well as their accomplishments. This being the case, enough of your precepts of *dharma*
—29.455—471.

33. Persons who are well-versed in *dharma* direct all their love (and devotion) to you, Oh *ātman* (soul) of all. For when you, the eternally dear Lord are available, what purpose can be served by husbands, sons and other relatives who are nothing but a source of trouble. Therefore, Oh Supreme Ruler ! Be pleased to be gracious unto us, Oh Lotus-eyed God !

34. Our heart which uptil now used to be engaged happily in our homes, has been easily enticed away by you; so too our hands which were occupied with our domestic work. Our feet refuse to move away a single step from the soles of your feet. Under these circumstances, how can we return to Gokula and (even if we are carried there) what possibly can we do there ?

35. Extinguish, Oh darling, with the flood of the nectar of Your lips[1] the conflagration (of passion) set ablaze in our hearts by you, with your beguiling smiles, sideglances and melodious music, otherwise, with our bodies consumed by the fire of separation, we shall, by meditating upon you (like *yogins*), attain to the position of your feet.

36. Oh lotus-eyed Lord who are affectionate and favourable to persons (like *yogis*, sages and cowherds like us) who dwell in forests ! Since the moment we happened somewhere (at some unknown place) to touch (but once) the soles of Your feet which are the delight of goddess Lakṣmī[2] we have been blessed by You and are now not at all able to stand before any other person, Oh dear Lord !

37. Although Śrī (the goddess of affluence and beauty) —to bask in whose favourable glance (at least once), gods make strenuous efforts,—has already secured a place on your bosom, she still aspires with Tulasī (the presiding deity of the

1. SG. clarifies that the fire of passion set ablaze is so intense and enormous that it requires a *flood* and not sprinkling of the nectar-drops for extinguishing it.

(ii) *SG.'s second interpretation* : Let the nectarine flood of your lips be crystallized into words and let it enter our ears and put out the fire of passion enkindled in our hearts.

2. Or which condescend to give (occasional) opportunity of touching the goddess Lakṣmī.

basil plant) and loves to secure the dust on Your lotus-like feet which it is the privilege of Your servants to enjoy. We also have similarly sought the dust under Your feet.

38. Do be propitious unto us, You soother of all afflictions. It is with the hope of (getting the opportunity of) adoring You that we quitted our homes (like *yogis*) and have approached the soles of Your feet, Oh adornment of mankind! Grant us who are burning with intense longing, excited by Your charming smiles and enchanting glances, the privilege of serving You.

39. Looking at Your countenance covered with curling locks of hair, with cheeks shining with refulgent earrings and with lips full of ambrosia, and with sideglances accompanied by charming smiles, and beholding Your mighty arms reassuring protection (to Your devotees) as also Your bosom that excites passion in the heart of goddess Śrī, we would like to be Your menial servants (lit. your slaves).

40. Oh darling! Breathes there a woman in all the three worlds who would not swerve from the noble path approved by the elite, when (she happens to be) enchanted with the ravishing melodious (modulations of the) music of Your flute and (chances to be) be-witched by gazing of Your form, the most charming in all the (three) worlds, even a glance which sends a thrill of joy through cows, birds, trees and beasts.

41. It is certain that your honour has specially incarnated for dispelling the fear and afflictions of Gokula even as the First Divine Person—god Viṣṇu—did as the Protector of the Celestial Region. Therefore, Oh friend of the distressed, place Your lotus-hand on love-fired breasts and (aching) heads of Your maid-servants."

Śrī Śuka continued :

42. Listening to the piteous prayer of the Gopīs, the Ruler of the Masters of Yoga laughed loudly. Although he was ever-revelling in his own self, out of mercy and grace he conferred bliss on them.[1]

1. VB. emphasizes the aloofness of Lord Kṛṣṇa who Himself being immersed in His own spiritual bliss, proceeded to delight the Gopīs (with no personal involvement).

43. With their countenances blooming under the gaze of their beloved Lord, the Gopīs gathered around Lord Kṛṣṇa (Acyuta) of glorious deeds, whose charming smiles radiated the splendour of his jasmine-like teeth. And he looked like the full moon surrounded by stars.

44. Being praised in songs (by the Gopīs) and himself bursting into a loud song, Lord Kṛṣṇa, adorned with the Vaijayantī wreath and leading a bevy of hundreds of beautiful damsels, wandered over the forest, gracing it (with his hallowed and charming presence).

45. Surrounded by Gopīs, he entered the cool sandy bed of the river and sported with them, while pleasant gentle breezes cooled by (their contact with) the waves of the Yamunā and charged with the fragrance of water lilies (blooming by the moonlight) were blowing.

46. Exciting amorous sentiment in the beautiful damsels of Vraja by stretching out his arms, embracing them, touching their hands, locks of hair, thighs, waists, bosom, by indulging in jokes and by pricking them gently with his nails, by his sportive glances and smiles, Kṛṣṇa gave delight to Gopīs.

47. Recipients of such a high honour from the noble-souled Lord Kṛṣṇa, the Gopīs got puffed up with pride and (each one of them) regarded (herself) as superior to all other women on the earth (in beauty).

48. Perceiving their conceit at their fortune (of being associated with the Lord) and their pride (of being the most beautiful woman), Lord Kṛṣṇa disappeared then and there, for curing them of that pride and showering Grace on them.

CHAPTER THIRTY*

Search after Kṛṣṇa

Śrī Śuka continued :

1. When the Lord suddenly disappeared, the damsels from Vraja, like she-elephants which have missed the leader of their herd, were deeply distressed, when they could not see him.

2. With their hearts captivated by the graceful movements, loving smiles, lustful glances as also by delightful discourses, amorous dalliances and frolics of the Lord of goddess Lakṣmī (Kṛṣṇa), those young damsels mentally identified themselves with him and began to emulate his various acts and sports.

3. Identifying themselves with Lord Kṛṣṇa and exhibiting Kṛṣṇa's sportful movements and amorous dalliances, the Gopīs, the beloveds of their darling (Kṛṣṇa), whose persons had become (as it were) the duplicates (of Kṛṣṇa) in deportment, graceful smiling, glancing, speech etc., declared (to each other) "I am Kṛṣṇa."

4. Singing aloud of Kṛṣṇa's glory in a chorus, they sought for him, like lunatics, from forest to forest, enquiring of trees about that Lord (the Supreme Man) who, like ether, was pervading all the creatures from within and without.

5. "Oh Aśvattha ! Oh Plakṣa ! Oh Nyagrodha ! (varieties of Indian fig trees). Have you seen the son of Nanda who has absconded, stealing away our hearts by his captivating smiles and bewitching glances ?

6. Oh Kurabaka, Aśoka, Nāga, Punnāga and Campaka trees ! Did the younger brother of Balarāma who humbles the pride of proud women by his smiles pass this way ?

7. Oh blessed Tulasī (Basil plant) to whom the feet of Lord Govinda (Kṛṣṇa) are so dear ! Have you seen Acyuta, so very beloved of you, wearing you (in a wreath) swarming with bees.

* This is ch. No. 28 in VJ. This ch. shows that none but Lord Hari by His nature possesses all *yogic* powers. It also shows the intensity of devotion of the Gopīs—VJ.

8. (Addressing various flowering trees) Oh Mālatī! Oh Mallikā! Oh Jāti! Oh Yūthikā! Was Mādhava (Lord of Lakṣmī, Kṛṣṇa) seen by you giving you delight by the touch of his hands, while passing by the way?

9. (Invoking other trees) Oh mango tree (of the *cūta* variety)! Oh Priyāla, Panasa (Jack-fruit tree), Asana, Kovidāra, Jambū (Rose-apple tree), Arka (the sun plant), Bilva (the wood-apple tree), Bakula, Āmra (a variety of mango tree), Kadamba and Nīpa trees and other trees on the bank of the Yamunā—Born as you are for the benefit of others! May you direct the path of Kṛṣṇa to us whose minds are vacant (due to separation from Hari).

10. What austere penance have you performed, Oh Earth, inasmuch as you appear resplendent with your hair standing on their ends through the thrill of joy, at the touch of the feet of Keśava (Kṛṣṇa)! But is this ecstasy due to (the touch of) Kṛṣṇa's feet just now or is it due to your being bestridden (formerly) by Lord Trivikrama (Viṣṇu, as Vāmana who covered the universe in three steps) or is it caused by the embrace of the Lord when incarnated as a boar (even before Vāmana-incarnation)?

11. Oh female deer! Here is permeated the fragrance of our leader's—Lord Kṛṣṇa's—garland of Kunda flowers tinged with (the scent of) saffron applied to the breast of his lady-love (when he hugged her). Did Kṛṣṇa pass this way along with his beloved, giving delight to your eyes by his graceful limbs Oh friend?

12. (To trees which bent low with the load of fruits) Oh trees! Did the younger brother of Balarāma, placing one (i.e. left) hand on the shoulder of his beloved and holding a lotus in the other (i.e. right) hand (to protect his beloved by warding off) the swarms of bees attracted by (the fragrance of) Tulasī and blinded by the intoxication (caused by the fragrance) which followed him—did Kṛṣṇa (ever) come here and was pleased to accept your low bows with glances full of affection (and appreciation)?

13. (Oh friends!) Ask these creepers which have embraced the arms (i.e. branches) of their husbands, the trees, as they certainly exhibit the thrill (sprouts or flowers) of joy at

the touch of his finger-nails while plucking a flower for his beloved)."

14.* Thus the cowherd women became bewildered in their vain search of Kṛṣṇa and raved in this way. With their hearts engrossed (and as if identical) with him, they began to emulate the divine sports of the Lord.

15. One of the Gopīs who imitated Kṛṣṇa sucked the breast of another Gopī who played the part of Pūtanā. Another Gopī emulating Kṛṣṇa, the baby, began to cry and kicked another Gopī who acted the part of a cart (*Śakaṭa*).

16. Acting the role of a demon (viz. Tṛṇāvarta) carried away another Gopī who behaved like an infant Kṛṣṇa, while a third crawled on all fours dragging the feet and thereby making a jingling sound of the anklets.

17. Two Gopīs enacted[1] the role of Balarāma and Kṛṣṇa while others played the part of cowherds. Out of them one struck a third gopī that played the part of *Vatsāsura* (a demon in the form of a calf), while another (acting as Kṛṣṇa) struck another (fourth) Gopī who enacted the role of the demon Baka.

18. One imitated Kṛṣṇa shouting out at cows from a distance, while another emulated him and played upon the flute, while others applauded her saying "Well done."

19. Another Gopī who mentally identified herself with Kṛṣṇa placed her arm on some other Gopī and while following her, told the other "Lo ! I am Kṛṣṇa. Look at my graceful gait."

20. "Don't be afraid of tempestuous winds and (driving) shower. Protection against them has been provided by me". Saying so, another Gopī strained herself and held up (a part of) her garment with one hand (as if it were the mount Govardhana[2]).

21. Treading on the head of another Gopī and mounting thereon (one Gopī) ordered, "Now that I, the wielder of

*VJ.'s text does not include 10 verses from this verse (i.e. vv. 14-23 both inclusive).

1. Historical present is used in some of these verses but for consistent use of tense, past tense is used in translation.

2. Cf. VP. 5.13-28.

the rod of punishment to the wicked, have incarnated, get out from this place, Oh wicked serpent."[1]

22. (Imagining that all the Gopas are surrounded by forest conflagration and to vouchsafe their protection) another Gopī said, "Oh cowherds ! Lo that raging forest fire. Shut up your eyes quickly. I shall speedily accomplish your welfare (rescue from fire)."

23. Tied to (a Gopī who represented) a mortar with a wreath by another (Gopī who acted the part of Yaśodā).

23-A* ["Now I bind the thief who has stolen butter and broken a number of (earthen) pots"]. And the lady with beautiful eyes (who was thus bound) covered her face (with hands) and feigned fear (put up a show of trembling with fear).

24. While they were enquiring of the creepers and trees of Vṛndāvana about Kṛṣṇa, they noticed in a certain part of the forest, the foot-prints of the Supreme soul (Kṛṣṇa).

25. "It is obvious that the footprints are definitely those of the noble-souled son of Nanda, as they are identified by the marks such as a flag, a lotus, a *vajra*, a goad and a barley seed"[2]

26. While they went ahead tracing his path by following those footprints, the poor women were sorely distressed at heart to find them interspersed with those of a young woman and spoke to each other.

27. "Whose foot-prints possibly these can be? Who can be this woman who walked in his company with his hand resting on her shoulder, even as a she-elephant with the trunk of her mate on hers.

28. Certainly the Supreme Ruler, the glorious Lord Hari, has been propitiated[3] by this lady. Hence, being pleased with her, Lord Kṛṣṇa took her to a rendezvous abandoning us all.

1. Cf. VP. 5. 13. 27.

* VR's text adds this half-verse.

2. Cf. VP. 5.13-32.

3. SG. : Here the name of that Gopī is Rādhā is indicated by the text : *rādhayati ārādhayati iti śrī-Rādhā iti nāmakaraṇaṁ darśitam*'. Although the text of the Bh.P. is silent on this point, all commentators of the Bengal school of Vaiṣṇavism presumed that she was Rādhā and have written interesting extensive commentaries on these verses.

29. Oh friends ! How blessed are the particles of dust under the Lotus-feet of Lord Govinda—the particles which god Brahmā, Śiva, and goddess Lakṣmī bore on the crowns of their head, for absolving themselves of the sins (which separated them from him. Let us do so, so that by placing the dust on our heads we shall be united with Kṛṣṇa).

30. But these foot-prints of hers cause distress to our hearts inasmuch as only she (out of all Gopīs) has stolen away Kṛṣṇa (who belongs to all of us) and enjoys his kisses in a secret place.

31. But here her foot-prints are not visible. Most probably, seeing that the tender soles of his beloved's feet are pricked with sharp and pointed blades of grass, her darling Kṛṣṇa has carried her on his shoulders.

31 A.* These foot-prints have been sunk more deeply (in the soil) as he was carrying the young woman. Have a look at these foot-prints of love-lorn Kṛṣṇa (obviously) weighed down under a heavy load.

31 B. (Going a few paces ahead, they observe :) It appears that here he set her down for gathering flowers (for putting them in her braid of hair).

32. (Proceeding still further) Here flowers are gathered by the Lover for his beloved. Behold these foot-prints which are not entire as he stood on tip-toe.

33. (Most probably) on this spot the lust-ful Lord has performed the decoration of the hair of his lady-love. He must have certainly taken his seat here for fastening the flowers in her braid.

34. It is with a view to demonstrate to the world the wretched plight of the love-stricken as well as the stone-hearted nature of women that the Lord sported with the lady even though he is ever delighted in his own blissful self, self-sporting Perfect Person unattracted by the amours of women.

35-36. Showing to each other the traces of Kṛṣṇa's foot-prints in this way, the Gopīs wandered in a despondent mood (concentrating on Kṛṣṇa). And the Gopī whom Kṛṣṇa

* 31-A Not found in the Text of ŚR and VB.

(in preference to other Gopīs, and) leaving others in the forest, had brought there, now began to regard herself as the most beautiful of all women. Thought she to herself, "the beloved Lord resorts to me only, abandoning all other Gopīs who too love him."

37. Thereupon, after going to a certain place in the forest, she, being affected with pride, told Śrī Kṛṣṇa, "I am not able to walk any further. Therefore (give me a lift and) take me whither-so-ever you please".

38. When requested thus, he told his beloved, "Mount on my shoulder" and he disappeared. And the lady lamented in repentance.

39. "Oh Lord! My darling! Oh most beloved one! Where have you gone? I am your miserable slave. Be pleased with me to reveal your Presence, Oh mighty armed Lord!"

40. While the (other) cowherd women went on tracing the path of the Lord, they noticed from a distance, their distressed friend bewildered through her separation from her darling.

41. Listening to her report as to how she was received with honour by Mādhava (Kṛṣṇa) and was humiliated by him through her own wickedness, they were extremely astonished.

42. They further probed into the forest (for Kṛṣṇa) so long as the moon-light was available. Seeing that darkness was setting in, they returned from that spot.

43. With their minds absorbed in him, they talked about Kṛṣṇa only; they imitated his movements and sang about his excellences. They became oblivious of their persons, as well as of their homes.

44. Returning to the sandy bank of the Yamunā, the Gopīs contemplated on Kṛṣṇa only. Anxiously waiting for his arrival, they sang of Kṛṣṇa in a chorus.

CHAPTER THIRTYONE[1]

Gopis' song[2] *(prayer for Kṛṣṇa's return)*

Gopis sang :

1. It is due to your birth here that the goddess of affluence and beauty (Lakṣmī) abides here permanently and the Vraja outshines in progressive prosperity. But dear Lord! We, your beloveds, who have with difficulty managed to be alive for your sake (in the hope of visualizing you) are searching for you in every direction. Be pleased to reveal yourself to us, Oh darling.[3]

2. Oh Lord of amorous enjoyment! Is this not killing us *en mass* by disappointing us, your gratuitous maid-servants, with your eyes that surpass (lit. steal) the splendour of the interior of a beautiful full-blown lotus in a translucent lake in the autumn, Oh Bestower of boons?

3.* Oh mighty Lord (lit. Bull among men)! We have been so often protected by you from death through drinking of poisonous water, from Aghāsura, the demon disguised as a boa-constrictor, from heavy showers, stormy winds and the fire of lightening, from the demon[4] (Ariṣṭa) in the form of a bull) and from the son of Mayāsura (the demon Vyoma)[5]

1. Ch. 29 in VJ.'s Text. According to VJ, this chapter shows that for those who are not eligible to study the *Vedānta* and yet aspire after *Mokṣa*, singing His glory is the way of propitiating the Lord. It brings about His Grace. This chapter describes Gopis' (women, not eligible to Vedic studies) way of propitiating the Lord. The Gopīs are addressing Kṛṣṇa directly, as He is all the while present in their hearts.

VR. The request for revelation may be treated as the burden of the song.

2. This is not a chorus but one Gopī after another (or one group of Gopīs after another) is expressing herself.

3. SG. states modestly that he explains the "crumbs" of the noble-soul ŚR who has deeply drunk the essence of the nectarlike song. SG quotes a Prākrit verse (Text corrupt) which means that a beloved does not survive her separation from her lover, but as their lives are entrusted to Him, they are alive.

*In VJ.'s text, ŚR's 6th verse is 2nd and ŚR's 2nd verse as 3rd.

4. Vide infra 10.36.16

5. Vide infra 10.37.28

and from perilous situations all over. (Why are you so indifferent to us now ? We still hope to secure your protection.)

4*. Oh friend ! As a matter of fact you are not the son of a Gopī (Yaśodā) but you are the witness, dwelling in the soul (i.e. hearts) of embodied beings. When prayed by god Brahmā for the protection of the universe, you appeared in the clan of Sātvatas (or the family of devotees). (Hence, it is improper for you to show indifference to your devotees).

5. Oh Leader of Vṛṣṇis ! Place on our head your lotus-like palm that graciously assures protection to those who resort to your feet through fear of *saṁsāra*—Your palm which bestows all desires and has espoused the hand of Śrī, the goddess of prosperity, Oh Beloved.

6. Oh Mighty Hero ! The Annihilator of the afflictions of the inhabitants of Vraja ! Oh friend whose beguiling smile humiliates the pride of your people (votaries) ! Be pleased to accept us who have been your bonded servants. Show unto us—poor women—your charming lotus-like countenance.

7. Be pleased to place on our bosoms your lotus-feet which totally dissipates the sins of those who prostrate themselves (in complete submission) at them (your feet) that (affectionately) follow the herbivorous animals (cows), which are the abode of Śrī, the goddess of beauty and prosperity, and which were placed on the hoods of the serpent Kāliya—and thereby remove completely the pangs of passion from our hearts.[1]

The anachronism is obvious. SG. defends it by saying that Gopīs developed omniscience due to their devotion to Kṛṣṇa. Hence, these future acts are quoted here. VB asserts that Gopīs being omniscient, the chronological sequence is not binding on them!

*. This is verse 5th in VJ. (as per Vṛndāvan edt.).

VJ : You are verily the delight of the Gopīs, Oh friend ! For the protection of the universe you have appeared in the family of Yadus (i.e. Sātvatas). You are the Inner Controller of all embodied creatures and witness to all (or you are ever realizing your ownself). You are worshipped by god Brahmā, the creator or the preceptor of the Universe.

1. ŚR, VR & VJ unanimously explain *Kṛndhi hṛcchayam* as *Kāmaṁ chindhi*—'cut down, destroy the passionate love in our hearts'. VB's imaginative explanation is interesting. For example—The Gopīs submit : 'Our breasts are not soft but you have trodden upon the hard hood of Kāliya. We may be uncultured but your feet followed cows. The request is made by all Gopīs and hence plural *kuceṣu*.

8. Oh lotus-eyed Lord ! With your melodious words consisting of charming expressions delightful (and appealing even) to the minds of the wise and with the nectar from your lips, revive us who are charmed with you and are swooning for you—and are but your slaves doing your biddings, Oh Valiant hero !

9. (We did not die of separation from you but are alive due to listening to your nectarlike stories).

Highly meritorious (due to their liberality in the previous existence) must be those persons[1] who extol your nectarlike stories which are not only life-giving to the afflicted but are superior to the nectar (itself), inasmuch as, they are highly eulogized by the knowers of the Brahman (to whom nectar is negligible) and which remove all sins, are the most auspicious to hear, and the source of all prosperity and are spread all over the world.[2]

10. Darling Kṛṣṇa ! Your hearty laughs, your loving oglings, your sports and pastimes so auspicious to contemplate on, and your enchanting jokes and acts in privacy all go down into our heart and agitate it, Oh Deceitful Love !

11. Oh Loving Lord ! When you go out of Vraja to graze the cattle, our heart gets agitated (with the thought that) your lotus-like beautiful feet will be pricked and pained by the gravel and stubs and blades of grass, Oh Darling.

12. When at the close of the day you now and then present your countenance overhung with dark-blue curly locks of hair, soiled with the dust raised by cows (in the forest), it appears like a lotus (surrounded by black bees and over-strewn with pollen), and thereby you provoke the passion of Love in our hearts (and do not satisfy it) Oh Cheat !

13. Oh delightful Enchanter ! Pray be pleased to place on our bosom your lotus-feet, bestowers of desires[3] to prostrating supplicants, worshipped by the lotus-born deity,[4] the very ornament of the earth (enhancing its beauty by footprints),

1. They are the most liberal persons on the earth (ŚR.)

2. *or* Those who sing of your glory broad-cast all over the world are the most munificent donors.

3. VB—*Kāmaṁ dyati khaṇḍayati* cuts down, removes *kāma*

4. God Brahmā—ŚR; goddess Lakṣmī—SG.

the most blissful ones which ought to be meditated in times of distress, Oh Remover of mental anguishes.

14. Oh Hero![1] Pray, condescend to grant to us the nectar of your lips which enhances the charm of amorous enjoyment and destroys all griefs—the nectar which has been enjoyed fully by the flute kissed by you in sounding, making people forget all other passions and attachments.

15. During day-time, while your Lordship is away wandering in the woods, and we are not able to see you, even a quarter of a moment is felt by us as an age. (But when you return in the evening we feel that) god Brahmā must be dull-witted in creating our eye-lashes which, while winking, deprive us even for a moment of the joy of looking at you, when we are eagerly gazing at your beautiful countenance, graced with curly locks of hair.

16. Oh crafty Deceiver! Who would abandon poor women like us who, being enchanted by the loud melodious music of a musical expert like you and who know that we are sure to come to you—us who have completely set at nought our husbands, children, followers, brothers and relatives and knowing your way, have sought your presence, Oh Acyuta!

17. Remembering your secret amorous promises and beholding your smiling countenance provoking the passion of love in our heart, your loving glances, your broad chest, the abode of Śrī (goddess of affluence and beauty), our hearts get excited with excessive longing every now and then, and becomes infatuated.

18. Darling Kṛṣṇa! Your incarnation is for dispelling the sins and miseries of the inhabitants of Vraja (viz. Gopas) and of the forests viz. sages, as well as for conferring the highest auspiciousness on the universe. Be pleased, therefore, to impart to us who entertain a strong yearning for you in our hearts, something of that balm (of your company) which will relieve all the mental anguish of your people (votaries).

19*. As your Lordship constitutes our very life, our

1. Hero in erotics—SG.
Hero in munificent gifts like *puruṣārthas*—VB.

*Deleted in VJ's text.

mind reels to think whether your lotus-feet on which you wander in the forest, are not pained while walking on the gravels etc., for (on our part) we, being afraid (of injuring your tender feet) place them gently on our hard breasts, Oh tender Darling !

CHAPTER THIRTY-TWO

Kṛṣṇa comforts Gopīs

Śrī Śuka said :

1. In this way (as described in the previous chapter), the Gopīs, yearning strongly to see Lord Kṛṣṇa went singing loudly, wailing loudly and at times raving incoherently, they wept loudly and piteously, Oh king.[1]

2. And (surprisingly enough) in their very midst appeared Lord Kṛṣṇa, the descendant of king Śūra, with his lotus-face beaming with smile, wearing a yellow garment, adorned with a wreath of flowers, capable of fascinating the god of Love (cupid) himself (with his charm).

3. Seeing their belovedmost Darling arrived,[2] all those women, though emaciated and weak at once sprang to their feet, with their eyes wide open with rapturous delight, even as the limbs of the body do on the return of the vital principle (*Prāṇa*).

3-A. *VR.'s Text* :

The more they drank the nectarine beauty of his countenance with the drinking vessels (in the form) of their eyes, the more unsatiated they grew (lit. they were not satiated at all), just as men of spiritual wisdom feel about his feet.

1. The beginning of the chapter shows that just as the Lord manifested Himself to the Gopis, He reveals himself to the possessors of spiritual means of getting divine wisdom—VJ.

2. SG. quotes VP. *tato dadṛśur āyāntaṁ vikāsi-mukha-paṅkajaḥ* and states that Kṛṣṇa revealed himself at a distance and then approached the Gopis. The above quotation is not traceable in the Gītā Press etc. of VP.

4. One of the Gopīs, in her ecstasy, clasped the lotus-hand of Kṛṣṇa with her palms, while another placed on her shoulder his arm smeared with sandal-paste.

5. Another slim and emaciated Gopī received in the hollow of her palms, the betel chewed by him, while another Gopī, feverish with love, placed his lotus-feet on her bosom.

6. Being beside herself with the agitation of unrequieted love, another Gopī knitted her eyebrows and continued to bite her lip and was looking at him as if she was subjecting him to a volley of side-glances.

7. Another Gopī gazed at his lotus-face with fixed unwinking eyes. Although she drank (his nectar-like face) to the full, she did not feel satiated like saintly persons who are never satiated serving his feet.

8. A certain other Gopī got him established in her heart through the pupils of her eyes, and closed the eyes (so as to prevent his exit). Then she (mentally) embraced him, and through that thrill, had all her hair standing on their ends like a *yogin* immersed in spiritual bliss.

9. All of them became satisfied and happy by the high festival of having the look of Keśava (Kṛṣṇa) and had their fever born of separation subsided, just as people do when they attain God-head or meet a person who has realized the Brahman or who reach Prājña in deep sleep.

10. Surrounded by the ladies who had shed off their sorrow (due to the separation from the Lord), the glorious immortal Lord Kṛṣṇa shone more brilliantly like the Puruṣa (Supreme Spirit) endowed with his spiritual powers[1].

11-12. The Supreme Lord repaired with them to the sandy bed of the Yamunā where swarm of blackbees were attracted by the gentle breeze charged with the fragrance of fully blossomed jasmine and *Mandāras*. The darkness of the night where-of was dispelled by flood of rays of the autumnal

1. These are variously enumerated by different commentators :

(1) ŚR—(a) *Sattva, rajas* and *tamas*

(b) spiritual knowledge and (physical and mental) strength essential for meditation.

(2) VR. : 24 *tattvas* forming the part of the astral body of a *jīva*.

(3) VJ. : various forms of Lakṣmī attending upon the Lord.

moon, rendering the scene all the more delightful; the soft sands whereof were (evenly) spread by the handlike ripples of the Yamunā[1]. (In this way, the Lord surrounded by the Gopīs appeared still more beautiful).

13. With their mental anguish completely dissipated by the extreme joy of seeing him, the Gopīs accomplished their desires to their heart's content, just as *Śrutis* (*Vedas* which pertain to the *karmakāṇḍa* or sacrificial and other rituals, are unsatisfied due to their inability to see the Lord but) have their purpose achieved (in the portion containing *jñāna-kāṇḍa* or spiritual knowledge leading to and resulting) in God-realization. With their upper garments coloured with the spots of saffron applied to their breasts, they prepared a seat for Kṛṣṇa, who was dearer to them than their self (or their indwelling soul).

14. The glorious Almighty Lord who is enthroned in the hearts of the masters of *yoga* took his seat on it. Assuming a personality which was the only receptacle of all the splendour and beauty in the three worlds[2], he shone splendidly in the congregation of Gopīs[3].

15. Offering warm respectful welcome to him who enkindled the passion of love, the Gopīs, with their eyebrows the sportfulness of which was enhanced by their smiles and playful oglings, and praising him while pressing his hands and feet placed on their laps, spoke to him slightly feigning anger.

Gopīs said :

16. Some show favour (in response) to those who resort to them, while others behave to the contrary (and favour those

1. VJ. reads : *Kṛṣṇehdyasta* etc. and interprets :

The sands whereof were scattered and made uneven by the sports of Kṛṣṇa—

(*Śrī Kṛṣṇa-mūrtikrīḍayā āyastāni ca taralāni cāta evācitāni itastato vikīrṇāni* /)

2. VJ. : Worthy of being enjoyed only by the goddess Lakṣmī who is adored and served by the three worlds.

VB : He assumed the best of the form suitable to the time, place etc. and manifested whatever was the worthiest.

3. SG. suggests that Kṛṣṇa assumed different forms each per Gopī and occupied the seat prepared by her and made her feel that it is her special privilege to receive Kṛṣṇa that way.

who do not resort to them), while (still) others do neither (and confer grace of favour on none). Oh Lord ! Be pleased to explain to us clearly about this.

The Lord replied :

17. Oh friends ! Those who love or resort to each other (the reciprocity of their love is with a selfish motive), strive to achieve purely their own purpose. Neither friendliness nor righteousness plays any part therein. This love is just for self-interest and nothing else[1].

18. Those who love even those who do not resort to them (or love them) in return, are really compassionate like parents. Here lies pure, blemishless righteousness as well as good will, Oh charming damsels (with beautiful waists).

19. There are some who do not love those who resort to them. How can they be expected to favour them who do not resort to them ? These belong to the following categories :

(1) They are sages immersed in the spiritual delight of *ātman* (the soul) (and are unconscious of the external world).

(2) They have accomplished the objects of their desires (and as such have no interest or longing for enjoyment and hence indifferent, though conscious of the external world).

(3) They are ungrateful (and incapable of appreciating obligations done to them).

(4) They are bent on hating their elderly people (father or teacher).

20. (When Kṛṣṇa dodged the implied accusation of Gopīs against him in explaining the above categories, the Gopīs smiled. Kṛṣṇa noticed it and explained).

As far as I am concerned, Oh friends (I do not belong to any of these categories because I am an extremely compassionate and the best friend of all), I do not respond immediately to their love and devotion (I do not reveal myself to them), so that they would ever continue to meditate upon me, just as a penniless man who has lost the money he

1. KD refuses to regard this as real worship or love : It is naked self-interest 32.17.172-80.

has earned, is absorbed in thinking about his lost treasure and would not be aware of anything else.

20.A *VJ's Text* adds :

In the same way both (the categories described above) continue to get from me the fruit or return in great or small measure (according to the intensity of their devotion to me) even as one obtains fruit from the *kalpa taru* (wishyielding tree).

21*. Oh fair damsels! In this way, it is with a view of seeing the intensity and constancy of your devotion to me that I remained with you invisible (and stayed with you listening to your expression of love about me) as you have, for my sake, renounced the conventional worldly sense of decorum, the injunction of the Vedas (for righteousness or otherwise) and your kith and kin. Oh beloved ones! It does not behove you to blame me, your Darling.

22. Even if the long life of celestials[1] be granted, it is not possible for me to repay adequately your devoted service to me with whom your relations are pure and faultless. And you have resorted to me and adored me cutting asunder the unbreakable ties that fetter you to your home. (The only way is:) May your righteousness be rewarded by your good deeds only.

*VJ : The Lord explains how to serve him on the plea of Praising the service rendered by Gopis :

Just as a penniless fellow who lost his wealth he could earn, is too much submerged in deep sorrow to be cognisant of anything else, you have dedicated to Me everything—worldly way of life, injunctions of the Vedas and your relatives; your devotional service shall not be fruitless. By nature I am beyond the ken of senses and hence was invisible to you—But it does not behove you to find fault with Me who am your darling.

1. The life of a god is 36000 human years but KD interprets *vibudhāyus* as the life-span of god Brahmā which is one *parārdha* years i.e. 100,000,000,000,000,000 years—32.22.260.

CHAPTER THIRTY-THREE

Description of Rāsa Krīḍā

Śrī Śuka said :

1. Listening to these soft fascinating words of the Lord, the Gopīs forgot the agony caused by separation from him and their bliss was enhanced by personal contact with him, Oh dear king.

2. There (on the sandy bank of the Yamunā) Lord Govinda inaugurated his *Rāsa Krīḍā*[1] (the play called *Rāsa*) with those jewel-like damsels (of superb beauty) who were so devoted and affectionate to him and who formed a circle with their arms interlocked (with those of Kṛṣṇa)[2]

3. Then commenced formally the festive dance called *rāsa*, beautified splendidly by the (moving) circle of Gopīs with Kṛṣṇa, the great Master of Yoga of inconceivable mystic powers (assumed as many forms as there were Gopīs and) entered in between every two Gopīs and with his arm placed around the neck of the adjacent Gopī, made each of the damsels consider to be nearest to him (and being embraced by him).

1. SG. quotes from Bharata's *Nāṭya- śāstra* : The dance in which a number of female dancers dance with their hands interlocked in the company of men who place their arms round the neck of the women-partners :

naṭair gṛhīta-kaṇṭhīnām anyānyāttakara-śriyām/
nartakīnām bhaved rāso maṇḍalībhūya nartatām//

2. SG. quotes *Bilva-maṅgala* which describes how Kṛṣṇa accompanied each Gopi as her dance-mate : "A circle of dancers was formed with Kṛṣṇa between two dancing ladies and a lady between two Kṛṣṇas. In the middle of such a circle of dancers Kṛṣṇa stood and played upon His flute.

aṅganām aṅganām antarā Mādhavo /
Mādhavaṁ Mādhavaṁ cā'ntareṇāṅganā //
ittham ākalpite maṇḍale madhyagaḥ /
saṁjagau veṇunā Devakī-nandanaḥ //

This is possible only to *Bhagavān* Kṛṣṇa with His *yogamāyā*. Hence the significance of the words *bhagavān* and *yogamāyām upāśritaḥ* in *Supra* 10.29.1

Vide infra V. 20 which states that Kṛṣṇa assumed as many forms as there were the cowherd-women.

Kṛtvā tāvantam ātmānaṁ yāvatīr gopa-yoṣitaḥ /

4. (As soon as Lord Kṛṣṇa thought of beginning the *rāsakrīḍā*) there thronged in the sky hundreds of heavenly cars of celestials along with their wives whose minds were carried away with curiosity (of seeing the *rāsa* dance).

5. At that time, kettle-drums were sounded and showers of flowers fell. The heads of Gandharvas accompanied by their consorts sang the noble and hallowing glory of the Lord.

6. There arose in the ring of *rāsa* (dancers), the (orchestral) din of the jingling bangles and anklets and the tinkling of the small bells of girdles of the ladies accompanied by their darling Lord.

7. Exceedingly beautiful shone the glorious Lord, the son of Devakī, in the midst of those pairs of damsels like unto a highly precious emerald[1] embedded in between a pair of gold beads.

8. With their measured treads of feet and (artistic) movements of their hands (in dancing), with their smiles and (gracefully) amorous dance of eyebrows, with bending waists and shaking breasts, with the fluttering of their garments, with ear-rings rocking on their cheeks, with drops of perspiration trikling down their face and with their braids of hair and girdles getting loosened (in the course of dancing), the dancing-mates of Kṛṣṇa glorified the Lord in songs and appeared beautiful like flashes of lightening illuminating a circle of clouds (as Kṛṣṇa assumed as many forms as the Gopīs in that circular movement of *rāsa*).

9*. In the course of dancing, the Gopīs, enamoured of loving devotion to Kṛṣṇa and thrilled with delight at the touch of Kṛṣṇa, sang at the pitch of their voices sweetened with different musical modes (*rāgas*) filling thus the whole universe with the music (of their song).

10. A certain Gopī sang in chorus with Kṛṣṇa in a higher pitch. Even though her notes of the gamut (*svara-jāti*) did not harmonize with that of Kṛṣṇa, she was applauded by him

1. SG. explains that although Kṛṣṇa was of sapphire-blue complexion, the brilliant-golden complexion of the Gopīs, He embraced, made Him appear like emerald.

*Commentators quote names of Gopīs. These names of the Gopīs involved in the dance are imaginary-unsupported by the text of the Bh.P.

with the words "Well-done", as he was pleased with her performance. When she proceeded to reach her highest pitch to the measured beat (*tāla*) well-known as *Dhruva* (*pada*), Kṛṣṇa showed great regard for her.

11. Thoroughly exhausted by (participation in) the *rāsa* dance and with her bangles slipping (from her wrists) and jasmine flowers dropping (from her braid), another Gopī caught hold by her arm, the shoulder of Kṛṣṇa who was standing by (i.e. flung her arms round him).

12. (It is reported that) another Gopī smelt how Kṛṣṇa's arm placed on her shoulder, was fragrant like a lily and was anointed with sandal paste, (and losing herself) she (actually) kissed it and was thrilled with it (with her hair standing on their ends).

13. To another Gopī who rested on Kṛṣṇa's cheek her own which was glowing with the brilliance of her own earrings rocking in the course of dancing Kṛṣṇa gave his half-chewed betel.

14. Another Gopi, standing by his side was fatigued with singing and dancing, making all the while a jingling sound of her anklets and girdle (while dancing) pressed to her bosom his blissful lotus-hand.

15. Obtaining Acyuta (the immortal God—Kṛṣṇa), the sole Darling of the goddess Śrī (Lakṣmī) as their beloved, the cowherd women with his arms round their neck extolled him in song and played (danced) with him.

16. The Gopa women with the beauty of their face enhanced by lotuses adorning their ears, cheeks beautified with their curly locks of hair, and drops of perspiration, with wreaths of flowers dropping from their (braids of) hair, danced with the glorious Lord accompanied with the musical instruments in the form of jingling bangles and anklets, at the ring of the *rāsa* dance where humming blackbees acted as songsters.

17*. Kṛṣṇa, the Lord of goddess Lakṣmī, sported with the beauties of Vraja by embracing them, pressing their palms, winsome oglings with free amorous gestures and hearty (loud)

* VJ. God is absolutely independent and above all prescriptions and prohibitions and can violate all canons of conduct !

laughter, even as a child would play with its own reflection (in the mirror).

18. Their senses were so overwhelmed with ecstatic joy at the contact with that Divine Personality that the women of Vraja whose wreaths and ornaments were loosened and falling, were too much beside themselves (with joy) to re-adjust their dishevelled locks of hair, their garments and brassiers, Oh Prominent Kuru!

19. While witnessing Kṛṣṇa's love sports, the celestial damsels were smitten with love and fainted. And even the Moon-god along with his retinue (of stars or *nakṣatras*) was too much amazed (to proceed with his movements and halted).

20. Though a reveller in his own Supreme bliss, the Lord assumed as many forms as there were Gopīs and delightfully disported[1] with each of them.

21. The merciful Lord wiped out affectionately, the sweat off their faces with his most blissful comforting hand as they were fatigued with overdancing with him, Oh dear king.

22. Adoring the Supreme Lord with the splendour of their cheeks enhanced by the brilliant gold ear-rings and curly locks of hair and with glances accompanied with nectar-like smiles, the Gopīs who (despite their fatigue in the *rāsa* dance) became enraptured by the touch of his finger-nails, burst out in singing his hallowing deeds.[2]

23. Like unto a king-elephant breaking down the dams and entering water in the company of she-elephants, the exhausted[3] Lord Kṛṣṇa who had transgressed the restraints (laid down by the Vedas and public decorum) became desirous of getting over the fatigue, and in the company of the Gopīs, entered the waters of the Yamunā (where he was) closely

1. VJ. reads 'rarāma'. The *Parasmaipada* form indicates the aloofness of the Lord in that *rāsa*

rarāmeti Vyatyayena para-dārābhimarśanena doṣo nāsti iti vakṣyamāṇam artham ihaiva sūcayati

2. These songs suggested the conclusion of the *rāsa* (Ve.)

3. SG. imagines that this adj. is used to indicate that the beauty of Kṛṣṇa's countenance was enhanced by droplets of swea appearing on it through fatigue.

followed by black-bees (humming melodiously) like the chiefs of celestial songsters, the Gandharvas, (as they were) allured by his garland (of *Kunda* flowers) squeezed by contact with the persons of the Gopīs (while embracing etc.) and was coloured with saffron applied by them to their breasts.

24. Oh dear Parīkṣit ! The Lord, who ever revels in his own blissful state, sported here like a king-elephant as he was profusely sprinkled over with water on all sides by the youthful damsels who were casting amorous glances at him, and were heartily laughing, while he was being praised by gods who were showering on him flowers from their aerial cars.

25. Like unto a young elephant exuding temporal fluid sauntering in the company of female elephants, the Lord, surrounded by a swarm of black-bees and a bevy of young ladies, roved in a grove on the bank of the Yamunā, where blew on all sides a gentle breeze bearing the fragrance of acquatic flowers as well as of the flowers on lands.

26. In this way, the Lord of accomplished desires to whom the bevy of young damsels were deeply attached and devoted, enjoyed all those nights (without losing a single minute without enjoyment—the night[1] illuminated by the rays of the moon and which formed the basis for all charming poetical works specially appropriate for autumnal season—but he controlled all his energy within himself (such was his control over Eros.)

King Parīkṣit said :

27. The Almighty Lord of the Universe along with his aṁśa-part (Balarāma) incarnated here to establish Dharma (righteous way of life) and the suppression of the vile way of life.

28. He is the Promulgator of the moral order. He is the ideal model of ethical standard and the Protector thereof. How did he act in direct contravention of it, in seducing sensually the wives of others ?

1. The plural number indicates that throughout His *Kiśora* period (from 11 to 15 years of age), Kṛṣṇa enjoyed the *rāsa*-dance every night-SG. This is a better interpretation than imagining that Kṛṣṇa extended that particular night for many days while Gopīs felt it to be a single night.

29. Oh holy sage of sacred vows ! Be pleased to resolve our doubt as to with what intention the Lord of Yadus who is said to have accomplished all his desires, perpetrated such censurable deed.

Śrī Śuka explained :

30. Transgression of the canons of righteousness and over-adventurism are found to have been committed by mighty rulers. But that does not amount to a blemish for a noble heroic soul, as in the case of omnivorous fire (which does not get polluted by consuming impure things).

31. An incapable weakling (dependent on his body) should never commit this (transgression) even mentally. A person imitating him foolishly meets destruction like a person other than Rudra (but imitating Rudra) does by swallowing the (*Halāhala*) poison churned out of the sea.

32. The words of the possessors of divine wisdom and might are always correct and authoritative, but not necessarily, so their acts (which may be emulated on certain occasions only). Hence an intelligent person should practice such course (of conduct) which is consistent with their own precepts.[1]

33. Such authoritative persons who are devoid of ego (*ahaṁkāra*) have no selfish ends to serve by virtuous behaviour or have no stakes to lose by acting to the contrary.

34. Need it be told that the Lord, the controller of all beings like the sub-human creation (birds, beasts etc.), human beings and celestials who, being fit to be governed by him (and are subject to his control), is not concerned with piety or impiety of the acts (the moral code of conduct of ordinary beings is not applicable to the Almighty).

35. The sages who are completely satisfied (and have become desireless) by serving the pollen-like dust of his

1. VR. : Therefore, an intelligent person should follow those acts of God which are consistent with His precepts. *OR* A prudent man should not emulate the acts of God which are against His precepts.

VJ. : An intelligent person should not practice what is said or regarded as contrary to Vedic injuctions.

lotus-feet and who have absolutely freed themselves by shaking off all the bondage of *karmas* by virtue of their Yogic Powers, behave according to their free will and are not bound (by their acts). How could there be any bondage to the glorious Lord who has assumed a personality at his own free will ?

36. He who dwells not only in these Gopīs but also in their husbands—nay in all embodied beings (as their Inner Controller), and who presides over all these, has as a sport, assumed the form of Kṛṣṇa in this world.

37. It is for showering Grace on all creatures that the Lord has put on a human form and participated in those sportful activities (like the *rāsa krīḍā*). By listening to these, a person may become attached to him exclusively (as a devotee).

38. The male inhabitants of Vraja were so much spell-bound by the deluding potency of the Lord that they always considered their wives ever present by their sides and they never felt any jealousy against Kṛṣṇa.

39. At the approach of the *Brāhma muhūrta* (i. e. dawn) the Gopīs, the beloveds of the glorious Lord, returned reluctantly to their homes with the permission[1] of the Lord.

40. He who reverentially listens to and rehearses the account of the amorous sport of Viṣṇu (i. e. his incarnation Kṛṣṇa) with the damsels of Vraja, conceives intense devotion to the Almightly Lord, attains spiritual wisdom and self-control, and soon overcomes the maladies of the heart (like lust and other passions).

1. SG.—*anu-moditāḥ*—who were all the while—(every minute of that night)—filled with joy by Kṛṣṇa (hence their reluctance to return).

CHAPTER THIRTYFOUR

Sudarśana emancipated and slaying of Śaṅkhacūḍa

Śrī Śuka said :

1. On one occasion, the cowherds had their curiosity aroused in participating in a pilgrimage to god (Śiva) and they set out in carts drawn by bullocks to a place known as Ambikāvana (the grove of goddess Pārvatī).

2. Having performed ablutions in the river Sarasvatī, they devoutly worshipped the god Śiva as well as the goddess Pārvatī with various articles of worship.

3. Most reverentially, they donated cows, gold, garments, honey, sweet-meats to Brāhmaṇas as gifts, praying "May god Śiva be propitious unto us."

4. The highly fortunate Nanda, Sunandaka and others observed a vow of subsisting on the waters of the river (the whole day) and passed that night on the bank of the Sarasvatī.

5. A certain big boa-constricter of that forest, being pinched with extreme hunger, came there by chance and began to swallow up Nanda who was asleep.

6. While being swallowed by the serpent, Nanda screamed out "Oh Kṛṣṇa, Kṛṣṇa, this big serpent is devouring me, Oh child! please save me who have approached you for rescue."

7. Hearing his shriek, cowherds suddenly awoke. Beholding Nanda swallowed by the serpent, they got bewildered and struck the serpent with fire-brands.

8. Though it was scorched by burning fuel, the serpent did not let go Nanda. At that time Kṛṣṇa, the Lord of Sātvatas, approached the reptile and touched it with his foot.

9. With all his sins absolved by the touch of the glorious Lord of Lakṣmī, he cast off his serpentine body and assumed a form that was worshipped by Vidyādharas.

10. The Lord (of senses), Kṛṣṇa, asked the man with resplendent personality decorated with a wreath of gold, as he reverentially bowed down to him.

11. "Who are you of miraculous form resplendent with supreme splendour? How is it that you lost your self-control and were forced into this disgustful form of life?"

The serpent (*now a Vidyādhara*) *answered* :

12. "I am a certain (famous) Vidyādhara known as Sudarśana. Endowed with divine splendour and excellent beauty, I ranged in my aerial car in all directions.

13. Puffed with pride of my beautiful form, I jeered at the ugly forms of the sages Aṅgiras. For my sin of deriding them, I was brought down to this species by them.

14. I now find that this curse was pronounced upon me to show me grace, by those merciful sages, inasmuch as I am absolved of all sins by being touched with foot by the preceptor of the world.

15. Oh destroyer of sins ! I am relieved of the curse by the touch of Your foot. You are the dispeller of the fears of beings who resort to you through fear of *saṁsāra*. Kindly give me permission to take leave of You.

16. Oh great *yogin* ! Oh supreme Person ! I approach you most humbly, Oh Protector of the righteous people ! Oh resplendent God ! Oh Supreme Ruler of the rulers of worlds ! Be pleased to grant me permission (to return to my region). Oh Acyuta ! Instantaneously at your very sight, I am released from the curse of the Brāhmaṇa.

17. A person who utters your name at once purifies all the listeners (of the Name) as well as himself. What more need be said that a person who is touched by your foot gets absolved of all his sins instantaneously."

18. Taking leave of Kṛṣṇa (the descendant of Daśārha) with these words, circumambulating him and playing obeisance to him, Sudarśana went to heaven and Nanda was thus rescued from that precarious situation.

19. Having seen the special personal glory of Kṛṣṇa, the inhabitants of Vraja with astonished minds, completed their religious observance of Śivarātri. They returned to Vraja reverentially discussing his glorious exploits.

20. On another occasion, Govinda (Kṛṣṇa) and Balarāma of wonderful prowess, sauntered in the forest at night in the company of damsels of Vraja.

21. Being melodiously extolled by damsels, who were deeply attached to them, with their persons well adorned and

beautifully painted with sandal-paste and pigments, they wore beautiful wreaths and were dressed in fine garments.

22. They hailed the advent of the night, as the moon and the stars were rising and appeared in view and as a gentle breeze was blowing over the bed of lilies to which were attracted swarms of bees intoxicated with the fragrance of jasmine flowers.

·23. Going simultaneously through the whole scale of musical notes with modulations of their voices, both of them presented vocal music which was auspicious and delightful to the mind and ears of all beings in the world.

24. Hearing that ravishing music, the cowherd women fell in a trance and were not aware of their garments slipping away from their persons, loosening of their braids and dropping of wreaths from them, Oh Protector of the people !

25. While they both were thus sporting as they pleased and singing at will like intoxicated persons, a servant of Kubera known as Śaṅkha-cūḍa approached them.

26. Before their very eyes (and in defiance of them), he dauntlessly drove the screaming young women who were under their protection, towards the north, Oh king !

27. Beholding their women crying out (for their succour), "Oh Kṛṣṇa ! Oh Balarāma" like cows when seized by a robber, the two brothers rushed in pursuit.

28. Shouting out the promise of protection, "Don't be afraid" the two brothers armed themselves with a Śāla tree and rushing hastily, they overtook the wretch of a *Guhyaka* (Yakṣa)

29. Terrified to see them both close on his heels like the time-spirit and god of death *incarnate*, the foolish fellow let the women go and took to his heels with the intention of saving his own life.

30. In order to deprive the Yakṣa of the jewel on his head, Kṛṣṇa pursued him wherever he ran, while Balarāma stayed on protecting the women.

31. Within a short distance, the Lord confronted him and with a blow of his fist sundered off his head along with the jewel.

32. Killing Śaṅkhacūḍa in this way and taking from him the brilliant gem, Kṛṣṇa gave it, out of affection, to his elder brother, before the very eyes of the damsels.

CHAPTER THIRTYFIVE

Gopīs' Song (in pairs of verses)

Śrī Śuka said :

1. When Kṛṣṇa departed to the forest (to tend the cattle), Gopīs whose hearts followed him, spent their days in great misery, loudly singing of his sportful pastimes.

The Gopīs said:

2-3. Oh Gopīs when Mukunda with his left cheek inclined to the joint of his left arm and with dancing eyebrows, applies the flute to his lower lip and begins to play on it with his tender fingers placed on its holes, the Sidddha damsels passing through their aerial cars along with their husbands, feel disconcerted with amazement at the melodious music, and feeling bashful to find that their hearts have been hit by the shafts of love, become infatuated and are not aware of the loosening of their garments.

4-5. Oh delicate ladies ! How wonderful is the phenomenon ! Listen. When this child of Nanda, with his smiles beaming like a wreath of sparkling pearls[1] and with the lightening-like (fickle yet lustrous) goddess of wealth (Lakṣmī) permanently abiding on his chest (as *Śrī-Vatsa*, plays melodiously) on his flute to bring solace and delight to the afflicted people, bulls in Vraja, deer and kine in their herds, from far afar, have their hearts captivated with the enchanting music of the flute and stand (listening to the music) with their

1. OR (1) smiles reflecting from the garland of pearls on His chest as His countenance is inclined towards it. (2) Whose laugh shines like a wreath of pearls on His chest (3) The lustre of which was spotlessly white like the laugh of pearls (*hārāṇāṁ hāsa iva viśadā sphūrtir yasya*)—ŚR.
VJ. reads.—*hāra-bhāsaḥ*—Looks brilliant with the pearl-garland.

ears erect and (holding unswallowed) half-chewed morsels of grass between their teeth (and look) as if they are asleep or drawn in picture.

6-7. (The melodious music of Kṛṣṇa's flute hypnotises even the non-sentient creation.)

When Lord Kṛṣṇa dresses himself like a wrestler with a tuft of peacock-feathers and tender leaves and anointed with mineral paints, and sometimes accompanied by Balarāma and cowherds calls the cows (through the melodious notes of his flute), (even the non-sentient) rivers stop flowing as if they are strongly longing to receive the dust of his louts-feet borne by the breeze. But they possess poor merits like us, inasmuch as, they (instead of getting the much-yarned-for dust) keep waving their arms in the form of waves and have the flow of water stopped (as we have our eyes bedimmed with tears).

8-9. When Kṛṣṇa,[1] who like the Ancient-most Person Nārāyaṇa, possesses unfading eternal splendour[2], (and whose heroic exploits were celebrated by his followers, (the cowherds[3]), ranges[4] in the forest, calls the cows which are grazing on the slopes of the mount Govardhana by uttering their names (musically) through his flute, the creepers and trees in the forest[5] as if mainfest the All-pervading Lord Viṣṇu abiding in them, by exhibiting their floral richness and wealth of fruit, laden wherewith the boughs of the trees are bowing down low and with their bodies thrilled with intense love spray forth a shower of honey.

1. This describes the effect of Kṛṣṇa's flute on the immovable or stationary creation like trees—ŚR., VR.

VJ. : Just as the most Ancient *puruṣa* Nārāyaṇa who lies on the cosmic waters, is being praised by sages like Sanaka with the Vedic *mantras* which are profusely evolved out of the mouth of Vāyu etc.

2. Or : the ever-lasting abode of Lakṣmī, the goddess of affluence, splendour and beauty.

3. Or : Gods and sages (in the case of viṣṇu)

4. VJ : The adj. *vanacara* includes all the incarnations including the Fish.

5. VJ. : applies this to the sages and *Yogīs* in the forest who perform austere penance in the forest; who realizing Lord Viṣṇu within their hearts, bow to Him with their hands and are imbued with eternal bliss.

10-11.* Lo! Look here when Kṛṣṇa with a charming *Tilaka* (a sacred mark on his forehead) heartily appreciates the enchanting high pitched humming-song of the swarms of black-bees intoxicated with the honey in the Tulasī flowers woven in his *Vanamālā* and emitting ethereal fragrance, and applies the flute to his lips (to breathe a song in response to their music), the cranes, swans and other acquatic birds living in the lake, with their hearts enticed away by the captivating music, approach Lord Hari and with their eyes closed and minds under perfect control, meditate on him (lit. sit close to him) in perfect silence.

12-13. When accompanied by Balarāma and beautifully decorated with floral ear-rings[1], Kṛṣṇa stands on the summits of mountains and that Lord of eternal Bliss fills the whole Universe by the fascinating music of his flute, Oh beautiful ladies of Vraja, even the cloud, being afraid in mind of showing disrespect to the great Lord, rumbles softly keeping time with the tune of his flute, spreads himself over him as an umbrella and covers the friend (of theuniverse) with a flower-like spray (or the invisible gods spray him with flowers).

14-15. (To Yaśodā who has joined these Gopis :)

Oh chaste lady! Your son is expert in the various games and sports played by cowherds. But when he applies his flute to his Bimba-fruit-like red lips and plays out varied original tunes in the art of flute-playing, the chiefs of gods of whom Indra, god Śiva and god Brahmā are prominent, listen to the delineation of the music in different pitch again and again.[2] Although these gods were experts in music, they failed to grasp the heart (the underlying principles or the nature of the fine points) of the music and stood confused.

16-17. When Kṛṣṇa of the noble gait of the king-elephants moves on playing on his flute, and soothing the pains caused to the earth at Vraja due to the *hoofs* of the cattle, by means of his feet similar to lotus-petals and beautified with the marks of a flag, a vajra (thunder-bolt), a lotus and a goad, we, with the stormy passion of love enkinded in

* This describes the effect of the music of Hari's flute on birds.

1. or with pearl necklaces.

2. or inclining their neck and mind to the direction whence the musical notes were coming—VR.

us by his sportful oglings, are reduced to the (stationary) state of trees and out of infatuation are not aware of the loosening of the braids of hair and the garment.

18-19. Sometimes, when wearing a wreath of beads[1] and counting the cows (in his charge thereby (with the beads), Kṛṣṇa, wearing a garland of Tulasī the fragrance of which is specially liked by him, sings playing on his flute, resting his hand on the shoulder of his affectionate friend, the she-deer, the mates of black-antelopes, with their hearts enticed away by the music of the flute, follow Kṛṣṇa, the ocean of excellences, and renouncing all desires to return home, stay by his side like the cowherd-damsels.

20-21. Oh sinless Yaśodā! When your child, Nanda's son, picturesquely dressed with the wreaths of *Kunda* (jasmine) flowers and surrounded by the cowherds and the wealth of the cattle, plays on the bank of the Yamunā, joking with his intimate friends, a gentle breeze (from the south) blows agreeably and pleasantly and offers him respect with its cool touch charged with the fragrance of sandal. And bands of demigods (like Gandharvas) performing the function of bards and minstrels, wait around him worshipping him with instrumental and vocal music and articles of worship.

22-23. Being compassionate to the people of Vraja and the cows, he held up the mount Govardhana. When after collecting his entire wealth of cattle, he returns home playing on his flute, his panygeric is being sung by his friends and his feet being worshipped by the old (gods like Brahmā and others) on the way, with his garlands covered over with the dust raised by the hoofs of the cows, here comes the Moon (the Lord of stars) born of Devakī's womb—a veritable feast to the eyes of Gopīs by his splendour, even in a fatigued condition,—he does so solely with the desire of fulfilling the wishes of his friends.

24-25. With his eyes slightly rolling with ecstatic joy, showing great regard to his friends and well-wishers, adorned

1. Adorned with jewel *Kaustubha*—*VJ*.

with a wreath of sylvain flowers, with his face pale like a slightly ripening *badara* fruit, and his tender cheeks beautified with the splendour of his gold ear-rings, here comes in the evening, like the Moon (the Lord of the night). The Lord of Yadus (Kṛṣṇa) with the sportive gait of an elephant-king, with a cheerful face relieving the day-long endless agony (of separation) of the cow-like Gopīs of Vraja (to relieve the cows of the daylong—as if interminable—heat of the sun).

Śrī Śuka said :

26. In this way, the highly fortunate damsels of Vraja with their minds and hearts absorbed in him, used to spend their days in delight singing the sportful activities of Lord Kṛṣṇa, Oh King Parīkṣit.

CHAPTER THIRTYSIX

Akrūra deputed to bring Kṛṣṇa and Balarāma to Mathurā

Śrī Śuka narrated :

1. Some time after this (festive occasion described in the last chapter), there arrived at Vraja, Ariṣṭa, a demon having the form of a bull, with a huge body and a big hump, tearing up and shaking the earth with his hoofs.

2. Bellowing with terrific harshness and breaking the earth with his hoofs, he rushed with his tail upraised, turning up mounds of earth with the ends of his horns.

3-4. Discharging dung and urine in small quantities at intervals, he came with his eyes fixed and staring. Oh dear Parīkṣit! At his violent and terrific roar, cows and women were so shaken with fear that they prematurely delivered their off-spring in miscarriage.

5. Noticing that demonic beast with sharp horns, cowherd men and women got terrified. And the cattle ran away in fear, deserting Gokula, Oh king.

6-7. Calling upon Kṛṣṇa, "Oh Kṛṣṇa, Kṛṣṇa", all of them sought the shelter of Govinda for their protection. Noticing the Gokula overwhelmed with fear and fleeing, Kṛṣṇa reassured them with the words, "Don't be afraid", and challenged that demon in the form of a bull, "You stupid wretched-most fellow ! What do you gain by terrifying the poor cowherds and cattle ?

8. When I am here to crush down the pride of strength of the wicked and evil-minded brutes like you." Challenging him thus, Kṛṣṇa stroked his arms and provoked the wrath of Ariṣṭa, by clapping his hands.

9. Kṛṣṇa waited spreading out his serpent-like mighty arm on the shoulder of a friend. The demon Ariṣṭa who was thus enraged, dashed at Kṛṣṇa in fury, furrowing the earth below with his hoofs and dispersing the clouds with his tail upraised.

10. Thrusting forward the ends of his horns and staring fixed with blood-shot eyes, the demon, trying to cow down Kṛṣṇa with his side-glances, darted at him even as the thunderbolt discharged by Indra.

11. Catching hold of the Asura by his horns, the glorious Lord pushed him back to a distance of eighteen paces as an elephant would do to drive back its rival.

12. Although pushed backward by the Lord, Ariṣṭa who was perspiring all over, and heaving sighs, sprang to his feet and in a wrathful frenzy, speedily dashed at Kṛṣṇa again.

13. As he rushed towards Kṛṣṇa, the Lord seized the demon by the horns and hurled him on the ground. Pressing him down with one foot, he wrung his body as one would wring and twist a drenched cloth. Pulling out one of his horns, he struck him and the demon dropped down on the earth.

14. Vomiting blood, discharging urine and dung, kicking up his legs and with eyes rolling under excruciating pains, he went to the abode of death. Thereupon, the celestials, showering flowers on him, sang hymns in praise of Hari.

15. Having slain the demonic bull and glorified by his

people (Gopas and gods), He, along with Balarāma, entered Gokula giving delight to the eyes of Gopīs.

16. When the Asura (demon) Ariṣṭa was killed by Kṛṣṇa of miraculous feats, the worshipful divine sage Nārada who was endowed with divine vision, intimated to Kaṁsa as follows :

17. "By Vasudeva who was apprehensive (about the safety of his children) were given in charge of his friend Nanda, Kṛṣṇa, the son of Devakī and Balarāma, the son of Rohiṇī, while the daughter (you tried to kill) was born of Yaśodā. It is by them both that your men (deputed to kill Kṛṣṇa) were slain."

18. Hearing that (revelation) Kaṁsa, the king of Bhojas whose mind was agitated with wrath caught hold of a sharp, sword, with a view to kill Vasudeva.

19. He was prevented from taking that action (lest knowing of their father's death Kṛṣṇa and Balarāma should abscond). But realizing that his (Vasudeva's) sons are (ordained by Providence as) the cause of his death, Kaṁsa got Vasudeva and his consort fettered with iron chains.

20. When the divine sage (Nārada) departed, Kaṁsa sent for Keśin and commissioned him with the order, "Let Balarāma and Keśava (Kṛṣṇa) be killed by you."

21. Then Kaṁsa, the king of Bhojas, summoned his ministers like Muṣṭika, Cāṇūra, Śala, Tośala and others, conductors of elephants and spoke to them :

22-23. Listen to this, Oh warriors, Cāṇūra and Muṣṭika. In the Vraja of Nanda dwell Balarāma and Kṛṣṇa, the two sons of Vasudeva. It is ordained that I should meet death at their hands. When both of them are brought here, they are to be done to death by you in the game of wrestling.

24. Let galleries of various designs, suitable to the arenas of wrestlers, be constructed. Let all people in the city (of Mathurā) and the villages, witness this freestyle wrestling.

Additional verses in the Text of VR and VJ.

24.1. Oh highly intelligent superintendent (or keeper) of my elephants ! Listen to this command of mine. Our Elephant, Kuvalayāpīḍa has the rut flowing from its temples.

24.2. It should be placed at the entrance of the arena with a heavy iron bar in its trunk. The two sons of Vasudeva (Ānaka-dundubhi) are to be killed.

24.3. But even the conductor of the elephant got agitated in mind and submitted, "How can I kill the two sons of the sister of His Majesty, the Lord of the earth ?"

24.4. When addressed thus by the elephant-driver, the wicked-minded Kaṁsa ordered him again, making all the assembled persons hear it for compliance.

Kaṁsa said :

24.5. Carefully listen to this command personally given by me. You should all hear it and bear it in mind. Listen to the reason why from the start, I have been a sworn enemy of these, even though they are my relatives.

24.6. On one occasion, my highly fortunate lotus-eyed mother who was in her youth, was wandering about in the garden of the palace, when a gentle cool breeze was blowing.

24.7-8. It was the spring time when the garden was beautified with full-blown Aśoka, Bakul, areca nuts and Punnāga trees, with humming and hovering swarms of black bees, resounded with the sweet cooings of cuckoos. It was attractive with the group of dancing peacocks and the herds of playful monkeys; it was lined with rows of Sāla trees.

24.9. While my mother of auspicious vows was sauntering there, she, who was well adorned and had taken her bath after menstruation, and was agitated with the passion of love, contemplated of her husband.

24.10-11. At that time a certain Gandharva, Drumila by name, was going through the garden, unseen by others. He noticed that she was alone and ready for the occasion. He being able to read the thoughts and intentions in the minds of all, understood what she was thinking about. He assumed the form of Ugrasena and resembled him in speech and smiles.

24.12. The Gandharva who entertained a lustful passion about that chaste lady and was love-striken, got her consent. Being perfectly ignorant about the reality, she accompanied and had a pleasant time with him in that forest grove.

24.13. That chaste lady somehow came to discover him to be somebody else during the act of intercourse. She was extremely distressed at heart and with her mind and eyes agitated demanded, "Who are you, Oh wretched cheat ? That a wicked person like you has perpetrated this deed condemned by the noble ?"

24.14. The long-armed Drumila tried to console her who demanded this of him. He gently explained, "Oh good lady ! We belong to a family of Gandharvas. We are equal to the celestials and are there beloved attendants.

24.15. Oh auspicious lady ! Please note that we (Gandharvas) are not easily accessible to females of the human species like you who are fit to be enjoyed by human beings only. And there is a lot of difference between men who are subject to birth, death and such other physical and mental ailments and the celestials (who are unaffected by them), Oh pretty woman !"

24.16. While he was talking thus, the lady with her mind overwhelmed with rage, interrupted, "Do you want to appease me now after perpetrating that nefarious act ?

24.17. In defiance of the deities presiding over water, fire, earth, air, the ether, the moon, the sun, and disregarding the presiding divinities of the cardinal points, Time-Spirit, the two twilights (the dawn and the dusk) and the Dharma itself, you have adulterated with me.

24.18. Like unto a restraint-less elephant emitting ichor and blind with passion, you, wretched fellow, have made me, who was like a pure, translucent lotus-pond in a forest, turbid and impure. You wrethed-most vile immortal ! Do you again dare to try to conciliate me ?"

24.19-20. While she was censuring him thus, he, being afraid of being imprecated, urged through fear, "Oh Lotus-eyed lady ! Sexual relation between immortals and women is of the regular order while that between men and celestial women is of the irregular order and is unnatural.

24.21. Hence, Oh lady with lotus fragrance, please note that I have not committed an offence. My semen shall not go waste. A son will be born to you.

24.22-23-24. He will be affluent, intelligent, highly energetic and daring. My words shall not prove vain and untrue." While he was speaking thus, my enraged mother who was deeply distressed at the loss of her irrecoverable chastity, exploded in wrath : "You have transgressed the bounds of *dharma* and have taken to different (sinful) course of conduct, and are a wicked sinner, a follower of the wrong (immoral) path, your son shall be cruel, characterised by criminality and void of good qualities. He will never receive the blessings of gods, Brāhmaṇas and sages".

24.25. While the lady was giving vent to her wrathful expression, the Gandharva became afraid that she would curse him and uttering the words. "He will be an enemy of your relatives", he disappeared.

24.26. After his departure, my blessed mother came back to her palace from the garden. And nobody else knew the incident.

24.27. In due course she became pregnant and delivered me at the proper time. On one occasion, the worshipful sage Nārada told me all this.

24.28. Since that time I hate these relatives who are wicked. You yourself are a witness here how they are always inimical to me.

24.29-30. As I am born of a Gandharva, it will not be sinful to kill the wickedly disposed Ugrasena, the evilminded Devaka, the crafty Vasudeva and their partisans and dependants. I, therefore, issue a command to you that they both (Kṛṣṇa and Balarāma) should be ruthlessly killed.

24.31. By performing the worship of god Yama, the deity of the other world with the offerings of the two boys (Kṛṣṇa and Balarāma) crushed to death by the mighty elephant, let them (Vasudeva, Ugrasena and others) follow their path (to the abode of death).

24.32-33.* Let Vasudeva, Ugrasena, that Nanda and Devaka, the cowherds and Yādavas and all of their followers and partisans witness with tearful eyes the killing of their own

* Vṛndāvana edition gives these 33 additional verses.

sons. Let all the people in the country be invited and let them witness the free style wrestling[1] (*svaira-saṁ-yugam*.

25. Oh conductor of my elephant! You are a good man: The elephant Kuvalayāpīḍa is to be posted by you at the entrance of the arena. See to it that my two enemies (Kṛṣṇa and Balarāma) are killed by it.

26. Let the sacrifice connected with the bow (*dhanur-yāga*)[2] be commenced with due formality on the fourteenth day (of the dark half[3]). Let the priests offer sacrificial animals as victims to the king of *bhūtas* (goblins) i.e. god Śiva who is the *bestower* of all boons (to god Śiva the bestower of boons and the ruler over all beings).

27. Having thus passed the orders, Kaṁsa who was adept in the technique of achieving his purpose sent for Akrūra, the prominent member of the Yadu clan. Taking his palm in his hand, he spoke to Akrūra.

28. "Oh leader of charitable persons![4] Devoted as you are to me, please do a friendly turn to me; for there is nobody else either in my clan of Bhojas or those of Yadus who will guard my interest.

29. Hence, Oh gentle friend, I depend on you as a means of accomplishing an important mission even as the mighty Indra does, depending on god Viṣṇu, achieve his object.

30. Go to the Vraja of Nanda. There dwell two sons of Vasudeva. Please fetch them both here in this chariot. Let there be no delay.

31. It is reported that gods who are dependents of Viṣṇu have ordained my death (at the hands of one of them). Bring both of them along with cowherds headed by Nanda (lest the boys should refuse to come). Instruct Nanda and others to bring

1. but *pauruṣam*— 'my prowess' interprets VR.

2. VB. explains : As against the Viṣṇu-power of Kṛṣṇa, Kaṁsa wanted to counter-balance it by propitiating god Śiva. The worship of god Śiva as presiding over the bow (which would thereby be victorious in fighting) is called *dhanuryāga* in *Śiva-tantra*.

3. VB states it to be the *Śivarātrī* day.

4. VB. : Akrūra used to give cows as gifts to Brāhmaṇas every day for a period of twelve years and his mother gave food in charity. Hence he is designated as *dānapati* (the leader of donors).

the tribute (curds, ghee etc.) so that they would be convinced that the *dhanur-makha* (sacrifice to Bow) is real and not a ruse to bring them.

32. When they are brought here, I shall get them killed by an elephant which is like the god of death. If they happen to escape (death from the elephant), I shall get them despatched by two wrestlers who are like thunderbolts.

33-34. When both of them are finished, I shall put to death Vasudeva and his brothers who will be grieving (the death of Kṛṣṇa and Balarāma) and massacre the clans of Vṛṣṇis Bhojas, Dāśārhas, and also my aged father Ugrasena who still dotes for sovereignty and his brother Devaka as well as all other enemies of mine.

35. It is after that that this earth will be rid of all thorns (free from enemies). My father-in-law Jarā-sandha will be like a father unto me and Dvivida (the monkey chief), a dear friend.

36. Śambara, Naraka and Bāṇa have entered into friendly alliance with me. Having killed all the kings siding with gods, I shall enjoy the earth.

37. In view of (the knowledge of) these facts, quickly bring the youngsters Balarāma and Kṛṣṇa inducing them to witness the bow-sacrifice as well as the beauty of Mathurā, the capital of Yadus.

Akrūra replied :

38. Oh king! What you intend to do is all for the good inasmuch as you try to avert the evil (viz. death). But one should maintain equanimity and try one's level best whether it results in success or failure. For it is the Providence which is the real cause (instrument) of success.

39. A man builds castles in the air (lit. one entertains very big plans) even though they are thwarted by the Destiny and thus experiences joy and sorrow. I shall, however, carry out your order.

Śrī Śuka said :

40. Having directed Akrūra (to go to Vraja) and sent away his counsellors, Kaṁsa entered his palace and Akrūra his home.

CHAPTER THIRTYSEVEN

Slaying of Asuras Keśin and Vyoma

Śrī Śuka said :

1. Demon Keśin who was deputed by Kaṁsa, assumed the form of a gigantic horse with the speed of the mind. Furrowing the earth with his hoofs, overcrowding the sky with clouds and heavenly cars dispersed by the waving of his mane and terrifying all creatures by his neighing he came to Nanda's Vraja.

1-A*. With big eyes, a terribly vast cavern-like mouth, an enormous neck resembling a large dark-blue cloud, the wicked-hearted Keśin, desirous of achieving the desired object of Kaṁsa, rushed to the Vraja of Nanda, making it tremble with fear.

2. Occupying a forward position, the glorious Lord challenged Keśin who was creating a panic among the inhabitants of his Gokula by his neighing and was disturbing the formation of clouds in the sky by his tail and was seeking a fight with him—at which Keśin roared like a lion.

3. Beholding Kṛṣṇa confronting him, that unapproachable formidable beast of terrific speed rushed at him with extreme rage, drinking up the heavens, as it were, with his wide open mouth (and turning round) kicked hard with his hind legs the Lord with lotus-eyes.

4. Dodging the Kick, Kṛṣṇa, the Lord (who is supra-sense perception) angrily caught hold of his two hind legs with his hands and whirling him round threw him contemptuously to a distance of hundred bows (cubits), even as Garuḍa would fling (an ordinary) serpent, and stood as before.

5. Regaining his consciousness, Keśin sprang to his feet. Opening his mouth wide in violent wrath, he fiercely attacked Hari. Smiling fearlessly, Hari thrust his left arm into Keśin's mouth as a serpent enters a hole.

* Not found in the text of ŚR but recorded in the texts of VR., VJ., VB. and SD. Gauḍīya Vaiṣṇava annotators follow ŚR and do not comment on it.

6. When Keśin tried to bite Kṛṣṇa's arms his teeth dropped down at the touch of the Lord's arm as if at the touch of red-hot iron. And the Lord's arm thrust in the interior part of his body went on growing immensely like dropsy, when neglected.

7. With his breath (passage) choked by the (disproportionately) swelling arm of Kṛṣṇa, he kicked up his legs, perspired profusely all over the body, and with its eyes rolling, discharging excretion, he fell down dead on the ground.

8. Extricating his arm from out of the body of Keśī (which was burst open at various places) like a ripe cucumber, the mightly-armed Kṛṣṇa was not even slightly touched with pride, even though he effortlessly killed his enemies, but was glorified in songs and showered over with flowers by the wondering gods.

9. Oh king! Thereafter the divine sage Nārada, the foremost of devotees of the Lord, approached Kṛṣṇa of noble behaviour and conferred with him in privacy as follows:

10. "Oh Kṛṣṇa (the enchanter of the world)! Oh Kṛṣṇa of incomprehensible nature ! Oh Lord of *yogī*! The absolute Ruler of the world! Oh Vāsudeva (the pervader of the universe) and the abode of all! Oh the most prominent among the Sātvatas (the Yādava clan) ! Oh Almighty Lord![1]

11. Like unto fire lying dormant in fuel, you alone are the Inner Controller of all beings. Remaining unrevealed, you abide in the hearts of every being as a witness to everything. You are the Supreme Person, the Controller of the universe.

12. Depending entirely upon your own Self, You evolved *guṇas* through your *Māyā* potency. The Almighty Lord of unfailing will power as you are, you create, protect, and devour (destroy) this universe with those *guṇas*.

13. Such as you are, you have incarnated yourself on the earth for the annihilation of the *daityas* (demons), goblins

1. ŚR. : Nārada glosses over the disclosure about Kṛṣṇa to Kaṁsa by telling Him, "You are the Almighty Lord specially incarnated for relieving the earth of its burden of Daityas. Now You be active, finish with them and protect the Universe."

and *rākṣasas* that have been born as kings and for protecting those who abide by the canons of righteousness (or your votaries.)

14. Fortunately enough this demon Keśin who assumed the form of a horse and terrifically frightened at whose neighing, gods (the eye-lid-less beings) deserted the heaven, has been easily killed by you, as in a sport.

15. Oh Omnipresent Lord! Day after tomorrow, I shall witness Cāṇūra, Muṣṭika and other wrestlers, as also the elephant (Kuvalayāpīḍa) as well as Kaṁsa slain by you in broad day-light.

16. Thereafter I shall see the slaying of the demon Pañcajana (who was a conch-dweller) Kālayavana, Mura and Naraka as well as bringing down (from heaven the celestial tree) Pārijāta after defeating Indra.

17. After that I shall witness your marriages with the daughters of warriors (like Bhīṣmaka, Rukmiṇī's father) by offering your personal valour as the dowry (i.e. by defeating the opposition) as also the absolvement of Nṛga[1] from sin at Dvārakā.

18. Thereafter I would see the recovery of the jewel Syamantaka and a spouse (Jāmbavatī) along with it and the restoration of his son to a Brāhmaṇa from the abode of Death.

19. (I shall see later) the destruction of Pauṇḍraka.[2] and burning down the city of Kāśī, the death of Dantavaktra and slaying of Śiśupāla, the king of Cedi in the great sacrifice Rājasūya, performed by Yudhiṣṭhira).

20. It will be my privilege to see whatever other heroic deeds your Lordship would perform while dwelling in Dvārakā and they shall be eulogised in songs by poets on the earth.

1. Nṛga—A king of Ikṣvāku race, famous for his gifts of cows to Brāhmaṇas. One day, due to oversight and without being aware of it, he gifted a cow which was already given by him to another Brāhmaṇa. For this sin, he was born as a Chameleon but was absolved of all sins at the touch of Kṛṣṇa and went to heaven—vide *infra* 10.64.10.

2. *Pauṇḍraka* : King of ancient Kārūṣa. His name was Vāsudeva. On hearing of Vāsudeva Kṛṣṇa, he sent him a message to surrender all his special royal emblem and worship him. Kṛṣṇa invaded Kārūṣa with a big army and killed Pauṇḍraka Vāsudeva who used to wield artificial Sudarśana discus etc. like Kṛṣṇa Vāsudeva.—vide *infra* 10.66.7-21

21. After that I shall see you in the form of Death or time-spirit intent on destroying the whole universe and the annihilation of Akṣauhiṇīs (Divisions) of armies with you in the role of Arjuna's charioteer.

22. We approach, for protection, the glorious Lord who is entirely constituted of perfectly pure knowledge and has all his purposes accomplished as he is well-established in his own blissful nature; whose will is never futile; and due to whose spiritual refulgence the stream of *guṇas* originating from Māyā is ever warded off.

23. I lay prostrate before you, the leader of Yadus, Vṛṣṇis and Sātvatas—the leader (yourself) who are the supreme Ruler, and who have brought forth all this varied creation (the phenomenal world of differences) through his own Māyā and have assumed a human form for the sake of sporting.

Śrī Śuka said:

24. In this way, the sage Nārada, the foremost among the votaries who was delighted to see him, paid obeisance to Kṛṣṇa, the Chief Yadus and departed with his permission.

25. And Lord Kṛṣṇa also, having killed Keśin in a fight, tended the cows along with other cowherds who were highly pleased with him for his heroic act and enhanced the joy and happiness of the inhabitants of Vraja.

26. On one occasion, while they were grazing the cattle on the table-land high up on the mountain, the cowherd boys played the game of hide and seek in which some *gopas* became thieves (or cattle-lifters) and others guards (or policemen).

27. At that time, some played the part of thieves while others became guards, while some others played the role of sheep (to be lifted). In this way they indulged in the game fearlessly, Oh King !

28. Vyoma, the son of the Asura Maya who was a past-master in black magic, assumed the form of a cowherd and playing the role of a cattle-thief carried away a great many cowherd-boys who acted the part of goats.

29. The mighty Asura threw each cowherd-boy so carried in the cave of that mountain, and closed its entrance

with a rock. In this way four or five boys remained (outside the cave).

30. Noticing the vile act of that Asura, Kṛṣṇa, the protector of the righteous, forcibly caught hold of him while kidnapping the cowherds, even as a lion would do to a wolf.

31. The mighty demon resumed his original form big like a mountain. Being suffocated with his grip, he wanted to extricate himself but could not do so.

32. Catching hold of him by both his hands, he dashed the Asura to the ground and killed him in the way of sacrificial beasts, while gods were witnessing it from heaven.

33. Having broken open the rock that blocked the entrance to the cave, he brought the cowherds out of that perilous situation. Glorified by gods and cowherds, he returned to his own Gokula.

CHAPTER THIRTYEIGHT

The Arrival of Akrūra to Gokula

Śrī Śuka said :

1. Having stayed at Mathurā that night[1] the highly intelligent Akrūra mounted a chariot and proceeded to Nanda's Vraja.

2. On his way, the highly fortunate Akrūra who was filled with extreme devotion to the lotus-eyed Lord reflected to himself as follows :—

3. "What auspicious act has been done by me ! What austere penance I have performed ! Or what gift to a deserving person has been donated by me, by virtue of which I am going to see Lord Kṛṣṇa today.

4. Just as recitation and study of the Vedas is impossible to a person born in the Śūdra class, I consider that gaining even the sight of Kṛṣṇa of excellent renown is very

1. Vide Supra 10.36.40.

difficult for me, inasmuch as my mind is addicted to sensual pleasures.

5. Perhaps that may not happen that way. Even though I may be a vile person, I may be blessed with the sight of the Immortal Lord Kṛṣṇa. Sometimes a person carried along with the current of time, may get to the other shore of *saṁsāra*.

6. To-day all my evils (sins) are destroyed, and my birth has achieved its highest objective in that now I shall bow down to the glorious Lord's lotus-feet which are contemplated by *yogins*.

7. Verily Kaṁsa has shown a great favour to me as, being deputed by him, I shall see the lotus-feet of Lord Hari who has now incarnated in this world and by the lustre of whose circle of toe-nails, people in the former ages have got over the darkness of *Saṁsāra* which is so very difficult to cross.

8. The Lord's feet are worshipped by gods Brahmā, Śiva and others, by goddess Lakṣmī, by sages and by Sātvatas (Yādavas or his devotees)—feet which wandered in the forest along with his companions for grazing the cows and which are tinged with the saffron applied to the breasts of Gopīs.

9. Verily, as the deer go round by my right side (an auspicious omen), I believe I shall certainly behold today the face of Mukunda (Kṛṣṇa) with its charming cheeks and shapely nose, its smiling glances and reddish lotus-eyes, covered over with curly locks of hair.

10. How strongly I do yearn that today I shall be blessed with the audience (vision) of god Viṣṇu, the abode of beauty and excellence, who by his own Divine will has incarnated as a human being for lightening the burden of the earth. In case it so happens, it will be undeniable that the very existence of my eyes has achieved its fulfilment.

11. Though he is merely the witness of the Cause and the effect, he is devoid of egoism. By virtue of his lustre (lustre-like Spiritual Knowledge), he has dispelled the darkness of ignorance or Nescience and the consequent notions of differentiation and misapprehensions resulting from it. By his will, he is, however, found to be sportively engaged in the

houses (of Gopīs, arbours of trees in the Vṛndāvana forest) in the company of Jīvas created in himself through his Māyā Potency which, under his supervision and control, invests them with the life-spirit, the senses and mind or intellect.

12. The words describing his excellent attributes, exploits and incarnations which are capable of destroying all the sins of the world and of conferring auspicious blessings, resuscitate, contribute to the beauty and secure sanctity to the world. But words which do not describe them (howsoever ornamental and elegant they be) are like decorations of a dead body.

13. The Almighty Lord who brings about the felicity and blessings to the great gods who abide by the injunctions laid down by him[1], has descended into the clan of the Sātvatas. It is reported that the Supreme Ruler now stays at Vraja spreading all around his glory, which, due to its being auspicious to all beings, is sung by gods.

14. Inasmuch as I have been witnessing auspicious omens from the dawn, I believe that to-day I shall certainly behold him—the one great goal of the noble souls, the Father (or the Preceptor) of the world, the most lovable and charming to the three worlds, a veritable grand feast to those who are blest with a sight—manifesting a form which is the coveted-most abode of the goddess Śrī.

15. And as soon as I see them, I shall immediately get down from the chariot and will certainly bow down directly to the feet of those two Almighty rulers of the Universe, the Prime Personalities—Kṛṣṇa and Balarāma whose feet have been merely intellectually grasped and meditated upon for Self-realization even by *yogis* (but have never been able to visualize them actually). Along with them I shall pay respects to their cowherd-friends and to all the beings residing in the forest of Vṛndāvana.

16. (Now he covets the touch of the Lord's hand and hopes that the Lord would fulfill his longing.) Will not that Omnipresent Lord place his lotus-palm on the head of mine who have prostrated myself at the soles of his feet—his hands

1. ŚR specifies these as *varṇāśrama-dharma*.

which have afforded protection to all men who being terrified of the serpent in the form of Time (or Death) seek resort to them? (I heartily yearn for this favour).

17. By offering worship to those very palms Kauśika (Indra who is reported to have worshipped it on an occasion) and the demon-king Bali (who offered water in token of the gift of three paces of land to the Dwarf-Viṣṇu) attained sovereignty over the three worlds and which, by their very (cool and) fragrant touch like the *Saugandhika* lotus (noted for its specially sweet smell) alleviated the fatigue of the damsels of Vraja during the *rāsa*-sport and thus refreshed them.

18. Though deputed by Kaṁsa, I am sure, he will entertain no hostile attitude to me as his enemy. For the Immortal[1] Lord is Omniscient and can see everything in the universe. Being the Supreme Soul (*Kṣetrajña*) he will see with his pure (unclouded and unprejudiced) vision what is desired inside and outside of the heart of everyone.

19. How strongly I yearn for it! If he, with a merciful eye, looks smilingly at me who am prostrate at his feet, who with folded palms have concentrated on the soles of his feet, I shall instantaneously get thoroughly absolved of all sins, and with all my fears of *saṁsāra* dispelled, shall enjoy exquisite joy and Supreme bliss.

20. Would that when he would, with his mighty arms, embrace me, his best friend and well-wisher, his clansman who look upon him exclusively as my God, my soul (body) will be highly sanctified immediately and the fetters of *karman* lie shattered thenceforth.

21. When, after enjoying the privilege of being embraced by him (lit. having a personal contact with him), I shall stand bowing down to him with folded palms and he will address me, "Uncle Akrūra", I shall feel that our coming into life (birth) has achieved its purpose. Fie upon the life of that being who is not respected in such a way by the worshipful Lord.

22. No one is beloved of him or an intimate friend of him nor is any one disagreeable, hateful or worthy of indiffe-

1. Lord with unfailing knowledge—VT.

rent treatment to him[1]. He however, attends upon his devotees just as the celestial wish-yielding tree grants[2] the desire of a person when he is resorting to it.

23. And moreover, his elder brother Balarāma, the best in the Yadu-clan, will embrace me with a smile. When I shall be humbly bowing with folded palms, he would take me by my hands and usher me into his house. When I shall be received with due formalities by all his relatives, he will enquire of Kaṁsa's behaviour towards his relatives and clansmen.

Śrī Śuka said :

24. Oh King, while Akrūra, the son of Śvaphalka was contemplating about Lord Kṛṣṇa, he arrived by his chariot at Gokula, when the sun was reaching the setting mountain (the western horizon)

25. In Vraja, he noticed the foot-prints of the Lord, the sacred dust of whose feet is respectfully received with their crowns (i.e. heads) by all the protectors of the worlds—foot-prints which are distinguished with the marks of a lotus, a barly seed, a goad and such other characteristics and are auspiciously ornamental to the earth.

26. His impatience heightened to its climax through the ecstasy of delight at their sight, his body thrilled with the excitement of love with his hair standing on ends, with his eyes bedimmed with tears (lit. tear-drops), he jumped from the chariot and exclaiming, "How blessed and rare are these particles of the dust from Lord's feet", he prostrated himself and rolled over them.

27. This is the real ultimate purpose of life (*puruṣārtha*) of all beings invested with a body that they emulate the ecstatic mental state and behaviour of Akrūra since the moment he received Kaṁsa's order to bring Kṛṣṇa, without any hypocrisy, fear or worry at the sight of Hari's image, hearing his glory etc.

1. Cf. *samo'haṁ sarva-bhūteṣu na me dveṣyosti na priyaḥ* etc.
—BG. 9.29.

2. grants according to merits the deserving fruit—VJ. (*sva-sva-yogya-phaladānena*)

28. There, in the enclosure meant for milking cows, he saw Kṛṣṇa and Balarāma wearing yellow and blue garments respectively and with eyes beautiful like lotuses in the autumn.

29. They were *Kiśora* (lads between eleven to fifteen years) in age, dark-blue and white in complexion (respectively), the abodes of beauty and affluence (also bearing *Śrī-vatsa* mark in the case of Kṛṣṇa), with mighty arms and charming countenance, prominent among the beautiful, possessing the might and prowess of young elephants.

30. The noble-souled pair of brothers ornamented the (ground in) Vraja with (the prints of) their feet marked with the (figures of) a banner, a Vajra, a goad and a lotus and their smiling eyes expressed compassion.

31. They had taken their bath and had their person besmeared with fragrant pigments (such as sandal-paste). They wore wreaths of flower and *Vana-mālās* and were immaculately attired. They expressed noble yet attractive playfulness.

32. They were the Foremost and the first ancient-most Persons, the cause of the world and the protectors thereof. They had descended on the world in their personal rays (*aṁśas*) as Balarāma and Kṛṣṇa for the good of the world.

33. By their personal splendour they dispelled the darkness of the directions (all over the world). They appeared respectively like a mountain of emerald and a mount of silver both chased in gold[1], Oh King !

34. So overwhelmed with devout affection was that Akrūra that he quickly jumped down from the chariot, and fell prostrate like a stick near the feet of Balarāma and Kṛṣṇa.

35. With his eyes flooded with tears of joy at the sight of the glorious Lord and with hair standing all over his body, he was not able even to introduce himself to them as his throat was choked with love and emotion.

1. The problem is how could the dark-blue Kṛṣṇa dispel darkness. VJ. says Kṛṣṇa was like the sun and the 'dark-splendour' (*Kṛṣṇa-prabhā*) of the sun dispels darkness.

VR. differs : Kṛṣṇa was like a big emerald set in the middle of gold while Balarāma was like a diamond inlaid in a dark background.

36. Being affectionate to those who have completely surrendered themselves to him, the Lord who understood him (as to who he was and the purpose of his arrival etc.), drew Akrūra near him with his hands, characterised with the mark of discus, and embraced him as he was pleased with him.

37. The noble-minded Balarāma embraced Akrūra who was bowing low before him. Holding his clasped palms by his own, he led him to his house along with his younger brother Kṛṣṇa.

38. After enquiring about his journey (whether he faced any troubles etc.) and offering him a high seat, Balarāma washed his feet with due formality and offered him articles of *Madhuparka* (such as honey, ghee, curds, water).

39. Having presented a cow to the guest and after massaging him as he was fatigued, the powerful Lord served to him with reverence, preparation of pure food with a variety of excellences.

40. When his meal was over, Balarāma, the expert in the highest *dharma* (viz. proper reception of guest) again delighted him by offering articles like fragrant betel-leaf, scenting his mouth, perfumes and sweet-smelling garland.

41. When the customary formalities were over, Nanda enquired : "Oh Dāśārha (Descendant of Daśārha) ! How do you manage to get on with the regime of ruthless Kaṁsa—you who are now no better than sheep tended by a butcher.

42. That blood-thirsty wicked Kaṁsa has killed the children of his cousin (sister) even while she was bitterly crying. We wonder what safety or happiness there could be to you, his subjects.

43. Having thus been honoured by Nanda in sweet words, Akrūra recovered from the fatigue of the journey by such polite enquiries.

CHAPTER THIRTYNINE

Akrūra returns with Kṛṣṇa and Balarāma

Śrī Śuka continued :

1. Seated comfortably on a couch and received with high respect by Balarāma and Kṛṣṇa, he (Akrūra) realized all the aspirations he cherished on his way to Gokula.

2. Is there anything unattainable to a person when the glorious Lord, the very abode of goddess Śrī, becomes propitious? However, those who are exclusively devoted to him expect nothing from him, Oh King !

3. When the supper was over, Lord Kṛṣṇa, the son of Devakī, enquired about the treatment meted out by Kaṁsa to his Kinsmen and his further plans in the matter.

The glorious Lord enquired :[1]

4. Oh gentle-natured uncle ! It is good that you have come. I hope you had a comfortable journey. May be well with you all. Are all our (near and distant) kinsmen[2] and friends un-harassed (by Kaṁsa) and free from ailments ?

5. Dear uncle ! It is certainly not very consistent on my part to enquire after the welfare of our kinsmen and that of their descendants (or of the subjects in general), so long as this co-called maternal uncle Kaṁsa, the very bane (lit. disease) of the family, is prospering.

6. Alas ! It is for my sake that my venerable parents, despite their innocence, had to undergo immense sufferings. It is for me that their sons were murdered and they had to remain in chains in the prison.

7. It is our good fortune that today we could have a sight of our relative—a sight I had been coveting for long, Oh gentle-natured uncle ! Be pleased to explain to us the purpose of your visit. Oh uncle.

1. The following four verses (4,5,6 and 7) are not found in VJ's text.

2. ŚR. explains : *jñāti*—near relatives. They are *sapiṇḍa*; *bāndhavas* are distant and hence *a-sapiṇḍa*

Śrī Śuka said :

8. When thus enquired by Lord Kṛṣṇa, Akrūra, the descendant of Madhu, described in details the history and rationale of Kaṁsa's deep-rooted hostility to the Yadu clan, his attempts on the life of Vasudeva.

9. He reported to Kṛṣṇa the message (inviting them on the pretext of *dhanur-yāga* and the proposed attempt on their life through Cāṇūra and others) and the mission for which he had been deputed as an emissary by Kaṁsa and what Nārada had narrated to Kaṁsa about his (Kṛṣṇa's) birth from Vasudeva.

10. On hearing the message from Akrūra, Kṛṣṇa and Balarāma, the vanquishers of hostile warriors, laughed loudly, and they communicated to their foster-father Nanda the command of the king Kaṁsa.

11. He (Nanda) on his part ordered the cowherds.: "Let all the yield of cows (such as milk, ghee) as well as presents (of various kinds) as tribute, be taken with you. Let the bullock-carts be kept ready.

12. Tomorrow we have to go to Mathurā where we shall be paying as tribute the choicest products of our cows' yield to the king. We shall also witness there a very grand festival for attending which (it is reported that) all the people from the country (of Śūrasena) are going." Nanda, the Gopa chief, got this order proclaimed all over his Vraja, through the security officer of the Vraja.

13. The cowherd women (to whom Kṛṣṇa was their very life) were deeply distressed at heart on hearing that Akrūra had come to Vraja to take away Balarāma and Kṛṣṇa to the capital city (Mathurā).

14. Some had the splendour of their countenance withered by the hot breaths due to the agony of heart caused by hearing that news. Some became so much beside themselves through overwhelming grief that they got their garments loosened, bangles dropping and braids of hair dishevelled.

15. Through their concentrated contemplation on Kṛṣṇa, some Gopīs got all the functions of their sense-organs ceased and became insensible to this external world, as if they had ascended to the realm of the Supreme Self.

16. Some other Gopīs lost their consciousness as they remembered the wonder-fully phrased speeches of Kṛṣṇa touching their very heart and expressed with warm loving smiles.

17-18. Musing over Kṛṣṇa's extremely graceful gait and manner of behaviour, his amiable smiles and loving glances, his witty repartee dispelling sorrows and his extra-ordinary exploits, the Gopīs terrified and distressed at the very thought of impending separation, met together in groups and with tears flowing over their cheeks (faces) and hearts absorbed in Kṛṣṇa, they complained :

Gopīs said :

19. Alas ! Oh Creator ! You have not the slightest compassion anywhere in you, inasmuch as, you bring together embodied beings in friendliness and love and unnecessarily separate them before they have accomplished their desired object. Your whimsical behaviour is childish (lit. like the purposeless behaviour of a child).

20. It is not a good act (in fact a wicked) act on your part that you, having first manifested to us the countenance of Kṛṣṇa covered over with ringlets of dark hair, charming due to its beautiful cheeks and prominent nose, beautiful with a beaming smile that dispelled all grief, now takes it away from our view.

21. You are really cruel as (disguising yourself) under the nomenclature Akrūra[1], you like an irrational person, are depriving us of our very eye given by you to us. It is with that we visualized the excellence of your creative capacity (completely exhibited) even in a part (limb) of Kṛṣṇa, the slayer of Madhu.

22. Alas ! What a pity ! The friendship of Nanda's son is of a momentary nature. He is so much fond of new company that he does not condescend to cast a glance at us who have been eagerly longing for him and who, being

1. You will say it is Akrūra and not I, who is taking away Kṛṣṇa. It is not possible for others to do this. It is you who have come here under the name Akrūra—ŚR.

beguiled by his enchanting acts, have openly accepted his slavery forsaking our homes, relatives, sons and husbands.

23. For the ladies of the city (Mathurā), their night will dawn very happily. All the benedictions have been (i.e. will be) definitely realized by them. For as Kṛṣṇa enters the city, they will drink (with their eyes) the countenance of the Lord of Vraja (Kṛṣṇa) full of intoxicating (yet) nectar-like smiles, the charm of which is enhanced by lovely side-glances.

24. Oh ladies ! Even if Mukunda (Kṛṣṇa) is self-controlled and independent and has his relatives in Vraja, how can he ever return to us, poor rustic women, when his mind is captivated by the sweet, soft words, and fascinated by the bashful smiles and amorous deportment of the ladies of Mathurā.

25. Today, certainly there will be a high feast to the eyes of Dāśārhas, Bhojas, Andhakas, Vṛṣṇis and Sātvatas and those who will see passing by the road (in the chariot) Kṛṣṇa, the son of Devakī, the consort of goddess Śrī (Lakṣmī), the very abode of excellences.

26. As this fellow wants to carry off Kṛṣṇa who is dearer than life itself to us, beyond the known paths (to a far-off land beyond our reach), without (in any way) consoling deeply-grieving persons (like us), Akrūra (not cruel) ought not to be the name of such a ruthless fellow who is (as a matter of fact) extremely cruel.

27. Look ! without feeling the slightest feeling (lit. witness) of sympathy or mercy he (Kṛṣṇa) has comfortably occupied his seat in the chariot; following him the haughty Gopas (cowherds) are hastily speeding up in their bullock carts. (This departure of Kṛṣṇa) is treated with indifference by the elders (of Vraja). It appears that hostile Destiny is working against us today.

28. Approaching Kṛṣṇa (the Lord of Lakṣmī) We shall dissuade him (from going). What can the elders of the family and relatives do unto us whose hearts have been rendered afflicted and melancholy by Fate, by bringing about separation from Mukunda (Kṛṣṇa) which is unbearable even for half a minute, (under such circumstances even death is no terror to us.)

29. Oh cowherd women! How can we get over without him the unending darkness of separation from him, with whom we felt like a moment the nights indulged in rāsa dance (and similar other sports) the charm of which was enhanced by his warm love, charming smiles, sweet whispers, playful glances and embraces?

30. How can we (even manage to) live without Kṛṣṇa who at the even tide, with Balarāma (the incarnation of Śeṣa) as his compassion, and surrounded by cowherds, used to enter Vraja, playing on his flute, and with his curly hair and wreaths of flowers soiled heavily with dust raised by the hoofs of the cattle, and captivate our hearts by casting at us his smiling side-glances?

Śrī Śuka said :

31. Talking to each other in this manner, and extremely distressed at the thought of separation from Kṛṣṇa, the women of Vraja whose hearts were deeply attached to Kṛṣṇa threw to winds their sense of bashfulness and cried loudly, (uttering his various names:) "Oh Govinda ! Alas Dāmodara! Oh Mādhava".

32.* When it was sun-rise, Akrūra finished his morning *Sandhyā* (prayer to the sun) and other religious duties, and drove his chariot (along with Śrī Kṛṣṇa and Balarāma) without paying any heed to the lamentations of womenfolk.

33. Cowherds, headed by Nanda, followed them closely in their bullock-carts taking with them abundant tribute in the form of pitchers full of the yield of cows (such as milk, curds, ghee).

34. The cowherd women also followed their beloved Kṛṣṇa feeling a bit delighted when he turned round and cast an affectionate glance at them and waited[1] for his command not to follow him.

*A ŚR. gives an additional verse here :

Krūram Akrūrataḥ śrutvā Kaṁsaṁ Kaṁsaniṣūdanaḥ |
gopī-manorathārāmaḥ sa-Rāmaḥ svapuraṁ yayau ||

Having heard from Akrūra (the report about) cruel Kaṁsa, Kṛṣṇa, the slayer of Kaṁsa, the delight of the Gopīs (by fulfilling their desires) went to his capital (Mathurā) along with Balarāma.

1. Waited for his reply to the message sent by them through an emissary and stood on an eminence within the range of his view—VT.

35. Perceiving that the Gopīs were deeply tormented at his departure, Kṛṣṇa, the Lord of Yadus, comforted them through a messenger that he would return soon.[1]

36. As long as the flag (of the chariot) was visible and as long as the dust raised by the chariot could be seen, they stood motionless like figures painted in pictures, as they had deputed their minds after him.

37. At long last, being disappointed at the return of Lord Kṛṣṇa, they too returned and for relieving themselves of the sorrow of separation, they spent days (and nights) in glorifying his deeds and pastimes in songs.

38. In his chariot swift in speed like the wind, the Lord along with Balarāma and Akrūra arrived (at noon) on the bank of the Yamunā that absolves one of all sins.

39. After (washing his hands and feet) performing the Ācamana (ritual sipping of water), he drank the sweet crystal-clear water of the Yamunā. Going near a grove of trees (where the chariot was standing), he got into it alongwith Balarāma.

40. Akrūra on his part seated them (comfortably) in the chariot, and (requesting them not to leave their seats as he was afraid of enemies) he took leave of them. Coming to the pool of Yamunā (known as 'Ananta tīrtha'), he performed ablution according to *śāstric* injunctions.

41. As he plunged into the river water reciting the ancient Vedic *mantras* (of *Agha-marṣaṇa*), that Akrūra (being of purified mind) saw therein both Balarāma and Kṛṣṇa together.

42. 'How is it that the two sons of Vasudeva who were seated in the chariot are down here ? In that case they must not be in the chariot.' With this suspicion, he emerged out of water and looked for them.

43. Perceiving both of them seated (in the chariot) as before, he took, a plunge again thinking, "Was my vision of them both in the water unreal ?"

1. VT. strongly objects to the interpretation : "I shall be sending you messages and thus see you through messengers though personally I cannot come", for this contradicts the words of Kṛṣṇa's special emissary Uddhava :

āgamiṣyatyadīrgheṇa kālena Vrajam acyutaḥ /

44-45. Again he saw in that very water, Śeṣa, the Lord of Serpents—a resplendent God with one thousand heads, with crowns adorning his one thousand hoods, wearing a blue garment, white as lotus-fibers, (enormous) like the white snow-clad mountain Kailāsa with its (golden) peaks. He was being praised by Siddhas, Cāraṇas and Gandharvas as well as by Asuras, with their heads bowed down in salutation.

46. He saw on Śeṣa's lap (coils) another (Supreme) Person (Lord Viṣṇu) bluish dark like a cloud in complexion, clad in yellow silken garment, with four arms, eyes reddish like lotus-petals and very serene and gentle in appearance.

47. He had a beautiful and gracious countenance with enchanting smiles and glances, well-shaped eyebrows, prominent nose, beautiful ears, charming cheeks and reddish lips.

48. He had long and mighty arms, high shoulders and broad chest—the home of the goddess Śrī, a conch-shaped neck, a deep navel and stomach shaped like a tender leaf with three folds.

49. He had well-formed loins and hips, pair of well-developed thighs like those of an elephant and a pair of beautiful knees and shapely shanks.

50. His ankles were prominent and were surrounded by the halo of light radiating from his reddish toe-nails. His lotus-feet were specially charming with petal-like tender toes and (a pair of) big toes.

51-52. He was shining brilliantly with a diadem, bracelets, armlets decked with the most precious jewels as well as with a girdle, a sacred thread, necklace, anklets and ear-rings. He held a lotus, conch, discus and a mace in each of his hands. He had the *Śrī vatsa* mark on his chest, and a resplendent *Kaustubha* gem was shining at his neck. He wore a garland of special sylvain flowers (called Vanamālā).

53-54. He was being praised in hymns with distinct words expressive of different sentiments, by his attendants, the prominent among whom were Sunanda and Nanda, by sages like Sanaka (and his three brothers Sanandana, Sanātana, Sanat kumāra), by the rulers of gods like god Brahmā, Rudra and others, by nine foremost of Brāhmaṇas (such as Marīci, Kāśyapa and others) and by the most prominent of the Lord's pure-hearted devotees like Prahlāda, Nārada and Uparicara Vasu.

55. He was waited upon personally by the deities like Śrī (presiding deity over affluence), Puṣṭi (goddess of nourishment), Sarasvatī (presiding over speech), Kānti (goddess of beautiful complexion and splendour), Kīrti (presiding deity of fame), Tuṣṭi (goddess of contentment), Ilā (the Earth goddess), Ūrjā (goddess of energy and strength), Vidyā (goddess presiding over spiritual enlightenment), Avidyā (the goddess of Nescience), by Śakti (Power) and Māyā (the deluding potency of the Lord).

56-57. He was extremely delighted to have the vision of that Lord and overwhelmed with intense devotion and thrilled with joy (with his hair standing on their ends) his eyes wet with tears of love, Akrūra of the Sāttvata clan summoned courage, and bowed down with his head. And folding his pair of palms, with concentrated attention, he slowly began to praise in voice choked with emotions.

CHAPTER FORTY

Akrūra's Hymn (in praise of the Lord)

1A. *VJ.'s Text adds* :

At this vision of the Lord, Akrūra's heart and senses became filled with divine joy and serenity. Bending his neck (head) down with devotion, he praised the Lotus-eyed Lord.

Akrūra said :

1. I bow down to you as you are the Prime cause of all causes (like *Mahat* etc. from which the Universe evolved). You are the veritable Nārāyaṇa (the Deity reposing over the cosmic waters), the In-dweller in all bodies, the First Principle not subject to change or modification. It is from the lotus sprouted from his navel that god Brahmā, the Creator of the Universe appeared. It is from him (Brahmā) that the universe was evolved.

2.* All the causes of the evolution of the world such as (the elements) the earth, water, fire, air, the sky and its originator-*ahaṃkāra*, the principle of cosmic intelligence called *mahat*, *prakṛti* (Primordial matter) and the cause thereof (viz. *Puruṣa*, the mind, the senses (and organs) and their objects and all the gods presiding over them, are all evolved out of your Supreme Person (*Śrī mūrti*).

3. These—god Brahma[1] and others—being material (or other-than-the spirit) do not know the essential nature of yours who are the real *ātman* (Supreme self). For god Brahmā is conditioned by or enveloped in the *guṇas* of *Prakṛti*. As such he is unable to congnize your essential nature which is beyond all *guṇas*.

4. Certainly, the righteous and practitioners of yoga worship you directly as the Supreme Person, the Ruler of the Universe-as the Indweller of the body (*Or* in the senses and organs of the bodies of every *jīva*), presiding over all material bodies (or the great elements like the ether, air, fire etc.), presiding over the bodies of god.

5. Some twice-borns (e g. Brāhmaṇas, Kṣatriyas) follow the path of action—*Karma mārga*, and betake themselves to the course of sacrificial performance. With the help of the knowledge of three Vedas (*Ṛk*, *Sāman* and *Yajus*), they worship none but you under the names and forms of different divinities in extensive sacrificial sessions.

6. Having renounced all activities[2] (pertaining to (*karma-mārga*, they have attained tranquillity and control of senses.[3] Such men of spiritual wisdom worship the Embodiment of

*. VR presents the *viśiṣṭādvaita* stance : He shows that this verse described the Lord both as the material cause as well as the efficient cause. "From Your Person Brahman characterised by *mūla-prakṛti* as his body is transformed into *mahat*, *ahaṁkāra*."

1. VJ : Jīva and others—Like inanimate things, even *jīva* cannot cognize your nature. The *jīvas* are observed with the false notion that the body and soul are identical or they themselves are the absolute masters.

VJ. These—Brahmā and others cannot cognize Your real nature as they are distinct and different from your self.

2. VR. : give up all Vedic rites performed for attaining their desires which give rise to egotism and passions

OR : realize that Vedic rites are a form of worshipping the Lord.

3. VJ. : Unswerving devotion of the Lord exclusively.

Knowledge through sacrifice in the form of spiritual knowledge i.e. meditation on the Lord).

7.* According to the injunctions laid by you (in the (*Pañcarātra āgama*) some consecrate their person[1] become absorbed in you and worship you as per procedure laid down by you (in the *Pañcarātra āgama*), as the One Deity abiding in many emanations (*Vyūhas* such as Vāsudeva, Saṅkarṣaṇa. Pradyumna and Aniruddha) or as one form (viz. Nārāyaṇa).

8. Others (i.e. devotees of Lord Śiva) adore you only in the form of Śiva[2] as per procedure ordained by god Śiva (*in Śaiva āgamas*) but with difference of details according to the teachers (of various Śaiva sects like *Kāpālika Kālāmukha*, *Pāśupata* etc.), Oh glorious Lord!

9.* Those who are votaries of other deities and have thus reposed their faith and devotion unto them (thinking these deities as different from you), all of them really worship you who pervade them all, Oh Supreme Lord.

10. Oh Lord ! Just as rivers with their sources in mountains and flooded by raining clouds enter into the sea from all directions, similarly all paths (of devotion and worship) lead ultimately unto you.

11. *Sattva*, *rajas* and *tamas* are nothing but modifications of your *Prakṛti* (potency). And everything from inanimate immovables to the highest deity Brahmā, are the products of Prakṛti and are woven warf and woof in Prakṛti[3] (and therefore not different from you. You pervade them all)

* After describing the paths of Karma, Sāṅkhya, and Yoga, he mentions *Pañcarātra* and *Śaiva* systems in verses 7 and 8.

1. ŚR. : as per Vaiṣṇavite and Śaivite procedures.

VR. : By the five consecrating rites prescribed in the *Pāñcarātra āgamas*.

SD.: quotes a verse enumerating the five *saṁskāras*: *Tāpaḥ puṇḍraṁ tathā nāma mantro yāgaś ca pañcamaḥ*

tāpa is branding with representations of discus etc., *Puṇḍra*—mark on the forehead (the rest is easy).

2. VB. In *Tāmasa Kalpa* Viṣṇu assumes the form of Śiva.

*. Cf. *Yepyanya-devatābhaktā yajante śraddhayānvitāḥ* |
tepi māmeva Kaunteya yajantyavidhipūrvakam ||

BG. 9.23.

3. ŚR : *Or* : and ultimately they merge into *Prakṛti* and *Prakṛti* unto you. In this way all gods etc. are absorbed in you.

12. Hail to you whose mind is perfectly unattached to everything even though you are the In-dwelling soul of everybody and witness to the intellects (minds) of all. This stream of *guṇas* (*saṃsāra*) created by your Nescience operates powerfully on gods, men, and subhuman beings.

13. Fire is regarded as your mouth, the earth as your feet, the sun as your eye, the sky as your navel, cardinal points as your ears, the celestial region (the firmament) as your head, Indra, the ruler of gods your arms, and oceans as your belly and the wind as your vital strength[1].

14. Trees and herbs are the hair on your body; the clouds are the locks of hair on your head; mountains are the bones and nails of your transcendental self; days and the nights are your winking; god Brahmā, the Creater of the world, is your generative organ, and rain shower is regarded as your semen.

15. Oh Immortal Supreme Self! You are the perfect immutable Person who can be comprehended by the mind only. On you are projected worlds teeming with beings along with the protectors of those worlds, just as acquatic beings move in water or insect exists in the *Udumbara* fruit (Indian fig).

16. Whatever forms you assume for your sportive activities in the world, dispel the afflictions and sorrows of people. Hence they sing your glories in joy.

17. I bow to you the Fish incarnation, the cause of the world who moved freely in the cosmic waters of the ocean of deluge. Hail to you who assumed the form of *Hayagrīva* (horse-necked god) for killing the demons Madhu and Kaiṭabha.

18. Salutations to you Oh gigantic Tortoise, the bearer of mountain Mandara (at the time of churning the ocean for nectar). I bow to you who have assumed the Boar form for the sportive activity of uplifting the earth (from the bottom of the ocean).

19. Oh Lord! The Dispeller of the fear of the righteous! I bow to you the wonderful man-lion. My salutations

1. VT. The verse shows how the Lord pervades all gods.

to you Oh Vāmana who have crossed the three worlds (in one step).

20. Salutations to you Paraśurāma, the chief of Bhṛgus who cut down the forest in the form of haughty Kṣatriyas. I salute to you, Oh Rāmacandra, the best of Raghus, who have killed Rāvaṇa.

21. Hail to you the Lord of Sātvatas ! Who manifested yourself in four divine emanations of Vāsudeva, Saṅkarṣaṇa (Balarāma), Pradyumna (Kṛṣṇa's son) and Aniruddha (Pradyumna's son).

22. Hail to you Lord Buddha ! Who are absolutely pure but who deluded Daityas and Dānavas (by your anti-Vedic teaching). I bow to you who assumed the form of Kalki and killed the kṣatriyas who were reduced to the stage of Mlecchas (*non-Aryans*).

23. Oh Glorious Lord ! This world of beings is deluded by your māyā potency and wanders in the path of *karma* (*saṁsāra*) with the false notion of me-and-mine i.e. of the body being his own self and property as his own.

24. And I am such a stupid person, Oh Lord Kṛṣṇa ! That I too wander (move in) my body, sons, house, wives, wealth, kith and kins etc. who are really unreal like dream but thinking them to be real.

25. I entertain a contrary notion towards things which are not eternal (e.g. fruit of *karmas*), are not the real self (viz. my body) as well as which are full of troubles (e.g. house, property) and regard them as eternal, real-self and full of happiness). I am enveloped in the darkness of ignorance and take pleasure in the opposite pairs like pleasure and pain and I do not know that you are the most dear to me.

26. Just as an ignorant person does not know that it is really water that is covered by weeds and other water-plants, and abandoning the real water, runs after a mirage, similarly I have turned my face away from you (and am pursuing unrealities like my body, house etc.)

27. Being of poor intellectual capacity and understanding, I am not able to control my mind which is perturbed by desire for enjoyment and activities to attain it, and am dragged here and there by uncontrollable senses.

28. Oh Lord ! I (who am as described above) have approached your feet which are not easily accessible to the unrighteous, regard (the accessibility of your feet) as an act of Grace on your part. Oh God with a lotus in the nevel ! Release from the cycle of births and deaths is possible if one's mind becomes attached to you through the service of saintly persons[1].

29. I bow to you who are the embodiment of Pure Consciousness and the Source of all knowledge. You are the Ruler (of factors e.g. Time-Spirit, Nature, Destiny) that control *Jīvas*; you are the very Brahman of infinite power.

30. Salutations to Lord Vāsudeva, the asylum of all beings. Oh Lord of sense-organs ! I bow down to you. Oh Lord ! Be pleased to protect me who have approached your feet.

CHAPTER FORTYONE

Kṛṣṇa's Arrival at Mathurā

Śrī Śuka said :

1. Having manifested his (original Viṣṇu) form in the water to Akrūra, the glorious Lord Kṛṣṇa withdrew it again, even while he was glorifying him,[2] like an actor (who instantly retires) after playing his role.

2. Noticing that the vision had disappeared, Akrūra emerged from water. He hastily performed the (mid-day) religious duties. He then returned to the chariot still wondering at the vision.

3. Lord Kṛṣṇa (the Controller of Senses) enquired, "have you seen anything miraculous either on the land or in the water or in the sky? I surmise (from your appearance) that you have perceived some such wonder.

1. ŚR. : It is through Your Grace that one gets the opportunity of rendering service to saintly persons which leads to attachment to you, resulting in Final Emancipation from *Saṁsāra*.

2. Despite Akrūra's continuation of praise. This shows Kṛṣṇa's indifference to praise (*anādare ṣaṣṭhī*) —VT

Akrūra replied :

4. "Whatever wonders are there on the earth, in the sky or in the water in this world exist in you who constitute the whole of the universe. What marvel can remain un-witnessed by me who have a direct vision of you?

5. Oh Supreme Lord! When I directly perceive you who accommodate all the marvels within you, what wonder, either on the earth, in the water or the sky could be witnessed by me."

6. Replying him in these words, Akrūra, the son of Gāndinī, drove the chariot and at the end of the day, he brought Balarāma and Kṛṣṇa to Mathurā.

7. People in the country-side who assembled at various stages on the way, became delighted to see the sons of Vasudeva (Balarāma and Kṛṣṇa) and were not able to take away their eyes from them.

8. In the meanwhile, Nanda, the cowherd, and other inhabitants of Vraja who came ahead of them (by a short-cut) stood waiting for them in a park near the city (Mathurā).

9. After joining them (Nanda and his group of cowherds) the glorious Lord of the world took Akrūra by hand while Akrūra was modestly bowing, and spoke to him as if with a laugh.

10. "You may go in advance with the chariot to the city and return home. We shall get down here and after resting for some time, shall go to the city."

Akrūra requested :

11. Oh Lord! I shall not enter Mathurā leaving you both here. It does not behove you, Oh Protector (of the world) who are so kind to your devotees, to forsake me who am your votary.

12. Be pleased to come. Let us go together. Oh Lord! You transcend sense-perception. Oh best of friends! Visiting our house along with your elder brother (Balarāma), with your friends and cowherds bless our home with your august presence.

13. Be gracious to sanctify our houses with the dust of your feet as we are after all householders (inevitably committ-

ing five types of sins[1]). For the ancestors and gods including the Fire-god get satisfied and propitiated with the water used for washing your feet (which is kept in a vessel or small reservoir in the courtyard of the house).

14. By washing the pair of your feet the great king Bali attained sanctifying fame, incomparable affluence and supreme sovereignty) as also the goal reached by absolute votaries.

15. The sacred waters (viz. the river Gaṅgā) that washed your feet have sanctified the three worlds, were borne by god Śiva on his head and by contact with which the sons of Sagara attained to the heaven.

16. I bow to you, Oh God of gods, Oh Lord of the universe, the listening and recital of whose glory bring spiritual merit; On the foremost one in the Yadu clan, Oh Nārāyaṇa of glorious reputation."

The glorious Lord replied :

17. It is after slaying Kaṁsa who is the enemy of our Yadu clan, that I shall visit your house in company of my elder brother (Balarāma) and shall bring delight to my friends.

Śrī Śuka said :

18. Akrūra who was thus replied, became rather disappointed. He, however, entered the city, reported (to Kaṁsa) the account of the mission assigned to him and returned home.

19. The next day in the afternoon, Lord Kṛṣṇa, accompanied by Balarāma and surrounded by the cowherds, entered Mathura with a view to see the city.

20. He saw the city Mathurā with high gate-ways and entrances made of crystals, with huge doors of gold beautified with gold arches. The granaries thereof were made of copper and brass. It was inaccessible due to deep moats around it. Its outskirts were made attractive with parks and beautiful gardens.

1. Manu enumerates five types of inevitable sins caused in the household work such as 'cooking on a stove', 'pounding', 'crushing', 'brushing up of vessel' etc. as follows:

pañca sūnā gṛhasthasya cullī peṣaṇyupaskarāḥ /
kaṇḍanī coda-kumbhaśca-Manu 3.66

21-22. It appeared beautiful with its quadrangles (where four roads meet) decorated with gold and with mansions of gold with suitable pleasure gardens attached to each of them. It was decorated with guild-halls of different classes of artisans and with buildings of other citizens. It was filled with the joyful cooing of pigeons and joyous notes of the peacocks perching on the window-grills and platforms, eaves (awnings) and seats (under trees) all inlaid with Vaiḍūrya (cat's eyes) diamonds, crystals, sapphires, corals, pearls and emeralds. Its streets, market places and quadrangles were profusely sprinkled with water and were strewn with flowers, sprouts, parched paddy and unbroken rice-grains.

23. He saw that it appeared beautiful for the entrances of houses were decorated with (auspicious objects such as) artistic pitchers full of water, sprinkled with curds and sandal, graced around with flowers and with rows of lamps and with tender foliage, inserted in the pitchers, with trunks of plantain trees and areca nut trees with bunches of fruit on the branches, and festive flags and buntings hoisted over them.

24. Oh King ! When Kṛṣṇa and Balarāma, the sons of Vasudeva, surrounded by their friends, entered the city by the royal road, women of that city hastily came out to have a look at them, and some eager ones climbed the terraces of their houses.

25. Out of haste some dressed themselves and put on ornaments in the wrong way; some forgot to wear the ornament in pair and put on one ear-ring (leaving the other ear ornamentless), and one anklet (leaving the other foot anklet-less) ; while others started (with only one eye painted with collyrium) without applying collyrium to the other eye.

26. Hearing the noise (as the sons of Vasudeva approached), some were so overjoyed that they set aside their dishes while taking meals; some besmeared with oil (preliminary to bath) came out (with oily appearance) without taking bath; some rose from sleep (and without taking any wash, ran up to see), while mothers suckling babies hurried forth (leaving their babies half-fed and crying).

27. With his noble gait and deportment like a mighty elephant in an intoxicated stage (exuding ichor), and with

his personality delighting (his consort) the goddess Śrī, the Lotus-eyed Kṛṣṇa provided a sumptuous feast to their eyes and captivated their hearts with his noble sportive smiles and glances.

28. The women of Mathurā whose hearts were already deeply attached to him (lit. were melted and rushed after him) through the reports they frequently heard about him, (regarding his excellences, prowess etc.) now espied him personally. They were honoured by being sprinkled with the nectar-like glances and fascinating smiles by him. They embraced that Embodiment of Bliss (mentally) as he entered through the gate-way of their eyes, occupied their hearts (and was in their 'possession'). They were so thrilled with joy that the hair on their body stood on their ends. They felt relieved of the endless agony of their hearts through pangs of separation (from him), Oh subjugator of enemies (e.g. lust, passions etc.)[1]

29. Climbing to the highest terraces of the mansions and with their lotus-like faces blooming with delight, the young damsels showered flowers on Balarāma and Kṛṣṇa.

30. At every stop Brāhmaṇas, being overwhelmed with joy, worshipped them with pots of water (to wash their feet), curds and rice-grains (to be applied to their fore-heads as an auspicious mark) and with wreaths, sandal-paste, perfumes and suitable presents (e. g. fruits, sweetmeats etc.)

31.* The ladies of the city (Mathurā) remarked to each other, "Oh ! What great penance must have been performed by cowherd women on account of which they had the privilege to behold at will these two brothers who are themselves a joyous festival to the eyes of the human world.

32. Beholding a certain washerman who was a dyer too coming that way, Kṛṣṇa, the elder brother of Gada[2] asked him to give the excellent, well-washed clothes.

33. "Please give us both suitable clothes becoming to our worthy status. The highest prosperity will certainly be yours for offering us these as gift."

1. ŚR adds : Oh King ! Don't be immersed in the erotic sentiment.

* Not found in VJ's Text.

2. Name of Kṛṣṇa's step-brother, son of Vasudeva and Deva-rakṣitā (Devakī's sister)—Supra 9.24.46-52.

34. Though requested by the glorious Lord who was perfect and possessed of plenty in every respect, the highly arrogant servant of the king (Kaṁsa) got angry and retorted with scorn.

35. "You ill-mannered, rustic hill-dwellers and foresters! Do you always ever wear such fine clothes? How do you have the audacity to overstep your limits and to desire to have the royal clothes.

36. Get ye gone, you childish fellow. If you really wish to live, you should never make such requests. Take care. The king's men verily arrest insolent people, beat them (soundly) and strip them of their belongings."

37. While he was thus swaggeringly boasting, Śrī Kṛṣṇa, the son of Devakī, got enraged and with his finger-tips he severed his head from his trunk.

38. All the servants of the washerman threw down the bundles of clothes and took to their heels in all directions. Kṛṣṇa took the clothes (he wanted).

39. Kṛṣṇa as well as Balarāma put on two pieces of garments (an upper and lower one) of their choice. They distributed the remaining to the (accompanying) cowherds and threw the rest on the ground.

40. Then a weaver was pleased with them and elegently dressed them both with rich multi-coloured clothes in a manner worthy of them.

41. With the variety of excellent clothes and decorations, Kṛṣṇa and Balarāma appeared brilliant and most beautiful like two young elephants, one white and the other dark, tastefully adorned for some festivel.

42. Being pleased with him, the glorious Lord Kṛṣṇa conferred on him the type of liberation called "similarity of godly form" (in the next world), and superb affluence, strength, wealth, memory and acuteness of sense organs in this world.

43. Then they proceeded to the house of a florist called Sudāman. Seeing them he respectfully rose to receive them and bowed, placing his head on the ground (i. e. lying prostrate before them).

44. He offered them seat and water to wash their feet. He worshipped both of them along with their followers (cowherds) by offering the articles of worship, wreaths of flowers, betel leaves and sandal paste.

45. He submitted, "The very object of our life has been fulfilled, Oh Lord, My race has been sanctified by you. And by your arrival my ancestors, gods and sages have been pleased with me.

46. Both of Your Honour are the ultimate cause of this Universe. It is by your rays that you have descended on this earth for its prosperity and protection.

47. Both of you are the friends and the soul of the world. Even though you are favourable to your devotees, you do not entertain discriminating outlook. You are equal unto all beings.

48. Therefore be pleased to lay down a command on Your servant as to what I should do for you. It is a high favour upon a human being that you direct him to do your service."

49. Oh Great King, Sudāman who was greatly pleased in mind, divined the wishes of them both and he presented them garland made of specially fragrant flowers.

50. Kṛṣṇa and Balarāma who were excellently decorated by the garlands, were greatly pleased with him and they, the great bestowers of boons, conferred on him, blessings as he bowed them respectfully and sought their protection.

51. He sought from them the boon of entertaining unswerving devotion unto them who constituted the soul of all, as well as friendship to their devotees and great compassion to all beings.

52. Having given him the boon as well as bestowing on him prosperity that would increase with his descendents and having conferred on him strength, longevity, glory and splendour, the Lord departed with his elder brother.

CHAPTER FORTYTWO

Description of the Wrestling Arena

Śrī Śuka said :

1. While proceeding ahead on the royal road, Kṛṣṇa espied a deformed young woman of charming countenance carrying a vessel containing sandal-paste and other unguents (for smearing and beautifying the body). He asked laughingly just to humour her.

2. "Who are you, Oh lady of shapely thighs? For whom is this vessel of unguents intended? Tell us the truth. Give us both some excellent unguents (out of these). (By this act of yours) you will soon be blessed with good luck."

The maid-servant said :

3. "Oh beautiful youth! I am a maid-servant called *Tri-Vakrā* (Deformed at three places viz. at the neck, the breast and the waist), but I am esteemed by (His Majesty) Kaṁsa in (the technique of) preparation of unguents). For the pastes and ointments prepared by me are very much liked by the king of Bhojas.-who else other than you both deserves to be anointed with this?"

4. Her heart being thoroughly captivated by their beauty, comeliness, bewitching smiles, sweet words and loving glances, she besmeared them thickly with the unguent.

5. Then with the upper part of their bodies painted with the unguent, the colour of which was different from that of the complexion of their persons, they both (Kṛṣṇa and Balarāma) appeared very much effulgent.

6. The glorious Lord who was very much pleased with her, decided to straighten up perfectly the hump-backed woman deformed at the three different places, though possessed of a charming countenance, and thereby to show (to the world) the fruit of having a sight of him.

7. Pressing the front part of her feet with his own feet, he held her chin with two fingers of his raised open palm and made her body perfectly straight.

8. Instantly, at the very touch of Kṛṣṇa, she became the loveliest young damsel with all limbs straight and proportionate and shapely, with big buttocks and heavy breasts.

9. Being thus gifted with excellent beauty and noble qualities, she thereupon felt the passion of love enkindled in her. And drawing him by the end of his upper garment, she requested him, beaming with a smile.

10. "Come, Oh hero! Let us go home. I cannot bear (the idea of going away) leaving you here, now. Please be propitious unto a woman whose mind has been agitated by you, Oh prominent one among men."

11. When solicited thus by the woman, despite the presence of even Balarāma, Kṛṣṇa cast a glance at him and at the faces of cowherds, laughed loudly and spoke to her.

12. "Oh lady with beautiful eye-brows! After accomplishing the object of my coming here (viz. killing of Kaṁsa) I shall certainly visit your house which relieves the pangs of hearts of men. You are the only resort of homeless wayfarers like us.[1]

13. After taking leave of her in sweet words, as he proceeded through the commercial area of the town (lit. through the streets of the Vaiśya community), he, along with his elder brother and followers was worshipfully received with various presents, betel-leaves, garlands of pearls and precious stones and perfumes by the guilds of merchants.

14.* The minds of the ladies of the merchant communities were so much agitated and overwhelmed with love that they forgot themselves. With loosened garments and braids of hair and slipping bracelets, they stood motionless as if painted in a picture.

15. Thereupon, enquiring with the people about the venue of the Bow-(Sacrifice), the Immutable Lord (Kṛṣṇa) entered the sacrificial-hall and saw the wonderful bow, beauti-

1. VJ. : God is not attached to anyone. But his devotees worship him and become his resort.

VR. : You deserve to be enjoyed.

* Untraced in VJ.'s Text.

ful (and big) like the rainbow (as it was studded with precious stones).

16. It was guarded by many men-at-arms, as it was worshipped and decorated with precious stones and valuables. Though he was prohibited by the attending guards, Kṛṣṇa forcibly caught hold of it.

17. Sportively picking it up with his left hand and fixing its string, Kṛṣṇa of formidable prowess, stretched it to the full and snapped it asunder in two in a second, as an intoxicated elephant would do to a sugarcane. And all men stood a-gazing (in astonishment).

18. As the bow was being broken, the crashing sound filled the sky, the space between the earth and heaven and all the quarters. Hearing that sound, even Kaṁsa was seized with terror.

19. The guards of the bow along with the attendants got enraged. Armed as they were, they were anxious to arrest him. Shouting "Let him be seized and bound down", they encircled him.

20. Perceiving those fellows of wicked intentions, Balarāma and Kṛṣṇa flared up in rage, and grasping the two pieces of the broken bow stick, soundly drubbed them all.

21. Having destroyed the battalion of soldiers despatched against them by Kaṁsa, they came out of the gate of the sacrificial hall. As they roamed along, they were delighted to see the affluence of the city.

22. Witnessing their marvellous prowess, splendour, fearlessness and handsome personality, the citizens of Mathura regarded them as two foremost ones among gods.

23. While both of them were thus wandering at will, the sun set. Kṛṣṇa and Balarāma surrounded by cowherds, returned from the city to the camp of their carts.

24. All the auspicious blessings anticipated (to happen to the citizens of Mathura) by the Gopīs who became afflicted with the pangs of (impending) separation from Kṛṣṇa at the time of his departure (from Vraja), materialised to be true at Mathura, in the case of those citizens who could gaze at the splendour of the elegant personality of Kṛṣṇa (The Supreme Person), the ornament of Manliness to whom Śrī, the goddess

of beauty and affluence, resorted for shelter disregarding other gods who sought her.

25. After washing their pair of feet, they partook of rice boiled in milk. With full knowledge what Kaṁsa intended to do the next day, they spent that night quite happily.

26-27. Kaṁsa, however, was struck with panic when he heard the report of the breaking of the huge bow and the massacre of the guards of the bow and the contingent of the army (deployed against them), and the marvellous sportive acts of Śrī Kṛṣṇa and Balarāma. The wicked-minded fellow, being terrified, remained sleepless for a long time, and saw both in sleep and while awake, many evil omens portending death.

28. Though his reflection in water or mirror was visible, he could not see his head in that reflection. Though no second luminary was in existence, he saw every planet (or lamp) in duplicate.

29. He espied holes in his shadow. Nor could he hear the whizzing sound of vital breath when the ears were closed. He felt that the trees he saw were of gold. Nor his footprints (in dust or sand) as he walked, were visible to him.

30. In dreams he saw himself clasped in embrace by dead persons (or goblins) and that he rode a donkey and gulped poison. He saw that he was wandering along with a garland of red flowers, and was smeared all over with oil and was naked.

31. He perceived such and other similar portends foreboding death, both in his dreams and in the waking state. Being terribly afraid of death, he did not get any sleep at all through anxiety.

32. When the night was over and the sun came up from the eastern waters, Kaṁsa caused (i.e. gave orders for) the grand celebration of athletic sports (such as wrestling of athletes etc.).

33. Men worshipped the wrestling arena. There was a fanfare of trumpets and beating of drums. The galleries were decorated with garlands, flags, buntings and ornamental arches.

34. Citizens and country people headed by Brāhmaṇas and Kṣattriyas entered and were comfortably seated, each

according to his position. Princes and royal personages also occupied their respective seats.

35. Surrounded by his ministers and at the centre of his tributary princes sat Kaṁsa on the throne, though his heart was aching with anxiety.

36. While the flourish of trumpets was being (occasionally drowned by the stroking of arms by athletes[1], the well adorned proud athletic champions occupied their seats alongwith their trainers.

37. Cāṇūra, Muṣṭika, Kūṭa, Śala and Tośala as well —all highly cheered up by the exciting music of the instruments presented themselves into the arena.

38. Cowherd Nanda and other cowherds who were invited by the king of Bhojas and who had offered their presents to him, took their seats on a separate dais.

CHAPTER FORTYTHREE

Killing of the elephant Kuvalayāpīḍa

Śrī Śuka said :

1. The next morning, Kṛṣṇa and Balarāma who had taken their bath and performed purificatory rites (as if to expiate the sin of killing their maternal uncle who, despite warnings of breaking the sacred bow, did not release their parents but wanted to kill them, heard the sound of the kettledrums and the shouting and beating of arms by wrestlers, went to see the tournaments, Oh repressor of enemies !

2. Arriving at the entrance of the arena, Kṛṣṇa beheld the elephant Kuvalayāpīḍa stationed there under the direction of the controller of the elephant.

3. Preparing himself for action by tightening the cloth worn round the loins, and tying up tightly his curly locks of

1. *mallānāṁ tāla-śca*
sva-bāhu-mūlaghātaḥ—VT

hair (with his upper garment) he spoke to the conductor of the elephant in a voice deep like thunder.

4. "You conductor of the elephant ! Make way for us. Hurry up. Clear out instantly. Else I shall send you along with your elephant to the region of Death."

5. Threatened thus, the driver of the elephant got enraged and goaded that already infuriated elephant looking like the god of Death at the end of the universe, to charge against Kṛṣṇa.

6. The big elephant vehemently dashed at Kṛṣṇa and seized him with his trunk. But slipping out of the coil of his trunk, Kṛṣṇa dealt him a blow and concealed himself betwixt his legs.

7. The enraged animal could not find Kṛṣṇa. Guided by his sense of smell, he reached his trunk to Keśava (Kṛṣṇa) who forcibly disengaged himself and rushed out of his grip.

8. Catching hold of the tail of that extremely mighty elephant, Kṛṣṇa easily dragged him to a distance of twenty-five bows (or one hundred cubit) even as Garuḍa would do to a cobra.

9. With his firm grip on his tail, he turned him to the contrary direction when he tried to turn to the right or to the left to catch hold of Kṛṣṇa, just as a boy would do to a calf to revolve it either this way or that.

10. Then he confronted the elephant at the very front and struck him down with his hand. He ran before the elephant with that much speed that he thought Kṛṣṇa to be in his grasp at every step and he made him tumble down.

11. While running sportively, Kṛṣṇa fell down on the ground, and promptly jumped aside. Thinking that Kṛṣṇa had fallen down (and lying there), the infuriated elephant struck the ground with his tusks (as Kṛṣṇa was not there).

12. Extremely enraged at the futility of his attack and being goaded on by the drivers, he dashed in rage towards Kṛṣṇa.

13. The glorious Lord, the slayer of demon Madhu, approached the attacking elephant, caught hold of his trunk and felled him on the ground.

14. Like a lion, Lord Kṛṣṇa pressed down the fallen elephant with his foot and extracting a tusk of that elephant killed him as well as his drivers.

15. Leaving the dead elephant there, Kṛṣṇa with one tusk in hand, entered the arena. With one tusk on his shoulder, with his body stained with drops of ichor and blood, Kṛṣṇa shone beautiful with his lotus-like face decked with pearl-like drops of perspiration'

16. Surrounded by several cowherds, Balarāma and Kṛṣṇa armed with an excellent weapon in the form of the tusk of the elephant, entered the amphitheatre.

17.* When, accompanied with his elder brother, Kṛṣṇa entered the arena, he appeared like a thunderbolt to the athletes, as a superman to men, the god of Love (Cupid) incarnate to women, a kinsman to cowherds, a chastiser to wicked monarchs, a child to his parents, the veritable Death to Kaṁsa, the king of Bhojas, as a weakling or an inadequate competitor to the ignorant, the Highest Principle (*Brahman*) to the Yogins and the Supreme Deity to Vṛṣṇis.

18. Seeing that the elephant Kuvalayāpīḍa was killed and both of them were still invincible, Kaṁsa with all his intrepidity and self-possession, felt extremely terrified at that time, Oh King.

19. The mighty-armed brothers with picturesque dress, strange ornaments, wreaths and wearing quaint garments, shone like two excellently attired brilliant actors on the stage and they captivated (and agitated the minds of the on-lookers with their brilliance.

* ŚR. explains that Lord Kṛṣṇa was a combination of different *rasas* (sentiments) according to the view point of the person concerned. He quotes a verse enumerating the order of *rasas*. He manifested :

raudro'dbhutaśca śṛṅgāro hāsayaṁ vīro dayā tathā|
bhayānakaś ca bībhatsaḥ śāntaḥ saprema-bhaktikaḥ||

VT. and VB. also in a lengthy commentary expound how Lord Kṛṣṇa represented all the *rasas*. For example : the ordinary citizens were so much surprised to see the Supra-human exploits of Kṛṣṇa (e.g. killing a big elephant singlehandedly without the use of weapons by his physical might) that it was a miracle to them (*adbhuta*)

20. The occupants of the galleries, both from the town and the country gazed at those two super-men. With their eyes and countenances beaming with an outburst of extreme joy, they as if drank the countenances of those brothers with their eyes but did not feel satisfied, Oh King.

21. They were as if drinking them with their eyes, licking them with their tongues, smelling them with their nose and clasping them in their arms.

22. They described to each other the details of what they actually saw (e.g. breaking of the sacrificial bow) and of what they heard (e.g. lifting of mount Govardhana) as if they were recollecting their personality (armed with the tusks of the elephant), excellences (such as bravery), sweetness (of smiling, manner of speaking etc.) and their extraordinary courage.

23. "These two brothers are the incarnations of the rays of the Almighty Lord Hari whose abode is cosmic waters, descended on the earth in the house of Vasudeva.

24. It is reported that this Kṛṣṇa was born of Devakī and taken to Gokula where, without being known by anyone, he grew up in the house of Nanda till that time.

25. By him Pūtanā, the demon in the form of a whirl-wind (Cakravāta), the two Arjuna trees, the Yakṣa (Śaṅkhacūḍa), Keśin, Dhenuka[1] and others of the same tribe were finished.

26. Cows along with cowherds were rescued by him from the forest-conflagration, the serpent Kāliya was subdued and Indra was humbled down with his pride ridden off.

27. The big mountain (Govardhana) was held up by him on his palm for seven days and Gokula was protected from (driving) showers, (tempestuous) winds and thunderbolts.

28. Looking with delight at his ever-cheerful appearance beaming with smiles, the Gopīs easily[2] got over their sufferings of various sorts.

29. People say that being protected by him in every respect, the race of Yadu became widely celebrated and will attain affluence, glory and influence.

1. It may be noted that Dhenuka was killed by Balarāma (vide 10.15.36) But people in Mathura heard a different report.

2. ŚR. alternately takes *āśramam* as qualifying *mukham* and interprets: the slightly 'fatigued countenance of Kṛṣṇa.'

30. This is his elder brother the splendid-looking Balarāma of lotus-eyes, by whom were killed Pralamba, Vatsaka (the demon who assumed the form of a calf) and Asuras like Baka and others[1]"

31. While people were talking thus (among themselves) and there was a flourish of trumpets, Cāṇūra addressed Kṛṣṇa and Rāma, and spoke as follows :

32. "Oh Kṛṣṇa, the son of Nanda ! Oh Balarāma ! Hearing that both of you are respected as great heroes, expert in wrestling, you have been invited by the king who is eager to see you.

33. Subjects who abide by the wish of the king in thought, word and deeds, attain to prosperity. And if they behave to the contrary, they meet with the reverse of it.

34. It is quite well known that since the age as cowherd-boys who tend calves, even grown up cowherds also take delight in sporting and wrestling in the jungle while pasturing the cows.

35. Hence, let all of us do what is liked by the king. All beings will be propitious unto us thereby, as the king personifies all beings."

36. Hearing that speech, Kṛṣṇa welcomed it. Considering that wrestling was desirable in his case[2], he gave a reply appropriate to the place and occasion.

37. "(Though we are not city-dwellers like you under Kaṁsa's direct control) we too, wanderers in the forest as we are, are the subjects of the king of Bhojas we shall always do what is agreeable to him. It will be a great favour unto us.

38. We are after all boys. We shall play with those who are equal to us in strength. Let there be proper type of wrestling. There should not be the slightest transgression of justice, Oh judges of the wrestling tournaments."

1. As it usually happens in hearsay information, people of Mathura seem to have mixed up matters, for Vatsa and Baka were killed by Kṛṣṇa.

2. VB. explains that the investiture of the sacred thread of Kṛṣṇa had not taken place. As such, though he was a Kṣattriya, he was ineligible to use arms. Hence (for killing them) wrestling was appropriate from the point of time and place or traditional usage.

Cāṇūra replied :

39. "Neither You nor Balarāma is a child nor a teenager (from eleven to fifteen years of age). You, by whom an elephant possessing the strength of a thousand elephants was killed as if in a sport, are the foremost amongs the powerful people.

40. Hence, Oh Kṛṣṇa (A scion of the Vṛṣṇi clan) You will have to wrestle with powerful athletes. There is no injustice in this case. You measure Your strength with me and let Balarāma wrestle with Muṣṭika."

CHAPTER FORTYFOUR

Slaying of Kaṁsa

Śrī Śuka continued :

1. (When the pairs (or wrestlers) were so determined) Lord Kṛṣṇa (the slayer of demon Madhu) of unflinching resolution caught hold of Cāṇūra and Balarāma, the son of Rohiṇī advanced towards Muṣṭika.

1-A* (Spurious—vide the foot-note)

2. With the ambition of vanquishing the opponent, they interlocked their hands and feet with those of the opponent and vehemently tugged each other (with all their strength).

3. While wrestling they struck each other with fore-arms with clenched fists[1], knees with knees, heads with heads and chests with chests.

*. D.S. Yande's edition of the Bh.P. Bombay 1928 adds this spurious verse. As Vṛndāvana edt. does not give it, I did not include it above :

āsphoṭya hastau hastābhyām ūrū caiva punaḥ punaḥ /
visṛjya bhūyaḥ saṅgṛhya parikramya parasparam //

It describes how the wrestlers stroked loudly their arms and thighs, closed upon each other and tried to dodge.

I regard it as 'spurious' as some standard annotators such as ŚR., VR., VJ., VB., VT. do not take its cognisance.

1. *tasmān muṣṭyupa-lakṣitatvena kathañcit muṣṭir eva vācyā*—VT

4. They mutually tried to overpower each other by whirling, squeezing into arms, dashing each other to the ground and by pouncing on each other or dodging by receding.

5. Fired with the ambition to vanquish the other, they subjected each other's bodies to sufferings by lifting up, by carrying away, dashing down on the ground and fixing the opponent to the spot.

6. Noticing that unequally-arranged fight between the weak boys and the powerful athletes, all the lady-spectators, being full of compassion, spoke (criticising) in groups, to each other, Oh king !

7. "Alas ! It is out and out injustice on the part of the royal assembly who revel in such unequal fighting between the weak and the strong opponents, despite the presence of the king as spectator.

8. What a great contrast is there between the athletes of adamant-like powerful bodies, enormous like the hills, as opposed to the two saplings (teenagers) of very delicate limbs and who have not even attained youth.

9. This is certainly the transgression of righteousness on the part of this assembly. One should never stay at all at a place where violation of religion and justice takes place.

10. An intelligent person who is aware of the faults of the members of attending an assembly, ought not to enter that assembly at all. Irrespective of his participation in the discussion of the assembly by remaining silent despite knowing the truth or making a non-factual statement), the attending member incurs sins.

11. Lo ! Have a look at the lotus-face of Kṛṣṇa. How his countenance appears adorned with droplets of perspiration and resembles a lotus covered with drops of water, as he whirls round his opponent.

12. Don't you see the face of Balarāma, with reddish eyes, flushed with rage against Muṣṭika, yet beautified with a defiant laugh.

13. Oh ! How blessed must be the lands of Vraja where this Ancient Person whose feet are worshipped by god Śiva and goddess Lakṣmī roams about in the guise of a human being, decorated with wreaths of quaint wild flowers, playing upon

his flute, tending cows in the company of Balarāma and goes out for playing games (Shame upon this assembly where he is maltreated thus).

14. What supreme type of penance the Gopīs must have practised that they drink with their eyes his personal charm which is the essence of beauty, neither equalled nor surpassed by anything, which is by itself too beautiful to be adorned by anything external which assumed novelty every moment and is very difficult to obtain, as it is the permanent absolute abode of glory, beauty, affluence and almightiness.

15. Blessed are the women of Vraja who, in the course of their every day activities like milking the kine, pounding corns etc. churning curds for butter, applying cow-dung to the ground, rocking the cradles, lullabying their babies, cleaning and sweeping the houses, glorify him in songs with their hearts deeply attached to him, with their throat choked with tears and who get whatever they wish with their minds absorbed in Lord Kṛṣṇa[1] (*or* who carry on all their activities while contemplating on Lord Kṛṣṇa).

16. Inexhaustible must be the fund of merits of those women of Vraja who, coming out on the street quickly on hearing him playing upon the flute, while going out of the Vraja in the morning and returning to Vraja in the evening along with the (herd of) cows, are able to behold his countenance beaming with smiles and radiating grace and compassion.

17. While the women folk were loudly discussing among themselves, the glorious Lord Hari, the Master of Yoga made up his mind to finish with the enemy, Oh Leader of Bharatas!

18.* Hearing the panicky discussion of women (full of apprehension), the parents (Vasudeva and Devakī) who were not aware of the (extraordinary) strength of their children, were overwhelmed with filial love and were agitated at heart (full of repentance for not instructing Akrūra not to bring children to Mathura).

1. *ŚR. urukramacittaṁ tenaiva yānaṁ sarva-viṣaya-prāptir yāsāṁ tāḥ* /

*. untraced in the text of VJ.

19. Acyuta (Kṛṣṇa) and Cāṇūrā fought with each other using diverse manouvers in wrestling. In the same manner did Balarāma wrestle with Muṣṭika.

20. It is reported that at every blow and stroke from the Lord's limbs (such as fisted fore-arms and knees) which were hard like strokes of Vajra (Indra's thunderbolt), the limbs of Cāṇūra got shattered and he fainted now and then.

21. With the swiftness of a hawk, the enraged Cāṇūra jumped up and clenching both hands into fists, struck the glorious Lord Kṛṣṇa (the son of Vasudeva) on the chest.

22-23. The Lord however did not budge an inch under that blow like an elephant when struck with a wreath of flowers), (on the contrary) catching hold of Cāṇūra by both his arms, he whirled Cāṇūra several times so violently as extinguished his life thereby and dashed him on the ground, where he lay stretched with ornaments and garlands scattered and hair dishevelled, like the flagstaff of Indra struck down.

24. Similarly Muṣṭika was violently slapped with his palms by Balarāma who was dealt a blow with his fist by Muṣṭika.

25. Trembling violently (in a swoon) and pressed hard (from within), he vomitted blood profusely through his mouth and fell down dead on the ground, like a tree uprooted by a stormy wind.

26. After this, Balarāma, the past master in boxing (lit. in dealing blows) sportively yet scornfully dealt a blow with his left fist and killed another demon Kūṭa who advanced to fight.

27. At the same time, Śala (who approached Kṛṣṇa to pull his leg) got his head knocked off by Kṛṣṇa's kick and the head of Tosalaka (who attempted the same simultaneously) had his head split in two (by Kṛṣṇa's kick) and both of them fell down lifeless on the ground.

28. When Cāṇūra, Muṣṭika, Kūṭa, Śala and Tośalaka were thus killed, the rest of the wrestlers, being anxious to save their own lives, ran away.[1]

1. Out of the various commentaries describing this wrestling, it appears that VB had a better idea of that art.

29. Then Balarāma and Kṛṣṇa dragged forth their cowherd-friends in the arena. And clasping them they sported. While the trumpets were flourishing, their anklets too jingled as (Kṛṣṇa and Balarāma) capered and danced.

30. With the exception of Kaṁsa, all spectators were overjoyed at the (athletic) feats of Balarāma and Kṛṣṇa. And all good people including prominent Brāhmaṇas cheered them up with the shouts "Bravo ! Well-done !".

31. It is traditionally reported that when the stalwart wrestlers, were killed and the rest took to their heals, Kaṁsa, the king of Bhojas, stopped the blowing of all trumpets and commanded as follows :

32. "Drive out from the city (Mathura) the two ill-behaved sons of Vasudeva. Confiscate the wealth of all Gopas (cowherds). Arrest and bind down the wicked-minded Nanda.

33. As to the evil-minded Vasudeva, the vilest of the vile, let him be put to death immediately along with father Ugrasena and his attendants who have sided with the hostile party."

34. While Kaṁsa was thus boastfully ordering, the indefatigable Lord Kṛṣṇa flared up in rage and with vehemence he sprang forth with agility to the high dias (occupied by Kaṁsa).

35. Perceiving Kṛṣṇa so approaching him as his veritable Death, the heroic Kaṁsa instantly sprang from his seat and grasped his sword and shield.

36. Like Garuḍa forcibly seizing a serpent, the formidable Lord of irresistible and terrible energy, instantaneously caught hold of Kaṁsa firmly, as he was moving about right and left, like a hawk in the sky.

37. Toppling down his crown and catching Kaṁsa by his hair, the Lord hurled him down from the high dias to the groundfloor of the arena. And on him jumped the absolute willed, (the weighty) support of the (heaviest of the heavy) universe, the veritable Lord Viṣṇu (the lotus-navelled God) himself.

Vj.'s text adds

37A. When Kaṁsa was thus thrown down and crushed by Kṛṣṇa, (the mightily heavy) abode of the three worlds and of absolute will power, Kaṁsa gave up his life in a second (the winking of the eyelid), Oh King.

38. And like unto a lion dragging an elephant, Lord Hari dragged him on the ground though lifeless, even while the world was witnessing it (aghast). Loud shrieks, screams and shouts expressing grief and horror burst forth from all the people, Oh King.

39. With a mind agitated with fright, he always visualized in front of him the Lord armed with a discus even while he was drinking, speaking, wandering, sleeping (nay even) breathing. Hence after death, he attained (identity with) that very form which is so very difficult (for others) to attain.

40. Kaṅka, Nyagrodhaka, and other eight younger brothers of Kaṁsa became enraged and attacked him with a view to repay the moral debt of their brother by avenging his death.

41. With the tusk of the elephant as a club (*parigha*) Balarāma, the son of Rohiṇī, struck down and finished all those who rushed fully prepared and with vehement impetuosity, as a lion kills beasts.

42. Kettle-drums were sounded in the heavens. Great divinities like Brahmā, Śiva and others were highly delighted and sang songs of glory, while showering flowers on him. And celestial women danced.

43. The widowed women, however, who were deeply grieved at the death of their husbands and friends came there beating their heads and eyes overflowing with tears, Oh great king.

44. Embracing their husbands lying dead on the ground the grieving ladies lamented loudly, shedding frequently profuse tears.

45. (They bewailed: "Ah! My Lord! My beloved, knower of *dharma*! Oh merciful Lord! Oh affectionate darling! By your death we, along with your home and progeny are as good as killed.

46. Oh foremost among men! Bereaved of you the protector, the city of Mathura does not appear beautiful as it is bereft of joyousness, festivals and auspiciousness.

47. Oh Lord ! You perpetrated utmost cruelty and harshness towards the innocents. Hence, you have been brought to such a plight. What oppressors of living beings can get happiness ?

48. For, this Kṛṣṇa is verily the beginning (creator), end (destroyer) and the protector of all beings. He who is insubordinate to him shall never get any happiness."

Śrī Śuka said :

49. Having consoled the ladies of the royal family, the glorious Lord who is the protector of the world, caused what is known as the formal obsequies and funeral rites of those who were killed.

50. Thereupon, Śrī Kṛṣṇa and Balarāma secured the release of their father and mother from their chains and touching their feet with their heads, paid respects to them.

51. Realizing that their sons who were bowing down are verily the Lords of the world, Devakī and Vasudeva being afraid (of a possible offence to them) did not embrace them.

CHAPTER FORTYFIVE

Restoration of Preceptor Sāndīpani's son

Śrī Śuka continued:

1. Noticing that his parents, Vasudeva and Devakī, had realized the truth (of their Divine Nature) prematurely (before enjoying the filial bliss in loving them as their children), the Supreme Person, Kṛṣṇa, cast over them his divine Māyā (the spell of his deluding faculty) which infatuates the world, so that this realization (of his God-hood) should not continue (as it would not give scope to their parental love and affect their affectionate filial behaviour).

2. Kṛṣṇa, the bull (prominent person) among the Sātvatas, approached along with his elder brother to his parents.

He bowed down with great modesty, and respectfully addressed them: "Oh Mother" and "Oh father."

3. "Father! Though both of you have been all along longing earnestly for it, we could not, at any time, give you the pleasure of witnessing the infancy, childhood and boyhood of your sons.

4. Unfortunate as we are, we had not the good luck of staying near you nor could we enjoy the bliss of being caressed by parents which children dwelling in their parent's home experience.

5. It is not possible for a mortal being, even within the full span of human life of hundred years, to repay the obligations of parents who brought forth and nourished his body whereby all the four objects in life (like *dharma*, *artha* etc.) are achieved.

6. If he (the son) be (physically and financially) competent but does not maintain them by rendering personal service or financial help, he is made to eat his own flesh (in hell) after his death, by servants of Yama.

7. He who, in spite of his competence (to support) his old mother, father, chaste wife and infant son, his preceptor, (learned) Brāhmaṇa and one seeking his resort, is as good as dead though breathing.

8. With our minds ever in terror of Kaṁsa and due to our inability to worship you both, all these days have been sheerly wasted away.

9. It behoves you, Oh father and mother, to forgive us, since we were dependants and unable to render service to you, even though you were mercilessly harassed by that wicked-hearted fellow Kaṁsa."

Śrī Śuka said:

10. Fascinated by the charming words of Lord Hari who, though the soul of the universe, had assumed a human form through his Māyā Potency, they placed him on their lap, embraced him and felt greatly delighted.

11. Oh King! Bound with ties of (filial) affection, they bathed him profusely with their tears. Being bewildered and

with their throats choked with tears and emotions, they could utter nothing.

12. Having thus comforted his parents, Lord Kṛṣṇa, the son of Devakī, (immediately) installed his maternal grandfather as the king of Yadus.

13. He addressed him (Ugrasena): "Oh great king! May Your Majesty be pleased to command us (Yadus) as well as the subjects (of the Śūrasena country). Owing to an imprecation from Yayāti, Yadus are not entitled to occupy a throne.[1]

14. When I attend upon you as your servant, even gods (and other supernatural beings) will submissively offer worship to you. What then to speak of other chiefs of human beings? They will definitely do so.

15-16. Lord Kṛṣṇa, the Creator of the Universe, brought back his kith and kin—Yadus, Vṛṣṇis, Andhakas, Dāśārhas, Kukuras and others, who being overcome with the fear from Kaṁsa, had fled to different directions and had undergone suffering in foreign lands. He consoled them, providing them with sufficient wealth and wherewithals and rehabilitated them in their homes.

17. Protected by the arms of Kṛṣṇa and Balarāma and with all their agonies removed by Kṛṣṇa and Balarāma, they enjoyed themselves in their homes with all their desire accomplished.

18. (Having the opportunity of) seeing daily the lotus-like countenance of Kṛṣṇa graced with splendour and beauty and beaming with smiles and compassionate looks, all of them were delighted.

19. Even aged persons thereof, who could drink with their eyes the nectarine beauty of his lotus-face, became rejuvenated with abundant strength and energy.

1. Despite Yadu's refusal to transfer his youth to his father for enjoying his mother (a serious moral problem), Yadu was given the southern part of his kingdom by his father (*vide Supra* 9.19.22). ŚR. explains: 'Though you belong to the Yadu clan, you will not incur any sin as you occupy the throne by my command.'

20. Thereupon, the glorious Lord Kṛṣṇa, the Son of Devakī, and Balarāma approached Nanda, and embracing him, spoke to him as follows, Oh King of kings.

21. "Father ! Both of us have been extremely fondled and nourished by you both (Nanda and Yaśodā) who have been highly affectionate to us. Parents cherish more love towards their children than to their own selves.

22. He is the real father and she is the (*de facto*) mother who nourish and caress like their own sons, other babes who are abandoned by their relatives, due to their incapacity to feed and protect them.

23. Father ! Now all of you return to your Vraja. After looking to the welfare and felicity of friends hereof, we shall come to visit you, our kith and kin who due to our separation from them are grieved through their love for us."

24. Having consoled Nanda along with the residents of Vraja in this way, the glorious Immutable Lord (Kṛṣṇa) respectfully worshipped them with garments, ornaments, utensils (of copper, brass etc. as milk-containers) and other gifts.

25. Nanda who was addressed thus (by Kṛṣṇa) was overwhelmed with filial love. With his eyes streaming with tears, he hugged them both and returned to Vraja along with Gopas.

26. Thereafter, Vasudeva, the son of Śūra caused as per *Śāstric* prescriptions, the ceremony of the investiture of the sacred thread[1] (essential for the status of the 'twice-borns') (of their sons) by his family priest Garga and other Brāhmaṇas.

27. After adorning the Brāhmaṇas with ornaments, he worshipped them and gave as *dakṣiṇā* (fee for performing this ceremony) cows with their calves, decorated with gold chains and other ornaments and covered with silk-cloth.

28. The noble-minded Vasudeva recollected the cows which he donated mentally, according to the constellation that was in ascendance at the time of the birth of Balarāma and Kṛṣṇa but (which he could not give, as they) were seized ille-

1. As the presence of mother is essential in the sacred thread ceremony, it is obvious that Balarāma's mother, Rohiṇī was brought from Vraja—VT.

gally and unrighteously by Kaṁsa. And he gave those cows also (which he intended to give).

29. Thereupon, being consecrated (through the investiture of the sacred thread) and attaining the status of the 'twice-borns', those two staunch observers of vows adopted the vow of celibacy (lit. vow pertaining to the *Gāyatrī mantra*) from the sage Garga, the family priest of Yadus.

30. Though both of them were the source of all lores, and the omniscient Lords of the worlds, they concealed their unclouded spiritual knowledge which is in-born and not borrowed from others, by behaving like common men.

31. Desirous of having a residence in a preceptor's house for their education, they approached (and served Sāndīpani who was originally a resident of Kāśī[1] but was now a citizen of Avantī.

32. The self-controlled brothers formally approached him with due humility and respect, and set a model of faultless behaviour with the teacher, (for others to emulate). Both of them who were respectfully treated, served their teacher with devotion, as if he were a god.

33. Being highly pleased with their pure-hearted devoted services, the eminent Brāhmaṇa teacher, Sāndīpani taught them all the Vedas along with their *Upaniṣads* (the philosophical works) and the accessory branches (viz. *Śikṣā*—phonetics, *chandas*—prosody, *Vyākaraṇa*—grammar, *Jyotiṣa*—Astronomy, *Kalpa*—science of Vedic ritualism and *Nirukta*—etymology).

34. He taught them Military science (lit. the Veda pertaining to archery) along with the mystic formulae (*mantras*) of discharging and retracting *astras* (missiles), *dharma-śāstra* (Law incorporated into the codes of Manu etc.), *Mīmāṁsā*, Logic and political science along with its six branches[2] (viz. techniques regarding peace-treaties, warfare, expedition, encampment, spreading sedition and dis-array among enemies and consolidation of alliance).

1. *Kāśyam*—belonging to Kāśyapa *gotra*.
2. ŚR. and VJ. quote the following verse enumerating these branches-
Sandhiṁ ca vigrahaṁ caiva yānam āsanam eva ca/
dvaidhī-bhāvaṁ saṁśrayaṁ ca ṣaḍ-guṇāḥ kavayo viduḥ //

35. Those two greatest among the great, who were themselves the progenitors of all lores mastered everything that the teachers uttered but once to them (while teaching), Oh protector of men !

36. Within a period of sixtyfour days and nights, those brothers, with controlled minds, mastered as many (i.e. sixtyfour[1]) arts and crafts, and persuaded their preceptor to accept whatever he liked as his fee of teaching.

1. ŚR. quotes a work *Śaiva tantra* enumerating the traditional sixty four *kalās*. Ardhamāgadhī Jaina canon enumerates 72 *kalās*. The resemblance between the two lists is significant from the point of social life in ancient India. Here the list of sixtyfour *kalās* as quoted by ŚR. and explained by VT is given.

1. *Gīta* (singing) 2. *Vādya* (instrumental music) 3. *Nṛtya* (dancing) 4. *Nāṭya* (histrionics) 5. *Ālekhya* (painting, and drawing) 6. *Viśeṣakacchedya* (painting various designs on the body) 7. *Taṇḍula-kusuma-bali-vikāra* (preparations of various designs with rice, flowers etc. in worship) 8. *Puṣpāstaraṇa* (preparing a bed of flowers 9. *Daśana-vasanā-aṅgarāga* (painting the teeth, limbs of the body and articles of dress with various figures). 10. *Maṇi-bhūmikā-karma* (paving of the floor with precious stones.) 11. *Śayana-racanā* (preparation of bed) 12. *Udaka-vādya* (*Jala-taraṅga* : a musical instrument with water pots), *Udaka ghāta* (steadying water enabling one to walk over it) 13. *Citra-yoga* (demonstration of miracles). 14. *Mālya-grathana-vikalpa* (preparation of wreaths and chaplets of flowers). 15. *Śekharāpīḍa-yojana* (preparation of ornaments of flowers for the ears etc.) 16. *Nepathya-yoga* (method of beautifying the body with clothes etc.). 17 *Karṇa-patra-bhaṅga* (drawing ornamental figures on the ears). 18. *Sugandha-yukti* (making of cosmetics and perfumes) 19. *Bhūṣaṇa-yojana* (making ornaments of different kinds). 20. *Aindrajāla* (Jugglery). 21. *Kaucumāra-yoga* (assuming various disguises) 22. *Hastalāghava* (sleight of hand) 23. *Citra-śākāpūpa-bhakṣya-vikāra-kriyā* (preparation of various sweet dishes). 24. *Pānakarasarāgāsava-yojana* (preparation of drinks of various tastes and colours). 25. *Sūcīvāya-karma* (needle work and embroidery). 26. *Sūtra-krīḍā* (Puppet-show by string-pulling), 27. *Vīṇā-ḍamaruka-vādya* (making musical instruments), 28. *Prahelikā* (solving conundrums—like cross-word puzzles); 29. *Pratimālā* (making replicas of things—) 30. *durvācaka-yoga* (uttering tongue-twisters), 31. *Pustaka vācanam* (fast reading of books (Mss) despite *lacunae*), 32. *Nāṭakākhyāyikā-darśanam* (Dramaturgy and writing plays or dramas), 33. *Kāvya-samasyā-pūraṇam* (completion of a verse from a part—generally containing an apparently illogical statement) to make a cogent statement out of it) 34. *Paṭṭikā-vetra-bāṇa-vikalpa* (Preparation of ligatures, canework, arrows), 35. *tarka-karma* (spindle work), 36. *takṣaṇam* (carpentry), 37. *Vāstuvidyā* (architecture), 38. *rūpya-ratna-parīkṣā* (evaluation and testing of valuable metals (silver, gold) precious stones), 39. *dhātuvāda* (Alchemy), 40. *maṇi-rāga-*

37. Noticing their miraculous capacity and greatness and their super human intelligence, the Brāhmaṇa, after consultation with his wife, sought (the restoration to life of) his son who died in the ocean at Prabhāsa (paṭṭaṇa in Saurāṣṭra), as his fee.

38. Complying with his request with the word, "So be it", those two great heroes (who could single-handedly fight with ten thousand warriors) and were of unlimited prowess, then mounted their chariot, arrived at Prabhāsa and going to the beach thereof, sat there for a moment. Having come to know of the arrival of those divine personages, the god presiding over the ocean, worshipped them with valuable presents.

39. The glorious Lord Kṛṣṇa spoke to him: "Let the son of my preceptor who was swallowed up by you in a big wave, be restored immediately."

The Presiding Deity of the sea replied:

40-41. "Oh refulgent Lord Kṛṣṇa ! I have never carried away that son of your preceptor. But there is a formidable demon called Pañcajana who moves through the waters. He is an asura who has assumed the form of a conch As a matter

jñāna (developing colours in precious stones), 41. *ākara-jñāna* (mining and mineralogy), 42. *Vṛkṣāyurveda* (botany), 43. *meṣa-kukuṭa-lāvaka-yuddha-vidhi* (arranging ram-fights, cock-fights), 44. *Śuka-sārikā-pralapana* (teaching parrots, etc. to imitate human speech), 45. *utsādanam* (Driving out an enemy—by a *mantra*), 46. *Keśamārjana-Kauśala* (hair-dressing and cleaning), 47. *akṣara-muṣṭikā-kathana*(reading closed letters and divining what is hidden in fists), 48. *mlecchita-kutarka-vikalpa* (reading books in foreign or barbaric-scripts), 49. *deśa-bhāṣājñāna* (knowledge of languages of the country i.e. Indian languages), 50. *Puṣṭa-śakaṭikā-nirmiti-jñāna* (knowledge of making a cart blossom), 51. *yantra-mātṛkā-dhāraṇa-mātṛkā* (magical formulae—with figures inscribed with letters and amulets to wear), 52. *sampāṭyam* (breaking hard substances like diamonds in different shapes), 53. *mānasī-kāvya-kriyā* (mind-reading in verse form), 44. *abhidhāna-kośa* (Lexicography), 55. *chandojñana* (knowledge of prosody), 56. *Kriyāvikalpa* (multiplying the number of objects by various devices), 57. *chalitaka-yoga* (playing tricks), 58. *Vastra-gopana* (showing one's clothes as more superfine), 59. *dyūta viśeṣa* (expertise in gambling), 60. *ākarṣa-krīḍā* (attracting remote objects= telekinesis). 61. *Bālakrīḍanaka* (playing children's games), 62. *Vaināyikī* (jugglery and practice kriyā dharmas), 63. *Vaijayikī* (foreknowledge of victory in debate), 64. *Vaitālikriyā* (control of goblins and evil spirits).

of fact, the boy has been carried away by him." Hearing that, the glorious Lord instantly plunged into the water, killed the demon (Pañcajana) but could not trace the child in his bowels.

42-44. Taking the conch which formed his body, he returned to his chariot. He went with Balarāma to Saṁyamanī, the beloved city of Yama, the god of death and blew his conch. Hearing the loud blast of the conch, Yama, the chastiser of all beings, offered them worship on a grand scale and with deep devotion. Bowing down in humility, he submitted to Kṛṣṇa who abides in the hearts of all beings, "Oh Viṣṇu who have assumed a human form out of sport! What can I do for you both ?"

The glorious Lord replied:

45. Oh great Ruler ! Even if the son of my preceptor is brought here due to the force of his *Karma*, bring him here in obedience to and under the sanction of my command.

46. The preceptor's son who, in compliance of his command, was brought back by the god of Death, was restored to their preceptor by those two eminent Yadus who requested him, "Be pleased to ask for any other boon."

The Preceptor (Sāndipani) said:

47. Child Kṛṣṇa ! The obligations of the preceptors have been richly and properly repaid by you both respectable pupils. What desire of your preceptor can remain unfulfilled ?

48. Oh heroes ! You return to your homes ! May your glory be purifying to the world ! May your memory and knowledge of the Vedas remain afresh here and hereafter.

49. Oh child parīkṣit ! Being thus permitted to return home, both of them returned to their capital in their chariot which had the speed of the wind and the thundering of the cloud.

50. All the subjects who missed Balarāma and Kṛṣṇa for many days, were highly rejoiced to see them both, like persons who have recovered their lost wealth.

CHAPTER FORTYSIX

Uddhava deputed for consoling Nanda

Śrī Śuka said:

1. Uddhava was the foremost counsellor of the Vṛṣṇis and the utmost beloved friend of Kṛṣṇa. He was a direct disciple of Bṛhaspati (the preceptor of gods and a founder of the political science) and was most intelligent.

2. On one occasion, holding Uddhava's hand in his own, Lord Hari, the destroyer of miseries of those who seek asylum in him, spoke to him—his most beloved votary of unflinching devotion.

3. "Oh gentle-natured Uddhava! Please do go to Vraja. Bring felicity to our[1] parents (Nanda and Yaśodā) by communicating my message to them. Please relieve the (mental) agony of separation from me of the Gopīs by conveying my special message to them.

4. They have entirely devoted their heart and soul to me and they regard me as their very life. For my sake they have given up their husbands and sons—nay their bodily requirements[2] as well.

4A. They are united with me in mind regarding me as their beloved-most, the climax of their love and their Lord.

I always support and give happiness to those who renounce all pleasures and interests and means to obtain them here and hereafter, and have over-ruled popular moral conventions for my sake.

5. Myself, the foremost of their beloved objects, being away at a distant place, the women of Gokula always brood over me and being overwhelmed with deep anxiety and grief caused by separation from me, they have become oblivious to everything else, dear friend!

6. It is due to my message assuring them of my return to visit them that the cowherd women whose heart and soul is

1. *v.l. nau*—of us both—VB.

2. 4-A. Some editions (e.g. Yande's Bombay edition) add this line here :

māmeva dayitaṁ preṣṭham ātmānam manasā gatāḥ /

absorbed in me are somehow managing to stay alive with great difficulty".

Śrī Śuka said :

7. Oh king ! When thus instructed, Uddhava received with respect and devotion the message of his Lord. Getting into his chariot, he drove fast to Nanda's Gokula.

8. While the sun was setting and his chariot was obscured with the thick cloud of dust raised by the hoofs of the cattle that were returning home, the blessed Uddhava reached Nanda's Vraja (and could contact Nanda without Gopīs being aware of his arrival).

9. It (the Gokula) was noisy to the roaring of maddened bulls (in rut) fighting with one another for cows in heat, and by rushing of cows with heavy udders to meet their calves.

10. It appeared beautiful with snow-white calves (briskly) frisking and capering here and there and with the musical notes of flutes and (whistle-like) sounds while milking the cows.

11. The Gokula appeared most resplendent with richly adorned Gopīs and Gopas, the former glorifying in songs the auspicious deeds of Balarāma and Kṛṣṇa.

12. It was charming with the habitations of the cowherds where the sacred fire, the sun-God, guests, cows, Brāhmaṇas, ancestors and gods were being worshipped with flowers, lights and fragrant frank-incense burnt before them (*OR* and which were beautified by garlands, lamps and burning frank-incense).

13. On all sides, it abounded in groves in full blossom and resounded with the sweet warblings and notes of birds and hummings of bees. It was beautified with ponds full of lotus-beds teeming with swans and Kāraṇḍavas (a species of ducks).

14. Seeing (and receiving) Uddhava, the beloved follower of kṛṣṇa, who had arrived there, Nanda was exceedingly delighted. He embraced him and worshipped him (with due formalities and respect) regarding him to be Vāsudeva (Kṛṣṇa) himself.

15. When he was served with rich dishes and was comfortably resting on a bed, and had been relieved of his fatigue by shampooing and such other services, Nanda enquired of him.

16. "Oh Highly blessed dear Uddhava ! Is our friend Vasudeva, the delight (or son) of Śūra happy and doing well, as he is now free (from imprisonment) united with his sons, wives and others and is surrounded by his friends and well-wishers ?

17. The wicked Kaṁsa who always hated the righteous and religious-minded Yadus, has fortunately been killed by his own sins along with his followers.

18. Does Kṛṣṇa remember us, his mother Yaśodā, his friends, well-wishers and other Gopas, Vraja of which he was the protector, cows, Vṛndāvana and mount Govardhana !

19. Will Kṛṣṇa, the Protector of cows, come at least once, to see his friends, kith and kin (hereof) ? Then alone we shall be able to see his charming countenance with a shapely nose, happy smiles and (loving) glances.

20. We have been protected from the forest conflagration, stormy winds and driving showers, the demon in the bullock form (Ariṣṭa), the serpent (Kāliya) and from perils and fatal accidents which were difficult to be avoided, by the highly noble-souled Kṛṣṇa.

21. Dear Uddhava ! When we remember the heroic exploits of Kṛṣṇa, his sportive glances, his smiles and talks, all our actions become slackened.

22. Even as we see the play-grounds, the river Yamunā, hills, forests and groves adorned with the foot-prints of Kṛṣṇa, our mind becomes absorbed in him.

23. As observed by Garga, I too regard that Balarāma and Kṛṣṇa are the most prominent divinities who have descended on this earth for accomplishing some important mission of gods.

24. Both of them easily killed, as in a sport, Kaṁsa who possessed the strength of ten thousand elephants, the two wrestlers (Cāṇūra and Muṣṭika) and the king of elephants. Kuvalayāpīḍa.

25. Like a king of elephants breaking down a sugarcane, Kṛṣṇa snapped the formidable bow three *tālas* (i.e. twentyseven spans) in length. And on one hand, he held up the mount Govardhana for a period of seven days.

26. By him were killed as in a sport demons like Pralamba, Dhenuka, Ariṣṭa, Tṛṇāvarta, Baka and others who have vanquished gods and *asuras*."

Śrī Śuka said :

27. Recollecting graphically again and again the sports and exploits of Kṛṣṇa, Nanda whose mind and intellect were deeply attached to Kṛṣṇa lapsed into silence, as he was overwhelmed with extreme longing and (felt choked up) with a flood of affection.

28. While Yaśodā was listening to the description of the exploits of her sons, she shed tears profusely and her breasts overflowed with milk through maternal affection.

29. Noticing such a supreme affection of Nanda and Yaśodā towards Lord Kṛṣṇa, Uddhava spoke with great joy to Nanda.

Uddhava said :

30. "Oh courteous bestower of honours ![1] Both of you are indeed the most praiseworthy among embodied beings in this world, inasmuch as you cherish such a deep love for Nārāyaṇa (Kṛṣṇa) who is the Creator of all beings.

31. For these two—Balarāma and Kṛṣṇa—are the primary (efficient and material) cause of the Universe ; they are the *Puruṣa* (spirit) and *Pradhāna* (Primordial matter). Permeating all beings, these two Ancient (beginningless) Lords control varieties of consciousness.

32. If at the time of death, a person concentrates his mind in him at least for a moment, he reduces to ashes all his (accumulated) *karmas* and (realizing the nature of his self) becomes identical with Brahman, (and attaining a form constituted of pure *sattva*) acquires the refulgence of the Sun, and instantly reaches the highest goal.

1. You gave us the honour of belonging to the fraternity of devotees of the Lord from Nārada down to a resident of Gokula—VT.

33. Both of you cherish utmost devotion unto him (Kṛṣṇa) who is the veritable Lord Nārāyaṇa himself, the cause (source) of all beings, and who has assumed a human form for some divine purpose. Oh noble-souled Nanda! What meritorious acts are yet to be achieved by you both!

34. At no distant date, the immutable Lord Kṛṣṇa will visit Vraja again. The glorious of the Sātvatas will accomplish whatever delights his parents.

35. Whatever Kṛṣṇa has promised you after slaying Kaṁsa, the enemy of Sātvatas, in the arena[1] he will accomplish it for you.

36. Please do not get depressed, Oh highly fortunate ones! You shall see Kṛṣṇa by your side. Just as the fire (latently) exists in fuel, he abides in the hearts of all beings.

37. (Please do not entertain doubt how he will leave his dear parents and come to you). None is extremely beloved of or disliked by him, for he is above attachments. None is superior or inferior or unequal to him as he is the same to all.[2]

38. He has no mother, no father, no wife, no children or other relatives. He has none who is his own or who is his non-self. He has no corporeal form at all.

39. He has no bound of *Karma*. But out of sport and for the protection of the righteous, he incarnates in good (e g. Rāma, Kṛṣṇa, bad (Fish, Boar) and mixed (e.g. Man-lion) types of species.)[3]

40. Though this unborn Lord is transcendental to and hence unaffected by *guṇas*, he assumes all the *guṇas* such as the *sattva*, *rajas* and *tamas*. It is out of sportiveness that he creates, maintains and destroys the universe by these means.

41. Just as the whole earth appears rotating to an eye that is rolling, the Soul is regarded as the Agent through the influence of *ahaṁkāra* (Ego) while it is actually the mind that is active.[4]

1. Vide.Supra 45.23
2. Not traced in VB
3. Incarnates among gods, humans and sub-human beings—VJ.
4. Not traced in VJ.'s Text.

42. This glorious Lord Hari is not merely a son of you both, but is the Sun, Soul, father, mother and the Almighty Ruler of all.

43. Without the presence of and apart from the Lord, there is nothing which is seen or heard of, has happened in the past or present or can happen in future: nothing immobile or mobile, great or small is different from or without the presence of the Lord. For only he is everything and real.

44. In this way, while Nanda and Kṛṣṇa's follower (Uddhava) were talking, the whole night passed away (without their being aware of it). (At dawn) the cowherd women got up, lighted the lamps, duly worshipped the presiding deities of their home e. g. the threshold, and began to churn their curds.

45. The Gopīs appeared splendid with their jewels shining refulgent in the light of lamps, as they pulled to and fro the cords of the churning-rod, with (jingling) rows of bangles on their hands, with their big hips, heavy breasts and pearl necklaces moving (in a rhythmic motion), with their cheeks refulgent with the radiance of the rocking ear-rings (while churning), and with their countenance decked with red saffron.

46. The sound of the singing damsels of Vraja glorifying loudly in songs the deeds of the lotus-eyed God (Kṛṣṇa) mixed with the (gurgling) sound of the churning of the curds, filled the heaven and thereby whatever was inauspicious in all directions was dispelled.

47. When the sun rose, and the Gopīs of Vraja saw a gold-plated chariot at the door of Nanda, they enquired whose chariot it was.

48. Has Akrūra, the accomplice of Kaṁsa who carried away lotus-eyed Kṛṣṇa to Mathura and thus accomplished Kaṁsa's purpose, come again ?

49. Is he going to bring about the gratification of his dead master by offering us i.e. our bodies or flesh as *piṇḍa* (offering to the deceased) to him. While the women were talking thus, Uddhava who had finished his bath and morning (religious) duties, arrived there.

CHAPTER FORTYSEVEN

Uddhava's Discourse on the Real Nature of the Lord, Return to Mathura

Śri Śuka said :

1-2. Observing that follower of Kṛṣṇa (viz. Uddhava) with (knee) long arms and eyes like (a pair of fresh-blown) lotuses clad in yellow (silk) raiment and wearing a garland of lotuses, with a lotus-like cheerful countenance, brightened with ear-rings set with resplendent jewels, all the damsels of Vraja, beaming with broad smiles, became extremely eager and curious to know who was that charming personality with fascinating looks, wearing dress and ornaments like those of Lord Kṛṣṇa, whence he came and his who's who. They surrounded him who had taken shelter under the lotus-feet of the Lord Kṛṣṇa of hallowing renown.

3. Ascertaining that he was the emissary of the spouse of goddess Lakṣmī (Kṛṣṇa) carrying a message for them, they bowed down to him with modesty. They received him courteously with bashful smiles, glances and sweet words. When he was comfortably seated, they enquired of him in great confidence (privately) :

4. "We learn that you are the attendant of Kṛṣṇa, the Lord of Yadus, who have arrived here and that your honour has been deputed by the Lord for bringing about the happiness of his parents.

5. Otherwise, we do not see that there is anything worth remembering for him in the Gokula. The ties of affection of relatives and kinsmen are extremely difficult to dissociate even for sages.

6. In the case of others (who are not relatives) the friendship is contracted for achieving a purpose and it lasts till the purpose is accomplished, as in the case of love shown by men to (good-natured, guileless) women or by black bees to flowers.

7. Courtezans abandon a penniless (lover) ; subjects, an incompetent king; students who have completed the course of Vedic studies, their preceptors and the priests in sacrifice, the sacrificer who has paid their fees for performance of sacrifice.

8. Birds leave off the trees the fruits of which are exhausted; guests, the house after finishing their meals; beasts, a forest that is burnt down; a paramour after enjoying the women though attached to him."

9. When Uddhava, the emissary of Kṛṣṇa arrived at Vraja, the Gopīs whose body, mind and speech were completely devoted to Lord Govinda (Kṛṣṇa) disregarded the worldly usages and etiquettes (in behaving with strangers).

9*-A. VJ.'s Text differs (vide the footnote).

10. Remembering vividly every now and then the sportive activities of their Kṛṣṇa during his infancy and childhood, they glorified his deeds in songs and also wept, casting off their sense of bashfulness.

11. A certain Gopī who was musing over her union with Kṛṣṇa, saw a bee about her and imagining that it was the messenger deputed to her by her Beloved Kṛṣṇa, addressed it as follows[1] :

The Gopī said[2] :**

12. Oh bee ![3] Oh friend of a rogue (Kṛṣṇa, a treacherous paramour) ! Don't touch our feet (and try to win our favour by submissive bows) with your beard-like tentacles

* VJ's text reads differently :

When Uddhava, the emissary of Kṛṣṇa, arrived at Vraja, he perceived that the Gopī's thereof had dedicated their mind, body of speech to Govinda so completely that they had lost the sense of worldly manners and etiquettes.

1. SG. and the annotators of Gauḍīya school of Vaiṣṇavism assert that this Gopī was Rādhā. SG quotes the *Agni P.* to support this view but the quotation is untraceable in the Gurumandal Calcutta edt. of the *Agni P.*

** Irrespective of the name of Gopī who sang this ode to the black bee, it is one of the best poetic outbursts of a love-lorn heart in Sanskrit literature. Gauḍīya Vaiṣṇavas regard this as the expression of "divine ecstasy" in the *mahābhāva* stage. This expression of intense love is called *Citrajalpa* and is discussed in their works on rhetorics. As VT. points out, this stage is superior to Mokṣa in blissfulness.

2. VJ. States that this address of a black bee is equally applicable to Uddhava. Thus *Kitava-bandhu* in v. 12 means 'A friend or relative of Kṛṣṇa who was a thief (stole butter etc.)

3. *madhupa*—One who has kissed the nectar-like sweet lips—VR.

tinged with the saffron of the wreath (of Kṛṣṇa) that was pressed down upon the (Saffron-painted) breasts of our rival women (of Mathura). Let Kṛṣṇa, the chief of Madhus whose messenger you are, as described above carry with him, the favours of the proud ladies (of Mathura). (Why his attempt to court rustic women like us!) which will become a butt of ridicule in the assembly of Yadus.

13. Being infidel like you who (after sucking the honey) immediately desert the (innocent, good-natured) flower, he made us drink but once the seductive, enchanting nectar of his lips. He instantly abandoned us. Alas! What a pity? How is it that the (notoriously fickle) goddess of wealth continues to serve his lotus feet (I presume that) her mind must have been transported by the fascinating talk of Kṛṣṇa of hallowed renown.

14. (Thinking that it is to gain her favour that the black-bee is humming a song of Kṛṣṇa's glory, she retorts).

Oh six-legged one![1] Why are you singing here, in such details, in front of us, homeless foreste-dwellers, the glory of the Ancient-most[2] person Kṛṣṇa the Lord of Yadus. (It is already too well known to us). Go hence. Let all his episodes be glorified in song in the presence of the female friends of Kṛṣṇa (the friend of Arjuna). Those lady-loves of Kṛṣṇa the agonies of whose breasts (and heart) are soothed by his embrace and other erotic acts will bestow on you your desired object.

15. Are there any women on the earth, in the celestial region or in the nether-world who are difficult to be won over by him with his alluring crafty sweet smile and the tempting dancing of his eyebrows? What are we after all to him, the

1. *Ṣaḍaṅghri*—Oh Uddhava you have mastered six *darśanas*, you attend to sixfold duties, you have trampled underfoot the six objects of enjoyment which obstruct the path of devotion.—VJ.

2. *Purāṇa*—

(i) *purā pūrvam eva ṇam nirvṛtti-rūpam*
sukha-rūpam . . sāmpratam duḥkha-karam /
which formerly gave pleasure to us but now brings grief—SG.

(ii) *pure vartamānam* 'Kṛṣṇa who is staying in the town'—VJ.

dust on whose feet is adored by goddess Lakṣmī ?[1] However (go and convey my message to him) that the epithet *uttama-śloka* (one of the most glorious renown) befits him who is on the side of the helpless and forlorn people like us.

16. (The black bee approached her feet as if to beg pardon). Get away. Take away your head from my feet. I know you thoroughly. Being an emissary of Mukunda (an expert in fraudulent courting) you are trained in the fine art of conciliation and winsomeness by means of sweet words. It is here at Vraja that he (ungratefully) deserted us who have abandoned our husbands, children, prospects of happiness in the next world (by conforming to social morality) for his sake. Inconstant at heart as he is, what is there to be gained by such reconciliation ?

17. (In his previous incarnation as Dāśarathi Rāma) Cruelhearted by nature, like a hunter, (desirous of eating the flesh of his kill), he (surreptitiously) hit with an arrow Vāli, the king of monkeys. Being dominated by one woman (his consort Sītā), he deformed another woman (Śūrpaṇakhā) who approached him with amorous purpose. Like a crow eating up *bali* (boiled rice etc. offered in *bhūta-yajña*), he (as Vāmana) ate up (accepted the worship offered by) King Bali and (ungratefully) bound him down (and threw him in a cave in the subterranean world.) Now enough of any friendship with that person of black complexion (Kṛṣṇa). But the wealth of his episodes is too (precious and sweet) to forgo.

1. *caraṇa raja...ka* : We are however not among the gullible women who fall a victim to his temptations. The term *uttama-śloka* is applicable to the partisans of the helpless—VR.

(ii) We are after-all forest dwellers. We only hear that the term *uttama śloka* is used for one who espouses the cause of the indigent and the helpless but that is not our experience (for he has no interest in us). VJ.

SG. is interesting. The gist is as follows :

Only low women (*kāḥ striyaḥ*) or all women fall a victim to him by his craftiness in enticing women. Goddess Lakṣmī may be worshipping the dust on his feet but none of us will stoop so low. Only a person of glorious renown deserves singing which he is not. *Or* He has become so closefisted (and hard-hearted) that he does not see us. (This is of course ironical).

18* In this world, many persons who have but once enjoyed a particle of his delightful sportive deeds which are (sweet as) nectar to the ears, have shaken themselves free from conflicting pairs of qualities (like love and hate, pleasure and pain). Reducing themselves to non-entities[1], they have at once forsaken their homes and members of their families in a bereaved state, and have adopted the ascetic way of life like that of birds (i.e. the way of life of *haṁsa* ascetics) and practice control of sense-organs[2].

19. Oh messenger of Kṛṣṇa ! Let other topics be discussed. For, like female deer, the gullible female mates of black-antelopes, which (mistakenly) believe in the enticing musical notes of the hunter (and get into a trap or are hit with an arrow), we innocent maid-servants of Kṛṣṇa trusted in his crafty professions of love as genuine, and have many times[3] seen and suffered from the acute pangs of love created by his amorous touch of nails.

20. Oh friend of our Darling Lord ! Are you redeputed by our Beloved that you have come again ? You are an honourable guest. Dear black-bee ! Please seek whatever you would like to have from me. Oh gentle-natured bee ! As his consort Lakṣmī is always by his side and has a place on his bosom, how are you going to take up from here to the side of the Lord, separation from whom is very painful and difficult.

21. Oh gentle black-bee ! Is the son of our Gopa-chief (i.e. Nanda,) now at Mathurā back from his preceptor's house ? Does he remember his father's house (i.e. his parents Nanda and Yaśodā) ? Does he ever refer to us his maid-servants, in his talk ? Would that (he return to Gokula and) place his arm fragrant with the (pigment of) *aguru*—sandal on the crown of my head (to soothe me)"

*. The SK wording of the text appears apparently a censure but it is a praise of the Lord in the deeper sense.

1. Go away out of sight like birds—SG.

2. *bahavaścaranti* : Just as birds fly through the support of the sky, the ascetics do so through the support of Lord Hari. These ascetics maintain their body for the Spiritual Knowledge.

bhikṣu-caryām : indriya-grāma-nigraham/ —SG.

3. Female deer suffer but once when hit by an arrow, but our sufferings are life-long.

Śrī Śuka said :

22. Having heard this (expression of ardent love for Kṛṣṇa, Uddhava consoled those Gopīs who were eagerly desirous of seeing Kṛṣṇa, with the messages of their Darling and addressed them as follows :

Uddhava said :

23. Oh Gopīs ! You have completely achieved all the objects in human life (e.g. *dharma, artha, kāma, mokṣa*) and are adored and praised by the world, inasmuch as your hearts are dedicated to the glorious Lord Vāsudeva.

24. Devotion unto Kṛṣṇa is engendered[1] by charitable gifts, observance of vows, austerities, performance of *homa* (sacrifice) muttering of a *mantra* or God's name, Vedic (scriptural) studies, self-control and such other meritorious acts.

25. It is fortunate of you that you, respectable ladies, have established such an unsurpassably supreme (standard of) devotion into the glorious Lord of hallowing renown as is extremely difficult even for sages.

26. You deserve congratulations as you have renounced (attachment to) your sons, husbands, your own persons, kith and kin as well as your homes, and have sought after the Supreme person Kṛṣṇa.

27. Oh highly blessed Gopīs ! Due to your separation from the Lord, you have accomplished an unflinching, absolute devotion unto Lord Adhokṣaja (Kṛṣṇa). You have certainly rendered a great favour unto me by giving me a glimpse of your ardent devotion to the Lord.

28. Let the message of your dear Lord which will bring delight to you be heard (alternatively). It is to convey this message that I, as a *confidant* of the Lord, have come here.

The Glorious Lord said :

29. As I pervade all as their Inner Soul, there cannot be any separation between you and me. Just as the five elements—the ether, air, fire, water and earth—are found in all

1. v.l., *bhaktir na sādhyate* 'Is not engendered'—VR.

beings, similarly, I abide (as the support) in the mind, vital breath, elements, conative and cognitive senses and qualities.

30. By the force of my Māyā Potency and in association with *bhūtas* (elements), the senses and the *guṇas*, I create myself (in various forms) within myself, protect them, and destroy them.

31. The Self (*ātman*) is absolutely pure, distinct, untainted and unconcerned with *guṇas*, an embodiment of consciousness and knowledge. He appears (as *Viśva*, *Taijasa* and *Prājña*) in the states of sleep, dream and wakefulness through mental states (and not directly) which are the creations of Māyā.

32.* . Ever alert and vigilant, a person should try to control that mind with which he broods over the objects of senses which are unreal like the objects seen in a dream, and runs after the senses (sense-object) even during wakefulness.

33. According to the opinion of the spiritually wise, the study of the Vedas, the Yoga (with its eightfold path), the Sāṅkhya teaching (discriminating between the soul and the non-soul), renunciation (*saṁnyāsa*),—austerities, control (over the senses), truthfulness—all these have mind-control as their goal, even as all the rivers terminate in the ocean.

34. It is with a view to attract your mind constantly to me while you eagerly meditate upon me, (and thus to secure our mental nearness) that I, though your beloved, am staying far away beyond the ken of your eyes.

35. The mind of women is not so much ardently drawn to and absorbed in their beloved while he lives near, just before their eyes, as and when he is staying far away.

36. As you have completely dedicated your entire heart resigning all its activities to me, and are constantly contemplating on me, you will attain me within a short time.

37. Those ladies who being detained at Vraja (by their husbands etc.) could not participate in the *Rāsa*) in the forest, have attained to me by contemplating on my exploits, Oh blessed ladies".

* Not traced in VJ.

Śrī Śuka said :

38. Having heard the message of their most beloved Lord, the damsels of Vraja whose recollections of Lord Kṛṣṇa were revived by it, became highly delighted and spoke to Uddhava.

The Gopīs said :

39. Luckily the tyrant Kaṁsa, the deadly enemy and persecutor of Yadus is killed along with his followers. It is a matter of good fortune that the immortal Lord (Kṛṣṇa) is living happily with his relatives who have obtained all their objects (through his grace).

40. (Some asked) : Does Kṛṣṇa, the elder brother of Gada who was adored by us with affectionate, bashful smiles and loving glances, impart the same delight to the women of the city (Mathura), Oh gentle Uddhava?

41. (Others asked) : Highly expert in erotics and beloved of excellent women as he is, how can he fail to (be won over) and bound down by their love when he is greeted with words (expressing love) and amorous gestures by them.

42. (Someone asked) : Does the Lord of cows (or of Gokula ever remember us, the rustic women, causally, in some context in the assembly of the urban women of Mathura, during his free talk of his past life, Oh piousone ![1]

43. (Others asked) : Does he ever remember those nights (at Vraja) when in Vṛndāvana grove lovely with blooming lilies and jasmines and resplendent with the full moon, he sported with us, his beloveds, and when in the ring of the Rāsa dance resonant with the jingling of anklets his charming stories were sung by us ?

44. (Some asked) : Will Kṛṣṇa, the descendent of Daśārha ever come here to enliven us who are tormented with grief on account of separation from him, by the life-giving touch of his limbs, like Indra refreshing woods (scorched with heat of summer) with rain-clouds.

45. (Others exclaimed) : Why should Kṛṣṇa (bother to) come here at all when he has obtained a kingdom, slain

1. The adj. implies that Uddhava being pious must tell the truth. —SG

all the enemies, will have married a number of princesses and is living happily in the company of his friends.

46. (Others gave out the fact of the matter)

What purpose of the Supreme Soul, the Consort of Lakṣmī (Kṛṣṇa) be served by us, the forest-dwellers or by others (princesses), when he himself has all his desires accomplished and is perfect (within himself).

47. Even the public woman Piṅgalā[1] has observed that desirelessness is the real happiness. Knowing that as we do, our longing and hope to meet Kṛṣṇa is difficult to overcome.

48. Who could detach one's mind from the secret talks one had with the Lord of hallowing renown from whose person Śrī seldom dissociates herself, even though he does not long for her ?

49-50. What a pity ! The river Yamunā, the mount Govardhana, the woodlands of Vṛndāvana, the cows, the musical notes of flutes—all associated with Kṛṣṇa with Balarāma as his companion—poignantly remind us again and again of Kṛṣṇa, the son of the Gopa Nanda, through his foot-prints which are the asylum of the goddess Lakṣmī. Alas ! It is simply impossible to forget him, Oh Uddhava.

51. Our hearts have been fascinated and spirited away with his seductive gait, enchanting laughter, sportive glances, and honeyed words. How can we forget him, Oh Uddhava ?

52. Oh Lord ! Oh Consort of goddess Lakṣmī ! Oh Lord of Vraja who destroyed our afflictions ! Oh Lord of cows ! Be pleased to lift up Gokula that is submerged in the sea of grief.

Śrī Śuka said :

53. Thereupon, the Gopīs whose agonies of separation from Kṛṣṇa, were removed by the message of Kṛṣṇa, realized that Kṛṣṇa the Supra-sensuous Lord was within

1. Piṅgalā—Name of a prostitute in Mithilā. Once she was disappointed as none came to her in spite of her waiting, she realized the bliss of transcending desires and hopes. Avadhūta regarded her as his preceptor *vide, infra* 11.7.34, 11.8. 22-44.

them—nay was identical with them—and they worshipped Uddhava with due respects.[1]

54. Uddhava stayed there for some months alleviating the grief of those cowherd women. He brought delight to the settlement of those cowherds (Gokula) by glorifying in songs the delightful stories of Lord Kṛṣṇa's sportive activities.

55. For as many days, Uddhava stayed at Nanda's Vraja, (they were so absorbed) in talking about Kṛṣṇa, those days of the residents of Vraja flitted away as if they were so many moments only.

56. Observing devoutly the river Yamunā, Vṛndāvana, mount Govardhana, the valleys and the blossoming trees, (where Kṛṣṇa roamed and sported and) which reminded the people of Vraja of Kṛṣṇa (causing thereby a longing to see him) that Servant of Hari spent that time in joyfulness.

57. Uddhava was highly pleased to notice the intense mental anguish of the Gopīs (as described above[2]) caused by their (longing for and) absorption of their minds in Kṛṣṇa, Uddhava paid his respects to them and (in justification of the bowing down to Gopa women by a Kṣattriya like himself and sang (of their glory) as follows :

58. "Only these Gopa women have really vindicated their worthiness of possessing a human body (life as a human being) since their heart is steeped in Supreme Love (and devotion) to Lord Kṛṣṇa, the protector of cows—a stage which those who are scared of *saṁsāra* (and aspire after liberation from it i. e. *mumukṣus*), the sages (who are *muktas* i. e. freed from the bondages of *saṁsāra*) and we (the devotees of the Lord) aspire. To a person interested in the stories of the Infinite Lord, what importance is there to the kinds of birth as a Brāhmaṇa (viz. physical heredity from Brāhmaṇa parents, ceremonial birth by means of investiture with the sacred thread and initiation in the sacred Gāyatrī *mantra* and ritua-

1. They worshipped Uddhava regarding him as if he was Lord Kṛṣṇa himself.—VJ.

2. vide Supra vv 4-21 and vv 39-52

listic birth with consecration for sacrificial performance)[1] *OR*, Of what use is the repeated birth as four-faced god Brahmā if one has no fascination or liking for the stories of the Infinite Lord[2].

59. What a contrast is this ! (On the one hand) these rustic forest-dwelling women condemned for adultery[3] (in the eyes of the public as they abandoned their husbands and offered themselves to Lord Kṛṣṇa) and their deeprooted intense absolute devotion to Lord Śrī Kṛṣṇa, the Supreme Soul, on the other. Certainly, the Almighty Lord himself bestows the highest beatitude upon his devotees who, even though ignorant, always remember him and resort to him, just as nectar, the king of medicines when used (unknowingly by an ailing patient, cures him).

60. Oh ! How covetable was the blissful Grace that was showered on the cowherd women of Vraja at the time of Rāsa dance when all their cravings and longings for getting themselves embraced by the mighty arm of the Lord were amply satisfied—A grace never enjoyed even by goddess Śrī who is always closely associated with his person, nor by the celestial damsels whose fragrance and splendour of complexion is like lotuses—What need be said of others ? (Much less can others expect it).

61. How strongly I desire to be one of these shrubs, creepers, plants or herbs of Vṛndāvana which have the good luck to come in contact with the dust on the feet of these cowherd women who forsook their relatives so difficult to abandon, and the traditional path followed by the noble and the good (which is equally difficult for chaste women to give up) and took to the path of devotion that leads to Lord Kṛṣṇa who is sought after by the Vedas.

1. This explanation is based on the 1st way dissolving the compound in the text :

ananta-kathā-rasasya : *Ananta+kathā+rasa*.

2. This will be the interpretation if the compound in text mentioned above is dissolved as *Ananta+kathā+a-rasa*—ŚR.

3. SG. regards this as a comparison between Gopīs and Uddhava who call themselves: *vayaṁ vyabhicāra-duṣṭāḥ*—we who are averse to pious deeds.

62. The Gopīs dispelled all the agonies of their heart by embracing Lord Kṛṣṇa's lotus-feet placed on their bosoms during Rāsa dance—the lotus-feet of the Lord which are adored by the goddess Śrī, god Brahmā and others who have accomplished all their desires, and by masters of yoga in their hearts.

63. I bow down again and again the dust under the feet of the damsels of Nanda's Vraja, whose loud singing of the stories of Lord Hari sanctifies the three worlds.

Śrī Śuka said :

64. Then, after taking leave of the Gapīs, Yaśodā and Nanda and bidding good-bye to Gopas, Uddhava, the scion of Daśārha, became ready to depart (on his return journey) and mounted his chariot.

65. When he just got out of his house, Nanda and others brought in their hands different presents (presumably for Kṛṣṇa and Balarāma) and with eyes dimmed with tears of love, spoke to him affectionately as follows :

66. "May all our mental activities be concentrated on the lotus-feet of Lord Kṛṣṇa. May our speech (oral activities) be ever engaged in uttering the name of the Lord and may our body (physical activities) be engaged in bowing to him (and doing such worshipful services).

67. Wandering whithersoever (or in whatever species of birth) we be, as a result of our *karman* (actions) or by the will of the Almighty Lord, may our love be constant in the Supreme Lord Kṛṣṇa in consequence of our auspicious deeds and charitable gifts (performed by us in our past lives)"

68. Thus honoured by the cowherds through their devotion to Kṛṣṇa, Uddhava returned to Mathura protected by Kṛṣṇa, Oh King Parīkṣit.

69. Lying prostrate before Kṛṣṇa, he reported to Kṛṣṇa the effusion of intense devotion of the people of Vraja (unto him), and handed over the presents (sent by the cowherds) to Vasudeva, Balarāma and King Ugrasena.

CHAPTER FORTYEIGHT

Visit to the Houses of Trivakrā and Akrūra

Śrī Śuka said :

1. Now knowing the earnest desire of the maid-servant Trivakrā who was pining with passionate love for him, the Almighty Lord, the In-dwelling soul of all, who is omniscient, went to her house with an intention to gratify her cherished desire.

2. The house was equipped with highly costly articles of furniture; was enriched with means of stimulating erotic passions, was decorated with garlands of pearls, flags, canopies, beds, seats, was perfumed with fragrant incenses, lights (emitting sweet scent), wreaths of flowers and perfumes.

Texts of VR and SD add :

2A. (It was beautified with beautiful paintings in various colours pertaining(or designed according) to *kāmaśāstra* (science of Erotics).

3. Beholding that he was coming, she (Tri-vakrā) in a flurry, quickly rose from her seat, went forward along with her female companions to pay him due respect, and warmly received him by offering a high, comfortable seat and other articles of worship.

4. Uddhava also was similarly received as a pious person, but he touched with his hand (to pay respects to) the seat offered to him, and sat on the floor. (To carry out his part as a man) Kṛṣṇa also, following the practice of the world, (got up from his seat and of his own accord quickly entered the bed-room furnished with costly bed.

5. Embellishing herself after bath, with cosmetics, fine clothes, ornaments, garlands of flowers, scents, betel-leaves chewing, nectarlike drinks and the like, she approached Kṛṣṇa, the Lord of goddess Lakṣmī—ogling him with amorous glances and bashful sportive smiles.

6. He called to his side that beautiful woman who was a bit nervous and hesitant through bashfulness, as it was their first meeting. He took her by the hand that was adorned with bracelets and made her sit on the bed. He gave that

charming lady her desired pleasure for the slight act of merit she had done, by offering him the pigment (at his request, while going to Kaṁsa for service).

7. Enjoying the fragrance of his feet, swept off the agonies in her breast and bosom specially tormented by love-fever, and those of her eyes as well, by (the soothing touch of) his feet. She clasped in her arms her beloved Kṛṣṇa, the embodiment of bliss who was now on her bosom and thus got rid of the suffering of separation she had gone through, for a long time.

8. Alas ! Having thus obtained in return for the offer of pigment the presence of the Lord of the Absolute state (who confers Final Beatitude), the Supreme Ruler of the Universe so difficult to attain, the unfortunate woman begged of him the following.

9. She said, "Oh beloved-most Lord ! Be pleased to stay with me for some days here in my house and give me the pleasure of your company. Oh lotus-eyed god ! I cannot forgo your company."

10. Having conferred upon her the boon as per her desire and having honoured her (with presents), the Lord of all the universe who respects others, returned with Uddhava to his (Vasudeva's) splendid palace.

11. Having propitiated the All-pervading Lord Viṣṇu, the Supreme Ruler of all rulers of the universe (like god Brahmā) who is so very difficult to be pleased, a person who seeks what is agreeable to the mind (viz. the pleasures of the sense) is certainly a man of perverted intelligence inasmuch as the so-called pleasures are trivial (and not worth craving).

12. With a desire to do a good turn to Akrūra in his interest and with the intention of sending him on some errand, Lord Kṛṣṇa accompanied by Balarāma and Uddhava went to the house of Akrūra.

13. Seeing from a distance that those greatest among foremost of men who were his own relations, were coming, he was overjoyed. He rose from his seat and went forward to receive them. He embraced them and honoured them.

14.* He bowed down to Kṛṣṇa and Balarāma (as he knew their divine nature, though they were his juniors in age) and was reciprocally respected by them. When they were comfortably seated, he worshipped them with due formalities

15-16. He washed their feet and sprinkled over his head that water (with which he washed them). He received them respectfully by presenting articles of worship such as rich clothes, excellent perfumes, wreathes of flowers and ornaments. He bowed them bending down his head and kneaded their feet after taking them in his lap. Modest and devoted as he was, Akrūra submitted Lord Kṛṣṇa and Balarāma as follows:

17. "How fortunate it is that the wicked Kaṁsa along with his followers has been killed by you both and this clan of yours has been not only rescued from the (seemingly) unending harassment and difficulties but is made prosperous as well.

18. Both of you constitute Pradhāna (Primordial matter) and Puruṣa (the self, in Sāṅkhya terminology). Both of you constitute (the material and efficient) causes of universe and are inherent in it. Without you neither cause nor effect can exist.

19. Oh Lord Kṛṣṇa who is the Supreme Brahman Itself ! Having evolved the universe through your potencies (such as *rajas* and others) you have entered into it (as its Indwelling Soul or Inner Controller) ! you appear as many in various innumerable forms which are within the ken of sight and hearing.

20. Just as the constituent elements like earth, water, fire etc exhibit themselves in various forms of beings mobile and immobile as through various species of creatures, so your honour who is the one, absolute, self-dependent Supreme self, manifest yourself in innumerable forms (in various species such as human beings, beasts etc. and in various stages of life such as child, youth etc. which are but your creations (and thus appear as many).

21. Through your potencies in the form of *guṇas* viz. *rajas*, *sattva* and *tamas*, you evolve, protect and dissolve the universe. But you are not bound or affected either by the *guṇas* or by the actions. Essentially constituted of pure knowledge and

* Not traced in VJ.'s text.

consciousness as you are, nothing could work as a limiting condition on you.

22. As physical body and other limiting conditions (which are supposed to subject the soul to limitations and bondage) are not observed predicable in your case, no birth or difference can be predicated of the soul in reality (much less so in the case of the Supreme Soul viz. your honour). There is no bondage or Liberation (*mokṣa*) therefrom for you. It is our lack of discrimination and ignorance which project these on you.

23. Whenever this ancient path (of religion prescribed in the Vedas promulgated by you for the good of the world is threatened with obstruction by the false heterodox creeds, your honour assumes a form (constituted) of pure, unalloyed *sattva guṇa* (for the re-establishment of the original Vedic path).

24. You are that Supreme Lord, now incarnated in the house of Vasudeva along with Balarāma, your partmanifestation, with the mission of removing the burden of the earth by slaying one hundred *akṣauhiṇīs* of kings born with non-celestial i.e. demonic *asura aṁśa* and also to enhance the glory of your (Yadu) race.

25. Oh Supreme Ruler ! Today our homes have been rendered highly blessed and fortunate indeed inasmuch as they are visited by you who are the creator and the preceptor of the world, the very embodiment of all gods, ancestors, beings and the kings and the water washing whose feet (viz. the river Gaṅgā) hallows the three worlds. Oh Supra-sensuous Lord !

26. What learned person would seek resort to any person other than you who are so beloved of your devotees, true of word, friendly and grateful and who bestow on all his votaries and friends who resort to you, their desired objects—nay his own self which is above decay or growth.

27. Oh Janārdana ! Luckily you, access to whom is very difficult even to the great masters of Yoga as well to the lords of gods, have become manifest to us. Be pleased to cut off cords your Māyā quickly (and immediately) regarding sons, wives, money, relatives and of our very body.

Śrī Śuka said:

28. The glorious Lord Hari who was worshipped and glorified by his votary Akrūra, spoke to him smilingly, and addressed to Akrūra hypnotising him as it were with his sweet and pleasant words.

The Lord said:

29. "You are our elderly relative (or preceptor), uncle. You are our ever praiseworthy relative. We are after all your children who are to be protected, nourished and looked after with compassion.

30. Highly blessed and most adorable persons like your honour should always be waited upon by persons desirous of achieving their *summum bonum*. For gods are always intent on achieving their own purpose (and are selfish), but saintly persons are never so selfish at all. (They oblige you without any expectation in return while gods won't grant you anything unless they are pleased by the offer of oblations in the sacrifice etc. Hence saints are greater then gods).

31* Not that the holy places (*tīrthas*) consisting of water and gods represented in earth and stone images do not purify but they do so after a pretty long time, while saintly persons sanctify one immediately at the first sight.

32. You are verily the worthiest of our friends. With the object of doing some good to pāṇḍavas and making enquiries (probing the real state of affairs) about them, please do go to Hastinapura.

33. We have heard that after the death of their father those grieving children along with their grief-striken mother were brought by the king Dhṛtarāṣṭra to his capital and they stay there.

34. It is certain that king Dhṛtarāṣṭra, the son of Ambikā who is both blind and of poor intellect, is under the control of his wicked son and does not treat them impartially.

* The term *Tīrtha* does not connote a storage of water but it is the deity presiding over them that is implied. The same is the case with images of gods made of earth or stone. But these deities have to be served for a long time to please them. But not so the saints—VJ.

35. Do go now and ascertain his present behaviour (with them) whether it be good or otherwise. After knowing the facts correctly we shall so manage (the situation) as will be conducive to the welfare and happiness of our friends."

36. Having briefed Akrūra (regarding his mission to Hastinapura) the glorious Almighty Lord Hari straightway returned to his palace along with Balarāma and Uddhava.

CHAPTER FORTYNINE

Akrūra's Mission to Hastinapura

Śrī Śuka said :

1-2. Having arrived at Hastinapura, the noted capital of the great and glorious kings of the Puru dynasty, he saw there Dhṛtarāṣṭra, the son of Ambikā along with Bhīṣma, Vidura, Kuntī : Bāhlīka along with his son Somadatta, Droṇa, the descendant of Bhāradvāja along with Kṛpa of the Gautama family, Karṇa, Suyodhana (i.e. Duryodhana), Aśvatthāman, the son of Droṇa, Pāṇḍavas and other friends thereof.

3. Having met his relatives in the appropriate manner (to establish closer contacts), Akrūra, the son of Gāndinī, was respectfully enquired about by them about their friends (at Mathura) and he also reciprocally asked them about their well being.

4. With a view to probe and know in depth the behaviour of the king whose sons were wicked and who was himself feeble-minded, and who was guided by the will of the wicked (like Śakuni), Akrūra stayed there many months.

5-6. Pṛthā (Kuntī) and Vidura completely reported to him all the wicked acts such as administering poison (to Bhīma) and others by Dhṛtarāṣṭra's sons who could not tolerate and felt jealous of Pāṇḍavas' majesty, prowess, physical strength, heroism, modesty and other excellent virtues as well as the love and loyalty the subjects had for them; they also told him what they intended to do (to harm Pāṇḍavas).

7. Approaching her brother (cousin) Akrūra who came to visit her, Kuntī (Pṛthā) remembered her birth-place and with her eyes full of tears enquired :

8. "Oh gentle Akrūra ! Do my parents (Śūrasena and Māriṣā), brothers (Vasudeva and others), sisters (Śruta-devā etc.), nephews (Kṛṣṇa, Balarāma and others), respectable ladies in the house (like Devakī and others) and female friends remember me ?

9. Does my nephew, the glorious Lord Kṛṣṇa, the protector of his dependants and affectionate to his votaries, and the lotus-eyed Balarāma ever remember the sons of their paternal aunt?

10. Would Kṛṣṇa care to comfort with words of consolation me who am grieving here in the midst of enemies like a female deer in the midst of wolves. Would he do so to my children who are now fatherless.

11. Oh Kṛṣṇa ! Kṛṣṇa ! Oh great *yogin* ! Oh Soul of the Universe ! Oh Creator of the world ! Be kind and protect me who have sought Your protection, Oh Govinda, I am suffering along with my children.

12. To persons who are afraid of death and of the cycle of births (*saṁsāra*), I do not see any other refuge except the lotus feet of yours—of the Supreme which confer Liberation from *saṁsāra*.

13. Bow to Kṛṣṇa, the pure Brahman (unalloyed with Māyā), the Supreme Soul, the Lord of Yogas, the very embodiment of *yoga* ! I have sought asylum in you."

Śrī Śuka said :

14. In this way, remembering her relatives, and Kṛṣṇa, the Ruler of the world, your paternal great-grand mother lamented loudly, in grief.

15. Akrūra who looked upon pleasure and pain with equanimity and Vidura of great glory, consoled Kuntī by telling her the divine parentage of her sons (and their mission to help Kṛṣṇa in the reduction of the burden of the earth).

16. When he was about to return to Mathura, Akrūra approached King Dhṛtarāṣṭra who practised discrimination between his sons and Pāṇḍavas and was specially partial and

attached to his sons. He communicated to the king in the midst of his relatives, the message of his well-intentioned relations such as Kṛṣṇa and others.

Akrūra said :

17. Oh son of Vicitravīrya ! You are the enhancer of the glory of the Kuru race ! But after the demise of your brother Pāṇḍu, you have now occupied the throne (in stead of installing Pāṇḍu's son--the legal heir—on the throne).

18. By governing the earth with piety (and as per code of righteous government), pleasing your subjects by your (spotless) character and behaving with strict impartiality with your relatives, you can still attain prosperity and good reputation.

19. If you act otherwise, you will be censured in this world and shall go to dark hell hereafter. You, therefore, treat impartially your sons and the Pāṇḍavas.

20. There is no possibility of having eternal companionship with anybody at any time in this world—not even with one's body. What need be said of contacts with one's wife and sons, Oh King.

21. A creature comes into being alone and it dies alone, all by itself. It is all alone when it experiences the fruits of good deeds or suffers the consequences of his evil actions.

22. Others who go under the name of sons (*lit.* one deserving nourishment) carry away the wealth accumulated by unfair means of this dull-witted fellow, as the brood of acquatic animals share waters.

23. A foolish person who unrighteously nourishes life, wealth, sons and others under the wrong notion that they are his own, finds himself deserted by them, for good, even when he has not yet accomplished his objective of enjoying them.

24. A person not knowing his real interest, being deserted by them (viz. wealth, sons etc. which he regarded as his own) carries the load of his sins himself as he is averse to religion and with his hopes of enjoyment, unfulfilled, he enters the hall of blinding darkness.

25. Oh King ! Realizing that this world is like a dream,

illusion or an idle fancy, you control your own mind by yourself and be impartial and serene, Oh Lord.

Dhṛtarāṣṭra replied :

26. Oh *Dānapati* (the most distinguished donor of charities) ! As your honour utters this sweet, salutary speech, I do not feel sated with it, just as a mortal would feel after obtaining the nectar.

27. Oh gentle-natured Akrūra ! Your sweet and righteous advice, however, does not get fixed in my fickle mind which is partial through affection towards my sons, any more than a flash of lightening into the mount Sudāman.

28. What human being can violate the decree of the Supreme Ruler who has now descended in Yadu's race for removing the burden of the earth.

29. Bow unto that Supreme Lord who, having created this universe by his Māyā of incomprehensible ways and having entered it afterwards (as the Inner Controller) he apportions the *karmas* and their fruits, and whose sportive acts which are very difficult to comprehend and who is the main cause and the ultimate goal of this wheel of transmigration (*saṁsāra*).

Śrī Śuka said :

30. Having thus gauged the mind of the king Dhṛtarāṣṭra and taking leave of his well-wishers and relatives, Akrūra of the Yādava clan, returned to Mathurā.

31. Oh Parīkṣit (the scion of the Kuru race) ! (After his arrival at Mathurā), he reported to Balarāma and Kṛṣṇa, the behaviour of Dhṛtarāṣṭra towards Pāṇḍavas—the maiu purpose of his deputation to Hastināpura.

CHAPTER FIFTY*

Settlement at the Fort of Dvārakā

Śrī Śuka said :

1. Asti and Prāpti were the two queens of Kaṁsa Oh prominent Bhārata. When their husband was slain, they were afflicted with sorrow. They went to their father's house.

2. Stricken with grief, they reported fully to their father Jarāsandha, king of Magadha, the cause of their widowhood.

3. Hearing that unpleasant account, he was filled with grief and indignation, Oh King Parīkṣit. He made a great endeavour to wipe out the Yādavas from the face of the earth.

4. Accompanied with an army of twenty-three *akṣauhiṇis* Jarāsandha besieged Mathurā, the capital of Yadus, on all sides.

5-6. Observing the army of Jarāsandha was surging forth like a sea overflowing its coastal limits, and that His capital was besieged by it and His own people were struck with panic, the glorious Lord Hari who assumed a human form with a special mission (of removing the burden of the earth) considered the measures suitable for the exigencies of that time and place and also the purpose of His incarnation (on the earth).

7-8. "I shall now destroy this army amounting to many akṣauhiṇīs consisting of infantry, cavalry, chariot-corps and elephants, in the service of Jarāsandha's tributary princes and brought together (and deployed) by Jarāsandha, King of Magadha, as this force is nothing but an accumulated burden to the earth. But Jarāsandha should not be killed, as he will again make efforts and mobilise more forces (and help disburdenment of the earth).

9. This incarnation of Mine is for this mission, viz. removal of the burden of the earth, protection of the righteous and the elimination of the wicked.

*Henceforth there is much divergence in the Texts of ŚR and VJ. For the convenience of readers, additional verses in VJ are translated in the footnotes and the additional special chapters in VJ are given separately as an *Appendix* to the X Skandha.

10. Another personality (e.g. the boor incarnation) has been assumed by me for the protection of the path of righteousness and termination of the unrighteousness when it becomes predominant, at times.*

11. While Kṛṣṇa was thinking in this way, there descended near him, from the sky, two chariots resfulgent like the sun, (each) equipped with military appurtenances (armour, banner etc.) and manned by charioteers.**

* (*Here the Text of VJ. gives the following additional verses*).

10.1 While Kṛṣṇa was pondering thus, the mighty king of Magadha with his big army, laid siege to Mathurā including its groves and parks.

10.2-4. According to the commands of Jarāsandha, the Magadhan king, Kaliṅga, Cekitāna, Dantavaktra, Vidūratha, Ulmuka, Veṇudāri, Śālva and the wicked-minded Śiśupāla, king of Caidyas, reached the, eastern gate (of Mathurā) and blocked it. Vinda, Anuvinda of Avanti, Virāṭa, Darada, Ekalavya, Bālhika and the king of Panjab (land of five rivers) besieged the southern gate.

10. 5-6. Directed by Jarāsandha, the powerful king Pauṇḍraka, Yudhāmanyu, Bṛhat-Kṣatra, Śālva, Bhūriśravas, Uttamaujas, Rukmi, Druma, Sudaksiṇa assailed the western gate and beleaguered the city of Mathurā.

10. 7-8. Drupada Śiśupāla, Trigarta, Jayadratha, Śakuni, Somadatta and the mighty Kuṇinda—all proud of their power—proceeded to the northern gate under the leadership of Jarāsandha and laid siege there, Oh prominent Bhārata.

10.9 Like a sea overflowing its coastal limits, they blockaded all the four gates. Uttering war-cries, blowing conches a number of times, they became ready for action and beat thousands of kettle-drums.

10.10. Hearing that tumultuous uproar of the combined forces of those kings at the gates, which resembled the roaring of the inundating oceans at the end of the universe, Kṛṣṇa was not at all disturbed in mind like a proud mighty lion on hearing the howling of a pack of jackals.

** The Vrindavana edition quotes in VJ.'s com. the following verses as *additions in VJ.'s text* :

11.1 (There appeared) the terrific yet beautiful discus Sudarśana of thousand spokes, and the auspicious heavy mace named *Kaumodakī* as it belonged to Nārāyaṇa who imparts delight and happiness to the world.

11.2 (There appeared) the most formidable bow called Śārṅga, bent at three points and equipped with a string; sword called Nandaka of sharp edge and pointed at the end; two light and attractive quivers with inexhaustible store of arrows.

12. Seeing their ancient celestial weapons appearing there of their own accord, Kṛṣṇa, the Supra-Sensuous Lord, spoke to Balarāma.

13. "Look, Oh respectable brother, the great peril that is threatening to befall Yadus, of whom you are the protector, Oh Powerful Lord. Behold, this chariot of yours has arrived along with your favourite weapons.

14. Getting into this vehicle, wipe out this (hostile) army and rescue your people from the impending disaster. Our incarnation is certainly for this purpose, Oh powerful Lord, that we should afford protection and felicity to the righteous.

15. Remove the burden of the earth now known as "the army of twentythree *akṣauhiṇis*" Having planned together thus, both the descendants of Daśārha (viz. Kṛṣṇa and Balarāma) put on their armours (armed with their respective weapons and accompanied with a small band of selected warriors mounted their chariots and sallied forth from the city of Mathurā.*

11.3 (The chariot was yoked with) horses called Saibya, Sugrīva, Meghapuṣpa and Balāhaka. And a heavy and sturdy plough and a club (pestle) for Balarāma.

11.4-A. These weapons alighted from the sky for using them in the battle.

15.1 Oh King Parīkṣit ! Accompanied with a small army consisting of many prominent Yadus well-armed and clad in coats of mail, both of them rushed out of the great city.

15.2 When Kṛṣṇa came out of his residence, he summoned all Vṛṣṇis and commanded them to defend forthwith the four gates of the city.

15.3 Kṛṣṇa deployed Vasudeva, Niśaṭha, Kṛtavarmā and Uddhava at the eastern gate, Oh descendant of Bharata !

15.4 Hari sent to defend the northern gate Ugrasena, Sudāman, Pṛthu and Vipṛthu.

15.5 Hari sent to the Western gate extremely powerful warriors Sātyaki, Gada, Prasena and Akrūra, the son of Gāndinī.

15.6-7 Kṛṣṇa of supremely heroic lustre, equipped with weapons of his choice, himself with Dāruka as his charioteer and with Balarāma to help him, sallied forth through the northern gate. The Lord of the universe blew out his conch of very loud sound, inspiring terror in Daityas and Dānavas.

16. Surrounded by a small force, both of them kṛṣṇa and Balarāma equipped themselves with their beautiful weapons and went out of the city. Hari with Dāruka as his charioteer came out of the city and blew conch.

17. It (the challenging conch-blowing) sent a cold shivering of shudder in the hearts of the armies of the enemy. Seeing them both, Jarāsandha said : 'Oh Kṛṣṇa ! Meanest of all men' (also 'to whom other men are inferior', 'the best among men').

15.8 Kṛṣṇa, the consort of goddess Lakṣmī, smilingly spoke to Dāruka who had occupied the front seat (of the chariot-driver), in the chariot.

The Glorious Lord directed :

Take the chariot to the place where Śiśupāla the king of Caidyas, and Jarāsandha, the king of Magadhas, have taken their positions, Oh knower of military duties (*dharma*). I shall thoroughly satisfy with my arrows, the (itch of fighting of all the) kings very proud of fighting.

Śrī Śuka continued :

15.9 Thus directed by the Lord, Dāruka quickly drove the horses to that spot and Govinda, the conqueror of inimical forces, roared like a lion.

15.10 Blaring out his conch, Balarāma also sent forth a roar like a lion that shuddered the hostile forces, causing nervous anxiety and fear in their hearts.

15.11 At the eastern gate there was a terrible fight between the Yadus and the (attacking) princes, eight princes (like Kaliṅga etc.) fighting with the four (such as Vasudeva and others). It was a miraculous sight indeed.

15.12 At the southern gate, there was tough fighting between Yadus who were inspired with confidence by Kṛṣṇa and the inimical princely forces.

15.13 At the western gate also the battle between formidable Yādava archers and the army of opposing princes was so thrilling that it made one's hair stand on their ends.

15.14 Fired with the ambition of conquering both the worlds (here and hereafter), Yadus, though beaten by princes valorous as the king of gods, did not recede from the battlefield, Oh King.

15.15 In that battle, god Viṣṇu (i.e. Lord Kṛṣṇa) beloved of the three worlds, an eminently brave member of the Yādava clan, reached the spot where the most terrible kings of Caidya (Siśupāla) and of Magadha (viz. Jarāsandha) were positioned.

18. I do not wish to fight with a young boy like you as you are alone. It is shameful (to fight with you). I won't fight with you who lay concealed so long (out of Kaṁsa's fear) you stupid fellow ! The murderer of relatives ! You go away (Fighting is not your profession) as you are a *gupta* (a man of Vaiś'ya community, as you are the son of the cowherd Nanda.

19. Oh Balarāma ! If you have faith and confidence in you, muster some courage and fight with me. Go to heaven leaving your body shattered with my arrows or kill me (if you dare).

The glorious Lord replied :

20. "Those who are really brave do not boast but display their valour. We do not take seriously the words of those who are delirious (or of unbalanced mind through grief due to the death of your son-in-law) or who are on the point of death (as you are now)."

21. Jarāsandha, the foster-son of the demoness Jarā, assailed both Balarāma and Kṛṣṇa, the descendants of Madhu, and surrounded them both, their detachment of soldiers, vehicles (chariots), flags, horses, charioteers with a big formidable army, just as a tempestuous wind would cover the sun with clouds or the fire with particles of dust.

22. Finding that the chariots of Kṛṣṇa and Balarāma which were distinguished by the ensigns with the figures of Garuḍa and Palmyra tree had become invisible in that battle, the women of Mathurā who occupied seats on the top of the ramparts, mansions and towers were struck with grief and fell in swoon.

23. Perceiving that his own army was sorely afflicted by incessant showers of extremely sharp arrows from the cloud-like inimical forces, Hari twanged His excellent bow called

Verse 18.1. ŚR. gives a complimentary interpretation of the line :

guptena hi tvayā'manda na yotsye yāhi bandhuhan /·

With you who, being the Inner controller of all beings, are beyond the ken of sight. Oh highly intelligent person ! You are the destroyer of *Avidyā* ! Be pleased to come (let me attain to you).

Śārṅga which was held in high esteem (lit. adored) by both gods and demons alike.

24. And taking out arrows from the quiver, and setting them on the bow, pulling the bow-string and discharging vollies of sharp arrows, he incessantly shattered down chariots, elephants, horses and infantry-men, whirling the bow like a fire-brand.*

* *Here VJ's Text adds the following verses* :

24.1 Then Kṛṣṇa applied to his mouth and loudly blew the conch Pāñcajanya, which, white like the moon in appearance, gave out a loud blast that spelt death to Daityas, and gave courage and comfort to Yādavas who were struck down with hosts of Kṣatriya forces.

24.2 Hearing the most defeaning terrible blast of the conch, the kings, at every point, lost courage at the terrific sound. The warriors on the Yādava side assisted by their army, raised their weapons and put down the army of opposing kings.

24.3 The Yādava warriors felt encouraged by Hari's twanging of the Śārṅga bow. They immediately rushed onwards against the enemies, discharged volleys of arrows and put to flight all the kings at the four gates.

24.4 Śiśupāla, the king of Caidya's, who bent his bow almost in a circle, challenged and threatened Kṛṣṇa saying, "Oh Kṛṣṇa! Stop, halt, Oh Kṛṣṇa."

24.5 Kṛṣṇa rushed at him showering on him innumerable sharp arrows washed with oil, from his bow which was bent practically into a circle.

24.6 Thereupon Śiśupāla, the son of Damaghoṣa, took out five terrible arrows. With four of them he hit the horses and with one the charioteer, quickly.

24.7 He quickly set ten arrows on the bow and discharged them at Kṛṣṇa, the slayer of the demon Madhu. He gave out a roar like a lion and all this happened as if like a miracle.

24.8 At that (Śiśupāla's exploit) Kṛṣṇa applauded him, crying out, "Well done! Bravo! Oh Śiśupāla, you are a great archer. You are a hero and a powerful one at that.

24.9-15 Now you wicked-minded fellow, see my expertness in archery by experiencing it personally." While Kṛṣṇa was speaking thus, all the kings simultaneously discharged and hit Kṛṣṇa with sharp arrows. Kṛṣṇa hit each of them with five shafts, dispatching the charioteer and four horses of each chariot to the abode of the god of Death. Kṛṣṇa, the delighter of the Yadus, pierced each of the kings with three arrows, on the chest, in the mouth and on the forehead, in the battle. The valiant leader of the Yadus quickly cut down the thirty bows of the thirty kings

25. The elephants fell down with their temples split up; a number of horses with their necks cut off with arrows fell down. The chariots stood with the horses, charioteer and the warrior killed and flag staff broken. The foot-soldiers had their arms, thighs and necks cut down.

26. There flowed forth hundreds of streams of blood issued from the shattered bodies of soldiers, elephants and horses which were teeming with (floating acquatic) serpent-like (hacked down) arms, rolling tortoise-like human heads, they were studded with islets of elephant-bodies and were infested with crocodiles in the from of (dead) horses.

27. Therein were hands and thighs of men like fishes, the locks of human hair like moss, bows like ripbles and weapons like bushes. The shields (or wheels) were like terrible whirl-pools and ornaments of big and costly precious stones formed the stones and sand in them.

28. By Balarāma of infinite prowess (who was) knocking down with his pestle the proud and powerful enemies in that battle, there started streams of blood which struck terror in the hearts of the cowards and inspired matrial delight and courage in the valiants.

29. Oh dear Parīkṣit ? That army impassable and terrible like an ocean of vast limitless (unfordable) expanse and directed (lit. protected) by Jarāsandha was completely annihilated. This was a supreme sportive feat of the sons of Vasudeva who were the Lords of the world.

with thirty shafts in that battle. He laughingly cut off the bow even of Śiśupāla, the son of Damaghoṣa, and with three shafts cut down the flag, his crown and the umbrella. Thereupon Kṛṣṇa, the descendant of Madhu, fitted ten Bhalla type of arrows on his Śārṅga bow. He drew the bow-strings up to the ear and hit Śiśupāla with them in the battle. The army of the *kṣatriyas* which was pierced with arrows became confounded.

24.16. The hostile army, the horses, charioteers and chariots of which were killed and destroyed, became helpless as there was nobody to save it, as if it was struck with tempestuous winds at the end of world which blows away hills, trees and creepers.

24.17. Keeping all the while the Magadhan army in view, Kṛṣṇa of ferocious valour, continued discharging arrows, blowing his conch and twanging his bow incessantly and moving it in a circle like a fire-brand, in the battle.

30. There is nothing surprising in the defeat of the hostile forces in the case of Kṛṣṇa of infinite excellence who, out of sportiveness, brings about by His will, the creation, protection and destruction of the three worlds. This is however an attempt to describe the story of the Lord who imitates the ways of the mortals.*

31. Like a lion powerfully seizing another lion, Balarāma took Jarāsandha a captive who, though extremely powerful himself, had lost his chariot and the whole of the army and was left alone alive.

32. With a view to achieve His purpose of (destroying demonic forces which would be mobilised by Jarāsandha) he forbade Jarāsandha's being bound with the nooses of Varuṇa and cords of human beings (by Balarāma) although Jarāsandha had put to death many enemies (in the past).

33-34. Released and allowed to go by Kṛṣṇa and Balarāma, the Protectors of the world, Jarāsandha who was highly respected by warriors, felt ashamed. He made up his mind (to retire from politics and) to perform penance. But on his way (to the forest) he was dissuaded by (his friendly) kings with expressions conveying the import of sacred texts (and quotations from *Śāstras*) as well as popular maxims and words of worldly wisdom. They convinced him by the argument:) "Your defeat by the Yadus is the consequence of the bondage of your *karma* (actions in past life)".

* *Here VJ.'s text adds* :

30.1. When all his army was annihilated and the remaining soldiers fled away, the extremely mighty Jarāsandha, alone in his chariot confronted Balarāma, the wielder of the plough (as a weapon).

30.2. Both of them were enormously big like mountains, proud like intoxicated elephants, fired with indignation and possessed of great strength. They fought with each other.

30.3. Jarāsandha who was overwhelmed with wrath, took up his heavy mace (*Gadā*) and turning it round a hundred times, hurled it at the chest of Balarāma.

30.4. Dodging the onward dashing *gadā*, big and heavy like a mountain peak, Balarāma, the wielder of a plough (as his weapon) smilingly made his attempt fruitless.

30.5. Having rendered the mace ineffective by striking it with his pestle, the wrathful Balarāma struck it against the chariot and killed his charioteer.

35. With all his army annihilated and himself slighted by the Lord by showing indifference to him, king Jarāsandha, the son of Bṛhad-ratha returned to Magadha with his heart weighed with despair and melancholy.

36. Kṛṣṇa also whose army was unscathed (as the wounds of his soldiers immediately healed with his nectarine glance and who had crossed over the ocean of the inimical forces (by crushing them), was applauded (with words "Well done! Bravo") and was showered over with flowers by gods.

37. He returned to his capital while his victory was being celebrated in songs by the congregations of the citizens of Mathurā and bards like Sūta, Māgadha and *Bandins* whose hearts were delighted with the total disappearance of the feverish panic (caused by the siege of Mathurā).

38. As the Lord entered the capital, conches, drums, kettledrums, trumpets were loudly and incessantly sounded and lutes, flutes and *mṛdaṅgas* were every now and then played upon.

39-40. The roads of the city were sprinkled with water. The population was jubilant. The city was decorated with flags and was resonant with the recitation of the Vedas. Ornamental arches with festoons suspended were erected all over the way. (By way of worship and reception) Kṛṣṇa was showered over with flowers and tender shoots by women; curds mixed with unbroken grains of rice were applied to his forehead and he was gazed with affection by the people with their loving eyes full of joy.

41. The Lord (Kṛṣṇa) presented to Ugrasena, the king of Yadus, all the spoils of the battle, the untold treasure (left behind by the flying army) and the ornaments and jewelry of the warriors (killed and hence) lying on the battle field.*

* The *Textus ornatior* of VJ. gives a number of additional verses and chapters. This additional material has made the Kṛṣṇa legend more comprehensive and attractive. Readers are recommended to read the additional verses in the footnotes and additional chapters which are given as Appendix to this Skandha.

From verse 41 here VJ. adds three more interesting chapters describing the repeated attacks of Jarāsandha in Mathurā and the journey of Kṛṣṇa and Balarāma to the South (probable to find a suitable place for the Yādavas at a safe distance from Magadha) and how Kṛṣṇa killed

42. In this manner Jarāsandha, king of Magadhas mobilised every time an army of the same (twentythree) number of *Akṣauhiṇis* and fought for seventeen times (in succession) with the Yadus who were protected by Lord Kṛṣṇa.

43. (In every expedition) the Vṛṣṇis completely destroyed the whole of his army through the dint of Kṛṣṇa's spiritual power. With his forces completely slaughtered and himself allowed to escape by the enemies, king Jarāsandha returned to his capital.

44. While the eighteenth invasion was imminent, there appeared in the interval, a Yavana hero (Kālayavana) who was despatched by Nārada.[1]

45. Kālayavana (who regarded himself as) the matchless hero in this world, heard (the report from Nārada) that Vṛṣṇis were his equals in war. He invaded and laid siege to Mathurā with three crores of Mlecchas(barbarians).

46-47. Seeing him (with that vast army), Kṛṣṇa who had Balarāma as His companion, conferred (with him), "Alas! A great calamity is bafalling Yadus on both sides (from Kālayavana and Jarāsandha. Today this *Yavana* with his vast army has completely beleaguered us. Jarāsandha, the king of Magadha also will be coming today, tomorrow or day after tomorrow.

48. If Jarāsandha, the son of Jarā, comes while both of us are engaged in fighting with this (Kālayavana), the mighty Magadhan king will massacre our clansmen or take them captive to his capital.

49. Therefore, let us construct today a fortress inaccessible to human beings (lit. bipeds) and keeping our kinsmen

Śṛgāla Vāsudeva, an ally of Jarāsandha at Karavīra (Kolhapur?). Followers of VJ.'s text are requested to read these chapters which are printed as an Appendix before reading the next (42nd) verse. That verse follows ch. 50. verse 24 in the Appendix.

1. According to VP. 5.23.6 it was in reply to the query of Kālayavana as to who is a match to him that Nārada mentioned the name of Yādavas. Nārada did not instigate him against Kṛṣṇa.

safe in that fort, we shall arrange for the killing of this Kālayavana."[1]

50. Having thus consulted with Balarāma, the Lord caused a fortress constructed in the (western) sea. In the fortress, he got built a city twelve *yojanas* (96 miles) in area and wonderful in every respect.

51. The building of the city exhibited the expertise in architecture and the skill in masonry of Tvaṣṭṛ, the architect of gods. The roads, quadrangles, streets (and residential areas) were constructed strictly in conformity to the prescribed tenets of the science of architecture (pertaining to city building).

52. In that city, gardens planted with celestial trees and creepers and wonderful parks were laid out. It was built with sky-scraping, gold-towered buildings and balconies of crystals.

53. It had barns built of silver and brass which were adorned with gold pitchers. The houses therein were of gold with jewelled domes and floors paved with gold and big emeralds.

54. It was provided with shrines with upper storeys dedicated to gods. It was thickly populated with persons belonging to the four classes of the society. It appeared beautiful with the palaces of the rulers of the Yadu clan.

55. For the sake of Hari, the great Indra transported his own assembly-hall Sudharmā and the celestial tree Pārijāta[2] resorting to which a human being is not subjected to the conditions (such as hunger, thirst, old age, death) affecting a mortal.

55-A *VJ's text adds* :

This city became a beloved resort of Lord Viṣṇu (Kṛṣṇa), the God of gods who resides on the milky ocean.

1. As per VP 5.23.1-4 Gārgya who was insulted by Yadus got a boon from Lord Śiva that his son (Kālayavana) would terrorise Yadus and would be invincible. To respect Śiva's boon, Kṛṣṇa did not kill him.

2. ŚR. explains this anachronism by stating that although Pārijāta was not brought at the time of building Dvārakā, the event that Kṛṣṇa brought it from Indra took place before this narration of the *Bhāgavata* by Śuka.

56. Varuṇa gifted (snow-) white horses with one black ear, swift like mind in speed.

56-A. *VJ.'s Text*

The Lord of waters presented to the God of gods one thousand such horses. Kubera, the presiding deity over treasures gave him eight treasures[1], while Guardian deities of the worlds submitted their special type of wealth to him.

56-B. *VJ.'s Text*

Similarly, guardian deities of other spheres presented him the wealth special to them.

57. When Lord Hari incarnated on the earth, Siddhas to whom all powers were given for the execution of their duties by the Lord, resubmitted all the powers etc, to him.

58. Having transferred all the people (his clansmen) there (to Dvārakā) by using his supernatural *yogic* powers and in consultation with Balarāma, the protector of the remaining population (of Mathurā), Kṛṣṇa issued out of the gates of Mathurā, wearing garland of lotuses completely unarmed.[2]

CHAPTER FIFTYONE[3]

Mucukunda's Eulogy of the Lord

1-3. The Yavana (Kālayavana) perceived Śrī Kṛṣṇa coming out (of the gates of Mathurā) like the rising Moon, most beautiful to look at, dark in complexion, clad in yellow silken garment, with the *Śri-vatsa* mark on his bosom, with his neck beautified with the pendant brilliant Kaustubha gem,

1. S.R. quotes the following list of eight treasures
padmas' caiva mahāpadmo matsya-kūrmau tathaudakaḥ |
nīlo mukundaḥ śaṅkhaś ca nidhayo'ṣṭau prakīrtitāḥ ||
2. Here ends chapter 53 in VJ.'s text.
3. Ch. 54 in VJ.'s text.

having four mighty (knee-) long arms and eyes reddish like a fresh-blown lotus, ever beaming with joyousness, with splendid, beautiful cheeks, bright with a smile and lotus-like countenance with dazzling alligator-shaped ear-rings.

4-5. "This exquisitely beautiful man characterised by *Śri-vasta*, four arms, lotus-like eyes and wearing a Vanamālā must be Vāsudeva (Kṛṣṇa). From the characteristic marks described in details by Nārada (I presume) he cannot be anyone else. But since he is armless and walking on foot, I too shall fight with him unarmed (and without using any vehicle)".

6. Resolving thus, the Yavana, with the intention of seizing him whom even the *yogin* cannot attain with difficulty, chased him who was running fast with his back towards the Yavana.

7. Showing himself to be within his grasp at every step, the king of Yavanas was taken far away to a distant mountain cave.

8. "Born as you are in the Yadu race, it is not proper for you to run away from the enemy". Reproaching him thus while pursuing, he could not overtake him (and catch hold of him) as his inauspicious *karmas* were not exhausted.

9. Even though he was thus vilified, the Lord entered a deep cave in the mountain[1]. Kālayavana also made his way into it and saw that another person was lying there asleep.

10. "Surely after luring me to such a long distance, he is (pretending to be) asleep like an innocent person." Thinking thus and regarding the sleeping man to be Kṛṣṇa, the stupid fellow kicked him

11. The man who was asleep for a long time became awakened. He slowly opened his eyes and looked in all directions and espied Kālayavana standing by his side.

1. VB. States that the cave is near Dhavalapura (Dholapur) at a distance of 10 yojanas from Mathurā. N.L. De identified it with a lake three miles to the west of Dholapur and states that on the site of the lake there was formerly a mountain—GDAM I.p. 132.

12. By the angry look of the enraged man (rudely awakened from sleep), there arose a fire out of Kālayavana's body and he was reduced to ashes in a moment.

King Parīkṣit asked :

13. What was the name of the man who (thus) killed the Yavana, Oh Brāhmaṇa sage ? From whom was he born ? What (extra-ordinary) prowess did he possess ? Why did he enter the cave for sleep ? What majestic lustre did he possess ?

Śrī Śuka narrated :

14. He was born in the race of Ikṣvākus and was a prominent son of Māndhātṛ. He was well-known by the name Mucukunda. He was friendly to Brāhmaṇas and always true to his words.

15. He was implored to ensure their protection (from demons) by the host of gods headed by Indra, as they were very much afraid of (and harassed) by Asuras. He accordingly afforded them protection for a long time.

16. Having secured (the services of) god Kārttikeya (son of Śiva) as their protector, they spoke to Mucukunda, "Oh King ! You may now retire from the onerous task[1] of protecting us.

17. Having given up your world kingdom from which all the thorns (miscreants and enemies) were wiped out by you, you have been protecting us in doing which you have given up all pleasures, Oh warrior.

18. Now none of your sons, queens, clansmen, ministers or your contemporary subjects survives as they are subjected to the influence of Time (and have died).

19. The glorious supreme immortal Lord, the Time-spirit is mightier than the mighty. He drives off all creatures easily as in a sport, as a herdsman would do his cattle.

20. May God bless you. Please ask of us any boon except the final emancipation. For the imperishable Almighty Lord Viṣṇu alone has the capability to grant it.

1. Though he was in heaven, Mucukunda was always engaged in fighting and had no respite to enjoy heavenly bliss—VJ.

21*-22. When the highly glorious king Mucukunda was thus addressed (by gods), (it is reported that) he respectfully bowed to gods[1]. He entered a cave (shown to him by gods) and reposed himself to enjoy the sleep granted to him by gods.

23. (The gods assured him) "He who would wake you up thoughtlessly while you are asleep (and thus disturb your rest), the stupid fellow be reduced to ashes the very moment he is woked at by you".

24. When the Yavana was reduced to ashes, the glorious Lord Kṛṣṇa, the most prominent Sātvata manifested himself to the intelligent king Mucukunda.

25-27. He perceived the Lord, of dark-blue complexion like a cloud, wearing a yellow silken garment, with the *Śrīvatsa* mark on the chest, lustrous with the refulgent *Kaustubha* gem, having four arms, appearing resplendent with the *Vanamālā* (a garland of forest flowers special to Śrī Kṛṣṇa), with a charming, kindly disposed countenance, beautified with radiant alligator-shaped ear-rings, captivating to the eyes of all human beings[1] with smiling looks expressing gracious love, endowed with youthfulness, noble in gait like a proud lion.

28. Being over-awed with his dazzling effulgence, the highly intelligent and wise king gently enquired of him as he was unapproachable due to his splendour.

Mucukunda said

29. "Who are you arrived here in this inaccessible mountain cave in a dense forest ? How is it that you go about in this forest full of thorns, on foot tender like lotus-petals ?

* According to Yande's (Bombay) edition.

1. *VJ.'s text adds* :

21.1 ... and he begged of them to grant him (the boon of) sleep lasting for a pretty long period inside a cave. When he was granted that boon, the noble-minded king Mucukunda being overcome with fatigue sought from them (undisturbed) sleep.

Vṛndāvana edition adds :

21.2. (Mucukunda requested as a boon :) 'Whoever disturbs my sleep should be instantaneously reduced to ashes, Oh most prominent gods'. The gods granted the boons saying 'Amen'.

1. v.l. enhanting to the eyes of the three worlds (VJ.)

30. You are the embodiment of majestic lustre of all those endowed with effulgence and luminosity. Are you the glorious Fire-god or the Sun-god or the Moon-god or the great Indra or the guardian deity of the world or any other divinity of that high status?

31. I regard you as the Supreme Person, Lord Viṣṇu out of the three Gods of gods (viz. Brahmā, Viṣṇu and Śiva) as you dispel the darkness of the cave (or remove ignorance in my heart) by your splendour as does the light of a lamp.

32. Oh most excellent person! If it pleases You, may your birth, exploits, family name be frankly disclosed to us who are sincerely desirous of hearing it (or who sincerely desire to render you service).

33. As for us we are Kṣattriyas of the Ikṣvāku race, Oh Tiger among men. I am, Oh Lord, known as Mucukunda, the son of Māndhātṛ (who was the son of Yuvanāśva).

34. Completely exhausted by vigil extending over a long period and with all the limbs of my body benumbed and overpowered with sleep, I lay enjoying un-interrupted sleep to my heart's content, from which I was rudely awakened by some unknown person, just now.

35. Even he has been reduced to ashes, verily by his own sins, indeed. It is after that your glorious personality, the destroyer of enemies, has been perceived by me.

36. Being bedazzled by your unbearable lustre, we cannot look at you for long. Our powers are ineffective in your presence, Oh blessed God. But you deserve to be honoured by all embodied beings (This much we can say about you)".

37. Thus respectfully addressed by the king, the glorious Lord, the Creator of all beings, laughed aloud and replied to him in a voice deep like the thundering of a cloud.

The Almighty Lord replied:

38. Dear King! my incarnations, exploits and epithets are innumerable. They, being infinite in number, it is not possible even for me to count them.

39. Possibly someone might reckon, through (a continuous period of) many lives, all the particles of dust over the

earth, but nobody can ever enumerate my excellences, exploits, designations and incarnations.[1]

40. Even great sages (like Parāśara, Vaiśampāyana etc.) who tried to describe my descent and exploits pertaining to the past, present and future in order, have not been able to reach the end.

41. However, listen to me as I narrate those pertaining to the present time, Oh dear king. Formerly, I was entreated by god Brahmā to protect the order of righteousness and for annihilation of Asuras who caused a burden to the earth.

42. I have descended in the race of Yadus in the house of Vasudeva. As I am born of Vasudeva, they call me Vāsudeva.

43. Kālanemi, born as Kaṁsa and the haters of the righteous like Pralamba and others have been killed by me. This Yavana is caused to be burnt by me through your fiery looks.

44. Having been earnestly and repeatedly implored by you in days gone by, I, that Vāsudeva, being fond of my votaries, have come over to this cave for showering my divine Grace on you.

45. Seek boons from me, Oh royal sage. I shall bestow on you all desired objects as no person that resorts to me (submitting himself completely to my Will) shall suffer misery any more.

Śrī Śuka said:

46. When addressed thus, Mucukunda bowed down to him. Remembering the words of Vṛddha Garga (predicting God Viṣṇu's revelation to him), he realized that he (Vāsudeva) was Lord Nārāyaṇa himself. Overwhelmed with joy, he submitted as follows:

1. Cf. *Viṣṇor nu kaṁ vīryāṇi pravocaṁ yaḥ pārthivāni vimame rajāṁsi* /—RV. 1.154.1, AV 7.26.1; VS. 5-18, TS. 1.2.13.3

Mucukunda said:

47. Oh Lord ! This person (i.e. I or human being) whether male or female is absolutely deluded by your Māyā (Deluding Potency). With his eye (or mind) concentrated on *saṁsāra* (*Or* being unable to realize that you alone are the Reality), he does not seek resort in you (as a devotee). For the sake of happiness, he is attached to the house including wife, children, wealth etc.) which is the source of all miseries and is thus deceived (in his search for happiness).

48. After securing the blessing of birth as a human being in this world—which, in itself, is very difficult to obtain—and that too with proportionate limbs (and soundness of mind) without any efforts (on one's part but through Divine Grace), a person who does not resort to the lotus-feet of the Lord, is, Oh handsome Lord, a wicked-minded (dull-witted) fellow who, like a beast desirous of eating grass falls into a grass-covered well (with no way out), sinks down in the dark deep well of domestic life.

49. All this life of mine has been fruitlessly wasted, Oh Invincible Almighty, for I behaved as a king elated with the pride of affluence and splendour of my royalty, identifying this mortal body as the Self and in endless anxiety due to my attachment to sons, wives, treasures, and lands.

50. Forgetting you altogether, I became incorrigibly haughty and lordly with the deep-rooted (ignorant) attachment to this inert body which is similar to an earthen pot or a wall (and thus totally different from the Soul), the inherent pride of being a god among men (king) surrounded by many military officers commanding division of chariots, elephants, cavalry-men and foot-soldiers and leading expeditions over the earth.

51. Like unto a hungry serpent, licking the corners of its mouth with its tongue, seizing upon and swallowing up a rat, you, the alert God of Death, surprisingly overtake a person who forgets you altogether, and is engrossed in pondering over the ways and means of achieving worldly plans which (even if frustrated) intensify the desire for worldly objects which (even after attainment) extremely increases the greed and thirst for them.

52. The mortal body which formerly moved in chariots plated with gold or rode on elephants and was designated (honorifically) as 'the god among men', is reduced to what may be called as excrement (if devoured after death by dogs, crows etc. in an undisposed condition), as worms (if interred in the grave) and as ashes (if cremated by fire) during the inevitable course of Time.

53. Having conquered (all kingdoms spread over the earth in) all directions, with the (possibility of future) wars forestalled, occupying the exalted imperial throne, being paid respects by his (former) equals, the man is reduced to the state of a pet (a beast for play) for women in his home which is characterized by sexual pleasures, Oh Almighty Lord.

54. Being devoted to the performance of austerities denying himself all pleasures of senses, he continues to perform righteous acts and donate gifts (in the present life) with the expectant desire, "I should become the king of heaven (Indra) or the sole sovereign ruler of the world. But this simply intensifies his thirst and is not conducive to real happiness.

55. When the time of release from the *saṁsāra* of a person wandering in the cycle of births and deaths, approaches then only companionship with saintly persons takes place, Oh Imperishable Lord. It is only after association with saints that the mind (being averse to attachment to all worldly objects turns to your devotion—you who are the Master of the high and the low.

56. That the bondage of attachment to kingship should be severed automatically (without any efforts on my part) is, Me-thinks your special divine Grace shown to me—the Grace devoutly solicited by saints of unflinching devotion to you and by kings who though they ruled over the entire earth, still wished to retire to the forest for penance.

57. Oh Omnipresent Lord ! I do not seek any other boon from you except rendering service to your feet, which is regarded as the most covetable blessing according to those who have renounced everything (and possess nothing of their own). Having propitiated you, the bestower of *Mokṣa* (Liberation), Oh Hari, what wise man would solicit a boon from you which will create a bondage to one's soul.

58. Hence, rejecting all blessings which are bound with the *guṇas* viz. *Sattva*, *rajas* and *tamas*, Oh Lord, I seek resort in you, the Supreme Person, the very embodiment of knowledge and consciousness unsullied by any taint, transcendent to all *guṇas*, the One without second.

59. For a very long time, I have been troubled in this world with fruits of action and have been afflicted with the *vāsanās* (effects left on the mind after enjoying fruits of actions) and am harrassed by six unsatiable (internal) enemies. Being unable to secure mental peace, I have with great difficulty approached your lotus-feet Oh Lord who are the Supreme Soul, free from fear and grief of death, Oh Lord ! Be pleased to protect me who am full of distress.

The glorious Lord said:

60. Oh Emperor of the entire world ! Oh great king, Your mind is free from impurities (like attachment, greed ete.) and judgment clear. For though you were tempted with boons (at your sweet will), you were not lured thereby.

61. It was with a view to test your unerring, vigilance that you were tempted with boons. Please know that the mind and intelligence of unflinching devotees is never changed by temptation of blessings.

62. The mind of those who are other than devotees and who control it by *Prāṇāyāma* (breath control) and other means, is not devoid of *vāsanās* (the subtle desires) and it is noticed that they are again attached to sense-objects.

63. You may roam over the earth at will after setting your mind on me. May your devotion unto me be everlasting and unflinching for ever.

64. In compliance of your duties as a Kṣattriya, you have killed living beings in hunting (fighting etc.). Expiate the sin committed by you by seeking my asylum and by meditation and performance of penance.

65. In the next birth you will be a prominent Brāhmaṇa, the best friend of all beings. Then you will certainly attain to me, the Absolute, Oh king.

CHAPTER FIFTYTWO

Kṛṣṇa and Balarāma escape to Dvārakā: Balarāma's marriage

Rukmiṇī's Letter to Kṛṣṇa

Śrī Śuka continued :

1. In this way, blessed by Kṛṣṇa, Mucukunda, the descendant of Ikṣvāku, circumambulated by the right Lord Kṛṣṇa, bowed to him and came out of the cave.

2. He noticed the dimunition of stature and form in men, beasts, creepers and trees and concluding that the Kali Age[1] had set in, he went to the northerly direction.

3. Endowed with faith and penance, free from attachment and cleared of doubts, the wise king concentrated his mind on Kṛṣṇa and entered the mount Gandhamādana[2].

4. He arrived at Badarikāśrama[3], the abode of Nara and Nārāyaṇa. Undergoing conflicting pairs of conditions (such as heat and cold, pleasure and pain) with tranquillity of mind, he propitiated Lord Hari with his austerities.

5. The Lord again returned to the city of Mathurā which was still besieged by the Yavana army. He annihilated the Yavana army and carried of their wealth as spoils to Dvārakā.

6.* While the wealth was being transported on the backs of men and oxen under the direction of the Imperishable

1. VT : Though the Kali age set in after Kṛṣṇa's departure from this world, he guessed that the advent of the Kali Age was imminent.

2. A part of Rudra Himālayas in the Kailāsa range. According to *Mbh.* and *Varāha P.* Badarikāśrama is situated on this mountain.—GDAMI p. 60.

3. Badrinath in Garhawal in U.P.

* *After this verse VJ.'s text reads* :

6.1 Thereupon king Jarāsandha, fierce like the universal fire at the end of the world, deployed his forces consisting of divisions of chariots, elephants, horsemen and foot-soldiers in crocodile-like formation within the wink of the eye and he surrounded Lord Kṛṣṇa in the midst of that formation.

6.2 Grasping the situation the ferocious Kṛṣṇa hastily uprooted a tree and struck down with it the elephants, chariots and horses in that battle.

Lord, Jarāsandha, commanding an army of twentythree *akṣau-hiṇīs* arrived on the scene.

7. Observing the violent onrush of inimical forces, Balarāma and Kṛṣṇa, the descendants of Madhu[1] adopted the human way of life and quickly began to run, Oh king.

8. Though really dauntless, they left the vast treasure (the spoils from the Yavana army) and simulating terrified cowards, they ran for many *yojanas* on foot, tender like lotus-petals.

9. Seeing both of them on the run, the powerful king of Magadhas laughed heartily and being ignorant of the deep designs and capacity of those two Lords pursued them with his army of chariots.*

6.3 Thus knocked down by Kṛṣṇa with the tree, elephants in the hostile army fell down dead on the ground like mountains struck down by Indra with his *Vajra* (Thunder-bolt).

6.4 There was left no trace of the chariots along with the occupants of the chariots, of the horses along with their riders, as if they were reduced to powder (in a grinding mill), Oh best among the Kurus.

6.5 Being infuriated, Balarāma knocked down with blows of his fist, intoxicated elephants, on the battle field, just as Indra, the King of gods, does to mountains with his thunderbolt.

6.6 The chariots (of the enemies) which were shattered down with the blows of Balarāma's fist, could not even be seen on the earth, Oh King, as they were reduced to powder like dry, withered leaves.

6.7 In the meanwhile, Jarāsandha noticed that all the wealth of the Yavana was being carried to Dvārakā and (pursuing it) and massacring the Yādavas (escorting it), seized it all. He then returned to the scene of the battle to encounter Balarāma and Kṛṣṇa, Oh scion of the Kuru race.

1. *VJ.'s Text adds here* :

7.1 Noticing Jarāsandha dashing towards them with his allied princes and their armies and themselves being showered with volleys of arrows like two cubs of elephants (*kari-potakau*) driven by heavy rainshower, and themselves were without any chariots, weapons, armours and soldiers.

* *Here VJ's text adds* :

9.1 Striking back, the two warriors took rest at Karavīrapura at night. When the sun rose, the two heroes ascended the mount Gomanta.

9.2-3. Climbing up mount Gomanta which was inhabited by Siddhas, Cāraṇas, Gandharvas and Vidyādharas, Balarāma and Kṛṣṇa hastily ascended its peak known as Pravarṣaṇa as clouds always shower

10. Being completely exhausted by (the strain of) running fast to such a long distance, they, however, ascended the lofty mountain peak known as Pravarṣaṇa where Indra the god of rain, always sends forth showers.

11. Surmising that they must have concealed themselves somewhere on the mountain and not being able to locate their place of hiding, they (Jarāsandha's men) set the whole mountain on fire on all sides with the fuel (the trees cut down by them during their search) strewn around.

rains there. They happily lived there subsisting on fruits and roots, Oh king.

9.4. Feeling elated and happy, Jarāsandha also pursued the two Mādhava brothers (Kṛṣṇa and Balarāma) and laid siege to the Gomanta mountain, surrounding it with his vast army.

9.5-7. He summoned his followers, the allied princes proud and irresistible in fight, such as (kings of) Kaliṅga, Kuñjarapati, the ruler of Śurāṣṭra (Kathiawar), Jayadratha the king of Sindhu (lower Sindh), Somadatta of the Kuru family, Śakuni the king of Gandhāra and Rukmi, the (crown) prince of Vidarbha, Sudakṣiṇa of Kāmboja and Virāṭa, the king of Matsyas. He commanded them to go up and fight from the east of Gomanta.

9.8-10. For scaling (and attacking) the mountain Gomanta from its southern side, Jarāsandha ordered the following kings—Drupada, the king of Pāñcālas, Damaghoṣa, the ruler of Cedis, Brahmadatta, king of Śālvas and Ekalavya, the chief of Niṣādas, Bāhlika, the foremost of Kurus and the unconquerable Yudhāmanyu, Vinda and Anuvinda of Avanti and Pauṇḍraka, the king of Kāśi.

9.11-13. To Druma, the ruler of Kimpuruṣas, Dantavaktra and his younger brother, the heroic king of Videhas and Bhūriśravas, Bṛhaccāpa, the ruler of Karuṣas and Śatadhvaja of Daśārṇa, Śaibya, the king of Suvīra (or Sauvīra, upper Sindh and Southern Punjab) and the great chariot warrior Darada,—To these King Jarāsandha of immeasurable dignity and splendour, commanded to ascend expeditiously the mount Gomanta from the west.

9.14-15. Despatching as vanguards Suśarmā of Trigarta, the mighty Veṇudārin, the immensely powerful Kulinda, the chiefs of Kekayas, Śiśupāla and the invincible monarch Bhīṣmaka, he himself quickly scaled up the mount from the northern side.

9.16. Having thus climbed mount Gomanta abounding in fruit-bearing trees of all seasons, they searched for Kṛṣṇa and Balarāma everywhere below the peak Pravarṣaṇa. Not finding Balarāma and Kṛṣṇa, they deforested the mount cutting down all the trees.

12. Thereupon, both Kṛṣṇa and Balarāma quickly (and with great velocity) leapt from the mountain peak which is eleven *yojanas* in height and had its sides burning, and descended on the plains below (beyond the army of Jarāsandha).

13. Without being noticed by enemy and his followers, those best sons of Yadu race returned to their capital Dvārakā which is surrounded by the sea as its moat, Oh king.

14*. Falsely believing that Balarāma and Kṛṣṇa must have been burnt (in that fire), the king of Magadhas withdrew his vast army and returned to his kingdom of Magadha.

15. It has been already narrated to you by me (*vide Supra* 9.3.27-36), that Kakudmin, the son of Revata, the celebrated king of Ānarta gave his daughter Revatī in marriage to Balarāma, as per direction of god Brahmā.

16. Lord Kṛṣṇa also married Rukmiṇī, the princess of Vidarbha and the daughter of Bhīṣmaka and who was an *aṃśa* (part-manifestation) of goddess Śrī in a *svayaṁvara* ('self-choice' type of marriage where the girl elects of her own free will, her husband).

17. Like Garuḍa, the son of Kaśyapa taking away the pitcher of nectar (defeating all the gods), Kṛṣṇa carried her away defeating instantly Śālva and other kings who were partisans and allies of Śiśupāla, the king of Cedis.

King Parīkṣit enquired :

18. It has been heard by us that the Lord married the beautiful looking Rukmiṇī, the princess of Bhīṣmaka as per *rākṣasa* form of marriage (wherein the girl is abducted per force in the teeth of opposition of relatives.)

* *After this adds VJ.'s Text* :

14.1. Having vanquished Balarāma and Kṛṣṇa, the foremost among the Yādavas in the eighteenth expedition, Jarāsandha had brought under his dominion all the directions (all kingdoms on the earth) and feeling proud of it, he lived in his own kingdom, Oh king.

14.2 The noble-souled Kṛṣṇa and Balarāma (the Mādhava brothers) entered the city of Dvārakā and lived happily in the company of their highly joyous relatives and were being praised day and night by bards and songsters like *Sūta*, *Māgadha* and *Bandins*.

End of ch. 55*th in VJ.'s Text*

For ch. 56 in VJ.'s Text vide the Appendix.

19. I desire to hear the story of Lord Kṛṣṇa of boundless power and energy, who defeated Jarāsandha, Śālva and others and carried away the girl, Oh worshipful sage.

20. Oh Brāhmaṇa sage ! The stories of Lord Kṛṣṇa are meritorious, sweet, ever-interesting, delightful and they wipe out the sins of the world. What person who knows the importance of listening to them, will be sated at hearing them.*

Śrī Śuka narrated:

21. There was a great king called Bhīṣmaka, a powerful monarch of the Vidarbhas. He had five sons and only one charming looking daughter.

22. The eldest son was Rukmi. After him was born Rukmabāhu and then Rukmakeśa, Rukma-mālin and the pious Rukmiṇī was their sister.

23. Listening attentively to the glorification of Lord Kṛṣṇa's beauty, prowess, excellent virtues and affluence as sung by the visitors to her palace, she regarded him as her worthy spouse.

24. Kṛṣṇa also made up his mind to marry her as he knew her to be a suitable wife due to her intelligence, auspicious characteristics, nobility of heart, beauty, high character and other excellences.

25. In spite of all brothers being desirous of giving their sister in marriage to Kṛṣṇa, Rukmi who hated Kṛṣṇa, came in the way of it and proposed Śiśupāla, the king of Cedis.

26. Grasping the situation, the beautiful princess of Vidarbha was deeply agitated at heart. She pondered over the problem and immediately despatched a trusted Brāhmaṇa to Kṛṣṇa with the mission of bringing him.

27. Arriving at Dvārakā, he was ushered into (Kṛṣṇa's presence) by the door-attendants where he saw the First (the most ancient) Person (in the world) seated on a throne of gold.

28. Seeing him come, Lord Kṛṣṇa who was always friendly to Brāhmaṇas, got down from his throne. Offering a

* Here *Vṛindāvana* edition gives the additional chapters 56 and a part of 57. These are translated in the Appendix.

(respectable) seat to the Brāhmaṇa, he worshipped him (as an honourable guest) as gods used to treat him.

29. When he had taken his meals and rested comfortably, Śrī Kṛṣṇa, the final asylum of the saintly people, approached him and massaging gently his feet with his hand, he quietly enquired of the Brāhmaṇa.

30. "Oh most prominent one among great Brāhmaṇas ! Is your righteous course of conduct traditionally approved by the elders, going on without any difficulty ? (I hope) you are (happy with it and) contented in your heart.

31. If a Brāhmaṇa adjusts himself in contentment, with whatever he gets by chance, but does not swerve from his course of righteousness, he is like a wish-yielding cow capable of granting blessings to all the world (*or* that righteous course of conduct serves as a wish-yielding cow to him)

32. Even Indra, the king of gods, if discontented, has to wander from one world to another restlessly.[1] But a destitute person, if contented, sleeps soundly without a touch of feverish anxiety to his body and mind.

33. I bow down again and again with my head to those Brāhmaṇas who are happy with the realization of their self[2], pious and the best friends and well-wishers of all beings, free from ego, serene and self complacent.

34. Are you all happy (with a feeling of security) under your ruler, Oh Brāhmaṇa ? That king is liked by me in whose country the subjects protected by him lead a happy life.

35. Please tell me the place from which you have come here crossing this (unfordable) sea and the object of seeing me. If it be no undivulgable secret, please tell us everything—what we should do for you?"

36. When such relevant queries were made courteously to the Brāhmaṇa by the Supreme Lord who had sportively assumed a human form, described to him in details (the situation which led princess Rukmiṇī to depute him to Lord Kṛṣṇa)*

1. v.l. *nāpnoti* : Even though he is the lord of gods he does not attain to higher worlds but suffers—ŚR.

2. *Or* : With what they get as a result of their destiny or *karmas*.

* Here VR.'s Text adds : (also VJ.)

36.1. I have been deputed to your presence, on best of men, by

Rukmiṇī said in her message :

37. Oh the most-beautiful Person in all the worlds! Having listened to your excellent qualities which enter into the heart through (the passage of) ears and remove all the feverishness of the body and the mind, and of your excellent charms ensuring all the cherished blessings to those who possess eyes, my heart sheds all bashfulness and enters in you, Oh Immortal Lord!

38. Oh Kṛṣṇa! Lion among men! What wise, judicious girl of very noble descent will not seek you as a husband at the proper time—you who are the most beautiful one among all men, and one's own compeer in family, character, personal charm, knowledge, youthfulness, affluence and splendour.*

39. I have, therefore, chosen you as my lord indeed. Oh Lotus-eyed dear lord! I have submitted my self unto you. Please do take me as your wife. Like a jackal polluting by his touch the lion's share of the prey, may not Śiśupāla, the king of Cedis come hastily and touch the hero's share (i.e. myself).

40. If the Supreme Lord, the Almighty, has been properly propitiated by me by religious deeds such as digging wells, performing sacrifices, giving donations, observance of religious rules and vows and the worship of gods, Brāhmaṇas and preceptors and such other deeds, may Lord Kṛṣṇa, the elder brother of Gada, come and marry me so that others like the son of Damaghoṣa (Śiśupāla) may not take my hands.

princess Rukmiṇī. Please listen to her message and let her prayer (and proposal) be implemented immediately there-after.

36.2. Placing the letter (written by Rukmiṇī) at his feet, he bowed down to him. The Lord of the world, with beautiful smiling eyes, took it up. The Lord, *Dharma* incarnate, read it attentively as if he was eagerly desirous to read it.

**VJ's Text adds* :

38.1. You are the glorious consort of goddess Lakṣmī, loved by Your devotees, the Supreme Controller of the Universe who are resorted to for protection by helpless people and as such also by me. Taking this into account, be pleased to grant the prayer of mine who am a servant of your lotus-like feet. Oh dearest Lord I have submitted myself to your feet.

41. Oh Invincible Lord ! May you come secretly with an army and generals to Vidarbha at the time of marriage which is to be celebrated very shortly. Defeat the armies of Caidya and Jarāsandha, the king of Magadha, and take me away as the spoil of your prowess according to the *Rākṣasa* form of marriage.[1]

42. 'How should I marry you who live in the precincts of the harem without putting your relatives to death ?' If this be the ground for hesitation, I shall suggest you an expedient. On the day preceding the marriage there is (in your family a traditional) procession to our family deity. In that, the bride to be wed goes openly to her deity.*

43. Oh Lotus-eyed Kṛṣṇa ! In order to remove their personal ignorance, great-souled persons like god Śiva desire to have the dust on your lotus-like feet for covering their person as a bath. If I do not have this favour from you, I shall give up my life by starvation and other severe observance of vows so that at least after a hundred births I shall be favoured with your Grace.**

The Brāhmaṇa said :

44. Oh Lord of Yadus ! These are the secret words of the message that I have bought for you. Please consider what is worth doing in this (exigency of the situation), and prompt action should be taken immediately after this.

1. This form of marriage is recommended for *Kṣatriyas*.

**VJ. adds here* :

42.1 Coming over there at that time with the four divisions of army such as chariots, elephants, cavalry and infantry, and having given a sound drubbing to kings of Śālva, Magadha, Cedi and others, may the Lord of Lakṣmī take me along with my maids of honour from the temple to his own capital and have there a formal marriage celebration (lit. taking of hands).

***VJ's Text*

Śrī Śuka said :

43.1 Pondering over all the contents of the letter as well as the oral message of the princess, Kṛṣṇa, the slayer of demon Madhu, looked at the Brāhmaṇa (to convey his message).

CHAPTER FIFTYTHREE

Rukmiṇī's Marriage : Rukmiṇī carried away by Kṛṣṇa.

Śrī Śuka said :

1. Hearing the message of Rukmiṇī, the princess of Vidarbha, Kṛṣṇa, the delight of Yadus, clasped the hand of the Brāhmaṇa and laughing heartily, he spoke to him.

The Lord said :

1 A. *VR.'s Text adds* :

Just as the most beautiful Rukmiṇī has ever fixed her heart on Me.

2. So also I too have set My heart on her. Hence I do not get any sleep at night. I know that it is due to Rukmin's hatred against me that my marriage with her is obstructed by him.

3. As one would capture a flame after churning the fuel, I will vanquish those wretched kings in a battle and take away (as prize) that faultlessly beautiful princess who is so devoted to me.

Śrī Śuka narrated :

4. Having ascertained (from the Brāhmaṇa) the constellation under which Rukmiṇī's marriage was to take place (viz. day after tomorrow at night, Kṛṣṇa, the slayer of the demon Madhu ordered his charioteer Dāruka to get his chariot ready forthwith.

5. Dāruka instantly brought up the chariot drawn by (the famous horses) Śaibya, Sugrīva, Meghapuṣpa and Balāhaka and stood before him with folded palms.

6. Taking up the Brāhmaṇa with him, Kṛṣṇa, mounted the chariot and with those swift horses (yoked to the chariot) he travelled from Ānarta[1] to Vidarbha within one night.

7. Due to his weakness of being over-affectionate to his

1. Gujarat and a part of Malwa with Kuśasthalī or Dvārakā as the capital—GDAMI p. 7.

son, the king of Kuṇḍina caused all the auspicious rites connected with marriage-ceremony, with a view to give his daughter to Śiśupāla.

8-9. The city had all its streets, roads and quadrangles profusely sprinkled with water. It was decorated with banners of various kinds and buntings and arches. It was crowded by men and women who were wearing garlands of flowers, fragrant ointments and dressed themselves with immaculate clothes. They perfumed their mansions with the fumes of aloe wood (*Aguru*) smoke.

10. Having worshipped the manes, gods and Brāhmaṇas with due formalities and giving them a heavy feast he caused the auspicious verses recited according to formalities (to bless the bride).

11. The bride of beautiful teeth who had taken a bath and had gone through the formal auspicious preliminaries (such as wearing an auspicious thread woven with a piece of gold) was clothed in a pair of brand-new silken pieces and was beautified with excellent ornaments.

12. For the protection of the bride (from evil influences), the most prominent Brāhmaṇas pronounced *mantras* from the Sāmaveda, the Ṛg-Veda and the Yajur-Veda. The family-priest of the king who was expert in the Atharva-Veda offered oblations to fire for the appeasement of evil stars (and the prosperity of the house).

13. The king who was prominent among those who were well versed in Śāstric prescriptions gave as gift to Brāhmaṇas gold. silver, clothes and sesamum seeds mixed with raw sugar and cows as well.

14. In the same way king Damaghoṣa, the ruler of Cedis, caused all the religious formalities conducive to the good of his son, by Brāhmaṇas who were expert in *mantras.*

15. Accompanied with regiments of elephants exuding ichor, chariots decorated with garlands of gold and with armies of cavalry and infantry, he came to the city of Kuṇḍina.

16. The king of Vidarbhas went out to receive him and worshipped him with all the formalities with a gladsome heart. He lodged him in a separated mansion which was reserved for that purpose.

17. There came thousands of kings who were the allies of Śiśupāla such as Śālva, Jarāsandha, Dantavaktra, Vidūratha, Pauṇḍraka and others.

18-19 All those enemies of Kṛṣṇa and Balarāma determined to see to it that the bride was secured for Śiśupāla. They decided among themselves, "In case Kṛṣṇa accompanied by Balarāma and other Yadus comes and tries to carry away the bride, we shall jointly put up a fight with him." Having made up their minds thus, all the kings came with all their forces and vehicles there.

20-21. Hearing the report of military preparations of the hostile kings, the glorious Balarāma who came to know of Kṛṣṇa's having gone alone to carry away the bride, apprehended a fight, and taking with him a very big army consisting of elephants, horsemen, chariots and foot-soldiers quickly rushed to Kuṇḍina, as he was overcome with brotherly affection.

22. The beautiful daughter of king Bhīṣmaka who was yearning for the arrival of Lord Hari and not seeing (any chances) of the return of the deputed Brāhmaṇa, began to think as follows :

23. "Alas ! Only one night has remained for the celebration of the marriage. I am afraid I am unfortunate with little merit (to my credit). The Lotus-eyed Lord has not come as yet, nor do I know its reason. The Brāhmaṇa who was my emissary with that message, has also not returned as yet.

24. Is it that the noble-souled Lord who made preparations for coming here has seen something censurable in me and hence does not come for the acceptauce of my hand ?

25. To me who am unfortunate, neither god Brahmā nor god Śiva is favourable and the fair goddess Pārvatī the spouse of god Śiva, that chaste daughter of Himālayas too seems to be averse to me."

26. While the girl whose mind was thus fixed on Lord Kṛṣṇa (as if carried away by him) was pondering thus, her eyes were bedimmed with tears. But as she knew what was proper for that particular time (viz. not shedding tears), she closed her eyes.

27. In this way, of the bride who was eagerly waiting for the coming of Lord Kṛṣṇa, the left thigh, arm, and eye began to throb indicating thereby auspicious and happy news.

28. That very excellent Brāhmaṇa who was directed by Kṛṣṇa (after his arrival in the park near Kuṇḍina) saw the glorious princess in the harem.

29. Seeing his cheerful countenance and gait with confident steps (indicating a success of his mission) the virtuous girl who was expert in guessing the indications, asked him with a broad smile.

30. He informed her that Kṛṣṇa, the delight of Yadus had arrived and assured her of his definite promise of taking her away (*supra* verse 3) and that he was brought in his chariot by Kṛṣṇa Himself.

31. Knowing definitely that he (Kṛṣṇa) had arrived (at Kuṇḍinapura), the princess of Vidarbha was over-joyed at heart. (In her exultation) she could not decide what gift or boon be conferred on the Brāhmaṇa for his highly valuable service. And she simply bowed down to him[1] (and later paid him sumptuously).

32. Learning that both Balarāma and Kṛṣṇa had arrived out of curiosity to witness the celebration of his daughter's marriage, king Bhīṣmaka went forth to receive them with a flourish of trumpets, taking with him proper articles of worship and presents.

33. (Being highly intelligent, he guessed that Kṛṣṇa had arrived for marrying his daughter for which he was quite willing). So he worshipped Kṛṣṇa with due formalities suitable after the arrival of the bridegroom and he brought *Madhuparka* (a preparation of honey and curds—a customary offer to a bridegroom after arrival on the eve of the marriage ceremony), excellent (lit. well-washed) garments and other desirable presents (of various kinds) and worshipped them as enjoined in scriptures.

1. ŚR. : *Or* : Rukmiṇī was an incarnation of Lakṣmī, the goddess of wealth. All people who pay respects to her are bestowed with all kinds of wealth. She decided, "When I, Lakṣmī, pay respects to this Brāhmaṇa, he will automatically become more affluent than all others."

34. The high-minded monarch arranged for a spacious, luxurious accommodation for them.

3-4A. *VJ's Text* :

It was quite spacious and suitable for them but in a garden on the outskirts of Kuṇḍinapura, as the city was overcrowded with kings like Jarāsandha and others.[1]

34. . . . He also arranged for the hospitable reception of Kṛṣṇa's followers and army, in a proper manner.

35. In this way, he received all other kings who arrived there, each according to his prowess, age, military power and affluence, catering to them all that they desired.

36. Hearing that Kṛṣṇa had arrived, the citizens of Kuṇḍinapura came to see him and (as it were) drank (to their heart's content the honey of beauty) of his lotus-face with both their eyes as if they were the joined palms for drinking).

37. (They spoke amongst themselves) : 'Only Rukmiṇī and no other girl deserves to be his consort, and he alone of faultlessly beautiful personality is the suitable consort for Rukmiṇī, the daughter of Bhīṣma.

38. May the Lord, the creator of the three worlds, be pleased with whatever little merit we possess and as his grace (showered on us) may the imperishable Lord Kṛṣṇa accept the hand of the princess of Vidarbha."

39. While the citizens who were attached to Rukmiṇī by bonds of affection, were speaking thus with one another, the bride, guarded by soldiers, started from the harem to the shrine of Ambikā (goddess Pārvatī).

40. Deeply contemplating on the lotus-feet of Lord Kṛṣṇa, she went on foot to see and worship the foliage-like tender feet of goddess Bhavānī.

40-A *VJ's. Text adds* :

Kṛṣṇa, the delight of Yādavas went there in the company of some selected followers.

41. The bride observed silence; she was accompanied by her mothers and was surrounded by her friends (maids of

1. Probably to avoid an outbreak of conflict if the two inimical camps are accommodated in the town.

honour). She was protected by the valiant royal guards clad in coats of mail and alert with their weapons uplifted.

41-A. *VJ's Text* :

And she was surrounded by aged chamberlains (eunuchs) with canes indicating their office, *Mṛdaṅgas*, conchs, drums, trumpets and kettle-drums were sounded (during the procession.)

42. She was accompanied by thousands of prominent courtesans carrying with them a variety of offerings and articles of worship and by Brāhmaṇa women (whose husbands were alive) tastefully adorned with garlands of flowers, perfumes (or sandal paste) excellent garments and ornaments.

43. Songsters singing songs and musicians playing on their instruments as well as bards and panegyrists like *Sūta*, *Māgadha* and *Bandins* surrounded the bride glorifying her in songs.

44. Arriving at the shrine of the goddess[1], she washed her lotus-like hands and feet. Purifying herself with sipping the water thrice as *ācamana*, she entered with a serene mind in the inner apartment—into the presence of the goddess Pārvatī.

45. Aged Brāhmaṇa ladies who were well-versed in the (pre-marital) rituals, guided the bride in the worship and paying respects to the goddess Pārvatī, the Consort of Śiva, along with god Śiva as well.

46. (Rukmiṇī prayed :) I constantly pay my respects to you Oh auspicious[2] Mother goddess, along with your children (Gaṇeśa and Kārttikeya). May Lord Kṛṣṇa become my consort. May this prayer of mine be granted.

47. She worshipped the goddess Pārvatī in several ways by sprinkling her with water, applying sandal-paste and unbroken rice-grains, varieties of incense, with (a rich variety of) clothes, garlands of flowers, ornaments, various kinds of articles of worship and offerings (variety of edibles) and with rows of lights (waving them round her).

1. VR.'s *v.l.*—she entered the shrine of the goddess.

2. *Śivā*—implies respects to Lord Śiva with whom she (the goddess) shares the name and person.

48. With similar articles she worshipped Brāhmaṇa women *Suvāsinis*—(whose husbands are alive) in the same way, offering them salt, *apūpa* (fried cakes), betel leaves, *maṅgalasūtra* (the sacred thread to be worn round the neck by *Suvāsinis*), fruits (of various kinds) and (pieces of) sugarcane.

49. The Brāhmaṇa ladies gave her some part (of what she offered as worship to the goddess Ambikā) and gave their blessings (in addition) along with them. Rukmiṇī bowed down to them and and to the queen-mother and accepted the things offered to her (as *prasāda*).

50. Completing (the observance of) the vow of silence she came out of the temple of Ambikā[1], clasping the hand of her servant (nurse) with her own hand resplendent with rings of precious stones.

51-53. The glorious warriors who assembled there found themselves tormented with the passion of love and became perplexed at seeing her, who like the deluding potency (Māyā) of the Lord, was enchanting to the warriors, with her beautiful slender waist, and countenance beautified with the ear-rings; she was sixteen years of age[2], wore a girdle of precious stones around her waist: had protruding breasts (showing attainment of womanhood); her eyes were unsteady, appearing as if afraid of her over-hanging locks of hair. Beaming with bright smile, her white jasmine-bud like teeth appeared reddish as they were tinged with the splendour of her red lips-red like the *Bimba* fruit. Her gait was like that of a royal swan and her feet were radiant with the splendour of jingling anklets.

54. Hypnotized on seeing Rukmiṇī who under the pretex of the religious pilgrimage (to the shrine of the goddess), had come to offer her beauty to Lord Hari, the kings whose

1. *VJ.'s Text adds*

50.1 Nearby was the shrine of Indra and (his consort) Śacī who were the family deities of the royal house of Vidarbha.

50.2 Rukmiṇī entered (the inner part of the shrine) in the presence of Śacī, the beloved of the lord of gods. She bowed to the feet of Śacī whose lotus-feet were not worshipped by her for a pretty long time. Then she issued out of that temple with many umbrellas being held over her and fanned by waving of a number of *chowries*.

2. *Śyāmā*—who had not attained puberty – ŚR., VR.

hearts were captivated by her sublime smile and bashful looks, dropped down their weapons (without being aware of it), and fell senseless on the ground even though they were mounted on elephants, chariots and horses.

55. At that time, she was eagerly awaiting the arrival of the Lord and hence was slowly moving (her feet resembling) a pair of lotus-buds. Removing aside her hair flowing over her eyes with her fingers, she cast bashful side-glances to have an over-view of the kings that assembled there. And Lo! she noticed him there.

56. Even while the enemies were looking on, Kṛṣṇa snatched away the princess who was desirous of ascending his chariot; he seated her in his chariot with the ensign of Garuḍa (emblem of Garuda on the flag) setting at nought the whole lot of Kṣattriyas assembled there. Kṛṣṇa, the Consort of Lakṣmī, then slowly (and fearlessly) departed from the place (to Dvārakā) with his forces headed by Balarāma, like a lion seizing his own share of prey from the midst of a pack of jackals.

57*. Other proud kings under the leadership of Jarāsandha did not tolerate this discomfiture and loss of reputation (by Kṛṣṇa's carrying away Rukmiṇī in the teeth of their opposition). They exclaimed: "Fie upon us who, although armed with bows, have been deprived of our reputation and glory by cowherds just as the lions are deprived of their kingly position by the deer."

CHAPTER FIFTY-FOUR

Celebration of Rukmiṇī's Marriage

Śrī Śuka said:

1. With these self-condemning words, all the highly indignant kings put on their coats of mail and mounting their own vehicles and surrounded by their respective armies hotly pursued Kṛṣṇa, equipped with bows in their hands.

* This is the Ist verse of the next chapter in VJ.

2. Beholding the on-rushing kings in pursuit, the generals of the Yādava army stood their ground to confront them, twanging their bows, Oh king.

3. Veterans of war (like Jarāsandha) who were riding on horse-back, the shoulders of elephants and seats in the chariots discharged volleys of arrows like innumerable clouds pouring showers of water on mountains.

4. Finding her consort's force covered with showers of arrows, the slender-waisted bride with her eyes agitated with fear looked at her Lord's face bashfully.

5. Laughing out that fear, the Lord assured her: "Don't be afraid, Oh fair-eyed maiden ! The inimical forces will be liquidated in no time by your soldiers''.

6. Not tolerating that prowess of the enemies, (the leaders of the Yādava army like) Gada, Balarāma and others shot down the horses, elephants and chariots (of the enemy) with their steel-arrows (*nārāca*).

7. And rolled down on the ground crores of heads of the occupants of chariots, horsemen and elephant-riders—all ornamented with ear-rings, crowns and head-gears.

8. And fell down on the grounds, their hands wielding swords, maces (*gadās*) and bows, and also fore-arms, thighs, feet, as well as the heads of horses, mules, elephants, camels, donkeys and (infantry-) men.

9. As their armies were thus being drubbed and slain by Vṛṣṇis ambitious of victory, the kings led by Jarāsandha turned back and fled away (from the battle field).

10. They all approached Śiśupāla who was gloomy, dispirited and with parched-up mouth, grieving as if his legally married wife was abducted.

The kings consoled him:

11. "Oh tiger among men ! Give up this despondency. In the case of embodied beings, pleasure or pain is never observed to be his permanent lot.

12. Just as a wooden doll dances according to the will of the showman (controlling it), the same way, due to his being controlled by God, the embodied being endeavours to pass through pleasure or pain.

13. Though backed by an army of twenty-three *akṣauhiṇis*, (every time) I suffered defeat at the hands of Kṛṣṇa in seventeen expeditions. But ultimately I was victorious in one (the last) battle.

14. I, however, do not feel aggrieved or elated by anything (defeat or victory) as I know that the world is controlled by time in combination with Providence.

15. Leaders of the army-commanders as we are, on this occasion also we were defeated by the small contingent of Yādavas under the protection of Kṛṣṇa.

16. The enemies became victorious this time as Time was favourable to them. We too shall vanquish them when the Time will be propitious to us."

Śrī Śuka said:

17. Thus consoled with enlightenment by his friends, Śiśupāla returned to his capital along with his followers, while the other allied kings who survived that battle went back to their respective cities.

18. The mighty prince Rukmī who hated Kṛṣṇa, could not tolerate the idea of his sister being married to Kṛṣṇa according to the *rākṣasa* from of marriage and with an army of one *akṣauhiṇi*, he hotly pursued Kṛṣṇa.

19. The mighty-armed, impetuous, determined Rukmī, clad in armour and armed with a bow, in his high indignation, took the vow in the hearing of all princes (before they departed).

20. "Upon my word I hereby solemnly declare that I shall not enter Kuṇḍinapura unless (and until) I bring back Rukmiṇī after killing Kṛṣṇa in the battle."

21. Announcing this, he mounted his chariot and commanded his charioteer: "Quickly drive the horses to the spot where Kṛṣṇa is, so that I shall have an encounter with him.

22. Today with my sharp arrows I shall vanquish the pride of valour of that cowherd (or: the protector of the Vedas), the most wicked-minded fellow (or: one who is gracious unto the wicked as well who has abducted per force my sister".

23. Not knowing the extent of (the infinite) power of the Lord, Rukmī, the wicked braggart pursued alone in a chariot and shouted out the words, 'Stop', 'stop' to Kṛṣṇa who (also) was driving alone in his chariot.

23A. He overtook Kṛṣṇa while he was crossing the divine river Narmadā. Being fully prepared for a fight, he repeatedly shouted out at him to stop.

24. With all the force at his command, he bent the bow (by drawing the bowstring) and hit Kṛṣṇa with three arrows and roared: "Wait minute here (Oh thief! My enemy), the disgrace to Yadu's family[1].

25. Where are you going clandestinely kidnapping my sister like a crow[2] stealthily picking up sacrificial oblation? I shall today subdue your pride, you dullard[3] who are a cheat and adopt crooked stratagems in fighting.

26. Surrender my younger sister (lit. a young girl) before you are not lying (in the dust) struck down by my arrows."[4] Smilingly Kṛṣṇa cut down Rukmī's bow and wounded him with six arrows.

27. He struck his four horses with eight shafts, the charioteer with two and his flag with three. Taking up another bow, Rukmī pierced Kṛṣṇa with five arrows.

28. Struck by the stream of arrows, the imperishable Lord Kṛṣṇa sundered Rukmī's bow. He again equipped himself with (still) another bow which too the Lord snapped.

29. Kṛṣṇa cut into splinters whatever weapon—whether a club studded with iron, spear, pike, sword and shield, lance and iron club—Rukmī took up (one after another).

30. Jumping down from his chariot with a sword in hand, the indignant Rukmī, determined to finish with Kṛṣṇa, rushed at him like unto a moth dashing at a fire.

1. As usual ŚR treats this as a compliment explaining the pun in *yadūnāṁ kulapāṁsana* as *yadūnāṁ kulapa, aṁsana*—"you Protector of Yadu's race, expert in destroying enemies".

2. ŚR takes *muṣitvā dhvāṅkṣa* as *adhvāṅkṣa* and interpretes "Like god Indra taking away his legitimate sacrificial oblations"

3. *manda*—stable, immovable—ŚR.

4. 26.A—*VJ.'s Text adds* :

Bending the bow by drawing the bow-string powerfully, he hit Kṛṣṇa with three arrows.

31. As he was advancing, Kṛṣṇa cut down his sword and shield into sesamum-like particles with his arrows and taking up his sharp sword, he rushed forth bent on killing Rukmī.

32. Beholding his attempt to kill her brother, the virtuous Rukmiṇī was overwhelmed with fear. Falling at the feet of her consort, she piteously[1] entreated:

(*VJ.'s Text*: *Rukmiṇī prayed*)

33. "Oh lord of Yoga of incomprehensible nature ! Oh God of gods ! The Protector of the world ! Oh embodiment of auspiciousness ! It does not behove you to kill my brother, Oh mighty-armed Lord.

Śrī Śuka said:

VJ's Text:

33-A. Praying him thus in frightened tones, the poor Rukmiṇī earnestly desiring to save her brother, clasped the feet of Kṛṣṇa, the Protector of the world.

34. The merciful Lord gave up his attempt (on Rukmī's life) as his feet were clasped by Rukmiṇī whose whole person was trembling with fear, whose mouth was parched up with grief, whose throat was choked (with emotions) and whose gold necklace was fallen, out of nervous anxiety.

35. Binding that evil-doer with a piece of cloth, he disfigured him by shaving his head (with the blade of his sword) keeping (intermittently) some part of the mustaches and hairlocks on the head. In the meanwhile, prominent heroes in the Yādava forces crushed and routed the extraordinary hostile forces, like elephants trampling down stalks of lotuses.

36. When they approached to the presence of Kṛṣṇa, they beheld Rukmī reduced to that (humiliating) plight, as good as dead (through shame). The mighty Lord Balarāma was moved with pity and releasing him, he protested to Kṛṣṇa.

(*VJ's Text*: *Balarāma reproved*:)

37. "This blame-worthy act, abhorrent to us (our race), has been perpetrated by you, Oh Kṛṣṇa, in shaving the mous-

1. v.l. *paṇḍitā*—omniscient—(VT)

taches and the locks of hair of a relative. Disfiguring a relative this way amounts to killing him.

38. (Addressing Rukmiṇī): In your grief and brooding over this deformity of your brother, please do not scorn us (as evil-minded people) Oh good lady. No other person is the giver of (i.e. responsible for) the pleaure or pain that comes to one's lot; for a person reaps the fruits of his own actions.

39. Even if a relative has committed an offence deserving death in retribution, he should not be killed by a relative. He should be discharged forthwith. What is the propriety of slaying a person again, when he stands killed by his own sinful acts.

40. God Brahmā has ordained this as the *dharma* (the code of conduct) for Kṣattriyas that even a brother should kill a brother (in the battle). What could be more terrible than this ? (Hence it is the *kṣattriya dharma* that is at fault and not we who abide by it, Oh lady).

41. (Turning to Kṛṣṇa) It is only the proud, blinded with the intoxicating influence of prosperity that offend relatives for the sake of kingdom, land, wealth woman, honour, authority or for any such consideration.

42. (Addressing Rukmiṇī) : It is an improper lookout on your part that you, like an ignorant person, think auspiciously and well of your brother who always bears ill-will towards all beings and ill of those who are your well-wishers[1].

43. "That some persons are friends, some enemies and some indifferent is the self-delusion created by Lord's *Māyā* (deluding potency) among persons who regard the body and the soul as identical.

44. For the Supreme Soul is one only in all corporeal beings. But he is mistaken as many by the ignorant, just as the luminary (the sun, though one, is regarded as many when it is reflected in different vessels containing water) or the sky (though one, is regarded as different when circumscribed in a

1. *ŚR* adds : It is certainly your improper outlook that you regard the auspicious or proper punishment meted out to your brother (by shaving him) as evil, even though your relative is ill-disposed to all beings.

pitcher (*ghaṭākāśa*) or within a room (*maṭhākāśa*) is looked upon as many (when in reality it is one).

45. This body constituted as it is of five material elements (like the earth, water, fire and others), vital elements (like sense-organs and their presiding deities) and the *guṇas*[1] and has a beginning and an end, is projected on the Soul (*ātman*) through ignorance (*avidyā*) which makes the embodied soul wander in the cycle of *saṁsāra*[2].

46. The soul has no union with or disunion from anything else (viz. the body), as nothing other than the soul exists at all, Oh good lady. The soul is the cause of such appearance, just as the sun is the cause of the perception of the sun by means of the eye and colour (but the sun bears no union or disunion with them)[3].

47. Changes such as birth (youth, death) and others pertain to the body and never to the soul, just as the waxing and the waning of the moon are attributable to the digits of the moon (which remains constant all the while). The death of the body is like the *amāvasyā* (*kuhū*) when the light of the moon disappears but the moon remains unaffected (in the same way the soul continues to exist despite the disappearance of the body).

48. Just as a sleeping man, in a dream, perceives himself, the sense objects of enjoyment and experiences the fruit (enjoyment) thereof, even though nothing of these exists in reality, similarly an ignorant person undergoes (the experience of this unreal) *saṁsāra*.

1. ŚR: and is thus conditioned by the triad—*ādhibhautika*, *ādhyātmika* and *ādhidaivika*.

2. ŚR. : The body is not pure due to conditioning circumstances.

3. (i) It is the power of illumination of the sun which shines all the while and has no contact with the eye and as such has neither union or disunion with the eye. Similarly, the Soul being of the nature of consciousness and existing in the past, present and future has no possibility of union or disunion with the body—VT.

(ii) The Supreme Soul is not bound or separated from the body coming into existence of which is dependent on Him, just as the Sun is unconnected with the eye or the colour, both of which depend on the sun for their function—VR.

49. Therefore, by means of the knowledge of reality eliminate completely your sorrow which is born of ignorance and which causes you pining and delusion. And be comforted and serene at heart, Oh lady, with bright smiles."

Śrī Śuka said :

50. When the beautifully slim lady was thus enlightened by the glorious Lord Balarāma, she overcame her mental depression and attained equipoise of her mind through reason.

51. Allowed to get away with life only, shorn of his power (or army) as well as of glory, brooding over his disfigurement and with his plans and ambitions frustrated, Rukmī built a big town called Bhojakaṭa[1] for his residence.

52. He resided there through indignation, as he formerly announced. "I shall not re-enter Kuṇḍina unless and until I have killed the wicked-minded Kṛṣṇa and brought back my younger sister".

53. Having vanquished all the monarchs in his way, the Lord brought Rukmiṇī, the daughter of Bhīṣmaka to his city, Dvārakā and married her as per *Śāstric* injunction, Oh Scion of the Kuru race.

54. There was a great festivity in every house in Dvārakā, the capital of Yadus, of the residents thereof, who were exclusively devoted to Lord Kṛṣṇa, the protector of Yadus, Oh king:

55. Men and women thereof were highly delighted. Adorned with ear-rings of highly polished jewels, they presented valuable gifts to the newly-wedded couple wearing excellent bridal dress.

56. The city of Vṛṣṇis (Dvārakā) shone splendidly with flags raised in honour of Indra, with a wonderful variety of garlands, cloths and ornamental arches decorated with jewels, provided with auspicious arrangement at every door of pitchers

1. *Bhojakaṭa* or *Bhojapur* is identified with Bhojapura, six miles to the south-east of Vidiśā. GDAMI 33. It was built to the north of the Narmadā as per *purāṇas* which thus support this identification. GDAMI 33 and 224.

full of water, insense of the *aguru* (agall ochum)burning and lamps.

57. Its streets were besprinkled with the exuded ichor (temporal fluid) of elephants of the great kings invited for the marriage, and entrances beautified with tall plantain trees and areca-nut trees.

58. Moving hastily here and there in confusion in that marriage, clansmen of Kurus, Sṛñjayas, Kaikeyas, Vidarbhas, Yadus and Kuntīs were happy to meet each other.

59. Hearing the episode of Kṛṣṇa's carrying away Rukmiṇī sung by the people everywhere, kings and princesses who attended the marriage became extremely wonder-struck.

60. Great was the exultation among the citizens of Dvārakā, Oh king, to see Kṛṣṇa, the Lord of goddess Śrī now married to Rukmiṇī who was no other than goddess Lakṣmī herself.

CHAPTER FIFTY FIVE

The Story of Pradyumna's Birth[1]

Śrī Śuka narrated :

1. As to Kāma[2], the god of Love, who was a portion of (the future) Lord Vāsudeva, was formerly burnt down through the wrath of god Śiva. Hence he (Kāma) resorted to him again for the restoration of his corporeal form.

* Ekanātha has written an excellent work in ovi metre on Rukmiṇī's marriage. Out of respect for Ekanātha, KD has incorporated it in his com. on this skandha (Harivaradā)

1. As SR and VR point out this chapter contains a chronological anamoly as it describes slaying of the demon Śambara by Pradyumna and his return to Dvārakā alongwith his wife Māyāvatī—incidents which took place long after Kṛṣṇa's marriages with Jāmbavatī, Satyabhāmā and others which are described in the subsequent chapters.

2. This refers to the incident when at the behest of god Indra, Kāma, disturbed god Śiva's spiritual concentration, with a view to tempt him to marry Umā and get rid of the menace of the demon Tāraka by procreating a son (the future Skanda). But contrary to expectations, Siva flared

2. That very god of Love was born of Rukmiṇī, the princess of Vidarbha, and (lit. from the semen of) Kṛṣṇa. He became celebrated as Pradyumna and was in no way inferior to his father (Kṛṣṇa) in any respects.

3. Knowing that the babe was his future enemy (slayer), the demon Śambara, the inveterate enemy of Kāma, who could assume any form at will, clandestinely kidnapped it even when it had not completed ten days (on the sixth-day)[1] and throwing it into the sea, he went home.

4. A huge powerful fish swallowed that babe. But along with others, that fish was caught into a big net by fishermen.

5. The fishermen brought it as a present to Śambara. The cooks carried it to the kitchen and cut that wonderful fish with a knife.

6. Finding a babe in its abdomen, they offered it into the charge of Māyāvatī[2]. As her mind was full of misgivings (about the child), the divine sage Nārada narrated to her all the details how it was born and how it was found in the bowels of that fish.

7. It is reported that she was Rati, the glorious wife of the god Kāma, waiting for the reincarnation of her consort whose body had been reduced to ashes.

up with anger at this disturbance and opened his Third eye—the fire out of which reduced Kāma to ashes (*Vāl. Ram.Bāla* 23.10-13). VT. and VR. argue that Pradyumna, the Third emanation (*Vyūha*) of the *Pāñcarātra* school is indestructible. VT. finds a *via media* by assuming two sets of deities—the ordinary—*Prākṛta* set to which category Kāma, the servant of Indra who tried to disturb Siva and got consumed by fire, belonged. The other set, viz. the four manifestations (*Vyūhas*) of Nārāyaṇa of which Pradyumna forms the third, is not implied here. The word—*tu* in the text *Kāmas tu* signified this distinction between the two categories, and emphasizes that it was the *Prākṛta kāma*, the *jīva* of whom sought birth from Kṛṣṇa.

1. *ṣaṣṭhe 'hni jātamātraṁ tu Pradyumnaṁ sūtikāgṛhāt/*
mamaiṣa hanteti mune hṛtavān kāla-Śambaraḥ //

VP. 5.27.3.

2. As explained below (VT) and in VP. 5.27.27ff., she was Rati, the wife of Kāma who was reduced to ashes by Śiva. Under the pseudonym Māyāvatī, she worked as the kitchen-in-charge of Śambara waiting for her re-union with her husband in his next birth.

8. She was entrusted with the charge of supervision (of the cooking of pulses and rice) in Śambara's kitchen. Having come to know that the child was her spouse Kāmadeva himself, she developed affection to that child[1].

9. Not long afterwards[2] Pradyumna, the son of Kṛṣṇa, attained youth and caused confusion in the heart of women who had a look of him.

10. Considering him as her husband, Rati was ogling at him with bashful smiles and raised evebrows aud approached with amorous purpose Pradyumna who with eyes longish like lotus-petals and knee-long arms was the most beautiful man in the world.

11. The respectable son of Kṛṣṇa (strongly) protested: "Oh mother ! You seem to have a perverted mind. Abandoning the motherly relation, you behave like a lustful woman."

Rati replied :

12. "Your honour is the son of Lord Kṛṣṇa taken away by the demon Śambara from (the lying-in-chamber in) your house. I am Rati, your (lawfully) married wife and you are (none else but) Kāma, the god of Love, my Lord.

13. This demon Śambara cast you into the sea when you were not even ten days old. A fish swallowed you up. It is from the bowels of the fish that your honour came out here, my lord.

14. This enemy of yours is irresistible and invincible as he is expert in hundred types of black magic (*māyā*). You, however, slay him by means of *māyā* powers like *mohana* (stupefaction) and others.

15. Being deprived of her child, your mother is wailing like a female osprey at the loss of her young one. Being overwhelmed with motherly affection for a child, she is anxious and miserable like a cow bereaved of her calf."

1. v.l.—noted in VT : 'Due to her Māyā power, even Śambara could not know the child'.

2. According to HV, Pradyumna's growth was wonderfully accelerated with specific medicines, etc.

16. Exhorting him thus, Rati, the past-master in deluding magical processes (*māyāvatī*), imparted to the noble-souled Pradyumna the knowledge of 'Supreme Illusion' (*Mahāmāyā*), capable of destroying all sorts of spells and magical processes and illusions.

17. Approaching Śambara, he challenged him for a fight, provoking a quarrel by insulting him with unbearable taunts.

18. Reproached with sharp words of abuse, Śambara, like a serpent trodden under foot, rushed out with a mace in hand and eyes reddened with indignation.

19. Vehemently whirling his mace, he hurled it at the noble-souled Pradyumna and gave out a roar, terrible like the stroke of a thunderbolt.

20. The glorious lord Pradyumna struck back the oncoming mace with his own and flying in rage, he dashed his own mace at the enemy, Oh king.

21. Resorting to the illusory method of warfare of Daityas as taught by Maya, the Asura, taking up a position in the sky, discharged on Pradyumna, the son of Kṛṣṇa, a shower of missiles.

22. Being troubled with the down-pour of missiles Pradyumna, the powerful hero, the son of Rukmiṇī, employed his Great Lore consisting of pure *sattva* which was capable of counteracting and annihilating all *Māyās* (illusive processes, spells, etc.)

23. Thereupon, the *daitya* (Śambara) used hundreds of magical spells (*māyās*) used by Guhyakas, Gandharvas, Piśācas (goblins), Nāgas and Rākṣasas but the son of Kṛṣṇa simply blew them out (i.e. easily destroyed them).

24. Raising his sharp-edged sword, he forcibly severed from Śambara's trunk his head with its copper-coloured beard (and moustaches) and adorned with a crown and earrings.

25. Showered over with heaps of flowers by the celestials who were eulogising him, Pradyumna was taken to his (home-) city (Dvārakā) through the sky by his spouse who was capable of coursing through the sky.

26. Like unto a cloud accompanied with lightening, he, with his consort, alighted from the sky into (Kṛṣṇa's) excellent harem crowded with hundreds of beautiful women, Oh king.

27-28. Beholding him, of a complexion dark-blue like a cloud, wearing a yellow silken garment, of extra-ordinarily long arms, reddish eyes, with an enchanting smile and charming countenance, with his lotus-face extremely graced with dark-blue curly locks of hair, the ladies thought him to be Kṛṣṇa himself and out of bashfulness concealed themselves immediately wherever they could.

29. Coming to a conclusion from the distinguishing characteristics between the two (such as absence of *Śrivatsa* that he was not Śrī Kṛṣṇa, the ladies approached him with great delight and wonderment as he was accompanied by a jewel-like beautiful damsel.

30. Then among them Rukmiṇī, the sweet-tongued princess of Vidarbha, of bluish (corners of) eyes, recollected her lost son and milk of maternal affection oozed out of her breasts.

31. "Who can this be a jewel among men? Whose son is this lotus-eyed one? What mother has borne him in her womb? Who is this damsel obtained by him?

32. If my son who being stolen away from the maternity chamber and thus lost, be alive somewhere, he would be his compeer in age, similarity of features, etc.

33. How could this boy inherit so much resemblance to the Lord wielding the Śārṅga bow in form (features), limbs, gait, tone of voice, smiles and way of looking.

34. Or, he must really be the same child whom I bore in my womb. I have begun to feel more affection for him and my left arm is throbbing."[1]

35. While Rukmiṇī, the princess of Vidarbha, was thus reflecting (to ascertain whether Pradyumna could be her son), Kṛṣṇa, of glorious renown, came there along with Devakī and Vasudeva.

1. This is regarded as an auspicious omen in regard to women, foreboding good tidings.

36. Though Kṛṣṇa knew the actual state of affairs, the Lord kept mum. It was Nārada who told all the story from his (Pradyumna's) kidnapping by Śambara.

37. Listening to that extremely miraculous account (of Pradyumna's life till then), the ladies of Kṛṣṇa's harem joyfully congratulated him upon his return after many years, like one returning to life from the realm of death.

38. Devakī and Vasudeva, Kṛṣṇa, Balarāma, Rukmiṇī and other women of the harem embraced the young couple and were transported with joy.

39. Hearing that Pradyumna who was missing so long has arrived, the citizens of Dvārakā exclaimed; How wonderful! How happy it is that the boy who (being missing) was as good as dead, has returned to life."

40. It is not wonderful that owing to his close resemblance to his father Kṛṣṇa, many times Pradyumna's (step-) mothers mistook him for Kṛṣṇa and resorted to seclusion (the passion of love was awakened in them). The very thought of the god of Love provokes passion. What of other women when Pradyumna, the god of love, who was the reflection of exact semblance of the Lord, the abode of goddess Lakṣmī, presented himself within the range of their sight?

CHAPTER FIFTY SIX

The story of Syamantaka jewel

(Kṛṣṇa's marriage with Jāmbavatī and Satyabhāmā)

Śrī Śuka said :

1. Satrājita[1] who had committed an offence against Kṛṣṇa, gave, of his own accord and making some special effort for it, his own daughter in marriage to Kṛṣṇa offering therewith the *Syamantaka* jewel (as an atonement for the offence).

1. The word is spelt both ways : *Satrājita* and *Satrājit*. The translation retains the spelling adopted in the original Sk. text.

King Parikṣit enquired :

2. What offence did Satrājita commit against Kṛṣṇa, Oh Brāhmaṇa sage ? Whence did he get the Syamantaka gem? Why did he offer his daughter in marriage to Hari?

Śrī Śuka narrated :

3. The Sun-god was an intimate friend of his own devotee Satrājita. The Sun-god was so much affectionate to and pleased with Satrājita that he presented to him the Syamantaka gem.

4. Wearing that gem about his neck and effulgent like the Sun-god, he could hardly be visible and recognized due to its dazzling lustre, Oh king.

5. Beholding him even from a distance, people felt blinded with his brilliant splendour and believing him to be the Sun-god, reported it to the Lord who was playing at dice.

6. "Salutations to You, Oh Nārāyaṇa, the Wielder of the conch, discus and mace ! Oh Lotus-eyed Dāmodara ! Oh Govinda, the Delight of Yadus.

7. Blinding the eyes of men with his lustre, here comes the Sun-god of scorching rays, with a desire to pay visit to you, Oh Protector of the world.

8. Prominent gods really try to seek the way (to find you) in all the three worlds. Having come to know today that you live undisclosed among the Yadus, the birthless Sun-god has come to see you, Oh Lord."

Śrī Śuka said :

9. Hearing the report of the ignorant people, the Lotus-eyed Kṛṣṇa laughed loudly and remarked : He is not the Sun-god but Satrājit dazzling with the jewel (*Syamantaka*).

10. Satrājit entered his affluent, splendid mansion beautified with auspicious objects (for the celebration of his successful return with the gem) and got the jewel properly installed by Brāhmaṇas in the shrine of his family deities.

11. Oh King ! Every day, the gem yielded eight *bhāras*[1] of gold. Where the gem is installed and worshipped, there is no danger from famines, epidemics, calamities, serpents, diseases, inauspicious things or from rogues.

12. He was solicited by Kṛṣṇa on one occasion for the gem, for presenting to Ugrasena, the king of Yādavas. But being greedy of wealth, he did not comply regardless of the consequences of such refusal (to the Lord's request).

13. One day, Prasena (the brother of Satrājit) wore that jewel of extra-ordinary lustre about his neck and mounting his horse, he went to the forest for hunting.

14. Having killed Prasena along with his horse, a lion snatched the gem from him (out of curiosity for the dazzling thing) and was entering his mountain cave when he was killed by Jāmbavat who desired to possess the gem.

15. In his den, he used it as a toy for his young son. Not finding his brother, Satrājit was greatly tormented.

16. (He expressed his suspicion :) "My brother is most probably murdered by Kṛṣṇa as he went out to the forest with the Syamantaka jewel round his neck". Hearing that, people passed on the rumour in whispers from ear to ear.

17. Hearing that rumour, the Lord accompanied by some citizens followed the track of Prasena (Prasena's horse) in order to wipe out the calumny imputed to him.

18. People saw that Prasena and his horse were killed by a lion in the forest and that the lion was killed by a bear on the side of the mountain.

19. Keeping outside the citizens (with instructions to wait), the Lord alone entered the den of the king of bears, though it was terrible and full of blinding darkness.

20. Seeing there that the excellent gem was used as a toy of a male child he determined to take it away and stayed there near the child.[2]

21. Seeing that extra-ordinary person (not seen before) the nurse of the child screamed out as in fear. Hearing that,

1. ŚR. quotes verses which show that one *bhāra* is equivalent to 8000 *Tolās* (1 *Tolā*=11.66 grams).

2. VB quotes a verse from *Purāṇas* as the nurses lullaby to the child, "The lion killed Prasena, the lion was killed by Jāmbavat. Oh tender child, don't cry. This Syamantaka is for you."

the enraged Jāmbavān who was the foremost among the mighty rushed at him, in rage.

22. Verily, in his indignation, he failed to understand Kṛṣṇa's greatness, and regarding him as an ordinary person he fought with him, his own Master (Rāma in previous incarnation), the Supreme Lord.

23. Like two hawks fighting for a piece of meat, the combat between them was tumultuous as they tried to overthrow each other by weapons, rocks, trees and arms.

24. There was a continuous combat for twenty-eight days (and nights as well) hitting each other with fists, harsh like the strokes of thunderbolt.

25. Jāmbavān was extremely wonderstruck as his joints and limbs were crushed and dislocated by the blows of Kṛṣṇa's fists and as his strength decreased and the body was full of perspiration.. He addressed to him :

26. "(Now) I know You to be Lord Viṣṇu, the Ancientmost Person, the Creator of the Universe and the Controller thereof Who constitute the energy, the power of endurance (mental strength) and physical power of all beings.

27. You are really the Creator of the progenitors of the Universe ; You are the Reality that underlies it (as the material cause of the created substances). You are the Time Spirit which controls and destroys the world. You are the Supreme Soul of all.

28. You are verily my Lord Rāma, at whose side-glances which were slightly enkindled with wrath, the whole ocean full of alligators, whales and other aquatic animals got agitated and was made to give way to you; Who built a bridge across the sea as if it was a memorial of your glory; who burnt down the city of Laṅkā and by whose arrows, the heads of demons rolled on the ground."

29-30. To his devotee, the king of bears who had thus realized the knowledge of his being the Supreme Spirit, Kṛṣṇa, that Imperishable glorious Lord, the lotus-eyed son of Devakī, touched (all over his body, out of compassion) with his bliss-bestowing hand (relieving all his fatigue, wounds and pain in the combat) and out of Supreme Mercy and Grace, spoke to him in a voice deep with affection.

31. "We (I and citizens of Dvārakā) arrived here at the entrance of your cave for the sake of the Syamantaka gem. (Though some of the false imputation of calumny is hereby removed), I have entered the den to wipe out completely the false accusation (of Prasena's murder) against me, by means of (i.e. by producing) this gem."

32. It is traditionally reported that thus addressed, Jāmbavān gladly offered his daughter Jāmbavatī in marriage to Kṛṣṇa, along with the Syamantaka gem, by way of worshipping him.

32A. *VR's Text adds* :

Lord Kṛṣṇa who is affectionate to his devotees, was worshipped (by Jāmbavān) with many other excellent precious stones. And the Lord instantly bestowed on him (or decided to confer upon him) the Supreme Emancipation from which there is no return to *saṁsāra*.

33. After Waiting (at the entrance of the cave) for twelve days and finding that Kṛṣṇa entered the cave but had not returned out of it, the people who accompanied him there, returned to their own city (Dvārakā) in grief.

34. When they heard the report that Kṛṣṇa had not issued out of the cave (for the last twelve days), Devakī (Kṛṣṇa's mother), queen Rukmiṇī, Vasudeva (Kṛṣṇa's father), his friends and kinsmen deeply grieved (his non-return).

35. Citizens of Dvārakā cursed Satrājit (for the disappearance of Kṛṣṇa). Deeply grieving, they devotedly worshipped the goddess Durgā (well-known by the name, Candrabhāgā),[1] the Supreme Illusive potency of the Lord, for the safe return of Śrī Kṛṣṇa.

36. (Possibly) due to the blessing of the goddess they received through their worship and prayers of the deity, Lord Hari manifested Himself along with his spouse (Jāmbavatī) and with his purpose (recovery of the Syamantaka gem) completely achieved, thus thrilling them with joy.

1. ŚR. remarks : *Candrabhāgāṁ nāma Durgām* suggests that his Text most probably read *Candrabhāgā* for *Mahāmāyā* and was *Upatasthus Candrabhāgāṁ Durgām*" etc. instead of the current one.

37. All of them were transported with ecstatic joy to find Kṛṣṇa as if returned to life after death and that too with a spouse and the Syamantaka gem about his neck.

38. Summoning Satrājit to the royal assembly, in the presence of the king (Ugrasena), the Lord narrated the story of the recovery of the gem and entrusted the gem to his (Satrājit's) care.

39. Deeply feeling ashamed, he took that Symantaka jewel. Casting down his head and full of repentance for his guilt (of traducing the Lord), he returned home.

40. Constantly brooding over the sinful act (of caluminating an innocent person like Kṛṣṇa) and being agitated and perplexed at his conflict with a powerful party, he pondered : "How can I wipe off this misdeed and misbehaviour? Or how will Lord Kṛṣṇa be propitiated and gracious unto me?

41. What course would lead to my well-being whereby people won't censure me who am really short-sighted, mean, foolish and greedy of wealth.

42. I shall offer him my daughter who is a jewel among women, as well as that Syamantaka gem to him. This is the proper expedient, otherwise no peace can be brought about (between us) by any other way."

43. As the tradition reports, by this reasoning process, he reached this decision. Taking personal initiative in the matter, Satrājit offered his daughter who was excellent in all respects as well as the Syamantaka jewel to him.

44. According to ritualistic formalities prescribed in the Śāstras the Lord married Satyabhāmā who was blessed with good disposition, charming beauty, generosity and other excellent virtues and had many suitors soliciting her hand.

45. (Declining the offer of the Syamantaka gem) the glorious Lord said, "We do not accept the Syamantaka gem. Let it be with you as you are the devotee of the Sun-god (the donor of the gift). We shall enjoy the yield of the gem (viz. gold. As you have no son. I am the legal heir for the gold yielded everyday by the gem).

CHAPTER FIFTY SEVEN

The Story of Syamantaka

(*Murder of Satājit for Syamantaka—Akrūra allowed to retain it*)

Śrī Śuka said:

1. Hearing the report of Pāṇḍavas and Kuntī having been burnt (in the house of lac at Vāraṇāvata[1]), Śrī Kṛṣṇa, the Ruler of Senses, though knowing the reality (about their escape to safety), went with Balarāma to the Kuru country (to its capital Hastināpura) as a formal condolence visit to relatives.

2. It is traditionally reported that as co-sharers in their grief, he met Bhīṣma, Kṛpa along with Vidura, Gāndhārī as well as Droṇa and exclaimed: 'Alas ! What a pity !'

3. Taking advantage of this opportunity (of Kṛṣṇa's absence), Akrūra[2] and Kṛtavarmā instigated Śatadhanvā[3], "Why should not the gem Syamantaka be seized (now, as Kṛṣṇa is away) ?

4. Satrājit who, having positively promised us his beautiful, jewel-like daughter, set us at nought and gave her in marriage to Kṛṣṇa. Why should not such a fellow follow his brother (to the land of death) ?"

5. His mind being thus thoroughly perverted and prejudiced, the wicked-most, sinful fellow with his span of life

1. *Vide MBH. Ādi.* ch. 147.

2. VT. takes pains to absolve Akrūra of his participation in the criminal conspiracy of murdering Satrājit. His explanation that being enraged at Satrājit's accusation of Kṛṣṇa, Akrūra wanted to kill him, is not convincing—as Satrājit offered both Satyabhāmā and Syamantaka to Kṛṣṇa and it was Kṛṣṇa who of his own accord requested Satrājit to retain the jewel with him. When matters were amicably settled, to instigate Śatadhanvā to murder Satrājit is certainly not creditable. And his subsequent absconding with Syamantaka and the production of the gem when cornered by Kṛṣṇa, reflects against the character of this 'one of the greatest devotees' of Kṛṣṇa.

3. One of the five sons of Hṛdika of the Yadu clan, and a brother of Kṛtavarmā (*vide supra* 9.29.27)

diminished (and was about to be terminated soon), murdered Satrājit out of greed, while he was asleep.

6. While the women (in the family) were screaming and wailing loudly and helplessly, he, like a butcher knifing a beast, finished with Satrājit and absconded, taking with him the gem Syamantaka.

7. Beholding her father thus slain, Satyabhāmā was stricken with grief and bewailed, 'Oh father! father I am undone' And she fainted.

8. Depositing that dead body in a trough full of oil (to prevent its decomposition), she rushed to Hastināpura. Tormented as she was, she reported the matter of her father's assassination to Kṛṣṇa who (being omniscient) already knew the facts (of the case).

9. Hearing that (tragic incident) Balarāma and Kṛṣṇa, both the Lords of the world, following the (customary) way of human beings bewailed, 'Alas, what a calamity has befallen us!', with eyes flowing with tears.

10. From Hastināpura, the Lord with his consort and elder brother returned forthwith to his capital and started to adapt measures to slay Śatadhanvā and recover the gem from him.*

* *Vj's Text adds*:

10.1. At this juncture, there arrived from the capital[1] of the Pāñcāla country, an emissary deputed by king Yajñasena (Drupada) announcing the self-choice (*Svayamvara*) type of marriage of his princess Yajñasenī (Draupadī).

10.2. Being invited there along with his brother, Srī Kṛṣṇa went to (Kāmpilya), the capital of Pāñcālas and saw there the teen-aged sons of Pāṇḍu.

10.3-4. Those princes were perfectly disguised as Brāhmaṇas and were not seen before. Accompanying them, after they had achieved their ambition through the exhibition of their prowess by hitting the mark (the test for winning Draupadī's hand), he arrived at a potter's residence. He paid respects to his paternal aunt (Kuntī) and took leave of prince Yudhiṣṭhira.

10.4A. And hastened back to Dvārakā to slay Śatadhanvā.

1. viz. Kāmpilya, the capital of South Pāñcāla, the kingdom of Drupada. It is now known as Kampil, 28 miles N.E. of Fathegaḍh in Farrukkhabad District, U.P.—GDAMI p. 88.

11. Knowing the punitive measures adopted by Kṛṣṇa, Śatadhanvā got afraid and being anxious to save his life, he begged of Kṛtavarmā's help. But he (Kṛtavarmā) replied:

12. "I will not offend Balarāma and Kṛṣṇa, the Lords of the universe. Who can hope to live in peace after committing an offence against them?

13. The great warrior Kaṁsa was forsaken by the goddess of wealth and prosperity due to his hatred of them, and had to leave this world along with his followers, while Jarāsandha had to take to flight in (each of the) seventeen expeditions losing even his own chariot."

14. Being thus refused help (by Kṛtavarmā), he entreated Akrūra for help. But he too replied: "What person knowing the might of these two Lords of the world, can dare to oppose them?

VJ.'s Text adds:

14. A. God Śiva whose abode is mount Kailāsa, used to bow down to Hari with his head. He (Hari) has vanquished Hamsa and Ḍimbhaka who have become arrogant and overbearing due to boons (got by them), in the battle. The great poisonous serpent (Kāliya) was expelled by him from the pool (in the Yamunā).

15. It is out of sport that he creates, maintains and destroys this Universe. People deluded by his *Māyā* (the Unborn) do not comprehend the activities of the Creator of the Universe.

16. As a boy of seven years, he uprooted a mountain and held it up on one hand easily, as in play, like a child holding an umbrella-like mushroom.

17. Salutations to the Glorious Lord Kṛṣṇa of miraculous deeds. I bow down to the Infinite Lord, the Prime Cause of the universe, the Indwelling Soul of all."

18. Thus refused help by Akrūra, Śatadhanvā deposited the great jewel with him and mounting a horse (or a mare) capable of going hundred *yojanas* a day, he took to flight.

19. Balarāma and Kṛṣṇa rode in their chariots carrying

the flag with the emblem of Garuḍa, pursued with very swift horses, the murderer of his father-in-law, Oh king.

20. Śatadhanvā left his horse that dropped down (dead through fatigue), in a park of Mithilā. Being afraid, he began to run on foot, Kṛṣṇa also, out of rage, followed him on foot.

21. The glorious Lord who pursued on foot beheaded him with his Sudarśana disk of very sharp edge, and he searched his upper and lower clothes for the Symantaka jewel.

22. Not finding the jewel on his person, Kṛṣṇa returned and spoke to his elder brother, "Śatadhanvā has been killed in vain, for the jewel is not on his person."

23. Then advised Balarama, "The jewel has been certainly deposited by Śatadhanvā with some person (at Dvārakā). You return to the capital and trace him (the person possessing the jewel).

24. I wish to see king Videha, my dearest friend." Speaking thus, Balarâma, the delight of Yadus, entered the city of Mithilā, Oh king!

25. Seeing him come unexpectedly, the king of Mithilā, being highly pleased in mind, immediately rose up to receive him, and worshipped duly his honourable guest with suitable presents and other articles of worship.

26. The powerful lord Balarāma spent some years in the city of Mithilā. He was duly honoured by the noble-souled Janaka with great affection. It was during that period that Suyodhana, the son of Dhṛtarāṣṭra, learnt the art of fighting with mace, at his feet.

27. Returning to Dvārakā, Lord Kṛṣṇa who wanted to please his beloved wife, reported the death of Śatadhanvā and also of his not finding the gem with him.

28. Thereupon, along with friends and well-wishers, the Lord caused to be performed all the obsequies of Satrājit his father-in-law who had been murdered.

29. Having heard the report of the slaying of Śatadhanvā, Akrūra and Kṛtavarmā, the instigators of the crime, were overwhelmed with fear and absconded (from Dvārakā).

30. When Akrūra left Dvārakā, there appeared evil portents to the citizens of Dvārakā and they frequently suffered

from physical and mental troubles as well as troubles caused by gods and elements (*Mahābhūtas*), so goes the tradition.

VJ.'s Text Adds:

30-A. Thereupon Śrī Kṛṣṇa inquired of old people of whom Ugrasena was prominent: "What is the reason that after such a long time. these ill omens and calamities are befalling us?"

31. Forgetting what I have spoken before, some chroniclers declare as above. But how is it possible that ominous portents will occur in the home-town of Lord Kṛṣṇa who is the abode of ascetics (capable of counteracting such evils by their very presence)?

32. Formerly, so the tradition goes, when the lord of rains did not send seasonal showers, the king of Kāśi gave his daughter Gāndinī in marriage to Śvaphalka (the father of Akrūra) who came there as a guest and there fell showers of rain in the kingdom of Kāśi.

33. His son Akrūra possesses the same (hereditory) miraculous powers. Wherever he stays, the rain-god sends showers at the proper season. No calamities or epidemics (like cholera) affect at that area.

34. Hearing the advice of the elders and considering that this (i.e. the departure of Akrūra) could be the cause (of these calamities, but the absence of the Syamantaka gem is the real cause), Śrī Kṛṣṇa managed to bring back Akrūra (to Dvārakā) and spoke to him.

35. Śrī Kṛṣṇa who knew the minds of all (understood that this great devotee does not covet to possess the Syamantaka gem, and must have certainly brought it with him) received him with deep respect, engaged him in delightful conversation, narrated to him some pleasantries and spoke with a smile:

36. "We already know that the brilliant gem Symantaka is in your possession since it was deposited with you by Śatadhanvā, Oh master of charities.

37. As Satrājita had no male issue, (legally) the sons of his daughter Satyabhāmā should offer water oblations and lumps of rice (to the departed soul), pay off his debts and inherit the remaining property.

38. As you observe vows properly, let the Syamantaka gem, however, remain in your possession, as it is difficult for others to retain it. But my elder brother (Balarāma) does not believe that I do not possess the gem (he suspects that I have it with me).

39. Please show to our relatives (the Symantaka gem) and bring peace of mind to them, Oh highly fortunate Akrūra. (You cannot deny the possession of the gem as) now-a-days your sacrificial performances on altars of gold are going on continuously (without any interruption or break)."

40. Pursuaded with such sweet words, Akrūra, the son of Śvaphalka, brought the gem wrapped up in a piece of cloth and handed over to him that gem which was resplendent like the Sun.

41. Having made Akrūra to show the gem to his relatives and clansmen*, he wiped out the blame and suspicion imputed to him by (producing) the gem (from Akrūra) and the Lord returned that gem to Akrūra.

42. He who reads, hears, contemplates this highly auspicious episode rich with the exploits of the glorious Lord Viṣṇu, the Ruler of the Universe—an episode which wipes out all sins—becomes free from evil reputation and sins, and attains ever-lasting peace.

* *Here Vj's Text adds* :

41.1. The ruler of the world cleared off the accusation levelled against Him and explained the details of the case to Balarāma who had been away so long and had returned for seeing the gem (and to convince himself personally).

41.2. But on seeing it, he regarded himself to be the proper person to possess it and coveted to have it, Oh prominent Kaurava. Satyabhāmā considered herself to be (legally) the proper heir eligible (to possess) that hereditary property.

41.3. Without knowing the mind of Hari, she confidently wished to possess it. Even Jāmbavatī desired to get that gem as it was given as dowry by her father (as such her claim was legal).

41.4. Knowing all these (covetous) claims, Lord Kṛṣṇa, the consort of goddess Lakṣmī handed over again the gem to Akrūra.

CHAPTER FIFTY EIGHT

Espousals of Lord Kṛṣṇa

Śrī Śuka said:

1. On one occasion, Śrī Kṛṣṇa, the most prominent one among men, went to Indraprastha (modern Delhi) to see Pāṇḍavas who were celebrated for their bravery and other virtues. The Lord of the goddess Śrī was accompanied by Sātyaki and others.

2. Seeing Lord Mukunda, the Supreme Ruler of all, coming, all the sons of Pṛthā (Pāṇḍavas) immediarely stood up and those warriors went to reċeive him just as the divinities presiding over senses do to the returning main vital respiration (as senses become active when respiration returns).

3. Those warriors embraced the Imperishable Lord and got all their sins removed by the contact with his person. Beholding his countenance, beaming with affectionate smile, all of them were transported with joy.

4. Having bowed down to the feet of Yudhiṣṭhira and Bhīma, he embraced Arjuna and was in their turn paid respects by the twin Nakula and Sahadeva.

5. When he was comfortably seated on an excellent throne, the dark-complexioned, recently-married Draupadī who was above censure (in spite of her marriage with five brothers), came there slowly and bashfully bowed down to him.

6. In the same way, Sātyaki was worshipped and paid respect to by Pāṇḍavas. Others also were equally received and they sat on their respective seats around Kṛṣṇa.

7. Approaching Kuntī, Kṛṣṇa paid respects to her. He was looked at with eyes full of affection and tears, and was as if embraced by her looks. He was inquired about the relatives. He made queries about her health and well-being as also of her daughter-in-law, and other relatives.

8. Remembering all the many sufferings they had undergone (at Vāraṇāvata and till their coming to the Svayaṁvara of Draupadī), her throat was choked with perplexing affection and eyes full of tears, she spoke to Kṛṣṇa who manifested himself in order to remove all the sufferings (of his devotees).

9. "Oh Kṛṣṇa, when remembering us, your relatives, my brother Akrūra was deputed to us by you, we had been happy since then. For we were blessed with a protector like you.*

10. You being the well-wisher and the very soul of the universe, do not entertain the deluding notion of partiality (calling someone as your own and disavowing relationship with others). You, however, abide in the hearts of those devotees who constantly remember you and destroy all their sufferings by your very presence therein.

Yudhiṣṭhira said:

11. "Oh Supreme Lord ! I do not know what righteous act has been performed by us inasmuch as you, who are not easily visible even to experts in Yoga, have manifested yourself to our view, in spite of our poor understanding".

12. Earnestly requested by the king (Yudhiṣṭhira), the All-pervading Lord happily spent the four months of the rainy season there, giving delight to the eyes of the citizens of Indraprastha.

* *Vj.'s Text adds* :

9.1 "I have been quite at ease and happy since the time you, without forgetting, specially came to visit us while we were (at Kāmpilya) in the Pañcāla country".

9. 2-3. When Kuntī spoke thus, Śrī Kṛṣṇa, the Supreme Master in Yoga, of his own accord told her : "Having seen your sons along with their bride while they were (then) living in-cognito in the Pāñcālas (in its capital city Kāmpilya) at the potter's house, I departed hastily on that very day.

9.4-6. For, I wanted to kill Śatadhanvā, the enemy (and murderer of Satyabhāmā's father. When that evil genius Śatadhanvā was killed (and the Syamantaka gem was not on his person), my elder brother, Balarāma, the wielder of a plough (as his principal weapon) got angry with me. Disregarding me, he went to the Videha country in despondent mood. I stayed in the city (of Dvārakā) all this pretty long period, anxiously waiting for his return. Due to the pressure of work, I did not go anywhere".

To him who was explaining thus (the reasons of not seeing her so long), Kuntī, with her heart filled with feelings of affection, spoke to Him.

13-14. One day[1], equipping himself with the Gāṇḍīva bow, two quivers with inexhaustible stock of arrows and putting on his armour, Arjuna, the victorious, mounted his chariot distinguished by the flag bearing a monkey-emblem, prepared himself for hunting. Arjuna, the destroyer of hostile warriors, accompanied by Śrī Kṛṣṇa, entered a dense forest infested with a number of tigers and wild beasts.

15. He hunted down with his shafts a number of tigers, boars, buffaloes, antelopes (called *ruru*), *śarabhas* (a fabulous eight-legged animal, capable of killing lions), bisons, rhinoceroses, hares and porcupines.

16. As the day for performing sacrifice (or the *Śrāddha*-performance) had arrived, the attendants carried away those beasts which were considered proper and pure as oblation to the sacrificial fire.

17. Having sipped the water thrice (as *ācamana*), those two dark-complexioned great (chariot) warriors drank the crystal-clear water and noticed a charming girl strolling about.

18. Arjuna who was deputed by his friend Śrī Kṛṣṇa, approached that beautiful damsel of well-set teeth and charming appearance and enquired of her:

19. 'Oh beautiful maiden! Who are you? Whose daughter are you? Whence have you come? What is the intention (of strolling here)? I believe you wish to have a spouse? Tell me everything, Oh beautiful lady.'

Kālindi replied:

20. I am the daughter of the Sun-god. I am performing austere penance with the desire of getting the boon-bestowing god Viṣṇu who is worth courting, as my consort.

21. I do not wish to seek as my spouse any other person than the god Viṣṇu, the abode of goddess Śrī, Oh hero. May

1. This episode must have taken place after the burning down of the Khāṇḍava forest by Arjuna. God Agni who was satisfied by consuming that forest, gave Arjuna the Gāṇḍīva bow and two inexhaustible quivers of arrows and the chariot with the monkey-flag. —*MBH Ādi* 224.3-20.

the glorious Lord Mukunda (Kṛṣṇa), the refuge of the helpless, be propitious unto me.

22. I am known as Kālindī. I dwell in the mansion constructed by my father under the waters of the Yamunā and I mean to stay there, till I am able to see the immortal Lord Acyuta."

23. Arjuna (the controller of sleep) reported it *verbatim* to Śrī Kṛṣṇa. He knew it already. He placed the girl in the chariot and approached Kṛṣṇa in the presence of Yudhiṣṭhira along with her.*

24. When Kṛṣṇa was requested to help in the matter, he immediately got an extremely wonderful and beautiful city built by Viśvakarmā for the sons of Pāṇḍu.

25.** While the glorious Lord stayed there with the desire of doing some good to his relatives (or devotees), he became the charioteer of Arjuna for consigning the Khāṇḍava forest to the Fire-god.

26. Being pleased with him, the Fire-god bestowed upon Arjuna the (Gāṇḍīva) bow, four white horses and the chariot (drawn by them), two quivers with inexhaustible stock of arrows and an armour impregnable by (the arms etc. discharged by) armed soldiers.

27. Maya (the Asura architect) who was rescued from the (forest-) conflagration, (built for his friend) and presented to his friend Arjuna an assembly-hall wherein Duryodhana had optic illusions and he mistook a sheet of water for a paved floor and *vice-versa*.

28. Taking leave of Yudhiṣṭhira and obtaining consent of his friends, he returned to Dvārakā accompanied by Sātyaki and others.

Here Vj's text adds :

23.1. While Kṛṣṇa, the Controller of sense-organs, was happily staying at Indraprastha, he sent for Viśvakarman, the master architect of that period.

23.2-3. He made Viśvakarmā to build a wonderful city with high ramparts, portals, towers, mansions, gates. It became celebrated as the city of Indra (*Indra-prastha*). He did so with the desire to oblige his ralatives. Accompanied with his relatives, he was permitted (to depart from Indraprastha).

25** A bit of anachronism : *vide* verse 13 above.

29. Thereupon, in the auspicious season when the day was propitious and an auspicious constellation of stars was in ascendance, he married Kālindī.

29-A. *VJ.'s Text adds*:

Who being endowed with charming beauty and youthfulness gave delight to the mind and the eye).
And he thereby enhanced the joy and auspicious prosperity of his own people.

30. Vinda and Anuvinda, (the princes) of Avanti who were subservient followers of Duryodhana, forbade their sister (Mitravindā from choosing Kṛṣṇa as her consort) in her *svayaṁvara*, even though she was devotedly attached to *him*.

31. Śrī Kṛṣṇa then forcibly carried away Mitravindā, the daughter of his paternal aunt, Rājādhidevī (*vide Supra*. 9.24-31) while all the kings (attending the *Svayaṁvara*) stood agazing.

32. There was a very pious king called Nagnajit ruling over Kosala (at Ayodhyā). He had an excellent daughter named Satyā (Nīlā) who was also known as Nāgnajitī (after her father's name).

33. Kings were not able to win her for marriage without subduing seven extremely dreadful, wicked bulls with pointed horns and which never brooked the very smell of (approaching) warriors. [The taming of these bulls was the condition precedent of being eligible for Satyā's hand].

34. Hearing that the princess could be won only by the subduer of those bulls, Lord Kṛṣṇa, the Protector of Sātvatas, proceeded to Ayodhyā, the capital of Kosalas, with a vast army.

35. With great pleasure, the king of Kosalas received him respectfully with due formalities, such as going forth to welcome, offering a seat etc. and worshipped him with very valuable presents and articles of worship, and in his turn he was reciprocally congratulated by Kṛṣṇa.

36. Beholding that a suitor who was agreeable and desirable to her in every respect had arrived in state, the princess of that great king fell in love with him, (who was the consort of goddess Lakṣmī). (She prayed:) 'If I have devoutly wor-

shipped the Lord by the observance of the vows, may this Śrī Kṛṣṇa be my spouse and all auspicious benedictions prove true.'

37. What should I do whereby that glorious Lord will be pleased with me—the Lord, the dust on whose lotus-feet is borne on their heads by the goddess Śrī, the lotus-born god Brahmā, god Śiva, the Lord of mount Kailāsa along with the protectors of different worlds; Who is the Supreme Ruler and who, from time to time sportively assumes various forms with the object of enforcing the Law (of righteousness) as ordained by him?"

38. And to Kṛṣṇa who was duly worshipped, the king submitted again: 'Oh Nārāyaṇa! The Lord of the World! What more service a poor person like me can render to you who are perfectly satisfied in your own spiritual bliss.'

Śrī Śuka said:

39. The Lord who was pleased with him and occupied a comfortable seat, smilingly addressed to the king in a voice deep like the rumbling of clouds.

The Lord said:

39-A. *VJ.'s Text adds*:

'Wise men opine that that suitor (bridegroom) is the best who does not propose his suit on any other occasion except at the time of *svayaṁvara* (self-choice-by the bride-type of marriage). Oh Lord of the earth! It is such a suitor who (proposes his suit) when he gets an invitation along with other kings who might participate for the same object (as suitors)[1].

40. Wise men have strongly censured all entreaties on behalf of a prince—even if he be an humble *kṣattriya* but is following the path of the duty prescribed by *śāstras*. It is out of a strong desire for securing your friendship that I am soliciting you for your daughter (in marriage). And we are not prepared to pay any price (for the same).'

1. *saḥ arthārthī tāṁ velāṁ kālaṁ vinā āhvayati ātmānam iti śeṣaḥ*—VJ.

The king said:

41. 'What other suitor (bridegroom) superior to you can there be in this world, Oh Lord—a bridegroom most covetable for the girl, as being the only abode of all excellent virtues and on whose bosom the goddess Śrī abides permanently inseparable.

42. But with a view to securing a suitable bridegroom to the maiden, we have already laid down a condition for testing the prowess of the suitor, O Prominent *Sāttvata*.

43. These are the seven bulls untamed and ungovernable, O warrior. A great many princes have been discomfited and got their limbs pierced and broken by them.

44. (How strongly I wish it) If these (bulsl) be tamed and controlled by you alone. O scion of the Yadu clan, your honour will be the desired-most suitor to my daughter O Lord of the goddess Śrī.'

45. Hearing the nature of the convention, the Lord fastened his girdle tightly. He divided himself into seven persons and controlled the bulls easily as if in a sport.

46. With their pride crushed and spirit broken, he tied them with ropes (after passing the cords through their noses) and he sportively drew them (after him) like unto a child drawing wooden toy-bulls.

47. The king was wonderstruck. With pleasure he offered his daughter in marriage to Kṛṣṇa. The Lord espoused her with due religious formalities as she was worthy of him.

48. The Queens were extremely delighted to find that their daughter secured her beloved Kṛṣṇa as her spouse and there was a high festival (on that occasion).

49. Conchs, drums and kettle-drums were sounded. Vocal and instrumental music along with expressions of benedictions by Brāhmaṇas were heard. Rapturously exulted men and women donned excellent clothes, and decked themselves with garlands and ornaments (on the joyous occasion).

50-51. By way of dowry the mighty king gave ten thousand cows, three thousand excellently dressed young women (as maid-servants) all decked with necklaces of gold-coins, nine thousand elephants, chariots hundred times the elephants, horses hundred times the number of chariots and men-servants hundred times the number of horses.[1]

52. With his heart overwhelmed with affection, the king of Kosalas sent the couple in a chariot escorted with a big army.

53. Although the kings were formerly worsted in their encounter with the Yādavas and the uncontrollable bulls they, out of extreme jealousy obstructed Kṛṣṇa on the way while he was taking the bride with him.

54. As those kings advanced discharging volleys of arrows, Arjuna, the wielder of the Gāṇḍīva bow, keen on obliging his relative, routed them as a lion would do to insignificant beasts.

55. On reaching Dvārakā along with the dowry, Lord Kṛṣṇa, the son of Devakī and the prominent leader of Yadus, passed his time in conjugal happiness with Satyā.

56. Śrī Kṛṣṇa married Bhadrā, the princess of Kekayas, the daughter of His paternal aunt Śrutakīrti (vide Supra 9.24. 30) as she was offered in marriage by her brothers Santardana and others.

57. Like unto Garuḍa swooping down upon the (pitcher of) nectar (in the teeth of opposition from gods), Kṛṣṇa, singlehandedly carried away Lakṣmaṇā, the princess of the Madraruler, who was endowed with auspicious marks, in her *svayaṁvara* (setting at nought the assembled suitor-princess).

58. Similarly, Śrī Kṛṣṇa had thousands (sixteen thousand) other spouses, all of whom were good-looking and whom he rescued from the prison of demon Narakāsura, the son of the goddess earth, after slaying him.

1. VR calculates them as follows :
9,000 elephants, 9000,00 chariots, 9000,00,00 horses, and 9000,00,00, men-servants.

CHAPTER FIFTY NINE

Narakāsura slain. The Pārijāta tree brought to Dvārakā

The king Parikṣit enquired :

1. Be pleased to narrate to me the great prowess of Kṛṣṇa, the wielder of Śārṅga bow as to how he killed the demon Naraka, the son of the earth-goddess and those damsels (subsequently married to Kṛṣṇa) came to be taken to captivity by him (Naraka).

Śrī Śuka said :

2. Kṛṣṇa was informed of the atrocious deeds of Narakāsura, the son of the Earth, such as snatching away his umbrella, the insignia of his Lordship of the heaven[1], depriving his mother Aditi of her ear-rings, his expulsion from Maṇiparvata, the peak of mount Mandara, the mountain of gods, through the complaint lodged by Indra[2]. He along with his consort (Satyabhāmā)[3] mounted Garuḍa and flew to Prāgjyotiṣapura[4] (the capital of Narakāsura).*

1. Naraka did not deprive Indra of his umbrella as complained by him, but that of Varuṇa *vide* verse 23 below. But ŚR. explains that that was an affront to Indra himself as he was the king of gods.

2. Cf. VP. 5.29.1 This chapter deals with the same episode. Hence the textual similarities.

3. ŚR. explains that Indra appraized Kṛṣṇa of these misdeeds while he was in the palace of Satyabhāmā. So to satisfy her curiosity, he took her with him. ŚR gives another reason : Satyabhāmā was an incarnation of the Earth goddess. When Narakāsura was born of the Earth through Viṣṇu's contact with her in the Boar (Varāha) incarnation, while lifting her up from the *rasātala*. He promised her not to kill Naraka without her consent. Hence Satyabhāmā—the mother earth—was taken by him as a consenting party.

4. Kāmarūpa or Kāmākṣyā in Assam (near Gauhati)—
—GDAMI p. 158.

**Vj.'s Text as given in the Vrindavana edition* :

2.1. While the highly blessed Kṛṣṇa was staying at Dvārakā, he was approached by Indra who came from the heaven in a distressed and despondent state of mind.

2.2. Lord Kṛṣṇa received him with due respect, consoled him (with a promise of help) and gave him leave to depart.

3. The city was well protected on all sides with inaccessible hilly fortifications and mounted missiles and weaponry and was unapproachable due to the moats of water and fire and belts of stormy winds and was covered on all sides by thousands of terrible and strong snares devised by the demon Mura.

4. He shattered down the hills with his mace, devastated the fortification of weaponry with his shafts, cut off the moats and belts with his discus and the wire-snares with his sword.

5. With the loud blast of his conch, He blew down the war-machinery (on the ramparts) and broke down the hearts of the proud warriors. Śrī Kṛṣṇa the wielder of the mace demolished the fortification with his heavy mace.

6. Hearing the (deafening) blast of the conch terrific like the thunders at the end of *yugas* (when the universe dissolves) the five-headed demon Mura who was sleeping under water, rose therefrom.

7. Raising up his trident, that dreadful demon extremely difficult to look at due to his glaring lustre like the Sun or the Fire (about to destroy the world) at the end of *yugas*, rushed at Kṛṣṇa, with his five mouths wide open as if to devour the world as a serpent would rush at Garuḍa.

8. Brandishing the trident with great velocity, he hurled it with all his might at Garuḍa and roared with all his five mouths. The loud roar filled the earth and the heaven, all the directions and the firmament in fact all the cavity of the Brahmāṇḍa (universe).

9. Thereupon powerfully hitting two arrows at the trident as it was dashing against Garuḍa, He cut it into three

2.3. He (Kṛṣṇa) arrived at the great city of the king of demons which was situated on a high peak of the Himālayas, and was inaccessible due to the moats, belts of water, fire and winds and was guarded by soldiers.

2.4. He quickly cut down the snares of Mura by his discus and the terrible rows of swords (round the fortification) with his sword.

2.5. Within the wink of an eye, Hari blew off the water by using the wind missile and extinguished the fire-belt with the missile of Varuṇa (creating downpour of water). And with the terrific blast of his conch, he broke down the spirit (heart) of the proud warriors.

and stuffed the demon's mouths with arrows. The demon (on his part) vehemently hurled his mace at Kṛṣṇa in that battle.

10. In that battle, the invincible elder brother of Gada (i.e. Śrī Kṛṣṇa) shattered, with his mace, the on-rushing mace to a thousand pieces. And as the demon was rusing at him with his arms raised-up, he easily severed off his heads with his discus.

11. With his heads dissevered, the demon fell lifeless into the water like a mountain with its peak cut off by the mighty Indra. Grieved at their father's death, his seven sons, enraged and impatient to avenge it, rushed at Kṛṣṇa fully prepared[1].

12. Directed by Naraka, the son of the Earth, the seven sons of Mura viz. Tāmra, Antarīkṣa, Śravaṇa, Vibhāvasu, Vasu Nabhasvān and the seventh Aruṇa, with their commander Pīṭha at their head, sallied forth to the battlefield, fully equipped with arms.[2]

13. Overwhelmed with rage, they advanced discharging volleys of shafts, swords, maces, darts, double-edged swords and javelins on the invincible Lord. As the tradition goes, the Almighty Lord of unfailing prowess reduced with his shafts the whole volley of weapons to sesamum-seed like pieces.[3]

14. He (Śrī Kṛṣṇa) despatched to the abode of the god of death all of them with Pīṭha as their leader, with their heads, thighs, arms, legs chopped off and their armours split open. Observing that his army commanders were massacred with the discus and shafts of Lord Kṛṣṇa, Naraka, the son of the

1. *VJ.'s Text differs* :

11—A. When the demon Mura was killed, a shower of flowers expressing joy at the event, fell on the head of Viṣṇu (i.e. Kṛṣṇa)

2. *VJ.'s Reading* :

12.1. Directed by Naraka and riding their chariots drawn by bulls, those warriors (sons of Mura) sallied forth from their homes. Overwhelmed with rage they discharged from their well-strung bow, weapons, like darts, *ṛṣṭis* (double edged weapons) and javelins at the unconquered Lord).

3. *VJ.'s Text adds* :

13.1. The remaining warriors then immediately sped to the great capital (Prāg-jyotiṣapura) and reported to Naraka that all sons of Mura were killed.

goddess Earth, could not control his rage and rushed out with his elephant-corps all exuding ichor and their pedigree traceable to Airāvata born (i.e. churned) out of the Milky ocean.*

15. Beholding Kṛṣṇa seated on Garuḍa along with his consort like a cloud emblazoned with a streak of lightening appearing just above the disc of the sun[1], Naraká discharged at him a *Śataghnī*[2]. All his soldiers simultaneously struck at him.

16.* With his sharp pointed arrows equipped with variegated feathers, the glorious Lord Kṛṣṇa, the elder brother of Gada, mowed down the army of Naraka cutting down the arms, thighs, necks and trunks of the soldiers simultaneously killing the horses and elephants.

17. (What a wonderful feat) O scion of the Kuru race! Hari cut down with three sharp arrows each of the weapons and missiles discharged (at Hari) by the hostile soldiers.

18. He was borne by Garuḍa who (on his part) struck down elephants with his wings, killing them with his bill, claws and wings.

19. Distressed by Garuḍa's attacks they retreated into the city. Seeing his army killed and routed by Garuḍa, Naraka continued to fight single-handed.

* *VJ.'s Text adds* :

14.1. Surrounded with thousands of chariots and elephants and accompanied by a vast army, Naraka arrived at the battlefield.

1. *VJ.'s Text* :

15.1 Beholding Kṛṣṇa—the Sun, the four-armed Kṛṣṇa wielding an excellent bow and a conch, the Kaumodakī mace and a disc (in each hand).

15.2. Espying Naraka dark blue like a cloud riding on elephant, Govinda blew his conch and roared like a lion.

15.3. The invincible army of the demon-king showered a volley of terrific arrows on the head of Kṛṣṇa. That son of the goddess Earth discharged at Kṛṣṇa his iron *Śataghnī* and he was struck with that blow.

15.4. It was a miracle when the volley of innumerable arrows discharged by Naraka were simultaneously splintered with his shafts smilingly despatched by the Lord.

2. A weapon used as a missile, supposed by some to be a sort of a rocket—ASD p. 545.

16* VJ.'s wording of the 1st half differs :

Then with volleys of sharp arrows decked with variegated feathers discharged at Naraka's army, the glorious Lord Kṛṣṇa, etc.

20. Naraka, the son of the Earth goddess struck Garuḍa with his *Śakti* (spear) which had beaten back even *Vajra* (Indra's thunderbolt). Though hit by it, Garuḍa did not budge (an inch) like an elephant struck by a garland of flowers.[1]

21. His attempt having been thus frustrated, Naraka, the son of the Earth goddess, took up his spear to strike at Kṛṣṇa, but before he could hurl it, Hari, with his discus (Sudarśana) of razor-like sharp edge, severed the head of Naraka who was riding on elephant.

22. The head still adorned with ear-rings and a beautiful crown, though lying on the ground was shining, splendidly 'Alas!' "Bravo! Well done" applauded the sages, while the lords of gods, showering flowers on Śrī Kṛṣṇa, eulogized him.

23. Thereupon the goddess Earth approached Kṛṣṇa and handed over to him a pair of ear-rings resplendent with jewels and chased in the purest gold (belonging to Aditi), accompanied with the necklace called Vaijayantī[2] and a garland of forest flowers (*vanamālā*), the umbrella (the royal insignia) of Varuṇa as well as a great jewel (or the peak of mount Mandara called *Maṇiparvata—vide* verse 2 above).

24. The goddess folded her palms, bowed down to him and with her heart full of sincere devotion extolled the Lord of the universe who is adored by gods.

1. *VJ.'s Text adds* :

20.1. Though deeply pierced with that *Śakti* (spear) Garuḍa did not move at all like an elephant struck with a garland, in that fight with Naraka.

20.2. Thereupon, taking up his bow Naraka discharged a shower of arrows on Kṛṣṇa, but Keśava cut them all with his shafts.

20.3. Noticing that Naraka had properly set an *ardha-candra* arrow (with semi-circular head) and was about to discharge by pulling the bow-string, Kṛṣṇa cut down his bow.

20.4. Then the son of the mother Earth picked up his heavy mace of hard iron, but Kṛṣṇa cut it with an arrow called *Kṣurapra* (an arrow with shoe-shaped sharp head).

20.5. After this, Naraka, the vanquisher of hostile forces hurled his sharp-edged axe at Viṣṇu (Kṛṣṇa) but he cut it down with his sword.

20.6. Then he threw at Kṛṣṇa seventyfive *Tomaras* (javelins) and Naraka, the destroyer of hostile heroes, roared like a lion.

20.7. Kṛṣṇa simultaneously cut down all the javelins with one arrow. It was simply a miracle, O Prominent Kuru.

2. VJ. takes *Vaijayantī* as 'garland of flowers of five colours' and *Vanamālā* as 'a big garland of flowers and leaves reaching the foot,' but VR regards both as one : *vaijayantyā vana-mālayā saha*.

The Earth-goddess prayed :

25. Salutations to you, Oh God of gods, Oh wielder of a conch, a discus and a mace ! I bow to you, Oh Supreme Soul who have assumed form in compliance with the wishes of your votaries.

26. Hail to You, O God with a lotus in the navel (and are thus the cause—creator—of the universe). I bow to You O wearer of the wreath of lotuses (signifying your glorious renown). Salutations to You, O God with lotus eyes (soothing the torments of the world). Bow unto You, O God with lotus feet (deserving adoration and service by the world).

27. Hail to the Lord of (the highest) divine faculties (such as omnipotence etc.), Vāsudeva—the resort of all beings and the All-pervading god Viṣṇu. You are the Supreme Person, present before all the evolutes[1], the Creator (or the Cause) of the Primordial matter (*Prakṛti*). I bow to you, Perfect Spiritual Wisdom incarnate.

28. Hail to you who are yourself unborn but are the Creator of this Universe; who are the Brahman itself of infinite potencies. You are the Inner Controller of the great and the small, the Master of all elements (or created beings), O Supreme Soul.

29.* O Lord when desirous of creating the universe you assume intense form of *rajoguṇa* (viz. the four-headed god Brahmā); for the dissolution of the world you support the *Tamoguṇa* (and assume the form of god Rudra). And for the continuance of the world, you assume the *sattva* (i.e. Viṣṇu form). You are no other than the Time (*Kāla*), the Primordial

1. ŚR. quotes a Śruti text to support this :
pūrvam evāham ihāsam iti tat puruṣasya puruṣatvam /

29*. VR : O omnipresent Lord ! When desirous of creation, you do so by entering the body of the four-faced god (Brahmā) characterised by *rajo-guṇa*. For destruction (of the universe) you enter into the person of Rudra, Kālāgni (Fire burning down the universe) etc. who are dominated by *tamas*. For protection of the world, you enter into the bodies of Manu and other in whom *sattva-guṇa* is predominant as well as by incarnating yourself directly. It is due to your presence in *Kāla* (The Time Spirit), Primordial matter (*Prakṛti*) and the individual Soul that you are designated as *Kāla* though distinct from them. VR. quotes :
aitad ātmyam idaṁ sarvam, tat satyam, sa ātmā —Chāndogya 6.8.7 etc.

matter (*Prakṛti*) and the supreme Spirit itself—yet you are distinct from them.*

30. You are one without a second. i.e. the earth (and other elements like) water, fire, wind and the sky, the five *tanmātras* (the subtle elements with their qualities such as sound, taste, touch, form and fragrance), the presiding deities over senses, mind, cognitive and conative senses, *ahaṁkāra* (Ego, I-ness), *Mahat* (the Principle of Cosmic Intelligence), the mobile and immobile creation all these are illusions imposed on you.

30-A. *Yande's Bombay edt. adds in the ft. note* (P. 857).

When I was lifted by you, O Lord, in your boar incarnation, this son (Naraka) was born of me in consequence of your contact. So you gave that son to me and now he has been struck down by you.

31. This (Bhagadatta) is his (Naraka's) son. He is afraid and hence I have brought him to your feet, as you remove all the miseries of those who are afflicted. Be pleased to protect him by placing on his head your lotus-like hand which washes off all sins and impurities.

Śrī Śuka said :

32. When the glorious Lord was entreated in these words by the goddess Earth in devotion and humility, the Lord vouchsafed him protection and entered the palace of Naraka, full of all affluence.

32A. *VJ.'s text adds*

Having installed him (Naraka's son, Bhagadatta) on his hereditary throne (lit. kingdom) and reappointed his ministers to their respective posts, Hari entered the series of compartments and dwelling units of Naraka's harem.

33. Hari found there sixteen thousand (and one hundred—) daughters of kings (Siddhas, gods, *asuras* etc.-) brought as captives after defeating various kings[1].

29* VB : emphasizes that God transcends the *guṇas*.

VJ. You are Kāla (the Time-Spirit) which gives effect to the Fate (*adṛṣṭa*) of beings. You are called Pradhāna as the exalted-most, Supreme Person and are so designated. *Or* You are *puruṣottama* and hence called *Pradhāna Puruṣa*.

1. ŚR. bases his interpretation on the basis of VP: 5'29.31 (regarding additional one hundred girls) but the second versequoted by him—

34.* Perceiving the great hero among men enter, the damsels were so fascinated with him that they mentally chose him as their desired-most beloved spouse brought to them by their Destiny.

35. "May this hero be my husband. May god Brahmā (or the Creator) approve and grant my prayer." With this devout feeling for him, all of them severally set their hearts on Kṛṣṇa.

36. Śrī Kṛṣṇa sent them all to Dvārakā in palanquins after they had taken their bath and put on excellent clean dress[1]. He also despatched along with them valuable treasure (of precious stones etc.) as well as chariots, horses and immense wealth.

37. Kṛṣṇa sent sixtyfour, white, four-tusked swift-footed elephants of Airāvata's pedigree to Dvārakā.

VJ.'s Text adds :

37-A. He gave to Bhagadatta one elephant, called Supratīka out of them and sent the rest to the shed.

38. Having gone to the palace of Indra and restored to Aditi her two ear-rings, he along with his beloved consort Satyabhāmā was worshipped by the king of gods along with his queen Indrāṇī.

39. Importunated by his consort, he uprooted the celestial tree Pārijāta and placed it on (his mount) Garuḍa. After defeating the celestials (who resisted the taking away of Pārijāta), he brought it to his capital Dvārakā.[2]

40. It was planted as an (additional) adornment to the garden of Satyabhāmā's palace. Covetously hankering after

deva-siddhāsurādīnāṃ nṛpāṇāṁ ca Janārdana |
hṛtvā hi so 'suraḥ kanyā rurodha nijamandire ||

is not traced in the Gītā Press edition.

34A.*—VJ.'s reading : Seeing him enter, the damsels who were all youthful, well-ornamented and of attractive features were fascinated with the great hero among men.

1. VT. explains that those girls led an austere life, wearing tawny-coloured clothes observing vows and fasts.

2. VJ,'s text elaborated this episode in two chapters. (ch. 65 and 66) which are translated in the Appendix as chapter 59-I and 59-II.

its fragrance and intoxiçating honey, black bees from heaven followed it.[1]

41. Indra touched the feet of Kṛṣṇa with the crests of his crown many times while he bowed to him and begged of him to accomplish his purpose (viz. the recovery of Aditi's ear-rings, Varuṇa's royal umbrella and others). But once his purpose was achieved, he fought against him. What a great ignorance on the part of gods! Fie upon that affluence!

42. Later on, the immutable Lord assumed as many forms as the number of damsels (brought from Naraka's harem) and on the same specific auspicious time, he simultaneously yet severally married each one of them in their respective mansions with due formalities (and still remained changeless and perfect).

VR.'s Text adds:

42A. Lord Hari grants all the wishes of his devotees. He is infinite and incomprehensible. What is miraculous therein that he was severally and simultaneously present with each of his spouse?

42B. Lord Kṛṣṇa who is the Supreme of all the masters of Yoga, is still visualized within, without and all around in hundreds and thousand forms by his devotees.

43. In their mansions which surpassed all comparisons and were endowed with super-abundant affluence, the imperishable Lord of incomprehensible activities remained present (all the while simultaneously). Though he was perfectly satisfied with his own bliss, he sported with those *aṁśas* (rays) of goddess Lakṣmī (viz. those newly wedded 16000 damsels) and like other house-holders attended to his house-hold duties.

44. Having obtained the consort of goddess Lakṣmī as their own spouse whose ways (or approaches to whom) are incomprehensible even to god Brahmā and others, those damsels continuously waited upon him with ever-increasing incessant delight, by means of their affectionate smiles, side-glances in their ever-new meetings and their bashful behaviour and speech.

1. This is described in ch. 67 of VJ.'s text which is translated in the Appendix at ch. 59-III.

45. Although hundreds of maid-servants were in their service, each of them personally rendered service to the Lord by rising up and advancing to receive him, offering him a seat and excellent articles of worship, washing his feet, offering betel-leaves, removing his fatigue and refreshing him by fanning, application of sandalpaste and garlands of flowers, and by combing his hair, arranging his bed, bath and catering to him refreshments (or presents) to him.

CHAPTER SIXTY

Conversation between Kṛṣṇa and Rukmiṇi (A Sweet Quarrel)

Śrī Śuka said :[1]

1. On a certain occasion, Rukmiṇī, the princess of Bhīṣma was waiting upon her consort, the Creator and the Preceptor of the world who was comfortably seated on her own bed while the maid-servants[2] were fanning.

2. That Unborn Lord, the Controller of the Universe, who, out of sport, creates, protects and destroys this universe,

1. VJ.'s text gives the introductory background in 4 verses.
King Parikṣit enquired :

1.1 Every one of the queens of Kṛṣṇa was devotedly attached to him from the bottom of her heart and every one of them was confident in her heart that she was the only beloved-most queen of Kṛṣṇa.

1.2 Was Kṛṣṇa equal to all in his love of them or was he specially attached to one (of them) ? As I strongly desire to know the fact of the matter, be pleased to narrate it to me.

Śrī Śuka said :

1.3 It is widely well-known to all that out of all his queens, Rukmiṇī, the princess of Bhīṣma, was the senior-most and the Lord was loving her the most of all.

1.4 On one occasion, a love-quarrel with her was provoked by Kṛṣṇa. I shall narrate to you the whole episode. Please listen to it, O descendant of the Kurus.

2. *Vide* verse 7 below.

was born in the race of Yadus for the protection (and enforcement) of the moral ordinances laid down by him.

3-6. O King! (In her mansion) Rukmiṇī was waiting upon her Consort, the Lord of the three worlds, as he was comfortably relaxing on a cushion, white like the foam of milk, on an excellent couch, in her inner apartment which was beautified with a canopy fringed with strings of lustrous pearls suspended from it and with refulgent precious gems as lamps. It (the apartment) was decorated with flowers and wreaths of jasmine resonant with the swarms of humming bees; it was lit up with silvery moon-beams that entered through the appertures of the latticed windows. From the garden a gentle breeze surcharged with the fragrance of Pārijāta wafted in, while the incense of the fumes of burning aloe wood escaped out of the eyeholes of the lattice.

7. The queen (Rukmiṇī) too from her (female) friend's hand the *chowrie* with a (gold) handle studded with gems and began to serve her Lord by fanning Him with it.

8. She was holding the *chowrie* in her hand adorned with rings and bracelets and was making a jingling sound with a pair of anklets studded with jewels. By the side of Lord Kṛṣṇa, she looked extremely charming with the lustre of necklace reddened with the saffron applied to her bosom covered in her upper garment and with her priceless girdle worn round her waist.

9. Gazing at her who was goddess Lakṣmī herself who was exclusively devoted to him and had assumed a form suitable to the form sportively adopted by him[1], Lord Hari, being very much pleased with her, smilingly spoke to her who appeared extremely charming with her countenance looking all the more beautiful with her curly locks of hair, ear-rings, gold necklace and her face splendidly beaming with nectar-like (sweet) smile.

1. *devatve deva-deheyaṁ manuṣyatve ca mānuṣīn /*
Viṣṇor dehānurūpaṁ vai karotyeṣātmanas tanum //

—VP. 1.9.145.

The Lord said :

10. O princess (of excellent beauty and virtue) ! You were desired and sought after by rulers of the earth whose affluence and power equalled to that of the divine protectors of worlds; were endowed with majestic splendour and were far-famed for their wealth, beauty of form, magnanimity and might.

11-12. O lady with beautiful eyebrows ! Why did you reject the prince of Cedi (Śiśupāla) and others who arrived (at your place) seeking your hand and were mad with intense love for you and to whom you were (already) agreed to be offered (in marriage) by your brother and father ? Why did you select us who were in no way their compeer—us, who being afraid of other Kings, have sought shelter in the sea, have contracted enmity with the powerful (monarchs like Jarāsandha) and have practically relinquished the royal throne.

13*. O damsel with lovely brows ! Women who (by marrying) follow the path of men whose ways are obscure and who generally follow paths untraversed by the (general) public, generally come to grief.

14. (Women generally approve of the rich even though they may not be good looking.) But we are have-nots and we are generally dear to people who possess nothing (and are poor). Hence affluent people generally do not resort to me, O lady with beautiful waist.

15. (It is advisable that) Marriage and friendship be contracted between those who are equal in wealth, heredity (or family prestige) sovereign power, beauty of form or future prospects but not between the inferiors or superiors.

16.** O princess of Vidarbha ! Without ascertaining the

*. The inner significance of these epithets seems to be as follows (as later brought out in Rukmiṇī's reply).

Women who seek us whose nature is incomprehensible and who do not follow the trodden-orthodox path of action, reach the abode of the Supreme Man. VR and VB give a similar (though somewhat different) explanations.

**Some epithets in the verse have double meaning :

guṇair hīnaḥ—without i.e. transcending the *guṇas* (*sattva*, *rajas*)

bhikṣubhir mudhā—who are eulogized by recluses disinterestedly (without any ulterior motive)

vide infra Rukmiṇī's reply—verses 34-48.

real situation, we who are really devoid of all qualities but are praised for nothing by beggars, have been selected by you due to your lack of foresight.

17. Even at this stage you may choose some prominent Kṣattriya hero who is suitable to you in every respect. You may thereby enjoy all the blessings both here and hereafter.

18. Kings like Śiśupāla, Śālva, Jarāsandha, Dantavakra and others—why even your elder brother Rukmī also—have been hating me (like an enemy), O lady with beautiful thighs.

19. In order to humiliate the pride of those haughty princes who are blinded with the arrogance of their prowess that you have been brought here by me who have to crush the pride of the wicked.

20. As a matter of fact, we do not hanker after women, children or wealth and are indifferent to the world. We are perfectly satisfied in our blissful Self. We are unconcerned to our body or to our household. Like a lamp we are simply a witness who have nothing to work for.

Śrī Śuka said:

21. Having spoken to her thus, the Lord who wished to remove the pride of Rukmiṇī who, due to her continuous association with him, regarded herself the beloved-most spouse of her Lord till then, became silent.

22. It is reported that at that time, on hearing this unpleasant speech, the like of which was never heard before —of her beloved, the Lord of the three worlds, queen Rukmiṇī shuddered at heart, began to tremble and shedding tears, sank into fathomless anxiety.

23. Scratching the floor with her shapely foot beautified with reddish nails; sprinkling profusely with tears darkened with collyrium, her breasts rendered reddish by the application of saffron, she stood there with her face cast down and her speech choked with excessive grief.

24. As her reason became benumbed and lost with excessive agony, fear and grief, the fan dropped from her hand which became instantly so much shrivelled and loose that bangels were slipping from them and her body suddenly became

unconscious and fell down with disheveled hair like a plantain tree uprooted in a stormy wind.

25. Observing that (indescribably powerful bondage of love of his beloved (owing to which) she could not understand the subtle significance of his joke, Lord Kṛṣṇa who was merciful by nature, took pity on her.

26. Quickly springing down from the couch, the four-armed Lord[1] lifted her up and gathering up her locks of hair, gently wiped her face with his lotus-hand.

27. He wiped out her eyes which were full of tears and her breasts soiled with her tears of grief. He hugged in his arms his chaste faithful consort who was exclusively and absolutely devoted to him, O king.

28. The Lord, who knew how to comfort and was past-master in offering consolation and is the last resort of the righteous and the saintly people comforted mercifully his broken-hearted queen whose mind was bewildered with the (harshness of the misunderstood) subtle joke for which she was the wrong target (*lit.* which she did not deserve).

The Lord consoled :

29. O princess of Vidarbha ! No. Please do not be displeased with me. I know that you are absolutely devoted and faithful to me. O beautiful damsel ! It is just with the desire of hearing your retort that I spoke that in jest.

30. It was just to behold your charming countenance with its lower lip throbbing with anger through love, with corners of eyes reddened while casting wrathful side-glances and the knitting of your beautiful eyebrows.

31. This is the highest benefit in the domestic life of the householders that they can spend some hours in joking and jesting with their beloved, O beautiful timid lady.

Śri Śuka said :

32. O king ! When that princess of Vidarbha was thus cajoled and comforted in these words by the glorious Lord,

1. The Lord manifested his four arms for the purpose of lifting her up, embracing her, wiping her face etc. ŚR.

she realized that it was nothing but his jocular speech and got over her fear of being abandoned by her dear Lord.

33. Beholding (attentively) the Lord's face through her beautiful affectionate side-glances accompanied with bashful smile, she addressed the most prominent of men, O descendant of Bharata.

Rukmiṇi said:[1]

34. Verily, what Your Lordship has said is factually correctnamely that I am not equal and similar to you who are endowed with infinite excellences (like greatness, beauty etc). There cannot be any comparison between you who are ever established in your own greatness, the glorious Lord of the trinity of gods (Brahmā, Viṣṇu and Rudra) and I who am *Prakṛti* (The Primordial Nature) consisting of three *guṇas* (*sattva*, *rajas* and *tamas*) and whose feet are resorted to by the ignorant.

35. O Supremely mighty Lord (or Lord of mighty strides in cosmic Form) ! It is true that you, being as it were afraid of *guṇas* (*sattva, rajas* or qualities e.g. sound, smell, etc.) abide in the sea[2] (i.e. shine eternally in hearts unfathomable like the sea). Being the Supreme Self, of infinite pure consciousness, you are ever hostile to wicked senses (or persons who are controlled by wicked propensities). And sovereignty has been spurned away as a position of blinding darkness by your servants. (Then what of you ?).

1. ŚR. quotes verses enumerating all the epithets Kṛṣṇa used to show his inferiority to Rukmiṇī in his jocular speech above and attempts to show the hidden meaning or the puns used in each which extol the real greatness of Kṛṣṇa as expounded in Rukmiṇī's speech here.

2. VR : What fear can exist for you who covered the three worlds in your strides? It was just to exhibit your intense love for me that you resorted to the sea which has 'sea-ness' like my father, the milky ocean. I being your beloved-most, you love everything related to me.

VJ. *samudra*—Body constituted of five elements. You abide fully refulgent (of the size of a thumb) in the heart of the body consisting of five elements.

36. The paths of sages who enjoy the honey of your lotus-like feet are not clearly understandable (discernible). And to men of bestial nature, they are certainly incomprehensible. Hence the way of their behaviour like that of the Supreme Ruler is extraordinary and supernatural. Such being the case, need it be said that your course of conduct must be much more so, O Almighty Lord.

37. Are you really *niṣ-kāñcana* (a have-not possessing nothing as your own) ? No. For there is none superior to you. Even god Brahmā and others who enjoy (sacrificial) offerings and worship (from others) offer worship to you. Persons who cater to the satisfaction of their senses and are blinded by their affluence do not know that you are the *Kāla*—the exterminator of all. Your worship is the dearmost to gods who enjoy oblations and (reciprocally) they are so to you.

38. You are indeed the embodiment of all the highest) purposes in human life, the very personification of the fruit thereof, with the desire of attaining which the wise and intelligent people renounce every thing, O Almighty Lord ! The association between your worship and them (the master-servant relation)[1] is quite proper. But not so that between a man and a woman who are attached to each other and are subject to pleasure and pain.

39. Your prowess and glory have been extolled by sages who have renounced the staff (the external index of being a recluse). You are the soul of the universe. You are ever willing to bestow your Soul (upon your votaries). Hence I have chosen you rejecting gods like Brahmā, Śiva, Indra whose blessings and positions are shattered down and destroyed by the (vehement) velocity of Time impelled by the slight movement of your brow. What of others (like Śiśupāla, Śālva and others mentioned by you).

40. O elder brother of Gada ! Your words (of having taken shelter at the sea through the fear of kings) are meaningless (as fear is impossible in your case). Oh Lord ! putting to flight all kings by the twanging of your Śārṅga bow, you carried me away like a lion which routing all beasts, appro-

1. VR calls it *Śeṣa-Śeṣī* relation.

priates his own prey. How can it be true that you became afraid of those kings and took shelter at the sea ?

41. Longing for you, great (*lit.* crest-jewels of) monarchs like Aṅga, Pṛthu (the son of Vena), Bharata (the son of Jayantī, the queen of Ṛṣabha), Yayāti (the son of Nahuṣa), gaya and others renounced their undisputed sovereignty over the whole world and entered the forest(for performing penance). Did they suffer here for having taken to the path leading to you, O Lotus-eyed one ?

42. What mortal woman with a clear vision that you, the abode of all excellences, are the real objective in life and has once enjoyed the fragrance of your lotus-feet which are extolled by saints and sages, which grants emancipation from *saṁsāra* to people and are the abode of the goddess Lakṣmī, will disregard them and take resort to another person who is ever subject to the fear of death and *saṁsāra.*

43. I resorted to you, the Supreme Ruler of the worlds, as a suitable partner, my very Soul who grant all wishes here and hereafter. May your feet which liberate from the false *saṁsāra* and protect those who resort to them, protect me who am wandering in the cycle of births.

44. O Imperishable Lord ! Annihilator of enemies ! May the kings (like Śiśupāla and others) listed by you be married to that unlucky woman to whose ears your stories sung in the assemblies of god Śiva and Brahmā, have not reached. For those kings (mentioned by you) behave like a donkey, an ox, a dog, a cat and a menial servant in the homes of their wives.

45. The stupid woman who has not tasted the fragrance of the honey in your lotus-feet will resort as a beloved to a living corpse covered from outside with skin, moustaches, beard, hair on the body, nails and filled inside with flesh, bones, blood, worms, refuse, flegm, bile and wind.

46. O lotus-eyed Lord ! You revel in your own self and you do not cherish any extraordinary outlook (i.e. any special love) for me. May my love to your feet be constant when for the advancement of the world you look at me (i.e. *Prakṛti*) with an excess of *rajas*, that itself is the highest grace on me.

47. O slayer of Madhu ! I do not regard your speech as without significance or false. For sometimes, as in the case of Ambā[1], some girls do set their hearts on somebody else (than the one for whom they are brought to marry).

48. In the case of an unchaste woman though married, her mind hunts after new persons. A wise man should not maintain i.e. marry an unchaste woman, for he falls both here and hereafter.

The Lord said:

49. O virtuous princess ! It is only with the desire of hearing this (from you) that you were deceived (by that jocular speech). Whatever you spoke after my speech i.e. the interpretation you have put upon it—is quite true and correct.

50.* Whatever blessings you seek from me shall always be fulfilled as you are absolutely devoted to me, O beautiful lady. But blessings sought from me lead to freedom from desires.

51. Your deep love to your husband and your fidelity to him has been proven, O sinless lady. Though I have tried to move you (and shift your allegiance) with my words, your mind (and fidelity) could not be alienated.

52. Those who, for the sake of conjugal happiness worship me, the bestower of emancipation from *saṁsāra*, by performing penance and observance of vows, and have given their hearts to sensual pleasure, are deluded by my Māyā.

53. Having attained to (i.e. propitiated) me, the Lord and Bestower of Liberation from *saṁsāra* as well as of wealth or worldly pleasures, those who long to have only worldly pleasures from me (and not me their Lord and Bestower) are really unfortunate, O proud lady. For, these pleasures can be obtained even in the hell or lower species of life. To men given to such sensual pleasures, life even in hell would be welcome and suitable.

1. Ambā, a princess of Kāśī, loved the king of Śālva even though Bhīṣma carried her away to marry his step brother Vicitra-vīrya.—*MBH Adi* 102.60-64.

* VJ. Whatever you long to have is always with you already. Hence you do not wish to attain any greatness or power. *Or* Whatever blessing you wish to have, you have it in me.

54. O deity of my house (and wealth) ! How glad I am that you have borne to me a constant attachment and devotion which liberates from *saṁsāra*[1] and which is very difficult to practise for the wicked and still more so for deceitful women actuated by wicked tendencies and given to the gratification of low sensual appetites.

55. O Proud lady ! In all the houses, I have not noticed such a loving wife like you who, at the time of your marriage disregarded all the suitor-monarchs assembled (at your place) and despached a Brāhmaṇa-emissary with a confidential message to me of whom you have merely heard good accounts only.

56. You have patiently borne oft-recurring occasions of grief (caused by us) such as the disfiguration of your brother after taking him captive in the battle (by me), the death of your brother (at Balarāma's hand) while playing at dice (in the gambling hall) on the occasion of (Aniruddha's) marriage.[2]

57. That a messenger with a secret clear-worded message was sent by you to secure me (as your consort), that you felt this whole world as void when (you felt that) I delayed and that then you wanted to cast away your body[3] as not worthy of any other person (except me). This supreme love of yours (is impossible for me to repay) we can receive you gladly, hailing you with joy.

Śri Śuka said:

58. In this way, imitating the human world in such amorous conversation, the glorious Lord of the Universe, though absorbed in his own spiritual Bliss, indulged in love-sport with Lakṣmī (in the form of Rukmiṇī).

59. In the same way, the Omni-present Lord, the Preceptor of the Universe was present severally in the mansions of all other queens as its Master and simultaneously carried out all the duties prescribed for house-holders.

1. Wealth in the form of Devotion characterised by Love which is itself of the nature of liberation from *saṁsāra*—VT.

2. An anachronism : *vide infra* ch. 61. 36.

3. vide Supra 29.36 :

Yarhyambujākṣa na labheya bhavat-prasādam |
Jahyām asūn vrata-kṛśān śatajanmabhiḥ syām ||

CHAPTER SIXTYONE

Aniruddha's Marriage : Rukmī Slain

Śrī Śuka said :

1. Each of the above-mentioned queens of Kṛṣṇa bore to him ten sons respectively who were in no way inferior to their father in qualities of head-and-heart.

2. Observing that Lord Kṛṣṇa did not move out of their mansion but was always at home, every one of the princesses, being ignorant of his divine nature, considered herself to be his most beloved wife.

3. Those damsels were enchanted with his countenance charming like a blooming lotus, (knee-) long arms, large beautiful eyes, glances expressive of winning affectionate smiles and sweet conversation, but reciprocally with all the charms at their command, they could not conquer and fascinate the heart of the Perfect One.

4. On the contrary, those sixteen thousand wives of Kṛṣṇa failed to agitate his mind with those shafts of the god of love, and other enticements conveying erotic messages by the movement of their eye-brows charming with the sentiment expressed by their smiles and stealthy side-glances.

VJ.'s Text adds :

4A. Even though their Lord occupied a high seat in their personal mansion, out of bashfulness due to their new union in marriage, those chaste and virtuous damsels cast from behind the pillars their side-glances through eyes full of love at their highly beloved consort, the Lord of saintly people, the sole asylum of the goddess of wealth.

4B. They laughed with joy when their eyes were closed from behind with his hands by their beloved while he was enjoying himself in their mansions. But being afraid of disturbing his passion of love for them, they waited only adjusting garments on their person though it may not be pleasant to him.

5*. Having obtained the consort of the Goddess of Wealth and beauty (Lakṣmī) as their own consort, the ways of approaching whom were incomprehensible even to god Brahmā and others those damsels enjoyed with ever-increasing joy and love his affectionate smiles, side-glances with a longing for union felt as ever new.

6. Although hundreds of maid-servants were in their service, each of them personally rendered service to the Lord by rising up, advancing to receive him, offering him a seat and excellent articles of worship, washing his feet, presenting him betel-leaves, removing his fatigue and refreshing him by fanning, application of sandal-paste and garlands of flowers and by combing his hair, arranging his bed, bath and catering to him refreshments.

7. Out of those (sixteen thousand, one hundred and eight) queens of Kṛṣṇa who bore him ten sons each, eight were previously mentioned as principal queens. I shall relate to you about pradyumna and other sons (of these eight queens).

8-9. Pradyumna being the eldest, Cārudeṣṇa, Sudeṣṇa, the chivalrous Cārudeha, Sucāru, Cārugupta, Bhadracāru and his younger brother Cārucandra, Vicāru, Cāru as the tenth—these sons were born of Rukmiṇī. They were in no respect inferior to their father Hari.

10-12. Bhānu, Subhānu, Svarbhānu, Prabhānu, Bhānumān, Candrabhānu, Bṛhadbhānu, and the eighth Atibhānu, Śrībhānu, Pratibhānu—these were the ten sons by Satyabhāmā. Sāmba, Sumitra, Purujit, Śatajit, Sahasrajit, Vijaya, Citraketu, Vasumān, Dravid, Kratu—these were the ten sons of Jāmbavatī. Sāmba and these others were all favourites of their Father.

13. Vīra (*v. l.* Bhānu), Candra, Aśvasena, Citragu, Vegavān Vṛṣa, Āma, Śaṅku, Vasu, Śrīmān, Kunti were the sons of Nagnajitī.

* ŚR. notes that verses 5 & 6 are extremely beautiful and they are an echo of those in a previous chapter (*Supra* 59. 44 & 45 with some modification.

14. Śruta, Kavi, Vṛṣa, Vīra, Subāhu, Bhadra, Ekala, Śānti, Darśa, Pūrṇamāsa, Avara and Somaka were the ten sons of Kālindī.

15. Praghoṣa (*v. l.* Prajaṅgha), Gātravān, Siṁha, Bala, Prabala, Ūrdhvaga, Mahāśakti, Sahas, Ojas and Aparājita were the sons of Mādrī (Lakṣmaṇā).

16. Vṛka, Harṣa, Anila, Gṛdhra, Vardhana and Annāda, as also Mahāṁśa, Pavana, Vahni and Kṣudhi were the sons of Mitravindā.

17. Saṅgrāmajit, Bṛhatsena, Śūra, Praharaṇa, Arijit, Jaya, Subhadra, Vāma, Āyus and Satyaka were the sons of Bhadrā.[1]

18-19. Dīptimān, Tāmratapta and others were born to Hari by Rohiṇī.[2] (She was the chief of the group of sixteen thousand and one hundred queens). A mighty son Aniruddha was born of Pradyumna by Rukmavatī the Princess of Rukmī in the city of Bhojakaṭa (while Pradyumna was there).

As the mothers of Kṛṣṇa's sons were sixteen thousand in number, the sons and grandsons of those sons numbered billions.

King Parīkṣit enquired :

20. Oh learned sage ! How is it that Rukmī who was vanquished in combat by Kṛṣṇa and was eagerly waiting for an opportunity to avenge, gave his daughter in marriage to his enemy's son ? Be pleased to narrate to me how the matrimonial alliance came about between these two deadly enemies.

21. For the *Yogins* can accurately and distinctly see the future, the past and the present as well as what is beyond the ken of senses, which is very remote and screened off (by something else).

Śrī Śuka narrated :

22. Being the actual embodiment of Anaṅga (the god of Love), he (Pradyumna) was selected by Rukmavatī in her *svayaṁvara* (self-election by the bride-type of marriage). Com-

1. It appears a slip on the part of ŚR. to equate her with Śaibyā-VT.
2. Obviously a similarity of name in the women of the same family.

pletely defeating the assembled kings single-handedly in his chariot, he carried her away.

23*. Although Rukmī, humiliated by Kṛṣṇa, was cherishing enmity against him (but) with a view to please his sister Rukmiṇī, he offered his daughter in marriage to his nephew.

24. It is reported that the mighty son of Kṛtavarmā married Cārumatī, the large (beautiful) eyed daughter of Rukmiṇī.

25. Though still nursing deep hostility to Kṛṣṇa and though aware of the violation of the restrictions of *dharma-śāstra*[1]

23* *Here VJ's Text adds* :

23.1. Rukmī who was humiliated by Kṛṣṇa (by deforming him after defeat) continued to (brood over and) nurse the enmity. By his penance, he propitiated god Śiva abiding on mount Śrī Śaila.

23.2-3. Rudra, the most prominent among boon-conferring gods, was propitiated by Rukmī by performance of penance. He asked Rukmī to seek a boon. He sought for a strong unbreakable bow which will be invincible for hosts of enemies and un-sunderable even to gods. "So be it", said the god Śiva and gave him the bow. But god Śaṅkara cautioned him thus :

23.4. "When you confront god Viṣṇu, this bow will desert you and will return to me. Not otherwise."

23.5 Telling him thus, god Śiva gave him the bow and disappeared. Having secured the boon, the king returned to his capital Bhojakaṭa.

23.6 With the help of the bow, Rukmī brought under his control all kings noted for their prowess in battle. Kṛṣṇa was the only exception.

23.7 With greed of retaining the possession of the bow, Rukmī did not even think of opposing Vāsudeva. Nor did he think of entering into faithful alliance with him, O great king.

23.8 Although he still cherished the enmity, he remembered the words of god Śiva. Pradyumna who was the veritable Manmatha (the god of Love) incarnate, was chosen by Rukmavatī in the *Svayaṁvara*.

23.9 Having vanquished in the battle, all the kings assembled there (for the *svayaṁvara*) single-handedly in his chariot, he carried her away. The great warrior Aniruddha was born of Rukmavatī.

23.10 Being directed by (Uṣā) Bāṇa's daughter, Citralekhā kidnapped him; and on account of him, the thousand-armed Bāṇa became a two-armed one.

1 Śrīdhara notes the popular objection that one should not dine with the enemy (*dviṣad annaṁ na bhoktavyam*) and not the real object of *dharma-śāstra* which discourages in-breeding by prohibiting cross-cousin marriages. VB quotes:

mātā pitāmahī yasya tathaiva prapitāmahī /
tisra eka-kule jātāḥ so'bhiśasto nigadyate //

in such a matrimonial alliance, Rukmī, with the desire of pleasing his sister to whom he was bound by the ties of affection, gave his grand-daughter Rocanā to Hari's grandson (Rukmī's daughter's son).

26. For the marriage ceremony, Rukmiṇī, Balarāma, Kṛṣṇa, Sāmba, Pradyumna and others went to the city of Bhojakaṭa.

27. When the marriage ceremony was over, some haughty kings like Dantavakra of Kaliṅga and others urged Rukmī, "Completely vanquish Balarāma in the play of dice".

28. Though ignorant of the game of dice, Balarāma is strongly addicted to it, O king." Thus advised, Rukmī invited Balarāma to play dice and played at dice.

29. In that game, Balarāma consecutively staked wagers of one hundred, one thousand, ten thousand (coins of gold) and Rukmī won them all. At that time the king of Kaliṅga laughed loudly at Balarāma, displaying his teeth—(an insult) with which Balarāma, the wielder of the plough, could not put up.

30. Then Rukmī staked one lakh (coins) as a bet which Balarāma now won. But resorting to deceit, Rukmī asserted, "I am the winner".

31. Agitated with anger like the swelling ocean under the full moon, the glorious Balarāma whose eyes were naturally reddish, became fiery with extreme rage and he staked a wager of ten crores (of gold coins).

32. As per rules of that game, Balarāma rightly won that bet. But Rukmī resorted to false pretext and said, "I have won the bet. Let the umpires declare their decision".

32-A. *VJ's Text* :

"So be it" said Dantavakra of Kaliṅga showing his teeth (grinning) at Balarāma. Balarāma boiled with rage but (controlled himself and) observed silence.

33. Thereupon a voice from the heaven declared. "As per rules of the game, the wager is properly won by Balarāma. What Rukmī says is false."

34. Ignoring the declaration from the heaven, Rukmī, being instigated by wicked kings and impelled so by his (impend-

ing) death, laughed loudly at Saṅkarṣaṇa (Balarāma) and spoke to him.

35. "You are after-all cowherds ranging over the forests and not experts at the play of dice. Kings like us play with dice and with arrows (i.e. fight) and not persons (cowherds) like you."

36. When thus humiliated by Rukmī and ridiculed by kings, Balarāma flew in rage and taking up an iron bar[1], struck Rukmī down in the assembly of kings.

37. He vehemently caught hold of the (flying) king of Kaliṅga on the tenth pace and angrily knocked out his teeth exhibiting which he laughed at him.

38. Other kings with their arms, thighs and heads broken, chopped off and bathed in blood when struck with the iron bar by Balarāma, fled away in terror.

39. When His brother-in-law Rukmī was slain, Hari being afraid of alienating the relation with his queen Rukmiṇī and brother Balarāma, expressed no remark for or against the incident.

40. Seating Aniruddha along with Suryā in an excellent chariot, Balarāma and others from the Dāśārha clan of whom Lord Kṛṣṇa was the mainstay, and who had accomplished all their objects, left Bhojakaṭa and journeyed to Dvārakā (Kuśasthalī).

CHAPTER SIXTY TWO[2]

Aniruddha taken captive by Bāṇāsura

The King Parīkṣit submitted:

1. The best of Yadus (Aniruddha) married Uṣā, the daughter of Bāṇa. On this occasion a terrible and very great combat took place between Lord Hari and god Śaṅkara. O

1. v.l. with the dice-board-VJ.
2. Not traced in VJ.'s Text.

great yogin! May you be pleased to describe to me in details this episode.[1]

Śrī Śuka narrated:

2. Bāṇa was the eldest of the hundred sons of the great-souled Bali who donated in charity the whole of the earth to to Lord Hari who presented himself before him in the form of Vāmana (a dwarf, a Brāhmaṇa boy).

3. Balī's own son Bāṇa was always engaged in devotion to god Śiva. He was respectable, generous, intelligent, true of word and firm in observance of vows.

4. Formerly, he used to rule over his kingdom from the beautiful city of Śoṇitapura[2] as its capital. By the grace of god Śiva even those celestials (the sworn enemies of *Asuras*) behaved with him as his servants. Endowed with a thousand arms as he was, he pleased god Śiva (the world-delighter) by playing upon musical instruments while god Śiva performed his Tāṇḍava[3] dance.

5. The glorious god Śiva, the Lord of all beings, worthy of seeking shelter, who is affectionate to his votaries, asked Bāṇa to seek any boon. Bāṇa begged of him to be the guardian deity of his capital.

1. The Vrindāvan edition records the following verse from the Text of VT. and other commentators of Gauḍīya Vaiṣṇava school.

1A. Bāṇa was the eldest out of the hundred sons of the noble-souled Bali. Being endowed with a thousand arms, he pleased god Śiva by playing on a musical instrument while the latter performed his Tāṇḍava dance.

2. Assames claim Tejapur as the Śoṇitapur of Bāṇa. But the route followed by Kṛṣṇa in his expedition against Bāṇa and its siege etc. (as given in *Harivaṁśa*), show that Śoṇitapur in Kumaun on the back of Kedār-gaṅgā about 6 miles from Uṣāmaṭha near Gupta Kāśi has better claims to be this Śoṇitapur-GDAM p. 189.

3. According to Bharata, the sage Taṇḍu was its initiator. But later as *Śabdārthacintāmaṇi* notes it came to be applied to all male dances and dancing by women was called *lāsya*. It implies violent type of dance in which Rudra indulges at the end of *yugas*. The violent effect of this dance is expressed in the Ist verse (Maṅgala) of *Matsya P.* as follows:

Pracaṇḍa-tāṇḍavāṭope Prakṣiptā yena dig-gajāḥ |
bhavantu vighna-bhaṅgāya Bhavasya caraṇāmbujāḥ ||

Matsya P. 1.1

6. On one occasion, Bāṇa who was madly elated with his prowess, touched with his crown brilliant like the sun, the lotus-feet of god Śiva who (as the presiding deity of his capital) was near to him and said:

7. "I bow to you, O great God, the preceptor and the highest Ruler of the world, the Wish-yielding tree fulfilling the desires of persons whose longings are not satisfied.

8. The (boon of) thousand arms conferred by you have resulted into a burden to me; for I do not find an equal combatant (against me in the three worlds excepting you).

9. With my arms itching for a fight and being impelled by eagerness to combat, I marched against the elephants (supporting the world) at the end of cardinal points, crushing down the mountains on the way. But being terrified, the elephants hastily took to flight, O Ancient-most Person".

10. Hearing this (arrogant speech), the glorious god Śiva got enraged and told him, "When your flag-staff (with the peacock ensign) shall be broken down automatically, your combat with some one equal to me will take place and it will humiliate (break down) your pride, O stupid fellow".

11. Thus snubbed, the Asura with perverse mentality became delighted and repaired to his place. The crooked-minded fellow was waiting for the fulfilment of Śiva's augery which indicated a crushing blow to his prowess.

12. He had a daughter called Uṣā. Virgin as she was, in dream, she enjoyed sexual pleasure with Aniruddha, the son of Pradyumna as her beloved consort whom she had never seen or heard of.

13. Not finding him there near her (after opening her eyes), she got up in a bewildered state, exclaiming "Where are you my beloved lord?", in the midst of her girl-companions and was exceedingly abashed.

14. Bāṇa had a minister called Kumbhāṇḍa. His daughter Citralekhā was her bosom-friend. Out of great curiosity, she enquired her friend Uṣā:

15. "Whom are you searching for, O friend with beautiful eyebrows? what is the nature of your desire? As far as I have observed, as yet there has been no suitor to your hand, O princess."

Uṣā narrated :

16. "In my dream I saw an unknown man of dark complexion, lotus-eyed, endowed with (knee-) long arms, wearing a yellow (silken) garment, captivating the hearts of women (capable of enjoying them).

17. I am seeking after him as my beloved Lord who having allowed me to drink the honey of his lips, has gone (to some unknown place) throwing me into the sea of misery even though I am still thirsty (after him)."

Citralekhā said :

18. "I shall remove (the cause of) your grief. If he who captivated your heart exists somewhere in the three worlds, I shall bring that man. Please tell me who it is."

19. Saying thus she drew graphic portraits (of elite youths) of gods, Gandharvas, Siddhas, Cāraṇas, serpents, Daityas, Vidyādharas, Yakṣas and human princes.

20. Out of human beings, she drew the portrait of Vṛṣṇi's : Ugrasena, Vasudeva, Balarāma, Kṛṣṇa. When she saw Pradyumna's portrait, she felt shy.

21. Seeing the carefully painted portrait of Aniruddha she looked down in shyness and exclaimed smilingly, "It is he. It is he." O Ruler of the earth.

22. Citralekhā who was endowed with *yogic* powers knew that he was the grand-son of Kṛṣṇa and through the air, she went to Dvārakā under the protection of Kṛṣṇa, O King.

23. Resorting to her *yogic* powers, she bore Aniruddha, the son of Pradyumna, who was sleeping on an excellent bed and brought him to Śoṇitapura and presented her beloved to her friend, Uṣā.

24. Beholding the most beautiful of beautiful persons, she was extremely rejoiced and in her private apartment which was inaccessible to the eyes of males, she enjoyed herself with the son of Pradyumna.

25. He was respectfully received with excellent garments, wreaths of flowers, perfumes, sweet incense, lights, high seat, with drinks, foods and other eatables, with sweet conversations and personal service.

26. Aniruddha who remained concealed in the princess's apartment, got his senses captivated by Uṣā whose love for him was ever increasing and he did not know how many days rolled away.

27. As she was thus enjoyed by the Yādava hero and lost her virginity, the attendants observed through marks which could be hardly concealed, that she was enjoying specially joyous life.

28. The servants reported to Bāṇa, "O King, from the behaviour of your daughter, we mark that she is casting a stain on your family.

29. Though we were cautiously guarding her, we do not know how such pollution took place in the apartment of your virgin daughter who was closely guarded and was beyond the reach of male eyes."

30. Thereupon Bāṇa who was sorely distressed to hear of his daughter's pollution, hastened immediately to the appartment of his daughter and saw there the best of the Yadus.

31. He saw Aniruddha who was the son of Kāma (Pradyumna), the most beautiful person in the world, dark in complexion, wearing a yellow garment, of lotus eyes, long and mighty arms and with his countenance brightened with the lustre of his ear-rings and locks of hair and was beaming with smiling looks.

32. Bāṇa was shocked to see Aniruddha playing at dice with his beloved daughter who on her part adorned herself with festle ornaments—and wearing between his arms a garland of Jasmine flowers, special to the season of spring, tinged with the saffron on her bosom during his contacts with her person seated in front of her.

33. Seeing Bāṇa enter surrounded with fierce looking soldiers, Aniruddha, the descendent of Madhu, took up an iron bludgeon and took position like Yama, the wielder of the rod determined to finish with any body that may approach him.

34. Like a great boar that kicks away the attacking dogs, he struck them down who attacked him on all sides with

the intention of arresting him. Beaten thus by him, they ran out of Uṣā's palace with their heads, thighs and arms broken.

35. The powerful son of Bali got angry with Aniruddha who was striking down his soldiers and he bound him down with *Nāgapāśa* (serpent-like cords).

36. Uṣā was overwhelmed with grief and despondency to see him bound with the cords of *Nāga* and wept loudly with tears flowing down her eyes.

CHAPTER SIXTYTHREE

Bāṇa Vanquished. Aniruddha brought to Dvārakā

Śrī Śuka said :

1. And thus passed away the four months of the rainy season, while the relatives of Aniruddha, (being unable to trace him) missed him and were grieving for him (for his disappearance), O descendant of Bharata !

2. Learning from Nārada, the report of Aniruddha's valorous fight and his imprisonment, Vṛṣṇis who looked upon Kṛṣṇa as their presiding deity, speedily marched against Śoṇitapura, the capital of Bāṇa.

3-4. Pradyumna, Yuyudhāna, Gada, Sāmba and Sāraṇa, Nanda, Upananda, Bhadra and others—all loyal followers of Balarāma and Kṛṣṇa—these prominent Sātvata heroes accompanied with twelve *akṣauhiṇīs* of army, laid close siege to the city of Bāṇa, on all sides.

5. Noticing that the parks of the city, fortifications, gates, balconies and towers were shattered down, Bāṇa was fired with rage and taking with him an equally strong army, sallied forth out of the city.

6. The worshipful god Rudra surrounded by the Pramathas and accompanied by his son Skanda, rode his big bull and fought with Balarāma and Kṛṣṇa for the sake of Bāṇa.

7. The combat that raged between Kṛṣṇa and Śaṅkara and the duel between Pradyumna and Guha (Kārttikeya) was

tumultuous, astounding and horripilating (making the hair stand on the ends).

8. There was an encounter between Balarāma with Kumbhāṇḍa and Kūpakarṇa; and a duel between Sāmba and the son of Bāṇa, and between Bāṇa and Sātyaki.

9. Great gods like Brahmā and others, sages, Siddhas, Cāraṇas, Gandharvas (celestial singers) heavenly damsels, Yakṣas came in their aerial cars to witness the wonderful battle.

10-11. With sharp-pointed shafts discharged from his Śārṅga bow, Kṛṣṇa put to flight the followers of god Śiva viz. goblins, Pramathas, Yakṣas, Dākinīs, Yātudhānas, Vināyakas, Vetālas, and ghosts, Mātṛkas, Piśācas Kūṣmāṇḍas and Brahma-rākṣasas.

12. God Śiva, the wielder of Pināka bow, discharged various kinds of missiles on Kṛṣṇa, the wielder of Śārṅga bow. Śrī Kṛṣṇa, without expressing any surprise, neutralised each and every missile of Śiva by his counter-missiles.

13. He nullified Brahmāstra with a Brahmāstra, Vāyavyāstra (missile creating stormy winds) with Parvatāstra (a missile surrounding the winds by mountain-like obstacles), the Agnyastra (the fire missile) with the rain missile and Rudra's special Pāśupata missile with his own Nārāyaṇāstra.

14. Then Śrī Kṛṣṇa stupefied god Śiva by making him yawn and lethargic with Jṛmbhaṇāstra (yawning missile) and in the meanwhile slaughtered Bāṇa's army with his sword, mace and arrows.

15. Skanda being pierced on all sides by the streams of arrows discharged by Pradyumna and bleeding in every part of the body, retreated from the battle on the back of his peacock.

16. Kumbhāṇḍa and Kūpakarṇa fell down pounded by the pestle of Balarāma and their armies with their leaders killed, ran away in all directions.

17. Noticing his army shattered and scattered in this way, Bāṇa became extremely enraged. He left his combatant Sātyaki, and in his chariot he rode to and attacked Kṛṣṇa.

18. Simultaneously bending five hundred bows, Bāṇa who was over-proud of his valour, applied a couple of arrows each on each of the bows.

19. The glorious Lord Hari simultaneously snapped all Bāṇa's bows, killed his charioteer, horses and shattered his chariot and blew his conch.

20. Bāṇa had a mother[1] (mother-like presiding deity) called Koṭarā. With a desire to protect the life of her son, she appeared before Kṛṣṇa completely nude with locks of her hair dishevelled.

21. Then (in that situation), Kṛṣṇa turned his face without casting a look at the naked deity. In the meanwhile, Bāṇa whose chariot was broken and bows cut down, retreated to his capital.

22. When all the army of Bhūtas (goblins etc.) fledaway, Jvara (Śiva's fever) having three heads and three feet, rushed at Kṛṣṇa burning down as it were, all the ten cardinal points.

22A. And he appeared in the battle in front of Kṛṣṇa.

23. Thereupon the refulgent god Nārāyaṇa had a look at that Jvara and let loose against him his own (Vaiṣṇava) Fever. In this way the Śaiyite and Vaiṣṇavite fevers fought with each other.

24. Severely beaten by the fever commanded by Viṣṇu, the Śaivite fever screamed loudly. He could not find any shelter from fear. Being terribly afraid, the fever commanded by Śiva sought refuge with Kṛṣṇa and folding his palm praised him.

Jvara prayed :

25. I bow to you, Lord of infinite potency, the controller of great gods (like Brahmā and others), the Soul of all (the universe). One without a second, (of the nature of) Absolute Consciousness, the Cause of the creation, subsistence and dissolution of the universe, you are what is known as the Brahman which is indicated by the Vedas (but not cognised directly), absolutely serene, subject to no modification.

26. (You, being beyond all attributes, are the Lord of all). The Time-spirit (that impels action), Providence (resultant from the *karma* or action), *Karma*, *Svabhāva* (the natural propensities as a result of *Karma*), substance (subtle elements),

1. The name of Bāṇa's real mother was Aśanā. VT clarifies that according to V.P. *Koṭarī* was the family deity of Daityas.

the body, Prāṇa (vital breath called *Sūtra*), the Ego, modifications (viz. eleven senses—10 conative and cognitive senses+1 mind, the internal organ) and the combination of these evolutes called the *Liṅga* or subtle body which sets in motion the stream of cause-effect relation like that of the seed and the tree—all is your Māyā. I seek shelter in you in whom there is negation of Māyā.

27. Sportively assuming various incarnations (as Fish, Tortoise, Boar etc.) you protect the gods, saintly persons who abide by the *dharma* (duties prescribed for their respective class and stage in life) and for their protection you exterminate those who deviate from the righteous path and live by committing violence. This incarnation of yours is intended for lessening the burden of the earth.

28. I am being consumed by the extremely unbearable, terrible, deadly cold fever created by your irresistible energy. Corporeal beings have to suffer, so long as they, remaining enmeshed in desires, do not take shelter at the soles of your feet.

The Lord said :

29. "Oh Triśira ! (three-headed fever) I am pleased with you. May your fear from my fear be set at rest. May he who remembers our conversation, be free from fear from you."

30. Thus ordered the Śaivite Fever bowed down to Lord Kṛṣṇa and departed. But Bāṇa mounting his chariot advanced and fought with Kṛṣṇa.

31. Then equipped with various weapons in each of his arm, Bāṇa who was extremely enraged, discharged a volley of arrows on the Lord with the discus as his weapon, O king !

32. While Bāṇa was discharging missiles, the Lord amputated with his discus, the sharp razor-like felly, the arms of Bāṇa, like branches of a tree.

33. While Bāṇa's arms were thus being lopped off, the worshipful god Śiva who was compassionate to his devotee approached Kṛṣṇa and requested him as follows :

Rudra submitted :

34. (It is not surprising that Bāṇa fights with you as he is unaware of your real nature, for you are the veritable

Brahman, the Supreme Light lying concealed in the Vedas (which are the Brahman revealed in verbal form). You reveal yourself to sages and hence those sages of pure heart realize you to be all-pervading and pure as the sky and (eternally) absolute.

35. You are indeed the Cosmic Man (*Virāṭ puruṣa*) that comprise within you (as parts of your body) all the universe. Thus the sky is your navel; the fire, your mouth; water, your seminal fluid; the heavenly region, your head; the cardinal points, your ears; the earth, your feet; the moon your mind; the Sun, your eye; myself (viz. Rudra), your Ego (*ahaṁkāra*); the seas, your belly; Indra (and other protectors of the world), your arms;

36. Herbs and plants are your hair on the body; clouds, the locks of your hair; god Brahmā, your intellect; the procreator of the worlds, your generative organ; and Dharma (the god upholding righteousness), your heart. (But this Bāṇa does not know this Cosmic Personality of yours).

37. This incarnation of yours, O Lord of undiminished glory and power (or who stay eternally in Go-loka), is for the protection of righteousness and for the prosperity of the world. All of us (protectors of various spheres) are delegated powers by you and hence we (can) protect the seven spheres of the universe.

38. You are the one without a second, the First Person (beyond all persons belonging to the three states), pure, self-luminous through knowledge, the cause of all but yourself without any cause, the controller (of the universe). Yet you manifest your self through your Māyā as an individual Soul (in every being be it gods, men or subhuman beings) and throw light on everything.

39. O Perfect Lord ! Just as the Sun, covered under his own shadow (viz. clouds, his creation) illuminates both the clouds as well as other forms, you, though the Self-luminous, get concealed under the *guṇas* (viz. Ego) and yet make all the *guṇas* and their products shine (with your light).

40. With their intellect deluded by your Māyā, men are attached to their sons, wives, houses and other belongings and they sink and come up again in the sea of misery (*saṁsāra*)

41. He who, after obtaining this human body (birth) through the Grace of the God, does not worship respectfully your feet, is certainly a self-deceiver fit to be pitied.

42. The mortal man who, for the sake of sense objects which are worthless and hollow, neglects you who are the beloved Soul and the Ruler of the world, consumes poison throwing aside the nectar.

43. I myself, god Brahmā, celestials and sages of pure heart have with all our heart and soul resorted to you who are the most beloved Soul and the controller of the world.

44. In order to get Liberation from *saṁsāra*, we seek asylum in you and worship you who are the cause of creation, subsistence and dissolution of the world, equal to all, serene, a beloved friend and deity. You are One without a second, the only goal, the one abode of all the world.

45. O god, this Bāṇāsura is my dear devotee deeply attached to me and much liked by me. Full protection has been promised by me to him. Therefore, may Your Grace be extended to him as you did in the case of Prahlāda, the king of Daityas.

The Lord said :

46. O worshipful Śiva ! We shall comply with whatever you have requested us and what is pleasing to you. Whatever you have decided (about Bāṇa) has my full approval.

47. This Asura is the son of Bali and as such I should not kill him. I have conferred a boon on Prahlāda that none of his descendants would be killed by me.

48. It was just to curb his arrogance that his arms have been lopped off by me. And his big army is annihilated because it was a burden to the earth.

49. The four arms that are left to him (Bāṇa) shall not suffer from age or destruction. From no quarters this Asura need entertain any fear and he shall be your attendant.

50. Having thus secured protection, the Asura bowed to Kṛṣṇa with his head and brought Aniruddha, the son of Pradyumna along with his bride, placing them in a chariot.

51. Placing in the van, Aniruddha and his bride who were clad in excellent dress, decked with ornaments and guarded by an *akṣauhiṇi* of soldiers, Kṛṣṇa set out with compliments from Rudra.

52. He entered His capital (Dvārakā) which was tastefully decorated with flags and ornamental arches, and had its streets and quadrangles thoroughly besprinkled with water. He was warmly received by the citizens, friends, relatives and Brāhmaṇas, with the blowing of conchs and sounding of drums and kettle-drums.

53. He who rising early at dawn, recalls and contemplates on the story of combat between Śrī Kṛṣṇa and god Śaṅkara and Kṛṣṇa's final triumph, will never meet any defeat in life.

CHAPTER SIXTYFOUR

The Story of Nṛga[1]

Śrī Śuka said :

1. On one occasion Sāmba, Pradyumna, Cāru, Bhānu, Gada and other princes of the Yadu clan went to a park for sports and entertainment.

2. Having played there for a long time, they felt very thirsty. While in search of water, they found a dry well and noticed a strange animal in it.

3. Observing that it is a lizard as big as a hill, they marvelled in their minds. Moved with pity, they tried to lift it out.

4. The boys tied the animal fallen (in the well) with leather thongs and ropes of fiber but were unable to lift it up.

1. Nṛga, a son of Ikṣvāku, was very famous for his generosity and performance of sacrifices (MBH, *Sabha* 8.8, *Vana*. 88.5-6, 121.1-2). Due to oversight, he gifted a cow twice for which he was cursed to be a chameleon (MBH *Anu*. 70.10-28, also *Vāl. Rām*. 7.24, 7.53).

Overcome with curiosity and surprise, they reported the matter to Śrī Kṛṣṇa.

5. The lotus-eyed glorious Lord Kṛṣṇa, the creator and protector of the world, went there (to the well). Peeping at it he sportively lifted it up by his left hand.

6. Being touched by the hand of the Lord of hallowing renown, the being instantly shuffled off his body of a chameleon and was transformed into a heavenly being adorned with wonderful ornaments, garments, and garland of flowers and distinguished by a complexion (bright) like molten gold.

6A. *VJ's Text adds* :

He bowed down to the lotus-feet of Lord Mukunda (Kṛṣṇa) with his head and lay prostrate before him.

7. Although Mukunda (Kṛṣṇa) was omniscient (and as such knew the reason), he enquired of him (the newly transformed god) with a view to making known to the public the cause of his birth in the species of lizards "Who are you, O glorious person blessed with most excellent personality. I believe you must be a great god.

8. My good friend ! What act of yours brought you to such a wretched plight which you certainly did not deserve. We are curious to hear your story. Be pleased to narrate it to us if you deem us worthy of being told."

Śrī Śuka said :

9. When the king (Nṛga) was thus accosted by Kṛṣṇa of infinite forms (Kṛṣṇa, the embodiment of Bliss), he bowed down to the Lord of Lakṣmī with his crown radiant like the Sun, and spoke:

Nṛga submitted :

10. O Lord ! I am a king called Nṛga, the son of Ikṣvāku. My name might have reached your ears if a list of liberal donors has been (at any time) mentioned to you.

11. What is there that is unknown to you who abide as a witness in the hearts of all ? And your vision and knowledge are unobstructed by Time. It is, however, in obedience to your command that I recount my history.

12. I donated as religious gift to Brāhmaṇas as many cows as there are sand-grains on the earth or as many as there are stars in the heavens or as many drops in the showers of rain.

13. All those cows were youthful, milk-yielding, possessed of good nature, of beautiful form and excellent breed. They were tawny in colour, had their horns plated in gold and hoofs in silver. They were gifted along with their calves all duly covered with silk garment, garlands and ornaments. And everyone of them was legitimately obtained by me (by paying their price in well-earned money).

14. I used to give them to youthful prominent Brāhmaṇas possessing excellent qualities and noble character; who, though coming from proverty-stricken families, were noted for their vow of truthfulness and were endowed with penance, learning or knowledge of the Vedas, spiritual lore and generosity.

15. I gave as religious gifts cows, lands, gold, houses, horses, elephants, girls (in marriage) alongwith maid-servants, a lot of sesamum seeds, silver, beds, garments, precious stones, utensils and furniture (necessary) for (unfurnished) houses as well as chariots. I performed a number of sacrifices and constructed wells, tanks and other works of social welfare.

16. (On one occasion) a cow belonging to a prominent Brāhmaṇa strayed and mingled in the herd of my cattle. Not being aware of this, it was gifted by me to another Brāhmaṇa.

17. As the cow was being taken away, the original owner of the cow saw it and asserted to him, "This cow belongs to me". The recepient of the cow as a gift argued, "The cow is mine, for king Nṛga has given it to me as a religious gift".

18. Both the disputant Brāhmaṇas, each trying to establish his claim, (approached me and) said, "You are the donor of the cow to me". The other asserted, "In that case, you have lifted my cow." And I became confused and embarrassed to hear their claims.

19. Caught in such a religious predicament, I tried to conciliate them with a humble entreaty. "I shall give a hundred thousand excellent cows (all better than this). Please give in exchange this cow.

20. Both of you be pleased to condone this fault which has been unknowingly committed by me—your humble servant. Be pleased to lift me up from this difficult situation whereby I shall be falling in a dirty hell.

21. The original owner of the cow declared, "I am not willing to accept (your offer at all) and he left. The other (new recepient owner) went away saying, "I do not wish to have ten thousand cows in exchange for this cow."

VR.'s Text adds :

21A. O Supreme Lord ! May be due to your Māyā power or your will expressed through force of time, I died. O Lord ! I narrate in your presence where I was taken away by the force of my destiny.

22. O God of gods ! In the meanwhile (after death) I was carried away by the messenger of Yama to Yama's abode. O Lord of the world ! I was asked there by the god of death :

23. "Would you like to reap the fruit of your evil acts first or would you like to enjoy the fruits of your meritorious acts first. I do not see the limit of the charitable and religious acts performed by you nor of the glorious world that you have attained thereby."

24. I said, "O god ! I shall first suffer for my inauspicious acts". He commanded, "Fall down" and immediately I fell and while falling, I found myself transformed into a lizard, O Almighty Lord.

25. O Keśava ! I am your servant (devotee) who have been friendly and charitable to Brāhmaṇas. I have been earnestly craving and striving to have your direct revelation. It is hence that my memory is still unblurred.

26. O Omnipresent Lord ! You are beyond the ken of sense perception. You are the Supreme Soul to be contemplated and visualized in their pure hearts with the help of the 'eye' (knowledge) of *Upaniṣads* by masters of *yoga*. (Such as you

are) I am amazed as to how you came directly within the range of my sight—I whose reason is blinded by extreme miseries—for, you are visualized by those who are to be emancipated from *saṁsāra* (Hence I believe I shall be released and this is my last birth).

27-28. O God of gods ! Lord of the world ! O Govinda (protector of cows or master of senses) ? O Supreme Man ! O Nārāyaṇa ! O Hṛṣīkeśa (the Master of Sense-organs; their prime mover) ! O Lord of hallowing renown ! O Infallible Lord ! O Immutable God ! O Kṛṣṇa ! Give me leave to return to my celestial state. O Lord ! (I pray) wherever I may be (i.e. in whatever species I be born) my mind have asylum at your feet.

29. Hail to you the source (creator) of everything ! The Master of Māyā potency ! The final resort (or abode) of all beings ! O Kṛṣṇa,[1] the Lord of all yogas, I bow down to you. (Though I am unwilling to part from you of above description, I take my leave of you to enjoy the fruits of actions conferred upon me by you".

30. Submitting to him this prayer, Nṛga circumambulated him and touched the feet of the Lord with his diadem. With his permission, he ascended an excellent aerial car, even as all people were looking on.

31. Lord Kṛṣṇa ! The son of Devakī, the God who is friendly to Brāhmaṇas—nay the very Dharma *incarnate*—spoke to person around him with a view to instruct those born in Kṣattriya class.

32. "The property of Brāhmaṇas, howsoever little it may be, if misappropriated, is indigestible even to the Fire-god (i.e. a person of immeasurable power and glory like the Fire god); what need be said that it is certainly so in the case of kings who, out of (empty) pride, regard themselves as the rulers (of the world).

33. I do not consider the most deadly poison *Halāhala* as the real fatal poison, as there is an antidote against it. But

1. ŚR. quotes a *Smṛti* (Purāṇic ?) source which interpretes Kṛṣṇa as *Brahman*.

Kṛṣir bhū-vācakaḥ śabdaḥ ṇaśca nirvṛti-vācakaḥ !
tayor aikyam param Brahma Kṛṣṇa ityabhidhīyate ||

the property of a Brāhmaṇa (if misappropriated) is the real poison, as it cannot be counteracted by any remedy in the world.

34. Poison kills (only one person viz.) the swallower. The fire is extinguished with water. But the fire ignited out of churning the *Araṇis* in the form of (misappropriated) Brāhmaṇa property burns the whole race along with its roots.

35. A Brāhmaṇa's property used without his (willing) permission (or with permission under duress) ruins three generations (the enjoyer, his son and grandson). But if usurped and enjoyed per force, it spells disaster to ten generations of ancestors (by forcing them to hell) and ten generation of successors after him.

36.* Kings blinded with the pride of their sovereign power and affluence, are incapable of seeing their own fall. Those kings who regard it good to covet Brāhmaṇa's property which is a veritable hell, are fools.

37-38. Those uncontrolled dictatorial monarchs, their descendants and relatives who deprive Brāhmaṇas of bountiful nature but with large family responsibilities, of their means of livelihood and their property are subjected to torture (*lit.* are cooked) in the hell called *Kumbhipāka*[1] for as many years as the number of particles of earth moistened by the tears shed by those Brāhmaṇas while crying.

39. He who confiscates the means of livelihood of a Brāhmaṇa irrespective of its being donated to him by himself or by another person, becomes a worm in the faeces for sixty thousand years.

40. (I strongly wish that) I may not come in possession of the wealth or property of a Brāhmaṇa (at any time and in any way), by coveting which people are cut short in their prime, kings become defeated and are deprived of their kingdoms and (after death) are born as formidable serpents.

* VR. construes differently: Those kings who regard it good to covet the property of a Brāhmaṇa are blinded by sovereign power and wealth, They do not foresee and think over their falling into the hell. They are extremely stupid.

1. One of the 28 hells in which the wicked are baked like potter's arthen-ware or are immersed in boiling oil.

41. O my kinsmen ! Abstain from hatred or injury (in retaliation) to a Brāhmaṇa who has offended you, attacked you or reproached you (with words of abuse). Always pay them your respects.

42. Just as I bow to Brāhmaṇas regularly with a calm and collected mind, similarly you also salute to them. He who fails to do so, shall be recepient of the punishment at my hands.

43. The property of Brāhmaṇa, even though misappropriated without being aware of it, brings about the downfall of the sinner just as the cow of the Brāhmaṇa brought about the fall of king Nṛga though he was ignorant of misappropriation."

44. Having thus taught (*dharma*) with the actual demonstration (of Nṛga's case) to the residents of Dvārakā, the glorious Lord Mukunda who hallows all (beings in all) worlds, entered his palace.[1]

CHAPTER SIXTYFIVE

Balarāma's Visit to Gokula—The Course of the Yamunā diverted

Śrī Śuka said:

1. (On one occasion) the glorious Lord Balarāma became eagerly desirous of seeing his friends and well-wishers (at Vraja). Mounting his chariot, he proceeded[2] to Gokula ruled over by Nanda, O the most prominent Kuru.

1. *Here VJ.'S Text adds*:

44.1 Association with the righteous persons will never fail to bear fruit, O King Parīkṣit. It was by virtue of his companionship with the pious that king Nṛga was released from hell (i.e. hellish life).

44.2 As with sacred places, everything done in relation to the righteous—their sight, touch, glorification, remembrance—brings about purification.

44.3 As you have listened to this, O chastiser of enemies, you should always (try to) adore the saintly people. If you desire to have the final emancipation, the property of a Brāhmaṇa should never be misappropriated by you.

2. *Pra-yayau*—went after wearing the dress of a Gopa (cowherd) —VT. It quotes HV. in its support and informs us that Balarāma went to convey the massage of Kṛṣṇa.

2. Balarāma was warmly embraced by Gopa men and women (at Vraja) who were yearning (to see him) for a pretty long period. He bowed to his (foster) parents Nanda and Yaśodā who welcomed him with blessings (and said):

3. "O Balarāma (of the Dāśārha clan)! May you, the Lord of the universe along with your younger brother Kṛṣṇa, protect us for a long time (just as you do to Yādavas)". With these words, they placed him on their lap, hugged him and bathed him with tears.

4. He paid respects to elderly Gopas with due formalities and was bowed down by his juniors in age. He met other Gopas (observing courteous exchanges) according to their age, friendly intimacy and according to their (respective) relations (with him).

5. He then approached the cowherds,[1] cut jokes and laughed with them, held them by hands, (expressed other friendly gestures). When he had taken rest and was refreshed, they gathered and seated themselves round him as he was comfortably seated.

6. The Gopas who had renounced their worldly pleasures for Śrī Kṛṣṇa of lotus—(petal-like) eyes were enquired about their health and of their relatives in a voice choked with emotions (and in faltering accents). They also reciprocally enquired about the health of Yādavas as per their relations).

7. "Are all our friends and relatives (at Dvārakā) hail and hearty, O Balarāma? Now that you are a married person blessed with children, do you (occasionally) remember us?

8. Luckily the wicked Kaṁsa has been slain and it is fortunate that all our friends and well-wishers are liberated (from his atrocious rule). It is really a matter of good luck that after killing and vanquishing your enemies, you have taken your abode in an inaccessible place (Dvārakā)".

9. Gopīs looked upon Balarāma's visit as an honour and paid respect to him (In spite of their pangs of separation from

1. VT. carefully collects evidence of the visits of Balarāma and Kṛṣṇa from VP. & HV. and points out that they used to visit at intervals when they happened to come to that side.

Kṛṣna) they beamed with a smile and asked, "Is Kṛṣṇa, the darling of ladies in the city (as against us—rustic women), happy?

10. Does he occasionally remember his friends, (like the Gopa-Dāman and others), father (Nanda) and mother (Yaśodā) at Vraja? Will he come at least once to see his mother (Yaśodā)? Does that mighty-armed Lord ever remember our modest service (or constant devotion to him)?

11. It is for his sake, O Balarāma that we abandoned our parents, brothers, husbands, sons, sisters and relatives whom it was hard to forsake.

12. Instantly he cut asunder. the bonds of friendship with us who were so beloved to him and he abandoned us forthwith. (The cause of our not preventing him from going was his fascinatingly sweet) words—what woman would hesitate to put forth faith in them?

13. (Some Gopīs asked): How would the wise and shrewd women of the town trust the words of that fickle-minded and ungrateful person? (Others replied:) When he provokes the passion of love in them by his fascinating words, his winning smiles and enticing looks, those women being overpowered with love, put faith in his wonderful speech.

14. (Some said): O Gopīs! What have we to do with the talk about him? Tell some other stories. (Drop all references to Kṛṣṇa). If his time can pass (happily) without us, our time (reciprocally) can do so without him (though in pangs of separation from him)".

15. Recalling in this way the smiles, sweet words, winsome looks, gait, loving embraces of Kṛṣṇa, those Gopa women wept bitterly.

16. The worshipful Lord Balarāma, past-master in the various ways of consoling, comforted them by conveying to them massages of Śrī Kṛṣṇa which were most soothing to their heart.[1]

1. *Sandeśaiḥ sāma-madhuraiḥ premagarbhairagarvitaiḥ /*
Rāmeṇāśvāsitā Gopyaḥ Kṛṣṇasyātimanoharaiḥ // VP. 5,24.20.

17. The glorious Lord Balarāma spent there (in Gokula) two months (of the spring season)—Caitra and Vaiśākha and entertained the Gopīs at night.

18. Surrounded by a bevy of ladies (Gopīs), Balarāma sported with them in the gardens on the bank of the Yamunā brightly illumined by the rays of the full moon as the gentle breeze charged with the fragrance of night lotuses was blowing.

19. The heavenly beverage called Vāruṇī[1], sent by god Varuṇa began to flow out from the hallow of a tree and filled with its fragrance the whole of the forest.

20. Inhaling the fragrance of that stream of honey (like beverage) wafted by the gentle wind, Balarāma went to that tree and drank it along with the women.

VR's Text adds :

20-A. Glorified in songs and himself bursting out in singing in the circle of beautiful women, he sported himself like Airāvata (Indra's elephant) in company of she-elephants.

20-B. Kettle-drums were sounded in the heavens, the heavenly beings showered flowers on them in delight. Gandharvas and sages glorified Balarāma's exploits in great joy.

21. Balarāma (the plough-armed) whose exploits were glorified in songs by the Gopīs, roved in an inebriated condition in the forest, with his eyes swimming in intoxication.

22-23. Adorned with a wreath of flowers and the special garland of five-coloured flowers called Vaijayantī, wearing one ear-ring only, with a smiling lotus-face beautified with dewy drops of perspiration, in an inebriated condition he commanded the Yamunā to come near him to enable him to indulge in water-sports. Being intoxicated, he thought that the Yamunā insolently disobeyed his order. Balarāma got enraged and forcibly dragged her with the pointed plough-share of his plough.

24. (He threatened her) : "You sinful one ! In total disregard for me you indifferently do not come despite my

1. VB. *Vāruṇī*, born while churning the ocean for nectar, was given to demons. Whatever tree she occupies gives out alcoholic beverage. VT. on the authority of HV. says that Vāruṇī was Varuṇa's daughter and hence not forbidden. Likewise she creates the beverage in the hollow of the Kadamba tree.

summons to you, but go your own way. By the tip of my plough I shall now divert you in a hundred ways".

25. When threatened thus, the river-goddess Yamunā became afraid and fell at his feet. Trembling with fear she spoke to the delight of the Yadus.

26. "O Balarāma, the Delight of the world! O mighty-armed hero! I did not know your prowess. O Lord of the world, (I now know) that it is with your one *aṁśa* (part) only, viz. Śeṣa that you support the universe.

27. O Soul of the universe so kind to his votaries! I have come to seek asylum in you, O glorious Lord. It behoves you to set me free (to flow in my own bed) as I did not know your supreme greatness."

28. Thus entreated, the mighty Balarāma then let go the Yamunā. And just like a king elephant entering water with his mates, he entered the waters (of the Yamunā) with the women (Gopīs).

29. After having sported to his hearts content (in the water), Balarāma emerged from her waters when Kānti[1] (a form of goddess Lakṣmī) presented to him two clothes of non-white (blue) colour, highly precious ornaments and an auspicious (brilliant) garland.

30. Putting on those blue garments, wearing the gold necklace, he shone like Airāvata, Indra's elephant, when painted and tastefully ornamented.

31. Even to this day, the Yamunā is seen to flow through the track (river bed) through which the Yamunā was dragged. It is an index of the great prowess of Balarāma of infinite prowess.

32. Balarāma's mind was fascinated with the sweet qualities of the young women of Vraja, so he felt all nights passed in sports at Vraja as one continuous night.

1. ŚR. quotes VP 5.25.16 and states that Kānti is a synonym of Lakṣmī while VT. regards her as a form of Lakṣmī, the Spouse of the second Vyūha Saṅkarṣaṇa.

CHAPTER SIXTYSIX

Slaying of Pauṇḍraka and others[1]

Śrī Śuka said :

1. When Balarāma had gone to the Vraja under Nanda's control, the ruler of the country called Karuṣa[2] being full of ignorance, sent to Kṛṣṇa a messenger declaring ' I am (the real) Vāsudeva.'

2. "You are the glorious Lord Vāsudeva, the ruler and the protector of the universe who have incarnated (for the protection of the world)". Thus flattered by foolish people, he really came to believe that he was the Imperishable Lord.

3. And the dull-witted fellow (being ignorant of the real greatness of Kṛṣṇa) sent an emissary to Lord Kṛṣṇa of inscrutable ways, at Dvārakā, even as an ignorant boy who is set up as a king by other (equally ignorant) children in children's play would do.

4. The messenger on his part arrived at Dvārakā and conveyed the following message of his king to the Almighty lotus-eyed Kṛṣṇa as he was attending the court-assembly.

5. " I am the only one Vāsudeva who have descended (as an incarnation on the earth) for showing compassion to all created beings. There is no other Vāsudeva. Hence you relinquish your false title.

6. O Sātvata ! Whatever emblems of ours (such as Kaustubha Vanamālā, conch, a discus etc.) you bear out of your stupidity, renounce them and come to me for shelter. If not, give a fight with me."

1. The same as Puṇḍra or North Bengal especially district of Malda and the adjoining area-*GDAMI*, pp. 95 & 161.

2. *Kauṭalīya Arthaśāstra* notes its fame for excellent elephants. D.C. Sircar however identifies Karuṣa with Shahabad region of South West Bihar (*SGAMI*-332-35). This explains Pauṇḍraka Vāsudeva's friendship with the King of Vārāṇasī and his stay at Vārāṇasī whence he advanced against Kṛṣṇa.

Śrī Śuka said :

7. Hearing that boasting of that puny-minded king Pauṇḍraka Ugrasena and other members of the assembly laughed loudly.

8. After jocular pleasantries, the glorious Lord replied (through the same) messenger. "O fool, I shall hurl my insignia (such as discus, mace etc.) at you, your emblems and supporters on the strength of which you brag thus (*Or* : I shall relieve you of all your artificial emblems like Sudarśana etc. on the strength of which you are boasting).

9. (As to your demand for my submission to you) It is you who will be the resort (prey) of dogs with that (braggart) mouth of yours shut. You will lie down dead on the battlefield surrounded by kites, vultures and other birds of prey, you fool."

10. The messenger conveyed that defiant censure to his master in full details. Śrī Kṛṣṇa also mounted his chariot, went to Kāśī (where Pauṇḍraka was staying with his friend, the king of Kāśī).

11. Hearing the intelligence of Kṛṣṇa's invasion, even the mighty car-warrior Pauṇḍraka quickly sallied forth from the town (Kāśī) with two *akṣauhiṇīs* of army under his command.

12. His friend, the king of Kāśī followed him to guard his rear with his army of three *akṣauhiṇīs*, O king. Hari espied Pauṇḍraka :

13-14. Who (Pauṇḍraka) was bearing the (replicas of Kṛṣṇa's arms such as) the (Pāñcajanya) conch, the (Nandaka) sword, the (Kaumodakī) mace, the Śārṅga bow; was distinguished by the Śrīvatsa mark (on the chest), was wearing (an artificial) Kaustubha gem and was decorated with Vanamālā. He was clad in two pieces of yellow silk and had an ensign of Garuḍa (on his chariot); he was adorned with a priceless crown and very costly ornaments and was wearing two radiant ear-rings of alligator-shape.

15. Seeing him seated (in the chariot) with an artificial dress similar to His own like an actor on the stage, Lord Hari burst into a heavy laugh.

VJ.'s Text adds :

15A. The battalion of archers of the king of Kāśī, equipped with strong bows, covered Kṛṣṇa with arrows within a moment, just as rain-clouds cover a mountain with water. Some of them were seated on elephants, some on horses and some mounted in chariots, all of them marched forward to the battlefront.

16. The enemies (mercilessly) attacked Hari with darts, maces, iron bars, javelins, *ṛṣṭis* (double-edged swords) different kinds of spears e.g. *Tomara*, swords and arrows.

VJ.'s Text adds :

16A. Another king, a friend of the ruler of Kāśī came to his help with three *akṣauhiṇīs* of army, in that battle.

17. Just as the cosmic fire bursting forth at the end of *yugas*, completely consumes all the categories of creatures, Śrī Kṛṣṇa with his mace, sword, discus and arrows, totally annihilated the armies of Pauṇḍraka and Kāśirāja consisting of elephant-divisions, cavalry, chariots and foot-soldiers.

18. That battlefield was scattered over with (parts and limbs of) chariots, horses, elephants, foot-soldiers, donkeys and camels which were cut down and amputated by his discus. Like the terrible dancing arena of Rudra, the battlefield shone, heartening only the brave.

19. Kṛṣṇa, the descendant of Śūra, (sarcastically) said to Pauṇḍraka, "O Pauṇḍraka, whatever weapons you asked me to surrender through your messenger, I now discharge at you.

20. I shall make you give up my epithet which you have falsely assumed, you ignorant fellow. And if I were not to desire to fight with you, I would seek you as a Protector today".

21. With this sarcastic reply (with reference to Pauṇḍraka's message with his emissary), he deprived Pauṇḍraka of his chariots with his sharp shafts. And just as Indra lopped of the tops (or wings) of mountain, he sundered off the head of Pauṇḍraka with his discus.

22. Similarly, he chopped off with his arrows the head of Kāśirāja from his body and made it fall down in the city of Kāśī like a lotus bud carried with it by wind.

23. Having thus killed the jealous Pauṇḍraka along with his friend Kāśirāja, he entered the city of Dvārakā while his nectarlike sweet exploits were being glorified in songs by Siddhas.

24. Due to the continuous contemplation of Hari, all the (Karma) bondages of Pauṇḍraka were completely annihilated. As he always put on a form similar to that of Hari, he became one with Hari.

25. Seeing the head adorned with ear-rings fallen at the palace-gate, people were puzzled as to what it was and whose head it was.

26. When they came to know that it was the head of their own king, queens, princes, relatives and citizens of Kāśī lamented loudly "Alas. We are undone. O king, O dear Lord, O Lord".

27-28. His crown Prince Sudakṣiṇa performed the funeral rites of his father. He determined, " I shall repay the debt of my father by killing his slayer". Sudakṣiṇa along with his family priest propitiated god Śiva with the deepest meditation.

29. In the holy place of Avimuktaka (or Kāśī), god Śiva who was pleased with him, offered him the boon (of his choice). He sought his desired-most boon, viz. the means to slay his father's slayer.

30-31 (Lord Śiva advised) : 'You should worship the fire known as *Dakṣiṇāgni*[1] (which is also called *ṛtvij*)[2] with the help of Brāhmaṇas according to the procedure prescribed for mastering black magic. That fire surrounded by Pramathas (goblins) will accomplish your purpose like a family priest (*ṛtvij*) appointed for a purpose, provided it is used against a person who is hostile to Brāhmaṇas and is hated by them. (This implies a warning not to use it against a friend of Brāhmaṇas like Kṛṣṇa). Observing strictly the prescribed vows, Sudakṣiṇa obeyed the directions of Śiva (for invoking the malevolent aspect of Dakṣiṇāgni) and directed it against Kṛṣṇa.

1. Out of the three fires maintained in the family, *Dakṣiṇāgni* is to be propitiated for the worship of manes and mastery over black magic (*abhicāra*).

2. *ṛtvij* is an epithet of Agni. vide ṚV 1.1.1 This is one interpretation.

32. As soon as the *abhicāra-prayoga* (sacrifice for mastery over black magic) was completed, there arose from the sacrificial pit, god Agni in person, but in his very terrific form. The locks of his hair, beard and moustaches were of red-hot copper. He was emitting flames of fire from his eyes.

33. He had a very grim appearance with large protruding tusks and staff-like long eyebrows. He was licking the ends of his mouth. He was naked and was brandishing a trident that threw out flames of fire.

34. Surrounded by goblins and setting ablaze all the cardinal points, he rushed against Dvārakā shaking the earth under his strides, with his legs tall as a palm tree.

35. Seeing that *Abhicāra* (malevolent) fire rushing towards them, all the citizens of Dvārakā were terribly afraid like wild beasts at the approach of the forest conflagration.

36. While the glorious Lord was playing dice in the assembly-hall, they ran to him overwhelmed with fear and prayed, "Protect us, O Lord of the three worlds, protect us from the fire that is burning the city".

37. Listening to the (report of that) public calamity and seeing the cause of their panic, the Lord, who is the shelter of his devotees, laughed loudly and assured them : Don't be afraid. I shall be your saviour".

38. The Almighty Lord who is a witness to whatever happens within and without all created beings, came to know it to be the *Kṛtyā* (female form of the malevolent force) of god Śiva and commanded his discus Sudarśana that was by his side, to destroy her.

39. The Sudarśana discus, the missile discharged by Lord Kṛṣṇa was dazzling like millions of Suns (combined). It was flaming forth like the cosmic fire destroying the universe (at the end of *yugas*). It was radiating its brilliant lustre in all directions, the heaven and the earth. It forthwith extinguished that *Abhicāra* fire.

40. Counteracted by the force of the missile (Sudarśana) of Lord Kṛṣṇa, the *Abhicāra* fire called *Kṛtyā* had all its force curbed down and blunted. As if slapped in the face, it turned back, approached Vārāṇasī and burnt down Sudakṣiṇa and his family-priests who directed the *Kṛtyā*.

41-42. Close on its heels, the discus of Viṣṇu entered the city of Vārāṇasī and reduced it to ashes along with its high towers, assembly halls, mansions, market places, towers, enclosures, treasuries, arches, stalls for elephants, horses, chariots, dining halls and kitchens and returned to Dvārakā again and stood by the side of Kṛṣṇa who does everything sportively.

43. The mortal being who listens to this attentively or relates this exploit of the most glorious Lord to others becomes completely absolved of all sins.

VJ.'s Text adds :

43A. Both of them (the narrator and listener of exploits) rid themselves of all sins including heinous ones like Brahmahatyā and when they cast off their body, they proceed to the heaven of Lord Viṣṇu.

CHAPTER SIXTYSEVEN

Balarāma slays Dvivida

King Parīkṣit said :

1. I long to hear again of the wonderful deeds of Balarāma, the possessor of infinite, immeasurable power and miraculous feats. Please narrate what other wondrous deeds he performed.

Śrī Śuka said :

2. There was a monkey called Dvivida, a friend of Narakāsura. He was a counsellor of Sugrīva and a brave and powerful brother of Mainda.

3. In order to avenge the death of his friend Naraka, he caused a great havoc in the country by setting on fire cities, villages, mines and cowherds' camps.

4. Sometimes he uprooted the hills and completely reduced to powder the whole of the Ānarta[1] country where Hari, the slayer of his friend, was living.

1. Western Gujarat with Dvārakā as its capital.

5. He was possessed of the strength of ten thousand elephants. Some times he used to stand in the midst of the sea and create a high tide by dashing up volume of seawater with his arms and drown the coastal area under water.

6. The wicked fellow broke down big trees in the hermitages of the great sages and desecrated the sacrificial fires with urine and excreta.

7. Like a wasp imprisoning a worm the naughty monkey shut up men and women in the valleys and caves of mountains and blocked their entrance with big stones.

8. In this way he wrought havock in the country and ravished women of noble birth. Once, hearing sweet enchanting music, he went to the Raivataka hill.

9. There he espied Balarāma, the Lord of Yadus, wearing a lotus-garland, charming in every limb, standing in the midst of a bevy of beautiful damsels.

10. While singing he was drunk with Vāruṇī and his eyes were swimming with intoxication. He had a brilliant personality and looked like an elephant exuding ichor.

11. The wicked monkey climbed the boughs of the trees and shaking the trees heavily made a chattering sound to attract their notice to his presence.

12. Beholding the insolence of the monkey those young damsels, the spouses of Balarāma, being fickle by nature and fond of fun, burst out into a heavy laughter.

13. In the teeth of Balarāma's presence, the monkey began to insult the damsels by twisting his eyebrows, making wry faces at them and showing them his hind part. Balarāma, the foremost among warriors, got enraged and hurled a big stone at the monkey.

14. But that wily monkey evaded the stone and (swooping down from the trees) took away the pitcher of wine (from Balarāma) and ridiculed Balarāma by laughing loudly and provoking Balarāma's wrath.

15. The wicked monkey dashed down the pitcher of wine, tore the clothes of women. Being puffed up with pride, he treated Balarāma with utmost contempt and caused him excessive annoyance.

16. Seeing his mischievous and arrogant behaviour and considering the havoc caused by him in the country, Balarāma flew in rage and took up his pestle and plough in hand, in order to kill the enemy.

17. Dvivida too was endowed with great strength. He uprooted a Śāla tree with his hand and rushing with great vehemence at Balarāma, struck his head with the tree.

18. The mighty Balarāma stood firm like a mountain. He caught hold of the tree (as its blow was) falling on his head and hit Dvivida with the pestle called Sunanda.

19. With his head crushed with the pestle, it became covered with a stream of blood. Dvivida shone with the torrent of blood like a mountain covered with a flow of liquid red chalk. In spite of that, he did not mind Balarāma's stroke.

20. He again pulled out another palm tree and removing all its leaves by dint of his physical power, he hit Balarāma in rage. But Balarāma splintered it into hundred pieces.

21-22. The monkey again struck him down with another palm tree which Balarāma cut into hundreds of pieces. Fighting in this way with the glorious Lord, he pulled out a palm tree to strike which was broken to hundreds of pieces. Uprooting trees on all sides, he denuded the forest into a treeless tract.

23. Being enraged, he discharged a shower of rocks on Balarāma all of which the wielder of pestle as his weapon, reduced to powder.

24. The leader of monkeys clenched his palm-like long arms into fists and approaching the son of Rohiṇī (Balarāma), he hit his chest with both the fists.

25. The ruler of Yādavas also threw down his pestle and plough and angrily hit with both of his hands on his (Dvivida's) collar-bones. And he fell down vomitting blood.

26. O king Parīkṣit (a tiger among the Kurus) ! As Dvivida fell down, the whole of the mountain along with its peaks and trees began to shake like a boat tossed with a tempest in the sea water.

27. There arose in the skies shouts of victory, salutation and approbation : 'Well-done', 'Well-done', from gods, *Siddhas*, prominent sages who were sending forth showers of flowers.

28. Killing in this way Dvivida, the scourage of the land (rendering it desolate), the glorious Lord Balarāma entered his city while he was being glorified in songs by the citizens.

CHAPTER SIXTYEIGHT

Hastināpura dragged by Balarāma

Śrī Śuka said :

1. O King Sāmba, the son of Jāmbavatī, who was always victorious in battles, carried away Duryodhana's daughter Lakṣmaṇā, at the time of her *svayaṁvara*.

2. Kauravas were extremely enraged at this, "This is a naughty boy. Setting us at nought, he per force carried away our daughter who did not want him (as a suitor).

3. Arrest and keep in confinement this unruly, wicked fellow. What can the Vṛṣṇis do? They are enjoying that territory conferred upon them by us and that too through our grace (we are the real masters of that land).

4. If, after hearing of the captivity of their son, they come here, the Vṛṣṇis will sue for peace with their pride humbled down like senses brought under control by breath-control (*prāṇāyāma*)."[1]

5. With this resolve, Karṇa, Śala, Bhūri, Yajñaketu and Duryodhana

5A. *VJ.'s Text* :

Along with Duḥśāsana, Śakuni who always gave wrong and wicked advice—all these disregarded Vidura and glorious Gāndhārī. . .

and with the approval of the Kaurava elders (like Bhīṣma) attempted to bind Sāmba.

6. Noticing that he was being pursued by Kauravas, the great chariot-warrior Sāmba, took up his beautiful bow and stood defiantly like a single lion turned at bay.

1. v.l. like serpents whose fangs are removed.—VJ.

7. Enraged and eager to take him captive, they shouted, 'Stop', 'Stop'. And under the leadership of Karṇa, those archers covered him with a volley of arrows.

8. Though surrounded by Kauravas, that scion of the Yadu race, the son of the incomprehensible Lord Kṛṣṇa, did not tolerate them like a lion attacked by insignificant beasts.[1]

9-10. Twanging his beautiful bow, he pierced simultaneously each of the six chariot-warriors like Karṇa and others, with equal number of shafts. He struck the four horses; with four arrows, the charioteers and the great archers in the chariots with one. All of them applauded his exploit.

11. Attacking him simultaneously, they deprived him of his chariot, each Kaurava warrior killing one of his four horses one his charioteer and the remaining warrior snapped his bow.

12. With great difficulty the Kauravas dislodged him from the chariot and took him captive. Victorious they entered their capital, with the boy as well as the maiden.

13. Hearing the news from Nārada's report, Yādavas got enraged, O King. And under the direction of Ugrasena, they made preparations of an expedition against the Kauravas.

14. But Balarāma pacified the Vṛṣṇi warriors who made full preparations of war. He was disposed to wash away the dirt (bitterness) of quarrels. He did not wish that there should be a feud between Kauravas and Vṛṣṇis.

15. In a chariot resplendent like the sun, he went to Hastināpura. He was accompanied with Brāhmaṇas and elderly persons of the family like the moon surrounded by planets.

16. Arriving at Hastināpura, he camped in a park outside the town. He deputed Uddhava to Dhṛtarāṣṭra to ascertain what they intended to do in the matter.

17. Uddhava formally paid respects to Dhṛtarāṣṭra, the son of Ambikā, Bhīṣma, Droṇa, Bāhlīka and Duryodhana and intimated to them the arrival of Balarāma.

1. v.l. He did not put up with the insult like a serpent beaten by a stick.

18. They were highly pleased to hear that Balarāma, their best friend had arrived. They warmly received Uddhava and taking into their hands auspicious presents, they went to Balarāma.

19. Approaching him they received him with due formalities and honours offering him *arghya* and a cow. Those of them who knew of his prowess bowed down Balarāma with their heads.

20. Hearing that their respective relatives were hale and hearty and enquiring after their welfare and health and such friendly talk, Balarāma declared fearlessly.

21. 'Listen attentively to what His majesty Ugrasena, King of kings, commanded you : Carry out his orders without delay.

22. (We hear) that a great many of you unjustly (according to the rules of warfare) combined and vanquished Sāmba who was fighting singlehandedly (as per canons of *dharma-yuddha*) and have taken him captive. With the desire of maintaining amity among relatives, I do tolerate this. (But now immediately bring him to us along with the bride)."

23. O Parīkṣit, Kouravas became deeply indignant to hear the speech of Balarāma who was endowed with immense power, prowess, energy and whose words expressed his inner strength. They said :

24. "O ! How wonderful it is ! Due to the inexorable force of time, a shoe covets to ride over the head that is served by a crown.

25. These Vṛṣṇis are related to us by conjugal ties (through Kuntī's marriage in our family). Condescended to share with us the bed, seat and food, the Vṛṣṇis are raised to royal status like us and are favoured with a royal throne.

26. It is due to our indulgence that they enjoy the royal insignia like *chowries*, fans, a conch, a white umbrella, a crown, a throne and a bed.

27. Now enough of those royal insignia to Yadus who go against their very donors like serpents made to drink nectar (Let us deprive the Yadus of those emblems) who prospered due to our grace are now giving orders to us shamelessly.

28. How could even Indra dare to take what is not given to him by Kauravas like Bhīṣma, Droṇa, Arjuna and others ? Can a ram dare to touch what is in the grasp of a lion (unless he gives it up out of grace) ?"

Śrī Śuka said :

29. Being elated with inordinate pride of their noble birth, their high relations, prosperity, those wicked unmannerly Kauravas addressed unspeakable words within the hearing of Balarāma and returned to their city.

30. Observing the wicked behaviour of Kauravas and hearing their unspeakable reproaches, Balarāma became indignant with wrath and was terrific to look at. Laughing loudly, he repeated to himself :

31. "Verily these wicked persons grown madly arrogant with pride of various kinds, do not desire to have peacefulness. Just as (beating with) a stick is the sure remedy to tame a beast, sound thrashing is the only means to bring these round.

32. It is after slowly appeasing the excited Yadus and indignant Kṛṣṇa that I came here with the intent of bringing about a peace with the Kurus.

33. These dull-witted wicked fellows are naturally inclined to quarrelling. These arrogant fellows have not only treated me scornfully but have used extremely reproachful words to me.

34-35. To them King Ugrasena, the ruler of Bhoja, Vṛṣṇi and Andhaka clans is not a sovereign ruler. Lord Kṛṣṇa, the Lord of goddess Lakṣmī whose orders are obeyed by Indra and other Lords of Spheres, He by whom the celestial assembly Sudharmā is occupied and the heavenly tree Pārijāta is brought (on the earth) and is enjoyed (according to these fellows) does not deserve a high royal seat.

36. Lord Kṛṣṇa whose pair of feet are directly worshipped by goddess Śrī in person, the Controller of all beings does not deserve the royal insignia (according to them).

37. The royal throne is extremely insignificant to him the dust on whose lotus feet is borne on the crowns of their heads by all the Lords of the various worlds (in the universe) and which sanctify sacred waters (like those of the Gaṅgā)

resorted to by holy men; and we—that is god Brahmā, Śiva, I (Saṅkarṣaṇa), and even goddess Śrī are but a part of His ray and always bear those particles of dust (on our heads).

38. We, Vṛṣṇis, enjoy the piece of land granted to us by Kurus! And we are nothing better than shoes and the Kauravas themselves the head!

39. What person capable of meting out punishment to others can tolerate the harsh and irrelevant words of those who are drunk with power and wealth and have become intoxicated and insolent?

40. Today I shall rid the earth of all the Kurus". With this determination, enraged as he was, Balarāma lifted up his plough as if to burn down the three worlds.

41. With the tip of the plough-share, he lifted up the whole city of Hastināpura and angrily began to drag it intending to throw it into the river Gaṅgā.

42. The city that was being dragged and falling into the Gaṅgā, began to rock like a boat. Finding the city so dragged, Kauravas were utterly confounded with consternation.

43. Anxious to save their lives along with those of their families, they placed forward Sāmba and (his spouse) Lakṣmaṇā and with folded palms sought shelter of that very Lord (Balarāma whom they had insulted).

44. 'O Balarāma, O Rāma. You are the support of all. We did not know your prowess. It behoves you to pardon the transgression committed by us who have been foolish and wicked-minded.

45. (You being the substratum of all) you yourself are perfectly independent but you are the cause of the creation, maintenance and destruction of the universe. It is true when they say that the three worlds are your toys and you are the player.

46. (Referring to the original state of Balarāma as the Serpent Śeṣa, the support of the worlds:) It is you! O Ananta (Serpent Śeṣa) of thousand heads, who easily hold up this globe of the earth on your head. At the end of the universe, you withdraw the universe within yourself and contain it. And repose on the cosmic waters as the only remaining unabsorbed existence without a second.

47. O glorious Lord! You assume the *Sattva guṇa* with the intention of maintaining and protecting the world. Hence your anger is only for teaching a lesson to all and not out of hatred or jealousy.

48. We bow to you who are the Inner Controller of all creatures, O omnipotent and immutable Maker of all! We have sought asylum in you. We offer our salutations to you.

Śri Śuka said :

49. Balarāma was thus propitiated to be gracious (unto them) by Kauravas who sought his refuge, for they were terrified as their capital city was rocking. Being highly pleased with them, he assured them protection with the words, 'Do not fear'.

50-51. Duryodhana was very affectionate to his daughter. As presents, he (Duryodhana) gave twelve hundred elephants, each sixty years old (in its prime of youth) and ten thousand horses, six thousand goldplated chariots shining like the sun and one thousand maid-servants each adorned with gold necklaces.

52. Glorious Balarāma, the prominent Sātvata, accepted it all and complimented by his friends and well-wishers, he set out with his son (Sāmba) and the daughter-in-law.

53. Returning to his capital Dvārakā, Balarāma met all his affectionate relatives and in the assembly of prominent Yādavas narrated what he did in the Kaurava country.

54. Even to this day the city shows the evidence of the exploit of Balarāma as it is elevated to the South and slopes down towards the Gaṅgā.

CHAPTER SIXTYNINE

Śri Kṛṣṇa's Household Life[1]

Śrī Śuka said :

1. Having heard that Narakāsura was killed and that Śrī Kṛṣṇa, a single individual as he was, married those numerous women, Nārada became eager to see how Kṛṣṇa managed to live with them all.

2. It is really miraculous that one person (Śrī Kṛṣṇa) possessing a single personality, could severally and simultaneously marry sixteen thousand women, each in a separate house.

3. Being curious to know this, the divine sage Nārada came to see this to Dvārakā which appeared beautiful with its parks and gardens in full blossom and was resonant with the notes of singing birds and humming of the swarms of bees.

4. It was resounded with the sweet warblings and melodious notes of swans and other waterbirds which swarmed the surrounding ponds and pools covered with full blown lotuses, lilies, *Kalhāras* and lotuses that bloom by day and by night.

5. (Nārada came to Dvārakā) which was thickly studded with nine hundred thousands of palatial buildings constructed with crystals and silver and was shining with excellent emeralds thickly set therein and furnished with articles (of furniture) plated with gold and adorned with jewels.

1. VJ.'s text introduces this chapter with three additional verses. It is after the 3rd verse of VJ. that the texts of ŚR and VJ. agree as from verse 1 above.

Śrī Śuka said :

1.1 Having vanquished all his enemies, Śrī Kṛṣṇa stayed there a number of days enjoying himself with those excellent women in this way.

King Parīkṣit asked :

1.2. How could one person—Janārdana—who has assumed a human form, give satisfaction to those sixteen thousand queens?

Śrī Śuka said :

1.3 Well. I shall narrate to you what may make the listeners wonder, as to how that one person Śrī Kṛṣṇa gave satisfaction to all the numerous queens.

6. The city looked beautiful with its streets, roads, quadrangles and market places in the city distinctly laid out ; with stalls, assembly-halls and shrines dedicated to gods. The roads, court-yards, foot-paths and threshholds of the city were profusely sprinkled with water. The heat of the sun in that city was warded off by everflying flags and pennants.

7. In that city, there was (a complex of palatial buildings known as) the harem of Lord Kṛṣṇa which was highly praised by all the presiding deities protecting different spheres (in the universe). In constructing that (palatial building complex), Tvaṣṭṛ, the celestial architect had exhibited all his architectural skill and ingenuity.

8. That part of the city was adorned with sixteen thousand palatial buildings of Kṛṣṇa's queens. Nārada entered into one of the big palaces out of them.

9. It was supported on columns of coral and the ceiling was of *Vaidūrya* (a precious stone). Its walls were of sapphire and its floor of unfading lustre was paved with the same precious stones.

10. It was also furnished with canopies specially designed by Tvaṣṭṛ from which wreaths of pearls were hanging and it (was provided) with seats and beds made of ivory and set with excellent jewels.

11. It was staffed with maid-servants adorned with necklaces of gold-coins and wearing costly apparel and with men-servants wearing coats, turbans, excellent dress and diamond-ear-rings.

12. O child Parīkṣit. Darkness in that place was dispelled by the lustre of clusters of jewels radiating light like lamps. In them, peacocks perching in picturesque (artificial) caves screamed loudly and danced gaily regarding (foolishly) the clouds of fumes of aloewood issuing out of the windows, to be the real clouds.

13. The Brāhmaṇa sage Nārada saw there Kṛṣṇa, the Lord of Sātvatas who was being fanned with a *chowrie* provided with a gold handle by his consort who in her turn was waited upon constantly by a thousand maid-servants who were all equal (to each other) in nature, beauty, age and excellent dress.

14. On seeing him, the glorious Lord, the foremost among those who observe the injunctions of Dharma, promptly got up from the bed of Rukmiṇī (the goddess Śrī), paid respects to his feet with his head adorned with a diadem. With folded palms, He made Nārada occupy his own (exalted) seat.

15. Though he himself was the Creator and Preceptor of the universe and the chief among the righteous, he washed Nārada's feet and bore that water on his own head. The epithet *Brahmaṇya-deva* (God who is friendly to Brāhmaṇas) is most appropriately applicable to him both in its implication and as a title. For the waters that wash his feet (viz. the river Gaṅgā) sanctifies the rest of the world.

16. Having worshipped the prominent divine sage (Nārada), the Ancient sage Nārāyaṇa, the friend and companion of the sage Nara, addressed him in measured words sweet like nectar and requested "O Lord Nārada! what service should we render to you?"

Nārada said:

17. "O almighty Lord! It is not at all wonderful in you who are the Protector of all the worlds that you entertain friendliness to all people as well as chastise the wicked (there is no contradiction in both these roles). You incarnate yourself at your own sweet will for conferring final Beatitude as well as for the maintenance and protection of the world. We realize this quite well, O Lord who are extolled as the highest one in the Vedas.

18. I have the good fortune of being blessed with the sight of the pair of your feet which in themselves are the blessed state of final Emancipation and which deserve to be meditated upon in their hearts by gods of unfathomable spiritual wisdom like Brahmā and others and which form the support to those who have fallen in the (dark) well of *saṁsāra* as a means to get out of it. (Hence I have accomplished my purpose). You, however, be pleased to favour me with unfailing, constant memory of your feet contemplating on which I shall move about in the world."

19. Thereupon, in order to fathom and know the Yogic power of the Lord of the masters of Yoga, that sage Nārada entered the mansion of another queen of Śrī Kṛṣṇa.

20. Even there he found Kṛṣṇa playing dice with his beloved consort Satyabhāmā and Uddhava. He was worshipped with utmost devotion by Kṛṣṇa by rising up to receive him, offering a comfortable seat and such other formalities.

21. Nārada was enquired of by Kṛṣṇa showing as if he was not cognisant of Nārada's arrival. He asked, "When did you come, O worshipful sage? We are after all imperfect beings. What service may we render to perfect (or persons established in the Self) sages like you?

22. O Brāhmaṇa sage! Be pleased to order us and make this life of ours blessed (by giving us an opportunity to serve you)". Nārada was extremely surprised. He rose up without a word and went to another house (of another queen of Kṛṣṇa).

23. Even there, he saw Lord Kṛṣṇa playing and fondling with his infant sons. Then in another house (of another queen), he saw him preparing for his bath.

24. At some houses, Nārada saw him offering oblations to sacrificial fire, at other places, he was seen worshipping God by performing five kinds of daily sacrifices (called *mahāyajñas*); at some houses, he saw him feeding the Brāhmaṇas with a feast and at another place, he found him taking food after offering oblations to the sacred fire.

25. At some houses, he was performing *sandhyā* (twilight prayer); at other places, he was contemplating the Gāyatrī observing complete silence. At some places, he was practising various skills in fencing with a sword and a shield.

26. At some other houses, he found Kṛṣṇa the elder brother of Gada riding horses, elephants or chariots. At some other mansions, he found him lying in bed. while being extolled by bards (*bandins*).

27. In a certain house, he was holding consultations with his counsellors like Uddhava and others; while at other places, surrounded by a bevy of courtesans, he was indulging in water-sports.

28. At some houses, he found him giving highly adorned cows to prominent Brāhmaṇas, while at others he saw him listening to the auspicious stories from *Itihāsa* and *Purāṇas*.

29. In a certain house, he was laughing by telling a joke to his beloved; in other places, he was carefully attending to Dharma, while at other places he was looking after matters pertaining to finance and at other places he was indulging in personal enjoyment.

30. At some houses he saw him sitting alone in meditation contemplating on the Supreme Lord transcendental to *Prakṛti*; at other places, he found him waiting upon the elders and the preceptors by offering them objects of enjoyment and articles of worship.

31. At some places, he was planning war against some kings, while at other places, he was negotiating peace; at some places he was conferring with Balarāma about the well-being of the saintly people.

32. At some place, he saw him celebrating the marriages of his sons and daughters at the proper age with brides and bridegrooms suitable to their status and royal fortune.

33. People were wonderstruck to see the enthusiasm of that Lord of Yoga in conducting festivities at the time of giving send off to children or welcoming those who returned (for example daughters going to their husbands' houses or returning therefrom after a long stay).

34. Sometimes he saw Kṛṣṇa worshipping all gods with elaborate sacrifices. Sometimes he was seen engaged in performing the *pūrta* duties of religion by digging wells, founding groves, constructing temples, etc., for public weal.

35. At some places, he saw Kṛṣṇa riding a pedigree horse from the Sindhu country and chasing a game. Sometimes followed by Yādava warriors, he hunted animals useful for sacrifice.

36. Somewhere he found him moving about *incognito* among his subjects, their houses, harems etc. with a view to understand the real feelings and plans of the people.

37. In this way, after observing this exhibition of Kṛṣṇa's vast Yogic powers, though he was following the human way of life, Nārada addressed him with a smile.

38. "O Lord of Yoga! Your Māyā is incomprehensible--nay not even easily cognisable—to the masters of Māyās.

But through the service of Your feet, our hearts are filled with the spiritual light. And we can comprehend your Yoga Māyā.

39. O Lord Kṛṣṇa! Be pleased to give me leave. I shall range all over the worlds overflowing with your glory, celebrating in songs your sportive acts which sanctify the world."

The Lord replied :

40. "Oh Brāhmaṇa sage. I am the promulgator of Dharma. It is I who practice it and grant my approbation to it. I have descended on this world for teaching it by my example. You need not get troubled, O child."

Śri Śuka said :

41. It is reported that Nārada saw one and the same Kṛṣṇa (present in all the houses of Kṛṣṇa's queens) performing the righteous duties of householders which purify them.

42. Having observed time and anon the vast display of the Yogic powers of Kṛṣṇa of infinite prowess, the sage who became formerly curious about it, was overwhelmed with great astonishment.

43. Nārada who was duly worshipped by Śrī Kṛṣṇa who showed His faith in *dharma*, *artha* and *kāma*, the three objects of human life, was greatly pleased with him. And constantly contemplating upon him only, he went his way.

44. O King! Following in this way the course of conduct as a human being, Lord Kṛṣṇa assumed different forms for the prosperity of the whole of the world; worshipped by the sixteen thousand beautiful damsels with their bashful, affectionate looks and smile, he spent his life delightfully (at Dvārakā).

45. He who celebrates in songs, listens to or expresses approbation for the exploits of Hari which it is impossible for others to perform but which Hari, who is the cause of creation, maintenance and destruction of the universe, has done, will get engendered in him the devotion to the Lord Almighty which will lead to the Final Beatitude.

CHAPTER SEVENTY

Kṛṣṇa's Daily Observances : Deputation from Captive Kings of Jarāsandha

Śrī Śuka said :

1. Now, at the approach of the dawning day, the queens of Mādhava, each of whom was sleeping with the arms of their Lord round their necks, cursed the cocks crowing at dawn, as they were nervously anxious about their (prospective) separation from him.

2. Aroused from sleep by the breezes wafting through Mandāra groves while the black bees were humming sweetly, birds began to sing and warble like bards to wake up Śrī Kṛṣṇa.

3. Closely hugged within the arms of her lover, even Rukmiṇī would not tolerate that extremely auspicious period (called *Brāhma muhūrta*) for fear of separation from his embrace.

4. Getting up in the *Brāhma* period (two hours before the sun-rise), Śrī Kṛṣṇa would wash his hands and feet and rinse his mouth. Sipping three spoonfuls of water as *ācamana*, he with a serene mind, used to meditate on the Self (*ātman*) who is beyond the range of darkness (i.e. *Prakṛti*).

5. He used to contemplate upon *Ātman* also designated as *Brahman*, Who is one without any limiting condition (*upādhi*), self-luminous, immutable; Who has been eternally free from the taint of *Avidyā* (Nescience) by virtue of His being established in His own self ; Whose existence and blissfulness of nature are revealed by His own potencies that bring about the creation, maintenance and destruction of the universe.

6. After meditation, he took bath in clean water after Śāstric injunctions. Putting on two garments, he performed the Twilight-prayer (*Sandhyā*), and other (prescribed observances. The prominent one among the righteous persons then offered oblations to sacrificial fire and silently repeated the *Gāyatrī mantra*.

7. He used to offer prayers to the rising sun and pour out water libations to gods, sages, his ancestors (*pitṛs*)—all of

whom were his own rays—and with a controlled mind, he used to worship the elderly persons and Brāhmaṇas.

8-9. To Brāhmaṇas who were adorned with ornaments, along with silken cloth, deer-hide (*Kṛṣṇājina*) and sesamum seeds, he used to give every day thirteen thousand and eighty-four cows, all of them docile, with horns capped with gold tops and hoofs plated in silver and necks adorned with pearl-necklaces, yielding abundant milk, with only one freshly yeaned calf, accompanied by their calves, beautifully caparisoned.

10. He used to pay respects to cows, Brāhmaṇas, elderly persons, preceptors and all beings who were his own manifestations, and he used to touch auspicious things (like a towny coloured cow, etc.).

11. He himself was one of the ornaments of the world. He used to adorn himself with his special garments (e.g. yellow silken loin cloth or *pitāmbara*) and adornments (e.g. the *Kaustubha* gem) and his special excellent garlands (e.g. the *Vanamālā*) and pigments.

12. Seeing the reflection of his face in liquid ghee and a mirror and cast his (first) glances at cows, bulls, Brāhmaṇas and gods, he used to take delight in granting the boons and desired objects to people belonging to all classes inhabiting in his city or dwelling in his harem (alike), and satisfying their requirements by supplying the needs of his counsellors and courtiers.

13. He would first distribute garlands, betel-leaves and sandal-pastes to Brāhmaṇas; then he would honour his friends, ministers and queens with them, and lastly he would accept them for himself.

14. By that time, the charioteer used to bring his most wonderful chariot drawn by Sugrīva and other horses and bowing down to him, he used to stand before him.

15. Thereupon, holding the charioteer's hand by his own, he used to mount his chariot along with Sātyaki and Uddhava, like unto the sun ascending the eastern mountain.

16. Gazed at by the ladies in the harem with their bash-

ful and affectionate looks and permitted unwillingly by them, he would proceed captivating their hearts with his bewitching smiles.

17. O king Parīkṣit then surrounded by all Vṛṣṇis, he would enter the assembly-hall called Sudharmā the occupants—members—of which are not subject to six 'waves' i.e. changes in human life (viz. hunger, thirst, grief, delusion, old age and death).

18. Seated there on an excellent, exalted throne, the Almighty Lord shone illuminating all the cardinal points by his personal lustre. Surrounded by lion-like prominent Yadus, Kṛṣṇa, the best of Yadus, appeared like the moon in the midst of the hosts of constellations and stars.

19. O King ! There, the court-jesters waited upon the Lord by providing amusements of various kinds. So did the masters in dancing with their manly dances as well as dancing girls with their special performances severally.

20. Bards — *sūtas*, *Māgadhas* and *Bandins* danced, sang and extolled him in accompaniment to tabors, lutes, tambourines, flutes, cymbals and conchs.

21. There were seated some Brāhmaṇas well-versed in the exposition of the Vedas. They elucidated Vedic verses as well as told the stories of ancient kings of sanctifying glory.

22. There arrived a stranger not ever seen before. With the permission of the Lord, he was ushered in his presence by the guards at the door.

23. Having bowed to the Supreme Lord Kṛṣṇa, he, with his palms folded, submitted to him the miserable plight of kings who were kept in captivity by Jarāsandha.

24. Those twenty thousand kings who did not submissively acknowledged Jarāsandha's sovereignty during his conquest of all the quarters (of the world), had been taken captive per force and are incarcerated at Girivraja (mod. Rajgir in Bihar).

(The message of the detained kings :)

25. "O Kṛṣṇa who attract the minds of devotees and of incomprehensible nature. You are the destroyer of the fear of those who seek resort in you. We are of poor intellect and are mortally afraid of *Saṁsāra*. We seek asylum in you.

26. We bow to that ever-vigilant Time-Spirit viz. you who are all powerful and who suddenly cut short the desire for long life of this world while it is deeply involved in doing prohibited acts and is careless and negligent in performing auspicious actions such as your worship and devotion as enjoined by you.

27. O Lord, You are the controller of the Universe. You have incarnated in this world by a ray of yours (i.e. Balarāma) for the protection of the righteous and chastisement and destruction of the wicked. We do not understand how somebody else (like Jarāsandha) transgresses your orders (with impunity) and why persons (though protected by you) still take to the path of their *Karmas* (and experience misery).

28. The happiness of Kingship contingent as it is on so many conditions, is an empty dream. We carry on the burden of *saṁsāra* (and the anxiety and responsibility of wife, children, etc.). with our body which is as good as dead and stands constantly in fear of death. We are extremely miserable inas much as we abandon the spiritual bliss which is obtainable from you by those who renounce all desires and undergo miseries due to (the inexorable force of) your Māyā.

29. The pair of feet of your Lordship destroy the miseries of those who surrender to them humbly. We are at present imprisoned. Be pleased to set us free from the bondage of *Karma* now called Jarāsandha, the king of Magadhas. Possessed as he is of the strength of ten thousand elephants, he singlehandedly took us, kings, captive and imprisoned us in his palace as a king of beasts (a lion) would do to sheep.

30. O Lord with uplifted discus (*Sudarśana*), Jarāsandha who was defeated by you eighteen times in the battle, has grown insolent by somehow defeating you in one of them. Though you possess infinite prowess you behave like a human being. But Jarāsandha is grinding us, knowing us to be your subjects. O unconquerable Lord, May you be pleased to do whatever you think proper to do (under these circumstances).

31. (The messenger concludes:) Thus the kings who are imprisoned by Jarāsandha are desirous of seeing your Lordship.

They have submitted themselves to the soles of Your feet. Be pleased to bestow happiness on those hapless kings.

Śrī Śuka said :

32. While the messenger of the kings was thus delivering the message of the kings, there manifested like the sun, the divine sage Nārada of supreme lustre, wearing gold-coloured matted locks of hair.

VR.'s Text :

32A. Nārada entered singing of the exploits and incarnations of his beloved Kṛṣṇa making Kṛṣṇa, his followers and the world as if melt (with the sweet music) and filling them with great delight.

VJ.'s Text :

32B. (Nārada came in) singing in sweet voice and expressions the delightful acts and incarnation of Lord Kṛṣṇa liquidating heaps of sins and filling the world with extreme joy.

33. Seeing him, the glorious Lord Kṛṣṇa, the Ruler of the rulers of the worlds, rose from his seat and bowed him with his head with great delight, along with the members of the assembly and his followers.

34. Having worshipped him with due formalities and seating him comfortably, he addressed him in sweet words, pleasing the sage with his devotion and sincerity.

35. He enquired, "Are all the three worlds now free from fear from all quarters? It is certainly a great advantage to us that your worship ranges over all the worlds (as we are thereby in a position to know what goes on in the world).

36. To be sure, nothing is unknown to you in all the creation of the Lord. We, therefore, enquire of you what Pāṇḍavas now intend to do.

Nārada replied :

37. O All-pervading almighty Lord, I have witnessed to a great extent a variety of your deluding potencies (*māyās*)[1]

1. VT : *Māyās* i.e. the creations or products of these *māyās* viz. a number of Brahmāṇḍas with all various gods such as Brahmās, Viṣṇus who possess their own *māyās* which are nothing but the powers imparted to them by you.— I have witnessed these etc.

which are inscrutable and insuperable, and which delude even god Brahmā, the great conjuror, the creator of the universe. O Perfect one ! By your powers you abide in all created beings and yet you remain with your splendour undisclosed like fire remaining latent in the logs of wood. (Although you are omniscient, you assume ignorance like a human being). Hence your query causes me no surprise.

38. Who is capable of knowing comprehensively what you intend to do, for you create as well as destroy this universe by your Māyā Potency. The universe appears to exist due to your Māyā (though it is unreal). I bow to you who are in essence distinct from everything else and are thus of incomprehensible nature.

39. O Lord ! I seek asylum in you who have enkindled the brilliant lamp (beacon-light) of your glory by sportively assuming various incarnations. This light is for those *jivas* who wander in the cycle of *saṁsāra* and do not know the way to Final Emancipation from the bondage of the body which is the source of all evil.

40. Though yourself the Supreme *Brahman*, you imitate the ways of human beings in the world. I, however, report to you what king Yudhiṣṭhira, the son of yourpaternal aunt and your devotee plans to do.

41. King Yudhiṣṭhira, the son of Pāṇḍu, aspires to be a sovereign ruler of the world. He, therefore, wishes to worship you with Rājasūya, the greatest of all sacrifices. You may therefore, be pleased to grant your approval (to their plan).

42. Gods, sages and illustrious kings will certainly attend that grand sacrifice with eagerness to see you.

43. O Lord ! Even (*cāṇḍālas* and other) outcastes become purified by listening to your stories, muttering your name or glorifying you and by contemplating on you who are Brahman *incarnate*. What need be said of those who perceive you directly and come in personal contact with you ?

44. Your glory which is absolutely pure has enveloped like a canopy all the quarters and has spread out all over the heavenly regions, the earth and the subterranean regions and it renders the world absolutely pure. O Lord ! Your very presence is auspicious to the world. The waters that wash your feet

are known as the *Mandākini* in the heavens, the *Bhogavati* in lower regions and as the *Gaṅgā* in this world and they hallow the universe.

Śrī Śuka said :

45. When Yādavas, the clansmen of Kṛṣṇa, being fired with the ambition of vanquishing Jarāsandha were not in a mood to approve of Nārada's words (but insisted on an expedition against Jarāsandha) instead of going to Rājasūya. Kṛṣṇa smilingly spoke in soft words to Uddhava, his devoted and loyal servant.

The Lord said :

46. "You are our best eye, a well-wisher and knower of the crux of political deliberations. Therefore, advise us what we should do under the circumstances. We believe in you and shall abide by your advice."

47. When thus called upon to tender advice by his Master, the Omniscient Lord, as if he were an ignorant person, Uddhava respected his order with his head, bowed down and replied (as follows) :

CHAPTER SEVENTYONE

Śrī Kṛṣṇa's visit to Indraprastha

Śrī Śuka said :

1. Having heard the words of the divine sage Nārada, and considering the views of the members of the assembly and that of Lord Kṛṣṇa, the greatly intelligent Uddhava spoke as follows :

Uddhava said :

2. O Lord ! As advised by the sage Nārada, you should render help to your cousins (sons of your paternal aunt) in the

performance of that sacrifice and also should extend protection to those (kings in the captivity of Jarāsandha) who desire to seek your shelter.

3. O Almighty Lord ! It is only the conquerer of all the cardinal points who is eligible to perform the Rājasūya sacrifice.

VR.'s Text adds :

3*A*. We should at first set out from this place to go to Indraprastha. It is there (at Indraprastha) that with Yudhiṣṭhira's permission, you should slay Jarāsandha for the sake of Yudhiṣṭhira. Hence, in my opinion, victory over the son of Jarā (i.e. Jarāsandha) will serve both the purposes.

4. We shall be achieving our great object by this act (of vanquishing Jarāsandha). And great glory will accrue to you by setting at liberty those imprisoned kings, O Govinda !

5. (To Yādavas who are eager to kill Jarāsandha, Uddhava cautions :) In physical strength that king (Jarāsandha) equals ten thousand elephants and as such, is irresistible to others who (regard themselves and actually) are mighty, except Bhīma who is his equal in strength.

6. It is only in a single combat that he can be conquered and not otherwise (with a powerful army), as he commands an army of one hundred *akṣauhiṇis*. He is friendly to Brāhmaṇas. And when requested by Brāhmaṇas, he would never refuse it.

7. Let Bhīmasena assume the guise of a Brāhmaṇa and approach him to beg of him single-handed combat with himself. There is not the slightest doubt that in your presence Bhīma will certainly kill him in that duel.

8. You are the formless Time-spirit who, as the Supreme Lord, are the real cause of the creation and destruction of the universe, while gods Brahmā and Rudra are mere instruments. So Bhīma will be the mere instrumental cause of killing Jarāsandha while (as a matter of fact) you are the real slayer.

9. (When Jarāsandha will be killed) the queens of those (released) kings will sing in their (respective) palaces your glorious act in slaying their own (common) enemy (who imprisoned their husbands) and of setting at liberty their husbands (who are dear to them as their own selves), just as Gopīs sing

of their deliverance (from the demon Śaṅkhacūḍa;) sages who resort to you for shelter glorify you for the rescue of the king of elephants (from the alligator), and the release of Sītā, the daughter of Janaka (from Rāvaṇa's captivity) and we who are protected by you, sing of your exploit in setting free your parents (Vasudeva and Devakī from the imprisonment of Kaṁsa).

10. O Kṛṣṇa! The killing of Jarāsandha will tend to serve many great objectives (purposes) with the fruition of the meritorious acts of the kings (resulting in their release and re-instatement on their thrones), and the fructification of the evil acts of Jarāsandha (resulting in his death and that of Śiśupāla as well). For performance of the Rājasūya sacrifice meets your approval.

Śrī Śuka said :

11. O King! This counsel tendered by Uddhava was so correct and good in every respect that the divine sage Nārada, Yādava elders and Śrī Kṛṣṇa as well, expressed their approval of it.

12. Thereupon the all-pervading glorious Lord Kṛṣṇa, the son of Devakī, sought the permission of his elders and preceptors and ordered his servants like Dāruka, Jaitra and others to prepare for the journey.

13. Having sent in advance, the ladies of his harem, sons, attendants and their kit, and after getting the formal permission of his elder brother Balarāma and Ugrasena, the king of Yādavas, Śrī Kṛṣṇa mounted his chariot brought to him by his charioteer and distinguished with the flag bearing the emblem of Garuḍa, O chastiser of enemies.

14. Thereupon, surrounded with his formidable army comprising of chariots, elephants, foot-soldiers and horsemen and led by their respective military leaders, Kṛṣṇa set out from Dvārakā filling all the quarters with the brilliant fanfare and tremendous sound of the beating of tabors, drums, kettledrums, conchs and horns or trumpets.

15. The devoted and virtuous queens of Kṛṣṇa, all clad in excellent garments, adorned with precious ornaments, pigments and garlands and well-guarded by attendants armed with

swords and shields--followed their husbands along with their sons in golden palanquins and vehicles borne by men and drawn by horses.

16. Mounting on vehicles and litters drawn by men, and on camels, oxen, buffaloes, donkeys, mules, carts and elephants and packing and loading their portable shelters of thatched cottages and tents, woollen blankets, cloths and other articles of their kit, on both sides of the animals, the attendants (of Kṛṣṇa) and courtesans all well-adorned, travelled in his train.

17. Like unto the sea grown agitated with roaring high waves and restless whales, the enormous army, dinning with loud noise and with its lofty flags, big banners, umbrellas, *chowries*, excellent weapons, ornaments, diadems (or helmets) and armours, was shining brilliantly under the bright rays of the sun.

18. Thereupon, the sage Nārada who was worshipped by Kṛṣṇa, the Lord of Yādavas, felt all his hearts and senses deeply satisfied and happy at the sight of Mukunda. After listening to his decision and accepting the reception offered to him, he bowed to Kṛṣṇa and meditating upon him (and thus installing him in his heart) he left Dvārakā, soaring up in the sky.

19. (When Nārada left) the Lord promised the messenger in a kindly tone : "O messenger ! You need not be afraid. May good betide you ! (I shall see to it that) Jarāsandha, the king of Magadhas, be killed."

20. Thus assured by the Lord, the emissary departed and reported in details to the kings all that happened. The kings longed to get their freedom restored and eagerly looked forward to Kṛṣṇa's actual appearance.

21. Having travelled through Ānarta[1], Sauvīra,[2] and Marus[3] and also Vinaśana[4], he crossed over mountains and rivers and passed by towns, villages, cowherd-settlements and quarries.

1. Gujarat and part of Malwa—GDAMI, p. 7.
2. N.L. De accepts Alberuni's identification of Sauvira with Multan and Jahrawar—Ibid, p. 183.
3. Marwar, a part of Rajasthan—Ibid, p. 127.
4. Near modern Sirsa in Kurukṣetra or Brahmāvarta—the land between the Sarasvatī and the Dṛṣadvatī—SGAMI, p. 49.

22. Later on, after crossing the river Dṛṣadvatī (Mod. Ghaggar) and the Sarasvatī, he passed through the Pañcāla country and the Matsya[1] region and arrived at Indraprastha.

23. Hearing the report of the arrival of Śrī Kṛṣṇa whose sight is very rare to ordinary human beings, king Yudhiṣṭhira who was friendly to all, was highly delighted and went out of the city (to receive him) along with his family priests and accompanied with his friends and well-wishers.

24. In the symphonic combination of vocal music (glorifying Kṛṣṇa in songs) and instrumental music and with the loud chanting of the *Vedas*, he eagerly approached Lord Kṛṣṇa just as senses do (i.e. are revived instantaneously) after the return of the chief *Prāṇa* (vital breath).

25. Having seen Śrī Kṛṣṇa, his dearest friend and relative after a long time, the heart of Pāṇḍu's son (Yudhiṣṭhira) melted with deep affection and he embraced him again and again.

26. Embracing with both of his hands the Person of Lord Kṛṣṇa, the sacred abode of the goddess Lakṣmī, the king Yudhiṣṭhira was purged of all sins. With his eyes overflowing with tears and the hair of his body standing on ends, he felt highly blessed and forgot all the delusions about the world.

27. Beaming with a smile and with all his senses and mind overwhelmed with the force of (overpowering) affection, Bhīma embraced his maternal cousin (son of his maternal uncle) and enjoyed great felicity. Arjuna and the twins Nakula and Sahadeva, with profuse tears of joy embraced Acyuta[2], the best of their friend and well-wisher.

28. Embraced by Arjuna and paid due respects by Nakula and Sahadeva, Kṛṣṇa saluted Brāhmaṇas and other elderly persons according to their seniority and other worth.

29-30. Paid respects by them, Kṛṣṇa reciprocally honoured Kauravas, Sṛñjayas, Kekayas, bards like Sūta and Māgadha

1. The territory of Jaipur including Alwar and some part of Bharatpur —GDAMI, p. 128.

2. SR. explains : While Arjuna bent to bow Kṛṣṇa, being equal in age, Kṛṣṇa held him up in his embrace while he was bowed down by Nakula and Sahadeva, his juniors.

and celestial singers, bards and court-jesters[1] praised him while others played upon musical instruments, like tabors, conchs, lutes, drums and horns or trumpets, danced and sang.

31. Lord Kṛṣṇa, the crest-jewel among persons with hallowing renown, was thus accompanied by friends and well-wishers who were eulogizing him. With them he entered the well decorated city of Indraprastha.

32. The roads of the city were sprinkled with scented water and the ichor that exuded from the temples of elephants in rut; it was decorated with variegated flags, golden arches and pitchers full of water (at the entrance of houses); it appeared beautiful with its well-washed citizens wearing new silken garments, ornaments, wreaths of flowers and perfumes as well as with young-women who were equally well-dressed, adorned and anointed in pigments.

33. Kṛṣṇa saw the capital of the king of Kurus (Yudhiṣṭhira) teeming with houses that were illuminated with a row of big lights, offerings of flowers, etc. It was charming on account of the latticed windows out of which were issuing out scented fumes, and flags were merrily flapping on the housetops which were decorated with domes of gold pitchers surrounded with big crests of silver.

34. As soon as the young damsels heard of his arrival, they immediately abandoned their domestic work and even their husbands in bed and flocked to the royal road (the main street) to see the one object worthy of drinking with (the goblets in the form of) eyes by the people, even though due to their eagerness to see him and in their haste, their locks of hair got dishevelled and the knots of silken garments, loose.

35. Women who climbed the terraces of their houses saw Kṛṣṇa along with his queens on the road that was crowded with elephants, horses, chariots and footmen. They showered flowers over him and embraced him with their hearts and extended a warm welcome to him with their profusely smiling looks.

1. The annotators differ slightly in assigning these musical activities among sūtas—upto Brāhmaṇas and court-jesters. VT. is uncertain, hence VR is followed.

36. Observing the queens of Mukunda (Kṛṣṇa) on the road accompanying their husband like constellations of stars surrounding the moon, the women of the town remarked to each other : (We don't know) what meritorious act must have been done by these consorts of Kṛṣṇa whereby this excellent-most personality (of Kṛṣṇa) extends (offers) delight to their eyes with his noble smiles and winsome amorous looks.

37. In the town, at every stage, citizens with auspicious things in their hands, approached Kṛṣṇa and worshipped him. So did the leaders of trade-guilds rid themselves of all sins.

38. Warmly received by ladies of the harem with their eyes blooming with joy and excited with eagerness, Kṛṣṇa entered the palace of the king Yudhiṣṭhira.

39. When Kuntī beheld her brother's son Śrī Kṛṣṇa, the Lord of the three worlds, her heart was full of delight and affection. She got up from the couch along with her daughter-in-law Draupadī and hugged him (affectionately).

40. Having brought Kṛṣṇa, the God of gods to his palace, with respect and devotion, king Yudhiṣṭhira was so beside himself with joy that he could not understand how to proceed with the formalities of worship (of such a respectable guest).

41. O king Parīkṣit ! Śrī Kṛṣṇa, however, bowed down to his paternal aunt Kuntī and paid respects to elderly ladies. He himself was bowed down by Draupadī and his sister Subhadrā.

42-43. Instructed by her mother-in-law Kuntī, Draupadī duly worshipped the queens of Kṛṣṇa such as Rukmiṇī, Satyabhāmā, Bhadrā, Jāmbavatī, Kālindī, Mitravindā. Śaibyā, and the pious Nāgnajitī and other women-guests, with garments, wreaths of flowers, ornaments, etc.

44. King Dharmarāja made comfortable arrangement of lodging for Śrī Kṛṣṇa and that of his queens, members of the army, followers and counsellors providing everyday with new objects of enjoyment.

45. Accompanied with Arjuna, Kṛṣṇa propitiated the Fire-god, offering him the Khāṇḍava forest for consumption. He rescued Maya (from the fire) who constructed a heavenly assembly-hall for king Yudhiṣṭhira.

46. With the desire of pleasing king Yudhiṣṭhira, Kṛṣṇa stayed many months at Indraprastha. Occasionally, surrounded by warriors, he rode out in a chariot with Arjuna for excursion and sport.

CHAPTER SEVENTYTWO

Jarāsandha slain

Śrī Śuka said :

1-2. (When Kṛṣṇa had spent a restful period for some days) on a certain occasion, king Yudhiṣṭhira was seated in his court-hall attended by sages, Brāhmaṇas, Kṣattriyas, Vaiśyas and his brothers, preceptors, elders of the family, clansmen and relatives. He addressed Kṛṣṇa within the hearing of them all.

Yudhiṣṭhira said :

3. O Lord Govinda ! I intend to adore you and your hallowed part-manifestations (in the form of Indra and other deities) by performing the noblest of sacrifice called the Rājasūya. May you be pleased (to help us) to accomplish this.

4. O lotus-navelled Lord ? Your feet destroy everything inauspicious. Those pious people who constantly worship them physically, contemplate on them mentally, and sing of them vocally attain emancipation from *saṁsāra*. They obtain even worldly blessings if they so desire but not others.

5. O God of gods ! Let the world, therefore, witness the supreme efficacy of the service of your lotus-like feet. O Lord ! Be pleased to demonstrate to the Kaurava and Sṛñjaya chiefs, the status reached and fruits reaped by those who worship you and by those who do not do so.

6. O Lord ! You are Brahman himself, the Inner Soul abiding in all beings. You eternally enjoy your essential state of blissfulness and look upon all as equal. Hence the notion of difference such as 'this is mine' and 'this is not mine' cannot

be predicated of you. Like persons betaking to the celestial wish-yielding tree, your grace is conferred on those who serve you and it is commensurate to the measure (and intensity) of their service, and there is no violation of this law.

The Lord replied :

7. O King! This resolution of yours is excellent. O destroyer of enemies? By performance of the Rājasūya sacrifice your auspicious fame (as the conqueror of all kings) will pervade the three worlds.

8. The performance of this sovereign sacrifice is desirable not only on behalf of us, your friends and well wishers, but also on behalf of sages, your ancestors, gods and all created beings.

9. Having defeated all the kings in the world and thus brought under control the whole of the earth, collect all the necessary articles of sacrifice and then commence the performance of this great sacrifice.

10. O King! These brothers of yours are born from the rays of the deities (such as Indra, Vāyu) who are the guardians of the worlds. And I, who am never won over by persons lacking self-control, have been conquered by you, by your control of mind and senses.

11. In this world, not even a celestial being can discomfit my devotee by his energy, glory, affluence or supernatural power, much less can an earthly being do so.

Śri Śuka said :

12. Having heard the approbatory speech of the Lord, king Yudhiṣṭhira became extremely delighted and his countenance looked cheerful like a fresh-blown lotus. He assigned the conquest of cardinal points (of the world) to his brothers who were imbued with the lustre and energy of god Viṣṇu.

13. He commanded Sahadeva to conquer the South along with Sṛñjayas and deputed Nakula to the West, and Arjuna to the North and Bhīma, in alliance with Matsyas, Kekayas and Madrakas to the East.

14. Conquering the kings with their might and energy, those warriors brought from those quarters immense wealth to king Yudhiṣṭhira who was preparing for sacrifice.

15. Hearing that Jarāsandha could not be conquered, Yudhiṣṭhira became anxious. They say that to Yudhiṣṭhira who was pondering (over the subjugation of Jarāsandha), Kṛṣṇa, the Primary Cause of the world, suggested the expedient suggested by Uddhava.

16. O Parīkṣit ? Thereupon, the three (warriors)—Bhīmasena, Arjuna and Kṛṣṇa—disguised themselves as Brāhmaṇas and went to Girivraja (the capital of Magadha) where stayed Jarāsandha, the son of Bṛhadratha.

17. Those three Kṣattriyas disguised as Brāhmaṇas, went to Jarāsandha's palace at the time of receiving unexpected guests (with no previous appointment). They begged of king Jarāsandha who was friendly and devoted to Brāhmaṇas and was a keen observer of the sacred duties of the householder.

18. O king ! Please know us as unexpected guests who have come over a long distance for soliciting a request. May god betide you ! Be, therefore, pleased to grant our request.

19. Is there anything unbearable to people with fortitude and endurance ? What act is there which the unrighteous would hesitate to do ? What is there that the generous cannot give away ? What person is a stranger or an enemy to those who look upon all as equals.

20. Whoever, endowed with capability to do so, does not, by means of this perishable body, achieve everlasting glory worthy of being sung by the righteous, is worthy of being pitied and censured.

21. Kings Hariścandra, Rantideva, Śibi, Bali, Mudgala (who lived on grains gleaned from fields), the legendary pigeon (who sacrificed its life for the hunter and the hunter (who emulated the pigeon's example) and many others attained to everlasting fame at the cost of this transient body.

Śri Śuka said :

22. From their tones, appearance, the scars on the forearms caused by the friction of bow-strings, Jarāsandha came to know that they belonged to the Kṣattriya class. He also

felt that he had seen them formerly somewhere. He began to think :

23. "These are certainly Kṣattriyas who have adopted the guise of Brāhmaṇas. I shall give whatever they beg of me even if it be my body which is difficult to part with.

24. The glorious fame of king Bali is heard glorified far and wide in all directions even though he was dislodged from his sovereign position by Viṣṇu in the disguise of a Brāhmaṇa.

25. The great king of Daityas, knowing full well that it was Viṣṇu in the form of a Brāhmaṇa and though prevented by his preceptor Śukra, he gave away the earth to Viṣṇu in the guise of a Brāhmaṇa who intended to deprive Bali of his sovereignty and splendour for the sake of Indra.

26. What is the good of this life of that wretched Kṣattriya who does not aspire to attain vast renown at the cost of this perishable, ever-waning body for the good of Brāhmaṇas."

27. Reflecting thus, the noble-minded king Jarāsandha spoke out to Kṛṣṇa, Arjuna and Bhīma, "O Brāhmaṇas. Choose whatever you desire to have. I shall give even my head to you."

Lord Kṛṣṇa replied :

28. "O great king. We are Kṣattriyas who have come here to seek a fight. We do not beg for food. We want a fight with you, in a single combat if it pleases you.

29. This is Vṛkodara (Bhīma) the son of Kuntī. This is his brother Arjuna. Please know me as Kṛṣṇa, their maternal cousin and your sworn enemy."

30. Thus informed by Kṛṣṇa, the king of Magadhas laughed loudly. Getting enraged, he declared, "you dull-witted fellows, (if you so seek it) I shall give a battle with you.

31. I shall not fight with a coward like you who get confounded in battles. Out of my fear, you abandoned your capital Mathurā and sought shelter in the sea.

32. This Arjuna is neither equal in age nor surpassing me in strength. And hence he is no match for me as a combatant. Bhīma is my equal in strength."

33. With these words, he handed over a huge mace to Bhīmasena and taking another tremendous mace for himself he went out of the town.

34. There on a level ground as the arena, the two warriors closed in fight against each other, both of them, being proud and furious in battle, hit each other with their maces hard like (Indra's) thunderbolt.

35. While they were making skilful wheeling manoeuvres to the right or to the left, the combat became spectacular like the one of actors on the stage.

36. O king! When the maces hurled at each other clashed each other, there arose a harsh and cracking sound *caṭ caṭ* resembling the clapping of Vajras (Indra's thunderbolt) or like the clashing of the tusks of two fighting tuskers.

37. Just as two twigs of the sun plant are reduced to pulp when two elephants, furious with rage, fight with each other with those twigs, those two maces hurled with full force of their arms dashed against each other and came in contact with each other's shoulders, hips, feet, hands, thighs and collar-bones and were reduced to powder.

38. When their maces were broken down in this way, those furious warriors among men pounded each other, boxing with fists as hard as iron. The noise produced by the blows of their palms as they struck each other was like that of two tuskers dashing against each other and was harsh like the striking of Vajra (or clapping of thunder).

39. Both Bhīma and Jarāsandha were equal to each other in training, strength and energy. They struck each other with unabated force. The combat however remained undecided.

40. In this way twentyseven days passed while they fought by day but behaved like friends at night (when the combat was over).

41. O king Parīkṣit! On one day Bhīmasena confessed to Kṛṣṇa, his maternal uncle's son, "O Mādhava (Descendant of Madhu), I am unable to vanquish Jarāsandha in the duel.

42. Śrī Kṛṣṇa knew the secret of the birth and death of the enemy and how the demoness Jarā conferred life on

Jarāsandha. He strengthened Bhīma by transferring his energy and began to consider.

43. He hit upon a plan of killing the enemy. Kṛṣṇa of infallible insight showed it to Bhīma symbolically by splitting a twig.

44. Bhīma, a prominent warrior of enormous strength understood the suggestion conveyed to him. He took hold of Jarāsandha by both his feet and felled him on the ground.

45. He pressed down one foot of the enemy with one of his feet and with his both hands he caught hold of the other foot and tore him in two from the anus, like an elephant splitting a branch of a tree.

46. Now people beheld the two separate parts of the body each with one foot, one thigh, one testicle, one hip, half the back, one breast, one shoulder, one arm, one eye, one eyebrow and one ear.

47. There was a great outcry, when the king of Magadhas was slain. Clasping Bhīma in their arms, Arjuna and Kṛṣṇa applauded him.

48. The glorious Lord Kṛṣṇa is the creator and protector of all beings. None could fathom his greatness and power. He installed Jarāsandha's son Sahadeva as the king of Magadhas on the throne and set at liberty kings kept in confinement by Jarāsandha, the king of Magadhas.

CHAPTER SEVENTYTHREE

Return of Kṛṣṇa and others to Indraprastha

Śrī Śuka said :

1. Twenty thousand eight hundred kings who were easily defeated in battle (by Jarāsandha) were kept confined in a valley surrounded on all sides by the mountain. (Released from captivity) they came out with unclean bodies and dirty clothes.

2. Emaciated with hunger and with mouths parched up and greatly reduced in bodies due to confinement for a long time, the kings saw Lord Kṛṣṇa of dark blue complexion like a cloud, wearing yellow silken garments.

3. He was bearing the mark of Śrīvatsa; had four arms. His eyes were reddish like the inner part of a lotus-flower and he was charming and gracious in appearance. He was adorned with brilliant alligator-shaped ear-rings.

4. He was holding a lotus in one of his hands and was wielding a mace, a conch and a discus (Sudarśana) in the remaining three arms. He was adorned with a crown, a necklace of pearls, bracelets, a zone and a pair of armlets.

5. His neck was shining with the excellent jewel Kaustubha and had a garland of forest-flowers (*Vanamālā*) hanging on his bosom. The kings appeared to drink him with eyes and to lick him with tongues.

6. They were as if smelling him with their noses and embracing him with their arms. They bowed to the Lord with their heads touching his feet and rid themselves of all sins.

7. At the sight of Śrī Kṛṣṇa they were so much overjoyed that they got over the languor and exhaustion caused by their incarceration. Folding their palms, the kings eulogized Hṛṣīkeśa (Śrī Kṛṣṇa, the Lord of all senses) in the following words :

The kings submitted their prayer :

8. We bow to you, O God of Gods. You remove the distress of those that seek shelter in you, O Immutable Lord, Being disgusted with the terrible *saṁsāra* we have resorted to you. Pray,. be pleased to protect us, O Kṛṣṇa.

9. O Lord ! Slayer of the demon Madhu ! We do not blame that Jarāsandha, king of Magadhas. It is really your Grace that we kings were deprived of our kingdoms, O Almighty Lord.

10. A king elated with pride of sovereignty and affluence does not attain the Final Beatitude, but being infatuated by your deluding potency (Māyā) looks upon the transient worldy fortune as permanent.

11. Just as children (or foolish people) mistake a mirage as a pool of water, persons without discriminatory power, ascribe reality to the everchanging Māyā which brings about modifications.

12. O Lord! Formerly we were blinded by our pride of kingship and affluence. In our ambition to conquer this earth, we competed with each other slaughtering mercilessly our own subjects. We were so madly proud that we did not think of death or of yourself, who were ahead of us.

13. O Kṛṣṇa! By your form called Time, of inexorable velocity and infinite prowess, we were despoiled of our former affluence and sovereignty. It is through your Grace that today we, with our pride completely destroyed, are contemplating on your feet.

14. We do not aspire after this mirage like sovereignty which is to be enjoyed by this ever-decaying body, a nursery of ailments). Nor do we seek to enjoy after death the fruits of our (religious or meritorious) actions (in heaven) which sound so pleasant to the ears, O Almighty Lord.

15. Pray, be gracious to teach us, that expedient whereby we shall never lose the memory of your lotus-like feet (and continue to contemplate on them) even while we are involved in the series of births and deaths.

16. We repeatedly pay our salutations to Lord Kṛṣṇa, the son of Vasudeva, the destroyer of the misery of *saṁsāra* (even of Daityas), the Supreme Self. You are the remover of sufferings of those who bow to you, O Govinda (Lord of Senses).

Śrī Śuka said :

17. O dear Parīkṣit! Thus eulogised by the kings who were now freed from captivity, the merciful Lord who affords protection to those who seek it, spoke to them in sweet language as follows :

The Lord said :

18. O monarchs! As desired by you, from now onwards your unflinching devotion unto me who am the Ruler of the

universe and the Self, abiding in all, shall grow strong and deep-rooted.

19. How glad I am at your correct resolution, O kings. What you expressed is the truth. For I have seen how growing pride of affluence and authority has a maddening effect on people.

20. Haihaya (Sahasrârjuna), Nahuṣa, Vena, Rāvaṇa, Naraka and other rulers of gods, demons and human beings have fallen down from their positions, in consequence of their arrogance, begotten of their prosperity and power.

21. Being thoroughly cognisant of the fact that everything that is created like the body (and other things connected therewith) is perishable, you worship me by performing sacrifices and be alert and protect your subjects in a righteous manner, O monarchs.

22. You secure the continuity of your family by begetting children. Bear up with equable mind, the weal and woe, prosperity and adversity, birth or death as it comes to your lot and carry on your life devoting your heart to me.

23. Remain indifferent to your body and things connected with it. Take delight in the spiritual bliss of the self and observe vows of self-discipline. Thus, concentrating your mind properly and steadily in me, you will ultimately attain to me who am the supreme Brahman.

Śri Śuka said :

24. Having enjoined the kings in the above manner, Lord Kṛṣṇa, the Ruler of the Universe ordered male and female servants to give them a bath.

25. He made Sahadeva (now the king of Magadha) to receive them respectfully, by giving them clothes, ornaments, wreaths of flowers and pigments worthy of kings.

26. When the kings had taken an excellent bath and put on their rich clothes and ornaments, they were served with dainty dishes and were offered various luxuries worthy of kings such as betel-leaves, etc.

27. Having been honoured by Mukunda, these kings, wearing brilliant ear-rings and freed from their distressful

conditions, looked resplendent like planets at the end of the rainy season.

28. Mounting them in chariots decorated with gold and jewels and drawn by good horses, and cheering up their hearts with sweet yet sincere words, they were sent to their respective countries.

29. The kings who were thus relieved of their hardships by the highly noblesouled Kṛṣṇa, returned contemplating on Kṛṣṇa, the Lord of the universe and his noble deeds.

30. (Arriving at their capitals) they told to their ministers (and subjects) the glorious deeds of that Supreme Person and carried on their life (and government) deligently as per instructions of the Lord.

31. Having slain Jarāsandha through the instrumentation of Bhīma, Keśava was worshipped by Sahadeva and accompanied with the two sons of Kuntī (Bhīma and Arjuna), he left for Indraprastha.

32. Having reached Khāṇḍavaprastha, these three warriors who had vanquished their enemies blew their conchs, thrillings their friends with delight and their foes with terror.

33. Hearing that sound, the citizens of Indraprastha became delighted in their minds. They concluded that Jarāsandha had been killed and king Yudhiṣṭhira also felt that he had accomplished his object.

34. Having bowed down to king Yudhiṣṭhira, Bhīma, Janārdana and Arjuna reported to him in details all they had severally done.

35. Having heard how compassion had been shown by Kṛṣṇa, Dharmarāja shed tears of joy and was too much overwhelmed with love to express a word.

CHAPTER SEVENTYFOUR

Yudhiṣṭhira's Rājasūya : Śiśupāla slain

Śrī Śuka said :

1. Having thus heard about the slaying of Jarāsandha and also about Lord Kṛṣṇa's supreme glory, king Yudhiṣṭhira was highly delighted. He addressed him as follows.

Yudhiṣṭhira said :

2. All the preceptors of the three worlds (like Sanaka and others) and all the great gods, the protectors of different worlds, do bear on their heads your commands when they have the privilege to receive that Grace which is rarely obtained by others.

3. O Lord of infinite prowess and glory ! That lotus-eyed personage like you bears and carries out commands of factually indigent persons who regard themselves conceitedly as rulers, is itself an extreme mockery unbecoming of you as below dignity.

4. But you are the Supreme Brahman like unto the effulgence of the Sun, the glory of the Brahman, the Supreme Self who is one, without a second is neither enhanced nor diminished by the performance of acts by you.

5. O unconquerable Lord of Lakṣmī ! Just as the beasts (or ignorant people) entertain the (perverse) notion of difference pertaining to their body indexed by such terms as "I and mine", "You and yours", even your devotees do not possess such a crooked notion of difference (Need it be said that it is totally absent in you ?)

Śrī Śuka said :

6. Addressing Kṛṣṇa thus and with his approval, Kuntī's son, Yudhiṣṭhira invited competent and worthy Brāhmaṇas who were proficient in the Vedas and the sacrificial ritual, to officiate as priests (at the Rājasūya sacrifice to be performed) in a period suitable for the celebration of such sacrifices such as the spring.

7-9. (Kṛṣṇa-) Dvaipāyana (Vyāsa), Bharadvāja, Sumantu, Gautama, Asita, Vasiṣṭha, Cyavana, Kaṇva, Maitreya, Kavaṣa, Trita, Viśvāmitra, Vāmadeva, Sumati, Jaimini, Kratu, Paila. Parāśara, Garga, Vaiśampāyana, Atharvan, Kāśyapa, Dhaumya, Paraśurāma (of the Bhṛgu clan), Āsuri, Vītihotra, Madhucchandas, Vīrasena, Akṛtavraṇa—these and many others were invited.

10. (And also were invited) Droṇa, Bhīṣma, Kṛpa and others, Dhṛtarāṣṭra with all his sons and the noble-minded Vidura.

11. Brāhmaṇas, Kṣattriyas, Vaiśyas, Śūdras whoever was desirous of seeing the sacrifice, and all kings and their ministers (and subjects) assembled there, O King.

12. Thereupon the Brāhmaṇas ploughed the sacrificial ground (where gods are to be worshipped with oblations) with gold ploughs and following the scriptural injunctions, they consecrated the king as the sacrificer.

13-15. As the tradition goes, all the utensils used in this sacrifice were of gold as they were at Varuṇa's Rājasūya sacrifice in ancient times. Indra and other protecting deities of different spheres, god Brahmā and Śiva along with their attendants, Siddhas and Gandharvas (celestial singers), Vidyādharas and big serpents, sages, Yakṣas, Rākṣasas, birds, Kinnaras, Cāraṇas, kings along with their queens—all of them were invited and they attended the Rājasūya sacrifice of Pāṇḍu's son, Yudhiṣṭhira.

16. They were not surprised at all, as they thought that such a performance is quite natural to the devotees of Kṛṣṇa (to whom nothing is impossible). The sacrificial priests who looked brilliant like gods, conducted for the king, the Rājasūya sacrifice according to *śāstric* injunctions, as the gods did for the sake of Varuṇa.

17. On the day fixed for extraction of the Soma juice, the king with serene mind duly worshipped the highly respectable Brāhmaṇas conducting the sacrifice as well as the judges of the sacrificial performance.

18. The members of the assembly could not arrive at a unanimous decision as to who should be regarded as worthy

of receiving the first honour of worship as there were many deserving claimants. At this juncture, Sahadeva spoke out.

19. "(It is my considered opinion that) the imperishable Lord Kṛṣṇa, the Lord and protector of Sâtvatas deserves this highest honour. For he is not only all deities but also Time, space, wealth and other things.

20. This universe is his manifestation. He constitutes the sacrifices. The sacrificial fire, oblations offered in the fire, the *mantras* recited at that time and the paths of knowledge and Yoga or devotion are meant for him.

21. He is One without a second; the universe is his manifestation O members of the assembly. Entirely dependent on himself and though himself unborn, he creates, protects and dissolves this universe.

22. It is through his Grace that people perform different actions, penances and *yogic* practices and everyone tries to achieve their high objects in life such as *dharma* (religious practices), *artha* (wealth), *kāma* (worldly enjoyment) and *mokṣa* (Final emancipation).

23. Therefore, this highest honour ought to be offered to Lord Kṛṣṇa who is the greatest of the great. It is thus by offering him the honour of the first worship in the assembly that we shall be honouring all created beings as well as ourselves.

24. He who desires to reap infinite merit in return for his gift should offer it to Lord Kṛṣṇa who constitutes the Soul of all created beings and looks upon all as his own self, (or attached to his devotees) quite serene (desireless) and absolutely perfect."

25. Sahadeva, who knew the supreme greatness of Kṛṣṇa addressed them in this way and observed silence. Hearing that all excellent and pious members of the assembly were satisfied and approved of the speech with the words "well said, well expressed",

26. Hearing the decision of the Brāhmaṇas and ascertaining the consensus (lit. what was desired in the hearts) of the members of the sacrificial assembly, king Yudhiṣṭhira was highly pleased. Overwhelmed with affection, he worshipped

Kṛṣṇa, the Lord of senses (as the foremost member of that assembly).

27. Then having washed the feet of Śrī Kṛṣṇa, he (Yudhiṣṭhira) along with his queens, younger brothers, counsellors and members of his family, delightfully bore on their heads (drops of) that water (with which he washed the Lord's feet) which was capable of purifying the world.

28. He worshipped him by offering yellow silken cloths, and very valuable ornaments. But he could not see him clearly as his eyes were flowing with tears (of affection and joy).

29. Seeing Kṛṣṇa so worshipped, all people (in the assembly) folded their palms and offered him salutations with the words *Namaḥ* (Bow to you), *Jaya* (Victory to you). And showers of flowers fell down (from the sky).

30. Hearing this (above-mentioned) shouts of salutation and victory, Śiśupāla, the son of Damaghoṣa, whose anger was provoked by the glorification of Kṛṣṇa's excellences, rose from his seat. He raised up his arm. Being enraged he fearlessly uttered harsh words (with reference to and) for the hearing of Lord Kṛṣṇa.

31. "The Vedic text that the Time-spirit is the real controller (capable of bringing about undesirable events) and that it is inviolable, is quite true. (For example, here, in this assembly) even the judgment of the elderly people has become vitiated by the prattling of an ignorant junior (like Sahadeva).

32. O leaders of the assembly ! You are the best judges of deciding who should be the proper recepient (of this highest honour). Please do not head the childish talk of that ignorant boy Sahadeva believing in which you consented that Kṛṣṇa deserved this honour.

33-34.* To the utter disregard of the leaders of this assembly who are endowed with austers penance, learning,

*. ŚR. takes pains to show that the inner meaning of these verses conveys the glorification of Lord Kṛṣṇa as Śiśupāla was his attendant in his original birth and as such he would naturally praise the Lord. It appears that members of the assembly shut their ears, thinking it to be defa-

observance of sacred vows,—members who have cleared all their sins by their spiritual knowledge; the great sages who are established in Brahman and who are worshipped even by the guardian deities of different spheres, how is a cowherd, a disgrace to his clan and family, considered eligible to receive this honour ? How can a crow deserve to receive Puroḍāśa (a sacrificial oblation) ?

35. He does not belong to any class of society, (*varṇa*), stage of life (*āśrama*) or nobility of birth. He has been excommunicated by (i.e. beyond the pale of) all *dharmas*. He behaves wantonly (against moral or religious code of conduct) and is devoid of virtues. How does he deserve worship ?

36. His family has been cursed by Yayāti (the founder of his clan) and is excommunicated by all good people. He is always indulged in drinking. How is he eligible for this worship ?

37. These marauders have given up their country (Śūrasena i.e. region around Mathurā)—a land frequented and inhabited by Brāhmaṇa sages; they have resorted to their citadel in the sea—a place destitute of Brāhmaṇas devoted to Vedic studies and harass all people from that strong-hold."

38. Śiśupāla whose fund of auspicious acts and merits was exhausted, spoke these and the like defamatory words to Kṛṣṇa. But the Lord did not respond at all as a lion does to the howling of female jackals.

39. Hearing that unbearable censuring of the Lord, the members of the assembly closed their ears and left the assembly, censuring Śiśupāla angrily.

40. He who does not leave the place even after hearing reproachful words about the Lord or about his devotees, becomes deprived of his merits and goes down to hell.

mation of the Lord; the clans of Matsya, Kekaya, Sṛñjayas did not understand this double meaning and wanted to attack Śiśupāla. And Lord Kṛṣṇa also did not understand his praise and beheaded his servant who was praising him in words of double meaning and marched against him with a sword (vide verses 38-43 below). In *supra* 3.18-3-8 where Hiraṇyākṣa upbraided Lord Viṣṇu in the boar form, ŚR. has tried to read Viṣṇu's praise in it, vide vol. I pp. 320-321.

41. Then sprang to their feet the indignant Pāṇḍavas, Matsyas, Kekayas and Sṛñjayas with their arms uplifted with the desire of finishing with Śiśupāla.

42. Undaunted by them, Śiśupāla took up his sword and shield and reproached the kings who sided with Kṛṣṇa in that assembly.

43. When matters came to such a stage the Lord himself stood up in the meanwhile and restraining his own partisans, angrily cut off the head of his advancing enemy with his sharp-edged discus—Sudarśana.

44. There was a great uproar when Śiśupāla was killed. In that bustle, the kings who were his followers ran away to save their lives.

45. Thereafter, like a meteor falling on the earth from the sky, there emerged an effulgent light from the body of Śiśupāla and entered the person of Vāsudeva while all beings stood as witness to it.

46. Pondering over the Lord with thoughts saturated with hatred and anger entertained for three consecutive lives, he (Śiśupāla) attained identity with the Lord, for it is one's own brooding which determines one's future state of life.

47. The emperor Yudhiṣṭhira gave liberal sacrificial fees to the priests who conducted the sacrifice and to the members of the sacrificial assembly. And having thus worshipped them all with due respect, he performed the closing ablution of the sacrifice (*avabhṛtha snāna*) according to the injunctions laid down in the *śāstras*.

48. After having accomplished the Rājasūya sacrifice successfully for king Yudhiṣṭhira, Kṛṣṇa, the Lord of the masters of Yoga, lived some more months at Indraprastha at the request of his friends.

49. Thereafter, Lord Kṛṣṇa, the son of Devakī, took leave of king Yudhiṣṭhira who was unwilling to let him go and returned to his capital along with his queens and counsellors.

50. The long narrative of how (Jaya and Vijaya) the two residents of Vaikuṇṭha (as the attendants of Lord Viṣṇu) had to undergo repeated births on the earth under the

curse of Brāhmaṇas (like Sanaka, etc.), has been described to you in details.[1]

51. When king Yudhiṣṭhira performed his closing ablution of the Rājasūya sacrifice he shone like Indra, the king of gods, in the assembly of Brāhmaṇas and Kṣattriyas.

52. All the gods, men and celestial beings (who attended the sacrifice) were duly honoured by the king. They went back to their respective place praising with joy Lord Kṛṣṇa and the Rājasūya sacrifice.

53. The sinful Duryodhana, the veritable Kali himself, who was a bane to the family of Kurus was the only exception. He could not bear the sight of the vast affluence and the royal splendour of Pāṇḍu's son (Yudhiṣṭhira).

54. He who sings of Lord Viṣṇu's glorious deed of slaying Śiśupāla (and Jarāsandha and others) and the release of the kings taken captive (by Jarāsandha) and the performance of the Rājasūya sacrifice is released from the bondage of all sins.

CHAPTER SEVENTYFIVE

Discomfiture of Duryodhana

King Parīkṣit enquired :

1-2. We have heard that all men, gods, kings and celestial beings who had assembled there for the Rājasūya sacrifice of king Ajātaśatru (Yudhiṣṭhira) were filled with joy to see its glorious accomplishment, O Brāhmaṇa sage. And Duryodhana was the only exception. Be pleased to explain to us. O worshipful sir, the reason of this.

The sage Śuka replied :

3. In the Rājasūya sacrifice of your illustrious grandfather, all his relatives attached to him with bonds of affection, accepted the responsibility of various departments and rendered him service (during the sacrifice).

1. *vide supra* Skandha VII. Ch.s 1-9.

4. Bhīma was the head of the culinary department, Duryodhana was in charge of treasury. Sahadeva was engaged in the reception department while Nakula was entrusted with the provision of supplies (of things required).

5. Arjuna was appointed to serve the elders and preceptors, while Kṛṣṇa was engaged in washing the feet (of the guests). Draupadī superintended service and catering of food while the noble-minded Karṇa was entrusted with conferring gifts.

6-7. Yuyudhāna, Vikarṇa, Hārdikya, Vidura and others as well as Bhūri and other sons of Bāhlika, Santardana and others were entrusted with different departments and duties in that great sacrifice. And all of them endeavoured to carry out their duties, as liked by King Yudhiṣṭhira, O great King.

8. When the priests, member of the assembly, persons of wide and deep erudition, intimate friends and relatives were properly honoured with sweet words, costly presents and sacrificial (and other religious) fees and when (the soul of) Śiśupāla entered the feet of Lord Kṛṣṇa, the Pāṇḍavas took the closing ablution of the Rājasūya sacrifice in the heavenly river, Gaṅgā.

9. During the celebration of the ceremony of the *avabhṛtha* bath, various instruments of music such as tabors, conchs, *paṇavas*, drums, kettle-drums and horns were sounded.

10. Dancing girls danced merrily. Bands after bands of songster engaged in vocal music. And sound of musical instruments like lutes, flutes and clapping reached the heaven.

11. With their flags and streamers of variegated colours (fluttering in the air) and accompanied with battalions of well-adorned soldiers, big elephants, chariots and horses, kings wearing wreaths of gold started (for the *avabhṛtha* bath).

12. With the sacrificer (Yudhiṣṭhira) in front of them followed the clans of Yādavas, Sṛñjayas, Kāmbojas, Kauravas, Kekayas and Kosalas shaking the earth with their armies.

13. The members of the sacrificial assembly, the priests and prominent Brāhmaṇas chanting the Vedas loudly followed him. And the gods, sages, manes (ancestors) and celestial singers (Gandharvas) sang the praise of Yudhiṣṭhira and showered flowers (on the procession).

14. Men and women who have adorned themselves richly with clothes, ornaments, garlands and perfumes sported smearing and sprinkling each other with oil and saffron-mixed water.

15. The courtesans sported being smeared by men and reciprocally smearing men with oil, milk, perfumed water, turmeric powder and thick saffron paste.

16. With a desire to witness this procession and festival ladies of royal families all well-escorted by guards went out in their vehicles (palanquins, chariots etc.) just as heavenly damsels crowded the sky in their excellent heavenly cars (to have a look at it). Those ladies when besprinkled by the friends of Śrī Kṛṣṇa (their maternal cousin) appeared still more beautiful with their faces blooming with bashful smiles.

17. With their syringes, the ladies of royal families sprinkled jets of coloured water on their brothers-in-law and friends. Their garments being moist, the limbs of their persons such as breasts, thighs, and hips were exposed to the view. In the excitement of watersport, the braids of their hair got loosened and flowers dropped down from them. By their attractive sportive activities, they provoked impious thoughts in impure-minded people.

18. The emperor ascended the chariot drawn by excellent horses and decorated with wreaths of gold. Accompanied by his consorts he looked resplendent like the sovereign sacrifice Rājasūya with the attendant ritualistic processes incarnate.

19. After performing the special sacrifice called *Patnisaṁyāja* and other rituals connected with the concluding bath (*avabhṛtha*), king Yudhiṣṭhira performed *ācamana* (sipped water thrice from his right palm) and as directed by the priest, he along with Draupadī took bath in the Gaṅgā.

20. Drums from the heaven as well as those from the earth were simultaneously sounded. Gods, sages, manes and human beings showered flowers on them.

21. Thereupon, persons belonging to all classes of society (*varṇas*) and stages of life (*āśrama*) took their bath there; for even persons who perpetrated the most heinous sins are absolved of them by such a bath.

22. Then King Yudhiṣṭhira put on two new silk cloths

and was well-adorned with ornaments. He then worshipped the sacrificial priests, the members of the (sacrificial) assembly, Brāhmaṇas and others by honouring them with clothes and ornaments

23. The king who was unflinchingly devoted to Nārāyaṇa duly honoured his friends, kinsmen, kings, friends, well-wishers and all others (who were present) in all respects.

24. Being adorned with jewelled ear-rings, wreaths of flowers, turbans, long coats, silk cloth and extremely costly necklaces, all men looked splendid like gods, while women, the beauty of whose countenance was enhanced by a pair of ear-rings and (overhanging) locks of hair, appeared charming with girdles of gold (round their waist).

25-26. Thereupon highly virtuous priests (*ṛtvijs*), members of that assembly, the reciters of the Vedas, Brāhmaṇas, Kṣattriyas, Vaiśyas and Śūdras as well as the princes who assembled to attend the sacrifice; as also gods, sages, manes and other beings, the guardians of the world along with their followers were duly honoured. They sought the permission to go and returned to their respective regions.

27. Even as a mortal being is not sated by drinking the nectar, people did not feel satiated by glorifying the splendid success of the Rājasūya sacrifice performed by that royal sage Yudhiṣṭhira who was but a humble servant of Lord Hari.

28. King Yudhiṣṭhira could not bear the idea of separation and affectionately importuned his friends, relatives, kith and kin and Lord Kṛṣṇa to stay longer.

29. Dear Parīkṣit ! The Lord despatched Sāmba and other Yādava warriors to Dvārakā. Being desirous of pleasing king Yudhiṣṭhira, the Lord continued to stay on with him.

30. In this way, with the help of Lord Kṛṣṇa, king Yudhiṣṭhira, the son of Dharma, crossed over the ocean of his cherished ambition (of performing the Rājasūya sacrifice) which was very difficult to be accomplished. And he was thus thoroughly cured of his fever of anxiety for proper performance of the Rājasūya.

31. On a certain occasion, Duryodhana was sorely troubled at heart to notice the glorious splendour of king Yudhiṣṭhira's harem and the grandeur of the Rājasūya (and

the eminent position attained thereby) by Yudhiṣṭhira whose heart was devoted to Lord Kṛṣṇa.

32. In that harem, all the affluence and royal splendour of kings of men, demon kings and Lord of gods accumulated and utilised by Maya, the architect of that palace, were shining resplendently. With all these, Draupadī, the princess of king Drupada, waited upon her spouses. The heart of Duryodhana, king of Kauravas, was attached to her and hence he was tormented (with jealousy).

33. At that time, thousands of consorts of Lord Kṛṣṇa were staying in that palace. Owing to the heaviness of their buttocks; they had to walk slowly and the anklets on their feet jingled sweetly. They were slender-waisted, and their (white) pearl necklaces became reddish with saffron applied to their breasts. And their beautiful countenances appeared still more attractive with their rocking ear-rings and curly locks of hair.

34-35. Once, in a part of that assembly constructed by Maya, emperor Yudhiṣṭhira, surrounded by his younger brothers and relatives and by Kṛṣṇa who was his eye (indicating what is in his interest or otherwise), was seated on a throne of gold like Indra, the Lord of gods himself. He was endowed with imperial glory and was glorified by bards.

VJ.'s Text adds :

35A. He was waited upon by prominent Brāhmaṇas coming from different parts of the country. Fanned with many white coloured *chowries*, the tiger among the kings (emperor Yudhiṣṭhira) shone like the Lord of gods in the heaven.

36. There entered the swaggering proud Duryodhana adorned with a crown and garlands with a sword in his hand. He was surrounded by his brothers and he was angrily railing at the guards at the door and others.

37. He was so much deluded by the skill of Maya that when there was a part of the floor, he mistook it for a sheet of water and drew up his clothes and fell on the floor and at places tumbled into water mistaking it (the sheet of water) as floor.

Vj's Text adds:

37A. He regarded the floor paved with sapphires as a pond of water and took up his clothes and all people laughed at him.

37B. When king Duryodhana was proceeding to a pond of water, he thought it to be crystal pavement and fell into that pond.

38. O dear Parīkṣit. Seeing that Bhīma laughed at him; so too laughed the ladies and other kings even though king Yudhiṣṭhira tried to check them. Kṛṣṇa approved of them.

39. Duryodhana felt abashed and he hung down his head. As if burning with rage, he silently left for Hastināpura. There was a great uproar (of dismay and regrets) among the pious members of the assembly. The foe-less king Yudhiṣṭhira was dejected in mind. The Lord who was bent on reducing the burden of the earth, remained silent. It was through his deluding potency that Duryodhana was led into these mistakes.[1]

40. O king, I have narrated to you what you asked me how Duryodhana's wickedness developed during the great sacrifice of Rājasūya.

CHAPTER SEVENTYSIX

Fight with Śālva

Śrī Śuka said :

1. O King! Now listen to the account of another miraculous deed of Kṛṣṇa, who, out of sport, assumed a human form. This concerns the killing of Śālva, the master of the aerial car Saubha.

1. According to ŚR., this delusion of Duryodhana was the 'seed' of removing the burden of the earth and Bhīma's laughter indicated Duryodhana's discomfiture. Hence, Kṛṣṇa kept quiet.

2. Śālva, a friend of Śiśupāla, had arrived (and was present) at the *Svayaṁvara* of Rukmiṇī. At that time (he), Jarāsandha and other partisans of Śiśupāla were vanquished by Yādavas.*

3. In the hearing of all the kings (present there) Śālva took a vow, "I shall eliminate all the Yādavas from this earth. Look at my bravery."

4. Having made this solemn declaration, the foolish king

* *Here VJ.' s Text adds the following verses.*

2.1 The Lord was desirous of lightening the burden of the earth. Contemplating over his self in himself, he remained silent. Thereupon the sage whose lotus-feet are adored by gods, revealed himself in the presence of the Lord of the world.

2.2. Nārada was welcomed by all the members of the assembly by going forward to receive and was duly worshipped by them. He was highly worshipped by Kṛṣṇa and he occupied a comfortable seat near the King.

2.3. With due formalities Dharmarāja bowed to him and enquired of him : "You have access every-where and you pay visits anywhere and at any time and are impartial (not attached to anyone), O Brāhmaṇa sage.

2.4-5. Who among all chivalrous kings ruling over many kingdoms in the world, is the warrior-prince that is engaged in war preparations all the while now ?". Hearing the question so posed by him, the sage Nārada replied.

Nārada said :

2.6. As the pride of all kings is crushed down by Kṛṣṇa of incomparable valour, they now live in their respective kingdoms with their activities curtailed and their glory lost.

2.7. There is, however, one Kṣattriya prince who is highly enterprising and is of wicked mind. He is born in the Śālva country and is a king with a powerful force of men and animals.

2.8. His brother Haṁsa, the son of Brahmadatta, was killed in the battle of the Yamunā by the high-souled Viṣṇu (Kṛṣṇa), the conquerer of the universe.

2.9. The enemy of Kṛṣṇa, with an ambition to repay the debt of his (dead) brother by avenging his death, went to Kuṇḍinapura and created an alliance with Rukmī and other princes for that purpose.

2.10. (The alliance was formed) with Śiśupāla, Druma and other kings, with Dantavakra as the prominent leader. But Jarāsandha and others were defeated in the battle.

1. V.l. entered the forest for performing Penance—VJ.

VJ.'s Text adds here :

4. A : When he departed and did not return for many years though his ministers waited for him, his younger brother was installed by them as the king, for they were in need of a monarch (to rule).

propitiated the Almighty god Śiva, subsisting himself only on a handful of dust (flour?) once a day.

5. At the end of the year, the glorious god Śiva, the consort of Pārvatī, who is easily propitiated in a short while, offered to bestow a boon on Śālva who had sought asylum with him.

6. As a boon, he prayed the god to grant him an aerial car which would go anywhere at his will and which should be impregnable to gods, Asuras, human beings, Gandharvas, serpents and Rākṣasas (demons) and which could strike terror in the heart of Vṛṣṇis.

7. "Be it so" said god Śiva, the Lord of mount Kailāsa. Commanded by Śiva. Maya, the conquerer of cities of enemies, constructed a city (like spacious aerial car) of steel, called Saubha and handed it over to Śālva.

8, Sālva obtained (in his possession) the aerial car that could move anywhere at his will and was shrouded in darkness and was inaccessible (to others).*

* *Here VJ's Text adds* :

8.1. He has now returned to his country which is militarily fully prepared with army and transport (horses, chariots, etc). Out of (all) princes, he is the only king actively preparing (for war), O king.

8.2. Having heard this report as detailed by Nārada, the affluent king Yudhiṣṭhira, the son of Dharma, quietly looked at the face of the glorious Lord Kṛṣṇa who was seated by his side.

8.3. Listening to that report, Śrī Kṛṣṇa, the essence of courage and fortitude, was not disturbed at all. Laughing a bit loudly he remarked, "So be it", That is the index of his greatness.

8.4. Having worshipped the sage and paying him respects with sweet words. he thought, "It is a good thing that he who was wanted and expected for a long time, has also come now."

8.5-6. Śri Kṛṣṇa, the Lord of Lakṣmī, immediately despatched Ugrasena, King of Yādavas, Yuyudhāna, Akrūra, Kṛtavarmā and other prominent Yādava warriors along with his contingent of army to defend Dvārakā (against the expected attack from Śālva.)

(End of the Eightyfourth chapter in VJ.'s Text)

Śrī Śuka continued :

8.7-8. While the noble-souled Govinda was thus staying at Indra-Prastha and king Yudhiṣṭhira along with his younger brothers had accomplished his purpose (the completion of the Rājasūya sacrifice), Śālva heard that his friend Śiśupāla, the son of Damaghoṣa and Jarāsandha had been killed and the Rājasūya had been completed and he got enraged.

9. Śālva laid siege to Dvārakā with a mighty army, O prominent Bharata. He razed to ground city parks, gardens, completely.

VJ. adds :

9.A He based his camp in the air over the city and fought.

10. He destroyed the city along with its towers, gates, mansions, balconies, terraces and places of recreation. Destructive weapons were showered from that formidable aerial car (a veritable floating city).

11. Heavily fell down (upon Dvārakā) huge stones, trees, thunderbolts, serpents, a shower of gravel (hail-stones ?). Terrific tornadoes swept (across the city) ; the cardinal points were darkened with heavy dust.

12. Just as the earth was (formerly) oppressed under the scourage of Tripura, the city of Kṛṣṇa was subjected to extreme harassment by Saubha and could not get any respite or comfort.

13. The glorious Pradyumna noticed how his people were subjected to distress. Encouraging them with words "Don't fear", the highly illustrious warrior mounted his chariot.

14-15. Sātyaki, Cārudeṣṇa, Sāmba, Akrūra and his younger brothers, Kṛtavarmā, Bhānuvinda, Gada, Śuka and Sāraṇa and other renowned leaders of the army followed him in their chariots equipped with bows and arms and accoutred in coats of mail and protected by chariots, elephants, cavalry and foot-soldiers.

16. Then there raged a battle between the army of Śālva and that of the Yādavas, tumultuous and horripulating like the (bitter) struggle between gods and Asuras (in ancient times).

17. Just as the sun (the hot-rayed luminary) dispells the darkness of the night instantaneously, Pradyumna, the son of Rukmiṇī destroyed in a moment all the black magical spells of Śālva, the master of Saubha, with his celestial missiles.

18. He pierced the commander-in-chief of Śālva's army with twenty shafts with gold feathers, iron tips and well-polished knots (known as *sannataparva*)

19. He struck Śālva with a hundred arrows and every

one of his soldiers with one shaft each, leaders of every battalion (or charioteers) with ten arrows and the horses with three each.

20. Observing that great and wonderful feat of the high-souled Pradymna, soldiers on both the sides applauded him.

21. But the aerial-car Saubha constructed by Maya had such a magical structure and contrivances that sometimes it appeared many, sometimes one, and at times it was invisible. It was thus very difficult for the enemies (Yādavas) to locate it or conceive its nature and whereabouts.

22. Sometimes Saubha was on the ground; sometimes it flew into the sky; at times it rested on the summit of a mountain; sometimes it floated on water; sometimes it whirled round like a fire-brand and was not stationary at any point—(and thus was impossible to locate).

23. So the leaders of the Yādava army discharged arrows at every such point where Śālva with his aerial car Saubha and his soldiers made their appearance.

24. With his floating city Saubha and his army being sorely oppressed by the arrows discharged by the Yādava enemies — arrows the touch of which was scorching like the fire and the sun and unapproachable like venomous serpents Śālva fainted.

25. Though the Yādava warriors were severely beaten by the volleys of weapons discharged by the leaders of Śālva's army, none of them deserted the battlefield or his respective (appointed) position, for they wanted to win both the worlds (viz. their sovereignty in the world if survived or heavenly happiness if killed) in the battle.

26. A minister of Śālva called Dyuman, a mighty warrior himself but who was previously heavily beaten (by Pradyumna), made a surprise attack on Pradyumna and striking him with a heavy iron mace, roared loudly.

27. Pradyumna's charioteer, the son of Dāruka (Kṛṣṇa's charioteer) who knew his duty (as a charioteer), carried away from the battlefield Pradyumna, the chastiser of enemies whose chest was gravely wounded by the stroke of the mace.

28. When Pradyumna, the son of Kṛṣṇa regained his consciousness after some time he blamed his charioteer, "Alas !

you have not done well in that you have removed me from the battle-field.

29. No person born in Yadu's race is known to have turned away from the battle-field except me who incurred the blemish through a weak-minded charioteer like you.

30. Having deliberately and obviously left the battlefield, what should I plead to my uncle Balarāma and father Kṛṣṇa when they meet me and enquire about my ability.

31. My brothers and sisters-in-law will jeer at me and openly ask me, "How did you fare with your enemies in the battle? How is it that you played the coward?"

The charioteer replied :

32. (It is) With full knowledge of my duty as a charioteer that I have done this, O longlived one. My Lord, the prescribed duty is that the charioteer should protect the warrior in times of peril and the warrior should reciprocally protect him.

33. Knowing this duty as a charioteer, I took you away from the battlefield as, when attacked by the enemy and struck down with a mace, you became unconscions in a Swoon.

CHAPTER SEVENTYSEVEN

Slaying of King Śālva

Śrī Śuka said :

1*. Pradyumna sipped water (as *ācamana*), clad himself in armour, equipped himself with a bow and commanded his charioteer, "Please take me to the side of Dyumat".

2. While Dyumat was slaughtering his (Pradyumna's) forces, Pradyumna checked him and with a smile, he pierced him with eight arrows.

1* *VJ.'s Text adds* before verse 1.

1.A. Hearing the words spoken by the charioteer, Pradyumna, the delight of Yadus re-armed himself with weapons and told his charioteer on the battlefield.

3. With four shafts he struck the four horses (of his chariot); he hit the charioteer with one; with two he snapped his bow and flag (staff) and with another shaft he cut off his (Dyumat's) head.

4. Gada, Sātyaki, Sāmba and other Yādava heroes slaughtered the army of Śālva, the master of Saubha. All the inmates of the aerial car Saubha fell down into the sea with their necks lopped off (from the trunk of their bodies).

5. In this manner the armies of Yādavas and Śālva went on striking at each other. That terrific and tumultuous battle continued for twenty seven days and nights without break.

6. On being invited by Yudhiṣṭhira, the son of Dharma, Kṛṣṇa who went to Indraprastha, stayed on there even after the completion of the Rājasūya sacrifice and slaying of Śiśupāla.

7.* He took his leave of the elders of the Kuru race, sages, Kuntī along with her sons. While he travelled to Dvārakā, he noticed very terrible portents.

4* *VJ reads*

4.A. Gada, Sātyaki, Akrūra, Sāmba, Śuka, Sāraṇa, Vasudeva and Ugrasena slaughtered the army of Śālva.

7* For verses 7-18 in ŚR.'s Text, VJ.'s Text reads the following verses (in *Vrindāvan edition*).

7.1. He noticed terrible evil omens prophesying war.

7.2. Taking leave of elders of the Kuru clan and sages and followed by Pāṇḍavas along with their ministers and accompanied by Brāhmaṇas, he set out from the city (Indraprastha).

7.3. After travelling for a short distance, he asked the citizens and the sons of Kunti to stop. He bade goodbye to the sons of Kunti who were bowing him down with tearful eyes.

7.4. He travelled in the westerly directions with his queens riding golden palanquins, accompanied with thousands of elephants, horses, chariots and foot-soldiers and followed by a battalion of princes.

7.5. Even Śālva who (i.e. whose force) was soundly battered retreated from the battlefield with his aerial car and returned to his own dominion.

7.6. While Śālva was going, Sāmba quickly pursued him and with his arrows he sent Śālva's minister Kṣemadhūrti to the abode of the god of death.

7.7. Pradyumna ambushed Śālva's most beloved general vininda while he was passing by the way and struck him with his arrows.

8. (On the way) he said to himself, "I have come here to Indraprastha accompanied by my elder brother Balarāma. The Kṣattriya princes, the allies of Śiśupāla must have surely attacked my city (Dvārakā), in our absence.*

9. After his arrival at Dvārakā he noticed the havoc wrought upon his subjects. He then entrusted the defence of the city to Balarāma. Perceiving the aerial car Saubha and the King of Śālvas, he commanded Dāruka.

10. "Quickly bring my chariot near Śālva, O charioteer. You need not be afraid (even though) this master of Saubha is skilled in the use of black magic in war-fare."

11. Dāruka, thus commanded by Kṛṣṇa, brought the chariot near Śālva. The friends and the enemy saw him enter the battle-field.

12. Śālva whose forces were practically wiped out, saw Kṛṣṇa enter the battle. At Kṛṣṇa's charioteer he darted a lance (that sped through the air) making a roaring sound.

7.8. Deeply pierced and wounded by Pradyumna, he took up a sword and shield and fought with Pradyumna, the son of Rukmiṇī. And it was a wonderful combat.

7.9. While he was making wonderful circular manouvers, the great Yādava warrior sundered his head off his body in that duel.

7.10. When its chief commanders were killed, the army lost its way and took to heels helter-skelter, with the main object of saving life.

7.11-13. The Eagle-bannered Lord Kṛṣṇa also hastily rushed to Dvārakā and found the mansions, balconies and towers in the city, in debris; the city gates, arches and ramparts broken down; main streets and quadrangles wiped out; parks and gardens devastated; and ponds and wells filled with stones; The recitation of Vedas and the sound 'Vaṣaṭ' (of priests offering oblations to fire) were silent. Kṛṣṇa was deeply troubled at heart and asked Kṛtavarmā how this devastation took place.

7.14. Hearing from Kṛtavarmā, the details how the King of Śālva wrought this ruin (of Dvārakā) Kṛṣṇa, the Lord of Yādavas announced his vow while all the Sātvatas (Yādavas) were listening.

7.15. "Just now I chase Śālva and enter Dvārakā only after killing that wicked Śālva and drowning his aerial car Saubha into the sea."

7.16-17. Lord Viṣṇu (Kṛṣṇa), the god with the emblem of Garuḍa on his banner, mounted his excellent chariot to which were yoked (the four famous horses) Śaibya, Sugrīva, Meghapuṣpa and Balāhaka; was equipped with various weapons and had Dāruka in front as the charioteer. He followed the track of Śālva with the speed of the mind and wind.

7.18. After crossing a long distance, He saw Śālva concealed under the waters of the sea but seated fully adorned in his aerial car Saubha.

* *VJ.'s Text adds* :

8-A. Pondering thus, the glorious Lord hastily arrived there coming to the battle-field, he saw Pradyumna and others.

13. Observing the lance rushing through the air with great speed and illumining all the quarters like a big meteor (or firebrand), Kṛṣṇa splintered it in hundred pieces with his arrows.

14. Hitting Śālva with sixteen shafts, he pierced the aerial car Saubha which was moving through the sky, with a volley of arrows just as the sun fills the space in the sky, with his rays.

15. Śālva wounded the left arm of Kṛṣṇa in which he wielded the Śārṅga bow. And the Śārṅga bow fell from Kṛṣṇa's hand. And it was indeed a miracle.

16. There was an outburst of wild outcry of consternation and wonder from all beings who witnessed it. The king of Saubha (i.e. Śālva) roared loudly and (boastfully) said to Kṛṣṇa:

17. "You stupid fellow! You abducted the fiancee of our brother-like friend (Śiśupāla) in our very presence and killed our friend in the assembly at the time of Yudhiṣṭhira's Rājasūya while he was unaware.

18. In your pride you (falsely) regard yourself as invincible. Only if you stand before me (in this battle), I shall, with my sharp arrows, send you to a place (Yama's abode) whence nobody returns."

The glorious Lord replied:

19. "You are vainly bragging, O dull witted one! You do not perceive the god of Death standing near you. Really valiant people do not indulge in idle prattling but exhibit their valour in fighting."

20. With these words Lord Kṛṣṇa, in extreme wrath, struck down Śālva on the collar-bone with his mace of terribly vehement force. (Under that blow) Śālva was thoroughly shaken and vomitted blood.

21. While the mace returned (to Kṛṣṇa) Śālva disappeared. Then within a short while a man approached him, bowed to him with his head and while sobbing told him, "I am sent by Devakī (with a message).

22. O Kṛṣṇa, of powerful arms. O Kṛṣṇa, so affectionate to parents! Your father is captured and dragged away

by Śālva even as a butcher does to an animal to be slaughtered."

23. Hearing this unpleasant news, Kṛṣṇa exhibited His human nature. Deeply troubled at heart, despondent and overcome with filial affection, he exclaimed like an ordinary mortal.

24. "How is it possible that unperturbable Balarāma who is invincible to gods and Asuras (together) was defeated by this despicable Śālva and my father was taken away as a captive. (Ultimately) Providence is all powerful."

25. While Govinda was uttering these words, Śālva, the Lord of Saubha, made his appearance bringing with him someone resembling Vasudeva and threatened Kṛṣṇa :

26. "This is your own father who brought you forth in this world and for whom you live. Before your very eyes, I shall slay him. Save him if you can, you childish fellow !"

27. Having threatened him thus, Śālva, the master of black magic cut off the head (of the semblance) of Vasudeva and taking it with him, he entered his aerial car Śaubha that was near him in the air.

28. By nature, Kṛṣṇa was the embodiment of pure knowledge. But even he was overwhelmed with human weakness and remained plunged for a while (for a *muhūrta*) in sorrow, due to his affection for his relative (father). Then that Lord of majestic lustre realized all that scene to be nothing but an illusion of *Asura* type spread by Śālva as per instructions of Maya.

29. Just as a person awakened from the dream finds the dream-scene vanished, that Immutable Lord Kṛṣṇa, after 'waking up' (disenchantment) from the illusory effect of Śālva's Māyā, found that there was neither the messenger nor the dead body of his father on the battlefield. Seeing his enemy ranging through the sky in his aerial car Saubha, he determined to kill him.

30*. In this way, O royal sage, some sages give an in-

*. Verses 23-28 give the view of inconsistent thinkers as ŚR. points out that Balarāma never went to Yudhiṣṭhira's Rājasūya.

consistent version. They do not remember that their words will prove contradictory.

31. Where are grief, delusion, attachment or fear which are possible to be found only in the ignorant ? How can these be presumed to affect the Absolute Lord, the master of Perfect knowledge, wisdom and Divine potencies of omnipotence, omnipresence.

32*. How could there be any possibility of Lord Hari being subjected to delusion—the Lord who is the shelter of those saintly persons who through the worship and service of his feet have obtained enlightenment in the knowledge of *ātman* (the self). With this knowledge of *Ātmavidyā*, these righteous people completely destroyed wrong notions existing from times

VR. From Vyāsa's words it is clear that Balarāma was in charge of Dvāraka in Kṛṣṇa's absence at Rājasūya. Śālva did not invade Dvārakā—in Kṛṣṇa's absence. VJ. emphasizes the impossibility of Hari being deluded by the magic spell.

* *VJ.'s Text adds* :

32.1. O Scion of the Kuru race! When Kṛṣṇa heard the words spoken by them, he began to strike down Śālva along with his aerial city Saubha.

32.2. Taking up his sharp discus Sudarśana, Kṛṣṇa charged it with the spell of the missile of the Fire-god and discharged it to destroy Saubha completely.

32.3. That discus charged with the spell of the missile of the Fire-god (pronounced on it) and hurled from the fore-hand of Nārāyaṇa (Lord Kṛṣṇa) and terrific with its flames went on burning upto the region of Brahmā.

32.4. All the celestials in their aerial cars felt scorched with the heat of the discus Sudarśana, cleared out of the sky and fled in all directions.

32.5. The Sudarśana discus dazzling like a hundred suns cut asunder the city of Saubha in two and again returned to the hand of Nārāyaṇa, O king Parīkṣi t.

32.6. Thus the city (of Saubha) lay shattered in the sea. But the irresistible Śālva made his appearance with a mace in hand. The wicked fellow hurled his mace at Kṛṣṇa.

32.7. Getting into the chariot brought up by the Daitya army—a chariot equipped with a heap of arms—Śālva discharged innumerable weapons on ·, e head of Kṛṣṇa and roared like a lion.

32.8. Hari split the mace hurled by Śālva, in three pieces with his arrows. He blew his conch Pāñcajanya and roared like a lion.

immemorial about the identification of the body with soul and thereby they have secured their own essential, infinite Lordly state.

33. While Śālva was vigorously attacking him with a volley of weapons, Kṛṣṇa, the descendant of Śūra, of unfailing prowess, wounded Śālva deeply with his arrows and shattered to pieces Śālva's armour, cut down his bow and the jewel on his head, and knocked down to pieces (Sālva's aerial car) Saubha.

34. Knocked down by the mace darted by Kṛṣṇa's hand, Saubha was splintered into thousands of pieces and fell into the water in the form of powder. Abandoning it, Śālva landed on the earth and raising his mace quickly rushed at Kṛṣṇa.

35. With a special kind of arrow called *bhalla*, Kṛṣṇa cut down Śālva's arm with the mace as he was rushing against him (to assault). In order to finish with Śālva, Kṛṣṇa took up his miraculous discus Sudarśana which was dazzling like the burning sun at the time of the destruction of the universe. (With the discus held up in the position of hurling), he shone resplendent like the Eastern mountain with the disc of the rising sun on its summits.

36. Just as (in ancient times) Indra chopped off the head of Vṛtra, Hari, with that very Sudarśana severed the head decked with a crown and ear-rings of Śālva of extensive capacity in black-magic. And there arose an outcry of grief (alas !) from his men.

37*. O king Parīkṣit ! When that sinful Śālva fell struck

**VJ.'s Text adds* :

37.1. Celestial drums were sounded and showers of flowers were let down. Glorified by the sages and by bards like Sūta, Māgadha and Bandins, Hari came to his capital Dvārakā, surrounded by his armies.

37.2. He entered the charming city decorated with a number of flags and other decorative work, and with clean quadrangles besprinkled with water.

37.3. He (Kṛṣṇa) was honoured by elderly Yādavas as well as by men in the city and the rural areas. He delighted the sixteen thousand queens who were over-whelmed with love for him. Thus the son of Devaki lived happily and in joy, O descendant of Kurus.

were sounded in heaven by gods. Then Dantavaktra angrily attacked him for avenging the deaths of his friends (viz. Śiśupāla, Śālva).

CHAPTER SEVENTYEIGHT

Dantavaktra and Vidūratha Slain :

Balarāma's Pilgrimage

*Śri Śuka said** :

1. The wicked Dantavaktra wished to demonstrate his friendship with Śiśupāla, Śālva and Pauṇḍraka who had gone to the next world (being killed by Kṛṣṇa). He wished to avenge their death by slaying Kṛṣṇa.

2. (Unaccompanied by an army or without riding a chariot) the foolish but mighty Dantavaktra rushed alone in rage with a mace in hand. Shaking the earth under his feet while walking, he confronted Kṛṣṇa.

3. Beholding him thus advancing, Kṛṣṇa quickly took up his mace and jumping down from his chariot, he resisted him as the seashore stops the flowtide of the sea.

4. Raising his mace, the foolishly arrogant king Kāruṣa (Dantavaktra) exclaimed : "How lucky it is ! I am glad that

* *VJ.'s Text adds at the beginning.*

1.1-1.2. : Having heard that Kṛṣṇa had gone to the bank of the Yamunā for the concluding bath (*avabhṛtha snāna*) of the Rājasūya sacrifice, Dantavaktra, the king of Kaliṅga, accompanied by his younger brothers and a big army consisting of elephant corps, quickly marched to ambush Kṛṣṇa while he would proceed to Dvārakā.

1.3-1.5 : Like unto a jackal obstructing a lion, the foolish Dantavaktra blockaded Kṛṣṇa who was accompanied by young Yādava princes, and was surrounded by the palanquins of his sixteen thousand queens, was followed by a group of kings, by a number of great sages, priests who officiate at sacrifices, family priests, preceptors and other Brāhmaṇas.

down with the mace and Saubha was smashed to pieces, drums you have come within the range of my sight to-day !"[1]

5*. O Kṛṣṇa ! You are the son of our maternal uncle[2]. But you are treacherous to friends (and have killed them). You Fish to slay me as well. Hence I shall kill you with my mace which is as hard as thunderbolt.

6. Being affectionate and loyal to my friends I shall pay off my debt (of friendship) to them by killing you, an enemy in the form of a cousin, just like a disease in one's body, O ignorant fool."[3]

1. As in the case of Śiśupāla's censure of Kṛṣṇa (vide *Supra* 10.74. 34-37) ŚR. gives another interpretation of Dantavaktra's reproachful speech implying Kṛṣṇa's glorification as Dantavaktra was Viṣṇu's attendant in Vaikuṇṭha.

ŚR's glorificatory interpretation of this verse :

Dantavaktra whose pride had already disappeared (at the sight of his master Viṣṇu in his original birth in Vaikuṇṭha) welcomed him, "How fortunate it is! How glad I am that your worship has presented yourself to my vision. It is certainly lucky ! Really very lucky!

*. *VJ.'s Text gives the following version* :

5.1. O Kṛṣṇa ! You are our maternal cousin but you are tracherous to friends and hunt after the wives of others. You are a traitor committing breach of trust, a murderer of relatives, fond of picking quarrels.

5.2. You have killed the son of my maternal uncle Pauṇḍraka in a battle. You have slain my cousins' brothers Rukmī and Śiśupāla. (It was Balarāma and not Kṛṣṇa who killed Rukmī).

2. Dantavaktra was the son of Śrutadevī, the sister of Vasudeva.

ŚR.'s interpretation of some adjectives to show that this is Kṛṣṇa's praise is far-fetched. For example the 2nd line in verse 5.

atastvāṁ gadayā manda haniṣye Vajrakalpayā is taken as *gadayā amanda haniṣye a-vajrakalpayā*

"O Lord capable of bearing anything! Bear up with the stroke of my gadā which is tender like a wreath of lotus.

3. ŚR.'s second interpretation of some adjectives in this verse :

ajña-(na vidyate jñaḥ yasmāt saḥ) Omniscient, *Vyādhi*—One who abides in the body as Inner Controller.

hatvā—Having arrived at the realization of your essential nature (*han* to go) *ānṛṇyam upaimi* : Pay off the debt of my ancestors (by realization of the Brahman).

"O Omniscient Lord ! Due to Sanaka's curse, I have become your cousin and enemy. But having realized your essential nature as one who abide as Inner Controller of all beings or facing you in the ways of Kṣattriyas, I shall pay off the debt of my manes."

7. Cutting to the quick Kṛṣṇa, with such harsh words like piercing an elephant with a goad, he hit Kṛṣṇa on the head with his mace and roared like a lion.

8. Though struck down with a mace in that battle, the descendant of Yadu (Kṛṣṇa) remained unshaken. Kṛṣṇa on his part hit Dantavaktra on the chest with his mace Kaumodakī.

9. With his heart shattered with the stroke of the mace, Dantavaktra vomitted blood through his mouth and he fell dead on the ground with his hair dishevelled and arms and legs outstretched.

10*. Just as it happened after the slaying of Śiśupāla, a very subtle ray of light emanated from the body of Dantavaktra and entered in the person of Kṛṣṇa — a wonderful sight indeed — while all beings were witnessing it.

11. Overwhelmed with grief for his brother, Vidūratha, Dantavaktra's brother, armed with a sword and a shield, came there having heavy sighs, but desired to kill Kṛṣṇa.

12. As he was advancing, Kṛṣṇa with his discus of sharp edge, severed off his head adorned with a diadem and ear-rings.

13-15**. Having thus demolished (the aerial car) Saubha and slain Śālva, Dantavaktra and his younger brother (Vidūratha) who were irresistible to others, Kṛṣṇa entered the decorated city of Dvārakā while his victory was being glorified

* *VJ.'s Text* : 10.1. Practically the same as verse 11 above.

10.2. He quickly jumped down from his chariot and brandishing his excellent sword and shaking the ground under his feet, he dashed against Kṛṣṇa.

10.3. When Kṛṣṇa cut off his sword with an arrow, he took up a terrible sharp-pointed *śakti*.

10.4. Determined to strike down Kṛṣṇa in the battle the foolish fellow darted towards him like an arrow discharged from a bow.

** *VJ.'s version* :

13-15.1. Having thus killed both Dantavaktra and Vidūratha in the battle, the Lord put to flight their army and captured their elephants (horses, etc.)

13.15.2. Kṛṣṇa again mounted his divine chariot *Puṣpa-ratha* which was tastefully decorated. He was accompanied by the Yādava clansmen and was praised by gods and men (in songs).

in songs by gods, men, sages, siddhas, Gandharvas (celestial singers), Vidyādharas, big serpents and by celestial damsels (*apsaras*), manes (ancestors), Yakṣas, Kinnaras and while he was being showered over with flowers and was accompanied by prominent Vṛṣṇis.

16*. In this way, the glorious Lord Kṛṣṇa, the master of Yoga and the Almighty controller of the Universe is ever victorious, though to the ignorant (lit. persons with the vision of brutes), he appears at times vanquished.

17. It is reported that when Balarāma heard of the war-preparations of the Kauravas against the Pāṇḍavas, he, being neutral** (with reference to the belligerent parties) went

16* *VJ.'s Text adds after verse* 16:

16.A. O descendant of Bharata ! The noble deeds of the Lord of hallowing renown are such as cannot be recounted in tens of thousands of years (even god Brahmā and others cannot do this, what of me ?).

16. B. O chastiser of enemies ! In this way the slayer of the demon Madhu (Śri Kṛṣṇa) began (the destruction of Rākṣasas) with the demoness Pūtanā and killed all the Asuras who were a burden to the earth.

(Here ends Chapter No. 101 in VJ.'s Text)

VJ.'s introduction :

Though the life of Balarāma is interwoven with that of Śrī Kṛṣṇa, two more chapters are added specifically to the life and deeds of Balarāma.

King Parīkṣit said :

1. I pay my obeisance to the Soul of the universe who through dint of his deluding potency brought about the destruction of the eighteen *akṣauhiṇīs* of army (in the Mahābhārata war) in equal number of days.

2. By listening to his stories and deeds in aggregate, my bewilderment, wonder and fear go on increasing again and again.

3. I consider that most probably my sinfulness which is difficult to cross has ceased to be. My senses are wide awake and the mind is extremely delighted and serene.

4. My hunger and thirst have subsided. My soul (mind) is filled with ecstatic delight. It is through your grace, O expert in religion (religious discourse) that I feel that I have accomplished all my objects in this world.

5. I, however, wish to hear from you something more. When Balarāma found that his friends (both Kauravas and Pāṇḍavas) were bent on fighting and that he could not prevent them from doing so, he went to perform ablutions in sacred places. O sage rich in penance ! Narrate to me what Balarāma did.

* KD. states that Balarāma, out of sympathy, wanted to intervene between the warring parties incidently, when he would reach Kurukṣetra in the course of his pilgrimage—78.146.

away on the pretext of a pilgrimage for performing ablutions in sacred waters.

18. After taking bath at Prabhāsa[1] and propitiating gods, sages and manes (*pitṛs*) by offering oblations of water and satisfying men (by serving them food), Balarāma, surrounded by Brāhmaṇas, went from the mouth of the Sarasvatī[2] to its source.

19*. (On the way) he visited various holy places like Pṛthūdaka[3], Bindusaras[4], Tritakūpa[5], Sudarśana[6], Viśāla, Brahmatīrtha,[7] Cakratīrtha and the spot where the Sarasvatī flows to the east[8].

1. Somanath or Verawal in Saurashtra. It is also called Devapattana. Somanath is one of the famous twelve *jyotir-liṅgas* of god Mahādeva. In its neighbourhood are the spots where Yādavas' internecine battle and death of Kṛṣṇa took place.

—GDAMI, p. 157.

2. It appears that at that time, the Sarasvatī was still flowing into the Gulf of Cutch i.e. The Arabian sea. There is a small river Rauṇākṣī, also known as the Sarasvatī in *Vāmana P.* (ch. 84) which falls in the sea near Prabhāsa. But the later description shows that Balarāma followed the course of the Vedic Sarasvatī to its source.

* It appears that no geographical sequence is followed in the description of this pilgrimage.

3. Pehoa in the Karnal district, Panjab. It is 14 miles to the west of Thanesvar. This *Tīrtha* is on the Sarasvatī, near the famous (*Brahmayonī Tīrtha*—GDAMI, p. 16. Vainya performed nine *aśvamedha* sacrifices at Pṛthūdaka (VT).

4. VT. states this to be the hermitage of the sage Kardama near Siddhapura in Gujarat. N.L. De identifies it with thr same : Sitpur to the northwest of Ahmedabad—GDAMI, p. 38.

5. Tritakūpa—A place near the Sarasvatī. In that well Trita fell and was taken out of it by god Soma (VT). Probably this refers to the incident supposed to be the basis of RV. 1. 105.

6. In Kurukṣetra, the same as Rāma-hrada—a sacred tank to the north of Thanesvar. ŚR identifies Sudarśana and Cakra Tīrtha.—GDAMI, p. 43, 166.

7. A certain Tīrtha on the Sarasvatī.

8. The Kurukṣetra Sarasvatī is called Prācī or Eastern Sarasvatī (*Padma P. uttara khaṇḍa* (ch. 67). N. L. De states that this name is specially applied to the Sarasvatī that issues out of the Puṣkara Lake—GDAMI, p. 187.

20. And passing through the various sacred places which were on the Yamunā and the Gaṅgā, he went to the Naimiṣa forest[1] where sages were holding a prolonged sacrificial session.

21. Having come to know that the distinguished guest was Balarāma, the sages who were engaged in the prolonged sacrifice, received him with due formalities, rose from their seats, bowed down to him and worshipped him.

22. Balarāma who was thus worshipped, took his seat along with his followers. He noticed that Romaharsaṇa, the disciple of the great sage Vyāsa, remained seated there, occupying a higher seat in front of the Brāhmaṇas.

23. Balarāma, the descendant of Madhu, got enraged when he found that Romaharṣaṇa, a sūta, did not rise from his seat to show reverence to him after his arrival, nor did he fold his palms to bow him and continued to occupy a higher seat in the presence of the Brāhmaṇas.

24. (He said to the Brāhmaṇas) "Why does this Sūta, a child of irregular marriage (between a Kṣattriya father and a Brāhmaṇa (mother) occupied a seat higher than Brāhmaṇas and us who are the protectors-of religion and social code of conduct. This evil-minded fellow deserves to be killed.

25-26. In spite of being a disciple of that worshipful sage Vyāsa and having studied many *smṛtis* (codes of righteous and religious conduct—social and personal) along with all the works on *Itihāsa* and *purāṇas*, he lacks self control, has no sense of discipline or modesty; he vainly pretends to be a learned man. His scholarship and learning do not contribute to his real excellence as in the case of an actor who lacks control over his mind and senses.

27. It is with this specific purpose that I have taken incarnation in this world, viz. those imposters and hypocrites who merely pretend to be religious should be done away with by me; for such people are more sinful than the unrighteous."

28. Balarāma had desisted from slaying even the wicked ones (as he was a pilgrim then). But as fate would have it,

1. Modern Nimsar on the left bank of the Gomati in the Sitapur district of U.P. It is 20 miles to the North-West of Lucknow.

—GDAMI, p. 135.

the mighty Lord spoke these words and pierced the Sūta with the end of a *Kuśa* grass.

29. Terrified and dismayed in their minds, all the sages screamed out exclaiming, "Alas ! Alas". They said to Balarāma, "O Lord ! You have perpetrated an irreligious and unrighteous deed.

30. O descendant of Yadu ! This elevated seat of a Brāhmaṇa has been offered by us to him as also, a long period of life and indefatiguate body till the sacrificial session lasts.

31. May be unknowingly but you have committed what amounts to be the sin of killing a Brāhmaṇa. (It is true that) being a master of Yoga, even the Vedic injunction against killing a Brāhmaṇa is not binding on you.

32. O purifier of the world ! If your worship, however, performs, of your own accord, the expiation for the sin of *Brahmahatyā* without being prompted to do so by others, you will be setting a noble example to others.[1]

The glorious Lord Balarāma said :

33. I shall expiate for this act of *Brāhmaṇa-cide* in order tc set an example to the world. Be pleased to prescribe to me the best course of atonement for such an act.

34. Be pleased to tell me whatever is expected by you for him—such as a long span of life, strength, sound-ness of sense-organs—and I shall accomplish it for him by my Yogic potency.

The sages replied :

35. O Balarāma ! May you be pleased to act in such a way as will preserve the infallibility of your missile (charged in the *Kuśa* grass), the efficacy of your prowess, the inevitability of death and that our boon (that the sūta should narrate the *purāṇas* to the end of our sacrificial session) also may not prove untrue.

1. *yad yad ācarati śreṣṭhas tat tad evetaro janaḥ |*
sa yat pramāṇaṁ kurute lokas tad anuvartate || —BG.3.2

Lord Balarāma said :

36. It is declared by the Vedas that it is one's own self that is born as a son.[1] His son Ugraśravas will now be the expounder of the Purāṇas and he will be blessed with a long life, bodily strength and keenness of senses (and intelligence).

37. O great sages ! Be pleased to tell me what else you wish to have and I shall accomplish it for you. O learned sages ! Please consider and advise me the course of expiation for the sin committed by me unknowingly.

The sages said :

38. There is a terrible Dānava, named Balvala, the son of Ilvala. On every *parva* (full-moon and new-moon) days, he comes here and pollutes the sanctity of our sacrifice.

39. He showers (on the sacred sacrifice) puss, blood, faeces, urine, wine and flesh. Please kill that wicked demon and that will be the most valuable service rendered to us by you, O descendant of Daśārha.

40. Thereafter, for twelve months you go round the Bhāratavarṣa and with a serene mind take bath in the sacred waters. Thereby being absolved of the sin, you will be purified.

CHAPTER SEVENTY-NINE

Balvala Killed : Balarāma's Pilgrimage

Śrī Śuka narrated :

1. O king Parīkṣit ! When the next *parva* (full moon) day came, a terrible, violent stormy wind swept over the place showering heavy dust and filling the whole atmosphere with obnoxious odour on all sides.

1. *aṅgād aṅgāt sambhavasi hṛdayād abhijāyase |*
ātmā vai putra-nāmāsi sa jīva śaradaḥ śatam||

—Kauṣītaki Up. 2.7.

Balarāma exhorts the sages to install Ugraśravas in the place of Romaharṣaṇa and all the boons promised to him by the sages will be now effective in the case of the son of Romaharṣaṇa.

2. Then there was a downpour of filthy things on the sacrificial ground, caused by Balvala, after which he appeared with a trident in hand.

3-4. Beholding that *asura* of gigantic body, extremely black like a heap of collyrium, with hair on the head, moustaches and beard like red-hot copper and a face terror-inspiring with its fierce tusks and terrific knit brows, Balarāma remembered (his weapons)—the pestle that shatters hostile forces and the plough which vanquishes demons. And both the weapons immediately presented themselves to him.

5. With the point of his plough, he pulled to the ground, Balvala who was ranging through the sky and full of indignation, he struck that sworn enemy of Brāhmaṇas on the head with a pestle.

6. With his forehead shattered and split open and bleeding profusely, the demon gave out a helpless yell and fell down to the ground like a mountain struck with Vajra and covered with liquid red chalk.

7. The sages applauded Balarāma (for this feat) and pronounced their unfailing benedictions. Those highly blessed sages sprinkled sacred waters on Balarāma (as *abhiṣeka*) as gods did to Indra when he killed Vṛtra.

8. They presented to Balarāma a celestial five-coloured *Vaijayantī* garland of unfading flowers (chiefly lotuses, two excellent pieces of cloth and very valuable ornaments.

9. Then with the permission of those sages, Balarāma, accompanied with Brāhmaṇas went to the Kauśikī[1] river. After taking bath therein, he proceeded to the lake[2] from which the Sarayū flows out.

10. From its source and travelling along the current of the Sarayū, Balarāma reached Prayāga. He took his bath there-

1. Modern Kośī running from Nepal by the western border of the Purnea district in Bihar. The river has been tamed by dams now. Was it in the *Kokāmukha tīrtha* where Balarāma took his bath? —SGAMI, pp. 278-80, 340.

2. The Purāṇas believe that the Mānasa lake is the source of the Sarayū. But the river rises in the mountains of Kumaun and after its junction with the *Kālī nadī*, it is called the Sarayū. Ayodhyā is on its bank.
—GDAMI, p. 181-82.

in, offered water oblations to gods (sages and manes) and proceeded to the hermitage of Pulaha.[1]

11-12. He bathed in the Gomatī, Gaṇḍakī, Vipāśā[2] the Śoṇa and visited Gayā and worshipped his ancestors. After taking his bath at the confluence of the Gaṅgā with the sea, he met Paraśurāma and paid his respects to him on the Mahendra[3] hill. He took bath in the seven branches of the Godāvarī, the Veṇā, the Pampā[4] and the river Bhīmā.

13. After paying a visit to the temple of Skanda, he went to Śrī Śaila[5]. The great Balarāma then visited the holy mountain Veṅkaṭa in the Draviḍa land.

14. Lord Balarāma then visited the city of Kāñcī[6] known as Kāmakoṣṇī[7] (Kāmakoṭī) and the great river Kāverī, he paid visit to the holy place known as Śrīraṅga[8] (Srirangam) where Lord Hari ever abides.

15. He then went to the Ṛṣabha[9] hill, a sacred place dedicated to Hari. He then visited Setu[10]—the dam built across the sea (by Rāmacandra) where people are absolved of very heinous sins.

1. The same as Śālagrāma, near the source of the Gaṇḍak —GDAMI, p. 161 & 174.

2. The Beas. It is difficult to plot the route followed by Balarāma as the *purāṇa* writer has vague idea of the geography of north India.

3. The range of hills extending from Orissa to the district of Madura. It is applied to Eastern Ghats in general—SGAMI, p. 61. N.L. De states that Mahendra hills separate Ganjam from the valley of the Mahanadi—GDAMI p. 119.

4. A tributary of the Tuṅga-bhadrā. It rises in the Ṛṣyamūka hills in Bellary district.

5. Also called Śrī Parvata (GDAMI, p. 193) It is a hill in the Nallamalur range and a famous Tirtha in Kurnool district of Andhra Pradesh.—SGAMI, p. 336.

6. Modern Conjeveram on the river Palar, 43 miles south-west of Madras. The eastern part of the town is called *Viṣṇu Kāñci* and western part as *Śiva kāñcī* —GDAMI, p. 86

7. N.L. De identifies it with Kumbhakonam but he is doubtful about it.—GDAMI, p. 86.

8. Śrīraṅgam, 2 miles to the north of Trichinopoly, Tamil Nad. Famous for its Viṣṇu temple (Śrī Raṅgam) —GDAMI, p. 193.

9. The Palni hills in Madura. They form the northern portion of the Malaya mountain. The hills are locally known as *Varāha Parvata*—GDAMI, p. 169.

10. The Adam's bridge between India and Ceylon Rameshwaram is the first island in this chain of islets. It is called *Saṅgama Tīrtha* also —GDAMI, p. 184.

16. Balarāma gave ten thousand cows to the Brāhmaṇas there. He then visited the rivers Kṛta-mālā, Tāmraparṇī and the mountain-chain called the Malaya (one of the seven important mountain ranges in India).

17. There he paid respects to the sage Agastya who was established on the mountain. After receiving blessings from him and with his permission, Balarāma went to the south-sea where he visited the goddess Durgā (Pārvatī), known there as Kanyā (at Kanyā Kumārī).

18. Next he visited the sacred place called Phālguna[1] and the lake called Pañcāpsaras (five celestial damsels) noted for the special presence of Viṣṇu. He performed ablution therein and gave ten thousand cows (to Brāhmaṇas).

19. Then Lord Balarāma went to Kerala, Trigarta.[2] (From thence he proceeded to the famous Śaivite holy place Gokarṇa where god Śiva is ever-present.

20. Having visited the shrine of Pārvatī (designated as Āryā) on the island, Balarāma proceeded to Śūrpāraka (Sopara, Dist. Thana, Maharashtra). After taking bath in the Tāpī, the Payoṣṇī[3] and the Nirvindhyā[4], he entered the Daṇḍaka forest.

21. (From that forest) he entered the river Narmadā on the banks of which is situated the city of Māhiṣmatī[5]. He performed ablution in the Manutīrtha and again returned to Prabhāsa.

22. Having heard from the Brāhmaṇas the report of the destruction of all Kṣattriya princes (participating) in the war

1. ŚR identifies it with Anantapur, fiftysix miles to the south-east of Bellary. Pañcāpsarā tīrtha is near it. VB. calls it 'Anantaśayana'. He states that the five divine damsels were restored to their original status by Arjuna. Hence it is called *Pañcāpsaras*.

2. North Canara in Karnataka—GDAMI, p. 205.

3. The Pain-gaṅgā. a tributary of the Godavari—SGAMI, p. 57.

4. The Newuj, a tributary of the Chambal flowing between the Betwa and the Kalisindh—SGAMI, p. 57.

5. Modern Maheshwar, forty miles to the south of Indore. It was the capital of Haihayas. In the Buddhist canon in the *Mahā Govinda sutta* (*Dīgha Nikāya* 29.36) it is called Māhissati and it was the capital of Avanti (Malwa).

between Kauravas and Pāṇḍavas, he considered it as the removal of the burden of the earth.

23. The scion (or the delight) of the Yadu's race (Balarāma) went to Kurukṣetra with the desire of preventing Bhīma and Duryodhana from their single combat with their maces on the battle-field.

24. As soon as Yudhiṣṭhira, the twins Nakula, Sahadeva and even Kṛṣṇa and Arjuna saw him, they bowed to him but they kept quiet, as they were afraid why he had come over there and what he wanted to say.

25. He saw both Bhīma and Duryodhana, with maces in hand, both highly enraged and bent on vanquishing the other, were making wonderful manoeuvres (in the combat with maces). He spoke to them :

26. "O king (Duryodhana), O Bhīma, both of you are warriors equal in strength. I think one of you is superior in physical strength while the other excels in training.

27. As both of you are equal in prowess, I do not see that either of you will be victorious or vanquished. Hence, such a fruitless combat should be stopped altogether.

28. O Parīkṣit ! The enmity of these two inveterate adversaries was so deepseated that neither of them accepted his advice, though it was salutary and significant. For they did not forget their mutual offensive words and the wicked deeds.

29. Considering that the combat was destined (as a fruit of their past acts and hence inevitable), Balarāma returned to Dvārakā. He was received there warmly by Ugrasena and other relatives who were glad at his arrival.

30. (Balarāma took him with all the necessary materials and assistants for performing sacrifices). He again visited the Naimiṣa forest. The sages, acting as his sacrificial priests, gladly helped Balarāma whose person was constituted of sacrifice (or sacrifices formed a part of his personality) and who kept himself aloof from the (Kaurava-Pāṇḍava) war, in the performance of all sacrifices.

31. The almighty Lord Balarāma imparted to them highly pure spiritual wisdom by virtue of which the sages re-

alized that the whole universe is in their Self and that their self pervaded all the universe.

32. Having performed the concluding bath of the sacrifice along with his consort Revatī and accompanied by his clansmen, relatives and friends, Balarāma who put on excellent dress and was well adorned, shone like the moon radiating its own (moon-) light.

33. Innumerable are other feats and exploits (of such a nature) of the mighty Balarāma who is infinite (or Ananta or the serpent Śeṣa himself) and incomprehensible by nature. He has assumed the form of a mortal being by his own Māyā potency.

34. He who remembers and contemplates over the feats of Balarāma who performed miraculous deeds, both in the morning and the evening, becomes a beloved of the infinite Lord Viṣṇu.

CHAPTER EIGHTY*

The Story of the Brāhmaṇa Śrīdāman[1]

King Parikṣit requested :

1. O worshipful sage ! We desire to hear of other glorious exploits of the noble-souled Kṛṣṇa of infinite powers and glory, O master.

2. What person (on earth) who has the power of discernment of what is excellent and the quintessence of things but has suffered sorely from the shafts of passions and desires, and had once the opportunity of listening to the holy and true

* VJ. : Before beginning the description of Kṛṣṇa's placid life at home in Dvārakā after the Mahābhārata war, VJ.'s text describes the interim activition of Kṛṣṇa such as visiting Dhṛtarāṣṭra, Gāndhāri and departure from Hastināpura. (for this refer Appendix, Chapter eighty-I.)

1. The text of the Bh. P. is silent about the name of the Brāhmaṇa. The name given here is on the strength of the colophon of the chapter.

stories of the Lord of hallowed renown, would desist from listening to them, O Brāhmaṇa sage ?

3. That is the only real speech (tongue) with which Lord's excellences are extolled. Those hands deserve their designation as hands which engage themselves in his service. That mind is worth its name which contemplates on him who abides in all the mobile and immobile creation. Only that ear (is the blessed and) deserves to be called such (viz. the ear) which listens to the holy stories of the Lord.

4. That head deserves to be called such as bows down to him as manifested in both mobile or immobile forms (or lays itself on the ground to bow to him and his votaries). That is the real eye which sees the Lord (in everything and everywhere). Those are the real parts of the body, which always resort to the waters that wash the feet of the Lord as well as those of his devotees (i.e. sprinkle themselves and get purified with those waters).[1]

Sūta said :

5. When the worshipful son of Bādarāyaṇa was thus requested by king Parīkṣit, Śuka whose heart is immersed in (the meditations of) the glorious Lord Vāsudeva, said.

Śri Śuka began to narrate :

6. There was a certain Brāhmaṇa friend of Lord Kṛṣṇa. He was a pastmaster in the knowledge of the Vedas (or the supreme Brahman), free from attachment to the objects of senses. He was perfectly serene in mind and possessed complete control over his senses.

7. Though he was leading the life of a householder, he subsisted on whatever came his way without asking or trying for it. He was (naturally) ill-clad and his wife also who was like him (had no sufficient clothing to cover her person) but was of the same spirit, had grown emaciated with hunger.

8. That poverty-stricken chaste lady who was devoted to her husband but whose body was trembling (with weakness)

1. VT. cautions that this sprinkling is limited to the limbs of the upper part (*nābher ūrdhvam*) of the body.

and with a withered countenance, approached her husband and submitted :

9. "Is it not a fact, O Brāhmaṇa, that Kṛṣṇa, the Consort of Lakṣmī incarnate, is a personal friend of your worshipful self? The glorious Lord, the leader of Sātvatas, is a friend and devotee of Brāhmaṇas and a worthy asylum to those who seek shelter in him.

10. Blessed Sir, be pleased to approach him who is the ultimate resort of the righteous and saintly people. He will (immediately understand your circumstances and) bestow abundant wealth on you, who are a poverty-stricken householder.

11. That Lord of Bhoja, Vṛṣṇi and Andhaka clans now resides at Dvārakā. If his lotus feet are remembered, he gives away even his own self (to them. He is so generous). Will not that father and preceptor of the world confer wealth and worldly desires on his devotees, as both these are not very important comparatively (as gifts to his votaries).

12. When he was thus softly entreated by his wife many times, the soft-natured Brāhmaṇa thought, "It will be a supreme blessing at least that I shall gain at the sight of the Lord of holy renown.

13. With these considerations, he made up his mind to go (to Dvārakā). (As it was customary not to see a king or a guest empty-handed, but to offer him something as a present) he said, "Is there anything in the house worth giving as a present to Kṛṣṇa? If so, give that with me, O blessed lady."

14. The lady solicited the (neighbouring) Brāhmaṇas to give her some *pṛthukas* (fried and beaten rice). Having secured four handfuls of such rice, she tyed them up in a rag and handed over them to her husband as 'Present' to Lord Kṛṣṇa.

15. With those handfuls of rice as present, the Brāhmaṇa travelled the city of Dvārakā anxiously thinking all the while, "How will it be possible for me to gain a sight of Lord Kṛṣṇa?"

16. Accompanied by other Brāhmaṇas, he crossed the three check posts of guards[1] and the defensive ramparts of the city

1. According to verse quoted by VT. a *gulma* or checkpost consists of nine elephants, nine chariots, twentyseven horsemen and fortyfive foot-soldiers.

and the mansions of Andhakas and Vṛṣṇis who followed the path of righteousness ordained by Lord Kṛṣṇa—which were inaccessible to other persons.

17. Out of the sixteen thousand palaces of the queens of Kṛṣṇa, the Brāhmaṇa entered one of them which appeared specially affluent and splendid, with the feeling of supreme bliss in merging with the Brahman.

18. Noticing from a distance that the Brāhmaṇa was coming, Lord Kṛṣṇa who then occupied a sofa with his beloved (Rukmiṇī), instantly rose from his seat, went forward to receive him and joyfully embraced him closely with both of his arms.

19. The lotus-eyed Lord felt extremely happy at the touch of the person of his beloved friend, the Brāhmaṇa sage and he shed tears of joy from his eyes.

20-21. Then he seated him on his own couch; and personally washed his feet and sprinkled his own head with the drops of water with which he washed the Brāhmaṇa's feet. O king Parīkṣit, the Lord who purifies the whole universe, smeared the Brāhmaṇa with excellent perfumes such as pastes of sandal aloe-wood and saffron.

22. Having worshipped his friend with perfumed fumes and rows of lamps, he offered him a cow as a gift, a betel-leaf (with its usual contents of areca-nut powder, cloves, etc.) and greeted him warmly with sweet words of welcome.

23. It is said that the queen Rukmiṇī herself, with a *chowrie* in her hand, fanned the ill-clad Brāhmaṇa of emaciated dusty body the veins of which were visible.

24. The ladies in the harem were really astonished to see that a semi-nude Brāhmaṇa is worshipped with so much affection by Lord Kṛṣṇa of such a spotless reputation.

25-26. (They commented): "What meritorious act must have been performed by this naked beggarly Brāhmaṇa, destitute of wealth and censured as worthless in the world, that he was greatly honoured by the preceptor of the three worlds, the abode of the goddess Śrī. But he discarded the goddess Lakṣmī who was occupying the sofa with him and embraced him as if he were his elder brother."

27. O king! Holding each other by the hand, they recounted to each other the sweet stories of the incidents that

happened while both of them lived together in their teacher's hermitage in their student days.

The glorious Lord enquired :

28. O dear Brāhmaṇa, expert in religion ! Please tell me if, after the completion of your course of education and after honouring your teacher with the payment of fee for education, you have married a wife suitable to you or have not done so as yet.

29. I learn that even as a householder, your mind is not interested in objects of enjoyment and being a learned man you are not so much after money.

30. Like unto myself who perform action to set example to the world, there are some people who discharge their duties without being affected by desires at heart and avoid the fascinations created by the celestial potency of the Lord.

31. Do you remember, O Brāhmaṇa, our stay in the house of our preceptor? It is there that a twice-born one knows everything worth knowing from his preceptor and ultimately reaches beyond the darkness (of *saṁsāra*).

32. Dear friend ! He from whom one is born (and thus invested with the body) is the first *guru* (preceptor). He from whom one becomes twice-born (by performance of the *upanayana*—investiture of the sacred thread) and becomes eligible for study of Vedas and performance of religious duties is the second preceptor. And one who imparts spiritual knowledge directly to persons belonging to all *āśramas* (stages of life)—is the Third *guru*(preceptor) and is veritably identical with me.

33. (Hence, those who resort to me as the preceptor giving enlightenment in spiritual knowledge, and cross the *saṁsāra* are the really intelligent ones) O Brāhmaṇa ! Those who, in this mundane existence, obtain oral instructions (in spiritual matters) from me as their preceptor, easily cross the ocean of *saṁsāra*, as they know the real essence in the order of *varṇas* (social classes) and *āśramas* (stages of life).

34. I abide in all beings as their Inner Controller. Just as I am pleased by rendering services (to the spiritual preceptor), I shall not be pleased (that much) by performance of sacrifices (or the duties of a householder's life), by birth in

cxcellent family, by the performance of the investiture of the sacred thread of *upanayana* (implying the observance of duties of a *brahmacārin* or a celibate person). Nor shall I be pleased so much with penance (in the *Vānaprastha* stage of life) or by the path of quietism (followed by *sannyāsins*).

35. Do you remember, O Brāhmaṇa, the incident which happened while we were staying at our preceptor's hermitage and were once sent by our preceptor's wife to bring fuel.

36. And how when we entered into the thick jungle, suddenly, out of season, there was an outbreak of a mighty violent storm, heavy down-pour of rain and terrible roaring of thunder over our heads.

37. In the meanwhile the sun set and all the quarters were enveloped in darkness and the undulations of the ground being covered under water we could not discern the high or the low level of the land.

38. Then failing to discern the direction to be followed and sorely beaten by the repeated violent blasts of wind and showers in the forest flooded with water, we were afraid and holding each other by hand, wandered here and there.

39. Having come to know of this after sunrise, our teacher Sāndīpani came in search of us with his disciples and found us in a bewildered condition.

40. He cried out, "O my children, you have undergone extreme hardships for our sake. Life or the soul is verily dearest to all. But you evinced devotion unto me disregarding even that (your life).

41. It is in this manner that a good disciple should repay his debt (of gratitude) to his preceptor, namely that he should offer with a sincere heart, whatever he has with him (including his very life).

42. O prominent among twice-borns ! I am really very much pleased. Let all your desires be fulfilled. May your knowledge of the Vedas never fail you either here or hereafter."

43. Many other such incidents took place during our residence in the house of our preceptor. It is by the grace of the preceptor that a man becomes perfect and eligible for supreme peace.

The Brāhmaṇa (Śrīdāman) replied :

44. O God of gods ! O Preceptor of the universe ! When we stayed in the preceptor's house, what was there that we did not accomplish through the help of you whose resolutions always turn out to be true.

45. O Almighty Lord ! Your person is constituted of the Vedas and you are the repository of all blessings; your stay in the house of the preceptor is certainly a wonderful imitation of the ways of the world.

CHAPTER EIGHTYONE

The Story of the Parched Rice

(The story of Śrīdāman continued)

Śrī Śuka said :

1. While Hari was conversing with the prominent Brāhmaṇa on such matters he, knowing as he did the minds of all beings, spoke to him smilingly.

2. Lord Kṛṣṇa was friendly to Brāhmaṇas and he was certainly the asylum of the pious. Looking at his dear Brāhmaṇa friend with an affectionate glance, he laughed loudly and asked in a joking mood:

The Lord said:

3. "What present have you brought for me from your house, O Brāhmaṇa? Even the slightest offering—a particle given with affection by my devotees is considered by me as very great, but even if a lot of presents are given to me by one who is not my votary, they are not conducive to my joy or satisfaction.

4. A person who devoutly offers me a leaf, a flower, a fruit or even water, I enjoy that which has been brought to me with devotion by a person of controlled and pure mind."

5. Even though the Brāhmaṇa was thus requested, he felt so much abashed that he did not hand over the present of

pṛthukas (parched, flattened rice) to the Lord of the goddess Śrī and simply hung his head, O king.

6-7. But the Lord can directly see what goes in the minds of all beings and he knew definitely the cause of Śridāman's visit. He thought to himself, "This Brāhmaṇa never approached me or worshipped me for money. This friend of mine has come here for pleasing his virtuous wife (in compliance of her entreaty). I shall bestow upon him wealth which is rare even for immortal gods.

8. Thinking thus within himself, he, of his own accord, snatched from under the clothes of the Brāhmaṇa, the parched flattened rice tied up in a rag (and brought by way of present to Śrī Kṛṣṇa) asking him, "What is it ?

9. My dear friend ! This present (parched rice-eatable) is exceedingly to my liking. These flattened parched rice will thoroughly satisfy me who am the Soul of the universe."

10. Saying thus, he ate handful of those rice and took another handful for eating when his consort Śrī (i.e. Rukmiṇī who was so devoted to him caught hold of the hand of the Supreme[1] Lord, (claiming that other handful of rice to herself).

11. "O Soul of the Universe ! This (handful of eaten rice) is more than sufficient in granting him all kinds of wealth and prosperity both here and hereafter. This much is quite enough for your satisfaction."

12. The Brāhmaṇa passed that night happily in the palace of Śrī Kṛṣṇa. He partook of the feast and drink and felt himself to be in the celestial world itself.

13. The next morning, he set out for his home. He was however, followed some distance by Lord Kṛṣṇa, the Creator of the Universe, the very embodiment of essential spiritual bliss who delighted him with his friendly talk.

14. But the Brāhmaṇa who was happy with seeing his great friend, returned home abashed on account of the mean-

1. ŚR. explains the significance of this prohibition to eat another handful as follows : one handful is enough to bestow on the poor Brāhmaṇa all the wealth and affluence. But by eating another handful, she will be at the service of the Brāhmaṇa (instead of Lord Kṛṣṇa)—a calamity she wanted to avoid.

ness of his heart as he did not get any money from Kṛṣṇa nor did he of his own accord request him for it.

15. (On the way, he said to himself): "How wonderful! The Lord is known for his friendliness to Brāhmaṇas which has been personally experienced by me, as the bearer of the goddess Lakṣmī on his bosom held me in close embrace—me who am the wretchedmost.

16. What a world of difference there is between me, a poverty-stricken sinner and Lord Kṛṣṇa, the abode of Lakṣmī. But I have been embraced by him with both of his arms because of my birth as a Brāhmaṇa (so kind and friendly he is to Brāhmaṇas).

17. Just like a brother, I was seated on the same sofa that was occupied by his beloved queen. Fatigued as I was, I was fanned by the Queen herself with a chowry in her hand.

18. I was adored like a god by Kṛṣṇa, the God of gods who treats Brāhmaṇas as his deities. He rendered me the highest service by personally shampooing my feet, applying sandal-pastes, etc.

19. Worship of his feet is the primary cause for men to be blessed with happiness in heaven or the bliss in the *Mokṣa* and all the affluence available either in this world or the nether-world and of mastery over all miraculous powers (*Siddhis*).

20. The Lord thought that if a penniless fellow (like me) should gain wealth, it would turn his head and would not remember me. It is with this consideration that the merciful Lord has not bestowed any wealth on me."

21. While he was musing thus, he arrived at the site of his home-stead. And Lo! It was surrounded on all sides by a palace several storeys high and resplendent like the sun, fire and the moon.

22. It was surrounded with wonderfully beautiful pleasure gardens and groves swarming with the melodiously warbling birds and with pools and tanks in which various types of lilies, lotuses, night-lotuses were in full blossom.

23. It was manned by well-adorned male attendants and beautiful female attendants with gazelle-like eyes. The

Brāhmaṇa could not recognise what it was, whose place it was and how was it that it was transformed so wonderfully.

24. While the Brāhmaṇa was pondering over that metamorphosis (of his humble home-stead) god-like glamorous men and women advanced to welcome the highly fortunate Brāhmaṇa with excellent vocal and instrumental music.[1]

25. Hearing that her husband had returned, the Brāhmaṇa's wife was transported with ecstatic delight. And in her joyous impatience, she hurriedly came out of the house (to receive him) like unto the goddess Lakṣmī incarnate coming out of her (heavenly) abode.

26. At the sight of her husband, the chaste lady had her eyes full of tears of love and eagerness. (Out of shyness) she closed her eyes and mentally paid respects to him and embraced him in her mind.

27. He was astonished to see his wife gloriously glamorous like a celestial damsel and shining (in her deportment) in the midst of maid-servants adorned with necklaces of gold coins.

28. Being beside himself with joy, he entered in the company of his wife, his own mansion which was furnished with hundred(s) of columns of precious stones and which resembled the palace of the great Indra.

29. His palace was furnished with beds white (and soft) like the foam of milk. The bedsteads were of ivory chased in gold and the fans and *chowries* had gold handles.

30. The seats were of gold provided with soft cushions. And wreathes of pearls were hanging from brilliant canopies.

31. The palace walls were of pure crystals studded with big emeralds and in them he saw excellent dolls of precious stones holding refulgent jewel lamps in their hands (to illumine the room).

1. VT in his com. on Verse 22-23 clarifies that when Śridāman stayed that night at Dvārakā and his wife in her humble cottage, this miraculous transformation of her cottage took place. When she got up and was astonished to see the change, the attendants explained how this metamorphosis was due to Lord Kṛṣṇa's, Grace. So in order that her husband should not feel confused, she instructed the attendants to receive him, etc.

32. Beholding such abundance of wealth, affluence and luxury, the Brāhmaṇa, with a dispassionate mind began to reflect upon that 'cause-less' un-sought-for windfall of wealth in his care.

33. "I am indeed unfortunate (from my childhood) and am confirmed in eternal poverty. But the cause of this unexpected prosperity can be traced to nothing else but the gracious visit (I had the privilege to obtain) of Lord Kṛṣṇa, the leader of Yadus, the master of infinite wealth.

34. My friend, the foremost of the Dāśārhas is infinitely liberal and is perfect in all blessings. Though he bestows abundantly upon his suppliants like the rain-god, he regards his gift as insignificant and nominal. Knowing the minds of his devotees he gives immense riches to them but does not promise them directly. (He is a silent but highly munificent donor).

35. Although what he gives is immensely abundant, he looks upon it as very little. And whatever insignificant is offered by his friends, he regards it as very great. That high-souled affectionate friend accepted with pleasure only a handful of the parched, flattened rice taken by me for him.

36. May I, in every future birth, be blessed with his good-will, friendship, love and service. May I have the fortune of associating myself with his devotees and may I cherish (ever-increasing) devotion to that abode of excellences and glorious powers.

37. For the Eternal Omniscient glorious Lord himself notices the downfall of the rich caused by the pride of their wealth, and does not wish to confer wonderful affluence, kingship and other spiritual powers or authorities on his devotee (even though he may solicit it) but grants them to the shortsighted ones.

38. Having come to this conclusion by intelligent thinking, the Brāhmaṇa who was devoutly and excessively attached to Kṛṣṇa, did not become much attached to those pleasures, but with the intention of renouncing them, he enjoyed those pleasures with his wife, but with little attachment to them.

39. To the Almighty Lord Hari, the God of gods, the

Lord and Protector of Sacrifices, Brāhmaṇas are his deities. To him, nothing is higher then Brāhmaṇas.

40. In this way, the Brāhmaṇa friend of the Lord realized that the Unvanquished Lord Kṛṣṇa is easily agreeable to the will of his devotees. His personal bonds (of ignorance or attachment) were cut asunder by the force of his intensive meditation. And in a short while, he attained to the Lord's region (Vaikuṇṭha), the highest goal of the righteous people.

41. A person who listens to this account of the grace showered on a Brāhmaṇa by the God who is friendly to Brāhmaṇas attains devotion unto the Lord and becomes free from the bonds of Karmas.

CHAPTER EIGHTYTWO[1]

Meeting of Vṛṣṇis and Gopas of Vṛndāvana

Śrī Śuka said :

1. On one occasion, while Balarāma and Kṛṣṇa were staying at Dvārakā, there occurred a complete eclipse of the sun, as it was at the time of deluge.

2. Being informed of it (beforehand astronomically), all (religious-minded) people from all sides went to the sacred place called Syamantapañcaka (Kurukṣetra) with the object of securing merits.

3. It was at that sacred place that Paraśurāma, the most prominent warrior, caused those big pools filled with the bloods of kings, while attempting to exterminate all Kṣattriyas from the earth.

4. Though the glorious Lord Paraśurāma was untouched by any *Karma* (despite his punitive action), in order to set a model example to people, he performed a sacrifice there for expiation of that sin (of killing Kṣattriyas) as an ordinary person will have to do.

1. The additional verses from VJ.'s Text are added here from Ch. 70 as printed on pp. 309-310 of the Vrindaban edition.

5. People from all over Bhāratavarṣa came to that most important place of pilgrimage.

VJ.'s Text adds :

5A-B. Śrī Kṛṣna accompanied with the palanquins of his sixteen thousand queens, by his sons, grandsons, multitudes of citizens, army-units, courtesans, she-elephants, by bevies of ladies from the city and other women-friends.

5-6. Vṛṣṇis as well as (elderly persons like) Akrūra, Vasudeva and Āhuka assembled to that sacred place to absolve themselves of their sins. And Gada, Pradyumna, Sāmba and others did the same.

7-8. Along with Sucandra (Rukmiṇī's son Cārucandra), Śuka and Sāraṇa, Aniruddha and the chief of the army Kṛtavarmā were posted for the protection of the city. With their chariots resembling celestial cars, with fleet horses springing like waves, with trumpeting elephants like thundering clouds and men appearing splendid like celestial beings (Vidyādharas), Yādavas who were adorned with wreaths of gold appeared extremely splendid and pompous on the way.[1]

1. *VJ.'s Text adds*:

8.1-2. With loud chantings of Vedic hymns and playing of instrumental music, and in accompaniment of the flourish of the sounds of conchs and beating of drums, they went on singing and repeating the name of Kṛṣṇa and Govinda continuously. In this way, they filled all the quarters with great noise as they went, O best of Kurus.

8.3. As they reached the holy place Syamantapañcaka, well known all over the three worlds, they built up hutments (dwelling places) with thatched roof, matting and wood (lit. with long grass and sticks).

8.4 Tents with blankets, deerskin and canvass were pitched up for kings. They were hundreds and thousands in number and had a variety of forms.

8.5 There arrived a number of kings, thousands of Brāhmaṇas, Vaiśyas and Śūdras and innumerable persons of lower castes.

8.6. And noble-souled sages of high reputation and of praiseworthy observance of vows, with preceptors, some maintainers of consecrated fire (*agni-hotrins*), some life-long celibate students and householders.

8.7. The blind, the deaf, the hunchbacks, dwarfs and physically handicapped people, persons with retarded intelligence, dumb persons—all are desirous of being absolved of their past actions.

8.8 All of them adorned their heads with the dust on the lotus-feet of Lord Kṛṣṇa, beautified with ornaments like bracelets, armlets (both on the lower and upper part of the forearm), garlands and ear-rings.

9. Like celestials ranging through the sky, along with their wives, they put on heavenly garlands, rich clothes. Arriving at Syamanta-pañcaka, those highly blessed people took their bath, observed a fast and were perfectly serene and self possessed in mind.

10. They gave to Brāhmaṇas gifts of cows covering them with clothes and adoring them with garlands and chains of gold. (And after the eclipse was over) the Vṛṣṇis again took a bath as per formalities in the pools created by Paraśurāma.

11-12. The Vṛṣṇis to whom Kṛṣṇa was their deity, served delicious food to prominent Brāhmaṇas and prayed, "May we be blest with constant devotion to Kṛṣṇa. With the permission of the Brāhmaṇas, they broke their fast. And they took rest according to their wish and pleasure under the dense, cool shade of trees. They interviewed their friendly kings and relatives who congregated there (for the same religious purpose).

13-14. They saw kings (their friends and relatives) of Matsya, Uśīnara, Kosala, Vidarbha, Kuru, Sṛñjaya, Kamboja, Kekaya, Madra, Kuntī, Ānarta and Kerala and hundreds of many other kings who were their allies or strangers. They met their friends and well-wishers like Nanda and other cowherds and Gopīs (cowherd women) who were anxiously longing to meet them.

15. Owing to overwhelming ecstatic joy of mutually looking at each other, their lotus-like hearts and faces became fully blossomed and full of splendour. They hugged each other in close embrace, with tears of joy trickling from their eyes; their hair stood on their ends; their voice choked with emotion and faltering—all of them were transported with joy.

16. Looking at each other with affectionate side-glances and exceedingly friendly smiles, the women also embraced each other closely, pressing against each other their breasts which were besmeared with saffron and their eyes full of tears of joy and affection.

17. After paying respects to the elders, they were bowed by their juniors. Welcoming each other, they enquired after the well-being (of their friends and relatives) and they told each other the stories of Kṛṣṇa.

18. When Kuntī saw her brothers, sisters, their sons, her parents, sisters-in-law and Śrī Kṛṣṇa, she felt relief as her grief soothed during her conversation with them.

Kunti said :

19. Dear (elder) brother ! I feel I am unlucky as no desire of mine becomes fulfilled. Or it may be that excellent-most brothers like you do not remember of me, even though I am entangled in calamities.

20. It appears that friends, relatives, sons, brothers—nay even parents—do not remember their own relative if the Fate frowns upon him.

Vasudeva replied :

21. Mother (a term of endearment for younger sister) ! Please do not blame us, who are ordinary mortals—toys or pawns in the hands of Providence. The world is completely under the control of the Almighty Lord and everyone acts or is compelled to act according to his will.

22. (As you know it) due to the harassment of Kaṁsa all of us had to flee and were scattered in all directions. Dear sister ! It is only recently that the Providence has rehabilitated us together.

Śrī Śuka said :

23. The kings who were duly worshipped by Vasudeva, Ugrasena and other prominent Yādavas felt deeply satisfied and delighted at the sight of Lord Kṛṣṇa.

24-26. (Those kings and prominent persons were) Bhīṣma, Droṇa, Dhṛtarāṣṭra, the son of Ambikā, Gāndhārī and all her sons, Pāṇḍavas and their queens, Kuntī, Sṛñjaya, Vidura, Kṛpa, Kuntibhoja, Virāṭa, Bhīṣmaka and Nagnajit, the mighty; Purujit, Drupada, Śalya, Dhṛṣṭaketu along with the king of Kāśī; Damaghoṣa, Viśālākṣa, the kings of Mithilā, Madra and Kekaya; Yudhāmanyu, Suśarmā, Bāhlīka along with his princes.

27. O king of kings ! These princes and those who were the allies of Yudhiṣṭhira were astonished to behold the per-

sonality of Lord Kṛṣṇa which was the abode of the goddess Śrī (of affluence and beauty) in the company of his queens.

28. Thereupon, the kings who were duly honoured by Balarāma and Kṛṣṇa were greatly delighted and eloquently praised Vṛṣṇis who were the relatives of Lord Kṛṣṇa and were under his protection.

29. (They complimented:) "O Ugrasena, the king of Bhojas! Inasmuch as you are lucky to have constantly the sight of lord Kṛṣṇa who is very difficult to be seen even by Yogins, you must deem to have accomplished the purpose of human existence among all men born in this world.

30. His spotless glory sung by the Vedas purifies the world; so does the water that washes his feet and his word, viz. the Vedic Śāstra[1]. The earth which has all its potential productive capacity burnt up by the Time-Spirit, has all her powers resuscitated by the touch of his lotus-feet. Hence, she yields to us all our desired objects.

31. The householder's life paves the way to hell. But though you lead that (householder's) life, Lord Viṣṇu himself who makes one unattached both to celestial life as well as salvation (*mokṣa*) stays in your houses, and you can see him, touch him, go after him, speak with him, sit close to him, eat with him, share the bed with him and have contacts and relations with him.[2]

Śrī Śuka said :

32. Learning that Yādavas of whom Kṛṣṇa is prominent, have arrived there, Nanda accompanied with Gopas and carts loaded with milk-products, came there with a desire to see them.

33. Seeing Nanda all the Yādavas were overjoyed and rose up to receive him, as the bodies do after the return of

1. VJ. : The *Śāstra* such as The *Brahmasūtras* issued out of Lord Kṛṣṇa's mouth purifies the world.

2. VJ. : You have really accomplished the highest purpose in your life as you are in direct contact with Lord Viṣṇu—The source of the bliss in the heaven and in the Mokṣa. He of his own accord has been in your house, so in your case householder's life will not lead to hell.

vital breath. Being extremely anxious to see him for a long time, they embraced him closely.

34. Vasudeva was especially pleased. Being overwhelmed with affection, he embraced him fast, remembering how Kaṁsa subjected him to harrowing persecutions and how he had to entrust his son to Nanda's care at his Gokula.

35. Śrī Kṛṣṇa and Balarāma embraced and bowed to their (foster) parents. But due to overwhelming affection, and the throat being choked with emotions (lit. tears of joy) they could not utter a word, O best of Kurus.

36. The highly blessed Yaśodā placed both the sons on her seat (v.l. on her lap) and clasping them together in her arms in close embrace, forgot her (longfelt) distress (of separation from them).

37. Remembering their close friendship with Yaśodā, both Rohiṇī and Devakī embraced her. With their voice choked with emotions (tears), they exclaimed in faltering tones.

38. "O queen of Vraja! Who can ever forget your everlasting (act of) friendship. Even if one attains to the fortune and status of the Lord of Heaven, the great debt (of your friendship) is unrepayable in this world.

39. Worshipful lady! These two children who had not seen their own parents, were entrusted to your filial care. They lived under your care like eyes protected by eye-lids without any fear from any quarter. You gave them protection, nourishment, loving care, caressing growth and development. For the good and righteous persons do not discriminate between a child who is theirs and the one who is not theirs.

Śrī Śuka said :

40. Having seen their beloved Kṛṣṇa after a pretty long time, they (yearned to gaze at him continuously without the interruption of winking of the eyelids and so) they blamed the Creator who created the eyelids and thus interrupted (even for a wink), his vision. Mentally they closely embraced him, who was ushered in their hearts through their eyes, and instantly became merged in him—an accomplishment not

within the easy reach of Yogins who always practice to attain one-ness with him through Yogic meditation.

41. (Kṛṣṇa assumed as many forms as there were Gopīs. And at night in a secluded place simultaneously met them all severally). When the Lord saw them in that (absorbed) state of meditation, he met each of them, in privacy, embraced them, enquired about their health and spoke to them smilingly.

42. "O friends ! Do you remember us who in order to serve the cause of our relatives have left Vraja and who were busy, as our heart was distracted elsewhere in annihilating the party of our enemies, and hence, were out of sight and have returned after a long time.

43. As a matter of fact, it is the will of the Almighty Lord which unites or disunites beings. Do you form a low opinion about us suspecting us to be ungrateful to you (despite your consistent friendliness during our stay at Gokul)? (Our absence was an act of God. Please do not misunderstand us).

44. Like unto the wind bringing together, or dispersing clouds, blades of grass, cotton, particles of dust, the Lord—the creator unites or disunites beings created by him.

45. It is a matter of great joy and fortune that the loving devotion entertained by you for me shall lead to my Self-realization and absorption in me, for it is only loving (and constant) devotion unto me that leads people to immortality i.e. Final Liberation.

46. O beautiful damsels ! Just as the elements such as the sky, water, earth, wind and fire constitute the inside and outside, beginning and the end of all material objects, I am really the beginning and the end of all beings permeating them all from within and without.

47. In this way all these elements constitute all (gross) products and beings (and are thus in them but they are not in the Soul). The Soul abides in them as the enjoyer and thus pervades them. You, therefore, observe clearly that both these (The soul and the elements) appear in me, but I as the Supreme Perfect Brahman transcend them, all.

Śrī Śuka said :

48. In this way, the Gopīs were initiated and instructed in the spiritual Lore by Lord Kṛṣṇa. By dint of constant contemplation on him, they destroyed the sheath of the subtle body (*jīva-kośa*) and became merged in him.

49. And they prayed : "O Lotus-navelled Lord ! May your lotus-feet worthy of being meditated upon in their hearts by masters of Yoga of unfathomable spiritual wisdom and which form as a support (or supporting plank) to get out of the well of *saṁsāra* to people who have fallen into that well, may these lotus feet ever remain manifest in our hearts even though we lead a domestic life in *Saṁsāra*.

CHAPTER EIGHTYTHREE

Narration of Their Marriage Episodes by Kṛṣṇa's Consorts

Śrī Śuka said :

1. The glorious Lord Śrī Kṛṣṇa who was the spiritual preceptor as well as the goal (to be attained), showered his grace on the Gopīs in that way (described in the previous Chapter). Thereupon (secondarily) he made enquiries about the welfare of Yudhiṣṭhira and all other friends and well wishers.

2. They were kindly enquired after and were duly honoured (with various presents). Their sins were destroyed at the very sight of the Lord's feet. With their minds full of joy they replied :

3. "O Lord, whence can anything inauspicious befall them who with (the goblets of) their ears, drink to their heart's content the nectar of your lotus-feet (making them forget all their griefs with its intoxicating effects)[1] the nectar which (after filling the heart of the great-souled persons and

1. *mādakatayā sarva-duḥkha-vismārakatvaṁ ca dhvanitam—VT.*

having been thoroughly enjoyed by them) flows out of the heart through their lips on some occasions (in the form of the glorification of his sportive actions). It is this nectar which rids all embodied beings of Nescience which is the root-cause of the repeated mundane existence (Lit. assuming bodies repeatedly).

4. We stand offering our salutions to *you only* (leaving all our attachment to our bodies and household properties[1]). By the effulgence of spiritual knowledge, you have shaken off (and are untouched by) the three states (of wakefulness, dream and dream-less sleep) produced by contact with the mind. Hence, you are a flood (or fathomless and limitless ocean) of blissfulness; you are the Absolute and infinite intelligence. You have assumed a (human) form through your Yogic potency for the protection of the Vedas (which were lost or whose influence disappeared) through the force of the Time-spirit. You are the ultimate goal (or abode) which the recluses of the highest order aspire to reach.

The sage (Śuka) resumed :

5. While people (like Yudhiṣṭhira and others) were glorifying in songs the praise of Śrī Kṛṣṇa, the crest-jewel among persons of hallowing renown (or the utterance of whose names is auspicious), the ladies of Andhaka (Yādava) and Kaurava families met together and narrated to each other the stories of Śrī Kṛṣṇa which are sung all over the worlds. Please listen as I shall describe them to you.

Draupadī asked :

6-7*. O Rukmiṇī who are never separate from Lord Kṛṣṇa, Bhadrā, Jāmbavatī, Kausalā, Satyabhāmā, Kālindī, Śaibyā, Rohiṇī[2], Lakṣmaṇā—O consorts of Śrī Kṛṣṇa, be pleased to tell us this—how did Śrī Kṛṣṇa who is the embodi-

1. *hitvā kim ātma-dhāma : ātmā śarīraṁ dhāma gṛhaṁ dehadaihika-sambandham parityajya*—ŚR.)

* 6-7 VT tries to defend the sequence in the names of Kṛṣṇa's queens but it is for metrical convenience that the seniority is not observed.

2. She was honoured like another Chief queen—ŚR.

ment of God himself, come to espouse you imitating the ways of ordinary mortals, through his own Māyā Potency.

Rukmiṇī replied:

8. Like a lion taking away its share (prey) from the herds of goats and sheep, the Lord carried me away, placing his foot on the heads (lit. covering with the dust of his feet the heads) of invincible warrior princes (like Jarāsandha, allies of Śiśupāla) who determined to make me over (in marriage) to Śiśupāla, stood (ready to fight) raising up their bows (and arms). May those feet of Lord Kṛṣṇa, the abode of Śrī (goddess of beauty and wealth), be available to me for worship, forever.

Satyabhāmā said :

9. In order to (disprove and) wipe out the charge (of murder of Prasena) imputed (to him) by my father whose heart was extremely grieved at the death of his brother (Prasena), the Lord vanquished Jāmbavān, the king of bears, and bringing back from him the (syamantaka) gem restored it to my father. Afraid of the consequences (of the false allegations made against Kṛṣṇa and in order to pacify him), my father offered me to him even though I was promised (to be given in marriage) to another (Akrūra).

Jāmbavatī said :

10. My father could not recognize him (Lord Kṛṣṇa) to be his (former) Master and deity, Rāmacandra, the husband of Sītā. He fought with him for twenty seven days. When he stood the test, my father came to know him, (to be no other than Rāmacandra). Then he (my father) took hold of his feet and offered me along with the jewel as a present. (O Draupadī) I am not very great. I am his female slave.

Kālindī said :

11. Having come to know that I am performing penance in the hope of (getting the privilege of) touching his feet, he approached me through his friend (Arjuna) and accepted

my hand in marriage. I am just a sweeper (a female servant) in his house.

Bhadrā said :

12. Attending my *svayaṁvara* and defeating my brothers and kings who offered resistance, my Lord carried me away to his capital (Dvārakā) just as a lion seizes away his share (prey) from a pack of hounds. May I have the good luck of washing the feet of him who is the abode of the goddess Śrī, in every birth.

Satyā said :

13. In order to put to test the prowess of the kings (who came as suitors for my hand), my father procured seven extremely mighty, energetic bulls with very sharp (pointed) horns. These bulls humiliated the pride of dauntless warriors. The Lord (however) quickly controlled them (by putting a string through their nose) and yoked them playfully as children do with lambs.

14. He won me as a prize for his prowess. He vanquished the kings who way-layed us and brought to Dvārakā me along with my maid-servants and an army of four divisions, (consisting of elephants, chariots, horses and infantry). May I ever be blest with the fortune of serving him.

Mitravindā said :

15. O Draupadī, my father of his own accord invited Kṛṣṇa who is my maternal cousin and as my mind was (attached to and) fixed on him, gave me in marriage to him along with my maids of honour and an *akṣauhiṇī* of army.

16. May I be blest with the opportunity of serving his feet (lit. touch of his feet) in every birth whenever I may be tossed by my Karman. That (touch of his feet) will confer on me the highest good (*Mokṣa*).

Lakṣmaṇā said :

17. O Queen (Draupadi)! By frequently hearing about the miraculous incarnation and deeds of the Lord as glorified by Nārada in songs and duly considering (to myself) that the

Lord is chosen as a consort by goddess Lakṣmī[1] discarding (Indra and other) guardians of the spheres,[2] I set my heart on him.

18. O chaste Lady, my father who is well known as Bṛhatsena is very affectionate to his daughter (to me). When he came to know my wish, he contrived a plan to fulfill it.

19. O queen, just as at the time of your *svayaṁvara* the device of an artificial fish was contrived with the desire of securing Arjuna (for you), in my case, the fish was covered from outside and only its reflection in water was visible.

20. Hearing of this *svayaṁvara*, thousands of kings experts in the secrets of missiles, archery and of arms and accompanied by their preceptors came from all sides to my father's capital.

21. They were received with honour by my father with due regard to their seniority in prowess and age. With their hearts set on me, they all took up the bow and the arrow kept in the assembly to hit the target.

22. Some kings who took up the bow were unable to string the bow and left it. Some (who could string the bow) could pull it upto their elbow (but were unable to fix the string on the other end) fell down struck by the bow.

23. Other warriors like the kings of Magadha (Jarāsandha) Cedi (Śiśupāla) Ambaṣṭha, Bhīma, Duryodhana and Karṇa were able to fix the string on the bow but could not know the location of the fish.

24. Arjuna became ready. He located the fish from its reflection in the water and discharged the arrow, but it just touched the fish at tangent and did not pierce through it.

25-26. When the proud kings found their pride crushed (thus humiliated), they retired to their seats. Lord Kṛṣṇa took

1. There is a pun on the following word :
Pacma-hastayā— (i) By goddess Lakṣmi (ii) By me with a lotus in hand.

2. *Lokapa*— (1) Guardians of spheres like Indra.
(2) Kings on the earth.
The second interpretation is : discarding other kings, I selected him with a lotus in my hand.

up the bow, strung it easily (as in a sport), fixed an arrow on it. Looking at the reflection of the fish in water (with that arrow) he felled it on the ground. At that time the sun was at the meredian.[1]

27. Drums were sounded in the sky while shouts of victory were raised on the earth. Gods were transported with joy and sent forth showers of flowers.

28. With anklets jingling sweetly at my feet (while I moved), dressed in a (specially prepared) rich silk *Sāri* and a similar costly upper garment decorated with a wreath of flowers in my braid (of hair) and holding forth a brilliant necklace of jewels wrought in gold in my hands, I entered the arena beaming with a bashful smile.

29. Lifting up my face beautiful with thick tresses of curly hair over-hanging and the cheeks illuminated by the brilliance of the ear-rings, I looked round at the (assembled) kings with a gentle smile and side-long glances and with my heart deep in love with the Lord, I (slowly approached him and) softly placed the necklace round his neck.

30. At that time *mṛdaṅgas*, tabors, conchs, drums and kettle-drums were sounded. Dancers (both male and female) began to dance and songsters began to sing.

31. When I selected Lord Śrī Kṛṣṇa (as my consort) the rival kings being overcome with lust for me, did not tolerate it, O Draupadī.

32. Placing me in the chariot drawn by (jewel-like) excellent four horses, the four-armed Lord, completely accoutered with armour, raised his Śārṅga bow and became ready to fight.

33. Dāruka (the charioteer) drove the gold plated Chariot while all the suitor-kings were merely looking on and he set out for Dvārakā with me, just as a lion proceeds (with his prey) through a pack of deer, O queen.

34. Like dogs trying to obstruct a Lion, those Kṣattriya princes, with a view to ambush him on the way, girded up their lions, raised their bows and pursued him.

1. The sun's position with *abhijit* is regarded as the auspiciousmost time conducive to achieve success in everything—ŚR.

35. With their arms, thighs and necks lopped off by the flood of arrows discharged from the Śārṅga bow, some kings fell in that fight while others withdrawing from the battle fled away from it.

36. Thereupon the Lord of Yadus (Kṛṣṇa) entered the city of Dvārakā (Kuśasthalī) which was specially decorated (for that occasion) with arches, banners and streamers which obscured (even) the sun—a city highly appreciated (for its beauty) both in the heaven and on the earth like the sun returning to his (glorious) residence Śrī Kṛṣṇa entered his Palace.

37. My father respectfully received and worshipped his friends, relatives and clansmen presenting them very costly clothes, ornaments, beds, seats and other articles.

38. Though my Lord is Perfect (and needs nothing) out of devotion, my father presented to him maid servants, all kinds of wealth, foot-soldiers, elephants, chariots, horses and very costly weapons.

39. (Abashed at her boastful description of her own marriage and to please her senior co-wives she concludes). All of us must have performed penance renouncing all attachments (in our previous life by virtue of which) we have the real privilege of being maid servants of our Lord who revels in his own blissful self.

The queens (representing 16000 *queens) said* :

40. Having killed Bhaumāsura along with his army in the battle, when the Lord came to know that Bhauma had kept in captivity the princesses of the kings vanquished by him during his expedition for the conquest of the earth, he set us free. Though he had all his desires accomplished, he was pleased to marry us who were constantly contemplating his lotus-feet which emancipate people from Saṁsāra.

41-42. O Chaste queen Draupadī ! We do not covet imperial sovereignty over the whole earth or kingdom of the celestial world or enjoyment of both the positions here and hereafter or the attainment of supernatural powers nor the exalted position of god Brahmā, *Mokṣa* (liberation from Saṁsāra) or residence in his eternal abode (known as *Salokatā*) but we love to bear on our heads the glorious dust on the feet of Śrī Kṛṣṇa (the wielder of the Kaumodakī mace)—the dust which is enriched with fragrance of the Saffron paste applied to the breast of goddess Śrī.

43. We earnestly crave for the touch of the feet of the great-souled Lord who tended cows—the touch which the Gopas and Gopīs of Vraja, women of Pulindas (hill-tribes), grass and creepers longed for.

CHAPTER EIGHTYFOUR

Vasudeva's Sacrifice[1]

Śrī Śuka said :

1. Listening to the bonds of intense love (expressed in the speeches) of his queens to Śrī Kṛṣṇa, the Soul of the universe, Kuntī, Gāndhārī, Draupadī, Subhadrā and other queens of the royal house along with all the Gopīs so devoted to Kṛṣṇa were greatly surprised and their eyes were filled with tears of joy.

2. While they were thus engaged in conversation, men with men and women with women, there arrived a number of sages with the desire of seeing Śrī Kṛṣṇa and Balarāma.

3-5. (They were as follows :) Kṛṣṇa-Dvaipāyana (Vyāsa), the divine sage Nārada, Cyavana, Devala, Asita, Viśvāmitra, Śatānanda, Bhāradvāja, Gautama, Paraśurāma along with his disciples, the worshipful Vasiṣtha, Gālava, Bhṛgu, Pulastya, Kaśyapa, Atri, Mārkaṇḍeya, Bṛhaspati, Dvita, Trita, Ekata, sons of god Brahmā (such as Sanaka, Sanandana and others) Aṅgiras, Agastya, Yājñavalkya and others.[2]

1. In the colophon the title of this chapter is *Description of Pilgrimage.*
2. Under 'others' VT. includes Parāśara, Maitreya, Vaiśampāyana, etc. Historically these were not contemporaries but the epic-writer credits them with inordinately long life or persons belonging to these *gotras* are implied. Biographical sketches of these have been given in the footnotes of the previous volumes of this work.

6. Beholding those sages who were universally respected, all the kings and others present there as well as Pāṇḍavas, Śrī Kṛṣṇa and Balarāma immediately rose from their seats to show respect and bowed to them.

7. Śrī Kṛṣṇa along with Balarāma and all others (present there) respectfully honoured the sages with sweet words of welcome, offering them seats, water to wash their hands and feet, flowers, incense, sandal paste, etc.

8. When they were comfortably seated, the glorious Lord, whose (human) form (incarnated in this world) was for the protection of *Dharma* (Religious order or path of righteousness) addressed them, while the great assembly was silently listening to him.

The glorious Lord (Śrī Kṛṣṇa) said :

9. How blessed are we ! Today we have attained completely the fruit (the highest objective) of having taken birth (in this world), as we have been blessed with a visit by masters of Yoga, the sight of whom is very difficult to obtain even for gods.

10. How can men whose (even concept of) penance is poor (limited to pilgrimage to sacred places, etc.) and who look upon the (stone or metal) images as God get the rare privilege of enjoying your sight, touching your feet), conversing with you, paying personal obeisance to you, worshipping your feet, etc. ?

11. Waters in sacred places consisting of sheets of water are not the real holy waters; the images made of clay and stones are not the real gods. It is after a long course of time that they purify people. But saints like you purify instantly by their very sight.

12. If the deities presiding over the fire, sun, stars, planets, earth, water, heavens, air, speech and mind are worshipped and propitiated they cannot wipe out the sin (i.e. ignorance in spiritual matters which is the root cause of sins) but promote the notion of diversity and difference. But the service rendered to persons of spiritual wisdom, even for a short time (a *muhūrta*) eradicates it completely.

13. He is really a donkey, carrying a fodder for the cattle[1] who looks upon this stinking dead body constituted of three humours (bile, phlegm and 'air') as the soul, regards wife and other relatives related to such a body as his own, believes a material image (of clay, stones, etc.) as an object of worship, and thinks that waters (absolve from sins and hence) are purificatory, but does not entertain such notions (of being saviours from sins) towards the spiritually wise.

Śrī Śuka said :

14. Hearing this speech of the glorious Lord Kṛṣṇa of unfailing infinite intelligence, which was very difficult to comprehend, the Brāhmaṇas got confounded and remained silent.

15. Pondering over for a long time, they realized that though he is the Supreme Controller of the universe, it is for teaching the world by his own example, that he behaved like an ordinary person (under God's control). And beaming with a smile, they addressed him.

The sages said:

16. We, the best ones among the knowers of Truth and the chief among the progenitors of the world, are deluded by your Māyā, (Though you are the Lord of the Universe) you keep your universal rulership concealed by your apparent human acts, showing to be controlled by God's authority. How wonderful is the behaviour of the Lord.

17. Though he is one and no activity can be attributed to him (or whose activities are not determined or ordained by his *Karmas*), he appears in many names and forms just as the earth though one has many names and forms (e.g. a pot, a pitcher and others) through her own products[2] and (though

1. *go-kharaḥ* : VC. quotes *Bṛhaspati Saṁhitā* which states : Persons, even though paid respects by kings, should be regarded as 'donkeys among brutes' (*gokharāḥ*) if they do not know the religion (*dharma*) of the glorious Lord and the secrets of *mantras*.

2. *Vācārambhaṇaṁ vikāro nāmadheyaṁ mṛttiketyeva satyam* /—*Chāndogya Up*. 6.1.4.

one) by himself he creates, protects and eats up (i.e. withdraws within himself) the universe but is not bound by any of these acts. O! How mysterious is the working of (you) the Perfect One, whose (birth and other) acts are merely an (outward) imitation of human beings (The real you are different).

18. Even though Your Lordship is the Supreme Person (transcendental to *Prakṛti* and *Puruṣa*,) from time to time, you assume the pure *sāttvika* form for the protection of your devotees, and for the chastisement and control of the wicked, and by your example, you maintain the path of the Vedas—and you are the embodiment of different castes (*varṇas*) and stages in life (*āśramas*).

19. The Veda constitutes your extremely pure heart. Through study, penance, self-control, you—the Brahman are realised there in both your manifest and unmanifest forms and your transcendental form is beyond the ken of these two.

20. O Lord Kṛṣṇa who are the Brahman yourself! As you are known through Śāstras (and Brāhmaṇas are the repository of these *Śāstras*) it is the Brāhmaṇas who form the best shrine as a means of realizing you. Hence, you are the most prominent amongst those who patronize the Brāhmaṇas and respect them.

21. Today in meeting you who are the shelter of all saintly persons, we have achieved the real benefit of our very existence, learning, penance and ability to see, as you are the highest consummation of all blessings.

22. Salutation to you, O glorious Lord Kṛṣṇa of boundless wisdom and intelligence. You are the Supreme Soul who have shrouded your glory by your yogamāyā (yogic deluding potency).

23. These kings in the assembly and your clansmen (Vṛṣṇis) who share life and enjoyment together with you do not know that you are the Almighty God, the Time-spirit and the Supreme Soul concealed under the veil of your Māyā.

24-25. Just as a person who is asleep does not (during that stage) remember his body in his wakeful stage and looks upon all objects (he sees in the dream) as real and supposes his self in the dream which is perceptible to the mind and exists in name only, to be real, similarly, (even while awake), a person loses his power of discrimination as his sense-activities are directed towards objects which exist in name only (and are not real) by your Māyā and his mind being deluded and bewildered, he does not realize you.

26. To-day we had the good fortune of seeking the feet of you (who are of the above description)—your feet which are the source of the sacred river Gaṅgā which absolves people of heaps of sins; which are enthroned in the heart by *yogins* whose *yogic* practices have been ripened and perfect. Those who have been able to wipe out evil proclivities or ego by means of overflowing tide of devotion have attained the highest stage of realizing you (or have secured resort in you). Hence, O Lord, be pleased to be gracious unto us your devotees."

Śrī Śuka said :

27. Having thus (prayed and) taken leave of Śrī Kṛṣṇa, the descendant of Dāśārha, Dhṛtarāṣṭra and Yudhiṣṭhira, the sages made up their minds to return to their respective hermitages, O royal sage.

28. Seeing that the sages were departing, the far-famed Vasudeva approached them, bowed them, clasped their feet and with great self-restraint, he requested them as follows :

Vasudeva said :

29. Salutation to you, O sages, in whom all deities abide.[1] It behoves you to listen to my request. Be pleased to advise me by adopting which course of *karma*, one can clear one's self of all *karmas*.

Nārada said :

30. It is not strange or wonderful that Vasudeva, regard ing Śrī Kṛṣṇa as a child, is desirous of being enlightened in spiritual knowledge and is asking us about the way of attaining to his spiritual good.

1. ŚR. quotes the following Vedic text in support of this supposition: *Yāvatīr vai devatās tāḥ sarvā veda-vidi Brāhmaṇe vasanti* /

31. In this world, over-familiarity in the case of mortals, breeds negligence or lack of reverence. Persons who live on the bank of the Gaṅgā discard the water of that very river and go to another place of sacred waters.

32. Kṛṣṇa's spiritual knowledge is not diminished by the force of Time which causes the creation and dissolution of the universe, nor by itself or by any external cause or action of *guṇas*.

33. His wisdom is unaffected by any affliction or hindrances (*kleśa*)[1] or the effect of *karmas* or flow of *guṇas*. He is the Almighty Lord, one without a second. But ordinary people regard him just like themselves[2] as he has shrouded himself under his own potencies, vital airs, etc., just as the sun is concealed by clouds, mists and eclipse, etc.

34. Then, O king, the sages, addressed Vasudeva (Ānakadundubhi) as follows while all including Acyuta and Balarāma, were hearing them.

35. "The cause of wiping out of *karmas* through performance of *karmas* has been seen (and declared) well by the good. One should devoutly propitiate and worship Viṣṇu, the Lord of sacrifices by performing sacrifice.

36. This course has been shown as the way to serenity of mind, an easy type of *Yoga* and *dharma* that brings delight to the soul, by wise sages who perceive with the eye of *śāstras*.

37. It has been regarded as the most auspicious course for householders of the twice-born castes, that they should devoutly worship the Supreme Person by sacrifices performed with pure self-earned wealth with fair means.

38. One should give up covetousness for wealth by spending it in the performance of sacrifices, and in gifts, the desire for wife and children by enjoying conjugal happiness in married life, the aspiration for celestial world and the pleasures

1. Patañjali enumerates the following *kleśas* :
Nescience (*avidyā*), feeling-of-personality or ego (*asmitā*), attachment (*rāga*), aversion (*dveṣa*) and will-to-live or fear of death (*abhiniveśa*).

2. VJ. Vasudeva being an ordinary person regards the Almighty Lord Kṛṣṇa just a common person like himself, as Kṛṣṇa has shrouded himself under his own potencies, etc.

5. O Supra-sensuous Lord ! Having created this universe of a diversified nature out of yourself, you enter it as its soul, the Indwelling Controller, and you, the eternal (unborn) Lord, become the active force (*Prāṇa*) and the cognitive force (*Jiva*) and maintain it.

6.* The powers with which *Prāṇa* and *Sūtra* are endowed and other forces which go to create the universe, are really the potencies of the Supreme Self, for these powers depend (for their existence on you and there is a great dissimilarity between (the nature of) *Prāṇa* and the Supreme Soul, (the former is physical or material while the latter is spiritual). The activity of *Prāṇa* and others is only apparent (the real motive force is you, just as the velocity of an arrow is not in the arrow itself but in the physical force of the man who discharged it.

7. The lovely light of the moon, the heat and glare of the fire, the brilliant splendour of the sun, the twinkling of stars and the streaks of lightning, the stability of mountains, fragrance which characterises the earth—all these special characteristics are as a matter of fact yourself only.[1]

8. The qualities of water, viz. satisfying the thirst, the life-giving effect, are yourself, O God. The waters themselves and their essential characteristics, viz. liquidity and taste are yourself. The energy of senses, the mental power (firm will-power), bodily strength, the activity of the body, the activities and the force of the wind are your qualities (though they are attributed to the wind element).

9. You are the space that is delimited by cardinal points; You are the quarters themselves and the ether with its characteristic the Subtle sound (*sphoṭa*) which is the *parā* form of speech. You are the sound *Om*, the *Paśyanti* form of speech. You are (the Madhyamā form of speech) and the articulate speech) (*Vaikhari*) which separates letter sounds and words which denote different objects.

6* The verses following these are the echoes of *Vibhūti Yoga*. *BG*. Ch.X.

1. *na tatra sūryo bhāti, na candra-tārakam, etc. tameva bhāntam anubhāti sarvaṁ, tasya bhāsā sarvam idaṁ vibhāti* /—*Kaṭha* Up. 5.15 *Śveta*. Up. 8.14. *Muṇḍaka* 2.2.10 *Śvetāśvatara*

Also Yadādityagataṃ tejo, etc. in *BG*.15.12.

47. Collyrium was applied to Vasudeva's eyes. His body was besmeared with butter. The sacrificial priests with due formalities consecrated with sprinkling water Vasudeva alongwith his eighteen queens, as the moon god was formerly consecrated in the company of his (twentyseven) consorts, in ancient times.

48. The consecrated Vasudeva who was clad in deerskin, appeared extremely splendid with his queens, all of whom were clad in silken garments and were excellently adorned with gold bangles, pearl necklaces, anklets and ear-rings.

49. Wearing silk garments and jewels, the priest, who officiated at Vasudeva's sacrifice along with the members of the sacrificial assembly, appeared splendid like the corresponding priests in Indra's sacrifice, O great king.

50. At that time, Balarāma and Śrī Kṛṣṇa (the former representing the *jiva* and the latter the Almighty Lord) the rulers of living beings, accompanied with their brothers, sons and consorts shone forth with all their supreme glorious powers (*vibhūtis*).

51. In every sacrifice, by performing with due rites and formalities, the *Prākṛta*[1] and *Vaikṛta* categories of sacrifices characterised by Agnihotra, he worshipped Lord Viṣṇu who is the controller and master of the materials for the sacrifice, the knowledge of *Mantras* employed and the formal act of performing the sacrifice.

52. Then at the appropriate time as prescribed in the Śāstras, Vasudeva gave to his sacrificial priests who were already adorned with ornaments, very richly[2] adorned cows, girls and land as the sacrificial fee.

53. Having made the sacrificer's wife to perform the *Samyāja* part of the sacrifice and after the rites of *avabhṛtha* ablution, the great sages who officiated at the sacrifice followed the *Yajamāna* (the performer of sacrifice) to the pools (created

1. ŚR. : *Prākṛta Jyotiṣṭoma, Darśa, Pūrṇamāsa, Vaikṛtta*: *saura sattra* and others going under the name *Agnihotra*.

2. The v.l. *mahādhanaḥ* means 'the extremely affluent Vasudeva'. VT. takes '*Mahādhanāḥ*' as qualifying *Dakṣiṇāḥ* and interpretes, 'sacrificial fees consisting of costly jewels, gold, money, etc.'

by and known after the name) of Paraśurāma and performed the concluding bath.

54. After taking his bath, Vasudeva richly adorned himself with ornaments and distributed clothes and ornaments to bards and his queens also gave gifts. He then entertained with food, people of all castes and communities and animals down to dogs to their complete satisfaction.

55-56. With rich liberal presents, Vasudeva honoured his relatives, their wives, and children—the princes and people of Vidarbha, Kosala, Kuru, Kāśi, Kekaya and Sṛñjayas; and also the members of the sacrificial assembly and the priests; various categories of gods, men, *bhūtas*, *pitṛs* (manes) and Cāraṇas. All of them took leave of Kṛṣṇa, the abode of the goddess Śrī and praising him and the sacrifice, returned to (their respective) home.

57-58. Dhṛtarāṣṭra and his younger brother Vidura, the sons of Pṛthā, Bhīṣma, Droṇa, Kuntī and the twins (Nakula and Sahadeva), Nārada, the glorious sage Vyāsa, friends, relatives and kinsmen with their hearts softened with friendly feelings, embraced their relatives of the Yadu clan and with heart heavy with the pangs of separation, left for their own states along with other people.

59. Highly honoured with extensive rich presents by Kṛṣṇa, Balarāma, Ugrasena and others, Nanda who was very affectionate to them, stayed on along with the Gopas (for some time more).

60. Having thus crossed the ocean of his desire (of performing sacrifices) with such an ease, Vasudeva was greatly delighted at heart. Surrounded by his friends and well-wishers, he took Nanda by the hand and said:

Vasudeva said :

61. O brother Nanda ! A bond called friendly affection has been forged by the Almighty Lord. I think it is very difficult even for valiant warriors and *yogins* to snap it asunder.

62. For, the great friendliness extended by the virtuousmost persons like you to ungrateful persons like us is unsurpassed and too valuable to be repaid. Though your friendliness bears no reciprocal return, it will never be withdrawn from us.

63. We, being ourself helpless and simply incapable of doing it, did not do any good turn to you. And now our eyes being blinded by the intoxication of affluence, we do not see you even when you are before us, O brother.

64. O respectable brother, royal fortune should not come to the lot of a person who aspires after the final beatitude, for his eyesight gets blinded by it and he does not recognize his people or relatives."

Śrī Śuka said :

65. In this way, the heart of Vasudeva was softened with the feelings of friendliness. Remembering the warm friendship borne by Nanda to him, tears welled-up in his eyes and he wept (with tears gushing down his cheeks).

66. With a view to giving the pleasure of his company to Vasudeva and out of deep affection from Śrī Kṛṣṇa and Balarāma, he postponed his departure from day to day and stayed on there for three months more, respectfully treated all the while by the Yadus.

67. During his stay, Nanda together with relatives (Gopas) and the inhabitants of Vraja (who accompanied him there) were catered to their heart's content, whatever they desired and wanted, by offering them valuable ornaments, silk cloths and other costly presents.

68. Taking with him all the valuable gifts presented to him by Vasudeva, Ugrasena, Śrī Kṛṣṇa. Uddhava, Balarāma and others, he took leave of the Yādavas and returned home (with a big Yādava army to guard him during his return journey).

69*. Nanda, Gopas and Gopīs whose hearts were attached

* *VJ.'s Text adds* :

69.1. Droṇa, Bhiṣma, Karṇa, Bāhlika, Vidura and others and Dhṛtarāṣṭra, along with his sons returned to their respective homes severally.

69.2. All other kings who had come there on a holy pilgrimage (stayed there for three months at the end of which) they returned to their respective kingdoms.

69.3. And the noble-souled Pāṇḍavas and Kunti, speaking in faltering accents (as their voice was choked with tears) accompanied with all their relatives, returned to Indraprastha, taking leave of Kṛṣṇa.

and fixed on the lotus-feet of Śrī Kṛṣṇa found themselves unable to retract them from there and returned to Mathurā.

70. When all the relatives departed (to their respective places), Vṛṣṇis who looked upon Kṛṣṇa as their Deity, noticed the approach of the monsoons and returned to Dvārakā.

71. On their return, they narrated to the people (who could not come to that pilgrimage) the great festival of the sacrifice performed by Vasudeva, the leader of Yadus and their meeting of friends and other incidents during the course of that pilgrimage.

CHAPTER EIGHTYFIVE

Restoration of his Elder Brothers by Kṛṣṇa
From the Realm of Death

The Son of Bādarāyaṇa (*Śrī Śuka*) *said* :

1. On one occasion, (after their return from the sacrifice at Kurukṣetra), Balarāma and Śrī Kṛṣṇa went (as usual) (to pay respects to their parents), and bowed down to Vasudeva. Vasudeva affectionately received them when they saluted his feet, and spoke to his sons as follows :—

2. Having heard the speech of the sages indicating the glorious powers of their sons and feeling a sense of confidence by their exploits, he affectionately addressed them and said.

3. O Kṛṣṇa! Kṛṣṇa! O great Yogin! O eternal Saṅkarṣaṇa! I (now) realize that both of you are the Supreme Persons (ruling over) *Prakṛti* and *Puruṣa*, the direct causes of the universe.

4. You are the place (Substratum), the agent and the instrument of the universe. You are its source and its object or purpose; whenever or whatever form it assumes is yourself. As and when this universe evolves, all the causes thereof including time and manner are the Almighty Lord yourself who control both the *Prakṛti* (to be enjoyed) and *Puruṣa* (the enjoyer) and transcend them both.

5. O Supra-sensuous Lord ! Having created this universe of a diversified nature out of yourself, you enter it as its soul, the Indwelling Controller, and you, the eternal (unborn) Lord, become the active force (*Prāṇa*) and the cognitive force (*Jiva*) and maintain it.

6.* The powers with which *Prāṇa* and *Sūtra* are endowed and other forces which go to create the universe, are really the potencies of the Supreme Self, for these powers depend (for their existence on you and there is a great dissimilarity between (the nature of) *Prāṇa* and the Supreme Soul, (the former is physical or material while the latter is spiritual). The activity of *Prāṇa* and others is only apparent (the real motive force is you, just as the velocity of an arrow is not in the arrow itself but in the physical force of the man who discharged it.

7. The lovely light of the moon, the heat and glare of the fire, the brilliant splendour of the sun, the twinkling of stars and the streaks of lightning, the stability of mountains, fragrance which characterises the earth—all these special characteristics are as a matter of fact yourself only.[1]

8. The qualities of water, viz. satisfying the thirst, the life-giving effect, are yourself, O God. The waters themselves and their essential characteristics, viz. liquidity and taste are yourself. The energy of senses, the mental power (firm will-power), bodily strength, the activity of the body, the activities and the force of the wind are your qualities (though they are attributed to the wind element).

9. You are the space that is delimited by cardinal points; You are the quarters themselves and the ether with its characteristic the Subtle sound (*sphoṭa*) which is the *parā* form of speech. You are the sound *Om*, the *Paśyanti* form of speech. You are (the Madhyamā form of speech) and the articulate speech) (*Vaikharī*) which separates letter sounds and words which denote different objects.

6* The verses following these are the echoes of *Vibhūti Yoga*. *BG*. Ch.X.

1. *na tatra sūryo bhāti, na candra-tārakam, etc. tameva bhāntam anubhāti sarvaṁ, tasya bhāsā sarvam idaṁ vibhāti* /—*Kaṭha* Up. 5.15 *Śveta*. Up. 8.14. *Muṇḍaka* 2.2.10 *Śvetāśvatara*

Also Yadādityagataṃ tejo, etc. in *BG*.15.12.

10. You are the real sense organ, the power revealing its special objects; You are also the presiding deities of the senses and their potency. You are the cognitive and retentive faculty of the Intellect. You are the co-ordinating power of different experiences inherent in *Jiva*.

11. You are the *Tāmasa* aspect of Ego (*Ahaṁkāra*) which is the root cause of the gross elements; the *Rājasa* type (*Taijasa*) of Ego, as the cause of the sense-organs; the *Sāttvika* kind of Ego (*Vaikārika*) which creates the deities presiding over the senses and the mind (and the *Pradhāna* or *Māyā* which makes *jivas* wander in the *Saṁsāra*[1] (*or* : You are the Chief *Prakṛti*, the cause of *Mahat* and other principles and which involves the *jivas* in *Saṁsāra*.)

12. Just as the material substance (e.g. gold) is the constant factor all through its various modifications (e.g. various ornaments like bangles, armlets, etc.), you are the constant factor abiding in all these perishable objects and are not subject to modification or decay.

13. The attributes of *Prakṛti* viz. *Sattva*, *Rajas* and *Tamas* and their products (such as *Mahat* and other principles) have been superimposed on you, the veritable Brahman, by your Yoga Māyā (but you are untouched by them)[2].

14. These created things, therefore, do not really exist, when they are not seen as projected on you (at the time of *Pralaya*) by *Yoga Māyā*; they are non-existent. (i.e. their very existence depends on you as the substratum on which they are superimposed). You abide in them (when you create and sustain the universe). Otherwise you remain unconnected with these modifications and abide in your absolute (blissful) state.

15. Those who are ignorant of the subtle course of yours who are the soul of all, and are present in this universe or Saṁsāra, which is a constant flow of *guṇas*, (wrongly identify themselves with their bodies through their ignorance and there-

1. VR : You constitute the *Karma* which makes *jīva* experience the fruit of the balance of his *Karmas*.

2. *Mayā tatam idaṁ sarvaṁ jagad avyakta-Mūrtinā* /
matsthāni sarva-bhutāni na cāham teṣvavasthitaḥ //
BG 9.4

by) get enmeshed by their Karmas, and continue to whirl in the *Saṁsāra*, as a consequence of those *Karmas*.

16. (I sincerely regret that) after having attained by a lucky chance, birth here (in Bhārata Varṣa) as a man endowed with vigorous sense-organs—which is really very difficult to obtain, I remained negligent about the main object of human life (viz. Pursuit of *Mokṣa*) through the influence of your Māyā and have wasted my life, O Lord.

17. Your Lordship binds down the whole of the world with bonds of affection to the body as being my own self and relations and belongings of the body (such as sons, etc.) as they are absolutely mine.

18. I realize that both of you are not our sons but directly the controllers of *Prakṛti* and *Puruṣa* (The Primordial Matter and individual souls). As you have stated (at the time of your incarnation in our prison-cell), both of you have taken this descent (in human form) for the annihilation of the Kṣattriya Kings who have become a burden to the earth.

19. O friend of the afflicted! I have, therefore, now sought asylum with your lotus-feet which dispel the fear of *Saṁsāra* of those who resort to them (your feet). Absolutely enough of this craving for objects of sense-enjoyment under the influence of which I looked upon this mortal body as my soul and you who are the supreme person, as my child.

20. Indeed, you did tell both of us in the lying-in-chamber, that you are, as a matter of fact unborn (not actually born) but for the protection of the order of righteousness (ordained by you), you reveal yourself as "born" from us (formerly as Sutapas and Pṛśni, Kāśyapa and Diti, now Vasudeva and Devakī) in every Yuga. You assume various forms like the sky and discard them (though you are one), O Lord whose glory is widely sung (in *Śrutis*). Who can comprehend the wonderful Māyā (Potency) of yours, O Omnipresent Lord?

Śrī Śuka said :

21. Hearing such a speech from his father, the glorious Lord, the leader of Sātvatas (Śrī Kṛṣṇa) smiled. Saluting his father with all humility, he replied in sweet words.

The Lord said :

22. Your speech is pregnant with philosophical significance, O father, and we accept it; as thereby you have expounded to us, your sons, the whole body of Philosophic principles.

23. I, you, this elder brother Balarāma, all these inhabitants of Dvārakā and all the mobile and immobile creation should be regarded as such (*Brahman*), O the greatest of Yadus.

24. The (Supreme) Soul is really one, self-illuminating, eternal, different and distinct from the body, devoid of any attributes; it is however due to his alliance with *guṇas* created by him and in bodies of various creatures produced out of those *guṇas*, that he appears diversified (as a man, a god, etc.), visible, momentary, identical with the body and possessed of attributes.

25. Just as the elements, sky, air, fire, water and earth become diversified (as small and great, manifest, and unmanifest, etc.) according to their products, so does the soul, though one, assume different forms and becomes many, manifest or unmanifest, small or great.

Śrī Śuka said :

26. In this way, O king Parīkṣit, Vasudeva who was thus enlightened by Kṛṣṇa became divested of the notion of diversity, remained silent and delighted at heart.

27. Devakī, the embodiment of all deities was there at this time (of conversation). She was wonderstruck, O prominentmost Kuru, to hear that her sons had brought back to life, the son of their preceptor.

28. Addressing Śrī Kṛṣṇa and Balarāma, Devakī, who remembered her sons killed by Kaṁsa, piteously appealed to them, with tears of grief flowing down from her eyes.

Devakī said :

29. O Balarāma, Delighter of hearts and of immeasurable prowess! O Kṛṣṇa, the Lord of the masters of Yoga! I recognize you both as the Lords of the progenitors of the universe and the First persons in the universe.

30. It is (traditionally) reported that both of you have been born of me for the extermination of Kings whose virtue

(or *Sāttvika* nature) is lost through the influence of the Time-spirit and who transgress the injunctions (you laid down for their behaviour) in the scriptures (*Śāstras*) and have proved to be a burden to the earth.

31. O Soul of the Universe (Śrī Kṛṣṇa) ! I resort to you for shelter to-day—you who bring about the creation , sustenance and dissolution of the Universe by your minutest part, viz. the particles of the *guṇas* (*Sattva, Rajas* and *Tamas*) which are evolved out of a part of Māyā which in its own way is an evolute of a part of Puruṣa who is but a part manifestation of you.

32. Both of you, being urged by Time and desired by your preceptor Sāndīpani to bring back to life his son who died long ago, you brought back his son from the region of *Pitṛs* (manes) i.e. the abode of death, and presented him to your preceptor as a homage (and thus paid the debt of your preceptorship)

33. You should similarly fulfil my desire as both of you are the Lords of the masters of Yoga. I desire to see, brought to life, my sons who have been killed by Kaṁsa, the King of Bhojas.

The sage Śuka said :

34. Directed thus by their mother, O Parīkṣit, Balarāma and Kṛṣṇa resorted to their Yogamāyā (Super-human Yogic potency) and entered the nether world called Suṭala.

35. Beholding both of them enter Sutala, King Bali recognised them to be the Deity, the Soul of the Universe and especially his own God (Lord Viṣṇu). His heart was overflowing with joy at their appearance. Instantaneously, he rose up from his seat and along with the members of his family, he prostrated himself before them.

36. He brought for those great-souled personages excellent seats. When they gladly occupied them, he washed their feet and sprinkled over his head as well as those of the members of the family present, that water which (as they say traditionally) purifies the world right from its creator, god Brahmā.

37. He worshipped them by offering extremely valuable cloths, ornaments, fragrant ointments, betel leaves, chauries

(waving around their faces) lamps, catering nectar-like sweet dishes and by submitting to their services his own self, his race and his wealth.

38. It is traditionally reported that Bali whose army equalled to that of Indra, the King of gods had his heart so much soaked with love for his God that he bore the Lord's feet on his head again and again. His eyes were bedimmed with tears of joy and his hair, standing on their ends. His voice being choked with emotions, he prayed in faltering accents.

Bali Prayed :

39. Salutations to you the Infinite (Lord Śeṣa) who are so vast (as to bear the universe on your hood). I bow to you Lord Kṛṣṇa, the embodiment of eternal bliss, the creator of the world, the expounder of the Sāṅkhya and Yoga *darśanas* (or the Paths of knowledge and *Bhakti*), the Supreme Soul, nay the very *Brahman* himself.

40. Even your sight is very difficult to obtain to all beings (even to the masters of yoga). It is through your Grace that (to some) it is not so very difficult, (just as now) you of your own accord have luckily blessed us with your visit even though we are dominated by *rajas* and *tamas* by nature.

41-42. We, Daityas, Dānavas, Gandharvas, Siddhas, Vidyādharas, Cāraṇas Yakṣas Ogres (Rākṣasas), goblins (Piśācas), the leaders of evil spirits like *bhūtas* and *Pramathas* and others of our ilk, bear continuous hostility to you who are the receptacle of pure *Sattva* (unsullied by *Rajas* and *Ṭamas*) and the very embodiment of scriptures (*Śāstras*).

42-A *VR's Text adds* :

That some people have attained to the different types of Liberation (from *Saṁsāra* known as *Sālokya* (residence in the Deity's abode), *Sāmipya* (vicinity to the Deity), *Sārūpya* similarity in form to the Deity) and *Sātmatā* (Coalescence with the Deity) is due to the disposition of their mind, O Lotus-eyed Lord.

43. Just as by virtue of unflinching devotion to you or by inveterate enmity to you (as in regard to Śiśupāla) or by deep passion of Love for you (as in the case of Gopīs), persons

have attained so much close union with you as could not be achieved by gods who possess *Sāttvika* nature.

44. O Lord of the masters of Yoga ! Even Masters of Yoga cannot comprehend the nature and the extent or the inscrutable functions of your Yoga-Māyā. What to speak of Daityas like us ?

45. Therefore, pray be propitious unto us—Graciously help me to get out of the dark well of house-holder's life which is different from the Shelter of your lotus-feet which are sought after by persons who are free from desires. Subsisting on whatever (fruit, etc. dropped automatically from the trees) I get at the foot of trees which afford shelter to all, I shall move about alone with a serene mind or (if association with others is necessary) in the company of pious people who are friendly to all.

46. O Ruler of all *jivas* ! Be pleased to impart your command to us and absolve us of all our sins. O Lord ! For a person who abides by your command faithfully is not subject to the injunctions and interdictions of the scriptures.

The glorious Lord said :

47. "In the first Manvantara, sage Marīci had six sons by his wife Ūrṇā. They were the gods (in that Aeon). They laughed at god Brahmā when they saw that he was ready to cohabit with his daughter.

48. On account of that 'misdemeanour' (as god Brahmā interpreted their laughter and cursed them), they were born in the race of Asuras as the sons of Hiraṇyakaśipu and were taken away by Yogamāyā.

49. They were born as sons to Devakī and were (immediately) murdered by Kaṁsa. Even now mother Devakī is lamenting for those children and they are now here with you.

50. For soothing the grief of our mother, we shall take them from this place to her. There they will be liberated from the curse (of Brahmā) and thus freed from the fever of affliction they will return to their celestial region.

51. Smara, Udgītha, Pariṣvaṅga, Pataṅga, Kṣudrabhṛt and Ghṛṇin—all these six (sons of Marīci) shall attain to their happy state again through my grace."

52. Having explained his mission to Bali, he took charge of those sons. Worshipped by Bali, both of them returned to Dvārakā and presented her (dead but now restored) children to the mother.

53. Seeking her children (so brought back to her), Devakī had her breasts filled with milk. Hugging them and placing them on her lap, she smelt their crowns repeatedly.

54. Overwhelmed with motherly affection at the touch of her children, and being over-joyed, she suckled them: she was too much deluded by Viṣṇu's Māyā by which the whole cycle of creation continues.

55. Having sucked the nectar of her milk which was left over there after Lord Kṛṣṇa's sucking, and due to the contact of the person of Lord Nārāyaṇa, they regained their self-knowledge.

56. Bowing to Kṛṣṇa, Devakī, their father Vasudeva and Balarāma, they ascended through the ethereal region to their places while all beings were witnessing it.

57. The divine Devakī was so much flabbergasted to see the arrival and departure of her dead children that she thought it to be the illusion created by Kṛṣṇa, O king.

58. O king Parīkṣit! Innumerable are these and such other miraculous exploits of Lord Kṛṣṇa, the Supreme soul of Infinite powers, O descendant of Bharata.

Sūta said :

59. He who devoutly and constantly listens to and recites to others this account of Lord Kṛṣṇa of eternal fame and glory—the account extolled by the venerable son of the sage Vyāsa which absolves the world of all sins, and which fills the ears of Lord's devotees with delight or is like ornaments to the ears of Lord's votaries, gets his mind concentrated in the Lord and attains to his region of eternal bliss.

CHAPTER EIGHTYSIX

Elopement of Subhadrā : The Lord's Grace on Śrutadeva

The King (Parikṣit) said :

1. O Brāhmaṇa sage ! We would like to know how (my grand-father, the ever victorious) Arjuna married the sister of Balarāma and Kṛṣṇa, as she was my grand-mother.

Śrī Śuka narrated :

2. While the mighty Arjuna was travelling over the earth for pilgrimage to sacred places, he arrived at Prabhāsa where he happened to hear about his maternal uncle's daughter (Subhadrā).

3. He further heard (the report) that Balarāma would like to give her in marriage to Duryodhana, while others opposed it. As he was desirous of securing her (as his wife), he disguised himself as a recluse bearing a triple staff.[1] and went to Dvārakā.

4. With a view to accomplishing his object, he stayed the months of the rainy season, at that place. He was now and then worshipped by the citizens as also by Balarāma who did not recognise him (and was unaware that he was Arjuna).

5. It is reported that one day, he was invited as a guest and brought to the palace by Balarāma, where he partook of sweet dishes served to him with devotion.

6. He espied there that youthful girl who captivated the hearts of warriors. With his eyes blooming with love, he set his heart agitated by passions, on her.

7. As soon as she saw him who was fascinating to the hearts of women, she also fell in love with him. She fixed her heart and gazed on him with smiles and bashful glances.

1. The three staffs indicate his control of mind, speech, and action. The word *daṇḍa* stands for restraint. The *Smṛtis* of *Manu* 12.10 and *Dakṣa* 7.30 declare that a man is called *tri-daṇḍī* who has restraint over speech, mind and body.

8. Brooding over her constantly, he was eager to get an opportunity to elope with her. As his mind was distracted with over-powering passion for her, he could get no peace of mind.

9. With the consent of her parents and Śrī Kṛṣṇa, that great warrior carried her away as she came out of the fort in a chariot to visit a shrine on the occasion of a great festival of gods.

10. Immediately after getting into the Chariot of Subhadrā, he took up his bow, routed all the soldiers who tried to obstruct him. Like a lion taking away his share, he carried her even as her Yādava relatives were screaming.

11. Hearing the report (of Subhadrā's elopement with Arjuna), Balarāma got enraged like an ocean on a full moon day. But he gradually calmed down when Kṛṣṇa and other well-wishers clasped his feet (and tried to pacify him).

12. Balarāma was pleased to send to the bride and bride-groom presents and marriage-gifts consisting of a big amount of money, articles of furniture, elephants, chariots, male and famale servants.

12A *VR's Text adds*:

Yādavas and Pāṇḍavas who were already relatives became very much delighted with mutual affection. Now listen to another anecdote of Kṛṣṇa's affection for two of his devotees.

Śrī Śuka resumed:

13. There was a great Brāhmaṇa, known by the name Śrutadeva. He felt to have accomplished all the goals in life by his unflinching single-minded devotion to Kṛṣṇa. He was serene, full of spiritual wisdom and un-attached to objects of pleasure.

14. He lived in the country of Videha, at Mithilā (its capital modern Janakpur). Though he was a householder, he carried out all his duties and responsibilities within whatever came to him without any effort.

15. Luckily, through the grace of God, he used to get just what was absolutely necessary for his bare maintenance

and nothing more. He was, however, quite contented with it and performed all his duties in the proper manner.

16. The protector (King) of that State, Bahulāśva by name, a descendant of Janaka was also free from egotism, dear Parīkṣit. Both Śrutadeva and Bahulāśva were beloved of Lord Kṛṣṇa.

17-18 Being pleased with both of them, the glorious Lord had his chariot brought by Dāruka. The almighty Lord rode the chariot and set out for the country of Videha (modern Tirhut or North Bihar) in the company of sages like Nārada, Vāmadeva, Atri, Kṛṣṇa (Kṛṣṇa-Dvaipāyana Vyāsa), Paraśurāma Asita, Āruṇi, I myself (Śuka), Bṛhaspati, Kaṇva, Maitreya, Cyavana and others.

19. At every stage in that journey, citizens and villagers received him on his arrival, with articles of worship and offerings in their hands, O king, just as they would do unto the Sun rising in conjunction with planets.

20. Men and women from the countries of Ānarta, Dhanva, Kuru, Jāṅgala, Kaṅka, Matsya, Pāñcāla, Kunti, Madhu, Kekaya, Kosal and Arṇa as well as others drank with their eyes his lotus-face illumined with noble smile and affectionate looks.

21. (As he proceeded), Kṛṣṇa, the Preceptor of the three worlds, conferred insight into and knowledge of the Truth and the state of fearlessness (i.e. Liberation from Saṁsāra) on people, the blinding darkness of whose vision had been completely dispelled by his gracious glances. Hearing on the way his own glory celebrated in songs by gods and men — his world — wide spotless (pure) glory which destroys inauspiciousness and sins—He slowly and leisurely journeyed to Videha.

22. Hearing Lord Kṛṣṇa's arrival (in Videha), villagers and citizens thereof became delighted and they came forward to welcome him with presents and other offerings in their hands.

23. When they saw Lord Kṛṣṇa of hallowing renown, their countenance, and hearts (as if) bloomed with ecstasy. With their palms folded on their heads, they bowed to him

and the accompanying sages of whom they had only heard before.

24. Believing that Kṛṣṇa, the Preceptor of the world had come there to shower his grace on him personally, both the king of Mithilā as well as the Brāhmaṇa Śrutadeva prostrated themselves at the feet of the Lord.

25. With their palms folded to pay obeisance, both the king of Mithilā (Bahulāśva) and Śrutadeva simultaneously invited Kṛṣṇa along with the sages accompanying him, to accept their hospitality.

26. The Lord accepted the invitation of both of them. With the desire of pleasing them both, he (assumed two forms and) entered (severally) the houses of them both, without being perceived by the other.

27-29. When Lord Kṛṣṇa and sages, whose even names never reached the unrighteous ears, visited his house, the high-minded Bahulāśva, the descendant of the family of Janaka brought excellent seats (and offered them). When they were comfortably seated, he paid obeisance to their feet with intense devotion. His heart was transported with joy and eyes were bedimmed with tears of joy. He washed their feet and sprinkled his own head as well as those of the members of his family with that water which purified the world. He then worshipped the Lord and sages whose minds were devoted to God by means of sandal paste, flowers, cloths, ornaments, fragrant incense, lamps and offered them oblations of water, cows and bulls.

30. When they were fed with sumptuous meal to their heart's content, he joyfully placed on his lap the feet of Viṣṇu (Kṛṣṇa). Pressing them gently, he spoke in sweet words pleasing them all, as follows :

The King (Bahulāśva) said:

31. "O all-pervading Lord ! You are the in-dwelling soul (*antaryāmin*) of all beings, the witness to everything and self-illuminating. It is hence that you revealed yourselves to us who remembered your lotus-feet.

32. You have often declared that neither your brother Balarāma (the incarnation of Śeṣa), nor your consort goddess

Śrī, nor your son (God Brahmā) is as dear to you as a person who is exclusively devoted to you. It is to vindicate the veracity of your statement that your Lordship has revealed yourself to our view.

33. What person cognisant of the knowledge that you offer your own self to those serene sages who regard nothing (even their bodies) as their own (and contemplate on you) will abandon your Lotus-feet?

34. You have incarnated in the family of Yadus for putting an end to the Saṁsāra of persons who are whirling in that cycle of birth and death. And you have extended your glory which can completely wash out the sins of the three worlds.

35. I bow to you, O glorious Lord Kṛṣṇa of unlimited wisdom and intellect; you are the divine sage Nārāyaṇa who quietly perform penance (for the happiness of the world).

36. O perfect lord ! Be pleased to stay in our house along with the sages for some days and purify this family of King Nimi by the dust of your feet."

37. Thus entreatingly invited by the king, the Lord, protector of the universe stayed for some days at Mithilā, bestowing happiness and well-being on men and women of Mithilā.

38. Like Janaka (the king of Mithilā), Śrutadeva was overjoyed to find that Kṛṣṇa had arrived and stayed in his house. It is traditionally reported that he was so much transported with joy that he waved his cloth and danced.

39. Bringing mats and seats of Kuśa grass, he seated them comfortably. He warmly greeted them with words of welcome. With great joy, he and his wife washed their feet.

40. With that water, that highly blessed Brāhmaṇa sprinkled himself and all the members of his family and relations. Feeling that he had accomplished all his ambitions in life, he was transported with ecstasy.

41. He propitiated them by worshipping them with whatever articles of worship he could procure, such as fruit and other articles (e. g. sandal-paste, flowers), cool water scented with the plant *Andropogon Muricatus* (called Vāḷā in Marathi), fragrant earth (musk?), Tulasī leaves, Kuśa grass and lotus

flowers and with food conducive to the promotion of *Sāttvika* qualities.

42. He tried to reason with himself, "O ! How wonderful ! How did this association of mine who am fallen in the dark well of household life, take place with Lord Kṛṣṇa and the gods on the earth (Brāhmaṇas) who have enshrined Lord Kṛṣṇa in their hearts and the dust on whose feet has the sanctity of holy waters."

43. When the guests were offered warm hospitality and were comfortably seated, Śrutadeva, along with his wife, children and relatives waited upon them and touching the feet of Kṛṣṇa, submitted to him as follows:—

Śrutadeva said:

44-45. "It is not only to-day that the Supreme Person has revealed himself to our vision but (long ago) when, having created the universe with his potencies, he had his presence therein by virtue of his personal power. But he has actually revealed to our vision to-day. Just as a man in the state of sleep mentally creates another dream world, world of his own through the influence of *Avidyā* on his mind (or by the force of your Māyā) and entering into that dream-world appears as objective reality.

46. You always shine in the hearts of those pure-minded persons who constantly listen to and speak about your glories: who always adore you and pay obeisance to you and converse with each other about you. (But it is my great fortune that you have manifested yourself within the range of my sight).

47. Even though you abide in the hearts of those whose minds are distracted by their Karmas, you are very far away from them and you cannot be comprehended by their mental powers such as Egotism (*Ahaṅkāra*). But you are quite nearest to those who have developed spiritual qualities by listening to and singing of your glories, contemplating on you, etc.

48*. Salutation to you who reveal yourself as the Supreme Soul (and confer liberation from Saṁsāra) to those who

48* (1) VR : Salutation to you who dispense both bondage and liberation from Saṁsāra. Those who know the Supreme Soul as he is, attain to know the (real nature of the) Soul as different from the body (and thus do not identify their body with their Soul) and who have allotted Saṁsāra (the cycle of births and deaths) to those who wrongly identify the body with the soul (and are thus separated from you). You control both the principles like *Mahat*, etc. which are the evolutes of *Prakṛti* and are thus 'caused' or products and the *Prakṛti* itself which is uncaused, but to both of these the *jiva* is subject (and hence he whirls in the *Saṁsāra*). By the force of your Māyā potency the vision of others is screened but yours is ever unobstructed.

49. As you are the Almighty Lord, be pleased to command us, your servants, what services we should render to you. Your very revelation to the view of men instantaneously puts an end to all their sufferings."

Śrī Śuka said:

50. They say that when the Lord heard Śrutadeva's appeal (as presented by him), the glorious Lord who annihilates all the agonies of those who bow and thus submit themselves to him humbly, took him by the hand and similingly spoke to Śrutadeva:

him. According to your will you ordain death to those who have not given their mind to you. You assume an incarnation for conferring grace on *Jivas* and not do so due to the force of Karmas. You are not partial in not bestowing Liberation from Saṁsāra on those whose vision is clouded by your Māyā and do not realize you properly.

(ii) VJ : It is beyond my capacity to propitiate you except by offering salutation to you who bestow all *Puruṣārthas* (desired objectives in human life) on those who comprehend the Paramātman correctly. You are all-pervading. You take up various forms according to your will. You pervade the gross universe which is the product (or evolute of Prakṛti) and also the subtle causeless i.e. eternal *Prakṛti*. It is due to your infinite Potency that your vision i.e. knowledge is always unobstructed.

(iii) VT : It is due to your grace that we came together and I could see you. For those who realize you, it is your *Śrī-Vigraha* (original form of God) which removes the fear of death. You control this transient world (which is a product) and your own region which is eternal. By the force of your Māyā the vision of those interested in this world is clouded but not of those who are related to your region.

The Lord said:

51. O Brāhmaṇa Śrutadeva! Please note that these sages who move with me purifying the people with the dust on their feet, have come here with the intention of conferring their grace on you.

52. Gods, sacred places and holy waters gradually purify people by their sight, contact and worship after a long period of time. But that is instantaneously accomplished just by the sight of these most exalted souls (the Brāhmaṇas—).

53. A Brāhmaṇa, by his very birth, is superior to all other beings. What needs be said of a Brāhmaṇa who is endowed with penance, learning, contentedness and devotion to me?

54. Even this Personality of mind endowed with four arms is not dearer to me than a Brāhmaṇa. A learned Brāhmaṇa is the very embodiment of Vedas while I, of gods. A proof (*Pramāṇa*) is Superior to what is to be proved (*Prameya*) as it depends on *Pramāṇa*. As Vedas are *Pramāṇa* and gods, the *Prameya*, the Superiority of the Vedas (and consequently of Brāhmaṇas) is automatically obvious.

55. Persons of evil mentality do not understand this truth. Out of jealousy they disregard their preceptor, me, Brāhmaṇas who are my ownself and entertain reverential attitudes to idols (and symbols, etc.) as adorable objects.

56. Perceiving me as the All-pervading Ātman everywhere, a Brāhmaṇa cherishes the idea that this universe consisting of mobile and immobile creation and the principles such as *Mahat* and others which constitute the universe, are nothing but my forms.

57. Therefore, O Brāhmaṇa Śrutadeva, worship these Brāhmaṇa sages with the same devotion and faith as you have in me. If this is done, I am directly worshipped but not by any other means even if it involves considerable expenditure of wealth and show of grandeur.

Śrī Śuka said:

58. Thus commanded by the Lord, he worshipped Kṛṣṇa and those excellent Brāhmaṇa sages as being the same (as one Ātman) with the same devotion and attained the goal of saints

(*Mokṣa*). Even king Bahulāśva of Mithilā also attained the same state.

59. O king Parīkṣit! The glorious Lord Kṛṣṇa who is devoted to his votaries stayed with his two devotees. Having enlightened them in the true path to *Mokṣa* as enunciated in the Vedas, he returned to Dvārakā.

CHAPTER EIGHTYSEVEN

Śruti Gītā

(Hyman of Praise by The Vedas)

Parīkṣit requested:[1]

1. O Brāhmaṇa sage! How is it possible for the Vedas, conditioned as they are with *guṇas*[2] and their products, to carry out their function directly with reference to the Supreme Brahman which is beyond specific indication and hence indefinable, devoid of *guṇas* and (beyond the range of perceptibility) is transcendental to the causal (cause-effect) relation.

1. Referring to the concluding verse of the last chapter—86.59—Parīkṣit doubted the competence and capability of the Vedas to declare or describe the Supreme Brahman.

2. ŚR explains: The Śruti texts are expressed in and consist of words. Words are characterised by their 'powers' technically known as *Mukhyā*, *Lakṣaṇā* and *Gauṇī*, or by their power by which it expresses, indicates or suggests the implication either by means of (i) *abhidhā* (denotation, the meaning belonging to the word by social consensus or convention (*Saṅketa*) which primarily made the word at all), (ii) *Lakṣaṇā* (the secondary signification. The standard SK. example is *Gaṅgāyām ghoṣaḥ*—'The cowherd colony is in or on the Gaṅgā'. Here *in* or *on* means not on the water-current of the river but on the bank of the river (technically called *Jahallakṣaṇā*). Or *Kuntāḥ Praviśanti* "spears enter" i.e. 'persons bearing the spears enter'. Something additional to the thing mentioned viz. spear-bearers is implied. *This is called a-Jahal-Lakṣaṇā*. The 3rd power of the word is *Vyañjanā*—'suggested or insinuated sense.' Thus if a cool breeze is implied by saying 'the cowherd colony is on the Gaṅgā', it will be *Vyañjanā*.

KD has explained in details ŚR's commentary adding his illustrations to elucidate it. Thus he gives the sub-division of *abhidhā* viz. *rūḍhi*, *yoga* and

Śrī Śuka explains:

2. The Almighty who is above limiting conditions and ever-liberated evolved the intellect, the senses, the mind and the vital breaths of all embodied beings (*Jīvas*) for the enjoyment of various objects, for bringing about their birth, for their transmigration to various other-worldly regions, for experiencing pleasures, etc. thereof and for their Final Liberation (where all speculation or ideation ceases to function). He created these for helping *Jīvas* attain their four objectives of life, viz. *artha*, *dharma*, *Kāma and Mokṣa*.

yoga-rūḍhi. Thus names of persons Rāma, John, etc. are by social convention (*rūḍhi*) but *nṛpati*. 'The protector of the people' 'a king' is etymological (*Yoga* or *Yaugika*). But *Pāṅka-ja* (born out of mud) may mean a lotus or a frog but is by *convention and etymology* used for a lotus flower. This is *Yoga-rūḍha*.

The thrust of Parīkṣit's submission is "How can Brahman which is transcendental to *Padārtha* can come with the range of words of Śruti.

As ŚR. succinctly states it : *evam padārthatvāyogād apadārthasya ca vākyārthatvāyogān na śruti-gocaratvam Brahmaṇaḥ* |

The position taken by other important annotators may be briefly summarised as follows :—

VR : The Supreme Brahman is indefinable either as a *cit* (conscious) or *acit* (unconscious, material) entity. It is beyond three *guṇas*. It is absolutely different and distinct from other intelligent or unintelligent existence. How could the *Śrutis* being verbal in nature, denote or describe *Brahman* directly.

VJ : The Supreme Brahman is indefinable, void of *guṇaṣ*, distinct from *Sat* and *asat* (The causal matter and its product). While Śrutis are words and as such can connote qualities or denote things having qualities. This being the case how could Śrutis speak of the Supreme Brahman? Did they directly describe it or indicate its properties ?

By Śuka's epithet—*Brahman*—VJ takes 'a sage whose all desires are accomplished.'

KD : Śuka concedes that when after the withdrawal of the universe, the *Prakṛti* ceases to be and there exists only formless, attribute less Brahman, this Brahman is beyond the power of Śrutis to decribe. But when the universe is created and the individual souls (*Jīvas*) which lay dormant or dissolved in the *Prakṛti* are granted their subtle-bodies (*liṅga Śarīra*) and are given scope to achieve their purpose in life, be it *dharma*, *artha*, *kāma*, or *mokṣa*, God is the Controller of Māyā and is hence called the Almighty Lord (*Prabhu*). To such *Jīvas*, *Śrutis* describe *That* (*Brahman*) *thou* (*art*) etc. But when the power of words ceases to be and the Śrutis find it beyond

3. This is the secret essence about the Brahman which is enshrined in the *Upaniṣads* and which is treasured up in their mind by the ancestors of our ancestors[1] (like Sanaka, Sanandana, etc.). He who faithfully and with devotion preserves it in the mind becomes rid of the limitation of the body[2] etc. and attains the *Summum bonum.*[3]

their capacity to speak about Brahman, they assume silence which is an eloquent guidanec (87.60-112).

VR: The controller of the universe invested the *Jīvas* (individual souls) with their bodies for favouring them with the opportunity of propitiating him as well as attaining their prosperity here and attainment of *Mokṣa* or *niḥśreyas* hereafter, and for gaining the knowledge of the self which leads to *mukti* (Final Emancipation), and removing the notion of difference about their essential nature. VR : alternately explains *Kalpanāya* as "for the sake of the sportive activities regarding the creation, etc. of the universe."

VJ : The Lord has created the intellect, the senses, the mind and the vital breath for *Jīvas* so that words (*mātrās*) indicate him directly that he is distinct from *Sat* and *asat* (or subtle and gross *Prakṛtis*) and in order that they should take to meritorious activities (*bhavārtham*) such as *svādhyāya* and *Pravacana*. The 'words' do not indicate attainment of heaven but obtaining merits for realization of the Supreme Self. VJ interpreres *Kalpanāya* as "for knowledge of the Supreme Self's (*Paramārtha jñānāya*).

VT : The Lord has created the intellect, the sense-organs, the minds and the vital breaths of various categories of *jīvas* like the human beings who were lying dormant or in a dissolved state along with the *Prakṛti* after the great *Pralaya* (dissolution of the universe) for the sake of understanding the Vedas and thereby to make them realize their Self (the principle of *jīva*) and for visualizing the Supreme Self (the *bhāgavat-tattva*) called here as *akalpana* (that which is devoid of *māyā*).

VB : The logically established view (*Siddhānta*) is that Brahman should be regarded of that nature as it is described in *Upaniṣads* (*Vedānta*). In the evolution of the world, the Lord created (1) Intelligence, (2) Sense-organs, (3) the mind and (4) vital breaths (*Prāṇas*) in this serial order and their respective function is (1) *mātrā* (2) another transmigration of the soul (3) for *ātman* and (4) *akalpana*. He insists that this order of the objects of Intelligence, etc. should be observed.

Sa kramo'trāpi grāhya evaṁ sarvopayogārtham, yato Bhagavāṁścatuṣṭayam utpāditavān, anenaiva sarvānupapattiḥ parihartavyā—iti Śukahṛdayam /

1. *Pūrveṣām purvajaiḥ* : (1) By Vāmadeva, Prahlāda and others—VR (ii) By God and others—VJ.

2. *akiñcana*—A person who regards nothing as worth praying for or worth attaining—VR..

3. *Kṣemaṁ gacchet*—Getting all his doubts resolved by pondering over the *Upaniṣads* should attain to the Lord.

4. Here, on this topic, I shall narrate to you in details an ancient legend concerning the great sage Nārāyaṇa and containing a dialogue between Nārada and the sage Nārāyaṇa.

5. On one occasion, during the course of his tour of the world, Nārada, the beloved of the Lord, went to the hermitage of Nārāyaṇa (i.e. Badarikāśrama), to visit that ancient sage.

6. It is reported that in this Bhārata varṣa, from the beginning of the Kalpa, the sage Nārāyaṇa has been engaged in performing penance coupled with righteousness, spiritual knowledge, self-control and mental tranquility for the prosperity of the people here and their spiritual good hereafter.

7. Nārada paid obeisance to Nārāyaṇa who was seated in his hermitage surrounded by sages, residents of the village called Kalāpa, and put him this very question, O scion of the Kuru family.

8. In reply to him, the glorious sage Nārāyaṇa, in the midst of the sages who were listening, told Nārada, the gist of the discussion on the *para Brahman*, which took place between the residents of Janaloka.[1]

The Venerable Lord (Nārāyaṇa) said:

9. O son of the Self-born god Brahmā, in the days of yore in Jana-loka, there was held a seminar on the *para Brahman* (i.e. it was a discussion in which participants both listened and spoke and thus shared their views and experiences about the nature of the *para Brahman* with others) among the mind-born sons of Brahmā who were sages observing life-long celibacy.

10. When you had been away to Śveta-dvīpa to see the the Aniruddha form of mine, a thorough and well-rounded discussion on the *para Brahman* took place—a discussion in which all the Śrutis were discussed, co-ordinated and synthesized. In that seminar this was definitely the very question you put to me.

1. This is fifth of the seven divisions of the universe and is situated above *Maharloka*.

11. Although they (The mind-born sons of Brahmā) were all equal in status from the point of learning, austere penance, virtuousness and so much unparalleled in abounding grace that to them friends, enemies and the indifferent ones were equal. They made one of them, viz. Sanandana as the expounder[1] while others became eager listeners.

11A *VR adds*:

I shall explain to you all your queries, O sinless one. Now listen to me.

Sanandana said:

12-13. After swollowing up (at the time of the *Pralaya*) all the universe created by him, the Supreme person along with all his (creative and protective) potencies (such as *prakṛti puruṣa, kāla*) was as if lying asleep (in his yogic trance). At the end of the period of Pralaya, Śrutis (i. e. the deities presiding over them which were created by his first exhalations at the beginning of the creation of the universe), awakened that Supreme person singing the hymns which appropriately described his true nature, just as bards and attendants of an emperor approach to wait upon him early in the morning while he is still asleep, and awaken him by singing sweet songs eulogising his famous heroic exploits.

Śrutis said :

14*. Be gracious to manifest your glorious exalted nature O invincible Lord. Be pleased to exterminate the beginningless

1. KD : This was a *Brahma-Makha* "sacrifice in the form of spiritual discussion." Just as in sacrifices. though the sacrificial priests know the whole of the Veda, the priests recite only that much portion of the Veda appropriate for the rite and that too pertaining to the part of the duty (*Kṣaṇa*) assigned to them, similarly, in this *Brahma-makha* although all of them were equal in all respects, they gave the *Kṣaṇa* of 'speakership' to Sanandana.

14* The gist of VR's lengthy explanation :

O invincible Lord, be pleased to free all beings from *Avidyā*, as you, being merciful by nature, take cognisance of only the good qualities ignoring the defects or evil qualities in beings (*Sā'parādha-janeṣvapi Kaścid guṇa-leśo'sti cet tam apekṣyā' nugrahaśīlas tvam* /). Avidyā, by the three *guṇas* causes the *jīvas* to whirl in *Saṁsāra* investing them with evil. You are all powerful and are endowed with six excellences (as enumerated in the *Viṣṇu P.*) implied in

Avidyā (Nescience) of all those beings which are vested with mobile and immobile bodies, as the *guṇas* (like *Sattva*, *rajas* and *tamas*) possessed by Avidyā are exhibited with the evil object (of obscuring the ever-blissful nature of the Soul). You are, by your very nature, endowed with all the powers, blissfulness and authority (and hence you have kept *Māyā* or *Avidyā* under control.) O Lord ! who as their indwelling controller evoke all the powers in all beings ! It is only the Veda which can describe you to some extent as (some times—such as at the beginning of creation) you (appeared to) work by way of sport in conjunction with Māyā but as a matter of fact you always abide in your ever blissful state of infinite knowledge and delight.

your epithet *Bhagavān*. You invest all powers in mobile and immobile corporeal beings. At the time of gross creation, when you work in association with *Prakṛti* and *Puruṣa*, Vedas can describe you.

VR : Concludes his Commentary stating his *Viśiṣṭādvaita* stance, as follows :—

anena Prakṛti - sambandha-mocakatva - niyata - tatsambandhāpādakatva - jñāpanāya sarva - kāraṇatvaṁ tasya nirvikāre' nupa-pannatvāttasmin cid - acid - vaiśiṣṭyaṁ viśiṣṭa - kāraṇatvādeva viśiṣṭa - kāryāṇām viśiṣṭa -kāraṇānyatvāt śarīrātma-bhāvācca kārya-śarīra. bhūta - cid-acid-vāci-śabdānāṁ viśesyātma - paryantābhidhāyakatvāc co'ktam

14-1. ŚR quotes the following Śruti (i.e. *Upaniṣadic*) texts attributing creation to the Supreme Person

(1) *Yato vā imāni bhūtāni jāyante / yena jātāni jīvanti / yat prayantyabhisaṁviśanti / tad vijijñāsasva—Taitt. Up.* 3.1.

Here creation, subsistence and dissolutions of all *bhūtas* is attributed to Brahman.

(2) *Yo Brahmāṇaṁ vidadhāti pūrvaṁ yo vai vedāṁśca prahiṇoti tasmai / taṁ ha devātma-buddhi-prakāśam mumukṣur vai śaraṇam ahaṁ prapadye—Śvetāśvatara Up.* 6.18).

Here god Brahmā's creation and his trustee-ship of the Vedas by the Supreme Man is mentioned.

(3) *Satyaṁ jñānam anantam Brahma /*
Yaḥ sarvajñaḥ sa sarva-vit / Taittirīya Up. 2,1r

The infinite knowledge and omniscience of the Reality is stated.

(4) *Ya ātmani tiṣṭhan ātmānam niyamayati /*

God's being the inner controller is described.

VJ : (*The gist only*) :

Be pleased to manifest your glory by being compassionate to your votaries. O invincible Lord ! Remove the screen to your will-power and do away with the cover of *Prakṛti* which obscures Jīva's qualities under the

15* The sages recognize that the universe that is perceived is the perfect *Brahman* (yourself) as it is the Reality (*Brahman*) that remains in the end (at the time of *Pralaya*). The *Brahman* is not

sufferings in *Saṁsāra*. Due to *Prakṛti* the inner qualities like infinite power, of Jīva which is your reflection, do not shine. You invest all beings such as Śrī, Brahmā, and others in this universe when you are associated with *Prakṛti* (which according to *Smṛtis* is one-eighth of the time of the dissolved state). The Vedas can follow you i.e. your commands and interdictions while during the stage of *Pralaya*, the Śrutis remain as mere hymns of your praise. VJ ends his com. with a quotation from Madhva Ācārya which affirms the equivalence of the Bh. P. with Śrutis.

15* (1) As *Pūrvapakṣa* ŚR quotes ṚV 8.44.16a. (which is repeated in all the Vedas e.g. *Tait. Saṃ*. 1.55.la. *Vāj. Sam*. 3.12*a*) and states that the Śrutis refer to Agni and Indra and not to me (*Para Brahman*). The *uttara pakṣa* (the reply) is given in this verse.

(2) *KD closely follows SS.*

(3) *Sudarśana Sūri and VR* :

When all the things evolved out of *Brahman* at the time of creation are withdrawn at the time of *Pralaya* and only *Brahman* (the cause of all things) remains. Just as earthen wares are created out of and ultimately reduced to the earth (their material cause), the gross perceptible universe is said to be *Brahman* from which the universe and all things included in it are created and of which they are constituted and within which they are withdrawn. Hence, the knowers (the seers of the Vedas) have devoted their mind and speech to you (who are the firm support). The foot-steps resting on bed-steads are as good as placed on the ground as the bedsteads have the earth (floor) as their support.

15*A. *VJ's Text reads the 1st half differently* :

You are beyond the eternal darkness called *Mūlaprakṛti*. It is through Vedas that your real nature is known. You are not subject to modifications. Hence, sages i.e. learned persons like Brahmā and others resigned their thoughts, words and actions to you. Just as the feet of men resting on the firm earth get full support and do not fall, the thoughts, words and actions of these sages do not prove untrue as you, to whom they have dedicated them, are the Supreme-most.

15* *VB* (*Summary*) :

The universe itself is *Brahman*—Śrutis and experience support this. When all modifications cease to be, *Brahman* remains. VB quotes *Yato vā imāni bhūtāni jāyante, etc.* (*Tait. Up*. 3.1.1). Just as earthen wares are made out of and ultimately reduced to earth, so it is *Brahman* out of which everything is evolved, and the reality that remains is *Brahman*. Hence, the seers of the Vedas have made you the centre of their thought, word and deed. Even misapprehensions are also intrinsically *Brahman* (*Bhramād api svī-kṛto Viṣayaḥ paramārthataḥ bhagavān eva bhavati* /) Just as foot-step placed anywhere rests in the ultimate analysis, on the earth.

subject to modifications. It is from the *Brahman* that the rising and setting i. e. evolution and dissolution of the universe of modifications take place, just as the clay (the material cause) remains constant though its modifications (the earthen-ware like pot, pitchers, etc.) are made and unmade. Hence, sages have concentrated their mind and speech on you and not on the modifications (things in the world). How can the feet placed by men (on stones, bricks etc.) not be regarded ultimately as rested on the *terra firma* itself. (Similarly, if *Śrutis* describe some modifications of yours, they ultimately describe you who form the basis, the substratum of them all).

16*. It is, hence, O Lord of Māyā (constituted of the three *guṇas* viz. (*Sattva*, *Rajas* and *Tamas*) that spiritually wise and thoughtful people immerse themselves into the nectarian sea of your stories which completely wash off the dirt (sins or impurities) of the entire world and have rid themselves of sins and (all types of) afflictions.[1] Need it be said, O Supreme Lord, that those who, by virtue of their self-realization, have cleansed all passions and evil propensities from their heart and have warded off the effects of Time (such as old age) will enjoy your state of eternal, infinite bliss ?

17*. Persons are alive (lit. bearers of life) in the real sense of the term only if they are your devoted followers, otherwise they are merely respiring bellows. It is due to your grace (i.e.

16* VJ : O Lord of three worlds ! Persons deeply learned in philosophy (*darśanas*) take a plunge in the sea of nectar of your stories which wash off the impurities of all people, have rid themselves of all the miseries of the world. Need it be said, O Supreme Lord, that the Liberated Souls whose afflictions from their hearts and the effects like birth, old age etc. caused by Time are wiped out by God himself and who resort to and worship you will enjoy the state of eternal, ihfinite bliss, have not to undergo any sufferings.

1. *ŚR quotes as an avthority .*

Yathā puṣkara-palāśa āpo na śliṣyanta evam evaṁ-vidi pāpaṁ karma śliṣyate

Chāndogya Up. 4.14.3.

17* VJ : It is by your entry into Brahmā, Rudra and other presiding deities of *Mahat*, *Ahaṅkāra* and other principles that they could create this Egg of the universe. Those who bore ill feeling towards you (*asuhṛdaḥ*) believe that everything is unreal. And their life is nothing but respiring like bellows and their exhalations are sighs expressive of their suffering in hell. The three

presence or interpenetration) that (insentient) Principles like *Mahat* (cosmic intelligence), Ahaṁkāra (cosmic 'I'-ness') and others could create this egg of the universe or body (macrocosm as well as microcosm). You are that Supreme Being that enter into and animate the five vestures of the body enshrining the soul (the virtues consisting of food, vital breath, mind *Vijñāna* and bliss) and assuming their form, he knows them all. But factually you are not connected with them and abide in the last (called *Brahma-puccha*[1] in *Tait. Up.* (2. 1. 5). You are distinct from the gross and the subtle—the ultimate eternal Reality which alone remains after the destruction of all others.

18*. Out of those paths (of Brahma-realization explored and laid down) by (ancient) sages[2], those whose eyes are blinded by gravel or *rajas* i. e. have gross outlook, contemplate Brahman as being at the abdomen (as presiding over the plexus called *Maṇipūra*, located at the navel). Followers of Āruṇi who have subtler vision contemplate Brahman in the cavity of the heart (at the plexus or nerve centre known as *Anāhata Cakra*). O infinite Lord, the meditator thence proceeds upward (by the channel or path called *Suṣumṇā*) upto the crown of the head (to the plexus called sahasrāra the exalted position of the lustre of Brahman[3]. He who reaches this position does not recede to fall again into the jaws of death.

categories the lowest i.e. human beings, middle i.e. sages and Gandharvas, the highest i.e. Indra and other gods and their leader god Brahmā knows and disseminates by his teaching the knowledge of your eternal, infinite, unparalleled blissful nature and your being transcendental to *Sat* and *Asat* (*sad-asataḥ Param*/). He is eligible to attain to a form similar to the Lord.

1. VR : has stoutly opposed the idea of *Brahmapuccha*. According to VR. : this verse emphasizes that the human life is useless if not devoted to the Lord. Persons who, though endowed with sound sense organs, indulge in enjoying objects of senses instead of engaging themselves in propitiating the Lord merely live and breathe like bellows.

2 VR : 1. *ṛṣi - vartamasu*—The paths of worship as prescribed in the Vedānta—VR.

3. *Paramaṁ dhāma*—The highest position is the centre between the eyebrows.

VR : classifies these worshippers as follows :—

(i) *Vaiśvānara-vidyā-niṣṭha* : Those who look upon gastral fire as a form of *Brahman*.

19*. You enter the various living species evolved by you, though as their (material) cause, you were already existing there. Of your own accord, you assume those forms like fire (lying dormant in the fuel and appearing similar to the size and shape of the fire-wood though as Fire it is undifferentiated one) and appear smaller or greater, higher or lower. Hence, persons whose judgment is clear and who do not expect any return (either here or hereafter) for their acts realize your true nature as being the only Reality, Pure, undifferentiated immutable in all these unreal forms.[1]

20. (The scriptures say) that the individual soul abiding in the body created and shaped by his former acts, is not limited by anything that may be termed as cause and effect. It is a part or ray of yourself who are endowed with all potencies. Having come to this conclusion regarding the nature of the individual Soul, wise men in this world, with unflinching faith and devotion, contemplate on your feet to which all righteous acts prescribed in the Vedas are dedicated and in consequence of which they attain to liberation from *Saṁsāra* (lit. State of getting no rebirth again).

(2) *Dahara—vidyā-niṣṭha*—Followers of Aruṇi who look upon God as being in the cavity of the heart (*hṛdaya-puṇḍarīkāntargatā'kāśar ūpaṁ tvām upāsate*)

(3) Those who follow the *parisara paddhati* i.e. the path of *suṣumṇā*.

(ii) 18* VJ : also classifies the contemplatists on Brahman as follows:—

(1) Possessors of subtle insight (*Kūrpadṛśaḥ Sūkṣma dṛṣṭayaḥ*) into Brahman and his attributes contemplate Brahman as *Udara* (*udarapūrṇam Brahman*) or Perfect, full, infinite, Brahman.

(2) Followers of Aruṇi meditate upon *Brahman* as *hṛdaya* (one abiding in the heart).

(3) The followers of the sage Maṇḍūka contemplate *Brahman* as *dahara* i.e. subtler than the sky and our vital breath lead to It. But those who follow the *Parisara* method and contemplate Brahman as passing from the heart through *Brahmanāḍī* to the crown of the head such meditators do not fall a victim to kṛtānta—God of death.

19* VJ (Only the difference is noted) quotes *Tantra Bhāgavata* as his authority. In the innumerable living species you are like *jīva* in them and assimilate yourself with those beings like fire in fire-wood. The Vital breath knows you. Great persons mentally go near you who are the eternal principle in the decaying forms and contemplate on you.

1. *Śvet Up*. 6.11.

21*. O controller of the universe ! You have assumed a corporeal form for shedding light on the true nature of the self which is difficult to comprehend. Those persons who have recouped from their exhaustion (caused by whirling in the cycle of *Saṁsāra*) by immersing themselves in the ocean of the nectarine stories of your glorious deeds and have renounced their homes (relatives, property, etc.) through their association with your swan-like votaries who take shelter in your lotus-feet, do not covet even for liberation from *Saṁsāra*.

22*. When the nest[1] (in the form of the body in which the soul dwells) follows the path that leads to you, it is useful as one's own self, well-wisher and a beloved person. Though you are always ready to help and are thus favourably disposed and the real well-wisher and loving, it is unfortunate that people of suicidal mentality do not take any delight or interest in you and do not worship you with some form of devotion. They wrong-

21* *KD* : gives a gist of this and states that the quality between God and the votary is synthesized into one-ness by intense devotion and exhorts to renounce the *Karmas*-religious rites prescribed by the Veda and engage oneself completely in the devotion to God.

(ii) *VJ* : O Lord whose essential nature is extremely incomprehensible those who have deeply studied the Vedas who have exhausted themselves in churning the extensively vast ocean of your glorious deeds and have been thereby released from *Saṁsāra*, have come to realize that you are the source of the Vedas and the "fruit" to be conveyed by them, and worship you by performance of sacrifices and meditation.

22* (1) *VR. construes differently* :

(i) If this nest i.e. the physical body is placed in your way (by devoting to your worship, etc.) you are just like the very soul, a well-wisher and a beloved person always ready to help.

(ii) KD : Poetically illustrates how a person forgets the Lord and engages himself into *Saṁsāra* and finally comes to grief. Hence, one should be absorbed in the devotion and worship of Ātman.

1. *Kulāya*—that which dissolves into the earth i.e. this physical body.

(iii) *VJ reads differently.*

Through the association of and for worshipping *sannyāsins* or Swan-like ascetics who are attached to your lotus-feet, some have renounced their houses, kith & kin and do not aspire to attain *Mokṣa* (liberation from *Saṁsāra*) which is the fruit of propitiating you, O Lord. They are devoted to you who are the most beloved one. They look upon this transient nest (This physical body) as good and dear and a selfless relative who guides by the path leading to you.

ly entertain attachment, etc. to the physical body which is so wretched and wander in this *Saṁsāra* which is extremely fearful.

23*. That state of yours which sages, the practitioners of rigorous Yogic path, contemplated in their hearts by restraining their vital breath, the mind and senses thoroughly, is also attained by your adversaries by constantly thinking of you, and also by the women (Gopīs of Vraja) whose hearts were enamoured of and attached to your mighty arms which were like the body of Śeṣa. The Lord of serpents, as well as we (the presiding deities of Śrutis) who realise you as equal to all and omnipresent and cling to your lotus-like feet, are the same (i.e. equal) in your eyes.

24*. Alas ! O Lord, how can one who has come into existence and passed away, at a later stage after you, can possibly presume to know you who existed anterior to all creation. It is from you that the sage (god Brahmā) was born. After Brahmā came into existence both the classes of deities (viz. (1)

23* VJ's Text combines the last two lines in verse 22 and the first two lines in verse 23 of ŚR's text. (The gist only) : Persons with wrong beliefs and course of meditation do not realise the Supreme Soul. Their minds being rooted in wrong notions suffer eternally in Hell and are invested with a condemned body from hell to hell. The enemies of sages who directed by *Mukhya Prāṇa* (Chief vital breath) know the way to *Mokṣa* and worship you as (present in) the *hṛdaya* (heart).

24* *KD* : You, being the author of the creation and dissolution of the universe, are anterior to all. Hence, you are beyond the comprehension of all. If we submit to your feet and follow the nine-fold path of devotion, you impart spiritual knowledge out of Grace. Hence, the path of devotion is the best of all. (HV Hari-Varadā) 87.488-510

(1) *VR* (*Summary*) :

devagaṇā ubhaye :—Two groups of sages : (i) Sanaka and others leading ascetic life and (ii) Marīci and others engaged in propagating species and world activity. When you withdraw even the *Śāstra* (Vedic Lore) within you and go to sleep, there is neither *Sat* (phenomenal intelligent being) nor *Asat* (phenomenal intelligent creation (the rest similar to ŚR).

(II) *VJ's Text* is a combination of the latter half of verse 23 and the first half of the present (No. 24) verse (only the gist of different interpretation is given.) You alone know your essential nature. The eternal Vedas seek the nectar of your lotus-feet but cannot properly comprehend you who are characterised by existence, consciousness and bliss. You are very kind to *Jīvas* who devoutly remember you.

ādhyātmika—deities presiding over sense-organs, mind and (ii) *ādhidaivika*—those presiding over the celestial world). When, withdrawing every thing within you, you go to sleep, at that time, there exists neither *Sat* (the gross phenomena) nor *Asat* (their subtle causes like *Mahat*, *Ahaṁkāra*, etc.) nor the product of these two viz. this psycho-physical organism called body, nor the velocity of Time, nor any *Śāstras* (*Śruti* texts) from which your nature can be known.[1]

25*. Those who postulate the evolution of the universe or being from non-being or the non-existent (as the Vaiśeṣika school does) or who believe in the cessation of the existent (twenty one types of miseries as *Mokṣa* or Liberation (as the *Nyāya school* does) or who posit the distinctness and plurality of Souls (as the Sāṅkhyas and Naiyāyikas, etc. do) and those who affirm that the fruit of (sacrificial and other) Karmas are real (as the followers of the Mīmāṁsā school hold)—all these propagate their misconceptions. It is due to ignorance about you (which leads persons to believe in the misconcept of diversity that the *Puruṣa* is comprised of the three *guṇas* or modifications of *Prakṛti*. It cannot exist in you as you are the embodiment of pure knowledge and absolute consciousness.[2]

1. *ko addhā veda ka iha pravocat /*
kuta ājātā, kuta iyaṁ visṛṣṭiḥ //
arvāg-devā asya visarjanenā
thā ko veda yata ābabhūva //—ṚV 10.129.6.

Also : *yato vāco nivartante aprāpya manasā saha /*—Tait. Up. 2.4.1

25* *KD* : elucidates ŚR's refutation of the view of Patañjali that the Brahman evolves out of *Asat* i.e. the *Jīva* attains Brahmahood though originally he did not possess it. He has incorporated the translation of the quotations from *Upaniṣads* (that are given below) into his lucid commentary.

VR : Only the difference from ŚR is noted as VR is a long Com. (second half) : Those who think that *Prakṛtis* of three *guṇas* and the *jīvas* (intelligent beings) are distinct and are not controlled by Supreme *Brahman* are under the influence of *Avidyā* (nescience). But you transcend *Prakṛti* and *Puruṣa* and yourself are Perfect, Infinite consciousness.

2. In refuting the other schools of thought the author of the Bh. P. based this verse on *Śruti* Texts like the following :—

(i) *Sad-eva somyedam agra āsīt / Chāndogya Up*. 6.2.1

(ii) *Brahmaiva san Brahmāpnoti/* - *Bṛhad. Up*. 4.4.6.

26*. All the universe including the Jīva, comprised of the three *guṇas* (modifications of Prakṛti) is a projection of the mind. It appears to have a real existence as it is superimposed on you. Those who have realized the *Ātman* (the soul) regard all this (subjective and objective) universe as *Sat*, i.e. really existent as it is the projection of the Ātman Himself. Just as persons seeking gold do not discard (ornaments which are) the modifications (of gold) as they are essentially gold, the knowers of the Self come to the conclusion that this Universe (both subjective and objective) is their very self as he (the *Ātman*) made it and then entered into it.

27**. Only those persons who devotedly serve (i.e. worship) you as abiding in all beings as their Indwelling soul, disregard-

(iii) *avidyāyām antare vartamānāḥ |*
svayaṁ dhīrāḥ paṇḍitam manyamānāḥ ||
Jaghanyamānāḥ pariyanti mūḍhāḥ |
andhenaiva nīyamānā yathāndhāḥ || Muṇḍaka 1.2.8.

ŚR was a follower of the *advaita* school of Śaṅkara. But like Śaṅkara, he was an ardent devotee at heart. After every verse of the *Śruti gītā* he composes one verse conveying the gist of that verse. At the end of his rendering in a verse the gist of this 25th verse, he expresses his ardent desire for Liberation by repeating the names of God who is both Śiva and Viṣṇu. He prays :

Śrīman Mādhava Vāmana Trinayana Śri Śaṅkara Śrīpate |
Govindeti mudā' vadan Madhupate muktaḥ kadā syām aham ||

26* (i) *VR* : The mind of all beings including that of a human being, constituted as it is of three *guṇas* which apparently shows to produce some effects cannot do so in your case (It cannot realize you). But your devotees who worship you and meditate upon you, purify their heart and realize that the Universe is *Sat*—a Reality as it is not different from *Paramātman* or *Brahman* —the universe, which is the effect or a synthesized whole of the subtle principles of sentient and non-sentient beings is *Brahman*.

(ii) *VJ's* : Text combines the last two lines of Verse 25 with the 1st two lines of the present verse :—To regard that the *jīva* is bound by three *guṇas* like Sattva and others is ignorance. Only the unrighteous postulate that your mind is constituted of three *guṇas*. Supra-human beings like gods with better insight, know that you transcend these *guṇas* and are an embodiment of supreme bliss and it is the *Jīvas* that suffer from miseries.

27** (I) KD : extends this devotion to the spiritual preceptors as well.

(II) VR : Out of mercy for those averse to you you control them like cattle and bring to the right path by teaching them the path of righteousness. Those who are not averse to you and are your votaries purify other ignorant persons.

ed Death and planting their foot on the head of Death attain Liberation (from the cycle of births and deaths). But to those who turn away their face from you, howsoever, learned they be, you bind them down like beasts by your commandments (of injunctions and interdictions ordained in the *Śrutis*). Only those who cherish devoted love to you purify themselves as well as others but not those who are averse to you !

28*. Being self-illuminating as the embodiment of knowledge as you are, you control the power of the sense-organs of all beings, though you yourself are devoid of senses[1] (in your formless aspect). Hence gods who are bound by Nescience (*Avidyā*) and who partake of the offerings oblated to them by men (under their dominance) offer worship and homage to you (just as tributary princes collect revenue from their subjects and pay tribute to their overlord, the emperor). The progenitors of the world execute the duties of their offices to which they are appointed through your fear[2] just as tributary kings do unto their emperor in this world.

(III) VJ.: the text is a combination of the last two lines of verse 26 and the first half of verse 27 of ŚR.

As gold is the material cause of an ornament of gold which is its modification and as such it is not discarded as separate from gold, the Lord who interpenetrated and illumined the universe after its creation has his own essential nature unchanged. The permeator of the universe is the same absolute God. Those who serve you as abiding in every principle of reality set their foot on the head of death and become Liberated.

1. (i) *a-pāṇi-pādo javano grahītā |*
Paśyatyacakṣuḥ sa śṛṇotyakarṇaḥ ||
sa vetti vedyaṁ na ca tasya vettā |
tam āhur agryam puruṣam purāṇam ||

—*Śvet. Up.* 3.19

28*. VR.: It is by your will-power that you bring about creation, etc. of the universe. You have all the powers of the sense-organs concentrated in your hands as you are the absolute.

2. *bhīṣa'smād vātaḥ pavate, bhīṣodeti sūryaḥ | bhīṣāśmād Agnīs' cendraś ca mṛtyur dhāvati pañcamaḥ |*

—*Tait. Up.* 2.7.1.

yathā'gneḥ kṣudrā viṣphuliṅgā vyuccarantyevam evā'smād ātmanaḥ sarve prāṇāḥ, sarve lokāḥ, sarve devāḥ sarvāṇi bhūtāni vyuccaranti |

Bṛhad. Up. 2.1.20.

29*. O Lord! You are eternally free and far beyond the reach of Māyā. But when you are pleased to sport with that beginningless Māyā or Avidyā by your mere glance (without coming into contact with her), all the mobile and immobile beings invested with their subtle bodies come into being.[1] But their bodies depend on the causal (latent) *karmas* of those beings which have come into existence by your (above-mentioned) glance. You are beyond the ken of sense-organs and the mind. Like the sky, you are impartial—equal to all. None kindred to you, none stranger.

[From the point of subtleness and impartiality] you are comparable to the Void[2] (*śūnya* in its positive aspect), incomprehensible to speech and mind.

30.** O Eternal Lord! If (it is postulated as Sāṅkhyas and schoolmen of similar views do, that) individual souls be infinite in number, each eternally existent and all-pervading, their being under control (of another i.e. you) is not possible.

29* (I) KD refutes 'voidness' conveyed by the term *śūnya*. *śūnya* means 'un-manifest' 'beyond the range of word'. He discusses fundamental problems about the nature and size (whether atomic or co-terminus with the body) of the soul. He discusses the concepts of 'bondage and 'liberation', 'plurality' and 'oneness' of the soul. (The discussion is too lengthy to be compressed in a foot-note].

asad vā idam agra āsīt / tato vai sad ajāyata /

—*Tait. up.* 2.7.1

(II) VR: (Summary only).

All beings mobile and immobile are invested with a body through which they are made to suffer agonies caused by *Prakṛti*. Emancipation from these sufferings is possible only by the gracious glance of the Lord. All sentient (and non-sentient) beings constitute your body. As nobody can be separate and distinct from you, you are their Proteetor. None is equal to you. Nothing pre-existed you. You are all-pervading like the sky and are not tainted by any contact.

(III) VJ.'s text combines verse 28 c, d and 29 a, b of ŚR's text. The gist of 29 a, b : VJ. quotes with approval Śāṇḍilya's opinion. If one were to hold that Liberation (from *saṁsāra*) is secured through the gracious glance of Viṣṇu, then it must be admitted that all beings whirl into *saṁsāra* due to the will of God.

30*. VR : (only the difference from ŚR is noted).

The view that that which permeates the universe is both the ruler and the ruled, is not correct and the holders of the view have failed to see the truth.

(It is illogical to hold that equals are sub-ordinate to equals.) And, hence, (the statement) that you control them or they are controlled by you is not possible. Their being controlled is possible only if the contrary is true (i.e. if the *jīvas* be limited or conditioned, finite and non-eternal). That (i.e. you or *Brahman*) which originates or produces as an evolute anything (viz. the *jīva* in this case) and thus forms its part (as the material cause) and is thus immanent in it, can control that evolute (the *jīva*). And this controlling power is not known to them who pose to know it[1], for it, being beyond the range of words and thoughts, what they come to know is defective.

31*. To postulate the creation of the *jīva* either from the beginningless *Prakṛti* (i.e. to regard the *jīva* as a product or transformation of *Prakṛti*) or from the eternal (birthless) *Puruṣa* or from a combination of both *Prakṛti* and *Puruṣa* is not tenable (for *Prakṛti* is *jaḍa*—inert—while the *jīva* is the intelligent, animating principle of life and as such it cannot be created by the inert *Prakṛti*. The second and the third alternative subjects *Puruṣa* to modifications). Just as bubbles are apparently formed out of interaction of water and air, *jīvas* apparently seem to come into existence through the *Prakṛti* and *Puruṣa* (as the material and instrumental causes. But the *Brahman* is the only reality and) the so-called creation of *jīvas* being unreal, they, with all their several names and forms, merge in you as the rivers merge into the sea (and lose their identity) or all juices (from various flowers collected by bees) get dissolved into (what is ultimately called) honey.[1]

1. *yasyāmataṁ mataṁ tasya, mataṁ yasya na veda saḥ /*
avijñātam 'vijānatām, vijñātam avijānatām //

—*Kena Up.* 2.3

(1) VR : Just as bubbles (temporary by nature) are created by the inter-action of water and wind (which are as compared with bubbles—permanent in nature), *jīvas* are formed from the combination of *Prakṛti* and *Puruṣa* both of which are birthless (eternal). It is due to your support that they bear different names and forms as a god, a man, etc. At the time of *Pralaya* (dissolution of the world) they merge in you leaving their names and forms as rivers do, etc.

(II) VJ : *Prakṛti* and *Puruṣa* are eternal, unborn and inseparable. Jivas come into existence conditioned with a body (like that of bubbles on water).

32*. Comprehending thoroughly that misapprehension (viz. the identification of the body with the Soul) has been implanted by your Māyā (leading to repeated births in Saṁsāra) intelligent and discerning persons cherish profound love and devotion to you who emancipate them from the cycle of births (and deaths). How can there be any fear of *Saṁsāra* to those who have resorted to you for refuge ? For your brow of three 'tyres' (i.e. Time or a year consisting of three seasons, viz. the summer, the rains and the winter) strikes terror constantly in the heart of those who do not seek asylum with you.

33. Persons who, neglecting the feet of one's spiritual preceptor, try to control the extremely restless, unbroken horse in the form of their mind, by trying to subdue the senses and controlling the breath, undergo great troubles for the means of controlling the mind, and are beset with hundreds of miseries in the *Saṁsāra*. Such persons are like merchants embarking on a voyage without securing the services of a helmsman (to pilot the boat.)

34. What (happiness) can men derive from one's kith and kin, sons, wives, wealth, houses, landed property, chariots and other vehicles—nay the very life-breath itself—when you, the very embodiment of every kind of blessing, are easily available by his side in the form of Ātman, ready to confer blessings on him who seeks asylum with you ? What thing in this *Saṁsāra* which is by its nature transient and essentially devoid of any substance, can give pleasure to a person who is ignorant of the above-mentioned truth (about your blissful nature) and endeavours to get sexual pleasure.

35**. Sages who have enthroned you on the lotus of their heart and hence the water with which their feet are washed, is

32. *VJ : How will your brows inspire fear of *Saṁsāra* in the hearts of those who completely submit themselves for your grace ?

VJ. **: Sages, gods and others who through holy scriptures realize that you alone are *Sat*, the Real, independent existence, and concentrate their heart on your lotus-feet which annihilate all sins, O Supreme Man, such persons do not even once approach the abode of Hara i.e. are not at all affected by *Ahaṁkāra* (Egotism).

It is noteworthy that VJ. specifically uses "Hara" and "Rudra" for *Ahaṁkāra*.

capable of destroying all sins, are completely free from lust and pride and they go on pilgrimage to various sacred places and holy waters on the earth. Those who have but once set their heart on you, the *Ātman*, the receptacle of everlasting bliss never again turn their mind to (the enjoyment of) the household life which robs man of his excellent virtues (like fortitude, serenity of mind, etc.)

36*. (The following is a refutation of the view of the Mīmāṁsakas regarding the reality of the world).

If you agree that as this (world) is evolved out of the Reality (*Brahman*), it must be real, (we say that) that is not the case. This (your) argument is fallacious. In some instances, no invariable concomitance is observed. (The effect does not necessarily follow the nature of the cause. e. g. A son is found different from the father.) In some cases, the so-called evolute is false (e. g. the "mis-perception" of a rope (a reality) as a serpent (which is unreal). Hence the world is not real like the (*Brahman*). If (you argue that the "mis-perception" of a serpent is caused by the presence of the rope and ignorance about the reality, similarly) the world is the product of both (*Brahman* and *Avidyā*), we reply that still the world is not real. It is superimposed on the Reality called *Brahman*. We appreciate the usefulness of this theory. The illusion theory is admitted as it explains the transactions of the phenomenal world, and such transactions are carried on by blindly following traditions. Your speech (Vedic texts promising reward for ritualistic acts such as performance of sacrifice, etc.) deludes through the manifold powers of words (such as *lakṣaṇā*, *vyañjanā*, etc.) persons who have become dullwitted by blind faith in Vedic rituals.[1]

36*. VR differs : If as you say, whatever is born of *Sat*—real existence —may not be real, you must show where this view fails and where it is totally disproved. The dull-witted followers of the path of Karma, are deluded through blind tradition.

1. : *tad yatheha karma-cito loko kṣīyate evam evā'mutra puṇya-cito lokaḥ kṣīyate* /

—*Chāndogya* Up. 8.1.6

Thus many Vedic texts do not subscribe to Mīmāṁsaka's contention that the Vedas advocate the path of Karma only.

37*. This phenomenal world was not in existence at the beginning before its creation. After the dissolution, the world shall cease to exist. In the intervening period, being superimposed on you, the Absolute Existence, it appears to be real. Hence, the world is compared with various modifications of material substances (e. g. bangles, armlets, crowns of gold, a pitcher or a dish of earth). It is like a figment of imagination with no basis in reality. But ignorant people regard it as the Reality.

38**. When the individual soul (*Jiva*) embraces Māyā under the influence of Nescience (Avidyā), he assumes her *guṇas* and wrongly identifies himself with the body, sense-organs etc. Thus losing (forgetting) his pristine glory and blissful nature, he succumbs to death (and is involved in the cycle of birth and death i. e., *Saṁsāra*). On the contrary, even as a serpent casts off his slough, you discard Māyā. Hence, you have preserved within you divine nature, infinite power and eight supra-human mystical powers. Thus you shine with your infinite power and glory.

39***. If the *Yogins* who try to control their senses do not exterminate the roots of passions from their heart, you, even though abiding in the hearts of these hypocrites, are not accessible to them, are like a diamond (necklace) worn round the neck but forgotten by the wearer. These *yogins*, after gratifying their own senses are flanked with miseries on both the sides, O Lord—One from Death i. e., *Saṁsāra* that has not been over-

* VR differs :

It is only the ignorant who believe that this universe did not exist before creation and it will be non-existent in future and, therefore, it is not existing at present also and that it is unreal like a figment of fiction.

** VR : (The gist only).

The *Jīva*, being deluded by Māyā is invested with a body (which is product of *Prakṛti*). Through the body he enjoys objects of senses and identifies himself with it and is subjected to death. He is thus robbed of his inherent knowledge and other qualities.

*** As usual VJ's text is a combination of verse 38.c.d and 32. a,b. : *Yogins* who are desireless and firm in the path of renunciation are blessed by the Lord with a life-free death and he grants them blissful *Mokṣa*.

come and on the other hand, from you who still remain unrealized.

40*. O glorious Lord (endowed with six excellences) ; he who has realized you, does not feel the effect of pleasure or pain as a consequence of meritorious or sinful acts as determined by you. Hence, he is not aware of the Vedic injunctions and interdictions which are binding on other embodied beings. (They are not binding on him as he has realized that the soul is distinct from the body.) You are every day ushered through the ears into the heart and are enshrined there in the hearts of men with sage advice and precepts transmitted from generation to generation. And you are ultimately attained by them as you are the final goal called *Mokṣa.*

41. Even lords of celestial regions (like god Indra, Brahmā) have not been able to fathom you or know your limit as you are Infinite. Even you have not done so, due to your infiniteness, as within you abide heaps of innumerable Eggs of Universes each along with its seven protective sheaths, which propelled by Time float about like particles of dust (driven by the wind) in the sky. Due to the infinite greatness of yours, Śrutis, finding that they end in you (as their goal), convey you indirectly by negating everything else than you.

The glorious Lord (*Nārāyaṇa*) *said :*

42. Having thus heard the exposition of the Śrutis regarding the Soul—Sanaka and other (mind-born) sons of Brahmā who had already accomplished their spiritual perfection, now worshipped Sanandana (who was their guide or resource person at the spiritual seminar).

43. The essence of all the *Vedas*, *Purāṇas* and *Upaniṣads* was in this manner churned out and extracted by those noble-souled Sanaka and other brothers who were the earliest creation of god Brahmā and who traversed through the sky.

44. O son of god Brahmā (Nārada) ! You bear in mind with faith this exposition about the (nature of the) soul which

40*. *eṣa nityo mahimā Brāhmaṇasya na karmaṇā vardhate no kanīyān*, etc.
—*Bṛhad Up.* 4.4.23

is capable of reducing to ashes all the desires of men and then you may move about, at will, anywhere in the world.

Śrī Śuka said :

45. Having received with faith and reverence what was thus expounded to him by the Sage Nārāyaṇa, Nārada, the self-controlled observer of life-long celibacy who could retain in memory what he had heard but once, and had already accomplished his purpose (in life), humbly submitted as follows :

Nārada submitted :

46. "Obeisance to that celebrated Lord Kṛṣṇa (Nārāyaṇa) of spotless hallowing glory, who assumes charming forms for the non-recurrence of birth (i. e. emancipation from *Saṁsāra*) of all beings.

47. Having thus respectfully bowed that first Sage Nārāyaṇa and his other high-souled disciples, Nārada straight-way arrived at the hermitage of my father, Kṛṣṇa Dvaipāyana.

48. He was warmly received by the worshipful sage Vyāsa. Seating himself comfortably, he described to him (Vyāsa) in details what he heard from the lips of the sage Nārāyaṇa.

49. O king Parīkṣit ! I have in this way replied to you in details the question that you put to me (by reporting to you the hymn sung by Śrutis) with a view to bringing out how far the *Brahman* which is attributeless and undefinable, can be reached by the mind.

50. One should constantly contemplate Lord Hari who keeps the Māyā at a distance from him due to his absolute state ; Who is the architect of the universe, planning its beginning, middle and end. He is the Controller of the unmanifest *Prakṛti* and of *Jīvas*. After creating the universe, He entered into it along with Jīvas and controls them. Having taken asylum with him, the Jīva protects himself against the Māyā. Having attained to him, the *Jīva* sheds his ignorance, just as a man who falls deep asleep loses the consciousness of his person (body).

CHAPTER EIGHTYEIGHT

God Rudra Saved

The King (Parikṣit) enquired :

1. Out of gods, Asuras or human beings, whoever worship (and propitiate) god Śiva who himself has renounced all worldly pleasures are blessed with wealth and enjoyment of pleasures, but not so in the case of those who are the votaries of Viṣṇu though he is the consort of the goddess of wealth.

2. We entertain a grave doubt and we desire to know (its solution) as to why the goal (i. e. the fruit achieved) of those who worship these two deities of different dispositions, is quite contrary to their expectation ? Why do the Devotees of the Lord of Lakṣmī do not get wealth and while those of Śiva become rich ?

Śrī Śuka said :

3. God Śiva is ever associated with his Śakti. He is invested with three *guṇas* viz. *Sattva*, *rajas* and *tamas* and is the presiding deity of the three types of (Cosmic) ego characterised by the *guṇas*, viz. *sattva* (or *vaikārika* ego, *rajas* (*taijasa* type of Ego) and *tamas* (or tāmasa type of ego).

4. Out of these three types of ego were evolved sixteen modifications or products (viz. mind from the *sāttvika* ego, ten sense-organs from *rājasic* type of *ahaṁkāra* and five *bhūtas* or elements from the *tāmasic* type of ego). He who adores one of these potencies is blessed with all types of earthly prosperity.

5. Lord Hari, on the other hand, is unaffected by and hence devoid of the attributes (of *Prakṛti*). He is the Supreme Person far beyond the range of *Prakṛti*. He is omniscient and is a witness to everything. A person who worships him becomes bereft of *guṇas*.

6. After the conclusion of the Horse-sacrifice, while listening to the exposition of the righteous duties, your grandfather, King Yudhiṣṭhira asked this very question to Kṛṣṇa.

7. The glorious Lord Kṛṣṇa who descended into the race of Yadu for blessing people with the *Summum bonum* (by

showing the way to *Mokṣa*) was very much pleased with that question and explained to him who was very desirous and eager to listen to him.

The Lord explained :

8. I gradually relieve a person of his wealth on whom I wish to bestow my grace. Then his own relatives, finding him penniless and hard-pressed with adversity and sorrow-stricken, forsake him (of their own accord).

9. When (he finds that) all his efforts with the desire of acquiring wealth have been futile, he becomes despondent and forms friendship with persons who are devoted to me. Then only I shower my grace on him.

10. My grace is the revelation of myself i. e. of Brahman. It is too subtle (to be comprehensible), Pure consciousness and infinite Reality (existence).

10A*. The intelligent person who realizes it as his own-self is liberated from *Saṁsāra.* Hence, people avoid me as one too difficult to be propitiated and turn to other gods (to worship).

11. Thereupon, having obtained sovereignty and prosperity from gods who are easily and quickly propitiated, they become arrogant, puffed up with pride and maddened. They forget the very gods who have bestowed boons on them and despise them.

Śrī Śuka said :

12. Gods Brahmā, Viṣṇu, Śiva and others are competent to pronounce a curse or grant boons. But dear Parīkṣit, God Śiva and Brahmā accord grace or curse instantaneously. (The moment they are pleased or displeased), but not so god Viṣṇu.

13. As an illustration of this, those versed in ancient lore cite the ancient legend how god Śiva after giving a boon to Vṛkāsura, found himself in danger.

10A* Additional half verse from the vṛndāban edition (Quoted from Bh. P. in Bengali script).

14. There was an Asura called Vṛka, the son of Śakuni. That wicked-minded fellow saw Nārada on the way and asked him which god out of the trinity (of Brahmā, Viṣṇu and Śiva) was easily and quickly propitiated.

15. Nārada advised him, "Do propitiate god Śiva and you will quickly accomplish your purpose. He gets pleased with slight merit and is enraged at the slightest offence.

16. When the ten-faced demon Rāvaṇa and Bāṇa eulogised him like bards, he bestowed on them unparalleled prosperity and sovereignty in consequence of which he found himself involved in serious troubles (Rāvaṇa uprooted mount Kailāsa, the residence of god Śiva and Bāṇa made him the protector of his capital city).

17. Being thus advised, that Asura began to propitiate god Śiva by offering to him the oblation of his own flesh chopped from his body, through the mouth of the fire-god, at the place called Kedāra in the Himālayas.

18. Out of desparation for not being able to visualize god Śiva (in spite of the sacrifice of his flesh), the Asura, on the seventh day, (took a bath in the holy waters of that place) and began to cut with sharp weapon his head with wet matted hair.

19. At that time the highly merciful god (with matted hair) who was brilliant like the fire-god, came out of the sacrificial fire. Just as we would do (to prevent our friends from suicide), he held both of his arms with his own and prevented him from that act. By the blessed touch of Śiva, his body became healed of wounds and perfect as before.

20. He spoke to him, "Dear Asura ! It is enough (desist from offering your head to me). Seek of me any boon you desire and I shall confer it on you. I am pleased even if water is reverentially offered to me by people devoted to me. You have unnecessarily tortured your body so cruelly.

21. That extremely sinful demon sought the god a boon that spelt terror to all living beings. (He requested as a boon:) "May every body die on whose head I shall lay my palm."

22. Hearing that prayer, Lord Śiva got depressed at heart (for a moment), O Parīkṣit. But laughingly he said,

"Yes. Be it so." and gave the boon which was like giving nectar to a serpent.

23. The Asura who was thus granted boon, was really desirous of laying his hand upon Gaurī (Pārvatī, the spouse of god Śiva). And they say that with a view to testing the efficacy of that boon, he advanced to place his hand upon the head of god Śiva himself. And god Śiva was seized with terror at his own act (of granting the boon.)

24. Agitated with terrific fear and trembling, he began to run fast to the northern direction with the demon pursuing (close on his heels). He ran traversing the whole of the earth, the heaven and the end of cardinal points.

25. Lords of gods did not know how to counteract or intervene and they kept quiet. At last Lord Siva went to Śvetadvīpa the ever-refulgent region of Viṣṇu lying beyond the sphere of darkness.

26. There abides Lord Nārāyaṇa in person, the ultimate resort of those who have renounced everything for the Lord, and hence have attained serenity of mind (by getting rid of passions like love, hatred, etc.) and have refrained from all forms of violence, an abode having attained which a person never returns to *Saṁsāra.*

27. Perceiving the predicament of god Śiva, the Lord who destroys all afflictions, assumed the form of a small boy by his Yoga-māyā and manifested himself at a distance.

28. Shining like fire by his refulgence and adorned with his girdle of *muñja* grass, deer-skin, staff and a rosary of Rudrākṣa beads and with *darbha* grass in his hand, he paid obeisance to the demon as if in deep humility.

The Lord said :

29. O son of Śakuni, evidently your honour is much exhausted. Have you come from a long distance ? Have rest for a short while (for a minute) (If proper care is taken of this body,) it fulfills all the cherished desires like the heavenly wish-yielding cow.

30. If the matter is fit for our ears, (i.e. if there be no objection in hearing of your intention) O mighty one, let me know on what you have set your mind. Generally a man desires

to accomplish his purpose with the help of his chosen assistants.

Śrī Śuka said :

31. When he was thus accosted in such nectar-showering words, the demon felt refreshed and confided to him (Viṣṇu) all that he had done before.

The glorious Lord (disguised as a Brahmacārin) remarked :

32. If this be the case, we do not believe in his (Śiva's) words; for he has been reduced to the State of a goblin (*Piśāca*) by the curse of Dakṣa, and is now the king of *Pretas* and *Piśācas* (evil spirits).

33. If you regard Śiva as the preceptor of the world and still have faith in him, O king of Dānavas, you may easily test the truth of his words this very moment, O dear Asura, by placing your palm on your head.

34. If the words of Śiva are found to be false, you straightway kill that liar so that he may not live to utter a falsehood again."

35. In this way his mind was changed by the wonderful and extremely soft, winning words of the Lord. And the wicked-minded fellow in utter forgetfulness placed his palm on his own head.

36. That very moment the Asura fell down with his head split up as if he was struck down with vajra (thunder-bolt). And there were applauding shouts like "Victory" "Salutations" and "Well-done" in the heavens.

37. When the wicked demon Vṛkāsura was killed, gods, sages, manes (ancestors) and Gandharvas let down showers of flowers and god Śiva was rescued from a dangerous situation.

38-39. To god Śiva who was thus saved, spoke the glorious Lord Viṣṇu: God Mahādeva ! This sinful fellow has been killed by his own sins. O Īśa (Controller of the world) ! What creature who has committed sin (or offence) against the great can possibly be safe and happy ? What need be said when the offence is committed against the controller of the universe and the father of the world like you ?

40. Whoever hears or relates this account of Liberation of god Śiva (from mortal danger) by Lord Viṣṇu, the Supreme Soul, who is the veritable sea of incomprehensible powers, becomes emancipated from *Saṁsāra* (the cycle of births and deaths) and becomes free from the danger of enemies as well.

CHAPTER EIGHTYNINE

Supremacy of Viṣṇu Vindicated :

Restoration to Life of Brāhmaṇa's Sons

Śrī Śuka said :

1. On one occasion, sages were engaged in performing a sacrificial session (of a long duration). O king, in that session a question was raised for discussion as to who of the trinity of the ruling gods (i.e. Brahmā, Viṣṇu, and Śiva) was the greatest.

2. In order to satisfy their curiosity, they deputed the sage Bhṛgu, the son of god Brahmā, to ascertain the truth. And he went to the assembly of god Brahmā.

3. In order to test the worth of that god, Bhṛgu, did not pay him homage or chant any hymn in his praise. The worshipful god Brahmā (took it as an affront and) was enraged with him, and was as if aglow with his burning wrath.

4. Considering that the insulting person was his own son, the self-born god Brahmā quenched the fiery wrath provoked in his mind, by restraining himself, just as fire is extinguished by water (which is its own product.)

5. From the assembly of god Brahmā, he repaired to mount Kailāsa (the abode of god Śiva). God Mahādeva was delighted (at his brother's surprise visit) and arising from his seat, he proceeded to embrace him.

6. But Bhṛgu showed no desire for it (avoiding him) with the remark, "you tread evil path, (flouting the authority of the Vedas" you have adopted the heretic way of life

and apply ashes of dead bodies from burning grounds). The tradition goes that the god flew in rage and with fiery eyes, he snatched up his trident and rushed forth to strike him.

7. His consort Pārvatī, however, fell at his feet and pacified him with sweet words. Thereupon Bhṛgu proceeded to Vaikuṇṭha where Lord Viṣṇu abides.

8-9. God Viṣṇu was then lying on the lap of the goddess Śrī (Lakṣmī). Bhṛgu kicked Him with his foot on his chest. The glorious Lord Viṣṇu, the resort of all saints, got up (in reverence) along with the goddess Lakṣmī. He alighted from the bed-stead and bowing down reverentially to the sage addressed him, "Welcome O Brāhmaṇa sage; please have some comfortable rest on the seat for a while. O mighty sage, it behoves you to forgive us, as we were not aware of your arrival.

10. "O great sage! Your feet are so very soft and delicate, my dear!" With these words he began to massage soothingly the feet of the Brāhmaṇa with his own hands.

11. "Be pleased to purify me along with my realm and the protectors of the world that are within me, with the water washing the feet of your worship—water which sanctifies even the holy waters of sacred places.

12. Worshipful sire! From to-day I have been the sole abode of goddess Lakṣmī. With my sins completely washed off by the touch of your feet (which symbolise knowledge) the goddess of prosperity (Lakṣmī in the form of *Śri Vatsa* mark) shall ever reside on my bosom."

12A. *Vj's Text.*

And let the mark (of your foot-print on my bosom) be known by the name *Śri Vatsa* from to-day."

Śrī Śuka said :

13. When Lord Viṣṇu addressed him thus, Bhṛgu felt deeply satisfied and happy with his melodious words in a deep low tone. He remained silent as his voice was choked with over-whelming feeling of devotion, his eyes, over-flowing with tears.

14. Returning to the place of that sacrificial session, Bhṛgu fully recounted to those sages who were well-versed in the Vedas, what he experienced (in the realm of the three gods).

15. Listening to that report the sages were wonder-struck and had their doubt (about the supremacy of the three gods) dispelled. They came to believe god Viṣṇu to be the Supreme-most god, who bestows tranquility and fearless State (*Mokṣa*).

16. For god Viṣṇu is directly the fountain head of righteousness, spiritual knowledge, renunciation (of four kinds) in association with eight kinds of mystical powers (*Siddhis*) and glory, which cleanly washes off the dirt (sins) of the soul.

17. He is called the highest goal of sages and of pious people who have completely renounced violence, are serene, endowed with equanimity of mind (or out-look of equality towards all) and non-attachment.

18. His beloved personality is constituted of pure *Sattva-guṇa*; Brāhmaṇas, his beloved deities. Persons of keen and subtle intellect who are of serene mind and who covet for no blessings, resort to him.

19. He has three forms which are invested of Māyā consisting of three *guṇas*: The Rākṣasa, the *Tāmasic* form, Asura, the *Rājasic* and gods, the *Sāttvic* form. (He is unattached to all these *guṇas* but) *Sattva* is the means of attaining the lore of Bhakti[1] and he is thus associated with *Sattva*.

Śrī Śuka said :

20. In this way, the Brāhmaṇas who were performing the sacrifice, came to this conclusion for dispelling the doubts of the people. By worshipping the lotus-feet of the Supreme Person, they attained to his blissful state.

Sūta said :

21. This story is the very nectar scented with the fragrance of the Lotus-mouth of Śuka, the son of the sage Vyāsa. It celebrates the glory of the Supreme Person of hallowing renown. It dispels the fear of the cycle of births and deaths (*saṁsāra*). The wanderer in this cycle of transmigration, who constantly drinks this nectar with the goblets of his ears, gives up fatigue of wandering through the paths of *Saṁsāra*.

Śrī Śuka began to narrate :

22. It is traditionally reported that on one occasion, at Dvārakā, the newly born son of a Brāhmaṇa woman died

immediately as he touched the ground (i.e. the moment she delivered the child, it expired), O descendant of Bharata!

23. The Brāhmaṇa took the dead body of the child and placed it at the gates of the royal palace and over-whelmed with grief and depressed in mind he wept bitterly and said.[1]

1. *VJ's Test supplied the back-ground with the following additional verses.*

23.1. On one occasion Śrī Kṛṣṇa embarked on performing a horse-sacrifice and he sent out a horse consecrated for the sacrifice, to go round the world.

23-2-3. Kṛṣṇa, the delight of Yādavas, sent Hārdikya, Kṛtavarmā, Yuyudhāna, Sātyaki, Cārudeṣṇa, sudeṣṇa, Pradyumna, Sāmba, Aṁśumant, Subhānu and a big army of Yādavas for the protection of the horse.

23.4. In a short period of time, they went round the earth and brought back the consecrated horse, O prominent Bharata.

23.5. Hearing the report that Lord Kṛṣṇa was desirous of performing a Horse-sacrifice, O Parīkṣit, sages who performed penance for a long time and observed their religious vows rigorously, came to attend it.

23.6-7. Having appointed sacrificial priests like *Hotṛ* (to recite the hymns and *mantras* from the *Ṛgveda*), *Adhvaryu* (the officiating priest expert in the *Yajurveda*), *Udgātṛ* (to chant the hymns from the *Sāmaveda*) and other priests to officiate over the sacrifice as per prescribed procedure, the glorious Lord Kṛṣṇa performed the ceremony of declaration of that day (of commencing the sacrifice) as the most auspicious (*Puṇyāha-maṅgala*) by sages and prominent Brāhmaṇas who were experts in the sacrificial lore and got himself consecrated for the sacrifice.

23.8. Kings and rulers of various countries who, with their refulgent crowns and diadems, looked brilliant like gods, came to attend upon him (at the sacrifice).

23.9. Pāṇḍavas and other kings who were eager to see the sacrifice and were invited by Kṛṣṇa came to Dvārakā, O King Parīkṣit.

23.10. While the glorious celebration of the horse-sacrifice was going on, Brāhmaṇas got thoroughly satisfied with the feasts and gifts of cloth, cows, land and gold.

23.11. Being initiated as a sacrificer, Śrī Kṛṣṇa saw to it that the prominent Brāhmaṇas got to their satisfaction all their desired objects as well as fed with whatever they wished to eat.

23.12-13. While kings occupied their respective seats all round and the cane-bearers, making a sound of the canes, were declaring "Silence please," a certain Brāhmaṇa with roots of grass (or a cane) in his hand, rushed in and standing at the gate of the sacrificial hall, raised-up his hands and cried out loudly in affliction. His throat was parched with hunger, face dried up, tears were flowing from his eyes and with distressed heart, he cried out thus:

24. "I have lost my child, because of the sin of a base kṣattriya (ruler) who is a hater of Brāhmaṇas, wicked-minded, greedy and voluptuous.

25. Subjects who serve a king who takes pleasure in violence, is of a bad character and has no control over his senses, perish by being subjected to perpetual impoverishment and unending miseries."[1]

26. In this manner, the Brāhmaṇa sage screamed out the same condemning appeal the second and the third time and left the dead body of the child at the royal gate.

27. Hearing that cry while he was near Śrī Kṛṣṇa Arjuna enquired with the Brāhmaṇa when his nineth child was lost.

28. "Is there no Kṣattriya in your house (i.e. in this city) who can wield a bow? These Kṣattriyas (Yādavas who cannot protect their subjects) are not better than Brāhmaṇas engaged in this sacrifice.[2]

29. The Kṣattriya (rulers) of that Kingdom where Brāhmaṇas being robbed of their wealth and being bereaved of their wives and children, have to grieve helplessly, are verily no better than actors on the stage who fill their belly by playing the role of Kṣattriyas.

30. O worshipful Sir, as both of you are so helpless here, I hereby undertake to protect the child that will be born of you. If I fail to fulfil my pledge, I shall enter fire (and burn myself down to death) and expiate myself of that sin."

1. *Here VJ's Text adds*:

25.1. Repeating this (above blame) again, the Brāhmaṇa screamed out again, out of extreme anguish.

25.2. Hearing that, self-respecting Arjuna rose from his high seat near Kṛṣṇa and approaching the Brāhmaṇa enquired.

25.3. "How many children have you O Brāhmaṇa? What is the trouble with you? You tell me everything unreservedly. I shall try to make you happy."

25.4. When (sympathetically) enquired thus, the Brāhmaṇa reported: "As soon as my child is born it is immediately taken away that very moment from the lying-in-chamber by some unknown agency, dear Sir."

2. These Brāhmaṇas are performing this sacrifice for these wretched Kṣattriyas who cannot protect their subjects—VJ.

The Brāhmaṇa remarked :

31. Saṅkarṣaṇa (Balarāma), Śrī Kṛṣṇa, Pradyumna the foremost archer and Aniruddha, an unparalleled hero have not been able to protect my child.

32. Even the Lords of the world found the achievement of this feat impossible. It is childish on your part to boast like this. We simply don't believe in it.

Arjuna said :

33. O Brāhmaṇa, I am neither Balarāma, nor Kṛṣṇa nor Kṛṣṇa's descendant. I am verily that Arjuna, the wielder of the bow famous by the name Gāṇḍīva.

34. Please don't underestimate my prowess, O Brāhmaṇa; even the three-eyed god (Śiva) was delighted with it. I shall defeat the god of death in battle and restore your progeny, Sire.[1]

1. *Here VJ's Text adds* :

34.1. Having inspired confidence in the Brāhmaṇa with this assurance O king, Arjuna requested Kṛṣṇa, "O Lord, please give me permission to go for (protecting the child of) the Brāhmaṇa.

34.2. You may continue your Horse sacrifice with these great men." To Arjuna who was requesting permission to go and who had equipped himself with his quivers and Gāṇḍiva bow, Kṛṣṇa spoke with a smile.

Lord Kṛṣṇa said :

34.3 "I shall have to come personally. It won't be possible (for you to protect the child), O Arjuna. The spirit that killed the child, appears to be extra-ordinary."

Arjuna replied :

34.4. Indra despite his alliance with the rulers of the spheres, was defeated by me at Khāṇḍava. The three-eyed god Śiva in the guise of a *Kirāta*, was pleased by me with my valour in a battle (with him).

34.5. The demons Nivāta-Kavacas, the residents of Hiraṇyapura, who could not be conquered even by Indra, were killed by me in a fight.

34.6. Can there be any evil spirit more powerful than that, O slayer of demons ? Why do you frighten me ? Please give me permission to go just now."

Śrī Śuka said :

34.7. Kṛṣṇa who was thus persuaded, gave permission to Arjuna to go. Arjuna, equipped with his (Gāṇḍiva) bow, went out of the sacrificial hall.

34.8. He ascended his spacious chariot with the banner of the monkey emblem hoisted over it. He placed the Brāhmaṇa in front of him and rode round the village.

35. The Brāhmaṇa, so confidently assured by Arjuna, went home pleased at heart, as he had heard the exploits of Arjuna.

36. When the time of delivery of his wife approached, that eminent Brāhmaṇa entreated Arjuna anxiously, "Pray protect my child from death."[1]

37. Arjuna sipped water (as *Ācamana*) and bowing to the great god Śiva, he invoked all his divine missiles and kept his bow Gāṇḍīva ready.

38. Arjuna as it were encaged the lying-in-chamber by creating a fence of arrows charged with *mantras* of various missiles on all side, above and below that chamber.

39. Then the wife of that Brāhmaṇa gave birth to a son who cried well (repeatedly), but in an instant, he bodily vanished through the sky.

40. Then the Brāhmaṇa censured Arjuna in the presence of Kṛṣṇa blaming himself, "Look at my folly, in placing faith in the empty bragging of an impotent person.

41. Who else can be capable enough to protect my child whom neither Pradyumna, nor Aniruddha, nor Balarāma nor Śrī Kṛṣṇa were able to protect.

42. Fie npon Arjuna, the boastful liar! Fie upon the bow of his who indulges in self-advertisement (self-flattery). The wicked fellow, out of his stupidity, brags to restore back what has been snatched away by Fate."

34.9 Arriving at the village of that Brāhmaṇa, he helped him get down from the chariot. When he heard that the Brāhmaṇa's wife had retired into the lying-in-chamber, Arjuna told him, O king.

Arjuna said :

34.10. "Go to your house, O Brāhmaṇa. I have given complete protection to you on all sides. Please go and comfort your wife who must be afraid."

1. *VJ's Text adds* :

36.1. When Arjuna was thus requested, he ascended his chariot and mounting the string on the Gāṇḍiva bow hastened to the proximity of the room of confinement.

36.2. The Brāhmaṇa also entered that lying-in-chamber and in a short while cried for Arjuna's help.

43. While the Brāhmaṇa sage was reproaching him, Arjuna used his mystical lore and quickly went to Saṁyamanī, the capital of the god of death (Yama).

44. Not being able to trace the child of that Brāhmaṇa he visited (and explored) the capital cities of the great gods like Indra, Agni, Nairṛta, Soma, Vāyu and Varuṇa and with his weapon ready, he went to the subterranean regions and to regions higher than the celestial region and many other regions.

45. As he could not trace the child and had failed to fulfill his pledge, he prepared himself to enter fire but was prohibited by Kṛṣṇa from doing so.

46. (Kṛṣṇa said) "I shall show you the sons of that Brāhmaṇa. Please do not disrespect yourself in this way. Those (who are censuring you now) will permanently establish (and sing of) our pure spotless glory.

47. Having comforted him with these words, the glorious Almighty Lord ascended his divine chariot along with Arjuna and sped towards the west.

48. Then passing over the seven island-continents and the seven oceans dividing those continents, the seven mountain-ranges and the *Lokāloka* mountain[1] (which divides the visible world from the region of darkness), he entered the region of darkness.

49. O prominent Bharata! In that pitch-black darkness, his horses, Śaibya, Sugrīva, Meghapuṣpa and Balāhaka lost their way and could not proceed.

50. Noticing their plight, Lord Kṛṣṇa, the Master of all experts in Yoga, discharged ahead his discus Sudarśana which was effulgent like one thousand suns shining simultaneously.

51. Piercing through that extremely horrendous, palpably thick all-pervading darkness, the effect of *Prakṛti* or created by the Lord himself with its exceedingly enormous lustre, the Sudarśana discus with the speed of the mind (quick like a thought or imagination) cut its way like the arrow of Rāma

1. A mythical mountain that encircles the earth and is beyond the seven continents and the encircling sea of fresh water. The sun's rays do not reach beyond that mountain.

discharged from the bow-string penetrated through hostile army.

52. Following the path cut by the discus, (the chariot reached the end of darkness), Arjuna saw that Supreme, Infinite, dazzling lustre beyond that dark-region (of *Prakṛti*). But his eyes became dazed and he closed the eyes.

53. Thereafter he entered water (the ocean) adorned with huge billows lashed up by powerful tempestuous gales. Verily he saw then a wonderful mansion highly resplendent with thousands of columns of brilliant jewels.

54. And in that mansion, he beheld the presence of the Serpent Śeṣa (Ananta) who was the most formidable yet wonderful to look at. He was radiant with brilliant jewels on each of his thousand hoods, with two fierce eyes. His body was white like the Himālayas but was black at the neck and in the tongue.

55. He beheld the all-pervading Lord of infinite powers resting on the soft and comfortable coils of serpent Śeṣa. The complexion of that most exalted Super-human being was dark like a cloud surcharged with water. He wore a yellow garment. He had a cheerful countenance and beautiful longish eyes.

56. The effulgence of the numerous precious jewels in his crown and the refulgence of his ear-rings enveloped (like a halo) and lit up his profuse curly locks of hair. He had eight long beautiful arms. He wore the brilliant Kaustubha gem round his neck and had the *Śrī Vatsa* mark (on his chest), and he was decorated with Vanamālā (a garland of five coloured forest flowers reaching upto the knees).

57. He was the Lord of Supreme gods who was attended upon by Sunanda and Nanda, the chief of his guards, by the discus Sudarśana and other weapons in a corporal form and by his four potencies, viz. *Puṣṭi* (grace), *Śrī* (splendour, beauty and affluence), *Kīrti* (Fame) and the Invincible potency (Māyā) and eight miraculous powers (*Siddhis*).

58. Śrī Kṛṣṇa bowed to the Infinite Lord who was himself in another form, Arjuna filled with awe at his sight, paid him obeisance. Both of them stood with folded palms. The Perfect Person, the controller of Brahmā and other lords (presi-

ding deities) of the spheres, smilingly addressed in a deep and sonorous voice to them.

59. "The sons of the Brāhmaṇa were brought by me desirous of seeing you both. Both of you have incarnated on the earth by your part-manifestations for the protection of righteousness. Having killed the demons who have become a burden to the earth as soon as possible, return to our presence.

60. Both of you are famous sages Nara and Nārāyaṇa who have already accomplished all blessings. But for the maintenance of the world-order, you both have set a model of righteousness for others to follow.

61-62. Thus commanded by the glorious Supreme Deity, those two dark-complexioned heroes (Śrī Kṛṣṇa and Arjuna) accepted the mandate, respectfully bowed to the Perfect Being, and taking with them the sons of the Brāhmaṇa returned with delighted hearts to their home by the same route they came. They restored to the Brāhmaṇa his sons grown up according to their age but similar in appearance as their father saw them (at the time of their birth).

63. Having visualized the shining region (known as Mahākālapura of Viṣṇu (or the glorious power of Viṣṇu, Arjuna was exceedingly astonished. He realized whatever prowess and manliness is possessed by a man is due to the grace of Śrī Kṛṣṇa.[1]

64. Displaying in this way many feats and exploits, Śri Kṛṣṇa, enjoyed worldly pleasures as well as worshipped the

1. *Here VJ's Text adds*:

63.1. Śrī Kṛṣṇa re-entered the sacrificial hall which was filled to its capacity with family priests, Brāhmaṇas and sacrificial priests, and eminent Kṣattriyas.

63.2. With the approval of the Brāhmaṇas, he went through the expiatory rites prescribed for moving out of the sacrificial precincts during the consecration period.

63.3 O excellent Kuru ! After completing the sacrifice according to *Śāstric* procedure, he satisfied the Brāhmaṇas granting all their desired objects. He worshipped the sacrificial priests and other sages.

63.4. Having performed the concluding bath (*avabhṛtha majjana*) in the great river Yamunā, the excellent member of the Yadu race passed his time happily in the company of great sages.

(Here ends the hundredth chapter in VJ's text)

Supreme Deity by performing great sacrifices on an exceedingly superior scale.

65. The glorious Lord was himself endowed with overflowing affluence, power, etc. just as god Indra showers down water profusely in the proper (i.e. the rainy) season, he also in due time incessantly bestowed all the desired-objects on his subjects, Brāhmaṇas and others.

66. He personally slew a number of unrighteous Kings and eliminated the remaining irreligious ones through Arjuna and others. He easily enforced abidance by the righteous path (and thus re-established *dharma*) all over the world through Yudhiṣṭhira and other virtuous Kings.

CHAPTER NINETY

The Song of Queens : Resume of Kṛṣṇa's Sports.

1-2. The Lord of the goddess Śrī (i.e. Śrī Kṛṣṇa) lived in great comfort and happiness in his capital city of Dvārakā. It was richly endowed with all types of affluence and prosperity. It was peopled with leaders of the Vṛṣṇi clan and by their women who were always dressed in immaculate, gorgeous garments. They were sparkling with the radiance of blooming youth. While they played with balls, etc. in their mansions, they appeared like flashes of lightning.

3. On the roads and streets, there was a heavy traffic—the highways being crowded with young elephants exuding ichor, well-adorned soldiers, richly caparisoned horses, chariots resplendent with burnished gold plates.

4. It was richly surrounded with parks and pleasure gardens beautified with rows of blossoming trees which were resounded with the musical notes and warblings of birds and humming bees.

5. Lord Kṛṣṇa who was the sole beloved consort of sixteen thousand queens, assumed as many various attractive

forms as he had queens and severally sported with them in their separate resplendent palaces of surpassing affluence.

6. The swimming pool in each of these mansions was full of crystal clear water scented with the pollen of full blown lotuses of various kinds such as *Kalhāra*, *Kumuda* and was loud with the warbling of birds.

7. Śrī Kṛṣṇa, the Lord of prosperity, entered the waters of those (swimming) tanks and sported freely. His bosom (*lit.* body) was smeared with the saffron paste applied on the breasts of his queens as they embraced him (during the water-sports).

8. His glory was then sung by Gandharvas and Sūtas; Māgadhas and Bandins were gleefully playing upon musical instruments like *mṛdaṅga*, kettle-drums, tom-toms and lutes.

9. Śrī Kṛṣṇa was being drenched with jets of waters discharged through syringes by his consorts who were laughing all the while. He, in return, profusely sprinkled water on them and thus he sported with his spouses like Kubera, King of Yakṣas, playing with Yakṣa women.

10. Their thighs and breasts became prominent to view through their wet *Saris* (garments). While they were sprinkling water on Kṛṣṇa, they advanced to him on the pretext of snatching away the syringe from him and embraced him. Due to a thrill of passionate desire (at the touch of Kṛṣṇa's person) their countenances beamed with great pleasure and they appeared brilliant and beautiful.

11. Śrī Kṛṣṇa got his garland (*Vanamālā*) tinged with saffron from the breasts of his consorts (while they embraced him). The knot of his locks of hair was loosened (during that amorous sport). Sprinkling and being sprinkled with water by his youthful wives, he sported with them like a king-elephant surrounded by she-elephants (spouting jets of water on him).

12. (At the end of the water-sport) Śrī Kṛṣṇa and his spouses gave (as gifts) their clothes and ornaments to the male and female dancers and those who lived by the profession of vocal and instrumental music.

13. While Śrī Kṛṣṇa was sporting thus, his (graceful) gait, (sweet) talk, (amorous) glances and (winning) smiles as well as his jokes, dalliances and embraces enchanted (and carried away) the hearts (of his queens).

14. So sang the queens of Kṛṣṇa as they being absorbed in him, remained speechless. While they were intensely thinking of the lotus-eyed Lord, they, sometimes, behaved like dullard and sometimes like a lunatic, uttered the following verses. Please listen.

The queens said :

15. "O she-osprey ! Lord Kṛṣṇa has covered his ever wakeful consciousness and has gone to sleep at night. Why don't you sleep ? Why have you lost your sleep and are wailing ? O friend, has your heart too been pierced deeply by the noble sportive glances of the Lotus-eyed Lord, like us ?

16. O *Cakravākī* (Red goose), at night you close your eyes but alas ! you continuously lament so piteously ! Is it because you cannot see your mate ? Or are you a female slave like us of the Lord and desire to wear on your braids of hair the garland that rolls on (and is touched by) the feet of Lord Kṛṣṇa.

17. O ocean, why is it that you roar and thunder incessantly and do not get any sleep at all ? Is it because you have been deprived of your beautifying ornaments like the gem Kaustubha and others ! you have been reduced to our irrecoverable stage (who are deprived of our beautiful painting on our breasts, etc. by contact with Śrī Kṛṣṇa at the time of amorous sports).

18. O moon, you have grown emaciated as you are a victim to the incurable disease of consumption. Hence, you are incapable of dispelling darkness with your rays. Is it due to your loss of memory, like us about the sweet secret talks indulged in by Lord Mukunda (Kṛṣṇa) that you have lost your power of expression ? At least you look like that to us. (We think it that way).

19. O Southern wind from mountain Malaya, what act unpleasant to you has been committed by us that you provoke the passion of love in our heart which is already torn and tattered by the side-glances of Śrī Kṛṣṇa ?

20. O beautiful cloud, (due to your similarity to Kṛṣṇa in complexion and his quality of removing the sufferings of the miserable—by showering your grace in the form of water)

you are really a beloved friend of the Lord of Yādavas (Śrī Kṛṣṇa) who is adorned with Śrīvatsa. Hence you, being attached to him with bonds of love like us, are lost in his meditation. Your heart too must be agitated with keen anxiety and is excessively anguished for him. You are, therefore, constantly remembering him and shedding profuse tears like us. Contact with Śrī Kṛṣṇa is really very painful.

21. O Cuckoo, blest with sweet notes! Your melodious cooing is so sweet like nectar that it will infuse life into the dead. You imitate the sweet voice and utterances of our beloved Lord. Please tell me what pleasant services, I may do to you to-day.

22. O generous-hearted mountain, you are the supporter of the earth. You neither move nor speak anything. It appears that you are deeply absorbed in thinking about some great object (or project). Do you long to place the lotus-feet of the delight of Vasudeva (Śrī Kṛṣṇa) on your breasts (Breast-like peaks) as we pine to do?

23. O rivers! O ye wives of the sea! (This being the summer) at present, your deep beds and pools are dried up; you have grown emaciated. Lotuses no longer beautify you. Just as we, being deprived of the amorous glances of our beloved consort, the Lord of Mathura, are robbed of our hearts and have become extremely lean and thin, you are denied the love-laden glances of your Lord in the form of rain showers (and are reduced to this plight).

24. (By chance there arrived a swan. Regarding it to be an emissary of Kṛṣṇa, one of the queens addressed it). Welcome, O dear Swan! Be seated. Have some milk to drink. Tell us some news about Śrī Kṛṣṇa the descendant of Śūra. We look upon you as a messenger (between us and Śrī Kṛṣṇa). Is the invincible Lord hale and hearty? Does he of fickle friendship remember what he confided and professed to us in our privacy? (If you say that he has deputed you as he remembers us) O insignificant emissary (who come from a faithless lover) why should we resort to him? (If he invites us to make friends as you say) convey our message when Śrī (the goddess Lakṣmī) who cheating us all, monopolised his company is not with him. If he says, "How is it possible that she who

is exclusively devoted to him can be avoided", ask him "Among all women is Śrī the only woman who is devoted to him ? Are we not so ?"

25. It is by virtue of such deep constancy and devotion to Kṛṣṇa, the Lord of the masters of Yoga that the consorts of Kṛṣṇa attained to the Supreme State of *Mokṣa*.

26. Kṛṣṇa's great glory is widely sung in exquisite poetry and songs. Even if (Kṛṣṇa's sports celebrated in songs are) heard, they irresistibly attract the minds of women. What need be said of those who had the privilege of seeing him directly ?

27. How is it possible to evaluate the greatness of the penance of those women who had the privilege to regard the Preceptor of the world as their husband and render him loving service by shampooing (pressing) his feet (and such other personal attention).

28. The Lord who was the asylum of the righteous and saintly people, himself followed the religious injunctions prescribed in the Veda and demonstrated (to the world) again and again that the objectives of human life, viz. religion (righteousness), wealth, enjoyment of worldly pleasures can be secured even in the householder's stage of life.[1]

1. *VJ's Text Adds* :

28.1-2. When Śrī Kṛṣṇa, the wielder of the Sudarśana discus was ruling over the world, the city of Dvārakā, the abode of the Vṛṣṇis, which was twelve *yojanas* in length, was densely peopled by Sages, Brāhmaṇas, Kṣattriyas, bards and was all the while (permanently) decorated (due to the festivals carried on there all the year round).

28.3-6. (In order to see Lord Kṛṣṇa) Sages of tranquil minds and always engaged in observing religious vows, used to come from sacred places like Piṇḍāraka[2], Kurukṣetra, Śālagrāma, Puṣkara, Vārāṇasi, Prayāga, Veṅkaṭa (Tirupati), Śrī-Parvata[3], from far off places like Gokarṇa and beautiful Candra-tirtha (the source of the Kāverī from Brahmagiri in

2. Near Golagar in Gujarat, sixteen miles to the east of Dvārakā. It was at this place that sages cursed Sāmba that he would give birth to a Pestle (*Musala*) which will destroy the Yādavas—Vide infra 11.1.

3. Śrī śaila in Karnul district of Andhra Pradesh. It has a temple of Mallikārjuna, one of the twelve *jyotir-liṅgas* of god Śiva. Nāgārjuna, the famous Buddhist philosopher, founder of Mādhyamika School, lived here.

29. Śrīkṛṣṇa who practised supremely ideal righteous way of life of a house-holder, had sixteen thousand and one hundred queens.

30. Of those jewels of women, eight queens of whom Rukmiṇī was the foremost and (the names of) their sons have been already detailed to you in order of seniority, O king!

31. Each of the (Sixteen thousand and one hundred) queens had ten sons from Kṛṣṇa. It means he had ten sons born from each queen. For the Lord's course was never futile (VT. clarifies that no sexual contact of Kṛṣṇa was unfruitful).

Coorg.) from Sahyādri, Bhṛgukṣetra (Broach), Kumāra-hill[1], from the banks of the holy Godāvarī, from the Narmadā, from Śūrpāraka (Sopara, Thana Dist. Maharashtra), Prabhāsa, the holy Badarikāśrama from the holy Naimiṣāraṇya and the inaccessible Brahmadurga[2].

28.7. The sages were of different categories (observing different types of vows): Some subsisted on water, some on mere air; some abstained from food altogether but all of them were firm in the observance of vows, some were clad in bark garments and deer-skin, some grew matted hair, while others had clean-shaven heads.

28.8. Some bathed thrice a day, some strictly observed the vow of silence, some were engaged in the study of the Vedas, while others in reciting praises and hymns to gods.

28.9. Some devoted their minds to contemplation, some determined on meditative trance. Some had only skin and bones in their persons, a bundle of veins and arteries.

28.10. O king Parīkṣit! These serene-minded sages came from all directions. These meditators on Reality always waited upon Lord Kṛṣṇa, O emperor.

28.11-12. The city of Dvārakā was resounded with the sounds of Kṣattriyas of mighty prowess and of Brāhmaṇas whom penance was the wealth, of Sūtas and Māgadhas who were devoted to singing the glories (of the Lord) and by the auspicious sounding (playing) of musical instruments and by the loud recitation of the Vedas (by Brāhmaṇas).

28.13. By virtue of the presence of the God of gods, Dvārakā became the most prominent of all sacred places and foremost among all holy places of (sacred waters) which wash off sins.

---

1. Probably Krauñcagiri, a hill at a distance of one mile from Tiruttani station of the Southern Railway. There is a temple of Kumāra or Kārttika-svāmin on the hill, GAMI, P. 107.

2. Probably the Brahmagiri hill near Tryambakeshwar Nasik District Maharashtra. The other claimant for this name is the hill in Coorg, the Source of the Kāveri. VJ is silent about the identification.

32. Although all those sons were of mighty Prowess, eighteen out of them were great "chariot-warriors" who achieved noble renown. Listen to their names :

33-34. (They are as follows) "Pradyumna, Aniruddha, (Cārudeṣṇa) Dīptimān, Bhānu, Sāmba, Madhu, Bṛhad-bhānu Citra-bhānu, Vṛka, Aruṇa, Puṣkara, Vedabāhu, Śrutadeva Sunandana, Citra-bāhu, Virūpa, Kavi and Nyagrodha.

VR's Text adds:

34.1. Trivakra's son Upakrośa was exclusively devoted to Kṛṣṇa. He was a direct disciple of Nārada. He adopted the vow of life-long celibacy.

34.2. The *Sāttvata Tantra* was composed by him. It has laid down Vaiṣṇavite purificatory rites for women, Śūdras and slaves (after which they are admitted to Vaiṣṇavism). By studying the *Tantra,* one attains Liberation from Saṁsāra.

35. Out of these sons of Kṛṣṇa (the enemy of Madhu), O Indra among kings, Pradyumna, the son of Rukmiṇī was the first and he was just like his father in all respects.

36. That great (chariot) warrior married the daughter of Rukmī. He begat by her (a son named) Aniruddha who possessed the might of ten thousand elephants.

37. Aniruddha, himself a grandson of Rukmī through his daughter, married the grand-daughter of Rukmī (through his son). Vajra was born of her and only he survived the destruction from the pestle (in the civil war among the Yādavas).

38. The name of Vajra's son was Pratibāhu whose son was Subāhu. From Subāhu was born Śāntasena and he begat a son called Śatasena.

39. No king born in this family (of Śrī Kṛṣṇa) was destitute of wealth or less prolific in progeny or short-lived or weak or inimical to Brāhmaṇas.

40. Even within the period of tens of thousand of years it is not possible to enumerate all those born in Yadu's family who became famous for their great deeds.

41. It is heard (by tradition) that there were three crores eighty eight hundred teachers for the children of Yadu's family.

42. Who can enumerate the number of the noble-souled Yādavas? King Ugrasena was attended upon by billions of warriors (lit. ten thousand times ten thousand lakhs) of sons.

43. Those very wicked demons who were killed in the wars between gods and demons, were born again as human beings. They became arrogant and troubled the people.

44. For their chastisement and control, gods were commanded by Hari and they descended in the race of Yadu. There were one hundred and one families of Yādavas.

45. The glorious Lord Hari was the guide and controller of all the Yādavas. All the Yādavas who obeyed his command and followed him prospered in every respect.

46*. The Vṛṣṇis dedicated their minds to Śrī Kṛṣṇa so completely that they were not conscious of their own self while doing bodily actions like sleeping, sitting, wandering, speaking, playing, bathing and other (acts of daily routine).

Additional verses in VJ's text.

46A. With the sacrificial material produced by his Yogamāyā, he performed sacrifices for twelve years at Kurukṣetra and thereby worshipped the Supreme Soul (which was identical with his self), the main substance or gist of all the Vedas.

46B. He was consecrated for sacrifice by Kṛṣṇa-dvaipāyana (Vyāsa), Viśvāmitra, Asita, Sāndīpani and Paraśurāma as the preceptors. The Lord of meritorious renown, his elder brother of pious reputation were worshipped by Uddhava.

47. (That Śrī Kṛṣṇa's renown is the holiest of all the holy places and Lord Kṛṣṇa is the best and most prominent of all gods is not wonderful). O King Parīkṣit, when the holy Lord (the holiest of the holy) incarnated in the family of Yadus, it made the holy water of the heavenly Gaṅgā that issues from the water (used for) washing his feet, inferior in holiness to his hallowing renown. (He is so great that) both who hated him or were affectionate to him attained to the

46* VR : VJ : Though they associated with Śrī Kṛṣṇa in activities such as sleeping, sitting, etc. with him, they did not realize that he was Lord Viṣṇu himself but thought him to be a prominent Yādava.

same state of being similar to him. Goddess Lakṣmī for whose favour gods and others are striving, has devoutly dedicated herself to him exclusively. His name whether heard or uttered (even once) dispels everything inauspicious. By him were taught the duties to every *gotra*. He wields in his hand the discus (Sudarśana) which symbolises the Time-spirit (which destroys all). Hence, it is not wonderful that he lightens the burden of the earth.

48. Victorious is Lord Kṛṣṇa who is the sole refuge of all people (and abides in each of them as their indewelling soul). (As a matter of fact, he is eternal and birthless). That he incarnated himself from Devakī is a matter of (ignorant) talk only. Though he is attended upon by prominent Yādava warriors it is with (the might of) his arms that he annihilated all unrighteousness.[1] He completely destroys the sins of all—the mobile and immobile (e.g. grass, creepers, trees and other beings. With his resplendently beautiful countenance and winning smiles, he enhances love in the women of Vraja and the cities (and makes them attain to *Mokṣa* by subduing carnal love.

48.A *VJ's Text adds* :

A man should continuously meditate upon Lord Hari, the Supreme Soul, who is the creator, sustainer and the destroyer of the universe; who after creating the universe entered into it (as the *Antaryāmin*-indwelling soul), who assumed the form of a sage (Vyāsa) and composed this compilation of Purāṇas; having attained to him Śiva gets rid of the bonds of *Prakṛti* and like a bird in sleep, becomes free from the attachment to his body and property and remains in a state of blissful conscious existence, with no fear of returning to birth or *Saṁsāra*.

49. He who is desirous of developing devotion to the (lotus) feet of Śrī Kṛṣṇa should listen to the stories of the sportive deeds of the Supreme Lord—the Lord who is trans-

1. *VJ's Text reads differently from this onwards*:
With his arms and lotus-feet set on the earth for lightening the burden of the earth. His personality is the abode of Lakṣmi. By his charming looks and smiling glances, he appeared like the God of Love to them.

cendental to *Prakṛti* and who for the vindication of the path of righteousness ordained by himself, has assumed different sportive forms (such as the Fish, the Tortoise and others) and performed (miraculous) sportful arts suitable to that form and capable of destroying all *Karmas*.

50. By attentively listening to, reciting and constantly meditating on the glorious stories of Lord Mukunda, a man attains to his region which is beyond the jurisdiction of the god of Death (or the Time-spirit) of irresistible force and for the sake of attaining which even the rulers of the earth renounced their (comfortable) house-holder's life (and their kingdoms) and betook themselves to the forest (and performed penance).

VJ's Text adds :

50A. He who devoutly and with faith listens to or narrates to others, the life and deeds of Lord Kṛṣṇa (as glorified by Śuka, the son of Vyāsa) of immortal and blissful glory which completely destroy the sin of the world and are a beautiful ornament to the ears of His devotees, can concentrate his mind on the glorious Lord and ultimately attain to his blissful region where there is no fear from any quarter.

X SKANDHA — APPENDIX

(Additional Chapters in VJ's Text
Ch. No. 50 in VJ's Text)

CHAPTER FIFTY—I.5

Jarāsandha's Second Expedition

Śrī Śuka said .

1-4. The mighty king Jarāsandha, the son of Bṛhadratha, who was day and night remembering and smarting under the previous discomfiture (by Lord Kṛṣṇa), invited all the allied princes in the third month (after the defeat) and inspired them to make preparations of war — with the allied forces of the kings of Matsya (mod. Alwar and parts of former states of Jaipur and Bharatpur)*, Mālava, of Cedi (Bundelkhand and adjacent part of Madhya Pradesh), Kuru, Pāñcāla (Rohilkhand but formerly the country from the foothills of the Himālayas upto the Chambal), Kerala, Kulinda (Garhwal and a part of Saharanpur district), Kuntala (Southern Maharashtra), Avanti (country round Ujjain), Kāśī, Gandhāra (former districts of Peshawar and Rawalpindi and Eusofzai country — now in Pakistan), Sṛñjaya, Kaliṅga (Major part of Orissa esp. the South of it). Kekaya (country between the Bias and the Sutlej), Andhra, Daśārṇa (Eastern Malva and Bhopal District), Vang (Western Bengal), Sindhu (lower part of Sindh), Madra (country between the Ravi and the Chinab), Trigartta (Jalandhar and a part of Lahore district), Sauvīra (upper Sindh and southern Punjab) and the warriors from the mountains — all making up an army of twenty-three Akṣauhaṇīs.

5. Accompanied by this army, he crossed the country of Magadha and proceeded towards the West (to Mathura). He, as it were, was dragging with him all the kings with their divisions of the elephants, cavalry, chariots and infantry.

* The identifications of the territories with their modern counterparts is as per N.L. De's GDAMI.

6. Having come to besiege Mathurā, he camped on the bank of the Yamunā, surrounded with the tents of a number of kings and camp followers.

7-8. He entertained himself listening to the eulogies sung by the bards such as *Sūtas*, *Māgadhas* and *bards* and rested. Hearing of the great preparations of war by the mighty king of Magadhas, Kṛṣṇa convened a conference and planned with Balarāma, Vasudeva, Uddhava, Akrūra, Śaineya, Āhuka and Sāraṇa.

9. Having properly planned the strategy at night in consultation with these, he summoned the best of his warriors at dawn before the sunrise.

10. The Lord of incomprehensible nature, divided his army consisting of the four divisions—elephants, horsemen, charioteers and foot-soldiers — in three detachments. Kṛṣṇa deployed these against the army of Jarāsandha, the king of Magadhas as follows :

11. Kṛṣṇa, the slayer of demon Madhu sent Balarāma, Hārdikya, Gada and Sāraṇa by the left side.

12. He sent by the right side Sātyaki, Vipṛthu, Pṛthu and Uddhava along with the army.

13. The Lotus-eyed Lord accompanied by some charioteers, himself entered the vast army of the king of Magadha directly from the front.

14. The army (of Jarāsandha) mixed up of numerous elephants, horses, chariots and foot-soldiers at random was unsuspectingly asleep on the bank of the Yamunā and was enjoying itself happily.

15-16. While the sun was rising on the eastern mountain and the darkness (of night) was being dispelled, and birds were warbling in their nests everywhere, and lotuses were blooming and swarms of bees were sweetly humming, Kṛṣṇa entered the terrible, invincible army of the king of Magadhas.

17. At that time, the horses (of the enemies) were unsaddled and tethered in a line here and there ; and at that time the elephants had no armour on their backs, O King!

18. The soldiers had not taken up their arms and even their hair were not tied. They had not put on their usual coats of mail, and were not riding their horses or vehicles.

19. The chariots were not yoked with horses and the flags were not raised (showing their unpreparedness). At this time, Kṛṣṇa wearing a yellow garment made his way into the army of the Magadhan king.

20. Seeing an army attacking them on three sides, all the kings became confused and were not able to know what to do.

21. Some warriors rallied together, while others fled away out of fear. Some soldiers took up their arms and counter-attacked the enemies (Yādavas) in the battle.

22. Some soldiers had their armours shattered while others had their legs, thighs and arms cut off. Some with their eyes grown red with anger attacked the enemies (the Yādavas).

23. Some soldiers of great valour rode the unsaddled horses and crushing the enemies in the battle, earned a bright, unblemished glory for themselves.

24. Kings suddenly roused from their sleep found the destruction of their army. Some of them put up a fight even without weapons essential for fighting.

25. Some deserted their camps and entered into deep forest. Some approached Jarāsandha, King of Magadhas and hailed, "Be successful in the battle."

26. Govinda entering the inimical forces single-handed in his chariot, killed a number of warriors who put up a fight with their weapons.

27. The mighty Balarāma also surrounded by a big detachment entered the Magadha army by the left side and routed the Magadhan forces.

28. The mighty armed Śaineya also attacked with his big army consisting of elephants, cavalry, chariots and infantry, by the right side and gave the enemy sound drubbing.

29. In this way, the army under the leadership and protection of the king of Magadhas was beaten on all sides, and being terrified, took to their heels in all the directions in a moment.

30. Sātyaki of the Vṛṣṇi clan pursued the army upto five *yojanas* and destroying the Magadhan force, he returned from the battle a victor.

31. Kṛṣṇa forcibly caught a number of elephants big like hills along with their accoutrement, *tomaras*, goads, etc. He collected as spoil chariots along with the weapons, flags and horses yoked to them and carried them to Mathura.

32. In that battle, Kṛṣṇa got as spoils innumerable umbrellas inlaid with gold jewels, numberless *chowries*, crowns, belts, gold armlets, earings and valuable clothes.

33. As per instructions of Kṛṣṇa, the slayer of Kaṁsa, Balarāma, the wielder of the plough as a weapon, brought a vast amount of spoil such as Jarāsandha's treasury, the vehicles, subjects, women of Jarasandha's harem, weapons and ornaments. He presented the wealth collected in the battle to Ugrasena, the king of Yadus.

CHAPTER FIFTY—II

Ch: 50 in Vj's Text

The Third Siege of Mathura: Jarāsandha's defeat

Śrī Śuka said:

1. Jarāsandha who boasted himself as a leader in battle was defeated by Kṛṣṇa, the destroyer of Madhu. He then proceeded to Śoṇitapura[1] to see Bāṇa, the son of Bali (for help).

2-5. Hearing that his friend defeated in the battle by Kṛṣṇa was coming with his circle of allied kings, Bāṇa of one thousand arms, the ruler of Dānavas went forward to meet and receive him with well-adorned elephants, caparisoned horses, chariots of various shapes, warriors, bevies of courtesans, bands of bards like *Sūta, Magadhas* and *bards* with flags and banners, umbrellas, auspicious trumpets and drums beating, with gold buntings or festoons, multicoloured lamps, pitchers

1. Assamese claim Tejapur as ancient Śoṇitapura, but from Harivaṁśa (ch. 174) it seems that the ancient Śoṇitapura is situated in Kumaun on the bank of the Kedār-Gaṅgā at a short distance from Gupta Kāśī—GDAMI p. 189.

and mirrors. They were extremely close friends and mutual sympathisers.

6. Both of them, solicitous as they were of mutual interests, paid respects to each other. Addressing Bāṇa, in the royal assembly, Jarāsandha spoke :

7. "Be pleased to note this, O king of Dānavas ! I was taken in (in a dastardly surprise attack) at night by the wicked-minded cowherd (Kṛṣṇa) of unrighteous behaviour and robber-like bravado-ness.

8. Many mighty rut-exuding (youthful) elephants and horses, and a number of chariots along with all the equipments and arms there-in were plundered by him.

9. These princely allies of mine did not tolerate (the idea of) my engaging him in a single-handed duel. I was prevented from doing so by these kings who participate in my joys and sorrows, victory and defeat).

10. I have now come here for your majesty's audience. O Lord (of Dānavas) ! Be pleased to render (some military) assistance (to us)." When addressed thus (and being acquainted with Jarāsandha's plight) Bāṇa, the son of Bali, took him (and his allies) to his own capital (Śoṇitapura).

11. He immediately arranged for the reception of the assembly of princely allies with a high feast, bath, beds, perfumes, and leaves of piper-betel (together with areca-nuts, catechu) for chewing after meals.

12-13. He honoured all the royal personages with presents. When Jarāsandha, the foster-son of Jarā, had enjoyed the reception, taken rest and seen the curiosities worth-seeing (in Bāṇa's Capital and comfortably occupied a golden seat after duly decorating himself (with princely ornaments), the king of Dānavas respectfully addressed the assembly of kings.

Bāṇa said :

14. O Jarāsandha ! Please do understand it. No empty promise is uttered by me. These elephants, these horses, this kingdom, all these subjects and whatever else is in my possession is absolutely at your disposal.

Śrī Śuka said :

15. Having promised thus, Bāṇa, the son of Bali, gave to the king of Magadha sixty thousand elephants, hundred thousands of chariots and one million horses swift in speed like the wind and the mind.

16. Bāṇa, the son of Bali, further gave him a contingent of three hundred Dānavas wellknown for their expertise in use of black magic in warfare, equal (in competence and military skill) to himself.

17. He also supplied him with innumerable palanquins of various types, umbrellas, *chowries*, ornaments, dress (clothes) as well as treasures (or utensils), beds, seats and such other requisites, O King.

18. Bāṇa ordered his ministers Kumbhāṇḍa and Kūpakarṇa, the best ones among the Daityas, to help Jarāsandha, O scion of the Kuru race.

19. What a great difference is between Lord Hari who is strong enough to annihilate the combined forces of all gods and Asuras in the world and the poor two ministers of Bāṇa, Kumbhāṇḍa and Kūpakarṇa ? (There cannot be any comparison at all).

20. Not comprehending the (Supreme) power of Viṣṇu, the kings being destined to meet death and encouraged (and instigated) by the king of Magadha, again made war-preparations against Yadus.

21. Taking leave of Bāṇa, the king of Magadha set out of Śoṇitapura. Accompanied with many kings and with four wings (viz. elephant-corps, cavalry, chariot-division and infantry) under his command, he reached Mathura in the course of some days.

22. He besieged that city of high towers, balconies, ornamental arches, wells, gardens and parks and massive fortification and blockaded its gates.

23. He tried to demolish the walls of the city with innumerable spearlike (pointed) rods, axes, pickaxes, clubs and stones hurled with catapults.

24. As the fortification of the city was being knocked down, Balarāma and Kṛṣṇa, enraged at the report of the return of Jarāsandha, the king of Magadhas, caused the beat-

ing of the war-drums (to alert all people summoning them to fight).

25-26. With Sātyaki, Kṛta-varman, Ugrasena, Gada, Āhuka and Vasudeva at the vanguard and accompanied by well-armed and fully provided armies of chariots, cavalry, elephant-corps and foot-soldiers, the two heroes of immense might and with perfectly undisturbed minds, rushed out like two ferocious lions.

27. Getting out of Mathura, the lotus-eyed Kṛṣṇa loudly blew out his big conch Pāñcajanya terrorising the enemies at heart (by its blast).

28-29. Thereupon broke out the fight between Yadus and Kṣatriyas. The Dānava ministers of Bāṇa, Kumbhāṇḍaka and Kūpakarṇa who were expert in the military use of black magic and possessed of great prowess, and accompanied with their Daitya army, fought with Vṛṣṇis with illusory tactics of warfare.

30. Perceiving that his army was suffering through the illusory magical method of fighting, he dispelled all the illusion within a wink of the eye by "Knowledge-missile" He then directed Sātyaki and Kṛtavarman, both of whom were eagerly desirous of fighting, and said :

31. "As both of you have an ardent desire for fighting, you give an extremely terrible fight with those two Daityas who are haughty and extremely desirous for fighting. Thus ordered, those two extremely powerful warriors immediately engaged in the bitterest fight, O King.

32. It is not at all a miracle how Lord Kṛṣṇa with one bow in the hand, single-handedly engaged a hundred Kṣattriyas in a battle, for Hari is verily the (Indwelling) Soul of all, O king.

33. Some elephants fell down dead with their trunks lopped off, and a large number of horses with their necks cut off lay down dead, O King.

34. The earth was scattered over with disjointed chariots shattered to pieces.

35. Soldiers with their bodies besmeared with blood and with their feet (legs), thighs and arms hacked down, fell like

Kiṁśuka trees full of blossoms (red flowers) lying uprooted with its main roots cut.

36-37. Volleys of arrows with feathers of kites and peacocks at the butts, polished with oil and well-knit by knots, with golden feathers and pointed arrow-heads were seen discharged from the Śārṅga bow, ten on each soldier, a hundred on every horse, a thousand at every chariot and ten thousand on each of the elephants of the hostile army. That was a tremendously aweful miracle to see.

38. Finding his army of fourfold divisions (infantry, cavalry, the chariot-corps and elephants) being soundly drubbed that way, Jarāsandha, the king of Magadha, driving in his chariot with the ensign bearing the emblem of a horse, attacked Balarāma,

39. Recollecting his previous enmity (due to his defeat by Balarāma), Jarāsandha was enraged at the sight of Balārma's great chariot with gold-plated yoke and palmyra ensign and dashed at him with a mace (*gadā*) in his hand and spoke (challenging him) as follows :

40. "Quickly take up your pestle (-like club) with which you desire to vanquish and conquer the enemies in the battle. Hurry up and demonstrate to me the power of your arms, before I strike you down with my mace.

41. Challenged in this way by the king of Magadhas, Balarāma, with his eyes fired with rage, grasped his terrible pestle brilliant like lightning, just as Yama, the son of the Sun-god, takes up his rod at the end of the world.

42. Brandishing in a circle the pestle for one thousand times, Balarāma, the wielder of the plough as his weapon, quickly discharged that pestle exuding fumes of fire and capable of subduing the pride of the enemies, and roared like a lion, O King !

43. Jarāsandha along with the horses, charioteer and chariot, became agitated by the pestle hurled by Balarāma's arm and found himself cheated in underestimating (Balarāma's strength).

44. Thereupon wielding his mace hard as iron and big like a hill-top, Jarāsandha, making the earth quake under his pace, rushed at Balarāma.

45. Balarāma, the son of Rohiṇī, perceived him rushing at him without a chariot. He too left his chariot on the battle-field and dashed at him on foot.

46. As all beings were witnessing it, Māgadha (Jarāsandha) overwhelmed with wrath, brandished his heavy mace made of hard iron, and attacking Balarāma, struck him down with the mace and roared.

47. Perceiving the on-coming mace hard as a rock striking against his chest, Balarāma caught hold of it by his left hand, O scion of the Kuru race !

48. Hurling aside the mace, he hit a blow with his fist Jarāsandha on his chest. The mighty son of Rohiṇī caught the powerful Jarāsandha in his arms.

49. Entwining between his legs the stomach of Jarāsandha, he held his neck under his arm-pit, whereupon both of them rolled on the ground.

50. While they were falling, Balarāma was on Jarāsandha O King. But within a moment, Jarāsandha of immense power brought him under him.

51. Both of the heroes, with their eyes red with anger, stood up and again caught hold of each other like two terrific elephants maddened with excuding ichor.

52. Those extremely enraged ferocious warriors intent on killing each other, dashed their chests against each other, and tried to drag (each other on the battle field).

53. Thus dragging each other in an area of ten thousand bows, they reduced to powder the trees and rocks that were in the vicinity, O King!

54. Jarāsandha the highly proud hero, disengaged himself and picked up his mace. Even the most powerful Balarāma of incomprehensible nature, stood up and taking his pestle in a moment began to strike him with it.

55. In that combat Balarāma struck Jarāsandha with his pestle, on his head, in between his chest and shoulders, on the shoulders, arms, navel thighs, knees, stomach and chest, many times.

56. The proud Magadha king hit hard Balarāma on the chest, neck, mouth, forehead, chin, shoulder, navel, hips as well as his sides simultaneously.

57. While Balarāma and Jarāsandha were striking down each other in the combat, the kings became nervous about fighting and were extremely troubled.

58. Thinking that the king of Magadhas was approaching death, they gradually lost their heart and became less inclined to fight.

59. Extremely powerful Sātyaki who was fighting Kumbhāṇḍa was pierced with three arrows by the minister of Bāṇa, in the battle.

60. The mighty-armed Sātyaki, being extremely hurt, heaved heavy breaths like an angry serpent. In order to kill Kumbhāṇḍa in the fight, he took five iron arrows.

61. Then a great uproar arose in the army of the Daitya minister, when Sātyaki of powerful arms, pulled the string to his ears and hit Kumbhāṇḍa, the minister of Bāṇa, in his navel, throat, forehead, chest and crown, O tiger in the Kuru race.

62-63. Thus pierced with the arrows, Kumbhāṇḍa fell down unconscious on his seat in the chariot. Seeing that he had lost his consciousness, the charioteer, grieved at heart, immediately carried him away from the battle in his chariot, O prominent Bharata !

64. Perceiving that Kumbhāṇḍa had left and was in the peril of life, Kūpakarṇa, the demon whom Kṛtavarmā engaged, left Kṛtavarmā and departed from the battle-field.

65. Both the demons left the battle-field without taking leave of the king of Magadhas, even though they were not relieved by him. Accompanied by their remaining army, both the daityas returned to Śoṇitapura by the same way they came.

CHAPTER FIFTY-III

(*Ch.* 52 *in VJ's text*) ; *Conquest of Karvirapura*)

Śrī Śuka said:

1. Finding that the army of Bāṇa had deserted them and they themselves were extremely troubled by the volleys of

weapons (from the Yādavas), the princes became dispirited, O excellent king !

2. Seeing that the dānava army had already departed, and the hostile princes were exhausted, and Kṛṣṇa was fighting on, Balarāma felt that his strength had increased.

3. In that combat, he caught hold of the lock of hair on Jarāsandha's head by his left hand and wanted to strike him on his head with his pestle.

4. At that moment, Balarāma heard a clear distinct incorporeal voice, loud like thundering clouds in the sky: "O Balarāma, Jarāsandha is not to be killed by you. Happily return from the battle."

5. Hearing that voice from the heaven, the mighty Balarāma left him and riding his chariot returned from the battle-field, praised highly by multitudes of Brāhmaṇa sages, Siddhas, bards and songsters.

6. Now Jarāsandha, the foster son of Jarā, hanging down his head and accompanied by kings who were defeated in the battle and surrounded with a small force that was left after being killed in the battle, retired from the fight and proceeded to his capital.

Śrī Śuka said :

7. Lord Kṛṣṇa of great splendour, covered the inimical forces with volleys of arrows and put to flight those kings, killing a majority of them in the battle.

8. He was followed by songsters and bards like Sūta, Māgadha and Bandins who were highly pleased with him, and were singing of his glory and by highly learned Brāhmaṇas who were loudly singing his panegyric.

9-12. Followed by these, the glorious Lord entered the city of Mathurā which was populated with citizens who were delighted and happy—a city with high walls of fortifications and lofty arched gates, decorated with flowing banners and with lighted lamps. As he entered by the royal road, he shone beautiful, showered over with flowers and with fried grains with folded palms by ladies occupying the tops of mansions. The citizens of Mathura who were eager to please them, presented to Kṛṣṇa and Balarāma, the descendants of Madhu, highly precious presents, excellent garlands, of flowers and ointments. Kṛṣṇa the prominent one among Yādavas, in this way passed by the royal road.

13-15. Entering the spacious assembly hall and occupying the excellent seat, the hero Kṛṣṇa, along with Balarāma and intelligent Sātyaki, was honoured by Yadus and Brāhmaṇas like Indra by gods in the heaven. Holding consultations with the intelligent statesmen and noble-souled old Yadus such as Ugrasena, Uddhava, Akrūra (to mention the prominent ones) who were present there, Lord Kṛṣṇa was allowed to go with Balarāma as his companion and helpmate.

16. Being desirous of seeing Gomanta, the best of mountains, and the great fortress at its top, both of them set out in the morning from Mathura and proceeded to the South.

17. The glorious Lord Hari accompanied by Balarāma crossed the Yamunā and passed through many countries, mountains, rivers and hills.

18-20. While passing by the way, they saw on a raised part of a forest an extra-ordinarily distinguished sage sitting at the root of a tree. The sage had a mass of matted hair on his head. He was clad in bark garments and the hide of a deer and had a *Kamaṇḍalu* (a water pot of a gourd) by his side. He was glorious like the Sun in lustre. He subsisted on spiritual knowledge and bliss and was surrounded with hundreds of disciples. Balarāma and Kṛṣṇa, the protectors of the world, were extremely glad to see him.

21. Both the heroes with due formality and alertness paid their respects to him. The glorious lord Kṛṣṇa spoke to the prominent sage as follows :

22. "I bow to you O Paraśurāma of the Bhārgava clan ! O glorious son of Jamadagni who regard penance as wealth ! We are known as Balarāma and Kṛṣṇa. Has our name ever reached your ears ?"

23. Bhārgava who was thus addressed by Vāsudeva gazed at the two descendants of Madhu (just to probe their spiritual nature). The noble Paraśurāma with his eyes blooming with affection spoke as follows :

24. "Welcome to you the best one among the Yadus

and to your noble-souled elder brother ! I know that you are the supra-sensuous Lord who are born in the Yadu clan.

25. You are the primary cause of all the effects (created things). You are the ancient-most person in this Universe. Salutations to you, O lotus-eyed Kṛṣṇa, the sole cause of all the worlds.

26. For what purpose are both of you whom the universe pays respects, have arrived here ?" When thus inquired by Paraśurāma, the son of Jamadagni, Balarāma and Kṛṣṇa spoke out.

27. "We desire to see Gomanta for the inaccessible fortress on its top, O powerful lord !" Hearing that, Paraśurāma, the son of Jamadagni, spoke to Kṛṣṇa.

28. "May it be so, O mighty-armed one ! You may go with your elder brother to Gomanta. At the foot of that hill, there is the city of Karavīra protected by Śṛgāla Vāsudeva, but he will not tolerate you (encroaching). After killing him in a battle, you can occupy the mount called Gomanta".

30. Thus instructed by Paraśurāma, the son of Jamadagni, Balarāma and Kṛṣṇa, the descendants of Madhu, took leave of the omniscient sage and proceeded to the southern direction. Both of them saw the mount Gomanta covered over with sky-scraping, big trees.

32. They also saw at its foot the city of Karavīra with high portals, ramparts varied in construction and wonderful mensions, palaces and towers.

33. Kṛṣṇa, the wielder of conch, discus and a mace loudly blew his conch. Hearing that blast of Kṛṣṇa's conch, Śṛgāla Vāsudeva became overwhelmed with rage and taking with him his massive army of the infantry, the cavalry, the chariots and the elephant corps, he attacked Balarāma and Kṛṣṇa, the delight of Yadus.

35. He as if completely covered those Mādhava brothers with a flood of (discharged) arrows. Seeing that formidable army, the two most prominent Yādava heroes fought with them on foot, in the battle, and made that army extremely agitated and troubled by volleys of arrows and threw it into confusion.

37. On seeing that, king Śṛgāla, full of rage, rushed against them both. Observing him approaching in his chariot with a bow in his hand, Lord Vāsudeva checked his progress just as the coast-line does to the flow-tide of the sea.

38. Both the mighty Vāsudevas who were extremely enraged fought with each other with the intention of finishing with the enemy.

39. As the fight proceeded that way, Lord Govinda in a moment cut off the head of Śṛgāla Vāsudeva along with its refulgent crown.

40. Seeing that their master was killed, the soldiers of his army who were still left alive, ran in all directions.

41. Thereupon, both Balarāma and Kṛṣṇa entered the big city of Karavīra.[1] Both of them were worshipped as their dear lords by Brāhmaṇas and merchants.

42. Under the guard of his soldiers, Kṛṣṇa arranged to send Śṛgāla Vāsudeva's elephants, horses, chariots, soldiers, treasures and wealth.[2]

CHAPTER FIFTY-IV

Kṛṣṇa Crowned : Jarāsandha's Defeat

Śrī Śuka said :

1-4. Balarāma and Kṛṣṇa ascended the prominent mountain Gomanta which was covered with lofty trees and creepers. It was thickly overgrown with Sāla, Tāla (palmyra), and Tamāla trees and was beautified with Priyāla and Aśoka trees. It was enriched with Kadamba, Nimba (Neema), Hintāla, Pūga, Punnāga trees. It appeared beautiful with groves of plantain trees and was resonant with cooing of joy-

1. Most probably Kolhapur in the Bombay State. But if Gomanta is Goa, the distance between the two renders the suggestions doubtful, unless the fort of Panhāla is identified with the Gomanta hill.

2. Here ends C. 52 of VJ.'s Text.

ful cuckoos. The trees thereof were shaken a bit by the swarms of humming bees and jumping monkeys. It appeared beautiful with palm trees the branches of which were binding down with the burden of their fruits. It was watered with a number of cataracts. It abounded in crystal water and cool dense shadows. They saw and enjoyed that beautiful landscape.

5. On the mountain, they went up the peak called Pravarṣaṇa where clouds always sent forth their showers without break.

6. Ascending that peak, those two great Yadus surveyed all directions. Enjoying themselves they lived on the best of the mountain, to their hearts' content.

7-8* In the meanwhile, in the milky ocean the best among oceans which is the abode of the God of gods, Viṣṇu, the wielder of conch, discus and a mace, the glorious mighty-armed Bali, the son of Virocana who visited it, took away the crown of the God of gods which was studded with costly jewels.

9. The crown was wonderfully wrought in a thousand rich sapphires (*Indranīla* stones) and was studded with hundred of precious *Gomeda* stones. It was shining with rubies, big blue precious stones and pearls.

10. It was richly set with *Puṣparāga* (a kind of precious stone) and corals. It was made of celestial gold. Having come to know that the diadem was taken away by the Dānava hero, Garuḍa, the king of birds, and the incharge protector of the city, instantly pursued him.

11. Overtaking the irresistible king of Dānavas on the way and putting up a terrible fight with him, he vanquished the prominent demon.

12. Taking away from him the crown, a veritable heap of jewels, which was brilliant like the Sun, he (Garuḍa) on his way back saw lord Hari, the son of Devakī.

8*. It is hard to believe that the great king Bali who donated his kingdom of three worlds to Viṣṇu in the form of a dwarf (Vāmana) could be tempted to steal the crown of Lord Viṣṇu whose greatest devotee he was.

13. He was sitting along with his elder brother on the beautiful and the best of mountains known as Gomanta. He immediately placed on his head that heavenly ornament—Viṣṇu's crown. Bowing down to his feet with his own head, he began to sing his praise.

Garuḍa said :

14. "I salute again and again lord Nārāyaṇa who has assumed a human form for some special mission, and who is extremely dear to all. My salutations to Nārāyaṇa who is the cause of the destruction of the enemies of gods and (as Inner Controller) is witness to the actions of everyone.

15. Being yourself the same Nārāyaṇa, you assume the form of god Brahmā and create all the Universe. As Nārāyaṇa, you protect it and ultimately assuming the form of Śiva (as his *ātman*) you destroy it, O glorious Lord.

16. I know that you are that god Viṣṇu, the Lord of all gods—who have incarnated on the earth as the scion of the Yadu race. I am Garuḍa, the son of Vinatā, your humble servant. O Lord ! Be pleased to command me what I should do."

Śri Śuka said :

17. Addressing the God of gods thus, Garuḍa, the king of birds, knelt before him on the ground, bowed him and stood before him with folded palms.

18. Seeing Garuḍa the prominent one among birds, Kṛṣṇa the greatest of Yādavas, with his countenance blooming with affection, touched his head (the best part of the body) with hands.

19. "You may go wherever you like, O blessed one. Come in time when you will be remembered by me." Commanding him thus, he discharged him. Balarāma and Keśava, the lords of the world, who subsisted on the fruits and roots and drank of waters from flowing streams, descended from the top of that mountain and arrived at Karavīrapura.

21. Having stayed there for four months both of them returned to the city of Mathurā taking with them a big army, O prominent one among Bharatas.

22. Hearing that king Śṛgāla was killed, Jarāsandha became overwhelmed with anger and surrounded with a vast army, he also came there, O great Kuru !

23. Balarāma and Kṛṣṇa battled with him for seven days. In that seven-day-war the king of Magadha with his enormous army was completely defeated.

24. He returned to the country of Magadha along with a number of Kṣatriyas. Balarāma and Kṛṣṇa who were expert in *Dharma*, entered the city of Mathurā along with their followers, while they were being praised by songsters and bards like Sūta and Māgadha.

(After this see Verse No. 42 in Ch. 50)

CHAPTER FIFTY-TWO—I

(After 56 in V.J.'s Text)

Kṛtavarmā Deputed to Hastināpura

Śrī Śuka said :

1-2. On one occasion Kṛṣṇa, the son of Devakī, in company of Balarāma and Sātyaki was being waited upon by kings of various countries in the royal assembly. He heard there from Brāhmaṇas, participants in a sacrificial session that Drupada, the king of Pāñcālas was taken captive by young sons of Kuntī in the battle, O scion of Kuru race.

3. On hearing that, the Imperishable Lord became glad at heart and deputed Kṛtavarmā to the city of Hastināpura to know the details.

4. On going to Hastināpura, Kṛtavarmā sought the audience of Bhīṣma, the aged grand-father of Kauravas accompanied by Droṇa, Vidura, Dhṛtarāṣṭra and Kṛpa.

5. He paid respects to king Yudhiṣṭhira along with his four brothers. Kṛtavarmā, the son of Hṛdika, paid special respects to Kuntī.

6-7. Yudhiṣṭhira on his part inquired about Kṛṣṇa, the slayer of Kaṁsa, as well as about his companions, about the killing of Kālayavana and victory over Jarāsandha, and the slaying of Vāsudeva, the uler of Karavīrapura as well as the building up of the city of Dvārakā in the sea.

8-10. On knowing the facts (about the above events) and the slaying of Haṁsa and Ḍibhaka and Brahmadatta the invincible, Yudhiṣṭ ira regarded that the sovereignty of the three worlds had permanently been secured in his hands. Kṛtavarmā was honoured by providing comforts, engagement in conversations and other ways of receiving the guest, by the sons of Pāṇḍu and by Kuntī whose eyes were overflowing with tears of affection. Kṛtavarmā took leave of his relatives and also of Kuntī.

11-12. He duly paid respects to the sons of his maternal aunt who were knowers of *Dharma*. He was permitted to leave by Bhīṣma, the son of Gaṅgā and by Dhṛtarāṣṭra, O sinless king ! He was also given leave by Vidura, Karṇa, the king of Aṅga, Droṇa, Kṛpa, by the intelligent Aśvatthāman as well as by Duryodhana.

13. Taking leave of them all, Kṛtavarmā departed from the city called Hastināpura and at the time of sunset, he arrived at Dvārakā, the head-quarters of Vṛṣṇis.

14. Entering the celestial assembly-hall which was attended by a number of kings he saw there Kṛṣṇa who was occupying a high seat of gold.

15. To Kṛṣṇa who was wearing a Vanamālā and who was being fanned with *chowries* by many servants, he reported in details everything as he saw or heard it.

16. Hearing the detailed report of what happened in the capital city Hastināpura of the Kauravas, Lord Hari, the Ruler of the world, learning of the valorous deed of the sons of Pāṇḍus became overwhelmed with joy.

CHAPTER FIFTYTWO-II

*Balarāma marries Revatī**

King Parikṣit said :

1. O great sage ! I wish to hear from you in details who was the king named Revata and how he was instructed by god Brahmā (to give his daughter in marriage to Balarāma).

Śrī Śuka replied :

2. Formerly (in the *Kṛta* Age), there was a king called Revata. He was expert in the essentials of *dharma* and *artha*. A glorious daughter was born to him whom he named Revatī.

3. He went to god Brahmā to consult him to whom he should give his daughter, as she was sought after by kings of various countries even though he did not propose her to anybody.

4. At that time in the assembly-hall of god Brahmā, two Gandharvas, Hāhā and Hūhū, were singing. They were experts in all the subtle excellent points in evolving music (such as presentation of the gamut in proper pitch and according to measured beats.

5. The king waited outside for some time expecting some interval in the musical concert. When it was concluded, he paid his respects to god Brahmā and sought his advice.

6. "O glorious Lord! This is my daughter. To whom I should give her in marriage ?" To him the lotus-born god Brahmā asked, "What prince you like most ?

7. Name to me all other rulers of the earth as well, O scion of the Kuru race !" Thereupon Revata enumerated to him the names of kings who were ruling over various countries.

8. Hearing the names of those kings, Brahmā laughed aloud and spoke to Revata, "O king ; Many *yugas* have elapsed since you came here,

9. While you were listening to the musical performance of these Gandharvas (which you are not eligible to hear) for a

* To be read after verse 15 of ch. 52 (original).
It appears to be an elaboration of *supra* 9.27-36.

moment. Where are those kings whom you regard suitable for your daughter, O king?

10. By this time, O tiger among kings, there are born two lords of the world in the house of Vasudeva. Those two descendants of the Yadu race are called Balarāma and Kṛṣṇa.

11. O king! Give your daughter in marriage to Balarāma out of them." When he was thus advised, the king paid obeisance to him and returned to his city.

12. He gave his beautiful daughter to Balarāma of mighty arms. But being born in the first (*Kṛta*) Age, she was of a big stature. Balarāma of powerful arms laid his plough on her shoulder and pulling her down made her of his equal stature.

CHAPTER FIFTY-FIVE

(VJ's Text — Chapter-68)

The Story of Pradyumna's Birth

The following are the additional introductory verses in VJ.'s Text:

Śrī Śuka said:

1-2. Having propitiated Śiva, the God of gods, the bestower of blessings on the world and having pleased the god residing on mount Kailāsa, with his penance, Lord Hari got a son from Rukmiṇī called Pradyumna. The hero was endowed with excellent beauty, generosity and other virtues. He was the god of Love (Kāma) re-incarnated after being burnt (by god Śiva).

The King Parikṣit said:

3. Be pleased to narrate to me what sort of son and of what name, Hari got after visualising god Śiva with the object of getting a son, and after securing the requisite boon.

CHAPTER FIFTY-NINE—I

(VJ.'s Text—Ch. 65)

The Pārijāta Tree Taken by Śrī Kṛṣṇa

Śrī Śuka said :

1. Having slain the extremely formidable demon Narakāsura, Śrī Kṛṣṇa, the exterminator of *dānavas*, mounted Garuḍa and set out of Prāgjyotiṣapura, O King.

2. While flying through the sky with his consort Satyabhāmā, Lord Viṣṇu (Kṛṣṇa) went to the capital of heaven to pay respects to Aditi, the mother of gods.

3. Arriving at the gates of heaven, god Viṣṇu (Kṛṣṇa) blew his highly resounding conch of great sound. Hearing that blast, the denizens of heaven approached to receive him with respectful offerings (e. g. water for washing feet and other articles of worship).

4. Worshipped by gods with devotion and humility and with their minds free from mental distress and fear, He entered the beautiful celestial palace of the Lord of gods.

5. There, Indra with his queen Śacī worshipped him presenting him jewels, celestial ornaments and clothes, perfumes and beautiful garlands.

6. Thereupon he proceeded with his spouse to the city of his mother Aditi. Noticing that her son Acyuta was coming, she received him.

7. Hari paid respects to her. With deep affection, she received with blessings the best of Yadus whom she had not seen for a long time.

8. Instructed by Kṛṣṇa, Satyabhāmā also, placed the earrings (of Aditi) at the feet of her mother-in-law and bowed down to her, O descendant of Kurus.

9. Having recovered her ear-rings she was deeply satisfied and hugged her daughter-in-law. With her eyes overflowing with tears of joy, Aditi, the beloved spouse of sage Kāśyapa, exclaimed :

10. There shall never be old age, deformity or discord with your beloved in your case through my gracious blessings. Positively rest assured, O auspicious lady !

11. Having taken their leave of the goddess Aditi and also of celestials, Keśava (Kṛṣṇa) accompanied with Satyabhāmā mounted Garuḍa and proceeded onwards.

12. While the god (Kṛṣṇa) and the goddess (Satyabhāmā) were being borne by the high-souled mighty Garuḍa, they beheld a wonderful garden sending forth excellently sweet scent. It was the Nandana garden so beloved to Indra, the husband of Śacī and hence well-guarded.

13. Noticing that garden full of divine fragrance and rich in blossoms, Satyabhāmā took Kṛṣṇa by hand and said, "O Keśava, I wish to enter into this wonderful garden and to indulge in sports for a while.

14. To respect her words (of request), Keśava got down from Garuḍa and entered the garden that was guarded by servants of Indra.

15. She saw there the heavenly trees resonant with the humming of intoxicated bees, bent down with the weight of fruits and thickly over-strewn with pollen dust of flowers.

16-17. The tender foliage of the trees was moving in gentle breeze and was rendered beautiful and attractive with sweet warbling birds. While sauntering therein, she happened to see the great Pārijāta tree. With her eyes full of wonder and curiosity, she asked Lord Kṛṣṇa, "What is the name of this tree ? It is really wonderful in all the three worlds."

18-20 The enjoyers of the fruits of this tree must be really lucky as they have all their desires fulfilled thereby. The space at its foot (roots) is paved with corals, its huge trunk is all gold ; it is covered with tender leaves of sapphires and platform round it is built of shining *Vaidūryas* (Lapis Lazuli). It blossoms forth in ruby-flowers and is laden with ripe fruits in the form of gomeda stones. It is shining with the flower-filaments of diamonds. It is beautified with hundreds of big branches of lustrous emeralds.

21. This tree has fascinated my heart thoroughly. If I am really loved by you, the tree should be taken away to our city (Dvārakā), O Lord of the world !

22. Seeing me sitting (resting) under the shade of this tree, your other queens would look upon me as your beloved-must spouse of all, O sinless Lord !"

23. When urged thus by his beloved consort Satyabhāmā, Kṛṣṇa, the son of Devakī, explained : "This tree is not to be removed from the Nandana garden, O gracious lady.

24. Formerly when this tree emerged while the milky ocean was being churned by gods and Asuras, this was given to Indra by all who participated all the fruits (or "jewels" evolved out of the churning of the ocean).

25. It is not proper for me to take this jewel of a tree away, setting at nought my friend Indra, the performer of hundred *Kratus*, O lotus-eyed lady, as I always follow the path of righteousness.

26. If an attempt for taking away this Pārijāta is made, a terrible fight with gods ambitious to gain victory is inevitable, O smiling beauty (lit. lady beaming with smiles) !"

27. When Satyabhāmā was thus addressed by the God of gods, Satyabhāmā retorted to Lord Hari, "Why do you frighten me with such deceptive arguments, O slayer of Kaṁsa ?

28. That unmannerly Śacī did not courteously receive me and honour me when I visited her. She is proud of her husband's prowess.

29. O Acyuta ! If I am really your beloved, this Pārijāta tree must be taken away at any cost. If I be not so (beloved), desist (from the attempt) immediately."

30. Thus importuned by Satyabhāmā, Kṛṣṇa ignored contemptuously the guards, uprooted the tree and placed it on Garuḍa.

31. The forest-guards then resisted Kṛṣṇa while some sped hastily to report to Indra the incident.

32. (They insistently protested) : "O Kṛṣṇa, Kṛṣṇa, this tree is worshipped by celestials. This must not be taken away. If you (just try to) take it away, you will instantly reap the fruit of that act.

33. You will never reach your capital with this tree, O Kṛṣṇa. You will find Indra (pursuing you) close at your back with his weapon (Vajra) raised (to strike you)."

34. Some forest guards quickly approached Indra who was sitting with his queen Śacī. Seeing him they reported, O King !

35. "Disregarding all gods including (Her majesty) Indrāṇī as well as your majesty, Kṛṣṇa's spouse has taken away the great tree Pārijāta.

36. While resisting her we prohibited her in clear terms. But that beloved spouse of Hari is so elated with the pride of her husband's prowess that she reproached us and carried away the tree."

Śrī Śuka continued :

37. Hearing this offensive report, god Indra looked at Śacī who was sitting by his side and like a serpent hit with a stick did not tolerate that insult.

38. Proclaiming immediate preparation for fighting and mobilising all his soldiers and summoning the guardians of various spheres for the battle, the Lord of gods marched out.

39. The army of gods followed Indra equipped with thunder-bolt and riding the excellent elephant Airāvata of four tusks.

40. The fire-god, securely accoutred in his panoply and riding his horse, armed himself with a terrific Śataghnī and a tail-like ladle, rode to the battle.

41. The valorous Yama (god of death) armed himself with his rod and riding his he-buffalo and accompanied with mahā-Kāla and others followed Indra with a view to fight.

42. Nirṛti of great splendour rode in his man-borne vehicle. The mighty-armed god, armed with a sword, set out for the battle, O King.

43. Varuṇa hastily mounted his alligator of terrible forms and with his noose raised in his hand started after Indra to fight.

44. The wind-god clad in coat of mail and armed with a *Tomara* (Javelin) rode his (swift) black-antelope and followed the Lord of gods to fight with Kṛṣṇa, the wielder of (Sudarśana) discus.

45. Kubera, in his palanquin carried by four men and armed with a *Mudgara* (a club) rushed out hastily with a desire to fight with Viṣṇu (Kṛṣṇa).

46. God Śiva, mounting his big bull and bearing a

sharp pointed trident and accompanied with an army of ten million goblins went with Indra for fighting.

47. Drums, conchs, *Mṛdaṅgas*, *Paṇavas*, Kettle-drums and *gomukhas* (a musical instrument), heavenly gold wind-instruments and innumerable cymbals were sounded.

48. With the thumping of iron tyres of chariot, harsh neighing of the horses, roaring like lions and loud striking of their arms, loud shouts of challenges for fighting.

49. And with hundreds and thousands of gods shouting, "Halt, stop : Where do you go ? Don't go."

50. Brandishing and waving their mass of arms and urging on their vehicles (for speed), hundreds and thousands of the gods were competing to be in advance.

51. With terrific twanging of the bow-strings and innumerable lusty shouts like lions, the impatient gods rushed forward to attack (Kṛṣṇa) as (a pack of) jackals rushing against a lion.

CHAPTER FIFTY-NINE

(*VI.'s Text Ch.* 66)

Satyabhāmā defeats Gods.

Śri Śuka continued :

1. Perceiving that gods are rushing forward to attack them, Kṛṣṇa, the Lord of the world, remarked to Satyabhāmā, "Here have arrived your guests, these gods".

2. While the Lord of gods was speaking thus, the warrior-gods despatched (against Kṛṣṇa) roared and discharged a volley of arrows on Kṛṣṇa, O descendant of Kurus.

3. Then, confused at the sudden calamity, Satyabhāmā took up the Śārṅga bow and with a volley of arrows cut off the shafts discharged by the warriors from heaven.

4. Thereafter advanced Kubera the Lord of wealth, surrounded by a number of Yakṣas and twanging the string of his palm-tree high bow plated with gold at both ends.

5. Discharging arrows with feathers of gold and now and then roaring like a lion, he rushed forward in the battle and shouted, "Stop, Stop."

6. Satyā (Satyabhāmā) hit forcibly his big belly with five sharp arrows that cut him to the quick, O King.

7. Being deeply wounded by her arrows in the battle, the god of wealth discharged three *bhalla* arrows at the beloved of Lord Hari and gave out a lusty shout.

8-9. Even before those shafts could reach her, she cut them with three arrows with crescent-shaped head. And the queen (Satyā) struck the forehead of Kubera, the Lord of Guhyakas, with eight *Vatsa-danta* (type of) arrows swift like the mind, O prominent Kuru. Extremely pained with those arrows, Kubera, the son of Pulastya, was over-whelmed with rage.

10-13. In that combat, he discharged twenty-one sharp arrows but Satyabhāmā, with her seven shafts, cut each of them into three pieces within half a second (wink of the eye). While they were in the air, Satyabhāmā, the beloved of Hari, flew into rage and cut into two the big bow of Kubera at its hold (in the middle) with an arrow with crescent-shaped head. Kubera, the Lord of riches picked up another bow and stringing it, discharged a volley of arrows, wrathfully breathing like a serpent. But queen Satyabhāmā with ease (as in a sport) cut down all those arrows with her *Sannataparva* shafts (of hard knots). It was a miracle as it were to see. Kubera, thereupon, wrathfully glared at Satyabhāmā.

15-16. "Look at my prowess I shall kill you outright today", growled he. With a desire to wipe out his defeat and humiliation and while all gods were gazing, he fixed an excellent arrow with a crescent-head on his bow tall as a palmyra tree, to kill queen Satyabhāmā.

17. Anticipating his plan (in mind), the consort of Hari cut his bow just in the middle (at its hold), with an arrow with a horse-shoe shaped sharp head, O best of Kurus.

18. Then Kubera, the protector of wealth took up his

formidable *Mudgara* (club) that terrified demons and brandishing it hundred times, hurled it at the queen (Satyā).

19. Kṛṣṇa with his left hand (easily) caught hold of that extremely terrible club as it was rushing towards her and seeing at him laughed loudly.

20. Thereupon, Kubera, the Lord of wealth retired from the battle and fled away. Kṛṣṇa spoke highly of his queen, embraced her with great regard.

21. When Kubera took to his heels in the battle with Kṛṣṇa, the enemy of Kaṁsa, Varuṇa raising his noose attacked Kṛṣṇa in a combat.

22. Perceiving the advance of Varuṇa who rode a crocodile, Garuḍa of formidable strength pounced upon him like a tiger springing on an ox.

23. Terrific was the fight between Garuḍa and Varuṇa, like the combat between Bali and Indra in the war between gods and demons.

24. Varuṇa, the Lord of waters, threw the noose about the neck of Garuḍa and angrily dragged him like one lion dragging another.

25. Lifting up Varuṇa, the Lord of waters with the ends of his wings and catching hold of the crocodile in his claws Garuḍa hurled them into the sea.

26. Having lost his mount and catching hold of his noose with great difficulty, Varuṇa ran away on foot from the battle-field to his abode whence he came.

27. When Varuṇa retired from the battle-field, the Wind-god and the Fire-god jointly attacked Kṛṣṇa, O the best of Kurus !

28. The Fire-god discharged five arrows, while the Wind-god fired three shafts. Their fight with Kṛṣṇa was wonderful to look at.

29. Thereupon, Govinda, exterminator of enemies, laughed loudly and pierced the Fire-god with one arrow and the Wind-god with seven.

30. Deeply and forcibly struck on the chest with one shaft with horse-shoe-shaped head, the Fire-god realized that Kṛṣṇa was extraordinary and quickly fled from the battle-field.

31. Noticing that the Fire-god had run away from the battle and that his whole body was bristling with arrows, he (the Wind-god) was overwhelmed with pain.

32. He realized that it was lotus-eyed god Viṣṇu who had appeared on the battle-field. He retired from the battle as he wanted to save his own life.

33. Thereupon mounting his he-buffalo and raising up his refulgent rod, Yama, with his eyes reddened with rage, attacked Kṛṣṇa in the battle.

34. Noticing Yama with his big rod raised up (to strike at him,) the lotus-eyed Kṛṣṇa hurled his mace at him and felled it from his hand.

35. The heavy blow of his mace on his rod made Yama's hand tremble. Turning his back, the god of death ran away with his buffalo, O scion of the Kuru race.

36. Beholding the discomfiture and retreat of Yama, Nirṛti was overwhelmed with fear and judging his power, did not come to fight.

37. But god Śiva of great heroic lustre, armed with a trident and mounting his bull, attacked Kṛṣṇa with his enormous army of goblins.

38. Those two mighty valorous heroes well-known in the world engaged in a terrible combat, each with an ambition to defeat the other.

39. Piercing Kṛṣṇa with ten arrows and Garuḍa with five, Śiva roared out in the battle, Stop, Stop.

40. Taking up his Śārṅga bow, Kṛṣṇa, the destroyer of cities of enemies, hit Śiva, the rider of the bull with thirty arrows simultaneously.

41. In that combat, Garuḍa, the destroyer of serpents, harassed the bull with his pointed bill, both of his claws and wings.

42. Discharging again fifty Nārāca arrows at him, Kṛṣṇa engaged Śaṅkara, the benign god who blesses the world, in the fight, O ruler of the world.

43. Śiva, got enraged and brandishing his sharp-pointed formidable-looking trident hurled it at Vāsudeva (Kṛṣṇa), O King.

44. Noticing the trident rushing at him, Kṛṣṇa hurled his heavy demon-destroying mace Kaumodakī at it, to ward it off.

45. It is traditionally reported that both the weapons — the Kaumodakī mace and the trident — buffeted each other in the sky and giving out huge flames both of them simultaneously fell into the sea.

46. Felling down the trident into the sea, the mace Kaumodakī returned to Viṣṇu's (Kṛṣṇa's) hand and the trident also to that of Śiva.

47. The serpent decorated god Śiva raised up his sharp sword and spurring his bull with his heals, he attacked Kṛṣṇa in the combat.

48. Promptly seizing the bull by his two horns, Garuḍa hurled god Śiva along with the bull to a distance of hundred bows (four hundred cubits).

49. Thereupon god Śiva, the wielder of trident with the bull as his mount, left the battle and speedily went back to his pce, O best of Kurus !

CHAPTER FIFTY-NINE—III

(VI.'s Text — Chapter No. 67)

Pārijāta planted in Satyabhāmā's Palace

Śrī Śuka continued :

1-2. Thereupon Indra, the King of gods put on his royal diadem, equipped himself with a quiver of arrows, armed himself with a bow, mounted on his huge elephant Airāvata and remembering the words of Śacī regarding the Pārijāta tree, attacked Kṛṣṇa in the battle, like an elephant attacking a lion.

3. Beholding him advance, Lord Hari, the conqueror of inimical cities, blew his high sounding conch filling all the quarters with the blast.

4. Attacking Kṛṣṇa and twanging his big bow, he hit Kṛṣṇa with an extremely pointed arrow with a sharp horse-shoe-shaped head in the combat.

5. Wounded on the chest with that *Kṣurapra* arrow by the King of gods, Hari laughed loudly and applauded him, "Welldone Indra! This is just like you (worthy of the King of gods.

6. Still again the King of gods set ten shafts on his bow (long and curved) like a great serpent and stretching the bow-string upto his ears, discharged them at Kṛṣṇa and his discus and roared like a lion.

7. In the meanwhile, Kṛṣṇa the noble-souled slayer of Kaṁsa cut into three all the arrows with one shaft in the mid-way (as they were coming), and hit Indra with ten excellently whetted shafts as if in a sport, O descendant of Bharata.

8. Those shafts pierced through Indra's body alongwith the armour and were seen coming out with great force smeared with blood.

9. Indra again set sixteen arrows on his bow and stretching (the bow string) discharged them, but Kṛṣṇa cut them with three shafts.

10. Still again with thirty shafts, Hari hit the King of gods in the battle and all those arrows struck deep in Indra's chest.

11. Indra then flew in rage like a serpent hit with a stick and with his goad he impelled his big elephant to attack Garuḍa.

12. Goaded on by Indra the elephant approached Garuḍa and dashed at his chest with his four tusks.

13. Thereupon, Garuḍa tormented the elephant called Airāvata with his bill, wings and claws, O descendant of Kauravas.

14. And while all beings were agazing, he raised his terrible Vajra which inspired awe among Dānavas and hurled it at Viṣṇu (Kṛṣṇa).

15. As that *Vajra*, the weapon of Indra, reached him, Viṣṇu, the slayer of Madhu caught it in his left hand and laughed loudly.

16. Being deprived of his weapon and his mount (elephant) tormented by Garuḍa, the King of gods retreated from the battle-field hanging down his head in shame.

17. Finding Indra frustrated in his object and intend-

ing to run, Satyabhāmā laughed loudly at the King of gods and said taunting.

Satyabhāmā said :

18. Come on Śakra. Don't retreat, O wielder of the thunderbolt. It is not proper for Śacī's dear lord to take to flight.

19. Your queen Śacī, the daughter of Pulomā, drunk with the pride of sovereignty and elated with the prowess of her husband as she is, will at once think low of you (and insult you) defeated as you are in the battle."

20. Hearing this taunting speech of queen Satyabhāmā, Indra looked her in the face and addressed to the slyly smiling queen.

Indra said :

21. Confronting on the battle-field the father and preceptor of the three worlds by whom are brought forth the gods, demons, the great serpents, Yakṣas, Siddhas, Gandharvas (the divine musicians), Kinnaras, goblins, ogres and others, who can avoid facing the humiliation of defeat ?

22. We who subsist on sacrificial oblations, expose our childishness by opposing the incomprehensible Lord, like the weakling of a calf appears to oppose its mother at the time of sucking her milk."

23. Having replied thus to Satyabhāmā, the daughter of Satrājit, Indra folded his palms, bowed to Lord Vāsudeva and prayed, O the best descendant of Bharata !

Indra prayed :

24. Hail to you O God of gods, the lotus-eyed Lord of Lakṣmī ! Be pleased to pardon me all my faults, O protector of the world.

25. You are kind and affectionate to those who seek resort to you. It does not behove you to abandon me of whom you are the sole asylum—me who am extremely foolish and uncontrolled.

26-27. The elephant Airāvata (my mount), the thunderbolt (my special weapon), this Pārijāta tree, sovereignty over gods and this Amarāvatī (my capital town)—in fact everything (in this universe) is under your control. I am your obedient servant. Whatever you wish to take away from this place may be taken away by you at will.

28. O Govinda ! I shall explain to you the fundamental reason of opposing you. You are now wholeheartedly interested in the mortal world.

29. If this wish-yielding tree Pārijāta is taken by you there, the earth becomes indistinguishable from the heavan.

30. It is hence that I opposed you, O tiger among the Yadus—O god, I may, therefore, be forgiven by you who know what should and what should not be done.

Śrī Śuka said :

31. Thus addressed by the king of gods, Janārdana, the the God of gods, w'th a smiling countenance, spoke to him, O the greatest Kuru.

The glorious Lord said :

32. "Absolutely no fault has been committed by you, O Indra. If any fault has been committed, it is mine, for there is no distinction between you and me.

33. Whatever is now done by you, irrespective of its being good or bad, has been committed by me, O thousand eyed god. Please do not brood over the matter at all.

34. This excellent-most Pārijāta tree will, as per my direction, come to the Nandana garden of its own accord, when I (departing from the earth) ascend to the heaven.

35. When the King of gods was thus addressed by Vāsudeva, O best of Kurus, the king of gods apologised to Kṛṣṇa, Satyabhāmā and Garuḍa.

36-37. May my son and your brother-in-law Arjuna, also known as Bībhatsu, be protected by you." Repeating this request again and again, Indra, getting leave to depart, got back his Vajra and returned to his capital with all protectors of different cardinal points. Kṛṣṇa, the delight of Yadus bade good-bye to Indra along with the protectors of all the cardinal points.

38-39. He ordered Garuḍa: Let us make a move to Dvārakā. Garuḍa, the enemy of serpents, easily bore Kṛṣṇa, Satyabhāmā and the Pārijāta tree and went to Dvārakā. He entered the beautiful city of Dvārakā adorned with many gates and portals.

40-41. It was brilliant, decorated with flags, buntings and festoons. Its floors were cleansed and besprinkled. He was worshipped with the attending prominent Yadus by offering him presents, betel-leaves, garlands, perfumes, pigments and unbroken grains of rice. He was saluted and greeted with flourish of trumpets and other instruments sounded on auspicious occasions, as well as with loud chantings of Vedic hymns.

42-43. Kṛṣṇa entered the heavenly assembly-hall *Sudharmā* which was attended by (a council of) elders. He bowed down to Āhuka (Ugrasena), Vasudeva and his elder brother Balarāma in order of seniority. He was duly honoured by them (reciprocally). In that assembly, he occupied an exalted seat of gold.

44. Kṛṣṇa appeared resplendent like Indra attended upon by prominent persons like Bṛhaspati and other protectors of the world in heaven.

45. Kṛṣṇa got the great tree Pārijāta planted in the palace of Satyabhāmā. It was surrounded on all side with pavements of precious stones.

46. Learning that the son of Devakī was coming with a big host of ladies, all the women of Yādava clan came there to see them.

47. Vasudeva as well as all ladies headed by Rohiṇī came to see Lord Kṛṣṇa, returned safe, hale and hearty after conquering the enemy.

48. Beholding that his mother in company of Devakī had come, Kṛṣṇa bowed down to them. They in their turn honoured him with blessings.

49. Similarly, seven beloved queens of Kṛṣṇa such as Rukmiṇī and others who were supremely beautiful and richly adorned, approached their Lord and paid respects to him.

50-51. Revatī, the beloved spouse of Balarāma, the famous Trivakrā, Durgā, Subhadrā and Tārā and other ladies of Bhoja, Vṛṣṇi and Andhaka clans with their faces blooming with joy and affection came to see, out of curiosity, Lord Kṛṣṇa who had returned hale and hearty after vanquishing the enemies and brought with him a bevy of ladies and Satyabhāmā as also the celestial Pārijāta tree brought from heaven.

53. All the ladies gathered there showered on Kṛṣṇa's head fried grains of rice, flowers and unbroken rice-grains and returned to their respective homes.

CHAPTER SIXTY-SIX—A

Slaying of Pauṇḍraka and others

(This corresponds to VJ.'s Text ch. 69. It gives the following additional verses in the Introduction)

Śrī Śuka said :

1.1-1.3 : It is reported that at that time there was a king called Pauṇḍraka, O scion of the Kuru race. Getting information of Kṛṣṇa's absence from Dvārakā, he laid siege to that citadel of Vṛṣṇis with a big army and subjected it to attacks. Balarāma, Sātyaki, Vasudeva, Uddhava, Ugrasena and other prominent Yādava warriors treated him (with their military preparations) in a manner suitable for a guest who comes at such a time.

King Parikṣit enquired :

1.4 Who was that Pauṇḍraka ? What country did he rule over ? Whose son was he ? Be pleased to narrate all this to me, O sage.

Śrī Śuka narrated :

1.5 The king of Kāśī had no male issue. He gave his daughter Sutanu to Vasudeva on condition of giving his kingdom as dowry.

1.6 A son with long arms and brilliant like the sun was born to them. He was called Pauṇḍraka. He was powerful, full of prowess and pride.

1.7-1.8 As he was the son of Vasudeva, he was called Vāsudeva. when he became a major the great glorious Vasudeva entrusted to him that kingdom (of Kāśī) along with the treasures, army, chariots and other vehicles. Then

Vasudeva married Kaṁsa's younger sister Devakī who was like a goddess.

1.9 Being interned by Kaṁsa, the king of Bhojas, Vasudeva could not even once visit Karavīrapura.

1.10 Being ever-conscious of the unbearable step-motherly relation and of having no brother of his own, the king of Kāśi lived in awe of Yadus.

1.11 Hearing the report of Kṛṣṇa's absence from Dvārakā, he stormed it at night but he was defeated by Balarāma and Śaineya (Sātyaki).

1.12 Having suffered a heavy loss of thousands of horses, elephants and foot soldiers, he quietly retreated in the latter part of the night to the city of Vārāṇasī.

1.13 When the night was over and the day dawned, Śrī Kṛṣṇa returned from Badarikāśrama by his mount Garuḍa and came to Dvārakā which was well defended by Balarāma.

1.14 He was received with flags and offered water to wash his hands and feet and the usual presents after arrival, by Yādavas, Vṛṣṇis and Andhakas who reported to him the whole story. Then he entered the council hall.

1.15 Once Pauṇḍraka the powerful king of Kāśī........

(After this follows verse 1-b in ŚR.'s Text in ch. 66)

CHAPTER EIGHTY-I

The Story of the Brāhmaṇa Sridāman

VJ.'s Text begins :

1-2A. When the mighty-armed Su (Dur) yodhana was struck down by the mace (of Bhīma) in the battle (and died subsequently), even the glorious Lord Govinda, having accomplished his desired object (of lightening the burden of the earth) made arrangement of leaving the desolate battle field.

2B-5. Kṛpa, Kṛtavarmā and the prominent chariot-warrior Aśvatthāman were the only three great warriors in the army of Su(Dur) yodhana. The survivors on the other (Pāṇḍava) side were the five Pāṇḍava warriors, the mighty Sātyaki, Yuyutsu, the son of Dhṛtarāṣṭra by a Vaiśya woman and other eminent people of whom Kṛṣṇa was prominent. As their leader and accompanied by elderly sages, he went to

Hastināpura for the condolence of Dhṛtarāṣṭra and he consoled Gāndhārī, Dhṛtarāṣṭra and the highly intelligent Vidura.

6-8. With difficulty he installed Pāṇḍavas to carry out their functions in governing their kingdoms. He was glorified by hosts of sages and bards like Sūtas, Māgadhas and Bards and was followed by sons of Pāṇḍu whose eyes were flowing with tears of joy. He took his leave of them, all of whom were sorry, missing him (after his departure). Hari returned to Dvārakā in a chariot brilliant like the Sun. With the loud blast of conchs and beatings of drums and the loud chorus of auspicious Vedic hymns and of incantation of *mantras* repeating the declaration of the day being auspicious he entered Dvārakā.

9-12. The city was decorated by the citizens with various kinds of arches and waving flags and fluttering banners and its grounds (streets, squares, etc.) were sprinkled and washed by them. He was attended upon by citizens who carried in their hands a specific kind of vessel tufted with tender shoots,[1] and by young prominent courtesans adorned with ornaments and by women of the cities and by Brāhmaṇas and their sons, grandsons and with brothers who brought in their hands lamps, mirrors, pots full of water, flowers, fruits, entire grains of rice.

13-14. Hari entered that excellent city on an auspicious day and was worshipped with due formalities. He entered the world-famous celestial assembly-hall *Sudharmā* and paid respects to Āhuka, Vasudeva, Balarāma and bowed to all mothers who were seated on high seats of gold.

15. He took his seat there and was duly worshipped by prominent Yādavas. Like unto the moon surrounded by the constellations of stars and planets in the sky, he shone there (in the assembly hall among the Yādava chiefs).

16-17. Day and night he was attended upon by the powerful monarchs who survived (the Mahābhārata war) and also by sons (of the monarchs killed) who were installed on the thrones of their respective kingdoms. Lord Kṛṣṇa, the support of the Universe, placed Yudhiṣṭhira in the front (of the world as the *bonafide* emperor, but through him) he governed righteously the earth whose burden had now been lightened.

1. Aṅkura-pūrita-pālika-pātra-viśeṣaḥ—VJ.

BIOTECHNOLOGY
Cracking New Pastures

BIOTECHNOLOGY: CRACKING NEW PASTURES

C. P. Malik
Aman Verma

Prints Publications Pvt Ltd
New Delhi

Published by

Prints Publications Pvt Ltd
Viraj Tower-2, 4259/3, Ansari Road,
Darya Ganj, New Delhi-110002
Tel. : +91-11-45355555
Fax: +91-11-23275542
E-mail : contact@printspublications.com
Website : www.printspublications.com

First Edition : 2022 (Hardbound)

ISBN: 978-93-936744-9-4

Price: ₹ 2995/-

Published and Printed by Mr. Pranav Gupta (Managing Director) on behalf of Prints Publications Pvt Ltd, New Delhi.

CONTENTS

Preface

The term 'BIOTECHNOLOGY' was coined in 1919 by Hungarian engineer Karl Ereky. Since then, biotechnology is one of the key technologies in benefiting the human race. It must be seen in the context of systems biology, synthetic biology, bioinformatics and nanotechnology, whose convergence will drive new products and technologies in the future. It is a disruptive technology whose potential is not well appreciated.

Breathtaking progress has been made in biotechnology in the past 50 years, especially in the past 20 years. The global biotechnology industry is now at the initiation of a technology curve whose growing potential seems limitless.

Biotechnology is the next driver of innovation and economic growth. This cutting edge technology is already beginning to usher in complex, rapidly emerging and far-reaching new changes in several areas, particularly food and nutrition, security, healthcare and environmental sustainability. It has sparked several discoveries. Developments in this area have radically altered our concept of healthcare with the arrival of numerous products that were unthinkable 20 years ago. Such is the pace of biotechnology that it can be anticipated in the coming years that even greater developments will occur. Thanks to the projects like Human Genome Project. The cost of this global collaborative project ran approximately around $3 billion. In 2006, the full genome of, James Watson was published in full, but the project cost just $300 million. There are companies offering to sequence personnel gene map for only $1,000 or so. It is predicted that the individual genome map would soon be available for $100 or around. This is one instance of the tremendous progress biotechnology is experiencing through some cutting edge technological tools. Such projects will open up opportunities for treatment of diseases at the individual basis. On top of this several of these developments owe their advances on computer software, electronic instrumentation, imaging, and several other enabling technologies.

The fundamentals of biotechnology remain, as always, same *i.e.* production of goods and services that are needed and can be provided with safety and reasonable cost. Keeping in view the remarkable advance being made in this growing discipline, we have attempted to highlight compendium of some of these enabling technologies and advances in a volume entitled *Biotechnology: Cracking New Pastures.*

Biotechnology has revolutionized the concepts in agriculture, food and industrial feed stocks in the recent past. Techniques to enhance agricultural productivity (green biotechnology) raise value added products and healthcare systems for better environments. Biotechnology has ushered tremendous changes in agriculture, medicine and cell biology.

India has enormous opportunities to exploit the potential of this new biology and this is attributable to several factors *e.g.* enormous genetic diversity in plants, animals, microbes;

strong coordinated system; and expertise in mathematical and computational areas. In fact genomics has opened new horizons for gene mining and allele mining, which are highly significant in various research areas especially in private breeding companies.

The present book *Biotechnology: Cracking New Pastures* discusses selected topics to provide the reader a sound knowledge of selected areas in different guises, ranging from Lectins, RNAi, Bacterial biosorption of heavy metals, Increasing yield potential of grain legumes, Science of Omics, Endophytic fungi; advances in DNA transfer to prions, Chemistry and Functions of NO, etc. Each topic is written by an expert and offers the most comprehensive and up-to-date information on pertinent topic. Most of these topics are sought after by researchers and students at the graduate as well as postgraduate levels. Each chapter discusses the current status.

The strength of the book is lavishly used images, and extensive literature citation in each chapter. Certain to become the standard reference for biotechnologists, molecular biologists, breeders, applied biologists, a must for teachers and students engaged in teaching and research in physiology and plant sciences, the book is the definitive source for those who are keen to remain updated with the recent advances in biotechnology. To give a snapshot of state-of-art research in the related area where things move faster than anywhere else is next to impossible, so it is inevitable that by the time the book goes into print, some developments will have superseded, those described here. Umpteen authors and co-authors have worked on this project, and although we tried to find a more or less uniform style, the authors with their unique views and values are still recognizable.

We would like to thank all those who have contributed to the making of this book, not the least those who contributed *via* frank discussions. We sincerely apologize unreservedly for any lapses, all of which are ours.

Finally, we would like to thank our families (CP Malik, his spouse Surakhsha; Aman, her husband Kuldeep Singh, daughter Anushka Singh) for their continued forbearance, support, encouragement and love throughout the compilation of this book.

Finally, we thank Mr. Pranav Gupta, Managing Director of Prints Publications Pvt Ltd, New Delhi, for believing in us and extending their support.

C P Malik
Aman Verma

LIST OF CONTRIBUTORS

Akhilesh Kumar
National Research Centre on Plant Biotechnology (NRCPB), IARI, New Delhi

Aman Verma
School of Life Sciences, Jaipur National University, Jaipur-302 025

B. K. Garg
Central Arid Zone Research Institute, Jodhpur - 342 003

Chitra Wadhwani
School of Life Sciences, Jaipur National University, Jaipur- 302 025

C. P. Malik
School of Life Sciences, Jaipur National University, Jaipur-302 025

H Wani Shabir
Department of Plant Breeding and Genetics, Punjab Agricultural University, Ludhiana-141 004

Jin Ho Joo
Department of Biological Environment, Kangwon National University, Chuncheon-200 701, Korea

Kartikeya Tiwar
School of Life Sciences, Jaipur National University, Jaipur- 302 025

K.R. Koundal
National Research Centre on Plant Biotechnology (NRCPB), IARI, New Delhi

Manjit S Gill
Department of Plant Breeding and Genetics, Punjab Agricultural University, Ludhiana-141 004

Mohammad Humayun Kabir
School of Biotechnology, Kangwon National University, Chuncheon-200 701, Korea.

Mukesh K Upadhya
School of Life Sciences, Jaipur National University, Jaipur- 302 025

Pushp Sharma
Department of Plant Breeding and Genetics, Punjab Agricultural University, Ludhiana-141 004

Rekha Kansal
National Research Centre on Plant Biotechnology (NRCPB), IARI, New Delhi

Ritu Mahajan
School of Biotechnology, University of Jammu, Jammu

Sang Eun Oh
Department of Biological Environment, Kangwon

Sarita Bhuradia
School of Life Sciences, Jaipur National University, Jaipur- 302 025

Varsha Chaturvedi
School of Life Sciences, Jaipur National University, Jaipur- 302 025

Yaksha Singh
School of Life Sciences, Jaipur National University, Jaipur- 302 025

1

LECTINS: THEIR PROPOSED BIOLOGICAL FUNCTIONS

REKHA KANSAL, AKHILESH KUMAR, K.R. KOUNDAL AND V.K.GUPTA

INTRODUCTION

Farmers still rely on the use of pesticides for crop protection against insect pests. However, the continuous use of chemical pesticides has added to environmental problems and has led to the development of resistance in many pests. This calls for alternative approaches for crop protection that lead to reduction of inputs in energy and chemicals and also will not generate harmful effects like pesticide residues (Jouanin *et al.* 1998). Consequently, plant genetic engineering may be exploited for development of insect resistant plants by insertion and expression of genes encoding entomopathogenic proteins. The use of transgenic plants carrying δ-endotoxin encoding genes from *Bacillus thuringiensis* is already in practice. More emphasis is now being laid towards the use of plant derived genes such as those encoding enzyme inhibitors and lectins that specifically inhibit insect pests. Lectins are currently receiving the maximum interest as insecticidal agents against sap sucking homopterans including aphids, leaf and plant hoppers.

The plant lectins are a heterogenous group of carbohydrate binding proteins which differ in their molecular structure and carbohydrate binding specificity (Barre *et al.* 2001). They are found in seeds and other tissues such as leaves, bark, stems, rhizomes, bulbs, tubers, *etc.* (Peumans and Van Damme, 1995; 1998). Because of the broad distribution and ease of isolation, plant lectins are the largest and the best characterized group among lectins. Rarely, lectins that differ in their sugar specificity have been found in the same plant (Table 1), especially in legumes and the Gramineae (Lis and Sharon, 1986 a, b).

Lectins are composed of several polypeptides which are encoded by related and linked genes of lectin genes family. Lectins play an important role in seed maturation, cell-wall assembly, defense mechanism and rhizobial nodulation of legume roots (Diaz *et al.* 1989). The lectins share extensive sequence homology and three-dimensional structural similarity but differ in carbohydrate specificity (Rouge *et al.* 1991; Sharon and Lis, 1990). Many of them have been purified and characterized with respect to their molecular structure, sugar binding specificity and biological role. More than 50 of them have been sequenced, mostly by protein sequencing methods (Peumans and Van Damme, 1999; Sharon and Lis, 1990; Van Damme *et al.* 1992, 1998). Yim *et al.* (2001) suggested the use of novel plant lectin libraries to discriminate in a highly specific manner among a variety of cell types. This technology might be very useful in a number of different applications requiring a high level of specificity in cell identification. Uses of plant lectins in bioscience and biomedicine have been reviewed by Pusztai *et al.* (2008).

Lectins other than those of the legumes also combine with carbohydrates, primarily by a network of hydrogen bonds and hydrophobic interactions. However, different amino acids are often employed for the same purpose, even for combination with the same ligand. In fact, essentially all side chains capable of forming hydrogen bonds with sugars do so in one lectin-carbohydrate complex or another (Table 1). Although carboxylic and carboxyamino acids are most common, basic and hydroxyamino acids, as well as aromatic ones, also participate in ligand binding. Because most saccharides are uncharged, ionic (charge-charge) interactions are not often found in lectin-saccharide complexes (Sharon and Lis, 2002).

HISTORY

Plant lectins were originally detected by the medical student Stillmark (1888), in the University of Dorpat/Estonia when he was working on his dissertation thesis on castor beans (*Ricinus communis* L.). At this time he described the presence of a toxic proteinaceous factor in extracts from castor beans, which also agglutinated red blood cells. To indicate the source in which it had been found the name ricin was given. Thus, historically, this fact is considered the true starting point of the research on plant lectins (Rudiger and Gabius, 1998). Soon after Stillmark's discovery, ricin and the related toxin from jequirity beans (*Abrus precatorius*, Leguminosae) played a fundamental role as model antigen in the pioneering studies of Paul Ehrlich. The first legume lectin isolated was concanavalin A from jack bean (*Canavalia ensiformis*) seeds. The prominent biochemist James B. Summer, well known for demonstrating that an enzyme (urease) is nothing but a protein, succeeded in purifying also the agglutinating principle from these seeds by crystallization and called Con A is able to interact with red blood cells as well as with starch, glycogen and mucins and these interaction can be prevented by low molecular weight carbohydrates such as sucrose.

DEFINITION

The term lectin (derived from a latin verb "legre" means "to select") was coined by Boyd many years later to emphasize the ability of some hemagglutinins to discriminate blood cells within the ABO blood group system (Boyd and Shapleigh, 1954). Presently, the term lectin is prevalent over that of hemagglutinin and is broadly one non-catalytic domain, which binds reversibly to a specific mono- or oligosaccharide (Peumans and Van Damme, 1998). Alternatively, lectins are also defined as proteins or glycoproteins of non-immune origin with one or more binding sites per subunit, which can reversibly bind to specific sugar segments through hydrogen bonds and Van der Waals interactions (Lis and Sharon, 1998). Both these definitions are very comprehensive and include non-agglutinating and some enzyme proteins (Van Damme *et al.* 1998, 1997) such as the class I plant chitinase, considered as a lectin because its single carbohydrate-binding domain is structurally distinct of its catalytic site and does not directly participate in the chitinolytic activity of this enzyme (Peumans and Van Damme, 1998). Obviously, chitinases cannot be called as agglutinins or phytohemagglutinins since they do not possess agglutination and/or glycoconjugate precipitation properties, as they are not multivalent carbohydrate-binding proteins. Another class of plant proteins which are also considered as lectins, according to the above definitions, is the type 2 RIPs (ribosome-inactivating proteins). Type-2-RIPs are the lectins that catalytically inactivate ribosomes or eukaryotes and therefore irreversibly shut down protein synthesis. They bind galactose, N-acetyl galactosamine and N-acetyl neuraminic acid.

OCCURRENCE

Generally, the richest sources for most lectins are the seeds or storage organ of plants. Apart from seeds in most plants studied so far there are few examples which show lectin presence.

Root : *Urtica, Phytolacca, Sambucus, Calystegia*

Tuber or Bulb : *Solanum, Galanthus, Scilla, Allium*

Bark : *Sambucus, Sophora, Robinia, Cytisus*

Leaves : *Aloe, Lactuca, Vicia unijuga, Viscum album*

Lectins are found in the protein bodies inside cells which proliferate at endoplasmic reticulum (ER) and transported *via* Golgi apparatus and originate by subdividing the vacuole. In addition to this intracellular site lectins have also been found in the cytoplasm and in intracellular space. The amount of lectin can vary markedly from one plant species to other. The data compiled on the basis of purification from various plants is given in Table 2.

BIOSYNTHESIS

The biosynthesis of most plant lectins studied so far proceeds *via* the secretory pathway. In brief, the lectin is synthesized at ribosomes attached to the ER, enters the lumen, and is further transported through the Golgi apparatus. In contrast to secretory proteins in a narrow sense, which moves to the cell membrane by vesicular transport and then leave the cell by exocytosis, lectins (other protein as typical storage proteins) end up in the vacuole.

TABLE 1 : Different lectins combining with the same ligand

Ligand	*Lectin*	*H-bonding residues*
Mannose	Con A	Asn, Asp
	GNL	Asn, Asp, Gln, Tyr
	MBP-A	Asn, Glu
Galactose	ACA	Asn, His, Thr
	ECorL	Asn, Asp
	Galectin 1	Arg, Asn, His, Glu

Con A, concanavalin A; GNL, *Galanthus nivalis* lectin; MBP-A, mannose binding protein A; ACA, *Amaranthus caudatus* agglutinin; ECorL, *Erythtrina corallodendron* lectin

TABLE 2 : Legume lectins: their carbohydrate specificity and amount in seeds

S.No.	*Plant Species*	*Carbohydrate specificity (Monosaccharides)*	*mg lectin per 100 g seeds*
1	*Canavalia ensiformis*	Man/Glc	2100
2	*Ricinus communis*	Gal	1400
3	*Vicia cracca*	Man/Glc	1400
4	*Phaseolus vulgaris*	No monosaccharide known	1200
5	*Glycine max.*	GalNAc/Gal	300
6	*Arachis hypogaea*	Gal	190
7	*Pisum sativum*	Man/Glc	140
8	*Dolichos biflorus*	Gal/Nac	110
9	*Lens culinaris*	Man/Glc	60
10	*Bauhinia purpurea*	GalNAc	28

Man, Mannose ; Glc, Glucose ; Gal, Galactose ; Gal N Ac, N-acetylgalactosamine

On the way from the site of synthesis to its final destination, a lectin is subject to a series of covalent modifications that are common for proteins on this route: the N-terminal signal sequence of about 20-30 amino acids responsible for initiating transmembrane passage is split off co-translationally as soon as sizeable segment of the newly synthesized protein has entered the lumen of the ER. The lectins are generally synthesised as a precursor, which subsequently, after an initial removal of an N-terminal signal peptide, is post-translationally processed into a mature protein. Depending on each specific lectin, the different precursors may or may not possess carbohydrate binding activity. In about two third of the molecules, the original N- and C-termini are then ligated, resulting in a circularly permuted protein (Loris *et al.* 1998).

CLASSIFICATION

Plant lectins are subdivided into five groups, according to the monosaccharide for which they exhibit the highest affinity: D-mannose/D-glucose, D-galactose/N-acetyl-D-galactosamine, N-acetyl-D-glucosamine, L-fucose and N-acetylneuraminic acid (Goldstein *et al.* 1997). Thus depending on the specificity toward a given monosaccharide, the lectin will selectively bind to one of the above sugars which are typical constituents of eukaryotic cell surfaces (Lis and Sharon, 1998).

Considering the overall structure of plant lectins, they are subdivided into four major classes:

1- Merolectins : Single carbohydrate-binding domain;

2- Hololectins : Di- or multivalent carbohydrate-binding sites;

3-Chimerolectins : Consisting of one or more carbohydrate-binding domain(s) plus an additional catalytic or another biological activity dependent on a distinct domain other than the carbohydrate-binding site;

4- Superlectins : At least two carbohydrate-binding domains but differ from the hololectins because their sites are able to recognize structurally unrelated sugars.

Although plant lectins are considered a very complex and heterogeneous group of proteins from the biochemical/physicochemical viewpoint yet sequence, structural information and molecular cloning of lectin genes enable subdivision of plant lectins in seven families of structurally and evolutionary related proteins: legume lectins; chitin binding lectins; type 2- RIPs and related lectins; monocot mannose-binding lectins; jacalin-related lectins; amaranthin lectin family and cucurbit phloem lectins (Murdock and Shade, 2002). With regard to their localization, plant lectins are generally most abundant in the seeds but they are also found in different vegetative tissues such as roots, leaves, bark, flowers, bulbs and rhizomes (Van Damme *et al.* 2000).

At present the most accepted classification is based on protein sequences which groups lectins into seven distinct families (Peumans and Van Damme, 1999) *viz.* the legume lectins, monocot mannose–binding lectins, jacalins, chitin-binding lectins, type 2-RIPs, amaranthins, and cucurbitaceae phloem lectins (Table 3). Among these, legume lectins are extensively studied lectin proteins, which are present in several hundreds of species of legumes. A database named Lectindb has been developed for plant lectins (Chandra *et al.* 2006).

LEGUME LECTINS

Although, among all the grain crops, legumes (also known as pulses) rank third after cereals and oilseeds in world production, but constitute an important dietary constituent for humans and animals daily diet. Grain legumes provide about a third of all dietary protein nitrogen and a third of processed vegetable oil for human consumption. Seeds of grain legumes contain at least 20-40% of protein (Wang *et al.* 2003) and in India it is the major source of protein, which people take in their daily diet. Thus, India stands top in the world for legume production (Table 4).

An important additional reason for the interest in legume lectins is their structural similarity to lectins from other sources, such as the galectins of animals. Typically, the members of this protein family consist of two or four subunits (or protomers), either identical or slightly different, each with a single, small carbohydrate-combining site with the same specificity.

TABLE 3 : Types of lectins and their source

S. No.	*Plant lectin type*	*Source*
1	Legume lectins	*Arachis hypogaea* (Peanut), *Canavalia ensiformis* (Jackbean-Con A), *Dolichos biflorus* lectin (DBL), *Lens culinaris* (lentil lectin), *Pisum sativum* (Pea lectin), *Glycine max* (soybean agglutinin), *Phaseolus vulgaris (PHA-L)* and *Dolichos lablab (Fril)*
2	Monocot mannose-binding (Bulb) lectins	*Galanthus nivalis* agglutinin (Snowdrop lectin) and *Allium sativum* (Garlic bulb lectin),
3	Cereal or Chitin-binding lectins	*Triticum vulgaris (WGA)*
4	Jacalin lectins	*Artocarpus integrifolia* (Jacalin), *Helianthus tuberosus* lectin (Heltuba)
5	Type 2-RIPs	*Ricinus communis* (Ricin B)
6	Amaranthin lectins	*Amaranthus caudatus* (ACA)
7	Cucurbitaceae phloem lectins	*Lagenaria siceraria, Cucumis melo*

TABLE 4 : Statistics of common Indian legume crops

Legume species (% of world production)	*Centre of origin*	*Production (MMT)*		*Major Producers (%)*	*India's rank in production*
		World	*Developing Country*		
Peanut (*Arachis hypogaea*)	South America	34.07	32.32	China (44)	Second
Common bean (*Phaseolus vulgaris*)	Central America	18.33	15.75	Brazil (17)	Second
Chickpea (*Cicer arietinum*)	Turkey	7.80	7.41	India (86)	First
Cowpea (*Vigna unguiculata*)	Ethiopia	3.68	3.64	Nigeria (65)	First
Pigeon pea (*Cajanas cajan*)	India	2.99	2.99	India (81)	First
Lentil (*Lens culinaris*)	Near East	2.94	2.94	India (33)	First
Green pea (*Pisum sativum*)	Peninsula	9.06	6.28	India (42)	First

(Source: FAO stat 2002)

They also contain one ion each of tightly attached calcium and manganese per subunit, which are required for carbohydrate binding. The subunits are of 25-30 kDa and are commonly composed of a single polypeptide chain of 250 amino acids. Most, but not all, are glycosylated and carry up to three asparagine-linked oligosaccharides per subunit (Imberty *et al.* 2000). The primary structures of the lectins of this family are remarkably homologous, with 20% of invariant amino acids and close to 20% of similar ones. The conserved amino acids include several of those that participate in hydrogen bonding or hydrophobic interactions with the monosaccharide held in the combining site and almost all residues that coordinate the metal ions. Currently, over 100 three-dimensional structures of more than 20 legume lectins, without as well as with various carbohydrate ligands, have been elucidated by high-resolution X-ray crystallography (Bettler *et al.* 2001). The legume lectin subunits, all of which are nearly super imposable, are in the shape of a dome. They consist largely of anti parallel sheets and possess a topology related to the jelly roll fold that is known as "the lectin fold" (Srinivasan *et al.* 1996). The same fold has been observed in a number of other proteins from diverse sources, including the mammalian galectins. The carbohydrate-binding sites of the legume lectins, similarly to those of other lectins, are in the form of shallow depressions on the surface of the protein. They are located at the top of each subunit and are accessible not just to monosaccharides but to oligosaccharides as well. The Ca^{2+} and Mn^{2+} are 4.25 Å apart and are in close proximity (9-13 Å) to the carbohydrate-binding site. The sites appear to be preformed because few conformational changes occur upon carbohydrate binding.

STRUCTURE

The first legume lectin structure to be solved was of concanavalin A (con A) (Baker, 1975; Hardman and Ainsworth, 1972). The structure belonged to 'jelly-roll motif' commonly found in viral coat proteins. It has a nearly flat six-stranded rear β-sheet and a curved seven-stranded front β-sheet. A short five membered β-sheet on top holds the two larger sheets together. In addition, a number of loops connecting the strands are also present. Two metal ions, calcium and a transition metal, found in all the legume lectin structures are essential for the carbohydrate binding. The metal ions are bound to four protein atoms and two water molecules. Till date more than 100 legume lectins have been isolated and out of them 50 have been sequenced. Among these, more than 20 legume lectins 3-D structure have been solved. Legume lectins consist of two or four subunits of 25-30 kDa, each with one Ca^{2+} and one Mn^{2+} required for activity. Their tertiary structures are super imposable; quaternary structures are different, possess diverse carbohydrate specificities and have a single combining site per subunit (Sharon and Lis, 2002).

One interesting aspect about legume lectin structures is their different quaternary association, independent of carbohydrate specificity. It is observed that small sequence dependent variations in tertiary structure lead to large changes in quaternary association (Manoj and Suguna, 2001). The dimeric structure found in the crystals of ConA, Pea lectin, Lentil lectin and Lathyrus lectin is termed as 'canonical dimer'. This dimer is formed by side-by-side arrangement of two monomers in such a way that the two rear β sheets form a contiguous 12-stranded β-sheet. However, this type of canonical dimer is missing in the crystal structures of *EcoRI*, *GSIV* and Peanut lectins. The dimers of these lectins posses back to back arrangement ('hand shake dimer') of the subunits (Srinivas *et al.* 2001).

All legume lectins have similar carbohydrate-binding sites (Loris *et al.* 1998). The four loops A, B, C, D, shown in red, purple, yellow and blue color in Fig. 1 associated with the concave face of the seven-stranded curved β-sheet at the top front side of the subunit form the binding site (Sharma and Surolia, 1997). The amino acid residues which bind metal ions (Ca^{2+} and Mn^{2+}) are highly conserved and the residues which constitute the sugar binding site are less conserved but similar in properties (Lis and Sharan, 1998).

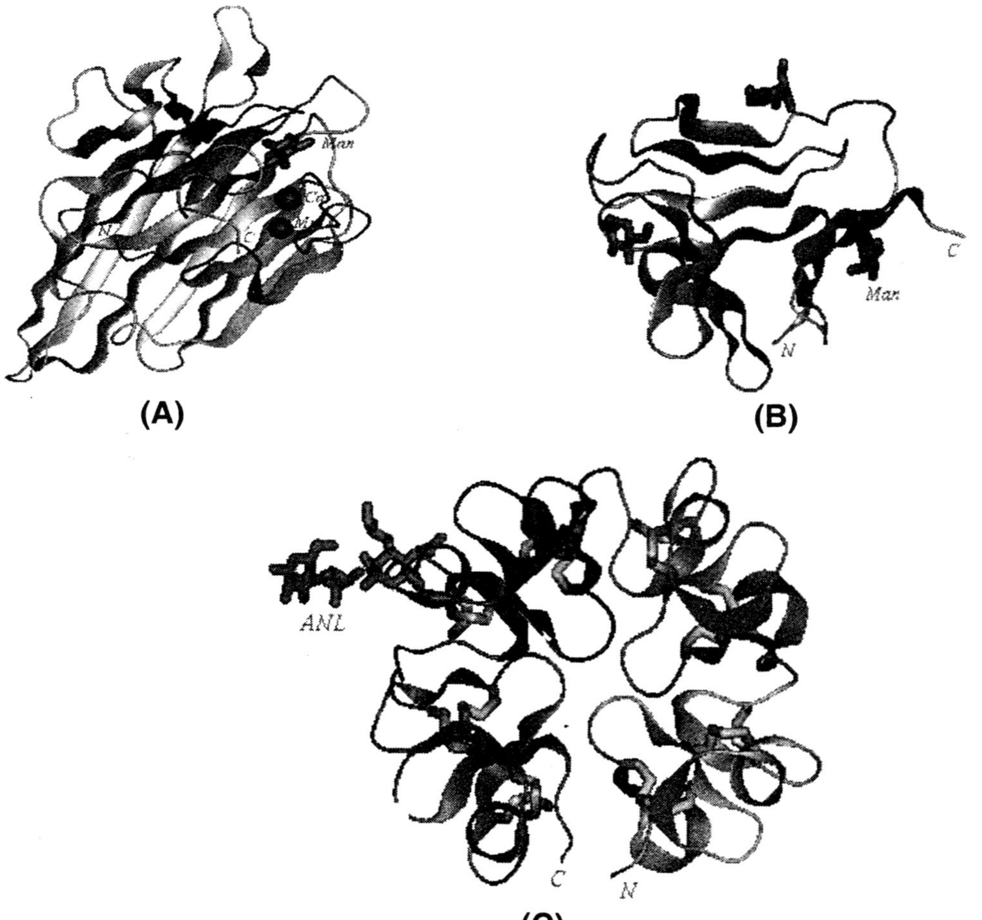

Fig.1. Crystal structures of subunits of, (A) Concanavalin A bound to mannose (Man), Ca and Mn are calcium and manganese ions, (B) *Galanthus nivalis* agglutinin (GNA) bound to mannose at three sites, (C) Wheat germ agglutinin bound to a-N-Acetyl Neuraminyl Lactose (ANL), disulfide bonds are shown in yellow.

The conserved residues Asp and Gly (or Arg) are from loops A and B, whereas Asn and the hydrophobic residues (Phe, Tyr, Trp or Leu) are from loop C. The size of the backbone of this loop is the primary determinant of carbohydrate specificity in legume lectins. The overall conformational changes observed upon sugar binding are small in legume lectins. The aligned sequences of legume lectins show 4 to 7 gaps in the binding loop D, admitting variation in the loop size (Sharma and Surolia, 1997). This partly explains the broad specificity of legume lectins compared to other lectin families.

ANTI-NUTRITIONAL PROPERTIES

A few lectins such as the lectin found in red kidney beans (the PHA lectin), are, however, known to damage the structure of the small intestine, or affect the pancreas and production of digestive enzymes when eaten by humans or animals. This is why kidney beans are always soaked and boiled before use, a process, which effectively destroys the lectin, making beans fit for human consumption. One of the most nutritionally important features of plant lectins is their ability to survive digestion by the gastrointestinal tract of consumers. This allows the lectins to bind to membrane glycosyl groups of the cells lining the digestive tract. As a result of this interaction a series of harmful local and systemic reactions are triggered placing this class of molecules as nutritative and/or toxic substances. Locally, they can affect the turnover and loss of gut epithelial cells, damage the luminal membranes of the epithelium, interfere with nutrient digestion and absorption, stimulate shifts in the bacterial flora and modulate the immune state of the digestive tract. Thus, they are also detrimental to numerous insect pests of crop plants although less is presently known about their insecticidal mechanism of action (Iika and Oliveira, 2004).

In addition to feeding studies made with transgenic potato themselves, several experiments included the addition of isolated purified lectins (Con A and GNA) to raw and cooked potato both in amounts similar to that in the transgenic potato and in amounts greatly in excess of those in the transgenic plant. One long term feeding study and several short-term studies were made with potato tuber expressing GNA. These showed, as expected, no discernable effect on growth. No comparable experiments were made with transgenic plants expressing the ConA in a concentration some 5000-times that found tuber expressing the ConA gene. Addition of isolated ConA at this concentration did cause a small depression in growth rate. However, lectins from different sources have different properties, and thus one lectin may be mitogenic, while another lectin is not. With the exception of several well-studied lectins, little is known about their precise effects when fed as part of the diet on the cells of the gut and immune system of mammals. Given the interest in the possible future introduction of lectin genes to provide pest resistance in crops, it is important that suitable tools are developed to evaluate the potential effect of lectins on animals, including any possible effect on the immune system.

PHYSIOLOGICAL FUNCTIONS

The wide distribution of lectins in all tissues of plants and their ubiquitous presence in the plant kingdom suggest important roles for these proteins. Despite their long history, the true physiological role of legume lectins is still not well understood. Sharon (2007) gave an overview of plant lectins including their physiological roles. Many hypotheses have been formulated in the course of the years but, at present, no physiological function for any legume lectin has been established with certainty. The difficulty in assigning a precise role arises from several of their features. The defining characteristic of all lectins is their carbohydrate-binding ability. This activity has been preserved during evolution, suggesting that it is essential for exploitation of their function. Nevertheless, some lectins possess additional activities that may be non-secondary in determining their following physiological role.

(*i*) In signal transduction

Several legume lectins, for instance, present adenine-combining sites able to bind active forms of the cytokinins, a major class of plant hormones. (Gegg *et al.* 1992) The specificity of adenine-binding sites has been maintained during evolution despite variations in carbohydrate specificity and tissue distribution. Therefore, it may be possible that in such cases proteins have a primary role unrelated to carbohydrates, *e.g.* hormone-binding, and that the carbohydrate-combining activity plays a regulatory or transducing function. In general, a single legume plant can contain a variety of lectins that may have evolved by gene duplication and become specialized for different roles in the plant (Etzler, 1992) Furthermore, despite being concentrated in plant seeds, lectins are also present in different tissues, where their function probably requires lower concentrations. Lectin plays a role in jasmonate/ethylene-responsive defense reaction. Plant lectins have not traditionally been thought to be inducible proteins but it has been found that lectin gene expression is induced by jasmonate and ethylene, consistent with defense role for this gene. Thus, in other words we can say that lectin is involved in endogenous developmental cues or external stresses (Lyou *et al.* 2009).

(*ii*) As plant antibodies

Early investigators noted the similarities of lectins to antibodies and asparagines that lectins might function as plant antibodies (Bird, 1959). One of the early events in the defence response of legumes is the production of phytoalexins (Dixon, 1995), whose synthesis is stimulated by the release of elicitors, many of which are oligosaccharides that arise from the breakdown of plant or pathogen cell wall components (Cote and Hahn, 1994). Therefore, lectins could participate in this step of the defense process either acting as receptors for elicitors or the elicitors in structures required by their receptors. It has been shown that the levels of *Dolichos biflorus* stem and leaf lectin, DB58, increase upon plant wounding (Etzler, 1998).

(*iii*) In symbiosis

Again, based on their carbohydrate-binding ability, lectins have also been thought to be involved in the establishment of symbiosis between nitrogen-fixing bacteria and plants (De Hoff *et al.* 2009; Etzler, 1986 and Sharon and Lis, 1989). Legumes are able to associate specifically and form symbiosis with soil bacteria of the rhizobia family, a phenomenon that makes them independent from soil nitrogen supplies. The idea that lectins are responsible for this association was advanced over 20 years ago and it has been the subject of much controversy. It has been suggested that root lectin recognized by bacterial receptor molecules is an important determinant of host plant specificity in *Rhizobium* legume symbiosis (Bohlool and Schmidt, 1974). Rhizobium adheres to the surface of differentiated root cells and is then internalized into the root hair to form nitrogen-fixing nodules. This symbiosis is specific in that certain species of Rhizobium can only associate with a particular species of legumes. It has been shown that bacteria that nodulate beans are agglutinated by bean extracts. Also, erythrocytes that can be agglutinated by the bean lectin bind to root hairs. Infact, nitrogen-fixing symbiosis is a multistep process that requires the formation of the root nodule, followed by the adhesion of the bacteria to the roots with the help of lectin (Mylona *et al.* 1995).

(*iv*) As toxins

It has been shown that plant lectins possess cytotoxic, fungitoxic, anti-insect and anti-nematode properties either *in vitro* or *in vivo* and are toxic to higher animals (Oka *et al.* 1997; Oliveira *et al.* 1994 and Ripoll *et al.* 2003); for example, the toxic effects of PHA, the lectin from *Phaseolus vulgaris*, on monogastric animals are well documented (Pusztai, 1991; Martinez-Aragon *et al.* 1995), and the expression in transgenic plants of genes encoding for the lectins GNA (from *Galanthus nivalis*; snowdrop), PSA (*Pisum sativum*; pea), WGA (*Triticum vulgare*; wheatgerm), ConA (*Canavalia ensiformis*; jack bean), AIA (*Artocarpus integrifolia*; jack fruit), OSA (*Oryza sativa*; rice) and UDA (*Urtica dioica*; stinging nettle) resulted in added protection against insect pests and/or phytopathogenic nematodes or fungi (Hilder *et al.* 1995; Hilder and Boulter, 1999; Powell, 2001; Ripoll *et al.* 2003). One of the most important features of plant lectins, compatible with the proposed defensive function, is the remarkably high resistance to proteolysis and stability over a large range of pH, even when they are out of their natural environment.

(*v*) In embryogenesis

Evidences exist for their involvement in embryogenesis, development and reproduction. Two lectin genes MsLEC1 and MsLEC2 from alfalfa cloned in antisense orientation and expressed in alfalfa lead to severe embryogenic, developmental and reproductive abnormalities (Brill *et al.* 2001).

(*vi*) As clinical tool

The lectins, proteins which characteristically bind with carbohydrate moieties, have been extensively studied in many biochemical and structural aspects in order to understand the molecular basis behind this non-catalytic event. At the same time, their clinical and agricultural potentials have been growing fast day-by-day. Over the last few decades, lectins have become a topic of interest to a large number of researchers owing to their potentially exploitable biological properties including antitumor, immunomodulatory and anti-insect, antifungal, antibacterial, anti-HIV, and mitogenic activities. Because of their sugar binding properties, lectins have been extensively studied and used as molecular tools for the study of carbohydrate architecture and dynamics on the cell surface, and have been exploited for such practical applications as distinguishing between normal and malignant cells, purification of glycoconjugate, and coating of drugs to enhance their gastrointestinal tract absorption. Although lectins, mainly those from legume plants, have been investigated for biological properties and plenty of studies concerning their physiological functions have been done in last decade (De Mejia *et al.* 2003; Frédérich *et al.* 2009; Islam *et al.* 2009; Rhodes, 1999). Kaur *et al.* (2005) isolated two mannose/glucose specific seed lectins from *Parkia biglandulosa* and *Parkia roxburghii* and characterized these for various physicochemical properties. *Parkia biglandulosa* lectin was found to be T-cell mitogen as revealed by IL-2 bioassay. These lectins showed anti-proliferative effect on two murine macrophage cancer cell lines *i.e.* P 388DI (50%) and J774 (70%). Liu *et. al.* (2009) have briefly presented the advances of plant lectins in elucidating their complex anti-cancer mechanisms implicated in apoptosis and autophagy. In addition, they have discussed the pre-clinical and clinical studies of plant lectins for their potential therapeutic applications.

(*vii*) In growth process

Probably, interaction with the hormone system determines the role of lectin in growth and development. Maximal lectin content was found in rapidly growing adventitious roots and leaf base of wheat seedlings. A possible mechanism is the involvement of lectins in inhibition of auxin-dependent catabolism of cell wall polysaccharides and growth by stretching. In the case of compatible pollination in petunia and onion plants, an increase in the content of lectins in the pistil sporophyte tissue was observed along with changing their carbohydrate specificity (Babosha, 2008).

(*viii*) As entomopathogenic protein

One of the possible physiological functions that have emerged is the defensive role of these carbohydrate-binding proteins against phytopathogenic microorganisms, phytophagous insects and plant-eating animals (Chrispeels and Raikhel, 1991; Gatehouse *et al.* 1995, 1996, 1997; Harper *et al.* 1995; Van Damme, 2008). Several lectin genes have been exploited for developing insect-resistant transgenic crops (Table 5). An essential feature of any active defense agent is the ability to specifically recognize the pathogen. Based on their carbohydrate-binding specificity and also considering their abundance in plant seeds and bark, lectins seem to possess all the necessary characteristics to exploit this function (Datta *et al.* 2000; Koundal *et al.* 2003; Qureshi *et al.* 2003, 2006; Sharma *et al.* 2004).

At present strategy employed by most of the worker is not only to use single genes, but also to use gene combinations whose products are targeted at different biochemical and physiological processes with in the insect. The availability of suitable promoters and effective insecticidal genes means that the application of transgenic technology can now be extended to the control of almost any order of insect in near future (Chakraborti *et al.* 2009; Datta *et al.* 2005; Hossain *et al.* 2006; Saha *et al.* 2006).

TABLE 5 : Applications of lectin genes in transgenic development

Transgenic plant	*Lectin gene used*	*Target insect*
Tobacco	Pea lectin	*Heliothis virescens*
	Snowdrop lectin (GNA)	*Myzus persicae* *Aulacorthum solani*
	Allium sativum leaf agglutinin (ASAL)	*Myzus persicae*
Potato	Snowdrop lectin (GNA)	*Myzus persicae* *Lacanobia oleracea*
Tomato	Snowdrop lectin (GNA)	*Lacanobia oleracea*
Rice	*Allium sativum* leaf agglutinin (ASAL)	*Nilaparvata lugens* *Nephotettix virescens*
Pea	Bean α-amylase inhibitor	*Callosobruchus malculatus* *Bruchus pisorum*
	Wheat germ agglutinin	*Callosobruchus maculatus*
Chickpea	*Allium sativum* leaf agglutinin (ASAL)	*Aphis craccivora*
Mustard	*Allium sativum* leaf agglutinin (ASAL)	*Lipaphis erysimi*
Sugarcane	Snowdrop lectin (GNA)	*Antitrogus consanguineus*
Cotton	Snowdrop lectin (GNA)	*Heliothis virescens*

Legume lectins represent the largest and most thoroughly studied family of these sugar-binding proteins. Over 100 members of this family are known, almost all isolated from seeds of the plants (Sharon and Lis, 2002). Because they are readily obtainable in purified form and exhibit an amazing variety of sugar specificities, these lectins are eminently suitable for tackling the question of how proteins bind carbohydrates. Lectin genes of plant origin have an added advantage, as when transferred, they are correctly transcribed, translated and processed in a plant host. Most of the lectin genes are devoid of introns and therefore, both genomic as well as cDNA clones can be mobilized for developing transgenic plants. Owing to the popularity of lectins as a tool in biochemistry, cell biology, medicine and plant biotechnology, an overview of lectins was presented in this chapter.

REFERENCES

Babosha AV (2008) Inducible lectins and plant resistance to pathogens and abiotic stress *Biochemistry* (Moscow) **73(7)**: 812-825

Baker JW Reeke GN Wang JL Cunningham BA and Edelman GM (1975) The covalent and three-dimensional structure of concanavalin A *J Biol Chem* **250**: 1513-1524

Barre A Bourne Y Van Damme EJM Peumans WJ and Rouge P (2001) Mannose binding plant lectins: Differential structural scaffolds for a common recognition process *Biochimie* **83**: 645-651

Bettler E Loris R and Imberty A (2001) 3D lectin databank www.cermav.cnrs.fr/databank.lectine

Bird GWG and Sang V (1959) Hemagglutinins in seeds *British Med Bull* **15**: 165

Bohlool BB and Schmidt EL (1974) Lectins: A possible basis for specificity in the *Rhizobium*-Legume root nodule symbiosis *Science* **185**: 269-271

Boyd WC and Shapleigh E (1954) Specific precipitating activity of plant agglutinins (lectins) *Science* **119**: 419

Brill LM Evans CJ and Hirsch AM (2001) Expression of MsLEC1 and MsLEC2 antisense genes in alfalfa plant lines causes severe embryogenic developmental and reproductive abnormalities *Plant J* **25**: 453-461

Chakraborti D Sarkar A Mondal HA and Das S (2009) Tissue specific expression of potential insecticidal, *Allium sativum* leaf agglutinin (ASAL) in important pulse crop chickpea (*Cicer arietinum*) to resist the phloem feeding *Aphis craccivora Transgenic Res* **18(4)**: 529-544

Chandra NR Kumar N Jeyakani J Singh DD Gowda SB Prathima MN (2006) Lectindb: a plant lectin database *Glycobiology* **16**: 938–946

Chrispeels MJ and Raikhel NV (1991) Lectins, lectin genes and their role in plant defense *Plant Cell* **3**: 1-9

Cote F and Hahn MG (1994) Oligosaccharins: structures and signal transduction *Plant Mol Biol* **26**: 1379-1411

Datta I Saha P Majumdar P Sarkar A Chakraborti D Banerjee S and Das S (2005) The efficacy of a novel insecticidal protein *Allium sativum* leaf lectin (ASAL) against homopteran insects monitored in transgenic tobacco *Plant Biotechnol J* **3(6)**: 601-611

Datta S Kansal R and Koundal KR (2000) Construction and screening of cowpea (*Vigna unguiculata* L.) cDNA library for lectin genes *J Plant Biochem Biotechnol* **6**: 67-71

De Hoff PL Brill LM and Hirsch AM (2009) Plant lectins: the ties that bind in root symbiosis and plant defense *Mol Genet Genomics* **282(1)**: 1-15

De Mejia EG Bradford T and Hasler C (2003) The anticarcinogenic potential of soybean lectin and lunasin *Nutr Rev* **61(7)**: 239-246

Diaz C Melchers LS Hooykaas PJJ Lugtenberg BJJJ and Kijne JW (1989) Root lectins as determinant of host plant specificity in the *Rhizobium*-legume symbiosis *Nature* **338**: 579-581

Dixon RA and Paiva NL (1995) Stress-induced phenylpropanoid metabolism *Plant Cell* **7**: 1085-1097

Etzler ME (1986) In: *The Lectins: Properties, Functions and Applications in Biology and Medicine*; Liener IE Sharon N and Goldstein IJ (eds.) Academic Press Orlando pp 371

Etzler ME (1998) From structure to activity: New insights into the functions of legume lectins *Trends Glycosci Glycotechnol* **10**: 247–55

Etzler ME (1992) Plant lectins: Molecular biology, synthesis and function In:*Glycoconjugates: Composition, Structure and Function*; Allen HJ and Kisailus EC (eds.) Marcel Dekker New York pp 521-539

Frédérich M Marcowycz A Cieckiewicz E Mégalizzi V Angenot L and Kiss R (2009) *In vitro* anticancer potential of tree extracts from the Walloon region forest *Planta Med* [Epub ahead of print]

Gatehouse AMR Down RE Powell KS Sauvion N Rahbe Y Newell CA Merryweather A Hamilton WDO and Gatehouse JA (1996) Transgenic potato plants with resistance to the peach potato aphid *Myzus persicae Entomol Exp Appl* **79**: 295-307

Gatehouse JA Gatehouse AMR and Fitches E (1997) Effects of snowdrop lectin (GNA) delivered *via* artificial diet and transgenic plants on the development of tomato moth (*Lacanobia oleracea*) larvae in laboratory and glasshouse trials *J Insect Physiol* **43(8)**: 727-739

Gatehouse AMR Powell KS Peumans WJ Van Damme EJ and Gatehouse JA (1995) Insecticidal properties of plant lectins: Their potential in plant protection In: *Lectins: Biomedical Perspectives*; Pusztai A and Bardocz S (eds.) Taylor and Francis London pp 35–38

Gegg CV Roberts DD Segel IH and Etzler ME (1992) Characterization of the adenine binding sites of two *Dolichos biflorus* lectins *Biochemistry* **31(30)**: 6938-6942

Goldstein IJ Winter HC and Poretz RD (1997) Plant lectins: Tools for the study of complex carbohydrates In: *Glycoproteins II*; Montreuil J Vliegenthart JFG and Schachter H (eds.) Elsevier Amsterdam pp 403–474

Hardman KD and Ainsworth CF (1972) Structure of concanavalinA at 2.4-A° resolution *Biochemistry* **11**: 4910-4919

Harper SM Crenshaw RW Mullins MA and Privalle LS (1995) Lectin binding to insect brush border membranes *J Econ Entomol* **88(6)**: 1197–1202

Hilder VA Powell KS Gatehouse AMR Gatehouse JA Gatehouse LN Shi Y Hamilton WD Merryweather A Newell CA and Timans JC (1995) Expression of snowdrop lectin in transgenic tobacco plants results in added protection against aphids *Transgenic Res* **4**: 18–25

Hilder VA and Boulter D (1999) Genetic engineering of crop plants for insect resistance a critical review *Crop Protection* **18**: 177-191

Hossain MA Maiti MK Basu A Sen S Ghosh AK and Sen SK (2006) Transgenic expression of onion leaf lectin gene in Indian mustard offers protection against aphid colonization *Crop Sci* **46**: 2022-2032

Iika M and Oliveira VT (2004) Antinutritional properties of plant lectins *Toxicon* **44 (4)**: 385-403

Imberty A Gautier C Lescart J P´erez S Wyns L and Loris R (2000) An unusual carbohydrate-binding site revealed by the structures of two *Maackia amurensis* lectins complexed with sialic acid-containing oligosaccharides *J Biol Chem* **275**: 17541–48

Islam B Khan SN Naeem A Sharma V Khan AU (2009) Novel effect of plant lectins on the inhibition of *Streptococcus mutans* biofilm formation on saliva-coated surface *J Appl Microbiol* **106(5)**: 1682-1689

Jouanin L Bonade-Bottino M Girard C Morrot G and Giband M (1998) Transgenic plants for insect resistance *Plant Sci* **131**: 1-11

Koundal KR Dash PK and Kansal R (2003) Plant defense proteins: Mechanism and potential of pest control through genetic manipulation *J Plant Biol* **30(2)**: 211-227

Lis H and Sharon N (1998) Lectins: Carbohydrate-specific proteins that mediate cellular recognition *Chem Rev* **98**: 637-674

Lis H and Sharon N (1986a) Lectins as molecules and as tools *Annu Rev Biochem* **55**: 35-67

Lis H and Sharon N (1986b) In: *The Lectins: properties, functions and applications in biology and medicine;* Liener IE Sharon N and Goldstein IJ (eds.) Academic press New York

Liu B Bian H and Bao J (2009) Plant lectins: Potential antineoplastic drugs from bench to clinic *Cancer Lett* doi:10.1016/j.canlet.2009.05.013

Loris R Hamelryck T Bouckaert J and Wyns L (1998) Legume lectin structure *Biochim Biophys Acta* **1383**: 9-36

Lyou SH Park HJ Jung C Sohn HB Lee G Kim CH Kim M Choi YD and Cheong JJ (2009) The Arabidopsis At LEC gene encoding a lectin like protein is up-regulated by multiple stimuli including developmental signal, wounding, jasmonate, ethylene, and chitin elicitor *Mol Cells* **27**: 75-81

Manoj N and Suguna K (2001) Signature of quaternary structure in the sequences of legume lectins *Protein Engg* **14**: 735-745

Martinez-Aragon A Cavallé C Frühbeck G Tosar A Santidrian S Stewart JC Rubio L and Pusztai A (1995) Identification and biological activity of lectins of different subunit composition isolated from *Phaseolus vulgaris* L var. athropurpurea *J Food Sci Technol* **68**: 375-381

Murdock LL and Shade RE (2002) Lectins and protease inhibitors as plant defenses against insects *J Agric Food Chem* **50**: 6605- 6611

Mylona P Mylona D Pawlowski and Bisseling T (1995) Symbiotic nitrogen fixation *Plant Cell* **7**: 869-885

Navjot K Jatinder S Kamboj SS Agrewala JN and Kaur M (2005) Two novel lectins from *Parkia biglandulosa* and *Parkia roxburghii*: isolation, physicochemical characterization, mitogenicity and anti- proliferative activity *Protein Peptide Lett* **12(6)**: 589-595

Oka Y Chet I and Spiegel Y (1997) Accumulation of lectins in cereal roots invaded by the cereal cyst nematode *Heterodera avenae Physiol Mol Plant Pathol* **51**: 333-345

Oliveira SM Dias-Baruffi SMO Thomaz LM Beltramini and Roque-Barreira MC (1994) Neutrophil migration-inducing lectin from *Artocarpus integrifolia J Immunol* **153**: 1798–1807

Peumans WJ and Van Damme EJM (1995) Lectins as plant defense proteins *Plant Physiol* **109**: 347-352

Peumans WJ and Van Damme EJM (1998) Plant lectins: specific tools for the identification, isolation, and characterization of O-linked glycans *Crit Rev Biochem Mol Biol* **33(3)**: 209-258

Peumans WJ and Van Damme EJM (1999) Seed lectins In: Seed Proteins Shewry PR and Casey R (eds.) Kluwer Academic Publishers The Netherlands 657-683

Powell KS (2001) Antimetabolic effects of plant lectins towards nymphal stages of the planthoppers *Tarophagous proserpina* and *Nilaparvata lugens Entomologia Experimentalis et Applicata* **99**: 71–77

Pusztai A Watt WB and Stewart JC (1991) A comprehensive scheme for the isolation of trypsin inhibitors and the agglutinin from soybean seeds *J Agri Food Chem* **39**: 862-866

Pusztai A Bardocz S and Ewen SW (2008) Uses of plant lectins in bioscience and biomedicine *Front Biosci* **13**: 1130-1140

Qureshi IA Dash PK Kansal R Srivastav PS and Koundal KR (2003) Isolation and characterization of a lectin from seeds of *Cicer arietinum Indian J Plant Physiol* **8**: 625-629

Qureshi IA Dash PK Kansal R Srivastav PS and Koundal KR (2006) Purification and characterization of an N-acetyl-D-galactosamine specific lectin from seeds of chickpea (*Cicer arietinum* L.) *Phytochem Anal* **17(5)**: 350-356

Rhodes JM (1999) Beans means lectins *Gut* **44(5)**: 593-594

Ripoll C Favery B Lecomte P Van Damme E Peumans W and Abad P (2003) Evaluation of the ability of lectin from snowdrop (*Galanthus nivalis*) to protect plants against root-knot nematodes *Plant Sci* **164 (4)**: 517-523

Rouge P Cambillu C and Bourne Y (1991) The three-dimensional structure of legume lectins In: Lectin Reviews Kilpatrick DC Van Driessche E and BogHansen TC (eds.) Vol.1 Sigma Chemical Co. St.Louis USA pp.143-159

Rudiger H and Gabius HJ (2001) Plant lectins: Occurrence, biochemistry, functions and applications *Glycoconj J* **18**: 589-613

Saha P Dasgupta I and Das S (2006) A novel approach for developing resistance in rice against phloem limited viruses by antagonizing the phloem feeding hemipteran vectors *Plant Mol Biol* **62(4-5)**: 735-752

Sharma M Sahni R Kansal R and Koundal KR (2004) Transformation of oil seed mustard *Brassica juncea* (L) cv Pusa Jai Kissan with snowdrop lectin gene *Indian J Biotechnol* **3**: 97-102

Sharma V and Surolia A (1997) Analyses of carbohydrate recognition by legume lectins: size of the combining site loops and their primary activity *J Mol Biol* **267**: 433-445

Sharon N and Lis H (1989) Lectins as cell recognition molecules *Science* **246**: 227-234

Sharon N and Lis H (1990) Legume lectins a large family of homologous proteins *The FASEB J* **4**: 3198-3208

Sharon N and Lis H (2002) How protein bind carbohydrates: Lesson from Legume lectins *J Agric Food Chem* **50(22)**: 6586-6591

Sharon N (2007) Lectins: carbohydrate-specific reagents and biological recognition molecules *J Biol Chem* **282(5)**: 2753-2764

Srinivas VR Reddy GB Ahmad N Swaminathan CP Mitra N and Surolia A (2001) Legume lectin family, the 'natural mutants of the quaternary state', provide insights into the relationship between protein stability and oligomerization *Biochim Biophys Acta* **1527**: 102–111

Srinivasan N Rufino SD Pepys MB Wood SP and Blundell TL (1996) A superfamily of proteins with the lectin fold Chemtracts *Biochem Mol Biol* **6**: 149-164

Van Damme EJ Smeets K Torrekens S Van Leuven F and Peumans WJ (1992) Isolation and characterization of alliinase cDNA clones from garlic (*Allium sativum* L.) and related species *Eur J Biochem* **209(2)**: 751-757

Van Damme EJ Van Leuven F and Peumans WJ (1997) Isolation, characterization and molecular cloning of the bark lectins from *Maackia amurensis Glycoconj J* **14(4)**: 449-456

Van Damme EJM Astoul CH Barre A Rougém P and Peumans WJ (2000) Cloning and characterization of a monocot mannose binding lectin from *Crocus vernus* (family Iridaceae) *Eur J Biochem* **267**: 5067-5077

Van Damme JM Smeets K Torrekens S Van Leuven F and Peumans WJ (1994) Characterization and molecular cloning of mannose-binding lectins from the Orchidaceae species *Listera ovata, Epipactis helleborine* and *Cymbidium* hybrid *Eur J Biochem* **221 (2)**: 769-77

Van Damme EJM Peumans WJ Barre A and Rouge P (1998) Plant lectins: a composite of several distinct families of structurally and evolutionarily related proteins with diverse biological roles *Crit Rev Plant Sci* **17**: 575-692

Van Damme EJM (2008) Plant lectins as part of the plant defense system against insects In: *Induced Plant Resistance to Herbivory*; Schaller A (ed.) Springer Science and Business Media pp 285-303

Wang W Peumans WJ Rougé P Rossi C Proost P Chen J and Van Damme EJ (2003) Leaves of the Lamiaceae species *Glechoma hederacea* (ground ivy) contain a lectin that is structurally and evolutionary related to the legume lectins *Plant J* **33(2)**: 293-304

Yim M Ono T and Irimura T (2001) Mutated plant lectin library useful to identify different cells *PNAS* **98(5)**: 2222-2225

2

PHYSIOLOGICAL ASPECTS OF DROUGHT TOLERANCE IN ARID LEGUMES

B. K. GARG

Clusterbean, moth bean, cowpea and horse gram grouped together as arid legumes are known to possess different mechanisms of drought resistance to survive and reproduce under drought-prone environments. The development of short duration and early maturing varieties that enable the crop to escape severe soil moisture deficits is of paramount importance in these legumes. Most of these legumes display several mechanisms of dehydration avoidance to maintain turgor potential for normal metabolic functioning under water deficits. These comprise maximization of water uptake through deep and extensive root systems and reduction of water loss by appropriate shoot attributes and osmotic adjustment for continued photosynthesis and growth at low water potentials. Significant genotypic differences exist for different physiological attributes and drought resistance traits which need to be better understood for selection and development of drought tolerant genotypes with higher yield potential under water limited conditions. These legumes are generally most sensitive to water stress at the flowering stage and genotypic differences at this critical stage are most important. Maintenance of higher leaf turgidity, net photosynthetic rate and stomatal conductance at similar stress levels, alongwith least alterations in leaf metabolites in moth bean was also reflected in its higher yield stability under water stress as compared to clusterbean and other legumes. In addition to drought tolerance characteristics, various improved cultural practices, optimum plant nutrition and adoption of drought ameliorative measures such as thiourea application must be considered to reduce drought impact and to obtain sustainable crop yields under arid environments. Arid legumes comprising cluster bean, moth bean, cow pea and horse gram are the integrated components of dryland farming, being the main stay of pulse and forage production in arid and semi-arid regions of the country. Their average productivity is, however, very low as they are confined and concentrated in arid areas having poor fertility soils and scanty and erratic rainfall leading to frequent droughts. Therefore, it is of paramount importance to identify and develop drought tolerant genotypes based on sound physiological mechanisms that influence the performance of these legumes under water deficits (Garg, 2003; Garg and Burman, 2002 a, b). Furthermore, appropriate crop management and improved cultural practices are equally important to reduce the hazards of drought for ensuring stable yields and increased water use efficiency under drought-prone environments of arid regions (Arnon, 1992; Turner, 1997 and Garg, 2002). The available information on physiological aspects of drought tolerance in these legume crops and some of the approaches for yield improvement under drought is discussed here.

DROUGHT RESISTANCE

Drought resistance refers to the ability of a crop to produce its economic product with minimum loss in water-deficit environment relative to the water constraint free management. According to Turner (1986) the ability of a crop to produce satisfactory in areas subjected to water deficits has been termed as drought resistance. Basically three mechanisms namely drought escape, drought avoidance and drought tolerance are involved in drought resistance (Levitt, 1980) while Turner (1986) suggested that they could be classified into three major categories, explained as follows :

(1) Drought escape

It is the ability of a plant to complete its life cycle before acute soil and plant water deficit develop. This is an important strategy of matching phenological development with the period of soil moisture availability to minimise the impact of drought where the growing season is short and terminal drought predominates. This mechanism involves rapid phenological development (early flowering and maturity), developmental plasticity (variation in duration of growth period depending on the extent of water stress) and mobilization of parenthesis assimilates to grain.

(2) Drought avoidance

It is the ability of plants to maintain relativity high tissue water potential inspite a shortage of soil moisture. Drought avoidance is achieved by maintenance of turgor through increased rooting depth, efficient root systems and internal hydraulic conductance and by reduction of water loss through reduced stomatal conductance, reduced absorption of solar radiation by leaf rolling and reduces evaporation surface *i.e.* leaf area reduction, cluster bean and moth bean survive under drought conditions by doing a balancing act between maintenance of turgor and reduction of water loss.

(3) Drought tolerance

It is the capacity of plants to withstand water deficit with low tissue water potential. Tolerance to dehydration is considered to arrive at the molecular level and depends upon membrane structure and enzyme activity. Basically it is due to the ability of the cells to maintain integrity of the cell membranes and prevent denaturation of proteins.

However, crop plants including arid legumes use more than one mechanism at a time to resist drought.

DROUGHT TOLERANCE ASSESSMENT

Drought is by for the most important environmental stress in agriculture and many efforts have been made to improve crop productivity under water limiting conditions. While natural selection has favoured mechanisms for adaptations and survival, breeding activity has directed selection towards increasing the economic yield of cultivated species. Meanwhile, fundamental research has provided significant gains in the understanding of the physiological and molecular responses of plants to water deficits but there is still a large gap between yield in optimal and stress conditions. A number of physiological studies have identified some traits for which presence or expression is associated with plant adaptability to drought-prone environments. However, a critical aspect in all studies dedicated to drought tolerance is the assessment of the degree of drought tolerance of different genotypes. In many studies the identification of tolerant and susceptible cultivars is based on few physiological measures related to drought response. The difficulty in identifying physiological parameters as reliable indicator of yield in dry conditions has suggested that yield performance over a range of environments should be used as the main indicator for drought tolerance (Voltas *et al.* 2005). Several indices were proposed to describe yield performance of a given genotype under stress and nonstress conditions or in comparison with the average yield or the yield of a superior genotype. Clearly there are only few studies on this line in the arid legumes (Garg, 2008). Some authors have expressed the yielding capacity with regard to an environment-related physiological trait, such as canopy temperature (Idso *et al.* 1981) or water potential (Karamanos and Papatheohari, 1999). Rizza *et al.* (2004) proposed on integrated "Water stress Index" (WSI) based on a simple soil water balance and the integrated reduction of plant transpiration relative to potentials transpiration. They related yield potential and adaptability of cultivars under water stress to the intercept and slope of the linear regression of yield versus WSI.

PHYSIOLOGICAL BASES FOR YIELD UNDER DROUGHT

The water content and the water potential of plant tissues are the most important physiologically relevant integrators of droughts effects on plant (Jones, 2007). Once a drop in water potential develops, responses of a wide range of physiological processes are induced, either directly or by plant hormones signalling changes in water status. Physiological traits relevant for the responses to water deficits and/or modified by water stress span a wide range of vital processes (Table 1). As a consequence, it can be expected that there is no single response pattern that is highly correlated with yield under all drought environments. Furthermore, different crop developmental stagers show different sensitivity to water stress which has also been found to be the case in arid legumes (Garg *et al.* 1998, 2005). Several studies have addressed yield under drought stress as a function of single physiological trait, in attempts to understand which metabolic processes or morpho-physiological traits are crucial in ensuring high yield performance under wide range of environments. But most of these studies relate to cereals crops like wheat, rice, maize and sorghum. Some attempts have been made in our laboratory to short list few of physiological traits contributing to high yield of arid legumes under stressful condition of Indian arid zone (Garg, 2003, 2008). However, it will be pertinent to mention here some of the single physiological parameters associated to yield in cereals which include-

(*i*) Stomatal conductance in wheat cultivars (Fisher *et al.* 1998)

(*ii*) Stay green in maize, rice and sorghum (Campos *et al.* 2004)

(*iii*) Osmotic adjustment (Morgan, 1986; Moinuddin *et al.* 2005)

(*iv*) Carbon isotope discrimination in C3 species (Farquhar and Richards, 1984).

TABLE 1 : Physiological traits relevant for response to drought condition (Adapted from Cattivelli *et al.* 2008)

Plant traits	*Modulation under stress*	*Effect relevant to yield*
Stomatal conductance	Decreases under stress	Less water consumption
Photosynthetic capacity	Reduction under stress	Calvin cycle enzymes, light reactions, biomass accumulation
Timing of phenological phases barley delayed in rice	Advanced flowering in wheat, duration, reduced grain number	Early/late flowering, maturity and growth
Starch availability	Inhibition of photosynthetic activity	Abortion, reduced grain number
Stem reserve utilization	Remobilization and compensation for reduced current photosynthesis	Higher remobilization for grain filling, high yield
Stay green	Resistance to premature senescence	Delayed senescence, post-flowering, drought resistance
Single plant leaf area	Reduced under stress	Plant size and related productivity
Rooting depth	Reduced total mass but increased root/shoot ratio	Higher/lower tapping of soil moisture
Osmotic adjustment	Slow response to plant water potential	Accumulation of solutes/ions, increased membrane stability
Antioxidative stress	Acclimatization of defence system	Protection against active oxygen species
Accumulation of stress-related proteins	Accumulated under stress	Protection of cellular structure and protein activities

However, these parameters have not received adequate attention in assessment of drought tolerance in arid legumes.

MOLECULAR MARKERS FOR DROUGHT TOLERANCE TRAITS

Many efforts have been dedicated in recent years to understand the genetic basis of physiological traits conferring advantages in dry environments, while less attention has been given to understanding the high yield stability in dry and wet environments. Single genes such as those controlling flowering time, ear type, plant height and osmotic adjustment may have important roles in adaptation to drought-prone environments. During the last 10 years, the application of QTL analysis provided very good opportunities to identify chromosomes regions controlling variations in almost all the physiological, morphological and developmental changes observed during plant growth in water-limiting conditions. Attention has particularly been paid to -

(1) Genetic variation of the osmotic adjustment.

(2) Genetic basis of stay green phenotype.

(3) The ability of roots to exploit deep soil moisture to meet ET demands.

(4) Reduction of leaf area to limit water use.

(5) Isotopic discrimination.

(6) Non-stomatal water loss from the leaves *e.g.* through the cuticle.

(7) Rate of leaf elongation in response to soil moisture and ET.

(8) Stress induces LEA proteins.

(9) Stomatal sensitivity to ABA.

(10) Overproduction of free proline.

However, most of their efforts have been made in crops like wheat, rice, maize, sorghum and some temperate legumes and at present there is no specific information on genetic basis of drought tolerance in arid legumes. As drought is a very complex phenomenon, use of above biotechnological tools for increasing efficiency of selection for drought tolerance in arid legumes is also advocated.

DROUGHT TOLERANCE IN ARID LEGUMES

In arid and semi-arid regions because of low and erratic rainfall, sowing is generally delayed until there is sufficient soil moisture for stand establishment. Thus, the most important characteristics that enable crop plants to yield satisfactorily are the matching of phenological development with soil moisture supply. In regions with a characteristics terminal drought, extension of crop production in drier regions has been accompanied by the development of short duration varieties that enable the crop to escape severe soil water deficits. In cluster bean and moth bean seed yields were significantly more in early flowering/ maturing genotypes under low rainfall conditions (Garg *et al.* 2003, 2004a and Vyas *et al.* 2003). Significant genotypic differences were observed in crop performance and various physiological attributes among early and late genotypes of moth bean under extreme dry conditions in the field (Vyas *et al.* 2003 a). Early flowering (30-31 days), genotypes such as RMO-40 and RMO-257 consumed soil moisture at a slower rate during vegetative stage and conserved it for the critical flowering stage. In contrast late flowering (45-50 days) genotypes consumed water at a faster rate during the vegetative stage. Consequently early flowering genotypes produced higher seed yield and exhibited greater WUE than late types. This was attributed to more efficient partitioning of photosynthates by early flowering genotypes. Observations on plant water status, NPK concentrations as well as Nitrogen Harvest Index (NHI) and Nitrogen Use Efficiency (NUE) also showed superiority of early genotypes over late genotypes under field drought conditions (Table 2).

TABLE 2: Seed yield, nitrogen uptake, nitrogen harvest index and nitrogen use efficiency of moth bean genotypes under field drought condition (Vyas *et al.* 2003)

Genotypes	*Seed yield ($kg\ ha^{-1}$)*	*N uptake ($kg\ ha^{-1}$)*	*NHI (%)*	*NUE (kg seed $kg^{-1}N$)*
		Early flowering		
RMO-40	723	16.04	35.2	45.1
RMD-117	495	11.77	37.8	42.1
RMO-224	644	14.88	46.8	43.3
RMO-225	481	11.05	50.9	43.5
RMO-257	443	9.73	50.9	45.5
Mean	557	12.69	44.3	43.9
		Late Flowering		
Jadia	408	17.88	32.4	22.8
FMO-1023-1	447	18.74	0.5	29.2
FMO-1096-1	385	1.72	27.9	35.9
Jawala	486	15.62	37.0	31.0
JMM-DBS-1	356	11.52	27.8	3.9
FMO-1118-1	443	16.68	31.1	26.6
IPCMO-880	345	12.27	31.2	28.1
FMO-1460-1	244	12.13	24.7	20.1
JMM-259	297	12.20	22.4	24.3
Mean	390	14.20	29.6	27.7

Likewise field studies undertaken with diverse early and late maturing genotypes of cluster bean under rainfed conditions for two consecutive years (1993- low rainfall, 1994- high rainfall) revealed significant genotypic differences in seed yield, WUE, nutrient uptake and leaf metabolism (Garg *et al.* 2003). The seed yield of early genotypes (RGC-936 and Suvidha) was significantly higher during low rainfall year while late genotypes (Maru guar and HG-75) out yielded early types during high rainfall year. WUE was 56.8% higher in early as compared to late genotypes during drought year. This was accompanied by higher NHI and NUE in early maturing genotypes indicating a better utilization of nitrogen (Table 3). Studies have further indicated that early genotypes of both these legumes maintain higher plant water status and experience less metabolic changes than late genotypes under water stress (Garg, 2003; Garg *et al.* 2001). For instance genotype CZM-32E of moth bean displayed higher drought tolerance capacity than cv. Maru moth due to maintenance of higher ψ plant and RWC, higher photosynthetic rate, higher nitrate reductase activity and better carbohydrate metabolism under different intensities of water stress (Table 4). Water stress had maximum adverse effect on seed yield at the flowering stage in genotypes Maru guar and FS-277 but at the pod development stage in cluster bean genotypes Suvidha, HFG-182 and JGC-19 (Garg *et al.* 1998). Different physiological and biochemical parameters also displayed higher metabolic derangements underwater stress at the flowering stage in all the genotypes. In moth bean early flowering genotypes (RMO-40 and CZM-99) consistently displayed less metabolic alterations than late genotypes (Maru moth and CAZRI moth-1) at vegetative and flowering stages but flowering stages more are sensitive to water stress. The maintenance of higher photosynthetic rate and better metabolic efficiency in early genotypes under water stress led to significantly less reduction in their seed yield and DMP as compared to late flowering genotypes (Garg *et al.* 2004a). Results of various studies on cluster bean, mung bean and moth bean indicated stress mediated changes in various leaf metabolites and enzyme activities which modulated the growth and yield of the legumes (Garg and Burman, 2002 a, b). It was found that under increasing water stress, normal GS-GOGAT system becomes less effective but GDH activity increases many fold indicating a shift in the pathway of ammonia assimilation which is an adaptive mechanism to detoxify the accumulated ammonia under acute water stress (Vyas *et al.* 1996; Garg *et al.* 1998). Evaluation of relative drought tolerance of arid legumes at vegetative and flowering stages revealed that moth bean displayed higher drought tolerance than cluster bean, mung bean and cowpea (Garg *et al.* 2005). Mung bean at the vegetative stage and cowpea at the flowering stage recorded maximum reduction in seed yield due to more alterations in various physiological and biochemical parameters. Maintenance of high leaf turgidity, net photosynthetic rate and stomatal conductance at almost similar stress levels (ψ plant) alongwith less alteration in leaf metabolites such as total chlorophyll, starch, reducing sugars, soluble protein and free amino acids in moth bean as compared to cluster bean and other legumes was reflected in its yield stability under water stress (Table 5). Further, higher plant water potential, leaf turgiscence and high photosynthetic rate on restoration of water supply to stressed plants showed high capacity of recovery in all the legumes, but it is more in case of moth bean. Osmotic adjustment is the active accumulation of solutes within the plant tissues in response to lowering of soil water potential (Morgan, 1983). The degree of osmotic adjustment varies with species and genotypic variation within a species has been demonstrated in a number of crops including several legumes (Turner, 1997). Osmotic adjustment has been shown to enable photosynthesis to be maintained at low leaf water potential, to delay leaf senescence, to improve floral survival and to improve yield under water limited conditions. A wide variety of organic solutes in plant tissues during water stress contribute to osmotic adjustment. Stress induced accumulation of free proline, free amino acids and reducing sugars has been observed in cluster bean and moth bean (Vyas *et al.* 1996; Garg *et al.* 1998, 2001, 2005) and other corps. However, cluster bean and pearl millet accumulate high levels of free proline as compared to moth bean and sesame plant under water deficits (Table 6). Over production of proline and glycine betaine which acts as osmo protectants and their correlation with stress tolerance has been well emphasised (Kishore *et al.* 1995). These studies indicated the possibility of genetic manipulation of proline over-production in drought resistant plants and control of osmoregulation in others. Most of the adaptations to drought have some limitations. A genotype of short duration usually yields less, compared to that of normal duration under better moisture availability (Garg, 2003). The mechanisms that confer drought resistance by reducing water loss (such as stomatal closure and reduced leaf area) generally result in reduced assimilation of carbon dioxide *i.e.* reduced photosynthetic efficiency.

TABLE 3 : Seed yield, harvest index, WUE and NUE of early and late genotypes of cluster bean under low and high rainfall condition (Garg *et al.* 2003)

Year	*Rainfall (mm)*	*Seed yield (kg ha⁻¹)*		*HI (%)*		*WUE (kg ha⁻¹ mm⁻¹)*		*NUE (kg seed kg⁻¹ N)*	
		Early	*Late*	*Early*	*Late*	*Early*	*Late*	*Early*	*Late*
1993	206	995	625	33.2	19.7	466	2.987	17.2	12.2
1994	279	660	800	116	12.7	1.83	2.38	11.7	10.5

Osmotic adjustment increases drought resistance by maintaining plant vigour but the increased solute concentration responsible for osmotic adjustment may have additional energy requirements at the cost of plant growth (Turner, 1986, 1997).

TABLE 4 : Water stress effects on water potential, net photosynthetic rate and starch in moth bean genotypes (Garg *et al.* 2001)

Water stress	*ψ plant(MPa)*			*Net photosynthetic rate (μ mol m-2s⁻¹)*			*Starch (mg g⁻¹ dw)*		
(d)	*V1*	*V2*	*V3*	*V1*	*V2*	*V3*	*V1*	*V2*	*V3*
0	- 0.60	- 0.70	- 0.70	8.0	8.4	11.8	131	127	146
3	- 0.90	- 0.95	- 0.90	4.2	3.5	9.4	77	120	128
6	- 1.25	- 1.20	- 1.10	2.7	2.6	5.2	60	73	77
9	- 1.50	- 1.35	- 1.30	1.5	1.7	4.2	55	57	71

YIELD IMPROVEMENT UNDER DROUGHT

Crop yields under drought can be improved by laying emphasis on integrated traits like seedling establishment, early growth vigour, developmental plasticity, leaf area maintenance, osmotic adjustment, high transpiration efficiency and mobilization of pre-anthesis stored reserves. In addition better crop management including appropriate planting dates, row spacing and plant populations, optimum fertilizer use and adoption of drought ameliorative measures may greatly help in alleviation of drought effects. In recent years several attempts have been made to minimise the detrimental effects of drought in cluster bean and moth bean which are briefly outlined here.

TABLE 5: Influence of drought at flowering stage on comparative performance, water status, photosynthesis and leaf metabolism of cluster bean, moth bean, mung bean and cowpea

(Garg *et al.* 2005)

Parameter	*Treatment*	*Cluster bean*	*Moth bean*	*Mung bean*	*Cowpea*
Seed yield	C	7.60	4.13	7.64	10.03
(g plant^{-1})	D	5.10	3.17	4.545	5.35
ψ plant	C	0.87	0.83	0.80	0.80
(-MPa)	D	1.90	1.93	1.87	1.77
RWC (%)	C	94.6	95.6	83.3	90.4
	D	65.4	95.6	83.3	90.4
Net photosynthesis	C	9.10	6.50	6.50	5.50
(μmol m^{-2} s^{-1})	D	4.48	4.80	2.51	2.61
Chlorophyll	C	9.79	9.96	9.77	9.97
(mg g^{-1} dw)	D	7.93	8.87	7.22	7.55
Reducing sugars	C	17.12	26.61	20.68	20.95
(mg g^{-1} dw)	D	33.04	27.984	22.75	24.68
Starch	C	18.06	219.2	308.4	210.1
(mg g^{-1} dw)	D	142.4	179.3	190.6	147.2
Soluble protein	C	89.6	61.8	74.1	75.0
(mg g^{-1} dw)	D	85.6	60.7	71.9	69.5

C-Control Plants; D-Droughted Plants

In cluster bean and moth bean seed yields were significantly more in early flowering/maturing genotypes under low rainfall situation. However, late genotypes provided higher yields under good rainfall conditions.

TABLE 6 : Influence of drought intensity on accumulation of free proline in certain arid zone crop plants (Garg, 2003)

Water stress levels	*Proline concentration (mg g^{-1}dw)*			
	Pearl millet	*Cluster bean*	*Moth bean*	*Sesame*
Control	0.75	0.47	0.38	0.45
Mild	3.26	3.91	0.71	0.62
Moderate	12.31	8.53	1.71	1.15
Severe	15.34	12.91	1.82	1.15

TABLE 7: Yield stability in moth bean and cluster bean through varietal intercrops (Kathju *et al.* 2003; Vyas *et al.* 2003)

Planting pattern	*Seed yield ($kg\ ha^{-1}$)*		*WUE ($kg\ ha^{-1}\ mm^{-1}$)*		*Net Photosynthesis ($\mu\ mol\ m^{-2}\ s^{-1}$)*	
	1995	*1996*	*1995*	*1996*	*1995*	*1996*
			MOTH BEAN			
Early (RMO-40)	744	825	2.66	2.26	11.3	19.2
Late (Maru moth)	528	1011	1.88	2.80	9.7	20.5
E + L	755	1188	2.72	3.32	12.3	22.0
			CLUSTER BEAN			
Early(Subidha)	833	986	2.89	2.66	22.7	26.8
Late (Maru guar)	717	1122	2.54	2.93	21.0	26.0
E + L	928	1172	3.20	3.16	23.6	27.8

1995: Low rainfall year (267 mm); 1996: High rainfall year (424 mm)

For stability of yield, planting of early and late genotypes of these legumes in 1:1 ration was found most appropriate under low as well as higher rainfall conditions (Table 7). The improved performance of mixed crop, particularly under low rainfall situation could be attributed to more efficient use of water, low initial canopy development and higher photosynthetic rates (Kathju *et al.* 2003; Vyas *et al.* 2003b). Hall (1988) indicated that varietal intercrops having alternate rows of early erect and medium spreading cowpea varieties improved the stability and productivity of cowpea under varying rainfall conditions of semi-arid Africa. Optimum plant population or row spacing is one of the major management variables under dry land conditions. In water deficit regions large canopy growth may be disadvantageous as it may exhaust the available soil moisture more rapidly from the root zone during drought.

TABLE 8 : Influence of thiourea of cluster bean (Garg *et al.* 2006)

Treatment	*Seed yield ($kg\ ha^{-1}$)*	*DMP ($kg\ ha^{-1}$)*	*Net Photosynthesis ($\mu mol\ m^{-2}\ s^{-1}$)*	*NRA ($mg\ NO_2\ g^{-1}\ dwh^{-1}$)*
Control	295	1172	10.3	348
Seed Treatment (Thiourea)	382	1409	13.1	512
Seed treatment + spray (Thiourea)	410	1512	13.5	581

Studies with cluster bean genotypes have shown that 40-45 cm row spacing was significantly better for achieving higher seed yields, WUE and NUE under arid conditions (Garg *et al.* 2002). In another study moth bean genotypes planted at 30 × 15 cm provided significantly higher seed yields, DMP and higher WUE as compared to 45 × 10 cm spacing (Burman *et al.* 2002). Addressing the soil fertility constraints can also alleviate drought stress effects on crop productivity in arid environments (Lahiri, 1980). The supply of phosphorus is particularly critical as declining water availability causes reduced phosphorus availability and absorption by moth bean and cluster bean under dryland conditions. Phosphorus application significantly ameliorated the detrimental effects of drought on water status, rates of net photosynthesis, contents of chlorophyll, starch, soluble protein and nitrate reductase activity in moth bean genotypes (Garg *et al.* 2004b). Consequently seed yield was significantly improved despite drought condition. Similarly application of potassium under soil moisture stress has been found to play a major role through its favourable influence on plant water relations, physiological processes like net photosynthesis and stomatal conductance and seed yields (Mengel and Kirkby, 1980). Maintenance of adequate potassium in the soil significantly improved plant water status, net photosynthesis, and yield of cluster bean under drought imposed at various developmental stages (Vyas *et al.* 2001). Similarly seed treatment with thiourea (500 ppm) followed by foliar sprays (1000 ppm) at vegetative and flowering stages significantly mitigated the detrimental effects of field drought in cluster bean through enhancement of photosynthetic efficiency and nitrogen metabolism (Garg *et al.* 2006, Table 8). Likewise, kinetin (5 ppm either as pre-sowing seed treatment or as foliar spray or both (at 25 and 40 DAS) significantly improved the growth, DMP, seed yield and WUE of cluster bean under field drought conditions (Burman *et al.* 2003). Combined application of phosphorus and thiourea has been found to act synergistically and improved growth and yield of cluster bean under simulated drought condition (Burman *et al.* 2004). This has been found to be mediated due to their favourable and additive effects on photosynthetic efficiency, leaf area development and nitrogen metabolism. The usefulness of thiourea application has also been demonstrated at farmer's fields (Garg and Burman, 2006) where seed treatment with 500 ppm thiourea followed by a single spray of thiourea (1000 ppm) at the pre-flowering stage significantly improved the growth and seed yield of cluster bean and moth bean (Table 9).

TABLE 9 : Influence of thiourea application on seed yield and DMP of cluster bean and moth bean genotypes at farmer's field (Garg and Burman, 2006)

Legumes	*Seed yield (kg ha^{-1})*		*Dry matter production (kg ha^{-1})*	
	Control	*Thiourea*	*Control*	*Thiourea*
		Moth bean		
RMO-40	507	569	1218	1320
CZM-99	450	521	1125	1254
		Cluster bean		
RGC-936	405	467	1416	1602
RGC-1003	438	543	1377	1994

It has been concluded that thiourea treatment can significantly enhance the productivity of both these legumes under arid conditions (Garg, 2007). Improvement in performance of a crop under water shortage can arise both from genetic changes to the crop that enable it to perform better in drought-prone environments and from agronomic changes that enable it to perform better under these constraints. It is evident that physiological manipulation along with good crop management is required for the most efficient use of limited rain water by different arid legumes. Thus, to face drought stress and to achieve sufficient and sustainable seed yield in the future, requires a multidisciplinary approach based on plant genomics, physiology, agronomy and modelling.

REFERENCES

Arnon I (1992) *Agriculture in Drylands - Principles and Practice* Elesiver, Amesterdam

Blum A (1988) Improving wheat grain filling under stress by stem reserved mobilization *Euphytica* **100:** 77-83

Burman U Garg BK and Kathju S (2002) Effect of spacing on seed yield and physiological traits in moth bean (*Vigna aconitifolia*) *Indian Journal of Agricultural Sciences* **72:** 76-79

Burman U Garg BK and Kathju S (2003) Influence of kinetin on photosynthesis,nitrogen metabolism and yield of cluster bean under moisture deficit conditions *Indian Journal of Plant Physiology* **8:** 287-291

Burman U Garg BK and Kathju S (2004) Interactive effect of thiourea and Garg BK and Burman U 2006 Yield improvement of cluster bean and moth bean by thiourea application under arid conditions *Journal of Arid Legumes* **3:** 51-54 phosphorus under simulated water stress *Biologia Plantarum* **48:** 61-65

Campos H Coper M Habben JE EDmeades GO and Schussler JR (2004) Improving drought tolerance in maize: a view from industry *Field Crop Research* **90:** 19-34

Cattivelli L Rizza F Badeck FW Mazzucotelh E Mastrangelu AM Francia E Mar C Tondelli A and Stanca AM (2008) Drought tolerance improvement in crop plants: An integrated view from breeding to genomics *Field Crops Research* **105:** 1-4

Farquhar GD and Richards RA (1984) Isotopic composition of plant carbon correlates with water-use efficiency of wheat genotypes *Australian Journal of Plant Physiology* **11:** 39-52

Fisher RA Rees D Sayree KD Lu ZM and Candon AG (1998) Wheat yield progress associated with higher stomatal conductance and photosynthetic rate and cooler canopies *Crop Science* **38:** 1467-1475

Garg BK (2002) Mechanisms of drought tolerance and strategies for yield improvement under drought *Current Agriculture* **26:** 15-21

Garg BK (2003) Physiological aspects of abiotic stress tolerance in arid legumes (in) *Advances in Arid Legumes Research* pp 347-354. A Hentry D Kumar and NB Singh (Eds) Scientific Publishers, Jodhpur

Garg BK (2007) Role of thiourea in improving the productivity or arid legumes *Journal of Arid Legumes* **4:** 1-5

Garg BK (2008) Physiology of drought tolerance of cluster bean and moth bean *Journal of Arid Legumes* **5:** 8-14

Garg and Burman U 2002a Moth bean physiology (in) *Moth bean in India* pp 87-102 D Kumar and NB Singh (Eds) Scientific Publishers, Jodhpur Garg BK and Burman U 2002b Physiology (in) *Guar in India* pp 63-83 D

Garg BK and Burman U 2006 Yield improvement of cluster bean and moth bean by thiourea application under arid condition *Journal of Arid Legumes* **3:** 51-54

Garg BK Burman and Kathju S (2004a) Effect of water stress on moth bean (*Vigna aconitifolia*) genotypes *Indian Journal of Plant Physiology* **9:** 29-35

Garg BK Burman U and Kathhju S (2004b) The influence of phosphorus nutrition the physiological response of moth bean genotypes of drought *Journal of Plant Nutrition and Soil Science* **167:** 503-508

Garg BK Kathju S and Burman U (2001) Influence of water stress on water relations, photosynthetic rate and nitrogen metabolism of moth bean genotypes *Biologia Plantarum* **44:** 289-292

Garg BK Burman U and Kathju S (2005) Comparative water relations, photosynthesis and nitrogen metabolism of arid legumes under water stress *Journal of Plant Biology* **32:** 83-93

Garg BK Burman U and Kathju S (2006) Influence of thiourea on photosynthesis, nitrogen metabolism and yield of cluster bean (*Cyamopsis tetragonoloba*(L.) Taub.) under rainfed conditions of Indian arid zone *Plant Growth Regulation* **48:** 237-245

Garg BK Kathju S Vyas SP and Lahiri AN (1998) Influence of water deficit stress at various growths stages on some enzymes of nitrogen metabolism and yield in cluster bean genotypes *Indian Journal of Plant Physiology* **3:** 214-218

Garg BK Kathju S Vyas SP and Lahiri AN (2002) Influence of spacings on performance, water use, nutrient uptake and nitrogen use efficiency of cluster bean under diverse rainfall conditions (in) *Human Impact on Desert Environment* pp 294-304 P Narain S Kathju Amal Kar and MP Singh (Eds) Scientific Publishers Jodhpur

Garg BK Kathju S Vyas SP and Lahiri AN (2003) Relative performance, evapotranspiration, water and nitrogen use efficiency and nitrogen metabolism of cluster bean genotypes under arid environment (in) *Advances in Arid Legumes Research* pp 212-220 A Hentry D Kumar and NB Singh (Eds) Scientific Publishers, Jodhpur

Idso SB Reginado R Reicosky D and Katfield J (1981) Determining soil induced plant water potential depression in alfalfa by means of infrared thermometer *Agronomy Journal* **73:** 826-830

Jones HG (2007) Monitoring plant and soil water status established and novel methods revisited and their relevance to studies of drought tolerance *Journal of Experimental Botany* **58:** 119-130

Karamanos AJ and Papatheohari AY (1999) Assessment of drought resistance of crop genotypes by means of Water Potential Index *Crop Science* **39:** 1792-1797

Kathju S Garg BK Vyas SP and Lahiri AN (2003) Sustainable production of moth bean through genotype management under arid environments *Journal of Arid Environments* **53:** 137-143

Kishore PBR Hong-Zong L Verma PAS and Miiao CH (1995) Over production of DELTA-pyrroline S-carbohylase synthetase increases proline production and confers osmo tolerance in transgenic plants *Plant Physiology* 108 1387-1394 D Kumar and NB Singh (Eds) Scientific Publishers Jodhpur

Lahiri AN 1980 Interaction of water stress and mineral nutrition on growth and yield (in) *Adaptation of Plants to Water and High Temperature Stress* pp 341-362 NC Turner and PJ Kramer (Eds) John Wiley, New York

Levitt J (1980) *Responses of Plants to Environmental Stress* Vol 2 Academic Press New York

Mengel K and Kirkby EA (1980) Potassium in crop production *Advances in Agronomy* **33:** 59-110

Moinuddin A Fisher RA Sayre KD and Reynolds MP (2005) Osmotic adjustment in wheat in relation to grain yield under water-deficit environments *Agronomy Journal* **97:** 162-1071

Morgan JM (1984) Osmoregulation and water stress in higher plants *Annual Review of Plant Physiology* **35:** 292-319

Rizza F Badeck FW Cattivelli I and Staca AM (2004) Use of a water stress index to identify barely genotypes adapted to rainfed and irrigated conditions *Crop Science* **44:** 2127-2137

Turner NC (1986) Adaptations to water deficits *Australian Journal of Plant Physiology* **13:** 175-190

Turner NC (1997) Further Progress in crop water relations *Advances in Agronomy* **39:** 1-51

Voltas J Lopez Coircoles H and Borras G (2005) Use of bipolar analysis and factorial regression for the investigation of superior genotypes in multi-environment trails *European Journal of Agronomy* **22:** 309-324

Vyas SP Kathju S Garg BK and Lahiri AN (1996) Activities of nitrate reductase and ammonia assimilating enzymes of moth bean under water stress *Science and Culture* **62:** 213-214

Vyas SP Garg BK Kathju S and Lahiri AN (2001) Influence of potassium on water relations, photosynthesis, nitrogen metabolism and yield of cluster bean under soil moisture deficit stress *Indian Journal of Plant Physiology* **6:** 30-37

Vyas SP Garg BK Kathju S and Lahiri AN (2003a) Relative drought tolerance of moth bean genotypes (in) *Advances in Arid Legumes Research* pp 394-397 A Henry D Kumar and NB Singh (Eds) Scientific Publishers, Jodhpur

Vyas SP Garg BK Kathju S and Lahiri AN (2003b) Genotypic management of cluster bean for sustainable production under arid environment *Indian Journal of Pulse Research* **16:** 104-107

3

RNA INTERFERENCE: ITS CONCEPT AND APPLICATION IN CROP PLANTS

GULZAR S SANGHERA, SHABIR H WANI, MANJIT S GILL, PREM L KASHYAP AND SATBIR S GOSAL

INTRODUCTION

Traditional plant breeding has been tremendously successful in improving the nutritional value of food and feed (Davies 2003). However this process is time-consuming and the limited genetic resources of most; crops have left little room for continued improvement by these means. There are many reasons for the limited genetic resources available for breeding (Hoisington *et al.* 1999). Two of the most important ones are:

(*i*) Loss of gene pools occurring during the domestication and breeding of crop plants (Lee 1998); and

(*ii*) Many of the natural gene traits that may be beneficial in one plant tissue such as seeds and fruits may be deleterious in other plant tissues such as vegetative tissues (Frankard *et al.* 1992 and Zhu and Galili 2003).

Over the past few decades breeding possibilities have been broadened by genetic engineering and gene transfer technologies as well as by gene mapping and identification of the genome sequences of model plants and crops. Directed efforts are now underway to use genetic engineering of metabolic pathways to alter plant nutrient levels (Galili *et al.* 2002). These efforts depend on a detailed understanding of plant metabolic pathways and constituent enzymes as well as on regulatory genes that control these enzymes. Modern technologies such as trancriptomics, proteomics and metabolomics are now proving to be important in understanding plant metabolic pathways and the role of key genes associated with their regulation. This can facilitate new insights into the complex metabolite neighborhoods that give rise to a given phenotype and may allow discovery of new target genes to modify a given pathway. Such genes can then be subject to new metabolic engineering efforts and applications.

The major strategy for transgenic enhancement of plant nutrient levels involves increasing the levels of expression of anabolic biosynthetic genes. Unfortunately the efficacy of this approach for crop engineering has been restricted by two main obstructions. First the introduction of extra gene copies can have the non-intuitive effect of decreasing expression from the introduced and homologous endogenous loci a phenomenon of gene silencing known as "co-suppression" (Napoli *et al.* 1990). Second feedback metabolic loops tend to maintain homeostatic nutrient levels. For example plants might respond to increased nutrient production induced by overexpression of biosynthetic genes by activating a degradation pathway that either negates nutrient accumulation or converts nutrients into undesirable metabolites (Karchi *et al.* 1994).

During the last decade our knowledge repertoire of RNA-mediated functions has hugely increased with the discovery of small non-coding RNAs which play a central part in a process called RNA silencing. Ironically the very important phenomenon of co-suppression has recently been recognized as a manifestation of RNA interference (RNAi) an endogenous pathway for negative post-transcriptional regulation. RNAi has revolutionized the possibilities for creating custom "knock-downs" of gene activity. RNAi operates in both plants and animals and uses double stranded RNA (dsRNA) as a trigger that targets homologous mRNAs for degradation or inhibiting its transcription or translation (De Bakker *et al.* 2002; Almeida and Allshire 2005 and Wadhwani *et al.* 2008) whereby susceptible genes can be silenced. This RNA-mediated gene control technology has provided new platforms for developing eco-friendly molecular tools for crop improvement by suppressing the genes responsible for various stresses and improving novel traits in plants including disease resistance and will be a promising future therapeutic agent to combat plant invaders. It has emerged as a method of choice for gene targeting in fungi (Nakayashiki 2005), viruses (Baulcombe 2004), bacteria (Escobar *et al.* 2001) and plants (Brodersen and Voinnet 2006) as it allows the study of the function of hundreds of thousands of genes to be tested (Godge *et al.* 2008). It can silence a gene throughout an organism or in specific tissues (Shahinul Islam *et al.* 2005) offer the versatility to partially silence or completely turn off genes work in both cultured cells and whole organisms and can selectively silence genes at particular stages of the organism's life cycle (Milhavet *et al.* 2003). Methods that introduce dsRNA into plant and animal cells have been enormously successful for decreasing cognate gene expression *in vivo* (Hannon 2002; Shi 2003 and Vaucheret *et al.* 2001). Due to all these elegant and unique features of RNAi our this chapter specifically focuses on the concept of RNAi current knowledge of its pathways and induction in plants and explore the possibilities for the applications of this technology in the improvement of plants with special reference to plant nutritional value and disease management.

Abbreviations: ABA abscisic acid; **ACMV** *African cassava mosaic virus;* **AGO** Argonaute; ***AtRdRP*** Arabidopsis RNA-dependent RNA polymerase ; **bp** base pair; **CaLCuV** *Cabbage leaf curl virus;* ***Chl*** chalcone synthase; ***CMV*** *Cucumber mosaic virus;* **CP**

coat protein; ***DCL*** dicer-like protein; **dpi** days post infection; **dsRNA** double-stranded RNA ; **ds-siRNAs** double-stranded small interfering RNAs; **eIF2C** elongation factor 2C; ***GFP*** green fluorescent protein; ***HC-Pro*** helper-component proteinase; **HIV** *Human immunodeficiency virus;* **hpRNAs** hairpin RNA; **kDa** kilo Dalton; **LISW** laser-induced stress wave; **miRISC** micro RNA-induced silencing complex; **miRNAs** microRNAs ; **mRNA** messenger RNA; **MSP** major sperm protein; **MSV** *Maize streak virus;* **MYMIV** *Mungbean yellow mosaic India virus;* **nt** nucleotide; **PME** pectin methylesterase; ***PolIV*** RNA *Polymerase* IV; **pri-tasiRNAs** primary transacting siRNAs; **PTGS** posttranscriptional gene silencing; ***PVX*** *Potato virus X;* **RDR** RNA-dependent RNA polymerase; **RDR** RNA-dependent RNA polymerase; **RISC** RNA-induced silencing complex; **RITS** RNA-induced transcriptional silencing complex; **RLC** RISC loading complex; **RMD** RNA-mediated defense; **RNAi** RNA interference; **rRNA** ribosomal RNA; **SARS-Cov** severe acute respiratory syndrome-associated coronavirus; **SDE** silencing defective; **SGS** suppressor of gene silencing; **siRISC** small interfering RNA-induced silencing complex; **siRNAs** Small interfering RNAs; **ssRNA** single-stranded RNA; **ta-siRNAs** transacting siRNAs; **T-DNA** transfer DNA; **TGMV** *Tomato golden mosaic virus;* **TGS** Transcriptional gene silencing; **TMV** *Tobacco mosaic virus;* **tRNA** transfer ribonucleic acid; **TRV** *Tobacco rattle virus;* **VIGS** virus-induced gene silencing

1. RNAi: THE CONCEPT

'RNA interference' refers collectively to diverse RNA-based processes that all result in sequence-specific inhibition of gene expression either at the transcription mRNA stability or translational levels. It has most likely evolved as a mechanism for cells to eliminate foreign genes. The unifying features of this phenomena are the production of small RNAs 21-26 nucleotides (nt) that act as specific determinants for down-regulating gene expression (Waterhouse *et al.* 2001; Hannon 2002; Pickford and Cogoni 2003) and the requirement for one or more members of the Argonaute family of proteins (Hammond *et al.* 2000). RNAi operates by triggering the action of dsRNA intermediates which are processed into RNA duplexes of 21-24 nucleotides by a ribonuclease III-like enzyme called Dicer (Fire *et al.* 1998; Bernstein *et al.* 2001 and Wesley *et al.* 2001). Once produced these small RNA molecules or short interfering RNAs (siRNAs) are incorporated in a multi-subunit complex called RNA induced silencing complex or RISC (Hammond *et al.* 2000; Tang *et al.* 2003). RISC is formed by a siRNA and an endonuclease among other components. The siRNAs within RISC acts as a guide to target the degradation of complementary messenger RNAs (mRNAs) (Hammond *et al.* 2000 and Tang *et al.* 2003). The host genome codifies for small RNAs called miRNAs that are responsible for endogenous gene silencing. The dsRNAs triggering gene silencing can originate from several sources such as expression of endogenous or transgenic antisense sequences expression of inverted repeated sequences or RNA synthesis during viral replication (Voinnet 2005) (Fig 1). When dsRNA molecules produced during viral replication trigger gene silencing the process is called virus-induced gene silencing (VIGS) (Lu *et al.* 2003). One interesting feature of RNA silencing in plants is that once it is triggered in a certain cell a mobile signal is produced and spread through the whole

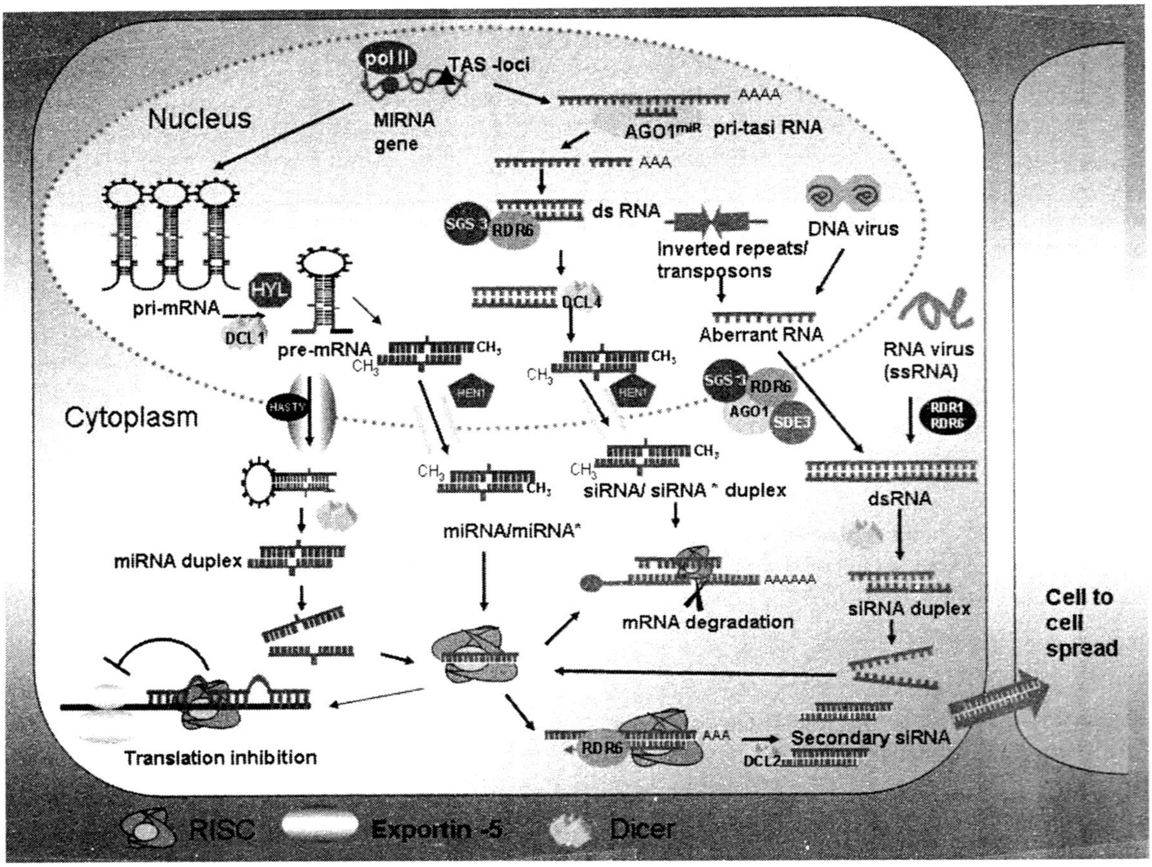

Fig. 1: Different RNAi pathways in Plants. 1).miRNA and tasi-RNA biogenesis regulating expression of MIRNA gene and TAS loci. With the help of DCL1 and HYL1,pri-miRNA is processed to short lived miRNA: miRNA* duplex in plants and are methylated by HEN1 within the nucleus. Thereafter, the miRNA is exported to the cytoplasm by HASTY and after maturation, methylated miRNA is incorporated into a RISC. In this complex, the miRNA is capable of targeting complementary RNAs for cleavage by AGO1, and also for translational repression. Similarly in second phase, trans-acting small interfering RNAs (ta-siRNA) duplexes can be set by miRNA-directed cleavage of the *TAS* transcript. One strand from each siRNA duplex is stably incorporated into RISC, and the other is degraded. siRNAs in RISCs guide cleavage of complementary RNAs. 2) Heterochromatic siRNAs, endogenous siRNAs/siRNAs from transgenes or viral RNA or DNA are generated through similar or partially overlapping pathways. Long double-stranded RNA, generated through the action of RNA-dependent RNA polymerases (RDRs), and iteratively processed by Dicer-like (DCL) proteins to yield multiple siRNA duplexes. One strand from each siRNA duplex is stably incorporated into a RISC, and the other is degraded. siRNAs in RISCs guide cleavage of complementary RNAs. Pol IV is involved in heterochromatic siRNA production in plants, either transcribing the genomic DNA to produce the single-stranded RNA or transcribing the double-stranded RNA to amplify the single-stranded RNA.

plant causing the entire plant to be silenced (Dunoyer *et al.* 2007). After triggering RNA silencing the mobile signaling molecules can be relay-amplified by synthesis of dsRNAs on the primary cleavage of product templates or by their cleavage into secondary siRNAs. This amplification leads to the transitory nature of silencing reaction that may spread along the mRNA though initiated by a locally targeted single siRNA (Klahre *et al.* 2002) and spreads in both the 5′ and 3′ directions (Tang *et al.* 2003). This bi-directional transition further have been witnessed by a process where both the 5′ and 3′ cleavage products of the initial target RNA act as aberrant mRNAs to trigger dsRNA synthesis (Herr *et al.* 2006) and induce secondary silencing reactions (Fig 2). This silencing process is also enhanced by the enzymatic activity of the RISC complex mediating multiple turnover reactions (Hutvagner and Zamore 2002 and Tang *et al.* 2003). Furthermore production of the secondary siRNAs leads to enrichment of silencing *via* its spread from the first activated cell to neighboring cells and systemically through the system (Himber *et al.* 2003). The cell-to-cell spread can be mediated as passive spread of the small RNAs

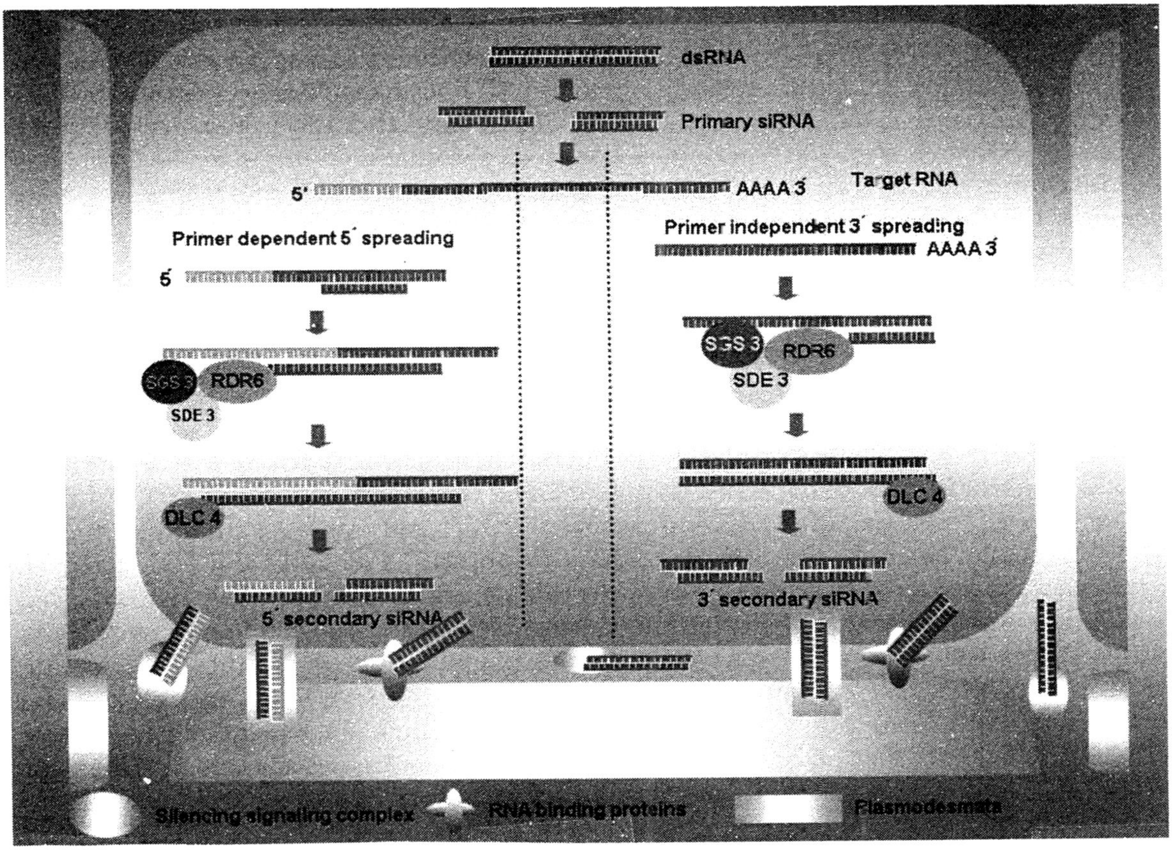

Fig. 2: Model depicting bi-directional mobilization of silencing signal in plant cell. In transitive RNA silencing the mobile signaling molecules relay-amplified by synthesis of dsRNAs into secondary siRNAs by a process where both the 5' and 3' cleavage products of the initial target RNA act as aberrant mRNAs to trigger dsRNA synthesis. siRNAs is produced as shown in scheme (1)showing primer dependent 5' spreading. Further dsRNA synthesis according to the scheme depicted in (2) primer independent 3' spreading. DCL4 appears as putatively involved in secondary siRNA biogenesis that induce secondary silencing reactions. The cell-to-cell spread can be mediated as passive spread of the small RNAs via plasmodesmata or by the silencing signal complex.

via plasmodesmata or by the silencing signal complex which is between 27 and 54 kDa (Kobayashi and Zambryski 2007). The systemic spread in phloem is mediated by the 24 nt siRNAs (Himber *et al.* 2003) unloading of the systemic signal appears to be mediated *via* plasmodesmata since it does not spread into meristematic cells (Voinnet *et al.* 2005). The discovery of RNA-binding protein (PSRP1) in the phloem and its ability to bind 25 nt ssRNA species add further to the argument that siRNAs (24-26 nt) are the key components for systemic silencing signal. The extent of cell-to-cell movement is dependent on the levels of siRNAs produced at the site of silencing initiation but is independent of the presence of siRNA target transcripts in either source or recipient cells (Li and Ding 2006).

2. KEY PLAYERS OF RNAi

RNAi is regulated by different RNA molecules like siRNAs and miRNAs that provide specificity to guide various activities of RNAi machinery including RNA cleavage (Elbashir *et al.* 2001; Llave *et al.* 2002; Hily and Liu 2007), translational repression (Doench *et al.* 2003) and methylation of chromatin (Volpe *et al.* 2002; Chan *et al.* 2004) and outlined in the Fig 1. The aforementioned RNA molecules have the potential to trigger gene silencing by acting as nuts and bolts of this machinery. dsRNAs are precursors of siRNAs whereas ssRNAs with stem-loop structures serve as precursors of miRNAs (pre-miRNAs). However both these RNA molecules are products of the single protein Dicer (Li and Ding 2006). These small RNA species can be divided into various classes which are briefly described in following sections.

2.1 SMALL INTERFERING RNA (siRNA)

This species of RNA is produced as populations from long dsRNAs that result from read through or bi-directional transcription of DNA repeats or transposon loci and from the action of host-encoded RNA-dependent RNA polymerases that synthesize complementary strands from cellular RNAs (Mourrain *et al.* 2000 and Dalmay *et al.* 2000). siRNAs are also generated from transgenic pan-handled transcripts that are used to provide experimental RNAi (Waterhouse and Helliwell 2003). Endogenous siRNAs either direct the endonucleolytic cleavage of homologous transcripts (transacting siRNAs) (Peragine *et al.* 2004 and Vazquez *et al.* 2004) or promote DNA methylation and heterochromatin formation at the genetic loci from which they originate (*cis*-acting siRNAs) (Xie *et al.* 2004) often resulting in transcriptional gene silencing (TGS). *Cis*-acting siRNAs are produced in the nucleus by DCL3 (dicer-like protein 3) whereas *trans*-acting siRNAs require DCL1 for their biogenesis (Xie *et al.* 2004).

2.2 MICRO RNA (miRNA)

It constitutes another class of endogenous small RNA. These molecules are excised by DCL1 from nuclear and non-coding precursor transcripts of approximately 70-200 nts in length which acquire a partial stem-loop structure (Dunoyer and Voinnet 2005). Mature miRNAs are cytoplasmic and direct the cleavage or translational repression of mRNAs that carry discrete complementary target sites (Bartel and Bartel 2003 and Bartel

2004). These miRNA sequences reside between protein coding genes or within introns (Bartel and Bartel 2003).

The first plant miRNA targets to be identified were a series of evolutionarily conserved transcription factors that control important developmental fates (Rhoades *et al.* 2002) but further advancement in the work indicates that miRNAs regulate many other biological processes (Jones-Rhoades and Bartel 2004; Sunkar and Zhu 2004). Moreover gene inversion or duplication events can generate species-specific miRNAs that probably contribute to the ability of plants to adapt to their environment (Allen *et al.* 2004 and Voinnet 2004).

2.3 TRANSACTING siRNA (tasiRNA)

tasiRNA is a class of plant endogenous sRNA which evolved from non-coding single-stranded transcripts called the pri-tasiRNAs. These are converted into dsRNA by RDR6–SGS3 giving rise to siRNAs produced as discrete species in a specific 21-nt phase (Peragine *et al.* 2004; Vazquez *et al.* 2004; Brodersen and Voinnet 2006). Much like plant miRNAs mature tasiRNAs guide cleavage and degradation of homologous cellular transcripts. The tasiRNA generating loci (TAS1–3) have been identified in *Arabidopsis* (Allen *et al.* 2005) but they probably also exist in other plant species and organisms that contain RNA dependent RNA polymerase (RDRs) such as *C. elegans* or *Neurospora crassa*. tasiRNA production involves an interesting mix of miRNA action and the siRNA biogenesis machinery (Brodersen and Voinnet 2006). Pri-tasiRNAs contain a binding site for a miRNA that guides cleavage at a defined point. The initial miRNA-guided cut has two important consequences. First it triggers RDR6-mediated transitivity on the pri-tasiRNA cleavage products allowing dsRNA production either 50 or 30 of the cleavage site (Allen *et al.* 2005) and secondly it provides a well defined dsRNA terminus which is crucial for the accuracy of a phased dicing reaction performed by DCL4 which produces mature tasiRNAs.

2.4 RNA DEPENDENT RNA POLYMERASE (RdRP)

As silencing is triggered by dsRNA conversion of ssRNA sequences to ds form is required for silencing of endogenous transcripts. In *Arabidopsis* this RdRP function is mediated by proteins encoded by the SILENCING DEFECTIVE1 (SDE1)/ SUPPRESSOR OF GENE SILENCING2 (SGS2) RdRP genes now referred to as RdRP6 (Xie *et al.* 2004) and the SDE3 RNA helicase gene (Mourrain *et al.* 2000; Dalmay *et al.* 2000b 2001 and Tang *et al.* 2003). These gene functions are not needed for virus-induced PTGS (Dalmay *et al.* 2000 and Voinnet 2001) or for PTGS of transgenes that are transcribed into sense-antisense RNAs forming dsRNA structures (Waterhouse *et al.* 2001 and Beclin *et al.* 2002). But host-encoded and pathogenesis-inducible RdRP identified as NtRdRP1 in tobacco (Xie *et al.* 2001) and as *AtRdRP1* in *Arabidopsis* (Yu *et al.* 2003) are known to enhance the silencing-based defense reaction against different RNA viruses. This suggests that the dsRNA accumulation may be the rate-limiting step in the silencing-based defense reaction.

One of the silencing pathways leading to DNA methylation is mediated by RNA *Polymerase* IV (Pol IV) RdRP2 and DCL3. In this pathway Pol IV and RdRP2 would synthesize dsRNA which is then be cleaved by DCL3 to generate siRNA. In one other pathway Pol IV acts together with AGO4 and one of the RdRP to produce specific siRNAs. These two silencing pathways are independent in the leaves but interdependent in the flowers (Herr *et al.* 2005). Synthesis of other small RNAs requires activity of specific RdRPs. At least tasiRNAs production also depends on RdRP6/SGS3 proteins (Allen *et al.* 2005).

2.5 DICER

Dicer is the key enzyme initiating the RNA-silencing process. It is a dsRNA specific Ribonuclease III-like endonuclease which cleaves the target dsRNAs into fragments of 21-24 nts leaving 3′-hydroxyl and 5′-phosphate ends and 2 nt 3′ overhangs at the termini of the duplex (Bernstein *et al.* 2001; Lau *et al.* 2001 see also Wadhwani *et al.* 2008). Dicer appears to interact with the RISC complex (see RISC assembly and Fig 4) and after cleavage the dsRNA fragments disassociate from dicer and become associated with the RISC. Only one strand of the miRNA fragments (the strand complementary to the target sequence) but either strand of the short lived ds-siRNAs are incorporated into the RISC where these RNAs function as sequence specific tags and target the silencing function to the homologous RNAs (Dunoyer *et al.* 2004).

Arabidopsis and rice genomes encode at least for four different dicer-like proteins (DCL1-DCL4) (Schauer *et al.* 2002). DCL1 produces miRNAs (Bartel 2004 and Chen *et al.* 2005) DCL3 produces 24 nt long siRNAs involved in DNA methylation and in heterochromatin formation (Xie *et al.* 2004) and DCL2 cleaves natural antisense transcripts into siRNAs (Deleris *et al.* 2006). DCL4 generates siRNAs of 21 nt which mediate viral RNA silencing (Dunoyer *et al.* 2005; Gasciolli *et al.* 2005; Herr 2005; Qi *et al.* 2005 and Xie *et al.* 2005). If DCL4 is not functional then DCL2 and DCL3 produce 22 and 24 nt-long siRNAs respectively from viral sequences but only siRNAs produced either by DCL4 or by DCL2 can mediate antiviral silencing. These dicers can restrict virus accumulation into inoculated leaves and DCL4 produce the silencing signal which can inhibit the virus spread because viral siRNAs are produced by DCL4 and DCL2 partially antagonizes the production of miRNAs by DCL1 at least in leaf and fully substitutes for DCL4 to produce viral siRNAs when DCL4 is inhibited by viruses (Bouche *et al.* 2006 and Dunoyer *et al.* 2007).

2.6 RNA INDUCED SILENCING COMPLEX (RISC)

In order to guide suppression of homologous targets the small (s) RNA duplex must become single-stranded which needs a less stable strand with the 5′ phosphate end of the helix that is incorporated as a guide RNA into an effector complex containing an Argonaute (AGO) protein (Schwarz *et al.* 2003 and Herr 2005). Two types of effector complexes *viz.* cytoplasmic and nuclear complexes have been described for induction of RNAi. Cytoplasmic complex known as (RISC) (Hammond *et al.* 2000) can mediate both mRNA cleavage and translational inhibition (Sigova *et al.* 2004). RISC is multi-subunit large assemblies of 250-500 kDa associated with the single stranded fragments of the si- or miRNA (Nykänen *et al.* 2001 and Omarov *et al.* 2007). However the nuclear complex known as RNA-induced Transcriptional Silencing (RITS) complex was first described in fission yeast for repressing DNA expression (Verdel *et al.* 2004). Both these complexes contain (AGO) proteins which are specific to each effector complex *e.g.* RITS have AGO4 and RISC involves AGO1 which are homolog of the translation initiation factor eIF2C (Hammond *et al.* 2000; Hall 2005 and Song and Joshua-Tor 2006).

2.7 ARGONAUTE PROTEINS

Argonaute proteins are the direct binding partners of siRNAs and form the core of RISC. These are about 100 kDa highly basic proteins comprising PAZ and PIWI domains. The PAZ domain which occurs also in the Dicer enzymes may mediate protein-protein interactions and facilitate binding with the Dicer complex. PAZ and PIWI domains are responsible for 3-2 nt overhang recognition and endonucleolytic activities respectively (Hammond *et al.* 2000; Hall 2005; Song and Joshua-Tor 2006). Due to their basic character the argonaute proteins bind RNAs (*e.g.* siRNAs) and guide them to functional complexes (Tang *et al.* 2003; Bartel and Bartel 2003; Dugas and Bartel 2004; Lecellier and Voinnet 2004; Matzke *et al.* 2004 and Vaucheret *et al.* 2004). It is now well known that AGO1 which has slicer activity is an essential component of RISCs and cleaves the target mRNAs which are homologous to the miRNA or siRNA sequences in the complex (Vaucheret *et al.* 2004; Baumberger and Baulcombe 2005; Qi *et al.* 2005; Ronemus *et al.* 2006) and AGO4 is essential for DNA and histone methylation in *Arabidopsis* (Fagard *et al.* 2000; Morel *et al.* 2002; Zilberman *et al.* 2003 and Irvine *et al.* 2006). In the absence of small interfering RNAs (siRNAs) NRDE-3 resides in the cytoplasm. NRDE-3 binds siRNAs generated by RNA-dependent RNA polymerases acting on messenger RNA templates in the cytoplasm and redistributes to the nucleus. Nuclear redistribution of NRDE-3 requires a functional nuclear localization signal for nuclear RNAi and results in NRDE-3 association with nuclear-localized nascent transcripts (Guang *et al.* 2008). Thus specific Argonaute proteins can transport specific classes of small regulatory RNAs to distinct cellular compartments to regulate gene expression.

2.8 OTHER PLAYERS OF RNAi

Hua enhancer 1 (HEN1) a dsRNA methylase (Park *et al.* 2002; Boutet *et al.* 2003 and Xie *et al.* 2004) is required for miRNA accumulation in *Arabidopsis* and for the methylation of miRNA duplexes (Yu *et al.* 2005). HEN1 can also methylate the 3′-OH of siRNAs with less efficiency when they are in duplexes with a 2 nt overhang and preferably of 23 nt. HEN1 is also involved in the production of siRNAs (Akbergenov *et al.* 2006 and Yang *et al.* 2006). HYPONESTIC LEAF 1 (HYL1) a dsRNA binding protein affects miRNA but not siRNA accumulation (Anantharaman *et al.* 2002; Han *et al.* 2004; Vazquez *et al.* 2004 and Wu *et al.* 2007). HYL1 function is also required for hormonal (auxin, ABA and cytokinin) responses (Lu and Federoff 2000). It is possible that other cellular proteins are also affecting the silencing processes. For instance enhanced pectin methylesterase (PME) can enhance the degradation of the viral RNAs and the RNA silencing mechanism (Dorokhov *et al.* 2006). Still some other proteins *e.g.* dsRNA binding proteins (Han *et al.* 2004; Vazquez *et al.* 2004 and Kurihara *et al.* 2006) SDE3

(Dalmay *et al.* 2001) and SGS3 (Mourrain *et al.* 2000) may operate with different DCL proteins in different RNA silencing pathways (Herr *et al.* 2006).

3. GENERAL APPROACHES TO SUPPRESS THE EXPRESSION OF UNDESIRABLE GENES

To reduce the levels of undesirable gene products two general approaches are commonly used: recessive gene disruption and dominant gene silencing. In gene disruption approaches the target sequence is mutated to eliminate either expression or function whereas dominant gene silencing methods induce either the destruction of the gene transcript or the inhibition of transcription. The advantages of the dominant gene silencing methodologies over the gene disruption approach are 2-fold. First dominant gene silencing is easier to manipulate genetically and to screen for subsequent transgenic plants. Second dominant gene silencing can be manipulated in a spatial and temporal manner using specific promoters. Among the dominant gene silencing approaches dsRNA triggered RNAi is the most powerful method (Smith *et al.* 2000); it is the most efficient in terms of the extent of gene silencing and the resulting silencing is almost as complete as in a gene knockout approach. It appears that dsRNA triggered RNAi directly bypasses the requirement for dsRNA synthesis via RDR which is likely the rate-limiting step in the plant RNAi pathway.

4. RNAi SILENCING TECHNOLOGIES IN PLANTS

Although dsRNA-triggered gene silencing was discovered in plants *via* crossing parents that overexpress sense and antisense RNA by (Waterhouse *et al.* 1998) and in animals (Fire *et al.* 1998), the first to apply this technology to plants was Chuang and Meyerowitz 2000. In this case dsRNAs were produced and triggered efficient silencing of flower identity genes using inverted repeats. This vector-based RNAi technology was further improved using an intron instead of a fragment of DNA as the linker by Peter Waterhouse and colleagues (Smith *et al.* 2000). These RNAi vectors were specifically designed to generate long dsRNA species with the same sequence as the target genes. Similarly vectors designed to express hairpin RNAs (hpRNAs) were also successfully applied to silence the corresponding target genes (Wesley *et al.* 2003 and Wadhwani *et al.* 2008). Since constitutive expression of dsRNA or hairpin RNA of some genes often leads to unexpected adverse effects on plant growth and development chemically inducible RNAi silencing vectors were developed to enable temporal and spatial control of gene silencing (Chen *et al.* 2003 and Guo *et al.* 2003). The application of such chemically inducible silencing systems to the study of plant functional genomics is significant but the large-scale use of chemicals for plant improvement is impractical and harmful to the environment. Tissue- or organ-specific control of gene silencing might be a better choice in developing plant RNAi technologies.

In plants three RNAi pathways occur that seem to be involved in a variety of regulatory and immune functions. The first pathway regulates gene expression by microRNAs (miRNAs) (Jones-Rhoades *et al.* 2006) and *trans*-acting smRNAs (ta-smRNAs) (Bartel 2005 and Vaucheret 2005). Both predominantly direct cleavage of near-perfect complementary target mRNAs (Vaucheret *et al.* 2004) but suppression of translation has also been observed in plants (Chen 2004). The working of miRNA based RNAi pathway (Fig 1) emerged after the expression of a specific gene "MIRNA" which is predominantly found within genomic segments previously known as intergenic regions (IGRs) (Jones-Rhoades *et al.* 2006). The expression of this gene begins with Pol II transcription to yield a primary miRNA transcript (pri-miRNA) that is capable of forming the characteristic imperfect "foldback" hairpin structure (Xie *et al.* 2005). The pri-miRNA transcript is cleaved by DCL1 in the nucleus with the help of the dsRBP HYPONASTIC LEAVES1 (HYL1) to produce the shorter precursor miRNA (pre-miRNA) dsRNA molecule. The first DCL1-catalyzed cleavage step in the miRNA biogenesis pathway is made just below the miRNA duplex region of the dsRNA stem loop (Lu and Fedoroff 2000). The miRNA duplex is then released from the pre-miRNA stem loop structure by the second cleavage step of the miRNA pathway which is again directed by the combined action of DCL1 and HYL1 (Vazquez *et al.* 2004). The two-nucleotide 3′ overhangs of the liberated miRNA duplex are methylated by the sRNA-specific methyltransferase HEN1. The duplex of siRNAs are also methylated by HEN1 and is assumed to protect all sRNA species from polyuridylation and degradation (Yu *et al.* 2005 and Yu *et al.* 2006). The miRNA duplex is then transported to the cytoplasm with several classes of miRNA relying on the action of the *Drosophila* Exportin-5 ortholog HASTY (HST) for this nuclear exportation step (Park *et al.* 2005). In the cytoplasm the mature single-stranded miRNA is loaded onto AGO1 the catalytic center of RISC to guide the slicer activity of AGO1 to repress the expression of complementary mRNA transcripts (Jones-Rhoades *et al.* 2006) which are predominantly mediated by transcript cleavage (Xie and Qi 2008).

In addition tasiRNAs also known to play significant role in RNAi pathway which arises from defined genetic loci (TAS loci) through miRNA-dependent biogenesis pathway (Vaucheret 2006) (Fig 1). The expression of tasiRNAs is initiated by Pol II transcription to yield TAS transcripts that contain miRNA target site(s). The miRNA-directed cleavage of a TAS transcript is thought to generate critical features that are recognized by RdRP6 (Allen *et al.* 2005). The cleaved TAS transcript is converted into dsRNA by RdRP6 a process that also requires the SUPRESSOR OF GENE SILENING 3 (SGS3) (Peragine *et* al. 2007). Successive cleavage of the resulting dsRNA by DCL4 produces a phased array of 21-nt siRNAs (Xie *et al.* 2005). Some of these siRNAs (the ta-siRNAs) are incorporated into RISCs to direct the cleavage of mRNA targets (Peragine *et al.* 2007).

The second cytoplasmic pathway protects cells against the invasion of foreign nucleic acids such as viruses and transgenes through the action of siRNAs that direct the cleavage of homologous RNAs (Lecellier and Voinnet 2004). Viruses engineered to contain an endogenous sequence can trigger silencing of the endogene which is termed 'virus-induced gene silencing' (VIGS) (Baulcombe 1999; Ruiz *et al.* 1998 and Godge *et al.* 2008) (Fig 2). This system involves a branched pathway that also converges on the production of dsRNA. Depending on the nature of the transgene and the virus dsRNA is either formed directly by intra- or intermolecular base pairing (hpRNA constructs IR transgenes) or indirectly through antisense transgenes or replication intermediates

(RNA viruses) or through the action of RdRP6 and other proteins (sense transgenes and DNA viruses) (Smith *et al.* 2000). The subsequent processing of the dsRNA into two classes of siRNAs (Hamilton *et al.* 2002) depends on different DCL activities (Tang *et al.* 2003). DCL3 produces the long siRNAs (24-26 nt) that involved in methylation and systemic silencing while DCL4 produces the short siRNAs (21 nt) (Dunoyer *et al.* 2005) that can either guide RISC-mediated RNA degradation or spread to adjacent cells where they trigger RdRP6-dependent systemic silencing (Himber *et al.* 2003 and Schwach *et al.* 2005).

The third nuclear pathway ensures genome integrity and defense against endogenously repeated DNAs transposons and retroelements. It is related to transcriptional gene silencing (TGS) because it involves DNA methylation and/or chromatin modification by endogenous heterochromatic siRNAs (Zilberman *et al.* 2003 and Chan *et al.* 2004). The key player of this RNAi pathway is heterochromatic siRNAs which are typically 24-nt small RNAs that are associated with genomic repetitive sequences such as transposons retroelements rDNAs and centromeric repeats (Hamilton *et al.* 2002 and Kasschau *et al.* 2007). Current model for heterochromatic siRNA biogenesis states that Pol IVa produces single stranded RNA transcripts from certain genomic loci including transposable elements and other repetitive regions (Lu *et al.* 2005). The Pol IVa transcripts move to the nucleolus where they are converted into dsRNAs by RdRP2 and subsequently processed by DCL3 to yield heterochromatic siRNAs in the nucleolar RNA processing center that colocalizes with Cajal bodies (Li *et al.* 2006). The heterochromatic siRNAs direct DNA and histone methylation in an AGO4-dependent pathway (Zilberman *et al.* 2004). The heterochromatic siRNA-directed DNA methylation also requires the Pol IVb (Herr *et al.* 2005) the SNF2-like ATPase DRD1 (Kanno *et al.* 2005) and the *de novo* cytosine methyltransferase DRM2 (Chan *et al.* 2004). Since AGO4 has been shown to physically interact with the largest subunit of Pol IVb and DCL3 AGO4 and Pol IVb colocalize in the nucleolar RNA processing center Pol IVb may be part the AGO4-containing RISC in the chromatin RNA silencing pathway (Li *et al.* 2006). It has been proposed that the AGO4/NRPD1b/siRNA complex directs target recognition for DRD1- and DRM2-dependent DNA methylation at specific loci (Pontes *et al.* 2006). AGO6 another member of the *Arabidopsis* AGO family has been shown to have partially redundant functions with AGO4 in heterochromatic siRNA-directed silencing (Zheng *et al.* 2007).

5. WORKING MODEL OF RNAi IN PLANTS

RNA interference was discovered in plants as a mechanism whereby invading nucleic acids such as transgenes and viruses are silenced through the action of small RNA molecules (Brodersen and Voinnet 2006). The most important biochemical features of RNAi pathways in plants include the formation of double stranded RNA; processing of dsRNA to small (s) 20–26nt dsRNAs with staggered ends; and inhibitory action of a selected sRNA strand within effector complexes acting on partially or fully complementary RNA or DNA. The present model for RNAi in plants (Fig. 3) includes three phases: initiation by producing small RNAs maintenance by assembly of effector complexes signal amplification and transitive silencing along with dissemination by non-cell autonomous silencing. These phases are briefly described as:

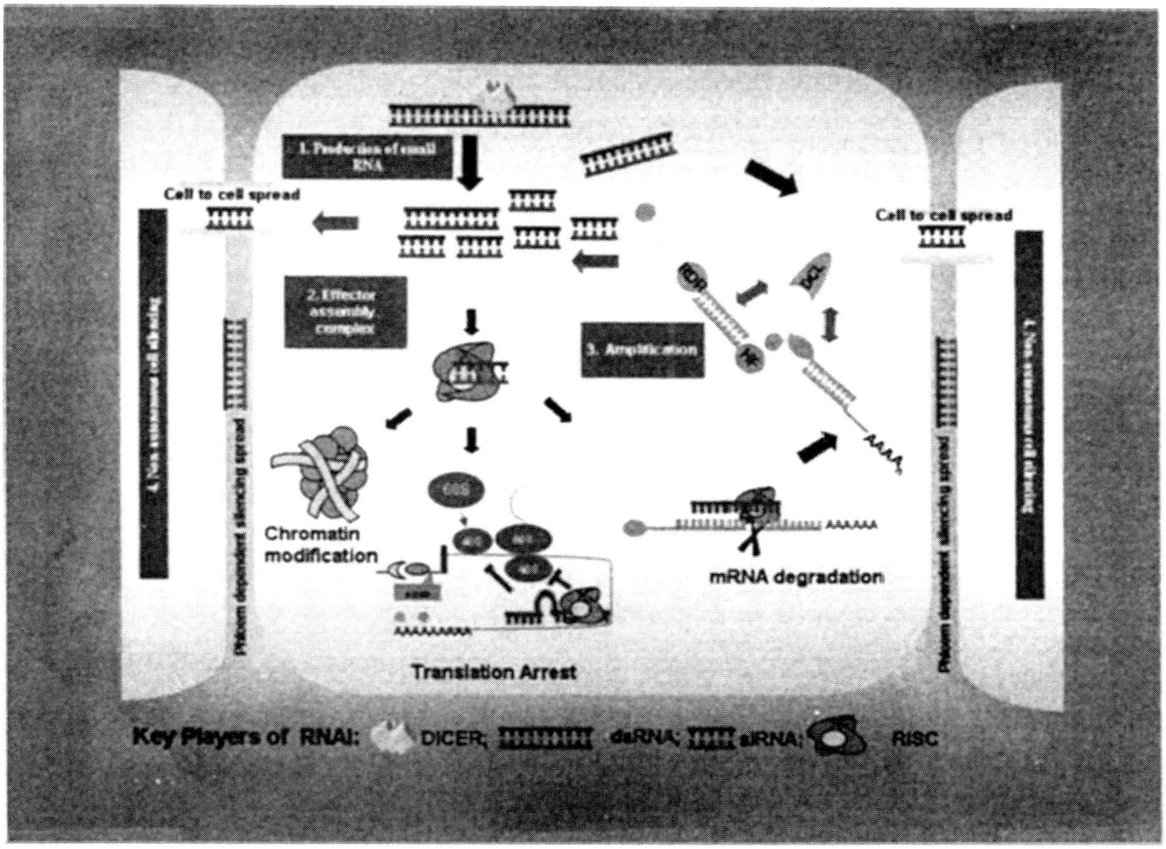

Fig. 3 Simplified working model of RNAi in plants. Most important steps include 1) Dicing leading to the production of small duplex RNAs (21-30 nt); 2) Assembly of effector complexes guiding chromatin remodeling, translational arrest and mRNA cleavages or degradation; 3) Amplification to generate new sources of dsRNA for dicing, leading to further silencing; 4) Non-cell autonomous cell silencing beyond the sites of silencing initiation via putative silencing signals.

5.1 PRODUCTION OF SMALL RNAs

RNA silencing begins with recognition of an RNA trigger by a type III endonuclease Dicer (Bernstein *et al.* 2001) leading to the production of small duplex RNAs 21 to 30 nts in length with the characteristic 2′nt overhang at the 3′ ends. Subsequently the small RNAs are loaded into an effector complex to guide specific RNA silencing (Tomari and Zamore 2005). Two types of RNA molecules have the potential to serve as a trigger of RNA silencing. dsRNAs are precursors of siRNAs whereas ssRNAs with step-loop structures serve as precursors of miRNAs (pre-miRNAs). *Arabidopsis* encodes DCL1-4 all of which recognize dsRNA triggers although the primary role of DCL1 is to process pre-miRNAs. Two classes of siRNAs of sizes 21 to 22 and 24 nt respectively are produced in

Arabidopsis plants and it is likely that the 21, 22 and 24 nt siRNAs are produced by DCL4, DCL2 and DCL3 respectively (Dunoyer *et al.* 2005; Gasciolli *et al.* 2005; Qi *et al.* 2005 and Xie *et al.* 2005). In *Arabidopsis* miRNAs and siRNAs are methylated at the 3′ end which is essential for protection of the small RNAs from degradation mediated by 3′-uridylation activity (Li *et al.* 2005 and Yu *et al.* 2005).

5.2 ASSEMBLY OF EFFECTOR COMPLEXES

To act as silencing triggers double-stranded siRNAs must be channeled through an ordered RISC assembly pathway that results in the selection of one strand and the destruction of the other (Pham and Sontheimer 2005). RISC which directs methylation of chromatin siRISC and miRISC which guide cleavage and translational arrest respectively of target mRNAs play a significant role in assembly of effector complexes (Fig. 4). All of these complexes contain one (guide) strand of the duplex small RNAs as

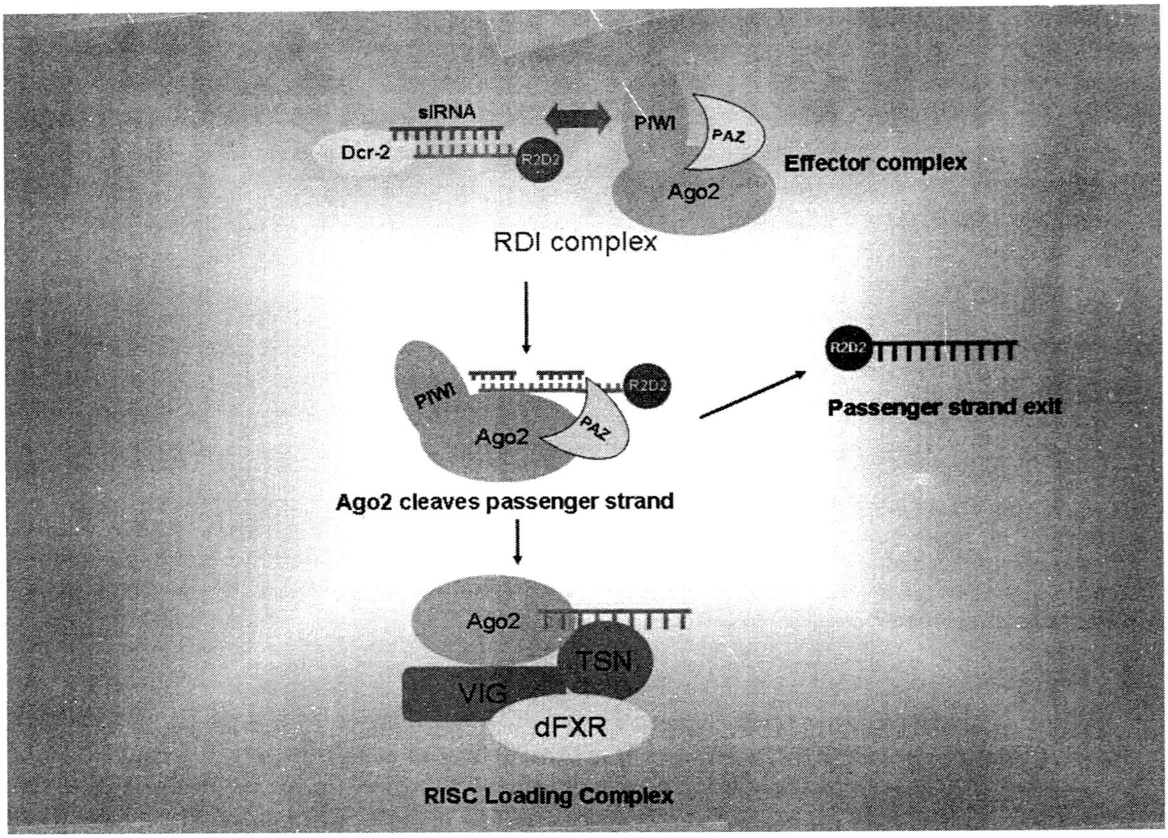

Fig. 4: Formation of RISC assembly complexes. The asymmetric siRNA molecule bound by Dcr2 and R2D2 which sense the stability at both ends of siRNA duplex. This initiation complex is known as RDI complex (Dcr2 –R2D2 initiation complex).Dcr2 is eventually exchanged with Ago2, which by virtue of its PIWI domain cleaves the passenger strand which results in the formation of an active RISC loading complex.

the specificity determinants and a member of the Argonaute protein (AGO) family (Li and Ding 2006). The PIWI domain of AGOs has structural similarities to RNaseH and the ability to cleave the target RNA base-paired with the guide strand siRNA called slicing has been demonstrated for *Arabidopsis* AGO1 (Baumberger and Baulcombe 2005 and Liu *et al.* 2005). It is likely that assembly of these effector complexes may follow a pathway in which siRISC assembly begins with binding of siRNA duplexes by the heterodimer of Dicer-2 and R2D2, a dsRNA binding protein with tandem dsRNA binding motifs in the RISC loading complex (RLC) (Tomari *et al.* 2004) (Fig. 4). Thus Dicer-2 is also required in RISC assembly downstream of siRNA production. Next RLC delivers the siRNA duplex into AGO2 which subsequently cleaves the passenger strand siRNA triggering its dissociation from the complex and activation of RISC that contains only the siRNA guide strand (Matranga 2005 and Rand *et al.* 2005).

5.3 AMPLIFICATION AND TRANSITIVE SILENCING

Fungi nematodes and plants encode eukaryotic RNA-dependent RNA polymerases (RdRP) that generate new sources of dsRNA for dicing leading to further silencing amplification. In both plants and *Caenorhabditis elegans*, RdRP amplification results in the spread of silencing along the target gene beyond the region initially targeted for silencing referred to as transitive RNAi (Sijen *et al.* 2001; Vaistij *et al.* 2002). RdRP genes are essential for RNA silencing in the germ line (*ego-1*) and somatic tissues (*rrf-1*) in *C. elegans* have been identified (Smardon *et al.* 2000 and Sijen *et al.* 2001). *Arabidopsis* encodes six RdRPs designated RdRP1–6 which together with individual DCLs control specific small RNA biogenesis pathways.

5.4 NON-CELL AUTONOMOUS SILENCING

The effects of RNA silencing can spread beyond the sites of silencing initiation *via* a putative specific silencing signal (Voinnet 2005). Two distinct steps have been observed in the spread of RNA silencing in plants. Accumulated evidences suggest a role for 21-nt siRNAs in the short-distance spread and 24-nt siRNAs in the phloem-dependent long-distance transport (Palauqui *et al.* 1997; Hamilton *et al.* 2002 and Himber *et al.* 2003). Although RdRP amplification is not required for the cell-to-cell spread extensive short-distance spread beyond 10 to 15 cells in plants requires the *RdRP6/DCL4* pathway and its product the 21-nt siRNAs (Himber *et al.* 2003; Dunoyer *et al.* 2005; Schwach *et al.* 2005). In contrast a predicted role for the 24-nt siRNAs (or their longer precursor dsRNA) produced by the *RdRP2/DCL3/AGO4* pathway in the long distance silencing spread remains to be rigorously examined. However both classes of siRNAs are found in the phloem indicating their potential to mediate silencing spread in plants (Yoo *et al.* 2004). Similarly it is also not clear if DNA methylation associated with the maintenance or persistent silencing of transgenes play a specific role in non-cell autonomous silencing.

6. METHODS TO INDUCE RNAi IN PLANTS

In RNAi research field one of the biggest challenges is the delivery of the active molecules that will trigger the RNAi pathway in plants. In this system a number of methods for delivery of dsRNA or siRNA into different cells and tissue include transformation with dsRNA-forming vectors for selected gene(s) by an *Agrobacterium* mediated transformations (Chuang and Meyerowtiz 2000 and Waterhouse *et al.* 2001); delivery cognate dsRNA of *uidA* GUS (β-glucuronidase) and TaGLP2a:GFP (green fluorescent protein) reporter genes into single epidermal cells of maize barley and wheat by particle bombardment (Schweizer *et al.* 2000) introducing a *Tobacco rattle virus* (TRV)-based vector in tomato plants by infiltration (Liu *et al.* 2002a); delivery of dsRNA into tobacco suspension cells by cationic oligopeptide polyarginine-siRNA complex; infecting plants with viral vectors that produce dsRNA (Dalmay *et al.* 2000a) and delivery of siRNA into cultured plant cells of rice cotton and slash pine for gene silencing by nanosense pulsed laser-induced stress wave (LISW) (Tang *et al.* 2006) are being used. Among these the most reliable and commonly used approaches for delivery of dsRNA to plants cells are agroinfiltration micro-bombardment and VIGS. These are discussed in the following sections.

6.1 AGROINFILTRATION

Agroinfiltration is a powerful method to study processes connected with RNAi. The injection of *Agrobacterium* carrying similar DNA constructs into the intracellular spaces of leaves for triggering RNA silencing is known as agroinoculation or agroinfiltration (Hily and Liu 2007). In most cases agroinfiltration is used to initiate systemic silencing or to monitor the effect of suppressor genes. In plants cytoplasmic RNAi can be induced efficiently by agroinfiltration similar to a strategy for transient expression of T-DNA vectors after delivery by *Agrobacterium tumefaciens*. The transiently expressed DNA encodes either an ss- or dsRNA which is typically a hairpin (hp) RNA. The infiltration of hairpin constructs are especially effective because their dsRNA can be processed directly to siRNAs while the constructs expressing ssRNA can also be useful to induce silencing (Johansen and Carrington 2001; Voinnet *et al.* 2001; Mlotshwa *et al.* 2002 and Tenllado *et al.* 2003) and for dissecting the mechanism of gene silencing especially concerned with its suppressors systemic silencing signal and also for simple protein purification (Johansen and Carrington 2001; Voinnet *et al.* 2001; Mlotshwa *et al.* 2002 and Tenllado *et al.* 2003). Besides they provide a rapid versatile and convenient way for achieving a very high level of gene expression in a distinct and defined zone.

6.2. MICRO-BOMBARDMENT

In this method a linear or circular template is transferred into the nucleus by micro-bombardment. Synthetic siRNAs are delivered into plants by biolistic pressure to cause silencing of GFP expression. Bombarding cells with particles coated with dsRNA or siRNA or DNA that encode hairpin constructs as well as sense or antisense RNA activate the RNAi pathway. The silencing effect of RNAi is occasionally detected as early as a day after bombardment and it continues up to 3 to 4 days post bombardment. Systemic spread of the silencing occurred 2 weeks later to manifest in the vascular tissues of the non-bombarded leaves of *Nicotiana benthamiana* that were closest to the bombarded ones. After one month or so the loss of GFP expression was seen in non-vascular tissues as well. RNA blot hybridization with systemic leaves indicated that the biolistically delivered siRNAs induced due to *de novo* formation of siRNAs which accumulated to cause systemic silencing (Klahre *et al.* 2002).

6.3. VIRUS INDUCED GENE SILENCING (VIGS)

Modified viruses as RNA silencing triggers are used as a mean for inducing RNA in plants. Different RNA and DNA viruses have been modified to serve as vectors for gene expression (Timmermans *et al.* 1994 and Pogue *et al.* 2002). Some viruses such as *Tobacco mosaic virus* (TMV) *Potato virus X* (PVX) and TRV can be used for both protein expression and gene silencing (Kumagai *et al.* 1995; Angell and Baulcombe 1999; MacFarlane and Popovich 2000 and Mallory *et al.* 2002). All RNA virus-derived expression vectors will not be useful as silencing vectors because many have potent anti-silencing proteins such as TEV (*Tobacco etch virus*) that directly interfere with host silencing machinery (Kumagai *et al.* 1995; Palmer and Rybicki 2001). Similarly DNA viruses have not been used extensively as expression vectors due to their size constraints for movement (Kjemtrup *et al.* 1998). However a non-mobile Maize streak Virus (MSV)-derived vector has been successfully used for long-term production of protein in maize cell cultures (Kumagai *et al.* 1995). Using viral vectors to silence endogenous plant genes requires cloning homologous gene fragments into the virus without compromising viral replication and movement. This was first demonstrated in RNA viruses by inserting sequences into TMV (Dallwitz and Zurcher 1996) and then for DNA viruses by replacing the coat protein gene with a homologous sequence (Kjemtrup *et al.* 1998). These reports used visible markers for gene silencing phytoene desaturase (*PDS)* and chalcone synthase (*CHS)* providing a measure of the tissue specificity of silencing as these have been involved in carotenoid metabolic pathway. The *PDS* gene acts on the antenna complex of the thylakoid membranes and protects the chlorophyll from photooxidation. By silencing this gene a drastic decrease in leaf carotene content resulted into the appearance of photobleaching symptom (Liu *et al.* 2002 and Turnage *et al.* 2002). Similarly over expression of *CHS* gene causing an albino phenotype instead of producing the anticipated deep orange color (Cogoni *et al.* 1994). As a result their action as a phenotypic marker helps in easy understanding of the mechanism of gene silencing. Table 1 shows some general characteristics for currently available virus-derived gene silencing vectors. Most viruses are plus-strand RNA viruses or satellites whereas *Tomato golden mosaic virus* (TGMV) and *Cabbage leaf curl virus* (CaLCuV) are DNA viruses. Though RNA viruses replicate in the cytoplasm, DNA viruses replicate in plant nuclei using the host DNA replication machinery. Both types of viruses induce diffusible homology-dependent systemic silencing of endogenous genes. However the extent of silencing spread and the severity of viral symptoms can vary significantly in different host plants and host/virus combinations. With the variety of viruses and the diversity of infection patterns transmission vectors and plant defenses it is not surprising that viruses differ with respect to silencing (Teycheney and Tepfer 2001). Because the continuing development of virus-based silencing vectors can extend VIGS to economically important plants it is useful to consider some of the characteristics of successful VIGS vectors.

TABLE 1 : RNAi effects on targeted region in some fungal plant pathogens.

Pathogen	*Targeted region*	*Result*	*References*
Magnaporthae oryzae	*eGFP*	Sequence specific degradation of mRNA	Kadotani *et al.* 2003
Cladosporium falvum	*cgl 1* and *cgl 2*	Blocking disease infection spread	Segers *et al.* 1999
Venturia inaequalis	*Multiple inverted repeats*	-	Fitzgerald *et al.* 2004
Fusarium graminearum	-	-	Nakayashiki 2005
Blumeria graminis	*Mlo*	Immunity	Schweizer *et al.* 2000

7. RNAi APPLICATION IN CROP PLANTS:

7.1. IMPROVEMENT OF PLANT NUTRITIONAL VALUE

Genetic engineering technologies have advantages over classical breeding not only by enlarging the scope of genes and the types of mutations to be manipulated but also by the ability to control the spatial and temporal expression patterns of the genes of interest. Control of spatial and temporal expression patterns is important because for many crops the tissue that is consumed as food (mostly seeds) is distinct from tissue that controls plant growth and productivity (mainly roots and shoots). However in many cases genes controlling specific traits do not operate in a tissue-specific manner but function in all or most plant organs. Therefore a mutation of a given gene that is good for the improvement of seed quality is often deleterious for the growth of other plant organs.

A well-studied example illustrating such a problem is increasing the level of lysine in plants. Lysine synthesis is strongly regulated by a feedback inhibition loop in which lysine inhibits the activity of dihydrodipicolinate synthase (DHPS) the first enzyme on the pathway specifically committed to lysine biosynthesis. Genetic mutations in the tobacco DHPS gene rendering its encoded DHPS lysine-insensitive cause lysine overproduction in all plant organs (Frankard *et al.* 1992 and Negrutiu *et al.* 1984). However although high lysine levels in seeds are beneficial increases in the level of this amino acid in vegetative tissues are undesirable because high levels of lysine cause abnormal vegetative growth and flower development that in turn reduces seed yield (Frankard *et al.* 1992 and Negrutiu *et al.* 1984). Targeting the expression of bacterial genes encoding lysine-insensitive DHPS to seeds of several transgenic model and crop plants using seed-specific promoters eliminated its undesirable effects in vegetative tissues resulting in plants with good growth characteristics and high lysine levels in their seeds (Falco *et al.* 1995; Karchi *et al.* 1994 and Mazur *et al.* 1999). Tissue-specific manipulation in transgenic plants holds importance not only for gene overexpression but also for gene suppression approaches. This is because traits of interest in plant organs that are consumed as foods may also be negatively regulated by different genes controlling a variety of factors such as:

(*i*) enzymes that either degrade or convert the desired metabolites into undesirable ones; and (*ii*) enzymes or cellular processes or regulatory factors that interfere with the production of the desired metabolite.

Such genes could be suppressed but their constitutive suppression might have adverse effects on plant growth and reproduction.

To date the utilization of the RNAi technology to enhance specifically the nutritional value of plant organs that are consumed as foods is progressively increasing with several published successful efforts suggesting that this approach has tremendous potential. The first is also associated with improving lysine level in seeds. Because lysine accumulation in plants is negatively affected by its catabolism (degradation), constitutive knockout of lysine catabolism using a gene insertion knockout approach accelerates lysine accumulation in seeds when combined with the seed-specific expression of a feedback-insensitive DHPS (Zhu and Galili 2003). However seeds of plants that have accumulated elevated lysine levels germinate poorly because the excess lysine levels produced in the seeds are not efficiently degraded during seed germination (Zhu and Galili 2003). Reduction of lysine catabolism specifically during seed development by an RNAi approach indeed improves seed germination (Zhu and Galili 2004).

Seed-specific RNAi approaches have also successfully been used to generate dominant high lysine corn by suppressing the expression of 22-kD maize zein storage proteins a group of abundant proteins in maize seed but poor in lysine content (Segal *et al.* 2003). Reduction of lysine-poor zeins by traditional breeding was only successful in screening recessive lysine-rich mutants called opaque mutants particularly opaque-2. Opaque-2 encodes a maize b-zip type transcriptional factor that controls the expression of a subset of storage proteins including the 22-kD zein storage protein. Albeit rich in lysine this opaque-2 mutant is not very useful in agriculture because of its other adverse effects on seed quality and yield. Down-regulation of the maize lysine-poor 22-kD zein gene *via* RNAi does not alter the general functions of the Opaque-2 transcription factor but generates quality and normal maize seeds with high levels of lysine-rich proteins and free lysine. Maize is mostly used in western countries for livestock feed but in many developing countries it is also a staple crop for humans. It is thus expected that high lysine maize developed using RNAi approaches will be of significant economical and humanitarian significance world wide and that a similar RNAi-mediated approach will be used to enhance the lysine content in seeds of other staple crops.

Another nutritionally important crop is cotton. Cotton is mainly used for fiber production and is an important crop not only in developed countries but also in many developing countries where malnutrition and starvation are widespread (Sunilkumar *et al.* 2006). In these developing areas the cottonseeds that remain after fiber extraction could be extensively used as sources of protein and calories but they are largely underutilized because they contain a toxic gossypol terpenoid. Gossypol is also produced in vegetative cotton tissues where it protects cotton plants from insects and other pathogens (Sunilkumar *et al.* 2006). Hence the suppression of its production should occur specifically in cottonseeds. Indeed transgenic cotton plants expressing an

RNAi construct of the δ-cadinene synthase gene of gossypol synthesis fused to a seed-specific promoter caused seed-specific reduction of this metabolite while its content in non-seed tissues was comparable to the control plants (Sunilkumar *et al.* 2006). These cotton plants are thus expected to have similar insect and pathogen resistance to that of wild type cotton but to produce seeds with higher nutritional value.

While insufficient food calories is one of the major causes of malnutrition in developing countries an excess of digested calories leads to obesity and other diseases in developed countries (Maskarinec *et al.* 2006). Foods rich in inefficiently digested carbohydrates such as fiber are therefore considered to be health promoting (Williams 1995). The major nutritional source of plant-derived carbohydrates is starch which is composed of amylopectin and amylose polysaccharides synthesized by two competitive pathways. Yet in cooked plant foods undergoing cooling before eating amylose molecules tend to efficiently form digestion-resistant complexes that are part of healthy dietary fiber (Crowe *et al.* 2000). Aiming to increase the relative content of amylose in wheat grains an RNAi construct designed to silence the genes encoding the two starch-branching isozymes of amylopectin synthesis were expressed under a seed-specific promoter in wheat (Regina *et al.* 2006). This resulted in increased grain amylose content to over 70% of the total starch content. When fed to rats in a diet as a wholemeal the high amylose grains had positive effects on indices of gastrointestinal health elucidating the potential of RNAi technology to improve human health particularly in developing countries (Regina *et al.* 2006).

A significant part of human diets both in developed and developing countries is composed of vegetables. Among the vegetables tomato fruits are relatively rich in a number of vitamins as well other health promoting metabolites such as flavonoids and carotenoids including the strong antioxidant carotenoid or lycopene which provides the tomato fruit with its typical red color. Carotenoids are synthesized by the same biosynthetic pathway that synthesizes chlorophyll and it has been shown that genes controlling the light-mediated regulation of the photosynthetic machinery also influence tomato fruit quality by altering the levels of carotenoids and flavonoids (Adams-Phillips *et al.* 2004). The tomato high pigment (hp-2) phenotype which accumulates elevated levels of carotenoids and flavonoids is due to mutations in the regulatory gene DE-ETHIOLATED1 (DET1) which represses several light-dependent signaling pathways (Levin *et al.* 2003 and Mustilli *et al.* 1999). Despite their positive effects on fruit quality hp-2 mutants generally possess abnormal growth and various vegetative phenotypes and so are transgenic plants in which the DET1 gene is constitutively silenced (Davuluri *et al.* 2004; Levin *et al.* 2003 and Mustilli *et al.* 1999). Such negative phenotypes are not unexpected taking into account the central regulatory function of the DET1 gene in light signaling and photosynthesis. Yet RNAi-mediated suppression of DET1 expression under fruit-specific promoters has recently shown to improve carotenoid and flavonoid levels in tomato fruits with minimal effects on plant growth and other fruit quality parameters (Davuluri *et al.* 2005). This exemplifies again how coupling the highly efficient RNAi gene suppression machinery with tissue specific promoters provides a highly valuable trait that is impossible to obtain by conventional breeding.

RNAi technology has also been successful in genetic modification of the fatty acid composition of oil. A hairpin RNA- (hpRNA) mediated RNAi method was used in cotton to down-regulate two key fatty acid desaturase genes encoding stearoyl-acyl-carrier protein Δ 9-desaturase and oleoyl-phosphatidylcholine ω 6-desaturase (Liu *et al.* 2002). Knockdown of these two genes in cotton led to the increase of nutritionally improved high-oleic (HO) and high-stearic (HS) cottonseed oils that are essential fatty acids for human heart health. It is almost certain that more cases of improved crops via dsRNA-triggered RNAi technology will be reported in the coming years. With more target genes of metabolic pathways discovered in the practice of nutritional genomics (Grusak 2002) in plants RNAi and miRNA technologies will become essential tools to manipulate plant macro- and micro-nutrients for human health. The readers are referred to Larkin and Harrigan (2007) for examples of the application of metabolic profiling to studying a diverse range of transgenically modified plants. It is evident that metabolic profiling platforms will have value in assessing changes in pathways associated with the production of important nutrients and plant chemicals including but not restricted to fatty acids amino acids carbohydrates carotenoids flavonoids and terpenses such as gossypol.

7.2. RNAi IN PLANT DISEASE MANAGEMENT

Despite substantial advances in plant disease management strategies our global food supply is still threatened by a multitude of pathogens and pests. This changed scenario warrants us to respond more efficiently and effectively to this problem. The situation demands judicious blending of conventional, unconventional and frontier technologies. In this sense RNAi technology has emerged as one of the most potential and promising strategies for enhancing the building of resistance in plants to combat various fungal bacterial viral and nematode diseases causing huge losses in important agricultural crops. The nature of this biological phenomenon has been evaluated in a number of host-pathogen systems and effectively used to silence the action of pathogen. Many of the examples listed below illustrate the possibilities for commercial exploitation of this inherent biological mechanism to generate disease-resistant plants in the future by taking advantage of this approach.

7.2.1. Management of Plant Pathogenic Fungi

RNA-mediated gene silencing (RNA silencing) is used as a reverse tool for gene targeting in fungi. Homology-based gene silencing induced by transgenes (co-suppression) antisense or dsRNA has been demonstrated in many plant pathogenic fungi including *Cladosporium fulvum* (Hamada and Spanu 1998) *Magnaporthae oryzae* (Kadotani *et al.* 2003) *Venturia inaequalis* (Fitzgerald *et al.* 2004) *Neurospora crassa* (Goldoni *et al.* 2004) *Aspergillus nidulans* (Hammond and Keller 2005) and *Fusarium graminearum* (Nakayashiki 2005) (Table 1) whether it is suitable for large-scale mutagenesis in fungal pathogens remains to be tested. Hypermorphic mechanism of RNA interference implies that this technique can also be applicable to all those plant pathogenic fungi which are polyploid and polykaryotic in nature. And also offers a solution to the problem where frequent lack of multiple marker genes in fungi is experienced. Simultaneous silencing of several unrelated genes by introducing a single chimeric construct has been demonstrated in case of *Venturia inaequalis* (Fitzgerald *et al.* 2004).

HCf-1 a gene that codes for a hydrophobin of the tomato pathogen *C. fulvum* (Spanu 1997) was co-suppressed by ectopic integration of homologous transgenes. Transformation of *Cladosporium fulvum* with DNA containing a truncated copy of the hydrophobin gene *HCf-1* caused co-suppression of hydrophobin synthesis in 30% of the transformants. The co-suppressed isolates had a hydrophilic phenotype lower levels of *HCf-1* mRNA than wild type and contain multiple copies of the plasmid integrated as tandem repeats at ectopic sites in the genome (Hamada and Spanu 1998). The transcription rate of *HCf-1* in the co-suppressed isolates was higher than in the untransformed strains suggested that silencing acted at the post-transcriptional level (Hamada and Spanu 1998). This was due to ectopic integration of the transgene next to promoters which initiate transcription to form antisense RNA and that this in turn determines down-regulation of HCf-1. But gene silencing was not associated with DNA cytosine methylation (Hamada and Spanu 1998). Similarly the silencing of *cgl1* and *cgl2* genes using the cgl2 hairpin construct in *Cladosporium fulvum* has also been reported (Segers *et al.* 1999) though the effect was possibly restricted to highly homolougous genes (exons of *cgl 1* and *cgl 2* are 87% identical). However the less homologus *cgl 3* (53% overall identity to *cgl 2*) was not affected as the target specificity always depends upon the actual sequence alignment and more over short regions of high density that led to unwanted off-targets effects. Such a strategy could be exploited for protecting the consumable products of vegetables and fruits crops from the post harvest diseases caused by different plant pathogens in future.

Fitzgerald and collegues (2004) using hairpin vector technology have been able to trigger simultaneous high frequency silencing of a green fluorescent protein (*GFP*) transgene and an endogenous trihydroxynaphthalene reductase gene (*THN*) in *V. inaequalis*. *GFP* transgene acting as easily detectable visible marker while the trihydroxynaphthalene reductase gene (*THN*) playing role in melanin biosynthesis. High frequency gene silencing was achieved using hairpin constructs for the *GFP* or the *THN* genes transferred by *Agrobacterium* (71 and 61% respectively). *THN*-silenced transformants exhibited a distinctive light brown phenotype and maintained the ability to infect apple. Silencing of both genes with this construct occurred at a frequency of 51% of all the transformants. All 125 colonies silenced for the GFP gene were also silenced for THN (Fitzgerald *et al.* 2004). Similarly multiple gene silencing has been achieved in *Cryptococcus neoformans* using chimeric hairpin constructs (Liu *et al.* 2002) and in plants using partial sense constructs (Abbott *et al.* 2002).

The first effort towards the systematic silencing of *Magnaporthe grisea* a causal organism of rice blast was carried out in by Kadotani *et al.* (2003) by using the enhanced green florescent protein gene as a model. To assess the ability of RNA species to induce silencing in fungus plasmid construct expressing sense antisense and hairpin RNA were introduced into an *eGFP*-expressing transformants. The fluorescence of *eGFP* in the transformants was silenced much more efficiently by hairpin RNA of *eGFP* than by other RNA species. In the silenced transformants the accumulation of *eGFP* mRNA was drastically reduced. But not methylation of coding or promoter region was involved. The small interfering RNA molecules of 19-23 nucleotides were observed in both sense and antisense strands of *eGFP* gene (Kadotani *et al* 2003). Later on Nakayashiki and collegues (2005) developed a protocol for silencing the *mpg1* and polyketide synthase-like genes. *mpg1* gene is a hydrophobin gene which is essential for pathogenicity as it act as a cellular relay for adhesion and trigger for the development of appressorium (Talbot *et al.* 1996). Their work on this host-pathogen system revealed that they were successfully able to silence the above mentioned genes at varying degrees by pSilent-1-based vectors in 70–90% of the resulting transformants. Ten to fifteen per cent of the silenced transformants exhibited almost "null phenotype". This vector was also efficiently applicable to silence a *GFP* reporter in another ascomycete fungus *Colletotrichum lagenarium* (Nakayashiki 2005).

7.2.2. Management of Plant Pathogenic Bacteria

One of the striking examples of bacterial disease management where RNAi showed a remarkable type of gene regulation was documented by Escobar *et al.* (2001). They developed a crown gall disease management strategy that targets the process of tumourogensis (gall formation) by initiating RNAi of the *iaaM* and *ipt* oncogenes. Expression of these genes is a prerequisite for wild type tumor formation. Transgenic *Arabidopsis thaliana* and *Lycopersicon esculentum* transformed with RNAi constructs targeting *iaaM* and *ipt* gene(s) showed resistance to crown gall disease. Transgenic plants generated through this technology contained a modified version of these two bacterial gene(s) required to cause the disease and was the first report to manage a major bacterial disease through RNAi. The extra genes recognize and effectively shut down the expression of the corresponding bacterial gene during infection thus preventing the spread of infection. The incoming bacteria could not make the hormones needed to cause tumors and plants deficient in silencing were hyper-susceptible to *A tumefaciens* (Dunoyer *et al.* 2007). Successful infection relied on a potent anti-silencing state established in tumors whereby siRNA synthesis is specifically inhibited. The procedure can be exploited to develop broad-spectrum resistance in ornamental and horticultural plants which are susceptible to crown gall tumorigenesis. This approach can be advocated for the effective management of those pathogens which multiply very rapid and results in tumor formation such as *Albugo candida Synchytrium endobioticum Erwinia amylovora etc.* The natsiRNA (nat-siRNAATGB2) was strongly induced in *Arabidopsis* upon infection by *Pseudomonas syringae pv tomato* and down-regulates a PPRL gene that encodes a negative regulator of the RPS2 disease resistance pathway. As a result the induction of nat-siRNAATGB2 increases the RPS2-mediated race-specific resistance against *P. syringae* pv *tomato* in *Arabidopsis* (Katiyar-Agarwal *et al.* 2006). Recently the accumulation of a new class of sRNA 30 to 40 nucleotides in length termed long-siRNAs (lsiRNAs) was found associated with *P. syringae* infection. One of these lsiRNAs AtlsiRNA-1 contributes to plant bacterial resistance by silencing AtRAP a negative regulator of plant defense (Katiyar and Agarwal *et al.* 2007). A *Pseudomonas* bacterial flagellin derived peptide is found to induce the accumulation of miR393 in *Arabidopsis*.

miR393 negatively regulates mRNAs of F-box auxin receptors resulting in increased resistance to the bacterium (*P. syringae*) and the overexpression of miR393 was shown to reduce the plant's bacterial titer by 5-fold (Navarro *et al.* 2006).

7.2.3. Management of Plant Pathogenic Viruses

Antiviral RNAi technology has been used for viral disease management in human cell lines (Bitko and Barik 2001; Gitlin *et al.* 2002; Jacque *et al.* 2002 and Novina *et al.* 2002). Such silencing mechanisms (RNAi) can also be exploited to protect and manage viral infections in plants (Waterhouse *et al.* 2001 and Ullu *et al.* 2002). The effectiveness of the technology in generating virus resistant plants was first reported to PVY in potato harbouring vectors for simultaneous expression of both sense and antisense transcripts of the helper-component *proteinase* (*HC-Pro*) gene (Waterhouse *et al.* 1998). The *P1/HC-Pro* suppressors from the potyvirus inhabited silencing at a step down stream of dsRNA processing possibly by preventing the unwinding of duplex siRNAs or the incorporation into RISC or both (Chapman *et al.* 2004). The utilization of RANi technology has resulted in inducing immunity reaction against several other viruses in different plant-virus systems (Table 2).

In phyto-pathogenic DNA viruses like geminiviruses non-coding intergenic region of *Mungbean yellow mosaic India virus* (MYMIV) was expressed as hairpin construct under the control of the 35S promoter and used as biolistically to inoculate MYMIV-infected black gram plants and showed a complete recovery from infection which lasted until senescence (Pooggin *et al.* 2003). RNAi mediated silencing of geminiviruses using transient protoplast assay where protoplasts were co-transferred with a siRNA designed to replicase (Rep)-coding sequence of *African cassava mosaic virus* (ACMV) and the genomic DNA of ACMV resulted in 99% reduction in Rep transcripts and 66% reduction in viral DNA (Vanitharani *et al.* 2003). It was observed that siRNA was able to silence a closely related strain of ACMV but not a more distantly related virus.

About more than 40 viral suppressors have been identified in plant viruses (Ruiz and Voinnet 2007). Results from some of the well-studied virus suppressors indicated that suppressors interfere with systemic signaling for silencing (Mlotshwas *et al.* 2002). During last few years the *p69* encoded by *Turnip yellow mosaic virus* has been identified as silencing suppressors that prevented host RDR-dependent secondary dsRNA synthesis (Chen *et al.* 2004). *P14* protein encoded by aureus viruses suppressed both virus and transgene-induced silencing by sequestering both long dsRNA and siRNA without size specificity (Merai *et al.* 2005). Multiple suppressors have been reported in *Citrus tristeza virus* where *p20* and coat protein (*CP*) play important role in suppression of silencing signal and *p23* inhibited intracellular silencing (Lu *et al.* 2004). Multiple viral components viral RNAs and putative RNA replicase proteins were reported for a silencing or suppression of *Red clover necrotic mosaic virus* (Takeda *et al.* 2005). In this case the RNA silencing machinery deprived of DICER-like enzymes by the viral replication complexes appears to be the cause of the suppression. *Pns10* encoded by *Rice dwarf virus* suppressed local and systemic S-PTGS but not IR-PTGS suggesting that *Pns10* also targets an upstream step of dsRNA formation in the silencing pathway (Cao *et al.* 2005).

TABLE 2 : Effects of targeted region of RNAi in various plant-virus systems.

Host system	*Virus*	*Targeted region*	*References*
N. benthamiana, M. esculenta	*African cassava mosaic virus*	*pds, su, cyp79d2*	Fofana *et al.* 2004
Barley, wheat	*Barley stripe mosaic virus*	*pds*	Holzberg *et al.* 2002; Scofield *et al.* 2005
Soybean	*Bean pod mottle virus*	*pds*	Zhang and Ghabrial 2006
Barley, rice, maize	*Brome mosaic virus*	*pds, actin 1, rubisco activase*	Ding *et al.* 2006
Arabidopsis	*Cabbage leaf curl virus*	*gfp, CH42, pds*	Turnage *et al.* 2002
P. sativum	*Pea early browning virus*	*pspds, uni, kor*	Constantini *et al.* 2004
N. benthamiana	*Poplar mosaic virus*	*gfp*	Naylor *et al.* 2005
N. benthamiana, S. tuberosum	*Potato virus X*	*pds, gfp*	Ruiz *et al.* 1998; Faivre-Rampant *et al.* 2004
Nicotiana tabacum	*Satellite tobacco mosaic virus*	*Several genes*	Gossele *et al.* 2002
N. benthamiana, N. tabacum	*Tobacco mosaic virus*	*pds, psy*	Kumagai *et al.* 1995
N. benthamiana, Arabidopsis, tomato, *Solanum* species, Chilli pepper, opium poppy, *Aquilegia*	*Tobacco rattle virus*	*Rar1, EDS1, NPR1/NIM1, pds, rbcS, gfp*	Liu *et al.* 2002b; Ratcliff *et al.* 2001; Brigneti *et al.* 2004; Chung *et al.* 2004; Hileman *et al.* 2005; Gould and Kramer 2007
N. benthamiana	*Tomato bushy shunt virus*	*gfp*	Hou and Qiu 2003
N. benthamiana	*Tomato golden mosaic virus*	*su, luc*	Peele *et al.* 2001
N. benthamiana, Lycopersicon esculentum N. glutinosa, N. tabacum	*Tomato yellow leaf curl China virus-associated b DNA satellite*	*pcna, pds, su, gfp*	Tao and Zhou 2004

(Modified after Godge *et al.* 2008)

Niu and colleagues (2006) used a 273-bp (base pair) sequence of the *Arabidopsis* miR159 a pre-miRNA transcript expressing amiRNAs against the viral suppressor genes *P69* and *HC-Pro* to provide resistance against *Turnip yellow mosaic virus* and *Turnip mosaic virus* infection respectively. In addition a dimeric construct harboring two unique amiRNAs against both viral suppressors conferred resistance against these two viruses in inoculated *Arabidopsis* plants.

Similarly Qu *et al.* (2007) used a different amiRNA vector to target the 2 b viral suppressor of the *Cucumber mosaic virus* (CMV); a suppressor that interacted with and blocked the slicer activity of *AGO1* had also shown to confer resistance to CMV infection in transgenic tobacco. A strong correlation between virus resistance and the expression level of the 2 b-specific amiRNA was shown for individual plant lines.

It is evident from above-mentioned reports that the RNA components such as single strand template RNA dsRNA and/or siRNA of the silencing pathways are the preferred targets of most viral suppressors. However plant viruses are known to have evolved a counter-silencing mechanism by encoding proteins that can overcome such resistance (Li and Ding 2006; Díaz-Pendón and Ding 2008). These suppressors of gene silencing are often involved in viral pathogenicity mediate synergism among plant viruses and result in the induction of more severe disease. Simultaneous silencing of such diverse plant viruses can be achieved by designing hairpin structures that can target a distinct virus in a single construct (Díaz-Pendón and Ding 2008).

Contrarily the RNAi system may cause an increase in the severity of viral pathogenesis and/or encode proteins which can inactivate essential genes in the RNAi machinery (Elbashir *et al.* 2001 and Li *et al.* 2002) that helps them in their replication in the host genome (Hannon 2002).

7.2.4. Management of Plant Parasitic Nematodes

Several major plant parasitic nematodes such as the root-knot (*Meloidogyne* spp.) and cyst (*Heterodera* spp.) along with other minor nematodes cause significant damage to important crops like legumes vegetables and cereals in most parts of the world and continue to threaten these agricultural crops. So a natural eco-friendly defense strategy that delivers a cost-effective control of plant parasitic nematodes is needed which is difficult to achieve through conventional approaches. However the birth of RNAi technology from classical *C. elegans* studies has shown the ways and means to explore the possibilities of this mechanism for protecting plants from nematode damage. In this context two approaches have been advocated one of them relies on targeting plant genes that are involved with the infection process and the second approach targets essential genes within the nematode. RNAi can be induced in *C. elegans* by feeding it dsRNA so it was reasoned that expressing hpRNAs containing sequences of vital nematode genes in the host plant might deliver dsRNA to a feeding nematode to incapacitate or kill it.

After the demonstration of gene silencing using siRNA duplexes in the nematode (Fire *et al.* 1998) the use of RNAi has rapidly emerged as the technique of choice for plant nematologists to put their efforts especially for nematode management in agriculture. RNAi-mediated suppression of a gene plays an indispensable role in hampering the nematode development and may adversely affect the progression of pathogenesis in direct or indirect ways. There are accumulating evidences for the efficacy of RNAi in plant parasitic nematode management and a wide range of genes have been targeted for silencing in cyst and root-knot nematode species (Table 3).

RNAi in the context of phyto-parasitic nematodes was used as early as the beginning of this century when stimulation of oral ingestion by second-stage juveniles of cyst nematodes *H. glycines G. pallida* (Urwin *et al.* 2002) and root-knot nematode *M. incognita* (Bakhetia *et al.* 2005) was achieved by using octopamine. Later on resorcinol- and

TABLE 3 : RNAi effect on targeted region of plant parasitic nematodes.

Nematode	*Targeted region*	*RNAi affect*
M. incognita	Cysteine proteinase	Delayed development, Decrease in established nematodes population
	Dual oxidase	Decrease in established nematodes population and fecundity.
	Splicing factor, Integrase	Reduction in gall formation and Female nematode population
	Secreted peptide 16D 10	Reduction in gall formation and established nematode population
H. glycines	Cysteine proteinase	Increased male: female ratio.
	C-type lectin	Reduction in established nematodes population
	Major sperm protein	Reduction in mRNA level
	Aminopeptidase	Decrease in established nematodes population and increase in male: female ratio.
	_-1,4-endoglucanase	Decrease in established nematodes population
	Pectate lyase , Chorismate mutase	Increase in male: female ratio.
	Secreted peptide SYV46	Decrease in established nematode population
G. pallida	Cysteine proteinase	Increase in male: female ratio.
	FMR Famide-like peptides	Motility inhibited
G. rostochiensis	Chitin synthase	Delay in egg hatch
	_-1,4-endoglucanase	Decrease in established nematodes population
	Secreted amphid protein	Reduction in invasion ability to locate and invade plant roots
Heterodera schachtii	*Suc* transporter genes	Reduction of female nematode development

(Modified after Karakas 2008)

serotonin-inducing dsRNA uptake by second stage juvenile of *M. incognita* was found to be more effective than octopimine (Rosso *et al.* 2005). The genes targeted by RNAi to date are expressed in a range of different tissues and cell types. The ingested dsRNA can silence genes in the intestine (Urwin *et al.* 2002 and Shingles *et al.* 2007) female reproductive system (Lilley *et al.* 2005) sperm (Urwin *et al.* 2002 and Steeves *et al.* 2006) and both subventral and dorsal oesophageal glands (Chen *et al.* 2005 and Rosso *et al.* 2005; Huang *et al.* 2006; Bakhetia *et al.* 2007). Uptake of dsRNA from the gut is a proven route to systemic RNAi in *C. elegans*. The systemic nature of RNAi in plant parasitic nematodes following ingestion of dsRNA suggests that they share similar uptake and dispersal pathways.

However RNAi of a *chitin synthase* gene expressed in the eggs of *Meloidogyne artiella* was achieved by soaking intact eggs contained within their gelatinous matrix in a solution containing dsRNA (Fanelli *et al.* 2005). The enzyme plays a role in the synthesis of the chitinous layer in the eggshell. Depletion of its transcript by RNAi led to a reduction in stainable chitin in eggshells and a delay in hatching of juveniles from treated eggs. Similarly RNAi targeting for *cysteine proteinase* transcripts did not reduce parasitic population of established nematodes on plants but result into the alteration of their sexual fate in favour of males at 14 days after invasion (Urwin *et al.* 2002).

On the other hand *H. glycines* exposed to dsRNA corresponding to a protein with homology to C-type lectins did not affect sexual fate but 41% fewer nematodes were recovered from the plants (Urwin *et al.* 2002). But treatment with dsRNA corresponding to the major sperm protein (MSP) had no effect on nematode development or sexual fate 14 days after treatment. In addition to this reduction in transcript abundance for targeted mRNAs in the infective juvenile and for MSP transcripts when males reached sexual maturity and sperm are produced was observed (Urwin *et al.* 2002). In further extension of such types of experiments showed efficient FITC uptake by soaking *M. incognita* 90-95% of individuals swallowed the dye when the target was a dual oxidase (an enzyme comprised with a peroxidase domain EF-hands and NADPH oxidase domain and potentially involved in extracellular matrix development). The effect of RNAi was observed when root knot nematode (RKN) juveniles were fed on dual oxidase-derived dsRNA the reduction in the number and size of established females at 14 and 35 days post infection with an overall reduction of 70% in egg production was observed (Bakhetia *et al.* 2005). RNAi has also been induced for a *chitin synthase* gene that is expressed in the eggshells of *M. artiella* after soaking its developing eggs in a dsRNA (Fanelli *et al.* 2005).

Heterodera schachtii induces syncytial feeding structures in the roots of host plants and this requires the up-regulation of *Suc* transporter genes to facilitate increased nutrient flow to the developing structure. Targeting these genes and down-regulating them with RNA silencing resulted in a significant reduction of female nematode development (Hoffman *et al.* 2008). Indeed tobacco plants transformed with hpRNA constructs against two such root-knot nematode genes have shown such an effect: the target mRNAs in the plant parasitic nematodes were dramatically reduced and the plants showed effective resistance against the parasite (Fairbairn *et al.* 2007).

8. CONCLUSIONS AND FUTURE OUTLOOK OF RNAi

RNAi and miRNA technologies of gene silencing are newly developed genomics tools that have great advantages over antisense and co-suppression due to their higher silencing efficiency and shortened time period for screening for the targeted plants. These technologies are particularly useful in conjunction with the practice of gene or pathway discoveries through nutritional genomics trancriptomics proteomics and metabolomics in plants to improve human health. The RNA silencing has practical use because of the ability to reduce gene expression in a manner that is highly sequence specific as well as technologically facile and economical having potential in agriculture specifically for nutritional improvement of plants and the management of mascotous plant diseases. However the major obstacles hindering its immediate applications include selection of targeting sequences and in the delivery of siRNA. The key issues are

(1) how to select silencing targets for a particular disease and

(2) how to efficiently deliver siRNAs into specific cell types *in vivo*?

Tissue or organ-specific RNAi vectors have already been proven to be useful for targeted gene silencing in specific plant tissues and organs with minimal interference with the normal plant life cycle. New-generation RNAi vectors the miRNA vectors have been developed with high silencing accuracy and fewer side effects in plants. Genetic engineering of highly nutritional food crops requires both gene silencing and counter-silencing technologies. Besides RNAi technology can be considered an eco-friendly biosafe and ever green technology as it eliminates even certain risks associated with development of transgenic plants carrying first generation constructs (binary vectors and sense and antisense genes). As witnessed from earlier strategies for obtaining viral resistant plants the expression of protein product from the transgene of interest risked hetero-encapsidation through protein-protein interactions between target and non-target viral gene product resulted in the development of a non-aphid transmissible strain of Zucchini yellow mosaic virus to aphid-transmissible strain from a transgene expressing a plum pox capsid protein (Lecoq *et al.* 1993). Since RNAi triggers the formation of dsRNA molecules that target and facilitate the degradation of the gene of interest as well as the transgene itself to avoid problems arising from the synthesis of gene sequences as well as non-coding regions of gene thus limiting undesirable recombination events. Keeping in view the potentialities of RNAi technology and lesson from classical examples demonstrated that why and how this technology has emerged to combat plant pathogens in the near future as it has already added new dimensions in the chapter of plant disease management. Further development of vectors that can suppress the RNAi pathway but overexpress transgenes in a tissue-specific manner will revolutionize this field. Such vectors could be based on various viral RNA silencing suppressors and their derivatives. Future directions will focus on developing finely tuned RNAi-based gene silencing vectors that are able to operate in a temporally and spatially controlled manner. However a better and comprehensive understanding of RNAi should allow future plant researchers to work effectively and efficiently in order to improve crop plants nutritionally and manage various mascotous intruders of crop plants.

REFERENCES

Abbott JC Barakate A Pincon G Legrand M Lapierre C Mila I Schuch W Halpin C (2002) Simultaneous suppression of multiple genes by single transgenes. Down-regulation of three unrelated lignin biosynthetic genes in tobacco. *Plant Physiology* **128:** 844-853

Adams-Phillips L Barry C Giovannoni J (2004) Signal transduction systems regulating fruit ripening. *Trends in Plant Science* **9:** 331–338.

Akbergenov R Si-Ammour A Blevins T Amin I Kutter C Vanderschuren H Zhang P Cruissem W Meins FJ Hohn T Pooggin MM (2006) Molecular characterization of geminivirus derived small RNAs in different plant species. *Nucleic Acids Research* **34:** 462-471

Allen E Xie Z Gustafson AM Carrington JC (2005) microRNA-directed phasing during *Trans*acting siRNA biogenesis in plants. *Cell* **12:** 207-221

Allen E Xie Z Gustafson AM Sung GH Spatafora JW Carrington JC (2004) Evolution of microRNA genes by inverted duplication of target gene sequences in Arabidopsis thaliana. *Nature Genetics* **36:** 1282-1290

Almeida R Allshire RC (2005) RNA silencing and genome Regulation. *Trends in Cell Biology* **15:** 251-258

Anantharaman V Koonin EV Aravind L (2002) SPOUT: a class of methyltransferases that includes spoU and trmD RNA methylase suprefamilies and novel superfamilies of predicted procaryotic RNA methylases. *Journal of Molecular Microbiology and Biotechnology* **4:** 71-75

Angell SM Baulcombe DC (1999) Technical advance: potato virus X amplicon mediated silencing of nuclear genes. *The Plant Journal* **20:** 357-362

Bakhetia M Charlton W Atkinson HJ McPherson MJ (2005) RNA interference of dual oxidase in the plant nematode *Meloidogyne incognita. Molecular Plant-Microbe Interaction* **18:** 1099-1106

Bakhetia M Urwin PE Atkinson HJ (2007) qPCR analysis and RNAi define pharyngeal gland cell-expressed genes of *Heterodera glycines* required for initial interactions with the host. *Molecular Plant-Microbe Interaction* **20:** 306-312

Bartel B Bartel DP (2003) MicroRNAs: at the root of plant development? *Plant Physiology* **132:** 709-717

Bartel DP (2004) MicroRNAs: genomics biogenesis mechanism and function. *Cell* **116:** 281-297

Baulcombe DC (1999) Fast forward genetics based on virus-induced gene silencing. *Current Opinion in Plant Biology* **2:** 109-113

Baulcombe DC (2004) RNA silencing in plants. *Nature* **431:** 356-363

Baumberger N Baulcombe DC (2005) Arabidopsis ARGONAUTE1 is an RNA Slicer that selectively recruits microRNAs and short interfering RNAs. *Proceedings of the National Academy of Sciences USA* **102:** 11928-11933

Beclin C Boutet S Waterhouse P Vaucheret H (2002) A branched pathway for transgene-induced RNA silencing in plants. *Current Biology* **12:** 684-688

Bernstein E Caudy AA Hammond SM Hannon GJ (2001) Role for a bidentate ribonuclease in the initiation step of RNA interference. *Nature* **409:** 363-366

Bitko V Barik S (2001) Phenotypic silencing of cytoplasmic genes with sequence specific double stranded short interfering RNA and its applications in the reverse genetics of wild type negative strand RNA virus. *BMC Microbiology* **1:** 34-44

Bouche N Lauressergues D Gasciolli V Vaucheret H (2006) An antagonistic function for *Arabidopsis* DCL2 in development and a new function for DCL4 in generating viral siRNAs. *The EMBO Journal* **25:** 3347-3356

Boutet S Vazquez F Liu J Beclin C Fagard M Gratias A Morel J B Crete P Chen X Vaucheret H (2003) *Arabidopsis* HEN1: a genetic link between endogenous miRNA controlling development and siRNA controlling transgene silencing and virus resistance. *Current Biology* **13:** 843-848

Brigneti G Martin-Hernandez AM Jin H Chen J Baulcombe DC Baker B Jones JD (2004) Virus-induced gene silencing in *Solanum* species. *The Plant Journal* **39:** 264-272

Brodersen P Voinnet O (2006) The diversity of RNA silencing pathways in plants. *Trends in Genetics* **22;** 268-280

Cao X Zhou P Zhang X Zhu S Zhong X Xiao Q Ding B and Li Y (2005) Identification of an RNA silencing suppressors from a plant double stranded RNA virus. *Journal of Virology* **79:** 13018-13027

Catalanotto C Azzalin G Macino G Gogoni C (2000) Gene silencing in worms and fungi. *Nature* **404:** 245

Chan SW Zilberman D Xie Z Johansen LK Carrington JC Jacobsen SE (2004) RNA silencing gene control *de novo* DNA methylation. *Science* **303:** 1336

Chapman EJ Prokhnevsky A I Gopinath K Dolja VV Carrington JC (2004) Viral RNA silencing suppressors inhibit the micro-RNA pathway at an interphase step. *Genes and Development* **18:** 1179-1186

Chen J Li WX Xie D Peng JR Ding SW (2004) Viral virulence protein suppresses RNA silencing-mediated defense but up regulates the role of microRNA in host gene regulation. *Plant Cell* **16:** 1302-1313

Chen Q Rehman S Smant G Jones JT (2005) Functional analysis of pathogenicity proteins of the potato cyst nematode *Globodera rostochiensis* using RNAi. *Molecular Plant-Microbe Interactions* **18:** 621-625

Chen S Hofius D Sonnewald U Bornke F (2003) Temporal and spatial control of gene silencing in transgenic plants by inducible expression od double stranded RNA. *The Plant Journal* **36:** 731-740

Chuang CF Meyerowtiz EM (2000) Specific and heritable genetic interference by double-stranded RNA in *Arabidopsis thaliana*. *Proceedings of the National Academy of Sciences USA* **97:** 4985-4990

Chung E Seong E Kim YC Chung EJ Oh SK Lee S Park JM Joung YH Choi D (2004) A method of high frequency virus induced gene silencing in chili pepper *Capsicum annuum* L. cv. *Bukang*). *Molecular Cell* **17:** 377-380

Cogoni C Macino G (1999) Homology dependent gene silencing in plants and fungi: a number of variations on the same theme. *Current Opinion in Microbiology* **2:** 657-662

Cogoni C Romano N Macino G (1994) Suppression of gene expression by homologous transgenes. *Antonie Leeuwenhoek International Journal of General Molecular Microbiology* **65:** 205-209

Constantin GD Krath BN MacFarlane SA Nicolaisen M Johansen IE Lund OS (2004) Virus-induced gene silencing as a tool for functional genomics in a legume species. *Plant Journal* **40:** 622-631

Covey SN Al-Kaff NS (2000) Plant DNA viruses and gene silencing. *Plant Molecular Biology* **43:** 307-322

Dallwitz MJ Zurcher EJ (1996) Plant viruses online. In: Brunt AA Crabtree K Dallwitz MJ Gibbs AJ Watson L Zurcher EJ (Eds) *Descriptions and Lists from the VIDE Database* CAB International UK 1484 pp.

Dalmay T Hamilton AJ Mueller E Baulcombe DC (2000) Potato virus X amplicons in Arabidopsis mediate genetic and epigenetic gene silencing. *The Plant Cell* **12:** 369-380

Dalmay T Hamilton AJ Rudd S Angell S Baulcombe DC (2000) An RNA-dependent RNA polymerase gene in *Arabidopsis* is required for posttranscriptional gene silencing mediated by a transgene but not by a virus. *Cell* **101:** 543-553

Dalmay T Horsefield R Braunstein TH Baulcombe DC (2001) SDE3 encodes an RNA helicase required for post-transcriptional gene silencing in *Arabidopsis*. *The EMBO Journal* **20:** 2069-2078

Davies WP (2003). An historical perspective from the Green Revolution to the gene revolution. Nutrition Reviews **61:** S124–S134

Davuluri G R van Tuinen A Mustilli A C Manfredonia A Newman R Burgess D Brummell D A King S R Palys J Uhlig J (2004). Manipulation of DET1 expression in tomato results in photomorphogenic phenotypes caused by post-transcriptional gene silencing. *Plant Journal* **40:** 344–354.

Davuluri G R van Tuinen A Fraser P D Manfredonia A Newman R Burgess D Brummell D A King S R Palys J Uhlig J (2005) Fruit-specific RNAi-mediated suppression of DET1 enhances carotenoid and flavonoid content in tomatoes. *Nature Biotechnology* **23:** 890–895.

de Bakker MD Raponi M Arndt GM (2002) RNA-meditaed gene silencing in non-pathogenic and pathogenic fungi. *Current Opinion in Microbiology* **5:** 323-329

de Boer SH (2003) Perspective on genetic engineering of agricultural crops for resistance to disease. *Canadian Journal of Plant Pathology* **25:** 10-20

Deleris A Gallego-Bartolome J Bao J Kasschau KD Carrington JC Voinnet O (2006) Hierarchical action and inhibition of plant Dicer-like proteins in antiviral defense. *Science* **313:** 68-71

Díaz-Pendón JA Ding SW (2008) Direct and Indirect Roles of Viral Suppressors of RNA Silencing in Pathogenesis. *Annual review of Phytopathology* **46:** 303-326

Dinesh-Kumar SP Anandalakshmi R Marathe R Schiff M Liu Y (2003) Virus-induced gene silencing. *Methods in Molecular Biology* **236:** 287-294

Ding XS Schneider WL Chaluvadi SR Rouf Mian RM Nelson RS (2006) Characterization of a Brome mosaic virus strain and its use as a vector for gene silencing in monocotyledonous hosts. *Molecular Plant Microbe Interaction* **19:** 1229-1239

Doench JG Petersen CP Sharp PA (2003) siRNAs can function as miRNAs. *Genes and Development* **17:** 438-442

Dorokhov YL Frolova OY Skurat EV Ivanov PA Gasanova TV Sheveleva AA Ravin NV Makinen KM Klimyuk VI Skryabin KG Gleba YY Atabekov JG (2006) A novel function for a ubiquitous plant enzyme pectin methylesterase: the enhancer of RNA silencing. *FEBS Letters* **580:** 3872-3878

Dugas DV Bartel B (2004) microRNA regulation of gene expression in plants. *Current Opinion in Plant Biology* **7:** 512-520

Dunoyer P Himber C Ruiz-Ferrer V Alioua A Voinnet O (2007) Intra- and intercellular RNA interference in *Arabidopsis thaliana* requires components of the microRNA and heterochromatic silencing pathways. *Nature Genetics* **39:** 848-856

Dunoyer P Himber C Voinnet O (2005) DICER-LIKE 4 is required for RNA interference and produces the 21-nucleotide small interfering RNA component of the plant cell-to-cell silencing signal. *Nature Genetics* **37:** 1356-1360

Dunoyer P Lecellier CH Parizitto EA Himber C Voinnet O (2004) Probing the microRNA and small interfering RNA pathways with virus-encoded suppressors of RNA silencing. *The Plant Cell* **16:** 1235-1250

Dykxhoorn DM Lieberman J (2005) The silent revolution: RNA interference as basic biology research tool and therapeutic. *Annual Review of Medicine* **56:** 401-423

Elbashir SM Lendeckel W Tuschl T (2001) RNA interference is mediated by 21 and 22-nucleotide RNAs. *Genes and Development* **15:** 188-200

Escobar MA Civerolo EL Summerfelt KR Dandekar AM (2001) RNAi-mediated oncogene silencing confers ressitance to crown gall tumorigenesis. *Proceedings of the National Academy of Sciences USA* **98:** 13437-13442

Fagard M Boutet S Morel JB Bellini C Vaucheret H (2000) AGO1 QDE-2 and RDE-1 are related proteins required for post-transcriptional gene silencing in plants quelling in fungi and RNA interference in animals. *Proceedings of the National Academy of Sciences USA* **97:** 11650-11654

Fairbairn DJ Cavalloro AS Bernard M Mahalinga-Iyer J Graham MW Botella JR (2007) Host-delivered RNAi: an effective strategy to silence genes in plant parasite nematodes. *Planta* **226:** 1525–1533

Faivre-Rampant O Gilroy EM Hrubikova K Hein I Millam S Loake GJ Birch P Taylor M Lacomme C (2004) Potato virus X-induced gene silencing in leaves and tubers of potato. *Plant Physiology* **134** 1308-1316

Falco S C Guida T Locke M Mauvais J Sanders C Ward R T Webber P (1995) Transgenic canola and soybean seeds with increased lysine. *Biotechnology* (NY) **13:** 577–582.

Fanelli E Di Vito M Jones JT De Giorgi C (2005) Analysis of chitin synthase function in a plant parasitic nematode *Meloidogyne artiellia* using RNAi. *Gene* **349:** 87-95

Fire A Xu S Montgomery MK Kostas SA Driver SE Mello CC (1998) Potent and specific genetic interference by double-stranded RNA in *Caenorhabditis elegans*. *Nature* **391:** 806-811

Fitxgerald A Van Kha JA Plummer KM (2004) Simultaneous silencing of multiple genes in the apple scab fungus *Venturia inaequalis* by expression of RNA with chimeric inverted repeats. *Fungal Genetics and Biology* **41:** 963-971

Fofana IB Sangare A Collier R Taylor C Fauquet CM (2004) A geminivirus-induced gene silencing system for gene function validation in cassava. *Plant Molecular Biology* **56:** 613-624

Frankard V Ghislain M and Jacobs M (1992) Two feedback-insensitive enzymes of the aspartate pathway in Nicotiana sylvestris. *Plant Physiology* **99:** 1285–1293.

Frederick Meins F Si-Ammour AJ Blevins T (2005) RNA silencing systems and their relevance to plant development. *Annual Review of Cell and Developmental Biology* **21:** 297-318

Fulci V Macino G (2007) Quelling: posttranscriptional gene silencing guided by small RNAs in Neurospora crassa. *Current Opinion in Microbiology* **10:** 191-203

Galili G Galili S Lewinsohn E and Tadmor Y (2002) Genetic molecular and genomic approaches to improve the value of plant foods and feeds. *Critical Reviews in Plant Sciences* **21:** 167–204

Gasciolli V Mallory AC Bartel DP Vaucheret H (2005) Partially redundant functions of Arabidopsis DICER-like enzymes and a role for DCL4 in producing trans-acting siRNAs. *Current Biology* **15:** 1494-1500

Gasciolli V Mallory AC Bartel DP Vaucheret H (2005) Partially Redundant Functions of DICER-like enzymes and a role for DCL4 in producing- acting siRNAs. *Current Biology* **15:** 1494 - 1500

Gitlin L Karelsky S Andino R (2002) Short interference confers intracellular antiviral immunity in human cells. *Nature* **4:** 418-430

Godge MR Purkayastha A Dasgupta I Kumar PP (2008) Virus-induced gene silencing for functional analysis of selected genes. *Plant Cell Reporter* **27:** 209-219

Goldoni M Azzalin G Macino G Cogoni C (2004) Efficient gene silencing by expression of double stranded RNA in *Neurospora crassa*. *Fungal Genetics and Biology* **41:** 1016-1024

Gossele VV Fache II Meulewaeter F Cornelissen M Metzlaff M (2002) SVISS-a novel transient gene silencing system for gene function discovery and validation in tobacco. *The Plant Journal* **32:** 859-866

Gould B Kramer EM (2007) Virus-induced gene silencing as a tool for functional analyses in the emerging model plant *Aquilegia* (columbine Ranunculaceae). *BMC Plant Methods* **12:** 6

Grusak M A (2002) Phytochemicals in plants: Genomics-assisted plant improvement for nutritional and health benefits. *Current Opinion in Biotechnology* **13:** 508–511

Guang S Bochner AF Pavelec DM Burkhart KB Harding S Lachowiec J Kennedy S (2008) An argonaute transports siRNAs from the cytoplasm to the nucleus. *Science* **321:** 537-541

Guo HS Ding SW (2002) A Viral protein inhibits the long range signaling activity of the silencing signal. *EUROPEAN MOLECULAR BIOLOGICAL ORGAN Journal* **21:** 398-407

Guo HS Fei JF Xie Q Chua NH (2003) A chemical-regulated inducible RNAi system in plants. *The Plant Journal* **34:** 383-392

Hall TTM (2005) Structure and function of Argonaute proteins. *Structure* **13:** 1403-1408

Hamada W Spanu PD (1998) Co-suppression of the hydrophobin gene *Hcf-1* is correlated with antisense RNA biosynthesis in *Cladosporium fulvum*. *Molecular and General Genetics* **259:** 630-638

Hamilton A Voinnet O Chappell L Baulcombe DC (2002) Two classes of short interfering RNA in RNA silencing. *The EMBO Journal* **21:** 4671-793

Hammond SM Bernstein E Beach D Hannon GJ (2000) An RNA-directed nuclease mediates post-transcriptional gene silencing in *Drosophila* cells. *Nature* **404:** 293–296

Hammond TM Keller NP (2005) RNA silencing in *Aspergillus nidulans* is independent of RNA-dependent RNA polymerase. *Genetics* **169:** 607-617

Han MH Goud S Song L Fedoroff N (2004) The *Arabidopsis* double-stranded RNA-binding protien HYL1 plays a role in microRNA-mediated gene regulation. *Proceedings of the National Academy of Sciences USA* **101:** 1093-1098

Hannon GJ (2002) RNA interference. *Nature* **418:** 244-251

Herr AJ (2005) Pathways through the small RNA world of plants. *FEBS Letters* **579:** 5879-5888

Herr AJ Jensen MB Dalmay T Baulcombe DC (2005) RNA polymerase IV directs silencing of endogenous DNA. *Science* **308:** 118–120.

Herr AJ Molnar A Jones A Baulcombe DC (2006) Defective RNA processing enhances RNA silencing and influences flowering of *Arabidopsis*. *Proceedings of the National Academy of Sciences USA* **103:** 14994-15001

Hileman LC Drea S Martino G Litt A Irish VF (2005) Virus induced gene silencing is an effective tool for assaying gene function in the basal eudicot species *Papaver somniferum* (opium poppy). *The Plant Journal* **44:** 334-341

Hilly JM Liu Z (2007) An Overview of small RNAs. In: Bassett CL (Ed) *Regulation of Gene Expression in Plants* Springer-Verlag Berlin pp 123-147

Himber C Dunoyer P Moissiard G Ritzenthaler C Voinnet O (2003) Transitivity dependent and -independent cell-to-cell movement of RNA silencing. *The EMBO Journal* **22:** 4523-4533

Hoffman Y Aflalo C Zarka A Gutman J James TY Boussiba S (2008) Isolation and characterization of a novel chytrid species (phylum Blastocladiomycota) parasitic on the green alga *Haematococcus*. *Mycological Research* **112:** 70-81

Hoisington D Khairallah M Reeves T Ribaut J M Skovmand B Taba S and Warburton M (1999) Plant genetic resources: What can they contribute toward increased crop productivity? *Proceedings of the National Academy of Sciences of the USA* **96:** 5937–5943.

Holzberg S Brosio P Gross C Pogue GP (2002) Barley stripe mosaic virus-induced gene silencing in a monocot plant. *Plant Journal* **30:** 315-327

Hou H Qiu W (2003) A novel co-delivery system consisting of a tomato bushy stunt virus and a defective interfering RNA for studying gene silencing. *Journal of Virology Methods* **111:** 37-42

Huang G Allen R Davis EL Baum TJ Hussey RS (2006) Engineering broad root-knot resistance in transgenic plants by RNAi silencing of a conserved and essential root-knot nematode parasitism gene. *Proceedings of the National Academy of Sciences USA* **103:** 4302-14306

Hutvagner G Zamore PD (2002) A microRNA in a multiple-turnover RNAi enzyme complex. *Science* **297:** 2056-2060

Irvine DV Zaratiegui M Tolia NH Goto DB Chitwood DH Vaughn MW Joshua-Tor L Martienssen RA (2006) Argonaute slicing is required for heterochromatic silencing and spreading. *Science* **313:** 1134-1137

Jacque JM Triques K Stevenson M (2002) Modulation of HIV-1 replication by RNA interference. *Nature* **418:** 435-438

James C (2006) http://www.gmocompass.org/eng/agri_biotechnology/gmo

Johansen LK Carrington JC (2001) Silencing on the spot. Induction and suppression of RNA silencing in the Agrobacterium-mediated transient expression system. *Plant Physiology* **126:** 930-938

Jones-Rhoades MW Bartel DP (2004) Computational identification of plant microRNAs and their targets including a stress-induced miRNA. *Molecular Cell* **14:** 787-799

Jones-Rhoades MW Bartel DP Bartel B (2006) MicroRNAS and their regulatory roles in plants. *Annual Review of Plant Biology* **57:** 19–53.

Kadotani N Nakayashiki H Tosa Y Mayama S (2003) RNA silencing in the pathogenic fungus *Magnaporthe oryzae. Molecular Plant-Microbe Interaction* **16:** 769-776

Kanno T Aufsatz W Jaligot E Mette MF Matzke M Matżke AJ (2005) A SNF2-like protein facilitates dynamic control of DNA methylation. *EMBO Reporter* **6:** 649–655.

Karakas M (2008) RNA interference in plant parasitic nematodes. *African Journal of Biotechnology* **7:** 2530-2534

Karchi H Shaul O Galili G (1994) Lysine synthesis and catabolism are coordinately regulated during tobacco seed development. *Proceedings of the National Academy of Sciences of the USA* **91:** 2577–2581.

Kasschau KD Carrington JC (1998) A counter defensive strategy of plant viruses: suppression of posttranscriptional gene silencing. *Cell* **95:** 461-470

Kasschau KD Fahlgren N Chapman EJ Sullivan CM Cumbie JS Givan SA Carrington JC (2007) Genome-wide profiling and analysis of Arabidopsis siRNAs *PLoS Biology* **5:** e57.

Katiyar-Agarwal S Gao S Vivian-Smith A Jin H (2007) A novel class of bacteria-induced small RNAs in Arabidopsis. *Genes and Development* **21:** 3123–3134

Katiyar-Agarwal S Morgan R Dahlbeck D Borsani O Villegas JA Zhu J Staskawicz BJ Jin H (2006) A pathogen-inducible endogenous siRNA in plant immunity. *Proceedings of the National Academy of Sciences USA* **103:** 47-52

Kjemtrup S Sampson KS Peele CG Nguyen LV Conkling MA (1998) Gene silencing from plant DNA carried by a geminivirus. *Plant Journal* **14:** 91-100

Klahre U Crete P Leuenberger SA Iglesias VA Meins F (2002) High molecular weight RNAs and small interfering RNAs induce systemic post transcriptional gene silencing in plants. *Proceedings of the National Academy of Sciences USA* **99:** 11981-11986

Kobayashi K Patricia Zambryski P (2007) RNA silencing and its cell-to-cell spread during Arabidopsis embryogenesis. *The Plant Journal* **50:** 597 - 604

Kumagai MH Donson J della-Cioppa G Harvey D Hanley K Grill LK (1995) Cytoplasmic inhibition of carotenoid biosynthesis with virus-derived RNA. *Proceedings of the National Academy of Sciences USA* **92:** 1679-1683

Kurihara Y Takashi Y Watanabe Y (2006) The interaction between DCL1 and HYL1 is important for efficient and precise processing of pri-miRNA in plant microRNA biogenesis. *RNA* **12:** 206-212

Larkin P J Harrigan G G (2007) Opportunities and surprises in crops modified by transgenic technology: Metabolic engineering of benzylisoquinoline alkaloid gossypol and lysine biosynthetic pathways. *Metabolomics* **3:** 371-382

Lau NC Lim LP Weinstein EG Bartel DP (2001) An abundant class of tiny RNAs with probable regulatory roles in *Caenorabditis elegans*. *Science* **294:** 858-862

Lecellier CH Voinnet O (2004) RNA silencing: no mercy for viruses? *Immunology Review* **198:** 285-303

Lecoq H Ravelonandro M Wips-Scheibel C Monsion M Raccah B Dunez J (1993) Aphid transmission of an non-aphid transmissible strain of *Zucchini yellow mosaic potyvirus* from transgenic plants expressing the capsid protein of plum pox potyvirus. *Molecular Plant-Microbe Interactions* **6:** 403-406

Lee M (1998) Genome projects and gene pools: New germplasm for plant breeding? Proceedings of the *National Academy of Sciences of the USA* **95:** 2001–2004.

Levin I Frankel P Gilboa N Tanny S Lalazar A (2003) The tomato dark green mutation is a novel allele of the tomato homolog of the DEETIOLATED1 gene. *Theoretical and Applied Genetics* **106:** 454–460.

Lewis BP Shih I Jones-Rhoades MW Bartel DP Burge CB (2003) Prediction of mammalian microRNA targets. *Cell* **115:** 787-798

Li C Pontes O El-Shami M Henderson I Bernatavichute Y Chan S Lagrange T Pikaard C Jacobsen S (2006) An ARGONAUTE 4-containing nuclear processing center colocalized with cajal bodies in *Arabidopsis thaliana*. *Cell* **126:** 93 – 106

Li F Ding SW (2006) Virus counter defense: diverse strategies for evading the RNA silencing immunity. *Annual Review of Microbiology* **60:** 503-531

Li J Yang Z Yu B Liu J Chen X (2005) Methylation protects miRNAs and siRNAs from a 3_-end uridylation activity in Arabidopsis. *Current Biology* **15:** 1501-1507

Lilley CJ Goodchild SA Atkinson HJ Urwin PE (2005) Cloning and characterization of a *Heterodera glycines* minopeptidase cDNA. *International Journal of Parasitology* **35:** 1577-1585

Liu H Cottrell TR Pierini LM Goldman WE Doering TL (2002) RNA interference in the pathogenic fungus *Cryptococcus neoformans*. *Genetics* **160:** 463–470

Liu Q Singh S P Green A G (2002). High-stearic and high-oleic cottonseed oils produced by hairpin RNA-mediated post-transcriptional gene silencing. *Plant Physiology* **129:** 1732–1743.

Liu J Carmell MA Rivas FV Marsden CG Thomson JM (2004) Argonaute2 is the catalytic engine of mammalian RNAi. *Science* **305:** 1437-1441

Liu Y Schiff M Marathe R Dinesh-Kumar SP (2002b) Tobacco *Rar1 EDS1* and *NPR1/NIM1* like genes are required for *N* mediated resistance to tobacco mosaic virus. *The Plant Journal* **30:** 415-429

Liu YL Schiff M Dinesh-Kumar SP (2002a) Virus induced gene silencing in tomato. *The Plant Journal* **31:** 777-786

Llave C Kasschau KD Rector MA Carrington JC (2002) Endogenous and silencing associated small RNAs in plants. *The Plant Cell* **14:** 1605-1619

Lu C Federoff N (2000) A mutation in the *Arabidopsis* HYL1 gene encoding a dsRNA binding protein affects responses to abscisic acid auxin and cytokinin. *The Plant Cell* **12:** 2351-2366

Lu C S.S. Tej S. Luo C.D. Haudenschild B.C. Meyers P.J. Green (2005) Elucidation of the small RNA component of the transcriptome *Science* **309:** 1567–1569.

Lu R Martin-Hernandez AM Peart JR Malcuit I Baulcombe DC (2003) Virus induced gene silencing in plants. *Methods* **30:** 296-303

MacFarlane SA Popovich AH (2000) Efficient expression of foreign proteins in roots from tobravirus vectors. *Virology* **267:** 29-35

Mallory AC Parks G Endres MW Baulcombe D Bowman LH (2002) The amplicon-plus system for high-level expression of transgenes in plants. *Nature Biotechnogy* **20:** 622-625

Maskarinec G Takata Y Pagano I Carlin L Goodman M T Le Marchand L Nomura A M Wilkens L R Kolonel L N (2006) Trends and dietary determinants of overweight and obesity in a multiethnic population. *Obesity (Silver Spring)* **14:** 717–726

Matzke M Aufsatz W Kanno T Daxinger L Papp I Mette MF Matzke JM (2004) Genetic analysis of RNA-mediated transcriptional gene silencing. *Biochimica et Biophysica Acta* **1677:** 129-141

Mazur B Krebbers E Tingey S (1999) Gene discovery and product development for grain quality traits. *Science* **285:** 372–375

McManus MT Sharp PA (2002) Gene Silencing in mammals by small interfering RNAs. *Nature Review Genetics* **3:** 737-747

Merai Z Kerenyi Z Molnar A Barta E Valcozi A Bistray G Havelda Z Burgyan J Silhavy D (2005) Aureusvirus P14 is an efficient RNA silencing suppressor that binds double stranded RNAs without size specificity. *Journal of Virology* **79:** 7217-7226

Milhavet O Gary DS Mattson MP (2003) RNA Interference in Biology and Medicine. *Pharmacological Reviews* **55:** 629–648

Mlotshwas S Voinnet O Mette MF Matzke M Vaucheret H Ding SW Pruss G Vance GB (2002) RNA silencing and its mobile silencing signal. *The Plant Cell* **14:** S289-301

Mocellin S Provenzano M (2004) RNA interference: learning gene knock-down from cell physiology. *Journal of Translational Medicine* **2:** 1-6

Morel JB Godon C Mourrain P Beclin C Boutet C Feuerbach F Proux F Vaucheret H (2002) Fertile hypomorphic ARGONAUTE (ago1) mutants impaired in post-transcriptional gene silencing and virus resistance. *Plant Cell* **14:** 629-639

Moss EG Tang L (2003) Conservation of the heterochronic regulator Lin-28 its developmental expression and microRNA complementary sites. *Developmental Biology* **258:** 432-442

Mourrain P Beclin C Elmayan T Feuerbach F Godon C Morel JB Jouette D Lacombe AM Nikic S Picault N Remoue K Sanial M Vo TA Vaucheret H (2000) *Arabidopsis SGS2* and *SGS3* genes are required for posttranscriptional gene silencing and natural virus resistance. *Cell* **101:** 533–542

Mustilli A C Fenzi F Ciliento R Alfano F Bowler C (1999) Phenotype of the tomato high pigment-2 mutant is caused by a mutation in the tomato homolog of DEETIOLATED1. *Plant Cell* **11:** 145–157.

Nakayashiki H (2005) RNA silencing in fungi: mechanisms and applications. *FEBS Letters* **579:** 5950-5970

Nakayashiki H Hanada S Nguyen BQ Kadotani N Tosa Y Mayama S (2005) RNA silencing as a tool for exploring gene function in ascomycete fungi. *Fungi Genetics and Biology* **42:** 275-283

Napoli C Lemieux C Jorgensen R (1990) Introduction of a chimeric chalcone synthase gene into petunia results in reversible co-suppression of homologous genes in *trans*. *The Plant Cell* **2:** 279-289

Navarro L Dunoyer P Jay F Arnold B Dharmasini N Estelle M Vionnet O Jones JD (2006) A plant miRNA contributes to antibacterial resistance by repressing auxin signalling. *Science* **312:** 436–439

Naylor M Reeves J Cooper JI Edwards ML Wang H (2005) Construction and properties of a gene-silencing vector based on Poplar mosaic virus (genus *Carlavirus*). *Journal of Virology Methods* **124:** 27-36

Negrutiu I Cattoir-Reynearts A Verbruggen I Jacobs M. (1984) Lysine overproducer mutants with an altered dihydrodipicolinate synthase from protoplast culture of *Nicotiana sylvestris* (Spegazzini and Comes). *Theoretical and Applied Genetics* **68:** 11–20

Niu QW Lin SS Reyes JL Chen KC Wu HW Yeh SD Chua NH (2006) Expression of artificial microRNAs in transgenic *Arabidopsis thaliana* confers virus resistance. *Nature Biotechnology* **24:** 1420-1428

Novina CD Murray MF Dykxhoorn DM Beresford PJ Riess J Lee SK Collman RG Lieberman J Shanker P Sharp PA (2002) siRNA-directed inhibition of HIV-1 infection. *Nature Mediterranean* **8:** 681-686

Nykänen A Haley B Zamore PD (2001) ATP requirements and small interfering RNA structure in the RNA interference pathway. *Cell* **107:** 309-321

Omarov RT Ciomperlik JJ Scholthof HB (2007) RNAi-associated ssRNA-specific ribonucleases in *Tombusvirus* P19 mutant-infected plants and evidence for a discrete srRNA-containing effector complex. *Proceedings of the National Academy of Sciences USA* **104:** 1714-1719

Palmer KE Rybicki EP (2001) Investigation of the potential of maize streak virus to act as an infectious gene vector in maize plants. *Archives of Virology* **146:** 1089-1104

Park M Y Wu G Gonzalez-Sulser A Vaucheret H Poethig RS (2005) Nuclear processing and export of microRNAs in *Arabidopsis. Proceeding of National Academy of Sciences. USA.* **102:** 3691-3696.

Park W Li J Song R Messing J Chen X (2002) Carpel factory a Dicer homolog and HEN1 a novel protein act in miRNA metabolism in *Arabidopsis thaliana. Current Biology* **12:** 1484-1495

Pasquinelli AE Reinhart BJ Slack F Martindale MQ Kuroda MI Maller B Hayward DC Ball EE Degnan B Müller P Spring J Srinivasan A Fishman M Finnerty J Corbo J Levine M Leahy P Davidson E Ruvkun G (2000) Conservation of the sequence and temporal expression of *let-7* heterochronic regulatory RNA. *Nature* **408:** 86-89

Peele C Jordan CV Muangsan N Turnage M Egelkrout E Eagle P Hanley-Bowdoin L Robertson D (2001) Silencing of a meristematic gene using geminivirus-derived vectors. *Plant Journal* **27:** 357-366

Peragine A Yoshikawa M Wu G Albrecht HL Poethig RS (2004) SGS3 and SGS2/SDE1/RDR6 are required for juvenile development and the production of trans-acting siRNAs in *Arabidopsis. Genes and Development* **18:** 2368-2379

Pham JW Sontheimer EJ (2005) Molecular requirements for RNA-induced silencing complex assembly in the *Drosophila* RNA interference pathway. *Journal of Biological Chemistry* **280:** 39278-39283

Pickford AS Cogoni C (2003) RNA-mediated gene silencing. *Cellular and Molecular Life Science* **60:** 871-882

Pogue GP Lindbo JA Garger SJ Fitzmaurice WP (2002) Making an ally from an enemy: plant virology and the new agriculture. *Annual Review of Phytopathology* **40:** 45-74

Pontes O Li CF Nunes PC Haag J Ream T Vitins A Jacobsen SE. Pikaard CS (2006) The Arabidopsis chromatin-modifying nuclear siRNA pathway involves a nucleolar RNA processing center *Cell* **126:** 79-92.

Pooggin M Shivaprasad PV Veluthambi K Hohn T (2003) RNAi targetting of DNA viruses. *Nature Biotechnology* **21:** 131-32

Qi Y Denli AM Hannon GJ (2005) Biochemical specialization within Arabidopsis RNA silencing pathways. *Molecular Cell* **19:** 421-428

Qu J Ye J Fang RX (2007) Artificial microRNA-mediated virus resistance in plants. *Journal of Virology* **81:** 6690-6699

Rand TA Petersen S Du F Wang X (2005) Argonaute2 cleaves the anti-guide strand of siRNA during RISC activation. *Cell* **123:** 621-629

Ratcliff F Martin-Hernandez AM Baulcombe DC (2001) Tobacco rattle virus as a vector for analysis of gene functions by silencing. *Plant Journal* **25:** 237-245

Ratcliff FG MacFarlane SA Baulcombe DC (1999) Gene silencing without DNA. RNA-mediated cross-protection between viruses. *Plant Cell* **11:** 1207-1216

Regina A Bird A Topping D Bowden S Freeman J Barsby T Kosar-Hashemi B Li Z Rahman S Morell M (2006) High-amylose wheat generated by RNA interference improves indices of large-bowel health in rats. *Proceedings of the National Academy of Sciences of the USA* **103:** 3546–3551

Rhilla R Singh RL Singh US Singh R Duveiller E Singh HB (2001) Recent advances in the management of plant diseases using chemical. *Indian Journal of Plant Pathology* **19:** 1-23

Rhoades MW Reinhart BJ Lim LP Burge CB Bartel B Bartel DP (2002) Prediction of plant microRNA targets. *Cell* **110:** 513-520

Ronemus M Vaughn MW Martienssen RA (2006) MicroRNA-targeted and small interfering RNAmediated mRNA degradation is regulated by argonaute dicer and RNA-dependent RNA polymerase in *Arabidopsis*. *Plant Cell* **18:** 1559-1574

Rosso MN Dubrana MP Cimbolini N Jaubert S Abad P (2005) Application of RNA interference to root-knot nematode genes encoding esophageal gland proteins. *Molecular Plant-Microbe Interactions* **18:** 615-620

Ruiz MT Voinnet O Baulcombe DC (1998) Initiation and maintenance of virus-induced gene silencing. *Plant Cell* **10:** 937-946

Ruiz-Ferrer V Voinnet O (2007) Viral suppression of RNA silencing: 2b wins the golden fleece by defeating argonaute. *Bioassays* **29:** 319-323

Schauer SE Jacobsen SE Meinke DW Ray A (2002) DICER-LIKE1: blind men and elephants in *Arabidopsis* development. *Trends in Plant Science* **7:** 487- 491

Schwach F Vaistij FE Jones L Baulcombe DC (2005) An RNA-dependent RNA polymerase prevents meristem invasion by potato virus X and is required for the activity but not the production of a systemic silencing signal. *Plant Physiology* **138:** 1842-1852

Schwarz DS Hutvagner G Du T Xu Z Aronin N and Zamore PD (2003) Asymmetry in the assembly of the RNAi enzyme complex. *Cell* **115:** 199–208.

Schweizer P Pokorny J Schulze-Lefert P Dudler R (2000) Double stranded RNA interference with gene functions at the single cell in cereals. *The Plant Journal* **24:** 895-903

Scofield SR Huang L Brandt AS Gill BS (2005) Development of a virus-induced gene silencing system for hexaploid wheat and its use in functional analysis of the Lr21-mediated leaf rust resistance pathway. *Plant Physiology* **138:** 2165-2173

Segal G Song R Messing J (2003) A new opaque variant of maize by a single dominant RNA-interference-inducing transgene. *Genetics* **165:** 387–397

Segers GC Hamada W Oliver RP Spanu PD (1999) Isolation and characteristaion of five different hydrophobin-encoding cDNA from the fungal tomato pathogen *Cladosporium fulvum*. *Molecular and General Genetics* **261:** 644-652

Shahinul Islam SM Miyazaki T Tanno F Itoh K (2005) Dissection of gene function by RNA silencing. *Plant Biotechnology* **22:** 443–446

Shingles J Lilley CJ Atkinson HJ Urwin PE (2007) *Meloidogyne incognita*: molecular and biochemical characterization of a cathepsin L cysteine proteinase and the effect on parasitism following RNAi. *Experimental Parasitology* **115:** 114-120

Sigova A Rhind N and Zamore PD (2004) A single Argonaute protein mediates both transcriptional and posttranscriptional silencing in *Schizosaccharomyces pombe. Genes and Development.* **18:** 2359-2367.

Sledz AC Williams BRG (2005) RNA interference in biology and disease. *Blood* **106:** 781-794

Smith N Singh S Wang MB Stoutjesdijk P Green A Waterhouse PM (2000) Total silencing by intron-spliced hairpin RNAs. *Nature* **407:** 319-320

Song JJ Joshua-Tor L (2006) Argonaute and RNA – getting into the groove. *Current Opinion in Structural Biology* **16:** 5-11

Spanu P (1997) HCf-1 a hydrophobin from the tomato pathogen *Cladosporium fulvum. Gene* **93:** 89-96

Steeves RM Todd TC Essig JS Trick HN (2006) Transgenic soybeans expressing siRNAs specific to a major sperm protein gene suppress *Heterodera glycines* reproduction. *Functional Plant Biology* **33:** 991-999

Storici F (2008) RNA- mediated DNA modification and RNA- template DNA repair. *Current Opinion in Molecular Therapeutics* **10:** 224-230

Sunilkumar G Campbell L M Puckhaber L Stipanovic R D Rathor K S (2006) Engineering cottonseed for use in human nutrition by tissue-specific reduction of toxic gossypol. *Proceedings of the National Academy of Sciences of the* USA **103:** 18054–18059

Sunkar R Zhu JK (2004) Novel and stress-regulated microRNAs and other small RNAs from *Arabidopsis. Plant Cell* **16:** 2001-2019

Takeda A Tsukuda M Mizumoto H Okamoto K Kaido M Mise K Okuno T (2005) A pant RNA virus suppressor RNA silencing through RNA replication. *The EMBO Journal* **24:** 3147-3157

Talbot NJ Kershaw MJ Wakley GE de Vries OMH Wessels JGH Hamer JE (1996) MPG1 encodes a fungal hydrophobin involved in surface interactions during infection-related development of *Magnaporthe grisea. Plant Cell* **8** :985-999

Tang G Reinhart BJ Bartel D Zamore PD (2003) A biochemical framework for RNA silencing in plants. *Genes and Development* **17:** 49-63

Tang W Weidner DA Hu BY Newton RJ Hu X (2006) Efficient delivery of small interfering RNA to plant cells by a nanosecond pulsed laser-induced wave for post transcriptional gene silencing. *Plant Science* **171:** 375-81

Tao X Zhou X (2004) A modified viral satellite DNA that suppresses gene expression in plants. *The Plant Journal* **38:** 850-860

Tenllado F Martinez-Garcia B Vargas M Diaz-Ruiz J R (2003) Crude extracts of bacterially expressed dsRNA can be used to protect plants against virus infection. *BMC Biotechnology* **3:** 3-14

Teycheney PY Tepfer M (2001) Virus specific spatial differences in the interference with silencing of the *chs-A* gene in non-transgenic petunia. *Journal of General Virology* **82:** 1239-1243

Timmermans M Das O Messing J (1994) Geminivirus and their uses as extrachromosomeal replicons. *Annual Review of Plant Physiology* **45:** 79-112

Tomari Y Du T Haley B Schwarz DS Bennett R (2004) RISC assembly defects in the Drosophila RNAi mutant armitage. *Cell* **116:** 831-841

Tomari Y Zamore PD (2005) Perspective: machines for RNAi. *Genes and Development* **19:** 517-529

Turnage MA Muangsan N Peele CG Robertson D (2002) Geminivirus-based vectors for gene silencing in *Arabidopsis. The Plant Journal* **30:** 107-117

Ullu E Djikeng A Shi H Tschudi C (2002) RNA interference: advances and questions. *Philosophical Transactions of the Royal Society of London British Biological Science* **29:** 65-70

Urwin PE Lilley CJ Atkinson HJ (2002) Ingestion of double-stranded RNA by pre-parasitic juvenile cyst nematodes leads to RNA interference. *Molecular Plant-Microbe Interactions* **15:** 747-752

Vaistij FE Jones L Baulcombe DC (2002) Spreading of RNA targeting and DNA methylation in RNA silencing requires transcription of the target gene and a putative RNA dependent RNA polymerase. *Plant Cell* **14:** 857-867

Vanitharani R Chellappan P Fauquet CM (2003) Short interfering RNA-mediated interference of gene expression and viral DNA accumulation in cultured plant cells. *Proceedings of the National Academy of Sciences USA* **100:** 9632-9636

Vaucheret H (2006) Post-transcriptional small RNA pathways in plants: mechanisms and regulations. *Genes and Development* **20:** 759–771.

Vaucheret H Vazquez F Crete P Bartel DP (2004) The action of ARGONAUTE1 in the miRNA pathway and its regulation by the miRNA pathway are crucial f or plant development. *Genes and Development* **18:** 187-1197

Vazquez F Gasciolli V Crete P Vaucheret H (2004) The nuclear dsRNA binding protein HYL1 is required for microRNA accumulation and plant development but not posttranscriptional transgene silencing. *Current Biology* **14:** 346-351

Vazquez F Vaucheret H Rajagopalan R Lepers C Gasciolli V Mallory AC Hilbert JL Bartel DP Crete P (2004) Endogenous transacting siRNAs regulate the accumulation of Arabidopsis mRNAs. *Molecular Cell* **16:** 69-79

Verdel A Jia S Gerber S Sugiyama T Gygi S Grewal SI and Moazed D (2004) RNAi-mediated targeting of heterochromatin by the RITS complex. *Science* **303:** 672–676.

Voinnet O (2001) RNA silencing as a plant immune system against viruses. *Trends in Genetics* **17:** 449-459

Voinnet O (2004) Shaping small RNAs in plants by gene duplication. *Nature Genetics* **36:** 1245-1246

Voinnet O (2005) Non-cell autonomous RNA silencing. *FEBS Letters* **579:** 5858-5871

Voinnet O Lederer C Baulcomb DC (2000) A Viral movement protein prevents spread of the gene silencing signal in *Nicotiana benthamiana. Cell* **103:** 157-167

Volpe TA Kidner C Hall IM Teng G Grewal SI Martienssen RA (2002) Regulation of heterochromatin silencing and histone H3 lysine-9 methylation by RNAi. *Science* **29:** 1833-1837

Wadhwani, C Malik C P Kaur B (2008) RNA interference: Small and Silent In Biotechnology-Perspectives and Prospects (Eds. Malik, C P, Wadhwani, C and kaur, B). MD Publications, New Delhi Pp187-254

Waterhouse PM Graham MW Wang MB (1998) Virus resistance and gene silencing in plants can be induced by simultaneous expression of sense and antisense RNA. *Proceedings of the National Academy of Sciences USA* **95:** 13959-13964

Waterhouse PM Halliwell CA (2003) Exploring plant genomes by RNA induced gene silencing. *Nature Review Genetics* **4:** 29-38

Waterhouse P M Wang M B Lough T (2001) Gene silencing as an adaptive defense against viruses. *Nature* **411:** 834-842

Wesley SV Helliwell CA Smith NA Wang MB Rouse DT Liu Q Gooding PS Singh SP Abbott D Stoutjesdijk PA Robinson SP Gleave AP Green AG Waterhouse P (2001) Construct design for efficient effective and high-throughput gene silencing in plants. *Plant Journal* **27:** 581-590

Wilda M Fuchs U Wossmann W Borkhardt A (2002) Killing of leukemic cells with a BCR/ABL fusion gene by RNA interference (RNAi). *Oncogene* **21:** 5716-5724

Williams C L (1995) Importance of dietary fiber in childhood. *Journal of the American Dietetic Association* **95:** 1140–1146

Wu F Yu L Cao W Mao Y Liu Z He Y (2007) The N-terminal double-stranded RNA binding domains of *Arabidopsis* HYPONASTIC LEAVES1 are sufficient for pre-microRNA processing. *Plant Cell* **19:** 914-925

Xie Z Allen E Fahlgren N Calamar A Givan SA Carrington JC (2005) Expression of Arabidopsis MIRNA genes. *Plant Physiology* **138:** 2145-2154.

Xie Z Allen E Wilken A Carrington JC (2005) DICER-LIKE 4 functions in *trans*-acting small interfering RNA biogenesis and vegetative phase change in *Arabidopsis thaliana. Proceedings of the National Academy of Sciences USA* **102:** 12984-12989

Xie Z Fan B Chen C Chen Z (2001) An important role of an inducible RNA-dependent RNA polymerase in plant antiviral defense. *Proceedings of the National Academy of Sciences USA* **98:** 6516-6521

Xie Z Johansen LK Gustafson AM Kasschau KD Lellis AD Zilberman D Jacobsen SE Carrington JC (2004) Genetic and functional diversification of small RNA pathways in plants. *PLoS Biology* **2:** E104

Xie Z Qi X (2008) Diverse small RNA-directed silencing pathways in plants. Biochimica et Biophysica Acta (in Press)

Yang Z Ebright YW Yu B Chen X (2006) HEN1 recognizes 21-24 nt small RNA duplexes and deposits a methyl group onto the 2_ OH of the 3′ terminal nucleotide. *Nucleic Acids Research* **34:** 667-675

Yoo BC Kragler F Varkonyi-Gasic E Haywood V Archer-Evans S (2004) A systemic small RNA signaling system in plants. *Plant Cell* **16:** 1979-2000

Yu B Yang Z Li J Minakhina S Yang M (2005) Methylation as a crucial step in plant microRNA biogenesis. *Science* **307:** 932-935

Yu D Fan B MacFarlene SA Chen Z (2003) Analysis of the Involvement of an inducible *Arabidopsis* RNA-dependent RNA polymerase in antiviral defense. *Molecular Plant-Microbe Interactions* **16:** 206-216

Zheng X Zhu J Kapoor A Zhu JK (2007) Role of Arabidopsis AGO6 in siRNA accumulation DNA methylation and transcriptional gene silencing. *EMBO Journal* **26:** 1691-1701.

Zhu X Galili G (2003) Increased lysine synthesis coupled with a knockout of its catabolism synergistically boosts lysine content and also transregulates the metabolism of other amino acids in Arabidopsis seeds. *Plant Cell* **15:** 845–853.

Zhu X Galili G (2004) Lysine metabolism is concurrently regulated by synthesis and catabolism in both reproductive and vegetative tissues. *Plant Physiology* **135:** 129–136

Zilberman D Cao X Jacobsen SE (2003) *ARGONAUTE4* control of locus-specific siRNA accumulation and DNA and histone methylation. *Science* **299:** 716-719

Zilberman D Cao X Johansen LX Xie Z Carrington JC Jacobsen SE (2004) Role of Arabidopsis ARGONAUTE4 in RNA-directed DNA methylation triggered by inverted repeats. *Current Biology* **14:** 1214-1220.

4

BACTERIAL BIOSORPTION OF HEAVY METALS

SEDKY H. A. HASSAN, YASSER MAHMOUD AWAD,
MOHAMMAD HUMAYUN KABIR, SANG EUN OH AND JIN HO JOO

Recently, water as an essential resource for all living organisms, is shown to confront high risks caused by heavy metals released from the industrial wastes runoff to water streams and river. So, realistic science approach has been directed towards biosorption of heavy metals from waste water and aqueous solution. Biosorption using biosorbents (*i.e.*, living or dead bacterial biomass, or other low cost biomaterials) has consider as a worldwide driven research in the field of water environment clean up technologies. Biosorbents have the abilities to bind metal pollutants and therefore, can remove the pollutants from water. This article report biosorption recent information and biosorbents efficiencies in heavy metals removal from contaminated compared to costly conventional methods water. In addition, brief reviewed of metal biosorption and bioaccumulation, biosorption mechanisms, factors affecting the biosorption and effect of pretreatment in addition to the future of biosorption will be discussed in the present review.

INTRODUCTION

Due to increasing concern for environmental safety, cooperative efforts are committed to clean up contaminated water not only for food safety which is recognized as of global interest but also for human health. Globally, it has been recognized that heavy metals pollution may be one of the most serious challenges confronting water as an essential natural resource for all living organisms.

Environmental pollution caused by metals has accelerated dramatically since the beginning of the industrial revolution (Nriagu, 1990). In South Korea, mine residues and waste have been abandoned on hillsides and discharged by rain directly to stream water and adjacent agricultural soils (Chen *et al.* 2000; Jung and Thornton, 1997). The heavy metals run off causes detrimental effects on surrounding soil and water bodies, and is menace to human health with outbreaks of diseases as itai-itai due to Cd accumulation in rice (Ok *et al.* 2007). Conventional methods as ion exchange, chemical precipitation, reverse osmosis and evaporative recovery are very expensive and/or often inefficient for the removal of heavy metal from the aqueous solution. Therefore, it is necessary to develop novel technologies for metal removal (Chong and Volesky, 1995).

Currently, using microbial biomass as biosorbents for, heavy metal removal from industrial waste streams has been considered as a potential alternative technology (Costa and Leite, 1991). Biosorption can separate dissolved metals out of diluted solution in high performance and rapid intrinsic kinetics. Therefore, it is an ideal treatment of high volume complex wastewater with low level (Edyvean *et al.*, 1997). Biosorption is also based on the use of sorbent (solid phase) which derived from different kinds of biomaterials or biomass. Moreover, it is obvious that natural ion exchange of biosorbents increased the adsorption capacity of metal on those biomaterials (Volesky, 2003). However, many researchers have worked on low cost adsorbents with high adsorption capacity as chitosan, zeolites, waste slurry and lignin. In addition, these inexpensive adsorbents show high removal capacities for each metal compared to activated carbon (Babel and Kurniawan 2003).

CONVENTIONAL TECHNOLOGIES FOR HEAVY METAL REMEDIATION

In the last few decades, it has become clear that conventional treatments of polluted sites is too expensive. So we should rely on other low-cost technologies with high efficiency to remediate heavy metals from contaminated water. However, in this review, different chemical and physical treatments will be discussed as conventional methods to remove heavy metals from industrial wastewater.

Conventional methods include chemical precipitation, chemical oxidation or reduction, ion exchange, filtration, electrochemical treatment, reverse osmosis, membrane technologies and evaporation recovery (Atkinson *et al.* 1998; Crini, 2006).

Regarding chemical precipitation is commonly used for heavy metal removal from water via addition of anion for metals participating in the form of suspended solid particles, and then these particles are removed by settling, filtration or centrifugation. However, precipitation lacks specificity and is ineffective in heavy metal ions at low concentration (Gray, 1999). In this concern ferrous sulphate, ferric chloride, aluminum sulphate and polyaluminium chloride are also used as coagulants in the pretreatment of currency printing ink wastewater (Nandy *et al.* 2003). Also, Electro-coagulation is also effective in removing dissolved metals from wastewater using an electrical current by neutralizing ions and then, metals become destabilized and precipitate in a stable form (Gray, 1999).

Ion exchange is an adsorption process that has the capacity to achieve ppb levels of heavy metals in aqueous solution through surface ions exchange of an ion exchange resin. However, ion exchange method is nonselective and is highly sensitive to solution pH and also, it is expensive compared to the other methods (Gray, 1999). Furthermore, membrane technology is used to separate heavy metals from wastewater without generating any pollution load. In this part, commercial nanofiltration membrane is used for cadmium and nickel removal from aqueous solutions (Murthy and Chaudhari, 2009). Moreover, nanofiltration gained its popularity in metal separation/rejection by reverse osmosis (RO) and ultrafiltration (UF) (Lamba *et al* 2002; Qin *et al* 2004). However, the cost of operation, maintenance in system application and necessary pretreatment is high.

Reverse osmosis and electro-dialysis involves the use of semi-permeable membranes for the recovery of metal ions from diluted wastewater. Whilst, in electro-dialysis, the selective membranes as alternation of cation and anion membranes are fitted between the electrodes in electrolytic cells, and therefore, the associated ion migrates under continuous electrical current, allowing the recovery of metals. On the other hand, fouling of membrane by slightly soluble components in solution and in wastewater which had high suspended solids are obviously disadvantages of this method (Huang and Koseoglu 1993).

Concerning adsorption process, metal ions are transferred and physically or chemically attached to the surface of a solid adsorbent (Volesky, 2003). Activated carbon and aluminosilicates are commonly used as adsorbents for metal removal. Also, a combination of activated alumina adsorption and micro filtration was used to treat contaminated water samples from Deloro water treatment plant containing 100 ppm arsenic (Motrazavi *et al.* 1993). Adsorption is an effective method for removal of low-level metal ions. However the regeneration might be expensive and could influence the performance of the adsorbent.

Unquestionable, activated carbon has been widely used in wastewater treatment but remains an expensive method whilst the greater cost as higher as its quality (Babel and Kurniawan 2003). On the other hand, these treatment methods may be ineffective or extremely expensive; mostly when the metals in solution ranged 1–100 mg/l (Nourbakhsh *et al* 1994).

In recent years, research is focused on developing eco-friendly and effective methods using biological treatments as biosorption to remove heavy metals from waste water in comparison to conventional treatment which not environmentally recommended and usually dependent on the concentration of the waste (Vijayaraghavan and Yun, 2008).

METAL UPTAKE BY MICROORGANISMS

Removal of heavy metal ions from polluted wastewaters by bacterial biomass has been studied extensively (Hassan *et al.* 2009 ; Kao W-C *et al.* 2008; Tuzen *et al.* 2008 ; Akhtar *et al.* 2007; Kadukova and Vircikova, 2005; Chaisuksant, 2003; Leung *et al.* 2001; Veglio *et al.* 1997; Akthar and Mohan, 1995; Fourest *et al.* 1994; Volesky, 2003, 1994, 1990). Microorganisms have the ability to remove heavy metals by two process; (1) biosorption "an energy-independent binding of metals to cell wall", and (2) bioaccumulation "an energy-dependent process of metal uptake into the cells" (Karna *et al.* 1999: Gadd, 1992).

Both living and non-living microbial biomass of bacteria, fungi and algae have been used in removing toxic metal ions (Kumar *et al.* 2008; Karna *et al.* 1999; Kumar *et al.* 1998; Volesky, 1990, 1994).

Metal removal by microorganisms is a complex process that depends on the chemistry of the metal ions, cell wall composition of microorganisms, cell physiology, and physicochemical factors such as pH, temperature, time, ionic strength and metal concentration (Hassan *et al* 2009; Gabr *et al* 2008; Kao W-C et *al*.2008; Tuzen *et al* 2008 ; Godlewska-Zylkiewicz 2006; Mapoleto *et al* 2005 ; Chaisuksant 2003; Goyal *et al* 2003 ; Volesky 2003; Klimmek *et al* 2001; Leung *et al* 2001). Metabolism-independent process of metal binding sites to the cell walls of bacterial biomass and external surfaces is the main mechanism present in the case of non-living biomass. Metabolism-independent or biosorption essentially involves adsorption process such as ionic and physicochemical adsorption. A variety of functional groups located on the bacterial cell walls are known to be included in metal biosorption. These involved carboxyl, amine, hydroxyl, phosphate and sulfhydryl groups. The removal of heavy metals by living and non-living biosorbents have been studied (Hassan *et al* 2009; Gabr *et al* 2008; Kadukova and Vircikova 2005; Mapoleto *et al* 2005; Chaisuksant 2003; Pardo *et al* 2003; Goyal *et al* 2003; Volesky 2003; Veglio *et al* 1997; Fourest *et al* 1994).

Although, metal biosorption by bacterial biomass occurs through complexation, coordination, physical adsorption, chelation, ion exchange, inorganic precipitation and/or a combination of these process (Akhtar *et al* 2007; Chen *et al* 2005; Kratochvil and Volesky 1998; Tsezos *et al*. 1995). Such process includes the active participation of several anionic ligands present on the biomass, like phosphoryl, carboxyl, carbonyl, sulfydryl and hydroxyl groups, was used to immobilize metal ions (Volesky, 2003). Also, the ability of any biosorbent depends on biomass characteristics, physicochemical properties of the heavy metals and the environmental conditions i.e., the solution pH, temperature, and interaction with other ions etc (Volesky 2003).

BIOACCUMULATION (METAL UPTAKE BY LIVING CELLS)

Bioaccumulation is an intracellular metal accumulation process by the living cells. This process involves metal binding on intracellular compounds, metal binding proteins, intracellular precipitation, methylation and other mechanisms. The uptake process usually involves adsorption of heavy metal ions at the bacterial cell wall or cell membrane through interactions with various functional groups and/or transport into the cell with subsequent transformation.

The term bioaccumulation describes an active process by living cells in which the removal of heavy metals depends on the metabolic activity of a living organism. It has been proved that, in some cases, that growing cells are able to remove metals continuously through internal detoxification mechanisms (Malik, 2004).

The activation energy for bioaccumulation, which is about 63 KJ/mol, corresponds to a biochemical process. This process involves transport of the metal across the cell membrane and its subsequent transformation (Davis *et al.* 2003; Veglio and Beolchini

1997; Blackwell *et al.* 1995). Most mechanisms of metal transport appear to rely on the electrochemical proton gradient across the cell membrane, which has a chemical and electrical potential, both of which are responsible for the transport of ionized solutes across membranes. The metal ion uptake is a function of cell age, composition of growth medium, contact time, pH of metal solution, initial metal ion concentration and concentration of cells in an aqueous solution. In addition, it seems that bioaccumulation is also dependent on the culture conditions and growth medium condition. Kinetics of bioaccumulation of metal ions is usually biphasic in nature: consisting of an initial rapid phase which can contribute up to 90% of the uptake and last for 10 to 30 minutes. The second phase is slower and has been found to last up to four hours (Kadukova and Vircikova, 2005). It can be inhibited by metabolic inhibitors such as low temperatures and lack of energy sources (Genter, 1996; Cho *et al.* 1994).

Biosorption is a quick process independent of presence of specific nutrients, while bioaccumulation is a slow and nutrient dependent. Living systems can be unreliable due to many problems of maintaining active biomass populations under high variable wastewater conditions. The extent of bioaccumulation is lower than that of the biosorption. Besides, bioaccumulation represents only 0.5–2% of dry cell weight (Raraz, 1995; Wood and Wang, 1985). From terminological point of view, bioaccumulation term is usually used for metal uptake by living cells, while biosorption is used for passive sequestering by dead cells (Volesky, 2003).

BIOSORPTION (METAL UPTAKE BY NON LIVING CELLS)

Biosorption can be defined as the ability of biological materials to accumulate heavy metals from wastewater through metabolically mediated or physicochemical pathways of uptake or a property of certain types of inactive, non-living microbial biomass to bind and concentrate heavy metals from even very dilute aqueous solution (Volesky, 2003; Fourest and Roux, 1992).

Biological materials (bacteria, fungi, algae and plant biomass) are known for their potential to adsorb heavy metals (Kratochvil and Volesky, 1998; Chang and Hong, 1994). Biosorption or bioadsorption is in fact a passive uptake of heavy metals by biomass.

Mechanisms of cell surface sorption are independent of cell metabolism; they are based upon physicochemical interactions between heavy metal ions and functional groups of the cell wall of microorganisms. The needed activation energy for biosorption is about 10–20 KJ/mol, which is in agreement with the physical nature of the process (Vijayaraghavan and Yun, 2008; Kadukova and Vircikova, 2005).

Biosorption is usually a rapid process responsible for metal removal by non-living biomass. It does not depend on temperature, metabolic energy, or the presence of metabolic inhibitors. Norton *et al.* (2004) reported that metal uptake is not significantly affected by biomass viability. Therefore, any metabolic activity process is currently considered to be a negligible part of biosorption.

Biosorbents in the waste materials discarded either from fermentation industries or from rubber plantaions or marine biomass as a source of raw biosorptive materials..

Therefore, the biomass can be either living or non-living but non living is preferred as it is easy to handle, and the processes is not growth dependent as well as it has no physiological constraints.

Consequently, biomass exhibits this property, acting just as chemical substance, as an ion exchanger of biological origin. It is particularly the cell wall structure of certain algae, fungi and bacteria, which was found responsible for this phenomenon (Volesky, 2003, 1990). Also, the microorganism's cell wall consists mainly of polysaccharides, lipids and proteins, which have many binding possibilities for metals. Such compounds possess numerous functional groups, including carboxylate, hydroxide, amine, imidazole, sulfate and sulfhydryl, with various charge distributions and geometries. So, these functional groups can selectively bind certain metal ions. In this part, binding is attributed to ion exchange, adsorption, complexing, microprecipitation and crystallization processes which occurrs on the cell wall (Sheng *et al.* 2004; Malik, 2004; Davis *et al.* 2003; Veglio and Beolchini, 1997; Blackwell *et al.* 1995). The cell wall constituents play an important role in metal sequestering due to the complexity of the used biomaterials. Also it is quite possible that some of these mechanisms act simultaneously, to a degree dependent on the biosorbent and the aqueous environment. Since this process is independent of the metabolism, binding of metals is very quick, up to 1 min (Delgado *et al.* 1998; Bustard *et al.* 1997) and mostly reversible (Veglio and Beolchini, 1997). Advantages and disadvantages of biosorption by non-living biomass are as follows :

Advantages

There are a number of advantages associated with the use of dead cells (Ahluwalia and Goyal, 2007; Tsezos *et al.* 1995). The dead microbial biomass is less sensitive to toxic heavy metals, and biosorption may not be inhibited by their presence. In contrast, inhibition of heavy metals removal due to the toxicity of these materials only occurs in the case of metabolically mediated accumulation by living cells. The advantages of biosorption of heavy metals using dead cells of bacterial biomass include the following features :

- Growth-independent. Nutrients are not required for the growth of bacterial cells. Therefore, there are no problems of feeding or metabolic products.
- Dead cells or non-living biomass is not subjected to toxicity limitation of cells.
- We can use the biomass from fermentation industries waste.
- There is no metabolic activity or physiological activity since the bacteria or fungal are dead cells.
- Low operational cost.
- Because non-living biomass behaves as an ion exchanger; the process is very rapid and takes place within few minutes to few hours. Metal loading on biomass is often highly efficient.

- Easily operating and controlling. We can control operating conditions such as pH, temperature, time and metal concentrations.
- Sterilization conditions are not required for this process.
- Pre treatment of bacterial biomass for improvement biosorptive capacity.
- Possibility of metal recovery.
- Regeneration and reuse of biosorbent.
- Biomass can be stored for a period of time.
- High efficiency of removal from dilute metal solutions.

Disadvantages

- The biological process improvement potential (e.g. through genetic engineering of cells) is limited because cells are not metabolizing. Because the production of the adsorptive agent occurs during pre-growth, there is no biological control over characteristic of biosorbent. This will be particularly true if waste biomass from a fermentation unit, is being utilized.
- There is no potential for biological altering the metal valency state, *i.e.*, less soluble forms are even for degradation of organometallic complexes.
- The major disadvantage of biosorption technology is that it has had limited practical applications to date and large scale production of the biomass has been established (Feng and Aldrich, 2004). This may be remedied in the future through progressive research and development as well as advanced pilot-scale projects.

The adsorption is easy to understand when it refers to a single metal situation; however, the assessment of sorption becomes complicated in a multi-ion situation which is generally encountered in effluent. Biosorption efficiency depends upon many factors including the capacity, affinity and specificity of the biosorbent and their physical and chemical conditions in effluents.

BIOSORPTION ISOTHERMS

Several studies on metal accumulation by microorganisms have been used the adsorption isotherms as a way to describe metal accumulation with metal concentration increase. The relationship between the amount of metal ion which is adsorbed on the cell (q_{eq}) and the metal ion concentration remaining in solution (C_{eq}), is described by an isotherm equation. Also, the isotherm represents the equilibrium distribution of metal ions between the aqueous and solid phase. Thereby, the equilibrium distribution is important in the determination of the maximum biosorption capacity. Several isotherm models are available to describe this equilibrium distribution. In addition, biosorption isotherm curve can be applied for plotting equilibrium concentration of heavy metals versus the adsorbed amount by bacterial biomass. The two most commonlly used models for describing this type of system are those given by Langmuir and Freundlich.

Langmuir isotherm

Langmuir adsorption isotherm is based on the following assumption (Volesky, 2003; Fourest and Roux, 1992):

(1) Metal ions are chemically adsorbed at a fixed number of well-defined sites,

(2) Each site can only hold one ion,

(3) All sites are energetically equivalent,

(4) There is no interaction between the ions,

(5) The maximum adsorption occurs when a saturated monolayer of solute molecules is present on the adsorbent surface,

(6) The energy of adsorption is constant,

(7) There is no migration of adsorbate molecules in the surface plane (localized adsorption).

Langmuir equation, which is valid for monolayer sorption on the surface containing definite number of identical sites and has been used extensively for dilute solutions, has the following form.

$$q_c = \frac{q_{\max} bC_c}{1 + bC_e} \quad \text{...(1)}$$

While, the linear form of Langmuir equation is

$$C_{eq}/q = 1/q_{max}b + C_{eq}/q_{max} \quad \text{...(2)}$$

Where q_{max} is the langmuir constant (mg/g) reflect the maximum adsorption capacity of the metal ion per unit weight of biomass to form a complete monolayer on the surface bound at high C_{eq}. The value of Langmuir constant b(L/mg), represents a ratio of adsorption rate constant to desorption rate constant, which also gives an indication of the affinity of the metal for binding sites on the biosorbent, q_{max} and b can be determined from the linear form of Langmuir equation Eqe (2) by plotting Ceq/qeq vs Ceq (Hassan *et al.* 2009; Norton *et al.* 2004; Volesky , 2003; Aksu and Dönmez 2001; Puranik and Paknikar 1999; Veglio *et al.* 1997; Chong and Volesky, 1995; Volesky and Holan, 1995).

Langmuir model was chosen to estimate the maximum adsorption capacity corresponding to complete monolayer coverage on the biomass surface. On the other hand, Freundlich model was chosen to estimate the adsorption intensity of the biosorbent towards the biomass.

FREUNDLICH ADSORPTION ISOTHERM

Freundlich expression is an empirical equation based on the sorption on a heterogeneous surface. Furthermore, Freundlich isotherm describes more complicated adsorption model where interactions occur between adsorbed molecules. It models monolayer adsorption on a heterogeneous surface and takes the following mathematical form:

$$q_{cq} = KC_{edl}^{1/n} \qquad \ldots(3)$$

The linearized form of this model is;

$$\ln q_{eq} = \ln K_f + 1/n \ln C_{eq} \qquad \ldots(4)$$

Freundlich equation generates an exponential shaped theoretical equilibrium curve and it is represented through eq. 3, where K and n are the Freundlich constants characterizing of the system. Equation 3, can be linearized in logarithmic form (eq. 4) and Freundlich constants can be determined.

Freundlich isotherm is also more widely used but provided no information on the monolayer adsorption capacity. In contrast to Langmuir model, Freundlich equation measures the adsorption capacity K_f, and the intensity of adsorption (n). (Hassan *et al.* 2009; Goyal *et al.* 2003; Volesky, 2003; Chong and Volesky, 1995; Mattuschka and Strauble, 1993; Aksu and Dönmez 2001; Puranik and Paknikar, 1999).

BRUNAUER–EMMETT AND TELLER (BET EQUATION)

BET isotherm is used occasionally and is represented multi-layer adsorption at heterogeneous sites with varying binding affinities at the adsorbent surface. Also, it assumed that a Langmuir isotherm applies to each layer (Kapoor and Viraraghavan, 1995; Morley and Gadd, 1995). Langmuir model assumed that the adsorption take place only on occupied adsorption sites (monolayer). On the other hand, BET model assumes that a number of adsorbate molecules layers are formed at the surface of sorbent and Langmuir equation can be applied to each layer. The equilibrium condition will therefore, involve several types of surfaces in the sense of molecules layers number on each surface. Also, multiple layering adsorption is similar to Langmuir model, the rate of adsorption on any layer is equal to the rate of desorption from that layer. The BET isotherm equation is:

$$Q_e = \frac{BC_cQ^0}{(C_s - C_e)\,[(1 + (B-1)\,C_e)/C_s]}$$

$$q_e = \frac{C}{(C_s - C)q_c} = \frac{1}{BQ^0} + \frac{B-1}{BQ^0}\frac{C}{C_s} \text{ (liner form)}$$

In which Q^0 is the metal uptake per unit weight of adsorbent in forming a complete monolayer on the surface, B is a constant relating to the energy of interaction with the surface. C_e is the measured metal concentration in solution at equilibrium and C_s is the saturation concentration of the solute.

BET and Freundlich models can be interpreted best at low concentration adsorbent/adsorbate interactions (Morley and Gadd, 1995). Kiran and Kaushik (2008) showed applicability example of BET model for Cr(VI) biosorption using *Lyngbya putealis* exopolysaccharides and they claimed that multilayer adsorption occurred in this system. In addition, Preetha and Viruthagiri (2005) applied BET model to describe the biosorption of Zn^{2+} by *Rhizopus arrhizus.*

Sips isotherm

Sips isotherm is an empirical model to study the adsorption process (Al-Asheh *et al.* 2000: Sips, 1948). It is the combination of both Langmuir and Freundlich isotherms, thus it is also known as Langmuir–Freundlich isotherm. Sips isotherm equation is given as below:

$$q_e = \frac{q_m (bC_e)^{1/n}}{1 + (bC_e)^{1/n}}$$

Where, qm is the total binding sites (mg/g), b is the median association constant (L/mg) and $1/n$ is the heterogeneity factor. Ce is the equilibrium concentration (mg/L), while qe is the adsorbed amount at equilibrium (mg/g). When 1/n<1, indicates the adsorbent has heterogeneous binding sites, while $1/n$ closer or even to 1 indicates homogeneous adsorbent (Al-Asheh *et al.* 2000).

Sips model assumes that the surface is homogeneous, but the sorption is a cooperative process due to adsorbate–adsorbate interactions.

Kumar and Porkodi (2006) concluded that the Sips isotherm provided best fitting of experimental data, followed by the Langmuir and the Redlich–Peterson isotherm equations. Oo *et al.* (2009) reported that the $1/n$ values for the adsorption of copper (II) (0.5737) and lead (II) (0.3252) confirmed with Freundlich isotherm which assumes heterogeneous adsorption. Sips isotherm provides a reasonably accurate prediction of heavy metal biosorption experimental results with high value of coefficient correlation ($R2$) (Apiratikul and Pavasant, 2008; Basha *et al.* 2008; Senthilkumar *et al.* 2007; Vijayaraghavan *et al.* 2006).

Redlich–Peterson isotherm

Redlich–Peterson isotherm contains three parameters and is an improvement over Langmuir and Freundlich isotherms. However, Redlich–Paterson is another empirical equation, which capable to represent adsorption equilibria over a wide range of concentration. This equation has the following form;

$$q_e = \frac{K_{RP} C_e}{1 + a_{RP} C_e^{\beta}}$$

In which, K_{RP} and d_{RP} are the Redlich–Peterson constants, and _ is basically in the range of zero to one. If _ is equal to 1, it reduces to Langmuir isotherm equation. while, in case where the value of d is much higher than one, Redlich–Peterson isotherm equation can be approximated by a Freundlich-type equation. Consequently, this equation is commonly used in the prediction of heavy metals bioadsorption equilibria data (Padmavathy, 2008; Preetha and Viruthagiri, 2007; Dursun, 2006; Ho 2006; Ho and Ofomaja, 2006; Vijayaraghavan *et al.* 2006).

NON-IDEAL COMPETITIVE ADSORPTION (NICA)

NICA is a multi-component competitive binding model that accounts for both ion-specific non-ideality and chemical heterogeneity of the biosorbent. Also, it has been used for, e.g. metal adsorption by bacteria (Plette *et al.* 1996) in addition to Scatchard plots have been used to show biosorption equilibria.

Often, either of these models is applicable to describe metal sorption by microorganisms (Table 1), but since the models were originally developed for other systems, they should be interpreted with a great care for such complex biological systems as microorganisms (Kapoor and Viraraghavan, 1995). For more information about the adsorption isotherms referred to the review of Gimbert *et al.* (2008).

TABLE 1 : Use of models to describe metal accumulation by microorganism

Organism	*Metal(s)*	*Model*	*References*
Pseudomonas cepacia	Cd, Zn	Langmuir	Savvaidis *et al.* 1992
Bacillus subtilis,	Cd, Zn, Cu	Langmuir	Cotoras *et al.*, 1992
Rhizopus arrhizus	Ag, Ni, Cu, Cd, Zn	Langmuir	Fourest *et al.* 1994
Rhizopus arrhizus	Cu	Langmuir	Brady and Tobin, 1995
Mucor hiemalis	Cr III	Langmuir	Pillichshammer *et al.* 1995
Aspergillus carbonarius	Cu	Langmuir	Al-Asheh and Duvnjak, 1995
B.megaterium, B. circulans,	Cr VI	Langmuir	Srinath *et al.* 2002
Chlorella kessleri	Cu	Langmuir	Kadukova and Vircıkova, 2005
Spirulina sp	Cd, Cu, Cr111	Langmuir	Chojnacka *et al.* 2005
Pseudomonas aeruginosa	Pb, Cd, Cu	Langmuir	Chang *et al.*1997
Citobacter strain MCMB-181	Cd, Zn, Pb	Langmuir	Puranik and Paknikar, 1999
Pseudomnas fluroescens	Ni	Langmuir	Lopez *et al.* 2001
Pseudomnas aeruginosa	Ni, Cu	Langmuir	Sar *et al.*1999
Sphaerotilus natans	Cu,Cd	Langmuir	Esposito *et al.*2001
Pseudomonas putida	Pb, Cd, Cu, Zn	Langmuir	Pardo *et al.*2003
Corynobacterium glutamicum	Pb	Langmuir	Choi and Yun, 2004
Arthrobacter sp	Ni, Pb, Cu, Mn	Langmuir	Veglio *et al.*1997
Arthrobacter sp	Cu, Cd,	Langmuir	Pagnanelli *et al.*2002
Zoogloea ramigera	Cu	Freundlich	Aksu *et al.*1992
Streptococcus equisimilis	Cr VI	Freundlich	Goyal *et al.*2003
Escherichia coli,		Freundlich	Mullen *et al.*1989
Thiothrix strain A1	Cu, Ni, Zn	Freundlich	Shuttleworth and Unz, 1993
Chlorella vulgaris	Cu	Freundlich	Aksu *et al.*1992

Organism	*Metal(s)*	*Model*	*References*
Bacillus sp	Pb, Cu	Freundlich, Langmuir	Tunali *et al.*2006
Pseudomonas putida	Cu, Zn	Freundlich, Langmuir	Chen *et al.*2005
Streptomyces coelicolor	Ni, Cu	Freundlich, Langmuir	Öztürk *et al.*2004
Enterobacter sp	Cu,Cd	Freundlich, Langmuir	Lu *et al.*2003
Candida sp	Cu	Freundlich, Langmuir	Aksu and Dommez, 2001
Ochrobacterium anthrobi	Cd, Cu, Cr111	Freundlich, Langmuir	Ozdemir *et al.*2003
Zoogloea ramigera	Pb, Ni, Cu,Fe111	Freundlich, Langmuir	Sag and Kutsal, 1995
Pseudomnas strain	U	Freundlich, Langmuir	Sar and Souza, 2001
Rhizopus arrhizus	Cd, Zn, Cu	BET	Morley and Gadd, 1995
Rhizopus arrhizus	Cu	BET	Gadd, 1988
Rhodobacter sphaeroides	Cd, Pb	NICA	Seki *et al.*1998
Algae Gelidium	Cu(II), Pb(II), and Cd(II)	Langmuir	Vilar *et al.*2007
Aspergillus niger	Cu(II) and Pb(II)	Langmuir, Freundlich and Redlich–Peterson	Dursun ,2006
	Cr(VI)	Langmuir and Freundlich	Mungasavalli *et al.*2007
Aspergillus sydoni			Kumar *et al.*2008
Bacillus cereus	Pb(II) and Cu(II)	Langmuir and Freundlich	Jian-hua *et al.*2007
Escherichia coli	Ni(II) and Cd(II)	Freundlich	Zhou *et al.*2007
Caulerpa lentillifera	Cu(II), Cd(II), and Pb(II)	Dubinin-Radushkevich, Sips	Apiratikul *et al.*2008
Caulerpa lentillifera	Cu(II), Cd(II), Pb(II), and Zn(II)	Langmuir and Freundlich	Pavasant *et al.*2006
Eichhornia crassipes	Cr(VI)	Freundlich	Choi and Yun, 2006
Penicillium janthinellum	Cr(VI)	Langmuir and Freundlich	Kumar *et al.*2008

Organism	*Metal(s)*	*Model*	*References*
Pseudomonas aeruginosa	Cr(III) and Cr(VI)	Langmuir and Freundlich	Kang *et al.*2007
Pseudomonas sp	.Cd(II), and Cr(VI)	Langmuir and Freundlich	Ziagova *et al.*2007
Rhizopus arrhizus	Cr(VI)	Langmuir, Freundlich and Redlich–Peterson	Preetha and Viruthagiri, 2007
Staphylococcusxylosus	Cd(II), and Cr(VI)	Langmuir and Freundlic	Ziagova *et al.*2007

FACTORS AFFECTING BIOSORPTION

pH in aqueous solution

For biosorption of heavy metal ions, pH is one of the most important environmental factors. Solution pH value strongly influences not only the site dissociation of the biomass surface, but also the solution chemistry of the heavy metals as hydrolysis, complexation by organic and/or inorganic ligands, redox reactions, precipitation, the speciation and the biosorption availability of the heavy metals (Esposito *et al.* 2001; Wang *et al.* 1997).

The biosorptive capacity of metal cations increases with increasing pH of the sorption system, but not in a linear relationship. On the other hand, extreme pH value can cause precipitation of metal complexes, so it should be avoided during experiments. As pH increases, functional sites on the microbial surface become deprotonated and may bind cationic metals instead. This results in the common trend of increasing accumulation with increasing pH. However, in many cases, the accumulation starts to decrease again at higher pH. Therefore, at low pH values the cell surface becomes more positively charged, then reducing the attraction between metal ions and functional groups on the cell wall. In contrast, higher pH results in facilitation of the metal biosorption, since the cell surface is more negatively charged. The metals will transform into hydroxide complexes at high pH values, however, it could not be considered as a biosorption behavior of the cells. Mapoleto and Torto (2004) proved that the biosorption capacity of Cd^{2+}, Cr^{3+}, Cr^{6+}, Cu^{2+}, Pb^{2+} and Zn^{2+} is dependent on pH. For all studied metal ions, the optimum pH values in all cases were found to be greater than 5. The optimum pH for Cd^{2+} and Pb^{2+} biosorption is 5.8. Also, Özer and Özer (2003) reported that optimal pH value for Pb^{2+} and Ni (II) ion uptake is 5.0 by *S. cerevisiae*.

Cr(VI) and some other metals such as arsenic are known to exist as anions meaning that the metal carry negative charge. These anions exhibit different pH features from metal cations. The biosorption was favourable at low pH for these anions. In this concern, cell wall ligands of bacterial biomass are protonated at low pH values, and compete significantly with metal binding. With pH increase, more ligands such as amino and carboxyl groups, would be exposed leading to attraction between these negative charges and the metals and hence increases in biosorption on to the cell surface. As the pH increased further, the overall surface charge on cells could become negative and therefore, biosorption of anions decreased again (Khambhaty *et al.* 2009; Wang and Chen, 2006; Park *et al.* 2005; Tewari *et al.* 2005).

Time

The biosorption process of heavy metal by bacterial biomass usually completes rapidly. The biosorption of metals as cadmium, cobalt, copper, zinc, lead, nickel, chromium and uranium by nonliving cells of bacterial biomass, is a rapid process and often reaches equilibrium within several minutes (Özer and Özer, 2003; Kapoor and Viraraghavan, 1997).

However, it is necessary to optimize the contact time, considering the efficiency of desorption and regeneration of the biomass. Gabr *et al.* (2008) optimized the sorption time for Pb(II) and Ni (II) by heavy metal resistant strain *Pseudomonas aeruginosa* ASU 6a. Besides, the result showed that a 30 min sorption period was the best option to ensure the metal removal from solution and good recovery from biosorbent. Similar results were observed by Hassan *et al.* (2009) who concluded that the optimum time for biosorption of Cu and Cd by *P. stutzeri* was 30 min.

IONIC STRENGTH (IS)

Since Na, K, Ca, Mg are present in many industrial wastewaters, it is useful to estimate the extent and interferes of light metals with biosorption of heavy metal by bacterial biomass (Goyal *et al.* 2003; Volesky 2003; Esposito *et al.* 2001; Pagnanelli *et al.* 2000). Most of light metals bind weakly to the negatively charged biomass particles, through electrostatic attraction in which a significant ionic strength effect may be observed in the presence of high concentration of light metals. Calcium, which may form specific, coordinate bonds, might be having stronger effect on heavy metal biosorption (Goyal *et al.* 2003; Volesky, 2003; Esposito *et al.* 2001; Pagnanelli *et al.* 2000). However, the effect of ionic strength can be explained via the competition of light metals with the heavy metals for electrostatic binding to the biomass. Kaewsarn (2002) reported that the effect of Na^+ on Cu(II) uptake was negligible at a concentration of 10 mM, and K^+, Mg^{2+} and Ca^{2+} reduced the removal efficiency by 4%, 11% and 13%, respectively. In addition, Chang and Hong, (1994) noted that the mercury uptake by *P. aeruginosa* decreased with the increment of ionic strength. Also, Cho *et al.* (1994) showed that no significant decrease in the binding of Cd^{2+} and Zn^{2+} occurred up to the ionic strength of 10^{-3} M. In contrast, Chaisuksant, (2003) illustrated that the presence of light metal ions (Na^+, K^+, Mg^{1+} and Ca^{2+}) in solution had an insignificant effect on cadmium and copper sorption capacity by pretreated biomass of marine alga *Gracilaria fisheri*. In general, the increaseof ionic strength decreased biosorption efficiency because of the increment of electrostatic charge (Volesky, 2003).

SURFACE AREA AND ITS EFFECT ON BIOSORPTION

The passive part of microbial metal accumulation can be influenced by surface properties such as charge and orientation of the metal binding functional groups on the cell surface. Microorganisms have a high surface area-to-volume ratio as their small size, and therefore this high surface area provide a large contact area that can interact with metals in the surrounding environment. Microbial metal accumulation has received much attention during the last years due to the potential use of microorganisms for cleaning metal-polluted water. However, less attention has been paid to the role of microorganisms for metal mobility in soil even though the same processes might occur there. Metal accumulation by microorganisms is influenced by the surface characteristics of microorganisms, but also themselves can lead to changes in the surface properties such as charge changes (Ivanov *et al.* 1996; Chen and Ting, 1995; Collins and Stotzky, 1992).

PRETREATMENT OF BIOSORBENT

Untreated or living cells of bacterial biomass may not be affected on heavy metal removal (Huang and Huang, 1996). Pre-treatment of bacterial biomass by some physical and chemical reagents may result in the improvement of biosorption capability (Galun *et al.* 1987). These types of pretreatments modify cell surface of bacterial biomass which is essential for biosorption either by removing or masking the groups as well as exposing more metal binding sites (Gupta *et al.* 2000). Furthermore, many physical pretreatment methods have been used such as heat treatment, autoclaving, freeze drying and boiling (Gabr *et al.* 2008; Göksungur *et al.* 2005; Seki *et al.* 2005; Mapoleto and Torto, 2004; Robles *et al.* 2000; Pethkar and Panikar, 1998). Chemical methods include the treatment with various organic and inorganic reagents, such as acid and alkali, methanol, formaldehyde, etc. Those methods are found to improve metal biosorption to some extent. Because of the important role of cell wall in the metal biosorption by non-viable cells, metal biosorption may be enhanced by heat or chemical sterilization or by crushing. Thus degraded cells would offer a larger available surface area and expose the intracellular components and more surface binding sites due to the destruction of the cell membranes (Errasquín and Vázquez, 2003; Robles *et al.* 2000). Autoclaved bacterial biomass caused a decrease in biosorption efficiency. The bioadsorption capacity of autoclaved *Mucor rouxii* decreased compared to the live fungus, and it can be attributed to the loss of intracellular uptake (Yan and Viraraghavan, 2000). Whistler and Daniel (1985) reported that the heat treatment could cause a loss of amino-functional groups on the fungal surface through the non-enzymatic browning reaction. In contrast, Galun *et al.* (1987) reported that *Penicillium* biomass pretreatment at 100°C for 5 minutes increased the biadsorption of lead, cadmium, nickel and zinc ias well as the increase was attributed to the exposure of latent binding sites after pre-treatment

The heat inactivation of the fungal biomass of *Lentinus edodes* was resulted in an increase in the biosorption capacity for mercury(II), cadmium(II) and zinc(II) metal ions compared to live cells (Bayramoglu and Arica 2008). Similar observations were reported for other biomasses, including fungi and yeast (Vilar *et al.* 2006; Bayramoglu *et al.* 2005; Brady and Tobin, 1995).

The findings obtained by Tunali and Akar (2006) indicated that pretreatment methods by heat or detergent or alkali altered the adsorption capacity of *B. cinerea* biomass which ranged from 1.75 ± 0.4590 to 12.98 ± 0.9623 mg g^{-1} biomass at 100 mg l^{-1} initial concentration of Zn(II) compared to the native biomass. The highest Zn(II) loading value (12.98 ± 0.9623 mg g^{-1}) was obtained by heat inactivated biomass, while pre-treatment detergent and sodium hydroxide treatments which increased the uptake of Zn(II) from 2.18 ± 0.6245 to 6.38 ± 0.6520 and 4.14 ± 1.0678 mg g^{-1}, respectively. The increase of biosorption rate was attributed to the activation and availability of more binding sites after pre-treatment. Preheating of biomass could cause a loss of amino-functional groups from the surface of bacterial or fungal biomass. Therefore, these functional groups are among the groups in the composition of polysaccharides which contribute to the binding of heavy metals (Yan and Viraraghavan, 2000).

The alkaline pre-treatment of bacterial biomass, including NaOH, KOH, NH_4OH, alkaline detergents or other alkaline reagents such as tolune, ruptures and destroy the cell walls of the microbes and exposes additional functional groups for metal ion binding, thus enhancing the biosorption capacity of biomass (Nadeem *et al.* 2008 ; Ochie, 2008 ; Tong 2007; Tan and Cheng, 2003;Ginisty *et al.* 1998).

Alkaline treatment destroys autolytic enzymes that cause purifications of biomass and removes both lipids and proteins that masked reactive sites. Sar *et al.* (1999) observed that metals (Cu^{2+} and Ni^{2+}) uptake capacity of lyophilized *Pseudomonas auruginosa* cells was enhanced when pretreated with NaOH, NH_4OH or toluene. Furthermore, Liu *et al.* (2004) reported that the effect of alkali or physical pretreatment increased the capacity for Zn(II) biosorption by the indigenous *T. thiooxidans* biomass compared to untreated biomass.

The acidic pre-treatment also improved the biosorption efficiency of bacterial biomass. Therefore, this may be due to the availability of more binding sites and elimination of impurities and ions that block heavy metals binding sites (Abbas *et al.* 2008; Gupta and Rastogi, 2008; Vijayaraghavan and Yun, 2008; Araujo *et al.* 2007). In addition Huang and Huang (1996) reported that acid pretreatment can strongly enhance the adsorption capacity of *Aspergillus oryzae* mycelia. It was assumed that the acid treatment may dissolve polysaccharide compounds in the outer layer of the fungal cell wall, thus producing additional binding sites. However, in the investigation by Kapoor and Viraraghavan (1995), acid pre-treatment of *A. niger* significantly reduced the biosorption of lead, cadmium, nickel and zinc.

Detergent treatments can increase the removal of metals from the solution, because the disruption of cell components increased cell permeability and exposed a wider variety of potential binding sites (Gadd, 1993).

Increased metal capacities of biosorbents due to the successful introduction of additional functional groups into the biomass cell wall were also reported by Seki *et al.*

(2005) and Marshall *et al.* (1999). Consequently, an improvement in the binding capacity of the alga *Lyngbya taylorii* (two- to six-fold) for Cd^{2+}, Ni^{2+}, Pb^{2+} and Zn^{2+} was observed upon phosphorylation (esterification of the hydroxyl groups of the polysaccharides) of the biomass (Klimmek *et al.* 2001). On the other hand, the blockage (via methylation) of negatively charged carboxylic groups resulted in an increase of the sorption amounts of anionic metallic species Cr (VI) and As (V), Pt (IV) (Seki *et al.* 2005; Parsons *et al.* 2003; Jianlong, 2002). Although, these treatments could change the properties of biological solids structure and therefore, their ability for biosorption. In this regard, freeze-drying does not seem to modify the structure of the wall cells (Pardo *et al.* 2003).

MECHANISM OF BIOSORPTION AND BIOACCUMULATION

The main biosorption of heavy metals mechanism is referred to non directed physico-chemical interactions that occur between dissolved metal ions in aqueous phase and cellular components of living or dead organisms which act as a solid phase. Involved interactions may be physical adsorption, ion exchange, complexation, coordination, microprecipitation, chelations crystallization or diffusion (Vijayaraghavan and Yun, 2008; Volesky, 2003; Yan and Viraraghavan, 2000; Volesky and Holan, 1995; Fourest and Roux, 1992; Gadd, 1988). Besides, the biosorption mechanisms of heavy metals showed that heavy metals are adsorbed by physicochemical interactions between metal ions and the bacterial surface. The different mechanisms of biosorption by bacterial biomass are shown in Figure 1.

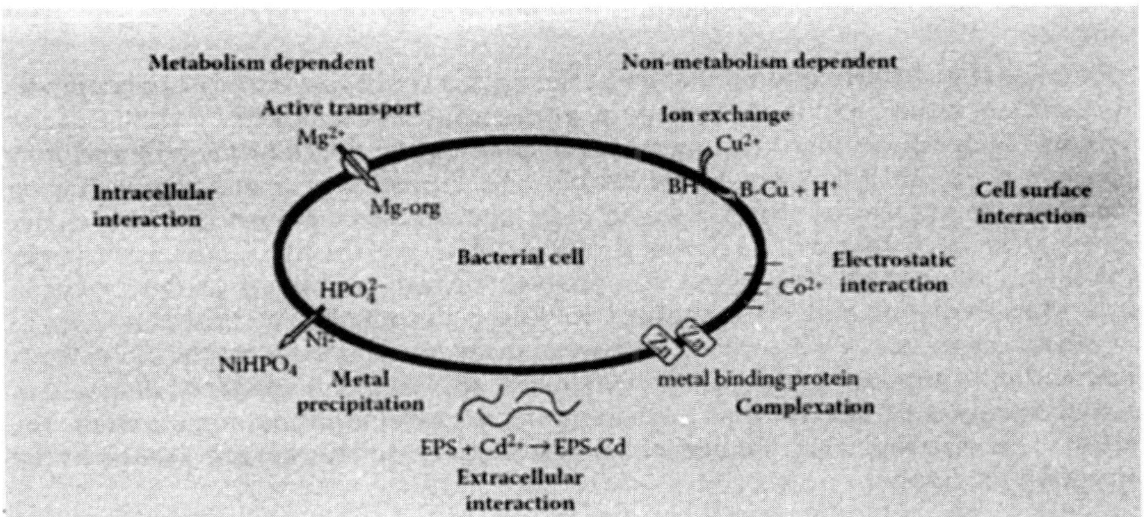

Fig. 1. Schematic diagram showing the different mechanisms of bacterial biosorption (Adapted from Prasad *et al. 2006*).

Binding of metals to cell surface components and intracellular accumulation were identified to proceed through two mechanisms in metals biosorption by living microorganisms (Gadd, 1993). The intracellular accumulation or metabolic processes may result in the accumulation of relatively large amounts of metal but these processes are slow and are mostly dependent on nutrients and environmental conditions (Malik, 2004). Also, cell surface and cell wall binding are a passive process and take place with both live and dead cells. Biosorption is very rapid, often less than a few minutes (Pardo *et al.* 2003) and these kinds of metal removal occur by ion exchange or physical adsorption processes involving specific chemical sites on cell wall which contained negative charge (Volesky and Holan, 1995). While, Akhtar *et al.* (2007) suggested that there are two phases of adsorption phenomenon were involved in biosorption of uranium in live *Trichoderma harzianum*: the first one, was related to physic sorption, and the second was due to both structural change and surface transformation. Besides, copper biosorption by live yeast *Saccaromyces cerevisae* was found to be biphasic and consisted of an initial, and rapid surface binding, then followed by a second slow intracellular uptake (Huang and Huang, 1996).

Gabr *et al.* (2008) reported some of the functional groups which contain negative charge like carboxylate, phosphate, sulfahydryle and amino groups which are present in cell wall of *P. aeruginosa* ASU 6a, and these function groups play an important role in biosorption of lead and nickel from aqueous solution. In addition, the cell wall of *P. aeruginosa* S22 contains proteins, lipids, which reflect the range of distinct potential complexation sites, such as carboxylate, phosphate, sulfahydryle and amino groups. Also amino acids as histadine, and cysteine, are reported to have strong affinity for metal ions (Komy *et al.* 2006). Aspartic acid and glutamic acid were also reported by Huange and Huang (1996) as amino acid residues might be responsible for metal adsorption.

Shumate *et al.* (1978) explored that metal ion uptake could react to form a precipitate, and discretely settled within the cells or as affine colloidal entrapped by extra cellular polymers. They also reported that metal ion may be transported into the cells and may react to form a product that remains within the cells. Furthermore, metal cations may be complexed by negatively charged sugar units at the end of polysaccharides chain. Besides, they cited that extra cellular polyphosphate groups associated with sugar metabolism, and complex metal ion by chelating through negatively charged oxygen atoms. Muraleedharan and Venkobachar (1990) used electron spin resonance spectra to study the mechanisms of biosorption. Moreover, the obtained spectra for the biosorbents before and after exposed to the metal solutions. In addition, they observed decrease in the concentration of free radicals with samples to metal solution compared to the control. This also indicated the participation of the negatively charged groups in the biosorption processes.

Another important mechanism which was involved in biosorption, is the ion exchange, where the cell wall of the biomaterial is generally regarded as a complex ion exchanger similar to commercials resins. It was reported that the cell walls contain a mixture of monovalent, divalent cations and that the displacement of one cation by another (e.g. H^+) is dependant on the strength o the individual ligand complex (Al-Asheh and Duvnjak, 1997).

BACTERIAL BIOSORPTION OF HEAVY METALS

Removal of toxic metal ions may contribute to the detoxification of polluted environments. Therefore, the investigation of metal uptake by bacteria is fundamental for the application of biosorption, since it gives information about metal ions removal efficiency in the process (Vegliό, and Beolchini, 1997). As a necessary factor for the design of equipment, the maximum adsorption capacity of bacteria is usually used by the parameter q_{max}. Table 2 shows the maximum biosorption capacity of heavy metals by bacteria reported in literature. However, the direct comparison of experimental data is not possible, due to differences in experimental conditions employed (such as; pH, equilibrium time, temperature, biomass concentration, heavy metal concentrations and the bacterial biomass). Even so, Table 2 provides some information to evaluate the possibile usage of bacterial biomass for the removal of heavy metal ions. Also, the biosorption capacity is not only dependent on the type of heavy metal ions, but also on the type of bacteria, due to the variations in cellular constituents.

TABLE 2 : Important results from the literature for metal biosorption by various bacterial biomass

Metal	*Biosorbent*	*pH*	*q_{max} (mg/g)*	*References*
Copper	*Bacillus sp. (ATS-1)*	5	16.3	Tunali *et al.* 2006
	Bacillus subtilis IAM 1026	5	20.8	Nakajima *et al.* 2001
	Enterobacter sp. J1	5	32.5	Lu *et al.* 2006
	Micrococcus luteus IAM 1056	5	33.5	Nakajima *et al.* 2001
	Pseudomonas aeruginosa PU21	5	23.1	Chang *et al.* 1997
	Pseudomonas cepacia	7	65.3	Savvaidis *et al.* 2003
	Pseudomonas putida	6	6.6	Pardo *et al.* 2003
	Pseudomonas putida	5.5	96.9	Uslu and Tanyol, 2006
	Pseudomonas putida CZ	4.5	15.8	Chen *et al.* 2005
	Pseudomonas stutzeri IAM 12097	5	22.9	Nakajima *et al.* 2001
	Sphaerotilus natans	6	60	Beolchini *et al.* 2006
	Streptomyces coelicolor	5	66.7	Öztürk *et al.* 2004
	Thiobacillus ferrooxidans	6	198.5	Ruiz-Manriquez *et al.* 1997
	Paenibacillus jamilae	6	7.8	Morillo *et al.* 2008
	Pseudomonas pseudoalcaligenes	5	48.4	Leung *et al.* 2001
	Pseudomonas aeruginosa AT18	5	113.64	Pérez Silva *et al.* 2009
	Pseudomonas stutzeri	5	33.16	Hassan *et al.* 2009
Cadmium	*Aeromonas caviae*	7	155.3	Loukidou *et al.* 2004
Cadmium	*Bacillus circulans*	7	26.5	Yilmaz and Ensari, 2005
	Enterobacter sp. J1	6	46.5	Lu *et al.* 2006

Metal	Biosorbent	pH	q_{max} (mg/g)	References
	Pseudomonas aeruginosa PU21	6	42.4	Chang *et al.* 1997
	Pseudomonas putida	6	8	Pardo *et al.* 2003
	Pseudomonas sp.	7	278	Ziagova *et al.* 2007
	Staphylococcus xylosus	6	250	Ziagova *et al.* 2007
	Streptomyces pimprina	5	30.4	Puranik *et al.* 1995
	Paenibacillus jamilae	6	20.4	Morillo *et al.* 2008
	Pseudomonas aeruginosa	8.5	6.18	Tuzen *et al.* 2008
	Streptomyces rimosus	8	64.9	Selatnia *et al.* 2004
Lead	*Bacillus sp. (ATS-1)*	3	92.3	Tunali *et al.* 2006
	Corynebacterium glutamicum	5	567.7	Choi and Yun, 2004
	Enterobacter sp. J1	5	50.9	Lu *et al.* 2006
	Pseudomonas aeruginosa	5	79.5	Chang *et al.* 1997
	Pseudomonas aeruginosa	5	0.7	Lin and Lai, 2006
	Pseudomonas putida	5.5	270.4	Uslu and Tanyol, 2006
	Pseudomonas putida	6.5	56.5	Pardo *et al.* 2003
	Streptomyces rimosus	6.5	135	Selatnia *et al.* 2004
	Streptoverticillium cinnamoneum	4	57.7	Puranik and Paknikar, 1997
	Paenibacillus jamilae	Not available	303.03	Morillo *et al.* 2008
	Pseudomonas aeruginosa	8.5	6.07	Tuzen *et al.* 2008
	Pseudomonas pseudoalcaligenes	5	271.7	Leung *et al.* 2001
	Pseudomonas aeruginosa ASU 6a	6	123	Gabr *et al.* 2008
Nickel	*Streptomyces coelicolor*	8	11.1	O¨ztu¨rk *et al.* 2004
	Streptomyces rimosus	6.5	36	Selatnia *et al.* 2004
	P. aeruginosa ASU 6a	7	113.6	Gabr *et al.* 2008
	Pseudomonas aeruginosa	8.5	5.25	Tuzen *et al.* 2008
	Escherichia coli	7	34.3	Kao *et al.* 2008
	Paenibacillus jamilae	6	17.6	Morillo *et al.* 2008
Zinc	*Paenibacillus jamilae*	6	12.31	Morillo *et al.* 2008
	Escherichia coli	7	659	Kao *et al.* 2008
	Pseudomonas aeruginosa AT18	7.-7.2	87.72	Pérez Silva *et al.* 2009
	Pseudomonas putida	7	6.9	Pardo *et al.* 2003
	Pseudomonas putida	5	17.7	Chen *et al.* 2005
	Streptomyces rimosus	3	30	Mameri *et al.* 1999
	Streptomyces rimosus	3	80	Mameri *et al.* 1999
	Streptoverticillium cinnamoneum	5.0-6.0	21.3	Puranik and Paknikar, 1997

FUTURE PROSPECTS

Bacterial biosorption of heavy metals, is an inexpensive technology to remediate or stabilize those pollutants from contaminated aqueous solution, and has received a great concern not only as effective adsorbents from low-cost biomaterials but also as bacteria had the abilities to adsorb different types of pollutants. In this concern, bacterial biomass (living/non-living cells) can be applied to the mixed contaminated water for the removal of several heavy metals within short time.

Biosorption is confronting a great challenge due to nontechnical pitfalls involved in the commercialization of technology (Volesky and Naja, 2005). Besides, biosorption has two future approaches for metal removal; first one is to use living cells as hybrid technology for pollutant remediation (Tsezos, 2001). However, the second is to develop effective commercial biosorbents (Volesky, 2007). Consequently, the application of biosorption using living cells has obtained attention compared to dead cells in addition to growing microbes as a useful alternative for heavy metal contaminants from industrial waste (Malik, 2004). The optimization of biosorption characteristics and physical conditions is required as additional trend for developing biomaterial immobilization as reuse, recycling and metal-microbes interactions (Wang and Chen, 2006).

During the last few years, various adsorbents have received a great attention as they have metal-binding capacities and are able to clean up heavy metals from contaminated water at low cost and local availability. Low cost biosorbents is utilized in detoxifying effluents of metal plating, mining and ore operations, beside numerous researches illustrated that biosorption is a beneficial alternative to conventional treatments for heavy metals removal from aqueous solution (Vijayaraghavan and Yun, 2008; Wang and Chen, 2006).

It is clear that biosorption of heavy metals is self-driven and don't disturb the sites in cleaning process. Also, biosorption could contribute to conventional methods as a second or pretreatments that enhanced the efficiency of heavy metal removal from industrial wastes and wastewater. Further researches are required to focus on low cost biosorbents as it is difficult to create a definite protocol that could be applied to any contaminated water and wastewater. So, each biosorbent must be customized and adapted to site-specific conditions. Modeling, regeneration and immobilization of biosorbents deserve indepth investigations.

REFERENCES

Abbas M Nadeem R Zafar MN Arshad M (2008) Biosorption of chromium (III) and chromium (VI) by untreated and pretreated *Cassia fistula* biomass from aqueous solutions. *Water Air Soil Pollut* **191**139-148

Ahluwalia SS and Goyal D (2007) Microbial and plant derived biomass for removal of heavy metals from wastewater *Bioresour Technol* **98:** 2243-2257

Akhtar K., Akhtar M.W. and Khalid A.M., (2007) Removal and recovery of uranium from aqueous solutions by *Trichoderma harzianum*. *Wat. Res.* **41:** 1366-1378

Aksu Z and Dönmez G (2001) Comparison of copper (II) biosorptive properties of live and treated *Candida* sp. *J Environ Sci Health* **36**: 367–381

Aksu Z, Sag Y and Kutsal T, (1992) The biosorption of Copper(II) by *C. vulgaris* and *Z. ramigera*. *Environ Technol* **13**: 579–586

Akthar M, Sastry K and Mohan P, (1996) Mechanism of metal ion biosorption by fungal biomass. *BioMetals.* **9**: 21–28

Akthar MN, Mohan PM (1995) Bioremediation of toxic metal ions from polluted lake waters and industrial effluents by fungal biosorbent. *Curr Sci* **69**: 1028-1030

Al-Asheh S and Duvnjak Z (1997) Sorption of cadmium and other heavy metals by pine bark. *J Hazard Mater* **56**: 35-51

Al-Asheh S and Duvnjak Z, (1995) Adsorption of copper and chromium by *Aspergillus carbonarius Biotechnol Prog* **11**: 638–642

Al-Asheh S, Banat F, Al-Omari R and Duvnjak Z (2000) Prediction of binary sorption isotherms for the sorption of heavy metals by pine bark using single isotherm data. *Chemosphere* **41:** 659–665

Apiratikul R and Pavasant P (2008) Batch and column studies of biosorption of heavy metals by *Caulerpa lentillifera Bioresour Technol* **99:** 2766–2777

Araujo GCL Lemos SG Ferreira AG Freitas H Nogueira ARA (2007) Effect of pre-treatment and supporting media on Ni(II), Cu(II), Al(III) and Fe(III) sorption by plant root material. *Chemosphere* **68:** 537-545

Atkinson BW Bux F and Kasan HC (1998) Considerations for application of biosorption technology to remediate metal-contaminated industrial effluents. *Wat SA* **24:**129–35

Babel S and Kurniawan T A (2003) Low-cost adsorbents for heavy metals uptake from contaminated water: a review *J Hazard Mater* **97:**219–243

Basha S Murthy ZVP and Jha B (2008) Sorption of Hg(II) from aqueous solutions onto *Carica papaya*: application of isotherms. *Ind Eng Chem Res* **47:** 980–986

Bayramoglu G Arica MY (2008) Removal of heavy mercury(II), cadmium(II) and zinc(II) metal ions by live and heat inactivated Lentinus edodes pellets. *Chem Eng J* **143**: 133-40

Bayramoglu G Celik G Yalcin E Yilmaz M and Arica MY (2005) Modification of surface properties of *Lentinus sajor-caju*mycelia by physical and chemical methods: Evaluation of their Cr^{+6} removal efficiencies from aqueous medium. *J Hazard Mater* **119**: 219–229

Beolchini F Pagnanelli F Toro L Vegliò F (2006) Ionic strength effect on copper biosorption by Sphaerotilus natans: equilibrium study and dynamic modelling in membrane reactor. Wat Res **40:**144–152

Blackwell KJ Singleton I and Tobin JM (1995) Metal cation uptake by yeast: a review. *Appl Microbiol Biotechnol* **43:** 579–584

Brady JM and Tobin JM (1995) Binding of hard and soft metal ions to *Rhizopus arrhizus* biomass, *Enzym Microb Technol* **17**: 791–796

Bustard M Donnellan N Rollan A McHale AP (1997) Studies on the biosorption of uranium by a thermotolerant, ethanol-producing strain of *Kluyveromyces marxianus*. *Bioprocess Eng* **17**: 45–50

Chaisuksant Y (2003) Biosorption of cadmium (II) and copper (II) by pretreated biomass of marine alga *Gracilaria fisheri Environ Technol* **24:**1501– 1508

Chang JS and Hong J (1994) Biosorption of mercury by the inactivated cells of *Pseudomonas aeruginosa* PU 21 (Rip 64). *Biotechnol Bioeng* **44**: 999–1006

Chang JS Law R and Chang CC (1997) Biosorption of lead, copper and cadmium by biomass of *Pseudomonas aeruginosa* PU21 *Wat Res* **31**: 1651-1658

Chen P and Ting Y (1995) Effect of heavy metal uptake on the electrokinetic properties of *Saccharomyces cerevisiae. Biotechnol Lett* **17**: 107–112

Chen XC Wang YP Lin Q Shi JY Wu WX and Chen YX (2005) Biosorption of copper(II) and zinc(II) from aqueous solution by *Pseudomonas putida* CZ1. *Colloids Surf B Biointerfaces* **46**: 101-107

Chen H M Zheng C R Tu C and Shen Z G (2000) Chemical methods and phytoremediation of soil contaminated with heavy metals. *Chemosphere* **41:** 229-234

Cho DY Lee ST Park SW and Chung AS (1994) Studies on the biosorption of heavy metals onto *Chlorella vulgaris. J. Environ. Sci Health Part A*; **29**: 389– 409

Choi SB and Yun YS (2006) Biosorption of cadmium by various types of dried sludge: an equilibrium study and investigation of mechanisms. *J Hazard Mater* **138:** 378–383

Choi SB and Yun YS, (2004) Lead biosorption by waste biomass of *Corynebacterium glutamicum* generated from lysine fermentation process *Biotechnol Lett* **26**: 331-336

Chojnacka K Chojnacki A and Gorecka H (2005) Biosorption of Cr^{3+}, Cd^{2+} and Cu^{2+} ions by blue green algae *Spirulina* sp.: kinticks, equilibrium and the mechanism of the process. *Chemosphere* **59**: 75-84

Chong KH and Volesky B (1995) Description of 2-metal biosorption equilibria by Langmuir-type models. *Biotechnol Bioeng* **47**: 451-460

Collins Y and Stotzky G (1992) Heavy metals alter the electrokinetic properties of bacteria, yeasts, and clay minerals. *Appl Environ Microbiol* **58**: 1592–1600

Costa ACA and Leite SGC (1991) Metal biosorption by sodium alginate immobilized *Chlorerella homosphaera Biotechnol Letter* **13:** 559-562

Cotoras D Viedma P Cifuentes L and Mestre A (1992) Sorption of metal ions by whole cells of *Bacillus* and *Micrococcus Environ Technol Lett* **13**: 551–559

Crini G (2006) Non-conventional low-cost adsorbents for dye removal: a review *Biores Technol* **97:** 1061–85

Davis T A Volesky B and Mucci A (2003) A review of the biochemistry of heavy metal biosorption by brown algae. *Wat Res* **37:** 4311–4330

Delgado A Anselmo AM and Novais JM (1998) Heavy metal biosorption by dried powdered mycelium of *Fusarium flocciferum*. *Wat Environ Res* **70**: 370–376

Dursun AY (2006) comparative study on determination of the equilibrium, kinetic and thermodynamic parameters of biosorption of copper (II) and lead(II) ions onto pretreated *Aspergillus niger Biochem Eng J* **28:** 187–195

Edyvean RGJ Williams CJ Wilson MW and Aderhold D (1997) Biosorption using unusual biomass. In: Wase, D.A.J. and Foster, C., Editors. *Biosorbents for Metals Ions*, Taylor & Francis, London, pp 165–181

Errasquín E L Vázquez C (2003) Tolerance and uptake of heavy metals by *Trichoderma atroviride* isolated from sludge. *Chemosphere* **50:** 137-143

Esposito A Pagnanelli F Lodi A Solisio C and Vegliό F (2001) Biosorption of heavy metals by *Sphaerotilus natans*: an equilibrium study at different pH and biomass concentrations. *Hydrometallurgy* **60:** 129-141

Feng D and Aldrich C (2004) Adsorption of heavy metals by biomaterials derived from the marine algae *Ecklonia maxima Hydrometallurgy* **73**:1-10

Fourest E and Roux JC (1992) Heavy metal biosorption by fungal mycelial by-products: mechanisms and influence of pH. *Appl Microbiol Biotechnol* **37:** 399–403

Fourest E Canal C and Roux J C (1994) Improvement of heavy metals biosorption by mycelial dead biomass (*Rhizopus arrhizus, Mucor meihi* and *Penicillium chrysogenum*) pH control and cationic activation. *FEMS Microbiol Rev* **14**: 325–332

Gabr RM Hassan SHA Shoreit AAM (2008) Biosorption of lead and nickel by living and non-living cells of *Pseudomonas aeruginosa* ASU 6a. *Int. Biodeterior. Biodegradation* **62:** 195-203

Gadd G (1992) Metals and microorganisms: a problem of definition. *FEMS Microbiol Lett* **100**: 197–204

Gadd GM (1993) Interactions of fungi with toxic metals. *New Phytol* **124:** 25-60

Gadd G M (1988) Accumulation of metal by microorganisms and algae. In: Rehm H, editor. Biotechnology: a complete treatise. vol. 6B, special microbial processes vol. 4. Verlagsgesellschaft, Weinheim: VCH; p 401– 430

Galun M Galun E Siegel BZ Keller P Lehr H and Siegel SM (1987) Removal of metal ions from aqueous solutions by *Penicillium* biomass: kinetic and uptake parameters. Water Air Soil Pollut **33:** 359–371

Genter RB (1996) Ecotoxicology of inorganic chemical stress to algae. Algal ecology. Praha7 Academic Press. (pp 403–468).

Gimbert F Morin-Crini N Renault F Badot P-M Crini G (2008) Adsorption isotherm models for dye removal by cationized starch-based material in a single component system: Error analysis. *J Hazard Mater* **157:** 34-46

Ginisty P Besnainou B Sahut C and Guezennec J (1998) Biosorption of cobalt by *Pseudomonas halodentrificans*: influence of cell wall treatment by alkali and alkaline-earth metals and ion-exchange mechanisms. *Biotechnol Lett* **20:**1035-1039

GodlewskaZylkiewicz B (2006) Microorganisms in inorganic chemical analysis. *Anal Bioanal Chem* **38:**114-123

Göksungur Y Üren S and Güvenc U (2005) Biosorption of cadmium and lead ions by ethanol treated waste baker's yeast biomass. *Bioresour Technol* **96:** 103–109

Goyal N Jain SC and Banerjee UC (2003) Comparative studies on the microbial adsorption of heavy metals. *Adv Environ Res* **7:** 311–319

Gray NF (1999) Water Technology, John Wiley and Sons, New York pp. 473–474.

Gupta VK Rastogi A (2008) Equilibrium and kinetic modelling of cadmium(II) biosorption by nonliving algal biomass *Oedogonium sp* from aqueous phase *J Hazard Mater* **153:** 759-766

Gupta R Ahuja P Khan S Saxena RK Mohapatra M (2000) Microbial biosorbents: meetings challenges of heavy metals pollution in aqueous solution. *Current Sciece* **78:** 967–973

Hassan SHA Kim SJ Jung A-Y Joo JH Oh SE and Yang JE (2009) Biosorptive capacity of Cd(II) and Cu(II) by lyophilized cells of *Pseudomonas stutzeri J Gen Appl Microbiol* **55:** 27-34

Ho Y (2006) Isotherms for the sorption of lead onto peat: comparison of linear and non-linear methods. *Polish Journal of Environmental Studies* **15:** 81–86

Ho Y and Ofomaja AE (2006) Biosorption thermodynamics of cadmium on coconut copra meal as biosorbent. *Biochem Eng J* **30:** 117–123

Huang C and Huang C P (1996) Application of *Aspergillus oryze* and *Rhizopus oryzae* for Cu(II) removal. *Wat Res* **30:** 1985-1990

Huang YC and Koseoglu SS (1993) Separation of heavy metals from **industrial waste** streams by membrane separation technology. *Waste Manag* **13:** 481-501

Ivanov A Khassanova L Collery P Khassanova Z Choisy C and Etienne JC (1996) Microorganisms as a tool of studying copper metal ions induced changes in electrophysical cell. *Properties Cell Mol Biol* **42,** 825–831

Jian-hua P Rui-xia L and Hong-xiao T (2007) Surface reaction of bacillus cereus biomass and its biosorption for lead and copper ions, *J Environ Sci* **19:** 403–408

Jianlong W (2002) Biosorption of copper (II) by chemically modified biomass of *Saccharomyces cerevisiae*. *Process Biochem* **37:** 847–850

Jung M C and Thornton I (1997) Environmental contamination and seasonal variation of metals in soils, plants and water in the paddy fields around a Pb-Zn mine in Korea. *Applied Geochm* **16:** 1377-1386

Kadukova J and Vircikova E (2005) Comparison of differences between copper bioaccumulation and biosorption. *Environ Int* **31:** 227-232

Kaewsarn P (2002) Biosorption of copper (II) from aqueous solutions by pretreated biomass of marine algae *Padina* sp. *Chemosphere* **47:** 1081–1085

Kang S Lee J and Kima K (2007) Biosorption of Cr(III) and Cr(VI) onto the cell surface of pseudomonas aeruginosa. *Biochem Eng J* **36:** 54–58

Kao W-C Huang C-C and Chang J-S (2008) Biosorption of nickel, chromium and zinc by MerP-expressing recombinant *Escherichia coli J Hazard Mater* **158:** 100-106

Kapoor A and Viraraghavan T (1995) Fungal biosorption an alternative treatment option for heavy metal bearing wastewaters: a review. *Bioresour Technol* **53:**195–206

Kapoor A and Viraraghavan T (1997) Heavy metal biosorption sites in *Aspergillus niger. Bioresour Technol* **61:** 221-227

Karna RR Uma L Subramanian G and Mohan PM (1999) Biosorption of toxic metal ions by alkali-extracted biomass of a marine cyanobacterium, *Phormidium valderianum* BDU 30501. *World J Microbiol Biotechnol* **15:** 729-732

Khambhaty Y Mody K Basha S Jha B (2009) Biosorption of Cr(VI) onto marine *Aspergillus niger:* experimental studies and pseudo- second order kinetics. *World J Microbiol Biotechnol* DOI 101007/s11274-009-0028-0

Kiran B and Kaushik A (2008) Cyanobacterial biosorption of Cr(VI): Application of two parameter and Bohart Adams models for batch and column studies. *Chem Eng J* **144:** 391-399

Klimmek S Stan HJ Wilke A Bunke G and Buchholz R (2001) Comparative analysis of the biosorption of cadmium, lead, nickel, and zinc by algae. *Environ Sci Technol* **35**: 4283–4288

Komy ZR Gabar RM Shoriet AAM Mohammed RM (2006) Characterization of acidic sites of *Pseudomonas* biomass capable of binding protons and cadmium and removal of cadmium via biosorption. *World J Microbiol Biotechnol* **22:**975–982

Kratochvil D and Volesky B (1998) Biosorption of Cu from ferruginous wastewater by algal biomass. *Wat Res* **32:** 2760-2768

Kumar KV and Porkodi K (2006) Relation between some two- and three-parameter isotherm models for the sorption of methylene blue onto lemon peel. *J Hazard Mater* **138: 633-635**

Kumar R Bishnoi NR Garima and Bishnoi K (2008) Biosorption of chromium(VI) from aqueous solution and electroplatingwastewater using fungal biomass. *Chem Eng J* **135**: 202–208

Kumar V Wati L Nigam P Yadav BS Singh D and Marchant R (1998) Decolorization and biodegradation of anaerobically digested surgarcane molasses spent wash effluent from biomethanation plants by white-rot fungi. *Process Biochem* **33:** 83-88

Kumar V Wati L Nigam P Yadav BS Singh D and Marchant R (1998) Decolorization and biodegradation of anaerobically digested surgarcane molasses spent wash effluent from biomethanation plants by white-rot fungi. *Process Biochem* **33**: 83-88

Lamba N Murthy ZVP Kumar R (2002) Membrane processing of an aqueous waste stream fromcatalyst manufacturing plant, *Sep Sci Technol* **37**: 191–202

Leung WC Chua H and Lo WH (2001) Biosorption of heavy metals by bacteria isolated from activated sludge. *Appl Biochem Biotechnol* **91:**171-84

Lin CC and Lai YT (2006) Adsorption and recovery of lead (II) from aqueous solutions by immobilized *Pseudomonas aeruginosa* PU21 beads. *J Hazard Mater* **137:** 99–105

Liu H-L Chen B-Y Lan Y-W and Cheng Y-C (2004) Biosorption of Zn(II) and Cu(II) by the indigenous *Thiobacillus thiooxidans Chem Eng J* **97:** 195-201

Lopez A Larao N Priergo J and Marques A (2001) Effect of pH on the biosorption of nickel and other heavy metals by *Pseudomonas fluorescens* 4F39. *J Ind Microbiol Biotechnol* **24:** 146– 151

Loukidou MX Zouboulis A I Karapantsios T D and Matis K A (2004) Equilibrium and kinetic modeling of chromium (VI) biosorption by *Aeromonas caviae Colloids and Surfaces A: Physicochem Eng Aspects* **242:** 93–104

Lu W-B Shi J-J Wang C-H Chang J-S (2006) Biosorption of lead, copper and cadmium by an indigenous isolate *Enterobacter* sp. J1 possessing high heavy-metal resistance. *J Hazard Mater* **134:**80–86

Lu Z H Dameron C T and Solioz M (2003) The *Enterococcus hirae* paradigm of copper homeostasis: copper chaperone turnover, interactions, and transactions. *Biometals* **16:** 137-143

Malik A (2004) Metal bioremediation through growing cells. *Environ Int* **30**: 261–278

Mameri N Boudries N Addour L Belhocine D Lounici H Grib H Pauss A (1999) Batch zinc biosorption by a bacterial nonliving *Streptomyces rimosus* biomass. *Wat Res* **33:**1347–1354

Mapoleto M and Torto N (2004) Trace enrichment of metal ions in aquatic environments by *Saccharomyces cerevisiae Talanta* **64**: 39–47

Mapoleto M Torto N and Prior B (2005) Evaluation of yeast strains as possible agents for trace enrichment of metal ions in aquatic environments. *Talanta* **65**: 930–937

Marshall WE Wartelle LH Boler DE Johns MM and Toles CA (1999) Enhanced metal adsorption by soybean hulls modified with citric acid. *Bioresour Technol* **69**: 263–268

Mattuschka B and Strauble G (1993) Biosorption of metals by a waste biomass. *J Chem Tech and biotechnology* **58**, 57-63

Morillo JA García-Ribera R Quesada T Aguilera M Ramos-Cormenzana A and Monteoliva-Sánchez M (2008) Biosorption of heavy metals by the EPS produced by *Paenibacillus jamilae World J Microbiol Biotechnol* **24:**2699–2704

Morley GF and Gadd GM (1995) Sorption of toxic metals by fungi and clay minerals. *Mycol Res* **99:** 1429–1438

Motrazavi S Volchek K and Whittaker H (1993) The removal of arsenic from water by adsorption and microfiltraion, proceeding of the 10th technical seminar on chemical spills, St John, New Brunswick, pp9-29

Mullen M D Wolf D C Ferris F G Beveridge T J Flemming C A and Bailey G W (1989) Bacterial sorption of heavy metals. *Appl Environ Microbiol* **55**: 3143-3149

Mungasavalli DP Viraraghavan T and Jin YC (2007) Biosorption of chromium fromaqueous solutions by pretreated *Aspergillus niger*: batch and column studies. *Colloids Surf A Physicochem Eng Aspects***301:** 214–223

Muraleedharan TR and Venkobachar C (1990) Mechanism of biosorption of copper (I) by *Ganoderma lucidum Biotechnol Bioeng* **35:** 320–325

Murthy ZVP Chaudhari L B (2009) Separation of binary heavy metals from aqueous solutions by nanofiltration and characterization of the membrane using Spiegler–Kedem model. *Chem Eng J* **150** : 181–187

Nadeem R Ansari TM Khalid AM (2008) Fourier Transform Infrared Spectroscopic characterization and optimization of Pb(II) biosorption by fish (*Labeo rohita*) scales. *J Hazard Mater***156:** 64-73

Nakajima A Yasuda M Yokoyama H Ohya-Nishiguchi H Kamada H (2001) Copper biosorption by chemically treated *Micrococcus luteus* cells*World J Microbiol Biotechnol* **17**:343–347

Nandy T Shastry S Pathe PP and Kaul S N (2003) Pre-treatment of currency printing ink wastewater through coagulation-flocculation process. *Water Air Soil Pollut* **148:** 15–30

Norton L Baskaran K and McKenzie T (2004) Biosorption of zinc from aqueous solutions using biosolids. *Adv Environ Res* **8**: 629-635

Nriagu J O (1990) Humans influence on the global cycling of trace metals. In: Heavy metals in the environment. Frame, J G, editor 1 CEP consultants Ltd Edinburg

Ochie A V (2008) Recent Progress on Biosorption of Heavy Metals from Liquids Using Low Cost Biosorbents: Characterization, Biosorption Parameters and Mechanism Studies. *CLEAN - Soil Air Water* **36:** 937 – 962

Ok Y S Lee H and Kim J G (2007) Enhanced uptake of Cadmium by native plant (*Artemisia princeps* var. Orientalis) using Ethylenediaminetetrascetic acid. *J Biol Sci* **7**: 681-684

Oo CW Kassim MJ and Pizzi A (2009) Characterization and performance of Rhizophora apiculata mangrove polyflavonoid tannins in the adsorption of copper (II) and lead (II). *Ind Crops Prod* doi:101016/jindcrop200903002

Özar A and Özer D (2003) Comparative study of the biosorption of Pb (II), Ni (II) and Cr (II) ions onto *S. cerviciae*: determination of biosorption heats. *J Hazard Mater* **100**: 219-229

Ozdemir G Ozturk T Ceyhan N Isler R and Cosar T (2003) Heavy metal biosorption by biomass of *Ochrobacterium anthropi* producing exopolysaccharide in activated sludge. *Bioresour Technol* **90:** 71-74

Öztürk A Artan T and Ayar A (2004) Biosorption of nickel (II) and copper (II) ions from aqueous solution by *Streptomyces coelicolor* A3 (2). *Colloids Surf B Biointerfaces* **34:** 105-111

Padmavathy V (2008) Biosorption of nickel(II) ions by baker's yeast: kinetic, thermodynamic and desorption studies. *Bioresour Technol* **99**: 3100–3109

Pagnanelli F Esposito A Veglio F (2002) Multi-metallic modelling for biosorption of binary systems. *Wat Res* **36:** 4095-4105

Pagnanelli F Petrangeli Papini M Trifoni M Toro L and Veglio F (2000) Biosorption of metal ions on *Arthrobacter* sp.: Biomass characterization and biosorption modeling. *Environ Sci Technol* **34**: 2773–2778

Pardo R Herguedas M Barrado E and Vega M (2003) Biosorption of cadmium, copper, lead and zinc by inactive biomass of *Pseudomonas putida Anal Bioanal Chem* **376:** 26-32

Park D Yun YS Jo JH Park JM (2005) Mechanism of hexavalent chromium removal by dead fungal biomass of *Aspergillus niger Wat Res* **39**:533–540

Parsons JG Gardea-Torresdey JL Tiemann KJ and Gamez G (2003) Investigation of trace level binding of $PtCl6^{2-}$ and $PtCl4^{2-}$ to alfalfa biomass (*Medicago sativa*) using Zeeman graphite furnace atomic absorption spectrometry. *Anal. Chim. Acta.* **478**: 139–145.

Pavasant P Apiratikul R Sungkhum V Suthiparinyanont P Wattanachira S and Marhaba TF (2006) Biosorption of Cu^{2+}, Cd^{2+}, Pb^{2+}, and Zn^{2+} using dried marine green macroalga *Caulerpa lentillifera Bioresour Technol* **97**: 2321–2329

Pérez Silva RM Rodriguez AA G_omez Montes De Oca JM Cantero Moreno D (2009) Biosorption of chromium, copper, manganese and zinc by Pseudomonas aeruginosa AT18 isolated from a site contaminated with petroleum. *Bioresour Technol* **100:** 1533-1538

Pethkar AV and Panikar KM (1998) Recovery of gold from solutions using *Cladosporium cladosporioides* biomass beads *J Biotechnol* **63:**121–136

Pillichshammer M Pumple T Eller K Klima J and Schinner F (1995) Biosorption of chromium to fungi *Biometals* **8:** 117-121

Plette A Benedetti M and Van Rimsdijk (1996) Comparative binding of protons, calcium, cadmium and zinc to isolated cell walls of a Gram-positive soil bacteria. *Environ Sci Technol* **30**: 1902-1910

Prasad M NV Sajwan K S and Naidu R (2006) Trace elements in the environment CRC Press Boca Racton

Preetha B and Viruthagiri T (2007) Batch and continuous biosorption of chromium(VI) by *Rhizopus arrhizus Sep Purif Technol* **57:** 126–133

Preetha B and Viruthagiri T (2005) Biosorption of zinc(II) by *Rhizopus arrhizus*: equilibrium and kinetic modeling, *Afr J Biotechnol* **4**: 506–508

Puranik PR and Paknikar KM (1997) Biosorption of lead and zinc from solutions using *Streptoverticillium cinnamoneum* waste biomass, *J Biotechnol* **55**: 113–124

Puranik PR Chabukswar NS and Paknikar KM (1995) Cadmium biosorption by *Streptomyces pimprina* waste biomass *Appl Microbiol Biotechnol* **43:** 1118–1121

Puranik PR and Paknikar KM (1999) Biosorption of lead, cadmium and zinc by *Citrobacter* strain MCM B-181: characterization studies. *Biotechnol Progress* **15**: 228-237

Qin JJ Wai MN Oo MH Lee H (2004) A pilot study for reclamation of a combined rinse from a nickel plating operation using a dual-membrane UF/RO process, ***Desalination*** **161:** 155–167

Raraz AG (1995) Biological and biotechnological waste management in materials processing. *JOM* 56–62

Robles LC Feo JC and Aller AJ (2000) Selective preconcentration of phenyl-mercury by living *Escherichia coli* and its determination by cold vapour atomic absorption spectrometry. *Anal Chim Acta* **423:** 255–263

Ruiz Manriquez A Magana PI López V Guzmán R (1997) Biosorption of Cu by *Thiobacillus ferrooxidans Bioprocess Eng* **18:**113–118

Sag Y and Kutsal T (1995) Biosorption of heavy metals by *Zoogloea ramigera*: use of adsorption isotherms and comparison of biosorption characteristics. *Chem Eng J* **60**:181–188

Sar P Kazy SK Asthana RK and Singh SP (1999) Metal adsorption and desorption by lyophilized *Pseudomonas aeruginosa Int Biodeterior Biodegradation* **44**: 101–110

Sar P and D'Souza S F (2001) Biosorptive uranium uptake by a *Pseudomonas* strain: Characterization and equilibrium studies. *J Chem Technol Biotechnol* **76**: 1286-1294

Savvaidis I Hughes M N Poole R K (*2003*) Copper *biosorption* by *Pseudomonas cepacia* and other strains. *World J Microbiol Biot* **19:** 117-121

Savvaidis I Hughes MN and Poole RK (1992) Differential pulse polarography: a method of directly measuring uptake of metal ions by live bacteria without separation of biomass and medium. *FEMS Microbiol Lett* **92**: 181-186

Seki H Suzuki A and Maruyama H (2005) Biosorption of Cr (VI) and As (V) onto methylated yeast biomass. *J Colloid Interf Sci* **281:** 261–266

Seki H Suzuki A and Mitsueda SI (1998) Biosorption of Heavy Metal Ions on *Rhodobacter sphaeroides* and *Alcaligenes eutrophus H16 J Colloid Interf Sci,* **197**: 185-190

Selatnia A Boukazoula A Kechid N Bakhti MZ Chergui A Kerchich Y (2004) Biosorption of lead (II) from aqueous solution by a bacterial dead *Streptomyces rimosus* biomass. *Biochem Eng J* **19:** 127–135

Senthilkumar R Vijayaraghavan K Thilakavathi M Iyer PVR and Velan M (2007) Application of seaweeds for the removal of lead from aqueous solution. *Biochem Eng J* **33**: 211–216

Sheng PX Ting YP Chen JP and Hong L (2004) Sorption of lead, copper, cadmium, zinc, and nickel by marine algal biomass: characterization of biosorptive capacity and investigation of mechanisms. *J Colloid Interf Sci* **275**: 131–140

Shumate H Strandberg G and Parrott J (1978) Biological removal of metal ions from aqueous process streams. *Biotechnol Bioeng Symp* **8:** 12–20

Shuttleworth K L and Unz R F (1993) Sorption of heavy metals to *Thiothrix* strain A1 *Appl Environ Microbiol* **59**:1274–1282

Sips R (1948) On the structure of a catalyst surface. *J Chem Phys* **16**: 490-495

Srinath T Verma T Ramteke PW and Garg SK (2002) Chromium (VI) biosorption and bioaccumulation by chromate resistant bacteria. *Chemosphere* **48**: 427–435

Tan T Cheng P (2003) Biosorption of metal ions with Penicillium chrysogenum *Appl Biochem Biotechnol* **104**:119-128

Tewari N Vasudevan P Guha BK (2005) Study on biosorption of Cr(VI) by Mucor hiemalis. *Biochem Eng J* **23**:185–192

Tong Mi (2007) Polymer modified biomass of baker's yeast for treating simulated wastewater containing nickel and lead. *Polymers for Advanced Technologies* **18:** 829 – 834

Tsezos M (2001) Biosorption of metals. The experience accumulated and the outlook for technology development. *Hydrometallurgy* **59**:241–243

Tsezos M Remoudaki E and Angelatou V (1995) Systematic study on equilibrium and kinetics of biosorptive accumulation. The case of Ag and Ni. Int. *Biodet Biodeg* **35**: 331-332

Tunali S and Akar T (2006) Zn (II) biosorption properties of *Botrytis cinerea* biomass. *J Hazard Mater* **131**: 137-45

Tunali S Akar T Safi Ozcan A Kiran I and Ozcan A (2006) Equilibrium and kinetics of biosorption of lead (II) from aqueous solutions by *Cephalosporium aphidicola. Sep Purif Technol* **47**:105–112

Tuzen M Saygi KO Usta C Soylak M (2008) *Pseudomonas aeruginosa* immobilized multiwalled carbon nanotubes as biosorbent for heavy metal ions. *Bioresour Technol* **99**:1563-1570

Uslu G and Tanyol M (2006) Equilibrium and thermodynamic parameters of single and binary mixture biosorption of lead (II) and copper (II) ions onto *Pseudomonas putida*: Effect of temperature *J Hazard Mater* **135**: 3187-3193

Veglio F and Beolchini F (1997) Removal of metals by biosorption: a review. *Hydrometallurgy* **44**: 301–316.

Veglió F Beolchini F and Gasbarro A (1997) Biosorption of toxic metals: an equilibrium study using free cells of *Arthrobacter* sp. *Process Biochem* **2**: 99-105

Vijayaraghavan K and Yun Y-S (2008) Bacterial biosorbents and biosorption. *Biotechnol Adv* **26**:266-291

Vijayaraghavan K Padmesh TVN Palanivelu K and Velan M (2006) Biosorption of nickel(II) ions onto *Sargassum wightii*: application of two-parameter and three-parameter isotherm models. *J Hazard Mater* **133**: 304–308

Vilar VJP Botelho CMB and Boaventura RAR (2006) Equilibrium and kinetic modelling of Cd(II) biosorption by algae *Gelidium* and agar extraction algal waste. *Wat Res* **40**: 291–302

Vilar VJP Botelho CMS and Boaventura RAR (2007) Modeling equilibrium and kinetics of metal uptake by algal biomass in continuous stirred and packed bed adsorbers. *Adsorption* **13**: 587–601

Volesky B Naja G (2005) Biosorption: application strategies. 16th Internat. Biotechnol. Symp.Compress Co., Cape Town, South Africa.

Volesky B (1990) Biosorption by fungal biomass. In: Volesky B, Biosorption of heavy metals. Florida: CRC press, (140–171).

Volesky B (1994) Advances in biosorption of metals: selection of biomass types. *FEMS Microbiol Rev* **14**: 291-302

Volesky B (2007) Biosorption and me. *Water Res* **41**:4017–29

Volesky B and Holan ZR (1995) Biosorption of heavy metals. *Biotechnol Prog* **11**: 235-250

Volesky B (2003) Sorption and biosorption BV Sorbex, Inc. Montreal-St. Lambert, Quebec, Canda

Wang J and Chen C (2006) Biosorption of heavy metals by *Saccharomyces cerevisiae*: a review, *Biotechnol Adv* **24**: 427–451

Wang CL Michels S PC Sawson C Kitisakkul S Baross J A Keasling J D and Clark DS (1997) Cadmium removal by a new strain of *Pseudomonas aeruginosa* in aerobic culture. *Appl Environ Microbiol* **63**: 4075-407

Whistler R and Daniel TR (1985) Carbohydrates. In Owen R Fennema (Ed.) Food Chemistry. 96-105

Wood JM and Wang H-K (1985) Microbial resistance to heavy metals. In: Irgolic KJ, editor: Environmental inorganic chemistry (proceedings). Deerfield Beach, Florida7 VCH Publishers; (pp. 487–512).

Yan G and Viraraghavan T (2000) Effect of pretreatment on the bioadsorption of heavy metals on *Mucor rouxii, Water SA* **26**: 119–124

Yan G and Viraraghavan T (2006) Effect of pretreatment on the bioadsorption of heavy metals on *Mucor rouxii Water SA* **26**: 119–124

Yilmaz EI Ensari NY (2005) Cadmium biosorption by Bacillus circulans strain EB1. *World J Microbiol Biotechnol* **21**:777–779

Zhou M Liu Y Zeng G Li X Xu W and Fan T (2007) Kinetic and equilibrium studies of Cr(VI) biosorption by dead *Bacillus licheniformis* biomass. *World J MicrobiolBiotechnol* **23**: 43–48

Ziagova M Dimitriadis G Aslanidou D Papaioannou X Tzannetaki EL and Liakopoulou-Kyriakides M (2007) Comparative study of Cd(II) and Cr(VI) biosorption on *Staphylococcus xylosus* and *Pseudomonas* sp. in single and binary mixtures. *Bioresour Technol* **98**: 2859–2865

5

INFLUENCE OF HERBICIDES ON BIOLOGICAL PROCESSES IN GRAIN LEGUMES

VIRENDER SARDANA AND PUSHP SHARMA

INTRODUCTION

Nitrogen is the most important nutrient required for plant growth. Its manufacturing requires non-renewable fossil fuel and thus its application in the form of chemical fertilizers is expensive, has low use efficiency and its use causes environmental pollution (Keeney 1982, Newbould 1989). Legumes are the integral part of cropping systems. Legumes globally play an important role in nitrogen cycling. Nitrogen fixation is carried out by legume-*rhizobia* symbiosis. Only *prokaryotes* have the ability to fix nitrogen biologically. Nitrogen fixed by various legumes in association with different species of *rhizobia* through the process of biological nitrogen fixation (BNF) is better alternative as it results in increased soil fertility, meets most of the N requirements of the crop and leaves substantial amount of N_2 in soil for utilization of subsequent crops in rotation (Peoples and Herridge 1990). These contribute about 25 per cent of the total nitrogen in grain legumes/pulses, 32 per cent in permanent grasslands and 29 per cent in forest ecosystems (Suhas *et al.* 2007). It is estimated that legumes contribute about 35×10^6 tonnes of biologically fixed nitrogen per annum (Burns and Hardy 1975, Paul and Clark 1996). Legumes vary in their ability to fix N_2 depending upon several factors (Giller and Wilson 1991, Peoples and Crasswell 1992, Wani *et al.* 1995).

Grain legumes or pulse crops are grown both in *kharif* and *rabi* seasons. The important *kharif* season pulses are pigeonpea (*Cajanus cajan* L. Millsp.), blackgram/ urdbean (*Phaseolus mungo* L. Hepper), greengram/moong (*Phaseolus radiatus* L. Wilczek), horsegram (*Macrotyloma uniflorum* L. Verdc), mothbean (*Phaseolus aconitifolia* J. Marechal) and cowpea (*Vigna unguiculata* L. Walp). The *rabi* pulses include chickpea (*Cicer arietinum* L.) lentil (*Lens culinaris* Medic), pea (*Pisum sativum* L), lathyrus (*Lathyrus sativus*

L.) and frenchbean (*Phaseolus vulgaris* L.). Greengram and blackgram are also grown in *spring/summer* season in northern India after harvest of sugarcane, wheat, potato, mustard etc. and during *rabi* season in the rice fallows in south-eastern and southern region.

Weeds constitute an important factor in crop production and their presence causes significant reductions in yields besides impairing quality of produce due to competition and allelopathic effects. At the global level, the losses caused by weeds exceed the losses from any other category of pests. Of the total losses to agricultural produce, weeds account for about 45 per cent in comparison to 30 per cent by insects, 20 per cent by diseases and 5 per cent by other organisms (Rao 1987). Infestation of weeds in pulses is more in the *kharif / rainy* season than during *rabi*. Important weeds associated with pulse crops in different seasons are listed in Table 1.

TABLE 1 : Major weeds of pulse crops

Classification of weeds	*Predominant weeds*
Kharif	
Annual grasses and sedges	*Echinochloa colonum, Echinochloa crus-galli, Eleusine aegiptiacum, Eleusine indica, Eragrostis sp., Dactyloctenium aegiptium, Digitaria sanguinalis, Panicum maximum, Setaria glauca,*
Broadleaf weeds	*Amaranthus viridis/spinosus, Celosia argentia, Cleome viscosa, Commelina benghalensis, Digera arvensis, Phyllanthus niruri, Physallis minima, Trianthema monogyna/portulacastrum, Tribulus terrestris,*
Perennials	*Cynodon dactylon, Cyperus rotundus, Saccharum spontaneum, Sorghum halepanse,*
Rabi	
Annual grasses and sedges	*Avena fatua/ludoviciana, Phalaris minor, Poa annua*
Broadleaf weeds	*Anagallis arvensis, Asphodelus tenuifolius, Chenopodium album, Cuscuta spp., Fumaria parviflora, Lathyrus aphaca, Medicago denticulata, Melilotus spp., Rumex dentatus/spinosus, Vicia spp.,*
Perennials	*Circium arvenses, Cynodon dactylon, Cyperus rotundus*

While the losses caused by insects-pests and diseases to standing crop and stored grains are visible, weeds invisibly rob the crop of essential and limited nutrients and compete for space, light, moisture etc. Use of herbicides for weed control (Tables 2 and 3) is an essential input in crop management and their role is gaining importance due to rising costs and non-availability of labour to carry out weeding. Presently, herbicides form the largest class of agro-chemicals.

Application of any agro-chemical including pesticides on crops may alter the equilibrium by direct toxic action on micro-organisms inhabiting the soil or may cause selective toxicity to a group of micro-organisms. Herbicides used to control weeds may adversely affect crop plants through their effect on growth, nodulation, nitrogen fixation, other physiological processes or economic yield by virtue of their toxic nature. Herbicide use may alter the biological equilibrium in soil (Grossbard 1976). As with other biocides, biological effect of herbicides often extends to non-target organisms in the environment. These unintended effects may inhibit or stimulate the activities of harmful or beneficial non-target organisms. These depressive or stimulating effects depend on the kind of chemicals, their concentration and environmental conditions.

TABLE 2 : Commonly used herbicides in pulse crops in India

Common name	*Chemical name*	*Trade name*	*Legumes in which mainly used*
Alachlor	2-chloro-N-(2,6-diethylphenyl) N-(methoxymethyl)acetamide	Lasso	Pigeonpea, green gram, black gram, cowpea, peas
Dinitramine	N^3-N^3-diethyl-2,4-dinitro-6-(trifluoromethyl)-1-3-benzenediamine	Cobex	-
Fluchloralin	*N*-(2-chloroethyl)-2,6-dinitro-*N*-propyl-4-(trifluoromethyl)benzenamine	Basalin	Pigeonpea, green gram, black gram, peas, lentil chickpea
Fluorodifen	2-nitro-1-(4-nitrophenoxy)-4-trifluoromethylbenzene	Soyex, Preforan	-
Isoproturon	*N,N*-dimethyl-*N*-(4-{1-methylethyl}phenyl)urea	Isopro-turon	-
Linuron	*N*-(3,4-dichlorophenyl)-*N*-methoxy-*N*-methylurea	Afalon, Lorex	Chickpea
Nitrofen	2,4-dichloro-1-(nitrophenoxy)benzene	TOK	-
Metolachlor	2-chloro-N-(2-ethyl-6-methylphenyl)-N-(2-methoxy-1-methylethyl) acetamide	Dual	Soybean
Oxadiazon	3-[2,4-dichloro-5-(1-methylethoxy) phenyl]-5-(1,1-dimethylethyl)-1,3,4-oxadiazole-2-(3 *H*)-one	TOK E 25	Pigeonpea, soybean, peas, chickpea, lentil
Oxyfluorfen	2-chloro-1-(3-ethoxy-4 nitrophenoxy)-4-(trifluoromethyl) benzene	Goal	Chickpea, lentil
Sethoxydim	2-[1-(ethoxyimino)butyl]-5-[2-(ethylthio)propyl]-3-hydroxy-2-cyclohexen-1-one	-	Green gram, chickpea

Common name	*Chemical name*	*Trade name*	*Legumes in which mainly used*
Pendimethalin	(N-(1-ethylpropyl)-3,4-dimethyl-2,6-dinitrobenzamine)	Stomp, Prowl	Soybean, green gram, black gram, chickpea, peas
Prometryn	*N,N*-bis(1-methyl)-6(methylthio)-1,3,5-triazine-2,4-diamine	Caparol, Gessagard	Peas
Diallate	S-(2,3-dichloroallyl-diisopropylthiocarbamate	Avadex	
Triallate	S-(2,3,3-trichloro-2-propenyl) bis(1-methylethyl)carbamothioate	Avadex, Far Go	
EPTC	S-ethyl dipropylthiocarbamate	Eptam	Pigeonpea, peas, chickpea
Terbutryn	*N*-(1,1-dimethylethyl)-N-ethyl-6 (methylthio)-1,3,5-triazine-2,4-diamine	Igran, Prebane	Pigeonpea, peas, chickpea
Imazaquin	2-[4,5-dihydro-4-methyl-4-(1-methylethyl)-5-oxo-1 *H*-imidazol-2-yl]-3-quinolinecarboxylic acid	-	Soybean
Imazamox	2-[4,5-dihydro-4-methyl-4-(1-methylethyl)-5-oxo-1 *H*-imidazol-2-yl]-5-methyl-3-pyridinecarboxylic acid	-	Peas
Imazethpyr	2-[4,5-dihydro-4-methyl-4-(1-methylethyl)-5-oxo-1 *H*-imidazol-2-yl]-5-ethyl-3-pyridinecarboxylic acid	-	Soybean, black gram, peas, lentil, faba bean
Bentazone	3-(1-methylethyl)-(1*H*)-2,1,3-benzo thiadiazin-4(3*H*)-one 2,2-dioxide	Basagran	Peas
Carbetamide	*N*-ethyl-2-[1{phenylamino}carbonyl) oxy]propanamide(R)-isomer	Legurame	
MCPA	(4-chloro-2-methylphenoxy) acetic acid	Chiotox, Rhomene, DOW MCP	
MCPB	4-(4-chloro-2-methylphenoxy) butanoic acid	Can-Trol, Thistrol	
Metribuzin	4-amino-6-(1,1-dimethylethyl)-3(methylthio)-1,2,4-triazin-5(4H)-one	Sencor	
Dalapon	2,2-dichloropropionic acid	Dowpon	
Dinoseb	2-(1-methylpropyl)-4,6-dinitrophenol	DNBP, Premerge, Basanite	

Common name	*Chemical name*	*Trade name*	*Legumes in which mainly used*
Methabenzthiazuron	*N*-(2-benzothiazolyl)-*N*,*N*-dimethylurea	Dosanex	
Chloroxuron	*N*-[4-(4-chlorophenoxy) phenyl]-*N*,*N*-dimethylurea	Tenoran, Norex	Soybean, peas
Fluazifop butyl	(R)-2-(4-[{5-(trifluoromethyl)-2-pyridinyl}oxy)phenoxy]propionic acid	-	Soybean, greengram, lentil
Fomesafen	5-[2-chloro-4(trifluoromethyl) phenoxy]-N-(methylsulfonyl)-2-nitrobenzamide	-	Green gram
Trifluralin	2,6-dintro-*N*,*N*-dipropyl-4-(trifluromethyl)benzenamine	Treflan	Pigeonpea, green gram, black gram, peas, chickpea

TABLE 3 : Commonly used herbicides and their time of application in pulse crops

Crop	*Herbicide (Time of application)*
Soybean	Pendimethalin (pre-em), Imazaquin (pre-plant), Imazethpyr (pre-plant, pre-em, post–em)), Metolachlor (pre-em), Trifluralin (pre-plant, pre-em), Oxadiazon (pre-em), Sethoxydim (pre-em), Chloroxuron (post-em), Fluazifop butyl (post-em)
Pigeonpea	EPTC, Trifluralin (pre-plant), fluchloralin (pre-em), Oxadiazon (pre-em), Terbutryn (pre-em), Bentazon (post-em)
Green gram	Fluchloralin (pre-plant, pre-em), Trifluralin (pre-plant, pre-em), Pendimethalin (pre-em), Fluazifop butyl (post-em), Fomesafen (post-em), Sethoxydim (post-em)
Black gram	Fluchloralin (pre-plant, pre-em), Trifluralin (pre-plant, pre-em), Pendimethalin (pre-em), Imazethpyr (post-em)
Peas	Diallate (pre-plant), Triallate (pre-plant, pre-em), EPTC (pre-plant) Fluchloralin (pre-plant, pre-em), Trifluralin (pre-plant, pre-em), Oxadiazon (pre-em), Pendimethalin (pre-em), Prometryn (pre-em), Terbutryn (pre-em), Bentazon (post-em), Carbetamide (post-em), Chloroxuron (post-em), Cyanazine (post-em), Dalapon (post-em), Dinoseb (post-em), Imazamox (post em), Imazethpyr (post-em), MCPA (post-em), MCPB (post-em), Metribuzin (post-em)
Chickpea	EPTC (pre-plant), Fluchloralin (pre-plant, pre-em), Trifluralin (pre-plant, pre-em), Oxadiazon (pre-em), Pendimethalin (pre-em), Terbutryn (pre-em), Oxyfluorfen (pre-em), Sethoxydim (post-em)
Lentil	Fluchloralin (pre-plant, pre-em), Oxadiazon (pre-em), Oxyfluorfen (pre-em), Fluazifop butyl (post-em), Imazethpyr (post-em)
Fababean	Imazethpyr (post-em)

EFFECT ON LEGUME CROPS

Germination and emergence

Pre-plant application of fluchloralin and pre-emergence application of pendimethalin or metolachlor @ 1.0, 1.5 and 2.0 kg/ha did not influence germination of chickpea, though higher dose reduced it marginally (Yadav *et al.* 2006). Pre–emergence application of oxyflourfen @ 1.68–6.72 kg/ha caused significant reduction (20%) in germination of pigeonpea (Semidey and Alimodovar 1987). Pahwa *et al* (1988) recorded inhibition in germination of pigeonpea with application of fluchloralin (0.75, 1.0 and 1.25 kg/ha), pendimethalin (1.0, 1.5 and 2.0 kg/ha) and fluazifop-p-butyl (0.5, 1.0 and 1.5 kg/ha) compared to control. Pendimethalin and trifluralin (1.1, 1.7 and 2.2 kg/ha) delayed emergence and caused severe injury to soybean seedlings at concentration of 1.7 and 2.2 kg/ha (Bollich *et al.* 1988).

Growth

Swelling of root tip is universally recognized morphological effect of dinitroaniline herbicides. The toxic effect occurs between times of radical and shoot emergence of seedlings from soil (Kolhe *et al.* 1984).

Root growth of soybean was retarded more than the top growth with application of trifluralin and threshold concentration for root growth was recorded to be 0.75 ppm (Ronald 1965). Bertholet and Clark (1985) also reported reduction in root length of soybean with trifluralin. Primary root length of pigeonpea was inhibited by fluchloralin, pendimethalin and fluazifop-p-butyl up to 45 DAS which recovered at later stages (Pahwa *et al.* 1988). Fluazifop-p-butyl caused maximum reduction in dry weight of roots per plant in pigeonpea at all concentrations in comparison to untreated control at 60 DAS (Pahwa *et al.* 1988).

Salvo *et al* (1991) observed that root and shoot growth of chickpea seedlings remained either unaffected or little affected by application of fluchloralin (0.5, 1.0 and 1.5 kg/ha), metribuzin (0.25, 0.5 and 0.75 kg/ha) and pendimethalin (0.75, 1.0 and 1.25 kg/ha). Pahwa *et al.* (1988) observed increase in fresh and dry weight of roots of pigeonpea at 45 DAS at lower concentration of fluchloralin and pendimethalin which decreased at higher concentration of herbicides.

Pahwa and Prakash (1992) reported that higher concentration of pendimethalin reduced root and shoot development of chickpea. Stem length and number of leaves of pigeonpea were reduced with application of herbicide, particularly fluazifop-p-butyl (Pahwa *et al.* 1988). Fresh and dry weights of shoots were significantly reduced with all the herbicides at initial stges, which regained at later stages particularly where fluchloralin was applied (Pahwa *et al.* 1988).

Pahwa (1972) reported reduction in length of roots and chlorophyll content of shoots of peas with pre-emergence application of dinitroaniline herbicides. Pre-emergence application of methabenzthiazuron and pendimethalin @ 1.2 kg/ha, diclofopmethyl @ 0.6-1.2 kg/ha, fluchloralin @ 0.5-1.0 kg/ha and oxyfluorfen @ 0.1-0.2 kg/ha decreased root length but not shoot length in peas (Prakash and Pahwa 1984). Reduction in fresh and dry weight of shoot of cowpea at initial stages and recovery at later stages on with fluchloralin application was also noticed by Prakash and Pahwa 1985.

Herbicides have been found to affect growth of crops like mungbean and peas (Prakash and Pahwa 1982, Pahwa and Prakash 1988). Nadasy *et al.* (2000) reported reduction in leaf area of soybean with application of metolachlor. Chaurasia (2001) and Murti *et al.* (2004) reported reduction in number of branches per plant and dry matter production in urdbean with application of pendimethalin and fluchloralin. Fluchloralin, pendimethalin and metolachlor @ 2.0 kg/ha caused significant reduction in number of branches per plant of chickpea than their lower dose (1.0 kg/ha) but was at par with untreated control (Yadav *et al.* 2006). All these herbicides except fluchloralin @ 1.0 kg/ha reduced leaf area of plants at 30 DAS compared to untreated plants (Yadav *et al.* 2006).

Lower doses of fluchloralin and metribuzin increased number of leaves per plant in blackgram (Pahwa and Prakash 1988). Majority of the herbicides have been observed to cause no inhibitory effect on bacterial population and activity at normal dosages of their application (Mohammad 1984, Tanski *et al.* 1984). However, dalapon (Kruglov *et al.* 1973) and diclobenil (Grossbard 1976) inhibited bacterial population at field dosages.

BIOLOGICAL NITROGEN FIXATION (BNF)

Herbicides applied for weed control may influence the process of BNF by affecting plant growth or by influencing N_2 fixing bacteria. These may also influence physiological processes of nodulation of *rhizobia* (Eberbach and Douglas 1989, Martensson 1992, Madhavi *et al.* 1994). Different strains of *rhizobia* can show differential response to herbicides. (Mallik and Tesfai 1983, Olson *et al.* 1984, Van Rensburg and Strijdom 1984, Kishinevsky *et al.* 1988, Mahmood and Mohammed 1991, Martensson 1992) due to their differential ability to detoxify the herbicide. The effect of pesticides including herbicides on nitrogen fixation in legumes has earlier been reviewed by Gaur (1980; Lal 1988 and Roberts 1992). Effects of herbicides on biological N_2 fixation have been reported in soybean (Rennie and Dubetz 1984, Mallik and Tesfai 1985, Bollich *et al.* 1985, 1988, Ozair and Moshier *et al.* 1988, Ozair *et al.* 1990, Yueh and Hensley 1993), fababean (Bertholet and Clark 1985, Haider *et al.*1991, Vidal *et al.* 1992, Martinez *et al.* 1996), kidneybean (Bethlenfalvay *et al.* 1979, Schenelle and Hensley 1989 1990), lentil (Sandhu *et al.* 1991, Sprout *et al.* 1992), chickpea (Kumar *et al.* 1981, Khokhar and Malik 1988, Pahwa and Praksah1992), lupins (De Felipe *et al.* 1987), groundnut (Kishinevsky *et al.* 1988), clovers (Brock 1972, Lindstrom *et al.* 1985, Martensson and Nilsson 1989, Eberbach and Douglas 1989, 1991, Clark and Mohanti 1991), peas (Singh *et al.* 1994, Gonzalez *et al.* 1996), *Trifolium repens sylvestre* (Fletcher *et al.* 1956, 1957).

MICROBIAL ACTIVITY AND NODULATION

Rhizobium

No effect: Fletcher (1960) observed no adverse effect of 2,4-D, MCPA, 2,4,5-DB or MCPB on growth of *Rhizobium trifolii* up to 25 ppm. Rhizobium population was not affected by trifluralin applied @1.0 kg/ha to soil (Olson *et al.* 1984). Methabenzthiazuron (1.0 and 1.5 kg/ha), pendimethalin (1.0 and 1.5 kg/ha) and terbutryn (0.6 and 1.2 kg/ha) caused no adverse effect on *rhizobial* growth in chickpea (Kumar and Kolar 1988) and lentil (Kumar and Kolar 1989). However, higher concentration was deleterious. Sandhu (1984) found no adverse effect of methabenzthiazuron and terbutryn on nodulation and rhizobial activity in lentil. Lewis and Hamner (1946) observed that 2, 4-D upto 1000 ppm failed to influence the activity of *Rhizobium leguminosarum*. N-serve application of 1-10 ppm caused little effect on *rhizobium* survival and nodulation in lucerne but higher rates caused morphological changes (McKell and Whalley 1964).

Dunigan *et al* (1972) observed that pre-emergence application of alachlor, chloramben, DCPA or post-emergence application of chloroxuron, dinoseb, linuron and prometryne at their recommended rates did not affect nodulation in soybean. Bentazone application had little or no effect on number of nodules, weight of nodules, root and shoot and also nitrogenase activity in soybean (Ozair and Moshier 1988, Ozair *et al* 1990). Terbutryn (0.6 and 1.2 kg/ha) caused no adverse effect on number of nodules in chickpea (Kumar and Kolar 1988), lentil (Kumar and Kolar 1989) and peas (Van Rensburg and Strijdom 1984). Renne and Dubetz (1984) found no adverse effect of recommended rates of chloramben, linuron, metribuzin and trifluralin on N_2 fixation in soybean. Similarly recommended doses of sethoxydim, alachlor, fluazifop butyl and metolachlor caused no adverse effect on N_2 fixation in soybean (Kucey *et al.* 1988). No marked differences in number of nodules per plant with application of pendimethalin and metolachlor @ 1.0 kg/ha were observed in peas (Singh and Wright 1999) and chickpea (Yadav *et al.* 2006). Ammonification and sulphur oxidation were slightly reduced by diquat dibromide, paraquat, dichloride and paraquat dimethyl sulphate at 0.25-0.50 ppm concentration in silty clay loam soil (Tu 1966).

Adverse effect: The antagonistic effects of herbicides reported by several workers in differerent legumes, *rhizobial* growth and nodule activities have been vividly summarised in Tables 4 and 5. Alachlor and metribuzin (Mallik and Tesfai 1985), paraquat (Clark and Mahanty 1991), trifluralin (Mallik and Tesfai 1985, Bollich *et al.* 1988) decreased nodulation when applied at their recommended rates. Even at recommended rate of application, some herbicides decreased the process of BNF (Bollich *et al.* 1988, Martensson and Nilsson 1989, Haider *et al.* 1991, Sprout *et al.* 1992) or N_2 fixation (Bethlenfalvay *et al* 1979, Cardina *et al.* 1986, Madhavi *et al.* 1993, 1994) possibly by influencing internal processes of plant even without any visual symptoms of phytotoxicity.

In symbiosis with legumes, as the *rhizobia* obtain their energy from the host plant, any adverse effect of a herbicide on plant may decrease the supply of carbohydrates. Herbicide may directly inhibit growth of *rhizobia* (Van Rensburg and Strijdom 1984, Martensson 1992) or may reduce their nitrogen fixation capacity.

Herbicides generally affect nodulation and N_2 fixation by influencing plant growth rather than directly affecting rhizobia (Brock 1972, Bethlenfalvay *et al.* 1979, Lindstrom *et al.* 1985, Martensson and Nilsson 1989, Sprout *et al.* 1992, Gonzalez *et al.* 1996). Paraquat significantly reduced the amount of N_2 fixed in soybean (Kucey *et al.* 1988).

Trifluralin and pendimethalin up to 2.2 kg/ha were reported to inhibit N_2 fixation by affecting acetylene reduction (Bollich *et al.* 1988). In another study, inhibitory effect of higher doses of herbicides on nodulation has been reported by Prakash and Pahwa 1982). Pahwa *et al.* (1988) observed increase in fresh and dry weight of roots, number, fresh and dry weights of nodules and leghaemoglobin content of nodules of pigeonpea at 45 DAS at lower concentration of fluchloralin and pendimethalin which decreased at higher concentration of herbicides.

Herbicides have been found to affect nodulation in crops like mungbean and peas (Prakash and Pahwa 1982, Pahwa and Prakash 1988, Singh and Wright 2000a). Earlier, Szabo (1964) and Avrov (1966) observed reduction in number and size of nodules of peas due to prometryne. Fluazifop-p-butyl caused maximum reduction in number of nodules per plant at all concentrations in comparison to untreated control at 60 DAS (Pahwa *et al.* 1988). Fluchloralin, pendimethalin and metolachlor @ 2.0 kg/ha caused significant reduction in number and dry weight of nodules per plant of chickpea than their lower dose (1.0 kg/ha) but was at par with untreated control (Yadav *et al.* 2006).

Trifluralin applied at normal rates reduced nodulation in soybean, gram and othe legumes (Dunigan *et al.* 1970, Brock 1972, Misra and Gaur 1974). Nodulation decreased in soybean with application of trifluralin (Yueh and Hensley 1993). Application of simazine (1.6-3.2 kg/ha) to chickpea (Kumar *et al.* 1981), simazine (2.0 kg/ha) to fababean (Haider *et al.* 1995) and prometryn (0.75 kg/ha) to kidneybean (Fischer and Tasistro 1981) decreased dry weight of roots and shoots as well as number and weight of nodules. Prometryn applied to peas @ 6g/kg soil decreased nodule weight and nitrogenase activity (Paromenskaya and Lebskii 1986, Singh and Wright 2000b). Misra and Gaur (1975) reported severe reduction in root nodulation, growth, yield and nitrogen uptake by groundnut due to simazine application. Terbutryn also decreased number and weight of nodules in groundnut (Van Rensburg and Strijdom 1984, Kishinevsky *et al.* 1988) and lentil (Sandhu *et al.* 1991).

Adverse effect of trifluralin (Udoh and Nelson 1986) and alachlor (Kao and Wang 1981) on nodulation in soybean has also been well documented. Luthra *et al.* (1983) reported reduction in N_2 fixation in pigeonpea with application of herbicides. Bollich *et al.* (1988) found inhibitory effect of triflurlin and pendimethalin on nodulation and N_2 fixation, whereas Akhtar *et al.* (1990) reported reduction in nodulation in soybean with increasing concentration of pendimethalin and fluazifop butyl. Similarly, the number and dry weight of nodules were reduced with herbicide application in soybean (Jain *et al.* 1990). Though lower concentration of herbicides did not cause marked reduction in nodulation, pre-plant application of pendimethalin (1.25 kg/ha) and trifluralin (1.08 kg/ha) and pre-emergence application of alachlor (2.88 kg/ha) and oxadiazon (0.875 kg/ha) reduced the period of nodulation and N_2 fixation in chickpea (Salvo *et al.* 1991). In drybeans, there was differential response of herbicides on nodulation (Schenella and Hensley 1990, Ahmad and Rashad 1996).

Specific nitrogenase activity (SNA) in drybeans was depressed with post-em application of bentazone @ 2.2 kg/ha without any adverse effect on number and weight of nodules even at three times higher concentration (Schnelle and Hensley 1990). Bentazone affected infection, nodule development and plant dry matter production but not bacteria population (Martensson 1992). Number and weight of nodules in birdsfoot tremoil (*Lotus corniculatus*) remained unaffected by dalapon but were reduced with application of 2, 4-DB (Garcia and Jordan 1967). Drastic reduction in plant dry weight as well as nitrogenase activity in lucerne (*Medicago sativa*), white clover (*Trifolium repens*) and peas (*Pisum sativum*) were also observed with increasing rate of bentazone from 0 to 10 ppm (Torstensson 1975). Simazine applied @ 0.1 ppm markedly reduced nodulation of legumes such as clover, lucerne and peas (Hauke Pacewiczowa 1969, 1970). Nodule formation in peas (*Pisum sativum*), beans (*Phaseolus lunatus*), red clover (*Trifolium pratense*), alfalfa (*Medicago sativa*) and kidney bean (*Phaseolus vulgaris*) was prevented with application of 2,4-D particularly sodium and amine salts (Carlyle and Thorpe 1947, Payne and Fults 1947). Reduced nodulation in white clovers (*Trifolium repens*) following application of MCPA was observed by Payne and Fults (1947) and Anderson and Baker (1950). Choudhri and Rajgopal (1958) observed reduction in nodule formation even at 10 ppm of 2,4,5-T, IPC and MH and the adverse effect increased with increasing concentration of herbicides. 2,4-DB alone or in combination with dalapon reduced N_2 fixation, number and dry weight of nodules of bird foot trefoil (Gracia and Jordan 1967). Dalapon alone reduced dry weight rather than number of nodules whereas 2,4-DB affected host plant rather than nodules.

The aniline, trifluralin and nitralin appear to have largely adverse effect on *rhizobia* and nodulation. Most of the triazines appear inhibitory even at the recommended rates of application. Hamdi and Tewfik (1969) observed inhibition in growth and nodulation of cowpea with recommended rates of trifluralin applied on the day of planting but stimulated when herbicide was applied 4 weeks before planting.

TABLE 4 : Effect of herbicides on *Rhizobial* growth

Crop	*Herbicide*		*Effect*	*Reported by*
	Name	*Dose*		
Peas	Linuron	0.75 kg/ha	Reduced population of soil bacteria	Singh *et al* (1994)
Peas	Methabenz thiazuron	1.31 kg/ha	Reduced population of soil bacteria	Singh *et al* (1994)
Peas	Pendimethalin	0.75 l/ha	Reduced soil bacterial population	Singh *et al* (1994)
Peas	Prometryn	1-2 kg/ha	Toxicity to rhizoshere Rhizobia	Bhalla and Chourasia (1985)
Peas	Simazine	0.9-1.5 kg/ha	Toxicity to rhizoshere Rhizobia	Bhalla and Chourasia (1985)

Crop	*Herbicide*		*Effect*	*Reported by*
	Name	*Dose*		
Peas	Methabenz thiazuron	1.05 kg/ha	Reduced rhizobial population	Bhalla and Chourasia (1985)
Pigeonpea	Simazine		Reduced rhizobium population of *Rhizobium* spp.	Madhavi *et al* (1994)
Pigeonpea	Oxyfluorfen		Reduced population of *Rhizobium* spp.	Madhavi *et al* (1994)
Lentil	Oxyfluorfen		Reduced population of *Rhizobium leguminosarum*	Madhavi *et al* (1994)
Lentil	Simazine		Reduced population of *Rhizobium leguminosarum*	Madhavi *et al* (1994)
Colver, lucerne, pea	Simazine	0.1 ppm	Reduced nodulation and yield. Higher rates decreased amino acid in protein and modified levels of free amino acid	Hauke-Pacewiczowa (1969, 1970)
Alfalfa	Simazine		Reduced population of *Rhizobium meliloti*	Madhavi *et al* (1994)
Alfalfa	Oxyfluorfen		Reduced population of *Rhizobium meliloti*	Madhavi *et al* (1994)
Groundnut	Simazine	2 ppm	Reduced nodulation, growth and yield	Misra and Gaur (1975)
Not specified	Simazine	0.1-1.0 ppm	Morphological changes in nodules. Decreased nodulation	Thomas and Hammond (1971) Dunigan *et al.* (1970)
Not specified	Prometryne	2.5-5.0 ppm	Initially decrease and subsequently increase in nodulation in light chestnut soils	Shkola (1970)
	2,-D	50 ppm	Suppression *R. leguminosarum*	Gaur and Misra (1972)
	2, 4-D	250 ppm	Reduction in population of *R. meliloti* and *R japonicum*	Gaur and Misra (1972)
	2,-D	1000 ppm	No effect on *R. leguminosarum*	Lewis and Hamre (1946)
	2,-D	400 ppm	Complete inhibition of *R. leguminosarum*	Carlyla and Thorpe (1947)

TABLE 5 : Effect of herbicides on nodulation and nodule activity in different crops

Crop	*Herbicide*		*Effect*	*Reported by*
	Name	*Rate*		
Soybean (*Glycine max*)	2,4-DB	0.23 kg/ha	Reduced number and weight of nodules and SNA	Mallik and Tesfai (1985)
	Alachlor	1.7 l/ha	Significantly reduced number and weight of nodules and SNA	Mallik and Tesfai (1985)
	Bentazone	1.1 kg/ha	Marginal reduction in number and weight of nodules and ARA and SNA	Ozair and Moshier (1988), Ozair *et al* (1990)
	Bentazone	2.8 ml/l	No effect on nodule weight but number and SNA decreased	Yueh and Hensley (1993)
	Glyphosate	1.12 l/ha	Reduced number and weight of nodules and SNA	Mallik and Tesfai (1985)
	Metolachlor	1.92 l/ha	No effect on number and weight of nodules	Greenfield (1991)
	Metribuzin	0.34 - 1.7 kg/ha	Significant reduction in number and weight of nodules and SNA	Mallik and Tesfai (1985)
	Prometryn	1.6-3.2 kg/ha	Reduced number and weight of nodules; increased SNA	Kumar *et al* (1981)
	Sethoxydim	29.4 ml/l	No effect on number and weight of nodules and SNA	Yueh and Hensley (1993)
	Trifluralin	0.96 l/ha	No effect on number and weight of nodules	Greenfield (1991)
	Trifluralin	0.56-2.8 l/ha	Reduced number and weight of nodules and SNA	Mallik and Tesfai (1985)
	Trifluralin	0.92-2.8 l/ha	Drastically reduced nodulation but increased SNA	Yueh and Hensley (1993)
Kidney bean (*Phaseolus vulgaris*)	Acifluorfen	0.44 kg/ha	Reduced nodule weight	Fischer and Tasistro (1981)
	Alachlor	13.3 l/ha	No effect on number and weight of nodules or SNA	Schenelle and Hensley (1990)

Crop	*Herbicide*		*Effect*	*Reported by*
	Name	*Rate*		
	Alachlor	1.92 l/ha	Reduced weight of nodules	Fischer and Tasistro (1981)
	Bentazone	2.2 kg/ha	No effect on number and weight of nodules but SNA declined	Schenelle and Hensley (1990)
	Bentazone	0.96 kg/ha	Nodule weight reduced by 86% over control	Fischer and Tasistro (1981)
	Bentazone	1.8 kg/ha	SNA declined	Bethlenfalvay *et al* (1979)
	EPTC	25.5 kg/ha	No effect on number and weight of nodules; slightly increased SNA	Schenelle and Hensley (1990)
	Linuron	0.75 l/ha	Reduced nodule weight by two third	Fischer and Tasistro (1981)
	Prometryn	0.75 l/ha	Drastically reduced weight of nodules	Fischer and Tasistro (1981)
	Trifluralin	6.7 l/ha	No effect on number and weight of nodules and SNA	Schenelle and Hensley (1990)
Lupins (*Lupines albus/ angushfolius*)	Cyanazine	1.75 kg/ha	Increase in SNA	Pozuelo *et al* (1989)
	Cyanazine	1.38 kg/ha	Drastically reduced SNA	De Felipe *et al* (1987)
	Linuron	1.38 l/ha	Drastically reduced SNA	De Felipe *et al* (1987)
	Metribuzin	0.5 kg/ha	Increase in SNA	Pozuelo *et al* (1989)
	Simazine	0.75 kg/ha	Enhanced SNA	Pozuelo *et al* (1989)
	Simazine	1.38 kg/ha	Drastically reduced SNA	De Felipe *et al* (1987)
	Trifluralin	0.85 l/ha	Increased SNA	Pozuelo *et al* (1989)
Red clover (*Trifolium pretense*)	Bentazone	25-200 mg/l	Reduced number of nodules	Martensson (1992)
White clover (*Trifolium repens*)	Bentazone	1.21 kg/ha	Reduced number of nodules	Clark and Mahanty (1991)

Crop	*Herbicide*		*Effect*	*Reported by*
	Name	*Rate*		
Alfalfa/ Lucerne (*Medicago sativa*)	Chlorsulfuron	2 g or more	Significant reduction in nodulation and SNA	Martensson and Nilsson (1989)
Lentil (*Lens culinaris*)	Fluchloralin	1.5 l/ha	Marginal to no effect on number and dry weight of nodules or SNA	Yadav *et al* (1990)
	Linuron	0.5-0.75 kg/ha	Reduced number and weight of nodules and SNA	Sandhu *et al* (1991)
	Methabenz thiazuron	1.05 kg/ha	No effect on number and weight of nodules; Slight reduction in SNA	Sandhu *et al* (1991)
	Methabenz thiazuron	1.0-1.5 kg/ha	No effect on number of nodules	Kumar and Kolar (1989)
	Metribuzin	0.5-0.75 kg/ha	Reduced number and weight of nodules and SNA	Sandhu *et al.* (1991)
	Metribuzin	2.2-4.4 ppm	Reduced number of nodules and SNA	Sprout *et al* (1992)
	Oxadiazon	0.5 l/ha	Marked reduction in number and weight of nodules and SNA	Sandhu *et al* (1991)
	Oxyfluorfen	0.15-0.20 l/ha	Reduced number and weight of nodules and SNA	Sandhu *et al* (1991)
	Pendimethalin	1.0 l/ha	No effect on number and dry weight of nodules and SNA	Yadav *et al* (1990)
	Pendimethalin	1.0-1.5 l/ha	No effect on number of nodules	Kumar and Kolar (1989)
	Terbutryn	0.6 kg/ha	No effect on number of nodules but weight of nodules decreased	Sandhu *et al* (1991)
	Terbutryn	0.6-1.2 kg/ha	No effect on nodules	Kumar and Kolar (1989)
Chickpea (*Cicer arietinum*)	Fluchloralin	0.5-1.5 l/ha	Reduction in number and weight of nodules and SNA at higher rates	Pahwa and Prakash (1992)
	Methabenz thiazuron	1.0-1.5 kg/ha	No effect on number of nodules	Kumar and Kolar (1988)

Crop	Herbicide		Effect	Reported by
	Name	Rate		
	Methabenz thiazuron	2.35-3.5 kg/ha	No effect on number and weight of nodules; reduction in SNA	Khokhar and Malik (1988)
	Metribuzin	0.25-0.75 ppm	Reduced number and weight of nodules and SNA at higher rates	Pahwa and Prakash (1992)
	Pendimethalin	1.0-1.5 l/ha	No effect on number of nodules	Kumar and Kolar (1988)
	Pendimethalin	0.75-1.25 l/ha	Reduced number and dry weight of nodules at higher rates; SNA increased	Pahwa and Prakash (1992)
	Simazine	1.6-3.2 kg/ha	Drastically reduced number and weight of nodules and nitrogenase activity	Kumar *et al* (1981)
	Terbutryn	0.6-1.2 kg/ha	No effect on nodule population	Kumar and Kolar (1988)
	Terbutryn	2-4 kg/ha	No effect on number of nodules but reduced weight of nodules and SNA	Khokhar and Malik (1988)
Peas (*Pisum sativum*)	Linuron	0.75 kg/ha	Reduced number and weight of nodules and SNA	Singh *et al* (1994)
	Imazethapyr	0.35-6.91 uM	Reduced number and weight of nodules	Gonzalez *et al* (1996)
	Methabenz-thiazuron	1.31 kg/ha	Reduced number and weight of nodules and SNA	Singh *et al* (1994)
	Prometryn	6 g/kg soil	Reduced nodule weight and nitrogenase activity significantly	Paromenskaya and Lebskii (1986)
	Pendimethalin	0.75 l/ha	Reduced number and dry weight of nodules and SNA	Singh *et al* (1994)
Faba bean (*Vicia faba*)	Linuron	1-4 kg/ha	Reduced weight of nodules and ARA	Haider *et al* (1991)
	Methabenz-thiazuron	2.5-4.0 kg/ha	Reduced nodule weight and ARA	Martinez *et al* (1996)
	Simazine	0.5-2.0 kg/ha	Reduced nodule weight and ARA at higher rates	Haider *et al* (1995)

ARA = Acetylene reduction activity, SNA = Specific nitrogenase activity

Favourable effect

Herbicide application may, sometimes, stimulate the metabolic and physiological processes (Berger and Heitefuss 1991). Nutman (1948) found enhanced rate of nodulation in dalapon inoculated red clover. At normal/recommended rates of application, prometryne increased number of nodules of *Phaseolus* roots (Rankov *et al.* 1966). Lower dose of simazine (0.75 kg/ha) increased specific nitrogenase activity in lupins (Pozuelo *et al.* 1989). Nitrogenase activity of soybean plants was 1.8 times higher with trifluralin application than unsprayed plants (Yueh and Hensley 1993).

Praksah and Pahwa (1984) reported increase in number of nodules per plant of pea with methabenzthiazuron (1.0 and 1.5 kg/ha), diclofopmethyl (0.6 kg/ha), fluchloralin (1.0 kg/ha), pendimethalin (1.0 and 1.5 kg/ha) and oxyfluorfen (0.1 kg/ha) in comparison to control. Prakash and Pahwa (1985) reported increase in N_2 fixation efficiency of nodules in cowpea with lower concentration of herbicides.

Application of fluchloralin (0.75, 1.0 and 1.25 kg/ha), pendimethalin (1.0, 1.5 and 2.0 kg/ha) and fluazifop butyl (0.5, 1.0 and 2.0 kg/ha) increased number, fresh and dry weight, leghaemoglobin content and N_2 fixation efficiency of nodules in pigeonpea at lower doses but decreased at higher doses (Pahwa *et al.* 1988). Pre-emergence application of pendimethalin @ 0.25 kg/ha to groundnut increased number of nodules per plant at 45 DAS but caused reduction at 1.0 and 1.25 kg/ha (Pahwa and Praksah 1990)

Azolla

Inoculation time of azolla in rice coincides with pre-emergence application of herbicides. It is apprehended that herbicides used for weed control at this stage may prove to be deleterious to Azolla under transplanted conditions (Moody and Janiya 1992; Gopalaswamy *et al.* 1994). Monuron applied as low as 1 ppm proved toxic to soil algae, *Stichococcus bacillaris* (Raud *et al.* 1959). Butyric acid form of MCPA was highly toxic to green algae whereas 2,4-D, 2,4,5-T and acetic acid form of MCPA up to 500 ppm were harmless (Shennan and Fletcher 1965). Janiya and Moody (1981, 1986) reported deleterious effect of herbicides on biomass production of azolla. Thiobencarb, propanil, butachlor, 2,4-D and piperopos caused significant reduction in fresh weight of azolla at 30 DAT; 2,4-D caused least suppression, propanil was more deleterious while thiobencarb was the most deleterious. Mixture of molinate-simetryn-MCPB was also highly damaging to azolla (Jainiy and Moody 1981). In an earlier study, reduction in growth and N_2 fixation in Azolla due to herbicide application was reported by Moody and Janiya 1972). Azolla is susceptible to butachlor, oxadiazon and thiobencarb but not to 2, 4-D (Srinivasan *et al.* 1993). Butachlor was highly toxic causing 65.0 per cent reduction while EPTC S-ethyl dipropyl thiocarbamate applied alone or in combination with 2,4-D ester caused reduction of 21.0-23.6 per cent. Hoist *et al.* (1982) reported reduction in growth and N_2 fixation of azolla with application of triazine, dinitroanaline and substituted urea herbicides at concentration of 0.1–10 ppm. Relative growth rate of azolla was significantly reduced by anilophos concentration above 1.0 ppm, whereas *in vitro* biomass production of azolla hybrids and wild cultures decreased with increasing concentration of anilophos with 1.5 and 2.5 ppm adversely affecting growth and biomass production while tolerance limit for butachlor and thiobencarb was found to be only 0.5 ppm (Gopalasamy and Kannaiyan 1997). High sensitivity to azolla at low concentration of herbicides under *in vitro* conditions might be due to its direct contact with herbicides.

Anderson and Domsch (1980) and Kumar *et al*. (1987) reported initial set back to microbial population and restitution after certain period of time. Magnitude of herbicide toxicity is governed by soil organic carbon status and amino acid contents in plants (Andreae and Good 1957). Such restitution can be ascribed to addition of organic matter to soil through decaying azolla fronds in advanced stages of growth resulting in activation of soil microflora. However, N content of azolla was not influenced by any of the herbicides viz; butachlor, EPTC, molinate, thiobencarb (Srinivasan *et al*. 1993).

EPTC either alone or in combination with 2,4-D ester resulted in significantly higher biomass and relative growth rate compared to control and thus can be safely applied in azolla dual cultured rice fields provided azolla inoculation is made 3 days after herbicide application (Srinivasan *et al*. 1993). Inoculation of rice crop with azolla at 12 days after herbicide (butachlor or anilophos) application resulted in higher biomass production than that inoculated 7 days after application of herbicide (Gopalasamy *et al*. 1994) ***Azotobacter*** : Sharma and Saxena (1974) reported that application of 2,4-D sodium salt (4-5 ppm) increased *Azotobacter* population in soil whereas higher concentration (.5 ppm) reduced it. Nair *et al*. (1957) concluded that growth of *Azotobacter* can be stimulated at lower concentration of 2,4-D. Piter (1981) observed stimulation in the growth of Azotobacter in the presence of pyramin (20 and 100 ppm). Diuron and 2, 4-D sodium salt stimulated *Azotobacter* population and 2, 4-D amine, atrazine, Destum and Sinbar showed good growth but asulox 40, Gramoxone, TotaCol, Paracot and Sirmate retarded growth of *Azotobacter* (Jadhav *et al*. 1988). MCPA application @ 2 kg/ha to lime rich soil caused no adverse effect on *Azotobacter* population while soils poor in lime, population of *Azotobacter* following MCPA application declined. Lenhard (1959) postulated that though higher concentration of herbicides than that normally used for weed control inhibits growth and respiratory metabolism in *Azotobacter*, the actual nitrification process may be affected at much lower concentration. Higher concentration of phenoxy herbicides can markedly inhibit growth and respiration of *Azotobacter* species (Colmer 1953). Herbicides such as monuron, neburon, diuron, dinoben, chlorazine, alipur, pebulate, 2, 4-DES, chloramben, pentanochlor and diphenamide caused greater inhibition on growth of *Azotobacter chroococcum* than *A. galophilium*.

Soil microbes

Soil fertility depends on the delicate balance of various types of micro-organisms. Mineral nutrient status of soil depends on activities of microbes in soil whose role in nutrient transformation is well established. The use of herbicides for weed in crops is well documented but the effect of these herbicides on soil fauna and beneficial microorganisms is less understood (Cullimore *et al*. 1977). Herbicide may disturb and alter the biological equilibrium in soil (Grossbard 1976) by influencing biological activities in soil (Gopalasamy *et al*. 1994, Singh and Dudeja 2007). Inhibitory or stimulatory effects depend on kind of herbicide, its concentration and period of incubation (Amakiri 1980). Some herbicides may show differential effect in different types of soils (Bollich *et al.* 1985). Dinitro aniline herbicides showed highest persistence in silty clay soil under normal tillage conditions and least persistence in sandy loam soils (Flom and Miller 1978).

McCall *et al.* (1962) observed reduction in O_2 uptake by microbes at higher rates of 2,4-D and PBA. EPTC temporarily depressed soil respiration (Chandra *et al.* 1968) while chlorpropham increased it (Stotsky *et al.* 1956, Teater *et al.* 1958). Soils low in organic matter is known to absorb less metribuzin resulting in greater availability for uptake by plants (Savage 1976, Sharom and Stephenson 1976, Lafleur 1979). Soybean injury to metribuzin increased with increase in moisture content (Coble and Schrader 1973). Bertholet and Clark (1985) also reported that metribuzin caused greater injury to faba bean in soils low in organic matter and in high rainfall areas.

Skrdleta *et al* (1964) reported inhibition in population of *Rhizobium* sp. with 2, 4-D and MCPA. Similarly Siduron suppressed growth of soil bacteria and *Azotobacter* but did not affect actinomycetes, filamentous fungi, soil ciliates and algae (Fields and Hemphill 1968). Avrov (1966) observed stimulatory effect of simazine on lupine nodule bacteria. Microbial population decreased soon after application of pendimethalin, increased after some time and then again decreased (Ponnuswamy *et al.* 1997). *Trichoderma harzianum* is used as a biocontrol agent. Since this fungus is inoculated with soil, it is likely to interact with herbicides which are applied to soil. Application of pendimethalin and alachlor significantly reduced the growth, survival and competitive ability of *Trichoderma harzianum* (Jayaraj and Radhakrishnan 2000). Effect of pendimethalin was more pronounced than alachlor. The fungus tends to regain its multiplication in later stages. Many workers have reported this kind of initial reduction in microbial population and its restitution after a period of time Anderson and Domsch 1980, Kumar *et al.* 1987, Gopalasamy *et al.* 1994). This phenomenon of restitution of growth might be attributed to gradual decomposition of the toxicant residues by microbial action and decomposition through physico-chemical reactions that take place in soil. Vintikova *et al* (1965) concluded that bacterial sensitivity was a property of microbial strains and was independent of plant species.

Sidhu *et al* (1985) reported suppressing effect of fluchloralin on soil microflora up to 7 days after application. Similarly, Patel and Patel (1998) observed significant reduction in bacterial as well as fungal population up to 10 days after application of fluchloralin @ 1.5 and 3.0 kg/ha. Pre-emergence application of pendimethalin @ 1.0 kg/ha significantly reduced population of bacteria, fungi and actinomycetes one day after treatment, whereas, glyphosate applied @ 1.0 kg/ha as post–emergence caused reduction of only fungal colony at one day after treatement (Nalayini *et al.* 2000). However, 30 days after treatment, there was no difference in the population of these microbes with pendimethalin and glyphosate. Kumar *et al* (1987), Nalayini and Sankaran (1992) and Selvamani and Sankaran (1993) reported similar facts. Since pendimethalin was applied directly to soil resulting in more amount of it reaching the soil than glyphosate which was applied on foliage of weeds; hence the inhibitory effects vary.

Actinomycetes were stimulated in the presence of herbicides 2, 4-D, Simazine, Bladex and NaTA (Desmukh and Shrikhande 1974). Application of 2, 4-D, Bladex and NaTA depessed bacterial and fungal populations in red clay loam soil whereas similar reduction bacterial population in black clay soil was observed with 2, 4-D only whereas fungal population was reduced with application of 2, 4-D, NaTA and Bladex (Desmukh and Shrikhande 1974). Dalapon is reported to have slight stimulatory effect on soil population (Hale *et al.* 1957, Worsham and Giddens 1957). Cole (1976) did not observe any adverse effect of long term application of atrazine on soil microbes. Giardina *et al.* (1979) observed no change in microbial population with application of 1% ammonium sulphate or 30 ppm atrazine. More harmful effect of herbicides on these organisms in red soils compared to black soil could be ascribed to the adsorption of herbicides on mineral colloids in the black soil. Earlier Magee and Colmer (1960) and Steinbrenner *et al* (1969) observed stimulatory effect of herbicides on population of actinomycetes. Fungal population was affected more than the bacterial population (Patel and Patel 1998). Nalayini *et al.* (2000) also observed that bacteria were influenced to lesser extent than actinomycetes.

BIOCHEMICAL PROCESSES

Application of trifluralin significantly decreased the amount of reserve protein *arginine* in the hypocotyls of mungbean (Mercado and Baltazar 1971). Dukes and Biswas (1967) recorded increase in carbohydrate content of peanut plants treated with trifluralin @ 5 and 10 ppm followed by gradual decrease with its increasing concentration. Total soluble carbohydrates and reducing sugars in cotyledons and embryo axis of treated seeds of different legume crops increased with application of pendimethalin @ 5, 10 and 25 ppm (Dhall 1992). Trifluralin did not cause marked reduction in protein synthesis (Mann *et al.* 1965). Higher rates of simazine decreased amino acid in the protein and modified the levels of free amino acids (Hauke Pacewiczowa 1969, 1970). Moreland *et al* (1969) reported that diuron inhibited RNA and protein synthesis in excised tissue of soybean.

There was significant reduction in activity of RNase and DNase enzymes during germination of pigeonpea with increase in dose (5, 10, 15 and 20 ppm) of trifluralin and pendimethalin (Pahwa and Bajaj 2000). Pendimethalin was more toxic than trifluralin.

DISEASES MANAGEMENT

Several pathogens survive on annual and perennial weeds. The capacity of a potential pathogen to induce disease may be reduced if the herbicide applied to combat weeds in crop fields proves toxic to that pathogen or put it at competitive disadvantage (Altman and Campbell 1977). Application of herbicides significantly increased germination of *Rhizobium bataticola* inoculated seeds of linseed (Ahmad and Vyas 1988) probably due to fungitoxicity of these herbicides (Ahmad 1982). Fields and Hemphill (1967) recorded depression in growth of certain bacteria with siduron. Fungi are more resistant to phenoxy herbicides as compared to bacteria. Paraquat was more fungitoxic to a range of organisms than other herbicides (Wilkinson and Lucas 1969). While

Houseworth and Tweedy (1972) reported fungitoxic potential of alachlor against *Fusarium oxysporum* and *Diplodia maydis*, Altman and Campbell (1977) observed disease reduction with 2,4-D. Gopalaswamy *et al.* (1994) observed reduction in population of bacteria, fungi and actinomycetes up to 20 days after application of herbicide. Paraquat, butachlor, alachlor and anilophos caused significantly more inhibition (18.2, 22.7, 32.9 and 36.2%) of fungal growth as compared to pendimethalin (49.4%) and 2,4-D (63.3%) when applied @ 25 ppm and control (85.0%) and the fungal growth decreased with increasing concentration of herbicides (Rai *et al.* 2000).

Stimulating effect of phenoxy herbicides on fungi has been reported (Anderson and Baker 1950, Roberts and Bollen 1955, Newman and Downing 1958). Thiobencarb (1.0 kg/ha) slightly stimulated bacterial population whereas population of fungi was markedly reduced with all the herbicides up to 20 days after applications followed by restitution after 30th day. Anilophos and butachlor though reduced bacterial population up to 20 days after application, the restitution occurred on 30th day (Gopalaswamy *et al.*1994).

Aspergillus and *Penicillium* were little affected by simazine and atrazine up to 1000 mg/kg except for slight delay in spore formation. Proliferation of *Aspergillus niger* was reduced by 2,4-D at 10-50 ppm whereas, picloram up to 50 ppm did not reduce fungal growth. Damping off of pea seedlings was less in autoclaved soil subsequently inoculated with *Pythium debaryanum* and to which DMPA @ 100 ppm was added than in inoculated soil without DMPA (Fields and Hemphill 1967). Addition of FYM @ 5t/ha significantly increased fungal population up to 30 days after application of fluchloralin as compared to control (Patel 1990, Patel and Patel 1998).

REFERENCES

Ahmad M (1982) *Studies on contol of plant diseases by herbicdes*. MSc (Agri.) thesis. Jawaharlal Nehru Vishwavidyalaya, Jabalpur (MP).

Ahmad M and Vyas SC (1988) Effect of herbicides on seed borne nature of fungi. *Pestology* **12(6)** : 8-9.

Ahmed AHH and Rashad MH (1996) Comparative studies on the effect of fusillade in corn and soybean plants. Bulletin of the Faculty of Agriculture, Univeristy of Cairo. pp. 570-610.

Akhtar M, Afghan S, Mahmood T, Abbas G (1990) Effect of pre and post emergence weedicides application on nodulation, growth and yield of soybean at different fertility levels. *Journal of Agricultural Research,* Lahore **28** : 29-37.

Altman J and Campbell CL (1977) Effect of herbicides on plant diseases. *Annual Review of Phytopathology* **15** : 361-385.

Amakiri MA (1980) Effect of herbicides on microbial population and activities in soil under teak (*Tectona grandis* LF) plantation. *African Agricultural and Forestry Journal* **42** : 420-426.

Anderson GR and Baker GO (1950) Some effects of 2,4-D in representative Idaho soils. *Agronomy Journal* **42** : 456-458.

Anderson JPE and Domsch KH (1980) Influence of selected pesticides on the microbial degradation of ^{14}C-Triallate and ^{14}C-Diallate in soil. *Archives of Environment Contamination Toxicology* **9** : 115-123.

Andreae WA and Good ME (1957) Studies on 3-indole acetic acid metabolism. IV. Conjugation with aspartic acid ammonia as processes in the metabolism of carbonic acids. *Plant Physiology* **32** : 566-572.

Andus IJ. (1976) Herbicide: Physiology, Biochemistry and Ecology. Vol. I. Academic Press, New York.

Avrov OE (1966) Effect of herbicides on nodule bacteria and nodule formation in legumes. Dokl Vses Akad Sel Khuz nauk No. **3** : 16-19 (*cf Soils and Fertilizers 29 : 454*).

Bakalivanov D and Bajchev A (1979) Effect of the herbicide Dalapon on soil micro organisms and its decomposition in a smolnitza. *Soils and Fertilizer* **44(1)** : 1073.

Berger A. and Heitefuss R (1991).Use of isoproturon alone and in combination with other compounds post-emergence in winter and spring on wheat and barley. II. Side effects on dehydrogenase activity, nitrogen formation and straw decomposition. *Weed Research* 31 : 1-18.

Bertholet J and Clark KW (1985) Effect of trifluralin and metribuzin on faba bean growth, development and symbiotic nitrogen fixation. *Canadian Journal of Plant Science* **65** : 9-21.

Bethlenfalvay GJ, Norris RF and Phillips DA (1979) Effect of bentazon, a Hill reaction inhibitor, on symbiotic nitrogen-fixing capability and apparent photosynthesis. *Plant Physiology* **63** : 213-215.

Bhalla PL and Chourasia KK (1985) Effect of herbicidal treatments on the growth and seed yield of garden pea (*Pisum sativum subsp. hortense* L). *Seeds & Farms (September)* : 32-42.

Bockman OC (1997) Fertilizers and biological nitrogen fixation as sources of plant nutrients: Perspectives for future agriculture. *Plant and Soil* **194** : 11-14.

Bollich PK, Dunigan EP and Jadi AWM (1985) Effects of seven herbicides on $N_2(C_2H_2)$ fixation by soybeans. *Weed Science* **33** : 427-430.

Bollich PK, Dunigan EP, Kitchen LM and Taylor V (1988) The influence of trifluralin and pendimethalin on nodulation, N_2 (C_2H_2) fixation and seed yield of field grown soybean. *Weed Science* **36** : 15-19.

Brock JL (1972) Effects of the herbicides trifluralin and carbetamide on nodulation and growth of legume seedlings. *Weed Research* 12 : 150-154.

Burns RC and Hardy RWF (1975) *Nitrogen Fixation in Bacteria and Higher Plants*. Springer-Verlag, Berlin.

Cardina J, Hartwig NL and Lukezic FL (1986) Herbicidal effects on crownvetch rhizobia and nodule activity. *Weed Science* **34** : 338-343.

Carlyle RE and Thorpe JD (1947) *Journal of American Society of Agronomy* **39** : 929 -936.

Chandra P, Furtick WR and Bollen WB (1968) The effects of four herbicides on micro organisms in nine Oregon soils. *Weeds* **8** : 589-598.

Chaurasia RM (2001) Effect of pendimethalin and fluchloralin on growth, nodulation and yield of urdbean. MSc (Ag) thesis. Narender Dev University of Agriculture and Technology, Kumarganj, Faizabad.

Choudhri RS and Rajgopal R (1958) Modern Development in Plant Physiology, Delhi University, India.

Clark SA and Mahanti HK (1991) Influence of herbicides on growth and nodulation of white clover, *Trifolium repens*. *Soil Biology and Biochemistry* **23** : 725-730.

Coble HD and Schrader JW (1973) Soybean tolerance to metribuzin. *Weed Science* **21** : 308-309.

Cole MA (1976). Effect of long term atrazine application on soil microbial activity. *Weed Science* **24** : 473-476.

Colmer AR (1953) Applied Microbiology **1** : 184-187.

De Felipe MR, Fernandez-Pascual M and Pozuelo JM (1987) Effects of the herbicdes lindex and simazine on chloroplast and nodule development, nodule activity, and grain yield in *Lupinus albus* L. *Plant and Soil* **101** : 99-105.

Deshmukh VA and Shrikhande JG (1974). Effect of some herbicides on soil microflora. *Journal of Indian Society of Soil Science* 22 : 300-303.

Dhall V (1992) Effect of pendimethalin on germination, early seedling growth and metabolism of pigeonpea, lentil, *Trianthema portulacastrum* and *Melilotus indica*. M Sc. Thesis, CCS Haryana Agricultural University, Hisar.

Domsch KH, Jagnow G and Anderson TH (1983) An ecological concept for the assessment of side effects of agrochemicals on soil microorganisms. *Residue Review* **86** : 66-103.

Dukes IE and Biswas PK (1967) The effect of trifluralin on the nucleic acid and carbohydrate content of sweat potato and peanuts. Abstract Weed Science Society of America. p. 59.

Dunigan EP, Allen LD and Frey JP (1970) *Losangles Agric* 13 : 6-7.

Dunigan EP, Frey JP, Allen Jr LD and McMahon A (1972) Herbicidal effects on the nodulation of glycine max (l) Merrill. *Agronomy Journal* 64 : 806-808..

Eberbach PL and Douglas LA (1989) Herbicide effects on the growth and nodulation potential of *Rhizobium trifolii* with *Trifolium subterraneum* L. *Plant and Soil* **119** : 15-23.

Eberbach PL and Douglas LA (1991) Effect of herbicide residues in a sandy loam on the growth, nodulation and nitrogenase activity (C_2H_2/C_2H_4) of *Trifolium subterraneum* L. *Plant and Soil* **131** : 67-76.

Fields ML and Hemphill DD (1967) The influence of DMPA on damping off of peas by *Pythium debaryanum* ATCC 9998. *Weed Science* **15** : 281-282.

Fields MI and Hemphill DD (1968) Effect of siduron and its degradation products on soil microflora. *Weed Science* **16** : 417-420.

Fischer A and Tasistro A (1981) Effect of certain herbicides upon the *Rhizobium phaseoli-Phaseolus vulgaris* symbiosis. In: *Theory and Practice of the Use of Soil Applied Herbicides*, Proceedings of the EWRS Symposium, Versailles, pp. 120-128.

Fletcher WW (1960) The effect of herbicides on soil microorganisms. In: *Herbicides and the Soil* (EK Woodford and GR Sagar, Eds), pp. 20-62. Blackwell Scientific Publications, Oxford.

Fletcher WW, Dickenson PB and Raymond JC (1956) The effect of certain hormone herbicides on the growth and nodulation of *Trifolium repens sylvestre* in aseptic culture. *Phyton* **7** : 121-130.

Fletcher WW, Dickenson PB, Forrest JD and Raymond JC (1957) The effect of soil application of certain substituted phenoxyacetic and phenoxybutyric acids on the growth and nodulation of *Trifolium repens sylvestre. Phyton* **9** : 41-47.

Flom DG, Miller SD (1978) Persistence of dinitroanaline herbicides. Proceedings of North Central Weed Control Conference **33** : 35-36.

Garcia M and Jordan DC (1967) Effect of herbicides on nodulation and N-fixation in birdfoor trefoil. *Bacteria Proc.* p. 8.

Gaur AC (1980) Effect of pesticides on symbiotic nitrogen fixation by legumes. *Indian Journal of Microbiology.* **20** : 362-370.

Gaur AC and Misra KC (1972) *Indian Journal of Microbiology* **12** : 45-46.

Geller IA and Khariton EG (1961) *Microbiologiya* **30** : 494-499.

Giardina MC, Giardi MT and Buffone R (1979). Soil enrichment studies with atrazine long term effects on degradation and microbiological composition. *Soils and Fertilizers* **44(3)** : 275.

Giller KE and Wilson KT (1991) *Nitrogen Fixation in Tropical Cropping Systems*. CAB International Wallingford.

Gonzalez A, Gonzalez-Murua C and Royuela M (1996) Influence of imazethapyr on *Rhizobium* growth and its symbiosis with pea (*Pisum sativum*). *Weed Science* **44** : 31-37.

Gopalaswamy G, Anthoni R and Abulkareem A (1994) Interaction of herbicides with *azolla* and soil microbes. *Indian Journal of Weed Science* **26(2)** : 28-34.

Gopalaswamy G and Kannaiyan S (1997) Influence of herbicides on the growth and biomass production of *Azolla* hybrids. *Indian Journal of Weed Science* **29(1&2)** : 53-57.

Gracia M and Jordan DC (1967) *Soils and Fertilizer* **30** : 476.

Grau CR (1977) Effect of dinitramine and trifluralin on growth, reproduction and activity of *Aphamomyces entelches, Phytopathology* **67** : 551-556.

Greenfield PL (1991) The influence of method of inoculation and certain herbicides on nodulation and seed yield of soybean. *South African Journal of Plant and Soil* **8** : 119-122.

Grossbard E. (1976) Effect of herbicides on the soil microflora. In: Herbicides – Physiology, Biochemistry, Ecology. Andus JJ (ed.). Academic Press, London. pp. 99.

Haider J, Fendrik I and Niemann EG (1991) Effect of linuron and dinosebacetate on *Vicia faba-Rhizobium leguminosarum* symbiosis. *Soil Science and Plant Nutrition* **37** : 601-609.

Haider J, Fendrik I and Niemann EG (1995) Effect of linuron and simazine on growth and N_2 fixation by *Vicia faba* L in a sandy soil. *Annals of Bangladesh Agriculture* **5** : 1-8.

Hale MG, Hulcher FH and Chappel WE (1957) The effects of several herbicides on nitrification in a field soil under laboratory conditions. *Weeds* **5** : 331-341.

Hamdi YA and Tewfik MS (1969) *Acta Microbiology* Pol 18 : 53-67.

Hauke-Pacewiczowa T (1969) Pam Pulawaki 37 : 241-259. (*cf Soils and Fertilizers 33(6) : 1970*).

Hauke-Pacewiczowa T (1969) Meded Rijksfae Landb Wet Gent 35 : 497-503.Pam Pulawaki 37 : 241-259. (*cf Soils and Fertilizers 34(5) : 1971*).

Hoist RW, Yopp JH and Kapusta G (1982) Effect of several pesticides on the growth and nitrogen assimilation of the *Azolla-Anabaena* symbiosis. *Weed Science* **30** : 54- 58.

Houseworth LD and Tweedy BG (1972) Effect of herbicides on soil borne pathogens. *Plant Disease Reporter* **40** : 52-56.

Jadhav JJ, Jadhav SK and Hapase DG (1988). Compatability of weedicides with *Azotobacter chroococcum*. *Pestology* **12(6)** : 24-26.

Jain HC, Tiwari JP and Jain NK (1990). Influence of herbicides on nodulation under different row spacings and seeding rates in soybean. Proceedings of Biennial Conference. Indian Society of Weed Science. p. 198.

Janiya JD and Moody K (1981) Effect of herbicides on azolla. *International Rice Research Newletter* **6(5)** : 23.

Janiya JD and Moody K (1986) Herbicides reduce azolla growth. *International Rice Research Newletter* **11(1)** : 28.

Jayaraj J. and Radhakrishnan NV (2000) Survival of the biocontrol agent *Trichoderma harzianum* in soil as influenced by certain herbicides. *Indian Journal of Weed Science* **32(1&2)** : 116-117.

Jordan TN, Baber RS and Barrentina WL (1978) Comparative toxicity of several dinitroaniline herbicides. *Weed Science* 26 : 72-75.

Kao TC and Wang CC (1981) Study on effect of herbicides on growth of *rhizobia* and development of root nodules. Journal of Agricultural Association, China, *Microbial Abstract* **17(2)** : 12-15.

Keeney DR (1982) Nitrogen management for maximum efficiency and minimum pollution. In: *Nitrogen in Agricultural Soils* (FJ Stevenson, Ed), pp. 605-649. American Society of Agronomy, Crop Science Society of America, and Soil Science Society of America, Madison, Wisconsin.

Khokhar SN and Malik BA (1988) Effect of herbicides on nodulation and nitrogenase activity of chickpea. *Pakistan Journal of Agricultural Research* **9** : 493-497.

Kishinevsky B, Lobel R, Lifshitz N and Gurfel D (1988) Effects of some commercial herbicides on rhizobia and their symbiosis with peanuts. *Weed Research* **28** : 291-296.

Kolhe SS, Mitra BN, Meur SK and Bhadauria SS (1984) Influence of pre-emergence herbicide on germination and growth parameters of paddy. *Indian Journal of Weed Science* **16** : 207-209.

Kruglov YuV, Gersh NB and Bui Benko NV (1973) The effects of metribuzin (a methyl urea) on soil biology. *Khim Sel'sk khoz* **11** : 294-299.

Kucey RMN, Chaiwanakupt P, Arayangkool T, Snitwongse P, Siripaibool C, Wadisirisul P and Boonkerd N (1988) Nitrogen fixation (^{15}N dilution) with soybean under Thai field conditions II. Effect of herbicides and water application schedule. *Plant and Soil* **108** : 87-92.

Kumar K and Kolar JS (1988) Relative performance of terbutryn, methabenzthiazuron and pendimethalin for weed control in chickpea (*Cicer arietinum* L.). *Journal of Research, Punjab Agricultural University* **25** : 534-538.

Kumar K and Kolar JS (1989) Effect of chemical weed control and Rhizobium inoculation on the yield of lentil. *Journal of Research, Punjab Agricultural University* **36** : 19-24.

Kumar K, Kolar JS and Bhandari SC (1987) Effect of terbutryn, methabenzthiazuron and pendimethalin on soil microflora in Bengal gram (*Cicer arietinum* L.) and lentil (*Lens culinaris*). *Indian Journal of Ecology* **14** : 52-58.

Kumar S, Pahwa SK, Promila and Sharma HR (1981) Effect of simazine and prometryn on the growth and nodulation of chickpea (*Cicer arietinum* L.). *Journal of Agriculttural Science* (Cambridge) **97** : 663-668.

Lafleur KS (1979) Sorption of metribuzin by model soils and agronomic soils: rates and equilibrium. *Soil Science* **127** : 51-55.

Lal S (1988) Effects of pesticides on Rhizobium-legume symbiosis. In: *Pesticides and Nitrogen Cycle*, Vol III (R Lal and S Lal, Eds), pp. 47-128. CRC Press, Inc., Boca Raton, Florida.

Lenhard GS (1959) African *Journal of Agricultural Science* **2** : 487-497.

Lewis RW and Hamner Cl (1946) Bulletin Michigan Experimental Station **29** : 112.

Lindstrom K, Polkunen J and Kansanen P (1985) Effect of dinoseb on nitrogen fixation of red clover (*Trifolium pretense*). *Soil Biology & Biochemistry* **17** : 865-869.

Lund ZF, Pearson RW and Buchanan GA (1970) An implanted soil mass technique to study the herbicide effects on root growth. *Weed Science* **18** : 279-281.

Luthra YP, Sheoran IS and Singh R (1983) Ontogenetic interactions between photosynthesis and symbiotic nitrogen fixation in pigeonpea. *Annals of Applied Biology* **103** : 549-556.

Madhavi B, Anand CS, Bharathi A and Polasa H (1993) Effects of pesticides on growth of *rhizobia* and their host plants during symbiosis. *Biomedical and Environmental Sciences* **6** : 89-94.

Madhavi B, Anand CS, Bharathi A and Polasa H (1994) Biotoxic effects of pesticides on symbiotic properties of rhizobial species. *Bulletin of Environmental* Contamination and Toxicology **52** : 87-94.

Magee LA (1958) Dissertation Abstract **19** : 413-414.

Magee LA and Colmer AR (1960) *Sugar Bulletin* 38 : 242.

Mahmood SM and Mohammed SH (1991) Effect of certain herbicides and insecticides on the growth of some *Rhizobium* species. *Assiut Journal of Agricultural Sciences* **22** : 243-259.

Mallik MAB and Tesfai K (1983) Compatibility of *Rhizobium japonicum* with commercial pesticides in vitro. *Bulletin of Environmental Contamination and Toxicology* **31** : 432-437.

Mallik MAB and Tesfai K (1985) Pesticidal effect on soybean-rhizobia symbiosis. *Plant and Soil* **85**: 33-41.

Mann JD, Jordan LS and Day BE (1965) A survey of herbicides for their effect upon protein synthesis. *Plant Physiology* **40** : 840-843.

Martensson AM (1992) Effects of agrochemicals and heavy metals on fast growing rhizobia and their symbiosis with small seeded legumes. *Soil Biology & Biochemistry* **24** : 435-445.

Martensson AM and Nilsson AK (1989) Effects of chlorsulfuron on *Rhizobium* grown in pure culture and in symbiosis with alfalfa (*Medicago sativa*) and red clover (*Trifolium pretense*). *Weed Science* **37** : 445-450.

Martinez J, Vidal D and Simon E (1996) Nitrogenase activity, nodulation and seed production in *Vicia faba* as affected by methabenzthiazuron. *Journal of Agricultural Science* (Cambridge) **127** : 319-324.

McCall TM, Arm TJ and Wiess AF (1962) Comparison of the effects of chemical and sweep tillage methods of summer fallow on some properties of Pullman silty clay loam. *Agronomy Journal* **54** : 404-407.

McKell CM and Whalley RDB (1964).Compatibilityof 2-Chloro-6(trichloromethyl) pyridine with *Medicago sativa* L inoculated with *Rhizobium meliloti*. *Agronomy Journal* **56** : 26-28.

Mercado BL and Baltazar AM (1971) Morphological and physiological responses of crops and weeds to trofluralin. VI Amino acids-trifluralin interaction in mungbean (Phaseolus aureus). *Phillipine Agriculture* **54** : 384-389.

Misra KC and Gaur AC (1974) Influence of simazine, lindane and ceresin on different parameters of nitrogen fixation by groundnut. *Indian Journal of Agricultural Sciences* 44 : 837-840.

Misra KC and Gaur AC (1974) Zbl Bakt Abt II 130 : 598-602.

Mohammed B (1984) Influence of alachlor and fluchloralin on the rhizosphere fungi of soybeans. *Journal of Maharastra Agricultural Universities* **9** : 303.

Moreland DE, Malhotra SS, Gruenhagen RD and Shokran EH (1969) Effects of herbicides on RNA and protein synthesis. *Weed Science* **17** : 556-563.

Moody K and Janiya JD (1972) The role of Azolla in weed control in rice. *Phillipines Journal of Weed Science* **19** : 79-102.

Murti R, Khan AK, Vaishya RD and Yadav PK (2004) Effect of some dinitroaniline herbicides on growth, nodulation, chlorophyll content and nitrate reductase activity of urdbean (*Vigna mungo* (L) Hepper). *Indian Journal of Weed Science* **36(1&2)** :124-126.

Nadasy E, Lehoczky E, Lucas P and Adam P (2000) Influence of different pre-emergence herbicides on the growth of soybean varieties. *Zeitschrift-furpflanzekrankheiten-Und-Pflanzenschutz, Sanderh* (Germany) **17** : 635-639.

Nair KS, Menon KMK and Mariakulandai A (1957) *Madras Agriculural Journal* **44** : 667-668.

Nalayini P and Sankaran S (1992) Effect of pre-emergence herbicides on soil microorganisms. *Indian Journal of Agronomy* **37** : 625-626.

Nalayini P, Kandasamy OS and Balasubramaniyan A (2000) Effect of pre-emergence and post emergence herbicides on soil microgflora. *Pestology* **14(10)** : 22-23.

Nelson DR, Belliville RJ and Porter CR (1984) Role of nitrogen assimilation in seed development of soybean. Plant Physiology **74** : 128-133.

Newbould P (1989) The use of nitrogen fertilizer in agriculture. Where do we go practically and ecologically? *Plant and Soil* **115** : 297-311.

Newman AS and Downing CE (1958) Journal of Agriculture and Food Chemistry **6** : 352-363.

Nutman PS (1948) *Annals of Botany* **12** : 81.

Olson BM, McKercher RB and Germida JJ (1984) Microbial populations in trifluralin-treated soil. *Plant and Soil* **76** : 379-387.

Ozair CA and Moshier IJ (1988) Effect of post emergence herbicides on nodulation and nitrogen fixation in soybean (*Glycine max*). *Applied Agricultural Research* **3** : 214-219.

Ozair CA, Moshier IJ and Chaudhry AH (1990) Green house evaluation of selected herbicides for their effect on soybean (*Glycine max*) growth, nodulation and nitrogenase activity. *Pakistan Journal of Botany* **22** : 197-203.

Pahwa SK (1972) Effect of some pre-emergence herbicides on weed control and physiology of pea (*Pisum sativum* L.). MSc thesis, Haryana Agricultural University, Hisar.

Pahwa SK and Bajaj K (2000) Effect of pre-emergence herbicides on the activity of ribonuclease and deoxyribonuclease enzyme during germination in pigeonpea and carpetweed. *Indian Journal of Weed Science* **32 (1&2)** : 21-24.

Pahwa SK and Prakash J (1988) Effect of some herbicides on growth, nodulation, leghaemoglobin and nitrogen content of soybean. Abstract in the Biennial Conference of Indian Society of Weed Science. pp. 45.

Pahwa SK and Prakash J (1990) Effect of pre-emergence herbicides on the growth and nodulation in groundnut (*Arachis hypogaea* L.). Proceedings of the Biennial Conference. Indian Society of Weed Science. p. 1.

Pahwa SK and Prakash J (1992) Effect of some herbicides on the growth, nodulation and nitrogen fixation in chickpea (*Cicer arietinum* L.). *Indian Journal of Plant Physiology* **35** : 207-212.

Pahwa SK, Prakash J and Sharma HR (1988) Effect of herbicides on the growth, nodulation and symbiotic nitrogen fixation in pigeonpea (*Cajanus cajan* (L.) Millsp.) *Crop Research* **1** : 131-140.

Paromenskaya LN and Lebskii VK (1986) Influence of the herbicide prometryn on symbiotic nitrogen fixation and morphology of pea nodules. *Microbiology* **54** : 655-658.

Patel PR (1990) Studies on the effect of herbicides on plant pathogenic and beneficial microorganisms in groundnut. MSc Thesis, Gujarat Agricultural University, Sardar Krushinagar.

Patel RB and Patel BK (1998) Effect of fluchloralin and farm yard manure on soil microflora. *Journal of Research, Gujarat Agricultural University* **24(1)** : 15-18.

Paul EA and Clark FE (1996) Soil Microbiology and Biochemistry, 2nd Edition. New York: Academic Press.

Payne MG and Fults JL (1947) *Agronomy Journal* **39** : 52-55.

Peoples MB and Crasswell ET (1992) Biological nitrogen fixation: Investments, expectations and actual contributions to agriculture. *Plant and Soil* **141** : 13-39.

Peoples MB and Herridge DF (1990) Nitrogen fixation by legumes in tropical and sub-tropical agriculture. *Advances in Agronomy* **44** : 155-223.

Piter SJ (1981) Herbicidal effect on some metabolic processes of *Azotobacter crococcum. Soils and Fertilizer* **44(11)** : 1055.

Pochon J, Tardieux P and Charpentier M (1960) *Compt Rend* **250** : 115-156.

Ponnuswamy K, Santhi P, Gopalasamy G and Mohammed Ali A (1997) Interaction of herbicides with soil microbes in cassava (*Manihot esculenta* Crantz). *Indian Journal of Weed Science* **29(3&4)** : 147-150.

Pozuelo JM, Fernandez-Pascual M, Lucas MM and De Felipe MR (1989) Effect of eight herbicides from five different chemical groups on nitrogen fixation and grain yield in *Lupinus albus* L. grown in semi-arid zones. *Weed Research* **29** : 419-425.

Prakash J and Pahwa SK (1982). Effect of some new herbicides on growth and chlorophyll content of mungbean. Abstract in the Biennial Conference of Indian Society of Weed Science. pp. 42-43.

Prakash J and Pahwa SK (1984) Effect of some new herbicides on growth of pea plants. *Pesticides* **18** : 56-58.

Prakash J and Pahwa SK (1985). Effect of some herbicides on growth, nodulation and chlorophyll content of cowpea (*Vigna unguiculata* (L) Walp) plants. *Haryana Journal of Agronomy* **1** : 39-41.

Raghuwanshi MS, Jain HC and Tiwari JP (1998) Influence of herbicides on nodulation under different seeding rates and row spacings in soybean. *Pestology* **22(11)** : 35-37.

Rai JP, Dubey KS and Sinha A (2000) Effect of some herbicides on the growth of *Rhizoctonia solani* Kuhn *in vitro*. *Indian Journal of Weed Science* **32(1&2)** : 112-113.

Rankov V, Elenkov E and Surelkov P (1966) Effect of some herbicides on development of nitrogen fixing bacteria. *Agrokhumisja* **4** : 115-120 (*cf Soils and Fertilizers* **29** *: 452*)

Rao VS (1987) *Principles of Weed Science*. Oxford and IBH Oxford Publishing Company Pvt Ltd, New Delhi, India.

Raud G, Tyssett C and Vacher b (1959) *Annals of Luise Pasteur* **96** : 242-244.

Rennie RJ and Dubetz S (1984) Effect of fungicides and herbicides on nodulation and N_2 fixation in soybean fields lacking indigenous *Rhizobium japonicum*. *Agronomy Journal* **76** : 451-454.

Rethinam p, Kesavan R and Purushothaman (1974) *Indian Journal of Microbiology* 14 : 149-151.

Roberts JE and Bollen WB (1955) *Annals of Applied Microbiology* **3** : 190-194.

Roberts JMF (1992) Effects of pest management systems on biological nitrogen fixation. In: *Biological Nitrogen Fixation and Sustainability of Tropical Agriculture* (K Mulongoy, M Gueye and DSC Spencer, Eds), pp. 97-108. Johan Wiley & Sons, Chichester.

Ronald ET (1965) Effect of trifluralin on soybean root development. Proceedings South Asia Weed Conference **18** : 652.

Salvo-Soares N, Souza-Paes M-Do-C-del, Cruz L, Martina ALM, Nagar V, Oliverira-Lombardi MLC, Lopes ES, Ambrosio LA, Novo M-do-C-de, Guz LSP, Lombardi MLC de O (1991). Effect of different herbicides on nodulation and nitrogenase activity in groundnuts. *Bragantia* **50** : 139-151.

Sandhu PS (1984) *Effects of sowing dates, phosphorus levels and herbicides on response of rhizobium in lentil*. Ph D Thesis, Punjab Agricultural University, Ludhiana.

Sandhu PS, Dhingra KK, Bhandari SC and Gupta RP (1991) Effects of hand hoeing and application of herbicides on nodulation, nodule activity and grain yield of *Lens culinaris* Med. *Plant and Soil* **135** : 293-296.

Savage KE (1976) Adsorption and mobility of metribuzin in soil. *Weed Science* **24** : 525-528.

Schenelle MA and Hensley LE (1986) Effects of pesticides upon nitrogen fixation and nodulation by dry beans. *Pesticide Science* **28** : 83-88.

Schenelle MA and Hensley DL (1989) Mode of action of bentazon in depressing nitrogen fixation by dry bean (Phaseous vulgaris). *Transactions of the Kansas Academy of Science* **92** : 149-154.

Schenelle MA and Hensley DL (1990) Effects of pesticides upon nitrogen fixation and nodulation by dry bean. *Pesticide Science* **28** : 83-88.

Selvamani S and Sankaran S (1993) Soil microbial population as affected by herbicides. *Madras Agricultural Journal* **80** : 397-399.

Semidey N and Alimodovar L (1987) Oxyflourfen : Canadian herbicides for weed control in pigeonpea. *Journal of Agricultural University, Puerto Rico* **71** : 277-285.

Shaheid SI (1971) Cytological and biochemical effects of the herbicide trifluralin on plant roots. Dissertation Abstarct B **31** : 4457.

Sharma LN and Saxena SN (1974). Influence of 2,4-D on soil micro organisms with special reference to *Azotobacter*. *Journal of Indian Society of Soil Science* **22** : 168-174.

Sharom MS and Stephenson GR (1976) Behaviour and fate of metribuzin in eight Ontario soils. *Weed Science* **24** : 153-160.

Shennan JL and Fletcher WW (1965) *Weed Research* **5** : 256-274.

Shkola AI (1970) Vest Sel Kho Nauk Am=lma-Ata 13 : 34-37.

Sidhu PS, Bhandari SC, Mehla SP and Gill HS (1985) Effect of fluchloralin, oxadiazon and pendimethalin on soil microflora and nodulation in groundnut. *Journal of Research, Punjab Agricultural University, Ludhiana* **22(1)** : 33-38.

Singh M and Dudeja SS (2007) Soil Plant Microbe interaction for ecologicl sustainability. *In: National Symposium on Legumes for Ecological Sustainability: Emerging Challenges and Opportunities*, held at Indian Institute of Pulses Research, Kanpur from November 35-5. p. 34.

Singh G and Wright D (1999) Effect of herbicides on nodulation, symbiotic nitrogen fixation, growth and yield of pea (*Pisum sativum* L.). *Journal of Agricultural Science* **133** : 21-30.

Singh G and Wright D (2000a) Effects of herbicides on nodulation and growth of two varieties of peas (*Pisum sativum*). *Acta Agronomica Hungarica* **50:** 337-348.

Singh G and Wright D (2000b) Effects of prometryn and trietazine/simazine on weeds, nodulation, nitrogenase activity and yield of pea (*Pisum sativum*). *Annals of Biology* **18** : 1-18.

Singh G, Kundra HC, Brar LS and Gupta RP (1994) Effect of herbicides on soil microorganism dynamics, *Rhizobium*-legume symbiosis and grain yield of pea (*Pisum sativum* L.). *Annals of Agricultural Research* **15** : 22-26.

Skrdleta V, Vintikova H and Srogl M (1964) Susceptibility of rhizobia to some seed killers. *Rostl Vyroba* **37** : 827-834 (*cf Soils and Fertilizers* **28** *: 50*).

Sprout SL, Nelson LM and Germida JJ (1992) Influence of metribuzin on the *Rhizobium leguminosarum*-lentil (*Lens culinaris*) symbiosis. *Canadian Journall of Microbiology* **38** : 343-349.

Srinivasan G, Pothiraj P and Choudhry GK (1993) Response of azolla (*Azolla pinnata*) to rice (*Oryza sativa*) herbcides. *Indian Journal of Agronomy* **38** : 156-158.

Steinbrenner K, Naglitsch AF and Schlight I (1960) Albrecht-Thaer-Arch 8 : 611.

Stotsky G, Marlin WP and Mortensen JL (1956) *Proceedings Soil Science Society of America* **20** : 392-396.

Suhas PW, Singh P, Sreedevi TK, Thang NV and Bangong T (2007) Increased resource conservation and improved livelihood through legume based cropping systems. *In: National Symposium on Legumes for Ecological Sustainability: Emerging Challenges and Opportunities,* held at Indian Institute of Pulses Research, Kanpur from November 35-5. p. 29.

Szabo I (1964) The effect of two herbicides on the soil microflora and root nodule formation in pea. Mosomagy, Agrartud Foisk Kosl **7** : Kem Talajt 26 : 33 (*cf Soils and Fertilizers* **28** *: 250*)

Tanski HH, Montonece L, Ervio LR, Junnila S and Ressala B (1984) The effects of chlorsulfuron, glyphosate, metribuzin and TCA on soil nitrification capacity and dehydrogenase activity in compartment. INRA publication, Paris No. 31.

Teater RW, Mortensen JL and Pratt PF (1958) Effect of certain herbicides on the rate of nitrification and carbon dioxide evolution in soil. *Journal of Agriculture and Food Chemistry* **6** : 214-216.

Thomas MA and Hammond HD (1971) *Ohio Journal of Science* 71 : 21-29.

Tortensson L (1975) Effects of bentazon and dinoseb on soil microorganisms and on the *Rhizobium-Leguminosae* symbiosis. *Swedish Journal of Agricultural Research* **5** : 177-183.

Tripathi B, Kumar CPC, Rangarajan T, Chandurkar PS and Vijayalakshmi (1993) Pendimethalin, metolachlor, residues in soil and their effect on soil microflora, weed spectrum and green peas (*Pisum* sativum L.). In: *Integrated Weed Management for Sustainable Agriculture*, Vol II, pp. 98-100. Proceedings of the International Symposium. Indian Society of Weed Science, Hisar, India.

Tu CM (1966) PhD thesis. Oregon State University. pp. 125.

Udoh DJ and Nelson LE (1986) Trifluralin induces chlorosis in soybean grown on clayey high ph soil. *Plant and Soil* **96** : 175-184.

Van Rensburg HJ and Strijdom BW (1984) Effect of herbicides on survival of rhizobia and nodulation of peas, groundnuts and Lucerne. *South African Journal of Plant and Soil* **91** : 135-138.

Vidal D, Martinez J, Bergareche C, Miranda AM and Simon E (1992) Effect of methabenzthiazuron on growth and nitrogenase activity in *Vicia faba*. *Plant and Soil* 144 : 235-245.

Vintikova H, Skrdleta V and Srogl M (1965) The sensitivity of nodule bacteria to herbicides. p. 264-268 (*In: Plant microbe relationships. Procedings Symposium Prague 1963 (cf Soils and Fertilizers* **28** *: 570).*

Wani SP, Rupela O Lee KK (1995) Sustainable agriculture in the semi-arid tropics through biological nitrogen fixation in grain legumes. *Plant and Soil* **174** : 29-49.

Wilcke E Sonderh Z (1968) *Pfla path Pfefraukh Pflschuts* **4** : 163-167.

Wilkinson V and Lucas RL (1969) Effect of herbicides on the growth of soil fungi. *New Phytology* **68** : 709-719.

Worsham AD and Giddens J (1957) Some effects of 2,2-dichloro propionic acid on soil microorganisms. *Weeds* **5** : 316-320.

Yadav K, Prasad V, Rai R and Ahmad N (1990) Effect of some herbicides on the nodulation and grain yield of lentil. *Journal of the Indian Society of Soil Science* **38** : 749-752.

Yadav PK, Khan AH, Murti R and Upadhyay RK (2006) Effect of herbicides on germination, growth and nodulation in chickpea (*Cicer arietinum*). *Indian Journal of Agricultural Sciences* **76** : 682-684.

Yueh LY and Hensley DL (1993) Pesticide effet on acetylene reduction and nodulation by soybean and lima bean. *Journal of the American Society for Horticultural Science* **118** : 73-76.

6

SCIENCE OF OMICS

RITU MAHAJAN

Cells are the fundamental working units of every living system. All the instructions needed to direct their activities are contained within the chemical called DNA (deoxyribonucleic acid). DNA from all organisms is made up of the same chemical and physical components. The DNA sequence is the particular side-by-side arrangement of bases along the DNA strand (e.g., ATTCCGGA). This order spells out the exact instructions required to create a particular organism with its own unique traits. The genome is an organism's complete set of DNA. Genomes vary widely in size: The smallest known genome for a free-living organism (a bacterium) contains about 600,000 DNA base pairs, while human genome has about 3.2 billion base pairs.

The sequencing of the first genome of a higher plant *Arabidopsis*, was available to public domain in 2001 and with new generations using more efficient sequencing machines (Marshall and Pennisi, 1998), the sequence of several other plant genomes may become available in the coming decade. In the wake of these sequencing efforts, plant research enters an exciting period in which genome-wide approaches are becoming an integral part of plant biology (Somerville and Somerville, 1999). This is reflected by the development of tools to exploit and further expand this wealth of information.

The term functional genomics can be referred to as the "development and application of global (genome-wide or system-wide) experimental approaches to assess gene function by making use of the information and reagents provided by structural genomics" (Hieter and Boguski, 1997). It involves the use of high-throughput methods for the study of large numbers of genes (ideally the entire set) in parallel. Gene "function" can be considered from several points of view: it can be mean biochemical function (e.g. protein kinase), cellular function (e.g. a role in a signal transduction pathway), developmental function (e.g. a role in pattern formation), or adaptive function (the contribution of the gene product to the fitness of the organism). Having identified a new sequence, the comparison with sequence databases is the simplest way to obtain (essentially biochemical) functional information.

Currently, about 50% of newly identified genes show sequence similarity to previously described genes. However, computerized analyses are generally not sufficient to define gene function with a high level of confidence, and experimental confirmation is needed in most cases. Indirect information on cellular or developmental function can be obtained from spatial and temporal expression patterns; for example, the presence of mRNA and/or protein in different cell types, during development, during pathogen infection, or in different environments. The sub cellular localization and post-translational modifications of proteins can be informative as well. Knocking out or over expressing the gene permits the gene sequence to be linked to a phenotype from which a cellular role or a role in development may be deduced. Finally, the fitness of plants carrying mutations or natural variants for the gene can be compared in different environments with wild-type plants to study the adaptive function.

SINGLE NUCLEOTIDE POLYMORPHISM (SNPs)

SNPs along with EST markers are the type of third generation markers, which are extensively used now days in various genomic studies. ESTs basically are used in functional genomics while SNPs are used in individual genotyping.

Single nucleotide polymorphisms or SNPs (pronounced "snips") are DNA sequence variations that occur when a single nucleotide (A, T, C, or G) in the genome sequence is altered (Gupta *et al*, 1999). For example a SNP might change the DNA sequence AAGGCTAA to ATGGCTAA.

So SNPs are the sequence based molecular markers.

This variation is due to **point mutation** at a given location. The mutation can be of two types:

1. **Transition:** In this case there is subtitution of a purine with other purine and a pyrimidine with other pyrimidine. This type of transition occurs basically at **CpG** islands. The methylated Cytosine gets deaminated to form Thymine base pair. This leads to the occurrence of SNP at a given location.
2. **Transversion:** Here in this case purine base gets substituted with a pyrimidine base and leads to occurrence of SNP.

Some important features of SNPs

- Two of every three SNPs involve the replacement of cytosine (C) with thymine (T).
- SNPs can occur in both coding (gene) and noncoding regions of the genome. Many SNPs have no effect on cell function and they do not form a mutant phenotype.
- When they are present in coding regions they may present at the third position of the codon and there is hence no effect on the phenotype. But when a nucleotide is

present at first and second position it they may lead to change in sequence of amino acid and hence leads to the mutant phenotype.

- When the SNP is present in coding region they may show 100% transmission with the trait. But when they are away from the gene or are present in the non-coding region they do not show 100% transmission with the trait.

The SNPs show intraspecific diversity all individuals of a same species have same DNA sequence but the differences occur at certain loci due to SNPs. In case of human beings 99.9% DNA is same but the difference is due to 0.1% SNPs. These SNPs make us individuals rather than identical clones.

Methods used for discovery and identification of new SNPs

Some of the methods available for the discovery of these SNPs are described in this section, although rarely one or more methods described later for SNP genotyping can also be used for SNP discovery.

These methods involve:

- **Locus specific PCR amplification**
- **Alignment among available genomic sequences**
- **Whole genome shotgun sequences**

Locus specific-PCR amplification

While using this method, locus specific PCR primers are synthesized from the genomic sequences available in the data banks and PCR amplification is undertaken using DNA samples from several individuals for which we want to find SNPs. PCR amplified products are sequenced and sequence differences are used for discovery of new SNPs. This method is not commonly used as it requires prior sequence information so this method can be used only for genomic regions with known sequences.

Alignment among available genomic sequences

Alignment of genomic and EST sequences is the most convenient method for discovery of SNPs, if genomic/EST sequences from a heterozygote or from more than one individuals of the same species are available in the databases. There are various data bases having full genomic as well as EST sequences. The alignment of sequences is automated through computer software, and will allow detection of SNPs. This alignment can be pairwise if two sequences are to be compared or multiple alignment if more sequences are there. However, a comparison of genomic sequences will detect SNPs, both in coding and non-coding regions, while that of ESTs will detect SNPs only in the coding region.

Whole genome shotgun sequences

In this approach, random clones from the genomic library prepared from a mixture of DNA from several individuals are sequenced. SNPs can be detected by alignment of sequences belonging to the same locus.

Methods used for genotyping individuals at SNP Loci

These are basically two terms. SNP discovery is the which involves the determination of new SNP at a given location while the term SNP genotyping involves the genotyping of the individuals for the SNPs which have already been discovered.

A number of methods for SNP genotyping are now available, although all of them may not be equally useful.

There are basically two classes:

- **Gel based methods:** These methods using agarose gel electrophores is done for genotyping.
- **Non gel based methods:** These methods do not involve the use of agarose gel electrophoresis rather fluorescent dyes are used here.

GEL based methods for SNP detection:

1. **RFLP and AFLP-based assay**: The presence of SNP Scan be detected by RFLP or AFLP conducted on PCR products, whenever such SNP generates or destroys a specific restriction site for an enzyme. The PCR product in this method is subjected to restriction digestion with individual enzymes. The detection is done by RFLP or AFLP to find the differences in patterns, which will be due to changes in the restriction sites.
2. **Single-strand conformation polymorphism:** Single strand conformation polymorphism (SSCP) technology detects allows detection of polymorphism which is to differences of one or more base pairs in the PCR products and is therefore suitable for SNP detection. The technique relies on the secondary structure being different for single strands derived from PCR products that differ by one or more nucleotides at an internal site The technique has been utilized for detection of SNPs in the genus *Picea* (spruce).
3. **Allele-specific amplification for SNP genotyping**: SNP Scan also be detected by designing allele-specific primers for individual SNP sites. Different fluorochromes are attached at the 5′ ends and the polymorphic nucleotides are attached at the 3′ ends of the two primers. These allele-specific primers, when used for PCR with pre amplified DNA as the template; the amplified product will be allele-specific and could be identified either on polyacryamide gel or on an automatic sequencer. This approach has been utilized for SNP genotyping in barley.

Non-gel based methods

1. **TaqMan assay**: In TaqMan assay an oligonucleotide TaqMan probe is labelled with a fluorescent reporter molecule (e.g. FAM or TET) at the 5′end and a quencher (e.g. TAMRA) at the 3′ end. The probe on hybridization to the template DNA is degraded at its 5′ end due to exonuclease activity of *Taq* polymerase (TaqMan), so that the reporter is released leading to a rise in fluorescence signal.

However, when due to the presence of a SNP, the probe mismatches with the template leading to failure in duplex formation. So no such degradation at the 5′ end of the probe is possible and there is no rise in fluorescence signal.

Fig. 1. TaqMan Assay

2. **Molecular beacons**: These are the hairpin shaped, oligonucleotide, hybridization probes which have quencher dye at 3′ end and reporter dye at 5′ end. When the beacon is hair pin shaped it will not give the signal but when the beacon does not find the SNP it will hybridize and give the signals.

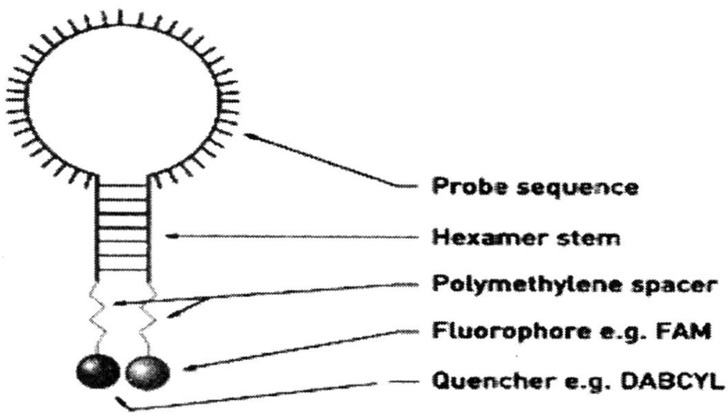

Fig. 2. Molecular Beacons

3. **Oligonucleotide ligation assay**: In this approach, two independent probes (one is 5′ biotinylated and the other is 3′ fluorescent-labelled) are used for hybridization with PCR product, so that when the probe matches the product then these two probes anneal with the PCR product and undergo ligation resulting in an oligonucleotide which is biotinylated at the 5′ end and fluorescent-labelled at the 3′ end. The ligation product, which is fluorescent labelled at the 3′ end, is captured on a solid streptavidin-coated matrix due to biotinylation at its 5′ end, and the signal is detected by autoradiography.

The SNPs are called **mother of all markers** as they have certain uses over others. These are:

- These are the most abundant type of molecular markers present and are spread on whole of the genome. and can be used to create high density maps and also can be used to tag the gene of interest
- These are codominant markers and can be used to distinguish heterozygotes from the homozygotes.

Limitations

- These are biallelic in nature, detects the population where only two alleles are present
- These are population specific and can be used only on one population.

Applications

- **Cultivar identification and evaluation of diversity**: SNP are used to identify level of intervarietal variation for each genome. In wheat, one SNP per 20 bp and in the maize genome, one SNP per 70 bp have been recorded in certain regions of these genomes.
- **Functional proteomics**: To identify the SNPs that modify proteins and protein active sites.
- **Gene therapy**: It involves the insertion of normal genes into germ cells or fertilized cells so as to create a beneficial genetic change.

DNA MICROARRAYS

DNA microarray technology has given rise to the study of functional genomics (Brown and Botstein, 1999; Lockhart and Winzeler, 2000). The entire set of genes of an organism can be microarrayed on an area as small as a fingernail and the expression levels of thousands of genes are simultaneously studied in a single experiment. DNA microarray technology allows comparisons of gene expression levels on a genomic scale in all kinds of combinations of samples derived from normal and diseased tissues, treated and nontreated time courses, and different stages of differentiation or development. Further computational analysis of microarray data allows the classification of known or unknown genes by their mRNA expression patterns. Global gene expression profiles in cells or tissues will provide us with a better understanding of the molecular basis of phenotype, pathology, or treatment.

DNA arrays or gene chips

- DNA arrays consists of large number of DNA molecules spotted in systemic order on a solid surface.
- Depending on the size of each spot on the array, DNA array can be categorized as microarrays (dia < 250μm and macroarrays (dia > 300 μm).
- When the solid substrate used is small in size, arrays are also referred as DNA chips or gene chips.

- DNA chips can be used as Variant Detector Array (VDAs) to look for DNA sequences that differ by single nucleotide polymorphism ("SNPs")

Based on type of probes

Chips are of two types:

- **Oligo chips**
  20 - 30bp
  - **sequencing**
  - **expression**
- **cDNA chips**
  < 2000bp
  - **expression**

On a glass surface, complementary DNAs (cDNAs) or gene-specific oligonucleotides can be spotted. Oligonucleotides can also be synthesized *in situ*.

***in situ* synthesis of oligonucleotide arrays**

Photolithography

This method was developed by Fodor *et al* (1991) and it is now referred to as the Affymetrix GeneChip system. In this method oligonucleotide arrays, DNA oligonucleotides are synthesized in situ onto the DNA chip using photolabile protecting groups and photolithographic masks are used to add the selective sequences of nucleotides (Lipshutz *et al.* 1999). This technique use phosphoramides, surface linker chemistry and combinatorial synthesis strategies.

Synthesis support: The synthesis support consists of a glass substrate derivatised with polylysine or aminosilane.

Masking: Photolithographic masks having apertures are used to cover the regions, where a particular nucleotide is not desired to be added.

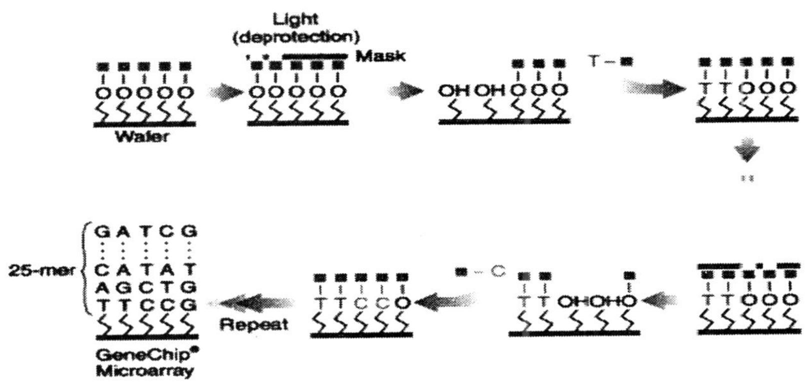

Fig. 3. Photolithography (Fodor *et al* 1991)

Illumination: The surface of solid support is illuminated, by illumination (wavelength more than 280nm) through micro apertures of the photolithographic masks, so that specific regions of the support are activated for synthesis.

Coupling: A 3'-O-phosphoramidite activated deoxynucleoside is protected with a group present to the surface that was illuminated and coupling occurs in the sites that were exposed to the light.

The selective photodeprotection and coupling cycles are repeated until the desired sets of products are available.

Ink jet

Ink jet is another technology can be used for *in situ* production of oligonucleotide microarrays.

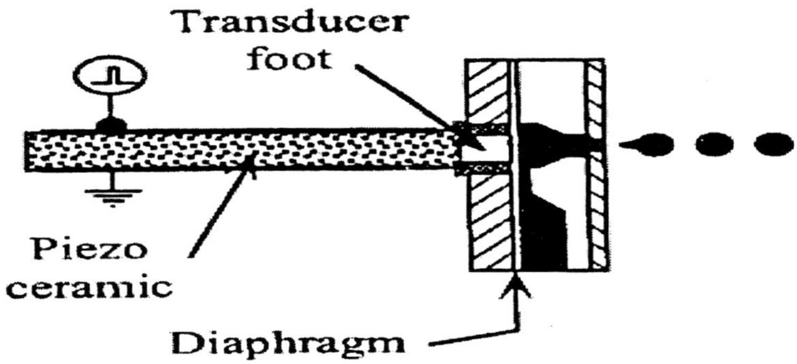

Fig. 4. Piezoelectric delivery method for microspotting

It involves direct delivery of tiny droplets of phosphoramidite solutions to precise locations on a surface rather than using lithographic masks. Piezoelectric delivery method is recently used for the manufacture of high-density oligonucleotide microarrays.

cDNA deposited arrays

In deposited arrays, which were developed by Pat Brown lab in Stanford University (Schena *et al* 1995) a high-speed spotting robot is used to affix PCR-amplified cDNA or synthesized oligonucleotides onto a chemically modified glass slide. Polylysine or amino silane is commonly used as a substrate for coating the surface of these glass slides. Mechanical microspotting allows transfer of premade substances onto a solid surface. This is done by capillaries, needles and tweezers. The inkjet printing method produces more uniform spots, which had been difficult to achieve with available pin spotting techniques.

cDNA vs. oligonucleotide as a target DNA

For reference, the term "probe" refers to the fluorescently labeled DNAs or RNAs and the term "target" refers to the DNAs on the slide. The definitions are reversed in some articles, especially when the Affymetrix GeneChip system is mentioned.

The oligonucleotide targets require only the sequence information of genes, and thereby can maximally exploit the genome sequences of the organism. The precise fold that changes from cDNA or oligonucleotide microarrays are not identical, but the general trends of changes and the fold differences are similar to each other when the same genes are compared in both array experiments. In oligonucleotide arrays, the design of oligonucleotides is very critical to the results and they should be designed very carefully. In cDNA arrays, there may be potentially confounding effects of cross-hybridization due to sequence homologies among members of a gene family. When oligonucleotides are used, they can be specifically designed to differentiate between highly homologous members of a gene family as well as alternatively spliced forms of the same gene (exon-specific). Oligonucleotide arrays can also be designed to allow detection of mutations and SNPs.

Hybridization

In two-color hybridization, fluorescently labeled cDNA probes, directly reverse-transcribed from two separate mRNA populations, are hybridized onto the target DNA fixed on the slide. One cDNA sample is labeled with Cy3 fluorescent dye, and the other sample with Cy5. Cy3 has advantage over Cy5 as Cy5 has strong fluorescent background and is sensitive to photobleaching. After hybridization and washing on a single array, the relative level in mRNA transcript for each gene is measured by the Cy5/Cy3 color ratio using a confocal laser scanner.

Applications

- **Detection of SNPs**: Use of SNPs offer great promise for rapid and highly automated gene sequencing and are extensively used as markers of choice.
- **Functional genomics**: Microarrays for gene expression analysis provide an integrated platform for functional genomics. Samples of mRNA from a variety of cells and tissues are used for microarray analysis that would yield information about specific changes in gene expression patterns. Novel expression profiles were identified for many sequences. DNA chips can also be used to distinguish the transcripts from individual members of multigene families.
- **Diagnostics and gene mapping**: Chips have been prepared to detect mutant alleles in CFTR (cystic fibrosis), BRCA 1 (cancer susceptible genes) and beta globulin genes.
- **DNA chips and agricultural biotechnology**: DNA chips with ESTs can also be used to collect data on expression in an agricultural crop under different conditions. This information can be of practical utility in agricultural biotechnology. Transgenic plants can be rapidly analyzed using microarrays on DNA chips, and expression pattern under different environmental conditions can be predicted at the gene level.
- **Proteomics**: Like genomics, proteomics is the study of protein-protein interactions. Protein linkage maps can be generated using genomic sequence

information. Protein-protein interactions can be studied using the yeast-two hybrid systems.

Limitations

- Post-transcriptional regulatory events cannot be detected.
- The expression patterns of individual members of closely related gene families may not be reliably detected.
- Sensitivity of detection of transcripts expressed at low levels.
- Most arrays are based on known genes and ESTs, which are currently biased towards most abundant genes.

CARBOHYDRATE MICROARRAYS

Carbohydrates, as components of glycoprotein, glycolipids and proteoglycans, play an important biological role as recognition markers through carbohydrate-protein interactions. For the most part, biophysical and biochemical methods have been used to analyze these bimolecular interactions. In contrast, less attention has been given to the development of high-throughput procedures to elucidate carbohydrate protein recognition events. Recently, carbohydrate arrays were developed and employed as a novel highthroughput analytic tool for monitoring carbohydrate-protein interactions. This technique has been used to profile protein binding and enzymatic activity. Carbohydrate microarray technologies are new developments at the frontiers of glycomics (Ratner, 2005). While conventional DNA and protein microarray technologies have been a boon to industrial and academic research, investigators interested in studying the biological role-played by glycans.

Carbohydrates and glycoconjugates are known to be involved in inflammation, cell-cell interactions, pathogen-host adhesion and signal transduction. With half or more of all proteins containing some carbohydrate modification, the challenges associated with their study have been a considerable hindrance to the field of glycobiology and to understanding of biology as a whole.

Carbohydrate recognition often consists of low affinity interactions between glycans and their associated binding partners. Therefore a successful microarray platform must be able to probe protein-carbohydrate, carbohydrate-carbohydrate and RNA-carbohydrate interaction with sufficient specificity to detect weak binding. To, achieve this glycan moiety should be displayed in fashion that is readily accessed by the analyte. Carbohydrate-modified surfaces are ideal for interrogating these weak interactions, as monolayers of sugars on the surface of chip to the multivalent display of glycan frequently found on the cell surface.

Factors for consideration

- Several factors must be taken into consideration while designing a microarray.
- A suitable surface must be selected for displaying the glycan library. This can include microtitre plates, glass slides, nitrocellulose and gold surfaces.

- A linking chemistry whether covalent or non-covalent binding must be adopted. For e.g. lipid modified glycans are required for non-covalent binding and amino and maleimido derivatised sugars for covalent attachment.
- A protocol must be developed for blocking potential sites for non-specific binding of analyte to surface.
- A method must be developed to detect weak binding events on the surface of the array.
- Probe is fluorescently labeled prior to hybridization and then the signal is detected.

Early microarray platforms

- **Wang and Feizi** (2003) utilized nitrocellulose surfaces for immobilization of carbohydrates and neoglycolipids to study microbial polysaccharides. The surface was blocked by BSA (Bovine Serum Albumin) to reduce non-specific binding.
- **Mrkish and his colleagues** (2003) covalently attached synthetically defined sugars to an array. They used linker-modified saccharides bound to derivatised self-assembled monolayers of alkanethiolate on gold surface. The arrays were used for on-chip enzymatic glycosylations and direct analysis of protein binding partners by MALDI-TOF MS.

The Consortium for Functional Glycomics currently possesses a library of more than 1,000 synthetic chips for microarray fabrication.

Biological applications

- Arrays of carbohydrates have been used to identify the glycan specificity of proteins, nucleic acids and intact cells.
- Glycochip has been employed to examine human serum for carbohydrate reactivity and to profile glycan-dependent enzymes and enzyme-inhibitors.
- The arrays have application in the study of HIV glycobiology as the virus surface has protein glycoprotein gp120, which plays a vital role in entry of host surface into the cell.
- Amino glycoside chips have been prepared to study the antibiotic resistance, antibiotic toxicity and to detect RNA binding.
- Efforts are there to develop glycochips against malaria, HIV and cancer.

Carbohydrate-binding proteins of the immune system-antibodies, selecting, a cytokine and a chemokine - and several plant lectins indicate that microarrays of carbohydrates (glycoconjugates, oligosaccharides and monosaccharides) will greatly facilitate not only surveys of proteins for carbohydrate-binding activities but also elucidation of their ligands. It is predicted that both naturally occurring and synthetic carbohydrates will be required for the fabrication of microarrays that are sufficiently comprehensive and representative of entire glycomes (Shin *et al*, 2004).

SERIAL ANALYSIS OF GENE EXPRESSION (SAGE)

With the advent of the human genome project, a vast amount of information about genes and gene structure is suddenly at our fingertips. But this information is limited. Every cell within an organism has the same genetic composition (with the exception of its gametes), and yet, obviously skin tissue is very different from nervous tissue. The DNA sequence cannot provide information about these differences, which represent the next level of complexity and organization within an organism: DNA expression. A method to efficiently count large numbers of mRNA transcripts by sequencing short tags, usually 10 bp in length. It uses a new analytical method of reliably matching SAGE tags to known genes. SAGE is a technique that allows rapid, detailed analysis of thousands of transcripts in a cell.

Principles

The basic concept of SAGE rests on two principles:

- A short nucleotide sequence tag (9-10bp) containing sufficient information to uniquely identify a transcript provided it is isolated from a defined position within the transcript.
- Concatenation of short sequence tags allows the efficient analysis of transcript in a serial manner by sequencing of multiple tags within a single clone. The number of times that a sequence of a given gene is found within the isolated clones represents the frequency of the transcript .

Serial Analysis of Gene Expression (SAGE), originally described by Velculescu *et al* (1995) counts polyadenylated transcripts by sequencing a short 14 bp tag at the genes 3'end, adjacent to the last restriction site (Polyak *et al*, 2001).

Basic steps in the SAGE protocol:

- Select cells for profiling.
- Isolate mRNA using magnetic beads and synthesize cDNA.
- Cut transcript with anchoring enzyme (NlaIII).
- Release 14 bp tags from the 3' end, adjacent to the last restriction site with tagging enzyme BsmF1.
- Pair and ligate tags to form ditags, and concatenate ditags into plasmids for automtic sequencing.
- Extract and count tags to calculate expression level of each transcript.

Once the cDNA has been created, it is then cleaved using an anchoring enzyme. The anchoring enzyme is a restriction endonuclease that recognizes and cuts specific 4 base pair (bp) DNA sequences. Since this enzyme requires only 4 specific nucleotides, it cleaves DNA molecules often, resulting in every cDNA that has been generated being cut at least once. The cut cDNA is then bound to streptavidin beads by virtue of its multiple thymidine ('T's) at its 3' end, thereby immobilizing it. At this point, we have multiple cDNAs bound to beads that are all of varying lengths, each with the same cut site and 5' overhang, because the anchoring enzyme recognizes the same 4 bp in all transcripts, but these 4 bp occur at different points within each transcript.

The sample of bound cDNAs is then divided in half and ligated to either linker A or B. These linkers are designed to contain a type IIS restriction site. Type IIS restriction endonucleases cut at a defined distance up to 20 base pairs away from their recognition sites. The type IIS restrictive endonuclease, also called the tagging enzyme, cleaves the cDNA to release it from its bound bead. Blunt ends are then created, so that neither the 3' nor 5' end has overhanging single-stranded sequences. Once this is achieved, the cDNA tags bound to linker A and B are ligated to each other to create ditags. These ditags have linker A on one end, linker B on the other, and both transcript tags are adjacent to one another in the middle. These ditags are then amplified by PCR, using primers that are complimentary to sequence in either linker.

Once the ditags have been amplified, they are then cleaved using the anchoring enzyme again. This has two effects: first, it releases the linkers from either end of the ditag, leaving only sequence from the two tags. Secondly, it creates sticky ends, or 3' and 5' ends that have overhanging, single-stranded DNA that can complimentary base pair with single-stranded DNA of another ditag. In this way, all of the ditags generated are linked, or concatenated to produce one long string of tags. This collection of tags is then introduced into a vector to be cloned and sequenced.

Problems with Gene Tags

There are several problems:

- The tags generated during SAGE are extremely short (13 - 14 bp). If the tag derived is from an unknown gene, it is difficult to investigate its potential function using such a short sequence. In cancer research, for example, the most attractive feature of SAGE is its ability to evaluate the expression pattern of thousands of genes in a quantitative manner without prior sequence information. This has lead to analysis of differential gene expression of cancer cells and their normal counterparts, and identification of several novel genes that could potentially play a role in tumourigenesis.
- Another problem with tags is tag specificity. There are instances in which multiple genes share the same tag, as there is an overlap in sequence between the two genes; using longer tag sequences can eliminate this problem. Increasing tag length to 18 bp in an attempt to increase tag specificity has been reported to yield a better representation of DNA expression.
- Another downfall of the SAGE technique is that typeIIS restriction enzymes (typically *Bsm*FI) do not always yield the same length of fragments. *Bsm*FI should yield exact 14 bp tags, but, depending on the temperature, the length of fragments produced varies. Since two tags are ligated tail to tail, it is hard to ensure each tag is 14 bp long in a ditag of 28 bp - the ditag could be consist of a 12 bp and 16 bp tag, a 13 bp and 15 bp tag, or any variation thereof. Maintaining the temperature at 65° C can minimize this problem.

Applications

- SAGE technique allows the rapid and detailed analysis including the relative abundance of all the transcripts in a given sample (cell or tissue).
- SAGE has been widely used in biological, medical, and pharmaceutical areas of research (Wakatsuki *et al*, 2001).
- SAGE has been used successfully to compare expression profiles between normal and diseased cells (Tuteja and Tuteja, 2004) or any two differentially treated samples.

EXPRESSED SEQUENCE TAGS (ESTs)

As one can imagine, finding a gene that codes for a protein, or proteins, is not easy. Traditionally, scientists would start their search by defining a biological problem and developing a strategy for researching the problem. Oftentimes, a search of the scientific literature provided various clues about how to proceed (Newman *et al*, 1994; Cooke *et al*, 1996; Yamamoto and Sasaki, 1997). Researchers would then work to isolate that protein, determine its function, and locate the gene that coded for the protein. Alternatively, scientists could conduct what is referred to as linkage studies to determine the chromosomal location of a particular gene. Once the chromosomal location was determined, they would use biochemical methods to isolate the gene and its corresponding protein.

An Expressed Sequence Tag is a tiny portion of an entire gene that can be used to help identify unknown genes and to map their positions within a genome.

ESTs are small pieces of DNA sequence (usually 200 to 500 nucleotides long) that are generated by sequencing either one or both ends of an expressed gene. The idea is to sequence bits of DNA that represent genes expressed in certain cells, tissues, or organs from different organisms and use these "tags" to fish a gene out of a portion of chromosomal DNA by matching base pairs. The challenge associated with identifying genes from genomic sequences varies among organisms and is dependent upon genome size as well as the presence or absence of introns, the intervening DNA sequences interrupting the protein coding sequence of a gene.

Gene identification is very difficult because most of our genome is composed of introns interspersed with a relative few DNA coding sequences, or genes. These genes are expressed as proteins, a complex process composed of two main two steps. Each gene (DNA) must be converted, or transcribed, into messenger RNA (mRNA), RNA that serves as a template for protein synthesis. The resulting mRNA then guides the synthesis of a protein through a process called translation. Interestingly, mRNAs in a cell neither contain sequences from the regions between genes, nor from the non-coding introns that are present within many genes. Therefore, isolating mRNA is key to finding expressed genes in the vast expanse of the human genome.

The problem, however, is that mRNA is very unstable outside of a cell; therefore, scientists use special enzymes to convert it to complementary DNA (cDNA). cDNA is a much more stable compound and, importantly, because it was generated from a mRNA in which the introns have been removed and cDNA represents only expressed DNA sequence. cDNA is a form of DNA prepared in the laboratory using an enzyme called reverse transcriptase. cDNA production is the reverse of the usual process of transcription in cells because the procedure uses mRNA as a template rather than DNA. Unlike genomic DNA, cDNA contains only expressed DNA sequences, or exons.

From cDNAs to ESTs

A "gene family" is a group of closely related genes that produces similar protein products. Once cDNA representing an expressed gene has been isolated, scientists can then sequence a few hundred nucleotides from either end of the molecule to create two different kinds of ESTs. Sequencing only the beginning portion of the cDNA produces what is called a 5' EST. A 5' EST is obtained from the portion of a transcript that usually codes for a protein. These regions tend to be conserved across species and do not change much within a gene family. Sequencing the ending portion of the cDNA molecule produces a 3' EST. Because these ESTs are generated from the 3' end of a transcript, they are likely to fall within non-coding or untranslated regions (UTRs), and therefore tend to exhibit less cross-species conservation than do coding sequences.

A UTR is that part of a gene that is not translated into protein.

ESTs are generated by sequencing cDNA, which itself is synthesized from the mRNA molecules in a cell. The mRNAs in a cell are copies of the genes that are being expressed. mRNA does not contain sequences from the regions between genes, nor from the non-coding introns that are present within many interesting parts of the genome.

ESTs as Genome Landmarks

Just as a person driving a car may need a map to find a destination, scientists searching for genes also need genome maps to help them to navigate through the billions of nucleotides that make up the human genome. For a map to make navigational sense, it must include reliable landmarks or "markers". Currently, the most powerful mapping technique, and one that has been used to generate many genome maps, relies on Sequence Tagged Site (STS) mapping. An STS is a short DNA sequence that is easily recognizable and occurs only once in a genome (or chromosome). The 3' ESTs serve as a common source of STSs because of their likelihood of being unique to a particular species and provide the additional feature of pointing directly to an expressed gene.

Limitations

- Low copy number genes
- Rare tissues
- Enrichment of 3′ ends
- Incomplete coverage of genes

PROTEOMICS

The term proteomics was coined in 1995 by an Australian postdoctoral fellow Marc Wilkins as a complement of genomics, the study of genes (Wilkins *et al* 1996). While the genome is a rather constant entity, the proteome differs from cell to cell and is constantly changing through its biochemical interactions with the genome and the environment In simplest term, it is the study of proteome, that refers to the collection of total set of proteins expressed in a cell at a given time, in an organism or Proteomics is the study of protein expression, regulation, modification, and function in living systems for understanding how living systems use proteins. Using a variety of techniques, proteomics can be used to study how proteins interact within a system or how protein expression changes in different parts of body, in different stages of its life cycle and in different environmental conditions as every individual has one genome and many proteomes.

The needs for proteomics research is necessary as in a cell there are certain genes that encode proteins with specific functions. The large increase in protein diversity is thought to be due to alternative splicing and about 200 different post-translational modifications of the proteins. This discrepancy implies that protein diversity cannot be fully characterized by gene expression analysis alone, making proteomics a useful tool for characterizing cells and tissues of interest. The proteome in any individual has a collection of 30-50% different gene products which are expressed at low levels, and its only proteomics which can convert proteins to peptides, followed by their conversion to amino acids which can be further determined and identified. Moreover the genome is static and the proteome reflects the cellular processes.

The study of proteomics is to obtain a global integrated view of:

- measurement of protein composition of organelles (spliceosome, phagosome, speckles etc.)
- normal and abnormal cellular processes
- protein-protein interactions
- protein-drug interactions
- determination of protein structure (NMR, X-ray, in silico etc.)
- identification of how and where proteins are modified (Post translational modifications)

Methods of studying proteins

1. **Two-dimensional gels and mass spectrometry**: Developed in late 1970s. Proteins from a sample are separated on the basis of charge and mass, and then analyzed by spectrometry (Henzel *et al* 1993). This method of detection is mainly used for cellular Proteomics. This is one of the established technology (can resolve 10000 spots per gel) used for studying proteins expressed at different levels. MS instruments consist of three modules: an ion source, which splits the sample molecules into ions; a

mass analyzer, which sorts the ions by their masses by applying electromagnetic fields; and a detector, which measures the value of an indicator quantity and thus provides data for calculating the abundances of each ion present. The technique has both qualitative and quantitative uses. MS can determine the isotopic composition of elements in a molecule, the structure of a compound by observing its fragmentation, can quantify the amount of a compound in a sample or study the fundamentals of gas phase ion chemistry. It is biased at detecting very small, very large and nuclear bound proteins and at the same time it is time consuming.

Similarly, MALDI, or Matrix-assisted laser desorption/ionization, is a soft ionization technique used in mass spectrometry. This technique allows the analysis of biomolecules (proteins, peptides, and sugars) and larger organic molecules (polymers and dendrimers). MALDI is used to ionize these molecules because they are very fragile and will usually fragment when ionized by other, more conventional ionization methods. A laser beam is used for ionization, and the biomolecule is protected by a matrix to prevent it from being destroyed, and to allow for optimal vaporization and ionization.

2. **Protein microarrays:** Protein microarrays are tools that can be used in many different areas of research, including basic and translational research. Proteomic arrays are typically high-density arrays (> 1000 elements/array) that are used to identify novel proteins or protein-protein interactions, to identify the substrates of protein kinases, or to identify the targets of biologically active small molecules (MacBeath and Schreiber, 2000). Silicon chips are coated with specific surface chemistries or known protein ligands, and proteins from a sample are fractionated on the chip, and then analyzed by mass spectrometry or chips are prepared with different surface chemistries, much like traditional protein chromatography columns, but in a flat array. To detect proteins that are bound to the array, the samples must be labeled directly with a fluorophore or a hapten. Alternatively, in some applications antibodies can be used to detect binding events, where antibodies are spotted onto the protein chip and are used as capture molecules to detect proteins from cell lysate solutions. For immunoproteomics approaches, antigen microarrays are used to detect disease associated changes in the autoantibody profiles.

The ultimate goal of proteomics is to the study biochemical activities of every protein encoded by an organism or proteome. Zhu *et al* (2001) made a landmark where they prepared the first proteome chip by cloning ~94% (>5800 of 6200) of the yeast open reading frames in a yeast expression vector which expressed the proteins as N-terminal GST-His x6 double tagged fusions. A high-throughput yeast protein purification method was developed to individually purify proteins. 80% of yeast proteins were full length and of sufficient quantity to be detectable by most assay types. The proteins were then purified using the GST tags and were then attached to Ni-NTA-coated glass slides using the HisX6 tags. In addition to identifying known interactions, 33 novel binding proteins were detected and 150 novel lipid-binding proteins were also identified. This study demonstrated that an entire proteome can be immobilized on a glass surface to directly screen for interactions with proteins and small molecules.

3. **Automated yeast two-hybrid screen**: Pioneered by Fields and Song in 1989, the technique was originally designed to detect protein-protein interactions using the GAL4 transcriptional activator of the yeast Saccharomyces cerevisiae. The GAL4 protein activated transcription of a protein involved in galactose utilization which formed the basis of selection (Hurt *et al* 2003). Since then, the same principle has been adapted to describe many alternative methods including some that detect protein-DNA interactions, DNA-DNA interactions. Joung *et al* (2000) use E. coli instead of yeast which facilitates the rapid analysis of larger libraries (due to the higher transformation efficiency and faster growth rate). Such methods also might be faster than phage display, which is an enrichment technique requiring multiple rounds of affinity purification and amplification and also allows studies of sequences (of much larger proteins) that are not readily displayed on a phage surface.

In general, in any two-hybrid experiment a protein of interest is fused to a DNA-binding domain and transfected in a yeast host cell bearing a reporter gene controlling this DNA-binding domain. When this fusion protein cannot activate transcription on its own, it can be used as "bait" or as a "target" to screen a library of cDNA clones that are fused to an activation domain. The cDNA clones within the library that encode proteins capable of forming protein-protein interactions with the bait are identified by virtue of their ability to cause activation of the reporter gene. So the yeast two-hybrid system is devised to identify genes encoding proteins that are physically associated with a given protein in vivo. Since the emergence of the two-hybrid approach in 1989, a number of improvements have been incorporated that have increased its applicability. A laboratory robot performs bioassay to find whether pairs or groups of interact (Albers *et al* 2004). A successful technique for rapid results in global proteomics but provides information only on binding partners and not on biochemical function. It can yield false-positive and false- negative results with no structural information.

4. **High-throughput crystallography**: The high-throughput protein crystallography beamline is a dedicated facility for determining the structure of protein crystals and undertaking initial assessment of more complex crystals. Single crystals are analysed using multiple wavelength anomalous dispersion (MAD). Hypothetical proteins from a sequenced genome are expressed, purified, and crystallized to obtain three-dimensional structure, then tested for their biochemical functions (Kim *et al* 2003). This technique is important to determine the three-dimensional structures of nonmembrane proteins for which sequence-based methods have been unable to predict a function. Membrane proteins were excluded because it is technologically challenging to produce them on a high throughput scale, so a subset of protein structures is designed that may be useful in elucidating protein function and that will contribute to our understanding of the sequence/structure relationship. This technique can be useful to uncover certain protein functions and also provide their structural information.

5. **Shotgun proteomics**: Shotgun proteomics using liquid chromatography-tandem mass spectrometry (LC-MS/MS) provides the most powerful analytical platform for global inventory of complex proteomes. It is a method of identifying proteins in complex mixtures using a combination of high performance liquid chromatography combined with mass spectrometry. In this method, the proteins in the mixture are digested and the resulting peptides are separated by liquid chromatography. Tandem mass spectrometry is then used to identify the peptides.

6. **Bottom up proteomics**: Bottom-up proteomics is the most mature and most widely used approach for protein identification and characterization. A method to identify proteins, characterize their amino acid sequences and post-translational modifications by proteolytic digestion of proteins prior to analysis by mass spectrometry. The proteins may first be purified by gel electrophoresis. Then the crude protein extract is digested directly, followed by one or more dimensions of separation of the peptides by liquid chromatography coupled to mass spectrometry. By comparing the masses of the proteolytic peptides or their tandem mass spectra with those predicted from a sequence database, peptides can be identified and multiple peptide identifications assembled into protein identification. Reversed-phase HPLC provides high-resolution separations of peptide digests with solvents that are compatible with ESI.

7. **Top-down proteomics**: In top-down proteomics, intact protein molecular ions generated by ESI are introduced into the mass analyzer and are subjected to gas-phase fragmentation. It is a method of protein identification that uses an ion trapping mass spectrometer so as to store an isolated protein ion for mass measurement and tandem mass spectrometry analysis. An obstacle to this approach is the determination of product ion masses from multiply charged product ions

Applications

Protein as a diagnostic tool: One of the most promising developments is the interaction between human genes and proteins resulting in identification of new drugs for the treatment of diseases. If a certain protein is implicated in a disease, its 3D structure provides the information to design drugs which then interfere with the action of the protein. A molecule that fits the active site of an enzyme, but cannot be released by the enzyme, will inactivate the enzyme. The identification of new drugs to target and inactivate the enzyme HIV-1 protease that cleaves a very large HIV protein into smaller, functional proteins. The virus cannot survive without this enzyme; therefore, it is one of the most effective protein targets for killing HIV (Sullivan *et al* 1998). In Alzheimer's disease, targeting the enzyme beta secretase (which causes plaque to build up in the patient's brain), slows the progression of the disease (Cole and Vassar 2008). Specific proteins can be used as biomarkers to diagnose disease. A number of techniques like western blot, immunohistochemical staining, enzyme linked immunosorbent assay (ELISA) or mass spectrometry allow us to test for proteins produced during a particular disease, which helps to diagnose the disease quickly.

Protein chips: Chip-based separation of proteins (David *et al* 2007) provide methods that are faster, automated and more convenient than conventional gel electrophoresis. A chip that held thousands of immobilized proteins could be used to detect protein-protein interactions quickly and easily (Kersten and Feilner, 2007). Zyomyx developed a high-density protein chips made of silicon, which is microfabricated to posts to create a 3-D substrate. This technology offers profiling biochipTM for high throughput, low sample volume protein studies. A human cytokine chip was the first product to be commercialized, while various other products and technologies are under development. The chips are expensive.

Determining the existence of proteins in complex mixtures: Earlier antibodies to particular proteins or to their modified forms have been used in biochemistry and cell biology studies or ELISA was used for quantative determination of protein amounts, but now more recent techniques such as Matrix-assisted laser desorption/ionization have been employed for rapid determination of proteins in particular mixtures.

Differential expression of proteins: Proteins expressed under normal conditions are compared to those under stressed conditions. The approach is quite similar to microarray analysis where the expression levels of proteins are significantly changed, indicating the potential role of the protein to the causation of the stress.

Proteins as messengers: The binding of one protein to other protein receptors so as to send a signal to the cell results in forming structural connections between cells and thus leading to study of interaction between the proteins.

***In vivo* isotopic labeling:** This is a common method used in comparative proteomics (Schwender and Ohlrogge, 2002). Here one set of samples is grown on a natural nitrogen source while the comparative sample is grown in the presence of the heavy isotope. The isotopic label can be introduced either as an amino acid (termed stable isotopic labeling in cell culture, SILAC) or by ^{15}N as the sole nitrogen source, typically in the form of $K^{15}NO_3$. Due to difference in masses of peptides from the two or three populations a direct comparison of MS peak intensities can be made for the two samples.

Proteomics is an extremely powerful technology but few limitations are:

- 2-D gels only work for hydrophilic (soluble) proteins. So membrane proteins simply don't run into the gel.
- 2-D gels are resolution sensitive. It's possible to resolve only hundreds to a few thousand spots on each gel whereas low abundance proteins may be masked by nearby abundant proteins on the gel.
- No two gels are exactly the same. So computers stretch the gel images (rubber-sheeting) to try to make them look as similar as possible before comparing them but now in DiGE (difference gel electrophoresis) (Unlu *et al* 1997; Tonge *et al* 2001) two protein samples are labelled with different fluorescent dyes, then mixed and run on the same gel. The gel is then viewed by fluorescence at two wavelengths. Though this technique is simple but very expensive.

Protein databases

A variety of protein sequence databases exist which play an important role as central comprehensive resources of protein information (Pruess *et al* 2006)

- UniProt (The UniProt Consortium comprises the European Bioinformatics
- Institute (EBI), the Swiss Institute of Bioinformatics (SIB), and the Protein Information Resource (PIR) and is the world's most comprehensive resource on protein information..
- PIR (Protein Information Resource to support genomic and proteomic research).
- Swiss-Prot (manually curated biological database of protein sequences) (Junker *et al* 2000)
- TrEMBL- computer-annotated supplement of Swiss-Prot that contains all the translations of EMBL nucleotide sequence entries not yet integrated in Swiss-Prot.
- PDB (Protein Data Bank is a repository for 3-D structural data of proteins and nucleic acids)
- NCBI (National Center for Biotechnology Information houses genome sequencing data in GenBank and an index of biomedical research articles in PubMed Central and PubMed, and information relevant to biotechnology)
- Human Protein Reference Database (manually curated scientific information pertaining to the biology of most human proteins).
- Proteopedia The 3D encyclopedia of proteins and other molecules.

METABOLOMICS

Metabolomics is the study of small metabolites present in biological system. It is species independent and can be applied on diverse array of plants. However, despite the immense technical challenges associated with analyzing a wide range of metabolites of varying concentrations, different techniques have been developed for their detection. These techniques are high throughput and are cheap on a per sample basis, making them ideal as rapid screening tools. The combination of high throughput and breath will help metabolomics in becoming a key tool in variety of fields in the years to come.

The history of metabolomics traces back to 2000-1500 B.C. when Chinese doctors use body fluids to determine the biological condition of patients in order to predict disease. In 1614 Santorio Sanctorius whose work was first to obtain physical data and provide quantitative basis of pathology, is considered to be the founding father of metabolic studies. Thomas Willis performed the first analysis of urine in 1674 and he found that people with diabetes mellitus and diabetes insipidus could be distinguished based solely upon the sweetness of their urine which was confirmed by Matthew Dobson in 1776.

The term metabolomics was coined by Oliver *et al* in 1998 and in 2006 a new approach called "Sniper" metabolomics was introduced which uses both chromatography and mass spectrometry in order to analyze metabolites. Metabolism and metabolomics share as their root the ancient Greek word, metabol, which means change. Metabolomics is an emerging field in analytical biochemistry and can be regarded as the end point of the "omics" cascade. Thus metabolomics is the quantitative measurement of the metabolic profiles of model organisms or metabolites to characterize their phenotype or phenotypic response to genetic or nutritional perturbations whereas metabonomics is the quantitative measurement of "total" metabolic response of vertebrates to pathophysiological situations (nutritional, xenobiotic, surgical or toxic stimuli).

Where genomics deals with the analysis of the complete genome in order to understand the function of single genes, the majority of functional genomics studies are currently based on the analysis of gene expression (transcriptomics) and comprehensive protein analysis (proteomics). However, changes in the metabolome are the ultimate answer of an organism to genetic alterations, disease, or environmental influences. Even the genome of a large number of plants has been sequenced but the function of majority of their genes is not cleared, because these genes are believed to involve in plant metabolism. By studying their sequence homology one can assign putative functions but cannot describe their biochemical functions. It is likely that at least some of metabolites fulfill important biological functions such as helping plants to survive in specialized ecological niches. To study function of such metabolites metabolite profiling is required. Metabolite profiling is an analytical method for relative quantization of a number of metabolites from biological samples (a specific tissue, a part of a tissue of interest or a mixture of different organs). The requirements and current strategies for the comprehensive and quantitative analysis of the molecular phenotype have been recently reviewed for all three levels of gene products (mRNA, proteins and metabolites), including thoughts on database requirements and informatics tools (Fiehn 2001).

Metabolomics techniques

The main aim of metabolomics is the quantification and identification of all metabolites of a given biological system under defined conditions. There are variety of methods that facilitates the study the metabolic alterations on comprehensive scale. No single technique or protocol can be used for metabolic analysis due to difference in metabolite concentrations. Thus the two dominant detection systems are nuclear magnetic resonance (NMR) and mass spectrometry (MS). An advantage of NMR is the linearity of quantitative responses on increasing metabolite concentrations, almost irrespective of the chemical compound class. Large signals in NMR can directly be interpreted as high level concentrations, whereas in MS quantitative responses strongly rely on the ionization potential of each metabolite.

Therefore, quantization in MS is limited to relative abundances of a given metabolite between samples, or requires calibration curves if absolute comparisons of different metabolites are needed. Thus MS is generally more favored than NMR due to four reasons: (i) MS is advantageous with respect to the capability to resolve complex mixtures of compounds, (ii) for most compounds, MS is far more sensitive than NMR,

(iii) due to the need for high end magnets, NMR instruments are usually far more expensive than most MS instruments and (iv) coupling of NMR to separation techniques such as liquid chromatography is far from straightforward. This leads to the main use of NMR as a tool for 'metabolite fingerprinting' in which we classify samples according to the origin or their biological relevance in order to maintain a high throughput (Fiehn 2002).

The most frequently used tool for profiling primary metabolites is Gas Chromatography coupled to mass spectrometry (GC-MS). Compounds screened by GC-MS profiling cover large parts of primary metabolism that are conserved across species, facilitating comparative studies between genetically and environmentally perturbed potato tuber systems (Roessner *et al* 2001). The most versatile method of separating compounds with wide range of polarity is LC. Semi-polar compounds, alkaloids, flavonoids can be separated by using reverse phase columns whereas hydrophilic columns are used for polar compounds like sugars, amino acids, vitamins, nucleotides etc. The mass detection of LC-MS is conditioned by the capacity of an analyte to ionize while being a part of complex mixture as only ions can be measured by MS.

Other elegant method of obtaining metabolite information is the use of 13C material (Mashego *et al* 2004). Nowadays, in stabilized (LC or GC)-MS setups, retention-time variation can be relatively low, allowing direct comparisons of chromatograms and the construction of metabolite databases (Moco *et al* 2006). The resolving power of much used Quadrupole (Q) MS instruments is 4 times less then Time-of- Flight (TOF)-MS and that of Fourier transform (FS)-ion cyclotron (ICR)-MS is 400 times greater than Q-MS (Moco *et al* 2007). Seifar *et al* (2008) developed a rapid, sensitive and selective ion-pair reversed-phase liquid chromatography–electrospray ionization isotope dilution tandem mass spectrometry (IP-LC–ESI-ID-MS/MS) for quantitative analysis of free intracellular metabolites in cell cultures. No recovery check of metabolites in the cell extraction step was needed because 13C-labeled extract was added to the cells before the extraction of intracellular metabolites. This effectively minimizes the extraction differences between the labeled and unlabeled analytes.

Advantages of Metabolomics:

- Identification of target organ, severity, onset, duration and reversal of the effects (time-course)
- Classify sample as "normal" vs "abnormal"
- Determine mechanisms of action within the organ
- Potential for identifying novel biomarkers of toxic effect
- Non-invasive
- No a priori decisions about samples need be made
- No sample processing necessary other than cold collection
- Complete time course data can readily be obtained
- Minimization of compound requirements

- Relatively fast analysis (200-300 samples/day)
- Useful tool for modeling physiological variation and exposure conditions

Applications

As a diagnostic aid: To determine the mode of action of various herbicides using GC-MS. The analysis of metabolic profiles from seedlings treated with median lethal (LC50) doses of acetyl CoA carboxylase (ACC) and acetolactate synthase (ALS) inhibitors, alongside untreated control seedlings, resulted in the visual discrimination of metabolite profiles of the different plants (Sauter *et al* 1991). Similarly used in tomato to catalogue the metabolite composition of developing tomato fruit where the influence of Hexose Phosphorylation diminishes during fruit development (Roessner *et al* 2003). Ma and Gang, 2006 studied difference in chemical curcuminoids between micropropagated and green house grown turmeric plants using GC-MS method.

Metabolic response to stress: An interesting area in plant system is the metabolic response of plants to various biotic and abiotic stresses. Thimm *et al* (2004) analyzed the effect of carbon starvation by exposing Arabidopsis plants to an extended night by metabolic profiling. Similarly Cook *et al* (2004) compared Ws-2 and Cvi-1 ecotypes to Arabidopsis lines over expressing CBF transcription factor genes, and this CBF over expression configured the metabolome of Arabidopsis in a way that resembles cold acclimation treatments.

Gene function: The technique has been used to explore the function of genes in plants, yeast and experimental animals. Metabolomic strategies have also been used to define gene function in the yeast. Allen *et al* (2003) studied extracelluler metabolites in *S. cerevisiae* to distinguish between the wild-type and mutant strains of yeast during different growth phases. Similarly, Nakagawa *et al* (2004) studied that in transgenic petunia plants over expression of a cDNA for a zinc-finger protein (LIF), alters cytokinin metabolism and plant forms.

Food Science: Plants are a fabulously rich source of diverse functional biochemicals and metabolomics is also already proving valuable in an applied context. By characterizing their biochemical composition, metabolomics will greatly assist in identifying the unexploited biodiversity available today (Kussmann *et al* 2007). Food quality is easily and rapidly deteriorated by a number of different pests, leading to major losses. Vikram *et al* (2004) studied the response of four different types of fungi applied to apples to study the effect of different metabolic responses during food storage.

Databases

There are different tools for visualization or databases that can be used to display the coupling of different "omics" data (e.g. KEGG (www.genome.jp/kegg), MAPMAN (gabi.rzpd.de/projects/ MapMan), KappaView (kpv.kazusa.or.jp/kappaview) and DOME (a database of OMEs). AraC is a tool to visualize biochemical pathways of Arabidopsis (Mueller *et al* 2003). MetaCyc (http://metacyc.org/) provides metabolic pathways and citations to 150 different organisms. MetNetDB is a metabolic and regulatory networkmap that contains a growing map of Arabidopsis entities (genes, RNAs, polypeptides, protein complexes and metabolites) and the catalytic and regulatory interactions between them. For identifying GS-MS signal an important databases is AMDIS (Automated mass spectral deconvolution and identification system) (www.amdis.net) and for MS and NMR Advanced Chemistry Development Labs (ACDLabs) is mainly used.

Limitations of Metabolomics:

- Requirement of specialized equipments
- Extensive expertise is required
- Information is limited to time- and dose-points taken
- High risk of false positive data
- Difficulty in separation of physiological (adaptive) and toxicological (adverse) effects
- Sensitivity of the assay
- Advisability of sub-fractionating metabolites (highly charged, neutral)
- Supplemental MS or other tests for final identifications (e.g., fructose and glucose)

CONCLUSION

Given the speed with which functional genomics, proteomics and metabolomics has advanced in the last decade, there are potential developments around the corner that will make much of the current technology redundant. There are some more advanced approaches currently being developed.

Together with the completion of the sequence of different plant genomes, a magnificent tool kit is becoming available that will dramatically improve the quality of research in all disciplines of plant biology (Bouchez and Hofte, 1998). This tool kit comprises large collections of knockout mutants in model organisms for systematic gene function searches and methods for the study of the regulation of entire sets of genes at the mRNA (transcriptomics) or protein level. A challenge in the next decade will be to build integrated databases combining information on such things as sequence, map position, mRNA and protein expression, mutant phenotypes, metabolism, and allelic variation. Also, intelligent software tools will be required for the efficient mining of this wealth of information and to construct intelligible models describing the complex molecular interactions that constitute the regulatory networks. EST sequencing and mapping or genomic sequencing of a few strategic crop species may suffice to facilitate the transfer of information from model species to the majority of crop plants, to be used for crop improvement in the future (Leung and An, 2004).

The science of omics has fundamentally altered the way in which we view plant biology, by providing the possibility of taking a global view of cellular processes. Sequencing programs are rapidly documenting the expressed genes of many species. Several functional genomic, proteomics approaches discussed in this chapter, address plant gene function on a large scale. Plants are combinatorial chemists par excellence, and understanding the principles that relate enzyme structure to function will open up unlimited possibilities for the rational design of new enzymes to generate novel biologically active natural products. Knowledge of the molecular genetics of plant natural product pathways will also facilitate the engineering of these pathways for plant improvement and human benefit. It is highly probable that the field of omics will continue to be driven by technological developments for the foreseeable future.

REFERENCES

Albers M, Kranz H, Kober I, Kaiser C, Klink M, Suckow J, Kern R and Koegl M 2004 Automated yeast two-hybrid screening for nuclear receptor-interacting proteins. *Mol Cell Proteomics* **4**: 205-213.

Allen J, Davey H M, Broadhurst D, Heald J K, Rowland J J, Oliver S G and Kell D B 2003 High-throughput classification of yeast mutants for functional genomics using metabolic footprinting. *Nat Biotechnol* **21**: 692–696.

Bouchez D and Hpfte H 1998 Functional genomics in plants. *Plant Physiol* **118**: 725-732.

Brown PO and Botstein D 1999 Exploring the new world of the genome with DNA microarrays. *Nature Genet* **21**: 33-37.

Cagney G, Amiri S, Premawaradena T, Lindo M and Emili A 2003 In silico proteome analysis to facilitate proteomics experiments using mass spectrometry. *Proteome Science* **1**: 5-7.

Cole L S and Vassar R 2007 The Alzheimer's disease _-secretase enzyme, BACE1. *Mol Neurodegeneration* **2**: 22-26.

Cook D, Fowler S, Fiehn O and Tomashow M F 2004 A prominent role for the CBF cold response pathway in configuring the low-temperature metabolome of Arabidopsis. *PNAS* **101**: 15243–15248.

Cooke R, Raynal M, Laudié M, Grellet F, Delseny M, Morris P C, Guerrier D, Giraudat J, Quigley F and Clabault G 1996 Further progress towards a catalogue of all Arabidopsis genes: analysis of a set of 5000 non-redundant ESTs. *Plant J* **9**: 101-124.

David A H, Jason P and Michael S 2007 Protein microarray technology. In: *Mechanisms of Ageing and Development* **128**: 161-167.

Feizi T 2003 Use of nitrocellulose surfaces for the immobilisation of carbohydrates and neoglycolipids. *Curr Opin Struc Biol* **13**: 637-645.

Fiehn O 2001 Combining genomics, metabolome analysis, and biochemical modelling to understand metabolic networks. *Comp Funct Genom* **2**: 155-168.

Fiehn O 2002 Metabolomics – the link between genotypes and phenotypes. *Plant Mol Biol* **48**: 155–171.

Fields S and Song O 1989 A novel genetic system to detect protein-protein interactions. *Nature* **340**: 245 – 246.

Fodor S P, Read J L, Pirrung M C, Stryer L, Lu A T, Solas D 1991. Light-directed, spatially addressable parallel chemical synthesis. *Science* **251**: 767-773.

Gupta P K, Roy J K and Prasad M 1999 DNA chips, microarrays and genomics. *Current Science* **77**: 875-884.

Henzel W J, Billeci T M, Stults J T, Wong S C, Grimley C and Watanabe C 1993 Identifying proteins from two-dimensional gels by molecular mass searching of peptide fragments in protein sequence databases. *PNAS* **90**: 5011-5015.

Hieter P and Boguski M 1997 Functional genomics: it's all how you read it. *Science* **278**: 601-602.

Hurt J, Thibodeau S, Hirsh A, Pabo C and Joung J 2003 Highly specific zinc finger proteins obtained by directed domain shuffling and cell-based selection. *PNAS* **100**: 12271–12276

Joung J K, Ramm E I and Pabo O Carl 2000 A bacterial two-hybrid selection system for studying protein–DNA and protein–protein interactions. *PNAS* **97**: 7382-7387.

Junker V, Contrino S, Fleischmann W, Hermjakob H, Lang F, Magrane M, Martin M J, Mitaritonna N, Donovan C and Apweiler R 2000 The role SWISS-PROT and TrEMBL play in the genome research environment. *J Biotechnol* **78**: 221-234.

Karas M and Hillenkamp F 1988 Laser desorption ionization of proteins with molecular mass exceeding 10000 daltons. *Anal Chem* **60**: 2299–2301.

Kersten B and Feilner T 2007 Generation of plant protein microarrays and investigation of antigen-antibody interactions. *Methods Mol Biol* **355**: 365-378.

Kim S H, Shin D H, Choi I G, Schulze-Gahmen U, Chen S and Kim R J 2003 Structure-based functional inference in structural genomics. *Struct Funct Genomics* **4**: 129-130.

Kussmann M, Affolter M, Nagy K, Holst B and Fay L B 2007 Mass spectrometry in nutrition: understanding dietary health effects at the molecular level. *Mass Spectrom Rev* **26**: 727-750.

Leung H and An G 2004. Rice functional genomics: Large scale discovery and applications to plant improvement. *Adv Agron* 82: 55-111.

Lockhart DJ and Winzeler EA 2000. Genomics, gene expression and DNA arrays. *Nature* **405**: 827-836.

Ma X and Gang D 2006 Metabolic profiling of Turmeric (*Curcuma longa* L) Plants Derived from *in vitro* Micropropagation and Conventional Greenhouse Cultivation. *J agric Food chem* **54**: 9573-9583.

MacBeath G and Schreiber S 2000 Printing proteins as microarrays for high-throughput function determination. *Science* **289**: 1760-1763.

Marshall E and Pennisi E 1998 Hubris and the human genome. *Science* **280**: 994-995.

Mashego M R, Wu L, Dam J C, Ras C, Vinke J L, Winden W A, Gulik W M and Heijnen J J 2004 MIRACLE: mass isotopomer ratio analysis of U-C-13-labeled extracts. A new method for accurate quantification of changes in concentrations of intracellular metabolites. *Biotechnol Bioeng* **85**: 620-628.

Moco S, Bino R J, Vorst O F, Verhoeven H A, Groot J C, Beek T A, Vervoort J J and Vos C H 2006 A liquid chromatography-mass spectrometry-based metabolome database for tomato. *Plant Physiol* **141**: 1205 - 1218.

Moco S, Bino R J, Vorst O, Verhoeven H A, Groot J, Beek T A, Vervoort J and Vos C H 2006 A Liquid Chromatography-Mass Spectrometry-Based Metabolome Database for Tomato. *Plant Physiol* **141**: 1205-1218.

Mrkish M and Su J 2002 A modified surface for microarrays and SPR. *Chem Biol* 41: 4175-4181.

Mueller L A, Zhang P and Rhee S Y 2003 AraCyc: a biochemical pathway database for Arabidopsis. *Plant Physiol* **132**: 453–460.

Nakagawa H, Jiang C, Sakakibara H, Kojima, Honda I, Ajisaka H, Nishijima T, Koshioka M, Homma T, Mander L and Takatsuji H 2004 Overexpression of a petunia zinc-finger gene alters cytokinin metabolism and plant forms. *Plant J* **41**: 512-523.

Newman T, Bruijn F J, Green P, Keegstra K, Kende H, McIntosh L, Ohlrogge J, Raikhel N, Somerville S and Thomashow M 1994 Genes galore: a summary of methods for accessing results from large-scale partial sequencing of anonymous Arabidopsis cDNA clones. *Plant Physiol* **106**: 1241-1255.

Oliver S G, Winson M. K, Kell D B and Baganz F 1998 Systematic functional analysis of the yeast genome. *Trends Biotechnol* **16**: 373–378.

Polyak K and Riggins G J 2001 Gene discovery using the serial analysis of gene expression technique: implication for cancer research. *J Clinic Onco* **19**: 2948-2958.

Pruess M, Kersey P, Kulikova T and Apweiler R 2006 Databases and resources for in silico proteome analysis. *Methods Biochem Anal* **49**: 397-414.

Ratner DM 2005. Advancing the burgeoning field of genomics. *Biotech* **17**: 8-11.

Roessner U, Hegemann B, Lytovchenko A, Carrari F, Bruedigam C, Granot D and Fernie A R 2003 Metabolic Profiling of Transgenic Tomato Plants Overexpressing Hexokinase Reveals That the Influence of Hexose Phosphorylation Diminishes during Fruit Development. *Plant Physiol* **133**: 84-99.

Roessner U, Willmitzer Land Fernie A R 2001 High-resolution metabolic phenotyping of genetically and environmentally diverse potato tuber systems. Identification of phenocopies. *Plant Physiol* **127**: 749–764.

Sauter H, Lauer M, Fritsch H 1991 Metabolic profiling of plants - A new diagnostic technique. In: *Synthesis and chemistry of agrochemicals II.* ACS Symposium American Chemical Society, Washington 288-299.

Schena M, Shalon D, Davis RW and Brown PO 1995 Quantitative monitoring of gene expression patterns with a complementary DNA microarray. *Science* **270**: 467-470.

Schwender J and Ohlrogge J B 2002 Probing in vivo metabolism by stable isotope labeling of storage lipids and proteins in developing *Brassica napus* embryos. *Plant Physiol* **130**: 347-361.

Seifar R M, Zhao Z, Dama J, Winden W, Gulik W and Heijnen J 2008 Quantitative analysis of metabolites in complex biological samples using ion-pair reversed-phase liquid chromatography–isotope dilution tandem mass spectrometry. *J Chrom* **1187**: 103–110.

Shin I, Cho J W and Boo D W 2004 Carbohydrate Arrays for Functional Studies of Carbohydrates. *Comb Chem Screen* **10**: 565-574.

Somerville C and Somerville S 1999. Plant functional genomics. *Science* **285**: 380-383.

Sullivan N, Sun Y, Binley J, Lee J, Barbas C F, Parren P, Burton D R and Sodroski J 1998 Determinants of human immunodeficiency virus type 1 envelope glycoprotein CD4 and monoclonal antibodies. *J Virol* **72**: 6332-6334.

Thimm O, Blasing O, Gibon Y, Nagel A, Meyer S, Kruger P, Selbig J, Muller L A, Rhee S Y and Stitt M 2004 MAPMAN: a user-driven tool to display genomics data sets onto diagrams of metabolic pathways and other biological processes. *Plant J* **37**: 914–939.

Tonge R, Shaw J, Middleton B, Rowlinson R, Rayner S, Young J, Pognan F, Hawkins E, Currie I and Davison M 2001 Validation and development of fluorescent two-dimensional gel electrophoresis proteomics technology. *Proteomics* **1**: 377-396.

Tuteja R and Tuteja N 2004. Serial analysis of gene expression: Application in human studies. *J Biomed Biotech* **2**: 113-120.

Unlu M, Morgan M E and Minden J S 1997 Difference gel electrophoresis: a single gel method for detecting changes in protein extracts. *Electrophoresis* **18**: 2071-2077.

Velculescu V E, Zhang L, Vogelstein B and Kinzler K W 1995 Serial analysis of gene expression. *Science* **270**: 484-487.

Vikram A, Prithiviraj B, Hamzehzarghani H and Kushalappa A 2004 Volatile metabolite profiling to discriminate diseases of McIntosh apple inoculated with fungal pathogens. *J Sci Food Agric* **84**: 1333–1340.

Wakatsuki T, Hada A and Ryo A 2001 Use of serial analysis of gene expression (SAGE) technology. *J Immun Methods* **250**: 45-66.

Wang D 2002 Tools of glycobiology. *Nat Biotechnol* **20**: 275-281.

Wilkins M R, Sanchez J C, Gooley A A, Appel R D, Humphery I, Hochstrasser D F and Williams K L 1996 Progress with proteome projects: why all proteins expressed by a genome should be identified and how to do it. *Biotech Genet Eng Rev* **13**: 19-50.

Yamamoto K and Sasaki T 1997 Large-scale EST sequencing in rice. *Plant Mol Biol* **35**: 135-144.

Zhu H, Bilgin M, Bangham R, Hall D, Casamayor A, Bertone P, Lan N, Jansen R, Bidlingmaier S, Houfek T, Mitchell T, Miller P, Dean R A, Gerstein M and Snyder M 2001 Global analysis of protein activities using proteome chips. *Science* **293**: 2101-2105.

7

INCREASING YIELD POTENTIAL OF GRAIN LEGUMES : PHYSIOLOGICAL DETERMINANTS IN RELATION TO CEREALS

PUSHP SHARMA AND VIRENDER SARDANA

Legumes have been recommended as a part of cropping systems since ancient times. The key benefit of legume, of course, is their ability to form symbiosis with specific bacteria that allows the fixation of atmospheric dinitrogen (N_2). The fixed N is used in legume plants to synthesize the essential amino acids, nucleic acids and other nitrogenous compounds required to sustain and grow plant tissue. The ability of legumes to fix atmospheric N_2 can make these species especially valuable assets in cropping systems.

In roughly, the past half century, however, the role of legumes in cropping systems has often diminished in favour of increasing emphasis on cereals. Rather than relying on N input to the cropping system from legumes in many parts of the world N fertilizer is applied in increasing amounts in the production of cereals. However, now, the continuous production of cereals with applications of large amounts of fertilizer is facing several constraints. For several perspectives, legumes can become critical components of alternate cropping systems, particularly if legume yields can be enhanced. In industrial countries, the abundant application of N-fertilizers to fields has raised environmental concerns and regulations have been established to control nitrogenous compounds in ground water and water ways. In developing countries, the opposite concern exists in the lack of manufactured N-fertilizer causing severe limitations in cereal yields. Nitrogen fertilizer availability in the developing countries is constrained by the cost of manufacture, distribution and credit for farmers to purchase fertilizer.

The high protein concentrations of legume tissues make them desirable as feed and food sources. The vegetative tissues of virtually all legumes are high in protein concentrations, which make them very desirable as forage for animals. Seeds of grain legumes are high in protein so that when digestive inhibitors in some species are inactivated, they are excellent foods. Human consumption of seeds of grain legumes is important world wide including common beans (*Phaseolus* sp.), Soybean (*Glycine max*), peas (*Pisum sativum*), Peanut (*Arachis hypogaea*), cowpea (*Vigna ungiculata*), chickpea (*Cicer orientinum*) and pigeonpea (*Cajanus cajan*).

To sustain legume production and stimulate expanded use of legume in cropping system, there is a need to further increase legume yield both in terms of plant mass and total plant N accumulation. The topics to be considered for possible improvement in order to increase yields include plant development, carbon assimilation, nitrogen assimilation and stress amelioration. Most of the work with legumes has been done with grain legumes pod/legumes, so much of the discussion will focus on pulse crops.

PLANT DEVELOPMENT

The basic scheme of temperature - driven plant development in legumes is not unlike that of cereal species. Rates of germination and emergence, leaf emergence and flowering are all quantitatively linked to the temperature to which the plants are subjected. Rates of development increase in an approximately linear manner until temperature becomes too high and results in inhibition of development. In addition many legumes are sensitive to the day length under which they develop. Growth related limitations are discussed hereby

Germination and seedling vigour

Grain legumes, pulses in general have slow growth rate at the time of germination and seedling stage. Most of the long duration pulses exhibit slow dry matter accumulation in the initial stages of growth. Due to slow development of leaf area, canopy, poor interception of solar radiation leads to slow growth rate, poor seedling vigour and ultimately yields. This has been well illustrated in chickpea and pigeonpea by Khanna-Chopra and Sinha (1990). Higher rates of germination and seedling vigour as reported in large-sized seeds of cowpea provides competitive advantage for sunlight in mixed cropping. Since pulses are often cultivated in mixed cropping systems, these attributes constitute a major hurdle in realizing higher yield potentials. Temperature extremities viz. both low and high decreases the rate of germination and thus, growth rates. Therefore, soaking of seeds prior to sowing increases the germination percentage and also reduces the time required for germination. Old seeds have higher germination percentage than new seeds, which is due to the presence of chemicals or hard seed coat. This leads to lower percentage of germination, seedling vigour and root/shoot ratio. Therefore, it is desirable to enhance seedling vigour.

Even the fresh hard seeds of lentil and mungbean exhibit lower germination, which can be improved by storing the seeds for some time before sowing.

Leaf area

More the leaf area, more will be the interception of solar radiation, higher will be photosynthetic activity and subsequently higher productivity. Most of the pulses have low leaf area index (LAI). Therefore, increase in the leaf area to some extent would enhance the transfer of photoassimilates to the sinks.

Seed weights at different nodes have been directly correlated with the leaf area at these nodes (Savithri *et al.* 1978), thus, clearly illustrating larger the leaf area more will be interception of light which leads to higher grain yield.

In most of the legume crops, the light interception by the canopy is low due to low leaf area. Leaf area increases gradually reaches maxima followed by a decline. So, LA and ultimately LAI varies with the age of plant. Leaf area of mungbean, averaged on genotypes was 58, 371, 683, 530 and 226 cm^2 $plant^{-1}$ at 15, 30, 45, 60 and 75 DAS (Prasad and Srivastava, 1999) and of late sown chickpea was 14, 82, 243, 379 and 288 cm^2 $plant^{-1}$ at 25 and 50 DAS, at flowering, 10 and 20 days after flowering (Ganguly *et al.* 1999). Leaf area is low at early stages of growth but also during reproductive phase LA declines drastically, leading to low photosynthesis and ultimately low yields. Increase in LA with irrigation has been reported by Sharma *et al.* (unpublished).

Therefore, selection of varieties based on their physiological pattern and manipulation of agronomic practices particularly time of sowing, plant population, planting geometry etc. can improve LAI and subsequently increase productivity per unit time. Little is known about the genetic regulation of development rate of plants. Some legumes are handicapped by especially slow production of leaves causing low crop growth during early stages of development Pigeonpea, for example, has small leaves that are produced at a slow rate so that the time to achieve full radiation interception is substantially delayed as compared to other species (Muchow, 1985). Consequently, major increase in yield potential of pigeonpea and other relatively small leaved species seem possible if the rate of leaf area development could increase.

Growth phenology

The phenology of grain legumes is strongly responsive to photoperiod (Summerfield and Roberts, 1985). Temperature not only affects the length of vegetative growth phase but also the initiation of flowering, by increasing the mean temperature during the vegetative phase, hastens flowering in mungbean (Poehlman, 1991) and chickpea (Sharma *et al.* 2005). Developing short duration varieties for multiple cropping systems and maximizing grain yield, the vegetative phase should be terminated with flowering and assimilates be channelized into pod production. It is also argued that early flowering plants are low yielders due to short stature, few nodes, smaller leaf area and shorter grain filling period as compared to the late flowering plants. So, the growth pattern of genotypes should be such that it suits best to the environment or the growing season for which it has been targeted. Longer reproductive phase results in the development of better sink for higher harvest index (Kumar *et al.* 2001). To improve and stabilize yield, efforts are needed to optimize the resources by manipulating both genotypes through breeding and environment via agronomic manipulation in order to exploit genetic potentials to the maximum and minimize environmental constraints on the realization of that potential (Lawn 1981). It is desirable, therefore, to match crop phenology to the climate/environment, which prevails during the growing season in a given location.

CARBON ASSIMILATION

Leaf photosynthetic potential of legumes seems to be as high as C_3 cereals. Measurements of leaf photosynthetic (P_n) rates of field grown soybean have been reported over 40 µmol $m^{-2}s^{-1}$ and a number of observations near or above 30 µmol $m^{-2}s^{-1}$ have been reported for field grown peanut (Bell *et al.* 1994). Photosynthetic rates (range) expressed as mg $CO_2dm^2hr^{-1}$ in some pod legumes are lentil (10-30), cicer (25-40), *Phaseolus vulgaris* (15-40) and cowpea (12-30.7), which are similar to wheat, barley and cotton in their photosynthetic rate but certainly poorer than those of maize, sorghum and millets. Several studies on the variability in photosynthesis rates in soybean (Sinclair 1980). Phaseolus vulgaris (Evans *et al.* 1973), chickpea (Shanthakumari and Sinha 1972) and mungbean (Sinha and Khanna unpublished) clearly show that varietal differences are common in these species. Further, photosynthetic rates changes considerably during the lifecycle of legumes. The fact that virtually no data has been reported on the leaf photosynthetic activity of other grain legumes under field conditions may offer an important research opportunity for characterizing growth and yield potential in other legume species.

While legumes are capable of high leaf photosynthetic rates, these rates contrast with cereals in that they are achieved only with a much greater investment in leaf N content per unit leaf area than required in cereals. For example, leaf N contents of soybean have shifted to about 0.7 g N m^2 greater levels as compared to rice to achieve comparable photosynthetic rates (Sinclair and Horie 1989). The additional leaf N in soybean seems to be needed to achieve photosynthetic rates comparable to C_3 cereals is seemingly disadvantage. The basis for this difference between cereals and legume has not been explained. There appears to be no evidence that photosynthetic biochemistry of legumes is less efficient than that of C_3 cereals. One hypothesis is that leaves of legumes simply store more protein than cereals because of the higher relative abundance on N in legume plants as a result of N_2 fixation. Consistent with this hypothesis is the presence in many legumes leaves of a layer of paraveinal mesophyll cells (Lansingh and Franceschi, 2000) that are rich in glycoproteins (Klauer *et al.* 1996). The paraveinal mesophyll cells have little photosynthetic capability and seem to function as storage and transport cells. The physiological role of the paraveinal mesophyll in legume leaves certainly deserves further attention as contributors of the carbon and N economy of these species.

Radiation use efficiency

The carbon assimilation capacity of the total crop can be effectively expressed by Radiation Use Efficiency (RUE), defined as the ratio of mass accumulated to cumulative intercepted total solar radiation. Sinclair and Horie (1989) calculated the potential RUE of soybean based on leaf photosynthetic capacity as being about 1.2 g MJ^{-1}. This estimate was lower than that anticipated for C_3 cereals (1.4 MJ^{-1}) as expected based on the difference in the higher energy content of the soybean mass. In practice, there have been only a few reports of soybean RUE as high as the 1.2 g MJ^{-1} suggested by Sinclair and Horie (1989). Most experimental observations have reported RUE values in the range of 0.65 to 1.15 g MJ^{-1} with a median of approximately 0.9 g MJ^{-1} (Sinclair 2004).

Field observations of RUE may frequently be lower than theoretical values because RUE is sensitive to many stresses which decreases leaf photosynthesis rate. Consequently, water deficit or biotic pests that result in decreased leaf photosynthetic rate will result in decreased RUE. Probably, the most important environmental factor decreasing RUE is water deficit. Soil dehydration that results in loss of leaf photosynthetic activity will result directly in a decrease in RUE. Especially, in legumes that may have shallower roots than cereals, the onset of decrease in RUE may occur early in the drying cycle.

Focused research to understand the commonly observed lower RUE than theoretically anticipated for legumes may lead to insights for increasing yields. Management or genetic options can be worked out to sustain high leaf photosynthetic rates of legume leaves and consequently sustained high RUE.

Photosynthetic efficiency

Increase in LAI may not be correlated with increased productivity because all the radiation captured may not be utilized into yield. It is the conversion efficiency which determines the efficiency of photosynthetic active radiations (PAR) which is converted into yield. Variation in photosynthetic efficiency has been observed in genotypes of many pulse crops (Table 1). Photosynthetic rate and RUBP-carboxylase activity were positively correlated with grain yield in chickpea (Pandey and Singh, 1996). Thicker leaves have higher photosynthetic capacity, which compensates for slower growth rate. Canopy structure to capture higher quantity of solar radiation could not be compensated for lower photosynthetic efficiency of pods relative to leaf in top podding pulses like mungbean, pigeonpea and cowpea as significant quantity of radiations are intercepted by flowers and pods. Due to lack of assimilate supply, yields are lowered as observed due to partial defoliation at different stages of growth (Sharma *et al.* unpublished) and shading during flowering (Saxena *et al.* 1983) Pulse crops are grown in mixed and intercropping system, therefore, shading of pulses could influence photosynthesis and productivity.

FLOWER AND FRUIT ABSCISSION

Large number of reproductive sinks viz. flowers, fruits and seeds, are produced in grain legumes. But, only a small fraction of them ends up in seed production. Due to physiological constraints, there is a large scale abscission of flowers and fruits. The major reason for low productivity of pulses is the poor realization of sink capacity due to flower and fruit shedding (Hebblethwaite *et al.* 1984). Plants are unable to meet the

TABLE 1 : Photosynthetic rates (P_n) rates and photosynthetic characteristics in pod legumes

Characters	*Species*	P_n *(mg $CO_2dm^{-2}hr^{-1}$)*
Photosynthetic rates (P_n)	Soybean	12-24
	Lentil	10-30
	Cicer	25-40
	Phaseolus vulgaris	15-40
	Cowpea	12-30.7
Photosynthetic characteristic		
Photosynthetic rates	Pod legumes	Normally 20-30
Temperature range		Optimum between 25°-30°C
Light saturation		10,000 lux
CO_2 compensation point		About 50 ppm
Photorespiration		Present
Main carboxylating enzyme		RUBP
Kranz anatomy		Absent

carbon and nitrogen demands of developing sinks. Thus, the greater requirement of C and N and also continuous translocation from vegetative parts leads to the senescence of vegetative tissues and reduction in the seed filling period, thus, lowering the yield. Intra-plant competition for assimilates between the reproductive and vegetative parts has been attributed by Gates *et al.* (1983) to higher flower and pod abscission. Other reasons for lower fruit and seed set in legume crops are briefly enlisted.

HORMONAL/NUTRITIONAL REGULATION

Sometimes pollination and fertilization occur but still the flowers abscise. Shedding of flowers with ovules is due to hormonal or nutritional imblance.

Pollination failure

Pulses are generally self-pollinated crops. Sometimes during flower development, under adverse climatic conditions, pollination does not occur and flowers wither away.

Environmental conditions

Environmental factors particularly temperature affects pollen germination, pollen tube growth and thus, fertilization leading to flower abortion in chickpea Sharma *et al.* 2005). Water stress too has similar effect on mungbean (Singh, 1990a). Lower pod set may also result from cloudy weather, low night temperature and soil moisture. Even if under conducive temperature's for pollen germination only a small percentage of flowers set fruit.

Availability of photoassimilates

Excessive production of sinks (flowers) but poor pod set is probably due to limited availability of assimilates. The analysis of carbon and nitrogen economy of chickpea and pigeonpea by Singh (1990b) has suggested the selection criterion for cultivars *i.e.* low photorespiration, delayed leaf abscission, efficient mobilization of C and N from stem and leaves, higher photosynthetic and N-fixing rates during seed filling phase, for maximizing the efficiency of photosynthates utilized for seed weight and protein production.

Insects : In summer mungbean, Thrips cause flower shedding as a result of which number of pods formed and grain yield declines significantly (Chhabra and Kooner, 1985).

Any of these factors or a combination might be true. In determinate genotypes, there is increased competition for photosynthesis between developing fruits and nitrogen fixing nodules and fruit setting is better than indeterminate genotypes. The degree of synchrony of flowering and pod set could increase the potential sensitivity of water supply during reproductive phase of growth in grain legumes.

It is well documented that growth regulators helps to enhance the productivity of legumes. This could be the direct or indirect effect on flower retention (Sharma *et al.* 2005).

SOURCE-SINK RELATION WITH YIELD

Large number of flowers are produced in most of the grain legumes but only a few of them produce pods and set seeds. There exist high sink potential to give higher yield but it is not realized. Major limiting factor for realizing higher yield was the insufficient supply of assimilates to the young pods during later part of the reproductive phase, leading to unfilled pods in higher proportion as observed in *Kabuli* chickpea (Pandey *et al.* 1978).

Yield parameters viz. pods, pod weight node^{-1}, number of seeds and seed weight in the late formed pods decline, which indicates the limited supply of assimilates/nutrients during pod filling. Towards the apex, both fruit and seed weight declines and some of the fruit do not contain seeds Flowers are produced continuously in indeterminate plants, but these flowers do not develop into fruits, even if these flowers produce fruits, seeds are not formed. This is due to the limitation of leaves (source) at the upper flowering nodes. Moreover, the first formed fruits and seeds may exert some regulatory effect on fruit formation and seed development by regulating leaf area or floral biology.

Though the N-content of vegetative phase is more than double even then the extra N is not translocated to seeds. The site(s) that limit translocation have not been identified though they appear to be at or close to the developing seeds for genetic manipulation of N translocation. Atkins *et al* (2005) have cloned an asparaginase and two seed amino acid transporters from developing lupin seed. Constructs from these genes coupled to a seed specific promoters lead to the generation of transgenic over expression and anti-sense lines where significant increase in pod set and seed number has been achieved.

The determinant growth habit has potential advantage as the competition from vegetative sink to reproductive sink is reduced, for assimilates, resulting in improved productivity.

Low biomass production is the potential constraint for higher productivity in short duration determinate type of pod bearing legumes, which could be increased by higher plant density (Gates *et al.* 1983). Higher biomass production and reduction in the number of late formed branches may help in increasing grain yield in indeterminate type of faba bean (Silim and Saxena, 1990). Sinha (1974) has reported that sink potential was only 15% in cowpea against 75% in wheat as per theoretical calculations. It was inferred that sink potential was more than adequate to give yields comparable with cereals. However, poor sink utilization/ seed filling could be due to poor photosynthesis, limitation in nitrogen fixation, canopy structure, hormonal regulation, soil properties, water management etc.

PARTITIONING OF ASSIMILATES

The translocation of photosynthates from source to developing sinks depends upon the crop duration particularly vegetative and reproductive phases. Actually, it is the relative partitioning of current assimilates and the extent of remobilization of stored assimilates to the reproductive parts, which matters. Generally, the partitioning will be more if reproductive phase is longer and remobilization of assimilates is significant from vegetative to reproductive parts. Remobilization accounts for a very small portions of seed and major contribution is from current assimilation. Extent of remobilization depends on duration and nature of the crop. Remobilization may not take place from stem and leaves but from pods, the latter contributes about 9-15% of seed weight in rainfed chickpea (Davies *et al.* 1999).

Partitioning of assimilates depends upon the photoperiod under cloudy weather conditions/adverse photoperiod, partitioning of assimilates to reproductive sinks is reduced and there is excessive vegetative growth. Optimum photoperiod results in termination of vegetative growth and initiates reproductive growth, prolonging the reproductive phase and diverts major part of current assimilates to the desirable reproductive sinks.

Indeterminate growth habit is common in grain legumes, with no distinction of vegetative phase as in cereals. Vegetative phase continues even during pod development as a result, there is stiff competition between the vegetative growth and pod/seed development for assimilates. This is an important character limiting yield in grain legumes. Shinano *et al.* (1993) reported low productivity in grain legumes was due to greater respiratory loss from shoots rather than N translocation to the reproductive organs. The substantial increase in productivity in cereals has been possible by increasing the HI than the increase in total biomass (Jain 1986). Similarly, the greatest potential for physiological improvement in productivity of tropical grain legumes lies with increasing the proportion of biomass partitioning into seed. Genotypes with high partitioning efficiency towards reproductive sink and higher dry matter production at pod formation have been recommended for breeding in pulse crops by Manian *et al.* (1989).

Increase in harvest index has been a major component of yield increase for cereals and a few grain legumes. Soybean, for example, commonly has a harvest index of approximately 0.40 or greater. For a number of grain legumes, harvest indices can be substantially below this level. Pigeonpea, for example, may have harvest index as low as 0.20 (Lawn and Troedson, 1990). Success with other crops in increasing harvest index indicates that such selection in breeding programmes could be a practical approach to achieve rapid grain yield increase in some legumes.

NITROGEN FIXATION

The capability of legumes to undertake symbiotic N_2 fixation is a critical distinguishing trait of legumes, and causes legumes to be a highly desirable component of many cropping systems. There are, however, several aspects of the N_2 fixation process that result in unique physiological considerations. One of these is the regulation of O_2 concentration in the nodule. Nitrogen fixation is catalyzed by nitrogenase, which is highly sensitive to oxygen and can be readily denatured when exposed to O_2. Therefore, the metabolic step leading to N_2 fixation is a paradox in that the reaction requires large amount of energy supported by oxidative respiration while the basic N_2 fixing enzyme is destroyed by the O_2 that is essential for respiration.

Nodules are well designed to meet the dual requirement of high O_2 supply rate for respiration within the nodule and maintenance of low O_2 concentration. The internal volume of the nodule where fixation takes place is surrounded by a shell, 2 or 3 cells thick, which acts as an O_2 diffusion barrier. The O_2 permeability of the barrier is variable and adjusts to maintain a low O_2 concentration in the internal volume of the nodule (Serraj *et al.* 1999), oxygen readily diffuses in the internal volume of nodules through a network of gas spaces. To facilitate diffusion of O_2 from the air spaces to the site of respiration within N_2 fixing cells, nodules of many species have O_2 transporters in these cells to which O_2 binds and facilitates diffusion. The transporter in grain legumes is "leghemoglobin" which gives the interior of healthy nodules a pinkish/red colour when they are cut open and the leghemoglobin is exposed to atmospheric oxygen concentration.

Amides and/or ureides are the nitrogenous compounds synthesized in nodules from ammonia produced in the primary step of N_2 fixation. Those grain legumes that transport ureides seem to have a higher N_2 fixation rates than those that transoport amides. Ureides are efficient for N transport since their C:N ratio is 1:1. However, the solubility of ureides is low (Sprent, 1980) and this fact may contribute to the requirement by ureide-transporting species of relatively high water fluxes out of nodules via the xylem (Serraj *et al.* 1999). Since, the source of the water for xylem outflow is phloem flow into the nodule, interruption of phloem flow into nodules results in rapid decreases in N_2 fixation rates. In addition, feedback of nitrogenous compounds from the mother plant exerts a control on nodule activity (Serraj *et al.* 1999). The tight regulation of nodule activity by water and nitrogen flow results in a close balance between N supply and N requirement to support plant growth.

In cropping situation, it would seemingly be beneficial to maximize N_2 fixation to increase yield and/or protein content of the plant products and to increase the production of fixed N for the overall cropping system. Currently, there is little information about what may be the ultimate limit on N_2 fixation rate. The highest N_2 fixation rate for soybean appears to be about 0.6 g N $m^{-2}d^{-1}$, which was reported for plants grown on a gravel hydrophonic culture in field (Harper, 1971). One possibility is that N_2-fixation rate in soybean might simply be limited by the rate of formation of vegetative storage 'compartments' in which to deposit the fixed N. One research approach to investigate maximizing N_2-fixation rate would be to undertake studies with legumes with large tubers (Tropical Legumes, 1979). These tubers might provide both energy reserves and storage capacity, to investigate the limit for maximum N_2 fixation rate.

Another major limitation on N_2-fixation rate when legumes are rotated with a cereal in a cropping system is the large amounts of N-fertilizer that may be applied to the cereal. High level of residual nitrate in the soil will inhibit nodulation and N_2 fixation activity (Streeter, 1988). Delayed nodule formation and initiation of N_2-fixation can result in a period after the soil nitrate is exhausted when there is little or no N_2 fixation. Consequently, there may be several weeks during critical stages of plant development when N supply within the plant is restricted and the legume suffers N-deficiency symptoms and loss of yielding capability.

There has been considerable interest in developing cultivars with N_2 fixation that is tolerant to residual nitrate for use following heavily fertilized cereals in cropping rotations. A goal has been to identify genotypes that can develop nodules in the presence of nitrate so that N_2-fixation activity is initiated prior to or as soon as the soil nitrate is exhausted. Several soybean genotypes have been identified that have less sensitivity of N_2-fixation rates to nitrate than most soybean (Serraj *et al.* 1992).

Another approach to enhance nitrate tolerance was the identification of genotypes that form unusually large numbers of nodules in the absence of nitrate. Even though nitrate resulted in the same relative decrease in these 'super nodulating' lines, as normal lines the number of nodules on these lines under nitrate treatment was still high (Carroll *et al.* 1985; Gremaud and Harper, 1989). However, the retention of a reasonable nodule population when subjected to nitrate has failed to result in yield increase (Maloney and Oplinger, 1997).

Nitrogen fixation in the species that transport ureides from the nodules to the shoot have been found to be extremely sensitive to soil water deficits (Serraj and Sinclair 2002). Nitrogen fixation rates in the ureide-transporting species e.g. soybean and cowpea, begins to decline as result of soil drying well in advance of any other physiological process. This sensitivity may in part be a consequence of the need for high water flux to and from nodules to sustain ureide transport. In addition, there appears to be an especially strong negative feedback from the shoot to roots (Serraj *et al.* 1999) involving elevated ureide concentrations that signal decreased N_2-fixation rates. Nitrogen fixation in amide transporting species, on the other hand, does not appear to be any more sensitive to water deficits than other physiological responses.

The sensitivity of N_2-fixation to drying soil has proved to be greater in ureide-transporting legumes than any other physiological processes in these plants (Serraj *et al.* 1999). This sensitivity has been confirmed in field studies employing various water-deficit treatments on a sandy soil with no residual N (Sinclair *et al.* 1987). So, nitrogen accumulation reflected N_2-fixation and the results were expressed relative to the well-watered treatment. It was inferred that in every water deficit treatment the relative nitrogen accumulation decreased to a greater extent than mass accumulation. Further, Purcell and King (1996) showed directly a loss of soybean yield as a result of N_2-fixation sensitivity to soil drying. In a field experiment, plots subjected to drought were either left with no added nitrate or nitrate was added. Those plots to which nitrate was added as a source of N during the drought had an 18% greater yield than the plots untreated with nitrate and dependent solely on N_2-fixation. Eight lines were found to have substantial N_2-fixation tolerance by Sinclair *et al.* (2000) in soybean. In addition, these eight tolerant lines were found to exhibit little feedback inhibition of N_2-fixation rates when supplied with high levels of ureides (Sinclair *et al.* 2003).

Nitrogen assimilation and partitioning

A large quantity of nitrogen is required for growth and yield in grain legumes. A part of this requirement is via biological nitrogen fixation (BNF). Nodulation and N_2-fixation is maximum during flowering and early pod development followed by a decline. This decline coinciding with greater need of N for developing sinks *i.e.* seed (Sharma and Sharma, 2008). During pod-filling stage, nodulation and nitrogen fixation is reduced due to the greater sink capacity *i.e.* preferential mobilization of assimilates for seed development, as a result less photosynthates are available for nodule growth and maintenance. Since, the current nitrogen fixation declines, the N-requirement of developing seeds are met by translocation of N from subtending leaves. Rubisco (the major enzymatic protein of leaves) is mobilized, resulting in reduction of photosynthetic efficiency of leaves (Grover *et al.* 1985).

Leaf area declines during pod development leading to leaf senescence because a large quantity of carbon and nitrogen is left unused. Poor mobilization of N from vegetative to reproductive parts, accompanied by inadequate BNF, leads to poor productivity in grain legumes. Although, pulses (also grain legumes) have the ability to draw adequate N from soil, BNF and remobilization from leaves, yet the greater N demand remains to be a major constraint for productivity. It is important to enhance the rate of photosynthesis during seed filling so that enough of carbohydrates are available for enhancing N uptake and its utilization for the development of seed (Ganeshaiah and Uma Shanker, 1987).

Pulses are considered as valuable food crops, because of high protein content in the seeds. Therefore, their nitrogen requirement is much higher as compared to cereals.

Nitrogen content in seed is several times higher than in other plant parts viz. leaves, stems, roots etc. The proportion of total nitrogen recovered in seeds exceeds grain HI *i.e.* NHI (Nitrogen Harvest Index). The level of nitrogen in the seeds ranges from 3-7% while in plant residues, it is 0.75-1.5%. Thus, for most grain legumes, a higher HI necessitates an even higher NHI.

Hence, the comparison of grain legumes with cereals is greatly unjustified. However, amino acid composition of grain legumes is complementary to cereals since they are relatively richer in lysine.

STRESS AMELIORATION

Major abiotic stresses affecting legume crops are impact of temperature, salinity, moisture, solar radiations and micronutrient deficiency.

Moisture stress

Grain legumes are highly sensitive to water stress. Drought leads to yield reduction because of less dry matter accumulation and increased abscission. In, general under water stress, there is decrease in leaf water potential, stomatal conductance, net assimilation of CO_2 and transpiration. Water stress imposed at flowering stage, leads to reduction in dry matter accumulation in different plant parts. Yield losses were higher when stress was imposed at flowering than at pod filling stage. However, cumulative effect of water stress at both the stages has been reported by Sekhon *et al.* (2004).

Water stress at initial stages limits sources, leading to the reduction in total biomass, whereas at reproductive phase (initiation of flowering, initiation of podding and both) leads to flower and pod abscission, thereby decreasing the sink strength. Significant reduction in leaf area, leaf area duration, relative leaf growth, specific leaf weight (SLW) and yield have been observed in mungbean and urdbean by Sharma *et al.* (unpublished). Genotypes having higher root dry matter, root length and volume are tolerant to drought. Irrigation increases dry matter accumulation than yield. Excess water enhances vegetative growth, thus, creating competition for developing desirable sinks. Flooding creates anoxia (oxygen deficiency) which leads to decline in LAI, nodulation, yield and yield attributes. However, irrigation applied at initiatiun of flowering, podding and at both the stages enhances leaf area and leaf characteristics, chlorophyll content, photosynthetic efficiency and ultimately yield as compared to stressed plants (Sharma *et al.* unpublished).

The special limitation of soil drying on N_2 fixation of ureide-transporting legumes, has been already discussed in this chapter. Besides N_2-fixation, growth and water loss by grain legumes varies with soil water content in the same pattern as observed for all crop species (Sinclair and Ludlow, 1986). There is no influence on plant gas exchange rates until only $1/3^{rd}$ of the transpirable water remains in the soil. At this $1/3^{rd}$ point, the plant gas exchange rates decreases approximately linearly until the stomata are closed. Once, there is no transpirable water remaining in the soil plants enter a survival phase in which they are no longer growing but continue to extract soil water at a very slow rate to maintain plant water balance and avoid desiccation. Interestingly, there are very large differences among grain legumes in the ability to survive these severe stress conditions. Soybean has a very poor ability to survive severe stress while pigeonpea can survive long term stress (Sinclair and Ludlow, 1986). However, Serraj and Sinclair (2002) argued that these differences in survival of severe drought are likely not to be particularly important in high production agriculture. If the total amount of available water is so limited to cause crop survival to be a concern, then yield potential is likely to be severely restricted and little or no yield can be harvested from such a crop. A water-deficit response in soybean is the slow wilting phenotype PI-416937. This genotype was identified as to maintain turgor with soil drying such that the plants wilted several days later than the other genotypes (Solane *et al.* 1990). The basis of this unique phenotypic expression is speculated to be a result of either deeper rooting in the soil or a water conservation strategy in which plants use water at a slightly lower rate than other lines depending on the environment through the growing season, such traits could be of considerable benefit in some dry seasons and result in little or no penalty in wet seasons.

Temperature

Legume production has been extended over a wide range of climates from cold, northern latitudes, to hot, tropical regions. Much of the expansion in the range of adaptation has resulted from empirical selection of superior performance of individual genotypes for new climate zones. There have, however, been research programs targeted specifically at identifying genetic variation within legume species for adaptation to various temperature regimes.

In peanut, cold night temperatures of less than 15°C resulted in lost leaf photosynthetic activity during the following day (Sinclair *et al.* 1994; Bell *et al.* 1994). Bell *et al.* (1994) studied eight genotypes and found significant differences in the influence of cold night temperature while the threshold for the negative influence of temperature did not seem to vary among genotypes, some genotypes (OAC Ruby and OAC Garroy) had smaller decreases in photosynthetic rates at lower temperatures than the other genotypes. These results indicated that selection in legumes for photosynthetic tolerance of cold temperature is possible.

Sink strength in terms of flower and pod formation are directly linked with temperature. Significant decline in bud and flower drop has been recorded in pigeonpea and chickpea under low temperatures (Singh *et al.* 1997). Time of sowing is directly related to temperature too. For example early sown pigeonpea attains highest LAI, intercepts maximum solar radiation, produces highest total dry matter and yield (Patel *et al.* 2000). Late sowings curtails vegetative period resulting in reduction in relative growth rates, biomass, yield and yield attributes (Singh *et al.* 2003).

Low temperature had adverse effect on the reproductive physiology in chickpea germplasm (Sharma *et al.* 2005). Pollen fertility was reduced significantly when the temperature falls below 3°C. Pollen germination, pollen tube growth and fertilization was hampered by the cold spell. Low temperature reduced flower retention. However, in the genotypes which flowered and set pods during cold spell, seeds could not develop because low temperature hindered the translocation. In cowpea, high night temperatures (>30°C) resulted in flower abscission (Warrang and Hall, 1984). The high night temperature was shown to result in indehiscence of anthers and low pollen viability. Out of 58 cultivars only three cultivars had high pod-set under high night temperatures (Warrang and Hall, 1983).

Under field conditions, it is hardly possible to separate the temperature and photoperiod effects. Therefore, attempt in the form of agronomic practices or breeding objectives which would confirm to the requirements of the location. On the basis of the studies carried out by Summerfield (1975, Personal Communication) has proposed the model (Fig.1) for the physiology of yield in cowpea and soybean in the tropics.

Solar radiations

Pod legumes particularly summer grown mungbean genotypes are higher yielders because of high solar radiation, higher crop growth rates (RGR, NAR), specific leaf weight (SLW), leaf area index (LAI) than in the rainy seasons with cloudy weather (Singh *et al.* 1985). There is a direct positive correlation between PAR interception and crop duration. There are adverse effects of shading on legumes in intercropping systems. Defoliation at different stages of crop growth limits source strength, reduces light interception, photosynthetic efficiency and yield in mungbean (Sharma, unpublished). Shading during reproductive stage has more severe effects on yield than vegetative phase (Hudge *et al.* 1993).

Salinity

Salinity invariably affects germination and growth of plants through a check on the nitrogen-fixing machinery, protein synthesis, carbohydrate metabolism, enzyme synthesis etc., which in turn have a tremendous negative effect on harvest index of the crops. Salt injury influences several physiological processes and productivity, which has gained immense importance in the last couple of years. It is the toxicity of ions penetrating cells as well as augmentation in the osmotic potential of the medium, which subsequently hinder the penetration of water into the roots (Munns and Keyser, 1981). The accumulation of salts within the plant tissues caused a disturbance in the plant growth and development thus, altering the degree of hydration of cytoplasm during the period of osmotic adaptations (Sands and Clarke, 1977). The extent of injury varied with plant species and within same species, it varied with the type of predominant ions, their concentration, the physiological stage of growth at which the plant encounters the saline stress. Various physiological processes, nitrogen fixation, growth and productivity of legumes in response to abiotic stresses has been vividly discussed by Sharma and Sardana (2008).

Nutrition

Both inadequate nitrogen supply via soil or BNF reduce biomass, leaf area, leaf area duration, nitrate reductase, grain nitrogen and total nitrogen per unit area (Bhattacharya and Ali, 2002) whereas nitrogen application enhances these characteristics along with the increase in chlorophyll, photosynthetic activity and nitrate reductase in nodules (Sekhon *et al.* 2002c). Nitrogen limitation in cropping system can be minimized by using legumes but often there remains a limitation on plant growth due to inadequate phosphorus. Certain legumes, however, appear to have the capacity to make a major contribution in improving the availability of P in rotational cropping system. Several species have been identified that exhibit substantial superiority in recovering soil P that is unavailable to other species. For example, Ae *et al.* (1990) reported that pigeonpea thrived on an Alfisol soil with most of the P bound to iron while maize, sorghum, pearlmillet and soybean died from P-deficiency within one month after sowing. Ishikawa *et al.* (2002) found that roots of pigeonpea encreated large amounts of citric and piscidic acid and these contributed to the mobilization of P in the soil. They concluded, however, that this mechanism was inadequate to account for all of the P taken up by the plant. The root cell-walls of pigeonpea contains a small molecule that has P-solubilizing abilities (Ae and Shen, 2002) and likely contributes to the recovery of bound P from the soil. Peanut also exhibited the same P solubilizing abilities, which was associated with survival on low P-available soil while maize, sorghum and soybean died. Ohwaki and Hirata (1992) also reported that chickpea exuded more citric and malic acid than five other legumes indicating that this species may be another good candidate for use on soils with low P availability.

In addition to differences among species in recovering non-soluble P, there are genotypic differences within species Lynch and Beebe (1995) compared 364 common bean genotypes under P-deficient conditions and found substantial differences in growth. It was confirmed in a comparison to the six contrasting cultivars of common bean that there were substantial differences in the ability to recover P from different forms of immobile P (Yan *et al.* 1996). Ishikawa *et al.* (2002) included four cultivars of pigeonpea in their study of P recovery from various sources and found distinct differences among genotypes, which depended on the form of immobilized P. Phosphorus application increased LAI, crop growth rate, chlorophyll content, lessened abscission of flowers and increased grain yield in mungbean (Garai and Datta, 2002), cowpea (Rao and Subramanian, 1990) lentil and field pea (Singh *et al.* 2001) by enhancing leaf water potential, stomatal conductance, light interception, water use efficiency and decreasing canopy temperature (Yadav *et al.* 1994).

Nutritional efficiency has been attributed to a number of mechanisms including root processes affecting availability of nutrients in rhizosphere, root structure and geometry, translocation from roots to shoot and foremost remobilization with shoots understanding the physiology, genetics and regional distribution of efficiency for a particular nutrient should assist in developing nutrient efficient varieties for productivity enhancement.

Expansion in legume production is likely to continue for the foreseeable. Protein demand will increase as human diets improve and/or shift to greater amounts of meats, virtually necessitating an increase in the production of all grain legumes. The increasing demand will result in a number of opportunities and challenges. The opportunities are to use innovative approaches to fully integrate grain, legume production into cropping system., Approaches which take full advantage of legumes ability to fix atmospheric nitrogen symbiotically. Following approaches/thrust areas should be looked into for increasing grain legumes productivity.

- Efforts are needed to redesign the varieties with appropriate growth habit and efficient source-sink kinetics. In grain legumes wild traits like photo-thermo sensitivity, indeterminate growth habit which causes intra-plant competition for photosynthate resulting into poor partitioning. It may be presumed that determinate types under good management would partition photosynthate to yield components with greater efficiency through early seedling vigour, faster leaf development, synchronous flowering, slow senescence and increased rate of dry matter production.
- All the heritable characters viz. morphological and physiological processes responsible for linear productivity in grain legumes can be manipulated by genetic manoeuvres to irradicate undesirable factors and incorporate desirable traits which minimize the adverse effect on yield.
- Indepth studies and systematic efforts are required for identifying desirable traits from the beginning *i.e.* higher seedling vigour, faster vegetative growth, higher response to nutrients, irrigation and other inputs, thermo and photoperiod insensitivity, improved root system, efficient partitioning, lower flower and fruit drop, synchronous maturity, more biomass production are the needs of all the pulse/legume crops.
- Understanding the physiological mechanisms that enable plant to adopt to various stresses via tolerance or avoidance mechanism, thus, maintaining growth by imparting stability to the membrane will help in selection of stress tolerant cultivars.
- In short duration, pod legumes increase in the reproductive phase, pod filling period, higher tolerance to water stress during reproductive phase in long duration pulses under rainfed conditions and under residual moisture in rabi pulses. Likewise resistance against waterlogging, high temperature (Kharif season), both high and low temperature (Rabi season), improved BNF capacity, resistance to insect-pest and pathogen should be attempted through selection, breeding and biotechnological tools.
- Inorder to genetically manipulate N translocation, constructs from the cloned genes coupled to a seed specific promoter should be used to generate transgenic over-expression and anti-sense lines. Atkins *et al.* (2005) have generated transformants using a flower specific promoter and significant increase in pod set and seed number has been recorded.
- The possible underlying mechanism particularly endogenous level of hormones responsible for the hormonal imbalance related to flower and fruit shedding requires outmost attention. Further role of plant growth substances in enhancing

sink strength, efficient assimilate partitioning and increasing yield is required to be studied in detail.

- Most productive genotypes could be identified through selection for yield in high productivity environments and for HI in low productivity conditions. This will impart the much desired respite to pulses against unfavourable environment via increase in inherent capacity for higher productivity.
- Development of dual-purpose grain legume cultivars with high N_2-fixation capability to produce a modest grain crop in the growth year for immediate economic benefit to the grower and to generate a reasonable amount of high N-content plant residue to be incorporated into the soil for use in the subsequent cereal crops.
- Full exploitation of some grain legumes to recover P from the soil could be a very important asset in many cropping situations. The challenges of fully exploiting legumes are likely to be focused on their sensitivity to a number of environmental stresses.

Continued success in increasing the productivity of grain legumes and their use in cropping systems will likely be well rewarded with improved economic and environmental viability of crop production over many areas of the globe.

REFERENCES

Ae N Arihara J Okada K Yoshihara T Johansen C 1990 Phosphorus uptake by pigeonpea and its role in cropping systems of the Indian subcontinent *Sci* **248** : 477-480

Ae N Shen RF 2002 Root cell wall properties are proposed to contribute to phosphorus (P) mobilization by groundnut and pigeonpea *Plant Soil* **245** : 95-103

Atkins CA Ferguson M Penny M Smith C 2005 Source and sink relationship in food legumes Abst. A-28. In 4th International Food Legumes Research Conference October 18-22, 2005 New Delhi, India

Bell MJ Gillespie TJ Ray RC Michaels TE Tollenaar M 1994 Peanut leaf photosynthetic activity in cool field environments *Crop Sci* **34** : 1023-1029

Bell MJ Gillespie TJ Ray RC Michaels TE Tollennr M 1994 Peanut leaf photosynthetic activity in cool field environments *Crop Sci* **34** : 1023-1029

Bhattacharya A Ali M 2002 Physiological traits and seed yield in chickpea under high nitrogen input *Legume Res* **25** : 9-14

Carroll BJ McNeil DL Gresshoff PM 1985 A supernodulation and nitrate tolerant symbiotic (NTS) soybean mutant *Plant Physiol* **78** : 34-40

Chhabra KS Kooner BS 1985 Problem of flower shedding caused by thrips, *Megalurothrips distalis* (Karnyl) on summer mung bean, *Vigna radiata* (L.) Wilczek and its control *Tropical Pest Management* **31** : 186-188

Davies SL Turner NC Siddique KHM Plumer JA and Leport L 1999 Seed growth of *desi* and *kabuli* chickpea (*Cicer arietinum* L.) in a short-season Mediterranean type environment. *Aust J of Exp Agri* **39** : 181-188

Evans AN 1973 Genetic improvement of *Phaseolus vulgaris* In Nutritional improvement of food legumes by breeding Protein Advisory Group, United Nations, New York

Ganeshaiah KN Uma Shankar R 1981 Auto-parasitization of leaves in pulses – N limiting or C limiting *Curr Sci* **50** : 942-944

Ganguly SB Bhattacharya A Singh DN 1999 Physiological studies in chickpea varieties : Physiological determinants and their relationship to productivity under late seeding *Ind J of Pulses Res* **12** : 65-74

Garai AK Datta JK 2002 Sources of phosphate fertilization and cycocel spray on some physiological attributes in seed yield in mung *Crop Res* (Hisar) **23** : 300-304

Gates P Smith ML Boulter D 1983 Reproductive physiology of *Vicia faba* L. In : The *faba* bean *Vicia faba* L. (ed PD Hebblewaite) pp. 133-142 London : Buntherworks

Gremaud MF Harper JE 1989 Selection and initial characterization of partially nitrate tolerant nodulation mutants of soybean *Plant Physiol* **89** : 169-173

Grover A Koundal KR Sinha SK 1985 Senescence of attached leaves regulated by developing pods *Physiol Plantarum* **63** : 87-92.

Harper JE 1971 Seasonal nutrient uptake and accumulation patterns in soybeans. *Crop Sci* **11** : 347-350

Hebblethwaite PD Scott RK Kogbe JOS 1984 The effect of irrigation and bees on the yield and yield components of *Vicia faba* L. In *Vicia faba* : Agronomy. Physiology and Breeding (eds PD Hebblethwaite TEK Dewkins MC Heath Ghock Wood) pp 71-93 The Hague : Martinus Nijhoft/Dr W Junk

Hudge VS Sardar MB Khan GM Chavan MH Shete DM 1993 Effect of low light on growth and yield in black gram *Annals of Plant Physiol* **7** : 182-186

Ishikawa S Adu Gyamfi JJ Nakamura T Yoshihara T Watanabe T Wagastsuma T 2002 Genotypic variability in phosphorus solubilizing activity of root exudates by pigeonpea grown in low-nutrient environments *Plant Soil* **245** : 71-81

Jain HK 1986 Eighty years of post Mendelian breeding for crop yield : Nature of selection process and further potential. *Ind J of Genet and Plant Breeding* **46** (Supplement) **30** : 30-53

Khanna Chopra R Sinha SK 1990 What limits the yield of pulses? Plant Processes or plant type . In : Proceedings of the International Congress of Plant Physiology Vol.1 (eds SK Sinha PV Sane SC Bhargava PK Agrawal) pp 268-278 New Delhi : Society for Plant Physiology and Biotechnology

Klauer SF Franceschi VR Ku MSB Zhang D 1996 Identification and localization of vegetative storage proteins in legume leaves *Am J Bot* **83** : 1-10

Kumar J Pannu RK Rao BV 2001 Development of a short duration chickpea for the subtropics *Int Chickpea and Pigeonpea Newsletter* **8** : 7-8

Lansingh AJ Franceschi VR 2000 The paraveinal mesophyll : a specialized path for intermediary transfer of assimilates in legume leaves *Aust J Plant Physiol* **27** : 757-767

Lawn RJ 1981 The potential contribution of physiological research to pigeonpea improvement In : Proc of the International Workshop on Pigeonpea Vol 1 (ed Nene YL) pp 151-164 Hyderabad : ICRISAT

Lawn RJ and Troedson RJ 1990 Pigeonpea : Physiology and yield formation : In The Pigeonpea (Eds. YL Nene SD Hall VK Sheila) pp 179-208 Wallingford : CAB International

Lynch JP Beebe SE 1995 Adaptation of beans (*Phaseolus vulgaris* L.) to low phosphorus availability *Hort Sci* **30** : 1165-1171

Maloney TS Oplinger ES 1997 Yield and nitrogen recovery from field grown supernodulating soybean *J Prod* Agric **10** : 418-424

Manian K Natarajaratnam M Ramaswamy P Balasubramanian M Sreerangaswamy SR 1989 Significance of dry matter production and its partitioning in horsegram genotypes. *Madras Agri J* **76** : 512-516

Muchow RC 1985 Canopy development in grain legumes grown under different soil water regimes in a semi-arid tropical environment Field crops *Res* **11** : 99-109

Munns DW Keyser HH 1981 Tolerance of rhizobia to acidity aluminium and phosphate *Soil Sci Soc Am J* **34** : 519-523

Ohwaki Y Hirata H 1992 Difference in carboxylic acid exudation among P-starved leguminous crops in relation to carboxylic acid contents in plant tissues and phospholipid level in roots. *Soil Sci Plant Nutr* **38** : 235-243

Pandey CS Singh M 1996 Genotypic variation in photosynthetic efficiency in relation to productivity in gram (*Cicer arietinum*) genotypes. *Ind J of Agri Sci* **66** : 466-469

Pandey RK Saxena MC Singh VB 1978 Effect of some growth regulators on yield and yield components of *Kabuli gram* (*Cicer arietinum* L.) *Pantnagar J of Res* **3** : 175-177

Patel NR Mehta AN Shekh AM 2000 Radiation absorption growth and yield of pigeonpea cultivars as influenced by sowing dates *Expt Agri* **36** : 291-307

Poehlman JM 1991 The Mungbean New Delhi Oxford & IBH Publishing Co. Pvt. Ltd.

Prasad S Srivastava JP 1999 Physiological analysis of yielding ability in mungbean *Ind J Pulses Res* **12** : 49-56

Purcell LC King CA 1996 Drought and nitrogen source effects on nitrogen nutrition, seed growth and yield in soybean *J Plant Nutrition* **19** : 969-993

Rao DG Subramanian VB 1990 Effect of P on nodulation N harvest index and growth : Correlation between nodulation and other plant parts in cowpea under well watered and dryland conditions *Ind J of Plant Physiol* **33** : 275-281

Sands R Clarke ARP 1977 Response of radiata pine to salt stress I water relations osmotic adjustment and salt uptake *Aust J Plant Physiol* **4** : 637-646

Savithri KS Ganapathy PS Sinha SK 1978 Fruit and seed development in mungbean (*Phaseolus aureus* Roxb) *J Agri Sci Cambridge* **90** : 551-556

Saxena NP Natarajan M Reddy MS 1983 Growth and yield of chickpea, pigeonpea and groundnut. In : Proc of the Symposium on Potential Productivity of Field Crops under different Environments (ed Y Yoshida) pp 281-305 Manila IRRI

Sekhon HS Sharma P Singh G 2004 Effect of irrigation on growth and yield on kharif mungbean (*Vigna radiata* (L.) Wilczek) genotypes *J Pl Sci Res* **20** : 102-105

Sekhon HS Singh G Sharma P Sharma AK 2002c Effect of *Rhizobium* inoculation and nitrogen on biological nitrogen fixation growth and yield of mungbean (*Vigna radiata* (L.) Wilczek) *Envi & Ecol* **20** : 282-290

Serraj R Drevon JJ Obaton M Vidal A 1992 Variation in nitrate tolerance of nitrogen fixation in soybean (*Glycine max*) Bradyrhizobium symbiosis *J Plant Physiol* **140** : 366-371

Serraj R Sinclair TR 2002 Osmolyte accumulation : Can it really help increase crop yield under drought conditions *Plant Cell Envir* **25** : 333-341

Serraj R Sinclair TR Purcell LC 1999 Symbiotic N_2 fixation response to drought *J Exp Bot* **50** : 143-155

Shanthakumari P Singh SK 1972 Variation in chlorophylls and photosynthetic rate in cultivars of Bengal gram (*Cicer arietinum* L.) *Photosynthetica* 189-194

Sharma P Sardana V 2008 Physiological processes nitrogen fixation growth and productivity of legumes in response to abiotic stresses. In Advanced Topics in Biotechnology and Plant Biology (eds. Malik CP Bhavneet K Chitra W) pp 323-398 MD Publishers Pvt. Ltd., New Delhi

Sharma P Sekhon HS Sandhu JS 2005 Cold tolerance studies in chickpea (*Cicer arietinum* L.) In : Proceedings of the 4th International Food Legumes Research Conference (IFLRC IV) p 86 October 18-22, 2005, IARI, New Delhi

Sharma P Sharma Poonam 2008 Biological Nitrogen fixation : Legume-Rhizobium physiology, phytohormones mediated response to nodulation and nitrogen fixation : In Advanced Topics in Biotechnology and Plant Biology (eds. Malik CP Bhavneet K Chitra W) pp 399-445 MD Publishers Pvt Ltd., New Delhi.

Shinano T Osaki M Tadano T Barrow NJ 1993 Comparison of production efficiency among field crops related to nitrogen nutrition and application. *Plant and Soil* **155-156** : 207-210.

Silim SN Saxena MC 1990 Composition of dry matter accumulation, partitioning and yield of determinate and indeterminate faba bean (*Vicia faba* L.). In Proc. of the *Int. Congress of Plant Physol* Vol. 1 (Eds. SK Sinha PV Sans SC Bhargava PK Agrawal) pp 289-298 New Delhi Society for Plant Physiol and Bichem.

Sinclair TR 1980 Leaf CER from post-flowering to senescence of field grown soybean cultivars *Crop Sci* **20** : 196-200

Sinclair TR 2004 Improved carbon and nitrogen assimilation for increased yield in "Soybeans" : Improvement, Production and Uses (ed J Specht R Boerma) (Am Soc Agronomy, Madison, WI)

Sinclair TR Bennet JM Drake GM 1994 Cool night temperature and peanut leaf photosynthetic activity Proc Soil Crop Sci Soc Florida **53** : 74-76

Sinclair TR Horie T 1989 Leaf nitrogen, photosynthesis and crop radiation use efficiency : A review *Crop Sci* **29** : 90-98

Sinclair TR Ludlow MM 1986 Influence of soil water supply on the plant water balance of four tropical grain legumes *Aust J Plant Physiol* **13** : 329-341

Sinclair TR Muchow RC Bennet JM Hammond LC 1987 Relative sensitivity of nitrogen and biomass accumulation of drought in field grown soybean *Agron J* **79** : 986-991

Sinclair TR Purcell LC Vadez V Serraj R King CA Nelson R 2000 Identification of soybean genotypes with N_2 fixation tolerance to water deficits *Crop Sci* **40** : 1803-1809

Sinclair TR Vadez V Chenu K 2003 Ureide accumulations in response to Mn nutrition by eight soybean genotypes with N_2-fixation tolerance on soil drying *Crop Sci* **43** : 592-597

Singh BB Singh DP Singh NP 1997 Genetic variability in pigeonpea germplasm for cold tolerance *Ind J of Genet and Pl Breeding* **57** : 425-430

Singh DN 1990a Influence of water on pollen germination and fruit set in mungbean. In : Proceedings of the International Congress of Plant Physiology Vol.1 (eds SK Sinha PV Sane SC Bhargava PK Agrawal) pp 320-322 New Delhi : Society for Plant Physiology and Biotechnology

Singh G Sekhon HS Sandhu JS Singh SJ Gumber RK Randhawa AS 2003 Effect of location and seed rate on three genotypes of mungbean *Tropical Sci* **43** : 116-120

Singh G Sekhon HS Sharma P 2001 Effect of *Rhizobium* vesicular arbuscular mycorrhiza and phosphorus on the growth and yield of lentil (*Lens culinaris*) and field pea (*Pisum sativum*) *Envir & Ecol* **19** : 40-42

Singh R 1990b Assimilation and partitioning of carbon and nitrogen during growth and development of grain legumes. In : Proceedings of the International Congress of Plant Physiology Vol.1 (eds SK Sinha PV Sane SC Bhargava PK Agrawal) pp 261-267 New Delhi : Society for Plant Physiology and Biotechnology

Sinha SK 1974 Yield of grain legumes. Problems and prospects. *Indian J. of Genet and Pl Breeding* **34** : 988-994

Solane RL Patterson RP Carter TE Jr 1990 Field drought tolerance of a soybean plant introduction *Crop Sci* **30** : 118-123

Sprent JL 1980 Root nodule anatomy, type of export product and evolutionary origin in some Leguminosae. *Plant Cell and Envir* **3** : 35-43

Streeter J 1988 Inhibition of legume nodule formation and N_2 fixation by nitrate *Crit Rev Plant Sci* **7** : 1-23

Summerfield RJ Roberts EH 1985 Grain legumes species of significant importance in world agriculture In A Handbook of Flowering Plants (ed Halery AH) pp 61-184 Boca Raton Florida CRC Press

Tropical Legumes : Resources for the Future 1979 National Academy of Sciences, Washington DC

Warrang MoA Hall AE 1984 Reproductive response of cowpea (*Vigna unguiculata* (L.) Walp) to heat stress II Response to night air temperature *Field Crops Res* 8 : 17-33

Yadav SK Chander K Kumar A 1994 Response of late sown gram (*Cicer arietinum*) to irrigation and phosphorus *Ind J of Agri Sci* **64** : 24-28

Yan X Lynch JB Beebe SE 1996 Utilization of phosphorus substrates by contrasting common bean genotypes *Crop Sci* **36** : 936-941

8

ENDOPHYTIC FUNGI : A BIOCONTROL AGENT

KARTIKEYA TIWARI, MUKESH K. UPADHYAY AND PAYAL LODHA

The control of pests and diseases affecting cultivable plants is made mainly by the use of chemical compounds. The use of agrochemicals to control insects and plant pathogens represents, however, a high risk to field workers, consumers and environment. They are responsible, for eliminating important species of insects that control other pests and microorganisms that are performing a critical role in the environment, inhibiting growth and multiplication of useful microbes. The natural and biological control is an alternative way that may contribute to reduce or even eliminate the use of chemical products in agriculture. The natural and biological control of agricultural pests gained more attention during the past decades especially through endophyte microorganisms. Therefore, this way to control pests are important to reduce the costs and protect the environment.

Petrini (1986) defined all organisms that colonize internal plant tissues are referred as endophytes and include everything from virulent foliar pathogens to mycorrhizals root symbionts. Fungi that cause visible symptoms of plant diseases have been separately classified as pathogens, regardless of the degree of penetration into the host plant's tissue. By default, fungi that cause asymptomatic infections entirely within the tissues of the host plants called endophytic fungi (Carroll, 1986). However, some mycologists also include fungi that inhabit plant organs at some point in their life cycle without causing apparent harm to their host, as well as latent internal pathogens (Petrini, 1992).

In the continual search by agricultural industries for new products, natural selection has been found to be superior to combinatorial chemistry for discovering novel substances from endophytic fungi that have the potential to be developed into new industrial products especially mycoherbjudes and pharmaceutical compounds. Since natural products are adapted to a specific function in nature, the search for novel secondary metabolites should concentrate on organisms that inhabit novel biotopes and endophytic fungi inhabit such a biotope. From the last 12 years, 6500 endophytic fungi from herbaceous plants and trees, screened for biological activities, and have isolated and determined the structures of the biologically active compounds. The potential role of the endophyte and its biologically active metabolites in its association with its host has been investigated by large number of workers (Barker *et al.* 1984; Prestidge *et al.* 1984; Ahmad *et al.* 1985). It may be hypothesized that the interaction of fungal endophyte–plant host is characterized by a finely tuned equilibrium between fungal virulence and plant defense. If this balance is disturbed by either a decrease in plant defense or an increase in fungal virulence, disease develops. Not only the endophytes synthesize metabolites to compete first with epiphytes and then with pathogens in order to colonize the host, but presumably also to regulate metabolism of the host in their delicately balanced association. The utilization of a biotope such as that of the fungal endophyte is one aspect of intelligent screening, another very important one is the taxonomy of the fungus in order to avoid redundant structural isolations.

The endophyte communities in angiosperms are frequently dominated by species of Diaporthales and those in gymnosperms by species of Helotiales. Divergence of angiosperms and gymnosperms coincides with the divergence of the Diaporthales and the Helotiales in the late Carboniferous about 300 million years ago, indicating that the Diaporthalean and Helotialean ancestors of tree endophytes had been associated, respectively, with angiosperms and gymnosperms; some are, however, opportunists and can cause disease after the host has been weakened by some other factor. Mutualism of tree endophytes is often assumed, but evidence is mostly circumstantial. The sheer impossibility of producing endophyte-free control trees impedes proof of mutualism. Some tree endophytes exhibit either a pathogenic or a putatively mutualistic behaviour depending on the situation. A wide diversity of microorganisms are present in most plant parts of both gymnosperms and angiosperms, especially the leaves where the tissue is apparently healthy, these may be endophytes, epiphytes or latent pathogens. The distinction among endophytes, epiphytes (those that live on the surface of plants) and phytopathogens (those that cause diseases to plants) is of pure didactic meanings. There is a gradient separating them and thus, it comes to a situation where it is a very difficult task to draw limits to discriminate each category. Endophytic microorganisms only received considerable attention in the last 20 years, when their capacity to protect their hosts against insects-pests and other pathogens. As endophytic fungi and bacteria started to be better analysed, it became clear that they could confer other important characteristics to plants, such as greater resistance to stress conditions (*i.e.* water), alteration in physiological properties, production of phytohormones and other compounds of biotechnological interest. In addition to the economical aspects, the study of endophytic microorganisms has strong academic interests, concerning the discovery of new microbial species, mainly when tropical hosts are investigated. It was demonstrated that the presence of these microorganisms in their respective hosts could result in the reduction of insect attacks. Webber (1981) was probably the first researcher to report an example of plant protection giving by an endophytic fungus, in which the endophyte *Phomopsis oblonga* protected elm trees against the beetle *Physocnemum brevilineum*. It was suggested that the endophytic fungus *P. oblonga* was responsible for reducing the spread of the elm Dutch disease causal agent *Ceratocystis ulmi* by controlling its vector, the beetle *P. brevilineum*. Gaynor and Hunt (1983) observed in several ryegrasses that high fungi infection is correlated with a decrease in the attack frequency of the Argentine steem weevil, *Listronotus bonariensis*. These authors also showed that these associations may be complex and factors like the level of nitrogen fertilizers may as well affect attack frequency. Lasota *et al.* (1983) had also correlated in the white spruce *Picea glauca*, death rate of the Homoptera *Adelges abietis* when galls are infected with the endophytic fungus *Cladosporium sphaerosperum*. In this review the major themes related to the control of insects-pests by endophytes will be addressed, together with the perspective of applying this knowledge to the development of a biological control by means of modern methods.

Endophytic microorganisms and their effect on insects

It was confirmed that the plant protection process promoted by endophytes is more complex than one might have expected. Although, in most of the published reports on the subject they show a mutualistic interaction, that is, positive in respect to the host and negative to the insects-pests and there are also reports of neutral or even antagonistic interactions. In addition to the reports mentioned above (Webber, 1981; Funk *et al.* 1983; Gaynor and Hunt, 1983; Lasota *et al.* 1983; Barker *et al.* 1984; Prestidge *et al.* 1984; Ahmad *et al.* 1985), that correlate endophytic fungi with negative effects towards insects, In fact, Clay (1989) stressed that, although many endophytic fungi have already been isolated from around 80 grass species of temperate countries, only six genera are the most frequent. The situation, since Clay's review (1989) about ten years ago, has gained minor changes. Ahmad *et al.* (1986) showed that the blue grass billbug *Sphenophorus parvulus* is less frequent on plants infected with endophytic fungi and verified the same results in grasses attacked by the Southern armyworm *Spodoptera eridania*. Saha *et al.* (1987), studying endophytes in fine fescue, verified that endophytic fungi from the genus *Acremonium* were associated with host resistance to *Blissus leucopterus hirtus* and the same observation was made by Mathias *et al.* (1990), in *L. perenne-A. lolii* interaction. Kindler *et al.* (1990) verified that *Acremonium* reduced the attacks of the aphid *Diuraphis noxia* in *Lollium* as well as in *Festuca* and the same observations were made by Clement *et al.* (1990; 1992). Kanda *et al.* (1994) reported the preference of larvae from the bluegrass webworm *Parapediasia teterrella* for diets with endophyte-free plants, to a point that the larvae would starve to death if only plants infected with *Acremonium* were available. In the field, endophyte-free species were severely attacked by insects, whereas those infected with *Acremonium* stayed almost free of insect larvae. As it will be seen in more details, endophytic fungi (Clavicipitaceae, Ascomycetes) synthesize alkaloids during plant infection, reducing the survival and the development of *S. frugiperda* in Graminae and Cyperaceae. The authors concluded that this is a general characteristic of infected grasses, that is, insect resistance and consequential improved performance of plants in nature. Considering other grasses, the studies are sparse. However, the host protection process displayed by endophytic fungi against insects seems to be general. For example, alcoholic extracts from *Poa ampla* infected or not with *Neotyphodium typhnium* were assayed against mosquito larvae. Only the extracts from the infected plants were effective against the insect, whereas the extract obtained directly from the fungi was not (Ju *et al.* 1998). Although plants other than grasses can be protected by endophytes, the data on these cases are not so conclusive nor numerous. Sherwood-Pike *et al.* (1986) described in oak (*Quercus* sp.), the role of the endophytic fungus *Rhabdocline parkeri* against the insect *Contarinia* sp. Petrini *et al.* (1989) found that the endophytic fungi *Phyllosticta* sp. and *Hormonema dematioides* were dominant in the balsam fir *Abies balsamea*. The first fungus colonized preferentially galled needles attacked by *Paradiplosis tumifex*, being a candidate for biological control. The examples given so far include researches performed in field and lab conditions, as well as comparisons between field and lab experimental data. Choice tests on diets composed of endophytes-free and infected plants are often used along with several choice combinations. Although, the majority of the works cited above are quite conclusive, the results do not always finish up in the control of insects by endophytes. As it will be shown, there are cases of neutrality or even improvement of insect performance in plants colonized by endophytic microorganisms.

Insect control displayed by endophytic fungi

Since the pioneer works in the field, the capacity of endophytic fungus to repel insects, induce weight loss, reduction of growth and development reduction and even to increase pest death rate, was correlated with toxin production. In several cases, it was shown that the mode of action of certain fungi was based on the capability to render the plant unpalatable to several types of pests like aphids, grasshoppers, beetles, etc (Carroll, 1988; Clay, 1988a; 1988b). Bacon *et al.* (1977) established for the first time a correlation between an endophytic fungi, *Epichloë typhina* and the toxicity of its host; It is now a fact that several toxins are produced by endophytic fungi and that these substances confer host protection against different herbivors. We suggest for more details on toxins the review of Bacon and Hills (1996) in which the most important toxins found in *L. perenne,* like ergot alkaloids of two types, ergopeptine and clavine and neurotoxines called lolitrems are described. It is not known if the precursor is converted in lolitrems by the plant or if the fungus is not capable of synthesizing it in pure culture but is able to do so while inside the plant. Examples of toxin production by endophytic fungi, notably those colonizing grasses are considerably abundant in the literature. In 1988, Prestidge and Gallagher established a relationship between the presence of the fungus *A. lolii* in *Lolium perenne* and the growth, survival and feeding behaviour of *Listronotus bonariensis* larvae. In this case, the reduction in insect attacks towards infected plants was due to a strong toxin, lolitrem B, also toxic to mammals. This toxin, once added to insect diets, reduced insect growth and survival. Its assimilation occurs by ingestion but not by absorption through the insect integument. In certain cases, the production of toxin by the endophytic fungi was a plausible explanation for interactions resulting in natural insect control. Thus, Clark *et al.* (1989) showed in *Abies balsamea* and red spruce *Picea rubens,* that from 900 samples of fungal isolates, five produced toxic substances and three of those produced powerful toxins that, once extracted and given to insects, caused death and decreased development rate of *C. fumiferana*. Few fungi generally produce alkaloids, mainly peramine and ergovaline. Peramine, lolitrem B and ergovaline were found in *Lolium* and *Festuca* infected with *Acremonium coenophialum* and *A. lolii* and in *Festuca longiflora* infected with *E. typhina*. Individuals of *Rhopalosiphum padi* and *Schizaphis graminum* did not survive in grasses containing the alkaloid loline. On the other hand, ergovaline did not affect both insect species. The methanolic extracts of *F. arundinacea* infected with *A. coenophialum*, contain lolines of fungal origin, which are able to alter feed behaviour and weight of insects-pests. Diets amended with extracts containing loline derivatives reduced weight and altered certain behaviours of *S. frugiperda* and *O. nubilalis*, notably in the first insect (Riedell *et al.* 1991). In certain cases, the production of toxin by the endophytic fungi was a plausible explanation for interactions resulting in natural insect control. Thus, Clark *et al.* (1989) showed in *Abies balsamea* and red spruce *Picea rubens,* that from 900 samples of fungal isolates, five produced toxic substances and three of those produced powerful toxins that, once extracted and given to insects, caused death and decreased development rate of *C. fumiferana*. Many other cases of insect control involving toxins produced by endophytic microorganisms can be found in the literature. Siegel *et al.* (1990) verified the presence of the alkaloids N-formil, N-acetil loline, peramine, lolitrem B and, ergovaline during plant attack by aphids. Several grasses infected with *Acremonium* spp. and *E. typhina* were analysed. Patterson *et al.* (1992) observed in *Lolium* and *Festuca* that the production of alkaloids by *Acremonium* reduced attacks of the Japanese beetle *Popilla japonica*. Other works find that ambient variations may affect toxin production by endophytic fungi. Breen (1992) verified that changes in temperature and seasons modify toxin levels in the plant. This is the case of the peramine toxin, produced in *L. perenne* by *A. lolii*. The antixenosis towards the aphid *S. graminum* is dependent on peramine and the endophyte concentration so, a natural consequence is that the effect on the insect-pest will also be modified. Two new active toxins against the Spruce budworm *C. fumiferana* were found in an unidentified endophytic fungus infecting the wintergreen *Gaultheria procumben* (Findlay *et al.* 1997). Alkaloids from *N. lolii* and *L. perenne* are capable of altering insect behaviour. Several of these alkaloids were added to the diet of adult individuals of the Coleoptera *Heteronychus aratur*. Peramine, lolitrem B, lysergol-type alkaloids, festuclavine and lisergic acid showed no effects on the insect. Ergovine showed moderate effects whereas ergotamine, ergovaline from the ergot-type alkaloid family seem to be responsible for the plant resistance (Ball *et al.* 1997b). Recently, Miles *et al.* (1998) showed that endophytic isolates of *Neotyphodium* sp. produce N-formilonine and a paxiline analogous in the host *Echinopogum ovatus*. These compounds show insecticidal activity against *L. bonariensis* and other insects. The majority of works related to toxin production was performed in grasses. However, Calhoun *et al.* (1992), for the first time, identified toxic products synthesized by endophytic fungi in woody plants and that were able to modify growth and death rates in larvae of the spruce budworm *C.*

fumiferana feeding on balsam fir. The endophytes in this case were identified as *Phyllosticta* and *Hormonema dematioides* and the toxic compounds were mainly heptelidic acid and rugulosine.

Modifications of endophytes

Environmental factors like temperature, hydric stress, soil pH, insect-pest resistance and other ecological parameters may also affect the endophyte concentration and toxin production. Breen (1994), idealized a model with all of these interactions affecting the increase or decrease in plant resistance to insects-pests in the presence of endophytes. Arechavaleta *et al.* (1989) had already verified in the *F. arundinacea* endophyte *A. coenophialum* that the production of ergo-peptide alkaloids increased in soil amended with nitrogen fertilizers and during a moderate hydric stress, which consecutively altered insect-pest control. A study about the interaction between nitrogen fertilization, pests and the endophytic fungus *A. coenophialum* showed that in a general manner, insects like *S. frugiperda* developed better in nitrogen fertilized plants not infected by the endophyte. However, considering this and other insects, the occurrence of *A. coenophialum* blocks insect development. The results, therefore, are quite variable and do not allow us to draw any general correlation between nitrogen fertilizer and endophyte-mediated pest control in *F. arundinacea* (Davidson and Potter, 1995). In the same manner, Bultman and Conard (1998) verified interactions among several factors like nutrient levels and plant damage during endophytic fungi control of *S. frugiperda* in the host *F. arundinacea*. The insect pupal mass was negatively influenced by the endophyte in low nutrient levels but the effect was negligible in plants highly fertilized. This study showed again that these interactions are complex and influenced by several factors, in this case by fertilizer application. The recent studies, in soil less cultivation conditions, conduced by Richardson *et al.* (1999) verified that the Chewings fescue *F. rubra* subspecies *commutata* showed differences in alkaloid contents in respect of endophyte colonization and amounts of several nitrogen sources. Fluctuation in the contents of the alkaloids ergovaline and peramine in colonized plants was verified, which will consecutively alter insect resistance. Clay *et al.* (1993), analized changes resulting from these plant-plant interactions in insect control and presence of endophytic fungi. They also analysed the effects of a member of the genus *Acremonium* in relation to attacks of *S. frugiperda* larvae to the tall fescue *F. arundinacea* and the red fescue *F. rubra* grown separately or mixed with other grasses. In general, insect attacks were reduced in hosts colonized by endophytes, because the plants were less chosen by the pests. However, different degrees of insect attacks were observed according to the plant associations analysed. These studies demonstrated that plant interactions wouldchange the effects of endophytic fungi in insect control.

Effect of endophytic entomopathogenic fungi on plants for pest control

It is widely known that Fungal species like *Metarhizium anisopliae, Beauveria bassiana* and others are often used in the biological control for agriculture insects-pest management. If these fungi inhabit plant tissues as endophytes, they will obviously be able to act in insect control. Even in situations where they are not present in the plant, artificial inoculation techniques may circumvent this obstacle. As discussed in this review that endophytic fungi that do not colonize insects and cause disease, may be used as a natural insect control as well as an effective insect control if they are artificially inoculated into plants and display characteristics against the pests. Unfortunately, works concerning this promising line of research are scarce and, when were conduced, involved a temperate climate system, as usual, where the pest control problem is not so urging as in plants. Clay (1989), in a review on the potential of insect control by endophytic fungi, stressed that insect biocontrol may be improved by the development of artificial inoculation techniques, as those developed by Latch and Christensen (1988). As endophytic fungi, notably members of the genus *Acremonium*, are able to control some insects-pests, it is important to know if they can be inoculated in endophytefree plants and, if they can transmit to the host the capacity to resist to certain pests. That was done with success by Koga *et al.* (1997), by infecting *F. arundinacea* and *L. perenne* seeds with the endophytic fungus *Acremonium* and, as a result, obtained plants resistant to the bluegrass webworm *P. teterrella*. It was observed that not only the inoculation worked well, but also the mutant fungus was kept in competition with wild type ones. These results demonstrated that inoculation of valuable strains for biological control will not only be used with success but, modified microorganisms, once inoculated into a host, will be able to coexist and even overcome wild type strains of the same species. An important point, at least in grasses, resides in the fact that several fungi species may be transmitted by seeds,where the biocontrol becomes able to be passed to the next.

Effects on the host plant physiology with impact on insect control

In certain plants, toxin production is not solely a fungal function. There are fungus-plant interaction factors acting on this production and toxins may be produced and dissipated throughout the host tissues. Evidently, it may result in insect control even if the endophyte is not present in the attacked sites. The development and nutrition of the moth *Plutella xylostella* larvae were studied in brassicas. Larvae were affected by the ingestion of leaves, before the endophytic fungus *Acremonium alternatum* reached these leaves. There were also differences in feed efficiency of males and females. Contrasting with their utility in insect control, toxin and mycotoxin produced by endophytic fungi may cause problems to cattle feeding on colonized plants. In *L. perenne* infected by *N. lolii*, peramine production plays a major role in controlling the Argentine stem weevil *L. bonariensis*. It was verified that with plant ageing, the amount of peramine decreases in leaves and reaches the lower levels during the inflorescence phase in eight fungus plant interactions (Ball *et al.* 1997a). Other seemingly simple interactions may occur like the increase of stroma induced by the endophytic fungus *E. typhina* in host plants, resulting in an increase in stroma-mediated transpiration and consecutively reduction in herbivorous insect attacks (White *et al.* 1993).

Molecular biology improved pathogenic properties of endophytes

The recombinant DNA technology has been applied as a tool to improve endophytic microorganisms, aiming to the introduction of new characteristics of agronomic interests as biological control of pests. Probably, Fahey (1991) described the first work directed at the introduction of a heterologous gene in an endophytic microorganism with the purpose of insect control. As a member of the biotechnological company Crop Genetics International, described the major steps in the construction of an endophytic bacterium with the purpose of insect control. This was achieved through the of an insecticidal toxin in the host plant. The genetically modified microorganism is able to secrete toxin inside the plant, protecting it against attacks of target insects. The author described several advantages of inoculating this bacterium into corn plants as a way of protecting it against insects: the product requires only one application in seeds or aspersion over young plants; there is no need for a large amount of the product because the bacterium multiplies after inoculation; the genetically modified bacterium stays restricted to the inner parts of the plant and thus, there is no dissemination to other plants; the process does not yield toxic compounds; this and other similar products require a shorter time to be technologically developed because it is easier to modify a microorganism than a plant; the modified microorganism is not transmitted to progeny seed of inoculated plants and therefore, from a commercial point of view, it must be acquired constantly; the process has wide applicability because it can be used for other plant species; bacteria multiplication is high inside the plant, the endophytic bacteria may be found inside hosts at high densities. Consequently, false positive results may be observed in plant transformation protocols involving, for instance, enzymatic activity detection. This was the case of Tor *et al.* (1992), while transforming plants of the genus *Discorea* with a vector expressing *Gus* (b - glucuronidase). Although, *Gus* activity was observed in putative plant transformants, this activity was due to endophytic bacteria inhabiting the plant material. The engineered bacterium exhibited insecticidal activity in artificial diets but not *in planta*. Lampel *et al.* (1994) used an improved integrative vector that, although showed some instability, resulted in toxin production *in planta* after all.These transformed bacteria were then inoculated in corn crops and showed to reduce damages caused by the European corn borer *Ostrinia nubilalis* (Tomasino *et al.* 1995). In a review on endophytic fungi from the genus *Acremonium*, Van-Heeswijck and McDonald (1992) launched the idea of using engineered endophytic fungi in the control of insects and diseases affecting *L. perenne*. Murray *et al.* (1992) introduced into a lolitrem B-deficient strain of *Acremonium* (designated 187B) a b –glucuronidase (*Gus*) gene. The transformation protocol yielded 700-800 transformants/mg DNA and transformants were successively introduced into *Lolium* where *Gus* activity was observed. In a similar manner, Tsai *et al.* (1992) developed a transformation system for *A. coenophialum*. Several genes from endophytic fungi and related to toxin production are now being cloned and studied in depth. Wang *et al.* (1999) cloned a gene coding for a DMAT Synthase (dimethyl tryptophane synthase) that is responsible for the first step in the synthesis of ergot by the fungus *Claviceps purpurea*. Genes related to the latter were identified in the endophytic fungi *Balansia obtecta* and *Neotyphodium* spp., known to produce, respectively, ergobalansine and ergovaline. Tudzynski *et al.* (1999) also cloned a gene (DMATS) of *C. purpurea* involved in the ergot synthetic pathway *in planta*. Young *et al.* (1999) found in *Epichloë* a cluster containing genes for the synthesis of mycotoxins like paxiline and lolitrem B. In our laboratory in the Escola Superior de Agricultura " Luiz de Queiroz", Universidade de São Paulo at Piracicaba, for some years we have been developing studies with endophytic microorganisms from banana, corn, citric plants, among others. Efficient transformation systems have been established for some of these endophytic microorganisms as well as protocols for reintroducing these microorganisms into plants.

CONCLUSION

Endophytic microorganisms were studied in more details only from the 80's onwards. Soon after that, they started to be recognized as being of great importance for the hosts, protecting the plants against pests, including among others, insects, nematodes and plant pathogenic fungi and bacteria. They also cause physiological modifications in their hosts, such as making them more resistant to hydric stress. The role of endophyes protecting plants against insects and diseases has been quite well studied. However, the research is based mainly on endophytes from hosts and, besides, the work has been concentrated in some genera of grasses. Apart from isolated studies, only more recently, efforts are being directed to endophytes from tropical plant hosts. This is a broad field of investigation that is almost entirely open to new findings. The results presented in this review show that, as expected, great diversity has been found among endophytes isolated from tropical hosts. They must, of course, play important roles as, for instance, protecting plants against pests and environmental stresses, as already found in temperate isolates of endophytes. Thus, it is expected that new ways of interactions between endophytes and their hosts will be certainly found. It is also expected that new biological agents produced by endophytes will be discovered with the increase of studies focusing on these fungi.

REFERENCES

Ahmad S Govindarajan S Funk CR and Johnson- Cicalese JM 1985 Fatality of house crickets on perennial ryegrass infected with a fungal endophyte *Entomologia Experimentalis et Applicata* **39**:183-190

Ahmad S Johnson-Cicalese JM Dickson WK and Funk CR 1986 Endophyte-enhanced resistance in perennial ryegrass to the bluegrass billbug *Sphenophorus parvulus Entomologia Experimentalis et Applicata* **41**:3-10

Arechavaleta M Bacon CW Hoveland CS and Radclife DE 1989 Effects of tall fescue endophyte on plant response to environmental stress *Agronomy Journal* **81**:83-90

Bacon CW and Hills NS 1996 Symptomless grass endophytes: products of coevolucionary symbioses and their role in the ecological adaptation of grasses In: Endophytic fungi in grasses and woody plants Redlin SC and Carris LM (edts) American Phytopathologycal Society Press St Paul pp 155-178

Ball OJP Barker GM Prestidge RA and Lauren DR 1997a Distribution and accumulation of the alkaloid peramine in *Neotyphodium lolli*-infected perennial ryegrass *Journal of Chemical Ecology* **23**:1419-1434

Ball OJP Miles CO and Prestidge RA 1997b Ergopeptide alkaloids and *Neotyphodium lolli*-mediated resistance in perennial ryegrass agains adult *Heteronynchus arator* (Coleoptera: Scarabaeidae) *Journal of Economic Entomology* **90**:1382-1391

Breen JP 1992 Temperature and seasonal effects on expression of *Acremonium* endophyte-enhanced resistance to *Schizaphis graminum* (Homoptera: Aphididae) *Environmental Entomology* **21**:68-74

Breen JP 1994 *Acremonium*-endophyte interactions with enhanced plant resistance to insects *Annual Review of Entomology* **39**:401-423

Bultman TL and Conard NJ 1998 Effects of endophytic fungus nutrient level and plant damage on performance of fall armyworm (Lepidoptera: Noctuidae) *Environmental Entomology* **27**:631-635

Bultman TL Borowicz KL Scneble RM Couldron TA and Bush LP 1997 Effect of a fungal endophyte on the growth and survival of two *Euplectrus* parasitoids *Oikos* **78**:170-176

Calhoun LA Findrlay JA Miller JD and Whitney NJ 1992 Metabolites toxic to spruce budworm from balsam fir needle endophytes *Mycological Research* **96**:281-286

Carroll G (1986) The biology of endophytism in plants with particular reference to woody perennials In: Microbiology of the Phylloplane Fokkema NJ and Van der Heavel J (edts) Cambridge University Press London UK pp 205-222

Carroll G 1988 Fungal endophytes in stems and leaves: from latent pathogens to mutualistic symbionts *Ecology* **69**:2-9

Clark CL Miller JD and Whitney NL 1989 Toxicity of conifer needle endophytes to spruce budworm *Mycological Research* **93**:508-512

Clay K 1988 Fungal endophytes of grasses A defensive mutualism between plants and fungi *Ecology* **69**:10-16

Clay K 1989a Fungal endophytes of grasses Their potential as biocontrol agents *Mycological Research* **92**:1- 12

Clay K 1989b Clavicipitaceous endophytes of grasses: their potential as biocontrol agents *Mycological Research* **92**:1-12

Clay K Marks S and Cheplick GP 1993 Effects of insect herbivory and fungal endophyte infection on competitive interactions among grasses *Ecology* **74**:1767- 1777

Clement SL Lester DG Wilson AD and Pike KS 1992 Behaviour and performance of *Diuraphis noxia* (Homoptera: Aphididae) on fungal endophyte-infected and uninfected perennial ryegrass *Journal of Economic Entomology* **85**:583-588

Clement SL Pike KS Kaiser WJ and Wilson AD 1990 Resistance of endophyte-infected plants of tall fescue and perennial ryegrass to the Russian wheat aphid (Homoptera: Aphidiae) *Journal of the Kansas Entomological Society* **63**:646-648

Davidson A W and Potter DA 1995 Response of plant-feeding predatory and soil-inhabiting invertebrates to *Acremonium* endophyte and nitrogen fertilization in tall fescue turf *Journal of Economic Entomology* **88**:367-379

Fahey JW Dimock MB Tomasino SF Taylor JM and Carlson PS 1991 Genetically engineered endophytes as biocontrol agents: A case study in industry In: Microbial Ecology of Leaves Springe Verlag New York pp 402-411

Findlay JA Buthelezi S Li GQ Seveck M and Miller JD 1997 Insect toxins from an endophytic fungus from wintergreen *Journal of Natural Products* **60**:1214-1215

Funk CR Halisky PM Johnson MC Siegel MR Stewart AV Ahmad S Hurley RH and Harvey IC 1983 An endophytic fungus and resistance to sod webworms: association in *Lolium perenne BioTechnology* **1**:189-191

Gaynor DL and Hunt WF 1983 The relationship between nitrogen supply endophytic fungus and Argentine stem weevil resistance in ryegrass Proceedings of the New Zealand Grassland Association **44**:257-263

Ju Y Sacalis JN and Still CC 1988 Bioactive flavonoids from endophyte-infected blue grass (*Poaampla*) *Journal of Agricultural and Food Chemistry* **46**:3785-3788

Kanda K Hirai Y Koga H and Hasegawa K 1994 Endophyte-enhanced resistance in perennial ryegrass and tall fescue to bluegrass webworm *Japanese Journal of Applied Entomology and Zoology* **38**:141-145

Kindler D Breen JP and Springer T 1990 Russian wheat aphid resistance in cool-season grasses *Journal of Economic Entomology* **84**:685-692

Lampell JS Canter GL Dimock MB Kelly JL Anderson JJ Uratani BB Foulke Jr JS and Turner JT 1994 Integrative cloning expression and stability of the *cryIA*(c) gene from *Bacillus thuringiensis* subsp *kurstaki* in a recombinant strain of *Clavibacter xyli* subsp *cynodontis Applied and Environmental Microbiology* **60**:501-508

Lasota JA Waldvogel MG and Shetlar DJ 1983 Fungus found in galls of *Adelges abietis* (L) (Homoptera: Adelgidae): identification within tree distribution and possible impact on insect survival *Environmental Entomology* **12**:245-246

Murray FR Latch GCM and Scott DB 1992 Surrogate transformation of perennial ryegrass *Lolium perenne* using genetically modified *Acremonium* endophyte *Molecular and General Genetics* **233**:1-9

Patterson CG Potter DA and Fannin FF 1992 Feeding deterrency of alkaloids from endophyte-infected grasses to Japanese beetle grubs *Entomology Experimental and Applied* **61**:285

Prestidge RA Zijpp S and Badan D 1984 Effects of Argentine stem weevil on pastures in Central Volcanic Plateau *New Zealand Journal of Experimental Agriculture* **12**:323-331

Richardson MD Cabrera RI Murphy JA and Zaurov DE 1999 Nitrogen form and endophyte-infection effects on growth nitrogen uptake and alkaloid content of Chewings fescue turfgrass *Journal of Plant Nutrition* **22**:67-79

Riedell WE Kieckhefer RE Petroski RJ and Powell RG 1991 Naturally-occurring and synthetic loline alkaloid derivatives: Insect feeding behaviour modification and toxicity *Journal of Entomological Science* **26**:122-129

Saha DC Johnson-Cicalese JM Halisky PM Heemstra MI and Funk CR 1987 Occurrence and significance of endophytic fungi in the fine fescues *Plant Disease* **71**:1021-1024

Sherwood-Pike M Stone JK and Carroll GC 1986 *Rhabdocline parkeri* a ubiquitous foliar endophyte of Douglas fir *Canadian Journal of Botany* **64**:1849-1855

Siegel MR Latch GCM Bush LP Fannin FF Rowan DD Tapper BA Bacon CW and Johnson MC 1990 Fungal endophyte-infected grasses: Alkaloid accumulation and aphid response *Journal of Chemical Ecology* **16**:3301-3316

Tomasino SF Leister RT Dimock MB Beach RM and Kelly JL 1995 Field performance of *Clavibacter xyli* subsp *cynodontis* expressing the insecticidal protein gene *cryIA* (c) of *Bacillus thuringiensis* against European corn borer in field corn *Biological Control* **5**:442-448

Tor M Mantell SH and Ainsworth C 1992 Endophytic bacteria expressing beta-glucuronidase cause false positives in transformation of *Dioscorea* species *Plant Cell Reports* **11**:452-456

Tsai HF Siegel MR and Schardl CL 1992 Transformation of *Acremonium coenophialum* a protective fungal symbiont of the grass *Festuca arundinacea Current Genetics* **22**:399-406

Tudzynski P Holter K Correia T Arntz C Grammell N and Keller U 1999 Genetics of alkaloid biosynthesis in *Claviceps purpurea*: evidence for a gene cluster *Fungal Genetics Newsletter* **46** (Supplement):140

Van-Heeswijck R and McDonald G 1992 *Acremonium* endophyte in perennial ryegrass and other pasture grasses in Australia and New Zealand *Australian Journal of Agriculture Research* **43**:1683-1709

Wang J Machado C Panaccione D and Schardl C 1999 Ergot alkaloid biosynthesis genes cloned from *Claviceps* and *Balansia Fungal Genetics Newsletter* **46** (Supplement):120

Webber J 1981 A natural control of Dutch elm disease *Nature London* **292**:449-451

White Jr JF Glenn A E and Chandler K F (1993) Endophyte-host associations in grasses XVIII-Moisture relations and insect herbivory of the emergent stromal leaf of *Epichloe Mycologia* **85**:195-202

Young C McMillan L and Scott B 1999 Molecular cloning of an indole-diterpenoid gene cluster from *Penicillium paxilii Fungal Genetics Newsletter* **46** (Supplement):121

9

DNA-DELIVERY METHODS TO RAISE TRANSGENICS

C P MALIK, SARITA BHURADIA AND AMAN VERMA

Genetic transformation occurs frequently in nature in prokaryotes. The transfer of genes from one organism to another is termed horizontal gene transfer (Richardson and Palmer, 2007). For example, bacteria can acquire virulence factors, as well as antibiotic resistance genes, which may lead to the breakdown of the efficacy of antibiotics. Horizontal gene transfers are rare in higher eukaryotes, but years ago scientists found that a pathogenic bacterium, *Agrobacterium*, could transfer genes from its genome to its plant hosts, where expression of the transferred genes caused crown gall disease (Chilton *et al.* 1977).

The development of *Agrobacterium*-mediated genetic transformation, and direct transformation by biolistics, *i.e.*, the high velocity delivery of DNA attached to metal particles, led to the first generation of transgenic plants and the rapid application of this technology to crop improvement.

GENETIC ENGINEERING AS A DRIVING FORCE FOR MODERN AGRICULTURE

Genetic engineering is a powerful tool for improving crop quality and productivity, and reducing information systems for biotechnology Plant Research labor and resource utilization of farming. For example, farmers saved up to an estimated 60% of costs for pest control by growing Bt (insect resistance) cotton in certain regions of the US in 1997, according to a USDA report (Price *et al.* 2003). The reduction of pesticide spray has many other advantages for both the environment and humans. Because of these and other benefits, the adoption of three primary GE crops (corn, cotton and soybean) for two traits, HT (herbicide tolerance) and Bt, has dramatically increased since the first commercial introduction in 1996. According to recent USDA survey the acreage of GE is shown in the Fig. 1 below.

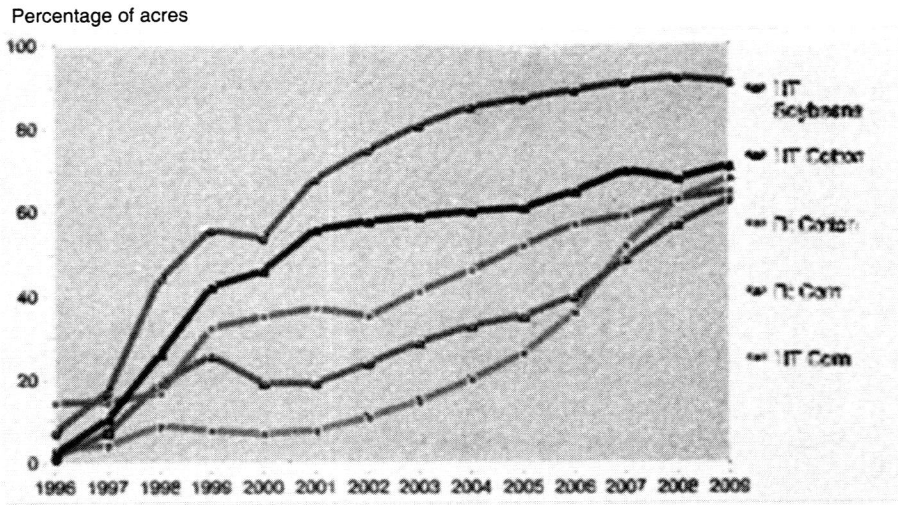

Data for each crop category include varieties with both HT and Bt (stacked) traits.
Sources: 1996-1999 data are from Fernandez-Cornajo and McBr'de (2002).

Fig. 1. Rapid growth in adoption of genetically engineered crops continues in the U.S.

Plant transformation is widely adopted as a technique to improve crop plant traits and to gain deep understanding how plants work. Successful plant transformation depends on the stable introduction of desirable transgene (s) into the genome of the plant. Several methods have been developed to accomplish this and many divergent crop plant species have been successfully transformed.

Two processes are involved to accomplish the genetic modification of plants and these comprise: the potential to transfer and integrate DNA into the genome of a host cell. The second process is the ability to regenerate fertile plants from the genetically transformed cell.

The first production of recombinant DNA molecule was accomplished in the early 1970's using restriction enzymes (Smith and Wilcox, 1970; Meselson and Yuan, 1968). Subsequently, the first stably transformed plants were reported in the early 1980's (Herrera-Estraella, 1983). Currently transgenic crops are increasingly becoming a dominant feature of the agricultural landscape of USA and other countries. In due course of time US Department of Agriculture animal and Plant Health Inspection Services permitted field trials of these engineered herbicide-tolerant varieties in the USA. With continued research transgenic plants have a pivotal role in crop improvement and are also being exploited in pharming industry (see Fig.1).

The first fertile transgenic monocot was developed through regeneration of transformed protoplast with naked DNA using electroporation or PEG techniques, including rice (Datt *et al.* 1990; Zhang *et al.* 1988; Zhang and Wu, 1988) and maize (Rhodes *et al.* 1988). For details refer to the reviews by Jones (2006) and Darbani *et al.* (2008).

Compared with traditional systems, plants have several advantages for the molecular pharming of pharmaceutuical proteins (Teli and Timko, 2004) and these are : low cost of production, rapid scalability, the absence of human pathogens and the ability to fold and assemble complex proteins accurately. Transgenic plants are widely used for large scale production of recombinant proteins like plantibodies and plantigenes.

As mentioned earlier, the genetic modification of plants depends on two main processes; first, the stable introduction of new genetic material into plant cells (transformation) and second, is utilization of tissue culture methods to regenerate transgenic plants from single transformed cell.

There are two types of gene delivery methods:

- Biological and
- Non-biological systems

Transgenic plant production process is a very complex and multistage procedure which involves three discrete phases:

- Delivery of exogenous DNA
- Stable integration of exogenous DNA into the genome of the host cells and
- Recovery of a viable transgenic plant

In the following we shall discuss the two systems:

BIOLOGICAL GENE TRANSFER

Agrobacterium-mediated transformation:

The first record of successful dicots transformation utilized oncogenic and disarmed strains of *Agrobacterium tumefaciens* and a range of explants types (Gasser and Fraley, 1989; Klee *et al.* 1987; Wordragen, and Dons, 1992). In the 1970's the rational gene transfer of exogenous DNA into crops using *A. tumefaciens* was revolutionary. However, regeneration for protoplast proved more difficult for many crops species and alternative more easily regenerable explants were developed. For instance, different explants were used in various species *e.g.* in tomato leaf discs (McCormick *et al.* 1986), in soybean cotyledon nodes (Hinchee *et al.* 1988) and immature cotyledons (Parrott *et al.* 1989) .

Agrobacterium was the logical and natural transformation candidate to consider since it naturally transfers DNA (T-DNA) located on the tumor inducing (Ti) plasmid into the nucleus of host plant cells and stably incorporated DNA into the plant genome (Chilton *et al.* 1977). In transgenic plant production methods the *Agrobacterium*-mediated transformation technique is the most widely used and powerful technique. However, many aspects remain to be unraveled *e.g.* genotype independent transformation of many economically important crop and forest species (Stanton, 2003; DeLa Riva *et al.* 1998). Through this method it is feasible to introduce large segments of DNA with minimal rearrangement and with fewer copies of inserted transgenes at high efficiency and with low cost (Gelvin, 2003; Gheysen *et al.* 1998; Hansen and Wright, 1999; Jones, 2006).

The development of *Agrobacterium* for plant transformation required the removal of oncogenic functions to generate disarmed strains and modification to permit the insertion of foreign DNA between the border sequences and to reduce the large size of the native Ti plasmid (which in *Agrobacterium* strain C-59 is 214233 bp (Goodner, *et al.* 2001). Two approaches have been used: one involves cis-integration of transgenes via homologous recombination or co-integration and in the other involves plant genetic engineering.

Agrobacterium-mediated transformations remain popular and the most effective among the most dicotyledons plants where *Agrobacterium* is naturally infectious.

Tissue culture/*in vitro* and in plants transformations: Transformation targets can be classified into two categories:

- Tissue culture and
- *in planta* methods

Tissue culture method utilizes the totipotency and plasticity of plant cells. This method depends on two principle routes by which plants can be recovered. These are somatic embryogenesis which is an asexual propagation process. Here somatic cells differentiate into embryos-like structures with shoot and root meristems. The other route comprises organogenesis in which the ability of some plant tissues *e.g.* hypocotyls, cotyledons, leaf bases or callus derived from them get reorganized into shoot meristems which can subsequently be rooted to generate complete plant (s). *In planta* method or germ line transformation methods depend on the ability to introduce naked DNA or T-DNA into gametes at the time of fertilization. In this way tissue culture is avoided. *Arabidopsis thaliana* can be transformed by several in plants methods including vacuum infiltration (Alough and Bent, 1998) transformation of germinating seeds (Feldmann and Marks, 1987) and floral dipping (Alough and Bent, 1998).

However, recently *Agrobacterium* inoculation of germinating seeds of rice has brought about transformation efficiency higher than 40%(Supertova *et al.* 2005) but ranged from 4.7 to 70% for the flower infiltration method and from 2.9 to 27.6% for the seedling infiltration method. For inoculation of manually impossible infection by viruses a method was developed called agro inoculations (Grimsley, 1990). The agro inoculation method invariably enhanced infection efficiency even when manual inoculation is possible (Hayes, *et al.* 1988; Biddens *et al.* 1989; Lesser *et al.* 1992). The optimization of agro infection –plant interaction is crucial for efficient transformation. Besides many other factors (the type of explants) are also important and they must be suitable to permit the recovery of whole transgenic plant (De la Riva *et al.* 1998; Frame *et al.* 2002; Zhang *et al.* 2003). The fundamental limitations of *Agrobacterium* based system led to the reduced ability of them to transfer DNA into monocots cells. Moreover, this system relies completely on the functioning of *vir*-proteins which target only the nucleic genome and not the organelle genome.

Viral-based transformation

Viral based transformation systems provide very high expression temporarily in plant cells. Potato virus X (Ruiz *et al.* 1998), barley stripe mosaic virus (Holzberg *et al.* 2002) and gemni virus vectors (Kjemtrup *et al.* 1998; Turnage et al,., 2002) are some of plant viral mediated transformants. They could be viral RNA or cDNA which can be used via dicot inoculation. This has proven to be the most efficient way of introducing cDNA-derived viral RNA into plants (see Jia *et al.* 2003 and references there in).Viral based transformation provide rapid and high level expression and this is the chief benefit of this technique. The main disadvantage of this technique is that they have less infectivity using average or large length transgene (Porta and Lomonossoff, 2002 Marillonnet *et al.* 2005).Other disadvantages are- large number of integrated transgene copies, chromosomal rearrangement, appearance of disease symptoms and low frequency of stable transformations.

Non-Biological Transformation Methods

Though *Agrobacterium* based transformations are preferred for most plant species there are some non-biological (NBM) based or direct gene transfer methods used chemically or physically for DNA uptake by the protoplast, intact cells or even whole plant. The NBM are potentially suitable for all species and all plants materials. They also do not require vector systems dependence. In the following we shall discuss some of the widely used NBM:

Particle bombardment/biolistic Method

The bombardment method was first described in 1987 for the production of transgenic (Sanford *et al.* 1987). Subsequently, the method has been found to be more useful for the transformation of recalcitrant cereals. A variation in the micro projectile transformation is an electric discharge Particle Acceleration Device (DPAD). Gene constructs for ballistic can be in the form of circular or linear plasmids or a linear expression cassette. Embryogenic cell cultures are likely the best explant to use for ballistic transformation because they can be spread out as uniform targets of cells and also they have high recovery potential (Kikkert *et al.* 2004). .Mannitol or sorbitol can be also effective as osmoticum in bombardment medium as they cause higher rates of stable transform ants for all suspension cultured cells (Kikkert *et al.* 2004). Particle bombardment has emerged as a reproducible method for rice transformation, in commercially important conifers species (*Picea glauca*), which was achieved via embryogenesis callus tissue as explants (Ellis *et al.* 1993), larch (Klimaszewska *et al.*1997) as well as *Pinus radiata* (Walters *et al.* 1998) and loblolly pines (Connett *et al.* 2002).

There are several **advantages** of this methodology compared with alternate propulsion technology and these have been discussed by McCabe and Christou, 1993, Darbani *et al.* 2008.

- The range of species and genotypes which can be engineered.

- High transformation frequencies.
- Elimination of cell death following hypersensitive responses to agro bacterium (Perl *et al.* 1996).
- No need to kill Agro bacterium after transformation.
- The use of linear expression cassettes called clean gene technology eliminates the possibility of plasmid backbone integration into the target (Fu *et al.* 2000).

Disadvantages

- The transformation efficiency might be lower than that with *Agrobacterium*
- It is more costly
- Intracellular targets are random and DNA is not protected.
- High frequency for complex integration pattern and multiple copy insertions that cause gene silencing and variation of transgene expression (Dai *et al.* 2001; Darbani *et al.* 2008). Efforts to reduce the incidence of recombination and reduction in the amount of DNA bombarded in each cell have led to the development of 'agrolistics'. This was developed to enhance efficiency of ballistics and yield simple integration patterns (Taylor and Fauquest, 2002). Agrolistics is a refinement to micro particle bombardment technology in which *vir* gene are co- bombarded.

Electrotransfection

Electroporation is the application of strong electric field pulses to cells and tissues and is known to cause some type of structural rearrangement of the cell membrane resulting in a temporary increase in porosity and providing a local driving force for ionic and molecular transport through the pores. In vitro introduction of DNA into cells is now the most common application of electroporation. There are several physical factors which are shown to affect the electrotranfection efficiency and these are created transmembrane potential by imposing pulse electric field, extent of membrane permeation, duration of the permeated state, mode and duration of molecular flow. Global and local concentrations of DNA forms of DNA and tolerance of cells to membrane permeation and the heterogeneity of the cells population (Hui,1995; Wearer, 1995).

Electroporation has several advantages over ballistic: it does not require the expensive particle gun apparatus associated consumable supplies and licensing and has worked well for stable transformations experiments (Shewry *et al.* 1994.). The efficiency of electroporation is relatively high: 6.25% for embryos and 54.6% for callus clusters, which is fully comparable with the eat results obtained for this species after micro bombardment (Deshayes *et al.* 1985). Despite apparent advantages of this technique, it is not used very often because of irreproducible results (sometimes!) and due to non-mendelian segregation of progeny. On an average this technique gives about 55% survival rate which up to 57% of the survivors expressed a marker gene (Songstad *et al.* 1995).

Silicon carbide fibers: This method is one of the recently developed methods to deliver DNA to plants. Physical and chemical characteristics 0f silicon carbide make them capable of penetrating the cells without killing them. There are several examples of SCMT success including maize (Kappler *et al.* 1992; Wang *et al.* 1995; Petalino *et al.* 2000), rice (Komatsu *et al.* 2006), wheat (Brisibe *et al.* 2000), tobacco (Kappler *et al.* 1990), and Agrostic stolonifera (Dalton *et al.* 1998). This system has several advantages and some are: rapid, inexpensive, easy to set up and effective on wide variety of cell types.

Among the disadvantages the main are: low rate of transformations,low efficiency, cell damage, inhalation of fibers as health hazards (Komalsu *et al.* 2006); Wang *et al.* 1995; Songstad *et al.* 1995). Liposome mediated transfection:

A derivation of PEG-mediated transfection is the liposome mediated transformations technique. Cationic liposome are positively charged lipids and are increasingly used for DNA uptake due to their favorable interaction with negatively charged DNA and cell membranes. In this approach foreign DNA must be encapsulated in a spherical lipid bilayer termed a liposome to prepare lipoplexes (Gad *et al.* 1990). After endocytosis (Fukunaga *et al.* 1983) the DNA is free to recombine and integrate into the host genome. Successful transfection based on the system was reported for tobacco (Dekeyser *et al.* 1990), wheat (Zhu *et al.* 1993 and potato Sawahel, 2002). The advantages of this method are that it is relatively non-toxic (Anonelli and Stadler, 1989), and is very simple to perform with readily available chemical reagents. This method is highly reproducible and efficient and requires no sophisticated apparatus (Antonelli and Stadler, 1990; Felgner *et al.* 1987). Wave and beam mediated transfection: Ultrasound for transfection has been widely used in animals cells and tissues. In this technique explants are suspended in a few milliliters of sonication medium in a microcentrifuge tube. Plamid DNA (and possibly carrier DNA) is then added and after rapid mixing the samples are ready for sonication. The cells are finally transferred to fresh growth medium, In this step, sound frequency and exposure time are determined for maximal uptake and efficiency (Lin *et al.* 2005). Ultrasound treatment increases membrane permeability (Bommannan *et al.* 1992) thereby felicitating the entrance of macromolecules into cells for transformation (Wyber *et al.* 1997). Stable transformations of tobacco by leaf pieces sonication was achieved via 1500 to 2000 fold longer time ultrasound treatment compared with protoplast sonication (Zhang *et al.* 1991).Another instance for intact tissue sonication based transformation is reported in potato tube discs subjected to ultrasonication (Scwahel, 1996). Sonication-assisted *Agrobacterium* mediated transformation (SAAT) is a new techno logy and the method involves subjecting the plant tissue to short periods of ultrasound in the presence of *Agrobacterium*. Trick and Finer (1993) reported that, in all tissues tested, the SAAT treatment greatly enhanced the level of transient expression. SAAT could be efficiently used for transformation of woody trees especially eucalyptus sp. (Monica *et al.* 2004). The method was newly developed and required further assessing for both of the different experimental conditions and plant species.

Injection based method: Microinjection is one of the most effective techniques of transforming animal cells and has been used for the transformation of plant cell as well (Banks and Evans, 1976). A pivotal feature of this technique is the use of low melting point (LMP) agarose both for holding protoplasts during microinjection and for their subsequent culture (Harwood and Davies, 1990). Several plant species such as tobacco (Schnorf *et al.* 1991), Petunia (Griesbach, 1987), oilseed rape (Neuhaus *et al.* 1987)and barley (Holm *et al.* 2000) have been transformed using microinjections. The injection of inheritable materials using a hypodermic syringe is called macroinjection. This is an approach to the delivery of exogenous DNA that could circumvent the expenses, time and genome stress associated with the transformation of cells in culture and subsequent plant regeneration. The technique has many advantages *e.g.* it is very precise from the delivery view point, is capable for the transformation of any protoplast or single cell system and has extremely high transformation efficiency. The chief disadvantage of this technique is the likelihood for the production of chimera plants with only a part of the plant having transformed. However, from this chimeric plant, transformed plants of single cell can be subsequently obtained. To overcome these problems pollen tube pathway (PTP) utilizing the normal fertilization cycle was developed to eliminate the regeneration phase and in this approach the stigma ia cut off and a drop of DNA solution is applied to the cut end of the style of recently pollinated plant florets. This procedure was used by Luo and Wa (1988) for the first time in rice. For more details a reference may be made to a review by Malik and Thind (1993). The procedure is extremely slow and requires expensive equipment and moreover it is very tedious. Transgene Integration and Gene targeting:

Molecular analyses of integration sites resulting from integrated DGT suggests that transgenes insert via double stranded illegitimate recombination, utilizing the plant's own DNA repair mechanism at a single cor sometimes more than one locus. The locus may contain one or more/multiple co[pies of the trangenes which may have undergone rearrangements and /or many have generated short length of "filler" DNA homologous to flanking plant genome DNA (Kohli *et al.* 1998; Suitashev *et al.* 2000; 2002).The processing transfer and integration of T-DNA into plant chromosomal DNA have been studied, both biochemically and in *Agrobacterium* strains containing mutant forms of the vir, chv, psc and Att alleles (for detailed reviews pl see Christie, 1997; Ward *et al.* 2002; Zupan *et al.* 1998; 2000). While the precise mechanism of T-DNA integration remains unclear, it is likely that DNA in the T-complex is made double-stranded just prior to integration *via* non-homologous end joining. The conventional way of overcoming the problem of transgene rearrangements high copy number or unintentional disruption of native genes is to generate a large number of lines and screen for single-copy events. However this unpredictability is a major concern for opponents of GM technologies, and gene targeting, by homologous recombination an alternative mofre precise method of genetic manipulation. It is commonly used in m ice in prokaryotes in the nuclear genomes of simple plants such as moss and the chloroplast genome (Capecchi 2001;

Evans *et al.* 2001; Smithies, 2001) but appears to operate at low frequency in higher plants. In over four million *Arabidopsis* plants transformed to induce two simultaneous mutations, only one was identified as a true gene targeting event without ectopic T-DNA insertions (Hanin *et al.* 2001). A more encouraging result was reported by Terada *et al.* (2002) who obtained sex rice plants in which the waxy gene had been disrupted by true homologous recombination with a frequency of 6.5 x 10^{-4}. With further development gene targeting technologies could provide a means through which any gene could be mutated and reintroduced into its original chromosomal location.

BENIGN METHODS OF SELECTION AND REMOVAL OF MARKER GENES:

Selectable marker genes are used routinely for research purposes, enabling highly efficient DNA cloning procedures in *E.coli,* yeast and plant transformation. However, perceived risks of horizontal and vertical gene transfer have made the use of such selectable genes undesirable especially where field trials are proposed and efforts have been made to develop benign selection systems or to reduce the dependence on selectable markers genes in the transformation process. The most widely adopted benign selection system utilizes the manA gene encoding phosphomannose isomerase (PM1) (Syngenta) which converts the predominant carbon source available to the plant, mannose-6-phosphate to fructose-6-phosphate for respiration (Joersbo, 2001; Joersbo *et al.* 1999). Not only are the untransformed cells deprived of a carbon source but also the unutilized mannose-6-phosphate accumulates and has additional negative effects including inhibition of glycolysis possibly due to phosphate starvation. PM1 selection method has been shown to be an effective selection system for crop species including wheat and maize (Negotto *et al.* 2000; Reed *et al.* 2001; Wang *et al.* 2001) and pearl millet (O'Kennedy *et al.* 2004).

In a small proportion of lines the co-bombardment of trait and marker genes on separate plasmids generates integrations into unlinked loci and the potential to identify progeny individuals that are null for the marker gene through segregation away from the trait gene. However, even in lines that have lost the plant selectable plasmids by segregation the bacterial selectable marker, origin of replication and plasmid by segregation, the bacterial selectable marker, origin of replication and plasmid backbone linked to the trait gene remain in the transgenic plant. In an attempt to overcome this, Fu *et al.* (2000) used DNA fragments comprising only the transgene expression cassette to transform rice biolistically. They found that, not only was the vector backbone eliminated from the plant line but also the proportion of low copy number structurally simple transgenic loci were enhanced. Purifying clean DNA fragment containing only the sequences necessary for transgene expression is not a trivial task and *Agrobacterium* T-DNAs should be inherently cleaned because in an ideal model, only the sequences delineated by the left and right borders are transferred.

TABLE 1 : Selected reports detailing the explant and A. tumefaciens strain/plasmid used in A. tumefaciens transformation of rice, maize, wheat and barley, PCE, pre-cultured immature embryos, EC, embryogenic callus cultures, E, fresh immature embryos.

Variety (S—Spring) (W—winter)	*Explant*	*Agrobacterium strain (vector)*	*Transformation Frequency (%)*	*Plant Selection*	*No. of plants reported*	*Ref.*
Wheat						
Bobwhite (S)	PCIE EC	C58 pMON18365	1.4-4.3	G418	>100	(Cheng *et al.* 1997)
Fielder (S)	PCIE	AGL0 pBGX1	1.8	GFP, Timentin, Bialaphos	4	(Weir *et al.* 2001)
Florida (W)	IE	AGL1 pAL154/156	0.3-3.3	PPT (c-phosphinothricin)	39	(Wu *et al.* 2003)
Cadenza (S)	IE	AGL1 pAL154/156	2.5	PPT (c-phosphinothricin)	5	(Wu *et al.* 2003)
Ceery-5 (S)	EC	LBA4404 pHK21	1.2-3.9	Glufosinate ammonium	17	(Khanna and Daggard, 2003)
Bobwhite (S)	PCIE, EC	C58 pMON18365	4.4	Glyphosate	3354	(Hu *et al.* 2003)
Bobwhite (S)	PCIE, EC	C58 pMON18365	4.8-19	Paromomcyin Glyphosate	154	(Cheng *et al.* 2003)
Bobwhite (S)	PCIE	C58 pPTN155	0.5-1.5	G418	13	(Haliloglu and Baenziger, 2003)
Barley						
Golden Promise (S)	IE	AGL1 pDM805	4.2	Bialaphos	5.4	(Tingay *et al.* 1997)
Golden Promise (S)	IE	AGL1 pBGXYNR: pBHXYNR	6.0	Bialaphos	24	(Patel *et al.* 2000)
Golden Promise (S)	IE	AGL1; AGL0 pWBVec82b	2-12	Hygromycin	63	(Mathews *et al.* 2001)
Schooner (S)	EC	AGL0; AGL1; LBA4404	0.5-2.9	Hygromycin; Biolaphos	19	(Wang *et al.* 2001)

		pTO134; pHPAVpol; pB2Pol				
Golden Promise (S)	PCIE	AGLO pBU-B3.5S.IG	1.7-6.3	Bialaphos	42	(Trifonova, Madsen and Olesen, 2001)
Golden Promise (S)	IE	AGLO pYF133	3.5	Hygromycin GFP	11	(Fang. Akula and Altpeter, 2002)
Golden Promise (S)	IE	H228 pNRG040	N/A	Bialaphos	42	(Horvath *et al.* 2003)
Golden Promise; Schooner; Chebec and Sloop (all S)	IE	AGL1 pWBVecB; pVecB-GFP; pVecB-Gusl	0.6-12.0	Hygromycin; GFP; GUS	34	(Murray *et al.* 2004)
Maize						
Funk's G90	Shoot apices	EHA1 TiBO542; pGUS3	N/D	Kanamycin; Carbenicillin	6	(Gould *et al.* 1991)
A118 and others	BC, IE	LBA4404 pSB131; pTOK233	5-30	PPT; Bialaphos	>100	(Ishida *et al.* 1996)
A118	IE	LBA4404 pNOV117	0.7-32	Mannose	>50	(Negrotto *et al.* 2000)
Hi II	IE	LBA4404 pSB11 Ubi bar/35SGUS	40	Bialaphos	>500	(Zhao *et al.* 2002)
Hi II	IE	EHA101 pTF102	5.5	Bialaphos	50	(Frame *et al.* 2002)
Hi II	IE	LBA4404 p108-p111, based on pSB11	0.50-25	Bialaphos	>100	(Gordon-Kamm *et al.* 2002)
A118, Hi II and hybrids	IE	LBA4404 pWCO38; pWCO39	N/D	Butafenecil; mannose	>2500	(Li *et al.* 2003)

Delivery method		*Transformation efficiency*	*Rang of transformable plant species*	*Tissue culture*	*Type of explant*	*Eqiupments*	*Others*
Agrobacterium-based method		High and stable	Many species, specially dicotyledonous	With and without tissue culture phase	Different intact cells, tissues or whole plant	–	Possibility of agroinfection, combination with sonication and biolistic methods and transgene size up to 150 Kb
Viral-based method		High and transient	Virus-host specific limitation	Without tissue culture phase	In-planta innoculation	–	Rapid, efficient PTGS, inducible expression and with mosaic status
Bombardment Biolistics based methods		High	Unrestricted	With and without tissue culture phase	Intact tissues or microspores	Very expensive apparatus	Efficient for viral infection complex integration patterns, without specialized vectors and backbone-free integration and transformation of YAC with insert up to 150 kb
	Agrolistic	High	Unrestricted	With and without tissue culture phase	Different intact explants or whole plant	Very expensive apparatus	Clean and precisely integration with reduced degraded transgene events
Electro-transfection	Electro-portation	Low to high	Unrestricted	With and without tissue culture phase	Protoplasts, meristens or pollen grains	+	Fast, simple and inexpensive in contrast with biolistics
	Electro-phoresis	Moderate	Unrestricted	Without tissue culture phase	Intact tissue on whole plant	–	Rapid and simple but yields shimeric
Lipofection		Low	Recoverable	With tissue	Protoplasts	–	High efficiency with combination of

			species from protoplast	culture phase			PEG based method, simple, non-toxic and positive correlation between efficiency and lipoplex size and highly reproducible
Silicon carbide mediated		Low to high	Unrestricted	With tissue culture phase	Variety of cell types	–	Rapid, inexpensive and easy to set-up
Injection based methods	Micro injection	High	Recoverable species from protoplast	With tissue culture phase	Protoplasts	Expensive micro-manipulator	Very slow, precise, single cell targeting possibility, requires high skill, the chimeric nature of transgenic plants and ability of whole chromoseome transformation
	Micro-injection PTP*	Low	Plants with sexual reproduction	Without tissue culture phase	Cametes	–	Rapid and simple
	Others	Low	Limited (with few species)	Without tissue culture phase	Immature embryos or meristems	–	Production of chimeric plants and damaging of cells
Wave or beam mediated transformation	Sonoporation	Low	Unrestricted	With and without tissue culture phase	Protoplast, cells, tissues and seedings	+	Effective to transfect by virus particles and able to increase the *Agrobacterium* based transformation efficiency
	Laser mediated	Low	Unrestricted	With tissue culture phase	Variety of cell types	+	Rapid and simple
Desiccation based method		Low	Unrestricted	With tissue culture phase	Rehydrated embryos	–	Simple

* Pollen-tube pathway, +; Necessary, –; Unnecessary

Other approaches to marker gene elimination involve the use of site specific recombinases or transpoases to excise or relocate the marker gene for elimination by segregation. These methods have proved successful in model dicot species (see review by Ebinuma *et al.* 2001; Hohn *et al.* 2001) and have been successfully applied in rice (Hoa *et al.* 2002) and maize (Zhang *et al.* 2003).

In a radically new approach to the removal of foreign DNA it has been demonstrated that analogs of the *Agrobacteriumn* T-DNA border sequences exist in plants (so called P-DNA) and that they can function to delimit T-strand synthesis and DNA transfer during the transformation process (Rommens *et al.* 2004).

MINICHROMOSOMES: THE NEXT GENERATION TECHNOLOGY FOR PLANT

The next generation – engineered minichromosomes

Despite many successes, genetic engineering has many limitations

- The technology used to create stacked gene var is not efficient. When stacking genes in inbred lines, the two genes located on different chromosomes will segregate at a ratio of 1:2:1 following first a genetic cross, and then self-pollinate to make each homozygous. This implies that one-sixteenth of the progeny will maintain the two homozygous stacked transgenes in the next generation. Gene stacking or pyramiding is also widely used in conventional crop breeding programs to combine multiple characteristic traits.
- Another difficulty is linkage drag, *i.e.* reduction in fitness of a cvr due to deleterious genes introduced along with the beneficial gene during backcrossing. This may occur because genes closely linked to the desired genes or transgenes are usually difficult to recombine during the transfer from one line to another. Hence several generations of backcrossing is usually required to introduce a good character gene to an elite cvr without linkage drag. This problem has created a bottleneck that limits the advancement of plant genetic engineering technology from the first generation of GE crops, characterized as 'input traits', to the next generation, characterized as 'output traits' (Halpin, 2005).

Recently Yu and co workers (Yu W *et al.* 2007.) have described an engineered minichromosome system that could be used as a genetic engineering platform for the expression of an almost unlimited number of genes intended to be inherited together as an independent unit. This engineered minichromosome technology should remove the bottlenecks mentioned above, and possibly lead to the second generation of genetic engineered crops.

Chromosome engineering and minichromosomes

Minichromosomes have been produced in yeast and mammalian cells through either *de novo* construction using the minimum constituent parts of chromosomes or telomere-mediated chromosomal truncation of existing Chromosome (Farr. 1991; Harrington *et al.* 1997) (Fig. 2).

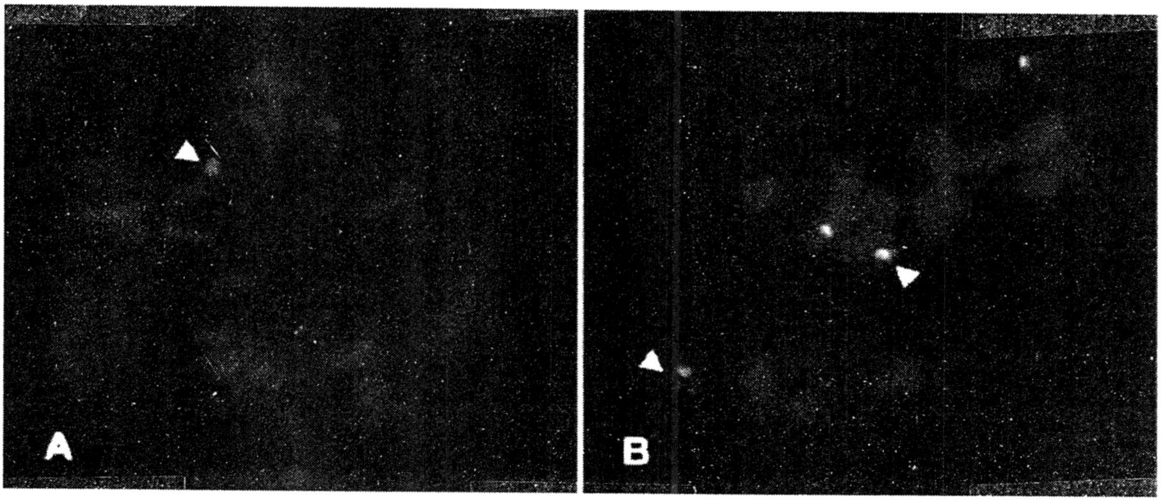

Fig. 2 Minichromosomes produced from maize B chromosome truncation. Arrows denote minichromosomes. B chromosome centromeres are labeled green with a B specific repeat probe. Transgenes carrying the truncating sequences and site specific recombination cassettes, as detected with the transgene probe, are red. Chromosomes are stained blue with DAPI. A) A minichromosome without the transgene (a copy of a stably integrated transgene is present on an A chromosome). B) Two minichromosomes with the truncating terminal transgenes (red) occurring in the same cell are shown, as well as two normal B chromosomes

However, these technologies for minichromosome construction were not successful in plants until recently when telomere-mediated chromosomal truncation in maize was reported, which causes chromosome fracture at the telomere sequence insertion site. An array consisting of 2.6 kb telomere repeats efficiently produced chromosomal truncations in maize. However, due to deficiencies in truncated chromosomes, recovery of chromosomes with large truncations is difficult to attain through the genetic transformation process. Moreover, genetic transmission of truncated chromosomes is unlikely; they are non-viable in the haploid gametophyte generation because they lack essential genes. However, the lethality of truncated chromosomes can be overcome either by using tetraploid materials in which the gametes will be diploid and the deficiency of truncated chromosomes would be compensated by additional copies of the homologs, or by using a non-essential chromosome, such as the maize B chromosome 5.

Yu *et al.* (2007) recovered a minichromosome formed by the truncation of chromosome 7 in a tetraploid plant. This minichromosome was transferred to a diploid background by repeated backcrossing and as stably maintained. By using the same set of constructs, they targeted the maize B chromosome with biolistic-mediated gene transformation. Truncated B chromosomes were recovered with much greater efficiency. The sizes of the mini B chromosomes ranged from very small to the size of the large B chromosome. These chromosomes from A and B chromosomes of maize were studied for their utility as utility as artificial chromosome for future genetic engineering in plants.

Attaching genes to minichromosomes

Minichromosomes generated by telomere truncation can have different configurations: those with transgenes and those without. This difference depends on the orientation of construct integration relative to the Centromere of the recipient chromosome, which is subsequently broken at the site of telomere integration. The transgene can segregate with either fragment of the broken chromosome. However, if the transgene is retained on the chromosomal fragment without a functional Centromere, which is essential for normal chromosome segregation during cell division, it will be lost after cell division. In this circumstance, minichromosomes lacking a transgene will be formed and could be selected if there are other transgenes in the same cell able to produce resistance to the selection agent in the transformation process (Fig. 2A). If the transgene is present on the fragment containing a centromere, it is then present on a minichromosome (Fig. 2B). In fact, both types of minichromosomes were recovered. Minichromosomes with attached transgenes were characterized in detail for mitotic and meiotic behaviors, transmission frequencies, gene expression, and the ability to use site-specific recombination.

All minichromosomes in the experiment were transmissible from generation to generation. They never paired with other chromosomes during meiosis, which minimized the chance of recombination with other normal chromosomes in the genome; thus all transgenes on the minichromosome can transmit as a unit. In addition, the research demonstrated that foreign genes could be expressed from maize B chromosomes, which otherwise are inert chromosomes with no essential genes (Fig. 3).

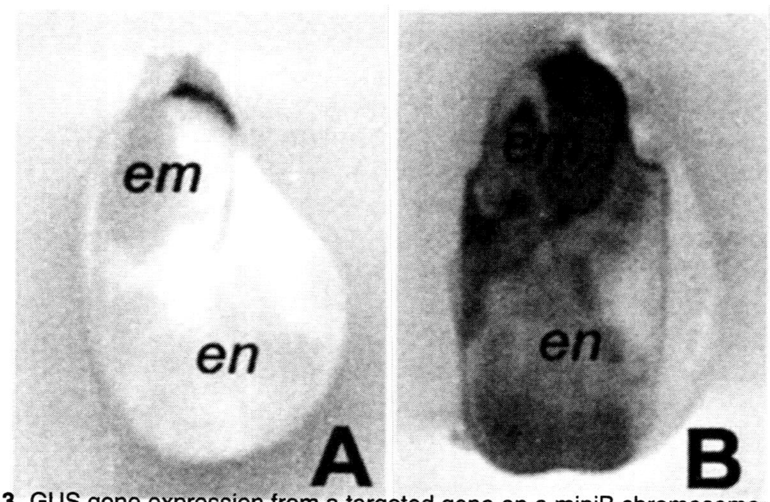

Fig. 3. GUS gene expression from a targeted gene on a miniB chromosome.

A) shows no GUS expression in the absence of the transgene. B) shows GUS gene expression in both embryo (em) and endosperm (en) of a mature kernel with a copy of the transgene on a miniB chromosome.

Minichromosomes from maize B chromosomes have other properties that make them exceptionally useful as artificial chromosome platforms. For example, mini-B chromosomes can accumulate to high copy numbers in the presence of normal B chromosomes, but remain stable in the absence of normal B chromosomes. This property might allow one to manage the copy number of the chromosome in order to increase gene expression from transgenes on the chromosome under appropriate circumstances.

Manipulation of genes on minichromosomes

Yu *et al.* (2007) also demonstrated that additional transgenes could be targeted to the minichromosome by site-specific recombination, which allowed the addition of subsequent genes. Yu *et al.*(2007) crossed a minichromosome containing a promoter less lox-DsRed gene, which encodes a red fluorescent protein, with another transgenic plant that expresses Cre, the recombinase for Cre/lox recombination, in a 35S promoter-lox-Cre cassette. Recombination occurred between the two chromosomes at the lox site, thus activating DsRed gene expression, and at the same time placing all genetic elements distal to the 35Slox- Cre gene onto the minichromosome5. The demonstration of the Cre/lox recombination system in the minichromosome facilitates further manipulation of foreign genes onto minichromosomes. By using other site-specific recombination systems (Yu W *et al.* 2006. Ow *et al.* 2007; Wright *et al.* 2005), Yu *et al.* predict they will be able to add, delete, or replace genes on minichromosomes in order to redesign existing engineered chromosome platforms. This new technology has numerous advantages over the current genetic engineering technology.

As noted above, an immediate application of minichromosome technology is to enable stacking of genes involved with herbicide tolerance and pest resistances. Future developments could facilitate any application that requires the inheritance of multiple foreign genes as a unit. One can now contemplate adding entire biochemical pathways to plants to confer new properties or to synthesize novel metabolites in mass quantities. With mini-B chromosomes, the quantity can be increased to maximize.

CONCLUSION

Plant genetic transformation applications and the desire for higher transformation efficiency have stimulated work on inventing and improving various methods. These applications are of specific benefit to molecular genetic studies, crop improvement and production of pharmaceuticals materials. *Agrobacterium* based methods are usually superior for many species including dicots and monocots. For some angiosperms and non-angiosperms biolistic is usually used.

Biolistic is by far the most widely used direct transformation procedure both experimentally in research and commercially. In addition, it has proven to be the most efficient technique.

In the past two decades several other methods have emerged with the view point that: more efficient method might emerge; the methods may turn out to be less expensive. Moreover, biolistic and *Agrobacterium* methods and patented, and securing a commercial license is trivial.

Chloroplast targeting is one of the advantages for direct transformation since high level recombinant protein expression for chloroplast targeting. This technique has also some drawbacks like low transformation frequency, prolonged selection pressure and green part dependence for transgene products.

In plants transformation methods are immensely attractive: however, this has proven to be effective and efficient in *Arabidopsis*.

Even though plant transformation can no longer be described as a new technology, it continues to evolve and leading to more facile and efficient transformation.

REFERENCES

Antonelli N and J Stadler 1989 Chemical methods for efficient direct gene transfer to maize cells: Treatment with polyethylene glycol or polybrene J Genet Breed **43**: 113-122

Briddon RW J Watts PG Markham and J Stanley 1989 The coat protection of beet curly top virus is essential for infectivity Virology **172** (2): 628-633

Chilton MD MH Drummond DJ Merio D Sciaky AL Montoya MP Gordon and EW Nester 1977 Stable incorporation of plasmid DNA into higher plant cells: The molecular basis of crown gall tumorigenesis Cell **11** (2): 263-271

Dai S P Zheng P Marmey S Zhang W Tian S Cher RN Beachy and C Fauquet 2001 Comparative analysis of transgeneic rice plants obtained Agrobacterium-mediated transformation and particle bombardment Mol Breed **7** (1): 25-33

Darbani B A Eimanifar CN Stewart and WN Camargo 2007 Methods to produce market-free transgenic plants Biotechnol J **2** (1): 83-90

Dekeyser RA B Claes RMU De Rycke ME Habets MC Van Montagu and AB Caplan 1990 Transient gene expressions in intact and organized rice tissues Plant Cell **2** (7): 591-601

De la Riva GA J González-Cabrera R Vázquez-Padrón and C Ayra-Pardo 1998 *Agrobacterium tumefaciens:* A natural tool for plant transformation Elect J Biotechnol **1** (3): 118-113

Deshayes A L Herrera-Estrella and M Caboche 1985 Liposome-mediated transformation of tobacco mesophyll protoplasts by an *Escherichia coli* plasmids EMBO J **4** (11): 2731-2737

Farr C et al 1991 Functional reintroduction of human telomeres into mammalian cells *Proc Nati Acad Sci USA* **88** 7006-10 *Genet* 15 345-55

Feldmann KA and MD Marks 1987 *Agrobacterium* mediated transformation of germinating seeds of *Arabidopsis thaliana*: A non-tissue culture approach Mol Gen Genet **208** (1): 1-9

Felgner P T Gadek M Holm R Roman HW Chan M Wenz JP Northrop GM Ringold and M Danielsen 1987 Lipofection: A highly efficient lipid-mediated-DNA transfection procedure Proc Natl Acad Sci **84** (21): 7413-7417

Frame BR H Shou RK Chikwamba ZI Zhang CI Xiang TM Fonger SE Pegg B Li DS Nettleton D Pei and K Wang 2002 *Agrobacterium tumefaciens*-mediated transformation of maize embryos using a standard binary vector system Plant Physiol **129** (1): 13-22

Griesbach RJ 1987 Chromosome-mediated transformation via microinjection Plant Sci **50** (1): 69-77

Grimsley NH 1990 Agroinfection Physiol Plant **79** (1): 147-153

Halpin C 2005 Gene stacking in transgenic plants - the challenge for 21st century plant biotechnology *Plant Biotechnol J* **3**: 141-55

Harwood WN and DR Davies 1990 Protoplast Microinjection Using Agarose Microdrops In: Method in Molecular Biology Pollard JW and JM Walker (Eds) Vol 6 The Human Press pp: 323-333

Herrera-Estrella L 1983 Transfer and expression of foreign genes in plants PhD Thesis Laboratory of Genetics Genetics University Belgium

Holm PB O Olsen M Schnorf H Brinch-Pederse and S Knudsen 2000 Transformation of barley by microinjection into isolated zygote protoplasts Transgenic Res **9** (1): 21-32

Holzberg S P Brosio C Gross and GP Pogue 2002 Barley stripe mosaic virus-induced gene silencing in a monocot plant J **30** (3): 315-327

Hui SW 1995 Effects of Pulse Length and Strength on Electroporation Efficiency In: Methods in Molecular Biology Plant Cell Electroporation and Electrofusion Protocols Nickoloff JA Vol 55 Humana Press Inc: Totowa NJ pp: 29-40

Jefferson RA Assaying chimeric genes in plants: The genes fusion system Plant Mol Biol Rep **5** (4): 387-405

Jones HD 2006 Advances in transformation technology in plant Biotechnology: Current and future applications of genetically modified crops John Wiley and Sons London (ed) NG Halford Pp 71-90

Kaeppler H DA Somers HW Rines and AF Cockburn 1992 Silicon carbide fiber-mediated stable transformation of plant cells Theor Applied Genet **84** (5-6): 560-566

Kikkert JR 1993 The Biolistic® PDS-100/He device Plant Cell Tissue Organ Culture 33: 221-226

Kikkert JR JR Vidal and BI Reish 2004 Stable Transformation of Plant Cells by Particle Bombardment/Biolistics In: Methods in Molecular Biology Transgenic Plants: Methods and Protocols Peña L (Ed) Vol 286 Human Press Inc: Totowa NJ pp: 61-78

Kjemtrup S KS Sampson CG Peele LV Nguyen MA Conkling WF Thompson and D Robertson 1998 Gene silencing from plant DNA carried by a geminivirus Plant J **14** (1): 91-100

Lesser RM V Ziegler-Graff A Reutenauer E Herrbach O Lemaire H Guilley K Richards and G Jonard 1992 Agroinfection as an alternative to insects for infecting plants with *Beet western yellows luteovirus* Proc Natl Acad Sci **89** (19): 9136-9140

Liu Y H Yang and H Sakanishi 2005 Ultrasound: Mechanical gene transfer into plant cells by sonoporation Biotechnol Adv wwwsciencedirectcom

Luo ZX and R Wa 1988 A simple method for the transformation of rice via pollen-tube pathway Plant Mol Biol Rep **6** (3):165-174

Marillonnet S C Thoeringer R Kandzia V Klimyuk and y Gleba 2005 Systemic *Agrobacterium tumefaciens*-mediated transfection of viral replicons for efficient transient expression in plants Natl Biotechnol **23** (6): 718-723

Meselson M and R Yuan 1968 DNA restriction enzyme from *E coli* Nature 217 (5134): 1110-114

Monica TV A Carlos and ER Gonzales 2004 Method for genetic transformation of woody trees European Patent EP1448777 2004 http://wwwfreepatents onlinecom/ EP1448777html

Neuhaus G G Spangeberg O Mittelsten-Scheid and HG Schweizer 1987 Transgenic rape seed plants obtained by microinjection of DNA into microscope derived embyoids Theor Applied Genet **75** (1): 30-36

Ow DW 2007 GM maize from site-specific recombination technology what next? *Curr Opin Biotechnol* **18** :115-20

Paszkowski J RD Shillito M Saul V Mandák T Hchn B Hohn and I Potrykus 1984 Direct gene transfer to plants EMBO J **3**: 2717-2722

Porta C and GP Lomonossoff 2002 Viruses as vectors for the expression of foreign sequences in plants Biotechnol Genet Eng Rev **19**: 245-291

Price GK et al 2003The size and distribution of marker benefits from adopting agricultural biotechnology *US Department of Agriculture*

Richardson AO & Palmer JD 2007 Horizontal gene transfer in plants *J Exp Bot* 58

Ruiz MT O Voinnet and DC Baulcombe 1998 Initiation and maintenance of virus-induced gene silencing Plant Cell **10** (6): 937-946

Sawahel W 1996 Ultrasound-mediated stable transformation of potato tuber discs Biotechnol Tech **10**: 812-824

Sawahel WA 2002 The production of transgenic potato plants expressing human U-interferon using lipofection-mediated transformation Cell Mol Biol Lett **7** (1): 19-29

Schaefer DJ 2002 A new moss genetic: Targeted mutagenesis in *Physcomitrella patens* Annu Rev Plant Biol **53**: 477-501

Shewry PR A tatham NG Halford JHA Barker U Hamnapel P Gallois M Thomas and M Kreis 1994 Opportunities for maniuplating the seed protein composition of wheat and bareley in order to improve qulity Transgenic Res **3** (1): 3-12

Smith HO and KW Wilcox 1970 A restriction enzyme from Hemophilus influenzae I Purification and general properties J Mol Biol **51** (2): 379-391

Songstad DD DA Somers and RJ Griesbach 1995 Advances in alterntive DNA delivery techniques Plant Cell Tissue Organ Culture **40** (1): 1-15

Stanton BG 2003 Agrobacterium-mediated plant transformation: The biology behind the gene-jockeying too Microbiol Mol Biol Rev **67** (1): 16-37

Taylor NJ and CM Fauquet 2002 Microparticle bombardment as a tool in plant science and agricultural biotechnology DNA Cell Biol **21** (12): 963-977

Teli NP and MP Timko 2004 Recent developments in the use of transgenic plants for the production of human therapeutics and biopharmaceuticals Plant Cell Tissue Organ Culture **79**: 125-145

Trick HN and JJ Finer 1997 SAAT: Sonication-assisted Agrobacterium-mediated transformation Transgenic Res **6** (5): 329-336

Turnage MA N Muangsan CG Peele and D Robertson 2002 Geminivirus-based vector for gene silencing in Arabidopsis Plant J **30** (1): 107-114

Yu W et al 2007 Construction and behavior of engineered minichromosomes in maize *Proc Natl Acad Sci U S A* **104** 8924-9

Wang K P Drayton B Frame J Dunwell and JA Thompson 1995 Whisker mediated plant transformation: an alternative technology *In Vitro* Cell Dev Biol Plant **31** (2): 101-104

Weaver J C 1995 Electroporation Theory In: Methods in Molecular Biology Plant Cell Electroporation and Electrofusion Protocols Nickoloff JA (Ed) Vol 55 Humana Press Inc: Totowa NJ pp: 3-28

Wright DA *et al* 2005 High-frequency homologous recombination in plants

Yu W et al 2006 Telomere-mediated chromosomal truncation in maize *Proc Natl Acad Sci USA* **103**: 17331-6

Zhang W S Subbarao P Addae A Shen C Armstrong V Peschke and L Gilbertson 2003 Cre/lox mediated gene excision in transgenic maize (*Zea mays* L) plants Theor Applied Genet **107** (7): 1157-1168

Zhu Z B Sun C Liu G Xiao and X Li 1993 Transformation of wheat protoplasts mediated by cationic liposome and regeneration of transgenic plantlets Chin J Biotechnol **9**: 257-261

10

NITRIC OXIDE (NO): A VERSATILE GASEOUS HORMONE

AMAN VERMA, C. P. MALIK, VARSHA CHATURVEDI AND V. K. GUPTA

INTRODUCTION

Umpteen research papers continue to flood the scientific journals with insights into the biological activity and potential clinical uses of nitric oxide (NO). The organization of redox signaling and the use of NO to transmit information, modulate biological processes or create cellular damage are highly complex. Recent reports provide an exceptional picture of NO production, regulation of NO bioactivity through detoxification reactions and of biochemical events through which NO transduces signals into cellular responses, especially during disease resistance. Furthermore, other exciting reports on NO function are in seed germination, seedling growth and reproduction support the view that NO is a 'do it all' molecule that plays a crucial role during the entire lifespan of the plant.

NO is seemingly emerging as an important endogenous signalling molecule in plants, mediates many developmental and physiological processes including xylogenesis, programmed cell death, pathogen defence, flowering, stomatal closure, and gravitropism (Lamattina *et al.* 2003; Neill *et al.* 2003; Delledonne, 2005; Lamotte *et al.* 2005). Experimental evidence in support of such signalling roles for NO has typically been obtained *via* the application of either NO or NO donors (NO itself is a reactive gas with a short half-life in air), *via* the measurement of endogenous NO and through the manipulation of endogenous NO content by chemical and genetic means. There are potential complications with using NO donors (Floryszak-Wieczorek *et al.* 2006) and undoubtedly technical problems associated with assaying the NO content of and release from plants (Planchet and Kaiser, 2006*a*, *b*). Moreover, in some situations, NO can be released in far higher amounts than would probably be required to effect biological responses which raises the question of how it can actually function as a biological signal. NO also have paradoxical effects. For example, it is growth promoting at low concentrations, but quite inhibitory or toxic at high concentrations (Beligni and Lamattina, 1999) and being reactive is perhaps unlikely to travel far between or even within cells. It may be that in the rush of enthusiasm to ascribe biological roles to NO some problems have been overlooked and with hindsight some of the experimental data may require re-evaluation.

This review focuses on NO evolution and its role in plants and perhaps, raises more questions than answers. The subsequent review (Verma *et al.* in press) shall discuss NO metabolism and its divergent roles in plants *e.g.* seed germination and seedling growth, cell growth and differentiation; organogenesis; flowering; pigment synthesis; Cell metabolism (photosynthesis, respiration, function of peroxisomes and senescence); We shall also discuss NO and its cross-talk with different plant hormones (IAA, GA, Cytokinin, ABA, Ethylene salicylic acid) as well as calcium. In recent years role of NO in overcoming different stresses has also been demonstrated and these include drought stress, salinity and temperature stress, heavy metal stress and UV-radiation and ozone stresses. The role of NO in biotic stresses shall also be included.

WHAT IS NO?

Until recently NO was known principally as a hazardous molecule that caused pollution and acid rain, and that destroyed the ozone layer and damaged ecological environments. After receiving negligible biological research interest for decades, the unique biological attributes of NO were finally becoming evident, and NO was chosen as "Molecule of the Year" by Science magazine in 1992. In 1998, the researchers Ferid Murad, Louis J. Ignarro, and Robert Furchgott were awarded the Nobel Prize recognizing their pioneering work with NO (The Nobel Prize in Physiology or Medicine 1998). While examining the effect NO generation and removal in plants of various chemicals on the artery wall, Furchgott observed the secretion of a substance in endothelium with a shorter activity half-life than acetylcholine (Furchgott RF, Zawadzki JV, 1980). Meanwhile Murad *et al.* (1979) reported that cGMP levels increased via activation of the enzyme guanylate cyclase (GC) during neurodilator- induced relaxation of smooth muscle cells. Based upon the convergence of findings by Furchgott (1988), the substance which caused relaxation of artery muscles was named "endothelium- derived relaxing factor" (EDRF). Four years after the adoption of this term, it became evident that EDRF was in fact NO when Murad, Ignarro and colleagues (1987, 1979), while working with nitrodilators and NO, discovered that these substances caused cGMP-related vasodilatation in smooth muscle tissue. The Nobel Prize recognizing NO research brought the NO molecule great attention in basic and clinical biomedical sciences. Today it is known that many cell types synthesize NO and that it mediates many physiological processes, such as neurotransmission, immunity, resistance, and regulation of the cell-cell communication.

Following this sudden surge of NO into biological research, its divergent effects in both animals and plants were examined. Previously the NO-related studies in plants were focused on its involvement in atmospheric pollution. NO release in plants and its effects on plant growth were defined for the first time in the 1970s [Anderson and Mansfield (1979); Klepper (1979)]. Subsequently, NO-related studies in plants were limited to those by a few pioneering researchers such as Leshem and Haramaty (1996) and Laxalt *et al.* (1997), until a remarkable rise in NO and plant biology studies [Beligni and Lamattina (2001a; b); Del Rio *et al.* (2004); Durner and Klessig (1999); Graziano and Lamattina (2005); Neill, *et al.* (2003); Neill *et al.* (2002b)] occurred when NO was demonstrated to play a role in plant defense mechanisms.

CHEMISTRY OF NO

NO is a colorless and gaseous molecule, which can easily diffuse through cell membranes due to its low molecular density and lipophilic quality. Furthermore, NO can act as a physiological messenger that interact strongly with other molecules and has a half life of just a few seconds (Durner and Klessig 1999; Neill *et al.* 2002a). As its electron structure is suitable for electron transfer, there are three inter-convertible forms of NO: the highly reactive, uncharged free radical ($NO^{\cdot}$) with an unpaired electron, the nitrosonium cation (NO^+) and nitroxyl anion (NO^-). $NO^{\cdot}$ rapidly reacts with O_2 to form NO_2, and rapidly breaks down into nitrite and nitrate in an aqueous solution. The highly reactive and destructive ion peroxynitride ($OONO^-$) is produced when $NO^{\cdot}$ reacts with superoxide (O_2^-) or H_2O_2. $NO^{\cdot}$ also reacts with iron and iron-containing proteins, thus forming iron-nitrosyl complexes. The highly promiscuous reactivity of NO and its ability to easily cross cell membranes make it a good signaling molecule in plants. NO^+ mediates electrophoretic attack on reactive sulfur, oxygen, nitrogen and aromatic carbon centers, with thiols being the most reactive group. Nitrosation of SH (*i.e.* S-nitrosation) centers of many enzymes or proteins have been described and such modification are reversible and protein-S-nitrosation↔denitrosation represents an important mechanism for regulation of signal transduction.

NO BIOSYNTHESIS

It is pivotal to elucidate the mechanisms by which NO is biosynthesized in plant cells. However, despite all the research efforts over the last 10 years or so, there remains much to be known. Most work has focused on two potential enzymatic sources of NO in plants, nitric oxide synthase (NOS) and nitrate reductase (NR), but recent research has also alluded to other potential sources of NO in different compartments of plant cells (Fig. 1). Prior to the complete sequencing of the *Arabidopsis* genome, early work on NO signalling in plants used pharmacological inhibitors of NO-generating enzymes to indicate the potential source of NO. In addition to non-specific inhibitors of NR, these inhibitors included compounds such as NG-nitro-L-arginine methyl ester (L-NAME) and NG-monomethyl-L-arginine acetate (L-NMMA), analogues of arginine expected to function as competitive inhibitors of NOS. Tungstate, that probably replaces molybdenum in the NR enzyme, has also been used as a potential NR inhibitor. The inhibition of physiological responses such as programmed cell death, stomatal closure or root growth by these compounds suggested that either NOS or NR were likely to be sources of endogenous NO (Neill *et al.* 2003). Early work by del Rio and colleagues (2002) used immunogold labelling to indicate that NOS-like enzymes were present in pea peroxisomes, but the cloning of a pea homologue of NOS was not reported.

Further, the peroxisomal NOS activity was biochemically characterized and arginine-dependent NO accumulation measured by chemiluminescence and electron paramagnetic resonance (EPR) spectroscopy (Corpas *et al.* 2004a). In addition, constitutive NOS activity, which appeared to be developmentally regulated, was detected in the leaves, stems, and roots of pea seedlings (Corpas *et al.* 2006). More recently, arginine-dependent, salinity-induced increases in NOS activity have also been demonstrated in olive (Valderrama *et al.* 2007). What still remains to be achieved, however, is the identification of genes encoding the enzymes responsible for these activities.

The first genetic evidence for a NOS-like enzyme in plants came from the work of Crawford and colleagues who identified an *Arabidopsis* orthologue of mammalian NOS, named AtNOS1 (Guo *et al.* 2003). The encoded protein, AtNOS1, had similarity to one from a snail that was possibly involved in NO synthesis. Importantly, AtNOS1 was shown to possess the biochemical characteristics of NOS in that it reduced arginine to citrulline when assayed with a commercial NOS-assay kit. More importantly still, a T-DNA insertion mutant, AtNOS1, was identified that produced much reduced levels of NO in guard cells and roots in response to ABA. Collectively, these data strongly suggested that AtNOS1 was truly a source of NO in *Arabidopsis.* Indeed, other studies also confirmed that the mutant, AtNOS1, was deficient in NO synthesis and action (He *et al.* 2004; Zeidler *et al.* 2004 and Bright *et al.* 2006).

However, the function of AtNOS1 as NOS has now been seriously questioned, with three parallel reports in 2006 discussing the problems associated with this concept. It now appears that AtNOS1 may not actually be a NOS at all. Certainly, it has been difficult to demonstrate typical NOS activity. Various researchers have been unable to reproduce the results of the earlier work and detect citrulline when using the arginine-to-citrulline conversion kit and working with either AtNOS1 or related enzymes from other species (Zemojtel *et al.* 2006). Other tests to detect NO arising from the activity of this enzyme have also failed (Crawford *et al.* 2006). The current view is that, although AtNOS1 may not be a NOS *per se*, it is somehow involved in NO synthesis or accumulation. Hence, a name change to *Arabidopsis thaliana* Nitric Oxide Associated 1 (AtNOA1) has been suggested (Crawford *et al.* 2006). AtNOS1, or as know called as, AtNOA1, has a conserved GTPase domain and because it is probably targeted to the mitochondria (Guo and Crawford, 2005), it has been speculated that it may be a GTPase involved in mitochondrial ribosome biogenesis. Presumably impaired AtNOA1 activity would then be expected to result in impaired mitochondrial function and thus, altered NO levels (Zemojtel *et al.* 2006). However, GTPase activity is yet to be shown for AtNOA1. Moreover, Guo (2006) argues that the lack of detection of NOS activity from

AtNOA1 and its homologues could be due to the fact that their NAD (P) H-dependent activity may be very low compared with that of their mammalian counterparts. It was also suggested that AtNOA1 may use the stable NO synthesis intermediate, N-w-hydroxyarginine (NOHA), rather than arginine to produce NO. Such an intermediate would not be detectable by the traditional NOS assay. In addition, it has been suggested that there may be other co-factors yet to be identified in plants which could be required to regulate AtNOA1 activity (Guo, 2006).

Realistically, these recent developments lead us back to square one: no plant *NOS* gene has yet been identified. They also highlight a major caveat in the field of NO research in that the traditional NOS assay kits that have been used for mammalian enzymes may not be appropriate for plants. Additional methods such as EPR spectroscopy and chemiluminesence to detect arginine-dependent NOS activity would be suitable alternatives (Corpas *et al.* 2004*a*). Nevertheless, the substantial pharmacological data resulting from the use of NOS inhibitors to inhibit biological responses and NO production do indicate that there must be enzymes in plants that are thus affected. By definition, these enzymes are NOS enzymes, but how they use arginine to make NO remains to be seen. Possibly a plant NOS will have little sequence similarity with its mammalian counterpart, but will still contain domains which allow its redox functions to occur. Such domains could even be located on different polypeptides which could be brought together following a signalling event. If such a scenario were to be correct, the identification of the NO-producing enzyme in plants could be more difficult than previously thought, but one may assume that the enzyme would have a redox function and contain binding sites for redox prosthetic groups such as flavin or haem.

Another enzymatic source of NO is NR. The primary function of the NR family of enzymes in plants is one of nitrogen assimilation by converting nitrate to nitrite. However, NR can also convert nitrite to NO *via* a NAD (P) H-dependent reaction. This was shown originally *in vivo* using mutant NR soybean plants (Dean and Harper, 1986), but has also been shown *in vitro* using purified NR and plant extracts (Rockel *et al.* 2002; Neill *et al.* 2003). The first genetic evidence of a physiological role for the generation of NO by NR was in ABA-induced stomatal closure in *Arabidopsis* (Desikan *et al.* 2002). NR uses nitrite as a substrate to generate NO. The inhibition of NR activity with tungstate inhibited both ABA and nitrite-induced stomatal closure and prevented NO generation (Desikan *et al.* 2002; Bright *et al.* 2006), thus implying that a NR-like enzyme did play a role in generating the NO normally required to produce these responses. Importantly, it has also been possible to show the inhibition of purified NR activity *in vitro* using tungstate (Bright *et al.* 2006). *Arabidopsis* contains two NR genes, *NIA1* and *NIA2*, which have a high degree of coding sequence similarity and result in two isoforms which are 83.5% identical at the amino acid level, but which show some localized areas of sequence divergence in the first 90 N-terminal amino acids and in various other regions within the two proteins. Use of the *Arabidopsis nia1nia2* NR double mutant confirmed a role for one or both of the encoded enzymes in guard cell responses to ABA (Desikan *et al.* 2002). The observation that nitrite did not induce NO generation in *nia1nia2* guard cells suggests that this requirement for NR reflected its *in vivo* capacity to produce NO from nitrite.

However, as pointed out by Crawford (2006), a lack of NR may have several effects on plant nitrogen metabolism and indeed Modolo *et al.* (2006) have reported that the arginine content of *nia1nia2* leaves is substantially reduced. Recent work using single NR mutants indicates that NIA1, which is usually present at a much lower abundance than NIA2, is the source of NO during ABA signalling (Bright *et al.* 2006). These data also suggest that the aberrant NO biology in *nia1nia2* is due specifically to the lack of NIA1 as opposed to generally aberrant nitrogen metabolism. Interestingly, Yu *et al.* (1998) similarly concluded that NIA1 and NIA2 have distinct signal transduction and nitrogen assimilatory roles. NO generation by NR is stimulated by hypoxic conditions and in spinach and maize NR-mediated NO generation can be modulated by the phosphorylation status of the NR (Rockel *et al.* 2002). Thus, a potential regulatory mechanism may exist *in vivo*. Increasing endogenous nitrite concentrations, either by dark treatment or by antisense-inhibition of endogenous nitrite reductase activity (Morot-Gaudry *et al.* 2002 and Rockel *et al.* 2002), increases NO emission. NR-mediated NO generation has also been demonstrated in roots with a potential physiological role that of mediating aerenchyma formation, having been suggested (Dordas *et al.* 2003).

As shown in tobacco, mitochondrial reduction of nitrite to NO can also be a major source of NO with tissue nitrite concentrations being a major limiting factor and NR function obligatory (Planchet *et al.* 2005). However, it is not clear whether or not this occurs in both leaves and roots (Gupta *et al.* 2005 and Modolo *et al.* 2005). In addition, soybean chloroplasts have recently been identified as a source of NO *via* arginine or nitrite (Jasid *et al.* 2006). However, in this case, the enzymes regulating both arginine and nitrite-dependent NO formation are not yet known. Apoplastic, non-enzymatic conversion of nitrite to NO at low pH has also been demonstrated in the barley aleurone layer (Bethke *et al.* 2004).

A plasma membrane-bound, root-specific enzyme, nitrite-NO oxidoreductase (Ni-NOR), may also function as a further source of NO. This enzyme was identified biochemically *via* its NO-generating activity. However, unlike NR, it does not use NAD (P) H as a cofactor, but uses cytochrome *c* as an electron donor *in vitro* and has a comparatively reduced pH optimum. However, neither its physiological role nor its genetic identity is yet known (Stohr and Stremlau, 2006).

Other enzymes may also be involved in NO production (Corpas *et al.* 2004b). For example, in animals, xanthine oxidoreductase (XOR), under hypoxic conditions, can produce NO in preference to H_2O_2 (Millar *et al.* 1998). However, Planchet and Kaiser (2006b) were unable to observe any NO production from recombinant xanthine oxidase. Interestingly, Arnaud *et al.* (2006) demonstrated a plastid-located, iron-induced NO burst in *Arabidopsis* that, although susceptible to inhibition by L-NAME, required neither AtNOS1 nor NR. Such novel NO sources await characterization.

HOW TO GET RID OF NITRIC OXIDE

It is likely that biologically active molecules such as NO are rapidly removed or metabolized following initial signalling events. It is also possible that increased rates of

NO accumulation or emission actually reflect reduced rates of removal rather than increased generation. Thus, the importance of determining how NO levels are controlled is of prime importance (Fig. 1B). Simple chemical reactions are often responsible for the removal of NO from solution. Nitric oxide is inherently unstable and will readily react with oxygen to form nitrite and nitrate. As described above, nitrite can act as a precursor to NO and may have some biological activity (Gladwin *et al.* 2005).

The free radical nature of NO implies that it will readily react with other radicals that might also be present. In both animals and plants, NO is often produced at the same time and in the same place as Reactive Oxygen Species (ROS) such as superoxide anions. Superoxide and NO will react in a stoichiometric manner to produce peroxynitrite ($ONOO^-$). Although it has been noted that plant cells, unlike animal cells, appear resistant to peroxynitrite (Delledonne *et al.* 2001), it may have intrinsic signalling properties. Whether or not this turns out to be the case, the level of NO can be instrumental in controlling ROS levels in cells and *vice versa*. It has been noted that the basal rates of NO production in leaves are often under-estimated because the NO reacts rapidly with superoxide anions (Vanin *et al.* 2004).

NO reacts readily and reversibly with either thiol groups in the cysteine residues of proteins or with the tripeptide glutathione (GSH) and protein S-nitrosylation may be a key facet of NO signalling. Glutathione concentrations are typically 2–3 mM in plant cells (Ball *et al.* 2004) and thus, formation of S-nitrosylated glutathione (GSNO) could have a large impact on the concentration of free NO. GSNO is metabolized by the enzyme GSNO reductase (Diaz *et al.* 2003; Fig. 1B) and this enzyme may be instrumental in controlling the bioavailability of NO and the formation of protein S-NO groups, thereby regulating such NO-regulated processes as, for example, plant pathogen defence responses (Feechan *et al.* 2005).

In addition to reacting with thiol groups, NO can also interact with transition metals, particularly iron which is often associated with haem as in guanylyl cyclase and it has long been recognized that NO can react with haemoglobins. Non-symbiotic haemoglobins (nsHbs) from barley, alfalfa, and *Arabidopsis* are known to react with NO resulting in its removal from solution. Nitrate is formed in a NAD(P)H-dependent reaction with the oxidized haem intermediate being rereduced by either the NAD(P)H or FADH or, as in the case of the barley haemoglobin, by methaemoglobin reductase (Perazzolli *et al.* 2006). *Arabidopsis* AHb1 is also S-nitrosylated (Perazzolli *et al.* 2004). Interestingly, nsHbs are induced by certain treatments where NO generation might be enhanced, for example, by low partial pressures of O_2 (Trevaskis *et al.* 1997) or by nitrate or nitrite and by NO itself (Wang *et al.* 2000; Ohwaki *et al.* 2005; Shimoda *et al.* 2005; Sasakura *et al.* 2006). Transgenic manipulation of AHb1 affects NO evolution, which, correlated with the ability to survive hypoxic stress (Perazzolli *et al.* 2004), indicates a physiological role for AHb1 in modulating NO levels. Further evidence for the endogenous NO-detoxifying action of Hb comes from work involving plant–microbe interactions. Boccara *et al.* (2005) showed that HmpX, an *Erwinia chrysanthemi* flavohaemoglobin and virulence determinant, removed NO. Infection with an HmpX-deficient mutant of *E. chrysanthemi* triggered high levels of NO coupled to the hypersensitive response in the host plant. Sasakura *et al.* (2006) showed that an nsHb in the actinorhizal plant *Alnus firma* is highly expressed in nodules and may serve to detoxify NO.

NO PERCEPTION

Undoubtedly plants perceive and respond to NO, the mechanisms by which such perception occurs still seek clarification. There is now considerable research interest concerning this question, but as no specific plant NO receptor has been identified, work in this area has taken its lead from mammalian research. The reactive nature of NO and its ability to interact with and modify many proteins suggests that there may turn out to be many 'NO perceptors' (Fig. 2). In animal cells, soluble guanylyl cyclase (sGC) has a key role in NO signalling. NO activates sGC by binding to its haem domain stimulating a transient rise in cGMP levels which, in turn, activates a number of targets. In plants, pharmacological studies using inhibitors of NO sensitive guanylyl cyclase have implicated cGMP downstream of NO and ABA signalling in guard cells (Neill *et al.* 2003). NO induces an increase in cGMP (Durner *et al.* 1998) and laboratory findings has shown that application of ABA or the NO donor SNP to guard cell-enriched preparations from *Arabidopsis* induces a small and transient increase in cGMP that can be prevented by the application of the GC inhibitor 1H-[1, 2, 4]-oxadiazolo-[4, 3-a] quinoxalin-1-one (ODQ) or the NO scavenger PTIO. Thus, a similar mechanism of NO stimulated cGMP synthesis may also operate in plants. A key signalling molecule downstream of cGMP is cyclic ADP-ribose (cADPR) (Wendehenne *et al.* 2001). In animal cells cADPR stimulates Ca^{2+} release *via* intracellular ryanodine receptor calcium channels (RYR) and it is possible that a similar signalling mechanism operates in plants. In tobacco, cADPR elevates the expression of the genes encoding phenylalanine ammonia lysase (PAL) and the pathogenesis-related protein 1 (PR-1) in a manner that is sensitive to RYR inhibitors (Durner *et al.* 1998). These genes are also NO-regulated and cADPR antagonists reduce the expression of PR-1 (Klessig *et al.* 2000). NO is known to cause increases in the level of free Ca^{2+} (Durner *et al.* 1998; Garcia-Mata *et al.* 2003). Thus, NO may signal through cGMP, cADPR, and Ca^{2+} to promote its effects. NO, cGMP, and cADPR have all also been shown to mediate ABA-induced stomatal closure (Neill *et al.* 2003; Garcia-Mata and Lamattina, 2002). The cPTIO inhibition during this process of the ABA-induced inactivation of the Ca^{2+} dependent inward rectifying K^+ channel and activation of the outward rectifying Cl^- channel (Garcia-Mata *et al.* 2003) strongly implicates NO and Ca^{2+} in the signalling cascade that may operate.

Mammals, vertebrates, insects, and many lower eukaryotes possess sGCs with a haem domain capable of binding NO. Bacterial sGCs contain a similar NO binding domain termed the H-NOX domain (Karow *et al.* 2004; Boon *et al.* 2006). However, plant homologues of the animal NO sensitive sGC have yet to be identified. The *Arabidopsis* guanylyl cyclase, AtGC1, is apparently not activated by NO (Ludidi and Gehring, 2003). Thus, the question remains as to how and by what signalling process NO induces a rise in the level of cGMP in plants and it may be that plant enzymes that generate cGMP in response to this gas are quite different from their mammalian counterparts. Indeed, a recent report has demonstrated that the *Arabidopsis* brassinosteroid receptor BRI1 contains a domain with guanylyl cyclase activity (Kwezi *et al.* 2007) indicating that there may well be more novel plant guanylyl cyclases awaiting discovery.

The redox chemistry of NO facilitates its reaction with iron–sulphur and haem groups which are present in a number of different proteins. In addition, NO may also signal its presence through other mechanisms such as either direct S-nitrosylation or indirect *trans*-nitrosylation of either protein cysteine residues or low molecular weight compounds such as glutathione or *via* peroxynitrite nitration of tyrosine residues (Fig. 2; Mur *et al.* 2006). In animals, S-nitrosylation has been shown to regulate a number of signalling processes, stuctural proteins, and metabolic pathways and has become established as the prototype redox-based, post-translational protein modification in the animal kingdom (Wang *et al.* 2006).

In plants, evidence is now beginning to emerge that S-nitrosylation may also play an important role in NO signalling. A number of proteins became S-nitrosylated when extracts of *Arabidopsis* cell cultures were treated with GSNO and SNO-containing proteins isolated by the biotin switch method (Lindermayr *et al.* 2005). The proteins identified were involved in a wide range of cellular processes. However, their *in vivo* S-nitrosylation and its biological significance remain to be seen. The *in vitro* activity of one of three recombinant methionine adenosyl transferase isoforms has been shown to be altered by S-nitrosylation in a manner dependent on the presence or absence of Cys-114

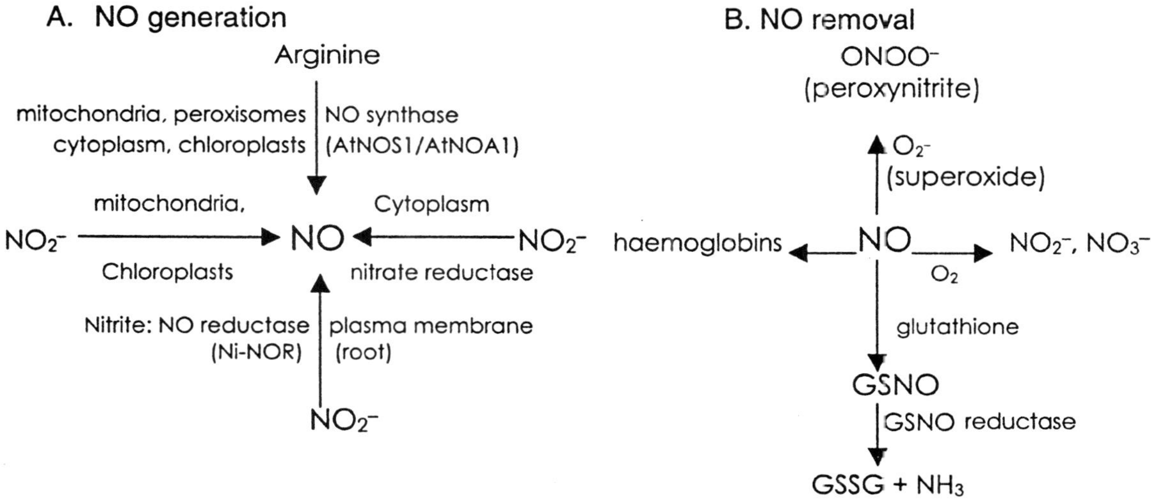

Fig. 1. NO generation (A) and removal (B) in plant cells. NO can be generated from arginine by NO synthase enzymes; AtNOA1 is required for this process in *Arabidopsis*. NO can also be produced from nitrite (NO_2^-) by nitrate reductase (NR), by nitrite:NO reductase (Ni-NOR) and *via* mechanisms yet to be fully defined in chloroplasts and mitochondria. NO reacts readily with oxygen and superoxide. NO is metabolized by reaction with haemoglobins and reacts with glutathione to form *S*-nitrosoglutathione (GSNO). GSNO is catabolized by GSNO reductase.

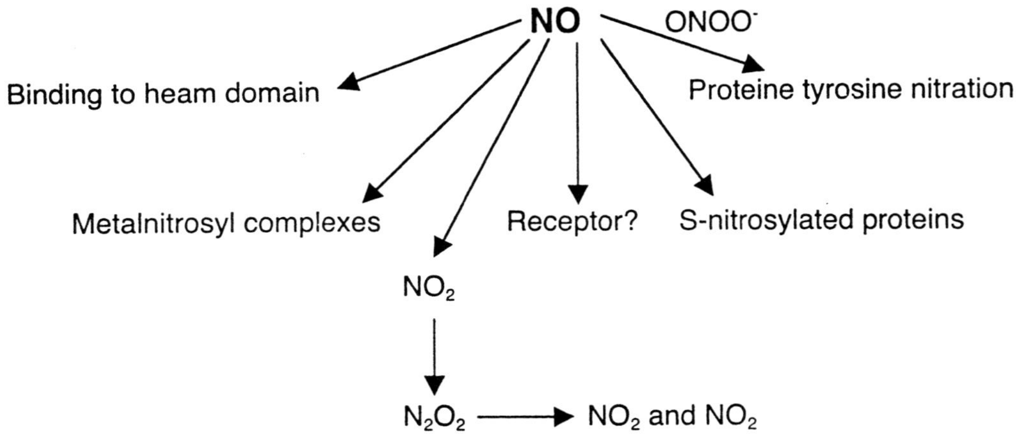

Fig. 2. Potential mechanisms of NO perception. NO may be perceived in plants by a number of mechanisms that differ depending on the cell type, intracellular location, biochemical microenvironment, and environmental stimuli. NO can bind to the haem domain in proteins such as guanylate cyclase and with metals to form metal-nitrosyl complexes. It can also react with the SH group of low molecular weight thiols such as glutathione to form *S*-nitrosoglutathione (GSNO) and, either directly or via GSNO, nitrosylate proteins to form S-nitrosylated proteins. S-nitrosylation induces conformational changes and is reversible. NO reacts with superoxide to form peroxynitrite which can then nitrate proteins on tyrosine residues. It is not yet known whether this reaction has signalling consequences.

(Lindermayr *et al.* 2006). Similarly, the activity of an *Arabidopsis* metacaspase appears to be dependent on the nitrosylation of a critical cysteine residue (Belenghi *et al.* 2007). Under lowered partial pressures of O_2 the mammalian RyR1 calcium channel also becomes S-nitrosylated on a specific Cys residue at physiologically relevant NO levels and in a manner dependent on the presence of calmodulin (Eu *et al.* 2000).

Should this occur in plants, it would have obvious relevance in terms of NO signalling and responses and there is some work suggesting that this may be the case in stomatal guard cells (Sokolovski and Blatt, 2004).

As protein S-nitrosylation can be mediated by GSNO, formed by the S-nitrosylation of GSH (Wang *et al.* 2006), the degree of protein S-nitrosylation and thus, 'NO activity', will be reflected in the availability of reactive GSNO. An *Arabidopsis* GSNO reductase, AtGSNOR1, has now been identified and its biological importance highlighted (Sakamoto *et al.* 2002; Diaz *et al.* 2003; Feechan *et al.* 2005). Loss-of-function mutations of this gene increased S-nitrosylation levels and disabled R (Resistance)-gene related defence responses against microbial pathogens (Feechan *et al.* 2005). Conversely, gain-of-function mutants were enhanced in their defensive ability. It was demonstrated that AtGSNOR1 positively regulated the signalling network controlled by the plant immune system activator, salicylic acid. In pea, both GSNO reductase activity and gene expression are decreased by cadmium stress (Barroso *et al.* 2006). Thus, there is definitely a case for S-nitrosylation being involved in signalling pathways which may include that for NO. Obviously the study of S-nitrosylation in plants is in its infancy and much work is required to determine on which specific proteins it occurs *in vivo* during the different physiological processes regulated by NO. Various proteins S-nitrosylation motifs have also been suggested based on the appropriate regions of animal proteins that are known to be affected. Wang *et al.* (2006) suggested the motif [HKR]-C-[VILMFWC]-x-[DE] as that targeted by NO and the motif [GSTCYNQ]-[KRHDE]-C-[DE] has been suggested as that targeted by GSNO. Scanning the *Arabidopsis* protein databases with these motifs yields 231 and 241 hits, respectively. While the proteins identified include a number of MAP kinases and other signalling proteins, none of those identified as being S-nitrosylated by Lindermayer *et al.* (2005) but are present in the lists of proteins generated. Thus, there is probably no substitute for laboratory-based investigations in this case. However, a number of potential, bioinformatically-generated targets could be examined in transgenic mutant complementation experiments where the highlighted Cys is either present or absent for nitrosylation in the complementing protein.

It is also possible that NO signals *via* the nitration of tyrosine residues. Tyrosine nitration is mediated by reactive nitrogen species such as the peroxynitrite anion ($ONOO^-$) and nitrogen dioxide (NO_2) which are formed during the metabolism of NO in the presence of oxidants such as superoxide radicals ($O_2^{\cdot-}$), hydrogen peroxide (H_2O_2), and transition metal centres (Radi, 2004). Although the peroxynitrite anion can cause tyrosine nitration *in vitro*, its role in this process has been questioned and alternative mechanisms have come to the fore that depend on the formation of NO_2 by the action of haem peroxidases on nitrite (Brennan *et al.* 2002). A number of recombinant *Arabidopsis* haemoglobins that exhibit peroxidase-like activity and differentially mediate nitrite-dependent protein nitration *in vitro* have been identified (Sakamoto *et al.* 2004). Endogenous protein tyrosine nitration has also been demonstrated, in mutant tobacco plants with greatly increased amounts of NO (Morot-Gaudry *et al.* 2002) and more recently in olive leaves where the amount of tyrosine nitrated proteins increased under salt stress (Valderrama *et al.* 2007). Thus, the extent and biological significance of protein nitration and whether or not what appears to be a non-reversible reaction can act as a signalling process, presumably in tandem with protein turnover, remains to be determined.

NO MOVEMENT

It is possible that NO can diffuse within a cell from a specific site of generation, say in the mitochondria, to other regions of the cell where it might induce an effect by interaction with specific target proteins. It is also possible that NO can diffuse out of the cell across the plasma membrane into adjacent cells and thereby create a small region of cells responding to NO. However, whether or not NO does diffuse within and between cells and if it does, how far it moves remains unknown. Given that cells clearly contain many proteins and other molecules that react with NO, it might be that such diffusion is limited. This could of course be the case unless the NO concentration were to be sufficiently high, not necessarily across the whole cell, but perhaps in a microlocale within the cell, so as to saturate, transiently at least, such 'NO-binding molecules' in its immediate vicinity. This would leave non-reacted NO free to diffuse across and out of cells. It is likely that cellular regions do have higher local NO concentrations either because they contain the biochemical machinery required for NO synthesis or because NO accumulates preferentially in such regions. For example, NO is more soluble in lipid than water and so may accumulate preferentially in membranes where its rates of reaction with any interacting molecules may be consequently higher (Liu *et al.* 1998). Different stimuli may activate NO synthesis either by different mechanisms and/or in different subcellular compartments and there may also be a directional focus. For example, a bacterium or fungal hypha may about only one region of a plant cell and the resultant signalling might activate NO generation in only a proximal and discrete region of the cell. If NO response proteins such as ion channels or second messenger-generating enzymes are also co-located then one could envisage local 'NO hot-spots' and NO signalling micro-domains. Although it may well be technically difficult to monitor NO transport, it may be informative to apply NO *via* a point source to the exterior or interior of a tissue and then to monitor real-time NO movement by, for instance, fluorescent imaging using a NO-sensing dye such as DAF-2DA.

An alternative, but not exclusive scenario for NO transport might be that its generation is elevated in discrete regions owing to localized stimulation resulting from the long-distance transport and site-specific accumulation of compounds such as the hormones ABA or IAA that can stimulate its production. Directional transport of IAA is well-known, particularly with respect to its role in mediating tropic responses to gravity and light. NO has been implicated in gravity signalling with localized NO accumulation being induced either by gravistimulation or asymmetric IAA application and prevented by the inhibition of IAA transport (Hu *et al.* 2005). The systemic transport of 'defence-signals' is activated by pathogen challenge and it may be that these signals also stimulate NO generation at sites distant from those of the initial pathogen perception.

Another possibility awaiting clarification is that NO precursors or 'NO storage compounds' may be transported with either NO generation or release occurring at distant sites in a manner analogous to the transport of the ethylene precursor ACC. GSNO has been suggested as one transportable form of NO and although it has not yet been unequivocally identified in plants, a recent report demonstrated cross-reactivity with an anti-GSNO antibody in pea collenchyma cells and immunofluorescence microscopy indicated that the GSNO content decreased dramatically under cadmium stress (Barroso *et al.* 2006). GSNO has recently been demonstrated in leaf vascular tissue and shown to increase under salt stress using confocal laser microscopy (Valderrama *et al.* 2007). Glutathione is also present at high (*e.g.* millimolar levels in wheat) concentrations in phloem cells (Bourgis *et al.* 1999). Arginine and nitrite could also serve as transported NO precursors. Nitrite concentrations in the phloem and xylem are unknown. However, whole tissue nitrite concentrations, which are typically 10–20 μM, can be transiently raised above this level (Rockel *et al.* 2002) which may be indicative of the movement of NO precursors. Arginine concentrations can be quite high (*e.g.* 250 μM in *Arabidopsis* leaves (Modolo *et al.* 2006) and 300–800 μM in melon phloem) and, interestingly, can be increased by ABA treatment (Mitchell and Madore, 1992).

NO GENERATION FROM PLANTS

There can be no doubt that NO is evolved from plants. Such evolution, measured as NO_x (a mixture of NO and NO_2), was first reported in the 1980s and shown to be increased by treatment with salicylic acid and various other compounds (Harper, 1981; Dean and Harper, 1986; Klepper, 1990). Wildt *et al.* (1997) measured NO emissions from several species and several other reports have demonstrated that NO evolution from plants can increase or decrease in response to treatments such as pathogen challenge, water stress, exposure to UV-B, the application of fungicides, and anoxic conditions (Lesham and Haramaty, 1996; Clarke *et al.* 2000; Magalhaes *et al.* 2000; Rockel *et al.* 2002; Hari *et al.* 2003; Conrath *et al.* 2004; Perazzolli *et al.* 2004; Mur *et al.* 2005, 2006). However, there are a number of technical and biological uncertainities with these measurements and quite varied rates of NO evolution have been estimated using a variety of different measuring techniques. Of course, it is also difficult to gauge the biological significance of the NO evolved. Typically, the rates of evolution are in the nmol g^{-1} h^{-1} range (Table 1). A key question is whether or not this NO evolution reflects increased concentrations of biologically active NO *in planta*. In some cases, this seems likely to be the case. For example, during responses to pathogen challenge there are good correlations between NO evolution and the biological responses that occur. Such correlations have been shown using either NO scavengers and NO synthesis inhibitors or virulent and avirulent pathogens. However, as pointed out by Planchet and Kaiser (2006*a*, *b*), estimates of intracellular NO content and rates of NO evolution do not always agree. For example, during anoxia NO is generated at a much higher level than is probably required for its cell signalling function. Such paradoxes remain to be resolved, but the concept of localized NO generation and action may partly explain them.

TABLE 1 : Some estimates of the rates of NO evolution from plants

Examples	*Level of NO ($nM\ g^{-1}FW\ h^{-1}$)*	*Treatments*	*Assay method*	*Reference*
Arabidopsis cultures	30–120	Control; *P. syringae*-challenged	Haemoglobin assay	Clarke *et al.* (2000)
Arabidopsis plants	0.1–1	Air; N_2	Chemiluminescence assay	Perazzolli *et al.* (2004)
Arabidopsis plants	3–17	Control	Gas chromatography	Magalhaes *et al.* (2000)
Tobacco leaves	5–20	Control; *P. syringae*-challenged	Laser photoacoustic detection	Mur *et al.* (2005)
Arabidopsis rosettes	5–30	Control; *P. syringae*-challenged	Laser photoacoustic detection	Mur *et al.* (2006)
Soybean cultures	12–600	Control; fungicide-challenged	Mass spectrometry	Conrath *et al.* (2004)
Spinach leaves	0.5–20	Air; N_2	Chemiluminescence assay	Rockel *et al.* (2002)

It is not known if NO released from one part of a plant can induce effects on either other parts of the same plant or on adjacent plants. Agricultural soils can also release substantial amounts of NO (Davidson and Kingerlee, 1997). Certainly, NO gas does have effects on plant biology. Indeed, the early work on NO concerned its effects as an air pollutant (Mansfield, 2002). NO is still an air pollutant today and plants in urban areas or close to traffic are likely to receive higher chronic and more acute exposures than those in rural areas (rural locations 7–70 nl l–1, urban 20–900 nl l–1; Environment Agency, 2006). The early work showed that NO at 50–500 nl l–1 (urban smog [NO] ≤5000 nl l–1) could retard growth and inhibit photosynthesis (Mansfield, 2002) and other studies have shown that trace amounts of NO in smoke can stimulate seed germination (Keely and Fotheringham, 1997).

NO INDUCED STOMATAL CLOSURE

Exogenous NO, supplied in the form of NO donors, was first shown to induce stomatal closure and reduce transpiration in species such as *Vicia faba, Salpichroa organifolia*, and *Tradescantia spp.* by Garcia-Mata and Lamattina (2001). Such findings were confirmed in epidermal peels or leaves of pea (Neill *et al.* 2002), *Arabidopsis thaliana* (Desikan *et al.* 2002), *etc*. Many different NO donors induce stomatal closure in a dose- and time-dependent manner, and their effects can be reversed by simultaneous co-incubation with the NO scavengers 2-phenyl-4, 4, 5, 5-tetramethylimidazoline-1-oxyl-3-oxide (PTIO) or 2-(4-carboxyphenyl)-4, 4, 5, 5-tetramethylimidazoline-1-oxyl-3-oxide (cPTIO) (Bright, 2006). Many such plant studies have used the NO donor sodium nitroprusside (SNP) that also generates cyanide. However, neither cyanide itself nor light-inactivated SNP induce stomatal closure (Bright, 2006), and cPTIO does not react directly with cyanide (Bethke *et al.* 2006). Moreover, the reaction product of cPTIO and NO, cPTI, which has some biological activity per se (Planchet and Kaiser, 2006b), does not inhibit ABA-induced guard cell movements. Thus, the effects mediated by NO donors such as SNP must indeed be due to the release and biological activity of NO.

The requirement for endogenous NO during ABA-induced stomatal closure has been demonstrated by both pharmacological and genetic approaches that either remove NO or prevent its generation and correlate stomatal responses with estimates of its accumulation. It has been shown that pea and *Arabidopsis* guard cells generate NO in response to ABA and that their treatment with PTIO both removes NO and inhibits ABA-induced stomatal closure. Similar guard cell responses have been shown in *V. faba* (Garcia-Mata and Lamattina, 2002). The treatment of *Arabidopsis* leaves with either L-NAME or tungstate, compounds that potentially inhibit NO generation from L-arginine or nitrite, inhibits guard cell NO production and stomatal closure (Bright *et al.*2006). Moreover, in the AtNOS1 and *nia1nia2* mutants, both ABA-induced stomatal closure and ABA-induced NO generation are impaired (Desikan *et al.* 2002).

Much of the aforementioned work has used the NO-sensitive fluorescent dye 4, 5-diaminofluorescein diacetate (DAF-2DA) and related compounds to detect the presence of NO. However, as highlighted recently by Kaiser and colleagues (Planchet and Kaiser, 2006*a*, *b*), DAF-2DA can generate art factual fluorescence arising from its reaction with

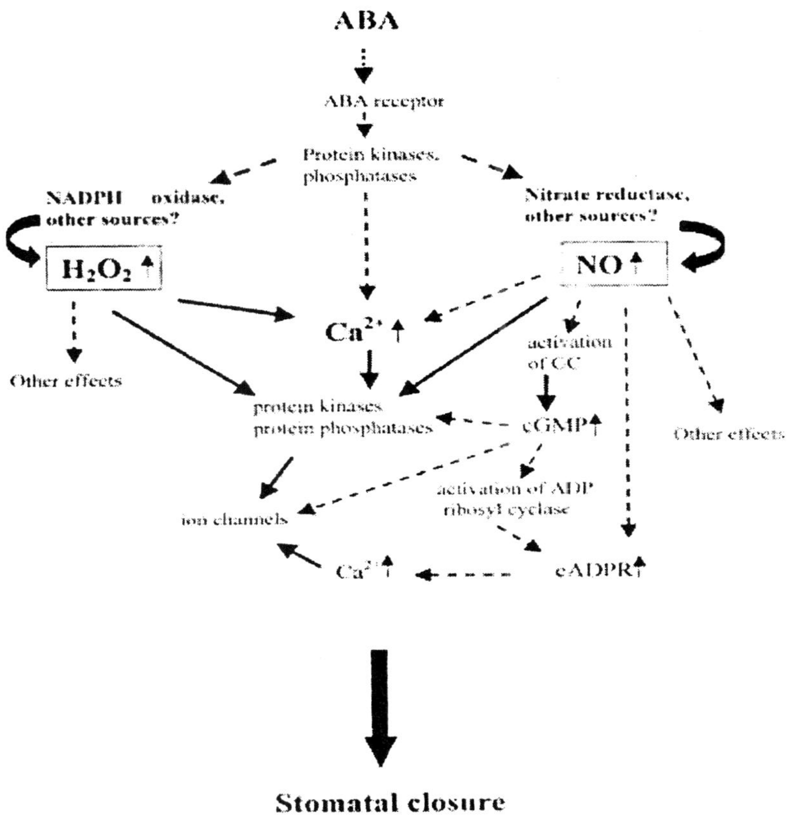

Fig. 3. The pattern and process of the ABA-induced signal transduction in plant cells

compounds other than NO. Nonetheless, the use of appropriate control dyes such as 4-aminofluorescein diacetate (4AF-DA), that do not react with NO, and the NO scavenger PTIO allows the conclusion that NO is truly being detected in guard cells. The use of other NO assays such as electron paramagnetic resonance spectroscopy or photoacoustic laser detection is difficult within the guard cell system. However, it has been possible to demonstrate ABA-enhanced NO generation in pea epidermal peels using the haemoglobin assay (Neill *et al.* 2002). Thus, information from various sources does demonstrate that ABA-induced stomatal closure requires NO generation and action (Fig. no. 3). Recent reports indicate that guard cells also generate NO in response to elicitor challenge (Melotto *et al.* 2006) and methyl jasmonate (MeJA) (Munemasa *et al.* 2007), treatments that both induce stomatal closure. As with the effect of ABA, in these cases the prevention of NO accumulation also inhibited the associated stomatal closure. Clearly there are several potential mechanisms by which NO could be generated in guard cells in response to ABA and other stimuli. ABA-induced stomatal closure and guard cell NO generation are both inhibited by potential NOS inhibitors such as L-NAME (Neill *et al.* 2002; Guo *et al.* 2003; She *et al.* 2004; Bright *et al.* 2006), and both stomatal closure and ABA-induced guard cell NO generation are impaired in the

AtNOS1 mutant (Guo *et al.* 2003 and Bright *et al.* 2006). Thus, whatever its exact function may turn out to be, the requirement for AtNOS1 (AtNOA1) is clear, as is a requirement for at least one mechanism that is inhibited by L-arginine analogues.

However, in *Arabidopsis* at least, there are also some reports indicating that ABA-induced NO synthesis in guard cells is mediated by NR. The NR substrate, nitrite, induces stomatal closure and NO production in a dose-dependent manner (Desikan *et al.* 2002; Bright, 2006; Bright *et al.* 2006). NO generation by NR is inhibited *in vitro* by tungstate, probably as a result of its competitive binding to the molybdenum-binding site in the enzyme. Tungstate also inhibits either ABA- or nitrite-induced NO generation and stomatal closure *in vivo* (Bright, 2006; Bright *et al.* 2006). The NR-deficient *nia1nia2* mutant, which contains only 0.5% of wild-type NR activity (Wilkinson and Crawford, 1993), exhibits neither guard cell NO synthesis nor stomatal closure in response to either ABA or nitrite, indicating that one or both of the two *Arabidopsis* NR isoforms are required. The observation that nitrite fails to induce NO synthesis in *nia1nia2* guard cells suggests that this requirement for NR reflects its *in vivo* ability to produce NO from nitrite. However, as raised by Crawford (2006), the lack of NR may have several effects on plant Nitrogen metabolism that could potentially limit NOS-like activity and, as mentioned previously, Modolo *et al.* (2006) have reported that levels of the NOS substrate, L-arginine, are substantially reduced in *nia1nia2* leaves. In resolving this issue, the *Arabidopsis* single mutants, *nia1* and *nia2*, have been used to study further the involvement of NR in guard cell NO synthesis during ABA-induced stomatal closure (Bright, 2006). Of the two isoforms, *nia2* accounts for 90% of the total nitrate assimilatory activity of NR in seedlings, while *nia1* accounts for the remaining 10% (Wilkinson and Crawford, 1991). The sequences of the *Arabidopsis* mRNAs encoding the two isoforms have ~70% identity and give rise to proteins which are 83.5% similar at the amino acid level (Wilkinson and Crawford, 1993). Both genes are probably expressed in guard cells (Bright, 2006). Guard cell NO synthesis and stomatal responses to ABA were examined in the loss-of-function T-DNA insertion mutant, *nia1::Ds* (Parinov *et al.* 1999), which has no *nia1* activity (Wang *et al.* 2004), and in the loss-of-function deletion mutant, *nia2-5* (Wilkinson and Crawford, 1991). Nitrite-induced stomatal closure was abolished in the *nia1::Ds* plants and ABA-induced stomatal closure was substantially reduced. NO accumulation in the guard cells of this mutant in response to these stimuli was effectively absent in comparison with that of the same cells of wild-type leaves. *nia1::Ds* stomatal closure in response to SNP was as for the wild type, indicating that these aberrant stomatal responses were not related to a general impairment in guard cell movement. In contrast to the *nia1::Ds* mutant, stomata of the *nia2-5* mutant behaved as those of wild type, closing in response to either ABA or nitrite, and their guard cells showed wild-type levels of NO accumulation after such stimulation. Thus, it would seem highly likely that the activity of *nia1*, but not *nia2*, is required for effective ABA signal transduction in guard cells during stomatal closure (Bright, 2006). This also suggests that the aberrant NO biology in the *nia1nia2* mutant is due specifically to a lack of *nia1* as opposed to generally aberrant N metabolism. Interestingly, some years ago Yu *et al.* (1998) also concluded that *nia1* and *nia2* have distinct signal transduction and nitrogen assimilatory roles. *nia1* and *nia2* have similar amino acid sequences, but there are distinct regions that differ between the two proteins. Thus, key questions must concern their subcellular localization, interacting protein partners, and activation characteristics.

NO SIGNAL TRANSDUCTION IN GUARD CELLS

Given that exogenous and endogenous NO induces stomatal closure, there must be some mechanism(s) by which NO is perceived in guard cells and the signal subsequently transduced into the alterations in membrane transport that effect ion and water movement across the tonoplast and plasma membrane. The small size, ready diffusibility, and reactive nature of NO perhaps make the ligand-specific, proteinaceous receptor interaction paradigm unlikely. On the other hand, the reactive nature of NO does make it likely that it reacts, directly or indirectly, with either several or perhaps many proteins. Thus, there may be a number of different 'NO perceptors' that exist in different cell types and during different physiological states. On the basis of mammalian work and emerging studies in plant systems, it is probable that both the transient activation of soluble guanylyl cyclase (sGC), which generates the second messenger cGMP, and the reversible modulation of protein activity *via S*-nitrosylation-induced conformational changes (Delledonne, 2005; Wang *et al.* 2006) are major components of NO signalling.

CGMP-DEPENDENT SIGNALING

The evidence that cGMP is an NO signalling intermediate has been obtained in several systems (Neill *et al.* 2003; Delledonne, 2005). Both salt and osmotic stress, two conditions which would both be expected to induce ABA synthesis, induced a rapid increase in the cGMP content of *Arabidopsis* seedlings (Donaldson *et al.* 2004). Using a sensitive radioimmunoassay technique, the cGMP content of pea epidermis and *Arabidopsis* guard cell fragments has been similarly measured as being in the pmol g^{-1} range, and transient increases in cGMP levels following either ABA or SNP treatment have been observed that could be prevented by co-incubation of the treated tissues with PTIO. Further evidence that cGMP can mediate the effects of ABA in stomatal guard cells has resulted from pharmacological work using the cell-permeable cGMP analogue 8-bromo cGMP (8BrcGMP) and inhibitors of NO-sensitive sGC such as 1H-[1, 2, 4] oxadiazolo[4, 3-a]quinoxalin-1-one (ODQ). The ABA- or NO-induced closure of pea (Neill *et al.* 2002) and *Arabidopsis* stomata was inhibited by ODQ. This inhibition could be prevented by co-incubation of the ABA-/NO-stimulated, ODQ-treated guard cells with 8BrcGMP. However, 8BrcGMP alone did not induce stomatal closure. Thus, it would appear that although an elevated level of cGMP is required for effective ABA-induced stomatal closure; additional signalling pathways stimulated by ABA must operate in concert for such an increase to mediate its effects.

In non-plant systems, cADP ribose (cADPR), an agent that mobilizes Ca^{2+} from internal stores, is a downstream messenger of NO. Nicotinamide, a potential inhibitor of cADPR synthesis, blocks ABA- and NO-induced stomatal closure (Neill *et al.* 2002).

Garcia-Mata *et al.* (2003) have also shown that NO-induced intracellular Ca^{2+} release and the regulation of guard cell plasma membrane K^+ and Cl^- channels are mediated by a cGMP- and cADPR-dependent pathway.

cGMP may also signal by binding to and directly activating cyclic nucleotide-gated ion channels (CNGCs) or by similarly activating cGMP-dependent protein kinases. To date, no cGMP-activated plant protein kinases have been identified, and the potential role of CNGCs in guard cell NO signalling awaits clarification.

Though cGMP has been unequivocally identified in various plant tissues (Neill *et al.* 2003) and pharmacological data indicate a role for it during stomatal closure, very little is known of the mechanisms by which cGMP might be turned over in plant cells. The one plant guanylyl cyclase gene (*AtGC1*) cloned from *Arabidopsis* encodes a protein which shows many domain differences from mammalian sGC, lacks a haem-binding motif, and is insensitive to NO (Ludidi and Gehring, 2003). The biological roles of *AtGC1* remain to be described and it may be that plants contain other enzymes capable of cGMP production. Interestingly and indicating that there may well be novel plant guanylyl cyclases awaiting discovery, a recent report has indicated that the *Arabidopsis* brassinosteroid receptor, *AtBRI1*, contains a domain with guanylyl cyclase activity (Kwezi *et al.* 2007). If cGMP is an intracellular plant signal, then mechanisms for its rapid degradation will exist. Plant cells do indeed possess cGMP hydrolysis activity and the *Arabidopsis* genome contains several genes for potential phosphodiesterases including that encoding a putative cGMP phosphodiesterase (Maathuis, 2006).

NO and its related species can oxidize, nitrate, or nitrosylate proteins (Mur *et al.* 2006; Wang *et al.* 2006). Peroxynitrite, formed by the reaction of NO with superoxide, can oxidize proteins on cysteine, methionine, or tryptophan residues or nitrate tyrosine residues to form nitrotyrosine. These post-translational modifications may well turn out to have roles in intracellular signalling and the subsequent physiological effects. For example, recent work indicates a role for protein tyrosine nitration in plant defence responses (Saito *et al.* 2006).

S-nitrosylation is the reversible covalent attachment of NO to the thiol group of cysteine residues forming an *S*-nitrosothiol (SNO) and may well be an ancient highly conserved cell signalling mechanism (Wang *et al.* 2006). Nitrosylation can occur either directly through the interaction of NO and other NO-related species with the cysteine group or indirectly by trans-nitrosylation where the NO is derived from *S*-nitrosglutathione (GSNO) or other *S*-nitrosylated proteins. Some recent studies indicate that this redox-based mechanism plays a pivotal role in plant biology and will, therefore, also be important with regard to NO signalling in guard cells.

S-nitrosylated proteins can be detected using the 'biotin switch assay' which is based on specifically biotin labelling any *S*-nitrosylated cysteines within proteins. This assay is useful for demonstrating the existence of potentially *S*-nitrosylated proteins but, like many assays, may be prone to identifying false positives. However, *S*-nitrosylation can be demonstrated unequivocally using mass spectrometry (Lindermayr *et al.* 2006). The biotin switch assay has been used to show the presence of *S*-nitrosylated proteins in plants and to demonstrate that specific proteins can be *S*-nitrosylated (Lindermayr *et al.* 2005, 2006; Wang *et al.* 2006; Belenghi *et al.* 2007). A large number of potentially *S*-nitrosylated proteins have been identified which include stress-related proteins, redox-related proteins, signalling proteins, cytoskeletal proteins, and proteins involved in photosynthesis and metabolism (Lindemayr *et al.* 2005). Moreover, conserved protein *S*-nitrosylation and GSNO-binding motifs are present in plant proteins (Wang *et al.* 2006), and the effects of *S*-nitrosylation on protein activity and plant physiology are now being addressed (Lindermayr *et al.* 2006; Belenghi *et al.* 2007). It would seem likely that all cells contain nitrosylated proteins and that the spectrum and levels of these, the 'nitrosylome', will alter during NO accumulation in, for example, guard cells after their challenge with ABA. In fact some evidence that this is the case already exists, and data published by Sokolovski and Blatt (2004) suggest that NO regulates outward rectifying K^+ channels in *V. faba* guard cells by *S*-nitrosylation.

DOWNSTREAM SIGNALLING

Alterations in the calcium concentrations of specific cellular compartments and reversible protein phosphorylation are two processes central to cell signalling. Thus, it is not surprising that NO is likely to affect these processes in guard and other cells. ABA and NO activate mitogen-activated protein kinases (MAPKs) (Desikan *et al.* 2004*a*; Pagnussat *et al.* 2004; Zhang *et al.* 2007), and MAPK activation has been suggested as a convergence point for guard cell H_2O_2 and NO signalling during ABA-induced stomatal closure (Desikan *et al.* 2004*a*). NO also activates other protein kinases such as the osmotic stress-activated kinase, NtOSAK, in tobacco (Lamotte *et al.* 2006). NO affects calcium mobilization (Lamotte *et al.* 2006), and Sokolovski *et al.* (2005) demonstrated a requirement for both protein phosphorylation and altered calcium flux in order for normal NO responses to occur in guard cells. Further evidence that NO signalling requires protein dephosphorylation results from the observation that stomata of the *Arabidopsis* ABA-insensitive phosphatase mutant, *abi1*, are insensitive to NO (Desikan *et al.* 2002).

NO AND H_2O_2

It is commonly observed that NO and ROS such as superoxide and H_2O_2 are generated in response to similar stimuli and with similar kinetics. NO and ROS can interact in various ways. For example, they can interact chemically as in the formation of compounds such as peroxynitrite. NO may also affect the activities of enzymes that alter ROS levels, and *vice versa*. Thus, they could both impact either negatively or positively on the same or related signalling pathways and thereby lead to additive and possibly synergistic responses. Stomatal closure in response to ABA is one such example where this occurs. ABA induces the production of H_2O_2. In *Arabidopsis* guard cells this is likely to arise from superoxide generated by the isoforms of NAD(P)H oxidase encoded by the genes *AtrbohD* and *AtrbohF* (Kwak *et al.* 2003; Desikan *et al.* 2004*b*; She *et al.* 2004). Consequently, the simultaneous presence of both superoxide and NO in the same location may lead to the generation of peroxynitrite anions (Neill *et al.* 2003). Peroxynitrite may well have unique signalling properties, but as yet there is no evidence that it affects guard cell movements, and the co-incubation of ABA-treated leaves with a peroxynitrite scavenger does not inhibit the induction of stomatal closure (Bright, 2006).

Lum *et al.* (2002) observed that exogenous H_2O_2 induced NO generation in the guard and other cells of *Phaseolus aureus* leaves. In a chemiluminescence-based assay, the H_2O_2 induced a substantial increase in an apparent NOS-like activity. This increase was reduced by using a potential NOS inhibitor. Interestingly, the H_2O_2-induced NO generation was inhibited by the calcium channel blocker verapamil. Thus, it is possible that Ca^{2+} ions may mediate this effect of H_2O_2. She *et al.* (2004) and He *et al.* (2005) also reported that H_2O_2 induced NO synthesis in *V. faba* guard cells and that again this accumulation could be reduced by a NOS inhibitor. Moreover, they found that both NO generation and stomatal closure stimulated by darkness or UV-B were dependent on guard cell synthesis of H_2O_2. Similarly, in *Arabidopsis*, H_2O_2 induces guard cells to synthesize NO which is required if the induction of stomatal closure is to follow (Bright *et al.* 2006). ABA-induced NO synthesis is dependent on prior H_2O_2 generation in both *V. faba* (Dong *et al.* 2005) and *Arabidopsis* (Bright *et al.* 2006). Removal of the H_2O_2 with antioxidants or inhibition of its synthesis by inhibiting NAD(P)H oxidase activity prevents NO generation and stomatal closure. Similarly, removal of the NO using PTIO prevents either H_2O_2- or ABA-induced stomatal closure. Guard cells of the *AtrbohD/F* double mutant (Kwak *et al.* 2003) also fail to make NO in response to ABA, as do those of the NR-deficient *nia1nia2* mutant. However, H_2O_2 stimulation of guard cell NO accumulation in the *Atnos1* (*Atnoa1*) mutant was as in the wild type (Bright *et al.* 2006). Thus, the requirement of AtNOS1 for NO synthesis must be epistatically upstream of H_2O_2 and its signalling effects. Regardless, the current evidence would suggest that H_2O_2 induces guard cell NO synthesis through the activity of NR. More detailed analysis has demonstrated that only the NIA1 isoform is required, as H_2O_2-stimulated NO generation is as wild type in the *nia2-5* mutant (Bright, 2006). Critically, it has been suggested that the presence of oxidants could increase the sensitivity of the DAF-2DA used in these studies. Thus, the implication is that increased concentrations of H_2O_2 might result in an increase in the fluorescence of this dye without any actual increase in the level of NO (Planchet and Kaiser, 2006*a*, *b*). While this is difficult to discount completely *in vivo*, it would appear that H_2O_2 does not increase the sensitivity of DAF-2DA *in vitro* (Bright *et al.* 2006). Furthermore, DAF-2DA fluorescence does not increase in the guard cells of the *nia1nia2* mutant following ABA or H_2O_2 challenge. The fact that this mutant generates increased H_2O_2 levels in guard cells in response to ABA strongly suggests that H_2O_2 does indeed induce NO production and that it this that is measured by the increased DAF-2DA fluorescence.

It seems that the ABA–H_2O_2–NO cascade is not restricted to guard cells. Zhang *et al.* (2007) have now demonstrated that it also operates in the mesophyll cells of *Zea mays* leaves and that the effects of ABA and H_2O_2 on the induction of antioxidant defences depended on NO generation and could be reduced using cPTIO or L-NAME.

While it is well established that H_2O_2 induces NO synthesis and accumulation, there is also a suggestion that NO may modulate H_2O_2 levels. Both She *et al.* (2004) and He *et al.* (2005) have reported that this was the case in *V. faba* guard cells. However, Dong *et al.* (2005), also working with *V. faba* guard cells, did not observe this phenomenon. NO does not appear to induce H_2O_2 generation in *Arabidopsis* guard cells (Bright *et al.* 2006) or in maize mesophyll cells (Zhang *et al.* 2007). Thus, there is argument as to whether or not this occurs, but feedback mechanisms and autocatalysis are part and parcel of signalling pathways, and it may be that such discrepancies simply reflect differences in the physiological states of the tissues examined.

STOMATAL CLOSURE DURING WATER STRESS

Although Magalhaes *et al.* (2000) reported decreased NO emission following wilting, other studies has shown that water stress causes enhanced NO synthesis and accumulation in guard cells (Leshem and Haramaty, 1996; Garcia-Mata and Lamattina, 2002; Gould *et al.* 2003). Recently such findings have been confirmed by Zhang *et al.* (2007) who showed that polyethylene glycol-induced water stress stimulated NO production in guard cells as a result of increased ABA synthesis. However, the effects of dehydration and turgor loss on the level and emission of NO in and from plants, respectively, certainly requires clarification. ABA synthesis is undoubtedly induced by turgor loss. Thus, the question arises as to whether or not NO plays a direct role in mediating drought-induced stomatal closure. Recent work indicates that NO is not required for rapid water stress-induced stomatal closure. Rapid dehydration of detached *Arabidopsis* leaves caused equally rapid stomatal closure. This was not inhibited by pre-incubation of the leaves in PTIO and occurred in both the *nia1* and *nia1nia2* mutants in the same way as in leaves from wild-type plants. The stomata of the *abi1* mutant do not close at all during this treatment, indicating that the stomatal closure response is active and ABA dependent. Thus, in contrast to the requirement for NO synthesis during ABA-induced stomatal closure in well-hydrated leaves, stomatal closure during rapid wilting may result from ABA signalling that bypasses the need for NO synthesis and perception. It may be different during stomatal closure induced in intact plants by a more gradual reduction in water potential, but it is worth noting that neither the *AtNOS1* nor the *nia1* mutants are wilty. Possibly the effects of NO differ depending on its concentration and the physiological state of the guard cell. For example, Sakihama *et al.* (2003) reported that NO donors actually caused stomatal opening when used at high concentrations. Similar results have been obtained in that, unlike low (0.1–50 μM) concentrations of SNP, high (0.5–1 mM) concentrations failed to cause stomatal closure (Bright, 2006). Another interesting occurrence that has yet to be explained concerns the interaction of ABA, ethylene, and NO signalling in guard cells. ABA, ethylene, and NO all induce stomatal closure when applied alone, but stomatal closure is reduced when either ABA or NO is combined with ethylene (Desikan *et al.* 2006), a situation likely to arise during the wilting of plants. Whichever, NO does appear to have ameliorative benefits in warding off the effects of drought. Garcia-Mata and Lamattina (2001) reported that prolonged SNP treatment provided plants with such beneficial long-term effects. Wheat plants watered with SNP and then exposed to water stress had higher relative water contents than those not receiving the SNP pre-treatment. Presumably the long-term exposure to NO in some way enables plants to retain more water during subsequent dry periods.

STOMATAL MOVEMENTS DURING LIGHT/DARK TRANSITIONS

The inhibition of stomatal closure by cPTIO when bean leaves are transferred into the dark coupled to increased fluorescence of dark-incubated guard cells stained with DAF-2DA indicates that NO is involved in light/dark-regulated stomatal movements (She *et al.* 2004). As also reported for pea leaves (Desikan *et al.* 2004*b*) and indicating the involvement of H_2O_2, this dark-induced stomatal closure could also be inhibited by the addition of ascorbate or exogenous catalase. Adding weight to the concept that NO is involved in dark-induced stomatal closure, stomata of the *Arabidopsis nia1* mutant fail to close after transfer from the light to the dark, and their guard cells show markedly reduced DAF-2DA fluorescence compared with those of the wild type which close after such treatment. Re-opening of *Arabidopsis* stomata on transfer from the dark to the light can be prevented by the addition of ABA or the NO donor SNP (Bright, 2006). The addition of the NO scavenger PTIO effectively prevents this ABA inhibition of re-opening. It is generally considered that the dark-induced cessation of photosynthesis allows the pH gradient between the chloroplast and cytosol to dissipate such that the cellular distribution of ABA changes, with more accumulating in the cytosol. At this point the redistributed ABA may induce stomatal closure directly in the guard cells or indirectly after its movement from the mesophyll to epidermal cells. These data suggest that stomatal closure on transfer from the light to dark involves a linear signalling process from H_2O_2 and NO and that their re-opening, either on transfer to the light or on return to conditions of hydration, may also be partly dependent on the metabolic removal of H_2O_2 and NO. The degree to which stomata close in the dark depends on numerous factors including the stomatal density and leaf age, the position of the plant in its circadian rhythm, the light intensity and quality of the preceding photoperiod, the ambient CO_2 concentration, the relative humidity and soil water availability, and whether the plant operates a C3, C4, or crassulacean acid metabolism (Caird *et al.* 2007). Thus, the involvement of NO with respect to these variables remains to be fully determined.

STOMATAL RESPONSES TO PHYTOPATHOGENIC BACTERIA

Gaining entry into subepidermal tissues is one of the first steps in the bacterial infection of plants, and it is often assumed that openings such as stomata serve as passive ports of entry for such pathogens. However, active stomatal closure has recently been described as part of the innate immunity of plants to bacteria (Melotto *et al.* 2006). For example, in what has been termed a pathogen-associated molecular pattern (PAMP)-induced basal defence mechanism, *Arabidopsis* guard cells are able to perceive *Pseudomonas syringae* cell surface molecules such as lipopolysaccharide (LPS) and flagellin which trigger NO synthesis and result in stomatal closure. Inhibitors of NO synthesis prevent this stomatal closure. In contrast to those of the wild type, stomata of the ABA-insensitive stomata mutant, *ost1-2*, or the ABA-deficient mutant, *aba3-1*, failed to close in response to LPS and flagellin. *Escherichia coli* also induced stomatal closure that was prevented by inhibitors of NO synthesis. Thus, it would appear that the ABA and/or NO signalling mechanism are required for stomatal closure during bacterial challenge. Interestingly, virulent pathogenic bacteria have a mechanism to overcome this barrier and cause stomata to re-open. Using mutants of *P. syringae* which were unable to elicit stomatal re-opening, Melotto *et al.* (2006) identified the phytotoxin coronatine (COR) as the bacterial virulence effector responsible for overcoming this barrier to infection. COR effectively prevented ABA-induced stomatal closure in wild-type *Arabidopsis*, but not in the COR-insensitive mutant, *coi1-20*. COR did not prevent ABA-induced NO synthesis in wild-type plants. Thus, it is likely that COR acts downstream of ABA and NO to prevent stomatal closure (Melotto *et al.* 2006).

NO AS AN ANTIOXIDANT AND PROTECTANT

Exogenous NO, applied *via* the roots in the form of SNP, has been shown to provide some protection against the oxidative damage associated with water stress (Garcia-Mata and Lamattina, 2001). Several other studies have also shown that exogenous NO ameliorates the oxidative stress induced by a range of abiotic conditions including those resulting from the presence of heavy metal ions, salinity, high temperatures, the presence of H_2O_2, dehydration, UV irradiation, and the presence of paraquat (Cheng *et al.* 2002; Hung *et al.* 2002; Uchida *et al.* 2002; Kopyra and Gwóźdź, 2003; Zhang *et al.* 2003, 2006; Hsu and Kao, 2004; Hung and Kao, 2005; Laspina *et al.* 2005; Shi *et al.* 2005; Wang and Yang, 2005; Yu *et al.* 2005; Tian *et al.* 2007). Some of the antioxidant effects of NO may be due to its direct interaction with ROS such as superoxide to form peroxynitrite that might then be scavenged by other cellular processes. In other cases NO may enhance the antioxidant capacity of cells by increasing the activities of antioxidant enzymes such as superoxide dismutase, which converts superoxide to H_2O_2, and catalase and ascorbate peroxidase, which both remove H_2O_2 (Cheng *et al.* 2002; Hung *et al.* 2002; Uchida *et al.* 2002; Kopyra and Gwó d , 2003; Zhang *et al.* 2007).

Whether or not endogenous NO has an antioxidant function is debatable. Guo and Crawford (2005) detected high levels of oxidized proteins and lipids in the *AtNOS1* mutant. *AtNOS1* has enhanced sensitivity to the oxidative stress induced by either methyl viologen or salinity that can be ameliorated by exogenous NO (M Zhao *et al.* 2007; MG Zhao *et al.* 2007). Moreover, in calli of stress-tolerant and stress-sensitive reed ecotypes, heat and salt stress induce endogenous NO generation in the tolerant, but not in the sensitive ecotype. NO enhanced stress tolerance in both ecotypes, but more so in the sensitive ecotype, and depletion of endogenous NO by cPTIO reduced survival in the tolerant ecotype. The enhanced antioxidant enzyme activity and stress tolerance associated with the ability of the tolerant ecotype to make NO was abolished by this cPTIO treatment (Zhao *et al.* 2004; Song *et al.* 2006). Similarly, in *Populus* callus and *Stylosanthes guianensis*, stress tolerance has been associated with endogenous NO synthesis (Zhou *et al.* 2005; F Zhang *et al.* 2007). Given that various stresses induce ABA and, as a consequence NO, and given that NO appears to enhance antioxidant enzyme activity, one might expect a signalling link between ABA, NO, and oxidative stress tolerance. In *S. guianensis*, ABA enhances the activity of antioxidant enzymes, and this is dependent on NO production (Zhou *et al.* 2005). Recent work by Zhang *et al.* (2007) has clearly demonstrated this link. Their data show that the enhanced MAPK activity and antioxidant gene expression and enzyme activity induced in maize leaves by ABA and H_2O_2 are in fact dependent on endogenous NO generation. Thus, the data indicate a key 'ABA–H_2O_2–NO–MAPK–antioxidant survival cycle' and suggest that during water stress ABA has several ameliorative functions that involve NO as a key signalling intermediate and which include the rapid induction of stomatal closure to reduce transpirational water loss and the activation of antioxidant defences to combat oxidative damage .

NO AND CA^{2+}: THE TWO MESSENGERS

Ca^{2+} is a ubiquitous second messenger. The fluctuations in the intracellular levels control an incredible number of processes. The specificity of Ca^{2+} signaling might be related to its extreme compartmentalization and its complex temporal and spatial distribution. The molecular systems for producing signaling events, namely Ca^{2+} channels and transporters, responds to an array of physiological stimuli including extracellular or intracellular messengers, membrane depolarization or hyperpolarization, and mechanical or thermal stimuli. Work on various animal cell types indicate that most of the channels and transporters involved in the control of Ca^{2+} homeostasis seem to be modulated by NO. NO acts either directly on channels and transporters, or indirectly *via.* interconnected secondary signaling cascades.

The list of transporters and Ca^{2+} channels directly regulated by NO by the means of S-nitrosylation on oxidation comprises Ca^{2+} -ATPase, store operated Ca^{2+} chaneels, voltage operated P/Q type and L type Ca^{2+} channels, CNGC and ryanodine receptors (RyRs; Stamler *et al.* 2001). RyRs are large, homotetrameric high conductance Ca^{2+} channels mediating the release of Ca^{2+} from the endoplasmic reticulum (Eu *et al.* 1999). RyRs are the targets of NO because they contain large number of sulfhydryls. For instance the skeletal muscle and cardiac RYRs (RyR1 and RyR2, respectively) contain 100 and 89 cysteines per 560-kDa subunit. Modification of RyR activity by NO might influence key physiological functions such as vasomotor control, muscular contraction, and insulin release. At molecular level, NO interacts with RyRs in a complex way since both activation and inhibition have been reported (Hart and Dulhunty, 2000). At physiological pO_2, RyR1 is activated by S-nitrosylation of a single cysteine residue (Cysteine 3635) located with in CaM binding domain. It is assumed that by S-nitrosylation cysteine 3635 reverses the inhibitory effect of CaM on RyR1 (Sun *et al.* 2001).

The indirect modulation of Ca^{2+} channels by NO is mainly mediated by cGMP. cGMP can mediate ion channel activity by two different mechanisms (1) direct action through its binding to cyclic-nucleotide binding sites of CNGCs, (2) indirect action mediated by PKGs (Ahern *et al.* 2002; Clementi, 1998). PKGs are widespread proteins that controls ion cahannels function, since virtually every type of ion channel contains PKG phosphorylation sites. Accordingly PKG mediated phosphorylation of Ca^{2+} channels, including the inositol 1, 4, 5-triphosphate receptor (IP_3R) and voltage dependent Ca^{2+} channels, has been proposed to account for the stimulatory and inhibitory effects of NO on Ca^{2+} mobilization (Clementi 1998). There is also increasing evidences that PKGs activate ADP-ribosyl cyclase, the enzyme catalyzing the cyclization of NAD^+ to cyclic ADP-ribose (c-ADPR). cADPR is a nucleotide showing Ca^{2+} mobilizing in a wide variety of cells. RyRs appears to be cADPR intracellular target; although it is not clear whether cADPR acts as a direct triggering molecule for the RYR mediated Ca^{2+} release or as a modulating factor. Activation of the cGMP/PKGs/cADPR cascade is a key pathway used by NO to activate RyRs in Sea urchin eggs and in various neuronal cell types.

The efficacy of NO in increasing intracellular Ca^{2+} concentration might have deep repercussions on cell metabolism and adaptation. It has been shown that the combined action of NO and Ca^{2+} lead to the activation of protein kinase-A dependent activation of CREB transcription factor capable of reprogramming the pattern of gene expression in neurons. NO and Ca^{2+} have to act in a very narrow time lapse for the activation to occur. Another important example of the cross talk between NO and Ca^{2+} is provided by Patel *et al.* 1999, who reported that increase in the frequency of Ca^{2+} oscillations in the rat liver cells, induced by the endothelial derived NO, stimulate metabolic activity in hepatocytes together with an increased blood flow resulting from the vasodilating effects of NO. The modulation of the Ca^{2+} signal by the NO is therefore critical for cellular and organ function.

PROTEIN KINASES AS TARGETS OF NO ACTION

During the last few years, an increasing number of protein kinases have been shown to be mediated by NO. NO activate all three mitogen activated protein kinase (MAPK) cascades, namely the stress activated protein kinase/c-Jun N-terminal kinase (SAPK/JNK) cascade, the stress activated p38 activated MAP kinase cascade and the ERK/MAPK cascade. The activation of ERK/MAPK module by NO has important implications. For instance, in stress conditions, this process leads to the inhibition of the proapoptotic protein Bad and to the expression of pro-apoptotic proteins (such as Bcl-2) and enzymes involved in the antioxidant defence. In neuronal cells, No induces the expression of immediate early genes through the ERK/MAPK pathway and plays a role in the synaptic plasticity. NO activates the MAPK cascade *via* the upstream S-nitrosylation of low molecular proteins including $p21^{ras}$, Rac1 and Cdc42. It has also been reported that NO can directly suppress JNK activation by S-nitrosylation, supporting pro-survival mechanisms. Similarly, NO inhibits the autokinase activity of JAK2 and JAK3, through oxidation of crucial dithiols to disulfide. Because JAKs transmit signals from almost all types of cytokine receptors, such inhibition may explain how macrophage produced NO affects the ability of certain lymphoid cells to proliferate in response to cytokine. Finally protein phosphates also represent targets for NO (Stamler *et al.* 2001). By direct interaction with phosphates, either activation or inhibition might occur, which will counteract or prolong activation of protein kinase activity. Taken together, these findings establish a role for protein kinase signaling pathways in the cellular response of NO.

NO AND PROGRAMMED CELL DEATH (PCD)

The most recent major advances in the study of programmed cell death (PCD) in plants include the observation that peptide inhibitors of caspases inhibit the hypersensitive response and NO has been shown to be required for the induction of disease related PCD. Mutant analysis has led to the cloning of the first genes involved in PCD related disease resistance, *LSD1* and *MLO*. Intrinsically programmed cell death is, by now, an accepted requisite for life in multicellular eukaryotes. Extra and intracellular inputs dictate whether cells find themselves in the right place, at the right time in development, and surrounded by the right neighbors (Ashkenazi and Dixit, 1998). If reinforcing microenvironmental signals are perceived, the cell lives and continues about its business. But when spatial and temporal signals clash, and the 'I'm OK, you're OK' monitoring system is perturbed, cells follow an intrinsic pre-set default pathway leading to their own death (Raff, 1992). Cells which beat the system, through mutations disarming the default death pathway(s), can become malignant. Conversely, it is well established that some cells are destined to die as part of normal developmental processes, or can be triggered to die quickly as part of a response to infection. This broad outline was established in animal systems. Recent data suggests that several fundamental aspects of this model can also operate in plants. Possible mechanistic overlap and molecular parallels between cell death control in plants and animals are under investigation. Definition of a 'program' is one which is intrinsically encoded by the plant cell. Hence, mutants who interrupt or induce cell death might define steps in pathways which either respond to, or regulate, cellular homeostasis. This definition, at first glance, could preclude cell death initiated by pathogen-produced toxins. But if that toxin has a specific cellular target, and that target performs a cellular task which is monitored for fidelity, then lack of fidelity in the process could trigger an intrinsic death program (Dangl *et al.* 1996; Greenberg, 1997; Pennell and Lamb, 1997; Wang *et al.* 1996). Programmed cell death (PCD) occurs at many points during plant development, but the most progress to date has been made using the hypersensitive cell death response (HR) to pathogen infection as a model. Whether the HR, per se, stops pathogen growth or whether it is a consequence of the mechanism(s) which does is not clear. It is very often correlated with disease resistance. As well, common disease symptoms — the outcome of a successful infection — also very often include the death of host cells. It is important to consider that the deaths engendered in these two outcomes could be mechanistically different; these differences might reflect the fact that in the HR the plant is controlling its own cellular destiny, whereas during the onset of disease symptoms it is the pathogen which may use interdiction of a normal cellular signaling pathway to further its goal of growth and propagation.

Many, but not all, programmed cell deaths in animals lead to a stereotyped cellular dismantling known as apoptosis. Apoptosis is the outcome of the integration of a wide range of signals, all of which feed into a conserved cysteine proteinase (caspase) cascade (Thornberry and Lazebnik 1998). This cascade is under constitutive negative regulation. If that regulation is removed, the default pathway is activation of caspases and orderly cellular dismemberment. Apoptosis, contrary to vernacular usage, is not synonymous with PCD, as there are other programs which can operate to initiate cell suicide in animal cells (*e.g.* [Schwartz *et al.* 1993]). Some facets of apoptosis are shared between kingdoms. Broadly, signals are transduced, ion fluxes occur, and specific proteinases are activated during plant cell death. Nuclear condensation and DNA cleavage first into large fragments, and subsequently into fragmented 'ladders', is observed in some, but not all cases of pathogen-induced PCD. The lack of apoptotic bodies in plants is not surprising, if their function is to facilitate phagocytosis of their contents by neighboring cells. There is no way for typical apoptotic bodies to pass through the cell wall. A recent study points out yet another difference between plant and animal versions of PCD processes. Tobacco cells pulsed with chemical inducers of PCD has a window within which they can reverse the program, even after chromatin condensation has begun (O'Brien *et al.* 1998). This is in contrast to the animal model where once initiated, there is no turning back from PCD. Proteins in the BCL2-CED9 family can either prevent or trigger PCD in animals (Adams and Cory 1998). No genes encoding BCL2 family members been unambiguously defined in public plant databases. Immunolocalization studies using antibodies to a human BCL2 family member, however, detected a BCL2-like epitope in leaves and meristematic tissues of tobacco and maize. BCL2 family members are mostly localized on the mitochondria in animals (Green and Reed 1998,). As might be expected, the BCL2-like plant protein localizes to mitochondria, nucleus and chloroplasts (Dion *et al.* 1997). An additional tool to uncover genes operative in the *BCL2* control pathway, perhaps including plant genes, was recently described [Xu Q and Reed JC, 1998)—yeast hybrid analysis was used to screen a human library for an inhibitor of BAX (a pro-apoptotic BCL2 family member), and homologues of this inhibitor were found in *Arabidopsis*, mouse, and *C. elegans*, implying possible mechanistic conservation. Overexpression of the animal anti-apoptotic BCL-XL, however, in transgenic tobacco did not inhibit HR (Mittler *at al.*, 1996). Animal viruses often encode proteins which inhibit caspase activation. When overexpressed in tomato and tobacco, the p35 protein from Baculovirus seems to inhibit both pathogen growth and disease symptoms caused by necrotrophic pathogens. Interestingly, growth of obligate biotrophs was not slowed although the eventual disease symptoms these pathogens produce were diminished. This result strongly suggests that induction of conserved mechanisms for apoptosis are used by virulent, necrotrophic pathogens to kill cells upon which they can then feed. Another preliminary study concludes that TMV induced HR was inhibited by p35 overexpression in tobacco and that mutation in p35 which abolish caspase inhibition also abolish this phenotype. A recent demonstration that plants induce a caspase-related proteinase activity preceding HR suggests that, among the many cysteine proteases in plants, at least one has the substrate requirements of an animal caspase (del Pozo and Lam E, 1998). In animals, the CED-4/Apaf1 proteins activate caspases and these are tethered by BCL-2 proteins until required (Zou *et al.*

1997). Enticing homologies between these proteins and a domain in plant disease resistance proteins has been noted (van der Biezen and Jones, 1998), further suggesting structural similarities between plant and animal cell death control.

SIGNAL TRAFFIC TO CONTROL HR CELL DEATH

The signal cascade leading to HR is triggered through recognition of a pathogen avirulence gene product by the appropriate disease resistance (*R*) gene (Hammond-Kosack and Jones, 1996), or by an elicitor of plant defense responses recognized by a specific receptor (*e.g.* [Nürnberger, *et al.* 1994]). Recognition of either type of signal initiates the overall resistance response, in association with an influx of Ca^{2+} ions from the extracellular space, anion fluxes leading to alkalinization of the extracellular milieu, an oxidative burst producing reactive oxygen intermediates (ROIs), defense gene activation, development of local and systemic disease resistance (Hammond-Kosack and Jones, 1996; Yang *et al.* 1997; Scheel, 1998). Measurements of increase in cytosolic calcium support the concept that it plays a very early role in this transduction chain (Xu and Heath, 1998). The overall order of these events seems to reflect the activation of multiple pathways, as inhibition of Ca^{2+} flux or oxidative burst prevents cell death but not defense gene activation (Jabs, *et al.* 1997). An exciting recent development is the identification of a MAP kinase which mediates a variety of input signals, is salicylic acid (SA) inducible, and leads to defense gene activation (Ligternik, *et al.* 1997; Zhang and Klessig, 1997; Zhang *et al.* 1998,). Interestingly, this kinase acts either upstream to or independently of the oxidative burst. This, or another, kinase cascade may end in the phosphorylation of a putative transcription factor for defense response genes (Dröge-Laser, *et al.* 1997). ROI are ordinarily generated during both metabolic and photoactivated processes, and damage the cell *via* uncontrolled oxidation of cellular components. Different ROI are produced within the cell, and, in combination with different sites of production, could drive cell death in a variety of cellular contexts. The oxidative burst initiated by pathogen attack results in superoxide synthesis, which can occur within regions of the cell wall adjacent to the pathogen (Bestwick, *et al.* 1997). Superoxide can spontaneously dismutate to the more stable product hydrogen peroxide (H_2O_2) or it can act as a localized signal molecule. H_2O_2 can serve multiple roles in plant disease resistance: as a direct antimicrobial activity; a component of structural defense through oxidative cross-linking of the cell wall; and as both an intra- and inter-cellular signaling molecule (Lamb and Dixon, 1997). Oxidative burst, in isolation, does not lead to cell death, but high levels of hydrogen peroxide (much greater than those produced during a typical oxidative burst) can kill cultured soybean cells (Levine *et al.* 1994). In addition, mutant bacteria which cannot trigger HR still generate a normal oxidative burst (Glazener, *et al.* 1996) and the oxidative burst is apparently not a sufficient signal for HR in the cowpea–cowpea rust fungus pathosystem (Heath, 1998). Nitric oxide (NO) can act to potentiate PCD in animals (Hausladen and Stamler, 1998) and important recent evidence supports a similar role for NO in plants (Delledone, *et al.* 1998; Durner, *et al.* 1998). If NO production is inhibited in cultured soybean cells or tobacco leaves, the HR is blocked and resistance to avirulent bacteria is moderately attenuated.

Furthermore, exogenous generation of NO and ROI synergistically promote cell death and induce gene expression of both PR1 (SA-dependent) and PAL (SA-independent) defense genes. How do these local events relate to the onset of systemic signals? Recent evidence suggests that ROI may also be rapidly induced at distal uninfected leaves (Alvarez, *et al.* 1998) following a local oxidative burst in infected leaves. The notion here is that rapid systemic signaling can be used as an early warning system which primes the SA-dependent systemic responses. The cell has numerous compounds and enzymes which serve to scavenge ROI before untoward damage can occur. These antioxidants are typically upregulated in times of oxidative stress (*e.g.* high light, ozone exposure). Ascorbate peroxidase (APX) uses ascorbate to detoxify hydrogen peroxide. APX is found throughout the cell, and is believed to be one of the main scavengers of peroxides. Like other antioxidative enzymes, the levels of APX declines in cells undergoing HR (Mittler, *et al.* 1998; Dorey, *et al.* 1997; Fodor, *et al.* 1997). Overproduction of APX in the chloroplast, however, does not protect tobacco against ozone induced damage (Torsethaugen, *et al.* 1997). Are there relationships between the set of signal events leading to HR and any case of developmentally controlled cell death? One highly developed system for analyses of PCD during development is tracheary element (TE) formation in trans differentiating *zinnia* mesophyll cells (Fukuda, 1996). Cell death during TE formation is not apoptotic and does not generate an observable oxidative burst. A calcium influx and perception of extracellular signals, mediated by a serine protease, however, are required for TE cell death (Groover, *et al.* 1997; Groover and Jones, 1998). Thus, most features of this developmental cell death differ from signaling in HR as outlined above.

SALICYLIC ACID (SA) AND THE POTENTIATION OF CELL DEATH

In tobacco and *Arabidopsis*, endogenous SA levels rise following pathogen attack and correlates with expression of pathogenesis-related (*PR*) genes as well as the onset of SAR. Exogenous addition of SA induces *PR* gene expression as well as heightening disease resistance (Ryals, *et al.* 1996). Yet, SA acts downstream of the oxidative burst and SA addition without pathogen triggers neither substantial increase in ROI nor cell death. A variety of experiments strongly support a model whereby SA and ROI (and probably NO) potentiate the overall HR and defense response (Fauth, *et al.* 1996; Kauss and Jeblick, 1996; Kauss and Jeblick, 1995; Shirasu, *et al.* 1997). Transgenic expression of salicylate hydroxylase (*nahG*) under the control of temporally different promoters demonstrates that SA accumulates during pre-necrotic phases of TMV infection in tobacco and that this accumulation is required to curtail viral spread (Mur, *et al.* 1997). SA pretreatment of parsley cell suspensions also potentiates subsequent induction of various defense genes by both elicitor-dependent and -independent modes. SA potentiated, pathogen-induced cell death is also supported by observations of reduced lag time to cell death from eight to four hours (Thulke and Conrath, 1998). The most likely scenario is that ROI production triggers both NO and SA synthesis. Superoxide and NO can combine to form the very dangerous peroxynitrite radical, and high levels of NOS activity could lead to more superoxide production (Dangl, 1998), resulting in an amplification which produces more SA and NO. It is critical to note that amplification mechanisms containing an extracellular component (ROI production or signals emanating from dying cells), must be negatively controlled by desensitization once a sufficient response has been reached. This desensitization could respond to gradients of ROI or SA around HR sites. For example, recent work suggests that although the levels of ROI and SA in live cells around HR sites are sufficient to induce defense gene transcription, they are not enough to trigger HR (Dorey, *et al.* 1998).

MISREGULATION OF HR CELL DEATH IN MUTANTS

A number of mutants misregulate cell death, suggesting that the wild-type function of the genes they define may be in PCD control. They are collectively termed 'lesion mimics' because their phenotypes are reminiscent of either HR or disease symptoms (Buckner, *et al.* 1998). Some lesion mimics map to disease resistance genes, suggesting that misregulation of R function can lead to inappropriate cell death. For example, the *Rp1 R*-gene locus in maize is prone to unequal crossing over that generates new fungal resistance specificities. Derivative alleles exist that cause lesioning in the absence of pathogen (Hu, *et al.* 1996). Some genes whose mutant phenotypes are increased disease resistance and propensity for cell death have been cloned. The *Arabidopsis LSD1* gene is a negative regulator of cell death which responds to a superoxide dependent signal. It encodes a zinc finger protein which may function as a transcriptional regulator (Dietrich *et al.* 1994; Dietrich *et al.* 1997). In barley, the *MLO* gene encodes a novel transmembrane protein (Büschges *et al.* 1997). In *mlo* mutants, defense pathways are primed; this leads to both a low level lesion phenotype and resistance against downy mildew. In contrast, *lsd1* mutants are generally resistant to virulent bacterial and oomycete pathogens. Thus, *MLO* negatively regulates subset defense response components active against one species of pathogen, while *LSD1* negatively regulates a potentially broader set. These two mutants are instructive because they suggest that defense systems are in part pre-existing and active in the absence of negative control. Mutations in negative regulators which interpret activation signal thresholds can lead to default cell death. In addition to negative regulators controlling the extent of HR, there are a number of lesion mimic mutants, mostly dominant, that induce the SA-dependent disease resistance pathway in *Arabidopsis*. These mutations can be sometimes genetically upstream of requirements for SA accumulation in defense gene induction and disease resistance (Hunt *et al.* 1997). Alternatively, they can function in the amplification loop of SA responses such that SA is both required for lesion formation and able to potentiate lesion formation (Weyman *et al.* 1995). There are also a number of constitutive disease resistant mutants which do not make lesions. In particular the *dnd* mutation is resistant to virulent pathogens in the absence of HR and makes a smaller and less obvious HR when challenged with avirulent pathogen (Yu *et al.* 1998). This phenotype is in keeping with classic examples of systemic tobacco mosaic virus resistance in tobacco and suggests that the potential normal requirement for HR in either local or systemic resistance can be bypassed. Do all mutants that trigger PCD define genes whose wildtype function is either in pathogen recognition or response pathways? *Les22* in maize was recently cloned and found to encode an enzyme in the porphyrin pathway (Hu *et al.* 1998). Mutation in this enzyme causes a build up of a photoactivatable intermediate, which generates ROI in response to high light. Additionally, this pathway seems to impinge on heme formation, which is required for catalase and APX function, resulting in an inability to detoxify the ROI produced. If leaves are protected from high light until they are fully developed, thereby lowering flux through this pathway, lesioning disappears. Thus, ROI resulting from metabolic perturbation of pathways can trigger PCD and yet not be involved in defense. The maize *LLS1* gene is a negative regulator of cell death, and encodes an enzyme believed normally to degrade a phenolic signal. The absence of this enzyme leads to cell death (Gray *et al.* 1997). Neither *Les22* nor *lls1* mutants induce disease resistance pathways. Mechanistically, this class of mutants suggests that cells sense metabolic perturbations and can follow a default pathway, normally under negative control, to cell death. Alternatively, these mutants result in accumulation of toxic compounds which then kill the cell. Lesion mimics can also result from transgene overexpression. Several recent papers illustrate how these may trigger the disease resistance pathway much as the lesion mimics upstream of SA accumulation described above. Transgenic tobacco plants with reduced levels of catalase form lesions and express PR genes in response to high light, and this death increases protection against TMV and Pseudomonas (Chamnongpol *et al.* 1996; Chamnongpol *et al.* 1998; Takahashi *et al.* 1997) in an SA-dependent manner (Du and Klessig 1997). Expression of the light driven proton pump bacterio-opsin in tobacco results in increased systemic SA levels, PR gene expression, and resistance to several pathogens (Mittler, *et al.* 1995). Expression of the same gene in potato imparted resistance to certain fungal isolates, but unexpectedly increased susceptibility to Potato Virus X (Abad *et al.* 1997). Hence, inducible artificial lesion mimics resulting from transgene expression may not be a panacea for disease resistance in agriculture, but may prove useful in certain cases.

Measurement of NO

Measurement of NO in biological specimens is difficult both because of the small amounts present (usually less than nanomolar) and the lability of NO in the presence of O_2. This instability is partially ameliorated by adding superoxide dismutase to the medium in which NO is to be measured (Archer SL and Cowan NJ, 1991). Superoxide dismutase (2000-4000 units) enhances the detection of NO from isolated pulmonary artery rings, presumably by decreasing the amount of superoxide anion present and thereby preventing the destruction of NO. NO is commonly measured by the chemiluminescence reaction with acid reflux (Palmer RMJ *et al.* (1987); Rees DD *et al.* (1989); Myers P *et al.* (1990); Amezcua JL *et al.* (1989); Chen WZ *et al.*(1989)) or without acidification (Menon N *et al.* 1989), by the diazotization of sulfaniic acid assay (Ignarro LJ *et al.* (1987); Tracey WR *et al.* (1990); Martin W *et al.* 1988; Schmidt HHHW *et al.* 1988), by electron paramagnetic resonance (EPR) with nitroso or hemoglobin traps (Arroyo C and Kohno M 1991; Greenberg, SS *et al.* 1990), and by spectrophotometric measurement of the conversion of reduced to met-hemoglobin (Kelm M *et al.* 1988; Kelm M and Schrader J 1988). These assays use one of three detection strategies: they chemically trap NO and measure either adduct (nitrosyl hemoglobin, NO-Hb), the conversion of reduced to methemoglobin, or the light emission (chemiluminescence) that occurs when ozone interacts with NO.

CHEMILUMINESCENCE ASSAY

This assay was originally developed to measure NO as an atmospheric pollutant (Zafiriou OC and McFarland M 1980), but when performed with acid and K! it is also an assay for nitrite (Aoki T 1990). Detection of NO is based on the observation that ozone interacts with NO to generate light. Luminescence, measured by a sensitive photomultiplier tube (PMT), is directly proportional to NO levels. The assay takes advantage of the low solubility of NO in aqueous solutions by measuring NO in the gas phase, whether the original sample was a gas or a liquid. If the specimen is liquid, the NO is driven into the gas phase by bubbling the solution with an inert gas under vacuum conditions, a process called "stripping?'. The gas above the liquid is called the "head space?'. Chung and Fung (1990) documented the predisposition of NO to exist as a gas. They found that when they injected NO into a physiological buffer, 83% immediately appeared in the head space. The specimen (gas or liquid) is injected into a glass purge chamber previously evacuated to 3 mm Hg to remove O_2 and stabilize NO. If the specimen is gaseous (Brien J *et al.* 1991) one can simply enter the sample into the reaction chamber without the need for stripping. Several components are necessary to measure NO using chemiluminescence. In addition to a PMT and ozone generator, one must have a sample chamber in which NO can be held, and if necessary stripped into the gas phase. A glass purge chamber (Sievers Research, Inc., Boulder, and Cob.) that has a fit in its floor to permit stripping of liquid specimens is useful for this purpose. This purge chamber has an inflow line for delivery of an inert gas to the fit and an outflow line to carry the gas in the head space to the reaction chamber. NO is "stripped" from the liquid to the gas phase by bubbling the specimen with an inert gas such as helium (12 ml/mm x 60 s).

Aoki T (1990) showed that the rate of stripping the liquid samples is an important determinant of NO measurement; flow rates of less than 8 mi/mm cause underestimation of NO due to incomplete stripping. If one is dealing with a gaseous specimen the stripping phase is omitted, greatly simplifying the assay. Once stripping is complete, the gaseous specimen is drawn through a "needle valve" into a reaction chamber. The opening size in the needle valve is adjusted to make the NO signal appear as a brief spike and avoid entrainment of foam from the sample. In the reaction chamber, ozone (generated internally by electrical discharge) is mixed with NO in front of a cooled, red-sensitive PMT. It is critical to avoid aspiration of foam or bubbles into the reaction chamber as this can coat the PMT and diminish its sensitivity. This precaution is especially important in dealing with biological specimens because proteinaceous material foams dramatically during stripping, limiting the assay's usefulness in specimens containing albumin or blood.

Assay calibration

Gaseous NO or aqueous solutions containing various amounts of NO (20-1000 pmol) are used to calibrate the photomultiplier tube. A calibration curve is produced by plotting the signal from the PMT (mV) vs. the known NO dose. This calibration curve is used to estimate the amount of NO present in biological specimens. The integration time, the period of time during which photons are counted before a value is presented and counting resumes, can be varied to optimize the assay for weak vs. strong NO signals. The optimal integration time should be short enough so the counts do not saturate the tube but long enough to detect small signals. Whereas an integration time of 0.06 is adequate for most experiments, use of an integration time of 0.25 s results in a more linear NO/chemiluminescence curve and greater sensitivity, albeit at the price of increased noise. A NO dose/chemiluminescence curve must be constructed for each integration time.

Sensitivity/detection threshold

Zafiriou and McFarland Aoki, T. (1990) reported that the chemiluminescence assay is sensitive to 10- M NO. However, most investigators find the sensitivity threshold for detection of NO is 20-50 pmol. Several authors have noted that the chemiluminescence/NO curve are linear between NO doses of 300 and 3000 pmol. The sensitivity of the assay for authentic NO is not dramatically affected by the use of reducing agents or acids if done properly, for unlike measurements in biological models, O_2 can be excluded and there should be little signal amplification due to recruitment of nitrite or other oxidation products.

Specificity

The specificity of the chemiluminescence assay depends on whether the sample is acidified or refluxed under strong reducing conditions (*e.g.*, in the presence of KI or NaI) before to measurement. If the assay is performed without acidification or NaI, the signals achieved in biological models are much smaller (usually by 1 log order) than those produced in the presence of acid and NaI (Menon N *et al.* 1991). In the absence of NaI and acid, chemiluminescence is almost exclusively due to NO. The few other substances that could elicit chemiluminescence (*e.g.*, H2S) are either nonvolatile or do not occur in biologic models. To be detected in this assay a molecule must first enter the head space, a fact that provides a good deal of specificity. NO has a high partition coefficient and tends to enter the head space whereas nitrite and nitroso thiols will remain in solution. Once in the gas phase, a substance must be capable of interacting with ozone to produce light. This requires that the substance have unsaturated or strongly polar groups (*e.g.*, sulfides, amines), characteristics that are rare in small molecules. Thus NO's unique chemical properties greatly enhance the specificity of the assay. Most authors report that the assay is entirely specific; however, it has been found that DMSO at high doses can cause a chemiluminescent signal. This is a potential problem because DMSO is used as a solvent for many drugs, including the endothelial-dependent vasodilator A23187. This problem can be resolved by interposing a red filter, which absorbs light at the wavelengths emitted by the interaction of ozone and sulfoxides, in front of the PMT and limiting the dose of DMSO used to less than 0.1 ml/I0 ml sample.

An alternative means of proving that a chemiluminescence signal is due to NO is to scrub the head space by passing the gas through a solution of 1 M Fe^{2+} before it reaches the reaction chamber. Fe^{2+} interacts with NO and reduces the signal strength several hundred fold if the signal was due to NO. A number of features of the chemiuminescence assay merit discussion.

DIAZOTIZATION ASSAY

This assay is the standard technique for measuring inorganic nitrite. It is discussed as a NO assay only because it has been used as such in the literature. This two-step assay is based on the observation that the adduct of nitroxides and sulfanilic acid interacts with N-(1-naphthyl) ethylenediamine, generating a product that is readily monitored by spectrophotometry.

Methods

The basic assay is designed to measure single samples, but it can be modified to give "on-line" results (Tracey WR *et al.* 1990). In the basic assay the sample is placed in a vessel containing 4 N HCI. An aliquot is withdrawn and incubated for 10 mm with a mixture of 2 N HC1 and sulfanilic acid (2 mg/ml). N- (1-naphthyl) ethylenediamine (1 mg/ml) is added, and after 30 mm absorbance at 548 nm is measured. The NO level can be calculated by comparing the observed change in absorbance to a NO/absorption calibration curve.

Utilization

Tracey *et al.* (1990) evaluated the ability of an automated version of the diazotization assay to detect authentic NO and attempted to correlate measured NO with EDRF activity in a parallel bioassay. In these studies the test fluid (either authentic NO or EDRF produced by stimulating cultured endothelial cells with bradykinin BK, adenosine triphosphate ATP, or A23187) was split, so that part was delivered to a bioassay (a denuded aortic ring) and the remainder to a spectrophotometer. The diazotization assay was performed en route to the spectrophotometer. Perfusate destined for the spectrophotometer (1.2 ml/min) was mixed first with 2 M HC1 and then sulfaniic acid (0.7 mg/ml) was added. This mixture was passed through a 3.5 mm delay coil and then N-(l-naphthyl) ethylenediamine (0.7 mg/ml) was added. All reagents were infused at 0.3 ml/mm. After passing through a 6 mm delay coil, the mixture entered the spectrophotometer and the absorbances at 548 nm were compared to baseline (the absorption measured with all reagents present, but before adding EDRF or NO). The detection threshold of the diazotization assay is roughly 10 to 106 M NO. In this assay, absorption at 548 nm should increase solely as a function of NO dose. In fact, when using this assay on authentic NO solutions, Tracy *et al.* (1990) found the magnitude of signal varied depended on the duration of NO bubbling used to prepare the authentic NO solution. The longer the solutions were bubbled with NO, the greater the signal noted by the diazotization assay. In contrast, the duration of bubbling had no effect on the vasodilator potency of the NO solution in bioassay. They then removed the NO from the test solutions by bubbling it with an inert gas and made the elegant observation that bioassay activity was, as expected, severely diminished; surprisingly, NO levels estimated from the diazotization assay were unaltered. They correctly interpreted these findings as evidence that a nonvolatile, hemodynamically inactive substance, probably NO, was accounting for much of the NO signal in the diazotization assay. It appears that despite the use of nominally O_2-free solutions, the small contaminating amounts of O_2 caused conversion of NO to NO, which was biologically inactive but was converted to NO during the diazotization assay by the acid pH.

Of even more concern, the administration of ATP, A23187, and BK decreased tension in aortic rings from 40 to 50% (as did authentic NO), but the EDRF failed to produce any signal in the diazotization assay. This indicates that either the diazotization assay is insufficiently sensitive to detect the amount of NO produced under these conditions or the endothelial relaxing factor in these experiments was not NO. It appears that the diazotization assay is not adequately sensitive to measure NO at submicromolar concentrations and is best considered a measure of nitrite and mixed nitroxides.

ELECTRON PARAMAGNETIC RESONANCE (EPR) ASSAY

NO is a gaseous, paramagnetic molecule with the unpaired electron in the _ orbital. The basic principle of detecting radicals by EPR spectroscopy is that at a discrete amount of energy (microwave frequency) and magnetic field strength, unpaired electrons are promoted to higher energy levels; relaxation from this state produces a characteristic spectrum. NO and NO_2 cannot be studied by simple EPR as the relaxation time of the stimulated electron to ground state is too rapid to be detected (Maples K *et al.* 1991). Spin traps are compounds that interact with the unstable radicals, producing a more stable adduct that can be detected by EPR. The spin traps that can be used to detect NO include the nitroxide compounds and hemoglobin. Nitroxide traps are relatively stabilized by the resonance of the unpaired electron. There are two types of nitroxide spin traps, the nitrones and the nitroso compounds. The nitroso compounds usually provide the best information about the identity of a radical, as the radical is added directly to the nitroso nitrogen, thereby increasing the information in the hyperfine splitting parameters (Buettner GR 1987). However, oxygen-based adducts of the nitroso compounds are unstable and one must usually rely on the nitrones for such studies. The identity of the radical, defined by EPR, is characterized by the magnitude and multiplicity of the hyperfine splitting of the spin adduct's spectra. The amount of radical present is proportional to the magnitude of the signal.

Methods for EPR using nitroxide traps

A commercially available spectrometer is used. The magnetic field is usually set at or near 330 mT, with a microwave power of 8-10 mW, frequency of 9 GHz, and modulation amplitude of 0.1 mT. Experiments need to be performed in darkness to prevent photolysis of the spin traps. When NO interacts with the nitroso compounds (*e.g.*, 2-methyl-2-nitrosopropane (MNP) and 3, 5, -dibromo-4-nitrosobenzene, DBNBS), a triplet signal is formed that can be characterized by its line width and hyperfine coupling constant.

Utilization

Although in principle this technique is simple, the attempt to detect NO using traps which themselves have - NO moieties is problematic. Arroyo and Kohno (1991) compared the specificity of multiple spin traps for NO and concluded that the nitroso spin traps (MNP, DBNBS) are better suited for the identification of NO-rebated signals than the nitrones (*e.g.*, 5, 5 - dimethyb-pyrrobine-N-oxide (DMPO). The spectra generated by the nitrones in the presence of NO appear to result from hydrolysis of the probes and provide an inaccurate estimate of NO levels. In fact, nitrones are unstable at acid pH and tended to yield NO-type spectra even in the absence of NO.

Hemoglobin is also useful as a spin trap because nitrosyl hemoglobin (NO-Hb) is readily measured by EPR. NO interacts with hemoglobin, producing both NO-Hb and methemoglobin (the NO-Hb interacts with oxygen, producing further methemoglobin) (Henry Y *et al.* 1991). The 77 K spectra of NOHb has a characteristic three-line, hyperfine signal that is not seen when hemoglobin is exposed to other nitro compounds (*e.g.*, NO, azide). A super-hyperfine structure (triplet of a triplet) is also detectable. The g values for NO-Hb are 2.060, 2.010, and 2.005, with values of 26.8 and 6.4 G. An advantage of using hemoglobin as a spin trap technique is the commercial availability of hemoglobin bound to agarose (Sigma, St. Louis, Mo.). This gel can be applied to columns suitable for EPR spectrometry, as described by Wennmalm *et al.* (1990). Quartz columns (length 15 cm, ID 3.8 mm) are lined with a hemoglobmn-agarose gel (created by dissolving 400 l of Hb-agarose in 1 ml of H_2O) and then excess material is washed free with 10 ml of H_2O. The hemoglobin is reduced (manifest as a change in color from brown to purple) by the addition of dithionite (10 mg/I ml H_2O). The column can then be exposed to the experimental specimen and analyzed by EPR at 77 K. Like the chemiluminescence assay, the EPR NO-Hb assay can measure NO itself, or by adding dithionite or acid to the specimen, can measure combined NO and nitrite. Greenberg *et al.* (1990) studied EDRF activity and NO production in femoral arterial rings using the N0-Hb EPR technique. The threshold for detection of authentic NO was I nM (spectra obtained at 77 K using a spectrometer operating at 9.42 GHz with 20 mW power and 100 kHz modulation frequency). They attempted to detect NO production in response to acetylcholine by using this technique, but found no signal in the effluent from acetylcholine-treated femoral arteries even though ACH and the authentic NO had produced similar relaxation in the bioassay. They concluded that ACH-induced vasodilatation was not mediated by NO in the canine femoral artery. The conclusion that ACH-induced vasodilatation does not (always) occur through production of NO is supported by studies of bovine and rat pulmonary arteries using the chemiluminescence assay. Wang *et al.* (1991) noted increased levels of NO-Hb in rats with endotoxic shock. They enhanced EPR-detection of NOHb by pooling the blood from several animals to increase the signal intensity. The signal-to-noise ratio was improved by subtracting the EPR spectra from the blood of control animals. They reported that levels of NO-Hb did not correlate with vascular tone, an observation made previously in studies that failed to find a correlation between dilator potency of the nitro vasodilator drugs and the blood levels of NO-Hb. The authors discuss the hypothesis that only that fraction of NO that reaches the lumen is available for interaction with reduced hemoglobin. The assay may therefore not have access to the pool of NO that determines vasodilator efficacy, namely, that which reaches the smooth muscle. However, this theoretical criticism applies potentially to all assays. One advantage of the N0-Hb assay over the chemibuminescence assay is the ability of the former to measure NO in blood, and unlike the diazotization assay, acidification is unnecessary, although acidification of the specimen will convert the NO-Hb EPR assay to a nitrite assay. Wennmalm *et al.* (1990) used the N0-Hb complex, as detected by EPR, to measure nitrite in humans after forearm ischemia. They added dithionite to specimens, there by converting nitrite to NO, and then measured EPR spectra using a spectrometer (microwave frequency 9.17 GHz, power 8 mW). Spectra were scanned from 3000 to 3500 gauss with a scan rate of 250 G/min. They established a "normal" venous nitrite level in humans of 0-0.6 mM and noted that ischemia greatly increased this level.

Westenberger *et al.* (1990) detected the NO adduct of Hb in the venous blood of rats with endotoxic shock using EPR (microwave power 10 mW at 9.20 GHz, modulation amplitude 8 G). In sepsis, NO-Hb accounted for as much as 0.8% of all hemoglobin. They found the typical three-line hyperfine splitting of 1.75 mT at g' 2.012 and 1.6 mT at g' 2.609 "characteristic of an unpaired electron coupled to nitrogen in a ferrous heme-NO complex". The authors identified a separate EPR signal at g' 6 that corresponded to the ferric heme in methemoglobin. Maples *et al.* (1991) found a linear relationship between the amount of NO inhaled and the intensity of the NO-Hb EPR signal in broncho-alveolar lavage fluid from human volunteers who intermittently inhaled low doses of NO (1.5-4 ppm, 20 mm every other day x 6). Unfortunately the equipment required to perform EPR is expensive and considerable expertise is necessary. In contrast, the chemiluminescence assay is easier to learn and much less costly. Furthermore, the interaction between NO and hemoglobin is pH dependent. Liu *et al.* (1987) showed that at alkaline pH there was significant impairment of EPR detection of NO-Hb adduct due to inhibition of the interaction between NO and Hb (hyperfine coupling was unchanged). Hemoglobin forms a fairly stable adduct with NO that is readily detected by EPR (Doyle MP and Hoekstra JW 1981). For those with the necessary equipment and expertise, EPR, particularly using hemoglobin as a trap, is a useful means of assaying NO.

METHEMOGLOBIN SPECTROPHOTOMETRY ASSAY

Unlike the EPR assay, this technique is based on the rapid oxidation of reduced hemoglobin (Fe^{2+}) to methemoglobin (Fe^{3+}) by NO rather than on the detection of NO-Hb. NO's oxidation of reduced hemoglobin occurs in less than 100 ms, suggesting the assay is sufficiently dynamic to study the time course of NO synthesis. The threshold for detection of NO using this assay is I nM.

Methods

Commercially available hemoglobin is 50-95% methemoglobin (Matsunaga K and Furchgott RF 1988) and must be reduced with a molar excess of dithionite. Once reduced, the hemoglobin gradually reoxidizes to methemoglobin. Although some authors have then purified the mixture by gel chromatography using a Sephadex column, this is not essential. NO is detected by observing the characteristic shift in the Soret absorbance peak of hemoglobin from 433 nm to 406 nm. Accumulation of oxyhemoglobin is not a problem in this assay due to the much higher affinity of hemoglobin for NO than O_2. Furthermore, oxyhemoglobin can be detected by its Soret peak (416 nm). Conversion of reduced to methemoglobin can be measured as the extinction difference at 401 and 411 nm (the isobestic point) (Schror, K *et al.* 1991).

Utilization

Ignarro *et al.* (1987) detected the production of NO or a related nitrosyl product from A23187-stimulated aortic endothelial cells by using this assay. They found that estimates of NO synthesis provided by the diazotization and methemoglobin assays were comparable. Kelm *et al.* (1988) measured the production of EDRF/NO by porcine thoracic aortic endothelial cells using a "difference spectrophotometric" variant of this assay. They used 2-4 ml of endothelial cells grown on beads as a source of EDRF and perfused this column of beads with medium containing 4 iM HbO_2. Methemoglobin production was measured as the extinction difference between the absorption maximum and isobestic point of reduced vs. met-hemoglobin. These authors measured NO in real time using a dual wavelength (401 and 411 nm), double-beam spectrophotometer equipped with a flow-through cell. They were able to document the production of NO beginning 15 s after stimulation of endothelial cells with bradykinin (peak production at I min). Kostic and Schrader (Kostic M and Schrader J 1992) used this assay to indicate that post ischemic myocardial hyperemia is due at least in part to increased production of NO. Schror *et al.* (1991) demonstrated increased NO-Hb in response to nitro vasodilators in the Langendorff rabbit heart. The advantages of the measurement of NO by monitoring methemoglobin production include the wide availability of spectrophotometers, avoidance of sample acidification, and the relative stability of the methemoglobin. Furthermore, as the reduced hemoglobin is present from the beginning of an experiment, NO synthesis can be measured continuously, removing the uncertainty as to when to sample for NO. However, unlike the non acidified chemiluminescence assay, which gains specificity from the volatility and water insolubility of NO, this assay might detect other nitrosyl groups in the sample.

GAS CHROMATOGRAPHY

Although NO can be detected by standard gas chromatography techniques, this assay is much less sensitive than chemiluminescence or EPR assays. Pai *et al.* (1987) used a Varian gas chromatograph with a Porapak Q column and electron capture detector to measure enzymatical by generated NO. They found that gas chromatography was much less sensitive than chemiluminescence assay, a difference that they attributed part to the sample processing methodology required for gas chromatography.

ALTERNATE NITRIC OXIDE ASSAYS

Mass spectroscopy

Gustafsson *et al.* (1991) recently used mass spectroscopy to measure NO in the breath of guinea pigs. They trapped NO as nitroso thio proline by bubbling the expirate through a degassed aqueous solution of thioproline (15 nM). The nitroso thioproline was extracted with ethyl acetate, and dried and derivatized by N-methyl-N-(tertbutyldimethylsilyl) trifluroacetamide in acetonitnile. Samples were placed on a CP-Sil-5-CB column interfaced with a mass spectrometer operating in the positive chemical ionization mode with isobutane. The derivatizedform of nitrosothioproline had a retention time of 4.76 mm. It is not clear whether this assay is more sensitive than measuring breath chemiuminescence. Indeed, in the same experiment breath NO was exposed to Fe (II) sulfate and the resulting nitrite was measured by chemiluminescence. The principle of trapping NO in degassed water for subsequent analysis, regardless of the technique, appears to a reasonable strategy for measuring exhaled NO. In addition, these experiments noted that in the rabbit, inhalation of physiologic levels of hypoxia (6% O_2) acutely decreased the amount of expired NO from normoxic levels of approximately 24 to 20 ppb.

MICROELECTRODE NO ASSAYS

There are currently two amperometric methods available for measuring NO from intact tissues and single cells. Shibuki (1990) recently reported the measurement of NO release in the cerebellum using a micro electrode. He modified a miniature O_2 electrode by sealing its fire-polished 150-250 tm tip with a thin chloroprene rubber seal so that only low molecular weight gases could enter. By introducing a platinum cathode within the pipette and holding it at positive voltage, it was possible to detect NO, a readily oxidized gas, by its oxidation at the electrode's surface. Pipettes were fibbed with 30 mM NaC1 and 0.3 mM HC1 (pH 3.5), and a Teflon-coated platinum wire was placed as close as possible to the membrane. A 200 im silver wire was the anode. The cathode was kept 0.9 V from the anode and the anode was grounded. The principle of the assay is that if the anode is grounded there should be no current. There was a linear relationship between current and NO concentration *in vitro* over a small range (1-3 tM NO). Using this electrode, Shibuki was able to measure NO release in rat cerebellar tissue elicited by electrical stimulation of the white matter. The author claims a nanomolar NO sensitivity for the technique with a rapid response time (seconds). If others duplicate this technique it may permit measurement of local production of NO in tissues.

Luis A.J. Mur *et al.* 2005 demonstrate the use of laser photoacoustic detection (LPAD) as a highly sensitive method to detect in planta nitric oxide (NO) production from tobacco (*Nicotiana tabacum*). The specificity of the photoacoustic signal for NO when adding gas or the NO donor, sodium nitroprusside, on injection into plant leaves, was demonstrated by its abolition with O_3 ($NO + O_3 \rightarrow NO_2 + O_2$). The utility of the LPAD method was shown by examination of a nonhost hypersensitive response and a disease induced by *Pseudomonas syringae* (*P. s.*) pv *phaseolicola* and *P. s.* pv *tabaci* in tobacco.

NO in plants

NO involved in various aspects of plant growth and development (Beligni and Lamattina 2000, Gouvea *et al.* 1997, Leshem *et al.* 1998) action of NO in plants has been mainly accomplished by exogenous application of NO donors in a wide range of plant systems. The concentration of NO release and the reducing power (Ramamurthi and Lewis1997). Various role of nitric oxide in growth and developmental processes, such as :

SEED GERMINATION

Exogenous application of NO and related nitrogen oxides have been reported as stimulators of seed germination and break dark imposed dormancy (Keenley and Fotheringham 1997, Giba, 1998). Seeds of *Paulownia tormentosa* need long periods of light to germinate. However, if seeds are supplied with 10 mM KNO_3, a single red light exposure was sufficient to induce germination (Grubisic and Konjevic, 1990). SNP and some other organic and inorganic nitrates also stimulated germination with a similar efficacy (Grubusic *et al.* 1992). The dark imposed dormancy of lettuce seeds could also be broken by either 100μM SNP or 100μM SNAP to the same extent as both GA_3 (Beligni and Lamattina, 2000). Thus, stimulatory effects of nitrate compounds in plants could be due to their reduction to NO and that phytochrome regulated dormancy breakage in photoblastic seeds was closely connected with redox changes (Grubusic *et al.* 1992). These effects of nitrite on seed germination suggest that soil nitrite is one of the factors determining seed germination (Neill *et al.* 2003).

CELL GROWTH AND DIFFERENTIATION

In the life cycle of a plant, light is known to inhibit the elongation growth of hypocotyls and internodes. NO donors are reported to significantly reduce hypocotyls growth and internode elongation in three different plants species (*Arabidopsis thaliana, Lactuca sativa and Solanum tuberosum)* grown in dark or under conditions of low light intensity (Beligni and Lamattina, 2000). Low micromolar concentrations of NO increased the rate of leaf expansion in pea and elongation of maize root segments (Leshem and Haramaty1996; Gouvea *et al.* 1997). NO also exerts effects on cellular differentiation, especially xylogenesis, and is currently regarded as a signal molecule in plant cell differentiation. Programmed cell death (PCD) is one of the most distinctive characterstics exhibited by the differentiating xylem in plants and is coordinated with the processes of secondary wall formation and lignification (Groover and Jones, 1999). NO has been shown to affect plant peroxidases involved in cell wall lignification in the xylem of *Zinnia* seedlings and *in vitro Zinnia* cell culture system. NO production remains characteristic of vascular tissue (predermined to die). The scavenging of NO by 2-phenyl-4, 4, 5, 5- tetramethyl imdazoline-1-oxyl-3-oxide (PTIO) inhibits tracheary element differentiation and increase cell viability (Gabaldon *et al.* 2005). In the second system, Gabaldon *et al.* (2005) used mesophyll cells of *Zinnia* leaves for studying transdifferentiation of cells into tracheary elements.

Cell respiration: High concentration of NO affects mitochondrial functionality in plant cells by reducing cell respiration due to strong inhibition of the cytochrome pathway (Zottini *et al.* 2002). They observed that treatment of suspension cultures of carrot cells with SNP (1 mM) decreased cell viability and cPTIO prevented the killing effect of NO, thus demonstrating that NO is responsible for cell lethality. In plants, in addition to cytochrome oxidase, a second terminal oxidase, termed the alternative oxidase (AOX) is also present. Unlike cytochrome pathway, which is coupled to oxidative phosphorylation, electron transport is shunted into the alternative pathway resulting in a nearly normal rate of respiratory O_2 uptake (Miller and Day, 1996). According to Millar and Day (1996), AOX pathway may play a role in NO tolerance in higher plants by lowering respiration dependent production of ROS under conditions where NO is overproduced (nitrosative stress).

PHOTOSYNTHESIS

Air pollution studies in plants have shown that NO inhibits photosynthetic CO_2 assimilation (Wellburn, 1990). Since NO is degraded to nitrite (or nitrate) in an aqueous solution under ambient air, But studies of Takahashi and Yamasaki (2002) suggest that nitrite is involved in the mechanism of NO dependent inhibition of photophosphorylation, and confirm that NO molecule itself has a suppressive effect on photophosphorylation by inhibiting electron transport activity in photosystem II. According to these authors, inhibitory effect of NO is due to the NO induced dissociation of bicarbonate from the specific sites of thylakoids. The sensitivity of photosynthesis against NO depends on the local concentration of bicarbonate within thylakoid membranes. NO also inhibited induced pH formation across the thylakoid membrane. This NO-induced inhibition was found to be temporary as the activity was completely recovered by removing NO.

Emission of NO from plants has been linked with the accumulation of nitrite in many cases (Mallic *et al.* 2000 a,b; Klepper, 1990, 1991).Nonetheless, nitrite is accumulated in the cells when photosynthetic electron transport (Shingles *et al.* 1996) or nitrogen metabolism (Mallic *et al.* 2000a,b) is not operational. The activities of nitrogen metabolism and carbon assimilation are interdependent (Huppe and Turpin, 1994). From these studies, it appears that NO acts a transmembrane messenger to alarm dysfunction nitrogen assimilation so that photosynthetic activity is down regulated.

CELL METABOLISM

NO also affect the functioning of cellular organelles like chloroplasts (Takahashi and Yamasaki, 2002), mitochondria (Zottini *et al.* 2002) and subcellular organelles like peroxisomes (del Rio, 2002). Chloroplast and mitochondria are important cell organelles for energy transduction in the processes of photosynthesis and respiration, respectively NO exerts its effect at various levels.

ROOT ORGANOGENESIS

Exogenously applied NO donors, such as sodium nitrite (SN), sodium nitroprusside (SNP), nitrosoglutathione (NGLU) and nitrocystein (NCYS) are reported to induce elongation of maize root tip segments in a dose- dependent manner (Gouvea *et al.* 1997). These workers suggested that NO is a putative elongation inducer and that IAA and NO donors conceivably share common steps in the signal transduction pathway, since both elicited the same plant response. Pagnussat *et al.* 2002 also demonstrated dependence of auxin- induced adventitious root formation in cucumber explants on NO. IAA treatment in cucumber explants induced a transisents increase in the level of endogenous NO in the basal region of the hypocotyls where new root meristems develop. Moreover, NO has been found effective in inducing adventitious root formation in woody species (Lamattina *et al.* 2003). Stohr (2001) reported involvement of plasma membrane- bound enzyme the nitrite: NO reductase in the formation of NO in plant roots. The presence of NO is also reported in root nodules (Mathieu *et al.* 1998). EPR analysis of soybean plants grown in the absence of nitrate showed the presence of leghemoglobin-NO (Lb-NO) complexes in root nodules. The concentration of Lb-NO complexes in root nodules. The concentration of Lb-NO complexes varied with age, being higher in younger nodules and almost absent in senescent ones (Mathieu *et al.* 1998) they suggested that NO binding to heme group of hemoglobin is essential to have a role in nitrogen fixation . Possibly, Lb-NO could react with O^{2-} and / or H_2O_2 to avoid ROS damage to the nodules and controlled levels of Lb-NO complex in active nodules could result in an equilibrium between oxy-Lb mediated oxygen transport and ROS formation. But according to Nathan (1992), NO exerts deletrious effect on the rate of nitrogen fixation. However, significance of the effect of NO during symbiosis is still far from completely understood.

FLOWERING

He *et al.* (2004) provided pharmacological, physiological, molecular and genetic data to demonstrate that NO represses the photoperiod and autonomous floral pathways in *Arabidopsis thaliana*. Treatment of *A. thaliana* plants with NO donor (SNP) enhanced the vegetative growth and significantly delayed flowering. Studies revealed that NO affects the genes that control both the autonomous and environmentally sensitive pathways that control flowering. NO suppressed CONSTANS and GIGANTEA gene expression and enhanced FLOWERING LOCUS C expression indicating thereby that NO regulates the photoperiod and autonomous pathways. Several genes affected by NO (CAB, CO and GI) are also regulated by light, the primary effect of NO may be on light signaling, and the effect on flowering may be secondary.

PIGMENT SYNTHESIS

NO donors are reported to stimulate de-etiolation and increase chlorophyll content in potato, lettuce, *Arabidopsis* and dark brown wheat seedlings (Beligni and Lamattina, 2000). Short term pulse of white light or red light cause 2-3 fold increase in the chlorophyll content of NO treated seedlings over control ones suggesting thereby a putative role for NO in de-etiolation (Beligni and Lamattina 2000). The magnitude of increase in chlorophyll was further elevated when seedlings were subjected to abiotic and biotic stresses, suggesting thereby a possible connection between NO, light and stress signaling pathways in plants. NO also increased chlorophyll content in leaves of pea, particularly in guard cells (Leshem *et al.* 1996) and retarded chlorophyll loss in potato leaves infected with *phytophthora infestans*. NO donors are reported to significantly increase chlorophyll content and chloroplast membrane density in maize plants growing under conditions of very low iron concentration (Granziano *et al.* 2002). It is well known fact that iron deficiency impairs chlorophyll biosynthesis and chloroplast development (Thoiron *et al.* 1997). It seems quite likely that enhanced chlorophyll content and vigor of N- fertilized crops is the result of increased availability of NO. It also enhances betacynanin synthesis in *Amaranthus caudatus*. The synthesis of anthocyanin and betacynanin is promoted by cytokinins and red light (Bamberger and Mayer 1990, Piatelli *et al.* 1969). Use of NOS inhibitors and NO scavengers blocked the Cytokinin induced pigment synthesis suggesting that NO is required to accomplish cytokinin function.

STOMATAL CLOSURE

ABA is an endogenous antitranspirants that induces stomatal closure, thereby leading to water conservation. Recently, NO has been identified as a mediator of guard cells ABA signaling (Neill *et al.* 2002a). Scavenging of NO or inhibition of NO synthesis reduces ABA induced stomatal closure. Garcia-Mata and Lamattina (2001) showed that exogenous application of NO as SNP reduced transpiration and induced stomatal closure in several species, such as *Vicia faba*, *Salpichera* and *Tradescantia*. NO- induced stomatal closure is likely to be a common phenomenon. The ABA induced stomatal closure was completely checked when epidermal peelings of pea leaves were treated with PTIO, a scavenger of NO (Garcia-Mata and 2002). They suggested involvement of NO as an endogenous signaling intermediate in ABA induced stomatal closure.

PEROXISOMAL FUNCTIONALITY

Peroxisom are subcellular organelles with oxidative type of metabolism, biochemical, immunological and immunocytochemical data provide evidence that plant peroxisomes contain NOS activity (per NOS) which is calcium-dependent, constitutively expressed, and immunorelated with the mammalian NOS (Barroso *et al.* 1999). The presence of NOS in peroxisomes, suggests that these organelles are a cellular source of NO. Inside peroxisomes, NO could react with oxygen radicals generated in peroximal matrix by xanthin oxidase to form powerful oxidants peroxynitrite which could regulate conversion of xanthin dehyrogenase into superoxide- generating xanthin oxidase (del

Rio *et al.* 1992). The level of measured NO was linearly dependent on the amount of peroximal protein (Corpus *et al.* 2004). NO can also react with reduced GSH to form S-nitrosoglutathione (GSNO), a reactive nitrogen oxide species (Wink *et al.* 1995). GSNO has been reported as a powerful inducer of defense genes (Durner *et al.* 1998).Presence of NOS in plant peroxisomes implies that these organelles could also have a function as a source of signal molecules like NO, superoxide radicals, hydrogen peroxide and GSNO.

SENESCENCE AND PROGRAMMED CELL DEATH

Cell death is an essential process during the plant's life cycle. Two modes of cell death are described in plants: Programmed cell death (PCD) and Necrosis. Two examples of PCD in plants, senescence and cell death associated with the hypersensitive response (HR); demonstrate range of forms that PCD can take place in plants. Senescence is a highly regulated process during which new metabolic pathways are activated and others are turned off (Pedroso *et al.* 2000).

PCD is genetically controlled and has characteristic feature of the apoptotic cell death in animals. These features include cell shrinkage, chromatin condensation and DNA fragmentation.

Necrosis, also a type of cell death results from severe and persistent trauma and is considered not to be genetically orchestrated (Loak, 2001).

Delledone *et al.* (2001) have shown that the interaction between NO and ROS can determine whether or not PCD is determined by NO: superoxide ratio. If level of superoxide is greater than NO, then NO reacts with superoxide to form peroxynitrite which does not results in PCD. On the other hand, Leshem *et al.* (1998) observed lower NO concentration in mature fruits than in green fruits, and senescing flowers compared with fresh flowers. To confirm this, the authors applied exogenous NO to flowers, fruits and vegetables and observed that NO delayed senescence and extended the post harvest life in all cases. If level of NO is greater than superoxide, then NO reacts with H_2O_2 to induce cell death. Treatment of tobacco cells with both H_2O_2 and NO together induced substantial increase in cell death with PCD characteristics (Neill *et al.* 2002 b).

TARGETING OF POLLEN TUBES TO OVULES

Prado *et al.* (2008) have investigated the role of NO in the process of pollen–pistil communication, using *Arabidopsis in-vivo* and lily *semi-vivo* assays. Cross-pollination between wild-type and AtNOS1 plants shows that the mutation affects the pistil tissues in a way that is compatible with abnormal pollen tube guidance. The presence of NO in an asymmetric restricted area around the micropyle is demonstrated. The pollen–pistil interaction transcriptome indicated a time-course-specific modulation of transcripts of AtNOS1 and two Nitrate reductases (nr1 and nr2), which collectively triggered a putative NO signaling pathway. It was also inferred that NO was necessary for micropyle targeting to occur. Activation of calcium influx in pollen tubes partially rescued normal pollen tube morphology, suggesting that this pathway is also dependent on Ca^{2+} signaling. A role of NO in modulating Ca^{2+} signaling was further substantiated by direct imaging the cytosolic free Ca^{2+} concentration during NO-induced reorientation, where two peaks of Ca^{2+} occurred. Taken together, these results provided evidence for the participation of NO signaling events during pollen–pistil interaction. Of special relevance, NO seems to directly affect the targeting of pollen tubes to the ovule's micropyle by modulating the action of its diffusible factors.

NITRIC OXIDE IN PLANTS AND CROSS TALK WITH VARIOUS PLANT HORMONES

Growth and development of plants is under the control of natural mobile biomolecules called plant hormones, which are transported from cell to cell and organ to organ to signal and coordinate various processes. Apparently, NO has emerged as an important bioactive molecule involved in regulation of a wide range of processes. Nitric oxide (NO) research is a new exciting field in plant biology. Yaacov Leshem, the pioneer in the study of nitric oxide in plants, has proposed that this bioactive molecule should be classified as a phytohormone which may function as a gaseous endogenous plant growth regulator (Leshem, 2001) have postulated NO to be a non-traditional regulator of plant growth.

Several studies have reported that NO can regulate processes related to plant growth and development, some of which are summarized in Table 1.

Exogenous application of different plant hormones has been reported to trigger endogenous production of NO (Lamattina *et al.* 2003), which could alleviate many stress symptoms in plants by contributing to cellular homeostasis. The small size and high diffusion rate of NO through biological membranes mean that NO fits the premises that hormones are easily transported.

NO AND INDOLE ACETIC ACID (IAA)

NO synthesis has also been found to be induced by auxin in cucumber roots (Pagnussat *et al.* 2002). The dependence of NO in auxin induced adventitious root development reflects the possibility that IAA and NO might share common steps in signal transduction pathway. A plasma membrane bound enzyme, nitrite: NO reductase

TABLE 1: Biological activities of nitric oxide in plants, Beligni and Lamattina, 2000.

Tissue or organ	*Physiological action*	*Species*	*Optimum concentrations*
Seeds	Induction of germination	*Paulownia tormentosa*, Lettuce,California chaparral(*Emmenanthe penduliflora*)	10^{-6}
	Inhibition of respiration after imbibitions	Soybean	10^{-6}
	Inhibition of aleuronic cell death	Barley	10^{-6}

Roots	Elongation	Maize	10^{-10}
	Induction of adventitious and lateral root formation	Cucumber, lavender (*Lavendula spp.*)	10^{-9} to 10^{-5}, 10^{-6}
Tuber	Tuberization	Potato	10^{-6}
Hypocotyls	Inhibition of growth in low light conditions	Lettuce, *Arabidopis thaliana*	10^{-6}
Stems	Inhibition of internodal growth in low light conditions	Potato	10^{-6}
Leaves	Induction of de-etiolation	Wheat, barley	10^{-6}
	Delay of senescence	Pea	$5\text{-}10^{-6}$
	Stoma closure	Wheat, *Vicia faba*	10^{-6}
	Leaf expansion	Peas	$5\text{-}10^{-6}$
	Induction of defensive responses	*Arabidopsis*, Tobacco	$2\text{-}10^{-6}$
	Inhibition of cell death	Potatoes	10^{-6}

(Ni-NOR) was reported in the formation of NO in plant roots (Stoher *et al.* 2001). But it remains to be tested whether NO is also involved in other IAA-mediated plant physiological responses.

NO AND GIBBERELEIC ACID (GA)

NO donors also reported to promote germination of photoblastic seeds in the dark to the same extent as both GA treatment or 5 min pulse of while light. But these seeds also germinate in light in presence of NO scavenger, suggesting that their mode of action to stimulate germination is different (Beligni & Lamattina, 2000).

NO AND CYTOKININS

Cytokinins have been shown to induce NO synthesis in tobacco parsley and *Arabidopsis* cell cultures (Tun *et al.* 2001,Chory *et al.* 1994). Some effects of cytokinins can be mimicked by NO. The synthesis betacyanins in *Amaranthus* seedlings is promoted by cytokinins and red light (Bamberger & Mayer, 1990). NO mimicked cytokinins action on pigment synthesis, suggesting that it act downstream of cytokinins to promote the response, or that NO is necessary to accomplish its function (Lamattina *et al.* 2003). NOS inhibitors and NO-scavenger block the effect of this hormone on betacyanin synthesis (Scherer & Holk, 2000). A novel role of cytokinins in the induction of programmed cell death has been recently proposed. It is possible that this cytokinins induced response is mediated by NO. It also triggers several responses in which hormone and phytochrome interact or act separately to give same response. Exogenous application of cytokinins inhibits hypocotyls elongation in manner similar to light treatment (Chory *et al.* 1994).

NO AND ABA

The recent discovery of NO involvement in ABA-induced stomatal closure represents a significant development in NO research. Studies of Garcia-Mata & Lamattina, (2002) in *Pisum sativum* and *Vicia faba* demonstrated at ABA induced NO production was essential for stomatal closure as removal of NO with scavenger PTIO substantially inhibited ABA-induced closure. However, ABA did not induce NO synthesis in *Arabidopsis* suspension cultures, indicating tissue specificity (Tun, *et al.*).

NO AND ETHYLENE

Ethylene, a gaseous hormone, plays an active role in plant responses from germination, cell expansion to stress responses and fruit ripening. The effect of NO and ethylene during maturation and senescence is antagonistic and an inverse relationship between endogenous content of these two gaseous molecules has been observed during fruit ripening (Leshem & Pinchasov, 2002). NO application extends post harvest life of horticulture produce by inhibiting ethylene production (Leshem *et al.* 1998). The administration of sildenafil, an inhibitor of cGMP-degrading phosphodiestrases, results greater inhibition of ethylene production and indicates that c GMP could be involved in the NO-induced inhibition of ethylene metabolism.

NO AND SALICYLIC ACID

NO action in plants is closely linked to salicyclic acid (SA). SA functions at multiple nodes in the defense signaling network to potentiate a variety of plant defense responses including oxidative burst. NO burst has been reported in tobacco and soybean plant tissues treated with a virulent bacterial pathogens or elicitors (Clarke *et al.* 2000 Pedroso *et al.* 2000). NO acts synergistically with SA as well as ROS to potentiate defense and according to song and Goodman, (2001) NO are at least partially required for function of SA.

FUNCTIONS OF NITRIC OXIDE IN BIOTIC STRESS

Indications that NO is involved in signalling defence responses during plant-pathogen interactions have been well documented in many experiments. The challenge of a pathogen very often leads to the induction of HR. There is some evidence that NO plays a key signalling role during HR, next to the accumulation of ROS and SA. Hypersensitive cell death *via* NO is a typical example of programmed cell death (PCD). It was shown that NO-donor treatment of plant tissue initiates chromatin condensation and DNA fragmentation. Moreover, NO-provoked cell death may be inhibited by animal caspase-1 inhibitor. Although studies confirm caspase activity in plants, and transgenic plants with an over expression of a caspase inhibitor-protein p35 and Op-IAP show the inhibition of HR, A plant cellular responses to infection are often correlated with rapid, localized cell death termed as HR at the site of infection. This is also said as (PCD) in the sense that it can be mimicked by plant mutant in the absence of pathogen. This rapid responses is followed by the acquisition of resistance to a range of pathogen at sides away from the original infection termed as systemic acquired resistance (SAR) (Alvarz *et al.* 1998; Hammond-Kosack & Jones, 1996). The responses to plant attack by the pathogens involves the activation of a wide variety of defenses in order to prevent pathogen attack which include the increased expression of various defense genes, such as that for phenyl-alanine ammonia lyase (PAL). PAL is the first enzyme in phenyl propanoid pathway involved in synthesis of phytoalexins with antimicrobial activities. They First induction of the involvement of NO in disease resistance came from the work on potato tuber (Noretake *et al.* 1996). They observed that treatment of the potato tuber tissue with NOC-18 (NO-donor) provoked an accumulation of phytoalexin riehitin, an endogenous antibiotic compound. The effect NOC-18 was counteracted by PTIO and free radial scavenger Tiron (Noritake *et al.* 1996). NO also protected chlorophyll levels in potato leaves infected with pathogen *Phytophthora infestans* (Beligni *et al.* 1997). Durner *and* Delledonne *et al.* (1998) demonstrated a regulatory role for NO as a plant defense signal against pathogen infection. They demonstrated that NO collaborates with ROS to trigger transcriptional activation of plant defense genes and HR. Injection of the animal NO synthase, its substrate and cofactor to tobacco leaves, a common marker for defense-gene transcription called PR-1 was activated through the accumulation of SA, an intermediate required for many disease resistance responses. SA is a crucial signal during plant-pathogen interactions and NO acts synergistically with SA as well as with ROS to potentiate defense response (Song and Goodman 2001). In *Arabidopsis* suspension cells, exogenous NO induced cell death at concentrations similar to those generated by cells challenged by avirulent bacteria (Clarke *et al.* 2000). In soybean and tobacco cell suspensions a simultaneous increase in NO and H_2O_2 activated cell death, whereas, an independent increase of only one of the above-mentioned factors induced cell death only slightly (Tuteja *et al.* 2004; Pinto *et al.* 2002) Moreover, cytological observations showed that either administration of NO-donors or a change in H_2O_2 level has no effect on elicitation of HR in infected oat cells, although both molecules were required for onset of death in neighbouring cells (Tada *et al.* 2004). The mechanism by which NO and H_2O_2 interact in killing is still largely unknown. However, chemical reaction between NO and H_2O_2 produce either singlet oxygen or hydroxyl radicals (Noronha *et al.* 1993), which can cause cell death. Reaction of NO with O_2 produces a highly toxic molecule for animal cells, peroxynitrite, mediating apoptosis. For plants ONOO is relatively non-toxic (Dellodone *et al.* 2001). However, it was found that in tobacco leaves ONOO induces PR-1 accumulation (Durner *et al.* 1999) and protein nitration modulating cell redox state. Early NO production, known as NO burst seems to be closely dependent on the genetic makeup of the plant (R genes) and of the pathogen (avr) (Bennett *et al.* 2005). As a confirmation of this fact, prompt nitric oxide production (30-45 min after inoculation) was recorded in non-compatible systems of P. s. pv. *Phaseolicola*-tobacco and P. s. pv. Tomato-*Arabidopsis.* This early "NO burst" directly preceded H_2O_2 generation and occurred approximately 6 h before the appearance of visible HR-type cell death symptoms. As a confirmation lack of NO emission was observed in plants inoculated with a mutant of the avirulent bacterium (hrp), incapable of supplying the avr protein to the plant (Mur *et al.* 2005). Phytoalexin accumulation is another event connected with plant resistance, in which NO seems to be engaged (Able *et al.* 2003). Treatment of potato tubers with exogenous NO stimulated the accumulation of rishitin. Additionally, the effect of inhibited synthesis of this compound was observed after the application of an NO-scavenger (Noritake *et al.* 1996). Independently, biosynthesis of specific phytoalexins was observed after NO treatment of soybean cotyledons (Modolo *et al.* 2002). NO may also participate in the onset of systemic acquired resistance (SAR), in tobacco exogenous NO induces the accumulation of salicylic acid-playing a fundamental role in SAR (Durner *et al.* 1998). Activation of PR-1 protein, obtained *via* NO, occurs with the participation of SA, since as it was shown in transgenic plants unable to accumulate SA (NahG), a similar effect was not observed. Moreover, disease spots caused by TMV on leaves pretreated with NO were considerably more reduced in comparison to those on transgenic ones. The application of inhibitors specific for animal NOS or NO scavengers reduced SAR (Song *et al.* 2001) Thus; these results suggest an important role of NO in the induction of a distal signalling network leading to enhance SAR in tobacco. Studies of effects of NO inhibitors in genetically well defined host pathogen interaction in response to *Pseudomonas syringe* showed promotion of disease infestation and bacterial growth. This clearly demonstrates that NO plays a key role in disease resistance in plants. Likewise, O-infiltration of NOS inhibitors L-NNA (N^W–nitro-L-arginine) or PBITU (5, 5′-1, 3-phenyl-bis(1, 2-ethanediyl)-bis- isothiourea) promoted the spreading of chlorosis accompanied by enhanced bacterial growth in leaves of *Arabidopsis* ecotype Col-O (Delledonne *et al.* 1998). A pathogen inducible NOS (iNOS) has been recently identified in tobacco and *Arabidopsis* (Chandok *et al.* 2003). They observed that plant iNOS has similar kinetic properties to its animal counterpart and also requires tetrahydrobiopterin, FAD, NADPH, Ca^{2+}, and calmodulin for its activity *in vitro*. Most of the available on NO detection during plant-pathogen interaction come from studies of infections by biotrophic pathogens. Rapid accumulation of NO has been observed in soybean and *Arabidopsis* suspension cultured cells in response to avirulent bacteria (Delledonne *et al.* 1998, Clarke *et al.* 2000); in tobacco leaves treated with fungal elicitor cryptogein (Foissner *et al.* 2000) and in potato tubers treated with an elicitor from *Phytophthora infestans* (Yamamoto *et al.* 2003). A direct contact of avirulent crown rust fungus with oat plants also induces production of NO at an early stage in the defense response (Tada *et al.* 2004). Further experiments are needed to examine the course of metabolism of NOS inhibitors or NO scavengers in plants to further assess the ability of NO to induce the SAR response.

FUNCTIONS OF NITRIC OXIDE IN ABIOTIC STRESS

The most important factors limiting the crop productivity are environmental stresses. At whole plant level, the effect of any stress is usually perceived as a decrease in photosynthesis and growth which is associated with alterations in carbon and nitrogen metabolism (Loggini *et al.* 1999). At molecular level, negative effect of stress is associated with generation of reactive oxygen species (ROS) which initiate several oxidative destructive processes and also triggers various signaling pathways (Neill *et al.* 2002 b, Varnova *et al.* 2002). Thus maintenance of appropriate ROS levels might represent survival response. Recently, NO has been found to be involved in diverse biological pathways where it has been proved to be protective against damages provoked by oxidative stress (Beligni and Lamattina, 1999). Favourable balance between ROS/NO is important for healthy plant growth (Bolwell 1999). Evidences showing that plant response to such stressor as drought, high or low temperature, salinity, heavy metals and oxidative stress, is regulated by NO.

DROUGHT STRESS

The major environmental constraints that limit crop productivity and performance is drought stress. It is highly desired to understand the underlying cellular processes that ameliorate the injurious effects of drought stress and conserve water in crop plants. Water deficit is associated with the accumulation of the plant hormone ABA which is found to induce NO synthesis in guard cells. Application of NO donors has been shown to ameliorate injurious effects of drought stress in several plant species (Garcia-Mata and Lamattina, 2001). NO donor reduced transpiration rates and stomatal aperture by 35, 30, and 65 % respectively, in *Tradescantia, Salpickroa organifolia* and *Vicia faba* (Garcia- Mata and Lamattina, 2001). This NO induced stomatal closure was correlated with increase in water content as a result of reduction in transpiration rate, stomatal aperture and ion leakage to the extent found in untreated leaves. ABA synthesis in wheat roots in response to water deficit was much higher in the presence of NO donors and ROS, which suggests synergistic action of ROS and NO (Zhao *et al.* 2001) as a confirmation of this fact, ABA accumulation under stress was blocked after the administration of ROS scavengers and a NOS inhibitor. The accumulation of NO also proved to be necessary in stomata of *Vicia faba* during ABA induced closure of stomata (Garcia-Mata *et al.* 2002) Close functional cooperation between signal molecules of ABA, H_2O_2 and NO was also confirmed by the recent reports. In the cited study it was shown that stress-induced ABA accumulation along with NO and the accompanying reaction of stomatal closure in *Arabidopsis* is additionally dependent on H_2O_2 synthesis (Desikan *et al.* 2006).

TEMPERATURE STRESS

NO participates also in plant response to high and low temperature stress. For example, high temperature treatment of lucerne cells resulted in an increase of NO synthesis, whereas, the application of exogenous NO increased cold tolerance in tomato, wheat and maize (Neill *et al.* 2003) Most probably the observed effects were related with the antioxidative action of NO, which elevates negative effects caused by the intensification of peroxidative metabolism in thermal stress (Neill *et al.* 2002). Application of NO donors mediated chilling resistance in tomato, wheat and corn (Lamattina *et al.* 2001). In *Brassica* species, SNP treatments ameliorated injurious effects of chilling stress imposed on the leaf disc under *in vitro* conditions by modulating the regulation of generation of peroxide radicals and activities of anti oxidants enzymes (Setia *et al.* 2005). Stress tolerance induced by NO reflects its antioxidants properties *via* suppression on high levels of ROS that accumulate following exposure to heat or chilling stress (Neill *et al.* 2002 b).

Very recently Malik *et al.* (2007) demonstrated that cool temperature ($32^0C/12^0C$) delayed initiation of fibers but addition of NO caused a shift in redoxbalance from a reduced state to an oxidative state in the initiating fibers of cotton ovules. Thus, IAA was sprayed to cause initiation of fibers at low temperature. NO is also shown to regulate the auxin degrading system during various phases of fiber growth. The role of NO in early initiation of fibers and their prompt elongation is inferred. NO also affected the activity of acid invertase, preventing sucrose accumulation during the elongation phase. Total sugars decreased with low temperature but NO restored their content. NO also promoted the activity of α-galactosidase indicating restoration of fiberwall synthesis during the elongation.

HEAVY METALS STRESS

Pretreatment of lupin (*Lupinus lutens*) seedlings for 24 h with 10 µM SNP resulted in efficient reduction of detrimental effect of heavy metal like cadmium and lead (Kopyra and Gwozdz, 2003). The protective effect of NO may be at least partly due to stimulation of SOD activity and / or direct scavenging of the superoxide anion.

SALINITY STRESS

NO-donor treatment of rice seedlings caused the effect of loss minimization (Uhida *et al.* 2002). In this case after the application of NO a stronger growth of plants was observed, along with the maintenance of appropriate PS II activity, an increase of antioxidative enzymatic activity and the expression of specific salinity stress resistance genes. On the other hand, prolonged stress conditions may result in an over production of NO and NO-derived products, leading to a range of specific responses, known as nitrosative stress. Recently, (Valderrama *et al.* 2007) indicated that in olive leaves salinity stress induced the production of RNS, *i.e.* NO, GSNO and RSNO, and in consequence, a rise in tyrosine-nitrated proteins, which are good markers of nitrosative stress.

UV-B RADIATION

Mackerness *et al.* 2001 showed also the participation of NO in plant response to UV-B radiation, demonstrating post-stress induction of CHS expression, an increase in NOS-type enzymatic activity and an elevation of NO level. Results of a study by Shi *et al.* 2005 suggest that NO may effectively protect plants against UV-B radiation, most probably through increased activity of antioxidative enzymes. It needs to be mentioned that NO-donor treatment of potato tubers prior to UV-B irradiation resulted in the development of almost 50% more healthy leaves in comparison to plants not subjected to NO.

OZONE STRESS

NO may also interact with atmospheric pollutant ozone. Treatment of *Arabidopsis* plants with ozone induced NOS activity that preceded accumulation of SA and cell death (Rao and Davis, 2001).

WOUNDING

According to Orozco-Cardenas and Ryan, 2002 demonstrated that injury itself does not induce NO synthesis; however, the application of exogenous NO inhibits the process of NO generation and the expression of wounding inducible genes during pathogenesis.

PHOTO-OXIDATIVE STRESS

Oxidative stress within chloroplast originates due to light dependent O_2 reduction. Artifically ROS can be generated with bipyridinum herbicides like diquat and paraquat (Dodge, 1994). These herbicides act at photosystem I as artificial electron acceptor (Beligni and Lamattiana, 2002). Their oxidation produces ROS which when produced in high amounts provokes severe damage in almost every cellular component. In natural conditions, superoxide is formed when electron transport within photosynthetic chain occurs in excessive amounts related to $NADP^+/NADPH$ ratio. During a photo-oxidant condition, ROS concentration in the cell can rise to such toxic levels to cause severe damage. Recently, NO has been reported as an important ROS scavenger, able to reduce the extent of chlorophyll loss, ion leakage, necrosis and defoliation caused by herbicides (Beligni and Lamattina, 1999; Dodge, 1994). Beligni and Lamattina (2002) observed marked reduction in diquat- triggered lipid peroxidation, ribulose 1, 5 bis- phosphate carboxylase/oxygenase (rubisco) and DI protein by two nitric oxide donors, SNP (100μM) and SNAP (200μM) in potato leaf pieces and isolated chloroplast . NO donors also protected the RNA against oxidative damage. These effects may, at least in part, be explained by its ability to directly scavenge ROS.

CONCLUSION

Clearly much remains to be discovered about NO action in plants. NO is undoubtedly made by plant cells and has a range of biological activities. Therefore, it would seem likely that the processes by which NO is made and removed are subject to regulation. Even though the details remain to be resolved, it is clear that various stimuli can increase the rate of NO production and that altering NO turnover in cells, either by modulating its production or removal, does have biological effects. NO is evolved from plants and the rate of evolution can be dramatically increased in response to various stimuli, but the physiological significance of such evolution is not clear. Increased NO evolution probably reflects increased cellular NO generation, but whether NO derived from different intracellular sources is evolved at different rates or from different cells is not known. There is clearly much to explore about NO.

Overall, much more work needs to be done before assigning the term plant hormone to NO. The endogenous variation of NO during the plant life cycle need to be monitored whether NO acts directly or indirectly through changes in the balance of plant hormones also needs to be determined. A mutational analysis of NO- regulated growth in *Arabidopsis* and the gene cloning of mutant phenotypes should be powerful tools to dissect the cross talk between NO and other chemical messenger. In the mean time, NO will surely go on surprising us with novel functions.

REFERENCES

Able AJ 2003 Role of reactive oxygen species in the response of barley to necrotrophic pathogens *Protoplasma* **221** 137–143

Adams JM Cory S 1998 The Bcl-2 protein family: arbiters of cell death *Science* **281** 1322-1326

Ahern GP Klyachko VA Jackson MB 2002 cGMP and S-nitrosylation: two routs for modulation of neuronal excitability by NO *Trends Neuro Sci* **25** 510-517

Alvarez ME Pennell RI Meijer PJ Ishikawa A Dixon RA and Lamb C 1998 Reactive oxygen intermediates mediate a systemic signal network in the establishment of plant immunity *Cell* **92** 773-784

Amezcua JL Palmer RMJ de Souza BM and Moncada S 1989 Nitric oxide synthesized from L-arginine regulates vascular tone in the coronary circulation of the rabbit *Br J Pharmacol* **97** 1019-1024

Anderson L Mansfield TA 1979 The effects of nitric oxide pollution on the growth of tomato *Environmental Pollution* **20** 113-121

Aoki T 1990 Continuous flow determination of nitrite with membrane separation/ chemiluminescence detection *Biomed Chromatogr* **4** 128-130

Archer SL and Cowan NJ 1991 Acetylcholine causes endothelium dependent vasodilatation but does not stimulate nitric oxide production by rat pulmonary arteries or elevate endothelial cytosol calcium concentrations *Circ Ret* **68** 1569-1581

Arnaud N Murgia I Boucherez J Briat J-F Cellier F Gaymard F 2006 An iron-induced nitric oxide burst precedes ubiquitin-dependent protein degradation for *Arabidopsis* AtFer1 ferritin gene expression *Journal of Biological Chemistry* **281** 23579–23588

Arroyo C and Kohno M 1991 Difficulties encountered in the detection of nitric oxide (NO) by spin trapping techniques A cautionary note *Free Radic Ret Commun* **14** 145-155

Ashkenazi A Dixit V 1998 Death receptors: signaling and modulation *Science* **281** 1305-1308

Ball L Accotto GP Bechtold U et al 2004 Evidence for a direct link between glutathione biosynthesis and stress defence gene expression in *Arabidopsis The Plant Cell* **16** 2448–2462

Bamberger E and Mayer AM 1990 Effect of Kinetin on formation of red pigment in seedlings of *Amaranthus retroflexus Science* **131** 1094-1095

Barroso J Corpas FJ Carreras A *et al* 2006 Localization of S-nitrosoglutathione and expression of S-nitrosoglutathione reductase in pea plants under cadmium stress *Journal of Experimental Botany* **57** 1785–1793

Barroso JB Corpas FJ Carrweas A Sandalio LM Valderrama R Palma JM Lupianez JA and del Rio LA 1999 Localization of nitric-oxide synthase in plant peroxisomes *J Biol Chem* **274** 36729-36733

Belenghi B Romero-Puertas MC Vercammen D Brackenier A Inze D Delledonne M Van Breusegem F 2007 Metacaspase activity of *Arabidopsis thaliana* is regulated by S-nitrosylation of critical cystein residue *J Biol Chem* **282** 1352-1358

Beligni MV and Lamattina L 1999 Is nitric oxide toxic or protective? *Trends Plant Science* **4** 299-

Beligni MV and Lamattina L 2000 Nitric oxide stimulates seed germination and de-etiolation and inhibits hypocotyls elongation three light-inducible responses in plants *Planta* **210** 215-221

Beligni MV and Lamattina L 2002 Nitric oxide interferes with plant photo-oxidative stress by detoxifying reactive oxygen species *Plant Cell Environment* **25** 737-748

Beligni MV Lamattina L 2001a Nitric oxide in plants: the history is just beginning *Plant Cell and Environment* **24** 267-278

Beligni MV Lamattina L 2001b Nitric oxide: a non-traditional regulator of plant growth *Trends Plant Sci* **6** 11 508-509

Bestwick CS Brown IR Bennett MHR Mansfield JW 1997 Localization of hydrogen peroxide accumulation during the hypersensitive reaction of lettuce cells to *Pseudomonas syringae pv phaseolicola Plant Cell* **9** 209-221

Bethke PC Badger MR Jones RL 2004 Apoplastic synthesis of nitric oxide by plant tissues *The Plant Cell* **16** 332–341

Bethke PC Gubler F Jacobsen JV Jones RL 2004 Dormancy of Arabidopsis seeds and barley grains can be broken by nitric oxide *Planta* **219** 847–855

Bethke PC Libourei IG Jones RL 2006 Nitric Oxide reduces seed dormancy in *Arabidopsis Journal of Experimental Botony* **57** 17-526

Boccara M Mills CE Zeier J Anzi C Lamb C Poole RK Delledonne M 2005 Flavohaemoglobin HmpX from Erwinia chrysanthemi confers nitrosative stress tolerance and affects the plant hypersensitive reaction by intercepting nitric oxide produced by the host *The Plant Journal* **43** 26–237

Bolwell GP 1999 Role of reactive oxygen species and NO in plant defense responses *Curr Opin Plant Biol* **2** 287-294

Boon EM Davis JH Tran R Karow DS Huang SH Pan D Miazgowicz MM Mathies RA Marletta MA 2006 Nitric oxide binding to prokaryotic homologus ofthe soluble guanylate cyclase 1 H-NOX domain *Journal of Biological Chemistry* **281** 1892–21902

Bourgis F Roje S Nuccio ML *et al* 1999 S-methylmethionine plays a major role in phloem sulfur transport and is synthesized by a novel type of methyltransferase *The Plant Cell* **111** 485–1498

Brien J McLaughlin B Nakatsu K and Marks G 1991 Quantitation of nitric oxide formation from nitro vasodilator drugs by chemiluminescence analysis of headspace gas *j PharmacoL Methods* **25** 19-27

Bright J 2006 Nitric oxide signalling in *Arabidopsis thaliana* guard cells Bristol UK: University of the West of England PhD thesis

Bright J Desikan R Hancock JT Weir IS Neill SJ 2006 ABA-induced NO generation and stomatal closure in *Arabidopsis* are dependent on H_2O_2 synthesis *The Plant Journal* **45** 113–122

Buckner B Janick-Buckner D Gray J Johal GS 1998 Cell-death mechanisms in maize *Trends Plant Sci* **3** 218-223

Buettner GR 1987 Spin Trapping: ESR parameters of spin adducts *Free Radic Biol & Med* **3** 259-303

Büschges R Hollricher K Panstruga R Simons G Wolter M Frijters A van Daelen R van der Lee T Diergaarde P Groenendijk J *et al* 1997 The barley Mlo gene: a novel control element of plant pathogen resistance *Cell* **88** 695-706

Caird MA Richards JH Donovan LA 2007 Night-time stomatal conductance and transpiration in C3 and C4 plants *Plant Physiology* **143** 4–10

Chamnongpol S Willekens H Langebartels C Van Montagu M Inzé D Van Camp W 1996 Transgenic tobacco with a reduced catalase activity develops necrotic lesions and induces pathogenesisrelated expression under high light *Plant J* **10** 491-504

Chamnongpol S Willekens H Moeder W Langebartels C Sanderman HJ Van Montagu M Inze D Van Camp W 1998 Defense activation and enhanced pathogen tolerance induced by H_2O_2 in transgenic tobacco *Proc Natl Acad Sci* USA **95** 5818-5823

Chandok MR Ytterberg AJ Van Wijk KJ and Klessing DF 2003 The pathogen-inducible nitric oxide synthase (iNOS) in plants is a variant pf the P protein of the glycine decarboxylase complex *Cell* **113** 469-482

Chen WZ Palmer RMJ and Moncada S 1989 Release of nitric oxide from the rabbit aorta] *Vasc Med BioL* **1** 1-6

Cheng F Hsu S Kao CH 2002 Nitric oxide counteracts the senescence of detached rice leaves induced by dehydration and polyethylene glycol but not by sorbitol *Plant Growth Regulation* **38** 265–272

Chory J Reinecke D Sim S Washbun T and Brenner M 1994 A role for cytokinins in de-etiolation of *Arabidopsis* det mutants have an altered response to cytokinins *Plant Physiol* **104** 339-347

Chung S and Fung H 1990 Identification of the subcellular site for nitroglycerin metabolism to nitric oxide in bovine coronary smooth muscle cells *Pharmacol Exp The'* **253** 614-619

Clarke A Desikan R Hurst RD Hancock JT Neill S J 2000 NO way back: nitric oxide and programmed cell death in *Arabidopsis thaliana* suspension cultures *Plant J* **24** 667-677

Clementi E 1998 Role of Nitric Oxide and its intracellular signaling pathways in the control of calcium homeostasis *Biochem Pharmacol* **55** 713-718

Conrath U Amoroso G Köhle H Sültemeyer DF 2004 Non-invasive online detection of nitric oxide from plants and some other organisms by mass spectrometry *The Plant Journal* **38** 1015–1022

Corpas FJ Barroso JB Carreras A *et al* 2004a Cellular and subcellular localization of endogenous nitric oxide in young and senescent pea plants *Plant Physiology* **136** 2722–2733

Corpas FJ Barroso JB Carreras A Valderrama R Palma JM Leon AM Sandalio LM del Rio LA 2006 Constitutive arginine-dependent nitric oxide synthase activity in different organs of pea seedlings during plant development *Planta* **224** 246–254

Corpas FJ Barroso JB del Rio LA 2004b Enzymatic sources of nitric oxide in plant cells: beyond one protein-one function *New Phytologist* **162** 246–248

Crawford NM 2006 Mechanisms for nitric oxide synthesis in plants *Journal of Experimental Botany* **57** 471–478

Crawford NM Galli M Tischner R Heimer YM Okamoto M Mack A 2006 Response to Zemojtel *et al*: plant nitric oxide synthase: back to square one *Trends in Plant Science* **11** 526–527

Dangl JL 1998 Plants just say NO to pathogens *Nature* **394** 525- 527

Dangl JL Dietrich RA Richberg MH 1996 Death don't have no mercy: cell death programs in plant–microbe interactions *Plant Cell* **8** 1793-1807

Davidson EA Kingerlee W 1997 A global inventory of nitric oxide emissions from soils *Nutrient Cycling in Agroecosystems* **48** 37–50

De Pinto MC Tommasi F and de Gara L 2002 Changes in the antioxidant systems as part of the signaling pathway responsible for the programmed cell death activated by nitric oxide and reactive oxygen species in tobacco Bright-yellow 2 cells *Plant Physiol* **130** 698-708

Dean JV Harper JE 1986 Nitric oxide and nitrous oxide production by soybean and winged bean during the *in vivo* nitrate reductase assay *Plant Physiology* **82** 718–723

del Pozo O Lam E 1998 Caspases and programmed cell death in the hypersensitive response *Curr Biol* **8** in press

Del Rio Corpas FJ Sandalio LM Palma MG and barroso JB 2002 Reactive oxygen species antioxidants systems and nitric oxide peroxisomes *J Exp Bot* **53** 1255-1272

Del Rio LA Corpas FJ Sandalio LM Palma JM Gomez M Barroso JB 2002 Reactive oxygen species antioxidant systems and nitric oxide in peroxisomes *Journal of Experimental Botany* **53** 1255–1272

Delledone M Xia Y Dixon RA Lamb CJ 1998 Nitric oxide functions as a signal in plant disease resistance *Nature* **394** 585-588

Delledonne M Xia Y Dixon RA Lamb C 1998 Nitric oxide functions as a signal in plant disease resistance *Nature* **394** 585-588

Delledonne M Zeier J Marocco A Lamb C 2001 Signal interactions between nitric oxide and reactive oxygen intermediates in the plant hypersensitive disease resistance response *Proceedings of the National Academy of Science* USA **98** 13454–13459

Delledonne M 2005 NO news is good news for plants *Current Opinion in Plant Biology* **8** 390–396

Desikan R Cheung MK Bright J Henson D Hancock JT Neill SJ 2004a ABA hydrogen peroxide and nitric oxide signalling in stomatal guard cells *Journal of Experimental Botany* **55** 205–212

Desikan R Cheung M-K Clarke A Golding S Sagi M Fluhr R Rock C Hancock J Neill S 2004b Hydrogen peroxide is a common signal for darkness and ABA-induced stomatal closure in *Pisum sativum* L *Functional Plant Biology* **31** 913–920

Desikan R Griffiths RHancock J Neill SJ 2002 A new role for an old enzyme: nitrate reductase-mediated nitric oxide generation is required for abscisic acid-induced stomatal closure in *Arabidopsis thaliana Proceedings of the National Academy of Sciences* USA **99** 16314–16318

Desikan R Last K Harrett-Williams R Tagliavia C Harter K Hooley R Hancock JT Neill SJ 2006 Ethylene-induced stomatal closure in *Arabidopsis* occurs via AtrbohF-mediated hydrogen peroxide synthesis *The Plant Journal* **47** 907–916

Diaz M Achkor H Titarenko E Carmen Martinez M 2003 The gene encoding glutathione-dependent formaldehyde dehydrogenase/GSNO reductase is responsive to wounding jasmonic acid and salicylic acid *FEBS Letters* **543** 136–139

Dietrich RA Delaney TP Uknes SJ Ward EJ Ryals JA Dangl JL 1994 *Arabidopsis* mutants simulating disease resistance response *Cell* **77** 565-578

Dietrich RA Richberg MH Schmidt R Dean C Dangl JL 1997 A novel zinc-finger protein is encoded by the *Arabidopsis* lsd1 gene and functions as a negative regulator of plant cell death *Cell* **88** 685-694

Dion M Chamberland H St-Michel C Plante M Darveau A Lafontaine JG Brisson LF 1997 Detection of a homologue of bcl-2 in plant cells *Biochem Cell Biol* **75** 457-461

Dodge A 1994 Herbicide action and effects on detoxification processes in Causes of Photoactive Stress and Amelioration of Defense Sytems in Plants pp 219-236 eds CH Foyer and PM Mullineaux (CRC Boca Raton FL : USA)

Donaldson L Ludidi N Knight MR Gehring C Denby K 2004 Salt and osmotic stress cause rapid increases in *Arabidopsis thaliana* cGMP levels *FEBS Letters* **569** 317–20

Dong Lu Zhang X Jiang J An GY Zhang LR Song CP 2005 NO may function in the downstream of H_2O_2 in ABA-induced stomatal closure in *Vicia faba* L *Journal of Plant Physiology and Molecular Biology* **31** 62–70

Dordas C Hasinoff BB Igamberdiev AU Manac'h N Rivoal J Hill RD 2003 Expression of a stress-induced hemoglobin affects NO levels produced by alfalfa root cultures under hypoxic stress *Plant J* **35** 763–770

Dordas C Rivoal J Hill RD 2003 Plant haemoglobins nitric oxide and hypoxic stress *Annals of Botany* **91** 173–178

Dorey S Baillieul F Pierrel M-A Saindrenan P Fritig B Kauffmann S 1997 Spatial and temporal induction of cell death defense genes and accumulation of salicylic acid in tobacco leaves reacting hypersensitively to a fungal glycoprotein *Mol Plant–Microbe Interact* **10** 646-655

Dorey S Baillieul F Saindrenan P Fritig B Kauffmann S 1998 Tobacco class I and II catalases are differentially expressed during elicitorinduced hypersensitive cell death and localized acquired resistance *Mol Plant–Microbe Interact* **11** 321-334

Doyle MP and Hoekstra J W 1981 Oxidation of nitrogen oxides by bound dioxygen in hemoproteins *j Inorg Biochem* **14** 351-358

Dröge-Laser W Kaiser A Lindsay WP Halkier BA Loake GJ Doerner P Dixon RA Lamb CJ 1997 Rapid stimulation of a soybean protein serine-threonine kinase which phosphorylates a novel bZIP DNAbinding protein G/HBF-1 during the induction of early transcription-dependent defenses *EMBO J* **16** 726-738

Du H Klessig DF 1997 Role for salicylic acid in the activation of defense responses in catalase-deficient tobacco *Mol Plant–Microbe Interact* **7** 922-925

Durner J and Wendehenne D and Klessing DF 1998 Defense gene induction in tobacco by nitric oxide cyclic GMP and cyclic ADP- ribose *Proc Natl Acad Sci* USA **95** 10328-10333

Durner J Klessig DF 1999 Nitric oxide as a signal in plants *Current Opinion in Plant Biology* **2** 369-374

Eu JP Xu L Stamler JS Meissner G 1999 Regulation of ryanodine receptors by reactive nitrogen species *Biochem Pharmacol* **57** 1079-1084

Fauth M Merten A Hahn MG Jeblick W Kauss H 1996 Competence for elicitation of H_2O_2 in hypocotyls of cucumber is induced by breaching the cuticle and is enhanced by salicylic acid *Plant Physiol* **110** 347-354

Feechan A Kwon E Yun B Wang Y Palls JA Loake G 2005 A central role for S-nitrosothiols in plant disease resistance *Proceedings of the National Academy of Sciences* USA **102** 8054–8059

Floryszak-Wieczorek J Milczarek G Arasimowicz M Ciszewski A 2006 Do nitric oxide donors mimic endogenous NO-related response in plants? *Planta* **224** 1363–1372

Fodor J Gullner G Adam AL Barna B Kömives T Király Z 1997 Local and systemic responses of antioxidants to Tobacco Mosaic Virus infection and to salicylic acid in tobacco: role in systemic acquired resistance *Plant Physiol* **114** 1443-1451

Foissner ID Wendehenne D Langebartels C Dürner J 2000 *In vivo* imaging of an elicitor-induced nitric oxide burst in tobacco *Plant J* **23** 817–824

Fukuda H 1996 Xylogenesis: initiation progression and cell death *Annu Rev Physiol Plant Mol Biol* **47** 299-325

Furchgott R 1988 In: Vasodilation: Vascular Smooth Muscle Peptides Autonomic nerves and Endothelium (PVanhoutte Ed) Raven Press NY 401–414

Furchgott RF and Zawadzki J V 1980 The obligatory role of the endothelium in the relaxation of arterial smooth muscle by acetylcholine *Nature* **288** 373-376

Gabaldon C Gomez RL Pedreno MA and Barcelo AR 2005 Nitric oxide production by the differentiating xylem of *Zinnia elegans* *New Phytol* **165** 121-130

Garcia-Mata C and Lamattina L 2001 Nitric oxide induces stomatal closure and enhances the adaptive plant responses against drought stress *Plant Physiol* **126** 1196-1204

Garcia-Mata C and Lamattina L 2002 Nitric oxide and abscisic acid cross talk in guard cells *Plant Physiol* **128** 790–792

Garcia-Mata C Gay R Sokolovski S Hills A Lamattina L Blatt MR 2003 Nitric oxide regulates K^+ and Cl^- channels in guard cells through a subset of abscisic acid-evoked signaling pathways *Proceedings of the National Academy of Sciences* USA **100** 11116–11121

Gladwin MT Schechter AN Kim-Shapiro DB *et al* 2005 The emerging biology of the nitrite anion *Nature Chemical Biology* **1** 308–314

Glazener JA Orlandi EW Baker CJ 1996 The active oxygen response of cell suspensions to incompatible bacteria is not sufficient to cause hypersensitive cell death *Plant Physiol* **110** 759-763

Gould KS Lamotte O Klinguer A Pugin A Wendehenne D 2003 Nitric oxide production in tobacco leaf cells: a generalized stress response? *Plant Cell and Environment* **26** 1851–1862

Govea CM CP Souza JF Magalhes AC and Martins IS 1997 NO- releasing substances that induce growth elongation in maize root segments *Plant Growth Regul* **21** 183- 187

Gray J Close PS Briggs SP Johal GS 1997 A novel suppressor of cell death in plants encoded by the Lls1 gene of maize *Cell* **89** 25-32

Graziano M Beligni MV and Lamattina L 2002 Nitric oxide improves internal iron avilalability in plants *Plant Physiol* **130** 1852-1859

Graziano M Lamattina L 2005 Nitric oxide and iron in plants: an emerging and converging story *Trends in Plant Science* **10** 4-8

Green DR Reed JC 1998 Mitochondria and apoptosis *Science* **281** 1309-1312

Greenberg JT 1997 Programmed cell death in plant–pathogen interactions *Annu Rev Plant Physiol Plant Mol Biol* **48** 525- 545

Greenberg SS Wilcox DE and Rubanyi GM 1990 Endothelium-derived relaxing factor released from canine femoral artery by acetylcholine cannot be identified as free nitric oxide by electron paramagnetic resonance spectroscopy *Circ Rex* **67** 1446-1452

Groover A DeWit N Heidel A Jones A 1997 Programmed cell death of plant tracheary elements differentiating *in vitro Protoplasma* **196** 197-211

Groover A and Jones AM 1999 Tracheary element differentiation uses a novel mechanism coordinating programmed cell death and secondary cell wall synthesis *Plant Physiol* **119** 375-384

Groover A Jones AM 1998 Tracheary element programmed cell death *Plant Physiol* **112** 1765-1782

Grubisic D and Konjevic R 1990 Light and nitrate interaction in phytochrome-controlled germination of *Paulownia tormentosa Planta* **181** 239-243

Grubisic D and Konjevic R 1992 The effect of organic nitrates in phytochrome controlled germination of *Paulownia tormentosa seeds Photochem Photobiol* **56** 629-632

Guo F Okamoto M Crawford NM 2003 Identification of a plant nitric oxide synthase gene involved in hormonal signaling *Science* **302** 100–103

Guo FQ Crawford NM 2005 Arabidopsis nitric oxide synthase1 is targeted to mitochondria and protects against oxidative damage and dark-induced senescence *The Plant Cell* **17** 3436–3450

Guo FQ 2006 Response to Zemojtel *et al* plant nitric oxide synthase: At NOS1 is just the beginning *Trends in Plant Science* **11** 527–528

Gupta KJ Stoimenova M Kaiser WM 2005 In higher plants only root mitochondria but not leaf mitochondria reduce nitrite to NO *in vitro* and *in situ Journal of Experimental Botany* **56** 2601–2609

Gustafsson L Leone A Persson M Wikiund N and Moncada S 1991 Endogenous nitric oxide is present in the exhaled air of rabbits guinea pigs and humans *Biochem Biophys Rex Commun* **181** 852-857

Hammond- Kosack KF and Jones RDG 1996 Resistance gene dependent plant defence responses *Plant Cell* **8** 1773-1791

Hammond-Kosack KE Jones JDG 1996 Inducible plant defense mechanisms and resistance gene function *Plant Cell* **8** 1773-1791

Hari P Raivonen M Vesala T Munger JW Pilegaard K Kulmala M 2003 Ultraviolet light and leaf emission of NO_X *Nature* **422** 134

Harper JE 1981 Evolution of nitrogen oxide(s) during *in vivo* nitrate reductase assay of soybean leaves *Plant Physiology* **68** 1488–1493

Hart JDE and Dulhunty AF 2000 Nitric Oxide activates or inhibits skeletal muscle ryanodine receptors binding on its concentration membrane potential and ligand binding *J Memb Biol* **173** 227-236

Hausladen A Stamler JS 1998 Nitric oxide in plant immunity *Proc Natl Acad Sci* USA **95** 10345-10347

He JM Xu H She XP Song XG Zhao WM 2005 The role and the interrelationship of hydrogen peroxide and nitric oxide in the UV-B-induced stomatal closure in broad bean *Functional Plant Biology* **32** 237–247

He Y Tang RH Hao Y Stevens RD Cook CW Ahn SM Jing L Yang Z Chen L Guo F Fiorani F Jackson RB Crawford NM and Pei ZM 2004 Nitric oxide represses the *Arabidopsis* floral transition *Science* **305** 1968-1971

Heath MC 1998 Involvement of reactive oxygen species in the response of resistant (hypersensitive) or susceptible cowpeas to the cowpea rust fungus *New Phytol* **138** in press

Henry Y Ducrocq C Drapier J Servent D Pellat C and Guissani A 1991 Nitric oxide a biological effector electron paramagnetic resonance detection of nitrosyl-iron-protein complexes in whole cells *Eur Biophys j* **20** 1-15

Hsu YT Kao CH 2004 Cadmium toxicity is reduced by nitric oxide in rice leaves *Plant Growth Regulation* **42** 227–238

Hu G Richter TE Hulbert SH Pryor T 1996 Disease lesion mimicry caused by mutations in the rust resistance gene rp1 *Plant Cell* **8** 1367-1376

Hu G Yalpani N Briggs SP Johal GS 1998 A porphyrin pathway impairment is responsible for the phenotype of a dominant lesion mimic mutant of maize *Plant Cell* **10** 1095-1105

Hu X Neill SJ Tang Z Cai W 2005 Nitric oxide mediates gravitropic bending in soybean roots *Plant Physiology* **137** 663–670

Hung KT Chang CJ Kao CH 2002 Paraquat toxicity is reduced by nitric oxide in rice leaves *Journal of Plant Physiology* **159** 159–166

Hung KT Kao CH 2005 Nitric oxide counteracts the senescence of rice leaves induced by hydrogen peroxide *Botanical Bulletin of Academia Sinica* **46** 21–28

Hunt MD Delaney TP Dietrich RA Weyman KB Dangl JL Ryals JA 1997 Salicylate-independent lesion formation in *Arabidopsis* lsd mutants *Mol Plant–Microbe Interact* **10** 531-536

Huppe HC and Turpin DH 1994 Integration of carbon and nitrogen metabolism in plant and algal cells *Annu Rev Plant Physiol MolBiol* **45** 577-607

Ignarro L Buga G Wood K Byrns R Chadhuri G 1987 Endothelium derived relaxing fadtor produced and released from artery and vein is nitric oxide *Proceedings of the National Academy of Science* USA **84** 9265–9269

Jabs T Colling C Tschöpe M Hahlbrock K Scheel D 1997 Elicitor- stimulated ion fluxes and reactive oxygen species from the oxidative burst signal defense gene activation and phytoalexin synthesis in parsley *Proc Natl Acad Sci* USA **94** 4800-4805

Jasid S Simontacchi M Bartoli CG Puntarulo S 2006 Chloroplasts as a nitric oxide cellular source Effect of reactive nitrogen species on chloroplastic lipids and proteins *Plant Physiology* **142** 1246–1255

Karow DS Pan D Tran R Pellicena P Presley A Mathies RA Marietta MA 2004 Spectroscopic characterization of the soluble guanylate cyclase-like heme domains from *Vibrio cholerae* and *Thermoanaerobacter fengcongensis Biochemistry* **43** 10203–10211

Kauss H Jeblick W 1996 Influence of salicylic acid on the induction of competence for H_2O_2 elicitation Comparison of ergosterol with other elicitors *Plant Physiol* **111** 755-763

Kauss H Jeblick W 1995 Pretreatment of parsley suspension cultures with salicylic acid enhances spontaneous and elicited production of H_2O_2 *Plant Physiol* **108** 1171-1178

Keeley JE and Fortheringham CJ 1997 Trace gas emission and smoke- induced seed germination *Science* **276** 1248- 1250

Kelm M and Schrader J 1988 Nitric oxide release from the isolated guinea pig heart *Eur J Pharmacol* **155** 317-321

Kelm M Feelisch M Spahr R Piper HM Noack E and Schrader J 1988 Quantitative and kinetic characterization of nitric oxide and EDRF release from cultured endothelial cells *Biochem Biophys Res Commun* **154** 237-244

Klepper L 1990 NO_x evolution by soybean leaves treated with salicylic acid and selected derivatives Pesticide *Biochemistry and Physiology* **39** 43–48

Klepper LA 1979 Nitric oxide (NO) and nitrogen dioxide emissions from herbicide-treated soybean plants *Atmospheric Environment* **13** 537–542

Klessig DF Durner J Noad R *et al* 2000 Nitric oxide and salicylic acid signaling in plant defense *Proceedings of the National Academy of Sciences* USA **97** 8849–8855

Kopyra M and Gwozdz EA 2003 Nitric oxide stimulates seed germination and counteracts the inhibitory effect of heavy metals and salinity on root growth of *Lupinus luteus Plant Physiol Biochem* **41** 1011-1017

Kostic M and Schrader J 1992 Role of nitric oxide in reactive hyperemia of the guinea pig heart *Circ Rex* **70** 208-212

Kwak JM Mori IC Pei ZM Leonhardt N Torres MA Dangl JL Bloom RE Bodde S Jones JD Schroeder JI 2003 NADPH oxidase AtrbohD and AtrbohF genes function in ROS-dependent ABA signalling in *Arabidopsis EMBO Journal* **22** 2623–2633

Kwezi L Meier S Mungur L Ruzvidzo O Irving H Gehring C 2007 The *Arabidopsis thaliana* Brassinosteroid Receptor (AtBRI1) contains a domain that functions as a guanylyl cyclase *in vitro* In: Public Library of Science ONE 2:e449 oi:101371/journalpone0000449

Lamattina L Garcia-Matta C M Graziano M Pagnussat G 2003 Nitric Oxide: The versatility of an extensive signal molecule *Ann Rev Plant Biol* **54** 109-136

Lamb C Dixon RA 1997 The oxidative burst in plant disease resistance *Annu Rev Physiol Plant Mol Biol* **48** 251-275

Lamotte L Courtois C Barnavon L Pugin A Wendehenne D 2005 Nitric oxide in plants: the biosynthesis and cell signalling properties of a fascinating molecule *Planta* **221** 1–4

Lamotte O Courtois C Dobrowolska G Besson A Pugin A Wendehenne D 2006 Mechanisms of nitric oxide induced increase of free cytosolic Ca^{2+} concentration in Nicotiana plumbaginifolia cells *Free Radical Biology and Medicine* **40** 1369–1376

Laspina NV Groppa MD Tomaro ML Benavides MP 2005 Nitric oxide protects sunflower leaves against Cd-induced oxidative stress *Plant Science* **169** 323–330

Laxalt AM Beligni M V Lamattina L 1997 Nitric oxide preserves the level of chlorophyll in potato leaves infected by *Phy- tophthora infestans European Journal of Plant Pathology* **103 643-651**

Lesham Y Haramaty E 1996 The characterization and contrasting effects of the nitric oxide free radical in vegetative stress and senescence of *Pisum sativum Linn foliage Journal of Plant Physiology* **148** 258–263

Leshem Y Y 1996 Nitric oxide in biological systems *Plant Growth Regul* **18** 155-159

Leshem Y 2001 Nitric Oxide in Plants (London UK: Kluwer Academic Publishers)

Leshem YY and Pincasov Y 2002 Noninvasive photoacustic spectroscopic determination of relative endogenous nitric oxide and ethylene content stoichiometry during the ripening of strawberries *Fragaria anannasa* (Duch) and avocados *Persea americana* (Mill) *J Exp Bot* **51** 1471-1473

Leshem YY Willis RBH and Ku VVV 1998 Evidence for the function of the free radical gas nitric oxide (NO) as an endogenous regulating factor in higher plants *Plant Physiol Biochem* **36** 825-833

Levine A Tenhaken R Dixon R Lamb CJ 1994 H_2O_2 from the oxidative burst orchestrates the plant hypersensitive disease resistance response *Cell* **79** 583-593

Ligternik W Kroj T zur Nieden U Hirt H Scheel D 1997 Receptor- mediated activation of a MAP kinase in pathogen defense of plants *Science* **276** 2054-2057

Lindermayr C Saalbach G Bahnweg G Durner J 2006 Differential inhibition of *Arabidopsis* methionine adenosyltransferases by protein S-nitrosylation *Journal of Biological Chemistry* 2811–7

Lindermayr C Saalbach G Durner J 2005 Proteomic identification of S-nitrosylated proteins in *arabidopsis Plant Physiology* **137** 921–930

Liu M Huynh B Payne W Peck HJ Dervartanian D and Legall J 1987 Optical EPR and M{246} ssbauer spectroscopic studies on the NO derivatives of cytochrome cdl from *Thiobacilluc deni{128}rficanx Eur j Biochem* **169** 253-258

Liu X Miller MJS Joshi MS Thomas DD Lancaster JR Jr 1998 Accelerated reaction of nitric oxide with O_2 within the hydrophobic interior of biological membranes *Proceedings of the National Academy of Sciences* USA **95** 2175–2179

Loake G 2001 Plant cell death: unmasking the gatekeepers *Curr Biol* **11** R1028- R1031

Ludidi N Gehring C 2003 Identification of a novel protein with guanylyl cyclase activity in *Arabidopsis thaliana Journal of Biological Chemistry* **278** 6490–6494

Luis AJ Mur I Edi Santosa Lucas JJ Laarhoven Nicholas J Holton Frans JM Harren and Aileen R Smith 2005 Laser Photoacoustic Detection Allows in Planta Detection of Nitric Oxide in

Tobacco following Challenge with Avirulent and Virulent *Pseudomonas syringae* Pathovars *Plant Physiology* **138** 1247-1258

Lum HK Butt YKC Lo SCL 2002 Hydrogen peroxide induces a rapid production of nitric oxide in mung bean (*Phaseolus aureus*) Nitric Oxide: *Biology and Chemistry* **6** 205–213

Maathuis JM 2006 cGMP modulates gene transcription and cation transport in *Arabidopsis* roots *The Plant Journal* **45** 700–711

Magalhaes JR Monte DC Durzan D 2000 Nitric oxide and ethylene emission in *Arabidopsis* thaliana *Physiology and Molecular Biology of Plants* **2** 117–127

Mallick N Mohna FH Rai LC and Soeder CJ 2000a Evidence for the non involvement of nitric oxide synthase in nitric oxide production by the green algae *Scendesmus Obliquus J Plant Physiol* **156** 423-426

Mallick N Mohna FH Rai LC and Soeder CJ 2000b impact of physiological stresses on nitric oxide formation by green alga *Scendesmus Obliquus J Microbial Biotechnol* **10** 300-306

Mansfield TA 2002 Nitrogen oxides: old problems and new challenges In: Air pollution and plant life—Bell JNB Treshow M eds Chichester UK: John Wiley and Sons Ltd 119–133

Maples K Sandstrom T Su Y and Henderson R 1991 The nitric oxide/heme protein complex as a biologic marker of exposure to nitrogen dioxide in humans rats and in vitro models *Am j llespir Cell Mol Biol* **4** 538-543

Martin W Smith J Lewis MJ and Henderson AH 1988 Evidence the inhibitory factor extracted from bovine retract or penis is nitrite whose activated derivative is stabilized nitric oxide *Br j Pharmacol* **93** 579-585

Mathieu C Moreau S Frendo P Puppo A and Davis MJ 1998 Direct detection of radicals in intact soybean nodules: Presence of Nitric oxide- Leghemoglobin complexes Free Radical *Biol Med* **24** 1242-149

Matsunaga K and Furchgott RF 1988 Interactions of light and sodium nitrite in producing relaxation of rabbit aorta *J PharmacoL Exp Ther* **248** 687-695

Melotto M Underwood W Koczan J Nomura K He SY 2006 Plant stomata function in innate immunity against bacterial invasion *Cell* **126** 969–980

Menon N Patricza J Binder T and Bing R 1991 Reduction of biological effluents in purge and trap micro reaction vessels and detection of endothelium-derived nitric oxide (edno) by chemiluminescence *j MoL Cell CardioL* **23** 389-393

Menon N Wolf A Zehetgruber M and Bing R 1989 An improved chemiluminescence assay suggests non nitric oxide mediated action of lysophosphatidylcholine and acetylcholine *Proc Soc Exp Biol Med* **191** 316-319

Millar AH and Day DA 1996 Nitric oxide inhibits the cytochrome oxidase but not the alternative oxidase of plant mitochondria *FEBS Lett* **398** 155-158

Millar TM Stevens CR Benjamin N Eisenthal R Harrison R Blake DR 1998 Xanthine oxidoreductase catalyses the reduction of nitrates and nitrite to nitric oxide under hypoxic conditions *FEBS Letters* **427** 225–228

Mitchell DE Madore MA1992 Patterns of assimilate production and translocation in muskmelon (*Cucumis melo L) Plant Physiology* **99** 966–971

Mittler R Feng X Cohen M 1998 Post-translational suppression of cytosolic ascorbate peroxidase expression during pathogeninduced programmed cell death in tobacco *Plant Cell* **10** 461-473

Mittler R Shulaev V Lam E 1995 Coordinated activation of programmed cell death and defense mechanisms in transgenic tobacco plants expressing a bacterial proton pump *Plant Cell* **7** 29-42

Mittler R Shulaev V Seskar M Lam E 1996 Inhibition of programmed cell death in tobacco plants during a pathogen-induced hypersensitive response at low oxygen pressure *Plant Cell* **8** 1991-2001

Modolo LV Augusto O Almeida IMG Magalhaes JR Salgado I 2005 Nitrite as the major source of nitric oxide production by *Arabidopsis thaliana* in response to *Pseudomonas syringae FEBS* Letters **579** 3814–3820

Modolo LV Augusto O Almeida IMG Pinto-Maglio CAF Oliveira HC Seligman K Salgado I 2006 Decreased arginine and nitrite levels in nitrate reductase-deficient *Arabidopsis thaliana* plants impair nitric oxide synthesis and the hypersensitive response to *Pseudomonas syringae Plant Science* **171** 34–40

Morot-Gaudry-Talarmain Y Rockel P Moureaux T Quilleré I Leydecker MT Kaiser WM Morot-Gaudry JF 2002 Nitrite accumulation and nitric oxide emission in relation to cellular signalling in nitrite reductase antisense tobacco *Planta* **215** 708–715

Munemasa S Oda K Watanabe-Sugimoto M Nakamura Y Shimoishi Y Murata Y 2007 The coronatine-insensitive 1 mutation reveals the hormone signalling interaction between abscisic acid and methyl jasmonate in *Arabidopsis* guard cells Specific impairment of ion channel activation and second messenger production *Plant Physiology* **143** 1398–1407

Mur LAJ Bi Y-M Darby RM Firek S Draper J 1997 Compromising early salicylic acid accumulation delays the hypersensitive response and increases viral dispersal during lesion establishment in TMVinfected tobacco *Plant J* **12** 1113-1126

Mur LAJ Craver TLW Prats E 2006 NO way to live; the various roles of nitric oxide in plant–pathogen interactions *Journal of Experimental Botany* **57** 489–505

Mur LAJ Santosa IE Laarhoven LJJ Holton NJ Harren FJM Smith AR 2005 Laser photoacoustic detection allows in planta detection of nitric oxide in tobacco following challenge with avirulent and virulent *Pseudomonas syringae* pathovars *Plant Physiology* **138** 1247–1258

Murad F Arnold WP Mittal CK Braughler JM 1979 Properties and regulation of guanylate cyclase and some proposed functions for cyclic GMP Adv Cyclic Nucleotide Res **11** 175–204

Myers P Minor RJ Guerra RJ Bates J and Harrison D 1990 Vasorelaxant properties of the endothelium-derived relaxing factor more closely resemble 5-nitroso cysteine than nitric oxide *Nature (London)* **345** 161-163

Nathan C 1992 Nitric oxide as a secretory product of mammalian cells *FASEB J* **6** 3051-3064

Neill SJ Desikan R Clarke A Hurst RD and Hancock JT 2002b Hydrogen peroxide and nitric oxide as signaling molecules in plants *J Exp Bot* **53** 1237-1242

Neill SJ Desikan R Clarke A and Hancock JT 2002a Nitric oxide is a novel component of abscisic acid signaling in stomatal guard cells *Plant Physiol* **128** 13-16

Neill SJ Desikan R and Hancock JT 2003 Nitric oxide signaling in plants *New Phytol* **159** 11-35

Neill SJ Desikan R Hancock JT 2003 Nitric oxide signalling in plants *New Phytologist* 15911–35

Noronha Dutra AA Epperlein MM Woolf N 1993 Reaction of nitric oxide with hydrogen peroxide to produce potentially cytotoxic singlet oxygen as a model for nitric oxide-mediated killing *FEBS Lett* **321** 1993 59–62

Nürnberger T Nennstiel D Jabs T Sacks WR Hahlbrock K Scheel D 1994 High-affinity binding of a fungal oligopeptide elicitor to parsley plasma membranes triggers multiple defense responses *Cell* **78** 449-460

O'Brien IEW Baguley BCMurray BG Morris BAM Ferguson IB 1998 Early stages of the apoptotic pathway in plant cells are reversible *Plant J* **13** 803-814

Ohwaki YKawagishi-Kobayashi M Wakasa K Fujihara S Yoneyama T 2005 Induction of class-1 non-symbiotic haemoglobin genes by nitrate nitrite and nitric oxide in cultured rice cells *Plant Cell Physiology* **46** 324–331

Orozco-Cardenas ML and Ryan CA 2002 Nitric oxide negatively modulates wound signaling in tomato plants *Plant Physiol* **130** 487–493

Pagnussat G Simontachi M Puntarulo S and Lamattina L 2002 Nitric oxide is required for root organogenesis *Plant Physiol* **129** 954-956

Pagnussat GC Lanteri ML Lombardo MC Lamattina L 2004 Nitric oxide mediates the indole-acetic acid activation of a mitogen-activated protein kinase cascade involved in adventitious root formation *Plant Physiology* **135** 279–286

Pai T Payne W and LeGall J 1987 Use of a chemiluminescence detector for quantitation of nitric oxide produced in assays of denitrifying enzymes *Analyt Biochem* **166** 150-157

Palmer RMJ Ferridge AG and Moncada S 1987 Nitric oxide release accounts for the biological activity of endothelium-derived relaxing factor *Nature (London)* **327** 524-526

Parinov S Sevugan M Ye S Yang W-C Kumaran M Sundaresan V 1999 Analysis of flanking sequences from Dissociation insertion lines: a database for reverse genetics in *Arabidopsis Plant Cell* **11** 2263–2270

Patel S Robb-Gaspers LD Stellato KA Shon M Thomas AP 1999 Coordination of calcium signaling by endothelial derived nitric oxide in the intact liver *Nature Cell Biol* **1** 467-471

Pedroso MC Magalhaes JR and Durzan D 2000 A Nitric oxide burst precedes apoptosis in angiosperm and gymnosperm callus cells and foliar tissues *J Exp Bot* **51** 1027-1037

Pennell RI Lamb CJ 1997 Programmed cell death in plants *Plant Cell* **9** 1157-1168

Perazzolli M Dominici P Romero-Puertas MC Zago E Zeier J Sonoda M Lamb C Delledonne M 2004 *Arabidopsis* non-symbiotic hemoglobin AHb1 modulates nitric oxide bioactivity *The Plant Cell* **16** 2785–2794

Perazzolli M Romero-Puertas MC Delledonne M 2006 Modulation of nitric oxide bioactivity by plant haemoglobins *Journal of Experimental Botany* **57** 479–488

Piatelli M Giudici de Nicola M and Castrogiovanni V 1969 Photocontrol of amaranthin synthesis in *Amaranthis tricolor Phytochemistry* **8** 731-736

Planchet E Gupta KJ Sonoda M Kaiser WM 2005 Nitric oxide emission from tobacco leaves and cell suspensions: rate-limiting factors and evidence for the involvement of mitochondrial electron transport *The Plant Journal* **41** 732–743

Planchet E Kaiser WM 2006a Nitric oxide (NO) detection by DAF fluorescence and chemiluminescence: a comparison using abiotic and biotic NO sources *Journal of Experimental Botany* **57** 3043–3055

Planchet E Kaiser WM 2006b Nitric oxide production in plants *Plant Signaling and Behaviour* **1** 46–51

Raff M 1992 Social controls on cell survival and cell death *Nature* **356** 397-400

Ramamurthi A and Lewis RS 1997 Measurment and modeling of nitric oxide release rates for nitric oxide donors *Chem Res Toxicol* **10** 408-413

Rao MV and Davis KR 1999 Ozone- induced cell death occur via distinct mechanisms in *Arabidopsis:* The role of salicyclic acid *Plant J* **17** 603-609

Rees DD Palmer RMJ and Moncada S 1989 Role of endothelium-derived nitric oxide in the regulation of blood pressure *Proc Natl Acad Sci USA* **86** 3375-3378

Rockel P Strube F Rockel A Wildt J Kaiser WM 2002 Regulation of nitric oxide (NO) production by plant nitrate reductase *in vivo* and *in vitro Journal of Experimental Botany* **53** 103–110

Ryals JL Neuenschwander UH Willits MC Molina A Steiner H-YHunt MD 1996 Systemic acquired resistance *Plant Cell* **8** 1809-1819

Saito S Yamamoto-Katou A Yoshioka H Doke N Kawakita K 2006 Peroxynitrite generation and tyrosine nitration in defense responses in tobacco BY-2 cells *Plant and Cell Physiology* **47** 689–697

Sakamoto A Sakurao SH Fukunaga K Matsubara T Ueda-Hashimoto M Tsukamoto S Takahashi M Morikawa H 2004 Three distinct *Arabidopsis* hemoglobins exhibit peroxidase-like activity and differentially mediate nitrite-dependent protein nitration *FEBS Letters* **572** 27–32

Sakihama Y Murakamai S Yamasaki H Involvement of nitric oxide in the mechanism for stomatal opening in *Vicia faba* leaves *Biologia Plantarum* 2003 **45** 117–119

Sasakura F Uchiumi T Shimoda Y Suzuki A Takenouchi K Higashi S Abe M 2006 A class 1 hemoglobin gene from Alnus firma functions in symbiotic and non-symbiotic tissues to detoxify nitric oxide *Molecular Plant–Microbe Interactions* **19** 441–450

Scheel D 1998 Resistance response physiology and signal transduction *Curr Opin Plant Biol* **1** 305-310

Scherer GFE and Holk A 2000 NO donors mimic and NO inhibitors inhibit cytokinin action in betalain accumulation in *Amaranthus Caudatus Plant Growth Regul* **32** 345- 350

Schmidt H H H W Nau H Wittfoht W Gerlach J PrescherK EKleinM M Niroomand Fand Bohme E 1988 Arginine is a physiologic precursor of endotheliumderived nitric oxide *Eur J PharmacoL* **154** 212-216

Schror K Forster S and Woditsch I 1991 On-line measurement of nitric oxide release from organic nitrates in the intact coronary circulation *Naunyn-Schmiedebergs Arch Pharmacol* **344** 240-246

Schwartz LM Smith SW Jones MEE Osbourne BA 1993 Do all programmed cell deaths occur via apoptosis? *Proc Natl Acad Sci* USA **90** 980-984

Setia N Setia RC and Aggarwal M 2005 Amelioration of temperature effects by NO in leaves of oil seed *Brassica Species J PlSci Res* **21** 191-194

She XP Song XG He JM 2004 Role and relationship of nitric oxide and hydrogen peroxide in light/dark-regulated stomatal movement in *Vicia faba Acta Botanica Sinica* **46** 1292–1300

Shi S Wang G Wang Y Zhang L Zhang L 2005 Protective effect of nitric oxide against oxidative stress under ultraviolet-B radiation *Nitric Oxide* **13** 1–9

Shibuki K 1990 An electrochemical microprobe for detecting nitric oxide release in brain tissue *Neurosci Rex* **9** 69-76

Shimoda Y Nagata M Suzuki A Abe M Sato S Kato T Tabata S Higashi S Uchiumi T 2005 Symbiotic rhizobium and nitric oxide induce gene expression of non-symbiotic haemoglobin in Lotus japonicus *Plant and Cell Physiology* **46** 99–107

Shingles R ROH MH and Mc Carty RE 1996 Nitrite transport in chloroplast inner envelope vesicles I Direct measurement of proton- linked transport *Plant Physiol* **112** 1375-1381

Shirasu K Nakajima H Rajasekhar VK Dixon RA Lamb CJ 1997 Salicylic acid potentiates an agonist-dependent gain control that amplifies pathogen signals in the activation of defense mechanisms *Plant Cellb* 261-270

Sokolovski S Blatt MR 2004 Nitric oxide block of outward-rectifying K^+ channels indicates direct control by protein nitrosylation in guard cells *Plant Physiology* **136** 4275–4284

Sokolovski S Hills A Gay R Garcia-Mata C Lamattina L Blatt MR 2005 Protein phosphorylation is a prerequisite for intracellular Ca^{2+} release and ion channel control by nitric oxide and abscisic acid in guard cells *The Plant Journal* **43** 520–529

Song F Goodman RM 2001 Activity of nitric oxide is dependent on but is partially required for function of salicylic acid in the signaling pathway in tobacco systemic acquired resistance Mol *Plant Microbe Interact* **12** 1458–1462

Song L Ding W Zhao M Sun B Zhang L 2006 Nitric oxide protects against oxidative stress under heat stress in the calluses from two ecotypes of reed *Plant Science* **171** 449–458

Stamler JS Lamas S Fang FC 2001 Nitrosylation: prototypic redox based signaling mechanism *Cell* **106** 675-678

Sto¨hr C Strube F Marx G Ulrich WR Rockel P 2001 A plasma membrane-bound enzyme of tobacco roots catalyses the formation of nitric oxide from nitrite *Planta* **212** 835–841

Stohr C Stremlau S 2006 Formation and possible roles of nitric oxide in plant roots *Journal of Experimental Botany* **57** 463–470

Sun J Xin C Eu JP Stamler JS Meissner G 2001 Cysteine- 3635 is responsible for skeletal muscle ryanodine receptors modulation by NO *Proc Natl Acad Sci* USA **98** 11158-111162

Tada Y Mori T Shinogi T and Yao N 2004 Nitric oxide and reactive oxygen species do not elicit hypersensitive cell death but induce apoptosis in the adjacent cells during the defense response of oat *Mol Plant Microbe Interact* **17** 245–253

Takahashi H Chen Z Du H Liu Y Klessig DF 1997 Development of necrosis and activation of disease resistance in transgenic tobacco plants with severely reduced catalase levels *Plant J* **11** 993-1005

Takahashi S and Yamasaki H 2002 Reversible inhibition of photophosphorylation in chloroplasts by nitric oxide *FEBS Lett* **512** 145-148

The Nobel Prize in Physiology and Medicine1998http://nobelprizeorg/ nobel_prizes/medicine/ laureates/1998/ [Last visited date: 080906]

Thoiron S Pascal N and Briat JF 1997 Impact of iron deficiency and iron re supplly during the early stages of vegetative development in maize (*Zea mays L) Plant Cell Environ* **20** 1051-1060

Thornberry NA Lazebnik Y 1998 Caspases: enemies within *Science* **281** 312-1316

Thulke O Conrath U 1998 Salicylic acid has a dual role in the activation of defence-related genes in parsley *Plant J* **14** 35-42

Tian QY Sun DH Zhao MG Zhang WH 2007 Inhibition of nitric oxide synthase (NOS) underlies aluminium-induced inhibition of root elongation in *Hibiscus moscheutos New Phytologist* **174** 322–331

Torsethaugen G Pitcher LH Zilinskas BA Pell EJ 1997 Overproduction of ascorbate peroxidase in the tobacco chloroplast does not provide protection against ozone *Plant Physiol* **114** 529-537

Tracey WR Linden J Peach MJ and Johns RA 1990 Comparison of spectrophotometric and biological assays for nitric oxide (NO) and endothelium-derived relaxing factor (EDRF): nonspecificity of the diazotization reaction for NO and failure to detect EDRF *J PharmacoL Exp TIler* **252**922-928

Trevaskis B Watts RA Andersson CR Llewellyn DJ Hargrove MS Olson JS Dennis ES Peacock WJ 1997 Two hemoglobin genes in Arabidopsis thaliana: the evolutionary origins of leghemoglobins *Proceedings of the National Academy of Sciences* USA **94** 12230–12234

Tun NN Holk A and Schere FE 2001 Rapid increase of NO release in plant cell cultures induced by cytokinin *FEBS Lett* **509** 174-176

Uchida A Jagendorf AT Hibino T Takabe T Takabe T 2002 Effects of hydrogen peroxide and nitric oxide on both salt and heat stress tolerance in rice *Plant Science* **163** 515–523

Valderrama R Corpas FJ Carreras A Fernandez-Ocana A Chaki M Luque F Gomez-Rodriguez MV Colmenero-Varera P del Rio LA Barroso JB 2007 Nitrosative stress in plants *FEBS Letters* **581** 453–461

Van der Biezen EA Jones JDG 1998 Homologus between plant resistance gene products and regulators of cell death in animals *Curr Biol* **8** R226-R227

Vanin AF Svistunenko DA Mikoyan VD Serezhenkov VA Fryer MJ Baker NR Cooper CE 2004 Endogenous superoxide production and the nitrite/nitrate ratio control the concentration of bioavailable free nitric oxide in leaves *Journal of Biological Chemistry* **279** 24100–24107

Vranova E Inze D and Van Breusegem F 2002 Signal transduction during oxidative stress *J Exp Bot* **53** 1227-1236

Wang H Li J Bostock RM Gilchrist DG 1996 Apoptosis: a functional paradigm for programmed plant cell death induced by a hostselective phytotoxin and invoked during development *Plant Cell* 8 375-391

Wang Q Jacobs J DeLco J Kruszyna H Kruszyna R Smith R and Wilcox D 1991 Nitric oxide hemoglobin in mice and rats in endotoxic shock *Life Sci* **49** 55-6O

Wang R Guegler K LaBrie ST Crawford NM 2000 Genomic analysis of a nutrient response in Arabidopsis reveals diverse expression patterns and novel metabolic and potential regulatory genes induced by nitrate *The Plant Cell* **12** 1491–14–509

Wang R Tischner R Gutierrez RA Hoffman M Xing X Chen M Coruzzi G Crawford NM 2004 Genomic analysis of the nitrate response using a nitrate reductase-null mutant of *Arabidopsis Plant Physiology* **136** 2512–2522

Wang Y Yun BW Kwon EJ Hong JK Yoon JY Loake GJ 2006 S-nitrosylation: an emerging redox-based post-translational modification in plants *Journal of Experimental Botany* 57 1777–1784

Wang YS Yang ZM 2005 Nitric oxide reduces aluminium toxicity by preventing oxidative stress in the roots of *Cassia tora L Plant and Cell Physiology* **46** 1915–1923

Wellburn AR 1990 why are atmospheric oxides of nitrogen usually phytotoxic and not alternarive fertilizers? *New Phytol* **115** 395-429

Wendehenne D Pugin AKlessig DF Durner J 2001 Nitric oxide: comparative synthesis and signaling in animal and plant cells *Trends in Plant Science* 6177–183

Wennmalm A Lanne B and Petersson A 1990 Detection of endothelial-derived relaxing factor in human plasma in the basal state and following ischemia using electron paramagnetic resonance spectrometry *Analyt Biochem* **4** 128-130

Westenberger U Thanner S Ruf H Gersonde K Sutter G and Trentz O 1990 Formation of free radicals and nitric oxide derivative of hemoglobin in rats during shock syndrome *Free Radic Rex Commun* **11** 167-178

Weyman K Hunt M Uknes S Neuenschwander U Lawton K Steiner H-Y Ryals J 1995 Suppression and restoration of lesion formation in *Arabidopsis* lsd mutants *Plant Cell* **7** 2013-2022

Wildt J Kley D Rockel A Rockel P Segschneider HJ 1997 Emission of NO from several higher plant species *Journal of Geophysical Research* **102** 5919–5927

Wilkinson J Crawford NM 1991 Identification of the *Arabidopsis* CHL3 gene as the nitrate reductase structural gene NIA2 *The Plant Cell* **3** 461–471

Wilkinson JQ Crawford NM 1993 Identification and characterization of a chlorate-resistant mutant of *Arabidopsis thaliana* with mutations in both nitrate reductase structural genes NIA1 and NIA2 *Molecular and General Genetics* **239** 289–297

Wink D A Cook JA Pacelli R Liebmann J Krishne M C and Mitchell J B 1995 Nitric oxide (NO) protects against cellular damage by reactive oxygen species *ToxicolLett* **82\83** 221-226

Xu H Heath M 1998 Role of calcium in signal transduction during the hypersensitive response caused by basidiospore-derived infection of the *Cowpea Rust fungus Plant Cell* **10** 585-597

Xu Q Reed JC 1998 Bax Inhibitor-1 a mammalian apoptosis suppressor identified by functional screening in yeast *Molecular Cell* **1** 337-346

Yamamoto A Katou S Yoshioka H Doke N and Kawakita K 2003 Nitrate reductase a nitric oxide-producing enzyme induction by pathogen signals *J Gen Plant pathol* **69** 218-229

Yang Y Shah J Klessig DF 1997 Signal perception and transduction in plant defense responses Genes Dev **11** 1621-1639

Yu CC Hung KT Kao CH 2005 Nitric oxide reduces Cu toxicity and Cu-induced NH_4^+ accumulation in rice leaves *Journal of Plant Physiology* **162** 1319–1330

Yu I-C Parker J Bent AF 1998 Gene-for-gene disease resistance without the hypersensitive response in *Arabidopsis dnd1 mutant Proc Natl Acad Sci* USA **95** 7819-7824

Yu X Sukumaran S Marton L 1998 Differential expression of the *Arabidopsis* NIA1 and NIA2 genes *Plant Physiology* **116** 1091–1096

Zafiriou OC and McFarland M 1980 Determination of trace levels of nitric oxide in aqueous solution *Analyl Chem* **52** 1662-1667

Zeidler D Zahringer U Gerber I Dubery I Hartung T Bors W Hutzler P Durner J 2004 Innate immunity in *Arabidopsis thaliana:* lipopolysaccharides activate nitric oxide synthase (NOS) and induce defense genes *Proceedings of the National Academy of Sciences* USA **101** 15811–15816

Zemojtel T Fröchlich A Palmieri MC *et al* 2006 Plant nitric oxide synthase: a never-ending story? *Trends in Plant Science* **11** 524–525

Zhang A Jiang M Zhang J Ding H Xu S Hu X Tan M 2007 Nitric oxide induced by hydrogen peroxide mediates abscisic acid-induced activation of mitogen-activated protein kinase cascade involved in antioxidant defense in maize leaves *New Phytologist* **175** 36–50

Zhang F Wang Y Yang Y Wu H Wang Di Liu J 2007 Involvement of hydrogen peroxide and nitric oxide in salt resistance in the calluses from *Populus euphratica Plant Cell* and *Environment* **30** 775–785

Zhang H Shen WB Xu LL2003 Effects of nitric oxide on the germination of wheat seeds and its reactive oxygen species metabolisms under osmotic stress *Acta Botanica Sinica* **45** 901–905

Zhang S Du H Klessig DF 1998 Activation of the tobacco SIP kinase by both a cell wall-derived carbohydrate elicitor and purified proteinaceous elicitins from *Phytophthora spp Plant Cell* **10** 435-449

Zhang S Klessig DK 1997 Salicylic acid activates a 48-kD MAP kinase in tobacco *Plant Cell* **9** 809-824

Zhang Y Wang L Liu Y Zhang Q Wei Q Zhang W 2006 Nitric oxide enhances salt tolerance in maize seedlings through increasing activities of proton-pump and Na^+/H^+ antiport in the tonoplast *Planta* **224** 545–555

Zhao L Zhang F Guo J Yang Y Li B Zhang L 2004 Nitric oxide functions as a signal in salt resistance in the calluses from two ecotypes of reed *Plant Physiology* **134** 849–857

Zhao M Zhao X Wu Y Zhang L 2007 Enhanced sensitivity to oxidative stress in an *Arabidopsis* nitric oxide synthase mutant *Journal of Plant Physiology* **164** 737–745

Zhao MG Tian QY Zhang WH 2007 Nitric oxide synthase-dependent nitric oxide production Is associated with salt tolerance in *Arabidopsis Plant Physiology* **144** 206–217

Zhao Z Chen G and Zhang C 2001 Interaction between reactive oxygen species and nitric oxide in drought- induced abcisic acid synthesis in root tips of wheat seedlings *Aust J Plant physiol* **28** 1050-1061

Zhou B Guo Z Xing J Huang B 2005 Nitric oxide is involved in abscisic acid-induced antioxidant activities in Stylosanthes guianensis *Journal of Experimental Botany* **56** 3223–3228

Zottini M Formentin E Scattolin M Carimi F LoSchiavo F and Terzi M 2002 Nitric oxide affects plant mitochondrial functionality *in vivo FEBS Lett* **515** 75-78

Zou H Henzel W Liu X Lutschg A Wang X 1997 Apaf-1 a human protein homologous to C elegans CED-4 participates in cytochrome c-dependent activation of caspase-3 **Cell 90** 405-414

11

PRIONS: THE LETHAL PROTEINS-REVISITED

C.P.MALIK, CHITRA WADHWANI, VARSHA CHATURVEDI AND YAKSHA SINGH

In a recent review Wadhwani and Malik (2007) discussed various aspects of Prions -the lethal proteins. The present discussion is aimed at looking at the prion diseases from a molecular point of view, taking into consideration the genetic as well as the transmissible and sporadic aspects of the diseases. The present appraisal intends to not only critically analyze the prion particle, ending in identifying the progress that needs to be made in the future, and above all, the major uncertainty of variant CJD.

INTRODUCTION

Prusiner (1981) coined the name Prion agents that cause a novel type of fatal brain diseases. Prions are Proteinaceous infectious agents of about 27 Kilo Daltons which (almost certainly) do not have a nucleic acid genome. It was reported to be present in amyloid fibrils in the brain. They resist inactivation by procedures that modify nucleic acid but respond to agents that disrupt proteins. Prion diseases are often called spongiform encephalopathies because of the post mortem appearance of the brain with large vacuoles in the cerebellum and cortex. Research on prion diseases has recently accelerated because the causative agents are not viruses or bacteria or fungi or parasites. The mounting experimental evidence has generated great interest in what appears to be a totally new kind of mechanism of disease. The main goal of present review is to understand the various aspects of these unique proteins partly. The prions are infectious proteins and on account of lacking a nucleic acid genome appear to be a Protein Life form More recently, Prions have come to the attention of a wide audience because they are the causative agents of neurological disorders such as BSE (Bovine Spongiform Encephalopathy) whose possible transmission to human has caused great concern in U.K and elsewhere. The exact nature of this etiological agent has been and still is a focus of scientific debate.

THE PRION PARTICLE

Perhaps, the best current working definition of a prion is a proteinaceous in acid (Prusiner, 1997). A wealth of data supports the infectious particle that lacks nucleic acid (Prusiner, 1997). A wealth of data supports the contention that scrapie prions are devoid of nucleic acid and seem to be composed exclusively of a modified isoform of PrP, designated PrPSc. The normal cellular PrP, denoted PrPC, is converted into PrPSc through a process whereby a portion of its α-helical and coil structure is refolded into β sheet (Pan *et al.* 1993). This structural transition is accompanied by profound changes in the physicochemical properties of the PrP. While PrPC is soluble in no denaturing detergents, PrPSc is not. PrPC is readily digested by proteases, whereas PrPSc is partially resistant (Oesch *et al.* 1985). Because prions appear to be composed entirely of a protein that adopts an abnormal conformation, it is not unreasonable to think of prions as infectious proteins (Pan *et al.* 1993; Telling *et al.* 1996). But we hasten to add that we still cannot eliminate the possibility of a small ligand bound to PrPSc as an essential component of the infectious prion particle. In a more broad view, prions are elements that impart and propagate variability through multiple conformers of a normal cellular protein. The species of a particular prion is encoded by the sequence of the chromosomal PrP gene of the mammal in which it last replicated. In contrast to pathogens with a nucleic acid genome that encode strain-specific properties in genes, prions seem to encipher these properties in the tertiary structure of PrPSc (Bessen and Marsh, 1994; Telling *et al.* 1996; Prusiner, 1997). The discovery that mutations of the PrP gene caused dominantly inherited prion diseases in humans linked the genetic and infectious forms of prion diseases and presented another hurdle for investigators who contain used to argue that prion diseases are caused by viruses. More than 20 mutations of the PrP gene are now known to cause the inherited human prion diseases, and no significant genetic linkage has been established for five of these mutations (Hsiao *et al.* 1989) (for review, see Prusiner, 1997). The prion concept readily explains how a disease can manifest as a heritable as well as an infectious illness. Moreover, the hallmark common to all of the prion diseases whether sporadic, dominantly inherited, or acquired by infection is that they involve the aberrant metabolism of the prion protein (Prusiner, 1991). Although PrPSc is the only known component of the infectious prion particles, these unique pathogens share several phenotypic traits with other infectious entities such as viruses. Because some features of the diseases caused by prions and viruses are similar, some scientists have difficulty accepting the existence of prions despite a wealth of scientific data supporting this concept (Chesebro and Caughey, 1993; Manuelidis and Fritch, 1996; Lasme´ zas *et al.* 1997; Chesebro, 1998).

PrP gene, PrPc Protein and its Isoform

Prion protein gene has been located on chromosome 20. It bears two exons separated by a single intron. Exon I and II are transcribed and the two RNA's ligated into a single mRNA coding for PrP protein. The latter is a cell surface glycoprotein. Normal Protein is a precursor of infectious several posttranslational events to become Prion Protein (PrP 27-30) which causes scrapie in sheep. In humans PrP is translated as a 253 amino acid protein that is translocated into the Endoplasmic reticulum (ER), where signal sequences at both amino (an ER entry signal) and carboxy (a glycosyl phosphatidylinositol) terminal ends are cleaved to produce mature PrP of 208 amino acids. In the ER, the GPI anchor is attached and two asparagine-linked glycosylation sites are core glycosylated. PrP then passes to the Golgi apparatus for trimming and modification of the sugars prior to transport to the exofacial membrane of the cell. In certain cases, PrP may exist in a transmembrane topology that may be specifically linked to the pathogenesis of the disease. PrP molecules arising from mutated genes probably do not adopt the disease conformation as soon as they are synthesized. Otherwise people become sick in early childhood. The mutation in the PrP gene renders the resulting proteins susceptible to flipping from an α-helical to β-sheet shape. Presumably it takes time until one of the molecules spontaneously flips over and still more time for disease PrP to accumulate and damage the brain enough to cause symptoms. In sucrose gradients, infectivity co migrates with rod shaped particles called amyloid fibrils found by electron microscopy in infected brains. Polyacrylamide gel electrophoresis of the proteins in the infectious fraction from sucrose gradients has revealed a single protein termed the prion protein (PrP) with a relative molecular weight 0f 27-30 kDa. Further analysis has revealed that the scrapie PrP or PrPSc is a glycoprotein. A great advance in the field came with the derivation of a monoclonal antibody that recognizes PrPsc. In addition to the prion associated protein that is readily detected in infected tissue, a cross-reacting normal cellular analogue (PrPc) has also been identified using this antibody. The latter protein has homologues in many animal species including mammalian and most likely avian. Purification and partial sequence analysis of PrPSc allowed the design of synthetic oligonucleotide DNA probes complementary to all possible codons that can encode the PrP amino acid sequence. These probes in turn, have led to the cloning of mRNA's encoding PrP and detection of such mRNA's in both normal and scrapie infected hamster tissues. Because DNA's of both normal and infected cells contain a single copy of a gene for this mRNA, it appears that PrP is a component of normal brain tissue that remains closely associated with scrapie agent infectivity during extensive purification. The amino acid sequence of the normal and scrapie PrP is the same and PrPc expressed in uninfected cells is the precursor for PrPSc. The ability of the PrPSc to form aggregates of fibers in the brain distinguishes it from the normal protein. Moreover, the normal protein is slightly smaller and more easily digested by proteinase K than is PrPSc The conformational differences between the two proteins distinguish them and are determined most likely at the plasma membrane or during transfer to lysosomes. It is the accumulation of PrPSc that causes brain cell damage, but whether PrPSc is the causative agent or a consequence of infection is still not known. It appears unlikely that the mRNA is itself the genome of the prion, since none of this RNA has been detected in spleens of infected mice where high levels of infectivity are found. The length of time for development of disease probably reflects the interval needed for production of this abnormal prion protein shape and recruitment of normal PrP into its unusual form. In experiments involving transgenic mice, a mutation was introduced into the DNA coding for the normal PrPSc so that the defect in this protein found associated with GSS was expressed. The animals developed scrapie-like lesions in the brain. Whether or not an infectious agent is also made is under study. In other experiments, transfer of the gene for the hamster PrPSc to transgenic mice made the animals highly susceptible to the hamster adapted scrapie strain. Disease involved the hamster (and not mouse) PrP. When, however, these mice were inoculated with the mouse scrapie strain, the brain pathology showed the presence of mouse PrP. These observations support the role of the protein in nerve cell pathology but do not resolve if PrP is a component of the causative agent or is required for its replication. Finally, it is interesting to note that, using anti-PrP antisera, researchers have found the PrP antigen in amyloid fibers not only in Scrapie infected brains but also in human brains of CJD victims. However, the role of this protein, if any, in the infectivity or pathogenesis of these diseases has yet to be proved, and morphologically similar structures have been observed in noninfectious neuropathies, including Alzheimer's disease. However, the fibers in the amyloid of Alzheimer's disease differ in amino acid sequence from these PrP.

Sterilization

Infectious particles possessing nucleic acid are dependent upon it to direct their continued replication. Prions however, are infectious by their effect on normal versions of the protein. Therefore, sterilizing prions involves the denaturation of the protein to a state where the molecule is no longer able to induce the abnormal folding of normal proteins. However, prions are generally quite resistant to denaturation by proteases, heat, radiation, and formalin treatments, although their infectivity can be reduced by such treatments. Prions can be denatured by subjecting them to a temperature of 134 degrees Celsius for 18 minutes in a pressurised steam autoclave. Ozone sterilization is currently being studied as a potential method for prion deactivation. Renaturation of a completely denatured prion to infectious status has not yet been achieved, however partially denatured prions can be renatured to an infective status under certain artificial conditions.

PRIONS SHOW THEIR GOOD SIDE

Zamponi and colleagues in a study published in *Journal of Cell Biology* 5 May, 2008, have inferred that normally functioning prions prevent neurons from working themselves to death. Diseases such as mad cow result when the prion protein adopts an abnormal conformation. This infectious form creates a template that induces normal copies of the protein to misfold as well. Scientists have long assumed that prions must also have a beneficial side but have been unable to pinpoint any such favorable traits.

In their work, the authors found that mice lacking the prion protein had overactive brain cells. Their neurons responded longer and more vigorously to electrical or drug-induced stimulation than did neurons that had normal prion protein. This hyperactivity eventually led to the neurons' death. The results might help explain why misfolded prions cause dementia: in the wrong conformation, the prion can no longer protect brain cells from deadly overexcitement.

INFECTIOUS AND NON-INFECTIOUS PRIONS HAVE CLEAR DIFFERENCES IN MOLECULAR STRUCTURES

Prions have been identified as the cause of "mad cow" disease (BSE). The culprits are "incorrectly folded" proteins that can "infect" healthy proteins. The molecular bases for such prion diseases are not yet fully understood. Why are some proteins infectious while others are not?

A team headed by Beat Meier (ETH Zurich, Switzerland) and Raimon Sabaté (University of Bordeaux, France) has examined two different forms of a prion-forming protein domain by means of NMR spectroscopy. In the journal *Angewandte Chemie 2008*, the researchers report that the infectious and non-infectious forms differ markedly in their molecular structure.

These are proteins that can fold in different ways. Pathogenic prions are dangerous because they can convert physiological, non-pathogenic molecules into the diseased form. Often, prions largely consist of β-sheet structures. These are accordion-like folded protein ribbons that can easily aggregate into thread-like structures (amyloid fibrils).

The research team took on the prion-forming domain of the fungal protein HET-s. At a pH value of 7—under physiological conditions—this domain forms infectious fibrils. In acidic solution, at pH 3, it also forms fibrils, but these are not infectious.

By using nuclear magnetic resonance spectroscopy (NMR), the team was able to get a closer look at this protein. NMR allows for the evaluation of interactions of the nuclear spins of specific atomic nuclei with each other and their chemical surroundings, which gives information about the structure and dynamics of molecules and molecular fragments. The spectra of the pH 7 and pH 3 versions of the prion differ significantly. Both are mainly arranged in the rigid β-sheet structure, but up close the structures diverge widely. Particularly striking is the fact that the infectious pH 7 form has highly flexible loops in addition to the rigid domains. These are absent from the non-infectious pH 3 prions.

The lack of infectiousness of the pH 3 fibrils is thus related to the fact that their molecular structure is significantly different from that of the fibrils formed at physiological pH as shown in fig:1

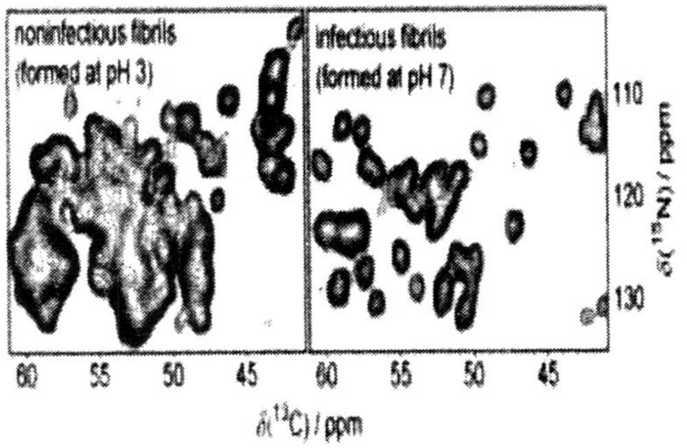

Fig.1. Magnetic resonance studies find clear differences between the structures of infectious and non-infectious prions.

PRION FINGERPRINTS DETECTED WITH GLOWING MOLECULE

Peter Nilsson *et al.* (2007) at Linköping University in Sweden, among other institutions found an effective and sensitive new method for detecting and characterizing prions, the infectious compounds behind diseases like mad cow.

Mad cow disease (BSE), which has caused the death of more than 200,000 cattle and 165 people in the U.K., has now abated. But other prion disorders are on the rise, and there is concern that new strains will infect humans. Prions are not readily transmittable from species to species, but once they have broken through the species barrier they can rapidly adapt and become contagious within the species. Intensive work is now underway to find new, more sensitive methods for detecting these potentially deadly protein structures and distinguish between various strains.

Methods are based on a fluorescent molecule, a so-called conjugated polymer. The research team infected genetically identical laboratory mice with BSE, scrapie (which afflicts sheep), and CWD (chronic wasting disease or "mad elk disease," which is epidemic in the central U.S.) for several generations in a row. Gradually new strains of prions emerge, making the diseases more fatal to the mice. Tissue samples from mice were examined using the fluorescent molecule, which seeks out and binds with prions. This is signaled by a shift in color. By tweaking the molecule, the team has been able to get it to show different colors depending on the structure of the prion each prion strain emits its own optical fingerprint.

This is an important difference compared with other techniques used to find prions, such as antibodies and the well-known stain Congo red.

The technique has also proven to work well on tissue sections from dead animals, such as cows infected with BSE. Now the scientists want to move on and look for alternative sample-taking methods for diagnosing and tracking prion diseases in humans in early stages.

The method would then be useful for screening blood products, since there is a risk that people can be carriers of prions without having any symptoms of disease. In the U.K. it was discovered that 66 people had received blood from blood donors who were infected with the human form of BSE (a variant of Creutzfeldt-Jakob disease, vCJD), and among them, four individuals have been shown to be infected (source: Health Protection Agency, Jan. 2007). We can directly see the structure of the prions and thereby deduce the disease, Nilsson developed the technique has been applying the technology to prion diseases. Prions and other defectively folded proteins give rise to similar disorders, such as Alzheimer's,

ACCELERATED METHOD TO DETERMINE INFECTIOUS PRION STRAINS

According to Lasmézas *et al. PLos ONE* (2009) some prion strains are pathogenic for humans and some are not, it's vital that we know the difference when we find them in the field and when we study them in the laboratory, The new method for distinguishing among various strains combines a transgenic mouse model with a rapid and sensitive cell-based procedure, There are about 20 prion strains known in mouse models. Different varieties of prion strains are identified in mouse models according to incubation time, clinical symptoms, and localization of brain lesions, accelerated incubation. A transgenic mouse line called Tga20 plays an important role, because it succumbs rapidly to prion disease .The prions primarily target the brainstem and the thalamus of this transgenic mouse, explaining why these animals have a shorter incubation time than their normal counterparts.

INFECTIOUS, TEST TUBE-PRODUCED PRIONS CAN JUMP THE 'SPECIES BARRIER'

Castilla *et al* (2009) in, *Cell* have shown that they can create entirely new strains of infectious proteins known as prions in the laboratory by simply mixing infectious prions from one species with the normal prion proteins of another species. Unlike conventional infectious microorganisms, the infectious agent in the case of prion diseases consists exclusively of a misfolded form of the prion protein.

These researchers now find that prion strains produced by combining normal hamster proteins with infectious mouse proteins can infect hamsters and *vice versa*. Although they are both rodents, prions from one of the two species normally don't readily infect the other, a common phenomenon amongst prions known as a species barrier.

The novel prions they produced not only look different, but they also produce symptoms in the animals that differ from any known strain found in nature they report. It is Surprising that the new barriers are crossed and new prions arise. There is the potential for a large variety of new infectious prions—some of which may have dramatic effects.

The infectious agent is a protein with a different shape from the normal protein. Those misfolded and misshapen proteins can spread by causing normal protein to change their shape. Those aberrant forms band together, forming fibrils.

Soto's *et al. in Science* (2005) have reported the generation of infectious prions by amplification of prion misfolding in the test tube. In those experiments, they used a technology called protein misfolding cyclic amplification (PMCA) that mimics some of the fundamental steps involved in the replication of infectious prions in living animals, but at an accelerated rate. The method involves placing small quantities of infectious prions with large quantities of the normal protein from the same species together, allowing the infectious form to imprint on the normal form and thereby replicate itself.

Now, they have demonstrated that the same method can generate new strains when infectious prions from one species are mixed with normal prion proteins from another species. The finding provides conclusive evidence that the imprinting of disease-causing prions on normal forms can overcome species barriers, and doesn't require any other infectious agent.

The new method might provide insight into the risk that other prion diseases could spread from one species to another, For instance, scientists don't know whether chronic wasting disease, a condition now on the rise amongst deer in some parts of the U.S., can be transmitted to humans or not.

Test tube studies like this one might help answer that question, and-- in the case that the deer prions can make the leap—such studies may inform scientists about what those prions might look like,. By studying any new prion strains created in mice with the human prion protein, scientists might also gain insight into the potential symptoms associated with those diseases.

"The data demonstrate that PMCA is a valuable tool for the investigation of the strength of the barrier between diverse species, its molecular determinants, and the expected features of the new infectious material produced," the researchers concluded. "Finally, our findings suggest that the universe of possible prions is not restricted to those currently known but that likely many unique infectious foldings of the prion protein may be produced and that one of the sources for this is cross-species transmission."

PRION DISEASES

A fifty-two year old man stepped into his shower, but could not recognize anything at all. Even his soap was a stranger. One year later, after losing his ability to speak and see he died. Shortly after his death, scientists proclaimed that he had died of variant Creutzfeldt -Jakob disease (Klein *et al.* 2007).

The prion diseases are fatal neurodegenerative disorders of humans and animals that are important because of their impact on public health and because they exemplify a novel mechanism of infectivity and biological information transfer. These diseases are caused by conformational conversion of a normal host glycoprotein (PrP^C) into an infectious isoform (PrP^{Sc}) that is devoid of nucleic acid. These diseases, grouped under the category of transmissible spongiform encephalopathies (TSEs), are the result of the misfolding of the normal host encoded cellular prion protein (PrP^c), to its pathogenic isoform, the scrapie protein (PrP^{sc}) in a post-translational conversion (Prusiner *et al.*1996).The PRNP gene, located on the short arm of human chromosome 20, is responsible for the creation of the normal prion protein (Prusiner *et al.* 1994).

Several polymorphisms occur in the PRNP gene, although the most important one is at codon 129, since it appears to affect the susceptibility to prion diseases (Belay *et al.*1992) Prion diseases have shown to afflict animals as well as humans (Chakra borty *et al.* 2005).

Prion diseases are fatal neurodegenerative disorders of humans and animals that are important because of their impact on public health and because they exemplify a novel mechanism of infectivity and biological information transfer. These diseases are caused by conformational conversion of a normal host glycoprotein (PrP^C) into an infectious isoform (PrP^{Sc}) that is devoid of nucleic acid.

In several cases, little physical data about the infectious agent exist, and the classification is essentially based on similarities in epidemiologic and pathologic findings. Both genetic and sporadic forms of the diseases have been categorized in Table 1.

Table 1: The Prion Diseases, the hosts and mechanism of pathogenesis

Diseases	*Host*	*Mechanism of Pathogenesis*
Kuru	Fore people	Infection through ritualistic cannibalism
iCJD.	Humans	Infection from prion-contaminated HGH, dura mater grafts, etc
vCJD	Humans	Infection from bovine prions?
fCJD	Humans	Germline mutations in PrP gene
GSS	Humans	Germline mutations in PrP gene
FFI C	Humans	Germline mutation in PrP gene (D178N, M129)
sCJD	Humans	Somatic mutation or spontaneous conversion of PrP^c into PrP^{Sc}?
FSI	Humans	Somatic mutation or spontaneous conversion of PrP^c into PrP^{Sc}?
Scrapie	Sheep	Infection in genetically susceptible sheep
BSE	Cattle	Infection with prion-contaminated MBM
TME	Mink	Infection with prions from sheep or cattle
CWD	Mule deer, elk	Unknown
FSE	Cats	Infection with prion-contaminated beef
Exotic ungulate encephalopathy M	Greater kudu, nyala, oryx	Infection with prion-contaminated MBM

Abbreviations: BSE, bovine spongiform encephalopathy; CJD, Creutzfeldt-Jakob disease; sCJD, sporadic CJD; fCJD, familial CJD; iCJD, iatrogenic CJD; vCJD, (new) variant CJD; CWD, chronic wasting disease; FFI, fatal familial insomnia; FSE, feline spongiform encephalopathy; FSI, fatal sporadic insomnia; GSS, Gerstmann-Straussler-Scheinker disease; HGH, human growth hormone; MBM, meat and bone meal; TME, transmissible mink encephalopathy.

PRION DISEASES IN ANIMALS AND HUMANS

Prion diseases, also called spongiform encephalopathies, are a group of closely related, fatal neurodegenerative disorders that affect mammals, including cows, sheep, and deer, as well as humans. Different strains of the infectious agent, called a prion, cause mad cow disease, chronic wasting disease, and different forms of scrapie and human Creutzfeldt-Jacob disease, Mad cow disease has had devastating consequences for bovine livestock populations, particularly in Europe, and for humans who have consumed contaminated beef products. There have been more than 200 recorded human fatalities worldwide due to mad cow disease. Creutzfeldt-Jacob disease, a low-incidence but always fatal disease, affects humans in all countries. Prions consist mainly or entirely of an abnormal form of a normal cellular protein. They multiply by converting their normal counterparts into a likeness of themselves, which may aggregate to form deposits called amyloid. Accumulation of different kinds of amyloid plays a role in a wide range of neurodegenerative diseases, including Alzheimer's and Parkinson's diseases.

Most mammalian species develop this disease such as the Scrapie in sheep, Transmissible Mink Encephalopathy (TME) in mink, Chronic Wasting Disease (CWD) in mule deer, Bovine Spongiform encephalopathy (BSE) in cows. Humans are also susceptible to several Prion diseases like Creutzfeldt Jacob Disease (CJD) (Creutzfeldt, 1920), Gerstmann Straussler scheinker syndrome (GSS), Fatal Familial Insomnia (FFI), Kuru and Alper's syndrome. Alper's syndrome is the name given to Prion diseases in infants. Prions related diseases are characterized by long incubation and a symptomatic period of illness followed by loss of motor control, dementia, paralysis and ultimately death (Huang *et al.* 2004).

Epidemiology

More than one etiological factor might be responsible for the diseases. Humans might be infected by prions in following ways:

1. Acquired infection

Diet and medical procedures such as surgery, growth hormones, corneal transplants etc. *i.e.* infectious agent implicated. Recently it has been shown that pathological prion proteins are deposited in the neuroepithelium of the olfactory mucosa in patients with sporadic CJD, *i.e.* even nasal secretions could be infectious (Monaco *et al.* 2003).

2. Inherited genetic mutations

Sometimes rogue prions are produced by genetic mutation that is why some cases of CJD, GSS and FFI in humans are inherited in an autosomal dominant fashion.

3. Sporadic prion diseases

Majority of the cases seem not to result from infection, but occur as a spontaneous disease with or without a genetic predisposition (Mastrianni, 2004).

4. RNA mutation

Researchers have suggested RNA mutation as a possible initial event in the etiology of sporadic prion diseases (Garcion *et al.* 2004).

A new variant of CJD has been identified which is designated vCJD, is transmitted to humans by indigestion of BSE-contaminated food products in Great Britain (Scott *et al.* 1999). The disease affects approximately one person per million per year, worldwide (Mckintosh *et al.* 2003). The disease has no preference for a particular gender (Brown *et al.* 1987) and nor is there a predilection for a particular ethnic group although certain mutations within the PrPc gene that causes familial diseases may be more restricted to certain groups, based on the origin of mutation (Mastrianni, 2004).

PRIONS: ON THE TRAIL OF KILLER PROTEINS

The animal and human prion diseases are characterized by their ability to cause an invariably fatal degeneration of the nervous system. When the brain tissue is viewed under a microscope, the sections have a sponge-like appearance. The classic neuropathological features of human prion disease include spongiform degeneration, gliosis, and neuronal loss in the absence of an inflammatory response. Scrapie was the first example of this type of disease and has been known for many hundreds of years. Kuruî is the condition, which first brought prion diseases to prominence in 1950's. It was found in geographically isolated tribes in Papua New Guinea. It spread through cannibalism because the people used to ingest brain tissue of dead relatives for religious reasons.

The symptoms of Kuruî are congestion of blood vessels in brain, cortical atrophy, vacuolization in neuronal cytoplasm and dendrites, which gives the neuropil a spongy appearance. Ultimately the cells misfire and become non functional (Hadlow, 1959). Clusters of brain cells die and the brain stops looking like brain. In mad cow disease the cows become so uncomfortable and itchy that they frantically rub up against anything they can, finally scrapping off most of the wool and hair. Inherited prion diseases like GSS and FFI show the deposition of amyloid plaques in the cortical and sub cortical regions of the brain. Impairment of movement is observed when cerebellum gets involved where as decrease in memory and mental agility shows the involvement of cerebral cortex. Porter and Porter (Porter *et al.* 1973) have reported lack of specific immune response to the puzzling agent. Essentially, the brain cells fall apart, leading to symptoms such as a progressive sub-acute or chronic decline in cognitive or motor function.

(*a*) Different prions affect different regions of the brain

Symptom depend on which region of the brain is affected as in figs. : 2 (a), (b)

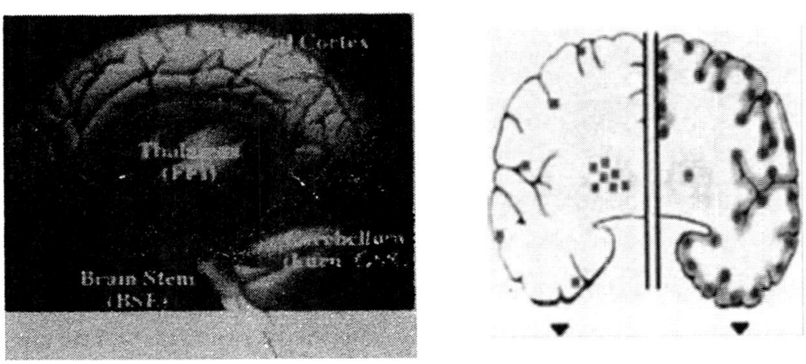

Fig 2. (a) and (b) Parts of brain being affected.

Cerebral cortex: When affected, the symptoms include loss of memory and mental acuity, and sometimes also visual impairment (CJD).

Thalamus: Damage may result in insomnia (FFI).

Cerebellum: Damage results in problems to coordinate body movements and difficulties to walk (kuru, GSS).

Brain stem: In the mad cow disease (BSE), the brain stem is affected.

(*b*) Spongy appearance of brain tissue

Mutations can result in different shapes of the prion protein that accumulates in different regions of the brain: In familial insomnia (FFI), mutated prions (violet squares) accumulate in the thalamus, with the result that the patients are unable to sleep. In Creutzfeldt-Jakob disease, the prion protein accumulates primarily in the cerebral cortex (red dots area). A precise diagnosis of a prion disease can only be made upon autopsy. The fig. 3 shows thin sections of diseased brains. FFI, with typical proliferation of astrocytes, the support cells of the brain, is shown to the left (arrows). CJD, with the characteristic spongiform appearance with vacuoles (arrows) is shown to the right. Due to their characteristic appearance, the diseases are known as the transmissible spongiform encephalopathies (TSEs) as they can be transmitted both experimentally and naturally. The TSEs consist of several closely related prion diseases, of which four similar diseases affect humans as shown in Fig. 3

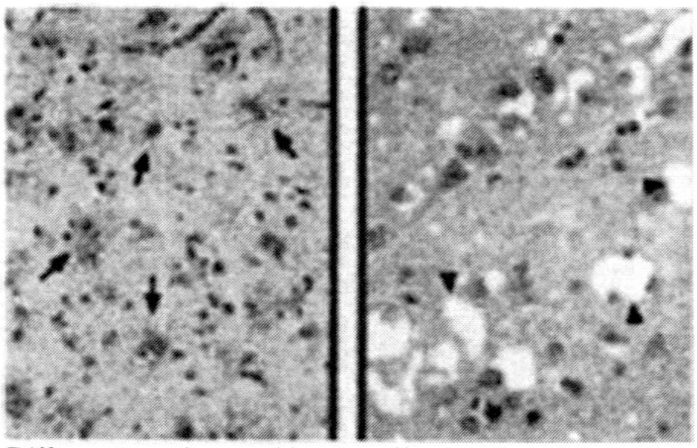

Fig 3. Different regions of brain affected by different prions.

1. Through horizontal transmission from e.g. a sheep to a cow (BSE).
2. In inherited forms, mutations in the prion gene are transmitted from parent to child *i.e.* familial.
3. They can arise spontaneously i.e sporadic (no known antecedent events).

Relevance

The prion diseases can affect both humans and animals, and it is invariably fatal due to the neurological damage it causes. Presently, there are no vaccines or medicines that will prevent the disease and, apart from nursing care, there are no treatments to halt or slow its inevitable course. The course of the disease is alarmingly rapid compared with other neurodegenerative disorders such as Alzheimer disease, Parkinson's disease and motor neuron disease.

Epidemiology and Clinical features of the different diseases

Background: The prion diseases are a large group of related neurodegenerative conditions, which affect both animals and humans. These diseases all have long incubation periods but are typically rapidly progressive once clinical symptoms begin. All prion diseases are fatal, with no effective form of treatment currently; however, increased understanding of their pathogenesis has recently led to the promise of effective therapeutic interventions in the near future.

Prion diseases are unique in that they can be inherited, they can occur sporadically, and they can be infectious. The first of these diseases to be described was Scrapie, a disease of sheep recognized for over 250 years. This illness, manifested by hyper excitability, itching, and ataxia, leads to paralysis and death. It is called Scrapie because of the tendency of affected animals to rub against the fences of their pens in order to stay upright, reflecting their cerebellar dysfunction.

Pathophysiology: A unifying feature of all the prionoses is their neuropathology.

These illnesses tend to affect the gray matter of the central nervous system (CNS), producing neuronal loss, gliosis, and characteristic spongiform change. The latter is a vacuolation of the neuropil, and to a variable degree, of the neurons. In addition, plaques with the typical staining properties of amyloid (eg, apple-green birefringence after Congo Red staining when viewed under polarized light) are observed in many of these conditions.

PRION RELATED DISEASES

Sporadic diseases include CJD, which occurs worldwide with incidence of about 1 in a million people. An example of an acquired disease is kuru, meaning shivering or trembling, which was discovered in Eastern Highlands of Papa New Guinea amongst members of the ForÈ tribe. It is also known as the laughing disease due to the facial grimaces it causes and is thought to be acquired through the ritual cannibalism of dead relatives who had caught the disease. There is also iatrogenic CJD and new variant CJD.

New variant CJD is commonly thought to result from eating food contaminated with the BSE agent.

Familial diseases are genetically inherited and include familial CJD, which accounts for about 15% of all CJD cases. Also inherited are GSS, with a global incidence of 1 in 10 million, and FFI, where insomnia is a major symptom, in addition to other symptoms including dementia. GSS diseases comprise dementing, ataxic and atypical GSS with neurofibrillary tangles. Included is the atypical prion disease, which does not easily fit the diagnostic criteria for prion disease. There are also several types of animal prion diseases affecting animals. This is explained by the fact that many are zoo animals possibly exposed to the agent in their feed.

HUMAN PRION DISEASES

In the care of patients dying of human prion disease, the precautions used for patients with AIDS or hepatitis are certainly adequate. In contrast to these viral illnesses, the human prion diseases are not communicable or contagious. There is no evidence of contact or aerosol transmission of prions from one human to another. However, they are infectious under some circumstances, such as ritualistic cannibalism in New Guinea causing Kuru, the administration of prion-contaminated growth hormone causing iatrogenic CJD, and the transplantation of prion-contaminated dura mater grafts. Familial CJD, GSS, and FFI are all dominantly inherited prion diseases; five different mutations of the PrP gene have been shown to be genetically linked to the development of inherited prion disease. Prions from many cases of inherited prion disease have been transmitted to apes, monkeys, and mice carrying human PrP transgenes.

Creutzfeldt-Jacob disease

Creutzfeldt-Jacob disease (CJD) occurs rarely throughout the world and typically presents as a dementia in either men or women at least 60 years old. Some cases are clustered in certain families, and the fact that some of these families also have an apparently higher incidence of Alzheimer's disease has led to the supposition that the two diseases may be related. Only CJD is readily transmissible to apes (and occasionally, rodents) however. CJD also appears to be transmissible to humans by contaminated products.

Coste E - Uro *et al.*(*PLos Pathog* , 2008) from the United Kingdom and France have identified four separate biochemical subgroups in a selection of cases of Creutzfeldt-Jakob disease. The study suggests that these subgroups could represent distinct prion strains in the most common human prion disease.

Prion diseases are transmissible neurodegenerative disorders characterized by accumulation of an abnormal isoform (PrPSc) of a host-encoded protein (PrPC) in affected tissues. Although considered a spontaneous disorder, the clinicopathological characteristics of sporadic Creutzfeldt-Jakob disease (sCJD) are variable and substantially influenced by a particular variation in the DNA of the prion protein gene (PRNP). Due to the strong influence of host factors on the characteristics of the disease, diversity of prion agents responsible for CJD remains extremely difficult to investigate.

In this study, using two new biochemical assays, the authors identified four distinct biochemical PrPSc subgroups in 41 sCJD cases. These subgroups correlate with the current sCJD sub classification. The subgroups were also found in 12 iatrogenic CJD (iCJD) cases from different countries. iatrogenic CJD occurs following human-to-human sCJD transmission. In contrast to the sCJD cases, however, there was no particular correlation with the PRNP codon in the iCJD cases, indicating that observed biochemical properties could be specific to the prion agent.

Creutzfeldt-Jacob disease (sporadic)

In a number of countries, there have been extensive epidemiological studies on the numbers of CJD cases. All of these countries obtained broadly the same results, approximating about 0.5-1 case per million. There is no significant case clustering other than in familial clusters. Cases are distributed apparently at random with a frequency related only to local population density. There is no evidence for case to case spread (other than with respect to iatrogenic CJD discussed below). There is now evidence of an association with local scrapie prevalence, since CJD is as common in scrapie free areas such as Australia and New Zealand, as it is in the UK, where scrapie is endemic. Despite the attention focused on links between BSE and CJD, the overall incidence figures do not appear to have risen more in the UK than in countries, which do not have BSE. Although an overall increase has been observed, it is likely to be due to increased accurate identification of cases due to increased attention, which is now focused on these diseases. This is especially relevant to the increased incidence noted in the elderly, where other dementing illnesses are common and could be confused with CJD. Occasional weak statistical associations with particular foodstuffs have been reported, although these have tended to disappear in subsequent years of the study and no consistent new risk factors have emerged. Despite this, concern has been expressed about a number of occurrences of CJD in UK dairy farmers.

Clinical features of CJD

According to Collinge & Palmer (1997) the core clinical syndrome of CJD is of rapidly progressive multifocal dementia usually with myoclonus. The onset is usually in the 45- 75 year age group with peak onset between 60-65 years. The clinical progression is typically over weeks progressing to akinetic mutism and death, often within two to three months. Around 70% of cases die in less than 6 months. Prodromal features include extrapyramidal signs, cerebellar ataxia, pyramidal signs and cortical blindness. About 10% of the cases present initially with cerebellar ataxia. Routine haematological and biochemical investigations are normal although occasional cases have been noted to have raised serum transaminases or alkaline phosphatase. There are no immunological markers and acute phase proteins are not elevated. They go on to mention that "Prospective epidemiological studies have demonstrated that cases with a progressive dementia and two or more of myoclonus, cortical blindness, pyramidal, cerebellar or extrapyramidal signs, or akinetic mutism with a typical EEG nearly always turn out to be confirmed as histological definite CJD if neuropathological examination is performed". This depends on neuropathological confirmation being "by demonstration of spongiform change, neuronal loss, and astrocytosis". PrP amyloid plaques are usually not seen with CJD, although the presence of protease resistant PrP can be demonstrated by immunoblotting of brain homogenates.

Iatrogenic CJD

Iatrogenic CJD is usually referred to as CJD despite cases arising from peripheral inoculation (not intracerebral) usually having a prominent cerebellar syndrome more reminiscent of Kuru (discussed later). Transmission may occur by any one of a number of routes involving accidental inoculation with human prions as a result of medical procedures; the routes involving the use of inadequately sterilised neurosurgical instruments due to the high heat resistance of the prion, dura mater and corneal grafting, as well as the use of gonadotrophin derived from the pituitary gland from cadavers. Iatrogenic CJD actively demonstrates the transmissible properties of the prion (described later). The first case was with a 55 year old woman who received a corneal transplant from a donor later found to have died from CJD. In such cases of neurosurgical transmission, the equipment was found to have been sterilised with 70% ethanol and formaldehyde vapour. This is normally enough for conventional agents, but is ineffective against prions. In view of this, the new sterilisation protocol involves immersion in 1 M NaOH for one hour to inactivate the prions.

New Variant CJD

Teenagers rarely get sporadic CJD, and when in 1995 two cases were reported in the UK, (Bateman, Britton) both were unusual in having Kuru-type plaques, which is only found in about 5% of CJD cases. Shortly after, a third young case emerged and a link was suggested with BSE. In the following months further cases emerged showing similar histological patterns which were unique from those observed with other prion diseases. These cases were named new variant CJD, despite being atypical in their clinical presentation with most cases not meeting the accepted clinical diagnostic criteria for probable CJD. Since the original reports, 124 cases of nvCJD have been diagnosed in Great Britain, 6 in France, 1 in Italy, and 1 in Ireland. These cases were extensively compared with other prion diseases and the lack of correlation seemed to confirm the arrival of a new strain of prion disease in the UK due to the incredibly small statistical probability of these similar cases occurring by chance. The symptoms of the new variant CJD start with behavioural and psychological disturbances, which include anxiety, depression, persistent pain in the limbs/face, withdrawal and behavioural changes which progress over neurological features later become apparent often after most patients have gone to see a psychiatrist due to the preliminary symptoms. Several weeks later, progressive cerebellar syndrome develops with gait and limb ataxia. Later dementia develops progressing to akinetic mutism; myoclonus was also seen in most patients and sometimes was preceded by choreoathetosis. The neuropathological appearances were very consistent with widespread spongiform change, gliosis and neuronal loss, most severe in the basal ganglia and thalamus, the most remarkable feature being the abundant PrP amyloid plaques in the cerebral and cerebellar cortex. The plaques consisted of Kuru like florid plaques (surrounded by spongiform vacuoles) and multicentric plaque types. The florid plaques were very unusual and seen previously only in scrapie, but were very consistent. There was also an extensive amount of PrP in the cerebral cortex, cerebellar cortex, and in the molecular layer of the cerebellum. The unusual young age of these patients and the link with BSE may point to a risk involving dietary exposure. The risk involved however is as yet undetermined, and will only be determined as time goes by and more or fewer cases are identified. This is due to the potentially long incubation time related to the species barrier.

Different (atypical) forms of CJD

These forms of the disease are well recognised, and around 10% of cases have a longer clinical course of over two years. These cases may be represented by people with heterozygous PrP polymorphisms. 10% of cases involve cerebellar ataxia rather than cognitive impairment, and are called ataxic CJD. Other types of CJD can include Heidenhain's variant of CJD, which refers to cases where cortical blindness predominates with severe involvement of the occipital lobes. There is also the panencephalopathic type of CJD where there is extensive degeneration of the grey matter; this was mainly reported in Japan. Amyotrophic variants of CJD have been described with prominent early muscle wasting and are usually seen in late disease when other features are established. However most cases of dementia with amyotrophy are not experimentally transmissible, and their relationship with CJD is not clear. It is possible that these are variants of motor neurone disease with associated dementia.

When evaluating a patient for possible sporadic CJD, the clinician should be guided by published case definitions; they are as follows:

Definite CJD

Characteristic neuropathology

Protease-resistant PrP by Western blot

Probable CJD

Progressive dementia

Typical findings on EEG

At least 2 of the following - Myoclonus, visual impairment, cerebellar signs, pyramidal or extrapyramidal signs, or akinetic mutism

Possible CJD

Progressive dementia

Atypical findings on EEG or EEG not available

At least 2 of the following-Myoclonus, visual impairment, cerebellar signs, pyramidal or extrapyramidal signs, or akinetic mutism

Duration less than 2 years

Kuru disease

The study of Kuru is immensely important for the understanding of these diseases, providing the most extensive clinical experience of acquired prion disease in humans, the epidemiology of Kuru clearly indicates the infectious, but non-contagious, properties of prions and provides extensive evidence that vertical transmission from pregnancies does not occur. Kuru reached epidemic levels in the ForÈ people in the Okapa district of the Eastern Highlands of Papua New Guinea (Gajdusek *et al.* 1957, Gajdusek, 1977) other areas affected included Keiagana, Kanite, Yate, Usurfa and Gima, which are in the close vicinity.

Work done by Gajdusek (1957) in an epidemiological survey, uncovered the link between the ritualistic cannibalism and the disease occurrence. This included the differential age and sex incidence which was due to the women and children preparing the food, and becoming exposed to the agent, as well as eating the less desirable brains and other internal organs, even the bones were pounded up to be eaten with greens later. The whole of the deceased sufferer was recycled by way of endo-cannibalism. This is a type of cannibalism. It could be termed 'transumption' as it is seen as disposing of the dead relative, recycling the remains back into the community, and most importantly as a spiritual and virtuous gift to the family members. These customs were thought to instill wisdom.

The ratio of occurrence was about 5 females to 1 male, with about 1% of the population affected. In the years after these practices were stopped, the only cases were from the older and not the younger people (who won't have been cannibals) indicating no evidence for vertical transmission, and due to the mortality rate much later, an incubation time of as much as 40 years or more.

The clinical duration had a mean of 12 months with a range of 3 months to three years, the course tending to be shorter in children. Cerebellar ataxia is the central feature with dementia usually absent (contrasting to CJD). Gross dementia can occur but is usually rare. There is a prodrome stage followed by three clinical stages which are:

1. *Prodromal stage:*

Kuru typically begins with prodromal symptoms consisting of headache, aching of limbs, and also joint pains which can last for several months.

2. *Ambulatory stage:*

At this stage there may be no objective signs of disease, but it can be self diagnosed as patients experience an onset of unsteadiness in standing or walking, or of dysarthria or diplopia. Gait ataxia worsens and patients develop a broad-based gait, truncal instability, and titubation. There is a postural tremor present which is coarse and accentuated by movement; patients characteristically hold their hands together in the midline to suppress this. Standing with feet together reveals clawing of toes to maintain posture. This clawing response is regarded as pathogonomic of Kuru. Therefore signs at this stage are of midline truncal ataxia, presumably due to paleocerebellar disease, which is reflected by the only clear macroscopic brain abnormality seen in Kuru, which is atrophy of the cerebellar vermis. As the gait ataxia and astasia worsens the patients require a stick, as ataxia progresses the patient passes to the next stage of the disease (Sedentary). The mean clinical duration of the first stage is around 8 months and correlates closely with total duration.

3. *Sedentary stage:*

At this stage patients cannot walk, but are able to sit. Walking attempts lead to a high steppage, wide based gait with reeling instability, and flinging arm movements in an attempt to maintain posture. Hyper-reflexia is seen, although usually plantar responses remain flexor and abdominal reflexes intact. Clonus is characteristically short lived. Athetoid and choreiform movements and parkinsonian tremors may occur. There is reduced muscle power but no paralysis, and obesity may be common at this stage but possibly linked to bulimia. Characteristically there is emotional lability and bizarre uncontrollable laughter, which has lead to the disease being referred to as 'laughing death'; one sufferer may start and this spreads throughout the group, although this is only a small aspect of the disease. Myoclonic jerking is rarely seen (unlike in CJD) in this stage which lasts about two to three months.

4. Tertiary stage:

Hypotonia and hyporeflexia develop and the terminal stage is marked by flaccid muscle weakness. Plantar responses remain flexor and abdominal reflexes intact. The patient is unable to sit unsupported, dysphagia occurs and the patients become incontinent. Inanition and emaciation develop and transient conjugate eye signs and dementia may occur with primitive reflexes developing in some cases. Brainstem involvement and both bulbar and pseudobulbar signs occur.

Respiratory failure and bronchopneumonia eventually lead to death. This final stage lasts one or two months. Often death may occur earlier due to the nature of the illness, for example the sufferers may role into a fire, and burn themselves when in the later stages of the disease. The sufferer is always very well cared for by their family. In the last five years, there have only been 18 deaths in the south ForÈ, with only one male death in 1998 and none yet in 1999, indicating the beginning of the end of the kuru epidemic.

INHERITED PRION DISEASES

Gerstmann-Straussler-Scheinker disease

This was first described by Gerstmann in the 1920s-30s as a peculiar heredo-familial disease of the central nervous system. The classical presentation is with a chronic cerebeller ataxia accompanied by pyramidal features, with dementia occurring later in a much more prolonged clinical course than that seen in CJD. The mean duration is around five years with onset usually in the third or fourth decades of life. The histological hallmark is the presence of the multicentric amyloid plaques. Spongiform change, neuronal loss, astrocytosis and white matter loss are also usually present. This is an autosomal dominant disorder and is caused by mutations of the PrP gene, which can now be classified within the spectrum of inherited prion disease. Interestingly, in several kindreds of GSS, extensive neurofibrillary tangle (NFT) formation is found (Ghetti, 1994). NFTs are an essential feature of Alzheimer disease, but are also observed in other neurodegenerative conditions.

Fatal Familial Insomnia

This disorder was first described in 1986 and is an autosomally dominant inherited sleep disorder. This presents itself as a progressive untreatable insomnia and autonomic dysfunction (i.e hyperthermia, hypertension, tachycardia, tachypnea, hyperhydrosis), dementia, and motor paralysis however, the phenotypic expression is very variable even within the same family. Thalamic atrophy is the main histological finding, with the anterior-ventral and medial dorsal thalamic nuclei being consistently affected, while the cortex shows moderate asterocytosis.

The age of onset is also variable, ranging from 18-60 years. Once symptoms begin, the course ranges from 6 months to 3 years. Because of the diversity of clinical presentations of this disorder, genotyping is very important for definitive diagnosis. Unlike other prionoses, spongiform change can be a minor feature or can be absent altogether. All patients with FFI have a missense mutation at codon 178 of the PrP gene where Asn is replaced by Asp, coupled with a Met at the polymorphic codon 129. The somewhat divergent clinical and neuropathological features of FFI, in comparison to other human prionoses, highlight the wide spectrum of disease associated with PrP dysfunction and suggest that other human illnesses have yet to be recognized as prionoses.

Familial CJD

This inherited disease occurs later on in life at a similar time to GSS with similar symptoms except for a more rapidly advancing dementia and an abnormal EEG.

CAUSES OF PRION DISEASES

Prion-related diseases are unique in that they can be related to infectious, sporadic, or familial causes:

Infectious causes

Kuru, a form of prion disease, occurred among the Fore people of the Eastern Highlands of New Guinea and was related to ritualistic cannibalism. The disease is believed to have started with the chance ingestion of body parts of a patient with sporadic CJD, followed by a serial passage of the disease Many cases of iatrogenic CJD have been reported. In clinical practice, CJD has been transmitted by surgical instruments, EEG electrodes, corneal transplants, dura mater grafts, human pituitary-derived gonadotrophins, and human-derived growth hormone.

Concerns that nvCJD could be transmitted by blood transfusion have not yet been borne out by a documented case. nvCJD in humans is presumed to have been caused by ingestion of beef products contaminated with BSE. BSE is presumed to have started because of the practice of supplementing the diets of calves and dairy cows with meat and bone products. These meat and bone products are thought to have been contaminated with scrapie material (from sheep) and/or with material from cattle with a sporadic form of bovine prion disease.

Recently, a number of cases of apparent sporadic CJD have occurred in the United States among young individuals (<30 y). The incidence of sporadic CJD among such young individuals has historically been about 1 case per billion populations. In the years

1979-1996, 4 cases of sporadic CJD were reported in the United States among individuals younger than 30 years. In the years 1997-2000, 5 cases have occurred in the United States among young patients. Two of these individuals came from adjacent counties in Michigan (ages at onset were 26 and 28 y), and 3 cases occurred among individuals who were known hunters of deer and/or elk.

Over the same period, a major outbreak of CWD occurred among the deer and elk populations in many western states. CWD is a form of prion disease that occurs naturally in the deer and elk population; however, the pathology has many similarities to BSE, including the presence of florid plaques. Significantly, transmission studies of CWD PrPSc in the laboratory have shown that it can cross the species barrier from deer to human PrP at about the same efficiency as the BSE prion agent. These observations have led to the speculation that limited transmission of CWD to humans has occurred recently in the United States.

Familial causes

The cause of familial forms of prion disease is related to mutations in the PrP gene. A number of mutations in the PrP gene are linked to autosomal dominant forms of prion disease. The diseases can also be related to infectious causes, such as nvCJD, that are thought to be related to ingestion of cattle products contaminated with BSE. The disease can also be related to a spontaneous conformational change in the normal PrPC to a PrPSc form. The PrPSc form has higher beta-sheet content and is self-propagating, inducing more PrPC to convert to the PrPSc form.

Sporadic causes

Sporadic CJD is the most common form of prion disease.

It probably arises as a spontaneous conformational change in PrPC to a PrPSc form.

The PrPSc form is then self-propagating, inducing more PrPC to convert to the PrPSc form.

ANIMAL DISEASES

Scrapie Disease

The oldest known prion disease, was described in 1759 (Leopold) and is characterized by the abnormal walk and scratching of infected sheep and goats. It is still found in parts of world despite attempts to eradicate the agent by destroying infected flocks. The disease is characterized by incoordination and unsteady gait, which becomes progressively worse until death. The infectious agent, in the form of extracts from infected brains has been passed experimentally to mice, hamsters, ferrets, mink and monkeys but apparantly is not infectious for chimpanzees or rabbits. The disease induced by the Scrapie agent in Mink is analogous to that in sheep and is indistinguishable from a Transmissible MinkEncephalopathy (TME) found naturally in in Mink. Likewise, Chronic Wasting Disease of mule deer and elk is similar both in pathology and known physical properties to the Scrapie agent. A condition in cattle, the so called ìMad Cow Diseaseî is believed caused by a prion transmitted in contaminated feed supplements derived from infected sheep and goats. Concern has been raised that this agent might also cause disease in humans eating contaminated meat. Scrapie was the first example of this type of disease to be noticed and has been known about for many hundreds of years. There are two possible methods of transmission in sheep:

1. Infection of pasture with placental tissue carrying the agent followed by ingestion, or direct sheep-lamb transmission *i.e.* an acquired infection.
2. Parry showed considerable foresight by suggesting that it is not normally an infectious disease at all but a genetic disorder. He further suggested that selective breeding would get rid of the disease.

Scrapie is classified as a slow infection. It is characterized by a prolonged incubation period of months, years or possibly decades in which the patient or the host animal is without symptoms. Once the illness begins, however, it progresses steadily and always leads to death. The name scrapie comes from the tendency of sheep that have the disease to scrape off much of their wool. The disorder has been known for more than 200 years, and by 1935 French workers had shown convincingly that it can be transmitted from one sheep to another by inoculation. This demonstration of transmissibility implies that the infectious agent is capable of reproducing itself in the host animal. The clinical and pathological signs of Scrapie are similar to those of Kuru and CJD. The initial symptoms are difficulty in walking and loss of coordination, indicating a functional disorder of the cerebellum. Other symptoms include irritability, excitability, restlessness, scratching, biting, and rubbing of skin, patchy loss of wool, loss of weight, weakness of the hindquarters and impaired vision. There is no sign of an inflammatory process or fever, and cell counts in the spinal fluid remain normal. This indicates that the immune system does not respond to the disease agent. Pathological effects brought on by the diseases are confined to the central nervous system. In some of the disorders numerous vacuoles give the brain tissue a spongy appearance. The natural mode of transmission in sheep is unclear, but scientists do know that it is transmitted by a filterable particle that is resistant to heat and formalin fixation. As yet there are no biochemical or cell culture assay systems for either Scrapie agent or any other of these agents. Transmission of the disease to mice or hamsters allows endpoint titration of biological activity to be performed, albeit slowly. With the finding that the interval from inoculation to onset of disease is inversely proportional to the dose of Scrapie agent injected intracerebrally into hamsters, it has become possible to assay samples with the use of four animals in 60 to 70 days- provided that the titers of Scrapie agent in the samples are sufficiently high. This assay has been used to help purify the infectious principle and investigate its structure on the molecular level. Variants of the Scrapie agent have been isolated from standard stocks by passage in mice and hamsters at limiting dilutions. Some of these exhibit different neuropathological effects, including markedly different incubation times and tissue tropism. These ìstrainsî seem to be stable and do not revert or interconvert with detectable frequency. The existence of such stable variants is most easily explained by the operation of a genetic mechanism based on the presence of a nucleic acid genome in the infectious agent. However as noted above, no such genome has been found and no virus like particles has been observed in infectious samples. The Scrapie agent (like viruses) passes through filters of 22 to 100 nm. It can be inactivated by strong alkaline solutions (1 M NaOH) but is highly resistant to nonionic detergents. Its resistance to nucleases and erlative sensitivity to proteases led to its consideration as an infectious protein (prion).

Timm Konold *et al.* BMC Veterinary Press (2008) from the Veterinary Laboratories Agency in Weybridge, UK, investigated the transmission of scrapie by feeding milk from scrapie-affected ewes to lambs that are genetically susceptible to contracting scrapie. The researchers were looking for the presence of the prion protein, PrPd, which is associated with the disease. Scrapie can be transmitted to lambs through milk, according to new research. The study provides important information on the transmission of this prion-associated disease and the control of scrapie in affected flocks. Scrapie is a fatal neurodegenerative disease of sheep and goats. Clinical signs include itchiness, head tremor, wool loss and skin lesions as well as changes in behaviour and gait. Eighteen lambs were fed milk from scrapie-affected ewes. Three of these lambs were culled and two were found to have PrPd in intestinal tissues. The prion protein was also detected in lymphoid tissue of the gut of the surviving lambs and in some control lambs mixed with the scrapie milk recipients after weaning.

This suggested that scrapie milk recipients were able to shed the infectious agent and infect other lambs. There was no sign of PrPd in tissue samples from a control group of 10 lambs (one culled and the rest alive), which were housed in the same building but fed milk from healthy ewes. The research will continue, to see whether the lambs with PrPd develop the disease as they get older. This work raises the possibility that other prion diseases could be transmitted in sheep *via* milk although it should have no direct implications for human health. Scrapie has been found in sheep and has not been shown to be transmissible to humans. BSE has not been found naturally in sheep and occurrence in sheep in the UK is considered to be unlikely. This research adds to our understanding of the transmission of prion diseases in sheep and would help to inform measures needed to protect human health if BSE were ever to be found in sheep.

Transmissible mink encephalopathy

Transmissible mink encephalopathy (TME) is a disease of farmed mink, probably caused by feeding on Scrapie-contaminated meat.

Chronic Wasting disease

Chronic wasting disease (CWD) is a Scrapie-like disease of obscure origin found in wild and captive mule deer and Rocky Mountain elk.

Bovine Spongiform Encephalophathy/Mad Cow Disease

BSE is a progressive neurological disorder of cattle which results from infection by an unconventional transmissible agent. From November 1986 until December 1995, an estimated 155,600 head of cattle in almost 33,000 herds were diagnosed with BSE in Great Britain. The epidemic peaked in January 1993 with almost 1,000 new cases per week. The nature of the transmissible agent is unknown but currently the most accepted theory is that he agent is a modified form of a prion protein. Scientists considered herd type, size and age structure, whether the animals had been in contact with sheep, and is so, whether Scrapie was present in the flock. Sheep were not present on 20% of the farms; therefore it was believed that the cattle food which was being supplemented with sheep bone meal was responsible for the outbreak. So far, the disease has been confined to the United Kingdom with only a few cases showing up outside. Those cases resulted in cows being exported from the U.K. Britain may have been at greater risk than other countries when the Scrapie agent unexpectedly moved from sheep to cattle, apparently sometime in the 1980s. Feed practices in Britain differ from those in other countries, and British farmers raise a large number of sheep-and hence Scrapie-infected carcasses-relative to cattle. Most of the herds affected are dairy, milk producing herds. The reason for this may be that dairy cattle eat more commercially produced food, and thus are more likely to ingest sheep ruminants. Beef cattle depend on grazing and vegetation for food. In 1996, scientists believed that there was a clear possibility that BSE might be infecting humans as well.

Pathogenesis

BSE has an incubation period of 2 to 5 years. Infection can show up in the brain, spleen, thymus, tongue, and gut. Cows infected with BSE appear alert but agitated, anxious and apprehensive. The cow takes a wide base stance, abdomen is drawn up, gait becomes abnormal and exaggerated, and causes tumbling and skin wounds. There are fine muscle contractions over the surface of the neck and body with occasional larger muscle jerks. The animal begins to lose weight and there are frenzied movements including aimless head butting. Disease is fatal for cattle within weeks to months of onset.

Epidemiology

At its peak the epidemic affected approximately one percent of adult breeding cows (annual incidence). The peak was in the winter of 1992/93 when a maximum of just over 1000 suspected cases a week were being reported. The incidence has subsequently fallen year by year at a rate of around 40% per year. The within head incidence has been monitored closely, as this is a good indicator of whether or not there has been spread of disease from cow to cow in the herd. This suggests that there has been little or no spread of infection from animal to animal (horizontal transmission). It is still unclear as to whether cows may become infected directly from the food or from asymptomatic mothers that have died. Post-mortem tests are the only type of diagnostic test which are currently available. Scientists examine the characteristic appearance of the brain under the microscope and also use electron microscopy techniques.

Nano-sensor For Better Detection of Mad Cow Disease Agent

Craighead Harold *et al. Analytical Chemistry* (2008) in New York are reporting development of a nano-sized sensor that detects record low levels of the deadly prion proteins that cause Mad Cow Disease and other so-called prion diseases. The sensor, which detects binding of prion proteins by detecting frequency changes of a micromechanical oscillator, could lead to a reliable blood test for prion diseases in both animals and humans the researchers say.

Prions are infectious proteins that can cause deadly nerve-damaging diseases such as Mad Cow Disease in cattle, scrapie in sheep, and a human form of Mad Cow Disease called variant Creutzfeldt - Jakob disease. Conventional tests are designed to detect the proteins only upon autopsy and the tests are time-consuming and unreliable.

In the new study, Harold G. Craighead and colleagues describe a high-tech, nano-sized device called a nano mechanical resonator array. The device includes a silicon sensor, which resembles a tiny tuning fork, that changes vibrational resonant frequency when prions bind. Its vibration patterns are then measured by a special detector. In experimental trials, the sensor detected prions at concentrations as low as 2 nanograms per milliliter, the smallest levels measured to date.

Feline spongiform encephalopathy

Feline spongiform encephalopathy (FSE) is a disease seen in domestic cats, and in a few other members of the cat family. The spongiform encephalopathies (feline and non feline) are assumed to be caused by feeding BSE-infected material to the animals in question, often in zoos. Mice, hamsters and monkeys have proved experimentally to be the most useful models of prion diseases.

Iron Is Involved In Prion Disease-associated Neuronal Demise

Imbalance of iron homeostasis is a common feature of prion disease-affected human, mouse, and hamster brains, according to Singh *et al. (PLos Pathogens,* 2009).These findings provide new insight into the mechanism of neurotoxicity in prion disorders, and novel avenues for the development of therapeutic strategies.

Unlike other neurodegenerative conditions, prion disorders are sporadic, inherited, and infectious, and affect both humans and animals; common examples are mad cow disease in cattle, scrapie in sheep, and Creutzfeldt-Jakob disease in humans. The causative agent is a misfolded protein referred to as PrP-scrapie that replicates itself by changing the conformation of neighboring copies of the same protein, namely the prion protein. Aggregates of PrP-scrapie are toxic to brain cells and cause a spongy-like appearance in diseased brains. Singh suggests that accumulation of PrP-scrapie alters the metabolism of iron in diseased brains. The imbalance of brain iron homeostasis worsens with disease progression, and is not an outcome of end-stage disease. Since iron is highly toxic when mismanaged, this condition is likely to contribute significantly to prion-disease associated neurotoxicity. The likely cause of this condition is loss of normal function of the prion protein in cellular iron metabolism demonstrated recently by Singh *et al.* combined with gain of toxic function by the redox-active PrP-scrapie complex; it was surprised to find that prion disease-affected brains are iron deficient despite a significant increase in their overall iron content. The group concludes that ferritin, a major iron storage protein, co-aggregates with PrP-scrapie in diseased brains and sequesters bound iron in the complex, creating a state of apparent iron deficiency. The brain cells respond to this condition by increasing their level of iron uptake, thus creating a vicious cycle of increased iron uptake in the presence of increased iron.These observations contribute to our understanding of how the prion agent causes neurotoxicity, and may enable the development of novel therapeutic strategies targeted at restoring brain iron homeostasis in prion disorders.

Prion Infectivity Found In White and Brown Fat Tissues Of Mice

Race *et al. (PLos Pathogen,s* 2008) from the National Institutes of Health and the Scripps Research Institute have found novel prion infectivity in white and brown fat tissues of mice. Prion diseases affect humans as well as wild and domestic animals. Distribution of prion infectivity in organs and tissues is important in understanding prion disease pathogenesis and designing strategies to prevent prion infection in animals and humans. Studies in animals including sheep, goats, cattle, deer, mink, hamsters and mice, have found prion infectivity mostly in nervous system tissues such as the brain and spinal cord. The tissues studied here in a mouse model demonstrate a proof of principle that white and brown fat tissues are sites of prion agent deposition and therefore may play a previously unrecognized role in prion infectivity and transmission of prion disease. It will be important to extend studies to prion-infected large animals, such as cattle, sheep, deer, and elk where they may be potential sources of contamination of human and domestic animal food chains. Results of the current and future studies may merit additional consideration of steps to eliminate from the food chain any fat from ruminants suspected of exposure to or infection with prions as shown in Fig.6 .

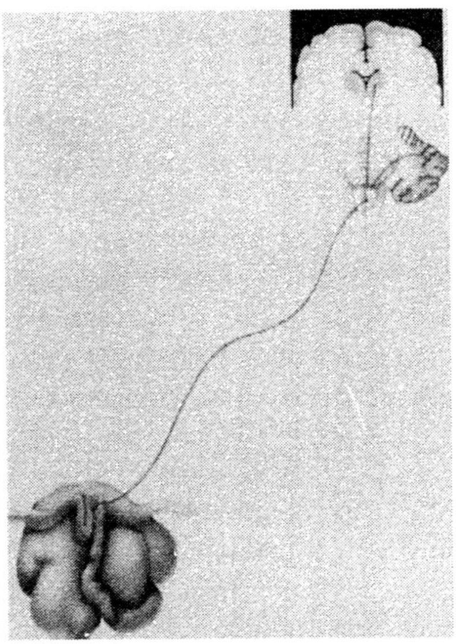

Fig. 5. Spread of infection across species barrier.

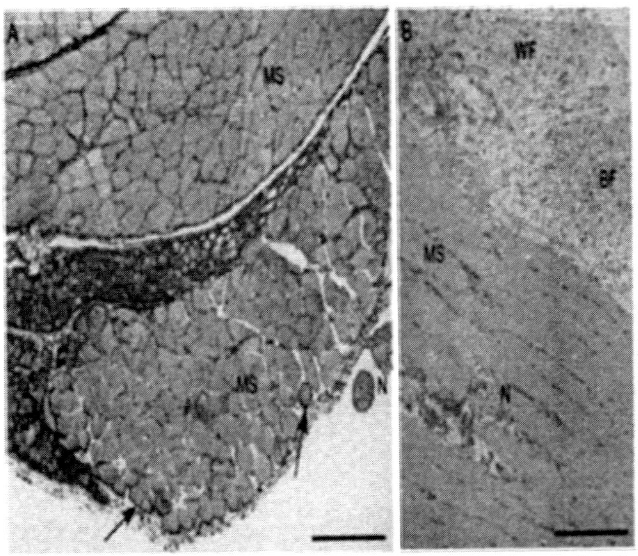

Fig. 6. PrP in white fat and adjacent skeletal muscle of Scrapie-Infected Mice.

Prion Discovery Gives Clue to Control of Mass Gene Expression

The common brewer's yeast of a new, infectious, misfolded protein -or prion -- by University of Illinois at Chicago molecular biologists raises questions about the roles played by these curious molecules, often associated with degenerative brain diseases like "mad cow" and its human counterpart, Creutzfeldt-Jakob.

Liebman and Patel propagated the new prion from a normal yeast protein called Cyc8. They note that like the Cyc8 protein, the prion of Cyc8 can affect the expression of a large number of yeast genes. Liebman *et al.* discovered that Cyc8 was a prion candidate using a genetic screen that looks for proteins that when overproduced can spur formation of new prions. To date, scientists have discovered only seven prions, six of which are only in fungi, including yeast. The latest two discovered, Cyc8 and another, identified as Swi1, The normal Cyc8 protein shuts down expression of more than 300 genes in yeast, including some genes that are involved in stress tolerance. Once Cyc8 is converted to a prion, it loses that function; This might provide some advantages under stressful conditions. Since the protein represses more than 300 genes, it's possible the prion form can activate the genes on a mass level." If an organism wanted to activate all the genes in a cell that the protein repressed, he said, 'Converting the protein into a prion would be an easy way to do it."

Patel and Liebman's are testing the protein to see if this molecular mechanism does in fact take place naturally. They're also studying the interaction of prions to determine if pre-existing prions facilitate or destabilize new prions.

Whether the actions of prions in yeast are analogous to mammalian models is not yet fully known, "There could be prions in humans that are not causing disease but have important effects on the cell or organism," said Liebman. "They may even be related to the ones we find in yeast. The more prions we learn about and study, the more information we learn from them -- how they arrive, what proteins are needed to maintain them. As we study other models, we have a better idea."

THE CJD-BSE CONNECTION

The prion disease of humans that causes the most concern is variant CJD (vCJD). The cause of this disease has not yet been determined. One theory is that humans may become infected with aberrant prions after ingesting meat from cows infected with BSE. This would require that aberrant prions from one species (cows) could serve as a template for refolding normal prions of another species (humans). This jump from one species to another involves crossing what is referred to as the species barrier. In a laboratory setting, prions have been shown to cross the species barrier. The onset of disease in these cases, however, is delayed compared to cases in which the infecting (aberrant) prions are from the same species as the new host. It is believed that the origin of the BSE outbreak in Europe (and especially Britain) was due to aberrant sheep prions crossing the species barrier to infect cows. During the 1970's there were changes made to the process used to render offal for a livestock feed additive. These changes created conditions that allowed prions to survive the rendering process. The sheep disease known as Scrapie is prion disease. It is believed that prions from Scrapie-infected sheep survived the rendering process and were passed on to cows that ingested infected feed. Once the prions were established in the livestock population the feed could have acted as a reservoir of infective prions. The practice of using rendered offal as an additive to livestock feed has been discontinued. Whether or not bovine prions can be passed to humans is unclear. Human prion diseases like vCJD have long incubation times (typically more than 12 years). The details of the transmission of prions from one species to another have not been fully elucidated.

Route of infection

When cows are fed with offals prepared from infected sheep, prions are taken up from the gut and transported along nerve fibers to the brain stem. Here prions accumulate and convert normal prion proteins to the disease-causing form, PrPSc. Years later, BSE results when a sufficient number of nerve cells have become damaged, affecting the behavior of the cows as shown in Fig.5

Evidence that proteins are infectious

Proteins are not normally termed infectious agents and unlike viruses, bacteria and other infectious organisms, the prions have no obvious nucleic acid. It has been proven that these are present with the disease symptoms, but do these actually cause the disease from step one- this was to be found out. The prion diseases themselves are known to be transmissible, from the early studies of CuillÈ and Chelle, when they set out to determine the infectivity of Scrapie in 1936, to the likely cannibalistic transmission of Kuru. Parallels were drawn to the possible infectivity of similar diseases such as CJD. The infectivity of these diseases was demonstrated by intracerebral inoculation of Kuru into chimpanzees by Gajdusek *et al.* (1966) and by similar ways with CJD by Gibbs *et al.* (1968). With this evidence it can only be said that the disease is transmissible and not strictly due to the prions. The strongest evidence was by Prusiner *et al.* (1982) where he further purified the prion by demonstration using 3000-fold enrichment for infectivity, and it was the only macromolecule that could be associated with infectivity. However some investigators think that the agent is merely the pathologic product which coincidentally purifies with the "Scrapie virus".

Despite these ideas, there is little evidence to support this view as fractions containing

<1 prion molecule per ID 50 have not been found, if it were to be found, it would indicate that prions are not required for infectivity. There is now a lot of evidence that the discovered 27-30 prion protein is a major and necessary component of the prion disease, this evidence includes:

- That during the co purification of PrP 27-30 and Scrapie infectivity using biochemical methods, the PrP concentration obtained is proportional to the prion titre.
- The kinetics of proteolytic digestion of PrP 27-30 and infectivity are similar.
- Co purification of the infectious prion and infectivity by immuno affinity.

- Chromatography is achieved, and? -Prion antisera neutralises infectivity.
- The novel prion protein is detected only in clones of cultured cells producing infectivity.
- The prion amyloid plaques are specific for prion diseases of animals and humans, and the deposition of the prion amyloid plaque is controlled at least partially by the prion protein sequence.
- There is correlation between the infectious prion and disease in humans and animals.
- Incubation time in mice is affected by base substitutions in the mouse prion gene-Mo-PrP.
- The existence of the species barrier (discussed later) due to amino acid differences in the protein causes a longer incubation time.
- There is genetic linkage between mutations in the prion gene (also discussed later) and the onset of disease, with a mutation at codon 102 linked with GSS development and a mutation in codon 200, or insertions of six additional octarepeats linked with familial CJD.
- Mice expressing prion genes with a point mutation similar to that of GSS develop neurological dysfunction, spongiform brain degeneration and gliosis.

From the evidence discussed at this point most scientists will believe that there is some involvement of prions in the infectivity and pathology of Scrapie, BSE and CJD, but the nature of the involvement was still to be found. Investigators suggest an answer to this with the prion concept.

THE PRION CONCEPT

It took quite a while for this idea of the prion protein to be accepted because it at first sight appeared to challenge some of the most fundamental ideas about molecular biology. Of course, people are used to the idea that infections are caused by bacteria, which are large and can be seen, and viruses, which can be sometimes rather more obscure. Now, here was a situation where there was an infection but apparently no virus, and viruses contain nucleic acid and this was just a protein. And people probably misunderstood in the first instance, and thought that a protein was making more copies of itself, whereas the fundamental dogma of molecular biology says that the information required to make proteins is contained in nucleic acid which then has to be converted into the production of proteins. Of course, it later became obvious that the prion hypothesis doesn't actually challenge the fundamental laws of molecular biology at all, because the DNA that is responsible for making the protein is in the host - the animal that was infected - and indeed it's in all animals and all people. What happens is the abnormal protein directs the conversion which produces more abnormal protein from normal protein, but not from nothing, it doesn't make it itself, it still has to be made originally under the instructions of nucleic acid. It's just the conversion of its shape, which is directed by the protein to another protein molecule. It wasn't as heretical as some people first thought, but it is wholly new, because it's a new way in which information can be transferred from one molecule to another without going through nucleic acid, which is the normal repository of information in biology.

THE PRION STRUCTURE

Proteins consist of stretches of amino acids. Some fold into alpha helices; others fold into beta pleated sheets. These shapes are maintained by hydrogen bonds. The sheets and helices then fold together further to form the protein's tertiary structure. A protein, such as the one illustrated here, can include both alpha helices and beta sheets and can consist of several subunits that combine to form the quaternary structure. Prions have one characteristic that makes them unique: they can exist in two different conformations at the level of secondary structure. There is an alpha-helical portion of secondary structure in a normal prion that is refolded into beta-sheet formation in an aberrant prion. The primary structure of the aberrant prion remains the same, but its secondary structure is different. As a result, its tertiary structure will be different as well. The isolated prion protein was found to be a product of a cellular gene on the short arm of chromosome 20 in humans and in a systemic region of chromosome 2 in mice. Studies then on the hamster and mouse models, after uncovering a protein designated PrP 27-30 (27-30K daltons) led to the eventual molecular cloning and complete sequence of prion protein cDNA (Oesch *et al.* 1985, Locht *et al.* 1986, Collinge & Palmer, 1997). The normal product (PrPc) of the prion gene (called PRNP in humans) is found to be expressed in most cell types, with expression at its highest predominantly in the brain. In 1987 investigations involving PrPc and PrP 27-30 started where an experiment involving bacterial-derived stearic acid treatment of the prion enabling it to react with antisera indicated that PrPc is anchored to the cell surface by a glycolipid, components of which include ethanolamine, *myo*-inositol, phosphate, and stearic acid as shown in fig. 9.

Later experiments involving PrPc indicated that PrPc is expressed as a glycosylphosphatidyl inositol-anchored glycoprotein found on the outer cell membrane (Stahl *et al.* 1987, 1990, 1992). However, this normal form can be distinguished from the infective prion found in diseased brain samples by its non-resistance to proteolytic hydrolysis (Borchelt *et al.* 1990). The infectious prion protein will now be termed as PrPsc and the normal prion protein, its function later to be discussed is now termed as PrPc (the "sc" stands for Scrapie and the "c" stands for cellular).

Different terminology of the two forms of the protein has also come into light. This is the PrPsens and PrPres; these names are given to prions, which are not structurally identical to PrPc or PrPsc. They may be truncated or recombinant forms, and are not exactly the same as the scrapie (sc) and cellular (c) forms, the 'res' indicates resistance to proteolytic degradation, and the 'sens' is for sensitivity to proteolytic degradation. There are therefore two different isoforms of the prion protein, one is expressed normally and one is present aberrantly. Initial studies on the different forms of the prion (Borchelt *et al.* 1990) found there were differences in the proteolytic resistance. Also demonstrated was that PrPc can be released from normal, and Scrapie infected neuroblastoma cells which were treated with phosphatidylinositol-specific phospholipase C (PIPLC), and also be labelled by a sulpho-NHS-biotin. Using pulse chase experiments [35S] methionine was found to incorporate almost immediately into PrPc. PrPsc however was incorporated at a much slower rate. PrPsc was not released by PIPLC, which suggested structural differences. It also enabled to monitor the amounts of both PrPc and PrPsc in the cell. Although this gave no real clues to the mechanisms involved, it further established the presence of two different forms of the protein. Mass spectrometry and amino acid sequencing studies were undertaken on the Scrapie prion protein, this was done using denatured PrPsc that was digested with endoproteases and isolated by HPLC. Analysis was done using mass spectrometry.

Edman sequencing and the primary structure of PrPsc was found to be identical to that of the PrP gene sequence, arguing that neither RNA editing nor protein splicing feature in the synthesis of PrPsc. Mass spectrometry was also used to identify any posttranslational modification-differences between the two isoforms, and none were found contending that PrPsc molecules do now differ from PrPc at the level of an amino acid substitution or a post-translational chemical modification (Stahl *et al.* 1993). However, the possibility of a small fraction of PrPsc being modified by a yet unidentified post-translational process could not be eliminated, or that PrPc carries a modification that is removed in the formation of PrPsc. It is probable then, that the differences are in the secondary andalso enabled to tertiary structures as shown in Fig.7

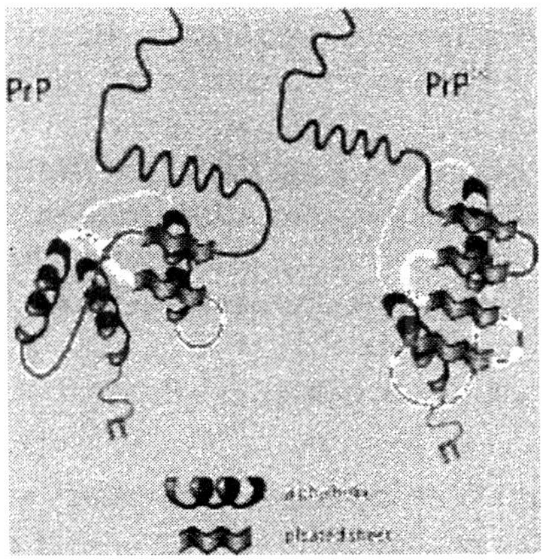

Fig. 7. A normal prion (left), compared to an aberrant, disease-causing prion (right).

The same amino acid sequence but two different structures

Work was then done on investigating the structure of the prion comparing PrPc to the structure of PrPc was found to have mainly a-helices and the structure of PrPsc was found to comprise mainly of b-pleated sheets. This was achieved using a pattern-matching approach (Cohen *et al.* 1985) and Fourier analysis of the primary sequence hydrophobocities to detect amphipathic regions, interestingly the secondarystructure showed some homology to that of the serum amyloid a proteins. The prion was linked with having a post-translational modification to yield amyloid A, which is more evidence for the prion involvement in amyloid plaque formation (Bazan *et al.* 1987). Later Pan *et al.* (1993) wrote a paper which described the conversion of a-helices to b-sheets as part of the formation of the scrapie prion proteins. Using Fourier Transform Infra-Red spectroscopy (FTIR) it was demonstrated that PrPc has high a-helix content (42%) and no -sheet content (3%), and PrPsc has high b-sheet content (43%) and low ahelix content (30%). Even higher b-sheet content is observed (54%) as compared to (ahelix content 21%) when using limited proteolysis to created N-terminally truncated PrPsc. This was confirmed by circular dichroism measurements. Pan *et al.* (1993) then remarked on the likeliness of a conformational transition being a fundamental event in the propagation of prions. Baldwin *et al.* (1994) produced a report which identified and confirmedthe differences between PrPc and PrPsc using spectroscopy to be conformational and even possibly transitional. For this FTIR spectroscopic methods were used, and also suggested the possibility of the transition of alpha to beta transition, they found that the N-terminal truncation of PrPsc by limited proteolysis did not destroy the prion infectivity. Instead, it increased the b-sheet content shifting the FTIR absorption to lower frequencies, which was typical of the cross b-pleated sheets of amyloids. Thus, the formation of PrPsc from PrPc involves a conformational transition in which one or more a-helical regions of the protein are converted to b-sheets. This transition was mimicked by synthetic peptides, allowing predictions of domains of PrP involved in prion diseases. Further evidence for the PrPsc formation from PrPc was shown in experiments involving the synthesis of a-helix peptides from regions of the prion protein, and their subsequent conversion to form amyloid peptides composed largely of b-sheets. Although this evidence is quite good, harder evidence was to follow (Gasset *et al.* 1992, 1993). Muramoto *et al.* (1996) performed studies on recombinant forms of PrPc. It is known that some truncation of the PrPc N terminus still permits conversion into the PrPsc isoform and so to assess whether additional segments of the PrP molecule can be deleted, the regions of the putative secondary structure were removed. It was found that removing a 36-residue loop between the second and third helix did not prevent formation of protease resistant PrP (PrPsc 106) that was also found to be soluble. Also, all the deletions of the 4 putative a-helical structures prevented PrPsc formation.

The results suggested that all of the proposed secondary structures are necessary for the conversion of PrPc into PrPsc and that the discovery of PrPsc 106 should facilitate structural studies of the prions and possible development of antibodies against PrPsc. A year later in 1997, studies investigating the possible posttranslational modifications involved with the PrPc conversion to PrPsc focussed on Scrapie infected ScN2a cells, where the metabolism of both PrP isolates involved cholesterol dependant pathways. It was demonstrated that both PrPc and PrPsc are attached to Trition X-100-insoluble, low-density complexes or "rafts". These "rafts" probably contain cholesterol due to their sensitivity to saponin. However, when extracted from solubility into insolubility using Triton X-100 at 37°C it was found that two different peaks of different densities were there, suggesting two populations of PrP-containing "rafts". This may permit the isolation of PrPc specific rafts. This suggested the possibility of "rafts" hosting the proposed PrPc to PrPsc formation, or if not some other aspect in the "life-cycle" of prions (Naslavsky *et al.* 1997).

The three dimensional structure of PrP

The three dimensional-structures for the cellular prion protein were predicted using was used, consisting of the prediction of secondary structures and of an evaluation of the packing of secondary structures. By using experimental and theoretical constraints four theoretical structures consisting of a-helix bundles were achieved. A group of amino acids was identified as being important for tertiary structural arrangement. Although the predicted structures gave a testable model, PrPc is thought now to have only three a-helix bundles (shown later). Possible inaccuracies could be in the computer programme or rather the experimental, theoretical constraints or data applied to the programme. Despite this, the structure of PrPc seems to be far more predictable than that of PrPsc (Baldwin *et al.* 1998). This is partially due to the very small amount of the natural protein isoforms isolated from the brain, and the solubility of PrP 27-30 in detergents that reduces infectivity even though the b-sheets can be regenerated. Despite this, the NMR (Nuclear Magnetic Resonance) experiments on recombinant protein can lead to a much better characterisation of the 3D structure of the prion proteins. In the studies involving the use of hamster and mouse models to elucidate the threedimensional structure, the hamster and mouse prion protein structure was compared, and is shown below. James *et al.* (1997) shows the hamster and mouse prion proteins superimposed, the mouse structure is more refined but shorter in length than the hamster prion, showing a close relation and therefore is a good model for transgenic studies (described later).

THE CONVERSION FROM PRPC TO PRPSC

The prion protein exists in two forms. The normal, innocuous protein (PrPc) can change its shape to a harmful, disease-causing form (PrPSc). The conversion from PrPc to PrPSc then proceeds via a chain-reaction. When enough PrPSc proteins have been made they form long filamentous aggregates that gradually damage neuronal tissue. The harmful PrPSc form is very resistant to high temperatures, UV-irradiation and strong degradative enzymes.

The wild type prion (PrPc) is found in the secretory pathway of cells expressing the protein (1) and moves to the plasma membrane where it is anchored by its GPI tail (2). There it may bind to an extracellular ligand (possibly copper) (3) before being cycledfrom the membrane into endocytic vesicles (4). At some point its cargo is released and the protein either passes to the lysozome for degradation or back to surface for another round of ligand binding. In this respect it resembles many other membrane-resident proteins.

The pathogenic form (PrPSc) also finds its way to endocytic vesicles where it coopts some of the wild type form to become pathogenic. PrPSc is resistant to degradation, a hallmark of the infectious form, so accumulates. Neurotoxicity is probably linked to the conversion event itself, perhaps through its interference with normal PrPc turnover, because there is considerable evidence to show that the accrued PrPSc is not inherently toxic. As shown in Fig.8

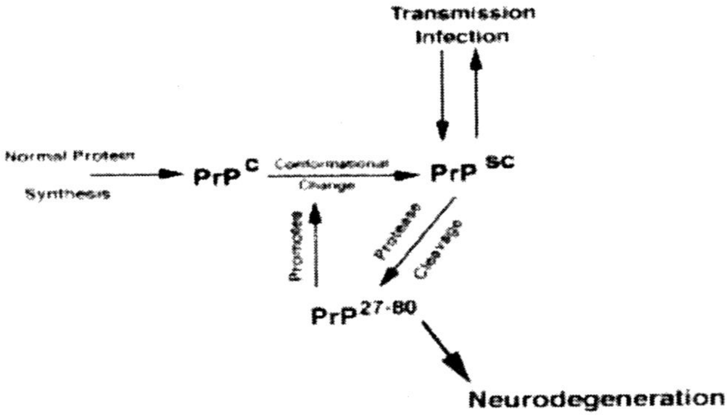

Fig. 8. Conversion of PrPc to PrPsc.

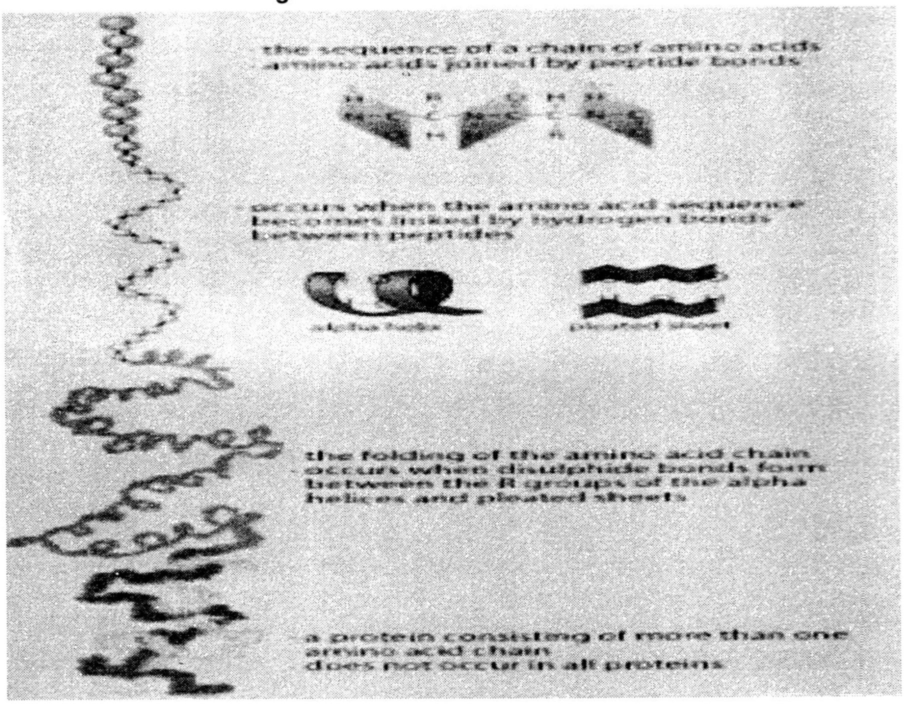

Fig. 9. Normal protein structure.

Infection of normal cells may occur when an aberrant prion acts as a template for the refolding of a normal prion into a new aberrant prion. It is thought that there is at least one more protein involved: the as-yet-unidentified Protein X. This protein is believed to mediate the folding from a normal into an abnormal prion.

When proteins are synthesized inside of a cell there are other special proteins (known as chaperones) that help in this process. Chaperones are proteins that bind to the newly synthesized protein or protein subunit, in order to ensure that the protein is properly folded into its secondary or tertiary structure. It has been hypothesized that Protein X is a type of chaperone.

The concept that a protein can transmit information (*i.e.* protein structure) is novel.

At the time that this idea was proposed, it was truly radical; it conflicted with many years of evidence showing that only DNA was capable of transmitting such information.

This does not mean that prion diseases cannot be genetic. If an individual happens to carry a gene that codes for a mutant prion, then all of the prions that their cells produce will be the abnormal, disease-causing prions. One such disease is familial CJD.

THE FUNCTION OF PRPc

Studies on transgenic mice to deduce the function of PrPc. From all the evidence put forward above, it seems certain that the production of the aberrant form of the PRNP gene product is responsible in some way for the pathogenesis of the disease. We do know that the PrPc protein is expressed as a glycosyl phosphatidyl inositol-anchored glycoprotein found on the outer cell membrane of neurons and to a lesser extent of lymphocytes and other cells (Stahl *et al.* 1987, 1990, 1992). However, the role of the normal cellular form of the prion is unclear and unproven. B eler *et al.* (1992) made studies on mice with inactive Prn-p genes (homozygously disrupted) and showed that the mice developed normally. The genes were disrupted by homologous recombination with a 4.8 kilobase DNA fragments in which codons 4 to 187 of the 254-codon open reading frame were replaced by a neomycin phosphotransferase (neo) gene under the control of the herpes simplex virus thymidine kinase promoter. Then were obtained mice heterozygous (Prn-p0/+) for the disrupted gene, the presence of which was confirmed by Southern analysis. Heterozygous mice were then mated to other heterozygotes to give a new population. Surprisingly, this population contained 24% Prn-p (0/0), 26% Prn-p(+/+) and 50% Prn-p(0/+) mice, surprising because they were all phenotypically the same, and Southern analysis confirmed these results. The Prn-p(0/0) mice were tested for many abnormalitiesin their behaviour, fitness and fertility and were all confirmed normal for at least 7 months, with no immunological defects. The reason that these results are surprising is that the Prn-p gene is highly conserved through evolution and so it might be thought that the function of this gene is vital to the organism. In contrast to B¸eler *et al.* (1992), more recent studies have reported that the prion protein is necessary for normal synaptic function (Collinge *et al.* 1994) and that altered circadian activity rhythms and sleep has been observed in mice also devoid of the prion protein (Tobler *et al.* 1996). One might ascertain from PrP knockout mice, that although there appears to be no symptoms, by looking closely at the behaviour of the mice they might be seen to differ phenotypically from the PrP-normal mice. It seems that the studies in 1992 may have missed the subtle phenotypic differences observed in later more focused studies. They suggest that because of the intriguing similarities to rhythm and sleep alterations in fatal familial insomnia, where there is a profound alteration in sleep and the daily rhythms of many hormones, the loss of function PrP may be related to the normal function of the prion protein. Essentially, it can be seen that the probable function of PrPc, being a well-conserved protein present in many mammalian species, may be involved in maintaining sleep continuity or regulating sleep intensity. Another study by Sakaguchi *et al.* (1996) looked at the long-term effects of the disrupted gene on mice. At about 70 weeks of age, the PrP-null mice all began to show progressive symptoms of ataxia. A rotorod test evidently showed up a lack of co-ordination in these mice. As they got older, their coordination became progressively worse and theyfrequently collapsed. Closer examination of the afflicted mice gave a good indication of what Prion Proteins would normally be doing when there is plenty of it in the brain. The cerebellum, the part of the brain responsible for movement and coordination, had shrunk by almost one third in the specifically bred Prion free mice and upon pathological investigation, there was an extensive loss of Purkinje cells in the vast majority of cerebellar folia. This suggests that PrP plays a role in the long-term survival of Purkinje neurons (Moore *et al.* 1999). It was also reported that neuroprotective functions of PrP include its antioxidative and anti-apoptotic properties (Brown *et al.* 2001, Kim *et al.* 2004, Wong *et al.* 2001). In addition to this a role in copper binding and delivery and a signally function has been supported with experimental evidence (Brown *et al.* 1997, Stockel *et al.* 1998, Brown *et al.* 1999, Mouillet-Richard *et al.* 2000). Recent studies on yeast have shown that the infectious prions linked to the disease, could help organisms adapt to tough situations. In yeast, some cells carry the normal type of proteins, whereas others harbor the infectious form, which accumulates in clumps and is passed on from one cell to another. Scientist has shown that the Prions in their infectious form help the yeast to adapt, changing their rates of survival when they were grown in various nutrients or temperatures. Prions may therefore offer a speedy way for yeast to evolve (Osherovich *et al.* 2002). In addition to this, the rouge Prion fibres are being analyzed to be used as templates for nanowires (Nanobiotechnology). Scientists have used a Prion protein from yeast to template the formation of metal wires approximately 100nm wide. While other biomolecules have been used in nanofabrication strategies, the researchers argue that the physical and chemical study of Prion proteins make them more likely to be able to withstand industrial metallization processes (Lindquist *et al.* 2003). Another study by Mabbott *et al.* (1997) has looked at the possibility of the involvement of T-lymphocyte activation as a role of PrPc, this is due to the fact that PrPc is a GPI anchored protein (membrane attached via a glycosylphosphatidyl-inositol anchor).Certain GPI anchored proteins on lymphocytes have previously been shown to play an important role in an early step of cell activation, and as the expression of PrPc has also been identified in lymphoid tissues, they hypothesized that PrPc like other GPI-anchored proteins may play a role in lymphocyte activation. In this study it was demonstrated that the PrPc is expressed on the surface of murine lymphocytes, and following mitogen stimulation the lymphocyte PrPc expression was significantly enhanced suggesting a role of PrPc in lymphocyte activation. Also Also the mitogen responsiveness in PrPc-deficient lymphocytes was significantly reduced in comparison to wild-type controls. Therefore, the results imply that PrPc is expressed on the extra cellular leaflet of the lymphocyte membrane and involved in lymphocyte activation.

Although this report does suggest a role for PrPc being involved in immune function it must be noted that the PrPc molecule is not the only GPI-anchored protein expressed on the surface of murine lymphocytes. Other examples include the Thy-1, Ly-6, CD58, CD- 59 and Oa-2 proteins.

Previous work demonstrates that the non-specific removal of all GPI-anchored proteins with a phospholipase C enzyme abrogates the ability of murine lymphocytes to respond to stimulation by the mitogen Con A, so there is evidence that the GPI-anchored proteins are involved with activation of lymphocytes. However, PrPc is predominantly produced in the brain and not predominantly in the peripheral organs and those expressing lymphocytes (spleen, thymus gland, lymph nodes, gut wall and bone marrow).

But, this does not necessarily mean the lack of lymphocyte involvement of PrPc. PrPc may be involved in a multiple role, for example it may have a role in the brain and a role related to lymphocytes, this would explain the highly conserved nature of the gene, as a mutation in the gene would be more likely to give a loss of function or there is the possibility that PrPc can be involved but in a coincidental way, as many other GPI-anchored proteins are known to have the same effect.

Work done by De Armond *et al.* (1997) has uncovered the possibility that glycosylation can modify the conformation of PrPc. Glycosylation could also affects the affinity of PrPc for a particular conformer of PrPsc, and there by determining the rate of nascent PrPsc formation and the specific patterns of PrPsc deposition. They postulated that variations in the complex carbohydrate structure in the CNS could account for selective targeting (*i.e.* the formation of PrPsc in particular areas of the brain being due to differences in PrPc/PrPsc affinity). The experiments were done using deletions of Asn-linked oligosaccharides of PrPc in transgenic mice.

Recently Ikeda *et al.* (1999) have performed experiments on cultured hepatic stellate cells, and by using immuno electron microscopy, have revealed that PrPc resides on the plasma membrane of stellate cells. Their results indicate that PrP expression is closely related to stellate cell activation associated with fibrogenic stimuli. This has helped elucidate the pathogenesis of liver fibrosis, and develop possible therapeutic strategies to prevent liver cirrhosis. PrPc is not expressed in the normal healthy liver, but it was found to increase dramatically in diseased livers associated with stellate cell activation.

Applications

Armed with a plausible idea of how pathogenesis could arise, the way in which copper is bound to the surrounding sequence becomes highly significant. The role of copper binding by the octarepeats is important as well as the significance of repeats and their conservation. More intriguing still is the idea that copper (or other metal ion) binding it may, in part, modulate the conversion event. The high affinity site is in the region of the protein that appears to determine some of the disease characteristics; it has to be found whether mutations known to affect these disease traits influence the affinity or range of metal ions that can be bound. Equally, if perturbation of copper metabolism is at the heart of the pathology, then intervention strategies that target copper directly may offer prospects for disease management.

The search for sensitive and robust diagnostics should also take account of the fact that metal ions may modulate the conformation of the protein; antibodies that can distinguish the metal dependent conformation of prion protein may be useful diagnostic reagents. Lastly, a role for a redox active metal in the TSEs may draw them into a larger group of neurological disorders, including Alzheimer's disease that may have a shared basis of action. In that case there is every hope that advances in any one field will be beneficial to a wide range of related diseases.

Alzheimer's Prevention Role Discovered For Prions

Another role for prion proteins, the much debated agents of mad cow disease and vCJD, has been identified. It appears that the normal prions produced by the body help to prevent the plaques that build up in the brain to cause Alzheimer's disease. The possible function for the mysterious proteins was discovered by a team of scientists led by Medical Research Council funded scientist Professor Nigel Hooper of the University of Leeds. Alzheimer's and diseases like variant Creutzfeldt - Jakob disease follow similar patterns of disease progression and in some forms of prion disease share genetic features. These parallels prompted Professor Hooper's team to look for a link between the different conditions. They found an apparent role for normal prion proteins in preventing Alzheimer's disease. Their experiments have shown that the normal prion proteins found in brain cells reduce the formation of beta-amyloid, a protein that binds with others to build plaques in the brain that are found in Alzheimer's disease, explains Professor Hooper. He continues: In vCJD, the normal version of prion protein, PrPc, found naturally in the brain is corrupted by infectious prions to cause disease. The normal function of PrPc has been unclear. Using cells grown in the lab, the team looked at the effect of high and low levels of normal prion protein on the successful formation of beta amyloid, the source of Alzheimer's plaques. They found that beta amyloid did not form in cells with higher than usual levels of PrPc. In comparison, when the level of PrPc was low or absent, beta amyloid formation was found to go back up again. Mice genetically engineered to lack PrPc were also studied. Again, this revealed that in its absence, the harmful beta-amyloid proteins were able to form. It appears that PrPc, the normal prion protein, exerts its beneficial effect by stopping an enzyme called beta secretes from cutting up amyloid protein into the smaller beta-amyloid fragments needed to build plaques. Further evidence for the protective role of normal prion proteins is provided by mutated versions that are linked to genetic forms of prion disease because beta-amyloid fragments are able to form when the normal prion protein is corrupted by genetic mutation. According to Professor Hooper their findings have clearly identified a role for normal prion proteins in regulating the production of beta-amyloid and in doing so preventing formation of Alzheimer's plaques. Whether this function is lost as a result of the normal ageing process, or if some people are more susceptible to it than others this is not known yet. The next step for this research will be to look in more detail at how the prion protein controls beta amyloid, knowledge that could be used to design anti-Alzheimer's drugs. Theoretically, if a way of mimicking the prion's function is found it would be possible to halt the progress of Alzheimer's. However, there's still a lot of work to be done in looking at levels of prions in the human system and how these alter with age.

INTO THE FUTURE, AND THE UNKNOWN INCUBATION FACTOR

It is certain that due to the attention received, and the dangers well illustrated in the media, and by scientists, prion research will progress extremely quickly in the next five years. Attention will be focused on the function of PrPc, the development of effective rapid diagnostic techniques, and the molecular studies on the mechanisms of replication to provide targets for the development of effective chemotherapeutic agents. Perhaps most importantly and perhaps the most elusive fact to find out, however, is the possible incubation time for vCJD in humans.

The only model for comparison is the rise and fall of the kuru epidemic in Papa New Guinea. The maximum incubation time for that disease (not transmitted across the species barrier) has shown to be maximally about 40 years, with the peak onset after a few years after successful inoculation with the agent, as children as young as four have been reported with the disease. The big question is, what will be the effect of species barrier between cows and humans (and possibly even sheep and humans in the case of BSE fed sheep) in the case of vCJD. No one seems to know, some people think the 20-30 or so cases so far are the tip of the iceberg, others think it is mostly over.

However, it may be encouraging to think that the BSE agent's ability to traverse the species barrier also may mean that it is also faster at crossing this barrier than other prion diseases and so expression would be sooner (years) rather than later (decades). One way or another, time will tell. At present there is no cure for Prion diseases and the kill rate is 100%. More research is necessary to understand these devastating infectious agents and create opportunities to evaluate therapeutic strategies for these unusual diseases.

REFERENCES

Baldwin M James T Cohen F Prusiner S 1998, The three-dimensional structure of prion protein: implications for prion disease *Biochemical Society Transactions* **26** 481-486

Baldwin M Pan K Nguyen J Huang Z Groth D Serban A et al 1994, Spectroscopic Characterisation of Conformational Differences Between PrPc and PrPsc - an a-Helix to b-Sheet Transition Philosophical Transactions of the *Royal Society of London Series B-Biological Sciences* **343** 435-441

Bazan F Fletterick R McKinley M Prusiner S 1987, Predicted secondary structure and membrane topology of the scrapie prion protein *Protein Engineering* **1** 125-135

Belay E.D and L B Schonberger 2005, The public health impact of prion diseases *Annu Rev Public Health* **26** 191-212

Beler H Fischer M Lang Y Bluethmann H Lipp H DeArmond S *et al* 1992, Normal evelopment and behaviour of mice lacking the neuronal cell-surface PrP protein *Nature* **356** 577- 582

Bessen RA and Marsh RF 1994 Distinct PrP properties suggest the molecular basis of strain variation in transmissible mink encephalopathy *J. Virol.* **68** 7859-7868

Borchelt D Scott M Taraboulos A Stahl N Prusiner S 1990, Scrapie and Cellular Prion Proteins Differ in Their Kinetics of Synthesis and Topology in Cultured Cells The *Journal of Cell Biology* **110** 743-752

Brown D 1999, senior scientists dismiss fears of CJD epidemic The Daily Telegraph March 27th

Brown D R 1999, Prion Protein expression aids cellular uptake and veratridine-induced release of copper *Jourl of Neuroscience Research* **58** 717- 725

Brown D R Clive C Haswell S J 2001, Antioxidant activity related to copper binding of native prion Protein *Jourl of Neurochemistry* **76** 69- 76

Brown P Cathala F Raubertan R F et al 1987, The epidemiology of Creutzfeldt-Jacob disease Conclusion of a 15 year investigation in France and review of the old *Literature Neurology* **37** 895- 904

Caughey B Chesebro B 1997, Prion protein and the transmissible spongiform cephalopathies Trendsin *Cell Biology* **7** 56- 62

Chakraborty C S Nandi S Jana 2005, Prion disease: a deadly disease for protein Misfolding *Curr Pharm Biotechnology* **6** 167-77

Chesebro B 1998, BSE and Prions: Uncertainities about the *Agent Science* **279** 42- 43

Christian Wasmer Alice Soragni Raimon Sabaté Adam Lange Roland Riek Beat H. Meier 2008, Infectious and Noninfectious Amyloids of the HET-s (218-289) Prion Have Different NMR Spectra. *Angewandte Chemie*

Christina J Sigurdson K Peter R Nilsson Simone Hornemann Guiseppe Manco Magdalini Polymenidou Petra Schwartz Mario Leclerc, Per Hammarström, Kurt Wüthrich, and Adriano Aguzzi 2007, "Prion strain discrimination using luminescent conjugated polymers" *Nature*

Cohen F Abarbanel R Kuntz D Fletterick R 1985, Turn Prediction in Proteins Using a attern *Matching Approach Biochemistry* **25** 266- 275

Collinge J Palmer M 1997, 'Prion Diseases' Oxford University Press

Collinge J Whittington M Sidle K Smith C Palmer M Clarke A Jefferys J 1994, Prion protein is necessary for normal synaptic function *Nature* **370** 295- 277

Craighead Harold G. 2008, "Prion Protein Detection Using Nanomechanical Resonator Arrays and Secondary Mass Labeling" *Analytical Chemistry*

De Armond S S_nchez H Yehiely Qiu Y Ninchak-Casey A Daggett V et al 1997, Selective Neuronal Targeting in Prion Disease *Neuron* **19** 1337-1348

Gajdusek D C 1977, Unconventional viruses, the origin, disappearance of Kuru *Science* 943-960

Gajdusek D C Zigas V 1957, Degenerative disease of the Central Nervous system in New Guinea: The endemic occurrence of ìKuruî in the native population N Engl *Journal of Medicine* **257** 974-978

Gajdusek D Gibbs C Alpers M 1966, Experimental transmission of a kuru-like syndrome to chimpanzees *Nature* **209** 794- 796

Garcion E Wallace B Pelletier L Wion D 2004, RNA mutagenesis and sporadic prion diseases *Journal of Theoretical Biology* **230** 271-274

Gasset M Baldwin M Lloyd D Gabriel J Holtzman D Cohen F et al 1992, Predicted a-helical regions of the prion protein when synthesised as peptides form amyloid *Proceedings of the National Academy of Sciences of the United States* of Americ **89** 10940- 10944

Gibbs T Gajdusek D Asher D Alpers M Beck E Daniel P et al 1968, Creutzfeldt-Jacob disease (Spongiform encephalopathy): transmission to the chimpanzee *Science* **161** 388- 389

Hadlow W J 1959, Scrapie and Kuru *Lancet* **2** 289- 290

Hsiao K Prusiner S 1990, Inherited human Prion diseases *Neurology* **40** 1820 1827

Huang F P Mac Pherson G G 2004, Dendritic cells and Oral transmission of Prion disease *Adv Drug Del reviews* **56** 901- 913

Ikeda K Kawada N Wang Y Kadoya H Nakatani K Sato M Kaneda K 1999, Expression of Cellular Prion Protein in Activated Hepatic Stellate Cells American *Journal of Pathology* **153** 1695-1700

James T Liu H Ulyanov N FarrJones S Zhang H Donne D et al 1997, Solution structure of a 142-residue recombinant prion protein corresponding to the infectious fragment of the scrapie isoform *Proceedings of the National Academy of Sciences of the United States of America* **94** 10086- 10091

Karapetyan *et al.* 2009, Prion Strain Discrimination Based on Rapid In Vivo Amplification and Analysis by the Cell Panel Assay. *PLoS ONE* **5**

Khosravani *et al* 2008, Prion protein attenuates excitotoxicity by inhibiting NMDA receptors. *J. Cell Biol.* **181** 551-565 [link]

Kim B H Lee H G Choi J K Kim J I Choi E K Carp R I Kim Y S 2004, The cellular Prion protein (PrPc) prevents apoptotic neuronal cell death and mitochondrial dysfunction induced by serum deprivation Brain Research *Molecular Brain Research* **124** 40-50

Klein Alec. 2007, "Hospitals Rethink Reuse of Brain Surgery Devices." Chicago Tribun Chicagoland Final *ed* sec News **12** Access World News.

Lasmezas CI Deslys J-P Robain O Jaegly A Beringue V Peyrin J-M Fournier J-G Hauw J-J Rossier J and Dormont D 1997 Transmission of the BSE agent to mice in the absence of detectable abnormal prion protein. *Science* **275** 402–405

Lindguist S L *et al* 2003, Prion templates Proceedings of Natural Academy of Sciences USA **100** 4527

Locht C Chesebro B Race R Keith J 1986, Molecular Cloning and complete sequence of prion protein cDNA from mouse brain infected with the scrapie agent *Proceedings of the National Academy of Sciences of the United States of America* **83** 6372- 6376

Manuelidis L Fritch W 1996, Infectivity and host responses in Creutzfeldt-Jakob disease *Virology* **216** 46- 59

Mastrianni J A 2004, Prion diseases *Clinical Neurosciences Research* **3** 469-480

Mckintosh E Tabrizi S J Collinge J 2003, Prion diseases *Journal of Neurovirology* **9** 183-193

Monaco S *et al* 2003, Prions: They really do get up your nose N Engl *Jour Med* **348** 711- 720

Moore R C Lee I Y Silverman G L Harrison P M Storme R Heinrich C Karunaratne A Pasternak S H Chishti M A Liang Y Mastrangelo P Wang K Smit A F Katamine S Carlson G A Cohen

F E Prusiner S B Melton D W Tremblay P Hood L E Westaway D 1999, Ataxia in Prion Protein (PrP) deficient mice is associated with up regulation of the novel PrP like Protein doppel *Journal of Molecular Biology* **292** 797-817

Mouillet-richard S Ermonval M Chebassier C *et al* 2000, signal transduction through Prion Protein *Science* **289** 1923-1928

Muramoto T Scott M Cohen F Prusiner S 1996, Recombinant scrapie-like protein of 106 amino acids is soluble *Proceedings of the National Academy of Sciences of the United States of America* **93** 15457-15462

Naslavsky N Stein R Yanai A Friedlander G Taraboulos 1997, Characterization of Detergent-insoluble Complexes Containing the Cellular Prion Protein and Its Scrapie Isoform *Journal Biological Chemistry* **272** 6324-6331

Oesch B Westaway D W‰lchli M McKinley M Kent S Aebersold R 1985, A cellular gene encodes scrapie PrP 27-30 protein *Cell* **40** 735-746

Osherovich L Z Weissman J S 2002 The utility of Prions Developmental *Cell* **2** 143- 151

Pan K.-M Baldwin M Nguyen J Gasset M Serban A Groth D Mehlhorn I Huang Z Fletterick RJ Cohen FE and Prusiner SB 1993.Conversion of-helices into-sheets features in the formation of the scrapie prion proteins. *Proc. Natl. Acad. Sci. USA* **90** 10962–10966

Porter D D Porter H G Cox N A 1973, Failure to demonstrate a humoral immune response to scrapie infection in mice *Journal Immunology* **111** 1407-1410

Prusiner S 1982, Novel Proteinaceous Infectious Particles Cause Scrapie *Science* **216** 136-144

Prusiner S B 1991, Molecular Biology of Prion Diseases Science **252** 1515-1522

Prusiner SB 1996, Molecular biology and pathogenesis of prion diseases. *Trend Biochem Sci.* **21** 482-7

Prusiner SB 1997, Prion diseases and the BSE crisis. *Science* **278** 245–251

Prusiner, SB 1994, Biology and genetics of prion diseases. *Annu Rev Microbiol.* **48** 655-86

Race B Meade-White K Oldstone MBA Race R Chesebro B 2008,Detection of Prion Infectivity in Fat Tissues of Scrapie-Infected Mice. *PLoS Pathog*, **4**

Sakaguchi S Katamine S Nishida N Moriuchi R Shigematsu K Sugimoto T *et al* 1996, Loss of cerebellar Purkinje cells in aged mice homozygous for a disrupted PrP gene *Nature* **380** 528 -531

Sciences USA 100 4527 Mabbott N Brown K Manson J Bruce M 1997, T-lymphocyte activation and the cellular form of the prion protein *Immunology* **92** 161-165

Scott M R Will R Ironsids J *et al* 1999, Compelling transgenic evidence for transmission of bovine spongiform encephalopathy Prions to humans *Proceedings of Natural Academy of Sciences* USA **96** 15137-15142

Singh *et al* 2009, Abnormal Brain Iron Homeostasis in Human and Animal Prion Disorders. *PLoS Pathogens* **3**

Stahl N Baldwin M Teplow D Hood L Gibson B Burlingame A Prusiner S 1993, Structural Studies of the Scrapie Protein Using Mass Spectrometry and Amino Acid Sequencing *Biochemistry* **32** 1991- 2002

Stahl N Borchelt D Hsiao K Prusiner S 1987, Scrapie Prion Protein Contains a Phoshatidylinositol Glycolipid *Cell* **51** 229-240

Stockel J Safar J Wallace A C *et al* 1998, Prion Protein selectively binds copper (II) ions *Biochem* **37** 7185-7193

Telling G Scott M Mastrianni J Gabizon R Torchia M Cohen F *et al* 1995, Prion Propagation in Mice Expressing Human and Chimeric PrP Transgenes Implicates the Interaction of Cellular PrP with Another Protein *Cell* **83** 79- 90

Timm Konold S. Jo Moore Susan Bellworthy and Hugh A. Simmons. 2008, Evidence of scrapie transmission via milk. *BMC Veterinary Research*

Tobler I Gaus S Deboer T Achermann P Fischer M R¸licke T *et al* 1996, Altered circadian activity rhythms and sleep in mice devoid of prion protein *Nature* **380** 639- 642

Uro-Coste E Cassard H Simon S Lugan S Bilheude J-M *et al.* 2008 Beyond PrPres Type 1/Type 2 Dichotomy in Creutzfeldt-Jakob Disease. *PLoS Pathog* **4**

Uro-Coste E Cassard H Simon S Lugan S Bilheude J-M *et al.* 2008, Beyond PrPres Type 1/Type 2 Dichotomy in Creutzfeldt - Jakob disease. *PLoS Pathog* **43**

Wadhwani C and Malik C.P 2007, Prions-the lethal proteins. In *Current advancres in Biotechnology.* Ed Malik C P Kaur B and Wadhwani C M D Publications New Delhi

Wong B S Liu T Li R Pan T Peterson R B Smith M A Gambetti P Perry G Manson J C Brown D R Sy MS 2001, Increased levels of oxidative stress markers detected in the brains of mice devoid of Prion proteins *Jour Neurochem* **76** 565- 572

12

NONI (*MORINDA CITRIFOLIA* L.) -A HOPE IN A BOTTLE

A. R. MALIK, S. H. WANI AND B. N. DAR

INTRODUCTION

Morinda citrifolia commercially known as 'Noni' grows widely throughout the pacific and is one of the most important traditional Polynesian medicinal plant. Noni is noted for its extremely wide range of environmental tolerance. It is found naturally in relatively dry to mesic sites or lowland areas in close proximity to shorelines, or as an important forest understory species in low elevation pacific island forests and rainforests. Noni has extensive range of environmental tolerances including exposure to wind, fire, flooding and saline conditions. Although not considered to be invasive to a degree that threatens ecosystems noni is treated as a weed in some settings, is very persistent and difficult to hill, and is one of the first plants to colonize harsh waste areas or lava flows. All parts of the plant have traditional and/or modern uses, including roots and bark (dyes, medicine), trunks (firewood, tools), and leaves and fruits (food, medicine). Noni is well suited for intercropping within traditional agroforestry subsistence farming systems or as a monocrop in full sun. The tree has attained significant economic importance worldwide in recent years through a variety of health and cosmetic products made from its leaves and fruits.

MAJOR COMPONENTS

A number of major components have been identified in the Noni plant such as scopoletin, octoanoic acid, potassium, vitamin C, terpenoids, alkaloids, anthraquinones (such as nordamnacanthal, morindone, rubiadin, and rubiadin- 1-methyl ether, anthraquinone glycoside), b-sitosterol, carotene, vitamin A, flavone glycosides, linoleic acid, Alizarin, amino acids, acubin, *L*-asperuloside, caproic acid, caprylic acid, ursolic acid, rutin, and a putative proxeronine (Levand and Larson ,1979 and Heinicke, 1985).

Noni fruit powder is high in carbohydrates and dietary fiber. According to the College of Tropical Agriculture and Human Resources at the University of Hawaii at Mānoa, a 100g sample of the powder contains 71% carbohydrate and 36% fiber. The sample also contained 5.2% protein and 1.2% fat (Nelson, 2006).These macronutrients evidently reside in the fruit pulp, as noni juice has sparse amounts of macronutrients. The main micronutrients of noni pulp powder include 9.81 mg of vitamin C per 1200mg sample, as well as 0.048 mg niacin (vitamin B3), 0.02 mg iron and 32.0 mg potassium (Nelson, 2006). Vitamin A, calcium and sodium are present in moderate amounts. When noni juice alone is analyzed and compared to pulp powder, only vitamin C is retained at a high level, 33.65 mg per 100g of juice (Nelson, 2006). Although the most significant nutrient feature of noni pulp powder or juice is its high vitamin C content, noni fruit juice provides only about half the vitamin C of a raw navel orange. Sodium levels in the noni juice blend (about 3% of DRI) (Nelson, 2006) are multiples of those in an orange. Although the potassium content appears relatively high for noni, this total is only about 3% of the recommended dietary allowance and so would not be considered excessive. Noni juice is otherwise similar in micronutrient content to a raw orange. Noni fruit contains a number of phytochemicals, including lignans, oligo- and polysaccharides, flavonoids, iridoids, fatty acids, scopoletin, catechin, beta-sitosterol, damnacanthal, and alkaloids. Although these substances have been studied for bioactivity, current research does not conclude anything about their effects on human health (Deng *et al.* 2007 and Mohd *et al.* 2007). Laboratory experiments demonstrated that dietary noni juice increased physical endurance in mice (Ma *et al.* 2007).

DISTRIBUTION

M. citrifolia is commonly assumed to have originated in Southern Asia and subsequently distributed by humans or other means into the islands of the Western pacific. The distribution of Noni is pantropical at latitudes of 19°W or S. The Indo-pacific distribution includes eastern Polynesia (Hawaii, lime Island, Marquesas, cook Islands), Melanesia (Fiji, New Guinea, Solomon Islands), western Polynesia (Samoa, Tonga, Rothmas and Tuvalu) and Micronesia (Pohnpei, guam, Palau the Marshall Islands and Northern Marianas), Indonesia, Australia and SouthEast Asia. Noni has also become naturalised on the open, shores of central and South America and on many islands of West Indies, the Bahamas, Bermuda, the Florida and parts of Africa.

Botanical description

The scientific name of Noni is *Morinda citrifolia* L. The botanical name for the genus was derived from the two latin words *morus*, mulberry, and *indicus*, Indian, in reference to the similarity of the fruit of Noni to that of true mulberry (*Morus alba*). The species name indicates the resemblance of the plant foliage to that of some citrus species. It belongs to family Rubiaceae (coffee family) and subfamily Rubioideae. Noni is the common name for *Morinda citrifolia* L and is also called great morinda, Indian mulberry,

Mengkudu (Malaysia), beach mulberry, Tahitian noni, cheese fruit or noni (from Hawaiian) in various cultures throughout the world.

The Noni plant is a small evergreen tree found growing in open coastal regions at sea level and in forest areas up to about 1300 feet above sea level. The plant is often found growing along lava flows. It's identifiable by its straight trunk, large, bright green and elliptical leaves, white tubular flowers, and its distinctive, ovoid, "grenade-like" yellow fruit. The fruit can grow in size up to 12 cm or more and has a lumpy surface covered by polygonal-shaped sections. The seeds, which are triangular shaped and reddish brown, have an air sac attached at one end, which makes the seeds buoyant. This could explain, in part, the wide distribution of the plant throughout the Polynesian islands. The mature Noni fruit has a foul taste and odour (Swanholm *et al.* 1959) and is not considered to be at risk in the wild.

GROWING HABITATS

Noni grows in shady forests as well as on open rocky or sandy shores. It reaches maturity in about 18 months and then yields between 4–8 kilograms (8.8–18 lb) of fruit every month throughout the year. It is tolerant of saline soils, drought conditions, and secondary soils. It is therefore found in a wide variety of habitats: volcanic terrains, lava-strewn coasts, and clearings or limestone outcrops. It can grow up to 9 metres (30 ft) tall, and has large, simple, dark green, shiny and deeply veined leaves.

The plant flowers and fruits all year round and produces a small white flower. The fruit is a multiple fruit that has a pungent odor when ripening, and is hence also known as *cheese fruit* or even *vomit fruit*. It is oval and reaches 4–7 centimetres (1.6–2.8 in) in size. At first green, the fruit turns yellow then almost white as it ripens. It contains many seeds. It is sometimes called starvation fruit. Despite its strong smell and bitter taste, the fruit is nevertheless eaten as a famine food (Krauss, 1993) and in some Pacific islands, even a staple food, either raw or cooked (Morton, 1992). Southeast Asians and Australian Aborigines consume the fruit raw with salt or cook it with curry. The seeds are edible when roasted. Noni is especially attractive to weaver ants, which make nests out of the leaves of the tree. These ants protect the plant from some plant-parasitic insects. The smell of the fruit also attracts fruit bats, which aid in dispersing the seeds.

ASSOCIATED PLANT SPECIES

The associated plant species include breadfruit (*Artocarpus altilis*), banana (*Musa* spp.), papaya (*Carica papaya*), plalms (e.g. betel nut palm, *Arecacatechii* and coconut, *Cocos nucifera*), pandanus (*Pandanus* spp.), beach hibiscus (*Hibiscus tiliaceus*), til (*Cordylinie fruticosa*) and piper species (e.g. kava, *Piper methysticum*). Some of these associated species are understory and some are overstory for Noni. It grows as a recent introduction around villages or in homegardens, in backyards and along streams and gulches.

USES AND PRODUCTS

Captain James Cook of the British Navy noted in the late 1700's that the fruit was eaten in Tahiti (Cheeseman, 1903). An 1866 publication in London explained that *Morinda citrifolia* fruit was consumed as a food in the Fiji Islands (Seemann and Flora, 1866). Later publications describe the use of this fruit as a food throughout the Pacific Islands, SouthEast Asia, Australia, and India. In Roratonga "the fruit was often eaten by the natives" (Cheeseman, 1903). Australian Aborigines were reported to be "very fond" of the fruit (Maiden, 1889). In Samoa, Noni fruit was common fare, and in Burma, the fruit was cooked in curries or eaten raw with salt (Morton, 1992). Merrill (1943) described *Morinda citrifolia* L as an edible plant in a technical manual of edible and poisonous plants of the Pacific Islands, in which the leaves and fruits could be used as emergency food. Abbott (1992) also reported that Noni had been used as a food, drink, medicine, and colorful dye. Very young leaves are cooked as vegetables and eaten with rice in Java and Thailand; mature leaves are wrapped around fish before cooking and then eaten with the cooked fish. The terminal bud is used as food. Dried leaves or fruits are used to make infusions and teas for medicinal use.

The medicinal history and accumulated scientific studies, to date, have revealed and confirmed the Polynesian's claim of the health benefits of Noni. The medical knowledge and pharmacopoeia of the Polynesians is now believed to have been fairly complex and modern scientific and medical communities are beginning to study the plants compiled from this knowledge base. The Polynesians utilized the whole Noni plant in various combinations for herbal remedies. The fruit juice is in high demand in alternative medicine for different kinds of illnesses such as arthritis, diabetes, high blood pressure, muscle aches and pains, menstrual difficulties, headaches, heart disease, AIDS, cancers, gastric ulcers, sprains, mental depression, senility, poor digestion, atherosclerosis, blood vessel problems, and drug addiction. Scientific evidence of the benefits of the Noni fruit Juice is limited but there is some anecdotal evidence for successful treatment of colds and influenza (Solomon, 1999). Allen (1873) reported some information on the ethnobotanical properties of Noni. He said that the fruit is used as deobstruent and emmenagogue. This is one of the earliest articles on the medicinal benefits of Noni. Isabel Abbott (1985), a former botanical chemist at the University of Hawaii, stated that, "People are crazy about this plant. They use it for diabetes, high blood pressure, cancer, and many other illnesses". Bushnell (1950) reported that Noni was a traditional remedy used to treat broken bones, deep cuts, bruises, sores, and wounds. Morton (1992) gave numerous references for medicinal uses of Noni. In addition, Polynesians are reported to have successfully used Noni to treat breast cancer and eye problems. Betz (1997), stated that "*Morinda citrifolia* has been tested for a number of biological activities in animal and anti-microbial studies." He reports that the dried fruit has smooth muscle stimulatory activity and histaminergic effects. In Hawaii, ripe fruits are applied to draw out pus from an infected boil. The green fruit, leaves and the root/rhizome have traditionally been used to treat menstrual cramps and irregularities, among other symptoms, while the root has also been used to treat urinary difficulties (McClatchey, 2002).

BIOLOGICAL ACTIVITIES OF NONI PRODUCTS

Antibacterial activity:

Acubin, *L*-asperuloside, and alizarin in the Noni fruit, as well as some other anthraquinone compounds in Noni roots, are all proven antibacterial agents. These compounds have been shown to fight against infectious bacteria strains such as *Pseudomonas aeruginosa, Proteus morgaii, Staphylococcus aureus, Baciillis subtilis, Escherichia coli, Salmonella,* and *Shigela.* These antibacterial elements within Noni are responsible for the treatment of skin infections, colds, fevers, and other bacterial-caused health problems. Extracts from the ripe Noni fruit exhibited moderate antibacterial properties against *Ps aeruginosa, M. pyrogenes and E. coli,* and were also shown to have moderate antibacterial properties against *Salmonella typhosa, Salmonella montevideo, Salmonella schottmuelleri, Shigella paradys,* and *Shigella paradys* (Bushnell, 1950).

Antiviral activity:

Umezawa (1992) found a compound isolated from Noni roots named 1-methoxy- 2-formyl-3-hydroxyanthraquinone suppressed the cytopathic effect of HIV infected MT-4 cells, without inhibiting cell growth.

Anti-tubercular effects:

Noni has been found to kill Mycobacterium tuberculosis. A concentration of extracts from Noni leaves killed 89 per cent of the bacteria in a test tube, almost as effective as a leading anti-TB drug, Rifampcin, which has an inhibition rate of 97 per cent at the same concentration.

Antitumor activity:

In 1994, Hirazumi, a researcher at the University of Hawaii, reported anticancer activity from the alcohol-precipitate of Noni fruit juice (noni-ppt) on lung cancer in C57 Bl/6 mice at the 83rd Annual Meeting of American Association for Cancer Research. The noni-ppt was shown to significantly prolong the life of mice up to 75 % with implanted Lewis lung carcinoma compared with the control group (Hirazumi *et al.* 1994). It was concluded that the noni-ppt seems to suppress tumor growth indirectly by stimulating the immune system (Hirazumi *et al.* 1996). Improved survival time and curative effects occurred when noni-ppt was combined with sub-optimal doses of the standard chemotherapeutic agents such as adriamycin (Adria), cisplatin (CDDP), 5 fluorouracil (5-FU), and vincristine (VCR), suggesting important clinical applications of noni-ppt as a supplemental agent in cancer treatment (Hirazumi and Furus, 1999). These results indicate that noni-ppt may enhance the therapeutic effect of anticancer drugs. Therefore, it may be of benefit to cancer patients by enabling them to use lower doses of anticancer drugs to achieve the same or even better results.

Anthelmintic activity:

An ethanol extract of the tender Noni leaves induced paralysis and death of the human parasitic nematode worm, *Ascaris Lumbricoides,* within a day (Raj , 1975). A botanist via Morton reported that Noni has been used in the Philippines and Hawaii as an effective insecticide (Morton, 1992).

Analgesic activity:

Betz (1997) reported that the Noni fruits posses analgesic and tranquilizing activites. A French research team led by Younos, tested the analgesic and sedative effects of extracts from the *Morinda citrifolia* plant. The extract did "show a significant, dose-related, central analgesic activity in the treated mice." They stated that "these findings validate the traditional analgesic properties of this plant." The analgesic efficacy of the Noni extract is 75 % as strong as morphine, yet non-addictive and side effect free (Younos *et al.* 1990).

Anti-Inflammation:

There have been recent applications for the use of oil from noni seeds (West, 2008). Noni seed oil is abundant in linoleic acid that may have useful properties when applied topically on skin, e.g., anti-inflammation, acne reduction, moisture retention (Letawe *et al.* 1998 and Darmstadt, 2002).

Hypotensive activity:

Dang Van Ho of Vietnam demonstrated that a total extract of the Noni roots has a hypotensive effect (Youngken, 1996). Moorthy and Reddy (1970) found that an ethanol extract of the Noni roots lowered the blood pressure in an anesthetized dog. Youngken's research team determined that a hot water extract of Noni roots lowered the blood pressure of an anesthetized dog (Davison,1927). A Hawaiian physician reported that Noni fruit juice had a diuretic effect (Asahina *et al.* 1994).

Immunological activity:

Asahina *et al.* (1994) found that an alcohol extract of Noni fruit at various concentrations inhibited the production of tumor necrosis factor-alpha (TNF- α, which is an endogenous tumor promoter. Therefore the alcohol extract may inhibit the tumor promoting effect of TNF-α.

Mental health and improved high frequency hearing:

A small human clinical trial of the effect of TNJ on auditory function and quality of life in the patients with decreased bone mineral density and auditory function has been conducted in UIC College of Medicine, Rockford, IL. This study showed that TNJ provided a positive benefit on mental health and improved high frequency hearing. The data suggests that increased amounts or extended duration of TNJ intake may be required to affect this disorder (Langford *et al.* 2002).

COMMERCIAL PRODUCTS

The primary commercial products from Noni include beverages (fruit juice, juice drinks), fruit powders (for manufacture of reconstituted juice or juice drink products made from dried ripe or unripe fruits), toiletries (lotions, soaps etc.), oil (from seeds), and leaf powders (for encapsulation or pills).The bark of the great morinda produces a brownish-purplish dye for batik making; on the Indonesian island of Java, the trees are cultivated for this purpose. In Hawaii, yellowish dye is extracted from its root in order to dye cloth (Thompson, 1971).

Noni as nutraceutical and functional food (NFF):

Noni can be used as a raw material for nutraceutical and functional food products. In Thailand, "Yor" leaves cooked with curry give a wonderful and nutritious dish. "Yor" fruits can be prepared as a Thai traditional salad "Somtumyor". Dried fruits or leaves powder boiled with water produces a tea, which is used to relief blood pressure, muscle pains and vomiting. There are more than 120 nutraceutical compounds identified in Noni (Solomon, 1999). Noni or Yor juice extract which is obtained from fermented Noni fruits is the most effective product that has helped relieved people ($n \geq 10{,}000$) from the suffering of about 22 conditions, such as arthritis, heart disease, diabetes, headache and muscle pain, high blood pressure, cancer, etc. (Solomon, 1999). Recently 'Noni' juice extract has been commercially processed and distributed internationally as a dietary supplement. Relatively unheard of 5 years ago, *M. citrifolia* has now exploded into nearly a billion-dollar industry.

ENVIRONMENTAL PREFERENCES AND TOLERANCES

Climate

Elevation range : 1-800 m, depending on latitude and environment.

Mean annual rainfall : 250-4000 mm.

Rainfall pattern : Noni can tolerate, a wide range of precipitation patterns, including summer, winter, bimodal and uniform.

Dry season duration (consecutive months with <40 mm rainfall) : At least 3-4 months depending on age, size of tree, temperature, relative humidity and soils.

Mean annual temperature: 20-35°C.

Minimum temperature tolerated: 12°C

Soils

Noni grows in a very wide range of soils and environments, with a notable ability to survive in harsh environments, such as those found on coral atolls or basaltic lava flows. It can also be found in solution pits or brackish tide pools near the coast, in limestone soils or outercroppings, on coral atolls, as a colonizing species of basaltic lava flows, as well as in native forests.

Soil drainage :

Noni tolerates a wide range of drainage conditions including seasonal waterlogging, but it prefers free, well drained soils.

Soil acidity :

It can grow in a wide range of acidity levels, from acidic to alkaline.

Special soil tolerances :

Noni tolerates shallow, saline, sodic and infertile soils.

StressTolerance

Mature, cultivated Noni can easily withstand drought for 6 moths or more. Wild noni plants growing in arid conditions can spend their entire lives in conditions of perpetual drought. The plant grows well in full sun. Noni can grow in a wide range of light intensities, from full sun to over 80 per cent shade. It can regenerate after fire by sprouting new foliage from roots or stems. Noni withstands and even thrives in brackish tide pools.It can also tolerate flooded conditions for long periods of time. It is very salt-resistant and tolerant of ocean salt spray. Noni is tolerant to extreme salinity in general and is thought to possibly gain nutritional benefit from the minerals contained in seawater. Although windy areas are not advised for commercial production, noni can grow in windswept locations however, yields and overall plant growth of noni in such areas are diminished.

Abilities

It has the ability to regenerate from shoots or root suckers rather than from seed, producing small thickets or groves. Noni is not considered to be self-pruning, although the woody branches of this plant are brittle and may be relatively easily broken during overly heavy fruiting loads or during high winds. Noni plants regenerate well, even after severe pruning, Noni may be cut back to the trunk (stumping) to promote the growth of a dense head of foliage.

GROWTH AND DEVELOPMENT

The growth rate is moderate, generally 0.75-1.5 m/yr, slowing as the tree reached maturity. Noni flowering and fruiting is continuous throughout year. Fluctuations in flowering and fruiting may occur due to seasonal effects (temperature, rainfall, sunlight intensity and duration). Noni does not compete well with grasses or with grassy weeds in deep soils as an agricultural monocrop. However, it is a good forest understory plant that can tolerate very harsh conditions and plant competition from forest trees, including allelopathic species. In fact, noni is one of the few plants that can thrive beneath the canopy of iron-wood (*Cstuarina equisetifolia*) trees.

PROPAGATION

Noni is relatively easy to propagate from seeds, stem or root cuttings and air-layering. The preferred methods of propagation are by seed and by cuttings made from stem verticals.

PROPAGATION FROM SEED

Noni seeds are reddish-brown, oblong-triangular, and have a conspicuous air chamber. They are buoyant and hydrophobic due to this air chamber and their durable, water-repellent, fibrous seedcoat. The seedcoat is very tough, relatively thick, and covered with cellophane-like parchment layers. A single large noni fruit can contain well over 100 seeds. Only soft, ripened noni fruits should be chosen for seed collection. The seeds must be separated from the fibrous, clinging fruit flesh. First, split the fruit by hand into smaller pieces. Separate the seeds from the flesh using a strong spray of water and a firm screen or colander, washing the pulp through the screen while retaining the cleaned seeds. Rubbing the fruit fragments on the screen by hand or with a blunt object can help force the fruit flesh through the screen. It may take 15 minutes or more of vigorous washing and rubbing to detach most of the flesh from the seeds.

Scarifying the hard seedcoat by nicking or puncturing it significantly reduces germination time, improves germination percentage, and promotes uniform sprouting. Whereas in nature the seedcoat must gradually decompose before water can enter, scarification overcomes this natural seed dormancy. Using a household blender to separate seeds from the ripened flesh can also result in nicking the seedcoats, or the seeds can be suspended in water and sub-seedcoats, or the seeds can be suspended in water and subjected to short pulses of blending. Noni seeds can be dried and stored, but the length of time they will remain viable is not known. After cleaning, spread the seeds out on newspaper and dry them in the shade or indoors for 2 or 3 days. Store the seeds in an airtight container at room temperature. Fresh Noni seeds can be planted immediately after extraction from the fruit. Some growers soak the seeds until they start to germinate, then plant them in containers, while others plant fresh seeds without pre-soaking treatments. Some growers just plant fruit fragments containing seeds directly into the field soil. Noni seeds require hot, wet conditions for optimum germination. Unscarified seeds need several months to a year before natural germination takes place, but this period can be reduced to a month or so using heat. The seeds can tolerate temperature of 100°F (38°C) perhaps even higher. Select the warmest spot in the nursery of greenhouse to germinate Noni seeds or heat can be supplied using nursery heating pads.

Generally Noni seedlings are grown in pots in full sun for a minimum of 9-12 months before they are transferred to the field. Seedlings upto a year old or more may also be planted. If Noni plants are transplanted too young they are most susceptible to weed competition, mechanical damage, and slug attack. Seedling and young plants grown from cuttings can be given liquid fertilizer once a month, or a controlled release fertilizer less often (depending on the formulation's release period). Balanced formulations such as 14-14-14 that also contain micronutrients (minor elements) are advised. Young plants also respond well to applications of dilute, liquid foliar fertilizers. As plants become established, granular, rapidly soluble formulations can be used. Noni is relatively salt-tolerant, and fertilizer burn is uncommon under normal conditions.

VEGETATIVE PROPAGATION

Cultivation of noni plants from stem cuttings (verticals or laterals) reduces the time required to obtain plants that are ready for transplanting. Cuttings from stems and branches will sprout roots readily under the proper conditions.

Select vigorous plants for propagation. Remove a branch or stem and check for fresh sap flow from the wound. If the sap flows readily, cuttings could be made from these materials. If sap does not ooze from the cut end, discard the material and select another plant, another location, or perhaps wait for a better time of year. Sap flow indicates a vigorous, actively growing plant with relatively high reserves of energy. Insert the cut end of the freshly cut Noni stem into a pot containing a general-purpose growth medium. Rooting hormone should improver or accelerate rooting of vegetative cuttings, but it is not necessary. As with seed germination, bottom heat enhances rooting, and an artificial, pathogen-free medium is preferred to untreated agricultural field soil. Select a location with partial shade and keep the cuttings well watered until rooting occurs. After rooting, move the plants into full sun and begin fertilizer applications. Noni plants may also be produced by air layering or by digging up plants that have sprouted from the root system of a mature plant.

SITE SELECTION

Avoid locations where other crops have been planted recently, due to the susceptibility of Noni to root-knot nematodes. Select a site in full of partial sun with well drained, well aerated soil. Avoid heavy soils, compacted areas, and flood-prone sites. Prepare a hole about the size of the pot and transplant carefully. In rocky location, "rip" the land (disturb or plow the subsoil) before grading to prepare a flat or gently sloping field.

PRUNING

Less than 3 years old should be pruned back after or during their first production of fruits. In the flowering years, the pruned plants will become bushy and because Noni trees can reach a height of approximately 20 ft, growers may wish to prune the plants to facilitate picking.

NUTRITION AND FERTILIZER

Young seedlings and transplants are given controlled-release fertilize formulations, while older, mature plants are given rapidly available granular formulations. Fertilizer should be applied away from the trunk at the "drip line" of the plant, the area where water drips from the edge of the leaf canopy

Noni plants of all ages respond well to sprays of foliar fertilizer. Noni flower and fruit production is very responsive to sprays of high-phosphorous foliar fertilizers (e.g., 10-45-10) and products (e.g., seaweed emulsions) containing nitrogen and minor elements.

Noni should be fertilized frequently using smaller amounts of fertilizer, rather than infrequently suing larger amounts. In high-rainfall areas, young plants up to a year old can be given $\frac{1}{2}$ pound per month of balanced fertilizer (14-14-14), and more mature plants can be given up to 1 pound per month. Effective organic fertilizers for noni cultivation include crushed coral, dolomite, K-mag 7-7-7, and composted chicken manure and macadamia nut husks. Some locations will benefit from yearly applications of lime, about 1 pound per plant.

IRRIGATION

Noni thrives with moderate irrigation and can survive extended drought once established and mature. When plants are less than 2-3 years old condition are dry, irrigate once or more a week, applying up 10 gallons per plant; for older plants, irrigate less frequently. Overwatering can accelerate damage from root-knot nematodes, cause root rot, and leach fertilize nutrients beyond the root zone.

CROP IMPROVEMENT

Among all the new innovations and activities, information technology and biotechnology ruled the world for the past two to three decades. In the field of Plant biotechnology, the technical advances have been tremendous and unique in their application as commercial tools to improve agriculture, sylviculture, horticulture and agro industries. Noni plants were taken for rapid multiplication using tissue culture techniques at the tissue culture lab in Chennai. Axillary buds were taken from young seedlings and after proper sterilization these buds were inoculated to Murashige and Skoog's medium containing various hormone combinations. After successful culture initiation at *in vitro* buds were subjected to rapid multiplication. An excellent rate of multiplication with enough elongation of the multiple shoots was achieved in the medium. After multiplication, shoots of 4cm in length and above were separated individually and inoculated to rooting media to produce roots. Enough roots were produced within 18 days *in vitro* (Subramani, 2006).

Other than micropropogation, Noni biotech division will also enter into new research area like:

- Cell culture to produce saline tolerant plants
- Micropropogation of elite clones
- Isolation and identification of cells *in vitro*
- Cell immobilization for production of nutraceuticals
- Bioreactor technology

PLANT DISEASES

Black flag of noni

A severe leaf and fruit blight occurs in the Puna district of the island of Hawaii. The disease is caused by the pathogen *Phytophtora botryose.* Symptoms include a black leaf and stem blight, stem or branch dieback, and a chocolate-colored or black fruit rot. The disease is favored by prolonged periods of wet weather. Control measures include pruning, weed control, and field sanitation.

Sooty mold

Sooty mold is a black, superficial growth of a nonparasitic fungus that utilizes the sugary exudates produced by soft-fungus insects such as scales and aphids. Sooty mold can easily be wiped off leaves by hand. Heavy infestation of the fungus can reduce photosynthesis, resulting in poor plant growth and reduced fruit size and quality. A soapy water spray can control sooty mold.

Noni root-knot disease

Noni root-knot is a disease of the roots caused by root-knot nematodes, *Meloidogyne* species. Above-ground symptoms include reduced vigor, plant stunting, and yellowing. Affected roots can be galled, swollen, cracked, and rotten. This disease can be minimized by using nematode-free transplants and by adding organic soil amendments such as composts containing chicken manure. Moderate irrigation and fertilizer use will also minimize the damage and reduce the magnitude of secondary root rot by saprophytic fungi and bacteria.

Stem rot

In stem rot, tissues at the base of the plant decay, resulting in stunted plants. The initial plant symptom is wilt, including leaf flagging, and drop. The disease arises from a complex of multiple causes including predisposing stresses (root-knot nematodes, flooding, stem injury) and stem-girdling decay by a soilborne fungus, *Sclerotium rolfsii.* Planting pathogen-free plants, selecting appropriate sites, and avoiding plant stress can minimize the occurrence and severity of stem rot.

INSECT PESTS

Pest attacks of cultivated noni can cause significant damage. Pests known to attack noni in Hawaii include aphids (*Aphis gossypii*), ants, scales (the green scale), mites (eriophyid mites), whiteflies (fringe guava whitefly), and slugs. Pest outbreaks are favored by monocultures of noni. Thus, intercropping with other species of nonhost plants can minimize the overall severity and frequency of pest attacks.

Eliminate weeds that are alternate hosts of noni pests to prevent outbreaks. Significant weed hosts of noni pest are identified by periodic inspections of both noni pests nearby weeds for the presence of pests such as aphids, scale, and whitefly. These and other soft-bodied insects can be effectively controlled with sprays of insecticidal soaps and oils. Mites can be controlled by pruning affected leaves and by applications of approved pesticides, such as sulphur. For slugs and ants, apply a temporary barrier at the base of the noni plant, such as copper tape (for slugs), or a sticky substance such as pine tar (for ants).

WEEDS

Noni transplants are susceptible to competition from weeds such a Guinea grass and sensitive grass (*Mimosa pudica*). Young noni plants should be weeded by hand until the stem is sufficiently large to withstand potential mechanical injury from mowers or string trimmers. Although weed mats can suppress weeds, they also inhibits granular fertilizers from penetrating to the roots zone, and heat can accumulate under the mat, which may favour nematode reproduction. Once noni plant are well established, competition from weeds is less damaging than when the plants are young. Care should be taken to eradicate weeds that are hosts of root-knot nematodes may be identified by inspecting their roots for the presence of the characteristic galls and swellings. Noni is susceptible to attack by dodder (*Cuscuta sandwichensis*), a parasitic weed. Dodder should be manually removed from infested Noni plants.

HARVESTING AND YIELD

Noni plants can begin to bear fruit about 9 months after planting. Fruits can be harvested at this early stage, although they generally are small and few. Some farmers choose to forgo harvest during the first and second years in favour of pruning back the branches instead. This pruning results in a bushy plant with more vertical and lateral branches and ultimately produces greater fruit yield.

In Hawaii, noni fruits may be harvested year round, although there are seasonal trends in fruit production that may be affected or modified by the weather and fertilizer applications. Fruit production may diminish somewhat during winter months in Hawaii. The expected yield from mature, healthy plants is 250-500 pounds per plant per year, depending on nutrition and plant spacing. However, yields at some locations can exceed 500 pounds per plant per year with good crop management. Fruits may be picked just before they begin to ripen fully and turn completely whitish-yellow on the tree. These fruits are suitable for shipping and will continue to ripen en route unless measures are taken to retard ripening. For processing locally, fresh fruits are picked when ripe, just before they fall naturally from the tree. Juice can be squeezed directly from the ripened fruits or allowed to drip from the fruits and ferment as in the traditional method.

AGROFORESTRY / ENVIRONMENTAL PRACTICES

Although Noni regrows well after pruning. Noni plants are generally not managed for mulch production in agroforestry situations. It is well suited for home gardens. A single plant is sufficient to meet the needs of one or more families. Noni can be used for boundary markers due to its persistence and ability to survive harsh conditions and extended periods of drought. The fruits and leaves are useful as animal feed or fodder (pets and livestock). Ripe fruits are a natural source of food for birds, rodents and insects. The flower nectarines are very attractive to honeybees. Noni is tenacious enough help to stabilize lands in harsh or unstable coastal environments. Although the naturalized *M. citrifolia* (the wild and cultivated Noni types) is considered by many to be a beautiful plant with shiny green foliage, some object to its use as an ornamental plant due to the strong and sometimes offensive odour of ripened fruits and because the fallen fruits attract many flies and other insects. The cultivated *M. citrifolia* variety 'Potteri' is a beautiful and functional ornamental plant with small fruits and green and white variegated leaves.

CONCLUSION

Morinda citrifolia assumed to have originated in Southern Asia has been used in folk remedies by Polynesians for over 2000 years, and is reported to have broad range of antibacterial, antiviral,antifungal, antitumor, antihelminthic, analgesic, hypotensive and immune enhancing effects. Noni plant has the ability to survive in harsh environments and wide range of acidity levels. It has rapid regeneration ability and can be propagated from seed,stem or root cuttings and air layering. Owing to its therapeutic and nutritional value, it can be considered as one of the most important medicinal plants.

REFERENCES

Abbott I A 1992 La'au Hawaii' traditional Hawaiian uses of plants v 3 Honolulu Hawaii: Bishop Museum Press; p 97- 100

Abbott A 1985 The geographic origin of the plants most commonly used for medicine by Hawaiians J Ethnopharmacol; **14**: 213-22

Allen WH 1873 London C Some information on the ethnobotanical properties of Noni (*Mor inda citr ifolia*) In: The useful plants of India

Asahina A Y Ebesu J S M Ichinotsubo D Tongson J and Hokama Y 1994 Effect of okadaic acid (OA) and Noni fruit extraction in the synthesis of tumor necrosis factor-a (TNF-a) by peripheral blood mononuclear (PBN) cells *in vitro The Procedings of the International Symposium of Ciguatera and Marine Natural Products* p 197-205

Betz J 1997 Pride Publishing Noni: Polynesia's natural pharmacy p 13

Bushnell O A Fukuda M Makinodian T1950 The antibacterial properties of some plants found in Hawaii *Pacific Sci* **4**: 167-83

Cheeseman T F 1903 The flora of raratonga the chief island of the cook group v 6 London: *Linnean Soc* p 261-313

Darmstadt G L Mao-Qiang M Chi E Saha S K Ziboh V A Black R E Santosham M Elias P M 2002 "Impact of topical oils on the skin barrier: possible implications for neonatal health in developing countries" *Acta Paediatrica* **91** (5): 546–554

Davison C 1927 Hawaiian medicine The Queen's Hospital Bulletin with Palama Clinic Section; **4**: 2-5

Deng S Palu A K West B J et al 2007 Lipoxygenase Inhibitory Constituents of the Fruits of Noni (*Morinda citrifolia*) Collected in Tahiti *J Nat Prod* **70**(5):859-862

Heinicke R1985 The pharmacologically active ingredient of Noni *Bulletin National Tropical Botanical Garden* **15**:10-14

Hirazumi A Furusawa E Chou S C and Hokama Y 1994 Anticancer activity of Morinda citrifolia (noni) on intraperitoneally implanted Lewis lung carcinoma in syngeneic mice *Proc West Pharmacol Soc* **37**: 145-6

Hirazumi A Furusawa E Chou S C and Hokama Y1996 Immunomodulation contributes to the anticancer activity of *Morinda citrifolia* (noni) fruit juice *Proc West Pharmacol Soc* **39**: 7-9

Hirazumi A and Furusawa E 1999 An immunomodulatory polysaccharide- rich substance from the fruit juice of *Morinda citrifolia* (noni) with antitumour activity *Phytother Res* **13**: 380-7

Krauss B H 1993 *Plants in Hawaiian Culture* Honolulu: University of Hawaii Press Honolulu

Langford J Doughty A Wang M Y Clayton L and Babich M 2002 Effects of *Morinda citrifolia* on auditory function and quality of life in patients with decreased bone mineral density and auditory function *J Complementary & Alternative Med* **15**:10-16

Letawe C Boone M and Pierard G E1998 "Digital image analysis of the effect of topically applied linoleic acid on acne microcomedones" *Clinical & Experimental Dermatology* **23** (2): 56–58

Levand O and Larson HO1979 Some chemical cons tituents of *Morinda citrifolia Planta Med* **36:** 186-7

Ma D L West B J Su C X Gao J H Liu T Z and Liu Y W 2007 Evaluation of the ergogenic potential of noni juice *Phytotherapy Res* **21**(11):1100-1101

Maiden J H 1889 Useful native plants of Australia including Tasmania Sydney: Tuner and Henderson Publisher p 45

McClatchey W 2002 "From Polynesian Healers to Health Food Stores: Changing Perspectives of *Morinda citrifolia* (Rubiaceae)" *Integrative Cancer Therapies* 1 (2): 110–120

Merrill E D 1943 Noni (*Morinda citrifolia*) as an edible plant In: Technical manual: emergency food plants and poisonous plants of the islands of the pacific Washington DC: US Government Printing Office

Mohd Z Z Abdul-Hamid A Osman A *et al* (2007) Isolation and identification of antioxidative compound from fruit of mengkudu (*Morinda citrifolia* L) *Inter J Food Properties* **10**(2):363-373

Moorthy N K and Reddy G S1970 Preliminary phytochemical and pharmacological study of *Morinda citrifolia* Linn Antiseptic **67**: 167-71

Morton J F 1992 The ocean-going Noni or Indian mulberry *(Morinda citrifolia* Rubiaceae) and some of its 'colorful' relatives *Economic Bot* **46**: 241-56

Nelson S C 2006 "Nutritional Analysis of Hawaiian Noni (Noni Fruit Powder)" *The Noni Website* Retrieved 15-06-2009

Raj R K 1975 Screening of indigenous plants for anthelmintic action against humanAscaris Lumbricoides: Part-II *Indian J Physiol Pharmacol* **19:** 47-9

Seemann B and Flora V 1866 A description of the plants of the Viti or Fiji is lands with an account of their history uses and properties London: L Reeve and Co p 1865-73

Solomon N 1999 The Noni Phenomenon Direct Source Publishing USA 43-47

Subramani J 2006 Crop Improvement in Morinda citrifolia Proc First National Symposium on Noni Research October 7-8 2006

Swanholm C E St John H and Scheuer P J 1959 A survey of alkaloids in Hawaiian plants *Pacific Sci* **13**: 295-305

Thompson R H 1971 *Naturally Occurring Anthraquinones* New York: Academic Press

Umezawa K1992 Isolation of 1-methoxy-2-foremyl-3-hydroxyanthraquinone from *M citrifolia* and neoplasm inhibitors containing the same Japan Kokai Tokyo *Appl*; 92/264: 311-17

West B J Jensen C J Westendorf J 2008 A new vegetable oil from noni (*Morinda citrifolia*) seeds *Inter J Food SciTech* **43**(11):1988-1992

Youngken H W Jenkins H J and Butler C L 1996 Studies on *Morinda citrifolia* L II *J Am Pharm Assoc* **49**: 271-3 57

Younos C Rolland A Fleurentin J Lanhers M C Miss L R and Mortier F 1990 Analgesic and behavioural effects of *Morinda citrifolia Planta Med* **56**: 430-4

INDEX

I

L

M

N

O

P

Q

R

S